DICTIONARY *of* SCRIPTURE *and* ETHICS

DICTIONARY *of* SCRIPTURE *and* ETHICS

JOEL B. GREEN
GENERAL EDITOR

JACQUELINE E. LAPSLEY, REBEKAH MILES, AND ALLEN VERHEY
ASSOCIATE EDITORS

a division of Baker Publishing Group
Grand Rapids, Michigan

Published by Baker Academic
a division of Baker Publishing Group
P.O. Box 6287, Grand Rapids, MI 49516-6287
www.bakeracademic.com

Printed in the United States of America

Library of Congress Cataloging-in-Publication Data
Dictionary of scripture and ethics / Joel B. Green, general editor ; Jacqueline E. Lapsley, Rebekah Miles, and Allen Verhey, associate editors.
p. cm.
Includes bibliographical references and index.
ISBN 978-0-8010-3406-0 (cloth)
1. Ethics in the Bible—Dictionaries. 2. Christian ethics—Biblical teaching—Dictionaries. I. Green, Joel B., 1956– II. Lapsley, Jacqueline E., 1965– III. Miles, Rebekah, 1960– IV. Verhey, Allen.
BS680.E84D53 2011
241′.2—dc23 2011017242

11 12 13 14 15 16 17 7 6 5 4 3 2 1

CONTENTS

CONTRIBUTORS

Adam, A. K. M. PhD, Duke University. Lecturer in New Testament, University of Glasgow. **Information Technology**

Adam, Margaret B. PhD candidate, Duke University. Visiting Assistant Professor of Theology, Loyola University Maryland. **Compassion**

Adams, Samuel L. PhD, Yale University. Assistant Professor of Biblical Studies, Union Presbyterian Seminary. **Sirach; Wisdom of Solomon**

Adeney, Frances. PhD, Graduate Theological Union. William A. Benfield Jr. Professor of Evangelism and Global Mission, Louisville Presbyterian Theological Seminary. **Comparative Religious Ethics**

Arnold, Bill T. PhD, Hebrew Union College—Jewish Institute of Religion. Paul S. Amos Professor of Old Testament Interpretation, Asbury Theological Seminary. **Divination and Magic**

Baker, Mark D. PhD, Duke University. Associate Professor of Mission and Theology, Mennonite Brethren Biblical Seminary. **Atonement**

Baker, William R. PhD, University of Aberdeen. Professor of New Testament, Cincinnati Christian University Graduate School. **Slander**

Bandstra, Barry. PhD, Yale University. Professor of Religion, Hope College. **Concubinage**

Banks, Robert. PhD, Cambridge University. Associate of the Centre for the Study of the History and Experience of Christianity, Macquarie University. **Time, Use of**

Bashaw, Jennifer Garcia. PhD candidate, Fuller Theological Seminary. **Martyrdom; Persecution**

Beach-Verhey, Timothy A. PhD, Emory University. Pastor, Faison Presbyterian Church. **Covenantal Ethics; Law, Uses of; Responsibility; Self-Denial; Vocation**

Beaton, Richard. PhD, University of Cambridge. Principal of De Pree Leadership Center, Associate Professor of New Testament, Fuller Theological Seminary. **Leadership, Leadership Ethics**

Berquist, Jon L. PhD, Vanderbilt University. Executive Editor for Biblical Studies, Westminster John Knox Press. **Incarnation**

Biddle, Mark E. DTheol, University of Zurich. Russell T. Cherry Professor of Old Testament, Baptist Theological Seminary at Richmond. **Sin**

Birch, Bruce C. PhD, Yale University. Professor of Old Testament, Emeritus, Wesley Theological Seminary. **Justice; 1–2 Samuel; Scripture in Ethics: Methodological Issues**

Blanchard, Kathryn D. PhD, Duke University. Assistant Professor of Religious Studies, Alma College. **Family Planning; Jealousy and Envy; Welfare State**

Bock, Darrell L. PhD, University of Aberdeen. Research Professor of New Testament Studies and Professor of Spiritual Development and Culture, Dallas Theological Seminary. **Blasphemy**

Boda, Mark J. PhD, Cambridge University. Professor of Old Testament, McMaster Divinity College. Professor, Faculty of Theology, McMaster University. **Haggai; Zechariah**

Boer, Theo A. PhD, Utrecht University. Associate of Ethics Institute, Utrecht University; Associate Professor of Ethics, Protestant Theological University, Utrecht. **Euthanasia**

Boyd, Greg. PhD, Princeton Theological Seminary. Senior Pastor, Woodland Hills Church, St. Paul. **Evil; Powers and Principalities**

Bratton, Susan Power. PhD, Cornell University; PhD, University of Texas at Dallas. Chair of Environmental Science, Professor of Environmental Studies, Baylor University. **Population Policy and Control**

Brawley, Robert L. PhD, Princeton Theological Seminary. Professor of New Testament Emeritus, McCormick Theological Seminary. **Acts; John; Luke; Mark; Matthew**

Bretzke, James T., SJ. STD, Pontifical Gregorian University, Rome. Professor of Moral Theology, Boston College School of Theology and Ministry. **Casuistry; Natural Law; Roman Catholic Moral Theology**

Brower, Kent. PhD, The University of Manchester. Senior Research Fellow and Vice-Principal, Nazarene Theological College. **Holiness; Legalism; Righteousness**

Brown, Nicholas Read. PhD candidate, Fuller Theological Seminary. Visiting Professor, Loyola Marymount University. **Sodomy**

Brown, William P. PhD, Emory University. Professor of Old Testament, Columbia Theological Seminary. **Creation, Biblical Accounts of**

Brownlee, Jay. Service User Representative, Scottish Personality Disorder Network. **Self-Harm**

Bruckner, James K. PhD, Luther Seminary. Professor of Old Testament, North Park Theological Seminary. **Health**

Burridge, Richard A. PhD, University of Nottingham. Professor, King's College London. **Apartheid; Discrimination**

Carnahan, Kevin. PhD, Southern Methodist University. Assistant Professor of Religion and Philosophy, Central Methodist University. **Deterrence, Nuclear; Military Service; Pluralism; Political Ethics**

Carroll R. (Rodas), M. Daniel. PhD, University of Sheffield. Distinguished Professor of Old Testament, Denver Seminary. Adjunct Professor, Seminario Teológico Centroamericano, Guatemala. **Aliens, Immigration, and Refugees; Amos; Micah; Old Testament Ethics**

Carvalho, Corrine. PhD, Yale University. Professor of Theology, University of St. Thomas. **Sanctuary**

Cates, Diana Fritz. PhD, Brown University. Associate Professor of Religious Studies and Ethics, The University of Iowa. **Vice**

Chapman, Stephen B. PhD, Yale University. Associate Professor of Old Testament, Duke Divinity School. **Ban, The; Deuteronomistic History; Holy War**

Charry, Ellen T. PhD, Temple University. Margaret W. Harmon Professor of Historical and Systematic Theology, Princeton Theological Seminary. **Happiness; Supersessionism**

Cherian, Jacob. PhD, Princeton Theological Seminary. Vice President and Dean, Southern Asia Bible College. **Tithe, Tithing**

Cheung, Luke Leuk. PhD, St. Andrews University, St. Mary's College. Dean, China Graduate School of Theology. **Fidelity; Integrity; Temptation**

Childs, James M., Jr. PhD, Lutheran School of Theology at Chicago. Edward C. Fendt Professor of Systematic Theology, Trinity Lutheran Seminary. **Greed**

Chilton, Bruce. PhD, St. John's College, Cambridge University. Bernard Iddings Bell Professor of Religion, Bard College. **Kingdom of God**

Clapper, Gregory S. PhD, Emory University. Professor of Religion and Philosophy, The University of Indianapolis. **Affections**

Cleveland, Lindsay K. PhD candidate, Baylor University. **Humanity; Nationalism**

Clifton-Soderstrom, Michelle. PhD, Loyola University Chicago. Assistant Professor of Theology and Ethics, North Park Theological Seminary. **Discipline**

Cochran, Elizabeth Agnew. PhD, University of Notre Dame. Assistant Professor of Theology, Duquesne University. **Disability and Handicap; Dishonesty; Honesty; Lust; Sloth; Utilitarianism**

Cohick, Lynn H. PhD, University of Pennsylvania. Associate Professor of New Testament, Wheaton College. **Headship**

Conklin-Miller, Jeffrey. ThD student, Duke Divinity School. **Excommunication**

Conley, Aaron. PhD candidate, Iliff School of Theology and University of Denver. MDiv, Truett Theological Seminary. **Restitution**

Cook, E. David. PhD, University of Edinburgh. Holmes Professor of Faith and Learning, Wheaton College. **Institution(s); Reproductive Technologies; Resource Allocation**

Corcoran, Kevin. PhD, Purdue University. Associate Professor of Philosophy. **Monism, Anthropological; Self**

Cosgrove, Charles H. PhD, Princeton Theological Seminary. Professor of New Testament Studies and Christian Ethics, Northern Seminary. **Libertinism; Moral Formation; New Testament Ethics; Scripture in Ethics: A History**

Couey, J. Blake. PhD, Princeton Theological Seminary. Visiting Assistant Professor, Gustavus Adolphus College. **Revenge**

Cox, D. Michael. PhD candidate, University of Dayton. **Character**

Creegan, Nicola Hoggard. PhD, Drew University. Senior Lecturer, School of Theology, Laidlaw College. **Gender; Women, Status of**

Day, Linda. PhD, Princeton Theological Seminary. **Esther**

De La Torre, Miguel A. PhD, Temple University. Professor of Social Ethics, Iliff School of Theology. **Conscientization; Liberationist Ethics; Praxis**

deSilva, David A. PhD, Emory University. Trustees' Distinguished Professor of New Testament and Greek, Ashland Theological Seminary. **Circumcision; Clean and Unclean; Deuterocanonical/Apocryphal Books; Hebrews**

Dillon, Dana L. PhD, Duke University. Assistant Professor of Theology, Providence College. **Dissent; Intention**

Dobbs-Allsopp, Chip. PhD, Johns Hopkins University. Associate Professor of Old Testament, Princeton Theological Seminary. **Lamentations; Poetic Discourse and Ethics; Song of Songs**

Donahue, John R., SJ. PhD, University of Chicago. Research Professor in Theology, Loyola University, Maryland. **Parables, Use of in Ethics**

Douglas, Mark. PhD, The University of Virginia. Associate Professor of Christian Ethics, Columbia Theological Seminary. **Anxiety; Ends and Means; Force, Use of; Imperialism; Media, Ethical Issues of; Security; Tyranny; Violence; War**

Dowdy, Christopher. PhD candidate, Southern Methodist University. **Mercy**

Downs, David J. PhD, Princeton Theological Seminary. Assistant Professor of New Testament Studies, Fuller Theological Seminary. **2 Corinthians; Hedonism; Materialism; 1–2 Timothy; Titus; Vices and Virtues, Lists of; Wealth**

Driggers, Brent. PhD, Princeton Theological Seminary. Associate Professor of New Testament, Lutheran Theological Southern Seminary. **Freedom**

Dryden, J. de Waal. PhD, Cambridge University. Associate Professor of Biblical Studies, Covenant College. **Jude; 1 Peter; 2 Peter**

Dufault-Hunter, Erin. PhD, University of Southern California. Assistant Professor of Christian Ethics, Fuller Theological Seminary. **Individualism; Orphans; Pornography; Sex and Sexuality; Sexual Ethics; Sociology of Religion; Spousal Abuse**

Duff, Nancy J. PhD, Union Theological Seminary, New York City. Stephen Colwell Associate Professor of Christian Ethics, Princeton Theological Seminary. **Alcohol; Just Wage; Singleness**

Duggan, Michael W. PhD, The Catholic University of America. Associate Professor of Theology and Religious Studies, St. Mary's University College. **Ezra; Nehemiah**

Eddy, Paul R. PhD, Marquette University. Professor of Biblical and Theological Studies, Bethel University. **Evil**

Edgar, Brian G. PhD, Deakin University. Professor of Theological Studies, Asbury Theological Seminary. **Play; Worldliness**

Edgar, David Hutchinson. PhD, Trinity College, Dublin. Chester Beatty Library, Dublin. **Desire; James**

Finger, Reta Halteman. PhD, Northwestern University. Assistant Professor of New Testament, Messiah College. **Widows**

Finger, Thomas. PhD, Claremont Graduate University. Scholar in Residence, Bethany Theological Seminary. **Eschatology and Ethics**

Freund, Richard. PhD, Jewish Theological Seminary. Director of the Maurice Greenberg Center for Judaic Studies, University of Harford. **Collective Responsibility**

Furnish, Victor Paul. PhD, Yale University. University Distinguished Professor Emeritus of New Testament, Southern Methodist University. **Galatians; Philemon; Philippians; Romans**

Goldingay, John. DD, Archbishop of Canterbury at Lambeth; PhD, University of Nottingham. David Allan Hubbard Professor of Old Testament, Fuller Theological Seminary. **Loans**

Gorman, Michael J. PhD, Princeton Theological Seminary. Dean and Professor of Sacred Scripture, The Ecumenical Institute of Theology, St. Mary's Seminary and University. **Abortion; Cruciformity**

Green, Barbara. PhD, University of California at Berkeley and Graduate Theological Union. Professor of Biblical Studies, Dominican School of Philosophy and Theology, Graduate Theological Union. **Jonah**

Green, Joel B. PhD, University of Aberdeen. Professor of New Testament Interpretation, Associate Dean for the Center for Advanced Theological Studies, Fuller Theological Seminary. **Almsgiving; Antichrist; Collection for the Saints; Healthcare Systems in Scripture; Hypocrisy; Koinonia; Loans; Repentance**

Greenman, Jeffrey P. PhD, University of Virginia. Associate Dean of Biblical and Theological Studies, Professor of Christian Ethics, Wheaton College. **Cardinal Virtues; Courage; Prudence; Seven Deadly Sins**

Greenway, William. PhD, Princeton Theological Seminary. Associate Professor of Philosophical Theology, Austin Presbyterian Theological Seminary. **Animals**

Grigg, Viv. PhD, Auckland University. International Director, Urban Leadership Foundation. **Urbanization**

Gupta, Nijay K. PhD, University of Durham. Instructor of Biblical Studies, Seattle Pacific University. **Neighbor, Neighbor Love; World**

Gushee, David P. PhD, Union Theological Seminary, New York. Distinguished Professor of Christian Ethics, Mercer University. **Baptist Ethics; Cruelty; Human Rights; Meekness; Omission, Sins of; Polygamy; Torture**

Gutenson, Charles E. PhD, Southern Methodist University. Chief Operating Officer, Sojourners. **Pacifism; Trinity**

Hall, Amy Laura. PhD, Yale University. Associate Professor of Christian Ethics, Duke Divinity School. **Agape; Parenthood, Parenting**

Haloviak, Kendra Jo. PhD, The Graduate Theological Union at Berkeley. Assistant Professor of New Testament Studies, La Sierra University. **Revelation, Book of**

Harrington, Daniel J. PhD, Harvard University. Professor of New Testament, Boston College School of Theology and Ministry. **Additions to Daniel; Additions to Esther; Baruch; Judith; Letter of Jeremiah**

Hartin, Patrick J. DTh (Ethics), DTh (New Testament), University of South Africa. Professor of Religious Studies, Gonzaga University. **Humility; Judgment**

Hatch, Derek C. PhD, University of Dayton. Instructor in Religious Studies, University of Dayton. **Technology**

Hawk, L. Daniel. PhD, Emory University. Professor of Old Testament and Hebrew, Ashland Theological Seminary. **Conquest; Joshua; Judges**

Hernández-Díaz, R. J. PhD Candidate, Iliff School of Theology and University of Denver. MA, Fuller Theological Seminary. **Class Conflict; Hatred**

Holt, Else K. PhD, Faculty of Theology, University of Aarhus. Associate Professor, Faculty of Theology, University of Aarhus. **Jeremiah**

Hoppe, Leslie J., OFM. PhD, Northwestern University. Adjunct Professor of Old Testament, Catholic Theological Union. **Poverty and Poor**

Horrell, David G. PhD, University of Cambridge. Professor of New Testament Studies, University of Exeter. **1 Corinthians; Ecological Ethics**

Hovey, Craig. PhD, University of Cambridge. Assistant Professor of Religion, Ashland University. **Blessing and Cursing; Libel; Speech Ethics**

Howe, Bonnie. PhD, Graduate Theological Union. Visiting Professor of Ethics and Biblical Studies, New College, Berkeley, Graduate Theological Union. **Accountability; Authority and Power**

Ignatkov, Vladimir. PhD, Fuller Theological Seminary. Seminary Research Specialist, Fuller Theological Seminary. **Consequentialism**

Iosso, Christian. PhD, Union Theological Seminary. Coordinator for Social Witness Policy, Presbyterian Church (U.S.A.). **Social Service, Social Ministry**

Jefford, Clayton N. PhD, The Claremont Graduate School. Professor of Scripture, Saint Meinrad School of Theology. **Apostolic Fathers; Didache**

Jervis, L. Ann. ThD, Wycliffe College, University of Toronto. Professor of New Testament, Wycliffe College, University of Toronto. **Suffering**

Jones, Beth Felker. PhD, Duke University. Assistant Professor of Theology, Wheaton College. **Body**

Jones, D. Gareth. MD, University of Otago; DSC, University of Western Australia. Professor of Anatomy and Structural Biology, University of Otago. **Death, Definition of**

Jones, Peter L. MTS, Brite Divinity School. Adjunct Instructor of Theology, Brite Divinity School. **Civil Disobedience**

Kallenberg, Brad J. PhD, Fuller Theological Seminary. Associate Professor of Theology, University of Dayton. **Character; Technology; Virtue Ethics**

Kärkkäinen, Veli-Matti. DrTheolHabil, University of Helsinki. Professor of Systematic Theology, Fuller Theological Seminary. **Ecumenism**

Keenan, James, SJ. STL, STD, Gregorian University, Rome. Professor of Theological Ethics, Boston College. **Conscience; Contrition; Double Effect, Principle of; Habit; Subsidiarity, Principle of**

Kelle, Brad E. PhD, Emory University. Associate Professor of Old Testament, Point Loma Nazarene University. **Hosea**

Kenney, Maria. Research Student, Durham University. **Continence; Food; Gluttony; Temperance**

Kiel, Micah D. PhD, Princeton Theological Seminary. Assistant Professor of Theology, St. Ambrose University. **Tobit**

Kiesling, Chris A. PhD, Texas Tech University. Professor of Human Development and Christian Discipleship, Asbury Theological Seminary. **Godliness; Moral Development; Right and Wrong**

Kilner, John F. PhD, Harvard University. Forman Chair of Ethics and Theology, Trinity International University. **Aged, Aging**

Kinghorn, Kevin. DPhil, University of Oxford. Associate Professor of Philosophy, Asbury Theological Seminary. **Free Will and Determinism; Moral Absolutes**

Kinghorn, Warren. MD, Harvard Medical School. Consulting Associate in Psychiatry, Duke University Medical Center; ThD Student, Duke University Divinity School; Staff Psychiatrist, Durham VA Medical Center, Durham, NC. **Guilt; Moral Psychology; Passions**

Kirk-Duggan, Cheryl. PhD, Baylor University. Professor of Theology and Women's Studies, Shaw University Divinity School. **Abuse; Emancipation**

Klein, Ralph W. ThD, Harvard Divinity School. Professor of Old Testament Emeritus, Lutheran School of Theology at Chicago. **1–2 Chronicles**

Kotva, Joseph J., Jr. PhD Fordham University. **Excellence; Loyalty; Oaths**

Lapsley, Jacqueline E. PhD, Emory University. Associate Professor of Old Testament, Princeton Theological Seminary. **Emotion; Empathy; Moral Agency; Narrative Ethics, Biblical; Priestly Literature; Ruth; Ten Commandments**

Laytham, D. Brent. PhD, Duke University. Professor of Theology and Ethics, North Park University. **Narrative Ethics, Contemporary**

Lee, Eunny P. PhD, Princeton Theological Seminary. Assistant Professor of Old Testament, Princeton Theological Seminary. **Ecclesiastes; Isaiah**

LeMon, Joel M. PhD, Emory University. Assistant Professor of Old Testament, Candler School of Theology, Emory University. **Psalms**

Leslie, Kristen J. PhD, The Claremont School of Theology. Associate Professor in Pastoral Care and Counseling, Yale Divinity School. **Sexual Abuse; Sexual Harassment**

Lewis, James W. PhD, Duke University. Associate Dean, Professor of Theology and Ethics, Anderson University School of Theology. **African American Ethics**

Logan, James Samuel. PhD, Princeton Theological Seminary. Associate Professor of Religion, Associate Professor and Director of African and African American Studies, Earlham College. **Prison and Prison Reform**

Long, D. Stephen. PhD, Duke University. Professor of Systematic Theology, Marquette University. **Cost-**

Benefit Analysis; Debt; Ecclesiology and Ethics; Markets

Longenecker, Richard N. DD, Acadia University; DSacTh, Wycliffe College, University of Toronto; PhD, New College, University of Edinburgh. Professor Emeritus of New Testament, Wycliffe College, University of Toronto. **Forgiveness; Household Codes; Reconciliation; Resurrection**

Lundberg, Matthew D. PhD, Princeton Theological Seminary. Assistant Professor of Religion, Calvin College. **Creation Ethics**

Lustig, B. Andrew. PhD, University of Virginia. Homes Rolston III Professor of Religion and Science, Davidson College. **Artificial Intelligence; Canon Law; Science and Ethics**

Luzárraga, Ramón. PhD, Marquette University. Assistant Director of the Institute of Pastoral Initiatives and Faculty of the Department of Religious Studies, University of Dayton. **Charity, Works of; Gambling**

Lynch, Elizabeth. PhD, University of Aberdeen. **Self-Harm**

Lysaught, M. Therese. PhD, Duke University. Associate Professor of Theology and Assistant Department Chair, Marquette University. **Confession; Infanticide; Infertility; Liturgy and Ethics; Penitence**

MacDonald, Gary B. PhD candidate, Southern Methodist University. Director of Advanced Ministerial Studies, Perkins School of Theology. **Deviance; Malice**

Maddalena, Julie Mavity. PhD Student, Southern Methodist University. **Self-Love**

Magallanes, Hugo. PhD, Drew University. Associate Professor of Christianity and Cultures, Southern Methodist University, Perkins School of Theology. **Exploitation; Latino/Latina Ethics; Liberation; Oppression; Preferential Option for the Poor; Solidarity; Wesleyan Ethics**

Malcolm, Lois. PhD, University of Chicago. Associate Professor of Systematic Theology, Luther Seminary. **Duty**

Markham, Paul N. PhD, Durham University. Adjunct Professor of Philosophical Theology, Asbury Theological Seminary. Director of WKU Alive Center for Community Partnerships, Western Kentucky University. **Conversion**

Marshall, Christopher. PhD, King's College, University of London. Associate Professor of Religious Studies, Victoria University of Wellington. **Capital Punishment; Crime and Criminal Justice; Justice, Restorative; Justice, Retributive; Punishment; Reward and Retribution**

McCall, Robin C. PhD student, Princeton Theological Seminary. **Holiness Code; Leviticus**

McCann, Dennis P. PhD, University of Chicago Divinity School. Wallace M. Alston Professor of Bible and Religion, Agnes Scott College. **Good, The**

McCarthy, David Matzko. PhD, Duke University. Associate Professor, Mount St. Mary's University. **Norms; Truthfulness, Truth-Telling**

McFee, Daniel E. PhD, Marquette University. Associate Professor of Religious Studies and Co-Director of the Evelyn Lincoln Institute for Ethics and Society, Mercyhurst College. **Benevolence; Values, Value Judgments**

McSwain, Larry L. STD, The Southern Baptist Theological Seminary. Associate Dean, Doctor of Ministry Degree Program; Professor of Leadership; and Watkins Christian Foundation Chair of Ministry; McAfee School of Theology, Mercer University. **Baptist Ethics**

Mein, Andrew. DPhil, Oxford University. Tutor in Old Testament, Westcott House, Cambridge. **Ezekiel**

Messer, Neil. PhD, University of Cambridge. Reader in Theology and Head of the Department of Theology and Religious Studies. University of Winchester. **Selfishness**

Middleton, J. Richard. PhD, Vrije Universiteit, Amsterdam. Professor of Biblical Studies, Roberts Wesleyan College. **Image of God**

Mikoski, Gordon. PhD, Emory University. Assistant Professor of Christian Education, Princeton Theological Seminary. **Practices**

Miles, Rebekah. PhD, University of Chicago. Associate Professor of Ethics, Perkins School of Theology at Southern Methodist University. **Children; Family; Feminist Ethics; Professional Ethics; Work**

Miller, Keith Graber. PhD, Emory University. Professor of Bible and Religion, Department Chair, Goshen College. **Adoption; Anabaptist Ethics**

Miller, Paul D. PhD Student, School of Religion, Claremont Graduate University. Adjunct Professor of Writing, Pitzer College. **Proselytism**

Moore, Joy Jittaun. PhD, Brunel University/London School of Theology. Associate Dean for Black Church Studies and Church Relations, Duke University Divinity School. **Race**

Moreland, J. P. PhD, University of Southern California. Distinguished Professor of Philosophy, Talbot School of Theology, Biola University. **Dualism, Anthropological**

Morrow, Maria C. PhD student, University of Dayton. **Penance**

Mott, Stephen Charles. PhD, Harvard University. Professor of Christian Social Ethics Emeritus, Gordon-Conwell Theological Seminary. **Justice, Distributive**

Muck, Terry C. PhD, Northwestern University. Dean, E. Stanley Jones School of World Mission and Evangelism, Professor of Missions and World Religions, Asbury Theological Seminary. **Religious Toleration**

Musser, Sarah Stokes. PhD student, Duke University. **Killing**

Nation, Mark Thiessen. PhD, Fuller Theological Seminary. Professor of Theology, Eastern Mennonite Seminary. **Conscientious Objection; Conscription**

Ogletree, Thomas W. PhD, Vanderbilt University. Frederick Marquand Professor Emeritus of Ethics and Religious Studies, Yale University Divinity School. **Law, Civil and Criminal; Love, Love Command**

Okello, Joseph B. Onyango. PhD, University of Kentucky. Visiting Assistant Professor of Philosophy of Christian Religion, Asbury Theological Seminary. **Deontological Theories of Ethics; Theodicy**

Olson, Dennis T. PhD, Yale University. Charles T. Haley Professor of Old Testament Theology, Princeton Theological Seminary. **Adultery; Deuteronomy; Exodus; Genesis; Law; Murder; Numbers; Torah; Vows**

O'Neil, William, SJ. PhD, Yale University. Associate Professor of Social Ethics, Jesuit School of Theology, Santa Clara University. **Natural Rights**

Paeth, Scott. PhD, Princeton Theological Seminary. Assistant Professor of Religious Studies, DePaul University. **Desertion; Teleological Theories of Ethics; Trade**

Parry, Robin. PhD, University of Gloucestershire. Editorial Director, Paternoster, an imprint of Authentic Media. **Prostitution**

Payne, Richard. MD, Harvard Medical School. Professor of Medicine and Divinity, Duke Divinity School. **Hospice**

Perdue, Leo G. PhD, Vanderbilt University. Professor of Hebrew Bible, Brite Divinity School. **Wisdom Literature**

Phillips, Susan S. PhD, University of California Berkeley. Executive Director and Professor, New College Berkeley, Graduate Theological Union. **Care, Caring**

Pinches, Charles R. PhD, University of Notre Dame. Professor of Theology and Religious Studies, University of Scranton. **Faith; Hope; Patience**

Pohl, Christine D. PhD, Emory University. Professor of Social Ethics, Asbury Theological Seminary. **Hospitality; Promise and Promise-Keeping**

Portier-Young, Anathea. PhD, Duke University. Assistant Professor of Old Testament, Duke Divinity School. **Daniel; 1 Maccabees; 2 Maccabees**

Post, Stephen. PhD, University of Chicago. Professor, Director of the Center for Medical Humanities, Compassionate Care, and Bioethics, Stony Brook University. **Altruism; Dementia; Sanctity of Human Life**

Powell, Mark Allan. PhD, Union Theological Seminary, Virginia. Robert and Phyllis Leatherman Professor of New Testament, Trinity Lutheran Seminary. **Generosity; Stewardship**

Premnath, D. N. ThD, Graduate Theological Union, Berkeley. Academic Dean and Associate Professor of Hebrew Bible, St. Bernard's School of Theology and Ministry. **Habakkuk; Joel; Malachi; Nahum; Obadiah; Zephaniah**

Pressler, Carolyn. PhD, Princeton Theological Seminary. Harry C. Piper Jr. Professor of Biblical Interpretation, United Theological Seminary of the Twin Cities. **Equality; Incest; Virginity**

Rae, Scott B. PhD, University of Southern California. Professor of Christian Ethics, Talbot School of Theology, Biola University. **Dualism, Anthropological**

Rasmussen, Larry L. PhD, Union Theological Seminary, New York City. Reinhold Niebuhr Professor Emeritus of Social Ethics, Union Theological Seminary, New York City. **Economic Ethics**

Ray, Stephen G., Jr. PhD, Yale University. Neal F. and Ila A. Fisher Professor of Theology, Garrett-Evangelical Theological Seminary. **Good Works; Harm**

Reed, Esther D. PhD, Dunelm, University of Durham. Associate Professor of Theological Ethics, University of Exeter. **Government**

Reese, Ruth Anne. PhD, University of Sheffield. Associate Professor of New Testament, Asbury Theological Seminary. **1–3 John**

Reuschling, Wyndy Corbin. PhD, Drew University. Professor of Ethics and Theology, Ashland Theological Seminary. **Divine Command Theories of Ethics; Egalitarianism; Evangelical Ethics; Manipulation**

Roberts, J. J. M. PhD, Harvard University. W. H. Green Professor of Old Testament Literature Emeritus. **Necromancy**

Roels, Shirley J. PhD, Michigan State University. Professor of Management, Calvin College. **Profit**

Rosner, Brian. PhD, University of Cambridge. Professor of New Testament and Ethics, Moore Theological College. **Idolatry**

Ross, Chanon R. PhD candidate, Garrett Evangelical Theological Seminary. **Goodness; Obscenity; Propaganda; Sex Discrimination; Terrorism**

Rynkiewich, Michael A. PhD, University of Minnesota. Professor of Anthropology, Asbury Theological Seminary. **Bribery; Colonialism and Postcolonialism; Culture; Land**

Sandoval, Timothy J. PhD, Emory University. Associate Professor of Hebrew Bible, Chicago Theological Seminary. **Proverbs**

Schlimm, Matthew R. PhD, Duke University. Assistant Professor of Old Testament, University of Dubuque Theological Seminary. **Perfection; Prisoners of War**

Schuurman, Douglas J. PhD, University of Chicago. Professor of Religion, St. Olaf College. **Gratitude; Moral Law**

Scoggins, David. ThM candidate, Fuller Theological Seminary. **Fundamentalism**

Sechrest, Love L. PhD, Duke University. Assistant Professor of New Testament, Fuller Theological Seminary. **Antinomianism; Prejudice; Racism**

Sedgwick, Timothy F. PhD, Vanderbilt University. Vice President and Associate Dean for Academic Affairs, Virginia Theological Seminary. **Anglican Ethics and Moral Theology**

Sensenig, Kent Davis. PhD candidate, Fuller Theological Seminary. Assistant Professor of Bible and Religion, Eastern Mennonite University. **Resistance Movements**

Seow, Choon-Leong. PhD, Harvard University. Professor of Old Testament Language and Literature, Princeton Theological Seminary. **Job**

Shuman, Joel James. PhD, Duke University. Associate Professor of Theology and Department Chair, King's College. **Anger; Foster Care**

Sider, Ronald J. PhD, Yale University. Professor of Theology, Holistic Ministry, and Public Policy, Palmer Theological Seminary. **Economic Development**

Siker, Jeffrey S. Professor and Chair, Department of Theological Studies, Loyola Marymount University. **Homosexuality**

Siker, Judy Yates. PhD, University of North Carolina. Vice-President and Professor of New Testament and Christian Origins, San Francisco Theological Seminary. **Anti-Semitism**

Simpson, Gary M. ThD, Christ Seminary-Seminex. Professor of Systematic Theology and Director, Center for Missional Leadership, Luther Seminary. **Fruit of the Spirit; Just-War Theory; Law and Gospel; Lutheran Ethics**

Smit, Dirkie. DTh, Stellenbosch University. Professor of Systematic Theology, Stellenbosch University. **Reformed Ethics**

Smith, Jordan. PhD, Florida State University. Lecturer in Biblical Studies, The University of Iowa. **Vice**

Smith-Christopher, Daniel. DPhil, Oxford University. Professor of Theological Studies, Loyola Marymount University. **Exile**

Sours, Sarah Conrad. PhD candidate, Duke University. Visiting Instructor, Southwestern College. **Asceticism; Quality of Life; Tolerance**

Spencer, F. Scott. PhD, University of Durham. Professor of New Testament and Preaching, Baptist Theological Seminary at Richmond. **Imitation of Jesus; Jubilee**

Stackhouse, Max L. PhD, Harvard University. De Vries Professor of Theology and Public Life Emeritus, Princeton Theological Seminary. **Business Ethics; Consumerism; Covenant; Democracy; Dirty Hands; Genocide; Globalization; Humanitarianism; Public Theology and Ethics; Rights; Taxation**

Stassen, Glen H. PhD, Duke University. Lewis B. Smedes Professor of Christian Ethics, Fuller Theological Seminary. **Beatitudes; Common Good; Just-Peacemaking Theory; Sermon on the Mount**

Stratton, Lawrence M. JD, Georgetown University; PhD, Princeton Theological Seminary. Lecturer in Human Studies, Waynesburg University. **Privacy**

Stubbs, David L. PhD, Duke University. Associate Professor of Ethics and Theology, Western Theological Seminary. **Theocracy**

Sumney, Jerry L. PhD, Southern Methodist University. Professor of Biblical Studies, Lexington Theological Seminary. **Colossians; Ephesians; 1–2 Thessalonians**

Swartley, Willard M. PhD, Princeton Theological Seminary. Professor Emeritus of New Testament, Associated Mennonite Biblical Seminary. **Mutual Aid; Peace; Sabbath; Slavery**

Swinton, John. PhD, University of Aberdeen. Chair in Divinity and Religious Studies, Professor in Practical Theology and Pastoral Care, University of Aberdeen. **Mental Health; Pedophilia; Self-Esteem; Self-Harm**

Tarpley, Mark A. PhD, Southern Methodist University. **Child Abuse; Childlessness; Justification, Moral; Orthodox Ethics**

Thobaben, James R. PhD, Emory University. Professor of Church in Society, Asbury Theological Seminary. **Civil Rights; Healthcare Ethics; Motive(s); Nihilism; Social Contract**

Tink, Fletcher L. PhD, Fuller Theological Seminary. Executive Director, Bresee Institute for Metro-Ministries, Nazarene Theological Seminary. **Conflict; Homelessness**

Tousley, Nikki Coffey. PhD candidate, University of Dayton. **Virtue Ethics**

Towner, Philip H. PhD, University of Aberdeen. Dean of The Nida Institute for Biblical Scholarship, American Bible Society. **Submission and Subordination**

Tran, Jonathan. PhD, Duke University. Assistant Professor of Theological Ethics, Baylor University. **Humanity; Nationalism**

Trimiew, Darryl. PhD, Emory University. Chair of the Department of Philosophy and Religion, Medgar Evers College. **Obligation**

Trull, Joe E. ThD, Southwestern Baptist Theological Seminary. Editor, *Christian Ethics Today Journal*. **Deception**

Van Til, Kent A. PhD, Marquette University. Assistant Professor of Religion, Hope College. **World Poverty, World Hunger**

Veeneman, Mary M. PhD, Fordham University. Assistant Professor of Biblical and Theological Studies, North Park University. **Death and Dying; Dependent Care**

Verhey, Allen. PhD, Yale University. Professor of Theological Ethics, Duke University Divinity School. **Bioethics; Ethics in Scripture; Marriage and Divorce; Suicide; Theft**

Vogt, Christopher P. PhD, Boston College. Associate Professor of Moral Theology, St. John's University, New York. **Ars Moriendi Tradition, Use of Scripture in**

Vondergeest, Craig. PhD, Union Theological Seminary, Virginia. Assistant Professor of Religion, Presbyterian College. **1–2 Kings**

Wadell, Paul J. PhD, University of Notre Dame. Professor of Religious Studies, St. Norbert College. **Friendship, Friendship Ethics**

Wagner, Amy Renee. PhD candidate, Loyola University Chicago. **Autonomy; Confidentiality**

Warner, Laceye C. PhD, Trinity College, University of Bristol. Associate Dean for Academic Formation and Programs, Associate Professor of the Practice of Evangelism and Methodist Studies, The Royce and Jane Reynolds Teaching Fellow, Duke University Divinity School. **Evangelism**

Weaver, Darlene Fozard. PhD, The University of Chicago. Associate Professor of Theology and Director of The Theology Institute, Villanova University. **Birth Control; Celibacy; Conception; Eugenics; Procreation**

Webb, Stephen H. PhD, University of Chicago Divinity School. Professor of Religion and Philosophy, Wabash College. **Vegetarianism**

Wenk, Matthias. PhD, Brunel University. Chair, Department of Theology and Pastor, InstitutPlus and BewegungPlus. **Holy Spirit**

Westmoreland-White, Michael. PhD, The Southern Baptist Theological Seminary. Outreach Coordinator, Every Church a Peace Church. **Golden Rule**

Wheeler, Sondra E. PhD, Yale University. Carr Professor of Christian Ethics, Wesley Theological Seminary. **Discernment, Moral; Enemy, Enemy Love; Property and Possessions**

Williams, Paul Spencer. MA, Oxford University. David J. Brown Professor of Marketplace Theology and Leadership, Regent College. **Capitalism**

Willis, Amy C. Merrill. PhD, Emory University. Assistant Professor of Religious Studies, Gonzaga University. **Dead Sea Scrolls**

Wilson, Jonathan R. PhD, Duke University. Pioneer McDonald Professor of Theology, Carey Theological College. **Pride; Virtue(s)**

Woodley, Randy S. PhD, Asbury Theological Seminary. Distinguished Adjunct Faculty, George Fox Evangelical Seminary. **Reparation**

Wright, John W. PhD, University of Notre Dame. Professor of Theology and Christian Scriptures, Point Loma Nazarene University. **Grace; Salvation; Sanctification**

Yamada, Frank. PhD, Princeton Theological Seminary. Associate Professor of Hebrew Bible and Director for the Center for Asian American Ministries, McCormick Theological Seminary. **Rape; Shame**

Ybarrola, Steven. PhD, Brown University. Professor of Cultural Anthropology, Asbury Theological Seminary. **Cross-Cultural Ethics; Ethnic Identity, Ethnicity**

ABBREVIATIONS

General

Akk.	Akkadian
chap(s).	chapter(s)
Eng.	English
Ger.	German
Gk.	Greek
Heb.	Hebrew
Lat.	Latin
mg.	margin
pars.	parallels

Divisions of the Canon

NT	New Testament
OT	Old Testament

Ancient Texts, Text Types, and Versions

LXX	Septuagint
MT	Masoretic Text
Vulg.	Vulgate

Modern Versions

CEB	Common English Bible
KJV	King James Version
MSG	The Message
NAB	New American Bible
NASB	New American Standard Bible
NEB	New English Bible
NET	New English Translation
NIV	New International Version
NLT	New Living Translation
NRSV	New Revised Standard Version
TEV	Today's English Version (= Good News Bible)
TNIV	Today's New International Version

Old Testament

Gen.	Genesis
Exod.	Exodus
Lev.	Leviticus
Num.	Numbers
Deut.	Deuteronomy
Josh.	Joshua
Judg.	Judges
Ruth	Ruth
1–2 Sam.	1–2 Samuel
1–2 Kgs.	1–2 Kings
1–2 Chr.	1–2 Chronicles
Ezra	Ezra
Neh.	Nehemiah
Esth.	Esther
Job	Job
Ps./Pss.	Psalms
Prov.	Proverbs
Eccl.	Ecclesiastes
Song	Song of Songs
Isa.	Isaiah
Jer.	Jeremiah
Lam.	Lamentations
Ezek.	Ezekiel
Dan.	Daniel
Hos.	Hosea
Joel	Joel
Amos	Amos
Obad.	Obadiah
Jon.	Jonah
Mic.	Micah
Nah.	Nahum
Hab.	Habakkuk
Zeph.	Zephaniah
Hag.	Haggai
Zech.	Zechariah
Mal.	Malachi

New Testament

Matt.	Matthew
Mark	Mark
Luke	Luke
John	John
Acts	Acts
Rom.	Romans
1–2 Cor.	1–2 Corinthians
Gal.	Galatians
Eph.	Ephesians
Phil.	Philippians
Col.	Colossians
1–2 Thess.	1–2 Thessalonians
1–2 Tim.	1–2 Timothy
Titus	Titus
Phlm.	Philemon
Heb.	Hebrews
Jas.	James
1–2 Pet.	1–2 Peter
1–3 John	1–3 John
Jude	Jude
Rev.	Revelation

Apocrypha and Septuagint

Add. Esth.	Additions to Esther
Bar.	Baruch
Jdt.	Judith
1–2 Esd.	1–2 Esdras
1–4 Macc.	1–4 Maccabees
Sg. Three	Song of the Three Young Men
Sir.	Sirach
Sus.	Susanna
Tob.	Tobit
Wis.	Wisdom of Solomon

Old Testament Pseudepigrapha

2 Bar.	*2 Baruch (Syriac Apocalypse)*
Ezek. Trag.	Ezekiel the Tragedian
L.A.B.	*Liber antiquitatum biblicarum* (Pseudo-Philo)
Let. Aris.	*Letter of Aristeas*
Pss. Sol.	*Psalms of Solomon*
T. 12 Patr.	*Testaments of the Twelve Patriarchs*
T. Ash.	*Testament of Asher*
T. Gad	*Testament of Gad*
T. Iss.	*Testament of Issachar*
T. Levi	*Testament of Levi*
T. Reu.	*Testament of Reuben*
T. Job	*Testament of Job*

Dead Sea Scrolls

CD-A	*Damascus Document*[a]
1QS	*Rule of the Community*

Rabbinic Tractates

Ber.	*Berakot*
Giṭ.	*Giṭṭin*
Menaḥ.	*Menaḥot*
Roš. Haš.	*Roš Haššanah*
Šabb.	*Šabbat*
Sanh.	*Sanhedrin*
Šebu.	*Šebuʿot*
Yoma	*Yoma* (= *Kippurim*)

Other Rabbinic Works

ʾAbot R. Nat.	*ʾAbot de Rabbi Nathan*
Rab.	*Rabbah* (+ biblical book)
Sipre	*Sipre*

Apostolic Fathers

Barn.	*Epistle of Barnabas*
1–2 Clem.	*1–2 Clement*
Did.	*Didache*
Diog.	*Epistle to Diognetus*
Herm. Mand.	*Shepherd of Hermes, Mandate(s)*
Herm. Sim.	*Shepherd of Hermes, Similitude(s)*
Ign. *Magn.*	Ignatius, *To the Magnesians*
Ign. *Rom.*	Ignatius, *To the Romans*
Pol. *Phil.*	Polycarp, *To the Philippians*

New Testament Apocrypha and Pseudepigrapha

Apos. Con.	*Apostolic Constitutions and Canons*

Papyri

P.Bod.	Bodmer Papyri

Greek and Latin Works

Ambrose

Hel.	*De Helia et Jejunio*
Vid.	*De viduis*
Virg.	*De virginibus*

Aristotle

De an.	*De anima*
Eth. nic.	*Ethica nichomachea (Nichomachean Ethics)*
Pol.	*Politica*

Athanasius

Inc.	*De incarnatione (On the Incarnation)*

Augustine

Civ.	*De civitate Dei (The City of God)*
Conf.	*Confessionum libri XIII (Confessions)*
Coniug. adult.	*De coniugiis adulterinis (On Adulterous Marriages)*
Corrept.	*De correptione et gratia (Admonition and Grace)*
Doctr. chr.	*De doctrina Christiana (Christian Instruction)*
Enarrat. Ps.	*Enarrationes in Psalmos (Commentary on the Psalms)*
Enchir.	*Enchiridion de fide, spe, et caritate*
Ep.	*Epistulae (Letters)*
Grat.	*De gratia et libero arbitrio (Grace and Free Will)*
Lib.	*De libero arbitrio (Free Will)*
Mor. eccl.	*De moribus ecclesiae catholicae (The Way of Life of the Catholic Church)*
Pat.	*De patientia (Patience)*
Perf.	*De perfectione justitiae hominis (Perfection in Human Righteousness)*
Serm. dom.	*De sermone Domini in monte (Sermon on the Mount)*
Tract. ep. Jo.	*In epistulam Johannis ad Parthos tractatus (Tractates on the First Epistle of John)*
Tract. ev. Jo.	*In evangelium Johannis tractatus (Tractates on the Gospel of John)*
Virginit.	*De sancta virginitate (Holy Virginity)*

Cicero

Tusc.	*Tusculanae disputationes (Tusculan Disputations)*

Clement of Alexandria

Exc.	*Excerpta ex Theodoto (Excerpts from Theodotus)*
Paed.	*Paedagogus (Christ the Educator)*
Quis. div.	*Quis dives salvetur (Salvation of the Rich)*

Diogenes Laertius

Lives	*Lives of Eminent Philosophers*

Epictetus

Diatr.	*Diatribai (Dissertationes)*

Gregory of Nyssa

Op. hom.	*De opificio hominis (On the Making of Man)*

Herodotus

Hist.	*Historiae (Histories)*

Irenaeus

Haer.	*Adversus haereses*

Jerome

Epist.	*Epistulae*

Josephus

Ag. Ap.	*Against Apion*
Ant.	*Jewish Antiquities*
J.W.	*Jewish War*

Justin Martyr

1 Apol.	*Apologia i (First Apology)*
2 Apol.	*Apologia ii (Second Apology)*
Dial.	*Dialogus cum Tryphone (Dialogue with Trypho)*

Lactantius

Inst.	*Divinarum institutionum libri VII (The Divine Institutes)*

Onasander

Strat.	*Strategikos (On the Duties of a General)*

Origen

Hom. Num.	*Homiliae in Numeros*
Princ.	*De principiis (First Principles)*

Philo

Alleg. Interp.	*Allegorical Interpretation*
Embassy	*On the Embassy to Gaius*
Migration	*On the Migration of Abraham*
Moses	*On the Life of Moses*
QG	*Questions and Answers on Genesis*
Sacrifices	*On the Sacrifices of Cain and Abel*
Spec. Laws	*On the Special Laws*

Plato

Resp.	*Respublica (Republic)*

Pliny the Elder

Nat.	*Naturalis historia (Natural History)*

Plutarch

Cato Maj.	*Cato Major (Cato the Elder)*
Mar.	*Marius*
Mor.	*Moralia*

Quintilian

Inst.	*Institutio oratoria*

Seneca

Ep.	*Epistulae morales*

Sophocles

Aj.	*Ajax*

Tertullian

Apol.	*Apologeticus (Apology)*
Idol.	*De idololatria* (Idolatry)
Marc.	*Adversus Marcionem (Against Marcion)*
Scap.	*Ad Scapulam (To Scapula)*
Ux.	*Ad uxorem (To His Wife)*

Thucydides

Pel. War	*The Peloponnesian War*

Other Authors

John Calvin

Institutes	*Institutes of the Christian Religion*

Thomas Aquinas

Comm. John	*Commentary on the Gospel of Saint John*
Comm. Phil.	*Commentary on Saint Paul's Letter to the Philippians*
ST	*Summa theologiae*

Secondary Sources

AARAS	American Academy of Religion Academy Series
AB	Anchor Bible
ACCS	Ancient Christian Commentary on Scripture
ACW	Ancient Christian Writers
AGJU	Arbeiten zur Geschichte des antiken Judentums und des Urchristentums
AJB	*American Journal of Bioethics*
AJIL	*American Journal of International Law*
AJMG	*American Journal of Medical Genetics*
AK	Arbeiten zur Kirchengeschichte
AnBib	Analecta biblica
ANESSup	Ancient Near Eastern Studies: Supplements
ANTC	Abingdon New Testament Commentaries
AOAT	Alter Orient und Altes Testament
AOS	American Oriental Society
AOTC	Abingdon Old Testament Commentaries
ASCE	*Annual of the Society of Christian Ethics*
ATANT	Abhandlungen zur Theologie des Alten und Neuen Testaments
AThR	*Anglican Theological Review*
ATR	*Australasian Theological Review*
AUS	American University Studies
BA	*Biblical Archaeology*
BBR	*Bulletin for Biblical Research*
BDB	Brown, F., S. R. Driver, and C. A. Briggs. *A Hebrew and English Lexicon of the Old Testament*. Oxford, 1907
BECNT	Baker Exegetical Commentary on the New Testament
BETL	Bibliotheca ephemeridum theologicarum lovaniensium
BibInt	*Biblical Interpretation*
BibSem	Biblical Seminar
BibW	*The Biblical World*
BIS	Biblical Interpretation Series
BJS	Brown Judaic Studies
BMJ	*British Medical Journal*
BPEJ	*Business and Professional Ethics Journal*
BTB	*Biblical Theology Bulletin*
BZAW	Beihefte zur Zeitschrift für die alttestamentliche Wissenschaft
BZNW	Beihefte zur Zeitschrift für die neutestamentliche Wissenschaft
CathM	*Catholic Mind*
CBET	Contributions to Biblical Exegesis and Theology
CBQ	*Catholic Biblical Quarterly*
CBQMS	Catholic Biblical Quarterly Monograph Series
CBR	*Currents in Biblical Research*
CC	Continental Commentaries
CEJL	Commentaries on Early Jewish Literature
CH	*Church History*
Chm	*Churchman*
ChrBio	*Christian Bioethics*
ChrCent	*Christian Century*
ChrCr	*Christianity and Crisis*
ChrTo	*Christianity Today*
CIT	Current Issues in Theology
CMQ	*Catholic Medical Quarterly*
ConBNT	Coniectanea biblica: New Testament Series
ConBOT	Coniectanea biblica: Old Testament Series
CSCD	Cambridge Studies in Christian Doctrine
CSHJ	Chicago Studies in the History of Judaism
CSIR	Cambridge Studies in Ideology and Religion
CSP	Cambridge Studies in Philosophy

CSPB	Cambridge Studies in Philosophy and Biology
CSR	*Christian Scholar's Review*
CSRT	Cambridge Studies in Religious Traditions
CTHP	Cambridge Texts in the History of Philosophy
CTR	*Criswell Theological Review*
CurTM	*Currents in Theology and Mission*
EgT	*Église et théologie*
EH	Europäische Hochschulschriften
ERS	*Ethnic and Racial Studies*
ESCT	Edinburgh Studies in Constructive Theology
ETL	*Ephemerides theologicae lovanienses*
ETMP	*Ethical Theory and Moral Practice*
EUS	European University Studies
EUSLR	Emory University Studies in Law and Religion
EvQ	*Evangelical Quarterly*
ExAud	*Ex Auditu*
ExpTim	*Expository Times*
FAT	Forschungen zum Alten Testament
FC	Fathers of the Church
FCB	Feminist Companion to the Bible
FCNTECW	Feminist Companion to the New Testament and Early Christian Writings
FOTL	Forms of Old Testament Literature
FRLANT	Forschungen zur Religion und Literatur des Alten und Neuen Testaments
GAP	Guides to Apocrypha and Pseudepigrapha
GBS	Guides to Biblical Scholarship
GG	God and Globalization
GT	Guides to Theology
HBM	Hebrew Bible Monographs
HBT	*Horizons in Biblical Theology*
HCR	*Hastings Center Report*
HNT	Handbuch zum Neuen Testament
HorTh	Horizons in Theology
HSM	Harvard Semitic Monographs
HTS	Harvard Theological Studies
HUT	Hermeneutische Untersuchungen zur Theologie
IBC	Interpretation: A Bible Commentary for Teaching and Preaching
IBMR	*International Bulletin of Missionary Research*
IFT	Introductions in Feminist Theology
IJPT	*International Journal of Practical Theology*
IJSE	*International Journal of Social Economics*
Int	*Interpretation*
IR	Introduction to Religion
IRSC	Interpretation: Resources for the Use of Scripture in the Church
IRT	Issues in Religion and Theology
ISBL	Indiana Studies in Biblical Literature
JAAR	*Journal of the American Academy of Religion*
JAMA	*Journal of the American Medical Association*
JBL	*Journal of Biblical Literature*
JBQ	*Jewish Bible Quarterly*
JECS	*Journal of Early Christian Studies*
JES	*Journal of Ecumenical Studies*
JETS	*Journal of the Evangelical Theological Society*
JHP	*Journal of the History of Philosophy*
JHS	*Journal of Hebrew Scriptures*
JJS	*Journal of Jewish Studies*
JLR	*Journal of Law and Religion*
JNES	*Journal of Near Eastern Studies*
JPastT	*Journal of Pastoral Theology*
JPC	*Journal of Pastoral Care*
JPE	*Journal of the Philosophy of Education*
JPSP	*Journal of Personality and Social Psychology*
JPSTC	JPS Torah Commentary
JPT	*Journal of Pentecostal Theology*
JPTSup	Journal of Pentecostal Theology: Supplement Series
JPsyC	*Journal of Psychology and Christianity*
JR	*Journal of Religion*
JRE	*Journal of Religious Ethics*
JRT	*Journal of Religious Thought*
JSCE	*Journal of the Society of Christian Ethics*
JSJSup	Supplements to the Journal for the Study of Judaism
JSNT	*Journal for the Study of the New Testament*
JSNTSup	Journal for the Study of the New Testament: Supplement Series
JSOT	*Journal for the Study of the Old Testament*
JSOTSup	Journal for the Study of the Old Testament: Supplement Series
JSP	*Journal for the Study of the Pseudepigrapha*
JSexR	*Journal of Sex Research*
JTS	*Journal of Theological Studies*
KD	*Kerygma und Dogma*
LAI	Library of Ancient Israel
LBS	Library of Biblical Studies
LCC	Library of Christian Classics
LCL	Loeb Classical Library
LHBOTS	Library of Hebrew Bible/Old Testament Studies
LLA	Library of Liberal Arts
LNTS	Library of New Testament Studies
LPT	Library of Protestant Thought
LTE	Library of Theological Ethics
MCL	Martin Classical Lectures
MdB	Le monde de la Bible
MNTS	McMaster New Testament Studies
ModTh	*Modern Theology*
MQR	*Mennonite Quarterly Review*
MTMA	Moral Traditions and Moral Arguments
MTS	Moral Traditions Series
NAC	New American Commentary
NCamBC	New Cambridge Bible Commentary
Neot	*Neotestamentica*
NIBC	New International Bible Commentary
NICNT	New International Commentary on the New Testament
NICOT	New International Commentary on the Old Testament

NIGTC	New International Greek Testament Commentary
NIVAC	NIV Application Commentary
NovT	*Novum Testamentum*
NovTSup	Supplements to Novum Testamentum
NPNF[2]	*Nicene and Post-Nicene Fathers*, Series 2
NSBT	New Studies in Biblical Theology
NSCE	New Studies in Christian Ethics
NTL	New Testament Library
NTM	New Testament Monographs
NTR	New Testament Readings
NTS	*New Testament Studies*
NTT	New Testament Theology
NTTS	New Testament Tools and Studies
OBT	Overtures to Biblical Theology
OECS	Oxford Early Christian Studies
OSTE	Oxford Studies in Theological Ethics
OTG	Old Testament Guides
OTL	Old Testament Library
OTM	Old Testament Message
OThM	Oxford Theological Monographs
OTR	Old Testament Readings
OTS	Old Testament Studies
OtSt	Oudtestamentische Studiën
PBM	Paternoster Biblical Monographs
PBTM	Paternoster Biblical and Theological Monographs
PL	Patrologia Latina [= Patrologiae cursus completus: Series latina]. Edited by J.-P. Migne. 217 vols. Paris, 1844–1864
PM	Philosophy and Medicine
PPA	*Philosophy and Public Affairs*
PR	*Philosophical Review*
ProEccl	*Pro ecclesia*
PRS	*Perspectives in Religious Studies*
PSB	*Princeton Seminary Bulletin*
QR	*Quarterly Review*
R&T	*Religion and Theology*
RA	Revealing Antiquity
RB	*Revue biblique*
RBS	Resources for Biblical Study
RelS	*Religious Studies*
RelSRev	*Religious Studies Review*
RevExp	*Review and Expositor*
RFCC	Religion in the First Christian Centuries
RFIA	*Review of Faith and International Affairs*
RGRW	Religions in the Graeco-Roman World
RMT	Readings in Moral Theology
SBJT	*Southern Baptist Journal of Theology*
SBL	Studies in Biblical Literature
SBLAB	Society of Biblical Literature Academia Biblica
SBLDS	Society of Biblical Literature Dissertation Series
SBLEJL	Society of Biblical Literature Early Judaism and Its Literature
SBLMS	Society of Biblical Literature Monograph Series
SBLSymS	Society of Biblical Literature Symposium Series
SBS	Stuttgarter Bibelstudien
SBT	Studies in Biblical Theology
SCE	*Studies in Christian Ethics*
SCJ	*Sixteenth Century Journal*
SEC	Studies in Early Christianity
SecCent	*Second Century*
SHANE	Studies in the History of the Ancient Near East
SHBC	Smith & Helwys Bible Commentary
SHCT	Studies in the History of Christian Thought
SHJ	Studying the Historical Jesus
SHS	Scripture and Hermeneutics Series
SJSJ	Supplements to the Journal for the Study of Judaism
SL	*Studia Liturgica*
SLMAHR	Studies in the Late Middle Ages, Humanism, and the Reformation
SMRT	Studies in Medieval and Reformation Traditions
SNTSMS	Society for New Testament Studies Monograph Series
SNTW	Studies in the New Testament and Its World
SocRel	*Sociology of Religion*
SP	Sacra Pagina
SPS	Studies in Peace and Scripture
SRRCC	Studies in the Reformed Rites of the Catholic Church
STI	Studies in Theological Interpretation
STR	Studies in Theology and Religion
SVTQ	*St. Vladimir's Theological Quarterly*
SwJT	*Southwestern Journal of Theology*
TCrS	Text-Critical Studies
TGl	*Theologie und Glaube*
THNTC	Two Horizons New Testament Commentary
ThTo	*Theology Today*
TS	*Theological Studies*
TSNABR	Bishop Henry McNeal Turner Studies in North American Black Religion
TTC	Theology for the Twenty-First Century
TUMSR	Trinity University Monograph Series in Religion
TW	*Theologische Wissenschaft*
TynBul	*Tyndale Bulletin*
UBT	Understanding Biblical Themes
UCOP	University of Cambridge Oriental Publications
UNT	Untersuchungen zum Neuen Testament
VT	*Vetus Testamentum*
VTSup	Supplements to Vetus Testamentum
WBC	Word Biblical Commentary
WestBC	Westminster Bible Companion
WesTJ	*Wesleyan Theological Journal*
WMANT	Wissenschaftliche Monographien zum Alten und Neuen Testament
WUNT	Wissenschaftliche Untersuchungen zum Neuen Testament
WW	*Word and World*

INTRODUCTION

JOEL B. GREEN, GENERAL EDITOR

Forty years ago, when James M. Gustafson surveyed the state of the discipline in Christian ethics, he called attention to the relation of Christian ethics and biblical studies and lamented the "paucity of material that relates the two areas in a scholarly way" (Gustafson 337). Many echoed Gustafson's complaint, both from within Christian ethics and from within biblical studies. The complaint prompted the development of a considerable literature, as both moral theologians and biblical scholars attempted to relate Scripture and ethics "in a scholarly way." Whatever else may be lamented about scholarly attention to the relation of Scripture and ethics, one can no longer lament a "paucity of material."

The growth of this literature is one reason for the *Dictionary of Scripture and Ethics*. Students need a reference tool that will survey the literature and provide an introduction to the ethics of Scripture, to the relevance of Scripture to contemporary moral questions, and to the paths by which one might make a way from ethics to Scripture and back again. Pastors need a reference tool that will survey the relation of Scripture and ethics in a way relevant to their tasks of preaching, teaching, and counseling. And specialists in biblical studies or in Christian ethics who want to enter a conversation with the specialists in the other discipline need a reference tool that will provide an account of particular features of the other discipline that are especially relevant to the conversation between disciplines.

A second reason for compiling the *Dictionary of Scripture and Ethics*, however, is that for all the scholarly attention to the relation of Scripture and ethics, it remains a labyrinth. Among some, and for a variety of reasons, the study of Scripture has little, if anything, to contribute to the study of moral theology. There are biblical scholars who regard it as no part of the task of their discipline to form or inform the way Christians understand and embody Scripture. And there are Christian ethicists who regard the biblical text as at best marginally important to the ways in which Christian ethics should be undertaken. On the other hand, there are some who regard the Bible as a timeless moral code that simply needs to be repeated and obeyed today. For still others, the biblical witness may be relevant today, but the trail from ancient Scripture to contemporary moral questions is an arduous one, best left to those who are experts on that trail, to a scholarly or ecclesiastical magisterium. And for yet others, including many scholars, the complexities and language of one discipline or the other make a meaningful conversation difficult, if not impossible.

Negotiating the Labyrinth

In some ways, reasons for the troubled relationship between the Bible and ethics are easy to understand. Straightforward attempts to follow the Bible on any number of issues have long been frustrated by changing contexts. The world of Leviticus is not the world of 1 Corinthians, and neither of these is our world. Even if the theological considerations of religious communities demand wrestling with the ramifications of these ancient texts for faith and life, it remains the case that, historically speaking, they were not written "for/to/about us." Within the Bible itself, we find attempts to reappropriate legal texts, for example, in new settings, and these interpretive impulses continued—and continue—in all sorts of attempts to comment on, apply, and embody these writings. Indeed, a common feature of ancient Judaism was "the realization that there was no pure teaching of Revelation apart from its regeneration or clarification through an authoritative type of exegesis" (Fishbane 4). Moving outside the interpretation of biblical texts among the biblical writers themselves, the translation of the Hebrew Bible into Greek (LXX) and the development of the targumic tradition served further to codify interpretive traditions. The Qumran scrolls evidence a vast exegetical enterprise, with two commitments not so much juxtaposed as intertwined: to the authority of the Scriptures and to their interpretation and embodiment in the community of the faithful. The traditions of midrashim that subsequently grew up around the Scriptures similarly engaged in a dialogue with the biblical texts, extending their meaning from the past into the present, with "readers fighting to find what they must in the holy text" (Boyarin 16). That is, precisely because of the status of the biblical texts as Scripture, their immediacy to contemporary readers was a nonnegotiable presupposition; their capacity to speak on God's behalf in the readers' present and to be embodied in their lives was crucial.

The rise of historical criticism brought to the surface another challenge: diversity within the biblical canon. How does one present a *biblical* perspective on a given question when the Bible contains within its covers diverse approaches to the same issue? One answer has been a kind of harmonization that makes all of the voices speak as though they were one, in spite of the fact that no single voice in Scripture, taken on its own, could ever be heard to speak in just that way. Another answer has been to allow one voice to speak for all. In Protestant circles, the voice of choice has typically been Pauline, especially as heard in Romans. When thinking of the theology of James or John or Jude, according to this strategy, one is more likely to hear the voice of the Pauline ventriloquist than that of James, John, or Jude. A third answer has focused on the search for the coordinating center of Scripture—"covenant," for example, or "reconciliation"—the effect of which has been to mute alternatives within the canon. A fourth has been to focus on Scripture's metanarrative, a unity that lies in the character and activity of God that comes to expression in various but recognizably similar ways in these various texts. Fifth, many have found in the diversity of Scripture a reason to reject outright the possibility of using Scripture as a normative source in theology and ethics.

Other issues challenge us. We find in the Bible puzzling texts, some that offend both our own sensibilities and those of our forebears. What are we to make of the imprecatory psalms, for example, or apparently divinely sanctioned violence within families or among peoples, or strained rhetoric and oppressive perspectives regarding the status and role of women? These are not new questions, but have long tested the interpretive ingenuity of the Bible's readers (Thompson). We face issues today about which texts from another time and place can hardly be expected to have anything to say, at least not in a direct way. The *Dictionary of Scripture and Ethics* does not pretend to resolve all of these problems but rather serves to codify the issues and to identify ways in which they are being acknowledged and addressed in contemporary discussion.

The *Dictionary of Scripture and Ethics* aims to provide a map that will locate and orient conversations about the relation of Scripture and ethics. With essays and contributors representative of the full array of relevant concerns, the *Dictionary of Scripture and Ethics* will become a useful, indeed essential, resource to which students, pastors, and scholars turn for orientation and perspective on Scripture and ethics. It may be too much to hope that this dictionary will provide a way out of the labyrinth, but it aims to provide a little light on the path. Then perhaps the confidence of the psalmist that "[God's] word is a light to [our] path" (Ps. 119:105b) may be restored in the church.

Organization

At the outset the *Dictionary of Scripture and Ethics* departs from a conventional alphabetical listing of entries by providing three introductory articles. These survey, respectively, ethics within Scripture, historical perspectives on the place of Scripture in moral theology, and methodological issues concerning the relevance of Scripture to contemporary moral theology. These articles provide an orientation for the volume and for its users. Many of the items surveyed in these introductory articles will be more fully developed in other entries of the dictionary, but the introductory articles will serve to set the more particular entries in a larger context. So, for example, the introductory essay on ethics within Scripture will be developed further and sometimes challenged by the separate entries on each of the biblical books and by additional articles on genres, codes, and so forth found within Scripture. Similarly, the introductory article on historical perspectives of the role of Scripture in moral theology will be supplemented and sometimes challenged by separate entries on different communities of interpretation, on different key figures in the history of moral theology, and on the history of interpretation of some important biblical and moral topics. Finally, the issues surveyed in the introductory article on methodological questions concerning the relevance of Scripture to moral concerns will be revisited by some of the entries both on Scripture and on particular moral issues.

Among the entries located within the alphabetical listings are three different kinds of articles.

There are, first, articles on the relation of ethics and Scripture. There are articles, for example, on certain modes of moral reasoning and the ways in which those modes of moral reasoning have shaped appeals to Scripture in Christian ethics. There are articles on distinctive communities and traditions of biblical interpretation and moral reflection, highlighting the ways in which such communities and traditions shape appeals to Scripture in Christian ethics. There are entries on some important hermeneutical and methodological considerations concerning the relation of Scripture and Christian ethics.

There are, second, articles on ethics within Scripture. These entries focus on the ethics of each of the books of the Bible and on the possible significance of each book for contemporary Christian ethics. They sketch some of the moral issues explicitly addressed in the book and some of the patterns of moral reasoning displayed in the book. They supplement the introductory essay on "Ethics in Scripture," but they are also supplemented by later articles on genres, collections, and passages found within Scripture. So, for example, one will find in addition to the entry on Matthew an entry on the Sermon on the Mount. The entry on Exodus might be supplemented by attention to entries in the alphabetical section on Law and the Covenant. In addition to articles focused on biblical books, however, articles attending to the ethics within Scripture will focus on passages that have played a particularly significant role in Christian ethics, for example, the Jubilee, the Golden Rule, and the Love Commandment; on the relevance of particular genres within Scripture to moral reflection; and on some of the material that may, as some have argued, have provided documentary sources for the canonical books.

The third type of article within the alphabetical listings is focused on issues in Christian ethics. These issues include both classical and contemporary issues. The entries include both major "orientation" articles on topics like bioethics, ecological ethics, economic ethics, political ethics, and sexual ethics, and shorter articles focused on more particular issues, like abortion, technology, capitalism, pacifism, and marriage. Again the more narrowly focused articles will supplement the broader "orientation" articles. Some of these articles begin with attention to Scripture and move toward attention to the contemporary discussion; some begin by introducing the contemporary issues and then retrieve biblical materials; but each entry works to join Scripture and ethics.

With its introductory essays, entries on the biblical books, major "orientation" articles, and different types of entries with their bibliographies and cross-references, the *Dictionary of Scripture and Ethics* will be a valuable resource for all of those students, pastors, and scholars who want Scripture to form and inform their moral reflection and conversation and want their study of Scripture to be formed and informed by an interest in ethics.

Bibliography

Boyarin, D. *Intertextuality and the Reading of Midrash*. ISBL. University of Indiana Press, 1990; Fishbane, M. "Inner-biblical Exegesis: Types and Strategies of Interpretation in Ancient Israel." Pages 3–18 in *The Garments of Torah: Essays in Biblical Hermeneutics*. ISBL. Indiana University Press, 1989; Gustafson, J. M. "Christian Ethics." Pages 285–354 in *Religion*, ed. P. Ramsey. Prentice-Hall, 1965; Thompson, J. L. *Reading the Bible with the Dead*. Eerdmans, 2007.

ETHICS IN SCRIPTURE

ALLEN VERHEY

Ethics may be defined as disciplined reflection concerning moral conduct and character. In Scripture, such reflection is always disciplined by convictions about God's will and way and by commitments to be faithful to God. Biblical ethics is inalienably theological. To sunder biblical ethics from the convictions about God that surround it and sustain it is to distort it. The fundamental unity of biblical ethics is simply this: there is one God in Scripture, and it is that one God who calls forth the creative reflection and faithful response of those who would be God's people.

That unity, however, is joined to an astonishing diversity. The Bible contains many books and more traditions, each addressed first to a particular community of God's people facing concrete questions of conduct in specific cultural and social contexts. Its reflections on the moral life, moreover, come in diverse modes of discourse. They come sometimes in statute, sometimes in story. They come sometimes in proverb, sometimes in prophetic promises (or threats). They come sometimes in remembering the past, sometimes in envisioning the future. The one God of Scripture assures the unity of biblical ethics, but there is no simple unitive understanding even of that one God or of that one God's will. To force biblical ethics into a timeless and systematic unity is to impoverish it. Still, there is but one God, to whom loyalty is due and to whom God's people respond in all of their responses to changing moral contexts.

Ethics in the Old Testament

Ethics in Torah

The one God formed a people by deliverance and covenant. The story was told in countless recitals of Israel's faith. The God of Abraham heard their cries when they were slaves, rescued them from Pharaoh's oppression, and made them a people with a covenant (e.g., Deut. 6:20–25; 26:5–9; Josh. 24:2–13). The covenant, like an ancient suzerainty treaty, acknowledged and confirmed that God was the great king of Israel and that Israel was God's people. (George E. Mendenhall provided the classic description of ancient treaties in relation to Torah.) And like those ancient treaties, Israel's covenant began by identifying God as the great king and by reciting God's kindness to Israel (e.g., Exod. 20:2). It continued with stipulations forbidding loyalty to any other god as sovereign and requiring justice and peace in the land (e.g., Exod. 20:3–17). And it ended with provisions for the periodic renewal of covenant and with assurances of God's blessing on faithfulness to covenant and the threat of punishment for violation of the covenant (e.g., Exod. 23:22–33).

The remembered story and the covenant formed a community and its common life. And if Gerhard von Rad is right, they also provided a framework for the gathering of stories and stipulations into larger narrative and legal traditions (J, E, D, and P; various codes), and finally, for the gathering of those traditions into the Torah.

Much of the Torah (usually translated "law") is legal material. Various collections (e.g., the Decalogue [Exod. 20:1–17; Deut. 5:6–21]; the Covenant Code [Exod. 20:22–23:19]; the Holiness Code [Lev. 17–26]; the Deuteronomic Code [Deut. 4:44–28:46]) can be identified and correlated with particular periods of Israel's history. The later collections sometimes revised earlier legislation. It was evidently not the case that the whole law was given at once as a timeless code. Rather, the lawmakers displayed both fidelity to the earlier legal traditions and creativity with them as they responded both to new situations and to God.

Although the Torah contains no tidy distinction between ceremonial, civil, and moral laws, the traditional rubrics do identify significant functions of the legal material. As "ceremonial," the legal materials in Torah struggled against temptations offered by foreign cults to covenant infidelity and nurtured a communal memory and commitment to covenant. As "civil," the Torah had a fundamentally theocratic vision. In this theocratic vision, the rulers were ruled too; they were subjects, not creators, of the law. Such a conviction, by its warnings against royal despotism, had a democratizing effect. As "moral," the statutes protected the family and its economic participation in God's gift of the land. They protected persons and their property. They required fairness in disputes and economic transactions. And they provided for the care and protection of vulnerable members of the society, such as widows, orphans, resident aliens, and the poor.

The legal materials never escaped the story or the covenant. Set in the context of narrative and covenant, the legal traditions were construed as grateful response to God's works and ways. Moreover, the story formed and informed the statutes. The story of the one God who heard the cries of slaves in Egypt stood behind the legal protections for the vulnerable (e.g., Exod. 22:21–23; Lev. 19:33–34).

The narratives of the Torah were morally significant in their own right. Artfully told, they rendered the work and the will of the God to whom loyalty was due. They put on display something of God's cause and character, the cause and character to be shared by the faithful people of God. Noteworthy among such narratives were the stories of creation. They affirmed that the one God of covenant is the God of creation too. This is no tribal deity; this is the one God of the universe. In the beginning there is a narrative prohibition of idolatry as compelling as any statute; nothing that God made is god. In the beginning there is a celebration of the material world and a narrative prohibition of anything like Platonic or gnostic dualism; all that God made is good. It was, in the beginning, an orderly and peaceable world. There is a narrative invitation to a common life of gratitude for the blessings of God. When the curse fell heavy on God's good creation, the one God would not let human sin or the curse have the last word in God's world. God came again to covenant and to bless, blessing Abraham with the promise that in him "all the families of the earth shall be blessed" (Gen. 12:1–3). The Yahwist's stories of the patriarchs not only trace the blessing of David's empire to that promise but also form political dispositions to use the technical and administrative skills of empire to bless the subject nations (Gen. 18–19; 26; 30:27–28; 39–41) (see Wolff).

Ethics in the Prophets

The one God who created the world, who rescued slaves from Pharaoh and made covenant with a people, spoke to those people through the prophets. The prophets came as messengers of the great king. They came with a particular word for a particular time, but they always reminded the people of the story and the covenant and called the people to respond faithfully.

Frequently, in resistance to unfaithfulness, they brought a word of judgment. The sum of their indictment was always the same: the people have violated the covenant (e.g., 1 Kgs. 19:10, 14; Hos. 8:1). Concretely—and the message of the prophet was always concrete—some specific idolatry or injustice was condemned as infidelity to the covenant. The infidelity of idolatry was never merely a cultic matter. The claims of Baal, for example, involved the fertility of wombs and land and an account of ownership. The prophetic announcement of God's greater power freed the people to farm a land stripped of claims to divinity but acknowledged as God's gift, and it required them to share the produce of that land with the poor. The infidelity of injustice was never merely a moral matter, for the one God of covenant demanded justice, and the welfare of the poor and powerless was the best index of covenant fidelity. So the prophets denounced unjust rulers, greedy merchants, corrupt judges, and the complacent rich. Their harshest criticisms, however, were aimed at those who celebrated covenant in ritual and ceremony but violated it by failing to protect the poor and powerless (e.g., Amos 5:21–24).

On the other side of God's judgment the prophets saw and announced the good future of God. God will reign and establish both peace and justice, not only in Israel but also among the nations, and not only among the nations but also in the whole creation. That future was not contingent on human striving, but it already made claims on the present, affecting human vision and dispositions and actions. The prophets and the faithful were to be ready to suffer for the sake of God's cause in the world.

Ethics in Wisdom

The will and way of the one God could be known not only in the great events of liberation and covenant, not only in the oracles of the prophets, but also in the regularities of nature and experience. When the sages of Israel gave moral counsel, they seldom appealed directly to Torah or to covenant. Their advice concerning moral character and conduct was, rather, disciplined and tested by experience.

Carefully attending to nature and experience, the wise comprehended the basic principles operative in the world. To conform to these principles was at once a matter of piety, prudence, and morality. The one God who created the world has established and secured the order and stability of ordinary life. So the sage could give advice about eating and drinking, about sleeping and working, about the way to handle money and anger, about relating to friends and enemies and women and fools, about when to speak and when to be silent—in short, about almost anything that is a part of human experience.

The ethics of the sage tended to be conservative, for the experience of the community over time provided a fund of wisdom, but the immediacy of experience kept the tradition open to challenge and revision. The ethics of the sage tended to be prudential, but experience sometimes could teach that the righteous may suffer, and that there is no tidy fit between piety, prudence, and morality (Job). The ethics of the sage tended to delight both in the simple things of life, such as the love between a man and a woman (Song of Songs), and in the quest for wisdom itself. Experience itself, however, could teach that wisdom has its limits in the inscrutable (Job 28), and that the way things seem to work in the world cannot simply be identified with the ways of God (Ecclesiastes).

Wisdom reflected about conduct and character quite differently than did the Torah and the prophets, but, like "the beginning of wisdom" (Prov. 1:7; 9:10), "the end of the matter" was a reminder of covenant: "Fear God and keep his commandments; for that is the whole duty of every one" (Eccl. 12:13). The beginning and end of wisdom kept wisdom in touch with Torah, struggling to keep Torah in touch with experience, and covenant in touch with creation.

Ethics in the New Testament

The one God of creation and covenant, of Abraham and Israel, of Moses and David, of prophet and sage raised the crucified Jesus of Nazareth from the dead. That good news was celebrated among his followers as the vindication of Jesus and his message, as the disclosure of God's power and purpose, and as the guarantee of God's good future. The resurrection was a cause for great joy; it was also the basis for NT ethics and its exhortations to live in memory and in hope, to see moral conduct and character in the light of Jesus' story, and to discern a life and a common life "worthy of the gospel of Christ" (Phil. 1:27).

Jesus and the Gospels

The resurrection was the vindication of Jesus of Nazareth as the Christ. He had come announcing that "the kingdom of God has come near" (Mark 1:15), that the coming cosmic sovereignty of God, the good future of God, was at hand. And he had made that future present; he had made its power felt already in his words of blessing and in his works of healing. He called the people to repent, to form their conduct and character in response to the good news of that coming future. He called his followers to "watch" for it and to pray for it, to welcome its presence, and to form community and character in ways that anticipated that future and responded to the ways that future was already making its power felt in him.

Such was the eschatological shape of Jesus' ethic. He announced the future in axioms such as "Many who are first will be last, and the last will be first" (Mark 10:31; Matt. 19:30; Luke 13:30). He made that future present by his presence among the disciples "as one who serves" (Luke 22:27; cf. Matt. 20:28; Mark 10:45; John 13:2–17). And he called the people to welcome such a future and to follow him in commands such as "Whoever wants to be first must be last of all and servant of all" (Mark 9:35; cf. 10:44). To delight already in a coming kingdom in which the poor are blessed was even now to be carefree about wealth (Matt. 6:25, 31, 34; Luke 12:22) and to give generously to help the poor (Mark 10:21; Luke 12:33). To welcome even now a kingdom that belongs to children (Mark 10:14) was to welcome and to bless them (Mark 9:37). To respond faithfully to a future that was signaled by Jesus' open conversation with women (e.g., Mark 7:24–30; John 4:1–26) was already to treat women as equals. To celebrate God's forgiveness that made its power felt in Jesus' fellowship with sinners (e.g., Mark 2:5; Luke 7:48) was to welcome sinners and to forgive one's enemies.

Because Jesus announced and already unveiled the coming reign of God, he spoke "as one having authority" (Mark 1:22), not simply on the basis of the law or the tradition or the regularities of experience. And because the coming reign of God demanded a response of the whole person and not merely external observance of the law, Jesus consistently made radical demands. So Jesus' radical demand for truthfulness replaced (and fulfilled) legal casuistry about oaths. The radical demand to forgive and to be reconciled set aside (and fulfilled) legal limitations on revenge. The demand to love even enemies put aside legal debates about the meaning of "neighbor." His moral instructions were based neither on the precepts of law nor on the regularities of experience, but he did not discard them either; law and wisdom were qualified and fulfilled in this ethic of response to the future reign of the one God of Scripture.

This Jesus was put to death on a Roman cross, but the resurrection vindicated both Jesus and God's own faithfulness. This one who died in solidarity with the least, with sinners and the oppressed, and with all who suffer was delivered by God. This Jesus, humble in his life, humiliated by religious and political authorities in his death, was exalted by God. When the powers of death and doom had done their damnedest, God raised up this Jesus and established forever the good future he had announced.

The Gospels used the church's memories of Jesus' words and deeds to tell his story faithfully and creatively. So they shaped the character and conduct of the communities that they addressed. Each Gospel provided a distinctive account both of Jesus and of the meaning of discipleship. In Mark, Jesus was the Christ as the one who suffered, and he called for a heroic discipleship. Mark's account of the ministry of Jesus opened with the call to discipleship (1:16–20). The central section of Mark's Gospel, with its three predictions of the passion, made it clear how heroic and dangerous an adventure discipleship could be. "If any want to become my followers, let them deny themselves and take up their cross and follow me" (8:34 [and note the allusions to martyrdom in 8:35; 10:38–39]).

Hard on the heels of that saying Mark set the story of the transfiguration (9:2–8), in which a voice from heaven declared, "This is my Son, the Beloved; listen to him!" It is striking that the voice did not say, "Look at him, all dazzling white." The voice said, "Listen to him." Silent during the transfiguration, Jesus ordered the disciples to say nothing of what they had seen until the resurrection, and then he told them once again that he, the Son of Man, "is to go through many sufferings and be treated with contempt" (9:12). Mark proceeded to tell the story of the passion, the story of a Christ who was rejected, betrayed, denied, deserted, condemned, handed over, mocked, and crucified, but still was the Son of God, the Beloved, and finally vindicated by God. The implications are as clear as they are shocking: Jesus is the Christ not by displaying some tyrannical power, not by lording it over others, but rather by his readiness to suffer for the sake of God's cause in the world and by his readiness to serve others humbly in self-giving love (cf. 10:42–44). And to be his disciple in this world is to share that readiness to suffer for the sake of God's cause and that readiness to serve others humbly in self-giving love.

The call to heroic discipleship was sustained by the call to watchfulness to which it was joined (13:33–37), by the expectation that, in spite of the apparent power of religious leaders and Roman rulers, God's good future was sure to be.

Mark's call to watchful and heroic discipleship touched topics besides the readiness to suffer for the sake of God's cause, and it illumined even the most mundane of them with the same freedom and daring. Discipleship was not to be reduced to obedience to any law or code. Rules about fasting (2:18–22), Sabbath observance (2:23–3:6), and the distinction between "clean" and "unclean" (7:1–23) belonged to the past, not to the community marked by freedom and watchfulness. The final norm was no longer the precepts of Moses, but rather the Lord and his words (8:38). In chapter 10 Mark gathered the words of Jesus concerning marriage and divorce, children, possessions, and political power. The issues were dealt with not on the basis of the law or conventional righteousness, but rather on the basis of the Lord's words, which appealed in turn to God's intention at creation (10:6), the coming kingdom of God (10:14–15), the cost of discipleship (10:21), and identification with Christ (10:39, 43–45). Mark's Gospel provided no moral code, but it did nurture a moral posture at once less rigid and more demanding than any code.

Matthew's Gospel utilized most of Mark, but by subtle changes and significant additions Matthew provided an account of Jesus as the one who fulfills the law, as the one in whom God's covenant promises are fulfilled. And the call to discipleship became a call to a surpassing righteousness.

Matthew, in contrast to Mark, insisted that the law of Moses remained normative. Jesus came not to "abolish" the law but to "fulfill" it (Matt. 5:17). The least commandment ought still to be taught and still to be obeyed (5:18–19; 23:23). Matthew warned against "false prophets" who dismissed the law and sponsored lawlessness (7:15–27). To the controversies about Sabbath observance Matthew added legal arguments to show that Jesus did what was "lawful" (12:1–14; cf. Mark 2:23–3:6). From the controversy about ritual cleanliness Matthew omitted Mark's interpretation that Jesus "declared all foods clean" (Mark 7:19; cf. Matt. 15:17); evidently, even kosher regulations remained normative. In Matthew's Gospel the law held, and Jesus was its best interpreter (see also 9:9–13; 19:3–12; 22:34–40).

The law, however, was not sufficient. Matthew accused the teachers of the law of being "blind guides" (23:16, 17, 19, 24, 26). They were blind to the real will of God in the law, and their pettifogging legalism hid it. Jesus, however, made God's will known, especially in the Sermon on the Mount. There, he called for a righteousness that "exceeds that of the scribes and Pharisees" (5:20). The Beatitudes (5:3–11) described the character traits that belong to such righteousness. The "antitheses" (5:21–47) contrasted such righteousness to mere external observance of laws that left dispositions of anger, lust, deceit, revenge, and selfishness unchanged. This was no calculating "works-righteousness"; rather, it was a self-forgetting response to Jesus' announcement of the kingdom (4:12–25).

Matthew called the community to play a role in moral discernment and discipline. The church was charged with the task of interpreting the law, vested with the authority to "bind" and "loose" (18:18), to make legal rulings and judgments. These responsibilities for mutual admonition and communal discernment were set in the context of concern for the "little ones" (18:1–14) and forgiveness (18:21–35), and they were to be undertaken with prayer (18:19). Jesus was still among them (18:20), still calling for a surpassing righteousness.

In Luke's Gospel, the emphasis fell on Jesus as the one "anointed . . . to bring good news to the poor" (4:18). Mary's song, the Magnificat (1:46–55), sounded the theme early on as she celebrated God's action on behalf of the humiliated and hungry and poor. In Luke, the infant Jesus was visited by shepherds in a manger, not by magi in a house (2:8–16; cf. Matt. 2:11–12). Again and again—in the Beatitudes and woes (6:20–26), for example, and in numerous parables (e.g., 12:13–21; 14:12–24; 16:19–31)—Jesus proclaimed good news to the poor and announced judgment on the anxious and ungenerous rich. Luke did not legislate in any of this; he gave no social program, but he insisted that a faithful response to this Jesus as the Christ, as the "anointed," included care for the poor and powerless. The story of Zacchaeus (19:1–10), for example, made it clear that to welcome Jesus "gladly" was to do justice and to practice kindness. Luke's story of the early church in Acts celebrated the friendship and the covenant fidelity that were displayed when "everything they owned was held in common" so that "there was not a needy person among them" (Acts 4:32–34; cf. 2:44–45; cf. also Deut. 15). Character and community were, and were to be, fitting to "good news to the poor."

The "poor" included not just those in poverty, but all those who did not count for much by the world's way of counting. The gospel was good news, for example, also for women. By additional stories and sayings (e.g., 1:28–30; 2:36–38; 4:25–27; 7:11–17; 10:38–42; 11:27–28; 13:10–17; 15:8–10; 18:1–8), Luke displayed a Jesus remarkably free from the chauvinism of patriarchal culture. He rejected the reduction of women to their reproductive and domestic roles. Women such as Mary of Bethany, who would learn from Jesus and follow him, were welcomed as equals in the circle of his disciples (10:38–42).

And the gospel was good news to "sinners" too, to those judged unworthy of God's blessing. It was a gospel, after all, of "repentance and the forgiveness of sins" (24:47), and in a series of parables Jesus insisted that there is "joy in heaven over one sinner who repents" (15:7; cf. 15:10, 23–24). That gospel of the forgiveness of sins was to be proclaimed "to all nations" (24:47); it was to be proclaimed even to the gentiles, who surely were counted among the "sinners." That story was told, of course, in Acts, but already early in Luke's Gospel the devout old Simeon recognized in the infant Jesus God's salvation "of all peoples" (2:31; cf., e.g., 3:6). The story of the gentile mission may await Acts, but already in the Gospel it was clear that to welcome this Jesus, this universal savior, was to welcome "sinners." And already in the Gospel it was clear that a faithful response to Jesus meant relations of mutual respect and love between Jew and gentile. In the remarkable story of Jesus' healing of the centurion's servant (7:1–10), the centurion provided a paradigm for gentiles, not despising but loving the Jews, acknowledging that his access to God's salvation was through the Jews; and the Jewish elders provided a model for Jews, not condemning this gentile but instead interceding on his behalf. In Acts 15, the Christian community included the gentiles without requiring that they become Jews; the church was to be an inclusive community, a welcoming community, a community of peaceable difference.

John's Gospel told the story in ways quite different from the Synoptic Gospels, and its account of the moral life was also quite distinctive. It was written that the readers might have "life in [Jesus'] name" (20:31), and that life was inalienably a life formed and informed by love. Christ was the great revelation of God's love for the world (3:16). As the Father loves the Son (e.g., 3:35; 5:20), so the Son loves his own (13:1). As the Son "abides" in the Father's love and does his commandments, so the disciples are to abide in Christ's love (15:9–10) and keep his commandments. And his commandment was simply that they should love one another as he had loved them (15:12; cf. 15:17). This "new commandment" (13:34) was, of course, hardly novel, but it rested now on a new reality: the love of God in Christ and the love of Christ in his own.

That reality was on display in the cross, uniquely and stunningly rendered by John as

Christ's "glory." The Son of Man was "lifted up" on the cross (3:14; 12:32–34). His glory did not come after that humiliating death; it was revealed precisely in the self-giving love of the cross. And that glory, the glory of humble service and love, was the glory that Jesus shared with the disciples (17:22). They too were "lifted up" to be servants, exalted in self-giving love.

The commandment in John was to love "one another" (e.g., 15:12) rather than the "neighbor" or the "enemy." John's emphasis surely fell on mutual love, on relations within the community. But an emphasis was not a restriction, and the horizon of God's love was the whole world (3:16). And as God so loved the world that he sent his Son, so Jesus sent his followers "into the world" (17:18; cf. 20:21). The mission of the Father's love seeks a response, an answering love; it seeks mutual love, and where it finds it, there is "life in Christ's name."

Paul and His Gospel

Before the Gospels were written, Paul had addressed pastoral letters to the churches. He always wrote as an apostle (e.g., Rom. 1:1) rather than as a philosopher or a code-maker. And he always wrote to particular communities facing specific problems. In his letters he proclaimed the gospel of the crucified and risen Christ and called for the response of faith and faithfulness.

The proclamation of the gospel was always the announcement that God had acted in Christ's cross and resurrection to end the reign of sin and death and to establish the coming age of God's own cosmic sovereignty. That proclamation was sometimes in the indicative mood and sometimes in the imperative mood. In the indicative mood, Paul described the power of God to provide the eschatological salvation of which the Spirit was the "first fruits" (Rom. 8:23) and the "guarantee" (2 Cor. 5:5). But the present evil age continued; the powers of sin and death still asserted their doomed reign. The imperative mood acknowledged that Christians were still under threat from these powers and called them to hold fast to the salvation given them in Christ. "If we live by the Spirit, let us also be guided by the Spirit" (Gal. 5:25).

Reflection about the moral life was disciplined by the gospel. Paul called the Romans, for example, to exercise a new discernment, not conformed to this present evil age but instead "transformed by the renewing of your minds" (Rom. 12:2). There is no Pauline recipe for such discernment, no checklist or wooden scheme, but certain features of it are clear enough. It involved a new self-understanding, formed by the Spirit and conformed to Christ (e.g., Rom. 6:11; Gal. 2:20). It involved a new perspective on the moral situation, an eschatological perspective, attentive both to the ways in which the power of God was already effective in the world and to the continuing assertiveness of sin and death. It invoked some fundamental values, gifts of the gospel and of the Spirit, notably freedom (e.g., 2 Cor. 3:17; Gal. 5:1) and love (e.g., 1 Cor. 13; Phil. 1:9). And it involved participation in a community of mutual instruction (e.g., Rom. 15:14). Discernment was not simply a spontaneous intuition granted by the Spirit, nor did it create rules and guidelines *ex nihilo*. Existing moral traditions, whether Jewish or Greek, could be utilized, but they were always to be tested and qualified by the gospel.

This new discernment was brought to bear on a wide range of concrete issues faced by the churches: the relations of Jew and gentile in the churches, slave and free, male and female, rich and poor. Paul's advice was provided not as timeless moral truths but rather as timely applications of the gospel to specific problems in particular contexts.

The Later New Testament

The diversity of ethics in Scripture is only confirmed by other NT writings. The Pastoral Epistles encouraged a "quiet and peaceable life in all godliness and dignity" (1 Tim. 2:2). It was an ethic of moderation and sober good sense, avoiding the enthusiastic foolishness of others who might claim the Pauline tradition, whether ascetic or libertine.

The subtle theological arguments of the book of Hebrews did not exist for their own sake; they supported and sustained this "word of exhortation" (13:22). The theological basis was the covenant that was "new" (8:8, 13; 9:15; 12:24) and "better" (7:22; 8:6), and the fitting response to that covenant was to "give thanks" and to "offer to God an acceptable worship with reverence and awe" (12:28). Such worship, however, was not a matter of cultic observances. It involved "sacrifice," to be sure, and that "continually," but the sacrifice that is pleasing to God is "to do good and to share what you have" (13:15–16). Hebrews 13 collected a variety of moral instructions, including, for example, exhortations to mutual love, hospitality to strangers, consideration for the imprisoned and oppressed, respect for marriage, and freedom from the love of money.

The Letter of James too was a collection of moral instructions, and a somewhat eclectic collection at that. There was no single theme in James, but there was an unmistakable solidarity with the poor (1:9–11; 2:1–7, 15–16; 4:13–5:6) and a consistent concern about the use of that recalcitrant little piece of flesh, the tongue (1:19, 26; 3:1–12; 4:11; 5:9, 12). James contains, of course, the famous polemic against a "faith without works" (2:14–26), and it seems likely that he had in mind a perverted form of Paulinism, but James and Paul perhaps are not so far apart. When James called for an active faith (2:22), readers of Paul might be reminded of Paul's call for a "faith working through love" (Gal. 5:6).

The ethic of 1 Peter was fundamentally a call to live with integrity the identity and community formed in baptism. The "new birth into a living hope through the resurrection of Jesus Christ from the dead" (1:3; cf. 1:23) was a cause for great joy (1:6, 8), but it was also reason to "prepare your minds for action" and to "discipline yourselves" (1:13). In 1 Peter the author made extensive use of what seem to have been moral traditions associated with instructions for baptism (and which are also echoed in other NT texts [see Selwyn]). The mundane duties of this world in which Christians are "aliens and exiles" (2:11) were not disowned, but they were subtly and constantly reformed by being brought into association with the Christian's new moral identity and community.

The Letters of 2 Peter and Jude defended sound doctrine and morality against the heretics who "promise them freedom" (2 Pet. 2:19). In 2 Peter is a carefully wrought catalog of virtues, beginning with "faith," ending with "love," and including in the middle a number of traditional Hellenistic virtues (1:5–8).

The Johannine Epistles, like the Pastoral Epistles and 2 Peter, defended sound doctrine and morality, but these epistles made their defense in ways clearly oriented to the Johannine perspective. To believe in Jesus—in the embodied, crucified Jesus—is to stand under the obligation to love. In Jesus' death on the cross we know what love is (1 John 3:16). And to know that love is to be called to mutual love within the community (e.g., 1 John 2:9–11; 3:11, 14–18, 23; 4:7–12, 16–21; 2 John 5–6).

The book of Revelation, like most other apocalyptic literature, was motivated by a group's experience of alienation and oppression. In the case of Revelation, the churches of Asia Minor suffered the vicious injustice and petty persecution of the Roman emperor. Revelation encouraged and exhorted those churches by constructing a symbolic universe that made intelligible both their faith that Jesus is Lord and their daily experience of injustice and suffering. The rock on which that universe was built was the risen and exalted Christ. He is "the firstborn of the dead, and the ruler of the kings of the earth" (1:5). He is the Lamb that was slain and is worthy "to receive power and wealth and wisdom and might" (5:12). The victory had been won, but there were still sovereignties in conflict. On the one side were God, his Christ, and those who worship them; on the other side were Satan, his regents, the beasts, and "the kings of the earth," and all those who think to find security with them. The bestiality of empire was on display, and it called for "patient endurance" (1:9; 2:2–3, 10, 13, 19; 3:10; 13:10; 14:12).

The conflict is not a cosmic drama that one may watch as if it were some spectator sport; it is an eschatological battle for which one must enlist. Revelation called for courage, not calculation, for watchfulness, not computation. And "patient endurance" was not passivity. To be sure, Christians in this resistance movement against the bestiality of empire did not take arms to achieve a power like the emperor's. But they resisted. And in their resistance, even in the style of it, they gave testimony to the victory of the Lamb that was slain. They were to live courageously and faithfully, resisting the pollution of empire, its cult surely and its lie that Caesar is Lord, but also its murder, fornication, sorcery, and idolatry (cf. the vice lists in 21:8; 22:15; see also 9:20–21). They were to be the voice of all creation, until "those who destroy the earth" would be destroyed (11:18), until the Lord makes "all things new" (21:5).

Ethics in Scripture are diverse, not monolithic. Yet, the one God of Scripture still calls in it and through it for a faithful response, still forms and reforms conduct and character and community until they are something "new," something "worthy of the gospel of Christ."

Bibliography

Barton, J. *Ethics and the Old Testament*. 2nd ed. SCM, 2002; Birch, B. *Let Justice Roll Down: The Old Testament, Ethics, and the Christian Life*. Westminster John Knox, 1991; Burridge, R. *Imitating Jesus: An Inclusive Approach to New Testament Ethics*. Eerdmans, 2007; Hays, R. *The Moral Vision of the New Testament: Community, Cross, and New Creation; A Contemporary Introduction to New Testament Ethics*. HarperSanFrancisco, 1996; Mendenhall, G. *Law and Covenant in Israel and the Ancient Near East*. Biblical Colloquium, 1955; Selwyn, E. *The First Epistle of St. Peter*. 2nd ed. Macmillan, 1947; Verhey, A. *Remembering Jesus: Christian Community, Scripture, and the Moral Life*. Eerdmans, 2002; von Rad, G. *The Problem of the Hexateuch and Other Essays*. Trans. E. Trueman Dicken. Oliver & Boyd, 1966, 1–78; Wolff, H. "The Kerygma of the Yahwist." Pages 41–66 in W. Brueggemann and H. Wolff, *The Vitality of Old Testament Traditions*. John Knox, 1975; Wright, C. *Old Testament Ethics for the People of God*. InterVarsity, 2004.

SCRIPTURE IN ETHICS

A History

CHARLES H. COSGROVE

Throughout the history of the church Christians have looked to the Bible for theological concepts by which to understand their moral obligations, commandments by which to live, values by which to order personal and social existence, patterns of life worthy of emulation, and insight into the dynamics of character formation. At the same time, the Bible has been used along with other sources of moral understanding (acknowledged and unacknowledged) and has been read in a wide variety of cultural contexts that have shaped the way it has been interpreted.

The Early Church

In the NT direct appeal to the Bible in ethical exhortation and instruction is not nearly as frequent as appeal to other authorities. In the Gospels, Jesus is the chief model and authority for ethics. Elsewhere too we find appeals to the example or teaching of "Jesus" or "Christ" or "the Lord Jesus," and so forth (e.g., Rom. 15:1–3; Phil. 2:5–11; Eph. 5:2; 1 Tim. 6:3; 1 Pet. 2:21–23). Other normative voices are civic authorities (Rom. 13:1–5; 1 Pet. 2:13–15); household authorities—masters (Col. 3:22; 1 Pet. 2:18), husbands (Eph. 5:22; Col. 3:18; 1 Pet. 3:1), and parents (Col. 3:20; Eph. 6:1); church leaders (Phlm. 8, 21; Heb. 13:17); common knowledge (Rom. 1:29–32; cf. 1 Cor. 5:1), including knowledge of one's duties (Rom. 13:6–7); and traditional Christian instruction in so-called vice and virtue lists (1 Cor. 6:9–10; Gal. 5:19–23). The Jewish Scriptures figure in ethical argument and exhortation sometimes independently and sometimes in connection with other sources and authorities.

The Mosaic law became a subject of great debate in the early church. Throughout the early period, appeals to Scripture as a rule for ethics were complicated by the fact that an increasingly influential wing of the church rejected the Mosaic law as a norm for the church or defended a complex (and perhaps sometimes confused and uncertain) understanding of its bearing on questions of behavior. For Paul, the law's authority as a rule for righteousness has terminated in Christ (Rom. 3:21–4:25; 10:1–13; Gal. 3:6–4:7). Nevertheless, the ethic of Christ coincides at points with Mosaic commandments; and love, which Christ commands, fulfills the central purpose of the law (Rom. 13:8–10; Gal. 5:13–14). Moreover, since Scripture was written for "us" (those in Christ who live at the end of the age), Paul reads Deut. 25:4 allegorically as a warrant for apostolic rights (1 Cor. 9:8–10) and interprets Ps. 69:9 christologically in describing Jesus' self-giving way as an example to be imitated (Rom. 15:3). Paul also bases instructions about nonretaliation on Deut. 32:35 and Prov. 25:21–22 (see Rom. 12:19–20), and in a few places he adduces cautionary moral examples from Scripture (1 Cor. 10:1–11; 2 Cor. 11:3).

The conviction that love is central to the Mosaic law was already taught by ancient Jewish rabbis. Mark and Luke attribute this belief to Jesus but imply that other Jewish teachers affirmed it as well (Mark 12:28–34; Luke 10:25–28). In Matthew, Jesus teaches that all the law and the prophets "hang" on the two Great Commandments (Matt. 22:40). One can understand Jesus' opinions in controversies over the law as instances of applying the love command as an interpretive rule (e.g., Matt. 12:1–8, 9–13). In the Sermon on the Mount, however, Jesus casts his teaching at several points in the form, "You have heard that it was said [in the law of Moses]. . . . But I say to you . . ." (Matt. 5:21–22, 27–28, 31–32, 33–34, 38–39, 43–44). Is this reinterpretation, which upholds the authority of the law but asserts that Jesus is the authoritative interpreter, or is it supersession of the law's authority, making Jesus the sole authority and rendering the law's specific commandments obsolete? Other parts of Matthew favor the first alternative (see Matt. 5:17–20; 8:4).

Jewish followers of Jesus had already been shaped by their upbringing in the synagogue, where Scripture (especially the Torah or Pentateuch) was central. Hence, much of the moral instruction of the early church takes for granted prevailing Jewish views about various moral subjects, including sexual ethics, concern for the poor, gender roles, the virtues that should characterize a godly person, and so forth. These assumptions occasionally become explicit in appeals to Scripture that rest on traditional Jewish interpretation (e.g., 1 Tim. 2:9–15). The Jewish heritage is especially evident in the most common form of direct moral appeal to Scripture, the example. Paul singles out Abraham as a man of steadfast trust in God (Rom. 4); so does Hebrews, mentioning other exemplary biblical figures as well (Heb. 11). James refers to the prophets and Job as examples of suffering and patience (Jas. 5:10–11). Negative examples are also adduced: Lot's wife (Luke 17:32); Israel (1 Cor. 10:1–11; Heb. 3:16–4:11); disobedient angels, Sodom and Gomorrah, Cain, Balaam, and Korah (Jude 6–11); Esau (Heb. 12:16); and Cain (1 John 3:12).

The Patristic Period

By the second century, the church possessed not only the Jewish Scriptures but also apostolic writings (Gospels, the letters of Paul, etc.) as guides for ethical reflection. On many topics the church fathers worked out views consistent with the ethics of Greek and Roman philosophers by claiming that the Greeks had stolen their ideas from Moses and by articulating a theory of natural law available to all human beings. The concept of natural law came from philosophy, but the fathers found support for the idea in Rom. 1.

The church also staked out distinctive positions on moral questions such as service in the army, abortion and infanticide, and sexuality. Regarding participation in the Roman army, Jesus' "disarming" of Peter in Gethsemane was a crucial prooftext (Matt. 26:52), taken as signaling a new era of nonviolence for God's people that superseded the old era, in which violence was sanctioned by God (Tertullian, *Idol.* 19). The *Didache* and the *Epistle of Barnabas* include abortion in lists of prohibitions modeled on the Ten Commandments (*Did* 2.2; *Barn.* 19.5). Later church teachers developed this position by working out theories of the embryo as a living person (with a soul), as evidenced by, for example, the fetal kick of John the Baptist (anonymous Christian cited in Clement of Alexandria, *Exc.* 50).

The fathers generally affirmed the Pauline rule of freedom from the Mosaic law but worked out their own understandings of it. By the middle of the second century Christians were distinguishing between commandments meant to be taken literally by the church and commandments meant to be interpreted only spiritually. According to Justin Martyr, some laws have enduring force because they are moral law; some concern the mystery of Christ; some were given because of Israel's hardness of heart and had only a temporary purpose (see Justin Martyr, *Dial.* 44; 46). According to the author of the *Epistle of Barnabas*, the Jews were deceived by an evil angel into interpreting the Mosaic laws of sacrifice and so forth literally (9.4), but Moses wrote "in the Spirit" (10.2, 9) for those who have heard the "voice of the Lord" (9.7) and are spiritually circumcised in their hearing (10.12).

At the same time, Jewish teaching remained an important influence in Christian ethical instruction—for example, in Christian adoption of the "two ways." Developed in Judaism as an interpretation of the two paths set forth in Deut. 30, the "two ways" concept assumed a variety of forms. Christian versions appear in *Did.* 1–5; *Barn.* 18–20; *Apos. Con.* 7. Book 1 of the *Didache* (*Did.* 1.1–6.2) is a paraphrase of teachings known to us from the Sermon on the Mount. Otherwise, the instructions in *Did.* 1–5 and *Barn.* 18–20 contain practically no material drawn directly from the oral Jesus tradition, the Gospels, or other first-century "apostolic" writings (such as the letters of Paul or James). But one can see forms of ethical expression found also in the Sermon on the Mount and the letters of Paul, particularly the vice and virtue list and the apothegm (a succinct moral directive sometimes briefly elaborated). By contrast, Scripture is used heavily in the moral instructions in book 7 of the *Apostolic Constitutions*, where the "two ways" teaching is explicitly traced to Deut. 30:15, the apothegm is the primary form of instruction, and specific apothegms are drawn from many different parts of the Bible.

Hostile attitudes toward Jewish conceptions of God, creation, and the moral life existed in some of the Christian groups who styled themselves "gnostics." At least some gnostics taught that the creator depicted in the Jewish Scriptures is an evil deity whose activity as creator and promulgation of the law through Moses brought human souls into spiritual darkness and servitude. A number of gnostic interpreters apparently regarded the Scriptures as in some sense authoritative and devoted considerable energy to interpreting Genesis, which offered them material for working out their spiritual-theological cosmologies of human origins. Some of this commentary survives in the *Apocryphon of John*, the *Hypostasis of the Archons*, and the *Tripartite Tractate*. It appears that gnostics took a dim view of sexuality and bodily appetites, which perhaps made a rigorous asceticism morally normative in most gnostic circles.

In the wider church, the Jewish Scriptures were studied as a source of moral instruction and a reservoir of moral examples. We see this already in *1 Clement*, which begins with a long moral discourse based on biblical examples of behavior to be imitated and avoided (*1 Clem.* 1–12). In a revealing description of what "preaching" meant in the second-century church, Justin Martyr mentions lengthy readings from "the writings of the prophets or the memoirs of his apostles," after which the "president" exhorts the people to imitate what they have heard (*1 Apol.* 67). In time, Christian schools were formed, which included moral instruction through study of biblical examples. Fourth-century Christian school exercises in "characterization" (*ethopoiia*) taught students to imagine what biblical figures might have said in moments of moral crisis (e.g., what Cain said after he killed Abel [P.Bod. 33] and what Abraham, Sarah, and Isaac said after God commanded Abraham to sacrifice Isaac [P.Bod. 20]). This was preparation for the day when the students, as preachers and teachers, would present biblical stories as compelling moral examples.

In addition to extracting moral examples from Scripture, Christian writers backed up their exhortations with one-sentence scriptural proofs. The purpose of these sentences probably was not so much to prove something as to restate the exhortation in scriptural language and thus give it greater motivational force. The use of short proof sentences from Scripture became a staple of Christian moral discourse for later writers, being used in all aspects of moral appeal. For example, in Basil's *Longer Rules*, Scripture sentences are adduced to reinforce a rule of practice, underscore the consequences of a certain action (as a warning or motivation), stress the requirement of right means to an end, and define appropriate ends.

Allusion and unmarked paraphrase of Paul, the Gospels (and oral Jesus tradition), and other earlier Christian writings are also extremely common in the apostolic and postapostolic fathers, many of whom saturate their discourse with phrases from Scripture. Apparently, it was assumed that the audience would detect most of the borrowing, in which case a high concentration of scriptural phrases gave the impression that the speaker's exhortation and instruction were simply the voice of the Bible, as if no interpretation were going on. In fact, the selection and disposition of the scriptural words as they were knitted together by the speaker's own formulations made for a highly interpretive use of Scripture.

Virtually all of the church fathers engaged in forms of allegorical interpretation, a method of exegesis based on the assumption that Scripture contains hidden (encoded) teaching. This often involved the discovery of instruction about the moral-spiritual journey of the individual soul. For example, commenting on the words "Come to Heshbon, let it be built" in a sermon on Num. 21:27 (*Hom. Num.* 13), Origen interprets "Heshbon" as the soul torn and emptied of its pagan beliefs and immoral habits, then rebuilt and outfitted with pious thoughts, correct understanding, and upright morals. As a general rule, the literal sense of the apostolic writings was regarded as the guide and control on allegorical interpretation. Some fathers spoke of a "rule of truth" or "rule of faith" as normative for interpretation (e.g., Irenaeus, Tertullian, Augustine). This rule, which included an ethical aspect, was regarded as expressing the essentials of apostolic teaching.

Some church fathers differentiated between higher and lower forms of Christian moral life. The idea is perhaps suggested already in *Herm.* 56.3 and *Did.* 6.2 (cf. Tertullian, *Ux.* 1.3). Advocates appealed to what they saw as evidence of such a distinction in the NT, in 1 Cor. 7:25–38; Rom. 3:3 (so Origen); Matt. 19:21 (so Ambrose). Ambrose and Augustine distinguished between "precepts" (mandatory for all) and "counsels" (freely chosen only by some), a distinction that became basic to the thinking of the medieval church (Ambrose, *Vid.* 12.72; 14.82; Augustine, *Virginit.* 15.15).

The fathers also took up specific moral issues, relying on various sources of inquiry in their day. These included, along with Scripture, "common knowledge" based on custom and cultural consensus and arcane knowledge based on specialized inquiry. For example, advocates of an ascetic lifestyle drew on philosophical asceticism, medicine, and Scripture in working out their teachings on fasting, sexual abstinence, and other forms of bodily self-denial. Often appeals to the various authorities were tightly interwoven. For example, Jerome counsels the widow Furia about how to ward off sexual desire by interpreting 1 Cor. 6:18 in the light of Galen's theory that certain foods stoke the body's internal heat, arousing passion (Jerome, *Epist.* 54.9). Similarly, Augustine seems to assume some current medical-philosophical conception of gestation when, commenting on Exod. 21:22, he says that the question of murder does not arise where the fetus is "unformed."

Augustine was the most important figure of the patristic period for the future of Christian theology and ethics in the Western church. He accepted the allegorical method but cautioned against excesses and insisted on respect for the letter. Augustine worked out what we would call an "ethic of interpretation," emphasizing that judgments about which interpretations of the text to embrace should be guided by love of God and neighbor, a view that manifestly reflects Matt. 22:40 (*Doctr. chr.* 1.36.40). Augustine also found a basis in Jesus' teaching for the principle that intent, as consent to an action and not simply desire, is the basic criterion for evaluating moral action. Hence, although adultery is wrong, it might be permissible in certain cases, such as when a wife yields to the sexual advances of a wealthy suitor in order to get money that her husband desperately needs to pay his taxes, provided she does not submit out of desire for the man (*Serm. dom.* 1.16.50).

The Medieval Period

The fathers developed the concept of the inspiration of Scripture by the Holy Spirit, and by the fourth century the basic contours of the canon were established. They also assumed that Scripture contains levels of meaning beyond the ordinary meaning of its words. The fifth-century theologian John Cassian formalized this hermeneutical tradition of multiple senses of Scripture into a fourfold scheme: historical (literal), allegorical (Christ and his church), anagogical (eschatological/heavenly), and tropological (having to do with the moral-spiritual formation of the soul). Thus, a number of fundamental interpretative assumptions were established in the early centuries of the church and taken over by the medieval church. To illustrate, in the Latin-speaking West the author (Lat. *auctor*) of Scripture was identified as the Holy Spirit and distinguished from the writer (Lat. *scriptor*) of a book of Scripture, the writer being a human being whom the Spirit used as an instrument. The concept of the unified authorship of Scripture justified interpreting passages far apart in time and place in the light of one another. Moreover, almost everyone assumed that Scripture contains secrets veiled under shadow and figure that could be discovered through allegorical interpretation. The plain sense set a certain limit on what allegorical exegesis could discover, but the latter also offered a way to find cherished philosophical concepts in biblical books that looked unphilosophical at the literal level. Greek moral philosophy, which focused on the formation of character, had been an influential conversation partner of the fathers. In the medieval period the allegorical method helped build a conceptual bridge between the unified authorship of Scripture and the newly rediscovered *Nicomachean Ethics* of "the Philosopher" (Aristotle).

The relation of Scripture to the world was also conceived differently than in the days when the church's relation to the world was essentially oppositional—as in early Christian apocalyptic but also in the pre-Constantinian church's sense of being an alien minority in a hostile world from which the path to martyrdom or the way of monastic and ascetic life was the noblest means of resistance and escape. The growth of the church in the fourth century and the changed political situation prompted a reconceptualization that affected how Scripture was read "historically" and "politically" in the early medieval period. In several works Eusebius had already woven scriptural history together with pagan history to form a salvation-historical narrative in which the Jewish patriarchs were cast as superior in understanding to their pagan counterparts. The Christian poet Prudentius viewed not only the Jewish but also the pagan past as preparatory (in a typological way) for the revelation in Christ and as part of a unified salvation history. Working in a similar vein, later minds not only read wider history in the light of Scripture but also interpreted Scripture in the light of wider history. Hence, in 492, responding to a crisis in which the current emperor claimed authority over the church in doctrinal matters, Pope Gelasius I argued that the emperors of Rome ceased to exercise priestly authority once Christ appeared, showing that Christ, the true priest and king, had in effect established a new relation between priestly and royal power. Apparently, Gelasius treated history and Scripture as both divinely authored, with Scripture providing clues to the meaning of history and history providing clues to the meaning of Scripture.

The new view of Christ's relation to temporal power encouraged the use of the OT for models of rulership (kingship), but the relation between church and state had to be worked out. Gelasius observed that in the past some persons, such as Melchizedek, were both kings and priests, but that when Christ appeared, the true king and priest (an allusion to the Christology of Hebrews), he established a separation of these offices. In the twelfth century, the conviction that Christ is the true and supreme king over the world inspired the idea that the pope is the vicar (representative) of Christ. This meant that whatever Scripture says of Christ could be applied to the pope as his vicar. Allegorical interpretation of the "two swords" text in Luke 22:38 proved that the priesthood possesses both spiritual and political authority. Hence, it became plausible to use OT stories of kings, along with other passages deemed to speak (literally or allegorically) about temporal power, in support of a pontiff's political aims and actions. Notable examples of this kind of self-serving exegesis are found in the "political" sermons of Pope Clement VI (1291–1352).

The Christ of the Gospels was also the model for the Christian life generally. Naturally, the proper way to imitate Christ was debated. One of the most pronounced discussions concerned the poverty of Christ. This interpretive conflict reached particular intensity in the fourteenth century between the Franciscans, who insisted that imitation required a vow of absolute poverty, and Pope John XXII, who rejected the claim that Jesus had ever embraced absolute poverty. Both sides appealed to a common fund of biblical passages. Central was how to understand the instructions in Matt. 10:9–10 to the disciples, when they are sent out on their mission, about taking no gold, silver, copper, and so on, a topic that led to the question of whether Pope John XXII had violated a "natural right" when he legally annulled Franciscan poverty in a series of bulls in 1322–23. William of Ockham's defense of the Franciscans helped to establish the concept of a natural right as a freedom, a notion that would outlive the debate about Christ's poverty.

In the medieval world, rules for the ordering of life under churchly authority, including moral behavior and discipline, were developed in what came to be known as "canon law," a loose body of authoritative tradition that was eventually systematized in the twelfth and thirteenth centuries in Gratian's *Decretum* and a collection of papal decretals assembled by Raymond of Peñafort under Pope Gregory IX. Sources included the Bible and Roman law as well as papal and conciliar decrees. In this era, but less so in subsequent development of canon law, the influence of the Bible was conspicuous. According to Gratian, the Bible reveals natural law, which is distinct from human custom, and in his *Decretum* the Bible figures prominently as a source of prooftexts.

The work of codifying and interpreting canon law differed from moral theology, the primary purpose of which was not to articulate and interpret rules but rather to give an intelligible account of the moral-spiritual formation of the soul in preparation for heaven and the beatific vision. This went back to Augustine, who also inherited from his Christian and pagan predecessors a view of ethics as virtue-centered and oriented to character formation. Hence, the great French scholastic Peter Abelard (1079–1142) opened his treatise on ethics (*Scito te ipsum*) with the statement "We regard morals as the virtues and vices of the mind that make us prone to good or bad deeds."

In the theological *summa* (a systematic compendium of theology), discussion of right action assumed the teaching of the church (codified in various bodies of canon law), which the scholars sought to interpret, not debate. The scholastics applied reason to moral questions in the light of Scripture and through interaction with other revered authorities—the church fathers and certain ancient philosophers regarded as sources of insight, to be reconciled where possible, not simply as debate partners.

Byzantine scholars transmitted ancient commentaries on Aristotle's *Nicomachean Ethics* and wrote their own commentaries on the same. The Byzantine interest in Greek philosophical ethics is also evinced in a Christianized version of Epictetus's *Enchiridion*, which served as a cherished introduction to ethics in the East, and Eastern moral exegesis of Scripture appeared in all kinds of works, including ascetical writings on prayer and spirituality. Nevertheless, Eastern Christian ethics did not become the subject of treatises but rather was treated almost exclusively as a dimension of theology, specifically, as a basic aspect of divine communion (or "deification").

The importance of the ancient Greek philosophical tradition for Western medieval scholars led to debates about whether philosophy (and philosophical ethics) could be legitimately pursued on its own terms as an inquiry separate from theological ethics and the revelation in Scripture. One advocate of this conceptual separation was Albert the Great, who wrote the first Latin commentary on the whole of Aristotle's *Nicomachean Ethics*. In conversation with Aristotle, Albert defined happiness as intellectual contemplation of immaterial, invisible realities achieved through detachment from earthly things through ascent to the divine.

In his commentaries on the *Nicomachean Ethics*, Albert quoted Scripture only rarely. For example, in his extensive treatment of chapter 10 in his first commentary on the *Nicomachean Ethics*, Albert quotes Scripture only about ten times. Far more frequent are quotations from the fathers and from more recent scholars (including other commentators on Aristotle). The relative absence of Scripture owes in part to the topics, which often do not lend themselves to easy prooftexting from Scripture, and above all to the nature of the discourse as Albert conceives it: a philosophical discussion based on reason with only minimal recourse to proofs from the Bible. This approach was typical of a good deal of philosophically oriented medieval discussions of ethics. Methodologically, philosophical ethics, unlike theological ethics, did not rely on Scripture and Christian tradition but rather was conducted on the basis of reason through commentary on classical philosophers such as Aristotle. Hence, the commentary on the *Nicomachean Ethics* by the great thirteenth-century philosopher and theologian Thomas Aquinas (*Sententia libri ethicorum*) does not refer to Scripture at all.

Scripture does play a role in Thomas Aquinas's *Summa theologiae*, including the second part, where he examines the conditions of moral existence and its philosophical foundations. Thomas begins with the purpose of human life and the nature of the moral life (human action, passions and habits, vice and virtue, law and grace), then goes on to examine specific virtues and vices. These include the primary "theological" (or "supernatural") virtues of faith, hope, and charity, along with the chief "natural" virtues of prudence, justice, fortitude, and temperance. Conceiving moral existence in terms of virtues and vices was a traditional approach, going back to the fathers and especially to Augustine, who derived the theological virtues from Scripture (with 1 Cor. 13:13 providing the hermeneutical key) and the natural virtues from the Greco-Roman philosophical tradition as mediated through Christian reflection.

The sections of Thomas's *Summa theologiae* dealing with ethics take the same form as other parts of the work. He presents logical analyses set forth in a consistent pattern of formal disputation (proposition, objections to it, his answer, and his replies to the objections) in which authorities are quoted from time to time. These authorities are Scripture, church fathers (Augustine, Ambrose, and others), certain ancient philosophers (especially Aristotle), and occasionally another source such as canon law. One or more of these authorities may be found in many arguments, but not every argument contains an appeal to authority. Quotations from Scripture appear in some objections, but most are found in Thomas's statement of his own view (in contraries, answers, and replies). These quotations are almost always a single sentence from the Bible: a declaration, often in the form of a *sententia* (apothegm) or treated as such; a statement about what God does (past, present, or future tense); or an exhortation that can be treated as expressive of a principle or as showing a relation between concepts. The scriptural sentences are used in various ways: as a major premise in an argument, as a supplemental proof of a conclusion of an argument, as a formulation of a contrary, as evidence for the meaning of a key word or concept, and as a basis for drawing an inference about a relation between concepts. Thomas rarely appeals to anything but the plain sense of Scripture, although he does not oppose the hermeneutic of multiple senses and argues that the ceremonial and judicial laws of the OT have figurative meanings. He also never debates the interpretation of a text but almost always treats the meaning of Scripture as self-evident; only very occasionally does he cite an authority for an interpretation of Scripture (e.g., *ST* II-I, q. 4, a. 2).

A different rhetorical form of ethical discourse is found in Abelard's *Scito te ipsum*, a logical-philosophical analysis of moral culpability in which Scripture figures not only as a fund of *sententiae* but also as a source of moral examples. Sometimes Abelard expounds the meaning of a scriptural sentence. He also sometimes brings together groups of scriptural statements and discusses their interrelation as he develops a point, always assuming the inherent unity of Scripture. It is apparent that Scripture profoundly shaped Abelard's thinking. At the same time, he depended on the scholastic tradition for concepts and questions for interpreting Scripture.

A common theme in scholastic ethics is the nature of love as the central moral teaching of the Bible. The NT and the fathers bequeathed to the later church the conviction that love is the highest affection and the supreme virtue. Augustine, on whom medieval thinkers heavily depended, sought to encapsulate this teaching in an epigram: "Love, and do what you will" (*Tract. ep. Jo.* 7.8). For Augustine, love was not simply a criterion for judging right from wrong but rather a "weight" in the heart that moves the will to a good purpose and ultimately to union with God (*Conf.* 13.9.10). In this sense, love is passional but in a spiritual sense, without bodily desire.

The idea that love, rightly understood, lacks sexual desire might have posed problems for the medieval efforts to interpret Song of Songs, but ever since Origen, that book had been interpreted as an allegory of spiritual love: Christ the bridegroom burning with celestial love for the church (or for the soul of each believer). Origen called that love *eros* (much less frequently *agape*) and thus inspired a spiritual eroticism of commentary on Song of Songs. Medieval divines interpreted Song of Songs on the basis of the fourfold reading of Scripture, which included a tropological (moral) sense. The tropological *modus* was variously understood as speaking in Song of Songs of the nuptials of the soul and Christ in a purifying spiritual ascent (Honorius); the soul's progression through faith, hope, and charity (Bernard of Clairvaux); the soul as a bride whom the Spirit makes "fertile with the offspring of the virtues" (the *Eulogium sponsi di sponsa* [PL 176, 987C]); and so forth. The medieval tradition of commentary on Song of Songs also saw a shift from expositions focused on the higher moral-spiritual life of the cloistered to interpretations that applied Song of Songs to the more general human struggle to order and direct desire.

The book of Psalms also offered expressions of the soul's ardent love for God and was revered as an innerbiblical corpus containing virtually everything found elsewhere in Scripture. That comprehensiveness was understood as including a moral voice in which David's colloquy with God is also David's dialogue with the church. David was seen as both a moral exemplar and a moral instructor. In commentary and preaching, as well as paraphrases and imitations of the psalms, David was taught as a model of compunction and penance, a source of soothing words to the soul in spiritual pain, and an example of justifiable individual and collective complaint in the midst of spiritual and temporal sufferings. Richard Rolle (1290–1349) extolled the psalms as medicine for the sick soul, urging recitation of them as a means to attain a vision of heaven. An instance of politically charged use of the complaint psalms is John Lydgate's rewriting of Ps. 136 in his *Defense of Holy Church* (1413–14). Lydgate encouraged readers to think of Henry V as a modern-day David who ought to remain vigilant against the political machinations of the Lollards.

The Reformation Era

The various branches of the Protestant Reformation championed the principle of *sola scriptura* and tended to be biblicistic in their approaches to theology and ethics. This biblicism led to reconceptualizations of the relation of church and society. Martin Luther's insistence that gospel and law are fundamentally different revived the old question of how Christians are to understand and make use of the Mosaic law. Reformers who represented what came to be known as the Lutheran and Reformed branches of Protestantism worked out a threefold use of the law: the law given to constrain behavior (the "first" or "civil" use); the law as God's means of convicting sinners and driving them to the mercy of the gospel (the "second" or "evangelical" use); and the law (or certain parts of law, the Ten Commandments above all) as moral law for the church (the "third" use). The third use of the law first appears in the writings of Philip Melanchthon. Luther seems generally to have affirmed it, although he did not emphasize or expound it. The third use became enshrined as an expression of Lutheran faith in article 6 of the *Formula of Concord* (1577) and was also embraced by John Calvin (*Institutes* 2.7.12), becoming a hallmark of Reformed theology.

Calvin's understanding of the third use of the law was closely connected with his conception of sanctification as a process of increasing conformity to the Ten Commandments. Calvin regarded the Ten Commandments as the most comprehensive revelation of moral principles in Scripture. Under their broad injunctions one could order all the more specific moral instructions of the Bible. Other Reformers gave pride of place to the Sermon on the Mount as the epitome of scriptural ethics, and everyone found a hermeneutical key in Jesus' teaching that all of Scripture "hangs" on the two Great Commandments, love of God and neighbor (Matt. 22:40). For Calvin, the double love command ought to guide the interpretation of individual commandments. For Luther, the double love command showed above all the unity of the law in love as a principle for distinguishing law and gospel.

Another area of fresh discussion was the Sermon on the Mount. Against tradition, Luther argued that this sermon presents not counsels of perfection for the few but rather a gospel ethic to which every Christian is to aspire. At the same time, the sermon defines the moral life of the kingdom of God, not the kingdom of this world—that is, not the social order, which must be governed by law and not by the gospel. The distinction between law and gospel and the doctrine of two kingdoms guided Luther's interpretation of Paul's teaching about civil authority in Rom. 13. According to

Luther, the word *person* (*anima* or "soul" in the Vulgate) in Paul's instruction "Let every person be subject to the governing authorities" (Rom. 13:1) includes the pope. Hence, the church does not stand above civil authority and must be obedient to it, at least in matters pertaining to worldly order (*To the Christian Nobility*).

Where Luther sharply distinguished temporal and spiritual authority as belonging to different spheres (different "kingdoms"), other Reformers assumed a greater unity between the two. Of particular significance is Huldrych Zwingli's notion that the ordination of civil authority, according to Rom. 13:1–7, includes the idea, or at least the possibility, that the Christian magistrate who hears the gospel will carry out his office according to God's will (*On Divine and Human Justice*). The concept of the Christian magistrate was a basic hermeneutical axiom in Zwingli's approach to civil authority, and he tended to think of the body of Christ (the *corpus Christianum*) as a unity entailing the whole of society. Accordingly, in his commentary on Jeremiah (1531), Zwingli proposed that when citizens and magistrate heed the gospel, "the Christian city is nothing other than the Christian church." Zwingli interpreted Matt. 18:15–20 (on dealing with an offender) as a basis for the Christian magistrate to exercise the right of excommunication, and he appealed to the fact that the OT spoke of rulers as "shepherds" to argue that the magistrate has a role in church discipline.

If Paul's teaching about law and gospel in Romans and Galatians became guiding canons for Luther and his followers, the concept of discipleship in the Gospels provided the hermeneutical key for the Anabaptists, who made up the bulk of the so-called radical wing of the Reformation. According to Anabaptists, the prescriptions of the Sermon on the Mount are not individual and aspirational goals but rather are divine commands for a disciplined ordering of community life. The Anabaptists stressed the moral transformation of the believer and rejected or downplayed the concept of original sin, emphasizing the teaching in Ezekiel that sons do not inherit the guilt of their fathers (Ezek. 18:4, 20). Christ, they said, makes believers ethically righteous, which is the main point of the only Anabaptist writing that directly discusses "atonement theory" (*On the Satisfaction of Christ* [c. 1530]). The Anabaptist focus on the example and teachings of Jesus as the template for community ethics led most Anabaptists to embrace pacifism (e.g., those influenced by Conrad Grebel and Menno Simons, but not Thomas Müntzer and his followers). Article 6 of the Schleitheim Articles of the Swiss Brethren (1527) summarizes the scriptural basis for nonviolence; almost all the prooftexts come from the example and teaching of Jesus. Moreover, on the basis of Jesus' teaching about discipleship (Matt. 6:19–34; Luke 12:33; 14:33) and descriptions of the community of goods in Acts 2:44–45; 4:32–5:11, Anabaptists also renounced private property (so the Hutterites and Swiss Anabaptists according to the Swiss *Congregational Order* of 1527) or at least put special importance on simplicity of life and care for the poor. Anabaptists understood the reference in Luke 4:18 to preaching good news to the poor as a crucial expression of the gospel, calling for a church of and for the poor. They also rejected the taking of oaths (on the basis of Matt. 5:33–37).

The Roman response to the Protestant Reformation involved the so-called Counter-Reformation, in which the Council of Trent (1545–64) played a crucial role. At this council the Roman Catholic Church reaffirmed but also revised its canon law, declared that both the Bible and unwritten traditions passed down from the apostles are to be revered as sources of truth, and stressed that the church must be regarded as superior in its judgments over private interpretation (*Decree Concerning the Canonical Scriptures*, Session IV [1546]). But responding to Protestant challenges was not the only concern of the Roman Catholic Church in the sixteenth century. A number of creative thinkers were working on their own questions in the domains of both theology and ethics. A subject bearing on biblical interpretation was "probabilism." Dominican theologian Bartholomew Medina, commenting on Thomas Aquinas, had formulated the following principle: "If an opinion is probable, it may be followed, even if the opposing opinion is more probable" (*Commentary on the Summa* I-II, 19.6). This view became a dominant topic of discussion among sixteenth- and seventeenth-century Roman Catholic divines. In matters of ethics probabilism touched individual moral freedom, and in *Apologema pro antiquissima et universalissima doctrina de probabilitate* (1663), Juan Caramuel analyzed examples of moral action in Scripture in an effort to show that an incipient probabilism is present in Scripture's judgment on those actions.

The Modern (and Postmodern) Era

By the late nineteenth century, questions of personal morality, domestic relations, contemporary social and political problems, the relation of church and state, the duties of citizenship, relations between nations, the proper role of government, the nature of justice, movements such as communism and socialism, questions of human rights, the poor, and so forth were ordered under a discipline of "Christian ethics" (in the Protestant world) or "moral theology" (in Roman Catholicism) distinct from the disciplines of biblical theology and dogmatic theology. This development was an eventual result from a momentous shift in the late eighteenth century when study of the Bible (in the universities of Europe) began to be separated from dogmatic theology as a distinct historical subject. According to the new conception, set forth programmatically by Johann Philipp Gabler in a famous address in 1787, specialists in biblical studies were to supply the theologians with critically established historical descriptions of biblical theology; the theologians, for their part, had the constructive task of translating biblical theology into contemporary thought forms. For Christian ethics, this meant applying the Bible to the questions of the day with awareness of the need for translation from the ancient world into the modern. Christian ethics and moral theology emerged as later disciplinary divisions. In practice, however, no strict division of labor was followed by individual scholars; one finds systematic treatments of ethics that depend on ethicists' and dogmaticians' own interpretations of Scripture, as well as historical studies of biblical ethics that are oriented to modern questions and concerns.

Nevertheless, there was growing agreement that while the Bible has a fixed sense (its historical sense), Christian ethics is a constructive discipline that must constantly evolve to grapple with new issues and to rethink old issues under changed conditions. At the same time, there was an increasing sense of a gap between the diverse moralities of Scripture and what seemed morally proper and rational to the modern mind. This posed a challenge to the Protestant project of basing theology and ethics directly on Scripture. Hence, for some, the Bible's perceived moral deficiencies called for defense through rational interpretation and explanation (e.g., J. A. Hessey, *Moral Difficulties Connected with the Bible* [1871]; Newman Smyth, *The Morality of the Old Testament* [1886]).

The new relation between biblical morality and contemporary moral thought was worked out in terms of new modes of inquiry set in motion by the Enlightenment, which solidified the Cartesian method of inquiry not only in science but also, in modified form, in other fields. In a way that almost defies historical analysis (because of the interaction over centuries of so many political and intellectual forces), the Bible helped create the conditions for the Enlightenment but also became an object of Enlightenment criticism, including criticism based on Enlightenment notions of religion. Advocates of the Enlightenment approach to knowledge championed reason against the authority of institutions (notably the church) and ancient books (the Bible and Aristotle). The recognition by seventeenth-century scientists (*philosophes*) that neither ancient philosophy nor Scripture offered adequate or accurate foundations for inquiries into cosmology, geography, geology, physical anthropology, and the like had led to a distinction between the scope (*scopus*) of philosophy (science) and the scope of Scripture. The province of science was empirical truth; the province of the Bible was the truth about God and salvation. In the eighteenth century this view was increasingly embraced by divines, including John Wesley. They regarded the Bible as authoritative for matters of faith and the moral life, not for knowledge about the physical world.

For some, however, the authority of the Bible was no longer absolute even for doctrine or ethics. Alexander Geddes (1737–1802), an early historical critic, concluded that the divine command that the Israelites exterminate the Canaanites (Josh. 1–3) was not really from God but rather was an invention of "some posterior Jew" (*The Holy Bible*, vol. 2 [1797], ii). This form of moral criticism of Scripture differed from the traditional view going back to the church fathers, who claimed that God had accommodated to "Jewish weakness" by encoding with allegory various practices commanded in the Jewish Scriptures that were later superseded in their literal sense by Christ. Geddes and other Enlightenment Christians treated the Bible like any other ancient book, subjecting it to the same moral criticism that they applied to Homer and other ancient writers. Geddes and other practitioners of what was called "higher criticism" also tended to differentiate the teachings of the OT from the "pure religion of Jesus," which they understood as essentially moral and rational (devoid of the supernatural and of traditional dogma). Intense interest in reconstructing the true history and true religion of Jesus behind the trappings of the Gospels led to numerous portraits of Jesus from 1750 through the early twentieth century, many of which cast Jesus chiefly as an enlightened moral teacher (so Joseph Priestley, G. W. F. Hegel, Ernst Renan, and Adolf von Harnack). The religio-moral authority of Jesus was largely taken for granted in these reconstructions, but the Bible was treated not as an authority but rather as a fallible historical source for recovering the life and teaching of Jesus. This shift from the assumption that authority resides in a text (Scripture) to the view that authority resides in history (in the Jesus of history or in God's activity in history) was one aspect of a broader theological problem posed by the Enlightenment: how could faith rest on the "accidents" of history and the uncertainties of historical knowledge?

For the majority of Christians who continued to accept the authority of Scripture, a number of ethical issues came to the fore as matters of intense debate in the nineteenth century. These included the question of whether the Bible supports slavery (a debate begun by abolitionists who began marshaling Scripture against defenders of the institution) and whether it teaches the subordination of women (to their husbands and to men in general). In working out their arguments from Scripture, women such as Elizabeth Wordsworth, Harriet Beecher Stowe, and Florence Nightingale used the concept of "progressive revelation" (developed by Enlightenment thinkers such as Gotthold Ephraim Lessing) to assign patriarchy (and other things in the OT that they found morally repugnant) to the primitive beginnings of biblical morality. Moreover, by assuming that the revelation of morality in Scripture is from the primitive to the more enlightened, they plotted an evolutionary trajectory that pointed beyond the limited egalitarian vision of the apostles (such as Paul) to perfect equality of the sexes as God's ultimate will.

The concept of progressive revelation in biblical morality was also embraced by abolitionists such as Francis Wayland to argue that the slaveholding of the patriarchs has less revelatory weight than NT teaching (notably the command of Jesus to love one's neighbor as oneself). Wayland and other abolitionists also developed a hermeneutic of "ethical implication," which seems to have owed something to principles of legal interpretation invoked in nineteenth-century debates about the US Constitution. They argued that the moral teaching of Scripture consists in what is commanded or prohibited in Scripture but also in what is required by or consistent with Scripture's explicit injunctions. Accordingly, they maintained that the system of slavery in America, because it did not recognize the parental rights of slaves, violated implicit ordinances of Scripture, namely, the duty of children to obey parents and of parents to care for and exercise authority over their children (Wayland, *Elements of Moral Science* [1856 edition]).

A good deal of nineteenth-century Protestant ethics entailed establishing Christian morality on the basis of theological doctrines and, with the aid of theophilosophical principles, working out positions on specific moral questions (e.g., in the influential works of Hans Martensen, G. C. A. Harless, and Isaak Dorner). Gabler's program assumed the existence of "universal concepts" by which to translate biblical theology into dogmatic theology. This idea appears to have controlled the constructive efforts of many nineteenth-century Christian ethicists who referred to the Bible only occasionally (and usually in the old prooftexting style of the medieval theologians that they claimed to have superseded) by referring generally to what Scripture "teaches." Thus, it is with breezy confidence that R. F. Weidner asserted (in an epitome of the Christian ethics of Martensen and Harless) that "the education of man for the Kingdom of God" is a basic teaching of Scripture about "the aim of history" (*Christian Ethics*, 2nd ed. [1897], 37). This and similar theophilosophical conceptions of the message of the Bible reflected an age devoted to the idea that history is evolving progressively through increasing enlightenment toward the earthly kingdom of God.

The end of the nineteenth century also saw the birth of the history-of-religions school, which put in question the presumed uniqueness of Israelite and early Christian religion in their ancient religious environments. Within the diverse theological movement known as neoorthodoxy, higher criticism's historical relativization of biblical ethics was met with different responses. For Rudolf Bultmann, who maintained that there is nothing in the ethics of the NT that an upstanding pagan would not have endorsed, the witness of the gospel, preserved most clearly in Paul, entails freedom not simply from the Mosaic law but from every human convention and moral norm. The Bible bears on ethics not by providing its material criteria but rather by disclosing a way of being characterized by radical faith, which Bultmann expounded through a Christian form of existentialism. Most neoorthodox theologians accepted the results of historical criticism and recognized that the moral teachings of the Bible are diverse, reflecting a variety of practices in different times and places and showing the influence of the beliefs of other ancient Mediterranean peoples. Hence, except within emergent fundamentalism, it was generally agreed that biblical morality had to be mediated through some kind of critical hermeneutic and could not be accepted naively.

In the twentieth century, the use of the Bible in ethics often entailed the assumption that Scripture speaks appropriately to the present not at its moral rule level (the level of specific prescriptions) but only at the level of its general ethical concepts—love, justice, mercy, peace, nonviolence, reconciliation, equality, and so forth (e.g., Paul Ramsey). Some who operated with this hermeneutical assumption attended to biblical rules (commandments and other moral instructions) by looking to the purpose behind the rule and treated that purpose as more important than the letter of the rule.

In addition to taking seriously the problem of the great cultural distance between the social worlds presupposed by biblical morality(ies) and those of the modern era, twentieth-century interpreters also approached biblical ethics with awareness of the apocalyptic assumptions under which NT writers framed their moral instructions. Many interpreters concluded that since the early Christians expected a near end of the world, their instructions about how to live ought to be understood as "interim ethics"—that is, an ethics for the time between the passing present order and the soon-to-arrive new creation. This concept was famously applied to the Sermon on the Mount by Albert Schweitzer but also influenced how Paul's practical instructions to his churches were viewed. Seeing NT ethics as largely interim ethics was another argument against appropriating its teachings at the rule level.

Some twentieth-century interpreters embraced the concept of eschatological transition (found in, e.g., 1 Cor. 7:29–31) and made it the basis of a "crisis ethic." Eschewing moral rules as alien to the gospel, they maintained that every believer is always living between the times and must discover God's will in the crisis created by the tension between the ever-present old and new. Bultmann worked out a crisis ethic through conversation with existentialist philosophy. Karl Barth maintained that ultimately the Christian is called to be obedient not to Scripture but rather to God's personal address, contending that the Bible's witness to God's revelation in Christ prepares one to hear God's command, but that the command is not found in Scripture and must be heard in the concrete situation. Others who adopted the eschatological framework maintained that believers are called to live between the times by embodying the radical ethic of Jesus. The church has to discern the way, but that discernment ought to hew closely to the specific patterns of life expressed in the teachings of the Sermon on the Mount and displayed in the paradigm of Jesus' life (so Stanley Hauerwas).

The scope and the purpose of Christian ethics also were in dispute. In the first half of the century it was largely assumed that, in addition to working out norms for personal ethics, the church has a responsibility to apply Christian ethical principles to society, a task requiring judgments about the bearing of biblical teaching on social and political questions. Advocates of "Christian realism" distinguished the personal from the social, arguing, for example, that the Sermon on the Mount presents an ideal suited to individual moral aspiration but impractical for social life. Social existence requires a realistic ethic of justice worked out in terms of broad biblical concepts, not concrete biblical prescriptions (so Reinhold Niebuhr). In the latter part of the twentieth century a number of influential voices began insisting that the church, not the individual or society, is the proper subject of Christian ethics. The church is called to be a distinct moral community that bears witness to the world by embodying the way of Jesus. The teachings of the Sermon on the Mount and other rigorous NT moral instruction were meant not as a general social ethic or a merely personal ethic but rather as an ethic for the church. For some, this understanding of ecclesial ethics was a way of rejecting the assumptions of Christendom (the notion of a unified Christian social order) in favor of the agonistic relation between the church and the world assumed by the NT (so John Howard Yoder, Stanley Hauerwas). Increasing religious pluralism and secularization made this way of thinking attractive for those who wished to conform their lives in Christian community as closely as possible to what they understood as NT patterns of faith and life without imagining that the church could or should shape the wider society in the image of the kingdom of God.

In Roman Catholic circles natural-law ethics tended to dominate, although after Vatican II there was greater interest in a renewal of moral theology nourished by study of Scripture (*Optatam Totius* §16). At the same time, critical academic study of Scripture was much more likely to receive the Vatican's imprimatur than in previous generations. Meanwhile in Europe (in the form of political theology) and in Latin America (in the form of liberation theology) the post–World War II period saw both Protestants and Catholics engaging Scripture with fresh interest in a Christian social ethics that would place the problem of the poor front and center. Latin American liberation theology espoused a new hermeneutical principle, contending that the Bible speaks not only on behalf of the poor but also from their perspective; hence, the poor are in the best social location to understand Scripture. This idea, called "the epistemological privilege of the poor," was allied to the conviction that social location (and precommitments) shapes interpretation of the Bible. The appearance of liberation theology in the Western academy ushered in an era of perspectival interpretation. Various scholars began stressing that the influence of social location is not a problem to be overcome but rather is a necessary condition of interpretation that should be formalized as part of the hermeneutic process (see, e.g., Tolbert and Segovia). At the same time, the field of hermeneutics was overwhelmed by theoretical challenges. Whether in the dialogical forms espoused by Hans-Georg Gadamer and Paul Ricoeur or the deconstructionist brands associated with Jacques Derrida and Paul de Man, philosophical hermeneutics confronted Christian ethics with questions about the semantic clarity of texts and the location of meaning in texts, radicalizing the kinds of questions that earlier generations of Christians had tackled in discussing, for example, allegorical interpretation, the perspecuity of Scripture, and probabilism.

The interaction between liberationist and philosophical hermeneutics raised fresh questions about both the interpreter and the biblical text as factors in the hermeneutic process. If the church fathers and most theologians of the medieval and Reformation eras had assumed that in order to interpret rightly one needed to be well formed spiritually, and if the Enlightenment and its heirs had tended to emphasize the power of reason and the importance of "method" in interpretation, an increasing number of late-twentieth-century interpreters focused on the process by which the socially (or ideologically) conditioned interpreter constructs meaning out of a (somewhat or radically) "indeterminate" biblical text under the impulse of a certain interest (or precommitment). Recognizing that in a situation of multiple interpretive possibilities and competing human interests the interpreter must be regarded as a moral agent led to reflection on the "ethics of interpretation" (Elisabeth Schüssler Fiorenza, Daniel Patte).

Biblical scholarship also became increasingly sensitive to the role of literary or oral "form" in textual communication and the importance of considering the nature and purpose of a biblical text before using it as a basis for conclusions about ethics. Hence, one asked whether poetic descriptions of God's knowledge of the person in the womb (Ps. 139:13–16) were being used appropriately if made the basis for inferences about the moral status of the fetus or whether references to animal life in poetic descriptions designed to extol the greatness of the Creator (Ps. 104) warranted philosophical inferences about the moral status of living things in Christian versions of deep ecology. At the same time, many biblical interpreters were also developing a fresh appreciation for the way Scripture, in the variety of its genres (and not only or even primarily in ethical prescriptions), bears on ethics by shaping community Christian identity and providing insight into moral formation.

By the close of the twentieth century, the role of the Bible in Christian ethics had become a highly complex theological and intellectual problem. Except in fundamentalist circles, one could no longer simply equate biblical ethics with Christian ethics. The diversity of moral perspectives in Scripture and the epochal difference between antiquity and modernity (or postmodernity) made it difficult to conceive the Bible as a direct source of Christian ethics. This problem was only exacerbated by a growing perception that Scripture was not only a weapon against ideology (as Latin American liberation theology generally treated the Bible) but also a purveyor of it (as some feminist biblical interpreters contended). Hence, by the dawn of the twenty-first century, almost all participants in the discussion agreed that the Bible is in some sense an authority for Christian ethics, but conceptions of that authority—its force and scope—continued to vary widely.

Bibliography

Althaus, P. *The Ethics of Martin Luther*. Trans. Robert C. Schulz. Fortress, 1972; Birch, B., and L. Rasmussen. *Bible and Ethics in the Christian Life*. Rev. ed. Augsburg, 1989; Cosgrove, C. *Appealing to Scripture in Moral Debate: Five Hermeneutical Rules*. Eerdmans, 2002; Curran, C. *American Catholic Social Ethics: Twentieth-Century Approaches*. University of Notre Dame Press, 1983; de Groot, C., and M. Taylor, eds. *Recovering Nineteenth-Century Women Interpreters of the Bible*. SBLSymS 38. Society of Biblical Literature, 2007; Estep, W. *The Anabaptist Story: An Introduction to Sixteenth-Century Anabaptism*. 3rd ed. Eerdmans, 1996; Ferguson, E., ed. *Christian Life: Ethics, Morality, and Discipline in the Early Church*. SEC 16. Garland, 1993; Fleming, J. *Defending Probabilism: The Moral Theology of Juan Caramuel*. Georgetown University Press, 2006; Gorman, M. *Abortion and the Early Church: Christian, Jewish, and Pagan Attitudes in the Greco-Roman World*. InterVarsity, 1982; Harakas, S. *Patristic Ethics*. Vol. 1 of *Wholeness of Faith and Life: Orthodox Christian Ethics*. Holy Cross Orthodox Press, 1999; Harnus, J.-M. *It Is Not Lawful for Me to Fight: Early Christian Attitudes toward War, Violence, and the State*. Herald Press, 1980; Hauser, A., and D. Watson, eds. *The Ancient Period*. Vol. 1 of *A History of Biblical Interpretation*. Eerdmans, 2003; Helmholz, R. "The Bible in the Service of Canon Law." *Chicago-Kent*

Law Review 70 (1995): 1557–81; Jones, D. *Reforming the Morality of Usury: A Study of Differences That Separated the Protestant Reformers*. University Press of America, 2004; Kuczynski, M. *Prophetic Song: The Psalms as Moral Discourse in Late Medieval England*. University of Pennsylvania Press, 1995; Luthardt, C. *Geschichte der christlichen Ethik*. 2 vols. Dörffling & Franke, 1888–93; Matter, E. *The Voice of My Beloved: The Song of Songs in Western Medieval Christianity*. University of Pennsylvania Press, 1990; Ogletree, T. *The Use of the Bible in Christian Ethics: A Constructive Essay*. Fortress, 1983; Shaw, T. *The Burden of the Flesh: Fasting and Sexuality in Early Christianity*. Fortress, 1998; Siker, J. *Scripture and Ethics: Twentieth-Century Portraits*. Oxford University Press, 1997; Swartley, W. *Slavery, Sabbath, War, and Women: Case Issues in Biblical Interpretation*. Herald Press, 1983; Tolbert, M., and F. Segovia, eds. *Reading from This Place*. 2 vols. Fortress, 1995; Walsh, K., and D. Wood, eds. *The Bible in the Medieval World: Essays in Memory of Beryl Smalley*. Basil Blackwell, 1985; White, R. E. O. *Christian Ethics: The Historical Development*. John Knox, 1981.

SCRIPTURE IN ETHICS

Methodological Issues

BRUCE C. BIRCH

All traditions that regard the text of the Bible as Scripture would agree that these texts should be important resources for Christian ethics. Yet there is little agreement on, and often little attention paid to, how Scripture and ethics relate. Although the literature on this relationship has grown significantly in the last two decades, the tendency in practice in the Christian life is to leave this relationship unexamined. Texts are only casually or haphazardly brought into conversation with formative or normative concerns for Christian ethics. This article seeks to raise some issues of perspective, foundational understandings, and methodological practice that might be helpful in constructing a more self-conscious relating of Scripture to the moral life in Christian practice. The views reflected here in brief draw on and are consistent with longer treatments of this subject in previous publications (Birch and Rasmussen; Birch, *Let Justice Roll Down*).

Perspectives on Biblical Ethics

It is helpful to think of different arenas within which questions of the relationship between the Bible and ethics can be raised. Each of these arenas poses different challenges and offers differing insights, but it is important not to confuse them or assume only one to be significant.

The World behind the Text

Some treatments of biblical ethics have focused on recovering, understanding, and critically assessing the morality of the biblical communities out of which the biblical texts were produced. Since these texts represent the witness of Israel and the early church stretching over more than fifteen centuries, the ethical systems of differing times, places, and groups reflected in the biblical text are diverse and complex.

Naturally, there has been considerable interest in recovering the morality of Jesus as the central figure in Christian faith, understood by most Christian traditions as God incarnate in human history. How Jesus lived, who he understood himself to be, and how his death and resurrection became the confessional foundation for the formation of the church make Jesus' own understanding of ethics crucially important. The popular slogan "What would Jesus do?" reflects this concern to use the ethics of Jesus as a model for moral conduct.

By the same token, entire denominational traditions have placed a high value on discovering and emulating the pattern of moral life practiced in the earliest church, especially as reflected in the book of Acts and the writings of Paul and other early church leaders in the NT Epistles. These NT writings often are treated as manuals of conduct for contemporary Christian life.

Efforts to discern and understand the ethics of Jesus or the early church may help to deepen our knowledge of the biblical communities that produced the witnesses of the biblical text. However, these communities were diverse and complex, and their testimonies in the biblical texts do not produce a single, unified ethic that can be emulated. There are four canonical Gospels, and each has a unique portrait of Jesus. There have been many notable efforts to recover the actual words and teachings of Jesus in a historical sense, and these have produced no uniform result. The writings of Paul and other NT authors reflect the unique circumstances of early congregations in differing time periods, and although all contribute to the resources for Christian ethics, there is once again no singular unified Christian ethic to be recovered and emulated.

With respect to the OT, the witness of Israel to its life lived in covenant with God is even more diverse and stretched over a longer period of time and historical circumstances. Efforts to find unifying themes throughout the OT texts or developmental patterns of moral conduct have been notably unsuccessful. We cannot produce a typical or complete history of ancient Israelite ethics. Different texts reflect different social strata and historical settings. Many recent studies have helped us to understand these glimpses of ancient Israel more fully in their own contexts, but there is no singular code of moral conduct to be emulated here. Instead, there is a richness of testimony of life lived in relation to God, both in obedience and disobedience. We may learn from these and be informed from them in our own moral efforts, and this methodology is addressed later in this article.

The Text as Canon

Another way to understand biblical ethics is to see it as the moral conversation contained within the texts collected, edited, recognized, and passed on as a canon of Scripture. For Christians, the canons of the OT and the NT (and, for Roman Catholic and Orthodox Christians, the Apocrypha) have been collectively passed on through the generations as foundational for Christian faith and practice, theology and ethics. As soon as these texts have been gathered into the collections of Law, Prophets, Writings, Gospels, and Epistles and given authority as scriptural canon throughout historical processes of collection and recognition, a new context is created for assessing the biblical resources for Christian ethics. Individual books and at times divergent voices within a single book may be studied for their moral witness, but also subject to study and reflection are the moral conversations that take place between books and texts within the canon. Tensions, agreements, convergences, continuities, and contradictions are now handed on from one generation to the next. One concern of biblical ethics is to listen carefully and critically to the moral witness of the entire canon.

The character of the moral conversation created by the formation of canon is to some degree an artificial construct that transcends the witness to any particular historical context in biblical times. Biblical ethics at this canonical level can be informed by what we can critically discover about the particularities of the world behind the text, but the canon itself forms a new context within which texts make their moral witness in a larger conversation. This canonical moral witness may or may not be capable of connection to concrete moral worlds behind the text (e.g., the entire book of Job reveals little about the world out of which its witness came).

The nature of the moral conversation may differ greatly within the canon. Sometimes continuities of moral witness may be observed, such as the consistent concern for the welfare of the poor and the dispossessed. New juxtapositions raise new issues for moral conversation. Why do we have four Gospel portraits of Jesus, and what does each contribute, singly and in juxtaposition, to the moral vision grounded in the life and witness of Jesus of Nazareth? What are the moral implications of encountering the universal God of creation before beginning the particular story of God's promise to Abraham? How is this altered further by Paul's extension of God's people to include gentiles as well as Jews? Sometimes the canon forces us to deal with moral tensions. For example, what is the proper role of faith to public civil authority? We must read both the story of Daniel and Rom. 13.

Biblical authority will be discussed more fully below, but here it should be said that a proper understanding of canon emphasizes that canon is not a definitive collection of timeless, divinely revealed truths. Canon is a collection of witnesses to an ongoing encounter with the presence of God in the lives of persons and communities. The canon is witness to a process of experiencing, witnessing, preserving, and passing on testimony to the experience of divine reality in a wide range of human contexts. Thus, the canon functions not as a static deposit of timeless truth, but rather as a partner in conversation with our own experience of God's presence in our lives. "The canon functions not in isolation from our own experience of God but precisely in the process of letting our own story be intersected by the biblical story and reflecting critically and acting faithfully in the church out of those intersections. The end result toward which we should strive is a deabsolutized canon which allows for the honoring of ancient witness to the degree that it reveals to us the basic truths of our faith while at the same time honoring the power and authority of our own experience of God" (Birch and Rasmussen 156–57).

The Text as Scripture in the Present

The canon of Scripture, both OT and NT, originated in ancient times, but these collections of texts and their voices have been passed on through the generations to the present as authoritative in some fundamental way for the moral character and conduct of contemporary communities of faith. Thus, biblical ethics can refer to critical reflection on these texts and the way in which they inform the moral life of contemporary Christians. Some of the issues and dynamics of this will be discussed below, but here we should note that studies focused on Scripture as a resource for contemporary ethics will not find there some uniform system or pattern of moral identity and behavior that can simply be adopted or imposed. Nor is it productive to force upon the canon some moral system formed outside the text.

It may well be that the canon invites readers into a process of moral conversation and discernment with a diversity of witnesses that communities of faith have passed on as valued dialogue partners. These texts do not invite us into a ready-made set of moral rules, norms, and conclusions. The process of conversation and discernment will yield diverse results: illumination and insight in one instance, but dialogic struggle and tension in another. In reading of Jesus' life and ministry, we may find models to emulate in practice and thought. But in reading of Israel's experience as God's people, we will encounter testimony to both obedient and disobedient life lived before God. The faithful moral alternative in one biblical context may not be the faithful choice in another. Differences between the biblical world and our own must be faced honestly, and the use of Scripture as an ethical resource cannot be a simple pattern of emulating ancient ways, nor will we find a single, unified moral code to merely adopt. What the canon represents is the judgment of generations of faithful communities that have found these texts worthy of moral contemplation and ethical reflection. They witness to the experience of relationship to God and the challenge of life as God's people in diverse contexts and circumstances. The moral authority of these texts is foundational for the moral character and conduct of contemporary communities of faith, but only in dialogue with the traditions that passed on these texts and with the best critical understanding of our own experience of God and the world we live in now.

Foundational Understandings

The relationship between Scripture and ethics is dynamic and multifaceted. The Bible is certainly no simple prescriptive manual, nor is it just distant historical background for the Christian life. The church's claim that the Bible is a living resource for the life of faith is a serious one, but to understand that relationship requires clarity about some foundational matters. The sections below discuss some of these, related to community, moral agency, biblical authority, and divine reality.

The Centrality of Community

The canon of Scripture is the product of community. Whatever the diverse origins of particular texts or books of the Bible, the communities of ancient Israel and the early church collected, preserved, debated, and passed on the particular collection of ancient faith witnesses that we know as the OT and the NT. As a resource for Christian ethics, the witness of these texts is fully available only in the context of contemporary faith communities.

The Bible is the story of a community of those who understood themselves to be God's people, both ancient Israel as God's covenant people and the early church as the body of Christ. For those communities, the moral life was never a matter of individual character and conduct alone. The moral life is lived in the midst of and held accountable by the faith community. Individual moral life is lived in the context of a community that understands itself to be called into being by the gracious activity of God, seeks together to discern the nature of the moral life, and holds its members accountable to one another. Israel, the early church, generations of the faithful, and the contemporary church in its diverse forms all serve as interpretive communities within which the Bible is both a witness to the experience of God's grace and a testimony with the power to mediate that divine grace to transform new generations.

The Bible is the church's book. The church is shaped by the story and testimony of the canon of Scripture. Both the church's identity and its ongoing activity are shaped in dialogue with the Bible as a foundational resource. This relationship between ecclesial community, the Bible, and the moral life has multiple dimensions.

The church acts as the shaper of moral identity. In the life of faith communities the stories of Israel, Jesus, and the early church are encountered in worship, teaching, and testimony. Here others are invited to make the biblical story a part of their own identity.

The church acts as the bearer of moral tradition. Differing ecclesial traditions give testimony to the power of the text of Scripture to shape Christian life and mission. We do not begin anew each time we open the pages of the Bible seeking resources for the moral life; others have gone before us, and we stand in rich streams of moral tradition as we seek to be faithful moral agents in our own time.

The church is the community of moral deliberations. Christians are not isolated readers of the text trying to discern the witness of Scripture to moral life. The life of faith communities provides contexts and forums for sharing both insights and challenges in claiming the biblical witness as central to moral life in our own world. Discernment happens not by heroic individual reflection but rather by sharing our deliberations with others in the effort to see how biblical witness to God's grace can help us discern that grace in the pathways of our own lives.

The church is the agent of moral action. There is always a place for the faithful ethical action of a committed individual, but those actions are a part of a larger active witness by ongoing historical communities. The power of even an individual act of moral witness is magnified by awareness of the larger church community of moral action to make God's grace visible in the world. And actions joined in systems of active witness can have remarkable transformative power.

The text of Scripture is where the originating and the ongoing interpretive communities meet. It is out of those intersections that the Bible has moral influence mediated through faith communities, both ancient and modern.

Moral Agency and Aspects of Christian Ethics

The Bible assumes that we, as humans created by God, are capable of moral responsibility. In the language of Christian ethics, we are created as moral agents, capable of being shaped by relationships to God and neighbor and capable of making moral decisions that affect those relationships. As such, the Bible also assumes that we can be held morally accountable for our lives as moral agents in the world, accountable for who we are and what we do as individuals and as communities. Moral agency encompasses both character and conduct, both our being and our doing. Here we will look at three aspects: (1) decision-making and action; (2) character formation; and (3) virtue, value, obligation, and vision.

For many, Christian ethics automatically suggests decision-making and action. In this dimension of Christian ethics the central question is: What are we to do? This can be applied to any of the many moral issues that face ancient or modern persons and communities. How is the Bible a resource for questions of moral conduct?

Over the centuries there have always been some tempted to make the Bible into a prescriptive code of conduct. This has never been very successful. At best, the result has been a picking and choosing of biblical texts that seem more usable in this way—for example, the Ten Commandments or the teachings of Jesus. But the simple truth is that the Bible never makes moral decisions for us, nor do biblical texts lay out strategies or courses of action. And biblical texts do not speak with a single voice. The commandment says, "Do not kill," but other laws in the Pentateuch allow capital punishment and waging of war. The teachings of Jesus include those often called his "hard sayings," radical demands of the kingdom that few can meet.

Many of our modern issues requiring moral discernment and action simply could not be anticipated by the biblical communities (e.g., issues of bioethics). Others appear in such radically altered modern contexts that moral response seems complex and unclear. The early church dealt with issues of economic disparity by owning and sharing everything in common, but this does not translate immediately into morally responsible decisions in a complex global economy where economic disparities are intertwined with complex sociopolitical systems.

Still, the Bible is an important resource for the ethics of doing as long as we do not expect the text to do our decision-making for us. The texts of Scripture do make clear broad moral imperatives that frame our moral decisions—for example, the constant concern for those marginalized in human community: the poor, the weak, the hungry, the outcast. Scripture offers images that challenge our moral imagination and consideration of moral alternatives (e.g., Jesus with the woman taken in adultery). The Bible supplies important principles, norms, and standards that can guide our decisions in particular contexts: justice, love, compassion, righteousness. We should note, however, that this does not let us off the hook in deciding what the most just or loving action might be in a given context. The Bible also makes clear that faithful life as moral agents is never lived in isolation; we are a part of God's people, called to hold one another accountable for our actions in the world and to regard the failure to act at all as a moral failure.

Christian ethics, however, involves more than what we do. It involves who we are to be. Alongside moral decision-making and action we must consider character formation, questions of identity, of "our basic moral perception." "Character formation is the learning and internalizing of a way of life formative of our own moral identity. It is our moral 'being,' the expression of who we are. . . . Character includes our basic moral perception—how we see and understand things—as well as our fundamental dispositions, intentions, and motives" (Birch and Rasmussen 190).

Moral character and identity are shaped by many elements: family, culture, relationships, particular experiences. But Christian moral character must have a fundamental relationship to the Bible. Christian moral agents are nurtured by relationship to the stories, hymns, visions, commandments, and teachings of the entire Scripture handed on and reflected upon by generations of God's people. In the life of Christian congregations we are exposed to the entire range of materials in Scripture, and this helps to shape our identity as people of faith and moral agents. This material shapes us in different ways both by the diversity of the texts themselves and by the way they are read, taught, and used in the lives of congregations and individuals.

While moral character and conduct, being and doing, provide a broad framework for the moral life and the Bible as a resource for Christian ethics, there are many other useful categories that provide nuance, perspective, and insight into the full complexity of moral agency. A full discussion of the Christian moral life would want to discuss categories such as virtue, value, obligation, and vision. Virtue focuses on qualities that mark us as Christian moral persons and communities (kindness, courage, humility, love, righteous anger, and others). Value tends to focus on qualities that mark the social embodiment of morality (justice, love, equality, peace). Scripture helps to name and form virtues and values, and these overlap in actual human experience. Obligation has to do with duties, commitments, and responsibilities that arise out of the decision to live our lives in the context of Christian community and the Scripture that foundationally defines its life. Some obligations are a part of the common frameworks that we share with others in our social contexts (e.g., family, citizenship, culture). Christian obligation arises out of our decision to be a part of the church, and then the Bible becomes a part of the resources that the church uses to shape its character and conduct in the world. Moral vision is the large picture of the moral drama that Scripture invites us into as partners with God in the redemptive activity of God's people. Moral vision is the category that suggests a framework anchored in the character and conduct of God that encompasses our being and our doing as Christian moral agents.

The Nature of Biblical Authority

The nature of biblical authority and how it functions in the life of Christian traditions and communities have been the subjects of considerable diversity of opinion, and this is one reason why Christian faith has such a variety of expressions. The Bible, understood as Scripture, is acknowledged by all Christian traditions as normative for the understanding and living of the Christian life. It shapes Christian identity and practice, as referenced in the preceding section. But how does the normative character of the Bible express itself? What is its relation to other authorities that also shape human moral life?

"Authority is not a property inherent in the Bible itself. It is the recognition of the Christian community over centuries of experience that the Scripture is a source of empowerment for its life in the world" (Birch and Rasmussen 142). To function in this way, however, the Bible must be understood as pointing beyond itself to the experience of the biblical communities with the character and activity of God. Authority rests not in the pages of the text, but rather in its function as a mediating witness to God, who called biblical communities of covenant and church into being and is still graciously active in our present experience.

Human moral life is shaped by many sources of authority. We become moral agents because we have been given identity and have been guided in our actions by a complex matrix of authoritative influences that are then shaped by us as individuals and members of various communities. These influences include family, nationality, ethnic identity, cultural context, formal and informal education, gender experience, signal life events, influential individuals in varied roles, and professed religious belief. The Christian moral life must include the Bible and its interpretive traditions as authoritative in some manner; otherwise, there is no basis on which to label our ethics as Christian. However, in Christian ethics the Bible, though always primary, is never self-sufficient. The Bible cannot be the sole source of authoritative influence, and thus it is never the exclusive authority for the moral life. Nevertheless, the Bible is indispensable for ethics to be labeled as Christian because it places us in a common tradition with other varieties of Christian experience throughout history and in today's world.

The Bible's primary and central role finds expression in a variety of ways because the Bible itself is an entire library of diverse texts. First and foremost, the Bible tells the story of who we are as the people of God connected historically to the communities responsible for the witness and preservation of the biblical texts. Centrally important within this entire biblical story is the story of Jesus, told in the diverse voices of the Gospels. But Jesus' story is connected both to Israel's story and to the early church's story. That story can model for the church both faithful and unfaithful moral life. To reflect on the biblical story is to aid us in discerning God's presence and activity in our own stories. For those who choose to be part of the Christian community, the Bible becomes an active dialogue partner in assessing and drawing on the other sources of moral influence in our lives. It is a matter of both content and process.

The authority of Scripture resides partly in its witness to a process of discerning and responding to the character and action of God in the life of the biblical witnesses. This in turn invites us to a similar process of discernment in our own time, guided by the way in which Scripture sensitizes us to the presence and activity of God here and now. But,

> attention to biblical authority as it mediates a process does not mean there is no continuity of biblical content to be claimed. . . . Our identity as the church is obviously shaped by images, concepts, and metaphors that are part of the Bible's content and not just witness to a process. But these cannot be regarded as revelatory deposits functioning as divinely sanctioned doctrine. The content must be constantly tested by the process. Which stories and images continue to manifest the redeeming power of God? Some matters of content are reassessed by the church, e.g., the biblical acceptance of slavery, Paul's admonition for women to keep silent in the church. Some matters of content are reasserted, e.g., God's preferential option for the poor and oppressed. Some matters of content remain central although our interactions with them may change, e.g., the gospel story of the life, death, and resurrection of Jesus. (Birch and Rasmussen 157)

Already implied in this brief discussion of biblical authority for Christian ethics is the recognition that the broad diversity of biblical material suggests various ways in which these materials are used and are experienced as authoritative. "Different types of biblical material must be appropriated in different ways. . . . The problem with most discussions of biblical authority is that they seem to imply a monolithic view of the Bible and its use. There is no single way in which the Bible is authoritative in ethical matters" (Birch, *Let Justice Roll Down*, 157). A constant moral imperative to care for the poor and dispossessed will carry authority in a contemporary ethical discussion in response to poverty. At the same time, diverse witnesses to the attitude of the faithful toward the power of the state will range as widely as the story of Daniel and the admonitions of Paul in Rom. 13. The authority of Scripture here is not to prescribe a course of action or even a line of response. It operates more to define a framework within which moral options in relating to the power of the state must be considered and weighed. Stories and hymns have authority in shaping the character of our lives as persons and communities that read and sing them and respond to the character of God revealed in them.

The Bible as the Scripture of the church forms the necessary authoritative framework within which ethical reflection must take place if it is to be Christian. Within that framework other moral influence can be engaged in dialogue and discernment. The God of the biblical text is still active in our own lives, our own faith communities, and our own religious experience. Hence, we must discuss the importance of witness to divine reality both in the biblical text and in our own time as a focus for Christian moral claims.

Divine Reality

For those who regard the Bible as Scripture, the texts that have been collected and passed on in the OT and the NT are witnesses to divine reality. They are the gathered testimonies of Israel and the early church to their experience of God in the life of Israel as God's covenant people; in the testimonies to the life, death, and resurrection of Jesus; in the formation and spread of the early church. Hence, Scripture as a resource for the Christian moral life mediates a divine reality that is assumed to be still present and active in the lives of contemporary confessing communities. Understanding who God is and how God has been active, what God wills and what God models, is essential to the Bible's role in Christian ethics.

The common popular view of the Bible's use in Christian ethics focuses on morality as obedience to God's revealed will. In its unexamined form this finds expression in those who think of the Bible as a prescriptive handbook for moral behavior. On closer examination, this always proves to be a highly selective sample of biblical texts. In more sophisticated forms the stress on revealed divine will has tended to identify a canon within the canon of texts regarded as serious expressions of God's will for how we are to conduct ourselves, guides to moral behavior and God's intention for us. The result has been emphasis on important texts such as the Decalogue, the preaching of the prophets, the teachings of Jesus, and the moral admonitions of Paul and other early church voices. Such texts are indeed centrally important, for the Bible does call us to live a life obedient to God's purposes for us, and for Christians, the teachings of Jesus in particular are important guides to moral conduct in lives that express love of God and neighbor.

However, God is much more than a lawgiver or a moral teacher in the Bible, and earlier we noted the limitations of the Bible in giving us moral instruction on what we are to do. It is more faithful to the range and diversity of biblical materials to focus on the character of God as well as the will of God, especially as revealed in divine activity related to the biblical communities of faith.

In addition to the roles of lawgiver and teacher, associated with the will of God as seen in, for example, the Decalogue and the teachings of Jesus, God plays many other roles in Scripture. These include creator, promise giver, deliverer, judge, redeemer, sovereign, and covenant partner. These roles do not appear in systematic discursive treatments in the biblical texts. They appear in stories of God's encounters and relationships with key biblical figures and ongoing biblical communities. They appear in relationships that the biblical stories tell us God has risked in divine presence within human history and divine encounters with individuals and communities that have given testimony in the biblical texts to these encounters.

Some scholars have appropriately highlighted the imitation of God (*imitatio Dei*) or of Christ (*imitatio Christi*) as a basis for ethics in the use of Scripture. Texts such as Lev. 19:2, "You shall be holy, for I the LORD your God am holy," or the entire emphasis of 1 John on loving as God has loved, make this moral imitation of God explicit. Many other texts name qualities of God's character that model moral character for God's people: love, righteousness, justice, compassion, faithfulness, service.

The Practice of Using Scripture as a Moral Resource

Beyond the scope of this article lies the complex set of practices that persons and communities must cultivate in light of the methodological perspectives discussed above. It is an ongoing process that stretches and matures through the Christian life. These practices include:

- *The development of critical skill in reading and understanding the biblical texts as fully as possible.* This is more than exegesis of individual and isolated texts; it is the development of patterns of reading that allows conversation between texts within the canon while honoring the full witness of each text. Fortunately, many useful tools are available to aid our reading, such as study Bibles, commentaries, concordances, dictionaries, computer programs, and Internet resources.
- *The practice of "reading in communion"* (see Fowl and Jones). Christian ethics is not informed by isolated individual reading of biblical texts so much as the reading together in community that takes place in the ongoing use of Scripture in the life of congregations. This is not simply the obvious practice of formal study of the Bible in various programs within the church; it also involves exposure to the Scripture in liturgy, preaching, hymns, and devotion. When this exposure to the biblical story is rich, the ongoing conversation in Christian community about the issues that challenge us will be informed by the implicit and explicit shaping of lives and decisions that comprise our identity as Christian moral agents in the world.

Clearly, the relating of Scripture to Christian ethics is a rich and complex conversation that is both historical and global. We are invited into the conversation not for the discovery of fixed moral truths, but rather to experience the moral power of life lived in the presence of God and as a part of God's people.

Bibliography

Barton, J. "Approaches to Ethics in the Old Testament." Pages 113–30 in *Beginning Old Testament Study*, ed. J. Rogerson. Westminster, 1982; idem. "The Basis of Ethics in the Hebrew Bible." *Semeia* 66 (1996): 11–22; idem. *Ethics and the Old Testament*. Trinity Press International, 1998; idem, "Understanding Old Testament Ethics." *JSOT* 9 (1978): 44–64; idem. *Understanding Old Testament Ethics: Approaches and Explorations*. Westminster John Knox, 2003; Birch, B. "Divine Character and the Formation of Moral Community in the Book of Exodus." Pages 119–35 in *The Bible in Ethics: The Second Sheffield Colloquium*, ed. J. Rogerson, M. Davies, and M. D. Carroll R. JSOTSup 207. Sheffield Academic, 1995; idem. *Let Justice Roll Down: The Old Testament, Ethics, and Christian Life*. Westminster John Knox, 1991; idem. "Moral Agency, Community, and the Character of God in the Hebrew Bible." *Semeia* 66 (1994): 23–41; idem. "Old Testament Narrative and Moral Address." Pages 75–91 in *Canon, Theology, and Old Testament Interpretation: Essays in Honor of Brevard S. Childs*, ed. G. Tucker, D. Petersen, and R. Wilson. Fortress, 1988; Birch, B., and L. Rasmussen. *Bible and Ethics in the Christian Life*. Rev. ed. Augsburg, 1989; Blount, B. *Then the Whisper Put on Flesh: New Testament Ethics in an African American Context*. Abingdon, 2001; Cahill, L. "The New Testament and Ethics: Communities of Social Change." *Int* 44 (1990): 383–95; Childs, B. *Biblical Theology of the Old and New Testaments: Theological Reflections on the Christian Bible*. Fortress, 1993; idem. *Old Testament Theology in Canonical Context*. Fortress, 1985; Clements, R. *Loving One's Neighbor: Old Testament Ethics in Context*. University of London Press, 1992; Eichrodt, W. "The Effect of Piety on Conduct (Old Testament Morality)." Pages 316–79 in vol. 2 of *Theology of the Old Testament*, trans. J. Baker. OTL. Westminster, 1967; Fowl, S., and L. Jones, *Reading in Communion: Scripture and Ethics in Christian Life*. Eerdmans, 1991; Hauerwas, S. *A Community of Character: Toward a Constructive Christian Ethic*. University of Notre Dame Press, 1981; idem. *The Peaceable Kingdom: A Primer in Christian Ethics*. University of Notre Dame Press,

1983; Hays, R. *The Moral Vision of the New Testament: Community, Cross, and New Creation; A Contemporary Introduction to New Testament Ethics.* HarperSanFrancisco, 1996; Hempel, J. *Das Ethos des Alten Testaments.* BZAW 67. Töpelmann, 1938; Janzen, W. *Old Testament Ethics: A Paradigmatic Approach.* Westminster John Knox, 1994; Knight, D. "Political Rights and Powers in Monarchic Israel." *Semeia* 66 (1994): 93–118; Matera, F. *New Testament Ethics: The Legacies of Jesus and Paul.* Westminster John Knox, 1996; Nasuti, H. "Identity, Identification, and Imitation: The Narrative Hermeneutics of Israelite Law." *JLR* 4 (1986): 9–23; Ogletree, T. *The Use of the Bible in Christian Ethics: A Constructive Essay.* Fortress, 1983; Otto, E. *Theologische Ethik des Alten Testaments.* TW. Kohlhammer, 1994; Rodd, C. *Glimpses of a Strange Land: Studies in Old Testament Ethics.* T&T Clark, 2001; Verhey, A. *The Great Reversal: Ethics and the New Testament.* Eerdmans, 1984; Wenham, G. "The Gap between Law and Ethics in the Bible." *JJS* 48 (1997): 17–29; idem. *Story as Torah: Reading the Old Testament Ethically.* OTS. T&T Clark, 2000; Wilson, R. "Approaches to Old Testament Ethics." Pages 62–74 in *Canon, Theology, and Old Testament Interpretation: Essays in Honor of Brevard S. Childs*, ed. G. Tucker, D. Petersen, and R. Wilson. Fortress, 1988; idem. "Sources and Methods in the Study of Ancient Israelite Ethics." *Semeia* 66 (1994): 55–63; Wright, C. *An Eye for an Eye: The Place of Old Testament Ethics Today.* InterVarsity, 1983; idem. *Old Testament Ethics for the People of God.* InterVarsity, 2004.

Abortion

Induced abortion (as opposed to spontaneous abortion, or miscarriage) is the deliberate termination of a pregnancy through the destruction and/or removal of the embryo or fetus.

Because recent discussion of abortion, even in the church, has almost universally considered it a political issue addressed within the framework of rights, the first task of Christian ethics is to make the question a truly theological and ecclesial one (Bauerschmidt; Hauerwas), reframing it within the fundamental scriptural framework of covenant faithfulness, or discipleship. How should being a baptized community of faith, hope, and love in Christ shape the way Christians approach abortion?

Recent theological approaches to abortion are parallel to the three traditional theological perspectives on war, though they are major areas on a spectrum, not precisely fixed points. (1) The position that sometimes designates itself "pro-life" or "right-to-life" is similar to the pacifist position, arguing that abortion is (perhaps with rare exceptions) unethical. Unlike pacifism, however, this position sometimes depends on asserting the innocence of the embryo/fetus. (2) The "justifiable abortion" position, existing in various forms (e.g., Steffen), resembles the just-war tradition: abortion is tragic but justified in certain circumstances. The criteria can relate to the status of the fetus/embryo (e.g., deformity, nonviability, threat to the woman's health) or to the situation of the pregnant woman (e.g., forced pregnancy; economic, emotional, or physical distress). Unlike just-war theory, the just-abortion argument usually recognizes the satisfaction of one criterion as sufficient rather than requiring the satisfaction of multiple criteria. (3) A third position—"pro-choice," "procreative choice," or "abortion rights" (e.g., Harrison)—is similar to the holy-war tradition in seeing the agent as sacred and capable of making a free, responsible decision without providing formal justification.

One cause of these various views is Scripture's apparent silence on the issue. This can lead to certain erroneous or misguided claims: that abortion was unknown in antiquity; that Scripture should have no role in the abortion debate; that Jews and Christians cannot formulate a robust position on the issue; or that Scripture's silence necessarily implies divine neutrality or approval, and that the faith community should follow suit.

The silence also leads people to look for texts to support their position. Abortion opponents often quote "choose life" (Deut. 30:19). They also appeal to texts about God's creation and call in the womb (Ps. 139:13–14a; Isa. 44:1–2; Jer. 1:5) and about fetal activity (Luke 1:41, 44) to argue that Scripture considers the embryo/fetus to be God's direct creation and indeed a human being. Those who disagree respond that, biblically, the embryo/fetus is akin to property that can be damaged (Exod. 21:22–23), and that human life does not begin until the first breath (Gen. 2:7). Each side accuses the other of prooftexting.

Some interpreters, recognizing the impasse created by appeals to such texts, have looked to broader scriptural themes for an implicit position on abortion or a framework for considering it. Abortion opponents have argued that scriptural themes such as creation as divine gift, the summons to welcome children, and the vision of *shalom* (part of a "consistent ethic of life") validate their position. Supporters of abortion/choice have argued for the voluntary and relational character of covenants in the Bible and stressed divine grace and forgiveness for poor decisions. They have also appealed to stewardship of creation and to choice ("*choose* life"), the former accenting human responsibility, the latter human freedom and liberation.

Critics of stewardship as justification for abortion have argued, however, that biblical stewardship does not include the deliberate destruction of creation, especially of human, or even potentially human, life. And critics of human freedom as justification for abortion point out that scriptural freedom is not absolute, that what is chosen is crucial. Moreover, they contend, liberation in Scripture is freedom *from* false deities, ideologies, and values, and freedom *for* joyful, bonded, covenantal service to God and others.

One significant aspect of the discussion is the witness of early Judaism (e.g., *Sibylline Oracles*, Philo, Josephus) and early Christianity against abortion, despite its absence from the Scriptures that have come down to us. (Rabbinic literature would permit abortion to save the woman's life.) Certain scriptural images and themes, including some noted above, shaped the symbolic world of Jews and then Christians; opposition to abortion, exposure, and infanticide became an ethical boundary marker for both groups in their pagan cultures. In explaining the biblical summons to love of neighbor, both *Did.* 2.2 and *Barn.* 19.5 (ca. 95–135) say, "Thou shalt not murder a child by abortion." Subsequent Christian writers echo the prohibition and treat the unborn as "the object of God's care" (Athenagoras, *Plea* 35) (see Bonner; Gorman, *Abortion*).

This historical witness demonstrates that Scripture can have a key role in the abortion debate even if exegesis alone, still less prooftexting, is insufficient. A hermeneutic is needed that recognizes the difficulty of the issue, expresses pastoral sensitivity, and preserves the basic requirements of covenant faithfulness. Recent work on metathemes in the Bible's moral vision, individual and corporate baptismal identity, virtue ethics, narrative, and analogy may provide a way forward.

Richard Hays suggests that the NT's central themes of cross, community, and new creation compel us to reframe abortion so that a problem pregnancy is not merely about an individual's decision. Rather, it is an occasion for the church to act together in generous, Christlike, sacrificial love to embrace the pregnant woman and her child *in utero* with spiritual and tangible support. Believers constitute one body (1 Cor. 12)—indeed, a family—and are called to bear one another's burdens (Rom. 12:5; Gal. 6:2). Such a view does not, however, eliminate personal responsibility, for the believer's body is not his or her own but God's, the temple of the Holy Spirit (1 Cor. 6:19–20). It is the locus and means of self-giving love for God and others (Rom. 6; 12:1–2).

Related to the communal and familial images is the overarching biblical motif of care for the needy (e.g., Matt. 25), including the widow and the orphan (Ps. 82:3–4; Jas. 1:27). The call to protect and provide for the vulnerable may be applied, by analogy, to the situation of both the woman and the developing child. Thus, a text that numerous ethicists (e.g., Bauerschmidt; O'Donovan; Hays) have seen as significant for the church's response to abortion is the parable of the good Samaritan. The attempt to identify the status of the other ("Who is my neighbor?") may imply that the inquirer desires to define certain others in such a way that they are incapable of placing a moral demand on the inquirer. Jesus transforms the question about the identity of the neighbor into a summons to actually be a neighbor. Analogously, the contemporary question of the personhood ("neighbor-hood") of the embryo/fetus should perhaps be reconstituted first of all as a question about the meaning of being a neighbor to the other(s) in need, both those already born and those not yet born. Furthermore, the parable suggests that when the question of identity or status is transformed, the summons to "go and do likewise" requires Jesus' disciples to be engaged in creative and potentially costly forms of community and ministry, and thus to recognize the neighbor by being a neighbor.

The result is an ethic of cruciform hospitality practiced by those baptized into the master story of Christ (Bauerschmidt; Hays; Stallsworth). Although this approach may not resolve every difficult case, it suggests that the relationship between Scripture and abortion is fundamentally about what kind of community of faith, hope, and love is needed for women and children, seen and unseen, to be welcomed into that community and into the world.

See also Adoption; Birth Control; Body; Children; Family Planning; Infanticide; Procreation; Sanctity of Human Life

Bibliography

Bauerschmidt, F. "Being Baptized: Bodies and Abortion." Pages 250–62 in *The Blackwell Companion to Christian Ethics*, ed. S. Hauerwas and S. Wells. Blackwell, 2004; Bonner, G. "Abortion and Early Christian Thought." Pages 93–122 in *Abortion and the Sanctity of Human Life*, ed. J. Channer. Paternoster, 1985; Channer, J., ed. *Abortion and the Sanctity of Human Life*. Paternoster, 1985; Gorman, M. *Abortion and the Early Church*. Wipf & Stock, 1998; idem, "Scripture, History, and Authority in a Christian View of Abortion: A Response to Paul Simmons." *ChrBio* 2 (1996): 83–96; Gorman, M., and A. Brooks. *Holy Abortion? A Theological Critique of the Religious Coalition for Reproductive Choice*. Wipf & Stock, 2003; Harrison, B. *Our Right to Choose: Toward a New Ethic of Abortion*. Beacon Press, 1983; Hauerwas, S. "Abortion: Why the Arguments Fail." Pages 295–318 in *Abortion: A Reader*, ed. L. Steffen. Pilgrim Press, 1996; Hays, R. *The Moral Vision of the New Testament: Community, Cross, and New Creation; A Contemporary Introduction to New Testament Ethics*. HarperSanFrancisco, 1996, 444–61; John Paul II. *The Gospel of Life*. Random House, 1995; Johnston, G. *Abortion from the Religious and Moral Perspective: An Annotated Bibliography*. Prager, 2003; O'Donovan, O. "Again: Who Is a Person?" Pages 125–37 in *Abortion and the Sanctity of Human Life*, ed. J. Channer. Paternoster,

1985; Religious Coalition for Reproductive Choice. "Prayerfully Pro-Choice: Resources for Worship." http://www.rcrc.org/pdf/Prayerfully.pdf; Schlossberg, T., and E. Achtemeier. *Not My Own: Abortion and the Marks of the Church*. Eerdmans, 1995; Simmons, P. "Biblical Authority and the Not-So Strange Silence of Scripture." *ChrBio* 2 (1996): 66–82; Stallsworth, P., ed. *The Church and Abortion*. Abingdon, 1993; Steffen, L. *Life/Choice: The Theory of Just Abortion*. Wipf & Stock, 2000.

Michael J. Gorman

Absolutes, Moral *See* Moral Absolutes

Abstinence *See* Alcohol; Gluttony; Sexual Ethics

Abuse

Abuse involves misuse, corruption, deceit, condemnation, vilification, violence, and excessive harm against one's self, another person, or another's relationships; it causes emotional battering, producing shame and disgrace. Abuse, a form of misbegotten anguish, engages the unauthentic self via unjust, immoral, despicable, reprehensible acts. Antithetical to beauty, truth, peace, and justice, abuse devastates, often allegedly for a higher good, such as ecclesial, national, or personal aggrandizement.

Abuse occurs in the OT in the context of family and national violence amid quests for leadership, liberation, and land acquisition. The Hebrew term *ʿālal* can mean "to abuse, act severely, harshly, ruthlessly; to make a fool or mockery of; to exploit, manipulate, dishonor, insult, defile, harm, or negatively have power over; to cause pain and/or shame." Sometimes God deals harshly with humanity—for example, the Egyptians (Exod. 10:2). A case of human abuse involves a Levite who gives his secondary wife/concubine to depraved men who gang-rape her (Judg. 19:25). With premeditation, he betrays and dismembers her and then sends her body parts throughout Israel, where violence invokes anarchy.

With similar sentiments, sexual abuse, often a hidden sin, involves aggression and hatred, objectifies and desecrates persons' mental, emotional, and bodily integrity, and robs them of their selfhood, victimizing them. See the incidents of Shechem's rape of Dinah (Gen. 34), Amnon's forced incest with Tamar (2 Sam. 13), and David's manipulation of Bathsheba (2 Sam. 11).

Wounded and denied an honorable death by his armor bearer, Saul commits suicide by falling on his own sword to prevent his Philistine enemies from abusing him (1 Sam. 31:4). Balaam's donkey makes a fool of him (Num. 22:29), and Jeremiah is mocked and ridiculed as a result of his prophecy against Judah and Jerusalem (Jer. 20:7–18). When King Zedekiah fears that Judeans will abuse him, Jeremiah counters that his obedience to God's voice will keep him safe (Jer. 38:19–20). Habakkuk laments God's silence as he cries out for help in the face of violence (Hab. 1:2–3).

In the NT, the Gospels reach their climax with Jesus' suffering and death prior to his resurrection appearances. In the book of Acts, Stephen, James, Peter, Paul, Silas, and others suffer abuse at the hands of the authorities (Acts 7:54–60; 12:1–5; 16:19–24). Elsewhere, Paul documents the abuse he endured as an apostle, which he interprets as a form of identification with the suffering of Christ (e.g., 2 Cor. 11:23–33). At the same time, he castigates the Corinthians for putting up with someone who "makes slaves of you, or preys upon you, or takes advantage of you, or puts on airs, or gives you a slap in the face" (2 Cor. 11:20). Here, the focus is less on the abuser (i.e., Christians from outside the Corinthian church who have come into it and exercised leadership contrary to Paul's ministry) and more on the Corinthians' apparent tolerance of this sort of exploitation. The author of 1 Peter addresses Christians whose lives are marked by slander and oppression from nonbelievers, and he urges them to follow the example of Jesus by not returning abuse for abuse (e.g., 1 Pet. 2:23; 3:9).

Cognizant of the Ten Commandments, with their call to honor God and respect the person and property of others, in concert with Jesus' admonition to love God and our neighbors as ourselves, Christian ethics calls us to respect appropriate boundaries, to do no harm, and not to give credence to abuse by keeping silent in the face of it.

See also Child Abuse; Cruelty; Incest; Killing; Oppression; Sexual Abuse; Spousal Abuse; Violence

Bibliography

Fewell, D. "Judges." Pages 73–83 in *Women's Bible Commentary*, ed. C. Newsom and S. Ringe. Exp. ed. Westminster John Knox, 1998; Fortune, M. *Sexual Violence: The Sin Revisited*. Pilgrim Press, 2005; Kirk-Duggan, C. *Misbegotten Anguish: A Theology and Ethics of Violence*. Chalice, 2001; idem. *Violence and Theology*. HorTh. Abingdon, 2006.

Cheryl Kirk-Duggan

Accountability

Moral responsibility is often spoken of in terms of accountability. Financial transactions and their consequences are recorded in account ledgers and other financial documents, and people use the logic and language of such accounting to think and talk about moral obligations and interactions and their consequences. This is true in both formal and everyday moral reasoning, as well as in scriptural moral discourse. For example, the letter to the Colossians speaks of a "record": "God made you alive together with him, when he forgave us all our trespasses, erasing the record that stood against us with its legal demands. He set this aside, nailing it to the cross" (Col. 2:13b–14).

The record being cleared is a handwritten certificate of indebtedness or an account sheet (*cheirographon*). The concept of moral debt and credit is implied: just as debits and credits are recorded in an actual ledger and accrue incrementally, so individual moral transactions—actions and failures to act—contribute to character and moral standing in incremental fashion. Moreover, just as a debtor has a responsibility to repay the creditor and, if the debt is not paid, must answer to an auditor or judge, so those who are guilty of "trespass" (*paraptōma*, "lapse") must answer to legitimate moral authorities. Thus, moral accountability combines concepts of moral transactions and accumulated consequences with the reporting function of accounting, giving an account or an explanation.

Accountability and Oversight

In the NT, the authority that household managers have over household accounts and affairs is often used to conceptualize both human moral responsibility and the ultimate authority—the right and responsibility—that God has to judge human behavior overall. This kind of oversight includes care and concern as well as the maintenance of household honor. Relationships in the household mirror and lay a foundation for order in the larger social structures of the state and in the church, the new household of God. Leaders in the churches are accountable for the consequences of their teaching (Matt. 23; Luke 20:47; Jas. 3:1). Human rulers are delegated by God to hold the community to moral norms, and rulers in turn are ultimately accountable to God (1 Pet. 2:13–17). Thus, accountability has social-political and ecclesial dimensions and is not confined to the personal and individual sphere. A structure of legitimate moral authority is implied; moral accounting implies moral authority.

Accountability and Moral Agency

In Scripture, ultimate accountability is sometimes spoken of in terms of a scroll or record book, but the canonical authors use several versions of the moral books. In the OT, the "Book of Life" lists the righteous (Pss. 1:1–3; 7:9; 11:7; 34:12; 37:17, 29; 55:22; 75:10; 92:12–14; 140:13). The Lord says to Moses, "Whoever has sinned against me I will blot out of my book" (Exod. 32:33; cf. Pss. 9:5; 69:28). In the NT, Philippians and Revelation also refer to a "Book of Life" holding the names of those slated for eternal life; erasure of one's name signifies loss of belonging or of citizenship in God's kingdom (Phil. 4:3; Rev. 3:5; 13:8; 17:8; 20:15; 21:27). In the Revelation to John, account books figure in the picture of final judgment: "The dead were judged according to their works, as recorded in the books" (Rev. 20:12; cf. Dan. 7:10).

In 1 Peter, yet another variation occurs; the accountable subject is a group of people, "the family of God" (4:17). This picture coheres with an OT theme that assumes group or communal responsibility (Exod. 32:9–10; Deut. 9:13–14). For contemporary readers steeped in cultures of expressive individualism, this can challenge assumptions about the scope of moral agency. Is membership in a large category—the righteous—nevertheless dependent on individual behavior? Some passages clearly speak of individual agency and a level of responsibility that includes scrutiny of each deed (1 Pet. 1:17). In other contexts, the emphasis is less on individual deeds and more on overall character or disposition over a lifetime, on the quality of faithfulness. In Rom. 4:3, Paul notes that "Abraham believed God, and it was reckoned [*logizomai*] to him as righteousness" (one meaning of *logizomai* is "to keep records of commercial accounts").

Final Accounting and Judgment

Strict accountability entails judgment (Exod. 32:33–34); the guilty are punished and the righteous rewarded. But there is throughout Scripture an alternative theme, in which the nurturing and gracious God provides mercy and pardon (e.g., Mic. 7:18–19), especially when there is repentance (e.g., Ezek. 18:23, 27–28, 32; 33:14–16). Thus, David writes, "Blessed are those whose sin the Lord does not count against them" (Ps. 32:2b TNIV; [cf. Ps. 103:10–12; Isa. 43:25; Jer. 50:20; Ezek. 20:44; Rom. 4:7–8; 2 Cor. 5:19; Rev. 14:5]).

Account as Story, Testimony

Sometimes accountability takes the form of testimony, of telling one's story to the judge. Thus, in Isa. 43:25–26, God calls the people to account: "I, even I, am he who blots out your transgressions, for my own sake, and remembers your sins no more. Review the past for me, let us argue the matter together; state the case for your innocence" (TNIV). The author of 1 Peter warns of a time when the unfaithful "will have to give an accounting to him who stands ready to judge the living and the dead" (4:5). Jesus portrays a scene of legal accountability and testimony gathering in the parable of the sheep and the goats, where behavior and dispositions toward the needy (or "the least of these brothers and sisters of mine") are linked to core character and ultimate destiny (Matt. 25:31–46).

Conclusion: Accountability and Justification

Accountability signifies that human behavior counts. It matters what people do to and for one another. Both individual and social well-being are at stake. People have moral obligations as individuals and in groups, including churches and nations, and there are consequences for failure to meet those obligations. Certain punishment is pictured as the natural consequence of moral debt (Exod. 32:34; Isa. 13:11; Jer. 21:14; 1 Pet. 2:14), yet the ultimate judge is God the Father, who "cares for you," and "will himself restore, support, strengthen, and establish" anxious Christians (1 Pet. 5:7, 10). The overall goal of judgment and punishment, of warnings about final accountability, seems to be corrective nurturing toward authentic goodness and wholeness of character, in both individuals and groups. The reality and seriousness of moral accountability are linked to the gravity and costliness of the gift of grace, of redemption (Eph. 2:3–10; Col. 2:13–14).

See also Collective Responsibility; Debt; Moral Agency; Responsibility

Bonnie Howe

Acts

The author of the Acts of the Apostles is unknown to us, but is likely the same person who wrote the Gospel of Luke. Although the tradition has identified the author as Luke, Paul's sometime companion (see, e.g., Phlm. 24), that proposal offers us little help in actually interpreting the narrative. Thus, the promise of the Spirit spans both volumes, but Paul in Acts is not coordinated with Paul's letters. God's kingdom is less prominent in Acts than in Luke; nonetheless, the risen Jesus, Philip, Barnabas, and Paul proclaim God's kingdom. Thus, believing communities are aspects of God's rule, so that in the following approaches ethics is not merely individual but communal.

(1) In Acts law identifies deficient behavior (2:23; 7:53; 13:39), enhances reputations (5:34), demonstrates piety (21:20, 24; 22:12), affects relationships between Judeans and gentiles (10:28), but does not prescribe praxis. One exception is the Jerusalem decree for gentiles to abstain from sexual immorality (15:29; 21:25).

(2) Acts advocates values that imply praxis. Magic (13:6–11; 19:19), divination (16:16), and idolatry (14:15; 17:16–31) are renounced; their counterpart is belief. Substantial importance falls on the use of possessions. Lying to God by defrauding the community in regard to possessions has drastic consequences (5:1–10). Trying to buy God's gifts is reprehensible (8:19–20). Holding everything in common and distributing according to need reflect how the community is related to God (2:44–45). Giving alms receives positive evaluations (10:4, 31; 24:17), although, for some interpreters, giving alms stands in tension with distributing according to need. The latter expresses parity, whereas benefactors and beggars perpetuate "paternalistic humanitarianism."

(3) Characters such as Peter, Paul, Lydia, Dorcas, Stephen, and Cornelius play such positive roles that many interpreters make them models of praxis. Some translations of 20:35 imply that Paul makes himself an "example." But Paul's statement is expressed using a Greek verb (no noun corresponds to "example") more adequately rendered "teaching by indication": "that by such work we must support the weak." Models serve as analogies for readers, but analogies break down when pushed toward their limits (e.g., raising the dead). Further, the characters themselves reflect the origin of what they do in God (3:12, 16). Still, readers can identify with characters in their deficiencies (Peter's reluctance to go to Cornelius [10:20, 28]) and can envision models of God in relation to humanity. If analogies are used to envision roles of ministry, a quotation from Joel clarifies that the first preachers included both women and men (2:11, 17–18).

(4) Acts construes a world centered on God, who is manifest in unusual phenomena: resurrection appearances, the coming of the Spirit with aural and visual analogies, speaking in tongues, divine plans for events and history. Praxis is repeatedly determined by interpreting Scripture or special revelation from the Spirit. God is strongly characterized as a God of power (1:7–8; 2:11) who changes relationships among people. Prominent among these is the surpassing of ethnic limits: "In every nation anyone who fears [God] and does what is right is acceptable to him" (10:35).

(5) Because Acts depicts the emerging identity of a new group, it is especially suitable for demonstrating the convergence of philosophical, feminist, and sociological theories concerning identity as a source for ethics. All three disciplines emphasize the relational character of identity. Identity

emerges in community, changes by social patterns, and is sustained in relationships of solidarity.

Pentecost is a case in point (chap. 2). Here it is possible to see how identity, as it is embedded in social identity, is a source for praxis. If a group number is small, a substantial factor of power is needed for social identity. The conferring of the Holy Spirit is described as the reception of such power (1:8). Moreover, when the Holy Spirit comes (2:1–4), then according to thematic development from Luke 11:13 through Luke 24:49, the group assumes identity as God's children who receive the promise of the Spirit from their divine parent. The essential component of the unfolding identity is their relationship with God.

An ethical consequence of this identity might, at first glance, be called "distributive justice." But distribution according to need differs from conventional distributive justice (2:44–45). Distributive justice presumes normal institutional structures. The early Jerusalem community establishes itself as an alternative to existing structures. No consideration is given to how important specific functions are for the common good, as alleged when executives are compensated out of proportion to employees. Conventionally, lower classes work for the benefit of higher classes; Acts reverses the exchange. People at higher levels sell their possessions for redistribution to people at lower levels. This is no longer distributive justice but "differential justice."

(6) Acts is often considered an accommodation to the Roman Empire. But new sensitivity to how empire is experienced raises awareness of how the believing community is an alternative to empire. Acts reflects how imperial power filters down through governors, client kings, and elite collaborators. Noticing the collaboration of the people and the intersection of government and religion in the case of Herod Agrippa I in 12:20–23 sharpens awareness of how virtually everyone (regrettably) collaborates with oppressive systems. Even opponents recognize that Paul and Silas, by proclaiming another king, Jesus, act against the emperor (17:7). When Paul's Roman citizenship protects him from being flogged, it demonstrates inequality in Rome's judicial system (22:24–25). When Paul speaks to Felix about justice and self-control (24:25), Felix's fear shows that Paul expounds not abstract virtues but criteria for imperial agents. Felix's desire for a bribe in 24:26 confirms the need. Finally, Paul's appeal to the emperor in 25:11 is not an expression of confidence in the notorious Nero, but is a way out of the collaboration between ruling Judean elites and Festus (25:9–12).

See also Almsgiving; Authority and Power; Colonialism and Postcolonialism; Divination and Magic; Ethnic Identity, Ethnicity; Holy Spirit; Kingdom of God; Koinonia; Luke; Women, Status of

Bibliography

Fowl, S., and L. Jones. *Reading in Communion: Scripture and Ethics in Christian Life.* Eerdmans, 1991; Hays, R. *The Moral Vision of the New Testament: Community, Cross, and New Creation; A Contemporary Introduction to New Testament Ethics.* HarperSanFrancisco, 1996; Johnson, L. *The Literary Function of Possessions in Luke-Acts.* SBLDS 39. Scholars Press, 1977; Matera, F. *New Testament Ethics: The Legacies of Jesus and Paul.* Westminster John Knox, 1996; Phillips, T., ed. *Acts and Ethics.* NTM 9. Sheffield Phoenix Press, 2005.

Robert L. Brawley

Additions to Daniel

The Greek version of Daniel contains the "Prayer of Azariah" (a communal lament/confession) and the "Song of the Three Jews" (a benediction) between 3:23 and 3:24, as well as the "Story of Susanna" (a detective story) and the "Story of Bel and the Dragon" (a parody on idolatry) at the end (chaps. 13 and 14 in most editions). The additions reflect in various ways the tensions between the two great attributes of God in the Bible: justice and mercy.

In his prayer made in the fiery furnace, Azariah addresses God directly ("O Lord, God of our ancestors") and acknowledges the justice of God in allowing Israel to be defeated and exiled at the hands of the Babylonians in the sixth century BCE. He goes on to appeal to the mercy of God and reminds God of his promises to Abraham. He suggests that "a contrite heart and a humble spirit" may now serve as an acceptable sacrifice and issue in Azariah's own (and Israel's) deliverance.

In their long benediction in the fiery furnace, Azariah and his companions, Hananiah and Mishael, first bless directly ("Blessed are you") the God of Israel and of all creation. Then they invite all creation to join in their praise ("Bless the Lord"), including what is in the heavens (vv. 36–41), what comes down from the heavens (vv. 42–51), what lives on earth (vv. 52–59), and various classes of humans (vv. 60–66). They end by blessing God for their own deliverance. The song is an eloquent statement in praise of God's mercy, and its invitation to all creation to join the chorus of praise has positive implications for ecological ethics.

The Susanna story combines sex, religion, and death. Two "dirty old men" (who are elders and judges in the Jewish community in Babylon) happen to see the beautiful, God-fearing Susanna bathing, and they lust after her. When she refuses their advances, they accuse her of adultery with "a young man." She is saved from execution only when God stirs in Daniel "a holy spirit," and he finds a way to prove the accusation false by separating the two men and showing that their testimony is contradictory. As a result, they (rather than Susanna) are condemned to death. The Susanna story illustrates the justice of God, the power of trust in God, and God's use of Daniel's wisdom. It has also initiated a long artistic tradition of erotic portrayals of the naked Susanna.

In the episode about Bel and the Dragon, Daniel engages in contests about who the living God is. Playing detective again, he exposes the folly of idolatry and affirms the sovereignty of the God of Israel, who has mercy on those who love and trust him in the midst of their sufferings. The Additions to Daniel are part of Catholic and Orthodox Christian Bibles.

See also Daniel; Deuterocanonical/Apocryphal Books; Idolatry; Justice; Mercy

Bibliography

Clanton, D. *The Good, the Bold, and the Beautiful: The Story of Susanna and Its Renaissance Interpretations*. LHBOTS 430. T&T Clark, 2006; Collins, J. *Daniel*. Hermeneia. Fortress, 1993; Harrington, D. *Invitation to the Apocrypha*. Eerdmans, 1999, 109–21.

Daniel J. Harrington

Additions to Esther

The Hebrew text of Esther presents theological and ethical problems. Not only is there no explicit mention of God, but it is also silent about circumcision, Sabbath observance, and food laws, which were major identifying markers in Diaspora Judaism. Moreover, Esther becomes part of the Persian royal harem and eventually enters a mixed marriage with the gentile king. These problems may partly explain why no fragments of it were discovered among the Dead Sea Scrolls.

The Greek version of Esther turns the theology implicit in the Hebrew text into an explicit theology by introducing God into the main narrative (2:20; 4:8; 6:13). It also contains six additional sections that Jerome gathered into an appendix and placed at the end of the book. These additions heighten the role of God and prayer, give greater prominence to Esther and her motivation, and ameliorate some of the ethical problems.

Additions A (Mordecai's dream) and F (its interpretation) place the crisis facing the Jews in a cosmic context and state the basic theme of the Greek version, "These things have come from God" (10:4). Also included are full texts of what purport to be the royal decree ordering the extermination of all Jews (addition B) and its cancellation (addition E). Addition A is early evidence for charges leveled by anti-Semites against Jews throughout the ages ("perversely following a strange manner of life and laws"), while addition E recognizes that Jews are "governed by most righteous laws" and are "children of the living God."

Addition C contains two lengthy prayers by Mordecai and Esther that serve to embed the story more firmly into the wider story of God and Israel. Mordecai appeals to God as ruler of the universe and the God of Abraham to spare Israel from destruction, thus linking the story to Israel's previous scriptural traditions. Esther prays to "the Lord God of Israel" for eloquence before the king. She claims to "hate the splendor of the wicked and to abhor the bed of the uncircumcised and of any alien." She swears that she has avoided the (unclean) food and drink served at the king's table. Whatever unseemly behavior she has undertaken has been done in the service of the greater good of rescuing her people from certain annihilation. Saving Israel overrides behaviors that might appear immoral to some. The emotional and psychological struggle that Esther undergoes is neatly captured in addition C when she enters the king's court unannounced and with God's help wins a favorable hearing and averts her people's crisis. Although the Greek version of Esther does not solve all the book's theological and ethical problems, it most likely was intended to make the story less morally offensive in some circles. The Greek version is part of Catholic and Orthodox Christian Bibles.

See also Anti-Semitism; Deuterocanonical/Apocryphal Books; Esther; Exile; Feminist Ethics

Bibliography

De Troyer, K. *Rewriting the Sacred Text*. TCrS 4. Society of Biblical Literature, 2003; Harrington, D. *Invitation to the Apocrypha*. Eerdmans, 1999, 44–54; Kahana, H. *Esther: Juxtaposition of the Septuagint Translation with the Hebrew Text*. CBET 30. Peeters, 2005.

Daniel J. Harrington

Adoption

In a tradition whose Scriptures speak repeatedly and favorably of adoption and whose founder was, in one or more senses, adopted, one would expect a perspective and practice of caring for abandoned and orphaned children by grafting them into families. That has been the case for the Christian tradition.

About 2 to 4 percent of families in the United States include an adopted child, and about one million children in the United States live with adoptive parents. At any given time in the United States alone, somewhere between 200,000 and 500,000 singles or couples are looking to adopt, and some 100,000 nonrelative adoptions take place each year, about half from out of the foster care system and about 20,000 from overseas.

The adoption of a child has enriched the lives of families of various faith traditions, but adopting children is a complex and multilayered phenomenon that raises a number of ethical issues. Motivations for adoption vary widely, from "saving" children, to expanding the faith, to recognizing children's "right to be adopted," to addressing the problem of infertility.

Adoption in Scripture

The first chapter of Genesis includes the divine mandate to the newly created humans to be fruitful and multiply (Gen. 1:28), a command repeated to Noah and his family as they set foot on dry land again after the flood (Gen. 9:1). Barrenness functions as the driving motif in many Hebrew narratives: Sarah and Abraham (Gen. 11:30; 16:1), the women of the house of Abimelech (Gen. 20:18), Rebekah (Gen. 25:21), Rachel (Gen. 29:31; 30:1), the wife of Manoah (Judg. 13:2), and Hannah (1 Sam. 1:2, 5–6). Rachel's plaintive plea to Jacob represents the anguish that many infertile couples still experience: "Give me children, or I shall die!" (Gen. 30:1).

Although there is no legal prescription regarding adoption in Hebrew law, we find several stories in the OT that involve adoption-like practices. Joseph becomes a foster parent to Jacob's sons Ephraim and Manasseh (Gen. 48:5). Hadad and the sister of Queen Tahpenes give birth to a son, Genubath, who becomes one of Pharaoh's children (1 Kgs. 11:20). Mordecai adopts Esther as his own daughter after her parents die (Esth. 2:7, 15). Most prominent among these adoptees is Moses, whose mother leaves him in a basket among the reeds to protect him from Pharaoh (Exod. 2:1–10). In a broader sense, the OT suggests that God adopts Israel (e.g., Jer. 3:19; 7:6–7).

Aside from these direct, familial, or metaphorical adoption references, the OT evidences a profound concern for widows and orphans, apparently including not only children whose parents are deceased but also those who are abandoned. In Exod. 22:22; Ps. 82:3; Isa. 1:17; and Hos. 14:3 we find the charge to the Hebrew people to exercise justice and mercy with widows and orphans, a prominent theme in other OT texts as well.

In the NT adoption becomes a central theological concept, particularly at the hands of the apostle Paul. Among Jesus' recorded sayings is a strong motif of honoring the spiritual family over the natural family (e.g., Matt. 10:34–38; Luke 9:57–62; 14:26).

In Galatians Paul says that new followers of Jesus once were enslaved to false gods, but "God sent his Son . . . so that we might receive adoption as children" (Gal. 4:4–5). Belonging to Christ, Paul says, makes believers "Abraham's offspring, heirs according to the promise" (Gal. 3:29).

In Rom. 8:14–17 Paul argues that all those who are led by the Spirit of God are children of God, who have received "a spirit of adoption." Later in the same chapter, Paul describes what earlier appeared to be a present reality (adoption) as an eschatological hope; although children of God have the firstfruits of the Spirit, "we . . . groan inwardly while we wait for adoption, the redemption of our bodies" (Rom. 8:23).

Ephesians 1:3–14 echoes many of the same adoption themes already mentioned in Paul's epistles: believers are "destined . . . for adoption as [God's] children through Jesus Christ" (v. 5), and they have "obtained an inheritance" through Christ (v. 11), being marked with the seal of the Holy Spirit as a "pledge of our inheritance toward redemption as God's own people" (v. 14).

Accentuating the theme of adoption even further in Christian Scripture are the descriptions of Jesus' relationship with his human parents and with God, which can be understood in some senses as adoption. Scripture suggests that although Joseph has nothing to do with Jesus' conception, he raises Jesus as his son, so much so that Matthew's genealogy traces Jesus' lineage through Joseph (Matt. 1:16).

Adoption Ethics

Appropriate contemporary Christian ethical thinking about adoption might begin with God's call to care for orphans as well as with ethicist Timothy Jackson's attention to the "right to be adopted" rather than potential parents' rights to have or to adopt children.

As with birth parents, adoptive parents never know how their children will develop. In the spirit of the biblical tradition, being a parent means being open to welcoming strangers, whether they come to families by birth, the foster system, or adoption.

With the preponderance of adoptions from overseas, Western families have become particularly sensitive to their nations' tragic histories of imperialism and colonialism, seeking to avoid replicating those behaviors in their adoption practices.

Contemporary Christians also debate who should be able to adopt. Should it be only married, heterosexual couples, or should single people and same-sex couples be able to adopt as well? Should adoption be restricted to parents of the same racial identity?

Children fostered or adopted into Christian homes should be made conscious of the blessing and embrace of God and introduced to Jesus, who took children upon his knee and called upon adults to be as litle children, and to welcome them. Physically, politically, and economically embodying this graceful reality to all children in our midst is essential for those who represent the God manifested in Jesus. If God's grace covers all God's children across the world, in every faith and nation, then Christian believers' treatment of their birth children as well as those of outsiders, strangers, and enemies—their young neighbors at the family gate—must reflect such grace.

See also Abortion; Birth Control; Childlessness; Children; Family; Foster Care; Orphans; Parenthood, Parenting

Bibliography

Bartlett, D. "Adoption in the Bible." Pages 375–98 in *The Child in the Bible*, ed. M. Bunge, T. Fretheim, and B. Gaventa. Eerdmans, 2008; Clapp, R. *Families at the Crossroads: Beyond Traditional and Modern Options*. InterVarsity, 1993; Jackson, T., ed. *The Morality of Adoption: Social-Psychological, Theological, and Legal Perspectives*. Eerdmans, 2005. Melnyk, J. "When Israel Was a Child: Ancient Near Eastern Adoption Formulas and the Relationship between God and Israel." Pages 245–59 in *History and Interpretation: Essays in Honour of John H. Hayes*, ed. M. Graham, W. Brown, and J. Kuan. JSOTSup 173. JSOT Press, 1993; Miller, T. *The Orphans of Byzantium: Child Welfare in the Christian Empire*. Catholic University of America Press, 2003; Miller-McLemore, B. *Let the Children Come: Reimagining Childhood from a Christian Perspective*. Jossey-Bass, 2003; Pertman, A. *Adoption Nation: How the Adoption Revolution Is Transforming America*. Basic Books, 2000; Post, S. "Adoption Theologically Considered." *JRE* 25 (1997): 149–68; Stevenson-Moessner, J. *The Spirit of Adoption: At Home in God's Family*. Westminster John Knox, 2003; idem, "Womb-love: The Practice and Theology of Adoption." *ChrCent* 118, no. 3 (Jan. 24, 2001): 10–13.

Keith Graber Miller

Adultery

In the Bible, adultery is the act of sexual intercourse between a man and a woman who is either married or engaged to be married ("betrothed") to another man. The gravity of the violation of marriage through sexual infidelity is shown by its proscription in the Ten Commandments (Exod. 20:14; Deut. 5:18) and its status within some biblical law traditions as a capital crime. Both the man and the woman caught in adultery are to be put to death (Lev. 20:10; Deut. 22:22 [by stoning]; cf. John 8:5).

The Bible does not explicitly explain the reasons for the gravity of adultery, but some inferences may be made. The Bible's creation narrative portrays the fusion of the man and the woman into "one flesh" as a divinely created, joyful, and precious gift that addresses human loneliness (Gen. 2:18, 23–25). The joining of the man and woman also provides the crucible for the birth of children and the future of succeeding generations (Gen. 4:1; 5:1–32). In ancient Israel's patrilineal society, in which the family line is traced through fathers and sons, it was important to ensure the identity of the father of every child. A negative consequence of adultery was that children born of an "illicit union" in the law of Deuteronomy were prohibited from admission into the worship assembly (Deut. 23:2).

A woman's sexuality was considered to be under the guardianship of a male (husband, father, or other male relative). Thus, adultery by one man was understood primarily as a shameful offense against another man (the woman's husband) and the honor of his extended family (Deut. 22:24). Some of the prophets also used adultery as a metaphor for covenant infidelity in the relationship of Israel and Israel's God (Hos. 2–4). The exclusivity required in the worship of God (Exod. 20:3) mirrored the exclusivity of relationship required in human marriage, thereby associating adultery within the human community with theological concerns about the faithfulness of the community in its relationship to God (Jer. 2:20–24, 33–35; 3:1–9; 23:10, 14; Ezek. 18:6, 11, 15; 22:11; 33:26).

A gender-based double standard existed in sexual matters in ancient Israel. Sexual fidelity to one man was required of an individual woman, but a married man could have sexual relations with his own multiple wives (Gen. 29:15–30) or with his own multiple concubines (Gen. 16:1–4; 30:3–13; 2 Sam. 5:13; 16:20–22) without incurring the charge of adultery. The double standard is also apparent in some of the laws concerning charges of adultery that could be brought by husbands against their wives but not by wives against their husbands. In Num. 5:16–28 a ritual of ordeal is commanded for cases where a husband brings a charge of adultery against his wife but has no evidence to support it. The law in Deut. 22:13–21 describes a case in which a groom brings a charge against his bride that she is not a virgin. If the case is proved true, the bride is executed. The parents may save their daughter if they present a bloody sheet from the marriage bed as evidence of their daughter's virginity. No provision exists for the bride to bring a similar charge against the groom.

Other biblical traditions mitigate these male-biased texts by condemning men, and not only women, caught in adultery. The prophet Malachi condemns adultery by married males not because it is an affront to another male's honor, but because the adulterer has been faithless to "the wife of your youth . . . though she is your companion and your wife by covenant. Did not one God make her?" (Mal. 2:14–15). The wisdom tradition likewise urges its male readers to be faithful and to rejoice in the "wife of your youth" and not to be enticed "by another woman" (Prov. 5:15–23). The prophet Hosea condemns "your daughters" who commit adultery, but then he commands that they not be punished, since their fathers also commit adultery and sleep with prostitutes (Hos. 4:13–14).

One of the Bible's most notorious stories of marital infidelity is King David's adultery with Bathsheba, the wife of one of David's own soldiers, Uriah. Bathsheba became pregnant, and David tried to cover up his adultery by having Uriah killed in battle. The prophet Nathan condemned David for his affair with Bathsheba and for his killing of Uriah, indicating that the child born of their union would die as a consequence of his sin (1 Sam. 11–12). The narrative clearly condemns David but not Bathsheba; however, the death penalty is not imposed.

The most significant NT narrative involving adultery is Jesus' rescue of a woman caught in adultery who was about to be stoned (John 7:53–8:11). When asked about the law of Moses concerning the stoning of adulterers, Jesus famously replied, "Let anyone among you who is without sin be the first to throw a stone at her" (John 8:7). In the Sermon on the Mount, Jesus broadens the scope of the adultery commandment to include even the one "who looks at a woman with lust" (Matt. 5:27–30) and even those who are divorced and then remarry another person (Matt. 5:32; cf. 19:9; Mark 10:11–12; Luke 16:18; see also Rom. 7:3). Elsewhere adultery is included in NT lists of prohibited acts (Rom. 2:22; 13:9; 1 Cor. 6:9; Jas. 4:4). As in the OT prophets, the writers of the NT use adultery as a broad metaphor for unfaithfulness and deceit (Matt. 12:29; 16:4; Mark 8:38; 2 Pet. 2:14).

Thus, adultery is severely condemned in both Testaments. While some legal traditions impose a penalty of death, other biblical traditions offer a degree of forgiveness and mercy, even though severe consequences inevitably follow instances of marital infidelity. Jesus' words broaden the scope of adultery to include all those who even lust for another, thereby placing a restraint on self-righteous accusations against others without also rigorous self-examination of one's own lapses of sexual purity and faithfulness.

See also Hosea; Lust; Marriage and Divorce; Sex and Sexuality; Sex Discrimination; Sexual Ethics; Ten Commandments; Women, Status of

Bibliography

Countryman, L. *Dirt, Greed, and Sex: Sexual Ethics in the New Testament and Their Implications for Today*. Fortress, 2007; Davidson, R. *Flame of Yahweh: Sexuality in the Old Testament*. Hendrickson, 2000; Kreitzer, L., and D. Rooke. *Ciphers in the Sand: Interpretations of the Woman Taken in Adultery (John 7.53–8.11)*. BibSem 74. Sheffield Academic Press, 2000; Lipka, H. *Sexual Transgression in the Hebrew Bible*. HBM 7. Sheffield Phoenix, 2006; Moughton, S. *Sexual and Marital Metaphors in Hosea, Jeremiah, Isaiah and Ezekiel*. OThM. Oxford University Press, 2008.

Dennis T. Olson

Advance Directive *See* Bioethics

Advertising *See* Media, Ethical Issues of

Affections

Affections are intelligent responses to the perception of value. Examples of specifically Christian affections include love for God and neighbor, joy over what God has done in Christ, grief over our sins, fear of offending the Lord, and gratitude for the gifts of life and salvation. Such affections are the necessary contents of the well-formed "heart"—the center of the human being.

Augustine and Aquinas, as well as Jonathan Edwards and John Wesley, saw affections as voluntary movements of the will, ascribable to God as well as to humans. This classic Christian psychology is distinguished from the views of the Stoics, who understood much of affectivity to be a function of mistaken judgments. Augustine and Aquinas saw the Stoics as being unable to distinguish between the virtuous "affections" and the vicious "passions." For the Christian tradition, the proper object of the heart makes all the difference: affections are actions of the rational soul, focusing on God and neighbor, whereas passions are actions of the irrational soul, taking as their object the prideful self.

Today, the terms *affections* and *passions* have fallen out of common usage, often in favor of "emotion" language. This is problematic for understanding what Aquinas and Edwards meant, as our modern concept of "emotion" has blinded us to what the tradition saw as essential to "affections."

As shown by Thomas Dixon, the "emotions" came into being as a distinct psychological category in the nineteenth century, replacing terms such as *appetites*, *passions*, *sentiments*, and *affections*. Along with this change in terminology came a change in conceptuality. The tendency to see emotions as independent mini-agents of their own started with David Hume and was reinforced by people such as Immanuel Kant and Arthur Schopenhauer, both of whom describe a tripartite model of the soul, where in addition to understanding and will, a third faculty of feeling (*Gefuhl* or *Empfindung*) was added. It is easy to see why modern thinkers, following such models, came to view our affective life as necessarily irrational and involuntary.

This is seen especially in Thomas Brown's influential *Lectures on the Philosophy of the Human Mind*, where his fundamental conceptual distinction was between "our intellectual states of mind and our emotions." Ever after this, finding the intellectual component in affectivity—something inherent in the classical emphasis on the differing objects of passions and affections—is virtually impossible, as emotions and the intellect are ruled separate by definition. "Emotions" from this point onward, then, not only tended to replace "affections" and "passions," but they came to be associated with positivist and reductionist theories, where they are seen as involuntary, noncognitive states.

This means that if we are to understand what people such as Augustine, Aquinas, Edwards, and Wesley meant by the "life of the heart," the "affections," and "heart religion," we must bracket out what our modern world has invited us to believe about "emotions" and conceive of affective reality in a different way. Fortunately, several thinkers have begun this process. Philosophers such as Martha Nussbaum and Robert Roberts see emotions as intelligent responses to the perception of value, not just as nonreasoning movements or unthinking energies that simply push the person around. In short, these philosophers are now reconstruing "emotions" in a way entirely consistent with the Christian tradition's view of the "affections," allowing Christians to recover the classical discourse of the heart and its affections.

Setting "affections" in its classical context, we see why Jonathan Edwards could say that "true religion" consists, in large part, in having "religious affections." Such affections, often described by the "fruit of the Spirit" (Gal. 5:22–24), are not mere involuntary, felt impulses, unexpectedly and irrationally popping into consciousness, nor are they, à la Friedrich Schleiermacher, some universally present feeling of absolute dependence. The religious affections are embodied recognitions of who God is and what God has done; they are patterned through the spiritual disciplines, informed by prayer, and shaped by Scripture and the sacraments. Although the felt awareness of these affections may come and go, the affections are most reliably shown not in episodes of feeling, available only through introspection, but in the overall shape of a life, something outwardly observable in community.

See also Emotion; Fruit of the Spirit; Galatians; Moral Formation; Passions; Practices; Sanctification; Wesleyan Ethics

Bibliography

Clapper, G. *John Wesley on Religious Affections*. Scarecrow Press, 1989; Dixon, T. *From Passions to Emotions: The Creation of a Secular Psychological Category*. Cambridge University Press, 2003; Edwards, J. *Treatise on Religious Affections*. Yale University Press, 1959; Nussbaum, M. *Upheavals of Thought: The Intelligence of Emotions*. Cambridge University Press, 2001; Roberts, R. *Emotions: An Essay in Aid of Moral Psychology*. Cambridge University Press, 2003.

Gregory S. Clapper

Affluence *See* Wealth

African American Ethics

While various terms have found currency (e.g., *Coloreds*, *Negroes*, *Blacks*, *Black Americans*), the term *African American* is used here to describe persons and communities who are the product of the dynamic intersection of two worlds: African and American.

Overview of the Emergence of African Americans

The task of how African Americans use the Bible in ethical deliberations and as a book from which ethical actions spring becomes much more problematic without a description of who African Americans are as a community of discourse.

Africa is the second-largest continent in terms of size and population. Africa by some counts is composed of more than fifty countries, and nearly a thousand languages and dialects are spoken by diverse tribes. Each tribe also has religious expressions intrinsic to its own histories and historical settings. Yet sub-Saharan and western Africa generally represent areas of Africa from which much of the history of African Americans is derived.

Despite the diversity of life in Africa, there is a legitimate sense that sociocultural and religious understandings can be filtered through a shared African worldview. The African worldview embraces a belief in a Supreme Being, although the Supreme Being is not viewed as necessarily active in everyday affairs. There are lesser divinities who serve as mediators and are active in the fabric of everyday life. The "spiritual" pervades all of life, so that the distinct notions of sacred and secular space make little or no sense. Further, in the African worldview harmony between the living and the dead is important. Rituals and ceremonies proliferate to assuage the displeasure of the gods and spirits who otherwise would disrupt the harmony that everyone desires.

Moreover, tribal life and tribal identity are corporate. The sense of self or personhood is embedded in the tribe or the community. An old Ashanti proverb captures this idea: "Because we are, I am." Appropriate rituals mark the passage of children into tribal membership and mark the passage of young males and females into their adult roles. The Western notion of radical individualism is alien to the African worldview. One is not a person apart from community or tribal affiliation. In the West there is the notion that one can be a person apart from any identification with a community. There is little need to romanticize Africa or its inhabitants, but it is necessary to recognize the integrity of the African view of life, lived in a context of freedom and self-determination.

The English made initial contact with the western part of Africa in the fifteenth century, and their assumptions and presuppositions about Africans found their way into the logic and practices that cemented the racist ideology of white supremacy. In the subsequent practice of enslavement, millions of enslaved Africans began the journey across the Atlantic and ended up in the thirteen colonies. For those who survived the treacherous journey, their existence required strategies of survival and resilience in a new place—a place not truly their home.

In the colonies and later the United States, enslaved Africans, suffering under the oppressive weight of slavery, responded in ways that constructed paths of freedom and advanced the claim of being created in the image of God. Inevitably, enslaved Africans confronted North American evangelical Christians, especially during the eighteenth and nineteenth centuries. The enslaved Africans' engagement with the beliefs of North American evangelical Christians teased out a hybrid but real form of Christianity consistent with the values of their native land and the lived realities of African life in the New World. Future encounters with North American Christianity, especially during the First and Second Great Awakenings, also had significant shaping force.

From the inception of the slave economy and its deleterious practices, the enslaved men and women of African descent learned by necessity to live both as Africans, to the extent possible, and as Americans. Enslaved Africans engaged the assumptions of a white Christianity that sought to subjugate their minds and bodies, including their interpretations of the Bible that served as a canonical authority for racist readings of the Scriptures.

Christian Ethics in an African American Context

African American ethics refers both to a discipline and a way of thinking and being in the world. The United States has experienced significant racial progress over these nearly four hundred years. At this writing, the people of the United States elected the nation's first African American president. In all dimensions of life, progress can be observed. Yet, the intransigence of racism and the entrenchment of its logic and assumptions still inform much of our corporate life. The importance of the African American community is essential to the multitude of moral and ethical conversations about the value of human life and the proper goal of our common strivings as humans on this earth. In this ongoing engagement, the interpretation of the Bible has been and still is central. A focus on this dimension of African American ethics represents the thrust of the remainder of this essay.

African American Communities' Distinctive Approaches and Appeals to Scripture in Ethics

No reader approaches texts without presuppositions; that is, no community of readers comes to the text as blank slates. African Americans, at least at the beginning, filtered their fundamental readings of the Bible through a hermeneutical lens colored by their engagement with the distorted and dehumanizing practices of slaveholders, buttressed by a pernicious racist ideology. In the context of Africans being uprooted from their sense of place and a world of meaning-making and being compelled to live in a strange land, enslaved Africans responded in ways that promoted a quest for liberation or freedom. This liberationist or emancipatory impulse was a central thread in how the Bible was read and a central tenet of interpretation (exodus motif; Jubilee Year [Lev. 25:8–55]; Isa. 25:6–9; 65:20–25; Amos 5:21–24; Mic. 6:6–8; Luke 4:18–19; Rev. 21:3–7). This impulse to pursue liberation is central, in varying degrees, to all subsequent African American readings of the Bible.

European contact with the continent of Africa included also the role of missionaries and merchants and their use of the Bible to support colonialist ideologies. Europeans and whites presented the Bible as the sacred text, interpreted as having universal claims on all peoples. The slaves, even during the initial period of contact between "whiteness" and "blackness," attempted, sometimes successfully, to offer alternative responses to racist ideologies. Thus, African American use of the Bible is a function of the lived black experience within North America, particularly in the United States.

African Americans read the Bible as marginalized outsiders (Evans 35). The distorted relationships between those viewed as masters and thus superior and those viewed as enslaved and thus inferior provided the conceptual space for alternative readings of Scripture. A way to understand this might be thus: the alternative readings sought to decenter dominant, dehumanizing discourses and biblical interpretations, while they sought also to center or move to the center those biblical interpretations designed to provide other visions of human flourishing. Specifically, alternative readings and interpretations provided a sense of racial empowerment, a basis for self-love, a platform for moral uplift, a structure for moral rearmament, and a promise of progress and a hopeful future.

Historically, African American readings of the Bible take into account the historical contexts in which the readers lived. While the list of African American scholars and practitioners who have addressed African Americans' use of the Bible is long, Vincent Wimbush provides a helpful typology that attempts to provide a history of African American interpretations of the Bible. Wimbush identifies six "circles of biblical imaginary." In his discussion are the implicit and explicit reminders that the circles of African American interpreters of the Bible are diverse and emerge during specific periods of history in the United States. The critique of American society, especially its expressions and practices of racism and the formative nature of its liberal democratic ethos, requires consistent attention to alternative, compensatory readings of the Bible.

At times, the voices of African Americans have been muted and their roles maligned by patriarchal practices of both white and black males. Yet, there is a cacophony of strident womanist voices that resist efforts to marginalize their readings and interpretations of the Bible and other texts. Their contributions are many and significant, speaking to the broad scope of African American experiences. Katie G. Cannon, Cheryl A. Kirk-Duggan, Marcia Y. Riggs, Cheryl J. Sanders, Emilie M. Townes, and a host of others represent contemporary scholars whose works promote the kind of sociocultural analysis needed in any engagement of the African American community with alienating discourses and practices in our national life.

The rise of the independent black church movement in the seventeenth and eighteenth centuries also gave birth to interpreters of the Bible who challenged racism and its social practices in the United States. The black church nurtured spokespersons who offered life-affirming biblical interpretation in addition to criticizing racist rhetoric and dismantling the evil of segregation.

Frederick Douglass and Jarena Lee represent bold nineteenth-century examples of African Americans who offered stinging critiques of American society and male patriarchy by engaging in a critical reading of the Bible. Yet, many decades later, the emergence of the Black Power movement in the twentieth century presented the African American community with an interpretive challenge to its readings and interpretations of the Bible. The appropriation of Black Power by the representatives of the black theology project (such as James H. Cone) presents a continuing challenge in the search for a broad agreement among African Americans regarding the place of socioeconomic and sociopolitical action in service to the ongoing quest for liberation. For black theologians such as Cone, Black Power is not alien to the gospel of Jesus Christ.

In his books, Cone not only addressed the quest for liberation but also repositioned it within a context where God is the "God of the Oppressed." Cone asks and answers this basic question: "What has the gospel to do with the oppressed of the land and their struggle for liberation?" (Cone 9). Cone maintains that theologians who fail to place that question at the center of their work have ignored the essence of the gospel. While some black theologians criticized Cone early on for placing his work within the systematic structure of European theology, the basic point is that tensions exist between black theology and the black Christian churches. Some African American scholars have expressed deep concern that black churches, in their desire to link up with white evangelical Christianity, have diminished their capacity of allowing Scripture to serve as a prophetic critique of all forms of racist ideology (Wimbush 84). This concern is seen within the worship life of many black churches as their sermons focus on "otherworldly" existence, thereby eclipsing the moral importance of life in the here and now.

This critical appraisal of black churches is a reminder that if the readings and interpretations of the Bible, and all aspects of worship, do not provide a critical analysis of social, economic, and political realities and inspire African Americans to seek life-affirming modalities of existence, then the African American church is being unfaithful to God and to the African American communities through time and space. While hearing this criticism clearly, black churches have often made their own criticisms of academic black theology. Specifically, it is argued that those who embrace the black theology project must seek a deeper analysis of, or at least be more attentive to, the ways that liberation is expressed by black churches in their preaching, singing, pastoral care, and other practices. The notion of liberation, for them, must be broadened to include the spiritual liberation from sin as a necessary component of the gospel. Some African American theologians fear that the increased participation of African Americans in holiness, pentecostal, and fundamentalist church groups will mean the loss of those liberative interpretations of Scripture that have historically sustained African Americans. Yet, more conservative Christians need not be antagonistic to the ongoing quest for liberation (e.g., Cheryl J. Sanders). African Americans as a community of discourse have embraced, and still embrace in many cases, various reading strategies that build bridges across all forms of human division.

A Way Forward: Some Concluding Thoughts

African American ethics takes up God's agenda of reconciliation as revealed in Scripture. The problem is how one promotes the biblical notion of reconciliation in the face of the continuing legacy of racism and racist ideology in the United States. The role of Scripture is formative for a community's life, through its practices and social embodiments of more truthful interpretations of the biblical story in all of its aspects. There is general historical agreement that ongoing reflection on the social and cultural realities in which all humans participate is a critical ethical dimension of our communal readings of the Bible.

African American ethics should not be marginalized by African American insistence that whites cannot understand the plight of African Americans. Such an insistence ensures a racial ownership of human experiences in a way that is not consistent with life lived with God's end in view. Likewise, even white Christians, whether labeled as liberal, conservative, or fundamentalist, must exercise vigilance against appealing to unexamined claims to universal and absolute interpretations of the Bible that effectively obscure the presence of African Americans and thereby render African American life invisible. Interpretation requires that a community be capable of welcoming the stranger who enters its midst. That is why it is important to engage diverse reading communities in order to humanize our lives together and to experience the real benefits of connecting with broader communities of discourse. Galatians 3:28 is a central verse for gifting our vision to seek the plurality of oneness in the church and world.

Finally, vigilance against uncritical participation in the nation's liberal democratic society is required. African American ethics suffers to the extent that faith becomes only an inward, individualistic experience. Aligning faith commitments to the logic and presuppositions of market capitalism, without proper vigilance, mutes the prophetic impulses necessary for liberation and transformation of lives and communities.

See also Discrimination; Emancipation; Jubilee; Justice; Liberation; Liberationist Ethics; Race; Racism; Reconciliation; Slavery

Bibliography

Andrews, D. *Practical Theology for Black Churches: Bridging Black Theology and African American Folk Religion.* Westminster John Knox, 2002; Blount, B. *Then the Whisper Put on Flesh: New Testament Ethics in an African American Context.* Abingdon, 2001; idem, ed. *True to Our Native Land: An African American New Testament Commentary.* Fortress, 2007; Cartwright, M. "Wrestling with Scripture: Can Euro-American Christians and African-American Christians Learn to Read Scripture Together?" Pages 71–114 in *The Gospel in Black and White: Theological Resources for Racial Reconciliation*, ed. D. Okholm. InterVarsity, 1997; Cone, J. *God of the Oppressed.* HarperSanFrancisco, 1975; Evans, J., Jr. *We Have Been Believers: An African-American Systematic Theology.* Fortress, 1992; Felder, C., ed. *Stony the Road We Trod: An African American Biblical Interpretation.* Fortress, 1991; Paris, P. *The Social Teaching of the Black Churches.* Fortress, 1985; Raboteau, A. *Slave Religion: The "Invisible Institution" in the Antebellum South.* Updated ed. Oxford University Press, 2004; Riggs, M. *Awake, Arise and Act: A Womanist Call for Black Liberation.* Pilgrim Press, 1994; Sanders, C. *Saints in Exile: The Holiness-Pentecostal Experience in African American Religion and Culture.* Religion in America. Oxford University Press, 1996; Thurman, H. *Jesus and the Disinherited.* Friends United Press, 1981; Usry, G., and C. Keener. *Black Man's Religion: Can Christianity Be Afrocentric?* InterVarsity, 1996; Walker, T., Jr. *Empower the People: Social Ethics for the African-American Church.* TSNABR 5. Orbis, 1991; Wilmore, G. *Black Religion and Black Radicalism.* Rev. ed. Orbis, 1983; Wimbush, V. *The Bible and African Americans: A Brief History.* Facets. Fortress, 2003.

James W. Lewis

Agape

The Greek word *agapē* in the LXX translates Hebrew words reflecting multiple facets of affection and commitment. The narrative complexity of the word comes alive with attention to the OT text as it came to be translated from Hebrew to Greek. The LXX translators used *agapē* to translate words as disparate as *'ahab*, often a form of intimately passionate love; *raḥam*, related to the Hebrew word for "womb," a poignantly physical attachment eliciting mercy toward another; and *dôd*, which indicates a joyful delight in another. Passages pair *agapē* with Greek versions of *ḥesed*, an abounding loyalty often linked to forgiveness; *ḥaseq*, which refers to being bound or attached to another; and *rāṣâ*, which refers to being pleased with another—all words that shape the meaning of *agapē* in particular contexts. *Agapē* is used in these instances both for God's love and our responsive stance toward God and neighbor, creating an intertextual meaning.

Scriptural study of agape helpfully complicates Western scholarship on Christian love. In his seminal work on agape in Western ethics, Gene Outka refers his readers back two generations to another progenitor. Referring to Anders Nygren, Outka suggests, "His critics have been legion, but few have ignored or been unaffected by his thesis. . . . One may justifiably regard his work as the beginning of the modern treatment of the subject" (Outka 1). Nygren began a particularly modern pursuit, that of crystallizing the import of agape around a vital essence or, as he puts it, "motif." His work set a scholarly trajectory to distill the term and make it universally applicable. Through purportedly "scientific analysis," agape could be made "indifferent to value" and thus readily available to Christians across time and place.

The effort made intuitive sense in postwar Western Europe. The scriptural command to love God, neighbor, stranger, and enemy had become central in Western European thought. The horrors of Nazi Germany and the retributive firebombing of German and Japanese cities had made tragically clear how ready leaders (and the led) were to set aside the command when circumstances dictated or allowed. By the time Nygren's *Agape and Eros* came out in English, the Western world was predictably ready for the crystal clarity and diamond-like beauty of Nygren's "scientific analysis" on agape. The truly loving agent whom Nygren distilled in his study was a serviceable ideal for a miserably misanthropic era: purely self-giving, shorn of particular context, capable of instant and unambiguous action for the sake of another, initiated by God alone, with no storied motivation on the part of the loving one.

A serviceable ideal is scarcely the whole story. Hans Frei is a crucial interlocutor when considering agape as an item of ethical study. Frei's genealogy of "mythophiles" helps to give context to the supposedly context-free studies of agape initiated by Nygren. Frei argues that to "paraphrase by general statement" the truth of Scripture is to "reduce it to meaninglessness." To search the manifold forms and contexts of the scriptural canon in order to find a "central ideational theme" is, according to Frei, to make a type of reader's category error. Frei explains that meaning in Scripture is "not *illustrated* (as though it were an intellectually presubsisting or preconceived archetype or ideal essence) but *constituted* through the mutual, specific determinations of agents, speech, social context, and circumstances that form the indispensible narrative web" (Frei 280). Efforts to summarize reliably the core of Christian love are susceptible to the same sort of attempt to find the core Jesus of history, or the perduring anchor of faith. To paraphrase one commentator, the search for the historical agape is likely to recover a picture that looks remarkably like the scholar searching.

Scriptural references to agape may link God's command to love one's neighbor to a story of God's anguish at the deep betrayal of God's people, or to God's liberation of a people betrayed by their own neighbors. Reading the texts together, in tension, may bring out a word of solace or a word of God's judgment. By way of assigned lectionary texts, attentively and cyclically read, a congregation may receive a command to love in conjunction with their origins as nameless nomads, or in the midst of a call to rage against and passionately love family members who have forsaken them, or in conjunction with a story demanding attention to the deviant, or alongside a summons to perceive with gratitude those who become more holy each day. *Agape* becomes a resonant term, one evoking not one particular stance but rather a web of scriptural stories and meanings.

Hosea may be a helpful example of the way agape is shaded in Scripture. God's stance toward Israel is one of profound memory and investment in this prophetic book. The book suggests that love for those who are closest and with whom memories are shared is at times painful and difficult, perhaps even more so than love for those who are distantly strange. The stranger in one's own bedroom may be harder to love than the one across an ocean. At the risk of paraphrasing, one might say that Hosea narrates the acute betrayal unique to intimacy, love, and deep memory. Because God's agape is entwined with God's enduring relationship with the people of Israel, God's anger is particularly passionate and even vengeful. As in the case of Jeremiah and Isaiah, Hosea's metaphors draw from the intensity of a lover's vulnerable connection to his beloved and from a mother's passion for disobedient children. God has known God's people from conception, heard their cries in Egypt, and held them as they toddled toward maturity. God remembers a people who accepted God's love with grateful, youthful abandon and cannot with this memory send them away when they seek other lovers. The book layers metaphor upon metaphor, with God summoning Israel to respond in repentance and renewed commitment, as God is Israel's true parent, lover, and spouse. God's agape here may seem scandalously foolish, even indecent. The word may appear here as a judgment on those who remain distantly engaged, as a word of admonishment on those who note with dispassionate regard the loved ones they are vulnerably to cherish.

In Exodus and Leviticus, Abraham's and Moses' descendants are to remember with gratitude the mercy that God has shown them even while they were wandering and murmuring, and thus they are to identify with and show mercy to the wanderer in their midst. A NT text that is helpfully read for features of agape is Luke's Gospel, as Luke's readers are set before a forgiving God and led to include even enemies in the scope of Israel's stance of mercy. Willard Swartley has described Luke's version of agape as an outrageous extension of the banquet tradition to those who might otherwise be seen as unfit to invite to the table (Luke 14:16–24). Echoing a strand of agape in the OT, that of God's searching for those who are scattered (Ezek. 34), Luke narrates a God who longs for those who are "in the wilderness" (Luke 15:4) due to oppression or rebellion. Although the parable of the nameless man on the highway may be read as a call to love universally, the Samaritan, an outsider, most clearly answers the call to love. This move may be read as a universalizing one, but it may also be read, perhaps simultaneously, as a recalibration of inside and outside, placing the stranger inside God's enduring covenant (Luke 10:29–37). The stories of lost sheep and small coins may newly adjust the vision of those interlocutors who deem themselves to be obviously above mere shepherds and surely better than a woman with a broom. The Lukan parables recast divine and human agape as abiding in the face of transgression. They go beyond this, even, to indicate that those who are lost are unique recipients of God's concern and, when found, a cause for God's delight.

Colin Grant suggests that the love evoked in agape is "identified only through the horizon of theological conviction and sustained through the apparatus of religion." Grant reads human agape as best cast in a context of "the divine extravagance of giving" (Grant 19). In this encyclopedic setting, wherein scholars each must sift through and explain particular, scriptural terms for the sake of clarity and brevity, one example of divine extravagance may be the lavish fecundity of Scripture itself—as it bears judgment, lament, joy, patience, resilience—for the daily task and manna of agape.

See also Altruism; Charity, Works of; Covenant; Enemy, Enemy Love; Grace; Love, Love Command; Neighbor, Neighbor Love

Bibliography

Frei, H. *The Eclipse of Biblical Narrative: A Study in Eighteenth and Nineteenth Century Hermeneutics.* Yale University Press, 1974; Grant, C. "For the Love of God: Agape." *JRE* 24 (1996): 3–21; Hall, A. L. "Complicating the Command: Agape in Scriptural Context." *ASCE* 19 (1999): 97–113; Heschel, A. *The Prophets.* Harper & Row, 1962; Nygren, A. *Agape and Eros.* Trans. P. Watson. Westminster, 1953; Outka, G. *Agape: An Ethical Analysis.* Yale University Press, 1972; Sakenfeld, K. D. *Faithfulness in Action: Loyalty in Biblical Perspective.* Fortress, 1985; Swartley, W. *The Love of Enemy and Nonretaliation in the New Testament.* Westminster John Knox, 1992; Vacek, E. *Love, Human and Divine.* Georgetown University Press, 1994.

Amy Laura Hall

Aged, Aging

Ethical actions and attitudes toward older people flow from an understanding of who they are. Two distinctive characteristics of older people stand out at various points in Scripture.

The Characteristic Wisdom

First, older people generally are wise. "Is not wisdom found among the aged?" Job asks rhetorically, and "Does not long life bring understanding?" (Job 12:12 TNIV; cf. 15:10; 32:7). "Elders" (normally elderly) are, therefore, in the best position to give good counsel based on the experience and memory of what God has done (e.g., Exod. 3:18; Deut. 32:7; Acts 15:2; 1 Pet. 5:5). In old age, people "still produce fruit" (Ps. 92:14), even if that simply means living a life of moral virtue (Titus 2:2–3) or praising God (Ps. 148:12). The more severe the limitations of old age, the greater the inspiration such examples are for the community. The mere presence of elderly people, in fact, is perhaps the best reminder that our own days will quickly pass—a reality that we must learn if we are to "gain a wise heart" (Ps. 90:12). Accordingly, a family that has lost all of its elderly members has been severely punished (1 Sam. 2:31). A city with men and women of "great age" is considered blessed (Zech. 8:4).

The difference that the wisdom of elderly counsel can make is nowhere more dramatically illustrated than in 1 Kgs. 12 (cf. 2 Chr. 10). There, a large assembly of God's people asks King Rehoboam to lighten their harsh workload. The king consults with two groups of counselors, one of old men and one of young men. His failure to heed the wise counsel of the old men leads to the dramatic breakup of God's kingdom into the two antagonistic kingdoms of Israel and Judah. Wisdom, then, generally is presented as a function of the life experience that only elderly persons have. Because it is also the product of righteousness and God's Spirit, however, it is possible occasionally for young people to have wisdom (Job 32:8–9; Eccl. 4:13) and older people to lack it (Job 12:20).

The Characteristic Weakness

A second characteristic of many elderly persons, at least at some point, is that they are weak. Old age is acknowledged in Scripture as a time of suffering and vulnerability (2 Sam. 19:35; Eccl. 12:1–7). It is a time of failing eyes (e.g., Gen. 27:1; 48:10; 1 Sam. 4:15; 1 Kgs. 14:4), failing feet (e.g., 1 Kgs. 15:23), and declining overall bodily health (e.g., 1 Sam. 4:18; 1 Kgs. 1:1). Knowing that insensitive people take advantage of the weakness of older people, the psalmist prays, "Do not cast me off in the time of old age; do not forsake me when my strength is spent" (Ps. 71:9; cf. 71:18).

Such weakness generally is characteristic of older people but not necessarily so. Elderly people, therefore, should not automatically be written off as mentally or physically incapable simply because of their age. God often breaks through stereotypes. Who would have thought that Sarah and Abraham would have a child in their very old age (Gen. 18:11–14; 21:5–7); or that the Shunammite woman would have a baby with her elderly husband (2 Kgs. 4:14–17); or that the elderly Zechariah and Elizabeth would have a child (Luke 1:7, 18, 24–25, 36–37)? Who would have expected Jacob to father Joseph at such an old age that Joseph became special for that reason (Gen. 37:3)? Although weakness often is present in older people, it must be discovered and documented, never assumed.

The Response of Respecting

Both the wisdom and weakness of elderly people call for ethical responses, namely, respecting and protecting. We respond appropriately to wisdom by respecting it and those who possess it. Evil societies sometimes are characterized by their lack of respect for older people (Deut. 28:50; 2 Chr. 36:17; Isa. 47:6). It is an evil day when "the youth will be insolent to the elder" (Isa. 3:5), when elders are shown no respect (Lam. 5:12). Those who are young are to resist the temptation to despise or speak harshly to those who are old (e.g., Prov. 23:22; 1 Tim. 5:1) and instead are to recognize gray hair (i.e., old age) as a crown of splendor (Prov. 16:31; 20:29).

People are to "rise before the aged," says the Lord, and "defer to the old" (Lev. 19:32). This particular command is one of seven commands in Lev. 19 whose importance is underlined by the conclusion, "I am the LORD." And this command regarding elderly people prefaces those words with the call to "fear your God." The point seems to be that obedience to this command in particular expresses a special reverence for God. By showing respect for those who are elderly, we are revering God.

The Response of Protecting

If we rightly respond to wisdom by respecting people who possess it, we appropriately respond to the relative weakness of elderly people by protecting them. God is frequently portrayed in biblical writings as the protector of those who are weak (Exod. 22:22–27; Pss. 35:10; 140:12), and God's people are challenged to be the same (Prov. 31:8–9; 1 Thess. 5:14). So it is not at all surprising to find God affirming, "Even to your old age I am he, even when you turn gray I will carry you" (Isa. 46:4).

That God says "even in old age" emphasizes that in a world enamored with strength and productivity it is all too easy to neglect older people. King David observed this phenomenon in his day, which is why he implores God to sustain him, as he puts it, "even when I am old and gray" (Ps. 71:18 TNIV). Because God is a sustainer of those who are old, it is natural to expect that godly people will be as well (e.g., Ruth 4:15). Community is built, to the benefit of all, when the needs of some provide others opportunity to serve and to witness the blessing of being served.

Elderly people are as worthy of staying alive and even receiving life-saving care as anyone else. In fact, whether a particular society values the wisdom and other contributions of older people is ultimately beside the point. All persons are God's creation in God's own image (Gen. 1:27) and are the objects of God's sacrificial love in Christ (John 3:16). God pours out the Spirit on those who are old as well as on those who are young (Joel 2:28;

Acts 2:17). The equal worth of all persons demands that all be respected and that those who are weak accordingly receive special protection.

Contemporary Challenges

This biblical outlook is at odds with some influential contemporary outlooks. For example, a utilitarian way of viewing people promotes whatever most people in society consider beneficial. In contemporary cultures that value people primarily in terms of their economic productivity, elderly people may not be given the same access to needed resources as younger people. This problem is compounded by its discriminatory impact on women. In the United States, for example, a large majority of older people are women. Scripture identifies the male/female distinction, along with slave/free and ethnic distinctions, as inappropriate categories used by one group to assert superiority over another (e.g., Gal. 3:28). Biblical writings exhort the community to provide special protection and care to older women in particular, who often are widows (e.g., Isa. 1:17; Jas. 1:27).

A biblical outlook is also at odds with the common human aspiration to live forever in this world. Genesis 3 introduces the suffering that unavoidably marks this world because of people's sinful self-centeredness. In response, God banishes humanity from the garden of Eden so that people cannot "take from the tree of life, and eat, and live forever" (Gen. 3:22). Far from mere punishment, this banishment is a wonderful example of God's mercy. In place of eternal life in this world of "bondage to decay" God offers an opportunity for forgiveness and the redemption of our bodies (Rom. 8:21–23). The resurrection of the crucified Jesus is God's victory over death and sin. That victory is a divine victory, not a technological victory. God's only begotten Son transforms death itself into the doorway to an immortality of joy (Rev. 21:4). Efforts to extend life become antagonistic to God's purposes if understood as part of a larger attempt to achieve immortality in this world. However, long life and health can be received as a blessing (Prov. 10:27; 16:31; Isa. 65:20). In response to God's gift and cause, our efforts to extend life through a variety of medical and other interventions can constitute a welcome participation in God's merciful involvement in a suffering world.

See also Death and Dying; Dementia; Dependent Care; Euthanasia; Family; Healthcare Ethics; Widows

Bibliography

Bailey, L. "Biblical Perspectives on Aging." *QR* 9 (1989): 48–64; Dulin, R. *A Crown of Glory: A Biblical View of Aging*. Paulist Press, 1988; Harris, J. *Biblical Perspectives on Aging: God and the Elderly*. 2nd ed. Haworth Press, 2008; Hauerwas, S., et al., eds. *Growing Old in Christ*. Eerdmans, 2003; Kilner, J. *Life on the Line: Ethics, Aging, Ending Patients' Lives, and Allocating Vital Resources*. Eerdmans, 1992; Mitchell, C., R. Orr, and S. Salladay, eds. *Aging, Death, and the Quest for Immortality*. Eerdmans, 2004; President's Council on Bioethics. *Taking Care: Ethical Caregiving in Our Aging Society*. U.S. Executive Office of the President, 2005; Sapp, S. *Full of Years: Aging and the Elderly in the Bible and Today*. Abingdon, 1987.

John F. Kilner

Alcohol

Drinking alcohol in moderation is neither prohibited nor identified as sinful in the Bible. Typically, consuming alcohol is portrayed as a commonly accepted social practice and a common element in religious rites. Alongside positive references to the moderate consumption of alcohol are numerous passages warning against the abuse of alcohol and condemning drunkenness.

Positive Images

The Bible presents an abundance of positive references to wine and strong drink, portraying the consumption of alcohol as a commonly accepted cultural practice (e.g., Judg. 19:19; 1 Tim. 5:23). Some well-known figures in the OT, such as Isaac, are depicted as drinking wine (Gen. 27:25), and in the NT Jesus served wine at Passover (Luke 22:20; 1 Cor. 11:25–26) and performed his first miracle by turning water into wine (John 2:1–11). Other positive references regard wine as a divine blessing (e.g., Isa. 25:6) and a lack of wine as God's curse (e.g., Deut. 28:39). Wine is given as a gift (e.g., 1 Sam. 16:20) and used in religious rites (e.g., Lev. 23:13), including the Last Supper, where the symbolic use of "cup" employs wine from the Passover meal (Luke 22:20; 1 Cor. 11:25–26). Wine is also employed as a standard for what is good, so that something can be "better than wine" (e.g., Song 1:2).

Negative Images

Almost all negative texts regarding alcohol warn against its abuse and condemn drunkenness (e.g., Isa. 28:1; Eph. 5:18). One NT text, however, speaks of abstaining from wine in order to prevent a brother or sister from stumbling (Rom. 14:21), and a few passages refer to vows of abstinence, although these apply to a particular group, such as the Levite priests (Lev. 10:9), or, as in the case of John the Baptist, a particular person (Luke 1:15), and are never required of the whole community.

Contemporary Arguments

Since the Bible clearly allows for moderate consumption of alcohol as well as the use of alcohol in religious rituals, on what basis have some Christians maintained that the Bible demands total abstinence from alcohol?

Christians who believe that the Bible teaches abstinence often claim that biblical references to wine indicate either unfermented grape juice or wine so diluted as to have virtually no intoxicating effect unless consumed in large quantities. The Hebrew and Greek words for "wine" and most especially for "strong drink," however, do not support these assertions. Furthermore, the claim for unfermented grape juice cannot be sustained by the logic of many biblical texts. Why would the Bible warn against drunkenness if "wine" refers to unfermented grape juice, which, by definition, cannot cause intoxication? After Jesus turned the water into wine at the wedding at Cana, why would the steward have marveled that the bridegroom brought out the good wine after the guests had become intoxicated if it did not contain alcohol (John 2:1–11)? The more common claim that references to wine and strong drink refer to drinks with extremely low alcohol content, thereby providing a necessary alternative to contaminated water, lacks linguistic and cultural evidence. In addition, it does not demand abstinence, but allows one to consume drinks with low alcohol content, especially when consumed for a specific purpose. A third argument, popular among nineteenth-century prohibitionists and sometimes employed today, is the "two wine" theory, which maintains that in the Bible the word *wine* sometimes refers to alcohol and other times indicates unfermented grape juice. Since the same word for wine is used in both cases, the "two wine" theory is impossible to support with unbiased linguistic arguments.

Making Biblical Claims

Although one cannot rightly maintain that the Bible forbids the consumption of alcohol, one also cannot claim that Christians who choose abstinence are only following personal or cultural preferences with no guidance from Scripture. Only by means of prooftexting can one say that a decision to refrain from drinking alcohol cannot be informed by the Bible. For instance, the Bible provides strong advocacy for the least of the brothers and sisters (Matt. 25:31–46) and exhorts us to define our own actions by their effect on others (Rom. 14:21). Given the potentially devastating financial, emotional, and physical effects of alcoholism and alcohol-related accidents, Christians can heed the biblical imperatives to love your neighbor as yourself (Lev. 19:18; Matt. 19:19) and to treat the body as a temple (1 Cor. 6:19–20) by choosing total abstinence. This choice is clearly informed by the Bible, even though the Bible does not explicitly prohibit drinking alcohol.

Hence, Christians who consume alcohol in moderation cannot claim that their teetotaling brothers and sisters have no biblical grounds for their decision to refrain from drinking. However, Christians who judge other Christians for allowing moderate consumption of alcohol have no biblical basis for their condemnation either. Perhaps the best scriptural guidance to inform Christian attitudes about drinking alcohol arises from the contrasting portrayals of John the Baptist, who exercised abstinence, and Jesus, who did not. The Pharisees condemned them both: "For John the Baptist has come eating no bread and drinking no wine, and you say, 'He has a demon'; the Son of Man has come eating and drinking, and you say, 'Look, a glutton and a drunkard, a friend of tax collectors and sinners!'" (Luke 7:33–34). Christians can, with John the Baptist and in allegiance to Jesus' concern for the least of the brothers and sisters, choose total abstinence, or they can, in line with numerous passages from the Bible as well as Jesus' own actions, choose to drink in moderation. Those who choose abstinence and those who choose moderation can together follow biblical teaching by fighting against the abuse of alcohol.

See also Asceticism; Body; Temperance

Bibliography

West, J. *Drinking with Calvin and Luther: A History of Alcohol in the Church*. Oakdown, 2005; Whitfield, D. "Alcohol and the Bible." http://chetday.com/alcoholandthebible.htm.

Nancy J. Duff

Aliens, Immigration, and Refugees

Migration has been a human reality throughout history. People move for many reasons, and the various labels assigned to them reflect these circumstances. The term *refugee* refers to those who are forced to abandon their place of origin because of a natural disaster or to escape a war zone or the threat of violent persecution. These persons seek asylum in a different place through their own efforts or through the intervention of international agencies such as the Office of the United Nations High Commissioner for Refugees, which works with governments and local organizations (often religious institutions) to resettle them. Ideally, treatment of refugees should follow internationally agreed conventions.

The term *immigrant* is used of those who leave home willingly and desire short- or long-term residence somewhere else. Most migrate in an effort to find employment and to provide their family a suitable life and future. Entry into a new land can be done according to proper protocols at established ports of entry or outside of that legal framework. Another category is "internally displaced persons," referring to those who remain within their national boundaries but change locations for the same reasons appropriate to refugee or immigrant status.

The twenty-first century is witnessing the movement of millions across borders. This demographic phenomenon impacts local and international economies, brings unforeseen pressures on law enforcement and the integrity of national borders, can strain educational and healthcare infrastructures, and is raising concerns about cultural identity in receiving countries. Living in a different culture creates challenges for the recently arrived populations as well. They wrestle with their own identity as they engage the complex problems related to their economic survival and accommodation to strange surroundings. Another affected sphere is religion. Refugees and immigrants around the world are revitalizing their traditions, Christian and non-Christian, and bringing fresh perspectives on the practice of their faith to their new lands.

Migration and the Bible

Migration and its effects are a major topic in both the OT and the NT. Then, as now, the reasons for migration vary. Many of those in the Bible who migrated would be categorized technically today as refugees or as forcefully displaced, but the descriptions of life and the theological reflection that those situations generated mirror the experiences of migrants everywhere. Scripture can offer distinct but interrelated messages to those who take in the outsider and to the newcomers. The majority culture that accepts refugees and immigrants learns that God loves the vulnerable. This divine concern should shape attitudes and orient actions on behalf of the stranger. Also, those who come from another place can be encouraged and empowered by God's commitment to the weak and by the biblical accounts of others of similar fate.

Biblical terminology. Several terms are used to refer to outsiders in the Bible. It is possible that each carries a discrete nuance. These distinctions are difficult to discern, however, because of the complexity of the biblical data and because of inconsistencies in the English versions. The same English word can be used for various Hebrew and Greek terms, and a particular Hebrew or Greek term is translated by different English words. The most common translations of the words in question are *alien*, *stranger*, *resident alien*, *foreigner*, and *sojourner*.

The relevant Hebrew terms in the OT are the nouns *nēkār*, *tôšāb*, and *gēr*, and the adjectives *nokrî* and *zār*. This variety in terminology implies that Israel differentiated among the outsiders in their midst. The terms *nēkār*/*nokrî* and *zār* can refer to something or someone who is foreign to Israel. These can be neutral designations (e.g., *nokrî* in Ruth 2:10; 1 Kgs. 8:41, 43), but frequently they carry a negative connotation of being a corrupting influence or a threat (*nēkār*/*nokrî* in Josh. 24:20; 1 Kgs. 11:1–8; Ezra 9–10; Neh. 13:23–27; Ps. 144:7; *zār* in Deut. 32:16; Prov. 22:14; Isa. 1:7). Those who are *nēkār*/*nokrî* are excluded from participating in certain rituals (Exod. 12:43) and from office (Deut. 17:15). Perhaps these were outsiders who did not seek to stay and integrate themselves into Israelite life and faith. The term *tôšāb* is harder to define. In the few places where *tôšāb* occurs, it often is in parallel with "hired servant" (Exod. 12:45; Lev. 25:6, 40) or *gēr* (Gen. 23:4; Lev. 25:23). In the latter case, some argue, the combination is to be construed as "resident alien" (Lev. 25:35, 47). The most significant term in the OT is *gēr*. The *gēr*, as its verbal root *gûr* suggests ("to take up residence"), is someone from elsewhere who settled down on a temporary or permanent basis. There are a series of provisions in the OT law for these individuals, who had made a commitment to become part of the community of Israel. It is impossible to determine whether this incorporation into national life was simply part of natural processes or if at some point formal procedures were established to make it official. As will become evident, the OT's contribution to discussions on refugees and immigrants is not limited to passages where these terms appear.

The relevant NT words are *xenos*, *paroikos*, and *parepidēmos*. These refer to people or things that may come from elsewhere and so appear to be out of place and have no status. The word *xenos* occurs four times in Matt. 25:31–46, where Jesus identifies the stranger with himself. *Xenos* and its verbal root, *xenizō*, can indicate something that is alien and unwelcome (e.g., Acts 17:20; Heb. 13:9). This word is the source of the English term *xenophobia*, which is the fear or dislike of someone foreign. It occurs in parallel with *paroikos* in Eph. 2:19 to refer to the relationship to the household of God that people have before they come to faith, and with *parepidēmos* in Heb. 11:13 to describe how past saints viewed themselves in the world. *Paroikos* and *parepidēmos* appear together in 1 Pet. 2:11. They may point to the legal standing in the

Roman Empire of the recipients of the letter as well as to their new spiritual reality in the world (cf. 1 Pet. 1:1).

Old Testament narratives. The place to ground discussion on refugees and immigrants is the creation of humankind in the image of God in Gen. 1:26–28. There are several interpretations of the meaning of the image. The ontological view holds that the image of God concerns what humans are and what they possess (an intellect, will, emotions, and a spiritual component). Some argue for a relational perspective, which holds that it refers to the unique communion with God available to humans through Christ, the supreme embodiment of the divine image (2 Cor. 4:4; Col. 1:15). A third view contends that the image is functional. It is humanity's special task to rule as God's vice-regents on earth. All three options assert that every person has worth. Outsiders also are created in the divine image. They too are valuable in God's sight and worthy of respect. Their giftedness as humans signifies that they have great potential. For these newcomers, the image communicates that there is no warrant to feel inferior as second-class persons. At the same time, there is a claim on their lives. The image can be a motivation for them to develop skills for the common good and to live responsibly as God's representatives in their adopted land.

The movement of individuals and groups begins in the opening chapters of Genesis. Cain is condemned to perpetual wandering for murdering Abel (Gen. 4:10–14). In the biblical narrative humanity is scattered at Babel, and this dispersal yields the multiplication of nations (Gen. 10–11). Nations have geographical boundaries (Gen. 10:5, 20, 30–31; cf. Deut. 32:8; Acts 17:26), but peoples have migrated across these for millennia. The story of the chosen people begins with Terah's move from Ur to Haran and Abram's subsequent pilgrimage from there to Canaan (Gen. 11:31–12:5). In other words, the history of the patriarch and his descendants is one born of migration (Gen. 23:4; cf. Deut. 26:5).

Many move to survive. Abraham, Isaac, and Jacob (and his sons and their families) sojourn temporarily in different places in their search for food (Egypt [Gen. 12; 42–46]; the Negev [Gen. 20]; Philistia [Gen. 26]). Jacob goes north to Aram to flee the wrath of his brother Esau and lives for a time with Laban and his family (Gen. 27–31). Moses leaves Egypt for many years to avoid trouble for killing someone; he marries a Midianite and names their son "Gershom," a word play on the term *gēr* (Exod. 2). Naomi and her family leave Bethlehem in a time of famine and cross the Jordan into Moab. Ten years later, now a widow and with both her sons dead, she moves back with Ruth, her daughter-in-law. Naomi the immigrant has returned home, and now Ruth is the immigrant. Survival is still the issue, however, and Ruth goes to the fields to glean alongside the harvesters of Boaz. Others are removed forcibly from their homes. Joseph is betrayed and sold into slavery. He overcomes difficult circumstances in Egypt, rises to become second to Pharaoh, and helps save that land from starvation (Gen. 37; 39–41). He prepares the way for his father and the rest of his clan to migrate to the Nile Delta and settle in Goshen (Gen. 47:1–12). Centuries later, thousands are taken into exile into several regions of Mesopotamia when Israel falls to Assyria in the eighth century BCE (2 Kgs. 17), and Judah to Babylon in the sixth century BCE (2 Kgs. 24–25).

Life in other lands could be harsh. After a time, the ruler of Egypt forgot Joseph's contributions and exploited the Israelites as slave labor for building projects (Exod. 1; 5). Egyptian sources describe measures (e.g., building a line of forts along the eastern frontier) to keep out certain groups seeking pasture and employment in the fertile regions of the Nile River. Inscriptional evidence indicates that some in Assyrian exile became domestic servants; others were assigned to work on farms or in construction. Psalm 137 voices the anger, shame, and homesickness of those forcibly removed from Judah by Babylon. Not everyone, though, endured such harsh fates. In Egypt some foreigners rose to prominence (Joseph [Gen. 41]; Moses [Exod. 1–2]). Daniel lived in the royal precincts, where he served several kings with distinction. Esther's uncle Mordecai seems to have been a man of some means, and this young woman became queen of the Persian Empire. Nehemiah was cupbearer to the Persian king Artaxerxes, a post that required absolute loyalty. Ezra and Ezekiel apparently ministered freely among their people in exile.

Another key issue, pertinent to both the host culture and migrant populations, is the accommodation of newcomers to their new situations. The OT narratives reflect a spectrum of assimilation processes and their effects. Some desire little acculturation. Ezra, for example, as a priest deeply committed to the law, seems to have assimilated little. He desires instead to return to his homeland and to reestablish life there according to the demands of the Mosaic covenant.

Others assimilate to a significant degree but do not totally forget their roots. Naomi goes back to seek the support of friends and kin in Bethlehem after the death of her husband and sons. Jeremiah instructs those in exile to plan for a long stay and to invest their lives in the place where they find themselves. This advice is accompanied by an exhortation to continue to trust in the God of Israel in light of a possible future return (Jer. 29:1–14). Daniel and his friends receive Babylonian names and are trained for service to the empire. Yet, even as they fulfill their duties, they maintain the dietary laws and openly testify to their faith, even at great personal cost (Dan. 1–6). Nehemiah is cupbearer to the king but still is attentive to news from his ancestral land. He leaves with the king's permission and support to rebuild the walls of Jerusalem. He revitalizes Jewish society as governor but after a time returns to his post in the Persian court.

Still others evidently experience almost total assimilation. Joseph is given an Egyptian name, marries an Egyptian, and has two sons by her (Gen. 41:45, 50–52). He is so acculturated that his brothers do not recognize him. Interestingly, Joseph had not forgotten his mother tongue and understands their conversation (Gen. 42–45). Following Egyptian custom, he embalms Jacob after his death, and the same is done to him (Gen. 50:2, 26). Moses is thought to be an Egyptian by the women at the well (Exod. 2:19). Ruth leaves her homeland and declares her intention to take on the identity of her mother-in-law's people (Ruth 1:16–17). Yet, as one who has recently arrived, Ruth must be coached by Naomi on how to navigate the different cultural mores and institutions (Ruth 2–3). Ruth marries Boaz and is fully accepted into the Israelite community. The closing lines of the narrative reveal that this immigrant woman is a key piece in the genealogy of David (Ruth 4:13–22). Esther is generations removed from the fall of Judah. Like many exiles, she had both a Jewish and a Persian name (Esth. 2:7). Mordecai, her relative, must have done well for himself financially and socially in order to have the right to sit at the city gate (e.g., Esth. 3:2; 5:9). That this prosperous foreigner did not do him homage infuriated Haman and motivated him to seek the destruction of all the Jews. Mordecai demonstrates loyalty to the king by uncovering an assassination plot (Esth. 2:21–23), even as he works through Esther to save their people (Esth. 4; 8–10). There is no indication that either contemplated returning to the land.

From these same narratives it is possible to reconstruct a continuum of responses of the host peoples: from Egyptian anxiety of being overrun by large numbers of foreign workers (and their violent effort to halt the growth of that population) and Haman's hatred of the Jews, to the ambivalent reception of Abraham (Gen. 12:10–20; 26:6–11), to the inclusion of Ruth by the Bethlehemites and the deep trust that Artaxerxes has in Nehemiah, and Nebuchadnezzar and Darius in Daniel. These diverse emotional reactions are accompanied by diverse political decisions and social arrangements. The treatment of immigrants, however they arrived, was an issue in the ancient world.

Finally, mention should be made of the ancient practice of hospitality toward strangers. The people of God practiced this openness toward others (e.g., Abraham [Gen. 18:1–8]) and also were beneficiaries of gracious treatment when they traveled elsewhere (e.g., Moses [Exod. 2:15–20]). Kindness toward the outsider reflected righteousness before God (Job 31:32).

The OT narratives can orient discussion about immigration and refugees in several ways. For example, they demonstrate that migration was a fundamental reality for many peoples of the Bible, even as it is today. It is not a recent or isolated phenomenon. Moreover, the kinds of forces that drive contemporary migration, such as basic human needs and military conflict, and the mistreatment that strangers sometimes endure are present in the biblical accounts. The different assimilation experiences in these accounts also mirror modern variations. An appreciation of the Scriptures as in large measure a collection of the stories of migrant and displaced peoples can sensitize today's receiving communities to the presence and plight of these persons in their midst. That the Bible contains migration accounts is helpful too for those who have migrated. In its pages the displaced discover individuals and circumstances with which they can identify. They are exposed to examples of how to live faithfully in potentially adverse situations (e.g., Joseph, Ruth, Ezra, Nehemiah, Daniel) in full confidence that God is with them no matter where they are on the assimilation spectrum and irrespective of the kind of welcome they experience in their new land.

Old Testament law. Sojourners (the term *gēr*), whether from another country or internally displaced, were especially vulnerable to the vicissitudes of life. This is evident in that they are classified with widows, orphans, and the poor as being most at risk. There were no governmental assistance programs such as we have today. The extended family was to provide a safety net in times of need. The difficulty for these outsiders was that they were separated from those kinship networks. Moreover, they were outside the local land tenure system, where property was passed on within the family through male heirs. In an agrarian peasant society such as Israel, these outsiders, without family and land, were at the mercy of the Israelites for sustenance, work, and protection.

The provision of food was a constant concern because sojourners depended on others for day-to-day living. They were at risk of being overworked and underpaid (or not paid at all). As outsiders, they might find themselves at a disadvantage in legal matters. Legislation in the OT responds to these challenges. Sojourners qualified, along with those other needy groups, for the gleaning laws at harvest time (Lev. 19:9–10; Deut. 24:19–22) and the triennial tithe (Deut. 14:28–29). They were to be given rest on the Sabbath (Exod. 20:10; Deut. 5:14) and be paid a fair wage on time (Deut. 24:14–15). No one was to take advantage of them in the courts (Deut. 1:16–17; 27:19). The prophets denounced those who oppressed the sojourner (Jer. 7:5–7; 22:2–5; Mal. 3:5).

The law does not stipulate specific penalties for not showing compassion toward the sojourner. Instead, it makes a moral appeal rooted in two primary motivations. First, the Israelites must never forget that they had been despised foreigners in another land. At one time, they had been workers in Egypt's oppressive system, but they had been redeemed by God's gracious, powerful hand. That is, as descendants of immigrants, they should be generous to the sojourners among them. That saga of migration was to define them, and the treatment of the outsider served as a measure of their faith in God (Lev. 19:34; Exod. 23:9). From the very outset of their escape from Egypt, outsiders had lived among them (Exod. 12:38). The Israelites themselves were sojourners still in that land of which God was the owner (Lev. 25:23). The second and more important reason to love the sojourner is that God does. God demands charity toward the weak, including the outsider (Deut. 10:14–19; cf. Ps. 146:6–9; Jer. 7:4–7; Zech. 7:8–10).

The legislation related to sojourners was generous, but mutuality was assumed as well. With these benefits came the expectation of accommodation by the outsider. The sojourner was expected to learn the laws of the land (Deut. 31:10–13; cf. Josh. 8:34–35). Penalties for violations were to be the same for native and outsider alike (Lev. 24:22; Num. 15:29). Participation in religious feasts (e.g., Exod. 12:48–49; 20:8–11; Lev. 16:29–30; Deut. 16:11, 14) required conversion, an awareness of procedures, and the ability to speak Hebrew. These laws point to a degree of assimilation into the local community. The prophets spoke of a future day when there would be a shared life with outsiders (Isa. 56:1–8; Ezek. 47:21–23).

This legal material remains relevant for the contemporary situation. As Scripture, the law is part of the divine revelation to the church, which must discern guidance from its demands. Even though these laws indeed were designed for Israel—its time, place, and culture—their significance reaches beyond that ancient people of God. Deuteronomy 4:5–8 states that Israel's legislation (and thus their laws regarding the sojourner) was a witness to the other nations of the character of God and the fundamental values that can make for a healthy society. Then and now, other nations will have their own particular legislation and socioeconomic configurations for outsiders, but the divine insistence on their care remains.

The New Testament. An examination of relevant material in the NT starts with Jesus himself. When he was a small child, Jesus and his family fled to Egypt to avoid Herod's rampage (Matt. 2:13–15). No information about the length of their sojourn in Egypt is provided, but at that time there was a large, long-standing Jewish community there. Jesus lived as a refugee in a foreign land, and so life in another place as a displaced person was part of his personal experience.

In his teaching Jesus never deals directly with the topic of migration. Nevertheless, at least two items are relevant. First, Jesus involved himself with those who were different and despised by the broader community. On several occasions he engaged the Samaritans, a people loathsome to many Jews. Jesus spoke with a Samaritan woman (John 4:7–26), and he uses a Samaritan as a paragon of righteousness in his response to the question "Who is my neighbor?" (Luke 10:29–37). This teaching is consistent with his call to reach out to the marginalized—gentiles, women, the poor, the sick, and those classified as sinners by the religious authorities.

The second point concerns Jesus' pronouncement in Matt. 25:31–46 about caring for the stranger (vv. 35, 38, 43–44). Advocates for refugees and immigrants often appeal to this passage to defend the rights of outsiders. This interpretation is possible but faces the problem that the referent is disputed. The occurrences of the qualification "the least of these" and "brothers" (Matt. 25:40, 45) may restrict these individuals to Jesus' disciples (cf. Matt. 10:42; 12:48–50; 18:6, 10, 14; 28:10). If this latter interpretation is the better one, then the "strangers" are followers who suffer for Jesus' sake at the hands of others.

The forced displacement of believers due to persecution is recorded in Acts. Many are scattered by the persecution headed by Saul (later called

"Paul"), himself a Diaspora Jew (Acts 8:1–5; cf. Rev. 1:9), and itinerant preachers apparently were a common phenomenon in the early church (cf. the missionary journeys of Paul; 1 Cor. 16:5–18; Gal. 4:13–14; Phil. 2:19–30; 3 John 5–10). There also are multiethnic churches with believers from various backgrounds and places of origin (e.g., Acts 13:1), a mix that produced tensions (Acts 15; Gal. 2; Eph. 2).

The NT Epistles reveal that all Christians are sojourners in a spiritual sense; their citizenship ultimately lies elsewhere (Phil. 3:20; Heb. 13:14). In 1 Pet. 1:1; 2:11 the author speaks of believers as "aliens" and "strangers." The addressees of this letter may have been literal exiles who had been moved by the empire. If so, that legal standing reflected in unique ways their spiritual status as Christians. In addition, hospitality toward others, whether fellow believers or unfamiliar persons, is a Christian virtue. All Christians are to be gracious to others (Rom. 12:13; Heb. 13:2; 1 Pet. 4:9; cf. Luke 14:12–14), and this quality should distinguish the leadership of the church (1 Tim. 3:2; Titus 1:8).

Migration, Theology, and Mission

Both the OT and the NT have much to teach concerning the migration of people. This survey has pointed out that refugees and immigrants are made in the image of God, that migration is part of human experience, that many biblical "heroes" were displaced persons, and that OT legislation was benevolent to the vulnerable in many concrete ways. The life and teachings of Jesus demonstrate the need for believers to consider the possibility that those who are different may be the very ones who can lead them to a deeper faith, while the NT Epistles call the church to care for the outsider. After all, every Christian is an outsider—a stranger—in the world. This extensive scriptural material should shape attitudes and actions toward outsiders. Today, many believers need to be reminded that they are descendants of immigrants and displaced people, and that to follow the God of the Bible means being gracious toward those whom he loves. How these biblical perspectives and moral demands take shape in personal behavior, church initiatives, and civil legislation that can promote human flourishing and the common good depends on the impact of the Christian ethical voice and involvement.

These multiple challenges for migrant populations, which contain many Christians, have spawned creative theological reflection. As in the days of the Jewish exile and during the early years of the church, displaced believers are wrestling in fresh ways with the person of God and the nature of faith. New ways of thinking are attempting to move beyond traditional theological categories and limited interpretations of the Bible that have not given enough attention to the views and experiences of marginalized peoples. Theologians and pastoral workers are turning to postcolonial studies, international law, the histories of migration, and sociological and anthropological work on ethnicity, hybridity, and transnationalism to better comprehend the situation of immigrants and refugees—that is, the modern-day human diaspora in an era of globalization. This diaspora theology seeks to speak from and for these people, whether to encourage those who suffer as victims of their circumstances or to orient those who see their displacement as an important moment in the worldwide work of the sovereign God. Inevitably, these efforts are leading to new appreciations and understandings of the character and mission of the church that will enrich theology and Christian practice.

See also Exile; Globalization; Hospitality; Image of God; Nationalism; Population Policy and Control

Bibliography

Brettell, C., and J. Hollifield. *Migration Theory: Talking across Disciplines*. 2nd ed. Routledge, 2008; Carroll R., M. D. *Christians at the Border: Immigration, the Church, and the Bible*. Baker Academic, 2008; Groody, D., ed. *A Promised Land, a Perilous Journey: Theological Perspectives on Migration*. University of Notre Dame Press, 2008; Hanciles, J. *Beyond Christendom: Globalization, African Migration and the Transformation of the West*. Orbis, 2008; Hoffmeier, J. *The Immigration Crisis: Immigrants, Aliens, and the Bible*. Crossway, 2009; Miller, P. "Israel as Host to Strangers." Pages 548–71 in *Israelite Religion and Biblical Theology: Collected Essays*. JSOTSup 267. Sheffield Academic Press, 2000; O'Neil, W., and W. Spohn. "Rights of Passage: The Ethics of Immigration and Refugee Policy." *TS* 59 (1998): 84–106; Pohl, C. "Responding to Strangers: Insights from the Christian Tradition." *SCE* 19 (2006): 81–101; Pontifical Council for the Pastoral Care of Migrants and Itinerant People. *The Love of Christ towards Migrants: Instruction*. Catholic Truth Society, 2004; Ramírez Kidd, J. *Alterity and Identity in Israel: The "Ger" in the Old Testament*. BZAW 283. De Gruyter, 1999; Rivera, L. "Toward a Diaspora Hermeneutics (Hispanic North America)." Pages 169–89 in *Character Ethics and the Old Testament: Moral Dimensions of Scripture*, ed. M. D. Carroll R. and J. Lapsley. Westminster John Knox, 2007; Smith-Christopher, D. *A Biblical Theology of Exile*. OBT. Fortress, 2002; Soerens, M., and J. Hwang. *Welcoming the Stranger: Justice, Compassion, and Truth in the Immigration Debate*. InterVarsity, 2009; Waters, M., and R. Ueda, eds. *The New Americans: A Guide to Immigration since 1965*. Harvard University Press, 2007.

M. Daniel Carroll R. (Rodas)

Almsgiving

Almsgiving in the NT refers to benevolent activity on behalf of the needy as an expression of genuine social solidarity—that is, of caring for and embracing those in need as if they were members of one's own kin group. Although the terminology of "almsgiving" is absent from the OT, Israel's Scriptures both call for the care of the needy (conventionalized in references to "the alien, the orphan, and the widow") and provide the theological footing of the practice in the Gospels and Acts. By way of more specific background, we can point to legislation concerning "gleaning rights" (Deut. 24:19–22), loans to the poor (Exod. 22:25; Lev. 25:35–37), and the tithe for the needy (Deut. 14:27–29).

Almsgiving is one of several responses among the Jews to the burdensome economic situation under Roman occupation (compare, e.g., the "community of goods" among the Essenes and in the Jerusalem church, banditry, and revolutionary activity against Rome). In addition to day-to-day economic struggles in an agrarian-based economy, war, failed crops, natural disasters, and taxes set the stage for the downward mobility of persons below the level of subsistence. However, neither Rome nor the regional governments supported by Rome made allowances for assistance in times of distress. The urban elite might provide benefaction in isolated instances, but the situation at the time of Jesus was characterized by the near absence of charitable practices in the Roman world. Jesus' commentary on the situation of the prodigal son living in need is thus a faithful barometer of socioeconomic realities: "no one gave him anything" (Luke 15:16).

Recognizing that economic sharing is embedded in social relations, we can see immediately the problem of "giving to the poor" in Roman antiquity. Often, giving to the needy was rank-specific, so as to allow those who had temporarily fallen on hard times to maintain their accustomed status. Otherwise, the practice of giving to the needy would exist outside of normal structures of reciprocity; that is, givers had nothing to gain from the gift because they could never be repaid and because giving to the destitute did not enhance one's social stature in public life. This is exactly the point of almsgiving, however. Thus, according to the Gospels, Jesus castigates the Pharisees and scribes because they shared none of their resources with the needy and engaged in acts of greed; in other words, their practices distanced them from the needy (Luke 11:39–41; 20:47). Similarly, in the Synoptic Gospels, Jesus directs a rich man to sell what he has and give to the poor (Matt. 19:21; Mark 10:21; Luke 18:22). He does not ask this rich man to embrace poverty per se, otherwise he could have counseled disinvestment without redistribution. Rather, in this scenario, to preserve one's wealth was to preserve one's social distance from the marginal. In another example, in Luke 19:1–10, a rich man, Zacchaeus, demonstrates his identity with the poor through almsgiving. Almsgiving, then, takes place apart from the normal structures of socioeconomic reciprocity and is not a measure of honor and status, except before God, who sees and rewards such practices (Matt. 6:1–18; Luke 6:27–36; 14:12–14; Acts 10:1–4).

In the early church, Clement of Alexandria (150–215 CE) is known for his unrelenting emphasis on almsgiving. Perhaps without engaging in sufficient critical reflection on how wealth is produced, Clement encouraged Christian participation in business affairs and entrepreneurial activity in the commercially oriented Alexandria so that Christians might be in a better position to assist the poor. For him, the solution to the problem of scarcity was, first, a renegotiation of consumption—"The best wealth is to have few desires" (*Paed.* 2.3)—and, second, for the wealthy to come to the aid of the needy.

Clearly, almsgiving should not be confused with such contemporary "acts of charity" as giving a small monetary gift to the homeless person one passes each day. In light of the social nature of economic sharing, giving small amounts to the needy and giving to those with whom one has no expectation of genuine relationship do not qualify as illustrations of almsgiving.

See also Charity, Works of; Economic Ethics; Koinonia; Tithe, Tithing

Bibliography

Hamel, G. *Poverty and Charity in Roman Palestine, First Three Centuries C.E.* University of California Press, 1990; Kim, K.-J. *Stewardship and Almsgiving in Luke's Theology*. JSNTSup 155. Sheffield Academic Press, 1998; Moxnes, H. *The Economy of the Kingdom: Social Conflict and Economic Relations in Luke's Gospel*. OBT. Fortress, 1988.

Joel B. Green

Altruism

Altruism is a broad sociological classification for other-regarding actions that emerged in the nineteenth century as a secular alternative to the language of charity, benevolence, and Christian love. Although it captures the other-regarding essence of generous behaviors, it is now so deeply identified with self-sacrifice that it hardly captures the ways in which a generous life contributes to the happiness and flourishing of altruists (e.g., as exemplified in 2 Cor. 9:7, "God loves a cheerful giver"). Moreover, it does not distinguish between the various forms of altruism. Altruism can be based on reason alone, on instinct, and on position or role expectation (e.g., a firefighter). Hence the Pauline words, "If I give everything I have to feed the poor . . . but have not love, I gain nothing" (1 Cor. 13:2–3). In other words, we can sacrifice ourselves for others, but in the absence of love, we have achieved little.

From the Christian perspective, the highest human expression of altruism is altruistic love, or agape. Love includes an emotional center that affirms others in a tenderness and concern, and that is palpable in things such as facial expression and tone of voice. Altruistic love is an intentional affirmation of the other, combining emotion and reason with action. Its agapic enhancement involves elevation by worldview (including biblical teachings) and the experience of divine love.

In the Christian tradition, forms of altruism that are widely extensive beyond kin, that are enduring over time, and that are purely motivated have some grounding in the work of the Holy Spirit. As it is written, "By contrast, the fruit of the Spirit is love, joy, peace, patience, kindness, generosity, faithfulness, gentleness, and self-control" (Gal. 5:22–23). Or as Jas. 1:17 reads, "Every generous act of giving, with every perfect gift, is from above, coming down from the Father of lights, with whom there is no variation or shadow due to change." And perhaps most centrally, in 1 John 4:19, "We love because [God] first loved us."

The Christian theological tradition has not embraced the language of altruism, which originated in a positivistic effort to displace the particularity of agape love. The historical tension between Christianity and secular altruistic science has severely limited the potential for dialogue between theology and science around agape love.

Altruism, even without the emotionally intense features that are associated with love, concerns the role of the other in moral experience. By the strictest definition, the altruist is someone who does something for the other and for the other's sake rather than as a means to self-promotion or internal well-being—for example, even the feeling of inner satisfaction. A more balanced definition would indicate that a sense of internal well-being as an indirect side effect of altruistic behavior does not imply that the agent's psychological motive is somehow impure and egoistic. Many philosophers have argued for the motivational reality of altruism, even if mixed with some subordinated egoistic desires to get what the self wants or needs, so long as the controlling aim is to give to the other what he or she may want or need. Psychological altruism exists when the agent seeks to promote the well-being of the other "at least primarily for the other person's sake" (Hazo 18). However, if altruistic acts are purely tactical, then there is no genuine psychological altruism present, and the action is primarily egoistic. In the broadest terms, the altruist no longer sees self as the only center of value, but discovers the other as other (Levinas; Wyschogrod) rather than as an entity in orbit around the self in its egoism. Claims of the self to ontological centrality are set aside.

Altruism is other-regarding, either with regard to actions or motivations; altruistic love adds the feature of deep affirmative affect to altruism; agape is altruistic love universalized to all humanity as informed by theistic commitments and the experience of the Holy Spirit. Pitirim Sorokin noted that the great sages of altruistic love seem to embody an attractive force of love that they have discovered as objectively existing in the universe, and that is associated with a Supreme Being or "Supraconciousness." Something is at work in love for all humanity that has connections with spirituality.

See also Affections; Agape; Benevolence; Care, Caring; Charity, Works of; Fruit of the Spirit; Selfishness; Self-Love

Bibliography

Hazo, R. *The Idea of Love.* Praeger, 1976; Levinas, I. *Totality and Infinity: An Essay on Exteriority.* Duquesne University Press, 1969; Sober, E., and D. Wilson. *Unto Others: The Evolution and Psychology of Unselfish Behavior.* Harvard University Press, 1998; Sorokin, P. *The Ways and Power of Love: Types, Factors, and Techniques of Moral Transformation.* Beacon Press, 1954; Vacek, E. *Love, Human and Divine: The Heart of Christian Ethics.* Georgetown University Press, 1994; Wycshogrod, E. *Saints and Postmodernism: Revising Moral Philosophy.* University of Chicago Press, 1990.

Stephen Post

Amos

The book of Amos perennially has generated interest because of its strong ethical message. Its strident condemnation of oppression and of religious ritual has resonated in diverse contexts over time. Many consider Amos and other prophets of that era—Isaiah, Micah, and Hosea—as the zenith of what has been called "ethical monotheism": they are champions of God's universal demand for justice. Recently, liberation theologies have found a valuable resource in Amos.

The book's heading (1:1) locates the prophet in the reign of Jeroboam II of Israel in the mid-eighth century BCE. This was a time of economic exploitation facilitated by the internal policies of the monarchy and international political and economic realities. The text is less interested in analyzing these underlying realities than in appealing to moral sensibilities concerning the plight of the needy, the arrogance of nationalism, and the nature of acceptable worship.

The book of Amos draws on various strands of theological traditions in ancient Israel. Its vocabulary and themes find echoes in the wisdom literature and the covenant demands of the law, while the concern for the sanctuaries and rituals suggests that the prophet was well acquainted with the religious world of that time. The moral voice of Amos is full of indignation and sarcasm, and the ethical realities presented in the book are complex and include every sphere of social life.

The exploitation of the poor is a key theme. They are sold into slavery because of debts and suffer undue taxation and unfair treatment in legal proceedings (2:6; 5:10–15; 8:4–6). In the midst of this injustice the comfortable enjoy abundance (3:15–4:3; 6:4–6; cf. Isa. 3:16–4:1; 5:8–25; Jer. 22:1–16). The well-to-do acquire their goods and status with violence toward the vulnerable (3:9–10; cf. Mic. 2:1–5; 3:1–4). The cruelty of the nations in warfare that is condemned in the opening chapter is evident within the borders of the people of God in the abuse of the unfortunate.

Although this socioeconomic criticism is aimed at those who take advantage of the weak, the prophet also turns his withering gaze against the nation as a whole. He mocks its military pretense. The litany of conflicts in chap. 1, the mockery of insignificant victories (6:13), and the announcement of comprehensive defeat in the near future (2:14–16; 3:11–12; 5:1–3, 16–17, 27; 6:8–14; 7:9, 17; 8:1–3, 9–10; 9:9–10) undermine Israel's confident posturing. Apparently, this pride in military power was shared by the entire populace. All crowded the sanctuaries to celebrate the national deity, whom they felt would ensure their safety. But the Lord God of hosts will have none of this worship that ignores oppression and takes his endorsement for granted (3:14; 4:4–6; 5:4–6, 18–27; 7:9; 9:1; cf. Isa. 1:10–20; 58; Jer. 7:1–11; Mic. 6:6–8; Mal. 3:2–5). The visions reveal that Israel is "so small" (7:1–6) and that its mighty fortresses actually have walls like "tin" (7:7–8 NET [not "plumb line," as in many translations]). The religious ideology that Amos so fiercely derides is defended by the high priest Amaziah (7:10–13). What made this uncritical and self-deceiving wedding of patriotism and religion even more insidious is that those who are the victims of the injustices of the nation cheer this perversion of the divine will along with the rest. They stubbornly accept that system and champion king and country (4:4–12).

The Lord desires that Israel seek and love the good and hate evil. This "good" is to be manifested concretely in the socioeconomic relationships of the community (5:10–15). It is to be the public display of righteousness and charity, which they have distorted and undermined (5:7; 6:12). God desires both just structures and a people of virtue. Ideally, they would have been nurtured in those ideals in their worship gatherings and would have had exemplars worth imitating in their leaders, but this is clearly not the case (4:1; 6:1; 7:9–10, 16–17; cf. Isa. 1:23; Ezek. 34).

The coming judgment is comprehensive. Some readers are troubled that all suffer the divine punishment. The text teaches, however, that sin and its recompense are not only individual or perfectly symmetrical. Judgments in history are not tidy. The personal and the social are interwoven, and the web of community ties complicates the nature of sin and chastisement. Transgression is systemic; it is embedded in social relationships in every sphere, and all are complicit at some level. The ideological distortions of faith also know no class, racial, or gender boundaries. Nations violate the norms of God on the international stage as well, as they go to war to acquire power, labor, and land (1:3–2:3; cf. Isa. 13–23; Jer. 46–51).

Amos teaches that everyone is guilty, especially the people of God whose knowledge and experience place them beyond excuse (2:11–12; 3:1–2; 9:7). At times, those who are innocent of some of these transgressions endure undeserved hardship. That is why the leaders are held most responsible for the plight and fate of their people. They make the domestic and foreign policies that affect everyone else and set a moral tone for society.

The broad, realistic ethical vision of Amos incorporates economics, politics, and religion. It involves individuals, social groups, and the entire nation in its censure. Yet this book also proclaims a future of peace, plenty, and a restored relationship with God and creation beyond the present injustice and the imminent wrath (9:11–15). Judgment is not God's final word. That future is an ethical hope that helps readers bear the contradictions of today and should motivate them to work to approximate that coming reality in the contemporary world.

See also Economic Ethics; Exploitation; Idolatry; Justice; Liberationist Ethics; Old Testament Ethics; Poverty and Poor; Wealth

Bibliography

Barton, J. *Understanding Old Testament Ethics: Approaches and Evaluations*. Westminster John Knox, 2003;

Brueggemann, W. *The Prophetic Imagination*. 2nd ed. Fortress, 2001; Carroll R., M. D. *Amos—The Prophet and His Oracles: Research on the Book of Amos*. Westminster John Knox, 2002; idem. "Seeking the Virtues among the Prophets: The Book of Amos as a Test Case." *ExAud* 17 (2001): 77–96; Dempsey, C. *Hope amid the Ruins: The Ethics of Israel's Prophets*. Chalice, 2000; Heschel, A. *The Prophets*. Harper & Row, 1962; Houston, W. *Contending for Justice: Ideologies and Theologies of Social Justice in the Old Testament*. Rev. ed. LHBOTS 428. T&T Clark, 2008; O'Brien, J. *Challenging Prophetic Metaphor: Theology and Ideology in the Prophets*. Westminster John Knox, 2008.

M. Daniel Carroll R. (Rodas)

Anabaptist Ethics

Christian discipleship, peacemaking, community, integrity, and fidelity to Scripture have been at the core of Anabaptist ethics for the past five centuries.

Anabaptists emerged in the volatile context of early sixteenth-century Europe, becoming part of the Radical Reformation (the "left wing" of the Protestant Reformation). Of central importance to many early Anabaptist leaders were the autonomy of the church from the state in matters of worship and religious practice; the necessity for baptism into the church to be voluntary, based on an adult commitment to follow in the way of Christ; the separation of Christians from the "worldly" realm of politics; and, for most surviving groups of Anabaptists, rejection of "the sword."

Anabaptists' direct spiritual descendants—today's Mennonites, Amish, and Hutterites, who number about 1.2 million around the world, with 60 percent of those in the southern hemisphere—are still shaped by their forebears' seminal sixteenth-century convictions, though they embody these sometimes-contested Anabaptist ethical principles in different ways in their contemporary contexts.

The Sermon on the Mount and Christian Discipleship

Because of their profound concern for ethics, Anabaptists did not fully embrace Reformer Martin Luther's call to salvation *sola fidei* ("by faith alone"), believing that such a view could degenerate into inattention to Christian living. Instead, they pointed toward a synergistic, salvific blending of divine action and human cooperation, perhaps more akin to a late-medieval Catholic view of God-infused transformation and active faith. True faith is lived out in life, they asserted, and all followers are called to follow Jesus Christ in all aspects of life. Early Dutch Anabaptist leader Menno Simons began all his treatises with an epigram from 1 Cor. 3:11: "For no one can lay any foundation other than the one that has been laid; that foundation is Jesus Christ."

Such faithful following was possible, early Anabaptists believed, because of the transformative grace of God and a slightly more optimistic view of human nature than was true for some of their Protestant counterparts. Menno Simons, after whom Mennonites were named, argued for what might be called "complex innocence" in childhood, a recognition of the absence of both faithfulness and sinfulness in children, but an "innocence," as he describes it, tempered with the acknowledgment of an inherited Adamic nature predisposed toward sinning.

Training children toward making commitments of faith and being faithful disciples was the ever-present goal of childhood nurture. Such a life of discipleship was impossible without experiencing a new birth, being converted and changed, and parents needed to guide their children toward such conversions and lifelong commitments. Voluntary baptism or *ana*-baptism (*re*-baptism, for those who had been baptized as infants in state churches) was construed as the beginning of the Christian life, not the end.

Sixteenth-century Anabaptists were known to live moral, upright lives, and they developed a reputation for being people of integrity and clean living. Often, early Anabaptist sermons included stories about the results of being good, with preachers telling virtuous-person narratives to inspire others also to be like Jesus. Such preaching was effective in the sixteenth-century context, where a large middle ground of people, whose intellectual leader was the Catholic humanist Erasmus, were attracted to this sort of moral preaching. Although Anabaptists were not self-consciously followers of Erasmus, many Anabaptist ideas and foundational scriptural texts can be found in his writings.

Although they did not formally recognize a "canon within the canon," early Anabaptists clearly gave priority to the NT over the OT and saw Jesus as absolutely central to understanding the biblical text, the key through which believers could interpret both Testaments. Most formative for Anabaptist ethics were the Synoptic Gospels, which most closely narrated the life and teachings of Jesus. Within those three Gospel accounts, Matthew's Sermon on the Mount (Matt. 5–7) and its Lukan counterpart (Luke 6) were most instructive, including Jesus' words about loving enemies, turning the other cheek, and sacrificial service to others. The Matthean Beatitudes (Matt. 5:3–12) are repeatedly cited in Anabaptist sources, often in relation to suffering and persecution.

Because a small number of sixteenth-century Anabaptists were violent, and because the pacifist

Anabaptists refused to obey civil authorities on matters such as infant baptism, they were perceived as a threat to social order. Within months after their beginnings in 1525, their first martyrs were killed, initially at the hands of Catholic authorities and later by Protestants. Over the course of the next century, thousands of Anabaptists were killed, and those in the movement fled to other lands and rural areas safe from the avenging arm of religious and civil authorities.

Hundreds of these martyr stories are told in a collection titled *Martyrs Mirror of the Defenseless Christians*, a huge volume in continuous publication since 1660 and still a staple in many Anabaptist homes. The text begins with the deaths of Jesus and Stephen and then traces a continuous history of faithful martyrs through the Waldenses, Albigenses, and the stories of hundreds of the Anabaptist martyrs.

The most influential story from *Martyrs Mirror* is of Anabaptist Dirk Willems, who in 1569 had been imprisoned for allowing people to be rebaptized in his home. After escaping from prison, he made it across an icy pond to safety, but an Anabaptist catcher in hot pursuit broke through the ice to his almost certain death. Instead of running ahead to safety, Willems returned to the precarious ice and saved the life of his persecutor, who then promptly arrested him. Soon afterward, Willems was burned at the stake. For generations of Anabaptists, the story seared its way into their sense of faith and faithfulness: believers are called to service to others, even if that means risking their own lives.

Another key section of the Sermon on the Mount that infuses early Anabaptist thought is the reference to truth-telling, integrity, and "the oath" (Matt. 5:33–37). The Anabaptist position on truth-telling has been rather absolutist throughout most of the tradition's history. In the 1527 Schleitheim Confession, the earliest Anabaptist confession of faith, one of the questions that early Anabaptists dealt with was swearing the oath. Although there were other problematic dimensions to swearing an oath (including swearing allegiance to a particular government), one of the problems with oath-swearing was that it suggested that the swearer was not being truthful all the time.

The Schleitheim Confession says, "Christ taught us similarly when He says: Your speech shall be yea, yea; and nay, nay; for what is more than that comes of evil." The implication was that Christian believers are always to tell the truth, not just when under an oath. For some contemporary Anabaptists, this is still an issue when they testify in court: if they are asked to swear, instead they simply "affirm" that they will tell the truth now—as always.

Early Anabaptists and their descendants also have drawn extensively on the Sermon on the Mount's call for nonresistance and loving one's enemies (see below). Often Anabaptists read such Christian teachings in a fairly straightforward, more or less literal manner, believing that such instructions should be embodied in their own lives. They understood the text simply to mean what it said, and they shaped their lives more around direct biblical teachings than complex theological expositions.

On Vocation

Pluralistic in both their sixteenth-century and twenty-first-century forms, early Anabaptists and their descendants have wrestled at length with the meaning of discipleship, the Christian obligation to engage or disengage "the world," the commitment to practice nonviolence, and the Christian's calling.

In the Christian church's first several centuries, those who committed themselves to the Jesus movement recognized the import of that decision of faith and calling—the way in which being a disciple of a crucified Christ could shape the entirety of their lives. As small, often marginalized, and intermittently persecuted communities of believers, being committed to Christ and the church often meant opening themselves to transformation and service as well as making sacrifices, taking risks, and closing occupational or vocational doors.

The meaning of Christian discipleship and the stratification of ordinary Christians and church leaders both underwent profound transformation in the years after the emperor Constantine came into power in 311/312 and new converts flooded into the now favored Christian church. Leaders, monks, and nuns became "the religious," those who had a sacred calling or vocation. Christian calling became truncated, referring largely to those who entered the priesthood or religious orders but generally devaluing the work of others outside those confines.

In the sixteenth century, Martin Luther rejected what he saw as a vocational double standard as well as his monastic vows, believing that true faith needed to be worked out in the complex and often difficult realities of life beyond monastery walls. He maintained that all stations in life in which it is possible to live honestly are divine vocations.

Although early Anabaptists generally appreciated Luther's honoring of more than monastic and priestly callings, they were suspicious that the content of a Christian's activity in a particular "station" or "office" seemed to come more from the "orders of creation" than from faith in Jesus. Tensions with civil authorities emerged over a range of issues, but particularly over the role of the Christian in governance.

Most Anabaptists were particularly critical of occupational roles that involved coercive force or violence, including any sort of political office; some were deeply suspicious of any work having to do with trade or commerce; others were worried even about the traditional assignment of special vocational status to "religious" occupations. The Anabaptists did not expect their convictions to be adopted by the whole society, but in the turmoil of the sixteenth century these radical practices and public pronouncements represented a threat to the stability of society.

Perspectives on the State

Building on the writings of Augustine as well as their contemporaries, most early Anabaptists agreed with Luther that the state was ordained to preserve order in a fallen world, adopting some version of a dualistic, two-kingdom understanding of the world. However, the surviving strains of Anabaptism parted ways with Luther on the issue of the Christian's role in the two kingdoms. For Luther, Christians stood squarely in the midst of both kingdoms: in their private, personal lives, they were in the kingdom of God, and in their public lives they were in the earthly kingdom. People were essentially split down the middle in their loyalties: Christian love called them to act in both kingdoms, abiding by the ethic of each when working in that realm and not expecting to effect much change in the earthly kingdom.

For most of the Anabaptists, it was the world, not individuals, that was split: faithful Christians lived in the kingdom of God and abided only by its ethics, and others were in the earthly kingdom. The Anabaptists acknowledged that God had instituted civil government, and therefore it should be obeyed, but only up to the point where the state's demands clearly contradicted God's authority. The foundational framework for Christians' relation to government was Acts 5:29 (obedience to God rather than human authorities) rather than the more socially conservative perspective of Rom. 13, which became the foundational passage for some other Protestant traditions.

Because of their understandings of the commandments of Christ, however, Anabaptists believed Christians could not kill, even when the state had legitimated killing in the cases of war and capital punishment. Therefore, although they believed that the state was divinely instituted, most Anabaptists said the true Christian could not participate in the government's work, because the civil realm required the use of violence for maintaining order and was therefore "outside the perfection of Christ," as the Schleitheim Confession says. Even Anabaptist leader Pilgram Marpeck, who served as a civil engineer, said, in effect, that one can be a Christian magistrate, but not for long; soon, one has to give up either the "Christian" or "magistrate" identity marker.

Commitments to Peace

Traditionally, the Anabaptists' peace position has been rooted in the biblical portrayal of Jesus' way of love and his willingness to suffer on the cross. Anabaptists generally have believed that Jesus' demonstration of love in all relationships should be normative for his followers. Often in Anabaptist history the faithful response to violence has been characterized as "nonresistance," a term derived from the Sermon on the Mount injunction to "resist not evil" (Matt. 5:39) but to turn the other cheek. For Mennonites, Hutterites, and Amish, nonresistance has been a way of being a faithful disciple of Jesus Christ, not a strategy for achieving peace.

Such a posture, espoused most articulately by Guy F. Hershberger in his mid-twentieth-century book *War, Peace, and Nonresistance*, was broader than simple conscientious objection or refusal to participate in warfare; nonresistance had implications for all dimensions of Christian life. Although many Anabaptists still use the language of "nonresistance," in the past sixty years, influenced in part by the successful activist movements of Mahatma Gandhi and Martin Luther King Jr., Mennonites and other Anabaptist descendants have debated the appropriateness of nonviolent resistance, sociopolitical activism, justice making, and "responsibility" in the political arena.

Influenced in part by Mennonite theologian John H. Yoder and other Anabaptist leaders, many twentieth-century Mennonites began to question the traditional church/world dualism of their faith heritage. Beginning in the 1960s, the language of the "lordship of Christ" over all the world (not just the church) began to be used in Mennonite circles. In Yoder's view, that theological shift justified and perhaps mandated a Mennonite "witness" to the state, asking the state to embody more fully the norms that Christ revealed, norms relevant for both individuals and institutions, including nations.

Others, such as Gordon Kaufman and J. Lawrence Burkholder, argued further for an Anabaptist embrace of "responsibility" as part of Christian discipleship, an ethic that could serve as a corrective to more naive forms of simply following Jesus in what is actually a complex, ethically ambiguous world. They and other Anabaptist thinkers in the last third of the twentieth century helped bring to the foreground Anabaptists' obligation to seek justice as well as practice love. Anabaptist thinkers and practitioners since their time have been attentive to justice concerns, particularly in the area of restorative (rather than retributive) justice, with some additional addressing of distributive justice.

In Yoder's classic *Politics of Jesus*, he argues that Jesus' ethic is a relevant social strategy for contemporary Christians: believers should create distinct communities through which the gospel works to change other sociopolitical structures. Yoder argues that "the ministry and the claims of Jesus are best understood as presenting to hearers and readers not the avoidance of political options, but one particular social-political-ethical option" that "is of direct significance for social ethics" (Yoder 11). In that Yoderian model, which has been picked up by Methodist ethicist Stanley Hauerwas and "baptist" James William McClendon, the church is called first "to be the church, not to change the world." The belief is that by focusing on forming faithful communities of believers, Christians will be able to live authentically and thereby also have a secondary, collective influence on reforming society.

In this more engaged spirit, recent Anabaptists also have not been content only to maintain a negative attitude toward war. Especially in North America, many have felt a need to do some corresponding positive act through which they could assist their countries and the world. Mennonite historian James C. Juhnke has contended that in the United States, the Mennonite tragedy was not that they became Americans so slowly, but that "they so desperately wanted to be good American citizens and could not fulfill the requirements without violating their consciences or abandoning the tradition of their forebears" (Juhnke 156). Juhnke attributes to this tension "whatever was creative in the Mennonite experience"—relief programs, development of positive alternatives to military service, and scattered criticism of American nationalism from a pacifist perspective.

In the contemporary context, Anabaptist concerns about warfare and violence have stimulated extensive development of peace studies and conflict-transformation programs in Anabaptist-related colleges and universities and have birthed creative peacemaking efforts in Mennonite denominational and interdenominational agencies, such as the Mennonite Central Committee (MCC). An active peacemaking group, Christian Peacemaker Teams (CPT) emerged in the 1980s with the support of the three historic peace churches. In hot spots such as Haiti, Hebron, Afghanistan, and Iraq, CPT sends small teams of workers to stand between hostile groups, document and report atrocities and violations of human rights, and actively intervene in violent situations.

How these various efforts at active peacemaking and social and political engagement will reshape contemporary Anabaptist ethics remains to be seen. Some notion of church/world separation likely will be maintained as Anabaptists sort through a number of possible models for embodying the faithful, peaceful way of Christ in the twenty-first century. It is quite possible that as Anabaptist themes are embraced by broader Christian thinkers and communities such as Stanley Hauerwas, Sojourners, and the "emergent church" movement, these people, publications, and bodies of believers will carry forward important Anabaptist convictions as much as or more so than do many of the ethnic institutional Anabaptist churches.

See also Beatitudes; Government; Just-Peacemaking Theory; Pacifism; Peace; Sermon on the Mount; Truthfulness, Truth-Telling; Violence

Bibliography

Bender, H. "The Anabaptist Vision." *MQR* 18 (1944): 67–88; Burkholder, J. *The Problem of Social Responsibility from the Perspective of the Mennonite Church*. Institute of Mennonite Studies, 1989 [1958]; Burkholder, J., and C. Redekop, eds. *Kingdom, Cross, and Community: Essays on Mennonite Themes in Honor of Guy F. Hershberger*. Herald Press, 1976; Driedger, L., and D. Kraybill. *Mennonite Peacemaking: From Quietism to Activism*. Herald Press, 1994; Friesen, D. *Artists, Citizens, Philosophers: Seeking the Peace of the City; An Anabaptist Theology of Culture*. Herald Press, 2000; Graber Miller, K. *Wise as Serpents, Innocent as Doves: American Mennonites Engage Washington*. University of Tennessee Press, 1996; Grimsrud, T. *Embodying the Way of Jesus: Anabaptist Convictions for the Twenty-First Century*. Wipf & Stock, 2007; Hershberger, G. *War, Peace, and Nonresistance*. Herald Press, 1944; Huebner, H. *Echoes of the Word: Theological Ethics as Rhetorical Practice*. Pandora, 2005; Juhnke, J. *Vision, Doctrine, War: Mennonite Identity and Organization in America, 1890–1930*. Herald Press, 1989; Klaassen, W., ed. *Anabaptism in Outline: Selected Primary Sources*. Herald Press, 1981; Koontz, G., and E. Yoder, eds. *Peace Theology and Violence against Women*. Institute of Mennonite Studies, 1992; Van Braght, T. *The Bloody Theater or Martyrs Mirror of the Defenseless Christians*. Herald Press, 1950; Wenger, J., ed. *The Complete Writings of Menno Simons*. Mennonite Publishing House, 1956; Yoder, J. *The Politics of Jesus: Vicit Agnus Noster*. 2nd ed. Eerdmans, 1994.

Keith Graber Miller

Anger

Anger is a passionate response to real or perceived insult or injury, to oneself or another. Christianity has been decidedly ambivalent about anger. Since the time of Gregory the Great, anger has been enumerated among the seven capital vices (better known as the seven deadly sins); however, Thomas Aquinas, whose explication of the seven deadly sins is generally regarded as exhaustive, allows that although anger carries with it the potential to do mortal harm it is not always a sin, for anger is among the passions with which people are created, and hence is not fundamentally evil. Thus, Thomas allows for the possibility of a righteous anger, properly constrained by right reason, which he says is praiseworthy. On this point he goes so far as to quote Chrysostom's assertion that in certain circumstances the failure to become angry is a sin (*ST* II-I, qq. 46–48).

The Pentateuch frequently portrays God as "angry" toward particular persons or groups of people. When God's anger is directed toward Israel, it usually is on account of some form of idolatry. Perhaps the paradigmatic example of this is found in the story of the golden calf in Exod. 32, where Moses both intercedes for Israel, asking an angry God not to destroy them for their idolatry, and then serves as the agent and mediator of God's anger, leading a retributive slaughter against the worst of the idolaters. Even in the Pentateuch, however, God's anger usually is depicted as diminutive in comparison to God's mercy. More, God's anger and mercy often are juxtaposed in the writings of the prophets, who cite God's anger as the cause of the misfortunes of Israel and Judah but also offer assurances that God's anger is temporary and of little consequence in comparison to God's steadfast love, which, the prophets assure, will soon be manifest in the restoration of God's people.

The psalms display something of this tension with respect to God's anger. On the one hand, the psalmist frequently asks God to remember his covenant and withdraw his anger, either from the psalmist personally or from the people of Israel. These psalms often conclude with an expression of confidence that God, because of his mercy, will eventually restore them to their rightful place as the people of God. On the other hand, the psalms of imprecation frequently evoke God's anger toward the psalmist's enemies, advocating their destruction in sometimes shocking terms.

The NT authors take a more cautionary approach to the matter of anger. They speak of God's anger, but they do so sparingly in comparison to their OT counterparts. Jesus is portrayed as becoming angry, most often toward his opponents among the scribes and Pharisees and the temple elites in Jerusalem. When addressing anger in general terms, however, NT texts are decidedly more circumspect. Anger is potentially a deterrent to faithful Christian life; it is contrary to the virtue of love (1 Cor. 13:5), it subverts faithful discipleship (Eph. 4:25–26, 31–32; Col. 3:7–9; Jas. 1:19–21), and divides the community and renders ineffective its witness to the gospel (2 Cor. 12:19–21). In several places the NT (following the wisdom of the OT) admonishes Christians to be "slow to anger." Christians tempted to anger would do well to heed the advice of the author of Ephesians, who says, "Be angry but do not sin; do not let the sun go down on your anger, and do not make room for the devil" (Eph. 4:26).

See also Patience

Bibliography

Fairlie, H. *The Seven Deadly Sins Today*. University of Notre Dame Press, 1979; Gaylin, W. *The Rage Within: Anger in Modern Life*. Simon & Schuster, 1984; Thurman, R. *Anger: The Seven Deadly Sins*. Oxford University Press, 2005.

Joel James Shuman

Anglican Ethics and Moral Theology

The English Reformation formed Anglicanism as a distinct tradition. The English reformers in the sixteenth century—most notably, Thomas Cranmer, Nicholas Ridley, and Hugh Latimer, all of whom were martyred—sought a reformation along the lines of continental Protestant Reformers. Besides the destruction of altars and monastic communities and the rejection and separation from the Roman Catholic Church, they emphasized the primacy of Scripture, the reading of Scripture in the vernacular in public worship, and justification by faith.

However, by the seventeenth century, the Church of England under Queen Elizabeth (1533–1603) saw a church that was both Catholic and Reformed. This was in part because the church was constituted by the people of England as both Catholic and Reformed rather than the church constituting the people as either Catholic or Reformed. Believing that a nation cannot endure and prosper without a common, established religion, Anglicanism emphasized common worship, tolerance of differing opinions, and increasingly dispersed authority. Dispersed authority, along with the elimination of mandatory, private confession and priestly absolution, meant an emphasis on individual conscience.

There was, in turn, an emphasis on practical piety, on forming the self in Christian faith. The practices of Christian faith were understood as matters of religious duties toward God and moral duties toward the neighbor and toward the self. These were referred to as matters of religion, justice, and temperance, or as the petition in the general confession in the 1552 *Book of Common Prayer* says, "to live a godly, righteous, and sober life."

This emphasis on practical piety pervades Anglican thought. For example, Richard Hooker's apology for the Church of England begins with God's order in which we participate through Christ, stressing later the experience of grace in the sacrament of Holy Communion over particular beliefs about the nature of the sacrament (*Laws of Ecclesiastical Polity*, book V, 1597). Jeremy Taylor (*The Rule and Exercises of Holy Living*, 1650; *The Rule and Exercises of Holy Dying*, 1651) and William Law (*A Serious Call to a Devout and Holy Life*, 1728), both notable influences on John Wesley (1703–91), speak of Christian faith as a way of life. Joseph Butler focuses on virtue (*Fifteen Sermons Preached at Rolls Chapel*, 1726). Fredrick Denison Maurice turns to piety as the experience of reconciliation (*The Kingdom of Christ*, 1838/1842). In the twentieth century, William Temple details Christian faith as self-offering (*Christus Veritas*, 1924), and Kenneth Kirk offers an account of Christian faith as the practices that lead to and from the vision of God (*The Vision of God*, 1931).

For Anglicans, "Scripture contains all things necessary to salvation" (Thirty-Nine Articles of Religion, article 6). But, as claimed by Richard Hooker, Scripture does not interpret itself: one must be "persuaded by other means that Scriptures are the oracles of God" (*Laws of Ecclesiastical Polity*, book I.XIV.1). For those who are persuaded, Scripture reveals the truth and way of salvation that come by Jesus Christ, including those things, such as the Trinity, which are not brought to full light without the use of reason. This reflects the broad realist tradition of most of Anglicanism. "They err," Hooker says, "who think that of the will of God to do this or that there is no reason besides his will" (*Laws of Ecclesiastical Polity*, book I.II.5). Anglican ethics and moral theology, in turn, are generally eudemonistic. In perceiving what is true, we act so as to become what we are meant to be and thereby achieve fulfillment, beatitude.

These theological and philosophical convictions reflect what has come to be described as an incarnational and sacramental theology, drawing from the prologue of the Gospel of John: "In the beginning was the Word [*logos*, the order of things]. . . . And the Word became flesh and lived among us" (John 1:1, 14). Concern is given to establishing the order of things as made known and effected by Jesus Christ. As with Richard Hooker, emphasis is given to participation in the divine order; or, as the Orthodox say, emphasis is placed on *theosis*, Athanasius's claim that "God became human that humans might become God" (*Inc.* 54.3).

Anglican ethics and moral theology have developed primarily along two foci. First, grounded in appeals to nature and forms of natural law, ethics is concerned with the end of life and the right ordering of society as a whole. Such work is that of a moral theology or casuistry seeking to provide moral teaching and guidance. Second, ethics is concerned about sanctification and the development of a virtue ethic. Of particular interest has been understanding conscience and an ascetical theology concerned with moral formation and sanctification as tied to spiritual disciplines. Within the Anglican tradition moral theology and ascetical theology are integrally related.

Given the first focus on the end and ordering of life, Scripture has, in Anglican ethics, served as a revelation of our supernatural end and as a moral guide for our present life. A biblical story and a covenant theology are assumed from Genesis to Revelation. Moral commands, most notably the Ten Commandments, reinforced the moral law as given in nature. So the Ten Commandments have been at the heart of the *Catechism of 1549* and the *Book of Common Prayer* (in all its editions). In terms of practical moral reasoning, Anglicans of the seventeenth century—the Caroline divines such as William Perkins, William Ames, Robert Sanderson, Joseph Hall, Jeremy Taylor, and Richard Baxter—developed a practical moral theology that combined the ascetical emphasis on sanctification and virtue with the examination of cases. Again, moral law was grounded in nature as well as given in divine commands found in Scripture. As casuists, these thinkers understood the need for adjudicating such commands or rules given the particular circumstances of cases. In fact, natural law assumptions of the day reflecting establishment views were taken for granted.

Given the second focus on sanctification and virtue ethics, Jesus Christ is the great exemplar, the prototype for what it means to be human. For example, Jeremy Taylor's most influential book in his own time was titled *The Great Exemplar* (1649). Drawing from the four Gospels, Taylor offers a spiritual reading of Scripture combining narrative, meditation, and prayer in order to focus the reader on the gracious work of God and on holy life as a life given in relationship to God. New Testament figures are icons that illumine the Christian life. From the faith of Mary to the wickedness of Herod, the character of this life is told in terms of Jesus' life and teachings.

Since F. D. Maurice and the rise of historical consciousness—from Charles Gore to archbishops William Temple and Michael Ramsey and the present archbishop of Canterbury, Rowan Williams—Christ has more frequently been understood as revealing the end of life as communion with God and the shape of such a life as self-offering to God and neighbor (Ramsey, *An Era in Anglican Theology: From Gore to Temple*, 1960). Such an understanding was also the theological ground for Anglican social thought with its critique of laissez-faire capitalism, fascism, and nationalism and its proposals for a Christian society (M. B. Reckitt, *Maurice to Temple*, 1947). As a theology of the cross, the canon of Scripture that interprets the rest of Scripture has at its center the Gospels, especially the Gospel of John, followed by Philippians and its kenotic understanding of Christ (Phil. 2:6–8). Scripture as read and understood in light of worship—given lectionary readings that are thematically tied to the liturgical year—offers the shape of the Christian life. As Anglican Dom Gregory Dix says, the shape of eucharistic worship is, like that of Christ, kenotic (*The Shape of the Liturgy*, 1948).

In the twentieth century, Kenneth Kirk draws together moral theology and ascetical theology. Begun in his book *Some Principles of Moral Theology and Their Application* (1920), Kirk's work concludes with the publication of his Bampton Lectures in 1931 as *The Vision of God*. Contextualizing moral commands in Scripture, Kirk grounds the moral life in the experience of its end in the vision of God as revealed in Jesus. Again, with Philippians and the Gospel of John as the primary sources, Jesus is the great exemplar, the prototype of what it means to be human.

The description of virtue and what is distinctive about Christian virtue grounded in the love of God could and did become removed from explicit reference to Scripture, as was the case with Butler's *Fifteen Sermons* and the English moral philosophy tradition represented by John Locke and David Hume. But as evident in Butler's more philosophical account of virtue and its grounding in the love of God (sermons 13 and 14), Scripture reveals the end of life and in Christ the character of such a life.

Parallel and in contrast to such development was an evangelical theology and ethic, beginning with John Wesley. While sharing common features with the broader Anglican tradition—for example, the place of piety and worship and the social character and obligations of Christian faith—the scriptural Christianity of evangelical Anglicans differed in taking a more positivist reading of Scripture as the revelation of the divine will. Emphasizing justification by faith and conversion, in terms of ethics the evangelical tradition read Scripture as a set of divine commands. In personal matters they were quite conservative; in social matters they were more radical reformers. For example, they assumed understandings of marriage and the prohibition against divorce, but condemned the slave trade and worked for specific reforms to address the conditions of the working poor. Most notable among these thinkers was William Wilberforce, whose thought is expressed in his 1797 publication of *A Practical View of the Prevailing Religious System of Professed Christians in the Higher and Middle Classes of This Country Contrasted with Real Christianity*.

Anglicanism remains a diverse tradition. This includes those dissenting from Anglican catholicity or comprehensiveness. Some evangelicals, for example, seek to complete the English Reformation along the lines of the continental Reformation. Some Anglo-Catholics, who seek a unity of faith and witness, share a common desire to establish more centralized authority. Each defines the breadth of Anglicanism as heterodox, in which truth is sacrificed to tolerance (which is then called comprehensiveness). In either case, there is fundamental disagreement about the truth of Scripture.

In terms of Christian ethics and moral theology, the divide between "conservatives" and "liberals" within Anglicanism may be understood as grounded in the difference between a voluntarist view of Scripture as the revelation of the divine will and ethics as a matter of divine command and a view of Scripture as historically and culturally shaped yet revealing a divine purpose and in Christ the character or virtues necessary for participation in the divine life. This is especially true in the highly contested area of human sexual ethics. On the one hand, Anglicans continue to deploy biblical critical studies to contextualize moral judgments and to understand them in light of broader ends. On the other hand, other Anglicans identify the authority of Scripture with specific moral commands.

The diversity of contemporary Anglican moral theology also includes reflection on Christian ethics in a postestablishment or postcolonial context. These include prophetic and countercultural accounts of Christian faith in relationship to culture and society. Still, predominantly—as with the nonviolent American theologian William Stringfellow and the nonviolent liberation theology of South African Desmond Tutu—Scripture offers a revelation of the end of human life while Christ is the exemplar or prototype of participation in that life—hence a continued focus on sanctification and a virtue ethic.

See also Casuistry; Divine Command Theories of Ethics; John; Natural Law; Philippians; Sanctification; Ten Commandments; Virtue Ethics

Timothy F. Sedgwick

Animals

Western European Enlightenment rationality of the seventeenth and eighteenth centuries made a fundamental distinction between the mental and the physical. This distinction categorically distinguished humans, the only physical beings with mind/spirit, from animals and the rest of brute nature. Notably, this distinction was also used to deny full personhood to women and to some peoples who purportedly lacked full possession of the reasoning capacities that signaled possession of mind. In terms of ethical consideration, then, mainstream Enlightenment rationality was decidedly androcentric, Eurocentric, and anthropocentric.

During the nineteenth and twentieth centuries, Western rationality's racism and sexism was largely recognized, and ongoing critique was initiated. But predominant Western rationality into the twenty-first century remains unwittingly anthropocentric. Consider, for instance, the category "animals." While in biology class humans are commonly categorized as animals, in common ethical, religious, and popular discourse "animals" is not understood to include humans. In accord with this predominant expectation, for instance, one would not expect to encounter theological anthropology under this entry for "animals." Indeed, in popular speech "animal" remains a term of derision when applied to a person. Or consider how ordinarily talk about animal experimentation would not be expected to include discussion of experimentation on humans.

Significantly, anthropocentrism even permeates modern Western environmentalism. The environment in question is typically the *human* environment. Animals are part of the environment and sometimes are even grouped with minerals, soil, and crops as resources to be preserved, managed, and sustainably harvested. Humans are not part of the environment. In accord with modern anthropocentric rationality, humans alone are thought to be above brute nature.

In place of the classic scriptural nexus "Creator/creatures/creation," then, modern Western Christians think in terms of the categorically different nexus of "God/humans/animals/nature." This fundamental shift in understanding decisively determines the very vocabularies and concepts out of which modern Westerners think. As a result, for instance, in the Adam and Eve creation narrative translators naturally translate a Hebrew word (*nepeš*) as "living being" when they apply it to humans and translate the same Hebrew as "living creature" when they apply it to the birds and beasts (Gen. 2:7, 19).

Within the parameters of this predominant modern Western conceptual framework, "things" such as animals disappear as subjects of direct divine and moral concern. Humans, as a categorically unique kind of being, are understood to be the sole proper subjects of direct divine and moral concern. "Nature," a category that includes everything that is not human, has only indirect or instrumental value. That is, natural objects, including animals, are considered valuable only insofar as they are valuable for humans.

In this fashion, anthropocentrism, not as a considered conclusion but as an unquestioned presumption, pervades mainstream modern rationality. To be sure, the way anthropomorphism plays to human pride and self-interest means that it has always influenced human reflection. In the wake of Enlightenment rationality, however, anthropocentrism gained unprecedented philosophical justification and began to exert unprecedented influence. Animals were simply rendered invisible as subjects of direct divine and moral concern as anthropocentrism was inscribed into modern Western rationality at a primordial level.

Not surprisingly, modern ethical and biblical reflection—and this obtains across the theological spectrum—has been decisively shaped by modernity's anthropocentrism. Consider, for instance, the account of Noah and the flood. In a recent work focused on biblical creation theology, one author, explaining the thematic significance of the actual shape of Hebrew narratives, points out that the central verses in Hebrew narratives are also often the thematic key to the story. Accordingly, Gen. 8:1, "God remembered Noah," would be the pivot-point for the story of Noah. However, Gen. 8:1 actually says, "God remembered Noah and all the wild animals and the domestic animals."

In the same way, it has long been standard to refer to "God's covenant with Noah" or the "Noahic covenant." Until recently, it was not thought significant or even noticed that the text repeatedly (six times in nine verses) specifies that God's covenant is not only with Noah but also "with every living creature that is with you, the birds, the domestic animals, and every animal of the earth with you, as many as came out of the ark" (Gen. 9:10).

Similarly, even as twentieth-century students of the OT were taught to attend to the significance of blessings, the blessing of the fishes and the birds in Gen. 1:22 and the call for land creatures to be fruitful and multiply in Gen. 8:17 typically were not really noticed. In the same vein, while the creation of humans in the image of God and the blessing of humans and the call for them to have dominion over the earth in Gen. 1:28 is surely one of the most famous passages of Scripture, the explicitly vegan giving of seeds and fruits exclusively for food to every creature with the "breath of life" in the very next verses (Gen. 1:29–30) receives scant notice.

As Western Christians have begun to become conscious of modernity's anthropocentrism, however, they have begun to notice God's delight in and blessing of nonhuman creatures in the seven days of creation narrative. They have begun to notice that the creation that God declares "very good" is expressly vegan. They have begun to notice that God covenants with all creatures and even the earth in what many now call the "rainbow" or "earth" covenant. Christians are attending anew to texts such as Ps. 148, where all creatures, from sun to birds to young men, are called on to praise God. They are noticing the wholly peaceable character of famous eschatological passages such as Isa. 11:1–10, the so-called Peaceable Kingdom passage, where "the lion shall eat straw like the ox," and no creature anywhere, whether human, domestic, or wild, will "hurt or destroy" on all God's holy mountain.

Conscious of modernity's anthropocentrism, Christians are noticing Jesus' background assertion that God attends to the death of each sparrow (Matt. 10:29). And they are noticing that Jesus rightly presumes that not even his theological opponents will dare to deny that it is good to break the Sabbath in order to rescue a sheep or an ox from a pit (Matt. 12:11; Luke 14:5). They are noticing that the "fire" of 2 Pet. 3:11–13 does not destroy the physical universe, loosing souls to be with God in some unearthly reality, but rather burns away all unrighteousness as it refines a "new heaven [i.e., a new sky] and a new earth, where righteousness is at home."

Examples revealing anthropocentric distortion of Scripture could easily be multiplied. But the clear effect of anthropocentrism vis-à-vis all these familiar texts is sufficient to make the problem evident. For as is now clear, modern Western philosophical, scientific, theological, ethical, and biblical understanding has been pervaded by an anthropocentrism that is alien to the Christian Scriptures. We must reevaluate not only Scripture and ethics but also theology, history, and worship in light of our newly found awareness that nonhuman creatures together with human creatures constitute a community of subjects of direct divine and moral concern.

Insofar as all the theological disciplines have developed decisively in the modern West, rigorous reorientation in the wake of our recent and ongoing awakening to anthropocentrism is vital. The issues raised are diverse and complex. Clearly, the Christian Scriptures differentiate between humans and other creatures. But what exactly are the differences? And what are their ethical implications? How do our major translations and mainstream interpretations of Scripture need to change in order to correct for modern anthropocentrism? And what are the theological and ethical consequences of making such a correction? What in the patristic writings and those of the Reformers have we failed to notice or misinterpreted because we have been looking unawares through anthropocentric spectacles? How are we to consider the place and capacities of nonhuman creatures in relation to worship, salvation, or heaven? When, if ever, is it permissible to kill, eat, wear, or experiment on nonhuman creatures? Are there ethically significant distinctions to be drawn among nonhuman creatures? If so, what are the criteria? What are Christians to think ethically and spiritually about pets, zoos, wilderness areas, pesticides, transgenic organisms, the "creation" and patenting of life, extermination of invasive species, human-caused extinction events, and varieties of hunting?

Anthropocentrism still reigns in early twenty-first-century scriptural interpretation, theology, and ethics. Nonanthropocentric focus on nonhuman creatures remains the purview of a small if fast-growing collection of scholars and advocates on the margins of mainstream theological discussion. But with ever-widening consciousness of the distorting influence of modern anthropocentrism, one can anticipate that the next few decades will see the emergence of significant areas of interpretive and ethical consensus about nonhuman creatures, as well as identification of edges of debate requiring ongoing research.

Although nonanthropocentric interpretation of Scripture and ethics remains in its infancy, one can identify three broad currents of thought: (1) the "land ethic" or "deep ecology," (2) "animal rights," and (3) "animal theology." The land ethic (c. 1948, Aldo Leopold) and deep ecology (c. 1972, Arne Naess) are biocentric and holistic. For Leopold, "a thing is right when it tends to preserve the integrity, stability, and beauty of the biotic community. It is wrong when it tends otherwise" (Leopold 224–25). This move beyond anthropocentrism, which becomes self-conscious in deep ecology, de-emphasizes individual animals, human or otherwise, and focuses instead on the health of biosystems.

Notably, this perspective may be reflected in Ps. 104. Nonetheless, it stands in tension with the vast majority of Scripture, which is overwhelmingly concerned with individual creatures. Christians will reject the position of a small minority of deep ecologists who refuse to distinguish ethically between amoebas and humans. Also, the land ethic and deep ecology should be distinguished from a metaphysical Darwinism (in contrast to a scientific Darwinism) that rejects moral ideals not consistent with biological realities, and that tends to invoke biological distinctions (e.g., capacity to reason, capacity for language) in the course of retaining modernity's categorical anthropocentrism.

Highly marginal nineteenth- and twentieth-century movements on behalf of animals rose to mainstream notice when Peter Singer's *Animal Liberation* (1975) captured the public imagination and stimulated the late twentieth-century "animal rights" movement. Singer's utilitarian argument turned upon the moral significance of animals' capacity to suffer. His frank description of the suffering of animals at human hands stirred widespread indignation and spurred overt resistance to anthropocentric disregard for the well-being of nonhuman animals. Appropriating the most powerful moral and international legal vocabulary available, the movement established itself around an appeal to animal "rights."

A Christian version of animal rights quickly materialized with Andrew Linzey's *Animal Rights: A Christian Assessment* (1976). The modern legal concept of "rights" is alien to Scripture, but globally it is a central ethical and legal category. Just as many Christians adopted the "rights" category on behalf of Christian ideals vis-à-vis humans, Linzey adopted the "rights" category vis-à-vis animals. By the 1990s, Linzey and other Christians had developed arguments using specifically scriptural and theological concepts, and as a result a variety of ethical positions predicated on "reverence for life," "creature care," and "love for all creatures" began to undergird Christian advocacy for "animal theology."

In contrast to biocentric perspectives, animal theology remains focused on individuals. In contrast to animal rights, animal theology is predicated on a nonanthropomorphic reading of Scripture and the Christian tradition. As illustrated above, the focus upon individual creatures and the inclusion of all creatures among a community of subjects who are loved by and worship God, and thus who are all subjects of direct divine and moral concern, is consistent with the mainstream of Scripture. However, scriptural, theological, and ethical debates over the precise contours of right regard for nonhuman creatures remain in their infancy. There is general agreement that anthropocentrism has distorted biblical interpretation, theology, and ethics, and that blatant mistreatment of nonhuman creatures is beyond the pale. But a mature, nonanthropocentric reading of Scripture and general consensus over right Christian response to a host of theological and ethical questions regarding nonhuman creatures are as yet the vital and still-to-be-realized product of this emerging sphere of scriptural, theological, and ethical reflection.

See also Bioethics; Creation, Biblical Accounts of; Creation Ethics; Ecological Ethics; Humanity; Vegetarianism

Bibliography

Leopold, A. *A Sand County Almanac*. Oxford University Press, 1987; Linzey, A. *Animal Gospel*. Westminster John Knox, 2004; Linzey, A., and D. Yamamoto, eds. *Animals on the Agenda: Questions about Animals for Theology and Ethics*. University of Illinois Press, 1998; Pinches, C., and J. McDaniel, eds. *Good News for Animals? Christian Approaches to Animal Well-Being*. Wipf & Stock, 2008; Waldau, P., and K. Patton, eds. *A Communion of Subjects: Animals in Religion, Science, and Ethics*. Columbia University Press, 2006.

William Greenway

Annulment *See* Marriage and Divorce

Antichrist

The term *antichrist* (Gk. *antichristos*) refers to the adversary of God and God's aims who is expected to appear in the end times. The term derives from the combination of the noun *Christos*, which means "anointed one" or "messiah," with the prefix *anti*, which means either "against" or "instead of." In this case, both senses of the prefix are important because almost all the relevant literature portrays the antichrist as one who is "against Christ," and some picture him also as a substitute for Christ. In the NT, the term appears only in 1–2 John (1 John 2:18 [2x], 22; 4:3; 2 John 7), but analogous figures appear in Rev. 13 (the beast from the sea), apocalyptic discourses in the Synoptic Gospels (e.g., false christs and false prophets in Mark 13:21–22), and 2 Thess. 2:1–3 ("the lawless one . . . destined for destruction").

The significance of the antichrist is tied to two traditions in Jewish and Christian thought: (1) the challenge of recognizing genuine agents from God, and (2) the crescendo of wickedness anticipated before God puts down the power of evil and actualizes his righteous aims in his kingdom.

First, distinguishing between true and false prophecy has long been controversial. For example, in Deut. 18:21 this question is raised: "How can we tell that a message is not from the LORD?" (NET). According to Deuteronomy, the truth of a prophetic word depends on whether it happens. Passages in the NT likewise emphasize the need to distinguish God's message from its counterfeits. In 1 John 4:1–3 the author warns that false prophets have gone out into the world. These people are false teachers who deny the Father and the Son (1 John 2:22) and refuse to accept that Jesus really came to earth as a human (1 John 4:2; cf. 2 John 7). Such people speak by "the spirit of the antichrist" (1 John 4:3) (see also Jer. 28:9; Mark 13:22; 1 Cor. 12:1–3). The issue persists in the early church, with the result that the *Didache* distinguishes between true and false prophets and apostles in terms of the doctrine they teach and the behaviors they practice, especially with regard to potential abuses of hospitality and money (*Did.* 11).

Second, ancient Jewish writings anticipate increased wickedness on the earth, sometimes together with the rise of an evil tyrant in opposition to God, in preparation for the end. For example, the book of Daniel describes a mighty ruler who wages war against God's holy ones (7:18–27), a king who will grow strong in power, cause fearful destruction, and destroy the powerful and the people of the holy ones (8:24). God must act against this ruler in order to break the power of evil and to establish his everlasting kingdom (7:27; 8:25). Similarly, in Mark's account of Jesus' warning about the end times, Jesus adds to his references to wars and earthquakes the coming of false prophets and false messiahs who will attempt to deceive the faithful through showy miracles and pronouncements. The most picturesque is Revelation's description of the beast from the sea, presented as the antithesis of Christ, with his counterfeit crowns (13:1; cf. 19:12), blasphemous names (13:1; cf. 19:11, 13, 16), power and authority (which the beast receives from Satan [13:2], but Jesus has from God [12:5, 10]), and a mortal wound that has been healed (13:3; cf. 1:18; 5:6). Clearly, the beast from the sea is Satan's agent of war against God's people (see 12:17–13:18) and as such is presented as the negative image of Christ.

Speculation about the antichrist continued in the early church. For example, in the *Epistle of Barnabas*, the beast of the fourth kingdom (Dan. 7:7–8) is the contemporary Roman Empire, identified with the increase in wickedness accompanying the last days (*Barn.* 4.1–5). *Didache* 16 anticipates the rise of false prophets together with a deceiver who will claim to be God's Son. In agreement with 1–2 John, Polycarp wrote that the antichrist is the spirit of false teaching (Pol. *Phil.* 7). Both in the NT, then, and in the early church it was possible to speak of the antichrist (or antichrists, in the case of 1 John 2:18) in the present tense while at the same time holding to the belief that the end time would see the emergence of the antichrist in his fullness.

See also Eschatology and Ethics; Revelation, Book of

Bibliography

Lietaert Peerbolte, L. *The Antecedents of Antichrist: A Traditio-Historical Study of the Earliest Christian Views on Eschatological Opponents*. SJSJ 49. Brill, 1996; McGinn, B. *Antichrist: Two Thousand Years of the Human Fascination with Evil*. HarperSanFrancisco, 1994.

Joel B. Green

Antinomianism

Antinomianism is an approach to Christian ethics that rejects behavioral standards of any sort as instances of a fixed and inflexible legalism. Antinomian practice maintains that Christians live without reference to norms as recipients of the free grace of God.

One can find teaching against antinomianism in the OT (e.g., Isa. 5:7, 13, 24–25; Hos. 4:6; 8:12; Mal. 2:7–8), and it is possible that the Epistle of Jude counters an early Christian antinomianism that is a distortion of Paul's understanding of freedom and grace (see vv. 4, 8, 16, 23). More discussion about antinomianism is focused on Matthew's approach to the law. Although some have speculated that Matthew's polemics are directed against antinomians as well as rabbis, others are more skeptical and see in Matthew a new and demanding form of religious practice. Jesus' teaching in the Sermon on the Mount does not replace the law, but rather fills out its intention (e.g., Matt. 5:27–32).

Paul's approach to these issues is the focus of contemporary debate between two broad lines of interpretation. Traditional interpretation holds that Paul's teaching is explicitly antinomian by opposing Spirit, gospel, and grace on the one hand, and law on the other. In this view, Paul attacks the law as the foundation of an unattainable system of works focused on self-achievement. Gaining in acceptance, however, is the idea that the traditional approach involves a mischaracterization of Judaism. Thus, a second group of interpreters maintains that grace was as central to the Judaism of Paul's day as it was in Paul's thought, and that both Judaism and Paul affirm that God's people will be judged according to their deeds (e.g., Rom. 2:6–16; 1 Cor. 3:12–15; 11:27–34; 2 Cor. 5:9–10; Gal. 6:7). This view sees Paul's opposition to the law as grounded not in human inability to obey God's commands (cf. Phil. 3:6), but rather in his conviction that works of Torah no longer mediate the grace of God to a single ethnic group (Rom. 3:28–30).

Today, the Christian's relationship to the law is a matter of continuing concern. The church continues to struggle to balance law and grace in the life of the community while acknowledging the essential nature of the law and the OT for moral reflection in the NT. Whether citing or alluding to the law in ethical instruction (Matt. 5:17; Luke 4:3–12), describing believers as "fulfilling" the law by walking by the Spirit (Rom. 8:4), or urging believers to comport themselves with the "law of liberty" (Jas. 1:25), the NT rejects the idea that the faithful are free to ignore divine standards of behavior in the law.

See also Law and Gospel; Legalism; Libertinism

Bibliography

Bassler, J. "Grace: Probing the Limits." *Int* 57 (2003): 24–33; Charry, E. "The Grace of God and the Law of Christ." *Int* 57 (2003): 34–44; Holloway, Z. "A Conceptual Foundation for Using the Mosaic Law in Christian Ethics—Part 2." *Chm* 120 (2006): 213–30; Loubser, G. "Paul's Ethic of Freedom: No Flash in the Galatians Pan." *Neot* 39 (2005): 313–37; Rowston, D. "The Most Neglected Book in the New Testament." *NTS* 21 (1975): 554–63; Westerholm, S. "Letter and Spirit: The Foundation of Pauline Ethics." *NTS* 30 (1984): 229–48; Yeago, D. "Gnosticism, Antinomianism, and Reformation Theology." *ProEccl* 2 (1993): 37–49.

Love L. Sechrest

Anti-Semitism

Anti-Semitism is hostility and/or prejudice against Jews and Judaism. Christian anti-Semitism, the specific topic of this entry, refers to the prejudice long held by Christians against Jews. The basis for this prejudice often is grounded in the NT, but a closer look at the Scriptures demonstrates the complexity of this issue both in antiquity and throughout history. Although the term itself implies discrimination against all Semites (Arabs and other Semitic-language-speaking peoples), it has been used exclusively in reference to Jews and Judaism.

Confusion of Terms

Although the term *anti-Semitism* would logically be a referent to hostility against any group of Semites, it is often and irregularly interchanged with the term *anti-Judaism*. The terms *anti-Jewish* and *anti-Semitic* are commonly used, though not uniformly. One common distinction associates "anti-Jewish" with the issue of Jews as a religious group and "anti-Semitic" with the issue of Jews as an ethnic group; however, inconsistent usage of this distinction has led to what Flannery calls "a semantical confusion that has often rendered rational discourse on the subject well nigh impossible" (Flannery 5). In the present article, the term *anti-Semitism* applies to all forms of anti-Judaism, but with the understanding that the term itself is more appropriately used only after its creation in the nineteenth century and only in reference to Jews and Judaism.

Anti-Semitism and the New Testament

One cannot read the NT without noting passages containing invective against the Jews and Judaism. The polemic ranges from subtle insult to stinging attack. Note, for example, Matt. 5:20: "Unless your righteousness exceeds that of the scribes and Pharisees, you will never enter the kingdom of heaven" (cf. Matt. 23:34–36; 27:25); John 8:42–44: "Jesus said to them [the Jews], 'If God were your Father, you would love me, for I came from God and now I am here. I did not come on my own, but he sent me. Why do you not understand what I say? It is because you cannot accept my word. You are from your Father the devil, and you choose to do your father's desires. He was a murderer from the beginning, and does not stand in the truth, because there is no truth in him"; Acts 7:51–53: "You stiff-necked people, uncircumcised in heart and ears, you are forever opposing the Holy Spirit, just as your ancestors used to do. Which of the prophets did your ancestors not persecute? They killed those who foretold the coming of the Righteous One, and now you have become his betrayers and murderers. You are the ones that received the law as ordained by angels and yet you have not kept it" (see also, e.g., Rom. 10:4; 1 Thess. 2:14–16).

Although these passages certainly demonstrate a clear hostility between early Jewish Christians and non-Christian Jews, it often is difficult to determine the degree to which such polemical language reflects an intramural or an extramural fight. It has become increasingly clear that early non-Christian Jews and Jewish Christians were engaged in disputes over what it meant to carry on the covenant traditions of the Jewish people. These quarrels are best viewed as being between rival siblings, each striving to define itself in a post-70 CE, post–Second Temple era, in which the only Jewish survivors are Pharisaic Jews (the precursors of rabbinic Judaism) and messianic Jews (the precursors of Christianity). So, if these and other similar NT passages do indeed reflect the kind of "in-house" conflict within first-century Judaism, why do they continue to be so problematic?

The problem, simply stated, is that these texts have been anachronistically applied to Jews and Judaism throughout two thousand years of history. Although the first-century controversy between messianic and nonmessianic Jews may have been a Jewish in-house dispute, for centuries the passages have engendered Christian "anti-Jewish" or "anti-Semitic" attitudes and actions and have been called forth as a defense or justification for atrocities of all kinds against the Jewish people and Judaism. What began as an internal conflict became the seedbed for Christian "anti-Semitism" throughout the history of Christianity. From the damning preaching of Melito of Sardis in the second century and John Chrysostom's "Eight Homilies against the Jews" in the fourth century, to the equally vicious condemnation by Martin Luther ("The Jews and Their Lies") in the sixteenth century, to the unspeakable horrors of the Nazi regime, NT passages (such as those listed above) have fueled the fires of prejudice and outrage against the Jews for putting Jesus to death (hence deicide) and for rejecting Jesus as the Messiah (damnable disbelief from the perspective of many Christians). In turn, Christianity has been accused of being anti-Semitic in origin. Indeed, Rosemary Radford Ruether has called anti-Judaism the "left hand of Christology." (For a concise review of the history of Christian anti-Semitism, see Saperstein.)

An Ongoing Dilemma

Recognition of the potential for harm inherent in these biblical passages has prompted biblical scholars to approach these texts in a variety of ways. Whereas pre–World War II biblical interpretation often promoted the idea of Christian supersessionism (Christianity as the replacement and completion of Judaism), the post-Holocaust context had to come to grips with the way such texts had been used to foment Christian hatred and persecution of Jews, culminating in the complicity of so-called Christian peoples in the horrors of the Shoah (the Holocaust).

Since the 1960s, however, various positive steps have been taken to address Christian anti-Semitism. In 1965 the Vatican II Council issued the historic document *Nostra aetate* ("In Our Time"), presenting important changes in the church's official teaching on Jews and Judaism. Jews were no longer to be viewed as "Christ-killers," and the Jewish religion was to be revered as an ongoing and living tradition. This was followed in 1974 by "Guidelines for Implementing *Nostra Aetate*," in 1985 by "Correct Ways to Present Jews and Judaism in Preaching and Catechism," and in 1998 by "We Remember the Shoah." These moves by the Roman Catholic Church included Pope John Paul II's historic visit to the Jewish synagogue in Rome (1986), where he referred to the Jewish people as "our elder brethren." The World Council of Churches has also made efforts to address the problem of Christian anti-Semitism. This is apparent in its 1967 publication "The Church and the Jewish People" as well as its 1982 "Ecumenical Considerations on Jewish-Christian Dialogue." The past thirty years have seen a number of statements from within Protestant Christianity as well. The United Methodist Church, Episcopal Church, Presbyterian Church USA, Evangelical Lutheran Church in America, American Lutheran Church, and United Church of Christ have issued statements regarding the inappropriateness of using the polemical passages of the NT as justification for hostility against Jews and Judaism as well as calling into question the practice of Christian proselytizing of Jews.

Although progress has been made in our reinterpretation of these texts, much work remains. In the world of the church, these texts too often continue to be ignored, thoughtlessly used, or explained away. Many Christians still consider Judaism to be incomplete and Christianity to be its fulfillment; too many Christians continue to stereotype Jews and Judaism as "Other," an inferior "Other." Clearly, these are unpleasant texts, but history has shown that we cannot afford to ignore them or dismiss them. In our increasingly pluralistic world, it is imperative that we wrestle not only with these "anti-Jewish" passages in the Christian canon but also with how they have been interpreted and misused. Only then can we begin to overcome a history of abuse. Contextual understandings of the NT writings within the formative period of early Jewish Christianity are imperative for all interpretations that seek to read these texts with responsibility and integrity.

See also Religious Toleration; Supersessionism

Bibliography

Boys, M. *Seeing Judaism Anew: Christianity's Sacred Obligation*. Rowman & Littlefield, 2005; Flannery, E. *The Anguish of the Jews: Twenty-Three Centuries of Antisemitism*. Paulist Press, 1985; Fredriksen, P., and A. Reinhartz. *Jesus, Judaism, and Christian Anti-Judaism: Reading the New Testament after the Holocaust*. Westminster John Knox, 2002; Ruether, R. *Faith and Fratricide: The Theological Roots of Anti-Semitism*. Seabury, 1974; Saperstein, M. *Moments of Crisis in Jewish-Christian Relations*. SCM, 1989; Siker, J. *Disinheriting the Jews: Abraham in Early Christian Controversy*. Westminster John Knox, 1991.

Judy Yates Siker

Anxiety

The term *anxiety* can mean several things. It is an emotion closely related to fear, worry, and dread; a basic human physiological response characterized by increased autonomic system activity to situations that combine danger and uncertainty, or an existential condition that shapes basic human interactions with the world and God. Though interrelated, each use of the term is freighted with distinct connotations for Scripture and ethics.

Anxiety as emotion is closely related to fear, but whereas fear is an emotional response to an identifiable danger, anxiety is a response to an unidentified threat or anticipated danger. Most expressions of this emotion (e.g., separation anxiety) are understandable responses to stressful situations and are likely to be evolutionary adaptations that, though uncomfortable, help those feeling the emotion to focus on the situation at hand, asking questions about both the situation and one's ability to successfully cope with it. Some expressions of the emotion, however (e.g., performance anxiety), can be disabling. More than any other person, Sigmund Freud brought anxiety to the fore; his understanding of its relation to the unconscious continues to impact contemporary understandings of the emotion. A universal emotion, anxiety nevertheless exhibits cultural variations: in a highly formal society, anxieties about breaking etiquette may be pronounced, while in a highly conformist society, it may be anxieties about being different.

The Scriptures usually encourage those feeling anxiety not to worry (explicitly in Matt. 6:25–34; Phil. 4:6; implicitly in Prov. 12:25), suggesting in these instances that anxiety is a manifestation of the human failure to trust in divine providence. There is, though, countertestimony to such encouragement in Scripture that recognizes either the mysteriousness of God's governance (as in Job) or the importance of learning to fear God rather than feel anxiety (e.g., Ps. 2:11). Although Christian ethicists have talked about the valued role of the emotions, including anxiety and fear, in ordering a moral life since antiquity, the attention to emotion in moral reasoning receded after the Enlightenment and has only just come back into focus as the result of work by various feminists, classicists, neurobiologists, and others. One exception to this is the use of the "anxious bench" in American evangelicalism since the early nineteenth century—a place where those considering becoming Christian sat so that others could pray for them to reorder their lives. One contemporary concern of social ethicists is that Christians challenge the social structures that promote undue anxiety.

Anxiety as a physiological response is closely connected to anxiety as an emotion but tends to be more positive about the possibilities for anxiety to stimulate moral action. According to behaviorists such as O. Hobart Mowrer, anxiety prepares us to deal with traumatic events before they occur. Since anxiety produces discomfort, we develop learned behaviors that help us either avoid or mitigate the impact of such events. Those behaviors may be premoral, but attention to this system provides insights into the early processes of moral development, as when children avoid dangerous or immoral behavior out of anxiety about possible consequences. Although anxiety as a physiological response helps order conventional moral life, Christians recognize that often they are called into anxiety-provoking situations—for example, practicing nonviolence at the risk of bodily suffering, reaching out to strangers or enemies at the risk of rejection, and generally refusing to live a life marked by the avoidance of suffering.

Anxiety as an existential condition has had the clearest and most dramatic impact in Christian ethics, due largely to the influence of Søren Kierkegaard, Reinhold Niebuhr, and Paul Tillich on twentieth-century Christian ethics. Kierkegaard not only foreshadowed the philosophical tradition of existentialism (as developed by Heidegger, Camus, Sartre, and others), which emphasizes angst in ethics, but also gave Niebuhr and Tillich a language for considering the complexities of the human condition. According to Niebuhr, the human ability to transcend the self gives an awareness of our own mortality; the tension between self-transcendence and finitude creates anxiety that should lead to creativity and trust but inevitably leads to sin. Tillich emphasized anxiety as an ontological (versus psychological) condition, the proper response to which is the courage to be. One of the seminal challenges to their approach, though, is to ask whether a Christian theological anthropology should be constructed around anxiety or gratitude.

See also Emotion; Freedom; Moral Development

Bibliography

Freud, S. *The Problem of Anxiety*. Psychoanalytic Quarterly Press, 1963; Hiltner, S., and K. Menninger, eds. *Constructive Aspects of Anxiety*. Abingdon, 1963; Kierkegaard, S. *The Concept of Dread*. Princeton University Press, 1968; Niebuhr, R. *Human Nature*. Vol. 1 of *The Nature and Destiny of Man*. Westminster John Knox, 1996; Tillich, P. *Reason and Revelation; Being and God*. Vol. 1 of *Systematic Theology*. University of Chicago Press, 1973.

Mark Douglas

Apartheid

Today most people believe that apartheid—the idea of separate development of people in their racial groups—was a terrible doctrine, evil, oppressive, and certainly unchristian. However, hard though it may be for those outside South Africa to understand, apartheid was a scriptural doctrine taught by the Dutch Reformed Church and backed by its excellent faculties of biblical studies in major universities. The biblical basis for apartheid was set out in the report *Human Relations and the South African Scene in the Light of Scripture* (1976). This is a challenge to those involved in biblical ethics, since both those who argued for apartheid and those in the liberation struggle used similar methods of exegesis to justify their opposing positions. This can be demonstrated by a brief consideration of the four main subgenres of ethical material in the Bible.

First, in terms of rules, the report interpreted God's command to "be fruitful and multiply" (Gen. 1:28) to include the separate diversity of peoples, as confirmed in Deut. 32:8–9 and Acts 17:26–27 with "the boundaries of their territories" (General Synod of the Dutch Reformed Church, *Human Relations*, 14–15). Also, commands forbidding the marriage of Israelites with other peoples were used to prohibit mixed marriages in South Africa under article 16 of the Immorality Act (General Synod of the Dutch Reformed Church, *Human Relations*, 93–99).

Second, contrasting principles were derived from Gen. 1:28: "separate development" (God made us all different), as argued by the Dutch Reformed Church (*Human Relations*, 14–15), versus "unity" (God made us one in our diversity), as argued by the liberationists. Similarly, the Dutch Reformed Church's treatment of Pentecost produced the principle of everyone hearing "God's great deeds in our own language" (Acts 2:10). However, Bax (128–30) criticized the exegesis in the Dutch Reformed Church report and produced the opposite principle of the Spirit at Pentecost "breaking down the barriers that separate humanity."

Third, the first French Huguenot settlers applied the paradigmatic narrative of the exodus story from slavery to a land flowing with milk and honey to their experience of escaping from persecution in Europe to the riches of the Cape area such as the Franschhoek Valley. However, they also applied the conquest material from Joshua and Judges to justify their oppression and slavery of the native peoples. This was further reinforced by the Boers' escape from the oppression of the British authorities in the Cape on the Great Trek culminating in their victory over twenty thousand Zulus at Blood River on December 16, 1838, subsequently kept as Covenant Day. However, the irony is that the same exodus paradigm lies at the heart of liberation theology and the black theology that influenced Desmond Tutu and Allan Boesak.

Finally, the overall worldview of biblical theology was used by both sides. Thus, the Dutch Reformed Church viewed its understanding of "human relations in the light of scripture" as based upon the whole scheme of creation-fall-incarnation-redemption, while the liberationists argued exactly the same for their understanding.

The fact that both sides could appeal to the same Scriptures using similar hermeneutical methods was a challenge at the time and remains so today. Despite the scriptural support for apartheid marshaled by the Dutch Reformed Church, the consequent oppression and bloodshed could not be justified. Thus, a decade later, its report *Church and Society* (1986) recognized that "the conviction has gradually grown that a forced separation and division of peoples cannot be considered a biblical imperative" (Dutch Reformed Church, *Church and Society*, 47). After the transition to majority democratic rule, Dominee Freek Swanepoel from the Dutch Reformed Church admitted to the Truth and Reconciliation Commission (TRC) that "the church had erred seriously with the Biblical foundation of the forced segregation of people. . . . We have indeed taught our people wrongly with regard to apartheid as a Biblical instruction" (TRC Faith Communities Hearings, East London, November 17–19, 1997). Thus, the pro-apartheid exegesis serves as a warning that we must read the Scriptures within an inclusive community of interpretation where the voices of those most affected by any interpretation are properly heard. Only then can such oppression carried out under the supposed aegis of biblical justification be avoided in the future (see Burridge 347–409).

See also Colonialism and Postcolonialism; Liberationist Ethics; Race; Racism

Bibliography

Bax, D. "The Bible and Apartheid, 2." Pages 112–43 in *Apartheid Is a Heresy*, ed. J. de Gruchy and C. Villa Vicencio. Lutterworth, 1983; Burridge, R. *Imitating Jesus: An Inclusive Approach to New Testament Ethics*. Eerdmans, 2007; de Gruchy, J. *The Church Struggle in South Africa: Twenty-Fifth Anniversary Edition*. Fortress, 2005; General Synod of the Dutch Reformed Church. *Church and Society: A Testimony of the Dutch Reformed Church*. Dutch Reformed Church Publishers, 1986; idem. *Human Relations and the South African Scene in the Light of Scripture*. Dutch Reformed Church Publishers, 1976.

Richard A. Burridge

Apocryphal Books *See* Deuterocanonical/Apocryphal Books

Apostolic Fathers

The Apostolic Fathers is a collection of late first- to mid-second-century texts that form a bridge between the NT and patristic literature. Typically included are the following: a letter by the church at Rome (*1 Clement*), a letter by Polycarp of Smyrna (*To the Philippians*) and an account of his martyrdom (*Martyrdom of Polycarp*), seven letters by Ignatius of Antioch, an anonymous letter attributed to Barnabas, an apology to Diognetus, a homily (*2 Clement*), a manual of instruction (*Didache*), and collected visions and teachings (*Shepherd of Hermas*).

Social ethics generally permeate these works. The NT directive to seek God's kingdom seems particularly evident. In *2 Clement*, Christians are exhorted toward mutual love (9.6) and righteousness (11.7). In *Shepherd of Hermas*, those who seek the seal of baptism must first be clothed in the twelve virtues and bear their names (*Herm. Sim.* 9.14–16). Several authors encourage the giving of alms and charity. Polycarp insists that alms deliver the giver from death (10.2), while the *Didache* urges charity for all who ask (1.5).

More broadly, the Apostolic Fathers arises at a transitional moment as the church discards its Jewish roots for more Hellenistic moorings. Of primary concern is the question of what ethics might be for Christians as they separate from the customary moral doctrines of the synagogue.

The authors of *1 Clement* and the *Didache* take a conservative view, envisioning an ethic that continues to cling to conventional Jewish ideals. The letter of *1 Clement* is written to correct a situation at Corinth in which younger elders have removed the established leadership of the church without due process. The author responds by offering Moses as a model by which leaders should execute their duties. The unique nature of this Jewish prophet serves as a key to how all Christians must live. There is nothing more divine than to live in order and harmony as is befitting God's will in the manner of patience, humility, righteousness, and self-control. Though explicitly directed toward Corinth's leadership, such attributes surface throughout the work as essential for the life of the larger community.

The *Didache* embraces a parallel position, offering the Decalogue as a foundation for correct Christian living. Prohibitions against acts such as murder, adultery, and theft form the structure of a desirable community ideal. At the same time, the *Didache* integrates warnings against lesser transgressions in order to protect the faithful from even greater sins. Included here are cautions against worldly practices such as magic, sorcery, abortion, infanticide, astrology, and idolatry (1.1–6.2). These sins typify the "way of death" and find analogous warnings in *Barn.* 18–20. The *Didache* counsels Christians to walk in the "way of life" instead, attending to the wisdom that paves its path. The "two ways" is popular within late Judaism and Qumran (see 1QS 3.13–4.26), as well as elsewhere among early Christians (see *Herm. Mand.* 6.1–2.10).

Other authors in this literature depart notably from any vision of ethics that depends on traditional Jewish norms, instead typically integrating elements of Hellenistic philosophy and instruction. The letters of Ignatius and the *Epistle to Diognetus* best illustrate this view.

Ignatius, bishop of Antioch, writes seven letters to churches in Asia Minor and Italy as soldiers take him to martyrdom in Rome early in the second century. He fears unstable leadership, Christians who would return the church to Judaism, and the threat of Docetism. These concerns push him toward a three-tiered model of institutional leadership that features a central overseer (bishop) and a cadre of supporters (deacons and presbyters). Like *1 Clement* and *Hermas*, both from Rome, Ignatius speaks of endurance, unity, and patience. He envisions church harmony to be an express result of compliance with the will of the bishop. The duty of Christians is to model their lives around the directives of God's duly ordained leaders, who provide regulation through correct liturgical practice and appropriate theological confession. For Ignatius, an ethical lifestyle means an existence of obedience.

The *Epistle to Diognetus* takes a more Stoic approach to Christian ethics. After indicating the various ways in which Christianity is superior to the foolish worship practices of Jews and the idolatry of pagans, the author argues that Christians live in the world much like a soul dwells within a body. They reside on earth, unseen, suffering wrong, loving those who hate them, and existing as immortal beings, appointed by God for the benefit of the mortal world (6.1–10). It is because they are citizens of another kingdom that believers in Christ quietly suffer injustice, become poor, and experience dishonor and slander. This concept ultimately became a foundation for Augustine's *The City of God* and has influenced Christian views of ethics in the West.

Between these extremes are several authors who combine Jewish and Hellenistic themes in their understanding of what it means to live an ethical lifestyle. The bishop Polycarp, for instance, is concerned for order and harmony within the church, much like his contemporary Ignatius and the author of *1 Clement*. In contrast to the latter text, however, he hesitates to incorporate OT texts when arguing on behalf of righteousness as a key to being Christian. His warnings to avoid any temptation toward slander, greed, and false testimony (4.3) and his admonitions to be gentle, steadfast, and enduring in patience (12.2) largely reflect NT themes and ideals, which find distinctive parallel in the teachings of Ignatius. Polycarp may actually seek to avoid a close connection with Judaism because of open hostility between the synagogue and church in Smyrna. The author of the *Martyrdom of Polycarp* ultimately accuses the Jews there of instigating his death.

Two other authors run beyond Ignatius and Polycarp in the use of OT texts in detailing an ethical lifestyle, though they make use of these materials in differing ways. The author of *2 Clement* composes an entire homily based on Isa. 54. In reflection of the prophet's words, Christians are encouraged to endure their suffering in patience with the hope of God's future reward. They are warned to avoid adultery, slander, and jealousy; they are enticed to be self-controlled, merciful, and kind (4.2). As transients in the world, Christians must live a holy and righteous life in order to obtain God's kingdom.

The *Epistle of Barnabas*, however, once more lays claim to the figure of Moses as an ideal for those who would be faithful to God. Unlike *1 Clement*, this author uses the prophet as a counterbalance to the faithlessness of the early Israelites. Whereas Moses acted with distinction in revealing the divine will for the chosen people, the Jews ultimately forsook their right to this covenant with God through their disobedience to the demands of that agreement. It is now for Christians to meet those same contractual demands in faith, thus to complete their true role as the people of God in a lifestyle of ethical piety.

The ethical agenda of the Apostolic Fathers is both broad and inclusive, featuring the essentials of traditional Jewish values and incorporating the best of Hellenistic moral concerns. The mixture of these elements is inconsistent, however, hinting at the diverse ways in which early NT values would ultimately become fixed within later patristic ethical values.

See also Almsgiving; Authority and Power; Didache; Martyrdom; Virtue(s)

Bibliography

Brändle, R. *Die Ethik der Schrift an Diognet: Eine Wiederaufnahme paulinischer und johanneischer Theologie am Ausgang des zweiten Jahrhunderts*. ATANT 64. Theologischer Verlag, 1975; Holmes, M., ed. and trans. *The Apostolic Fathers: Greek Texts and English Translations*. 3rd ed. Baker Academic, 2007; Jefford, C. *The Apostolic Fathers and the New Testament*. Hendrickson, 2006, 73–106; McDonald, J. *The Crucible of Christian Morality*. RFCC. Routledge, 1998.

Clayton N. Jefford

Armaments *See* War

Ars Moriendi Tradition, Use of Scripture in

The Ars Moriendi ("art of dying") tradition is a genre of devotional literature written to help Christians face death faithfully. Although some writings on how to die well predate them (e.g., Jean Gerson's *De arte moriendi* [c. 1408]), two anonymously written texts—*Tractatus artis bene moriendi* (c. 1415), and its abridged version, the *Ars moriendi*—are commonly recognized as the earliest works in the Christian Ars Moriendi tradition. Both enjoyed enormous popularity across Europe into the sixteenth century. They reflected the belief that one's disposition at death decisively determined one's eternal fate, depicting the deathbed as a place where Satan tempts the dying to faithlessness, despair, impatience, pride, and avarice. The texts offer practical strategies for avoiding each temptation.

The *Tractatus* makes little use of Scripture, drawing more heavily on liturgical texts and authorities such as Augustine and various popes.

Even when it instructs readers to model their dying after Christ, the text makes no direct references to the Gospels, merely naming five actions of Christ on the cross to be imitated.

Erasmus's *Preparing for Death* (1533) is far superior to the medieval *Ars moriendi*. Its focus shifts from dispensing techniques for outwitting Satan toward highlighting the need to live virtuously throughout life in order to die well. Erasmus's work is saturated with scriptural content; he draws especially on Pauline letters and other epistles to argue that trust in God's mercy and faith in the saving power of Christ's death and resurrection are the keys to sustaining hope in the face of death.

Erasmus uses biblical narrative (e.g., Jesus in the garden of Gethsemane) much more effectively when calling upon Christians to imitate Jesus in dying. He also highlights many passages about forgiveness (e.g., Luke 15:11–32; 18:10–14) in order to inspire readers to express forgiveness (a crucial task for the dying) and to strengthen their hope in God's mercy.

During the sixteenth and seventeenth centuries, several distinguished theologians contributed to the Ars Moriendi tradition. Their use of Scripture varied widely, typically reflecting the theological commitments of each author. Thomas Lupset's humanistic *Way of Dying Well* (1534) is devoid of scriptural references, reflecting his confidence in reason and natural law, whereas Thomas Becon's *The Sicke Man's Salve* (1561) cites Scripture to support almost every point. A notable Roman Catholic work is Robert Bellarmine's *The Art of Dying Well* (1619), which focuses primarily on the sacraments and the cultivation of virtue but draws heavily on Scripture to support this emphasis. Bellarmine highlights Luke 12:35–37 as a reminder that death could come at any time, encouraging readers to prepare themselves to meet the Lord by living righteously. Texts stressing the relative unimportance of a world that is passing away (e.g., 1 Cor. 7:31; 2 Cor. 4:17–18) are also emphasized.

Perhaps the most sustained instance of scripturally grounded reflection upon death in this genre is William Perkins's *A Salve for a Sicke Man* (1595). Perkins considers the claim in Ecclesiastes that the day of death is better than the day of birth (Eccl. 7:1). Perkins proceeds systematically, considering whether death is natural or a punishment for sin, how death could be regarded as welcome when Jesus prayed to be spared from death (Luke 22:42), and many other questions. Perkins's main conclusion is that the sting of death is sin (1 Cor. 15:56); Christians should lead lives of repentance and trust in God's mercy in order to remove their fear of death.

Holy Dying (1651) by Jeremy Taylor is notable for its seamless integration of Christian and classical sources. Taylor calls readers to follow the way of the cross if they would learn to live well and die well. Christians should avoid a life of ease and instead, "Let your laughter be turned to mourning and your joy to dejection" (Jas. 4:9). Taylor asserts that those who fail to learn patience by enduring smaller hardships throughout life will find it nearly impossible to die well. He encourages readers to see suffering as a form of chastisement for sin; one endures suffering as a form of mortification of the flesh so that one's spirit might ultimately be saved (1 Cor. 5:5).

Taylor draws most heavily on Scripture in three sections on prayer and virtue. He says that one becomes patient by learning to trust that God hears the afflicted (Ps. 6:9) and shows mercy toward those who trust in the Lord (Pss. 17; 27; 31). The section on faithfulness draws more deeply from the NT, calling readers to believe in God's promise of salvation through Jesus Christ and to be confident that all sinners have Jesus as their advocate before God (1 John 2:1–2). The section on charity returns to the psalms (especially Ps. 71), offering expressions of love for God while calling to mind God's mercy.

Taylor's use of Scripture is emblematic of the way the Ars Moriendi tradition matured beyond its medieval roots. The tradition draws on a wide variety of texts that capture the central tenets and themes of Christian faith in order to make the case that only a lifetime's pursuit of deep, vibrant faith can prepare one to die well.

See also Aged, Aging; Death and Dying; Hospice; Suffering; Virtue(s)

Bibliography

Atkinson, D., ed. *The English Ars Moriendi*. Peter Lang, 1992; Beaty, N. *The Craft of Dying: A Study in the Literary Tradition of the Ars Moriendi in England*. Yale University Press, 1970; Eire, C. *From Madrid to Purgatory: The Art and Craft of Dying in Sixteenth-Century Spain*. Cambridge, 1995. Erasmus. "Preparing for Death." Pages 389–450 in *The Collected Works of Erasmus*, vol. 70, ed. J. O'Malley. University of Toronto Press, 1998; O'Connor, M. *The Art of Dying Well: The Development of the Ars Moriendi*. Columbia, 1942; Taylor, J. *Holy Living and Holy Dying*. Ed. P. Stanwood. Clarendon, 1989. Vogt, C. *Patience, Compassion, Hope, and the Christian Art of Dying Well*. Rowman & Littlefield, 2004.

Christopher P. Vogt

Artificial Insemination

See Reproductive Technologies

Artificial Intelligence

Artificial intelligence is the science and engineering of making "intelligent" machines. While the term is currently invoked at the interface of several fields, including computer science, nanotechnology, and robotics, it also enjoys a longer history as a theme in the world's literature, mythology, and religious traditions (McCorduck). From the "golden robots" of Hephaestus to the golem stories in Jewish lore, from the dreams of Dr. Faustus to the cautionary tale of Mary Shelley's *Frankenstein*, from the cinematic adventures of Buck Rogers to Stanley Kubrick's darker vision in *2001: A Space Odyssey*, the history of such musings provides a richer framework for assessing recent technical developments.

On the one hand, the issues raised by the aims of computer science to create artificial intelligence touch on, and at times overlap with, religious questions concerning human responsibility and accountability raised by technology in its broadest sense: what theological vision informs our judgments about the appropriateness of human efforts to alter or transform nature? Two basic interpretive perspectives, both informed by Scripture, have emerged in the Christian tradition. The first, more literally conservative in its implications, stresses the essential giftedness of creation and cautions us against reducing it to merely instrumental status. The second framework, recently elaborated in the language of humans as "created co-creators" (e.g., Hefner; Peters), appears more dynamic and open-ended in its willingness to view human efforts to transform nature, including human nature, as an appropriate exercise of our creativity. The realm of artificial intelligence also finds some parallels with recent developments in synthetic biology, whose express aim is to engineer new forms of biological life "from the ground up" that have never existed before in evolutionary nature. On the other hand, the realm of artificial intelligence also poses novel issues, because recent efforts to replicate human intelligence challenge us to reflect anew about the status of *homo sapiens* as a distinct form of consciousness and agency in the world. Such reflections include both descriptive and prescriptive issues, which in turn require careful theological scrutiny.

At the descriptive level, definitional questions continue to plague discussions. What do we mean by "intelligence" in the first place? Which functions or capacities are central to the way that intelligence is defined? Moreover, even if particular human capacities such as computation or memory retrieval can be mimicked in programmable machines, whether such functions can ever eventuate in an "awareness" that parallels human self-consciousness remains a matter of deep dispute among philosophers of mind.

From a scriptural perspective, questions about human uniqueness are centrally captured by a twofold emphasis in the Christian tradition: humans are made "in the image of God" and must be understood as unitary creatures comprising body, soul, and spirit. Both themes provide important correctives to certain tendencies at work in popular discussions of science, including artificial intelligence. The theme of *imago Dei* refers to our capacity to reason, but it also is tied to other attributes of God that we are meant to reflect: freedom, compassion, and covenantal love (*ḥesed*), and the capacity for relationship with others (Campbell). Any account of artificial intelligence that seeks to reduce or minimize the range of such human capacities in order to draw simplistic parallels between humans and machines will be deeply impoverished. The second theme, that of our unitary nature as creatures of body, soul, and spirit, suggests that any effort at thoroughgoing materialism will, of necessity, fail to honor the robust scriptural vision of our human nature and destiny as creatures who live the "already but not yet" character of the resurrection's promise.

See also Dualism, Anthropological; Humanity; Image of God; Monism, Anthropological

Bibliography

Campbell, C. "Cloning Human Beings: Religious Perspectives on Human Cloning." Paper commissioned by the National Bioethics Advisory Commission (1997): http://bioethics.georgetown.edu/nbac/pubs/cloning2/cc4.pdf; Hefner, P. *The Human Factor: Evolution, Culture, and Religion*. Augsburg Fortress, 1993; McCorduck, P. *Machines Who Think: A Personal Inquiry into the History and Prospects of Artificial Intelligence*. 2nd ed. A. K. Peters, 2004; Peters, T. *Playing God? Genetic Determinism and Human Freedom*. 2nd ed. Routledge, 2002.

B. Andrew Lustig

Asceticism

Asceticism is the programmatic use of suffering or self-denial for spiritual or moral growth. It may include abstinence (e.g., from food or sex), renunciation (e.g., of property, political power, marriage, or social contact), or the deliberate self-infliction of pain (e.g., self-flagellation or the application of noxious substances).

Scripture and Tradition

Scripture is not univocal on this matter, its voices ranging from the approving to the suspicious. Aside from the general fast commanded for the Day of Atonement (Lev. 16:29; 23:27), there is little in the way of divine commandment to fast (see, perhaps, Joel 1:13–15; 2:12–15), unless one sees the impact of the various Sabbath regulations as a kind of economic asceticism (Exod. 23:10–12; Lev. 25).

More commonly, ascetic practices are narrated as voluntary and commendable. Fasting, the wearing of sackcloth, and the application of ashes are often associated with spiritual preparation (Matt. 4:2; Luke 4:2; Acts 13:3; 14:23), mourning (Gen. 37:34; 2 Sam. 1:12; 3:31–35; Esth. 4:3), petition (2 Sam. 12:16–23; Ezra 8:21; Neh. 1:14), penance (2 Kgs. 19:1; Jon. 3:5–8), or subservience (1 Kgs. 21:27; cf. political subservience in 1 Kgs. 20:31).

Ascetic practices are also associated with vocation. Samson, Samuel, and John the Baptist are obliged to follow the (normally voluntary) ascetic practices of Nazirites (Judg. 13; 1 Sam. 1:11; Luke 1:15; cf. Num. 6). In the NT, following Christ is so strongly linked with suffering—political persecution, sacrificial sharing, and personal restraint—that one may argue that Christians have a general vocation of suffering, the cultivation of which through practices of self-denial is not unwarranted (e.g., Matt. 5:10–12; 10:38; 16:24; Luke 9:23; John 15:19–20; Acts 4:34–35; 5:41; Gal. 5:19–24; Phil. 1:29; 1 Thess. 5:5–7; 1 Tim. 3:2–3; Heb. 13:13; 1 Pet. 4:1–2).

Accordingly, church history is replete with examples both of "heroic" self-denial and of a suspicion toward legalistic or immoderate asceticism. Ascetic practices are associated predominantly with the monastic tradition, beginning with the ascetic feats of the desert monastics (e.g., Anthony the Great, Simeon the Stylite), continuing with the Cenobitic monastic orders, most particularly among mystic theologians (e.g., Teresa of Avila, John of the Cross, Francis of Assisi) emphasizing the imitation of Christ's passion.

The prophetic tradition, however, includes fasting among those religious rites vitiated by economic injustice or religious insincerity (Isa. 1:10–17; 58:4–7; Jer. 14:12; Amos 5:21–24; Mic. 6:6–8; Zech. 7; cf. Jesus' critique of the Pharisees in Matt. 23:23; Luke 18:11–13). Aside from a preparatory forty-day fast, Jesus' public ministry is not characterized by asceticism; his apparent sociality (Matt. 11:19; Luke 7:34) and his followers' lack of fasting (Mark 2:18 pars.) arouse controversy. The early church seems to have practiced fasting (Acts 13:3; 14:23) and other voluntary asceticism (Acts 21:20–26), but Paul urges those who adopt any kind of ascetic practice not to allow it to cause dissension (Rom. 14; 1 Cor. 7:5).

Thomas Aquinas, similarly, insists that abstinence be practiced "with due regard" for the moral and physical health of the individual and the needs of the community (*ST* II-II, q. 146, a. 1), and Protestants have largely jettisoned the association of asceticism with vocation, eschewing mandatory celibacy and poverty for ordained clergy.

Contemporary Situation

Many moderns find themselves to be heirs of William James, who, in *The Varieties of Religious Experience*, approves of moderate practices of self-denial as promoting a sort of healthy temperance and moral robustness yet regards with suspicion anything that does not observe "the golden mean." Following James, many find themselves willing to acknowledge the medical and psychological benefits of moderate self-denial while still associating (what are seen as) extreme ascetic practices with psychological disorder.

Political critiques of Western capitalism, however, suggest that our success in the acquisition of wealth, knowledge, and power has led to an inability to sympathize with those who are suffering. What we think of as "reasonable" comfort, on this read, has been too heavily influenced by habits of consumption and leisure. Self-denial becomes a means both of solidarity with those who have no choice whether to suffer and of retraining one's understanding of "reasonable" freedom from suffering.

Certainly, contemporary Christians can affirm wholeheartedly the medical, psychological, ecological, and moral benefits of disciplined self-denial. Yet the weight of Scripture and tradition suggests that Christians may need to be willing to imitate Christ in ways that are more threatening and unpalatable in a world that too easily strives for the dangerously comfortable.

See also Celibacy; Continence; Food; Self-Denial; Temperance; Vegetarianism

Bibliography

Bynum, C. *Holy Feast and Holy Fast: The Religious Significance of Food to Medieval Women*. University of California Press, 1987; James, W. *The Varieties of Religious Experience*. Penguin Classics, 1983; Sölle, D. *Suffering*. Augsburg Fortress, 1984.

Sarah Conrad Sours

Astrology *See* Divination and Magic

Asylum *See* Aliens, Immigration, and Refugees

Atonement

The ethical implications of the cross are significant and numerous. Jesus modeled giving oneself for others and responding to violence not with more violence but with forgiveness. This article explores the ethical import of the saving work of the cross and resurrection of Jesus.

Atonement in the Old Testament

The atonement has ethical implications even when its meaning is stated simply as forgiveness of sin and restoration of relationship with God. When God gave the law to the people of Israel, it included instruction on what to do when they broke the commandments. So too, biblical ethics today must address the issue of failing or falling short. The law, however, included sacrifices as a means of atonement not just to liberate from guilt and shame but also to restore relationship with God. Human alienation from God is the fundamental cause and result of sinful actions. To restore that relationship is therefore central to enabling ethical living.

To understand the full depth of atonement in the OT, and thus in the NT as well, it must be placed within the context of God's covenants with Adam, Abraham, and Israel through Moses. A covenant is a formal arrangement of mutual loyalty between two parties that states the nature and purpose of the covenant, the obligations of the parties, and consequences for failure to meet those obligations. Covenants were common in the ancient Near East at all levels, from covenants between nations to familial covenants. God's covenants in the OT had both formal and familial characteristics. Within a covenantal context people are not considered just or righteous based on an abstract standard or legal code; they are considered just or righteous if they are faithful to their covenantal obligations to other people and to God. In this covenantal context law and justice have a strong relational character. For instance, when one commits a wrong against another, the offender does not simply pay a fine or a penalty but makes a payment of restitution to the victim as a step toward renewing the relationship (e.g., Lev. 6:1–7; Num. 5:5–10).

God provided Israel instruction for sacrifices for a variety of purposes, including cleansing, purifying, and removing guilt. Placing them all in their covenantal context brings to light important observations. Fundamentally, the purpose of sacrifice was not to placate God but to restore broken covenantal relationships. Integral to the sacrificial act was an attitude of repentance and obedience, identifying with the animal and offering oneself to God (e.g., Lev. 1:4; 4:4; 6–7; 17; Ps. 32; Isa. 6:1–8). Through the prophets God communicated strong displeasure with sacrifices not linked with changed ethical behavior (Isa. 1; Amos 5:21–24). Atonement was not a matter of God's simply overlooking the sin because of the sacrifice; rather, an actual restoration of interpersonal covenant relationships took place.

Atonement in the New Testament

The OT provides key observations for understanding atonement in the NT. Atonement is real change, from alienation to restored relationship. Biblical justice and ethics are relational, horizontal and vertical, individual and corporate, and restorative rather than retaliatory. Through the lens of God's covenants with Adam, Abraham, and Israel, God proves to be a just God by working to bring salvation and thus be faithful to covenant commitments. On the human side, Jesus, in a substitutionary way, both suffers the covenantal sanction that Israel deserves and fulfills covenant obligation by living faithfully in ways Israel has failed. Jesus thus "enables a new objective situation, namely, the end of exile and the construction of a new kind of temple, indwelt by God's own Spirit" (Vanhoozer 400).

The atonement is foundational to ethical behavior through liberating from guilt and shame, restoring relationship with God, and giving the church the same Spirit who enabled Jesus to lay down his life for others. It is a mistake, however, to see the atonement only as precursor to ethics. To empty the atonement of its ethical character would potentially weaken an individual's and a church's concept of Christian ethics. If proclamation of salvation through the cross does not include an ethical dimension, it is too easy to see ethical living as a second step, or even an optional appendix, to the core message of Christianity. For this reason, it is imperative to allow the covenantal character described above to shape one's understanding of the atonement and to follow the NT in using a diversity of imagery to communicate various aspects of the saving significance of the cross. We will look at some of that imagery, highlighting its ethical import.

Imagery of redemption and ransom implies liberation from enslavement or captivity (e.g., Mark 10:45; Rom. 3:24; Gal. 3:13; Col. 1:13–14; 1 Tim. 2:6; Heb. 9:15; 1 Pet. 1:18). The ethical dimension of the Christian life is strengthened through following the NT writers in proclaiming atonement not just as liberation from sin and death but also as liberation for righteous living (Rom. 6:18). God "has rescued us from the power of darkness and transferred us into the kingdom of his beloved Son" (Col. 1:13). Peter reminds his readers that they were ransomed from their futile ways and exhorts them to therefore rid themselves of all malice, guile, insincerity, envy, and slander (1 Pet. 1:18; 2:1).

The Pauline proclamation of salvation coming through union with Jesus has a similar dynamic—saved from, saved for. Through Adam came death and sin; through Christ came life and righteousness (Rom. 5:12–21). Paul portrays righteous ethical living not only as a result of the atonement but also as its means. Cohering with the covenantal dynamic observed above, salvation comes through Jesus' faithful obedience. He lives justly in our place, and through union with him we are justified.

Justification in a covenantal biblical context means not only to be declared free from guilt but also to be restored to right relationship. To be justified has ethical import through addressing the root cause of sin by healing our broken relationship with God. Through the covenantal lens justification also has a social dimension. To be restored in covenant relation to God also brings one into relationship with others—the covenant people of God. This social dimension is evident in that in the letters where Paul uses justification imagery, Galatians and Romans, he is addressing Christian communities struggling with questions of ethnic tension and identity. Who belongs, and on what basis do they belong? To use justification imagery to proclaim the saving significance of the cross reminds us of the central role of justice, right relationships, in Scripture. It also reminds us that restored relationship with God includes incorporation into the people of God. An expectation of ethical obligations to others within this community flows from this imagery.

Reconciliation imagery of the atonement also has vertical and horizontal dimensions with ethical implications. It is not God who needs to be reconciled to humans, but humans who need to be reconciled to God. Yet God takes the initiative and works through the cross and resurrection to make friends out of enemies (Rom. 5:10). Once again we see the "saved from, saved for" dynamic. "All this is from God, who reconciled us to himself through Christ, and has given us the ministry of reconciliation" (2 Cor. 5:18). It is not only through the cross that God models the same thing that Jesus and NT writers call us to do—love our enemies (Matt. 5:44; Rom. 12:14–21; 1 Pet. 2:21–23). Horizontal reconciliation, making peace between alienated people, is integral to and enabled by the atonement. The author of Ephesians, referring to the division between gentiles and Israel, writes that Christ "is our peace; in his flesh he has made both groups into one and broken down the dividing wall, that is, the hostility between us" (Eph. 2:14). Jesus takes two peacemaking initiatives: he tears down the barrier of division, and he creates people with a new identity. He brings interethnic peace through the cross by creating in himself "one new humanity," members together of the "household of God" (Eph. 2:11–22). Thus we are called to live out this reality and to follow his peacemaking example.

The NT provides rich and diverse atonement imagery. A weakness, however, of limiting thinking about and proclamation of the atonement to this imagery is that it too easily isolates the atonement from the life Jesus lived. Jesus' crucifixion was the consequence of a life in the service of God's purpose and in opposition to competing social, political, and religious powers. For instance, Luke's theology of the atonement is communicated not through a collection of images but rather through a lived-out drama of salvation. Ethics, a way of life, is central to the drama.

> Jesus embodied the fullness of salvation interpreted as status reversal; his death was the center point of the divine-human struggle over how life is to be lived, in humility or self-glorification. Though anointed by God, though righteous before God, though innocent, he is put to death. Rejected by people, he is raised up by God—and with him the least, the lost, the left out are also raised. In his death, and in consequence of his resurrection by God, the way of salvation is exemplified and made accessible to all those who will follow. (Green and Baker 77)

Luke's theology of the atonement enriches our understanding of the ethical character of other NT imagery. For instance, it adds concreteness to the imagery that through the cross God "disarmed the rulers and authorities and made a public example of them, triumphing over them in it" (Col. 2:15). Through the saving work of the cross and resurrection we are freed from the enslaving powers of death and alienation of "the present evil age" (Gal. 1:4). Some of these powers are the same that Jesus faced, such as mammon, ethnic prejudice, economic and political oppression, cultural practices that define some people as of greater value and status than others, and a religiosity of exclusion. Other powers are more contemporary, such as consumerism and technology. The cross and resurrection free us to follow the ways of the kingdom of God and to obey God without fear of the consequences of disobeying these powers. They have been exposed. Jesus repeatedly confronted a religiosity of exclusion, climaxing at the cross. God, through the resurrection, validated Jesus' stance against the alienating power of religion. The ethics of the kingdom does not have a bounded character that creates a community of exclusion. The purpose of this ethics is not to define who is "in" and who is "out" but rather to challenge and guide people brought together through their covenant relation with God to more fully walk in the way of Jesus and be the people and community that God created them to be.

Finally, the revelatory aspect of the cross is of both saving and ethical significance. The cross reveals the character and depth of human sin—what we are called to repent of. Jesus' life and death reveal what it means to live authentically as humans created in the image of God—the life we are called to live. The cross and resurrection reveal that God is a God of radical grace and self-giving love. The ethical direction found in Scripture is an expression of that love.

See also Covenant; Cruciformity; Forgiveness; Judgment; Justice; Peace; Reconciliation; Righteousness

Bibliography

Baker, M., ed. *Proclaiming the Scandal of the Cross: Contemporary Images of the Atonement*. Baker Academic, 2006; Driver, J. *Understanding Atonement for the Mission of the Church*. Herald Press, 1986; Dunn, J., and A. Suggate. *The Justice of God: A Fresh Look at the Old Doctrine of Justification by Faith*. Eerdmans, 1993; Green, J. B., and M. D. Baker. *Recovering the Scandal of the Cross: Atonement in New Testament and Contemporary Contexts*. InterVarsity, 2000; Shelton, R. *Cross and Covenant: Interpreting the Atonement for 21st Century Mission*. Paternoster, 2006; Vanhoozer, K. "The Atonement in Postmodernity: Guilt, Goats and Gifts." Pages 367–404 in *The Glory of the Atonement: Biblical, Historical and Practical Perspectives*, ed. C. Hill and F. James III. InterVarsity, 2004; Volf, M. "The Social Meaning of Reconciliation." *Int* 54 (2000): 158–72.

Mark D. Baker

Authority and Power

Authority and power are connected, contested, controversial concepts. "Power" denotes the energy and effective force residing in a person, role, or institution, while those in "authority" have a rightful charge to decide, to lead, and sometimes to enforce decisions. We speak of "spheres" of authority and "centers" of power, and we think in terms of vertical hierarchies, of being "under" authority or of having authority "over" someone or something.

Authority and power have long been topics of discussion and a locus of struggle in philosophy and theology, but such struggle gained intensity and verve in the twentieth century and continues into the twenty-first. For ethicists, both secular and theological, questions concerning who or what has legitimate authority, including moral authority, loom large. Philosopher Charles Taylor observes that people in modern secularized societies differ from those in earlier contexts—for example, those of the Scriptures and the early church, the medieval church, and even the churches of the Reformation—in the ways people imagine themselves in relation to authority and in the ways we picture what it means to have power or resist it. No longer do people assume that temporal powers directly correspond to supernatural ones, or that earthly power or office signifies divine appointment or delegation.

In every generation there will be voices counseling obedience to authorities, ecclesial and secular. But the more nuanced and interesting stances have come from those in the trajectory of the apostle Peter, who, in the face of imperial prohibition of his teaching ministry, declared, "We must obey God rather than any human authority" (Acts 5:29). This has been a pivotal question: how do we discern in the moment whose authority is legitimate and when established structures should be resisted or reformed? Moreover, as the Christian gospel has spread around the globe, new voices and perspectives on Christian ethics and scriptural interpretation have entered the conversation. Significant shifts have come from those theorists offering critiques of power and querying dominant authorities. It is beyond the scope of this article to cover the entire global spectrum, but this article does focus on contemporary critical voices, some of them from the "margins."

Authority and Power in Scripture

The biblical narratives turn time and again to stories of struggle around authority and power. In the biblical witness, God has ultimate authoritative power. In the beginning, God speaks, and the world is created. In relationships with creation and with people, God displays the character of completely legitimate, loving authority graciously wielded. Through steadfast love (*ḥesed*) God demonstrates noncoercive exercise of power that is trustworthy and just. The narratives also tell of misused power and illegitimate authority: false prophets and ungodly generals, judges, kings, and priests. In stark contrast, Jesus comes humbly exercising divine power on behalf of others.

Old Testament. In the grand narrative of the OT, God displays authority and power via various roles: father and mother, lawgiver and judge, shepherd and gardener, king, warrior, conqueror, deliverer, authoritative voice. In each role, the distinctive character of God's authority and power is displayed. The voice of God speaks, and creation responds. As household head, God provides powerful nurturing, blessing, and honor. As judge, God distinguishes the righteous from the unrighteous, the just from unjust, and pronounces consequences for actions. As shepherd, God gives powerful guidance and protection. The military commander God wages war on the unjust, defends the cause of the poor and oppressed, and makes a safe place in which his people may dwell in *shalom*. The OT God as authorizing power delegates responsibilities to human beings: Adam is empowered to name the animals and to care for the garden; Abraham to father a nation set aside for God; priests to bless and intercede; judges to mediate; kings and governors to rule; military leaders to command; prophets to speak.

Moses preeminently embodies God-given authority characterized by several of these key roles: he is a shepherd, lawgiver, mediator, judge, general, and prophet. As the narrative progresses, questions arise: shall the people of God have a temporal king? How will the power of an unjust or ungodly king be confronted and circumscribed? There is perennial strife between priestly temple authorities and other temporal structures. More prophets arise, and while the false ones coddle ungodly rulers, godly prophets speak truth to power and to the people. Thus, the prophetic voice becomes an authoritative channel of divine correction and guidance. Throughout the grand narrative God's steadfast love (*ḥesed*) remains a major OT theme, the prevailing character of God's power and authority. That power is displayed as God liberates his people from bondage, and continues as God announces and demonstrates his purpose to heal the nations, to re-create and redeem humankind and indeed all of creation.

New Testament. Jesus is the Lord (*kyrios*, "ruler"), the king, the new Moses—both prophet and priest. He wields Spirit-authorized power (*dynamis*, "power") as he confronts earthly and cosmic powers. His healing ministry displays authority over material and spiritual powers and restores marginalized individuals to honorable places in their families and communities. Thus familial structures are recast, tyrannical political power is defanged or relativized, and oppressive religious authorities are confronted (Luke 20:45–21:4). A question arises: by what authority (*exousia*, "authority") is Jesus doing these things (Mark 11:28)? In the process of making disciples, Jesus models authoritative, gentle shepherding of God's people. He displays noncoercive power and authority that invites and does not force, that frees and then empowers. New associations are formed, and new power and authority structures are built, as the new family of God is to be governed by love that is self-giving (*agapē*) and fraternal (*philadelphia*).

The NT Epistles evidence struggles among early Christians regarding how to define and exercise their new power and authority within the church, in the face of established temporal authorities (temple and empire), and in a world full of spiritual "authorities" and "powers." Paul's teaching that Christ's rule is total and preeminent (Eph. 1:21; Col. 1:16) fits the ancient Near Eastern conceptual world, in which earthly authorities correspond to—mirror and express—cosmic, supernatural powers (Eph. 1:21; 2:2; 6:12). In his character and message, the apostle Paul follows Jesus' example of self-giving leadership and of empowering the lowly (1 Cor. 1:26b–29). Paul urges believers to rely on the power of God (*en dynamei theou* [1 Cor. 2:5]); on this power the church is founded. And Paul wishes to pattern his own ministry and the shape of the church on the example of Jesus Christ's humble obedience (Phil. 2:5–11).

Authority and Power in Contemporary Ethics

In twentieth-century Christian ethics, authority and power came to be seen as matters of personal and group identity and agency strongly flavored by sociopolitical and economic factors, and Scripture often was interpreted in that light as well. Social analysts noticed effects of dominative power—"power-over"—but they also pointed to its transformative capacity, and in ethics these social theories, especially conflict theories, shaped the focal moral questions. Accordingly, the next sections review some key secular theories, then trace their influence in contemporary Christian ethics of power and authority. Readers desiring to move beyond the thumbnail sketches provided here would do well to consult *Comprehending Power in Christian Social Ethics*, Christian social ethicist Christine Firer Hinze's more complete survey and assessment.

Influential social theories. The vision that philosopher and social scientist Karl Marx (1818–83) had of ideal society implies a normative judgment that dominative power over others is illegitimate and ultimately will wane as the people find and assert their collective power. Marx's penetrating critiques of oppressive power-over, especially in capitalist systems, so focused attention on the systemic social and economic aspects of power that today the concepts of power and authority are almost invariably framed in those terms, even by non-Marxist thinkers.

German lawyer, political economist, and sociologist Max Weber (1864–1920) raised questions about the nature of social power and of the place of the individual agent in the modern rationalized, "disenchanted" world that has undergone "demagicalization." For him, rationalization itself is the greatest force shaping life in the modern world—the force that dictates that the norms for actions will be based on measurability, systematicity, and effectiveness. Many Christian ethicists work with or adapt Weber's taxonomy of social authority, which identifies certain ideal types categorized according to their spheres of authority.

Political philosopher Hannah Arendt (1906–75) distinguished between authority and power and saw legitimate, positive power in the human capacity to "act in concert" rather than via coercive command and lockstep obedience (Arendt 143). Arendt thus departed from the Western philosophical tradition, which she thought framed power as rule, hierarchical power-over. Arendt grounded her view of authority in the ancient Roman concept of *auctoritas*, authority foundational to a community and arising out of character, wisdom, and skill rather than relying on coercion or persuasion (Hinze 140). As Arendt critiqued contemporary society, she saw almost no structures operating in the public sphere with noncoercive authority.

French philosopher Michel Foucault (1926–84) shifted analyses of power away from the market and property metaphors, by which it was viewed as a substance of measurable and exchangeable commodity (Hinze 113). By contrast, Foucault pointed to "power relations," dynamic and multifaceted forces that operate in human societies, with potential for positive transformative impact. He saw power as operant in human relations at a personal level but even more significantly at systemic, social, and political structural levels, where it manages to subjugate and direct people's actions. Foucault thought that freedom from repressive and abusive power relationships comes only via awareness and resistance.

Power and authority in twentieth-century Christian ethics. Twentieth-century Christian ethicists and theologians interacted with these and other secular sociopolitical theories to develop Christian perspectives on the roles of individual agents in communities and in the political arena. Analyses of power relations and the nature of legitimate authority were key topics.

In the 1930s, French Roman Catholic neo-Thomist and personalist philosopher Jacques Maritain (1882–1973), whose ideas became influential especially in Latin America, developed a distinctively Christian vision of the common good created when power and authority structures enable whole persons—spiritual and material beings with relationships to God—to flourish. In his vision, power-over can be beneficent when authorities recognize the sovereignty of God and adhere to proper norms, and in that case they have a right to be obeyed. When political authorities become oppressive or self-serving, they fail to fulfill their proper, essential roles and are rendered illegitimate.

The emergence of fascism in Europe presented exactly the kind of challenge that Maritain's ethic attempted to address. The divine command ethic of Swiss Reformed theologian Karl Barth (1886–1968) was forged and tempered in that context as well. The Barmen Declaration, which Barth drafted, declares Jesus Lord ("Führer"), pointedly rejecting "other lords." German theologian Dietrich Bonhoeffer (1906–45), a student of Barth, wrestled with how to maintain a faithful church even in Nazi Germany. He thought it important to distinguish between spheres of authority, to separate the church from the world. While Bonhoeffer strove against the secular kingdom in which he lived, he prized and cultivated the life of the Confessing Church, within whose fellowship he counseled humility and gentleness. Bonhoeffer acted on his convictions as he chose to participate in a plot to assassinate Hitler, for which the Third Reich executed him.

In the wake of World War II, Christian theologians assessed the churches' roles in the buildup of the Third Reich and the execution of that conflict. German theologian Dorothee Sölle said that it was no longer appropriate to found a Christian ethic on the concept of obedience to authority and asked, "Is it possible to imagine a moral philosopher or theologian who would use the word 'obedience' as if nothing had happened? . . . The dangers of the religious ideology of obedience do not end when religion itself loses its spell and binding power. The Nazi ideology with its antireligious leanings proves the point that after disenchantment of the world, to use Max Weber's phrase, there is still domination and unquestioned authority and obedience" (Sölle x, xiii). Sölle called for a historically aware, contextualized theological ethic of power and authority grounded in Jesus' example of the self-aware yet selfless human being free to live for others.

For German American Protestant theologian Paul Tillich (1886–1965), the concept of power is linked with core theological issues of the nature of human identity (*imago Dei*) and the nature of reality itself (ontology). Love and justice are foundational relations, and both are fundamental to redemptive power. Beginning with the Genesis story of the fall of humankind, Tillich sees a human tendency toward conflict and abuse of power resulting from the estrangement accompanying the exposure of our finitude, our lack of omnipotence and omniscience. Tillich critiqued other Christian ethicists for missing the relationship between power and love; he envisioned "creative justice" issuing from a collective life where in particular situations love, power, and formal justice were applied, symbolized by the (transhistorical, immanent) kingdom of God. Still, he recognized a tragic necessity in human life for hierarchies and social structures that will at times be coercive (Hinze 202–3). Tillich's analysis of power and authority was influential in the work of Reinhold Niebuhr and Martin Luther King Jr., and it has traces in the thought of some Christian feminists.

American Reinhold Niebuhr (1892–1971) saw political will to power as both pervasive and potentially malevolent, rooted in human pride and ego assertion. As with Bonhoeffer, Niebuhr's model for Christian participation in the sociopolitical arena was colored by a Lutheran two-kingdoms theology in which there is unavoidable tension between life in the secular world and life in the kingdom of God. He saw God's spirit working within history but cautioned that progress toward realization of the kingdom would be slow. Niebuhr spoke of kingdom ethics as an "impossible possibility" (Niebuhr 2:246–47).

Martin Luther King Jr. (1929–68) wrote, "Power, properly understood, is the ability to achieve purpose. It is the strength required to bring about social, political, or economic changes. In this sense power is not only desirable but necessary in order to implement the demands of love and justice" (King 37). Grounding his call for social justice in scriptural mandates and images, and steeped in personalist theology and the thought of Tillich and Niebuhr, King articulated a version of Black Power that critiqued both "immoral power" and "powerless morality." Properly fused, power, love, and justice could be transformative.

Liberation perspectives on power and authority. The final three decades of the twentieth century witnessed the development of liberation theologies in response to oppressive social and political conditions and structures. These theologies from the "underside" focus attention on concrete social, economic, cultural, and relational contexts and seek to critique the power relations operative in each sphere. For liberationists, the central moral problem is systemic oppression in its particular local form, not a formal, theoretical problem or difficulty with belief in the modern era, as it was for Tillich and Niebuhr.

For Peruvian Dominican priest and theologian Gustavo Gutiérrez (b. 1928), biblical grounding for the call to liberation is deep in the exodus story and the kingdom of God, which Jesus announced and ushered in. God is on the side of the poor, working for their liberation, and Christians are accordingly called to solidarity with and action on behalf of the oppressed. The crisis of oppression has spiritual, institutional, and historical dimensions, and the liberating solidarity and praxis called for will also need to address each of those spheres. Similarly, Argentine Methodist theologian José Míguez Bonino speaks of "the active solidarity of love" that empowers the oppressed to break free from dominative and dependent social, economic, and political arrangements. Cuban American ethicist Miguel De La Torre says, "Solidarity that comes from making an option for the poor is crucial not because Christ is *with* the marginalized but, rather, Christ *is* the marginalized. In the words of the Apostle Paul, 'Remember the grace of our Lord Jesus Christ who for [our] sake, although rich became poor, so that [we] might become rich through the poverty of that One' (2 Cor. 8:9)" (De La Torre 57).

In the vision of Christian feminist ethicists, the notion of authority is revised and recast. Patriarchal and sexist authority structures and assumptions of power are rejected in favor of egalitarian models. For American Baptist womanist ethicist Emilie Townes (b. 1955), "The concept of power that comes from decision and responsibility is one that entails the ability to effect change and to work with others. This power requires openness, vulnerability, and readiness to change" (Townes 86). Letty Russell (1930–2007) wrote of empowerment of individuals in concert with others and of power that authorizes legitimate power: "Authority might be understood as legitimate power only when it opens the way to inclusiveness and wholeness in the household of faith" (Russell 61). Moreover, willingness "to work for God's covenant purpose of justice, *shalom*" is what qualifies people for inclusion in the power circle (Russell 36). Elisabeth Schüssler Fiorenza (b. 1938) moves the description and discussion of power beyond power-over associated with empire to "power for," affecting transformation. Beverly Harrison (b. 1932), influenced by her teacher Reinhold Niebuhr, offered a Christian feminist power analysis: "Evil is the consequence of disparities of power because where disparity of power is great, violence or control by coercion is the dominant mode of social interaction. Evil, on this reading, is the active or passive effort to deny or suppress another's power-of-being-in-relation. When power disparities are great, those 'in charge' cease to have to be accountable to those less powerful for what they do. Societies in which . . . some groups have vast and unchecked power and others are denied even the power of survival, are unjust societies" (Harrison 154–55). Harrison cautioned, "We act together and find our good in each other and in God, and our power grows together, or we deny our relation and reproduce a violent world where no one experiences holy power" (Harrison 41).

See also Autonomy; Conquest; Egalitarianism; Equality; Liberation; Liberationist Ethics; Powers and Principalities; Resistance Movements; Submission and Subordination; Tyranny

Bibliography

Arendt, H. *Crises of the Republic: Lying in Politics, Civil Disobedience, On Violence, Thoughts on Politics and Revolution*. Harcourt Brace, 1969; De La Torre, M. *Doing Christian Ethics from the Margins*. Orbis, 2004; Harrison, B. *Making the Connections: Essays in Feminist Social Ethics*. Ed. Carol Robb. Beacon Press, 1985; Hinze, C. *Comprehending Power in Christian Social Ethics*. AARAS 93. Scholars Press, 1995; King, M. L., Jr. *Where Do We Go from Here: Chaos or Community?* Beacon Press, 1967; Niebuhr, R. *The Nature and Destiny of Man: An Interpretation*. 2 vols. Charles Scribner's Sons, 1941–43; Russell, L. *Household of Freedom: Authority in Feminist Theology*. Westminster, 1987; Sölle, D. *Creative Disobedience*. Trans. L. Denef. Pilgrim Press, 1995; Townes, E. *A Troubling in My Soul: Womanist Perspectives on Evil and Suffering*. Orbis, 1993.

Bonnie Howe

Autonomy

The term *autonomy*, from the Greek *auto* ("self") and *nomos* ("law"), refers to the right of self-direction. It requires agency (the capacity to act as one intends) and liberty (freedom from external control). Originally a political term applied to self-governing nations, *autonomy* now more commonly applies to an institution or individual following a self-chosen plan. The autonomy of ethics indicates the independence of moral thinking from other influences, such as religion, culture, and tradition.

Ethicists as early as Aristotle addressed the political autonomy of the city-state; individual autonomy gained prominence much later, in the work of Immanuel Kant. Kant defined autonomy as the capacity to make moral decisions based on universalized maxims, without regard to external circumstances, potential outcomes, or personal desire.

Since Kant, the concept of autonomy has been applied in practical ways. In the helping professions, carefully crafted policies protect patient autonomy, preserving human dignity and preventing abuse where imbalance of power exists. In healthcare ethics, for example, informed consent protects patients' rights to make decisions about their own health. In business and legal ethics, practices such as performance reviews and judicial action hold individuals and institutions accountable and assume the ability to self-regulate behavior. Politically, acknowledging self-government means rejecting paternalism.

Despite the importance of autonomy to contemporary ethics, however, theological ethicists caution that overemphasis on autonomy may lead to unchecked individualism, reduce human relationships to contractual obligations, and especially undermine human dependence on God.

Extending autonomy to the point of individualism is a modern Western tendency, whereas many other cultures subordinate the autonomy of the individual to the well-being of the community. This may create tension when, for example, Western healthcare ethics emphasizes patient autonomy to the extent that it disregards practices of corporate decision-making (common in many Latin American cultures) or protecting patients from the gravity of their situation (as in some Asian cultures).

Scripture affirms individual autonomy but also values community. The divine image and likeness of God in human beings (Gen. 1:26–27) bestows human dignity and demands our honor and respect for self and others. At the same time, human beings exist in community with God and with other persons. Only God has absolute autonomy in the sense of being free from all authority; human autonomy is always in the context of appropriate submission to God and to human authorities (Matt. 9:8; Rom. 13:1–4; 1 Thess. 4:8).

Indeed, Scripture always speaks of human autonomy against the background of our total dependence on God. The Bible also has much to say about how we use our freedom and toward what end. Romans 6 equates freedom from sin with freedom for righteousness, for example. The author of 1 Cor. 9 says that he is free but makes himself slave to all. Autonomy that is consistent with Scripture is not freedom to indulge one's self-interests, but rather freedom from all that hinders one's service to God and other persons.

See also Freedom; Healthcare Ethics; Image of God; Individualism; Moral Agency; Self

Bibliography

Beauchamp, T. L., and J. F. Childress. "Respect for Autonomy." Pages 99–148 in *Principles of Biomedical Ethics*. Oxford University Press, 2009; Kant, I. *Foundations of the Metaphysic of Morals*. Trans. M. Gregor. Cambridge University Press, 1996; Schneewind, J. *The Invention of Autonomy: A History of Modern Moral Philosophy*. Cambridge University Press, 1998.

Amy Renee Wagner

B

Ban, The

The OT term *ban* (Heb. *ḥerem*) often refers to the destruction of booty and/or slaughter of captives after a military victory. It denotes the state or condition of Yahweh's exclusive ownership and mandates the complete withdrawal of something from human use by its physical destruction or conveyance to priests or a temple treasury (Lev. 27:28–29; Num. 18:14; Josh. 6:19, 24). War *ḥerem*, attested in other ancient Near Eastern cultures, predates Israelite history and varies in biblical depictions. In the OT, this ban serves as a prohibition of personal gain from battle and is thus an expression of God's sovereignty as well as a protection against idolatry (Exod. 22:20 [22:19 MT]). Deuteronomic tradition restricts the ban to the indigenous residents of Canaan, none of whom are to be spared (Deut. 7:1; 20:17). The depiction of the ban during Israel's journey to the land (Deut. 2–3; cf. Num. 21, 31) foreshadows rather than extends this restriction (Deut. 3:21). Deuteronomy's rationale for *ḥerem* is the prevention of spiritual corruption (Deut. 7:1–5; 20:16–18). Outside of Canaan, terms of peace are to be offered first; only if peace is rejected are captured males to be killed. Women, children, livestock, and spoil may also be kept by the Israelites in this case (Deut. 20:10–15). Several narratives illustrate a similar understanding (Josh. 2; 6–7; 10–11; 1 Sam. 15). The command to blot out the Amalekites (Exod. 17:14–16; Deut. 25:17–19) is presented as a supplementary directive rather than as *ḥerem* per se, but 1 Sam. 15 does invoke *ḥerem* in the context of an Amalekite battle. Although it targets an entire people for destruction, this action also ironically limits slaughter (since, according to 1 Sam. 15, the last Amalekite is dead). Later Deuteronomistic tradition directs the ban toward apostate Israelite cities (Deut. 13:6–18). Post-Deuteronomistic traditions mostly ascribe *ḥerem* to God alone and no longer to Israel (Isa. 34:2, 5; Mal. 4:6 [3:24 MT]; Mic. 4:13 is a notable exception). God may even initiate the ban against Israel (Isa. 43:28; Jer. 25:9). Zechariah 14:11 prophesies the end of *ḥerem* at the day of the Lord.

The extent to which the ban was ever historically enacted by Israel in battle is disputed. By setting the ban primarily within the context of Israel's entry into the land, the canonical OT presents it largely as a time-bound, nonrepeatable practice. By devoting lives and property to God through destruction, the OT does not mean to glorify vengeful slaughter, but rather to confess God as the sole source of victory. Nevertheless, the ban shockingly sanctions the killing of captives and noncombatants, and later appeals to this biblical tradition have sometimes used it to promote religiously motivated genocide. Yet modernity is arguably just as brutal in conducting profane war that seduces the strong into believing that they are masters of their own destiny.

See also Holy War

Bibliography

Hoffman, Y. "The Deuteronomistic Concept of Herem." *ZAW* 111 (1999): 196–210; Holloway, J. "The Ethical Dilemma of Holy War." *SwJT* 41 (1998): 44–69; Nelson, R. "Herem and the Deuteronomic Social Conscience." Pages 39–54 in *Deuteronomy and Deuteronomic Literature: Festschrift C. H. W. Brekelmans*, ed. M. Vervenne and J. Lust. BETL 133. Leuven University Press, 1997; Stern, P. *The Biblical Herem: A Window on Israel's Religious Experience*. BJS 211. Scholars Press, 1991.

Stephen B. Chapman

Banking *See* Business Ethics; Economic Ethics

Baptist Ethics

Baptists were born in the sixteenth century out of an environment of intolerance created by the demands of political power for religious conformity in a state-governed church, the Church of England. John Smythe (c. 1554–1612) and Thomas Helwys (c. 1550–1616) were English dissenters who formed a congregation in Amsterdam in 1609, establishing one branch of core ethical values for Baptists that emphasized individual liberty expressed in free interpretation of Scripture and religious practice, opposition to the control of religion by the state, and local congregational autonomy.

Baptists emerged in England, but they found their most fruitful soil for the expressions of their freedom in the frontier spirit of America. The expansiveness of the New World provided opportunity for the individualism of Baptist liberty to thrive, for if one encountered intolerance in one place, there was the opportunity to move to another. Roger Williams (1603–83) was a Baptist briefly, founded the first Baptist church in America in Providence, Rhode Island, but, more important, set forth the Baptist commitment to religious liberty in early documents of the church, the state of Rhode Island, and his writings. He was the first to use metaphors of separation between church and state. Liberty and separation of powers between church and state are inherent Baptist principles from Williams, which he applied to all humanity.

Through most of the eighteenth and nineteenth centuries, the focus of Baptist ethics was on the twin themes of religious liberty and separation of church and state, along with a highly individualistic ethic of personal morality that eventually embraced the temperance movement and other issues such as gambling, family solidarity, and, for some Baptists, the abolition of slavery. Isaac Backus (1724–1806) and John Leland (1754–1841) were among the most fervent early American Baptists to use their influence in advocacy with government leaders for religious liberty. Leaders such as these played a key role in pressing for the breakthrough church/state arrangement established in the First Amendment to the United States Constitution.

Baptist ethics are highly individualist in that the core values of Baptist faith allow for wide variances in understanding Christian faith and are deeply suspicious of coercion in matters of religious conscience. Added to these values is the historical reality that Baptists lack the towering theological authority of the Reformed tradition embodied in the works of Martin Luther and John Calvin.

But Baptists are distinctive and demanding in their insistence on the essential principles of radical discipleship, emphasizing the lordship of Jesus Christ as the only authority for true faith, with the Scriptures as the revealed truth of Jesus' life and teaching and the final written authority for faith and practice. Derived from these sources of authority, Baptists affirm the religious liberty of each Christian to interpret Scripture under the leadership of the Holy Spirit, reject creedal formulations of how Scripture must be interpreted, and insist on the autonomy of each congregation that gathers for worship and ministry. The final affirmation of these principles is the necessity of confessing faith in Christ as an informed adult decision, hence the practice of baptism usually by immersion only and the rejection of the baptism of infants.

The consequence of these principles is wide latitude in the application of faith to social and political issues. Such individualism and congregational autonomy often result in Baptists taking opposite sides on the same ethical issues. Given the lack of specific requirements of education for the ordination of clergy by most Baptists, ethical stances often are rooted in simplistic lay understandings that lack the nuances of a rational, clearly articulated approach to issues.

Further reinforcing diverse perspectives on ethics, Baptist congregationalism rejects ecclesiastical structures that can establish broadly accepted and enforceable policy. Baptists organize themselves voluntarily into fellowships, associations, and state and national conventions or unions, and many cooperate in international organizations, most notably the Baptist World Alliance (BWA). Because of this nonauthoritarian polity, Baptists tend to organize along racial, ethnic, national, and regional groups. There are fifty-six identifiable Baptist groups in North America, the greatest concentration in the world. The Southern Baptist Convention (SBC) is the largest of these, with more than 16 million adherents. The BWA, founded in 1905, is the most inclusive of these groups (the SBC withdrew from the BWA in 2004), having 214 unions and conventions comprising 37 million baptized believers and 105 million participants worldwide.

Each fellowship, association, union, or convention has distinct processes for addressing ethical issues. Normally, Baptists address ethical issues through resolutions passed at annual meetings. No resolution by any group is binding on any individual or congregation, but these declarations do express the sentiments of the group gathered at a given time. Such resolutions speak *to* Baptists and seldom *for* them. Among the most progressive groups, social action committees or Christian life committees give leadership to the denominations in making ethical pronouncements. Within the BWA, the Commission on Christian Ethics studies ethical issues of international importance and issues statements of analysis of a wide variety of matters, including environment, terrorism, human trafficking, poverty, and racism. A new administrative division was formed in 2008, the Division of

Freedom and Justice, to focus on universal human rights and connect more fully with the United Nations as a nongovernmental organization.

In spite of this decentralized approach to ethics, for much of the twentieth century Baptists were at the forefront of social activism within the progressive movement of the United States. None has been more influential in the early development of a clearly stated theological formulation of Baptist ethics than Walter Rauschenbusch (1861–1918). His *Christianity and the Social Crisis* (1907) became one of the most widely read books in religion in America in the early decades of the twentieth century. His *Theology for the Social Gospel* (1917) remains the classic theological formulation for a progressive Christian social ethic in spite of the intense critique and rejection of his insights by the fundamentalist movement of the 1920s and neoorthodox theologians of the mid-twentieth century.

Rauschenbusch rooted his theology in Jesus as a prophetic deliverer of the kingdom of God, a here-and-now reality of the reign of God in human life. As such, the kingdom is a social reality with the central virtue of love manifested to all that comes into being by divine initiative. The kingdom is not a static reality, but grows organically to affect all dimensions of life, whether family, government, economy, or the church. He also expanded the individual Baptist understanding of sin to include social sins of exploitation, accumulation, and greed, especially as these were manifested in the abuses characteristic of unfettered industrial capitalism. If sin is social, then so must be salvation as society is transformed through the actions of love in the social system. The church's call is to be an agent of participation in bringing kingdom activism to bear in the world.

The influence of Rauschenbusch can hardly be overestimated when one considers the impact of his thinking through the lineage of a host of Baptists who both embraced and reinterpreted his ideas. Baptist seminaries have been a major conduit of these ideas, with noted teachers of ethics applying his insights in their own cultural milieu. These included especially Crozer Theological Seminary—where Martin Luther King Jr. completed his bachelor of divinity degree—Andover Newton Theological Seminary, Southern Baptist Theological Seminary, and Southwestern Baptist Theological Seminary. Much of the ethical consciousness of Southern Baptists was developed in these latter two seminaries, where Henlee Barnette (1911–2004) and T. B. Maston (1897–1988) were respective conduits of King's ideas.

African American Baptists have made major contributions to the field, with early leadership in education and social action provided by Nannie Helen Burroughs (1879–1961), who led black women as the primary leader of the Woman's Convention of the National Baptist Convention for sixty-one years, established the National Trade and Professional School for Women and Girls, and called women to participate in a host of social and political organizations. Marian Wright Edelman (1939–), as founder and leader of the Children's Defense Fund, has extended her tradition as the leading spokesperson in America for social policy that enhances the needs and rights of children.

Ethical consciousness was on the agenda of black Baptists throughout the twentieth century, with primary leadership given by Howard Thurman (1899–1981). He authored twenty books, cofounded one of the early interracial congregations in America, served as faculty and chaplain at several prestigious educational institutions, and worked as an advisor to the major leaders of the modern civil rights movement. His friend and colleague Benjamin E. Mays (1896–1984) was a leading voice for civil rights as president of Morehouse College in Atlanta, Georgia, a mentor of Martin Luther King Jr., and a major civic leader in the Atlanta community.

No Baptist offered a more powerful voice for the cause of ethical concerns than Martin Luther King Jr. (1929–68). A third-generation son of Baptist preachers, he was the founder of the Southern Christian Leadership Conference and the primary advocate of nonviolent civil disobedience based on the teachings of Jesus and Gandhi. King's leadership in the civil rights movement resulted in the Nobel Peace Prize in 1964, following which he became an outspoken critic of the war in Vietnam and an advocate for a guaranteed minimum income for the poor as a founder of the Poor People's Campaign. King's corpus of published sermons and books as well as the numerous biographies and analyses of his work make him the most famous Baptist ethical activist in modern history.

Baptists as a whole have been largely conservative in their ethical perspectives in regard to personal life, with strong affirmations of the importance of a personal morality rooted in deep piety, the family as the model of moral behavior and the source of ethical guidance, the importance of temperance in relation to alcohol, opposition to the use of drugs, and living out one's faith with integrity in daily life and work. Much of the Baptist ethic is rooted in personal responsibility for each follower of Christ to embody behavior reflective of biblical norms.

In social ethics, on the issue of abortion the position has largely been one of a pro-life perspective with concessions by some for therapeutic abortions, with minority Baptist voices such as former Southern Baptist Theological Seminary ethics professor Paul Simmons strongly affirming a prochoice stance as a religious liberty issue. Baptists generally have been broadly supportive of birth control, but some very conservative Baptists have begun to reject the practice. Most Baptists have been cautious on bioethical issues, including therapeutic cloning, in-vitro fertilization, and end-of-life issues surrounding euthanasia.

Baptists have not been notable in their leadership on other issues concerning violence and sanctity of life. The majority tends to favor capital punishment, though strong voices oppose it. In regard to war, the just-war position has been predominant, with mostly unqualified support for American wars, especially among Baptists in the South. A small antiwar voice can be heard from the Baptist Peace Fellowship of North America. Strongly patriotic, only minority voices can be found in pacifist positions, though notable Baptists have been a part of the Fellowship of Reconciliation, including British leader Muriel Lester (1885–1968), Clarence Jordan (1912–69) and J. Martin England (1901–89) of Koinonia Farms fame, and Howard Thurman. Primary leadership for the emerging paradigm of just peacemaking has come from Glen Stassen (1936–), now at Fuller Theological Seminary.

The issue of slavery and race has been the most divisive one for Baptists, having prompted a major schism between Northern and Southern Baptists in 1845. Although popular attitudes often have been embarrassingly discriminatory, even to the present, significant progressive leadership has come from white Baptists in support of the black leadership described above. The SBC approved a resolution in support of *Brown v. Board of Education* in 1954 and more recently, on the occasion of its 150th anniversary in 1995, approved a repentant resolution confessing past injustices and requesting forgiveness for racism. Most Baptist leaders exhibit acute awareness of the painful history of racial division and discrimination and seek opportunities to heal old wounds, as occurred with the New Baptist Covenant meeting of 2008, an interracial gathering that brought together thousands of Baptists.

One issue that continues to unite Baptists in America to some extent is religious liberty and separation of church and state. The Baptist Joint Committee for Religious Liberty (BJCRL) advocates for legislation and frequently addresses court cases and social policy. On the one hand, the BJCRL, comprising representatives of fifteen broadly diverse Baptist bodies, is reflective of a broad commitment to religious issues in the nation's capital. On the other hand, the SBC no longer supports the BJCRL and articulates at least a different version of the Baptist commitment to religious liberty.

This serves as a reminder that the schism that rent the SBC beginning in the late 1970s was largely instigated by differences over ethical issues. After the fundamentalist-conservative takeover of the SBC, which was essentially finalized by the early 1990s, conservative stances on issues such as women's roles, abortion, and homosexuality became required of all who would serve the SBC in any official capacity. Those Baptists who opposed these developments, many of them eventually aligning with the new Cooperative Baptist Fellowship (founded in 1991), did not always disagree with conservative SBC leaders on the substance of their ethical views (though they sometimes did), but often appealed to Baptist commitments to freedom of conscience, the autonomy of the local church, and separation of church and state as the reason for their resistance to developments in the denomination. In the end, their arguments were in vain, and the schism between fundamentalist-conservative and moderate-conservative Southern Baptists became irreparable.

This means that since the late 1970s, Baptist social ethics has been split between a conservative approach tightly aligned with the Christian Right, a more progressive approach drawing its main inspiration from figures such as Rauschenbusch and King, and a harder to define approach that seeks to avoid focusing on social or political issues, in part because of the divisiveness of these issues. The conservatives have tended to gravitate toward Republican politics, and the progressives toward the Democrats—the former saw Ronald Reagan as the apotheosis of Christian political leadership, while the latter embraced Jimmy Carter. This quite definite split certainly has defined the recent history of Baptist social ethics in the United States, especially in the South, and has made it more difficult to identify a shared "Baptist" ethical vision. Perhaps twenty-first-century cultural, political, and religious developments will eventually heal this breach.

See also Abortion; African American Ethics; Alcohol; Anabaptist Ethics; Civil Rights; Evangelical Ethics; Fundamentalism; Gambling; Individualism; Just-Peacemaking Theory; Kingdom of God; Nationalism; Race; Racism; Religious Toleration; Sanctity of Human Life; Slavery; Temperance

Bibliography

Gaustad, E. *Roger Williams*. Oxford University Press, 2005; Leonard, B. *Baptists in America*. Columbia University

Press, 2005; McSwain, L., ed. *Twentieth-Century Shapers of Baptist Social Ethics*. Mercer University Press, 2008; Shurden, W. *The Baptist Identity: Four Fragile Freedoms*. Smyth & Helwys, 1993; Stassen, G., and D. Gushee. *Kingdom Ethics: Following Jesus in Contemporary Context*. InterVarsity, 2003; Stricklin, D. *A Genealogy of Dissent: Southern Baptist Protest in the Twentieth Century*. University of Kentucky Press, 1999.

Larry L. McSwain and David P. Gushee

Baruch

The book of Baruch is attributed to the scribe and secretary of Jeremiah, Baruch the son of Neriah (Jer. 36:27–32; 45:1–5). It is sometimes called 1 Baruch to distinguish it from the apocalypses 2 Baruch (Syriac) and 3 Baruch (Greek) as well as 4 Baruch (Paraleipomena of Jeremiah). Its Greek version appears in LXX manuscripts, though parts of it may have been composed in Hebrew. Most scholars place its composition in Palestine in the second or first century BCE, though its narrative setting is sixth-century Babylon. Its major concerns are why the exile took place and how Israel might repent and so continue as God's people. In dealing with those questions, the book adopts and develops the theological scheme of sin, exile, repentance, and return found in Deut. 28–33 and Jer. 26–33. The major ethical problem that it raises is the adequacy of that schema as an explanation of ancient Israel's national tragedy.

The four major parts of the book differ in their literary forms: the narrative framework (1:1–14), the exiles' prayer (1:15–3:8), the meditative poem about searching for wisdom (3:9–4:4), and the poem of consolation (4:5–5:9). What unifies these four pieces are the theological convictions that the exile was the consequence of Israel's sins, that what God wanted from his people was their repentance and renewed willingness to live according to the Torah, and that God would then return Israel to its great city (Jerusalem) and temple.

The narrative framework introduces Baruch and the exiles in Babylon and portrays what follows as their letter to Jews who were remaining in Jerusalem. The community's prayer (based on Dan. 9) recognizes the exile as God's just punishment for the people's sins and appeals to God's mercy and goodness and to the glory attached to God's name as reasons why they might be allowed to return from exile to their homeland and to renew their covenant with God. The poem about searching for wisdom (echoing Job 28) reflects on how hard it is to obtain real wisdom and affirms that it can be found in the Torah. The poem of consolation (based on Isa. 40–66) acknowledges that the exile was just punishment for Israel's sins but also offers encouragement and hope about returning to Jerusalem and the renewal of God's people. Thus, the book as a whole moves from the people's confession of sin and sadness over the exile, through a meditation on God's mysterious ways and an equation between wisdom and the Torah, to hope for return from exile.

The language, images, and theological ideas in Baruch are deeply rooted in the OT. The complex of sin, exile, repentance, and return is a communal application of the "law of retribution." According to that principle, wise and righteous persons prosper while foolish and wicked persons are justly punished in this life. Though taken for granted in many parts of the Bible (especially in the Deuteronomistic History, the Prophets, and Proverbs), this "law" is criticized and contested in the books of Job and Ecclesiastes. In Baruch it is accepted as a premise and serves as the starting point for interpreting Israel's communal exile in the sixth century BCE, for urging the people's moral renewal, and for holding out hope for a national revival.

The major question raised by the book of Baruch is whether this explanation of Israel's national tragedy in the sixth century BCE is truly adequate. Modern scholars tend to explain these events mainly in political, socioeconomic, and historical terms. The book's theological appeal to the schema of sin, exile, repentance, and return can be criticized as too easily blaming the victims or can be explained away as a futile attempt to make sense out of what has happened (an example of cognitive dissonance). However one might judge the adequacy of Baruch's explanation of the Jewish exile in the sixth century BCE, attempts to apply it or something like it to the Shoah (Holocaust) of twentieth-century Europe raise difficult ethical questions. These include the lack of correlation between the Jewish people's alleged "sins" and their "punishment," and the religious claims made by some about the providential significance of Zionism and the modern State of Israel.

See also Deuterocanonical/Apocryphal Books; Exile; Isaiah

Bibliography

Feuerstein, R. *Das Buch Baruch: Studien zur Textgestalt und Auslegungsgeschichte*. EUS 32/614. Lang, 1997; Harrington, D. *Invitation to the Apocrypha*. Eerdmans, 1999, 92–102; Wright, J. *Baruch ben Neriah: From Biblical Scribe to Apocalyptic Seer*. University of South Carolina Press, 2003.

Daniel J. Harrington

Beatitudes

The Beatitudes are sayings of Jesus found in Matt. 5:3–12, as the introductory section of the Sermon on the Mount. They set the theme of the sermon as deliverance coming with the kingdom of God (Matthew uses "kingdom of heaven" to avoid overusing the holy name of God). They are also found in a shorter version in Luke 6:20–22, at the beginning of the Sermon on the Plain. This article addresses the Matthean version of the Beatitudes.

Robert Guelich has shown that the Beatitudes frequently quote Isa. 61, which announces the deliverance that comes with God's reign. The Beatitudes are not like ideals in wisdom literature, "more concerned with 'worldly well-being' growing out of a life lived in conformity with the principles of God and the wise"; they are like "beatitudes in prophetic literature . . . addressed to those who because of their faithfulness would be saved from the last judgment and enter the new age" (Guelich, "Matthean Beatitudes," 417). Like Isaiah, Jesus is saying that we are being made participants in God's deliverance, and therefore we are joyful.

The first part of each beatitude is usually translated as "Blessed are . . . ," but the Greek word *makarios* usually means "joyful," here in celebration of the coming of God's deliverance. Joy is one of the marks of the reign of God in Isaiah's teachings, and Jesus regularly cites Isaiah when he proclaims the reign of God. We see the connection better when we translate each beatitude as "Joyful are . . ." The second part of each beatitude names a characteristic of those who experience deliverance in the coming reign of God.

The first and third beatitudes refer to the same key word in Isa. 61:1, *ʿănāwîm*, which means "poor, oppressed by the rich and powerful, powerless, needy, humble, lowly, pious." It connotes both the economically poor and the humble before God. We could follow Clarence Jordan's exegesis and translate them as "the poor and humble before God, whose wills are surrendered to God" (Jordan 21–22, 24–25). The conventional translation "poor in spirit" and "meek" can be confusing. The Greek word translated "meek" (*prays*) is used in the Bible of Moses (Num. 12:3 LXX) and Jesus (Matt. 11:29; cf. 21:5), both of whom had the strength to confront the ruling authorities of their times. That is hardly what the English word *meek* has come to mean. Guelich writes, "For Matthew, the *poor in spirit* are those who find themselves waiting, empty-handed, upon God alone for their hope and deliverance while beset with abuse and rejection by those in their own social and religious context" (Guelich, *Sermon on the Mount*, 75).

The second beatitude, mentioning "those who mourn" (Gk. *penthountes*), refers to being sad because of a loss, but also repenting. Jesus calls us to repent because the kingdom of God is at hand. Christians who pray for God's reign to come become aware that our lives and society are far from God's reign. They want to end the sinning and serve God. The prophet Amos pronounces God's judgment on those who do not mourn: they oppress the poor and crush the needy, and then they say, "Bring something to drink!" (Amos 4:1). God proclaims, "Woe to those who . . . are not grieved over the ruin of Joseph! . . . I will turn your feasts into mourning" (Amos 6:1, 6; 8:10).

The fourth beatitude refers to hungering and thirsting for restorative justice. "Righteousness" in our culture means "being a good and respectable individual," which is not the meaning of the Hebrew *ṣĕdāqâ* that stands behind Jesus' teaching: justice that restores rightness and community to the excluded and oppressed.

In the fifth beatitude, being "merciful" indicates being generous in doing deeds of deliverance.

In the sixth beatitude, the nature of our "heart" is seen in how we relate to people. Being "pure in heart" means that one has integrity, is willing God's will in one's being and doing.

The seventh beatitude refers to *eirēnopoioi*, "peacemakers," as in the English translation.

The eighth and ninth beatitudes concern those who are persecuted for their struggle to follow Jesus and to achieve restorative justice.

The third part of each beatitude celebrates the promise of participation in God's coming reign: theirs is the kingdom of heaven, they will be comforted by God, inherit the earth, be filled, receive God's compassion, see God, be called "children of God," and have the kingdom of heaven and great reward in God. Jesus says that we have this now, but in the size of a mustard seed.

See also Imitation of Jesus; Kingdom of God; Sermon on the Mount

Bibliography

Crosby, M. *Spirituality of the Beatitudes: Matthew's Challenge for First World Christians*. Orbis, 1981; Galilea, S. *The Beatitudes: To Evangelize as Jesus Did*. Trans. R. Barr. Orbis, 1984; Guelich, R. "The Matthean Beatitudes: 'Entrance-Requirements' or Eschatological Blessings?" *JBL* 95 (1976): 415–34; idem. *The Sermon on the Mount: A Foundation for Understanding*. Word, 1982; Hamm, D. *The Beatitudes in Context: What Luke and Matthew Meant*. Michael Glazier, 1990; Jordan, C. *Sermon on the Mount*. Rev. ed. Judson, 1974; Lambrecht, J. *The Sermon on the Mount: Proclamation and Exhortation*. Michael Glazier, 1985.

Glen H. Stassen

Benevolence

Benevolence is an intentional disposition to perform good deeds or charitable acts. It is the disposition that corresponds to acts of beneficence. Genesis 1:10–12 emphasizes God's benevolence in the acts of creation. Other OT passages exhort benevolence and link it to both wisdom and societal justice (Deut. 15:11; Prov. 14:21; Isa. 1:17; Mic. 6:8). Jesus commands benevolence as a demonstration of agapic love (Matt. 5:43–48; 7:12). Throughout the NT benevolence toward believers and nonbelievers connotes both a descriptive (Acts 2:42–47; 4:32–35; 6:1–4; Rom. 15:25–26; 1 Cor. 16:1–3; 2 Cor. 8:1–4; 1 John 3:17–18) and normative (Acts 20:35; Rom. 12:13; 2 Cor. 9:12–13; Gal. 6:10; 1 Tim. 5:3–16; Jas. 1:27) dimension of Christian life.

Modern discussions regarding benevolence center on the nature of benevolence (whether it is disinterested or self-interested), its origins (whether they are divine or natural), and its content (see Flescher and Worthen). Recent scientific literature has suggested that benevolence contributes to human well-being and health (see Post). Comparative religious studies have documented widespread exhortations to benevolence and beneficence (see Neusner and Chilton). Evolutionary naturalism has suggested adaptive fitness as a reason for benevolent behavior (see Sober and Wilson).

See also Agape; Altruism; Good, The; Koinonia; Value, Value Judgments

Bibliography

Flescher, A., and D. Worthen. *The Altruistic Species: Scientific, Philosophical, and Religious Perspectives of Human Benevolence.* Templeton Foundation Press, 2007; Neusner, J., and B. Chilton. *Altruism in World Religions.* Georgetown University Press, 2005; Post, S. *Research on Altruism and Love: An Annotated Bibliography of Major Studies in Psychology, Sociology, Evolutionary Biology, and Theology.* Templeton Foundation Press, 2003; Sober, E., and D. Wilson. *Unto Others: The Evolution of Unselfish Behavior.* Harvard University Press, 1998.

Daniel E. McFee

Bestiality *See* Sexual Ethics

Betting *See* Gambling

Bigamy *See* Marriage and Divorce

Bioethics

Bioethics is a relatively new word, fashioned in the 1970s from the Greek words *bios* ("life") and *ēthikē* ("ethics"). It refers to the interdisciplinary inquiry concerning the moral questions prompted by developments in the life sciences and healthcare. It includes medical ethics, which focuses on the conduct and character of those who provide healthcare, but it also includes the use of healthcare by patients or consumers, the ethics of research on human subjects, the ethics of animal research, the ethics of public health practices and policy, the relation of ecological issues to health, and a whole range of other issues related to the life sciences. A number of entries in this volume treat various special topics within bioethics.

Bioethics sometimes is traced to developments in the mid-twentieth century. At the end of World War II, stories of medical research prompted both great horror and great hope. The Nuremberg Tribunal disclosed the horrific stories of Nazi experimentation on human subjects, but the development of penicillin saved the lives of many soldiers and prompted the hope that medical research could bring a triumph over dreaded diseases as dramatic as any victory in war. The postwar success of the "March of Dimes" against polio nurtured that hope. Soon, developments in medical research and technology prompted a series of dramatic moral questions, leaving the public sometimes horrified, sometimes hopeful, and frequently confused. In the 1960s came revelations of the abuse of human subjects in medical research within the United States. The same decade saw the first heart transplant, the first pediatric intensive care units, the clinical use of respiratory support to prolong life, the advances in genetics that made it possible to diagnose individuals, including fetuses, as either affected by or carriers of certain genetic traits, and more. The questions were inescapable: May we use some people to learn how to care for other people? How can we take a beating heart from someone without killing that person? How should we decide who gets a scarce medical resource? Now that we can keep someone alive on a respirator, must we? Now that we can diagnose a fetus with Trisomy 18 and abort, may we? Who should live? Who should decide? And who should pay?

The new powers of medicine inevitably led to new questions, but the questions inevitably were moral questions, questions that could not finally be answered by science alone. By the 1970s, an interdisciplinary conversation had started about these questions, and bioethics was born. It is more accurate, however, to say that bioethics was resuscitated. There were, after all, long and worthy traditions of reflection concerning the ordinary human events of suffering and dying, giving birth and caring, not only among physicians but also within religious communities. Theologians were important contributors to those initial conversations, in part simply because they had traditions on which to draw (Smith). Bioethics, however, was quickly secularized as people looked for arguments that would be universally persuasive. It typically examined particular cases or public policies in the light of four presumably universal principles: respect for persons, beneficence (doing good), nonmaleficence (doing no harm), and justice. Even the theologians who contributed to the continuing conversation frequently sounded more like followers of Kant or Mill than followers of Jesus.

There has been, however, a revival of interest in theological reflection on bioethics, and for two reasons. The first reason was the growing suspicion that even the four principles mentioned above mean different things within different particular moral traditions and communities. The criticism of Enlightenment foundationalism by philosophers such as Alasdair MacIntyre encouraged Christian theologians to speak candidly as Christians in public discourse. Still more important, however, was the recognition that within the church many faithful people wanted to live and die and give birth and care with Christian integrity, not just with impartial rationality. The church was recognized as an important community of moral discourse and discernment concerning bioethics.

Faithful Christian reflection about bioethics sets the questions prompted by developments in medical science and technology within the context of Christian convictions and practices. One of those convictions is the authority of Scripture, and one of those practices is reading Scripture as somehow normative for the Christian life. Conversations about bioethics within the church will from time to time (and again and again) turn to Scripture for wisdom and guidance.

Attending to Scripture: Some Problems

When Christians turn to Scripture for guidance in bioethics they quickly encounter problems. The first problem is that Scripture is silent about heart transplants and respirators, about genetic diagnoses and in-vitro fertilization. It is folly to expect Scripture to provide direct answers to moral questions posed by the developments in contemporary science and technology.

The second problem, however, is that when Scripture does speak about biology or about human sickness and healing, its words seem sometimes, well, quaint. Reading Scripture, Christians confront again and again a strange biology and a strange world of sickness and healing. There is Jacob's success as a herdsman in producing speckled sheep by whittling white spots on sticks where the animals bred (Gen. 30:25–43). There is the bronze serpent on a pole with healing power (Num. 21:4–9), later destroyed by Hezekiah because it had evidently become an idol and a charm (2 Kgs. 18:4). There is King Asa being chided by the Chronicler for seeking "help from physicians" for his diseased feet (2 Chr. 16:12). There is again and again the assumption of a causal connection between sin and sickness. It is there, for example, in the promise of God after the exodus, "If you will listen carefully to the voice of the LORD your God, and do what is right in his sight, . . . I will not bring upon you any of the diseases that I brought upon the Egyptians" (Exod. 15:26). And it is there again in a sick man's lament, "There is no soundness in my flesh because of your indignation; there is no health in my bones because of my sin" (Ps. 38:3). From our own world of sickness there are many unanswered questions: What is the diagnosis? What is the prognosis? Is there a doctor in the house? In Scripture, however, there is no concern with a medical diagnosis or with securing the aid of a physician or even with getting a couple of aspirin (which the Sumerians had discovered at least a millennium earlier). There are different expectations of the sick in Scripture: not to send for a physician or a magician, but simply to be a penitent and a supplicant before God. It would be easy to multiply examples. Yet to be mentioned are the NT exorcisms, for example, or the assumption that diseases and psychoses can be traced to the power of demons. It is a strange world of sickness in Scripture.

The third problem is the diversity of voices within Scripture. As we have noted, many passages assume a causal connection between sin and sickness, but Job rejected the assumption and resisted the accusations of his friends. And Jesus too evidently rejected the putative connection between a man's blindness and either his own sin or his parents' sin (John 9:2–3). And while the Chronicler chided Asa for consulting physicians, in the Apocrypha the sage Jesus ben Sirach effortlessly integrated physicians and their medicines into Jewish faith in God the healer. "Honor physicians for their services," he said, "for the Lord created them. . . . The Lord created medicines out of the earth, and the sensible will not despise them" (Sir. 38:1, 4). There are different voices also about the causes of disease, whether "the hand of the LORD" (1 Sam. 5:6) or natural causes (Sir. 31:20–22; 37:27–31) or the power of demons, the explanation that took center stage only in the NT.

Enough has been said here to evidence the need for caution as Christians turn to Scripture for wisdom about medicine and bioethics. But one other problem deserves brief consideration. It is a problem not with Scripture but with us as readers of Scripture. Appeals to Scripture have sometimes led to foolishness, not to wisdom. Appeals to Scripture, it must be admitted, sometimes have done a great deal of harm. When Gen. 3:16, "In pain you shall bring forth children," was quoted to oppose pain relief for women in labor, a great deal of harm was done. When some Dutch Calvinists refused to have their children immunized against polio because Jesus said, "Those who are well have no need of a physician" (Matt. 9:12), a great deal of harm was done. When the Bible was quoted to argue that AIDS was God's punishment for homosexual behavior, a great deal of harm was done. These are abuses of Scripture, to be sure, but people have nevertheless been harmed—notably, women and children and those on the margins, seldom "righteous" adult males. The abuse of Scripture is one more reason to be cautious when we turn to Scripture.

Hermeneutical Issues

The necessity for caution should prompt attention to hermeneutical issues. Acknowledging that Scripture is *somehow* authoritative also for bioethics, we must give attention to *how* it is authoritative. Scripture's authority for bioethics has been construed in various ways. It sometimes has been taken to provide "a system of divine laws" (Frame 10; see also Payne) that supplies a moral handbook for bioethics. Sometimes its moral authority has been construed as the requirement to love one's neighbor, and then love itself has been variously construed either as a principle of "equal regard" or as an ideal of beneficence (and social utility). Sometimes Scripture is taken to reveal certain "goods" that belong to human flourishing. And sometimes it has been construed as the revelation of God's character and way, to which Christians must respond faithfully. Alongside the diversity of Scripture stands the diversity of ways of reading it as normative for bioethics.

Two hermeneutical proposals, however, are widely accepted. First, the Bible provides neither a medical textbook nor a moral handbook for contemporary bioethics (contra Frame; Payne). We may not simply repeat its words today as if they provided a timeless moral code for the new powers of medicine. Second, the story has hermeneutical priority. The wholeness of Scripture is fundamentally a narrative wholeness. Every part of Scripture must be read as a part of that whole, and appeals to Scripture must be tested by whether they fit that whole.

The Story of Scripture

Scripture gives us a story. It is a story that renders God's character and reveals God's will and way with God's people. It is a story of God's people too, a story that Christians own as their own, that can form their character and conduct, that is constitutive of Christian identity and determinative for Christian discernment. In our own strange world of sickness and medicine, we read the Bible and remember our story, struggling to discern how to perform it faithfully in sickness and in health and with the new powers medicine gives (see Verhey 39–67).

A story of creation. The story begins, of course, "in the beginning." In the beginning God created all things. Because God made all things, nothing that God made is God. There is a prohibition of idolatry in the creation narrative no less than in the Decalogue. Whatever we are to say about health and the new powers of medicine, this much is clear from the beginning: we may not make idols of them. The suspicion of idolatry has been a consistent characteristic of biblical reflection about health and medicine from the Chronicler to the early church and down the centuries to this very day.

We tend to think that we have outgrown idolatry, that it is a sin of "primitive" people, but the temptations to idolatry are no less present to the modern world than to the ancient world. Anywhere a good exists, it can evoke an extravagant and ultimate loyalty and prompt extravagant and final expectations. And health and healing are very real goods. They touch us near the center of our hopes and fears, where we live and die, give birth and shudder in pain.

Health is a good gift of God, but it can be a very demanding idol. The beginning of the story should make Christian bioethics a little suspicious of the "cult of health" in our culture, a cult within which hospitals and exercise facilities are the temples and doctors and dieticians are the priests. To be sure, few bend the knee before Asclepius or Gula, the ancient gods of healing, but the high god in the contemporary pantheon of idols may well be technology, especially medical technology with its healing power. Patients kneel at this shrine when they visit the doctor's office to petition for a piece of medical wizardry to be provided with technological grace. Francis Bacon (1561–1626) may have been a Puritan, but the project of modernity that bears his name, with its reduction of knowledge to power over nature and its extravagant confidence in technology as the faithful savior, is idolatrous (on "the Baconian project," see McKenny).

Children too are good gifts of God, but they are not gods. When undertaken with the presumption that human fulfillment and flourishing depend on having children "of one's own," assisted reproductive technologies are idolatrous. When such technologies are joined to genetic knowledge in an effort to make perfect children, the project is folly. And when that project is undertaken with the presumption that children are the hope of the future, it is idolatrous. God's power and grace are the hope of the future—also for our children.

There is a second implication of the creation story: God made all things, and made all things good. God said as much in the story, of course. The gnostics could not bear this story. They thought the soul, or spirit, to be good because it has a good source, and the body to be evil because it has an evil source. Contemporary dualists are more likely to say that the body counts for little, and that the soul, the mind, the capacity for reason and choice are what really count. But the creation story is a narrative prohibition of this dualism too. The story should make Christian bioethics a little suspicious not only of the Baconian project but also of that other pillar of modernity, Cartesian dualism.

We are, from the beginning, embodied creatures, "embodied souls or ensouled bodies," as Paul Ramsey used to say, not to be reduced either to biological organisms or to disembodied souls. The implications of this embodiment for bioethics are legion. When we ask, "Who counts as a person?" whether at the beginnings or the endings of life, embodiment resists the reduction of "personhood" to capacities for agency. When we would be attentive to suffering, embodiment reminds us that neither the technical expert who reduces the patient to manipulable nature nor the bioethical expert who reduces the patient to capacities for agency can really understand suffering, for people suffer neither as mere organisms nor as ghostly minds but as embodied selves. And when we would procreate, embodiment resists reducing human procreation either to mere biology or to a free contract transcending our bodies.

A story of human sin. Creation, of course, is not the end of the story. The story continued and the plot thickened with human sin. And hard on the heels of sin came death—not mortality, it must be said. Mortality is simply given with the creation, the simple sign that we do not have life the way God has life. But the threatening horror of death, the threat of alienation from our own bodies and from our communities and from God—that came hard on the heels of human sin. And sickness became the "forerunner and messenger" (Barth 366) of death, and of its threats.

The story of human sin, of human pride and sloth, is a story still on display—sometimes in the use of the new powers of medicine and sometimes in the refusal to use them, and it surely is relevant to bioethics (Elshtain).

A story of blessing. Human sin left an ugly mark on the world God made good; the "curse" fell heavy upon it. But God would not let sin and sickness or death and the curse have the last word. God came again to covenant and to bless. It is a long story. God called Abraham and blessed him, called him to be a blessing to the nations (Gen. 12:1–4), and the blessing of God would reach "far as the curse is found." The blessing of God, as the stories of the ancestors make clear, reaches into the ground in wells of water, into the womb with Isaac (whose Hebrew name refers to "laughter"), and into sociality in the ancestors' willingness to make covenants of peace. The blessing of God includes health, but it cannot be reduced to health as if health were the *summum bonum.* In these stories, moreover, the blessings are wrought in part by ancient technologies: well-digging, farming (Isaac [Gen. 26]), herding (Jacob [Gen. 30]), and public administration (Joseph [Gen. 41]). The fault is not in technology. Technology can bring blessing, can help to lift the curse a little. But the fault is not in nature either. The fault is still traced to human sin. And although technology can bring blessing, it is not the final solution. It too can be co-opted by pride and greed. The Tower of Babel, symbol of humanity's highest spiritual aspirations and greatest technological accomplishments, makes that clear enough.

When some slaves cried out to God, God heard those cries and answered them with the promise of liberation, and that promise included deliverance from "the diseases [of] the Egyptians" (Exod. 15:26). God sealed that promise with his word and with his name, "I am the LORD who heals you" (Exod. 15:26). This verse Karl Barth called "the divine Magna Carta in all matters of health" (Barth 369), strange for its assumption of the connection of sin and sickness but stunning for its promise of health in God's good future.

It is a long story, but at the center of that story, and at the center of the Christian canon, is Jesus of Nazareth. God came yet again to covenant and to bless.

The center of the story: Jesus. Jesus came announcing that the good future of God was "at hand" (Mark 1:15), and he already made that future present and its power felt in his works of healing and in his words of blessing. He suffered and died, but God raised him up. The stories of Jesus as healer, preacher, sufferer, and risen have formed the Christian tradition about medical care from the beginning and should continue to form a Christian bioethics.

In his healing ministry Jesus made known God's cause. When the dead were raised and those who were thought in the first century to be "like dead" or under the power of death were healed (Luke 7:22–23), the power and the purpose of God were disclosed. God's cause is life, not death; God's cause is human flourishing, including the flourishing we call "health," not sickness. The memory of Jesus and the hope for God's good future require that bioethics celebrate life, not death, but enable it to meet even death with courage and hope. In memory of Jesus and in hope the Christian community will delight in human flourishing, including the human flourishing we call "health," but also will be able to endure, with confidence in God, even the diminishing of human strength we call "sickness."

The Christian community today may praise God for medicine, for its research and new powers. It may not idolize either health or medicine, but it may, following the wisdom of Jesus ben Sirach, see medicine as a gift of God the creator. And it may also, in memory of Jesus, construe medicine as a servant of God the redeemer, as a healing ministry today, as a way God's future may still be given token. Physicians and nurses within the Christian community may construe their professions as callings, indeed as holy callings, and themselves as disciples of the healing Christ. To condemn medicine because God is the healer would be like condemning governments because God is the ruler or families because God is the father. Of course, if medicine pretends to be messianic, if it presumptuously thinks of itself as the ultimate healer, then its arrogance may be and must be condemned, just as the arrogance of governments and families that make pretentious claims to ultimacy may be and must be condemned. A modest medicine may be granted its modest and honorable place under God and alongside other measures that protect and promote life and health, including good nutrition, public sanitation, a clean environment, and the like.

The healing ministry of Jesus was a sign of God's triumph not only over the power of death but also over the power of Satan. Although exorcisms seem strange and alien to many of us, "possession" was widespread in the ancient Mediterranean; at least the demonological understanding of sickness and psychosis was widespread, and Jesus evidently shared that understanding. He explained his exorcisms neither as collusion with Satan nor as magic but as the good future of God made present and real: "If it is by the finger of God that I cast out the demons, then the kingdom of God has come to you" (Luke 11:20). His exorcisms were of one piece with God's final triumph over the powers of evil and already diminished Satan's dominance.

To remember this Jesus and to welcome the good future of God is to celebrate his exorcisms and somehow to make the stories of exorcism our own. That does not mean that we must account for pathologies and psychoses in the strange and alien categories of the first century, as the power of demons at work. The texts are not addressed to twentieth-century scientific and clinical questions and may not be used to prescribe either the way to understand such suffering today or the way to provide therapy. The stories are strange, but they can remind contemporary bioethics that God will triumph over all that hurts and harms and demeans persons and over all that destroys human community. The exorcisms also disclose something of God's cause. One decisive characteristic of "possession" was precisely that—possession. The sick had no control of themselves; they were possessed, subject to the power of the demons; their speech and action had no genuine connection with who they were. A second decisive characteristic of possession was isolation. The sick were separated from their community, alienated from the very ones who would care if they could. The strong man in Mark 5, for example, "lived among the tombs; and no one could restrain him any more, even with a chain" (5:3). But Jesus healed him, restored him to self-control (5:15), and said, "Go home to your friends" (5:19). The exorcisms freed persons to be themselves and to be with others. They restored persons to their own identity and to their community. The cause of God made known in Jesus' healing ministry is human flourishing, and the human flourishing made known in the exorcisms involves integrity and community.

Bioethics must respect the integrity and the community of the sick. In Christian community and in memory of Jesus, physicians may use their best medical skills and knowledge to explain what is happening in and to the sick. However, they must use those skills and that knowledge in ways that honor God and serve God's cause, including not only life and health but also the integrity of the sick and their community with those who are well. We remember Jesus and anticipate God's future by standing with those who lack control over their own lives, who lack control over themselves, by standing with the weak and the powerless, and by standing against whatever and whoever hinders and frustrates their freedom to be or to act in ways that have integrity with their identity. Sometimes sickness threatens such freedom, and then medicine can serve God's cause by using its powers. But sometimes medicine itself can threaten the powers of persons to live (or die) with integrity or within community, and then medicine can serve God's cause only by not using its powers. When, for example, medicine can only prolong one's dying, or when by its technological interventions it can only rob the dying of dignity and separate the dying from the human companionship of friends and family, then medicine must acknowledge that the moral limit to its powers comes long before the technological limit of its powers.

The healing ministry of Jesus is remembered in the Gospels and still remembered in the churches. It should form a people, and a medicine among those people, disposed to protect life, not to practice hospitality to death; disposed to sustain health, not to welcome sickness; disposed to respect the embodied integrity of people, not to run roughshod over their freedom and identity; disposed to nurture community, not to isolate and alienate the sick.

Jesus was not just a healer, however; he preached "good news to the poor" (Matt. 11:5; Luke 4:18; 7:22). His words of blessing to the poor and his compassion for them were no less a token and a promise of God's good future than his works of healing (e.g., Luke 6:20). In memory of Jesus, bioethics must be attentive to the needs of the poor. That memory too should form a people, and a medicine among those people, disposed to insist on justice for the poor and to practice kindness toward them. The needs of the poor are not all (or even mainly) medical; even their health-related needs are not all (or even mainly) medical. A Christian bioethics should include a concern to so order our communities that no one is doomed to an untimely death resulting from the lack of things such as clean air and pure water, adequate nutrition, periodic rest from labor, and security from violence. The need for medical care may seem relatively insignificant against the background of that list of more fundamental human needs. But the poor do have needs for medical care, and the need for medical care never seems insignificant when you have it. A Christian bioethics will surely include a concern to provide secure access to a decent standard of healthcare for those who need it, including the poor.

Jesus was not only the healer, not only the preacher of good news to the poor, but also the one who "suffered under Pontius Pilate, was crucified, dead, and buried." This too has important implications for Christian bioethics. The first implication is simply that although life and health are good gifts of God, they are not the greatest goods. On the one hand, life and the flourishing we call "health" belong to the creative and redemptive cause of God. The signs of it are breath and a blessing, a rainbow and God's own sanction, a commandment and a healing ministry, and finally, of course, an empty tomb. Life and its flourishing must, therefore, be recognized and celebrated as goods, as goods against which we may not turn without turning against the cause of God. They are to be received with thanksgiving and used with gratitude. Acts that aim at death and suffering do not fit this story, do not cohere with devotion to the cause of God or with gratitude for the gifts of God. On the other hand, life and its flourishing are not the ultimate goods. They are not "second gods" (Barth 392). Jesus walked a path steadily and courageously that led to his suffering and to his death. Therefore, Christians may not live as though either survival or ease, their life or their health, were the law of their being. Sometimes life must be risked, let go, given up. And sometimes health must be risked and suffering shared for the sake of God's cause in the world. The refusal ever to let die and the attempt to eliminate suffering altogether are signs not of faithfulness but of idolatry. And if life and its flourishing are not the ultimate goods, neither are death and suffering the ultimate evils. They need not be feared finally, for death and suffering are not as strong as the promise of God. One need not use all one's resources against them, but only act with integrity in the face of them.

The second implication is truthfulness. Without the cross—this reminder of human suffering and of the silence of God, this testimony of the anguish and the helplessness even of Jesus—the church is always at risk of distorting the good news into a kind of Pollyanna triumphalism and then of self-deceptively ignoring or denying the sad truth about our world. There is a spiritual enthusiasm that supposes that faith provides a charm against sickness and sadness, that prayer works like magic to end our suffering and grief, and that Scripture will put ambiguity to flight. But there is also a technological enthusiasm that supposes that some new piece of medical wizardry will finally rescue the human condition from its vulnerability to death and suffering. Jesus knew better. He taught his disciples not how to avoid suffering but how to share it.

This points to the third implication: compassion, both God's compassion and our calling. The good news is that God shares the suffering. The good news is that Jesus made the human cry of lament his own cry (Ps. 22:1; Matt. 27:46; Mark 15:34). When Christians remember the cross, they acknowledge the sad truth about our world, but also they celebrate the glad tidings that God cares, that God does not abandon the sufferer. To those who suffer, the story of Jesus provides an unshakable assurance that they do not suffer alone, that they are not and will not be abandoned, that Jesus suffers with them, that God cares. But a Christian bioethics will also call the community to share the suffering of others. The presumption that we can altogether eliminate suffering has sometimes led to abandoning (or eliminating) the patient when medicine cannot eliminate the suffering. A Christian compassion will neither kill nor abandon a patient. It will care even when, or especially when, medicine cannot cure (see Verhey 99–144).

Finally, there is a fourth implication for bioethics in the memory of Jesus' suffering, an implication that eminent historian of medicine Henry Sigerist called "the most revolutionary and decisive change" in the tradition of medicine: in memory of Jesus the sick were ascribed "a preferential position" (Sigerist 69–70). Christians are trained by the memory of Jesus' suffering and death to see in the sick and suffering—in their weakness and vulnerability, in their loneliness and pain—the very image of their Lord and to see in their care for them (or their abandoning them) an image of their care for Christ (or their abandonment of Christ). The classic text is Matt. 25:31–46, in which Jesus says, "Just as you did it to one of the least of these . . . , you did it to me."

The end of the story: already and not yet. This healer, this preacher of good news to the poor, this one who suffered under Pontius Pilate, was raised up as the "first fruits of those who have died" (1 Cor. 15:20). It was the promise of God's good future, of that day on which God "will wipe every tear from their eyes. Death will be no more; mourning and crying and pain will be no more, for the first things have passed away" (Rev. 21:4).

That good future, however, is not yet, still sadly not yet. In the meantime, although moral ambiguities are inescapable, Scripture can illumine both the enduring problems and the novel quandaries of health and healing, even it if does not tell us precisely what to do. In memory of Jesus the healer, and in hope, a Christian bioethics will not celebrate death or suffering as good; it will celebrate the powers God gives to intervene sometimes in a person's premature dying and to relieve a person's unnecessary suffering. In memory of Jesus the preacher of "good news to the poor," and in hope, a Christian bioethics will not delight when such powers, and the simpler things on which life and health depend, are not shared fairly and generously with the poor. In memory of Jesus who suffered and died, and in hope, a Christian bioethics will call on the community to practice Christ's compassion, signaling Christ's presence and care to those beyond cure on their own.

See also Abortion; Care, Caring; Death, Definition of; Death and Dying; Disability and Handicap; Dualism, Anthropological; Eugenics; Euthanasia; Health; Healthcare Ethics; Healthcare Systems in Scripture; Hospice; Infertility; Monism, Anthropological; Quality of Life; Reproductive Technologies; Sanctity of Human Life

Bibliography

Barth, K. *Church Dogmatics*. Vol. III/4. Trans. A. Mackay et al. T&T Clark, 1961; Elshtain, J. *Who Are We? Critical Reflections and Hopeful Possibilities*. Eerdmans, 2000; Frame, J. *Medical Ethics: Principles, Persons, and Problems*. Presbyterian & Reformed, 1988; Lammers, S., and A. Verhey, *On Moral Medicine: Theological Perspectives in Medical Ethics*. 2nd ed. Eerdmans, 1998; McKenny, G. *To Relieve the Human Condition: Bioethics, Technology, and the Body*. State University of New York Press, 1997; Payne, F. *Biblical/Medical Ethics: The Christian and the Practice of Medicine*. Mott Media, 1985; Reich, W., ed. *Encyclopedia of Bioethics*. 5 vols. Rev. ed. Simon & Schuster Macmillan, 1995; Sigerist, H. *Civilization and Disease*. Cornell University Press, 1943; Smith, D. "Religion and the Roots of the Bioethics Revival." Pages 9–18 in *Religion and Medical Ethics: Looking Back, Looking Forward*, ed. A. Verhey. Eerdmans, 1996; Verhey, A. *Reading the Bible in the Strange World of Medicine*. Eerdmans, 2003.

Allen Verhey

Birth Control

Birth control encompasses a range of practices associated with heterosexual genital sexual relations for the purpose of avoiding or terminating pregnancy. Birth control methods that prevent fertilization or implantation of fertilized ova are commonly known as "contraception." Contraception includes hormonal contraceptives, spermicidal agents such as copper intrauterine devices, and barrier methods such as condoms and diaphragms. Natural or behavioral forms of birth control differ from artificial contraception and include *coitus interruptus* (penile withdrawal from the vagina prior to ejaculation) and abstaining from vaginal intercourse. Abstinence might be total or only from vaginal sex, either permanently or restricted to fertile periods during a woman's menstrual cycle. Such periodic abstinence is often reductively referred to as the "rhythm method," a term that fails to indicate various methods, some very effective, for tracking fertility symptoms. Abortion and sterilization provide other birth control options. Emergency contraception involves taking a high dose of oral contraceptive within seventy-two hours of unprotected vaginal sex to prevent ovulation or fertilization. Male and female condoms and some forms of abstinence can also reduce the likelihood of some sexually transmitted diseases.

Aside from total sexual abstinence, all methods of birth control involve some risk of failure. Success rates vary considerably depending on the method and require responsible use. Artificial contraception, abortion, and sterilization also risk various side effects such as allergic reactions, weight gain, abnormal bleeding, and blood clots.

The earliest known forms of birth control included abstinence, *coitus interruptus*, natural resources used as spermicides, and cervical caps. Only in 1843 did scientists learn that conception occurs when sperm fertilize ova. In the United States the Comstock Act (1873) prohibited the distribution of "obscene" materials through the mail, including information about and devices for contraception and abortion. Margaret Sanger (1879–1966), a noted advocate for contraception, was charged with violating Comstock laws on several occasions. In 1918 legal paths opened for therapeutic uses of contraception. Sanger founded the American Birth Control League, the precursor to Planned Parenthood, in 1921. Sanger and others helped Gregory Pincus fund research to develop hormonal birth control in the form of an oral contraceptive called "the Pill." In 1960 the Food and Drug Administration approved the Pill. In *Griswold v. Connecticut* (1965) the Supreme Court ruled that laws against contraception violate the right to marital privacy. By this time, millions of women were taking the Pill. Its unsurpassed popularity as a birth control method, relative safety, and reliability contributed to profound changes in the West regarding the role of women in social and economic life.

Scripture and Tradition

Genesis provides one of the earliest references to birth control and the only explicit mention of it in Scripture (Gen. 38:8–10). Judah instructs Onan to father a child with his brother's widow. Onan instead "spills his seed on the ground." God is displeased and puts Onan to death. While some opponents of birth control cite this passage to support their position, others argue that Onan's offense is not *coitus interruptus* but rather his deliberate failure to perform his levirate duty.

Scripture does offer larger perspectives on human life, sexuality, marriage, and family that bear on the ethics of birth control. God is the author of life, calling humans to be fruitful and multiply (Gen. 1:28). Scripture also exhorts care for orphans (Exod. 22:22; Jas. 1:27) and stewardship over creation and one's resources. These latter themes can inform reflection on limiting biological offspring in order to welcome genetically unrelated children, serve the needy, or reduce overpopulation. Yet faith in divine providence, as evidenced in God's care for the lilies of the field (Matt. 6:25–34), can dispose Christian couples to accept unplanned children in hospitality and joy.

Several church fathers, such as Jerome and Augustine, opposed birth control. Opponents of birth control speak of the church's unbroken tradition of teaching against the practice. Christian communities were indeed united in their formal opposition to birth control, though there were complex pastoral practices in tension with Christian teaching in the early twentieth century (see Tentler). At the 1930 Lambeth Conference the Anglican Church approved birth control in limited circumstances, the same year Catholic teaching in *Casti connubii* declared its moral wrongness. Protestant traditions now variously approve of birth control and sanction it. Some evangelical Protestants eschew even behavioral forms of birth control and seek large numbers of biological offspring to build the kingdom of God, as in the Quiverfull movement (see Ps. 127:3–5).

According to Pope Paul VI's 1968 encyclical *Humanae vitae*, procreative responsibility includes a couple's thoughtful and prayerful discernment regarding the timing and spacing of children. However, not every means of regulating births is morally fitting. Catholic teaching about contraception is based more on natural-law arguments (and appeals to tradition) than scriptural arguments. The Catholic position is both principled, in that contraception is judged intrinsically wrong regardless of the agents' intention, and consequentialist, in that contraception's intrinsic violation of the human good is expected to yield damaging consequences such as promiscuity and male degradation of women.

The means employed for regulating births, argues *Humanae vitae*, must accord with the dignity of marriage and the marriage partners and therefore must respect the integrity of conjugal love. Christian tradition has long attributed two values to conjugal love, a unitive potential (it is capable of expressing and fostering intimacy between sexual partners) and procreative potential. Couples respect the integrity of conjugal love in every genital sexual encounter by never deliberately separating these values. Birth control methods for therapeutic reasons can be morally acceptable if the infertility that they cause is foreseen but not directly intended.

Humanae vitae met with much controversy and open dissent from a number of Catholics, particularly in the West. Opponents argue that conjugal love should be fruitful but reject the claim that each and every genital sexual act must be open to the possibility of procreation. Rather, fruitfulness should characterize the couple's relationship as a whole. The Catholic magisterium continues to teach that many forms of birth control are wrong even as pastoral and lay practice in the West often departs from this teaching; birth control remains a polarizing issue between conservative and liberal Catholics.

Ethical Issues

Some feminists argue that birth control is necessary for women's freedom from patriarchal control of reproduction. Others argue that patriarchy renders contraception yet another instrument aimed at making women available for male sexual satisfaction and attenuates men's reproductive responsibility.

Ethical issues surrounding birth control extend into legal disputes: whether healthcare workers who morally oppose contraception and abortion should be legally required to provide employees with health insurance that includes contraceptive coverage, offer emergency contraception, fill prescriptions for birth control, and at least provide information about and referrals for contraception and abortion. Given the possibility of sexual assault, any female of childbearing age is vulnerable to the possibility of unintended pregnancy brought about by rape. Although Catholic teaching prohibits the use of artificial contraception, US bishops assert women's right to defend themselves against pregnancy following rape, which opens a door for Catholic hospitals to provide emergency contraception.

Access to birth control bears on moral issues such as women's social equality, economic development for the poor, eugenics, and genocide. On one hand, access to birth control seems vital for personal reproductive responsibility, and the collective economic development that typically follows increases women's education and employment opportunities; on the other hand, access to birth control can function as an instrument of social control. Sanger, for instance, supported negative eugenics, limiting reproduction of "undesirable" populations. Black suspicion of government-sponsored birth control clinics developed during the 1960s. In 1967 the Pittsburgh chapter of the NAACP charged Planned Parenthood with promoting racial genocide through birth control. Given the range of issues that birth control impacts, relevant scriptural resources include those that speak to women's status, treatment of the poor, conscience, and the scope of secular authority.

See also Abortion; Adoption; Conception; Eugenics; Family Planning; Feminist Ethics; Orphans; Parenthood, Parenting; Population Policy and Control; Procreation; Reproductive Technologies; Roman Catholic Moral Theology; Sexual Ethics

Bibliography

Grisez, G. *Living a Christian Life*. Vol. 2 of *The Way of the Lord Jesus*. St. Paul's/Alba House, 2008; Maguire, D. *Sacred Rights: The Case for Contraception and Abortion in World Religions*. Oxford University Press, 2003; Noonan, J. *Contraception: A History of Its Treatment by the Catholic Theologians and Canonists*. Harvard University Press, 1966. Paul VI. *Humanae Vitae*. United States Catholic Conference, 1968; Smith, J. *Why* Humanae Vitae *Was Right: A Reader*. Ignatius Press, 1993; Tentler, L. *Catholics and Contraception: An American History*. Cornell University Press, 2004; United States Catholic Conference of Bishops. *Ethical and Religious Directives for Health Care Services*. 5th ed. United States Catholic Conference of Bishops, 2009.

Darlene Fozard Weaver

Blasphemy

In the OT and in Judaism, to use the divine name of God in an inappropriate way is blasphemy and is punishable by death (Lev. 24:10–16; *m. Sanh.* 6.4; 7.5; Philo, *Moses* 2.203–206). At the base of these ideas about blasphemy lies the command of Exod. 22:28 not to revile God or the leaders he appointed for the nation. In Second Temple Judaism, blasphemy covered a wide range of activity. In the Mishnah, *m. Sanh.* 7.5 defines a procedure for examining a charge and limits the offense to using the very name of God disrespectfully. Later rabbis debated whether the use of an alternative name qualifies as blasphemy (*m. Šebu.* 4.13; *b. Šebu.* 35a; *b. Sanh.* 55b–57a; 60a). Warnings were issued in such cases, but such usage does not appear, at least in the rabbinic period, to have carried an automatic death sentence.

There are acts of blasphemy. These include the use of substitute titles and a whole range of actions offensive to God. Acts of blasphemy concentrate on idolatry, a show of arrogant disrespect toward God, or the insulting of his chosen leaders.

Often those who blasphemed verbally also acted on their feelings. God manages to judge such offenses. Examples in Jewish exposition are Sisera, against God's people (Judg. 4:3; *Numbers Rab.* 10.2); Goliath, against God's people and worship of Dagon (1 Sam. 17; Josephus, *Ant.* 6.183); Sennacherib, against God's power (2 Kgs. 18–19; cf. Isa. 37:6, 23); Belshazzar, disrespect for God's presence (Dan. 3:29 Q [96]; Josephus, *Ant.* 10.233, 242); Manasseh, against the Torah (*Sipre* 112); and Titus, defaming the temple (*b. Giṭ* 56b; *'Abot R. Nat.* B 7). Acting against the temple is also blasphemous (1 Macc. 2:6; Josephus, *Ant.* 12.406).

There are a few texts involving Jesus and blasphemy. First, in Mark 2:7 Jesus is charged with blasphemy for forgiving sin. The charge revolves around Jesus directly exercising an exclusively divine prerogative (cf. Exod. 34:7). Here Jesus gives forgiveness without any cultic requirements, an approach pointing to Jesus' own authority.

In Mark 3:29 Jesus warns about blaspheming the Spirit, as opposed to other sins and blasphemies. Those who blaspheme the Spirit (i.e., deny what God does through Jesus) are guilty of an "eternal sin."

Finally, in Mark 14:53–65 Jesus is examined by the Jewish leadership, and his reply, appealing to a combination of Ps. 110:1 and Dan. 7:13–14, leads to a charge of blasphemy pronounced by the high priest and approved by the assembly. For them, Jesus' blasphemy operated at two levels. First, Jesus claimed that he would exercise comprehensive authority from God's side. Although Judaism might contemplate such a position for a few (*1 En.* 62; Ezek. Trag. 69–82), the leaders did not think that this Galilean teacher was a candidate. As a result, his remark would have been seen as a self-claim that was an affront to God's presence. Second, Jesus implicitly attacked the leaders by claiming to be their future judge (or by claiming a vindication by God). They held him in violation of Exod. 22:28, which commands that God's leaders not be cursed. Jesus' claim that their authority was nonexistent and that they would be judged represented a total rejection of their authority. The resurrection was evidence for Jesus in this difference of opinion.

See also Speech Ethics

Darrell L. Bock

Blessing and Cursing

Blessing and cursing are specific forms of performative speech. They enact their words rather than refer to something independent of them. They speak in both the optative and imperative moods, wishing and bestowing either good or evil. The speaker thereby intends a way of acting in addition to revealing an inner disposition (such as anger or love). It is too simple to equate receiving a blessing with reward. In the Bible, blessings often show themselves in material goods (Prov. 10:22). But Israel is subject to God's blessings and curses only because of Abraham's antecedent covenant (Deut. 11:26–28; 29:19–20) and the gift of land (Exod. 3:8). In Christian worship, liturgical blessings often follow the people's offering and God's return gift in the Eucharist. Every blessing is grace and gift, overflowing with goodness and boundless love.

Acting rightly is a fruit of the blessing to which it is tied. Against the Pelagian heresy (obedience merits a blessing), God's initiative makes human obedience possible. Furthermore, obeying per se is a blessing activity, even while not exhausting the blessing. This befits the excessiveness of divine goodness. Since blessing is the vehicle of the blessing (performative rather than indicative speech), an ethical act is never a complete blessing on its own, either in its intrinsic rightness or in its effects. The Beatitudes (Matt. 5:3–11) are not commands to specific ways of being (meek, poor in spirit), but rather indications of what God's kingdom is like so that any effects ("they shall see God") are themselves just as much blessings as are lives characterized by a particular ethic ("pure in heart"). Human blessing of God or of one another is always, respectively, either a gift returned or passed on. David thus blesses God at the gifts offered for building the temple: "Blessed are you, O Lord. . . . For all things come from you, and of your own have we given you" (1 Chr. 29:10, 14).

Cursing should be understood in relation to this, as terminating the reciprocity of blessing's gift. A curse calls down evil on God or others and refuses to return the initial blessing of life and speech. Since everything created is good (Gen. 1:31), it is not permitted even to curse the devil, who is a creature (Sir. 21:27). And since the purpose of human speech is to adore God (Augustine, *Enarrat. Ps.* 98.9), cursing God is blasphemy. The NT prohibits the cursing of enemies (Rom. 12:14), to whom God's love has been reasserted in Christ's abundant blessing to humanity. For Thomas Aquinas, cursing must intend not evil, but good (*ST* II-II, q. 76, a. 1–2), such as conforming with justice and so, paradoxically, with the logic of blessing. Cursing sin is therefore permitted, as is the cursing of inanimate objects (e.g., Gen. 3:17; Mark 11:14), only insofar as they are used to punish sin and enable larger blessing.

See also Beatitudes; Blasphemy; Enemy, Enemy Love; Speech Ethics

Craig Hovey

Body

The status of the body in Christian ethics has long been an ambivalent and debated one. A stark and hierarchical dualism between body and soul or between flesh and spirit is popularly assumed to provide a sound biblical basis for dealing harshly with the realities of embodiment and physicality. On the opposite end of the spectrum, the reductive materialism of empiricist science would shrink human existence to bodily existence, denying the human being as a spiritual creature in relationship to God. Yet the witness of Scripture in relation to questions about human bodies is far less simple than facile assumptions of dualism or materialism would suggest. Any seeming opposition between body and soul is made problematical by a careful reading of relevant biblical passages and by a biblical theology that recognizes the central importance of the body within the greater narrative of redemption. Many aspects of human life once believed to be purely spiritual are implicated in embodiment, but human life cannot be reduced to physical life in ways that underwrite treating human bodies as machines or commodities. The place of the body in Scripture challenges both hierarchical dualism and simplistic materialism. Both of these challenges entail important moral implications.

Scholars of the OT warn against imposing modern conceptual categories on a text that comes to us from a context very different from our own. The case of the understanding of bodies in the OT is one in which contemporary Westerners may be especially prone to import their own understandings of the body into the biblical text. We should not assume that the Hebrew *bāśār*, translated "flesh" or "body," exists in opposition to or is a problem for *nepeš*, often translated as "soul," in the way that the body is constructed as burden or prison in opposition to the soul in Western thought. The anthropology of the OT focuses on the whole human being in relationship to God. In the book of Psalms that relationship includes soul and body together. In Ps. 16:9 the "soul rejoices" and the "body also rests secure." In Ps. 31:9 the supplicant's grief includes both body and soul. Old Testament regulation of bodily life is an important part of observing the law. Fluids and discharges that are part of being a physical creature are regulated as part of the nation's obedience to God. This regulation is part of Israel's identity and often relates to the health and justice of the community as God's people. Rules about the body reveal the body's individual and corporate meaning. It is regulated to protect health and to direct people, individually and communally, toward God.

The primary NT referent for the word *body* is the physical body of Jesus of Nazareth. Jesus teaches against fearing the death of the body, not because the body is unimportant, but because the greater fear is "him who can destroy both soul and body in hell" (Matt. 10:28). The eye, as the lamp of the body, must be healthy lest "the whole body be full of darkness" (Matt. 6:23). The body is "more than clothing" (Matt. 6:25; Luke 12:23), and so the listener ought not to worry about what to wear. This lack of worry is not because the body is unimportant, but because the body has a greater purpose.

In Jesus' ministry, salvation embraces the body, allowing no separation between physical and spiritual needs. We see this in his mission statements, his ministry of healing, and profoundly in the Last Supper. There is a connection between the ordinary physical body of Jesus of Nazareth and the bread he breaks with his disciples shortly before his death. Christ's command "Take, eat; this is my body" (Matt. 26:26; cf. Mark 14:22; Luke 22:19) is central to a biblical understanding of the place of the body in Christian ethics.

There is considerable discussion in the literature of the use of the terms *sōma* ("body") and *sarx* ("flesh") in Paul's letters. There is a consensus, however, that Paul's understanding of the opposition between flesh and spirit is something very different from the body/soul dualism of Western thought. Paul was a Jew and thus was influenced in his understanding of the human being by the OT perspective. The Pauline *sarx* can be a value-neutral reference to the stuff of the physical body. Thus, it is often used to refer to the body of Jesus. The Pauline *sarx* can also be the whole human being under the condition of sin. When Paul speaks of the moral difficulties of life in the flesh, he is not referring to bodily life as such. Instead, he speaks of the whole of human life when it is controlled by sin. "While we were living in the flesh, our sinful passions, aroused by the law, were at work in our members to bear fruit for death" (Rom. 7:5). When one comes to the text of Paul's letters assuming hierarchical body/soul dualism, it is easy to suppose that the problem of flesh is simply that the body is evil, a weight that pulls the human being away from God. Paul does not use *sarx* in this way.

The great conflict in Paul's thought is not between the physical and the immaterial. It is not between body and soul. Rather, it is between the human being captive to sin and the human being controlled by the Spirit. Both ways of being human include the body. The Spirit is opposed not to the body but to sin, and "if the Spirit of him who raised Jesus from the dead dwells in you, he who raised Christ from the dead will give life to your mortal bodies also through his Spirit that dwells in you" (Rom. 8:11). The interesting moral question, then, is not "How can I be freed from my body?" but "What will my body look like when the Spirit gives it life?"

In 1 Cor. 15 the hope for the resurrection body is contrasted to the body as it is now known. The body now is the seed; the resurrection body is that which will grow. It is sown a *sōma psychikon*, raised a *sōma pneumatikon* (1 Cor. 15:44). The NRSV translation of *sōma psychikon* as "physical body" is unfortunate. It underwrites the tendency to assume that Paul is speaking here of body/soul dualism. Many translations instead describe the body that is sown as a "natural body." The contrast between the present and the resurrection is not between flesh and spirit but between bodies under the condition of sin, directed by the human desire, and the hope to which Paul points his reader, bodies under the leadership of the Spirit. The history of interpretation of this passage has been unrelentingly physical. Against gnostic visions, the hope of the resurrection body has been seen in the Christian tradition as maintaining material continuity with the *sōma psychikon*. The "flesh and blood" that cannot inherit the kingdom (1 Cor. 15:50) is not the physical body but human life under the condition of sin. In 2 Cor. 5:8 Paul says that "we would rather be away from the body and at home with the Lord," but this is a statement about the fragility of bodily life under sin and the dominion of death. Again, the "earthly tent" is the body under sin, not physicality itself. "For while we are still in this tent, we groan under our burden, because we wish not to be unclothed but to be further clothed, so that what is mortal may be swallowed up by life" (2 Cor. 5:4). The force of the interpretive tradition brings together 1 Cor. 15 and 2 Cor. 5 to claim a hope that the material stuff of the body will be changed but also will be in continuity with materiality as it is now known.

The body is for God. It is "not for fornication but for the Lord, and the Lord for the body" (1 Cor. 6:13). What follows is vital. The resurrection of the Lord is tied to the resurrection of humans in general, and for this reason, the life of the body takes on tremendous moral significance. The bodies of the Corinthians are "members of Christ" (1 Cor. 6:15). Union with a prostitute results in becoming "one body with her," and union with the Lord results in becoming "one spirit with him" (1 Cor. 6:16–17). There is something mystical at work here. The violation involved in fornication is anything but trivial. It involves sin "against the body itself" (1 Cor. 6:18), the body that is "a temple of the Holy Spirit" (1 Cor. 6:19). Holiness includes both body and spirit (1 Cor. 7:34). A key locus for a biblical ethics of the body might be 1 Cor. 6:20: "For you were bought with a price; therefore glorify God in your body."

In formulating a biblical ethics of the body, we must understand that individual bodies participate in far greater realities; they are in Adam or in Christ. "We, who are many, are one body in Christ, and individually we are members one of another" (Rom. 12:5). The "sharing in the body of Christ" in the broken bread (1 Cor. 10:16) makes all who partake into one body. "Discerning the body" at the supper is so important that eating and drinking without doing so results in judgment and even in weakness, illness, and death (1 Cor. 11:27–30). The twelfth chapter of 1 Corinthians is an important text for understanding the corporate body as the body of Christ. Paul reflects on the one body into which all are baptized and draws out the implications of the church as one body with many members. Dale Martin points out that although the analogy of the social body usually supported conservative hierarchy in the ancient world, "Paul's rhetoric questions this hierarchy" (Martin 94). In the body of Christ, the members need one another. A variety of gifts are given, and they are mutually interdependent. The parts of the social body that seem weakest are indispensable.

The body, individual and corporate, is integral to holiness. Paul images people who are "always carrying in the body the death of Jesus, so that the life of Jesus may also be made visible in our bodies" (2 Cor. 4:10). The body is something in which Paul can "carry the marks of Jesus branded on" it (Gal. 6:17). "He will transform the body of our humiliation that it may be conformed to the body of his glory, by the power that also enables him to make all things subject to himself" (Phil. 3:21). Paul's body is for God. He disciplines the body so that he "should not be disqualified" (1 Cor. 9:27). The holiness of the body, however, cannot be only about disciplining it. It has far greater positive than negative implications. In fact, "severe treatment of the body" can have "an appearance of wisdom" (Col. 2:23) but only indulges sinful desires. Sanctification includes all the aspects of the human life, as Paul prays for "spirit and soul and body" to be "kept sound and blameless" (1 Thess. 5:23).

Many major theological loci ought to illuminate a biblically grounded understanding of the body's relation to ethics. The doctrine of creation suggests that all those things Christians claim about creation as a whole also ought to be claimed about the body: as creation is good, so is the body. As creation is fallen, so the body is fallen as well. Creation, including the body, is completely dependent on the sovereign God. Human bodies should not be despised or idolized. The body is a good gift, one that should honor the giver.

Christian doctrine about what it means to be human, often referred to as theological anthropology, takes seriously the biblical picture discussed above when making claims about the constitution of the human being. The vast majority of the Christian tradition has understood the human being as a psychosomatic unity of body and soul. While not accepting hierarchical or moral dualism, most of the interpretative tradition has assumed that the human being is constituted both spiritually (either by a soul or by a soul and a spirit) and physically (by a body). The emphasis in recent theological discussion has been to point away from understanding this dual constitution as a moral dualism in which the physical body is negative and only the spiritual is valued. Attempting to be faithful to the place of the body in Scripture has led to a variety of efforts among contemporary philosophers and theologians to find language that denies both popular dualism and reductive materialism. In this vein, contemporary theologians have used various philosophical categories to speak about human psychosomatic unity. Some have reclaimed the language of Thomas Aquinas in which "the soul is the form of the body," and it is impossible to understand the human being without accounting for the body. John Cooper advocates a "holistic dualism" in which body and soul are seen as integrally knit together though still separable. Advocates of nonreductive materialism take the materialist emphases of contemporary science as instructive and claim that the human being *is* the body even while remaining a spiritual creature. These ways of articulating a philosophical rejection of moral dualism emphasize the unity of the spiritual and the physical in the human being and so value the body as constitutive of human life before God.

The church is the body of Christ. At the least, ecclesiology suggests that God's work for and with people includes the body, both individually and corporately. In the life of the church the human body is important, as is the way human beings relate to God through the body's senses. References to the body in the Letter to the Ephesians unfold the connections between ecclesiology and the body. The head of the church (Eph. 5:23; cf. Col. 1:18) is Jesus Christ, who holds the body together and "promotes the body's growth in building itself up in love" (Eph. 4:16). The saints are to be equipped "for the work of ministry, for the building up of the body of Christ" (Eph. 4:12). Christ as head of the church body nourishes it, holds it together, and "grows it with a growth that is from God" (Col. 2:19).

In the sacraments materiality meets materiality, water and wine meet flesh and blood, and something spiritual occurs. The existence of the sacraments is an affirmation of the importance of the body to Christian practice and piety. Prayer and liturgy include the body. The postures of prayer, the psychosomatic acts of worship, are at the heart of God's purpose for bodily creatures.

Christology is central to a Christian ethics of the body. In the incarnation the Word becomes flesh (John 1:14). Jesus took on all that it means to be human. Thus, in Jesus, God has a body. The body of Jesus Christ is the site of the reconciliation of humanity (Col. 1:24). Sanctification is accomplished through "the offering of the body of Jesus once for all" (Heb. 10:10). Jesus "bore our sins in his body on the cross" (1 Pet. 2:24). It is crucial to confess that Jesus has come in the flesh (1 John 4:2; 2 John 7). The particular body of Jesus, crucified and risen, is key to a biblical understanding of the body in general. In Jesus, the resurrection of the body is seen as both continuous with and discontinuous with his body before he died. The resurrection is a fleshy thing. The risen Jesus seems to walk through doors, but also he eats fish and carries the marks of his crucifixion. The resurrection of Jesus is the model for Christian hope. It is the model for what human beings might hope for the body to be. This means that salvation always includes the body.

The nature, role, and value of the human body are central to many moral questions. Embodiment is key to human life, and human beings as psychosomatic unities are always embodied in all aspects of the moral life. Classic moral emphases surrounding the body generally focused on questions about the propriety and purpose of asceticism and issues surrounding sexuality. Many people assume that Christian ethics is mostly about restricting the bodily pleasures of sexuality and eating. These strands certainly exist in the moral tradition, but careful theologians have always nuanced such positions. If pleasures of the body are restricted, it is not because the body itself is bad; it is because those pleasures, when misdirected, may point the human being away from God. In the best of Christian tradition the goods of bodily life have been ordered and subject to discipline but also embraced as God's good gifts.

So, in the case of sexuality, the good of marriage has always been upheld against gnostic opposition. Christian marriage is a way to glorify God in the body. In the embodied difficulties and vulnerabilities of married life, God provides one opportunity for sanctification. Christians also need to think about celibacy as a way of being embodied for the glory of God. Instead of constructing singleness as a dualistic calling that rejects the goods of the body and the importance of the body in life before God, we must see the single life much like married life. So singleness is a way of directing the body, with all its passions and desires, to God's purposes. Where sinners want their bodies to be for themselves alone, a means of unfettered personal gratification, Christians have ways of seeing the body as being turned outward, toward God and others. Thus, both marriage and singleness are bodily vocations, ways of living an embodied life in relationship with and for God.

Where hierarchical dualism would disparage and belittle the body, a Christian ethics of the body will grant enormous significance to all aspects of bodily life. Far from being insignificant, the ordinary, physical, daily realities of embodied life matter to God. Materiality and material life are not to be shunned. Material life must be embraced, treasured, and nurtured for God's glory. What we eat and how we eat it matters. Sexuality matters. Housework and manual labor, childbearing and childrearing, creative work and material beauty—all of these matter for the moral life. They are goods to be directed, in the power of the Holy Spirit, toward God's glory.

Where militant naturalism would reduce the body to a collection of material stuff, a Christian ethics of the body will act on the truth that the body is itself always spiritual. The body is spiritual because it is God's good creation central to human relationship with God. A Christian ethics of the body will, then, resist treating the body just as we treat any other material stuff. It will resist acting on the body as one more commodity in a system of consumer capitalism. The body is not a product to be bought and sold. It certainly is not a commodity to be controlled by the highest bidder. This will be important as Christians approach questions about both the beginning and the end of human life. It will also be important in a Christian analysis of products aimed at the body: plastic surgery, the wares of the beauty industry, and medical technologies. Christian ethics of the body must resist a pragmatic, utilitarian account of the body that treats it as a machine to be used.

In failing to see the body as God's good gift meant for God's glory, both hierarchical dualism and reductive materialism devalue the body. This devaluation can result in either extreme asceticism or extreme self-indulgence. Denigration of the body can be seen in the abuse of particular bodies, disgust for female or male embodiment, or in downplaying the importance of the physical life. Devaluing the body is seen in both overly restrictive and in viciously permissive sexuality, in the disordered eating that leaves the body wasting away and in the disordered eating that leads to obesity. The right valuing of the body recognizes it, within the economy of God's work in the world, as a good gift. This right valuing celebrates the life of the body while directing all aspects of that life, including eating and sexuality, toward the glory of God. More recent questions centered on the body and the moral life might do well to keep this classic perspective in mind. The bodily life is very good, but, like all of life, it is subject to the condition of sin and so is in need of redemption. The incarnation and resurrection of Jesus push the ethicist to think about how redemption, holiness, and the moral life must always include the body.

How will the Spirit enable the service and glorification of God in the bodies of human beings? As we seek to answer this question in the Christian moral life, at least four areas are suggestive (see Jones). The Spirit transforms human bodies, individually and corporately through (1) bodily spiritual discipline, (2) the fruit of the Spirit nurtured in church practice, (3) embodied human love, and (4) embodied witness. Spiritual discipline acknowledges human psychosomatic unity in the moral life. As Christians engage in embodied disciplines such as prayer, reading Scripture, fasting, and works of mercy, the moral effects are embodied in their lives. Embodied church practices—hearing the word, feeling the water of baptism, tasting the supper—are used by the Spirit to grow moral fruit in our very embodied lives. When we hear, feel, taste, and see, we are transformed in love, joy, and peace. Human beings love one another as bodies. Our passions are embodied. The way we care for one another is embodied. The opportunity to love other human beings is an embodied opportunity to serve and to glorify God. The Spirit transforms our bodies into material witnesses. The Christian moral life is a life meant to reach out to the world, to share the good news of Jesus Christ with the weak and the broken. It is as bodies that we reach out, that we proclaim and live the gospel. Evangelism reaches out to the needy bodies beloved by God through embodied witness.

See also Asceticism; Celibacy; Dualism, Anthropological; Food; Gender; Health; Healthcare Ethics; Holiness; Humanity; Incarnation; Martyrdom; Monism, Anthropological; Passions; Procreation; Resurrection; Sanctity of Human Life; Self; Sex and Sexuality; Sexual Ethics; Singleness

Bibliography

Bauerschmidt, F. *Julian of Norwich and the Mystical Body Politic of Christ*. University of Notre Dame Press, 1999; Brown, P. *The Body and Society: Men, Women, and Sexual Renunciation in Early Christianity*. Columbia University Press, 1988; Brown, W., N. Murphy, and H. Newton Malony, eds. *Whatever Happened to the Soul: Scientific and Theological Portraits of Human Nature*. Fortress, 1998; Bynum, C. *The Resurrection of the Body in Western Christianity, 200–1336*. Columbia University Press, 1995; Coakley, S., ed. *Religion and the Body*. CSRT 8. Cambridge University Press, 1997; Cooper, J. *Body, Soul, and Life Everlasting: Biblical Anthropology and the Monism-Dualism Debate*. Eerdmans, 1989; Cullmann, O. "Immortality of the Soul or Resurrection of the Dead? The Witness of the New Testament: The Ingersoll Lecture for 1955." Pages 9–53 in *Immortality and Resurrection: Death in the Western World; Two Conflicting Currents of Thought*, ed. K. Stendahl. Macmillan, 1965; Green, J. *Body, Soul, and Human Life: The Nature of Humanity in the Bible*. STI. Baker Academic, 2008; Gundry, R. *Soma in Biblical Theology: With Emphasis on Pauline Anthropology*. SNTSMS 29. Cambridge University Press, 1976; Isherwood, L., and E. Stuart. *Introducing Body Theology*. IFT 2. Pilgrim Press, 1998; Pope John Paul II. *The Theology of the Body: Human Love in the Divine Plan*. Pauline Books, 1997; Jones, B. *Marks of His Wounds: Gender Politics and Bodily Resurrection*. Oxford University Press, 2007; Martin, D. *The Corinthian Body*. Yale University Press, 1995; Rogers, E. *Sexuality and the Christian Body: Their Way into the Triune God*. Blackwell, 1999; Shults, F. *Reforming Theological Anthropology: After the Philosophical Turn to Relationality*. Eerdmans, 2003; Shuman, J. *The Body of Compassion: Ethics, Medicine, and the Church*. Westview, 1999.

Beth Felker Jones

Brain Death *See* Death, Definition of

Bribery

A bribe is "something of value that passes between two parties to induce the bribe-taker to use his position inappropriately to the advantage of the bribe-payer" (Wrage 14). The English word *bribery* is represented by no single Hebrew or Greek word.

The English word *bribe* has been used to translate several Hebrew words: *šōḥad*, *kōper*, *mattānâ*, and *šillŭm*. These Hebrew words also appear in other biblical contexts where they have been translated by words such as *gift*, *present*, *ransom*, *satisfaction*, *reward*, and *offering*. Other narratives describe what appears to be bribery—for example, someone taking money to deceive someone else—but none of these words is used as a descriptive adjective in those passages. The exegete must always look to the context to understand how the word should be translated.

A few direct admonitions against bribery are scattered through the law (Exod. 23:8; Deut. 16:19), wisdom literature (Pss. 15:5; 26:10; Prov. 17:23), and the prophets (Isa. 1:23; 5:23; 33:15; Amos 5:12; Mic. 3:11). These laws warn rulers and judges against accepting gifts and follow the logic that since God does not take bribes to pervert justice (Deut. 10:17), neither should they.

The law prohibits a gift that "blinds the officials, and subverts the cause of those who are in the right" (Exod. 23:8) and warns, "You must not distort justice; you must not show partiality; and you must not accept bribes, for a bribe blinds the eyes of the wise and subverts the cause of those who are in the right. Justice, and only justice, you shall pursue" (Deut. 16:19–20). As with the advice given in Prov. 17:23 and the accusation in Amos 5:12, the issue throughout Scripture seems to be the acceptance, not the offering, of a gift that "perverts justice" or would "push aside the needy in the gate."

The NT has no word for bribery and no direct admonitions against it. There are cases of persons taking money to pervert justice: Judas Iscariot (Matt. 26:14–16), the guards at Jesus' tomb (Matt. 28:12), and the witnesses against Stephen (Acts 6:11–14). There is also a case of a governor expecting money before rendering a judgment: Felix (Acts 24:26).

The biblical question is not whether gifts are exchanged with an expectation of return gifts or favors. That is a constant of life. Rather, the biblical concern is whether the transaction disadvantages the poor and weak in society. Indeed, this is recognized in proverbs and in cases. Proverbs notes rather neutrally, "A bribe is like a magic stone in the eyes of those who give it; wherever they turn they prosper" (17:8). If proverbs are good advice, the theme continues: "A gift opens doors; it gives access to the great" (18:16); and "A gift in secret averts anger; and a concealed bribe in the bosom, strong wrath" (21:14).

However, the application of this criterion follows biblical values, not our contemporary values. There are two cases of a king sending a gift to another king to entice the latter to attack an enemy. Asa sent a gift to Ben-hadad of Aram, enticing him to attack Baasha of Israel, which he did (1 Kgs. 15:18). Ahaz sent a gift to Tiglath-pileser, who attacked the army of Damascus and killed Rezin (2 Kgs. 16:7–9). Neither the good king Asa nor the evil king Ahaz is judged for this use of gifts. Instances such as these lead some to dismiss the Bible as containing too many inconsistencies to serve as a moral guide on this issue (Noonan).

It is unlikely that Scripture has in view all gift-giving. Central to all culture is reciprocity (Mauss), and the form that reciprocity takes (direct, indirect, delayed, equal, unequal) helps shape society (Lévi-Strauss). Gift-giving without incurring an obligation is rare in, if not absent from, human nature (Sahlins). In many places, such as Papua New Guinea, the local languages rarely have a phrase for "thank you" because words are never an adequate response to the thought and work that it takes to provide a gift. Only a return gift or action, carefully chosen and properly timed, is appropriate.

In many places in the world it is impossible to do business without first building social relationships through gift exchanges (not one, but several in a properly escalating cycle). The Japanese concept of *On*, for example, involves asymmetrical gift-giving that is intended to build obligations that last for generations. This is a classic case of the general rule that a quickly offered equivalent return gift completes the obligation and thus destroys the relationship, while unequal gifts mean that the relationship will continue because something is still owed.

What is identified as gift-giving by some and as bribery by others continues to be an ethical issue in international trade and even international aid. Bribery can take several forms, and it spills readily over into corruption. Government officials can be induced to do or not do their job, as in the case of the Enron failure in America or Suharto's record of $35 billion in a lifetime (Wrage 4, 11). Low-level officials can be bribed to look the other way, as the Russian police did in an act of bribery that permitted armed Chechnyans to pass through checkpoints to reach the town where they took control of a Russian school and eventually killed 344 people, more than half of them children (Wrage 19–20). International aid program officials can be induced to move food and supplies in one way or another, as in the UN Oil-for-Food Program, which left the decisions about oil customers and food suppliers in the hands of the Iraqi government, which proceeded to demand bribes for contracts (Wrage 86–87).

While some imagine that bribery and fraud in economics and politics is an issue only outside the West, big cases continue to explode on the scene in the United States. At this writing, the governor of Illinois has been impeached for inviting bribes in exchange for a nomination to fill a US Senate seat left open by the presidential election outcome. At the same time, one of the most profitable investors on Wall Street has been indicted for running the largest Ponzi scheme ever without raising alarm in the Securities and Exchange Commission, which is charged with oversight of investment firms.

Only by examining the cultural context on one side, around issues of whether the gift is voluntary or coerced (Adeney 162), whether it speeds up what should be done anyway or changes an outcome from a legal to an illegal practice, and whether the decision disadvantages the poor (because they lose out or because they cannot afford the gift), and by examining the biblical context on the other side, around issues of higher laws such as love, justice, and mercy, will Christians be able to make decisions about what constitutes a bribe and what constitutes a gift. This is the hermeneutical task of the church (Hays).

See also Business Ethics; Loans; Poverty and Poor; Wealth

Bibliography

Adeney, B. *Strange Virtues: Ethics in a Multicultural World*. InterVarsity, 1995; Hays, R. *The Moral Vision of the New Testament: Community, Cross, and New Creation; A Contemporary Introduction to New Testament Ethics*. HarperSanFrancisco, 1996; Mauss, M. *The Gift: The Form and Reason for Exchange in Archaic Societies*. Trans. W. Halls. W. W. Norton, 2000 [1925]; Noonan, J., Jr. *Bribes*. Macmillan, 1984; Sahlins, M. *Stone Age Economics*. Aldine, 1972; Wrage, A. *Bribery and Extortion: Undermining Business, Governments, and Security*. Praeger Security International, 2007.

Michael A. Rynkiewich

Burial and Cremation *See* Death and Dying

Business Ethics

The seeds of this relatively new field of applied ethics were planted long ago, but they have begun to flower only in the last couple of generations as one of several areas of ethics and the professions in a more highly differentiated global civil society than the ancient and early modern worlds could have imagined. In fact, the world economic situation is now so vast and complex, and some of its crises so deep, that business ethics must reexamine its foundations. No longer can it rely only on the maxims of the ancient classics or on the libertarian theories of Adam Smith or turn to the critical liberationist theories of Karl Marx. Today, most are democratic capitalists or social democrats, and even these must take a longer, wider, and deeper view of our situation—that is, take social-historical, comparative-civilizational, and religiously based ethical motifs into account at every point.

Business in the sense of production of goods for trade and peaceful exchange for mutual enrichment has, of course, been conducted on a modest scale for as long as we can trace the interactions of weavers, potters, and toolmakers with hunters, herders, and farmers. Further, bartering "markets" have been frequent in exchanges between primal societies almost as long.

Ancient trade routes crisscrossed Asia, Africa, Europe, and the Middle East long before Europeans arrived in the Americas, and we now know that such routes also connected pre-Columbian civilizations in what is now Latin America using silver and gold as media of exchange, and that wampum was a form of extratribal currency among the first peoples of North America. These facts indicate that goods were prepared for trade, and that there was enough of an ethic in place for it to be peacefully conducted from very early on in human history. Where there were written languages, we can find traces of moral advice about being diligent in work, honest in dealings, modest in desires for things, prudent in the use of resources, and aware that wealth and plenty, if not ill-gotten, are divine blessings to be enjoyed with thankfulness. Also, we are to honor those who recognize that it is a duty to give alms for the poor, to leave grain in the fields for gleaning by those who lack such resources, and to care for the widow and orphan who are left without a provider, as repeatedly commanded in the Bible.

Elsewhere, we also find references to a *jus gentium*, a cross-cultural ethic of "fairness" mixed with warnings against its violation, suggesting that a common morality functioned to regulate trading between peoples from different societies, although *caveat emptor* ("let the buyer beware") also was a warning in the marketplaces. Indeed, Greco-Roman and early Christian authors thought that these pointed to a *lex natura* that, like the wisdom literature of the Bible, seems to assume that all people can recognize morally just and unjust forms of trade and human relationships. And, the OT books of law and prophecy contain many references to the importance of being trustworthy in "dealings" and many warnings about treacherous and false dealings with the neighbor and the exploitation of the weak (see Stackhouse et al. 37–198).

In the modern West, and increasingly around the world in developing societies, business reflects a growing distinction between the institutions that produce for immediate use, such as nuclear or extended family households or primal communal villages, and chartered firms or incorporated industrial or financial institutions, whose task it is to produce goods and services for an impersonal market in a commonwealth. This has entailed removing production from the household or local community, shifting it to the latifundium (an early plantation or landed estate as a form of agribusiness with intensive manual labor) or to the more recent factory, which left the family or clan as consuming units of items purchased by wages or salaries.

Moreover, the modern West saw in the growing urban centers a remarkable increase of civil institutions, often mothered by church-related institutions (especially monastic and charity organizations), which won the legal right of self-governance and the provision of goods and services independently of familial ties and political regime. These created a great number of incorporated institutions that generated the social space for modern civil society and served an ever-wider public. Socially, this has meant that paralleling a separation of church and state has also been a separation of corporation and state, although the moral influence of religion has continued in indirect, sometimes attenuated forms in familial, political, and economic life.

These institutions developed the pluralistic fabric of modern civil society on which modern business depends. However, they are essentially built not to increase wealth but rather to increase the quality of life. These include schools and universities, hospitals and clinics, think tanks and research centers, artistic associations and singing societies, museums and orchestras, service and advocacy organizations, political parties and humanitarian institutions, and especially religious bodies that draw our attention to nonmaterial, socially transcending values.

The history of the development of the pluralistic spheres of society reveals that the church—which itself declared its independence from tribal particularity, imperial authority, and the ultimacy of material things—founded or fostered these other spheres of civil society in cultures where it gained influence. Similar effects were only partly realized by the temple, the synagogue, and the mosque. The other spheres under Christian influence often enhanced the creation of wealth indirectly by the nurture of values that shape how and why people work, relate to others, and understand what is to be treasured, but they betray their central purposes if they are used primarily for personal or group gain. The professionals in these other spheres do not want to become "merely a business," and often they see business as little more than an organized form of greed, self-interest, and materialistic preoccupation. Yet these same professionals and their institutions must be financially supported, directly through business- or government-based grants or indirectly through invested funds or the donations of the employees of those who work in government or in that sphere of society that is now called "business," located primarily in for-profit corporations that are embedded in a complex of civil institutions on which they depend.

At the same time, most of the nonprofit institutions that exercise increased influence in now globally oriented civil societies have a business office, comptroller or treasurer, fund-raising and budgeting staff, or accounting division to manage the relation of income to expenses, to allocate resources, and to manage property, insurance, employee benefits, and salary ratios. In fact, the management of nonprofit organizations has become a profession in itself, and both for-profit and nonprofit institutions, like families and governments, must obey one primary negative law of business: if output exceeds intake, upkeep becomes downfall.

As these institutions of civil society have increased in number and influence in highly differentiated societies, much of ethical reflection has developed in directions that are no longer rooted in theories of personal virtue, even if that remains critical in regard to the character of business leaders and employees. Still, ethical reflection has become more and more rooted in first principles of moral law, some of which have become incarnated in civil and criminal law and in the particular excellencies that are required to perform the various tasks associated with the specific purposes of particular institutions. Where this is the dominant mode of ethical reflection, the case study tends to be the focus. At its best, the key question becomes how to make executive decisions under a given set of conditions that can resolve apparent conflicts between what is right and what is good for the firm and how to do good while doing well. At its worst, the question becomes how to make decisions so as to avoid prosecution or bankruptcy.

Although traditions of deontological and teleological ethics from the Enlightenment have been applied to medical, law, architectural, and engineering schools during the last several centuries, only in the last half century have most institutions of higher learning rapidly developed departments of business or management stressing ethics. Indeed, the post–World War II period has seen the founding, funding, and rapid expansion of graduate schools of business and management, many of which aspire to match the excellence implied by the classical professions, usually with required courses in business ethics. This flurry of development indicates that this sphere of life has its own distinctive ethos that is having increased pervasiveness in modern and modernizing societies. Its ethos is one to which the first principles of right and wrong must be applied, and ends are defined in the context of a sphere of society that must be dedicated to the creation of wealth that serves the commonwealth as well as rewards the owners, managers, and employees of the business who deploy their wealth, skills, and energy to create an ever-generating enterprise. This will, of course, demand an adaptive system that produces goods and services for changing the world, makes a reasonable profit, and makes it over a long period of time—a condition that rules out methods or gimmicks that offer the illusion of big profits in the short term (such as Ponzi schemes) and whose moral base is something deeper than efforts to avoid getting caught.

To this end, a large industry in its own right, the production of textbooks for teaching ethics, has been developed. These books testify to the fact that a number of areas need moral attention. The best of these texts treat areas such as conflicts of interest, the boundaries of collusion and competition, corporate governance, advertising, accounting, marketing, pay scales, working conditions, personnel, customer and community relations, ecological responsibility, racial discrimination, sexual harassment, affirmative action, socially responsible investments, and issues related to legal demands in regard to usury, contracts, property rights, bribery, health and safety regulations, liability, taxation, and so on (see Beauchamp et al.; Hoffman et al.).

Furthermore, there is a history of moral reasoning in the intervening years between the *jus gentium* of ancient pre-Christian reflections and modern management training, for there are long-recognized ethical principles and images of good and evil that are conveyed by economic motifs. Beyond the commands to cultivate the earth and to be good stewards of the natural and cultural resources, to relieve poverty and want by direct sharing and the reduction of debts that keep the poor in thrall, even when done as a matter of shrewd self-interest (Luke 16:9), there are famous stories such as that of the good Samaritan, a religiously suspect trader who surpasses the orthodox religious leaders in actual compassion

(Luke 10:25-37); the prodigal son, a wastrel who could graciously be restored to his family when he recognizes his foolish ways (provoking the jealous anger of his obedient, hardworking brother) (Luke 15:11-32); the generous owner of the vineyard who paid part-time workers a full wage in their need (Matt. 20:1–16); and servants who multiplied the wealth entrusted to them by the master by trading in the marketplace versus those who took no such risks (Matt. 25:14–30 // Luke 19:11–27). These stories are widely acknowledged to be exemplary parables for those who are to have priority in the kingdom of God, but it is of great interest that business themes are used to illustrate this.

It must be admitted that there is no systematic treatment of business ethics in the Scriptures, and that there are occasional assumptions about slavery (Philemon), the end of the world (Matt. 24 pars.), and the demand for communistic practice in the church (Acts 4:32–5:11) that, if taken as normative (as occasionally has been tried), would make business practices inhumane, immoral, and/or impossible. Moreover, there are stern warnings about making money the focus of life (e.g., Luke 12:15–34), and most translations of the NT keep the word *mammon* from the Aramaic, since that word for money has taken on the meaning of a false god that some believe can save one from meaninglessness, emptiness, and death by trusting it above all. It is not money or wealth that is the root of all evil, but rather the love and idolatry of money (e.g., 1 Tim. 6:10).

Still, there are passages in the Bible and traditions in Christian spirituality that support the development of a business ethic for a complex economy, just as there are passages in the Scriptures and traditions of other religions that enhance or inhibit that possibility (see Hill; Miller; O'Brien and Paeth). In order to discern such elements, we must recognize that business does not constitute the whole of an economy. The form of governance (e.g., constitutional democracy versus tyranny or mass populism) makes a great difference in terms of the kind of business life that can be developed, as do both the laws governing property, inheritance, taxation, and the ease of forming corporations. The same is true of pervasive cultural attitudes toward nature and human nature and thus toward the kinds of technology and social relations that are thought to be legitimate. And the ethical principles guiding politics, law, technology, and human relations are influenced greatly by the dominant religious orientations that shape the whole society. That is why, for instance, different societies guided by different religions develop different kinds of business habits and institutions and why they adapt to global trends in divergent ways (see Harrison et al.; Berger et al.).

In short, business ethics can be taught in ways that are highly practical with specific case-oriented discussions of how to make managerial decisions that calculate the best possible or the least harmful results with the lowest level of damage to the business enterprise. Or business ethics can be taught as a way of examining civilizational dynamics, since business is fatefully intertwined with whole societies—indeed, intertwined today with the developing global civil society that has had a series of severe crises in the twentieth century and now in the twenty-first. If the latter choice is made, business ethics will be more historically, sociologically, and religiously based. It is the presumption of this choice that only it can start to overcome the pathologies that derive from irresponsible practices and unjust institutions while preserving the benefits of modern business.

See also Capitalism; Consumerism; Debt; Economic Development; Economic Ethics; Globalization; Just Wage; Koinonia; Leadership, Leadership Ethics; Professional Ethics; Profit; Wealth

Bibliography

Beauchamp, T., et al., eds. *Ethical Theory and Business Practice*. 8th ed. Prentice Hall, 2008; Berger, P., et al. *Many Globalizations: Cultural Diversity in the Contemporary World*. Oxford University Press, 2002; Harrison, L., et al. *Culture Matters: How Values Shape Human Progress*. Basic Books, 2000; Hill, A. *Just Business: Christian Ethics for the Marketplace*. IVP Academic, 2008; Hoffman, M., et al., eds. *Business Ethics: Readings and Cases in Corporate Morality*. 4th ed. McGraw-Hill, 2002; Miller, D. *God at Work: The History and Promise of the Faith at Work Movement*. Oxford University Press, 2006; O'Brien, T., and S. Paeth. *Religious Perspectives on Business Ethics: An Anthology*. Rowman & Littlefield, 2006; Stackhouse, M. *Globalization and Grace*. GG 4. Continuum, 2007; Stackhouse, M., et al., eds. *On Moral Business: Classical and Contemporary Resources for Ethics and Economic Life*. 2nd ed. Eerdmans, 1995.

Max L. Stackhouse

C

Calling *See* Vocation

Canon Law

"Canon law" refers to that body of ecclesiastical rules that focus on the church's structure, order, and discipline rather than on theological matters of doctrine, dogma, and belief. The word *canon* derives from the Greek *kanōn*, translated as "rod" or "ruler," a "standard by which things are measured," or, more broadly, a "rule of conduct." As such, canon law is best construed in dynamic terms; the precedents for church structure and discipline date from the first century of Christian thought and practice, but canon law has evolved significantly over time.

During its first three centuries, the Christian church drew fundamental rules for common worship and structure from the writings of the NT (e.g., Matt. 18:15; 28:19; Acts 2:38; Eph. 5:21–23; 1–2 Timothy; Titus; Jas. 3:5; 1 Pet. 5:1–3). Handbooks with guidelines for worship, order, and discipline were also circulated within particular Christian communities. The *Didache* (c. 100), written for the Syrian Christian community, contains directives concerning baptism, practices of fasting and prayer, Sabbath obligations, and the consecration of bishops and deacons. Similar collections include the *Traditio apostolica* (c. 218), the *Didascalia apostolorum* (c. 250), and the *Canones ecclesiastici apostolorum* (c. 300). The authority of these early sources derived mainly from their apparent apostolic pedigree rather than from particular claims of centralized juridical authority.

By the early third century, local ecclesiastical councils in Spain, France, Italy, and North Africa were convened to formulate norms for all of Christendom. Beginning with the Council of Nicea in 325, ecumenical or "universal" councils were convened to formulate fundamental doctrines, especially on matters of Christology. In addition, these councils adopted canons that were now deemed binding for all episcopal jurisdictions. After Constantine's conversion and the recognition of Christianity in the Roman Empire, canons adopted by subsequent councils reflected the confluence of NT precedents with Roman legal processes and perspectives. By the mid-fifth century, the church in the West emphasized the primacy of Rome, and so-called papal decretals on disputed questions were viewed as dispositive.

By the turn of the fifth century, canonical norms were being circulated in a confusing variety of sources and languages. In response, Dionysius Exiguus, a Greek scholar working in Rome, provided a uniform translation and comprehensive collection. The *Collectio Dionysiana* included fresh translations of conciliar canons, organized chronologically, as well as a compilation of papal decretals. During the papacy of Hadrian I in the Carolingian period, that collection was amplified in an influential subsequent version, the *Collectio Dionysiana-Hadriana*. At nearly the same time in the Eastern church, the *Nomokanon*, with a prologue written by Patriarch Photios in 882, provided an extended and updated collection of earlier versions. Because Orthodox churches remained autocephalous, their versions of the canons seldom included the papal decretals central to Western canon law.

With the Great Schism of 1054, the traditions of canon law in the West and East diverged radically. During the medieval period, two thinkers were especially influential for the ongoing tradition of canon law in the West. John Gratian of Bologna, in a work later called the *Decretum* (c. 1140), offered a comprehensive collection of nearly four thousand canons. Gratian also interspersed his own commentary and critique on disputed questions. By introducing this spirit of dialogue with traditional sources, Gratian inaugurated the pedagogical model for subsequent canon law jurisprudence in law schools at the newly founded universities. The second important text was St. Bernard's *Breviarium* (c. 1190), which provided a comprehensive collection of extant papal decretals. The *Breviarium* was organized into five broad subject areas: judge, court, clergy, marriage, and crime. Virtually all subsequent revisions of canon law in the West until the twentieth century retained Bernard's five-part structure of organization.

The scandals of the later medieval church, with major abuses in the selling of church offices for both financial and political motives, were key background features to the Reformation. In his initial protest at Wittenberg in 1520, Martin Luther burned books of canon law to indicate his rejection of human laws not based on Scripture. Over time, however, most Reformers recognized the need for church order and discipline and in effect devised their own canons in service to those objectives. By contrast, Henry VIII maintained the corpus of canon law as a framework for Anglican polity, but he argued that the tradition derived not from papal authority but from well-settled patterns of English custom and practice.

The Catholic Counter-Reformation found its fullest expression in the declarations of the Council of Trent, which ended in 1563. Trent clarified and restated fundamental dogmas and identified heresies, but it also adopted major decrees that led to the reform of ecclesial structures, especially regarding qualifications for ordination and pastoral responsibilities of bishops. In the wake of Trent, canon law was further extended and applied to issues that arose in the missionary outreach of various religious orders to the colonies.

The modern period has included two major efforts at revising canon law, which had last occurred under official papal jurisdiction in the early fourteenth century. Unlike the earlier versions surveyed here, which were largely collections of extant laws, the 1917 revision was promulgated as the first actual code of canon law. Rather than simply assembling prior collections, the new code rewrote the laws in systematic and streamlined fashion. By doing so, it served as the standard for seminary teaching until the time of the Second Vatican Council. During the papacy of Paul VI, work on updating the 1917 code began anew, with the revised code that remains in current use finalized in 1983. Its fourteen chapters outline the general norms of church governance, the rights and responsibilities of various vocations and offices, guidelines for the administration of the sacraments, and specific standards for adjudicating conflicts when they arise.

See also Didache; Ecclesiology and Ethics; Roman Catholic Moral Theology

Bibliography

Beal, J., J. Coriden, and T. Green. *New Commentary on the Code of Canon Law*. Paulist Press, 2002; Catholic Church. *Code of Canon Law*. Canon Law Society of America, 1983; Coriden, J. *An Introduction to Canon Law*. Rev. ed. Paulist Press, 2004; Van de Wiel, C. *History of Canon Law*. Eerdmans, 1992.

B. Andrew Lustig

Capitalism

Capitalism is the dominant form of economic organization in the modern world. It involves the private ownership of the means of producing wealth and the exchange of goods and services, land, labor, and capital via markets. In the last two hundred years capitalism has spread throughout the world, so that we can now speak of global capitalism. Despite the ubiquity of capitalism, however, its definition remains highly contentious. A major reason for this is the tendency, in the discussion of capitalism, to conflate descriptive definitions of the market with politically motivated ideologies of capitalism generated for a prescriptive purpose. This tendency has hampered the ethical debate about capitalism and influenced the various ways that Christians have used Scripture to reflect ethically upon it.

The Emergence of Capitalism

Although capitalism often is contrasted with socialism, in which the state owns the means of production and regulates distribution of that production, historically it first emerged in Britain in the eighteenth century following a long transition from the feudal order generally associated with the Middle Ages. Under feudalism, laborers typically were "tied" to the land, itself owned inalienably by the nobility and managed within a complex web of obligation and duty. A series of legal changes and cultural shifts broke these relationships such that land and labor could be subject to private sale, contract, ownership, and control. Capitalism is therefore often regarded as synonymous with "free markets" because it requires that both land and labor (the primary means of production, which together generate capital goods) be freely bought and sold in a market, as well as goods and services.

In addition to these structural changes, capitalism required and encouraged a new kind of motivation in economic activity, oriented toward growth. German sociologist Max Weber famously explained the origin of this new motivation in terms of the impact of Protestantism, especially in its Calvinist form. Economic activity had long been understood as an aspect of human social interaction and therefore the proper object of moral and ethical inquiry. Since the early church, the pursuit of wealth had been regarded with suspicion and the distribution of wealth as a matter of justice (González). Ordinary workers tended to respond to an increase in income by reducing the amount of time spent at work rather than by accumulating large surpluses. By treating business success as a sign of divine favor and acceptance of the fruit of work, Calvinism legitimated the deliberate pursuit of wealth by the ordinary believer and the accumulation of surplus needed to finance capitalist development. This "spirit" of capitalism soon lost touch with its religious root, however, leaving behind a secularized "work ethic," rationally oriented toward growth but without any grounding in Christian ethics.

The economic theoretical defense of capitalism began with the publication of Adam Smith's *Wealth of Nations* in 1776. Observing the dramatic changes in economic behavior occurring in Britain, Smith sought to explain them systematically. He did so within the academic framework of moral philosophy (and in this sense was in continuity with Christian tradition) but shifted the context of economic inquiry from justice to prudence (or practical wisdom). Like many of his contemporaries, Smith saw scarcity as the primary economic problem. His analysis sought to show how conflict over resources between self-interested parties could be harnessed by the price system in a free market to generate a harmonious result. In other words, liberty (the free market) would secure justice (a harmonious result) because self-interested parties would be free to act prudently (i.e., rationally, in their own interest). His theology therefore is not Christian but Deist or Stoic. This did not prevent some nineteenth-century Anglican and United States Baptist theologians from proclaiming the emergent laissez-faire capitalism as evidence of divine providence acting via Smith's "invisible hand" to bring good out of evil. Catholic and other Protestant theologians protested this collapse of economic justice into the operations of deregulated markets, but to no avail.

The secularization of economic thought continued throughout the nineteenth century. Academic study of economic behavior moved from being a branch of theology and moral philosophy to being an aspect of political economy and, finally, with the publication of Alfred Marshall's *Principles of Economics* in 1890, to being an autonomous social science, self-consciously modeled on the natural sciences. Based on the characteristically modern distinction between "facts" and "values," a theoretical and methodological difference was established between "positive economics," which described, evaluated, and established economic "laws" and "normative economics," which was concerned with issues of public policy arising from the result of the operation of those laws. A version of John Stuart Mill's "utilitarianism" became the ethical theory underpinning this new science of choice in which economic agents are understood and modeled as rational individuals in the sense that they arrange means to meet their preferred ends. Economics claims to be "ethically neutral" because agents can choose any end that they wish. Agents then act to maximize utility (the benefits of pursuing their chosen ends, less the costs). The aggregate of this behavior is coordinated by the price system and (with certain heroic but frequently made assumptions) can be measured in proxy form by the sum value of market transactions as gross domestic product (GDP). The growth of GDP has thus become a policy goal because GDP functions as a proxy for growth in overall utility or happiness.

Mainstream economic theory (sometimes referred to as the "neoclassical synthesis") has become the primary defender of capitalism in the twentieth century, arguing that it alone provides the conditions that meet economic theoretical requirements for maximum economic efficiency and therefore achieve maximum social utility or welfare. This powerful economic theoretical defense has reinforced the definitional confusion about "capitalism" and the tendency to conflate discussion such that "capitalism," "market economy," and "economics" are treated as near synonyms. Since the middle of the twentieth century, these terms have gradually been pried apart, and this has made the ethical task of engagement with capitalism easier.

Scripture and Ethical Engagement with Capitalism

For much of the twentieth century, ethical engagement with capitalism by Protestants capitulated to the fact/value distinction embedded in modernity. Protestant use of Scripture, whether in support or in critique of capitalism, was essentially willing to offer ethical principles derived from Scripture as more or less corrective directions to normative economic policy while leaving the positivist analytical framework unchallenged. A "minimal" or "indirect" role for Scripture became the norm in ethical reflection (see Smith). Scripture might inform economics at the most general level, such that "love of neighbor" functions to influence policy, or possibly in a little more detailed form via "middle axioms," principles about economic life derived thematically from Scripture and then applied to questions of public policy by economic specialists. In this way, even the division of labor between theologians and economists reflected the acceptance of a fact/value distinction in ethical reasoning about the economy.

The locus of scriptural reflection on the economy also tended to shift in these Protestant readings from the early church and medieval Catholic reflection on the bans on interest and the requirements to lend to the poor (derived mainly from reflection on the law and the Gospels) toward the creation mandate for humanity to work and be fruitful as stewards of the earth. Liberation theology insisted instead that Scripture be read from the sociopolitical perspective of the poor and, especially in its Catholic form, tended to identify salvation with socioeconomic liberation.

Toward the middle of the twentieth century, critiques of the neoclassical economic defense of capitalism began to emerge from within the economics profession itself. Joseph Schumpeter, for example, pointed out that markets actually exhibit a process of monopolistic "creative destruction" rather than the more benign perfect competition assumed by mainstream theory. More recently, Joseph Stiglitz has shown that the need for "perfect information" if a market exchange is to fulfill the theoretical requirements of mainstream analysis will never be achieved in practice. Such critiques have undermined the theoretical basis for deregulated markets as generators of maximum social welfare. Along with the crumbling of its neoclassical economic defenses, support for capitalism has been eroded by growing evidence of its social and environmental costs.

The typical response to these challenges by defenders of capitalism has been a renewed insistence that capitalism works, that there is no real alternative, and that a deregulated market system is the only way to preserve a free society. In this way, the true character of capitalism has begun to be unmasked. Rather than being a scientific description of the way things are, capitalism is increasingly understood as a liberal political ideology of the market. Increasingly, commentators have observed the influence of this ideology on market behavior (Nelson), ethical discourse about the relationship between Scripture and economics (Gay), and the corporate and individual behavior of the Christian church (Cavanaugh). Capitalism, like socialism, is increasingly seen as a Christian heresy (Milbank).

In parallel with these critiques, evangelical and reformed Protestants have developed renewed critiques of capitalism and of the mainstream economic theory supporting it. The claim to obtain certain knowledge through application of a rigorous method is false (Wolterstorff). Therefore, the fact/value distinction in economics is false, and Christian beliefs must enter into all aspects of economic theorizing. This methodological critique and a strong ethical critique of the utilitarian foundations of mainstream economics have led many Christian economists to develop alternative models that typically have focused on the strengthening of mediating institutions between the individual and the state, and alternative motivations for economic action beyond the maximization of profit or utility (Tiemstra).

This rather belated Protestant critique of modernity has paved the way for a far more formative and direct role for Scripture to play in ethical reasoning about the economy. For example, close readings of Lev. 25 and related texts concerned with the socioeconomic structure of ancient Israel have enabled distinctions to be drawn between a general biblical endorsement of enterprise and markets for goods and services, restrictions on the operation of labor markets, and more extensive limitations on the scope of land and capital markets (see Wright).

An enterprise economy with a wide (and more or less inalienable) distribution of wealth-creating assets and a narrowed degree of inequality in order to ensure social inclusion and community participation has been described as a "relational market economy" (Schluter). This vision coheres well with Catholic visions of "distributism," and in both cases this emerging Christian consensus contrasts the societal objective and anthropology of capitalism with that of Scripture and Christian tradition without needing to reject markets as the primary arenas for economic exchange. Rather than pursuing utility maximization through wealth generation, economic activity must be inhabited by and oriented toward the goal of friendship with God and one another through relational justice and peace (*shalom*). The challenge facing Christians in the twenty-first century is to put these scriptural and ethical reflections on capitalism into practice in the life of the church and to advocate them for society as a whole.

See also Business Ethics; Collection for the Saints; Common Good; Consumerism; Cost-Benefit Analysis; Debt; Economic Ethics; Globalization; Greed; Koinonia; Loans; Markets; Property and Possessions; Trade; Wealth

Bibliography

Cavanaugh, W. *Being Consumed: Economics and Christian Desire*. Eerdmans, 2008; Gay, C. *With Liberty and Justice for Whom? The Recent Evangelical Debate over Capitalism*. Eerdmans, 1991; González, J. *Faith and Wealth: A History of Early Christian Ideas on the Origin, Significance, and Use of Money*. Harper & Row, 1990; Hay, D. *Economics Today: A Christian Critique*. Eerdmans, 1991; Long, D. S. *Divine Economy: Theology and the Market*. Routledge, 2000; Milbank, J. *Theology and Social Theory: Beyond*

Secular Reason. Blackwell, 2006; Nelson, R. *Economics as Religion: From Samuelson to Chicago and Beyond*. Pennsylvania State University Press, 2003; Schluter, M., and J. Ashcroft. *Jubilee Manifesto: A Framework, Agenda and Strategy for Christian Social Reform*. Inter-Varsity, 2005; Smith, I. "God and Economics." Pages 162–79 in *God and Culture: Essays in Honor of Carl F. H. Henry*, ed. D. Carson and J. Woodbridge. Eerdmans, 1993; Tiemstra, J. "Christianity and Economics: A Review of the Recent Literature." *CSR* 22 (1993): 227–47; Waterman, A. "Economists on the Relation between Political Economy and Christian Theology: A Preliminary Survey." *IJSE* 14, no. 6 (1987): 46–68; Wolterstorff, N. *Reason within the Bounds of Religion*. Eerdmans, 1984; Wright, C. *Living as the People of God: The Relevance of Old Testament Ethics*. Inter-Varsity, 1983.

Paul Spencer Williams

Capital Punishment

Capital punishment has been a feature of every major civilization since the dawn of history, and usually it has been afforded religious sanction. Biblical Israel is no exception. The death penalty is entrenched in OT law and narrative, and it is attested, though not necessarily endorsed, in NT teaching as well. Given the diversity and complexity of biblical material on the subject, it is unsurprising that Christian opinion on capital punishment is divided. On the one hand, the support of churches for the elimination of the death penalty often has been a critical factor in those countries that have abolished it. On the other hand, strong approval for capital punishment among conservative religious voters is a significant factor in explaining why the United States stands alone among Western democracies in retaining its use.

In assessing the implications of the biblical material for Christian ethics, several considerations need to be carefully weighed. There is the exegetical question of what certain passages mean, especially Gen. 9; John 8; Rom. 13. There is the hermeneutical question of whether NT teaching ratifies or fundamentally revises OT practice. There is the theological question of whether a picture of God as judge or God as redeemer should serve as the controlling paradigm. There is also the philosophical question of what we mean by "justice" and how the retributive or restorative dimensions of justice should be balanced. Finally, there is the pragmatic question of whether capital punishment is harmful or beneficial to society.

Basically at issue for Christian ethics is whether Scripture prescribes capital punishment as a timeless principle of social life or whether its sanction in biblical times should be understood as historically contingent and radically subverted by the logic of the gospel. Different conclusions on this question stem mainly from varying interpretations of three main features of biblical teaching: (1) the institution of the death penalty in Gen. 9; (2) the endorsement of capital punishment in Mosaic law; (3) the moral, judicial, and political implications of NT teaching on forgiveness, reconciliation, nonviolence, and love of enemy. We will examine each of these in order.

(1) Genesis 9:6 is often viewed as a clear-cut authorization for the taking of human life as an act of retributive justice: "Whoever sheds the blood of a human, by a human shall that person's blood be shed; for in his own image God made humankind." Three reasons often are given for the eternal validity of this injunction: as part of the covenant with Noah, it is intended for the whole human race, not just for the people of Israel; its rationale of respecting the *imago Dei* in human beings grounds the punishment in the very order of creation (Gen. 9:6; cf. 1:27); and its refusal to envisage alternative penalties, such as monetary restitution, indicates that life-for-life is intended to be an unalterable criterion of justice (see Exod. 21:12, 23–25; Lev. 24:21; Deut. 19:19–21).

It is debatable, however, whether the text should be construed primarily as an abstract judicial principle. It is perhaps better seen as a statement of God's personal prerogative ("I will require") to act against those who refuse to show reverence for human life. Viewed against the backdrop of unrestrained vengeance before the flood (Gen. 4:23–24; 6:11–13), the injunction places a strict limitation on the legitimate grounds for extinguishing human life. Putting someone to death is appropriate only for culpable acts of homicide, and the penalty should fall on the guilty party alone, not on the family or clan. The Noahide context need not be taken as a sign of immutability. If the early Christians concluded that the food restrictions in Gen. 9:4 were no longer obligatory in the Christian era, at least for Gentiles (Acts 15:29; cf. Mark 7:19; Rom. 14:14; 1 Cor. 8:8–9; 10:25), the same could be true of the death penalty in Gen. 9:5–6.

(2) Mosaic law, in its final form, stipulates the death sentence for up to three dozen offenses. In addition to murder and certain types of manslaughter (Exod. 21:12–14; Num. 35:9–28; Deut. 19:11–13), it is prescribed for a wide range of interpersonal, religious, and sexual crimes, including kidnapping (Exod. 21:16; Deut. 24:7), rebellion against parents (Exod. 21:17; Lev. 20:9; Deut. 21:18–21), idolatry (Exod. 20:3–5; Deut. 13:1–16), perjury in capital cases (Deut. 19:16–19), blasphemy (Lev. 24:10–23), breach of the

Sabbath (Exod. 31:14; Num. 15:32–36), adultery (Lev. 20:10–16; Num. 5:11–30; Deut. 22:22–24), homosexual intercourse (Lev. 20:13), bestiality (Exod. 22:19; Lev. 20:15–16), and rape of a married woman (Deut. 22:25–29). Offenders were most commonly executed by stoning (Lev. 24:14, 16; Num. 15:35; Deut. 22:24; Josh. 7:25), although burning, beheading, impalement, and shooting with arrows are also recorded in the OT.

That such a variety of offenses were punishable by death does not necessarily mean that executions were excessively commonplace in ancient Israel. (Nor does it validate subsequent Christian practice of similarly prescribing death for matters such as witchcraft, adultery, blasphemy, sodomy, and bestiality, as was the case in, e.g., Puritan colonies in America.) It is important to understand that biblical law is not legislation in the modern sense. We are not dealing with hard-and-fast regulations that had to be rigidly applied in every situation. The various stipulations of the Torah are better seen as representative examples of legal reasoning, built up steadily over time and in a variety of circumstances, from which key values and principles could be drawn for application to other, different situations.

Biblical law had a more pronounced pedagogical or educational function than does modern law. It was addressed primarily not to the legal establishment but rather to the whole community (cf. Deut. 29:10–12), spelling out in direct and memorable terms what life in covenant relationship with God required. The purpose of attaching the ultimate penalty of death to certain behaviors was to mark them out as especially serious. It served to get people's attention, to issue a solemn warning against the destructive consequences of particular misdeeds, especially those that breached the central covenantal principles articulated in the Decalogue (violations of seven of the Ten Commandments carry the death penalty in biblical legislation). But this does not mean that death was invariably, or even typically, exacted for actual offending. The many narrative episodes in the Bible where people guilty of capital offenses are not executed disabuse us of the notion that the penalties were applied inflexibly. Substitute penalties often were acceptable, although not for such grave wrongs as premeditated murder (Num. 35:31; Deut. 19:13), enticement to idolatry (Deut. 13:8; cf. 19:13), and perjury in capital cases (Deut. 19:19–21). Moreover, when the death penalty was inflicted, it carried a religious and atoning significance, not merely a judicial one. It signified the community's action to purge the ritual pollution of sin from its midst lest it spread like a deadly contagion (e.g., Deut. 13:5; 17:7, 12; 19:19).

It is noteworthy that over time, pentateuchal law elaborated a variety of processes and procedures to prevent the accidental or deliberate miscarriage of justice in capital cases. The very high standard of proof demanded a very thorough investigation of the evidence (Deut. 17:4). Stringent efforts were made to root out false witnesses, and the deliberate falsification of evidence itself was punishable by death (Deut. 19:16–19). Multiple witnesses usually were required in capital cases (Num. 35:30; Deut. 17:6; 19:15), and the prohibition on substitute penalties prevented the wealthy from purchasing immunity (Lev. 27:29; Num. 35:31; Deut. 19:13). A distinction also was drawn between deliberate murder and accidental manslaughter, with cities of refuge being created where those guilty of accidental homicide could seek asylum from avenging kin (Exod. 21:12–13; Num. 35:9–34; cf. Deut. 4:41–43; 19:1–10; Josh. 20:1–9).

In later Jewish jurisprudence, as reflected in the Mishnah tractate *Sanhedrin*, procedural rules and evidential requirements in capital cases became so stringent that, were they followed strictly, it would have been virtually impossible to impose the death penalty. Since the institution is inscribed in Scripture, it could not be explicitly repudiated. But there was a pronounced tendency in early Judaism to oppose it in practice, if not in principle. Executions still occurred, but as the NT itself attests, the trend over time was to view the death penalty in the Bible as an indication of the seriousness of sin rather than as an obligatory or literal requirement.

(3) New Testament references to capital punishment are limited in number. Some texts are simply descriptions of, or allusions to, current practice (e.g., Luke 19:27; 23:40–43; John 19:11; Acts 25:11). Interpreters sometimes have construed these scattered narrative allusions and proverbial sayings (e.g., Matt. 26:52; Rom. 1:32) as signaling implicit acceptance of the death penalty in principle. But this is highly contestable, not least because capital power in the NT is more often than not directed against the righteous, including Jesus himself, rather than the wicked. The striking down of Ananias and Sapphira (Acts 5:1–11) also tells us nothing about attitudes toward state-administered capital punishment.

Even Paul's celebrated statement that the governing authority "does not bear the sword in vain" and is "the servant of God to execute wrath on the wrongdoer" (Rom. 13:3–5) does not necessarily validate capital punishment. Here "sword" probably is a symbol or metaphor for the coercive authority of the state in general, not a specific reference to judicial execution. Certainly in Rome's case the governing authorities made profuse use of the literal sword in asserting the state's authority, as Paul knew well and simply presumes as a historical fact. But it is not the state's power to kill that Paul underwrites with divine sanction; rather, it is the state's normative role in restraining evil and rewarding the good (Rom. 13:3–4). This function may include, but certainly does not require, use of the death penalty.

Two other NT passages have a significant bearing. One is Matt. 5:38–48, where Jesus repudiates the *lex talionis*, or "law of retaliation," as the governing norm of conduct for his followers. In biblical law the *lex talionis* encapsulates the important principle of equivalence: any redress claimed for a harm done must not exceed the level of harm suffered by the victim (Exod. 21:20–25; Lev. 24:19–22; Deut. 19:18–21). The death penalty functioned under this principle (a life for a life), where it served to "purge the evil one from your midst" (Deut. 19:19). But Jesus apparently renounces the death-dealing application of this principle, summoning his hearers not to resist the evil one violently but instead to act with love toward even their enemies.

The other passage is John 7:53–8:11. This is the only place where Jesus is expressly asked to adjudicate on a capital crime (cf. Lev. 20:10; Deut. 22:23–24), and it is surely significant that he does so negatively. Evidently, all the legal prerequisites for a "just" execution of the adulterous woman were in place (otherwise, his opponents would scarcely have used the episode to test his fidelity to the law [John 8:6]). But Jesus refuses to condone the woman's execution, not simply on legal grounds but rather on moral and religious grounds. "Let anyone among you who is without sin be the first to throw a stone at her" (John 8:7). Stoning was the legally prescribed mode of execution for the crime of adultery (Lev. 20:10; Deut. 22:22–24), yet Jesus urges that it is only those without sin who are properly qualified to discharge it. Although a variety of other arguments can be mounted against the death penalty (e.g., the dangers of wrongful conviction, its discriminatory impact on minority communities, its failure as a deterrent, and its brutalizing impact on those who carry it out), arguably it is this moral argument that remains the most potent. Ultimate jurisdiction over human life belongs only to Christ, the sinless one.

See also Crime and Criminal Justice; Enemy, Enemy Love; Forgiveness; Image of God; Justice, Restorative; Justice, Retributive; Punishment

Bibliography

Ballard, B. "The Death Penalty: God's Timeless Standard for the Nations?" *JETS* 47 (2000): 471–87; Bohm, R. *Deathquest III: An Introduction to the Theory and Practice of Capital Punishment in the United States*. 3rd ed. Lexis Nexis, 2007; Charles, J. "Crime, the Christian and Capital Justice," *JETS* 38 (1995): 429–41; idem. "Outrageous Atrocity or Moral Imperative? The Ethics of Capital Punishment." *SCE* 6 (1993): 1–14; House, H., and J. Yoder. *The Death Penalty Debate*. Word, 1991; Marshall, C. *Beyond Retribution: A New Testament Vision for Justice, Crime and Punishment*. Eerdmans, 2001; Megivern, J. *The Death Penalty: An Historical and Theological Survey*. Paulist Press, 1997; Wright, C. *Walking in the Ways of the Lord: The Ethical Authority of the Old Testament*. Apollos, 1995; Yoder, J. *The Christian and Capital Punishment*. Faith and Life Press, 1961.

Christopher Marshall

Cardinal Virtues

The four cardinal (Lat. *cardo* means "hinge, pivot") virtues are prudence (practical wisdom), justice, temperance (or self-control), and fortitude (or courage). These natural virtues are distinguished from the theological virtues of faith, hope, and love (1 Cor. 13:13).

The cardinal virtues originate in classical antiquity rather than biblical context. Nowhere in Scripture are these virtues discussed as a group, although each one is commended repeatedly, especially in OT wisdom literature. The cluster is found in OT apocryphal books. Wisdom 8:7 states, "If one loves justice, the fruits of her works are virtues; for she teaches moderation and prudence, justice and fortitude, and nothing in life is more useful for men than these" (NAB). Also, 4 Macc. 1:18 states, "Now the kinds of wisdom are rational judgment, justice, courage, and self-control." These four dimensions of moral virtue were developed in Plato's *Republic* and became a central feature in Stoic moral thought. In the classical context, these virtues were applied primarily to the political and military aspects of public life. Many Christian writers have adapted this moral vocabulary primarily as a way to guide lay people in their civic responsibilities.

The first theological treatment of them is found in Ambrose, who coined the term *cardinal virtues*. Ambrose recasts them as animating principles for the active Christian life by arguing from episodes in the lives of major OT fathers. For instance, Ambrose claims that all four virtues were displayed by Noah in building the ark (Gen. 6) and by Abraham in the story of his testing at Mount Moriah

(Gen. 22). Ambrose proceeds to provide a detailed exposition of each cardinal virtue as consonant with explicit biblical teaching. Augustine continues the transformation of pagan virtues by reframing true virtue as "nothing else than perfect love of God" with heart, mind, soul, and strength. He considers the four cardinal virtues as four forms of love: "Temperance is love keeping itself entire and incorrupt for God; fortitude is love bearing everything readily for the sake of God; justice is love serving God only, and therefore ruling well all else, as subject to man; prudence is love making a right distinction between what helps it toward God and what might hinder it" (*Mor. eccl.* 15.25). Thomas Aquinas develops a sophisticated account in which the four virtues are cardinal because they properly regulate human intellect, will, and passions, which must be well ordered to make possible right moral action. Roman Catholic tradition has emphasized the importance of the cardinal virtues considerably more than has Protestantism, which often has highlighted the question of the relation of divine grace to natural moral virtues acquired by human effort.

See also Character; Courage; Habit; Justice; Prudence; Temperance; Vices and Virtues, Lists of; Virtue(s)

Bibliography

Ambrose. *On the Duties of the Clergy*, book 1; Augustine. *The Way of Life of the Catholic Church*; Barton, J. *Understanding Old Testament Ethics: Approaches and Explorations*. Westminster John Knox, 2003, 65–74; *Catechism of the Catholic Church*, 1803–11; Cessario, R. *The Virtues, or, The Examined Life*. Continuum, 2002; Keenan, J. "Proposing Cardinal Virtues." *TS* 56 (1995): 709–29; Pieper, J. *The Four Cardinal Virtues: Prudence, Justice, Fortitude, Temperance*. University of Notre Dame Press, 1966; Plato. *Republic*, Book 4, 427–34; Thomas Aquinas. *Summa theologiae*, I-II, q. 61.

Jeffrey P. Greenman

Care, Caring

Care is relational, epistemological, theological, and constitutive of our behavior, selves, and communities. People care, and they act in ways that are caring. Caring confers meaning on persons, ideas, and things, shaping knowledge and action along lines of moral understanding and ethical comportment. What shows up as care varies from culture to culture, though care is understood across cultures as having to do with sustaining life and world. Care is central to Christian belief and life.

The word *care* is not an explicitly or restrictively religious one. It bears meaning beyond biblical and theological contexts, connoting orientation toward what matters, respectful attention to the nature of the cared for, reaching out to something other than the self, and a disposition toward benevolent action for the cared for. There is a moral weight to caring that involves concern and responsibility for whom or what is cared for, as when we speak of being burdened by "the cares of the world." (This weight lends a double edge to care, one captured well by the German word *Sorge*, which can be translated "care" or "anxiety.") Caring has to do with being engaged attentively and responsively and entails disposition as well as practice.

Within moral theory, the ethics of care (denoted as such since the middle of the twentieth century) contrasts with moral systems that accord primacy to reason, justice, and virtue and often is conceptualized, in origin and essence, as private and contextual rather than public and abstract. "To be a morally good person requires, among other things, that a person strives to meet the demands of caring that present themselves in his or her life"—this represents the imperative affirmed by care ethicists. Furthermore, "for a society to be judged as a morally adequate society, it must, among other things, adequately provide for care of its members and its territory" (Tronto 126). While invoking this universal standard of morality for persons and societies, the ethical theory itself is one of contextualized care for and of those entities that are cared about.

The ethics of care has been associated with and advanced by feminist ethicists (see, e.g., the writings of Carol Gilligan, Nel Noddings, Patricia Benner, Sara Ruddick, Joan Tronto, and Virginia Held), although some moral philosophers outside the field of feminist ethics have considered questions of care (e.g., Martin Heidegger, Michel Foucault, Charles Taylor, and Lawrence Blum).

Christianity (at its best) traverses the boundaries of ethical systems, presenting a radical ethic in which care is central to social and political life as well as to personal relationships for men and women. Scripture claims that justice and mercy meet in the One who is love and truth (as seen throughout Scripture—e.g., Ps. 85; Isa. 42; 1 John). An article of Christian faith is that humanity depends on a caring God in whose image we are created. Institutions of caregiving have flourished in the Christian era—hospitals, schools, orphanages—in response to the expanding recognition of God's image in others. On individual and social levels, however, the stance and action of care are prone to perversion. Modern philosophical and political questions concerning care have drawn attention to manipulative, disempowering, and contemptuous relations that masquerade as care. Psychological concerns have been raised about codependent, parasitic, or authoritarian interpersonal relations that purport to be caring. Counterfeits of caring relationships invite scriptural, ecclesial, and ethical examination.

Regarding Scripture

Scripture opens with the story of creation by God, about whom the first mention has to do with relating to the world in which we live. God is not described in terms of personality or attributes but rather is shown in caring activity. In the beginning God hovered over creation as a hen broods on her nest. God then spoke the world into contrasting elements that God deemed good, culminating in humankind, made male and female. As creator, God enacts one of the paradigmatic roles of care, that of the parent. We learn in Gen. 1 that God made people in God's image, blessed them, and then commissioned them with care for the earth and all that it entails. God so loved the world that the Word was made flesh, dwelt among people, and then suffered death so that we might have abundant life. Christian Scripture ends in the book of Revelation with Jesus' invitation to his children to come into new and eternal life with him. God will dwell with mortals, will wipe every tear from their eyes, and will give water as a gift to the thirsty (Rev. 21:3–6). All of Scripture reverberates with God's care for humankind and asserts that we have no understanding of God apart from this relationship. Our understanding of ourselves rests on God's creation and communication, and our orientation toward others is shaped by the image in which we and they are formed.

God cares. A distinguishing attribute of the God of Scripture is loving-kindness, *ḥesed* in Hebrew (this word is core to Hasidism and is a key concept in Kabbalah, the mystical branch of Judaism). The crux of care, as well as the complexity of the concept, is captured by this ancient word. Generous, active loving-kindness is a fundamental quality of God's nature and of God's relationship with people. It is indicative of the *imago Dei* in human beings, and Scripture draws attention to those, such as Naomi's daughter-in-law Ruth, who exhibit it. Loving-kindness is not prescribed or obligatory; it is surprising, responsive, creative, remarkable, generous, good but not required, inspiring of covenant but not determined by covenant, risky, and sometimes in conflict with other loves and commitments (see Andersen).

In Christian Scripture, the connection between care and sacrificial service fuses in the person of Jesus Christ, who is God's self-donation for the world God so loves and the exemplar for our lives of Christian discipleship and care. The Word became flesh and dwelt among us so that we might know God and know how we should then live. Through encounter with this ultimate expression of God, we are invited to follow Christ, imitating him in loving care for our neighbor and world (*imitatio Christi*). The mark of the Christian is love—love received and then extended. "'Care' is God's gift to human beings, and within this gift is embodied both the call and capacity to be the community of care" (Green 165). It is this flow of grace that is essential for care and guards against its perversions as dryly dutiful action or self-aggrandizing exploitation.

The Gospels show that Jesus gives sacrificially, and he also receives. He prays for strength, retreats for refreshment of his soul, and accepts the love that others give him. Jesus seeks care and receives it from God. He also seeks and receives from people. As God is relational throughout Scripture, so is Jesus. He has friends, family, and community. He responds to others in the contexts of their relational lives, weeping for those who are bereft, restoring the healed to their communities, and leaving his own restorative solitude, for example, for the sake of a desperate mother (Mark 7:24–30). In modern times and cultures that applaud seeming independence and self-determination, practices of receiving care are devalued to a greater extent than those of caregiving and self-care, though those too do not receive the regard or reward given to entrepreneurial, commercial, and political endeavor. Even so, the church's avowal that God is love rings true and steady despite clamorous claims of prosperity, certitude, popularity, and dominance.

Jesus' teaching is never detached from his person. We are invited, first and foremost, to follow a person, not a rule or methodology. Central to Jesus is his caring stance and action in the world. Sharing the Passover meal with his friends on the eve of his death, Jesus contrasts the ways of power in the world with the way he has come to show and encourage. He says, "But I am among you as one who serves" (Luke 22:27). From him, who came among us as a servant, we are to learn how to serve. Jesus lived in a competitive society marked by status divisions related to birthright, gender, lineage, accomplishment, and purity (moral, physical, and social). Yet he stepped over those divisions, not only through association but also in caring for the marginalized and ostracized—the poor, widowed, young, ill, foreign, shamed, demented, disabled, and hopeless. Moreover, stepping into a task assigned only to Gentile male slaves, women, and children, Jesus washed the feet of his closest followers (John 13:1–17) (see Green 149–67).

God and Jesus are called "shepherd," the one who tends the flock, seeks the lost sheep, guides the sheep to the fold, protects, feeds, plays music for, and gathers the flock together by the sound of his voice. The shepherd watches over the sheep, attends to them, and knows each one's particular needs. The scriptural exemplars of care are ones of serving, shepherding loving-kindness.

Deus caritas est

"God is love, and those who abide in love abide in God, and God abides in them" (1 John 4:16 [in Latin Bibles this "love" is *caritas*]). Love is central to Christian faith. Faith is relational, and from that love relationship arises the Christian's ethical commitment to love of neighbor. The NT Greek word *agapē* generally was translated as *caritas* in Latin (and "charity" or "love" in English). Thomas Aquinas developed the doctrine of *caritas* in the thirteenth century, understanding this love as both a gift of grace by Christ, who calls us "friends" through the Holy Spirit dwelling in us, and as a transforming virtue that perfects our natural love as our heart is stretched increasingly by God's great love for all. The "all-embracing friendship with God . . . is intimate, transforming, and includes all our neighbors" (Carmichael 128). As one writer on Christian spirituality claims in loud italics, "*Love* describes the manner of our life. *Care defines the mandate of our life*" (Howard 338).

Today the word *charity* is associated with impersonal and/or hierarchical giving to another. In our postmodern, psychotherapeutic age detached, principled, or ideal motivated care is suspect. Such caring action, often seen as the Christian ideal, may rely on the goads of guilt and shame that "do not inspire people to care in the same way as being moved by the other does, and they are dangerous" (Taylor 183). Belittlement of the one cared for coupled with self-aggrandizement of the one caring, skewed attachments associated with codependency, and various forms of anxious striving may infect charity and render it harmful. Because of these and other considerations, contemporary moral discourse has distinguished *charity* from *care*, despite the words' shared etymological and religious roots, and dismissed the former in favor of the latter. As one philosopher says, "Some people suggest that caring is close to the Christian virtue of *caritas*, but *caritas* is equivalent to charity. Care, however, is not the same as charity—when we take care of our children we are not being charitable—and being caring is not the same as being charitable. Valuing care is entirely independent of any religious foundation, and is the stronger for this" (Held 44).

This contemporary criticism of impartial charity contrasts with early twentieth-century (modern era) theological criticism. The modern view was critical of selfish and desiring *eros*, as distinguished from the preferable altruistic *agapē* or *caritas*. In this earlier view, forcefully articulated by the Swedish Lutheran theologian Anders Nygren, preferential loves, such as *eros* and *philia* (friendship), are tainted by self-interest, whereas charity is dispassionately revealed and divinely granted (Carmichael 4, 174–76). Benedict XVI, in his first papal encyclical, *God Is Love—Deus Caritas Est* (2006), reconciles these contrasting loves (preferential *eros* and divinely just *agapē*) within God's redeeming love through Jesus Christ. He says that charity extended by Christians must rest in "an encounter with God in Christ which awakens their love and opens their spirits to others" (Benedict XVI 41). Personal love is elicited by an encounter with the God who is love.

Soul Care

The words *care* and *cure* share origins in the Latin word *curare*, meaning "to cure, take care of, take trouble for, be solicitous." The early church employed the expression *cura animarum* ("cure of souls") to include the tasks involved in the care of persons as well as the stance of caring or solicitude toward a subject. The church offered the gospel, which healed broken and sick souls, and, in keeping with the church's commission to cure souls, clergy in several Christian traditions are given the appellation "curate." Over time and reflecting a broader Enlightenment shift, spiritual ministrations have been referred to less as the cure of souls and more and more as care of souls. With the development of scientific and therapeutically effective techniques that effected cures of diseases and disorders, the words *cure* and *care* became increasingly separate in meaning, with the former denoting objective skills and the repairs they effect, and the latter having to do with subjective concern and compassion.

The care of souls has a long history, secular as well as sacred. Ancient Greek philosophy grew in a religious environment that lacked dogmatic cohesion and theological rigor. Philosophy assumed the moral direction of daily life, and the philosophers were the *curatores animarum*, tending the divine element in human nature that, for Socrates and Plato (and their successors in Greece and Rome), was immortal and superior to the body (see McNeill). The care of souls entailed right teaching, holding a mirror for the self-examining soul, direction in right living, and the formation of the soul toward good and away from evil. Western psychotherapies that developed in the mid-twentieth century can be seen as heirs of a care of souls separate from religious doctrine, practice, and community.

Most religions, including Judaism, Hinduism, Buddhism, Islam, and Christianity, manifest ways of caring for souls that transmit the truth of the religion as well as ethical understandings of how to live within that truth. In some cases the care assumes the form of authoritative guidance, and in others the care focuses on compassion, accompaniment, and drawing out the experiences and values of the recipient of caring attention.

In contemporary Christian parlance, soul care, under the overarching umbrella of Christian spirituality, is claimed as the province of pastoral care and counseling and also of spiritual direction. Pastoral care is the ministry of care and counseling offered by pastors, chaplains, and church leaders to those in their congregations and communities. This care can range from home visitation to formal counseling sessions. Pastoral care is a broad domain of compassionate concern enfolding a wide range of possible tasks. Pastoral caregiving may be expressed in the choice of sermon topics and the crafting of worship as a pastor attends to the deepest needs of the congregation. It may be expressed through the cultivation of lay leaders, educational opportunities, or hands-on caregiving. Pastoral care can extend to the community beyond the church, as Jesus called us to care for the "least of these," and it may involve inspiring the congregation to "repair the world." Pastoral care concerns the well-being, salvation, education, and spiritual formation of the congregation as well as the presence of the church as light and salt in the world at large.

Pastoral counseling is an occasional ministry of pastors and also a formal practice of specialized professionals trained in the field and customarily offering pastoral counseling as their primary vocation. Spiritual direction is an ancient art of helping another person attend to God's word and address and then live in response to that. These Christian listening arts rest on practical theology, that branch of theology that attends to how we order our everyday lives—in all their aspects, such as work, family, relationships, and citizenship—according to the moral meanings derived from Scripture and Christian theology. Rooted in the Christian faith, pastoral care concentrates on the comfort, thriving, and sanctification of those being served.

Social Care and Flourishing

Christians, like all humankind, have been implicated in social evils—slavery, poverty, discrimination, and oppression. People are prone to selfishness, and when Christianity is the established religion of a society, it may preferentially opt for the privileged majority. However, the Christian gospel stands in critical relation to established institutions, holds a realistic view of human sinfulness, calls us to spiritual integrity of belief and action, and requires hope from us for the salvation of people and the transformation of the world, by God's grace. One political scientist states, "The Christian record in the annals of reform, it must be granted, is not impressive. . . . Nevertheless, Christianity in essence is not conservative" (Tinder 153). We are called to transform the world and practice care as we participate in God's history.

Individuals rely on the flow of grace from God through us in caring action to others. Christians communally—the body of Christ—are to work with God's Spirit in discerning that movement toward grace expressed in care. In the hope for environmental and social reform, as in the desire to care for one in need of care, Christians are to pray, listen, and, following Christ, take action in loving-kindness. Christianity requires hope and humility. In bowing before God, creator and redeemer of the world, the follower of Christ is to bend ear, eye, and helping hand toward the receiver of care. We are called to care.

Critics of care accuse would-be caregivers of contempt for the one in need, of presuming to know best what the receiver ought to receive. This is not the kind of caring that Jesus exhibited. In Jericho Jesus responded to a man calling to him from the sidelines as Jesus and his followers walked en masse down the dusty main street. In the midst of the bustle and roar of the crowd, Jesus stopped. He turned toward the blind man and asked, "What would you have me do for you?" Care requires these movements: stopping, turning, attending, and listening. This is true in one-on-one caregiving as well as in our care for broader social concerns. We listen for God and listen to the other. This attitude of social care and transformation rooted in love of God and neighbor has been identified as a prophetic stance. Hope in God's loving sovereignty sustains our disposition of care and undergirds our caring action.

As persons, we are formed, informed, and transformed by care, that which we receive as well as that which we extend. As contemporary psychology has turned its attention toward health and flourishing, more and more studies indicate the health and life satisfaction benefits of "prosocial" behavior, constituted of acts that demonstrate empathy, caring, and morality. In our social climate, in which flourishing is regarded as good and as a state worth striving for, caring action and love are subjected to less critical scrutiny and contempt. To the Christian, it comes as no surprise that we flourish when living in accord with the image and example of our caring God, to whose Spirit, word, and body we turn for guidance and correction in our own efforts to love and care.

See also Agape; Altruism; Charity, Works of; Compassion; Feminist Ethics; Imitation of Jesus; Love, Love Command; Neighbor, Neighbor Love

Bibliography

Andersen, F. "Yahweh, the Kind and Sensitive God." Pages 41–88 in *God Who Is Rich in Mercy: Essays Presented to Dr. D. B. Knox*, ed. P. O'Brien and D. Peterson. Lancer Books, 1986; Benedict XVI. *God Is Love—Deus Caritas Est: Encyclical Letter.* United States Conference of Catholic Bishops, 2006; Browning, D. *The Moral Context of Pastoral Care.* Westminster, 1976; Carmichael, L. *Friendship: Interpreting Christian Love.* T&T Clark International, 2004; Green, J. "Caring as Gift and Goal: Biblical and Theological Reflections." Pages 149–67 in *The Crisis of Care: Affirming and Restoring Caring Practices in the Helping Professions*, ed. S. Phillips and P. Benner. Georgetown University Press, 1994; Held, V. *The Ethics of Care: Personal, Political, and Global.* Oxford University Press, 2006; Howard, E. *The Brazos Introduction to Christian Spirituality.* Brazos, 2008, 337–69; McNeill, J. *A History of the Cure of Souls.* Harper, 1951; Taylor, C. "Philosophical Reflections on Caring Practices." Pages 174–87 in *The Crisis of Care: Affirming and Restoring Caring Practices in the Helping Professions*, ed. S. Phillips and P. Benner. Georgetown University Press, 1994; Tinder, G. *The Political Meaning of Christianity: The Prophetic Stance—An Interpretation.* HarperSanFrancisco, 1991; Tronto, J. *Moral Boundaries: A Political Argument for an Ethic of Care.* Routledge, 1993.

Susan S. Phillips

Care of the Aged *See* Care, Caring

Care of the Disabled *See* Care, Caring

Care of the Dying *See* Care, Caring

Casuistry

At first glance, the inclusion of "casuistry" may seem perplexing in a reference work on Scripture and ethics. Many would argue that the moral methodology associated with casuistry is the antithesis of a biblically nourished Christian ethics. Yet even the biblical bumper sticker "WWJD?" ("What Would Jesus Do?") is a form of casuistry. However, one has to approach any casuistry, biblical or otherwise, carefully. "WWJD?" has often been justifiably critiqued as presenting an impossible moral guide to imitate, for who could respond as Jesus did to a wine shortage at a wedding reception or to a storm at sea threatening a boatload of disciples? But seen in the light of casuistry, this practical question might take on a more helpful cast, since countless examples from Jesus' earthly ministry, the life of the young church, as well as evidence from the OT, give ample testimony to the long Jewish and Christian traditions of grappling with complex moral situations through casuistry. Casuistry is simply the application of moral principles, values, precedents, and/or models to cases.

The term comes from the Latin word *casus* ("case") and dates back to the seminary manuals of moral theology for training of priests in the hearing of confessions used from the late Middle Ages to the mid-twentieth century. An illustrative case, called a *casus conscientiae* ("case of conscience"), was outlined and then answered in light of the morally relevant principles, giving also appropriate counsel and a fitting penance to aid the penitent in countering sin and in living a more upright life. Pedagogically, this case method approach still is widely used in a variety of practical and professional contexts, from business to medicine to the legal profession.

For centuries, traditional Roman Catholic casuistry was grounded in an overly static understanding of the natural law, which in turn led to a rather impersonal, inflexible, and deductive mode of moral analysis that treated ethics as if it were a branch of mathematics. The deductive approach held that one could easily isolate a few morally relevant principles and then simply read the individual features of a concrete case in light of these principles. This resulted in neat and uniform applications, but it often failed to take into account crucial distinctive features of the individual cases. Many of the illustrative cases seemed improbable at best (e.g., the fictitious couple Titius and Bertha) and bizarre at the worst (e.g., what to do if a particle of the consecrated host should become trapped in one's false teeth). Such casuistry was tied to a view of moral theology that focused on fulfilling laws, often canon law, which were seen as the foundation of the Christian moral life, at least for Roman Catholics.

After the Second Vatican Council (1962–65), Catholic moral theology tried to become more explicitly biblical, and this new approach was accompanied by a turn to a more personalist model of ethics that privileged an inductive and existential approach to moral analysis. On the Protestant side, work such as Joseph Fletcher's "situation ethics" proposed that doing the most loving thing was the key moral norm. Such works simultaneously condemned casuistry and exemplified a casuistry that applied the principle of "the greatest good for the greatest number" to cases. In the wake of these developments, traditional casuistry declined, but it did not entirely vanish. Vestiges can still be found in the acrimonious debates over the moral legitimacy of contraception, just war, or terminating a pregnancy to save the life of the mother. More recently, a number of moral theologians, both Catholic and Protestant, have argued for a rehabilitation of casuistry, employing a more nuanced inductive approach to moral reasoning that would better account for the individual's concrete situation. Even the old *casus conscientiae* ("case of conscience") recognized that in the final analysis, the ultimate criterion for judging moral decisions is the individual acting within the sanctuary of his or her own conscience. In this search for trying to do one's best to act on and promote the good while avoiding or minimizing evil, some form of casuistry seems inescapable. A casuistry informed somehow by the biblical materials may and should contribute to that search.

See also Canon Law; Roman Catholic Moral Theology

Bibliography

Bretzke, J. "Navigating in a Morally Complex World: Casuistry with a Human Face." Pages 169–90 in *A Morally Complex World: Engaging Contemporary Moral Theology*. Liturgical Press, 2004; Jonsen, A., and S. Toulmin. *The Abuse of Casuistry: A History of Moral Reasoning*. University of California Press, 1988; Keenan, J., and T. Shannon, eds. *The Context of Casuistry*. MTMA. Georgetown University Press, 1995; Spohn, W. *Go and Do Likewise: Jesus and Ethics*. Continuum, 1999.

James T. Bretzke, SJ

Celibacy

Continence is abstinence from genital sexual activity. Continence may be practiced within and apart from marriage. Celibacy is a commitment to refrain from marriage and, accordingly, sexual relations. Celibacy therefore has moral dimensions that distinguish it from involuntary sexual inactivity and from periodic or even permanent abstinence within marriage. The celibate renounces the vocation of marriage to embrace another, as when Jesus says that there are "eunuchs for the sake of the kingdom of heaven" (Matt. 19:12).

Ethical issues surrounding celibacy include whether it is "unnatural" and will contribute to psychosexual dysfunction; whether it is morally or spiritually superior to married life; and whether it is essentially related to or incumbent upon Christians who are ordained or consecrated in service to the church.

Scripture and Tradition

In many places Scripture commends marriage and procreation (e.g., Gen. 1:28; 2:18–24; Matt. 19:5–6). Christian approval of celibacy departs from the norms of Jewish culture and Roman law. Celibacy challenges social hierarchies grounded on marriage and kinship. It permits more egalitarian and inclusive access to religious distinction and leadership. Celibacy points to the transfiguration of human relations in the kingdom of God (Matt. 22:30 pars.).

The most extensive scriptural treatment of continence and celibacy is 1 Cor. 7. Paul approves of temporary marital continence for devotional reasons but says that regular conjugal relations can prevent sexual immorality (1 Cor. 7:5, 8–9, 36). Paul's preference—not God's command—is that others be celibate as he is (1 Cor. 7:10). In light of his apocalyptic expectations, he encourages Corinthians to remain as they are (1 Cor. 7:26–31). Then Paul says that married people are anxious to please their spouses, whereas unmarried persons are anxious to please the Lord (1 Cor. 7:32–35). Will Deming argues that these verses do not support sexual asceticism. Rather, 1 Cor. 7 figures in debates between Stoics and Cynics regarding avoidance of civil institutions such as marriage. Only later in Christian tradition does sexual asceticism become the primary aim of celibacy.

Another Pauline passage figures in arguments about the more specific question of clerical celibacy. The principle *unius uxoris vir* (1 Tim. 3:12) acknowledges the presence of married clergy in early Christian communities, a fact that some use to challenge mandatory clerical celibacy. However, Christian Cochini and others posit apostolic origins for clerical celibacy in this very principle, interpreting it and patristic sources as requiring permanent continence for married priests. That continence, they argue, expresses a felt obligation to leave everything and follow the Lord (Luke 18:28–30), which only later became expressed in ecclesiastical law regarding celibacy.

These laws began to appear around the fourth century. The Council of Elvira (c. 306) required continence for priests, deacons, and bishops. Yet the Council of Nicea (325) refused to restrict priesthood to celibates, and the Synod of Gangra (c. 358) denounced the view that celibacy is superior to marriage. Aided by growing monasticism, Lateran Council II (1139) made clerical celibacy mandatory.

Protestant reformers argued that clerical celibacy is neither required nor superior to marriage, citing 1 Tim. 4:1–5 and Heb. 13:4, which affirm the goodness of marriage against its detractors. The Council of Trent (1545–63) reasserted mandatory clerical celibacy but characterized it as a church discipline rather than divine law, meaning that the requirement can be relaxed. Vatican Council II (1962–65) affirmed mandatory celibacy. Pope Paul VI subsequently celebrated celibacy as an unreserved response to Christ that manifests Christ's love for the church.

Contemporary Debate about Clerical Celibacy

Declining vocations to the priesthood and clergy sex abuse scandals prompt some to argue against mandatory clerical celibacy. Heinz-Jürgen Vogels enlists Matt. 19:11 and argues that celibacy is a gift, a distinct call that may or may not accompany a priestly vocation. Catholic priests in Eastern churches can marry, and married (male) Protestant clergy who convert to Catholicism may be ordained as Catholic priests. If in such instances married priests can serve effectively, why require celibacy for priests originally ordained in Western churches?

At its best, celibacy can direct sexual energy toward more inclusive interpersonal bonds, free the celibate for greater devotion to God in prayer and service, and facilitate the celibate's psychic healing and integration. Although it is easily undervalued or used comparatively to denigrate marriage, celibacy remains a valuable witness in the church.

See also Continence; Marriage and Divorce; Sexual Ethics; Singleness; Virginity

Bibliography

Cochini, C. *Apostolic Origins of Priestly Celibacy*. Ignatius Press, 1990; Deming, W. *Paul on Marriage and Celibacy: The Hellenistic Background of 1 Corinthians 7*. Eerdmans, 2004; Pope Paul VI. *Encyclical Letter on Priestly Celibacy: Sacerdotalis Caelibatus*. United States Catholic Conference, 1967; Vogels, H.-J. *Celibacy: Gift or Law? A Critical Investigation*. Sheed & Ward, 1993.

Darlene Fozard Weaver

Character

Character denotes the particular set of qualities, both natural and acquired, that serves to identify a person or community. These qualities are relatively stable and will be manifest as a consistency of action that can be termed "integrity." Accordingly, in the context of Christian ethics, character names an established disposition (or set of dispositions) with respect to the particular conception of the human good exemplified by Christ. Such character is developed over time and, as such, can be formed either toward or away from virtues, understood as those intellectual and affective habits that enable the pursuit of excellence. Conceptually, then, attention to the notion of character accents the dynamic and intentional process of formation that shapes the predispositions of an individual's moral and intellectual terrain.

Character in the Old Testament

The first source of Christian thought on character is the OT, with its rich vocabulary of related terms (e.g., *'ĕmûnâ*, "integrity" [1 Sam. 26:23]; *'ōraḥ*, "way of living" [Job 34:11; Ps. 119:9]; *tām*, "integrity" [Ps. 26:1]; *'āšûr*, "step" [Ps. 44:18; Prov. 14:15]; *'ĕmet*, "faithfulness, reliability" [Neh. 7:2]; *derek*, "way" [Ps. 50:23; 2 Kgs. 22:2; cf. Deut. 5:33]; *'šēm*, "name" [Ps. 41:5; Prov. 22:1]). The OT narratives are of particular importance because they, in providing the historical, communal, and theological context for the scriptural conception of character, are inextricably bound with biblical modes of characterization. In other words, the correlation of narrative and character highlights the ways the character of biblical persons and communities is displayed through narrative and, in so doing, situates narrative as the fundamental category for a biblical concept of character. This correlation has prescriptive implications for contemporary believers because the kind of character esteemed by the biblical authors, and therefore enjoined upon the community that recognizes the scriptural text as authoritative, takes its bearings from the sweep of the narrative. For example, antebellum slave preachers frequently read themselves and their congregations into the exodus narrative. By situating themselves inside the story, these antebellum preachers challenged their hearers to cultivate character appropriate to the controlling narrative. Thus, in telling and retelling the story of the exodus, they not only nurtured a powerful social memory but also fostered in themselves and their communities an image of salvation that included the call first to trust patiently in the deliverance of God their liberator and then to receive from God formation into a distinctive way of life. In such cases, the narrative scripts the lives of those who read the biblical world as their own, thereby determining the kind of character that will be formed in them. In sum, biblical narratives are both descriptive and determinative of character.

The formative power of these stories underscores the fact that biblical narratives were written in and for the community of God's people. The result is a notion of peoplehood (Jer. 7:23; 1 Pet. 2:9–10) in which a particular community is bound together in a particular time and place by a sense of its distinctive identity, shared memory, and unique vocation in the world. More than the aggregation of discrete stories about individuals in relationship with God, the biblical narrative is the story of a covenant people into which individual stories are variously nested within the stories of others and that of the community. As a result, members of the community, whose individual stories are embedded within the communal narrative, derive their sense of meaning and coherence from the larger narrative. Accordingly, character in the OT is frequently a quality of the community in which the individual participates. The people are in covenant relationship with God, and the particular character that God expects of Israel—one marked by traits such as justice, mercy, and humility (Mic. 6:8), and ideally instantiated by the king—is defined with reference to that communal relationship. The biblical story of God's dealings with his people, therefore, is both logically prior to and determinative of the individual's story. Correlatively, there is no individual story apart from the narrative of God's people, since to join God's people means being swept up by grace into this larger drama, receiving eyes to see the world through this narrative and to live accordingly in the world depicted in the Bible.

Finally, the OT wisdom literature (represented by Job, Proverbs, and Ecclesiastes, as well as the apocryphal books Sirach and the Wisdom of Solomon) also constitutes an important locus for reflection on character. This literature contends that the abundant human life is found by walking in the "path of life," guided by the wisdom that begins with the fear of the Lord (Prov. 9:10). The aim of such wisdom goes beyond simple rule-following to embrace the formation of responsible moral character, by which one is conformed to the underlying order of the world, itself a reflection of the wisdom by which God created the world (Prov. 3:19).

Classical Account of Character

The classical account of the acquisition of character through human activity is that of Aristotle (fourth century BCE), whose influence helped shape the linguistic world in which the NT emerged. Distinguishing between virtues of intellect and virtues of character, Aristotle's *Nicomachean Ethics* explains that the latter are acquired through habit, a relationship that explains the similarity of the two words in Greek: *ēthos* ("character") and *ethos* ("habit") (Aristotle, *Eth. nic.* 1103a15–18). Since character results from the repetition of particular activities, Aristotle concludes that we are responsible for our character. Accordingly, the pursuit of virtuous character constitutes a way of life in which the whole of an individual's life is transformed. That is, the self is the subject of a process of formation that is both the means to and the goal of that formation. There is an undeniable degree of circularity in Aristotle's account of character: one can be a virtuous person only by acting as a virtuous person would act (which includes right intention and desire); at the same time, one can become a virtuous person only by having regularly acted virtuously (Hauerwas, *Community of Character*, 139). Nonetheless, given the reciprocal relationship between our actions and our character, such circularity may be unavoidable: our actions shape our character, even as our character constrains the set of available alternatives that we are able to see and to enact.

Character in the New Testament

Although *ēthos*, the technical Aristotelian term for *character*, occurs only once in the NT ("Bad company corrupts good character" [1 Cor. 15:33 TNIV]), the NT is suffused with the concept (though often reflecting the greater influence of the Jewish, rather than Greek, tradition of thought), which recurs through a variety of related terms (e.g., *dokimē*, "character" [Rom. 5:4; Phil. 2:22]; *tropos*, "way of life" [Heb. 13:5]; *katastēma*, "behavior" [Titus 2:3]; *semnos*, "honorable, of good character" [Phil. 4:8; 1 Tim. 3:8, 11; Titus 2:2]). More important, even where such terms are absent, the notion of character is present through the closely related NT concept of discipleship. In other words, character formation is at the heart of the numerous NT passages dealing with discipleship (and the related notions of training, obedience, and sanctification), which is understood as a training process by which the character of Jesus comes to be formed in the lives of his followers. Thus, Jesus says that the disciple who has been fully trained becomes like the teacher (Matt. 10:24–25 // Luke 6:40). Such mimesis goes far beyond slavish imitation, consisting instead of the cultivation of the skill to make a host of subtle judgments and to attend to the world in a particular way. The result of this process of formation is a new way of life that entails the embodiment of Jesus' character in one's own time and place, a way of life that is partly constitutive of salvation itself, since "salvation" refers to more than a change in juridical status, embracing also an increasing participation in the abundant new life of the body of Christ. As John Howard Yoder says, "When God lets down from heaven the new Jerusalem prepared for us, we want to be the kind of persons and the kind of community that will not feel strange there" (Yoder 207). Discipleship entails the transformation of the self, effected through the repetition of particular practices—for example, the Eucharist, prayer, evangelism, hospitality, care for the poor, confession, forgiveness, worship—which, when properly undertaken, help to fashion the Christian's character in the likeness of Jesus.

A strong indication of the concern for character in the NT is found in Jesus' discussion of a tree and its fruit (Matt. 7:16–20 // Luke 6:43–44; cf. Matt. 12:33). Teaching his disciples that a tree is known by its fruit, Jesus closely identifies a person's (or community's) character with the fruit of his or her (or the community's) actions while maintaining that a tree can be made good. In other words, character can be properly formed (just as it can be deformed) so as to produce good fruit. Contrary to much popular understanding, then, character cannot be reduced to interior, private values, since, being intrinsic to the person, character cannot be lightly or easily chosen or changed. This observation suggests the paradoxical nature of character, which is not only deeply individual but also social and is at once both retrospective and prospective. Retrospectively and socially, Jesus' teaching suggests that character can be read off the history of past actions that a person trails behind: "You will know them by their fruits" (Matt. 7:16). Prospectively and individually, the character that one has developed significantly determines and delimits the available actions that one sees, desires, and even is able to perform: "A good tree cannot bear bad fruit, nor can a bad tree bear good fruit" (Matt. 7:18).

Furthermore, by linking character and actions, Jesus' teaching challenges any divorce between the individualistic and social components of discipleship, and together with it a host of related dichotomies, including those sometimes thought to exist between belief and practice, doctrine and ethics, and spirituality and morality. To overcome such false dichotomies is to realize that one's thinking about beliefs and doctrine is bound with one's character, such that deficiencies in the latter will inevitably cripple the former. Holy thinking demands holy living, and vice versa. This truth was recognized by the early church fathers, as witnessed by Athanasius, who wrote the following in the fourth century: "For the searching and the right understanding of the Scriptures there is need of a good life and pure soul, and for Christian virtue to guide the mind to grasp, so far as human nature can, the truth concerning God the Word. One cannot possibly understand the teaching of the saints unless one has a pure mind and is trying to imitate their life" (Athanasius, *Inc.* 57).

Perhaps the most systematic treatment of character belongs to the thirteenth-century theologian Thomas Aquinas, who adapted the newly rediscovered Aristotelian account of the acquisition of character, radically and fundamentally transforming it according to the Christian gospel. Whereas the content of Aristotelian virtue had been defined according to the natural end, or *telos*, of the flourishing Greek city-state, resulting in a set of virtues disposed to the maintenance of the status quo, Thomas held that the true end of human life is supernatural and eschatological—that is, eternal life with God (*ST* I-II, q. 2, a. 8). As a result, the content of Thomistic virtue differs markedly from that of Aristotle, as epitomized by Thomas's choice of martyrdom as the paradigm of courage (as opposed to Aristotle's paradigm, the soldier) and of charity as the heart of all the virtues. Moreover, Thomas maintained that perfect virtue—that is, virtue proportionate to the supernatural end—cannot be acquired through merely human action but rather must continually be received as a gift of God's grace.

Although the church fathers and many medieval theologians acknowledged the strong connection, implied by Jesus, between character and actions, thereby rejecting any bifurcation between the inner and the outer, this insight sometimes was abandoned or repudiated altogether by later thinkers. For example, Martin Luther's reaction against the Roman Catholic Church led him initially to emphasize punctilious acts of obedience over the habitual formation of character—a view that he reconsidered at the end of his life (Gaebler). Moreover, his suggestion that Christians are simultaneously righteous and sinful (*simul jus et peccator*), though intended to give assurance in the face of ongoing struggles with sin, has, in practice, sometimes eviscerated the motivation for holiness, since one can rest content in the present reality of forensic justification. Thus, the possibility of a disjunction between the inner and the outer, anticipated by the voluntarism of the thirteenth-century nominalists (e.g., John Duns Scotus, William of Ockham [see Oberman]), increased during the early modern era, only to be radicalized by later philosophers, especially Descartes and Kant.

Conclusion

The biblical concept of character sketched above strongly indicates that character formation is a necessary precondition for growth in theological knowledge. That is, formation precedes knowledge, just as doing often precedes comprehension. This pattern is not surprising, since in the Gospels the call for the disciples to follow Jesus precedes their understanding of his ministry. (That Jesus' progressive healing of the blind man in Mark 8:22–26 is bookended by explicit references to the disciples' lack of understanding [Mark 8:17–21; 9:31–32] may suggest that spiritual vision too is attained progressively.) In the same way, 2 Pet. 1:5 exhorts its hearers to support their faith with "virtue" (*aretē*), and their already developing virtue with increasing knowledge (cf. Col. 1:10). In this light, Scripture ought not be taken as a mere repository of principles and rules whose truths are uniformly accessible to all regardless of character. On the contrary, Jesus says that those whose hearts are dull and whose ears are hard of hearing cannot understand his message (Matt. 13:15). Instead, Scripture offers an alternative vision of the world that, by the power of the Holy Spirit, gives those who follow Jesus eyes to see and so to live differently. Thus, Heb. 5:14 differentiates between Christian novices and the mature, "whose faculties have been trained by practice to distinguish good from evil." By grace and practice, the character and vision of these mature Christians have been formed, and they can now see how to live truthfully in the world because they see the world and themselves as they really are. In short, since knowledge cannot be separated from character, proper understanding of oneself and the world requires conversion, by which one comes to see the world anew through the lens of God's revelation in Jesus.

Finally, the role of Scripture with respect to character is manifold. First, Scripture presents the grand narrative that governs and norms Christian formation. Second, Scripture relates the stories of Christianity's exemplary characters and, most important, the story of *the* exemplary character in the drama, Jesus, the *dramatis persona* in whom the Author himself is present and who therefore reveals the fullness of the divine dramatic intention. Third, the dynamic interplay between Scripture and character occurs most properly in the context of the believing community. Since an understanding of Scripture cannot be divorced from questions of character and individual stories are always woven into a wider communal tapestry, any individual act of exegesis is always implicated in a much larger context than the discrete encounter between the text and the isolated reader. On the contrary, the reading of Scripture is bound up with the communal life of the interpreters, the character of which will, to a large extent, determine one's ability to read Scripture (whether well or poorly). Finally, any account of biblical character must underscore the centrality of God's grace. Thus, the sort of communal formation of Christic character requisite for the right reading of God's word is itself both a task and a gift of God's grace. In other words, the transformation of believers into a people of character can happen only by the power of the Spirit, who, as Eph. 2:22 shows, fills not only individual believers but also the community as a whole (thus early theologians such as Augustine and Cyprian insisted that there is no salvation outside the community of God's people [*ad extra ecclesiam nulla salus*]). Accordingly, 2 Cor. 3:18 notes that believers are being transformed into the image of Jesus by the work of the Spirit. Similarly, Col. 2:19 asserts that the growth experienced by the body of Christ (as a whole) as it comes to maturity under its head is from God. Character, then, is not something that Christians achieve on their own; it is bound up with the transforming mercies of God.

See also Conversion; Moral Formation; Narrative Ethics, Biblical; Practices; Sanctification; Virtue Ethics

Bibliography

Brawley, R., ed. *Character Ethics and the New Testament: Moral Dimensions of Scripture*: Westminster John Knox, 2007; Brown, W. *Character in Crisis: A Fresh Approach to the Wisdom Literature of the Old Testament*. Eerdmans, 1996; idem, ed., *Character and Scripture: Moral Formation, Community, and Biblical Interpretation*. Eerdmans, 2002; Frei, H. *The Eclipse of Biblical Narrative*. Yale University Press, 1974; Gaebler, M. "Luther on the Self." *JSCE* 22, no. 2 (2002): 115–32; Hadot, P. *Philosophy as a Way of Life: Spiritual Exercises from Socrates to Foucault*. Blackwell, 1995; Hauerwas, S. *A Community of Character: Toward a Constructive Christian Social Ethic*. University of Notre Dame Press, 1981; idem. *Vision and Virtue: Essays in Christian Ethical Reflection*. University of Notre Dame Press, 1974; Murphy, N., B. Kallenberg, and M. Thiessen Nation, eds. *Virtues and Practices in the Christian Tradition: Christian Ethics after MacIntyre*. Trinity Press International, 1997; Oberman, H. "Luther and the Via Moderna: The Philosophical Backdrop of the Reformation Breakthrough." Pages 21–43 in *The Two Reformations: The Journey from the Last Days to the New World*, ed. D. Weinstein. Yale University Press, 2003. Yoder, J. *The Royal Priesthood: Essays Ecclesiological and Ecumenical*. Eerdmans, 1994.

D. Michael Cox and Brad J. Kallenberg

Character Ethics *See* Virtue Ethics

Charity, Works of

The phrase "works of charity" is commonly used to speak of works demonstrating faith, hope, and love for God through love of neighbor. This article uses the phrase "works of love" instead of "works of charity" because it avoids the popular stereotype in which "charity" is limited to mean aid to the poor.

The love that Christians practice is love centered on the other. In practice, the Christian works to ensure that the neighbor secures justice in the Aristotelian sense, whereby the other receives what is rightly due. Agape includes mercy to the neighbor, specifically compassion to the other in times of suffering and need, to the point of helping the neighbor bear the burdens of suffering and overcome its causes. All this helps the neighbor to flourish as a human being made in the image of God. Christian love is an engaged relationship to the other that is transformative to all involved. It is not a detached Stoicism whereby everyone is treated according to a high ethical standard with a clinical and dispassionate sense of equality.

Since the patristic period, Christianity has possessed a rich and unbroken tradition in which works of love are understood to be the practice of the greatest of the theological virtues. The reason for this lies with the human intellectual and volitional motivation to love one's neighbor precisely because that person is made in the image and likeness of God and in so doing to directly imitate God's love for that person. Eastern Orthodox theology describes love of neighbor as an icon of the love that unites the one, triune God, reproducing in an analogous way the perichoretic bonds of love shared by Father, Son, and Holy Spirit.

The biblical warrants used to identify love as the greatest of theological virtues begin with the unbreakable link that the Gospels make between love of God and love of neighbor. The Synoptic Gospels present the two great commandments of Jesus (Matt. 22:34–40; Mark 12:29–31; Luke 10:25–28), which are traditionally understood to be the fount of this virtue because Jesus commanded that his followers link the love of God with love of neighbor. Leviticus 19:18 adds love of neighbor to the Decalogue, which is evidence for Jewish antecedents for Jesus' message, but the NT makes clear that "neighbor" includes all people, even one's enemies, as Jesus' parable of the good Samaritan (Luke 10:29–37) illustrates. Elsewhere in the NT, love of neighbor is elevated to the status of the single best thing a Christian can do for God. In his letters, Paul identifies love of neighbor as *the* fulfillment of God's commandments (Rom. 13:9–10; Gal. 5:14); he holds it up as the sole means by which Christians can test the genuineness of their love (2 Cor. 8:8); he celebrates it as the most excellent act that a Christian can do (1 Cor. 13:13). Beyond Paul, 1 John 4:7–21 declares that God's love for us must be reciprocated through love of neighbor as a prerequisite for one who hopes to perfect this love through a life lived with God. Conversely, the author baldly declares that those who do not love do not know God. James 1:27 privileges love as a requirement for the practice of religion that is worthy before God through the example of caring for widows and orphans.

Patristic theology used these and other like-minded biblical warrants to support two arguments for love as the primary theological virtue. First, to practice the theological virtue of love requires that one already possesses the other two theological virtues: faith and hope. In other words, acts of love toward one's neighbor and God concretely demonstrate faith or one's trust in God by depending on God for grace to help overcome barriers of sin that attenuate practicing the virtues. Acts of love confess the hope or expectation of God's fulfillment of promises made in revelation by cooperating with God's vision. The repeated practice of love for neighbor deepens and refines the Christian's love for God, and that in turn deepens and refines the practice of faith and hope. Consequently, faith and hope find perfection, understood to mean completeness, in the practice of love. Second, the theological virtue of love is primary because it is the only theological virtue to possess an eschatological dimension. Patristic thought argues that faith and hope are theological virtues necessary only in this life to open one to trust and hope in God. On the one hand, with the afterlife and the glorified state in which the Christian is in the direct presence of God, these virtues are no longer needed. On the other hand, love remains perfected because the bond of love between God and the Christian is unmediated in this glorified state.

The eschatological dimension of the works of love contains ethical demands for Christian living in the present. Patristic theology identified Matt. 25:31–46, Jesus' judgment of the nations, as the source of these demands, which Roman Catholics know as the corporal works of mercy. Debate exists as to their origins as well as the identity of "the least of these" with whom Jesus sided. Lactantius demonstrated that the pagan Stoics knew these works of mercy. Biblical scholars have argued either for an independent development of the corporal works of mercy in Jewish thinking, given the numerous exhortations to practice mercy in the OT, or that these Stoic ideas entered Matthew's Gospel by means of a Hellenized Jewish cultural context. Regardless of its origins, and despite the fact that many patristic thinkers were influenced by Stoicism, that philosophy's dispassionate, detached approach to the works of mercy was ultimately rejected by most Christians. Jesus' example of engaged love for the people whom he encountered and ministered to decided the issue. And despite the existence of a tradition in which "the least of these" is understood to be fellow Christians, patristic theologians established the majority consensus: the judgment of the nations should be interpreted to mean that Jesus expects all Christians to serve their neighbor, Christian or not, especially the poor, as a requirement for salvation.

Medieval theology built upon this patristic legacy. Thomas Aquinas, in the *Summa theologiae*, closed his treatise on the theological virtues with a discussion on love (he is explicit that *charity* and *love* are synonymous terms) and its works. His argument for love as the greatest theological virtue, using 1 Cor. 13:13 as his starting point, is threefold. First, love is closer to its proper object, God, than are faith and hope. God does not need to have faith or hope in God's self. Those are virtues that only humans need to possess to have a loving relationship with God. Second, faith and hope could exist as virtues without love, but they could never become perfected virtues because without acts of love, faith and hope have no means by which they can be practiced. Third, Thomas agrees with patristic thought that love possesses the eschatological dimension by which it continues to exist in the afterlife in the state of God's glory. All things move toward their proper object, and love's proper object is the apprehension of the good. The good that is sought is not just moral perfection; it is the completeness of being that lacks nothing. Only God satisfies this understanding of the good. Therefore, in the glorified state God being perfectly known can be perfectly loved.

Roman Catholic and Orthodox theology continues to build on the patristic and medieval understanding of the works of love. Love is still understood to be the chief theological virtue, wherein love of neighbor translates to love of God, perfects faith and hope, and is the sole theological virtue that remains in the kingdom of God. Catholics continue to hold the corporal works of mercy of Matthew's Gospel as a core ethical teaching, a spearhead of Roman Catholic evangelization in that converts usually encounter the church not primarily through its preaching, but through its myriad works in education and social welfare. Works of love continue to serve as a motivator for vowed religious life; examples of orders that focus on the works of love as core to their spiritual charism include the Franciscans, the Vincentians, the Sisters of Charity, and the Sisters of Mercy.

Protestants feature the works of love as an integral part of their theology but often disagree with Catholics and Orthodox as to its proper place. Protestant understandings of the works of love are bound up with the doctrine of justification. Following Martin Luther, many Protestants reorder the theological virtues by placing faith as the primary virtue, through which hope and love find justification before God. Contrary to patristic and medieval theology, Luther thought it presumptuous to think that works of love presuppose faith. Given the pervasiveness of sin, it is difficult for humans to know if a work of love could be done out of love for God. Luther observed that believers and unbelievers alike can perform acts of love for any reason. Therefore, only God is capable of identifying a good work. Luther concluded that the only thing that a person can do is turn to God in faith and then, being justified, enlightened, and fortified by grace, receive the assurance that any and all works of love are good works in the service of God. John Calvin agreed. He acknowledged the virtues in his *Institutes*, but he saw them as worthless without the preeminence of faith to ensure that they led a person to God. He maintained that virtues are, at best, an aid to faith. John Wesley understood the works of love in Christian life by melding ideas from patristic thought and Reformed pietism. Therefore, he is misunderstood as having departed from the priority of faith argued by Luther and Calvin. He did not. Works of love, which Wesley identified as works of mercy, he understood to be the Christian's demonstration of gratitude to God's justification, which only God can initiate as a free gift and the person cannot merit alone. But his theology took a turn toward Arminian thought when he argued that works of love also demonstrate a free and open response by the believer to God's prevenient grace prior to conversion and a willingness to grow in God's grace after.

Christians disagree about the correct place of works of love in Christian theology and life, but all hold that such works are essential in the practice of faith. The variety of ministries that Christian churches have sponsored through the centuries stands as concrete expression of their shared faith, hope, and love for God.

See also Agape; Altruism; Cardinal Virtues; Enemy, Enemy Love; Good Works; Imitation of Jesus; Love, Love Command; Neighbor, Neighbor Love; Self-Love

Bibliography

Augustine. *Faith, Hope, and Charity*, 117–22; idem. *On the Trinity*, 8.10; idem. *Second Discourse on Psalm 31*; Bayer, O. *Martin Luther's Theology: A Contemporary*

Interpretation. Eerdmans, 2008; Chrysostom, J. *Homilies on the First Letter to the Corinthians*, Homily 34; idem. *Homilies on the Gospel of Matthew*, Homilies 61, 79; Collins, K. *The Theology of John Wesley: Holy Love and the Shape of Grace*. Abingdon, 2007; Jerome. *Commentary on Matthew*, 4.25.40; Keenan, J. *The Works of Mercy: The Heart of Catholicism*. Sheed & Ward, 2005; Lactantius. *Divine Institutes*, 6.10, 12; Leo the Great. *Sermons*, 45, 3; 91, 2; Luther, M. "Sermon: Twenty-Sixth Sunday after Trinity." Pages 379–95 in vol. 14 of *Standard Edition of Luther's Works*, ed. J. Lenker. Lutherans in All Lands, 1905; Partee, C. *The Theology of John Calvin*. Westminster John Knox, 2008; Thomas Aquinas. *St. Matthew*. Vol. 1, part 3 of *Catena Aurea: Commentary on the Four Gospels Collected Out of the Works of the Fathers*. John Henry Parker, 1842, 763–64, 865–68; idem. *Summa theologiae*, I-II, q. 62, a. 1–4; q. 64, a. 4; q. 65, a. 35; q. 66, a. 6. Ware; K. *The Orthodox Way*. St. Vladimir's Seminary Press, 1990.

Ramón Luzárraga

Chastity *See* Sexual Ethics

Child Abuse

The term *child abuse* can have a broad range of meanings, from failure to prevent immediate harm to a child to active forms of abuse, including emotional, psychological, sexual, and physical abuse. However, identifying exactly when child abuse has occurred is a much more debated question among Christian ethicists. One common example centers on whether corporal punishment is a form of child abuse.

Until the early 1990s, the topic of children and the issue of child abuse were largely overlooked in the field of Christian ethics, despite significant attention in other fields such as psychology and sociology. Since then, Christian ethicists have engaged the issue of child abuse at a number of different levels. Interests have included issues such as human rights for children, international child labor abuse, clergy abuse, Internet predators, and child neglect by parents and society. Areas of Christian ethical reflection in relationship to child abuse have included original sin and the nature of a child, the moral agency of the child, and the spiritual formation of the child.

The use of the Bible in relationship to child abuse has produced a wide range of responses; however, much of the attention has focused on the question of corporal punishment as it relates to the physical abuse of children. Further, the issue of child abuse often has centered exclusively on younger children. Questions surrounding emotional, psychological, and sexual abuse, particularly in older children, are in need of further consideration.

In addition, the Bible has come under criticism by some as an authoritative text that implicitly and explicitly facilitates child abuse. Two commonly mentioned examples are the sacrifice of Abraham's son Isaac and God the Father's sacrifice of his only-begotten Son, Jesus. Further, scriptural passages such as Prov. 13:24, "Those who spare the rod hate their children, but those who love them are diligent to discipline them," and Heb. 12:5–11, which parallels God and fathers as those who discipline their children, are viewed by some scholars as a parenting manual for corporal punishment. Even more, texts such as Exod. 20:12, which states that children should honor their parents, are seen as holding the potential for perpetuating multiple forms of child abuse.

On the one hand, those who make a case for this negative view of the Bible in relationship to child abuse note that a literal reading of the Bible and a view of the child as inherently sinful are catalysts for a perspective that calls for the breaking of the will and the submission of the child to the parents. On the other hand, supporters of this approach to children point to the emphasis placed in Scripture on physical discipline and obedience of children to their parents. Perhaps part of the difficulty in this debate is that the Bible apparently provides contradictory perspectives on the nature of children, depending on which passages one selects and what interpretive hermeneutic is applied to the Scripture.

One such example in which the Bible is used as a resource to assist victims of child abuse is found in the work of Scott Marshall. Marshall points to passages such as Lev. 18:6–18, where children are protected from sexual abuse, and Matt. 18:1–6, in which Jesus welcomes children into the midst of his adult disciples. Other passages that affirm God's love for children as gifts and blessings further promote a positive account of the role of children within the Bible. Further, Donald Capps uses the image of the garden to recast the theological framework for viewing the raising of children in a more positive perspective.

The fact remains that Christian ethicists and biblical studies have only begun to engage the assortment of issues and questions that surround child abuse within their respective disciplines and, even less, as they interact with one another. Difficult questions remain to be sorted through as the nature and role of children become increasingly urgent issues, especially in light of greater awareness of global child abuse in its myriad forms.

See also Abuse; Children; Discipline; Exploitation; Moral Agency; Parenthood, Parenting; Sexual Abuse

Bibliography

Bunge, M., ed. *The Child in Christian Thought*. Eerdmans, 2001; Capps, D. *The Child's Song: The Religious Abuse of Children*. Westminster John Knox, 1995; Marshall, S. "Honor Thy Father and Mother: Scriptural Resources for Victims of Incest and Parental Abuse." *JPC* 42 (1988): 139–48; Pais, J. *Suffer the Children: A Theology of Liberation by a Victim of Child Abuse*. Paulist Press, 1991.

Mark A. Tarpley

Childlessness

In addition to infertility, there are at least five other important aspects of childlessness that Christian ethicists must consider. First, voluntary childlessness continues to rise in part because of the postponing of childbirth to later years due to career concerns and/or marrying at a later age. Second, childlessness is related to miscarriages. Third, childlessness among same-sex unions continues to become an increasingly significant question. Fourth, the desire of singles for children is becoming an important issue. Fifth, continued medical advancements not only provide us with a greater understanding of infertility but also offer many alternative fertility options to couples unable to conceive children. These new medical findings offer both hopeful possibilities and difficult ethical decisions.

In Scripture, childlessness provides the backdrop for narratives that invoke elements ranging from shame, power, rivalry, and jealousy to promise, providence, and redemption. The biblical examples of Sarah, Rebecca, Rachel, and Hannah as well as the NT figures of Elizabeth and Mary illustrate some of these different elements in what are often referred to as "barren mother" type-scenes. What is revealed in these narratives is the complexity of the human person and human relationships as it relates to childlessness and the divine-human encounter in a life of faith. In addition to the type-scene approach, Jeanne Stevenson-Moessner's recent work has extended the idea of childlessness to include God as the adoptive parent as a powerful biblical metaphor for Christian living.

The way in which the biblical witness and the contemporary ethical landscape interact on the question of childlessness raises a number of challenging ethical questions, many of which depend on how one approaches the biblical text, understands the nature and purpose of children and family structures, and approaches bioethical issues. For example, some ethicists see childbearing and children as an essential characteristic of marriage, while other ethicists give priority to the relational character of marriage and reduce the emphasis on childbearing. Despite these difficulties, general agreement can be found rooted in the biblical witness that God is an important partner in working through the issue of childlessness in which God and the couple or individual must struggle together within a community of faith.

See also Abortion; Adoption; Bioethics; Children; Conception; Concubinage; Family; Family Planning; Homosexuality; Infertility; Marriage and Divorce; Parenthood, Parenting; Procreation; Reproductive Technologies

Bibliography

Cook, J. *Hannah's Desire, God's Design: Early Interpretations of the Story of Hannah*. Sheffield Academic Press, 1999; Havrelock, R. "The Myth of Birthing the Hero: Heroic Barrenness in the Hebrew Bible." *BibInt* 16 (2008): 154–78; Magnuson, K. "Marriage, Procreation, and Infertility: Reflections on Genesis." *SBJT* 1 (2000): 26–42; Stevenson-Moessner, J. *The Spirit of Adoption: At Home in God's Family*. Westminster John Knox, 2003; Wildes, K., ed. *Infertility: A Crossroad of Faith, Medicine, and Technology*. PM 53. Kluwer Academic Publishers, 1997.

Mark A. Tarpley

Children

As people of faith reflect today on the lives of children and on the responsibilities that adults bear for them, they often turn to Scripture as a resource. At the same time, critics have charged that some problems faced by children today, such as child abuse, are caused in large part by teachings about children both in Scripture and in subsequent reflection on Scripture throughout the Christian tradition (Greven; Miller). In moral reflection on children today and the challenges that they face, is Scripture a helpful resource or part of the problem? What does Scripture say about children?

In the OT, children are often described as a joy and a gift. A blessed man is depicted with many children who are like arrows in his quiver or olive shoots around his table (Pss. 127:3–5; 128:3–6), and the births or promises of children are seen as blessings and gifts (Gen. 13:16; 15:1–7; 1 Sam. 1:19–20). God's blessing of Abraham centers on the promise of many descendants (Gen. 12:1–3; 15:5). In Gen. 1:28, Adam and Eve receive their first blessing and first directive: "Be fruitful and multiply." Likewise, the absence of children was a cause of great sorrow throughout both Testaments. Abraham, Sarah, Rachel, Hannah, and Elizabeth grieved over barrenness and longed for children (Gen. 16; 21:1–7; 29:31; 30:1–24; 1 Sam. 1–2; Luke 1).

Children were included in the covenant. As a sign of the covenant, male infants were to be circumcised (Gen. 17:10–14). God also speaks to and works through children in special ways. The boy Samuel heard God calling his name (1 Sam. 3:1–20). Joseph had prophetic dreams (Gen. 37).

David, the youngest son, was called to defeat the giant Goliath (1 Sam. 17).

Children were viewed not only positively as a blessing and a delight. Even from conception and birth, a child was sinful (Ps. 51:5). Children were also foolish and lacking in the wisdom expected of adults (2 Kgs. 2:23–24; Prov. 22:15; Isa. 3:4–5; Wis. 12:24–25; 15:14). Because of both children's value within the community and their ignorance, adults had a special responsibility to teach children (Deut. 6:2–7; Prov. 1:8; 3:1; 6:20). Children, who were to honor and be obedient to their parents, also needed the parents' firm discipline (Prov. 3:11–12; 13:1, 24; 22:15; 23:14).

Adults had special responsibility to provide not only for their own children but also for orphans, including the orphans of foreigners (Exod. 22:22; Deut. 10:18; 24:17–21; Isa. 1:17; 10:2; Jer. 22:3). Harming or failing to care for the orphan is condemned (Deut. 27:19; Job 6:27; 22:9; Ps. 94:6; Jer. 5:28). Children sometimes were adopted and raised by another family or a member of the extended family, as in the case of Moses and Pharaoh's daughter as well as Esther and Mordecai (Exod. 2; Esth. 2:7).

Throughout both Testaments, God is described as a father (Deut. 32:6; Isa. 63:16; 64:8; Jer. 3:4, 19), and God as father models appropriate paternal care for children: loving, providing, defending, rebuking, encouraging, and forgiving. God's parental care extends not just to his Hebrew children, but to all people.

The few passages in the NT Epistles related to children tend to focus on the ordering of the household. In Eph. 6 and Col. 3, children are instructed to obey their parents, and then, immediately following, fathers are instructed to "not provoke your children" (Eph. 6:4; Col. 3:21). Instead, fathers should "bring them up in the discipline and instruction of the Lord" (Eph. 6:4). In both cases, these passages come between similar instructions about obedience of wives to husbands and slaves to masters. Similarly, 1 Tim. 3 and Titus 2 center on the order of the household, listing among the requirements for bishop or deacon the importance of managing one's children well so that they are "submissive and respectful in every way" (1 Tim. 3:4). In Hebrews, adults are instructed to submit to and respect the discipline given by God just as children are to submit to the discipline provided by their parents (Heb. 12:5–11). Generally absent from the Epistles and from Acts is the strong, continuous OT focus on children as a blessing as well as the radical claim found in the Gospels that children provide a model for adults.

In the Gospels, as in the Epistles and the OT, children are instructed to honor and obey their parents (Matt. 15:4; 19:19; Mark 7:10; 10:19; Luke 18:20). Likewise, Jesus picks up other themes of the OT concerning children. Children are a blessing and a part of the covenant community, and adults have special responsibilities to children.

In some respects, however, Jesus' words are strikingly different and more radical than the teachings of the OT and especially the NT Epistles and the wider Greco-Roman context. Jesus not only heals children (Matt. 9:18–26 pars.) but also blesses them and takes the more radical step of pointing to them as models for adults (Mark 10:13–16 pars.).

Jesus uplifts children as those to whom the kingdom of God belongs and insists that unless adults become as children, they will never enter the kingdom (Mark 10:13–16 pars.). Those who wish to be great are especially admonished to become humble like a child (Matt. 18:1–4). When one welcomes children, one welcomes Christ (Matt. 18:5 pars.). Moreover, children can have special knowledge (as in the OT). In Matthew, it is not the religious leaders but the children who recognize the identity of Jesus and shout, "Hosanna to the Son of David" (Matt. 21:14–16). In response to the anger of the priests and scribes, Jesus alludes to Ps. 8:2: "Out of the mouths of infants and nursing babies you have prepared praise for yourself" (Matt 21:16 NASB).

The value of children is also emphasized in the NT narrative by God's coming into the world in the form of an infant. Before God took on the nature of an adult, God had assumed the nature of an infant and child. Moreover, even within the being of God we find the relationship between parent and child; the internal relations of the Trinity are expressed in the familial language of the love of son for father and father for son.

Although Jesus spoke of children as valuable and as models for adults, he expressed ambivalence about familial relationships, including the relationships between parents and children. In Matt. 19:29, for example, we find Jesus saying, "Everyone who has left houses or brothers or sisters or father or mother or children or fields, for my name's sake, will receive a hundredfold, and will inherit eternal life."

Many of the teachings about children found in the Epistles and the Gospels stand in sharp contrast. Whereas the Epistles give greatest attention to the ordered relationship between parents and their own children, Jesus focused more on the relationship between faithful people and children generally, not simply or necessarily those who are biologically related. Whereas the Epistles emphasize hierarchical relationships within the family and the obligation of fathers to provide care and discipline for their children and for the children, in turn, to be obedient to their parents, Jesus lifts up children as models for adults.

These teachings about children from the OT and the NT provide the basis for subsequent Christian reflection on children. Several issues have been predominant. First, the more radical Gospel themes about children as models for adults have generally been neglected in favor of an emphasis on authority and order. Christian thinkers have frequently drawn on the fifth of the Ten Commandments, to honor parents, as well as admonitions from the NT Epistles for children to obey their parents (especially their fathers) and for fathers to properly order their households and discipline their children.

For example, Martin Luther, reflecting on the fifth commandment, insists that children should "revere their parents as God's representative" and honor them "as the most precious treasure and the jewel on earth" (Luther 23, 30). Obedience to parents is a greater work than almost any other. It should please children to obey their parents because this obedience "is so highly pleasing to the Divine Majesty and to all angels, and vexes all devils, and is, besides, the highest work which we can do, after the sublime divine worship" (Luther 26). Even almsgiving and care of neighbor are not as important as honoring and obeying one's parents.

Another common topic of discussion in Christian reflection on children has been the nature of children. In most of the Christian tradition (as in the Jewish tradition), children are seen as a great blessing and gift. John Calvin and John Wesley, for example, drew on Ps. 127:3 to insist that children are a blessing from God. Friedrich Schleiermacher wrote of the blessings that come through dealing with children and youth; interaction with the young, "more than anything else, keeps us fresh and cheerful" (Schleiermacher 46).

When Augustine and the Pelagians argued about the nature of children, they set the framework and even vocabulary for much subsequent discussion in the Christian tradition. When the Pelagians insisted that children are born with capacities for good and, like Adam, take on sin over time, Augustine countered by insisting that from conception a child inherits the original sin of Adam, which had been passed down from one generation to the next. Before children have actual opportunity to sin, they are in a state of noninnocence. Only through baptism would children be cleansed from the guilt of original sin. A key passage of Scripture in the discussions of original sin from Augustine and Pelagius through much of the Christian tradition is Rom. 5:12: "Therefore, just as sin came into the world through one man, and death came through sin, and so death spread to all because all have sinned." Reflecting on this passage, Augustine wrote, "As infants cannot help being descended from Adam, so they cannot help being touched by the same sin, unless they are set free from its guilt by the baptism of Christ" (Augustine 335).

Thomas Aquinas, Martin Luther, John Calvin, John Wesley, and many others in Western Christianity incorporated, in part, this Augustinian understanding of original sin in children. In many cases, they also softened it. John Wesley, for example, insisted that all bore the guilt of the original sin, but that through prevenient grace all humans experienced a restoration of some of the capacities lost in the fall. Late in life, Wesley even suggested that by prevenient grace the guilt of original sin was erased as soon as any child was born.

These claims about the nature of children are linked to another set of discussions about parental responsibilities for children. Children, as special blessings from God and as beings who are immature and even sinful, deserve and need special care. Parents are admonished to care for, instruct, and discipline their children. From John Chrysostom and Thomas Aquinas to John Calvin and Jonathan Edwards, the role of parents in caring and disciplining children is paramount.

Of course, not all parents are able or willing to care for their children, and in these cases the responsibility falls on others—other individuals, churches, or the state, for example. The concept of subsidiarity, originating in Catholic moral theology, provides one example of how to order these various responsibilities. Applying the concept of subsidiarity to the care of children, one would hold that ideally children should be cared for by those at the most immediate local level, the family. If the family fails to care for the children, then the responsibility falls to other local groups such as churches or local civic organizations. If these smaller groups fail to care for children, then the responsibility falls to the state.

Recent decades have seen a resurgence of interest in children as fitting topics of sustained theological and ethical reflection. Some of these discussions continue the themes addressed in Scripture and in the Christian tradition: What responsibilities do individuals and social groups have for children? What is the nature of a child, and, given that nature, how should children be formed? How is the household to be ordered, and how are children best disciplined?

Christians today face other topics that are not so familiar. The desire for children is echoed in Scripture, but some of the reproductive techniques used to get those children are new and present moral challenges unknown centuries or even decades earlier. Some Christian denominations have opposed, for example, in-vitro fertilization and donor insemination; others have given support. Moreover, the desire to form and nurture healthy children is a familiar theme, but the capacity to shape children before birth through genetic engineering and genetic selection is also new and presents challenges to Christian communities. New technologies for birth control and for the termination of pregnancies have also changed the moral landscape in relation to children.

Although the responsibility that adults bear for children is a key theme of Scripture and the subsequent Christian tradition, the affirmation of the inherent "rights of children" is a more recent way of framing and reshaping the discussion. What rights do children have, and how do these rights shape their relationships with their families and societies? How does the right to bodily integrity and autonomy shape the relationship between parent and child? If one affirms that children have rights to healthcare, food, housing, and education, who is responsible for the protection of these rights and the provision of the things necessary to fulfill them? What responsibilities do Christians have to secure these rights for children around the world, half of whom live in poverty? Because of the global nature of the economy, poverty in one country is often linked to the consumption and investments of people in other countries. What responsibility do Christians have for consuming and investing in ways that are life-giving for children around the world?

To return to the question with which this article began, have the OT and the NT and their interpretation over time been helpful or harmful to children? Some themes in Scripture are clearly beneficial, such as the claims that children are a blessing, a special responsibility, and even a model for adults. Other themes are thought by some to be damaging for children, such as the claim that infants and children are somehow guilty of sin (even original sin). Bonnie Miller-McLemore, however, argues that a robust and nuanced understanding of sin can help adults today reflect on and care for children more faithfully. According to Miller-McLemore, many recent reflections on children and childrearing (e.g., in the field of psychology) are so committed to the idea of children's innocence that they have difficulty accounting for the complexity of children's moral and spiritual lives, including their struggles with selfishness and malice. She argues that Christian teachings about sin would help account for and take more seriously the complex lives both of children and parents. Miller-McLemore's work is one example of a recent trend among mainline Christian scholars to look more closely at Scripture and the Christian tradition for resources to reflect on and help children (see also Bunge; Bunge, Fretheim, and Gaventa; Jenson).

See also Child Abuse; Discipline; Family; Foster Care; Household Codes; Infertility; Orphans; Parenthood, Parenting; Reproductive Technologies

Bibliography

Augustine. "Letter 157." Pages 319–53 in vol. 20 of *The Fathers of the Church*, ed. R. Deferrari. Catholic University of America Press, 1953; Bunge, M., ed. *The Child in Christian Thought*. Eerdmans, 2001; Bunge, M., T. Fretheim, and B. Gaventa, eds. *The Child in the Bible*. Eerdmans, 2008; Couture, P. *Seeing Children, Seeing God: A Practical Theology of Children and Poverty*. Abingdon, 2000; Greven, P. *Spare the Child: The Religious Roots of Punishment and the Psychological Impact of Physical Abuse*. Vintage Books, 1990; Hall, A. *Conceiving Parenthood: American Protestantism and the Spirit of Reproduction*. Eerdmans 2007; Jenson, D. *Graced Vulnerability: A Theology of Childhood*. Pilgrim Press, 2005; Luther, M. *The Large Catechism*. Trans. R. Fischer. Fortress, 1963; Miller, A. *For Your Own Good: Hidden Cruelty in Child-Rearing and the Roots of Violence*. Farrar, Straus & Giroux, 1983; Miller-McLemore, B. *Let the Children Come: Reimagining Childhood from a Christian Perspective*. Jossey-Bass, 2003; Schleiermacher, F. *The Christian Household: A Sermonic Treatise*. Trans. D. Seidel and T. Tice. Edwin Mellen Press, 1991.

Rebekah Miles

Choice *See* Free Will and Determinism

1–2 Chronicles

The sixty-five chapters of 1–2 Chronicles make this work one of the longest in the OT. Written in the first half of the fourth century BCE in Jerusalem, Chronicles urges wholehearted dedication to the second temple, its clergy, and its liturgical rites. Chronicles could also be characterized as a retelling of the history of the monarchy in Jerusalem, from David to Zedekiah, to which is prefaced a genealogy beginning with Adam and continuing to a list of the descendants of the twelve sons of Israel (Jacob). There is also a list of the descendants of King Saul and an account of his death.

David and Solomon are presented by the Chronicler in an idealized fashion. They presided over a united people of God and were responsible for the building of the first temple and establishing its regular clergy and services. David's generosity toward the construction of the temple knew no bounds and provided an excellent example for the other leaders of the people (1 Chr. 29:1–9). In his prayer at the dedication of the temple Solomon urged God to respond to calamities such as drought, famine, sickness, and especially military defeat by hearing the people when they repent and forgiving them (2 Chr. 6:24–35). In response to the prayer, Yahweh promised that if the people humble themselves, pray, seek his face, and repent, he will hear them, forgive their sin, and heal the land. This promise provides a pattern for human and divine activity in many points of Judah's history, especially in the case of Hezekiah, who serves as a second David and Solomon.

This idealized portrait of David and Solomon contrasts sharply with the description of these kings in the books of Samuel and Kings. No mention is made in Chronicles of David's adultery with Bathsheba, his murder of Uriah, his son Amnon's rape of his half-sister Tamar and David's weak response to this crime, and Absalom's revolt and his death under questionable circumstances. David's long contest with Saul (1 Sam. 16–30) is passed over in silence, and Yahweh turns the kingdom over to David in 1 Chr. 10:13 with no mention of the civil war with Ishbaal or the death of Abner and Ishbaal under questionable circumstances (2 Sam. 2–4). Similarly, the book does not discuss the seven hundred wives or three hundred concubines of Solomon, let alone their leading him astray to serve other gods (1 Kgs. 10:28–11:40). Even Solomon's journey to sacrifice at the "high place" at Gibeon (1 Kgs. 3:2–6) is cast in a different light, since according to the Chronicler the tabernacle was located at Gibeon (2 Chr. 1:3–6). Here, Solomon did not become king through the conniving of Nathan and Bathsheba, who took advantage of David's weakness in his final illness, nor is there any mention of the attempt by Adonijah, Solomon's brother, to usurp the throne. Rather, David, in full command of his powers, designated Solomon as king in fulfillment of the oracle of Nathan (1 Chr. 17:15; 22:9–10), and he cited a divine oracle designating Solomon as the king chosen by Yahweh (1 Chr. 28:6–7, 10). David's sin in regard to the census is retained, but David also acknowledged his guilt and decided to fall into God's hands because God's mercy is great (1 Chr. 21). There is no evidence that the Chronicler meant to silence the books of Samuel and Kings or even replace them. Instead, he stressed qualities of David and Solomon and of their rule of a united Israel that spoke directly to the issue that necessitated his writing. They were dedicated to the temple, generously supported it, and followed God's will in erecting it.

Hezekiah is one of several kings who reformed worship in the temple (cf. Asa, Jehoshaphat, Joash, Manasseh, and Josiah) and removed idols and other forms of syncretism. Hezekiah and Josiah also invited remnants from the north to participate in worship in Jerusalem, foreshadowing the same inclusive view of Israel that runs throughout Chronicles.

In the book of Kings, Manasseh is described as the worst king of Judah and is responsible for misleading the people to misbehave more than the nations that preceded them in the land (2 Kgs. 21:1–9 // 2 Chr. 33:1–10). Because of this behavior, exile had become inevitable, despite the outstanding behavior of Manasseh's grandson Josiah (2 Kgs. 21:11–16; 23:26; 24:3–4). In Chronicles, however, the sinful Manasseh was taken captive to Babylon, where he repented, humbled himself, affirmed monotheism, and was graciously restored to his throne by Yahweh. Back in Jerusalem, Manasseh also carried out a number of reforms and restored the altar of Yahweh and offered on it sacrifices of well-being and of thanksgiving (2 Chr. 33:11–17). Whatever one's ethical behavior, therefore, repentance and forgiveness are possible, and Manasseh is described as a model for Judah itself when it goes into exile.

The Chronicler was faced with a serious ethical dilemma as he wrote his book. The postexilic province of Yehud, in which he lived, was a small territory, about three times the size of the city of Chicago, with a population of fifty thousand or less, perhaps as small as twenty thousand. Yehud was therefore a tiny entity in the mighty Persian Empire, which extended from Libya and Egypt in North Africa in the west and to India in the east. Some in his audience no doubt wanted to throw off the hegemony of that empire, but the Chronicler recognized that the return of the exiles from Babylon to Palestine and the building of the second temple took place because Yahweh had used King Cyrus to bring these policies about. The Chronicler seems to have accepted the rule of the Persians as inevitable, at least for his time, and advocated his views on the temple, its clergy, and its rituals within this overall support for the Persian Empire. In our time, when many employ postcolonial insights in interpreting the Bible, the ethics of the Chronicler's position is debatable. The Chronicler, as in many of our own ethical choices, seems to have settled for what was realistically possible.

While in many parts of the Bible faithfulness is followed by reward or well-being and unfaithfulness by punishment, in Chronicles these rewards or punishments are more immediate and individual, normally taking place within a person's lifetime. There is no accumulated sin or merit as in the books of Kings. The doctrine of retribution places high value on moral or ethical decisions. That doctrine, of course, also has its problems, as the book of Job persuasively argues, when apparently righteous persons are not rewarded. Others argue that the doctrine of retribution can contribute to a feeling of works-righteousness. Some argue that the Chronicler is less concerned to demonstrate strict relations between acts and consequences than to emphasize Yahweh's benevolence and mercy toward the people (cf. 1 Chr. 22:12; 29:18; 2 Chr. 30:18).

The focus on temple worship and the rights of its clergy might suggest that the Chronicler had a very wooden idea of piety and the religious life. But we need to note how often the word *joy* is used in his history and how warmly he can speak of faith: "Believe in the LORD your God and you will be established" (2 Chr. 20:20).

See also Exile; 1–2 Kings; Old Testament Ethics; 1–2 Samuel

Bibliography

Japhet, S. *I & II Chronicles*. OTL. Westminster John Knox, 1993; Klein, R. *1 Chronicles*. Hermeneia. Fortress, 2006; Knoppers, G. *1 Chronicles 1–9*. AB 12. Doubleday, 2004; idem. *1 Chronicles 10–29*. AB 12A. Doubleday, 2004.

Ralph W. Klein

Church *See* Ecclesiology and Ethics

Church and State *See* Government

Circumcision

Circumcision is a rite practiced in a number of West Semitic cultures, involving some modification of the foreskin of the penis. As practiced in Israel, the rite involved the complete removal of the foreskin and was most often performed on the eighth day after a boy's birth. It was a necessary mark of belonging to God as part of the chosen line of Abraham, and as a member of the covenant people that receive (and, in part, are the realization of) God's promises (Gen. 17:9–14). The fact that this rite of "belonging" could be performed only on male Israelites raises questions about how a woman's place in the covenant people was understood to be secured, whether by her relationship to an Israelite man (a father or husband) or by some other means.

Circumcision, together with covenant membership, was not strictly related to biological descent. Those who are not "Abraham's seed" by birth could become such through circumcision (Gen. 17:12; Jdt. 14:10; Josephus, *Ant.* 13.9.1; 13.11.3).

Election, of which circumcision is an outward sign, carried ethical responsibilities. God chose Abraham so "that he may charge his children and his household after him to keep the way of the LORD by doing righteousness and justice" (Gen. 18:19). In recognition of this ethical dimension, Jewish authors often assert that outward circumcision is insufficient of itself to guarantee the reception of covenant blessings. These authors call for the metaphorical application of circumcision to other parts of the body, including ears, lips, heart, and inclination, images that refer to hearing God's commandments correctly, speaking the truth about God's decrees, and "loving God" faithfully (which meant faithfully observing the covenant stipulations [Deut. 10:16–17]). Such behavior showed the internalization of the outward sign of circumcision (Jer. 9:25–26).

During the Hellenistic period, serious cultural and political pressures were brought to bear against physical circumcision. Greeks despised the practice as a barbaric mutilation of the human form. As a result, Jews who were eager to blend in with the Greeks and other gentiles around them and to participate (naked, as was the custom) in Greek cultural practices and networking opportunities such as the athletic games in the gymnasium (2 Macc. 4:13–15) even performed epispasm in order to reverse the effects of circumcision (1 Macc. 1:14–15). A ban on circumcision was rigidly enforced during the most fevered period of Hellenization (1 Macc. 1:44–61). Nevertheless, most Jews of the period maintained their commitment to physical circumcision as the necessary rite for entering the covenant people.

Particularly in the face of ridicule and cultural prejudice, Jews began to formulate more advanced moral interpretations of physical circumcision to defend the practice. Philo of Alexandria (d. c. 50 CE) provides the fullest example of such reflection (see especially *Spec. Laws* 1.1.1–1.2.11; *QG* 3.48). In addition to benefits of hygiene, ritual purity, and fertility, he argued that circumcision trims the excess of sexual pleasure by removing the protective covering that keeps the glans beneath more sensitive. The rite thereby enacts, and thence continues to symbolize, the Jew's commitment to master the full range of the passions and to limit self-indulgence so that those passions do not subvert the Jew's commitment to the ethical virtues prized by Jews and Greeks alike (*Spec. Laws* 1.2.9; see also *QG* 3.48). This connects the rite with the positive value placed on self-mastery in much of the ethical literature of the period (4 Maccabees provides a readily accessible example). The ethical meaning of circumcision here, which for Philo ennobles and promotes the continued practice, becomes for Paul a substitute for circumcision. In the letter in which Paul argues most vociferously against the necessity of circumcision for joining the people of promise, he concludes by spelling out how the gift of the Holy Spirit enables the mastery of the passions that, for Philo, circumcision symbolized and began (Gal. 5:13–26).

In addition, circumcision nurtures humility before God as the giver of all life, a visible reminder that we are not ourselves the authors of life, even of our own offspring (*Spec. Laws* 1.2.10; see also *QG* 3.48). The rite, Philo explained, was a remedy for human pride in the face of life and death; from the point of insemination, circumcision called men (especially) to acknowledge God's sovereignty over all life.

Philo's figurative understanding does not lessen his commitment to physical circumcision (*Migration* 89–93). The same view would not prevail within the early Christian movement. Aware of the prophetic and Deuteronomic emphasis on the indispensability of the "circumcision of the heart," Paul argues that such inward circumcision is alone necessary, since it is what God truly seeks and approves in a human being (Rom. 2:25–29; see also *Barn.* 9.4–5). Paul declares three times that "neither circumcision nor uncircumcision" carries any value (1 Cor. 7:19; Gal. 5:6; 6:15), wholly replacing this outward sign with a focus on the ethical transformation that genuine discipleship entails. Christians were circumcised with "a circumcision not effected by hands" in the "putting off of the body of the flesh" by dying and being buried with Christ in the rite of baptism, thus being raised to new life from a state of being "dead in trespasses" (Col. 2:11–13). The ontological-ethical implications of baptism (see most especially Rom. 6:1–11) reprise the ethical implications of circumcision: dying to the passions of the flesh and the deeds to which they drive us, deeds that are not consonant with righteousness and justice, so as to use our bodies henceforth as tools of justice.

See also Covenant

Bibliography

Collins, J. "A Symbol of Otherness: Circumcision and Salvation in the First Century." Pages 163–86 in *"To See Ourselves as Others See Us": Christians, Jews, and "Others" in Late Antiquity*, ed. J. Neusner and E. Frerichs. Scholars Press, 1985; deSilva, D. *4 Maccabees*. GAP. Sheffield Academic Press, 1998; Fox, M. "The Sign of the Covenant: Circumcision in Light of the Priestly *'ot* Etiologies." *RB* 81 (1974): 557–96; Goldingay, J. "The Significance of Circumcision." *JSOT* 88 (2000): 3–18; Hall R. "Epispasm and the Dating of Ancient Jewish Writings." *JSP* 2 (1988): 71–86; Sasson, J. "Circumcision in the Ancient Near East." *JBL* 95 (1966): 473–76.

David A. deSilva

City, Cities *See* Urbanization

Civil Disobedience

"Civil disobedience" is a modern phrase coined by Henry David Thoreau for which there is no simple consensus definition. Examples that often inform attempts at definition include the movements associated with Mohandas Gandhi and Martin Luther King Jr. Other attempts include the possibility of violent resistance within civil disobedience. As a broad working definition, "civil disobedience" refers to the deliberate disobedience of a law in order to preserve one's moral integrity, protest, bring attention to an injustice, and/or catalyze the process of change in a bad law or policy.

Ethical-theological analyses of disobedience proceed on the assumption that there are two distinct yet overlapping general spheres of law and authority, one (human law) being subordinate to the other (God's law), and that conflicts between these spheres are possible. This conflict is present in, for example, the plight of Daniel (see Dan. 6), his choice being presented as one between obeying God's law or a human law. There is a general presumption, however, that those subject to any law should obey that law (see Rom. 13:1–8; Titus 3:1; 1 Pet. 2:13–16). The burden of proof, the demonstration that a conflict actually exists and calls for civil disobedience in some instance, therefore, rests with the disobedient.

At least one distinction is critically necessary in considerations of civil disobedience. Laws that oblige one to do what God forbids or prevent one from doing what God commands are thereby deemed bad and should be disobeyed. These instances call for direct civil disobedience—disobedience of the bad law. The refusals by the Hebrew midwives to obey Pharaoh's murderous command (Exod. 1:15–21) and by Peter and the apostles to stop preaching (Acts 4:18–19; 5:27–29) exemplify, respectively, both aspects of direct civil disobedience. Indirect civil disobedience involves disobeying a law that one would normally respect in the course of protesting some other law or policy deemed bad, as exemplified by Esther's disobedience on behalf of the Jews (Esth. 4:11, 16).

Disagreements in evaluating particular instances of civil disobedience today often involve (1) establishing the immorality of a law or policy, (2) differing conceptions of the nature and role of moral norms, and/or (3) the proper method of weighing conflicting norms when deliberating possible actions. These complexities and difficulties are exemplified in current debates among opponents of abortion laws in the United States who ask, for example: what actions of indirect civil disobedience are justified in relation to a law that does not command but permits the sin of others?

Further general principles should also inform reflection on civil disobedience today.

1. One must be diligent about the facts and context in question to satisfy the burden of proof.
2. Civil disobedience should be considered a last resort, especially in relatively just, liberal societies.
3. The moral objections to the injustice of the bad law or policy in question must outweigh the moral objections to civil disobedience generally as well as the particular act of civil disobedience chosen and its consequences.
4. One should expect and accept punishment for breaking the law, which strengthens the moral force of a given instance of civil disobedience by reflecting one's commitment to the rule of law and normal civil obligations.

See also Authority and Power; Civil Rights; Conscientious Objection; Dirty Hands; Dissent; Duty; Government; Martyrdom

Bibliography

Bedau, H., ed. *Civil Disobedience in Focus*. Routledge, 1991; Coleman, G. "Civil Disobedience: A Moral Critique." *TS* 46 (1985): 21–37.

Peter L. Jones

Civil Rights

Civil rights are individual or group protections from threats, especially of violence or deprivation of freedom, that should be enumerated and established by the state. Civil rights, in the specific sense of the term, developed in the Western liberal political tradition, although certainly other political theories also prohibit arbitrary actions of formal and informal authorities that harm some or all individuals in a society. It is generally assumed that civil rights are not something granted by society; rather, they are intrinsic to the individual or natural human order. In other words, the general assumption is that the social-contract description was not the invention of civil rights but rather a revealing of something essential for the thriving of human community and individuals. Until fairly recently, these rights were defined as "negative"—that is rights of noninterference. Civil rights theories almost always include (1) some claim about the inherent nature of the rights-holder, (2) some assertion that rights check the behavior of the majority and/or more powerful, and (3) some description of rights protection as a primary function of the state.

Civil rights tend to be asserted using deontological language; rule utilitarian reasoning can generate a prima facie standard of rights but not the "trumping" authority of rights over utility. What civil rights theories do not have in common is agreement on (1) who is included among rights-holders, (2) the extent of specific rights, (3) how rights should be prioritized, and (4) the ultimate source of rights.

The two major impediments to realized civil rights are bigotry acted out in the populace and intentional deprivation for self-serving purposes by those in power.

Recently, civil rights as a category has been expanding, both in the sense of specific rights being "added" or "discovered" and in the analytical ethical sense. The latter is most evident in the increasing use of the three-generation model.

- First-generation rights are negative rights or rights of noninterference (e.g., freedom of speech, assembly, religious exercise).
- Second-generation rights are positive rights or rights of entitlement (e.g., food, healthcare, education).
- Third-generation rights are rights of groups (e.g., right to self-determination for ethnic groups, solidarity claims for classes of people, the right of development; these allow the abrogation of prima facie individual rights for the sake of the collective rights).

Traditionally, only the first-generation rights were deemed actual civil rights. Now, the expanded understanding is used by some United Nations affiliates, nongovernmental organizations (NGOs), and nation-states (notably South Africa). This more recent analytical model is sometimes justified with the language of the French Revolution: liberty (first-generation negative rights), equality (second-generation rights of entitlement), and fraternity (third-generation rights of the community). Third-generation rights do not readily fit traditional Western social-contract theory, since the moral agent ceases to be the human individual and becomes instead the human as a subset or component of the group.

An example of the three-generation model can be constructed using selection for employment. The right to apply for a job and be fairly considered would be deemed first-generation (this would include affirmative action, narrowly understood). The right to a job, but not necessarily that particular one, would be a second-generation right. If, instead of affirmative action, there was an actual quota for hiring by ethnic or gender category, that would be a third-generation right for the purported disenfranchised group.

The understanding of civil rights has been marked by punctuated change, with the greatest shifts starting in the eighteenth century and often associated with social trauma. The United States was declared to exist on July 4, 1776. In the founding document, the Declaration of Independence, Thomas Jefferson and his coauthors appropriated, with a slight change, John Locke's language of rights to life, liberty, and property from the *Second Treatise on Government*. All individuals were entitled to life and liberty, though in practice these rights were limited by the claim that some could not properly exercise them (on the basis of gender, ethnicity, property ownership, and status as a slave). The enforcement of civil rights was also restricted by citizenship status and by the nation-state's borders (both limits on enforcement still remain to a great extent). Each individual was also at liberty, theoretically, to pursue his or her own goals, with "happiness" understood as the contentment that comes from satisfying the individual telos or human purpose. Importantly, it was the pursuit of happiness, not happiness itself, that was deemed a right. Using a social-contract construct, the Declaration of Independence and the US Constitution emphasized negative rights (especially in the Bill of Rights).

Two other influential social arguments about rights occurred in the eighteenth century. With its heritage of the Magna Carta and common law, a debate raged in Great Britain over the degree to which rights could or should be extended to or protected for those at various levels of society. In particular, "rights" language was increasingly used to protect the recently urbanized who had been forced off land due to the application of the enclosure laws and industrialization, those seeking religious freedom, and, as in the United States, those enslaved.

The French social argument about rights, while similar, placed a far greater emphasis on the social location of the rights-holders, specifically in debates about the property holdings and obligations to the poor of the various "estates." The social contract in France, paralleling arguments in Jean-Jacques Rousseau, was based on the "general will" (*la volonté générale*), by which the whole was deemed more than the sum of the individual parts. In other words, civil rights could be held not only by individuals but also by groups or, importantly, by "the" group (the state).

In the mid-nineteenth century in the United States the civil rights of individuals came into conflict with sovereignty claims or so-called states' rights. The Civil War was directly or indirectly about which government entity (federal or state) had the authority to enumerate civil rights and about the authority of the government (at any level) to limit the negative rights of particular classes of people. In order to morally allow ethnospecific slavery and the ethnic cleansing of the indigenous population, some persons living within the national borders had to be defined as being out of or at the edge of the human race; had they not been so defined, they would have been entitled to civil protection under the social contract. After the end of the Civil War in 1865 and the adoption of the Fourteenth Amendment in 1868, legal protections were extended to all individuals (again, this was theoretical, as women and indigenous people remained in lower statuses and application was inconsistent).

Women were included in voting rights in the United States with the ratification of the Nineteenth Amendment in 1920, a consequence of the suffragette movement (first-wave feminism) in the late nineteenth and early twentieth centuries. This group of women, some from socially liberal traditions and some from evangelicalism, commonly were associated with the temperance movement. They argued that the rights of women would strengthen families and the society at large. A smaller segment of the movement, associated with birth control and eugenics efforts, used both "rights" and "utilitarian" language.

The next major shaping of civil rights in the United States occurred during the Great Depression, in the late 1920s and the 1930s. New Deal political language, in response to economic malaise and building on early twentieth-century labor organization formulas, added entitlements or positive rights to those rights that the state was obligated to protect. Franklin Roosevelt famously declared in his 1941 State of the Union message that all people were entitled not only to negative rights but also to freedom from want, implying a governmental obligation to positively satisfy the physical needs of citizens to the extent possible.

The post–World War II civil rights movement was primarily a response to the limitation of individual legally acknowledged rights by nonfederal governmental entities and, to a lesser extent, private organizations. School boards used "separate but equal" arguments based on the 1896 *Plessy v. Ferguson* reasoning, county commissions skewed literacy tests for voting, and public accommodations were restricted on the basis of "color." Jim Crow laws, coupled with the broader cultural passivity toward or even affirmation of those laws, created onerous burdens on a specific class of persons. Events, though, seemed to weave together to make the enforcement of civil rights inevitable. The insistence that African American soldiers be allowed to fight in World War II, the 1954 *Brown v. Board of Education* case led by the NAACP, activity by the Brotherhood of Sleeping Car Porters and the National Council of Negro Women, as well as shifts in professional sports, promoted civil rights in accord with the post–Civil War constitutional amendments. The final implementation of legal protection for civil rights regardless of ethnicity was cemented by the civil rights movement proper with actions directed by Martin Luther King Jr. and the Southern Christian Leadership Conference as well as those led by the Congress of Racial Equality, the Student Nonviolent Coordinating Committee, and local boycott groups. King drew on experiences in South Africa and in India under Gandhi, and, in a way not seen since the urban social crusaders of the early twentieth century, he appropriated religious language. Specifically, King used just-coercion theory (see King's "Letter from a Birmingham Jail") and "beloved community" language in asserting the necessity of coercive nonviolent action. In essence, the American civil rights movement was a recollection of the negative-rights assertions of the postbellum amendments and the insistence that the governments, at the various levels, protect citizens as members of the social contract.

In the 1960s and through the 1970s the language of rights changed, with a far greater emphasis on positive rights and identity politics. The anticolonial revolutions of the post–World War II decades provided language that shaped civil rights arguments in the so-called developed world. A heavy emphasis on "liberation" arguments and the uniqueness of various group perspectives shaped debates over women's rights and gay rights, and, most important at a theoretical level, pushed the discussion of civil rights away from dichotomous to multilayered thinking. At the end of the twentieth century in the United States it was generally recognized that civil rights is not only a matter between blacks and whites but also a legitimate concern for other ethnic groups as well as groups defined by other characteristics. What certainly was not agreed upon, however, was what constituted a group deserving of distinct protection, as arguments about abortion, gay marriage, and animal rights have indicated.

Civil rights in a narrow social-contract sense is neither rejected nor supported directly in Scripture. What is quite evident in the OT is that all persons are due just treatment. However, this is an assertion not so much about the recipient as about the nature of those who serve. When respect for the sojourner is commended, the appeal is to the moral character of individuals and the called community, not a claim about political order among strangers. In the writings of the prophets there is a great deal about oppression, especially by corrupt political leaders, but once again this critique is developed primarily on the basis of the character that the unjust are supposed to have but do not. Injustice by the Israelites is often associated with idolatry and failure to live out the deep purpose or telos of being the people of God. Christians can legitimately understand civil rights as middle-axiom expressions of a moral good of the nation-state that they share with nonbelievers, but they should not equate civil rights with biblical justice as outlined by the OT prophets. The latter is far "thicker," having to do with the nature of being God's people, whereas the former is "thin" and a minimum reasonably expected for all societies.

In the NT there is no statement about civil rights. Nonetheless, the treatment of Jesus, and its obviously unjust character, has been recognized as a foil for what should be available to all, especially fair judicial proceedings. Paul asserts his rights as a citizen, although this is not a general claim about human status but rather one about his Roman political status (Acts 16:38; 22:22–29; 25:10–11). Paul makes a claim to rights in the church on the basis of his ecclesial authority, but these are not civil rights (1 Cor. 9). When Paul elsewhere urges Philemon to respect and care for Onesimus, he does so on the basis of brotherliness among the faithful, seemingly echoing the Johannine familial declaration that those who accept Jesus have the "right" to be named the children of God (John 1:12–13). Similarly, the change in status initiated by belief in Christ creates equality before God that is to be respected by other believers but does not apply in the same way to nonbelievers (Gal. 3:28). In these examples, however, as well as in the Sermon on the Mount and Paul's statements about lawsuits (1 Cor. 6), it seems that although Christians have rights before God that should be respected by other believers, it is best not to appeal to such rights within the church. Arguably, "rights" language should not be a primary ecclesial language, but rather familial and agapic language.

Nonetheless, although the theory is not explicitly presented in Scripture, civil rights are based on assumptions, in part, historically derived from Christianity. This does not mean that other cultural groups did not have similar positions, but that the historic line can be traced from Scripture through Catholic natural-law theory through Reformation individualism to the dialectic tension between revivalist evangelicalism and the British Enlightenment. The common assumption was that all humans have worth before, and indeed bear the image of, their Creator. Thus "endowed," their natural rights warrant civil protection. The nation-state is to politically and legally treat all alike, allowing each to pursue his or her own telos rather than assuming that there is a telos for the society defined by authorities into which all individuals must fit.

See also Aliens, Immigration, and Refugees; Civil Disobedience; Deontological Theories of Ethics; Discrimination; Egalitarianism; Equality; Happiness; Human Rights; Law, Civil and Criminal; Natural Law; Natural Rights; Rights; Social Contract

James R. Thobaben

Class Conflict

Class conflict (or class struggle) refers to a type of tension and antagonism among social groups differentiated along political and economic lines.

The issue of how to respond faithfully to class conflict generated heated debates between Latin American theologians and the Catholic Church beginning in the 1960s. Latin American theologians argued for the indispensability of Marxist-style class analysis in uncovering appropriate biblical and ethical responses to the chronic poverty and widespread economic injustice the people of their parishes and communities suffered (Gutiérrez; Míguez Bonino). Cardinal Joseph Ratzinger (later Pope Benedict XVI), prefect for the Congregation of the Doctrine of the Faith, declared that a singular focus on class conflict limits ethical options to capitalism or Marxist socialism and reduces all of theology, Scripture, and Christian reality to political-social praxis.

This specific debate on class conflict was precipitated and fueled by a lengthy tradition. In the Bible, the principle of justice as redress addresses the material inequalities that lead to class conflict (Mott). The Jubilee system is the preeminent example of this biblical principle of redress. During the Jubilee Year, all land is returned to the family of origin (Lev. 25:25–28). This principle is rearticulated in the law, wisdom literature, and the prophets as well as the NT injunctions to forgive debt (Matt. 6:12; 18:23–35; Luke 7:41–43; Rom. 13:8).

During the Reformation, Martin Luther unwittingly provided theological grounding for class conflict in Germany between the peasants and the ruling class. Luther's emphasis on the priesthood of all believers and the doctrine of justification by faith, along with his advocacy for the translation of the Bible into the vernacular, served as a challenge to traditional authority that culminated in German peasant revolts. The church hierarchy was convinced that Luther's message bred only discord and conflict, even though Luther openly opposed the revolt.

The debate between Luther and the Catholic Church about class conflict was recapitulated on the cusp of the twentieth century. In *Rerum novarum* (1891) Pope Leo XIII condemned class conflict as contradictory to fundamental Christian beliefs (O'Brien and Shannon). Leo tried to nudge European Catholics away from counterrevolution and toward political participation and social reform. Forty years later, with confidence in reform shattered by World War I and a worldwide depression, Pope Pius XI also condemned class conflict in *Quadragesimo anno* while simultaneously calling for an honest discussion of differences and inequality that abstains from hatred (O'Brien and Shannon). The Protestant movements of roughly the same time period underwent parallel shifts. Washington Gladden, a key figure in the social gospel movement, wanted the church to be conscious of issues of wealth, inequality, labor unions, and socialism without taking sides in class warfare (Dorrien 65–67).

By the mid-twentieth century, both Catholics and Protestants attempted to distance the church from the difficulties of class conflict. Many observers now agree that they failed to address in a constructive or compelling way the structural and institutional problems that provided impetus for class conflict. Liberal Christianity, in its Catholic and Protestant forms, was too middle class to challenge existing social relationships. A transformative Christianity was needed, one that learned from Marx's theory of class conflict and his critique of the capitalist modes of production and distribution, in the struggle on behalf of and with the poor (Dorrien 246).

Some theological reactionaries, disillusioned socialists, and postmodernists claim that class conflict has lost its significance and explanatory power. These theorists fail to realize that class conflict inspired and formed the basis of social theory rooted in power. Many social theorists and ethicists are now convinced that society is best understood as conflicts between more powerful groups that use their power to exploit groups with less power. Liberation theologies attempt to theorize these broader social, cultural, and geopolitical movements based on conflicts of power. What began as a debate over class conflict has given way to new ethical methodologies and scriptural hermeneutics that form a more adequate basis for Christian theological and ethical reflection within pluralistic, multicultural, and postmodern societies.

See also Liberationist Ethics; Poverty and Poor; Preferential Option for the Poor

Bibliography

Dorrien, G. *Social Ethics in the Making: Interpreting an American Tradition*. Wiley-Blackwell, 2009; Dussel, E. *Philosophy of Liberation*. Trans. A. Martinez and C. Morkovsky. Orbis, 1985; Gutiérrez, G. *A Theology of Liberation: History, Politics, and Salvation*. Trans. C. Inda and J. Eagleson. Orbis, 1973; Míguez Bonino, J. *Christians and Marxists: The Mutual Challenge to Revolution*. Eerdmans, 1976; Mott, S. *Biblical Ethics and Social Change*. Oxford University Press, 1982, 65–72; O'Brien, D., and T. Shannon. *Catholic Social Thought: The Documentary Heritage*. Orbis, 1992, 12–79.

R. J. Hernández-Díaz

Clean and Unclean

The labels "clean" and "unclean" presuppose an overarching conception of a proper order (the cosmos in a state of "purity") and of disruptions to that order ("pollution"). Purity and pollution were meaningful concepts for Greeks, Romans, Egyptians, and most other ancient peoples, but in the scriptural tradition we encounter these concepts primarily as formulated within ancient Israelite and early Jewish society.

God commanded the priests to "distinguish between the holy and the common, and between the unclean and the clean" and to teach the Israelites how to do the same (Lev. 10:10). Something or someone in the normal state, as the cosmic order presupposed in the Torah defined "normal," is clean. Bodies that did not leak were clean. Animals that looked and behaved the way animals should (e.g., sea creatures that had fins and scales, like fish ought to have, rather than legs like land animals or hides like land snakes) were clean. The label "unclean" applies when something crosses the line into abnormality. The ordinary spaces and things that are appropriate to the everyday world of human interactions are described as "common." "Holy" describes those spaces or things set apart from the ordinary to belong in some special way to God.

Concerns about purity and pollution were driven by the awareness of the special power of the divine to bless or to curse, to help or to harm. The divine was "other"—holy. People intuited that, in God's presence, certain things were appropriate and others inappropriate. Isaiah's vision of God brought immediate awareness of what was inappropriate (hence, "unclean") in his own life and in the people among whom he lived (Isa. 6:1–8): "I am lost, for I am a man of unclean lips" (Isa. 6:5). To enter the presence of the Holy One in a state of uncleanness was to invite disaster upon oneself, possibly upon the whole nation. Codifying the clean and unclean, and developing processes for containing and eliminating defilement, allowed humans to know when and how to approach the Holy One suitably and safely, giving access to the source of blessing and help (Lev. 26:3–12).

The purity codes of ancient Israel (as also of Greece and Rome) made no hard-and-fast distinction between ritual and ethical categories of defilement. Eating certain meats; committing incest, adultery, or bestiality; and idolatry all constitute pollution that would cause the Holy Land to reject the Israelites. Avoiding unclean foods (Lev. 11) and pursuing justice in relationships (Lev. 19) were facets of the holiness required of the people in order for them to remain in the land of a Holy God. A purification offering was offered for certain moral offenses and for the pollution incurred through childbirth. The more serious pollution taboos (murder, certain sexual deviations, and idolatry), for which there is no purification, fall within modern ethical categories. Separating out the Torah's moral and ritual requirements, however, was a Christian innovation. For the Jew, concerns about purity and pollution—about enjoying ongoing favorable encounters with God—enforced both ritual and ethical cleanness.

Israel's obligation to "make a distinction between the clean animal and the unclean" bears witness to God's act of distinguishing between Israel, the people whom God selected for God's self, and the nations, whom God regarded as inappropriate for such association and hence as "unclean" (Lev. 20:22–26). Observing dietary laws, in turn, helped maintain the social boundaries of Israel as a distinct people, God's special (holy) possession. Other facets of the purity codes, in turn, mirror the concern with maintaining boundaries, such as the labeling of leaking bodies or bodies with broken skin as unclean. Others extend the mirroring of God's actions begun in Lev. 20:22–26. As God rested on the seventh day, so too Jews rest from work on that day, mirroring and witnessing to the God of creation (Exod. 31:12–17). Law-observant Israel becomes a living reflection of the character of the Holy God in the midst of the world, a holy island of order in the midst of the gentiles' aberrations.

Around the turn of the common era, Jews (especially in Greek-dominated environments) began to pursue ethical reinterpretations of the laws concerning clean and unclean. The *Epistle of Aristeas*, for example, reads the dietary laws symbolically, suggesting that their primary interest is providing ethical guidance. Clean animals represent traits of the virtuous person, such as meditating upon wisdom (ruminating) and discerning between right and wrong (the cloven hoof) (*Let. Aris.* 150). Unclean animals represent vices popularly associated with these animals, such as violence with carrion birds or sexual looseness with the weasel (*Let. Aris.* 144–48). The author of 4 Maccabees regards the dietary laws as an exercise regimen designed to develop the virtue of self-control (4 Macc. 1:31–35). The ethical meaning did not, however, replace ritual observance.

The early Christian movement advanced a more exclusively ethical redefinition of purity and of the holiness that reflects God's character and that enables people suitably to approach the Holy God. Jesus rejected the concern over what foods one ingested in favor of a concern with what attitudes, intentions, and words one projected: "It is not what goes into the mouth that defiles a person, but it is what comes out of the mouth that defiles" (Matt. 15:11). Speech defiles the person, if that speech embodies immoral intentions, destroys reputations, or pollutes relationships (Matt. 15:19).

Pauline Christianity particularly understood God to be creating a new holy people from all nations. Since God's presence became available both to Jews and Gentiles by the Holy Spirit, Christian leaders concluded that "in cleansing [the Gentiles'] hearts by faith [God] has made no distinction between them and us" (Acts 15:9), decisively reversing the Levitical command that Jewish Christians "make a distinction" between clean and unclean, between themselves and people of other races (Lev. 20:22–26). Since the "dividing wall of hostility" (Eph. 2:14) that separated ethnic Jews from Gentiles was being torn down by God in Christ (Acts 10:1–11:18; Eph. 2:11–20), the Levitical purity regulations that replicated and reinforced that boundary also came to be regarded as superseded. At the same time, Christian leaders drew new lines of social separateness, again couched in discussions of foods that were inappropriate for the Christian to ingest. The new unclean meat was meat from animals sacrificed to idols, and this facilitated the creation of barriers against participating in the idolatrous worship that surrounded Christians in the Greco-Roman world. Pollution taboos thus still reinforced the group's distinctive identity and ethos.

Writers used the language of "clean and unclean" to foster a new moral separateness between disciples and their past lives and also, by implication, the ongoing social practices that they had rejected. "Fornicators, idolaters, adulterers, male prostitutes, sodomites, thieves, the greedy, drunkards, revilers, robbers—none of these will inherit the kingdom of God. And this is what some of you used to be. But you were washed, you were sanctified" (1 Cor. 6:9–11). The disciples' purification in baptism set them apart from their pagan past. The conceptual boundary between the holy and the unclean reinforces the inappropriateness of returning to that lifestyle and promotes the disciples' commitment to preserve the purity of the new life intact (see also Eph. 4:19).

The conceptual categories of clean and unclean came to be applied to moral considerations throughout the early church, such as sexual license (e.g., Eph. 4:19; 5:3–5; Jude 7–8), disruptions of congregational harmony (Phil. 2:14–15; 2 Tim. 2:21–23), and greed and the vices that accompany competition for this world's goods (Jas. 4:1-4). This is fully in keeping with the Hellenistic Jewish tendencies (although Philo and the author of 4 Maccabees still observed the Torah in its particulars) as well as Greek and Latin ethical philosophers, as when Epictetus urges his students not to defile the indwelling deity "with unclean thoughts and filthy actions" (*Diatr.* 2.8.13). There is an overall movement toward the view that God is ultimately concerned about the cultivation of justice and other virtuous practices and the elimination of immoral practices and destructive attitudes. Such renders people fit to stand in the presence of the Holy God in anticipation of a favorable reception.

Postindustrial societies may lack the religiously motivated conceptions of purity and pollution found in ancient Israel, but they also draw fixed lines between people, whether on the basis of microbes or hygiene, or along social-spatial and ethnic lines. The redrawing of purity maps in the scriptural and parabiblical tradition, especially the shift from social and ritual pollution to ethical lapses, poses an ongoing challenge to examine personal, cultural, and social purity lines and to conform them to two basic principles. The first is to keep these lines porous, extending love, kindness, and human connection to other people in any condition, mirroring God's commitment to compassionate redemption. The second is to remain separate from the true pollution that alienates people from the Holy God, namely, continued involvement in attitudes and practices that poison relationships and inhibit the universal experience of justice and *shalom*.

See also Holiness Code; Hope; Priestly Literature

Bibliography

deSilva, D. *Honor, Patronage, Kinship and Purity: Unlocking New Testament Culture*. InterVarsity, 2000; Douglas, M. *Purity and Danger: An Analysis of Concepts of Pollution and Taboo*. Routledge & Kegan Paul, 1966; Levine, B. *Leviticus*. JPSTC. Jewish Publication Society, 1989; Milgrom, J. *Leviticus 1–16*. AB 3. Doubleday, 1991; Nelson, R. *Raising Up a Faithful Priest: Community and Priesthood in a Biblical Theology*. Westminster John Knox, 1993.

David A. deSilva

Cloning *See* Bioethics

Coercion *See* Authority and Power

Cohabitation *See* Marriage and Divorce

Collection for the Saints

The collection for the saints refers to the monetary gift Paul raised among predominantly gentile churches on behalf of "the poor among the saints at Jerusalem" (Rom. 15:26). Although reluctant to ask for financial support of his own apostolic ministry, Paul appears in his letters as a relentless advocate on behalf of the economic situation of the Jerusalem believers. References to the collection are centered in the Pauline Epistles: Rom. 15:25–32; 1 Cor. 16:1–4; 2 Cor. 7:14–9:15; Gal. 2:9–10. Acts mentions the Pauline collection only in passing (24:17), but does refer to an earlier, parallel gift from the Antiochene Christians to Jerusalem (11:27–30).

The economic grounds for the relative poverty of the Jerusalem Christians are unknown. Some have postulated that the disinvestment of capital and economic distribution among the church's members led to its impoverishment, but this is a problematic reading of Acts 2:42–47; 4:32–5:11. Disinvestment was voluntary, not required; the ways in which income from disinvestment might have been deployed in economic development in Acts have not been adequately explored; and a number of earlier interpreters sought to discredit the practices of economic koinonia described in Acts as a way of discrediting Marxism and/or communism. In fact, we have no evidence supporting the conclusion that Jerusalem's economic koinonia was a failed experiment. It is more likely that the economically depressed situation in Jerusalem was the consequence of the usual combination of natural calamities facing an agrarian-based economy (e.g., drought, famine) and the lack of any state-generated assistance under Roman administration.

What is particularly fascinating about Paul's efforts on behalf of the Jerusalem poor is the range of arguments and motivations he brings to the task of encouraging "cheerful" giving (cf. 2 Cor. 9:7) among his predominantly gentile churches. This is evidenced already in the array of terms by which he refers to the collection: *charis* ("favor, grace, benefaction" [1 Cor. 16:3; 2 Cor. 8:4, 6, 7, 19; cf. 8:1, 9; 9:14]), *leitourgia* ("religious service" [2 Cor. 9:12]), *eulogia* ("blessing" [2 Cor. 9:5–6]), *koinōnia* ("fellowship" [Rom. 15:26; 2 Cor. 8:4; 9:13]), and *diakonia* ("service, support" [Rom. 15:31; 2 Cor. 8:4; 9:1, 12, 13]), in addition to *logeia* ("collection [of money]," used only twice in the NT [1 Cor. 16:1–2]). Clearly, the apostle works with no dichotomy between economics and faith, and indeed he understands economic sharing in preeminently theological and relational terms.

The collection is a classic example of embodied ethics. The collection is a Christian practice, noted for Paul's emphasis on giving as regular, proportional, personal, and voluntary (1 Cor. 16:1–4; 2 Cor. 9:5), and is rooted in and expressive of the gospel. Thus, at one level, it is an act of love and service toward others, a profound reflection of Christ's incarnation (2 Cor. 8:9), a participation in God's own generosity (2 Cor. 9:6–15), and a demonstration of faith (e.g., 2 Cor. 8:24; 9:13). Scripturally, Paul grounds this economic counsel in God's provision of daily manna (2 Cor. 8:15; see Exod. 16:11–31), an object lesson in Israel's history demonstrating God's provision of daily sustenance and the uselessness of hoarding one's surplus.

At another level, the collection is a tangible expression of the unity and equality of Jew and gentile in Christ. Economic sharing without any hint of repayment characterizes persons and communities who understand themselves in familial terms, unified in heart and purpose as well as economics. For Paul, it is critical to demonstrate that the gentile mission had as its consequence not the proliferation of churches but the growth of the one church. This point is of special interest, since gift-giving in antiquity, in an even more formalized sense than is true today, generally was a means of broadcasting one's honor and placing others in one's debt. Not only is this interpretation of gift-giving absent from Paul's message, it is also actually undermined. If anything, the debt Paul recognizes is that of the gentiles: "For if the Gentiles have come to share in their [i.e., the Jerusalem saints'] spiritual blessings, they ought also to be of service to them in material things" (Rom. 15:27). More pointedly, Paul emphasizes the values of mutuality and equity with regard to the gospel and so, by implication, with respect to economic status within and among Christian communities. Thus, to the Corinthians he writes that they should aim for equality (*isotēs*, "fair balance" [2 Cor. 8:13–14]). And this is motivated by recognition of the unrivaled generosity of God.

See also Koinonia

Bibliography

Bassler, J. *God and Mammon: Asking for Money in the New Testament*. Abingdon, 1991; Downs, D. J. *The Offering of the Gentiles*. WUNT 2:248. Mohr Siebeck, 2008; Georgi, D. *Remembering the Poor: The History of Paul's Collection for Jerusalem*. Abingdon, 1992; Nickle, K. *The Collection: A Study in Paul's Strategy*. SCM, 1966; Wheeler, S. *Wealth as Poverty and Obligation: The New Testament on Possessions*. Eerdmans, 1995.

Joel B. Green

Collective Responsibility

Moral responsibility is one of the fundamental questions of philosophy. According to major philosophical theories, individuals are judged morally responsible for their own actions. In antiquity there was a major debate over this issue, and it is found in biblical texts from the OT through the NT. Establishing the biblical basis for the concept of collective responsibility is not easy. In Exod. 20; 34; Num. 14; Deut. 5 the concept of "visiting the iniquity of the parents upon the children" is found, and it is interpreted as allowing for multigenerational divine punishment. The concept is also often found in Hittite texts.

The passage in Exod. 34 suggests that there are no conditions or mitigating circumstances for the visiting of the sins of parents on their children. The standard of collective responsibility is found in what modern biblical criticism identifies as early and later pentateuchal materials (ninth through eighth centuries BCE) and is also assumed in narratives and legal materials of the OT (e.g., Josh. 7:24–25; 2 Sam. 21:1–9). The standard of collective responsibility was challenged in prophetic and in late biblical texts. The challenge is found in Lam. 5:7 and also in Job 21:19–21 (and Job 27:14), where the book of Job takes collective responsibility as a matter of debate. The standard apparently was modified by the time of the sixth-century prophets Ezekiel (18:1–4) and Jeremiah (31:29), where the exile of the Judeans as punishment for all future generations of Judeans is challenged. In addition, Ezekiel (3:18–20) seems to be against what might have been a standing counterpart to intergenerational punishment: intergenerational merit, a concept that will reemerge in importance in the rabbinic period and early Byzantine Christian sources. Modern biblical criticism assumes that the debate over the idea of intergenerational punishment meted out by God took place by the end of the seventh century BCE (the Deuteronomistic law code) because in Deut. 24:16 there is a standard of individual responsibility (similar to Ezekiel and Jeremiah) in the Pentateuch.

The mixture of the two positions (collective versus individual responsibility) continues from the period of the OT through the intertestamental period (third century BCE through the first century CE). In Wis. 3:10–4:6; Sir. 41:5–7; Jdt. 7:19–20; *4 Ezra* 7:118 the standards of both collective and individual responsibility mixed together and sometimes are presented in the same verse (as in *2 Bar.* 54:15–19). An active continuation of the issue is found in various Dead Sea Scrolls. The Deuteronomy scroll *4QDeuteronomy*[n] has the "visiting the iniquity of the fathers upon the sons" citation, and other Dead Sea Scrolls texts contain references to a concept apparently derived from this biblical verse. The scrolls even refer to a time of *HaPequdah*, the multigenerational punishment or purification process. In addition, an eternal purification process is mentioned in the scrolls that stretches backward through the generations. It is found throughout the general rules of the community, but also in a liturgical text known as *Words of the Luminaries*[a] (4Q504). Intergenerational punishment is also found in *4QHosea Pesher*[a] (4Q166), and the *Damascus Document* contains multiple references, as do the *Thanksgiving Hymns*, the *Wisdom Poems*, and the *4QPurification Rules*.

The first-century CE Jewish writers Philo and Josephus make little or no reference to the standard of collective responsibility despite having comprehensive interpretations of the biblical citations where the idea appears. In the same period, the Targumim (Aramaic renderings of the Hebrew texts) wrestle with the two conflicting concepts and resolve them in a variety of ways.

One clear first-century use of the concept of collective responsibility appears in the NT. The text is crucial to any discussion of the concept. Its appearance in the NT implies that the standard of "visiting the iniquity of the parents upon the children" was still relevant in the time of the Gospel writers. Matthew, describing the events leading to Jesus' crucifixion, reports, "When Pilate saw that he could do nothing, but rather that a riot was beginning, he took some water and washed his hands before the crowed, saying, 'I am innocent of this man's blood; see to it yourselves.' Then the people as a whole answered, 'His blood be on us and on our children'" (Matt. 27:24–25). This verse in Matthew gains importance because it does not appear in the other Gospel accounts of the crucifixion, and the fact that this scene is paralleled in Luke and Mark without this exchange between Pilate and the crowd is relevant. The verse in Matthew is often cited in church literature and sermonizing starting in the Byzantine period as part of anti-Judaic arguments (and even in nineteenth- and early twentieth-century anti-Semitic polemics) justifying ill treatment of Jews living in later periods. It is important to note that the Ante-Nicene church fathers (first through the third centuries CE) cite the two biblical standards from the OT of divine punishment of the individual and multigenerational punishment in different ways in discussing the concept of theodicy.

See also Anti-Semitism; Covenantal Ethics; Moral Agency; Punishment; Reparation; Responsibility

Richard Freund

Colonialism and Postcolonialism

Although the most immediately relevant colonial period that shaped our times is the era of European expansion into the world (1492–1960), the practice is linked to empire, and empire has a long history, both in Scripture and in the world. Colonialism involves exploration, conquest, suppression, and exploitation, though the colonialist ideology is often more positive (for a helpful distinction between hegemony and ideology, see Comaroff and Comaroff). In the period of European expansion colonial ideology was often cast in biblical language in order to provide an ethical justification for colonial practices.

The colonial practices of Egypt, Assyria, Babylonia, the Medeo-Persian Empire, the Greek Empire, and the Roman Empire are referenced in Scripture, with appropriate chastisements for excesses (e.g., Exod. 14:23; Jer. 50:18). But Walter Brueggemann has suggested that Israel itself took on the practices of empire as he contrasts the Mosaic community with the Solomonic community. The warnings of the prophets against the oppression of the alien and the poor of the land have as their setting the tendency for Israelites to act as colonialists in a colonial world (e.g., Exod. 22:21; Lev. 19:33–34; Jer. 7:5–6; Ezek. 22:29).

The European colonialists, beginning in the sixteenth century, took up the same justifications for colonial expansion and exploitation. The colonizers thought that they had a mandate from God, similar to the mandate that they understood Israel to have had in the conquest of Canaan. The narrative assumed that the colonizers were Christians and thus, like Moses and Joshua, were more righteous and deserving than the colonized, who were considered to be heathens deserving punishment or extinction (for discussion of the identification of the colonized with Canaanites, see Warrior). These arguments were used to justify practices such as confiscating land, enslaving inhabitants, removing children from their parents, destroying culture and tradition, and reforming society along European lines.

Colonial critique grew from the 1930s on through the 1960s with writers such as Césaire, Fanon, and Memmi, while the postcolonial critique began with the identification of neocolonialism as a stage of economic dependence, following Marx, masked by the appearance of political independence (Nkrumah). In the field of literature, the postcolonial critique began to expose the hegemony of the West in its attempt to define the other (Said), revealing a colonization of the mind (Thiong'o) more insidious than the colonization of the land and the body. At the time that the colonized, or even the formerly colonized, accepts the terms and logic of the colonizer, the hegemony (in the scheme of Comaroff and Comaroff) is already in place.

"Decolonizing the mind" involves exposing the hegemony, resisting the ideology, and finding a voice and a venue for an alternative point of view, primarily through colonial discourse analysis. One ethical issue is representation; that is, who is speaking for the subaltern (Spivak)?

Postcolonial critics resist the continuing hegemony of colonialism by writing against, reinterpreting, and rewriting colonial literature. Instead of writing from the perspective of the conquering colonizer, critics began to write from the perspective of the victim. But this "victims of progress" perspective was quickly discarded in favor of imagining the oppressed as agents in their own right who are actively resisting, subverting, and modifying flows of colonial goods, ideas, and persons.

The ethical question, framed by Albert Memmi, is one of identification. On whose side does one stand: with the colonizer or with the colonized? Memmi argued that only by choosing to be on the side of the colonized can the colonizer find liberation. To pretend to make no choice is to benefit from the privileges of the colonizer without taking responsibility for the enduring consequences.

See also Conquest; Cross-Cultural Ethics; Culture; Dissent; Exploitation; Imperialism; Political Ethics

Bibliography

Ashcroft, B., G. Griffiths, and H. Tiffin. *The Empire Writes Back: Theory and Practice in Post-Colonial Literature*. Routledge, 1989; Bhabha, H. *The Location of Culture*. Routledge, 1994; Brueggemann, W. *The Prophetic Imagination*. Fortress, 1978; Césaire, A. *Discourse on Colonialism*. Trans. J. Pinkham. Monthly Review Press, 1972 [1950]; Comaroff, J., and J. Comaroff. *Of Revelation and Revolution: Christianity, Colonialism, and Consciousness in South Africa*. Vol. 1. University of Chicago Press, 1991; Fanon, F. *Black Skin, White Masks*. Trans. C. Markmann. Grove Press, 1967 [1952]; idem. *The Wretched of the Earth: The Handbook for the Black Revolution That Is Changing the Shape of the World*. Trans. C. Farrington. Grove Press, 1963; Memmi, A. *The Colonizer and the Colonized*. Trans. H. Greenfeld. Beacon Press, 1965 [1957]; Nkrumah, K. *Neo-Colonialism: The Last Stage of Imperialism*. Nelson, 1965; Said, E. *Orientalism*. Pantheon Books, 1978; Stanley, B., ed. *Missions, Nationalism, and the End of Empire*. Eerdmans, 2003; Spivak, G. "Can the Subaltern Speak?" Pages 271–313 in *Marxism and the Interpretation of Culture*, ed. C. Nelson and L. Grossberg. University of Illinois Press, 1988; Thiong'o, N. *Decolonizing the Mind: The Politics of Language in African Literature*. Heinemann, 1986; Warrior, R. "Canaanites, Cowboys, and Indians: Deliverance, Conquest, and Liberation Theology Today." *ChrCr* 29 (1989): 261–64; Young, R. *Postcolonialism: An Historical Introduction*. Wiley, 2001.

Michael A. Rynkiewich

Colossians

The Letter to the Colossians addresses a church troubled by teachers who argue that salvation is not secure without a visionary experience in which believers observe and participate in the angels' worship of God. They urge the Colossians to adopt a regime of rituals and practices that produce such experiences. In response, the letter assures its readers that those "in Christ" have all spiritual blessings and that no imitation of, or deference to, angels can enhance one's relationship with God.

Ethics is central to the message of Colossians. Near the beginning, the letter says that the purpose of receiving knowledge of God is to live a life worthy of God (1:9–10). This letter focuses on both the status that baptism confers and the demand to live in a particular way it imposes. The image of "putting off" the old way of life and "putting on" a new life conformed to Christ echoes baptismal language (3:8, 12). Thus, Colossians inseparably links the blessings received in baptism with ethical living. Proper living is not simply a consequence of receiving salvation; it is a gift that believers receive in baptism.

Colossians 3:1–4 defines "seeking the things above" as ethical living. This introduction to a section on ethics tells believers that they "have been raised with Christ." Here, being raised with Christ does not signal exaltation but rather indicates that believers must pattern their lives after Christ because God has given them new life in him. Therefore, all aspects of life should conform to being in Christ.

Colossians' explication of this new life is consistent with some elements of first-century ethical thought but opposes other elements of it. Many contemporaneous moralists condemned most of the vices listed in 3:8. Some of the virtues mentioned in 3:12 (particularly humility), however, run counter to cultural values. Colossians evaluates all ethical values by whether they are consistent with being "in Christ."

The household code of 3:18–4:1 gives direct instructions to wives and husbands, children and parents, slaves and owners. Similar registers of instructions appear in Ephesians, 1 Timothy, Titus, and 1 Peter. The concerns reflected in them go back to Aristotle's comments on household management (*Pol.* 1.3), but probably there was no precise literary form that these tables imitate.

The household code of Colossians is problematic because its apparent support of slavery and hierarchy within marriage seems to violate its previous ethical instructions. Unlike most moralists of the first century, the author of Colossians assumes that men and women in Christ should adopt the same virtues. Furthermore, in 3:11 the author proclaims that status markers make no difference in the church, but the code seems to reestablish them. The solution to this tension lies in recognizing the first-century church's position in relation to the broader culture. This code addresses wives, children, and slaves in households that have unbelievers as their heads. In such circumstances these subordinates had no choice but to fulfill their expected roles. All Colossians can do is redefine the meaning of their submission in ways that point to the incongruity between this ordering of relations and life in Christ. For example, wives are to submit "as is fitting in the Lord" (3:18). This phrase redefines submission so that it is proper for everyone, not just wives (if we take 3:11 seriously). This reading gains support from 3:19, which tells husbands not to be embittered toward their wives (the NRSV translation "never treat them harshly" is incorrect). Similarly, slaves are designated as heirs, and masters are told that they are slaves.

Such statements counter the code's apparent call for conformity to first-century expectations. Thus, it enjoins those required to conform to do so but also to know that their forced subordination does not reflect God's will.

Colossians' treatment of ethics suggests that believers should look to the identity that they have been granted in Christ and the character of God for criteria to evaluate all the values, structures, and expectations of their culture.

See also Household Codes; New Testament Ethics; Vices and Virtues, Lists of

Bibliography

Bevere, A. *Sharing in the Inheritance: Identity and the Moral Life in Colossians*. JSNTSup 226. Sheffield Academic Press, 2003; Meeks, W. "'To Walk Worthily of the Lord': Moral Formation in the Pauline School Exemplified by the Letter to Colossians." Pages 37–58 in *Hermes and Athena: Biblical Exegesis and Philosophical Theology*, ed. E. Stump and T. Flint. University of Notre Dame Press, 1993; Standhartinger, A. "The Epistle to the Congregation in Colossae and the Invention of the 'Household Code.'" Pages 88–121 in *A Feminist Companion to the Deutero-Pauline Epistles*, ed. A.-J. Levine and M. Blickenstaff. FCNTECW 7. T&T Clark, 2003; Sumney, J. *Colossians*. NTL. Westminster, 2008.

Jerry L. Sumney

Coma *See* Bioethics

Commandments *See* Ten Commandments

Common Good

The notion of the common good has long been central to Catholic social teaching and has had several connotations.

First, there is reference to the good of all people, all classes, and of each individual (Korzen and Kelley xxi, 4–18). The most influential papal encyclical for social teaching, Pope Leo XIII's *Rerum novarum* (1891), on justice for workers, says, "Civil society exists for the common good, and hence is concerned with the interests of all in general, albeit with individual interests also in their due place and degree" (§51). The common good is referred to twenty-five times in Pope John XXIII's *Mater et magistra* (1961), and forty-eight times in his *Pacem in terris* (1963), often as the "common good of all" (§§48, 56, 58) and the "universal common good" (§§7, 100, 125, 133, 134, 135, 137, 138, 139, 140) of all persons (see McCann in McCann and Miller). Its clear meaning for social justice is seen in the United States Catholic Bishops' *Economic Justice for All*, which cites "common good" thirty-four times. This is echoed by the climax of the US Pledge of Allegiance, "with liberty and justice for all."

The human dignity of all persons in Genesis reverberates throughout the encyclicals as a basis for the common good. *Pacem in terris* (§3) begins by quoting two psalms (8:1; 104:24) and Gen. 1:26, which states that God created humankind in his own image and likeness, endowed them with intelligence and freedom, and made them lord of creation. The document's first pronouncement is "Peace on earth . . . can be firmly established only if the order laid down by God be dutifully observed" (§1). This is both biblical and natural-law basis for the "universal common good." Additional support for the common good from the Ten Commandments, the book of Jonah, and the letters of Paul is developed by McCann and Miller.

Workers and all humans, body and soul, with special attention to less fortunate persons, including immigrants and political refugees, and underdeveloped countries should share in the common good (*Pacem in terris* §§91–108, 121–25) (see Hollenbach, esp. 93). *Gaudium et spes* (1965), promulgated by Pope Paul VI, emphasizes a special obligation to make ourselves neighbors to abandoned elderly persons, underpaid foreign laborers, refugees, suffering children, and hungry persons, quoting Jesus' words in Matt. 25:40: "Just as you did it to one of the least of these who are members of my family, you did it to me." *Mater et magistra* (§§43, 78–80, 139) associates the common good with economic rights of all citizens, especially the weaker—workers, women, and children. Public and universal authority "must have as its fundamental objective the recognition, respect, safeguarding and promotion of the rights of the human person" (*Pacem in terris* §139). Pope Benedict XVI writes, "Anyone who needs me, and whom I can help, is my neighbor. . . . Jesus identifies himself with those in need, with the hungry, the thirsty, the stranger, the naked, the sick and those in prison. 'As you did it to one of the least of these my brethren, you did it to me' (Mt 25:40)" (*Deus caritas est* §15).

Therefore, the common good requires government intervention, incentive, and regulation to stop the powerful from aggrandizing far more than their fair share for themselves. It requires that governments "increase the degree and scope of their activities in the economic sphere" and "devise ways and means and set the necessary machinery in motion for the attainment of this end"; otherwise, there occurs "unscrupulous exploitation of the weak by the strong" (*Mater et magistra* §§54, 58 [see also *Pacem in terris* §§63–66]). John Paul II says that we need to pay attention to the universal common good because of "the structures of sin" in the world (see McCann and Miller 142–43).

Nations need to provide employment for as many workers as possible, to maintain a balance between wages and prices, to make the goods and services for a better life accessible to as many persons as possible, to limit the inequalities between different sectors of the economy, to have regard for future generations, and to give effectively to the economically underdeveloped nations (*Mater et magistra* §§79, 150–65). However, this must be balanced by freedom and private initiative of individuals (*Mater et magistra* §§57, 66).

The good is "common" in the sense that we are created to share it, as by nature social beings, in solidarity, with interpersonal communion, unable to live or develop human potential unless related to others (*Gaudium et spes* §§12 [based on Gen. 1:26–27, 31; Ps. 8:5–6], 25).

The common "good" includes the sum total of those conditions of social living whereby people are able to achieve the kind of life that God has created us for, including bodily, economic, moral, and spiritual development, our own perfection, human dignity and development, with individual members encouraged to participate in the affairs of the group (*Mater et magistra* §§65, 149). The perfectionist teleology of *Mater et magistra* shifts to an invocation of dignity and human rights in *Pacem in terris*, *Gaudium et spes*, and *Dignitatis humanae* (O'Neill 173).

Catholic moral theologian David Hollenbach argues in *The Common Good and Christian Ethics* that we will not solve the glaring injustices to the poor and their children in inner cities and we will not act justly toward the hungry of the world unless we identify with them as our children and members of our human family. He also commends the public role of black churches in advocating civil rights and economic justice for all, and the inclusive understanding of the common good in the activities of evangelical Christian groups such as the Sojourners community and leaders such as Richard Mouw, president of Fuller Theological Seminary. Hollenbach is right that evangelicals are increasingly emphasizing the common good. The recent book *Toward an Evangelical Public Policy* is replete with references to "the common good," and its summary, "For the Health of the Nation," strikingly resembles the 2003 statement by the United States Roman Catholic bishops, *The Challenge of Faithful Citizenship: A Catholic Call to Political Responsibility*. Other Christian traditions are increasingly adopting the "common good" because they sense its helpfulness for healing the politics of division and injustices caused by ideologies of private self-interest that divert normal human compassion from caring for other humans (Korzen and Kelley).

See also Government; Image of God

Bibliography

Hollenbach, D. *The Common Good and Christian Ethics*. NSCE 22. Cambridge University Press, 2002; idem. *The Global Face of Public Faith: Politics, Human Rights, and Christian Ethics*. Georgetown University Press, 2003; Korzen, C., and A. Kelley. *A Nation for All: How the Catholic Vision of the Common Good Can Save America from the Politics of Division*. Jossey-Bass, 2008; McCann, D., and P. Miller, eds. *In Search of the Common Good*. T&T Clark, 2005; O'Brien, D., and T. Shannon, eds. *Catholic Social Thought: The Documentary Heritage*. Orbis, 2006; O'Neill, W. "Babel's Children: Reconstructing the Common Good." *ASCE* 18 (1998): 161–76; Sider, R., and D. Knippers, eds. *Toward an Evangelical Public Policy: Public Strategies for the Health of the Nation*. Baker, 1995.

Glen H. Stassen

Common-Law Marriage

See Marriage and Divorce

Common Ownership

See Property and Possessions

Comparative Religious Ethics

Comparative religious ethics as an academic discipline arose in the late nineteenth and early twentieth centuries as scientific and intellectual disciplines became increasingly specialized. A branch of comparative religion—more specifically, comparative theology—comparative religious ethics systematically reflects on differences and common values across religious traditions that have an impact on the treatment of moral concerns by various religions.

Comparative religious ethics as a biblical practice has a much longer history, one that must be teased out from biblical texts quite foreign to modern ethical discourse. Using the Bible in comparative religious ethics today presents a host of challenges—contextual, methodological, and theological.

Today, a new form of comparative religious ethics is emerging. This new form is based on the realities and demands of globalization and cultural relativism. That emerging systematic study of ethics across religions seeks application to global moral issues and practical results in society.

History of Comparing Values across Religions

As new religions developed, they drew from older religions for values. For example, Buddhism drew from Hinduism, Christianity from Hebrew religion, and Islam from Christianity. Those values were inextricably linked to the cosmic, philosophical, theological framework of the religion and the society in which the religion thrived. Hinduism and Buddhism sourced their ethical systems in reincarnation, karma, and a cosmology of cyclical time in a world of illusion. Chinese religions drew from a basis of relational and familial responsibilities operating within a cosmology of cosmic forces that included ancestors. Many indigenous religions linked natural events to human behavior in a world animated by spirits at every level. Monotheistic religions—Judaism, Christianity, Islam—focused ethical discourse in revelation, individual responsibility, and a cosmology of linear time in a world created by an all-powerful God. Greek ideas of practical reason and a hierarchy of matter and spirit also influenced Christian theologies in the West. As religions changed, older traditions adapted to fit new social and religious locations.

During the seventeenth century, the European Enlightenment's rejection of church authority moved the discourse around values from Christian theology to the spheres of reason and law. Human reason could evaluate values, and human law could establish precedents that adjudicated between good and evil. An emphasis on human freedom to choose the good ends moved the focus of ethics onto the means of accomplishing those ends. With the subsequent development of scientific disciplines, religious studies established a niche for theological, philosophical, and ethical comparison across religions. As modern science gained influence, an evolutionary understanding of development led to the construction of a hierarchy of religions from primitive to modern, a hierarchy that influenced comparative religious ethics as it developed as an area of study.

During the eighteenth and nineteenth centuries, as Western missionaries took Christianity across the globe along with European colonization, discourse among Christians and those of the religion of the society that they entered became common in some places and remained impossible in others. In Sri Lanka, Christian missionaries debated Theravada Buddhists in public forums. In South America, by contrast, the native peoples were not considered fully human by the Spanish invaders, so comparing values was not possible. Exceptions such as the arguments of Bartolomé de las Casas for the humanity and freedom of choice of the natives were rare. Generally, the natives were considered subhuman, needing to be conquered so that Christianity could be imposed upon them.

In 1893, at the World Parliament of Religions in Chicago, some debate among participants from various religions occurred. Comparison of religions on moral issues and values began to be brought into courses on world religions as they developed in universities during the first half of the twentieth century. Courses in comparative religious ethics per se became part of university curricula in the second half of the twentieth century in Europe and the United States. Those courses systematized ethics among religious traditions in Christian theological frameworks. Categories of God, sin, creation, soul, salvation, and others were applied to all religions for analysis.

Three Stages of Comparative Religious Ethics

The development of comparative religious ethics went through three stages with distinct differences in content, objectives, and methods.

Stage one. As Western expansion brought religions into close proximity, the comparative study of religion arose in the late nineteenth and early twentieth centuries. Two contrasting foci were prominent at that time. The first was a form of debate that we know as apologetics. Comparisons of religions focused on Christian theological categories—for example, good and evil, personal responsibility, a good God, and a created world. The Bible was used to support that evaluative framework. Those measures were used to evaluate the moralities of other religious traditions. The goal of the discourse was to convince those of a different religion of the veracity and worth of Christianity.

The second, nearly opposite, focus was on the scientific development of university disciplines. Sociology, anthropology, and history of religions attempted to do objective research that produced results that could be universally applied. That movement influenced theology as well. As the interdisciplinary project of comparative religion developed, an anti-Christian bias grew along with it. The use of Western theological categories of comparison continued to be used but were now separated from the religion of Christianity and considered to be universal categories of religious study.

Stage two. The second stage, beginning in the post–World War II era, focused on commonalities among religious traditions. The shattering experiences of World War I and World War II demonstrated the need for international agreement on the ethics of war, the sanctity of human life, and equity among peoples. During this modern phase of comparative religious ethics the search for universals predominated. Human reason and international law became sources for delineating values of human freedom and dignity, values that came to be considered universal in the West. Those sources for international discourse and the values that they generated were rooted in Enlightenment philosophical and Christian theological perspectives.

The 1948 United Nations Declaration on Human Rights (UNDHR) was an example of this type of comparative religious ethics. Persons from different religions and regions of the world worked together to craft a document that focused on the necessity and reasons for according each person rights that stemmed from being human. Although a Western individualistic focus predominated, views of representatives from various religious traditions from around the globe were heard.

That document led to a larger conversation as later documents that augmented the UNDHR brought those other voices more centrally into the conversation. In the 1990s religious scholars dialogued about ways that religious values could be added to the UNDHR, values that identify human rights and responsibilities from within frameworks of different religions. The resulting Declaration of Human Rights by the World's Religions (1998) offers ongoing opportunities for religious scholars to contribute to a global ethic of human rights. The Bangkok Governmental Declaration (1993) stressed the uniqueness and diversity of human-rights views across Asia. Those documents brought out the communal nature of human rights and the importance of balancing human rights with responsibilities. The creation of such documents by scholars of various religions highlights the importance of religions adding their voices to human-rights discourse.

Stage three. The third stage of comparative religious ethics comes with the postmodern turn. A general realization that traditions and views of morality grow up in particular contexts shapes this view. Ethics are placed in the context of traditions that are tied to historical narratives and present societal conditions. In this view, all knowledge is interpreted, understood from a particular perspective. An interpretive process that recognizes the gaps between text and context and the differences between ethical views of different traditions complexifies the work of comparative religious ethics. In dialogue with those of a different religion, both differences and common values are sought as discourse explores the substantive traditions of each religion. A certain degree of ethical relativism enters the dialogue as participants realize the limitedness of any perspective and its ties to social and historical location.

Using the Bible in Comparative Religious Ethics

Many religions use their sacred texts to help them establish values and evaluate moral behavior. Ways to do this vary: Hindu and Greek texts offer stories of the gods that model both laudable and sometimes less-than-honorable ways of acting. Hebrew and Islamic texts convey commands that people are encouraged to follow. Christian and Taoist texts outline a way of life that leads to harmony and well-being. Native American and traditional African religions show paths to identification with natural forces that increase one's ability to perceive the good. The content and style of communications differ, as do the underlying cosmologies of those religions, making direct comparison difficult.

Categories of analysis for comparative religious ethics have been developed in the West, influenced by the Judeo-Christian heritage and the Enlightenment philosophical framework of Europe and the United States. The Bible has been the text sourcing the framework used in comparative religious ethics until the late twentieth century. An awareness of major themes used in the Bible in ethics is essential to understanding that influence.

The idea of obedience to God's command, particularly the Ten Commandments, as the law of God was central for the people of Israel. The Ten Commandments provided the standard for evaluating both ritual and moral behavior of proponents of other religions during OT times. When neighboring societies practiced religions that focused on other gods and customs foreign to the Torah, priestly and prophetic voices condemned them. Correspondingly, when people from those societies acted in accordance with the commandments, they were praised. An unreflective comparative morality privileged Hebrew beliefs.

As Christian theologies developed, what Jews called the greatest commandments were linked, becoming the basis for Christian morality. The love of God and neighbor, as explained and modeled by Jesus' life, became a standard for evaluating beliefs and behaviors of those within and beyond the Christian church. The concepts of God's good creation corrupted by sin, of the person created in God's image, and of responsibility to a social order in covenant with God became important themes. The apostle Paul's Epistle to the Romans reinterpreted the OT law to demonstrate the importance of Jesus' death in appropriating the grace of God. His letters also emphasized a Stoicism borrowed from the Greeks that was incorporated in Christian understandings of moral behavior. Through the centuries those themes focused both Christian theological understandings of the good and Christian appraisals of other religions and their ethical systems.

During the thirteenth century, Thomas Aquinas's rediscovery of Aristotle's thought influenced Christian theological understandings of the good, the good end, and the role of reason or natural law in the analysis of moral behavior. During the Enlightenment, Immanuel Kant linked the love of God and neighbor to Aristotle's practical reason, thus reformulating that Christian theme in philosophical terms. The resulting critical standard required treating every person as an end in themselves. The Reformation brought to the fore notions of God's love and the human responsibility to respond to God's love.

The individualism that grew up through the Reformation and the Enlightenment was also rooted in a biblical idea of the worth of human beings. Both creation and redemption narratives provided theological sources for the idea of the worth, even sacredness, of the person. Those ideas led to the emphasis on freedom, dignity, and human rights that are central to contemporary Western views.

As colonial expansion brought Africans to the United States, a theology of liberation developed among slaves that drew from OT exodus narratives and prophetic voices. In the twentieth century, the Bible has been used in liberation and feminist theologies and as a moral reminder that draws on societal values shaped for centuries by Christian traditions.

Challenges and Responses for Contemporary Comparative Religious Ethics

The challenge of method: Categories of analysis. In the first two stages of comparative religious ethics—apologetics and scientific study, and the search for universals—practices of other religions were evaluated on the basis of Christian theological categories. The modern search for universals, without using the Bible, still resulted in a set of values that found their roots in Christianity and the Enlightenment. The sanctity of the individual; the focus on freedom, democracy, and human rights; the emphasis on reason; and an evolutionary idea of development of religions are some of those modern Western values.

As the academic discipline of comparative religious ethics developed, the importance of the third stage—recognition of context as determinative for ethics—became apparent. It became clear that using Christian theological and Western philosophical categories for comparing moralities across religions privileged Christian and other monotheistic religions and Western values. The evolutionary framework of religious studies further marginalized non-Western religions as that developmental framework ranked religions from "primitive" to "modern."

The development of philosophical hermeneutics and the critique of ideology in the mid-twentieth century deepened the dilemma for comparative religious ethics. Scholars recognized Western theologies, philosophies, and science as contextual and historically located systems of thought rather than universal verities. That began a search for different ways to organize comparisons of ethics across religions.

Finding patterns of response to moral issues across religions and organizing them is one way to move from using categories from Western frameworks to a more equitable method of analysis. Cultural responses are identified and compared not on the basis of an abstract idea or notion of the good, but according to how those moral responses resemble one another and differ from one another.

Seeking a cross-cultural rationality is another response to the problem of method. Although reason is developed contextually and historically, looking for commonalities across cultures in how they reason about morality or develop ethical systems is a fruitful approach.

A third way go about organizing comparative religious ethics is through identifying commonalities and honoring differences without arranging them in a broader framework.

Identifying shared categories and values provides a forum for discussion of ethics across religions. For example, monotheistic religions can discuss shared values in a framework of belief in one God who created the world and called it good. Jewish, Islamic, and Christian traditions differ in their views of Jesus but agree that one God exists and cares about humanity. Although different views of revelation exist between Islam and Christianity, both hold the belief that God conducts self-revelation to humankind. All three religions purport that God desires submission and obedience to divine commandments. Those overlapping areas allow for a systematic and wide-ranging discussion of religious ethics among Judaism, Islam, and Christianity.

Recognizing differences in overarching frameworks and values—for example, ideas of good and evil, right and wrong, and qualities of character that lead to human flourishing—also fosters conversation among different religions. Hinduism organizes values in a framework that understands the physical world to be illusion, whereas Christians understand the physical world to be God's creation. Those ideas influence the ways Hindu and Christian scholars organize comparisons of moralities. Scholars can avoid imposing their framework on the comparative discussion of ethics. Agreeing to disagree on the shared basis of the perspectival nature of all knowing leads not only to religious tolerance but also to imagining new paths for ethics in the contemporary world.

Through identifying commonalities and honoring differences, a comparison of substantive traditions with different frameworks becomes possible. A multidimensional hermeneutic allows for toleration of the views of others and self-criticism of one's own tradition and thus makes room for productive change. Defining shared values or universal norms by scholars from different religions and regions of the world forms one prong of this method. Defining moral norms and practices in each religious tradition, identifying areas of disagreement, and figuring out how to live with enduring differences forms another prong of that methodology.

The challenge of context: Cultural and ethical relativism. The recognition of context as determinative for ethics broadens here to include a range of views on cultural relativism that has developed in the past fifty years. Some scholars suggest an incommensurability of values across cultures and religions. If knowledge is proscribed by social location and interpreted from that standpoint, no universal framework for values is possible. Scholars from different traditions have little basis for conversation or agreement in this view. Other scholars take a milder view of cultural relativism, arguing that knowledge can be broadened by interaction with those of other traditions.

As scholars realized how much social location influenced knowledge, cultural relativism both helped and hindered comparative religious ethics. The understandings of socially located knowledge helped to identify the Western bias in how comparisons of ethical systems across religions developed. This has led to respectful discussions of substantive traditions with real differences rather than attempts to craft universals on principles alone. Cultural relativism has hindered the idea of universal truth or values that go beyond cultural understandings. A kind of nihilism about what is good and true can result from an extreme relativizing of knowledge. That can hinder discussions across traditions because in that view each religion holds a socially located framework and set of values that are valid for itself and are not transferable to other contexts.

In response, some argue that when Western "universals" are recognized as situated knowledge, a more valid search for commonalities and ethical values across traditions can occur. Others argue that knowledge gained through dialogues across traditions can revitalize traditions. Finding that a tradition's values may not be universal can be helpful to human flourishing. Both those responses assume a "soft" relativism that allows for social change through interaction.

The dialogue itself forms a new context in which imaginative and constructive ethical discourse can occur. In that new context, comparisons of religious ethics take on the character of interpreted knowledge. Dialogue geared to understanding can deepen appreciation of the values and ways of organizing the good in other traditions. That understanding can also reshape the view of one's own tradition.

Another response to the challenge of relativism is a narrative approach to comparative religious ethics. Rather than compare categories of analysis or address questions of the universality or relativism of any particular tradition's approach to ethics, listening to the narratives of those in other traditions forms the basis of this method. Sharing stories of major religious figures, such as Abraham, Siddhartha, Jesus, and Muhammad, can bring the ethics of different religious traditions into focus in a personal way. More recent figures can also be used to compare and contrast ways of formulating ethical principles and ideas across traditions. Using substantive narratives from religious texts and religious leaders fosters a different kind of discussion, one that is less oriented to systematization and more oriented to mutual understanding.

The challenge of approach: The demands of globalization. Those positive responses are not only hopeful but also necessary in an age of globalization. People of different religions mingle together in societies that once were monolithic, producing conflict around moral and cultural issues. The world needs some basis for resolving such conflict. Market economies merge and influence global financial health, presenting ethical issues for nations and corporations. Some agreement on trading practices, economic expansion, and protecting the environment seems necessary. Global mobility and wars that produce international refugees create situations that demand resolution.

Seeking answers to those dilemmas moves comparative religious ethics from a scholarly activity to one that involves political, social, and economic entities across societies. Cooperation and some shared values among religious traditions are necessary for peace. Protecting the environment is necessary for human flourishing. And competing goods must be weighed and evaluated from different religious perspectives. The emerging comparative religious ethics works to address those issues. It recognizes the importance of questions of religious identity and authority, values of equality and difference among peoples, the management of marriage and family life, as well as issues of economic globalization, human rights, and conflict and violence. Those have become urgent issues that require comparative religious ethics to analyze and evaluate, and to search for solutions to issues affecting people from many religious traditions. In addition to scholarly debate and analysis, agreements and action are now sought.

Going about that task requires identifying areas of convergence among religions without placing them in a hierarchy. Recognizing and honoring differences is also a response necessary for extending those convergences and identifying others. When traditions clash on values, withholding judgment may be necessary. Continuing discussion despite critical difference can broaden the horizons of traditions involved. Seeking interaction with political voices in societies, nongovernmental organizations, corporations, and disciplines such as philosophy, hermeneutics, sociology, and anthropology in addition to ethics and religious studies can also foster emerging comparative religious ethics.

Conclusion

Method, context, and approach are each addressed in the emerging discourse in comparative religious ethics as interpreted knowledge. A two-pronged method addresses questions of shared or universal values despite differing philosophical and religious frameworks and sifts through agreements and disagreements by studying substantive traditions. A recognition of the importance of context and perspectival interpretations seeks to form broader contexts of dialogue across traditions, dialogue that fosters creative solutions to contemporary problems. Those new conversations address not just theoretical issues, but actual problems resulting from globalization, seeking practical solutions to those problems that would lead to harmony and human flourishing.

See also Cross-Cultural Ethics; Globalization; Natural Law; Natural Rights; Pluralism; Religious Toleration

Bibliography

Adeney, F., and A. Sharma, eds. *Christianity and Human Rights: Influences and Issues*. State University of New York Press, 2007; Bauman, Z. *Postmodern Ethics*. Blackwell, 1993; Fasching, D., and D. Dechant. *Comparative Religious Ethics: A Narrative Approach*. Blackwell, 2001; Little, D., and S. Twiss. *Comparative Religious Ethics*. Harper & Row, 1978; Morgan, P., and C. Lawton, eds. *Ethical Issues in Six Religious Traditions*. 2nd ed. Edinburgh University Press, 2007; Schweiker, W., M. Johnson, and K. Jung, eds. *Humanity before God: Contemporary Faces of Jewish, Christian, and Islamic Ethics*. Fortress, 2006; Sullivan, W., and W. Kymlicka, eds. *The Globalization of Ethics: Religious and Secular Perspectives*. Cambridge University Press, 2007; Taylor, C. *Sources of the Self: The Making of the Modern Identity*. Harvard University Press, 1989; Wolfe, R., and C. Gudorf, eds. *Ethics and World Religions: Cross-Cultural Case Studies*. Orbis, 1999.

Frances Adeney

Compassion

God's Faithful Compassion

The OT recounts God's compassion with thanksgiving and praise, while expressing the confidence and hope that this divine compassion will continue to be upon God's people throughout all time. The Hebrew word *rāḥam* and its variants describe God's love, mercy, and abundant care. God's compassion is like the tender parental love and care for a dear child (Ps. 103:13; Isa. 49:15), but much greater. The breadth and depth of God's love perdures in constancy in the face of the people's persistent unfaithfulness. God's acts of compassion include forgiveness (1 Kgs. 8:50; Mic. 7:18), comfort (Isa. 49:15), patient presence (Isa. 30:18), loving-kindness (Ps. 145:8), and the restoration of justice (Jer. 13:14).

God listens to the needs of the people and responds with compassion (Exod. 2:27). God promises to have compassion on his servants (Deut. 32:36). The writer of Lamentations claims confidence in God's sure compassion, even and especially when God has first brought suffering (3:32). Isaiah calls for joyful responses to the fact that God does and will show compassion on those who wait for him to provide comfort and justice (30:18; 49:15). The psalms are replete with thankful proclamations of God's past compassion (78:38), desperate pleas for God's present compassion (6:2), and sure predictions of God's compassion to come (135:14). Although God's compassion appears more frequently in the OT than human compassion, God calls the people to practice compassionate justice through care for one another (Lev. 25:35–37 [the Jubilee]), for animals (Deut. 25:4), and for resident aliens (Exod. 23:9).

God's Compassion through Jesus Christ

In the NT, God manifests compassion in Jesus Christ, who constantly reaches out with works of healing and ministry to the needy, the suffering, and the outcast. Jesus responds in love and mercy to those whose pain, loneliness, and faith are strong. His compassion moves him to pour out healing care, forgiveness, and comforting presence, even to the point of his death and beyond in resurrection and ascension. Jesus is moved with compassion (*splanchnizomai*) when he sees the hungry crowds waiting with no food, and he provides them all with bread and fish (Matt. 9:36). He is similarly moved when he sees a widow following as her dead son is being carried to the grave (Luke 7:13), and after telling her not to weep, he brings her son back to life. The sick and afflicted cry out to him for mercy (*eleeō*), and he heals them. He is touched by the same feelings that we experience, and he sympathizes with our weaknesses, though without succumbing to temptation as we do (Heb. 4:15). Throughout, God stands as the source of all mercies (*oiktirmos*) (2 Cor. 1:3), sharing that mercy and love for us with the gift of his Son, Jesus Christ (Eph. 2:4). In God's infinite compassion, God gives the embodiment of divine compassion in human form.

Compassion of the Passible and Impassible God

During the last century, relational and openness theologies have expressed concern that traditional understandings of divine compassion describe a God who is detached from the suffering of creatures. Instead of claiming that God is both compassionate and unchanged by that compassion, this view champions a God who suffers with those who suffer, who (in the OT) responds with an emotional compassion not unlike human compassion (only greater), and who (in the NT) suffers and dies as God in Jesus Christ's crucifixion. In this way, God is passible, subject to the shifting circumstances that affect creatures.

The notion of a passibly compassionate God appeals to those looking for a present, accessible God who addresses contemporary pain, disaster, and evil by sharing in creaturely pain. They draw on biblical interpretation that emphasizes the way God's feelings and actions are described anthropomorphically, especially in the OT. The accompanying NT interpretation emphasizes the unity of the Trinity and the oneness of the hypostatic union more than the particularity of Christ's human and divine identities. The resulting presentation of God allows for the God of Israel and of the Trinity to respond in suffering compassion, in the time and space of creatures' lives.

In contrast, a contemporary reclamation of the early church's understanding of God as passible in a way that does not negate divine impassibility claims that all anthropomorphic images of God rest on the prior and foundational character of God as impassible, as unchanged and undiminished by the pain and death of the created world. Early hymns proclaim the mysterious and immanent presence of God, who compassionately cares for, suffers with, and comforts his people, without the changes that characterize human physical and emotional feelings. This understanding of God as passible and impassible emphasizes the effectiveness of Christ's compassionate ministry, suffering, death, and resurrection without imposing the human nature of Christ onto Christ's divine and divinely shared impassible nature.

Ethics of Compassion

Contrasting assessments of the compassionate God can lead to different emphases in the ethics of human compassion. A commitment to God's passibility recognizes that some problems are too great for God to change, and it focuses on human agency to bring about compassionate social change here and now. A commitment to God's impassibility places less emphasis on the capacity of human agency to effect change, and it focuses on human compassion that reflects and points toward God's ultimate power to bring eternal justice. Nonetheless, both the primarily passible and the primarily impassible interpretations of God claim his compassion for creation as a constant and determinative mark of his relationship with humans and all of creation. The compassion that God shows to his chosen people in the OT models the compassionate justice that God's prophets exhort his people to embody. Both interpretations require Christians to imitate, albeit imperfectly, Jesus Christ's divinely human compassionate ministry to the lost, hungry, poor, and suffering.

In word and activity, Christ issues an ethical call to the people of God to care for the needy with compassionate kindness, which the Samaritan did for the victim of a violent robbery (Luke 10:33), but which the rich man failed to do for the ill and impoverished Lazarus (Luke 16:19–21). This compassionate discipleship is not an attitude or feeling, but rather involves living with the poor as the poor, sharing all possessions, and extending familial commitments of care to strangers and enemies. The book of Acts shows how the earliest Christians try to live into Jubilee compassion, even in the face of persecution. The NT Epistles urge those who follow Christ to clothe themselves with "compassion, kindness, humility, meekness, and patience" (Col. 3:12), to suffer with and care for prisoners (Heb. 10:34), and to help those in need (1 John 3:17).

Today's responses to God's call for human compassion include liberation theology's solidarity with the poor, feminist ethics of care, feminist and womanist attention to trauma, pacifist and just-war ethics of peacemaking, animal care ethics, ecological ethics, and ethics that look to spread God's compassion universally.

See also Care, Caring; Feminist Ethics; Trinity

Bibliography

Fretheim, T. *The Suffering of God: An Old Testament Perspective*. Fortress, 1984; Moreno, J. "Evangelization." Pages 564–80 in *Mysterium Liberationis: Fundamental Concepts of Liberation Theology*, ed. I. Ellacuria and J. Sobrino. Orbis, 1993; Sanders, J. *The God Who Risks: A Theology of Providence*. InterVarsity, 1998; Sears, D. *Compassion for Humanity in the Jewish Tradition*. Jason Aronson, 1998; Webb, S. *On God and Dogs: A Christian Theology of Compassion for Animals*. Oxford University Press, 2002; Weinandy, T. *Does God Suffer?* University of Notre Dame Press, 2000; Welch, S. *A Feminist Ethic of Risk*. Augsburg, 2000.

Margaret B. Adam

Conception

Biblical authors did not possess the knowledge that we now have regarding human reproduction, nor could they have foreseen the reproductive technologies available today. Scripture assumes, for example, that conception occurs through heterosexual intercourse. Scripture does provide a vision of the origins of human life that may orient and inform ethical reflection on reproduction and the moral value of human life in its earliest stages.

Genesis describes the creation of the first humans. God fashions Adam from the earth (Gen. 2:7) and Eve from Adam's rib (Gen. 2:21–23). Thereafter, humans are conceived through intercourse, except for Jesus, who is conceived by the Holy Spirit (Matt. 1:18; Luke 1:26–38). Natural reproduction falls under the governance of God, the maker of life. God alone opens (Gen. 29:31; 30:22) and closes (Gen. 20:18; 1 Sam. 1:5) wombs. Scripture conveys both God's sovereignty as the Lord of life and God's intimate knowledge of us in passages that speak of God forming us in our mother's wombs: "You knit me together in my mother's womb. . . . In your book were written all the days that were formed for me, when none of them as yet existed" (Ps. 139:13b, 16b). All human life originates within God's plan of salvation history, yet in various places Scripture tells of divine appointment from the womb. Jeremiah is called by God from the beginning: "Before I formed you in the womb I knew you, and before you were born I consecrated you" (Jer. 1:5). From within Elizabeth's womb John the Baptist heralds the arrival of Jesus (Luke 1:41, 44) and is the prophet of the Most High who prepares the way of the Lord (Luke 1:57–80). Paul writes to the Galatians that God had set him apart and called him before he was born (Gal. 1:15). The general witness of Scripture is one of awe or wonder at the mysterious origins of life under the providential sovereignty of God (Eccl. 11:5). Scriptural emphasis on God's initiative and authorship rather than human will relativizes parental claims to offspring (see 2 Macc. 7:22–23) and emphasizes that life is a gift given by God.

Scriptural perspectives on conception bear on ethical issues such as abortion, desirable conditions for reproduction, and assisted reproductive technologies. Human life undoubtedly begins at conception, but Christians disagree regarding the moral status of prenatal human life. The Catholic magisterium argues for a right to life from conception until natural death, whereas ethicists such as Beverly Wildung Harrison differentiate the moral status of pre- and postnatal human life. Circumstances surrounding one's conception—rape, incest, assisted reproduction, within marriage or by casual sex—sometimes contribute to stigmas given religious warrant (see Witte). Oliver O'Donovan argues that extracorporeal conception distorts the parent-child relationship into that of creator and artifact, though moral analyses of assisted reproduction would also need to consider biblical attitudes toward fecundity, infertility, kinship, and healing.

See also Abortion; Birth Control; Family Planning; Procreation; Reproductive Technologies; Sexual Ethics

Bibliography

Harrison, B. *Our Right to Choose: Toward a New Ethic of Abortion*. Beacon Press, 1983; John Paul II. *Evangelium Vitae*. United States Catholic Conference, 1995; O'Donovan, O. *Begotten or Made? Human Procreation and Medical Technique*. Oxford University Press, 1984; Witte, J., Jr. "Ishmael's Bane: The Sin and Crime of Illegitimacy Reconsidered." *Punishment and Society: The International Journal of Penology* 5 (2003): 327–45.

Darlene Fozard Weaver

Concubinage

The word *concubine* derives from the Latin *concubina*, itself derived from *concumbere*, meaning "to lie with" (*com* = with + *cubare* = to lie down). The NRSV consistently translates the Hebrew term *pîlegeš* (37x in the OT) as "concubine." The word *pîlegeš* has no cognates in the other Semitic languages in the region. It may be a loanword based on the Greek term *pallax* (variants *pallakē*, *pallakis*) meaning "concubine," perhaps penetrating

Israelite culture via the Philistines, who were Aegean in origin (Rabin). The *Oxford English Dictionary* defines *concubinage* as "the cohabiting of a man and a woman who are not legally married," while stating under *concubine* that this position was legally recognized in Hebrew and Islamic societies. This inconsistency reveals the difficulty of defining the notion with precision. In biblical context, concubines had a recognized place within the social system. But the legal codes of the OT do not specify the conditions and requirements of either proper marriage or concubinage; a sketch of what constitutes concubinage, the reasons it existed, and why it was permitted must be constructed on the basis of narrative texts. An additional difficulty arises with the common Hebrew noun *ʾiššâ*, which basically means "woman" but often is rendered as "wife" where translators think it contextually appropriate; readers should remember that translating *ʾiššâ* as "wife" and *ʾîš* as "husband" may be overly restrictive because Hebrew has no specific term for "wife" or "husband" (as is true of Greek as well).

There is no consensus in biblical studies regarding the social status of the concubine. Tal Davidovich identified four definitions represented in the scholarly literature. A concubine is (1) a secondary wife acquired by purchase or as booty in war who is midway in status between primary wife and maidservant (Deut. 21:10–14); (2) a maidservant whose function was to perpetuate her master's line by bearing sons (Gen. 16:2–4 [*šipḥâ*, "slave-girl"]; 30:3 [*ʾāmâ*, "maid"]); (3) a woman who lives in a bonded relationship with a man within his household without legally being married to him (by analogy with Hellenistic and Roman law); and (4) a woman married to a man but who still lives in her father's house, so-called matriarchal matrimony (Judg. 8:3). Likewise, there is no consensus regarding the status and rights of children issuing from a concubine relationship. Biblical evidence supports a range of options, from equal inheritance rights, to lesser rights than children of primary wives, to no inherent property rights.

Texts from the wider Middle East do not settle the issues. Middle Assyrian law (late second millennium BCE) regulates concubinage and inheritance. A citizen may declare before witnesses that his concubine is to be his wife; then when he dies, his concubine's sons will receive a share of his estate (Pritchard 183, no. 41). In Roman law, *concubinatus* was an enduring monogamous relationship. It was an alternative to legal marriage, often exercised when the man had higher social status (Treggiari). Because *concubinatus* was not legal marriage, offspring would not automatically inherit their father's estate. In postbiblical Jewish law, a Jewish woman who lives monogamously with a Jewish man without the legality of a *ketubah* (marriage contract) is a concubine. Only one talmudic source addresses the legal difference between wives and concubines. Reflecting on David's wives and concubines, *b. Sanh.* 21a says that a wife has *kiddushin* (betrothal) and *ketubah*, whereas a concubine has neither; little else is said in the Talmud. By the early centuries CE, Jews virtually ceased practicing concubinage (Adler).

In distinction from Roman law, Hebrew concubinage was not a mutually exclusive alternative to marriage, but when practiced, it was a supplement to marriage. A man could have one or more wives and have one or more concubines at the same time. Concubinage seems to have been mostly the prerogative of community or state leaders. In the OT, patriarchs, tribal chieftains, and kings are those who took concubines: Abraham had Keturah (1 Chr. 1:32), Abraham's brother Nahor had Reumah (Gen. 22:24), Jacob had Bilhah (specifically identified as a concubine in Gen. 35:22), and Caleb had two concubines, Ephah and Maacah (1 Chr. 2:46, 48).

Sarah's maidservant Hagar is not identified specifically as a concubine, but she was Egyptian, apparently a slave, and clearly was not equal in status with Sarah; there is no evidence that concubines were necessarily slaves. There is evidence that offspring of concubines were viewed as potential rivals of the children of primary wives, as was the case with Hagar's Ishmael as well as Abraham's other concubines' sons (Gen. 25:6), and Gideon's son Abimelech (Judg. 8:29–31).

Biblical writers sometimes note that certain dishonorable men consorted with concubines or were the sons of concubines; it might be worth asking why. Reuben consorted with his father's concubine Bilhah (Gen. 35:22) and brought dishonor upon himself (Gen. 49:3–4). The concubine of Esau's son Eliphaz bore Amalek (Gen. 36:12), and Amalek was Israel's most heinous tribal enemy. The book of Judges associates two concubines with disreputable figures; in both cases the concubine is from an outside clan or tribe. While Gideon had seventy local sons by many wives, Gideon's concubine was from Shechem, and she bore him Abimelech, who went on to declare himself king (Judg. 8–9). An unnamed Levite from Ephraim took a concubine from Bethlehem. After he allowed her to be ravaged and raped to death by an unruly mob of Benjaminites, he cut her in pieces

(Judg. 19–21); this lengthy story is told to stigmatize the Benjaminites.

Kings assembled collections of royal women for a variety of reasons, including the making of diplomatic alliances, as war trophies, and as court helpers such as singers, weavers, and dancers. Not all held the same rank once they entered the king's household. Some women held the rank of wife (*'iššâ*), others were royal concubines, and still others were maidservants. Among the kings who took concubines, Saul took Rizpah (2 Sam. 3:7; 21:11), and David had at least ten concubines (2 Sam. 15:16; 20:3) in addition to wives. Absalom slept specifically with David's concubines whom he had left behind (2 Sam. 16:21–22). Solomon had three hundred royal concubines from foreign lands in addition to his seven hundred princess wives. Rehoboam had eighteen wives and sixty concubines (2 Chr. 11:21). Curiously, only kings reigning from Jerusalem are mentioned as having concubines, none from the kingdom of Israel. Concubines were considered royal assets, and any attempt by someone other than the king (e.g., Adonijah [1 Kgs. 2:21–22]) to sleep with them was considered an attempt to usurp the throne. Since the children of royal concubines were reckoned among the group of royal offspring and shared rights with the children of royal wives (Davidovich), controlling reproductive access to concubines protected the lines of office and inheritance. Overall, there is no moral criticism of concubinage as a social practice. While the Deuteronomistic History criticizes Solomon for taking a thousand wives, it was not because of their number or because they included concubines, but because they turned his heart from exclusive devotion to Yahweh (1 Kgs. 11:1–13).

In the NT, the word *concubine* is never used, and there is no specific reference to concubinage. The only possible indirect allusion comes in the Pastoral Epistles where qualifications for church officers are specified. Bishops, deacons, and elders should be "married only once" (1 Tim. 3:2, 12; Titus 1:6)—literally, be a "man/husband of one woman/wife." The NRSV may be misleading insofar as this text does not specifically rule out marrying more than one woman, but says only that a man may have but one woman at a time. This qualification for office may be specifying serial monogamy and perhaps was formulated in this way in order to align with Roman marriage practice, and it may be a move away from the Jewish tolerance of polygamy and concubinage; however, there are other interpretions of this prescription.

See also Family; Marriage and Divorce; Polygamy

Bibliography

Adler, R. *Engendering Judaism: An Inclusive Theology and Ethics*. Beacon Press, 1999; Davidovich, T. *The Mystery of the House of Royal Women: Royal Pīlagšîm as Secondary Wives in the Old Testament*. Uppsala Universitet, 2007; Levin, S. "Hebrew pi(y)legeš, Greek παλλακή, Latin paelex: The Origin of Intermarriage among the Early Indo-Europeans and Semites." *General Linguistics* 23 (1983): 191–97; Page, S. "Marital Expectations of Church Leaders in the Pastoral Epistles." *JSNT* 50 (1993): 105–20; Pritchard, J. *Ancient Near Eastern Texts Relating to the Old Testament*. 3rd ed. Princeton University Press, 1969; Rabin, C. "The Origin of the Word Pīlegeš." *JJS* 25 (1974): 353–64; Treggiari, S. *Roman Marriage: Iusti Coniuges from the Time of Cicero to the Time of Ulpian*. Oxford University Press, 1991.

Barry Bandstra

Concupiscence *See* Sexual Ethics

Confession

Confession in Scripture, tradition, and Christian ethics encompasses four deeply intertwined meanings: confession of praise, thanks, sin, and faith. By tracing confession in Scripture, we come to see worship as Christian ethics.

In Scripture

Two terms translate as "to confess" in Scripture: *yādâ* (or *tōdâ*) in Hebrew and *homologeō* (and *exomologeō*) in Greek. Old Testament notions of confessing entail a sense of action—casting forth thanks or praise for blessings, casting transgressions out of the self or community, or throwing out into the world claims of allegiance to the God of Israel. The word *yādâ* first occurs in Scripture on the lips of Leah (Gen. 29:35), who proclaims that in praise of God for the birth of her fourth son, she will call him "Judah," whose name means "praise." In the OT 80 percent of the occurrences of *yādâ* mean "thanks" or "praise"; most of these appear in the psalms, songs for communal worship.

The remaining occurrences of *yādâ* in the OT split about evenly between confession of sin and confession of God's name. With the covenant comes the obligation to confess uncleanness, transgressions, or unrighteousness (Lev. 5:5). Central to the worship of God by the people of Israel (Ps. 32:5), such confession is highly embodied, being intertwined with the bodies of sacrificial animals or the scapegoat, understood to literally carry the sins of the community into the desert (Lev. 16:21). Via confession, righteousness dislodged from among God, individuals, and community by human action is restored.

These same meanings carry over into the NT, but with a decisive shift in emphasis. The word *homologeō* also signifies confession of praise, thanks, sins, or faith, but faith emerges as primary. Deriving from the roots *logos* ("word") and *homou* ("together"), *homologeō* entails a more verbal sense, suggesting "to speak" and "to agree." Contrary to the OT, almost 75 percent of the time *homologeō* or *exomologeō* in the NT refers to confessing the name of the Lord Jesus or confessing faith in Christ Jesus (e.g., Matt. 10:32; John 9:22; Rom. 10:9). Such confession entails conversion to a new way of life among God's people and repentance for and confession of one's earlier sins.

In the Christian Tradition

"Confession" retains these multiple, interconnected meanings throughout Christian history. Augustine's *Confessions* is the exemplar par excellence. But due to the NT influence, confession of sin and faith come to dominate. The practice of confessing sins, rooted in Judaism, remains central to the early church (Jas. 5:16; *Did.* 14.1), fundamental to conversion, a precursor to baptism, and key for reconciliation within the Christian community. Confession of sin becomes central to the eventual sacrament of penance, a practice rejected as a sacrament by the Reformation but retained in the Roman Catholic and Orthodox traditions. The practice of general confession of sin remains a central component of most Christian liturgies.

Protestant traditions come to highlight confession of faith. In the NT "to confess" primarily refers to a public witness to the faith, even to the point of martyrdom. Confessions were relatively simple in the early church ("Jesus is Lord"), becoming more complex with the christological controversies, culminating in the creeds. Similarly, the sixteenth and seventeenth centuries saw the emergence of official statements of doctrine in the Protestant churches, of which the Lutheran Augsburg Confession was the first (1530).

Confession, Worship, and Christian Ethics

Tracing this history of confession highlights the deep wisdom of the Judeo-Christian tradition: worship is ethics (see Hauerwas and Wells). To praise and worship God is a moral act, the primary act of justice, according to Augustine (*Civ.* 19). To confess Jesus as Lord, to confess the God of Abraham, Isaac, and Jacob as the one God, is to enact the first commandment; confession, therefore, is the ground of all the commandments of the Torah and the new covenant. To confess is to commit an act of truth, not just verbally, mentally, or propositionally, but with one's life and actions. For to confess the Lord entails conversion, becoming a member of God's people, a complete change of life. It requires an ongoing practice of truthfulness about ourselves, especially of where we fall short, and of confession and reconciliation. As the OT attests, confession is a bodily action, something that we do not only with our words but also with our bodies and lives.

See also Conversion; Faith; Forgiveness; Liturgy and Ethics; Martyrdom; Penance; Reconciliation; Repentance; Sin

Bibliography

Hauerwas, S., and S. Wells. *The Blackwell Companion to Christian Ethics*. Blackwell, 2006.

M. Therese Lysaught

Confidentiality

A confidential relationship is one in which a person pledges not to disclose information shared within the relationship to outside parties. Confidentiality assumes that persons have the right to decide whether, when, and in what manner their personal information is made public. This assumption may be implicit (as in marriage or close friendship, where privacy is presumed) or explicit (as when the law protects confidentiality between doctors, lawyers, psychologists, clergy, or other professionals and their clients).

Consequentialist arguments for confidentiality include enabling trust in interpersonal relationships and allowing persons to seek advice or receive needed care more freely. Institutionally, confidentiality allows an organization to test ideas, protect proprietary concepts, and gain a competitive edge. Deontologically, maintaining confidentiality is related to the duties of promise-keeping and respect for the autonomy of the person. The duty of keeping confidence may be overridden, however, if keeping confidence would cause or allow harm to the person sharing the information, to an outside party, or to society at large.

The Bible—particularly in the wisdom literature—warns against both passing on and receiving gossip (see Prov. 11:13; 20:19; 2 Cor. 12:20) and commands "do not disclose another's secret" (Prov. 25:9). Keeping confidence makes one "trustworthy in spirit" (Prov. 11:13); violating confidentiality brings "shame" and "ill-repute" (Prov. 25:10).

See also Privacy; Professional Ethics; Promise and Promise-Keeping; Speech Ethics

Bibliography

Bok, S. *Secrets: On the Ethics of Concealment and Revelation*. Pantheon Books, 1983; Corey, G., M. Corey, and P. Callanan. *Issues and Ethics in the Helping Professions*. 7th ed. Brooks Cole, 2006.

Amy Renee Wagner

Conflict

Conflict is the state of dispute, disagreement, or open clash between opposing groups or individuals, ideas or interests. It may suggest antagonism or opposition even to the point of hostility and violence. War itself is often referred to as "armed conflict."

Antonyms are *accord*, *harmony*, and *unity*. In Scripture, the Hebrew word *šālôm* connotes the opposite of conflict. The very essence of the biblical revelation is that the world was created in *šālôm*, out of God's unified being, but then it subsequently fell into hostility to divine purposes, which has resulted in perpetual conflict within creation and between God and creation.

Attending to Scripture

The word *conflict* is used only occasionally in recent translations of Scripture. Equivalent words are many, including *strife*, *contention*, and *quarreling*. Titus 3:9 in the NIV employs three parallel words: "But avoid foolish controversies and genealogies and arguments and quarrels about the law, because these are unprofitable and useless."

Yet the entire Bible is the narrative of a God who confronts cosmological rebellion with its resultant conflict that spills out of the supernatural realm into the created world. Satan, the embodiment of heavenly rebellion, is displaced and seeks an alternate kingdom on earth. As a result, Adam and Eve, the human prototypes deceived by Satan into overt disobedience, seek their own self-centered interests, seeding the ongoing conflict among humans, between humans and God, and between humans and the rest of creation.

The mission of Scripture is to present a redemptive plan of salvation that will engage not only the human race but also the entire cosmos. From the fall until the final restoration of all things in the apocalyptic vision of Revelation, conflict prevails in all aspects of life. In Revelation, conflict erupts into cosmic war and the final defeat of Satan.

One word used throughout Scripture to describe the contentious powers is *evil*, which itself is cloaked in a wide variety of literary garments. Evil operates in three dimensions: the world, the flesh, and the devil. The "world" suggests the corrupted influence of created institutions, often born to good purposes but over time becoming self-serving, manipulative, and systemically evil. The "flesh" refers to the principle of carnality, the human compulsion to sinning at the personal level. The "devil" refers to satanic influences unexplained by the others but penetrating throughout the cosmos. In 1 Pet. 5:8 the author counsels believers, "Discipline yourselves, keep alert. Like a roaring lion your adversary the devil prowls around, looking for someone to devour." All three dimensions are alluded to in Eph. 2:1–2: "You were dead through the trespasses and sins [personal evil] in which you once lived, following the course of this world [systemic evil], following the ruler of the power of the air [cosmological evil]."

Conflict, in this debilitative sense, then, is the clash for control and possession between the two competing, though unequal entities, God and Satan, played out at the macrocosmic level. The authorized military conflicts of the OT and Christ's warning, "Do not think that I have come to bring peace to the earth; I have not come to bring peace, but a sword. For I have come to set a man against his father, and a daughter against her mother, and a daughter-in-law against her mother-in-law" (Matt. 10:34–35), must be seen in the light of the larger cosmological conflict (see also Luke 22:38).

The covenantal relationship between God and his chosen people was intended to introduce an era of peace and tranquility in a "promised land" that would serve as a "light to the Gentiles." The ceremonial laws were prescribed for the orderly functioning of society and the squelching of conflict. The Jubilee laws further sought to rectify relationships and reset economics that were out of kilter, potentially stirring strife. The establishment of cities of refuge offered redemptive measures for those guilty of manslaughter and other crimes.

However, conflict is also generally experienced at the microcosmic level in a wide variety of expressions and settings. Scripture shows a variety of interpersonal conflicts: between Abraham and Lot's herdsmen (Gen. 13:6–7), between Laban and Jacob (Gen. 31:36), between Jesus' disciples (Luke 22:24), between Greek and Hebrew Jewish Christians (Acts 6:1), between Paul and Barnabas (Acts 15:39), among the members of the Corinthian church (1 Cor. 3:1–3; 6:1–7). Some of these conflicts were settled amicably and creatively.

Not all conflict is derived from Satan or evil impulses. Some is provoked out of the "stuff of life." It may be unpredictable or the result of the natural order of things gone awry. Paul, without identifying the source of his conflict, says, "For even when we came into Macedonia, our bodies had no rest, but we were afflicted in every way—disputes without and fears within" (2 Cor. 7:5). The writer of Ecclesiastes suggests that there is a cycle of life's core experiences, "a time for every matter under heaven . . . a time for war, and a time for peace" (Eccl. 3:1, 8). He concludes ironically,

"I have observed the burden that God has given to people" (Eccl. 3:10 NET). Indeed, in many scriptural passages God seems to be the initiator of conflict for the purposes of disciplining or testing the faithful or punishing the disobedient. In the classic case of Job, both Satan and God seem to be agents of his suffering. One witness says, "The fire of God fell from heaven and burned up the sheep and the servants, and consumed them; I alone have escaped to tell you" (Job 1:16). Job's wife, herself conflicted, prods him, "Curse God, and die" (Job 2:9).

All change and growth involve a level of conflict. Its sources are less important than its resolution. Conflict unresolved can result in "barred gates" (Prov. 18:19 NET) between people, in severe "penalties" (Gal. 5:10), and in "evil practices" (Jas. 3:16 NET). Conflicts tend to escalate and pass down from generation to generation, wreaking havoc along the way.

Scripture offers a variety of suggestions to resolve conflict. Proverbs 15:18 advises that "those who are slow to anger calm contention." Another proverb warns against meddling "in the quarrel of another" (Prov. 26:17). Proverbs 30:33 discourages any escalation of anger. The sage states, "The beginning of strife is like letting out water; so stop before the quarrel breaks out" (Prov. 17:14).

Jesus highlighted the role of peacemakers in the Beatitudes, indicating that they will be called "children of God" (Matt. 5:9). And the apostle Paul writes, "If it is possible, . . . live peaceably with all. Beloved, never avenge yourselves, but leave room for the wrath of God" (Rom. 12:18–19). The practice of deferring or submitting to one another or to the authorities is seen in numerous passages (Eph. 5:21; Phil. 2:3; Heb. 13:17). Scriptures also highlight forgiveness as a principle of conflict resolution: "Bear with one another and, if anyone has a complaint against another, forgive each other; just as the Lord has forgiven you, so you also must forgive. Above all, clothe yourselves with love, which binds everything together in perfect harmony" (Col. 3:13–14).

At the core of the gospel is the appeal to and anticipation of unity. Jesus offers it in his farewell speech to his disciples: "Peace I leave with you; my peace I give to you. I do not give to you as the world gives" (John 14:27). Later he says to his disciples, "This is my commandment, that you love one another as I have loved you. No one has greater love than this, to lay down one's life for one's friends" (John 15:12–13); then, he prays to God that his followers "may become completely one, so that the world may know that you have sent me" (John 17:23). The day of Pentecost was marked by the "one accord" of those assembled in the upper room. The linguistic divisiveness of Babel was replaced by unified understanding under the miracle of the Holy Spirit (Acts 2). Paul reiterates the theme of unity, urging believers to live "with all humility and gentleness, with patience, bearing with one another in love, making every effort to maintain the unity of the Spirit in the bond of peace" (Eph. 4:2–3).

The Tradition and Scripture

Peter resolved his internal conflict over the role of the gentiles through lessons learned in a dream and his subsequent encounter with the centurion Cornelius. His ethnocentrism, born of his Jewish religious perspective, dissolved in the reality that "God shows no partiality, but in every nation anyone who fears him and does what is right is acceptable to him" (Acts 10:34–35). Similarly, the council at Jerusalem confronted its brewing schism successfully on the matter of the inclusion of gentiles as fellow believers, after hearing evidence, studying the Scriptures, acknowledging the spiritual realities of their foreign guests, and negotiating a legal compromise (Acts 15). This action allowed the church to move beyond its Jewish roots to become an international religion.

With successive waves of persecution, many early Christians chose to exclude themselves from society, opting to live as hermits, ascetics, and monks apart from society in the Egyptian desert, precisely to avoid worldly temptations and confrontation with political authorities. Later, with the growth of monasticism, it was believed that separation from the world would not only reduce conflict but also allow for the practice of communal spiritual disciplines unimpeded by society.

Sadly, the history of Christianity is replete with conflict. The struggle to define orthodoxy resulted in a succession of councils that marginalized heretics and splintered the church into various factions, primarily between Eastern and Western branches. The Reformation of the sixteenth century brought new conflict with the emergence of Protestantism in its myriad forms, sometimes battling for supremacy, often in overt competition for the lives and souls of adherents. In modern times, Christians have killed Jews, Catholics and Protestants have engaged in fratricide, and Christians and Muslims regularly die at one another's hands. Most wars of the twentieth century have seen large expenditures of life primarily within so-called Christian nations, attesting to the fact that the unity and peace that Christ appealed for has been tragically dishonored.

However, there have been notable exceptions. Among the various denominations are "peace churches" that have long advocated Christian pacifism. Most of these are from the Anabaptist stream—the Religious Society of Friends (Quakers), Mennonites, Amish, Church of the Brethren. In recent years there has been a movement of "restorative justice," taking its lessons from biblical principles, including the text of Matt. 5:21–26, which encourages a process of confrontation and reconciliation between the aggrieved party and the aggressor before spiritual gifts are offered. With increased population and its demands, conflicts arise at all levels. Christians need a discerning spirit to determine both the nature of the conflict and the options available for resolution.

See also Anabaptist Ethics; Anger; Class Conflict; Desire; Evil; Just-Peacemaking Theory; Peace; Powers and Principalities; Violence; War

Bibliography

Jewett, R. *Captain America and the Crusade against Evil: The Dilemma of Zealous Nationalism*. Eerdmans, 2004; Lederach, J. *Building Peace: Sustainable Reconciliation*. United States Institute of Peace, 1998; Miller, M., and B. Gingerich, eds. *The Church's Peace Witness*. Eerdmans, 1994; Rothman, J. *Resolving Identity-Based Conflict in Nations, Organizations and Communities*. Jossey-Bass, 1997; Sande, K. *The Peacemaker: A Biblical Guide to Resolving Personal Conflict*. Baker Academic, 2004; Smock, D. *Interfaith Dialogue and Peacebuilding*. United States Institute of Peace Press, 2002.

Fletcher L. Tink

Conquest

The nation of Israel participates in two wars of conquest within the pages of the OT. The first is a war of invasion in which the nation attempts to dispossess the indigenous peoples of Canaan (Josh. 1–21). The second is war of imperial expansion, in which the new king, David, defeats rival kings and dominates the peoples of the region (2 Sam. 8:1–14; 10:1–12:31; 1 Chr. 18:1–13). The conquest of Canaan is presented as an obedient response to the commands of God, whereas David's wars focus on the exploits of the king, with only an oblique reference to divine involvement (2 Sam. 8:1–14; 10:1–19; 1 Chr. 18:1–13).

The Davidic campaigns must be read in light of 1–2 Samuel's ambivalent portrait of David and apprehensions about the way kings use power (2 Sam. 11). The account of David's wars reflects a discomfort that is expressed by a tendency to cast the conflicts as defensive operations. The subjugation of the Philistines likewise is rendered as a necessary response to aggression (2 Sam. 5:17–25) but is of a different order, as it continues the conquest of Canaan. Here, in contrast to the accounts of David's external wars, the Lord assumes a prominent role in defeating Israel's last enemy in the promised land (cf. Josh. 13:2–3).

Joshua's conquest of Canaan is more problematic. The book of Joshua depicts Israel's occupation of Canaan as an invasion initiated by God and prosecuted in strict obedience to divine directives. Among these directives are commands to "put to the sword" the land's inhabitants and "utterly destroy all that breathe." The narrative repeatedly reports that Israel did exactly that, leaving no survivors (6:21; 8:22; 10:1, 28, 30, 31, 34, 37, 39; 11:8, 11, 12, 14, 20, 21). The massacres are reported with cold detachment and with no expression of remorse save that Israel failed to finish the job.

The Theology of Conquest

Central to the theology of the conquest is the depiction of the Lord as divine warrior. The Lord fights for Israel and defeats the vastly more powerful peoples of Canaan in order to fulfill his promises to the patriarchs. In the book of Joshua, the Lord wins victories for Israel by collapsing walls (6:20), divulging a stratagem (8:2), pelting Israel's enemies with stones (10:11), and even stopping the sun at Joshua's request (10:12–14). The paradigmatic battles at Jericho, Ai, Gibeon, and Hazor begin with assurances that the Lord is with Israel and has given their enemies into their hands (6:2, 16; 8:1, 18; 10:8; 11:6). The Israelites in turn slaughter the defeated peoples as an act of obedience to God.

A few biblical texts imply that the conquest is divine retribution for the sin of the Canaanites (e.g., Gen. 15:16; Deut. 9:4–5), but this assertion appears nowhere in the conquest narratives themselves. Rather, these narratives emphasize the manifestation of God's power and faithfulness. The Lord invades Canaan because he had promised the land to Abraham. God confirms that he is able to give the land by defeating the peoples of the land. The Lord thus lays claim to the land by right of conquest and gives it to Israel. The conquest narratives thus legitimate Israel's claim to the land by presenting it as a gift from its divine conqueror.

Approaches to the Problem of the Conquest

Faithful readers have grappled in various ways with the divinely ordained violence that infuses the conquest. Some early rabbinic interpreters speculated that more Canaanite cities might have been spared if they had asked for peace rather than resisting the invaders, while others declared that the commands to wipe out the Canaanites (e.g., Deut. 7:1–4) were no longer binding because the Canaanites no longer existed. The early Christian commentator Origen deflected attention from the genocidal violence by transforming the book of Joshua into an allegory of the Christian's battle to overcome sin and experience the fullness of salvation. The gnostic heretic Marcion, on the contrary, pointed to Joshua as evidence for his contention that the savage God of the OT could not possibly be the same deity as the God of grace and salvation who sent Jesus Christ.

A large body of traditional interpretation, particularly in Protestant circles, has sought to rehabilitate the conquest materials by avoiding the question of divinely sanctioned violence and extracting moral norms from Israel's example. In this way, Joshua can be held up as an exemplary figure of faith, courage, perseverance, and leadership, most notably in his declaration, "As for me and my household, we will serve the LORD" (Josh. 24:15). In a similar fashion, Israel's conduct of the war can be viewed, both positively and negatively, as an object lesson for virtues such as obedience, perseverance, zeal, and holiness. Zealously obedient Israelites succeed in winning great victories through God; sluggish and diffident Israelites fail to receive God's promise or complete the task God has assigned to them.

The rise of a historical consciousness in the nineteenth century allowed interpreters to situate the problem of divine violence within a developmental framework. From a humanistic perspective, the conquest traditions could then be understood as an early and primitive expression of Israel's religious thought in contrast to the more mature sentiments of peace and mercy reflected in later texts. From a theological perspective, this took the form of the notion of progressive revelation, the idea that God entered ancient Israel's experience at the level of its own understanding and then gradually led the nation to a higher spiritual and moral vision. Here again, the conquest materials could be understood as reflecting an early, more "worldly" vision that, although a necessary first step, faded in relevance as God revealed a more excellent way during the history of Israel's life as a people. With this in mind, it also could be argued that the biblical conquests actually reflect a more humane prosecution of war when set against the brutal practices and thinking of the other cultures of the ancient Near East.

The idea of progressive revelation provided a means for viewing God's participation in conquest as a necessary accommodation at an early stage of Israel's religious and moral understanding. In short, God had to enter and identify with a violent world in order to establish the basic understanding of human dignity that would form the foundation for more refined ethical sensibilities. Ordering the Israelites to slaughter their enemies outright (as opposed to torturing them) could thus be seen as an expression of this program. By directing the conquest and proscribing plunder, God was removing decisions about war from human beings and teaching that wars could not be justified by the desire for plunder. By fighting Israel's battles and demanding strict obedience, God was teaching the Israelites important lessons of trust and revealing his power and sovereignty. By commanding Israel to wipe out the Canaanites, God was reinforcing the imperative that Israel honor and preserve its unique covenantal relationship and obligations.

Although this approach accords well with an incarnational theology whereby God identifies with a particular people at a particular time, it entails significant problems. There are few dependable means for determining which biblical texts are early and which are late, and it is not at all clear that the OT as a whole reflects a progressive development of theology or morality. Furthermore, it has become difficult to maintain that Israel's wars of conquest were any more humane than those of the surrounding cultures, or that the Canaanites were more "deserving" of annihilation than anyone else.

A more recent approach recognizes that the conquest narratives, particularly the book of Joshua, do not speak with one voice. Rather, the narratives reflect a long and complex process of composition that bears the traces of many theological perspectives as Israel reworked traditions of its violent origins in the light of its own experience of salvation and suffering. Militant rhetoric and claims to land by right of conquest are given full voice, as they express essential elements of Israel's self-understanding. Other materials, however, present an opposing perspective that undercuts the rhetoric of nationalist triumphalism, humanizes both invaders and victims, and emphasizes the priority of mercy and inclusiveness. Read as narrative, the conquest does not so much offer a template that conveys universal ethical norms as provide a testimony that carves out ways of thinking about how to live as the people of God within a violent world.

See also Genocide; Holy War; Joshua; Killing; Land; 1–2 Samuel; Torture; Violence

Bibliography

Craigie, P. *The Problem of War in the Old Testament*. Eerdmans, 1978; Davies, E. "The Morally Dubious Passages of the Hebrew Bible: An Examination of Some Proposed Solutions." *CBR* 3 (2005): 197–228; Goldingay, J. *Israel's Gospel*. Vol. 1 of *Old Testament Theology*. InterVarsity, 2003; Hawk, L. "Conquest Reconfigured: Recasting Warfare in the Redaction of Joshua." Pages 145–60 in *Writing and Reading War: Rhetoric, Gender, and Ethics in Biblical and Modern Contexts*, ed. B. Kelle and F. Ames. SBLSymS 42. Society of Biblical Literature, 2008; Warrior, R. "A Native American Perspective: Canaanites, Cowboys, and Indians." Pages 135–43 in *Voices from the Margin: Interpreting the Bible in the Third World*, ed. R. Sugirtharajah. 3rd ed. Orbis, 2006.

L. Daniel Hawk

Conscience

Two contemporary distinctions are instructive for understanding developments in teachings regarding the conscience. The first differentiates the superego from the conscience; the second considers its function.

John Glaser describes the superego as an internalized principle of "pre-personal censorship and control" by which parents and guardians are able to keep their children safe, hygienic, socially acceptable, and obedient to authority. The superego, formed to keep children in check when their parents are not present, warns children against hurting their siblings, themselves, or anyone else. In anticipating their absences, parents often "lay down the law" by warning and, if necessary, subsequently punishing their children so as to demonstrate that parents always govern their children's activity. Because traces of the superego remain in adults as vestiges of external power and authority, many confuse the inhibiting force of the superego with the conscience. The call to conscience is a liberating call to love God and neighbor. Rather than exercising a prepersonal control, conscience calls us to act justly, to mature responsibly, and to govern ourselves wisely.

The second distinction concerns conscience's two-directional movement. The first is the judicial or consequent function, in which conscience operates subsequent to an action. In most of these instances, conscience estimates our actions negatively, whence the expression and experience of a "guilty" conscience. The second is a later development, by which conscience operates antecedent or prior to an action, legislating our activity. In this sense we speak of being guided by our conscience to act. Eric D'Arcy attributes this development to the apostle Paul.

In the NT four texts are particularly important. The judicial function of conscience appears in 1 Tim. 4:1–2, where liars have by their activity seared their consciences. In Rom. 2:14–15 conscience again has a judicial role, bearing witness to whether the gentiles adhere to the law inscribed in their hearts. But Paul adds that conscience may not only accuse but also excuse, and that like the inscribed law, conscience is found in each and every person. In Heb. 9:14 the legislative activity of conscience appears when our consciences are freed from dead works by the blood of Christ so as to serve the living God.

The most sustained scriptural discussion on conscience is in 1 Cor. 8–10, in the context of food offered to idols. One should abstain from eating "for the sake of conscience"—not for one's own conscience but for the conscience of the "weak" person who may have scruples on this matter. Here Paul recognizes conscience as legislative, but he insists on two other components. Conscience could judge as an exercise of one's understanding of faith that food offered to idols has no moral or faith claim on the Christian, and that therefore the Christian is free to ingest it. However, Paul flags the conscience of the weak and argues that to avoid causing scandal, the judgment of a conscience acting in the liberty of faith should heed the needs of the not yet formed. Here the communal responsibility of personal conscience emerges, particularly on the occasion of those actions that might cause scandal—that is, lead into sin.

In the scholastic era two "debates" capture the developments of teachings on conscience. The first concerns what is later known as an "erroneous" conscience. Bernard of Clairvaux (1090–1153), distrusting human judgment and believing that the root of sin is ignorance, argued that actions contrary to the law, even when done out of ignorance, were bad. Thus, if lying is always wrong, then a person not knowing this teaching who lies to protect another still sins.

Peter Abelard (1079–1142) held that the will, in particular its consent, determines actions as good or bad. If one is in error but does not consent to it, there is no sin. Thus, if one told a lie in order to protect the life of another but did not know that all lies were sin, Abelard would call the action good. Faced with the question of whether an action from a sincerely erroneous conscience is a sin, Bernard would answer affirmatively; Abelard, negatively.

At the Council at Sens (1140) Bernard accused Abelard of nineteen errors, among them the position that whatever is done out of ignorance ought not to be ascribed as morally blameworthy. Whether this was Abelard's opinion remains uncertain, but the opinion was condemned.

Without referring to the debate, Thomas Aquinas (1221–74) asked whether a person could ever disobey the conscience and not sin. He answered no (*ST* I-II, q. 19, a. 5). But then he asked whether following an erroneous conscience made the person good. He answered by asking whether, regarding the ignorance, one could have known otherwise. If the answer was yes, then the person was responsible for the erroneous conscience; if no, then the person was not responsible. Thus, if the person could have known that all lies were wrong, Thomas would have found the person culpable or bad. But if the person never learned that all lies were wrong and lied to protect someone, Thomas would call the lie wrong, but the person "excused" (*ST* I-II, q. 19, a. 6).

William of Ockham (1287–1347) adopted Thomas's argument but added that one who exercises the conscience responsibly, even if it is erroneous, is good. Ockham, unlike Abelard, recognized that ignorance is sometimes blameworthy, but, like Abelard, he recognized the goodness of an erroneous conscience acting in good faith.

By the sixteenth century most moral theologians agreed with Thomas that a dictate of conscience must be followed under pain of sin, and that an erroneous conscience in good faith is, at least, excused from blame. In 1690 Pope Alexander VIII condemned all those who taught that an invincibly ignorant conscience did not, at least, excuse.

Regarding the primacy of conscience, in his *Commentary on the Sentences of Peter Lombard*, Thomas confronted Lombard's teaching that one ought not to follow one's conscience when at odds with church teaching. Thomas straightforwardly rejected Lombard: "Here the Master is wrong" ("hic magister falsum dicit" [*In IV Sententiarum* d. 38, q. 2, a. 4]); we ought to die excommunicated rather than violate our conscience.

Contemporary church teachings uphold the primacy of conscience without compromising the responsibility to heed church teachings. Vatican II's *Gaudium et spes* (§16) provides five instructive points. First, conscience always relates itself to the law inscribed in our hearts: the voice of conscience summons each person to love good and avoid evil. Second, the intimacy one has with God is found in the conscience: "The conscience is the most secret core and sanctuary of a person. There we are alone with God, Whose voice echoes in our depths (John 1:3, 14). In a wonderful manner conscience reveals that law which is fulfilled by love of God and neighbor (Eph. 1:10)." Third, all persons have a conscience, and by our fidelity to it we "Christians are joined with the rest of humanity in the search for truth." Fourth, that search requires all persons "to be guided by the objective norms of morality." Fifth, the teaching closes on the matter of erroneous conscience: "Conscience frequently errs from invincible ignorance without losing its dignity. The same cannot be said for those who care but little for truth and goodness, or for a conscience which by degrees grows practically sightless as a result of habitual sin."

See also Moral Formation; Roman Catholic Moral Theology; Sin

Bibliography

Collins, R. *First Corinthians*. SP 7. Liturgical Press, 1999; D'Arcy, E. *Conscience and Its Right to Freedom*. Sheed & Ward, 1961; Dwyer, J. "Vatican II and the Dignity of Conscience." Pages 160–73 in *Vatican II, The Unfinished Agenda: A Look at the Future*, ed. L. Richard et al. Paulist Press, 1987; Eckstein, H.-J. *Der Begriff Syneidesis bei Paulus: Eine neutestamentlich-exegetische Untersuchung zum "Gewissensbegriff."* WUNT 2/10. Mohr Siebeck, 1983; Fuchs, J. *Christian Morality: The Word Becomes Flesh*. Georgetown University Press, 1987; Glaser, J. "Conscience and Superego: A Key Distinction." *TS* 32 (1971): 30–47; Gooch, P. "'Conscience' in the New Testament." *NTS* 33 (1987): 244–54; Hogan, L. *Confronting the Truth: Conscience in the Catholic Tradition*. Paulist Press, 2001; Keenan, J. "Can a Wrong Action Be Good? The Development of Theological Opinion on Erroneous Conscience." *EgT* 24 (1993): 205–21; Lottin, O. "La valeur normative de la conscience morale." *ETL* 9 (1932): 409–32; Patrick, A. *Liberating Conscience: Feminist Explorations in Catholic Moral Theology*. Continuum, 1996; Pierce, C. *Conscience in the New Testament: A Study of Syneidesis in the New Testament*. SCM, 1955; Potts, T., ed. *Conscience in Medieval Philosophy*. Cambridge University Press, 2002.

James Keenan, SJ

Conscientious Objection

Conscientious objection refers to a person's principled opposition to required military service.

Attending to the Scriptures

"You have heard that it was said, 'You shall love your neighbor and hate your enemy,' but I say to you, Love your enemies and pray for those who persecute you. . . . For if you love those who love you, what reward do you have?" (Matt. 5:43–46). In this text and in Matt. 5:9 peacemakers are said specifically to bear identity as children of God.

The teaching to love enemies is reiterated in various terms throughout the NT (Yoder; Swartley). One of Paul's ways of naming this is to say that our true worship of God is to "present [our] bodies as a living sacrifice, holy and acceptable to God" (Rom. 12:1), connecting such worship to specific and costly behaviors on the part of followers of Jesus, including love of enemies (Rom. 12:14–21). Moreover, we know that the fruit of the Spirit—"love, joy, peace, patience, kindness, generosity, faithfulness, gentleness, and self-control" (Gal. 5:22–23)—is to be manifest in our lives even, or perhaps especially, in the midst of a world that so often is violent.

All of this is to say that conscientious objection is not merely a simplistic adherence to the teaching "love your enemies." Rather, it is a realization that Jesus, through his life and teachings, radicalized the call to love God and neighbor (Matt. 22:37–39), showing that love of one another includes strangers, the poor, the hated, and the hating (i.e., enemies). It also includes the awareness that "we must obey God rather than any human authority" (Acts 5:29).

The Tradition and Scripture

Most scholars are agreed that the early church fathers taught that Christians are to love their enemies in concrete ways and specifically said that Christians were not to kill their enemies by serving as combatants in the military. This was true until the time of the emperor Constantine (312–37). From that point forward, a minority within the church has continued to agree with the earlier position. From the sixteenth-century forward, there have been continuous Christian traditions that as a whole formally affirmed this position.

The just-war tradition, with roots in Plato and Cicero, had its Christian beginnings with Augustine (354–430). Since then, this has been the dominant Christian position. This tradition over time developed elaborate criteria for determining whether wars were justifiable and whether specific behaviors within even justifiable wars were justifiable. Thus, logically the tradition (and theories based upon it) should have produced conscientious objectors to many of the wars fought by the countries within which Christians attached to this tradition have existed. Individual instances could be given, but overall the record seems not to be good. United States church leaders in the just-war tradition must ask themselves why they have not pushed for laws that provide the option of selective conscientious objection, if in fact that should be an option for Christians whom they shepherd (Walters).

Contemporary Application

Some have argued that, in light of the destructive capability of modern weapons, along with the growing awareness of our global community, pacifists and just-war adherents should be together much more often than apart in their "conscientious objection." Additionally, one might also suggest that some of the recent developments in the field of Christian ethics, perhaps especially virtue theory, should help us to see that since all Christians are "in Christ," "followers of Jesus," given "the fruit of the Spirit," and called to be a "peculiar people," then all Christians are to be peacemakers who love their enemies as well as their neighbors. And thus all Christians must be both conscientious participants and, at points, conscientious objectors within the countries and cultures that they inhabit—for the glory of God and for the sake of the whole world, which God loves.

See also Anabaptist Ethics; Conscription; Enemy, Enemy Love; Government; Just-Peacemaking Theory; Just-War Theory; Military Service; Pacifism; Peace; Resistance Movements; War

Bibliography

Bell, D. *Just War as Christian Discipleship: Recentering the Tradition in the Church Rather Than the State*. Brazos, 2009; Brock, B. *Against the Draft: Essays on Conscientious Objection from the Radical Reformation to the Second World War*. University of Toronto Press, 2006; Holmes, A., ed. *War and Christian Ethics*. 2nd ed. Baker Academic, 2005; McDonald, P. *God and Violence: Biblical Resources for Living in a Small World*. Herald Press, 2004; Swartley, W. *The Covenant of Peace: The Missing Peace in New Testament Theology and Ethics*. Eerdmans, 2006; Walters, L. "A Historical Perspective on Selective Conscientious Objection." *JAAR* 41 (1973): 201–11; Yoder, J. *Nevertheless: Varieties of Religious Pacifism*. 2nd ed. Herald Press, 1992; idem, *The Politics of Jesus: Vicit Agnus Noster*. 2nd ed. Eerdmans, 1994.

Mark Thiessen Nation

Conscientization

The term *conscientization* (a translation from the Portuguese *conscientização*) refers to something initially conceived as pedagogy for adult learning and literacy, a strategy of education whose goal was liberation. It has come to signify the process by which the disenfranchised become aware of how the racism, sexism, and classism embedded within social, political, and economic structures contribute to their suffering and oppression. Those who are oppressed, upon becoming conscious of how these structures operate to privilege a small elite group at their expense, discover their ability to transform these structures toward a more just arrangement. Hence, conscientization contains a strong political component. In the work of educator Paulo Freire, whose use of conscientization is a central theme in his theory of praxis, the term is defined as "the process in which men, not as recipients, but as knowing subjects, achieve a deepening awareness both of the socio-cultural reality which shapes their lives and their capacity to transform that reality" (Freire, *Cultural Action*, 27). To question and to challenge oppressive structures through conscientization is a learning process prevalent among those who participate in theologies of liberation.

The conscientization process is one where former "objects" become "subjects" of their own destiny by breaking through the normalized and accepted reasons given for their marginalization by those whom society privileges. Conscientization humanizes the disenfranchised, who had been seen only as "objects," through the use of their personal experiences to expose and unmask the contradictions within the prevailing social structures and the justification for maintaining those structures. It is a process by which the influential consciousness of the dominant culture, made universal and legitimate for everyone, including the oppressed, is replaced with the thoughts and values of the marginalized. Their newly found identity and the situation of their social location become the starting point for all critical analysis, including religious and theological thought. Upon evaluating the information based on the social location of the oppressed, subsequent formulation of actions to change the world becomes possible.

For those who participate in theologies of liberation, conscientization is an essential theme for bringing about a liberation rooted in the social location of the marginalized. Those whom society privileges with wealth and power are incapable of bringing about the liberation of the oppressed. Only the marginalized can work out their salvation, their liberation, in fear and trembling. But conscientization is not limited to the oppressed. Oppressors too are locked into structures that dehumanize them due to their complicity with repressive structures. The hope exists that oppressors can also find liberation through a conscientization that recognizes that even though the prevailing social structures privilege them, through the process of solidarity with the disenfranchised, working with them for a more just social order, they can reclaim their humanity and thus their salvation.

Conscientization can be understood as an awakening where the marginalized progress toward a critical consciousness. No longer is their consciousness submerged. This raising of consciousness provides the ability to intervene within a reality that until now has been masked by the false consciousness imposed by those from the dominant culture, a false consciousness based on myths that normalized and legitimized the dominance of oppressors. Not surprisingly, conscientization challenges how Christian ethics, theology, and biblical hermeneutics are constructed by the dominant culture because of their complicity with the social structures that privilege them.

See also Class Conflict; Liberation; Liberationist Ethics

Bibliography

Freire, P. *Cultural Action for Freedom*. Harvard Educational Review, 1970; idem, *Pedagogy of the Oppressed*. Trans. M. Bergman Ramos. Rev. ed. Continuum, 1993.

Miguel A. De La Torre

Conscription

Compulsory enlistment for military service (conscription) has been practiced in most cultures since the beginning of human history. However, universal conscription seems to have become a reality (and then only in certain times and places) only since the French Revolution.

Attending to Scripture

The first war mentioned in the Bible is in Gen. 14:1–12. Four Mesopotamian kings and their soldiers are portrayed as ransacking five cities lying on the plain of the Dead Sea area. Abraham rallies a militia of 318 men who rescue the captives and the booty (Gen. 14:13–16). This ad hoc form of "conscripting" soldiers appears to be the norm before the monarchical period of Israel's history (sometimes for purposes of defense, sometimes for aggression).

By the time of 1 Sam. 8, many Israelites had become uncomfortable with the vulnerability of the ad hoc nature of tribal militia. Elders approach Samuel, saying that they want a king to govern them, to be "like other nations" (1 Sam. 8:4–5). God, however, does not want Israel to be like other nations; he is to be their only king. And yet, given their persistence, God tells Samuel to let them have their king, which will mean, among other things, conscription: "[The king] will take your sons and appoint them to his chariots and to be his horsemen, and to run before his chariots; and he will appoint himself commanders of thousands and commanders of fifties" (1 Sam. 8:11–12). Thus begins a new way of Israel's living with and protecting its peoplehood under the monarchy.

However, Israel is persistently told that they are not to be like other nations. This is expressed most clearly in their deliverance from slavery—determining the future of Israel as a people—in which the Israelites are not to lift a weapon to protect themselves (Exod. 14:14). God alone will deliver them (Exod. 15:3, 18). Trusting in God, in specific terms, appears through virtually every strand of OT literature (Lind).

Thus, the call for the covenantal community to trust in God is a persistent theme across both Testaments. In the NT, however, it is radicalized and redefined in light of Jesus, the Messiah. Closely connected to the teaching to trust God is to love even enemies (Matt. 5:43–48; 6:7–15; cf. Rom. 12:14–21). Tied to these teachings is a major shift from the OT to the NT in understanding peoplehood; in the NT, identity is not tied to specific real estate (Brueggemann; Lohfink). In fact, in some strands of the NT, Christians are called very specifically to think of themselves "as aliens and exiles" (1 Pet. 2:11), an identity that sets them as a people apart from the other nations.

Thus, in the NT, followers of Jesus are not in the business of conscripting. The question therefore is this: how is conscription a reality and an issue in the NT? Although a few (Roman) soldiers appear in the NT, they basically have bit parts, though bit parts used for specific purposes—mostly to remind Jews that God might work through other peoples, even hated Romans (who were, after all, the oppressors of first-century Jews). Of none of the soldiers do we have details beyond initial encounters. In the midst of this, Christians are to trust that God would use pagans ruling over them for God's own purposes of keeping order in society (Rom. 13:1–7; 1 Pet. 2:13–17).

The Tradition and Scripture

Up until the fourth century, Tertullian spoke for the virtually unanimous views of the early church fathers when he said, "The Lord, by taking away Peter's sword, disarmed every soldier thereafter" (*Idol.* 19). Echoing the NT call to love enemies, the early church fathers believed that Christians should say no to conscription in the army.

By the time of the emperor Constantine (312–37), this way of thinking began to shift; by the time of the emperor Theodosius I (379–95), one could be in the military only if one were a "Christian."

From that time forward, in the Western world, though the church as church has generally not conscripted (moments in the crusades might be exceptions), the church has most often considered serving in the military, including conscription, for one's own nation as something also done for God. However, throughout the history of the church there have been Christians (and since the sixteenth century, ongoing traditions) who have seen killing, even in the military, as a violation of the covenant with the God revealed in Jesus Christ and therefore have refused conscription.

See also Conscientious Objection; Government; Military Service

Bibliography

Brueggemann, W. *The Land: Place as Gift, Promise, and Challenge in Biblical Faith*. 2nd ed. Fortress, 2002; Cahill, L. *Love Your Enemies: Discipleship, Pacifism, and Just War Theory*. Fortress, 1994; Hobbs, T. *A Time for War: A Study of Warfare in the Old Testament*. Michael Glazier, 1989; Hunter, D. "A Decade of Research on Early Christians and Military Service." *RelSRev* 18 (1992): 87–94; Lind, M. *Yahweh Is a Warrior: The Theology of Warfare in Ancient Israel*. Herald Press, 1980; Lohfink, G. *Jesus and Community: The Social Dimension of Christian Faith*. Fortress, 1984; von Rad, G. *Holy War in Ancient Israel*. Trans. and ed. M. Dawn. Eerdmans, 1991.

Mark Thiessen Nation

Consequentialism

Consequentialism is an umbrella term for a variety of ethical theories united by the idea that the consequences of an action are the primary consideration for moral choices.

Consequentialists are concerned with maximizing good consequences. But what counts as "good"? Many different answers have been given to that question. The good might be understood in relation to biological survival, social well-being, individual well-being, or simply entertainment value. Many earlier consequentialists defined the good as pleasure (quantitative utilitarianism). Pleasure, however, turned out to be no less ambiguous a notion than notion of the good. It too required further specification. Eventually it was replaced with personal well-being, which was taken to include personal freedom (qualitative utilitarianism), beauty and knowledge (ideal utilitarianism), or a combination of different intrinsic, nonmoral values (pluralistic utilitarianism).

Besides the question of what counts as "good," however, there was a second question: good consequences for whom? Again, many different answers have been given: good for one's self, good for one's immediate community, good for the greatest number. This distributive question has, moreover, prompted criticism of the view that the primary consideration for moral choices should be the consequences of the action. John Rawls, for example, has insisted that it is insufficient simply to maximize good consequences; we must also assure a fair distribution of the good consequences and of the burdens of achieving them. Fairness requires equality, not just maximizing the net aggregate of good consequences. Even Rawls, however, appeals to consequences when testing fairness, for the test of "presumptive equality" is whether any inequality works out in the long run (or has the consequence) that the less well-off members of society benefit.

Finally, consequentialism faces the challenge of calculation. For the decision-making process, it is important to be able to measure and calculate good and evil consequences against a commonly accepted scale. So far, there is no satisfactory account of such a scale. Moreover, correct calculation requires accuracy of prediction. For an accurate result, consequences must be assessed in their totality and relationship with one another. This is difficult, if not impossible; especially with long-term predictions there is always a chance of unforeseen consequences, or that consequences currently regarded as good will produce an undesirable result in the future.

Despite these criticisms, consequentialism remains appealing by its conformity with the common view of what rationality requires, the weighing of costs and benefits, and the individual's concern with values such as health, income, and status. Thus far, however, only a few Christian theologians have adopted a position that is primarily concerned with consequences. William Paley's theological utilitarianism is one example; Joseph Fletcher's situational ethics is another, quite different, example. More have objected to attention to consequences as a temptation to surrender Christian integrity (notably John Howard Yoder and Stanley Hauerwas). The primary reason for such limited interest is the lack of conformity between consequentialists' accounts of the good and the traditional interpretation of Scripture. Christians view life in terms of grace and relationships rather than rationalistic calculations. They emphasize the lack of individual power and of control over one's own end. They focus on those who are poor and weak rather than rich and successful. And they believe that the destiny of the universe is, ultimately, God's responsibility.

See also Deontological Theories of Ethics; Good, The; Happiness; Utilitarianism

Vladimir Ignatkov

Conservation *See* Ecological Ethics

Consumerism

Everyone is a consumer, but not everyone is caught up in consumerism in its morally ambiguous usages. A positive use of the term *consumerism* has to do with laws and institutions developed to protect consumers from fraud, deception, or adulterated products. Such protections find theological roots in biblical mandates such as those against unjust weights and measures in the marketplace (e.g., Deut. 25:13–16). The ancient tradition knew that commerce and trade cannot be conducted if there are no trustworthy standards in buying and selling. The Better Business Bureau, the Consumer's Guide, and the US Food and Drug Administration are examples of modern proconsumerism institutions in this tradition.

Today, however, the term *consumerism* usually is applied in a negative sense to that portion of the population that appears to be compulsively on the hunt for more and more "things," especially those that are commercially produced, heavily advertised, and fashionably made. Consumerism in this sense is related to but not identical with greed, avarice, miserliness, or covetousness in that these dispositions indicate a preöccupation with possessions as a source of security for the egocentric self, an attitude that tempts them to displace a confidence in God's providential care and a concern for the needs of the neighbor (e.g., Deut. 5:21; Matt. 6:19–21).

Consumerism differs from these vices because it is connected with the social practice of "shopping for pleasure" by those with discretionary wealth in cultures that have large commercial establishments—department stores, shopping malls, and, now, online marketing firms. Some call it an addiction like gambling, or a disease, "affluenza" (see de Graaf, Wann, and Naylor), although careful shoppers with limited means and driven by necessary prudence can also get caught up in these behaviors.

Consumerism in these senses has been called an "informal ideology": "informal" because unlike socialism, capitalism, and libertarianism, it has no developed social philosophy; and "ideology" because it is used as a "soft" attack on modern commercial life. It advocates a simple lifestyle, avoiding both a direct attack on capitalism and the use of a discredited socialist ideology. A formal ideology claims to offer an account of human nature, meaningful belief, and ethical action that can, does, and should guide public policies, personal behavior, and the course of history. Consumerism offers none of these, although critics project some of them onto it.

The "informal ideology" is thus lodged as a moral protest against, especially, corporate policies and marketing practices that push customers to purchase more. Common to this use are several hypotheses as to what drives consumerism. One is that it is based on the false assumption that happiness can be attained through the purchase of goods that satisfy wants and not needs. However, the boundaries between wants and needs are movable, and many social scientists recognize that these behaviors have to do with the level of development of a society. We can see this in many areas, from clothing fashions, to home decor, to automobile styles, but it is perhaps most obvious today in communication technology. Having access to a telephone and a radio was not imagined even as a want for most of human history until they became first a luxury for the few, then a need for the many. Today, access to a television, computer, and increasingly a cell phone is a desired want and a need for equipped participation in modern education, economy, politics, and culture in developed societies. Such wants and needs can prompt a prepossessing fascination with, excessive attention to, and obsessive purchases of new devices—consumerist behavior in the negative sense.

Others use the term *consumerism* primarily as an accusation against materialism, with a presumed zero-sum relationship between materiality and spirituality. The more that material goods matter in one's life, the less spiritual one must be; and the more spiritual one is, the less one will be concerned about material well-being. Some religious orientations see this distinction as the central reality of faith, and most religions recognize a place for this accent, but they also hold that spirituality can be present in the material realities of life. Ritual practices such as marriages and festivals are nearly always seen as spiritual and involve physical pleasures and material expression.

Christianity in particular holds that the creator God saw the material creation as good, that the very spiritual Christ became incarnate in the very material Jesus, and that the Holy Spirit animates the kingdom of God, which is working in the sustaining and redeeming dynamics of human history. Indeed, Scripture teaches that those who are in Christ not only will pray for the people and seek to convert them or deepen their faith but also will make significant contributions, as they are able, to feed the hungry, clothe the naked, and heal the sick—all of which require spiritually motivated material activities. And whereas the "rich man" turns away sadly when asked to give up everything for a life of discipleship, Jesus' disciples are promised houses, families, and lands (with all the material troubles that these may imply) as well as eternal life (Mark 10:17–30 pars.). Further, Jesus seems to have enjoyed eating and drinking with those who had much. Thus, as John Schneider has argued, the accusation that consumerism is evil because it finds meaning associated with material goods faces theological-ethical contradictions.

Critics of consumerism often blame advertisers for the ways in which some people get trapped into compulsive buying. There is surely some truth in this accusation. At least since the publication of Vance Packard's *The Hidden Persuaders* (1957), a suspicion of mass advertising, with its manipulation of images, has grown. Advertising often gives little information about the product while it portrays accessories of power, sex, or success. This selling of products by subliminal images or clever sound bites is held to be a form of systematic deception, even mind control. It could be called a form of adulteration of the product by symbolic means.

The question as to how much power advertisers actually exercise, however, has often been raised. The automobile industry has attempted to sell cars through heavy advertising, some of which informs the buyer about the product's value and some of which attempts to establish a symbolic meaning to the brand. But the notorious historic failures of the Nash, the Studebaker, and the Edsel and of contemporary Detroit automakers to provide people with cars that they will buy (no matter how extensive the advertising) suggest limits to advertising's power.

Leigh Eric Schmidt's fascinating study *Consumer Rites* shows how some holidays (e.g., Christmas, Mother's Day, Valentine's Day) became greater occasions for shopping and advertising than others (e.g., Easter, Father's Day, and the Fourth of July). He suggests that certain values must be present in society and be affirmed by advertising if a holiday is to be successful as a shopping day. Shopping is more value-laden than both the economic models of rational decision-making and the critics of consumerism recognize, and on closer examination, the values are not all bad. Who can condemn the giving of gifts to loved ones? However, in times of recession or depression the material expressions of those values have to be reduced, and the results are dire.

An intriguing view of why this is so can be found in Colin Campbell's *The Romantic Ethic and the Spirit of Modern Consumerism*. He echoes Max Weber's famous *The Protestant Ethic and the Spirit of Capitalism*, which argued that the governing religious value system in a society has profound implications for how an economy works, and that Protestantism generated a work ethic and a rationalizing spirit that fostered the production of wealth. Campbell says that Weber was right about production but that he failed to explain modern patterns of consumption.

Campbell turns to the rise of the Romantic ethic that grew out of pietistic evangelical movements present in several branches of Protestantism as well as in a cultural rebellion against the rationalism of the Enlightenment. Both of these accented a spiritual "imaginative hedonism" and an "ethic of feeling" seeking the renewal of vitality. This introduced fragments of a system of belief that culturally became the "spirit of consumerism." In this spirit, it is a duty to seek that which revitalizes sentiment and induces desires for a new, deeper source of what is authentic. Thus, beside the disciplined life that generated modern production was a movement that catered to the felt need for transforming inner experience.

Today, consumerism is tied to production in ways that derive from this development, as Peter Berger has seen. If consumers do not buy for whatever reason—distrust of the system, sudden collapse of credit, threat of unemployment, decisions to be frugal, and so on—producers have to reduce production. Thus, efforts are made to get everyone to become consumers so that production, now global, can flourish again. An unambiguous condemnation of consumerism only contributes to our woes.

See also Capitalism; Desire; Economic Ethics; Greed; Idolatry; Materialism; Profit

Bibliography

Berger, P. "Vice and Virtue in Economic Life." Pages 75–94 in *Christian Social Ethics in a Global Era*, ed. M. Stackhouse. Abingdon, 1995; Campbell, C. *The Romantic Ethic and the Spirit of Modern Consumerism*. Basil Blackwell, 1987; Cavanaugh, W. *Being Consumed: Economics and Christian Desire*. Eerdmans, 2008; de Graaf, J., D. Wann, and T. Naylor. *Affluenza: The All-Consuming Epidemic*. Berrett-Koehler, 2005; Miller, V. *Consuming Religion: Christian Faith and Practice in a Consuming Culture*. Continuum, 2005; Packard, V. *The Hidden Persuaders*. McKay, 1957; Schmidt, L. *Consumer Rites: The Buying and Selling of American Holidays*. Princeton University Press, 1995; Schneider, J. *The Good of Affluence: Seeking God in a Culture of Wealth*. Eerdmans, 2002; Stackhouse, M. "Reflections on Consumerism in a Global Era." *BPEJ* 12, no. 4 (2005): 37–45.

Max L. Stackhouse

Continence

Continence is the determined exertion of the will toward the control of one's appetites, particularly the bodily appetites for food, drink, and sex. The NT Greek word *enkrateia*, meaning "self-control," is synonymous with "continence" and is employed by many contemporary translations of Scripture. Continence often is confused with temperance, but in fact it is qualitatively different.

The Classical Tradition

Although Socrates understood continence to be a cardinal virtue, it was Aristotle who distinguished it from the virtue of temperance because of its need for strict bodily control over the appetites (*Eth. nic.* 1102b13–28; 1145b8–20). The Stoics highly valued its role in subjugating the appetites and desires to reason and emphasized its connection to asceticism.

Usage in Scripture

The Greek word *enkrateia* (and its opposite, *akrasia*) and its cognates appear in the NT primarily in the Epistles. The usage is somewhat problematic because in some versions, particularly the KJV, the translation consistently indicates "temperance" (e.g., Titus 1:8), which is a clear departure from the Greek position of distinguishing the two terms. This is likely due to the conflation of "temperance" and "self-control" that prevailed during the past four centuries.

The Epistles use the term in three main ways. It refers to various forms of abstinence from sexual activity. Within marriage, *enkrateia* in regard to sexual relations is recommended only as an occasional activity, for devotion to prayer and for a prescribed time; otherwise, one may fall into temptation because of *akrasia* (1 Cor. 7:5). The unmarried should practice continence as they can, but they may marry if it cannot be sustained (1 Cor. 7:9). This continence is portrayed not as a superior choice to proper sexuality within marriage, but rather as an acceptable alternative, whether temporary or permanent.

It is also linked to training, self-discipline, and fruitful victory. Athletes practice self-control as they prepare for the race (1 Cor. 9:25). In 2 Peter it is connected with knowledge and endurance, among others, as guarantors against ineffective and fruitless ministry (2 Pet. 1:6–8); and it is a commonsensical requirement for bishops, who are "God's stewards" (Titus 1:7–8).

Perhaps most important, *enkrateia* is one of the gifts of the Spirit, received when one has "crucified the flesh with its passions and desires" (Gal. 5:23–24). This is a clear departure from the classical position, in which continence was the cause, not the result, of ethical purity.

Development in the Christian Tradition

Moving beyond both the classical and scriptural models, the patristic writers stressed the sexual aspect of continence, particularly its connection to chastity. This emphasis found expression in the ecclesiastical requirements of virginity and marital celibacy. One notable exception was Augustine, who broadened its scope beyond the sexual (see *On Continence*). He saw *continentia* as a linchpin of the Christian moral life, and his own conversion included a visitation from a "chaste woman" whom he named "Lady Continence." He called continence "the virtue of the soul," whose spheres of influence are the flesh, the mouth, and the heart, declaring, "By continence we are gathered together and brought back to the One, from whom we have dissipated our being into many things" (*Conf.* 10.21.40).

Thomas Aquinas made something of a bridge between the two traditions (see *ST* II-II, q. 155). In reinstituting the Aristotelian catalog of virtues, he followed Aristotle's subordination of continence to temperance "as the imperfect to the perfect." Yet he also acknowledged the sexual aspects emphasized by the early church when he associated continence with chastity, virginity, and widowhood. Although the Reformation sought to abolish mandatory clerical celibacy, the discipline remains in the Roman Catholic Church.

Contemporary Applications

Although often confused with temperance, continence is actually its subordinate. Continence relies on strength of will to curb the appetites, which are seen as unruly and in need of a tight rein. This internal struggle makes continence secondary to temperance, which arises from a well-ordered and thus harmonious relationship between the appetites, the will, and reason. Incongruity between the outer appearance and the inner state is a sign of continuing discord and thus a sign of continence.

This distinction may have a clarifying effect on the view and treatment of addictions, eating disorders, and the like. "Dry drunks" achieve tenuous sobriety; anorexics eat little while ignoring their ravenous hunger. The desired action is present, but the inner turmoil remains.

See also Fruit of the Spirit; Temperance; Vices and Virtues, Lists of; Virtue(s)

Bibliography

Brown, P. *The Body and Society: Men, Women, and Sexual Renunciation in Early Christianity.* Columbia University Press, 1988; Heid, S. *Celibacy in the Early Church: The Beginnings of a Discipline of Obligatory Continence for Clerics in East and West.* Trans. M. Miller. Ignatius Press, 2001; Rorty, A. "Akrasia and Conflict." *Inquiry* 23 (1980): 193–212; Schlabach, G. "Love Is the Hand of the Soul: The Grammar of Continence in Augustine's Doctrine of Christian Love." *JECS* 6 (1998): 59–92.

Maria Kenney

Contraception *See* Birth Control

Contract *See* Covenant

Contrition

In the first question of *Supplementum* of the *Summa theologiae*, Thomas Aquinas defines contrition as an "assumed sorrow for sins, together with the purpose of confessing them and of making satisfaction for them" (see *ST Supp.*, q. 1–5). He raises an objection about the suitability of the definition by noting that contrition is given by God, and that what is given is not assumed. Therefore contrition is not assumed. He responds to his objection noting that the form of the act of contrition comes from God alone, but the substance comes from our free will and from God, who operates in everything.

Thomas's reply to the objection captures the difference between Roman Catholic theology and Lutheran theology; the latter would see the assertion of free will as, at best, undermining the grace of God.

The *Catechism of the Catholic Church*, referring to the Council of Trent, upholds the teaching that the two dimensions of contrition—sorrow for sin and resolve against sinning again—constitute the first act of the penitent in the sacrament. On the nature of that sorrow, Catholics differentiate perfect contrition, which is sorrow for the injury that the sin brings to the love of God, from imperfect contrition or attrition, which is sorrow that one's final destiny might be lost on account of the sin. Either contrition suffices.

In the OT, contrition is, along with humility, an important disposition (e.g., Ps. 51:7; Isa. 57:15; 66:2). It is modeled in David's prayer in Ps. 51. Together with the fear of the Lord, it is missing as a response to past sins on the part of God's people in Jer. 44:10. In the NT, Paul recognizes a "godly grief" that "produces repentance" among the Corinthians (2 Cor. 7:8–12).

See also Penance; Penitence; Reconciliation; Repentance

Bibliography

"Contrition." Paragraphs 364–65, 1451–54, in *Catechism of the Catholic Church*. Liguori Publications, 1994.

James Keenan, SJ

Conversion

Religious conversion is a topic of broad interest. Not only do biblical scholars and theologians study the phenomenon but social scientists also show a great interest in exploring this notable experience. Conversion is often cited as the central point of Christian religious identity—the moment at which or the process through which one becomes Christian. The experience is sometimes connected to Jesus' instruction to Nicodemus, "Very truly, I tell you, no one can see the kingdom of God without being born from above" (John 3:3). Thus, the conversion experience is taken to be of central importance to both soteriology (doctrinal issues concerning salvation) and a proper understanding of Christian discipleship.

Conversion connotes a turning or reversal of course. The Hebrew term *šûb* refers primarily to the orientation of a people or the corporate response to a divine initiative. In the OT this term designates both a movement away from and a turning toward. In this way, conversion is understood to be an explicitly goal-oriented change toward God's will for God's people (see John 3:7–10). Here the issue is not response to individual sin but rather repetitive rejection of God's covenant by the people of Israel. Therefore, in the OT conversion is not understood in an evangelistic sense to refer to change in religion or personal faith; the primary concern, rather, is the maintenance of covenantal relationship.

As in Greek literature more widely, so also in the NT, the concept of conversion typically is associated with the term *metanoia* ("repentance") and its verbal form, *metanoeō* ("to change one's course"), or *epistrophē* ("a turning [toward]") and its verbal form, *epistrephō* ("to turn around"). On the basis of word usage alone, however, a whole range of issues important to the interpreter remains ambiguous. Is conversion an event, a process, or both? Is conversion a cognitive category, a moral category, or both? What is the relationship between "rejection of one way of life for another" and "embracing more fully the life one has chosen"—both easily illustrated connotations of *metanoia*? Is conversion a crossing of religious boundaries? Of course, the concept of conversion often is present where no such terms are used.

Conversion in the NT often entails the recognition of and participation in the kingdom of God. In this sense, Mark's summary of Jesus' proclamation is programmatic: "The time is fulfilled, and the kingdom of God has come near; repent, and believe in the good news" (Mark 1:15). This transformation of this nature has both personal and social ramifications. The Gospels and Acts include a number of "conversion accounts," such as those of Levi (Luke 5:27–32) and Paul (Acts 9:1–20), and texts in which the demands of repentance are highlighted (especially Luke 3:1–17), but we find in the NT no normative conversion scheme or pattern. What we do find is that from the standpoint of the overarching theme of soteriology, human response, which includes *metanoia*, is necessary for individuals to appropriate for themselves God's offer of salvation, and that conversion refers to a change of thinking and believing that is itself inseparably tied to behavioral transformations (e.g., Luke 3:7–14). These behavioral changes, which include welcoming into the community those whom God has accepted, are necessary for and instrumental in the establishment of the Christian community, as is recounted in Acts. In many cases, the emphasis of the conversion account is less on a crisis event and more on a sustained participation with a divinely ordained community. Indeed, in Luke-Acts, where the language of conversion especially congregates, the purpose of Jesus' coming was "to guide our feet into the way of peace" (Luke 1:79), the gospel is the "way of salvation" (Acts 16:17), and the community of Jesus' followers is known as followers of "the Way" (Acts 9:2; 19:9, 23; 22:4; 24:14, 22), with the result that conversion is cast in the form of a "journey."

In biblical and theological studies conversion has increasingly been understood in sociological terms. Nicholas Taylor, for example, has sketched a model of conversion in the early Christian world that involves conviction, conformity, and community socialization. Donald Gelpi presents conversion as a "social process" consisting of seven stages: (1) settlement within a particular social context that sets the tone for the conversion experience, (2) experience of personal crisis, (3) personal crisis leads to religious quest, (4) religious quest leads to a connection with an advocate of a particular religious tradition, (5) interaction within the religious community, (6) religious commitment, and (7) recognition of the consequences of the religious commitment. In addition, findings from the biological neurosciences have led to interesting work related to religious conversion (Markham). These scientific perspectives provide support for a process-oriented view of conversion that moves beyond basic religious experience and takes seriously sociomoral reorientation. Significant religious change is usually a complex process involving personal, social, cultural, and religious forces that impact an individual's life in a number of ways (Rambo).

Conversion is noted not only for producing interior change related to belief and conviction, then, but also for generating a significant ethical predisposition toward social transformation. Bernard Lonergan spoke of the multidimensional character of religious conversion by identifying the intellectual, religious, and moral elements of the overall phenomenon. Gelpi then expanded Lonergan's typology to include the sociopolitical dimension that emphasizes a particularly important aspect of the conversion experience related to social transformation.

This social transformation is intimately connected with Jesus' proclamation of the kingdom of God. In this context, there is a tension between God's role in the conversion experience and the subsequent mandate for the convert. Not only is there a change in religious allegiance but there is also an acquired transformation in motivating desires. As one's life comes to be characterized by Christian virtues, the primary concern for the convert becomes the love of God and the love of neighbor, especially the neighbor in need. Therefore, to experience Christian conversion is not simply a juridical fact; rather, it is a holistic experience taking place within the context of a particular religious tradition that is marked by the acquisition of virtues having both internal and external significance.

Bibliography

Gaventa, B. *From Darkness to Light: Aspects of Conversion in the New Testament*. OBT 20. Fortress, 1986; Gelpi, D. *The Conversion Experience: A Reflective Process for RCIA Participants and Others*. Paulist Press, 1998; Lonergan, B. *Method in Theology*. University of Toronto Press, 1990; Markham, P. *Rewired: Exploring Religious Conversion*. Wipf & Stock, 2007; Rambo, L. *Understanding Religious Conversion*. Yale University Press, 1993; Taylor, N. "The Social Nature of Conversion in the Early Christian World." Pages 128–36 in *Modelling Early Christianity: Social-Scientific Studies of the New Testament in Its Context*, ed. P. Esler. Routledge, 1995.

Paul N. Markham

1 Corinthians

First Corinthians was written by Paul, from Ephesus (1 Cor. 16:8), sometime between 49 and 55 CE. The authenticity of the letter is not seriously doubted, and most scholars accept its literary unity. It forms part of an ongoing communication between Paul and the Corinthian community. After his initial visit to Corinth, Paul has already written a letter (1 Cor. 5:9), and the Corinthians have written to Paul (1 Cor. 7:1). First Corinthians responds to this written communication and also to oral reports that have been brought to Paul (1 Cor. 1:11; 11:18). Further (more anguished) visits and letters follow 1 Corinthians (2 Cor. 2:1–4; 10–13) before an apparent reconciliation restores the relationship sufficiently for Paul's collection project (1 Cor. 16:1–4; Gal. 2:10) to be revitalized and completed (Rom. 15:25–27; 2 Cor. 8–9).

The character of 1 Corinthians as a response to issues raised in both letter and oral report makes it full of topics of ethical (and sociological) interest but also makes it a letter in which it is hard to discern an overall direction and focus of argument. More than any other Pauline letter, 1 Corinthians is full of Paul's responses to specific issues of conduct and conflict, full of ethics in a broad sense. The opening four chapters are dominated by the theme of divisions at Corinth. Chapters 5–7 deal with issues of sexual ethics and marriage, chapters 8–10 with the question of food offered to idols. Chapters 11–14 broadly deal with issues relating to the worship of the community: head coverings for women (11:2–16), the Lord's Supper (11:17–34), and the proper use of spiritual gifts (chaps. 12–14). Chapter 15 addresses the subject of the resurrection, while chapter 16 deals with various practical matters and greetings. It is notable that at least two of these major ethical sections (chaps. 8–10; 12–14) are structured in an A-B-A pattern in which the central section presents a paradigm for ethical action that fundamentally informs the response to the topic under discussion: Paul's example in renouncing his rights for the sake of others (9:1–23) is a model to the Corinthian "strong" (8:9–13); love (13:1–13) is a crucial foundation for the proper exercise of any spiritual gift.

Scholars have debated what are the main sources of influence on the ethics of 1 Corinthians. Some have argued that the Jewish Scriptures and interpretative traditions fundamentally shape the pattern of Paul's instruction. Others have pointed out parallels between Paul's treatment of ethical topics (such as sex and marriage) and the discussions of such issues in popular Greco-Roman moral philosophy, especially among Stoics and Cynics. There are significant differences of view on such matters, but it seems reasonably clear that Paul's moral thought is shaped both by the Jewish scriptural tradition and by the philosophical discussions of his day; it is the relative weight and specific influences that are harder to determine. But whatever the influence of such sources and ethical traditions, it is clear that Paul reconfigures such influences around the central key to his ethics: Christ. Even here there are various possible strands to disentangle. Some have argued that Jesus' teaching specifically permeates and informs Paul's ethical instruction. First Corinthians is indeed unusual among the Pauline letters in including three of the four most widely agreed references to Jesus' teaching in Paul's writings: 7:10–11, referring to the teaching on divorce (Mark 10:2–12 // Matt. 19:3–9; Matt. 5:31–32 // Luke 16:18); 9:14, alluding to the mission charge instructions (Matt. 10:10 // Luke 10:7); and 11:23–24, citing the tradition of Jesus' words at the Last Supper (Mark 14:22–25 pars.). Possible echoes of Jesus' teaching also include 13:2 (cf. Matt. 17:20; 21:21). Yet clear use of Jesus' teaching seems strikingly minimal as an influence on the substance and presentation of Paul's ethics. More fundamental would seem to be Paul's Christology, in that he presents Christ both as the basis for unity and diversity in the community—"You are the body of Christ" (12:26)—and as the paradigm of self-giving and other-regard (10:33–11:1).

In an important rhetorical analysis of 1 Corinthians, Margaret Mitchell argues that the fundamental "thesis" of the letter is found in 1:10, in the appeal for ecclesial unity. Her analysis of the following sections of the letter as "proofs" in support of this central argument seems occasionally forced, but the notion that the letter is focused around this theme of community unity is well founded. Indeed, some of the language Paul uses, especially in the opening chapters, seems close to the language of ancient political discourse dealing with factionalism and rivalry. Others have pushed a political-ethical reading of 1 Corinthians further, arguing that Paul is seeking to strengthen the *ekklēsia* as an alternative society, standing in contrast and opposition to the imperial society ruled by Rome. David Horrell has argued that the metanorms of Paul's ethics, in 1 Corinthians and elsewhere, can be summarized as those of corporate solidarity and other-regard. Paul uses the ideas of the body of Christ, incorporation into Christ, and so on as a basis for community unity, but he equally stresses the need for this to be a diverse community. Even on some topics of ethical dispute, most notably concerning food offered to idols, he does not set out a ruling on the specific practice that is correct. Rather, he appeals for the practice of Christlike other-regard, which respects the interests and perspective of the other.

In terms of its relevance and contribution to contemporary ethical discourse, the appropriation of 1 Corinthians can operate at various levels. Christians study Paul's teaching on marriage and divorce, for example, to inform contemporary views on the subject. Some of the specific topics, such as food offered to idols, may be less directly relevant in Western contexts, but they are highly relevant in countries such as China and Indonesia, where Christians struggle to negotiate a stance regarding customs such as offerings to ancestors. On a broader level, Paul's way of doing ethics and the moral norms that inform this may be found instructive as a model for Christian ethics. The strongly christological basis to Paul's ethics means that he presents, in Alasdair MacIntyre's terms, a particular kind of tradition-specific and narratively founded ethics, while his concern to foster a corporate unity within which a (circumscribed) diversity of convictions and practices may be sustained bears some similarity to the central project of political liberalism.

See also 2 Corinthians; Ecclesiology and Ethics; Idolatry; Marriage and Divorce; Narrative Ethics, Biblical; Narrative Ethics, Contemporary; New Testament Ethics; Sexual Ethics

Bibliography

Adams, E., and D. Horrell, eds. *Christianity at Corinth: The Quest for the Pauline Church*. Westminster John Knox, 2004; Deming, W. *Paul on Marriage and Celibacy: The Hellenistic Background to 1 Corinthians 7*. SNTSMS 83. Cambridge University Press, 1995; Furnish, V. "Belonging to Christ: A Paradigm for Ethics in First Corinthians." *Int* 44 (1990): 145–57; Horrell, D. *Solidarity and Difference: A Contemporary Reading of Paul's Ethics*. T&T Clark, 2005; Meeks, W. "The Polyphonic Ethics of the Apostle Paul." *ASCE* (1988): 17–29; Mitchell, M. *Paul and the Rhetoric of Reconciliation: An Exegetical Investigation of the Language and Composition of 1 Corinthians*. HUT 28. Mohr Siebeck, 1991; Rosner, B. *Paul, Scripture and Ethics: A Study of 1 Corinthians 5–7*. AGJU 22. Brill, 1994; Wenham, D. *Paul: Follower of Jesus or Founder of Christianity?* Eerdmans, 1995.

David G. Horrell

2 Corinthians

The letter known as 2 Corinthians is not, in fact, the second letter that Paul sent to the Christian community in Corinth. It was preceded by at least two earlier epistles from the apostle to Corinth: one missive (unfortunately, no longer extant) mentioned in 1 Cor. 5:9; the other the canonical letter called "1 Corinthians." The text of 2 Corinthians itself gives some indication that it may consist of two (or more) originally separate epistles, for there is a marked shift in tone between chapters 1–9, which are largely conciliatory in nature, and chapters 10–13, which reflect a context of hostility and tension between the apostle and some opponents whom Paul somewhat sarcastically labels "super-apostles" (2 Cor. 11:5; 12:11). In its canonical form, however, 2 Corinthians offers a rich resource for reflection on the nature of Christian ministry and community.

One of Paul's major concerns in 2 Corinthians, and perhaps the point at which the letter raises the most questions for contemporary ethical reflection, is found in the apostle's attempt in chapters 8–9 to persuade the Corinthians to renew their support of the relief fund that Paul was organizing among the gentile churches of his mission for impoverished members of the Jewish Christian community in Jerusalem (see Rom. 15:25–32). Procedures for organizing this collection are explained in 1 Cor. 16:1–4, where Paul seems confident of the Corinthians' participation in the offering. In between the writing of 1 Corinthians and 2 Corinthians, however, Paul and the Corinthians had experienced no small conflict (see 2 Cor. 1:15–2:13), a clash (perhaps motivated by charges of financial impropriety leveled against Paul) that seems to have led the Corinthians to suspend their efforts to gather a collection for Jerusalem. There are indications in 2 Corinthians that Paul's opponents in Corinth seized on this controversy by charging Paul with financial impropriety (2 Cor. 11:7–15; 12:11–21).

Thus, 2 Cor. 8:1–9:15 is written with the goal of cautiously encouraging the Corinthians to resume their support of the relief fund for needy believers in Jerusalem. In this section Paul employs a striking variety of rhetorical appeals to accomplish this aim: (1) he emphasizes the example of the Macedonians, who have generously contributed to the fund in spite of their own deep poverty (8:1–6); (2) he highlights the paradigmatic grace (*charis*) of the incarnate Lord Jesus Christ, "who became poor for your sake, although he was rich, so that by his poverty you might become rich" (8:9); (3) he draws upon the principle of "equality" (*isotēs*) to promote a sharing of financial resources among believers in different economic and geographical locations (8:14); (4) he suggests that both he and the Corinthians will be shamed if believers come from Macedonia to Corinth and find the undertaking unfinished (9:1–5); (5) he paints an agricultural metaphor to suggest that giving to the collection is like sowing seed, a metaphor that emphasizes the generative activity of God in the act of human beneficence (9:6–10); and, finally, (6) he punctuates this appeal by indicating that true generosity results in thanksgiving and praise to God, the one from whom all benefactions ultimately originate (9:11–15). In his appeal Paul consistently underscores the point that the fulfillment of mutual obligations within the Christian community results in praise, not to human donors, as the dominant ideology of patronage in his cultural context would have suggested, but to God, the one from whom all benefactions come. Even the very human action of raising money for those in material need originates in "the surpassing grace of God" (*hē hyperballousa charis tou theou*) and will result in "thanks to God" (*charis tō theō*) (2 Cor. 9:14–15).

Paul therefore challenges the Corinthians to conceptualize their beneficence as an act of worship, offered in praise to God. In this profoundly theocentric vision of gift-giving within the community of faith, the willing generosity of the Corinthians is empowered by and patterned after the grace of God in Christ. Moreover, in appealing to the principle of financial equality between the Corinthians and impoverished believers in Jerusalem (8:13–15), Paul assumes that believers with more abundant resources will work to address the needs of those who require assistance, even as the Corinthians might someday require aid from Jerusalem (8:14).

Other motivations surely were behind Paul's efforts to organize a collection for Jerusalem, not the least of which was the apostle's goal of demonstrating an ecumenical solidarity between the gentile churches of his mission and the Christ-believing community in Jerusalem (cf. Rom. 15:25–32). Yet, to the extent that the contribution was aimed at meeting the very real financial needs of destitute believers in Jerusalem, readers today might ask themselves how individual and congregational resources can be used to support brothers and sisters in Christ who are experiencing economic distress. In a world of increasing disparity between the rich and poor—to say nothing of the extent to which globalization and technology have made these inequalities both manifest and also seemingly inescapable—the attempt to embody the kind of ecclesiological equality called for in 2 Cor. 8–9 is no easy task. Paul's own logic would seem to preclude the development of any kind of fixed rule for resource sharing (2 Cor. 8:8, 12; 9:5–7). Nonetheless, faithfulness to the message of 2 Corinthians will not allow those whose lives are shaped by the narrative of the incarnate Christ to stand by while massive inequality exists among churches. What is needed is not a law for giving but rather the empowering grace of the God who still stands behind all human generosity.

See also Collection for the Saints; 1 Corinthians; Economic Ethics; Generosity; Grace; Koinonia; New Testament Ethics

Bibliography

Cherian, J. "Toward a Commonwealth of Grace: A Plutocritical Reading of Grace and Equality in Second Corinthians 8:1–15." PhD diss., Princeton Theological Seminary, 2007; Downs, D. J. *The Offering of the Gentiles: Paul's Collection for Jerusalem in Its Chronological, Cultural, and Cultic Contexts*. WUNT 2/248. Mohr Siebeck, 2008; Wheeler, S. *Wealth as Peril and Obligation: The New Testament on Possessions*. Eerdmans, 1995, 73–89; Young, F., and D. Ford. *Meaning and Truth in 2 Corinthians*. Eerdmans, 1988.

David J. Downs

Cost-Benefit Analysis

Perhaps the greatest revolution of the modern era was not the American, French, or Bolshevik, but that of the accountants. Harvard economist Joseph Schumpeter recognized this when he stated that the invention of "double-entry bookkeeping" produced a "rational cost-profit calculation" that then subjugated everything, including our "philosophies," "picture of the cosmos," "concepts of beauty and justice," and "spiritual ambitions," to its "conqueror's career." Schumpeter gives the Christian scholastics credit for recognizing that a new spirit, one threatening the Christian faith, was behind this simple practice (Schumpeter 123–24). Is he correct?

Insofar as everything is given a number and placed within a cost-benefit ratio, Schumpeter was right. Such quantification fits well a utilitarian ethic where everything is assigned a number establishing its "usefulness" to its owner. That number is often determined by an economic theory called "marginalism," which asks at what cost will someone forgo exchanging for a certain product and use that money for something else. This gives things their "value" and forms an "economy."

The word *economy* comes from two Greek words: *oikos* ("household") and *nomos* ("law, rule, norm, principle"). *Economy* is an ancient term that seeks the norms or principles by which a "householder" rules a household. The householder could be the head of a family, a city, or an empire, or even God. This is why theologians use the term "economic Trinity" to explain how the triune God orders or "rules" life for creatures. Scripture is our primary witness for discovering that rule. Both Scripture and a cost-benefit analysis give us *nomoi*, or principles, that form an economy. How do they relate?

No single and definitive answer can be given to that question, but we do find practical wisdom in Scripture that suggests a tension between them. This is found in the commandment, "Remember the sabbath day, and keep it holy. Six days you shall labor and do all your work. But the seventh day is a sabbath to the LORD your God; you shall not do any work. . . . For in six days the LORD made heaven and earth, the sea, and all that is in them, but rested the seventh day; therefore the LORD blessed the sabbath day and consecrated it" (Exod. 20:8–11). This gives one of the basic *nomoi* of Scripture. Our labor is to imitate God. We keep the Sabbath by resting in order to hear God's word, assuming that nothing can equal the "value" that it brings.

Keeping the Sabbath does not prohibit cost-benefit analyses, but the command does call into question the "conqueror's career" of that logic. Take, for instance, three of its *nomoi*: "time is money," "24/7," and the "virtue" of efficiency. Benjamin Franklin's admonition that "time is money" suggests that we can always give time a value and determine if how it was "spent" was worth it. Yet time spent in worship and rest is not an investment that can be quantified and analyzed based on a return. If someone said, "I consider keeping the Sabbath an investment. I give of my time and expect a good return—eternity, streets of gold, all the wealth I can imagine," I think most Christians would recognize that this fails to keep the Sabbath. We give God glory and imitate God's actions in our labor because God is worthy of our worship. Moreover, for most Christians, Sunday is the Sabbath, which is a new day, an eighth day now made possible by Jesus' resurrection. It is an eschatological day that cannot even fit within the seven-day economy. It cannot be defined by the axiom "time is money." To expect an efficient economy where commodities are available 24/7 is to deny Sabbath rest and return to Egypt. Rest is the promise that we hope to inherit, as the book of Hebrews repeatedly witnesses. Jesus' parables also challenge the conquering career of a cost-benefit analysis when he tells us that having found the kingdom, we recognize that nothing can be equaled to it, not even life itself.

The ethics of the scriptural economy suggests not only that the Lord's Day resists the servitude of the cost-benefit analyses but also that it is virtuous to do so. The goodness of family, sex, adoption, organ donation, friendship, and much more cannot yet, and should not, be fully defined by the cost-benefit economy. Some economists think that adoption and organ donation would be more "efficient" if we were to adopt that logic. They are most likely correct. But not everything should be bought and sold. As the cross of Christ reveals, charity is not always "efficient." This is why the Lord's Day is a protest against the cost-benefit ratio. It shows us a different vision, a divine economy.

See also Capitalism; Economic Ethics; Sabbath

Bibliography

J. Schumpeter. *Capitalism, Socialism, and Democracy.* Harper, 1942.

D. Stephen Long

Courage

Courage, or fortitude (Lat. *fortis* means "strong"), is classified as one of the four cardinal virtues, alongside temperance, justice, and prudence. In classical antiquity, courage (Gk. *andreia*) was understood to be a settled quality of personal character that expressed moral excellence (*aretē*) by acting rightly in fearful or dangerous situations. Ancient philosophical discussions of courage usually are related to expounding the "manly strengths" appropriate to military contexts, where fear of death in battle is assumed. The most influential interpretation was given by Aristotle, who argued that courage is "a mean with regard to fear and confidence." Whereas the coward flees in the face of danger and the rash person dashes into it without adequate forethought, the courageous person avoids these extremes by fearing "the right things and for the right purpose and in the right manner and at the right time" for the sake of that which is noble. Aristotle held that only those who "fearlessly confront" a noble (or beautiful) death on the battlefield are courageous in the proper sense. The ability to face evil things in everyday life such as disgrace, poverty, disease, lack of friends, or ordinary death can be called courage only in a "metaphorical" sense and is not counted as "true" courage.

In Scripture, courage is associated with the boldness and confidence that is grounded in God's presence, protection, guidance, and empowerment. In the OT, Yahweh is the singular source of courage for his people. The basic formula is "Do not be afraid, for I am with you" (Gen. 26:24). In times of vulnerability God's people are exhorted to trust in God, who pledges to defend them. Yahweh is depicted repeatedly as the basis of courage for the Israelites at key turning points in their history. The Israelites and their leaders are exhorted "to be strong and courageous" not for the sake of what is noble but rather for the sake of fidelity to God's purposes and promises. A prominent example is when Joshua receives Yahweh's assurance of protection ("No one shall be able to stand against you all the days of your life") and presence ("As I was with Moses, so I will be with you") as he leads the people into the promised land (Josh. 1:5). Yahweh's faithfulness to Israel is the foundation for the exhortation, "Be strong and courageous. Do not be frightened or dismayed, for the LORD your God is with you wherever you go" (Josh. 1:9). Similarly, when faced with the Assyrian attack on Jerusalem by Sennacherib, King Hezekiah tells his military officers, "Be strong and of good courage. Do not be afraid or dismayed before the king of Assyria and all the horde that is with him; for there is one greater with us than with him. With him is an arm of flesh; but with us is the LORD our God, to help us and to fight our battles" (2 Chr. 32:7–8).

In the NT, the presence of Jesus and intervention of the Holy Spirit are the sources of courage. For example, when Jesus is walking on the Sea of Galilee, the disciples are terrified, but he assures them by revealing his identity: "Take heart, it is I; do not be afraid" (Matt. 14:27). His followers repeatedly demonstrate courage by risking their reputations or lives for the sake of fidelity to Jesus and his purposes. After the death of Jesus, "Joseph of Arimathea, a respected member of the council, who was also himself waiting expectantly for the kingdom of God, went boldly to Pilate and asked for the body of Jesus" (Mark 15:43). In the book of Acts, the Holy Spirit empowers Jesus' followers for audacious, costly witness to Christ: "When they had prayed, the place in which they were gathered together was shaken; and they were all filled with the Holy Spirit and spoke the word of God with boldness" (Acts 4:31). At the height of Paul's conflict with the Sanhedrin, "the Lord stood near him and said, 'Keep up your courage! For just as you have testified for me in Jerusalem, so you must bear witness also in Rome' " (Acts 23:11). Through the prayers of the saints and the work of the Holy Spirit, Paul hopes that by "speaking with all boldness, Christ will be exalted now as always" through his ministry, even to the point of death (Phil. 1:20). Paul asks the Ephesians to pray for him that he will "make known with boldness the mystery of the gospel" (Eph. 6:19). Courage is expected from the Christian community: "Keep alert, stand firm in your faith, be courageous, be strong. Let all that you do be done in love" (1 Cor. 16:13–14). Here, courage is associated with the spiritual and moral strength of those who stand firm in the proclaimed word of God, whose energies are focused on the church's mission on Christ's behalf, and whose conduct is oriented by love (*agapē*).

Courage is depicted not as a natural virtue but rather as a gift of God's grace given to enable his people to faithfully serve him and share in his mission to the world. In contrast to classical antiquity, the Bible presents courage as motivated by the pursuit of God and his glory. These themes are developed by the Christian moral tradition. The martyrs of the early centuries of Christianity became prime exemplars of heroic courage. Those who refused to compromise their faith and were willing to die for Christ's sake demonstrated courage in its highest sense. Augustine reframed all the cardinal virtues as forms of love, hence, "Fortitude is love bearing everything readily for the sake of God." Thomas Aquinas draws heavily on Aristotle but rejects military heroism as the paradigm of courage. Instead, Thomas argues that martyrdom most truly exemplifies courage, which he understands as a form of endurance that bears with difficulty and stands fast in the face of danger. He interprets martyrdom as a form of sacrificial love, which is oriented to the divine good, namely, the love of God, and inspired by the gift of the Holy Spirit, modeled after Christ's example and fulfilling the biblical declaration, "No one has greater love than this, to lay down one's life for one's friends" (John 15:13).

See also Character; Habit; Justice; Prudence; Temperance; Virtue(s)

Bibliography

Aristotle. *Nicomachean Ethics*, book 3, chaps. 6–9; Augustine. *Of the Morals of the Catholic Church*; Hauerwas, S. "The Difference of Virtue and the Difference It Makes: Courage Exemplified." *ModTh* 9 (1993): 249–64; Ruether, R. "Courage as a Christian Virtue," *CrossCurrents* 33 (1986): 8–16; Thomas Aquinas. *Summa Theologiae*, I-II, q. 45; II-II, qq. 123–40; Yearly, L. *Mencius and Aquinas: Theories of Virtue and Conceptions of Courage*. State University of New York Press, 1990.

Jeffrey P. Greenman

Covenant

It surely was a moment of inspiration when the ancient Hebrews first recognized that certain relationships found in human history reflected the ways in which God both relates to creation and offers a model for how humans should relate to one another. The English word *covenant* comes from a medieval term with Latin roots (*con* + *venire*). It implies that distinct parties can come together to give and receive promises or to form associations by agreement on common laws or for common purposes. This term is used as a translation of the OT Hebrew *bĕrît* and the Greek *diathēkē* (= last will and testament) and, some say, *dikaiōma* ("covenantal decree") in the Greek NT. Words akin to these have also been found in all the languages into which the Bible has been translated. Over time, for the most part, *covenant* became differentiated in usage from those words meaning a two-party agreement made solely on human terms, for it implies the presence of the divine as a third party in a principled bonding.

Covenantal relations tend to have one of two forms. The vertical form has to do with the way God calls a person or a people into a divine-human relationship with stipulations. Examples can be found in ancient suzerainty treaties in which powerful rulers promise to protect a people and the people take an oath of loyalty. While some traditions have held that by analogy human relationships must also have this stratified "sovereign-subject" relationship, others argue that if God is the Lord, no mere human authority can be. Thus, they accent a horizontal, more democratic meaning of covenantal relationship, found in a bond wherein the parties agree to walk together in the ways of God, who is invoked as the source of that relationship, witness to that pledge, and the seal of its sanctity. This normative relationship can be found in some marriages and communities of worship, advocacy, or service as well as in social movements that accent democracy rather than monarchy. Both models have a passive element and an active element. A person or a group finds it impossible to avoid being drawn into a relationship but also finds it good to be there and thus wills to affirm its demands.

There are historical, theological, and ethical debates as to who is to be included in these relationships, for the word *covenant* is not introduced in the scriptural record until the survivors of the legendary flood in the story of Noah's ark offer thanks to God. Then, God offers a covenantal promise to Noah, his descendants, and the earth itself that floods will never again wreak such destruction (Gen. 9:8–17), even if humans deserve it. Humanity is given a new start, and the earlier commands to Adam and Eve are repeated, now in an expanded environmental inclusion. As in the earlier mythic story, humans are to be fruitful and multiply, to exercise dominion over the plants and animals of the earth, and to avoid that which contains the spirit of life—that is, blood (Gen. 9:1–7). These parallels have suggested to some that from the beginning creation is laden with covenantal meanings that have to do with the "covenant of works," or "cultural mandate" (Gen. 1:28–30). At stake are questions of whether sinful humanity is to take covenantal responsibility for the re-creative (technological) cultivation of "nature," and whether all the peoples of the earth are to be seen as potential participants in covenantal living.

A more historical covenant was made by God with Abraham, who became the father figure of the Semitic peoples, as new encounters between Jews, Christians, and Muslims have reminded us. From among all the peoples of the earth, Abraham was called to leave his native home and to go to a promised land that was to become the territory of Israel. Abraham also was warned that his people would later become slaves in Egypt (Gen. 15; Deut. 30). This set the stage for a theology of history in which the most important covenantal event of the OT took place, the Sinai covenant (Exod. 19–24). The escaped slaves from Egypt were made a united people by the giving of the covenant at Sinai and called to be witnesses to the universal moral laws of the Ten Commandments before all the peoples of the world.

The question of the primacy of the vertical or the horizontal form of covenantal relations in human affairs was, however, unresolved. Was it to be a horizontal, covenanted "league" of tribes led by charismatic "judges" who would resist the threat of tyranny that a concentration of power and authority brings (1 Sam. 8), or was it to be a vertical covenant led by a monarch, representing God's relationship with the people of Israel (2 Sam. 7)? The question is not only political, for many kinds of human relationships can be covenantal. The interplay of vertical authority and horizontal mutuality has been, and continues to be, debated in every sphere of life: friend-friend, husband-wife, parent-child, nation-nation, teacher-student, employer-employee, judge-jury of peers, marketer-customer, doctor-patient, clergy-laity, and so on. A common feature is that each may become an ethical outworking of the divine-human covenantal relationship. In brief, covenant, as Daniel Elazar has argued, seems ever to involve a "constitutionalization of relationship" that actualizes a dimension of what is divinely desired for the potentialities at the deepest levels of existence.

The biblical record acknowledges that the best possibilities are seldom realized. False prophets, faithless priests, and feckless politicians used their authority to exploit the weak instead of guiding the people in covenantal faithfulness, as was their task. Thus Israel began to worship false deities, violate moral laws, and pursue ungodly ends. It was only when the record of the covenant was rediscovered at the time of Josiah that a major effort at renewal was launched (2 Kgs. 22–23). In the books of Jeremiah and Ezekiel God promises a new covenant, one to be written on the hearts of the people and never forgotten.

The NT is substantially about the fulfillment and radicalization of the covenantal traditions in Christ. Although the texts that refer to covenant are relatively few, the covenantal themes are pervasive, and the patterns of moral life that are commended both follow the general contours of covenantal ethics and give them a new spiritual base. One can hear in the Sermon on the Mount of Matthew's Gospel the echoes of the Mosaic covenant, although the logic of command and obedience is given an inner logic of blessing and love. And Luke traces the genealogy of Jesus back to the implicit covenant of Adam more than to the covenants of David's kingship or Abraham's genetic heirs, setting the stage for a worldwide mission. The Communion meal becomes the enactment and symbol of the new covenant. Further, Jesus is treated in many places as the fulfillment of prophecy, as the final sacrifice supplanting the blood of priestly offerings, and as the King of kings who is also the Prince of Peace. All who are in Christ are bound into a covenanting community that prophetically advocates justice for all, pastorally heals and nurtures every neighbor, and politically takes responsibility for shaping public life according to their gifts. Jesus inaugurates a new spiritual movement in human history, the reign of God, which surpasses the authority of Moses and supplants ethnic and imperial authority. It takes place within persons, in communities of conviction, and in the very dynamics of history that point toward a new Jerusalem, to which all the peoples of the world can bring their gifts, and in which the promises of covenant will be consummated.

See also Atonement; Covenantal Ethics; Egalitarianism; Obligation; Old Testament Ethics; Sermon on the Mount

Bibliography

Allen, J. *Love and Conflict: A Covenantal Model of Christian Ethics*. Abingdon, 1984; Baker, J. *Heinrich Bullinger and the Covenant: The Other Reformed Tradition*. Ohio University Press, 1980; Elazar, D. *Covenant and Polity in Biblical Israel: The Covenant Tradition in Politics* 4 vols. Transaction Publishers, 1991–98; Hillers, D. *Covenant: The History of an Idea*. Johns Hopkins University Press, 1969; Mendenhall, G. "Covenant Forms in Israelite Tradition." *BA* 17 (1959): 50–76; Miller, P. "Creation and Covenant." Pages 155–68 in *Biblical Theology: Problems and Perspectives*, ed. S. Kraftchick, C. Myers, and B. Ollenburger. Abingdon, 1995; Stackhouse, M. "The Moral Meanings of Covenant." Pages 249–64 in *The Annual of the Society of Christian Ethics, 1996*. Georgetown University Press, 1996; Wright, N. T. *The Climax of the Covenant: Christ and the Law in Pauline Theology*. Fortress, 1993.

Max L. Stackhouse

Covenantal Ethics

As a religious and moral image, covenant has a rich and variegated but erratic history. At certain times it has taken center stage in the moral imagination of Jews and Christians. But at other times it has faded into the background of their religious and moral lives, almost disappearing from the pool of metaphors and symbols that order human experience and interaction. Nevertheless, it has persisted and appears to be experiencing a bit of a renaissance in contemporary theology and ethics, particularly in the American context.

Three features of covenant make it appropriate for retrieval in the contemporary period. First, while the Bible contains a variety of significant symbols, metaphors, and images for understanding God and his way with the world, covenant runs as a bright thread through the Scriptures, offering one way of weaving discordant elements into a unified narrative. Second, not only does covenant play a central role in Scripture, it also has always provoked engagement with those outside the boundaries of the Jewish and Christian communities, which is attractive to theologians and ethicists attempting to negotiate the complexities of faithfulness in a pluralistic cultural and religious context. Finally, covenant has a special relevance in the American context because of the significant role this powerful image has played in the religious, political, cultural, and economic history of the United States, largely through the early but important influence of Reformed Protestant Christianity. Given these features, covenant has become an important means for resisting the radical individualism that infects contemporary, Western (particularly American) culture without reverting to hierarchical and homogeneous models of human community.

Covenant is a significant theme within the OT. God's covenant with Israel at Mount Sinai is the heart of Hebrew identity. It is the touchstone for their sense of themselves and their place in the world as well as their conception of God and his way with the world. Fundamental to their covenantal self-understanding is the experience of being the undeserving recipients of God's gracious providence and love. The account of the Ten Commandments in Exodus begins with a brief preamble and historical prologue: "I am the Lord your God, who brought you out of the land of Egypt, out of the house of slavery" (Exod. 20:2). Obedience to the commandments (Exod. 20:1–17) and the Book of Covenant (Exod. 20:22–23:33) are presented not as a condition for God's graciousness, but rather as an appropriate response to it. Blessings and curses are embedded in the covenant stipulations (Exod. 20:5–7, 12), but the character of the covenant is shaped more by gratitude for blessings received than by fear of threats made. God chose Israel, and the law shaped their life together by reminding them of their absolute dependence on God and their mutual dependence on one another. They were bound to God and one another through a covenant initiated by God's gracious providence.

While the people of Israel are identified as a "treasured possession" and a chosen people (Exod. 19:5; Deut. 7:6), the covenantal imagination resists exclusivism and nativism. A wider array of covenants placed God's relationship with Israel in a more universal context: the covenant with Noah and all the creatures of the earth (Gen. 9:10) shows that God's gracious and provident way transcends his relationship with Israel; God's covenant with Abraham (Gen. 12:1–4) aims the covenant with Israel at a more cosmic and universal intention: "in you all the families of the earth shall be blessed" (Gen. 12:3); finally, the laws of the covenant provoked generosity toward foreigners and strangers as the true measure of covenant identity and faithfulness: "you shall not wrong or oppress a resident alien, for you were aliens in the land of Egypt" (Exod. 22:21). Far from promoting a special and exclusive relationship between God and his chosen people, covenant describes God's way with the whole world and orients the chosen people toward a universal mission and cause: God's whole creation and universal kingdom.

The OT prophets and the witness of the NT reinforce and rearticulate these fundamental covenant themes. The prophets accused the people of Israel and Judah of forsaking the covenant that they had made with God. Despite Israel's faithlessness and forgetfulness, however, they held out the promise of renewal through God's continuing graciousness. "The days are surely coming, says the Lord, when I will make a new covenant with the house of Israel and the house of Judah" (Jer. 31:31). The ministry and mission of Jesus Christ drew on this promise of a new covenant. Jesus' summary of the law reflects and directly quotes the covenant tradition of Israel: "'You shall love the Lord your God with all your heart, and with all your soul, and with all your mind.' This is the greatest and first commandment. And a second is like it: 'You shall love your neighbor as yourself.' On these two commandments hang all the law and the prophets" (Matt. 22:37–40). Jesus' ministry among the excluded and marginalized—sinners, the sick, foreigners—drew on and reinforced the covenantal vision of God's graciousness, choosing an enslaved, alien people as God's own. Jesus' words at the Last Supper reflect the hope and promise of a new covenant: "This cup that is poured out for you is the new covenant in my blood" (Luke 22:20). Throughout his letters, the apostle Paul presents God's actions in Jesus Christ as embodying both continuity and discontinuity with the original covenant. Most important, Christ universalizes the covenant, moving it beyond the people of Israel to all people (Gal. 3:13–14, 23–28), and internalizes it, making it a matter of the spirit rather than the letter of the law (2 Cor. 3:6). From the Gospels of Jesus Christ to the letters of the apostle Paul, the NT interprets Jesus' life, ministry, death, and resurrection in the light of God's covenant with Israel. Like the OT, the NT maintains a focus on God's graciousness, but it presses the covenant toward a more inclusive community and emphasizes Jeremiah's hope that the new covenant will be written on the heart rather than on stone.

Despite the importance of the covenantal imagination in the scriptural witness, it remained in the background of Christian theological and ethical reflection until the Protestant Reformation. For a variety of reasons, more hierarchical and organic metaphors and images took prominence of place in medieval Christendom. But as the feudal orders of church and empire began to disintegrate, the emergence of more egalitarian, independent, and pluralistic social structures also required a new moral imagination. At the same time, renewed attention to Scripture in the Reformation era provided the opportunity to reinvigorate long-neglected biblical images. In the hands of various theologians and philosophers, particularly those shaped by the Reformed churches in Switzerland, England, Scotland, and the Netherlands, covenant became an important resource for reimagining human relationships with God and one another. Religious leaders such as Heinrich Bullinger (1504–75) in Zurich, Johannes Althusius (1557–1638) in the Netherlands, William Ames (1576–1633) in England, and Samuel Rutherford (1600–1661) in Scotland developed a covenantal approach to theology but also applied this image to the political and social spheres of life. Whether reforming ecclesiastical or civil structures, they moved in the direction of limiting power, dispersing authority, and federating diverse and relatively independent agencies. Their self-consciously theological, covenantal thinking played an important role in the development of modern conceptions of social and political life that founded their legitimacy upon mutually binding promises made by relatively free and equal partners. Without a doubt, these religiously inspired social movements influenced the more secular social contract philosophy of thinkers such as Thomas Hobbes (1588–1679) and John Locke (1632–1704).

In the American context, religiously inspired covenantal approaches and more secular social contract influences intermingled to shape the social, political, and cultural order that became the United States of America. Because the colonists were building civic and ecclesiastical orders from the ground up instead of reforming existing structures, the American experiment was uniquely suited for the expression of covenantal ideas. From the very beginning, covenants were a part of the religious and civic order in the American colonies. The Plymouth Colony and the Massachusetts Bay Colony were founded on a covenantal basis. The leaders of the New England colonies generally were adherents to the federal theology in one form or another. Their leadership put in place not only institutional structures but also modes of thought that had a profound effect on future political and civic developments. The intellectual and political lineage of James Madison, the undisputed father of the US Constitution, can be traced back to the covenant tradition through his teacher at the College of New Jersey (now Princeton University), John Witherspoon, a Presbyterian clergyperson and theologian. James Madison's contributions to the *Federalist Papers* are seen by many as a profound expression of covenantal social thought in secular form. After this early formative period in American life, the covenantal imagination receded into the background once again, though its influence on America's institutions and ethos persisted.

Covenantal ethics as an approach to contemporary theology and social philosophy emerged in the United States in the middle of the twentieth century. The theology and ethics of H. Richard Niebuhr (1894–1962) provided an important impetus for the recovery of covenant as a significant image for religious, political, and social life, particularly within Protestant Christianity. The philosophy of Martin Buber (1878–1965) played a similar role, from a Jewish perspective, provoking renewed attention to the dynamic, interdependent nature of human beings. Along with other proponents of covenant, Buber and Niebuhr inspired a generation of Christian theological ethicists, including Paul Ramsey, Joseph Allen, James Luther Adams, William Everett, William F. May, Clinton Gardner, Robin Lovin, Philip Wogaman, Charles McCoy, and Max Stackhouse. Noted Jewish social philosophers such as Michael Walzer and Daniel Elazar also tapped the image of covenant for resources to reconceptualize contemporary political thought and social ethics. Unlike the sixteenth-century revival of the covenantal imagination, however, its contemporary renaissance has emerged as an alternative not to a hierarchical and organic conception of human life, but rather to radical individualism and social contract liberalism.

While the covenantal and social contract traditions had once made common cause in the transition from the medieval to the modern order, these two related moral images now find themselves at odds. The covenantal imagination provided a way to resist some of the utilitarian and atomistic aspects of contemporary individualism without abandoning the liberal and egalitarian impulses of modernity. As a polemical matter, the differences between these two images, rather than their similarities and shared origin, are emphasized. The contractual model of human existence emphasizes the autonomous agent who enters into limited contracts for the sake of self-interest. The moral legitimacy of the contract is based simply on the consent of the parties, which guarantees the presence of mutual self-interest. A covenantal understanding of human existence, however, conceives relationship as more fundamental than autonomy. Human existence, according to a covenantal vision, is not a matter of equal exchanges in a fair marketplace but rather is characterized by receiving gifts and responding with gratitude. All beings (including human beings) are bound to one another in relationships of unavoidable interdependence within the ultimate context of their absolute dependence on Being Itself. Covenant, in distinction from contract, is triadic rather than simply diadic; while the contracting parties must contend only with one another, the covenanting partners find themselves unavoidably engaged with a transcendent moral order that cannot be thwarted or ignored. Whether done so willingly or grudgingly, the interdependent structures of existence must be accepted; otherwise, as the biblical prophets proclaimed, disaster awaits. The covenant can be (and often is) rejected or betrayed, but not without undermining the very things thereby sought.

Both contract and covenant base social relationships on the binding force of mutual promises. The social contract model, however, assumes that people have no responsibilities that they do not voluntarily accept. Individuals are, first of all, independent and autonomous. Covenant, however, assumes that these mutual promises simply acknowledge and embrace relationships of interdependence that already exist and cannot be avoided. Thus, whereas contracts are focused simply on the negotiated agreement of the two parties, covenants must always take broader realities and implicit responsibilities into account. Whereas a contractual view will see an agreement between employer and employee as legitimate to the extent that it is entered voluntarily, a covenantal view requires that other questions be asked as well. For example, does this agreement reflect and accept the deeper obligations of mutual interdependence that exist before and beneath it? From a contractual perspective, therefore, questions of whether the agreed upon wage is just or sufficient are short-circuited. But from a covenantal perspective, an agreement that does not provide a living wage is illegitimate, whether it was made voluntarily or not. Similarly, from a social contract perspective, a just law is one that reflects the will of the people. But from a covenantal perspective, the will of the people does not necessarily qualify as a just law. The problem with Jim Crow laws in the American South, for example, was not simply that they did not reflect the will of all the people—no law can meet such a rigorous standard—but that they betrayed the fundamental nature and dignity of humans bound in relationships of mutual dependence on one another. American political culture, therefore, continues to reflect a fundamentally covenantal conception to the extent that the will of the people can be overruled by the Supreme Court, and labor contracts must meet minimal standards such as the minimum wage and workplace safety.

In his now classic work *Love and Conflict: A Covenantal Model of Christian Ethics*, Joseph L. Allen distinguishes between the inclusive covenant and the many special covenants. He argues that while people enter into a variety of special covenants with various people for different reasons—familial, civic, economic, religious, and cultural—these always take place within the context of and are subordinate to the inclusive covenant. The conviction of a universal covenant certainly reflects the biblical witness that God created everything good, with its own inherent worth and dignity, and placed all creatures in relationships of mutual interdependence under his gracious and sovereign providence (Gen. 1:1–2:3). It also suggests, however, the character of the reality that confronts all people in all places, times, and cultures. For this reason, covenantal ethics is attractive to many contemporary theologians and social philosophers seeking what Max Stackhouse calls a "public theology." Acknowledging that all human ways of knowing and valuing are shaped by particular, inherited images, narratives, and cultural contexts, covenant provides a way out of the closed circle of religious fideism and private interests into a robust moral discourse about what we owe to one another in a world shared in common.

Today, the covenantal imagination is being investigated along a variety of trajectories applied to a variety of spheres. Biblical scholars are further elaborating our understanding of the covenantal theme within Scripture. Historians continue to investigate its role in the development of modern political, economic, civic, and family spheres, particularly in the American context. Cross-cultural studies are comparing it with other cultural images and resources around the world. And theological ethicists and social philosophers are applying the insights of the covenantal imagination to the problems of political life in a pluralistic context, economic life in the age of the business corporation, marriage and family life in an increasingly liberalized social order, medical ethics in an era of patient autonomy, professional identity and ethics in an individualistic society, civil society in an increasingly fragmented context, and the environment in the age of global warming and the degradation of nature. This rich but often neglected moral and religious image is, once again, providing provocative resources and lines of inquiry for moral discourse for a new and quite different time.

See also Covenant; Fidelity; Social Contract

Bibliography

Allen, J. *Love and Conflict: A Covenantal Model of Christian Ethics*. University Press of America, 1995; Bellah, R. *The Broken Covenant: American Civil Religion in Time of Trial*. Seabury, 1975; Elazar, D. *The Covenant Tradition in Politics*. 4 vols. Transaction Publishers, 1995–98; Everett, W. *God's Federal Republic: Reconstructing Our Governing Symbols*. Paulist Press, 1988; Hillers, D. *Covenant: The History of a Biblical Idea*. Johns Hopkins University Press, 1964; Lovin, R. "Covenantal Relationships and Political Legitimacy." *JR* 60 (1980): 1–16; May, W. *The Physicians' Covenant: Images of the Healer in Medical Ethics*. Westminster, 1983; McKenzie, S. *Covenant*. UBT. Chalice Press, 2000; Mount, E., Jr. *Covenant, Community, and the Common Good: An Interpretation of Christian Ethics*. Pilgrim Press, 1999; Niebuhr, H. "The Idea of Covenant and American Democracy." *CH* 23 (1954): 126–35; idem. *Radical Monotheism and Western Culture*. Harper & Row, 1960; Stackhouse, M. *Covenant and Commitment: Faith, Family, and Economic Life*. Westminster John Knox, 1997; Walzer, M. *Exodus and Revolution*. Basic Books, 1985.

Timothy A. Beach-Verhey

Covetousness *See* Jealousy and Envy

Creation, Biblical Accounts of

There are at least five self-contained accounts of creation in the OT: Gen. 1:1–2:4a; Gen. 2:4b–3:24; Job 38–41; Ps. 104; Prov. 8:22–31. In the NT, the prologue to John's Gospel (1:1–18) also counts as a bona fide creation narrative. In addition, many other biblical texts describe creation one way or another, such as Eccl. 1:3–11 and portions of Isa. 40–55. The ethical implications of each of these texts are examined below.

Genesis 1:1–2:4a

Due to its canonical placement, Gen. 1:1–2:3 (known as the Priestly account of creation) enjoys pride of place in the Bible. Structured around seven days, the account describes a steady process of creation initiated and governed by God's word, beginning with light and concluding with life. God, moreover, does not entirely work alone: in several instances the waters or the land are enlisted to aid in the creative process (1:9, 11, 20, 24). The result is a world of ordered complexity that accommodates and sustains the rich panoply of life, each "according to its kind." Light, sky, seas, and land are established first, followed by the creation of particular agents and living creatures within these domains: stars, birds, marine life, and land animals, including humans. Some have particular functions or mandates: the sun and the moon determine the seasons and religious festivals (1:14). Marine and aviary life receive the blessing to multiply (1:22). Humans are charged with the responsibility of exercising "dominion" (1:28). The outcome of every stage in the creative process is declared "good" by God, climactically so at the completion of creation (1:31). Such approbation acknowledges creation's integrity and self-sustainability, from seeds to reproduction. The climax of creation, however, is not the sixth day, with the creation of humankind, but rather the seventh day (2:1–3), when God ceases to create, thereby allowing creation, under human "dominion," to thrive on its own. The Exodus version of the Decalogue bases the Sabbath commandment on God's resting on the seventh day (Exod. 20:11; cf. Deut. 5:15).

Creation in Gen. 1 is a cosmic temple in which the holy seventh day corresponds to the temple's holiest of holies, the inner sanctum (1 Kgs. 8:12–13; see Exod. 40:34–35). While God remains outside creation, humans, created "in the image of God," reside within (Gen. 1:27). Elsewhere in the Bible, the term *image* designates a statue or engraving that represents God, explicitly forbidden in biblical tradition (e.g., 2 Kgs. 11:18; cf. Exod. 20:4; Lev. 19:4; Deut. 4:15–18). Genesis 1, however, applies the language of *image* to humans, who bear God's presence in the world and are commanded to exercise "dominion." For an ancient agrarian society, such a command gave divine warrant to cultivate the land and harness its fertility for sustaining life, human and nonhuman (Gen. 1:29–30). Stewardship, thus, is an appropriate way of making sense of "dominion" in Genesis for today.

Genesis 2:4b–3:24

Whereas creation in Gen. 1 begins in a primordial soup (*tōhû wābōhû* [1:2]), the second creation story, known as the Yahwist account, begins with a dry stretch of land. The soil takes center stage in this narrative, for from it God, like a potter working with clay, creates a human being, the *ʾādām*. From such a simple narrative beginning, a wordplay is born: the *ʾādām* is created out of the *ʾădāmâ*, the "ground." Just as the English word *human* is derived from the Latin *humus*, the meaning of *ʾādām* carries with it the sense of "groundling." If God is king of the cosmos in Gen. 1, God is king of the compost in Gen. 2. God animates the first human being not by divine touch (contra Michelangelo), but rather by mouth-to-nose resuscitation. In Gen. 2, creation is intimately physical.

In the Yahwist account of creation, God plants a garden for the *ʾādām* and gives him the task of serving and preserving it (2:15). The divine farmer entrusts the garden to the human farmer. Thus, the *ʾādām* becomes the servant of the soil, in contrast to the royal, nearly divine elevation of humanity in Gen. 1. There is nothing in the garden to be "subdued." Indeed, the ground and the "groundling" form a fruitful partnership, a kinship by which the *ʾādām* is sustained and the soil yields its productivity. But as fruitful as the garden is, God finds that the life of the human farmer is "not good" (2:18). The *ʾādām* needs a companion, and so God creates out of the ground the animals to see if a coequal can be found. Having failed, God resorts to a more invasive procedure: the woman is created from the *ʾādām*'s own flesh and blood, and only then does the *ʾādām* become a "man" (*ʾîš* [2:23]). Such a creation by no means implies subordinate status for the woman, but rather indicates coequality and mutuality with the man, hence the marriage etiology in 2:24.

Life in the garden embodies mutuality and harmony, meaningful work and intimacy. It is marred, however, by the couple's attempt to grasp divine power and wisdom. The man and the woman are deemed unfit to care for the garden and are expelled. They suffer the curse of pain and alienation (3:14–19). But God's curse, as a consequence of the couple's disobedience, is no mandate. The garden story does not command subordination and conflict any more than it mandates crop failure. Rather, it recognizes that the blessed life of mutuality, intimacy, and harmonious work is far more difficult to embody outside the garden. Nevertheless, the garden's ethos remains binding.

Job 38–41

God's answer to Job presents a vividly panoramic view of creation. Beginning with earth and all stars and concluding with monstrous Leviathan (to which a whole chapter is devoted), creation in the book of Job is testimony to God's providential care, which extends far beyond what is familiar to humans. God, for example, makes it rain "on a land where no one lives . . . to satisfy the waste and desolate land" (38:26–27). Creation's focus here is on the wilderness, where the wild things are, from ostriches to aurochs. There, each creature has its freedom and vitality, each valued and cherished by God. Unlike Adam, to whom the animals were brought to be named in the garden, Job is shown the natural habitats of these wild creatures and taught their names. Although creation extends far beyond human reach, God points out that Job is inextricably linked to the wild: "Look at Behemoth, which I made just as I made you" (40:15). In God's answer, Job discovers his link to the wild even as the wild remains untouched by him. And so it should. Creation near and far is full of vitality and variety, dignity and terrible beauty.

Psalm 104

Psalm 104 matches Job 38–41 almost animal by animal, from the lion to Leviathan (minus Behemoth). In addition, trees are celebrated, including the majestic cedars of Lebanon. The psalm's broad focus is on creation's habitational integrity. Each animal has its home, from the lion's lair to the coney's rock and the stork's juniper. Creation is not just habitat for humanity; it is habitat for diversity, including even habitat for divinity (104:2b–3a). God provides for all, and the products of nature provide joy for human beings (104:14–15). Dominion has no place in this psalm (cf. Ps. 8); humans are simply counted among the host of living creatures, all exercising their right to live in God's manifold world. The psalmist delights in the sheer variety of creatures and habitats that fill creation (104:24), a delight that God also shares (104:31b). Psalm 104 is God's fanfare for the common creature.

Proverbs 8:22–31

Wisdom presents herself as the consummate eyewitness to God's work in creation. She recounts how God constructed the world, ensuring its integrity. As for her place in creation, personified Wisdom claims to have been "brought forth" (i.e., birthed) prior to anything else created (8:24–25). Wisdom is God's cosmic child, and as a child she plays with both God and creation (8:30–31). Creation, in short, is fashioned for Wisdom's enjoyment. Humanity, on the other hand, is scarcely mentioned, except at the very end as Wisdom's play partner, the object of her delight, along with God. Humans exist for Wisdom's sake, for her delight. Wisdom's playful delight requires humans to live up to their biological name, *Homo sapiens* (the "wise human"), and also to be *Homo ludens* (the "playing human").

Ecclesiastes 1:3–11

Although not a creation account proper, the opening chapter of Ecclesiastes presents a unique snapshot of creation in perpetual motion, from rising generations and flowing streams to circling sun and blowing wind. And yet for all its frenetic activity, the earth remains the same (1:4b). There is "nothing new under the sun" (1:9). Change is a mirage. Creation, moreover, is fraught with "vanity" (Heb. *hebel*), making life futile and fleeting. As for humanity's place and role in a world of *hebel*, the ancient sage warns against getting swept up in the relentless, all-consuming quest for "gain." In Qoheleth's eyes, creation presents a lesson, but it is a negative one. As the world is full of expended effort, all for naught, so humans cannot grasp anything permanent and profitable, no matter how hard they try. *Hebel* always wins. Instead, the sage commends a nonprofit existence: "There is nothing better for mortals than to eat and drink, and find enjoyment in their toil. This also, I saw, is from the hand of God" (2:24). To pause amid the toil and to savor the simple gifts of sustenance—themselves the fruits of creation—is the highest good for humans. In his own way, the sage advocates a life of simplicity and joy. He is not a hedonist, not one to strive for pleasure as one strives for gain. No, Qoheleth commends a life of grateful acceptance.

Isaiah 40–55

Known as Second Isaiah, this corpus of prophetic poetry is filled with references to creation, all bound up with the prophet's bold historical pronouncements of release for the exilic community. As much as Qoheleth denounces anything new, the prophet of the exile heralds the new. In Isaiah, history and creation are inseparably wedded. God stretches out the heavens as a tent or curtain (40:22; 42:5) and hammers out the earth as a firmament (42:5b; 44:24b). God creates both light and darkness, weal and woe (45:6b–7; cf. Gen. 1:3). Incomparably transcendent, God stands alone as creator of all. All in all, God did not create the earth "a chaos [*tōhû*], he formed it to be inhabited" (45:18). As the heavens are stretched out, so God commands Zion to "enlarge the site of your tent" and to "let the curtains of your habitations be stretched out" in order to accommodate Zion's lost children, the returning exiles (54:2–3). Creation prefigures Israel's restoration in the land, inaugurated by a new exodus (43:16–23). This is indeed something "new" (42:9; 43:19; 48:6). Released from exile, Israel will never be the same; so also creation. Indeed, the prophet likens Israel's restoration to new botanical growth (41:17–21; 45:8; 55:10–11). God's saving word is a creative word.

John 1:1–18

The word that initiates creation in Gen. 1 reaches its creative fullness in the prologue to John's Gospel. Rewriting Gen. 1, especially the first three verses, John lifts up the divine "Word" (*logos*) that was present "in the beginning" and, at the same time, brings it down to earth, fully enfleshed (1:1, 14). Drawing from Prov. 8, John identifies Christ with primordial Wisdom, who was "with God" (1:1 [cf. Prov. 8:30]) and who "enlightens everyone" (1:9). As "light" was the first of God's primordial acts in Genesis, light in John is the sign of God's glorious effulgence "coming into the world" (1:4–5, 8–9). As in Genesis, light and life are interconnected (1:4). In Gen. 1, God fashions creation by divine word, but no indication is given as to when or how God will enter the cosmic temple, if ever. For John, however, the Christ event marks God's formal entrance into creation, once and for all (1:9–10). The evangelist establishes a broad theological arc extending from Genesis to John, from the creator God to the incarnate Christ, the "light of the world" (8:12). In John, God's creative "Word" is God's incarnational presence in the world (1:14).

Each in its own way, these creation traditions claim the world as God's creation and acknowledge creation's God-given worth and integrity, its goodness and its beauty. As God's cosmic temple, creation bears a sanctity that must not be profaned. Humankind, the accounts attest, is creation's royal steward and loyal servant, its most powerful agent and most grateful recipient. As God's "images," humans are called to reflect God's life-affirming ways, to embody the God who cares for all creatures and seeks their well-being. In the biblical narrative, the one who most fully exercises divinely ordained "dominion" is Noah, who preserves the diversity of all creation. The world that "God so loved" is nothing less than cosmic (John 3:16).

See also Animals; Creation Ethics; Ecological Ethics; Humanity; World

Bibliography

Brown, W. "The Moral Cosmologies of Creation." Pages 11–26 in *Character Ethics and the Old Testament: The Moral Dimensions of Scripture*, ed. M. D. Carroll R. and J. Lapsley. Westminster John Knox, 2007; idem. *The Seven Pillars of Creation: The Bible, Science, and the Ecology of Wonder*. Oxford University Press, 2010; Davis, E. *Scripture, Culture, and Agriculture: An Agrarian Reading of the Bible*. Cambridge University Press, 2009; Fretheim, T. *God and World in the Old Testament: A Relational Theology of Creation*. Abingdon, 2005.

William P. Brown

Creation Ethics

Issues of creation ethics are pressing in today's world as society increasingly recognizes creation's ecological fragility. Many now even characterize the situation as a crisis that threatens the survival of all creatures on earth. This crisis is closely related to the problem of poverty, as ecological degradation is often worst in areas inhabited by the poor. Yet many worry that environmental regulations may have the unfortunate effect of stultifying the economic development especially needed by the poor. In view of this balancing act, what responsibilities do Christians have to care for the well-being of nature in relation to human flourishing?

These critical issues of Christian ethics depend significantly on the biblical and theological questions surrounding the Christian understanding of the world as creation. What does it mean for the world to be "creaturely"? Is the created order meaningful beyond its role as the environment in which humans live? What does the creaturely status of human beings—we are creatures in ontological kinship with the nonhuman creaturely world—entail for the moral life?

God as Creator

Creation by definition is the gracious work of God, the Creator king. This key theme of creation as God's kingdom is established in the keynote creation accounts of Gen. 1–2 and is sounded by various other biblical texts (e.g., Ps. 24:1). Reflecting the full-bloom monotheism of the exilic period, Deutero-Isaiah affirms God's status as the Creator of all (Isa. 40:26; cf. Jdt. 9:12). God's position as sole maker and therefore king of all creaturely reality is itself one of the key biblical-theological themes that informs ethical considerations, for the line that differentiates appropriate behavior from idolatrous living runs along the Creator/creature distinction. Living rightly and faithfully requires the embrace of one's creaturely status rather than an idolatrous straining for the prerogatives that belong to God alone (see Gen. 3). This theme runs throughout the biblical canon, as echoed in the apostle Paul's theological account of human sin: "They exchanged the truth about God for a lie and worshiped and served the creature rather than the Creator" (Rom. 1:25). By contrast, true worship acknowledges God's status as Creator, as seen, for example, with the twenty-four elders of Revelation (4:11). In short, to live properly is to accept creaturehood rather than confuse oneself or other creatures with the Creator God.

The Status of Creation

Though subordinate to God as Creator, creaturehood is not a diminishment, but rather bears great dignity and goodness. The first Genesis creation account is particularly clear in its assessment of the high value, worth, and dignity of the created order. Throughout the formative days of creation, the various categories of creaturely being are regarded by God as "good," with the final refrain assessing the whole work of creation with a resounding "very good" (Gen. 1:31).

From Jesus' pronouncement that "it is not what goes into the mouth that defiles a person, but it is what comes out of the mouth that defiles" (Matt. 15:11) to Paul's assertion that "everything is indeed clean" (Rom. 14:20), the NT strongly affirms the goodness of creation (e.g., Rom. 11:36; 1 Tim. 4:4). This goodness theme is advanced most definitively through the promise of a renewal of all creation, a hope present in OT prophetic literature (Isa. 65:17–25) but portrayed most strikingly through Revelation's vision of a "new heaven and a new earth" (Rev. 21:1). There the divine king of creation promises to renew all of reality: "See, I am making all things new" (Rev. 21:5).

The NT as a whole interprets this promise through Jesus. His role as mediator of the original divine work of creation (see Col. 1:15; Heb. 1:2; cf. Rev. 3:14) and his redemptive incarnation in the dust and history of creation itself will culminate in a renewal of all creation. In short, the world's enduring goodness is not just a creational claim, but ultimately is a christological and soteriological claim: "God so loved the world that he gave his only Son, so that everyone who believes in him may not perish but may have eternal life" (John 3:16). While the second half of this venerated verse brings the idea to a rather anthropocentric close, we should not ignore the first half's insistence that it is the Creator king's love for the whole *kosmos* that precipitates the incarnation's validation of the goodness of creation (cf. Rom. 8:21).

The Role of Humankind

Among God's creatures it is seemingly only humans who have had a difficult time accepting creaturely limits and respecting the goodness of creation. This sinfully inflated sense of humanity was bolstered by certain understandings of the exalted status of humans as bearers of God's image. In Gen. 1 God creates humanity with the following words:

> "Let us make humankind in our image, according to our likeness; and let them have dominion over the fish of the sea, and over the birds of the air, and over the cattle, and over all the wild animals of the earth, and over every creeping thing that creeps upon the earth." So God created humankind in his image, in the image of God he created them; male and female he created them. God blessed them, and God said to them, "Be fruitful and multiply, and fill the earth and subdue it; and have

> dominion over the fish of the sea and over the birds of the air and over every living thing that moves upon the earth." (Gen. 1:26–28)

While various interpretations of what exactly constitutes the divine image have been proposed, this text often was assumed to be teaching that humans are overlords of the nonhuman creation, possessing the divine mandate to exercise domination over a wild, dangerous, or dormant nature.

Given this prominent interpretation of the *imago Dei*, coupled with Jewish and Christian roles in fostering the development of modernity, especially the scientific revolution and industrialization, the Christian religion has often been accused of complicity in the making of the ecological crisis. Lynn White Jr. famously argued in 1967 that Christianity, in aiding the rise of modern science, gave unchecked blessing to the exploitation of the earth, in no small part through its exalting humanity at the expense of the nonhuman created world. The degradation of creation is often also associated with particular movements or attitudes within Christian history, such as the world-denying gnostic Christianity that emerged early on and has afflicted the church even into the present, or forms of escapist eschatology that regard the material world as bound for destruction and therefore in need of little human concern here and now. While the precise degree of Christian culpability is debatable, it is difficult to avoid the conclusion that the church often has provided biblical and theological warrant for the despoiling of nature.

A more nuanced interpretation of the *imago Dei* concept, however, as suggested by biblical scholarship, points in a very different direction (see, e.g., Middleton). In the ancient Near Eastern world, an "image" (Heb. *ṣelem*) often referred to a statue that represented and demarcated a king's dominion. This background suggests that human beings, as dignified divine image-bearers, are called to be living, breathing representatives of the reign and concerns of God the king. As those who "have dominion," humans have only representative dominion and are called to serve as stewards of the true king, caring for and preserving the king's domain—that is, God's creation. "Be fruitful and multiply" and "subdue the earth," then, cannot rightly be taken as license for humans to adopt haphazard or anthropocentric conceptions of their relationship to the rest of creation, but actually are mandates to dwell caringly in the world as faithful stewards of God, bringing forth the fruits of the created order in a way that sustains its well-being in honor of the true Creator king.

In view of the NT portrayal of Jesus as the true "image of the invisible God" (Col. 1:15), the work of stewardly image-bearing takes on even crisper contours. Sin fosters an inappropriate and destructive living out of the image-bearing task. It is thus only through Jesus Christ, the sinless one who is the true image of God, that we can get our clearest idea of appropriate image-bearing and creaturely existence. Among other things, Jesus' inauguration of the kingdom of God through proclamation and healing, his faithful attendance to the "least of these" (Matt. 25:31–46), and his self-effacing journey to the cross of reconciliation provide christological soundings for creation ethics, although they are undoubtedly items that require careful translation into the arena of environmental considerations. If a degraded natural order, for instance, qualifies as a creational "least of these," then the church's image-bearing witness to Jesus' ministry may require significant attention to the well-being of nature, by analogy to the naked, hungry, and imprisoned.

Jesus' full embrace of creatureliness, despite his divine prerogatives, should also inform creation ethics. The christological hymn of Phil. 2:5–11 makes the point with its incarnational overtones: the one who by nature is God did not, ironically, like the first Adam, grasp after that equality, but rather accepted the servant status of a creature, even unto suffering and death. The moral and spiritual punch line of the text, of course, is that we who are not God, but by nature are creaturely servants of God, are called to reject our idolatrous strivings. In short, to live faithfully is to live as creatures, without deifying ourselves or exalting ourselves above other creatures. In this broad sense, we are called to follow the pattern of Christ, who embraced his incarnational creatureliness through his faithfulness to the calling of the Father by the leading of the Spirit.

Sustainability, Stewardship, and the Spirit

If the *imago Dei* is centrally a matter of human responsibility before God to conserve and cultivate the goodness of creation—to tend the creational kingdom on behalf of the Creator king—then a key motif for creation ethics is sustainability. The created order, at least the one planet over which humans currently have influence, should be protected because the triune Creator desires it—every facet of it—to flourish in its created goodness. While this means that human flourishing cannot rightly be pursued apart from its environmental impact, it also means that nonhuman environmental considerations cannot wholly trump questions of human well-being, especially concerns of the poor. In a sinful world, creation ethics, with its goal of sustainability, will always be a realm of difficult choices. At the same time, seeing the issue as a holistic set of ecological considerations should remind us that the well-being of humanity and of nonhuman nature are fully bound up with each other as one system of nature and one created kingdom of God. While nature depends significantly on humankind for its flourishing, especially given modern technology's provision of unprecedented human control over nature, humankind itself cannot flourish apart from nature, which has given rise to human life and provides us the resources for human sustainability.

How can stewardship and efforts toward sustainability be encouraged in the church? One recent family of theological proposals points to the immanence of the Holy Spirit in creation as a theme that can help to counterbalance the modern industrial desacralization of nature. Some of these proposals contend in very strong terms that the Spirit is the "Earth God," who dwells within the created world, penetrating all life and filling it with divine sanctity (Wallace). Others suggest that the person of the Spirit is the "womb" of creation, with all of creation existing "in" the Spirit (Moltmann). These proposals presuppose that a greater sense of the Spirit's presence and investment in creation will help the church avoid the temptation to see nature as mere "stuff" that we can use according to our whims. The difficulty with such proposals is how to invest creation with appropriate divine sanctity without blurring the clear biblical and monotheistic line between Creator and creation.

The Epistle to the Romans provides guidance in this regard. Paul speaks of the Spirit's indwelling of the adopted children of God as the ground of hope for future human renewal, despite our current sufferings (Rom. 8:17–18). Paul then connects the present suffering and future-minded hope of human beings to the situation of creation as a whole:

> For the creation was subjected to futility . . . in hope that the creation itself will be set free from its bondage to decay and will obtain the freedom of the glory of the children of God. We know that the whole creation has been groaning in labor pains until now; and not only the creation, but we ourselves, who have the first fruits of the Spirit, groan inwardly while we wait for adoption, the redemption of our bodies. (Rom. 8:20–23)

Paul's analogy between the suffering of believers and the "groaning" of creation as a whole, with the Spirit's presence and intercession filling the space between persecuted present and redemptive future for believers (Rom. 8:26–27), is highly suggestive of the Spirit's broader redemptive indwelling of the whole creation. Thus, the Spirit's role in sanctification is closely linked to the Spirit's work in the larger renewal of creation. To live faithfully in creation, then, is to live as a creature in the Spirit, recognizing that the Spirit's presence and work, through Christ, extend to the whole of creation.

Led by the Spirit's redemptive role in the Christian life and in recognition of the Spirit's renewing presence in creation, where should Christians direct their efforts in the area of creation ethics, especially its environmental considerations? One focus in contemporary discussions emphasizes Christian political responsibility: Christians should support policies that enhance the sustainability of the created order. They should advocate actively for programs and practices that respect the integrity of creation and foster its inhabitability for all creatures.

Along with political advocacy, the approach to Christian ethics articulated by thinkers such as Stanley Hauerwas suggests an additional mind-set. It reminds the church simply to be itself, to be a distinctive community of witness that lives the life of Christ and pursues creaturely faithfulness while recognizing that the well-being of creation ultimately depends on God. On this approach, rather than relying only on grand measures such as the marshaling and channeling of political power, the church is called to start small (to do "one thing," as Hauerwas puts it)—to pursue creative stewardship in day-to-day matters as an expression of faithfulness, to remember the particular "least of these" (whether imprisoned neighbor, hungry and homeless person, or polluted park) in the local church's midst—as a witnessing parable of the Creator God's concern for all of creation.

See also Animals; Creation, Biblical Accounts of; Ecological Ethics; Humanity; Image of God; Stewardship

Bibliography

Gunton, C. *The Triune Creator: A Historical and Systematic Study*. ESCT. Eerdmans, 1998; Hall, D. *Imaging God: Dominion as Stewardship*. Eerdmans, 1986; Hauerwas, S. *The Peaceable Kingdom: A Primer in Christian Ethics*. University of Notre Dame Press, 1991; Middleton, J. *The Liberating Image: The Imago Dei in Genesis 1*. Brazos, 2005; Moltmann, J. *God in Creation: A New Theology of Creation and the Spirit of God*. Fortress, 1993; Plantinga, R., T. Thompson, and M. Lundberg. *An Introduction to Christian Theology*. IR. Cambridge University Press, 2010, 147–94. Wallace, M. *Finding God in the Singing River: Christianity, Spirit, Nature*. Fortress, 2005; White, L. "On the Historical Roots of Our Ecologic Crisis." *Science* 155 (March 10, 1967): 1203–7.

Matthew D. Lundberg

Credit *See* Loans

Cremation *See* Death and Dying

Crime and Criminal Justice

The Bible has much to say about crime and criminal justice, and what it says has obvious importance for Christian ethical reflection on the subject. But there are considerable complexities in appraising and appropriating the biblical witness.

One immediate difficulty is that criminal legislation in the OT is diverse and scattered. The various criminal codes undoubtedly reflect growth and development over time and reveal the impact of changing historical circumstances. It is also the case that legal outcomes recorded in the narrative literature of the Bible do not always correspond with outcomes specified in the relevant laws. This is partly because biblical law is not legislation in the modern sense; it is a compilation of representative legal problems from which guidelines could be derived for specific cases, not a body of hard-and-fast regulations that cover every eventuality. Judges were guided by oral precedent and individual circumstance as well as by written stipulations. The imperative was to "pursue justice and only justice," not simply to apply the written word woodenly (Deut. 16:18–20; 17:8–13).

The theoretical basis of the biblical legal system is also quite different from that of the modern Western world. Modern law distinguishes between torts and crimes as well as between civil and criminal jurisdictions. These distinctions are not evident in biblical law. Similarly, in modern law what makes a particular act a crime is that it violates a specific law, instigated by the state, that prohibits the act and that prescribes a penalty for its commission. The deed is classified as criminal because it is considered to be an offense against the community as a whole, with society acting collectively through its institutional mechanisms to repress the behavior. In biblical law, by contrast, responsibility for prosecuting offenses typically rested with the victim or the victim's family rather than with a public body. The courts regulated appropriate forms of recompense depending on the degree of moral culpability involved and the nature of the harm inflicted, but the initiative rested with the injured party.

Where victims suffered pecuniary losses or material damages, they were entitled to full restitution (Exod. 21:33–36; 22:5–6; Lev. 24:18, 21), plus varying levels of compensation if the offense involved theft or deliberate misappropriation (Exod. 22:1, 4, 7, 9; Lev. 6:1–7; Num. 5:5–8; Prov. 6:30–31). Financial reparation was also considered appropriate for some interpersonal offenses (Exod. 21:22; 22:16–17; Deut. 22:29; Lev. 19:20). For more serious and intentional bodily harms, such as wounding or homicide, victims were entitled to pursue personal vengeance, though they might accept a ransom in lieu of retaliation (Exod. 21:28–32; cf. 2 Sam. 12:13; 14:11). In these cases, the *lex talionis* governed the level of repayment that could be exacted: "life for life, eye for eye, tooth for tooth, hand for hand, foot for foot, burn for burn, wound for wound, stripe for stripe" (Exod. 21:20–25; Lev. 24:19–22; Deut. 19:18–21; cf. Gen. 9:5–6). This dramatic formula expresses, with maximum memorability, the basic judicial principle of proportionality: the penalty exacted must not patently exceed the injury inflicted (cf. Gen. 4:23–24).

In cases of culpable homicide, the "life for life" provision was intended literally (Gen. 9:5–6; Exod. 21:12; Lev. 24:21; Num. 35:31). As well as underscoring the unique value of human life, the principle ruled out vicarious or collective punishments that might trigger spiraling blood feuds between families or clans (Deut. 24:16; 2 Kgs. 14:6; Ezek. 18:1–32). Responsibility for carrying out the death sentence rested, in the first instance, with the victim's avenging kinsman, "the redeemer of blood" (Num. 35:19; Deut. 19:12), though others might sometimes act in his stead (2 Sam. 4:11). In instances of lesser physical injuries, the "like for like" statements in the *lex talionis* typically were understood to mandate not actual physical mutilation but compensation of equivalent financial (or moral) value to the loss suffered (cf. Exod. 21:18–25; Deut. 19:15–21). Notwithstanding its vivid concrete language, therefore, the *lex talionis* represented a canon of proportionate restitution, not a sanctioning of imitative retribution.

In general terms, capital crimes were considered a stain on the entire community, a defiling of the land, and an occasion of collective responsibility before God (Lev. 18:26–28; 26:3–45; Deut. 19:10; 21:1–9). It was as if certain crimes produced a kind of environmental pollution that might spread contagiously unless the offender was "cut off" from the community by death or exile (Exod. 31:14–15; Lev. 7:2; 18:7–29). The whole community—"all Israel"—participated in punishing the offender (Lev. 24:14–16, 23; Num. 15:35–36; Deut. 17:7; 21:21; Josh. 7:25; 1 Kgs. 12:18; 2 Chr. 10:18), thereby physically removing and symbolically purging the source of contamination from its midst.

This highlights another important distinction between biblical law and modern law: crime in the

Bible is considered to be a transgression against God, not simply an offense against the secular state. The law is given directly by God, so that to violate any of the law's commandments is to sin against the lawgiver (Ps. 51:1, 4). Law and morality are one. The law's stipulations, moreover, apply equally to everyone in the community, regardless of class or social status (Exod. 23:2–3; Lev. 19:15; Deut. 1:16–17; 24:17–18). In other ancient Near Eastern legal collections it was the king or state that promulgated the law, and the social status of the parties and the economic impact of certain behaviors played a determinative role in evaluating harms and allocating penalties.

The religious grounding of biblical law is particularly visible in the criminalizing of a range of distinctively religious behaviors, such as blasphemy, sorcery, idolatry, breach of the Sabbath, and various cultic transgressions. These rank among the most serious forms of criminal wrongdoing, carrying the death penalty. The probable reason why certain sexual activities, such as adultery, also attracted severe punishment of both parties is that they too were considered to be an abomination to God, not simply a violation of the husband's rights (Gen. 20:6; 39:9).

In considering the nature and content of biblical criminal law, it is important to remember the pedagogical purpose of biblical law. The law was addressed to the entire covenant people (Deut. 29:10–12), not just to the legal establishment, and the religious rationale given for proscribing certain behaviors (e.g., Lev. 19:13–14; 33–37), and the gradation of penalties that attached to them, were intended to inculcate certain values, priorities, and ideals into the mind of the community. It is here that the significance of biblical criminal law for contemporary Christian ethics is mainly to be found. The death penalty was intended to mark out certain behaviors as especially serious, even though death was by no means invariably exacted. Instructively, the death penalty is never imposed for violating property rights, but only for crimes against persons and for deliberate breaches of loyalty to God. This underscores the unique value attached in the Bible to human life and relationships above property and possessions, and to the absolute necessity of Israel maintaining its exclusive devotion to God.

The NT does not contain its own corpus of criminal laws. Its frequent, though largely incidental, references to criminal justice matters are predominantly reflective of prevailing Jewish and Roman legal practice, which it often views in a critical light. Yet NT teaching on justice, love, and forgiveness furnishes the indispensable yardstick for assessing the relevance and application of OT criminal legislation today.

See also Capital Punishment; Justice, Restorative; Justice, Retributive; Law; Law, Civil and Criminal; Punishment

Bibliography

Drapkin, I. *Crime and Punishment in the Ancient World*. Lexington, 1989; Gorringe, T. *God's Just Vengeance: Crime, Violence, and the Rhetoric of Salvation*. CSIR 9. Cambridge University Press, 1996; Jones, M. *Criminals of the Bible: Twenty-five Case Studies of Biblical Crimes and Outlaws*. FaithWalk, 2006; Marshall, C. *Beyond Retribution: A New Testament Vision for Justice, Crime and Punishment*. Eerdmans, 2001; idem. *The Little Book of Biblical Justice: A Fresh Approach to the Bible's Teachings on Justice*. Good Books, 2005; Mendelsohn, S. *The Criminal Jurisprudence of the Jews*. Sepher-Hermon, 1991; Wenham, G. "Law and the Legal System in the Old Testament." Pages 24–52 in *Law, Morality, and the Bible: A Symposium*, ed. B. Kaye and G. Wenham. InterVarsity, 1978; Wright, C. *Walking in the Ways of the Lord: The Ethical Authority of the Old Testament*. InterVarsity, 1995.

Christopher Marshall

Cross-Cultural Ethics

If ethics is fundamentally about discerning good from bad, then cross-cultural ethics is about how the concepts of good and bad, as well as moral obligations, are understood in different cultural contexts. There are several elements to examine in order to adequately understand cross-cultural ethics from a Christian perspective. First, what do we mean by "culture," and how does ethics relate to this concept? Second, how do the ethical precepts of Scripture fit with the apparent fact that people from distinct cultures define "good" and "bad" in different ways? Finally, given the above, how can someone learn how the "good" is understood in different cultural contexts?

We begin with culture. For many people "culture" is defined as a list of traits such as customs, language, clothing, food, and traditions. In fact, the first published definition of "culture" by an anthropologist took this "trait list" approach: "Culture or civilization . . . is that complex whole which includes knowledge, belief, art, law, morals, custom, and any other capabilities and habits acquired by man as a member of society" (Tylor 1). In more recent years, symbolic/interpretive anthropologists have moved away from this approach and view culture as the meanings that individuals give to the world around them. From this perspective, we are constantly using our cultural understandings to interpret what is happening in a particular context at a particular time and then using those interpretations to generate social behavior

(Spradley). As a leading anthropologist put it, as humans, we are "suspended in webs of significance [that we ourselves have] spun" (Geertz 5).

We interpret the world in a distinct way as the result of growing up in a specific culture; that is, we are enculturated into a meaningful universe. It stands to reason, then, that individuals brought up in other cultures will interpret the world differently than we do, a fact demonstrated both by innumerable anthropological studies and missionary accounts, and by our personal experiences with those from other cultures. These differences can range from minor (e.g., among those in our own society) to major (e.g., among those from cultures with fundamentally different assumptions about reality). Regarding the latter, anthropologists have distinguished between two basic types of societies that reflect these different assumptions: egocentric and sociocentric. In egocentric societies it is assumed that all individuals are alike, and each one represents all of humanity. A person contains motivations and drives, can act as an individual independently from others, and possesses qualities such as generosity, kindness, and integrity. In sociocentric societies it is assumed that a person does not possess intrinsic qualities but rather is defined by concrete roles and situations. A person is not an autonomous self but instead is defined by his or her actions and prescribed roles (Robbins).

These cultural differences obviously have an impact on how "good" and "bad" are defined and can lead to actions being interpreted in very different ways from what perhaps was intended. One of the key problems is that we take for granted our cultural understandings of the world. We then assume either that others view the world in the same way or, if they do not, that their understandings are inferior or wrong. In other words, we are naturally ethnocentric. This often leads to cross-cultural misunderstandings and conflict. A few years ago, a group of students from the United States went to China with a Christian organization. China is a country that would be classified as sociocentric, whereas the United States is, in general, egocentric. The students were placed with Chinese roommates at a university with the intention of getting to know them and sharing their faith. The students soon became frustrated because they felt that their Chinese roommates were not being open and honest and, worse yet, were being duplicitous. The students came to this conclusion because when they would ask their roommates' opinion about something, the roommates would respond, "We Chinese think . . ." What the students from the United States failed to realize was that they were asking an egocentric question ("What do *you* think?") in a sociocentric culture, and they were receiving a sociocentric response ("*We* Chinese think . . .") that they interpreted through their egocentric filter as being closed and duplicitous.

While we need to be careful not to overly essentialize cultures (i.e., assume that everyone from a particular culture is the same in their "essence"), understanding these foundational differences can aid us in understanding cross-cultural ethics. Reflecting on the findings of anthropological studies, Christian anthropologist Paul Hiebert states, "It became increasingly clear that people live not in the same world with different labels attached to it but in radically different conceptual worlds" (Hiebert 15). In addition, since almost all societies today are multicultural, we need not travel very far, if at all, to encounter these cultural differences. Thus, developing the tools to understand other value systems and ethical reasonings is crucial for Christians around the world.

Given the close proximity of cultural diversity, the question arises as to how Christians should respond to values of "good" and "bad" that might be quite different from their own. One approach is to assume that our ethics are scriptural and therefore absolute and universal, and all Christians, regardless of their cultural backgrounds, would have to agree if they are being biblical. The obvious problem with this approach is that Christians from other cultures, who also equate their ethical standards with those of Scripture, will interpret ethical issues in ways that reflect their cultural assumptions, just as ours do. In other words, our culture provides us with the framework to evaluate motivations for actions as well as how our actions may be interpreted by others. Anthropologist Richard Lee learned this lesson the hard way. He had been living among the Ju/wasi of the Kalahari, and since his research focused on the subsistence patterns of these hunter-gatherer people, he felt that he could not share with the local people any of the food he had brought. Lee knew that the Ju/wasi with whom he lived thought that he was stingy with his food, so at Christmas time he decided to buy a very large ox from local herders, have it butchered, and share it among the local residents. Much to his surprise, and shame, all of the Ju/wasi whom he talked with about the purchase and coming event belittled him for having bought such an old and scrawny animal. The ridicule was so great that Lee began questioning his own judgment: was this, in fact, a large and fat ox? What Lee eventually learned was that among the Ju/wasi, a largely egalitarian people, anyone who boasts of a big kill is "put in his place" to prevent such a person from thinking of himself as a "big man" or chief or seeing others as inferior. It is a way to try to maintain the ethic of equality. So although Lee saw his motivation as a desire to give back to the community that had allowed him to live among them and do his research, the local people, interpreting his action through their cultural lens of egalitarianism, saw it as boastfulness, which led to their cultural (ethical) response of publicly humiliating him.

Many years ago I was traveling through Turkey with two American companions when we stopped at a bank to exchange some money. While one of my friends was working on the transaction, my other companion and I sat on a small sofa with a coffee table in front of us and two chairs on the other side. Shortly after our arrival, a Turkish man came in and sat in one of the chairs across from us. As we were talking my friend put his foot on the edge of the coffee table, as some Americans are prone to do. Suddenly the Turkish gentleman stood up, said something to us in Turkish that we did not understand, and then proceeded to swat my friend's foot off of the table. We were dumbfounded. What had just happened? What had we done to merit, in our minds, such a violent act? As we discussed what happened, the best we could come up with using our own cultural understanding was that Turks must not like people putting their feet on furniture. A few days later, we learned that my friend's action was a grave insult to Turks and, it turns out, in many other cultures in various parts of the world. My friend had shown the Turk the bottom of his shoe. In those cultures this act conveys the meaning of something like, "You are worth less than the scum on the bottom of my shoe." We were also unaware that in Turkey, as in other parts of the world, there is a strong value of honor and shame, and a person or group will go to great lengths to maintain honor. What my friend had unknowingly done by showing this man the bottom of his shoe was challenge his honor, and by slapping my friend's foot off the table he was reestablishing it. Not every Turk would have reacted in this same way, but probably all Turks, based on their system of ethics, would have interpreted my friend's act as an insult.

One of the benefits of a cross-cultural approach to ethics is that it helps us to see our own values from a different perspective. Like the proverbial tip of the iceberg, most of our cultural meanings are below the surface of consciousness; they are implicit, taken for granted. Exposure to how people from other cultures give meaning to the world around them can help us to reflect more deeply on our own values in comparison. As a simple example, I recall my reaction when I went to cinemas in Brazil. Before the beginning of each movie there was a short film that played the Brazilian national anthem while showing scenes of the flag and other aspects of Brazilian nationalism. My initial reaction was that this demonstrated a chauvinistic patriotism that was completely inappropriate in a movie theater. However, as I reflected on this, I came to realize that we do the same thing in the United States. Before virtually every sporting event someone sings the national anthem while everyone in attendance stands, faces the flag, and many put their hands over their hearts to show fidelity to flag and country. Prior to my Brazilian experience I never gave this a second thought; it just seemed "natural" to me as the way sporting events began. But seeing this act in Brazil brought my own culture's practice to the surface and caused me to reflect on why we have such a practice and what it might convey to those not from our country. In other words, my cross-cultural experience helped me to take something familiar and view it as somewhat strange, whereas what I initially viewed as strange in Brazil became more familiar to me as I saw how it related to my own practices.

A more serious and difficult cross-cultural ethical issue is bribery. Westerners have a very difficult time with bribery and almost universally see it as an immoral and corrupt practice. On a recent visit to Africa, the president of the United States, Barack Obama, cited bribery (among other things) as an antidemocratic and tyrannical practice. But again, it depends on what we mean by "bribery" and what its purposes are. The OT, for example, condemns certain kinds of bribery—for example, that which is used to exploit or oppress the poor; however, in the OT bribery is condoned in other contexts—for example, as a means of establishing a relationship between two or more parties, and especially as a means of obtaining justice (Adeney; Noonan). As Bernard Adeney states, "A single perspective on bribery cannot be forced on the Bible, because different verses were written at different times for different contexts and different people" (Adeney 153). Likewise, the contemporary practice must be understood within its particular sociocultural context. In some countries "bribes" are considered part of civil servants' salary structure and are a necessary supplement to meet the basic needs of their families. Here again it might prove helpful to reflect on our own practice of tipping in the United States. We understand that waiters and waitresses typically are not paid well by the owners and so rely on tips from customers to supplement their salaries. Although we think nothing of paying 15 percent or more for service in a restaurant, many international students whom I have talked with view this as a form of extortion. Interestingly, these same students often come from countries where paying "bribes" is a natural part of everyday transactions. This is not to condone all forms of bribery, for many are considered quite wrong and corrupting in all societies, but only to point out that when it comes to understanding ethical issues in other cultures, we must carefully examine and understand the meaning that any given action has in its cultural context.

Given the complexity involved in cross-cultural ethics, how might a Christian effectively approach the subject? To understand ethics cross-culturally, it is necessary to have a good understanding of at least three cultural categories: the biblical, our own, and the one(s) we are crossing into. Of the three, the most important yet most difficult to understand will probably be our own because, as we have noted, so much is just implicitly understood. However, if we fail to get a good grasp of our cultural assumptions, we will be unable to accurately distinguish biblical ethical principles from our own, wrongly assuming the two to be identical. In addition, we will be able to view other cultural beliefs and actions only through the lens of our own interpretive framework, thereby applying ethnocentric meanings to the motivations and behaviors of others. One way to better understand our cultural assumptions is to learn how people from other cultures see us (Cooke; DeVita and Armstrong). Fundamentally, we must develop good hermeneutical skills in order to not only "rightly divide the word of truth" but also to correctly interpret the "good" and the "bad" in their cultural contexts.

See also Bribery; Colonialism and Postcolonialism; Culture; Ethnic Identity, Ethnicity; Moral Absolutes; Pluralism; Sociology of Religion

Bibliography

Adeney, B. *Strange Virtues: Ethics in a Multicultural World*. InterVarsity, 1995; Cooke, A. *Alistair Cooke's America*. Basic Books, 2009; DeVita, P., and J. Armstrong. *Distant Mirrors: America as a Foreign Culture*. Wadsworth, 2001; Geertz, C. *The Interpretation of Cultures: Selected Essays*. Basic Books, 1973; Hiebert, P. *Transforming Worldviews: An Anthropological Understanding of How People Change*. Baker Academic, 2008; Lee, R. "Eating Christmas in the Kalahari." *Natural History* 78, no. 10 (1969): 14–22; Noonan, J. *Bribes*. Macmillan, 1984; Robbins, R. *Cultural Anthropology: A Problem-Based Approach*. 4th ed. Thomson/Wadsworth, 2006; Spradley, J. *The Ethnographic Interview*. Holt, Rinehart & Winston, 1973; Tylor, E. *Primitive Culture*. Putnam, 1920 [1871].

Steven Ybarrola

Cruciformity

The word *cruciformity*, formed from *cruciform* ("cross-shaped") and *conformity*, means "conformity to Christ crucified." Cruciformity is the spiritual-ethical dimension of the theology of the cross found throughout the NT and the Christian tradition. Paradoxically, because the living Christ remains the crucified one, cruciformity is Spirit-enabled conformity to the indwelling crucified and resurrected Lord. It is therefore the activity of the triune God, reshaping all relationships and responsibilities to express the self-giving, life-giving love of God displayed on the cross. Thus, cruciformity is also theoformity, or becoming like God. Although it often includes suffering, at its heart cruciformity, like the cross, is about faithfulness and love.

Several OT motifs anticipate NT cruciformity, especially the call to be "holy as I am holy" and the pattern of humiliation and exaltation quintessentially embodied in God's servant (Isa. 53). Such themes become explicitly cruciform in the call of Jesus, grounded in his own example and epitomized in Dietrich Bonhoeffer's famous words, "When Christ calls a person, he bids them come and die." In the Synoptic Gospels, Jesus summons disciples to a life of "taking up their cross" (Mark 8:34 pars.), analogous to his death. It consists of self-denial—losing oneself as the path to finding oneself—in witness to the gospel; hospitality to the weak and marginalized, represented by children; and service to others rather than domination (Mark 8:31–37; 9:31–37; 10:32–45 pars.), all with the possibility of suffering (Mark 13:9–13 pars.). The image of a servant/slave is captured by John's Gospel in the vivid story of Jesus washing the disciples' feet, a parable of Jesus' death and a summons to similar acts of loving service (John 13:1–17, 31–35). The community is empowered by the indwelling Christ—that is, by the Spirit—to perform deeds of love and to endure hatred and suffering (John 14:15–16:33).

Cruciformity is most fully developed by Paul as a narrative spirituality with an inherent dynamic deriving from the story of Christ (Phil. 2:6–11). The basic cruciform pattern is "although [x] not [y] but [z]," where [x] refers to status, [y] to selfish exploitation, and [z] to self-giving concern for others. Christ displayed his identity as the embodiment of God's self-giving, life-giving love in his incarnation (2 Cor. 8:9; Phil. 2:7) and death (Rom.

15:3; Phil. 2:8). The presence of Christ, by the Spirit, empowers believers to fulfill Jesus' threefold call: bearing faithful witness even to the point of suffering (Phil. 1:12–30; 1 Thess. 1:2–8; 3:1–10); identifying with the weak as an expression of God's cruciform wisdom and power (Rom. 15:1–2; 1 Cor. 1:18–2:5); and seeking the benefit of others rather than self (1 Cor. 8:1; 10:23–11:1; 13:5; Phil. 2:1–5, 25–30). This is a community ethic, in which all are cared for even as all forgo their own special interests. Cruciformity is ultimately a spirituality of hope because the pattern of Jesus, from suffering/death to resurrection/glorification, is also the metapattern for believers and indeed all creation (Rom. 8:17–39; 2 Cor. 4:16–18; Phil. 2:6–11; 3:21).

For ministers of the gospel, the cruciform imperative is intensified. Paul sees manual labor, physical and emotional suffering, adaptability, and nondominating power as analogous to the story of Christ and as worthy of imitation, especially by apostles (1 Cor. 9; 11:1; 2 Cor. 11:1–12:10; 1 Thess. 2:7–12). Cruciform ministry is life-giving for others (2 Cor. 4:8–15).

Elsewhere in the NT, cruciformity appears with special emphasis on faithfulness in suffering. The church's model of courage, nonretaliation, and hope is Jesus the high priest and pioneer (Heb. 12:1–3), the unblemished lamb and suffering servant (1 Pet. 1:18–23; 2:19–25; 3:8–17; 4:12–5:11), the faithful witness and Lamb of God (Rev. 1:5; 2:10, 13; 5:12–13; 7:9–17).

Objections to cruciformity take two forms: charges of inappropriateness and of inadequacy. The former is a response to interpretations of cruciformity that are unhealthily individualistic, masochistic, and/or unequally applied to women. The latter leads some to propose "Christoformity" to supplement or replace cruciformity. However, cruciformity is a communal, life-giving, and egalitarian spirituality; moreover, it never requires the neglect of other christological themes (incarnation, earthly ministry). It simply means that the cross is central and definitive.

See also Imitation of Jesus; Kingdom of God; New Testament Ethics

Bibliography

Bonhoeffer, D. *Discipleship*. Augsburg Fortress, 2001; Ehrensperger, K. *Paul and the Dynamics of Power: Communication and Interaction in the Early Christ-Movement*. T&T Clark, 2007. Gorman, M. *Cruciformity: Paul's Narrative Spirituality of the Cross*. Eerdmans, 2001; idem. *Inhabiting the Cruciform God: Kenosis, Justification, and Theosis in Paul's Narrative Soteriology*. Eerdmans, 2009; Hays, R. *The Moral Vision of the New Testament: Community, Cross, and New Creation; A Contemporary Introduction to New Testament Ethics*. HarperSanFrancisco, 1996; Moltmann, J. *The Crucified God: The Cross of Christ as the Foundation and Criticism of Christian Theology*. Fortress, 1993; Yoder, J. *The Politics of Jesus: Vicit Agnus Noster*. 2nd ed. Eerdmans, 1994.

Michael J. Gorman

Cruelty

Cruelty occurs when human beings willfully violate the vulnerability of sentient creatures through the wanton infliction of suffering. The English word *cruelty* derives from the Latin *cruor*, denoting gore or spilled blood, suggesting that a primary dimension of cruelty is found in physical abuses. Yet there are many nonphysical forms of cruelty, such as emotional, mental, psychological, and spiritual cruelty. Each modifier points to specific aspects of the self that can be harmed, a reminder of the profound vulnerability of every dimension of creaturely life.

Cruelty's moral affront cuts most deeply when its wantonness and the vulnerability of its victims are most obvious, as when a child is victimized for sport. Cruelty at its worst is undertaken for its own sake, for the perverse pleasure of causing suffering. Here cruelty connects quite profoundly to degradation; the victim is degraded by victimization, the perpetrator degraded by abandoning human decency. Power relations are also an inescapable factor in cruelty, as its victims normally are powerless in relation to their victimizers.

Both international and United States law ban "cruel, inhuman, and degrading treatment" of those detained in war. The combination is significant. Cruelty is by definition inhuman and degrading; it falls short of the behavior that human beings should either undertake or suffer and thus marks a diminishment of human dignity.

Cruelty unexpectedly became a prominent issue in American life during the administration of President George W. Bush (2001–9) in relation to the detention and interrogation policies employed in the "war on terror." Binding domestic and international obligations were rejected or redefined in an effort to extract information from prisoners by using harsh, previously banned interrogation strategies. The sordid details of what occurred reaffirmed for many moral and legal analysts that the legitimate "ends" of national security cannot justify any and every "means" of detention and interrogation, and that the United States must recommit to avoiding cruelty in its security policies. This example also suggests that an act can be considered cruel even if significant reasons can be offered to justify it.

The Bible is sometimes accused of permitting or even mandating cruelty, as in texts authorizing and describing holy war against the Canaanites (e.g., Josh. 8:10–29), as well as some of the more imaginative forms of suffering for enemies described in the imprecatory psalms (e.g., Ps. 137:8–9). God's wrath against the church's enemies is anticipated vividly in Revelation, including unforgettable images of torment (Rev. 18–20).

Yet there are also moral teachings in Scripture that forbid the doing of harm, especially to the most vulnerable, such as widows and orphans (Exod. 22:22), children (Matt. 18:6), the physically infirm (Lev. 19:14), and animals (Prov. 12:10). The Bible's central commands to love and do justice constitute the antithesis of cruelty, Jesus' cruel crucifixion absorbs and negates cruelty, and the early church became known for its stark rejection of the cruelty common to the Greco-Roman world.

See also Abuse; Authority and Power; Ends and Means; Evil; Holy War; Humanitarianism; Human Rights; Sanctity of Human Life; Suffering; Torture; Violence

Bibliography

Baumeister, R. *Evil: Inside Human Cruelty and Violence*. W. H. Freeman, 1999; Hallie, P. *Cruelty*. Wesleyan University Press, 1982.

David P. Gushee

Culture

Culture is a more or less integrated system of knowledge, values, and feelings that people use to define reality (worldview), interpret their experiences, and generate appropriate strategies for living; a way of living that people learn from others around them and share with others; the means by which people are able to adapt to their spiritual, social, and physical environments; and the resource from which people draw to innovate as their environments change.

For most anthropologists, following the lead of the symbolic, structuralist, and ethnosemantic schools, culture is not behavior but rather a particular organization of symbols, categories, and concepts that give meaning to the world. In the history of interpretation of Scripture, culture often is reduced to "customs" as if only a few odd bits of behavior separated people, and frequently dismissed as "evil" if those rituals and practices diverge from the perspective of the writer. However, the notions of culture, ethnocentrism, and relativity are present in nascent form in Scripture.

Several questions arise concerning the use of Scripture for ethics. The first is whether Scripture is authoritative for ethical decision-making, given the variety of cultural contexts in Scripture, the cultural distance between Scripture and the reader, and the bewildering cultural variety among contemporary Christian communities that might want to access Scripture for moral guidance. The second question is, if Scripture does have relevance for contemporary ethical questions, how is Scripture to be accessed? The third question is, who is in a position to access Scripture for a particular community?

A reading from a cultural standpoint reveals the source of culture in the blessings and activities of God in the first chapters of Genesis. There God creates, separates, and evaluates—three activities that are at the base of cultural differences (Douglas). God spends a lot of time naming things and then invites Adam to name things too. The establishment of categories of things is followed by economic, political, legal, and ritual provisions: eat this food, have dominion, do not eat this, walk with me. God presages ethics by declaring that "this is good" but that something else "is not good." God creates difference, an "other" with just enough similarity to be recognized but just enough difference to be interesting. Finally, God establishes rules for things such as marriage and residence, "Therefore a man leaves his father and his mother and clings to his wife, and they become one flesh" (Gen. 2:24), as well as other rules of conduct, "Of the tree of the knowledge of good and evil you shall not eat" (Gen. 2:17).

God has a consistent command throughout Scripture: "Be fruitful and multiply, fill the earth . . . and be a blessing wherever you go." This leads to linguistic and thus cultural diversity (Gen. 10), though the humans resist (Gen. 11:1–9). Israel receives the same instructions (Gen. 12:2; Jer. 29:4–7), as does the church (Acts 1:8; cf. Acts 8:1–4). However, there is always reluctance to bless an enemy (book of Jonah) or to consider others as part of the family of God (Isa. 19:24). Although there is evidence that the Israelites are typical people of the land with Palestinian customs, the rhetoric that contrasts the customs of the Israelites with the customs of the nations is sharp in the historical narratives and is even more acute in the Apocrypha, where the practices of the Greeks are dubbed as "strange customs."

The contest between cultures (*ethos* in the Greek NT) continues in the critique of the practices of Jesus (Matt. 9:3; Mark 2:24; Luke 23:2) and Paul (Acts 16:21; 18:13; 21:21) and creates a major problem for the early church (Acts 15). Is the good news rooted in Hebrew culture so that it can grow only in that context, or is it possible to plant the gospel in Greco-Roman culture so that a gentile Christianity might emerge? More simply, gentiles asked, "Do we have to become Jews in order to become followers of Christ?"

Many of Paul's letters wrestle with ethical issues rooted in cultural differences. In the issue of eating meat that has been sacrificed to idols, each side claims to know what the rule is. Paul reminds his readers in Corinth, "Knowledge puffs up, but love builds up. Anyone who claims to know something does not yet have the necessary knowledge" (1 Cor. 8:1–2). Instead of making a ruling, Paul handles each case separately, and he appeals for all to submit to the formation of the community of the king, Jesus Christ.

Writing to the issue of cultural differences over what food to eat and what day to celebrate, Paul even reaches a point resembling cultural relativity: "Let us therefore no longer pass judgment on one another, but resolve instead never to put a stumbling block or hindrance in the way of another. I know and am persuaded in the Lord Jesus that nothing is unclean in itself; but it is unclean for anyone who thinks it unclean" (Rom. 14:13–14).

But the "culture wars" were far from over (Gal. 2:1–21). The tension between establishing a separate community (a peculiar people) and proclaiming the gospel to all was played out as Christianity moved from one culture to another.

Eugene Nida called Paul's position, that "nothing is unclean in itself, but is unclean for anyone who thinks it unclean," "relative cultural relativity" because Paul was not operating in a vacuum (Nida 282). Paul wrote to a community committed to Christ. Some have interpreted "commitment to Christ" as agreement with a set of principles that exist as absolutes outside of culture, but others doubt that such principles even exist (Adeney 265n6). This reveals two fundamentally different approaches to Scripture and the contextualization of the gospel.

Toward one end of the continuum are those who believe that absolutes are what Scripture says, and that absolutes can be generalized from scriptural prohibitions. Toward the other end are those who believe that it is story (narrative) and not propositions that carries the message of Scripture, and that there is no such thing as a pure gospel without cultural trappings. On the latter account, all we have are examples of the gospel transforming specific cultures. Thus, in ethical reasoning, one does not work out principles and propositions to follow, but rather one learns to inhabit the stories of Scripture in order to live out of them into one's social settings.

The classic work on the relationship between the gospel and culture is H. Richard Niebuhr's *Christ and Culture*, in which he established five ideal types: Christ against culture, the Christ of culture, Christ above culture, Christ and culture in paradox, and Christ the transformer of culture. The simplicity of the categories that Niebuhr used and the arguments he expounded can be criticized, but the approach continues to frame the current "culture wars" or perceived opposition between gospel and culture. Followers of Lesslie Newbigin founded the Gospel and Our Culture network (gocn.org), which, among other things, continues the debate about the relationship between gospel and culture.

But is it really a contest? Kathryn Tanner avers that cultural creativity and diversity are subsumed in the unity of the theological task or mission (Tanner 152–57). That is, it is possible to be Christian only within a certain cultural context and against certain cultural others. Thus, culture is necessary to communicate the gospel and the medium in which the gospel grows and takes shape. The question is when to affirm culture, when to confront culture, and how the gospel transforms (in a deeper sense than Niebuhr meant) culture.

The question on the mission field, and perhaps in the congregation, is not whether the gospel will exist within culture, but rather whose culture will carry the gospel. In ethical matters it is the local congregation within a specific culture that is in a position, with the guidance of the Holy Spirit, to define ethical issues, including the definition of sin (Dye). Local elders, perhaps with the assistance of the missionary, work with Scripture to build a hermeneutic bridge: discover the story, place it in the larger context of Scripture, discern the meaning, translate the meaning into their situation, and work back down again to the issue on the ground. This is the equivalent of dynamic equivalence translation, but done with ethical issues.

Bernard Adeney provides an example. "You shall not boil a kid in its mother's milk" (Exod. 23:19), taken at a literal level, might not be a difficult ethical injunction for people who do not eat sheep or goats. But, raising the issue up a hermeneutic layer, we find that this text is an injunction against a magical fertility rite common in ancient Canaanite religions (Adeney 81). Sorcery is an intentional attack on an individual and on the formal structure of society. We have built half of the bridge. The theological task is to bring the injunction down to an ethical imperative that makes sense in the local culture. It could be an injunction against sorcery or one against gossip that tears at the fabric of society.

It is this method of case studies that led anthropology to develop a code of ethics for fieldwork (Rynkiewich and Spradley) and that should be, along with living in the story, at the heart of Christian ethics for the local congregation or mission field (Wolfe and Gudorf).

See also Colonialism and Postcolonialism; Cross-Cultural Ethics; Discernment, Moral; Ethnic Identity, Ethnicity; Moral Absolutes

Bibliography

Adeney, B. *Strange Virtues: Ethics in a Multicultural World*. InterVarsity, 1995; Clifford, J. *The Predicament of Culture: Twentieth-Century Ethnography, Literature, and Art*. Harvard University Press, 1988; Douglas, M. *Purity and Danger: An Analysis of the Concepts of Pollution and Taboo*. Routledge, 1966; Dye, W. "Toward a Cross-Cultural Definition of Sin." *Missiology* 4 (1980): 27–41; Geertz, C. *The Interpretation of Cultures: Selected Essays*. Harvard University Press, 1988; Newbigin, L. *The Gospel in a Pluralist Society*. Eerdmans, 1989; Nida, E. *Customs, Culture and Christianity*. Harper, 1954; Niebuhr, H. R. *Christ and Culture*. Harper, 1951; Rynkiewich, M., and J. Spradley, eds. *Ethics and Anthropology: Dilemmas in Fieldwork*. Wiley, 1976; Tanner, K. *Theories of Culture: A New Agenda for Theology*. Fortress, 1997; Wolfe, R., and C. Gudorf, eds. *Ethics and World Religions: Cross-Cultural Case Studies*. Orbis, 1999.

Michael A. Rynkiewich

Cursing *See* Speech Ethics

D

Daniel

As war captives exiled to the court of Babylon, Daniel, Azariah, Hananiah, and Mishael are chosen for service to the conquering king, trained in Babylonian sciences, and given new names (1:3–7). Yet they abstain from the king's food and wine, relying for sustenance not on imperial patronage but on divine providence (1:8–16). Six stories portray their trials and success (chaps. 1–6). God grants them wisdom (1:17; 2:19–23) as they rise to power (2:46–49; 3:30; 5:29; 6:4, 29). Daniel interprets dreams, solves riddles, and speaks hard truth to raging, proud, and drunken kings (chaps. 2; 4; 5). The heroes give their bodies over to death rather than worship the king's idol (chap. 3) or abandon the practice of prayer (chap. 6). God delivers them (3:25–29; 6:23).

Symbolic visions follow (chaps. 7–12): a parade of beastly empires, exposing the monstrosity of warring and rapacious kings who deal out deception and death; the fiery throne of the Ancient of Days; judgment against the beastly empires; and eternal dominion given to one like a human being (chap. 7); and future persecution, when some will betray the covenant while wise teachers of Judea fall to sword and flame (11:30–36). By their witness and self-sacrifice these teachers will make the many righteous and wise (11:33–35; 12:3). The angel Michael will take his stand in this anguished time to set the faithful free (12:1). Many of the dead will rise: some to eternal life, others to eternal disgrace (12:2).

The visions were written and joined to the stories during this persecution. In 167 BCE the Seleucid king Antiochus IV Epiphanes, ruler over Judea, banned the practice of Jewish faith, commanding Jews to sacrifice on alien altars, eat defiling foods, and profane their holy days and sanctuary. He burned Torah scrolls. Those who refused his commands he killed (1 Macc. 1).

In response, the book of Daniel promotes an ethic of nonviolent resistance and civil disobedience. Its politics is theopolitics, viewing all human rule in the light of divine rule. Daniel's critique of empire highlights its violence, greed, ambition, and deception. The vision of one like a human being promises the alternative of humane rule in which God's holy people participate in and imitate the justice of God's rule (7:13–14, 18, 27). The author's belief in God's deliverance and confidence in their angelic champions excluded the path of armed resistance. Instead, the book exhorts its readers to hold fast to the covenant and give public witness to truth even in the face of death.

Daniel is the first biblical book to articulate a belief in the resurrection of the dead, assuring its readers that God honors the covenant promises even when appearances say otherwise. God's faithfulness encourages their own. At the same time, when faced with the choice between worshiping an idol to preserve their life or dying in faithful service to God, the heroes Shadrach, Meshach, and Abednego (here called by their Babylonian names) give no consideration to outcomes (3:15–18). They do not need to believe that God will save them in order to do what is right.

The ethics of the book of Daniel draws on Israel's sacred traditions, including the Torah of Moses and the prophets (9:6–13). Daniel himself consults the scroll of Jeremiah (9:2); the author identified the wise teachers with Isaiah's suffering servant. Traditional prayers of penitence modeled appropriate confession of sins (9:3–21). Myths of the divine warrior who defeats the beasts of chaos and death provided a powerful symbolic framework for critiquing the empires and asserting God's power and will to save (chap. 7). At the same time, the book of Daniel draws on and engages traditions from other cultures. Israel adapted the divine warrior myths from Canaanite tradition. Daniel recasts the Babylonian art of interpreting dreams, drawing it within the purview of God's revelation. The apocalyptic worldview so central to the book's moral vision similarly adapts elements from Persian and Babylonian religious traditions. The visionary critique of empire borrows techniques from prophetic resistance literature elsewhere in the Hellenistic world. The multiple sources of Daniel's moral vision testify to a dynamic process of acculturation, affirming the authority of Israel's native traditions while speaking a new authoritative word into a new cultural moment.

The book of Daniel's activist stance demands engagement with the powers of the earth. While the visions engage in radical critique of empire, aiming to position the faithful outside its web of deception, the stories show the heroes enmeshed in imperial structures of power. They serve in the courts of Babylon, exercise rule, and accept the king's patronage. They participate in the moral economy of the empire and speak their critique from within. What is empire today? Does the contemporary reader stand inside or outside? How does one defend against royal and self-deception in the exercise of power?

Finally, how do those who seek to actualize Daniel's theopolitics, as many have done, avoid reinscribing structures of domination? Over the centuries, Daniel has been used to demonize nations, regimes, and religious traditions, fanning hatred and fueling violence among those who would inaugurate the eternal rule of Daniel's holy ones. The book's nonviolent ethic, recognition of our complicity in the imperial economy, and emphasis on a posture of humble penitence speak against such interpretations. Its call to martyrdom challenges believers in every age.

See also Colonialism and Postcolonialism; Eschatology and Ethics; Exile; 1 Maccabees; 2 Maccabees; Martyrdom; Old Testament Ethics; Pacifism; Powers and Principalities; Resurrection; Theocracy

Bibliography

Barton, J. "Theological Ethics in Daniel." Pages 661–70 in *The Book of Daniel: Composition and Reception*, vol. 2, ed. J. Collins and P. Flint. Brill, 2002; Fewell, D. *Circle of Sovereignty: Plotting Politics in the Book of Daniel*. Abingdon, 1991; Goldingay, J. "Daniel in the Context of Old Testament Theology." Pages 639–60 in *The Book of Daniel: Composition and Reception*, vol. 2, ed. J. Collins and P. Flint. Brill, 2002; Pace, S. *Daniel*. SHBC. Smyth & Helwys, 2008; Rowland, C. "The Book of Daniel and the Radical Critique of Empire. An Essay in Apocalyptic Hermeneutics." Pages 447–67 in *The Book of Daniel: Composition and Reception*, vol. 2, ed. J. Collins and P. Flint. Brill, 2002; Smith-Christopher, D. "The Book of Daniel." Pages 19–152 in *The New Interpreter's Bible*, vol. 7, ed. L. Keck. Abingdon, 1996.

Anathea Portier-Young

Deadly Sins *See* Seven Deadly Sins

Dead Sea Scrolls

Between the years 1946 and 1956, the caves near the Dead Sea surrendered nearly nine hundred scrolls dating from the period 150 BCE–70 CE. Of these scrolls, 222 were of biblical and apocryphal materials, and 670 were of a nonbiblical nature. The nonbiblical materials contain treatises, hymns, and commentaries on Scripture that are sectarian in origin and character, as well as some nonsectarian and presectarian materials. The consensus view holds that the Jewish sect of the Essenes, or some subset of the Essenes, lived in the nearby installation at Qumran as a priestly introversionist community and produced the scrolls as a critique of larger Second Temple Judaism, though this view has been subject to revision or outright rejection in some quarters. Sectarian works from the Dead Sea Scrolls include the *Damascus Document* (CD), which may be a narrative of the community's formation that tells of the coming of the Teacher of Righteousness and the community's self-imposed exile to "Damascus" or the Dead Sea wilderness. It also provides codes of everyday conduct for members who appear to live in scattered towns. The *Rule of the Community* (1QS being the most complete copy of the document) is a guide for the community's leader, the *Maskil*, on how to form sectarian character. Its codes of admission and conduct assume that its readers are males living communally (and perhaps celibately) with other males. A key portion of this document, the "Two Spirits Treatise" (1QS 3.13–4.26), describes the ongoing battle between two angels and their followers: the Prince of Light and the children of righteousness versus the Angel of Darkness and the children of injustice. Both of these warring angels were created by God. Other important sectarian documents include legal works such as the *Halakhic Letter* (4QMMT), which describes explicit differences between the sect of the temple cult on issues of purity; the *War Scroll* (1QM); the *Hodayot*, or thanksgiving hymns; and a commentary (pesher) on Habakkuk (1QpHab), which reinterprets Habakkuk in light of the conflict between the Teacher of Righteousness and the Wicked Priest (the high priest of the Jerusalem temple cult?).

The *Rule of the Community* expresses the ethical desideratum of the community to be that of seeking God wholeheartedly and doing what is just according to the divine commandments mediated by Moses and the prophets (1QS 1.1–3). This would seem to establish the Torah as the source for moral knowledge and deliberation. This is not an especially distinctive articulation of ethical thinking within early Judaism, but the *Rule of the Community* and other sectarian documents from the Dead Sea Scrolls define and nuance this ethical ideal in distinctive ways.

The community associated with the Dead Sea Scrolls understands the Torah to be a divinely revealed and rigorous code of covenantal demands rather than a divinely revealed narrative of Israel's origins. Narrative and story are not the chief means of character formation in the scrolls. Instead, the community prides itself on its unique ability and authority, over and against common readings of mainstream Judaism, to interpret the Torah commands according to the divine plan. This divine plan for humanity features a profoundly dualistic view of the cosmos and created order in which God has created both good and evil angels who fight for the hearts of humanity. Even the members of the community are subject to both angels, but sectarian formation is designed to strengthen the power of the righteous angel within each member.

The scrolls indicate a complex view of human virtue and character. Sectarian discourse explicitly valorizes the qualities of obedience to the covenant, moral and ritual purity, humility to the point of self-abnegation, intelligence, discreet concealment of God's mysterious plan, and hatred of the "sons of darkness" (1QS 1.1–7a; 4.3–5; 10.1–11:22). These virtues, however, are not personal; they are not a matter of individual disposition or choices. They result from the confluence of external forces, including the rivalry of the angelic forces, the divine election of the individual, and the community environment and its discipline that nurtures these virtues (Newsom). Moreover, although the individual is accountable for deeds and actions and subject to reproof, the *Rule of the Community* does not value a morally autonomous self. The self is to be submissive and receptive. The member's ability to be obedient, however, is the result of, on the one hand, God's previous allotment of the two angels within the member and, on the other hand, God's eschatological provision of a spirit of holiness, which has already been realized, in part, within the community.

This distinctive articulation of covenant ideals underwrites particular issues of ethical practice in the sectarian documents. A stringent dedication to moral and ritual purity characterizes the sectarian writings and demands the separation of the community from outsiders and their contaminated items. Outsiders include not only foreigners but also Jews not belonging to the sect—that is, all those belonging to common Judaism. This radical principle of purity goes hand in hand with the cosmic dualism of the sect and leads the community to fear and avoid others and to anticipate their destruction at the eschaton. Thus restorative justice and a concern for "the other" are not among the ethical norms of the community. Nevertheless, certain scrolls indicate the circumstances under which "the stranger" or the resident alien may become part of the community, though the resident alien is never permitted full status (Harrington).

The use of wealth and assets is a recurring theme in the sectarian and presectarian scrolls and is tied to the ideal of "covenantal fidelity" (Murphy). Both the *Damascus Document* and the *Rule of the Community* critique the economic systems of Second Temple Judaism that fostered wealth and arrogance. These documents suggest that the community was to be an alternative economic community where usury was prohibited and resources were distributed to help the poor and needy within the group in accordance with the demands of Torah. The Torah laws concerning wealth and tithes are also reinterpreted and extended. For example, the command of Deut. 6:5 to "love God with all one's strength" is understood to mean that members are to give all of their assets—property, wealth, food—to the entire community.

Marriage practices are also a concern of the sectarian materials, which resist and denounce polygamy for the sake of gaining wealth and discourage divorce. Marriage with foreign women is denounced for reasons of purity.

The contents of the *War Scroll* raise the question of whether the scrolls view war and violence as legitimate tools in the cause of purity and covenant fidelity. Certainly, there were groups within Second Temple Judaism that conceptually and actively embraced the use of physical violence for political ends, yet the view of the sectarians remains ambiguous. The *War Scroll* describes an eschatological holy war between angelic factions—the sons of light and the sons of darkness—and understands that humans will participate in this battle, at the end of which enemy factions (including the Romans) will be utterly destroyed. Moreover, this battle, which draws on "holy war" traditions, serves the purpose of ensuring the purity and righteousness of the children of light in accordance with Torah commands. Yet this battle remains future. So although the community embraced the concept of war and violence, even divine violence, as legitimate tools, the community that lived at Qumran did not necessarily directly engage in the war against the Romans that took place during the 60s CE (Elliott).

The ethical ideals of the scrolls are often important for the way in which they shed light on NT and early Christian convictions and practices such as communal property and the distribution of resources to benefit those in need (see Acts 2:42–47; 4:32–37). More generally, the sectarian attempts to build an alternative community raise for the reader's consideration both the moral promises and the problems that inhere in any radical community's attempt to resist the dominant culture of its time.

See also Covenant; Divine Command Theories of Ethics; Eschatology and Ethics; Free Will and Determinism; Holy War; Koinonia; Narrative Ethics, Biblical; Priestly Literature

Bibliography

Elliott, M. "Retribution and Agency in the Dead Sea Scrolls and the Teaching of Jesus." Pages 191–206 in vol. 1 of *The Destructive Power of Religion: Violence in Judaism, Christianity, and Islam*, ed. J. Ellens. Praeger, 2004; Harrington, H. "Keeping Outsiders Out: Impurity at Qumran." Pages 187–203 in *Defining Identities: We, You, and the Other in the Dead Sea Scrolls*, ed. F. García Martínez and M. Popović. Brill, 2008; Murphy, C. *Wealth in the Dead Sea Scrolls and in the Qumran Community*. Brill, 2002; Newsom, C. *The Self as Symbolic Space: Constructing Identity and Community at Qumran*. Brill, 2004; Smith, B. "'Spirit of Holiness' as Eschatological Principle of Obedience." Pages 75–99 in *Christian Beginnings and the Dead Sea Scrolls*, ed. J. Collins and C. Evans. Baker Academic, 2006; VanderKam, J., and P. Flint. *The Meaning of the Dead Sea Scrolls: Their Significance for Understanding the Bible, Judaism, Jesus, and Christianity*. HarperSanFrancisco, 2004.

Amy C. Merrill Willis

Death, Definition of

Although death gives the appearance of finality, its definition is problematic because it reflects a complex interplay of social, professional, and ethical forces. Over the centuries, new scientific discoveries in resuscitation, suspended animation, and experimental physiology have played crucial roles in contributing to the uncertainties associated with the definition of death. Conventional attempts to describe death as "when the soul leaves the body" presuppose a dualistic view of human beings and sit uneasily alongside the notion of embodied personhood.

Prior to the advent of sophisticated technologies of rescue and intensive care in the 1960s, patients were declared dead when breathing and cardiac activity had stopped, on the grounds that failure of this single vital organ system led to death of the entire organism. However, once the technology became available to maintain these functions artificially, a clearly defined boundary between life and death disappeared. This, in turn, raised the intensely practical issue of when life-sustaining treatment should be discontinued—a matter of considerable relevance for grieving relatives and those involved in managing the distribution of scarce resources for intensive care. In addition, the advent of organ transplantation and, with it, the need for viable, intact organs from cadavers necessitated a precise determination of when death occurs. Since dependence on cardiac activity no longer served this purpose, an alternative had to be found, and this led to the elaboration of brain-based criteria of death.

Brain death was first described in 1959 as *coma dépassé* (a state beyond coma). The concept of brain death is now widely accepted and is entrenched in legislation and practice guidelines in most countries (Ad Hoc Committee of the Harvard Medical School to Examine the Definition of Brain Death; Conference of Medical Royal Colleges and Their Faculties in the United Kingdom).

In 1981 a core document, *Defining Death*, established the central significance of brain death while not abandoning cardiopulmonary criteria of death. According to this document, "An individual who has sustained either (1) irreversible cessation of the circulatory and respiratory functions, or (2) irreversible cessation of all functions of the entire brain, including the brain stem, is dead" (President's Commission for the Study of Ethical Problems in Medicine and Biomedical and Behavioral Research 2). As the concept of brain death has been developed, two definitions have emerged.

The longer-standing and more generally accepted definition is "whole-brain death." This refers to death of all parts of the brain: the cerebral hemispheres (the brain's higher centers responsible for consciousness and higher cognitive functions) and the brain stem (the lower part of the brain responsible for maintaining most of the homeostatic functions essential for life). Confirmation is provided by a flat electroencephalogram (EEG), with absence of circulation to the brain as an important criterion. Such a patient is dead, whether or not there is maintenance of function of some organs, such as the heart, by artificial means.

The "whole brain" definition of death is a biological concept of death, in the sense that there is no material difference between the death of a dog, cat, or human being. Generally accepted as this definition is, debate still surrounds it because death of the brain does not mark the irreversible loss of the integrated functioning of the various subsystems and hence may not signify death of the whole organism. However, it is difficult to see why an individual is considered to be alive simply because that individual is "breathing" with the aid of a respirator.

More recently, a second definition has emerged, "higher-brain death," marking death of the cerebral hemispheres even when the brain stem continues to function. An individual in this state has lost the capacity for consciousness and the ability to think, feel, and be aware of others, but can still breathe.

The practical significance of this debate comes to a head when confronted by patients in a persistent vegetative state (PVS), which is the clinical manifestation of higher-brain death. The patient is wakeful and yet not aware (Royal College of Physicians), retaining an irregular sleep/wake cycle and many basic reflexes, but without any self-awareness or recognition of external stimuli. Nutritional support can preserve multiple organ systems in the PVS patient but cannot restore the patient to conscious life. In this sense, no treatment is available for these patients, although there are a few cases in the literature of limited recovery of mental functioning. Such cases appear to be rare, and the pressing ethical question is considered to be whether the patient as a person is alive in any meaningful sense. If not, should all forms of medical treatment, including hydration and nutrition, which are keeping the body functioning, be withdrawn? In adult PVS patients such termination is accepted by a variety of medical societies and interdisciplinary bodies after an agreed period of time, generally six to twelve months or longer. Appropriate consent by the families is essential, as is a definitive clinical diagnosis of PVS (American Academy of Neurology; British Medical Association; Royal College of Physicians).

To date, advocacy of the "higher brain" definition is limited to academic scholars; it has not been approved by any medical society and has not been adopted into law in any country or jurisdiction. Nevertheless, it raises penetrating questions about what it means to be alive as a human being, whether the notion of personhood is one that should be taken into account in ethical decision-making, and focuses attention on the qualities that make us persons.

The major contrast between the "whole brain" and "higher brain" definitions of death is an emphasis on the loss of bodily integration in the former case, and a loss of consciousness in the latter. Debate centers on whether the most fitting emphasis is the irreversible loss of bodily capacities in general, or the irreversible loss of specified capacities characteristic of the personal life of human beings (Bernat).

The theological contribution to this debate has been muted. The rabbinic tradition lends greatest support to a definition of death as indicated by the absence of breath at the nostrils, though an alternative position requires both the absence of respiration and cardiac activity. The emphasis on breath as determinative is supported by reference to Gen. 7:22 ("all in whose nostrils was the breath of the spirit of life" [NASB]) and is allied with the acceptance of whole-brain death as a form of physiological decapitation (Rosner). The focus on the brain rather than the heart poses challenges for Christian thinking, as does the role given to personhood in ethical decision-making. Never before have we had to think about the status of a living body in the absence of a living brain. For Christians, this focuses attention on what it means to be, and/or to function, in the image of God and demands an analysis of this issue far beyond anything previously undertaken.

See also Death and Dying; Dependent Care; Euthanasia; Healthcare Ethics; Quality of Life; Science and Ethics

Bibliography

Ad Hoc Committee of the Harvard Medical School to Examine the Definition of Brain Death. "A Definition of Irreversible Coma." *JAMA* 205 (1968): 337–40; American Academy of Neurology. "Position Statement on Laws and Regulations Concerning Life-Sustaining Treatment, Including Artificial Nutrition and Hydration, for Patients Lacking Decision-Making Capacity." *Neurology* 68 (2007): 1097–1100; Bernat, J. "A Defense of the Whole-Brain Concept of Death." *HCR* 28, no. 2 (1998): 14–23; British Medical Association. *Withholding and Withdrawing Life-Prolonging Medical Treatment: Guidance for Decision Making*. 3rd ed. British Medical Association, 2007; Conference of Medical Royal Colleges and Their Faculties in the UK. "Diagnosis of Death." *BMJ* 1, no. 6159 (1979): 332; President's Commission for the Study of Ethical Problems in Medicine and Biomedical and Behavioral Research. *Defining Death: Medical, Legal and Ethical Issues in the Determination of Death*. Government Printing Office, 1981; Rosner, F. "The Definition of Death in Jewish Law." Pages 210–21 in *The Definition of Death: Contemporary Controversies*, ed. S. Youngner, R. Arnold, and R. Schapiro. Johns Hopkins University Press, 1999; Royal College of Physicians. "The Vegetative State: Guidance on Diagnosis and Management." Royal College of Physicians, 2003.

D. Gareth Jones

Death and Dying

Death is the process by which the natural body ceases to function physically. The term *death* has been used medically in somewhat different ways over the course of the last several decades. Traditionally, death was determined by the cessation of the heart. Medical advances over the course of the past century have led to debate over how to define death.

The Uniform Determination of Death Act (UDDA) of 1980 states, "An individual who has sustained either (1) irreversible cessation of circulatory and respiratory functions, or (2) irreversible cessation of all functions of the entire brain, including the brain stem, is dead." It further states that a determination of death must follow accepted medical standards. The UDDA was adopted by the American Medical Association in 1980, the American Bar Association in 1981, and subsequently adopted by a majority of states in the United States.

Since the UDDA, there has been much discussion as to how death should clinically be understood. For example, Robert Veatch has pointed out that although the term *brain death* is commonly used in a somewhat separate way from *death* (i.e., an individual suffered brain death one day and died the next day), brain death should be defined as clinical death such that one who suffers brain death can be said to be dead. David Kelly notes that the term *brain death* is used clinically to explain to a patient's family that that individual is genuinely dead even though cardiovascular activity continues. Before the existence of medical technology that forces the heart and lungs to function when the brain does not, brain death would have meant instant cessation of heart and lung function. It is currently debated whether a definition of death that requires the cessation of all brain function is actually necessary, as neurologists since the 1970s have observed that isolated brain cells could potentially continue to function even if integrated supercellular brain function had ceased. This has led some to argue that one could measure death with similar accuracy by defining it as an irreversible loss of consciousness.

These types of issues have led to debate about how to understand the status of individuals who are in a persistent vegetative state (PVS). Because the UDDA makes clear that the irreversible cessation of all brain activity is needed for a determination of death, PVS and permanently comatose patients are not dead by current legal standards in the United States, as they have not lost function of the brain stem. At the same time, they have lost all neocortical brain function and thus will never recover higher-brain functioning, even though the heart and lungs continue to function without mechanical intervention. This leads to controversy over whether nutrition and hydration can be withdrawn from these patients. The controversy would be ended if the definition of death were broadened to include such patients, but it is not clear that society is willing to, or ought to, claim that breathing bodies are dead. Kelly argues that to declare such patients dead would simply be to avoid the ethically complex questions surrounding the withdrawal of care for these individuals.

These definitions of death become theologically complicated when questions are raised regarding medical care for the dying. Such questions can be connected to issues surrounding the meaning of personhood and the inherent dignity of the human being.

The Roman Catholic Church has argued consistently against both euthanasia and physician-assisted suicide, calling for the provision of ordinary care (such as nutrition and hydration) at the end of life, while allowing for the withholding of extraordinary care (though usually not the withdrawal of such care). This position is rooted in the understanding of human dignity, which is prominent throughout Catholic social teaching. Human dignity is inherent in all people because all are made in the image of God and because the life of each human being is given freely by God. The Catholic Church holds that the inherent dignity of all human beings calls for the protection of life at all stages, from conception through death.

Pope John Paul II draws on this understanding of human dignity when he asserts in *Evangelium vitae* that the current culture of death, which understands a life that requires greater care as either useless or burdensome, has fundamentally failed to see the inherent value in every human life regardless of disease, age, or handicap. This view of human dignity is critical when considering "death with dignity" movements that claim that in order to die with dignity, one must be given the ability to choose the time and manner of his or her own death. Human dignity, in Catholic social teaching, though, is inherent. As a result, one can never lose one's own dignity, and thus the Catholic Church advocates the protection of life even at its end.

The OT does not often comment on the meaning of death. In *Evangelium vitae*, John Paul II looks to Gen. 3 to argue that death was not part of God's original plan for humanity. He argues that death and suffering come about as a result of sin, and thus death and suffering are a part of our common human experience.

The Gospel of John comments on death as part of human existence, which comes into the world as a result of sin. Similar to its dualisms of light and darkness and righteousness and sin, there is a clear dualism of life and death in John's Gospel. Death is seen as a given in this world, but with the coming of Christ, life has come into the world so that all might escape death and experience eternal life.

The apostle Paul also clearly makes a connection between death and sin. Paul uses *thanatos* ("death") and related words at times to refer to the cessation of earthly life. More frequently, though, he discusses death in the context of that which comes to humanity as a result of human sin. "Death" and "sin" (*hamartia*) are often used in relationship to each other, and this is particularly apparent in Rom. 6. There, Paul acknowledges human death as the consequence of sin. In the same passage, though, Paul also talks about the death of Christ.

Paul's understanding of death is different from Greek views of the period. Whereas some Greek schools of thought looked to the flight of the soul from the body that it might find freedom in the spiritual realm, Paul looks to the final destiny of humanity as the resurrection of the body rather than a state in which the soul is separated from the body. Paul often describes the state of death as sleep (*koimaomai* [1 Cor. 7:39; 11:30; 15:6, 18, 20, 51; 1 Thess. 4:13–15]), but it is important to remember that sleep was a common way to describe death in both Greek and Hebrew literature. Paul does indicate some kind of intermediate state in 2 Cor. 5:8, where he speaks of being away from the body and at home with the Lord, which would further raise questions about Paul's understanding of death as sleep.

A thorough account of the understanding of death in the Bible cannot be offered apart from a discussion of the resurrection. The Nicene-Constantinopolitan Creed, recited every week by millions of Christians, states, "We look for the resurrection of the dead and the life of the world to come." It is clear in the NT that death is not the end for the Christian. For Christians, the future will ultimately bring the redemption of the body in the form of resurrection. Paul talks about the centrality of the resurrection to teaching about Christ in 1 Cor. 15, where he states, "If there is no resurrection of the dead, then Christ has not been raised; and if Christ has not been raised, then our proclamation has been in vain and your faith has been in vain. . . . If Christ has not been raised, your faith is futile and you are still in your sins. . . . If for this life only we have hoped in Christ, then we are of all people most to be pitied" (1 Cor. 15:13–14, 17, 19). This is not the only place where Paul addresses this issue. In 1 Thessalonians, Paul writes, "But we do not want you to be uninformed, brothers and sisters, about those who have died, so that you may not grieve as others do who have no hope. For since we believe that Jesus died and rose again, even so, through Jesus, God will bring with him those who have died" (1 Thess. 4:13–14).

In *Surprised by Hope*, N. T. Wright argues that the medieval depictions of heaven and hell (as found in Dante's *Divine Comedy*) that have been so influential on Western ideas of life after death are not supported by the language of the NT. Wright argues that when Jesus refers to "God's kingdom" in his preaching, he is referring not to the destiny of humanity after death, but rather to God's rule coming on earth in the same way as it is in heaven. At the end of Revelation, Wright observes, what is depicted is not bodiless souls en route to heaven, but rather the new Jerusalem coming down to earth. Because of this, life after death for the human being is ultimately an embodied existence. Wright argues that there are clear implications for how human beings are to live in the temporal realm. Human beings are called to partake in the building of the kingdom of God.

Wright wants to be clear that human beings cannot build the kingdom of God by their own efforts, but he also claims that God brings about the kingdom through the work of human beings. If the eschaton is characterized by the coming of the new heaven and the new earth, human beings are called to build for the creation. He writes, "Every act of love, gratitude, and kindness; . . . every minute spent teaching a severely handicapped child to read or to walk; every act of care and nurture, of comfort and support, for one's fellow human beings or for that matter one's fellow nonhuman creatures . . . —all of this will find its way, through the resurrecting power of God, into the new creation that God will one day make" (Wright 208).

Death is not something that simply happens to human beings at the end of life; it is something that also has the potential to affect how individuals understand themselves and relate ultimately to God in the course of their lives. Paul Tillich appropriates the ideas of Martin Heidegger regarding the human being facing death. For Heidegger, the human being is one who should be *Sein-zum-Tode* ("being-toward-death") in order to be authentic. Heidegger argues that the experience of the human being is one that is aware of the reality of death both as something encountered in those we know and also as something that happens in the wider world. Death is thus "a familiar event." At the same time, Heidegger notes that it is easy for one to tacitly acknowledge the reality of death and then move beyond it. As discussion of death arises, it is easy to quickly acknowledge one's own mortality and then just as easily see oneself as currently not involved. But to be truly authentic, Heidegger claimed, a human being must live in light of an awareness of the reality of his or her own death. Tillich appropriates this idea for Christian theology and describes the human awareness of death or finitude as the beginning of the process of asking questions about God. Tillich held that the experience of finitude, or human awareness of the possibility of nonbeing, raises the question of God in the minds of human beings. Human beings, he claims, are aware of their own finitude, but are at the same time able to conceptualize infinitude in a way that leads them to questions about God. As a result, for Tillich, awareness of one's own mortality is what leads to a questioning about and awareness of God.

The writings of Tillich, Heidegger, and Wright show not only that the end of one's life brings ethical questions in and of itself but also that the reality of death will have, or at least should have, a profound impact on one's ethical decisions well before the event of death itself.

See also Death, Definition of; Euthanasia; Healthcare Ethics; Image of God; Quality of Life; Resurrection; Sanctity of Human Life

Bibliography

Berkman, J. "Medically Assisted Nutrition and Hydration in Medicine and Moral Theology." Pages 143–72 in *Medicine, Health Care and Ethics: Catholic Voices*, ed. J. Morris. Catholic University of America Press, 2007; Breck, J. *The Sacred Gift of Life: Orthodox Christianity and Bioethics*. St. Vladimir's Seminary Press, 1998; John Paul II. *The Gospel of Life—Evangelium Vitae: On the Value and Inviolability of Human Life*. Times Books, 1995. Kelly, D. *Contemporary Catholic Health Care Ethics*. Georgetown University Press, 2004; Ladd, G. *A Theology of the New Testament*. Rev. ed. Eerdmans, 1993; Morris, J. "Death and Dying." Pages 127–41 in *Medicine, Health Care and Ethics: Catholic Voices*, ed. J. Morris. Catholic University of America Press, 2007; O'Donovan, O. "Keeping Body and Soul Together." Pages 223–38 in *On Moral Medicine: Theological Perspectives in Medical Ethics*, ed. S. Lammers and A. Verhey. 2nd ed. Eerdmans, 1998; Paul VI. *Gaudium et Spes: Pastoral Constitution on the Church in the Modern World*. Pages 164–237 in *Catholic Social Thought: The Documentary Heritage*, ed. D. O'Brien and T. Shannon. Orbis, 1992; Veatch, R. "The Impending Collapse of the Whole-Brain Definition of Death." *HCR* 23, no. 4 (1993): 18–24; Verhey, A. *Reading the Bible in the Strange World of Medicine*. Eerdmans, 2003. Wright, N. T. *Surprised by Hope: Rethinking Heaven, the Resurrection, and the Mission of the Church*. HarperOne, 2008.

Mary M. Veeneman

Debt

In the year 2000, the Roman Catholic Church declared "Jubilee." Many within the church sought forgiveness for the massive indebtedness of poor countries to wealthier ones. This declaration and call reminded Christians and all persons of good will of God's economy found in Lev. 25, which states that not only people but also the land should keep a Sabbath to the Lord. The land can be tilled for six years, but in the seventh year it is to lie fallow. Then, after seven times seven years, on the fiftieth year, a "Jubilee" is to be declared. It is a year of return and renewal. Debts are relieved, and property is returned.

The Jubilee did not prohibit loans and indebtedness, but it contextualized debt within God's mercy. We are all sojourners whom God redeems out of God's generosity. No one, therefore, could permanently own what belonged to another, for God was the true owner of everything. God states, "The land shall not be sold in perpetuity, for the land is mine; with me you are but aliens and tenants" (Lev. 25:23). For this reason, any debt was to be of a limited time and related to actual services or goods that could be exchanged. Debt was not to be a way of life. Debts are to be forgiven.

The biblical prohibition against usury also regulated debt within the context of hospitality and mercy. Loans were not to be given out at interest. This too is part of the legislation of the Jubilee: "If any of your kin fall into difficulty and become dependent on you, you shall support them; they shall live with you as though resident aliens. Do not take interest in advance from them, but fear your God; let them live with you. You shall not lend them your money at interest taken in advance, or provide them food at a profit. I am the Lord your God, who brought you out of the land of Egypt to give you the land of Canaan, to be your God" (Lev. 25:35–38). As God freely brought Israel out of Egypt and prepared a land for them, so they were to treat their own kin in a similar fashion. Similar judgments are found in Exod. 22:25; Deut. 23:19–20; Ps. 15:5. Although most of these judgments dealt primarily with how Israel treated its own kin, the church fathers read Luke 6:36 as Jesus affirming and expanding this type of economy.

Jesus strengthens the prohibition against certain forms of credit and interest by telling us,

> If you love those who love you, what credit is that to you? For even sinners love those who love them. If you do good to those who do good to you, what credit is that to you? For even sinners do the same. If you lend to those from whom you hope to receive, what credit is that to you? Even sinners lend to sinners, to receive as much again. But love your enemies, do good, and lend, expecting nothing in return. Your reward will be great, and you will be children of the Most High; for he is kind to the ungrateful and the wicked. Be merciful, just as your Father is merciful. (Luke 6:32–36)

We find here another example of how Jesus fulfills the law. He does not view it as bare prohibitions or permissions, but orders it toward its true end. Law is not an end in itself, but a means to embody the holiness by which all of creation becomes God's habitation. Loans are means to love even enemies.

For much of Christian tradition, this passage was understood to be a statement about political economy. Usurious interests on loans were prohibited by both reason and faith. Most ancient philosophers claimed that such loans violated the nature of things. Money does not naturally fructify, so to assume that it could increase without any relation to things that actually did was unnatural. For Christians, faith illumined reason. Jesus' statement was heard in the context of both what is naturally obvious—money does not fructify—and what has been received in faith. Jesus affirms and strengthens this when he states, "Do good and lend, expecting nothing in return." Eventually, Christian tradition made a distinction between genuine profit and interest. A loan could be made and profit received if the loan was used for a licit increase in goods. Animals and plants do fructify. If someone becomes a debtor to engage in an enterprise in which an increase came about, then the creditor and debtor could share in legitimate profits. But interest could not be charged prior to the actual profit or loss. This would be to sell "time," and it is not something that can be sold. Nonetheless, Jesus poses an important question about the nature of loans, credit, and debt in his recontextualizing of the tradition: "What credit is that to you?"

Most loans are for the purpose of a gain, a "credit" to one's account. But here Jesus puts this assumption into question and asks if living solely from such exchanges really is a credit, a favor, or benefaction (*charis*). He does not then deny that transactions should have benefits. He avoids any "Kantian" disinterestedness whereby ethics is defined by doing one's duty without reciprocity. Nor is this teaching similar to Adam Smith's butcher, brewer, and baker who look only to self-interest and thereby serve the common good through unintended consequences. This is not the credit that imagines a blessed future. Of course we have a legitimate self-interest; that is a necessary feature of Christian ethics. We should desire to live and have that same desire for others. This desire to be requires living out of "credit" (faith), for none of us can sustain his or her own life. Jesus therefore affirms a proper reward when we lend expecting no return: "Your reward will be great, and you will be children of the Most High; for he is kind to the ungrateful and the wicked. Be merciful, just as your Father is merciful." Loans and our expectations of them signify what we will be, as well as how our being relates to the good and to the blessed Trinity. How we exchange shows how we are or are not like God. The point of Jesus' teaching is that exchange is to be turned into communion.

Debts are based on contractual obligations that can easily be determined. They do not invite us to live as friends or to commune in one another's lives. The relation with a mortgage company is based solely on such a contractual obligation. It is a form of exchange, which is not inherently wrong, but it is not a form of communion that makes the world more holy. Such a relation knows only the barest of legal obligations; once those obligations are finished, we have no need of each other. Communion entails something much more than this. It assumes that no nice cost-benefit calculation can be made. The relation between debtor and creditor does not keep them at a distance from each other; instead, the relation brings them together such that they literally share in each other's lives. The paradigmatic example of this is the Eucharist, where God and creatures share in each other's lives, a sharing made possible only because God in Jesus becomes fully human and divine, two natures that remain unchanged but now indivisibly joined in one person. In the kingdom of God, all our relations will be like this. We will not have the alien character of the debt relation. For this reason, we are to pray every day, "Forgive us our debts as we forgive those indebted to us."

See also Economic Ethics; Greed; Jubilee; Loans; Poverty and Poor; Wealth

D. Stephen Long

Decalogue *See* Ten Commandments

Deception

Deception, the act of deluding or misleading others, is an important ethical issue in the Bible and in moral discourse. In Scripture, deception basically constitutes a false witness and is condemned (Exod. 20:16). The crux of the ethical question is whether a person, in order to achieve a morally good result, is justified in being misleading or engaging in outright lying.

Some of the Bible's best-known heroes are commended for lying or deceiving in order to achieve a greater good. For example, the book of Exodus begins with the oppression of the alien Hebrews in Egypt, focusing on Pharaoh's plan to diminish their numbers by instructing midwives to execute every Israelite male at birth (Exod. 1:15–16). But the midwives, because they "feared God," allowed the infant boys to live. Then they reported to Pharaoh why the Hebrew males escaped execution: "The Hebrew women are not like the Egyptian women; for they are vigorous and give birth before the midwife comes to them" (Exod. 1:19). The truth is obvious: the Hebrew midwives lied to the Egyptian king in order to prevent the murder of innocent babies. Most who read this story consider the midwives heroes.

Perhaps the best example of "righteous deception" is the story of Rahab, the prostitute of Jericho who aided two spies from Joshua's invading army, hiding them in her house (Josh. 1–2). When the king of Jericho sought the foreigners, Rahab concocted a grand lie, claiming that the men had fled: "Where the men went I do not know" (Josh. 2:5). Not only were Rahab and her household saved when Joshua conquered Jericho (Josh. 6:17) but also she is lauded twice in the NT as a hero of the faith (Heb. 11:31; Jas. 2:25).

From the beginning of serious ethical discourse by early Greek philosophers, the "truth" question has been central. Socrates and Plato believed that truth was predetermined by the gods and thus was inviolable. Aristotle, however, asserted that truth, or the ultimate good, was determined by the end result of an act. From these two streams of thought came two major categories in ethics: deontology, or the ethics of obligation, which asks, "What is right?" and teleology, or the ethics of consequences, which asks, "What is the good that I seek in this act?"

As an absolutist, Immanuel Kant believed that in order to be ethical one must speak the truth without exception. Truth-telling is a moral obligation that must be followed. No matter if the goal is to avoid a wrong or to achieve a good, to lie or deceive is always wrong because it violates basic ethical obligations.

A consequentialist (e.g., Martin Luther, Dietrich Bonhoeffer) would argue that often, especially when conflicting moral values are involved, the end result is relevant to the right moral choice. Not that the choice is ideal, but it may be the best of all the options available—the greatest good when the choice involves, for example, saving a life.

In light of the few biblical examples of "righteous deception" and the strong moral norm of truthfulness, it seems reasonable to conclude that lying or deception may be permitted as a lesser evil in exceptional circumstances, but truthfulness is the overriding principle in most instances.

See also Consequentialism; Deontological Theories of Ethics; Dishonesty; Ends and Means; Fidelity; Honesty; Teleological Theories of Ethics; Ten Commandments; Truthfulness, Truth-Telling

Joe E. Trull

Deformity *See* Body

Dehumanization *See* Humanity

Dementia

Dementia can be caused by a variety of diseases, the most prevalent of which is Alzheimer's disease, a progressive and irreversible condition that can be loosely described in terms of stages of loss. Yet researchers also refer to Alzheimer's as a disease of "fluctuation," for there are occasional good mornings when an affected individual seems surprisingly insightful, even when very deep into the disease progression. Thus, there is a resurrection of a sort even for the most deeply forgetful.

A number of Christians have pioneered the path of love for persons with dementia. Methodist minister Tom Kitwood, who directed the Alzheimer's Care Center at the University of Bradford in the 1990s, did more than any other leader to encourage humane care for this population. In his widely influential book *Dementia Reconsidered: The Person Comes First*, Kitwood described the power of agape love within the context of dementia care. He viewed such love as a constellation of tenderness, closeness, and the calming of anxiety and bonding. Kitwood and Kathleen Bredin developed indicators of well-being in people with severe dementia: the assertion of will or desire, usually in the form of dissent despite various coaxings; the ability to express a range of emotions; initiation of social contact (e.g., a man with dementia has a small toy dog that he treasures and places it before another person with dementia to attract attention); affectional warmth (e.g., a woman wanders back and forth in the facility without much socializing, but when people say hello to her, she gives them a kiss on the cheek and continues her wandering). All is never lost in the deeply forgetful, Kitwood argues, and they clearly fall within the inclusive scope of agape love.

Memory is, of course, a wonderful evolutionary gift, and we rightly treasure it, but its diminishment is no cause to devalue moral status. In his *Confessions*, Augustine wrote these elegant words about the majesty of memory—lines that have echoed over the centuries in Western thought:

> All this goes on inside me, in the vast cloisters of my memory. In it are the sky, the earth, and the sea, ready at my summons, together with everything that I have ever perceived in them by my senses, except the things which I have forgotten. In it I meet myself as well. I remember myself and what I have done, when and where I did it, and the state of my mind at the time. In my memory,

> too, are all the events that I remember, whether they are things that have happened to me or things that I have heard from others. (*Conf.* 10.8)

Memory, which remains in many ways mysterious, is one of the miracles of neurological evolution and is the source of all the connections between past and present experience that allow us to have self-identity and autobiography. Note that for Augustine, it is the temporal glue between past and present that allows us to "meet myself as well."

Augustine's assertion was that all human beings have a kind of spiritual dementia due to the fall of humankind away from a state of original oneness with God. We are all equally unable to remember that oneness, except for a "still faint glow" of that original union when we knew perfect happiness. We are all, in this sense, demented, and we all need to be reminded of God through the Christian community with its ritual of remembrance in the Lord's Supper. Forgetfulness is no cause for exclusion, but is cause for a community of recollection that provides prosthetic support for those who cannot recall whose they are or who they are. By extension, the Christian community should support persons with Alzheimer's disease as well as their caregivers, reminding the forgetful of who they are and of the worthiness of their lives despite their faded memories.

Many non-Christian philosophers tend to exclude the deeply forgetful from moral consideration because of their diminished cognitive powers, but they do so without any real experience of proximity, caregiving, and observational proximity over time. It is said that people with severe cognitive disabilities are not persons because they cannot project into the future. This general idea of personhood emerged from John Locke of Christ Church College, Oxford University. Locke wrote of the person as a being able to "consider itself, the same thinking being, in different times and places." Yet, because Locke was a physician and a Christian, it is hard to imagine this philosopher of the Enlightenment resting comfortably with the current exclusionary application of his ideas. Since when does the ability to project plans into the future define who counts in the eyes of God? Children of the Enlightenment vastly overrate the moral significance of rationality and intentionality. A half century ago, Christian ethicist Reinhold Niebuhr pointed out the crucial snobbery of rationalist elitism: "Since the divine principle is reason, the logic of Stoicism tends to include only the intelligent in the divine community. An aristocratic condescension, therefore, corrupts Stoic universalism. In the thought of Jesus men are to be loved not because they are equally divine, but because God loves them equally" (Niebuhr 53). Agape love assumes a universalism that is not compromised by memory disorders.

Hypercognitive values systems confer worth only on those who are cognitively strong (Post, *Moral Challenge* [2nd ed.]). Stephen Post coined the term *hypercognitive* in 1995 to underscore a persistent bias against the deeply forgetful that is especially pronounced in modern philosophical accounts of the "person" (Post, *Moral Challenge* [1st ed.]). Such systems have less to do with "pure" reason than with existential fears of forgetfulness, cultural norms of economic productivity, imperious and baseless utilitarian calculations, and arrogance. Modern utilitarians, for instance, have no particular moral authority in the eyes of caregivers when it comes to definitions of personhood or happiness, especially with regard to the cognitively imperiled. Utilitarians see persons with dementia as useless, couple this with the idea that no action is intrinsically wrong, and assert a narrow hypercognitive definition of personhood; thus the destruction of the deeply forgetful is almost assured, at least in principle. Yet family members are not influenced by such academic theories. Even Peter Singer, the arch-utilitarian proponent of painlessly killing the senile of mind, is by all reports an honorable and compassionate man who has cared well for his mother, who had Alzheimer's disease.

See also Agape; Altruism; Benevolence; Care, Caring; Dependent Care; Disability and Handicap; Image of God; Utilitarianism

Bibliography

Kitwood, T. *Dementia Reconsidered: The Person Comes First*. Open University Press, 1997; Kitwood, T., and K. Bredin. "Towards a Theory of Dementia Care: Personhood and Well-Being." *Ageing and Society* 12 (1992): 269–87; Niebuhr, R. *An Interpretation of Christian Ethics*. Meridian Books, 1956; Post, S. *The Moral Challenge of Alzheimer Disease*. 1st ed. Johns Hopkins University Press, 1995; idem. *The Moral Challenge of Alzheimer Disease: Ethical Issues from Diagnosis to Dying*. 2nd ed. Johns Hopkins University Press, 2000; Singer, P. *Practical Ethics*. Cambridge University Press, 1993.

Stephen Post

Democracy

The term *democracy* applies to a polity or form of governance in which members of a body participate in the decisions that affect the whole by voting on issues that demand a common policy (direct democracy) or by electing those who will make such decisions (representative democracy). This political definition, however, omits other social factors that also are democratic: provisions that protect civil society institutions from oppression by the majority; guarantees that each person have access to education, employment, and medical care; a free press; a pluralism of political parties; and freedom of religion. Such polities are held to be most fitting to the human condition.

Historically, republican polities also attempted to avoid the threats of monarchy, which can easily become imperial or tyrannical, and of populism, which can become "mobocracy" or anarchist. Republican advocates resisted monopolistic power and anarchy by accenting the rule of law as administered by jurists, legislators, and state leaders who became the guardians of the well-being of society. The temptations of republican thought were oligarchy (rule by the few) or plutocracy (rule by the wealthy). In recent centuries, with the spread of constitutions placing governments under law, democratic and republican theories and practices have blended. Most democracies are now actually democratic republics (or republican democracies). In fact, several limited monarchies with strong parliaments are counted as democratic. Consequently, various examples of democratic orders find their commonality in their support of electoral representation, government under law, human rights, regulated economies, social welfare, and, especially, religious freedom.

The biblical records, and thus most streams of Christian and Jewish tradition, have examples of all these possibilities. The Bible celebrates David's creation of an empire—a point not lost on historic Christian royalty and on the Holy Roman Empire particularly. But it also contains passages opposing both monopolistic power and those appeals to "the freedom of the gospel" that tended to justify libertine behavior, as we find in some gnostic tendencies and in some contemporary liberationist advocacy.

No book of the Bible represents anything like Plato's *Republic*, Aristotle's *Politics*, Cicero's *Laws*, or any modern treatise on polity, or offers a direct theological legitimization of democracy. Nevertheless, Christian thought has drawn on biblical themes that point toward an affinity for the compound that we call, today, democracy. Humans have a dignity, for each is created in the image of God, and with it are given the capabilities and the mandate to care for and cultivate the earth and to create cultures. However, when they distorted the gifts God gave them, they fell into sin and had to face the harsh realities of historical existence and their own sinfulness. Still, they were preserved by God's providence and were called to form covenanted societies under God's law and for God's purposes. They anointed leaders: prophets to preach justice, priests to nurture faithful worship, and kings to defend the community from violence and crime—although false prophets, unfaithful priests, and wicked monarchs were and are a perennial pitfall. They hoped for a messiah who would redeem the world from evil and be the truest prophet, the most faithful priest, and the righteous, peaceful king of kings.

Indeed, when Jesus came and was recognized as the Messiah, the church was formed as the exemplar of a just, loving, and realistic polity and as a witness to the coming reign of God. All who are in Christ or aspire to be like Christ are called to be prophetically, pastorally, and politically responsible for the whole society. In a long and complex history, various branches of the church developed distinct polities for how to best accomplish this, each citing preferred biblical passages as warrants for its normative status and advocating a parallel order in society.

Most scholars of this history identify three types of polity: hierarchical, federated, and locally independent. In time, most churches adopted elements of these types into their predominant model. Thus, strong hierarchical traditions developed councils, embraced subsidiarity, and supported constitutionally limited governments with locally rooted parliaments externally. Federated polities formed centralized bureaucracies and supported congregational initiatives for service or advocacy and representative democracies in society. And independent churches have formed unified publishing and lobbying wings that support religious freedom and moral causes. All advance and legitimate democracy today and see it as a temporal implication of the gospel for the sustaining of the common life in this world.

See also Authority and Power; Government; Theocracy

Bibliography

Dillistone, F. *The Structure of the Divine Society*. Westminster, 1951; Dulles, A. *Models of the Church*. Doubleday, 1974; Elazar, D. *The Covenant Tradition in Politics*. 4 vols. Transaction Publishers, 1995–98; Long, E., Jr. *Patterns of Polity*. Pilgrim Press, 2001; Nichols, J. *Democracy and the Churches*. Westminster, 1951; Stackhouse, M. *Public Theology and Political Economy: Christian Stewardship in Modern Society*. Eerdmans, 1987; Troeltsch, E. *Protestantism and Progress: A Historical Study of the Relation of Protestantism to the Modern World*. Beacon, 1958, 89–127; Witte, J. *Law and Protestantism: The Legal Teachings of the Lutheran Reformation*. Cambridge University Press, 2002.

Max L. Stackhouse

Denial *See* Speech Ethics

Deontological Theories of Ethics

In ethical theory, the phrase "deontological ethics" is often used synonymously with "duty-based ethics," since the term *deontology* is derived from the Greek word for "duty." Hence, a deontological theory of ethics properly entails a duty-based ethical theory. Broadly speaking, ethical theorists distinguish between two major types of deontological theories: act deontology and rule deontology.

Theories of act deontology, also called "particularism," contend that particular situations or circumstances faced by a given individual determine the course of action that the individual in question should follow. In other words, if one is faced with a particular situation *S*, one must be certain about the facts of *S*, which in turn will enable one to determine a particular course of action *A*, which one is subsequently obligated to follow.

Thus, it is quite possible, for example, for the particularist to suggest to Mr. Smith that he love his neighbor John for mowing his lawn, while at the same time advise another neighbor, Ms. Brown, to hate John for performing the same act of mowing her lawn. It might just be that John's act of mowing the lawn contributes to the overall beauty of the neighborhood, a situation that pleases Mr. Smith immensely. However, John's act of mowing the lawn also causes Ms. Brown's allergies to flare up, thereby aggravating Ms. Brown. This shows that theories of act deontology do not commit themselves to universal rules of ethics. Their view is that such universal or general rules are not only unavailable; they are also impractical, if they exist at all.

Theories of act deontology are further subdivided into two categories: intuitionism and decisionism. Intuitionists are extreme act-deontologists because they insist on deciding, via intuition, what the right course of action ought to be for every particular situation. The intuitionists consult their conscience without subscribing to any preexisting moral rules, and without basing their decision on the consequences that might be caused by that decision. Aristotle's doctrine of the mean sometimes has been placed in this category. But there are good reasons for contending that, overall, Aristotelian ethics is more virtue-based than duty-based.

E. F. Carritt and H. A. Pritchard are listed by many ethical theorists as modern examples of intuitionists. Joseph Butler is sometimes considered an intuitionist as well, though some theorists prefer to categorize his views as decisionist. For example, William Frankena regards Butler as an intuitionist, but Louis Pojman places him in the decisionist category. Irrespective of his placement, Butler contended that all humans have a conscience capable of determining the rightness or wrongness of actions in all situations. For this reason, argued Butler, general rules for determining the rightness or wrongness of actions are unnecessary. Instead, human conscience intuitively instructs all humans on the right thing to do or the right course of action to follow.

Decisionists, however, stress the importance of decision rather than intuition. They contend that the rightness of one's actions is decided or determined by the choice that one makes. It is not decided by any preexisting rules or laws; rather, it is decided by the act of choosing. Prior to choosing, the act in question is neither right nor wrong. Moreover, the more choices an agent makes in particular ethical situations, the more the agent develops general rules that would prove useful in deciding future courses of actions. However, these general rules should not override particular decisions concerning the course of action to be followed.

Theories of act deontology have been severely criticized by ethical objectivists for being too relativistic. An ethical objectivist believes that objective moral laws exist and are universally binding on all people. According to the objectivist, theories of act deontology provide no standard for deciding the rightness or wrongness of actions. By suggesting that particular situations dictate the course of action to be followed, the decision is left entirely on the agent. But according to the ethical objectivist, morality is something into which humans must learn and grow. A morally immature person needing instruction on a specific course of action to be followed will thus be helpless when faced with situations that call for ethical decisions to be made.

For example, many Christian ethicists are also objectivists and will therefore reject act deontology, for they contend that the Bible is their standard for faith and conduct. In other words, they make their moral decisions based on insights drawn, directly or indirectly, from Scripture (see 2 Tim. 3:16–17). This comes in sharp contrast with act deontology, which fails to provide any standard for making moral decisions.

Second, a given theory of act deontology is deemed self-defeating in the following sense. It must base its highly relativistic view on some underlying objective principle in order to reject the objectivity of morality. For example, consider its underlying ethical principle: given a particular situation *S*, one must get the relevant facts of *S* in order to determine a given course of action *A*. The ethical objectivist could quite conceivably contend that this principle is objective because it is general and universal, thereby applying to all ethical situations that the agent might face in the future. If so, the principle itself is undercut by the act-deontologist's contention that general rules or principles of ethics are unavailable.

Theories of rule deontology, by contrast, contend that general rules for morality are available. Thus, general rules such as "We must always tell the truth" are accepted by the rule-deontologist. Moreover, the rule-deontologist maintains that such rules are morally binding whether or not they have good consequences. The consequences do not determine the rightness or wrongness of the course of action to be pursued; neither is the course of action derived from or determined by particular situations as suggested by act deontology. Rather, one decides the right course of action based on the general rules. Hence, the standard for determining right and wrong is nonteleological, or for that matter, nonconsequentialist in essence.

Examples of rule-deontologists are Samuel Clarke, Richard Price, Thomas Reid, W. D. Ross, and Immanuel Kant. Consider, for example, the views of W. D. Ross. He drew distinctions between what could be called "actual duty" and "prima facie duty." According to Ross, the former refers to the actual right thing to do. Put differently, it refers to and involves the course of action that one is obliged to follow in some certain situation. According to Ross, under such circumstances there are exceptions to the rules governing what one ought to do. However, under prima facie duty it is possible to prescribe moral rules that are binding without exceptions.

For example, a prima facie rule can be stipulated as follows: one must always keep the promises one makes. Whereas this is the sort of rule that one must try to obey constantly, certain considerations could override it. For example, suppose Elaine borrows one hundred dollars from Peter and promises to repay him in about a month. But a week later, Elaine contracts a debilitating disease whose treatment not only renders her incapable of going back to work but also wipes away, in a matter of days, all of her savings to the extent that she cannot afford to buy food or pay bills. It would perhaps be immoral, under these circumstances, for Peter to ask for his money from Elaine. Thus, the prima facie duty to always keep one's promises can be quite legitimately overruled by another prima facie obligation: one individual should not subject another individual to deeper stress if the latter is already overwhelmed by circumstances beyond his or her control.

The most famous rule-deontologist perhaps is Immanuel Kant. In agreement with Aristotle, Kant believed that human reason is the source of morality. But he disagreed with Aristotle's claim that the goal of human reason is happiness. Kant believed that instinct did a better job than reason in producing happiness. Kant postulated, as an alternative, that the goal of reason is to produce a morally good person. He contended that humans ought to act in a certain way because acting in that way is the right thing to do, regardless of the consequences that follow that act.

But how does one determine the rightness of a given act *A*? Kant suggested what he called the "categorical imperatives" as the formula for determining the right thing to do. The first categorical imperative, called the "formula of universal law," proposed the following principle: act in such a way that you can at the same time will or desire that it become a universal law; that is, when deciding whether to lie, one should ask the following questions: "Do I want to live in a world where everyone tells lies? Can I live consistently in a world where everyone tells lies?" Reason informs the reasonable person that the answer to these questions is no. Hence, at least one universal law exists: we must always tell the truth.

The second categorical imperative, called the "law of humanity," proposed the following: always act, whether in your own person or in the person of another, in a manner that treats everyone as ends, not merely as means. Kant is suggesting that humans should treat one another as humans, not merely as tools. Thus, if Elaine borrows money from Peter on the promise to repay it in two weeks, she will be treating Peter merely as a tool if she breaks that promise.

The third categorical imperative, called the "law of autonomy," is really an enforcement of the first categorical imperative. Kant suggests, under this law, that maxims that do not follow the formula of universal law ought to be rejected. Kant believed that reason enables one to see that these three laws are morally binding on all people. One has a duty to follow them, regardless of the consequences they produce. If a given course of action is not consistent with any of these laws, it conflicts with duty, for Kant believed that only actions done from duty have moral worth. Moreover, they have their moral worth in the maxim according to which they were determined; that is, the three categorical imperatives give moral worth to the actions they prescribe.

First, for Kant, actions that conflict with duty have no moral worth. These include actions such as murder, adultery, and theft. Second, some actions are consistent with duty, but they have no moral worth because one has no immediate inclination to do them. For example, one pays taxes not because of an immediate inclination to do so, but rather because of a desire to avoid penalties. Or one performs acts of kindness not because of an immediate inclination to do so, but rather because of a desire to be elected to some public office.

Third, Kant also believed that some actions are consistent with duty, but they have no moral worth because the agent in question has an immediate inclination to perform the act. For example, one spreads joy to all people specifically because it is pleasurable to do so. Or one does not commit suicide because one's life is comfortable on the whole. Here, one is inclined to do what one already wants to do. For Kant, this sort of action has no moral worth.

To clarify what he meant by an action having moral worth, Kant drew attention to actions consistent with duty but contrary to immediate inclination. Examples of such actions include a person refraining from suicide even though his life is painful, or a teller not stealing money from her bank even though she is severely broke and could use the money if it was made available. In both instances, the agent in question is doing what duty demands. But the agent is also fighting off a contrary inclination, a temptation of sorts. According to Kant, such actions have moral worth precisely because they involve successfully fighting off such temptations, whether severe or mild. Kant's aim was to emphasize the importance of doing the right thing not because the rightness is determined by external reasons such as pleasure, happiness, or the good of the community; rather, one does the right thing because it is the right thing to do.

In light of these considerations, Kant defined duty as the necessity of an action done out of respect for the law—law here understood as the three categorical imperatives. Thus, for Kant, if a certain course of action in a given situation is consistent with the three categorical imperatives, one is duty-bound to follow that course of action.

Rule deontology seems to succeed where act deontology fails. It recognizes that ethical rules can be universalized in a way that enables the agent to make relevant ethical decisions. Also, Kantian deontology seems to place a high value on human reason. It recognizes that humans are rational creatures, and that the dictates of their reason ought to be respected. However, two common criticisms have been raised against rule deontology. First, it leaves the agent quite helpless when confronted by ethical dilemmas. For example, Kant's contention that it is never right to lie suggests that one must always tell the truth even when such truth-telling puts one's life in danger. Lying to protect a life from death, according to Kant's theory, is wrong.

A second criticism commonly raised against rule deontology is its apparent lack of motivation to follow a certain course of action. Whereas it locates the reasonableness of a certain course of action, it fails to give the agent the required motivation to follow that course of action. For example, an alcoholic could know by reason that it is wrong to sustain the habit of drunkenness, but the alcoholic's rational faculties fail to provide the motivation to stop drinking. The rule-deontologist, however, could respond to this critique by referring to Kant's definition of duty: the necessity of an action done out of respect for the law. The rule-deontologist could say, for example, that respect for the law is motivation enough to make the agent perform the necessary action. The Christian ethicist could counter by suggesting that since humans are, by nature, fallen creatures, they are incapable, by their own volition, of obeying or, for that matter, respecting any moral laws. To be sure, Christians will invoke Titus 2:11–12, contending that morality is made possible only by the grace of God.

See also Consequentialism; Duty; Moral Absolutes; Right and Wrong; Teleological Theories of Ethics; Virtue Ethics

Bibliography

Butler, J. *Five Sermons Preached at Rolls Chapel; and, A Dissertation upon the Nature of Virtue*. LLA 21. Liberal Arts Press, 1950; Denise, T., N. White, and S. Peterfreund, eds. *Great Traditions in Ethics*. 12th ed. Thomson-Wadsworth, 2008; Frankena, W. *Ethics*. 2nd ed. Prentice-Hall, 1973; Kant, I. *Groundwork of the Metaphysics of Morals*. Trans. and ed. M. Gregor. CTHP. Cambridge University Press, 1997; Pojman, L. *Ethics: Discovering Right and Wrong*. 5th ed. Thomson-Wadsworth, 2006; Rashdall, H. *The Theory of Good and Evil: A Treatise on Moral Philosophy*. 2nd ed. 2 vols. Oxford University Press, 1924.

Joseph B. Onyango Okello

Dependent Care

Dependent care involves care for individuals who are in some way unable to care for themselves, whether due to problems of age, health, or finance. The dependent individual might be a member of the family of the caregiver or the community of the caregiver, or the relationship might be legal and contractual.

The issue of dependent care, though not discussed as such in the Bible, is seen throughout both Testaments. In the giving of the Mosaic law, the people of Israel are directed to care for the widow, the orphan, and the outcast in their midst. Exodus 22:22–23 tells the people of Israel, "You shall not abuse any widow or orphan. If you do abuse them, when they cry out to me, I will surely heed their cry." The covenant curses outlined in Deut. 27 include the statement, "Cursed be anyone who deprives the alien, the orphan, and the widow of justice" (Deut. 27:19). The Decalogue command, "Honor your father and your mother" (Exod. 20:12), requires children to care for their aging parents.

The OT wisdom literature refers to children as a gift (Ps. 127:3–5) and talks about the importance of disciplining them (Prov. 13:1, 24). Additionally, the wisdom literature is clear about the need for children to obey their parents (Prov. 28:24; 30:17). These passages make clear the need for parents to care for children wisely (which includes proper discipline) and the need for children to honor their parents (which includes caring for them in their old age).

When the prophets speak out against the people of Israel on behalf of God, one of the primary complaints raised concerns the way in which they failed to care for the marginalized, which includes both children and the elderly. Zechariah evokes the Mosaic law in stating, "Thus says the Lord of hosts: Render true judgments, show kindness and mercy to one another; do not oppress the widow, the orphan, the alien, or the poor; and do not devise evil in your hearts against one another" (Zech. 7:9–10). Dependent care, even though not directly addressed as such, is addressed across the entire OT. Law, wisdom, and prophets all call for care for the vulnerable in society. The obligation falls not only on family members but also on the whole of society.

The OT notion of justice, which transcends many contemporary notions of justice, requires not only that one refrain from treating the vulnerable badly, not only that people care for other family members but also that the whole society provide care for the vulnerable and dependent.

The ethic of care for those who depend on others (including the poor and the marginalized) continues in the NT. Ephesians 6:1–4 emphasizes the need for children to obey parents and for parents to raise children with godly instruction, which implies proper care of dependents, whether children or elderly parents. James writes, "Religion that is pure and undefiled before God, the Father, is this: to care for orphans and widows in their distress, and to keep oneself unstained by the world" (Jas. 1:27). Luke-Acts has a particular emphasis on the idea that God shows no partiality and calls all classes of people, whether in the upper echelons of society or on its margins. This is seen in Luke's use of Isa. 61:1–2 in the account of Jesus' rejection at Nazareth (Luke 4:16–30). In this text, Jesus proclaims that his mission is to bring good news to the poor, to proclaim the release of captives, and to let the oppressed go free (Luke 4:18).

Perhaps most important in the NT is a clear emphasis on God as Father and the need of all for care from God. In the Sermon on the Mount, Jesus exhorts his hearers not to worry about life's various needs: "Therefore do not worry, saying, 'What will we eat?' or 'What will we drink?' or 'What will we wear?' For it is the Gentiles who strive for all these things; and indeed your heavenly Father knows that you need all these things. But strive first for the kingdom of God and his righteousness, and all these things will be given to you as well" (Matt. 6:31–33). The apostle Paul says that all who follow Christ are children of God, and that the Holy Spirit bears witness to this when we call out to God as Father (Rom. 8:12–17).

The fact that dependent care is a communal obligation and not just a familial one bears upon some contemporary issues related to dependent care. One such issue is that the burdens of dependent care are often borne especially by women. The demands of dependent care can affect their relationships to both other persons and their work. Gloria Albrecht observes that the common assumption is that childrearing is the responsibility of women such that women are expected to take time away from work to care for children either full time if possible or when a child is sick or without childcare. This means that it is women whose work suffers when childcare plans fall through or become complicated due to illness. Further, the burdens of eldercare also fall disproportionately on women.

There is another problem: the burdens of dependent care often are assigned to poor women. Women who are employed in high-paying jobs typically rely on lower-income women to provide childcare or eldercare. Albrecht writes, "All over the world, poor women from the periphery leave their own families to care for the children of women (and men) in the overdeveloped world" (Albrecht 83). In essence, Albrecht claims, middle- and upper-income women secure the well-being of their families at the expense of lower-income women. Albrecht's claims are furthered by Arlie Hochschild's *The Second Shift*, which explores the ways in which women who work full-time carry a greater burden of household work (dubbed by Hochschild "the second shift") than their male partners. This too, following Albrecht's argument, could be alleviated for higher-income families through the reliance on lower-income individuals, most of whom are women.

Albrecht also observes that in the United States the lowest-paid jobs do not provide a living wage. As a result of this, some workers, though employed, are forced to use public assistance in various forms (Medicaid, WIC, and housing subsidies are the most commonly used). When this is done, "the cost of labor has been *socialized*—not to the benefit of the common good but to the benefit of profit-making corporations" (Albrecht 89).

Both Testaments make clear that we are called to give care to those who need it, and to do so with social responsibility. If middle- and upper-income families procure their own work-life balances at the expense of poor families, those situations are characterized by the very lack of justice condemned by the prophets. Ada María Isasi-Díaz argues that without justice, religious beliefs and practices could be the "opium of the people" as Karl Marx claimed. Isasi-Díaz looks to the work of Margaret Farley to claim that true justice flows from a commitment to persons and mutuality. When we realize that there is something in us that binds us to others (even if the other does not explicitly realize it), then we are able to continue to pursue justice without losing sight of the reasons it is sought in the first place. This is the kind of justice, and mutuality in caregiving, to which biblical religion calls us.

See also Care, Caring; Economic Ethics; Feminist Ethics; Healthcare Ethics; Welfare State

Bibliography

Albrecht, G. *Hitting Home: Feminist Ethics, Women's Work, and the Betrayal of "Family Values."* Continuum, 2002; Hochschild, A. *The Second Shift*. Penguin Books, 2003; Isasi-Díaz, A. "Justice and Love Shall Kiss." Pages 163–96 in *A Just and True Love: Feminism at the Frontiers of Theological Ethics; Essays in Honor of Margaret A. Farley*. University of Notre Dame Press, 2007; Ladd, G. *A Theology of the New Testament*. Rev. ed. Eerdmans, 1993; Rendtorff, R. *The Canonical Hebrew Bible: A Theology of the Old Testament*. Trans. D. Orton. Deo Publishing, 2005. Verhey, A. *Remembering Jesus: Christian Community, Scripture, and the Moral Life*. Eerdmans, 2002.

Mary M. Veeneman

Depravity *See* Sin

Desertion

Desertion is the abandonment of military duty without the permission of one's superiors and with the intent of not returning. In the American and English common law traditions, it encompasses the act of being "absent without leave" (AWOL). To desert in a military context can include leaving one's post contrary to orders, abandoning one's unit to avoid battle, or otherwise failing to fulfill one's military responsibilities.

From a moral perspective, desertion is the failure to fulfill one's obligations to one's nation or its military institutions. These obligations may arise out of a general sense of patriotic duty or out of an explicit promise or oath that one has made to participate in military service. This can be understood deontologically as a matter of pure principle, in the sense that one's obligations are a matter of unconditional obedience to a moral law. It can also be understood teleologically, in the sense that desertion can jeopardize the possibility of victory, costing lives and possibly resulting in conquest of one's nation. It can also be understood to be a failure of virtue, insofar as it can be understood as evidence of cowardice in the face of the possibility of death or serious injury.

However, desertion has also been understood as an act of protest by soldiers against unjust or immoral wars. During the Vietnam War, for example, a significant number of US soldiers deserted, in some cases leaving the country to avoid prosecution, understanding this to be an act of conscience. Similar acts of desertion as a form of protest have taken place in the Iraq War. Desertion as the refusal to fight an unjust war can thus be understood not as a failure to fulfill one's moral obligations, but as obedience to a higher moral obligation. This concept is embedded in the Nuremberg Principles, which affirmed the obligation of soldiers to act morally even in the face of immoral commands. By the same token, the right of conscientious objection is recognized under international law to permit individuals to refuse to fight in wars that they deem to be immoral.

In the biblical context, desertion is usually described as the abandonment by soldiers of their posts (e.g., 2 Kgs. 7:4; 1 Chr. 12:19), but the concept is also used in English biblical translations to describe the abandonment of God by Israel, as well as the forsaking of Israel by God. It is also used to describe the abandonment of Jesus by his disciples. Paul uses the idea of desertion or abandonment to describe the rejection of the gospel by the early Christian communities, through their lack of faith or immoral actions. In these cases, the idea of desertion is not used in the specifically military sense, but it does depend on the same underlying assumption that individuals have an obligation of faithfulness to God that through idolatry and sinful action they fail to fulfill.

See also Conscientious Objection; Duty; Military Service; War

Bibliography

International Law Commission. "Principles of International Law Recognized in the Charter of the Nürnberg Tribunal and in the Judgment of the Tribunal." *Yearbook of the International Law Commission* (1950), vol. 2, paragraph 97; United Nations Office of the High Commissioner for Human Rights. "Conscientious Objection to Military Service: United Nations Commission on Human Rights Resolution 1998/77." Adopted April 22, 1998.

Scott Paeth

Desire

Desire, as a human orientation toward other people, objects, or states of being, appears as a characteristic attribute of human existence. Discussion of desire engages the appropriateness or otherwise of the objects of desire and its contribution to human well-being. In the OT, desire is generally not seen to carry a negative or positive ethical quality in itself; this depends on the circumstances in question and the object of desire. The NT writers, by contrast, frequently offer a more negative view of human desire. This may well be due to the influence of negative attitudes toward desire in influential strands of Greco-Roman moral discourse at the time.

Desire in the Old Testament

A sense of desire is expressed by several Hebrew terms, usually the stem *'wh*, although *ḥšq* and *ḥpṣ* can also connote longing for or setting one's heart on a desired object or person.

Desire for another human being is almost always expressed as the desire of a man for a woman (e.g., Gen. 34:2–3, 8; Deut. 21:11; 2 Sam. 11:2–4; 13:2), as one might expect within the androcentric culture of the time. Although the violent consequences that such sexual desire can lead to are ethically negative, there is no implication that the desire in itself is wrong, and so desire can lead to marriage (Deut. 21:11–13) and is portrayed as appropriate in the acclamation of royal marriage in Ps. 45:11. The positive potential of such relational desire is further shown in the expression of God's desire for Israel (Deut. 10:15).

The exception to the portrayal of male actors desiring passive females is in Gen. 3:16, where God tells Eve that her "desire" (Heb. *tĕšûqâ*, a rare term) will be for her husband, who, however, will rule over her, as the apparent primordial harmony of Adam and Eve is replaced by yearning and domination.

An uncomplicated sense of moral differentiation in relation to desire is implied by the book of Proverbs' references in general terms to the desires of the righteous and the wicked: the desire of the righteous leads to good (Prov. 11:23), and the wicked desire evil (Prov. 21:10), with the expectation that the righteous will receive their desire (Prov. 10:24; 13:12, 19). A similar sense is reflected in some of the psalms: the king who trusts God receives his desire (Ps. 21:1–7), whereas the wicked receive nothing (Ps. 112:10).

Desire in Greco-Roman Moral Thought

The role of desire, as humans pursued happiness or the good life, received greater systematic consideration from Greek and Roman philosophy than it did in the OT. Aristotle argued that desire, at a general level, had a role to play in ethical conduct, in assigning good to some external object as an impulse to action, while at the same time he criticized the commonly observed excessive desire for such objects as wealth and status.

For Epicurus and his followers, happiness was attained in a tranquil life, to be pursued by differentiating empty desires, which led to a disturbed and anxious life, from those "natural" desires that usually could be fulfilled in a modest and proportionate way. To the Stoics, however, desire was one of the passions that distracted people from happiness by focusing on some external object as good, whereas, in reality, only virtue was good. Desire was not in harmony with the rationality of the universe, which enabled the intentional selection of worthwhile action, and so humans needed to be free of desire and other negative passions in order to realize their well-being.

Desire in the New Testament

Some later Jewish writings, including 4 Maccabees, Philo, and Josephus, show the influence of Greco-Roman reflection on desire, particularly the negative Stoic attitude. In the NT, "desire" is represented by the Greek word *epithymia*, the same word the Stoics used in their negative assessment; particularly in the epistolary texts, it tends to be portrayed in a negative light.

On the one hand, the noun *epithymia* rarely occurs in the Gospels, though the cognate verb *epithymeō* is used several times, with less negative overtones, to depict a sense of longing (Matt. 13:17; Luke 16:21; 17:22; 22:15). On the other hand, the negative role of desire is highlighted in the intensification of the command against adultery in the Sermon on the Mount (Matt. 5:28), and in the Markan version of Jesus' parable of the sower, where desire for other things is one of the thorns that choke the word (Mark 4:19).

In Romans and Galatians, Paul associates desire with mortal human existence, unable to resist the power of sin (Rom. 1:24; 6:12; 13:14; Gal. 5:16, 24). Those who belong to Christ, empowered by the Spirit, are able to overcome desire in a fashion not entirely dissimilar to the way the training of philosophy equips the Epicurean or Stoic to deal with desire. A similar outlook is evident in Ephesians and Colossians (Eph. 2:3; 4:22; Col. 3:5). This is carried through in the Pastoral Epistles also (1 Tim. 6:9; 2 Tim. 2:22; 3:6; 4:3; Titus 2:12; 3:3), often in the context of emphasis on Christian teaching (1 Tim. 6:2b–3; 2 Tim 3:7; 4:3; Titus 2:1–10).

The Johannine tradition also portrays desire negatively, as a worldly quality in contrast with God's will (1 John 2:16–17). A negative attitude is also typical of the General Epistles: desire is worldly, "of the flesh," characteristic of the ignorance of believers' former lives (1 Pet. 1:14; 2:11; 4:2–3; 2 Pet. 1:4; 2:18). For James, one's own desires lead to sin and death (Jas. 1:14–15), by contrast with God's gift of birth by the "word of truth" (Jas. 1:17–18).

See also Emotion; Greed; Lust; Passions

Bibliography

Brennan, T. *The Stoic Life: Emotions, Duty, and Fate.* Oxford University Press, 2005; Brenner, A. *The Intercourse of Knowledge: On Gendering Desire and "Sexuality" in the Hebrew Bible.* BIS 26. Brill, 1997; Ellis, J. *Paul and Ancient Views of Sexual Desire: Paul's Sexual Ethics in 1 Thessalonians 4, 1 Corinthians 7, and Romans 1.* LNTS 54. T&T Clark, 2007; Engberg-Pedersen, T. *Paul and the Stoics.* Westminster John Knox, 2000; Nussbaum, M. *The Therapy of Desire: Theory and Practice in Hellenistic Ethics.* MCL 2. Princeton University Press, 1994; Sorabji, R. *Emotion and Peace of Mind: From Stoic Agitation to Christian Temptation.* Oxford University Press, 2000; Trible, P. *God and the Rhetoric of Sexuality.* Fortress, 1986.

David Hutchinson Edgar

Determinism *See* Free Will and Determinism

Deterrence, Nuclear

Nuclear deterrence is a strategy for dissuading enemy attack by threatening retaliatory nuclear strikes. During the Cold War, deterrence was associated with the possibility of "mutual assured destruction" if superpowers exchanged nuclear war. This led the American Catholic Bishops in 1983 to claim that they were members of "the first generation since Genesis with the power to virtually destroy God's creation."

Moral problems with deterrence follow from two claims: (1) use of nuclear weapons would necessarily bring about evils disproportionate to any potential good realized and/or would entail the direct targeting of noncombatants; and (2) it is inherently evil to threaten (or intend) disproportionate acts of war or the direct targeting of noncombatants. Defenders of nuclear deterrence must deny some part of these claims.

Some contend that the language of "inherent evil" is inadequate for determining moral duties in the situation. In some cases, they argue, it is necessary to choose the lesser of two evils.

Others, while granting that nuclear war entails inherent evil, deny that deterrence entails inherent evil. Some deny that threatening an immoral act is itself immoral. This leads to the idea of the "bluff," in which a state threatens nuclear retaliation but has no intent to carry it out. Bluffing, however, faces serious logistical problems. It is almost impossible to realistically threaten without requiring that some participants intend retaliation. Another argument focuses on the distinction between intending deterrence and intending the deployment of nuclear weapons. Deterrence is a strategy, the outcome of which depends on multiple parties. It is wrong, this argument holds, to equate having a deterrent strategy with having a nuclear war.

Others argue that the deployment of nuclear weapons does not necessarily entail inherent evil. Some argue that there is no technological necessity of disproportionate evil in the deployment of nuclear weapons. Others use the doctrine of "double effect" to argue that as long as intended targets are military, any proportionate number of unintended noncombatant casualties could be morally tolerated in a nuclear strike. These arguments have been critiqued, however. Even if not technologically necessary, would not the use of nuclear weapons inevitably lead to disproportionate evil in practice? Can one viably deploy double effect when the actual destruction is so massive and the strategy of deterrence depends on the massiveness of this destruction? Finally, would the threat of a limited nuclear war function sufficiently as a deterrent?

See also Consequentialism; Deontological Theories of Ethics; Double Effect, Principle of; Ends and Means; Just-War Theory; War

Bibliography

Hollenbach, D. *Nuclear Ethics: A Christian Moral Argument.* Paulist Press, 1983; O'Donovan, O. *Peace and*

Certainty: A Theological Essay on Deterrence. Eerdmans, 1989; Ramsey, P. *The Just War: Force and Political Responsibility*. Rowman & Littlefield, 2002; United States Conference of Catholic Bishops. *The Challenge of Peace: God's Promise and Our Response*. United States Catholic Conference, 1983; Walzer, M. *Just and Unjust Wars*. Basic Books, 1977.

Kevin Carnahan

Deuterocanonical/Apocryphal Books

The Apocrypha is a collection of Jewish writings dating somewhere between 250 BCE and 100 CE, written in Hebrew, Aramaic, or Greek, and composed across a wide geographic area. Although the texts were written by devout Jews, their collection into a discrete corpus is the result of Christian reading practices and positive evaluation of this material. The core of the collection includes two historical books (1–2 Maccabees), wisdom literature (Wisdom of Solomon, Sirach [also known as Wisdom of Ben Sira and as Ecclesiasticus]), additions to or rewritten versions of Jewish scriptural books (1 Esdras, Greek Esther, Greek Daniel [which includes the stories of Susanna and of Bel and the Dragon, as well as Prayer of Azariah and Song of the Three Young Men], Baruch, Letter of Jeremiah), and two edifying tales (Tobit, Judith). Current collections (e.g., the NRSV) also include two liturgical pieces (Ps. 151, Prayer of Manasseh), another specimen of historical fiction (3 Maccabees), an apocalypse (2 Esdras), and an essay promoting the Jewish "philosophy" (4 Maccabees).

The canonical status of these books has been a matter of debate from the beginning. Several of the Apocrypha have left a clear impression on the writings of the NT, though without ever being explicitly recited or referred to as Scripture. Many church fathers throughout the first four centuries of the church's history continued to read and invoke these texts, increasingly as scriptural authorities in their own right, though with famous objections being raised to such usage (e.g., by Jerome, who championed the use of the Jewish canon and the Hebrew form of the Jewish scriptural texts as the Christian OT).

Currently, Eastern Orthodox communions and the Roman Catholic Church regard at least the core collection of these books as Scripture, with the former also including Prayer of Manasseh, Ps. 151, and 3 Maccabees. The term *deuterocanonical* is used in these contexts to affirm the canonical status of this collection while acknowledging the fact that their composition and collection followed subsequently, for the most part, on the composition and collection of the Hebrew canon. During the Reformation it became a hallmark of Protestant churches to exclude these books from the Christian canon, although several leaders of the Reformation themselves were reluctant to see them fall into obscurity. Martin Luther, for example, commended (and included) them in his translation of the Bible as "both useful and good to read," though not of equal authority with Scripture, and the Church of England stipulated in the sixth article of religion that they be "read for example of life and instruction of manners." This last statement is particularly salient here, as it is precisely as ethical literature that the deuterocanonical/apocryphal books have been most widely read and valued.

The Mosaic covenant—the stipulations and terms outlined in the Pentateuch—provides the overarching framework for ethics throughout this literature. Nearly every text reflects explicitly on this covenant as a divinely given, clearly articulated matrix of specific ethical directives and of personal and corporate motivations to embrace these directives. "Wisdom," the ethical ideal in Sirach, Wisdom of Solomon, and Baruch, for example, has come to be identified with "the book of the commandments of God, the law that endures forever" (Bar. 4:1 [cf. Sir. 24:1–23; Wis. 16:6; 18:9]). The person whose behaviors and practices align with the stipulations of Torah is the "ethical" person (Sus. 3), whereas the person who transgresses the same exhibits ethical failure. As a result of the covenantal framework, the scope of concern throughout this literature tends to be particularistic, focused on the good of the Jewish people as a whole and, within it, the individual Judean. There are limited universalistic strains (e.g., Wis. 11:23–12:2; 13:1–7), but these are often swept aside (e.g., Wis. 12:10–11; 13:8–9).

The covenant curses and blessings outlined in Deut. 28–30 are a constant reference point for analyzing social and political conditions, diagnosing ethical failure, and pointing the way toward reform and restoration both of the individual and the nation. Motivations to ethical action tend to be drawn from the consequences laid out in the Deuteronomic model: obedience leads to divine blessing, disobedience to experience of divine wrath and punishment, repentance and renewed obedience to renewed experience of divine aid and restoration (see, e.g., Jdt. 5:17–20; Bar. 1:15–22; Sg. Three 5–13; 2 Macc. 4:7–17; 6:12–17; 4 Macc. 3:20–4:21; 18:3–4). Using this model, authors can appeal to individual self-interest: ethical action is a means to an end, most expedient for the doer in terms of leading to honor, advantage, and enjoyment of particular goods valued in society. This is common in Sirach and Tobit, as, indeed, it is in the advice literature of the period more generally. Authors can also appeal to the good of the nation: ethical action is most expedient for the commonwealth, whether on the basis of the covenant blessings and curses (the actions that God would take in response to the people's alignment with covenant stipulations) or with a view to natural consequences (e.g., demonstrating the nobility of the nation's way of life to others, or rallying resistance against a tyrant by a demonstration of courage and commitment). In both instances, the rewards and punishments may be anticipated in the natural course of one's lifetime or national fortune, or in the postmortem existence of the individual or eschatological future of the nation.

Ethical action, however, is also urged as a proper response to God, an expression of commitment to God and loyalty to God for the experience of God's past gifts. In 4 Maccabees, for example, a Torah-observant life productive of virtue is a means of living so as to best honor God, using the gift of human faculties well and in line with God's best intentions for it (4 Macc. 2:21–23). The commitment to do so even in the face of great hardship, even martyrdom, may be motivated by the hope for postmortem reward or fear of postmortem punishment (4 Macc. 9:8–9; 13:14–17; 15:2–3), but it is motivated also by the awareness that it is a proper and just return to God for the gift of life itself (4 Macc. 13:13; 16:18–19). Ethical action is what is due God.

The covenantal framework elevates the nation's (and the individual's) relationship with God and experience of God's favor (past, present, and future) as the ground for the meaningfulness of and motivation for ethical action. Right ethics begins with right piety. Hence, attention is given throughout the literature to debunking idolatry (see Letter of Jeremiah; Bel and the Dragon; Wis. 12:1–14:31) and maintaining commitment to the one God, the God who gave and enforces the covenant and its legal, ethical, ritual code. The author of Wisdom of Solomon explicitly reflects on the failure to experience this relationship with the one God: the filling of the religious vacuum with idolatry—creating relationships with false gods—has resulted in the moral chaos observable in gentile society at both the personal and social level (Wis. 13:1–14:31). Perversion of piety leads to perversion of thinking, feeling, craving, and action in every arena. In an earlier section of the book (possibly by a different author) the source of this ethical mayhem is sought in the failure of individuals to look beyond death to seek immortality through virtuous living, choosing instead to grasp at whatever fleeting pleasures they can, at whatever cost to others it entails. Looking at death as the end of existence elevates the wrong goals and means to their attainment (Wis. 1:16–2:24).

The Jews' commitment to monolatry and to the particular practices prescribed by Torah frequently led to tension with non-Jewish groups (and authorities) in regard to the latter's political and civic ethics (see, e.g., Add. Esth. 13:4–5; 3 Macc. 3:3–7, 21–23). The literature bears witness to strenuous debates and a significant diversity of response within Judaism regarding how to address this, many Jews advocating significant compromise, even capitulation on these points, in order to appear as "good citizens" and enjoy the benefits thereof (e.g., 1 Macc. 1:11–15; 3 Macc. 2:31–33). The deuterocanonical/apocryphal books, not surprisingly, consistently promote fidelity to the minority culture's ethical code, even where this incurs reproach or open hostility. Moreover, there are some stunning examples of innercommunal reinforcement of ethics, whether through giving assistance preferentially to the righteous poor, using charity as a means to promote alignment with the covenant (Tob. 2:2; 4:6; Sir. 12:1–7), or through enforcing the covenant violently—for example, by circumcising Jewish boys left uncircumcised by their apostate parents and lynching or executing apostate Jews (1 Macc. 2:42–48; 3:5–8; 3 Macc. 7:10–16).

Where fidelity to the covenant and the faithful performance of its stipulations are threatened, both violent and nonviolent resistance are commended as ethical responses. The books of 1–2 Maccabees are especially interested in military and diplomatic action as a component of faithful response to Torah and thus support violent resistance (see, e.g., 1 Macc. 2:15–28, 39–48; 3:1–26; 2 Macc. 8:1–16:37). Considerable space, however, is also given in these texts to commending nonviolent resistance even to the point of death (1 Macc. 1:60–63; 2 Macc. 6:1–7:42). The book of 4 Maccabees commends the ideal of the witness who resists apostasy, foreign domination, and religious repression but does so by suffering courageously in the face of repressive violence rather than by practicing violence. Although essentially advocating a violent solution to political and religious repression, the book of Judith presents a special ethical problem, celebrating the use of deceit and seduction as a valid ethical means to secure the safety of the nation (Jdt. 8:1–13:20), a means even sanctioned by God (Jdt. 9:13). Judith's strategy, however, is analogous to other uses of "craftiness" in wartime situations. Moreover, the ancient Mediterranean world tended to regard not the use of deceit, but rather being duped by deceit, as the point of failure.

A few texts within this collection merit special note for their contribution to ethical reflection. The book of Sirach contains the essential curriculum of a Jewish sage who maintained a school in Jerusalem in the decades around 200 BCE. This sage's literary legacy gives a window into early Jewish reflection on negotiating life in the household, in the larger society, even in the international sphere to advantage. It covers a wide variety of ethical and practical topics, including ethical speech, friendship, forgiveness, etiquette, caution in regard to ambition, moderation and self-control, household management, family duties, sexual ethics, the virtue of humility, the importance of mutual accountability, generosity, and practicing charity and social justice. A critical problem in Sirach concerns his view of women, which is largely negative and derived from his culture's obsession with female sexuality. As is reflected in the views of other authors in this collection, sexual exclusivity is the sine qua non of female virtue (see Jdt. 13:16; 4 Macc. 17:1; 18:6–9 [although in these books women are clearly regarded as capable of other virtues, notably courage and unyielding covenant loyalty]). However, Sirach expresses a clear lack of faith that women will reliably keep to the ideal, bringing anxiety and disgrace upon their fathers and husbands instead (Sir. 26:10–12; 42:11). Nevertheless, on many issues Sirach makes important ethical advances. The book promotes forgiveness of others on the basis of hoping for God's forgiveness of oneself. Also, it uses the commandments as a ground for ethical reflection, extending, for example, the prohibition against murder to include other acts of social or economic violence. Finally, it commends generosity toward all, especially the poor, as a reflection of God's character and thus of the donor's kinship with the divine. In all this, the author anticipates the ethics of Jesus of Nazareth.

The text of 2 Esd. 3–14 is a Jewish apocalypse from the late first century, usually referred to as *4 Ezra* (2 Esd. 1–2 and 2 Esd. 15–16 are slightly later Christian additions, called *5 Ezra* and *6 Ezra*, respectively). The author of this text sharply poses the ethical problem of the individual's seeking to live up to the ideal of the covenant while dominated by the tendency toward transgression that seems, from lived experience, to grip the human race (both Jews and gentiles) in a stranglehold. Like Paul, he looks to the story of Adam and Eve as the beginning of sin and, indeed, as the episode that forever predisposes their descendants toward vice (2 Esd. 3:22; 4:30; 7:118–119; cf. Sir. 25:24; Wis. 2:23–24). Nevertheless, moral responsibility is not in any way abated. The contest against the evil inclination may be difficult, and the stakes indeed high, but each person must fight well in this contest so as to walk aligned with God's law and arrive at the promised blessings beyond death (2 Esd. 7:127–130). The author thus reaffirms the conclusion at which Sirach had arrived three centuries before: ethical achievement or failure remains a matter of the individual's choice and responsibility (Sir. 15:11–20).

A product of the Hellenistic Diaspora, 4 Maccabees is the text within this collection most explicitly and fully devoted to well-defined ethical issues. Addressing a common subject of Greek and Latin philosophical ethics, the author presents Torah observance as a disciplined lifestyle that promotes self-mastery in regard to the "passions"—the emotional responses, volitional cravings, and physical sensations that pose an ongoing danger to consistent ethical action—with the result that the pious Jew attains the ethical ideals prized by the Greco-Roman philosophical culture (justice, courage, temperance, prudence, piety). Martyrdom is interpreted as both the ultimate sign of such self-mastery and the realization of the freedom of the wise person from all external compulsion. Sages can be injured only insofar as they consent to depart from their moral principles. The book is a fine example of religious ethical discourse that is also fully informed by, and engaged in, the larger Greco-Roman conversation.

The deuterocanonical/apocryphal books provide essential windows into the ethical interpretation of the received tradition and the ethical developments within Judaism in the postprophetic period. As such, they also provide essential background to any study of the ethics of the early Christian writings, and, indeed, the impact of the Apocrypha on the ethics of the early and ongoing Christian movement is significant. Whatever the canonical status of these texts might be in the eyes of the interpreter, any thorough investigation of biblical ethics must take this literature into account.

See also Additions to Daniel; Additions to Esther; Baruch; Freedom; Idolatry; Judith; Letter of Jeremiah; 1 Maccabees; 2 Maccabees; Martyrdom; Orthodox Ethics; Passions; Sirach; Tobit; Wisdom of Solomon

Bibliography

Charles, R. *The Apocrypha and Pseudepigrapha of the Old Testament*. 2 vols. Oxford University Press, 1913;

Collins, J. *Between Athens and Jerusalem: Jewish Identity in the Hellenistic Diaspora*. 2nd ed. Eerdmans, 2000; idem, *Jewish Wisdom in the Hellenistic Age*. Westminster John Knox, 1997; deSilva, D. *4 Maccabees*. GAP. Sheffield Academic Press, 1998; idem. *Introducing the Apocrypha: Message, Context, and Significance*. Baker Academic, 2002; Harrington, D. *Invitation to the Apocrypha*. Eerdmans, 1999; Helyer, L. *Exploring Jewish Literature of the Second Temple Period*. InterVarsity, 2002; Maldwyn, H. *The Ethics of Jewish Apocryphal Literature*. Robert Culley, 1909; Metzger, B. *An Introduction to the Apocrypha*. Oxford University Press, 1957.

David A. deSilva

Deuteronomistic History

The books of the Former Prophets (Joshua, Judges, 1–2 Samuel, 1–2 Kings) have become known by this title in accordance with an influential theory proposed by German OT scholar Martin Noth. Noth viewed the Former Prophets, together with Deuteronomy, as composing a unified, large-scale literary corpus whose primary purpose was to provide an explanation for Israel's sixth-century defeat and exile. With this goal in mind, a single editor-like exilic author had combined numerous preexistent traditions. The author, commonly referred to as the Deuteronomist, had creatively shaped the telling of this history (DtrH), highlighting certain aspects and glossing over others, dividing it into discrete periods and inserting into its continuous narrative a number of salvation-historical speeches by various characters or the narrator himself (Josh. 1:1–9; 12:1–6; 23:1–16; Judg. 2:11–3:6; 1 Sam. 12:1–15; 1 Kgs. 8:14–53; 2 Kgs. 17:7–23). These speeches cumulatively tracked the action of the overarching story and reinforced the author's theological perspective.

Despite some objections, subsequent scholarship at first upheld Noth's thesis strongly, although gradually with the proviso that the DtrH had instead been created in stages and by more than one hand. Building on the work of Rudolf Smend, many German scholars argued that the original exilic edition of the DtrH had been supplemented by two further layers of material, one focusing on the activity of prophets (DtrP) and another, later, layer exhibiting a characteristic emphasis on nomistic/Torah piety (DtrN). Following Frank Moore Cross, US scholars tended to adopt a two-stage view in which the first edition of the DtrH ($DtrH^1$) was produced in the preexilic period as Josianic propaganda, then modified after Josiah's death and Judah's downfall in order to conform to these newly disastrous circumstances ($DtrH^2$). However, the entire notion of a DtrH is now being criticized, with a new generation of scholars stressing the untidiness of the material, the presence of pluriform perspectives, the substantial differences between the individual books, and the possibility of even later postexilic dates for these books' composition and literary development. Yet, there is still no gainsaying the presence of Deuteronomy-like elements in each of the books, especially the motif of "other gods" (e.g., Deut. 6:14) and the repeated references to an approaching exile (e.g., Deut. 28:63–64).

The primary literary effect of the complex's disastrous conclusion is to create irony at the intersection between individual narratives and the wider story. For example, the stirring exploits of local heroes nevertheless fail to achieve permanent change (Judg. 2:16–23). Some episodes that might at first appear commendable are eventually revealed to be examples of Israel's sinful decline (Judg. 11:29–40; 19). So too praise of certain kings and the institution of the kingship itself (2 Sam. 7; 1 Kgs. 8) now occur within a broader literary frame in which monarchy is viewed as a primary reason for Israel's downfall (Deut. 17:14–20; 1 Sam. 12:12–15; 2 Kgs. 17:8; 21:10–15). While not quite as bleak as Noth envisioned (as Gerhard von Rad pointed out, God's promise to Israel is "forever"; the exiles will survive), the DtrH does indeed justify the righteousness of God by laying the blame for Israel's destruction squarely with Israel.

Israel, Land, and the Nations

The book of Joshua begins with Israel's armed occupation of Canaan at God's direction. The narrative gives an initial impression of a speedy, violent, and total conquest (Josh. 10; 21:43–45). God not only sanctions this warfare but also participates in it (Josh. 5:13–15; 10:6–11; 11:6–9). Disturbing is not only the lack of greater sympathy for the land's inhabitants but also the way that this portion of the Bible has provided ideological cover for numerous land grabs in history (e.g., the United States' takeover of Native American land, the Afrikaners in South Africa, the Ulster Scots in Northern Ireland). The litany of "utter destruction" in Josh. 10–11 reads almost like a celebration of genocide. Here again, however, Israel's violent loss of the land at the conclusion of the DtrH later casts doubt on Israel's earlier manner of occupying it. The effectiveness of the conquest is in fact subverted in the course of the narrative through passing references to its gradualism (Josh. 11:18–20; see also Deut. 7:22: "little by little"; cf. Exod. 23:30) and incompleteness (Josh. 13:1–13; 15:63; 16:10; 17:12–13; Judg. 1). Moreover, the narrative's only extended episode of urban conquest depicts a style of warfare more liturgical than actual: Jericho's walls are brought down by a priestly parade rather than siege works (Josh. 6). In the end, although violence in God's name is never rejected, a distancing is evident. Various battles have their outcomes reported without the details of the engagements being specified. By associating the "conquest" so closely with Israel's unique territorial inheritance, the narrative makes this primal instance of dispossession unrepeatable (i.e., there is only one "promised land"). Even more suggestively, Israel's ultimate loss of the land reinforces a conditional message of responsibility (Deut. 29; Josh. 23:6–13), even a sense of futility (Josh. 23:15–16; but cf. Deut. 30), with respect to Israel's privileged hold on its geographic claim.

The other peoples within the land and in the nations outside Israel are often portrayed as threats and enemies. Yet beginning with Rahab (Josh. 2; 6) and continuing in figures such as the queen of Sheba (1 Kgs. 10), the widow of Zarephath (1 Kgs. 17), and Naaman (2 Kgs. 5), the DtrH also depicts non-Israelites who come to know God through their interactions with Israel—a theme further emphasized by the placement of Ruth between Judges and 1 Samuel in the Christian canon. Additionally, the DtrH subverts Israel's ethnic distinctiveness by portraying Israelites who are more similar to foreigners than different, even if that similarity is interpreted as a mark of unfaithfulness (e.g., Samson, Solomon). In this way, the DtrH also illustrates and extends the Genesis account of how God is using Israel to bring blessing to "all the families of the earth" (Gen. 12:1–3; cf. 1 Kgs. 8:41–43). Or in a saying attributed to Rabbi Hizkiyah in the Zohar, a medieval Jewish text, "The blessed Holy One cast Israel into exile among the nations only so that the other nations would be blessed because of them, for they draw blessings from above to below every day."

Responsible Leadership

The book of Joshua also makes clear from the outset that Israel's leaders must submit to the rule of law (Josh. 1:7–9; cf. Deut. 17:14–20). Human authority can change within a spiritual succession (e.g., Moses to Joshua, the judges, Saul to David, Elijah to Elisha), but biological succession is viewed with intense suspicion (Judg. 8:22–23; 1 Sam. 2; 8:1–3). "Absolute monarchy" is not found in the DtrH. Instead, God is considered Israel's true king (Judg. 8:23; 1 Sam. 7; cf. Isa. 6:5), and human leadership is treated as fundamentally derivative of divine authority (God is supposed to "choose" those in leadership). Furthermore, kings and other leaders are held accountable within a variety of wider social contexts and interactions, such as Israel's tribal structure, moral tradition, legal system, priestly customs—and even outsider figures possessing specialized knowledge (e.g., the wise woman of Tekoa [2 Sam. 14]) or ability to communicate directly with God (e.g., the prophet Elijah [1 Kgs. 17–19; 2 Kgs. 1–2]). Still, the quality of leaders and the character of their leadership matter greatly to the health of the nation and to the furtherance of God's purposes in the world. God's leaders can be outnumbered (1 Sam. 14:6–15) and physically unprepossessing (1 Sam. 17) because they draw their true strength from ruling justly (2 Sam. 23:3). "Power politics" and coercive policies (1 Kgs. 5:13–18) are rejected in favor of a pious openness ("heart" [Josh. 24:23; 1 Sam. 16:7]) to the prophetic word (Josh. 24:2; 1 Sam. 15:22–23).

Indeed, prophetic figures begin to predominate in the course of the DtrH until Israel's destiny becomes almost a tug-of-war between righteous prophets and unrighteous kings. Only two kings receive unqualified praise (Hezekiah [2 Kgs. 18:5–6]; Josiah [2 Kgs. 23:25]), and both have reigns featuring a reform of Israelite worship in which prophets play a leading role (Isaiah [2 Kgs. 19–20]; Huldah [2 Kgs. 22:14–20]). The DtrH sponsors a view of history in which Israel's prophets all finally offer a common message (2 Kgs. 17:13) and stand within a succession begun by Moses (Deut. 18:15–22). In this perspective, law and prophecy are complementary rather than competitive authorities, particularly in the constraint that both provide to royal power. The Latter Prophets are significantly less inclined to ground moral imperatives in legal warrants (they instead usually emphasize spiritual/moral values such as "righteousness" and "covenant faithfulness"). The theological unity of law and prophecy is therefore a crucial Deuteronomistic insight and one that lies at the origin of the eventual shape of the OT canon (i.e., "the law and the prophets").

Human Dignity

Particularly striking throughout the DtrH is the richness of its individual characters, especially since their literary characterization typically is handled with great economy of means (e.g., little physical description, infrequent use of affective/emotional terms). Yet figures such as Delilah, Hannah, Jonathan, Abigail, Joab, Bathsheba, Jehu, and Jezebel are fascinating for their complexity and lifelikeness. Although the DtrH operates with a strong sense of divine involvement in history, human nature is depicted as varied, human choice as real, and human freedom as precious. Even the catastrophe at the end of the DtrH underscores the value God places on human freedom; otherwise, given the stakes, why give Israel any choice? God is correspondingly portrayed as having the capacity for direct action (1 Sam. 25:38) but more customarily acting through human judgments (2 Sam. 17:14). Even though human figures are shown to be embedded within social groups and contexts, each individual has access to God and therefore a concomitant dignity. In a classic story about the abuse of royal power (1 Kgs. 21), the rights of Naboth, an ordinary Israelite, are upheld against Ahab's covetousness. Jezebel's plot against Naboth turns on the bearing of false witness—in other words, the suppression of Naboth's ability to function as a trustworthy moral agent. The irreducible worth and complexity of individual moral character explain why the DtrH does not demonize its villains and presents its heroes unvarnished.

Women are often the victims of horrible mistreatment in the DtrH's narratives (Judg. 1:12–15; 11:29–40; 19; 21; 1 Sam. 1; 2 Sam. 13; 2 Kgs. 15:16), yet they can be simultaneously portrayed as fully realized human agents possessing a personal dignity equivalent to that of men (Judg. 1:14–15; 11:36–40; 1 Sam. 1:12–18). Women are not completely restricted to the domestic sphere, and occasionally they become leaders in warfare (e.g., Deborah, Jael), politics (e.g., Abigail, Michal, Bathsheba), and government (e.g., Jezebel, Athaliah, the queen of Sheba). Although Israelite women are for the most part apparently excluded from central positions of political power, the DtrH's overall perspective is surprisingly egalitarian rather than misogynistic. Ironically, even episodes of victimization can reinforce this egalitarian perspective by calling attention to the unfairness of the social structures in which women's moral agency and spiritual freedom are eclipsed (1 Sam. 1; 2 Sam. 3:12–16).

Even so, Israel is finally depicted as more than the sum of its individuals. At the heart of the DtrH is the challenge facing the people of Israel to *be* a people. That they are exiled *as* a people (2 Kgs. 24:14–16; 25:11) is a feature of the story pointing beyond itself to Israel's continuing communal future on the other side of divine judgment.

See also Ban, The; Deuteronomy; Exile; Holy War; Joshua; Judges; 1–2 Kings; Land; Law; Old Testament Ethics; 1–2 Samuel

Bibliography

Ellul, J. *The Politics of God and the Politics of Man*. Eerdmans, 1972; Klein, L. *The Triumph of Irony in the Book of Judges*. JSOTSup 68. Almond, 1988; Noth, M. *The Deuteronomistic History*. 2nd ed. JSOTSup 15. JSOT Press, 1991; Pleins, J. *The Social Visions of the Hebrew Bible: A Theological Introduction*. Westminster John Knox, 2001; Römer, T. *The So-Called Deuteronomistic History: A Sociological, Historical and Literary Introduction*. T&T Clark, 2005; von Rad, G. *Old Testament Theology*. 2 vols. Harper & Row, 1962–65; Wenham, G. *Story as Torah: Reading Old Testament Narrative Ethically*. Baker Academic, 2000.

Stephen B. Chapman

Deuteronomy

The book of Deuteronomy (meaning "a copy of the law" or "second law," from the Greek translation of 17:18) is presented as the last set of instructional sermons from ancient Israel's elderly leader Moses to a new generation of Israelites who are at the border preparing to enter the promised land of Canaan.

Core Ethical Assumptions in Deuteronomy

Many parts of Deuteronomy repeat or reinterpret earlier laws and narratives in the Pentateuch, especially the laws of the Covenant Code in Exod. 20:22–23:19. About 50 percent of the Covenant Code laws in Exodus are repeated with small but significant variations in Deuteronomy. The book of Deuteronomy often adds its unique theological stamp to this material, shaped especially by Deuteronomy's emphasis on "oneness": (1) Israel's relational loyalty to one God alone; (2) the identity of Israel as one people set apart from the nations; (3) the requirement of one centralized place of worship to which all Israel gathers in festivals; (4) adherence to one Torah, which all Israel is called to obey.

Deuteronomy's central confession is the Shema (from the first word of the Hebrew text, meaning "hear"): "Hear, O Israel: the Lord is our God, the Lord alone," followed by the command "You shall love the Lord your God with all your heart, and with all your soul, and with all your might" (Deut. 6:4–5). Jesus coupled this verse with Lev. 19:18 to describe the Great Commandments, which summarize all the law of Moses (Matt. 22:36–40; Mark 12:28–34; Luke 10:25–28).

Scholars have associated Deuteronomy's requirement for the centralization of worship in ancient Israel with the reforms of King Hezekiah and King Josiah, who cleansed the Jerusalem temple and destroyed worship sites and altars outside Jerusalem (2 Kgs. 18:3–6, 22; 22–23). These royal reforms seem to coincide with Deuteronomy's decree that all offerings of grain and animal sacrifices and all celebrations of holy festivals are to be held in the one "place which the Lord your God will choose" (Deut. 12:5, 13, 18, 26; 14:23; 15:20; 16:6, 11, 15–16; 17:10; 31:11). Although Deuteronomy centralizes sacrifice and worship in one place, it maintains that God's sovereignty and concern for holiness extend to the whole land and to every family within Israel.

Deuteronomy refers to itself frequently as "the book of the *tôrâ*" (1:5; 4:8, 44; 17:18–19; 27:3, 8, 26; 28:58, 61; 29:20, 28; 30:10; 31:9, 11–12, 24; 32:46). Some have translated *tôrâ* for Deuteronomy as referring to the polity or constitution of the people of Israel. Its emphasis on law, obedience, and allegiance to God alone suggests its role as a core legal foundation for the identity and organization of Israel as the people of God. Others have also noted the strong educational or instructional meaning associated with the Hebrew term *tôrâ* along with the frequent references in Deuteronomy to members of an older generation teaching a new generation (4:1, 5, 10, 14; 5:31; 6:1; 11:19; 31:19; 32:2; 33:10). Thus, Deuteronomy as *tôrâ* may be understood as a program of ethical, political, and theological catechesis achieved through a variety of formational strategies: narratives (chaps. 1; 9), laws (6:1; 12–26), rituals (chaps. 16; 26), poetic song (31:19; 32), oral recitation (31:9–13), and exemplary models of character (Moses in chap. 34).

Deuteronomy and the Sabbath

The Sabbath commandment in 5:12–15 and its further explication in the sabbath laws of 14:22–16:17 underscore the strong connection between the worship of God and concern for care and justice for the vulnerable members of the community. Regular worship of God on weekly Sabbaths and annual festivals is combined with the sharing of offerings with the most vulnerable members of the community (the poor, widows, orphans, landless Levites). The Sabbath laws also include the cancellation of all debts every seven years and the required freeing of slaves after seven years of service (15:1–6, 12–18). The Sabbath laws also hold in creative tension the ideal that there will "be no one in need among you" (15:4) with the realism that "there will never cease to be some in need on the earth" (15:11). This tension creates the need for structural provisions for the periodic cancellation of debts as well as more spontaneous and voluntary acts of charity and support to the poor (15:7–11).

Other Ethical Resources

Deuteronomy's laws also set in motion creative tensions between proper respect for authority (5:16) and provisions that ensure that those in leadership remain worthy of respect and authority (16:18–18:22). These same laws also prescribe a delicate balance between centralized leadership and distributed authority (see also 1:9–18). Ecological concern for the care of animals and vegetative life is evident in several laws (5:14; 20:19–20; 22:1–4, 6–7). Deuteronomy uses the metaphor of "circumcising the foreskin of the heart" to hold together the need for humans to strive to be obedient (10:16) and the promise that God will work within humans to create obedience (30:6).

One of the most ethically challenging texts in Deuteronomy is the law of holy war in 20:1–20, which commands the Israelites to kill "everything that breathes" (v. 16) when they enter the land of Canaan (see Josh. 6:21). In the end, however, Israel was unable or unwilling to carry out the law, as Israel allowed some Canaanites to remain alive in the land (Rahab [Josh. 2; 6]; the Gibeonites [Josh. 9; Judg. 1:21, 27–36]). Thus, God abandoned the strategy of holy war and allowed the Canaanites to remain in the land as a perpetual test of Israel's obedience in the face of the ongoing temptation to worship other gods (Judg. 2:19–23; 3:1–5).

See also Authority and Power; Ban, The; Conquest; Holy War; Idolatry; Law; Old Testament Ethics; Sabbath; Ten Commandments; Torah

Bibliography

Hamilton, J. *Social Justice and Deuteronomy: The Case of Deuteronomy 15*. SBLDS 136. Scholars Press, 1992; Levinson, B. *Deuteronomy and the Hermeneutics of Legal Innovation*. Oxford University Press, 1997; McDonald, N. *Deuteronomy and the Meaning of "Monotheism."* FAT 2/1. Mohr Siebeck, 2003; Millar, J. *Now Choose Life: Theology and Ethics in Deuteronomy*. Eerdmans, 1998; Miller, P. *Deuteronomy*. IBC. Westminster John Knox, 1990; Olson, D. *Deuteronomy and the Death of Moses: A Theological Reading*. Fortress, 1994; Vogt, P. *Deuteronomic Theology and the Significance of Torah: A Reappraisal*. Eisenbrauns, 2006.

Dennis T. Olson

Development, Moral *See* Moral Development

Deviance

Deviance is the characteristic or state of departing from common standards or established norms. Deviance especially refers to the violation of social mores concerning life and relationships, and, particularly, sexual behavior. Often used in a pejorative sense, it signals societal disapproval and condemnation and is associated with shame and definitions and theories of crime.

Sociological theories of deviance often focus on its place in social control. These include learning theories, which generally state that people inculcate norms of conformity and deviance through intimate reference groups, which can include family, church, workplace, friends, and media;

strain or anomie theories, which explain deviant behavior resulting from conflicts between social goals and the availability of legitimate means to reach those goals; control theories, which outline the development of self-control that keeps persons from acting on deviant tendencies or desires through internal constraints, such as conscience and morality, and external constraints, such as law enforcement and religious authority; and labeling theories, which hold that deviance is a process of social power in which a person or behavior is considered deviant only when it is labeled as such by persons or groups with social authority. Labeling theory was influenced by conflict theory, such as that of Karl Marx, whose work explains deviance as a construct of power within economic class conflict in which those with productive property exert their power over societal influencers—for example, religion, education, criminal justice—in order to protect their own interests.

Identifying the norms that define deviant and conforming behavior can be a complex undertaking, given that it is often assumed that the relevant social standards vary both within and among cultures. Behavior that is considered deviant in one group or culture may be considered acceptable or even praiseworthy in another, making it difficult to talk of application of universal or absolute norms to determine deviance. Postmodern social theory has paid particular attention to such complexity, calling into question the production of norms from conventional moral and legal authority and suggesting that discussion of norms or deviance is valid only within a relative group rather than throughout a culturally diverse society. Other theorists have looked to norms formed around issues of harm to person or property, justice, and human flourishing that may be applied more broadly in human society.

Within the religious community, deviance often centers on the place of the sinner, who violates central doctrines; the heretic, who rejects elements of the faith; and the apostate, who abandons the faith for an alternative set of religious values. In the codes of the OT, deviant acts viewed as a threat to the whole community—such as apostasy and blasphemy (Exod. 20:2–5; Lev. 24:10–14; Deut. 17:2–7), female sorcery (Exod. 22:18), and various sexual offenses (Lev. 18:6–23)—carry the greatest penalties. Sexual norms also play a prominent role in defining deviance in lists of virtues and vices in the NT, which include adultery, fornication, male prostitution, and sodomy (e.g., Matt. 15:19; 1 Cor. 6:9–10; Rev. 22:15). Such biblical lists are frequently used in defense of contemporary proscriptions concerning homosexuality, yet ongoing societal, ecclesial, and scholarly debates regarding the deviance of homosexual practice expose hermeneutical complexities in defining norms and mores across cultures and history.

While conventional wisdom and social-scientific study often have posited with religion a role as sustainer of societal moral order, at times religion has challenged secular culture, providing a source of deviant behavior rather than acting as an instrument of social control. The theme appears in the Bible as well, such as Jesus' defiance of purity laws (e.g., Matt. 8:1–4 pars.), his incitement of the synagogue crowd at the beginning of his Galilean ministry (Luke 4:28–29), and the marginal status of believers in the Roman Empire documented, for example, in 1 Peter or Revelation.

See also Clean and Unclean; Cross-Cultural Ethics; Holiness Code; Norms; Vice; Vices and Virtues, Lists of

Bibliography

Clinard, M., and R. Meier. *Sociology of Deviant Behavior.* 13th ed. Thompson/Wadsworth, 2008; Dinitz, S., R. Dynes, and A. Clark. *Deviance: Studies in Definition, Management, and Treatment.* Oxford University Press, 1975; Harrington, A. *Modern Social Theory: An Introduction.* Oxford University Press, 2005; Stark, R., and W. Bainbridge. *Religion, Deviance and Social Control.* Routledge, 1997; Talbott, R. "Nazareth's Rebellious Son: Deviance and Downward Mobility in the Galilean Jesus Movement." *BTB* 38 (2008): 99–113.

Gary B. MacDonald

Didache

The *Teaching of the Twelve Apostles*, or the *Didache* (Gk. *didachē* ["teaching"]), is an early Christian manual of instruction whose origins remain unknown. Most scholars date the work to the late first or early second century, with a provenance somewhere between Egypt and Syria. Familiarity with limited themes from Paul and the sayings of Jesus, mainly as reflected in the Gospel of Matthew, is evident throughout. The text plausibly divides into three parts: the teaching of the "two ways" (chaps. 1–6), various liturgical and ecclesiastical instructions (chaps. 7–15), and concluding apocalyptic warnings (chap. 16).

Many Christians by the turn of the second century sought to create a new ethic with origins that lay outside of the synagogue. Against this tendency, the *Didache* appeals to those NT authors who endorse a functional ethic from within Judaism. Two primary elements from this more Jewish perspective appear here: a concern for eschatology and the "two ways."

The language of eschatology emerges randomly throughout the latter half of the work. One hears a call for the coming of God's kingdom and that heaven's work be done on earth, as illustrated by the Lord's Prayer (8.2). So too, supplication is offered for the ingathering of the church from the ends of the earth (9.4) and from the four winds (10.5). In light of the Lord's dominion, appropriate liturgical practices and good conduct in how peripatetic prophets are received are encouraged. A brief apocalyptic piece (chap. 16), reminiscent of Paul (1 Thess. 4:13–18) and Mark 13, concludes the text. Here the faithful of God are warned to be careful, to gather frequently, and to avoid false prophets as lawlessness increases before that day when the Lord comes from the skies with the sound of a trumpet. Typical of apocalyptic literature generally, this final warning intends for the listener to live ethically in the hope of eternal reward. It casts a shadow of urgency over the entire collection of teachings, much as Revelation does for the larger canon of Christian Scripture.

Apart from the broad community ethic associated with proper liturgical and ecclesiastical practice, the *Didache* is particularly interested in the question of individual ethics. This is evident in the opening line of the work: "There are two ways, one of life and one of death" (1.1). The "two ways" perspective developed from OT roots (Deut. 30:15; Jer. 21:8) into a common late Jewish directive (see *T. Ash.* 1.3–9; 1QS 3.13–4.26) whose branches extended into the NT (see Matt. 7:13–14). The Apostolic Fathers preserve this teaching in *Did.* 1–6, *Barn.* 18–20, and *Herm. Mand.* 6.1–2.10, revealing broad usage of this moral standard throughout the early second-century church. The "two ways" are often associated with angels of light and darkness in literature, though not so in the *Didache*.

The "way of life" in the *Didache* follows two principles. The first is the double command to love God and neighbor, thus directing the listener toward observance of the Shema (Deut. 6:4) coupled with a charge to respect other people (Lev. 19:18). This link is variously attributed to the teachings of Jesus elsewhere in the tradition (Matt. 22:37–40 pars.). Within broad rabbinic practice, to love God and neighbor is equivalent to satisfying the requirements of the Torah generally. To meet this essential requirement of God is to fulfill one's obligation to live righteously. The text also contains a negative form of the so-called Golden Rule to describe the appropriate treatment of neighbors: "Whatever you do not wish for yourself, do not do to another." Among the NT Gospels, only Matthew equates the double command and Golden Rule with "the law and the prophets" (Matt. 7:12; 22:40).

The second rule to which the Didachist turns for the essential framework of the "two ways" is the Decalogue. Here the author warns the listener to avoid murder and adultery, idolatry and theft, and the like. These sins are primary snares of the "way of death" (chap. 5). In similar fashion, the *Didache* lists prohibitions against practicing worldly sins, such as magic, sorcery, abortion, hypocrisy, arrogance, astrology, and so forth. Such transgressions are stepping-stones to greater sins. Following rabbinic technique, the Didachist cautions against these lesser indiscretions in order to erect a fence around the more vital teaching of the Decalogue itself. Here the listener discerns an early Jewish-Christian argument for the need to respect the teachings of Torah and to practice an ethic pleasing to both God and humanity.

Secondarily inserted into the "two ways" segment are injunctions from the early church known as the "ecclesiastical interpolation" (1.3b–2.1a). Included here are instructions to bless, pray, and fast for one's enemies, to love one's opponents, to resist aggression, and to give gladly and not receive. Parallel teachings appear in the sermon materials of Matt. 5:38–48 and Luke 6:27–36, which may be the source for these sayings in the *Didache*. The presence of this insertion suggests that the *Didache* reflects an evolving community ethic. It is built on an early Jewish foundation featuring eschatological promise and warning, a "two ways" directive of the Shema and a command to love one's neighbor, an exposition of the Decalogue with a defensive hedge against secondary offenses, and the late addition of Jesus' teachings on the nature of sacrificial love. The agenda is expressly Jewish in form, though essentially Christian in flavor.

The *Didache* was widely known among later patristic writers, most of whom abandoned the shape of its ethics, undoubtedly because of the author's emphasis on a decidedly Jewish perspective.

See also Apostolic Fathers; Eschatology and Ethics; Golden Rule; Love, Love Command; Ten Commandments

Bibliography

Balabanski, V. *Eschatology in the Making: Matthew, Mark, and the Didache*. SNTSMS 97. Cambridge University Press, 1997, 180–209; Kloppenborg, J. "The Transformation of Moral Exhortation in *Didache* 1–5." Pages 88–109 in *The Didache in Context: Essays on Its Text, History, and Transmission*, ed. C. Jefford. NovTSup 77. Brill, 1995; Osborn, E. "The Love Command in Second Century Christian Writing." *SecCent* 1 (1981): 223–43; Rordorf, W. "An Aspect of the Judeo-Christian Ethic: The Two Ways." Pages 148–64 in *The Didache in Modern Research*, ed. J. Draper. AGJU 37. Brill, 1996.

Clayton N. Jefford

Dirty Hands

In the play *Les mains sales* (*Dirty Hands*), first performed in 1948, Jean-Paul Sartre presents a situation set in the resistance to the Nazi occupation of France during World War II. Underground fighters face circumstances wherein every action that they could undertake violates common morality, betrays a loyalty, or brings harm to others but appears to be the right thing to do. This portrayal is intended to expose the guilt of those who justify doing evil for good purposes and to challenge those moral philosophies that view ethics as essentially about the inviolability of universal principles. It is a dramatized existentialist argument against idealist (especially Kantian) theories and, by implication, against ideals formed by divine command. These are held to be impossible, wrong, or irrelevant in contexts where every option is tragic.

The problem is not new. Abraham was caught between obedience to God's command and his love for his son Isaac. David had to slay some ten thousands of enemies to establish a relatively peaceful regime. Elijah had to risk life and reputation to confront false prophecy and political power, as did Christ later on. But the most famous example is Pilate, who tried to wash his hands publicly to declare his innocence of the crucifixion of Jesus. And Paul instructs everyone to "live peaceably with all," and then writes just a few lines later that rulers are authorized by God to be "a terror to evil" conduct (Rom. 12:18; 13:3). These examples of biblical realism do not allow believers to hold that morality is simply a matter of following the universal and inviolable rules.

This realism is manifest in the classic traditions of Augustine and Aquinas and in the teachings of the Protestant Reformers, who thought that the innocence that the monastic life sought to protect and the perfection to which the sectarians aspired were unrealistic and pretentious. One cannot avoid sin by avoiding the complexities of the common life. Indeed, faithful living in society sometimes requires actions on the part of those called to particular roles that are otherwise forbidden. Thus, Luther wrote that soldiers "can be saved." And Calvin argued that the lower magistrates, who ordinarily are required to obey the higher officers, can confront them and even use force to reestablish a more just order if the higher magistrates conspire against the people and betray basic justice (*Institutes* 4.20.29–30). The contextual and consequential aspects of ethics cannot be neglected, even if ethics inevitably also is about following principles of right and wrong.

In the twentieth century, fascism in Western Europe and communism in the East brought the double threat of a militantly race-based neopaganism in the one and a militantly class-based secularism in the other. These engendered worldwide confrontations and apparently necessary uses of bribery, deception, spying, unsavory alliances, and secret operations—sometimes with assassinations, intensive interrogations, and the development of nuclear weaponry. Reinhold Niebuhr, as much as any other single figure, renewed theological reflection on such matters in the name of "Christian realism." He challenged the chauvinist nationalism that tempted secular realists to idolatry, and he challenged the idealism that had come to dominate much religious thought and resisted taking military actions against fascism and communism. Nationalism was too easily justifying any and all means, and idealism too quickly claiming its innocence.

Forms of secular realism had emerged in political science, rooted in the political theories of Machiavelli and Hobbes at the time of the Reformation. They argued that political leaders often were required to use evil means in order to serve the common good and to establish or maintain a polity that constrains chaos. The father of modern social thought, Max Weber, echoed these themes when he announced in 1918 that politics was about the accumulation of influence and coercive power and the potential use of force in a given territory. This monopoly on violence is granted so that a viable polity can be established to enhance and defend a society's well-being and its members' welfare. Those who seek to be politically effective and oppose the sometimes necessary and legitimate uses of force so that they can remain morally pure are likely to be politically irresponsible. They should return to the monastery.

During the Cold War, noted political theorist and moral philosopher Michael Walzer posed the issues again, raising many of the points already mentioned, but adding his own insights in a way that gave rise to contemporary debates about the Middle East conflicts and the use of torture. He recognized that the problem of "dirty hands" does not appear only in politics; every sphere of life has its own contextual factors that seem to demand actions that are, ordinarily, wrong. But the focus remains on politics because coercive force is intrinsic to it, and the threats of mass destruction may require a justifiable use of counterforce. Some actions may be wrong, and the one who does them may be morally guilty even if they are "the right thing to do."

Christian Ethicist Scott Paeth recently applied Walzer's arguments to current debates on torture. He cites one of Walzer's illustrations. Should a politician (in this case, a male) who believes that torture is wrong authorize the torture of a rebel who knows when and where bombs are scheduled to explode? Walzer argues that if he does, he commits "a moral crime," but his awareness of and "his willingness to bear . . . his guilt is evidence . . . that he is not too good for politics and that he is good enough. . . . It is by his dirty hands that we know him" (Walzer 169). Paeth sees in Walzer's argument the basis for criticism of US policies that led to Abu Ghraib and Guantanamo, for those authorizing the alleged torture have shown no willingness to acknowledge guilt. His argument also reflects the theological insight that responsible living requires humility, contrition, and forgiveness. To deny this is to falsify ethical reality.

Bibliography

Levinson, S., ed. *Torture: A Collection*. Oxford University Press, 2004; Luther, M. "Whether Soldiers, Too, Can Be Saved." In *The Christian in Society III*. Vol. 46 of *Luther's Works*, ed. R. Schultz. Fortress, 1967; Niebuhr, R. *The Nature and Destiny of Man*. Scribner, 1941; Paeth, S. "'Dirty Hands' Revisited: Morality, Torture and Abu Ghraib." *JSCE* 28, no. 1 (2008): 163–81; Sartre, J.-P. *Dirty Hands*. In *Three Plays*. Knopf, 1949; Walzer, M. "Political Action: The Problem of Dirty Hands." *PPA* 2 (1973): 160–80; Weber, M. "Politics as a Vocation." Pages 77–128 in *From Max Weber: Essays in Sociology*, trans. and ed. H. Gerth and C. Mills. Routledge, 1977.

Max L. Stackhouse

Disability and Handicap

The field of "disability studies" emerged in Britain and North America in the 1980s and 1990s. For the most part, scholars who work in this field use the term *disability* to refer to a chronic physical or cognitive condition that impairs someone, and the expression *persons with disabilities* to signify people affected by this condition. The disability community generally prefers the term *persons with disabilities* to *disabled persons* because the latter seems to call into question the full humanity of persons with disabilities. The use of the term *handicap*, in turn, functions as a means of highlighting society's lack of support for persons with disabilities; disabilities, scholars suggest, are not conditions that inherently "handicap" a person's ability to flourish, but these conditions do function as handicaps within a society that fails to address adequately the needs and experiences of persons with disabilities.

In recent decades attention to the experience of persons with disabilities has raised challenges about the portrayals of disability in Scripture. Although the Bible does not specifically speak about "disabilities" as contemporary scholars understand them, scriptural depictions of the "blind," the "deaf," and the "lame," along with other physical and mental impairments, have implications for how contemporary Christians understand the nature of disability. The introduction to a recent volume on portrayals of disability in Scripture contends that accounts of physical and cognitive difference in Scripture have contributed to a "continuum of attitudes" regarding disability, and that many of these attitudes are "still reflected in the present" (Avalos, Melcher, and Schipper 4).

Moral and theological reflection on disability raises several questions that draw Scripture and ethics together. We can examine many of these questions by relating disability to three theological topics: the nature of personhood, the contours of the people of God, and the meaning of suffering.

Disability and Personhood

The notion that humans are conceived in God's image is an important scriptural affirmation (Gen. 1:26–27). Through the centuries, Christians have debated the precise sense in which humans exist in God's image. Some theologians have historically associated the image of God with human reasoning or with the capacity for rational judgment. Others link the idea of *imago Dei* to the human body and specifically focus on our physically "upright" nature, which distinguishes us from many animals. Abraham Berinyuu argues that both conceptions of *imago Dei* are problematic for persons with cognitive or physical disabilities. These accounts of the *imago Dei* imply that persons with disabilities are less than fully human, and that their disabilities prevent them from imaging God. Berinyuu contends that, more recently, appeals to God's image have been used to substantiate the idea that all persons have a fundamental dignity and are worthy of respect. He expresses concern, however, that this affirmation implicitly places a greater burden on persons with disabilities to be perfect and puts them in a position where they are blamed when they fall short of perfection (Berinyuu 202–5).

Berinyuu's concern that particular interpretations of *imago Dei* exclude persons with disabilities runs parallel to misgivings expressed by many Christian ethicists that certain arguments in bioethics imply that persons with disabilities are less than fully human. Many scholars suggest that the discourse central to medical ethics and bioethics seems to promote and foster a narrow understanding of what it means to be human, an understanding tied to a specific vision of health and self-determination. For example, Mark Kuczewski suggests that many conversations in contemporary bioethics tend to focus on new technologies that fix or prevent medical conditions and that foster a vision of ideal humans as autonomous, self-directed agents. Such an account of human nature indicates that dependence on others is a quality to be shunned, and that persons with cognitive or physical disabilities are not fully human because they exhibit this dependence.

Berinyuu argues that we can overcome the problems inherent in positions that deprive persons with disabilities of full humanity by looking to the incarnate Jesus Christ as a model for understanding what it means to be human. An affirmation of Christ as the image of God points to an understanding of this image as fully consonant with weakness and vulnerability. The notion of the crucified Christ as God's "disabled body" (an insight originally offered by Nancy Eiesland) points to ways in which a focus on Christ gives rise to an understanding of personhood consistent with experiences of disability. Christ becomes disabled through his crucifixion and death, and Martin Albl suggests that as subsequent generations of followers seek to die and be raised in Christ, they are choosing to participate in Christ's disability; we see this theme in several Pauline Epistles (Rom. 6:3; 8:17; 2 Cor. 4:10; Gal. 2:19; Phil. 3:10).

Disability and the People of God

A study of disabilities in Scripture also raises a question about the status of persons with disabilities in relation to the people of God. Amos Yong observes that many Scripture passages associate disability with an impurity or defilement that is incompatible with God's holiness. Leviticus 21:16–23 excludes persons with disabilities from approaching God's sanctuary and making a sacrificial offering. And from 2 Sam. 5:8b we may infer that "the blind and the lame" will not be able to enter Jerusalem, although both Anthony Ceresko and Jeremy Schipper argue that this statement functions as a rhetorical strategy for emphasizing the irony in the shifts of fortune that David experiences. The opposition between disability and holiness is reinforced by passages that characterize disability as a condition that makes healing a prerequisite for cleanliness. For example, several passages in the OT imply a connection between disability and sin (Deut. 28:15–68; Pss. 6; 32; 38; 51; 102; 143). Some narratives in the Gospels connect disability to the activity of demons or evil spirits (Matt. 9:32–33; 12:22–24; 17:15–18; Luke 13:11). Blindness functions as a metaphor in Matt. 23 and John 9 for the foolishness of the Pharisees, and NT Epistles likewise contain frequent references to disability as a metaphor for an immoral or wicked character (Rom. 11:7, 25; 2 Cor. 4:4; Eph. 4:18; 2 Pet. 1:9; 1 John 2:11) (Yong 19–28).

Although many Scripture passages characterize disability as a condition that requires healing, others affirm that the blind and the lame will be part of God's eschatological community without explicitly indicating that these persons must be healed prior to inclusion (Isa. 33:23b; Jer. 31:8–9; Mic. 4:6–7; Zeph. 3:19). Moreover, Mikeal Parsons draws from Luke 13; 19; Acts 3–4; 8 to argue that a major emphasis of Luke-Acts is an affirmation that all persons should be included in the eschatological community, regardless of physical appearance. He contends that Luke's narrative challenges the assumption that physical appearance and moral character are linked (Parsons 298–303). It seems clear, then, that there exists a scriptural witness to the idea that persons with disabilities should be included in God's people.

But what should this inclusion look like? Many Scripture passages treat persons with disabilities (along with others who are marginalized within society) as persons who are objects of God's particular care and who deserve special compassion from God's people. Texts such as Job 29:12–17; Jer. 31:8; Zeph. 3:19, along with Jesus' healing ministry (see, e.g., Mark 5:1–20; 10:46–52; Luke 5:17–26; 7:11–17; 8:49–56; 9:37–43; 13:10–13; John 5:1–18), support this idea that God cares for those who have disabilities. But from the vantage point of contemporary disability studies, such passages can appear to treat persons with disabilities as passive objects of pity, an image that runs counter to their empowerment. Contemporary theologians advocate the pursuit of ecclesial practices that embrace the experience of persons with disabilities so that their participation in the church may go beyond being recipients of charity. Stanley Hauerwas contends that the character of the church should be a central moral focus for all Christians, in part because Christians all need to learn to care for the "other" without discriminating (even unintentionally) against persons whom we perceive to be other than ourselves (Hauerwas 172). Yong discusses specific practices through which Christians can work to incorporate persons with disabilities into the ministry of the church through the assistance of the Holy Spirit. He argues that attentiveness to disability requires rethinking the meaning and nature of the sacraments, worship, and discipleship to be open to taking seriously the humanity of persons with disabilities, particularly cognitive disabilities (Yong 193–226).

Disability and Suffering

From the vantage point of the Christian tradition, the meaning of suffering may not appear to be of exclusive import to a conversation regarding disabilities. Several passages in Scripture recognize suffering as part of all humans' experience. But reflection on the meaning and purpose of suffering is helpful for understanding both the biblical witness regarding disability and the possible contributions of Christian theology to contemporary conversations in ethics. Scholars attentive to disability have suggested that Christ's healing narratives are ambiguous because they treat disability as a condition that must be overcome in order for someone to have a fulfilling and purposeful life. But the broader witness of Scripture points to an account of suffering as an experience consistent with taking part in God's ministry. This affirmation is important because, as ethicists are increasingly recognizing, a belief that persons with disabilities suffer has troubling consequences for practices in contemporary healthcare ethics.

Although many Christians affirm that God does not cause or intend suffering, several narratives in Scripture show that God is able to bring about good even in the midst of suffering. The Scriptures proclaim that the incarnate Jesus Christ suffered, and that this suffering was redemptive for humanity. Christ suffered physical pain during the crucifixion and the emotional pain of abandonment by his friends. Christ's endurance of suffering is foundational for humanity's redemption, for their forgiveness of sin and reconciliation with God, and this suffering provides us with meaning and hope in the midst of our suffering, giving us a sense that when we suffer, we are taking part in an experience that God in Christ endured as well (Rom. 8:16–25).

The scriptural demand for justice challenges Christians to fight forms of discrimination that cause suffering. Many scholars point out that much of the suffering experienced by persons with disabilities is rooted not in the disability itself but rather in their struggle to work within a society in which they experience discrimination (Hauerwas 172). But insofar as some measure of suffering may be inherent in some disabilities, the biblical affirmation that suffering may be redemptive counters theologically troubling arguments that arise in healthcare ethics at the beginning and end of life. One example of this sort of argument often takes place when a prenatal test demonstrates that the genetic makeup of an embryo prefigures cognitive disabilities such as Tay-Sachs disease or Down syndrome. Parents often are encouraged to terminate a pregnancy in these circumstances, partly on the grounds that a child with a disability is likely to suffer more than most. If parents choose to bring the child to birth, some ethicists suggest, they will be producing more suffering in the world. Hans Reinders argues that this perception of suffering is harmful because it implicitly suggests that the world would be a happier place if people with disabilities had not been born (Reinders 160).

A narrative that understands suffering to have a redemptive value challenges the cultural perception that suffering makes one's life less meaningful or worthwhile and should be avoided at all costs. The Scriptures witness to the idea that God's redemptive activity can occur even, perhaps especially, in the midst of suffering.

See also Bioethics; Healthcare Ethics; Image of God; Mental Health; Narrative Ethics, Biblical; Narrative Ethics, Contemporary; Sanctity of Human Life; Suffering

Bibliography

Albl, M. " 'For Whenever I Am Weak, Then I Am Strong': Disability in Paul's Epistles." Pages 145–58 in *This Abled Body: Rethinking Disabilities in Biblical Studies*, ed. H. Avalos, S. Melcher, and J. Schipper. Semeia 55. Society of Biblical Literature, 2007; Avalos, H., S. Melcher, and J. Schipper, "Introduction." Pages 1–12 in *This Abled Body: Rethinking Disabilities in Biblical Studies*, ed. H. Avalos, S. Melcher, and J. Schipper. Semeia 55. Society of Biblical Literature, 2007; Berinyuu, A. "Healing and Disability." *IJPT* 8 (2004): 202–11; Ceresko, A. "The Identity of 'the Blind and the Lame' in 2 Samuel 5:8b." *CBQ* 63 (2001): 23–30; Eiesland, N. *The Disabled God: Toward a Liberation Theology of Disability*. Abingdon, 1994; Hauerwas, S. *Suffering Presence: Theological Reflections on Medicine, the Mentally Handicapped, and the Church*. University of Notre Dame Press, 1986; Kuczewski, M. "Disability: An Agenda for Bioethics." *AJB* 1 (2001): 36–44; Parsons, M. "The Character of the Lame Man in Acts 3–4." *JBL* 124 (2005): 295–312; Reinders, H. *The Future of the Disabled in Liberal Society: An Ethical Analysis*. University of Notre Dame Press, 2000; Schipper, J. "Reconsidering the Imagery of Disability in 2 Samuel 5:8b." *CBQ* 67 (2005): 422–34; Yong, A. *Theology and Down Syndrome: Reimagining Disability in Late Modernity*. Baylor University Press, 2007.

Elizabeth Agnew Cochran

Discernment, Moral

Although moral discernment is an activity of central importance in the Bible, it is not in any simple sense used as a biblical term. There is no single word in Hebrew or Greek consistently translated as "discern" or "discernment." Conversely, the English word *discernment* renders various Hebrew and Greek words, even within a single translation.

Multiple models of discernment are offered in the OT, corresponding to how God's will is made known in different contexts. Guidance is frequently given to the patriarchs in dreams and visions, and Joseph (Gen. 40–41) and later Daniel (Dan. 1:17–2:45) are identified as men of discernment based on their ability to interpret dreams in times of crisis. After the promulgation of covenant law, discernment is identified with careful adherence to the commandments and precepts of God. The trait called "discernment" or "prudence" throughout wisdom literature combines moral, religious, and practical insight. Psalms and Proverbs are full of prayers and petitions for such discernment, closely related to piety and the fear of God. Likewise, it is discernment that enables the judges and the kings of Israel to offer true judgments and wise leadership, as in the "understanding mind" for which Solomon prays and thus wins the favor of God (1 Kgs. 3:7–14). In addition, there is special discernment including foresight bestowed on the prophets for leading the people in times of crisis and catastrophe. Framed as the word of God coming to the prophet, this is regarded as a distinctive gift, and it is as seers specially called by God that the great prophets exercise their authority. Discernment is understood to include the ability to discriminate between true and false teachings and true and false prophets, guidance for which is given in the law. Finally, prophets such as Joel and Jeremiah speak of God bestowing moral vision and insight on God's people as a whole, so that the gift of discernment becomes more widespread (Joel 2:28–29), and the wisdom and holiness of divine law may be secured in the heart of all Israel (Jer. 31:33–34).

The narratives of the NT display similar variety, including special discernment through dreams and visions (e.g., Joseph's dreams [Matt. 1:20–21; 2:13, 19–20], Zechariah's vision in the temple [Luke 1:8–20], Peter's vision at Joppa [Acts 10:9–16]) and particular revelations of the Holy Spirit granted to individuals, especially in relation to recognizing the Christ (e.g., Elizabeth on Mary's visit [Luke 1:41–45], Simeon and Anna in the temple [Luke 2:25–38]). The descent of the Spirit at Pentecost is explicitly linked to Joel's prophecy of a general dispensation of spirit-bestowed insight (Acts 2:16–18). In Paul's letters, discernment is spoken of both as a general aspect of the life of faith among those led by the Spirit and as a particular spiritual gift dispensed for the sake of the whole community (1 Cor. 12:10). Thus, Paul can make being led by the Spirit a defining characteristic of those who belong to Christ (Rom. 8:9) and urge believers to be transformed by the renewing of their minds so that they can "discern the will of God" (Rom. 12:2). It is the Spirit alone who can make known the things of God (1 Cor. 2:10–16), and it is to the Spirit's presence in him that Paul appeals when offering moral judgment and advice beyond the word of the Lord to the churches (e.g., 1 Cor. 7:40).

The richness and diversity of biblical models of moral discernment are reflected in the later development of Christian moral theology. Appeals to revelation through dreams and visions do not abruptly disappear, but they do become more problematic as successive generations try to define and transmit a coherent faith and way of life. Orthodoxy insists on testing individual judgment and revelation by the standard of apostolic teaching and by the consensus of the community gathered in prayer and worship. Over time, a more formal interpretive tradition arises, along with a casuistry that applies general biblical principles (one may not do evil so that good may come [Rom. 3:8]) to particular cases. In the developed forms of virtue ethics, visual metaphors for moral life such as vision, illumination, and discernment itself come to full flower, with the definition of the preeminent moral virtue of prudence as a cultivated ability to see truthfully. This tradition retains the underlying unity of moral and spiritual life found in biblical models, grounding moral judgment and insight in the practices of the faith. It has regained prominence in recent decades.

See also Holy Spirit; Moral Formation; Virtue(s)

Bibliography

Hollinger, D. *Choosing the Good: Christian Ethics in a Complex World*. Baker Academic, 2002; Porter, J. *The Recovery of Virtue: The Relevance of Aquinas for Christian Ethics*. University of Notre Dame Press, 1990.

Sondra E. Wheeler

Discipline

In Scripture, "discipline" refers to correction, teaching, and punishment initiated and carried out by persons in positions of authority for the sake of one in need. Scripture refers explicitly to two kinds of authoritative relationships with regard to discipline: those between God and God's people, and those between parents and children. However, Paul's letters refer to discipline more broadly in the context of relationships within the church.

Discipline is a necessary component of loving God and for the development of good character. The writer of Hebrews captures the yield of discipline as the "peaceful fruit of righteousness"

(Heb. 12:11). Discipline should not be confused with mere punishment. The goal of discipline is to engender obedience and love and to share in God's holiness (Heb. 12).

In some cases, discipline is welcomed. For example, the wisdom literature contains numerous references to discipline as the way to inculcate virtues such as justice, equity, righteousness, prudence, knowledge, insight, understanding, courage, kindness, honesty, and piety. The constellation of virtues that emerges from living under discipline saves persons from evil and for life and the favor of the Lord. In other cases, discipline is refused, most often due to foolishness or the inability to hear and obey. The OT describes persons in such cases as destined to walk in the ways of darkness. Retrieving the familial metaphor, Hebrews goes so far as to say that those who do not share in God's discipline are not his children. This analogy refers to the fact that discipline legitimates one's identity as belonging to someone. Connecting discipline with identity retrieves the Gospel usage of disciples as called by Christ to become followers of him.

The Christian tradition includes the following under discipline: (1) discipline connotes a whole way of life that gives shape to authority and accountability within the church and serves as a witness to the world; (2) discipline covers practices that adhere to various forms of asceticism, to specific codes such as holiness codes and household codes, and to ethical mandates such as the Ten Commandments and the Beatitudes; (3) discipline includes punishment for wrongdoing in order to form persons for love.

Most simply, discipline is about the community of faith habituating persons to become disciples of Jesus Christ in all aspects of life. It also calls individuals to submit to Christian formation and to the disciplines that bring about Christian character. The end of Christian discipline is a community that witnesses to the good news that Christ has died, Christ has risen, and Christ is coming again.

See also Accountability; Asceticism; Beatitudes; Holiness Code; Household Codes; Practices; Punishment; Ten Commandments

Bibliography

Berkman, J. "Being Reconciled: Penitence, Punishment, and Worship." Pages 95–109 in *The Blackwell Companion to Christian Ethics*, ed. S. Hauerwas and S. Wells. Blackwell, 2004; Bonhoeffer, D. *The Cost of Discipleship*. SCM, 1959; Foster, R. *A Celebration of Discipline: The Path to Spiritual Growth*. HarperCollins, 1978; Norris, K. *Acedia and Me: A Marriage, Monks, and a Writer's Life*. Penguin Books, 2008.

Michelle Clifton-Soderstrom

Discrimination

Traditionally, to be "discriminating" is a sign of good taste, and ethics requires us to discriminate good from bad, fair from unfair, and so forth. Much Jewish law is based on discrimination—for example, to distinguish what is clean and may be eaten from that which is forbidden (Lev. 11). Equally, Jesus' parables of judgment include images of discrimination between wheat and weeds, good fish and bad fish, or sheep and goats (Matt. 13:24–30, 36–43, 47–50; 25:31–46).

However, discrimination as currently defined concerns the exclusion of a person or group of persons based solely on class or category. It is an unacceptable practice in contemporary social ethics. It is illegal in the workplace, and to be suspected of discrimination in any form can be disastrous. Equally, the OT asserts that the justice of God does not discriminate between people. Unlike some humans, God does not take bribes and is impartial; literally, "he does not wonder at, or respect, someone's face" (Deut. 10:17; 2 Chr. 19:7). Israel's judges and leaders are similarly instructed not to show partiality (Lev. 19:15; Prov. 18:5; see also Job 34:19). It is a mark of other gods and other nations to show partiality, especially to the wicked (Ps. 82:1–2). Divine impartiality is also found throughout deuterocanonical literature, where "the Lord is the judge, and with him there is no partiality" (Sir. 35:15; see also Wis. 6:7; *T. Job* 4.7–8; 1 Esd. 4:39). Jouette Bassler demonstrates how divine impartiality is axiomatic throughout the OT, postcanonical and rabbinic literature, as well as in Philo. Significantly, however, it is not applied to the relationships between Jews and gentiles (Bassler 185).

In the NT, this impartiality of God develops significant ethical implications. Here, God is also described as "the one who judges all people impartially," using the same image about having regard for someone's face (1 Pet. 1:17). This idea appears at the start of Peter's speech to Cornelius: "I truly understand that God shows no partiality" (Acts 10:34)—God is no "respecter of people's faces." Earlier, the Spirit tells Peter to go and meet Cornelius's envoys *mēden diakrinomenos* (Acts 10:20), which at first sight could simply mean "not hesitating." However, in Peter's later reports the same verb clearly means "without discriminating" (Acts 11:12), and that God has made no distinction "between them and us"—that is, Jews and gentiles (Acts 15:9).

This application of divine impartiality to the social, racial, and religious distinctions within the ancient world had radical ethical implications.

Jewish and Greco-Roman beliefs in the impartiality of God did not prevent widespread discrimination in societies where only free adult males of a certain standing had rights. Thus, Jewish men thanked God in their morning prayers for the three blessings: God did not make them a gentile, a slave or peasant, or a woman (*t. Ber.* 7.18; *y. Ber.* 13b; *b. Menaḥ* 43b). Similarly, various Greek philosophers are credited with the statement of gratitude that they were born "a human being and not a beast, a man and not a woman, and a Greek not a barbarian" (Diogenes Laertius, *Lives* 1.33; Plutarch, *Mar.* 46.1; Lactantius, *Inst.* 3.19.17).

Such attitudes were worked out in practical codes prescribing obedience from the inferior to the superior, such as wives to husbands, slaves to masters, or children to parents. Although similar "household codes" are found in the NT (Col. 3:18–4:1; Eph. 5:21–6:9; see also 1 Pet. 2:13–3:8), significantly they contain a degree of mutual submission "to one another out of reverence for Christ" (Eph. 5:21), which provides duties also for the husbands, masters, and fathers.

However, Gal. 3:28 provides the clearest statement of nondiscrimination, which cuts across all ancient social barriers: "There is no longer Jew or Greek, there is no longer slave or free, there is no longer male and female; for all of you are one in Christ Jesus." As Douglas Campbell states, "Paul baldly negates three standard bifurcations of society . . . concerning ethnicity, slavery, and/or gender" (109). Similar statements are found in 1 Cor. 12:13; Col. 3:11; and behind the structure of 1 Cor. 7:17–28.

Racial Discrimination—Neither Jew nor Greek

Arguing against the Judaizers from Jerusalem in Galatians, Paul uses the standard Jewish idea that "God shows no partiality," taking account of a person's face (Gal. 2:6). However, it is significant that, as he builds his argument about the relationship of Jews and gentiles, he breaks through into the radical application of such divine impartiality to this key racial, cultural, and religious divide to affirm that "there is no longer Jew or Greek . . . in Christ Jesus" (Gal. 3:28). This radical insight lies at the heart of Paul's argument in the opening chapters of Romans that both Jews and Greeks are accountable to God and face judgment, apart from the law or under the law, "for God shows no partiality," using the Hebrew image again (Rom. 2:11) (see Bassler 121–70).

Unfortunately, the subsequent history of relations between Christians and Jews reveals a sad story of far too much discrimination and persecution, from the early church through the pogroms of the Middle Ages to the Holocaust, while the consequences of this history are still felt in the relationships of Jews, Arabs, Palestinians, and all in the Middle East today. Nonetheless, Paul's insight stands against all forms of racial discrimination and was a source of inspiration in the civil rights struggle and also in the campaign against apartheid (see Burridge 347–409).

Social Discrimination—Neither Slave nor Free

The couplet about slave and free is repeated in 1 Cor. 12:13; Col. 3:11, yet Paul seems surprisingly "relaxed and non-committal about the institution of slavery itself" (Longenecker 54). In 1 Cor. 7:21–24 the issue is subordinated to eschatological pressure, and elsewhere Paul returns the runaway slave Onesimus to Philemon, although his subversive rhetoric appeals to a new relationship (Phlm. 16–24). God's impartiality is applied to slavery in the household codes (Eph. 6:9; Col. 3:25), and this is later picked up in *Did.* 4.10; *Barn.* 19.7. Paul's Christology probably does most to undermine slavery, both his self-description as "slave of Christ" (see Martin 147–49) and his appeal to the imitation of Jesus, who emptied himself to take "the form of a slave" (Phil. 2:5–7).

Once again, however, the church took a long time to accept the implications of nondiscrimination regarding slavery, as it continued to be justified from the early fathers through to Augustine (see Longenecker 60–65) and on to the nineteenth-century abolitionist controversies and the American Civil War (see Swartley 31–37, 278–79). In today's world, where it is thought that more people are enslaved than any time previously, not to mention the huge inequalities between the developed and developing nations, this remains a challenge.

Sexual Discrimination—Neither Male nor Female

It is significant that although issues of sexuality and gender were not relevant to Paul's argument in Galatians, he cannot help himself running on to apply his nondiscriminatory principle to "no longer male and female," evoking the language of Gen. 1:17. While some other passages in the Pauline corpus appear to be negative about women (e.g., 1 Cor. 11:2–16; 14:33–36), Paul's letters often end with commendations of women as his "co-workers" (Rom. 16:1–7; 1 Cor. 16:19; Phil. 4:2–3).

As with our other two areas, the Christian tradition includes a sad history of discrimination against women, particularly regarding their role in church leadership. Galatians 3:28 lies at the heart of current debate, with some arguing that the equality espoused relates only to its context of baptism (3:27), while others apply it also to ministry; Longenecker (92) suggests that those who stress creation tend toward subordination, whereas emphasizing redemption leads to more equality. Similar arguments also apply to the related issues regarding divorced ministers and homosexuals. Some argue that the common prohibition on the ordination of homosexuals is another form of discrimination, like apartheid or slavery or repression of women, and most laws against discrimination apply to sexual orientation as much as other areas. Others respond that biblical and theological considerations require that this area be treated differently. Campbell (112–31) applies his theological model of understanding Paul's gospel to the implications of Gal. 3:28 for the "case study" of "gay ordination." He argues that homosexuality is not an issue of the first order over which churches should be splitting.

Thus, the issue of discrimination remains a challenge for those seeking to apply the Scriptures to ethics. As we recognize the blind spots and history of oppression in the Christian tradition, so there may be areas that we do not perceive today but that, under guidance of the Spirit, future generations will come to see as discrimination.

See also Anti-Semitism; Apartheid; Civil Rights; Ethnic Identity, Ethnicity; Liberationist Ethics; Race; Racism; Sex and Sexuality; Slavery; Women, Status of

Bibliography

Bassler, J. *Divine Impartiality: Paul and a Theological Axiom*. SBLDS 59. Scholars Press, 1982; Burridge, R. *Imitating Jesus: An Inclusive Approach to New Testament Ethics*. Eerdmans, 2007; Campbell, D. *The Quest for Paul's Gospel: A Suggested Strategy*. JSNTSup 274. T&T Clark, 2005; Longenecker, R. *New Testament Social Ethics for Today*. Eerdmans, 1984; Martin, D. *Slavery as Salvation: The Metaphor of Slavery in Pauline Christianity*. Yale University Press, 1990; Swartley, W. *Slavery, Sabbath, War and Women: Case Issues in Biblical Interpretation*. Herald Press, 1983.

Richard A. Burridge

Dishonesty

Scripture frequently condemns dishonesty, opposing this quality to God's truthful and righteous nature. For example, Deut. 25:16 presents dishonest behavior as abhorrent to God. Writings of the prophets characterize Israel's dishonesty as a sign of its failure to uphold its part in the covenant with God (Isa. 59; Jer. 8; Ezek. 22). The NT Epistles caution against false prophets (2 Cor. 11:13; Gal. 2:4; 2 Thess. 2:11; 1 John 4:1) and contrast humanity's "false" character with God's truthfulness (Rom. 3:4; Heb. 6:18). These texts suggest that God's people should be committed to true actions and true speech. Truthfulness in deeds and language helps to preserve the relations of human beings with God and among themselves.

At the same time, several passages in the OT suggest the plausibility of arguing that prudential deception is morally justifiable and even praiseworthy. For example, 1 Sam. 19 recalls instances when Jonathan and Michal practice deception to protect David from Saul. This motif of deception among persons under God's protection is reiterated throughout the book of Genesis. Jacob and his mother, Rebekah, secure Jacob's birthright by deceiving Jacob's father, Isaac (Gen. 27). Jacob later "outwits" his father-in-law, Laban, and acquires much of his property through questionable means (Gen. 30:25–31:42). Jacob's sons deceive and murder a group of Canaanites to avenge their sister's sexual assault (Gen. 34). These and other examples seem to indicate that calculated and strategic acts of deception are not incompatible with the character of God's chosen people.

It is not clear that these scriptural stories function to endorse prudential dishonesty. Trickery is also associated with more clearly problematic figures such as Cain (Gen. 4:9) and can ultimately be traced back to the serpent in Eden, who tricks Adam and Eve into eating the fruit of the garden (Gen. 3:1–7). But these stories do demonstrate the complexity involved in defining honesty and dishonesty. The historical Christian tradition has acknowledged this complication and allows for some distinction to be made between intentional falsehood and occasional trickery. Augustine denounces falsehood as immoral but is willing to praise Jacob's deception of Isaac on the grounds that Jacob's actions signify the truth that he is the proper recipient of Isaac's inheritance. John Chrysostom goes further. He aligns some instances of trickery with prudential wisdom and argues that deception can be justified when it is done judiciously for someone else's interest (*On the Priesthood*). Jerome similarly defends occasional acts of dishonesty on the grounds that lies can be well intentioned and have good effects (*Apology against Rufinus*).

See also Deception; Honesty; Integrity; Truthfulness, Truth-Telling

Bibliography

Griffiths, P. *Lying: An Augustinian Theology of Duplicity*. Brazos, 2004; Ramsey, B. "Two Traditions on Lying and Deception in the Ancient Church." *The Thomist* 49 (1985): 504–33.

Elizabeth Agnew Cochran

Dissent

Dissent is a considered judgment that departs from authoritative doctrine of the church. Generally marked by an acceptance both of the authority of the church and of the binding nature of Christian doctrine, true dissent objects to a particular point of teaching without seeking separation from the church and its authority.

Although dissent often has been seen as a threat to church authority, church unity, and authentic doctrine, it also has been understood as a crucial tool spurring the church to needed reform and even supporting the development of doctrine. Dissent is neither heresy nor schism, though it can lead to either and has led to both.

Attending to Scripture

The key scriptural model for dissent is the story of Paul's disagreement with Peter over the imposition of Mosaic law upon gentile converts to Christianity, told in both Acts 15 and Gal. 2:11–21. Paul's own account makes clear that he saw Peter and James, in their separating themselves from gentile Christians, as "not acting consistently with the truth of the gospel" (Gal. 2:14). Although Paul made his case boldly, he also traveled to Jerusalem to submit the question to the authority of the church (Acts 15:6).

The church as described in Scripture, though not without dissension and differences, had remained united as a single body, in accord with the prayer of Christ (John 17:22–23) and his reconciling power (2 Cor. 5:14–19). Paul was committed to the truth of the gospel, but he also was committed to the unity of the church and recognized Peter and the other apostles as having particular authority within it. Likewise, Peter and the apostles listened to Paul's witness regarding the way the Spirit moved in the gentile church. Three key characteristics—respectful dissent, discerning ecclesial authorities, and all parties being committed to both the truth of the gospel and the unity of the church—allow for the church to move through dissent toward a deeper appropriation and embodiment of the truth of Christ.

Contemporary Context

The church today is marked more by disagreement than by dissent in the scriptural sense, largely because two of the areas of deepest disagreement among Christians involve who holds legitimate authority over doctrinal matters and what constitutes unity sufficient for the oneness of the church. In the absence of clear consensus or clear authority on these matters, disagreement often becomes mere difference of opinion, either within a broad and vague unity or across denominational divides. Because of the relationship between dissent and authoritative teaching, ecclesial bodies with more clearly defined structures of authority and more explicitly proclaimed doctrinal positions are more likely to have dissent develop and be maintained over time. In the context of widespread Catholic dissent from the papal teaching on contraception, Juan Arzube (204) has argued that the legitimacy of dissent depends on three criteria: the competence of the dissenter, the dissenter's sustained effort to assent to the authoritative teaching, and the continued conviction in conscience of the contrary opinion.

See also Authority and Power; Conscience; Freedom; Loyalty

Bibliography

Arzube, J. "Criteria for Dissent in the Church." Pages 202–5 in *The Magisterium and Morality*, ed. C. Curran and R. McCormick. RMT 3. Paulist Press, 1982; Curran, C., and R. McCormick, eds. *Dissent in the Church*. RMT 6. Paulist Press, 1988.

Dana L. Dillon

Divination and Magic

Magic may be defined as manipulation of supernatural powers in order to control events of nature or life circumstances. However, scholars of the subject recently have focused on the inadequacy of this definition and disagree on the distinction between magic and religion generally. The difficulty arises in the privileging of one's religion by attributing illegitimate magic to one's enemies, thus defining "otherness." Magic and divination therefore are used in antiquity as a polemic to distinguish one's own convictions, which were assumed to be religious, revelatory, and legitimate, from the activities of one's enemies, said to be magical and idolatrous. As a branch or subdivision of magic, divination is the art of deciphering and interpreting signs, which are said to reveal the future. This article considers these definitions for ancient Western Asia generally before taking up the question of divination and magic in the Bible.

Divination and Magic in the Ancient World

Early scholarly explanations of magic in the ancient world were related to developments in biblical theology. It was assumed that magic and divination derived from foreign influences and were in direct opposition to orthodox Yahwism of the OT, and further that there was a stark contrast between ancient Near Eastern religion as naturalistic and Israelite religion as historical. However, distinctions between ancient Israelite religion and the religions of other peoples of the ancient Near East often have been overstated. For example, a false dichotomy often has been assumed between fertility or nature religion and Israel's historically based religion. More recent investigations have turned to sociology and anthropology, which have criticized the assumption that magic was a primitive form of religion or a degeneration of religion (Jeffers 1–16; Dolansky). Such approaches have called into question any strict distinction between religion and magic that privileges the former, and have analyzed magic and divination as part and parcel of religious intermediations between the human and the divine.

Although dichotomies between biblical "historical" religion and ancient "naturalistic" religions must be discarded as overly simplistic, it remains true that biblical religion was distinctive in at least one central point. In a word, ancient Near Eastern and Greco-Roman religion was polytheistic and largely mythological, whereas biblical religion is monotheistic, largely enclosed in a narrative framework (Brichto 57). We may further observe, derived from this central difference, that ancient religions located ultimate power not with the gods but in an impersonal force beyond the deities to which even the gods themselves were susceptible. Thus, magic is central to ancient religion, as witnessed by the use of spells and incantations as a means for even the gods to exert power over one another and over nature.

This last point explains also the connection between magic and ritual in ancient religion. Magic and divination should be analyzed from the perspective of cosmology (Schmitt 67–106). In the ancient worldview, the cosmos is ordered at creation in a system of correspondences that are preserved in rituals. Thus ritualistic magic is humanity's wish for order in an otherwise chaotic universe, in a belief system that assumes that the ritual has a correspondence in heaven. Frequently, magicians were credited with extraordinary powers related to the use of words, audible pronouncements or inscriptions, which were believed to work automatically. Thus, magicians at times were characterized as bearers of the power of speech whose words were put into effect virtually immediately (for examples, see several of the articles in Mirecki and Meyer). Special words or phrases could be secret or be special names of gods or angels. Magical curses were not words bearing an innate power, as was once thought, but were performative utterances or illocutionary speech-acts in which the articulation of the words themselves involved performing an act (Aitken 13–17; Thiselton). Mesopotamian and Hittite theorists maintained a clear distinction between black or malicious magic (sorcery) and white or defensive magic, which was considered a gift of the gods (Black and Green 124–25).

The ancient world had a number of specialists, diviners, enchanters, magicians, and oracular practitioners, and many divinatory techniques. Of these, dreams were perceived as encoded revelations of the highest order. Message dreams require no interpretation, for in them a god or other figure appears in order to communicate by spoken word. In symbolic dreams, however, the dreamer observes enigmatic visual images that require oneiromancy, or dream interpretation (Noegel). For ancient Egyptians, dreams were a portal to the divine realm, requiring great technical skill to interpret them. Hence, the Egyptians produced dream manuals as early as the thirteenth century BCE, listing various dream possibilities and their corresponding good or bad meanings.

Many other divinatory techniques are attested in the ancient world, all based on the conviction that the various parts of the universe reflect a whole that is interconnected (Jeffers 144–96). Most ancients accepted the movement of the stars and planets as reflecting divine will, so that nearly all sought omens from celestial phenomena (astrology). But any phenomenon could be associated with a reflection of divine dispositions, providing a medium for divine communication. The moment in time when a priest sacrifices an animal to a deity was perceived as especially noteworthy because the ritual of the sacrifice provided a heightened sense of the nexus between the gods and the human realm. Over the centuries, the assumption of regularity in divine communication led to observations of unique or unusual patterns in the animal's organs, so that details of the animal's liver (hepatoscopy) or entrails (extispicy, with special interest in the gall bladder, kidneys, and lungs, as well as abnormal fetuses) were analyzed for omens in Mesopotamia beginning in the late third millennium BCE (cf. Ezek. 21:21). These observations were recorded for posterity and passed along from generation to generation, leaving a significant body of literature on the subject. Clay liver models have been found at Babylon, Alalakh, Mari, and Hazor, some inscribed with omens and instructional formulas for students of hepatoscopy.

In addition to these, the ancients showed interest in other mediums of divination, such as hair patterning, bird flight patterns, meteorites, or unusual weather patterns. We have examples of divination by means of water (hydromancy), invocation of the spirits of the dead (necromancy), the use of wood as a medium of divination (rhabdomancy), and several others (Jeffers 144–96). In later literature, Greek *mageia* ("magic"; Lat. *magia*) and related words derive from Persian *magus*, designating a person from an ancient Medo-Persian tribe with priestly functions (Graf 20). With the rise of Hellenism, the interest in magic and divination continued throughout the Mediterranean world, yielding numerous texts of ritual power, featuring amulets, incantation bowls, and other artifacts thought to aid the practitioner in addressing medical, demonic, or social problems.

Divination and Magic in the Bible

Internal evidence in the Bible on magic and divination is complex. We find condemnation of them in terms that acknowledge their effects, and yet other references that view certain magic-like practices positively. Even in the pentateuchal prohibitions, magic is condemned not because it is illusory or imaginary and thus ineffective; on the contrary, the Bible assumes that it is real and effective. The causes for magic's rejection must therefore be sought in the Bible's alternative worldview, its articulation of the very nature of God, and its understanding and definition of a proper relationship with God. Such causes for the ban on magic are not embedded in the distinctiveness of biblical religion as historical vis-à-vis the naturalistic religions of the ancient world. Rather, the very nature of God and God's means of revelatory communication with humans precludes the possibility of manipulation. God reveals only what God chooses to reveal to humanity, and no amount of magic or divination can wrest more from God.

The OT does not have a word *magic* per se, but rather condemns in vociferous language those who practice magical rites and ritual power. The Pentateuch contains a number of texts cataloging magical practices thought to be abominable to God and worthy of exile for all those who practice them. The most complete list is Deut. 18:10–11: "No one shall be found among you who makes a son or daughter pass through fire, or who practices divination, or is a soothsayer, or an augur, or a sorcerer, or one who casts spells, or who consults ghosts or spirits, or who seeks oracles from the dead." The concept of child sacrifice is clear enough, but the precise definition of the others is in doubt (for more on what follows, see Jeffers 25–101; Schmitt 107–22, 339–45). The term *qesem* is a technical one for divination generally, and it probably serves as the general term for which the specifics are detailed in what follows. The concept of soothsaying (Poel of *ʿānan*) was a subtype of divination likely involving an oracle, although its precise ritual or practice is unknown (cf. Isa. 2:6; 2 Kgs. 21:6; Mic. 5:12). The practice of augury (Piel of *nāḥaš*), again a general term, probably denotes the taking of omens or the ability to read signs in natural phenomena. The difference between practicing sorcery (Piel of *kāšap*) and the casting of spells (verb *ḥābar*, noun *ḥeber*) is not entirely clear. The ancient versions suggest that a sorcerer (LXX, *pharmakos*; Vulg., *incantator*) is an herbalist, using herbs while reciting incantations, although scholars today are not agreed about the accuracy of these translations. The spellbinder was assumed to have power over words to cast spells on others, binding them by his power. Whatever the similarities or differences between sorcery and spell-binding, both have moved from seeking discernment and guidance to exercising control over another.

The final abomination mentioned in Deut. 18:11 is necromancy, or consultation of the dead, which is known from other ancient cultures. The OT terminology for this practice is obscure, but a few details may be deduced from the recurrence of these terms elsewhere in the Bible. The Deuteronomic prohibition denounces those who consult "mediums" and "spiritists" (*ʾôb* and *yiddĕʿōnî*), or the NRSV's "ghosts" and "spirits." The first of these appears to have signified the deified spirit of one's ancestor at first, and subsequently the ancestral image in a more transient, preternatural manner. The second term, "spiritist," seems to denote the necromantic practices involved in communicating with the deceased ancestor, and used together with "medium" it serves to give definition to the ancestor cult generally (Arnold 200–201). We have evidence that necromancy was practiced irregularly in Israel itself.

These magical practices condemned in Deut. 18:10–11 are also prohibited in Exod. 22:18; Lev. 19:26, 31; 20:6, 27. Thus, the legal portions of the Pentateuch are univocal in renouncing magical practices. But other internal evidence in the OT, including that of the Pentateuch itself, is much more accepting of magic and divination. So, for example, Laban learned "by divination" that God had blessed him through his nephew Jacob (Gen. 30:27). The nature of Laban's divination is not given, but the verb used of his activity (Piel of *nāḥaš*) is one of those condemned in Deuteronomy and has a corresponding noun form used of Balaam's practice of looking for omens (Num. 24:1). Moreover, this is the same word used of Joseph, who is said to use a cup "for divination" (Gen. 44:5, 15). The use of vessel inquiry, or lecanomancy, may have been a variation of hydromancy or the ability to discern the will of the gods by gazing on the surface of oil on water. No matter the divinatory specifics, we find no condemnation of Laban, Balaam, or Joseph for these practices.

In addition, dream interpretation is highly valued as an acceptable means of prophecy in the Joseph novel (Gen. 37:5–9; 40:5–19; 41:1–36). Dreams occurred elsewhere in Genesis, where they served as a kind of *deus ex machina*, in which God makes decrees or proclamations (Gen. 20:3–7; 28:12–17; 31:10–13). Such message dreams did not require interpretation, and they seldom functioned as prophecies of future events or as acceptable means of Israelite prophetic divination. In Joseph's case, the dreams are symbolic rather than the message type, and they clearly need interpretation. Significant for his Egyptian context, Joseph credits God with the giving of useful interpretations of dreams that are otherwise unintelligible (Gen. 40:8; 41:16).

Another divinatory practice in the OT, far from renounced but instead encouraged, is cleromancy, the casting of lots. This practice is listed as one of three methods acceptable for seeking God's guidance, the others being dreams and prophecy (1 Sam. 28:6). The lots of the OT, the "Urim and Thummim," were housed in the priestly breastpiece attached to the ephod (Exod. 28:28–30). Although their precise nature is in doubt, they were likely cubic stones of different colors, perhaps marked "yes" and "no." They were thus an adaptation of the use of lots, which was a common custom from everyday life in the ancient world useful for making impartial decisions, much as our coin toss today (Tarragon). In Israel, they served as a divinely sanctioned method of divination in which they functioned not so much to understand the future as to bring one's deeds into conformity with the will of God. The legitimate use of cleromancy was thus used by the historian of David's rise in 1 Samuel to contrast him with Saul's use of necromancy (Arnold).

In Exodus, Moses and Aaron are able to perform the same ritual power as the Egyptian "magicians" (*ḥarṭummîm*, an Egyptian loanword designating a priestly official [Exod. 7:11]). The magical techniques of Moses and Aaron are the same as their Egyptian counterparts, except that their deity is more powerful. The magic rods of the Egyptian court are turned into snakes to match the miracle performed with Aaron's staff, only to be consumed by Aaron's staff (Exod. 7:12). The Egyptians could also turn water to blood, so that even this miracle failed to persuade Pharaoh to release the Israelites (Exod. 7:22). The Egyptians were also able to match Moses and Aaron with frogs (Exod. 8:7), but they came to the end of their abilities with gnats, whereby they were forced to admit, "This is the finger of God!" (Exod. 8:19). In this way, the Egyptians themselves admit that they are only magicians, whereas the Israelites are instruments in the hand of God, who is performing signs and wonders beyond mere magic.

Some scholars have attempted to explain the inconsistency of prohibiting yet permitting magic by means of evolutionary processes, in which a gradual decline of such practices may be traced historically in ancient Israel. More likely, however, portions of the OT are polemical in nature, denigrating the use and effectiveness of foreign divinatory practices while accepting the validity and usefulness of similar practices in the hands of Israelite protagonists.

The techniques and practices of other ancient Near Eastern prophetic communication are often indistinguishable from Israelite practices. As can be said of Moses and Aaron and their use of techniques quite similar to those used by the Egyptian magicians, so in Genesis the use of dream interpretation is not entirely different from the rest of the ancient world. Rather, the biblical heroes hold to a different conception of divinity. So while the techniques may be similar or even the same, the difference is in Joseph's (or Moses' or Daniel's) understanding of God. The genius of the narrator's use of dream interpretation in the Joseph novel is the way the text stresses the superiority of the Yahweh-inspired court diviner from within the tradition of such diviners (Cryer 183).

The NT contains much less direct evidence related to divination and magic. In Acts 8:9–11, Simon of Samaria is accused of practicing magic (verb *mageuō*) and amazing the people of the city with his powerful magic (noun *mageia*). But when the city was evangelized by Philip, the people turned away from Simon and turned to Christ, and even Simon himself was baptized and was amazed by the "signs and great miracles" taking place under Philip's ministry. Similarly, Bar-Jesus (aka Elymas), a Cyprian magician (*magos*), attempted to oppose the work of Barnabas, Paul, and John on the island (Acts 13:6–8). Paul renounced Bar-Jesus as the "son of the devil" and struck him with blindness (Acts 13:9–12). At Ephesus, the seven sons of Sceva the high priest were among those who "practiced magic" (*prassō ta perierga*) according to the instruction of certain books, most likely exorcism, although the evil spirit mocked them ("Jesus I know, and Paul I know; but who are you?") and overpowered them (Acts 19:13–19). Sorcerers are listed among the wicked to be punished in Revelation (21:8; 22:15; cf. 9:21), and sorcery is included in a list of vices in Gal. 5:20. Thus, the distinction between legitimate, God-directed miracles and illegitimate magic took root early in Christian thought. Today, Christians eschew magic both because of these explicit prohibitions in both Testaments, and because of the general understanding of magic as an illegitimate attempt to manipulate God.

This understanding of magic and divination, derived as it is from the alternative worldview of the Bible in distinction to manipulative uses of magic in antiquity, should also inform contemporary perspectives on prayer and spiritual formation. Prayer in the Bible is relational ("If you abide in me . . ." [John 15:7]), communal, and based on confession and forgiveness (Jas. 5:15–16), but never manipulative. Whether it is Abraham, Moses, or Daniel (Gen. 18:16–33; Deut. 9:25–29; Dan. 9:2–23), the supplicant's hope is based on prior relationship with God. Prayer is thus vital to the formation of Christlikeness in the life of the believer, whereas reliance on magic is detrimental to one's relationship with God.

See also Blessing and Cursing; Necromancy

Bibliography

Aitken, J. *The Semantics of Blessing and Cursing in Ancient Hebrew.* ANESSup 23. Peeters, 2007; Arnold, B. "Necromancy and Cleromancy in 1 and 2 Samuel." *CBQ* 66 (2004): 199–213; Black, J., and A. Green. *Gods, Demons, and Symbols of Ancient Mesopotamia.* University of Texas Press, 1992; Brichto, H. *The Names of God: Poetic Readings in Biblical Beginnings.* Oxford University Press, 1998; Cryer, F. *Divination in Ancient Israel and Its Near Eastern Environment: A Socio-Historical Investigation.* JSOTSup 142. JSOT Press, 1994; Dickie, M. *Magic and Magicians in the Greco-Roman World.* Routledge, 2001; Dolansky, S. *Now You See It, Now You Don't: Biblical Perspectives on the Relationship between Magic and Religion.* Eisenbrauns, 2008; Graf, F. *Magic in the Ancient World.* Trans. F. Philip. RA 10. Harvard University Press, 1997; Jeffers, A. *Magic and Divination in Ancient Palestine and Syria.* SHANE 8. Brill, 1996; Mirecki, P., and M. Meyer, eds. *Magic and Ritual in the Ancient World.* RGRW 141. Brill, 2002; Noegel, S. *Nocturnal Ciphers: The Allusive Language of Dreams in the Ancient Near East.* AOS 89. American Oriental Society, 2007; Schmitt, R. *Magie im Alten Testament.* AOAT 313. Ugarit-Verlag, 2004; Tarragon, J.-M. de. "Witchcraft, Magic, and Divination in Canaan and Ancient Israel." Pages 2071–81 in vol. 4 of *Civilizations of the Ancient Near East*, ed. J. Sasson. Scribner, 1995; Thiselton, A. "The Supposed Power of Words in the Biblical Writings." *JTS* 25 (1974): 283–99.

Bill T. Arnold

Divine Command Theories of Ethics

Divine command theories of ethics have in common the belief that commands that prescribe what humans ought or ought not to do have their source in God, who is the divine commander. Divine command theories are often classified in metaethical theories called "theological voluntarism," in that the normative and moral status of commands is right because God wills them. The legitimacy of commands is rooted in God's authority and sovereignty and God's own moral excellence, thereby making divine commands the foundation of morality and an integral part of understanding and participating in God's moral will. In order for God's commands to be ascertained, they must be communicated to humans in ways that are understandable, through natural law, divine revelation, the human conscience, or a personal encounter, given that they assume an obedient response. In most divine command theories God does not override human free will or coerce blind obedience. Human responsibility remains an important part of divine command theories because commands are constitutive of social practices (Adams 249) that bind God to humans, humans to God, and humans to one another in acts of promising and fulfilling obligations vital for maintaining relationships. God is not an arbitrary giver of commands but instead issues commands out of love and grace as a way to guide humans into right living. God's commands are viewed as purposeful and trustworthy because God is believed to be so. These commands are issued to humans who are free to follow or reject them. Obedience to God's commands enables humans to fulfill moral obligations and incur benefits that allow them to thrive, whereas disobedience has consequences that bring harm to persons and communities.

Scripture is an essential source in most divine command theories for understanding commands issued by God to humans and ascertaining the will of God. Scripture functions in two primary ways. Scripture contains literal rules and commands issued by God, making them obligatory for humans to understand and follow. The quintessential example often referenced is the Decalogue (Exod. 20:1–17; Deut. 5:6–21). God's moral will is contained in specific directives that tell persons what to do or what not to do, with the expectation of obedience. Scripture is also the command of God in a more general sense. Scripture expresses the will of God in all its various genres and guides humans in understanding how to fulfill the greatest commandments as summarized by Jesus: "'You shall love the Lord your God with all your heart, and with all your soul, and with all your mind.' This is the greatest and first commandment. And the second is like it: 'You shall love your neighbor as yourself.' On these two commandments hang all the law and the prophets" (Matt. 22:37–40).

Divine command theories of ethics share affinities with deontological theories of ethics in that moral content is contained in rules and emphasis is given to following these rules for fulfilling moral requirements. Divine command theories may also encompass aspects of teleological theories of ethics because God's commands are viewed as purposeful and a means for ordering human life and furthering God's purposes for the world. In obeying divine commands, we participate in divine goodness. Divine command theories may also encompass aspects of virtue ethics in that obedience to God's commands inculcates and shapes affections, desires, and behaviors, enabling humans to grow in wisdom and right living.

Divine command theories have been an important part of Christian moral thought due to affirmations of God's sovereignty and goodness, the primary role of Scripture as a means of God's communication, and the capacity that humans have to understand the requirements of God. The following persons represent divine command theories because of their understanding that God's will for humans is realized through obedience to divine commands, even though some of them could not be given the label "divine command theorist," given the later classification of these theories in the historical development of ethical theory.

Augustine

Augustine of Hippo (354–430), influential in shaping much of Western theology and ethics, upheld the idea of God's goodness as the end to which humans should aspire. Although humans may possess the will and reason to understand the good, the reality of sin necessitates a Divine Master whose divine law provides the order and peace needed for one's internal state as well as for ordered communities. In obeying the Divine Master there is true freedom and justice that come when human societies reflect the eternal order, or the city of God, as opposed to the disorder and chaos caused by sin in the earthly city. Obedience to God is also the means of control over the appetites of the body and vices of the soul. A will misdirected away from the good is the source of sin, evil, and vice. The will directed back toward God becomes more virtuous and more loving as it submits to God's eternal law as the ultimate good. Like most patristic thinkers, Augustine assumed that Scripture had authority because it was composed by the Divine Spirit (Augustine, *Civ.* 11.3) and therefore contained the commands of God.

John Calvin

The Protestant Reformer John Calvin (1509–64) espoused a high view of the sovereignty of God from which came his particular understanding of the purpose of divine commands. For Calvin, God has the divine right to command. The commandments are an integral part of God's covenant with humanity, and obedience is an expression of worship. Obedience to divine laws, especially those codified in the Decalogue, is the means by which humans glorify God, grow in holiness, and ensure justice and righteousness. The "two tables of the law" provide a dual focus for human obedience to God as the sovereign giver of commands. The first table includes the commands to worship God alone, while the second table contains the commands by which humans are to treat others. In this way, the divine commands of God provide instruction for "inward spiritual righteousness" and "outward decency" (Calvin, *Institutes* 2.8.5). God's commands are purposeful and perfect and are offered as gifts, as "allures," that assist humans in understanding the will of God and for living holy lives. By obeying the commands, humans not only avert God's judgment but also please God and are rewarded accordingly.

Karl Barth

Karl Barth (1886–1968), the Swiss neoorthodox theologian, believed that the ultimate command of God has been offered in Jesus Christ, who calls persons to a life of obedience patterned after him, thereby concretizing the commands of God. Barth's understanding of God's commands is based on two key theological propositions. The first is that God has the right and freedom to issue commands to humans. Humans lack the capacity to understand what God requires because God is "wholly Other." God therefore took the initiative in Christ by demonstrating what is required of humans. In Christ, not only are the requirements of the law fulfilled but also God provides all that humans need to freely respond and obey. In saying yes to Christ, the living Word, we say yes to God. The second proposition is that the law is a form of grace. The commands are gifts of grace that enable persons to obey the mandates of the gospel by loving God and loving others as Christ did. Recipients of grace are motivated by love and gratitude to God expressed in their obedience to divine commands. Obedience is not the end but instead the means by which humans are restored to divine likeness and reconciled with God and with others. The commands of God continue to come to humans through the preached word, the written word, and the living Word, which call persons to concrete responses to Christ manifested in obedience.

Philip Quinn

American philosopher and theologian Philip J. Quinn (1940–2004) supported divine command theory based on philosophical theology, Scripture, and the two greatest commands of Jesus. Like most divine command theorists, Quinn relied on a metaphysical image of divine sovereignty that extends into all realms of life, including the moral. God's commands rest on God's own moral truths, which God has and knows to be morally superior because of omniscience inherent with divinity. God's intellect, or what God knows to be good, and what God wills for humans to do are integrated and made known in divine commands. Divine commands are expressions of God's own wisdom as the all-knowing Sovereign and reflect the will of God. Quinn also supported a divine command theory of ethics by an appeal to Scripture, which is replete with commands that God gives to humans. Both the OT and the NT assume God as commander who issues instructions through the various genres of Scripture that direct humans in fulfilling their moral obligations through obedience. Jesus' two great commandments—to love God with all our heart, soul, and mind, and to love our neighbor as ourselves—are given to humans precisely because it is against our nature to do so. We must be commanded to fulfill the requirements of God against our inclinations. This kind of commanded love is foundational for Christian ethics.

Richard Mouw

Philosopher and theologian Richard Mouw provides a comprehensive contemporary articulation of divine command theory that expands the concept in important ways. Though affirming the Reformation tenet of *sola scriptura*, Mouw does not confine the command of God to the imperatives found in Scripture. Instead, commands ought to be interpreted and understood in light of the entirety of Scripture so that we may understand the character of God, ascertain God's creative and redemptive purposes, and comprehend the kinds of persons we should aspire to be. In doing so, we learn to "conform to what God requires" (Mouw 10), which encompasses far more than just obeying an isolated command in the Bible. Mouw also acknowledges the narratival dimensions of God's commands in Scripture. Divine command theory ought not to be set at odds with other construals of the moral life, such as narrative or virtue ethics, but instead includes them. Divine command theory does and should encompass the larger narrative of God's commands and locates them in a larger framework of morality. Obedience then becomes a willing and joyful means by which moral character is shaped, virtues are learned, and moral preparedness is developed. It is important, according to Mouw, that our understanding of God as divine commander be informed by a trinitarian understanding of God lest our view of the purpose, direction, and shape of the commands of God be one-dimensional and misunderstood. God the Father graciously provides divine legislation in Scripture and nature (Mouw 150); Jesus is the perfect embodiment of a life of obedience that fulfilled all that God requires; the Holy Spirit makes doing the will of God possible.

Scripture and Divine Commands

Scripture, seen as a primary way in which God's will is communicated to humans, plays a prominent role in divine command theories. Five considerations are important for ascertaining the relationships between Scripture and divine command theories.

First, divine command theorists, like all persons, have a priori assumptions about God that inform an understanding of Scripture's purpose as a means by which God communicates and commands, even as Scripture shapes our views of what God is like. Plato's "Euthyphro dilemma" poses a particular challenge for divine command theories: is something right because God commands it, or does God command it because it is right? Divine command theorists assume a view of the God of Jewish and Christian traditions revealed in the Scriptures as a good and just Sovereign, motivated by love, grace, and mercy for all that is created, and whose own goodness becomes the grounds for moral excellence and right living. The answer given by divine command theory to the dilemma is simply yes because of the bond between God's character and commands, which cannot be separated. The commands of Scripture are right because God commands them, and God commands them because they are right. Divine commands are right because they come from God, they are trustworthy because God is trustworthy, and God graciously gives them to humans because they are right and good to follow.

Second, divine command theories acknowledge the hermeneutical and interpretive dimensions to commands in Scripture. All commands are located in a larger narrative context, whether that be the immediate context of a particular text or biblical book, the canonical context, or the overall narrative context and purposes of Scripture. What one may be commanded to do in Scripture is not always self-evident without requisite attention to the contexts of commands. What God requires is communicated in forms other than imperatives. For example, the requirement to "do justice, and to love kindness, and to walk humbly with your God" is contained in prophetic material (Mic. 6:8). Jesus' command, "Go and do likewise" comes after a story about the actions of a merciful Samaritan (Luke 10:25–37). Paul orders the believers at Philippi, "Make my joy complete: be of the same mind, having the same love, being in full accord and of one mind" (Phil. 2:2). This requirement for Christian behavior is premised on the example and attitude of Jesus (Phil. 2:5–8). Failure to take seriously the interpretive contexts of commands minimizes the purposes, the telos, to which commands are directed and flattens the requirements by relegating morality to merely obeying a rule or principle as the sum total of what God requires.

The third issue relates to the relationship between the OT and the NT often framed in the question "How do we determine which commands must be obeyed and which ones are no longer binding?" This question may arise from a perception that there is disjunction between the OT and the NT, and that the law codes of the OT are irrelevant and arcane. It also caricatures the OT as law and the NT as grace, with the unfortunate consequence of breaking the relationship between the two. However, in Christian moral thought, when looking to Scripture for guidance, we must understand divine command theory in a covenantal ethical context. God initiates a covenant with humans as a gift of grace from which ensues loving responses of obedience to God and covenantal obligations to other persons. The commands of Scripture must be embedded and interpreted in this covenantal framework in order to help us understand how to think and act as God's people and how to maintain conditions of justice and peace that the commands enable persons to do. Jesus affirmed that he did not come to abolish the law but rather to fulfill it (Matt. 5:17–20). His teaching, recorded by Matthew in the Sermon on the Mount, bears marked resemblance to the requirements of the law in the OT and must have been recognized by Matthew's Jewish audience. Jesus reminds people of the stringent moral obligations and the commands of God in the context of grace. This new covenantal framework, like the previous one, carries with it obligations to obey the commands of God as a response of grace and do exceedingly more than the law requires.

Fourth, divine command theories must confront the dilemma posed when there are conflicts between the commands of God and when what one might be commanded to do is morally problematic and even evil. Divine command theories do not assume that humans are not to question and discern what commands require. Commands are interpreted in light of an overarching narrative of God's priorities and what God is doing in and through the contexts in which commands are located. Humans do make prima facie determinations about which requirements are self-evident in light of the character and purposes of God. Extracting commands from narrative contexts, such as God's command to Abraham to sacrifice Isaac (Gen. 22:1–19) or to the Israelites to exterminate groups of people (Deut. 7:1–6) requires discernment to understand both the placement of these narratives in light of God's history with God's people and how these narratives are normative for Christian faith and practice in light of the gospel.

Fifth, divine command theories are moral frameworks that locate the commands of Scripture in the good purposes of God. This reaffirms the relationship between God and Scripture. Scripture's authority is related to God's, and God offers the gift of Scripture to enable humans to freely discern, wonder, ponder, and continually explore what God requires of them. Obedience to divine commands is not the end but rather a means by which God's purposes and goods are realized. Since divine commands are related to God's character and are located in the larger narrative of Scripture, they serve multiple purposes beyond just grudging and coerced obedience. God's commands are gifts of grace to humans who freely choose, gifts intended to aid them in decision-making, discernment, and character formation. Divine commands, broadly conceived, offered in Scripture enable humans to participate in God's goodness and good work, train them in ways of righteousness and justice, enable them to practice doing things that shape their affections, and, in doing so, manifest the good will of God in lives that seek to fulfill what God requires.

See also Covenant; Covenantal Ethics; Deontological Theories of Ethics; Love, Love Command; Moral Law; Narrative Ethics, Biblical; Narrative Ethics, Contemporary; Teleological Theories of Ethics; Ten Commandments; Virtue Ethics

Bibliography

Adams, R. "Divine Commands." Pages 249–76 in *Finite and Infinite Goods: A Framework for Ethics*. Oxford University Press, 1999; Barth, K. *Church Dogmatics*. Vol. II/2. Trans. A. Mackay et al. T&T Clark, 1957; Hare, J. *God's Call:*

Moral Realism, God's Commands, and Human Autonomy. Eerdmans, 2001; Miller, P. "Divine Command and Beyond: The Ethics of the Commandments." Pages 12–29 in *The Ten Commandments: The Reciprocity of Faithfulness*, ed. W. Brown. Westminster John Knox, 2004; Mouw, R. *The God Who Commands.* University of Notre Dame Press, 1999; Quinn, P. *Divine Commands and Moral Requirements.* Clarendon, 1978; Porter, J. "Trajectories in Christian Ethics." Pages 227–34 in *The Blackwell Companion to Religious Ethics*, ed. W. Schweiker. Blackwell, 2008; Schweiker, W. "Divine Command Ethics and the Otherness of God." Pages 155–70 in *Power, Values and Conviction: Theological Ethics in the Postmodern Age.* Pilgrim Press, 1998; Spohn, W. *What Are They Saying about Scripture and Ethics?* Paulist Press, 1995.

Wyndy Corbin Reuschling

Divorce *See* Marriage and Divorce

Donations, Organ *See* Bioethics

Double Effect, Principle of

Paul rejected the principle "Let us do evil that good may come" (Rom. 3:8). Nevertheless, there are complexities still to be considered. Cutting open a living human being, for example, might be regarded as an evil. But what if a skilled surgeon does it in order to save the life of a patient? What if the consequence of the surgery is the patient's death? What if the result of the surgery is certain to be, if not death, some other evil, say, dismemberment; may the surgery still be done? Perhaps sometimes we should do evil that good may come. In defense of Paul's rejection of this principle and in response to the complexities involved, over long centuries the tradition of moral reflection in the church developed the principle of double effect.

Although Joseph Mangan, like others, argued that Thomas Aquinas first coined the principle of double effect, Josef Ghoos proved that the principle is a seventeenth-century summary insight of moral cases resolved during the conquests of the sixteenth century. After a century of casuistic questions, moralists began looking for commonalities among their case solutions and so articulated principles (such as double effect, material cooperation, and lesser evil) to help them in their new manuals of moral theology. In the sixteenth century Bartolomeo Medina (1528–80) and Gabriel Vasquez (1551–1604) began to name the common factors among the similar cases. Finally, John of St. Thomas (1589–1644) articulated the factors into the conditions of the principle as such.

Since the seventeenth century, the principle has referred to an act with two effects, one right and one wrong, that can be performed when four conditions are met. Those conditions address, respectively, the object of activity, the intention, the material cause of the act, and proportionate reason. They are listed as follows:

1. The object of the action is right or indifferent in itself; it is not intrinsically wrong.
2. The wrong effect, though foreseen, cannot be intended.
3. The wrong effect cannot be the means to the right effect.
4. There must be proportionate reason for allowing the wrong effect to occur.

Two of the most frequently cited cases used to illustrate the principle are the destruction of military targets in civilian areas and the administration of painkillers to dying patients. Many moralists declared that instances of the first case were morally permissible if they conformed to the principle's four conditions. Often they considered it permissible that a munitions factory, absolutely necessary for an enemy's war on others, be destroyed even if it is found behind enemy lines in civilian areas. They would add that the target is not the civilians but rather singularly the factory, and that collateral damage needs be held to a minimum. These arguments have been held since 1570, but later in the moral manuals they were incorporated as instances of the later developed principle. During World War II, the Vietnam War, and the Iraq War, the principle's application has come under scrutiny precisely because some tried to justify bombing civilian areas *as* military targets by using the principle, but those attempts were universally rejected.

The second instance concerns administering painkillers to alleviate the pain of the terminally ill even if such administration compromised the patient's life. This case has been much less controversial, and its solution was sanctioned by Pope Pius XII. Moralists often commented that it is pain relief, not the death of a patient, that is the object of the moral administration of such pain relief.

In recent years a few writers, especially the German theologian Peter Knauer, have argued that the first three conditions are incidental to the principle, and that all moral reasoning can be reduced to the fourth condition, proportionate reason. For them, the principle is an early expression of proportionate reasoning or what today is known as "proportionalism." This method holds that moral arguments are resolved simply by weighing the proportionality of values and disvalues in conflict. Bruno Schueller objected that the principle is sensible only within a moral method, deontology, which asserts the possibility of the first condition:

the object is not intrinsically wrong. The principle arises only in a method that already declares that the direct attack on civilian populations or the direct killing of a patient is wrong per se.

See also Casuistry; Deontological Theories of Ethics; Euthanasia; Intention; Just-War Theory; War

Bibliography

Ghoos, J., "L'Acte à double effet, étude de théologie positive." *ETL* 27 (1951): 30–52; Keenan, J. "The Function of the Principle of Double Effect." *TS* 54 (1993): 294–315; Knauer, P. "The Hermeneutic Function of the Principle of Double-Effect." Pages 1–39 in *Moral Norms and Catholic Tradition*, ed. C. Curran and R. McCormick. RMT 1. Paulist Press, 1979; Mangan, J. "An Historical Analysis of the Principle of Double Effect." *TS* 10 (1949): 41–61; McCormick, R. "The Principle of Double Effect." Pages 413–29 in *How Brave a New World? Dilemmas in Bioethics*. SCM, 1981; Pius XII. "Address to Delegates to the Ninth National Congress of the Italian Society of the Science of Anesthetics." *CathM* 55 (1957): 260–78; Schueller, B. "The Double Effect in Catholic Thought: A Reevaluation." Pages 165–91 in *Doing Evil to Achieve Good: Moral Choice in Conflict Situations*, ed. R. McCormick and P. Ramsey. Loyola University Press, 1978; Ugorji, L. *The Principle of Double Effect: A Critical Appraisal of Its Traditional Understanding and Its Modern Reinterpretation*. Peter Lang, 1985.

James Keenan, SJ

Drinking *See* Alcohol

Drunkenness *See* Alcohol

Dualism, Anthropological

Anthropological dualism refers to a view in which a human being consists of both a material entity, the body, and an immaterial entity, either the mind or the soul, that is related to the body but not identical to it. Also known as substance dualism, this view is committed to the claim that the soul is an immaterial entity that grounds personal identity through time and change. Two versions of dualism are most common. The more traditional, Cartesian dualism, comes from the philosophy of René Descartes. On this view, the mind is the immaterial substance externally related by a causal relation to the body, which is merely a physical entity. The mind is the immaterial entity that contains the capacities for mental function. A second version is known as Thomistic dualism. This form of dualism emphasizes the soul, not the mind, and sees the mind as a faculty of the soul. For the Thomistic dualist, the soul contains the capacities for biological and mental functioning. In this view, the soul is more closely and intimately related to the body than it is in the Cartesian version.

Both versions of dualism acknowledge what is known as functional holism—the view that the person is a functioning body/soul complex and a deeply integrated unity with a complicated and intricate array of mutual functional dependence and causal connection. Ontologically, the dualist holds that body and soul are different entities, though for most of a person's earthly and eternal life they function as a fully integrated unity. Dualists hold that it is possible for a person to live in a disembodied state, and that the Bible teaches that between death and the return of Christ and final resurrection believers live in an intermediate, disembodied state, awaiting receipt of a resurrection body at the general resurrection.

Anthropological dualism was the dominant view among theologians and the church until the mid-late twentieth century. Dualists argue that a commonsense reading of several key biblical passages supports their view. In 2 Cor. 5:1–10 Paul affirms that "to be absent from the body is to be at home with the Lord" (v. 8). Paul is assuming here what he has already laid out in 1 Cor. 15, which is a general resurrection of the dead (vv. 52–54), in which for those who have died "in Christ" there is some time that elapses prior to inheriting a resurrection body. The best way to make biblical sense of Paul's teaching that if he is "absent from the body, he is at home with the Lord" is to posit an "intermediate state" in which the believer lives "at home with the Lord" in a temporarily disembodied state. Dualists suggest that this view best explains several other NT passages that indicate an intermediate state, such as Jesus' statement to the thief on the cross, "Today you will be with me in paradise" (Luke 23:43), and Paul's statement that his "desire is to depart [from this life] and be with Christ" (Phil. 1:23).

Dualists insist that the soul gives a person continuity of personal identity through time and change. This suggests that regardless of the stage of bodily development in the womb or breakdown in approaching death, one is still a person with rights to be respected, thus making both abortion and assisted suicide/euthanasia morally problematic.

See also Abortion; Body; Healthcare Ethics; Humanity; Image of God; Monism, Anthropological; Resurrection; Sanctity of Human Life

Bibliography

Cooper, J. *Body, Soul, and Life Everlasting: Biblical Anthropology and the Monism-Dualism Debate*. Eerdmans, 1989; Goetz, S. "Substance Dualism." Pages 33–74 in *In Search of the Soul: Perspectives on the Mind-Body Problem*, ed. J. Green. 2nd ed. Wipf & Stock, 2010;

Moreland, J., and S. Rae. *Body and Soul: Human Nature and the Crisis in Ethics*. InterVarsity, 2000; Swinburne, R. *The Evolution of the Soul*. Rev. ed. Oxford University Press, 1997.

Scott B. Rae and J. P. Moreland

Duty

A duty is something that we are required to perform or avoid because of the binding force of moral or legal obligation. As a moral principle, duty flows from and gives expression to the fact that we are located within a "web of moral relations" that entails obligations to others, to oneself, and, for believers, ultimately to God.

A sense of duty is found in a range of ancient writings (e.g., from Egypt, Babylonia, India, China, Greece, and Rome). In Greco-Roman thought, the Stoics rooted the principle of duty in the assumption that all human beings share a capacity to reason, which enables them to judge what is good or bad based on a natural law that inheres in the universe and not on the basis of human passions or physical desires. All individuals, therefore, participate as fellow citizens within a community of rational beings (regardless of the accidents of birth) that entails duties to God, to oneself, to one's family members and friends, to the civic order, and even to strangers.

The biblical framework for understanding duty is God's covenant with Israel. As God's partner in covenant, Israel is to keep the Ten Commandments, which specify what is owed God and what is owed other human beings (e.g., to honor one's parents, to avoid murder, adultery, theft, and so on), as well as a range of precepts regarding worship practices and, among other things, obligations to family, to workers and slaves, to the larger communal order (e.g., through a tithe) and those less fortunate (e.g., widows, orphans, and strangers), and even to animals. Prophetic literature reiterates the requirements of God's law, calling people to avoid worshiping idols and perpetrating injustice on the poor.

Jesus came not to destroy the law but to fulfill it (Matt. 5:17). Summarizing the two great "love commands" found in the OT—"Love the Lord your God with all your heart, soul, mind, and strength" and "Love your neighbor as yourself"—Jesus' teaching is rigorist and eschatological. Proclaiming the imminent kingdom of God, Jesus calls his disciples to deny themselves and take up their cross and follow him, a call that may entail forgoing normal kinship ties and giving one's wealth to the poor.

Paul's letters presuppose that all people can, through conscience, discern God's law in both creation and in Scripture. Nonetheless, because of the power of sin, all are in need of God's redemption in Jesus Christ so that we can fulfill the law in a life of "faith working through love" (Gal. 5:6). Similarly, the Johannine literature stresses how God's love for us in Jesus Christ is embodied in our love for one another.

Among classical theologians, Thomas Aquinas argues that as rational beings, humans can perceive and enact the natural law, which is coterminous with God's revealed law. In addition, through grace Christians can fulfill the "new law" written in their hearts, the law of "faith working through love," and, for some, even the "counsels of the perfection" (chastity, poverty, obedience). Stressing sin's power over reason, the Reformers draw attention to the way God's commandments confront us with our duty. Insisting that we do not earn salvation by good works but rather are justified by faith in Christ alone, they also abolish any distinction among Christians, viewing one's vocation (e.g., as a parent or in a particular occupation) as the location for faith to be worked out in love.

Immanuel Kant also maintains that the moral law confronts us with duty. Unlike God, who embodies the holy law in God's holy will, we are imperfect beings who are not fully able to determine ourselves according to the dictates of practical reason. Nonetheless, Kant seeks to ground the principle of duty in human reason alone. Making the principle of duty the principle of ethics, he argues that a person's moral worth is defined by performing one's duty solely for duty's sake, regardless of personal inclinations and without calculating the advantages or disadvantages of anticipated consequences. Thus, duty is a "categorical imperative," which as "unconditioned"—that is, not determined by anything else—must always take the form of a universal principle. In Kant's "kingdom of ends" we are to act in such a way that we treat the humanity in our own person and in the person of everyone else always as an end and never merely as a means.

G. W. F. Hegel seeks to overcome Kant's distinction between "duty for duty's sake" and the goods that our actions might attain by arguing for an organic community based on universally valid principles of reason where the needs of individuals and the community can be reciprocally met and the content of one's moral duty is defined by one's position in the community (e.g., as parent, citizen, teacher, merchant). The British Hegelian F. H. Bradley characterized this ethics as an ethics of "my station and its duties."

Countering the modern tendency to subordinate the principle of duty to the principle of rights (e.g., the rights to life, liberty, property), David Selbourne argues that the civic order, as a web of moral relations, entails not only rights but also general and particular duties to one's self (e.g., self-restraint, avoiding self-harm, earning a livelihood, gaining education), to other human beings (e.g., to one's children, parents, spouses, and other family relations, to both friends and strangers, and to past and future generations), to the civic order (e.g., paying taxes, military or jury duties, and public service in general), and to animals and the natural world.

What grounds the principle of duty? Presupposing the idea of a conscience, an inner sense of what is right and wrong, some ground the principle of duty in reason alone, whereas others ultimately ground it in God's nature or will. For Christians, God's love manifest in Jesus Christ is the basis for presenting their bodies as a "living sacrifice, holy and acceptable to God" and for being transformed by the renewing of their minds so that they can discern God's will—"what is good, acceptable, and perfect" (Rom. 12:1–2).

See also Conscience; Deontological Theories of Ethics; Divine Command Theories of Ethics; Law; Obligation; Promise and Promise-Keeping; Righteousness; Ten Commandments

Bibliography

Bradley, F. *Ethical Studies: Selected Essays*. Liberal Arts Press, 1951; Kant, I. *Lectures on Ethics*. Trans. L. Infield. Harper & Row, 1963; Selbourne, D. *The Principle of Duty: An Essay on the Foundations of the Civic Order*. University of Notre Dame Press, 2001.

Lois Malcolm

Dying, Care of

See Care, Caring

E

Ecclesiastes

Moral formation is an important goal of wisdom literature, and Ecclesiastes is no exception. The title derives from the Greek translation of the Hebrew word *qōhelet*, which means "gatherer of an assembly" and functions as a pen name for the author. According to the epilogue, Qoheleth was a sage who "taught the people" (12:9 [hence the NRSV rendering "Teacher"]). But the teachings of this sage, marked by incongruities and radical skepticism, have perplexed readers, both ancient and modern. Qoheleth himself was perplexed by what he observed in the world, repeatedly declaring that "all is vanity [*hebel*]." The Hebrew word *hebel* literally means "vapor" or "breath" and is used as a metaphor for the ephemeral, incomprehensible, and unreliable dimensions of life, whatever is beyond the grasp of mortals. Because of the ubiquity of this motif (thirty-eight occurrences), many conclude that Qoheleth is a thoroughgoing cynic who despairs of finding anything good in life. Others, however, highlight the equally persistent counterpoint of joy that runs throughout his discourse with ever-increasing urgency and verve. There is a growing recognition that the book cannot be reduced to either one of these sentiments; indeed, the contradictions are part and parcel of its message.

Observation of moral incongruities leads Qoheleth to overturn all notions of human certitude. However, he does not give up his quest to determine what is good (2:3). He presses on to address fundamental questions: What does it mean to be human? How should one live in a world beyond human control?

In reconstructing his moral vision, Qoheleth critically engages traditional sources: wisdom teachings, Torah, Solomonic traditions, as well as other ancient Near Eastern literature. A hallmark of the wisdom tradition, however, is its empirical, contextual, life-centered approach to moral reflection. Qoheleth accordingly gives considerable authority to his own perception and experience. Under the guise of the wise king par excellence, he sets out on an ambitious program to investigate "all that is done under heaven" (1:13). His favorite verb is *r'h* ("to see, experience"), and he is most often the explicit or implicit subject. Qoheleth reports what he sees: injustice and oppression (3:16; 4:1; 8:9), the unpredictability of divine economy (2:26; 6:1–3), contradictions between traditional precepts and reality (7:15; 8:10–14; 9:11–13). He communicates his findings through literary vehicles that capture the imagination: memorable proverbs, gripping anecdotes, evocative poems. In short, the sage employs all the resources of the wisdom tradition, both its method and its forms, to lend weight to his teachings and to recast traditional profiles of wisdom.

Another element in Qoheleth's account of the moral life is the fear of God (3:14; 5:6; 7:18; 8:12–13; 9:2; 12:13). Rejecting sentimental religiosity, Qoheleth emphasizes the vast distance between God and humanity. Creation is ordered by God, and norms for the good life are a part of this design. But its logic is hidden from mortals, for God is wholly other (3:11; 5:2). God's inscrutable determination of events and the contingencies of an unpredictable world impinge on human agency, so that humans must relinquish control. They can respond only to what happens, moment by moment (3:1–15; 7:13–14). That is not to say that foresight is useless (10:10). Qoheleth does value wisdom, but he also exposes its limits and vulnerabilities. His teachings are therefore built on humble grounds that recognize both the tragic limitations and the joyous possibilities in humanity's "portion."

Qoheleth's ethic of enjoyment is all the more compelling because of its unflinching realism. Enjoyment entails perceiving things rightly; it is "seeing the good" or "seeing well" (2:1; 3:13; 5:17; 6:6, 9; 7:14; 11:9). The verb *r'h* connotes not only observation but also the meaningful integration of what one "sees." And Qoheleth urges his audience to encounter fully both the good and the bad (7:14a). He endorses not a hedonistic ideal that is intent on avoiding pain and maximizing pleasure, but rather an authentic and full-blooded experience of the world.

Enjoyment is described also in terms of the basic pleasures that sustain life: eating, drinking, working, sleeping, being with one's beloved (2:24–26; 3:12–13, 22; 5:17–19; 7:14; 8:15; 9:7–10; 11:7–12:1). Qoheleth thus presents a material and concrete understanding of the good life. Enjoyment is located resolutely in the fulfillment of fundamental needs, including not only physical but also vocational and relational pleasures. These are the things that God provides in order to make and keep human life human. They describe in concrete terms the desirable goals of life.

By associating enjoyment with basic needs, Qoheleth opposes the insatiability of the human appetite that can lead to destructive consumption. Enjoyment therefore has important socioeconomic implications. Indeed, the book's preoccupation with such issues is suggested by its frequent use of commercial terms. Although the debate about the book's provenance is ongoing (with recent scholarship converging on the postexilic period), Qoheleth clearly addresses an economically volatile context in which opportunities for wealth existed alongside risks of financial disaster. To hedge against possible loss, people toil away for more and more in an obsessed attempt to find some security or advantage. The acquisitive impulse that Qoheleth observes takes on a heightened virulence in contemporary culture, shaped by its technology of mass communication in service to a consumerist ethos. In contrast, Qoheleth's ethic of joy commends the habit of contentment. Enjoyment is not about the pursuit of more, but rather is the glad appreciation of what is already in one's possession by "the gift of God." Likewise, his work ethic is intimately connected with life's simple joys, not the pursuit of an elusive profit (Brown, "Whatever Your Hand Finds to Do").

Moral formation takes place in community; Qoheleth, however, seems to dwell in isolation, with communal concerns absent from his self-referential monologue. Nevertheless, a communal vision may be teased out from what he bemoans in his reflections. When he observes the plight of the oppressed, what disturbs Qoheleth is not only the fact of oppression but also that those who suffer have "no one to comfort them" (4:1). He also laments the absurdity of a solitary miser who toils away, with no companion to share in his riches (4:7–8). The focus of Qoheleth's despair is the unmitigated isolation of these individuals. In contrast, two are better than one (4:9–12).

A social dimension is also implicit in his most common metaphor for enjoyment, eating and drinking, which in the moral world of the OT takes place in the context of community. Qoheleth, admittedly, does not describe communal meals, but his rhetoric concerning the proper use of food suggests that an individual's enjoyment must never come at the expense of neighbor. He condemns irresponsible forms of feasting, which impede a person's capacity to fulfill social obligations (10:16–20). In contrast, the ethical life is characterized by a different kind of recklessness. The exhortation to "send out your bread upon the waters" (11:1–2) is a call to perform charitable deeds with abandon, and it constitutes an important expansion of Qoheleth's ethic of enjoyment. One must enjoy the bread in one's possession; one must also gladly release it for the benefit of others.

See also Old Testament Ethics; Wisdom Literature

Bibliography

Brown, W. *Character in Crisis: A Fresh Approach to the Wisdom Literature of the Old Testament*. Eerdmans, 1996; idem, "'Whatever Your Hand Finds to Do': Qoheleth's Work Ethic." *Int* 55 (2001): 271–84; Christianson, E. "The Ethics of Narrative Wisdom: Qoheleth as Test Case." Pages 202–10 in *Character and Scripture: Moral Formation, Community, and Biblical Interpretation*, ed. W. Brown. Eerdmans, 2002; Fox, M. *A Time to Tear Down and a Time to Build Up: A Rereading of Ecclesiastes*. Eerdmans, 1999; Seow, C.-L. *Ecclesiastes*. AB 18C. Doubleday, 1997; idem. "Theology When Everything Is Out of Control." *Int* 55 (2001): 237–49.

Eunny P. Lee

Ecclesiasticus *See* Sirach

Ecclesiology and Ethics

What role does the church play in ethics? Perhaps nothing shifted so drastically from the eighteenth and nineteenth centuries to the twentieth century in theological and biblical scholarship than the answer to this question. Alfred Loisy, Roman Catholic modernist theologian, encapsulated much of the earlier century's scholarship when he wrote in the early 1900s, "Jesus foretold the Kingdom, and it was the Church that came" (Loisy 166). The formation of the church had been viewed as a deviation from Jesus' proclamation. Jesus proclaimed the kingdom of God and a "radical monotheism" that relativized all earthly social institutions. Rather than proclaiming what Jesus proclaimed, the church proclaimed Jesus himself. Much of nineteenth-century scholarship claimed that the creation of the church was actually a mistake. Rather than an egalitarian, inclusive kingdom, we have a hierarchically structured church that took the exclusive right to mediate Jesus' presence to the world. Some scholars referred to this as "early Catholicism" and sought to get behind it to the "original Jesus." This "deviant" tradition culminated in Bishop Cyprian of Carthage's famous statement, "Outside the church there is no salvation."

Perhaps the most extreme version of the eighteenth- and nineteenth-century scholarship could be found in Hermann Reimarus's original quest for the historical Jesus. Reimarus (1694–1768) was a deist and biblical critic who wrote some "fragments" about Jesus' life that were not published until after his death by the philosopher Gotthold Lessing in 1774–78. Reimarus distinguished between Jesus' and the apostles' teaching. Jesus, using Jewish hyperbole, taught the coming of the kingdom and the need for repentance. The coming of the kingdom was neither a mysterious nor supernatural reality, but an allegory by which Jesus sought to change the social and political institutions of his day. The apostles then altered the simple moral and political message of Jesus. They had left everything to follow him, hoping to receive the kingdom that he promised. But they misunderstood its nature. His death left them hopeless. In turn, they invented the resurrection, proclaimed themselves leaders over the new community, and secured their future (albeit not very well, since many died as martyrs!) by creating the church.

Few nineteenth-century scholars went as far as Reimarus, but his critical scholarship raised questions that haunted those who came after him, the fundamental one being this: can we trust the apostles and the biblical witness to present Jesus, or should we get "behind" it to the original witness himself? The apostles and those who wrote the Scriptures had a stake in the story ending in a particular way. Was it not in their interest to see the "church" as the conclusion to the story? If so, then should we not treat the church with a "hermeneutic of suspicion," which is a way of interpreting that asks whose interest is served by telling a story in a particular way? By treating this interest with suspicion, we might discover better what actually happened than by being taken in by those who tell the story such that it serves their interest. This has led to a principle for interpreting Scripture called the "criterion of dissimilarity." In one version, it suggests that the authentic, original Jesus more likely will be found when we encounter a dissimilarity between what he said and what it was in the interest of those who formed the church to say.

The preoccupation with Reimarus's question led to a skeptical conclusion concerning Jesus' teaching on ethics and its relationship to the church. At best, the church was irrelevant to his ethics; at worst, it betrayed them. This is why Loisy penned his memorable lines. The church prohibited the realization of Jesus' radically inclusive and egalitarian ethics by usurping the kingdom that he proclaimed. For some, this meant that the church was a hindrance to Jesus' ethics. The kingdom could best be found outside the church in the secular realm.

What I have been describing is a rather bald view of the dominant biblical and theological scholarship of the eighteenth and nineteenth centuries on the relation between the church and ethics. It is bald in the sense that the critique of the church is seldom as straightforward and thorough as one finds in Reimarus or in Loisy's statement. However, this description is no caricature, and many scholars in both the church and the academy still uncritically accept the questions and even the answers that this scholarship raises. Yet, a sea change has occurred since this scholarship dominated. That sea change can be found in this statement by Karl Barth: "The Word did not simply become any 'flesh,' any man humbled and suffering. It became Jewish flesh" (Barth 166). Much earlier scholarship treated Jesus' Jewish context as insignificant. In fact, the criterion of dissimilarity separated Jesus not only from the community established in his name (the church) but also from the community within which he lived (Judaism). Thus, the authentic Jesus would also be found in those sayings in which his words clashed with the interests of Judaism in his day. But why should we find the authentic Jesus by treating with suspicion everything that would fit him within either Judaism or the community established in his name? Only if we see Jesus as some kind of modern heroic individual whose life makes sense in opposition to the communities around him would this work. By remembering that Jesus was Jewish, we gain better insight into both the claims that the early Christians made about who he was as well as the significance of his mission that led those persons to make such claims. When we remember that he lived and fulfilled his mission within this Jewish context, we will also come to the conclusion that the church was not a mistake, but essential to the fulfillment of his mission.

Who Was Jesus?

Christianity arose because first-century Jews worshiped Jesus as God. That they did so is relatively uncontroversial. When they did so and what it means remain, and most likely always will be, contested. The clearest testimony to Jesus' divinity comes in the Gospels themselves. It is explicit in the Gospel of John when it climaxes with Thomas confessing before the risen Christ, "My Lord and my God" (John 20:28). For some, this is evidence of a gradual development in the first-century understanding of who Jesus was. The early witnesses point in this direction but do not state it so explicitly. John's Gospel is thought to be a late document, perhaps written at the turn of the century. Of course, other unambiguous testimony is found elsewhere in Scripture that demonstrates that early Christians worshiped Jesus as God. In the Gospel of Matthew, the women leaving the tomb with joy to proclaim the resurrection to the disciples met Jesus on the way. We are then told, "And they came to him, took hold of his feet, and worshiped him" (Matt. 28:9). Other statements about Jesus' divinity include Phil. 2:6; Col. 1:15, although they are much more contested. Hebrews 1:3 likewise presents Jesus as the "exact imprint" of the Father.

Whether all these passages present Jesus as consubstantial with God as the church formulated it at Nicea and Constantinople in the fourth century is certainly up for debate, but that Jesus early on was worshiped is not. What does it mean that Jesus was worshiped? First-century Judaism was no monolithic religion. No "catechism" existed suggesting that it contained what all Jews should believe. So if Jesus was worshiped as divine, was it possible that he was considered to be some kind of intermediary being, along the lines of odd biblical characters such as Enoch and Melchizedek? Was he viewed as an angel, or as the personification of wisdom? And if so, would it have been unusual for first-century Jews to worship these characters? Of course, as is true of every age, scholars are divided about the answers to these questions. I find compelling those biblical scholars who argue that Jewish "radical monotheism" makes it unlikely that Jesus, had he been an intermediary figure, angel, or personification of wisdom, would have been worshiped. That first-century Jews worshiped Jesus means that they saw God present in him. Just as God dwelled with Israel in the ark of the covenant in the tabernacle, so now God "tabernacles" (John 1:14) with us in the person Jesus Christ. Jesus' body functions as the site where divinity and humanity live together in an intimate unity, which is similar to the function of the ark as it was first present in the tent of meeting and then in the temple. That in Jesus we find "true God" and "true humanity" united forever in one person leads us to recognize that the church, which is the continuation of this body, is essential for Christian ethics.

What Did Jesus Do?

Jesus proclaimed the kingdom of God, called people to repentance, gathered twelve disciples, and headed toward Jerusalem, where he was arrested, tortured, and crucified. His disciples then proclaimed him risen from the dead. They continued to go to synagogue, but they included him in their worship. Why they did this can best be seen in the context of Jewish eschatology. It held forth the hope that God's glory would return to Jerusalem, indwell the temple, and restore Israel so that Jews could live as God's people, making themselves and the land "holy" as God intended when they were given the Torah. When Jesus gathers twelve disciples and heads toward Jerusalem, what he is doing makes best sense against this Jewish expectation. When he arrives in Jerusalem and overturns the tables in the temple and claims that he will destroy it, this expectation has taken an odd twist. If Jewish hope held forth the expectation of the return of God's glory to the temple, then why would Jesus call it into question by claiming in this parabolic way that it was doomed? John's Gospel, which unlike the Synoptics sets this event at the beginning of Jesus' ministry, gives us insight into it. Only after the resurrection did his disciples recognize that the destruction and rebuilding of the temple signified that Jesus' material body was now the site of God's glory. This is why he said he would "rebuild" the temple in three days (John 2:19–22). The dogmatic tradition understands this as the foundation for the church. Jesus' body is the site of God's glory, now mediated through history by Word and sacrament constituting those who receive this mediation as the ongoing presence of his body. This is called the "threefold form" of the body of Christ. First is his material, historical risen body that is no longer present to us as it was to his disciples. Jesus ascended to the Father and sends the Spirit to mediate his presence. It is mediated through the second form, his Word and sacrament, which is why we call the Eucharist or Lord's Supper "the body of Christ" and Scripture the "Word of the Lord." When we receive these forms, which then require discipleship or following after Christ, we become a third form of his body, the church. It is also called "the body of Christ." All of this, of course, is thoroughly biblical language. But it could be confusing for it suggests a multiplicity to Christ's body. Is his body the risen, ascended body? Is it the Word and Sacrament? Or is it the church gathered in his name? The answer is yes, and with that answer we begin to understand the importance of ecclesiology for ethics.

Ecclesiology and Ethics

The church makes Christian ethics possible because only through it can Christians participate in Christ's body, receiving his righteousness, without which a *Christian* ethics makes no sense. This revises what is meant by the term *ethics*. Usually it is understood as an achievement that people can attain through their own natural powers. Aristotle, for instance, thought that everything had an end or purpose for which it was naturally inclined. This natural inclination brought with it the natural means to be able to attain its end. Just as an acorn has within it what is necessary to become an oak tree, so the human person naturally has the means to achieve his or her end. Although both the acorn and human person required the proper environment in which to pursue that end, this environment was still natural to the pursuer. Christian ethics can learn a great deal from Aristotle as well as most traditions of ethics, but it requires something more. A Christian ethic requires a supplementation that is more than natural in order for human creatures to achieve their end, for the end of the Christian life is not to achieve some natural end but to dwell with God. This is done by making God's name holy. The end of the Christian life is found in the prayer that Jesus taught us to pray: "Our Father who art in heaven, hallowed be thy name. . . ." Christian ethics seeks to make God's name holy in all our natural, ordinary activities so that God and creatures can dwell together as God intends. This cannot be done without using the natural means at our disposal. As one Jewish teacher quipped, "Any God who won't tell you what to do with your pots and pans and genitals isn't worth worshiping" (Hauerwas and Willimon 20). God uses the natural means that God created to make his name holy. But *God* uses these natural means, which requires that they become something more than natural. How can this be?

Jesus' perfect obedience alone fulfills the requirement that we make God's name holy. Anselm of Canterbury explained this well. He addressed the question how God could redeem the world through the suffering and death of an innocent man. Was this not a worse offense than the offense that caused the fall in the first place? Anselm responded, "Therefore God did not compel Christ to die, when there was no sin in him, but Christ himself freely underwent death, not by yielding up his life as an act of obedience, but on account of his obedience in maintaining justice, because he so steadfastly persevered in it that he brought death on himself" (Anselm 113). Christ's obedience was not simply his willingness to offer up his life as a sacrifice; it was more his perfect act of obedience in fulfilling the justice of God. He was willing to live as God intended human creatures to live even to the point of the cross. The cross was the indirect effect of Jesus' direct willing of obedience to the Father. It is this obedience that restores the harmony to a fallen creation.

For Anselm, then, God is not a pure power over the creation who could just snap his fingers and will that the harmony be restored. God cannot merely wink at the disruption of his good creation and act as if all is well. The work that makes it harmonious must still be accomplished in order for God to dwell in his creation as he intended. This dwelling took place first in the garden of Eden, but after the fall God no longer lives with creatures in that harmony. God, however, does not abandon them; God elects a people and dwells with them in the ark of the covenant in the tabernacle, which itself is modeled after the garden. God's presence then dwells in the temple, behind the temple veil in the holy of holies. For Christians, this presence of God, God's glory, returns to Jerusalem in the incarnation, mission, crucifixion, and resurrection of Jesus. He calls and institutes twelve apostles, equipping them to be his body in the world. Whoever receives them receives him. They are filled with the Spirit at Pentecost and reverse the curse of Babel. Harmony, unity, and peace are restored. God dwells with them.

So what does this mean for ethics? Christian ethics is not figuring out the proper method for making moral decisions. It is not a utilitarian calculation of the consequences of actions. Nor is it a commitment to law or a system of laws. It is not a casuistic analysis of difficult cases, or the cultivation of virtue within some generic community. All these ethics have their place, and Christian ethics can learn, and has learned, something from each of them. Christian ethics is about discovering that site where God dwells with creatures and creatures with God so that we can participate in the harmony and restoration of God's good created order, thereby making God's name holy. That site is Christ's body, which is the church. It is what Christ accomplished in his work, and he summons us to participate in it. This does not mean, of course, that Christian ethics asks nothing more of us than that we go to church, say our prayers, and return to our everyday lives as if nothing has happened. To meet the glory of God in church is to be met with a power that can only transfigure. We have not truly been to church until we are bedazzled with that transfiguration. The similarity between the theophany that occurs when God dwells in the tabernacle and Jesus' transfiguration manifests the relation between these two sites:

> Then the cloud covered the tent of meeting, and the glory of the Lord filled the tabernacle. Moses was not able to enter the tent of meeting because the cloud settled upon it, and the glory of the Lord filled the tabernacle. Whenever the cloud was taken up from the tabernacle, the Israelites would set out on each stage of their journey. (Exod. 40:34–36)

> And he was transfigured before them, and his face shone like the sun, and his clothes became dazzling white. Suddenly there appeared to them Moses and Elijah, talking with him. Then Peter said to Jesus, "Lord, it is good for us to be here; if you wish, I will make three dwellings here, one for you, one for Moses, and one for Elijah." While he was still speaking, suddenly a bright cloud overshadowed them, and from the cloud a voice said, "This is my Son, the Beloved; with him I am well pleased; listen to him!" (Matt. 17:2–5)

We "set out on the journey" once we are dazzled by the light.

See also Holy Spirit; Kingdom of God

Bibliography

Anselm of Canterbury. "Why God Became Man." Pages 100–183 in *A Scholastic Miscellany: Anselm to Ockham*, ed. E. Fairweather. LCC. Westminster, 1956; Barker, M. *The Gate of Heaven: The History and Symbolism of the Temple in Jerusalem*. SPCK, 1991; Barth, K. *Church Dogmatics*. Vol. IV/1. Trans. G. Bromiley. T&T Clark, 1988; Bockmuehl, M. *Jewish Law in Gentile Churches: Halakhah and the Beginning of Christian Public Ethics*. Baker Academic, 2000; Hahn, S., ed. *Temple and Contemplation: God's Presence in the Cosmos, Church, and Human Heart*. Vol. 4 of *Letter and Spirit*. St. Paul Center for Biblical Theology, 2008; Hauerwas, S., and S. Wells, eds. *The Blackwell Companion to Christian Ethics*. Blackwell, 2004; Hauerwas, S., and W. Willimon. *The Truth about God: The Ten Commandments in Christian Life*. Abingdon, 1999; Lohfink, G. *Does God Need the Church? Toward a Theology of the People of God*. Trans. L. Maloney. Liturgical Press, 1999; Loisy, A. *The Gospel and the Church*. Fortress, 1976; Long, D. S. *Christian Ethics: A Very Short Introduction*. Oxford University Press, 2010.

D. Stephen Long

Ecological Ethics

The rise of ecological awareness and environmental concern is a relatively recent phenomenon. Rachel Carson's hugely influential book *Silent Spring*, which drew attention to the impact of chemical pesticides in particular, was published in 1962 and has been credited with initiating the modern environmental movement. The environmental pressure groups Greenpeace and Friends of the Earth were formed in 1971. By the beginning of the third millennium, with an increasingly well-established scientific consensus regarding the likely impact of global warming caused by human activity, ecological issues had acquired a high public prominence and come to the center of ethical and political debate.

As with all such contemporary ethical challenges, Christian theologians turn to Scripture for wisdom and instruction. Already in 1954, with remarkable prescience, Joseph Sittler articulated the need for a "theology for earth," a theology that would rekindle a positive view of the earth as bound up in God's redemptive work. In a famous 1961 address to the World Council of Churches, calling for ecumenical unity, Sittler drew attention to the potential of the cosmic Christology of Col. 1; such a Christology offered a doctrinal basis for drawing the whole of creation into the orbit of God's redemptive purposes.

It was, however, the significant critical challenges to the biblical and Christian tradition that prompted reconsideration of the Bible's ecological implications. In particular, much discussion has focused on the issues raised by a now classic article by Lynn White Jr. published in 1967 and frequently cited and reprinted ever since. White argued that the (Western) Christian worldview, rooted in the creation stories and the notion of humanity made in God's image, introduced a dualism between humanity and nature and established the notion that it was God's will that humanity exploit nature to serve human interests. Thus, Christianity bears "a huge burden of guilt" (White 1206) for introducing the anthropocentric Western worldview that has permitted and promoted the active and aggressive conquest of nature for human ends. White does not explicitly cite biblical texts, giving only an overview of the biblical creation story, and his arguments concentrate much more on the historic development of Christian thought and early science during the period in which he specializes, the medieval era. Nonetheless, his forceful critique of the impact of the biblical tradition, especially the "dominion" text in Gen. 1:26–28, has stimulated a range of (often defensive) responses from biblical scholars.

Another important critical challenge focused on the impact of biblical eschatology. Some prophetic and apocalyptic texts present images of cosmic destruction associated with the coming "day of the Lord" (e.g., Joel 1:15; Amos 5:18–20; 1 Thess. 5:2–3). Catastrophes and natural disasters are depicted as a necessary precursor—the so-called messianic woes—to the final day of salvation (e.g., Mark 13). And Paul depicts Christians being "caught up" to meet the returning Lord in the air (1 Thess. 4:16–17). Particularly difficult from an ecological perspective is 2 Pet. 3:10–13, a text that not only describes a forthcoming cosmic conflagration but also encourages believers to be "hastening the coming of the day of God" on which this destruction will take place. From such texts, along with the enigmatic apocalyptic scenarios depicted in the book of Revelation, have developed various forms of contemporary Christian eschatology. For example, some evangelical Christians anticipate a "rapture" of Christians from the earth prior to a time of great tribulation; some urge that the return of Christ will happen suddenly and may well be imminent. Such visions of the future have been popularized in hugely successful books such as Hal Lindsay's *The Late, Great Planet Earth* (1971) and the "Left Behind" series of the 1990s by Tim LaHaye and Jerry B. Jenkins. It is not hard to see that such beliefs can engender the view that preserving and caring for the earth is not a priority, and there is some evidence that, at both governmental and individual levels, this has influenced decisions and policies in the United States. Indeed, a few fundamentalist writers have explicitly opposed environmentalism, depicting it as part of a (satanic) neopagan New Age movement and as promoting an unbiblical and unchristian pantheism. Again, these views raise critical questions about the kind of attitudes toward the environment that the Bible stimulates and supports.

The rise in awareness of ecological issues and the more specific challenges posed to the biblical tradition have engendered various kinds of engagement with Scripture. One prominent approach has been a primarily apologetic one eager to show, contrary to the criticisms of White and others, that Scripture does not legitimate ruthless exploitation of the environment and offers positive resources for ecological ethics. Other approaches have taken a more critical stance toward the Bible in their development of an ecological hermeneutic.

Apologetic Responses: Recovering Scripture's Ecological Wisdom

Lynn White's early critique has stimulated a number of treatments of the dominion text in Gen. 1:26–28. Biblical scholars have argued that this text, in its original historical context, does not envisage any kind of mandate for technological domination of nature to serve human purposes. Indeed, studies of the history of the impact of this text have concluded that it is only in the period of the sixteenth-century Renaissance, with the rise of modern science, that dominion comes to be seen as a human vocation—to "play the role of God in relation to the world" (Bauckham 167). In relation to the eschatological texts, the most common apologetic strategy has been to argue that the texts envisage the transformation of the earth, not its total destruction, such that there is continuity between "old" and "new" creation (see Finger).

In terms of the positive interpretation of these challenging texts, the most influential approach to Gen. 1:26–28 has been to read it as implying a human responsibility for stewardship of the earth. This approach picks up the use of kingly language in this text and interprets it within the broader treatment of kingly rule in the OT. This kingly rule, it is argued, was not (at least ideally) about exploitation and domination but rather about a responsibility to ensure the well-being and flourishing of those under the king's care. Other texts are important in developing a focus on stewardship as well, notably Gen. 2:15, from the second creation account, where the human is placed in the garden "to till and keep it." Indeed, the stewardship model of humanity's relationship to the earth has become a central plank in many attempts to construct a biblical ecological ethic and, more recently, in a realignment of evangelical leaders and bodies behind a more environmentally conscious vision of Christian responsibility. There are, however, those who question the value of stewardship as a central category for an ecological ethic, highlighting its primarily economic and managerial imagery and suggesting that it conveys too anthropocentric and hierarchical a view of humanity's relationship to the earth (e.g., Palmer).

Unsurprisingly, among the various eschatological texts it is those that depict a positive future transformation of creation that tend to loom large in ecological discussion; such texts seem to offer more positive potential for engendering ecological ethics than do the difficult texts such as 2 Pet. 3:10–13, which require some apologetic treatment. Some prophetic visions, notably in the book of Isaiah, depict a future peace that encompasses animals as well as humans, restoring an original peaceable, nonpredatory creation (cf. Gen. 1:29–30). Isaiah's famous and influential vision of the messianic age anticipates a time when "the wolf shall live with the lamb, the leopard shall lie down with the kid. . . . The cow and the bear shall graze, their young shall lie down together; and the lion shall eat straw like the ox" (Isa. 11:6–7; cf. 65:25). This, along with a promise of justice and liberation for the poor and oppressed, is what the establishment of righteousness will mean. These visions, then, have provided biblical resources for those who argue that Christian ethics should include a concern not only for human welfare but also for the peace and well-being of all creation. In the NT undoubtedly the favorite text among ecotheologians is Rom. 8:19–23. Here, in encouraging hope among the Christians at Rome, Paul states that the whole creation yearns to be set free from its bondage to decay and to share in the freedom of the children of God. In other words, the whole of creation is bound up with humanity in God's liberating and redeeming purposes. In contrast to texts such as 2 Pet. 3, Rom. 8 does not speak of cosmic destruction followed by renewal but rather implies a process of eschatological transformation in which the children of God—redeemed humanity—have a central place: creation anticipates sharing in their glorious liberty.

Other biblical texts also contribute significantly to what is perhaps the key shift of focus generated by the interest in ecological questions: a broadening of the traditional anthropocentric concern with human salvation and human relationship to God toward an emphasis on the whole of creation as bound up in God's loving and saving purposes. As is common in the history of engagement between Scripture and ethical issues, new and changing contemporary contexts have brought new questions to the agenda and different biblical texts to the center of attention. Alongside those already mentioned, important texts for ecological ethics include the following. Genesis 9:1–17, despite its description in Bible translations and commentaries as "God's covenant with Noah," is strikingly emphatic about the fact that this covenant is made with every living thing, with the whole earth. Some of the psalms, especially Pss. 104; 148, depict creation as a witness to the glory and greatness of God (Ps. 104; cf. Pss. 19:1–6; 136:5–9) and as called to join in praise of God (Ps. 148; cf. Pss. 66:1–4; 96:1; 97:1; 98:4–9). The latter theme is greatly expanded in the Greek additions to the book of Daniel (Sg. Three 35–68 at Dan. 3:23), taken up into liturgy as the Benedicite. The idea that all of creation is called to praise God might suggest an ecological reformulation of the classic Westminster Catechism: it is not only humanity's chief and highest end "to glorify God and fully to enjoy him forever" but also the whole creation's. The closing chapters of the book of Job (Job 38–42), in the speeches that God thunders from the whirlwind to an ultimately subdued Job, have been seen to offer a powerful critique of the notion that humanity is supreme in creation and of unique importance to God. Instead, God presents a catalog of the wonders of the nonhuman world, all of which exist in relation to God without any reference to their significance for humans. There is here, it seems, a clear decentering of humanity. In the NT, along with Rom. 8:19–23, Col. 1:15–20 offers strong support for the idea that God's reconciling work in Christ encompasses the whole cosmos, not only human beings. The phrase *ta panta* ("all things") runs repeatedly through this christological hymn, with Christ as the one in, through, and for whom all things were created, and through whom "God was pleased to reconcile to himself all things." The Gospels offer less directly relevant material, since Jesus does not comment on such themes, but his teaching on God's care for the birds and flowers (Matt. 6:26–28; 10:29; Luke 12:6, 24) is often cited as showing God's care for the whole of creation. Jesus' frequent use of imagery from nature and agriculture in his teaching is also held to indicate his awareness of and harmony with the natural world.

By drawing attention to such texts and their potential ecological significance, and by defending other texts against the critical charges of Lynn White and others, biblical scholars and ecotheologians have sought to show how the Bible can offer wisdom and instruction relevant to shaping human attitudes to the nonhuman world, foundations for a Christian ecological ethics.

Ecojustice Principles: The Earth Bible Project

A rather different approach to interpreting the Bible in the light of contemporary environmental issues has been developed by the Earth Bible Team, based in Adelaide, Australia, and published between 2000 and 2002 in an initial five-volume series under the general editorship of Norman C. Habel. In contrast to the approach of many "green" evangelicals, the approach taken by the Earth Bible Team reflects both a desire to avoid "cherry picking" merely a few favorite ecofriendly texts and a criticism of the view that the Bible is, or can be shown to be, ecofriendly. Habel, for example, commenting in 2000 on "the vast array of works on ecotheology that have flooded the market in the past 20 years," argues that "the vast majority of these works assume that the Bible is environmentally friendly and quote biblical passages uncritically to support the contention that an ecological thrust is inherent in the text" (Habel, *Readings*, 30–31). The team's approach does not by any means entail a denial that there is ecologically valuable and instructive material in the Bible, but it does require that an engagement be critical, ready also to expose and resist the material that is anthropocentric and negative toward the earth. The approach is guided by a series of "ecojustice principles" that provide a basis for the critical evaluation of biblical texts from the perspective of a commitment to ecojustice:

1. *Principle of intrinsic worth*: The universe, Earth, and all its components have intrinsic worth/value.
2. *Principle of interconnectedness*: Earth is a community of interconnected living things that are mutually dependent on one another for life and survival.
3. *Principle of voice*: Earth is a subject capable of raising its voice in celebration and against injustice.
4. *Principle of purpose*: The universe, Earth, and all its components are part of a dynamic cosmic design within which each piece has a place in the overall goal of that design.
5. *Principle of mutual custodianship*: Earth is a balanced and diverse domain where responsible custodians can function as partners, rather than rulers, to sustain a balanced and diverse Earth community.
6. *Principle of resistance*: Earth and its components not only suffer from injustices at the hands of humans, but actively resist them in the struggle for justice. (Habel, *Readings*, 24)

These principles developed "in dialogue with ecologists" deliberately avoid specifically biblical or theological terms in order to "facilitate dialogue with biologists, ecologists, other religious traditions . . . and scientists" (Habel, *Readings*, 38). The biblical texts are then read in the light of these ecojustice principles and found to warrant positive recovery or negative resistance according to whether and how they cohere with the principles.

For example, Habel rejects any attempt to "soften" the meaning of Gen. 1:26–28. This text legitimates harsh control of the earth and its other creatures by humans (Habel, "Geophany," 46–47). As such, it forms an unfortunate intrusion into the story of the beginnings of life on earth (Gen. 1:1–25), in which life emerges through a fruitful collaboration between God and Earth (capitalized as a character by Habel). Other writers in the series expose and criticize the anthropocentrism that they find in certain biblical texts (e.g., Ps. 8) while also drawing attention to the geocentric perspectives that can be found (e.g., Job 38–42). The work of the Earth Bible Project, continuing in a Society of Biblical Literature seminar on ecological hermeneutics, represents the most sustained and methodologically self-conscious attempt to engage with the Bible from an ecological perspective. The published volumes cover a wide range of biblical texts. Yet there are questions to be raised about how the approach connects with the approaches and concerns of Christian theology and ethics, as will become clear below.

Ecological Theology and Ethics

Both of the approaches surveyed above can be subjected to criticism in the quest to articulate a cogent basis for engaging Scripture in ecological ethics. The apologetic approach, as Habel's criticism suggests, tends to imply the claim that the Bible's message is one of positive value and concern for the environment—a claim notably embodied in *The Green Bible*, published in 2008. This claim is problematic in at least two respects. One is in its failure to acknowledge fully the extent to which certain "difficult" texts resist any retrieval for the ecological agenda; attempts to show otherwise remain unconvincing. The other is in its tendency to obscure the extent to which what is presented as "biblical teaching" is not simply a repetition of "what the Bible says," despite claims to the contrary, but rather is a particular construal of certain biblical texts prioritized over other biblical texts and read in the light of a particular understanding of the reader's contemporary context. For example, the claim that stewardship constitutes the biblical view of humanity's responsibility toward creation, encapsulated in Gen. 1:26–28, and that readings that see that text as legitimating human domination of nature are "distortions" of its meaning (e.g., Hill 38, 42) fails to acknowledge the extent to which both views are a particular and (more or less) plausible interpretation of this text and others. One reading emerged in the context of Enlightenment optimism about the possibilities for progress with the application of human knowledge, while the other arises in the context of much more recent awareness of the extent to which human activity has had destructive and unforeseen consequences for the complex and interdependent ecosystems that we inhabit.

The approach taken by the Earth Bible Team is preferable to the extent that it recognizes the variety within the biblical texts and acknowledges that some texts will remain problematic from an ecological perspective. Instead, the team presents the ecojustice principles as a statement of ethical commitment that guides the engagement with the biblical texts. There is a major difficulty with this approach, however, at least in terms of an approach to doing Christian theology: authority effectively lies not with the Bible or the Christian tradition but rather with the ecojustice principles. It is these that encapsulate a set of norms to inspire and instruct human belief and action. Why, then, should Christians find these principles persuasive enough to serve as a basis for ethical commitment and critical evaluation of the Bible? From where do these principles derive? Do they represent a specifically Christian theology and ethics, a rearticulation of the Christian tradition? It is evident that the Earth Bible Team does not want to present the principles in this way (see above). Instead, the principles seem to represent a summary of modern, scientifically informed, ecojustice commitments, something formed independently of the Christian and biblical traditions, in which case the Bible becomes pretty much dispensable.

What would seem to be needed, at least as a model for engaging Scripture in contemporary Christian theology and ethics, is an approach that falls somewhere between these two alternatives. One example of such an approach has been outlined, specifically in the context of an attempt to develop an ecological hermeneutic, by Ernst Conradie. For Conradie, it is important to appreciate how appropriation of the Bible in Christian theology is shaped by heuristic or doctrinal keys—justification by faith in the Lutheran tradition, liberation in liberation theology, stewardship in some recent ecotheology, and so on. The crucial point is that these doctrinal keys "are not directly derived from either the Biblical texts or the contemporary world but are precisely the product of previous attempts to construct a relationship between text, tradition and context." These doctrinal keys are made in the ongoing encounter between reader and text and in the attempt to fuse the distant horizons of both. As such, these keys have a "double function. . . . They provide a key to unlock the meaning of *both* the contemporary context *and* the Biblical texts and simultaneously enable the interpreter to establish a *link* between text and contemporary context" (Conradie 306). Just as any key offers a positive new way to construct relevant meaning from the Bible, so also, Conradie insists, it will inevitably "distort" both text and context, perhaps ideologically—that is, in legitimating and concealing the interests of dominant social groups. Doctrinal keys therefore should be subject to a hermeneutic of suspicion. But precisely by identifying them as doctrinal or hermeneutical keys, rather than as simply what the text "says," this critical suspicion is invited.

Such an approach invites an engagement with the biblical texts that is exegetically serious but also acknowledges such an engagement to be, inevitably, a constructive and creative act shaped by the perceived priorities of the contemporary context. To function as a form of constructive Christian theological engagement does not imply that such a reading must avoid any criticism of biblical texts. It does mean, however, that there will be some positive construction of doctrinal keys, formed in the encounter between reader and text, which in turn may serve as a criterion for critical appropriation. Just as Luther found in Paul's writings a message of justification by faith through grace alone, which then became the hermeneutical and theological heart of the Lutheran tradition, shaping a whole tradition of (critical) biblical interpretation and theological doctrine, so our own context, with its ecological crises and environmental pressures, may inspire new kinds of engagement with the Bible, new readings with new doctrinal keys at their heart.

From this kind of interpretive perspective we can begin to see how some of the ideas found in the biblical texts mentioned above might contribute to an ecological reconfiguration of Christian theology and ethics. The creation story of Gen. 1 repeatedly insists that everything that God made is "good" (1:10, 12, 18, 21, 25, 31), and the covenant of Gen. 9 binds God in eternal commitment to the whole earth (9:12–16). The psalms convey the idea that all creation shares the vocation to join in praise of God, while the book of Job punctures any human arrogance and self-importance. The eschatological visions of the prophetic literature depict a creation restored to peace and fertility, while the inaugurated eschatology of the NT texts suggests that the whole creation is already bound up in the transforming work of God in Christ, a reconciliation of the whole cosmos, and that Christians have a responsibility to embody and promote the realization of this goal. Bringing such texts into central focus can help to reshape the theological tradition such that creation becomes not merely the stage for the drama of human salvation but also fully involved in the process and eager to share in its outcome.

This does not, of course, resolve the difficulties of the biblical texts that appear to run counter to any commitment to care for the earth, but it does represent a self-conscious approach to interpretation that, like other theological traditions in the past, chooses to place certain biblical themes and motifs at the heart of its constructive enterprise. Luther famously found the Epistle of James of rather doubtful value compared with Romans and Galatians, with their exemplary presentation of the gospel message of justification by faith; similarly, in the light of the ecological challenges that face us, certain biblical texts may prove more valuable and important than others in constructing an ecological theology and ethics.

When it comes to the specific task of doing ecological ethics, it should be clear that what the Bible has to offer is general and theologically embedded orientations rather than guidance on specific issues. If, for example, we regard stewardship as a doctrinal key that emerges from a constructive ecological reading of Scripture, then this will imply a certain view of the relationship between humankind and nature and a certain model of God-given ethical responsibility. However, it will tell us very little about what stewardship might require in practice regarding specific dilemmas or questions. Similarly, if we find the idea of creation's praise a compelling theological theme, then this will shape and inform a sense of creation's value and purpose. It would seem to imply an imperative to foster and sustain creation's beauty and diversity. But again, this provides little by way of specific guidelines when it comes to decisions about particular situations. More significantly still, despite the ecotheological weight placed on eschatological texts such as Rom. 8:19–23, there is no explicit or direct ethical instruction evident in the conviction that God is in the process of bringing about the renewal and liberation of the whole creation. To be sure, one can well argue that the role that Paul ascribes to the children of God—the ones whom creation longs to see revealed—implies a responsibility on their part. But this responsibility, and any ecological dimensions to it, are not stated in the text and thus must be developed by contemporary interpreters.

This does not mean that specific ethical guidance on matters of ecological relevance cannot be derived from an engagement with Scripture. For example, the Torah's regulations for compassionate treatment of agricultural animals (e.g., Deut. 22), allowing a Sabbath rest for the land and making provision for a Jubilee Year (Lev. 25), and so on are potentially significant for a contemporary ecological ethics in general and a model of agricultural sustainability in particular. Andrew Linzey is among those who argue that the eschatological visions of a restored nonpredatory paradise (Isa. 11:6–9; cf. Gen. 1:29–30) provide a biblical basis for Christian vegetarianism: Christians should anticipate and work toward this vision of a nonviolent creation, and abandoning the killing of animals for food is one possible and significant step in this direction (Linzey 125–37). Christopher Southgate, drawing particularly on Rom. 8, argues that human efforts to end the extinction of species would be an appropriate response to the vision of the liberation of creation, in which the children of God take the responsibility associated with their freedom and glory in Christ (Southgate 124–32). But in these and other examples ecological ethics emerges from a reading of Scripture strongly informed by science, philosophy, theology, and contemporary ethics.

This is unsurprising, for ecological ethics is one area of Christian ethics where scientific insight has crucially formed our awareness of the very modern issues that we face—issues arising from, among other things, a vastly expanded human population, industrialization, and globalized consumer capitalism. These issues, and scientific awareness of them, are absent from the biblical writers' purview. In this area of contemporary ethics, at least, sufficient guidance cannot be found from the Bible alone but rather must come from a careful and constructive engagement between Scripture, contemporary science, and the traditions and approaches of Christian theology and ethics.

See also Animals; Bioethics; Creation, Biblical Accounts of; Creation Ethics; Eschatology and Ethics; Jubilee; Stewardship; Vegetarianism

Bibliography

Bauckham, R. *God and the Crisis of Freedom: Biblical and Contemporary Perspectives*. Westminster John Knox, 2002; Berry, R., ed. *The Care of Creation: Focusing Concern and Action*. InterVarsity, 2000; Bouma-Prediger, S., and P. Bakken, eds. *Evocations of Grace: The Writings of Joseph Sittler on Ecology, Theology, and Ethics*. Eerdmans, 2000; Conradie, E. "The Road towards an Ecological Biblical and Theological Hermeneutics." *Scriptura* 93 (2006): 305–14; Finger, T. *Evangelicals, Eschatology, and the Environment*. Evangelical Environmental Network, 1998; Habel, N. "Geophany: The Earth Story in Genesis 1." Pages 34–48 in *The Earth Story in Genesis*, ed. N. Habel and S. Wurst. Sheffield Academic Press, 2000; idem, ed. *Readings from the Perspective of Earth*. Sheffield Academic Press, 2000; Hill, B. *Christian Faith and the Environment: Making Vital Connections*. Orbis, 1998; Horrell, D. *Ecology and the Bible*. Equinox, 2010; Horrell, D., C. Hunt, and C. Southgate. "Appeals to the Bible in Ecotheology and Environmental Ethics: A Typology of Hermeneutical Stances." *SCE* 21 (2008): 219–38; Linzey, A. *Animal Theology*. SCM, 1994; Palmer, C. "Stewardship: A Case Study in Environmental Ethics." Pages 67–86 in *The Earth Beneath: A Critical Guide to Green Theology*, ed. I. Ball et al. SPCK, 1992; Southgate, C. *The Groaning of Creation: God, Evolution, and the Problem of Evil*. Westminster John Knox, 2008; White, L. "The Historical Roots of Our Ecologic Crisis." *Science* 155 (1967): 1203–7; Wilkinson, L., et al. *Earthkeeping: Christian Stewardship of Natural Resources*. Eerdmans, 1980.

David G. Horrell

Economic Development

A basic reality motivates modern thought and action on economic development. The contemporary world has large numbers of both very wealthy and desperately poor people. Thanks in part to modern science and technology, well over one billion people today enjoy food, housing, education, healthcare, and recreation unknown to even the aristocrats of earlier centuries. At the same time, the World Bank reports that one billion people try to survive on one dollar a day and almost two billion people on two dollars a day. They struggle with inadequate food, housing, healthcare, and education. Many conclude that economic development to enable the poor to enjoy a decent life is both a moral imperative and a technological possibility.

There is not, however, widespread agreement on the definition of economic development. For many in the 1960s and 1970s, economic development meant economic growth measured by an increase in a nation's gross domestic product (GDP). Human reason using science and technology was to be the means to economic development, understood as rising personal incomes, growing GDP, increasing industrialization, and technological improvement.

It soon became clear, however, that poverty results from more than just the lack of the right tools for effective agricultural and industrial production. Inadequate worldviews and unjust structures also produce poverty.

In 1990, David Korten defined development as "a process by which the members of a society increase their personal and institutional capacities to mobilize and manage resources to produce sustainable and justly distributed improvements in their quality of life" (Korten 67). Korten considered inadequate three earlier attempts at development: relief programs to feed hungry people, community development efforts to nurture faster economic growth, and structural change to create more just, sustainable socioeconomic systems. Without denying significant value in these efforts, Korten advocated mobilizing people's movements to energize and drive change.

In 1999, Nobel Prize–winning economist Amartya Sen published *Development as Freedom*. "The expansion of freedom," he argued, is "the primary end" and "the principal means of development" (Sen xii). Sen understands poverty to be the "deprivation of basic capabilities," not merely a very low income. Development, therefore, requires the emergence of five types of freedom.

Political freedom means civil rights and democratic political processes. Political freedom is both good in itself and a factor in avoiding poverty. Widespread famine, Sen notes, has never occurred in a democracy because politicians know they would lose the next election. *Economic freedom* involves genuine opportunities that persons have to own property and freely decide what to produce, sell, and consume. *Social freedom* requires societal choices that provide such things as education and healthcare for all so that all have the actual freedom to live better lives. *Transparency freedoms* refer to societal structures (courts, political processes, economic systems) that are transparent and open rather than corrupt. *Protective security or freedom* means a social safety net to prevent persons from experiencing abject misery, even starvation and death.

All these freedoms, Sen argues, are both essential to economic growth and also good in themselves. Therefore, comprehensive development requires the expansion of all these freedoms.

Sen's view of development as freedom is helpful. But his understanding of freedom is highly individualistic. The freedom that Sen desires is "more freedom to lead the kind of lives we have reason to value" (Sen 14). For Christians, that does not provide an adequate goal for economic development. Sinful persons often choose destructive things. We need a goal for development that transcends the personal preferences of sinful individuals.

In 1999, Bryant Myers (then vice president at World Vision International) included a crucial spiritual component in his book *Walking with the Poor*. Poverty is not only the lack of food, power, and Sen's various freedoms. Poverty, as Jayakumar Christian rightly argues, also arises from spiritual deprivation: the sinful God-complexes of the powerful and rich who oppress the poor, misguided worldviews, the marred self-image of the poor, and the destructive activity of unseen fallen spiritual powers.

The spiritual component that Myers adds is crucial. To suppose that human reason via science and technology can save us is naive. Only God can save us. To look for lasting transformation only at the level of community development, structural change, or even people movements is one-sided. We must also understand the spiritual factors that disempower the poor. Spiritual transformation is essential if our development work is to be truly Christian and genuinely sustainable.

Worldviews that persuade the poor fatalistically to accept their oppression and believe the oppressor's view of their worthlessness must give way to a biblical worldview where the God of the poor demands justice for all and creates every person in the very image of God. The transforming power of personal faith in Christ can restore marred self-identity, transform broken persons, and energize work for justice. Spiritual transformation is a crucial component of genuine development.

Myers is also helpful in insisting that a Christian understanding of the kingdom of God provides the best context for understanding the goal for genuine development. The ultimate goal is not just fewer people who are chronically malnourished, although that is enormously important. The ultimate goal is not community development and more just structures, although both are essential. The ultimate goal is not more personal freedom for individuals, although the Creator who chose to make every person in the divine image and grant them freedom wills genuine freedom for everyone. The ultimate goal is *shalom*—right relationships with God, neighbor, earth, and self.

The NT teaching on the kingdom of God shows that this divine *shalom* has broken into history decisively in the person and work of Jesus Christ and will come in its fullness at Christ's return. Christians know where history is going. Christians know that at some time in the future Christ will return to establish complete *shalom*, the fullness of right relationships. Therefore, Christian development seeks to move persons, communities, nations, and the whole world in that direction. "This kingdom frame is inclusive of the physical, social, mental and spiritual manifestations of poverty, and so all are legitimate areas of focus for transformational development that is truly Christian" (Myers 113).

That is not to say that economic development includes everything that is included in God's *shalom*. Rather, it is that part of *shalom* that pertains to economic life. But it is only within the larger framework of the fullness of *shalom* that we can properly understand economic development and the means to promote it.

We can deepen our understanding of economic development if we reflect further on poverty and its causes, God's special concern for the poor, and the nature of economic justice.

There are many causes of poverty (Sider, chap. 7). Some poverty results from sinful personal choices. Wrong choices about drugs, sex, work, and marriage clearly contribute to poverty. Some poverty is caused by natural disasters. The proper response is immediate aid so that people do not starve. Some poverty results from the lack of proper technology. To correct this, we use technological solutions such as developing better agricultural methods.

And some poverty results from great inequalities of power that have produced unjust systems and unfair structures. Continuing poverty among native peoples around the world is to a large degree the result of oppressive (often European) colonizers who seized their land and destroyed their way of life. In developing countries, local powerful landowners often use their power to oppress workers. In every nation, those with the most power abuse that power to write laws and operate government and business in ways that disadvantage the weakest. And globally, the richest, most powerful nations shape the patterns of international trade in ways that regularly benefit them and sometimes increase poverty for others. Structural change is the only adequate solution to systemic injustice.

Finally, as we have seen, spiritual blindness and oppression also create poverty. Rebellion against God and God's ways leads to bad choices and bad systems that create poverty. Fallen spiritual powers seek to destroy God's good creation. Effective economic development will work to correct all these causes of poverty.

Understanding the many complex causes of poverty, however, does not mean that we should indefinitely expand our definition of poverty. I doubt that it is helpful to say that "poverty is the absence of shalom in all its meanings" (Myers 86). Is the very wealthy landowner oppressing his workers poor? Is the proud, arrogant, promiscuous heiress poor? In many ways, very wealthy people are "poor in spirit." They certainly need to be changed by the gospel. But it does not advance clarity of understanding to call all that poverty. Terms such as *pride*, *injustice*, and *sexual promiscuity* are more helpful.

It is instructive to remember that the biblical words for the poor have an overwhelmingly economic component. The most common Hebrew words for the poor (*ʿānî*, *ʾebyōn*, *dal*) connote a beggar imploring charity; a thin, weakly impoverished peasant; or an economically impoverished person who has been wrongly oppressed. The primary NT word (*ptōchos*) refers to a beggar who is completely destitute and therefore must seek help from others. Only occasionally in the Scriptures do the words for the poor refer to "spiritual poverty" (Sider 41, 100–101). In biblical teaching, the understanding of poverty is primarily economic. Retaining that framework does not mean that we ignore the vast array of other things that violate *shalom* and displease God, but it does mean that we use other names—pride, injustice, hypocrisy, racism, adultery, and so forth—to refer to them.

Essential to a biblical concept of economic development is a clear understanding of God's special concern for the poor. There are literally hundreds of verses in the Bible about this. The Scriptures teach that God acts in history to lift up the poor (Deut. 26:5–8); God acts in history to pull down rich, powerful people who get rich by oppression or who refuse to share (Jer. 5:26–29); ministering to the needy is, in some mysterious way, actually ministering to Christ our Lord (Matt. 25:35–40); failure to embrace God's concern for the poor means that self-confessed Christians are not really God's people at all (Matt. 25:41–45) (Sider, chap. 4). Few preachers talk as much about God's concern for the poor as the Bible does.

Finally, we need a definition of economic justice if we are to know how to shape Christian development programs. The Bible does not demand equality of income or wealth; wrong choices rightly have negative economic consequences. But the Bible does demand equality of opportunity up to the point where every person and every family has access to the productive resources so that if they act responsibly they can earn their own way and be dignified members of their community.

We can see this norm for economic justice if we examine the OT teaching about the land. Since Israel was an agricultural society, land was the basic capital—the basic asset for producing wealth. When the people of Israel moved into the land of Canaan, God ordered that every family receive its own land (Josh. 18:1–10). Then when the kings of Israel slowly centralized land ownership, the prophets pronounced God's judgment and predicted national destruction (Isa. 15:5–8; Amos 5:4–5, 10–12; 7:10–17). But the prophets also promised a future messianic day when every person would own land again (Mic. 4:4). In an agricultural society, land is the basic capital. In an information society, it is education and knowledge. In every society, good economic development will promote a situation where all have access to the productive resources so that if they act responsibly, they can earn a decent living and be dignified members of their society.

The word *poverty* refers not to everything wrong with the human condition but rather to a cluster of deficiencies related to a lack of essential material resources (food, clothing, etc.), societal resources (education, healthcare, etc.), social power, and the inner brokenness caused by such deprivations. The causes of these deficiencies, however, are complex: personal and social, mental and structural, material and spiritual. Similarly, the term *economic development* does not signify everything that we need for human flourishing, but almost everything we need for full *shalom* relates somehow to economic development. Furthermore, we do need transcendent norms to show us what economic justice is and how economic development fits within the larger goal of full *shalom*. With the kingdom that Jesus inaugurated, we can now have the firstfruits of that dawning *shalom*. With his return, we will enjoy its fullness.

See also Economic Ethics; Land; Poverty and Poor; Wealth; World Poverty, World Hunger

Bibliography

Christian, J. "Powerless of the Poor: Toward an Alternative Kingdom of God Based Paradigm of Response." PhD diss., Fuller Theological Seminary, 1994; Korten, D. *Getting to the 21st Century: Voluntary Action and the Global Agenda*. Kumarian Press, 1990; Myers, B. *Walking with the Poor: Principles and Practices of Transformational Development*. Orbis, 1999; Schlossberg, H., V. Samuel, and R. Sider. *Christianity and Economics in the Post–Cold War Era: The Oxford Declaration and Beyond*. Eerdmans, 1994; Sen, A. *Development as Freedom*. Knopf, 1999; Sider, R. *Rich Christians in an Age of Hunger: Moving from Affluence to Generosity*. 5th ed. Thomas Nelson, 2005.

Ronald J. Sider

Economic Ethics

Biblical Assumptions

The striking and unitary vision of *oikos* ("household") in ancient Christianity and the biblical assumption of the integrity of creation provide the grounds for the understanding and practice of economics and economic ethics in Scripture.

***The vision of* oikos.** The word *economy* (Gk. *oikonomia*) shares the same Greek root, *oikos*, with *ecology* and *ecumenics*. The word *oikos* refers to the house and household, whether the family household, the "households of faith" of the early Christians, or the earth itself as the world house. The *oikoumenē* (whence "ecumenics" and "ecumenical") is the whole inhabited earth or imperial claims to it. (The Roman Empire at the time of Jesus and Paul referred to itself as the *oikoumenē*.) The emphasis of *oikoumenē* falls on the unity of the household. All belong to the same family. This unity lies across the expanse of inhabited terrain. Thus did the Christian households of faith (*oikoi*) include a conscious effort to stand for the whole church in each place, scattered as it was on three continents around the Mediterranean basin. This identity and mission required instruction, called *oikeiosis*, and borrowed from the Stoic notion of appropriation. It was appropriation in the sense of making something one's own, whether as a member of the family, society, the human race collectively, or the world (*cosmos*) as a whole.

The Christian householder was the *oikonomos*, literally "the economist," the one who knows the house rules (*oikos* + *nomos* ["law"]) and cares for the material well-being of its members. Thus, *oikonomos* sometimes is translated as "steward" or "trustee."

Household dwellers are *oikeioi*. Their task too is the mutual upbuilding of community and sharing the gifts of the Spirit for the common good (1 Cor. 12–13), a good that included meeting one another's material needs (Acts 2:44). This is designated *oikodomē*, the continual upbuilding of the *oikos*. Such care requires intimate knowledge of community structures and dynamics. It requires knowing the household's laws and logic, which is exactly what "ecology" means (*oikos* + *logos*).

Oikos is, then, the root notion of economics, ecology, and ecumenics as interrelated dimensions of the same world. Economics involves knowing how things work and managing "home systems" (ecosystems) in such a way that the material requirements of the whole household of life (*oikoumenē*) are met and sustained.

The integrity of creation. This ancient unitary Christian vision accords with the seamlessness, or integrity, of creation in the OT. The underlying assumption of the Scripture and teaching that Jesus knew is that creation is both the handiwork of God and the household of God. Creation is the dwelling place, the abode, of God's creating, redeeming, and sustaining Spirit; the transcendent God is "home" here, as are humans and all life. Early Christian theologians even referred to the way by which creation is upheld and redeemed as the "economy of God" (*oikonomia tou theou*).

The same seamlessness, or integrity, continues with the conviction that this vast *cosmos* is a shared home. All are born to belonging, and all—human beings and nonhuman creatures as well—are coinhabitants who live into one another's lives and die into one another's deaths in a complex set of relationships that sustain the life of creatures and the land.

Creation's shared life and integrity are assumed everywhere in the Old and New Testaments. In the Genesis account, *ʾādām* ("Adam") is formed by God from fertile soil, *ʾădāmâ* (Gen. 2:7). The English equivalent is "human from humus." There is a difference, however, since in the Genesis account all other creatures are also created from *ʾădāmâ*, and they share, with humans, the same breath of God that animates all life. Though differentiated by "kind" (Gen. 1:21), all creatures are also kin by virtue of their common origin and shared destiny.

Within this earthy humus order, human earth creatures are designated *šōmĕrê ʾădāmâ*, "guardians of earth," its custodians and preservers. "Stewards" can be an appropriate translation, provided it moves beyond "good management" to capture the Hebrew sense that humans belong to the land itself as those who serve it. "To till and keep" (*lĕʿobdāh ûlĕšāmrāh*) the garden is the primordial task given to humans by God, the human vocation itself (Gen. 2:15). The Hebrew here connotes not only working the soil as a cultivator but also working *for* it, attending to its needs as creation worthy of service (Davis 31). This is economy and ecology combined as sacred work. Not by chance, the words *cultivation*, *culture*, and *cultus* ("worship") share the same root.

When humans abdicate this task, and the integral relationship between God, fertile soil, and human earth creatures is broken by wayward humans, the ground itself is cursed ("because of you" says Gen. 3:17). The first of many instances of this violation of creation's integrity is the death of Abel at the hands of Cain. Strikingly, it is not Adam and Eve who cry out, according to the text, but *ʾădāmâ* (Gen. 4:10). And the consequence of this primal violence is that the ground "will no longer yield to you its strength" (Gen. 4:12).

Cain's response is further testimony to creation's many-sided wholeness. To be alienated from *ʾădāmâ* is a punishment heavier than he can bear. "Today you have driven me away from the soil," he says to God, "and I shall be hidden from your face; I shall be a fugitive and a wanderer on the earth" (Gen. 4:14). Cain, alienated from his very origins, fertile soil, is homeless on earth and estranged from God.

Differently said, the biblical testimony is that the flourishing and degradation of human life is of a piece with the flourishing and degradation of the land. The human economy belongs to the economy of nature as part and parcel of it. Human injustice bears destructive consequences for the whole community of life, whereas righteous living yields abundance. Economic, ecological, ecumenical justice assures the survival and continuation of flourishing life.

The first covenant in Scripture strikes this same chord. Usually identified as the Noahide covenant, it is better understood as God's covenant with earth. It comes after the escalation of human violence from Cain to Lamech causes God to regret the course of the initial creation and begin anew, after the flood. The first covenant accompanies this new beginning. "God said, 'This is the sign of the covenant that I make between me and you and every living creature that is with you, for all future generations: I have set my bow in the clouds, and it will be a sign of the covenant between me and the earth. When I bring clouds over the earth and the bow is seen in the clouds, I remember my covenant that is between me and you and every living creature of all flesh' " (Gen. 9:12–15a). Noah, strikingly identified as "a man of the soil" (Gen. 9:20), hears the covenant with creation articulated by God no fewer than four times, the last of which underscores yet again this covenant as the covenant "between me and all flesh that is on the earth" (Gen. 9:17).

The flourishing and degradation of the earth hinges on keeping or violating this divine covenant with creation—a theme as strong in the prophets as it is in Genesis. The prophets' discourse for this commonly centers on the life of righteousness. Righteousness is both "inner" and "outer," a matter of character and conduct, and of practice and policy as well as piety. Righteousness is synonymous with a just way of life, right living in good institutions. It is right relations with all that is—God, one another, the land, and the rest of nature. Righteousness achieved is known by its fruits—the fullest possible flourishing of all life.

A passage from Jeremiah must suffice to illustrate the harmony and the abundance that flow from keeping creation's covenant and observing the ways that God has commanded Israel. This passage envisions all nations streaming to Zion's mountain, itself rising from the redeemed plain.

> They shall come and sing aloud on the height of Zion,
> and they shall be radiant over the goodness of the LORD,
> over the grain, the wine, and the oil,
> and over the young of the flock and the herd;
> their life shall become like a watered garden,
> and they shall never languish again. (Jer. 31:12)

Paralleling the visions of creation redeemed are the prophetic warnings of consequences that flow from the violation of creation. In a likely reference to the consequences of violating the covenant of God with earth ("the everlasting covenant" of Gen. 9), Isaiah writes,

> The earth dries up and withers,
> the world languishes and withers;
> the heavens languish together with the earth.
> The earth lies polluted
> under its inhabitants;
> for they have transgressed laws,
> violated the statutes,
> broken the everlasting covenant. . . .
> The city of chaos is broken down,
> every house is shut up so that no one can enter.
> There is an outcry in the streets for lack of wine;
> all joy has reached its eventide;
> the gladness of the earth is banished.
> Desolation is left in the city
> the gates are battered into ruins.
> For thus it shall be on the earth
> and among the nations,
> as when an olive tree is beaten,
> as at the gleaning when the grape harvest is ended. (Isa. 24:4–5, 10–13)

Hosea's account of what happens goes like this:

> Hear the word of the LORD, O people of Israel;
> for the LORD has an indictment against the inhabitants of the land.
> There is no faithfulness or loyalty,
> and no knowledge of God in the land.
> Swearing, lying, and murder,
> and stealing and adultery break out;
> bloodshed follows bloodshed.
> Therefore the land mourns,
> and all who live in it languish;
> together with the wild animals
> and the birds of the air,
> even the fish of the sea are perishing.
> (Hos. 4:1–3)

Not to be missed in this consistent account of earth's flourishing or destruction at human hands is the presence or absence of economic justice. Selling the righteous for silver, the needy for a pair of shoes, and trampling "the head of the poor into the dust of the earth" while pushing "the afflicted out of the way" (Amos 2:6–7) is the kind of exploitation that cries out to heaven and elicits from God a refusal to accept even the sacred offerings of worship: "I hate, I despise your festivals, and I take no delight in your solemn assemblies" (Amos 5:21).

Isaiah has different words for much the same:

> Ah, you who join house to house,
> who add field to field,
> until there is room for no one but you,
> and you are left to live alone
> in the midst of the land!
> The LORD of hosts has sworn in my hearing:
> Surely many houses shall be desolate,
> large and beautiful houses, without inhabitant.
> (Isa. 5:8–9)

But this is not all. The work of economics and of economic ethics, which in biblical terms means cultivating the material conditions for the continuation and flourishing of life, goes beyond the creation and covenant accounts of Genesis and the warnings of ecological collapse and the visions of abundance in the prophetic literature. Torah economic legislation is extensive and includes the Sabbath, sabbatical, and Jubilee laws that mandate rest for the animals and the land together with human laborers. This allows the economy of nature to regenerate and renew on its own terms (see Lev. 25). The wisdom literature, to choose yet another body of texts, argues that material moderation is good, inequities are destructive, and enough is best. "Give me neither poverty nor riches; feed me with the food that I need, or I shall be full, and deny you, and say, 'Who is the Lord?' or I shall be poor, and steal, and profane the name of my God" (Prov. 30:8b–9). And the Bible closes, after the radical critique of imperial Rome by John of Patmos, with redeemed nature in the new Jerusalem. Trees of life line the banks of crystalline waters that flow from the throne of God, with fruit for each month and their leaves "for the healing of the nations" (Rev. 22:1–2). Not least, "nothing accursed will be found there" (Rev. 22:3). Here is the reversal of the ground cursed by human violence in Gen. 4. John's images nicely capture the integrity of creation reflected in the early Christian cosmology of *oikos* and the seamlessness of creation that marks Scripture from its opening to its close.

Modern Economics

With these biblical notes in hand, we turn to modern economics, the political economy of industrial capitalism (and, until 1989, of state-sponsored socialism). The year 1750 often is designated as the onset of the Industrial Revolution and modern economics because it marks the advent of that which made the modern industrial era possible: the use of accessible, compact, stored energy in the form of fossil fuels—first coal, then oil, then natural gas, and now all three.

Fossil fuels meant compact, stored energy. Armed with appropriate technologies and long-distance trade, humans no longer needed to live, as their ancestors did, in sync with the rhythms of renewable energy sources and their requirements—solar cycles, hydrological cycles, and the imperatives of the land and seasons in one's home locale. With stored, compact energy humans could create a built environment to replace the more immediate dependence on the unbuilt environment, which, in that fateful split-off of modernity, came to be called "the natural environment," as though human beings and the built environment of the human *oikos* were of another order altogether, no longer nature. "Organization" displaced "nature" and "city" displaced "country" as the dominant human environment, habitat, and home, or so we thought. In fact, what we came to *think* was "human" and "nature" as different entities and realms.

Fossil fuels thus made possible the transformation from "an organic, ever-renewing, land-based economy to an extractive, nonrenewing, industrial economy," the one that now reigns as "a controlling presence throughout the entire planet" (T. Berry, *Evening Thoughts*, 107). Fossil fuels also made it possible to solve one of the three nagging problems that every economy must address: production. No human economy has come close to solving the problem of production for so many people as has industrial/postindustrial capitalism. None has been so successful in harnessing Prometheus's gift of fire for mastering nature and subjugated cultures for human well-being (some humans far more than others, to be sure). None has generated wealth on a scale that even approaches modern economic orders. The very definition of a "mature" modern economy is an economy of growth that sustains high mass consumption (Rostow). And no economy has so effectively channeled other forces—science, technology, culture, law—into a way of life whose very understanding of the good life is the life of goods created and used in a world of our own design and making. For good reason, then, the modern era became synonymous with progress, and progress was associated above all with economic growth and prosperity.

But all this came at a price. On this end of the great transformation from feudal to modern, nature is no longer conceived as a communion of subjects, as it was in the primordial visions of humans and as it remains in the traditions of some indigenous peoples. Nature is a collection of commodified objects readied for human use (Swimme and Berry 243).

This change in conceptual worlds, economic practices, and a way of life was famously described by Max Weber as "the disenchantment of the world." The world was no longer "enchanted"; that is, it no longer bore mystery, spirit, divinity, or holiness. Nature was rendered a utilitarian object, a vast repository of resources, rather than a community of living subjects. Its meaning and value, as object and commodity, were thus separated from the meaning and value attached to human lives. In fact, humans here conferred value on nature, in contrast to an earlier notion that humans discovered its inherent or intrinsic value as cocreation. This setting apart of nature for its unqualified utilitarian use, together with its treatment at the hands of modern economic processes, belonged to a broader process of modernity that Weber called "rationalization." Rationalized actions and interactions are motivated by and based on considerations of efficiency and calculation. This contrasts with actions and interactions motivated by and based on custom and tradition (as sufficient authority). While rationalized organization of life has taken place in many domains of the human enterprise as a mark of modernity, it has triumphed in economic life above all (Weber). The consequence is devalued and secularized nature, subject to the canons of calculation and efficiency and the ways of corporate business and commodification for market exchange. Nature became "it" rather than "thou," with the primary relationship to human subjects being that of use.

The rationalized, disenchanted world made possible by fossil fuels and the industrial notion of nature as objective resources allowed a way of life built on two illusions. Modern humans thought that they could bypass the rhythms and requirements of nature that preindustrial populations had to observe and adapt to season in and season out. They could have their own built environment, created in their own image, and soon they rarely even bothered to ask about nature's demands for regeneration and renewal on its own complex, leisurely, and nonnegotiable terms. Moderns seemingly forgot that every human economy is always and everywhere a part of the *oikonomia* of nature.

Bypassing nature's rhythms and requirements for its own regeneration on its own terms made possible the second illusion: modern humans could bring nature under their control and liberate humankind from futility and toil. We now know that planetary processes are not just more complex than we think; they probably are more complex than we can ever think. They certainly are more complex than humans can master and control.

Life lived inside these two illusions—when coupled with massive supplies of stored energy and the powers of modern science and technology tied to the industrial paradigm of extraction, production, and consumption, exclusively for human ends—has had the following consequences for nature's economy. The rest of planetary nature, beyond human beings, no longer has an independent life, since no precincts of other-than-human nature, from genes to grasslands to glaciers, are exempt now from human impact and change. Humans have become one of evolution's "forcings" and are among the planet's weather makers. So dramatic is the shift in relationships between humans and Earth that Earth now belongs to the human story, whereas for all of human history until the modern era, humans belonged to Earth's story. Nature now belongs to the empire of its most aggressive species. It is not an obedient subject, however.

The uninvited blow to both these illusions of modern political economy—that humans can control nature, and nature's own rhythms and requirements can be bypassed in favor of human organization and habitat—is accelerated, with extreme climate change resulting in the decline of every major life system. Climate change, itself a consequence of burning fossil fuels on a scale that we now know has destabilized both the atmosphere and the biosphere, is the most far-reaching event to happen to the planet in thousands of years. Present and coming changes to the planet and its economy are comparable to the changes of a major geological era, yet they are happening within the span of a human lifetime and at the hands of humans. The plundering power of the modern global economy has made this possible, as had the consuming power of a population that grew from less than two billion to more than six billion within the course of a single century.

Climate change and ecosystemic degradation have also brought into sharp relief the failure of modern economics to adequately address two areas every economy must: distribution and sustainability.

Distribution. The modern economy sits inside a world first globalized in the wake of Columbus in the Age of Discovery. Here was the first wave by which the economy went global. It did so as the movement of conquest and colonization, commerce and Christianity across the two great oceans, the Atlantic and Pacific. These four—conquest and colonization, commerce and Christian missionizing—were viewed together by conquering European powers as "civilization," which then took up residence in the form of neo-European societies planted on all continents except Antarctica. As this vast network of settlement and trade eventually became the new economy of industrialized capitalism and socialism, it became the means by which mass wealth was generated in some quarters while mass poverty was generated in others. The benefits of the globalizing economy took the form of unprecedented affluence unequally distributed both within and between nations and regions. Reform movements to address modern social and economic injustice sprang up from the very beginnings of capitalism's injustice. They continue to this day. Fair distribution has yet to be achieved. The poverty of billions remains, despite unprecedented powers of production.

Sustainability. Attention to sustainability exposes the mismatch of what Wendell Berry calls "the Big Economy" (the modern human economy) and "the Great Economy" (the economy of nature). These economies suffer a fateful mismatch of metabolisms ("metabolism" refers to the physical and chemical processes necessary to sustain life).

Nature's economy is the first, fundamental, and sustaining condition of human lives and all other lives. Every human economy is always, everywhere, and absolutely dependent on nature's economy. It is inevitably part of nature's economy and subject to its dynamics, possibilities, and limits. Yet the embeddedness of the big (human) economy in nature's great economy hardly made an appearance in modern economic theory or practice until recently. Brilliant economists, business leaders, and politicians thus worried about economic growth without worrying about water, for example, or without paying attention to a warming atmosphere and encroaching habitat destruction. Species extinction, to choose another example, was never a topic in economic theory, and biodiversity rarely was, despite its indispensable role. These subjects did not fit the worldview and metabolism of dynamic global capitalism, with its outsize appetite, its focus on short-haul gains, its hyperactive product innovation and turnover, its growth-seeking markets, its drive for profits, and its assumption that nature's value is that of resources capable of commodification for market exchange. Such metabolism works in ways that outstrip the metabolism of nature's economy, a metabolism that is enormously intricate, without beginning and without end, complex, interlaced, slow, nonlinear, and long-haul. And it was the modern economy's unconstrained use of fossil fuels that let us change the metabolism of the human economy so dramatically as to escalate production and consumption to levels that are unsustainable for nature. (If Alan Durning is correct, global consumer classes produced and consumed as many goods and services in the half century following 1950 as did people throughout the entire period of history prior to that date [Durning 38].) Yet nobody other than indigenous persons spoke up to say that modern progress cannot be genuine progress if it is progress borrowed against the health of the Earth and the well-being of future generations.

The Present Transition

The mismatch of economic metabolisms, revealed by climate change and degraded life systems, forces the question of whether the current economy of global capitalism can be "ecologized" on a mass, "ecumenical" scale. While the answer is not yet clear, the need for an economic transition out of the fossil-fuel interlude is clear. The "great work" of this and coming generations, to use Thomas Berry's words, is to effect "the transition from a period of human devastation of the Earth to a period when humans [are] present to the planet in a mutually beneficial manner" (T. Berry, *Great Work*, 3). Or, to recall the foregoing treatment of the Christian vision of *oikos*, the question is whether Earth's global human economy can be rendered compatible with ecumenical and ecological Earth.

If such compatibility is to be achieved, major shifts in economics and economic ethics are needed.

The aim of economic life will need to shift from maximizing the production of goods and services to a three-part agenda of production, relatively equitable distribution, and ecological regenerativity. All economic activity will need to operate within the ecological limits of the planet. This means that all economic activity will be ecologically sustainable at minimum and regenerative at best. "Eco-nomics" replaces economics and ecology by joining both.

The economic paradigm will reject growth and high consumption as the lone indicator of mature economies. This paradigm does not preclude growth as a good, but it does insist that growth be ecologically sustainable or regenerative for the long term, that it reduce rather than increase the wealth and income gaps within and between nations and regions (climate change will exacerbate these inequalities, with those contributing least to climate change probably suffering the most), and that it bolster rather than undermine local communities and cultures to draw wisely from their cultural and biological diversity.

The new economic paradigm will also reject freedom as unrestrained political and market individualism and will cultivate freedom as thriving in community in ways that contribute both to personal well-being and the common good.

The chief obstacles to an effective transition from the fossil-fuel era will not likely be technological. Sustainable and regenerative technologies already exist in part and can be elicited with the proper political-economic incentives. The chief obstacles will be the political, economic, and sociocultural dimensions of ways of life that remain addicted to fossil fuels, fail to recognize the limits of planetary systems, assume that happiness and fulfillment are based on never-ending material consumption of goods and services, and think and invest for short-term rather than long-term ends in a political economy that operates with a metabolism different from that of nature.

An effective transition must also take into account the well-being of future generations, the future generations of both human and other life. Edith Brown Weiss's discussion of "generational rights" is suggestive as a way to answer the ethical question of what one generation owes the next. She posits three principles for intergenerational equity that can be guiding economic principles. Each generation "should be required to conserve the diversity of the natural and cultural resource base" so that future generations have the means to exercise their values and solve their problems. This is the "conservation of options" principle. Each generation should also be required "to maintain the quality of the planet so that it is passed on in no worse condition than that in which it was received." This is the "conservation of quality" principle. Each generation should provide its members with "equitable rights of access to the legacy of past generations and should conserve this access for future generations." This is the "conservation of access" principle (Brown Weiss 202).

In the end, the most basic issue for economics and economic ethics is how we live, and for what; it is at this crucial juncture that moral and religious convictions and commitments are vital to a successful transformation and transition. The answer does not lie in trying to retrieve and replicate the economy and economic ethics of the biblical communities. Theirs was a pastoral world initially and its urbanized versions later. The planet was large and richly endowed, with a small human population. Ours is an industrial and postindustrial planet—"hot, flat, crowded," humanly dominated and environmentally degraded (Friedman). That said, the *oikos* conception of Earth, with creation's integrity at its core, is perhaps more timely than ever, given its understanding of the interrelated domains of ecology, economy, and earth ecumenicity. Certainly, a spirituality and ethic for the long haul is needed, one that receives life as a gift of the Creator, knows our (*humus*) place in creation, and knows as well the significance of our striving, even in the face of inevitable corruptions, losses, and defeats. Not least, the very purpose of economics in the biblical world remains the same and carries new force on this side of modern economics: to cultivate and meet the material conditions for the continuation of life.

See also Capitalism; Creation Ethics; Ecological Ethics; Globalization; Jubilee; Land; Markets; Materialism; Population Policy and Control; Sabbath; Stewardship; Technology; Wealth; World Poverty, World Hunger

Bibliography

Berry, T. *Evening Thoughts: Reflecting on Earth as Sacred Community*. Ed. M. Tucker. Sierra Book Club, 2006; idem. *The Great Work: Our Way into the Future*. Bell Tower, 1999; Berry, W. "Two Economies." Pages 54–75 in *Home Economics: Fourteen Essays*. North Point Press, 1987; Brown Weiss, E. "Our Rights and Obligations to Future Generations for the Environment." *AJIL* 84 (1990): 198–207; Davis, E. *Scripture, Culture, and Agriculture: An Agrarian Reading of the Bible*. Cambridge University Press, 2009; Durning, A. *How Much Is Enough? The Consumer Society and the Future of the Earth*. Earthscan, 1992; Friedman, T. *Hot, Flat, and Crowded: Why We Need a Green Revolution—and How It Can Renew America*. Farrar, Straus & Giroux, 2008; Rostow, W. *The Stages of Economic Growth: A Non-Communist Manifesto*. 3rd ed. Cambridge University Press, 1990; Swimme, B., and T. Berry. *The Universe Story: From the Primordial Flaring Forth to the Ecozoic Era—A Celebration of the Unfolding of the Cosmos*. Harper Collins, 1992; Weber, M. *The Protestant Ethic and the Spirit of Capitalism*. Charles Scribner's Sons, 1906.

Larry L. Rasmussen

Ecumenism

Ecumenism is the work and search for the unity of Christian churches. The term *ecumenism* derives from the Greek word *oikoumenē* (e.g., Luke 2:1; Acts 11:28), which means "the whole inhabited world." Closely related to this word is the use of the term *ecumenical* with reference to ancient "ecumenical councils" such as that of Nicea (325) and the "ecumenical" patriarchate (of Constantinople).

Biblical Vision of Unity

The prayer of Jesus in John 17:21 for the unity of his followers based on the unity between the Father and the Son, "so that the world may believe," is the biblical passage most often used in regard to ecumenism. It highlights the integral relation between mission and ecumenism as well as the trinitarian basis of unity. Another key NT text is Eph. 4:4–6, the most elaborate account of the unity of the church. The idea of the oneness of the people of God is based on the similar OT idea of the oneness of their God (Deut. 6:4).

The NT often speaks of the church's unity with the help of the term *koinōnia*, usually translated as "fellowship" (Acts 2:42; 1 John 1:3) or "sharing" (Phil. 3:10). It signifies sharing at spiritual, sacramental, social, emotional, and economic levels.

There is a dynamic tension in the NT between the idea of the unity of the one church of Jesus Christ and the plurality of (local) churches. From the beginning of the church there has been a plurality of expressions of Christian faith. The ancient creeds declare faith in one (holy, apostolic, and catholic) church despite rampant divisions (Nicene Creed [381]), a conviction having its ultimate reference point in the eschatological vision of the mutual indwelling of God and God's people (Rev. 21:3).

Ecumenical Movement

While the roots of ecumenical consciousness go far back in history, exemplified by Cyprian's *Unity of the Catholic Church* (third century), the Edinburgh Missionary Conference of 1910 marks the beginning of the modern ecumenical movement. The establishment of the World Council of Churches in 1948—"a fellowship of churches" rather than a church—involved a coming together of missionary, doctrinal (Faith and Order [1927]), and socioethical (Life and Work [1925]) initiatives. Much of the ecumenical work also happens through bilateral and multilateral dialogues between churches, other ecumenical initiatives, and grassroots ecumenism in local churches and among individual Christians.

The ultimate goal of the ecumenical movement, "visible unity," is ambiguous. Among the models of unity the most obvious is "organic unity," the merging together of churches. Currently, the most promising one is "unity in reconciled diversity." Whatever "visible unity" may mean, all agree that it does not mean the kind of "world church" that would subsume all churches under one entity. Common witness and service, mutual acknowledgment of ministries, and the sharing of sacramental fellowship are integral parts of the goal of visible unity.

While in its most common senses the goal of ecumenical work is the unity of the Christian churches, there are those who also advocate the idea of the unity of all humankind.

See also Ecclesiology and Ethics; Ephesians; Holy Spirit; Koinonia; Love, Love Command; Reconciliation

Bibliography

Kinnamon, M., and B. Cope, eds. *The Ecumenical Movement: An Anthology of Key Texts and Voices*. Eerdmans, 1997; Lossky, N., et al., eds. *Dictionary of the Ecumenical Movement*. WCC Publications, 1991; Meyer, H. *That All May Be One: Perceptions and Models of Ecumenicity*. Eerdmans, 1999; Pannenberg, W. "Unity of the Church—Unity of Mankind: A Critical Appraisal of a Shift in Ecumenical Direction." *Mid-Stream* 21 (October 1982): 485–90; "World Council of Churches." http://www.oikoumene.org/.

Veli-Matti Kärkkäinen

Egalitarianism

Egalitarianism is the belief in the equality of all persons regardless of race, ethnicity, nationality, class, gender, disability, sexual orientation, or age because all persons are created in the image of God. Unlike in hierarchy, where status and privilege are ascribed based on differences, egalitarianism advocates that all individuals are owed dignity and opportunities to utilize their talents and skills for self-fulfillment and to contribute to the greater good of societies. Commitments to egalitarianism extend into policies and practices that acknowledge and protect human dignity, guarantee fundamental human rights, and provide equal access to economic and social goods necessary for human flourishing. Egalitarianism is confronted with conflicting notions of equality and a recognition that people differ in abilities, skills and talents, and aptitudes. However, egalitarianism challenges the prejudicial nature of these differences, which creates hierarchies that attribute value and privilege to certain persons while excluding others based on differences.

Egalitarianism is informed by a biblical-theological narrative that affirms the fundamental equality of all persons. Humanity's creation in the image of God is a critical starting point (Gen. 1:27). While there are disputes as to what the image of God is, at its most basic level it implies that God created humans, and that God bestows dignity and value on humanity that must be recognized by all human beings. Egalitarians affirm that men and women are created equal by God, not just in essence but in status, and stand in mutual, nonhierarchical relationships with each other and in their responsibilities to care for the created order (Gen. 1:26–31; 2:18–25). The first humans function as types for God's intentions in all human relationships. People are equal before God and in relationship to other persons. Moreover, humans are created in and for social relationships and communities, the maintenance of which requires the full participation of all persons in using their gifts and talents for the common good. The first humans were given responsibility to care for the creation with no hierarchical differentiation in status in carrying out their God-given responsibilities (Gen. 1:26–30). Egalitarianism is also informed by overarching themes of the NT, particularly Jesus' elevation of women, liberation for the poor, and the confronting of divisive racial barriers. Jesus interacted directly with women and addressed women as individuals, including them in the community of disciples (Luke 8:1–3; 10:38–41; John 4:1–26). Jesus involved himself with those on the margins of society, such as Samaritans, prostitutes, disabled persons, and those with diseases that made them social outcasts (e.g., Matt. 4:23–25; 8:1–4; 21:14–17; Luke 7:36–50; 17:11–19; 19:1–9). In the new community of disciples, gender, class, racial, and ethnic barriers were challenged by the example of Jesus and the moral demands of Christian faith for practicing *koinōnia* (Acts 2:42–47; 4:32–37; 6:1–6; 10:1–22; 15:1–30). Although it appears that the biblical writers sometimes accommodated gender, racial, and class barriers, egalitarians believe that the overall direction of Scripture requires a radical shift in perspective that acknowledges the fundamental equality of all persons, especially in the church, as summarized by the apostle Paul:

"There is no longer Jew or Greek, there is no longer slave or free, there is no longer male or female; for you are all one in Christ Jesus" (Gal. 3:28).

Egalitarianism has been a particularly contested ideal in many churches between hierarchalists and complementarians on the one hand, and egalitarians on the other, usually centered on the relationships between husbands and wives and on women's roles in ministry. Hierarchalists and complementarians interpret a divinely created and sanctioned hierarchy of men and women in the creation accounts, whereas egalitarians affirm a divinely created and intended mutuality between men and women as the more proper interpretation of the creation narratives in Genesis. In regard to marriage, instead of the subordination of wives to husbands, egalitarians believe that the ideal in Scripture is mutuality (Eph. 5:21). Of particular importance for egalitarianism is the belief that God calls women to use their gifts in ministry, with no restrictions based on gender, for the good of the church.

See also Equality; Gender; Headship; Image of God; Justice; Women, Status of

Bibliography

Bauckham, R. "Egalitarianism and Hierarchy in the Bible." Pages 116–27 in *God and the Crisis of Freedom: Biblical and Contemporary Perspectives*. Westminster John Knox, 2002; Mill, J. S. "The Subjection of Women." Pages 123–229 in *The Basic Writings of John Stuart Mill*. Modern Library, 2002; Rawls, J. *A Theory of Justice*. Harvard University Press, 1972; Van Leeuwen, M. *Gender and Grace: Love, Work and Parenting in a Changing World*. InterVarsity, 1990; Webb, W. *Slaves, Women and Homosexuals: Exploring the Hermeneutics of Cultural Analysis*. InterVarsity, 2001.

Wyndy Corbin Reuschling

Emancipation

Emancipation involves both terminology and thematic development in Scripture. Theologically, in the OT, emancipation largely pertains to God's liberation of God's chosen people related to covenant, land, and relationship in perpetuity (Gen. 12:1–3). Tension, turmoil, and trepidation occur when Israel/Judah disobeys God and divine judgment ensues, wherein Israel winds up in bondage or exile (Judg. 2; 6; 20; 23; Jer. 7; 52). In the NT, Jesus Christ comes as anti-imperial liberator, who as God's son announces God's rule and the good news: the resurrected Christ comes to emancipate, to set people free from sin (Rom. 6; 8). To emancipate means to liberate from control, restraint, bondage, involuntary servitude, or another's power, to set free from controlling influence, traditional mores, or beliefs. To emancipate involves liberation whereby one becomes manumitted from slavery or servitude. In Scripture, emancipation or lack thereof results from divine and/or human choice.

God chooses to exercise his sovereign freedom; that is, God selects and elects, thus emancipates, whom he chooses, for his purposes. For Paul, citing Exod. 33:19, God's election reflects God's deepest character of mercy, for divine injustice is an impossibility (Rom. 9:14–15): divine righteousness and divine wrath are two sides of one revelation. Human choice to sin exacts a problematic human predicament, which itself rejects God. Human misconduct leads to human self-destruction. God does not coerce, but instead allows humans to follow their own desires, and the resulting alienation estranges persons from God and neighbor. Where the law informs humankind of sin, only God can emancipate, can provide salvific righteousness.

Sometimes emancipation evolves as deliverance: a response to bondage (Gen. 37; 39–50). At the end of Joseph's saga, God remains hidden and responds during the exodus event, when God chooses to do so, revealing his radical grace and freedom: the source of divine deliverance of those who suffer, are exploited, oppressed, poor (Exod. 3:8; Ps. 12:5). God emancipates Israel, his elect, from Egypt's oppressive despot and toward new covenantal relationship with God. Throughout Exodus, God purposefully hardens Pharaoh's heart and punishes all of Egypt, guilty and innocent alike (Exod. 12:29), problematizing divine liberation; after all, did Israel's God not also create the Egyptians and Canaanites?

Intriguingly, Scripture does not explicitly state that slavery is wrong, and many cultures have used the Bible to justify involuntary servitude. Biblical laws in Deut. 15:12–18; Exod. 21:2–11; Lev. 25:39–45 provide parameters regarding dynamics of enslavement, especially regarding debt, along with prescriptions regarding the Sabbath Year and the Jubilee Year. Jubilee begins on the Day of Atonement and occurs every fifty years. In Sabbath and Jubilee Years issues of property and family relate to personal liberty and thus to liberty for the nation. Even in Philemon, Paul does not explicitly critique slavery, but rather invites Philemon to treat Onesimus as more than a slave, as a beloved brother (v. 16). Paul sees freedom as an opportunity to serve, even self-sacrifice for others. The price of this sacrifice may be costly, as he connects freedom to the cross. Although this is problematic for those often made subservient, Paul may be suggesting so-called traditionally feminine values for everyone. Personal and communal emancipation calls for living balanced, just lives, being neither victim nor perpetrator. For the faithful, emancipation signifies living as an authentic self for others out of the freedom of being a child of God.

See also Freedom; Jubilee; Liberation; Philemon; Slavery

Bibliography

Birch, B. *Let Justice Roll Down: The Old Testament, Ethics, and Christian Life*. Westminster John Knox, 1991; Campbell, W. "The Freedom and Faithfulness of God in Relation to Israel." *JSNT* 13 (1981): 27–45; Osiek, C. "Galatians." Pages 423–27 in *Women's Bible Commentary*, ed. C. Newsom and S. Ringe. Westminster John Knox, 1998; Schenker, A. "The Biblical Legislation on the Release of Slaves: The Road from Exodus to Leviticus." *JSOT* 78 (1998): 23–41; Stagg, F. "The Plight of Jew and Gentile in Sin: Romans 1:18–3:20." *RevExp* 73 (1976): 401–13.

Cheryl Kirk-Duggan

Embodiment *See* Body

Emigration *See* Aliens, Immigration, and Refugees

Emotion

There is nothing ethereal or otherworldly about the Bible: it depicts God's relationship with the world, particularly with Israel and the church, in all its messiness and materiality. And so it is no surprise that every human emotion (and presumably every divine emotion, although this is less certain) makes an appearance in the Bible.

For millennia in the West, emotions have been seen as opposed to reason and clear thinking. Recently, however, scholars from fields as diverse as philosophy and neuroscience have begun to press the case for the vital importance of emotions to rational thought and moral decision. Indeed, for these scholars, appropriate emotional responses are necessary for, and in part constitutive of, good moral decision-making.

Many passages in the Bible support the crucial importance of emotions for ethics both for human beings and for God. In Exod. 2, for example, Pharaoh's daughter is moved by the sight of the infant Moses and delivers him from death. Similarly in the NT, Jesus on several occasions acts out of compassion (Matt. 20:34; Mark 1:41; John 11:33), as does a Samaritan in one of his parables (Luke 10:33). One must be cautious in considering the ethical implications of the biblical material, however. Although many posit that emotions are universal to human experience, the expression of emotion (sentiment) is culturally determined. As such, some expressions of emotion appear with only certain kinds of subjects in the Bible. For example, men and God are overtaken by anger, whereas women and subordinates are not (van Wolde).

Considerable attention has been focused on the emotions associated with God in the Bible. God's initial election of Israel, for example, is born of an inexplicable love that cannot be reduced to "reasonable" explanations (Deut. 7:7–8; Hos. 11:1). God's anger, though troubling to many readers of the Bible, is ethically significant: the divine wrath is closely associated with God's passion for justice (Fretheim). God's anger at injustice (a frequent catalyst for divine wrath) reveals the *pathos* of God—that is, God's intimate involvement in the world. If God is not angered by the consequences of human sinfulness, then God apparently has little interest in the fate of the world.

See also Affections; Anger; Empathy; Love, Love Command; Moral Agency; Passions

Bibliography

Damasio, A. *Descartes' Error: Emotion, Reason, and the Human Brain*. Quill, 2000 [1994]; Fretheim, T. "Theological Reflections on the Wrath of God in the Old Testament." *HBT* 24 (2002): 1–26; Lapsley, J. "Feeling Our Way: Love for God in Deuteronomy." *CBQ* 65 (2003): 350–69; Nussbaum, M. *Love's Knowledge: Essays on Philosophy and Literature*. Oxford University Press, 1990; idem. *Upheavals of Thought: The Intelligence of Emotions*. Cambridge University Press, 2001; van Wolde, E. "Sentiments as Culturally Constructed Emotions: Anger and Love in the Hebrew Bible." *BibInt* 16 (2008): 1–24.

Jacqueline E. Lapsley

Empathy

Empathy (which entered into English from the German *Einfühlung*, "feeling into") is the emotional appreciation of another's feelings, thoughts, and experiences, yet without obliterating the line between self and other. It does not have long or deep roots in the philosophical tradition, only appearing relatively recently in nineteenth-century German discussions of aesthetics and in the romantic tradition. Many scholars from diverse fields today, however, such as Martha Nussbaum in philosophy and Antonio Damasio in neuroscience, take empathy to be necessary for good moral decision-making; indeed, it is partially constitutive of rationality. Pity differs from empathy in that it designates a desire to see someone better off, but generally it does not entail entering imaginatively into the subjective experience of another; it frequently involves an attitude of condescension.

Although many people show empathy in numerous OT passages (e.g., Pharaoh's daughter in Exod. 2:6), it is God's empathy for his people that is most powerfully on display in the OT. Divine empathy for Israel's suffering is apparent from the very beginning of the relationship between Yahweh and corporate Israel: God tells Moses to confront Pharaoh because "I have seen the misery . . . ; I have heard their cry. . . . I know their sufferings" (Exod. 3:7; cf. 2:25). Later, during the exile, the nadir of Israel's corporate life, the empathy of God is movingly expressed: "They will neither hunger nor thirst, nor will the desert heat or the sun beat upon them. [God] who has compassion on them will guide them and lead them beside springs of water" (Isa. 49:10 TNIV [the NRSV wrongly translates *raḥam* as "pity"]). God "feels into" Israel's suffering and is acting to end it (cf. Isa. 49:13, 15).

The NT continues this attention to empathizing with those who suffer. Jesus feels compassion (e.g., *splangchnizomai*) for both crowds of people (Matt. 9:36; 14:14; 15:32; Mark 6:34; 8:2) and individuals (Matt. 20:34; Mark 1:41; Luke 7:13) in distress on numerous occasions. Sometimes they are in distress because they are leaderless and in confusion (Matt. 9:36; Mark 6:34), sick or afflicted (Matt. 14:14; 20:34; Mark 1:41), or hungry (Matt. 15:32; Mark 8:2). In the parable involving the Samaritan and the victim of an assault and robbery, it is significantly the reviled Samaritan who shows empathy for the injured man along the roadside (Luke 10:33) and is a role model for the listener. Likewise in the Pauline Letters there is a strong emphasis on an empathic identification with the suffering of others, in imitation of Christ. Christian theology draws on the rich and abundant images of empathy throughout both Testaments for its theological reflection on the identity of both God, who cares passionately about the divinely created world, and of human beings, who are to imitate that empathic care.

See also Compassion; Emotion; Love, Love Command; Mercy; Moral Agency; Passions

Bibliography

Jervis, A. *At the Heart of the Gospel: Suffering in the Earliest Christian Message*. Eerdmans, 2007; Nussbaum, M. *Upheavals of Thought: The Intelligence of Emotions*. Cambridge University Press, 2001.

Jacqueline E. Lapsley

Employment *See* Work

Ends and Means

If we treat ends as the goods that one pursues and means as the actions that one takes in pursuing them, then two truths have always followed. First, nobody pursuing the project of practical moral reasoning utterly ignores one or the other. Even the fiercest focus on one or the other is softened by the project of putting means-ends reasoning to practical moral use.

Second, however, means and ends sit in tension with each other: a good end does not justify any means being used to achieve it, and purposeful inattention to the consequences of an action is tantamount to refusing accountability. People are called neither to treat good ends as justifying any means nor to do right that evil may result.

Scripture attests to an emphasis on means in some places (e.g., the law given at Sinai and Jesus' teachings in the Sermon on the Mount) and an emphasis on ends in other places (e.g., David's claim on the holy bread in 1 Sam. 21:1–7 and Jesus' teaching that a tree is known by its fruit in Matt. 12:33–37). However, it would be hermeneutically naive to uproot these texts from their larger contexts, theologically distorting to treat any one of them as the lens through which to view all biblical teachings on morality, and, therefore, ethically misguided to use them in defense of a particular method of moral engagement.

In the face of the second truth, many scholars have shaped systems for moral engagement that emphasize one far more than the other. The clearest example of a means orientation is found in the work of Immanuel Kant, who recognized that the desire for a good did not justify it. Founding his moral system on a process of a priori reasoning, Kant emphasized the obligation to act only in such a way that one could will that one's action could be universalized. And the clearest example of an ends orientation is the thought of John Stuart Mill, who argued that one should always act in such a way as to produce the most good.

Though neither Kant nor Mill developed his system of moral reasoning in particularly theologically astute ways, there have been Christian ethicists whose moral projects functioned in ways analogous to those of Kant and Mill. Paul Ramsey, for instance, used the idea of covenant fidelity to advance a strongly means-oriented approach to Christian ethics, and Joseph Fletcher argued that a Christian always has the obligation to act in the way that produces the most love.

Over the past several decades, ethicists have returned to a focus on the first truth: means and ends interpenetrate each other. This has been due in part to the increased attention that new (or very old) forms of moral inquiry have received: feminist and liberationist ethicists, virtue ethicists, pragmatists, and persons influenced by H. Richard Niebuhr's notion of "the responsible self" have contributed to new discussions about the complex interplay between means and ends as a way to avoid monistic reductionisms.

See also Consequentialism; Deontological Theories of Ethics; Divine Command Theories of Ethics; Justification, Moral; Responsibility; Teleological Theories of Ethics; Utilitarianism

Mark Douglas

Enemy, Enemy Love

The word *enemy* most frequently translates *'ôyēb* in Hebrew, meaning "one who hates." In the NT, *echthros* is the only word translated "enemy," and it is the consistent choice in the LXX, where it occurs more than four hundred times. Not formally defined in the canon, *enemy* is interpreted by rhetorical or poetic parallel with phrases such as "those who hate us" or "those who persecute you." It is used of both personal and national enemies.

The love of enemies is both commanded and enacted by Jesus in the NT. The imperative is issued most famously in his Sermon on the Mount, where loving and praying for one's enemies is offered as the crucial form of imitation that makes one a child of the heavenly Father (Matt. 5:44–45; cf. Luke 6:27–28, 35). Among the traditional "seven last words" of Christ on the cross is the prayer, "Father, forgive them; for they know not what they are doing," recorded in some manuscripts of Luke's Gospel (23:34). The parable that we call "the parable of the good Samaritan" takes much of its point from the traditional animosity between Jews and Samaritans, making the inclusion of enemies as neighbors to be loved the force of Jesus' directive, "Go and do likewise" (Luke 10:37).

However, admonitions to love enemies are not limited to the Gospels or even to the NT. Paul's instructions for the treatment of enemies in Romans, "If your enemies are hungry, feed them; if they are thirsty, give them something to drink" (12:20), are taken directly from Proverbs (25:21–22), which addresses not only conduct toward enemies but also inward attitudes toward them: "Do not rejoice when your enemies fall, and do not let your heart be glad when they stumble" (24:17).

The general imperative is fleshed out in various stipulations of the law (e.g., "When you come upon your enemy's ox or donkey going astray, you shall bring it back" [Exod. 23:4]) and repeatedly shown in narrative—for example, the reconciliation between Esau and Jacob (Gen. 33:4); the reunion of Joseph with the brothers who had sold him into slavery (Gen. 45:5); the young girl stolen into slavery who advised that Naaman the Syrian go to Elisha to be healed of his leprosy (2 Kgs. 5:2).

Above all other instances is the example of God's own patient love for enemies, manifested not only in his ever-renewed mercy on unfaithful Israel but also in his readiness to embrace traditional rivals such as Egypt and Assyria (Isa. 19:18–25; Jonah). Finally, Christ died for us while we were yet sinners (Rom. 5:8), having made ourselves enemies of God. As forgiven and reconciled people, Christians are made ambassadors of God and are entrusted with the work of reconciliation exemplified in the practice of loving enemies. However, the scope of this practice and its implications for public and political life are perennially contested.

See also Cruciformity; Love, Love Command; Neighbor, Neighbor Love; Sermon on the Mount

Bibliography

Cahill, L. *Love Your Enemies: Discipleship, Pacifism, and Just War Theory*. Fortress, 1994; Jones, L. *Embodying Forgiveness: A Theological Analysis*. Eerdmans, 1996; Stassen, G. *Just Peacemaking: Transforming Initiatives for Justice and Peace*. Westminster John Knox, 1992; Yoder, J. *The Politics of Jesus: Vicit Agnus Noster*. 2nd ed. Eerdmans, 1994.

Sondra E. Wheeler

Environment *See* Ecological Ethics

Envy *See* Jealousy and Envy

Ephesians

Ephesians addresses a more general audience and a less specific situation than any of the undisputed Pauline Letters. By its time, arguments about the place of gentiles in the church had cooled, so the letter's emphasis on unity is less polemical than what we find in Galatians. The arguments in Ephesians remain so general that many see it as a kind of circular letter. Its emphasis on unity makes Ephesians a letter that focuses on innerecclesial relations.

This ecclesial focus dominates the ethical outlook of Ephesians. The constant theme within its exhortations is conduct in relation to fellow believers. When the letter calls readers to tell the truth to their "neighbors," the motivation is that "we are members of one another" (4:25). Ephesians does not attend to the effects that church members' lives have on outsiders. This letter ties proper ethics to proper teaching; living the Christian life helps one maintain correct doctrine (4:13–16). Ethical behavior lies at the heart of Christian existence; the believer's purpose is to do good works (2:10).

Most of the recommendations in Ephesians about Christian ethics are consistent with first-century cultural values. Among the few places where it differs are its recommendation of humility as a virtue (4:2) and its commendation of manual labor (4:28). The household code in Ephesians exemplifies its acceptance of cultural structures; it adopts the cultural expectations of first-century household life but gives them Christian groundings. (Ephesians may address households in which the head of the household is a believer, which sets it apart from those addressed in Colossians and 1 Peter.) Ephesians differs from the surrounding culture in the grounds that it proffers more than in the values that it promotes.

Still, Ephesians insists that the church remain distinct from the world. Succumbing to vices contradicts the believer's status as a participant in Christ (4:21). Believers must stop living as they did when they were "gentiles" or one of the "children of darkness" and must adopt a manner of life consistent with who God is and what God has done for them (4:17–18; 5:6–10). Thus, believers must forgive one another because God forgave them in Christ (4:32), and they must live in love because Christ loved them (5:2).

The emphasis in Ephesians on a distinctive manner of life promotes group solidarity by separating the church from the world. Perhaps Ephesians wants the church to differ from the world by actually living by the shared virtues and avoiding the acknowledged vices. This letter asserts that believers can live by higher standards because God enables them to do so. The number of times Ephesians calls believers saints ("holy ones") (1:2, 15, 18; 2:19; 3:8, 18; 4:12; 5:3; 6:18 [additional references to holiness appear in 1:4; 2:21; 5:27]) demonstrates the importance that it gives to fulfilling the demand to live righteously. Other Pauline Letters regularly call believers "saints," but none use this title as often as Ephesians does. Holy living is an essential element of Christian life for Ephesians.

The foundational admonition in Ephesians is "Be imitators of God, as beloved children" (5:1). Believers' lives should reflect who God is. Calls to imitate a god were not uncommon among first-century moralists. Further, this exhortation fits the grounding of ethics found in OT passages that urge the people to be holy because God is holy (e.g., Lev. 11:44; cf. 1 Pet. 1:16). Ephesians identifies Christ, particularly his self-giving death, as the clearest revelation of the character of God that believers are to imitate (4:32–5:2).

The partially realized eschatology of Ephesians comes to expression in its ethics. Believers put off the "old person" at conversion; now they must put on the "new person" that is appropriate to this new life. This "new person" is created by God in righteousness and purity (4:22–24). This notion coheres well with the initial and theme-setting exhortation of Eph. 4–6: "Live worthily of the calling with which you were called" (4:1). Living ethically is an essential element of a life that is consistent with what God in Christ has done for believers, whom God has made as "beloved children."

See also Ecclesiology and Ethics; Eschatology and Ethics; Holiness; Household Codes; New Testament Ethics; Sanctification

Bibliography

Best, E. *Essays on Ephesians*. T&T Clark, 1997; Darko, D. *No Longer Living as the Gentiles: Differentiation and Shared Ethical Values in Ephesians 4.17–6.9*. LNTS 375. T&T Clark, 2008; Lincoln, A. *Ephesians*. WBC 42. Thomas Nelson, 1990; Malan, F. "Unity of Love in the Body of Christ: Identity, Ethics and Ethos in Ephesians." Pages 257–87 in *Identity, Ethics, and Ethos in the New Testament*, ed. J. van der Watt. BZNW 141. De Gruyter, 2006.

Jerry L. Sumney

Equality

Liberal Western understandings of equality, while rooted in the classical period of Greece, are nonetheless distinctly modern. Articulated by late seventeenth-century philosophers (e.g., John Locke) and given momentum by the revolutionary democratic movements of the eighteenth century, the ideal of the inherent equality of all persons has achieved axiomatic status in Western politics (one person, one vote) and law (equal standing under the law). Yet the notion of equality remains complex and contested. Who is included in the "all men" said to be "created equal" by the Declaration of Independence? The "all" that originally comprised only white, male, heterosexual property owners has expanded only partially and with great struggle. In the early twenty-first century, addressing radical global economic inequalities may be among the most pressing issues concerning whom "all men" includes.

Womanist and feminist ethicists have, in differing but overlapping ways, raised questions: Equal to whom? Whose norms determine the nature of equality? They argue that formally equal legal standing and formally equal access to resources under laws and institutions created by and for men fail to take into account genuine differences (e.g., childbearing and childrearing experiences of women) and thus lead to substantially unequal results (Riggs).

Ethical, philosophical, and political debates also reflect deep differences concerning "what" ought to be equal, opportunities or outcomes, and what equal opportunities or equal outcomes might look like, especially in the economic sphere. Also contested are how society ought to balance equality with other core ethical values such as efficiency and whether equality is of instrumental or intrinsic value.

As the term is used in modern and postmodern ethical discussion, *equality* is not a particularly biblical concept. Some scholarly reconstructions posit that gender roles in premonarchical Israelite tribal society or the earliest Jesus movement and house churches were more egalitarian than the biblical texts suggest (Meyers; Schüssler Fiorenza), but during the monarchical and postmonarchical periods, when the OT was decisively shaped, ancient Israel was a patriarchal society. Its basic social unit was the *bêt ʾāb*, the "father's household," in which authority and status were distributed according to gender, generation, and class (free or slave, patron or client). Biblical laws, proverbial instructions, and narratives largely (though not entirely) encode gender, generational, class, and ethnic asymmetries that both reflect and support the patriarchal social order.

Nonetheless, some of the multiple voices that make up the Bible do provide support for ethical affirmations of human equality. The priestly assertion that God created humankind, male and female, in God's own image stands as a radical and bedrock challenge to the attribution of unequal ontological status to any group. Paul refuses to validate traditional distinctions among Christians; baptismal unity results in the fundamental equality of Christians: "There is no longer Jew or Greek, . . . slave or free, . . . male and female; for all of you are one in Christ Jesus" (Gal. 3:28).

The OT understanding of land both contributes to and potentially corrects modern views of economic equality. In ancient Israel, land represented not only the basic economic resource but also security, freedom, and, in an experiential sense, identity (e.g., 1 Kgs. 21). Efforts to limit economic inequality are visible in the Sabbath laws that mandate the periodic cancellation of debts (Deut. 15:1–11) and limit the term of debtor slaves to seven years (Exod. 21:2–6; Deut. 15:12–18), and especially in the Jubilee laws. Leviticus 25 calls for land sold outside the family to be returned to its original owners every fifty years. Scholars debate whether these laws actually were put into practice, but certainly they do offer a clear vision of economic redistribution.

A NT model of shared resources is found in the book of Acts, which asserts that among believers, "no one claimed private ownership of any possessions, but everything they owned was held in common" (4:32 [see also 4:34–37; 5:1–11]).

See also Egalitarianism; Feminist Ethics; Image of God; Jubilee; Koinonia

Bibliography

King, P., and L. Stager. *Life in Biblical Israel*. LAI. Westminster John Knox, 2001; Locke, J. *Second Treatise on Government*. Ed. C. Macpherson. Hackett, 1980; Meyers, C. *Discovering Eve: Ancient Israelite Women in Context*. Oxford University Press, 1988; Rawls, J. *A Theory of Justice*. Rev. ed. Harvard University Press, 1999; Riggs, M. *Awake, Arise, and Act: A Womanist Call for Black Liberation*. Pilgrim Press, 1994; Schüssler Fiorenza, E. *In Memory of Her: A Feminist Theological Reconstruction of Christian Origins*. Crossroad, 1983.

Carolyn Pressler

Eschatology and Ethics

Over the last century, eschatology's influence on ethics has shifted several times in ways that parallel changes in biblical studies. These shifts can be traced in both disciplines' treatments of "the kingdom of God." Through the centuries, Christians have differed over the extent to which this kingdom is present or future, earthly or heavenly, and partially or fully actualized. Yet they have often forgotten that God's kingdom was the major theme of Jesus' ministry, until the nineteenth-century European "quest for the historical Jesus" rediscovered this fact.

Developmental Eschatology

The questers noticed that Jesus' sayings pictured this kingdom both developing in history and arriving catastrophically at its end. Living in a Europe dominated by confidence in progress, they considered the latter sayings as primitive fancy but the former as Jesus' true perspective. Albrecht Ritschl interpreted Jesus' mission, person, and deity in terms of bringing God's kingdom. Yet this kingdom of God sounded much like Kant's moral "kingdom of ends" (where all persons are ends in themselves, not means for others' ends). In many versions of this developmental eschatology, even Jesus' radical teachings could be applied to society: those about nonviolence to ending war (Kant's "perpetual peace"), those on accepting marginalized persons to expanding democracy, and Jesus' critique of riches and favor for the poor to socialist and labor movements.

Meanwhile, across the Atlantic, the kingdom of God had symbolized America's destiny ever since the Puritans sought to erect it in the wilderness. Nineteenth-century evangelical revivals sparked numerous social changes—for example, abolition, prison reform, temperance, and suffrage. The millennium (Rev. 20:4–6), which most Americans had expected to arrive shortly after Jesus' catastrophic return, was increasingly interpreted as a period of rapid worldwide progress that would precede his coming (this scheme was called "postmillennialism").

By the late nineteenth century, the coming of God's kingdom on earth became a dominant theme in American Christianity. Walter Rauschenbusch was incorporating German exegesis and theology into a "social gospel" for mainline churches. Here, God's kingdom was dynamically present and future, but it was entirely earthly, lacking any historical consummation. On both sides of the Atlantic this developmental eschatology envisioned the West leading the way.

Catastrophic Eschatology

Late in the nineteenth century, however, this immanent eschatology received a double blow. In North America, many evangelicals, finding it excessively optimistic, turned to newly crystallized premillennial schemes. The most influential of these, dispensationalism, interpreted eschatological texts literally and noticed that NT "kingdom" language diminishes rapidly after the Synoptic Gospels. Dispensationalists reinstated catastrophic eschatology and insisted that neither Jesus' teachings nor God's kingdom could become operative in this evil world. Premillennialists downplayed or discouraged social-ethical activism and predicted that world affairs would worsen rapidly, heralding Jesus' return.

Meanwhile in Europe, Johannes Weiss, Albert Schweitzer, and others were interpreting Jesus' sayings in a far different but still fairly literal fashion. They also held that Jesus' eschatology was catastrophic, but they considered him mistaken. Jesus intended his teachings only for a brief "interim" before the end, not as ethics for continuing societies. God's kingdom, then, had no real significance for Christian ethics.

World War I seemed to vindicate both premillennialism and this shift in biblical studies. Europe was experiencing a cataclysm like the one that Jesus anticipated. But could some kind of ethics be retrieved even from this eschatology?

The answer was yes, although it was done by prioritizing neither God's kingdom nor Jesus' teachings but rather the last judgment. As Karl Barth put it, God, first through Jesus and then through the war, had pronounced a decisive no against all human efforts to erect God's kingdom, especially by the West. Nevertheless, God also pronounced a yes and bestowed a righteousness that humans could partially experience, but it was rooted in eternity and could not undergo continuous historical development. Barth and others largely transferred the judgment, negative and positive, from the historical future into the present and reduced its cosmic scope mainly to personal encounters.

According to Rudolf Bultmann, Jesus' announcement of time's end and eternity's inbreaking had nothing to do with history's flow. Properly demythologized, it meant that God can, in the present, undo the past that binds us existentially and set us free and open toward our individual futures. Bultmann and Barth insisted that God calls us to moral decisions in specific situations in concrete ways. General rules can never tell us how to decide.

Inaugurated Eschatology

The biblical theology movement. By the 1930s, however, Weiss and Schweitzer's exegesis had long been under scrutiny. Hans Windisch noticed that some of Jesus' radical teachings are not apocalyptic but rather are concrete wisdom sayings incorporated into an eschatological framework (e.g., Matt. 5:29–40, 44–45; 6:19–21, 25–31). C. H. Dodd and Joachim Jeremias removed, as later accretions, most narrative and historical features from the Synoptic parables and claimed that Jesus taught not a catastrophic eschatology but rather a "realized" one. By the 1950s, most biblical scholars had concluded that God's kingdom, for Jesus, was "already" inaugurated but "not yet" consummated. Consequently, his teachings held some significance for continuing historical life.

Many of these scholars, influenced by Barth and neoorthodoxy's biblical orientation, were developing a "biblical theology." Biblical theology stressed the unity—better, unity in diversity—of the entire Bible. God, it claimed, is revealed through history, not mainly in moments of encounter, whether existentially or from eternity. Old Testament scholars such as Walther Eichrodt traced the development of a universal eschatological vision, especially through the prophets.

John Bright re-presented biblical history (or *Heilsgeschichte*) as a whole in his book titled *The Kingdom of God*. By "kingdom" Bright meant both the earthly process, with its social and political dimensions, and an eschatological vision that inspired but also critiqued the former, sometimes severely. Catastrophic eschatology's demonic powers became the energy behind sociopolitical forces that killed Jesus. They were defeated by his resurrection, which released the energies of the new age. These are available to the church, though it still struggles against the powers. It can oppose them, in part, through social and political channels, but primarily by "being the church," a community that actualizes and expresses God's "already" present but "not yet" fully realized kingdom.

Biblical scholars had developed a third eschatological paradigm that was impacting ethics. Here, the kingdom of God, as in catastrophic eschatology, broke into history by divine initiative, sharply judging all societies. Human effort could not construct it. Jesus' life and teaching, in their radical thrust if not every detail, shaped its ethics. Christians were to respond to this kingdom and make it tangible, as in developmental eschatology, yet not so much by transforming macrostructures as through their individual and communal lives, in concrete ways and settings, incarnating, by the energies of the new age, alternatives to the old age's destructive patterns.

Ethics of hope, reversal, and liberation. From the 1970s on, as massive apocalyptic evils increasingly threatened the world, this eschatologically informed ethics enjoyed wide appeal. It is expressive, not simply cognitive. It denounces current evils. It calls for decisions and for commitments to new ways of life. Such an ethic is more concerned with developing moral character and embodying social alternatives than with elaborating general rules or decision-making procedures.

This approach informed the "theology of hope." For neoorthodox ethics, biblical expressions such as "God's name" and "God's word" indicated divine self-revelation in the present. Wolfhart Pannenberg and some biblical colleagues argue that such themes almost always referred to partial, indirect revelations through historical events. It was these events that pointed toward God's self-manifestation, but only at history's end, and "proleptically" at Jesus' resurrection.

Jürgen Moltmann shows that God's speech in biblical narrative usually conveyed promises, and that a promise-fulfillment schema overarched it. Both Pannenberg and Moltmann stress that God's words were received not only by faith but also by hope, which propelled their recipients toward the future to overcome whatever opposed it.

Moltmann highlights the opposition between Jesus and his political and religious enemies and the agony of his resulting crucifixion. His social ethics, which also draw on neo-Marxism, critique many social structures and favor the oppressed. Pannenberg, however, emphasizes humankind's eschatological unity and promotes transformation of current structures.

Ethicists who appropriated this third paradigm were attracted by what Allen Verhey calls "the great reversal" (in a 1984 book so titled) of the old age's social hierarchies, such as the rich over the poor, men over women, and "the righteous" over "sinners." Verhey highlights the Synoptic Gospels but traces these themes and many current ethical implications through the NT. Wolfgang Schrage also developed a detailed NT ethic from its internal eschatological vantage point. Thomas Ogletree carefully delineated Scripture's role in this sort of approach. He suggests that it fosters a "dialectical" ethics: neither withdrawing from society nor seeking its overall transformation (as in the catastrophic and developmental paradigms) but rather living provisionally within its structures and focusing on specific issues.

Liberation theologies, especially from Latin America, include an eschatology that denounces current structures and announces a future released from them. The exodus from Egypt provides a primary biblical paradigm. Jesus exercised a "preferential option for the poor" and proclaimed liberation from all aspects of poverty: degradation and despair as well as economic need. In his death, Jesus identified with the poor in their oppression; his resurrection releases power to renew all of life.

These theologies often incorporate some neo-Marxist socioeconomic analysis. They emphasize the systemic nature of oppression and usually conceive God's kingdom as a worldwide socioeconomic reality opposed by globalizing capitalism. Full liberation apparently would require macrorevolution. But liberation theologies also inspire more limited changes through local base communities.

Recent New Testament ethics. This third paradigm also draws heavily from the apostle Paul. According to Christiaan Beker, Paul highlights Jesus' resurrection, which inaugurated God's triumph over the world's power structures and bestowed the firstfruits of the new creation. Paul's eschatology includes the dynamic vindication, manifestation, and universal sweep of God's righteousness but also a continuing dualism against opposition. His eschatology arouses a hope that inspires struggle against injustice, but only according to Jesus' cruciform pattern. This hope points not toward an endlessly open future but rather toward a real coming triumph. It calls for action but also for receptivity, prayer, meditation, and adoration.

Ever since Windisch, NT scholarship has recognized that many ethical and wisdom sayings appear in eschatological contexts. The highly publicized Jesus Seminar considers these contexts catastrophic and Jesus, once his authentic words are extricated from them, a wisdom teacher. Bruce Chilton and J. I. H. MacDonald, however, return ethics to eschatological contexts by restoring to the parables of the kingdom those narrative features that Dodd and Jeremias removed. So construed, many parables point toward an alternative world or an eschatological future and call for immediate ethical responses. Numerous ethical and wisdom sayings reappear within the eschatological horizon. This ethics is more a matter of creative response to God's eschatological inbreakings than of precise following of Jesus' teachings.

For N. T. Wright, however, Jesus' teachings outline a radically different way of being the true Israel in real-life Palestine, including nonviolence as a response to Roman oppression. John Howard Yoder argues, from an Anabaptist perspective, that Jesus intended these for continuing historical existence.

Although loving enemies and disregarding wealth might seem impractical, they can be practiced in daily life. Individuals, indeed, might find this lifestyle unsustainable. Yet it can be followed corporately, through mutual effort and assistance, in the church, which in turn can render its social implications visible. Yoder identifies expressions of this ethic throughout the NT, not just in the Synoptics—for example, in appeals to Jesus' way of the cross. However, since evil powers permeate social structures, only through cruciform discipleship will God's kingdom come to light.

Stanley Hauerwas expands many of Yoder's points, especially that Christian ethics is taught and practiced in the church. Consequently, he adds, ethics are developed and transmitted more through traditions and narratives than through rational argument, and it is more concerned with developing character, or virtues, than with general norms.

Richard Hays's comprehensive *Moral Vision of the New Testament* probes the eschatological perspectives of all four Gospels. He begins, however, with Paul, whose outlook he finds highly eschatological, and who, he maintains, alludes to Jesus surprisingly often. Hays wrestles with hermeneutical issues and applies his findings to concerns such as war, homosexuality, and abortion. Hays organizes his findings around three "focal images": community, cross (or cruciform existence), and new creation, all of which are main themes of inaugurated eschatology.

If Jesus' teaching is crucial to this third paradigm, one would expect to find numerous ethical treatments of his Sermon on the Mount. David Gushee and Glen Stassen, however, complain that none exists, and they provide a lengthy treatment covering numerous current moral issues. Stassen proposes, intriguingly, that Jesus did not begin by commanding impossible ideals (e.g., one should never be angry [Matt. 5:22]). Instead, Jesus first described a vicious behavioral cycle (covering all of Matt. 5:22) and then outlined practices to transform this cycle (Matt. 5:23–26 [e.g., "Come quickly to terms with your accuser"]).

In conclusion, although differences between the developmental and the catastrophic paradigms, and their partial resolution in an inaugurated paradigm, affect more issues than Jesus' teachings about God's kingdom, no other eschatological topic seems more central to ethics. Closely related is the question of whether eschatological sayings concern a wholly future, transcendent, or inner/subjective realm or whether they interconnect with concrete, this-worldly ethical teachings. Inaugurated approaches often connect them by conceiving eschatology not as apocalyptic (as in the previous sentence) but rather as akin to the prophetic. Eschatologically informed ethical texts envision a divinely initiated, radically different future, but one that transforms earthly life.

See also Anabaptist Ethics; Cruciformity; Fundamentalism; Hope; Imitation of Jesus; Judgment; Kingdom of God; Liberationist Ethics; Salvation

Bibliography

Beker, C. "The Challenge of Paul's Apocalyptic Gospel for the Church Today." *JRT* 40 (1983): 9–15; Bright, J. *The Kingdom of God: The Biblical Concept and Its Meaning for the Church*. Abingdon, 1953; Chilton, B., and J. I. H. McDonald. *Jesus and the Ethics of the Kingdom*. SPCK, 1987; Hays, R. *The Moral Vision of the New Testament: Community, Cross, New Creation; A Contemporary Introduction to New Testament Ethics*. HarperSanFrancisco, 1996; Moltmann, J. *Theology of Hope: On the Ground and the Implications of a Christian Eschatology*. Trans. J. Leitch. Harper & Row, 1967; Ogletree, T. *The Use of the Bible in Christian Ethics: A Constructive Essay*. Fortress, 1983; Pannenberg, W. *Ethics*. Trans. K. Crim. Westminster, 1981; Pannenberg, W., et al., eds. *Revelation as History*. Trans. D. Granskou. Macmillan, 1968; Rauschenbusch, W. *A Theology for the Social Gospel*. Abingdon, 1917; Schrage, W. *The Ethics of the New Testament*. Trans. D. Green. Fortress, 1987; Sobrino, J. *Jesus the Liberator: A Historical-Theological Reading of Jesus of Nazareth*. Trans. P. Burns and F. McDonagh. Orbis, 1993; Stassen, G., and D. Gushee. *Kingdom Ethics: Following Jesus in Contemporary Context*. InterVarsity, 2003; Verhey, A. *The Great Reversal: Ethics and the New Testament*. Eerdmans, 1984; Wright, N. T. *Jesus and the Victory of God*. Fortress, 1996; Yoder, J. *The Politics of Jesus: Vicit Agnus Noster*. 2nd ed. Eerdmans, 1994.

Thomas Finger

1 Esdras *See* Orthodox Ethics

2 Esdras *See* Orthodox Ethics

Esther

The book of Esther depicts the threatened annihilation of the Jewish population in the ancient

Persian Empire. After the current queen, Vashti, is banished, the Jew Esther is selected as the new queen by King Ahasuerus. Her relative Mordecai angers Haman, the second in command, who plots in revenge to have all the Jews killed. Esther convinces the king to overturn that decree, the Jews experience victory, and the Jewish holiday of Purim is established.

The book features characters who live by a compromised code of ethics: the negligent and overindulging Ahasuerus, the egotistical and vengeful Haman. When such individuals hold high social positions, personal inadequacies are shown to have the potential for widespread deleterious impact. The well-being of large segments of society (the nation's wives, its young women, and ultimately all Jews) is sacrificed for the happiness of a few (the king, his premier, and his officials). Prejudice and discrimination are given the royal stamp of approval. Against this, the courage and moral fiber of the characters who, in spite of the personal cost, resist wrongdoing and injustice (Vashti, Esther, Mordecai) are highlighted.

Particularly challenging for interpreters of the book is the violence that it depicts; most question whether such bloodshed is necessary, whether Jewish lives cannot be preserved without the loss of non-Jewish lives. Within the constraints of a story world in which royal decrees are irrevocable, there are seemingly few narrative options. Readers must take care not to allow narrative violence to condone real-world violence. The holiday of Purim is established to celebrate not a bloody victory but instead the people's relief of no longer living under mortal threat. This remembrance engenders generosity, as the people are charged to practice charity to those in need.

Present-day concerns lead us to utilize the book of Esther for contemporary ethical discourse in matters that lie outside the story level proper. Most significant, we must acknowledge that we read the book after the Shoah as well as other acts of genocide throughout modern history that, unlike in the story, were chillingly successful in their attempts for ethnic annihilation. If twentieth-century gentiles had followed the example of the book's Persian population and had chosen to side with the Jews and the other persecuted populations, perhaps the massacres of the Third Reich would not have occurred. In addition, concern for gender equality renders problematic the clearly patriarchal and hierarchical social system depicted in the book. Lacking a view of full personhood for women, female worth is measured by how much women "please" men, and despite Esther's superior political abilities, final power rests in male hands.

See also Narrative Ethics, Biblical; Old Testament Ethics

Bibliography

Day, L. *Esther*. AOTC. Abingdon, 2005; Fox, M. *Character and Ideology in the Book of Esther*. 2nd ed. Eerdmans, 2001; Goldman, S. "Narrative and Ethical Ironies in Esther." *JSOT* 47 (1990): 15–31; Laniak, T. *Shame and Honor in the Book of Esther*. SBLDS 165. Scholars Press, 1998; Mosala, I. "The Implications of the Text of Esther for African Women's Struggle for Liberation in South Africa." *Semeia* 59 (1992): 129–37.

Linda Day

Ethnic Identity, Ethnicity

Ethnicity is a relatively recent concept and focus of studies in the social sciences, first appearing in the *Oxford English Dictionary Supplement* in 1972. The term *ethnicity* comes from the Greek word *ethnos*, commonly translated as "nation" or "people" in the NT. Ethnicity has been defined in a variety of ways by scholars, but the key elements are (1) reference to common ancestors (fictive or metaphoric kinship), (2) a sense of distinctiveness (what makes "us" different from "them"), and (3) the idea that ethnicity and ethnic identity are relevant only when two or more ethnic groups are involved in the same social system (Eriksen; Hicks). Since ethnic identity has to do with individuals' perceptions of being a "people," the belief in common kinship is foundational to that identity. What makes a group distinctive from others can be drawn from a wide range of symbolic elements that may include, but is not limited to, what one wears, eats, believes, and/or the language one speaks.

Constructing Ethnicity

A class of students drawn from many of the different ethnic groups throughout China might say that what made their group distinctive was religion (many of them might be Muslim), clothing (some might wear distinctive outfits related to their group), language, and food (one group might be different because they do not eat dog). For the Basque people in northern Spain and southern France, their distinct language, Euskara, is a key symbol to their identity. This is seen in their traditional self-identifying term, *Euskaldun*, which means "speaker of Euskara," and the name of their homeland, *Euskal Herria*, which means "the land where Euskara is spoken." These symbolic elements, then, are used to create and often maintain the boundary between "us" and "them" (Barth).

One reason why ethnicity escaped the scrutiny of scholars for so long is that, according to the then-dominant modernization theory, these preindustrial allegiances should have given way to the integrative forces of modern society and broader national or class identities (van den Berghe; da Silva). In other words, traditional group loyalties to family, tribe, and clan would be replaced by interest-based loyalties to class, party, or state. However, the very processes of modernization—for example, urbanization, industrialization, education, improved communication technologies, including transportation—often had the opposite effect; increased contact through improved communication systems and urbanization led to a greater sense of distinctiveness and mobilization along ethnic lines than in the period prior to modernization (Connor).

Two seminal works published in 1963 challenged the modernizationist assumptions and had a great influence on the development of the study of ethnicity and ethnic identity. The anthropologist Clifford Geertz, surveying conflicts in the newly independent states of Asia and Africa, proposed that the problems were largely caused by competing allegiances between ethnic groups and the state, or more precisely, between what he termed "primordial sentiments" and civil politics. Many of these new states were inherently unstable because individuals tended to be loyal to their primordial groups (e.g., family, clan, ethnic group) rather than to the state government. Based on what we continue to see in some of these states today, Geertz was not only insightful but also rather prophetic. But lest we think that ethnic identities and conflicts are something relegated to the new states in Africa and Asia, the second influential publication of that year focused on these issues in the United States, specifically New York City. Nathan Glazer and Daniel Patrick Moynihan, authors of *Beyond the Melting Pot*, empirically challenged the assimilationist assumption of that most cherished metaphor of ethnicity in the United States. Summing up the main idea behind Israel Zangwill's 1908 play *The Melting Pot*, the authors state, "The point about the melting pot is that it did not happen" (Glazer and Moynihan 290).

These two works were influential in ushering in an era of heightened interest and scholarship on ethnicity and ethnic identity that has persisted to this day. The field, however, has continued to develop over the years, with ethnic identity now being studied within the context of broader movements, particularly globalization and transnationalism. There are many aspects to globalization, but certainly a key one has to do with the increased migration of people from less productive to more productive areas. In one sense, this is not new (studies conducted by the Manchester School of anthropology in the 1940s and 1950s focused on the social transformations taking place as the result of migration and urbanization in Africa), but what is new is the extent of this migration, particularly from certain parts of the world. In addition, beginning in the 1990s, anthropologists and other social scientists began studying the contexts that migrants came from, their adaptive strategies in the host country, and their continued ties with "home" (i.e., transnationalism). Globalization and transnationalism have called into question the idea of nicely bounded cultural (ethnic) groups and have replaced this with an emphasis on hybridity and creolization—the mixing of cultures and identities (Vertovec). As a result, although ethnic identity remains an important area of research and scholarship, it is understood to be much more complex and contingent than was previously thought.

Ethnicity, Scripture, and the Church

Nationalism, understood as an ideological movement, certainly is a modern phenomenon, but ethnicity and ethnic identity are found in antiquity (Smith). We read in the OT of groups such as the Canaanites, Cushites, Hittites, and Egyptians, to name but a few. We witness the ethnogenesis (creation) of a people, the Israelites, through Abraham, and we see God's jealousy for his people. In the NT we encounter a more complex multicultural context than often is assumed. We tend to think of the world at that time as divided between two or three groups: Jews, Greeks, and perhaps barbarians. However, when we look at the day of Pentecost alone, we find no fewer than thirteen languages referenced, which is a good indicator of distinct cultures and identities.

Issues pertaining to ethnicity and the church are found in the book of Acts as well as in many of Paul's letters. For example, Acts 15 tells of the Jerusalem council, in which the leaders of the church came together to decide if gentiles had to adopt Jewish customs once they became Christ followers. In other words, was the church going to be bound by the culture of one ethnic group (i.e., the Jews), or was it adaptable to other cultures and identities as well? The leadership decided on the latter, based largely on the testimony of how God had been working in powerful ways among the gentiles.

From that time onward, Christians and the church have had to grapple with what Andrew Walls calls a paradox: "The very universality of the Gospel, the fact that it is for *everyone*, leads to a variety of perceptions and applications of it" (Walls 46). Unfortunately, the church has had a difficult time with this paradox, often erring in one of two ways: either baptizing its nationalism with Christianity, thereby confusing its ethnic/ national identity and culture with the gospel, or totally rejecting any identity other than "Christian," which turns out to be just another version of cultural chauvinism, since, as Walls intimates, what being a Christian looks like will vary according to the cultural context. People are never "just Christians"; they are Christians from particular cultures and with particular identities. Maintaining the tension between the universal nature of the gospel and its particular cultural and identificational manifestations (i.e., unity in diversity) has been, and continues to be, a major challenge for the church.

See also Colonialism and Postcolonialism; Cross-Cultural Ethics; Culture; Globalization; Imperialism; Nationalism; Race; Urbanization

Bibliography

Barth, F. "Introduction." Pages 9–38 in *Ethnic Groups and Boundaries: The Social Organization of Culture Difference*, ed. F. Barth. Little, Brown, 1969; Connor, W. "Nation-Building, or Nation-Destroying?" *World Politics* 24 (1972): 319–55; da Silva, M. "Modernization and Ethnic Conflict: The Case of the Basques." *Comparative Politics* 7 (1975): 227–51; Eriksen, T. *Ethnicity and Nationalism: Anthropological Perspectives*. 2nd ed. Pluto Press, 2002; Geertz, C. "The Integrative Revolution: Primordial Sentiments and Civil Politics in the New States." Pages 105–57 in *Old Societies and New States: The Quest for Modernity in Asia and Africa*, ed. C. Geertz. Free Press of Glencoe, 1963; Glazer, N., and D. Moynihan. *Beyond the Melting Pot: The Negroes, Puerto Ricans, Jews, Italians, and Irish of New York City*. MIT Press, 1963; Hays, J. *From Every People and Nation: A Biblical Theology of Race*. InterVarsity, 2003; Hicks, G. "Introduction: Problems in the Study of Ethnicity." Pages 1–20 in *Ethnic Encounters: Identities and Contexts*, ed. G. Hicks and P. Leis. Duxbury Press, 1976; Smith, A. "The Problem of National Identity: Ancient, Medieval, and Modern?" *ERS* 17 (1994): 375–99; van den Berghe, P. *Class and Ethnicity in Peru*. Brill, 1974; Vertovec, S. "Introduction: New Directions in the Anthropology of Migration and Multiculturalism." *ERS* 30 (2007): 961–78; Walls, A. *The Missionary Movement in Christian History: Studies in the Transmission of Faith*. Orbis, 1996.

Steven Ybarrola

Eugenics

Eugenics is the attempt to improve one's offspring or the human race by promoting "good" genetic features (positive eugenics) and eliminating genetic "defects" and "degeneracy" (negative eugenics). Eugenic endeavors range from encouraging careful selection of a reproductive partner or voluntarily refraining from reproduction to forced sterilization and direct extermination of those deemed "unfit" to live and reproduce.

Francis Galton, Charles Darwin's cousin, developed modern eugenics. The American biologist Charles Davenport, whose work the Carnegie Institute supported, was key to the international spread of eugenics. Governments, scientists, leading institutions such as the American Medical Association, and many religious leaders advocated eugenic policies. Margaret Sanger urged contraceptive access as one way to reduce "dysgenic" reproduction. Various states legalized involuntary eugenic sterilization, laws that the Supreme Court upheld in the 1927 decision *Buck v. Bell*. Christine Rosen argues that religious adherents who advocated the modernization of their faith communities were those most likely to support eugenics. Proponents of the social gospel movement found eugenics amenable to their sense of responsibility for realizing the kingdom of God on earth. Fellow believers such as G. K. Chesterton did speak against eugenic programs.

Modern eugenics is most closely associated with Nazi Germany and the horrors of the Holocaust. After World War II, many eugenic ideas and programs were rejected. However, eugenics persisted in other forms, such as immigration policies and laws against miscegenation.

Advocates of modern eugenics enlisted Scripture to support their positions. As Rosen details, some preachers saw the great flood described in Genesis as a divine eugenic cleansing. They linked human races to Noah's three sons, Shem, Ham, and Japheth, from whom all humans presumably descended after the flood, and argued for a racial hierarchy based on Noah's cursing of Ham (Gen. 9:24–27). The election of Israel as a people set apart and covenantal purity codes were read as code for eugenics. Galton himself likened the eugenist to the good and faithful servant found in the parable of talents (Matt. 25:15–30). In the hands of eugenists, this parable becomes a warrant for genetic stewardship.

Eugenic programs that segregate, sterilize, and exterminate "unfit" populations are incompatible with the scriptural affirmation that God creates humans in the divine image (Gen. 1:27). While God did elect Israel as a covenant partner, remembrance of their delivery from oppression should prompt compassionate and just treatment of aliens (Lev. 19:33–34). Eugenic programs betray the example of Christ, who reached out to lepers and other marginalized persons (e.g., Mark 1:40–45).

Increasing knowledge about human genetics, reproductive technologies, and prenatal genetic diagnosis foster what some call a "new eugenics." Knowledge of the human genome and technologies developed to improve human life through genetic intervention are not inherently bad. They extend the reach of human power and raise ethical questions regarding the scope and limits of human responsibility for ameliorating suffering. Scriptural perspectives on human dignity and equality, parenthood, procreation, sickness, suffering, and technology should inform morally appropriate exercises of genetic technologies.

See also Bioethics; Image of God; Reproductive Technologies; Sanctity of Human Life

Bibliography

Chesterton, G. K. *Eugenics and Other Evils*. Cassell, 1922; Dyck, A. "Eugenics in Historical and Ethical Perspective." Pages 25–39 in *Genetic Ethics: Do the Ends Justify the Genes?* ed. J. Kilner, R. Pentz, and F. Young. Eerdmans, 1997; Galton, F. "The Possible Improvement of the Human Breed under Existing Conditions of Law and Sentiment." *Popular Science Monthly* 60 (January 1902): 218–33; Hall, A. *Conceiving Parenthood: American Protestantism and the Spirit of Reproduction*. Eerdmans, 2008; Rosen, C. *Preaching Eugenics: Religious Leaders and the American Eugenics Movement*. Oxford University Press, 2004.

Darlene Fozard Weaver

Euthanasia

The word *euthanasia* is composed from the Greek words *eu* ("good") and *thanatos* ("death"). For centuries, it referred to a "good death" in general—that is, a death free from agony or suffering and for which one was well prepared. From the early nineteenth century, however, it came to refer more specifically to medically assisted dying in the case of severe suffering with or without a patient's request. In the first half of the twentieth century, the term frequently was used in the context of eugenics. Hitler's infamous euthanasia program led to the killing of tens of thousands of handicapped and elderly people. In some discussions the term still carries this connotation.

The term is most commonly used in the context of a terminal disease and hardly ever refers to the voluntary killing of people without a medically classifiable disease. In the Netherlands, in 1995 the first country in the world to legalize euthanasia, the requirements include not only severe suffering but also a patient's request. About 90 percent of all euthanasia cases in the Netherlands are performed on patients suffering from cancer with a prospect of six weeks or less to live.

The difference between euthanasia and assisted suicide lies in the identity of the actor initiating the death: the doctor in the former, the patient in the latter.

Of all forms of killing a human being, euthanasia is considered by many as the least controversial. From an ethical point of view, it is important to observe that the Bible does not imply "vitalism"—that is, the view that life should be prolonged at all costs. "Dying well" may imply a recognition that an illness has won, and that time and resources should be spent on spiritual and palliative care rather than on intensive medical treatment with little chance of success. There is reason to assume that the suffering underlying a euthanasia request may sometimes even be caused by aggravating medical interventions. Insofar as a "right to die" refers to a right to refuse invasive and futile medical treatment, this right is relatively uncontroversial.

Despite the fact that the Bible rejects vitalism, despite the seriousness of human suffering, and even though a euthanasia request may be well informed and sincere, euthanasia remains problematic from an ethical point of view. A society allowing the intentional and direct killing of some of its citizens may have difficulty in drawing a line between use and abuse, between those who are eligible and those who are not. The availability of euthanasia may hamper attempts to develop efficient and accessible palliative care. The last stretch of a human life may not only be tragic and burdensome but also may provide opportunities for spiritual growth, valuable social encounters, and reconciliation. Even for many of the physicians who are willing to perform euthanasia, the act remains emotionally burdensome. In a sense, euthanasia can be seen as an act that destroys one's autonomy altogether rather than as an expression of an autonomous wish. The Bible does speak highly of the capacity of humans to actively engage in their own destinies, but this autonomy has its proper place within the context of respect for life. The Bible contains several accounts of people yearning for death (e.g., Elijah, Paul), but not a single passage justifies a decision to actively kill oneself or to ask others to do so. Although occasional acts of suicide in the Bible are not explicitly condemned, descriptions of their context reveal the utterly tragic character of such decisions.

Discussion continues concerning the appropriateness of the distinction between "active" and "passive" euthanasia. Although refraining from life-support treatment may in some cases be as problematic as active euthanasia, most sources in the Christian tradition agree that the active killing of a person, other things being equal, is more problematic than a decision to let "nature take its course." Another point of debate is whether a death that is the side effect of painkillers and sedatives can be called "euthanasia." The tradition of natural law, through the "principle of double effect," stresses the difference between death through active and intentional means, and death that is the side effect of another action. If a medication necessary to provide relief for pain and anxiety causes death, and if the intention is merely to make comfortable rather than to kill, such a decision may be justified.

In the past two decades, new medications against pain, anxiety, itch, extreme fatigue, and nausea have helped healthcare workers to provide more efficient palliative care. Experience from the Netherlands shows that palliative sedation—that is, inducing a deep sleep until the moment of a patient's natural death—has become increasingly acceptable as an alternative to euthanasia. There is reason to believe that new developments in palliative care will cause a further decrease in the demand for euthanasia. At the same time, the quest for assisted suicide in cases in which there is no physical and terminal disease is not likely to decrease.

See also Death and Dying; Healthcare Ethics; Hospice; Suffering; Suicide

Bibliography

Biggar, N. *Aiming to Kill: The Ethics of Suicide and Euthanasia.* Darton, Longman & Todd, 2004; Boer, T. "Recurring Themes in the Debate about Euthanasia and Assisted Suicide." *JRE* 35 (2007): 529–55; Gorsuch, N. *The Future of Assisted Suicide and Euthanasia.* Princeton University Press, 2006; Keown, J. *Euthanasia, Ethics, and Public Policy: An Argument against Legalisation.* Cambridge University Press, 2002.

Theo A. Boer

Evangelical Ethics

Evangelical ethics reflects the moral commitments, positions, and practices that one derives from the gospel, the *euangelion* of Jesus Christ, by considering questions of moral obligations, ultimate goods, and virtues in light of God's purposes for humankind revealed in the Scriptures. Evangelical ethics often is associated with the subculture of American Protestantism known as evangelicalism, a movement that emerged out of the modernist versus fundamentalist controversies of the early nineteenth and twentieth centuries, particularly around disagreements on the authority of the Bible. This more recent context in the United States, along with the influence of the European Reformation emphasis of *sola scriptura*, explains the centrality of Scripture in evangelical ethics. Evangelicalism clusters around a set of beliefs about the authority of Scripture; the birth, death, and resurrection of Christ; the necessity of conversion to Christ; and a sense of mission in the world. Although evangelicalism is not an ecclesiastical tradition, it is descriptive of beliefs shared in many theological trajectories of the Protestant Reformation and has much in common with those committed to the gospel of Jesus Christ and the authority of Scripture for faith, practice, and moral norms found in African American ethics, Anabaptist ethics, Baptist ethics, Reformed ethics, and Wesleyan ethics.

Historical Perspectives and Contemporary Expressions

One early expression of evangelical ethics was offered by Carl F. H. Henry in *The Uneasy Conscience of Modern Fundamentalism* (1947). Henry articulated a foundation for evangelical ethics in response to the separatist tendencies of fundamentalist Christians who retreated from society after the controversies between fundamentalists and modernists. Henry represented "neo-evangelicalism," reflective of the efforts to recover a former social ethic embraced by early evangelicals. The recovery of ethical concern by neo-evangelicals was based on a commitment to mission and evangelism at the heart of its movement and a desire to morally influence American culture. These neo-evangelicals desired to reclaim a heritage of social engagement and moral concerns characteristic of the eighteenth and nineteenth centuries in the United States, when evangelicals were involved in organizing missions, relief work, and education; addressing issues such as abolition of slavery, temperance, child labor, women's suffrage; and alleviating squalid urban conditions. Henry's work provided a basis for evangelical ethics that spurred on diverse social engagements, moral concerns, and commitments of evangelicals well into the second half of the twentieth century.

Henry's work contained certain assumptions that would come to characterize the ways in which Scripture was used in evangelical ethics. One was the emphasis on evangelism. Scripture's message was seen as stressing personal salvation, with an emphasis on social justice as secondary to a person's conversion to Christ. The individual ethic of a person was seen as the key to transforming the moral ethos of a society. This minimized attention to larger social concerns, except for such issues as abortion, which later propelled evangelicals into public engagement with the US Supreme Court decision in *Roe v. Wade* in January 1973 that overturned state laws prohibiting abortion. This bifurcation between personal evangelism and social justice was addressed by a gathering of evangelicals (including Henry) who wrote and endorsed "The Chicago Declaration of Evangelical Social Concern" in November 1973. The Chicago Declaration called for evangelicals to repent of their complicity in social injustices and to address racism, poverty, economic injustice, sexism, militarism, nationalism, and materialism. The Chicago Declaration became the impetus for the founding by Ron Sider of Evangelicals for Social Action. Its mission to promote holistic ministry and work for social transformation is based on a commitment to the gospel of Jesus Christ reflective of evangelical ethics.

Another legacy that came to characterize evangelical ethics was the equating of conservative theological positions with traditional social views and public policies. The Bible was used to buttress those positions and views. The emergence of Sojourners in 1970, formed by a group of students at Trinity Evangelical Divinity School during the Vietnam War, and its initial publication, *The Post-American*, challenged that equation and explored the relationship between Scripture, faith, social policies, and political action. With its official founding in 1971 by Jim Wallis and its subsequent move to Washington in 1975, Sojourners continues to provide an important voice for an evangelical ethic in its publication, *Sojourners*, and its advocacy for just social policies that address, based on Scripture, the needs of the poor and oppressed.

Stephen Charles Mott represents another early important expression of evangelical ethics. His book *Biblical Ethics and Social Change* (1982) influenced seminary students, particularly those who would later pursue graduate work in Christian ethics. Mott laid the foundation for a "biblical theology of social involvement" by providing an overview of the biblical theme of the kingdom of God in Scripture and its implications for love, justice, and strategies of social transformation.

Evangelicalism remains diverse and includes a variety of ethical perspectives and positions. Since Scripture is a primary source for ethics in evangelicalism, and since evangelicalism is diverse, there are various perspectives on Scripture's use in ethics. Important work is being done today by evangelical ethicists in their attempts to bring Scripture, Christian tradition, theological claims, and ethical theories to bear on contemporary issues such as hospitality, immigration, bioethics, nonviolence, just peacemaking, human rights, torture, consumption of resources, social justice, environmental concerns, and poverty.

Scripture in Evangelical Ethics

Scripture is a key source for moral guidance and ethical reflection in Christian ethics in general, but it is of singular significance in evangelical ethics, where there is a strong theological commitment to the authority of Scripture for faith and practice. The more difficult issue is to understand how Scripture is normative in ethics and how it offers moral guidance, given its complexity and various genres and also the methodological diversity in the application of its teachings to our contemporary contexts. Ethical theories provide various emphases and alternatives for understanding moral obligations such as rules, principles, virtues, and consequences. Evangelical ethics is predisposed to utilize Scripture for understanding one's duties, for determining positions on ethical issues, for establishing overarching moral commitments and themes codified as principles, and for character formation and growth in virtue. While these methods have provided clear ways for the use of Scripture in ethics, they also present some difficulties that can be addressed by new possibilities in biblical interpretation for understanding the relationship between Scripture and ethics.

Most typically, evangelical ethics approaches Scripture from a deontological perspective. The Bible is viewed as God's revelation to humankind and contains the rules and prescriptions by which people should live. God, as ultimate authority, issues commands through Scripture that all humans are obligated to obey, and in doing so they fulfill their moral obligations. This method of using Scripture emphasizes its perspicuity, its straightforward meaning in communicating what humans are obligated to do out of duty to God and to other persons. The rules and principles of the Bible are seen as clear, timeless, and universal, applicable to all persons in all contexts.

Evangelical ethics frequently employs Scripture to establish positions on moral issues. Given the inclination in evangelical theology to see Scripture as exhaustive, united in message, complete in what it communicates about God's intentions, and adequate to address every issue that humans will encounter, evangelicals look to Scripture to find a right position on a moral problem, enabling them to support a particular position on an issue by appealing to Scripture.

Sometimes evangelical ethics uses Scripture to determine overarching themes and moral commitments and to establish principles by which to live, often described as moral absolutes. Whereas God is viewed as the divine commander and Scripture is God's rule book for ascertaining what one is to obey from a deontological perspective, using Scripture to find principles by which to live assumes a natural moral order and purpose to the world that God intends humanity to follow. Using the Bible to ascertain moral principles assumes that the principles found in Scripture are easy to understand and what God expects of humanity is clear. By following God's principles found in Scripture, life will be lived well and good will prevail. Some examples of moral principles derived from Scripture to guide behavior are truth-telling and keeping promises, the Golden Rule, loving one's neighbor as oneself, and following established norms for sexual morality.

And often evangelical ethics makes use of Scripture for personal growth and the development of character. Evangelicals look to Scripture for modeling character traits that are pleasing to God for the purpose of becoming a better Christian and, therefore, for becoming more moral and virtuous. Underlying this method is the assumption that in reading Scripture one grows closer to God, which often is seen as the ultimate purpose of one's life. In growing closer to God, one becomes more righteous and more cognizant of how to please God. Scripture is an important aid to this process of spiritual growth. It is a method that privileges one's own morality and personal piety as contributors to the overall ethos of one's community. This method of using Scripture tends to prioritize one's being over one's action, heard in the rhetoric that God cares more about who we are than what we do.

While evangelical ethics provides clear, straightforward, and simple methods for using the Bible in ethics, these methods are also problematic in certain areas. Although Scripture does contain rules and prescriptions, it also contains many other genres that offer moral guidance in forms other than commandments. Simply looking to Scripture to find a rule to follow tends to reduce the ways in which Scripture offers moral guidance through narratives, prophecy, poetry, wisdom literature, epistles, and apocalyptic material. Scripture itself is complex, akin to the complexity of moral decision-making, and it requires various ways of using it to provide guidance for ethics. Another methodological problem in relying on the Bible for prescriptions is the interpretive difficulty in determining which rules should be followed and which ones can be ignored. Given evangelicalism's commitment to the plenary inspiration of the Bible, all that is offered in Scripture is authoritative and normative for theology and ethics, even rules often deemed morally problematic. Therefore, the use of Scripture to determine rules to follow and commands to obey is not as easy as it first appears without the requisite attention to the contexts and narratives in which the commands of Scripture are embedded.

Using Scripture to establish positions on ethical issues also presents hermeneutical and methodological difficulties. The ethical issues that confront people today are not the same as those that confronted people living in the contexts in which biblical texts were written and delivered. Our modern, scientific, and technological societies have presented us with a host of issues that are foreign to the ethical sensibilities of communities described in the Bible and those who first received these writings. Moving from Scripture to a stance on issues not specifically addressed in the Bible presents its own set of challenges for the use of Scripture in evangelical ethics, given the propensity and desire for clear, straightforward biblical answers to complex questions. While the Bible does offer moral guidance in the form of principles, the interpretive challenge remains in evangelical ethics in determining which principles are to be given priority and how these principles are to be lived out in highly complex and diverse contexts. So although neighbor love and the Golden Rule may be binding ethical principles, how to enact these moral commitments is another matter, requiring additional tools of ethical analysis. And although character and virtue are important aspects of Christian moral formation, the use of the Bible in evangelical ethics often attends to individual morality and tends to reduce complex moral issues to problems of personal ethics. The Bible often functions as a private book of devotion and virtue, hiding both the social contexts within which the Scriptures were written and our social contexts, which require more complex means of moral analysis.

A Richer Role for Scripture in Evangelical Ethics

Scripture's use in evangelical ethics can play a richer role with some methodological shifts in emphases that will not undermine the importance of the Bible but will elevate it by giving greater attention to the myriad ways in which morality and ethics are guided by Scripture. The growing interest in reading the Scripture as a narrative can provide a more communal and theological grounding for evangelical ethics that will increase its efficacy to more than just finding moral rules and principles by which to live. Narrative ethics will help evangelicals in their use of Scripture to make important connections with how one is to live and act in light of the overall story that one believes the Scriptures to tell. In this way, evangelical ethics may become more biblical in its justification of certain attitudes and behaviors in light of an expanded understanding of what Scripture is and what it is meant to do.

The use of the Bible in evangelical ethics has been influenced by Western individualism. This influence has minimized the social dimensions of Scripture as texts about the complexities of human communities. A recovery of the communal dimensions of Scripture and its location in ecclesial contexts may correct the over-personalization of Bible reading in evangelical ethics and help to recover the importance of the church as a location of Christian moral formation. This shift may expand the use of Scripture beyond a narrow reliance on duty, principles, and positions to one that sees the rich interaction between the reading and appropriating of Scripture by Christian communities and the formation of morality within the context of the church as a "community of moral discourse, deliberation and discernment" (Verhey 15–20). The renewed interest in a theological interpretation of Scripture can help evangelical ethics make important connections between theology and ethics, as can the renewed interest in the centrality and normativity of Jesus Christ for Christian ethics. Jesus' message and inauguration of the kingdom of God and its embodiment in Christian communities provide a moral framework for both personal and social ethics that can renew evangelical ethics, for imagining the shape and direction of the moral life consonant with the purposes and visions of God discovered when reading the Scriptures, and for informing choices about how to live and why.

See also African American Ethics; Anabaptist Ethics; Baptist Ethics; Deontological Theories of Ethics; Divine Command Theories of Ethics; Golden Rule; Individualism; Narrative Ethics, Biblical; Narrative Ethics, Contemporary; Reformed Ethics; Wesleyan Ethics

Bibliography

Cosgrove, C. *Appealing to Scripture in Moral Debate: Five Hermeneutical Rules*. Eerdmans, 2002; Dayton, D. *Discovering an Evangelical Heritage*. Harper & Row, 1976; Fedler, K. *Exploring Christian Ethics: Biblical Foundations for Morality*. Westminster John Knox, 2006; Grenz, S. *The Moral Quest: Foundations of Christian Ethics*. InterVarsity, 2000; Hollinger, D. *Choosing the Good: Christian Ethics in a Complex World*. Baker Academic, 2002; Mott, S. *Biblical Ethics and Social Change*. Oxford University Press, 1982; O'Donovan, O. *Resurrection and Moral Order: An Outline for Evangelical Ethics*. Eerdmans, 1994; Reuschling, W. *Reviving Evangelical Ethics: The Promises and Pitfalls of Classic Models of Morality*. Brazos, 2008; Spohn, W. *What Are They Saying about Scripture and Ethics?* Paulist Press, 1995; Stassen, G., and D. Gushee. *Kingdom Ethics: Following Jesus in Contemporary Context*. InterVarsity, 2003; Verhey, A. *Remembering Jesus: Christian Community, Scripture, and the Moral Life*. Eerdmans, 2002.

Wyndy Corbin Reuschling

Evangelism

The concept of evangelism can provoke vigorous responses among those who confess Christ and those who do not. Among Christians, responses to the language of evangelism vary from passionate commitment to antagonistic resistance. Perhaps because of an early desire to translate *evangelism* accessibly into English, the term has been too narrowly construed as preaching by a few rather than as witness through practices of love of God and neighbor, including verbal proclamation, by the baptized in and through communities of faith. A closer look throughout Scripture reveals evangelism embodied in the words, practices, and lives of individuals and communities for the purpose of witnessing to, and inviting others to share in, God's reign and salvation in Jesus Christ.

A generally accepted translation of the Greek term *euangelizomai* is "proclaim the gospel, or good news, of salvation in Jesus Christ." The content of the gospel is Jesus, his ministry, life, death, and resurrection. However, as many have noted, although the news of the gospel is ultimately good, it can be difficult for some to hear at first, particularly those comfortably embedded in habits and systems of sin. Another nuance related to a more textured understanding of evangelism is the realization that God is the author of salvation. Although God often invites human participation to share the gospel and initiate persons into God's reign, it is God who saves.

The OT is seldom seen as a source for evangelism, but as Christian Scripture it contains significant foundational themes to the gospel. God invites Israel into covenant relationship, to which Israel responds by living according to the Torah, often represented by the Ten Commandments, which include practices of love of God and neighbor. Although Israel can be seen as an exclusive and sometimes fierce enemy, a central theme in the OT is Israel's witness to the nations of its relationship to God through the covenant. Israel is more often portrayed as a light to the nations through which all may receive the blessings and salvation offered by Israel's God, Yahweh, creator of the universe.

In the NT, Jesus is the Son of God, the Messiah, Emmanuel ("God with us"), sent to Israel and all the nations to bring God's reign and salvation from sin. Inviting others to share in God's reign and the salvation offered by God in Jesus Christ through the Holy Spirit occurs throughout the NT in words and in lives. Indeed, Jesus, as message and messenger, gave his life on the cross to redeem a fallen creation. Although a verbal proclamation of Jesus' message of salvation remains at the heart of evangelism, throughout the Gospels the ministry of evangelism is consistently embodied. When the baptized feed the hungry, tend the sick, and visit the imprisoned, while also verbally narrating the gospel, the salvation of Jesus Christ is not merely told, but is shared, as we participate in evangelism by inviting others to share in God's reign and receive salvation in Jesus Christ through the Holy Spirit.

See also Kingdom of God; Proselytism; Salvation

Laceye C. Warner

Evil

Evil in the Old Testament

The primary term for "evil" in the OT is *rāʿ*. This root can have a moral connotation ("evil, wicked") or a nonmoral connotation ("worthless, trouble, calamity"). As a moral concept, *rāʿ* signifies any activity or state of affairs that is contrary to God's will. In this usage it is closely associated with the Hebraic concept of "sin" (*ḥāṭāʾ*, "to miss the mark"), a term that denotes any activity that violates covenantal faithfulness (Gen. 2:9; Prov. 11:21; 12:13). Evil resides in and springs from the human heart (Gen. 6:5; Prov. 6:14; Eccl. 8:11; Jer. 17:9) and issues forth in a wide variety of sins mentioned throughout the OT, including idolatry (Deut. 4:25), murder (2 Sam. 12:9), and adultery (Deut. 22:22).

Yet, in sharp contrast to the individualistic, secular mind-set of most modern Westerners, the OT does not limit moral evil to human individuals, but also reflects a belief in corporate/structural evil. Without denying the responsibility that individuals bear for their own evil choices, the OT depicts families, tribes, and nations as organic wholes in which individuals are held morally responsible for one another. Hence, when Achan sinned, for example, his whole family was punished and all of Israel suffered (Josh. 7). Similarly, when the wealthy of a nation systematically oppress the poor, the entire nation is vulnerable to God's judgment (Amos 4:1–3; 5:11–12).

While much more subdued than other ancient Near Eastern cultures, the culture of the OT also reflects the understanding that nonhuman agents can be evil and can bring about evil. Thus, for example, the OT mentions various evil spirits (e.g., *šēdîm* [Deut. 32:17; Ps. 106:37] and *śĕʿîrîm* [Lev. 17:7; 2 Chr. 11:15]) as well as various evil spirits that Yahweh uses to judge people (Judg. 9:22–25; 1 Sam. 16:14, 22) (Boyd, *God at War*, 79–83). So too the OT adopts and transforms the ancient Near Eastern understanding of cosmic evil, which scholars commonly refer to as the *Chaoskampf* (chaos struggle) motif. Thus we read about Yahweh battling against threatening hostile waters (e.g., Pss. 29:3–4, 10; 74:10, 13; 77:16; 104:6; Prov. 8:29; Job 7:12; 9:8; 38:8–11; Isa. 51:9–11; Nah. 1:4; Hab. 3:8, 15) as well as menacing cosmic monsters such as Leviathan (Ps. 74:13–14; Job 3:8; 41:1–34; Isa. 27:1), Rahab (Job 9:13; Ps. 89:9–10), and Behemoth (Job 40:15–24) (Wakeman; Day; Boyd, *God at War*, 73–113). Yahweh also must contend with rebellious gods who, though created to form his heavenly council (e.g., 1 Kgs. 22:20; Job 1:6; 2:1; Pss. 82:1; 98:7) and constitute his mighty army (2 Sam. 5:23–24; 2 Kgs. 2:11; 6:16–17; Pss. 34:7; 68:17; 82:1–8; 103:20; Dan. 7:10), have rebelled and now work at cross-purposes with him (e.g., Gen. 6:1–4; Ps. 82; Dan. 10:12–13, 20–21; cf. 1 Kgs. 11:35; 2 Kgs. 3:26–27; 23:13) (Wink 87–127). It is evident that evil in the OT is a cosmic and spiritual reality, as well as a reality of the human heart.

While the OT consistently celebrates the goodness, faithfulness, love, and mercy of God (e.g., Exod. 34:6–7; Deut. 32:4; 2 Sam. 22:31; Pss. 48:1, 9; 89:1–2; 92:15), several texts have led some scholars to conclude that, at least in the earlier stages of Hebrew religion, Yahweh's character included an evil element (Kluger 10; Westermann 16). For example, in Isa. 45:7 Yahweh declares, "I form light and create darkness, I make weal and create woe [*rāʿ*]; I the Lord do all these things" (cf. Amos 3:6; Lam. 3:37–38). As a number of scholars have pointed out, formidable difficulties accompany this view, and in any case these passages are easily understood simply to assert, in specific instances, that it is Yahweh alone who brings blessings and judgments ("calamities") in response to covenant faithfulness or unfaithfulness (Lindstrom).

Evil in the New Testament

The primary terms for "evil" in the NT are *ponēros* and *kakos*. As with the Hebrew term *rāʿ*, both terms can have either a moral or nonmoral connotation. And, as in the OT, when used with a moral connotation, both terms are closely related to the concept of "sin" (*hamartia*, "missing the mark"). The "mark" or moral goal in the NT is best captured by the concept of *agapē*—other-oriented, self-sacrificial love for God and neighbor (Matt. 7:12; 22:36–40; 1 Cor. 13).

The NT goes far beyond the OT in emphasizing the inner, attitudinal nature of both right-relatedness and sin, as seen, for example, in Jesus' six antitheses of the Sermon on the Mount (Matt. 5:21–48). In this sense, the concept of sin is used to denote instances of attitudinal and/or behavior transgression or trespass whereby right-relatedness and *agapē* love are violated for self-centered purposes. According to Paul, all humans have "sinned" in this sense and thus stand under God's judgment and in need of salvation (Rom. 3:23). Reflecting the OT understanding of corporate solidarity, Paul traces this condition back to Adam and Eve's rebellion, when evil first entered the world (Rom. 5:12).

With the advent of the apocalyptic worldview in the centuries leading up to the NT era, the OT view of cosmic evil was greatly intensified and expanded. Thus, Paul views sin not only as a matter of individuals "missing the mark" but also even more fundamentally as a cosmic power that holds all humans in bondage (e.g., Rom. 3:9; 6:6–12; 7:7–20, 23, 25). So too the NT views humans as held in bondage to a variety of evil principalities and powers (e.g., Rom. 8:38; 1 Cor. 15:24; Gal. 4:3, 8–9; Eph. 1:21; 3:10; 6:12; Col. 1:16; 2:8, 10, 15; cf. 1 Pet. 3:22) to such an extent that the entire present age can be construed as fundamentally "evil" (Gal. 1:4; Eph. 5:16). Creation itself is viewed as afflicted and corrupted with evil, waiting for its day of redemption (Rom. 8:19–22).

Significantly, the NT strongly emphasizes that Satan is the ultimate originator and expression of evil. For this reason, Satan is referred to as "the evil one" (*ho ponēros* [Matt. 5:37; 6:13; 13:19; John 17:15; Eph. 6:16; 2 Thess. 3:3; 1 John 2:13–14; 3:12; 5:18–19]), who rules the world (John 12:31; Eph. 2:2; 1 John 5:19) and is depicted as the one ultimately behind all sin, sickness, and death (John 8:44; Acts 10:38; Heb. 2:14). Individual and social evils are thus understood in the NT to be aspects of the kingdom of darkness and its ruler, Satan.

Jesus came to overthrow this kingdom of darkness and to liberate humanity and creation from its oppression, thereby reconciling all of creation to God (1 Cor. 15:20–28; Col. 1:19–20; Heb. 2:14; 1 John 3:8) (Boyd, "Christus Victor"). Understood against the backdrop of the apocalyptic worldview, Jesus' life, ministry, teachings, and especially his death and resurrection are seen as aspects of his messianic war against, and ultimate victory over, Satan, the powers, demons, and human sin (Boyd, "The Kingdom").

Having been liberated, followers of Jesus are called and empowered to manifest his victory in the midst of a world that remains oppressed. As with Jesus, "our struggle is not against enemies of blood and flesh, but against the rulers, against the authorities, against the cosmic powers of this present darkness, against the spiritual forces of evil in the heavenly places" (Eph. 6:12). Our mandate is to reflect God's character and will in our lives and resist sin, social/structural evil, and the kingdom of darkness that fuels it. The promise of God is that there is coming a time when Christ's victory over evil will be fully manifested throughout the earth. When God's kingdom is fully established on the earth, evil will be no more, and God shall be "all in all" (1 Cor. 15:28; cf. Eph. 4:10).

See also Eschatology and Ethics; Goodness; Institution(s); Powers and Principalities; Sin; Theodicy

Bibliography

Boyd, G. "Christus Victor View." Pages 23–49 in *The Nature of the Atonement: Four Views*, ed. J. Beilby and P. Eddy. InterVarsity, 2006; idem. *God at War: The Bible and Spiritual Conflict*. InterVarsity, 1997; idem, "The Kingdom as a Political-Spiritual Revolution." *CTR* 6 (2008): 23–42; Day, J. *God's Conflict with the Dragon and the Sea: Echoes of a Canaanite Myth in the Old Testament*. UCOP 35. Cambridge University Press, 1985; Eichrodt, W. *Theology of the Old Testament*. Trans. J. Baker. 2 vols. OTL. Westminster, 1961; Kluger, R. *Satan in the Old Testament*. Trans. H. Nagel. Northwestern University Press, 1967; Lindstrom, F. *God and the Origin of Evil: A Contextual Analysis of Alleged Monistic Evidence in the Old Testament*. Trans. F. Cryer. Gleerup, 1983; Wakeman, M. *God's Battle with the Monster: A Study in Biblical Imagery*. Brill, 1973; Westermann, C. *Isaiah 40–66*. Trans. D. Stalker. OTL. Westminster, 1969; Wink, W. *Unmasking the Powers: The Invisible Forces That Determine Human Existence*. Fortress, 1986.

Greg Boyd and Paul R. Eddy

Excellence

Of the four NT verses that reference *aretē*, a common term in Hellenistic ethics, three are significant: Phil. 4:8; 2 Pet. 1:3, 5. *Aretē* ("excellence, virtue") concerns skills and qualities of character, acquired over time through practice and effort, that enable persons to live well and/or perform their proper function. The reasons for the term's near absence in the NT are unclear. Perhaps Wolfgang Schrage is correct that it was viewed as overly individualistic.

In Phil. 4:8, Paul affirms "excellence" or "virtue" within a list of admirable traits that would have been familiar in Greek culture. Paul does not assume that the church and broader culture are always at odds. Instead, Paul calls the church to recognize what is true, honorable, just, pure, pleasing, commendable, excellent (*aretē*), and praiseworthy, wherever these qualities are found. In context, this is not a blanket affirmation of the surrounding culture; it is instead a call to discerning appropriation of moral insight, whatever its source. The community is to consider or "think about" these matters in light of Paul's own example and under the rule of the "God of peace," who guards their hearts and minds (Phil. 4:7–9).

In 2 Pet. 1:5, *aretē* occurs within a carefully constructed catalog of qualities toward which we are to exert "every effort." The readers are encouraged "to support" their faith with virtue (*aretē*), knowledge, self-control, endurance, godliness, mutual affection, and love. Allen Verhey rightly notes that this list is interesting due both to a heavy use of Hellenistic vocabulary and to a conception of moral growth in the Christian life via progress in qualities of character. This assimilation of Greek virtues is nevertheless grounded in a response both to God's generosity in providing "everything needed for life and godliness" and to Christ's own "goodness" (*aretē*) (2 Pet. 1:3).

The paucity of NT references to *aretē* suggests to some that the NT lacks interest in or is incompatible with a virtue- or character-oriented approach to ethics. Such a conclusion could be devastating to the contemporary interest in virtue-oriented approaches among many Christian ethicists, but it reads too much into the term's infrequency. Both Phil. 4:8 and 2 Pet. 1:3–7 show openness to virtue or character language and thought patterns. Moreover, without calling them such, Paul made frequent use of lists of virtues and vices (Rom. 1:29–31; 13:13; 1 Cor. 5:10–11; 6:9–10; 2 Cor. 12:20–21; Gal. 5:19–23), and he pictured the Christian moral life in a virtue-like way: as a race requiring effort, self-control, and training (1 Cor. 9:24–27; Phil. 3:11–17; cf. Gal. 2:2; Phil. 2:16). Similarly, again without naming it such, Matthew espouses excellences or virtues such as humility, justice, and integrity (Matt. 5:6–8). Indeed, Benjamin Farley's survey suggests that much of the biblical material is rightly read as promoting specific excellences or virtues, including faith, justice, patience, and hope. As the NT references to *aretē* indicate, the caveats to this affirmation of virtue-thinking are that it should be a discerning appropriation, grounded in grace, and guided by worthy examples such as Paul's and by Christ's own moral excellence.

See also Character; Teleological Theories of Ethics; Vices and Virtues, Lists of; Virtue(s); Virtue Ethics

Bibliography

Farley, B. *In Praise of Virtue: An Exploration of the Biblical Virtues in a Christian Context*. Eerdmans, 1995; Kotva, J. *The Christian Case for Virtue Ethics*. Georgetown University Press, 1996; Schrage, W. *The Ethics of the New Testament*. Trans. D. Green. Fortress, 1987; Verhey, A. *The Great Reversal: Ethics and the New Testament*. Eerdmans, 1986.

Joseph J. Kotva Jr.

Excommunication

Excommunication is the exclusion of a person from participation in the fellowship, worship, and particularly the sacramental life of a religious community. It can name a series of practices (e.g., cursing, banning, shunning) that entail the separation and potentially complete social ostracizing of an individual for the sake of minimizing the threat that this person's moral failure or heretical belief presents to the purity and holiness of the community. The practice of excommunication may appear strange within a modern context of denominationalism and individualism where the church is often more concerned with attracting members than disciplining them. Also problematic is the potential for abusive practices associated with excommunication, in view of the ease with which community discipline has been and can be used for less-than-holy ends.

Scriptural roots and guidance for such practices are found in both Testaments. In the OT, Adam and Eve's expulsion from the garden of Eden and the exile of the covenant community reflect the tradition of the "curse and ban," God's punishment of those individuals or groups that violate the terms of the covenant. Closely related are the laws of ritual purity that ensure the holiness of the community via the separation of the "clean" and the "unclean." Although neither tradition unambiguously constitutes excommunicative practice, both certainly influence later developments of more explicit and structured forms of excommunication in the first-century synagogue, some coinciding with the birth of Christianity as Christians themselves are excommunicated (see John 9:22; 12:42; 16:2). Similar disciplinary practices appear to develop in the early church, particularly evident in Paul's encouragement to exclude those who propagate false teachings (Gal. 1:9) or introduce morally problematic practices (1 Cor. 5:9–13).

However, such exclusions must be held in the light of Jesus' key teaching on excommunication and community discipline in Matt. 18 and the broader witness of his ministry, which overcame the ritualized definitions of clean and unclean. In his embrace of the "sinner," Jesus redefines the nature of holiness, located not in the purity of the community that excludes the unclean but rather in the new "social wholeness" of a reconciled community that embraces the outsider, practices repentance, offers forgiveness, and seeks to extend fellowship (2 Cor. 2:5–11). The character of God's gracious intent is revealed in this and makes visible the mercy that tempers God's judgment; even Adam and Eve are not given the death they deserve but instead continue their story in God's grace and presence, albeit in a new way. Excommunication serves the disciplinary purpose of encouraging repentance and restoration, but it does not nullify the promise of God's grace signified in baptism.

In this context, excommunication finds its place not as censure, or even as insurance of community holiness, but primarily as a description of the world outside the church: dis-membered, excommunicated, and as such, that which the church hopes to overcome in its graceful offer of community constituted by the disciplined hard work of forgiveness, reconciliation, and the sharing of a meal hosted by Jesus and to which all are invited.

See also Accountability; Discipline; Exile; Holiness Code; Punishment

Bibliography

Bonhoeffer, D. *The Cost of Discipleship*. Rev. ed. Macmillan, 1963; Brower, K., and A. Johnson, eds. *Holiness and Ecclesiology in the New Testament*. Eerdmans, 2007; Hein, K. *Eucharist and Excommunication: A Study in Early Christian Doctrine and Discipline*. EH 23/19. Herbert Lang, 1973; Jones, L. *Embodying Forgiveness*. Eerdmans, 1995; Vodola, E. *Excommunication in the Middle Ages*. University of California Press, 1986.

Jeffrey Conklin-Miller

Execution *See* Capital Punishment

Exile

The central issue in discussions of the ethics of exile is how the ethical examples of biblical characters and the values counseled in exilic texts are inevitably contextualized in the events and setting of conquered Israel and Judah. Exilic ethics, therefore, are advised under conditions of subjugation and subordination. A preliminary illustration of the importance of this contextualizing of exilic ethics is the behavior modeled by Abram/Abraham in the famous case where Abraham feared for his life and thus advised deception (Gen. 12:13). If this passage is dated to the time of the postexilic period (so Brett), then it must be read as a "subcultural" or even "survival" ethic—that is, misinforming the authorities for the sake of survival. Such ethical behavior may not be exemplary for "institutionalized" or "mainstream" ethics (the determination of which is always the privilege of the powerful), but may well be considered wise behavior in the context of subordination to hostile power. Therefore, any discussion of the ethical significance of biblical behaviors modeled or counseled in exilic texts cannot be separated from consideration of the events themselves.

Assessing the Historical Impact of the Exile

The historic importance of the exile and its impact on the life and faith of ancient Israel have not been matters of universal agreement in the last century of biblical scholarship. Charles Torrey, for example, famously wrote that the exile "was in reality a small and relatively insignificant affair" (Torrey 285). Early in the twenty-first century, however, as a result of both new archaeological work and recent interdisciplinary study of biblical texts (especially when read in comparison with literature on refugee studies, post-traumatic stress disorder, and minority existence), the situation has dramatically changed. In his most recent survey of archaeological work, Oded Lipschitz refers to material evidence of "Nebuchadnezzar's desire to eliminate Jerusalem as a religious and political center" and summarizes what he calls "the totality of the devastation" (Lipschitz 80). He concludes, "The demographic evidence thus supports the previous hypothesis that Jerusalem remained desolate throughout the time of Babylonian Rule" (Lipschitz 218). The total population of Judah at the end of the Iron Age is estimated at 108,000, but at the beginning of the Persian period at 30,125 (Lipschitz 270). It should not be surprising, then, that Rainer Albertz begins the most comprehensive recent summary of the exilic period in biblical history and literature with these words: "Of all the eras in Israel's history, the exilic period represents the most profound . . . [and] radical change. Its significance for subsequent history can hardly be overstated. Here, the religion of Israel underwent its most severe crisis" (Albertz 1).

A more radical transformation in biblical scholarship is hard to conceive. The events themselves are easily summarized. The short-lived "united" monarchy of ancient Israel existed from about 1020 BCE to the death of Solomon in about 722 BCE. After Solomon's death, the Hebrew tribal territories split into rival political entities: the northern "state" of Israel, and the southern "state" of Judah, based in Jerusalem. Before long, however, the assertion of power from Mesopotamian regimes to the east eroded any sense of independence on the part of these small, rival states in Palestine (not only Judah and Israel but also Damascus, Moab, Edom, Ammon, and others). The Neo-Assyrian Empire conquered the northern state of Israel in 722 BCE, and Sennacherib also devastated Judah in 701, but Judah was not fully conquered and made into a Neo-Assyrian province as the north certainly was. Still, the devastation of colonial control by Assyria had its continued impact on Israelite and Judean territories.

A century later the rising power was the Neo-Babylonian Empire. In their military attempts to possess Egypt, the Babylonians needed the corridor down the Mediterranean coast clear and under control; thus, Judah was "in the way." Judah, at first, surrendered to Babylon in 597 BCE, after a siege, and a number of prisoners of war were exiled into separate communities in the Babylonian heartland. Ten years later, the remaining Judean political vassal of Babylon, Zedekiah, tried to revolt with promised assistance from Egypt, and the results were catastrophic. The deportations associated with the Babylonian conquests of Judah are normally referred to as "the Babylonian exile." Substantial Diaspora communities were permanently planted in the eastern regions of Mesopotamian and Persian territories from the sixth century BCE onward, and remained well into the modern period. The biblical literature from the time of the Babylonian conquests consists of writings from both the homeland and the Diaspora, and often it reflects relations between the two kinds of communities (homeland and Diaspora). However, given the universal agreement that the writings that would later be canonized into the Jewish and Christian Scriptures were gathered, widely edited, and many actually written after the devastations of the sixth century BCE, the Bible as we now read it is largely the product of the conditions of Diaspora and occupation.

With regard to the Neo-Babylonian policies, David Vanderhooft surmises that Nebuchadnezzar's western ventures had monetary motivations as well (Vanderhooft 82, 209). Furthermore, following the Babylonian Empire, the Persian "economy" was also a system for the hoarding of precious metals facilitated by a massive tax and labor (Frye 114–15). These realities continue right through to the Hellenistic period under the Ptolemies and Seleucids (Green 187). Irrespective of the very real differences between the political and ideological regimes from 587 to 164 BCE and into the Roman period, any discussion of biblical ethics must be attentive to the stubborn realities of ancient imperial designs toward power and control over wealth, territory, and human resources.

Situating an Ethics of Exile

A number of ethical issues are raised when biblical literature of the period is read in a social context featuring these sociopolitical dynamics. First, there is the problem of "public transcripts" and "private transcripts" (Scott 1985; 1990), which refers to ideas that may be discussed within a minority community, as opposed to those ideas intended for public consumption. As Eftihia Voutira and Barbara Harrell-Bond illustrate, this has been an important emphasis in refugee studies: "To be a refugee means to learn to lie" (Voutira and Harrell-Bond 216). One of the most important arenas for ethical debate, therefore, is the relation of the subordinated to the powerful.

It hardly seems necessary to emphasize that such perspectives would dramatically change a modern reading of, say, the stories of Dan. 1–6. These can be read naively as mere counsels to faithfulness, but in their context they also must be read as stories of religious and social resistance to assimilation. Furthermore, the Daniel stories clearly represent a counsel to be highly suspicious of imperial power as well as a call to maintain identity in a hostile social and political environment.

Finally, the notion that the stories of Daniel suggest vaguely "positive" evaluation of emperors should not be easily taken to mean that the biblical texts reveal positive feelings about living in the shadows of empires. Even the case of Nehemiah, whose role as "cupbearer" often is cited as an example of the potential for success among Diaspora Jews, must be carefully reconsidered in historical context. How much of an honor is it to be chosen to be the taster of food for the emperor, thus the one who will die first if anyone tries to poison the emperor? This is hardly a success story; rather, it merely reveals the ambiguity of living under a regime and the expendability of minorities, and it reveals Hebrew stories that must calculate public relations as an element of domination.

In sum, the ethics of exile must be explicated in the context of oppression and fear. If not, then such ethical reflection is insufficiently biblical. With these foundational observations in place, then, the following are suggested as potentially important ethical themes arising from a consideration of exilic contexts and literatures of the Bible.

Communal solidarity and definition. It is widely noted that the language of the Mosaic legal tradition changes rather significantly from the earlier Covenant Code (Exodus) to the more compassionate language used in the Deuteronomic Code (dated, at the earliest, to the reign of Josiah, 640–609 BCE, but amended to include references to exile [e.g., Deut. 28:49–68]). Among the more compelling aspects of the Deuteronomic Code are counsels to mutual aid—care for fellow Hebrews (and even non-Hebrews) typified especially by a concern for the indigent (widow, orphan, foreigner). Many laws instituting care for the poor are unique to the later law code (e.g., gleaning [Deut. 24:19], provisions for hunger [Deut. 24:20]) and suggest an increased social solidarity among the Hebrew people that may well be tied directly to a sense of common threat in the Assyrian and Babylonian periods.

Another aspect of communal solidarity is the behavior of community members toward one another. There is evidence that this was an increasingly serious concern in the exilic and postexilic contexts. The specific Greek (LXX) addition to Daniel known as the book of Susanna is a clear case of internal conflict and corruption within the community. We know that such issues of internal corruption and behavior also continued to be serious issues right into the Roman period, where such concerns arguably define the conflicts between Jesus and his followers on the one side, and hostile members of his own tradition on the other, who see his teachings as inviting trouble from Roman authorities (e.g., John 11:48).

Later Persian and Hellenistic literature, such as the book of Tobit, also maintains a strong emphasis on service to others within the community (see Tob. 4:13–18). Again, much of the context of the NT ethics of Jesus is illuminated by this emphasis on communal solidarity (see Horsley and Silberman).

Solidarity and group identity. The importance of group cohesion in circumstances of oppression can hardly be overemphasized. Any minority must attend to issues of identity and definition. How are "we" to be defined in distinction from variously identified "others"? In the exilic biblical literature, however, there are clear signs of debate with regard to the ethics of this process of self-identity and maintaining faithful communities. For example, Ezra's concern for the "purity" of the exilic community (e.g., the "pure seed" [Ezra 9:2]) clearly reflected an emphasis on maintaining separations and boundaries that maintained identity in circumstances of exile and minority existence. The matter of actually divorcing all foreign wives, however, appears to have stirred debate, given that we have contrary views stated in postexilic biblical literature as well, most famously the story of Ruth (whose obvious status of acceptance in the story is a direct violation of Ezra's own counsel against Moabites [Ezra 9:1]) and in the counsel of the late texts of Isaiah (Isa. 56:3). Clearly, a major ethical issue involved the definition of, and integrity of the boundaries of, the "authentic" people of faith. The problem of conversion is obviously a related issue, and it haunts any reading of the book of Jonah or of Isa. 19, where even Assyrians and Egyptians will be included in the future definition of the people of God. There are a variety of texts suggesting exilic hopes that foreigners will learn to be well disposed toward Hebrews and Hebrew faith, even if falling short of a campaign of conversion (e.g., Zech. 8:22–23). But actual converts did exist, and thus how converts are to be treated (e.g., book of Ezra: rejection; book of Ruth: acceptance) is another ethical issue of relations with foreigners that continues to define the ethics of communal identity and integrity clear through the Hellenistic period (e.g., in works such as the noncanonical *Joseph and Aseneth*) and even into the NT debates between Paul and the so-called Judaizers, as outlined in Acts 15–16.

Violence and nonviolence in relation to outsiders. The issue of how "we" relate to "them" finds its utmost expression in the problem of violence. For example, the postexilic warning in Prov. 1 about being tempted to lives of urban crime (Prov. 1:10–19, esp. v. 13) is suggestive of the temptations toward banditry and criminal behavior in the Diaspora or under occupation. But this can also be expressed in the more acceptable language of nationalism and language of "restoration" (1 Maccabees is clearly restorationist). How to relate to non-Hebrews when living as a minority or under occupation is a major ethical debate reflected in exilic and postexilic biblical texts. There are texts that suggest Hebrew involvement in violence, as well as texts calling for apocalyptic punishment by God and angels of destruction (the apocalyptic tradition).

Angry exilic texts calling for vengeance against foreigners (e.g., Ps. 137; Jer. 50–51; Obadiah) are not, however, the only voices of counsel in the postexilic literature. The story of Jonah profoundly holds out the hope of a transformation of the enemy (and thus Hebrew nonviolent involvement in instigating that transformation), a tendency that seems closely related to the call of Isa. 49:6 to be a "light to the nations." Furthermore, Jeremiah's letter to the exiles (Jer. 29:4–23) has often been read as a counsel against fomenting revolution in the Diaspora. In this letter, Jeremiah cites the well-known exemptions from military activity (Deut. 20) to proclaim an armistice on the Diaspora communities, and then he concludes this section of the letter by counseling that these Jewish minority communities should "seek the peace [*šālôm*] of the city where I have sent you" (Jer. 29:7). It is likely that a disagreement on violent revolution versus nonviolent involvement was at the heart of the policy disputes illustrated by the public debates between Hananiah and Jeremiah in Jer. 28.

Resistance and cooperation in regard to governing authorities. How far can a member of a minority cooperate with the governing authorities? The positive values are continued life, potential prosperity, and even influence (1 Kgs. 8:50 clearly hopes for this) against the dangers of assimilation and loss of identity and thus also faith. Diaspora stories such as Esther, Nehemiah, and Daniel hold out the possibilities of some kind of advancement and prosperity even under the conquerors' regimes (even if the stories are not taken literally), but they all also raise the dangers of assimilation and loss of faith and identity. Potential for influence goes from the minimal desire to simply be left alone (thus 1 Kgs. 8:50) to the possibility of actually influencing public policy in relation to Hebrew existence (Esther).

Discovering a common ethical language. Finally, it is interesting to note the widespread use of the wisdom genre in postexilic texts. The inclusion of large amounts of foreign wisdom sayings in Israelite works (e.g., Egyptian wisdom in Prov. 22–23; Platonic thought in Wis. 9:15) suggests that the writers of these works we now identify as "wisdom literature" were, at the very least, involved in dialogue with non-Hebrews. This may well explain the pious but hardly uniquely Israelite character of the ethical maxims of wisdom literature: it is, rather, universal in scope and application and represents a sector of Israelite society that was finding a common ethical language for discussion with non-Hebrews. This would further explain the common counsel of the wisdom literature to reasoned discussion as opposed to short-tempered (and ill-considered) violence (e.g., Prov. 16:7; 17:9, 14, 22; 24:5–6; 25:15; Eccl. 9:13–18a). The influence of wisdom traditions carries through the Hellenistic period and into the NT writings as well (e.g., Matt. 7:24–27; James).

The ethics of exile in biblical literature consists of a discussion of ethical models and counsels of behavior that cannot be separated from the lived realities of subjugation and occupation. Such a context helps to explain the emphasis in exilic and postexilic biblical literature on a matrix of interrelated ethical issues such as communal solidarity, relations with outsiders, and relations to the dominant power.

See also Additions to Daniel; Daniel

Bibliography

Albertz, R. *Israel in Exile: The History and Literature of the Sixth Century B.C.E.* Trans. D. Green. SBL 3. Society of Biblical Literature, 2003; Brett, M. *Genesis: Procreation and the Politics of Identity*. Routledge, 2000; Frye, R. *The Heritage of Persia*. Weidenfeld & Nicolson, 1962; Green, P. *Alexander to Actium: The Historical Evolution of the Hellenistic Age*. University of California Press, 1990; Horsley, R., and N. Silberman. *The Message and the Kingdom: How Jesus and Paul Ignited a Revolution and Transformed the Ancient World*. Fortress, 2002; Lipschitz, O. *The Fall and Rise of Jerusalem: Judah under Babylonian Rule*. Eisenbrauns, 2005; Scott, J. *Domination and the Arts of Resistance: Hidden Transcripts*. Yale University Press, 1990; idem. *Weapons of the Weak: Everyday Forms of Peasant Resistance*. Yale University Press, 1985; Smith-Christopher, D. *A Biblical Theology of Exile*. Fortress, 2002; Torrey, C. "The Exile and the Restoration." Pages 285–340 in *Ezra Studies*. LBS. Ktav, 1970 [1910]; Vanderhooft, D. *The Neo-Babylonian Empire and Babylon in the Latter Prophets*. HSM 59. Scholars Press, 2002; Voutira, E., and B. Harrell-Bond. "In Search of the Locus of Trust: The Social World of the Refugee Camp." Pages 207–24 in *Mistrusting Refugees*, ed. D. Valentine and J. Knudsen. University of California Press, 1996.

Daniel Smith-Christopher

Exodus

The book of Exodus recounts God's liberation of the Israelites from slavery and their departure from Egypt (chaps. 1–15), the challenges of the journey through the wilderness (chaps. 16–18), the establishment of a special covenant relationship between God and Israel at Mount Sinai (chaps. 19–24), the breaking and restoring of the covenant in the incident of the golden calf (chaps. 32–34), and the building of the tabernacle as a visible sign of God's holy presence in the midst of the Israelite community (chaps. 25–31; 35–40).

Ethical Issues in Exodus 1–15

Women and civil disobedience. Exodus begins with the Bible's first instance of peaceful civil disobedience against an oppressive empire. The two Hebrew midwives refuse to carry out Pharaoh's orders to kill the male babies of the enslaved Hebrew minority community (1:8–22). Women—including Pharaoh's daughter, who disobeys her own father's decrees (2:1–10)—also figure prominently in rescuing the baby Moses.

The use of violence for the sake of social justice? Moses secretly kills an Egyptian supervisor who was beating a Hebrew slave (2:11–15). Was Moses justified in this act of violence for the sake of social justice? Both Jewish and Christian interpreters have differed widely in answering that question. The biblical text itself does not render a clear verdict one way or the other, inviting readers to contemplate the complex ethical issues involved.

The ten plagues: Justice and ecology. God sends a series of ten plagues upon the Egyptians in an effort to persuade Pharaoh to let the Israelites go (chaps. 7–13). These anticreational plagues that disturb the natural order and balance of nature may be understood as ecological disasters that are the consequences of Pharaoh's human injustice, which disturbs the moral order of the cosmos (Fretheim 105–11).

The hardening of Pharaoh's heart: Human freedom and divine determinism. Exodus brings the theme of God's "hardening Pharaoh's heart" (9:12; 10:1, 20, 27; 11:10; 14:4, 8) together with other texts that speak of Pharaoh's "hardening" his own heart (7:22; 8:32; 9:34). The motif of the hardening of the heart appears to hold human free will and divine determinism together in complex interplay. But at some point later in the plague sequence, Pharaoh's sin becomes so engrained that he reaches a point of no return. It is then that God hardens Pharaoh's heart.

God's liberation of the poor or of Israel? The story of God's liberation of slaves living under oppressive conditions in Egypt has been a defining narrative for many exponents of liberation theology and postcolonial criticism of the Bible. The exodus story, they argue, reflects the dynamics of oppressive empires and God's preferential option for the poor. Others argue that the biblical form of the exodus story is primarily not about God's preference for the poor in general but rather for the people of Israel in particular. Yet Israel's laws do refer to Israel's experience in Egypt as a motivation for justice and generosity to slaves, the poor, resident aliens, and other marginalized members of the society (22:21; 23:9; Deut. 15:12–15).

The Ten Commandments—Exodus 20:1–17

The centerpiece of the covenant on Mount Sinai is the Decalogue, or Ten Commandments. The first and most important commandment demands singular loyalty: "You shall have no other gods before me" (20:3). This is followed by a ban on all graven images or idols (20:4–6), which Israel would soon disobey in the incident of the golden calf (32:1–24). Other commandments prohibit the misuse of God's name, require the observance of a Sabbath day of rest every seven days, and obligate children to honor their parents. The commandments conclude by prohibiting murder, adultery, stealing, bearing false witness against a neighbor, and coveting what belongs to a neighbor (20:7–17). The commandments hold together obligations to God with obligations to humans and also to nonhuman creation (20:10).

The Covenant Code—Exodus 20:22–23:19

Most scholars argue that these laws are some of the oldest laws of the Bible. They resemble other law codes of the ancient Near East in their form of case law with conditional statements followed by consequences or penalties. These laws cover a wide range of quite specific circumstances within an ancient society. Since they follow immediately after the more generalized Ten Commandments, the Covenant Code functions as an illustrative exposition of how the Ten Commandments might be applied in specific rulings. The juxtaposition of the Decalogue and the Covenant Code signals the need for ongoing legal and ethical interpretation and application to specific contexts.

The Golden Calf—Exodus 32–34

Israel's first great sin is to make and worship a golden calf while Moses is away on top of Mount Sinai with God. The disobedience is so severe that God initially plans to destroy all Israel (32:10). However, Moses successfully intercedes with God so that God does not completely destroy the Israelites (32:11–14). Moses also convinces God to reveal something deeper about the divine character and goodness that has not been seen before. In the process, God reveals his name and character, shown to be grounded much more in his love, faithfulness, mercy, and forgiveness (34:6–7) than previous presentations of God's name and character in Exodus indicate (see 3:13–16; 20:5–6; 23:20–21). However, obedience to God's newly reformulated laws continues to be required, and consequences remain in effect for acts of disobedience (34:7, 10–28).

See also Civil Disobedience; Colonialism and Postcolonialism; Covenant; Ecological Ethics; Free Will and Determinism; Idolatry; Law; Liberation; Liberationist Ethics; Old Testament Ethics; Preferential Option for the Poor; Sabbath; Slavery; Ten Commandments; Violence

Bibliography

Fretheim, T. *Exodus*. IBC. Westminster John Knox, 1991; Levenson, J. "Exodus and Liberation." *HBT* 13 (1991): 134–74; Meyers, C. *Exodus*. NCamBC. Cambridge University Press, 2005; Olson, D. "The Jagged Cliffs of Mount Sinai: A Theological Reading of the Book of the Covenant (Exod. 20:22–23:19)." *Int* 50 (1996): 251–63; idem. "Violence for the Sake of Social Justice? Narrative, Ethics, and Indeterminacy in Exodus 2:11–15." Pages 138–48 in *The Meanings We Choose: Hermeneutical Ethics, Indeterminacy and the Conflict of Interpretations*, ed. C. Cosgrove. JSOTSup 411. T&T Clark International, 2004; Pixley, G., and C. Boff. "A Latin American Perspective: The Option for the Poor in the Old Testament." Pages 207–16 in *Voices from the Margin: Interpreting the Bible in the Third World*, ed. R. Sugirtharajah. Orbis, 2006.

Dennis T. Olson

Exploitation

The basic premise of exploitative activity is intrinsically related to notions of power, control, and dominion and how these are utilized by moral agents in their relationship with others. Exploitation assumes a relationship between two or more moral agents—the exploiter and the exploited—and it is in this dynamic relationship that power is instrumental in defining exploitation.

From the perspective of biblical ethics, all power comes from God (Matt. 6:13; John 19:11; Rom. 13:1), and God is by definition all-powerful; therefore, power itself is not morally pernicious, but the way that power is exercised determines the moral value of it. How, then, does God employ power? In answering this question, some have argued that the biblical narrative contains cases in which God uses power in an exploitative manner. Examples cited by those who follow this approach include God asking Abraham to offer his son in sacrifice, God's role in the story of Job, and God's influence in directing Jesus to his death at the cross. In the interpretation of these stories the common denominator is that power is being employed exclusively for the benefit of the powerful—God—and thus the ones with "inferior" power become victims of exploitation. In response to this interpretation, others have suggested that in these and other stories God does not obtain personal benefit, nor does God make a profit for personal gain, but rather God respects the will of moral agents and does not coerce them to do what is being asked, and what God is doing is asking a question in a framework of respect in a given relationship. It is in this last approach that the essence of exploitation becomes evident, which is the use of power by a moral agent—person, institution, and/or state—to obtain personal benefits at the expense of others by coercing them against their will and in some instances by inflicting physical harm.

Exploitation calls for an analysis of power, first to determine the power differential among participants, and second to determine if one or more agents are employing their privileged position to impose their agenda and/or will on others. However, it is important to note that in the biblical narrative exploitation is not exclusive to relationships between individuals and/or institutions, but also includes the environment. Although the environment itself is not a moral agent, having neither individual nor corporate will, institutions and individuals are in many ways in relationship with the environment. When they use their power as dominion and control for self-centered reasons and to obtain personal benefit, these practices constitute exploitative acts against nature and should be deemed morally wrong and as reprehensible as other practices including individuals and institutions.

See also Authority and Power; Manipulation; Submission and Subordination

Bibliography

Allen, J. *Love and Conflict: A Covenantal Model of Christian Ethics*. Abingdon, 1984; Hinze, C. *Comprehending Power in Christian Social Ethics*. AARAS 93. Scholars Press, 1995; Wink, W. *Engaging the Powers: Discernment and Resistance in a World of Domination*. Fortress, 1992.

Hugo Magallanes

Ezekiel

The book of Ezekiel is the third major prophetic work in the OT, attributed to Ezekiel son of Buzi, a Jerusalem priest deported to Babylonia by Nebuchadnezzar in 597 BCE. The book falls into three parts: chapters 1–24 are mainly oracles of judgment against Jerusalem and Judah, chapters 25–32 are oracles against the nations, and chapters 33–48 are principally taken up with promises of restoration, including the visions of the dry bones (37:1–14) and the new temple (40–48). The book is punctuated by dramatic visions of God, which set the scene for the prophet's call in exile (1:1–28), then describe Yahweh's abandonment of his temple to destruction (8–11) and return to his new dwelling place at the heart of a perfected Israel (43:1–9).

Sources and Assumptions

Ezekiel's ethic is fundamentally one of obedience to God's will revealed in "statutes and ordinances" (5:6–7; 11:12, 20; 18:17; 20:11; 36:27). Ezekiel draws on a range of earlier traditions, but the priestly influence is preeminent, and Ezekiel is much more positive about worship and ritual than are prophetic predecessors such as Amos and Micah. The prophet's personal commitment to purity is evident in his claim never to have defiled himself with unclean food (4:14). His moral language is heavily dependent on priestly forms of speech; his arguments often resemble priestly case law (14:1–11, 12–20; 18:1–32 [cf. Lev. 17; 19]); and his analysis of Israel's behavior is full of ritual concepts such as defilement, profanation, and purification. From the perspective of exile, where all Judah's old certainties are crumbling, Ezekiel succeeds in keeping the temple as a focal point for communal values and aspirations (Mein). As a priest, Ezekiel places a high value on hierarchy and order (especially visible in 40–48), and honor and shame also play a significant part in the prophet's worldview. Indeed, the logic of the book (seen in a nutshell in 36:16–32) is that Yahweh has been shamed by Israel's disobedience, and that both judgment and salvation are "for the sake of my holy name" (36:22).

Moral Issues

Ezekiel's oracles of judgment condemn Judah's failings in three main areas: cultic apostasy, political faithlessness, and social injustice. However, the main purpose of these oracles is not social analysis but rather theodicy. Ezekiel's task is to persuade the exiles that the current disaster is fully under Yahweh's control, indeed that it is Yahweh's only possible response to Jerusalem's grievous sins. In turn, the oracles of restoration promise a divine re-creation of both individuals and national institutions that will preclude the possibility of disobedience.

Responsibility is perhaps the key ethical theme in the book. Ezekiel 18 overturns the exiles' claim that their current troubles are not their fault but rather that of their parents. By setting out a test case in which each of three related individuals—a wicked father, a righteous son, and a wicked grandson—is judged on the basis of his own sins, Ezekiel challenges his hearers to take responsibility for their own situation. Past scholarship saw Ezekiel as the great herald of individual responsibility, moving beyond more "primitive" notions of corporate responsibility and punishment visible in both the Decalogue and the Historical Books. Ezekiel's contribution probably is more modest than a wholesale ethical revolution; rather, he takes ideas of individual responsibility that had long prevailed in legal proceedings and applies them afresh to the matter of divine judgment (Joyce).

Jacqueline Lapsley notes a tension in Ezekiel between different understandings of the moral self. The calls to repent (14:6; 18:32) presuppose that human beings have the capacity to do good and to reform themselves, whereas the promise of the new heart (11:19; 36:26) is both more deterministic and more pessimistic about the possibility of human virtue. It is the deterministic view that ultimately predominates in the book, as we see a shift from Jerusalem's responsibility for judgment to Israel's passivity in the face of restoration. Andrew Mein sees this theological shift as also reflecting the social experience of Ezekiel's hearers, who have moved from positions of power and responsibility in Jerusalem to live with the much more limited moral possibilities of life in exile.

The force of Ezekiel's rhetoric at times raises its own moral difficulties. This is most true of the two chapters (16; 23) in which Jerusalem is portrayed as a promiscuous wife, guilty of adultery and murder, destined for shame and brutal punishment. The rhetoric works by placing Ezekiel's (probably male) hearers in the position of a shamed and degraded woman and thereby shocking them into accepting their guilt. At the same time, it implies that women's sexuality is wild, defiling, and in need of control, and feminist critics warn that an ethical reading of these metaphorical texts must take into account their potential to perpetuate male dominance and even to justify violence against real women.

Contribution

Ezekiel's readers have sometimes been ambivalent about the prophet's contribution to ethics. Recent concerns about gender follow on earlier criticism of the prophet's emphasis on ritual. However, Ezekiel's very strangeness helpfully marks the distance between our world and that of the texts and reminds us that biblical prophecy does not approach ethics in a sanitized, theoretical way. The oracles arise out of the pain and confusion of the Babylonian deportations and the destruction of Jerusalem. Driven by an absolute conviction of God's holiness and power, the prophet articulates views of responsibility, free will, and social order that are still contested in contemporary ethical discourse.

See also Feminist Ethics; Free Will and Determinism; Old Testament Ethics; Priestly Literature

Bibliography

Block, D. *The Book of Ezekiel*. 2 vols. NICOT. Eerdmans, 1997–98; Darr, K. "Ezekiel's Justifications of God: Teaching Troubling Texts." *JSOT* 55 (1992): 97–117; Joyce, P. *Divine Initiative and Human Response in Ezekiel*. JSOTSup 51. JSOT Press, 1989; Lapsley, J. *Can These Bones Live? The Problem of the Moral Self in the Book of Ezekiel*. BZAW 301. De Gruyter, 2000; Matties, J. *Ezekiel 18 and the Rhetoric of Moral Discourse*. SBLDS 126. Scholars Press, 1990; Mein, A. *Ezekiel and the Ethics of Exile*. OThM. Oxford University Press, 2001; Odell, M. *Ezekiel*. SHBC. Smyth & Helwys, 2005; Odell, M., and J. Strong, eds. *The Book of Ezekiel: Theological and Anthropological Perspectives*. SBLSymS 9. Society of Biblical Literature, 2000.

Andrew Mein

Ezra

The books of Ezra and Nehemiah are considered a single volume in the Jewish canon. Ezra-Nehemiah recounts events in Judah during two distinct periods, of approximately a quarter century each, in the postexilic era. The first (538–515 BCE) covers the return of the Jews from Babylon and the subsequent reconstruction of the temple (Ezra 1:1–6:22). The second (458–433 BCE) covers Ezra's commission to teach the Torah in Jerusalem and the appointment of Nehemiah as governor (Ezra 7:1–Neh. 13:31).

The narratives of both the temple reconstruction and Ezra's marriage reform serve to identify the authentic Israel after the exile as consisting of the families of Judah and Benjamin along with the Levites and priests, who returned to Judah from Babylon (Ezra 1:5; 2:1–67; 4:1; 10:9). The "people of the land," foreigners who remained in the territory throughout the exile, must have no part in the reconstituted community. Zerubbabel, the leader, and Joshua, the priest, forbid them from working on the temple project, while Ezra demands that Judahite men sever marriage ties with foreign women (Ezra 4:1–3; 6:21; 10:2–3, 10–11). Ezra's marriage reform aims at preserving the "holy seed" by separating the exiles, who returned to Judah, from all outsiders (Ezra 9:1–2; 10:6–9, 44).

The book of Ezra invites reflection on the rights of refugees to return to their native territories and reconstitute their communities. Although underwritten by the Persian authorities, Ezra's reform is an exercise in ethnic self-determination. The text, however, sustains only one voice in a debate among various factions that claimed membership in the reconstituted Israel of the postexilic era. The author asserts the rigorist position of those "who tremble at the words/commandment of God" (Ezra 9:4; 10:3) by narrowly defining the community as consisting of the exiles from the families of Judah, Benjamin, and Levi. The reader needs to contemplate, however, the protests from the people of the land who are the subject matter of the correspondence between regional authorities and the Persian administration (Ezra 4:1–2, 7–22; 5:3–6:12). More important, a modern reader must protest the absence of any advocacy on behalf of the women and children whom the leaders banish from the community (Ezra 10:44).

Ezra's marriage reform extends beyond earlier tradition insofar as the Torah does not stipulate that Israelites must divorce their foreign wives. However, his reform appeals to the Deuteronomic laws excluding Ammonites and Moabites from the assembly of Yahweh and prohibiting Israelites from marrying foreigners who reside in the land (Ezra 9:1–2, 11–12; 10:10; cf. Deut. 7:1–4; 23:3–6). These precepts would rule out the marriage of the Moabite Ruth into the Judahite family of Elimelech and ultimately to Boaz (Ruth 2:1; 4:7–17). Indeed, Ezra would have banished from the reformed community Ruth and her son Obed, ancestors of David. The story of Ruth suggests a vision of inclusivity in contrast to the exclusivity of Ezra's covenant community.

See also Nehemiah; Old Testament Ethics; Ruth

Bibliography

Blenkinsopp, J. *Judaism, the First Phase: The Place of Ezra and Nehemiah in the Origins of Judaism*. Eerdmans, 2009; Grabbe, L. *Ezra-Nehemiah*. OTR. Routledge, 1998; Williamson, H. *Ezra and Nehemiah*. WBC 16. Word, 1985.

Michael W. Duggan

F

Faith

Theologically, faith expresses the fundamental disposition or response of the human person to God. Faith in God sets the standard for other faiths, sometimes unseating them: "Trust [*bāṭaḥ*] in the LORD with all your heart, and do not rely on your own insight" (Prov. 3:5).

In Hebrew, the basic sense of *ʾmn*, from which we get not only *ʾĕmûnâ* ("faith") but also "amen," is "to be dependable." Various forms of *ʾĕmûnâ* occur forty-eight times in the OT and are variously rendered as "truth," "faithfulness," and, occasionally, "faith." Nevertheless, the concept of faith, linked also with "trust" (*bāṭaḥ*), is foundational to all the biblical writings.

The Greek noun *pistis* (verb *pisteuō*; adjective *pistos*) is used more than 240 times in the NT, with various nuances. Sometimes the verb *pisteuō* is rendered "to believe," which connotes assent to certain truths. Yet one might hold a truth but lack faith. So James warns, "You believe that God is one; you do well. Even the demons believe—and shudder" (2:19). James's concern is that faith not be merely cerebral or internal: "Faith [*pistis*] by itself, if it has no works, is dead" (2:17).

Catholic tradition especially conceives faith (with hope and love) as one of three theological virtues. Since virtues are habits, settled dispositions to act, faith must do work. Moreover, virtues are something we "have"; faith dwells in us, transforming us. So Jesus urges his disciples to "have faith," which proves difficult, especially in crisis. In a storm Jesus says to them, "Why are you afraid, you of little faith?" (Matt. 8:26). Certain other characters in the Gospels have faith more easily. Jesus tells a centurion who is certain that Jesus can heal his servant, "In no one in Israel have I found such faith" (Matt. 8:10). If the disciples can come to have faith, beginning small like a mustard seed, it can deepen and grow powerful, moving mountains (Matt. 17:20).

Faith's growth comes also with spreading, as it forms faith communities that extend through time. This nuance is extended in the NT letters when the definite article is twinned with *pistis*, as in "I have kept the faith" (2 Tim. 4:7)—as we say today, "the Christian faith" or "our faith tradition." Although a Christian's faith involves more than assent to certain truths, it nonetheless requires such assent. Christian faith eschews the modern notion "faith in myself"; faith is always shared, and it is passed on from the apostles. So Paul wants to make sure that the members of the church in Philippi are "standing firm in one spirit, striving side by side for the faith of the gospel" (Phil. 1:27). Faith in this sense is a stronghold, or a shield (Eph. 6:16), that protects and surrounds an individual, rooting that person in the church. In the words of the Roman Communion Rite: "Lord, look not on our sins, but on the faith of thy church."

The notion of shared faith mitigates the dispute, sometimes portrayed as dividing Protestant and Catholic Christians, of faith's relation to works, especially in connection with salvation. Paul presses that we are reconciled to God "not by works of the law but through faith in Jesus Christ" (Gal. 2:16). Abraham models faith, not only because he "believed God, and it was reckoned to him as righteousness" (Gal. 3:6) but also because he acted on a promise. "Works-righteousness" lacks faith not by working, but by purporting to achieve salvation by its own effort, which is idolatrous for both Catholics and Protestants. Not only is faith received from God (Eph. 2:8) but also we know it from our forebears, as the litany in Heb. 11 recalls: "by faith Abraham . . . offered up Isaac" (v. 17), "by faith [Moses] kept the Passover" (v. 28), and so on. Christian faith always depends on a prior gift, but it must live anew in each age.

The book of Hebrews also provides the basic definition of faith as a requisite Christian virtue. "Faith is the assurance of things hoped for, the conviction of things not seen" (Heb. 11:1). Here, two seemingly opposed elements combine: surety of knowledge, yet without verification. Faith involves knowledge; it is a virtue in the intellect (Thomas Aquinas [on faith, see *ST* II-II, qq. 1–16]). Moreover, true faith requires that we rely on this knowledge with a certainty that supports daily life and action. Faith has the property of "endowing the believer with knowledge that would not be available to him by the exercise of his own powers" (Pieper 44–45). Yet faith's knowledge is "not seen" (i.e., verified) but comes "by hearing" (Rom. 10:17; 2 Cor. 5:7), which requires trusting another's word. This makes it in one sense less "perfect"; unlike love, faith (and hope) will disappear in the future, when we know God directly, seeing "face to face" (1 Cor. 13:12). Yet this makes faith key in our world since it accesses supernatural reality. Love remains the greatest of the theological virtues, but faith is its gateway. On Simone Weil's definition, "Faith is the experience that the intelligence is enlightened by love" (Grant 38). Far from opposing reason, faith activates thought, for it sends the mind searching (Pieper 52), striving to perceive the world in love's new light. The new vision of faith, however, can never be compelled; faith remains always the free response of the human person to God that must be renewed with each generation. Jesus' question remains forever valid: "When the Son of Man returns, will he find faith on earth?" (Luke 18:8).

See also Hope; Love, Love Command; Vices and Virtues, Lists of; Virtue(s); Virtue Ethics

Bibliography

Grant, G. "Faith and the Multiversity." Pages 35–70 in *Technology and Justice*. University of Notre Dame Press, 1986; Kierkegaard, S. *Fear and Trembling: A Dialectical Lyric*. Trans. A. Hannay. Penguin Books, 1985; Luther, M. *The Freedom of a Christian*. Trans. M. Tranvik. Fortress, 2008; Pieper, J. "On Faith: A Philosophical Treatise." Pages 13–85 in *Faith, Hope, Love*. Trans. R. and C. Winston. Ignatius Press, 1997.

Charles R. Pinches

Fall, The *See* Sin

False Witness *See* Speech Ethics

Family

Scripture is, in many ways, an unlikely source for a twenty-first-century ethic of family. The coarse and patriarchal life of households in ancient Israel bears little resemblance to the life of most families in the West today. And the ambivalence toward family found in the NT in the words of both Jesus and Paul is not an obvious source for a constructive ethic of the family.

In the OT, the closest Hebrew equivalent to the English word *family* is *bêt 'āb*, the "father's household." This multigenerational household was the basic unit of society. Although the *bêt 'āb* took on different forms, there was significant continuity through much of the history of ancient Israel. Millennia ago in small towns and open country in Israel, several family units, linked by kinship and mutual interdependence, lived together, normally, in a group of small houses made of mud bricks or in tents made of animal pelts.

Within this larger household or grouping of houses lived a patriarch, his wife or wives, their dependent children, and their adult sons and families, older relatives, and sometimes others such as orphans or servants. Within each of the small houses in the compound lived a father and mother, their young children, and perhaps an elderly relative or an orphan. Some scholars suggest that within the average smaller house lived six people. When the patriarch died, the oldest son took his place in the compound.

Each house, consisting of just a few rooms, connected with the other houses to form a larger family compound, the *bêt 'āb*. These larger households generally were self-sufficient, producing through agriculture and animal husbandry their own food and the materials for clothing. The various members of the household worked together, and all, including children, had responsibilities. The household was the center not only of economic production but also of teaching, religious life, moral instruction, and protection. The *bêt 'āb* included not just the people and their houses, but also the animals, the crops, and, above these, the land itself. The needs of the household as a whole took precedence over the needs and desires of individuals within it. Moreover, the patriarch of the family was responsible for the care not only of his own family but also of widows and orphans who were without family.

Each father's house (or, more accurately, each grouping of houses) joined with other households to form a clan. Within the clan people learned the customs and laws. Within the clan justice was meted out when those laws were violated. Clans taken together formed a tribe. Although the twelve tribes of Israel were thought of as large family units, the kinship was often more symbolic than genetic.

The *bêt 'āb* of ancient Israel could hardly be more different from postindustrial families. Unlike households of ancient Israel, approximately 25 percent of the households in many Western nations are made up of only one person, and most of the remainder consist of a couple alone or an individual family unit often isolated from extended family, sometimes by hundreds or thousands of miles. These family units are rarely self-sufficient but rather relate to and depend on a global network of food producers and other businesses, often half a world away. Families in the West rely on an array of other institutions to provide legal and judicial services, protection, and teaching. Their relationship to the land often is tenuous, as is their relationship to extended family. Roles within the family, whether by gender or by one's position within the family, are much more egalitarian and fluid today.

As strange as this biblical pattern of family life might seem to our twenty-first-century context, some of the explicit biblical advice is even stranger. If a son strikes or curses his parents, the consequences could be deadly. Deuteronomy 21:18–21 offers to parents a method for handling chronically rebellious sons who defy correction: "His father and his mother shall take hold of him and bring him out to the elders of his town at the gate of that place. . . . Then all the men of the town shall stone him to death." Those who curse or strike their mother or father likewise will be "put to death" (Exod. 21:15, 17). It may be that these penalties were rarely enacted, but their existence in the canon is unsettling to modern sensibilities nonetheless.

Even some of the more reasonable advice is suspect today. The advocacy of corporal punishment is at odds with much contemporary childrearing advice and practice. Many recent studies suggest that corporal punishment may be linked to slightly higher rates of violence in adulthood. Several dozen countries have enacted laws prohibiting the use of corporal punishment. Increasing numbers of parents in the United States forgo its use.

And then there are the stories of the families themselves. Siblings do not present a pretty picture in much of Scripture. Barely out of Eden, the first set of brothers starts things off poorly when Cain kills Abel. Jacob tricks his brother Esau out of his inheritance. Joseph's older brothers sell him into slavery. David's son Amnon lures his sister Tamar into his quarters and then rapes her.

Nor do parents and children always behave in exemplary fashion. Jephthah sacrifices his daughter to make good on a rash promise. Absalom plots against his father, David. Rebecca conspires against her husband and their son Esau, and Lot's daughters seduce their father. Even the honored patriarchs engage in questionable family behavior. Abraham casts out Hagar and their son, Ishmael, in Gen. 21, and in the very next chapter he lifts the knife in readiness to sacrifice Isaac.

And then there is Jesus. He left his own family, and when the disciples followed Jesus' call, they did the same. Jesus was, literally, a man without a household. "Foxes have holes, and birds of the air have nests; but the Son of Man has nowhere to lay his head" (Matt. 8:20; Luke 9:58).

Leaving one's family is not simply praised in the NT, it is also rewarded. When Peter exclaims to Jesus that the disciples have left everything, Jesus counters that those who have left their houses, wives, brothers and sisters, parents and children, and even their fields will be rewarded a hundredfold and will, besides, receive eternal life (Matt. 19:27–39; Mark 10:28–30; Luke 18:28–30).

Jesus insists that his reign brings not peace to families, but division and alienation. Jesus sets "father against son and son against father, mother against daughter and daughter against mother, mother-in-law against her daughter-in-law and daughter-in-law against mother-in-law" (Luke 12:49–53). Jesus also distances himself from his own family. When his mother and siblings call for him, Jesus insists that his true family consists of those who follow him (Mark 3:31–35). Throughout the Gospels Jesus places loyalty to God above loyalty to family.

Jesus' ambivalence about family finds parallel in Paul's hesitation about marriage. In 1 Cor. 7 Paul uplifts celibacy as the better path while acknowledging that for Christians who find it difficult to abstain from sexual activity, marriage is preferred.

There are, of course, many positive sayings and stories about the family in both Testaments. Children are seen as a blessing and a source of joy in life (Pss. 127:3–5; 128:3–6). The faithful are enjoined to provide for the basic needs of their families; failure to do so is a sign of unfaithfulness. For example, 1 Tim. 5:8 says, "Whoever does not provide for relatives, and especially for family members, has denied the faith and is worse than an unbeliever." The head of the family is also responsible for providing guidance and discipline to the household (Eph. 6:4). This guidance was central for the formation of Christian children and a Christian household.

Many contemporary readers are troubled by NT texts describing the proper order of the household. Wives are instructed to submit to their husbands, and husbands to love their wives. Children are enjoined to obey their parents, and fathers to discipline their children. Slaves, a part of the household, are to obey their masters, and masters are to treat slaves fairly (Eph. 5:21–6:9; Col. 3:18–4:1; see also 1 Tim. 3:1–13; Titus 2:1–10).

In the NT Epistles, familial language is often used to refer to the church (Gal. 6:10; Eph. 2:19), and throughout Scripture the family is a key metaphor for the family of God or the household of faith. Old Testament scholar Leo Perdue goes so far as to say that the family or household was the primary metaphor of the OT. Perdue writes,

> Throughout its history, ancient Israel's major understandings of God, creation, the nation, the nations, and morality were forged in large part by the social character and experience of the family household. Many of the key metaphors for imaging God, Israel, the land, and the nations originated in the household. . . . Indeed, the household not only grounded OT theology in Israel's social reality but also became the primary lens through which to view the character and activity of God, the identity and self-understanding of Israel in its relation to God, the value and meaning of the land . . . and Israel's relationship to the nations. (225–26)

Key scriptural themes about family have been picked up within the Christian tradition. For example, the ambivalence about marriage and family found in the NT and Paul's preference for celibacy formed the basis for vows of celibacy among priests, monks, and nuns in Catholicism. Many theologians who explicitly value marriage, such as Augustine and Thomas Aquinas, see it as less than a life of celibacy.

For all the ambivalence about family within the Christian tradition, the family was also seen as a key site of Christian formation. For the Eastern Orthodox, the family is, before all other things, a school for Christian faith. There are two paths to Christlikeness or deification: one in the monastery, the other in the household. John Chrysostom described the household as "a little church." The household is not a second-tier way of life beneath the monastery. "It is possible," Chrysostom wrote, "for us to surpass all others in virtue by becoming good husbands and wives" (Bunge 64). Others throughout Christian history have described the family as a "little church" or a "domestic church."

The NT theme of the proper ordering of the household comes up repeatedly in Christian reflections on the family. Thomas Aquinas, John Calvin, and many other theologians draw on texts from the NT Epistles to talk about the relationships of submission and obedience within the household. This theme is troubling for many people today who live in societies that emphasize equality and the rights and agency of the individual. Critics charge that the emphasis on submission and obedience in the family is subject to abuse and even can be, in and of itself, distorting.

From this perspective, the optimism of theologians like Chrysostom about the key role of the family in Christian formation can seem naive. If one sees the hierarchical nature of Christian family life as necessarily distorted, then any idea of the family as a primary locus of good Christian formation would have to be balanced by an awareness of the very real possibility of being badly formed within that hierarchical family.

Indeed, some scholars have seen the Christian family as a root cause of violence and distortion. Philip Greven, for example, explores the religious—largely Christian—roots of corporal punishment against children and insists that the resulting damage to the human psyche is devastating.

Recent criticisms of the family as a place of brutality and conflicting power interests sound very familiar to anyone who reads Scripture. What with all the intrafamilial jealousy, deceit, betrayal, assault, rape, abuse, and killing, it is difficult to find a model family in Scripture. And yet it is through this highly flawed body that God appears to be working throughout Scripture. God forms Adam and Eve as a family and instructs them to bear children. God's promises and covenants generally are made within the context of families. The people of Israel are organized by family groupings. In the Gospels, Jesus' birth is described through the ancestral families from which he came. The people of Israel, the disciples, the church, and even the Trinity are described in familial language. Scripture gives witness to God's redemptive work through families, to the brutal failure of many families to live up to God's commands, to the devastating consequences of failed families, and, ultimately, to God's power to work with and in spite of the best and worst of families to bring about God's redemptive purposes.

For all the differing themes in Scripture and the Christian tradition regarding family, there is an underlying unifying claim: families, however important to survival and even to faithfulness, are never the primary sites of human loyalty. That belongs alone to God, the one who created families, who sustains them in their failure, and who continues to work redemptively with and in spite of families.

See also Adoption; Celibacy; Children; Household Codes; Marriage and Divorce; Orphans; Parenthood, Parenting; Sex and Sexuality; Spousal Abuse

Bibliography

Anderson, H., et al., eds. *The Family Handbook*. Westminster John Knox, 1998; Balch, D., and C. Osiek, eds. *Early Christian Families in Context: An Interdisciplinary Dialogue*. Eerdmans, 2003; idem. *Families in the New Testament World: Households and House Churches*. Westminster John Knox, 1997; Browning, D., et al. *From Culture Wars to Common Ground: Religion and the American Family Debate*. Westminster John Knox, 1997; Bunge, M. *The Child in Christian Thought*. Eerdmans, 2001; Cahill, L. *Family: A Christian Social Perspective*. Fortress, 2000; Carr, A., and

M. Van Leeuwen, eds. *Religion, Feminism, and the Family*. Westminster John Knox, 1996; Greven, P. *Spare the Child: The Religious Roots of Punishment and the Psychological Impact of Physical Abuse*. Knopf, 1990; Perdue, L. "The Household, Old Testament Theology, and Contemporary Hermeneutics." Pages 223–58 in *Families in Ancient Israel*, by L. Perdue et al. Westminster John Knox, 1997; Post, S. *More Lasting Unions: Christianity, the Family, and Society*. Eerdmans, 2000; Rubio, J. *A Christian Theology of Marriage and Family*. Paulist Press, 2003; Ruether, R. *Christianity and the Making of the Modern Family*. Beacon Press, 2000; Thatcher, A. *Theology and Families*. Blackwell, 2007; Waters, B. *The Family in Christian Social and Political Thought*. OSTE. Oxford University Press, 2007; Witte, J., M. Green, and A. Wheeler, eds. *The Equal-Regard Family and Its Friendly Critics: Don Browning and the Practical Theological Ethics of the Family*. Eerdmans, 2007.

Rebekah Miles

Family Planning

Decades after the invention of the birth-control pill, family planning remains a contentious topic among both Catholics and Protestants. Some Christians take for granted the wisdom of using technological means to limit family size; others see large families as obedience to God. In Scripture, husbands sometimes take concubines as a remedy to barrenness (Gen. 16; 30), though the practice is never explicitly recommended. The only example of contraception occurs when Onan takes Tamar, the wife of his dead brother, as his own, as required by law (Deut. 25:5–10), but then "spills his semen on the ground" rather than produce an heir for his dead brother (Gen. 38:9).

Church bodies universally rejected contraception until 1930, when Anglican bishops agreed that contraceptive devices could be used where there was a "clearly felt moral obligation" between married people to limit family size for unselfish purposes. Most mainline Protestant bodies followed suit. In 1968, Paul VI reiterated the traditional Catholic prohibition against all but "natural family planning" (abstinence during fertile periods), which many Catholics and some Protestants continue to practice.

All Christian traditions maintain that children are gifts from God, which means that procreation should be neither undertaken nor forgone without serious consideration. The infertile, meanwhile, may take some small comfort in the affirmation that (in Barth's words) "the Child who alone matters has been born for them too."

See also Abortion; Birth Control; Childlessness; Conception; Marriage and Divorce; Population Policy and Control; Procreation; Reproductive Technologies

Bibliography

Barth, K. *Church Dogmatics*. Vol. III/4. Trans. A. Mackay et al. T&T Clark, 1961, 265–76; Blanchard, K. "The Gift of Contraception: Calvin, Barth, and a Lost Protestant Conversation." *JSCE* 27, no. 1 (2007): 225–49; Noonan, J. *Contraception: A History of Its Treatment by the Catholic Theologians and Canonists*. Belknap Press, 1986; Paul VI. *Humanae Vitae*. United States Catholic Conference, 1968.

Kathryn D. Blanchard

Feminist Ethics

Feminist reflection, whether in the scholarly disciplines of feminist ethics, feminist theology, or feminist psychology, for example, centers on ethical commitments to the well-being of women and criticism of those ideas and structures that inhibit or fail to enhance the well-being of women. Lisa Cahill insists that, for all the differences among various kinds of feminist ethics, they are held together by "a universal moral imperative: Justice for women!" (Cahill, "Feminist Ethics," 184).

Many feminists have also been advocates of justice for others who are oppressed, including children, ethnic or religious minorities in the United States and around the world, and gay and lesbian people. These commitments have led to the exploration of many topics, including social and economic justice, racism, and homophobia. Although feminist ethicists have addressed a wide array of issues, some issues with particular import for women have received greater attention—for example, abortion, domestic violence, children and parenthood, sexuality and reproduction, household labor, gender discrimination in the workplace, and sexual abuse.

The primacy of moral questions in feminist disciplines generally means that there is no hard-and-fast distinction between feminist ethics and other feminist disciplines. For example, Carol Gilligan is in the field of psychology, but her work was groundbreaking in feminist ethics. Likewise, most of the scholarship in feminist theology centers on ethical questions. And typologies of Christian feminist ethics typically include thinkers such as Rosemary Radford Ruether, who ordinarily is classified as a theologian.

Feminism and Scripture interact as some feminists explore the intersection between women's well-being and the OT and the NT. They ask how Scripture and its interpretation over time have served to promote ideas and social structures that enhance and/or inhibit the well-being of women. Moreover, how might the Bible now be interpreted to promote women's flourishing?

Although the whole of Scripture has been subject to the interpretive gaze of feminists, some texts have received greater attention and analysis. These include egalitarian texts (e.g., Gal. 3:28; Acts 2:17–18; Joel 2:28–29); texts that have often been used to support the subordination of women (e.g., 1 Cor. 11; Eph. 5; 1 Tim. 2); biblical stories of courageous women (e.g., Deborah, Esther, Judith, the women at Jesus' tomb); stories of women who were subject to abuse and injustice (e.g., Tamar [2 Sam. 13], Jephthah's daughter [Judg. 11]); stories of Jesus' interactions with women (e.g., Mary and Martha [Luke 10:38–42], the Samaritan woman [John 4:4–42], the adulterous woman [John 7:53–8:11]); stories and sayings of Mary the mother of Jesus, especially the Magnificat (Luke 1:46–55); texts concerning the reign of God and those calling for justice (e.g., the books of Isaiah and Amos); and texts concerning divine wisdom personified as Sophia (e.g., Prov. 8; Wis. 7).

The work of feminist biblical scholars has been driven in part by ethical norms and commitments. Elisabeth Schüssler Fiorenza, for example, insists that the goal of her critical feminist biblical interpretation is not simply to "understand" Scripture; rather, she seeks to "change" not only the way Scripture has been interpreted but also oppressive social and political institutions. She adopts the metaphor of "struggle" as her hermeneutical lens for interpreting Scripture (Schüssler Fiorenza 78–79).

Within the field of feminist ethics, many scholars operating from a secular framework do not consider Scripture at all. Of course, among many feminist religious ethicists and theologians, Scripture is a key topic. In the early years of feminist theology, feminists sometimes were placed into two categories: those who sought to reform the Jewish and Christian traditions, and those who sought to separate from them. Over the years, the major work in feminism and Scripture has been done by those who are in the "reformist" group. The reformist project has become so broad and diverse, however, that it is rarely described now as a category or type unto itself.

Many feminist ethicists, whatever their interest in Scripture, share some common assumptions. In addition to the commitment to the well-being of women and the subsequent affirmation of that which promotes women's well-being, many feminist ethicists share a common appeal to the experiences of women (all women or a particular group of women) as a source and norm for moral reflection.

This appeal to women's experience is connected to a common judgment that traditional ethical reflection is flawed because until recently it has been done almost exclusively by males, especially elite males, working out of elite male experience. These ethicists have, unwittingly, made male experience primary and thereby, consciously or not, have devalued female experience and in the process harmed or failed to enhance the well-being of women. Moreover, as the field of ethics was shaped almost exclusively by male experience, the whole of ethical reflection became distorted. The field of ethics is poorer, the argument runs, when shaped only by privileged males.

Carol Gilligan provides a classic example of the argument that ethics is weakened when male and not female experience is taken into account. Gilligan challenged Lawrence Kohlberg's theories about moral development. His original research had been done almost exclusively on men and boys, and Gilligan noticed that when women and girls were interviewed using Kohlberg's process, they tended to be scored at a lower level of moral development. Gilligan argued that Kohlberg's stages were seriously flawed because they claimed to show a pattern of human moral reflection, when in fact they overlooked the experiences of women. Working from research on groups of women, Gilligan came up with an alternate and complementary model of the stages of moral development. Kohlberg's research on men highlighted and gave priority to an ethic of justice with a concern for abstract rights, whereas Gilligan's research led her to emphasize an ethic of care involving assessments of complex responsibilities within particular concrete relationships. Emerging from these criticisms of Kohlberg, Gilligan and others put forth an alternate model that has attracted many supporters: a feminist ethics of care.

Gilligan's arguments, though quite popular, are in no way monolithic among feminist ethicists; indeed, they have been widely disputed. Working from the one simple fact that until recently the scholarly field of ethics was the nearly exclusive domain of men, feminists have developed a broad array of criticisms and alternatives. Different feminists have criticized traditional ethics for various offenses, including these: attaching greater importance to traits often associated with men (e.g., rationality, independence) and ignoring or giving less value to traits often associated with women (e.g., empathy, interdependence); creating an ideal moral person that was, unwittingly, made in the image of men, not in the image of women or people generally; not extending to females the moral rights and responsibilities of males (or privileged males, in any case); not considering women as full moral agents; neglecting to address fully issues in the so-called private sphere that are thought to be of particular importance to women (e.g., children, reproduction, birth control, and household labor); giving greater prominence to styles of moral reasoning typically associated with men and ignoring or devaluing those typically associated with women; developing moral theories or frameworks that show women as morally immature; and promoting or failing to work against social injustice toward women and others.

While feminist ethicists generally agree that traditional ethics has been weakened by the dominance of men and the absence of women, they disagree dramatically on the particulars. For example, while some feminists, as noted above, criticize traditional ethics for overvaluing male traits and devaluing female traits, other feminists deny that there are such things as male and female traits.

Indeed, different types of feminists and feminist ethicists can be distinguished in part by what they think is wrong with traditional ethics and what should be done to compensate for that weakness. Susan Parsons offers a typology of feminist ethics that has become a standard, particularly among Christian feminist ethicists. Parsons describes three types of feminist ethicists: liberal, social constructionist, and naturalist. In the case of the second and third types, they are shaped in response to criticism not only of traditional ethics but also of earlier models of feminist ethics.

Liberal feminism, like liberalism generally, is confident about the human capacity to discern both our true human nature and the rights that derive from that nature (Parsons, chaps. 2–3). The moral task of justice is to work so that all humans have the freedoms and material support that are their proper rights. Liberal feminism, then, takes the liberal discussion and insists that these same rights be extended to women. A classic example of this liberal feminist voice is the eighteenth-century writer Mary Wollstonecraft. A more recent example within the Christian tradition is found in the early work of Rosemary Radford Ruether, who uplifts as her primary norm "the full humanity of women," insisting too that this feminist norm is in keeping with what she claims is the key strand of Scripture: the "prophetic liberating tradition." This prophetic tradition, seen throughout Scripture, especially in Isaiah, Jeremiah, Amos, and the Synoptic Gospels, is a mechanism offered in Scripture for the critique of Scripture and subsequently of the entire Christian tradition.

Parsons's second type of feminist ethics, social constructionist, is shaped by its criticism of the liberal model, including liberal feminism, which is censured for its naïveté about the human capacity to discern some universal human nature and rights (Parsons, chaps. 4–5). All claims about human beings, as well as the very formation of human beings, are radically shaped and constructed by social context. In attempting to discern some common human nature by which moral judgments could then be made, liberals are arrogantly and arbitrarily making their own socially constructed model of the self normative for all. They are also turning a blind eye to the differences that concrete, social factors of human life, such as class, ethnicity, and gender, make in the formation of humans and of ideas about humanity. Feminist theologians operating out of this perspective, such as Sharon Welch, have no compelling reason to seek, as Ruether does, a biblical norm that would offer moral leverage for making claims about human rights and freedoms. A key criticism of this position is that it lacks moral leverage that would help women and others as they seek to evaluate and transform various social structures and ideas (Parsons, chaps. 4–5).

Parsons's third type, naturalist feminist ethics, finds that critical leverage in claims about human life (Parsons, chaps. 6–7). Unlike liberal feminist ethics, naturalist feminist ethics grounds its moral claims not in reference to a common humanity known by reason, but in the concrete lived experience of embodied, relational human beings. Lisa Cahill provides a minimalist naturalist ethic. Claims about human nature from various sources, including, for example, biology, the social sciences, Christian theology, and Scripture, are important for moral reflection. In contrast to many liberal positions, as well as some other naturalist positions, one holds these claims about human nature lightly or tentatively. Within this position, Scripture is an important resource alongside others.

Mary Daly offers a more radical naturalist position, calling for women to be attentive to their own experiences and their processes of moral reflection as women. Women's experience is the source of an alternative ethic that can both shape women's lives for good and provide a place from which to judge dominant male ethics and social structures. Because of her sharp distinction between male and female experience and the contrasting ethics that emerge from these two types of experience, Daly has been accused of a naive essentialism. Daly's understanding of the place of Scripture in her work can be summed up in an exclamation she is reported to have made: "Who the hell cares what Paul thought!" (Haney 4).

Some naturalist positions, like Daly's, have been criticized not only for affirming significant differences between men and women but also for failing to note the great differences that exist among women themselves. Just as feminist theologians and ethicists criticized male ethicists for claiming that their own experiences as men reflect those of human beings generally, so some African American and Latina women have criticized European American feminists for claiming that their own particular experiences reflect those of women generally.

Within the field of mujerista ethics and theology, for example, Latina women are engaged in moral reflection out of their experiences as, and in the interests of, Latina women. Ada María Isasi-Díaz writes, "A mujerista is someone who makes a preferential option for Latina women, for our struggle for liberation" (Isasi-Díaz 61).

African American women in the field of womanist ethics have reflected on the experiences of African American women and on the moral implications of those experiences. For example, in *Black Womanist Ethics*, Katie Cannon argues that the dominant ethic of Western culture assumes a level of freedom or agency unavailable to many African American women. Cannon describes an ethic of endurance that helps African American women and their communities survive and continue the struggle in the face of limited choices and oppression of many kinds. Womanist ethicists have addressed other ethical issues with particular import for many African Americans. For example, in *Breaking the Fine Rain of Death*, Emilie Townes examines the way that the healthcare system and some industry practices (e.g., disproportionately placing toxic waste dumps near poor, African American neighborhoods) have compromised the health of many African Americans.

Mujerista and womanist theology and ethics, emerging partly out of and in response to feminist theology and ethics, are fields of inquiry in their own right, distinct in many ways from feminist theology and ethics. There are also many distinctions among various kinds of mujerista and womanist ethicists. These two complex fields provide examples of the way feminist theology and ethics, which began with moral reflections on the experiences of women and on behalf of women, gave rise to many different kinds of theologies and ethics emerging from the experiences of women in a variety of contexts. These diverse theologies and ethics include some that do not even specifically mention the words *feminist*, *womanist*, or *mujerista*. With this explosion in the varieties of women's theologies and ethics, it becomes difficult to make absolute, fixed statements about the nature, aims, and scope of feminist ethics. Indeed, the impact of feminist ethics has been so widespread that most contemporary ethical models, whether written by men or women, whether feminist or not, have been shaped in part by feminist ethics.

See also Gender; Women, Status of

Bibliography

Cahill, L. *Between the Sexes: Foundations for a Christian Ethics of Sexuality*. Fortress, 1985; idem. "Feminist Ethics, Differences, and Common Ground: A Catholic Perspective." Pages 184–204 in *Feminist Ethics and the Catholic Moral Tradition*, ed. C. Curran, M. Farley, and R. McCormick. RMT 9. Paulist Press, 1996; Cannon, K. *Black Womanist Ethics*. AARAS 60. Scholars Press, 1988; Daly, M. *Gyn/Ecology: The Metaethics of Radical Feminism*. Beacon Press, 1978; Farley, M. *Just Love: A Framework for Christian Sexual Ethics*. Continuum, 2008; Gilligan, C. *In a Different Voice: Psychological Theory and Women's Development*. Harvard University Press, 1982; Haney, E. "What Is Feminist Ethics? A Proposal for Continuing Discussion." Pages 3–12 in *Feminist Theological Ethics: A Reader*, ed. L. Daly. Westminster John Knox, 1994; Isasi-Díaz, A. *Mujerista Theology: A Theology for the Twenty-First Century*. Orbis, 1996; Newsom, C., and S. Ringe, eds. *Women's Bible Commentary*. Westminster John Knox, 1998; Parsons, S. *Feminism and Christian Ethics*. NSCE 8. Cambridge, 1996; Ruether, R. *Sexism and God-Talk: Toward a Feminist Theology*. Beacon Press, 1983; Russell, L., ed. *Feminist Interpretation of the Bible*. Westminster, 1985; Schüssler Fiorenza, E. *Sharing Her Word: Feminist Biblical Interpretation in Context*. Beacon Press, 1998; Townes, E. *Breaking the Fine Rain of Death: African American Health Issues and a Womanist Ethic of Care*. Continuum, 1998; Traina, C. *Feminist Ethics and Natural Law: The End to the Anathemas*. Georgetown University Press, 1999; Welch, S. *A Feminist Ethic of Risk*. Fortress, 1990.

Rebekah Miles

Fetishism *See* Sexual Ethics

Fidelity

The word *fidelity* is derived from the Latin *fidelitas*, meaning "faithfulness, loyalty, trustworthiness."

Fidelity of God

In the OT, the fidelity of God is expressed in the terms being "merciful," "gracious," "faithful," and abounding in "steadfast love." The God of Israel is distinctively characterized as being faithful, denoting not only that Yahweh is committed to maintaining and confirming his covenant with his people (Deut. 7:2; 1 Kgs. 8:23) but also that he is truthful, as he is true to himself and has proved himself to be faithful to his people (Exod. 34:6–7; Ps. 89:1–4; Isa. 49:7). Yahweh is absolutely trustworthy and dependable, and so is his word (1 Kgs. 8:26; 2 Chr. 6:17), as evidenced in blessings that Israel received. God's people, in time of adversity, often appealed not so much to the power of Yahweh as to his promises of fidelity (2 Sam. 15:20; Ps. 36:7–10). Since Yahweh's fidelity also means self-consistency, being faithful to himself, he is also insistent on human accountability for wrongdoing (Exod. 34:7). God's name is "Jealous" (Exod. 34:14). Yahweh will tolerate no compromise in Israel's fidelity to him. Idolatry is strictly forbidden (Deut. 32:21). In the midst of judgment for Israel's apostasy, there is still hope because of Yahweh's restoring fidelity (Lam. 3:21–23). Yahweh will heal Israel's disloyalty and faithlessness (Jer. 3:22).

In the NT, the covenant God is the one who always remains faithful to his promise (2 Cor. 1:18–22; Heb. 6:15–20). He is the benevolent Father, whose generous mercy and abundant grace allow his children to experience needed forgiveness and to fulfill the righteousness that he demands (Matt. 5:45–48; 7:7–12; Rom. 5:15–21; Jas. 1:5). This new relationship of God's people with their Father in heaven is made possible only through Jesus, the obedient Son of the Father (Matt. 11:27 // Luke 10:22; Gal. 4:6).

Response to the Fidelity of God

As the covenant partner of Yahweh, Israel is called to respond in fidelity to the initiator of the covenant (Josh. 24:14; Ps. 119:30). Just as Yahweh is a faithful God, Jerusalem should be a faithful (*'āman*) city (Isa. 1:21, 26), which is essential for its continual existence. Its obligation of fidelity is summarized in the Shema: "You shall love the Lord your God with all your heart, and with all your soul, and with all your might" (Deut. 6:5). Fidelity and duty are inseparable. Israel is to imitate God's fidelity in the practice of justice and holiness (Lev. 19:2–4; Deut. 10:17–19). Infidelity is more than a failure to obey God; it is choosing to obey forces hostile to God, allying and even surrendering oneself to another rival source of power (Exod. 17–18; Deut. 13:6–10). The prophetic writings provide many examples of defections of fidelity among the Israelites (e.g., Isa. 1:2–4), though there are also many exemplars of faithfulness (e.g., Moses, Hezekiah, Daniel).

In the NT, the eschatological and saving act of God (Mark 1:15) demands undivided loyalty (Mark 12:29–30 pars.), taking priority over duties of marriage and family (Matt 19:12; Mark 3:31–35 pars.). Discipleship means following Jesus, with no distraction, no rival, and no compromise. Jesus himself is the paradigm for discipleship. He showed fidelity as the Son of God in the face of temptation from Satan (Matt. 4:1–11 // Luke 4:1–13) and exemplified perfect fidelity to the Father to the point of dying on the cross (Matt. 6:10; 26:42).

Christ's act of righteousness brings about justification of humankind (Rom. 5:18). The "faithfulness of Christ" (e.g., Rom. 3:22, 26; Gal. 2:16, 20) refers to the faithfulness of Christ in dying on the cross, through which the promise of salvation comes to fulfillment. In Hebrews, Jesus' faithfulness is seen as what qualifies him as the high priest who offers himself up as atoning sacrifice in heaven (Heb. 5:7–10). His fidelity to God is the ultimate paradigm for all who hold fast to the confession of Christ (Heb. 3:1–6), inspiring and enabling them to be faithful to the end (Heb. 12:1–3).

Communal Fidelity

Israel is a community of persons bound together in loyalty in covenantal membership to one another. Proper human behavior involves proving oneself to be trustworthy, upright, and faithful in human relationships (Prov. 19:22). The essence of true friendship is loyalty (Job 6:14).

The very opposite of the community faithfulness demanded by social structures, as in family and kinship, is faithlessness, disloyalty, or treachery, which the OT prophets condemn (Jer. 12:6; Mal. 2:10–11). An offense of faithlessness against a fellow member of the covenant family amounts to an act of infidelity against God. God's demand for marital fidelity is interwoven with his demand of covenant faithfulness from Israel (Mal. 2:10–16).

The demand for community fidelity is expressed in terms of justice (e.g., Hos. 5:1; Mic. 3:1), righteousness (e.g., Isa. 33:5; Mic. 6:8), faithfulness (e.g., 1 Sam. 26:23; Jer. 5:1), and mercy (e.g., Hos. 12:6). All these are characteristics of Yahweh, whom Israel worships. Being a member of God's people means turning away from idol worship (1 Thess. 1:9–10) to wholehearted devotion to the living God. Believers are those who love God (2 Thess. 3:5; Jas. 1:12) and live in obedience to his word (Rom. 1:5; 2 Thess. 2:15; 1 John 2:5–7). They belong to God and Christ, living under the lordship of Christ (1 Cor. 1:2; Eph. 4:15).

Jesus summarized the whole law in the double love command: love of God and love of neighbor (Matt. 22:37–40 pars.). The commandment to love one another echoes throughout the NT (e.g., John 13:34–35; 1 Cor. 13; Eph. 4:2; 1 Pet. 1:22; 4:8; 1 John 3:11). Again, Christ's sacrificial love is the paradigm for loving relationship in the Christian community (John 15:12; Eph. 5:1–2; 1 John 3:16). The demand for community fidelity is this embracing love and mercy, which, as in the OT, are the very character of God (Matt. 5:48 // Luke 6:36).

See also Covenant; Idolatry; Integrity; Love, Love Command; Temptation

Bibliography

Brueggemann, W. *Theology of the Old Testament: Testimony, Dispute, Advocacy*. Fortress, 1997; Gerhardsson, B.

The Testing of God's Son (Matt. 4:1–11 & par.): An Analysis of an Early Christian Midrash. ConBNT 2. Gleerup, 1966.

Luke Leuk Cheung

Flesh *See* Body; Sin

Flourishing, Human *See* Happiness; Salvation

Food

Food is the physical material taken into the body in order to sustain human life. Food issues are complex. In Scripture, the readings pertaining to food are varied and not always congruent. Jesus, the self-proclaimed Bread of Life (John 6:35), declared that humanity shall not live by bread alone (Matt. 4:4) and also chose bread as the symbol of his body (Matt. 26:26). In its production, preparation, distribution, and consumption, food lies at the nexus of nature, health, justice, culture, and sustainability issues.

Attending to Scripture

Food is first and foremost part of the created order and is therefore good (Gen. 1:31). God intends for all creatures to have food, and enough of it; witness the bounty of the garden of Eden (Gen. 1:29) and the promised land, flowing with milk and honey (Exod. 13:5), grain, olives, and new wine (2 Kgs. 18:32). Food can reveal the presence of God and his emissaries, as when Abraham and Sarah welcome the angels with a midday feast of bread and barbeque (Gen. 18:1–8). Food can also reveal God's provision and power, as when the Israelites survive on manna and quail (Exod. 16) or when the widow of Zarephath feeds Elijah from a infinite store of oil and flour (1 Kgs. 17). Jesus transforms a modest meal into dinner for thousands (John 6:1–14), and it is over a meal that the risen Christ reveals himself to his disciples (Luke 24:28–31) and reconciles himself to Peter (John 21).

Throughout Scripture, food is both essential and perilous, viewed as potentially imparting the sacred; by its ingestion, one pursued either holiness or degradation. It can detract from God's plans for us, as when Adam and Eve eat the forbidden fruit (Gen. 3) as well as when the newly liberated Israelites long for the cucumbers and melons of their captivity (Num. 11:5). In the wilderness, Jesus reminds Satan that food alone will not sustain us (Matt. 4:4). Yet because food is necessary for life, its presence indicates the desire to both continue and celebrate that life. Scripture shows that the purpose of food is unitive, not divisive, as when the early church ate together as an act of worship (Acts 2:46–47). Paul encouraged believers not to quibble over food details, such as whether a meal's main course had come from pagan sacrifice (1 Cor. 10:23–32), and he exhorted them to remember the purpose of their meal—not gluttony and inequity but sharing and fellowship (1 Cor. 11:19–22). Food also figures prominently in many commemorative situations, including Passover and the Last Supper, where the very body and blood of Christ reside in the ordinary bread and wine (Luke 22:14–20).

The Tradition and Scripture

Food has been central to the life of the church from its inception. Inaugurated with the bread and wine, the early church had regular fellowship meals (Acts 2:43–47). Yet food rapidly lost its positive standing for the church and came to be viewed as hazardous (see Grimm). The first monastics practiced fasting in their asceticism, viewing food as potentially dulling their hunger for God. Food was also seen as potentially connected to sex and thus morally suspect. The medieval injunctions against gluttony also highlight its potential for distraction from the spiritual life. John Wesley echoed these concerns, denouncing what he called an "elegant epicurianism"; rather, one should "despise delicacy and variety and be content with what plain nature requires" (Sermon 50).

Contemporary Application

As stated before, food issues are complex. Those who approach the topic thoughtfully find a plethora of questions regarding the health, feasibility, and integrity of current food practices. As an area of growing moral awareness, food justice requires simultaneous attention to many (often competing) concerns. Consumers need access to food that is affordable, palatable, nutritious, and safe. Producers need access to production systems that are nonexploitative, nonhazardous, and financially just. The "consumed" deserve a system of participation that is humane for the animals and sustainable for the environment.

There is currently a groundswell of interest in food issues. The growing presence of urban gardens, backyard vegetable plots, farmers' markets, and participation in community-supported agriculture all indicate an increasing dedication to pursuing health, justice, and relationship in our food choices. Among the blessings flowing from this commitment is the joyful rediscovery of ourselves, not merely as reconnected with the goodness of nature but also as literal cocreators in partnership with the creator God.

In the celebratory spirit of the Scriptures, food is one of the most powerful intersections of nature and culture (see Coff). As part of the created order, food is fundamentally natural; yet in its procurement, preparation, and presentation, it both shapes and reflects cultural mores. Many of these bear the blight of sinfulness. We demand constant access to exotic foods that bear an enormous carbon footprint; we expect lavish fare at budget prices. Yet when the relational aspect of food is recognized and honored, there is also much to celebrate. The rituals attendant to food preparation can provide a measure of stability and rootedness to our increasingly disconnected culture, as families reconnect at the end of the day by cooking and sharing the evening meal, and through the annual preparation of holiday meals and the passing down of cherished family recipes. How greatly it would honor God and God's creation if the practices surrounding food began to live up to its honorific as *tov me'od*, "very good."

See also Animals; Culture; Health; Justice

Bibliography

Berry, W. *Bringing It to the Table: On Farming and Food*. Counterpoint, 2009; Capon, R. F. *The Supper of the Lamb: A Culinary Reflection*. Modern Library, 2002; Coff, C. *The Taste for Ethics: An Ethic of Food Consumption*. Springer, 2010; Feeley-Harnik, G. *The Lord's Table: The Meaning of Food in Judaism and Early Christianity*. Smithsonian Institution, 1994; Grimm, V. E. *From Feasting to Fasting: The Evolution of a Sin*. Routledge, 1996; Jung, L. S. *Food for Life: The Spirituality and Ethics of Eating*. Fortress, 2004; Schlosser, E. *Fast Food Nation*. Harper, 2005.

Maria Kenney

Force, Use of

Use of force describes those actions in which some type of power is used to overcome resistance and compel someone or something into a particular form of behavior. Typically, such power includes either the use of or the threatened use of violence. However, not all coercive acts imply violence; both scriptural (e.g., 2 Cor. 12:11) and contemporary usages (e.g., a workers' strike) include nonviolent actions.

Given the wide variety of Greek and Hebrew words used to describe the use of force and the range of scriptural contexts in which force is used, it is impossible to specify either a single biblical conception of the use of force or a uniform theological perspective on the criteria that would allow persons to distinguish legitimate and illegitimate uses of force. However, one may use a variety of distinctions in analyzing or qualifying its use. These include:

- *Whether the use of force, in itself, is good, bad, or neutral.* Those who, following Immanuel Kant, treat any use of coercive power as tantamount to violating another's sovereignty, rights, or freedom will view the use of force as morally problematic (although perhaps justified). Those who, following Hegel, view power as de-centered and flowing dialectically through systems are more likely to treat the use of force as morally neutral or even beneficial. Whether one views the use of force as a failure of diplomacy or an aspect of its work turns, in part, on this distinction.
- *Whether all uses of force imply violence.* Any actions that include violence or the threat of violence bring with them a wide range of questions about morality, legitimacy, and efficacy. Answers to those questions have led some persons to favor nonviolence. However, not only do some forms of nonviolence (e.g., nonviolent resistance) make claims about their coercive efficacy, thereby bringing them under the purview of explorations into the use of force, but also some patterns of action that are not necessarily founded on moral concerns (e.g., economic sanctions and boycotts) are also premised on their coercive power.
- *Who may use force.* Since the rise of the modern nation-state and its claim to maintain a monopoly on violence, most attention to the moral questions that surround the use of force have been focused on the way force is used by the state, whether in military, policing, or penal contexts. The state acts as a surrogate for individuals, families, and communities who may otherwise feel obliged to use force themselves. However, this monopoly is not total; for instance, individuals may legally use force to defend themselves, and communities may hire private security firms to patrol their neighborhoods.
- *Whether God uses or approves of the use of force.* While a theologically construed understanding of the use of force will follow from one's understanding of divine action, it is also the case that moral claims about the use of force can shape one's understandings of God and God's actions.

In most instances, individuals are less likely to face the question of whether to use force than that of how to respond to its use.

See also Authority and Power; Justice; Just-Peacemaking Theory; Just-War Theory; Pacifism; Security; Violence

Mark Douglas

Forgiveness

Forgiveness is the act of granting a free pardon or giving up a claim of requital for an offense or debt.

It has to do with personal relations between one who has been wronged and a wrongdoer, though it is expressed in language that is judicial. In the act of forgiving, the cost or penalty for a wrong, whether actual or perceived, is borne by the forgiver and not by the one forgiven.

The Biblical Theme and Language of Forgiveness

Forgiveness by God of repentant sinners is a central theme in the OT. At Mount Sinai God proclaimed himself to be "merciful and gracious, slow to anger, and abounding in steadfast love and faithfulness, . . . forgiving iniquity and transgression and sin" (Exod. 34:6–7). Levitical legislation had as its purpose God's forgiveness of his people's sins (Lev. 4:20, 26, 31, 35; 5:10, 13, 16, 18; 6:7; 19:22; Num. 15:25, 26, 28). The psalmists repeatedly praise God for the fact that he forgives his people's sins (Pss. 86:5; 103:2–3; 130:4). The cry of Israel's prophets often incorporated some such request as "O Lord, hear; O Lord, forgive; O Lord, listen and act and do not delay!" (Dan. 9:19) or "O Lord GOD, forgive, I beg you!" (Amos 7:2).

In the Synoptic Gospels the themes of repentance and forgiveness are highly important features. They appear particularly in (1) Zechariah's prophecy about the future ministry of his infant son John, which includes the statement that he "will give knowledge of salvation to [God's] people by the forgiveness of their sins" (Luke 1:77); (2) the characterization of the ministry of John the Baptist as proclaiming "a baptism of repentance for the forgiveness of sins" (Mark 1:4 // Luke 3:3; cf. Matt. 3:7–8, 11; Acts 13:24; 19:4); (3) the prayer that Jesus taught his disciples to pray (the so-called Lord's Prayer), which includes the coupling together of God's forgiveness of sins and his people's forgiveness of others (cf. Luke 11:4 // Matt. 6:12); (4) Jesus' ethical teaching, which includes the specific commands "If there is repentance, you must forgive" and "If the same person sins against you seven times a day, and turns back to you seven times and says, 'I repent,' you must forgive" (Luke 17:3–4); (5) Jesus' words at the Last Supper as given in Matthew's Gospel: "This is my blood of the covenant, which is poured out for many for the forgiveness of sins" (Matt. 26:28); (6) Jesus' prayer on the cross for those who crucified him as expressed in Luke's Gospel: "Father, forgive them; for they do not know what they are doing" (Luke 23:34); and (7) Jesus' postresurrection words to his disciples as given in Luke's Gospel: "Thus it is written, that the Messiah is to suffer and to rise from the dead on the third day, and that repentance and forgiveness of sins is to be proclaimed in his name to all nations, beginning from Jerusalem" (Luke 24:46–47).

These twin themes, repentance and forgiveness, also appear prominently in the book of Acts: (1) in Peter's preaching on the day of Pentecost, which concluded with an appeal and a promise: "Repent, and be baptized every one of you in the name of Jesus Christ so that your sins may be forgiven; and you will receive the gift of the Holy Spirit" (Acts 2:38); and (2) in the second defense of Peter and "the apostles" before the Jewish Sanhedrin, which includes the following significant proclamation: "God exalted [Jesus] at his right hand as Leader and Savior that he might give repentance to Israel and forgiveness of sins" (Acts 5:31).

In the Johannine literature, however, the term *forgive* (in its verbal form) appears only in words of Jesus in John 20:23 and then in 1 John 1:9; 2:12. Paul's letters too are almost devoid of references to "repentance" (the noun appears only in Rom. 2:4, "God's kindness is meant to lead you to repentance," and 2 Cor. 7:9–10, "your grief led to repentance") and to "forgiveness" (the noun appears only in the quotation of Ps. 32:1 in Rom. 4:7, and in Eph. 1:7 and Col. 1:14). Yet in Luke's depictions of Paul's ministry in Acts there are a number of places where Paul is presented as (1) calling for "repentance" (cf. Acts 13:24; 17:30; 26:20), (2) proclaiming God's "forgiveness" through the work and person of Jesus (cf. Acts 13:38; 26:18), and (3) speaking generally of his preaching of the Christian gospel as a proclamation of "repentance" (cf. Acts 20:21).

Paul's Emphases on "Peace with God," "Reconciliation," and Being "in Christ"

In speaking of God's salvation, Paul frequently used the Jewish and Jewish Christian forensic expression *justification* and/or *righteousness*, which translate as a single term in Hebrew and in Greek (see especially Rom. 1:17; 3:21–22, 24; 5:1, 16–21; 2 Cor. 5:21). But he also seems to have viewed his own relational, participationist, and personal experiences of "peace with God" (cf. Rom. 5:1), "reconciliation" (Rom. 5:11; 11:15; 2 Cor. 5:18–20), and being "in Christ Jesus" (Gal. 3:26–28) as far more theologically significant, personally compelling, and ethically life changing than could be conveyed by the traditional soteriological terms *repentance* and *forgiveness*. So in his gentile mission Paul focused in his proclamation on the themes of "peace with God," "reconciliation," and being "in Christ" rather than just "repentance" and "forgiveness," evidently believing that the language of "peace," "reconciliation," and being "in Christ" not only connoted features that were more theologically profound and ethically significant but also resonated better with his gentile audiences in his gentile mission.

The Twofold Dimension of Forgiveness in Scripture

In the OT and the postbiblical traditions of Judaism, when forgiveness is spoken about, a twofold dimension is always understood and sometimes explicitly brought to the fore: (1) God's forgiveness of people, and (2) the need for people to forgive one another. For example, Sir. 28:2 reads, "Forgive your neighbor the wrong he has done, and then your sins will be pardoned when you pray" (cf. *T. Gad* 6.3–7). A later rabbinic tractate expressly states, "God forgives the one who forgives his neighbor" (*b. Roš. Haš.* 17a). This twofold emphasis is also at the heart of the prayer that Jesus taught his disciples: "Forgive us our sins, for we ourselves forgive everyone indebted to us" (Luke 11:4; cf. Matt. 6:12).

Such a twofold dimension is dramatically illustrated in two parables that Jesus told his disciples. The first is the parable of the unforgiving servant, which is a story of a servant who had been forgiven a very large debt by his master but could not find it within himself to forgive a much smaller amount owed him by one of his fellow servants. The result was that the unforgiving servant was thrown into prison by his master until he could pay his own debt (Matt. 18:23–35), with the parable concluding with these ominous words: "So my heavenly Father will also do to every one of you, if you do not forgive your brother or sister from your heart" (Matt. 18:35). The second is the parable of the prodigal son and his brother, which is a story about a son who requested from his father his "share of the property" that would eventually belong to him, went off to "a distant country," and there "squandered" his inheritance in "dissolute living," but later repented and returned home, where he was forgiven by his father and joyfully received back home. But the story does not end there, as Jesus went on to tell about the older brother, who, sadly, could not bring himself to forgive or welcome back his younger brother and thus, by his lack of forgiveness toward his brother, made himself an outcast in his own family (Luke 15:11–32).

As in the twofold dimensional nature of love, which we have received from God and are to express to all people, the presence of God's forgiveness in our lives is affirmed by our forgiveness of one another. Conversely, the failure of forgiveness on our part toward others signals the lack of our own reception of God's forgiveness. The experiences of God's love and of God's forgiveness carry their own intrinsic and inevitable compulsions. For just as Jesus taught his disciples "By this everyone will know that you are my disciples, if you have love for one another" (John 13:35), so the message of the Christian gospel is that those who have experienced God's forgiveness will also be forgiving, that their lives will reflect and their relations with others will express the essence of the "good news" of forgiveness that God in his love and Jesus in his work have effected on behalf of all people.

See also Atonement; Justice, Restorative; Peace; Reconciliation; Repentance; Salvation; Sanctification; Sin

Bibliography

Bash, A. *Forgiveness and Christian Ethics*. Cambridge University Press, 2007; Burridge, R. *Imitating Jesus: An Inclusive Approach to New Testament Ethics*. Eerdmans, 2007; Gerhardsson, B. *The Ethos of the Bible*. Trans. S. Westerholm. Fortress, 1981; Hays, R. *The Moral Vision of the New Testament: Community, Cross, New Creation; A Contemporary Introduction to New Testament Ethics*. HarperSanFrancisco, 1996; Matera, F. *New Testament Ethics: The Legacies of Jesus and Paul*. Westminster John Knox, 1996: Taylor, V. *Forgiveness and Reconciliation: A Study in New Testament Theology*. Macmillan, 1941; Verhey, A. *The Great Reversal: Ethics and the New Testament*. Eerdmans, 1984.

Richard N. Longenecker

Formation, Moral *See* Moral Formation

Fornication *See* Sexual Ethics

Fortune Telling *See* Divination and Magic

Foster Care

Foster care is a living arrangement in which children reside, under the supervision of a (usually publicly funded) child welfare agency, in a private household other than that of their biological parents. The modern institution of foster care has its roots in the child welfare movement of the mid-nineteenth century, when a growing dissatisfaction with institutional orphanages led to the temporary or permanent placement of children in private homes. Scripture does not directly address the subject of foster care as such, although both OT and NT writers speak to analogous arrangements frequently and at some length, making the care of children, especially orphans, an integral part of the common life of God's people.

The Torah frequently exhorts Israel to show hospitality to the strangers among them in memory of the fact that Israel was once a stranger among the Egyptians, who were less than hospitable (Exod. 22:21; 23:9; Lev. 19:34; Deut. 10:19). Orphans in particular are to be made recipients of hospitality (Exod. 22:22). After David had conquered Saul and his allies, he welcomed Saul's grandson (and Jonathan's son) Mephibosheth into his household as a gesture of kindness and respect (2 Sam. 9:1–12).

In the Gospels Jesus calls into question the absolute authority and significance of the biological family (Matt. 12:46–50 pars.), subordinating its importance to that of the community of his followers. Jesus also speaks from the cross and makes one of his disciples responsible to care for his mother after his death (John 19:25–27). Perhaps Jesus' clearest call for his followers to participate in practices like foster care is found in the parable of judgment in Matt. 25:31–46, where Jesus informs those being judged that the basis on which they are to be judged is whether they have offered or failed to offer succor to "the least of these who are members of my family."

Paul explains that persons baptized into Christ have been united to Christ and one another as members of Christ's body (Rom. 6; 1 Cor. 12), a uniting that entails particular social commitments to the membership. Among the community's gifts, he says, is hospitality to strangers (Rom. 12:13). The call to hospitality is echoed in the Pastoral and General Epistles, the strongest statement of which is in Jas. 1:27, which makes hospitality to orphans and widows a litmus test for Christian faithfulness: "Religion that is pure and undefiled before God, the Father, is this: to care for orphans and widows in their distress, and to keep oneself unstained by the world."

See also Adoption; Children; Family; Hospitality; Orphans

Bibliography

"Adoption History Project." http://www.uoregon.edu/~adoption/; Cahn, N., and J. Hollander, eds. *Families by Law: An Adoption Reader.* New York University Press, 2004; Shuman, J., and B. Volck. *Reclaiming the Body: Christians and the Faithful Use of Modern Medicine.* Brazos, 2006, 78–93.

Joel James Shuman

Freedom

A traditional Epiphany prayer reads, "Set us free, O God, from the bondage of our sins, and give us the liberty of that abundant life which you have made known to us in your Son our Savior Jesus Christ." This captures well the scriptural view of freedom, which differs considerably from Western, post-Enlightenment thinking on the topic. Whereas Western modernity understands freedom as the autonomous decision of the individual will, Scripture sees it as harmony with the divine will, a divine-human communion enabled by divine deliverance from bondage. One might argue that the scriptural view is an outdated product of antiquity, but Christian theology insists otherwise: true freedom is "a response rather than an initiative, as one accepts the invitation to fulfill the original orientation" of one's desire for God (Burrell 49; see also Hütter). In short, freedom is the realization of the creature's divinely intended telos, the "abundant life" of union with the Creator. As Augustine notes, "There is no true liberty except the liberty of the happy who cleave to the eternal law" (*Lib.* 1.32).

The OT's most foundational story describes divine liberation in precisely this way. God frees the Israelites from bondage in Egypt (Exod. 1–18); yet the true telos of that freedom comes on Mount Sinai, where God's covenant summons them to collective obedience (Exod. 19:1–Num. 10:10). While source-critical analysis might yield a different chronology—the law emerging well after the wilderness sojourn—this only serves to underscore the significance of the story in its final form. Regardless of historical chronology, in other words, Scripture insists that the very founding of Israel is its having been freed to live in harmony with God. Psalm 119 reflects this same dynamic: "Redeem me from human oppression, that I may keep your precepts" (v. 134).

The NT claims that this freedom has been fully revealed and realized in Jesus Christ. In certain Pauline Letters, for instance, the elucidation of key christological themes concludes with ethical exhortations (see especially Romans, Galatians, Ephesians, and Colossians). So the very structure of the letters suggests that conformity to God (through Christ) is the very telos of the deliverance gained (through Christ). Nowhere is this clearer than in Gal. 5:13–14: "You were called to freedom, brothers and sisters; only do not use your freedom as an opportunity for self-indulgence, but through love become slaves to one another. For the whole law is summed up in a single commandment, 'You shall love your neighbor as yourself.'" Likewise, the Gospels' presentation of Jesus includes not only acts of deliverance but also repeated calls to conformity to his entirely self-giving life (e.g., Mark 8:34–35; John 13:1–20). This freedom to love—or, better, freedom *as* love—is hardly the self-autonomy lauded by so much of Western culture; yet it is, according to the dominant scriptural pattern, the very form that salvation takes.

Moreover, for Scripture, divine deliverance is never a purely individual or spiritual matter. It carries sociopolitical connotations as well. In the first place, as liberation theologians have insisted for decades, both Testaments insist that God's salvation entails freedom from sociopolitical bondage (see De La Torre). So, for instance, God frees the Israelites from violent enslavement in Egypt, while Jesus frees the infirm and outcast from their physical and social oppression (in line with the classic prophetic concern for "justice," lifting up the poor and needy). Thus to be "set free . . . from the bondage of our sins," as the Epiphany prayer puts it, entails the transformation of oppressive social patterns. It is freedom not only from "my" sins but also from "our" sins.

Whatever the precise form of divine liberation, the possibility of its telos—communion with God—begins within and is sustained by a divinely created community. While in the OT this community is Israel, in the NT it is the church, the "body of Christ" (1 Cor. 12:27; Eph. 4:12). The Synoptic Gospels set as the church's vocation the extension of Jesus' public ministry of liberation into the world. When they describe the sending out of apostles on mission, for instance, they make sure to model that mission on the liberating activities of Christ himself (Matt. 9:35; Mark 6:13; Luke 9:1–2). Yet the church extends Jesus' ministry only because it is, first and foremost, a community gathered around Christ, the very agent of divine liberation, just as Jesus calls the disciples to "be with him" (Mark 3:14) and "abide in" him (John 15:1–17). As Paul writes, "Where the Spirit of the Lord is, there is freedom" (2 Cor. 3:17). And when he exhorts the Philippians, "Work out your own salvation with fear and trembling" (Phil. 2:12), Paul does not make salvation a human work. Rather, he lifts up the church as the communal locus of salvation, where Christ's abiding presence empowers members to live out their freedom from sin in the only way possible: transformed interpersonal relations modeled on Christ's own self-emptying (e.g., Phil. 2:1–11). The book of Revelation, written to Christians persecuted by Rome for their allegiance to Christ, envisions this freedom in its ultimate form: the martyrs surround God in heavenly worship, "day and night without ceasing" (Rev. 4:8). Far from a mere promise, this eschatological vision describes what worship effects here and now (see Campbell): true freedom from bondage, the realization of creation's telos in submission to its Creator. The church, after all, is but a witness to the freedom intended for all of creation (Rom. 8:18–25; 1 Cor. 15:20–28; Rev. 21:1–22:7).

See also Autonomy; Emancipation; Free Will and Determinism; Individualism; Liberation; Moral Agency; Salvation; Slavery

Bibliography

Burrell, D. "Can We Be Free without a Creator?" Pages 35–52 in *God, Truth, and Witness: Engaging Stanley Hauerwas*, ed. L. Jones, R. Hütter, and C. Ewell. Brazos, 2005; Campbell, C. "Apocalypse Now." Pages 151–75 in *Narrative Reading, Narrative Preaching: Reuniting New Testament Interpretation and Proclamation*, ed. J. Green and M. Pasquarello Jr. Baker Academic, 2003; De La Torre, M. *Reading the Bible from the Margins*. Orbis, 2002; Hütter, R. "What Is So Great about Freedom?" *Pro Ecclesia* 10 (2001): 449–59.

Brent Driggers

Free Will and Determinism

There are various senses in which we might talk about a person being free—for example, a patient who is cancer-free or a prisoner who is set free. Most of the debate in philosophical and theological contexts involves the sense of freedom needed to ground moral responsibility and personal relationships, as well as whether the thesis of determinism undermines human freedom.

Contemporary Debate

In spelling out the conditions for morally significant freedom, two rival accounts, or definitions, of freedom have developed over time. The differences between these rival accounts are most readily seen when we consider their respective reactions to the thesis of determinism. Determinism is a claim about how the world operates. Specifically, the world is viewed as a series of causal chains: one event causes the next event, which itself then causes a further event, and so forth. The analogy of an unwinding clock is sometimes used here: one cog moves another cog, which then moves another cog. Once any event occurs in a deterministic world, the next event in the causal chain necessarily occurs; there is nothing within our world with any kind of "power" that could change the inevitable outcome of unfolding events. Would determinism, if true, undermine genuine human freedom? Our two rival accounts of freedom give contrasting answers.

Compatibilists view genuine freedom as a matter of doing what you want to do or value doing. On the compatibilist account, it is irrelevant whether a person's desires and values are ultimately determined by a long chain of events that began before the person was even born. Indeed, compatibilism draws its name from the fact that its conditions for a free act are compatible with that act being causally determined. Incompatibilists, on the other hand, insist that the thesis of determinism does preclude the possibility of genuine human freedom. Typically, incompatibilists offer a positive account of freedom, called "libertarian" freedom, which stipulates that although our desires and beliefs may motivate us to act and give us reasons to act, these reasons must not causally necessitate a particular action if that action is to be freely chosen. In identifying the inadequacy of compatibilist freedom, some libertarians have focused on the alleged need, when we make free choices, to have had the ability to have chosen differently. Other libertarians have focused on the slightly different point that if we are to be responsible for an action we perform, we need to be ultimately responsible for it.

The question of ultimate responsibility allows us to see most clearly the contrasting ways compatibilists and libertarians understand moral responsibility for sin. Theological determinists, who affirm that God determines all events in our world, will, of course, want to offer the standard Christian affirmation that humans are morally responsible for the sinful acts that they freely perform. Accordingly, theological determinists will need to rely on a compatibilist understanding of freedom. Libertarians, however, insist that if God is the one who ultimately decides which events we will and will not perform, then it is God, not us, who is responsible for the actions that we perform. Put another way, if God initiates a causal chain of events that inexorably leads to my performing a certain act, then the link in the causal chain that immediately precedes my action may well be my own irresistible desire to perform that action. But if I truly had no ability to alter the chain of events God set in motion, then surely the blame for my actions lies outside myself.

In response to this focus on ultimate responsibility, compatibilists will want to emphasize that if a person's action is preceded by a morally objectionable desire to perform that action, then that person has acted from a morally objectionable state of mind. It may perhaps be an interesting question how I came to have the desires and values I presently have. And ultimately this question could fully be answered only with a complete understanding—something that we could never realistically have—of all our past choices, childhood influences, DNA, and so forth. But what is important for moral responsibility is whether, at the time of performing the action, I truly desired and valued that action. If so, then that action is truly mine, and I can rightly be held responsible for it.

The libertarian at this point may argue that even if we suppose that responsibility for an action accrues to the immediate (rather than ultimate) cause of an action, this would mean that we, not God, are responsible for any praiseworthy acts that we perform. The theological determinist here may acknowledge a certain asymmetry in how responsibility accrues for human actions: humans (as the immediate cause of their actions) are responsible for their sinful acts, while God (as the ultimate cause of their actions) is responsible for their meritorious acts. Still, the theological determinist may insist that this is precisely the kind of asymmetry we should expect, on an understanding of divine election where the elect are lifted out of their sinful patterns by the sheer grace of God.

Libertarians face their own problems of coherence, specifically on the question of how we might possibly explain how people are able to "break free" from the natural laws that seem to operate in our world and initiate their own causal chains. Frequently, libertarians will appeal to the idea of "agent causation," whereby we, as irreducible "agents," can cause events to occur (without ourselves being caused to do so). This agent-event causal relationship is perhaps no more mysterious than the kind of event-event causal relationships that operate routinely within our world. And at any rate, Christians are already committed to the idea of agent-event causation with their affirmation that a personal God created our world.

Biblical Evidence

On the surface, plenty of passages can plausibly be used to support either the theological determinist or the libertarian position. The psalmist declares, "In your book were written all the days that were formed for me, when none of them as yet existed" (Ps. 139:16), and we read in the NT that God "destined us for adoption as his children through Jesus Christ, according to the good pleasure of his will" (Eph. 1:5) (see also Job 23:13–14; Ps. 65:4; Isa. 43:7; Mark 13:22; Acts 13:48; Rom. 9:11–24; Eph. 2:8–9). Yet, God speaks through the prophet Jeremiah about Israel refusing to accept certain plans that God had for them: "In vain I have struck down your children; they accepted no correction" (Jer. 2:30). And we are reminded in the NT that God is "not wanting any to perish, but all to come to repentance" (2 Pet. 3:9) (see also Deut. 30:11–19; Josh. 24:15; Isa. 53:6; Matt. 23:37; John 5:40; Rom. 2:5–8; Rev. 22:17). In accounting for passages that seem difficult for whichever position one takes on theological determinism, we will want to ask questions such as whether the context of the passage suggests that metaphysical claims are being made or that suggestive affirmations aimed at spiritual formation are being offered.

If we conclude that Scripture affirms theological determinism, then an interpretation of the Christian doctrines of predestination and election become straightforward: God determines, as a matter solely of God's discretion, that certain individuals will be reconciled to himself through Jesus Christ. If we conclude that Scripture affirms human libertarian freedom, then the doctrines of predestination and election will need to be understood differently. For instance, scriptural references to predestination may be understood corporately—that is, God sovereignly choosing the nation of Israel and the gentiles for certain roles in God's unfolding plan for humankind, with our responses as individuals to God's redemptive plan not being predestined. Alternatively, these references might be understood in terms of God predestining from all eternity the means of our salvation (i.e., through Christ), as opposed to predestining the specific people who will freely avail themselves of these means. Or, we might understand predestination in terms of God intending for all people a final destiny of eternal life with him (i.e., writing everyone's name in the book of life), with God's conditional promise to us being that if we persevere, "I will not blot your name out of the book of life" (Rev. 3:5).

Debate within the Tradition

Although there have been historic divisions within the Christian tradition over theological determinism, the Second Council of Orange (529 CE) marked out the Christian orthodox position as one where God must initiate and draw us into a relationship with him if we are to respond positively to him. The historic debate then becomes whether God's grace is irresistible, or whether there remains room for libertarian freedom. The early church fathers seemed widely to affirm something akin to what we call libertarian freedom today. Justin Martyr talked of God creating us with the "power to turn to both [vice and virtue]" (*2 Apol.* 7); Origen agreed that "it is within our power to devote ourselves either to a life that is worthy of praise, or to one that is worthy of censure" (*Princ.* 3.1.1); Irenaeus maintained that "all *men* are of the same nature, able both to hold fast and to do what is *good*; and, on the other hand, having also the power to cast it from them and not to do it" (*Haer.* 4.37.2); and Tertullian described a person's freedom in terms of God having "conferred upon him both tendencies [to good and evil]; so that, as master of himself, he might constantly encounter good by spontaneous observance of it, and evil by its spontaneous avoidance" (*Marc.* 2.6).

The weight of opinion on the nature of human freedom shifted quite dramatically at the turn of the fifth century with the influential writings of Augustine. Augustine's emphasis that all good things ultimately emanate from God led him to describe God's grace as "that by which alone men are delivered from evil" (*Corrept.* 3), and Augustine has been widely interpreted as therefore denying human ability to choose between good and evil. Although the Eastern church did not follow Augustine on this point, Western theologians predominantly did align themselves with the Augustinian view that humans can will the good only if their wills are determined by God. This trend continued in the Western church until at least the time of the early fourteenth-century writings of John Duns Scotus. Duns Scotus affirmed that humans have the capacity to choose between pursuing personal happiness and acting charitably out of a concern for justice, and he provided technical arguments as to why the will "has the potentiality to determine itself to either alternative" (165). This more libertarian understanding of human freedom was widely affirmed within the Roman Catholic Church by the time of the Protestant Reformation, with the Council of Trent specifically declaring that a person is able to respond to God's invitation "by agreeing to, and cooperating with His grace, which he could resist" (Denzinger 1791); it continues to be the accepted Roman Catholic position today. By contrast, John Calvin and other Protestant Reformers, who aligned themselves with Augustine on many issues, tended to emphasize strongly a theological deterministic worldview, which allows room for compatibilist freedom but not libertarian freedom. Continuing the pattern of the past few centuries, some Protestants today continue to affirm Calvin's theology, while others affirm a more libertarian-oriented theology, as articulated by Jacobus Arminius.

See also Accountability; Autonomy; Freedom; Grace; Moral Agency; Responsibility

Bibliography

Augustine of Hippo. *On Rebuke and Grace*. Pages 471–91 in vol. 5 of *The Nicene and Post-Nicene Fathers*, ed. P. Schaff. T&T Clark, 1991; Denzinger, H., ed. *Enchiridion symbolorum: Definitionum et declarationum de rebus fidei et morum*. 31st ed. Herder, 1957; Duns Scotus, J. *Duns Scotus on the Will and Morality*. Ed. A. Wolter. Catholic University of America Press, 1986; Irenaeus. *Against Heresies*. Pages 315–567 in vol. 1 of *The Ante-Nicene Fathers*, ed. A. Roberts and J. Donaldson. Eerdmans, 1981; Justin Martyr. *Second Apology*. Pages 188–93 in vol. 1 of *The Ante-Nicene Fathers*, ed. A. Roberts and J. Donaldson. Eerdmans, 1981; Origen, *De principiis*. Pages 239–304 in vol. 4 of *The Ante-Nicene Fathers*, ed. A. Roberts and J. Donaldson. Eerdmans, 1981; Swinburne, R. *Responsibility and Atonement*. Clarendon, 1989; Tertullian. *Against Marcion*. Pages 269–475 in vol. 3 of *The Ante-Nicene Fathers*, ed. A. Roberts and J. Donaldson. Eerdmans, 1981.

Kevin Kinghorn

Friendship, Friendship Ethics

Friendships are relationships based in attraction in which persons are drawn together by the recognition of, and desire to share, something good and appealing in each other. The distinctive mark of friendship is that each person not only wishes for the good of the other (benevolence) but also actively works to achieve it (beneficence) and, because of affection for the friend, finds joy in doing so. Friends have similar interests, beliefs, goals, cares, and commitments. And because they like each other, they enjoy spending time together engaged in the goods and activities that uniquely characterize their friendship. The deeper and more substantive those goods and activities are, the richer and more promising will be the possibilities of the friendship. Finally, because friendships require openness and trust and involve some degree of intimacy and vulnerability, they cannot be sustained without virtues such as loyalty, justice, and perseverance.

Friendship ethics is an approach to the moral life guided by the conviction that the good is something that people pursue in company with others who also want to become good. Working in the tradition of Aristotle, and later Thomas Aquinas, philosophers and theologians who embrace this model argue that humans are social creatures who acquire the virtues and grow in the various habits and practices of goodness in and through the best and most formative relationships of their lives. They contend that the moral life is most properly understood as a quest for the unique human happiness that is found in goodness—for Christians in the unsurpassable goodness of God—but insist that such an adventure can be neither undertaken nor sustained without the guidance and support of friends. Thus, friendships not only make the moral life more pleasant or appealing but also are the form of life that makes it possible.

Friendship in Scripture

Although there is no detailed, systematic account of friendship in Scripture, there are numerous references to friendship and unmistakable esteem for friendship. Luke Timothy Johnson calls friendship a "prominent" and "pervasive" theme in the NT (Johnson 158–59). The esteem for friendship can be seen throughout Scripture, in the poignant portrayals of the friendships of Ruth and Naomi and of David and Jonathan, in the friendship that Jesus had with Martha and Mary and their brother Lazarus, and most especially in the friendship that developed between Jesus and his closest disciples. Indeed, on the eve of his crucifixion Jesus used the language of friendship to describe the bond that had formed between him and those closest to him. He spoke of those disciples not as servants or slaves but as friends, because just as all close friendships involve the sharing of confidences, Jesus had confided to them everything the Father had disclosed to him (John 15:15). Moreover, the unity characteristic of friendships is echoed in the farewell address of Jesus when he prayed that the communion that exists between him and his father might extend to those who follow him (John 17:22–23). And in the intimate exchange between the risen Jesus and Peter, when Jesus three times asked Peter if he loved him, the Gospel records Peter's avowal of love with the Greek word *phileō*, indicating friendship (John 21:15–17).

Likewise, wisdom literature is interspersed with references to friendship. Of Wisdom it is said that "in every generation she passes into holy souls and makes them friends of God, and prophets, for God loves nothing so much as the person who lives with wisdom" (Wis. 7:27–28). And Sirach offers insightful counsel on friendship when it cautions readers on the difference between fickle friends and genuine ones, calls for friends to be tested and tried before being trusted, and laments that many who claim to be friends flee when sorrow and adversity visit their friend (Sir. 6:6–13). But after warning readers about counterfeit friendships, the text concludes by exulting in the preciousness of friendship, comparing the faithful friend to a sturdy shelter, a treasure, and "life-saving medicine" (Sir. 6:14–17).

In the NT, Acts describes the communal life of the first Christians in terms akin to friendship (2:44–46). Just as the classical tradition of friendship emphasized the shared life of friendships, the harmony among friends, and that friends had "one soul" between them, Acts records that the first Christians "were together and had all things in common" (Acts 2:44), and that they were "of one heart and soul" (Acts 4:32). But the fellowship among the early Christians went beyond the classical accounts of friendship developed by Plato, Cicero, and Aristotle because it did not depend on social and economic equality. The unity among Christians was rooted not in similar social, economic, or political status, but in Christ and the Spirit (Johnson 162). And unlike the patron-client relationships that created obligations and indebtedness, in these Christian communities the wealthy shared what they had with those who may have been poor, but who were their equals in Christ (Acts 2:44–45). Thus, if a classic definition of friendship was that friends held things in common, in the early church this was normatively expressed through the sharing of material possessions. Beyond Acts, Paul utilized the classical tradition of friendship in his emphasis on the Christian life as a fellowship that is nurtured and sustained by precisely the practices that preserve friendships (e.g., honor, encouragement, kindness, support, fraternal correction, forgiveness) and is weakened by attitudes and behavior inimical to friendship (e.g., envy and discord).

Moreover, the entire biblical story of salvation can fittingly be read as a chronicle of God's befriending love. In creating humans in the divine image and sanctifying them in grace, God calls men and women to friendship with one another and to friendship with God. The covenant that God makes with Israel bespeaks both the affection and intimacy characteristic of friendships, and the expectations and responsibilities that are part of friendships. Also, Israel's infidelity exposes the betrayal and pain that sometimes accompany friendships, while God's patience and forgiveness demonstrate how strained and broken friendships can be healed. In his incarnation, Jesus is God's friendship with us "in person," and through his life, ministry, death, and resurrection, Jesus transcended the conventional limits of friendship by extending God's friendship to everyone—not just to social equals (Aristotle, *Eth. nic.* 8.1158b–1159a), but indeed even to the enemies of God (Carmichael 39). And through the Spirit, God is the friend who dwells in the hearts of all humans and who steadfastly accompanies them through life.

Friendship in the Tradition

The significance that friendship might have for the Christian life was most fully and richly explored in the fourth century when patristic theologians who had been classically educated in Greek and Roman philosophy and literature sought to incorporate the best of those traditions into their writings on the Christian life. Theologians such as Basil of Caesarea, Gregory of Nyssa, John Chrysostom, Gregory of Nazianzus, Ambrose, Jerome, and Augustine recognized that there was much in classical accounts of pagan friendship that could be adapted to the Christian life (White 4). For example, if Aristotle and Cicero held that friends shared the same good, then for Christian friends the shared good was life together in Christ. Or if the telos, or goal, of friendships for Aristotle and Cicero was prosperity in Athens or Rome, for Christians it was everlasting friendship with God and the saints in heaven. Thus, Christian friends sought one another's good when they helped one another grow in the new life of grace by acquiring and imitating the virtues of Christ. Because friendships grounded in Christ helped the friends grow in love of God and love of neighbor, they were seen as sanctifying ways of life. Indeed, far from distracting the friends from their love for God, such friendships helped them to remain focused on God and taught them that they experienced God's love not apart from their friendships, but through them. And if the classical tradition claimed that friends shared "one soul" between them, these patristic writers argued that the intimacy and unity possible in friendships among Christians were immensely greater and more enduring because Christians became one through the grace and love of God. Finally, these writers taught that the limits and fragility of earthly friendships were transcended in heaven. Eternal life marked not the end of friendships but rather their perfection, because in heaven all the friends of God will love one another and together will love and enjoy God.

The role of friendship in the Christian life was further explored in Aelred of Rievaulx's *Spiritual Friendship*, a twelfth-century treatise that is a Christian reworking of Cicero's *De amicitia* (*On Friendship*). Aelred was a Cistercian monk and abbot of Rievaulx, a monastery in northeastern England. He wrote *Spiritual Friendship* to show his fellow monks what good friendships should be in the monastic life and how they could aid their religious vocations. Aelred believed that good friendships should serve one's life in Christ. He distinguished spiritual friendships from other relationships by declaring that Christ is an active partner in a spiritual friendship, just as present to the friendship as the friends are to each other. For Aelred, spiritual friendship is life together in and with Christ, but also for the sake of Christ. Through spiritual friendships people live out their baptisms, imitate Christ, and thus become friends of God. Furthermore, given what is at stake in these relationships, Aelred taught that spiritual friends should be carefully selected and should manifest specific qualities of character such as faithfulness, trustworthiness, and stability. But once entered into, the relationships should end only if they become detrimental to a person's relationship with God.

A century later, Thomas Aquinas took the tradition further by defining charity (*caritas*), the central virtue of the Christian life, as friendship with God. Unlike Aristotle, who held that men and women could never be friends with the gods because the disparity between the gods and humans was too great, Thomas taught that God shares or "communicates" the divine love and happiness with every person, and that gift makes a life of friendship with God possible (*ST* II-II, q. 23, a. 1). To live in friendship with God is the vocation of every human being, Thomas reasoned, because only in God do people find the goodness, happiness, and beauty that will make them content and complete. Furthermore, a life of charity or friendship with God is an inherently communal way of life because individuals grow in the goodness and holiness of God only in fellowship with others. And a life of friendship with God is a distinctive and challenging way of life clustered around certain practices or virtues, which Thomas called the acts or effects of charity: joy, peace, mercy, kindness, almsgiving, and fraternal correction (*ST* II-II, q. 28–33). These practices characterize the life of charity and illustrate what living in friendship with God actually entails. Finally, the life of charity is centered in Christ because Christ is the perfect manifestation not only of God's friendship with humans but also of what it would mean for men and women to live in perfect friendship with God. For Thomas, Christ mentors persons in a life of friendship with God through the sacraments, particularly the Eucharist.

Contemporary Developments

After the thirteenth century, friendship not only faded from theological speculation but also was derided as the antithesis of genuine Christian love. First, once the Christian moral life began to be viewed primarily in the language of laws, duties and obligations, commands, and obedience, and not as a quest for happiness and goodness through the virtues, there was little role for friendship in it. Second, instead of seeing friendship as a context for learning the distinctive Christian love, *agapē*, friendship became viewed not only as a lesser or defective kind of love, but even as a pagan or ungodly expression of love. Compared to *agapē*, friendship's fatal flaw was that it is a preferential and selective love rooted in likeness and attraction, and a love that requires reciprocity. By contrast, Christian love was judged to be inclusive, universal, and offered to every person, even one's most persistent enemies, regardless of whether it is returned. The classic treatment of this understanding of the relationship between friendship (*philia*) and Christian love (*agapē*) is Anders Nygren's *Agape and Eros* (Swedish original, 1930–36). In contrast to friendship, Nygren famously defined *agapē* as spontaneous, uncalculated and unmotivated, absolutely universal and unconditional, and not dependent on the worth or goodness of the recipient.

Nygren's trenchant analysis largely displaced friendship as a subject for theological inquiry until the publication of Gilbert Meilaender's *Friendship* (1981) and the revival of virtue ethics. This, along with feminist ethicists' emphasis on the relational character of life, renewed interest in, and appreciation for, the place of friendship in the moral life. In response to Nygren, theologians who espouse friendship ethics argue that friendship's focus on the well-being of the other makes it a fitting setting for learning and growing in Christian love. In addition, the virtues and qualities of character that are essential for friendship (e.g., generosity, justice, faithfulness, attentiveness, thoughtfulness, forgiveness) are precisely the habits that Jesus extols in the Gospels. And as Thomas Aquinas's explication of charity testifies, far from narrowing one's world, friendships centered in Christ challenge Christians to expand the circle of love to embrace all of one's neighbors, who are loved and befriended by God, whether they be family members, close friends, strangers, or enemies. Thus, when seen through the lens of friendship, the Christian moral life becomes a richly human, deeply hopeful, but also magnanimously challenging way of life.

See also Agape; Benevolence; Charity, Works of; Happiness; Moral Development; Moral Formation; Neighbor, Neighbor Love; Virtue(s); Virtue Ethics

Bibliography

Aelred of Rievaulx. *Spiritual Friendship*. Cistercian Publications, 1977; Aristotle. *Nichomachean Ethics*. Trans. M. Ostwald. Bobbs-Merrill, 1962; Carmichael, L. *Friendship: Interpreting Christian Love*. T&T Clark, 2004; Hunt, M. *Fierce Tenderness: A Feminist Theology of Friendship*. Crossroad, 1992; Johnson, L. "Making Connections: The Material Expression of Friendship in the New Testament." *Int* 58 (2004): 158–71; Meilaender, G. *Friendship: A Study in Theological Ethics*. University of Notre Dame Press, 1981; Nygren, A. *Agape and Eros*. Trans. P. Watson. Westminster, 1953; Wadell, P. *Becoming Friends: Worship, Justice, and the Practice of Christian Friendship*. Brazos, 2002; idem. *Friendship and the Moral Life*. University of Notre Dame Press, 1989; White, C. *Christian Friendship in the Fourth Century*. Cambridge University Press, 1992.

Paul J. Wadell

Fruit of the Spirit

"The fruit of the Spirit" is Paul's metaphor (Gal. 5:22) that he places in contrast to his metaphor "the works of the flesh" (Gal. 5:19). Flesh and Spirit are contrasting powers or "desires" that produce opposing ways of human life together (Gal. 5:17). Paul designates love as the Spirit's first fruit.

Having highlighted this initial contrast of powers, Paul illuminates subsequent contrasts that have ethical import. Second, therefore, "works" in the plural contrasts with "fruit" in the singular. Flesh produces an unhindered plethora of obvious works that divide people from one another and thus hinder people from inheriting God's kingdom. Paul stresses the chaotic plurality of these works, which is comparable to the swamp of evils unleashed on the world when Pandora proverbially opened the box. Spirit, however, produces a singular "fruit" that issues in a flourishing life together led by the Spirit.

Paul's third contrast comes in Gal. 5:18, where life together "led by the Spirit" is distinguished from life together "subject to the law." On the one hand, for Paul, the law has its source in God and thereby is itself always good. Yet, law always intrinsically embodies a distinctive coercive element in order to gain even a semblance of flourishing human life together. On the other hand, Paul's organic metaphor of fruit stresses the effective yet noncoercive force field of life together in the Spirit. The notion of fruit recalls Jesus' words "every good tree bears good fruit" (Matt. 7:17). Because the Holy Spirit is free and freeing (2 Cor. 3:17; Gal. 5:1), Augustine and those influenced by him stress the spontaneity of the Christian life in the Spirit in contrast to the coercive character of a life together subject to God's law.

With these three contrasts framing Paul's metaphor of fruit of the Spirit, questions often arise about how to think through Paul's lists that follow the powers of flesh and Spirit. It is unlikely that Paul is using any ancient commonplace list of vices or virtues, or that he is giving some kind of specifically Christian comprehensive listing of vices or virtues. Some interpreters have thought that Paul is referencing three groups of three virtues, but others have rightly found that idea not persuasive or fruitful for ethical reflection. That Paul says "and things like these" and "such things" (Gal. 5:21, 23) indicates the illustrative and thereby nonexhaustive nature of these listings.

One significant suggestion made first by Augustine and taken up again by Martin Luther, among others, is that Paul places love as the first fruit of the Spirit because love is really the only virtue of Christian life together. In this view, love issues from faith in Christ, which is created by the Spirit (Rom. 5:5; 1 Cor. 13; Gal. 5:6). Christ becomes the one form of Christian faith and freedom—"Love one another as I have loved you" (John 15:12) (see Bonhoeffer). Indeed, this "as I have loved you" "expands into all" (Luther 93) aspects of the Christian life together producing, forming, and norming whatever other subsequent virtues are needed in order to serve neighbors and their neighborhoods and communities. Whether the neighbor is within or without the Christian church appears unimportant (Rom. 13:8–10; Gal. 5:13–14). Love seeking justice operates like a pluripotent stem cell becoming through Christian discernment whatever set of virtues neighbors, neighborhoods, and communities need for their welfare, thus setting out the breadth of Christian vocation in God's world.

The Augustinian-Lutheran trajectory opens a more discernment-oriented model of Christian ethical reflection that focuses on the necessities and needs of neighbors and their neighborhoods and communities. This contrasts with the "third use of the law" model of Christian ethical reflection, initiated by Philip Melanchthon and John Calvin, which focuses Christian ethical reflection more on identifying, following, and applying the particulars of biblical injunctions and commands. On the one hand, the "fruit of the Spirit" approach to ethical reflection based on discerning love seeking justice for the neighbor resonates with the centrality of prudence within classical and medieval natural law approaches to ethics, still championed by many contemporary Roman Catholic moral theologians. On the other hand, the "third use of the law" approach, which looks to biblical laws and NT injunctions as superior rules that guide Christian life, has largely rejected Christian natural-law reasoning.

See also Galatians; Love, Love Command; Vices and Virtues, Lists of; Virtue(s)

Bibliography

Bonhoeffer, D. "Ethics as Formation." Pages 76–102 in *Ethics*. Fortress, 2005; Boyce, J. "The Poetry of the Spirit." *WW* 20 (2000): 290–98; Grabill, S. *Rediscovering the Natural Law in Reformed Theological Ethics*. Eerdmans, 2006; Longenecker, R. *Galatians*. WBC 41. Word, 1990; Luther, M. *Lectures on Galatians, 1535*. Ed. J. Pelikan. 2 vols. Concordia, 1963–64; Martyn, J. *Galatians*. AB 33A. Doubleday, 1997; Plumer, E. *Augustine's Commentary on Galatians*. OECS. Oxford University Press, 2003; Porter, J. *Nature as Reason: A Thomistic Theory of Natural Law*. Eerdmans, 2005.

Gary M. Simpson

Fundamentalism

In the popular press, any movement that takes religion seriously might be labeled "fundamentalist." Scholars, however, seek more careful definitions, and contemporary Protestant fundamentalism emphasizes (1) the historical tenets of the Protestant Reformation (e.g., salvation by faith alone, the Bible as the sole authority in faith and practice); (2) evangelism; (3) personal transformation through relationship with Christ; (4) absolute biblical inerrancy; (5) premillennial dispensationalism, emphasizing the present fulfillment of end-times scenarios depicted in Scripture; (6) separatism, an unwillingness to bend on numerous doctrinal points; and (7) an aggressive, almost hostile approach to engaging the secular public. Fundamentalism shares the first three points with evangelicalism; the last four are more typically exclusive to fundamentalism.

Fundamentalist ethics focus on applying Scripture as literally as possible within a biblical-theological framework—that is, an understanding of the meaning of the Bible as a whole that logically links and emphasizes scriptural teachings that transcend multiple biblical texts. The primary debates within fundamentalist ethics, and between evangelicals and fundamentalists, reach back to the diverse biblical-theological frameworks that different groups use when reading Scripture. At its most literalist expression, one finds Greg Bahnsen and Rousas Rushdoony, whose theonomy or reconstructionism advocates the literal application of Mosaic law (e.g., capital punishment for blasphemy or adultery). Pat Robertson and Jerry Falwell have provided more popular and less literal voices; both are highly selective in the ethical issues they engage, choosing those issues that fundamentalists and non-Christians most disagree about (e.g., abortion, homosexuality, prayer in schools, creationism) over issues allowing for more common ground (e.g., domestic violence, adultery, alcoholism).

Fundamentalism combines a Christendom model of biblical faith and practice with an "age of reason" worldview: the nation as a whole, not only the church, is to follow biblical guidelines as closely as possible, while the Bible shapes, informs, and, perhaps most important, limits the reach of scientific and intellectual inquiry. Fundamentalists emphasize ethical issues that they believe most clearly show the manner in which society as a whole has strayed from scriptural precepts. The features of fundamentalists' use of Scripture in ethics most unique to them are (1) the selective retrieval of ethical mandates from Scripture, which cause the highest level of friction between the fundamentalist community and a secularizing public; (2) the frequent emphasis on OT models in which commands to national Israel are transposed to contemporary nations; (3) the deliberate use of combative language in the public sphere, designed to challenge the broader nonfundamentalist public; and (4) the use of eschatological/end-times scenarios to guide recommendations in international relations and foreign policy, particularly with regard to the Middle East, promoting uncompromising support for the modern Israeli state even beyond that of most Jewish lobbies.

Fundamentalist ethical applications of Scripture are by far the most widely known and reported both in the general media and throughout most Christian communities, exercising enormous influence even in churches and organizations that reject fundamentalist ethics. This is at least partly because fundamentalist ethics provides simple, straightforward approaches to difficult questions, and fundamentalists find it easy to "out-Bible" their Christian opponents, citing numerous scriptural verses that purportedly stand behind their claims.

See also Eschatology and Ethics; Evangelical Ethics; Moral Absolutes

Bibliography

Marsden, G. *Understanding Fundamentalism and Evangelicalism*. Eerdmans, 1991; Marty, M., and R. Appleby. *The Fundamentalism Project*. 5 vols. University of Chicago Press, 1991–95; Ryrie, C. *Dispensationalism*. Moody, 1995.

David Scoggins

Funerals *See* Death and Dying

G

Galatians

In this letter Paul expresses astonishment that certain unnamed teachers who seem to have insinuated themselves into his Galatian churches are persuading some members of those congregations to abandon the gospel that he had proclaimed to them. He is concerned, especially, that those gentile believers have been deceived into thinking that they must submit to various requirements of the Jewish law, including circumcision and the kosher table. The apostle seeks to refute this false teaching by asserting the divine origin of his law-free gospel and reminding the Galatians of its central affirmations.

Paul emphasizes that he proclaims Jesus Christ as the crucified Son of God (2:20–21; 3:1, 13–14), and that Christ's saving death has inaugurated a "new creation" (6:15) that believers experience as rectification ("justification" [2:16, 17, 21; 3:24; 5:4]) and freedom (2:4; 5:1, 13). Because "God shows no partiality" (2:6), this is "good news" for gentiles as well as for Jews (2:7–10; 3:28; 6:16).

What Paul means by the new creation, rectification, and freedom is expressed more concretely in a series of images. Believers are no longer enslaved to the "present evil age" (1:4), the law (3:23), the "elemental spirits of the world" (4:3), or their own desires (5:16–17). Having been "baptized into Christ," they are also "clothed" with him (3:27) and adopted as God's children (3:26; 4:1–3). They are therefore, even as gentiles, "Abraham's offspring, heirs according to the promise" (3:14–20, 29). Moreover, as "children of [God's] promise" (4:28), they have received God's Spirit (3:2, 5, 14; 4:6), by whom they are enabled to live out in the present the rectification already accomplished and to await with hope its ultimate fulfillment (5:5–6, 16–18, 22, 25; 6:8).

The explicit ethical appeals of this letter, which are concentrated in 5:13–6:10, are anticipated in the declaration that what matters most is not "circumcision" or "uncircumcision"—one's relationship to the law—but "faith made effective through love" (5:6 NRSV mg.). For Paul, faith is elicited by God's love as it has been revealed in the faithfulness of God's Son, "who loved . . . and gave himself" for others (2:20). And faith is expressed concretely as believers become agents of God's love in the world. Accordingly, the appeals in 5:13–6:10 highlight several ways in which the selfless love of Christ ought to be active in the lives of those who belong to him. Paul seems to be thinking especially of the perilous situation in the Galatian churches, where disputes about circumcision and other Jewish practices were turning Christian against Christian (5:15, 26 [note also, in 5:19–21, the inclusion of vices such as "strife," "quarrels," "dissensions," and "factions" in his listing of "the works of the flesh"]).

The introductory appeal (5:13) urges the Galatians not to use their freedom to serve their own interests (literally, "the flesh"), but, paradoxically, to bind themselves to one another "through love," as "slaves" are bound in service to their masters. Over against those who hold that gentile believers must adopt Jewish practices, Paul declares that the whole law is summed up in the one commandment to love the neighbor (5:14 [cf. "the law of Christ" in 6:2]). His summons to "live by the Spirit" (5:16–25) is also a call for the outworking of faith in love, for he regards love as the first and all-inclusive "fruit of the Spirit." No less important, his concluding appeal (6:10) to "work for the good of all" enlarges the field of love's service to include even those who stand outside the "family of faith."

Three significant convictions inform and support the ethical appeals in this letter. (1) What matters most is not one's adherence to religious rites and rules, but the "new creation" that God has inaugurated through Christ's death on the cross (6:14–15) and "faith made effective through love" (5:6). (2) Those who have been "baptized into Christ" understand that one's true identity is not contingent on religious, ethnic, social, or sexual status (3:27–28), but on one's standing before God and in Christ (e.g., 2:19–20). (3) Life before God and in Christ is simultaneously life in the Spirit, through whose empowering presence believers are guided in the ways of love (5:16–25). These same convictions, variously developed and expressed, are evident throughout all of Paul's letters.

See also Fruit of the Spirit; Love, Love Command; Vices and Virtues, Lists of

Bibliography

Barclay, J. *Obeying the Truth: A Study of Paul's Ethics in Galatians*. SNTW. T&T Clark, 1988; Hays, R. "Galatians." Pages 181–348 in *The New Interpreter's Bible*, vol. 11, ed. L. Keck. Abingdon, 2000; Martyn, J. *Galatians*. AB 33A. Doubleday, 1997.

Victor Paul Furnish

Gambling

Gambling is playing any game of chance and probability, involving the voluntary wagering of money or sometimes property to win a monetary prize or item of value larger than the amount of the original wager. According to this definition, gambling is not found in the Bible.

Readers of the Bible sometimes mistake the casting of lots for gambling. Most instances of casting lots in the OT are examples where the ancient Israelites employed this practice to ask God to make a decision. Issues including the possession of land (Josh. 18:6, 8, 10; Neh. 11:1), how sacrifices to God are to be made (Lev. 16:8; Neh. 10:34), which persons would serve God in a specific ministry (1 Chr. 24:31; 25:8; 26:13–14), and deciding the guilt or innocence of persons (1 Sam. 14:42; Jon. 1:7) found resolution this way. The NT features this means of casting lots only once (Acts 1:26), when the apostles asked God if either Matthias or Justus would succeed Judas and join their ranks.

Other examples of casting lots in the Bible portray it as a convenient means for people to make a decision or determine the possession of slaves and property. Examples of this practice in the OT include the Persian leadership casting lots to determine the day they would execute their planned genocide against the Jews (Esth. 3:7; 9:24), and another situation where unspecified conquerors of Israel cast lots to determine who would take possession of Jerusalem (Obad. 11) and take Israelite nobles as slaves (Nah. 3:10). Another passage (Ps. 22:18) foreshadows the sole, and arguably most infamous, example of this other method of casting lots in the NT. All four Gospels portray the men responsible for crucifying Jesus casting lots to determine who would take possession of his tunic (Matt. 27:35; Mark 15:24; Luke 23:34; John 19:24).

Neither is the parable of the talents (Matt. 25:14–30; Luke 19:12–27) an example of gambling in the Bible. The servants in the parable are engaged in acts of investing the master's money. Admittedly, sound investment practices possess a degree of uncertainty that gives it a resemblance to gambling, but the similarity ends there. Good investors invest with a level of risk that is judged manageable. A highly skilled card player can use applied mathematics to increase the odds of a winning hand, but the level of risk remains intolerable for a responsible investor.

No explicit prohibition or endorsement of gambling can be found in the Bible because casting lots or using talents both lack one or more of its features. Nothing is wagered, and most outcomes are not left to chance but rather to God or individual prudential judgment. Therefore, it is not surprising that while Protestant and Orthodox churches generally prohibit gambling in all its forms, they rarely employ the Bible in their arguments opposing it. In those instances where the Bible is employed against gambling, it is used to support arguments that warn against its destructive personal and social effects. Gambling's negative effects, in particular addiction and coveting the material gain of easy money either in the form of personal winnings or tax revenues at the expense of the majority of gamblers who lose money, are put forward as examples that violate Jesus' commands to love God and neighbor (Mark 12:29–31). Gambling is viewed as also violating biblical principles of the responsible stewardship of resources to meet the legitimate needs of others (Eph. 4:28).

Official Roman Catholic teaching is drawn from virtue ethics, which Catholics understand is in agreement with the ethical principles found in the Bible. Gambling is not viewed as intrinsically evil as long as the wagering is free of corruption and does not involve high stakes, understood as endangering one's ability to provide for personal needs and the needs of others. Within these parameters, justice is maintained because players are receiving the due consequences for their free participation in games of chance.

See also Debt; Economic Ethics; Greed; Stewardship

Bibliography

Beardslee, W. "The Casting of Lots at Qumran and in the Book of Acts." *NovT* 4 (1960): 249–52; Catholic Church, *Catechism of the Catholic Church*. 2nd ed. Libreria Editrice Vaticana, 2000, §2413; Kitz, A. "The Hebrew Terminology of Lot Casting and Its Ancient Near Eastern Context." *CBQ* 62 (2000): 207–14; Peck, J., and E. Alsgaard, eds. *The Book of Resolutions of The United Methodist Church*. United Methodist Publishing House, 2008, 553–56; Stapleford, J. *Bulls, Bears, and Golden Calves: Applying Christian Ethics to Economics*. IVP Academic, 2002, 158–71.

Ramón Luzárraga

Gender

The use of the term *gender* as distinct from *sex* came to prominence within contemporary feminist literature wishing to emphasize the social constructedness of male and female roles and images. If the nineteenth century discovered the constructedness of class and its hidden oppressions, the twentieth century can be said to have discovered gender and the similar hiddenness of binding expectations encapsulated in social mores, language, law, and sacred Scripture. A new literature and a new discipline of gender studies have emerged that comprise the study of social constructions surrounding roles that might once have been thought to be biologically prescribed; this might include either an analysis of subtle socialization and social pressures on men and women to act and take up gender-appropriate roles and occupations or a study of the media portrayal of image. Gender questions in the church have focused on feminist issues and on those surrounding headship and homosexuality.

Attending to gender not only reveals oppression but also brings to light hidden strengths and capacities. Thus, one of the central insights of twentieth-century feminism was that women's perspectives had not been noticed. In her book *In a Different Voice*, Carol Gilligan discovered a new way to understand human morality, that which looks through a lens of care for others and not only the (equally valid) lens of impartial justice. Women were more likely to use the ethics of care, yet all empirical research to that time had attended only to the moral thinking of males.

There has long been discussion about the relative input of biology and culture in the making of human society and ethics. Yet even the biological categories are ill defined; at least 1 percent of humans are of indeterminate sexuality. For these individuals, questions surrounding gender and identity may be particularly vexing, as they are for those whose sense of gender does not correspond to their biological sex. The church has struggled in this area, seeking to find an elusive biblical truth beneath the morass of social identity construction, and either justifying or condemning homosexual practice and ordination.

With the unmasking of hidden oppressions comes also an awareness that power is closely tied to social differentiations of every kind. This is of interest theologically because Christ has called his followers to identify and to resist evil, and because Christ's teaching (most clearly in Matt. 5) always subverted and resisted humanly constructed privilege. Important also has been the gender of God and the maleness of Christ; Yahweh is without gender, but any analysis of gender and theology quickly notes that God has become engendered within the tradition. Feminist theology has attended to questions of gender in common worship, prayer, and theology, where the use of male pronouns for God and humanity has produced what Brenda Brasher calls a "partitioned sacred canopy." In the contemporary evangelical church, discussion about the roles of men and women has focused on the biblical motif of headship. For many women, the gendered nature of their church experience has been so overwhelming as to make Christian faith untenable.

Others have tried to redeem this state of affairs, pointing to trajectories of resistance in the narratives of Scripture, to surprisingly subversive language for God (e.g., Prov. 1:20; Isa. 42:14), and to Jesus as one who undermined gender expectations and social power structures in decisive ways (Mark 7:27). They would also point to the undermining of gender roles wherever the Holy Spirit has worked in new and surprising ways in biblical history and in the church.

All these discussions can be understood as seeking to discover what a virtuous life might look like for all. The diversity of answers—from submissive wife to God-filled teacher, from male hero to gentle provider or equal partner—reflects the fractured nature of the church today. That gender and "God" language are still considered to be largely nonconstructed in the church at large makes for added confusion in this area. Reflection on gender has indeed opened a can of theological worms, but it also has exposed hidden sin and shown the depth of Jesus' redemptive overturning of human constructions of privilege.

See also Body; Creation, Biblical Accounts of; Equality; Feminist Ethics; Headship; Homosexuality; Marriage and Divorce; Sex and Sexuality; Sex Discrimination; Sexual Harassment; Virtue(s); Women, Status of

Bibliography

Cranny-Francis, A., et al. *Gender Studies: Terms and Debates*. Palgrave MacMillan, 2003; Gilligan, C. *In a Different Voice: Psychological Theory and Women's Development*. Harvard University Press, 1982; Storkey, E. *Created or Constructed? The Great Gender Debate*. Pasternoster, 2000; Young, I. *Justice and the Politics of Difference*. Princeton University Press, 1990.

Nicola Hoggard Creegan

Generosity

Generosity is the virtue of unselfish giving or, by implication, giving that exceeds expectations. Although the related concept of goodness is prominent in the OT, the majority of explicit biblical references to generosity are found in the NT; half occur in the letters of Paul.

Generosity is, first, an attribute of God. The Bible describes God as one who "gives to all generously and ungrudgingly" (Jas. 1:5). Paul speaks of "the generous act of our Lord Jesus Christ" (2 Cor. 8:9) and sees a specific connection between divine generosity and impartiality (Rom. 10:12). Such a connection may also be implied in Jesus' parable of the generous landowner (Matt. 20:1–15), in which indiscriminate generosity is presented as scandalous. Specifically, the Bible portrays God as generous in providing humanity with the gifts of nature (Gen. 1:29–30; Matt. 5:45), in offering forgiveness of sins (Ps. 86:5; Rom. 5:6–8), and in responding to prayer (Matt. 7:7–11).

Human generosity is said to derive from God, as an attribute of godliness. Extraordinary generosity may be a gift of the Spirit given to some (Rom. 12:6–8), but generosity is also a fruit of the Spirit produced in all believers (Gal. 5:22). For this reason, "every generous act of giving" may be said to come from God (Jas. 1:17).

Although there is slight reference in the Bible to humans being generous toward God (as in offering generous sacrifices [Exod. 35:5]), the emphasis with regard to human generosity is on that which is shown to other people. The primary biblical interest, furthermore, lies in the economic realm. Hypothetically, people might be generous with regard to many things (their time, their affection, etc.), but in fact the virtue of generosity is almost always expressed in the Bible with reference to charitable financial giving, particularly on behalf of the needy (e.g., Prov. 22:9). In the psalms, such generosity is closely linked to both righteousness (Ps. 37:21) and justice (Ps. 112:5).

The Bible offers numerous examples of generous people: Zacchaeus (Luke 19:1–10), a poor widow (Mark 12:41–44), the women who provided for Jesus and his disciples (Luke 8:1–3), Barnabas (Acts 4:36–37) and other members of the Jerusalem church (Acts 2:46), Cornelius (Acts 10:2), the Macedonian believers (2 Cor. 8:1–2), and many others. Paul, in particular, exhorts believers to be generous (2 Cor. 8:7), not only because of the benefit that their giving provides to others but also because such charity proves the genuine character of their faith and brings glory or thanksgiving to God (2 Cor. 9:11–13 [cf. Matt. 5:16]).

The rich have a particular obligation to be generous (1 Tim. 6:17–18), but the Bible often attributes generosity to persons who are not wealthy (Mark 12:41–44; 2 Cor. 8:2). This leads to an important observation: generosity is not simply to be equated with extravagant giving, as motive is a significant factor. Jesus denounces those who make large gifts in order to enhance their prestige (Matt. 6:1); such people would not be called generous, no matter how large the gift might be. Accordingly, Christian piety and tradition often have linked the virtue of generosity with anonymity (Matt. 6:2–4). Although there may be warrants for sometimes recognizing the generosity of certain givers (see Mark 12:43–44; 2 Cor. 8:1–6), a desire to obtain such recognition should not be a motivating factor.

Christian teaching on generosity has emphasized the aspect of motive in other respects as well. Truly generous giving is distinct from that which might derive from an attempt to appease God or from a desire to heighten one's position or influence within a community. Generosity is always to be associated with altruism. In particular, the hope that Christian giving will lead to material prosperity (as divine compensation) derives from a selfish materialism that Scripture regularly rebukes (e.g., 1 Tim. 6:9–10). This is not to deny the biblical promises that God rewards generosity (Prov. 11:25; Luke 6:38) but rather to emphasize that only unselfish giving is rewarded. The ironic teaching of Jesus is, essentially, "Expect nothing in return, and your reward will be great" (Luke 6:35; cf. 14:14).

Christian teaching also has extolled generosity to strangers and/or enemies. Jesus indicated that there is nothing special about people who do good to their own kind (Luke 6:33); his followers were to be known as people who give to everyone and do good to all, even those who hate them (Matt. 5:42–48; Luke 6:30–36). Jesus' parable of the good Samaritan illustrates precisely this point: those who understand what Jesus means by "love your neighbor" will open their purses and use their money generously to meet the needs of people who do not affirm or even respect their religion (Luke 10:33–35).

Finally, generosity in Christian tradition is usually thought to imply an element of sacrifice: the rich who give out of their surplus are not being generous (cf. Mark 12:44). Thus, Christian stewardship sometimes draws a distinction between, on the one hand, proportionate giving that provides an appropriate level of support for one's religious community, and, on the other hand, sacrificial giving that goes beyond what would be reasonably expected. The former is responsible (what everyone should do), but only the latter is to be regarded as generous. The virtue of generosity involves giving in an unexpected manner and at a sacrificial level that exceeds what common sense would deem appropriate.

See also Almsgiving; Altruism; Motive(s); Virtue(s); Wealth

Bibliography

Blue, R., with J. Berndt. *Generous Living: Finding Contentment through Giving*. Zondervan, 1997; Grimm, E. *Generous People: How to Encourage Vital Stewardship*. Abingdon, 1992; Hinze, D. *To Give and Give Again: A Christian Imperative for Generosity*. Pilgrim Press, 1990; Hoge, D., et al. *Money Matters: Personal Giving in American Churches*. Westminster John Knox, 1996; Powell, M. *Giving to God: The Bible's Good News about Living a Generous Life*. Eerdmans, 2006; Westerhoff, J. *Grateful and Generous Hearts: A Pilgrim's Stewardship Adventure*. Morehouse, 1997.

Mark Allan Powell

Genesis

The book of Genesis recounts stories of God's creation of the world and the beginning of human civilization (chaps. 1–11) as well as the stories of the first generations of the ancestors of ancient Israel as they interacted with other nations, beginning with Abraham and Sarah (chaps. 12–50). God elects the line of Abraham and Sarah as God's special people in order to bless them and so that they might be a blessing to "all the families of the earth" (12:1–3).

Human Community, the Image of God, and Human Vocation

In contrast to the polytheism of surrounding cultures, ancient Israel's story of origins portrays their one God as responsible for all creation (1:1). God creates humans as social beings in community, "male and female" (1:27). God creates the humans "in the image of God" with a vocation to "have dominion" over the earth's creatures (1:26–28; 5:1–2), a royal dominion like Israel's kings, who were obligated to care for the most vulnerable members of their society (Ps. 72; Ezek. 34).

The "Goodness" of Creation and the Persistence of Evil

In the book of Genesis, God repeatedly pronounces the creation "good" and "very good" (1:4, 10, 12, 18, 21, 25, 30), affirming the value of the material world. The "goodness" of creation includes the gifts of Sabbath rest every seventh day (2:1–3; cf. Exod. 20:8–11), sexuality and procreation among God's creatures (1:22, 28; 2:21–25), and the provision of abundant food (1:30; 2:9, 16; 9:1–4).

To call the creation "good," however, does not indicate idealized perfection. The primeval and watery forces of chaos and evil (1:2) are not eliminated in creation but rather pushed to the margins though still present (1:6–7; 7:11). Similarly, the serpent that tempts the humans (Eve and Adam, "who was with her" [3:6]) to eat the forbidden fruit was a "wild animal that the Lord God had made" (Gen. 3:1), not an evil or satanic deity invading God's creation from the outside.

Moral Ambiguity in the Human Characters of Genesis

As with the creation generally, the main characters in Genesis are good but also flawed. Adam and Eve are innocent and without shame (2:25), but eventually they disobey God (3:1–19). Noah is "righteous" before the flood (6:9), but after the flood things go awry (9:20–27). Abraham passes God's dramatic "test" of trust and obedience (22:1, 12), but he also endangers others in order to protect his own safety (12:10–20; 20:1–18). Jacob was favored and blessed by God (25:23; 28:13–15), yet he deceives, swindles, and cons his way to success and wealth (25:29–34; 27:1–40). Joseph graciously forgives his brothers (45:4–15; 50:15–21), but he also enslaves starving Egyptians and confiscates their land (47:13–26; see also 15:13; 16:3–6). Joseph's actions suggest that the Hebrews are as morally capable of enslaving and oppressing others as the Egyptians are (Exod. 1:8–14).

Violence and Glimpses of Reconciliation in Genesis

The use or threat of human violence spurred by jealousy or revenge is a constant motif present throughout Genesis. Cain murders his brother, Abel (4:8–16). Lamech threatens excessive revenge (4:23–24). Human violence is a primary reason for God sending the worldwide flood (6:11). After the flood, Nimrod arises as the world's first warrior (10:9). Abraham defends against the military attacks of four kings (14:1–24). The inhabitants of the city of Sodom threaten Lot and his visitors with rape and violence (19:1–11). Abraham nearly kills his own son Isaac (22:1–19). Esau resolves to kill his twin brother, Jacob, for stealing his birthright (27:41; 32:6–7). A "man" wrestles and injures Jacob (32:22–32). Jacob's sons kill all the male inhabitants of Shechem in retaliation for the rape of their sister Dinah (34:25–31). Joseph's jealous brothers conspire to kill him before changing their minds and selling him as a slave (37:18–19). Years later the brothers fear that the now-powerful Joseph will inflict violent revenge against them (45:3; 50:15–21). In the midst of these ongoing threats and acts of violence, Genesis also offers important glimpses of reconciliation and peacemaking amid conflict (12:10–20; 13:5–13; 20:1–18; 21:22–34; 26:1–11, 17–33; 30:1–21; 31:43–55; 33:4–11; 38:24–36; 45:1–15; 50:15–21).

Ethical Topics in Genesis

Numerous important and often controversial ethical issues arising from the Genesis narratives include the question of gender equality or inequality (1:27; 3:16; cf. Gal. 3:28; 1 Tim. 2:11–15), capital punishment in the case of human murder (4:8–16; 9:5–7), the historical use of Noah's curse of Ham and Canaan as justification for African American slavery (9:24–27), the debate over whether the cultural and linguistic diversity at the end of the Babel story was a gift or punishment (11:1–9), the question of whether the sin of Sodom was homosexuality or inhospitality and violence (19:1–11), and the justification of using violence in response to the rape of Dinah (34:1–31). Interpreters have long wrestled with the question of how a loving God could command a father, Abraham, to kill his own son, Isaac, as a test of faith and obedience (22:1–19). In light of the urgency of current ecological concerns and global warming, the creation narratives of chapters 1–2 provide an important resource for ongoing ethical and religious reflection on the care of the earth and the relationships of God, humans, and the environment.

See also Capital Punishment; Creation, Biblical Accounts of; Creation Ethics; Ecological Ethics; Evil; Food; Forgiveness; Gender; Homosexuality; Image of God; Jealousy and Envy; Murder; Old Testament Ethics; Sabbath; Sex and Sexuality; Sin; Sodomy; Violence; Women, Status of; Work

Bibliography

Fretheim, T. "Genesis." Pages 317–674 in vol. 1 of *The New Interpreter's Bible*, ed. Leander Keck. Abingdon, 1994; Habel, N., and S. Wurst, eds. *The Earth Story in Genesis*. Pilgrim Press, 2000; Levenson, J. *Creation and the Persistence of Evil: The Jewish Drama of Divine Omnipotence*. Princeton University Press, 1994; idem. *The Death and Resurrection of the Beloved Son: The Transformation of Child Sacrifice in Judaism and Christianity*. Yale University Press, 1993; Olson, D. "Untying the Knot? Masculinity, Violence, and the Creation-Fall Story of Genesis 2–4." Pages 73–86 in *Engaging the Bible in a Gendered World: Essays in Honor of Katharine Doob Sakenfeld*, ed. C. Pressler and L. Day. Westminster John Knox, 2006; Trible, P. *God and the Rhetoric of Sexuality*. OBT. Fortress, 1978.

Dennis T. Olson

Gene Therapy *See* Bioethics

Genetic Counseling *See* Bioethics

Genetic Screening *See* Bioethics

Genocide

The modern term *genocide* applies to ancient, historic, and contemporary atrocities for which there is no ethical justification. The term was coined by Polish jurist Raphael Lemkin in 1944 with the Holocaust in mind. It was adopted as a "crime against humanity" by some fifty nations of the United Nations in a "Convention on the Prevention and Punishment of the Crime of Genocide" in 1958 as a supplement to the Declaration of Human Rights, and it was approved (with reservations) by many other nations, including the United States, by 1998, the fiftieth anniversary of the declaration. The International Criminal Court, founded in 2002, is authorized to try persons from any signatory on the charge of committing actions intended "to destroy in whole or in part a national, ethnic, racial, or religious group as such" (article 2). This formulation has been criticized, however, for it is not clear whether it differs from or includes pogrom, massacre of political dissidents, class warfare, ethnic cleansing, or goon-squad terrorism designed to force people to leave a territory but not designed to exterminate a people.

The list of genocidal atrocities from world history makes even the most optimistic humanist have second thoughts about human nature and "original sin." No century or region is exempt. Even the "short century" from World War I to the fall of the Berlin Wall has a bloody record that includes the Ottoman Turks' massacre of the Armenians (1915–17); the Nazis' treatment of Jews, Gypsies, and Slavs (1930s–40s); Stalin's purges (1930s); the attacks on the Ibo of Nigeria (1966); the Tutsi-Hutu conflicts (1972, 1994); the "killing fields" of the Khmer Rouge in Cambodia (1975–78); and the Iraqi chemical bombing of the Kurds (1988), to mention only the most notorious. Ongoing charges of genocide are made regarding Serbia, Bosnia, Kosovo, and Darfur. In each case, a people is dehumanized, killer groups are organized, and responsibility is denied.

Those who draw their ethical views from Scripture must face the fact that the ancient Israelites' treatment of the Canaanites (see especially Josh. 1–12) is not far removed from genocide and is often understood as "holy war" (or "righteous arms"). As Joshua describes it, during the "conquest" and, later, when Israel was under pressure from desert tribes on one side and coastal Philistines on the other, the people of the exodus undertook wars of extermination that were bloody, frequent, and celebrated.

European settlers in North and South America as well as South Africa sometimes have used biblical passages to justify their conquests of indigenous peoples. However, Scripture and Christian doctrine concerning God's care for all peoples and concerning just and unjust wars have generated condemnation of such policies and legitimated the passing of international laws for the criminalization of genocide.

See also Conquest; Joshua; Killing

Bibliography

January, B. *Genocide: Modern Crimes against Humanity*. Twenty-First Century Books, 2006; Jones, A. *Genocide: A Comprehensive Introduction*. Routledge, 2006.

Max L. Stackhouse

Globalization

Modernity was marked by the rise of the nation-state; the development of postfeudal national economies; the growth of international cultural, scientific, and technological exchange; and the spread of religious pluralism, activist missions, and democratic ideals. It also saw an increase of colonialism, imperialism, and militarism while promising an era of perpetual peace and progress based on what were presumed to be universal humanistic values and secular reason. The promise was only ambiguously fulfilled, and the benefits of modernity have been limited by the postmodern fragmentation of older stablilities and the sense of loss of comprehensive meaning and values. That has brought both reactions against the disruptions of traditional beliefs and social orders and, more important, the emergence of vast new patterns of interdependence, the resurgence and reformation of religious traditions, the articulation of universal moral principles such as human rights, and acts of humanitarian intervention that compromise national sovereignty and exceed secular reason.

This new interdependence is today commonly called "globalization," and the economic effects of the dynamics driving it often are taken to be its causes, although economic interest is only one among a host of causes and is not new. In fact, multiple causes—religious, moral, social, technological, and cultural—have made economic changes both possible and in some cases necessary. Thus, if the dynamic to which globalization points is to be understood, multiple levels of interactive causation shaping a new postmodern public have to be recognized.

The term *globalization* was introduced in the 1950s by social theorist Roland Robertson as a worldwide set of dynamic changes that is creating a comprehensive context that influences every local context, all peoples, all nations, and the ecology of the earth itself. And it is demanding ethical responses. This dynamic has precedents in many Western developments prior to modernity, largely spurred by Christian convictions, although there is evidence of parallel trends in some non-Western religions and societies, especially where universalistic elements in classic worldviews prompted them to adopt or adapt similar patterns to become agents of globalization.

Specialists in various fields, however, treat the globalizing changes in terms of their own disciplines and often tend to attribute the dynamics to the factors that most interest them. Thus, economists (and both business leaders and critics suspicious of business) treat globalization as an economic dynamic. They see capitalist practices and institutions (which some celebrate and others excoriate) that can leap over the borders of nations to find raw material and customers to whom goods or services are sold (some say benefiting many, and others say impoverishing more). The debates over the facts are intense, but the best evidence strongly suggests that the growth of new middle classes is the chief result. Capitalist economies, however, are not autonomous. They depend on laws that legitimize and regulate corporations as employers and owners of capital, on ever-changing technological means of production that alter the ecosphere and involve the responsible management of nature, and on a literate labor force willing and able to work in industrialized settings—all of which require a relatively stable and open political environment, with educational systems and communications networks that allow people to exchange information, goods, and services over great distances.

More general definitions seek perspectives that are based in more comprehensive fields of study and a philosophy or theology of history. It is likely that contemporary globalization is essentially a civilizational shift, signaling a change like the shifts from tribal societies to feudal then urban societies, and then to the industrialized nation-states of modernity, now being superseded—though these forms of society continue to exist and have differing degrees of difficulty in adjusting to the multitude of globalizing influences. Each historic shift was shaped by both economic and political factors and by dominant religious and ethical transformations of culture and society. Such forces are now forming the infrastructure of what could become a new, transnational civil society—potentially a global civilization. It would be decidedly dynamic, incredibly complex, and increasingly inclusive if not fully equitable in its distribution of benefits. However, those who have attempted to study globalization as a comprehensive shift argue that more people gain from it than lose, a fact that continues to encourage the globalizing forces, even if those in tribal or peasant societies often are left behind.

To be sure, this partially formed global civil society, as messy, pluralistic and conflictual as it is, is developing without its being under the control of any single nation-state, although the hegemonic power of the West is notable and the least advantaged segments of the world's population often turn to local state intervention in every sector of social life to seek inclusion in the global dynamics so that they can gain from them and be protected from disruptive changes. More developed lands, especially the United States, Great Britain, the European Union, and Japan, plus increasingly China, India, Russia, and Brazil, are rapidly adapting to the changes demanded, taking advantage of the opportunities afforded, and thus reinforcing the developments and arrangements that intensify globalizing developments. These lands are also among the first to be negatively affected when global interactions falter due to rising energy costs or the failure of complex financial institutions, and their difficulties affect those least able to cope.

Thus, the effects of these dynamic trends are not entirely rosy, nor are they only economic in nature. Diseases such as HIV/AIDS, crime based in drugs and human trafficking, terrorism using suicide or car bombs, the threats of biological or nuclear weaponry, the lack of access to educational or healthcare institutions, the effects of ecological degradation and climate warming, and the personal and social disruptions caused by unstable family life—all these are global trends most severely felt by those people otherwise left behind by globalizing dynamics.

For all its distresses, however, today's globalization may only be one of a series of historic transformations of culture now reaching the whole world. For after humanity spread to most parts of the earth and developed distinctive local religions and societies, some began to find ways to develop links among them. Driven by cultural curiosity, a desire for adventure, religious zeal, hopes to learn from others, a quest for profitable trade, a lust for power, and a love for the exotic, people created routes of travel between west and east, north and south. For instance, combinations of material and ideal interests drove merchants and adventurers, monks and literati, to develop and use a variety of treks collectively called the old Silk Road that joined Turkey with China, with connecting routes in the West to Europe, Arabia, and Africa, and in the East to Korea and Japan. For centuries, goods, ideas, gold, and pieties were exchanged, and civilizations were enriched.

Centuries later, new technologies, fostered by the view that nature was fallen and needed repair and that transformations could more nearly approximate a promised cosmopolitan city, supplanted old, and camel caravans were replaced by clipper ships and then steamships. These accelerated the exploration of the continents and the colonization of new portions of the globe. They also facilitated the expansion both of slavery and missionary activity in unprecedented numbers. As morally repugnant as slavery was and as noble in intent as missionary work was, new unintended cultural syntheses were generated and wider visions of humanity became more common in the long run, prompting the formation of myriad "nongovernmental organizations" dedicated to humanitarian aid. New worldviews were created as it became more possible to speak of a common "humanity" with aspirations for human rights, emancipation, development, and the modernization of education, medicine, social life, and religious freedom.

Today's globalization may be another such wave of development, marked by new means of communication from jumbo jets to the Internet, new prospects of bioengineering and ecoengineering, and new interchanges between cultures and religions. The increased ability to control the biophysical world, including the capacity to destroy it, forces all peoples to consider what values, principles, and purposes should drive our responses to globalization's promises and perils. It is widely recognized, for example, that those now left out of the promises must be given special attention and the option of selectively adopting those aspects of globalization that are appropriate to their needs.

Equally striking is the dramatic resurgence of the world religions. This suggests that a quest for a guiding ethical and spiritual worldview is widely sought, one that can render a compelling, overarching vision of morals and meaning for our time, and one that is sufficiently complex that it can take account of the incredible complexities of many cultures and societies while being sufficiently simple to capture the loyalties of the world's peoples.

A biblical perspective on globalization would surely be able to draw from the several universalistic themes that run as golden threads throughout the Scriptures and have stamped subsequent history. Clearly, the creation story conveys the fundamental idea that God created the heavens and the earth, filled them with the potential for life, and saw them as good. It also conveys the idea that humanity is created in the image and likeness of God, thus with a conferred dignity and both commissioned and empowered to develop creation's potential in a stewardly fashion that accords with God's laws and purposes. Indeed, men and women are given a "cultural mandate" to form a society and a culture that builds on and enhances what is given in nature while observing the moral limits established by the Creator. The paradigmatic father and mother of humanity, like all their descendants, did not observe the limits and were cast out of the state of innocence into historical existence, as are all subsequent generations. Still, the residue of God's primal dignity, commission, and empowerment remains: sinful humans are to be agents of development toward a just, flourishing community.

A second set of universal themes runs throughout the Bible: peoples and persons are called to guide the rest of humanity to righteous living and serving the common good, even in the midst of evils, tragedies, and betrayals. The Hebrews are led from slavery to freedom, and then they are given universally valid commandments that can guide all people in their ethical duties to God and to neighbors. And prophets, priests, and political leaders are raised up and anointed to preach, teach, and organize the common life so that the people become aware of and faithful to God's providence when life goes bad. Indeed, the people so led come to expect that a messiah will be sent from God to heal the sinfulness that makes things go bad and to inaugurate a new era in civilizational history.

And, finally, Jesus is sent into the world to begin the new era, one that reflects the fact that Christ has taken all the sins of the world on himself in such a way that his life, death, and resurrection point to the reality of the reign of God working within and among humanity. It is the discernment that invites all who get the point of this event to accept a new commission to go unto all the world and proclaim the gospel of redemption from sin and evil—a redemption that has already happened in principle and will culminate in its full realization in a new heaven and a new earth and filled with a new complex civilization, the new Jerusalem, to which all the nations will bring their gifts. Here is the outline of the promising vision toward which a biblically based, fundamental public theology of history may well point when it considers globalization. If so, our ethics in the meantime, before the final possibilities are realized, will be shaped to enhance those aspects of globalization that bear such a promise, reform those aspects that could but do not at this time, and repudiate those developments that inhibit or block the world's movement in this sanctifying direction.

See also Capitalism; Class Conflict; Colonialism and Postcolonialism; Creation Ethics; Culture; Ecological Ethics; Economic Development; Emancipation; Human Rights; Kingdom of God; Pluralism; Religious Toleration; Technology; Urbanization; World; World Poverty, World Hunger

Bibliography

Berger, P., and S. Huntington, eds. *Many Globalizations: Cultural Diversity in the Contemporary World.* Cambridge University Press, 2002; Bhagwati, J. *In Defense of Globalization.* Cambridge University Press, 2003; Friedman, T. *The World Is Flat: A Brief History of the Twenty-first Century.* Farrar, Straus & Giroux, 2005; Huntington, S. *The Clash of Civilizations and the Remaking of the World Order.* Simon & Schuster, 1998; Küng, H. *A Global Ethic for a Global Politics and Economics.* Oxford University Press, 1997; Mandelbaum, M. *The Case for Goliath: How America Acts as the World's Government in the Twenty-first Century.* Public Affairs, 2005; Raschke, C. *GloboChrist: The Great Commission Takes a Postmodern Turn.* Baker Academic, 2008; Rifki, I. *Spiritual Perspectives on Globalization: Making Sense of Economic and Cultural Upheaval.* Skylight Paths, 2004; Robertson, R. *Globalization: Social Theory and Global Culture.* Sage, 1992; Stackhouse, M., et al. *God and Globalization.* 4 vols. Continuum, 2000–2007; Stiglitz, J. *Making Globalization Work.* W. W. Norton, 2007; Wolf, M. *Why Globalization Works.* Yale University Press, 2004.

Max L. Stackhouse

Gluttony

Gluttony is the excessive and/or inappropriate intake of something, principally food and drink. Considered one of the seven deadly sins, it received considerable censure during the Middle Ages but has been largely ignored in the contemporary moral landscape.

Gluttony is often confused with greed, another deadly sin, as both involve issues of inappropriate gathering and intake of something (food, money, information, etc.). The difference lies in the underlying motivation, gluttony being driven by the pleasure of the consumption itself (usually of food), and greed stemming from the pleasure and security derived from acquisition and hoarding (usually of money).

Attending to Scripture

Given the attention paid to gluttony through much of Christian history, there is a surprising paucity of references to gluttony in the Bible. The ones present, however, are decidedly severe in tone. Proverbs characterizes gluttony as unwise and leading to poverty and instructs the reader to "put a knife to your throat if you have a big appetite," as the delicacies of a ruler are deceptive (Prov. 23:2–3).

Such diverse books as Deuteronomy, Proverbs, Philippians, and Titus associate gluttony with disobedience, drunkenness, rebellion, and even death. Contrasted with wise children who keep the law, the "companions of gluttons shame their parents" (Prov. 28:7). Gluttony is practiced by the rebellious son who deserves to be stoned to death (Deut. 21:18–21). People for whom "their god is the belly" are focused on earthly things and will end up in destruction (Phil. 3:19). And the disreputable Cretans are dishonest, lazy, and vicious in addition to being gluttons; moreover, they are teaching a corrupted truth "for sordid gain" and must be sharply rebuked (Titus 1:10–14).

The sole Gospel reference (Matt 11:18–19 // Luke 7:33–34) is more characterization than definition, with Jesus labeled a glutton by "the people of this generation" as an apparent attempt to discredit his ministry because of his association with unacceptable people.

The Tradition and Scripture

The idea of gluttony as sin was known to the early church. For example, Chrysostom issued a (regrettably anti-Semitic) denunciation of those who consumed without remorse. The Middle Ages saw the height of attention to the vice, notably as one of the seven deadly sins. Gregory I named gluttony "the enemy dwelling within us" that can lead to loss of all the virtues through lust for food. Thomas Aquinas follows Gregory in defining gluttony as five paths to error in eating: hastily, sumptuously, daintily, too much, greedily. Yet he goes further and identifies gluttony with "turning away from our final end" and "abandoning our true destiny," which accounts for it being a mortal sin. In taking more food than is needed, gluttons sin against both themselves and others.

Attention to gluttony as sin faded during the Renaissance, and by the eighteenth and nineteenth centuries, its designation as a deadly sin began to be replaced by an increasingly medical vocabulary. At present, the language of addiction and "eating disorders" has almost entirely replaced the traditional concept of gluttony.

Contemporary Applications

As many in the Western world become increasingly overweight, a reexamination of the ethical significance of gluttony becomes more important. Although medical and addiction models are helpful, they fail to fully describe both the roots and the consequences of disordered eating. People today would do well to remember the medieval concern about gluttons being incapacitated by their food and to consider that human bodies are the temples of the Holy Spirit.

There is also a causal connection between gluttony and injustice: what we consume, others cannot. This transcends questions of mere volume. As the Western world grows more accustomed to having a stunning variety of foodstuffs from which to choose at any moment, Thomas Aquinas's injunction against eating daintily and sumptuously assumes a new importance. Both overeating and dieting drain resources that might have gone to care for others.

Finally, although eating is normally a communal activity, through gluttony it can become isolating. Through gluttony "we place ourselves apart, even at a table of sharing" (Fairlie 155). With table fellowship being a central activity for the church both present and ancient, such breaking of communion reinforces the serious nature of this once-deadly sin.

See also Alcohol; Body; Desire; Food; Seven Deadly Sins; Temperance

Bibliography

Fairlie, H. *The Seven Deadly Sins Today*. University of Notre Dame Press, 1979; Hill, S. "'The Ooze of Gluttony': Attitudes Towards Food, Eating, and Excess in the Middle Ages." Pages 57–70 in *The Seven Deadly Sins: From Communities to Individuals*, ed. R. Newhauser. SMRT 123. Brill, 2007; Olson, J. "Once a Deadly Sin: A Reassessment of the Sin of Gluttony." ThM thesis, Western Seminary, 2000; Prose, F. *Gluttony*. Oxford University Press, 2003; Thomas Aquinas. *Summa theologiae* II-II, q. 148.

Maria Kenney

Godliness

The Bible makes it unequivocally clear that God is holy and just, entirely free from moral evil. His invitation to humanity, even after their treasonous act(s) of rebellion, is to consecrate life in radical responsiveness to his suffering love on their behalf and to reflect his just character in relationships with others. Godliness denotes devotion to God, characterized by a life of conformity to his character and determination to honor him in conduct.

The OT word that denotes godliness, *hāsîd*, occurs thirty-four times and refers to what is holy, good, godly. In the OT, true godliness is associated with covenant loyalty, steadfastness, faithfulness: "for there is no longer anyone who is godly; the faithful have disappeared" (Ps. 12:1); "the LORD has set apart the faithful for himself" (Ps. 4:3); "And what does the one God desire? Godly offspring" (Mal. 2:15).

The relevant NT terminology, from the *euseb-* family, occurs as follows: fifteen times as a noun, three times as an adjective, twice as an adverb, and twice in verb form. The predominant use of this word signifies piety, devotion, or reverence. Although the whole of the Scripture shapes the significance of this concept, the terminology of *godliness* appears especially in the Pastoral Epistles (thirteen times), where it describes the Christian life. In the NT world, the term *godly* commonly described respect for Greek and Roman gods and for the orders of society. This may explain the infrequent use of the term in the LXX and in large portions of the NT.

In the letters to Timothy and to Titus, we find that a person who wishes to arrive at knowledge of the truth must be of pure mind and heart, good conscience, and sincere in faith. In Eden, the serpent brought a lie into a world that had been counseled against experimenting with the knowledge of good and evil. The serpent's deception introduced falsehood into human relations and doubt about the goodness of God. As God's Spirit in creation hovered over darkness and spoke to bring order out of chaos, so does his Spirit and speech (especially "the word made flesh" in Jesus [John 1:14]) reconstitute hearts and minds today, enabling them to come to a knowledge of truth.

Godliness, then, is fundamentally ascertained by intercourse with and enablement by the Spirit of God, something more than ethical reasoning or principled moral living. Frequently, the Pastoral Epistles couple life and doctrine, godliness and knowledge of truth, piety and contentment. Conversely, the ungodly are those who depart from truth, become embroiled in meaningless controversies, and abandon the faith. Their lives are marked by preoccupation with pleasure, gossiping and boasting; they succumb to deception, and a searing of the conscience. Furthermore, we read of a formal godliness that outwardly appears religious but that carries no power (2 Tim. 3:5). J. I. Packer observes three errors that recur in the church's pursuit of godliness: (1) legalism that emphasizes ethical effort to the neglect of faith and worship; (2) antinomianism that emphasizes faith and worship to the neglect of ethical behavior; and (3) formalism that emphasizes external behavior to the neglect of motivation (Packer 410). Essential to NT godliness is the divine knowledge and power of Christ, which supplies "everything needed for life and godliness" (2 Pet. 1:3). Such godliness unites faith, ethics, and transformation of the inner desires.

The Pastoral Epistles provide young leaders with moral directives that give shape to godliness. The implication is that one can be "trained in godliness" (1 Tim. 4:7), and that godliness will manifest itself in concrete acts often considered from the vantage point of their social impact. The writer's exhortations include aiming at love, submitting to the Scriptures, praying for those in authority, showing modesty in dress, being hospitable to guests, managing well one's children and the affairs of one's household, giving thanks, showing respect to elders and masters, employing one's spiritual gift, exercising purity toward the young, willingly enduring suffering, avoiding quarrels and profane speech, shunning youthful passions, and doing good works. The practice of such godliness is typically subversive and countercultural. In fact, 2 Tim. 3:1–9 warns that godlessness will characterize the last days, which bring distress, corruption, and counterfeit faith. Godlessness is destructive of persons, families, and society, and it is especially reprehensive when those appointed to spiritual leadership abandon it as the rule of their life. In navigating such turbulent waters, the loyal child of God can drop anchor in the eschatological hope of eternal life. Godliness, then, holds promise for this life and for the life to come, fitting the former with contentment and the latter with immortality.

See also Holiness; 1–2 Timothy; Titus

Bibliography

Packer, J. I. "Godliness." Pages 410–11 in *New Dictionary of Christian Ethics and Pastoral Theology*, ed. D. Atkinson and D. Field. InterVarsity, 1995.

Chris A. Kiesling

Golden Rule

The Golden Rule is the designation for Jesus' command to his disciples in the Sermon on the Mount: "[Therefore] in everything do to others as you would have them do to you; for this is the law and the prophets" (Matt. 7:12; cf. Luke 6:31).

Mark 12:31 and Rom. 13:9 similarly indicate that the law is summed up by the command "You shall love your neighbor as yourself," a quotation from Lev. 19:18. This suggests that Jesus' formulation likewise refers to Lev. 19:18.

The appearance of "therefore" in Matt. 7:12 indicates that the Golden Rule is based on God's trustworthiness and mercy in Matt. 7:11. Similarly, Mark 12:31; Luke 6:31–36; and Lev. 19:18 link the Golden Rule with God's gracious mercy as the Lord. God does not merely reciprocate; God initiates.

Versions of this principle are found in many world religions. For example, in Hinduism there is the saying "This is the sum of duty: do not do to others what would cause pain for you" (*Mahabhbharata* 5.1517); in Confucianism, "Do not do to others what you would not have them do for you" (*Analects of Confucius* 15:23); in Buddhist writings, "Hurt not others in ways you yourself would find hurtful" (*Udana-Varga* 5.18); in ancient Greek philosophy, "May I do to others as I would they should do unto me" (Plato, *Laws* II); in Judaism, in addition to Lev. 19:18, "Do not do to your neighbor what is hateful to you; this is the whole Law, all else is commentary" (*b. Šabb.* 31a), and "What you hate, do not do to anyone" (Tob. 4:15).

The Golden Rule thus functions, both in Jesus' teaching and elsewhere, as an overarching principle of initiating what one wishes others to reciprocate. It seeks to form in persons an other-centered view of the universe. Parents and teachers have used it to help form virtues of caring and hospitality. The early church received this precept in both negative and positive formulations (Luz 427).

The parallels in many different moral systems suggest to many that this precept fits the created order and is evidence of "general revelation" (apart from the special revelation in Scripture) or "natural law." Removed from the context of the rest of Jesus' teaching on God's mercy and trustworthiness as guiding norm, the Golden Rule is neither unique nor the most radical of Jesus' teachings. It and other religious moral standards stand in stark contrast to the laissez-faire ethic of the marketplace that makes self-interest the guiding virtue.

See also Comparative Religious Ethics; Imitation of Jesus; Sermon on the Mount

Bibliography

Bauman, C. *The Sermon on the Mount: The Modern Quest for Its Meaning*. Mercer University Press, 1985; Luz, U. *Matthew 1–7*. Trans. W. Linss. CC. Fortress, 1992; Schrage, W. *The Ethics of the New Testament*. Trans. D. Green. Fortress, 1987; Stassen, G. *Living the Sermon on the Mount: Practical Hope for Grace and Deliverance*. Jossey-Bass, 2006; Verhey, A. *The Great Reversal: Ethics and the New Testament*. Eerdmans, 1984.

Michael Westmoreland-White

Good, The

In attempting to survey the meaning of "the good" for a dictionary devoted to Scripture and ethics, it may be useful to recall that our ancestors frequently referred to the Bible itself as the "Good Book," as do many people today. What is the meaning of "the good" in the Good Book? What can we learn from the more than six hundred passages in, for example, the NRSV, that contain the word *good*? The range of meanings evident in these biblical passages generally reflects ordinary uses of the term, but they are clearly prephilosophical in content. They presuppose common sense and do not seek to clarify "the good" in distinction from other moral categories, such as "right" or "appropriate," or to develop some kind of value theory or alternative philosophical hypothesis, certainly not before actually using these terms to communicate basic moral attitudes and assert specific moral judgments. Such observations might lead to the conclusion that the Bible does not teach ethics, if by "ethics" one means what postanalytic moral philosophy seeks to clarify and regulate. Scriptural ethics, nevertheless, is not an oxymoron, for the ways in which moral terms are used in the Bible actually provide, if not a normative basis for criticizing postanalytic moral philosophy, a rich field for investigating whether and how such philosophical theories are relevant for understanding either biblical perspectives on morality or criticizing the way of life emergent from them.

Perhaps the most philosophically provocative discussion of "the good" occurs in the conversation between Jesus and the rich man (Mark 10:17–22; pars. Matt. 19:16–22; Luke 18:18–23). Addressed politely as "Good Teacher," Jesus responds with an unsettling question: "Why do you call me good?" And then he asserts, "No one is good but God alone." Nevertheless, the young man's question, "What must I do to inherit eternal life?" elicits a reply, "You know the commandments . . . ," to which Jesus' inquirer responds, "Teacher, I have kept all these since my youth." Mark then recounts how the conversation ended: "Jesus, looking at him, loved him and said, 'You lack one thing; go, sell what you own, and give the money to the poor, and you will have treasure in heaven; then come, follow me.' When he heard this, he was shocked and went away grieving, for he had many possessions."

All three Synoptic Gospel accounts turn this incident into a meditation on the cost of discipleship and whether the rich can ever become true disciples, but Matthew's version (19:16–22) omits Jesus' refusal to be addressed as "Good Teacher." Instead, the rich young man simply asks, "Teacher, what good deed must I do to have eternal life?" Jesus replies, "Why do you ask me about what is good? There is only one who is good." After their brief exchange regarding the commandments, in which the young man seeks advice on which ones to focus, Jesus says, "If you wish to be perfect, go, sell your possessions and give the money to the poor."

Both versions of the story are significant for analyzing what "the good" might mean in scriptural ethics. In Mark's rendering, Jesus relativizes all ordinary meanings of the good by judging them according to the single and transcendent norm of God's own goodness. That God's goodness is and ought to be the touchstone of any and all human good echoes down through the whole of the Bible from the very first chapter of Genesis, where after each step in creating the universe God is imagined as observing the effects of his own word and declaring them "good . . . good . . . good . . . very good."

Mark's account, second, links the good not only with the reality of God but also with the Decalogue, the "Ten Words" given by God to Moses as part of the sequence of events renewing the covenant between God and Israel (Exod. 20:1–17). As a practical matter, Jesus' response to the rich man confirms that God has indicated what is good for humanity in the Ten Commandments. Read against the categories of modern philosophical ethics, Jesus' response seems to support a robustly theocentric value theory warranting the priority of deontological moral reasoning over merely teleological or utilitarian considerations. The good ultimately must be understood in terms not of what ordinary people find desirable or undesirable, but rather of what, as James Gustafson puts it, God enables us to be and to do. But there is more to the story.

Mark's account, third, violates the boundaries of any conventional understanding of deontological ethics. After all, the rich man confesses himself to be an ideal moral agent, even according to the Bible's own standard: he has kept all the commandments from boyhood on. What he yet lacks is not named, but it is suggested in an unexpected directive: "Go, sell what you own, and give the money to the poor, and you will have treasure in heaven; then come, follow me" (Mark 10:21). Serious students of scriptural ethics have been trying to comprehend the meaning of that command ever since. It seems a direct assault on all reasonable standards of human decency, mutual regard, and common sense—in short, everything that people take for granted about what is good. Interpreted literally, as Clement of Alexandria (150–215 CE) already pointed out, it entails committing financial suicide, thereby putting not only one's own life in jeopardy but also that of one's family. That the rich man went away sad is quite understandable.

But if not interpreted literally, what does this command mean? The riches that this man could not part with are tokens of what people generally regard as the good. He is wealthy either by inheritance, or good fortune, or sheer ingenuity and hard work. Now he is invited to regard the good that these represent as an obstacle to acquiring the one thing that is good beyond any other good: eternal life. Whatever else it may signify, eternal life is a good that cannot be possessed. There may be others related to it—our personal relationships, for example—but such goods are not objects to be acquired or exchanged for other goods; they are invitations to be accepted and adhered to. They shift the meaning of happiness or success toward an open-ended loyalty or commitment, what Christians recognize as faithfulness. Hence, Jesus' final words to the rich man: "Then come, follow me."

What is at stake in Jesus' subversive discourse on the good is not only difficult to describe but also nearly impossible to live by consistently. No wonder that the Synoptic Gospels move so quickly into a moralistic reflection on the problems of rich people. Jesus' saying is quoted at this point: "It is easier for a camel to go through the eye of a needle than for someone who is rich to enter the kingdom of God" (Mark 10:25; Matt. 19:24; Luke 18:25). Even so, the challenge posed by "Come, follow me" is not specific to rich people or, if you will, people blessed with more than their share of the good. If the ultimate good—eternal life—is to be pursued, the rich man and any other serious seekers must acquire the habits of mind and heart that will enable them to regard all goods no longer as possessions. If Jesus' invitation is to be accepted, the all-too-human sense of entitlement regarding whatever we experience as good must be abandoned.

Matthew's redaction of this story is one way of attempting to conceptualize what the rich young man still lacks. He renders the good as an abstraction and contrasts it with what is perfect. "If you want to be perfect, go, sell your possessions, and give the money to the poor; and you will have treasure in heaven" (Matt. 19:21). Becoming perfect means finding a way to get beyond being good. Perfection, in Matthew's Gospel, is not simply a superlative, as in "good, better, best." In his rendering of the Sermon on the Mount, Matthew remembers Jesus saying, "Be perfect, therefore, as your heavenly Father is perfect" (Matt. 5:48). What is meant by "perfection" in this context is unclear, for although the term suggests completion or accomplishment in other biblical writings, here it is identified with God's own reality. Nevertheless, in Matthew's redaction, Jesus does preface his invitation with the supposition, "If you want to be perfect. . . ." The "eternal life" sought by the rich young man not only demands more than conventional standards of goodness, it also invites the reader to an open-ended personal relationship with Jesus, a fellowship intending spiritual transformation: "Then come, follow me."

What this story ultimately suggests regarding the role of the good in scriptural ethics is that what people commonly regard as good is not to be taken at face value. God is the source of all goodness, as well as any genuine insight into its nature. Achieving such an insight and living by it consistently means learning to set aside our own preferences and embrace God's will for us. It means following God's way, which may require us to surrender everything that we value as good as we seek a home in God's presence. This challenge communicates no information that was not already implicit in the biblical story as a whole. It merely underscores the point made in the book of Micah the prophet: "He has told you, O mortal, what is good; and what does the LORD require of you but to do justice, and to love kindness, and to walk humbly with your God?" (Mic. 6:8). That humanity's good requires people to act justly and love mercy may or may not be common sense. But the invitation to "walk humbly with your God," if accepted, sets people on a path where common sense itself, and all the world's moral philosophies responsive to it, may have to be surrendered if we are to reach our ultimate good. As a result, once the biblical meanings of "the good" are taken seriously, any ethics claiming to be scriptural is likely to appear oblique, if not obtuse, from the standpoint of conventional moral philosophy.

See also Godliness; Imitation of Jesus; Perfection

Bibliography

Girard, R. *The Girard Reader*, ed. J. Williams. Crossroad, 1996; Gustafson, J. *Can Ethics Be Christian?* University of Chicago Press, 1977; Hauerwas, S. *The Peaceable Kingdom: A Primer in Christian Ethics*. University of Notre Dame Press, 1991; Kirk-Duggan, C. *Refiner's Fire: A Religious Engagement with Violence*. Fortress, 2000; McCann, D., and P. Miller, eds. *In Search of the Common Good*. TTC. T&T Clark, 2005; Spohn, W. *What Are They Saying about Scripture and Ethics?* Rev. ed. Paulist Press, 1995.

Dennis P. McCann

Goodness

In traditional Christian theology, goodness is a transcendental predicate of being. This means that things are understood to be true, beautiful, and good insofar as they participate in God, who is the *summum bonum*, or ultimate good. Augustine was one of the chief articulators of a Christian understanding of God as the highest and unchangeable good from which all other good things, spiritual and corporeal, appear. Augustine both utilized and critiqued Platonic philosophy to explicate the nature of the good, but his identification of God as *summum bonum* comes from Scripture.

Attending to Scripture

Goodness plays a central role in Scripture's story of creation, fall, and redemption. In Gen. 1 God describes all creation, including humanity, as "very good." Additionally, human beings hold a special place in creation as the "image of God" (Gen. 1:26, 31). The first person, Adam, is given the special duty of tending the garden and naming all the other creatures. However, in Gen. 3, Adam and Eve are tempted into wanting more than their privileged place in creation by the serpent, who tells them that they will obtain the knowledge of God if they eat of "the tree of the knowledge of good and evil" (Gen. 3:3–5). The "original sin" of Genesis is the attempt to know good from evil independently of God in order to obtain equality with God. The opening stories of Genesis identify how God is the a priori ground by which creatures can know goodness because goodness derives from God. Jesus echoes this truth in Mark 10:18 (cf. Luke 18:19) when he declares, "No one is good but God alone."

Philippians describes the reversal of original sin. Whereas Adam and Eve conceived equality with God as something to be grasped, Jesus "did not regard equality with God as something to be exploited. . . . He humbled himself and became obedient to death—even death on the cross" (Phil. 2:6, 8). Jesus' obedience exemplifies a right relationship between creature and the Creator and demonstrates how knowledge of goodness comes by living faithfully to God.

Attending to Tradition

Augustine argued against pagan understandings of goodness in order to "make clear the great difference between their hollow realities and our hope, the hope given us by God" (*Civ.* 19.1). Whereas pagans identify the *summum bonum* with temporal and immanent realities, Augustine sees faith, as described in several scriptural passages, as restoring our dependence on God for knowledge of the good: "Scripture says, 'The just man lives on the basis of faith' [cf. Hab. 2:4; Rom. 1:17; Gal. 3:11; Heb. 10:38]. For we do not yet see our good, and hence we have to seek it by believing; and it is not in our power to live rightly, unless while we believe and pray we receive help from him who has given us the faith to believe that we must be helped by him" (*Civ.* 19.4). For Augustine, redemption is a matter of faith because faith restores the Creator/

creature distinction wherein we acknowledge our dependence on God for knowledge of the good. Otherwise, humanity falls prey to idolatry and identifies goodness with carnal pleasures, false doctrines, and errant philosophies that characterize the "City of Man."

For Augustine, Plato (and the Platonists), more than other philosophers, came closest to identifying the *summum bonum* with God. "Now this Sovereign Good, according to Plato, is God. And that is why he will have it that the true philosopher is the lover of God" (*Civ.* 8.8). Nevertheless, without the benefit of Scripture and faith in God, even the Platonists lacked knowledge of true goodness.

In modernity, the term *ethics* names the attempt to discern good from evil through access to universal and objective reason rather than through particularity and dogma. Modern ethics is the legacy of Immanuel Kant. Dietrich Bonhoeffer argued against modern ethics, saying, "The knowledge of good and evil seems to be the aim of all ethical reflection. The first task of Christian ethics is to invalidate this knowledge" (quoted in Long 122). Bonhoeffer said this because the task of Christian ethics is not discerning good and evil through universal principles; rather, the goal of Christian ethics is to restore human desire to its original focus, which is God. In other words, the task of Christian ethics is not merely discerning right from wrong, but recovering a desire for the goodness that is God. Christians come to know goodness through the conversion of their desire back toward God. Doxology forms us in the way of goodness.

See also Deontological Theories of Ethics; Virtue(s)

Bibliography

Long, D. S. *The Goodness of God: Theology, Church, and the Social Order*. Brazos, 2001.

Chanon R. Ross

Good Works

A genealogy of the idea of "good works" within the Christian tradition begins with Christian readings of the OT and the practices of the Jewish community that were deeply embedded in many early Christian communities. This is given witness by the Gospels (e.g., Matthew) and several epistles (e.g., James, 1–2 Peter). This early influence on Christian understandings of the place of works is most clearly seen in the activities of the apostles in the book of Acts. In this text we find significant focus on caring for the weakest both in the church and in the wider community. We also find in the Pauline epistles the ever-present presumption that acts of charity are a presumed dimension of the Christian life (2 Cor. 8:1–15).

The idea of good works has had a contested, albeit significant, place at the center of the Christian theological and scriptural traditions since the beginnings of the church. The category has primarily found its place in Christian theological reflection on the role that good works play in the scheme of salvation. Scripture offers multiple assessments of the importance of human actions (works) as they bear on salvation. On the one hand, there is the assessment of the Pauline tradition in which faith is the most important element of human response to the gospel, to which works give witness (Rom. 3:19–26), while on the other hand we have what might be called the Jamesian tradition, which holds that works demonstrate faith (Jas. 2:14–18). These differing approaches to the question of the place of good works in the scheme of salvation have created what might be termed a moral field of vision for the Christian tradition in the West, particularly after the Reformation. Prior to the Reformation it was fairly well accepted that a substantial dimension of the Christian life was good works (e.g., acts of mercy) that demonstrated one's cooperation with the workings of grace (cooperating grace) toward one's salvation. During the Reformation this particular formulation of the relationship between works and salvation was severely critiqued by Martin Luther and others who insisted that it was solely by grace through faith that salvation was found.

Two key questions have been asked about good works: What role do they play in the drama of salvation? How is that role adjudicated? There was certainly a diversity of thought in the early church about this relationship, yet there emerged a central position that held that good works in some way cooperated with the grace of God such that they had salvific import both for the individual Christian and for the cohort of the faithful more generally (Thomas Aquinas, *ST* II-I, q. 111, a. 1). Cooperating grace then becomes the primary way to make sense of good works in the grand scheme of salvation. This concept of cooperating grace also maintains the creative tension within Scripture between faith and works and underlines the reticence of the formers of the biblical canon to elevate one category at the expense of the other.

Within this discussion, a contested point in Western Christianity was the issue of how the merit derived from the work of the saints would accrue to the benefit of the faithful and who would mediate its benefit. While it had long been believed that the lives of those who were exceptionally faithful provided a surplus of grace on which the church could draw, this understanding was enshrined in church doctrine by Pope Clement VI only in 1343. Although this doctrine was developed as an encouragement to the faithful to live lives of abounding grace and good works, it, like all practices, was open to misuse. One of the most glaring of these abuses was the practice of granting indulgences. These indulgences were given by the church. Drawing on the surplus of grace accrued by the faithful, the church could shorten another person's time in purgatory. Perhaps the most significant abuse was when, through the work of persons such as John Tetzel, indulgences became a fund-raising tool for the church. While the practice itself became problematic and a source of substantial criticism, it was the underlying assumption that would spark schismatic controversy: the idea that the church was the primary dispenser of grace in the world. It is naive to suggest that the controversy around indulgences was the cause of the schism that came with the Reformation, but clearly it set the Protestant church(es) on a trajectory that would hold the salvific nature of works in substantial suspicion.

The best-known image of the Reformation is likely that of Martin Luther nailing his ninety-five theses to the door of the church in Wittenberg, all of which have to do with calling the church to task over its understanding of the workings of grace. At the center of Luther's protest is the concern that tying salvific benefit to the surplus grace accrued by the saints undermines trust in the sufficiency and power of God's grace for salvation. In place of this trust there is the fear that one's works will never be good enough to merit salvation, and that the church's interposition of itself does not resolve this matter. In fact, by contending that it holds within itself the treasury of grace, the church, in Luther's estimation, takes the gaze of the faithful away from God and focuses it squarely on the church in a way that invites idolatry and creates a type of bondage. The Reformation traditions have as their centerpiece a reinterpretation of the workings of grace in the scheme of salvation. This reorientation necessarily meant a reinterpretation of the salvific character of good works.

There are multiple interpretations of the place of good works in the economy of salvation, four of which might be identified as the major trajectories of thought that have come to characterize the Christian tradition in the West after the Reformation. The first trajectory, which is most closely associated with Roman Catholic tradition, recognizes that while salvation is finally the work of God, the Christian still materially cooperates with the workings of grace as such by good works. This is the continuing tradition outlined above. The second trajectory, most often identified with the ecclesial movement begun by Martin Luther, holds that works are the evidence of gratitude for the gift of grace from God. In themselves, they have little if any salvific significance, save in forming a life of gratitude that is pleasing to God. The third major trajectory interprets good works as a sign of God's electing grace that allows the continued perseverance of the saints in their good works in the face of the trials and temptations of life. This trajectory is most closely associated with the Reformed tradition. The fourth trajectory understands good works as being the way in which Christians pattern their lives after Christ and thereby give evidence of their faith and the working of the Spirit in their lives. This trajectory is most closely associated with the Anabaptist and Pietist traditions. It is important to note here that while the salvific significance of good works has stood as one of the points of contention between these trajectories of Western Christianity, there are significant ways that agreement can be found regarding the centrality of good works for the Christian life.

Perhaps the signature convictions that underlie both the magisterial and the radical elements of the Reformation are that faith alone justifies, and that grace alone is salvific. These commitments are summed up in the two phrases that have come to characterize the Reformation as a whole: *sola gratia* and *sola fide*. While the ranges of movements that emerge from the Reformation share these two points in common, there are differing points where each of these three trajectories (trajectories two, three, and four above) places its emphasis. To gain a fuller sense of the textures of these beliefs and their distinctiveness in the traditions of Western Christianity, some delineation is necessary.

In what may be termed the Lutheran trajectory, there is not a total denigration of good works, but certainly there exists a substantial suspicion of their place in the scheme of salvation. This suspicion is captured in the familiar phrase "works righteousness," which usually refers disparagingly to an understanding that good works have salvific consequence in and of themselves. It would be wrong, however, to presume that the interpretation of works in this trajectory is wholly negative. It is rather the case that good works are interpreted as signs of gratitude from those who rightly consider the depths of God's love shown in the sacrifice of Christ. The distinct textures of this interpretation are that this gratitude for God's grace evident in

Christ's sacrificial love is the central locus around which its piety and liturgical life are built.

The Reformed trajectory, like the Lutheran tradition, holds that good works are not in and of themselves salvific. They are, however, linked to salvation in a different way. The Reformed tradition's focus on both the sovereignty of God and the electing nature of grace interprets the capacity to persevere in good works as a sign of the electing grace of God working in the lives of the faithful. Good works in this scheme are probable evidence of election to salvation and therefore are linked closely with it. So, instead of good works preceding, cooperating, or simply responding to God's grace, their perduring presence in the life of the faithful follows the salvifically electing work of grace. This is a significant reason that the trajectories of the faith that emerge from this stream of the Reformation seemingly focus an inordinate amount of attention on the conduct of the faithful.

The final trajectory is that which emerges from what historians describe as the Radical Reformation. This tradition interprets good works in their relation to the conduct of the everyday life of the faithful. In the scheme of salvation in this trajectory the focus is on sanctification as a means to participate with grace in its salvific work. This is often spoken of in plain terms as walking in the way of Jesus. Doctrinal pronouncements recede in the scheme of things. Unlike the other two trajectories, the matter is more one of how the faithful conduct their lives in view of the examples and teachings of Jesus found in Scripture. Clearly, in the broad field of vision outlined in the preceding trajectories, the focus here is on visible holiness as a sign of the progressive work of sanctification in the lives of the faithful. Faithfulness is not a matter of propositional correctness or dogmatic purity—frequent features of the preceding trajectories—but rather the capacity to both witness to and reflect Jesus in the everyday materiality of one's life.

The preceding discussion has sought to distinguish the ways that good works might be conceived in the dominant streams of the Western Christian tradition. In observing these differences it is important to note, however, that while we have been focusing on the particular emphases that traditions place on good works, we cannot presume that any particular tradition represents a pristine example of any given trajectory. It is rather the case that discrete traditions represent the normalization of a particular emphasis, but within it will be found echoes of the other trajectories. For instance, while it is clearly the case that the emphasis of the Lutheran tradition is on a dogmatic point—salvation is *sola fide*—it is also the case that there was and is a strong thread of pietism that runs through many Lutheran communities. Similarly, although the Wesleyan traditions contain a significant focus on the idea of Christian perfection—visible holiness, as evidenced by the way one's life reflects the love of God made known in Jesus Christ into the world—there generally remains a commitment to dogmatic formulations. Likewise, in the traditions that might be closely associated with the Reformed trajectory there still remains a strong commitment to the cultivation of Christian character—visible holiness—even though God's sovereignty and grace are the only truly effective forces in the scheme of salvation. These examples demonstrate that in the broad stream of the Christian tradition in the West we find a plurality of understandings of the relationship between good works and salvation. Far from calling into question the value of good works in God's scheme of salvation, the trajectories reviewed above ask not whether good works are essential, but rather how they are essential to the Christian life.

See also Anabaptist Ethics; Charity, Works of; James; Lutheran Ethics; Reformed Ethics; Roman Catholic Moral Theology; Wesleyan Ethics

Bibliography

Oden, T. *The Good Works Reader*. Eerdmans, 2007; Sider, R. *Good News and Good Works: A Theology for the Whole Gospel*. Baker, 1999.

Stephen G. Ray Jr.

Government

For Christians, the question of government is how the church should understand the lordship of Christ in regard to earthly powers. If Jesus Christ is "King of the ages" (1 Tim. 1:17) and "King of kings and Lord of lords" (Rev. 19:16), and if "he disarmed the rulers and authorities . . . triumphing over them" (Col. 2:15), what does this mean for Christian living with respect to civil and political authorities? The question of government can, of course, be directed internally to the spiritual life of persons. So, for instance, Ignatius of Loyola describes his spiritual exercises as being for "the ordering of one's life," and a Charles Wesley hymn describes the believer as "govern'd by the word of truth." When focused on external aspects, however—the relation to Christ of those authorities who administer the law, execute judgment and punishment, collect taxes, and so on (see Rom. 13:1; 1 Pet. 2:13)—the question of government is contentious from almost every conceivable angle.

New Testament Texts

An initial problem is the seeming inconsistency of NT texts. Paul's instructions to his audience in Rom. 13:1–7 to "be subject to the governing authorities" because they are "God's servants" sit uneasily with texts that appear to designate earthly rulers as destroyers of the earth who set themselves for destruction (e.g., Rev. 6:15–17; 18:9–10).

Some NT texts affirm the need for earthly government to deal with wrongdoers and repeat the injunction to believers to be subject to rulers and authorities (e.g., Titus 3:1; 1 Pet. 2:13–19). In the Gospels, Jesus' reply to the Pharisees and Herodians about the payment of taxes implies that some kind of earthly rule is part of the universal human experience of divine providence: "Give to the emperor the things that are the emperor's" (Mark 12:17 pars.). Jesus gives little ground to the Zealot politics of violence (John 18:11; cf. Luke 22:35–38), implying instead that earthly government has a justifiable place within divine providence. He appears to accept the right of government to expect its citizens to meet certain obligations for the sake of good order. The saying in Mark 12:17 depends for its effectiveness on a distinction between the limited jurisdiction of earthly government and the supreme authority of God.

By contrast, other texts call the churches to oppose the "beast rising out of the sea" (Rev. 13:1) and the harlot of Babylon (Rev. 19:2), two figures commonly understood to represent the political tyranny and economic exploitation of Rome. Paul describes civil magistrates as those considered to be "of no account" in the church (1 Cor. 6:4). Earthly government is "doomed to perish" (1 Cor. 2:6). His presentation of Jesus Christ as almost an anti-Caesar, the promise of whose coming again in glory carries a huge political charge, seems to delegitimate rather than legitimate earthly government. Paul's Letter to the Romans, notes Jacob Taubes, opens with a declaration of Jesus Christ as "Son of God with power" (Rom. 1:4). This is reminiscent of Ps. 2, an enthronement psalm: "You are my son. . . . Ask of me, and I will make the nations your heritage, and the ends of the earth your possession" (Ps. 2:7–8). Such allusions, Taubes says, present the gospel as a declaration of war against Rome; Jesus' political order is universal but based on love and forgiveness, not law or ethnicity.

Methodological Issues

Also contentious are methodological claims about how to address the topic. Biblical scholars are sometimes so suspicious of the motives hidden in the politics of biblical texts that it becomes difficult, even impossible, to ask questions about their meaning today. Some, for instance, probe the extent to which parts of the Pentateuch, the Deuteronomic literature, and even the psalms are propaganda documents for the Davidic empire, Aaronide priests, or other interest groups (P. R. Davies; Keith Whitelam). Feminists remind us of the missing voices (e.g., women, ethnic minorities, people of low social class) in documentation that justifies the scope of secular government and recounts its history (Elisabeth Schüssler Fiorenza). Some literary scholars draw our attention to how biblical accounts of the possession and rule of the promised land have legitimized violent forms of secular government (Regina Schwarz). All remind us that any account of government is likely to be constructed from the point of view of those who made it. Biblical texts about government must be examined in terms of self-interest and power; interpretation is vulnerable always to ideological abuse.

Issues in Western Christian Tradition

A further thread of contention requires comment. It concerns government as "either/or" or "both/and" (1) a consequence of sin and (2) integral to the state of nature before the fall and directive toward the good. Unfortunately, the Latin West did not always hold these two meanings (or ministries) of government together adequately and tended to fall into dichotomized ways of thinking with far-reaching consequences for relations between the church and earthly powers.

Augustine, and some later Protestant traditions, tended to view earthly government as comprising measures to curtail the corruption of human nature, essentially coercive, law-based, and focused on punishment and restraint of the wicked. Augustine speaks of government in terms of the checking of anger and restraint of lust: "This is accomplished only by compulsion and struggle [*cohibendo et repugnando*]: it is not a healthy, natural process [*ex natura*], but, thanks to guilt, a weary one" (*Civ.* 14.19).

Thomas Aquinas, and some later Roman Catholic traditions, tended to view earthly government as, potentially at least, an expression of human nature in its goodness. Arguing from final causes, Thomas emphasizes the true role of earthly government as directive, in the sense of ordering those governed toward the ultimate end (Gk. *telos*) of created existence in God:

> For as "it belongs to the best to produce the best," it is not fitting that the supreme goodness of God should produce things without giving them their perfection.

> Now a thing's ultimate perfection consists in the attainment of its end. Therefore it belongs to the Divine goodness, as it brought things into existence, so to lead them to their end: and this is to govern. (*ST* I, q. 103, a. 1, *sed contra*)

The aim of the common good necessitates political dominion. The natural order as established by God in the universe requires this directive influence.

That Thomas Aquinas drew frequently on Augustine indicates that differences between them are not as deep as sometimes implied (e.g., *ST* I, q. 96, a. 4). John Calvin (1509–64) later insists that the tasks and burdens of civil government are both necessitated by sin and integral to the "order established by God" (*Institutes* 4.21.1). Yet the contrast recalls much about the politics of Western Christianity in the Middle Ages, notably the power struggles between the papacy and the Holy Roman emperors in the eleventh and twelfth centuries about the investiture of bishops and popes (i.e., whether the pope had the power to depose the Catholic rulers of medieval Europe) and the "two realms" or "two swords" theologies that tended to separate church and state.

"Two realms" or "two swords" theology often is associated especially with Martin Luther's *An Open Letter to the Christian Nobility* (1520), in which his attempts to disentangle Christianity from "theopapacy," or supremacy of church over the state, gave a relative autonomy to civil authority in its checking and punishment of the wicked. His clear distinction between the day-to-day roles and responsibilities of spiritual and temporal authorities echoes Augustine's supposition that need for political dominion arose with the requirements of temporal peace and felicity amid resentment, murder, and destruction (*Civ.* 15.3–4).

Eastern Orthodoxy

Nor has Eastern Orthodoxy always negotiated these tensions well. Its theology of government is sometimes difficult to disentangle from a complex history of the supremacy of the state over the church, exemplified by the subordination of the Russian Orthodox Church to the state in the eighteenth and nineteenth centuries, beginning with the reforms of Peter I. The concept of *symphonia*, however, a mutuality of submission and cooperation, remains a guiding aspiration. Emperor Justinian's Novella 6 (535) spoke of the blessings of both as flowing from the same divine source. The *Epanagoge*, or legal compendium from the Byzantine era (867–1056), written probably by Patriarch Photius I, described this *symphonia* of priestly and imperial earthly government as comparable to the harmony of body and soul. This relationship never existed in a pure form. At the least, however, and in similarity to aspects of Augustinian and Thomist theology, it offers a way to conceive of the tension between coercive and directive modes of government.

The Powers That Be

Today, a pressing issue that remains for Christians thinking about government is why many were silent when the Nazi regime took over the church in the early 1930s. Ernst Käsemann, a NT scholar critical of the church's weakness before Nazism, warned that Rom. 13:1–7 can open doors "not only to conservative but also to reactionary views even to the point of political fanaticism" (Käsemann 354). Uncritical evaluations of other texts might also risk an apparent licensing of acquiescence in the face of tyranny. Old Testament traditions of theocracy (1 Sam. 8), Israelite acceptance of kings only when divinely anointed (2 Sam. 1:14; 1 Kgs. 1:39; 2 Kgs. 11:12), and affirmations such as "By me kings reign, and rulers decree what is just; by me rulers rule, and nobles, all who govern rightly" (Prov. 8:15–16) might be deemed susceptible to this kind of interpretation.

Possible responses include "intertextual moves" that relativize one text against others, and "evaluative moves" that ask the reader to derive criteria from the entire canon by which to distinguish good government from bad. Some NT scholars in South Africa, for instance, have urged awareness of how reading a biblical text is an event that gives rise to choices with respect to the reading of extrabiblical texts (e.g., the Kairos Document [1985]) and questionable political situations. Bernard Lategan draws attention to Paul's phrase "because of conscience" (Rom. 13:5) and explores how the ambiguity of the words and imaginative involvement of the reader in moving between the text and present-day contexts become the stimulus for evaluative judgments (Lategan 166–68). This approach reminds readers that, in liberal democratic societies especially, the governed bear some responsibility for their government.

Another related response is to read contested NT texts through a contextual political lens and draw links between the Roman Empire and government today. Richard Horsley, for example, has emphasized how Paul's proclamation of the gospel placed the corrupt Roman imperial order under the judgment of God and thus attracted opposition and imprisonment (Acts 17:7; 1 Cor. 2:6–8; 6:1–4; 15:24; Phil. 1:7; 2:17; 1 Thess. 1:10; 2:2). His point is that Paul's challenge with respect to the imperial cult and the kind of paganism that it entailed puts questions to present-day readers about objects of worship and loyalty. Some, such as Walter Wink, urge readers to see Jesus' message of liberation as an invitation to name, unmask, and critically engage the "powers that be" today.

Principalities and Powers

Easy to overlook these days is the extent to which NT texts are colored by the cosmic dimensions of Christ's subjection of "the powers" (1 Cor. 15:24; Eph. 1:20–22; 3:10; 6:11–12; Col. 1:16; 2:8–10, 15; 1 Pet. 3:22). First-century readers were familiar with the spirit world of the OT (e.g., 1 Sam. 28:7–8; Isa. 24:21; Dan. 10:1–9), Near Eastern cosmology, Greco-Roman astrology and belief in *daimones*, emperor deities, and so on. Note the multiple references to Christ's lordship over the spiritual powers of the universe (e.g., Rom. 8:38; 1 Cor. 15:24–27; Eph. 6:12; Phil. 2:10). A central aspect of NT discussion of government is precisely this victory. In 1 Cor. 6:2, for instance, believers at Corinth are reminded that the saints will judge the world and its angels. That Jesus Christ is an agent of cosmic history and not merely a teacher of moral precepts is a core NT witness.

So what? Twenty-first-century political theologians are unlikely to win a serious hearing with arguments based on a cosmic struggle between the forces of light and the forces of darkness. Present-day readers are not likely to conceive of these powers as angels, *daimones*, or deities. Arguably, however, there remain quasi-metaphysical (suprapersonal) realities behind the government(s) that citizens experience, not least of which are spiritual battles with objects of worship other than the triune God. Despite different ways of making sense of their rhetoric, biblical texts resist retreat from theological questions about the spiritual powers behind structures of government (perhaps the veneration of material goods, market forces, and the accumulation of capital) and insist that disciples of Christ engage with earthly structures of government wary of "the elemental spirits of the universe . . . not according to Christ" (Col. 2:8).

Provisional Observations

From this difficult history, three important areas of agreement may be discerned. First, earthly government is at no time unrelated to the history of redemption. Neither Pharaoh (Rom. 9:17) nor Herod nor Pontius Pilate (Acts 4:27) was beyond the scope of divine providence. Cyrus, the Persian ruler, is nothing less than the Lord's "anointed" with a role in the redemption of the people of Israel (Isa. 45:1). A limited deference to political powers is often assumed in biblical texts due, we may suppose, to the necessary tasks of government that they perform.

Second, earthly government is integral to the "all things" (Gk. *ta panta*) that will be subject to Christ (Matt. 25:31–35; 1 Cor. 15:24–28) and are already "under his feet" (Eph. 1:22). As eschatological judge who will judge all nations, the Son of Man assumes a role that elsewhere in Scripture belongs to Yahweh Elohim (Zech. 14:5); the peoples and those in government will be judged according to the good or evil they have done with respect to welcoming the stranger, feeding the hungry, and much more.

Third, the divine origin and destiny of earthly government obligate Christian people to pray for its peace and order and for its rulers (1 Tim. 2:1–2). God delights when the steps of his peoples are "ordered" (Ps. 37:23 [*kûn*, meaning "directed aright" or "made steady"]; cf. Isa. 9:7; 1 Cor. 14:40 [*kata taxis*]). The Divine Liturgy of John Chrysostom, widely used in orthodoxy since the fifth century, and many other liturgies around the world pray for those in public service that they may "govern in peace," and that through the faithful conduct of their duties the faithful may live serenely and in holiness.

See also Anabaptist Ethics; Authority and Power; Civil Disobedience; Lutheran Ethics; Orthodox Ethics; Political Ethics; Powers and Principalities; Resistance Movements

Bibliography

Horsley, R., ed. *Paul and the Imperial Roman Order*. Trinity Press International, 2004; Käsemann, E. *Commentary on Romans*. Trans. and ed. G. Bromiley. Eerdmans, 1980; Lategan, B. "Reception: Theory and Practice in Reading Romans 13." Pages 145–70 in *Text and Interpretation: New Approaches in the Criticism of the New Testament*, ed. P. Hartin and J. Petzer. NTTS 15. Brill, 1991; McConville, J. *God and Earthly Power: An Old Testament Political Theology, Genesis–Kings*. LHBOTS 454. T&T Clark, 2006; Morrison, C. *The Powers That Be: Earthly Rulers and Demonic Powers in Romans 13,1–7*. SBT 29. SCM, 1960; Taubes, J. *The Political Theology of Paul*. Ed. A. Assmann et al. Trans. D. Hollander. Stanford University Press, 2004 [1993]; Wink, W. *The Powers That Be: Theology for a New Millennium*. Doubleday, 1998.

Esther D. Reed

Grace

"Grace" or "favor" describes the personal character out of which "gift" comes. Perhaps this relationship appears most clearly in the commonality in Greek between "grace" (*charis*) and "gift" (*charisma*). Grace entails (1) divine empowerment for particular types of human accomplishment; however, within the structure of the biblical witness, this empowerment is grace only because it is grounded in (2) a more primary, embodied instance of divine favor as God's own life in Jesus Christ (Fairbairn).

As we turn to the OT, "grace" is found in the oft-repeated formula, "If I have found grace in your eyes . . . ," the condition that enhances social receptivity. Within the narrative order of the Scriptures, however, the first occurrence of "grace" occurs at the beginning of the Noah narrative (Gen. 6:8). God's grace, seen in Noah, saves humanity, radically altering the path toward destruction arising from the pervasiveness of human evil (Gen. 6:7). After finding God's grace, Noah is declared to be blameless and just (Gen. 6:9). Similarly, "grace" frames the narrative following Israel's apostasy in Exod. 32. While Moses receives the design for right worship of God (Exod. 25–31), Israel itself falls into idolatry (Exod. 32). Moses invokes God's grace to preserve Israel from the divine judgment (Exod. 33:12–16); God affirms his grace to Moses and Israel (Exod. 33:17–23). Moses invokes God's grace for forgiveness of sin in the second giving of the stone tablets of the Torah (Exod. 34:9). God "passed before" Moses, proclaiming, "The LORD, the LORD, a God merciful and gracious, slow to anger, and abounding in steadfast love and faithfulness" (Exod. 34:6). The reiteration of the revelation of the divine name in the face of Israel's sin ties the name "Yahweh" to grace itself as a name for God. The second giving of Torah, then, manifests the actuality of the divine grace. God's grace not only forgives but also empowers Israel to live faithfully for God.

The use of the term *grace* at these two crises provides an underlying, often silent pattern throughout the biblical narrative: at each time when divine judgment is due but deferred or displaced, grace comes, not to annul God's justice, but rather to provide the conditions for humanity to fulfill God's intent for God's creation. After Gen. 6:8, the rest of the biblical drama is an outworking of God's grace for all creation; after Exod. 33, all the subsequent story of Israel, in its many failings (and occasional successes), remains the story of God's grace.

These two key OT scenes provide a pattern that finds its fulfillment in the NT. Divine grace grants life from death in the face of sin. Ultimately, this grace is not "something," but God, "the Lord," who is directly encountered in Jesus. Grace opens life past death to live in the eternal that is the triune God. As John Behr has observed, early Christians turned to the Jewish ancestral writings to understand the suffering and resurrection of Jesus Christ: "In this it is not so much scripture that is being exegeted, but rather Christ who is being interpreted by recourse to the scriptures" (17).

A crucial link in the Scriptures between God, grace, and Jesus Christ appears in John 1:14–18: "And the Word became flesh and lived among us, and we have seen his glory, the glory as of a father's only son, full of grace and truth" (v. 14). As Martin Hengel writes, "From v. 14 the Logos has to retreat because he is now identified with an *historical person*, a man through whom his mystery is disclosed: 'grace and truth came through *Jesus Christ*' (v. 17)" (Hengel 271). Thomas Aquinas articulated the logic of the relationship between God, grace, and Jesus in this passage: Jesus "was full of grace insofar as he did not receive any special gratuitous gift from God, but that he should be God himself" (*Comm. John*, chap. 1, lecture 8, §188).

The Pauline writings provide a locus classicus for the use of "grace" within the Scriptures. In Rom. 5:12–21 Paul uses "grace" as a cipher to speak of the center of his thought: the faithful obedience of Jesus Christ as the act of God for our redemption. Here Paul describes the obedience of Jesus as the "grace of God" (Rom. 5:15). As Luke Timothy Johnson remarks, "The obedience/faith of Jesus is itself the expression of God's gift of grace to humans and, therefore, the way in which (in this present time, apart from the Law) God's way of making humans righteous is revealed" (89). In Ephesians, "grace" can function as a brief sign for this christological content (see Eph. 1:6; 2:5–8; 4:7).

Because "grace" names God's favor seen in the faithfulness of Jesus (2 Cor. 8:9), Paul keeps possible antinomian impulses in the concept at bay (Rom. 6:1–23; Gal. 2:19–21; 5:4). As seen in the obedience of Christ, God's grace demands human participation. As one "stands" in the gospel (1 Cor. 15:1), one must also "stand" in "this grace" (Rom. 5:2). As grace comes in Christ, so living "in Christ" means that one lives in grace as a member of the ecclesia. As grace is cruciform in Jesus, it manifests the same character in those who receive grace through faith (Phil. 1:7).

Grace therefore takes on the sense of the human empowerment that comes from participation in Christ by the Spirit. The grace of God in Christ helps the church, via its individual members, to take on the cruciformity of Christ. By grace (*charis*) one receives the gifts (*charismata*) of the Spirit to form the body of Christ in the world (Rom. 12:1–13:10; 1 Cor. 12).

Hebrews and 1 Peter share a similar structure for grace as found within the Pauline writings. In Hebrews, "grace" names the beneficence of God

(4:16) seen in Jesus' death for all (2:9); the "Spirit of grace" will, ironically, bring punishment against those who spurn the sacrifice of the Son of God (10:29). One must therefore be strengthened in grace (13:9) and thus obtain it in the future by avoiding bitterness (12:15). For 1 Peter, "grace" envelops the believer's life through Christ's death by the Spirit in preparation for an end in God. The author of 1 Peter emphasizes the eschatological end of God's grace (5:10) as the end "that Jesus Christ will bring you when he is revealed" (1:13). This final grace presupposes the grace of Jesus' sufferings and subsequent glory (1:10). In the meantime, divine favor reaches to those who manifest its christological form (2:19; 5:5). Therefore, grace provides the context in which the believers are to "stand fast" (5:12). Believers participate in God's favor to sustain them as "sojourners and aliens" in preparation for the eternal life that will come ultimately through Christ.

See also Covenant; Cruciformity; Love, Love Command; Salvation

Bibliography

Behr, J. *The Mystery of Christ: Life in Death*. St. Vladimir's Seminary Press, 2006; Fairbairn, D. *Grace and Christology in the Early Church*. OECS. Oxford University Press, 2003; Hengel, M. "The Prologue of the Gospel of John as the Gateway to Christological Truth." Pages 265–94 in *The Gospel of John and Christian Theology*, ed. R. Bauckham and C. Mosser. Eerdmans, 2008; Johnson, L. "Romans 3:21–26 and the Faith of Jesus Christ." *CBQ* 44 (1982): 77–90; Thomas Aquinas. *Commentary on the Gospel of St. John: Part I*. Trans. J. Weisheipl. Magi Books, 1980.

John W. Wright

Gratitude

In both Scripture and Western ethics gratitude is crucial to the motive and practice of the moral life. In a general sense, gratitude is a virtue that acknowledges one's benefactor and the benefits themselves and desires to honor that benefactor by offering reciprocal gifts and services as is fitting and possible. Cicero says that gratitude is the greatest virtue and the source of all other virtues. Seneca notes that there was never anyone so wicked as not to approve of gratitude and detest ingratitude. Debate arises concerning whether one can ever repay a debt of gratitude. Immanuel Kant holds that one can never fulfill the sacred duty of gratitude. Aristotle teaches that some debts can be repaid, while others cannot. One who receives kindness from a friend can respond in turn, but one can never repay the debts owed to the gods, parents, and philosophy teachers. Unpayable debts stem from the greatness of the benefit received and from the asymmetry in status and resources between benefactor and recipient. Because gifts create a sense of indebtedness and a desire to reciprocate, Nietzsche and Derrida deny that there are "free" gifts. A gift is really a kind of Trojan horse, a covert form of self-interest and an attempt to elevate the status of the giver.

In Christian ethics gratitude is the summative core of a believer's response to God's gracious gifts freely given by God in Christ and freely received in faith. Calvin defines faith as a firm "knowledge of God's benevolence toward us" (*Institutes* 3.2.7). Gratitude is the fitting response to the gifted character of life and to God as the giver and source of every good gift (Jas. 1:17). Life is not merely a loan; it is the Creator's gift. New life in Christ is not a task; it is the Redeemer's preeminent gift. Once faith makes one aware of God as the source of all gifts, one can only respond with thanksgiving. As Barth says, "Grace and gratitude belong together like heaven and earth. Grace evokes gratitude like the voice an echo. Gratitude follows grace like thunder lightning" (42). Rather than being a calculated payment of a legal demand, gratitude is a spontaneous and free offering of worship and service to God. The Heidelberg Catechism places the whole of the Christian life under the heading of gratitude. Prayer and obedience express thanks to God. As Meister Eckhart observes, if the only prayer you said in your whole life was "Thank you," that would suffice.

In Scripture, gratitude is bound up with sacrifice, love, justice, prayer, and obedience. References to "giving thanks" permeate the psalms and other parts of the OT. Gratitude is behind all true obedience to God's commandments. The "laws of Israel and all the concrete demands addressed by God" to individual Israelites "are simply developments and specific forms of this one law, demands not to withhold from the God of the covenant the thanks which is his due, but to render it with a whole heart" (Barth 42–43). The NT abounds in references to God as giver and identifies giving thanks as the appropriate response to God and his gifts. In the central practice of the NT church, the Eucharist, the church acknowledges the "gift" (*charis*) of Christ's atoning sacrifice by "thanksgiving" (*eucharistia*). Since all efforts to live in the Spirit and to obey God's will are united as the giving of thanks for God's greatest gift, the moral life is solidly grounded in a religious foundation.

Christian ethics understands gratitude as a virtue and a moral practice, but it also reaches deeper than the moral realm. It grounds all moral action and disposition of the Christian moral life in the religious roots of the heart. Gratitude is one of the fundamental affections of human life in general and of the religious life in particular. Sin is ingratitude, a persistent refusal to acknowledge God as the giver of all good gifts. If sin is ingratitude, then obedience is gratitude. For it is "right and fitting" to give thanks.

See also Faith; Godliness; Humility; Virtue(s)

Bibliography

Barth, K. *Church Dogmatics*. Vol. IV/1. Trans. G. Bromiley. Charles Scribner's Sons, 1956; Calvin, J. *Institutes of the Christian Religion*. Trans. F. Battles. Ed. J. McNeill. LCC 20, 21. Westminster, 1960; Saarinen, R. *God and the Gift: An Ecumenical Theology of Giving*. Liturgical Press, 2005.

Douglas J. Schuurman

Greed

Instances of greed in the world of business have become all too commonplace in our day. Too often the greed of top leadership has led to the downfall of organizations with disastrous consequences for stakeholders dependent upon them. Countless numbers have lost jobs and investments on which they were dependent for retirement. The pain of financial failure is felt also when greed for gain leads to deceptive practices in selling products to people who cannot afford them and who then end up in default or even bankruptcy.

Scandalously large financial packages for top executives, often without reference to actual performance, provide another contemporary example of avarice. Arguably, the desire of some special interests to protect their wealth and power has frequently been a barrier to the common good in matters such as environmental and healthcare legislation.

Of course, not all in the business world are greedy, nor is greed a trait found exclusively among the wealthy. Greed as the excessive desire for goods and wealth, stinginess and hoarding, and covetousness of that which belongs to others are traits found throughout the human community. Furthermore, the notorious expressions of greed in our own time are matched by similar ones over the entire course of human history. The Bible is witness to this fact. The OT prophets repeatedly condemn those who oppress the poor by their greed. They are those who, according to Isaiah, "join house to house, who add field to field, until there is room for no one" (Isa. 5:8). He goes on to confront those "who write oppressive statutes, to turn aside the needy from justice and to rob the poor of [God's] people of their right, that widows may be your spoil, and that you may make orphans of your prey!" (Isa. 10:1–2). The Epistle of James speaks harshly of the rich who have padded their wealth through exploiting and defrauding their laborers (Jas. 5:4). Jesus challenges a rich young man to see how his wealth stands between him and devotion to God (Matt. 19:16–22), and in the Sermon on the Mount he warns, "You cannot serve God and wealth" (Matt. 6:24). In 1 Tim. 6:17–19 the wealthy are admonished not to be "haughty" or to trust in riches but rather to accumulate the wealth of good works, generosity, and readiness to share.

We are told in 1 John 3:17 that failure to help the neighbor in need when one is able to is inconsistent with Christian love. Greed in its self-centered concern for riches, great or small, fails the test of neighborly love by ignoring those in need and refusing to share. This is the thrust of the parable of the rich man and Lazarus in Luke 16:19–31, which is preceded by an indictment of the Pharisees as "lovers of money" (Luke 16:14). As the fruits of greed are contrary to the way of love, so also they are contrary to justice. This is the message of the parable of the rich fool recorded in Luke 12:16–21. The rich man is condemned not for having the wealth of a good harvest but rather for hoarding his goods without regard for the needs of the community. This stands in stark contrast to the communal justice of Acts 2:44–45; 4:34–35. Although the economy and culture of Luke's day differ dramatically from our own, it is not difficult to see some parallels. The concentration of wealth and power in the hands of a relatively small percentage of the population nationally and globally raises serious questions about the state of economic justice.

It is instructive that the Greek word *koinōneō*, meaning "to share," is in the same word family as *koinōnia*, meaning "community" or "communion" (see Rom. 15:26). Greed is the enemy of community, and community with God and one another in Christ is the promise of God's kingdom, anticipated in the church's eucharistic fellowship as the body of Christ (1 Cor. 10:16–17; Eph. 1:22–23). Sharing in this foretaste of the feast to come, Christians, then, are called to anticipate God's future through a life of sharing the wealth that is a trust from God (Ps. 24:1) and through advocacy on behalf of economic justice and the needs of the many.

See also Business Ethics; Koinonia; Property and Possessions; Resource Allocation; Wealth

Bibliography

Meeks, M. *God the Economist: The Doctrine of God and Political Economy*. Fortress, 1989; Moxnes, H. *The*

Economy of the Kingdom: Social Conflict and Economic Relations in Luke's Gospel. Fortress, 1988; Rosner, B. *Greed as Idolatry: The Origin and Meaning of a Pauline Metaphor*. Eerdmans, 2007; Schimmel, S. *The Seven Deadly Sins: Jewish, Christian, and Classical Reflections on Human Psychology*. Oxford University Press, 1997.

James M. Childs Jr.

Guilt

Guilt is generally understood in two correlative senses, the objective sense and the subjective sense, which do not always occur together. Objective guilt is a determination of one's standing before a law or norm from the point of view of an external judge. For example, one may be found, after a trial, "guilty." Subjective guilt is the self-reproach often experienced after one's perceived violation of a law or norm, and it has an important and complex relationship with shame. Most modern schools of psychotherapy, particularly in the psychoanalytic tradition, give important place to subjective guilt and to the behavioral and emotional strategies used to assuage it. In both the OT and the NT, however, subjective guilt plays at best a supporting role to objective guilt, which itself can be understood only in the context of the scriptural witness about sin. Sin is described in the biblical texts in complex and various ways. In the OT the connotation is generally one of missing the mark (e.g., Prov. 19:2), betrayal of covenant (e.g., Jer. 11), or ritual impurity (e.g., Lev. 19:5–8). The NT continues these uses and emphases. Particularly in the Pauline epistles, sin is a power that enslaves and can lead to estrangement from God. In Scripture guilt (as with the Heb. *'āšām* [e.g., Gen. 26:10]) is nearly always understood as the objective condition of having sinned; subjective guilt, insofar as it is clearly evident in texts such as Ps. 51, is understood as the recognition of this objective condition. No one in Scripture, including Paul in the anguished self-examination that he undertakes in Rom. 7, suffers from "false" guilt, understood as subjective guilt without its objective correlate.

Although the Catholic penitential manuals recognized a phenomenon known as "scrupulosity," in which penitents were inappropriately preoccupied with their own sinfulness, it was not until the rise of modern psychotherapy that subjective, rather than objective, guilt became a dominant theme in pastoral care and practice. Sigmund Freud (1856–1939), who understood himself as an atheist for whom religion was, at best, a projection of deep human needs for parental comfort and care, played a major role in this. For Freud, objective guilt before God in the biblical sense could not exist, since there simply was no God and therefore no divine law or covenant to break. Religiously oriented guilt, therefore, could only be subjective and so must be explained either as a collective species memory of a primal patricide or, more intelligibly, as a projection of guilt feelings experienced in more mundane contexts, such as the child's early relationship with parents and other authorities. This is the foundation of the self-censoring superego. Subjective guilt lacked its objective correlate and therefore was understood to be false; the relevant task of the psychoanalyst was to facilitate in the patient the reduction of subjective guilt through the interpretation and conscious recognition of its psychological determinants. In this respect, speaking very generally, Freud set a precedent for most of the modern psychotherapies, including those that do not trace their lineage to Freud and are in fact quite hostile to psychoanalysis.

Few would doubt that the modern psychotherapies have provided many important insights into human psychological functioning, including the recognition of biologically mediated syndromes such as obsessive-compulsive disorder, which can manifest as overwhelming ruminations of guilt. It remains important, however, for Christians to remember that in Scripture sin, not subjective guilt, is the primary enemy to be overcome. In Scripture subjective guilt is, after all, not a curse but rather a blessing for those who respond to it by returning to the covenant. In Scripture sin is a deadly, objective, self- and world-destroying reality; subjective guilt, standing as a sign of that reality, is therefore a movement of grace intended to bring the sinful individual or people back into right relationship with God, who loves and graciously forgives. Thus, the modern Christian therapist or moralist may appreciate the modern psychologies but must not lose sight of the fact that in Scripture the goal of "therapy" for guilt is not its assuagement per se but rather is right standing in the covenant community of the holy and yet gracious God.

See also Confession; Conscience; Contrition; Covenant; Repentance; Shame; Sin

Bibliography

Biddle, M. *Missing the Mark: Sin and Its Consequences in Biblical Theology*. Abingdon, 2005; Freud, S. *Civilization and Its Discontents*. Trans. and ed. J. Strachey. Norton, 1961; Pieper, J. *The Concept of Sin*. Trans. E. Oakes. St. Augustine's Press, 2001; Plantinga, C. *Not the Way It's Supposed to Be: A Breviary of Sin*. Eerdmans, 1995.

Warren Kinghorn

H

Habakkuk

Apart from the reference to the name *Habakkuk*, very little personal information concerning the prophet is found in the book.

From a literary perspective, the book is striking for its incorporation of diverse materials: the dialogical section (1:1–2:4), prophetic invective in the form of the woe oracles (2:5–20), and a psalm (3:1–19). The diversity of the materials has also given rise to discussion of the literary integrity of the book. The sections, however, are arranged in such a way as to provide a coherent argument and message.

In the opening verses Habakkuk laments the condition of his society (1:2–4). The prophet sees and hears destruction and violence all around. Strife and contention are on the rise. The wicked oppress the righteous. Key to the complaint is the abandonment and perversion of justice, mentioned twice in 1:4. The response to the lament comes in the form of an assurance that Yahweh is sending the Chaldeans to take care of the situation (1:5–11). Surprised by this response, Habakkuk protests with another lament that questions how God can be silent when the wicked swallow those more righteous than they (2:1–5). The prophet is told to record the vision and wait patiently for its fulfillment. The series of five woe oracles (2:5–20) is directed at those who plunder the people (vv. 6–8), those who derive gain at the expense of others (vv. 9–11), those who build a town with bloodshed (vv. 12–14), and those who degrade their neighbors (vv. 15–17). This could very well apply to native rulers as much as foreign powers because of the open-ended nature of the references. The ethical challenge of 1:2–4 and 2:5–20 has timeless value in that these passages isolate specific actions and behaviors that contribute to injustice, oppression, and violence within a community. Chapter 3 celebrates the victorious march of Yahweh coming in rescue of Yahweh's people.

From an ethical perspective, two other issues are pertinent: first, the frustration of facing a reality where evil seems to thrive; second, the question of what a faithful person should do in such a situation. The key to handling the frustration in the former issue is the realization that God is working out God's purposes. To those pondering the latter question Habakkuk offers a word of hope for living between promise and fulfillment. One can lead a meaningful life through faithfulness only by placing one's life under God.

See also Justice; Old Testament Ethics; Theodicy

Bibliography

Brown, W. *Obadiah through Malachi*. WestBC. Westminster John Knox, 1996; Floyd, M. *Minor Prophets: Part 2*. FOTL 22. Eerdmans, 1999; Mason, R. *Zephaniah, Habakkuk, Joel*. OTG. JSOT Press, 1994; Roberts, J. *Nahum, Habakkuk, and Zephaniah*. OTL. Westminster John Knox, 1991.

D. N. Premnath

Habit

At the beginning of the second book of the *Nicomachean Ethics* (1103a14–b1), Aristotle states that moral virtues are acquired through habits, *habitus*. He differentiates habits from nature. Acts that follow from nature necessarily proceed as they should. Habits require a certain repetition of practices by an agent to dispose the agent internally to act in a particular way externally. The habit is not contrary to nature, but rather is a further determination of one's natural dispositions toward certain ends.

When Augustine referred to habit, he tended to emphasize the routine of habit, and rather than using *habitus* generally turned to *consuetudo* or custom. While not having a negative view of these habits, he saw Christianity as making the human new by God through charity. Moreover, because the virtues of pagans are inevitably not true virtues, what makes the Christian truly virtuous is the grace or gift of charity. The old self formed by custom is changed by God's gratuitous entrance into our lives; through charity, Christians become disposed to God and neighbor and grow in true, Christian virtue.

Regarding Thomas Aquinas, Servais Pinckaers emphasizes the difference between habit and virtue by noting that only a virtue having perfected a habit allows a person to enjoy what he or she does. Bonnie Kent shows, however, that Thomas depends on habits in order to explain the virtues. He treats the habits extensively (*ST* I-II, qq. 49–54) so as to discuss the virtues. As he turns to the virtues, the first article of the treatise argues that human virtue is a habit (*ST* I-II, q. 55, a. 1).

Thomas locates habits not only in our passions but also in our will, arguing that a disposition to act in a certain way does not compromise the will's ability to choose (*ST* I-II, q. 50, a. 5). In his overall project to show how grace perfects nature, he also argues that while evidently the acquired or cardinal virtues (prudence, justice, temperance, and fortitude) are perfected habits, the infused or theological virtues (faith, hope, and charity) are perfect habits instilled in us by God. The latter habits take the human being to an end that exceeds the proportion of the human but does not contradict the nature of the human. God does not act against the nature that God created, but rather brings it to perfection (*ST* I-II, q. 51, a. 4).

See also Character; Moral Formation; Practices; Virtue Ethics

Bibliography

Kent, B. "Habits and Virtues." Pages 116–30 in *The Ethics of Aquinas*, ed. S. Pope. Georgetown University Press, 2002; Pinckaers, S. "Virtue Is Not a Habit." *CrossCurrents* 12 (1962): 65–82; Prendeville, J. "The Development of the Idea of Habit in the Thought of Saint Augustine." *Traditio* 28 (1972): 29–99.

James Keenan, SJ

Haggai

The book of Haggai records the words of a prophet from the late sixth century BCE and the response of the community to which he spoke. The prophetic message addresses a community living in the early phase of the restoration of Judah after the devastating Babylonian era that saw the destruction of Jerusalem and the exile of Judah's elite.

At several points the book draws on the Deuteronomic theology of blessing/curse (e.g., Deut. 28–30) in which disobedience invites God's disciplinary curse (Hag. 1:1–11; 2:15–19a), while obedience God's blessed reward (2:19b). Blessing/curse is expressed predominantly in terms of present physical privation and abundance. At two places in the book (2:6–9, 20–23), however, blessing takes on a universal (approaching eschatological/apocalyptic) tone as Yahweh promises subjugation of the nations. At one place in the book the priestly ethical vision dominates as the prophet identifies the altar and its sacrifices as unclean due to past disobedience (2:10–14).

The moral issue in the book of Haggai is singularly the failure of the people to begin reconstruction on the temple in Jerusalem. In this, Haggai stands in stark contrast to other prophetic books associated with preexilic/exilic prophets where the temple was attacked as a center of Israel's disobedience and its leadership as its chief offenders. In Haggai the rebuilding of the temple so dominates the ethical vision of the prophet that the remnant concept, articulated in Hebrew tradition as that purified group that would emerge from the exile, is described as those who took up Haggai's challenge in 1:12–15.

Motivation for ethical response in Haggai has both negative and positive dimensions. On the negative side is the cessation/avoidance of curse (Deuteronomic) and uncleanness (Priestly). On the positive side is the hope of blessing through abundant agricultural provision and international hegemony (2:6–9, 15–23), the promise of God's presence (1:13; 2:4–5), and the pleasure and glory of God (1:8).

The book of Haggai expresses a balance between the human and divine dimensions of ethical response. The people's obedient response to the prophet through the fear of the Lord identifies them as the remnant (1:12), but this obedience is accompanied by a divine work of "stirring up the spirit" of both leaders and people (1:14).

Drawing on a diversity of OT ethical traditions, the book of Haggai makes temple reconstruction a moral imperative. In the early phase of restoration after exile, the first step in ethical renewal would be the creation of a place for Yahweh's manifest presence to foster the foundational covenant relationship between Israel's God and his people.

See also Deuteronomistic History; Ezra; Malachi; Old Testament Ethics; Priestly Literature; Zechariah

Bibliography

Boda, M. *Haggai, Zechariah*. NIVAC. Zondervan, 2004; Boda, M., and M. Floyd, eds. *Tradition in Transition: Haggai and Zechariah 1–8 in the Trajectory of Hebrew Theology*. Continuum, 2009; Kessler, J. *The Book of Haggai: Prophecy and Society in Early Persian Yehud*. VTSup 91. Brill, 2002; Merrill, E. *Haggai, Zechariah, Malachi*. Moody, 1994; Petersen, D. *Haggai and Zechariah 1–8*. OTL. Westminster, 1984; Taylor, R., and E. Clendenen. *Haggai, Malachi*. NAC. Broadman & Holman, 2004; Tollington, J. *Tradition and Innovation in Haggai and Zechariah 1–8*. JSOTSup 150. JSOT Press, 1993.

Mark J. Boda

Handicap *See* Disability and Handicap

Happiness

Both the Roman Catholic and the Westminster catechisms begin by pointing the believer toward a happy life with God. According to the Roman Catholic catechism, "He calls man to seek him, to know him, to love him with all his strength" (Catholic Church 7). And the Westminster Larger Catechism states, "Man's chief and highest end is to glorify God, and fully to enjoy him forever" (McLeod 1). Doctrinally, it straddles soteriology and eschatology, being associated with contentment and enjoyment of God here and now and also perfection of the soul and the eternal vision of God in heaven.

Happiness in the Bible

There is no singular biblical doctrine of happiness. It is, however, a strong theme running through the OT. Several Hebrew words are translated as "happy," the most common of which is *'ašrê*. Some form of it appears in ten books, most frequently in Psalms and Proverbs. It is associated with marriage and family life but most often describes Israel's relationship to God: "Happy are the people to whom such blessings fall; happy are the people whose God is the LORD" (Ps. 144:15). The word *'ašrê* can refer to enjoyment of one's family, but it has the connotation of privilege or good fortune that Israel is God's and, further, that obedience to the commandments by revering the Lord, taking refuge in him, and obeying his law are the stuff of a happy life. It is the first word of the Psalter, "Happy are those who do not follow the advice of the wicked, or take the path that sinners tread, or sit in the seat of scoffers" (Ps. 1:1), where it refers to enjoying a righteous life by following the commandments and drinking in the wisdom of God. Happiness is the experience not of transient pleasant emotions but rather of sustained flourishing as a result of living wisely and being carefully guided by reverence for God.

The Beatitudes in both Matthew and Luke begin with the first word of the Psalter through its Greek translation in the LXX, *makarios*. Most English translations use "blessed" rather than "happy" in this spot, although they use "happy" when translating the same word in the Psalter. "Blessed" conveys the sense of being privileged or fortunate for those who have the wisdom to live righteously, following the commands of God, now modified by Jesus in the Sermon on the Mount. Despite the translation disparity, the point in both Testaments is that blessedness is a flourishing that comes from a way of life commended either directly by God (in the OT) or through Jesus (in the NT).

Happiness is rather hidden from the English reader in the NT because "blessed" may suggest that the disciple is granted this status rather than being an active participant in the obedient godly life, as is clear in the OT. *Makarios* appears in the NT most often in Matthew and Luke but also in Romans and Revelation, among other writings. The point here is that happy/blessed are those who follow God/Jesus and heartily take up the way of life that God commends. The commandments generally are not punctilious but rather are principles of righteousness that shape character.

Happiness in the Theological Tradition

Happiness was of great interest in ancient philosophy because most agreed that everyone wants to be happy. However, there was disagreement about what happiness is and how it is achieved. Various moral philosophies taught different pathways to it. Of these, Stoicism, Platonism, and much later Aristotelianism significantly influenced Christian thinking on the topic. Although they borrowed, Christians significantly qualified what they took from the Greek moralists by promoting heaven and hell in order to motivate the moral life.

In the fourth century, both Greek and Latin Fathers set the framework for a Christian doctrine of happiness by insisting that it is found in God. Life in and with God as far as possible in this life is urged but can only be perfected in the next. Gregory of Nyssa (*Life of Moses*) and the young Augustine of Hippo (*On the Happy Life*) counseled moral "ascent" into the goodness, beauty, and wisdom of God or, otherwise stated, the knowledge or experience of God that brings contentment and calm to the soul, even if such a state cannot be sustained or exhaustively attained. Both were christologically centered; knowledge, love, and enjoyment of God are attained only by locating oneself in Christ.

As he grew older, Augustine became more impressed with the difficulties and inevitable sufferings of life and concluded that we can but taste happiness here, and that only sporadically. Such a fitful experience creates dissatisfaction because we want sustained happiness, and dissatisfaction cancels happiness. In his great final work (*City of God*) Augustine concluded that complete and stable bliss is possible only in heaven and only for the saints, those who have lived faithfully in the bosom of the church. This set the pattern for later Western eschatology that saw this life largely as a vale of tears, with Christian hope yearning for relief in heaven.

A Stoic inheritance was insistence that happiness is not reducible to having health, wealth, reputation, or power but rather is a spiritual good. Boethius passed the idea to Thomas Aquinas, who synthesized many Christian sources of truth with Greek, Roman, Arab, and Jewish ones. The most important of these was Aristotle, whose work was recovered for the Christian West during Thomas's lifetime. Thomas's task was to wrest Christian thought away from the neo-Manichaeanism of his day. He reestablished Christianity firmly on the doctrine of creation, setting the church against disparagement of the body and material well-being.

Aristotle's *Nichomachean Ethics* sets the virtuous life in the context of happiness. It inspired Thomas Aquinas to do the same. He made a small but significant place for material temporal happiness at the head of his treatment of the Christian life. Material well-being in this life prepares and whets the appetite for the vision of God—that is, perfect knowledge of God by the saints forever.

The Christian doctrine of happiness has been primarily noetic and eschatological and only infrequently material and temporal. Yet the foundation exists for developing a vibrant Christian doctrine of happiness as the enjoyment of God enjoying us as we advance the well-being of creation in obedience to the way of life that is carved out in Scripture through the narrative of Israel and Jesus Christ.

See also Beatitudes; Eschatology and Ethics

Bibliography

Aristotle. *Nichomachean Ethics*. Trans. C. Rowe. Ed. S. Broadie. Oxford University Press, 2002; Augustine. *Concerning the City of God against the Pagans*. Trans. H. Bettenson. Penguin Books, 1972; idem. "The Happy Life." Pages 165–93 in *Augustine of Hippo: Selected Writings*, ed. M. Clark. Paulist Press, 1984; Catholic Church. *Catechism of the Catholic Church*. Continuum, 2002; McLeod, A., ed. *The Larger Catechism, Agreed upon by the Assembly of Divines at Westminster*. Whiting & Watson, 1813; Thomas Aquinas. *Treatise on Happiness*. Trans. J. Oesterle. Prentice-Hall, 1964.

Ellen T. Charry

Harm

An immediate way to think about the idea of harm is the disturbance of someone's or something's well-being. When used in religious language, however, the idea of harm means something more than passing or superficial injury. This is seen clearly in the understanding that animates the use of the word by the writers of Scripture. From its earliest usage in the OT, harm was used to evoke an image of grievous injury just short of death that is inflicted on someone (e.g., Gen. 42:38). As a sign of past good will, the words "I brought no harm to you" are invoked, thus reinforcing the gravity of the matter (e.g., Gen. 26:29). This framing of the word *harm* as referring to matters of substantial import is even attributed to the workings of God (e.g., Exod. 32:12; Jer. 25:6). Two significant points can be drawn from these scriptural references. The first is that the act of harming others is taken very seriously by the writers of Scripture because of their sense that God takes it very seriously. One need only reflect on the Decalogue to see that the only thing more grievous to God than harm brought to others is idolatry. The first four commandments seem directed at the predisposition of the heart. The last, and majority, of the commandments have to do with disordered relationships that bring about malicious and unnecessary harm. These actions when done by humans almost always give evidence of what Augustine would describe as a heart whose passions are disordered.

This idea of harm as the fruit of the disordered heart has a second theologically significant dimension when applied to groups. It is clearly the sense of Scripture that when unnecessary pain and suffering become the daily lot of the weakest within a society, evil has become mundane. It is precisely the everydayness of the suffering of the weak that the prophets railed against and to which the healing dimension of Jesus' ministry was directed. The significance here is that the moral vision of Scripture is once again made clear by the propensity of remembrance found in the Torah and in the Gospels. Several points can be taken from this plenitude of reference to God's judgment on suffering. Perhaps the most important one is that God is understood to be concerned not only about grievous bodily harm but also about the mundane, everyday harm that desensitizes the heart and spirit of the faithful and leads them to ambivalence in the face of evil and idolatry. This is the importance of the category of harm. Harm, understood in a theological manner, is the evidence of a heart, a people, or a nation that has turned from proper relationship to God and neighbor.

See also Self-Harm; Sin; Violence

Stephen G. Ray Jr.

Hatred

In general, hatred refers to an emotion of intense dislike or loathing. It is often considered a basic and innate emotion in the same class as antipathy, disgust, and malice.

A distinction can be made between hatred that does or does not involve propositions, attitudes, and beliefs. When it does not reflect these characteristics, it is regarded as "nonmoral" hatred, as in the instinctual behavior of human infants and animals. When these characteristics are present, it is regarded as "moral" hatred, insofar as it is based on a belief of the other's inferiority or evil—an idea encapsulated by the Nietzschean concept of resentment (or "ressentiment") (Nietzsche 19–28).

In the OT, hatred (Heb. *śānēʾ*) can have as its object human beings, such as Joseph's brothers' hatred for him (Gen. 37:5), or the hatred of evildoers (Pss. 5:5; 26:5; 139:21). Hatred can also be aimed at ideas or attitudes, as in the hatred of evil and idolatry (Isa. 1:14; 61:8; Jer. 44:4; Amos 5:21), bloodshed (Ezek. 16:37), wisdom (Prov. 8:35), or even sex (Deut. 22:13; 2 Sam. 13:15).

In the NT, hatred (Gk. *miseō*) suggests a broader semantic range than its English equivalent. For example, Jesus warns his followers, "Whoever comes to me and does not hate father and mother, wife and children, brothers and sisters, yes, and even life itself cannot be my disciple" (Luke 14:26). Jesus is not looking for disciples with a strong emotional disgust toward their family and life; that would be monstrous. In the context, Jesus is concerned with allegiance and the cost of discipleship (Fitzmyer 1059–67).

Within contemporary ethical discussions, Howard Thurman (74–88) has described the anatomy of hatred: it begins when people encounter each other without fellowship, progresses to an unsympathetic knowledge, expresses itself as malice, and finally transforms into actively seeking the harm of the other. Walter Wink (13–31) has argued that hatred and the violence derived from it have become the ethos of modernity and the religion of the United States.

As Thurman explains, hatred's ultimate manifestation is violence, often in the form of so-called hate crimes and hate speech, and genocide, ethnic cleansing, or war. Liberation theologies of various stripes emerged primarily in response to structural and institutional forms of hatred/violence along gender, class, and color lines. Womanists in particular have been at the forefront of challenging the intersection of various forms of hatred (Floyd-Thomas).

While contemporary ethicists have attended to manifestations of hatred, the prevalence of hatred suggests that hatred itself requires more detailed theoretical attention in both biblical interpretation and ethics.

See also Anger; Emotion; Love, Love Command; Malice; Violence

Bibliography

Fitzmyer, J. *The Gospel According to Luke*. 2 vols. AB 28, 28A. Doubleday, 1981; Floyd-Thomas, S. *Mining the Motherlode: Methods in Womanist Ethics*. Pilgrim Press, 2006; Nietzsche, F. *On the Genealogy of Morals*. Trans. H. B. Samuels. Dover, 2003; Thurman, H. *Jesus and the Disinherited*. Beacon Press, 1996; Wink, W. *Engaging the Powers: Discernment and Resistance in a World of Domination*. Fortress, 1992.

R. J. Hernández-Díaz

Headship

The metaphorical use of the term *head* in English implies leadership and authority. The term *head* (Gk. *kephalē*; Heb. *rōʾs*) is found repeatedly in the Bible, usually indicating the physical part of the body, but it can be used metaphorically in Hebrew to mean "chief" or "ruler." At issue for Christian ethics is precisely what this metaphor communicates in Greek.

Over the centuries, Christian exegetes have argued or assumed that the metaphor *head* carried the sense of authority, especially as it related to Christ and the church, and men and women. These views were consistent with the prevailing culture's patriarchal convictions that men ruled women because characteristics in each made this arrangement beneficial for both. The key NT texts cited include 1 Cor. 11:3; 12:21; Eph. 1:22; 4:15; 5:23; Col. 1:18; 2:10, 19; 1 Pet. 2:7 (see also Acts 4:11, citing Ps. 118:22).

Several observations should be noted. First, most metaphorical uses of the word *head* are found in Paul's Letters. Second, this use is not limited to male/female relationships. It also describes Christ's relationship to the church or functions within a saying, such as "Your blood be on your own heads" (Acts 18:6 [see also Rom. 12:20]). Third, metaphorical and literal uses of *head* can coexist in the same passage, as is evident in 1 Cor. 11. Finally, the issues of the Trinity (the nature of the Godhead) and gender relationships, although seemingly unrelated at first glance, are connected in the debate because 1 Cor. 11:3 links them in the phrase "the head of every man is Christ, and the head of the woman is man, and the head of Christ is God" (NIV).

As late as the 1950s, the dominant position on headship was that Paul intended a hierarchical relationship between men and women at home and in the church. The antiwar and equal rights movements that pervaded the 1960s in the United States sent shock waves through the culture. Front and center was the second wave of feminism that addressed questions about women's participation in the workplace (equal pay for equal work) and the church (ordination). The phrase "separate but equal" was deemed a fraudulent claim, and traditional assumptions that women are unfit to hold leadership positions became harder to defend. From these contentious times grew a renewed interest in the meaning of *head* within the NT. Moreover, a strong appreciation of individual or group perspectives, including those of women, minorities, and majority-world Christians, raised two important hermeneutical points: (1) the place of the reader is important, though it should be open to critique by the biblical text, and (2) the social ramifications of one's opinion should be considered as part of the final assessment of that position's accuracy.

Three important developments grew from this reexamination. First, a new metaphorical meaning for *head* in Greek was put forth: it meant "source," "preserver," or "fountainhead," not "leader." These alternative meanings were not inherently hierarchical, but rather stressed mutuality and nurturing (Bilezikian). This argument met with strong resistance (Grudem), but most recent discussions generally favor a third option: understanding *head* metaphorically to mean "preeminence" or "representative" (Thiselton). In this latter sense, *head* might serve as a synecdoche for the whole; thus, in 1 Cor. 11:3 Christ represents man as the new Adam and represents God to humanity as his "head." The clause concerning man and woman could be interpreted to mean that man as the head represents his family, including women, a standard assumption of the culture of Paul's day, or that man was first or preeminent in terms of the creation order (11:8–9).

Second, a methodological shift away from examining discrete passages in isolation to focusing on the historical setting of the Greco-Roman world, as well as a full-orbed assessment of Paul's theology, set the stage for new advancements. Recognizing the honor/shame culture of the NT world helps place Paul's description of marriage within its social milieu, enabling interpreters to distinguish modern cultural assumptions from those governing ancient social relationships. Appreciating the central place eschatology plays in Paul's theology and ethics exposes the interplay between being a new creature in Christ and living out that new life in the Roman Empire. Thus, in 1 Cor. 11:3–16 we find the honor/shame culture impacting Paul's concern that the church present itself with socially modest hairstyles or head coverings (both men and women are addressed here) as well as the insistence that in Christ, men and women are interdependent; neither can claim authority over the other (Cohick). In Eph. 5:23 Christian marriage is first presented as mirroring the patriarchal culture, with wives submitting to their "head," or husbands. Yet within a few verses the eschatological reversal inherent in the gospel challenges the assumptions of leadership as assertions of power and rights. Instead, power is reconfigured as sacrifice.

Third, further exploration into the use of metaphor suggests that a given term might carry several metaphorical meanings; each sense is to be gained by a close analysis of the immediate argument. An author might create a metaphor to expose or enhance a new position; in this case, the context, not a lexicon, is most helpful.

Not only Paul's eschatology but also his understanding of the relationship between the Father and the Son play a key role in ascertaining at least one meaning of *head*. First Corinthians is the key epistle, specifically 3:23; 11:3; 15:28. The debate centers on the Son's subordination to the Father—whether we have an eternal, essential subordination or one that is directly linked with the incarnation. Paul's arguments in context suggest that his main purpose is to highlight difference within order and mutuality. The Father and the Son share a single soteriological purpose and perform different tasks to accomplish that goal, including the incarnation of the Son. An additional question is whether or how gender relationships should mirror those of the Godhead. The practical answers should reflect the mutuality of the Trinity, even as they maintain gender particularity; the difficulty comes in living out differences without attaching value distinctions.

See also 1 Corinthians; 2 Corinthians; Egalitarianism; Ephesians; Eschatology and Ethics; Trinity; Women, Status of

Bibliography

Bilezikian, G. *Beyond Sex Roles: What the Bible Says about a Woman's Place in Church and Family*. Baker, 1985; Blankenhorn, D., D. Browning, and M. Van Leeuwen, eds. *Does Christianity Teach Male Headship? The Equal-Regard Marriage and Its Critics*. Eerdmans, 2004; Cohick, L. "Prophecy, Women in Leadership and the Body of Christ." Pages 81–97 in *Women, Ministry and the Gospel: Exploring New Paradigms*, ed. M. Husbands and T. Larsen. InterVarsity, 2007; Grudem, W. "The Meaning of *Kephalē* ('Head'): A Response to Recent Studies." Pages 425–68 in *Recovering Biblical Manhood and Womanhood: A Response to Evangelical Feminism*, ed. J. Piper and W. Grudem. Crossway, 1991; Johnson, A. "A Meta-Study of the Debate over the Meaning of 'Head' (*Kephalē*) in Paul's Writings." *Priscilla Papers* 20, no. 4 (2006): 21–29; Thiselton, A. *The First Epistle to the Corinthians*. NIGTC. Eerdmans, 2000.

Lynn H. Cohick

Health

Defining "Health"

In Scripture, health is understood by means of a person's relationship to God (see, e.g., Isa. 1:4–6; 30:26; Matt. 9:12–13). It is fundamentally theological and relational.

Health is not specifically defined in Scripture, and contemporary definitions of healthy persons and communities often are askew from scriptural perceptions of wholeness and health. In 1948, the World Health Organization (WHO) defined a healthy person in three parts: "physical, mental, and social well-being." A fourth "spiritual dimension" was added in 1984. These categories prevail in most contemporary medical discussions. The scriptural tradition has a more integrated and relational view of human health and wholeness. God, represented in the WHO word *spiritual*, is not simply a "fourth element" to be added as a supplement, but rather is the center of the matter.

Sickness and Healing

The most common method for describing health in Scripture is to study narratives concerning illness and the curing of disease (Brown; Wilkinson). Studies of illness and healing in biblical texts are valuable resources for understanding the varieties of relationships between God, God's agencies of healing, and human health. Several caveats, however, should be noted.

Scripture presents a wide spectrum of relationships that result in health or the loss of health. Careful relational and theological readings of individual texts of illness and healing are required. Sometimes the loss of health or strength is a result of human fault (e.g., Gen. 3:16–19; Exod. 15:26; Num. 12:9–16). Sometimes the innocent suffer or die because of someone else's sin (Gen. 20:3–9, 18; 2 Sam. 12:14–23), or the community may suffer for the sins of its leaders (Isa. 5:26–30; Hab. 1:5–11). Deuteronomic texts warn of the relationship between breaking the Sinai commands and suffering (Deut. 28:14–68). Some measure of health may be returned by confession of sin, forgiveness, and reconciliation, as in Ps. 103:2–3: "Bless the LORD, . . . who forgives all your iniquity, who heals all your diseases" (cf. Ps. 107:17–22).

Suffering is not always the result of someone's sin. When Job lost everything and his friends urged him to repent of his hidden sins, God considered the friends' theology erroneous (Job 42:7–9). Jesus sometimes forgave sins in his healing acts (Luke 5:17–26) but denied that a connection between health and righteousness or illness and sin was always present (Luke 13:1–5; John 9:1–3, 41).

The bodily resurrection of Jesus is the primary fact that undergirds all NT themes of health and healing (1 Cor. 15:2–23). The reversal of the domination of death establishes transforming hope (Rev. 21:3–7). In this hope death is not removed, but is muted by the possibility of peace in the midst of dying through the presence of the risen one. The deadness of Jesus before the resurrection has extended this peace even to places of extensive and horrific public deaths (Ford 202–6). Although this may not be called a "cure," the hope and peace of the presence of Christ in the midst of devastation may be a proleptic experience of health.

Approaches to Health and Ethics

Approaches to studying health through scriptural categories are diverse. John Wilkinson investigates *shalom* as an overarching concept for understanding the relational aspects of health. Michael Brown treats sickness and healing theologically, focusing on God as the healing source in the context of Near Eastern physicians and magic. John Pilch addresses the problem of the various meanings of language of health, illness, sickness, healing, and cure across anthropological and cultural lines.

Hector Avalos develops the historical thesis that the sociological, economic, and religious position of the Christians in the first centuries made the church the best healthcare provider in the Greco-Roman context. Kenneth Vaux traces Hebrew, Greek, Christian, and apocalyptic thought and action as the inspirations of modern science and biomedicine. Theological ethics has focused on the idolatry of health in contemporary religious culture (Shuman and Meador).

A focused treatment of health and biblical theological ethics is offered by Allen Verhey, who argues that Scripture gives us a story, not a definition of health. The narrative renders God's character, will, and way with God's people. Character and good conduct are formed through remembering the story and struggling to perform it in the present. The center of this living is "in memory of Jesus," whose victory over death, Satan, and sin makes "human flourishing" possible (Matt. 25:31–46) (Verhey 31–40).

Health and Shalom

The Torah, Prophets, Writings, Gospels, and Epistles are deeply, if not primarily, concerned with the ongoing and ultimate health of God's good creation. The Hebrew word *shalom* is sometimes used as a comprehensive term for describing human health and wholeness (e.g., Wilkinson). It is generally translated "well-being" or "health." Its meanings include "to be complete," "to lack nothing" (material prosperity), "to be whole," or "sound" (as in, "a sound bone"). It can also refer to safety and security for the weakest in a community, translated "Be not afraid." Another meaning refers to fellowship and contentment, especially in relation to God and the community, rooted in the Levitical *shalom* ("peace" or "fellowship") offering.

Some scholars argue for a much narrower definition of health within the broader context of God's purposes (Verhey 43 n. 18). The biblical perception of health, however, is necessarily broad, in contrast to current medical and technological perceptions, though not as broad as the biblical concept of salvation or as general as the term *shalom*.

The Shema

A simple yet comprehensive description of human health in Scripture is present in the Shema. It provides focus and a contextualized vocabulary that elucidates the assumed anthropology of biblical texts: "Hear O Israel: The LORD is our God, the LORD alone. You shall love the LORD your God with all your heart [*lēbāb*], and with all your soul [*nepeš*], and with all your might [*mĕʾōd*]" (Deut. 6:4–5).

The Hebrew words translated "heart, soul, might" are multidimensional, comprehensive concepts that describe a healthy, whole, created human turned toward loving God (Bruckner). These concepts provide an interior geography of human life and health. Contrary to English perceptions, their meanings do not correspond to the commonly made distinction of "body, mind, soul" or to the "physical, mental, social, spiritual" categories of the WHO; rather, they address the matrices of the human will (*lēbāb*), human relationships (*nepeš*), and human vitality (*mĕʾōd*) as gifts of God. Jesus recited the Shema (Mark 12:29–30; Luke 10:27) but added the word *mind* (*dianoia*), necessary because the Greek word *kardia* ("heart") is insufficient to express the total Hebrew concept of *lēbāb* ("heart-mind"). This foundational commandment provides a window into human health in both the OT and the NT.

Health of the Human "Heart"

The first matrix of human health represented in the Shema is "You shall love the LORD your God with all your *lēbāb*." The term *lēbāb*, translated "heart," is more accurately "heart-mind." In English, the heart is considered the seat of the emotions, whereas in Hebrew the *lēbāb* is the seat of decision-making, thought, and the will. It is the locus of mental-emotional health, the integration of a person's passion and intelligence.

When a person's intellect and passions are at odds, the heart-mind is divided. The integration of one's intelligence and passions may be used for good or evil, but its integration is the first element of a healthy heart-mind. Resisting God is described as being "hard-hearted" (stubborn) or "fat-hearted" (rebellious) (Exod. 7:13; Ps. 95:8; Mal. 2:2). The Shema and its broader Sinaitic context offer three foci for a healthy *lēbāb*: learning the instruction given at Sinai, choosing to act on the instruction, and integrity.

Health of the Human "Soul"

The second matrix of human health represented in the Shema is "You shall love the LORD your God with all your *nepeš*." The word *nepeš* refers to a physical life within a matrix of relationships or a living physical being in relation to others. The common meaning of the English word *soul* misses the necessary relational and physical aspects of *nepeš*. Hebrew thought is not dualistic (for a contrast with pervasive modern Cartesian dualism, see Green 48–50). The human did not become a being (or creature) abstractly or differentiated from its body, but physically and in relation to God, who breathed in the first breath (Gen. 2:7). Adam became a *nepeš*; he was not supplied with one.

The "health of a soul" (*šālôm nepeš*) is measured by the recognition that its existence in time is physical and limited. The NT opposes popular notions of an inherent eternal disembodied soul that persists beyond the grave. Resurrection is physical and is initiated by God (e.g., Luke 24:37–43; John 20:27).

The psalmist laments, using the expression "O my soul" (*napšî* [Pss. 42:5, 11; 43:5]), describing a soul (*nepeš*) that has become sick through alienation from God, the community, and self. This loss of well-being (*shalom*) is expressly relational (Gaiser).

Work and worship (*ʿābad*) constitute the first dimension of a healthy soul. One's daily employment, observance of the Sabbath, and "serving" the Lord are integrated and central in the biblical witness (1 Cor. 6:20). When the ethics of daily action and worship became separated in Israel, the prophets expressed God's outrage (Jer. 44:3–5; Amos 5:21–24). Justice and righteousness (*ṣĕdāqâ*) form a second dimension of the health of the soul. The reputation of a *ṣaddîq* ("righteous person") includes mercy to the poor, God's passion and delight (Exod. 22:21–27; Jer. 9:23–24). Health for individuals, the community, and the environment depends on such actions (Deut. 20:19; Hos. 4:1–3; Joel 2:21–22) (see Bruckner).

Health of Human Vitality

The third matrix of human health represented in the Shema is "You shall love the LORD your God with all your might [*mĕʾōd*]." If "might" (*mĕʾōd*) was simply a category of physical strength, several other Hebrew words might have been used (*ʿōz*, "powerful"; *ḥāzāk*, "strong"; *kōaḥ*, "mighty in battle"). Rather than indicating physical, personal, or political power, *mĕʾōd* indicates a quality of strength such as energy, vigor, or vitality. Rabbinic literature projects this toward fiscal health.

The concept most closely associated with this kind of strength is *ḥāyâ* ("to live"). It denotes vitality, vigor, and a quality of thriving at the beginning of physical life (Gen. 2:7); the vigor of the Hebrew women who successfully resisted Pharaoh's genocide (Exod. 1:19); and the unexpected flowing of "living water" (*mayyim ḥayyîm*) of the artesian spring redug by Isaac (Gen. 26:19). Jesus compares himself to this kind of living water (*hydōr zōn*) as the source of all vitality (John 4:10; 7:38; cf. Isa. 12:3; Jer. 17:13).

The Shema sets human health and flourishing solidly within a narrative of human dependence on God (Deut. 5:6; 6:12, 21; see also Gen. 2:7). Limitation and disability stand as the context of human health as represented in the Shema. One's limitation before God is found in the very substance of one's healthy "heart" (*lēbāb*), "soul" (*nepeš*), and "might" (*mĕʾōd*).

The context of the Shema is the call to love God, which precludes treating health itself as an ultimate good (*summum bonum*). It may even mean relinquishing one's life or physical well-being for the love of God (Isa. 53:4–12; Matt. 5:10–12; 16:25). The passage concludes with a strong warning against idolatry, particularly the gods of health and success (Deut. 6:11–15).

Medical science deals primarily with seeking cures through diagnosing physical symptoms, researching physical causes of illness, and administering physiological treatments. In the search for a broader definition of health, we find that Scripture provides an anthropology grounded in a patient's heart-mind decisions (*lēbāb*), relational dimensions of illness and health (*nepeš*), and a broad range of resources for restoring or sustaining a person's vitality (*mĕʾōd*).

See also Body; Dualism, Anthropological; Healthcare Systems in Scripture; Monism, Anthropological

Bibliography

Avalos, H. *Health Care and the Rise of Christianity.* Hendrickson, 1999; Brown, M. *Israel's Divine Healer: Studies in Old Testament Biblical Theology.* Zondervan, 1995; Bruckner, J. "A Theological Description of Human Wholeness in Deuteronomy 6." *Ex auditu* 21 (2005): 1–19; Ford, D. *Self and Salvation: Being Transformed.* CSCD 1. Cambridge University Press, 1999. Gaiser, F. "The Emergence of the Self in the Old Testament: A Study in Biblical Wellness." *HBT* 14 (1992): 1–29; Green, J. *Body, Soul, and Human Life: The Nature of Humanity in the Bible.* Baker Academic, 2008; Pilch, J. *Healing in the New Testament: Insights from Medical and Mediterranean Anthropology.* Fortress, 2000; Shuman, J., and K. Meador. *Heal Thyself: Spirituality, Medicine, and the Distortion of Christianity.* Oxford University Press, 2003; Vaux, K. *Being Well.* Challenges in Ethics. Abingdon, 1997; Verhey, A. "Health and Healing in Memory of Jesus." *Ex auditu* 21 (2005): 24–48; Wilkinson, J. *The Bible and Healing: A Medical and Theological Commentary.* Eerdmans, 1998.

James K. Bruckner

Healthcare Ethics

For more than two thousand years healthcare ethics has addressed moral questions that can be roughly divided into four categories:

1. professional character, including more recently the commutative justice of practitioners;
2. distributive justice, specifically who will get healthcare and how it will be rendered;
3. definitions of human nature, thus establishing boundaries of treatment;
4. how sickness, injury, and death are to be medically and socially interpreted.

For millennia, the first category of concern was dominant, with healthcare ethics being essentially professional etiquette, both toward patients and with other practitioners, coupled to a duty to be knowledgeable of the given corpus. During the past half century, distributive and commutative justice and human nature questions have risen to prominence. Though rarely as the central issue of healthcare ethics, the fourth category has been addressed in a variety of ways over the centuries through first-person narratives, medical fiction, medical anthropology and sociology, and in religious theodicies (e.g., Talcott Parsons on the "sick role"; Paul Brand on pain).

These four categories of ethical concerns have been addressed in various ways and to varying degrees as the social interpretation of the healer has changed. Broadly, the development of healthcare in the West can be broken into four overlapping eras: priestly practitioner, guild-member practitioner, licensed professional practitioner, and practitioner in a morally pluralistic society. A fifth era may be currently manifesting itself, that of the healthcare practitioner as bureaucrat. Though it might be the vanity of the moment, it does seem that because of technological development, organizational transformation, and the pluralizing of societal morality, the social understanding of the practitioner and healthcare ethics is changing far more rapidly and steeply now than in the not-so-distant past.

In virtually all tribal societies, shamans function as healers, often in association with their priestly role (though sometimes there are independent healers with limited religious or magical power). Healing is a pragmatic task requiring engagement of spiritual forces, perhaps combating evil or placating deities. Importantly, for most shamanistic communities disease is not seen as a physical process readily distinguished from the spiritual, since the differentiation of natural and supernatural is at most a matter of a few degrees, not a fundamental distinction. The moral behavior of practitioners, then, is defined primarily by diligent precision in ritual practice. Truth-telling is the moral duty to reveal the impact of the spirit world on the sick individual, and vice versa. Usually, the general defining of "person" is not as important as the specific defining of community membership, with all (or almost all) society members having access to the shaman, with greater or lesser amounts of compensation for services rendered. A component of shamanistic ethics lingers in late modern healthcare, with expectations for caregiving rituals and roles, and sometimes a "belief" in the intrinsic healing power of the provider.

In the West, both under Semitic religions and Greek philosophy, disease came to be defined as simultaneously a spiritual and physical reality, with the recognition that although the supernatural and natural are entwined, they can be analytically distinguished. Especially in the rise of the healthcare guild-like schools, this meant that religious aspects of care were distinguished from and, sometimes, subordinated to empirically verified (or so thought) techniques. The earliest, and arguably most influential, guild ethical code is that attributed to Hippocrates, a physician of the late fourth and early fifth centuries BCE. Hippocrates may have been part of the Asclepius tradition—the physicians who considered their "art" to be based on the example of the physician-deity—but he broke with it at a significant point in emphasizing the natural etiology of diseases even while not denying a deep underlying spiritual reality. The oath that bears Hippocrates' name seems to be aligned to large degree with the Pythagoreans or schools holding similar moral positions, given the explicit opposition to abortion and euthanasia, as well as the emphasis on confidentiality. The Hippocratic oath also requires that the practitioner recognize having a moral obligation both to patients and to the guild members.

Galen, in the second century CE, transformed medicine by incorporating various schools of thought into a comprehensive humoral theory that remained dominant for thirteen hundred years. Galen's theories satisfied not only the medical minds of the early Middle Ages but also the religious, since he accepted monotheism and a notion of "type" that coincided with the neo-Platonic idea of forms; nor did he fall out of favor in the late Middle Ages when Aristotle was reintroduced, since he had relied on Aristotelian philosophy, especially on the natural law. While folk healers dominated actual practice outside the circles of the elites, the educated healthcare providers were legitimated by and helped legitimate the medieval Christian social order. The guilds passed on ethical standards and knowledge of basic healthcare practices to members, while demanding loyalty and asking for personal integrity based on broader Christian morality. Galen, as well as Hippocrates before him, emphasized the significance of the relationship between patient and provider and the moral obligations of the physician to know the corpus and to support like-minded practitioners; as early as the sixth century, a Christianized Hippocratic oath was in use (see Galen; Verhey 7; W. H. S. Jones; D. Jones).

Perhaps one thousand years before Hippocrates, the Hebrews came out of Egypt. The Mosaic law does not mention healthcare provider as a distinct vocational category, but priests did function secondarily as public health officials—although, as has been often and correctly noted, the primary concern of the Levitical code was not physical health but rather the "holiness" or distinctness of Yahweh's people (see, e.g., Douglas). In Exod. 15:26, Yahweh claims the title "healer" in a manner not entirely unlike his claim to kingship (1 Sam. 8). King Asa, who lived in or about the tenth century BCE (though the Chronicler writes much later), is condemned or at least demeaned for seeking help from physicians rather than Yahweh (2 Chr. 16:12). Still, by the time of the Assyrian invasion and then the exilic and postexilic prophets, the role of physician as a distinct provider of healing services seems to have been acknowledged. This corresponds, roughly, with the period of similar developments occurring in the Greek world. In Jer. 8:22, the physician is used as a positive metaphor for the provider of spiritual balm. Isaiah seems to assert that being a physician or healer is a worthy calling, in that such is included with leading and providing food as necessary social functions (Isa. 3:7).

After the blending of cultures instigated by Alexander, medicine was more formally endorsed in Jewish society, and with that came healthcare ethics. In the book of Sirach, the author notes that although some diseases baffle physicians (Sir. 10), the profession itself is honorable and an instrument of God (Sir. 38). Sirach 38:1–5 says,

> Honor physicians for their services,
> for the Lord created them;
> for their gift of healing comes from the Most High,
> and they are rewarded by the king.
> The skill of physicians makes them distinguished,
> and in the presence of the great they are admired.
> The Lord created medicines out of the earth,
> and the sensible will not despise them.
> Was not water made sweet with a tree
> in order that its power might be known?
> And he gave skill to human beings
> that he might be glorified in his marvelous works.
> By them the physician heals and takes away pain;
> the pharmacist makes a mixture from them.
> God's works will never be finished;
> and from him health spreads over all the earth.
> My child, when you are ill, do not delay,
> but pray to the Lord, and he will heal you.
> Give up your faults and direct your hands rightly,
> and cleanse your heart from all sin.
> Offer a sweet-smelling sacrifice, and a memorial portion of choice flour,
> and pour oil on your offering, as much as you can afford.
> Then give the physician his place, for the Lord created him;
> do not let him leave you, for you need him.
> There may come a time when recovery lies in the hands of physicians,
> for they too pray to the Lord
> that he grant them success in diagnosis
> and in healing, for the sake of preserving life.
> He who sins against his Maker
> will be defiant toward the physician.

Jesus speaks of physicians neutrally in invoking the popular proverb about physicians healing themselves (Luke 4:23). However, he also states, "Those who are well have no need of a physician, but those who are sick" (Matt. 9:12 pars.), thus creating a positive analogy between the physician and himself as the spiritual physician. Jesus does not criticize the woman who spent all her money on medical treatments that were ineffective, nor does he commend her for having done so (Mark 5:25–26; cf. Matt. 9:20; Luke 8:43); the same can be said about both healing miracles at the pools. Luke is described as the "beloved physician" in Col. 4:14, which, though perhaps not an endorsement of medical care, clearly does not condemn it. Although the representation of healthcare seems generally positive, the subject is only minimally addressed and is clearly overshadowed by Jesus' own healings. The specific ethical conclusions that can be drawn from the NT about healthcare ethics particularly are that (1) the physician is supposed to provide efficacious care, (2) the physician is to be honored for integrity in caregiving, and (3) the physician is supposed to act in a manner consistent with the broader values of the faith community. Other particular healthcare issues must be considered using more general NT standards and virtues.

In the ante-Nicene period, most, though not all, Christian writers supported the legitimacy of physicians, adopting the attitude of the broader culture. In the Byzantine region, medicine remained a distinct profession honored with patron saints (the Diocletian martyrs, Damian [apothecary], and Cosmas [physician]), while in the West, as the empire declined, so did the status of professionally educated healers. Physicians were few, with folk empiricists serving the vast majority of the population. Monastics provided much of the formalized apothecary, dental, and surgical care until 1163, when the shedding of blood was deemed improper for monks by papal edict.

Because of the rise of universities, the Crusades, and trade moving more readily into Islamic regions and beyond, as well as increased urbanization, the medical profession, refreshed by earlier Greek and Islamic supplements for Galen, was firmly reestablished and served most levels of urban society. Various trade-level healthcare professions as well as university-educated physicians vied for authority and status. Perhaps the most important change in healthcare morality in the West, though, was due to the rise of hospitals, first in association with monastic communities, and then funded by municipalities. While in most hospitals care was provided as hospitality—that is, as an act of charity—the existence of hospitals also implied a justice claim for healthcare, though "justice" was understood in terms of a rightly ordered society, not individual rights. Also, public officials did attempt to provide public health services as a matter of civic duty, though the limits of charity as well as public determination were tested by the great plagues.

By the 1600s, medical professionals in English-speaking lands could be clearly distinguished into apothecaries, midwives, chirurgeons (sometimes overlapping barbers, because of the availability of sharp tools, and often performing dental tasks), and physicians (formally educated and continuing to use purgatives, bleeding, etc. to balance the humors even while the foundational rationalist or "dogmatic" theories were being slowly reshaped by experimental discoveries). Rules developed for healers as part of the broader development of professions in Western societies at the end of the Middle Ages (in association with the rise of capitalism, the rise of the nation-states, and the differentiation of religious and secular institutions). Given that healers had guilds of their own, moral standards varied to some degree with the kind of healer one happened to be; still all were expected to be honest in billing, have a respectful attitude toward those in one's company or guild, and make a reasonable effort to learn from new scientific discoveries (though actual treatment development was often delayed by decades). Christian leaders in this period both endorsed rigorous science and offered challenges to the rising professional class. For instance, John Wesley's most popular book during his lifetime was a home treatment manual, *The Primitive Physick*, and both Cotton Mather and Jonathan Edwards publicly endorsed inoculation as both physically efficacious and morally desirable for the informed believer and the society (it cost Edwards his life when he died from an infection). The public, which was also becoming more educated, continued to have doubts about the skills of practitioners and sometimes their moral character. This came to a head in 1788 in New York in riots over medical "resurrectionists," those who stole corpses for dissection; the profession continued to assert the need for bodies for education and the public remained skeptical well into the late nineteenth century.

As the professions formalized and crept toward government licensure, tendencies for guild secrecy were slowly replaced by public declarations of professional moral standards, which also served to distinguish "regular" medical practice from that of "irregulars" (i.e., folk empiricists and those educated under other theories of health such as homeopathy and chiropractic). Thomas Percival, as part of the normalization of the profession and in response to what he considered inappropriate behavior by his professional peers, published *Medical Ethics; or, A Code of Institutes and Precepts, Adapted to the Professional Conduct of Physicians and Surgeons* in 1803. Percival is quite clear that as practitioner medical skills rest on science, so practitioner morality rests on religion.

> An intimate acquaintance with the works of Nature raises the mind to the most sublime conceptions of the Supreme Being; and at the same time dilates the heart with the most pleasing views of Providence. The difficulties that necessarily attend all deep enquiries into a subject so disproportionate to the human faculties, should not be suspected to surprise a Physician, who, in his practice, is often involved in perplexity, even in subjects exposed to the examination of his senses.
>
> There are, besides, some peculiar circumstances in the profession of a Physician, which should naturally dispose him to look beyond the present scene of things, and engage his heart on the side of Religion. He has many opportunities of seeing people, once the gay and the happy, sunk in deep distress, sometimes devoted to a painful and lingering death, and sometimes struggling with the tortures of a distracted mind. Such afflictive scenes, one would imagine, might soften any heart, not dead to every feeling of humanity, and make it reverence that Religion, which alone can support the soul in the most complicated distresses; that Religion, which teaches to enjoy life with cheerfulness, and to resign it with dignity. (Percival 159 [quoting from lectures by John Gregory])

A code of ethics, largely based on Percival, was formally endorsed by the American Medical Association in 1847 and a committee on ethics established in 1858. The Hippocratic oath resurged, providing strong moral incentive for and against specific behaviors as an expression of professional (in the full sense of "professing") character. The Hippocratic oath and the code of ethics served the guild of practitioners by making a public declaration of standards, but it was not until the Flexner Report in 1910 that healthcare practice and education were genuinely held accountable to the public (though that too also served to restrict the supply of provider types, thus serving the economic interests of the dominant professions). This was the period of the licensed professional practitioner.

After World War II, the Nazi war crimes (especially the extermination of those with disabilities and medical experimentation on human subjects), along with revelations that the United States had allowed its own deadly experimentation in the Tuskegee Syphilis Study and had, prior to the war, its own eugenics advocates among cultural elites, led to public questioning of the ability of physicians to regulate their own behavior. This concern was exacerbated in the 1960s with the thalidomide crisis, the Willowbrook Study (on disabled children), reports about various military studies on soldiers, increasing use of complex technology (in particular that used in neonatal units), and uncertainty about the procurement and distribution of solid organs for transplant. Coupled with the rise of "rights" language in association with the civil rights movement, and growing moral relativism best exemplified in the situation ethics of Joseph Fletcher, healthcare ethics moved from being a matter of professional code, character, and etiquette to a society-wide debate on the appropriate way to develop, distribute, and use healthcare at micro- and macrolevels. The language of patients' rights, founded on the status of the individual as "person," was broadly introduced in *The Patient as Person* by Paul Ramsey, a Protestant ethicist. Although some Christian consideration of the core bioethical issues had occurred in the previous two decades, especially in Catholic circles, this book triggered full engagement of what was then mainline Protestantism. The term *person* was quickly picked up for use in a variety of sometimes contradictory ways—for example, someone to be protected from being "hooked up to machines" that might "imprison the soul," or a vulnerable individual in the nursing home who deserved decent care, or the individual patient entitled to information rather than paternalistic disregard. Also, the word *person* was used to counter the utilitarianism of situation ethics and of so-called lifeboat ethics. The growing public debate quickly focused in academic centers heavily weighted toward philosophy, including the Hastings Center and the center at Georgetown University, and within a decade the religious voices that had raised issues for public consideration had been all but displaced from the broader discourse.

Utilitarianism yoked, paradoxically, to subjectivism was offered as an alternative means for addressing bioethical concerns. One of the clearest examples was the ruling in *Roe v. Wade*, regardless of the effort to couch the argument in "rights" language. In response, not to the legalization of abortion but to the inadequacies of the subjectivist moral approach especially for biomedical research ethics, a distilled version of just-war theory tied into American social-contract theory and usually called "principlism" was formulated and offered to the broader healthcare community in the 1979 Belmont Report. Various interpretations of principlism were implemented by ethics committees in hospitals and institutional review boards in research facilities and academic medical centers. Principlism draws on social-contract theory and classical philosophical liberalism (this is not the same as mid-twentieth-century social liberalism) for the principle of autonomy (the ethical equivalent of the political concept of liberty). It pulls from the Hippocratic oath the principle of nonmaleficence ("First, do no harm"), and from social liberalism and Protestant progressivism the principle of beneficence (some versions combine beneficence and nonmaleficence into one category). The principle of justice is included, though often in vague ways, sometimes referring to justice in distribution, drawing from New Deal and Great Society arguments, and sometimes as pure procedure, drawing from classical social-contract arguments. Principlism allows discussion of healthcare and research ethics, but in the end it has not provided a basis for clear resolution of conflicts, with a few notable exceptions. Autonomy was and is the most functionally important of the principles of principlism and has successfully been used to define commutative justice obligations of practitioners, specifically moral boundaries for confidentiality, privacy, informed consent, and the right of refusal of treatment. It has been notably less effective in resolving differences over abortion and end-of-life decision-making, and in resolving micro- and macrodistribution conflicts.

This inadequacy has been countered since the 1990s in several different ways. Some organizations, in an effort to endorse social pluralism by promoting moral pluralism, are again encouraging a self-contradictory subjectivist version of utilitarianism (self-contradictory because utilitarianism depends on measurability and comparability); such is best understood as a revival under new terminology of situation ethics. Others have offered stricter versions of utilitarianism. The two most prominent are "interest-based" and supposedly "non-speciesist" utilitarianism (e.g., Peter Singer) and state-endorsed utilitarianism with formal metrics that include "quality of life" (e.g., "quality-adjusted life years"). Some versions of the latter seem all but inevitable under any form of strictly managed care, be it market-driven or governmentally managed, with the practitioner being increasingly identified with the bureaucratic role of rationer.

A reaction against this bureaucratizing tendency, especially from Christians, has taken two forms. One is a call to return to clear deontological moral reasoning with an emphasis on rights, especially the right to life, and on the practitioner's reasonable freedom of conscience in treatment decisions. This, though not emphasizing principlism, does share with it an emphasis on social-contract language. Another reaction has been a renewed concern for the character of the practitioner (e.g., Edmund Pellegrino, David Thomasma) and, sometimes, the character of the patient (e.g., Stanley Hauerwas). Both emphases, rights and virtue, seem to be needed as healthcare continues to rise in cost and outside management of the patient-practitioner relationship seems unavoidable.

In the near future, Christians should expect some continuing attempt to marginalize them on the grounds that their view about the right to life is simply one voice among many, even though that argument makes the notion of rights nonsensical.

Also, the continued debate about how healthcare is distributed, including whether it is a positive right or entitlement, should be expected. Equally important, non-Western concerns will need to be addressed, specifically the impact of HIV/AIDS and how Christians from areas without a history of social-contract theory address healthcare ethics. Perhaps most important in the long run, increasing conflict over the manipulation of human genetics for eugenic purposes should be expected, especially now that assisted reproductive technologies are so well developed.

See also Bioethics; Eugenics; Euthanasia; Healthcare Systems in Scripture; Hospice; Natural Law; Professional Ethics; Quality of Life; Resource Allocation; Sanctity of Human Life; Social Contract

Bibliography

Douglas, M. "The Abominations of Leviticus." Pages 41–57 in *Purity and Danger: An Analysis of the Concepts of Pollution and Taboo.* Routledge & Kegan Paul, 1966; Galen. "The Best Doctor Is Also a Philosopher." Pages 30–34 in *Galen: Selected Works.* Trans. P. Singer. Oxford University Press, 1997; Jones, D. "The Hippocratic Oath: Its Contents and the Limits to Its Adaptation." *CMQ* 54, no. 3 (2003): http://www.catholicdoctors.org.uk/CMQ/Aug_2002/hippocratic_oath.htm; Jones, W. H. S. *The Doctor's Oath: An Essay in the History of Medicine.* Cambridge University Press, 1924; Percival, T. *Medical Ethics; or, A Code of Institutes and Precepts, Adapted to the Professional Conduct of Physicians and Surgeons.* 3rd ed. Parker, 1849; Ramsey, P. *The Patient as Person: Explorations in Medical Ethics.* Yale University Press, 1970; Verhey, A. *Reading the Bible in the Strange World of Medicine.* Eerdmans, 2003.

James R. Thobaben

Healthcare Systems in Scripture

"Healthcare system" refers to the network of beliefs, resources, institutions, and strategies in the maintenance of health and the identification and treatment of sickness. Integral to a healthcare system are assumptions about the etiology and diagnosis of sickness, judgments concerning acceptable and unacceptable options for therapeutic intervention in cases of sickness, and a person's capacity to access healthcare options.

Scripture refers to the restoration of health by a number of options, including the body's capacity to self-heal, prayer and other forms of divine entreaty, and such therapeutic interventions as the intercession of a gifted healer, care within the household, use of traditional medicaments, or employment of a professional physician. The Bible explicitly rejects recourse to magic and generally views physicians with disdain. This is largely because, within Scripture, healing practices are guided by the recognition that Yahweh alone is the source of life and, therefore, the source of renewed health.

Perspectives on Sickness and Healing

Medical anthropologists understand that different societies construct in varying ways how their members think about and respond to sickness and healing. One society identifies a certain condition within the boundaries of its definition of health, while another views that same condition as sickness. Moreover, different societies provide different accounts of sickness, with each both identifying the etiology or cause of the sickness and indicating the therapeutic interventions necessary for recovery of health. One widely used classification of sickness introduces three categories (Hahn).

First, "disease accounts" focus on the body of the individual as the source of sickness. Patients are treated as individuals, with the site of disease sought in the structure and function of bodily organs and functions. Biomedical interventions serve as the primary mode of therapy.

Second, "illness accounts" identify patients as embodied persons in a nest of relationships. The cause and treatment of sicknesses thus require attention to persons in their social environments, with recovery of health measured not only in biomedical but also in relational terms.

Third, "disorder accounts" focus not only on the patient's body and social networks but also on the cosmic order of things. "When the universe is unbalanced, sickness may be manifested in particular locales and individual patients" (Hahn 28).

Of course, this is a catalog of ideal types, with actual accounts of sickness and recovery blurring the lines between these categories. The importance of such a classification rests in our recognition that, for most of our contemporaries in the modern West, sickness is understood in terms of disease accounts—indeed, our healthcare systems are dominated by biomedical diagnoses and therapies—whereas related legislation or narrated episodes of sickness and healing in the biblical materials are typically illness or disorder accounts.

As an example, consider the case of "leprosy," which in the Bible is rarely if ever true leprosy (Hansen's disease), but instead includes any of a number of skin conditions. Leviticus 13–14 commands that persons diagnosed by a priest (acting as a kind of healthcare consultant) as lepers be quarantined. In this case, "leprosy" is not life threatening from a biomedical point of view, nor is this skin disease contagious. Instead, the contagion is ritual impurity. "Leprosy" thus exemplifies how religious, social, and physical considerations coalesce in a single diagnosis. Cases of exorcism similarly correlate what might appear to moderns as discrete spiritual, social, mental, and physical factors, both in the presentation of the disorder and in its resolution (see, e.g., Luke 8:26-39).

The integration of measures of human well-being is crucial to a world in which healing and sickness are indicators of Yahweh's favor and displeasure. Although one cannot argue that health is necessarily the direct result of God's favor or that sickness is necessarily the direct result of divine punishment, it is true that for ancient Israel there could be a causal link from sin to sickness (see, e.g., Deut. 28; 1 Kgs. 13:1–25; Prov. 3:28–35; 11:19; 13:13–23; 1 Cor. 11:29–30).

Healthcare Practices

Healthcare practices in Israel centered in the home, where the sick were kept, and where care might take the form of maintaining vigil and soliciting the help of Yahweh through prayer and fasting (e.g., 2 Sam. 12:15–23). Women in childbirth received the aid of midwives (e.g., Gen. 35:17; 38:28). Only rarely do physicians appear in the OT. When they do, they are typically seen as negative alternatives to Yahweh (e.g., 2 Chr. 16:12; Jer. 8:22–9:6) or as persons offering worthless advice (Job 13:4). In the OT, faithfulness to Yahweh explicitly excluded magic (or sorcery, the manipulation of the spirits) as a remedy, in preference to divine intervention and care (e.g., Lev. 19:26–28; Deut. 18:10–14; Ezek. 13:17–18). This is consistent with the biblical portrait of Yahweh as the God to whom Israel must be exclusively loyal. It is also consistent with the state of medical knowledge in antiquity and thus with the mysteriousness of the human body and its processes, which encouraged hope in magic and/or miracle.

Physicians. Prejudice against physicians is not unique to the OT world. For example, Cato's advice to his son to stay clear of doctors, preferring instead "a little book of prescriptions for curing those who were sick in his family" (Plutarch, *Cato Maj.* 23.3–6), reflects a Roman preference for traditional healing practices over Greek medicine as well as Cato's rejection of fee-based, professional medicine. In rural areas of the Roman Empire, snake charmers and healers with magical powers were the norm. In pandemic times, however, all eyes turned toward the gods for defense and salvation.

Physicians were sufficiently common in the NT world that Jesus could allude to their activity metaphorically (e.g., Mark 2:17 pars.). Only the wealthy could afford the care of a trained physician, however, and village people were especially vulnerable to the abuse of charlatans. Mark 5:26 is illustrative: "She had endured much under many physicians, and had spent all that she had; and she was no better, but rather grew worse." Not surprisingly, then, Jesus' followers were advised against charging for their healthcare interventions: "Cure the sick, raise the dead, cleanse the lepers, cast out demons. You received without payment; give without payment" (Matt. 10:8 [cf. *Did.* 11]).

Village and rural folk depended less on persons who publicly professed the physician's oath, and they found the prospect of divine healing especially attractive (e.g., Acts 5:16). Hospitality might take the form of healthcare (e.g., Luke 10:30–35; Acts 16:33–34), and the author of 1 Timothy reflects medical tradition when he advises "a little wine for the sake of your stomach and your frequent ailments" (5:23 [for a registry of practical medicaments, see Pliny the Elder, *Nat.* 23–32]). Relative wealth could not certify medical competence, however. Medical treatises might sneer at root cutters, drug sellers, and purveyors of amulets and incantations, but even the best physicians understood little of the ways of the body.

Agents of healing. Throughout the OT, Yahweh's role as healer is paramount: "I am the LORD who heals you" (Exod. 15:26 [see also, e.g., 2 Kgs. 5:7; Isa. 57:19]). The prophet Ezekiel portrays Yahweh as healer of the weak, the sick, and the lost (Ezek. 34:16). Yahweh binds up and heals the wounded (Job 5:17–18).

In the NT, the role of God as healer is continued, but now healing is a sign of the inbreaking kingdom of God. According to the book of Acts, God worked deeds of power through Jesus so as to accredit him as God's authorized agent of salvation (2:22); likewise, the Lord "testified to the word of his grace by granting signs and wonders to be done" through Paul and Barnabas (14:3). Others may participate in God's healing activity, but this does not detract from the identification of Yahweh as the source of healing.

In the OT, prophets sometimes were portrayed as agents of healing. Elijah was instrumental in restoring a widow's son to life (1 Kgs. 17:8–24), and Elisha instructed Naaman, commander of the Syrian army, how to be cured of leprosy (2 Kgs. 5:1–15). According to the Synoptic Gospels, Jesus' disciples participated in his ministries of healing and exorcism (Mark 6:7–13 pars.), and in Acts, the apostles and other witnesses healed in the name of Jesus (e.g., 3:1–10; 9:34; 16:16–18). In 1 Cor. 12, Paul lists the gifts of healing and working of miracles as manifestations of the work of the Spirit in the life of the church. In his letter, James directs those who are sick to call for the elders of the church to pray over them, anointing them with oil in the name of the Lord (5:15–16). Correlating confession and healing, James emphasizes healing as integral to the integrity of the Christian community.

See also Divination and Magic; Health

Bibliography

Albl, M. "'Are Any among You Sick?' The Health Care System in the Letter of James." *JBL* 121 (2002): 123–43; Avalos, H. *Health Care and the Rise of Christianity*. Hendrickson, 1999; Hahn, R. *Sickness and Healing: An Anthropological Perspective*. Yale University Press, 1995.

Joel B. Green

Heaven and Hell *See* Judgment

Hebrews

The Epistle to the Hebrews is an anonymous sermon written by a member of the Pauline missionary team (as the author's acquaintance with Timothy suggests [13:23]). Since the author speaks of the Levitical sacrifices continuing to be offered in the present (9:9; 10:2), he probably wrote prior to the destruction of the Jerusalem temple in 70 CE. He addresses a congregation composed of both gentile Christians, for whom instruction in monotheism and the Jewish apocalyptic worldview would have been necessary (6:1–3), and Jewish Christians, with whom the author obviously shares deep roots in the Scriptures. These Christians previously suffered significant rejection at the hands of their neighbors (10:32–34), but some appear now to be in danger of drifting away from their formerly bold stance (2:1–2; 3:12–13; 4:1, 11; 10:24–27, 35–36), perhaps longing once again for some measure of acceptance by their non-Christian peers (the "fleeting pleasures of sin" [11:25]).

The chief ethical contribution of the sermon is the context that the author invokes for making ethical choices: the experience of God's generosity and kindness through Jesus Christ and the concomitant obligation to respond with gratitude in the form of witness, honor, and service (13:15–16). The ideals of the virtuous receiving and returning of favors taught by Greek and Roman ethicists are brought to bear on Christian discipleship, calling the audience not to take God's grace for granted, but to make their choices and lifestyle a consistent witness to their appreciation for God's favor. God's gifts call for appropriate response (6:4–8; 12:28) even when costly, since Jesus' display of favor on their behalf was costly in the extreme (13:12–14). Acts of service and encouragement offered to other members of the community (6:9–10; 10:24–25) are important responses. Choices that reflect a low estimation of Christ's death, most notably allowing one's desire for acceptance within non-Christian society to mute one's Christian witness and drawing back from investing oneself in the lives of fellow Christians, reflect a failure to respond nobly and gratefully (10:23–34). The author has in mind a particular challenge facing the congregation, but the canonical status of his sermon holds this question before disciples in all situations: what is the course of action that will most fully witness to my appreciation for God's favor, and offer the return that would be most pleasing to God (11:6; 12:28; 13:20–21) and most in keeping with the purposes inherent in redemption, as informed by the Judeo-Christian tradition? He urges his audience to replace their desire for "more" (which threatens their ethical integrity) with contentment and confidence in God's ongoing help (13:5–6)—an exhortation that remains a potent challenge to materialist societies.

Fear of divine judgment and retribution, such as would fall on the ungrateful or disloyal, is here an appropriate motivation for ethical decision (2:1–2; 6:4–8; 10:26–31; 12:25–29; 13:4). Such fear helps liberate disciples from the fear of death (2:14–15), which warps and limits ethical choice. Hardships incurred as a result of virtuous action or refusal to violate the bond of gratitude toward God are redeemed by the author as the crucible for character formation (5:8–9; 12:4–11).

The author is very much aware of the social dimension of ethical choice. Those whose approval we seek and whose censure we long to avoid directly influence the ethical decisions we make. The author seeks to exclude concern for one's estimation in the eyes of people not committed to the Christian way of life as a motivation for choice. This is prominent in the examples he praises in 10:32–34; 11:8–16, 24–27, 35–38; 12:1–3. Instead, he directs attention to the company of those who have fulfilled God's just requirements well in their lives—the praiseworthy heroes of the tradition and, above all, Jesus (12:1–2)—as those whose applause is worth seeking. He also encourages mutual investment and accountability in order to provide essential support for empowering individual disciples to make appropriate, often costly, ethical decisions (3:12–13; 5:11–6:1; 10:34; 12:15–16; 13:1–3).

The author is best known for his commendation of faith as an ethical virtue that guides disciples' actions (11:1–12:3). Faith acts with a view to long-term gain, even at the cost of short-term pain. Faith also entails courageous commitment

(3:7–4:11; 10:36–39). Faith thus combines the cardinal virtues of wisdom and courage. Faith responds with trust and obedience to the divine word, with a view to attaining the divine promises, and so becomes productive of the other ethical virtues.

See also New Testament Ethics

Bibliography

Attridge, H. *Hebrews*. Hermeneia. Fortress, 1989; Croy, N. *Endurance in Suffering: Hebrews 12:1–13 in Its Rhetorical, Religious, and Philosophical Context*. SNTSMS 98. Cambridge University Press, 1998; deSilva, D. *Despising Shame: The Social Function of the Rhetoric of Honor and Dishonor in the Epistle to the Hebrews*. SBLDS 152. Scholars Press, 1995; idem. *Perseverance in Gratitude: A Socio-Rhetorical Commentary on the Epistle "to the Hebrews."* Eerdmans, 2000; Johnson, L. *Hebrews*. NTL. Westminster John Knox, 2006; Koester, C. *Hebrews*. AB 36. Doubleday, 2001; Witherington, B., III. *Letters and Homilies for Jewish Christians: A Socio-Rhetorical Commentary on Hebrews, James and Jude*. InterVarsity, 2007.

David A. deSilva

Hedonism

Hedonism is a philosophical perspective that views pleasure or happiness as the ultimate good in human life. The ethical corollary of this position is that actions should be aimed at the maximization of pleasure and the avoidance of pain. This philosophical tradition can be traced back at least as far as the Athenian philosopher Epicurus (341–270 BCE), who argued that the pursuit of pleasure is "our primary and natural good" (Diogenes Laertius, *Lives* 10.128–129). Although Epicurus himself seems to have advocated some moral temperance, especially in the willingness to forgo temporary pleasure if it will bring long-term suffering, he and his followers gained a reputation for licentiousness (see Diogenes Laertius, *Lives* 10.6–7). The classic utilitarianism of Jeremy Bentham and John Stuart Mill represents an outworking of this ancient philosophical tradition.

The English word *hedonism* derives from the Greek *hēdonē*. In the biblical tradition *hēdonē* often is employed with pejorative connotations with reference to illicit desire or cravings (Luke 8:14; Titus 3:3; Jas. 4:1, 3; 2 Pet. 2:13), although the usage is not uniformly negative (see, in the LXX, Num. 11:8, where *hēdonē* denotes the "pleasant" taste of cakes; see also Prov. 17:1; Wis. 7:2; 16:20). In 1 Cor. 15:32 the apostle Paul seems to reflect popular critiques of Epicurean philosophy when, citing an earlier text from Isa. 22:13, he writes, "If the dead are not raised, 'Let us eat and drink, for tomorrow we die'" (on the language of "eating and drinking" in anti-Epicurean writings, see Plutarch, *Mor.* 1098C; 1100D; 1125D). Both Isa. 22:13 and contemporary anti-Epicurean polemic criticize libertine behavior, and Paul draws on this critique in order to challenge the Corinthians to live moral lives in light of the resurrection of Christ (1 Cor. 15:30–34). In Scripture, the pursuit of personal pleasure is at odds with the cruciform existence characteristic of those called to embody the narrative of the cross (e.g., Phil. 2:5–11).

Yet, different definitions of pleasure can lead to different applications of hedonistic philosophy. For example, popular Reformed pastor John Piper has argued for a theological perspective called "Christian hedonism." Assuming that the desire for happiness is universal, Piper contends that human beings ought to pursue, rather than avoid, the fulfillment of this desire. The deepest and most enduring satisfaction, however, is found only in God. Therefore, the pursuit of pleasure is part of worship and virtue. Piper reframes the opening statement of the Westminster Shorter Catechism: "The chief end of man is to glorify God by enjoying him forever." Far from being a call to self-indulgence, however, this system emphasizes worship, obedience, and love for others as a means to obtain true pleasure. Piper's position has been criticized from within the Reformed tradition for offering a hedonistic account of moral justification that has more in common with contemporary philosophy than with the language and logic of Scripture and for a tendency to minimize the themes of self-abandonment and suffering found throughout the NT (so Mouw).

See also Cruciformity; Desire; Happiness; Libertinism; Utilitarianism

Bibliography

Feldman, F. *Utilitarianism, Hedonism, and Desert: Essays in Moral Philosophy*. Cambridge University Press, 1997; Mouw, R. *The God Who Commands*. University of Notre Dame Press, 1990; Piper, J. *Desiring God: Meditations of a Christian Hedonist*. 3rd ed. Multnomah, 2003.

David J. Downs

Holiness

God is holy. This description dominates the OT picture of God. It is the intrinsic character of God, who alone is holy in essence. All other objects, places, and beings are holy only in relationship to the holy God. Since holiness is God's alone, it evokes images of otherness, transcendence, and mystery. A range of cognate ideas also attaches to it: purity, separateness from sin, life, glory, light, radiance, perfection, sanctification. God's holiness cannot tolerate impurity or sinfulness and so is understood to be dangerous. The purification demands established in Leviticus enable God's people to dwell in the presence of this holy and dangerous God (see Lev. 10:1–2). Hence, any approach to God must be with clean hands and a pure heart (Ps. 24:3–4).

Although holiness requires purity, holiness and purity are not identical. A profane person, object, or place could be either clean or unclean. Concentration on separation, danger, and purity can lead to legalism and external performance, which misses the dynamic of holiness that runs through the whole story of God. God reveals his holiness in action. Scripture read canonically points to the holy triune character of God. God is Being-in-Communion—the Holy Trinity—existing in the lively dynamic of unending holy love. God's people are called to be holy as God is holy, reflecting the holy character of the triune God, who creates humans as beings-in-communion made in the image and likeness of God (Gen. 1:28).

Christian ethics and theology are inextricably linked. Christian ethics takes its orientation from the story of God in Scripture as it is supremely revealed in Christ and illuminated in the community of believers through the presence and work of the Spirit. It describes how God's holy people should live. Since it is derived from relationship to the holy God and is the outflow of God's love poured into believers' hearts through the Spirit, it can never be reduced to personal piety or any other human achievement. Still less can Christian ethics be based on the shifting shape of culturally determined morality.

Israel as the Holy People of God

Right from Adam's disastrous choice to assert independence from God, God has called people to be on his rescue mission. The story begins in earnest with Abraham (Gen. 12:1–3), who is called to walk before God and be blameless (Gen. 17:1); it continues with the deliverance of Israel from Egyptian oppression. From this downtrodden people God creates a kingdom of priests and a holy nation (Exod. 19:6). Because Israel is God's own possession, it is to be holy as God is holy (Lev. 19:2). The Holiness Code (Lev. 19–26) gives details of how this call is to be articulated in the community. Much of this has to do with boundaries—separation from idolatry, limitations of sexual relationships—between profane and sacred, clean and unclean. God leads the people of Israel and dwells in their midst, symbolized by the pillar of cloud by day and fire by night that connects to the holy of holies, around which is arrayed his holy people. In turn, Israel is called to exclusive worship of God, but little attention is given to personal piety. Rather, they are addressed as a people living in community with most of the communal practices of holy living summarized in the command "Love your neighbor as yourself."

Scripture details Israel's failure in its calling. Because God's holiness and righteousness are inextricably intertwined, his holy people are to act righteously (see Isa. 5:7, 16). But holiness becomes synonymous with separation as an end in itself, centered on ritual and performance, against which the prophets rage. Israel begins to see its election as a right based on God's irrevocable promises to David (2 Sam. 7:14), while ignoring their conditionality so clearly set out in Torah (Deut. 28–30). So Israel does not maintain its exclusive fidelity to Yahweh; instead, it embraces idolatry. It forgets its past (Deut. 6:21; 7:6–8; 10:18–19), so it does not care for the alien, the poor, and the dispossessed. Instead, it tramples the poor into the dust and robs widows and orphans (Amos 2:6–8; 4:1; 5:10–12, 23–24), clearly a breach of God's holiness (Amos 4:2). It fails to proclaim the name of Yahweh in the nations; instead, its sins are the same as the surrounding nations (Amos 1–2), so the curses of Deuteronomy are realized in exile and the holy name of God is profaned in all the earth (Ezek. 36:20). But God rescues Israel from exile in a display of his holiness before the nations (Ezek. 36:32). In sum, Israel begins to view holiness as exclusivity and separation rather than as service; it no longer models God's love and justice.

The return from exile brings a renewed concern for holiness. The reforms of Nehemiah confirm the focus on separation as the denotation of holiness. The people must return to a high level of exclusiveness and purity. Boundaries between Israel and the gentiles that were seriously eroded during the monarchic period and the exile need to be reestablished in line with the priestly ideals of the Torah. The returnees even divorce their foreign wives (Ezra 10). Ethnic purity as separation from surrounding nations becomes crucial.

The return from exile was not as glorious as promised. With the exception of the period following the Maccabean revolt, Israel never returned to the idealized picture of David's reign. Questions about how the holy God could once again dwell among his people remained. So, holiness movements arose.

Jesus and the New People of God

Jesus, John, the Pharisees, and the Qumran community share this desire for renewal of the holy people of God. The Pharisees believe that holiness demands separation within society and seek to maintain and extend pockets of priestly purity so that the whole people would be a kingdom of priests. The Qumran community considers the temple hopelessly corrupt and looks for a new temple, so they withdraw from society to live a life as God's righteous remnant, making atonement for the land and people (1QS 8.10). Strict obedience to the Torah as God's command must be initiated. Nevertheless, outward obedience must be matched by inward holiness for the men of perfection (see 1QS 8.1–14).

Jesus and John the Baptist before him are in this reforming tradition, but the story of the holy God's redeeming interaction with the created order comes into focus through the life, death, resurrection, and ascension of Jesus. The story of Jesus overlays the story of Israel and illuminates it as God's way to bring Israel's story to its goal of blessing to all.

Jesus is re-creating the holy people, centered on him, "the Holy One of God" (Mark 1:24; John 6:69). This reshaped remnant is doing the will of God, pressing back to the foundations of loving God with one's whole heart and the neighbor as oneself. This holiness has little to do with purity as an end in itself; rather, it is contagious. Boundaries are breached, and people are transformed and restored to the community. This contagious holiness is observed most clearly in Jesus' hospitable dining with sinners and their transformation into participants in the mission of God.

The Gospel of John takes this theme of hospitality even further. The disciples of Jesus, then and now, are invited to share, through mutual indwelling, in the very life of the Holy Trinity (John 17; see also 2 Pet. 1:4). The hospitality of God in welcoming people into this relationship is to be mirrored in their lives of hospitality in community. Jesus redefines holiness primarily in terms of compassion, transformation, and mission, not separation. Purity remains significant so boundaries are not obliterated. However, transformation and single-minded commitment to God and his mission to the world are paramount, not boundary maintenance.

Paul ties holiness intimately to the death and resurrection of Jesus, who is the embodiment of God's whole salvific purpose for the entire created order. Those who are reconciled to God in Christ are saints, a reconfiguring of the people of God around the crucified and risen Christ. Believers are holy "in Christ" because Christ is holy. They are also called to imitate Christ.

Since Paul thinks that his converts are already new creatures in Christ, they are to reflect this new existence as God's holy people. This people, predominately gentiles, are called to be saints, holy ones in their contingent contexts. No longer divided on ethnic grounds but one new people in Christ (Eph. 2:11–22), they embody the call of God to Israel. They are to be agents of God's reconciliation in the world (2 Cor. 5:18–21) as Israel was called to be, saints in both communal and personal terms with an identity solely determined by being in Christ. The scriptural continuity of God's call of a holy people is implicit in Rom. 12:1–2; 13:10; 15:15–18. An explicit intertextual link is made between Lev. 19:2 and Exod. 19:5–6 in 1 Pet. 1:15–16; 2:9–10.

All of Paul's theology is ethical theology; all of his instruction is theological ethics, grounded in his belief that his audiences are called to become what they are in Christ through the Spirit. Thus, Paul would consider the division between justification and sanctification as artificial. These people, therefore, are not only holy in an objective sense due to their location in Christ; they are holy, called to live cruciform lives, shaped by the cross and resurrection of Christ, empowered by the Spirit to act in God's mission and reflecting his being before the world. This regularly means being countercultural, resisting idolatry and impurity because they are the temple of the Holy Spirit, who dwells in them. Especially in the context of the Roman Empire they are called on to articulate the lordship of Jesus in the face of competing claims.

The Holy Church

The church affirms the centrality of holiness in its creedal identity: it is "one holy catholic and apostolic church." But the underlying theme of separation persisted in ways that challenged the inclusive call for all who follow Christ to be his holy people. Holiness became more closely identified with those attached to monasteries or who withdrew from society (the desert fathers) so that there were, in effect, two classes of people in the church: laity and priestly. In that sense, this was a revisiting of the model of priesthood in the OT, but without the notion that all in the church were the holy people of God except in formal identification and specifically Christian liturgical contexts such as the Eucharist. Those in holy orders (the term itself shows the emphasis), such as ordained monks and clergy, were expected to be holy and devote themselves to holy practices: prayer and fasting (including, in the West, celibacy), which were not part of the routine life of the laity. In the mystery of the Trinity and the Eucharist the church experiences God's holiness. The veneration of icons, relics, and saints became important for the church in both the East and the West. The tension between corruption and holiness, however, was present in the minds of people, with the excesses of the church in Rome frequently cited as examples. Reform movements did arise with some effect (Lollards, Waldensians), but the idea of holiness became attached to office in the church rather than to character expressed in behavior.

The Reformation presented a more lasting challenge in the West. The slogan "justification by faith alone" was raised against a system that seemed to offer performance-based salvation and acquired merit. But the Reformers returned to Paul's "the righteous shall live by faith" to counter this view. Holiness, like righteousness, was alien to humans; it is God's alone, and never human achievement. Even the elect remain *simul iustus et peccator*; they are holy because they are clothed in Christ. The unintended consequence was that this concentration on justification eclipsed the call to and prospect of sanctification.

John Wesley recovered the catholic notion of sanctification and linked it again with the Reformation emphasis on justification. Wesley was also influenced, primarily through his Anglicanism, by aspects of Eastern thought. He saw his calling, and that of the Methodists who followed him, to be "spreading scriptural holiness across the land." Methodism itself spawned a range of inheritors, including Pentecostalism, the Keswick (or Higher Life) movement, the Salvation Army, and the various holiness movements with their emphasis on entire sanctification.

At their best, the holiness movements functioned as renewal movements. They practiced their faith in ministering to the poor and the oppressed and became an important revivalistic influence. They moved away from Methodism because they believed that it had lost its emphasis on holiness. But as they expanded, some teaching encouraged a formulaic approach to sanctification; its detractors saw it as legalistic or proclaiming a sinless perfectionism or even as Pelagian. Trenchant criticisms of the whole holiness movement were raised from within conservative Reformed circles.

Recent contributions from Catholic, Orthodox, and Reformed theologians have shown that the recovery of an emphasis on personal and corporate holiness is not a narrow sectarian interest. With increased attention to the story of God in Scripture and his call of a holy people, greater emphasis is now placed on holiness as the identifying characteristic of the people of God. Human holiness is increasingly seen as relational, in personal and corporate terms, and wholly derived from and dependent on the revelation of and in relation to the triune God. Legalists who continue to confuse purity and holiness still exist with a performance target approach to personal holiness, but the message of contagious holiness in the people of God is making its contribution to a renewal of Christian personal and communal ethics. Macroethical issues—social justice, poverty, racism, and war—are now seen as concerns of God's holy people as much as personal piety and microethical concerns.

A kingdom of priests and a holy nation as the identity of God's people is far more than a descriptive tag. The lives of God's people in community are to reflect the life of the Holy Trinity, a life of perpetual love. Postmodern Christians are challenged to reflect the holiness of the triune God in all aspects of their communal and personal lives. This demands a variety of responses, but the outworking of ethical practice is always to be rooted in the holiness of the triune God. Embodying that holiness in the public square frequently requires a countercultural approach. In that way, the community of God's people will fulfill its calling to be the agent of God's redemptive purpose in mission to Adam's rebellious race and the disrupted created order.

See also Clean and Unclean; Cruciformity; Holiness Code; Holy Spirit; Legalism; Perfection; Sanctification; Wesleyan Ethics

Bibliography

Barton, S., ed. *Holiness: Past and Present*. T&T Clark, 2003; Blomberg, C. *Contagious Holiness: Jesus' Meals with Sinners*. NSBT 19. InterVarsity, 2005; Borg, M. *Conflict, Holiness and Politics in the Teachings of Jesus*. New ed. Trinity Press International, 1998; Brower, K., and A. Johnson, eds. *Holiness and Ecclesiology in the New Testament*. Eerdmans, 2007; Deasley, A. *The Shape of Qumran Theology*. Paternoster, 2000; Douglas, M. *Purity and Danger: An Analysis of Concepts of Pollution and Taboo*. Routledge & Kegan Paul, 1978; Gammie, J. *Holiness in Israel*. Fortress, 1989; Harrington, H. *Holiness: Rabbinic Judaism and the Graeco-Roman World*. Routledge, 2001; Orsuto, D. *Holiness*. Continuum, 2007; Peterson, D. *Possessed by God: A New Testament Theology of Sanctification and Holiness*. NSBT 1. Apollos, 1995; Webster, J. *Holiness*. Eerdmans, 2003; Wells, J. *God's Holy People: A Theme in Biblical Theology*. JSOTSup 305. Sheffield Academic Press, 2000.

Kent Brower

Holiness Code

"Holiness Code" is a designation for the collection of laws in Lev. 17–26. These laws are the most definitive texts of the "Holiness School," which, while clearly related to the material of the Pentateuch associated with the Israelite priesthood (called "P"), are now widely agreed to postdate and supplement the P material. Despite this general agreement, the precise dating of the Holiness

Code remains disputed. Many scholars argue that it comes from a period prior to the Babylonian exile (586 BCE), while others contend that the Holiness School material is exilic or even, in part, postexilic.

The Holiness Code's Relevance to Contemporary Issues

The rigid laws found in the Holiness Code often strike contemporary readers as pedantic and arcane. A closer reading, however, reveals that its laws touch on some of the biggest social and ethical issues of our time. In the context of ongoing debates about marriage and adoption rights for gay and lesbian couples, the code's injunction against male homosexuality (Lev. 18:22; cf. 20:13) may be its most oft-cited law. Agricultural laws (e.g., Lev. 19:23; 25:2–7) and the code's strong interest in the effects of human sinfulness on the land (Lev. 18:28; 20:22; 25:18–19) invite reflection on the ethics of how we treat the earth. Laws designed to provide for the poor and disenfranchised (e.g., Lev. 23:22; 25) have direct implications for the ever-growing problems associated with socioeconomic disparity around the world today. And the establishment of the Year of Jubilee—that is, every fiftieth year, in which God specifies that Israel's fields are to lie fallow, land that has been sold is to revert to its hereditary owner, and enslaved Israelites are to be granted manumission (cf. Lev. 25:10–55)—has given rise to contemporary social efforts such as the ONE campaign, an organization devoted to debt relief, healthcare, and the alleviation of extreme poverty in developing nations.

Democratized and Relational Holiness

The name "Holiness Code" derives from Lev. 19:2, which serves as the ontological motivation for the laws therein: "Speak to all the congregation of the people of Israel and say to them: 'You shall be holy, for I the LORD your God am holy.' " Although it is never explicitly defined by the biblical text, holiness has its source in Yahweh, and Yahweh bestows it upon people (Lev. 21:8), space, time, and things (e.g., Lev. 21:23; 22:15–16). Baruch Levine has suggested that holiness is not so much Yahweh's nature as it is a description of the ways Yahweh acts, in justice and righteousness. Also, because God is holy, God is set apart from that which is common. Israel's priests are expected to imitate God's holiness. This view of holiness is common to both the P material of the Pentateuch and the Holiness School.

The Holiness Code makes clear by the nature of its laws that holiness is realized in active terms, through one's ethics and behavior. In this way, the very name of the collection implies that ethics—specifically, the establishment of a community-wide ethic based on the unique worldview of the Holiness School—is the Holiness Code's central concern. The instructions given by God in these laws relate to the holiness of Israel in all aspects of life: in its interactions with God, within the community, with other nations, with the land itself, and even with objects, times, and spaces. The fundamental goal of the laws is the establishment of a community that is holy, even more than the sanctification of individuals, but neither can exist apart from the other.

The Holiness Code departs from the earlier Priestly material of Leviticus and the rest of the Pentateuch by requiring the aforementioned combination of ethical behavior and distinctness not merely of Israel's priests, but of all the people of Israel. Robert Kugler has referred to this trend within the texts of the Holiness School as the "democratization" of holiness, and nowhere is it more evident than in the Holiness Code. The Israelites' emulation of God's holiness is intended to mark them as uniquely God's own. The Holiness Code goes further than P too by suggesting that Israel's actions have, in turn, a consecrating effect on God (Lev. 22:32); in other words, there is a reciprocal quality to holiness. Moreover, in imitating God's holiness, Israel is to serve as an example for its neighbors to follow, even as it maintains the careful boundaries that delineate holy from common. In these ways, "holiness" must be understood as a relational concept.

The confluence of ritual and moral law in the Holiness Code is one of its most distinctive qualities. The P material of Leviticus is almost wholly concerned with the proper practice of ritual requirements in Israel. Failure to follow proper ritual procedures results in a person or thing becoming ritually impure—a state that may be contagious to other people or things, and that renders the impure person or thing dangerously unfit to be in the presence of holiness. In the Holiness Code, though, a person may also contract impurity for transgressing a moral injunction. But the resulting impurity is also moral as well as ritual; it carries with it a stigma of sinfulness that is absent in ritual impurity. Moreover, whereas ritual impurity can be removed by ritual means, such as washing (e.g., Lev. 15:5–8), moral impurity can be removed only by punishment (e.g., Lev. 20:2–5) or by acts of atonement (e.g., Lev. 19:20–22).

Exclusivism and the Threat of Exile

The steady buildup of moral impurity in the community defiles not only the people but also the sanctuary (Lev. 20:3) and the land (Lev. 18:28). At the time of the Holiness Code's inception, Israel was keenly aware of the real threat of exile. Israel had experienced it at the hands of Assyria, and, depending on the dating of the code to which one subscribes, the same threat was either imminent or fully present from Babylon. It is hardly surprising that the code's most severe punishment for breaking many of its laws is not death, but *karet*: exile from the community (the punishment occurs thirteen times [e.g., Lev. 17:10; 18:29; 20:3]). To be "cut off" (Heb. *kārat*) from the community threatens not just the offender's life but also the extinction of his or her whole family line, so that the offender's existence will not even be remembered once he or she is dead. Therefore, the implied punishment of national exile in Lev. 20:22 ("You shall keep all my statutes and all my ordinances, and observe them, so that the land to which I bring you to settle in may not vomit you out" [cf. Lev. 18:26–28]) carries with it the very real threat of national extinction. The establishment and preservation of a clear national identity for Israel in the face of that threat, then, is also a principal aim of the Holiness Code. Israel's social and historical circumstances demanded that a definition of holiness include a strong measure of exclusivism. This does not mean that Israel was isolated from its ancient Near Eastern neighbors; they interacted with their neighbors and shared many aspects of culture with the nations around them. But the Holiness Code seeks to develop and codify Israel's theology and ethics in ways that are uniquely Israelite, distinctively different from those of their neighbors.

For most (though not all) modern-day readers, the threat of community dissolution is not as immediate as it was for Israel at the time the Holiness Code was established. Indeed, maintaining the goal of strict distinctness may well pose problems for communities of faith that seek instead to reach out to their neighbors. In part because so many of the Holiness Code's laws are presented in incontrovertible terms, there is a temptation to treat them, or at least some of them, as simple moral absolutes. But to separate the injunctions of the Holiness Code from, first, the culture and circumstances that birthed them and, second, the unique theological worldview that undergirds them is to strip them of their meaning and purpose. It is true that some of the Holiness Code's laws, such as the laws prohibiting incest in Lev. 18, dovetail with the social mores of our time. But others do not. For instance, the injunction in Lev. 19:19 against wearing clothing made out of two different materials is not widely practiced, and may even seem absurd, in the modern era. And yet the principles underlying both these types of laws are identical. Recognizing and practicing careful divisions in everyday life is necessary, in the Holiness worldview, in order to maintain safe distinctions between holy and common, and between Israel and its environs. Today, however, while the first distinction is laudable, the second may be problematic. The Holiness Code invites contemporary readers to reflect on the meaning of holiness and how it is to be manifested, ethically and morally, within their own communities of faith. When dealing with the specific laws of the Holiness Code today, we must consider the extent to which an ethic of exclusivism figures into our community's definition of holiness.

See also Clean and Unclean; Holiness; Homosexuality; Incest; Leviticus; Moral Absolutes; Moral Law; Old Testament Ethics; Poverty and Poor; Priestly Literature; Sanctification; Sanctuary; Sexual Ethics; Sin; Torah; World Poverty, World Hunger

Bibliography

Bono [Paul David Hewson]. Keynote address at the 54th National Prayer Breakfast, February 2, 2006: http://www.americanrhetoric.com/speeches/bononationalprayerbreakfast.htm; Joostens, J. *People and Land in the Holiness Code: An Exegetical Study of the Ideational Framework of the Law in Leviticus 17–26*. VTSup 67. Brill, 1996; Klawans, J. *Impurity and Sin in Ancient Judaism*. Oxford University Press, 2000; Knohl, I. *The Sanctuary of Silence: The Priestly Torah and the Holiness School*. Fortress, 1995; Kugler, R. "Holiness, Purity, the Body, and Society: The Evidence for Theological Conflict in Leviticus." *JSOT* 76 (1997): 3–27; Levine, B. *Leviticus*. JPSTC. Jewish Publication Society, 1989; Milgrom, J. *Leviticus*. 3 vols. AB 3, 3A, 3B. Doubleday, 1991–2001; idem. *Leviticus: A Book of Ritual and Ethics*. CC. Fortress, 2004; Wright, D. "Holiness in Leviticus and Beyond: Differing Perspectives." *Int* 53 (1999): 351–64.

Robin C. McCall

Holy Spirit

Throughout Scripture and the Jewish-Christian tradition the Holy Spirit has been considered as a positive ethical impetus on the community of believers as well as on the individual.

Old Testament Perspectives

It is notoriously difficult to determine whether references in the OT to the Hebrew term *rûaḥ* indicate God's Spirit, a human spirit, or simply "a wind from before the LORD." This difficulty should not be overemphasized, since the OT authors are not always interested in clearly differentiating between "wind" as a mysterious power used by God (Exod. 14:21; Num. 11:31), a human spirit as acted on by God (2 Chr. 36:22; Ezra 1:5; Job

10:12), and God's Spirit or a spirit sent by God as acting on people (Num. 11:25; Deut. 34:9; Judg. 9:23; 1 Sam. 16:15; 2 Kgs. 19:7; Ps. 51:10–11; Ezek. 11:19; 36:26–27). Many of these references simply wish to evidence the manifestation of God's active involvement in this world and among his people, as in Gen. 1:2: the Spirit is the manifestation of God's creative power that overcomes the forces of chaos and brings forth life (also Job 33:4; Ps. 104:30; Isa. 40:13; Ezek. 37:9). In contrast, where the Spirit is withdrawn, life ceases (Gen. 6:3).

Presenting the Spirit as life-giving power, it comes as no surprise that the OT speaks again of the Spirit when it expresses its eschatological hopes for the restoration of the people of God and this world. Some OT passages depict this ethical renewal as the result either of a direct outpouring of the Spirit on the people (Isa. 32:15–18; 44:1–5; Ezek. 37:1–14) or of the ministry of the Messiah/Servant, who will, through the Spirit, restore justice, peace, mercy, and the fear of God among Israel (Isa. 11:1–4; 42:1–4; 62:1–4). Joel 2:28–32 describes the eschatological renewal in social categories, implying that the outpouring of the Spirit will lead to a renewed social order: Israel's leaders ("old men") as well as those marginalized in society ("menservants and maidservants") have something to say. Similarly, Isaiah identifies the results of the Spirit's outpouring (either by way of the anointed Messiah/Servant or directly on the people) in terms of peace, justice, and mercy (Isa. 11:1–4; 32:15–18; 42:1–4; 44:1–5; 62:1–4; cf. Zech. 3:1–10; 4:6; 12:10). Ezekiel anticipated a renewed Torah obedience as a consequence of God's giving of his Spirit, and as a result thereof, the people will live safely in the land (Ezek. 36:27; 37:14).

The eschatological and ethical dimension of the Spirit in the OT seems to be a logical outcome of the notion of *rûaḥ* as *Spiritus Creator*. The ethical renewal fostered by the Spirit is defined mainly in social categories (justice, peace, mercy). While Ezek. 36:27 speaks of an "intrapersonal" renewal through the Spirit, the aim is the restoration of Torah obedience among God's people so that they may "live in the land" (Ezek. 37:13–14).

The OT reflects little interest in neatly defining the exact role of the divine and the human spirit in the anticipated renewal. A somewhat more developed argument on that is presented in the later sapiential tradition, in which the Spirit often was related to wisdom, which in turn leads to Torah obedience (e.g., Wis. 9:17–18; Sir. 4:11–19; 39:6–8). Other than within the sapiential tradition, it is much debated whether the writings of Second Temple Judaism reflect the Spirit as a positive ethical influence on the people of God (cf. Menzies; Turner; Wenk, *Community-Forming Power*).

New Testament Perspectives

Paul's letters. There is no doubt that for Paul the Spirit is both the origin and the norm of the believer's new life (e.g., Rom. 8:4–6; Gal. 3:2). This norm, expressed with the phrase *kata pneuma*, "according to the Spirit," is both pneumatologically and eschatologically motivated.

Gordon Fee understands Paul's antithesis of flesh versus Spirit not as a constant struggle within the believer, but as contrasting two modes of existence: *kata pneuma*, "according to the Spirit," refers to the believer's new eschatological existence, and *kata sarka*, "according to the flesh," to a person's preconversion existence. Thus, with the "flesh versus Spirit" antithesis Paul contrasts two modes of existence, and his exhortation not to live according to the flesh is directed toward those who entered the new eschatological life in the Spirit but now argue for a life based on Torah obedience, which implies living again according to the norms of the past—the flesh (Fee 816–22).

Paul can exhort his readers, whose existence is "in the Spirit," to "walk/live according to the Spirit" (Rom. 8:4–12; Gal. 5:13–6:10)—an expression of the indicative/imperative motive. The Spirit's presence in the life of believers empowers them to live according to the Spirit, however, not in such a way that the Spirit's impetus is understood as the transmission of a substance, but rather in relational terms; the Spirit is drawing the believer to communion with God and the people of God. This communion in turn leads to the ethical transformation of the individual (Rabens).

Not all of Paul's ethical exhortations are supported with a pneumatological argument. He explicitly links the Spirit with the call for mutual love (2 Cor. 6:6; Gal. 5:13–6:10; Phil. 2:1–2; Col. 1:8; 1 Thess. 4:8–9) (Horn), and thereby the Spirit is related to the very center of Pauline ethics: love (Rom. 13:8–10; 14:1–15:13; 1 Cor. 13) and renunciation of status (Gal. 5:6). Love will cross the boundaries between people in a horizontal way, and the renunciation of status will cross social boundaries in a vertical way between people of high and of low social status (Theissen 412). Hence, the Spirit is the Spirit of community (2 Cor. 13:13; Eph. 2:22; 4:3–6), and to destroy this community is, for Paul or one of his followers, to grieve the Spirit (Eph. 4:30).

To what extent does Paul's discussion of the charismata (Rom. 12:3–8; 1 Cor. 12–14) contribute to his Spirit-ethic emphasis? In the Pauline churches every person, regardless of social and/

or ethnic background and gender, had the right to say something; the Spirit is thereby instrumental in overcoming social boundaries between people. Hence, charismatic experiences have direct implications for the social structure and life of a group—a fact recently addressed by Pentecostal scholars (Petersen; Villafañe; Wenk, "Holy Spirit").

The question as to what extent Paul's "pessimistic anthropology" (Rom. 1:18–3:20) is just the other side of his positive view regarding the Spirit's involvement in the ethical life of the believer has yet to be addressed more thoroughly.

The Lukan writings. Luke clearly understood the Spirit as empowering believers for mission and inspiring prophetic speech, but it remains debated whether Luke understood the Spirit also as a positive ethical influence on the community of believers. Max Turner finds that Luke's perception of the Spirit "is dominated by his broader intention to portray the ministry of Jesus, and the Church which results, as the fulfillment of God's promises savingly to restore his people Israel and make her a light to the nations" (Turner 428). This appraisal accounts for Luke's two programmatic OT quotations at the beginning of each volume (Isa. 61:1–2 in Luke 4:18–19; Joel 2:28–32 in Acts 2:17–21). Both quotations agree in their eschatological and social-ethical vista as well as in their pneumatological emphasis. While Luke's Gospel narrates the life and ministry of the Spirit-anointed Messiah, Acts presents the life and ministry of the Spirit-anointed community as the continuation "of all that Jesus began to do and teach" (Acts 1:1); the Spirit outpouring on the day of Pentecost signals the executive power of Jesus by which he restores Israel and reigns over his church. This in turn leads to a community that surpasses the Hellenistic ideals of friendship. Further, Luke's redactional changes in the temptation narrative (Luke 4:1–15) seem to imply that he understood the Spirit to assist Jesus in his contest with the devil.

Emphasizing that Luke understood the Spirit as the Spirit of prophecy, one must also consider that the very same Spirit-inspired proclamation was at the same time understood to realize God's saving and restoring work. When the Spirit-anointed Messiah is expected to proclaim the good news to the poor (Luke 4:16–30), he is thereby expected to achieve the eschatological Jubilee Year and the new exodus. Hence, the Spirit's role in prophecy cannot be limited to the inspiration thereof but also comprises its intentioned result (Wenk, *Community-Forming Power*, 120–48, 200–221). Further, both in his Gospel and in the book of Acts, Luke depicts the Spirit not only as inspiring prophetic words but also as instrumental in preventing or overcoming schisms, as well as in bringing together people who otherwise would avoid each other; Luke 1:39–45 narrates how through the work of the Spirit a reversal of the social status takes place; the elderly, honorable Elizabeth confirms and praises the young, pregnant Mary as the mother of her Lord. Through the prophetic word the generally admitted definitions of shame and honor were overcome and the social roles newly defined, as reflected in the Magnificat (Luke 1:4–52). In the conversion stories in Acts 8–11 the Spirit is primarily described as initiating a communication process that due to religious and ethnic prejudices would otherwise never have taken place. In each story the Spirit's manifestation led to a redefinition of the community of the people of God, including now those traditionally perceived as outsiders (Samaritans, gentiles, a gentile eunuch, and a former persecutor of the church). Therefore, the Spirit became foundational for redefining the symbolic universe of the church (Wenk, *Community-Forming Power*, 274–308).

The Johannine writings. For John, life, the word of God, and the Spirit of God are closely related to one another (John 3:5–7, 34; 6:63). Since both the word and the Spirit are life-giving, it seems natural to him to combine this with the metaphor of living water (John 3:5–7; cf. Isa. 32:15–18; 43:19–21; Zech. 14:8). In John 7:37–39 the living water flowing from Jesus (or believers?), and thereby bringing forth new life, is equated with the Spirit (cf. Rev. 22:17). The Spirit is both the word and the water that accomplishes the eschatological cleansing as anticipated in Ezek. 36:25–26. In Jesus' Farewell Discourse (John 13–17) the Spirit guarantees the disciples the continuing presence of God—the Spirit is the new Paraclete for the disciples, taking the place of Jesus—and in John 20:19–23 the Spirit becomes the guarantee for the disciples' mission to be the continuation of Jesus' restoring and life-giving ministry (cf. John 16:5–16).

Although the Johannine writings represent a pneumatological wealth, it is difficult to speak of a pneumatologically motivated ethics. First, John's ethic is predominantly christologically motivated, and thus the Spirit will reveal Christ, remind the disciples of all that Jesus taught (John 14:15–31; cf. 1 John 2:26–27), and enable them to continue the ministry of Christ. Second, while often referring to the commandments in plural (e.g., John 14:15, 21; 15:10), John actually shows interest only in the mutual love (Theissen 73), which in turn is predominantly christologically sustained (John 13:34; 15:9–14; 17:23).

Contemporary Theology

Pneumatology is no longer the foster child of theology. Pentecostal scholars increasingly realize the potential of pneumatology for social ethics, but Michael Welker argues that the charismatic movement is overly preoccupied with the sensational, and therefore such Spirit experiences are of no relevance for a secularized society. He perceives the Spirit's work more in the various liberation theologies. According to Welker, the Spirit is the answer to both the pluralism and the individualism of our time: revealed in pluralism, the Spirit holds together the diversity. More appreciative of a nexus between charismatic experiences and social renewal is Jürgen Moltmann's pneumatology. For Moltmann, the Spirit both originates and preserves life; the Spirit is the one who intercedes on behalf of those confronted with injustice.

See also Fruit of the Spirit; New Testament Ethics; Old Testament Ethics; Trinity

Bibliography

Fee, G. *God's Empowering Presence: The Holy Spirit in the Letters of Paul.* Hendrickson, 1994; Hildebrandt, W. *An Old Testament Theology of the Spirit of God.* Hendrickson, 1995; Horn, F. "Wandel im Geist: Zur pneumatologischen Begründung der Ethik bei Paulus." *KD 38* (1992): 149–70; Menzies, R. *The Development of Early Christian Pneumatology: With Special Reference to Luke-Acts.* JSNTSup 54. Sheffield Academic Press, 1991; Moltmann, J. *The Spirit of Life: A Universal Affirmation.* Fortress, 1992; Neve, L. *The Spirit of God in the Old Testament.* Seibunsha, 1972; Petersen, D. *Not by Might, nor by Power: A Pentecostal Theology of Social Concern in Latin America.* Regnum, 1996; Rabens, V. *The Holy Spirit and Ethics in Paul: Transformation and Empowering for Religious-Ethical Life.* Mohr Siebeck, 2009; Theissen, G. *Erleben und Verhalten der ersten Christen: Eine Psychologie des Urchristentums.* Gütersloher Verlagshaus, 2007; Turner, M. *Power from on High: The Spirit in Israel's Restoration and Witness in Luke-Acts.* JPTSup 9. Sheffield Academic Press, 1996; Villafañe, E. *The Liberating Spirit: Toward an Hispanic American Pentecostal Social Ethic.* Eerdmans, 1993; Welker, M. *God the Spirit.* Fortress, 1994; Wenk, M. *Community-Forming Power: The Socio-Ethical Role of the Spirit in Luke-Acts.* JPTSup 19. T&T Clark, 2004; idem. "The Holy Spirit as Transforming Power within a Society: Pneumatological Spirituality and Its Political/Social Relevance for Western Europe." *JPT* 11 (2002): 130–42.

Matthias Wenk

Holy War

The term *holy war* is a misnomer; war is never called "holy" in the Bible. Language ascribing war to Yahweh does appear in the OT (Exod. 17:16; Num. 21:14; 1 Sam. 17:47; 18:17; 25:28), therefore the expressions *Yahweh war* and *divine war* are preferable. Many OT battle accounts feature divine involvement. Some wars, especially in the context of Israel's entry into the land, are portrayed as divinely authorized (Exod. 17:8–16; Deut. 7:1–6). Soldiers and weapons can be consecrated to the task (1 Sam. 21:5; 2 Sam. 1:21) and religious vows are associated with fighting (Num. 21:2; Judg. 11:36; 1 Sam. 14:24). God is sometimes described as a warrior (Exod. 15:3; Ps. 24:8; Isa. 42:13; Zeph. 3:17), commanding heavenly troops or "hosts" (1 Sam. 17:45; Isa. 13:4; Joel 2:11; cf. Rev. 12:7–9) and employing celestial chariotry (2 Kgs. 6:17; Ps. 68:17; Hab. 3:8). Such traditions ground Israel's security in God's sovereignty instead of human war craft. God reigns supreme in every aspect of life and death (Deut. 32:39–42). God is Israel's true king (Exod. 15:18; Judg. 8:23; Ps. 146) and ultimately responsible for Israel's defense (Pss. 47–48; Isa. 31:4–5). Faith in weapons (Josh. 24:12; Ps. 76:3), horses and chariots (Ps. 33:17; Isa. 31:1–3), or even international treaties (Isa. 30:1–5) is deceptive. Although heroes' exploits can be celebrated (Judg. 3:15–30), Israel's faith in God subverts the importance of bigger (1 Sam. 17), stronger (Ps. 33:16), or more numerous (Deut. 20; Judg. 7; 1 Sam. 14) warriors. The exodus serves as the fundamental paradigm: God fights on Israel's behalf, which limits rather than encourages militarism on the part of Moses and the people (Exod. 14:13–14; cf. 2 Chr. 20). However, exodus and exile are also held together: God will fight *against* the Israelites if they are disobedient (Num. 14:42–43; Isa. 5:25–30; 9:8–10:11; 63:10; Jer. 21:5–6; Lam. 2:5). Even the "ban" (Deut. 7; 20; Josh. 6–7), the committal of booty and captives to destruction, can be viewed as a prohibition of gain from battle and another reminder that victory comes from God alone. Retribution is properly left to God (Deut. 32:35; cf. Rom. 12:19). Thus, this biblical tradition has sometimes been interpreted as a warrant for pacifism. However, Israel is never barred from war, and some OT traditions acknowledge that Israel and other nations can assist in the martial administration of God's retributive justice (Num. 31:3; 1 Sam. 7:7–11; Ps. 18:34; Jer. 50–51).

Considerable tension exists between the pursuit of warfare in the OT and the NT emphasis on love of enemies (Matt. 5:44). Yet the NT also uses military language to describe God's war against worldly powers (1 Cor. 15:24–28), Jesus' role in that divine campaign (2 Thess. 1:6–10; Rev. 19:11–16), and the Christian life as spiritual battle (Matt. 10:34–36; 2 Cor. 10:3–5; Eph. 6:10–20; Heb. 11:32–34). Because war in the Bible repeatedly exhibits cosmological imagery (Josh. 10:9–11; Judg. 5:20–21; Pss. 18:14–15; 77:16–20), divine war should be understood theologically as a disruption of the created order and thus the withdrawal of God's compassionate oversight (cf. Rom. 1:18–32) rather than God's positive will for humankind. Peace is the Bible's overriding eschatological goal (Ps. 46:9; Isa. 2:4; 11:1–9; Zech. 9:9–10). Tragically, biblical passages relating to war are nonetheless misused to justify ethnic cleansing and genocide.

See also Ban, The; Conquest; Exile; Justice, Retributive; Just-War Theory; Military Service; Peace; Powers and Principalities; Violence; War

Bibliography

Craigie, P. *The Problem of War in the Old Testament*. Eerdmans, 1978; Kang, S.-M. *Divine War in the Old Testament and in the Ancient Near East*. BZAW 177. De Gruyter, 1989; Lind, M. *Yahweh Is a Warrior: The Theology of Warfare in Ancient Israel*. Herald Press, 1980; McDonald, P. *God and Violence: Biblical Resources for Living in a Small World*. Herald Press, 2004; Niditch, S. *War in the Hebrew Bible: A Study in the Ethics of Violence*. Oxford University Press, 1993.

Stephen B. Chapman

Homelessness

Homelessness is the state of being without a home or without adequate or reliable housing. A secondary meaning suggests the spiritual dimension of homelessness in the sense of the longing to be at home with God.

Attending to Scripture

Within the Bible, there are four senses in which home as a spiritual reality is offered, then lost or never attained: heaven, Eden, the land of Israel, and the new Jerusalem. Heaven, the abode of God, is described as eternal. Eden was created by God as home for the first human couple. It provided all conditions for harmonious and productive living, the *shalom* that would connote the character of God himself. After the fall, Adam and Eve and their offspring lived in a state of perpetual exile. Indeed, the human race is forever seeking its "paradise lost."

Abraham and later the children of Israel were promised a land of their own—a territorial home—as part of the covenantal agreement. Later, Jerusalem and its tabernacle ("the place of dwelling"), and subsequently the various versions of the temple, were designated as locations where God would take up residence with his people (Deut. 12:11; 14:33; 2 Chr. 36:15). However, due to their sinfulness and failure to live up to the terms of the covenant, they were exiled, and the temple was ravaged.

Scripture also includes references to the poor who lack a physical home. The judgment on Sodom included the condemnation that the town "had pride, excess of food, and prosperous ease, but did not aid the poor and needy" (Ezek. 16:49). In Isa. 58:7 the prophecy declares that part of true worship of God is to "bring the homeless poor into your house."

These themes continue in the NT, most notably in Jesus' parable of the sheep and the goats where he declares, "I was a stranger and you did not welcome me" (Matt. 25:43). Jesus' condition on earth is described as temporary homelessness—born in a borrowed manger (Luke 2:7), no place to lay his head (Luke 9:58), and buried in a borrowed tomb (Luke 23:50–55). Paul describes the state of the early disciples as one in which they are "poorly clothed and beaten and homeless" (1 Cor. 4:11). Homelessness in Scripture is both a spiritual state and a present, physical reality.

The Tradition and Scripture

Throughout Christian history, these two contrasting images of homelessness have continued. The first is the state of the pilgrim or sojourner. In the second century CE, the *Epistle to Diognetus* describes Christians in this manner: "They live in their own countries, but only as aliens; they participate in everything as citizens, and endure everything as foreigners. Every foreign country is their fatherland, and every fatherland is foreign. . . . They live on earth, but their citizenship is in heaven" (*Diog.* 5:5–9).

Christians throughout the history of the church have also thought of homelessness in a more literal sense, drawing on biblical injunctions that have motivated both Jews and Christians to assist the homeless, the stranger, and the poor (Lev. 25:35–43; Deut. 15:7–8; Prov. 14:31; 19:17). In postbiblical testimony, the bishop Irenaeus (c. 180 CE) ordered his followers to "deal thy bread to the hungry willingly, and lead into thy house the roofless stranger" (*Haer.* 4.17.3).

Clement of Alexandria, along with his successor Origen, commanded Christians to actively seek those who needed their gifts and compassion. If there were questions about the legitimacy of the need, these men believed that generosity should trump doubt. Around 200 CE, Tertullian encouraged followers to give even to the poor person who does not ask. In keeping with the biblical challenge, "How does God's love abide in anyone who has the world's goods and sees a brother or sister in need and yet refuses help?" (1 John 3:17), the later Christian writings of Origen, Clement, and *Shepherd of Hermas* condemned neglect of the poor.

During the Middle Ages, many abbeys and monasteries provided shelter for wayfarers and the homeless, treating them as "guests." More recently, Christian efforts to help the homeless have included the Salvation Army, Habitat for Humanity, church-based shelters and programs designed for the homeless, and Christian advocacy groups working to change government laws and polices that affect the homeless.

See also Almsgiving; Charity, Works of; Hospitality; Koinonia; Poverty and Poor

Bibliography

Albahyari, R. *Visions of Charity: Volunteer Workers and Moral Community*. University of California Press, 2000; Baumohl, J., ed. *Homelessness in America*. Oryx Press, 1996; Elliott, J. *A Home for the Homeless: A Sociological Exegesis of 1 Peter, Its Situation and Strategy*. Fortress, 1981; Fuhr, M. *No Place to Stay: A Handbook for Homeless Outreach*. Self-published, 1996; Pohl, C. *Making Room: Recovering Hospitality as a Christian Tradition*. Eerdmans, 1999; Polakow, V., and C. Guillean. *International Perspectives on Homelessness*. Praeger, 2001; Rouner, L., ed. *The Longing for Home*. University of Notre Dame Press, 1996; Yankoski, M. *Under the Overpass: A Journey of Faith on the Streets of America*. Multnomah, 2005.

Fletcher L. Tink

Homosexuality

The term *homosexuality* refers to a primary relational and sexual orientation toward a member of the same sex, in contrast to heterosexuality (primary orientation toward a member of the opposite sex).

Since the late 1960s the status of persons with a homosexual orientation within religion and society has been one of the most debated and divisive issues to arise, whether for Christian ethicists, biblical scholars, mental health professionals, biologists, advocates of ballot initiatives, legislative bodies, or denominational deliberations (both in the United States and abroad). The use of the term *homosexuality* itself has been much debated in public discourse, and many individuals who identify themselves as having an orientation to the same sex prefer the designation LGBT (lesbian/gay/bisexual/transgendered), particularly because it includes a broader and more nuanced range of orientations than simply homosexuality. The modern debate and discord over homosexuality has often been identified as beginning with the rise of the gay rights movement in the aftermath of the Stonewall Riots in New York City in 1969, a movement that has slowly but surely resulted in increased civil rights and legal protections for LGBT individuals, including marriage in some states. A fundamental question within the church has been whether the full inclusion of LGBT persons of faith represents a prophetic movement of God's Spirit parallel to the full inclusion of women and racial/ethnic minorities in the church, or whether it represents a movement away from fidelity to a normative understanding of human sexuality as revealed in Scripture and tradition. The place of reason and experience as sources of authority and revelation that both contextualize and relativize understandings of Scripture and tradition on homosexuality has also been an issue of much debate and disagreement among ethicists and biblical scholars alike.

Translating Words and Cultures

Six texts in the Bible deal directly with homosexual sex: the story of Sodom and Gomorrah in Gen. 19:1–10; the Holiness Code in Lev. 18:20; 20:13; Paul's statements in Rom. 1:26–27, and his passing remarks in 1 Cor. 6:9; 1 Tim. 1:10 (though some question Pauline authorship of the latter book). The interpretive challenge in each text has to do with the translation of Hebrew words from the OT and Greek words from the NT, as well as with the translation of ancient cultures for modern times.

The translation issue in Gen. 19 revolves around the desire of the Sodomites to "know" (*yādaʿ*) the visitors whom Lot is hosting (v. 5). The Hebrew term *yādaʿ* can also have overtones of sexual intercourse, which seems to be the intention in this passage. While the NRSV translates the Hebrew phrase as "that we may know them," the NAB translates it as "that we may have intimacies with them," and the NIV as "that we can have sex with them." The passage clearly suggests sexual violence, indeed homosexual rape, as a way for the Sodomites to dominate the foreign men visiting their town. Lot correctly sees their desire as a wicked thing and offers his two daughters to the mob as a lesser evil than violating his duty of offering hospitality to his guests. Little do the Sodomites know that these guests are angels sent by God to destroy the city. The Sodomites' wicked desires only confirm God's judgment. But does the passage indicate that all forms of same-sex relations or desires are evil in the sight of God? Certainly, homosexual rape is condemned, but it seems quite a step to condemn all forms of homosexual expression on the basis of this passage about sexual violence. This would be tantamount to condemning all forms of heterosexual expression because King David was guilty of adultery with Bathsheba, the wife of Uriah. For this reason, many ethicists and biblical scholars do not view Gen. 19 as having probative value for the debate over homosexuality in the modern world.

The issue in Lev. 18:20; 20:13 has less to do with translation and more to do with the larger context of the Holiness Code, which sets forth strict rules for the Israelites as they are about to take possession of the promised land. They must not engage in any of the idolatrous activities of the Canaanites, the former occupants of the land. The difficulty here is translating cultures, since Leviticus also bars practices such as cross-breeding animals, sowing two kinds of seed in one field, wearing garments made of two different materials, rounding the hair on one's temples, marring the edges of one's beard, or receiving a tattoo (19:19, 27–28; 21:5), cultural practices that today Christians see as having no particular significance for religious faith, even though the prohibitions are in the Bible. In addition, Leviticus provides a rationale for neither the prohibition in general (18:20) nor the extreme punishment in particular (20:13). Are modern people of faith to pick and choose among the various Levitical prohibitions and punishments? If so, on what basis? Thus, although the Levitical codes clearly condemn same-sex relations, the larger context of these prohibitions, as well as the penalty of death, have complicated how such condemnation should be understood or enacted today within the Christian community.

The most significant biblical passage to address the question about same-sex relations is Rom. 1:24–27. This is the only biblical passage that discusses both male and female same-sex activity. The passage emphasizes individuals with "degrading passions," "burning with lust," and engaging in "unnatural" activities that are shameful and perverse. The presumptions about excessive lust and the violation of natural law are important to highlight in this context. In what ways are homosexual desires more lustful than heterosexual desires? Paul's understanding appears to be that only male-female relations are natural. In the twenty-first century, however, the question about what is "natural" or "unnatural" in regard to human sexuality has become rather controversial. Some argue that individuals are born with a sexual orientation of which they become aware as they mature, and that both heterosexual and homosexual orientations are natural, even though the vast majority of individuals are heterosexual. Others would argue that God's intention was for all humankind to be heterosexual, and that homosexuality is a result of human sin that affects even our DNA. In this view, homosexual persons cannot be blamed for their orientation, but nonetheless they must refrain from acting on it. In the Roman Catholic tradition this view is clearly expressed in the papal encyclical *The Pastoral Care of Homosexual Persons* (1986). A related difficulty is that neither Paul nor his contemporaries within the patriarchal context of antiquity had any concept of sexual orientation as a way of understanding human sexuality.

In 1 Cor. 6:9–10 we again come upon a crucial translation issue. The passage occurs in the context of a vice list that includes behaviors contrary to God's will. Paul states that "wrongdoers will not inherit the kingdom of God," referring to "fornicators, idolaters, adulterers, male prostitutes, sodomites, thieves, the greedy, drunkards, revilers, robbers." The translation issue arises with the Greek terms *malakoi* and *arsenokoitai*, which the NRSV renders as "male prostitutes" and "sodomites." A literal translation would be something like "soft people" and "men who go to bed," though clearly something far more colloquial is meant—perhaps "male prostitutes and the men who hire their services"? The range of standard translations indicates how difficult the passage is: "boy prostitutes nor sodomites" (NAB), "male prostitutes nor homosexual offenders" (NIV), "both participants in same-sex intercourse" (CEB), "male prostitutes, homosexuals" (NLT), "passive homosexual partners, practicing homosexuals" (NET), "homosexual perverts" (TEV), and "nor effeminate, nor abusers of themselves with mankind" (KJV). The use of "sodomites" by the NRSV is unfortunate because it presumes a connection between the story of Gen. 19 and 1 Cor. 6 (1 Tim. 1:10 involves similar issues). Similarly, the use of "homosexual" is problematic because it suggests that the biblical authors had an understanding of homosexuality that parallels our contemporary understanding, resulting in potentially anachronistic readings of Scripture.

The cultural question has to do with what forms of homoerotic activity Paul knew about in his day. Like most Jews of his day, he seems to presume heterosexual expression as the norm, though his own preference is for celibacy (1 Cor. 7:7). As best we can tell, Paul would have known about pederasty and prostitution. Does his condemnation of these forms of same-sex relations in the first century indicate a blanket condemnation of all forms of same-sex relations in our time with our understanding of human sexuality? This question points to a larger debate in modern Christianity for which the issue of homosexuality has become a litmus test. The debate is between different groups of Christians who line up on different sides of a range of issues. What is the authority of Scripture, and how should it be interpreted? To what degree has God created humans with normative and essential standards of sexual ethics that transcend time and space? What role do human experience and reason play in discerning the leading of God's Spirit? Are same-sex relations to be condemned as a violation of God's revealed will, or are they to be celebrated as another expression of God's revealed will for human sexuality?

Those with a high view of Scripture and the continuity of tradition tend toward a more conservative approach to these questions. In this view, a homosexual orientation is not itself a sin, but it is a cross to bear and a desire that must be resisted. This approach emphasizes that the Bible makes no room for a positive evaluation of same-sex relations, and that the constant teaching of the church has been to condemn all forms of homosexual expression. Homosexuality is seen as a disordered condition that can, in some cases, be changed and corrected through various forms of therapy and counseling. For some who hold this view, homosexuality is not necessarily an orientation but rather a chosen set of behaviors contrary to God's will.

Those who value human reason and experience as interpretive guides for a contextual understanding of Scripture tend toward a more liberal or progressive approach to such questions. In this view, a same-sex orientation is simply a different orientation from heterosexuality and is intrinsically no better or worse, and certainly not sinful. Those advocating a more inclusive approach to LGBT individuals often appeal to the disciplines of psychiatry and biology as important resources for aiding our developing understanding of human sexuality in contrast to the biblical prohibitions of same-sex relations. The term *homosexuality* itself was coined in the late nineteenth century in German psychological literature. Definition and understanding of the term have evolved and changed over the last century. The first *Diagnostic and Statistical Manual of Mental Disorders* (*DSM-I*, published in 1952 by the American Psychiatric Association [APA]) identified "homosexuality" as a sociopathic personality disorder, while *DSM-II* (1968) defined it as a sexual deviation. In 1973 the APA revised *DSM-II* so that the general category of "homosexuality" was eliminated and replaced by "sexual orientation disturbance." This was a controversial change because it indicated a clear shift within the psychiatric community, which increasingly viewed a homosexual orientation as nonpathological, whereas the individual's struggle to accept his or her homosexual identity became the psychiatric problem to be addressed. This change was codified in *DSM-III* (1980, revised 1987), and in *DSM-IV* (1994, revised 2000) "homosexuality" was removed and replaced with the more generic and relatively vague "gender identity disorder," referring to individuals with significant anxiety about their sexual or gender identity.

Other questions have to do with whether it is important that Jesus said nothing directly about same-sex relations in any of his recorded teaching. Did he simply presume the cultural norms of his day, even though apparently he was celibate? Is Jesus' reference in Mark 10:1–12 to Gen. 1:27; 2:24 a tacit endorsement of heterosexual marriage between one man and one woman? Do the different approaches to marriage sanctioned in the Bible (multiple wives, concubines, levirate marriage) suggest openness to changing understandings of marriage and sexuality?

Homosexuality and Ecclesial Communities

Both the Roman Catholic Church and most Protestant denominations have conducted multiyear studies on homosexuality and have issued lengthy findings that often encourage more understanding and acceptance of LGBT persons within the church but stop short of endorsing anything other than heterosexual marriage as God's intention for appropriate human sexual expression. Significantly, within the Roman Catholic Church the primary issue revolves around procreation, to which all human sexual expressions must be open. In this view, then, by definition sexual relations between people of the same gender are immoral because they cannot create new life. By contrast, within most Protestant denominations the primary issue revolves around ordination and the question of whether ordained LGBT individuals can appropriately model Christian marriage. Thus far, most denominations have answered this question in the negative. The primary exception to this is the United Church of Christ and the Episcopal Church in America and in Canada. The Metropolitan Community Church (founded in 1968) is the most open denomination toward the full inclusion of LGBT persons. Within the Roman Catholic Church the question of ordination has nothing to do with marriage, since priests are by definition celibate.

And so the debates over homosexuality continue in one Christian community after another, with people of good faith holding firmly to their respective views on both sides of this clear divide. The debate over the status of homosexual persons within the church has a corollary with the larger societal debates over issues such as same-sex marriage, the constitutionality of laws limiting the rights of homosexual persons, and the call from various constituencies for full acceptance of LGBT individuals within society at large. The Bible serves as a key touchstone for this conversation within the church, though its interpretation, relevance, and application in relation to homosexuality remain points of significant contention, especially as interpreters seek to correlate and integrate the biblical witness with other sources of authority—tradition, reason, and experience.

See also Sexual Ethics

Bibliography

Alison, J. *Faith Beyond Resentment: Fragments Catholic and Gay*. Crossroad, 2001; Grenz, S. *Welcoming but Not Affirming: An Evangelical Response to Homosexuality*. Westminster John Knox, 1998; Jones, S., and M. Yarhouse. *Homosexuality: The Use of Scientific Research in the Church's Moral Debate*. IVP Academic, 2000; Nissinen, M. *Homoeroticism in the Biblical World: A Historical Perspective*. Fortress, 1998; Rogers, J. *Jesus, the Bible, and Homosexuality: Explode the Myths, Heal the Church*. Rev. ed. Westminster John Knox, 2009; Siker, J., ed. *Homosexuality and Religion: An Encyclopedia*. Greenwood Press, 2007; idem, ed. *Homosexuality in the Church: Both Sides of the Debate*. Westminster John Knox, 1994; Sullivan, A. *Virtually Normal: An Argument about Homosexuality*. Vintage Books, 1996; United States Conference of Catholic Bishops. *Always Our Children: A Pastoral Message to Parents of Homosexual Children and Suggestions for Pastoral Ministers*. United States Catholic Conference, 1997; Via, D., and R. Gagnon. *Homosexuality and the Bible: Two Views*. Fortress, 2003; White, M. *Stranger Beyond the Gate: To Be Gay and Christian in America*. Plume, 1995.

Jeffrey S. Siker

Honesty

Scripture upholds honesty as a quality closely related to excellence of character. The habitual practice of honesty is necessary for harmonious relationships. The Scriptures associate honesty not only with truth-telling but also with the pursuit of justice and faithfulness in interpersonal interactions. Through pursuing an honest character, we embody our respect for the moral ordering of the cosmos and its everyday realization in familial and political structures.

Scriptural texts promote a rigorous ethic of commitment to the truth for the sake of justice. God is "just" and "without deceit" (Deut. 32:4), and honesty preserves just social relations among God's people. The OT characterizes honesty as essential to properly ordered relations within society. For example, the commandment "You shall not bear false witness against your neighbor" (Exod. 20:16) emphasizes the importance of honesty for social institutions and interpersonal relationships (Swezey). Honesty in social interactions is a means through which Israel lives out the divine covenant (see Josh. 7:11) and preserves communal order. The stability of the political and familial order depends on truthfulness, and numerous passages connect deceitful actions to familial discord (e.g., Gen. 37–44; Prov. 6). Perhaps for this reason, the scriptural texts sometimes link breaches of honesty to violence and disruption: the suffering servant is morally righteous because he does not take part in violence or deceit (Isa. 53:9; 1 Pet. 2:22), Hosea connects lying to violence (Hos. 12:1) and bloodshed (Hos. 4:2), and Proverbs links "a lying tongue" with "hands that shed innocent blood" (Prov. 6:17).

Both the Old and New Testaments present honesty as a witness to God's own goodness. Because God is truth (Ps. 43:3; cf. John 14:6), honest and true actions are means through which God's followers are faithful to the divine character. A commitment to truth challenges us to avoid hypocrisy (1 Cor. 5:1–8; Jas. 3:6–10) and to live in a manner consistent with the truth that God gives us, like the seeds that grow in good soil and bear fruit (Luke 8:15). We image God's own goodness and truthfulness when we choose to be "doers of the word" and not merely hearers of it (Jas. 1:19–26).

In light of this strong commitment to honesty, it might seem that all instances of dishonesty are to be rejected. A lack of honesty is associated with God's enemies. Scripture affirms God's abhorrence of deception (Josh. 7:11; Job 15:35; Pss. 5:6; 10:7; 24:4; 32:2). Deceit is characteristic of God's enemies (Prov. 26:24; Isa. 57:4; 2 Cor. 11:13; Acts 13:10; Col. 2:8; Rev. 21:27) and is associated with persons who do "evil" (Ps. 109:2; Prov. 12:20; Sir. 37:3; Isa. 32:7; Rom. 1:29; Heb. 3:13). John 8:44–45 associates lying and truthlessness with the devil and opposes these actions to God.

At the same time, however, Scripture points to a more complex view of honesty that may allow for the temporary distortion of the truth for the sake of serving God in a more ultimate sense. For example, the prostitute Rahab allows Joshua's Israelite spies to stay in her home and then deceives the king of Jericho about their whereabouts (Josh. 2:1–6). She chooses these actions because she believes that Israel's God is indeed God, and that God wants the Israelites to live in Jericho (Josh. 2:8–14). Although her faithfulness to God leads her to deceive her own people, tradition celebrates her actions and their motives. James 2:25 presents Rahab's actions as works through which she has been justified before God.

Rahab's story suggests that dishonesty may sometimes be justified as an expression of true love for God. Thomas Aquinas offers a similar view of truth and the vices that oppose it. For Thomas, truth is a virtue related to justice. Like justice, truth is important for social interactions and also promotes equality to some degree. Vices that oppose truth include lying, dissimulation, hypocrisy, boasting, and irony. But Thomas allows for the possibility that these vices might be overridden by charity. He argues that the severity of these vices should be determined through considering their consequences for social relations. Although these vices are opposed to truth, they are not always mortal sins; rather, they are mortal sins when they oppose charity by compromising love for God or for one's neighbor (*ST* II-II, qq. 109–13).

This complex view of honesty has important implications for contemporary reflection on whether deception is ever morally justifiable—for example, in a situation in which honesty might lead to harm being done to another person. Because we can postulate hypothetical situations in which lying might seem morally acceptable, it may seem that a rigid commitment to strict truthfulness presents an ideal that it is impossible for humans to achieve on earth, an ethic of perfection that may have to be compromised as we face sin and evil. Some twentieth-century ethicists such as Reinhold Niebuhr read the Sermon on the Mount as presenting an ideal impossible for humans to emulate in a world tainted by original sin, and a case could be made for reading scriptural condemnations of dishonesty as part of this "impossible ideal." In addition to Rahab's story, other OT figures, including Jacob, Tamar, and Joseph, prudentially exercise deceit and trickery, and their actions do not seem to be censured (see Gen. 27; 30; 38; 44).

Regardless of conclusions we might draw about the feasibility of exercising complete honesty, the scriptural witness cautions against the problems that deceit and falsehood pose not only for personal holiness but also for community relations. More often than not, acts of deceit are unequivocally associated with evil, impurity, and opposition to the good. This overall commitment to honesty is rooted in a belief in God's own truth and goodness and in the unity of truthfulness and love.

See also Deception; Dishonesty; Integrity; Oaths; Ten Commandments; Truthfulness, Truth-Telling

Bibliography

Swezey, C. "Thou Shalt Not Bear False Witness against Thy Neighbor." *Int* 34 (1980): 405–10.

Elizabeth Agnew Cochran

Hope

According to Eccl. 9:4 NIV, "Anyone who is among the living has hope [*biṭṭāḥôn*]" (or "trust"). So Thomas Aquinas calls hope a "passion" that arises naturally in us; like fear, hope is something that we share naturally with the "dumb animals" (*ST* I-II, q. 40, a. 3). Unlike fear, however, hope responds not to the threat of evil but rather to the potential attainment of a good, which is difficult but not impossible. Hope pulls us into a future; it locates us within a story or a journey that is ineluctably tensed (Hauerwas and Pinches 126).

For Christians, hope is more than simply natural; it is also a theological virtue that stands between faith and love ("These three remain: faith, hope [*elpis*] and love" [1 Cor. 13:13 NIV]). Natural hope propels us into a future, but which future that is matters greatly for the theological virtue. Natural hope can picture a false world. On the road to Emmaus the disciples say mournfully to the unrecognized Jesus, "We had hoped [*ēlpizomen*] that he was the one to redeem Israel" (Luke 24:21). In subsequent conversation Christ must school their hope with understanding. Proper hope requires an informed faith. As the prophets point out for Israel, if hope is faithless, wrongly directed, it deserves to be lost. So Ezekiel's dry bones say, "Our bones are dried up, and our hope [*tiqwâ*] is lost" (Ezek. 37:11). False hope must be lost before true hope, and life, can be built.

Prophetic warnings against Israel's false hopes apply today. No one lives without hope. Yet the need encourages the error, especially among a people softened by comfort. So 1 Tim. 6:17 cautions the rich not "to put their hope in wealth." And Pope Benedict XVI argues that Christian hope has been displaced today by an idea of "progress" from Francis Bacon (1561–1626). "Hope too, in Bacon, acquires a new form. Now it is called: *faith in progress*" (Pope Benedict XVI 42–43). Bacon hoped that art would triumph over nature, so "overcoming all forms of dependency" (Pope Benedict XVI 43). By contrast, Christian faith rests in Christ, who suffered in dependent love.

As essentially "tensed," hope is laced throughout the biblical story, which moves back and forth between promise and fulfillment. Hope steadies us in the movement, the "steadfast anchor of the soul" (Heb. 6:19). Tied to "endurance" (*hypomonē*) or "patience" (*makrothymeō*), hope watches and waits—no easy task. ("Hope" mistakenly refers to what is expected as a matter of course: "Who hopes [*elpizei*] for what is seen?" [Rom. 8:24].) The good that we attain by hope is difficult, says Thomas, and requires training and exercise. In fact, security "lessens the character of hope: for the things in which a man fears no hindrance, are no longer looked upon as difficult" (*ST* I-II, q. 40,

a. 8). Biblically, we can claim no better example than Abraham, who clung tenaciously to God's promises: "Hoping against hope, he believed" (Rom 4:18). Commenting further, Paul "boasts" in the "hope of sharing the glory of God," which links for him with difficulties faced: "We boast in our sufferings, knowing that suffering produces endurance, and endurance produces character, and character produces hope" (Rom. 5:2–4).

Christian hope never stands alone; it is supported by, is almost interchangeable with, faith and love. In Hebrews, for instance, we are told that "faith is the assurance of things hoped for" (Heb. 11:1). Yet distinctions between the three virtues can be drawn. As good habits, virtues can be identified by bad habits or vices that oppose them. Hatred opposes love, and unbelief contrasts with faith. Yet when we lose hope, we fall into despair. By despair, Thomas says, "a man ceases to hope for a share in God's goodness" (*ST* II-II, q. 20, a. 4). Despair he identifies as the most dangerous sin. A person might act out of hatred or unbelief, but despair saps a person of all motivation. Those who lose hope lose their own stories and spiral into utter isolation.

Hope picks such people up and sets them on a path; it induces them "to seek for good things." Initially, the search is individualized because, according to Thomas, "hope regards directly one's own good, and not that which pertains to another." Schooled by love, hope expands beyond the self. "If we presuppose the union of love with another, a man can hope for and desire something for another man, as for himself" (*ST* II-II, q. 17, a. 3). Eschatologically, God's future is not merely mine but the whole of creation's, now groaning but awaiting its full redemption in Christ (Rom. 8:22).

Indeed, as essentially tensed, as surrounded by faith and love, as centered in the resurrection, hope looks always toward the eschaton, the "hope of eternal life that God, who never lies, promised before the ages began" (Titus 1:2). Hope fills the span between one coming of Christ and the next. Yet this sharply focuses Christian hope. The Messiah coming to reign is the Messiah who already came to suffer and die. The Lamb is worthy to open the scroll precisely because, as the heavenly chorus says to him, "You were slaughtered and by your blood you ransomed for God saints from every tribe and language and people and nation" (Rev. 5:9). Schooled theologically, Christian "hope of glory" (Col. 1:27) can never turn triumphal—a point as much relevant now as in the future kingdom. As John Howard Yoder insists, proper theological hope should shelter the church from the "Constantinian temptation" to bring the kingdom by force; only as such can it expose the pretentious hopes of the age that pin the meaning of history to something other than the crucified Christ, "our hope" (1 Tim. 1:1).

See also Eschatology and Ethics; Faith; Idolatry; Security; Virtue(s); Wealth

Bibliography

Benedict XVI. *Saved in Hope (Spe Salvi): Encyclical Letter of the Supreme Pontiff Benedict XVI*. Ignatius Press, 2008; Hauerwas, S., and C. Pinches. *Christians among the Virtues: Theological Conversations with Ancient and Modern Ethics*. University of Notre Dame Press, 1997, 113–28; Yoder, J. *The Original Revolution: Essays on Christian Pacifism*. Herald Press, 1977, 140–76.

Charles R. Pinches

Hosea

This OT book is associated with Hosea, son of Beeri. Hosea was a prophet active during the turbulent, final years of the northern kingdom of Israel (ca. 750–720 BCE). He is best known for the stories of his marriage to Gomer (1:2–9), and the book uses the prophet's broken family as a metaphor for the people's relationship with God. Yet the bulk of Hosea (chaps. 4–14) contains divine judgments against Israel's political and religious leaders for various kinds of wrong behavior and calls the people to return to faithfulness in light of God's love. Metaphors drawn from family, agricultural, and animal realms address the people's life before God. Ethical engagement with the book requires an exploration of these metaphors, especially the ways they fund an alternative imagination for their hearers' perception of reality.

The prophet's words focus on the moral failures of the people in their fidelity toward God and others (e.g., 4:1–3). Although often thought to be associated with the worship of the Canaanite god Baal, Hosea's criticisms are more typically concerned with the hypocrisy of the leaders of the community, especially kings (7:5–7; 8:4–10) and priests (4:4–6), accusing them of worshiping God ostensibly yet refusing to follow God's desires in the social and political dimensions of the community's life. In Hosea's view, the health of the kingdom depends on ethical leadership that comes from a sense of fidelity to God and generates faithfulness among the people. The book places these ethical demands in the broader context of God's enduring love for the people (2:14–23; 11:1–9; 14:4–8), which offers the ability to return to God for reconciliation.

The ethical discourse of Hosea poses difficulties for contemporary readers. In addition to depicting a punishing God, much of Hosea's language and imagery, especially in the marriage metaphor of chapters 1–3, is patriarchal, using female characters and experiences to represent sin and describing acts of physical abuse and sexual violence as symbols for divine judgment. In modern contexts so rife with domestic violence, such actions, even when depicted as a means toward reconciliation, can lead to views of God that produce destructive behavior, especially toward women and children. One can emphasize the ancient cultural context of these images or use other biblical depictions of God as correctives, but raising questions about such imagery and the import that it might have in contemporary society is a necessary part of ethical reflection on Hosea.

Not limited to its original context, Hosea's language and metaphors speak into any situation in which politics, economics, and religious ideology have become intertwined to serve the interests of the economically and socially advantaged. In the same way that the prophet challenged the royal and social elite of his day, the book offers an ongoing word of judgment against the co-opting of religious beliefs and practices in the service of social, political, military, and economic systems that injure the vulnerable and tear at the fabric of the community. Such a word of judgment, however, remains in the context of an enduring divine love, which permits the hopeful possibility of redemption from the destructive systems of power, greed, and violence.

See also Covenant; Idolatry; Old Testament Ethics

Bibliography

Keefe, A. *Woman's Body and the Social Body in Hosea*. JSOTSup 338. Sheffield Academic Press, 2001; Kelle, B. *Hosea 2: Metaphor and Rhetoric in Historical Perspective*. SBLAB 20. Society of Biblical Literature, 2005; Simundson, D. *Hosea, Joel, Amos, Obadiah, Jonah, Micah*. AOTC. Abingdon, 2005.

Brad E. Kelle

Hospice

The concept of hospitality has long been central to Christian life, and at its heart it means welcoming the stranger. The words *hospitality*, *hospital*, and *hospice* are derived from the Latin root *hospes*, meaning "guest." The modern hospital derives from the ancient practices of religious societies that set up houses for the ill traveler, which typically were adjacent to places of worship. For example, St. Bartholomew's Hospital, founded in London in 1123, cared for those with incurable diseases and the dying. Beginning at about the time of the Renaissance and progressing into modernity, the objectives of hospital care changed so that by 1544 St. Bartholomew's would no longer admit patients if they had incurable conditions. In 1842 the term *hospice* came to describe a place for the terminally ill, and an institution was created in Lyon, France, for these purposes.

Hospice care (offering palliative care for the terminally ill) engages the terminally ill and their families to " improve quality of life . . . through the . . . treatment of pain and other problems, physical, psychosocial and spiritual" (Bond 2008). St. Christopher's Hospice, founded by Cicely Saunders in London in 1967, serves as a model for the modern hospice.

Hospice in its ancient and modern versions derives from the Christian response to the challenges of caring for the sick and dying. Scripture, in particular the Gospels, gives several examples of responses to Jesus' suffering and dying, ranging from abandonment to full engagement. Jesus is abandoned by his fearful and despairing disciples before his death and crucifixion ("Then all the disciples deserted him and fled" [Matt. 26:56]), much as doctors and even friends and family sometimes isolate, ignore, and abandon their patients and loved ones in institutions as they become frail and enter the end of life. Other Gospel passages do not portray abandonment, but rather depict individuals who could not fully engage the suffering, remaining at a safe distance from Jesus and his tormentors (Matt. 27:55–56; Mark 15:40). Finally, there are the scriptural examples of those who were fully present, exemplified in Jesus' mother, her sister, Mary the wife of Clopas, Mary Magdalene, and the Beloved Disciple, who bore witness at the cross (John 19:25–26).

Contemporary concepts of hospice emphasize the practice of true compassion by being present with the dying, not just in hospitals and institutions, but most often in the home. Hospice is not a site of care but rather a practice of compassionate and caring presence that gives caregivers that sacred privilege to walk with those who are suffering, as did Simon of Cyrene with Jesus (Matt. 27:32; Mark 15:21; Luke 23:26). By having the strength to be present, hospice caregivers can transform suffering by forming a community that can sustain "the sufferer in the face of pain, anger and despair" (Schmidt 2005).

See also Ars Moriendi Tradition, Use of Scripture in; Death and Dying; Dependent Care; Healthcare Ethics

Bibliography

Bond C., V. Lavy, and R. Woolridge. *Palliative Care Toolkit: Improving Care from the Roots Up in Resource-Limited Settings*. Help the Hospices, 2009; Clemens K.,

B. Jaspers, and E. Klaschik. "The History of Hospice." Pages 18–23 in *Oxford Textbook of Palliative Medicine*. Oxford University Press, 2005; Schmidt, S. "Not in the Medical Records." Center for Christian Ethics at Baylor University, 2005. http://www.baylor.edu/christianethics/SufferingarticleSchmidt.pdf.

Richard Payne

Hospitality

Offering hospitality to strangers is central to the gospel and to the Christian moral tradition. Throughout much of the church's history hospitality has been a normative feature of Christian identity and ministry. Old Testament stories and law, as well as Jesus' life, death, parables, and practices, witness to its centrality. The importance of hospitality in the formation and growth of the early church suggests its continuing relevance for the people of God. Though variously understood and often undermined, hospitality remains important in Christian practice and tradition.

Within hospitality are located moral and practical concerns about care for vulnerable strangers, those with whom potential hosts have no natural bonds, but for whom their lack of welcome could be dangerous or cruel. Particular biblical texts have shaped a normative understanding of hospitality that emphasizes recognition of, and care for, those persons who are left out of society's benefits and are disconnected from life-giving relationships.

Hospitality in the Old Testament

God is portrayed as a generous and protective host in a number of biblical texts; to be hospitable is part of God's character (Exod. 16:4–36; Deut. 10:17–18; Pss. 91; 146:9). The people of God are expected to view themselves as aliens or sojourners, dependent on God's care and provision (Gen. 15:5–16; Lev. 25:23; 1 Chr. 29:14–15). In addition, faithful Israelites are commanded to care for sojourners and other vulnerable persons in their midst, remembering their own experience of having been mistreated strangers in Egypt (Exod. 22:21; Lev. 19:33–34; Deut. 10:19; 24:14–22).

Throughout the ancient world hospitality was commonly understood as the practice of welcoming strangers into one's household for short-term refreshment and shelter. Hosts were responsible to feed and to protect those guests who had come under their roof. Acts of hospitality by individuals or by familial households are important parts of numerous OT narratives and often are evidence of the righteousness of the host. In many cases, welcoming a stranger brings the host into close contact with messengers or purposes of God, and these encounters are filled with blessing and promise.

Abraham and Sarah welcome three strangers and give them honor, food, and a place to rest (Gen. 18). Sometime during this visit, they learn that the strangers are angels who have come with the promise that a son will be born to the couple in their old age. This is the most important OT story for the Christian hospitality tradition (see Heb. 13:2), but others are central as well: Rahab's provision of sanctuary to the Israelite spies (Josh. 2), Elijah's experience of hospitality at the hands of a foreign widow during a famine (1 Kgs. 17), and Elisha's regular welcome in the home of a Shunammite woman (2 Kgs. 4:8–37). In each one of these stories, the host is blessed through the presence of the guest(s) (see also 1 Sam. 25).

A few stories are more ambiguous, however. In Gen. 19, Lot's hospitality to two strangers is contrasted with the response of the men of Sodom, whose inhospitality and degradation show that the city is ready for judgment. In order to protect his male guests from sexual violation, Lot offers his daughters to the crowd to "do to them as you please," raising troubling questions for contemporary readers about the vulnerability of women and their status as protected persons during that time. Similarly, the story of the Levite's concubine in Judg. 19 is a terrible reminder that a community's understanding of who is deserving of the protection of hospitality can be very limited.

Certain ambiguities in the practice of hospitality arise from tensions that are present within the notion of covenant loyalty to Yahweh, evident in Israel's responses to different kinds of strangers. Because the God of Israel cares for sojourners, the sojourner (*gēr*, *tôšāb*) in Israel is to be protected and to receive the same kind of provision as widows and orphans. Sojourners or resident aliens and Israelites are to be treated similarly in the courts (Deut. 1:16–17; 24:17–22). Some are included in religious celebrations and, as they adopt the faith of the Israelites, are incorporated into the community (Exod. 12:43–49; Num. 9:14; Deut. 16:9–15; 26:1–15). Those strangers who leave behind their communities, religious identities, and political ties receive particular care in Israel, especially when their economic circumstances are fragile.

Other kinds of strangers are treated differently, however. The Israelites are instructed to exclude persons who might threaten their identity or unity. Those strangers or foreigners (*nēkār*, *nokrî*, *zār*) who continue to worship other gods, maintain connections with their home communities, or interact with Israelites primarily as merchants or traders do not generally receive welcome. Because of Yahweh's demand for exclusive loyalty in commitment and worship, strangers who might distract from that loyalty are excluded (Exod. 23:28–33; 34:10–16; Deut. 7:1–11; 18:9–14; Josh. 23:12–13; Ps. 106:34–39). While hospitality is at the heart of the covenant in terms of Yahweh's welcome to Israel and to vulnerable strangers, covenantal commitments simultaneously require the community to care for vulnerable sojourners and to be wary of strangers who might undermine loyalty to God alone.

In the wisdom literature, the righteous person is portrayed as hospitable, especially in caring for strangers and others in need. Job defends his righteousness by saying, "The stranger has not lodged in the street; I have opened my doors to the traveler" (Job 31:32). In the prophets, Isaiah describes the kind of worship that God desires as including care for the destitute and welcoming the homeless stranger into one's home (Isa. 58:6–7). The word of the Lord through Isaiah promises that the foreigner who loves the Lord will find welcome in "a house of prayer for all peoples" (Isa. 56:3, 6–7).

Hospitality in the Gospels

In the incarnation God becomes vulnerable to human welcome (John 1). Jesus is portrayed as stranger and guest as well as host in the Gospels. He experiences the marginality, vulnerability, and rejection of the stranger while proclaiming welcome to all who desire to come to him and to enter the kingdom of God. His hospitality is expansive and personal, offering welcome to those who are lost, sick, rejected, and in need. As both guest and host, Jesus challenges prevailing but often hidden socioreligious patterns of exclusion.

The Gospel of Luke is particularly rich with images of Jesus' experiences of hospitality. Born into a family in need of shelter, he later describes himself as having "nowhere to lay his head" (Luke 2:7; 9:57–58). He is frequently a guest in the homes of Pharisees (Luke 7:36–50; 14:1–24), friends (Luke 10:38–42), and sinners (Luke 5:27–32; 19:1–10). These shared meals provide an important setting for his teachings on divine and human hospitality.

Numerous Gospel stories show Jesus serving as a host; he feeds crowds gathered on hillsides, and he breaks bread with his disciples and cooks breakfast for them after his resurrection (Matt. 14:13–21; 15:32–39; 26:26–29; Mark 6:30–44; 8:1–10; 14:22–25; Luke 9:10–17; 22:7–23; John 6:1–14; 13:1–20; 21:1–14). On the road to Emmaus Jesus begins his interaction with two followers as a stranger, is invited by them to become their guest, and in breaking bread together, he becomes their host (Luke 24:13–35).

God hosts the children of Israel as they wander in the wilderness, supplying manna daily to meet their needs. In John 6:31–59, Jesus describes himself as the bread of life, the manna. Understanding Jesus as both host and bread draws together dimensions of hospitality from the OT and the NT with eucharistic practice.

Two texts from the Gospels are particularly important to understandings of hospitality in the Christian tradition. In Luke 14:12–14, Jesus challenges the tendency to offer hospitality to persons from whom one might expect to receive benefit or reward, and he tells his host to welcome to his dinner parties "the poor, the crippled, the lame, and the blind," those who cannot repay the favor. In doing so, human hosts imitate the generosity of God, who welcomes into the kingdom those same vulnerable groups (Luke 14:15–24). Such a host could expect God's reward.

Matthew 25:31–46 is the most important biblical text for the Christian hospitality tradition. In addressing his disciples' questions about how they will recognize the end of the age and his return, Jesus encourages them to prepare for it by living in response to him in the present. By explicitly linking care for the "least of these" with care for himself, Jesus draws the closest possible connection between hospitality to vulnerable persons and strangers and offering welcome to the Son of Man. Despite interpretive difficulties within the text itself, the passage is prominent in most discussions of hospitality throughout Christian history and ties entry into the kingdom to the practice of hospitality in this life.

Hospitality in the Early Church

The life-transforming significance of Jesus' costly welcome becomes the basis for practice within early Christian communities. Paul writes in Rom. 15:7, "Welcome one another, therefore, just as Christ has welcomed you, for the glory of God." The early churches struggled with how to respond to differences within their communities related to religious background, sensitivity to former cultural practices, and social and economic status. Reminding them of the acceptance and welcome they had received in Christ, Paul urges the Roman church to model in their shared life a similar sacrificial welcome to one another and to strangers (see also Rom. 12:13).

In early Christianity the practice of hospitality was important in addressing social and cultural differences within the communities, in responding to the physical needs of strangers and fellow believers, in strengthening corporate identity, and in providing household-based settings for community gatherings and worship (Riddle). Shared meals in which poor people could be fed and a distinctive Christian identity could be forged and reinforced were a particularly important, though difficult, dimension of hospitality (Acts 2:44–46; 10:1–11:18; 1 Cor. 11:17–34; Gal. 2:11–14; Jas. 2:1–13). Hospitality as a practice of congregational life was well fitted to the needs of the early congregations, especially as believers traveled to escape persecution and to spread the gospel.

Certain passages suggest that hospitality was expected of every believer (Rom. 12:13; Heb. 13:2; 1 Pet. 4:9), but that it was also a specific requirement for leadership in God's household (1 Tim. 3:2; 5:10; Titus 1:8). That the early church encountered some difficulties with hospitality is evident from the instruction in 1 Pet. 4:9 to practice it "without complaining" and from Paul's comments that he, unlike false apostles, did not burden the communities (2 Cor. 11:8–9; 12:14–18; 1 Thess. 2:9). Although the practice of hospitality was central in the early Christian communities, two categories of persons were denied welcome. Both claimed to be believers. Those who persisted in immoral lifestyles and those who propagated false teaching were excluded (1 Cor. 5:9–11; 2 John 9–11).

In the NT Epistles, the primary focus of hospitality was on strangers, though often the strangers welcomed would have been other Christians in need. *Philoxenia*, one of the key terms for hospitality in the NT, combines the Greek word for "the love or affection of those connected by kinship or faith" (*phileō*) and the word for "stranger" (*xenos*).

The Distinctive Character of Christian Hospitality

Hospitality remained important in the first several centuries of the church, especially in meeting the needs of the local poor, strangers, and pilgrims. Efforts to make hospitality more predictable and more widely available gave rise to hospitals and hospices. Its importance in monastic life is especially evident in the *Rule of Benedict* from the sixth century (chaps. 53, 61). The possibility of welcoming Jesus in the guise of a stranger was held in tension with a commitment to creating a distinctive and separated way of life.

In most ancient cultures the provision of hospitality to strangers was highly regarded as an expression of mutual aid. In some societies it was also a deliberate means by which relationships were forged and reinforced through reciprocal benefits. Particularly in the fourth and fifth centuries, Christian writers rejected this more calculating approach to hospitality and offered an understanding that was based on Jesus' teaching in Matt. 25:31–46; Luke 14:12–14.

Christian hospitality was to be distinguished from conventional practice by the welcome offered to the "least," those who could not be expected to be able to repay the favor. Lactantius, Jerome, and John Chrysostom, among others, rejected "ambitious" hospitality or hospitality done for "advantage" as inadequate for Christians. The emphasis on welcoming needy strangers became the normative understanding of hospitality in the Christian tradition.

Nevertheless, Christians found the practice of hospitality to be useful and to their advantage during many periods, especially because of the blend of intimacy and power that it often represented. Despite ongoing critiques of the misuse of hospitality, by the late Middle Ages, even in the church, it was associated with power, luxury, and indulgence. There were some efforts during the Reformation and early modern period to recover earlier understandings of hospitality, but by the eighteenth century, the term had been emptied of most of its moral meaning in the West. Although many of the activities and institutions associated with hospitality continued, understandings and practices of hospitality were fragmented across multiple spheres of life and increasingly distanced from the Christian tradition.

The practice of hospitality regained some moral standing in the twentieth century. In the 1930s, the Catholic Worker movement used the language of hospitality to describe its commitment to sharing life with those who were homeless and destitute. More recently, it has been important as a term in philosophical and theological discussions of recognition and responses to "otherness." Some denominations have used the concept to frame church responses to homosexuality (e.g., "welcoming and affirming" congregations). At the political level, hospitality has been connected to offering sanctuary or asylum, especially to refugees. In social ministry it has been retrieved in efforts to move away from anonymous or humiliating provider-recipient models of assistance toward more mutuality and respect. In response to the marginalization of certain populations (e.g., people who are poor, homeless, or with disabilities), hospitality has been emphasized in drawing persons into community. In recent efforts to retrieve the traditions and practices of the ancient church, hospitality has been an important bridge between contemporary and ancient reflections on the Eucharist, shared meals, justice, inclusion, and responding to social and ethnic differences.

See also Aliens, Immigration, and Refugees; Homelessness; Hospice; Imitation of Jesus; Koinonia

Bibliography

Greer, R. *Broken Lights and Mended Lives: Theology and Common Life in the Early Church*. Pennsylvania State University Press, 1986; Koenig, J. *New Testament Hospitality: Partnership with Strangers as Promise and Mission*. OBT 17. Fortress, 1985; Oden, A., ed. *And You Welcomed Me: A Sourcebook on Hospitality in Early Christianity*. Abingdon, 2001; Pohl, C. *Making Room: Recovering Hospitality as a Christian Tradition*. Eerdmans, 1999; Riddle, D. "Early Christian Hospitality." *JBL* 57 (1938): 141–54; van Houten, C. *The Alien in Israelite Law*. JSOTSup 107. Sheffield Academic Press, 1991; Volf, M. *Exclusion and Embrace: A Theological Exploration of Identity, Otherness, and Reconciliation*. Abingdon, 1996.

Christine D. Pohl

Household Codes

Many commentators have noted that the exhortations to wives and husbands, children and parents, and slaves and masters in Eph. 5:22–6:9 and Col. 3:18–4:1 not only are comparable in content but also are similar in form, and further that cognate materials are found in 1 Pet. 2:18–3:7 (see also 1 Tim. 2:8–15; 3:2–4; 6:1–2; Titus 2:9–10). Martin Dibelius first proposed that this type of ethical material should be understood as stemming from the ancient Greek "household codes" (Ger. *Haustafeln*)—rules concerning the management of a household in a patriarchal family—which continued to exist widely in the Greco-Roman world and were simply incorporated by the NT writers (see further Weidinger). That thesis, with further elaborations and some variations (particularly with regard to rationale), has since been espoused by many scholars.

The oldest example of such an ancient *topos* (conventional theme, topic, or form) appears in Aristotle's *Politics*, a fourth-century BCE work on moral philosophy:

> There are by nature various classes of rulers and ruled. For the free rules the slave, the male [rules] the female, and the man [rules] the child in a different way. All possess the various parts of the [human] soul, but they possess them in different ways. For the slave has not got the deliberative part at all; the female has it, but without full authority; while the child has it, but in an undeveloped form. (*Pol.* 1.1260a.9–14)

Aristotle's identifications of those who "by nature" are to be considered "those who rule" vis-à-vis "those who are ruled" had a continuing influence on all Greco-Roman political, religious, and ethical thought, coming particularly to expression in the Stoic "duty codes" and the writings of the Hellenized Jewish philosopher-theologian Philo.

Scholars have taken diametrically opposed positions with respect to the parallels between Greco-Roman household codes and NT exhortations regarding family relations. Many have argued for a direct genealogical relationship and further have claimed that the appearance of such household codes in the NT indicates a departure among early believers in Jesus from a dependence on the Spirit's guidance in favor of a regulated (possibly an institutionalized and/or even a secular) form of church governance. Others have insisted that the parallels between the household codes of antiquity and the family-related statements of the NT are not very close and so may be discounted.

However, parallels need not always be viewed as genealogical in nature but rather may be understood as simply analogical in nature—that is, as resemblances in certain particulars between things otherwise unlike, with those resemblances often stemming from similar situations. Although the NT writers (particularly Paul) may have known of existing Greco-Roman household codes, experienced the same situations addressed by these pagan codes, and used the forms of those codes in speaking to the same family situations, the NT exhortations regarding wives/husbands, children/parents, and slaves/masters would then be seen as more analogical in nature than strictly genealogical and as more distinctly Christian than pagan.

Important to note in the NT exhortations regarding relations between members in a Christian family are at least three significant matters. First, all NT exhortations are based on how the addressees have experienced the new spiritual reality of being "in Christ" and in the "body of Christ"—themes of great importance in the NT, particularly in Ephesians and Colossians—and not on the dictates of "nature" (as in paganism) or certain principles that may be derived from God's creation (as in Judaism). Second, the exhortations of Eph. 5:22–6:9 are introduced by the words of 5:21: "Submit [participle of the verb *hypotassō*] to one another out of reverence for Christ," with the verb "submit" not restated in 5:22 (though carried over from 5:21), which suggests that in a Christian family there is to be some type of personal submission of all the members to one another. Third, whereas in the Greco-Roman household codes the privileges of "ruling" were granted to husbands, parents, and masters and the responsibilities of "submitting" and "obeying" were assigned to wives, children, and slaves, in the family exhortations of the NT there appears a large measure of "mutuality" (i.e., a sharing of status, responsibilities, and sentiments) between wives and husbands, children and parents, and slaves and masters, with both parties in each of the three sets being exhorted to do what is right "in the Lord" on behalf of the other. Together, these three distinctive features signal a very definite advance in NT ethics over every ethical system or series of exhortations that are based on "nature" or certain perceived orders in God's creation.

See also Authority and Power; Children; Colossians; Ephesians; 1 Peter; Slavery; Submission and Subordination; 1–2 Timothy; Women, Status of

Bibliography

Balch, D. *Let Wives Be Submissive: The Domestic Code in 1 Peter*. SBLMS 26. Scholars Press, 1981, 1–20; Clarke, W. "Die Haustafeln." Pages 157–60 in *New Testament Problems: Essay, Reviews, Interpretations*. London, 1929; Crouch, J. *The Origin and Intention of the Colossian Haustafel*. FRLANT 109. Vandenhoeck & Ruprecht, 1972; Dibelius, M. *An die Kolosser, Epheser, an Philemon*. 3rd ed. HNT 12. Tübingen, 1953 (see especially the excursus following Col. 4:1); MacDonald, M. *The Pauline Churches: A Socio-Historical Study of Institutionalization in the Pauline and Deutero-Pauline Writings*. SNTSMS 60. Cambridge University Press, 1988, 102–11; Verner, D. *The Household of God: The Social World of the Pastoral Epistles*. SBLDS 71. Scholars Press, 1983, 16–23; Weidinger, K. *Die Haustafeln: Ein Stück urchristlicher Paränese*. UNT 14. Leipzig, 1928.

Richard N. Longenecker

Hubris *See* Pride

Human Dignity *See* Humanity

Human Experimentation *See* Bioethics

Humanitarianism

This activist form of humanism derives from both a sense of duty to aid others and a claimed right to intervene in troubled situations to mitigate suffering. It is historically rooted in faith-based traditions of almsgiving, charity, philanthropy, generosity, and loving care for the neighbor in need—indeed, for the stranger and even the enemy. Monastic and diaconal centers and leaders have long been advocates for the poor, provided homes for orphans, and offered havens for the sick or handicapped, many trying to live out the implications of Jesus' words, "Just as you did it to one of the least of these who are members of my family, you did it to me" (Matt. 25:40).

In the New World, as Johan Neem has recently documented, eighteenth-century Puritans formed voluntary associations as parachurch "corporations" for education, missions, and medical care outside the direct control of the state. Further, Gary Bass has gathered numerous reports of the role that "liberal" movements played in the nineteenth century to stop the bloodshed of ethnic conflicts or to aid the victims of natural disasters, gaining popular support by the increased impact of the press and populist celebrities with a cause. These influenced public opinion and developed the skills of citizens to form grassroots movements that shaped political policies and tax laws for nonprofit organizations.

The twentieth century saw the advent of world wars, hot and cold, which brought injury and displacement to millions. Humanitarian organizations multiplied and presented themselves as based on a religiously and politically neutral set of values that derive from "natural" human sympathy. Taking advantage of historic legal provisions in democratic states that allowed the easy incorporation of eleemosynary (motivated by mercy or pity) institutions and the new possibilities of working internationally, a fresh amalgam of motivations and values has taken massive organizational form in the contemporary world. In his work on the Red Cross, Jean Pictet identified "seven core principles" of genuine humanitarianism that are widely discussed: humanity (for all persons), impartiality (based on need, not status), neutrality (not taking sides in conflicts), independence (of any institution that may benefit), voluntary (noncoercive and nonprofit), unity (seeking cooperation), and universality (worldwide in reach).

Such ideals have mobilized a multitude of large rescue, relief, service, development, or advocacy organizations widely known today. These are based primarily in the West, usually organized in one country as a nongovernmental organization (NGO) that works internationally (e.g., Greenpeace, Médecins Sans Frontières), attached to a religious body (Catholic World Relief, Church World Service), or as a self-consciously interfaith organization (Oxfam), even if they work with government programs (USAID), intergovernmental programs (UN High Commission for Refugees), or transnational corporations (Save the Children, CARE).

No one knows how many people are helped by these organizations, but surely it involves millions. And no one knows how many workers serve in these organizations, but at any given time it surely is in the tens of thousands. Few can challenge their moral commitment, dedication, or quality of service, but they have been challenged regarding their relationships to what many consider to be "nonhumanitarian" organizations—that is, political, military, economic, and resurgent religious institutions. A trenchant treatment of these issues can be found in the book *Humanitarianism in Question*, key issues of which can be summarized.

Political Issues

Most humanitarian organizations seek to be apolitical in the sense that they do not seek governmental change. Yet, in some places it is impossible for NGOs seeking to meet the needs of the victims of floods (as in Myanmar) or famine (as in North Korea) or disease (as in Zimbabwe) to act freely. Such governments want the material goods that NGOs bring but also want to retain control of their distribution, in ways believed to reinforce tyrannical control and exacerbate the problems that the people face, or they refuse access. In some cases, the NGOs need protection from contending parties because the provision of food, medicine, and shelter is seen by one side or the other to be aiding the enemy or makes it seem that the NGOs are agents of that side. In other cases, the home governments of states from which the NGOs come have a political interest in the resources or policies of a country being served and seek to co-opt the NGOs, perhaps by supplying needed goods in return for priorities that fit with governmental interests.

Military Issues

The political issues sometimes overlap with overt military issues. The classic doctrines of just and unjust war, rooted in the Christian tradition and adopted in parts of international law, generally speak of the conditions that make it justifiable for a nation to resist unjust aggressors, but recent moral developments regarding human rights and genocide have prompted new thinking about the propriety of "humanitarian military intervention." The cases of atrocities in Rwanda, where action was not taken; of Kosovo, where it was taken by a multinational force, NATO, that also took over humanitarian efforts; and of Iraq, where some arguments and efforts of this sort were tried through contracted corporations, have blurred the traditional lines of distinction.

Economic Issues

These appear first in raising the money for humanitarian organizations. Funding may come from governments or military organizations, as mentioned, from foundations that sometimes bend the purposes of the humanitarian group to the foundation's priorities, or from mass voluntary giving, which requires large-scale fund-raising from private donors, some percentage of which goes back into further fund-raising that both educates the public and limits the amount that goes to the needy. Economic issues also arise from the bureaucratization needed to run organizations of scale and thus the professionalization of staff. And they arise from the question of whether profit-oriented organizations can do a more efficient job of serving the needy and investing in the productive possibilities found among people in need and capitalizing on their need for jobs, goods, and services.

Religious Issues

It is a serious question whether humanistic conceptions of duty, right, and care can sustain these institutions over time in a global environment or whether political, military, and economic issues will absorb such efforts. The dreams of socialist humanism seem to have faded, and the capitalist view that a market economy would automatically generate a humane world of interdependent plenty seems to be tarnished. If these utopian humanisms are inaccurate, it is reasonable and biblical to assume that participation in efforts to help the neighbor in need will require a faith-based compassion, working with and among, but also in addition to, the common organizations of civilization.

See also Almsgiving; Benevolence; Compassion; Economic Ethics; Generosity; Hospitality; Neighbor, Neighbor Love; Political Ethics; Sanctity of Human Life; World Poverty, World Hunger

Bibliography

Barnett, M., and T. Weiss, eds. *Humanitarianism in Question: Politics, Power, Ethics*. Cornell University Press, 2008 (see especially the chapters by M. Barnett, C. Calhoun, and S. Hopgood); Bass, G. *Freedom's Battle: The Origins of Humanitarian Intervention*. Knopf, 2008; Lyman, P., and P. Dorff, eds. *Beyond Humanitarianism: What You Need to Know about Africa and Why It Matters*. Council on Foreign Relations/Foreign Affairs, 2007; Neem, J. *Creating a Nation of Joiners: Democracy and Civil Society in Early National Massachusetts*. Harvard University Press, 2008; Pictet, J. *The Fundamental Principles of the Red Cross*. Henry Dunant Institute, 1979; Stackhouse, M., and P. Paris, eds. *Religion and the Powers of the Common Life*. Vol. 1 of *God and Globalization*. Continuum, 2000 (see especially the chapters by D. Shriver and W. Schweiker).

Max L. Stackhouse

Humanity

Overview

"Humanity" refers to the whole (including differences regarding language, ethnicity, nationality, gender, etc.) of those who are created human, and more figuratively the essence of that which is created human. In the first case, one can speak of "humanity" as the collective of humankind. In the second case, "humanity" refers to a shared nature or essence, which then warrants certain kinds of moral considerations (e.g., one can speak of "universal human rights" and, conversely, "crimes against humanity"). Any account of ethics directed toward particular ends (i.e., teleological ethics) will hold as critical definitions of "humanity," since one's understanding about what constitutes humanity will determine the specific ethical warrants required of, from, and about humanity. From Aristotle's account of the virtues, through Augustine of Hippo and Thomas Aquinas, to natural-law theory, ethical deliberation involves continuity between doing and being, or living commensurate with one's nature or essence. Due to the eschatological shape of Christian theology, the constitution of humanity and, hence, its ethical meaning require attention to both what humanity was created to be and to which end it is directed. For Christian ethics, then, denoting the ethical import of "humanity" requires a substantial review of biblical literature that begins with foundational accounts of the created nature of humanity and its articulation throughout the biblical narrative culminating in "the new humanity." Even moral systems less reliant on teleological modes of argument still hold at their center notions of humanity. For example, the monumentally important eighteenth-century philosopher Immanuel Kant prioritized a specific conception of humanity within the duty-oriented, or deontological, structure of his ethics.

Scripture

In the OT, the Hebrew word *ādām* can denote a particular human or humanity in the generic sense (e.g., Gen. 1:26; 2:7; 5:1, Isa. 52:14). The word *ādām* is also used as the proper name for Adam (Gen. 4:1). Like the OT, in the NT "human" (Gk. *anthrōpos*, *anthrōpinos*) indicates what is characteristic of humanity in distinction from God (e.g., Acts 17:25; Rom. 3:5; 6:19; 1 Cor. 2:13; 9:8; Gal. 3:15; Phil. 2:7) and other creatures (e.g., Jas. 3:7; 2 Pet. 2:16; Rev. 9:7; 18:13).

The OT introduces humanity in its opening accounts of the origin of all things as God's creation. In the first account (Gen. 1:1–2:3), God formed and filled the universe with an order characterized by the division of realms (heavens/earth, sky/waters, land/sea) and their inhabitants (sun/moon, plants/trees, birds/aquatics, wild animals/creeping things). This order of harmonious difference extends finally to the creation of humanity, differentiated by male and female. As with the other living creatures, God blessed them, commanded them to "be fruitful and multiply," and gave them vegetation for food. God distinguished humanity by making them in God's own image and by giving them dominion over all other creatures. God declared all creation good and blessed the seventh day, on which he rested.

The second account (Gen. 2:4–25) focuses on the creation of humanity and its relation to the other realms and inhabitants of the earth. God formed the first human (Heb. *ādām*) "from the dust of the ground [*adamah*]" with the "breath of life." God placed this human in the garden of Eden, where he willed that vegetation grow and receive water from a river and tending from the human. God declared it "not good" for the human to be alone, so he formed animals and birds out of the ground and gave them to the human to name. God created a partner from the side of the human, who called the partner "woman" (*'iššâ*) and himself "man" (*'îš*) (Gen. 2:23). The relationship between the two humans is oriented to the union of man and woman becoming one flesh (Gen. 2:24).

Together, these accounts reveal the place and purposes of humanity within creation, which are repeated and developed throughout Scripture: humans were made in the image of God, "a little lower than angels" (Ps. 8:5; Heb. 2:7), and were given dominion over the other creatures and the task of tending to God's creation in partnership with other humans in order to foster harmonious relationships of delight and rest among God, humans, and the rest of creation (cf. Exod. 20; Lev. 25–26; Deut. 5; Heb. 4).

God's purposes for humanity and all creation were distorted by Adam and Eve, the first man and woman, when they distrusted and disobeyed God, pridefully refusing to accept the limitations of their creatureliness by eating from the forbidden tree of the knowledge of good and evil (Gen. 3). This fall of humanity perverted the harmonious difference of the created order, so that rather than honoring God and submitting to his will, humans usurp God's role in seeking to possess divine knowledge independently; as a result, rather than cooperating with others in relationships of reciprocal love and service, individuals assert their own innocence and blame others; rather than stewarding creation as God's image-bearers for God's glory, humans exploit creation for their own distorted ends. Finally, all humans face death, which God warned was the consequence of eating from the forbidden tree.

After the fall, human sin multiplied, resulting in violence, injustice, and suffering (Gen. 4–6). God was grieved by human wickedness and judged humanity to have fallen so far from his intention for them that God sought to remove humanity and all living creatures from the earth by causing a great flood. God's judgment proved restorative when God looked favorably on Noah, who was "righteous and walked with God," and God willed to preserve creation through him (Gen. 6–8). God promised to preserve the creation and so to maintain his plan to bring about his purposes for all of creation through humanity.

However, humanity persisted in their wickedness and attempted to live independently of God, evinced by the construction of the tower of Babel (Gen. 11). In response, God introduced a further distinction between humans beyond that of male and female: nations of people bound together by shared language and land. God set apart one nation beginning with the call of and promise to Abraham and Sarah to be his people through whom he would bless all nations (Gen. 12). Reminiscent of the creation of humanity in Eden, God's call involves land and human fruitfulness, but this time God commands them to go into a land of their own, rather than the whole earth, and promises, rather than commands, the fruitfulness and multiplication of them and their descendants. As God chose Noah through whom to preserve all creation, so he chose Israel, the descendants of Abraham and Sarah, through whom he promised to "bless all nations" and to restore all creation to his initial purposes.

From this point forward in Scripture, until the NT Epistles, the fundamental distinction within humanity is that between Israel and the nations, eventually called "Jews" and "gentiles." God delivered the Israelites from Egyptian bondage and confirmed God's covenant with them (Exod. 13). God, through Moses, gave them the Torah as a charter specifying his relation to them as their only God and instructing them how to live as his people set apart to be a "priestly kingdom and a holy nation" and to serve as an example to all nations of true humanity characterized by "wisdom and discernment" (Exod. 19:6; Deut. 4:6). Israel was distinct insofar as God chose them to live in covenant relationship with him and enabled them to do so by providing the law's instruction of the way of life to follow and that of death to avoid, as well as the means to achieve forgiveness for their sins (Deut. 30:19; Lev. 4–5).

Yet Israel remained fallen like all humanity, of whom the psalmist says that they do not "seek after God. They have all gone astray. . . . There is no one who does good" (Pss. 14:2–3; 53:1–3 [cf. Rom 3:10–12]). That humanity's sin is a perversion of God's good order for creation is indicated by the link between human sin and the barrenness of the land (Hosea, Habakkuk) and God's punishment of Israel through exile from the land he had given to them and/or enslavement to foreign rulers (Neh. 9:16–37). Israel's cycle of disobedience and return to the Lord parallels that of humanity's fall and the goal of delight and rest in God toward which he purposed creation. Israel could not fully attain to this goal because, while their partial obedience to the law recovered their humanity to a degree, the law in itself could not transform the heart to bring about complete obedience, nor could it defeat death and so give life. Thus, Israel was hindered not only from within but also from without by powers of death that enslave and pervert his order (Job 2; Isa. 24:17). Despite the perversion of creation, humanity and the earth remained God's good creation and a reflection of God's glory (Isa. 6:3) toward which he had love and compassion.

God raised up prophets through whom he declared that he was "about to do a new thing" that would restore the created order by making rivers in the desert, wild animals to honor him, and God's people to declare his praise (Isa. 43:19–21). God promised to make a new covenant with Israel, to "remove the heart of stone from their flesh and give them a heart of flesh" (Ezek. 11:19) and put the "law within them and . . . write it on their hearts" (Jer. 31:33).

The story of God's restoration of creation through the chosen people of Israel culminates in the NT in the person of Jesus of Nazareth, Israel's "Messiah, the son of David, the son of Abraham" (Matt. 1:1). Jesus proclaimed, "The time is fulfilled, and the kingdom of God has come near; repent, and believe in the good news" (Mark 1:15). In his teaching and actions Jesus revealed the full meaning of the laws and institutions that God gave to the people Israel, and he demonstrated God's intention to bring restoration to all of creation by fostering human community, healing the sick, and proclaiming the forgiveness of sin and the gift of eternal life in God's kingdom of peace. Jesus revealed that Israel's enemies are the enemies of all humanity, namely sin and death. According to the Gospels, he taught that no one could enter God's kingdom without being born again of water and the Spirit (John 3:5), eating his flesh and drinking his blood (John 6:53), exceeding in righteousness (Matt. 5:20), doing the will of the Father (Matt. 7:21), and becoming like a child (Matt. 18:3).

The NT Epistles interpret Jesus' teaching in light of his death, resurrection, and ascension and his commission of the church in the power of the Holy Spirit. Paul speaks of Jesus as the one prefigured by Adam (Rom. 5), the last Adam (1 Cor. 15:45), and the new humanity (Eph. 2:14–16). Adam is regarded as the representative human, in whom all humanity participates by virtue of their own disobedience and eventual death. As a human, Jesus shared in the death of Adam; however, as the uniquely obedient and innocent human, Jesus did not share in Adam's sin but rather became sin for the sake of humanity (2 Cor. 5:21). Jesus absorbed the powers of evil in his mortal body, such that they died in his death and he triumphed over them in his resurrection to new life (Col. 2:15), the first of God's redeemed creation. Thus, Jesus is the last Adam—the last representative of humanity, whose resurrected life declares the ultimate defeat of death and evil and the gracious offer of God's life-giving Spirit for participation in God's new creation (2 Cor. 5:16–17).

In Jesus the consequences of the fall are undone: "In Christ God was reconciling the world to himself" (2 Cor. 5:19), and "he died for all so that those who live might live no longer for themselves, but for him who died and was raised for them" (2 Cor. 5:15 [cf. Rom 6:4]) and that they might "exercise dominion in life through the one man, Jesus Christ" (Rom. 5:17). Jesus has truly defeated sin and death, but this can be only a partial reality for humans. Until Jesus returns, raises the dead, and transforms mortal bodies into resurrection bodies, humans can only partially experience Jesus' victory through participation in his resurrection body and the life of the Spirit (Rom. 8; 1 Cor. 15). This participation occurs through baptism into Jesus' death and resurrection, whereby humans are born again through incorporation into the one body of Christ, which is the church.

The church is the "new humanity" of formerly opposed humans now reconciled in Christ (Eph. 2:15–16). Paul explains, "There is no longer Jew or Greek, there is no longer slave or free, there is no longer male and female; for all of you are one in Christ Jesus" (Gal. 3:28). The church participates in the new creation, where the distinctions between humans that are the result of the fall, including nations and slavery, are abolished. With respect to males and females, the created distinction remains, while the fallen opposition is removed. God's intended order of harmonious difference is restored in the church, where males and females live in cooperative partnership and where each member is gifted by the Holy Spirit for the good of the whole (1 Cor. 12). The church is to function like a body in which all share a corporate life as "members of one another" with Christ as the head (Gal. 3:28; Eph. 4:25).

The church is sustained as Christ's body through the Lord's Supper, wherein the church partakes of the body and blood of Christ (1 Cor. 11:17–34). Paul instructs his churches to "put on the Lord Jesus Christ" (Rom. 13:14 [cf. Gal. 3:27]) and so live in accord with their union with Christ, since by baptism they "have stripped off the old human with its practices and have been clothed with the new human, which is being renewed in knowledge according to the image of its creator" (Col. 3:9–10 [translation mine]). As Israel was called to be God's holy people, so the church is called to be holy and blameless, set apart as an example of true humanity.

The Ethics of Humanity

Any mode of Christian ethics needs to be mindful of the biblical narrative in order to situate human action and existence in terms of how Scripture portrays the origins and destiny and goods and challenges related to the biblical depiction of humanity. Of course, interpreting Scripture in relationship to a consistent portrayal of humanity has itself involved controversy. Debates regarding the humanity of Jesus Christ have remained a constant over the church's long existence. These efforts to delineate the relationship between Christ's divinity and humanity and both in relation to a general conception of humanity hold important implications for all manner of practical ethical considerations, such as worship, the sacraments, martyrdom, the church's relationship to the world, and many more. The creedal affirmation of Christ's "full humanity" involves broad implications for how one might understand the moral expectations demanded of humanity, given the prevalence of sin in relation to Christ's recapitulation of humanity as described by early patristic literature. Some have argued that the fall of humanity necessarily requires that Christian ethics take a "realistic" approach to moral possibilities (e.g., in the case of war and the likelihood of earthly justice). However, others have argued that the effects of sin on humanity can be mitigated through varying modes of divinization (classical Eastern Orthodoxy) or sanctification (Roman Catholicism and Methodism), such that the life and death of Jesus as embodied in the NT church as God's new humanity demonstrate the generatively broad horizon of ethical possibility.

In recent years, definitions of humanity have played a role in almost every important ethical question. From global capitalism to artificial reproductive technology to "rights" language, Christian ethicists have leaned into various notions of humanity in order to postulate Christian postures toward various issues in contemporary Christian ethics. Because many approaches to Christian ethics rely on naturalist or essentialist modes of argumentation, the nature of humanity has proved to play a critical role within several highly contested and complex topics in Christianity ethics. For example, the question of human ontology (the study of essence, nature, or being) continues to hold a prominent role in questions related to the human fetus. One popular strategy has been to attach "humanity" to the fetus (i.e., to grant the fetus the ontological status of a human), which then anathematizes certain medical procedures (e.g., abortion, artificial reproductive technologies, stem-cell research), following the suggestion that humanity as such deserves respect and consideration. Even if one steers clear of essentializing arguments, one can adjudicate such issues depending on how one understands humanity. Even if one does not grant the fetus human ontological status, one could still problematize medical and technological interventions such as stem-cell research by arguing against the commodification of humanity. Yet conversely, one could just as likely argue for the moral avocation of stem-cell research by way of another kind of claim about humanity, that respecting the uniqueness of humanity in the created order warrants precisely the kinds of medical and technological interventions that stem-cell research represents.

Because "humanity" is featured so variously in the Bible, and because the theological tradition has proffered so wide an array of interpretations of those various iterations, depending on how one interprets Scripture, one will position oneself in relation to these complex issues. Also, as explicated by recent developments in hermeneutics, one's position in relation to these complex issues determines one's interpretation of Scripture on such issues. This latter point demonstrates the significant roles that communities and practices play in the formation of moral imaginations and habits. The rise of postmodern philosophy as the grid through which to develop approaches not only to contemporary moral concerns but also to ancient sources and texts (such as Scripture and historical interpretations of Scripture) has led to an emphasis on hermeneutic communities of discourse that inculcate individuals into various modes of reading Scripture and the tradition. With the idea that linguistic habits frame ethical deliberation and action, contemporary Christian ethics has placed heavy emphasis on the interrelation among liturgy, language, and moral law. In turn, this has meant recouping descriptions of humanity as necessarily theological and hence scriptural. Rather than a freestanding and even secular definition of "humanity," the scriptural portrayal of the creation of humanity in the image of God locates Christian ethics as a discipline internal to the doxological life of the church.

See also Bioethics; Image of God; Sanctity of Human Life

Bibliography

Arendt, H. *The Human Condition*. University of Chicago Press, 1958; Hauerwas, S., and S. Wells, eds. *The Blackwell Companion to Christian Ethics*. Blackwell, 2004, 68–81; Lauritzen, P. "Report on the Ethics of Stem Cell Research." http://www.bioethics.georgetown.edu/pcbe/reports/stemcell/appendix_g.html; Shuman, J., and B. Volck. *Reclaiming the Body: Christians and the Faithful Use of Modern Medicine*. Brazos, 2006; Wright, N. T. *The Climax of the Covenant: Christ and the Law in Pauline Theology*. Fortress, 1993; idem. *Jesus and the Victory of God*. Fortress, 1997; idem. *The New Testament and the People of God*. Fortress, 1992; idem. *The Resurrection of the Son of God*. Fortress, 2003.

Lindsay K. Cleveland and Jonathan Tran

Human Nature *See* Humanity

Human Rights

The notion of human rights is both simple and enormously complex; millions understand it well enough to claim that they have rights or that their rights have been violated, and yet scholars, lawyers, and presidents debate the meaning of human rights endlessly and without resolution. Indeed, a significant contingent, including some Christian scholars, doubt whether the idea makes any sense at all.

The core of the idea of human rights is the belief that simply by virtue of being human, persons must be treated in certain specific ways and must not be treated in certain specific ways by their fellow humans. Something inherent in and fundamental to the meaning of human existence requires a minimum standard of treatment (or existence) for all persons.

At one level, then, human rights as a concept prescribes moral or even legal obligations related to how human beings treat one another. If a person has a human right not to experience X (e.g., torture, abuse, restrictions on free speech), then all other appropriately positioned persons, including collectivities such as governments, are morally obligated to refrain from doing X to that person; indeed, they are morally obligated to act in such a way as to prevent X from being done to that person or any person. The term *negative rights* sometimes is used to describe those acts that people have a legitimate claim to not have inflicted upon them.

More expansively, if a person has a human right to experience Y (quality education, healthcare, rest, leisure), then all other appropriately positioned persons, including governments, are morally obligated to act in such a way as to ensure that Y is available to that person. Here human rights specify not just how people must or must not be treated, but more broadly describe the conditions in which they live or the experiences or benefits they must enjoy. These *positive rights*, often articulated in modern human-rights theories and treaties, are more difficult both to specify and to enforce. Some theorists emphasize negative rights over positive rights or to the exclusion of positive rights.

A dialectic of rights and duties characterizes human-rights theory. Any person who possesses a right can legitimately claim that all other persons possess a duty in relation to the protection or advance of that right. Thus, any elaborate moral or legal structure that acknowledges a range of human rights simultaneously acknowledges a range of moral and legal duties to see to the recognition and advance of those rights.

A hallmark of human-rights theory is its universality. Simply by virtue of being human, each and every person has human rights. Each right that I claim for myself is a right that I am simultaneously claiming for every other self. Each duty that I believe falls on all to recognize and advance my rights is a duty I place on myself to recognize and advance the rights of all others.

In this way, a commitment to human rights serves as a remarkable force for the recognition of human equality and the improvement of the lot of those whose lives are most miserable. For example, when the signers of the Declaration of Independence declared that everyone has "the right to life, liberty, and the pursuit of happiness," they offered their words in a context in which only free white men of property had full political rights. Their "rights talk" exceeded their "rights practice," but it set into motion a long historical process by which ever more previously disenfranchised groups claimed the rights long articulated by that document.

Rights claims are moral claims, but they often become legal claims as well. Human-rights theories assume that governments do not create rights but only recognize rights that are independent and prior to the existence of governments. People have rights by virtue of being human; governments are obligated to recognize those rights. Not only is it impermissible for governments to violate those rights but also governments must sanction those individuals and groups that do violate human rights. In most nations, as well as in international law, human rights are now recognized as properly enforceable by legal means where this is necessary. Legislatures pass laws specifying particular human rights as well as penalties for their violation. International tribunals, such as the International Criminal Court, seek to deter and to punish the gross violation of human rights by individuals, governments, and nations.

A final feature of human-rights theory is the notion of inalienability. This essentially means that certain human rights are so basic, so fundamental to human existence or human dignity, that they may under no circumstances be lost, given away, taken away, or forfeited. For example, if personal liberty from enslavement is an inalienable right, it means that persons can neither sell themselves nor be sold or owned by others under any circumstances. Yet some rights are indeed forfeitable. For example, a person's freedom of movement can be forfeited if that person commits crimes that require imprisonment as punishment or to protect the community.

Biblical Considerations

Debate over the idea of human rights among Christian theologians and ethicists is partly rooted in the fact that no explicit theory of human rights is offered in Scripture. Biblical materials do, however, offer a wide range of resources that fit easily with the kind of human-rights commitments just outlined. In fact, it is not too much to claim that they are the ultimate foundation of such commitments. The fundamental biblical grounding for human rights is the worth of the human person before God, our creator, sustainer, and redeemer.

It is striking how often human-rights documents, such as the Universal Declaration of Human Rights (1948) or the International Covenant on Civil and Political Rights (1966), ground their specific human-rights claims in the "inherent dignity of the human person." But they do not further elucidate the origins of this purported inherent dignity. It is a majestic claim lacking any warrant other than, as in the Universal Declaration of Human Rights, its role in serving as "the foundation for freedom, justice, and peace in the world." In other words, belief in the inherent dignity of the human person serves a critically important instrumental role in creating the conditions for a better world. We have to believe in human rights because the consequences of failing to do so, as with the Nazi regime in Germany in the last century, are so grotesque.

However, the fact that an idea has good consequences does not necessarily mean that one should believe it. Contemporary international and secular human-rights declarations seem to many religious observers to be drawing silently on borrowed theological capital. Some would go further and claim that belief in human rights is incoherent, at least apart from biblical revelation. The surest ground for belief in inherent human dignity is a transcendent one. Christians and Jews believe that human beings are of equal and immeasurable worth because of specific biblical claims, laws, and teachings about how human beings are to be viewed and treated, and because the broader biblical narrative paints a picture of God's involvement with human beings that elevates the worth and value of the human person. The incarnation—in which God takes flesh in Jesus Christ, ministers to society's outcasts, teaches the obligation of love and mercy to all, suffers at the hands of humans, and dies for our salvation—serves as the ultimate grounding of Christian belief in the sanctity, dignity, and rights of each and every human being.

Noting the difficulty or even incoherence of secular warrants for rights claims, the lack of an explicit theory of human rights in the Bible, and the late emergence of a well-developed theory of human rights in Western culture, some Christian thinkers have rejected the idea altogether as an Enlightenment fiction.

Biblically, a rejoinder to this rejection of human rights can be offered as above. Historically, recent studies have traced "human rights" language farther and farther back into Western history, well before the Enlightenment period. Baptists are especially proud to note that pre-Enlightenment (early seventeenth century) Baptist leaders such as Richard Overton made arguments for human rights based on Scripture and on their painful experiences of religious persecution—a reminder that religious liberty lies very near the core of most understandings of human rights.

Toward the Future

Today, a large number of Christian groups exist to advance human rights in areas such as national security, modern-day slavery, sex trafficking, prison reform, genocide, abortion, and women's rights. They often find themselves in partnership with human-rights groups grounded in secular commitments or other religious faiths. Such partnerships offer a significant opportunity for holistic Christian moral witness and collaborating with others for the common good.

See also Baptist Ethics; Civil Rights; Humanity; Image of God; Incarnation; Natural Law; Natural Rights; Rights; Sanctity of Human Life; Social Contract

Bibliography

Claude, R., and B. Weston. *Human Rights in the World Community: Issues and Action*. University of Pennsylvania Press, 2006; Donnelly, J. *Universal Human Rights in Theory and Practice*. 2nd ed. Cornell University Press, 2002; Hayden, P. *The Philosophy of Human Rights*. Paragon House, 2001; Reed, E. *The Ethics of Human Rights: Contested Doctrinal and Moral Issues*. Baylor University Press, 2007; Wolterstorff, N. *Justice: Rights and Wrongs*. Princeton University Press, 2007.

David P. Gushee

Humility

Humility is a biblical social value describing one's relationship with God and one another. From a social-scientific perspective, humility captures the importance of remaining within one's own social position. Humble persons do not appropriate what is not part of their status in life. John the Baptist is the clearest illustration of this biblical virtue of humility: "I baptize you with water for repentance, but one who is more powerful than I is coming after me; I am not worthy to carry his sandals. He will baptize you with the Holy Spirit and fire" (Matt. 3:11). John acknowledges his social status in regard to the "one who is to come." He is "not worthy to carry his sandals."

Humility of God's People in the Old Testament

Israel first learned the virtue of humility through their experience of God's almighty power in delivering them from slavery in Egypt. In acts of worship they continued to express their relationship to God. There they remembered God's mighty deeds and showed dependence on God for who they were and for God's continued blessings. The psalms are eternal testaments to their humble dependence on God. Their attitude of humility in worship reflects the humble attitude that David adopted before the ark of the covenant on its entry into Jerusalem (2 Sam. 6:16–22). David's joyful spirit of abandonment before God reflected his joy in acknowledging that all he had and was came from God. In contrast to David's attitude stands the biblical story of the Tower of Babel. There, humans were unwilling to accept their status in relation to God, instead making themselves to be more than they were by striving to become gods. This clearly violated their social status and resulted in God's punishment (Gen. 11:1–9).

In the OT, two important examples of humility emerge. Moses was "very humble, more so than anyone else on the face of the earth" (Num. 12:3). Another example is the suffering servant in the book of Isaiah, who accepted his social status as an outcast among his people (53:1–12). By being true to their roles, they were used by God to accomplish his will.

Humility of the Son of God

Jesus is the humble Messiah announced in the book of the prophet Zechariah (9:9). Jesus' entry into the city of Jerusalem illustrated his submission to the Father. He did not claim for himself arrogant regal powers: "Look, your king is coming to you, humble, and mounted on a donkey" (Matt. 21:5). A king rode into battle on a horse, whereas a donkey (used for transporting things) was an animal of peace. Elsewhere, Jesus expresses his humility: "Take my yoke upon you, and learn from me; for I am gentle and humble in heart, and you will find rest for your souls" (Matt. 11:29).

Jesus did not come seeking his own glory (John 8:50). He humbled himself even to the extent of washing the feet of his disciples. "For I have set you an example, that you also should do as I have done to you. Very truly, I tell you, servants are not greater than their master, nor are messengers greater than the one who sent them" (John 13:15–16).

Humility of Jesus' Followers

For Paul, humility lies at the heart of Jesus' nature. Although Jesus was in the form of God, he was willing to take on the lowliness of human nature (Phil. 2:6–11). Such should be the attitude of every follower (Phil. 2:5). Paul values this virtue of humility and gentleness (2 Cor. 10:1).

The Epistle of James describes the life of a follower as characterized by a humility inspired by God's wisdom (3:13–17). Humility is the true attitude of a believer toward God (4:10).

Throughout the biblical writings humility is a fundamental virtue because it upholds and fosters the essential relationship that exists between the individual, the community, and God. Jesus' central concern for his followers was that they respect the honor of God and others (Matt. 23:12; Luke 18:14). As Augustine said, "Where there is humility, there is love" (*Tract. ep. Jo.* prologue).

See also Meekness; Pride

Bibliography

Elmer, D. *Cross-cultural Servanthood: Serving the World in Christlike Humility*. InterVarsity, 2006; Malina, B. "Humility." Pages 118–20 in *Handbook of Biblical Social Values*, ed. J. Pilch and B. Malina. Rev. ed. Hendrickson, 1998; Spencer, F. "Metaphor, Mystery and the Salvation of Israel in Romans 9–11: Paul's Appeal to Humility and Doxology." *RevExp* 103 (2006): 113–38.

Patrick J. Hartin

Hunting *See* Animals

Hypocrisy

Hypocrisy is a pattern of thinking, believing, feeling, and behaving that conceals what is true. In contemporary English the word *hypocrisy* refers to a range of behaviors and character flaws that we might describe in terms of playacting, duplicity, and insincerity. It is unfortunate that English Bibles generally translate *hypokritēs* as "hypocrite" and *hypokrisis* as "hypocrisy" (e.g., Matt. 6:2, 5, 16; 23:13, 15; Luke 12:1, 56; 13:15; 1 Tim. 4:2), as the Greek terms are more nuanced than these transliterations might suggest. In theatrical dialogue among the ancient Greeks our terminology referred to actors on a stage, without necessarily entailing any pejorative sense. This usage was known in the time of Jesus, though whether he had been exposed to the Greek theater is debated. In the LXX our terminology is used with reference to persons who are godless, not so much because of their insincerity but because they lack insight into God's character and purpose (e.g., Job 34:30; 36:13). Similar usage in the NT explains the collocation of "hypocrisy" with "lawlessness" (*anomia*) in Matt. 23:28, or with "wickedness" (*kakia*) and other vices in 1 Pet. 2:1.

To be sure, some biblical texts do provide evidence of hypocrisy as a form of playacting or showy performance. This is particularly true in the Gospel of Matthew, where showy spirituality (almsgiving, prayer, fasting) is condemned as hypocrisy (6:2, 5, 16), or where Jesus, quoting Isa. 29:13, unveils the pretentiousness of the Pharisees (15:7–9). In other instances, however, the charge of hypocrisy is transparently tied to lack of insight into the ways of God. Whereas in the former case we may think in terms of a lack of integrity between one's character and one's behavior, in the latter case we find no such disjunction. In the latter case, hypocrisy is not "claiming one thing and doing another," but rather is wayward dispositions displayed in wayward practices. For example, when Paul reports his indictment of Peter, Barnabas, and others on account of their hypocrisy (Gal. 2:11–14), he is not asserting that their claim to follow the gospel was fraudulent, but rather that they had failed to understand fully and to embody in their lives the far-reaching character of the gospel. Similarly, when Jesus labels his opponents as "hypocrites" in Luke 13:15, he is incriminating them not for playacting but for their failure to understand the purpose of God's command, "Observe the sabbath day and keep it holy" (Deut. 5:12). As "lord of the sabbath" (Luke 6:5; cf. 13:15), Jesus understands how to faithfully implement Sabbath legislation. Just as "the Lord your God brought you out [of slavery in the land of Egypt] with a mighty hand and an outstretched arm" (Deut. 5:15), so on the Sabbath

Jesus laid his hands on the bent-over woman and freed her from her long-standing bondage to Satan (Luke 13:10–17).

Both of these uses of "hypocrisy" can be understood in terms of lack of conformity with what is true. Whether one knowingly "says one thing but does another" or unknowingly misrepresents the truth, both behaviors camouflage the character and ways of God.

See also Integrity; Truthfulness, Truth-Telling

Joel B. Green

I

Idolatry

Idolatry refers both to the worship of other gods (Exod. 20:3; Deut. 5:7) and to the worship of images (Exod. 20:4; Deut. 5:8). Disagreement over the division of the Ten Commandments belies the close relationship between the two: the Jewish, Roman Catholic, and Lutheran traditions take what non-Lutheran Protestants count as the first two commandments together. Either way, "not making an idol" extends and applies to "having no other gods." While both senses of idolatry are valid, the biblical authors generally do not distinguish between the worship of other gods, the worship of images, and the worship of Yahweh using images. A pagan deity was sometimes thought to be present in its image (e.g., 2 Kgs. 19:18, where the kings of Assyria are said to have "hurled their gods into the fire").

In the Bible there is no more serious charge than that of idolatry: "The central theological principle in the Bible is [the refutation of] idolatry" (Halbertal and Margalit 10). Both disdainful polemic and extreme measures of avoidance are directed against idolatry throughout. Idolatry also plays a central role in the Bible's overarching narrative, and its capacity for an extended or figurative meaning makes the concept of idolatry fruitful in a range of contexts. Barton asserts that a "central task of theology is the critique of idolatry" (1). Understanding idolatry is also critical for Christian ethics.

Idolatry and Salvation History

The history of Israel is the story of the nation's struggle with idolatry. Despite dire warnings from Moses (Deut. 4:15–19; 7:1–5), the Israelites worshiped foreign gods, not only in Egypt (Josh. 24:14) but also again in the promised land (Judg. 2:11–13; 17–18). Idolatry continued to be a snare in the days of David (1 Sam. 19:11–17) and especially Solomon (1 Kgs. 11:1–8), whose sin forced the division of the kingdom (1 Kgs. 11:9–13). With few exceptions, idolatrous practices flourished in both Israel and Judah, and many prophets inveighed against the pollution of idols. The exile in Babylon renewed the confrontation, with Daniel and a few friends standing firm. And in the postexilic period Malachi, Ezra, and Nehemiah, to remove the temptation of idolatry, opposed marriages with foreigners.

The promises of a new covenant in Isaiah and Ezekiel envision God's people being cleansed and anointed with the Spirit and the removal of Israel's idols (e.g., Ezek. 36:26–36). Further, Isa. 45:5–6 reveals God's determination to be known among the nations as the true and living God. In the NT, those who continue to worship idols are excluded from the kingdom of God (Rev. 9:20), and Jesus emerges as the incarnate icon (or image) of God (*eikōn tou theou* [2 Cor. 4:4]).

The Effects of Idolatry

The Bible critiques idolatry in four complementary ways, each of which underscores its foolishness: idolatry frustrates, contaminates, and degrades its worshipers, who eventually incur the jealous judgment of God. These four effects are the reverse of what the true and living God does for those who trust in him: he saves, purifies, transforms, and justifies them.

Futility. "What use is an idol once its maker has shaped it—a cast image, a teacher of lies? For its maker trusts in what has been made, though the product is only an idol that cannot speak! Alas for you who say to the wood, 'Wake up!' to silent stone, 'Rouse yourself!' Can it teach? See, it is gold and silver plated, and there is no breath in it at all" (Hab. 2:18–19). The main premise of the biblical injunction against idolatry is that idols are ineffectual. Idol worship leads only to the disappointment and embarrassment of those who trust in them; idols are gods that fail (Ramachandra). Many pagans believed that certain benefits, such as fertility, rain, health, and guidance for certain decisions, resulted from worshiping idols. Correspondingly, OT idol polemic proclaims the powerlessness and deceptive nature of idolatry (1 Kgs. 18:27; 2 Kgs. 19:16–19; Pss. 115:4–8; 135:15–18;

Isa. 37:17–20; 41:23–24; 44:9–20; Jer. 14:22; 10:3–4; Hos. 8:4–6). The same theme continues in the NT. Paul condemns idolatry as foolish and futile (Rom. 1:21–22) and idols as "dumb" (1 Cor. 12:2).

Impurity. "Are not those who eat the [pagan] sacrifices partners [*koinōnoi*] in the altar?" (1 Cor. 10:18). Along with being worthless, in the OT and ancient Judaism idols are regarded as the "gods of the nations" (a frequent OT phrase) and consequently as "unclean." In the Jewish and Christian worldviews, idolatry was the defining characteristic of the gentiles. Opposition to idolatry was, in effect, an exercise in redrawing group boundaries (e.g., Dan. 3; 6). Postbiblical Jewish texts indicate that such concerns continued (*Jub.* 22:16–17). Paul's missionary goal was that gentiles "turn to God from idols" (1 Thess. 1:9). Consistently for Jews and Christians, a major reason to "flee idolatry" (1 Cor. 10:14) was to avoid the contamination of gentiles.

Likeness. "Those who make them [idols] and all who trust them shall become like them" (Ps. 135:18). Just as idols "have eyes but cannot see, and ears but cannot hear" (Ps. 135:16–17), so those who worship them become spiritually blind and deaf as part of God's disciplinary punishment (Meadors). "What you revere, you resemble, either for ruin or restoration" (Beale 11). Isaiah 6:9–13, a judgment on idolatry and a passage frequently alluded to by later OT and NT authors, lays out this principle: "Keep listening, but do not comprehend; keep looking, but do not understand" (Isa. 6:9). The same judgment of the "hardening of the heart" can be traced across the NT. In Rev. 9:20–21, for instance, idolatrous unbelievers are anesthetized with spiritual insensitivity, conforming to their lifeless idols.

Judgment. "A jealous and avenging God is the Lord" (Nah. 1:2). The theological ground for the judgment of idolatry, which appears throughout the Bible, is the jealousy of God. The belief that idolatry arouses God's jealousy is introduced in the second commandment (Exod. 20:5; Deut. 5:8–10; cf. Ezek. 16:38, 42; 23:25; see also Exod. 34:14, where it is the explanation of the divine name "Jealous"). The warning in 1 Cor. 10:22 ("Are we stronger than he?") echoes this teaching (Rosner, *Paul*, 195–203). God's jealousy, based on his love for those he has redeemed at great cost, motivates him to judge his people.

The Nature of Idolatry and Ethics

Idolatry carries a broader sense than literal obeisance to false gods. Ancient Jews took the commandment "You shall have no other gods before me" to be foundational to the rest of the Decalogue and in some sense all-embracing: "Whoever professes idolatry denies the Ten Words . . . whoever denies idolatry, professes all of the Torah" (*Sipre Num.* 111; cf. *Sipre Deut.* 54). Martin Luther taught in his catechisms that the first commandment casts its bright light over all the others and is the source and fountain from which all the others spring. Within the OT an extended or figurative sense of idolatry is evident in the prophets. As elusive as it may be, a definition of the concept of idolatry that goes beyond the literal is worth pursuing.

Idolatry makes the contingent absolute. For many, idolatry is a confusion of creation and the Creator (e.g., Barth) or the attribution of ultimate value to anything other than God (e.g., Niebuhr). Idolatry is a danger whenever we forget that we are created beings. Romans 1:23 is often cited in support: "They exchanged the glory of the immortal God for images resembling a mortal human being or birds or four-footed animals or reptiles." Reinhold Niebuhr (178) argues that a person who refuses to acknowledge the need for self-transcendence is in danger of replacing God with that which is finite and contingent. The versatility of this approach makes it popular in Christian ethics and preaching; idolatry occurs when we treat something other than God as ultimate.

For Vinoth Ramachandra, idolatry occurs when we "elevate some aspect of the created order to the central place that the Creator alone occupies" (107). In his sights are the gods of science, nation, ethnicity, sexuality, and so on. The sin of idolatry becomes a danger "when we forget that these are human creations" (109). Timothy Keller describes "the human heart" as an "idol factory" that takes good things like a successful career, love, material possessions, even family, and turns them into ultimate things: "Our hearts deify them as the center of our lives, because, we think, they can give us significance and security, safety and fulfillment, if we attain them" (xiv).

Idolaters love, trust, and serve idols. In the attempt to define idolatry, a fruitful complement to the concept of a contingent creation and the absolute God is to take a more inductive approach: in the Bible, what do idolaters do with their idols, what does the charge of idolatry consist of, and to what is the sin of idolatry compared?

One major conception of idolatry appears in the prophets, in whose writings God is seen as king and his people as his subjects. As king, he demands trust and confidence in his ability to provide for and protect those under his care. In the marital (Jer. 13; Ezek. 16; 23; Hos. 2) and political models idolatry consists of an attack on God's exclusive rights to human love and devotion and trust and service, respectively. In the OT, these same responses, in two different directions, characterize both idolaters and worshipers of God. In Ezek. 14:3, 7, for instance, people take "idols into their hearts," whereas the Shema calls on Israel to "love the LORD your God with all your heart" (Deut. 6:5). In Ps. 115:8–11 idolaters trust in their idols, whereas Israel and all those who revere God are called to trust in him. And in Judg. 10:13–16 the Israelites who served "other gods" repented, rejected those gods, and returned to serve the Lord. With this in mind, the most explicit target for the metaphorical charge of idolatry in the Bible is greed.

The way is paved for the condemnation of greed as a form of idol worship in the common OT warning that wealth may lead to apostasy. A person who has riches might disown God, saying, "Who is the LORD?" (Prov. 30:8–9). In the NT, Jesus insisted that people serve either God or mammon (i.e., riches, possessions), but not both (Matt. 6:24 // Luke 16:13). The apostle Paul condemned greed as idolatry (Eph. 5:5; Col. 3:5). He also believed that some people's god is their belly (Rom. 16:18; Phil. 3:19); in pagan moral philosophy the "belly" was a catchword for a life controlled by pleasures (Sandnes).

The comparison of greed with idolatry is best explained in relation to the Bible's consistent profiling of the idolater and the greedy person in terms of misdirected love, trust, and service, noted above (Rosner, *Greed as Idolatry*). Both idolaters and the greedy "set their hearts" on inappropriate objects. Both "rely on," "trust in," and "look to" their "treasures" for protection and blessing. Both "serve" and "submit to" things that demean rather than ennoble the worshiper.

The saying about mammon in Matthew and Luke confirms that the figurative versatility of the comparison of greed with idolatry allows for these three interpretations: "No one can serve two masters; for a slave will either hate the one and love the other, or be devoted to the one and despise the other. You cannot serve God and wealth" (Matt. 6:24). Misdirected love and service are signaled in the verbs "love" and "serve," along with the synonym "devotion" and the antonyms "hate" and "despise." The third response of trust is evident in the following context of Matt. 6:25–34, where Jesus points to the birds and the lilies in order to inspire trust in God's providential care and to calm anxiety about material things that provoke us to seek them obsessively.

See also Clean and Unclean; Desire; Greed; Ten Commandments

Bibliography

Barton, S., ed. *Idolatry: False Worship in the Bible, Early Judaism and Christianity*. T&T Clark, 2007; Beale, G. *We Become What We Worship: A Biblical Theology of Idolatry*. InterVarsity, 2008; Halbertal, M., and A. Margalit. *Idolatry*. Trans. N. Goldblum. Harvard University Press, 1992; Keller, T. *Counterfeit Gods: The Empty Promises of Money, Sex, and Power, and the Only Hope That Matters*. Dutton, 2009; Meadors, E. *Idolatry and the Hardening of the Heart: A Study in Biblical Theology*. T&T Clark, 2006; Niebuhr, R. *The Nature and Destiny of Man: A Christian Interpretation*. Charles Scribner's Sons, 1949; Ramachandra, V. *Gods That Fail: Modern Idolatry and Christian Mission*. InterVarsity, 1996; Rosner, B. *Greed as Idolatry: The Origin and Meaning of a Pauline Metaphor*. Eerdmans, 2007; idem. *Paul, Scripture and Ethics: A Study of 1 Corinthians 5–7*. AGJU 22. Brill, 1994; Sandnes, K. *Belly and Body in the Pauline Epistles*. SNTSMS 120. Cambridge University Press, 2002; Wright, C. *The Mission of God: Unlocking the Bible's Grand Narrative*. InterVarsity, 2006.

Brian Rosner

Image of God

Central to most Christian theological ethics is the idea that humans are made in the image of God (Lat. *imago Dei*). The idea first occurs in the Bible in Gen. 1:26–28, where God creates humanity (both male and female) in his "image" and "likeness" (parallel terms) and grants them the task of subduing the earth and ruling over the animals. The idea of creation in God's image is not, however, widespread in Scripture, found explicitly in only four other texts (Gen. 5:1–3; 9:6; 1 Cor. 11:7; Jas. 3:9). Most biblical occurrences of the *imago Dei* refer to Christ as the image par excellence or to the salvific renewal of the image in the church.

The Image of God and the Cultural Mandate

Although the idea that humans are created in God's image is rare in the OT, its meaning is clarified by other creation texts that portray the original human purpose. The *imago Dei* crystallizes the functional or missional view of humanity found in texts such as Gen. 2 and Ps. 8.

In Gen. 2 God plants a garden in Eden and places the first human there with the task of tilling and keeping the garden (2:15). Agriculture therefore is the first communal, cultural project of humanity. Since it is the Creator who first planted the garden, it could be said that God initiated the first cultural project, thus setting a pattern for humans, created in the divine image, to follow. Whereas Gen. 2 focuses on agriculture, Ps. 8 highlights animal husbandry as the basic human vocation. Humans are crowned with royal honor and granted rule over the works of God's hands, including various realms of animal life (Ps. 8:5–8). Here the domestication of animals is regarded as a task of such dignity and privilege that through it humans manifest their position of being "a little lower than God" (Ps. 8:5), an expression that begins to move in the direction of God's image/likeness.

Genesis 1:26–28 combines these two themes: humans are created to subdue the earth (similar to tending the garden in Gen. 2) and to rule over the animal kingdom (as in Ps. 8). And they are to accomplish these tasks as God's representatives or delegates on earth, entrusted with a share in his rule, which is the upshot of being made in God's image (Gen. 1:26–27). In the ancient Near East the king was thought to be the living image of the gods on earth, representing the gods' will and purpose through his administration of society and culture. In Gen. 1 the entire human race is appointed to this privileged role. The human task of exercising communal power in the world, initially applied to agriculture and the domestication of animals, results in the transformation of the earthly environment into a complex sociocultural world. Thus, Gen. 4 reports the building of the first city (4:17) and mentions the beginnings of cultural practices and inventions, such as nomadic livestock herding, musical instruments, and metal tools (4:20–22). This transformation of the world (the so-called cultural mandate) accomplished by God's human image on earth is a holy task, a sacred calling, in which humanity reflects the Creator's own lordship over the cosmos.

Just as God constructed the cosmos (heaven and earth) by wisdom, understanding, and knowledge (Prov. 3:19–20), so humans require this very same triad of qualities when they build a house (Prov. 24:3–4). This makes sense of the portrayal of Bezalel, who is put in charge of constructing the tabernacle. Bezalel is filled with God's Spirit (the same Spirit who attended creation in Gen. 1:2) and also with wisdom, understanding, and knowledge (Exod. 31:2–5; 35:30–35)—the same qualities that God exhibited when he made the world. The human embodiment of good artisanship in earthly construction projects thus recapitulates God's own building of the cosmos, which was also a developmental project, transforming an original unformed and unfilled mass (Gen. 1:2) into a complex world, over six days.

The Image of God and the Mediation of Divine Presence

The assumed parallel in the Bezalel account between the creation of the world and tabernacle construction (as macrocosmos and microcosmos) suggests the background picture of the created order as a temple, a sacred realm over which God rules. This picture is explicit in Ps. 148, which calls on a variety of heavenly and earthly creatures (148:1–4, 7–12) to praise their creator (148:5–7, 13–14), as if together they constituted a host of creaturely worshipers in the cosmic sanctuary. According to Isa. 66, heaven is Yahweh's throne, and the earth is his footstool (66:1a). Thus, the text questions why anyone would build an earthly "house" for God (referring to postexilic rebuilding of the temple), since God has already created the cosmos (66:1b–2). Why construct sacred space—a place to worship God—when all space is already sacred?

In the cosmic sanctuary of creation humans are the authorized "image" of God. Just as the physical cult statue or image in an ancient Near Eastern temple was meant to mediate the deity's presence to the worshipers, so humans are the divinely designated embodied mediators of the Creator's presence from heaven (where Yahweh is enthroned) to earth, thus completing the destiny of the cosmic temple, so that God might fully indwell the earthly realm, much as the glory of Yahweh filled the tabernacle when it was completed (Exod. 40:34–35). Although the Spirit of God was, indeed, hovering over creation at the beginning (Gen. 1:2), as if God was getting ready to breathe his presence into the world, when the Creator rests on the seventh day (Gen. 2:1–3), the world is not yet filled with God's glory. The issue is not human sin, at least not yet. The key point is that the mediation of God's presence on earth is precisely the historical vocation of humanity as the *imago Dei*, a vocation that has only just been assigned (and not yet carried out) in Gen. 1.

Human Violence and the Image of God

The incursion of sin tragically compromises the human calling to image God. From the primal disobedience in the garden (Gen. 3) through the first murder (Gen. 4), humans misuse their power to image God and so shut off earth from God's full presence. Indeed, human violence (which is fundamentally the misuse of the power of *imago Dei*) escalates, until the earth becomes filled with violence (Gen. 6:11) rather than with the presence of God. This violence leads to the flood (Gen. 6:13), which is a restorative operation meant to cleanse the earth.

The incursion of sin into God's good creation does not, however, obliterate the *imago Dei*. God's creation of both male and female in his "likeness" is reiterated (Gen. 5:1–2), and this image/likeness is passed on to future generations (Gen. 5:3). After the flood, God reaffirms the creation of humans in his "image," and this affirmation grounds the sanctity of human life (Gen. 9:6). The postfall persistence of the *imago Dei* is assumed also in Jas. 3:9, which, like Gen. 9:6, undergirds a specific ethical implication, challenging those who would bless God yet curse a person made in the divine "likeness." This NT text echoes the OT wisdom tradition that people somehow represent their maker, so that oppression or kindness shown to the poor and needy are equivalent to insult or honor shown to God (Prov. 14:31; 17:5; cf. 22:2). A similar idea lies behind Jesus' claim in the parable of the sheep and the goats (Matt. 25:31–46) that whatever works of love a person performs to "one of the least of these" is done to him (Matt. 25:40).

The Image of God and the Ethical Use of Power

The ethical significance of the *imago Dei* cannot be limited, however, to the injunction to honor God by respecting his image on earth. Persons made in God's image are not simply the recipients of ethical action; they are also called to act, imaging God's own use of creative power.

According to the creation account that forms the immediate context for the *imago Dei*, God creates without vanquishing any primordial forces of chaos (in contrast to ancient Near Eastern creation myths such as *Enuma Elish*), since to do so would enshrine violence as original and normative. Instead, God painstakingly develops the initial, unformed watery mass (Gen. 1:2) into a complex, well-constructed world. Not only is each stage of this creative process portrayed as "good" (Gen. 1:4, 10, 12, 18, 21, 25); when creation is complete, it is "very good" (Gen. 1:31). The human use of power in God's image is also to be nonviolent and developmental.

In ancient Near Eastern religious practice sacrifices were understood as providing food for the gods and were thought necessary to guarantee fertility of crops and flocks on earth. However, the God of Genesis freely blesses animals and humans with perpetual fertility (Gen. 1:22, 28) and grants food to both for their sustenance (Gen. 1:29–30). Most significantly, the biblical Creator does not hoard power as sovereign ruler of the cosmos but instead gladly assigns humanity a share in ruling the earth as his representatives (Gen. 1:26–28). God's own generous exercise of power for the benefit of creatures thus provides the most important model for the human exercise of power.

There are implications here for environmental stewardship, grounded first of all in the fundamental kinship that humans share with all other creatures (we do not transcend creation) and in the fact that all existence is a gift from the generous Creator. That humans have only a delegated, derivative authority in the world, and that the Creator's own use of power is the normative model for dominion further suggest that human rule over the earth and the nonhuman creatures is to be characterized by generosity and care.

However, we cannot stop with environmental stewardship, narrowly conceived. While the picture of the human vocation in Gen. 1:26–28 certainly grounds care for the earth, the Bible intends something much broader by its association of the *imago Dei* with the exercise of cultural, developmental power. In the biblical worldview, all cultural activities and social institutions arise from interaction with the earth. Thus, so-called creation care should not be treated as an ethical agenda separate from attending to the social structures that we develop, including governments, economic systems, technological innovations, forms of communication, and the urban and suburban landscapes in which we live and work. Such a separation may well result in the absence of critical ethical reflection on the defining human calling to develop culture and our contemporary need to work for its healing in a broken world.

Ethical reflection on human culture must take into account the fact that no human being is granted dominion over another at creation. The process of cultural development is meant to flow from a cooperative sharing in dominion. This provides a normative basis to critique interhuman injustice or the misuse of power over others, both in individual cases and in systemic social formations. More specifically, since both male and female are made in God's image with a joint mandate to rule (Gen. 1:27–28), this calls into question the inequities of patriarchy and sexism that arise in history. And since the *imago Dei* is prior to any ethnic, racial, or national divisions (see Gen. 10), this critiques ethnocentrism, racism, and any form of national superiority. That God's intent from the beginning is for a cooperative world of *shalom*, generosity, and blessing is evident most fundamentally from the Creator's generous mode of exercising power at creation, which ought to function as an ethical paradigm or model for gracious and loving interhuman action.

The Renewal of the Image and the Flooding of Earth with God's Presence

Since human sin/violence has impeded and distorted (but not obliterated) the calling to be God's image on earth, God has intervened in history to set things right, initially through the election of Abraham and his descendants as a "royal priesthood" (Exod. 19:6), that they might mediate blessing to all families and nations (Gen. 12:3; 18:18; 22:18; 26:4; 28:14). Israel's vocation vis-à-vis the nations therefore is analogous to the human calling as *imago Dei* vis-à-vis the earth. Indeed, the redemption of Israel constitutes the beginning of God's renewal of the image, a process that would ultimately spread to the entire human race. Likewise, the tabernacle is God's initial move to dwell on earth among a people who are being redeemed. But one day, "the earth will be filled with the knowledge of the glory of the LORD, as the waters cover the sea" (Hab. 2:14 [cf. Isa. 11:9]).

After a long and complex history of redemption, God's saving action culminates in the coming of Jesus, the paradigm *imago Dei* (2 Cor. 4:4–6; Col. 1:15; Heb. 1:3), God with us (Matt. 1:22–23), the one who completely manifested God's character and presence in the full range of his earthly, human life (John 14:9). As the second Adam, Jesus fulfilled through his obedience (even unto death) what the first Adam compromised by disobedience (Rom. 5:12–19).

And the risen Jesus, vindicated through resurrection, has become the head of the church, an international community of Jew and gentile reconciled to each other and to God and indwelt by God's Spirit. The church is thus the "new humanity" (a much better translation than "new self"), renewed in the image of God (Eph. 4:24; Col. 3:9–10; cf. 2 Cor. 3:18) and called to live up to the stature of Christ, whose perfect imaging becomes the model for the life of the redeemed (Phil. 2:5–11; Eph. 4:7–16, 22–24; 5:1; Col. 3:5–17). Indeed, one day the church will be conformed to the full likeness of Christ, which will include the resurrection of the body (1 Cor. 15:49; 1 John 3:2).

Whereas the church is God's temple (1 Cor. 3:16–17; 6:19; 2 Cor. 6:16; Eph. 2:21) indwelt by the Holy Spirit as a foretaste of that promised future, the day will come when "all the earth shall be filled with the glory of the LORD" (Num. 14:21) and "God will be all in all" (1 Cor. 15:28). Thus, at the end of the book of Revelation, when the curse is removed from the earth (a reversal of Gen. 3:17), God's dwelling can no longer be confined to heaven; rather, God's throne will be permanently established on a renewed earth (Rev. 21:3; 22:3), and those ransomed by Christ from all tribes and nations will reign as God's priests forever (Rev. 5:9–10; 22:5). This climactic fulfillment of the cultural mandate and the *imago Dei* is portrayed through the figure of the new Jerusalem, which is both holy city and redeemed people, representing the renewal of communal urban culture, a righteous, embodied polis.

In the present, as the church lives "between the times," those being renewed in the *imago Dei* are called to instantiate an embodied culture or social reality alternative to the violent and deathly formations and practices that dominate the world. By this conformity to Christ—the paradigm image of God—the church manifests God's rule and participates in God's mission to flood the world with the divine presence. In its concrete communal life the church as the body of Christ is called to witness to the promised future of a new heaven and a new earth in which righteousness dwells.

See also Animals; Authority and Power; Creation Ethics; Ecological Ethics; Egalitarianism; Humanity; Sin

Bibliography

Anderson, B. "Human Dominion over Nature." Pages 111–31 in *From Creation to New Creation: Old Testament Perspectives*. Fortress, 1994; Bird, P. "Sexual Differentiation and Divine Image in the Genesis Creation Texts." Pages 5–28 in *The Image of God: Gender Models in Judaeo-Christian Tradition*, ed. K. Børresen. Fortress, 1995; Hall, D. *Imaging God: Dominion as Stewardship*. Eerdmans, 1986; Janzen, W. *Still in the Image: Essays in Biblical Theology and Anthropology*. Faith & Life Press, 1982; Middleton, J. *The Liberating Image: The* Imago Dei *in Genesis 1*. Brazos, 2005; Middleton, J., and B. Walsh. "The Empowered Self." Pages 108–42 in *Truth Is Stranger Than It Used to Be: Biblical Faith in a Postmodern Age*. InterVarsity, 1995.

J. Richard Middleton

Imitation of Jesus

Tradition

Bishop and martyr Ignatius of Antioch attests to an early second-century commitment to total imitation of Christ, even unto death: "Allow me to be an imitator [*mimētēs*] of the suffering of my God" (Ign. *Rom.* 6.3). Throughout Christian history, devout disciples have sought to embody Jesus' holy teachings and actions, none more radically than Francis of Assisi, the renowned medieval itinerant preacher whose consuming Christlike life and ministry culminated in bearing stigmata of the crucified Christ in his hands, feet, and side (cf. Gal. 6:17).

However, despite these and other notable examples of those who closely emulated Jesus, by and large the imitation of Christ did not become a major tenet in the mainstream of Christian thought. More emphasis fell on Jesus' uniqueness as the "only begotten" Son of God and as the atoning Savior than on his universality as moral guide and exemplar. Luther and other Protestants worried that *imitatio Christi* promoted a "works righteousness" path to salvation inimical to *sola fide* (faith alone). Calvin noted that "the Lord did many things which he did not intend as examples for us" (*Institutes* 4.19.29), and that "it is not right to take all his actions indiscriminately as objects of imitation" (commentary on John 13:14)—in particular, Jesus' one-time, forty-day fast in the wilderness, his healing the paralyzed and raising the dead, his imparting the Spirit to his followers, and his sacrificial death on the cross.

The greatest impetus for imitating Jesus has come not through official church dogma and theological exposition, but rather through more popular piety and reflection. Two classic devotional works have been especially influential. *The Imitation of Christ*, by German Brethren teacher and Augustinian monk Thomas à Kempis (1380–1471), presents a series of meditations on Christian spirituality flowing from the conviction that "we ought to imitate [Christ's] life and manners" and let "our chiefest endeavor be to meditate upon the life of Jesus Christ . . . to conform [our lives] wholly to the life of Christ" (1.1.1–2). Thomas's reflections center on mystical union with the indwelling Christ and emulation of Christ's humility, simplicity, self-denial, and cross-bearing.

In His Steps, by American Congregationalist pastor and social activist Charles M. Sheldon (1857–1946), takes the form of a novelistic series illustrating "social gospel" values. Whereas Thomas's work primarily probes the inner life illuminated by Christ's presence, Sheldon's examines the outer life imitating Christ's conduct in the world. Inspired by the week's sermon text from 1 Pet. 2:21 ("Christ also suffered for you, leaving you an example, so that you should follow in his steps") and a visit from a "shabby-looking tramp," fictional pastor Henry Maxwell challenges his congregation to "pledge themselves earnestly and honestly for an entire year not to do anything without first asking the question, 'What would Jesus do?'" The narrative traces the struggles of the pastor and the parishioners to practice what Jesus would do in their community, concentrating on alleviating social ills such as poverty, lack of healthcare, unemployment, and alcoholism. Sheldon's "What would Jesus do?" motto reemerged with fresh vigor among Christian youth at the end of the twentieth century, advertised in various "WWJD?" paraphernalia and applied rather amorphously to a wide range of personal as well as social issues.

Scripture

The language of "imitation" is fairly rare in the NT: the verb *mimeomai* ("to imitate") appears four times, and the noun *mimētēs* ("imitator") six times. In only two cases is the imitation of Christ specifically in view, and both times it is secondary to other emphases: "Be imitators [*mimētai*] of me [Paul], as I am of Christ" (1 Cor. 11:1); "And you became imitators [*mimētai*] of us [Paul and associates] and of the Lord" (1 Thess. 1:6). Ephesians 5:1 stands out, exhorting God's "beloved children" to "be imitators [*mimētai*] of God," particularly practicing gracious forgiveness to one another "as God in Christ has forgiven you" (Eph. 4:32). Otherwise, objects of proper imitation include faithful ancestors (Heb. 6:12), Christian ministers (1 Cor. 4:16; 2 Thess. 3:7, 9; Heb. 13:7), churches (1 Thess. 2:14), and "what is good" (3 John 11).

However, the importance of imitating Jesus as a principal goal of Christian discipleship reaches beyond mimetic terminology.

Gospels and Acts. Jesus' primary call to discipleship in the Gospels, "Follow me," shocks in its simplicity and audacity. It comes with no preparation or negotiation, no curriculum or instruction manual. It demands abrupt and total response, leaving everything behind to follow Jesus (literally) on his homeless itinerant mission ("no place to lay his head" [Matt. 8:19–20; Luke 9:57–58]), which culminates in crucifixion. Along the way, Jesus' disciples discover his majestic glory, power, and authority as their Lord and God, requiring their wholehearted service, obedience, and worship. So following Jesus is more than an apprenticeship in Christian practice or learning how to live as Jesus lived.

But it is no less than that. Blazing the trail as the incarnate Son of God, Jesus expects his followers to reflect his character and perpetuate his mission: "A disciple is not above the teacher, but everyone who is fully qualified will be like the teacher" (Luke 6:40); "For I [your Lord and Teacher] have set you an example, that you should do as I have done to you" (John 13:15). In particular, Jesus calls his disciples to imitate his "fishing for people" (Mark 1:17), serving at table (Luke 22:24–27), washing one another's feet (John 13:12–15), and, especially, denying oneself and taking up the cross (Matt. 10:38–39; 16:24–26; Mark 8:34–36; Luke 9:23–25; 14:27). In the Johannine tradition, Jesus stresses his followers' vocation to love one another "just as I have loved you," with the supreme models of Jesus' love being his humble service and voluntary surrender of his life for his "friends" (John 10:11–15; 13:1, 12–17, 34–35; 15:12–15; cf. 1 John 2:5–11; 3:11–24; 4:7–12). Apart from specific charges to imitate Jesus within the Gospels, their primary genre as ancient Hellenistic biography (*bios*) suggests an overarching purpose of presenting the words, deeds, and full character of Jesus as worthy of emulation (see Burridge).

In both the Gospel of John and the book of Acts, the indwelling Holy Spirit plays a vital role in enabling Jesus' disciples to recall his words and further his work after his ascension (John 14:15–26; 15:26–27; 16:5–15; 20:20–23; Acts 1:4–8; 2:1–4, 17–21, 38–39; 4:31; 8:14–17; 10:44–48; 19:1–7). In Acts, Spirit-filled leaders such as Peter, Stephen, and Paul closely parallel (imitate) the ministry of Jesus in prophetic witness, miracle-working, persecution, and martyrdom (e.g., 3:1–10; 4:8–22; 6:8–10; 7:55–60; 9:32–42; 14:8–10; 20:7–12, 22–23). Potentially, however, the gift of "the Spirit of Jesus" (16:7) is for "everyone whom the Lord our God calls to him" (2:39).

Pauline and other New Testament writings. Although generically distinct from the Gospels and containing scant references to Jesus' earthly life, the letters of Paul still assume the metanarrative of Christ's coming into the world as the paradigm of Christian conduct. The hymn in Phil. 2:6–11 concisely plots Christ's story as a self-emptying appropriation of full human identity in the lowly "form of a slave" characterized by humility and obedience "to the point of death—even death on a cross" and vindicated by divine exaltation. Introducing this hymn, Paul exhorts the Philippian believers to "let the same mind be in you that was in Christ Jesus" (2:5). Although some have argued that Paul simply calls for assenting belief in Christ's work, a concomitant concern for imitating Christ's self-giving, cross-bearing disposition and behavior should not be diminished. The surrounding context in 1:27–2:16 stresses the humble attitudes ("mind") and actions that the Philippians should display, and Paul's own brief autobiography in 3:4–11 remarkably follows Christ's pattern: "suffering the loss of all things" and striving to know and "gain" Christ most fully by "becoming like him in his death."

This focus on emulating Christ's selfless, even sacrificial, service fits the pattern of discipleship in the Gospels and Acts and is explicitly reinforced elsewhere in Paul and other NT texts. As Christ "did not please himself" and "though he was rich, yet for your sakes he became poor," so we should set aside our own interests and resources to help the weak and needy among us (Rom. 15:1–3; 2 Cor. 8:8–9). The footsteps (1 Pet. 2:21) and footrace (Heb. 12:1–2) of Jesus, which we are called to follow, proceed along a track of unjust suffering culminating initially in crucifixion, but ultimately in God's justice and glory (Heb. 12:1–4; 1 Pet. 2:20–24).

Assessment

The imitation of Jesus in tradition and Scripture stresses a thoroughgoing, wholehearted response of discipleship to Jesus as sovereign Lord and suffering servant more than adherence to a set of characteristics or rules of conduct. Guidance and strength for following the Lord Jesus in today's world come from the foundational portraits of Jesus in the NT and the abiding Spirit of Jesus within individual believers and the community of faith.

Responsible imitation of Jesus must critically distinguish exemplary from exceptional dimensions of Christ's character and calling, being especially mindful of two things: Jesus' peculiar cultural-historical context in first-century Palestine, which necessarily complicates judgments concerning "what Jesus would do" two millennia later, and Jesus' inimitable spiritual-vocational identity as the redeeming Savior and Christ, accomplishing for us what we cannot do by ourselves. Moreover, we must remain alert to power dimensions inherent in an ethic rooted in the imitation of Jesus (see Adam; Castelli). Who determines what Jesus would do or have us do today? Coming from less faithful and proven authorities than the apostle Paul, mandates to "be imitators of me, as I am of Christ" (1 Cor. 11:1) raise dangerous prospects of exalting oneself and exploiting others.

See also Love, Love Command; Martyrdom; Power and Authority

Bibliography

Adam, A. "Walk This Way: Repetition, Difference, and the Imitation of Christ." Pages 105–23 in *Faithful Interpretation: Reading the Bible in a Postmodern World*. Fortress, 2006; Burridge, R. *Imitating Jesus: An Inclusive Approach to New Testament Ethics*. Eerdmans, 2007; Castelli, E. *Imitating Paul: A Discourse of Power*. Westminster John Knox, 1991; Longenecker, R., ed. *Patterns of Discipleship in the New Testament*. Eerdmans, 1996; Miles, M. "Imitation of Christ: Is It Possible in the Twentieth Century?" *PSB* 10 (1989): 7–22; Segovia, F., ed. *Discipleship in the New Testament*. Fortress, 1985; Shuster, M. "The Use and Misuse of the Idea of the Imitation of Christ." *Ex auditu* 14 (1998): 70–81; Spencer, F. " 'Follow Me': The Imperious Call of Jesus in the Synoptic Gospels." *Int* 59 (2005): 142–53; idem. *What Did Jesus Do? Gospel Profiles of Jesus' Personal Conduct*. Trinity Press International, 2003; Swartley, W. "Discipleship and Imitation of Jesus the Suffering Servant: The Mimesis of New Creation." Pages 356–76 in *Covenant of Peace: The Missing Peace in New Testament Theology and Ethics*. Eerdmans, 2006; Webster, J. "The Imitation of Christ." *TynBul* 37 (1986): 95–120.

F. Scott Spencer

Immigration

See Aliens, Immigration, and Refugees

Imperialism

The concept of imperialism refers to the attitudes and practices associated with one country's attempt to extend power into and maintain power over other countries through military conquest, political or economic control, cultural hegemony, or some combination thereof. Or, as Michael Hardt and Antonio Negri suggest, it is the attempt to expand national sovereignty beyond national borders. It is marked not only by hierarchical relationships between countries but also by expansionist and supremacist attitudes within dominant countries.

The term *imperialism* goes back only as far as the nineteenth century, when it was used to describe Napoleon's military ambitions and Disraeli's more complicated goal of spreading English "civilization" to the rest of the world, but the concept extends much further back in time. By definition, empires exercise imperialism, and empires go back to the fourth millennium BCE, including ancient civilizations such as Assyria, Babylonia, Persia, Greece, and Rome. The consensus among biblical scholars is that most of the OT as well as the NT and the Talmud were written by Jews and Christians living under the power of foreign empires. It is unsurprising, then, that the contexts and languages of those empires shape Scripture, which in turn shapes these faiths. Indeed, much of Jewish and Christian history is marked by the movements of the two faiths through empire, and much of Jewish and Christian theology can be described through attention to the two faiths' participation in and reactions to imperialism.

The relation of these faiths to imperialism is not uniform, however. Richard Horsley has helpfully outlined a typology of the ways religion and empire might relate: religion might reinforce the claims of empire by providing a theological justification for its existence and work; it might subvert empire by uncovering its idolatries and offering in its stead theopolitical alternatives; and it might define an empire. Like all typologies, Horsley's warrants further specification (there are many kinds of empire and many ways religion can reinforce, subvert, or define empires) and risks overinterpretation of its subject matter so that too much weight is given to the shaping of religions by their connections to empire. As a heuristic device, however, these three types are helpful because each type is visible in the Christian and Jewish texts and traditions.

- *Religion reinforces imperialism.* Interpreted weakly, Scripture reinforces imperialism, as when Isa. 45 refers to the Persian king Cyrus as God's anointed to release the exiles, or when Paul, in Rom. 13, suggests that even Roman authority comes from God. More strongly, any number of empires have benefited from the blessings of powerful segments of the Christian church—for example, Constantinian rule as described by Eusebius, the British Empire of the nineteenth century as described by evangelical missionaries, and, more controversially, the United States "empire" at the beginning of the twenty-first century as described by the Religious Right.
- *Religion subverts imperialism.* Having never been written from the perspective of imperial power, Scripture regularly subverts imperial ambitions. Jesus uses the language of empire to describe the kingdom of God, thereby undermining Roman pretenses to eternal power. Apocalyptic literature is so marked by a vision in which established empires are overturned that some biblical scholars suggest that anti-imperialism is a defining mark of apocalypticism.
- *Religion defines empire.* The Holy Roman Empire of Charlemagne could not be described without immediate reference to Christendom as the basis for imperial rule. Islam, with which Judaism and Christianity have both contended, is defined by the joining together of an imperial politic and religious way of life, as is, eschatologically, the new Jerusalem as well.

Because the relationships between the political and the spiritual are so complex, some theologies join several of these approaches. Augustine, for example, provides both a language for reinforcing imperialism and a vision of the world that undermines it in his *City of God*. More recently, postcolonial theologians and post-Marxist scholars have paid close attention to the claims, dangers, and, in some instances, possibilities of imperialism. Indeed, contemporary attention to ancient empires on the part of biblical scholars reveals both hermeneutical discoveries about the power of old imperialisms and stimulates new insight into American imperialism.

See also Colonialism and Postcolonialism; Conquest; Nationalism; Political Ethics; Powers and Principalities; Propaganda

Bibliography

Avram, W., ed. *Anxious about Empire: Theological Essays on the New Global Realities*. Brazos, 2004; Etherington, N. *Theories of Imperialism: War, Conquest, and Capital*. Barnes & Noble, 1984; Hardt, M., and A. Negri, *Empire*. Harvard University Press, 2000; Hobson, J. *Imperialism: A Study*. Allen & Unwin, 1938; Horsley, R. *Paul and Empire: Religion and Power in Roman Imperial Power*. Trinity Press International, 1997; idem. *Religion and Empire: People, Power, and the Life of the Spirit*. Fortress, 2003;

Pui-lan, K., et al., eds. *Empire and the Christian Tradition: New Readings of Classical Theologians*. Fortress, 2007; Said, E. *Culture and Imperialism*. Vintage Books, 1994.

Mark Douglas

Incarnation

As a doctrine, incarnation refers to the reality of God in human form and substance as Jesus Christ, as well as the process by which this embodiment occurred. As a concept, incarnation can point more widely to other noncorporeal entities that take on bodies or material forms.

Scripture and Doctrine

Central to the scriptural understanding of incarnation is the prologue to John's Gospel, especially the affirmation that "the Word" was with God and was God (John 1:1), the proclamation that "the Word became flesh" (John 1:14), and the identification of the Word with the light (John 1:7–9) about which John the Baptist testified, who was Jesus. Also of key importance is an early Christian hymn, quoted in the Letter to the Philippians, describing Jesus being "in the form of God" (Phil. 2:6), but also "being born in human likeness" and "being found in human form" (Phil. 2:7). The understanding that Jesus was both human and divine received little attention in the rest of the NT, but Christian theology of the subsequent centuries struggled extensively to explain this dual identity or nature of Jesus. The equation of Jesus and God raised numerous objections that the NT's few references could not easily overcome. Chief among these questions were concerns such as Jesus' preexistence, the significance of Jesus' death or God's death on the cross, and the process and timing of Jesus' becoming human or becoming divine.

Of the early church's many explanations, trinitarian theology came to the fore within the church's first few centuries as the dominant theory and then as the orthodox view. The idea of the Trinity is that God exists as three persons within one deity. Jesus is regarded as the second of these persons but coexistent with and equal to God the Father and God the Spirit. As such, Jesus can be called God the Son, or God incarnate.

This theology of Trinity finds expression in the church's classic creeds. For instance, the Nicene Creed of 325 (with revisions in 381) describes Jesus as "the only Son of God, eternally begotten of the Father, God from God, Light from Light, true God from true God, begotten not made, of one Being with the Father" (International Consultation on English Texts). Further, "by the power of the Holy Spirit, he [Jesus] became incarnate from the Virgin Mary, and was made man." This solution emphasizes the unity of Jesus and God ("of one Being," "true God") while affirming that Jesus came from God ("from God," "begotten"), and seeing humanity as something into which God the Son entered ("was made man").

Despite numerous challenges in every era, this formulation remains as the classic expression of Christian understanding of God's incarnation in Jesus. However, there are a number of arguments against trinitarianism based on different definitions of the divine essence, substance, or form that Jesus and God share or the human essence, substance, or form that distinguishes Jesus from other divine persons of the Trinity. Others have approached the problem of the incarnation in terms of difficulty in discerning literal versus symbolic language and reality when dealing with abstractions such as God's nature and essence. Other scholars have argued against the trinitarian incarnation because of its exclusivism, especially with regard to other religions. Significant divergent theories of incarnation include adoptionism (Jesus was human at birth, but then God elevated him and accepted him as divine; often, this is argued with reference to Luke 3:22 or other Gospel parallels), Docetism (concepts of Jesus as only seeming to be human, such as some gnostic belief), binitarianism (the doctrine that God and Jesus are divine but that the Spirit occupies a secondary and nonequal role), Oneness Pentecostalism (a twentieth-century movement seeing God as one spirit with three manifestations rather than three persons), as well as pantheistic or panentheistic approaches (emphasizing God's presence in many or all parts of creation rather than as a separate independent entity). Nevertheless, the incarnation of God in Jesus is usually understood as a requirement and hallmark of true Christian faith.

Other Developments in Scripture

Although Scripture provides few passages that discuss incarnation as an essential relationship of God and Jesus or as a philosophical explanation of Jesus' nature, in many instances Scripture discusses God's embodiment. Often, OT texts depict God with arms (e.g., Deut. 26:8; Ps. 89:13; Isa. 62:8; Jer. 21:5), legs (Gen. 3:8), face (Exod. 33:11; Ps. 80:7), breath (Gen. 2:7; Job 4:9), and other physical features (Exod. 33:23). Ancient Israel's neighbors believed in gods who inhabited material objects, but Israel denied this practice of idolatry. Further, Israel's later neighbors believed in multiple deities with human features and form, and some of the OT may reflect associated thoughts. Certainly, Israel used the language of embodiment to speak of God as in a form that humans would recognize. Perhaps this was poetic and metaphorical anthropomorphizing, but in many places the OT texts read sensibly if one imagines a God who is physically present in recognizable form.

Likewise, the NT speaks of the "body of Christ" (Rom. 12:5; 1 Cor. 12:12, 27; Eph. 3:6; 4:12; 5:23, 29; Col. 3:15) as the group of believers who survive after Jesus' death, resurrection, and ascension. In Jesus' absence, Christ's body remains. Although the Christian tradition usually understands this as metaphor, the concept of Christ's body shares in common with many other biblical texts an understanding of God's enduring physical presence with humanity.

Contemporary Applications

The incarnation is a classic Christian doctrine with almost two thousand years' history of theological debate, much of which has been conducted in rarefied discourse. However, at least two contemporary streams of Christian ethical reflection interact with incarnational and embodied understandings.

Through incarnation, God chose to be present in human form, in a human body. This emphasis on God's embodiment empowers ethical consideration of how people treat the human body. Paul understood the human body as a temple or dwelling place for God's spirit (1 Cor. 6:19), and incarnational theologies bolster this concept. There is a hallowedness or sacredness to the human body, which was created in God's own image and which God blessed and pronounced good (Gen. 1:27–28). The goodness and sacredness of the human body stand in contrast to a theological history of denigrating the body as an unworthy vessel and as sinful flesh, reflecting a fallen humanity that cannot be good. Thus, recent incarnational theologies correct this theological devaluation of the body and lift up the body as something that God esteems, treasures, and even chooses as habitation. This approach provides a theological grounding for an understanding of the sanctity of human life. At present, Christians do not agree about the particular ramifications of the body's goodness. For some, the sanctity of life means a pro-life, antiabortion, and antieuthanasia stand; for others, the sanctity of life argues against the death penalty and gun ownership. Even in the midst of these disagreements, persons of faith are finding increasing common ground on several embodied concerns: a struggle against hunger, a refusal of slavery, a disavowal of war's horrors, and a rejection of torture. Incarnation shows us an embodied God who resists acts that defile, devalue, or damage human bodies.

Embodiment theologies also lead persons of faith to new awareness of the ways our societies have divided themselves along bodily lines. The sins of racism and sexism have been grounded in denigrations of certain types of bodies, and recognition of divine embodiment allows renewed energies against these historic and pervasive sins. At the same time, we have a growing realization that humans have idealized certain bodily forms and discriminated against those whose bodies do not fit social norms. This occurs in cases of sexual orientation, disability (itself a contested term), inherited conditions, diseases and syndromes (including HIV/AIDS), bodily modifications (ranging from tattoos to transgendered persons), as well as other situations. Faith communities struggle now with inclusivity, and these issues remain an important area for ethics and social change.

See also Body; Humanity; Image of God; Sanctity of Human Life; Trinity

Bibliography

Berquist, J. *Controlling Corporeality: The Body and the Household in Ancient Israel*. Rutgers University Press, 2002; idem, *Incarnation*. UBT. Chalice Press, 2000; Betcher, S. *Spirit and the Politics of Disablement*. Fortress, 2007; Boring, M. *Truly Human, Truly Divine: Christological Language and Gospel Form*. CBP Press, 1984; Copeland, M. *Enfleshing Freedom: Body, Race, and Being*. Fortress, 2009; Hick, J., ed. *The Myth of God Incarnate*. Westminster, 1977; Jantzen, G. *God's World, God's Body*. Westminster, 1984; Kim, Y. *Christ's Body in Corinth: The Politics of a Metaphor*. Fortress, 2008; McFague, S. *The Body of God: An Ecological Theology*. Fortress, 1993; Molnar, P. *Incarnation and Resurrection: Toward a Contemporary Understanding*. Eerdmans, 2007; Moore, S. *God's Gym: Divine Male Bodies of the Bible*. Routledge, 1996; O'Collins, G. *Incarnation*. Continuum, 2007; Segal, A. "The Jewish Milieu." Pages 116–39 in *The Incarnation: An Interdisciplinary Symposium on the Incarnation of the Son of God*. Oxford University Press, 2002; Torrance, T. *Incarnation: The Person and Life of Christ*. InterVarsity Academic, 2008.

Jon L. Berquist

Incest

Incest taboos—prohibitions against sexual intercourse or other sexual contact between close kin—are both widely attested across cultures and variable. Which relationships are restricted, how seriously the taboos are taken, and the primary concerns underlying the prohibitions differ from group to group.

The NT seems to take OT incest prohibitions for granted; only one NT passage explicitly addresses the topic (1 Cor. 5:1–5). In the OT, legal texts delineate prohibited pairings (Lev. 18:6–19; Deut. 22:30 [23:1 MT]), define the punishment for incest violations (Lev. 20:11–12, 14, 17), and curse undetected offenders (Deut. 27:20, 22–23). Leviticus 18:6–19, the most comprehensive of the legal texts, first bars sexual intercourse between a man and anyone "near of kin" (*šĕʾēr bĕśārô*, lit., "flesh of his flesh," defined by Lev. 21:2 as father, mother, son, daughter, brother, and unmarried sister) and then explicitly identifies twelve prohibited consanguinous (blood) and affinal (by marriage) relatives. Reflecting the patriarchal structure of ancient Israelite families, the prohibitions cast males as subjects and females as objects.

Numerous OT narratives recount relationships prohibited in Lev. 18. Some implicitly condemn incest. Genesis 19:30–38 stigmatizes Moabites and Ammonites by portraying them as descended from Lot and his daughters. Reuben and Absalom are disparaged for sleeping with the concubines of their fathers (Gen. 35:22; 49:4; 2 Sam. 16:21–22), while Ham is cursed for looking on the "nakedness" of his father (Gen. 9:20–25). Other stories depict as neutral or even positive marriage to a half-sister (Gen. 20:12; see also 2 Sam. 12:13), sexual intercourse between a man and his daughter-in-law (Gen. 38), and marriage between a man and his aunt (Exod. 6:20). The diversity of Israelite attitudes toward incest is also attested by the law of levirate marriage (Deut. 25:5–10), which directly contradicts the prohibition against a man marrying his brother's wife (Lev. 18:16). Perhaps Lev. 18 (a relatively late text) represents legal reform; perhaps the tensions between the different texts reflect diverse opinions of different social circles in Israel.

In modern times, incest continues to be a matter of deep ethical concern. The focus of current ethical and psychological discussions of the topic has shifted, however. Old Testament authors sought to protect boundaries within families in order to prevent pollution, to limit conflict between males, and to protect male rights to women's sexuality, since "her nakedness" is really "his nakedness" (see Lev. 18:16). Today, while few would approve of incest between consenting, equally powerful adults, the discussion centers primarily on the abusive nature of the majority of incest cases and the grievous emotional, psychological, and (at times) physical harm done to the victim. In contrast to the OT laws, incest is viewed not as a violation of the "nakedness" of the father, grandfather, brother, and so on, but rather as a violation of the less powerful and thus vulnerable family member. Ethical critique of such abuse finds support not only in the incest laws, but especially in prophetic denunciation of exploitation of the powerless and in Jesus' care for the hurt and the oppressed.

See also Holiness Code; Sex and Sexuality; Sexual Abuse; Sexual Ethics

Bibliography

Brenner, A. "On Incest." Pages 113–38 in *A Feminist Companion to Exodus to Deuteronomy*, ed. A. Brenner. FCB 6. Sheffield Academic Press, 1994.

Carolyn Pressler

Individualism

The term *individualism* refers to the tendency across a broad array of spheres—politics, religion, psychology, philosophy—to make the individual person and the individual's fulfillment the locus of concern and measure of success. In secular ethics or moral philosophy, for example, each person becomes the final arbiter of what is true, good, and moral. Individualism also describes an ethos or belief system within cultures such as the United States that have historically protected and promoted individual liberty and the pursuit of each person's own vision of happiness. As such, individualism arguably supports political and economic values that Westerners consider self-evidently invaluable, such as representative democracy, economic creativity and expansion, and concepts of equality and personal liberty. However, this viewpoint and language has largely fallen out of favor in the postmodern academic milieu. Some social and moral philosophers aver that individualism's natural fruits are seen in the relativism that marks modern ethical discussion, in self-centered psychology and a "me first" culture, and in the fragmentation of societies now marred by isolation, loneliness, and greed.

Overall, the term *individualism* is best understood as a cultural value or bias, remarkably fruitful in Western civilization, that, despite heated discussions, is unlikely to be entirely displaced even as it is necessarily critiqued and honed by the discussions from within and outside the church. Utilized from within the Christian story, individualism provides a useful lens and acts as an interpretive key. It helps us read our culture, understand its development, and, when we are aware of its potential pitfalls, question ways we frame moral questions. Awareness of the bias of individualism can also help us read Scripture so that we remain tethered to important ethical commitments as we approach questions of morality. Just as no one tool proves sufficient for all needs, the biblical witness must correct individualism so that the church can truthfully witness as the body of Christ within individualistic societies.

Christian ethicists, especially those concerned with political theology, debate whether individualism can or should be rescued, as well as its legacy in political and moral theory. Understood as raw selfishness, atomism (i.e., the self as independent of others), or egoistic self-promotion, surely it should be rejected. But many Christians argue that a focus on the individual also upholds the protection and flourishing of persons. For many Christians and non-Christians, individualism as a belief in the value of each person encourages and nourishes justice, particularly as it is enshrined in the conception of natural or human rights. On the one hand, Christians can affirm an individualist lens in social and personal ethics if it focuses our attention on persons qua persons, created in the image of God with accompanying inherent dignity and individual responsibility (Gen. 1:26–28). On the other hand, if it is the primary lens through which we read human experience or determine morality, individualism skews our vision and fails to account for our relationality, our nature as beings who finally become individual "selves" only in community with others and with God.

Many philosophers, social theorists, and ethicists agree that Christianity historically fostered individualism, although they disagree about whether this development is positive or negative. These arguments highlight how individualism determines and frames ethical issues. From Augustine's deeply personal autobiography (*Confessions*) through the Reformation and its emphasis on conscience and a personal relationship with God, Christianity coupled with Western culture laid the groundwork for the ethos of individualism, especially the sense that persons are moral agents. Although secular humanism developed during the Renaissance and blossomed in the modern period, its confidence in the human person and preoccupation with the individual as the locus of concern in literature, politics, and economics probably would not be possible apart from Christianity's supporting role.

Within ethics, no single philosophy encapsulates the attractiveness and limitations of individualism as does the ethics of Immanuel Kant. He eloquently and powerfully argued for the autonomy of the individual, and his work remains one of the most influential articulations of morality today. Kant asserted a duty-based morality that focused on an individual's motivation; as a rational being, each person discerns the universal principles on which he or she ought to act. In order to be truly free, each must act as an autonomous (self-governing) person; Kant insisted on the value and dignity of every person. His rich work undergirds modern concepts of individual rights, personal liberty, and self-determination.

Some Christian ethicists find Kant's influence to be damaging on a number of fronts. They assert that "rights" language unwittingly birthed a society of individuals who seek entitlements and protect themselves in competitive or even violent self-promotion and possessiveness. This is evidenced not only in economic and political spheres but also in intimate ones, such as bioethics (as in the right to reproduce or the right to choose abortion) and sexuality (such as the right to sexual satisfaction or personal fulfillment in marriage). Community becomes difficult if not impossible in such an environment, encouraging each individual to pursue personal good at others' expense.

They also question Kant's conception that individuals are capable of, or should even strive for, disembodied and impartial rationality. Rather, we must consciously approach questions of morality shaped by our commitments, especially our faith. Additionally, if Christians affirm Kantian autonomy as the ideal mode of ethical reflection, the church forfeits a central countercultural aspect of its witness: we find our freedom and truest end not in self-determination but in submission to Christ and one another (Luke 17:33; John 12:25; Rom. 6:17–18; 2 Cor. 10:5–6).

Others consider such worries overblown, a caricature of Kant and the Enlightenment's legacy. They commonly accuse critics of being sectarians who enjoy the fruit of these concepts themselves while denying its protective framework for social justice to others. Christian criticism of individuality and in particular of human rights leaves the weak and marginalized, whom God commends to the church for particular care and concern, at the mercy of those who falsely claim that traditional ideals and community trump individual well-being, as in theologies that justified slavery, patriarchy, colonialism, anti-Semitism, and apartheid. Aspects of individualism provide the language and rationale for Christians and others to seek each human's flourishing within personal and social spheres. It does not demand denial of shared or common goods, nor does valuing the individual necessarily result in possessiveness or atomism.

Like any cultural value, individualism often presses out of its proper place and claims too much of our loyalty. Only if Christians maintain a critical distance from cultural biases can they find the wisdom to critique or support such values. From within the Christian story, such knowledge comes through humility before God, Scripture, and others; from such a location we must temper individualism so that it becomes a tool for nourishing just and truthful communities.

See also Collective Responsibility; Common Good; Democracy; Feminist Ethics; Human Rights; Image of God; Political Ethics; Self

Bibliography

Bellah, R., et al. *Habits of the Heart: Individualism and Commitment in American Life*. 3rd ed. University of California Press, 2007; Hauerwas, S., and S. Wells. "How the Church Managed before There Was Ethics." Pages 39–50 in *The Blackwell Companion to Christian Ethics*, ed. S. Hauerwas and S. Wells. Blackwell, 2004; idem. "Why Christian Ethics Was Invented." Pages 28–38 in *The Blackwell Companion to Christian Ethics*, ed. S. Hauerwas and S. Wells. Blackwell, 2004; Mount, E. *Covenant, Community, and the Common Good: An Interpretation of Christian Ethics*. Pilgrim Press, 1999; Mouw, R. "Individualism and Christian Faith." *ThTo* 38 (1982): 450–57; Taylor, C. *Sources of the Self: The Making of Modern Identity*. Harvard University Press, 1989; Wuthnow, R. *American Mythos: Why Our Best Efforts to Be a Better Nation Fall Short*. Princeton University Press, 2008.

Erin Dufault-Hunter

Inequality *See* Equality

Infanticide

Infanticide refers to intentional practices that cause the death of newborn infants or, secondarily, older children.

Scripture and the Christian tradition are unequivocal: infanticide is categorically condemned. Both Judaism and Christianity distinguished themselves in part via their opposition to widespread practices of infanticide in their cultural contexts. Are Christian communities today likewise distinguished, or, like many of their Israelite forebears, do they profess faith in God while worshiping Molech?

Infanticide in Scripture

Infanticide stands as an almost universal practice across history and culture (Williamson). Primary justifications often cite economic scarcity or population control needs, although occasionally infanticide flourished in prosperous cultural contexts (Levenson).

Infanticide or, more precisely, child sacrifice forms the background of much of the OT. Jon Levenson argues that the transformation of child sacrifice, captured in the repeated stories of the death and resurrection of the beloved and/or firstborn son, is at the heart of the Judeo-Christian tradition.

The Israelites found themselves among peoples who practiced child sacrifice, particularly sacrifice of the firstborn son. In Deut. 12:31 it is said of the inhabitants of Canaan that "they even burn their sons and their daughters in the fire to their gods" (cf. 2 Kgs. 3:27). As early as Gen. 22, Abraham finds himself commanded to sacrifice Isaac. To Abraham's ears, God's command is perfectly logical, since the gods of the Canaanite peoples require this. But to sacrifice his only son, born to him in his old age, unlikely to be replaced, rendering God's promise impossible to fulfill? Here, at the very beginning of Scripture, God begins to transform the notion of deity, showing the character of the true and living God; Yahweh is a God of life, not death.

Alongside child sacrifice, the OT presents a second form of infanticide. Immediately after Genesis, Exodus opens with Pharaoh's attempt to limit the Israelite population by killing every male child (Exod. 1–2). The contest between Yahweh and Pharaoh ends only when Yahweh slays all firstborn creatures in Egypt not protected by the blood of the lamb (Exod. 11:4–12:39). At the end of this story, Yahweh commands the Israelites, "Consecrate to me all the firstborn; whatever is the first to open the womb among the Israelites, of human beings and animals, is mine" (Exod. 13:2). The firstborn remain Yahweh's, but they live. When Yahweh gives Israel the covenant, child sacrifice is named an abomination and specifically prohibited (Lev. 18:21; Deut. 18:10; cf. 2 Kgs. 17:31; 23:4, 10).

Yet child sacrifice continues. Many Israelites, particularly their kings, wanted it both ways, to worship Yahweh but also to worship the gods of the neighboring peoples. Ahaz "even burned his son as an offering" (2 Kgs. 16:3), as did Manasseh (2 Kgs. 21:6) and the people of Israel in conjunction with their worship of Baal and Molech (Lev. 18:21; 2 Kgs. 17:17; Jer. 7:30–31; 19:5; 32:35; Ezek. 16:20–21, 36). Infanticide, in other words, was deeply enmeshed with idolatry, particularly the worship of Molech, a chthonic deity, a god of the dead or of death. By practicing child sacrifice, the Israelites entered into a "covenant of death" (Muers).

The NT opens with echoes of Exodus. In a twisted parody of pharaoic self-aggrandizement, Herod orders all male children younger than two years of age in and around Bethlehem to be killed (Matt. 2:16–20). Again, at the center of the story is idolatry: the magi come to properly worship the newborn child; Herod, a Jew, not only refuses to worship God's anointed, the one who proves to be God's only and firstborn beloved son, but also, when his ruse of wanting to worship the child fails, seeks to kill him.

Infanticide in the Christian Tradition

The early church (in continuity with its Jewish identity) continued adamantly to oppose the

Greco-Roman practice of infanticide. The ancient Greeks and Romans rejected child sacrifice as barbarous, yet they widely practiced infanticide via strangulation or exposure of newborns, particularly of girls or children with deformities. Here infanticide was practiced primarily for economic reasons, at the whim of the paterfamilias. Christian witness against infanticide (and abortion) spans the patristic context (e.g., *Did.* 5.2; *Epistle of Barnabas* 19:5; also the authors Tertullian, Athenagoras, Minucius Felix, Justin Martyr, Lactantius, Ambrose). Infanticide became a capital offense after the Roman Empire's conversion to Christianity (Valentinian I [374 CE]), although offenders rarely were prosecuted.

Infanticide Today

Despite the constant teaching of Christianity, infanticide continued as a social practice in the Christian West (Milner). It remains an issue today, not only in China and India, where ultrasound technology has augmented traditional practices of female infanticide, or in contexts of impoverished countries. Direct killing of infants or children by parents is deemed almost the epitome of sociopathology, yet an increasing number of socially accepted practices entail or permit the death of children: embryo research, embryonic stem-cell research, preimplantation genetic diagnosis, abortion, withholding treatment from "defective" neonates, and euthanasia of disabled children.

Analysis of these issues exceeds the parameters of this article. Many would reject the analogy between these practices and infanticide, since most involve the killing of humans not yet born, those categorized as "nonpersons." Yet arguments favoring these practices mirror those made in the Roman context: economic burden, parental autonomy, reduction of suffering. Proponents would more vehemently reject parallels to child sacrifice. But in light of the rhetoric of fear that is often used to justify these practices, as well as the salvific and utopian claims made on their behalf, Christians and their communities must ask questions. How are these practices contemporary forms of idolatry? In what ways do these practices enmesh participants in a "covenant with death"? Might it be that we, who live in the most prosperous culture ever, profess faith with our lips while sacrificing our children on the altars of Molech?

See also Abortion; Bioethics; Children; Euthanasia; Idolatry; Population Policy and Control; Sanctity of Human Life

Bibliography

Levenson, J. *The Death and Resurrection of the Beloved Son: The Transformation of Child Sacrifice in Judaism and Christianity*. Yale University Press, 1993; Milner, L. *Hardness of Heart/Hardness of Life: The Stain of Human Infanticide*. University Press of America, 2000; Muers, R. "Idolatry and the Future Generations: The Persistence of Moloch." *ModTh* 19 (2003): 547–61; Williamson, L. "Infanticide: An Anthropological Analysis." Pages 61–75 in *Infanticide and the Value of Life*, ed. M. Kohl. Prometheus Books, 1978.

M. Therese Lysaught

Infertility

Infertility refers to the biological inability to conceive and bear children. Stories of "barrenness" (the term used in some translations of the Bible) figure prominently in Scripture. This biblical witness challenges some contemporary assumptions about infertility and childbearing, especially when these stories are read theologically.

Barrenness in Scripture

The Bible contains stories of eight (initially) barren women: Sarah (Gen. 15–23), Rebekah (Gen. 24–25), Rachel (Gen. 29–35), Manoah's wife (Judg. 13), Hannah (1 Sam. 1–2), Michal (2 Sam. 6), a Shunammite woman (2 Kgs. 4), and Elizabeth (Luke 1). Then, as now, most of these women grieved their infertility. Shame and a sense of failure are compounded by their context: barrenness of land and womb was considered a sign of God's judgment, a curse for lack of righteousness or covenantal fidelity (Job 3:7; 15:34); fecundity was a sign of God's favor and blessing, a reward for righteousness (Exod. 23:36; Lev. 26:3–9; Deut. 7:12–14; Isa. 54:1). Moreover, Israel understood itself as being called to procreate, to fulfill God's original commandment, repeated in the context of the covenant to make Abraham's descendants as numerous as the stars, to "be fruitful and multiply" (Gen. 1:28; 35:11). Failure to conceive had personal and corporate implications.

Almost all these women are righteous, even exemplary; thus, their barrenness confounds. Like contemporary women, some of these biblical women try to engineer offspring (via concubines, maidservants, and mandrakes), but the long-term outcomes of these efforts are generally problematic.

Eventually all but Michal give birth to sons: Isaac, Jacob and Esau, Joseph and Benjamin, Samson, Samuel, and John the Baptist. Each of these stories is a key moment in salvation history. Adding the stories of Miriam, Mary, and others, one might say that, with rare exception, when God wants to do something in salvation history, someone gets pregnant. Someone gets pregnant when God wishes to establish the people of Israel, deliver Israel from the Philistines or Egyptians, transition Israel from judges to kings, herald the coming of the Messiah, or become incarnate. These stories attest that God works redemption through creation, through women (their bodies, agency, and work). Echoing the cross, these stories proclaim that God begins among the least and marginalized, confounding human wisdom by working redemption through something considered accursed.

Children in Christian Tradition

Elizabeth is the last barren woman mentioned in Scripture. With Jesus comes the fullness of redemption, and stories of miraculous birth disappear from the biblical narrative. Unlike the Jewish tradition, very early in its history Christianity adopts childlessness through vowed virginity as an ideal for both men and women. Apocalyptic notes in the Gospels caution women against bearing children because of the coming tribulation (Mark 13:17–19 pars.; Luke 23:28, 30–31) and appear even to bless the barren (Luke 23:29; cf. Wis. 3:13–14; Isa. 56:3–5; Jer. 16:1–4). Biological ties are relativized, as the church becomes one's new family. As Paul makes clear, for Christianity, redemption no longer comes through procreation but rather through adoption (Rom. 8:15, 23; Gal. 4:5; Eph. 1:5) (see Wilson).

Although childlessness became a new ideal, marriage remained the norm for most Christians. Children became understood as the primary purpose for marriage, and reproduction an obligation of those in the married state. Consequently, throughout Christian history barrenness has remained a stigma, a source of shame and grief.

Contemporary Application

These biblical stories of women righteous yet barren should dispel the misunderstanding of infertility as a punishment or curse. Should infertile Christians use reproductive technologies—fertility drugs, surrogacy, in-vitro fertilization? Although Scripture gives no commandment for or against such measures, the stories of barrenness do caution against trying to engineer children. The children who eventually come are, completely, gifts. Even then, many of the mothers (Sarah, Manoah's wife, Hannah, Elizabeth) return their children to God, for God's service. Christian reflection on reproductive technologies (and procreation) must consider this.

Such reflection must also take seriously the new paradigm of redemption: adoption. Since God now makes us his children via adoption, we may say that Christians are called to take adoption as a new paradigm for discipleship. Christian communities, above all, are called to live this new paradigm, to become exemplars of adoption. Even today, churches tend to exacerbate the pain of infertility by being excessively family- and child-oriented. Pastors should consider carefully how preaching and practices that privilege biological procreation impact infertile women and couples, and they should begin to restructure their congregations into places that embody the example of the God who adopts us all into the kingdom.

See also Adoption; Childlessness; Children; Procreation; Reproductive Technologies

Bibliography

Dresner, S. "Barren Rachel." *Judaism* 40 (1991): 442–51; Havrelock, R. "The Myth of Birthing the Hero: Heroic Barrenness in the Hebrew Bible." *BibInt* 16 (2008): 154–78; Ryan, M. "Faith and Infertility." Pages 150–70 in *Ethics and Economics of Assisted Reproduction: The Cost of Longing*. Georgetown University Press, 2001; Stimming, M. "Endless Advent." *ChrCent* 117, no. 34 (Dec. 6, 2000): 1273–75; Volf, M. "The Gift of Infertility." *ChrCent* 122, no. 22 (June 14, 2005): 33–36; Wilson, S. "Blessed Are the Barren: The Kingdom of God Springs Forth from the Empty Womb." *ChrTo* 51, no. 12 (Dec. 1, 2007): 22–28.

M. Therese Lysaught

Information Technology

Information technology comprises the various devices and systems for storing and manipulating digital data: computers, the internet, the world wide web, digital audio and video recording, and so on. As such, it involves technologies of storage and communication that are not unprecedented (from clay tablets to papyrus letters to books) but do have capacities and intensities that set them apart from their antecedents.

The prevalence of information technology in many contemporary cultures (and its increasing prominence around the globe) engages ethical questions in a variety of dimensions. Information technology raises familiar ethical topics in an unfamiliar context, new ethical questions intrinsic to the capacities of digital culture, and ethical questions relative to the costs of digital technology.

Familiar Problems

The ethical status of information technology touches on many familiar ethical problems in a radically different context: sexual desire and its appropriate bounds, control of words, and violence, to name but three. These topics, already subject to controversy in the physical world, take on different contours in digital interactions. The simulated sexual actions of a digital extension of someone's persona (an "avatar" or "toon") would constitute transgressions of biblical injunctions against chastity if committed in a physical environment, but since digital interaction involves no physical contact, no opportunity for procreation, and a significantly different pattern of "knowing" one's partner, the biblical rationale for prohibiting such relations requires new nuances. The global reach and the relative permanence of words transmitted online heighten the dangers associated with control of the tongue (or in this case, "control of the keyboard"). And although biblical restrictions on the use of violence have vivid application in physical environments, they lose much clarity in a digital world in which no physical damage is incurred, no life is lost. And although God's people apparently have always kept records (sometimes contrary to God's express command [see 2 Sam. 24]), the extensive databases of contemporary information technology combine an uncomfortably intrusive degree of personal detail and the risk that these databases may fall into malicious hands or inadvertently be made public. All these scenarios mimic situations in the physical world for which the traditions of Christian ethics have developed strong mandates, but they alter the function of the particular terms in which those mandates have been framed. It would seem extraordinarily odd to most Christians if one were to forbid believers to play chess against one another, but chess represents a highly stylized form of mortal conflict not different in many respects from a game that sets armed toons against one another in arena combat. Thus, ethical evaluation of digital interactions should attend to the specific distinctions between physical and digital environments; digital actions are not simply the same as the physical actions they represent.

Intrinsic Problems

Information technology poses a variety of ethical challenges for which Scripture provides no obvious precedents. For instance, the various opportunities for anonymity and self-representation challenge models of identity that depend on physicality and location. An infamous cartoon claims, "On the Internet, no one can tell you're a dog," but myriad possibilities for self-representation and concealment raise questions concerning the obligation to identify oneself truly online and whether that "true" identity is determined by the accidents of physical appearance or by other criteria. By the same token, digital technologies afford the possibility of withholding the agent's identity; users may sense themselves to have escaped the constraint of having their behaviors associated with their identities (although true online anonymity is more difficult to attain than casual users are apt to assume). A biblical ethic would acknowledge that God, the creator of heaven and earth, cannot be misled by online anonymity, but also that anonymity obscures temporal moral deliberation for both the agent and all other interested parties.

The complications concerning identity online affect deliberations about the reality of digital presence. Some of the earliest judgments concerning information technology stress the alleged danger of supposing that online interactions provide a legitimate substitute for physical interactions. The hasty fear that digital environments may supplant cherished aspects of physical interaction—"replacement panic"—skips past the distinctions between digital and physical presence, to the impoverishment of both modes (neither of which constitutes a functional replacement for the other, each of which offers opportunities alien to the other). On the one hand, the question "Are you Internet friends or real friends?" reveals an anxiety about presence that would have undermined, for example, the apostle Paul's letters as vehicles of his pastoral guidance, or even God's word spoken through the prophets.

On the other hand, the interconnected environment of digital technologies brings a heightened sense of principles that resonate with biblical ethics. For instance, the experience of temporal transience can tempt people to imagine that their impulsive transgressions disappear into an undetectable nothingness comparable to the presumably anonymous actions of digital avatars, whereas Scripture affirms that nothing escapes God's attention and judgment. Likewise, the online proximity of persons from every people, language, tribe, and nation provides a more vivid example of variegated communities than do most physical environments. The "intermingled" online environment provides both an anticipation of the integrated community of the kingdom of God and a vehicle by which one may advance that cause.

Opportunity Costs

A further ethical consideration for information technology involves the hidden costs of vesting an increasing proportion of cultural resources in this exceptionally complex system. A simple webpage may seem quite inexpensive, but it depends for its existence and usefulness on a robust supply of electrical energy, on an energy-intensive server farm to host the page, on intricate networks of digital communication to direct packet traffic to and from the site, and on the rapidly obsolescent computers that design and read the page. Although the Web and other digital technologies certainly contribute to a degree of heightened well-being around the world, all the resources that sustain this single webpage might otherwise be put to uses that offer more immediate benefits to needy people. The choice to adopt and maintain information technologies entails a concomitant choice not to direct the requisite resources to other purposes. More precarious still, the cultural prominence of information technology tends to occlude these costs (either by directing attention away from them or by making them seem "necessary").

Conclusion

A scriptural ethic of information technology needs to balance the various implications of this new environment. Since these capacities are relatively novel, attempts to arrive at a stable balance probably will teeter to unsatisfactory extremes for a numbers of years. A duly humble observer will remember that we have no command of the Lord on these matters. At the same time, these new challenges follow millennia of deliberation on prior technologies for processing information. A parchment codex might have cost more in the fourth century than a simple laptop computer does today, and medieval chroniclers have transmitted the tax records and genealogical data of many people who did not approve or give their permission. By reasoning carefully from clearer, more familiar circumstances, however, Christians will find guidance for theologically commendable uses of digital technology.

See also Dirty Hands; Friendship, Friendship Ethics; Integrity; Pornography; Violence

Bibliography

Adam, A. "Technology and Religion." In *An Introduction to Religious Studies*, ed. Paul Myhre. St. Mary's Press, 2009; Borgman, A. *Power Failure: Christianity in the Culture of Technology*. Brazos, 2003; idem. "This Is Not a Bible: Dispelling the Mystique of Words for the Future of Biblical Interpretation." Pages 3–20 in *New Paradigms for Bible Study: The Bible in the Third Millennium*, ed. R. Fowler et al. T&T Clark, 2004; Weinberger, D. *Small Pieces, Loosely Joined: A Unified Theory of the Web*. Basic Books, 2002.

A. K. M. Adam

Institution(s)

Scripture does not use the word *institutions*. Nevertheless, there are social realities that organize and order community life and practices and that reflect our modern understanding of institutional structures of social order and cooperation. There were and are institutions and institutional practices related to marriage and the family, education, government, economic exchange, and healthcare. These institutions are formed by human communities, often through various authorities, to facilitate human social functioning and to meet both general and specific human needs. Institutions operate through structures, develop a culture of their own, make and enforce rules governing cooperative human behavior, and may take on a life of their own. They enforce their rules in ways that range from fines and incarceration to gossip, social exclusion, and ostracism. Their impact may be for good or evil.

Scripture expresses concern for how the nature, operation, and impact of social structures affect the people within and outside such institutions. Today we have formal institutions such as churches, schools, governments, businesses, and healthcare organizations as well as informal institutions such as marriage and the family. These express social purposes, have some kind of permanence, and make and enforce rules governing cooperative human behavior.

Marriage is one example of an institution warranted by Scripture. God instituted marriage and the family for human good (Gen. 2:18–25), but human sin deeply affected it (Gen. 3). We are fallen people living in a fallen world. Our institutions too are marked by sin and the fall. Marriage is, however, not the only institution found in Scripture or the only one founded in God's will but distorted by human sin. The OT indicates that three forms of human structural relationships were grounded in God's will: the prophet, the priest, and the king were God-appointed (1 Sam. 10:1; Isa. 6:1–13). They gathered institutional power and social organization around their offices.

Even before the development of these particular roles, however, the patriarchs had gathered communities of God's people together and organized and led them. Egyptian pharaohs had institutional power and exercised that power for both good and evil. Joseph and Moses had interacted with that institutional power, served in its context, and finally challenged its oppressive power (Gen. 39–50; Exod. 2; 5–12). Theocracy—the rule of God—was mediated through leaders such as Moses and Joshua bringing the people of God to the promised land and settling there. When the settlement was threatened by both anarchy within and the Philistines without, the people called for the institution of kingship. It was an ambiguous request, marked on the one hand as a rejection of God's rule and by the desire to be like other nations, and on the other hand by God's provision against the Philistine threat (1 Sam. 8–12). And monarchy would be an ambiguous institution in Israel. God allowed and selected the first kings but warned of how such institutions would and did oppress the people (1 Sam. 8:11–18).

Religious institutions, like the political institutions, also had early beginnings. And like the political institutions, they were marked by ambiguity. God created religious institutions associated with the tabernacle and temple as structures for worship, sacrifice, and meeting with God (Exod. 35–47; 1 Kgs. 6–7). God chose the priests, but even religious power led to abuse (1 Sam. 2:12–17).

The prophets sometimes challenged kings, authorities, priests, and merchants with the word of God, reminding them to exercise justice and mercy and rule according to God's will (1 Kgs. 12; 18), but there were false prophets who served the political interests of the king or were paid for saying what someone wanted to hear.

The moral failures of Judah's political, religious, and economic institutions contributed to its defeat and exile. The prophets regarded it as the judgment of God. The exile led to new ways of relating to foreign institutional power. Nehemiah, Esther, Daniel, Shadrach, Meshach, and Abednego worked to fulfill God's will and the good of his people within institutional structures of other nations (Neh. 2; Esther; Dan. 1). They both exercised power and related to authorities for good. Nevertheless, there was also an acknowledgment of the oppressive power of these institutional structures and the brutality of empire.

Jesus met resistance from institutional power throughout his life. From Herod's murderous response to the announcement of his birth to his trial and crucifixion by a Roman procurator, political institutions resisted his work and ministry. From early struggles with priests and with the scribes and Pharisees who had institutionalized power and misused their authority (Mark 11:30; Luke 11:39) to the call for his death, religious institutions too resisted his work. The question of power (*exousia*) was at the heart of the struggle (Matt. 27:62; Mark 15; John 11:47–53).

The founding of the church brought new forms of institutional relationships. The appointment of Matthias as a replacement for Judas Iscariot (Acts 1:15–26) and of deacons to oversee the daily distribution of food among the disciples (Acts 6:1–6) shows how institutional structures began to emerge in the early church. The council of Jerusalem (Acts 15) dealt with what institutional requirements of food and sexual behavior were expected from gentile converts and the extension of early church mission.

Acts describes how the early church leaders dealt with authority and institutional powers in various ways. For example, Peter, in his response to the Jewish council, insisted on obedience to God rather than to human demands (Acts 4:19–20), while Paul, in his appearances before various authorities culminating in his appeal as a Roman citizen for trial before Caesar (Acts 25:11–12), had no qualms about using institutional rights. Paul also, of course, suffered at the hands of authorities (Acts 16:16–40; 18:12–17). Institutions remained ambiguous.

Without denying that ambiguity, Paul and Peter both insisted that Christians should pray for and support human authorities as God-appointed to restrain evil and reinforce good (Rom. 13:1–7; 1 Pet. 2:13–17). There is a struggle between good and evil in this world (Eph. 6:12), and institutions are implicated in that struggle, sometimes on the side of some good to be done or preserved and sometimes on the side of horrific oppression. Institutions are ultimately responsible and answerable to God for their uses of power, for what they do and how they function. In the book of Revelation the brutality of imperial institutions is on display, and resistance is called for in the struggle between God's reign and Satan (Rev. 8–18).

Historically, Christianity has struggled both with its own institutional forms (e.g., denominationalism) and with the power of secular institutions to shape human life. Debate about the exact forms and applications of the church and a stress on the qualities required of leaders is hardly new (1 Tim. 3:2; Titus 1:5, 7). Religiously based and secularly grounded institutions are both responsible to God for how they operate and for the effects they have on human society and individuals. Institutions are necessary, but because we operate in a fallen, sinful world and are fallen human beings, these institutions are marked by moral ambiguity. Intended for good, they will tend to oppress those whom they should serve and to claim ultimate power and authority for themselves rather than God.

Modern moral reflection weighs the nature and function of institutions and the good and evil impact that they have on human well-being. Truth and openness should be the marks and mode of human operations and communities. Institutions inevitably are sinful; some talk of structural sin affecting those who work for and are affected by them. With increasing concern about the social, economic, and environmental impact of institutions, moralists have introduced the notion of "stakeholders." Ecological concerns and economic and political abuse should require that all stakeholders have some say in the community's discernment concerning how institutions operate. They should not simply be controlled by government or left to their own devices or serve only the interests of shareholders and owners. Theologians have stressed the importance of good stewardship in human affairs, in religious, financial, and political organizations. If God is the Creator, then how we use properly what God has given, what ends we seek to achieve and what means we use matters.

Institutions are created by humans in order to facilitate living together. They are expressions of the needs, structure, and values of communities. They organize formally and informally how people live their lives and the common life. And they are ambiguous. Christian communities throughout Scripture attended centrally to God and to God's will for humans when they have dealt with institutions. The church often has played a prophetic role in relation to institutions. In some contexts it has become an established part of national life and fulfills a role within government (e.g., the Lords Spiritual in the House of Lords of the British Parliament, the chaplains of the US Congress, and the role of prayer in Parliament and Congress; broadcasting where religious broadcasting has a privileged role as a requirement; and national events such as coronations, inaugurations, national funerals, and public responses to national tragedies such as 9/11). The danger is that the church becomes indistinguishable from secular authorities and is not free to order itself and follow its God-given tasks or to act as a prophetic voice to society and its institutions. Nonestablished churches may play a role in faith-based initiatives serving the common good. Institutions are ultimately permitted by God for human good and ought to fulfill God's will and purposes.

See also Authority and Power; Business Ethics; Ecological Ethics; Economic Ethics; Government; Political Ethics; Powers and Principalities

Bibliography

Lash, N. *Voices of Authority*. Wipf & Stock, 2005; Scott, W. *Institutions and Organizations: Ideas and Interests*. 3rd ed. Sage Publications, 2008.

E. David Cook

Integrity

The word *integrity* is derived from the Latin *integritas*, meaning "wholeness and completeness, being indivisible and inviolable." It is one of the most important moral qualities of a person's character, particularly in a leader. Persons of integrity do not compromise their own virtue whatever the coercion. Often, breaches of integrity are achieved through some kind of compartmentalization, and in the case of religion by reducing one's faith to certain religious activities, ignoring the fact that faith should encompass all areas of life.

Integrity in Relation to God

In the OT, the concept of integrity is for the most part expressed by the word group *tmm* (concept of perfection). This word group denotes characteristics of unity, wholeness, completeness, blamelessness, purity, sincerity, honesty, and consistency, which reflect authenticity and trustworthiness. Noah is the first person whose moral character is described as both "righteous" (*ṣaddîq*) and "blameless" (*tāmîm*). Job is similarly described, meaning that he is blameless, innocent, and pious (Job 1:1, 8; 2:3, 9). He refused to accept his friends' accusations because he knew that they were false. His heart or conscience is his witness (Job 27:4–6). He insisted that he had never been deceitful, and God is the one who knows his "integrity" (*tûmmâ*) (Job 31:5–6). Eventually, Job's integrity was vindicated (cf. Jas. 5:11).

Another notable example in the OT is the prophet Jeremiah. Jeremiah had made himself the most unwelcome man in Jerusalem by predicting a Babylonian victory. Although he would rather believe that Judah would defeat its enemy, he could not speak otherwise because "there is something like a burning fire shut up in my bones" (Jer. 20:9). He was unlike those false prophets who sought to give the people what they wanted to hear. Another OT prophet, Daniel, is also a man of unimpeachable integrity. Daniel (and his friends) refused to compromise his devotion to the only true God, even to the point of death (Dan. 3:8–30; 6:1–28).

Integrity is not just commitment to achieve one's intention; if it were, the perpetrators of genocide, for example, who are committed to what they are doing, would be persons of integrity. The nature of one's commitments is central to one's integrity. According to the biblical tradition, integrity is a wholehearted commitment to love God and to do his will as expressed in his commandments. Such is also the calling of all Israel (Deut. 18:13). Joshua charged Israel to serve God in "sincerity" (*tāmîm*) and "faithfulness" (*'ĕmet*) (Josh. 24:14). Hence, to have integrity is to walk in the way of perfection (e.g., Pss. 15:2; 119:1; Prov. 11:20), to be entirely faithful to God. Human integrity has its ground in one's loving relationship with God (Deut. 6:4–5), living in his presence, accountable to him. Such a person will act in all areas of life in accordance with this deepest commitment and core motive. Paul, when attacked by his opponents, defended his integrity by appealing to his fear of the Lord as the motive behind all his actions (2 Cor. 5:11).

Integrity in Relation to Neighbors

The wholehearted commitment to love God entails love for all people. Persons of integrity are loyal to their promises and genuinely honest in their dealings with others. They are consistent not only in fulfilling their role entrusted to them by the society but also between their values and conduct. They are whole and trustworthy.

Grounded in the teaching of Jesus, the Epistle of James expounds on the importance of growth in wholeness or perfection in an individual as well as in a community. Hearing God's word without making a corresponding response in action (Jas. 1:22) and claiming to have faith while being without works (of mercy) (Jas. 2:14–25) are symptoms of duplicity, the very opposite of integrity. It is the same as claiming to have love for God while having no love for brothers and sisters (1 John 4:19–20). James calls such people "double-minded" (*dipsychos*) (Jas. 1:8; 4:8), wavering in all decisions in life (Jas. 1:8). James, representing Jesus' teaching in the Sermon on the Mount (Matt. 5:33–37), warns against duplicity of speech: "Let your 'Yes' be yes and your 'No' be no" (Jas. 5:12), not saying one thing yet meaning another. To do otherwise inevitably involves deception of some kind.

Self-deception is not only a symptom of duplicity; it also often makes duplicity possible. Not all "self-deception" is bad or sinful. It becomes a problem when such self-deception originates with evil inclination and becomes part of people's overall belief structure. It is the very character of lies to cover them up with more lies. Self-deception can pollute judgment in all areas of life, corrupting their entire structure of meaning. It will then continue to shape people's motivation for behavior and becomes a component in their habitual patterns of thought and feeling. A form of self-deception can be seen in Jas. 1:23–24, which speaks of people who look at themselves in a mirror and, after going away, immediately forget what they were like. James 1:26 speaks of the same kind of self-deception: those who think that they are religious but lack the kind of expression approved by God. By their false assumption they "deceive their hearts." Such deception is also found in one's pretense to be a friend of God in praying to him, yet in reality being a friend of the world and thus an enemy of God (Jas. 4:4). Such dividedness or "splitting" not only finds its consequence in the individual self, in one's relationship with God, but also is evident in the "splitting" within the Christian community, with members not trusting but instead fighting against one another (Jas. 2:1–16; 4:1–3, 11; 5:9). James also warns against hypocritical judging (Jas. 4:11–12), as did Jesus (Matt. 7:1–5), which eventually destroys trust and splits a community.

People can also collude with one another through self-deception to reinforce gross social and institutional injustice through socialization. Such failure to act persistently on one's core commitments—that is, to endure in faith (Jas. 1:3–4; 5:7–11)—often is a result of lack of wisdom, weakness of will, self-deception, and cowardice, which issue in disintegration, hypocrisy, dishonesty, unreliability, indifference, and impiety. This lack of integrity is caused by people's inability to resolve the conflicts of their own desires.

The Way to Integrity

God is the only one who is fully self-integrated, whose intentions and actions perfectly correspond. God can vow by his own name, showing his promises to humans to be doubly certain (Heb. 6:13–18). Jesus proves himself to be self-integrated as he overcomes temptations in compliance to the will of the Father, with which he fully identified. He acts in a way fully reflecting his sense of who he is, the Father's obedient Son in the power of the Spirit. God not only is perfect but also demands that his people be perfect (Matt. 5:48; cf. Lev. 19:2). God's grace and love are the indispensable integrative power that fulfills and completes a love in human beings (1 John 2:5). God is the one who guarantees that integrity is possible, and that it will finally be fulfilled in the eschaton (Jas. 1:4, 12). Jesus, as the perfecter of faith, will lead believers in this way of perfection and integrity through faith (Heb. 12:2).

The way to integrity involves people being willing to confront themselves, accepting rather than evading their responsibilities. Change is possible when people acknowledge that some past behaviors are wrong or unacceptable. Self-examination may involve repentance, as one stands before God in total transparency, admitting one's sinfulness and duplicity (Jas. 4:7–10). The importance of such self-examination is found also in Paul's teachings on having a clear conscience (2 Cor. 1:12; 1 Tim. 1:5, 19; 3:9).

Self-examination is not just reflecting on ourselves by ourselves; it involves reflecting persistently and openly on ourselves in the light of

Scripture, as the metaphor of the mirror in Jas. 1:22–25 illustrates. Such self-examination should not merely be done individually. The messianic community should also be a community of discernment (Jas. 5:13–17). Believers are to listen to God and his word in humility, listen to themselves and to one another, and act in accordance with the knowledge coming from such listening (Jas. 1:19). The community that accepts this challenge to pursue such commitment will enter into the deep process of integrity to which it is invited.

See also Character; Deception; Dishonesty; Fidelity; Perfection

Bibliography

Bauckham, R. *James: Wisdom of James, Disciple of Jesus the Sage*. NTR. Routledge, 1999; Musschenga, A. "Education for Moral Integrity." *JPE* 35 (2001): 219–35; Schweiker, W. "Consistency and Christian Ethics." *ATR* 90 (2008): 567–74.

Luke Leuk Cheung

Intelligence, Artificial *See* Artificial Intelligence

Intention

Intention names the end, purpose, or goal toward which an agent works in any voluntary action. Since the Scholastic period, intention has been considered, along with the object of an act and its circumstances, to be one of the "fonts of morality"—the three key aspects that constitute a moral act and that should be considered in order to offer an adequate evaluation of a moral act. The intention of the agent must be considered in evaluating the morality of an act, although it must never be considered in isolation from the act itself.

Attending to Scripture

Although Scripture gives little explicit attention to intention, it shows a concern with the interior dispositions of agents in ways that the tradition would come to associate with intention. Throughout Scripture, God not only judges actions but also "tests hearts and minds" (Ps. 7:10).

Several precepts of the Mosaic law explicitly distinguish between wrongful acts that happen accidentally and those done intentionally (Exod. 21:12–14; Num. 15:23–24). With increased purposefulness in a wrongful act comes increased punishment; lack of intentionality likewise decreases punishment. In such passages, the act is primary, but the intentionality (or lack thereof) can increase or mitigate the evil and the agent's accountability for it. Legal, prophetic, and wisdom texts in the Bible repeatedly express concern about the interior dispositions of persons. In particular, the law prohibits the coveting of both wives and property (Deut. 5:21), the prophets call the people to genuine conversion of the heart (Ezek. 11:19) rather than the outward show of sacrifice or worship (Isa. 1:13–15) or minimalist compliance with the law (Amos 8:5–6), and the psalms echo God's desire for pure and humble hearts and spirits (Ps. 51:18–19). This concern with the interior dispositions of the agent is intensified throughout the NT, especially in Jesus' Sermon on the Mount in Matt. 5–7. Jesus forbids not only murder but also anger (5:22), not only adultery but also lust (5:28). Though the acts are still forbidden, evil is located not in the act alone but also in the agent. Moreover, Paul, in Rom. 3:8, expressly condemns those who suggest doing evil so that good might come. This verse often has been held up in the tradition as a rejection of the idea that the intention of a good end might justify an act that is evil in itself. These and other biblical texts set the stage for development around the question of how the intention of the agent, the object of the act, and other circumstances contribute to the identity and moral evaluation of any act.

The Tradition

Augustine's "On Lying" explicitly makes the role of intention a central area of concern in establishing the morality of an act. Augustine defines lying as speaking a falsehood with the intention to deceive. He carefully establishes both of these components of the act: the exterior act of speaking falsehood, and the interior disposition of the will to deceive. Speaking falsehood might be storytelling or making a mistake; it is the intention together with the act itself that fully constitutes the act as a lie.

Drawing from Augustine but going beyond him, Peter Abelard is the first to suggest that the intention of the will is the primary morally relevant fact of an act, over and against performing the act. In his *Ethics*, Abelard considers several cases where an act that appears to be universally forbidden occurs without incurring sin (e.g., a woman forced into sex, a man having sex with a woman whom he mistakenly believes to be his wife). From such cases, Abelard argues that precepts that seem to forbid certain acts (murder, adultery, lying) are better understood to prohibit not the performance of the acts, but specifically the intention to commit the acts. The intention or consent of the will is the source of the evil, not the act itself. Thomas Aquinas insists that both the external act and the end intended by the agent matter to the constitution of the act as to the sort of act it is. Although some think that Aquinas stresses the external act so strongly as to resist inclusion of the agent's intention as more than a significant circumstance, Servais Pinckaers has suggested that this emphasis, which occurs primarily in Aquinas's early work, should be understood as his attempt to correct the overemphasis on intention by Abelard and Lombard. Pinckaers notes that, although the young Aquinas follows Lombard's language as he considers the substance and accidents of the act, he later shifts to the language of form and matter. In other words, for Aquinas, the end intended as the object of the interior act of the will and the external act that is the object of whatever power the will moves to act are related to one another as form to matter, and both are part of the substance of the act (*ST* II-I, q. 18, a. 6). Also note that Aquinas places his analysis of the act within the larger context of the person being ordered to an end in union with God. Crucial to his analysis of human action, therefore, is how the agent intends (or fails to intend) to be moved toward that final end by this act. Thomas never loses sight of the idea that both the intention and the act have roles in constituting the essence of human action.

Contemporary Application

Christians have always been tempted to allow the intention of a good end to trump scriptural prohibitions of certain acts. Can we not consider lying to be a good, not an evil, when it spares feelings or saves lives? Can we not understand killing to be a good, not an evil, when it secures the peace or protects human rights or even ends the suffering of one terminally ill patient? These questions, asked as we consider simple daily decisions as well as larger social questions such as war, abortion, and euthanasia, push us toward ignoring the commands of Scripture in the name of our own good intentions. Although our intentions do matter in establishing the morality of our actions, a good intention cannot make an evil act good, or a forbidden act permissible. Our analysis of action must never attend to the agent's intent to the exclusion of the act, nor to the act apart from the agent's intent. The two must be considered together for a full picture of the moral implications of any act.

See also Accountability; Deontological Theories of Ethics; Desire; Double Effect, Principle of; Moral Agency; Motive(s)

Bibliography

Augustine. "On Lying." Pages 382–425 in *Seventeen Short Treatises of St. Augustine, Bishop of Hippo*, ed. and trans. J. Parker. Oxford University Press, 1982; Pinckaers, S. "A Historical Perspective on Intrinsically Evil Acts." Pages 185–235 in *The Pinckaers Reader: Renewing Thomistic Moral Theology*, ed. J. Berkman and C. Titus. Catholic University of America Press, 2005.

Dana L. Dillon

Interest *See* Loans

Interim Ethic *See* Sermon on the Mount

In-Vitro Fertilization *See* Reproductive Technologies

Isaiah

This book takes its name from Isaiah of Jerusalem, a prophet whose ministry spanned the reigns of four Judean kings in the eighth century BCE. However, portions of the book address a much later and much different context in Israel's history, suggesting that it is a composite work. Chapters 1–39 deal primarily with the events and circumstances of Isaiah's day; because of rampant corruption and social injustice, the prophet announces that divine judgment is imminent, and that it will come at the hands of Assyria, the reigning world power. A dramatic shift occurs in chapters 40–55 ("Second Isaiah"), which proclaim a message of comfort and restoration to a people who have long been exiles in Babylon (597–539 BCE). Although stylistically similar, chapters 56–66 ("Third Isaiah") seem to presuppose yet another context, in which the exiles are back in their homeland but struggling to reestablish themselves as a viable community. Recent scholarship, however, has emphasized not only the diversity of this corpus but also its unity. Indeed, it appears that material spanning some 250 years was intentionally edited and shaped to create a thematic/theological coherence. The current form of the book, thus, has an overarching theme that highlights the drama of God's judgment of Israel for its national sin and the promise of a glorious restoration to follow.

For Isaiah, the moral life is grounded in the character and will of God, who is sovereign over all creation and passionately involved in Israel's life. Because Judah and its leaders are at odds with God, the word of the Lord, through the mouth of the prophet, confronts the wayward people with a life-or-death choice: if they forsake evil and learn to do good, they will enjoy life on the land; if not, devastation will come (1:16–20; cf. 58:1–14).

To discern and articulate God's will, Isaiah draws from Israel's religious heritage, including traditions about Zion that celebrate the supremacy of God and the inviolability of God's chosen city. In

Isaiah's theological ethic God's supremacy relativizes, indeed dwarfs, all other claims to power, so that prideful rebelliousness becomes the cardinal moral offense (2:11–22; 3:16–17). Humble obedience and trust are the virtues that the prophet prizes above all (7:3; 26:3–4; 30:15; 32:17; cf. 57:15; 66:2). This fundamental orientation impacts all spheres of life, even international relations. Hence, with Assyria making its westward move, Isaiah counsels the kings of Judah (Ahab in 8:11–15; Hezekiah in 37:6–7) to trust in God, not in diplomatic relations, to protect Jerusalem (30:1–15). Indeed, Assyria is merely the rod of divine judgment (10:5–19), and Judah must temporarily submit to it. Although the Zion tradition promised that God would always defend Jerusalem from its enemies, Isaiah turns that ideology on its head, arguing that because the city had become morally defiled and unfit for God's presence, God would purify it in judgment to make it habitable once more (4:2–6; 29:1–24).

Of course, obedience to God also has implications for Judah's internal relations. Instead of caring for the poor and vulnerable members of society as Torah required, Isaiah's audience was guilty of oppression and miscarriages of justice (1:16–23; 3:13–15; 5:8–24; 10:1–2; 29:21). Land ownership was a focal issue. Family-based land was a vital source of material support, critical for the living of a good life, and Isaiah bewails the destructive conduct of those who amass property at others' expense (3:14; 5:8). Moreover, he condemns not only the exploitation of the vulnerable but also the habitual drunkenness of the ruling class, which breeds misjudgment (5:11–13, 22–23; 28:1–13). The moral failure has implications for Judah's religious life. Isaiah categorically denounces its worship practices as detestable (1:10–15), because a right relationship with God cannot be cultivated without a right relationship with one's neighbor.

Chapters 40–55 address a broken people on the other side of judgment. This corpus engages ethics less directly, and its moral vision must be discerned in the way the prophetic voice breaks through the despair of the exiles and awakens them to renewed trust. The material continues Isaiah's emphasis on God's sovereign power but declares that it is now redemptively focused on Israel. Hence, the poet employs both hymnic and disputatious forms to make a passionate appeal for the exiles to trust God instead of Babylon (40:12–31). Even Cyrus the Persian, the emancipator who would take down Babylon and release its captives, is called a servant of God (44:28; 45:1). The prophet also draws from exodus and creation traditions to construct vividly the possibility of a new beginning (see Brown). In short, he marshals his theological resources and vast literary skills to inspire faith and move the people to action (their homeward journey).

At the same time, the enigmatic figure of a humble servant who brings forth justice and healing adds an important qualification to the message of deliverance. The "Servant Songs" (42:1–9; 49:1–6; 50:4–11; 52:13–53:12) suggest that justice is established through one who is willing to suffer for others. They also suggest that Israel's release from exile is not just for Israel's sake but has a larger purpose that embraces the nations. This gives meaning to Israel's suffering. It is not a sign of divine abandonment; rather, the servant's suffering was God's surprising way of bringing salvation to all.

Chapters 56–66 reflect the crisis of a people back in Jerusalem struggling to rebuild a city and form a community. And this section of the book also makes some important ethical claims. First, it renews Isaiah's earlier insistence on obedience to Torah that rises above self-serving scrupulosity (58:1–14; 59:1–15). As before, the focus is on proper administration of justice and tending to the needs of the weak. Second, its conception of community is remarkably inclusive, so that even those formerly excluded from the religious community now share in the new life together (56:3–8).

Finally, in spite of the harsh realities of resettlement, the accent is on the gracious promises of God, surely to be fulfilled (see especially chaps. 60–62; 65:17–25; cf. 40:8; 55:11). Eschatological visions occur throughout the book (2:4; 11:6–9; 35:1–10) but are all the more pronounced at its culmination. They present an alternative vision of reality in which God's good purposes—*shalom*, security, fruitfulness, and joy—will prevail over all creation. This hope fuels the moral life. The glorious vision summons the people to a way of living that is commensurate with it and contributes to its realization.

The book ends, however, with a cautionary word of judgment against the rebellious (66:24). Jerusalem, the renewed city, is a wondrous gift from God, but it does not merely descend from heaven. It requires human agents to build it, and that inevitably entails dissension and conflict. Although the book has a decided movement from judgment to hope, the reference to corpses and unquenchable fire stands as an acknowledgment of (and warning against) human strife that continually imperils God's (re)creation.

See also Eschatology and Ethics; Exile; Old Testament Ethics

Bibliography

Barton, J. "Ethics in the Book of Isaiah." Pages 67–77 in vol. 1 of *Writing and Reading the Scroll of Isaiah: Studies of an Interpretive Tradition*, ed. C. Broyles and C. Evans. VTSup 70/1. Brill, 1997; Brown, W. "I Am about to Do a New Thing: Yahweh's Victory Garden in Second Isaiah." Pages 229–69 in *Ethos of the Cosmos: The Genesis of Moral Imagination in the Bible*. Eerdmans, 1999; Brueggemann, W. *Isaiah 40–66*. WestBC. Westminster John Knox, 1998; Childs, B. *Isaiah*. OTL. Westminster John Knox, 2001; Goldingay, J. *Isaiah*. NIBC. Hendrickson, 2001; Mays, J. "Justice: Perspectives from the Prophetic Tradition." *Int* 38 (1983): 5–17; Oswalt, J. "Righteousness in Isaiah: A Study of the Function of Chapters 55–66 in the Present Structure of the Book." Pages 177–91 in vol. 1 of *Writing and Reading the Scroll of Isaiah: Studies of an Interpretive Tradition*, ed. C. Broyles and C. Evans. VTSup 70/1. Brill, 1997.

Eunny P. Lee

J

James

James is widely recognized as a text in which ethical exhortation receives greater prominence than more abstract reflection on doctrinal matters. There is no scholarly consensus as to whether the letter should be seen as deriving from James, the brother of Jesus and leader of the early Jerusalem church, or as a pseudonymous work from the latter part of the first century.

The opening verses introduce the key theme of undivided commitment to God in all circumstances. Such faithful commitment goes hand in hand with a God-given wisdom that is characteristic of life lived in harmony with the requirements of God's order of the universe (1:5–8; 3:13–18).

The demands of God's will for humankind are expressed by a variety of terms, including "the word of truth" (1:18), "the implanted word" (1:21), "the perfect law of liberty" (1:25; 2:12), and "the royal law according to the scripture" (2:8). The use of legal terminology to express God's will indicates a positive appropriation of the Jewish sense of law as expressing God's order. It seems likely, however, that such references are colored by an early Christian perspective influenced by the traditions of the sayings of Jesus, given a number of close parallels between the language and concerns of James and of the sayings of Jesus in the Gospels (e.g., Jas. 1:5 and Matt. 7:7; Luke 11:9; Jas. 1:9–10; 4:10 and Matt. 23:12; Luke 14:11; Jas. 1:17 and Matt. 7:11; Jas. 2:5 and Luke 6:20; Jas. 3:1 and Matt. 12:36–37; Jas. 5:1 and Luke 6:24–25; Jas. 5:2 and Matt. 6:19–20; Jas. 5:12 and Matt. 5:34).

The requirement for unqualified dependence on God embraces all aspects of human life. In three central discursive sections of the text, human attitudes and judgment (2:1–13), actions (2:14–26), and speech (3:1–12) are held up for scrutiny, and real or potential shortcomings in the addressees' conduct are exposed against the standard of faithful commitment to God (2:1, 5–6, 14–17).

The sense of dependence on God is consolidated by a strong conviction of the effectiveness of faithful prayer (1:5–8; 5:13–18), together with the portrayal of God as one whose inherent character is to give (1:5, 17–18). God's benefactions themselves appear to be part of that relationship of committed dependence on the part of believers: the one who doubts or who asks with dubious motives will not receive (1:6–8; 4:3).

A strong element of dualism informs the ethical exhortations of James, typified by the contrast between friendship with the world and friendship with God (4:4); the readers are urged to resist the devil (4:7), and, humbly accepting God's complete sovereignty, they will receive God's reward. An eschatological dimension to such admonitions seems clear (2:5; 5:7–11), but the text's concerns should also be seen as relating to the immediate circumstances of its readers.

In particular, the context of trials or testing of faith is invoked in 1:2–4, 12–15. Such testing may well relate to the adverse socioeconomic situations elicited by the author a number of times in the letter (1:9–11, 27; 2:2–7, 15–16; 5:4). The contrast between the negative portrayal of the rich and the sense of God's favor to the poor and humble is striking. In a world of scarce resources, where a high degree of social and economic control was exercised through the relationship between patron and client, the negative view of the rich may be closely related to the imperative of undivided commitment to God: God, not any agent of the transient, human, earthly order, is the one who gives unstintingly and who should be relied on in all circumstances. Human conduct should involve solidarity with the victims of the oppressive and ungodly structures of the present earthly order (1:27; 2:1–9, 14–17) and a renunciation of its values and status symbols (3:13–18; 4:13–5:6).

The ethical message of James is uncompromising. The faith of the Christian inevitably carries the demand of undivided commitment to God in lives lived in accordance with God's will. The importance of prayer in acknowledging God's sovereignty and provision is highlighted, as is the call to solidarity with those burdened by the oppressive structures of the human social order.

See also Eschatology and Ethics; Generosity; Hospitality; Justice; New Testament Ethics; Orphans; Poverty and Poor; Speech Ethics; Wealth; Widows; Worldliness

Bibliography

Bauckham, R. *James: Wisdom of James, Disciple of Jesus the Sage*. NTR. Routledge, 1999; Hartin, P. *A Spirituality of Perfection: Faith in Action in the Letter of James*. Liturgical Press, 1999; Hutchinson Edgar, D. *Has God Not Chosen the Poor? The Social Setting of the Epistle of James*. JSNTSup 206. Sheffield Academic Press, 2001; Jackson-McCabe, M. *Logos and Law in the Letter of James: The Law of Nature, the Law of Moses, and the Law of Freedom*. NovTSup 100. Brill, 2001; Wachob, W. *The Voice of Jesus in the Social Rhetoric of James*. SNTSMS 106. Cambridge University Press, 2000.

David Hutchinson Edgar

Jealousy and Envy

In common parlance, the words *jealousy* and *envy* often are used interchangeably, though subtle distinctions can exist between them. The word *jealousy*, or *zeal* (Gk. *zēlos*; Lat. *zelosus*), has a potentially positive sense in that it arises from love. One who is jealous is one who loves something or someone and wishes to guard it vigilantly; the focus of jealousy is the object that is loved. The word *envy*, however, comes from the Latin *invidia* ("to look upon"), and more often than not it has a negative connotation (i.e., to look upon with ill will). The focus of envy is the competitor; particularly when a desired object is perceived as being so scarce as to create a zero-sum game, hostility and malice may arise against the rival who appears to stand in one's way. In spite of the etymological differences in these two words, even the ancient texts are unsystematic in distinguishing them, so it is prudent to treat them together.

Attending to Scripture

Although the words *envy* and *jealousy* do not always appear in the biblical narrative, the qualities that they name play an important role. Eve and Adam are tempted to eat the forbidden fruit in hopes that it will make them "like God" in wisdom (Gen. 3:1–7). Their son Cain's decision to murder his brother, Abel, is presented as a passionate response to God's acceptance of Abel's offering and rejection of Cain's (Gen. 4:1–8). Scripture presents these inauspicious beginnings of humankind as being rooted in a human tendency to "look upon" the possessions of rivals with unjust desire. The OT history books are, accordingly, full of deception and bloody strife, both international and intrafamilial, arising from the desire to crush those who obstruct one's aspirations to power or prestige (Sarah and Hagar [Gen. 16; 21]; Joseph and his eleven brothers [Gen. 37]; Saul and David [1 Sam. 18:12]; Absalom and David [2 Sam. 15]).

If the biblical narrative presents envy as one of the main roots of humankind's ongoing downfall, it is therefore unsurprising that Scripture often warns against it (Job 5:2; Prov. 3:31; 23:17). In the wisdom tradition, human envy (*qin'â*) is presented as more destructive than wrath and anger (Prov. 27:4). In the Gospel accounts, envy on the part of the powerful—the feeling of "displeasure and ill will at the superiority of another person"—is cited as one of the main causes of Jesus' humiliating arrest, trial, and death (Hagedorn and Neyrey). Early Christian writers generally presented envy and jealousy (*phthonos* or *zēlos*) as sure signs of godlessness and wickedness (Rom. 1:29; Jas. 3:14–16), and linked them to other antisocial behaviors, including wrath, backbiting, and murder (2 Cor. 12:20; Gal. 5:21). One particular form of envy is greed (or covetousness), which arises with regard to material goods and is a form of idolatry (Col. 3:5).

In contrast, Scripture sometimes represents jealousy as the right of the powerful. The God of Moses commands, "You shall not make for yourself an idol . . . for I the Lord your God am a jealous [*qannā'*] God" (Exod. 20:4–5; Deut. 5:8–9). In his zeal for Israel, God plays the role of Israel's jealous husband, in vivid and sometimes horrifying detail (Hos. 2–3; Jer. 2–3; Ezek. 16). The ancient Hebrews also had special rituals for testing the fidelity of wives whose husbands were overcome by "a spirit of jealousy [*qin'â*]" (Num. 5:11–31). Paul, the apostle to the gentiles, writes, "I am jealous [*zēlō*] for you with a godly jealousy [*zēlos*]; for I betrothed you to one husband, so that to Christ I might present you as a pure virgin" (2 Cor. 11:2). Thus, whereas envy against one's rival is never justifiable and always creates trouble, a certain amount of righteous jealousy of the powerful toward their possessions is presented as helpful to maintaining divine and social order.

The Tradition and Scripture

Early Christian thinkers such as Origen, Clement of Alexandria, and Athanasius were clear in their denial of the possibility of envy in God. God is completely good and perfect, lacking nothing; since envy arises from a perceived lack it is therefore impossible for God (Petterson). More precise distinctions between envy and jealousy were drawn in the Middle Ages. Thomas Aquinas treats the two topics as entirely separable. Envy, he says, "is sorrow for another's good," especially insofar as that good "threatens to be an occasion of harm" to oneself (*ST* II-II, q. 36, a. 1–4). As such, envy usually arises between people in fairly similar situations who find themselves in close competition (the commoner, e.g., does not envy the king, nor vice versa). The envious desire to surpass a rival is a mortal sin because it is contrary to charity—the desire for the neighbor's good.

But jealousy or zeal, Thomas purports, is a passion that can be either righteous or evil. It "arises from the intensity of love [rather than of hatred]," and "an intense love seeks to remove everything that opposes it" (*ST* I-II, q. 28, a. 4). With regard to jealousy, therefore, its rightness or wrongness is determined by its subject and object. The zeal that arises from a vicious person's disordered love (such as envy or concupiscence) is problematic, but a virtuous person can be zealous for something truly good, such as God or friendship. Unlike envy, jealousy does not necessarily entail a lack of something and a concomitant desire to wrest that thing away from someone else. On the contrary, jealousy assumes that one already (rightly) possesses some good and refers to an attitude of loving vigilance toward it.

Part of the reason these terms are often closely associated seems to be the fact that they sit on the same fine line between virtue and vice, between the possibility of justification and the dangers of inordinate self-love. The act of looking upon something with a desire to grasp it for oneself is obviously related to a host of sins, including covetousness, ingratitude, immoderate love, idolatry, and pride. But envy does not necessarily entail the desire to take a good away from someone else (one might envy a friend's having a spouse and children, even if one does not desire those particular children or spouse). Likewise, even when jealousy may be justified (as in the case of one's property or family), it often fosters destructive behavior rather than acts of kindness and mercy.

Contemporary Application

In psychology, both jealousy and envy can be broadly characterized in terms of threats to self-esteem, although scientists draw distinctions as well. Envy might be considered a primal urge or emotion that "occurs when a desired advantage enjoyed by another person or group of persons causes a person to feel a painful blend of inferiority, hostility, and resentment" (Smith and Kim 60). Envy's "more sophisticated" or "domesticated" cousin, jealousy, builds on this primal emotion by adding some degree of rational valuation or justification (Burke).

Experience demonstrates that jealousy and envy, whether oriented toward money or material property, prestige or honor, or a spouse or lover, have similarly unedifying tendencies. In the long history of humankind, zealous desire for wealth or power has inspired theft and colonialism; zealous love of country or religion has justified xenophobia and genocide; and zealous demands for loyalty (e.g., of a spouse) or honor (e.g., of manhood) have sanctioned countless acts of unspeakable violence. Inherent in envy is an underlying posture of self-centeredness that regards one's own good as being of supreme importance. Although jealousy can be intellectually justifiable when directed toward something greater than or outside oneself (such as God or country), more often than not it leads to the overwhelmingly negative effects of rivalry, hostility, bitterness, anxiety, resentment, abuse, and intolerance. Christians' time therefore is better spent in cultivating humility than in justifying jealousy. The antidote to these negative emotions is found in love (1 Cor. 13:4) and fear of God (Exod. 18:21).

See also Seven Deadly Sins

Bibliography

Burke, N. "On the Domestication of Envy." *Psychoanalytic Psychology* 17 (2000): 497–511; Hagedorn, A., and J. Neyrey. " 'It Was out of Envy That They Handed Jesus Over' (Mark 15:10): The Anatomy of Envy and the Gospel of Mark." *JSNT* 69 (1998): 15–56; Petterson, A. "A Good Being Would Envy None Life: Athanasius on the Goodness of God." *ThTo* 55 (1998): 59–68; Smith, R., and S. Kim. "Comprehending Envy." *Psychological Bulletin* 133 (2007): 46–64.

Kathryn D. Blanchard

Jeremiah

The book of Jeremiah presents poetic oracles, sermons, and discourses in Deuteronomistic style, and narrative material from the last days of Judah and Jerusalem before the final assault of the Babylonians in 587 BCE. Chapters 1–25 contain oracles of judgment and doom, arranged in thematic collections, introduced by prose sermons (Stulman), and ending with a prose oracle of judgment against the whole world. Chapters 26–45 consist primarily of prose narratives that illustrate the kings' and the people's lack of reception of the prophetic warnings and its consequence, the fall of Jerusalem. Chapters 46–51 present oracles against the nations that surround Judah; chapter 52 repeats the narrative of the fall of Jerusalem, 2 Kgs. 24–25. Two poetic collections deserve special interest, the so-called Confessions of Jeremiah (11:18–12:6; 15:10–21; 17:14–18; 18:18–23; 20:7–18) and Book of Consolation (chaps. 30–31).

Jeremiah traditionally is dated to the late monarchic and early exilic periods. The prophet is believed to have received his calling in 627 BCE (1:5–19); his death is untold in the biblical text. The dating and authorship are disputed in recent scholarship, since a valid distribution of authentic and redactional layers is considered to be uncertain at best. The differences between the Hebrew (MT) and the Greek (LXX) versions also warrant that Jeremiah be read on the background of and as a witness to an innertextual theological discussion that ran for at least four centuries after the time of the prophet.

The basic message of Jeremiah is that the people have abandoned the covenantal relationship with Yahweh (in English Bibles, "the LORD"), their only God, and have followed foreign gods. Therefore, God will send foreign armies to wage war against them. By and large, as opposed to Amos, for example, social, cultic, or moral conduct is not the primary concern in Jeremiah. Ethical questions are subsumed under the covenantal headline, ethical or moral transgressions being viewed as consequences of apostasy.

Our primary direct source to ethics in Jeremiah is the so-called Temple Sermon in Jer. 7. The prophet urges the people to amend their ways and their doings (7:3), summed up in acting justly one with another; not oppressing the alien, the orphan, and the widow; not shedding innocent blood in this place (i.e., the temple/the land); and not following other gods (7:5–6). These recommendations represent the basic Deuteronomic ethos of protecting vulnerable social groups in society, so closely contingent with common ancient Near Eastern law. As examples of the people's transgressions, the prophet uses a short version of the Decalogue (cf. Deut. 5). He accuses the people of stealing, murdering, committing adultery, swearing falsely, making offerings to Baal, and going after other gods, and then believing that their trust in cultic observance will save them nevertheless (7:9–10). True observance of the law is manifested in keeping both the religious and the ethical commandments.

Accusations of ethical misdemeanors (e.g., greed for unjust gain [8:10]) are raised against the ruling classes, most of all the kings. In chapter 22, a collection of oracles about the monarchy, King Jehoiakim is accused of building his house by unrighteousness and injustice, making his neighbor work for nothing, and thus transgressing his social responsibility. Moreover, his house is built with excessive luxury, as a spacious house with paneling in painted cedar, in order to show off royal opulence. By contrast, his father, King Josiah, is touted as an example of good governance. He lived more modestly, and he implemented justice and righteousness and took care of the cause of the poor and needy, whereas Jehoiakim's "eyes and heart are only on dishonest gain, for shedding innocent blood, and for practicing oppression and violence" (22:17). Thus, the ethical demands made of a ruler in Jeremiah are in accordance with the Deuteronomistic ideal, which puts limitations on royal authority and admonishes the king not to acquire several wives or silver and gold in great quantity, in order to keep his heart with the Lord, "neither exalting himself above other members of the community nor turning aside from the commandment" (Deut. 17:20).

All in all, modesty seems to be an ideal in Jeremiah, and drunkenness, for example, being seen as a disgraceful state that makes the offender vulnerable to punishment, a potent display of divine rage (Jer. 25:15–29).

In the late oracle Jer. 31:31–34, the Lord promises that some day in the future he will make a new covenant with the house of Israel and the house of Judah: "I will put my law within them, and I will write it on their hearts; and I will be their God, and they shall be my people." The new covenant is aimed at creating a relationship between God and his people that is not subject to the uncertainties and damage afforded by the human propensity to sin. The knowledge of the Lord, internalized in the people, will lead to a life of justice and righteousness. In the NT, this new covenant is understood as fulfilled in the Lord's Supper (e.g., 1 Cor. 11:25), and the idiom has named the two biblical collections, the Old and New Testaments (Gk. *diathēkē*; Lat. *testamentum*).

From a modern perspective, Jeremiah can be an unpleasant book to read, given its violent and sexually offensive language. The relationship between God and God's people often is pictured in metaphors of war, cruelty, environmental catastrophes, and matrimonial violence. Israel, which once was God's wife, is portrayed as a wild ass in heat and as a whore, whose master has every right to punish her (chap. 2). For this reason, criticism is raised from both feminist and ideological-critical exegetes against some parts of the message of Jeremiah. Only in a few chapters, primarily in the Book of Consolation, do we find testimony of a forgiving God who cares for the exiled people. In the end, however, the powerful image of God crying like a mother for daughter Zion (8:18–22) adds a nuance of feminine empathy to the image of the OT God as an angry sovereign.

See also Covenant; Exile; Idolatry; Land; Old Testament Ethics

Bibliography
Stulman, L. *Jeremiah*. AOTC. Abingdon, 2005.

Else K. Holt

Job

The question of ethics is implied at the outset of the book of Job as the narrator speaks of Job's character: he is a man who is "blameless and upright" and who "fears God and turns away from evil" (1:1, 8; 2:3). This fourfold affirmation suggests that Job was the quintessential faithful and ethical person—personally (blameless) and socially (just), religiously (fearer of God) and morally (one who avoided wrong). Despite Job's meticulous actions to ensure that nothing ever goes wrong (1:5), however, a capricious agreement in heaven leads to a series of misfortunes that befall him and his family (1:6–2:9). In particular, he is afflicted "with loathsome sores . . . from the sole of his foot to the crown of his head" (2:7), a poignant spectacle because that precise affliction is found elsewhere only as a curse for those who violate the covenant (Deut. 28:35). The rest of the book then debates two key issues: the relevance of the doctrine of retribution in this case, and the proper response in the face of such suffering.

Job's afflictions lead his friends to suspect that something must be amiss in his conduct, even if they do not know what that might be. Their best response is that he should not blame God but rather look deeper within himself, and even if he fails to discover the problem, he should turn to God anyway in praise and in hope of divine forgiveness and restoration. It is the traditional response that we find already in the various "exemplary sufferer" texts from elsewhere in the ancient Near East. The premise is that it is impossible that anyone be without sin, so in the face of unexplained suffering, one should simply count on divine mercy (cf. 1 John 1:8–9). One must look beyond oneself, beyond any efforts to prove one's faithfulness and just conduct, and count instead on God's faithfulness and just conduct.

The reader knows from the prologue, though, that Job is suffering not because of any wrong that he has committed. Job himself, while not denying the possibility that he might have erred, is unwilling to simply accept the premise of traditional doctrine. He sees his friends not as comforters but as tormentors. In his rebuke of them he offers a profound ethic of friendship: "To one who is discouraged, steadfast love comes from one's friends, even if that one may have abandoned the fear of Shaddai" (6:14 [all translations mine]). For Job, God has seemed like an enemy. Whatever "steadfast love" (the biblical term for unwavering loyalty) Job will experience now, therefore, will come not from the deity directly; it will have to come from friends, if it comes at all. In times of deep despair, when God seems utterly inimical, when faith seems impossible, true friendship that does not depend on one's confessional stance, friendship that does not depend on one's theology, may be the very manifestation of grace. In Job's view, though, the friends are not true and cannot be trusted: "Surely you are not [confounded? trustworthy?], for you see trauma and you feared" (6:21).

The allusion to fear harks back to the "fear" in 6:14, where Job speaks of a friendship that manifests steadfast love to one who is desperate, even if that one should forsake "the fear of Shaddai." Job is suggesting that his friends are the ones who fear, not in the sense of being pious, but in the sense of being timid. They fear simply because they have seen Job's trauma, meaning not just his physical condition, but, even more, his apparent abandonment of piety. They fear the blatant theological contradiction that Job embodies in his broken self. Job has portrayed himself as a theological "whistleblower," who is not afraid to face the truth and "tell it like it is," whatever the consequences of doing so (6:10). In that sense, he is not a fearer, and perhaps because of that the friends might have regarded him as impious, one who does not fear. To Job, however, people who are afraid of confronting the tough, faith-shattering questions are not fearers of God. Rather, they are simply fearers, theological cowards, for they fear the truth.

There are profound theoethical reflections like this scattered throughout the book. The most important passage in this regard, though, is Job's oath of innocence in chap. 31, where he goes through a detailed list of crimes that may be committed by anyone, and he denies them all. Yet what is important is not the list itself, what one should or should not do, but how Job goes about his ethical reflection.

He begins with a series of possible sexual offenses, beginning with lust. He claims that he not only has been proper in his conduct, but he even has covenanted with his eyes not to desire (31:1). He speaks thus not only of guilt that is visible, exterior; he speaks rather of interiority (cf. Matt. 5:27–28). Importantly, the basis of such a profound commitment is theological: "What is the portion of God above? What is the lot of Shaddai on high?" (31:2). That is, God has assigned each individual a portion, an area of responsibility (so the Hebrew term implies), and one must honor that assignment.

What Job sets forth in 31:1–12 is his defense of his integrity. He is, therefore, unwittingly corroborating the narrator's and God's judgment that he is blameless. Yet he is also "just"—that is, proper as regards his treatment of others (31:13–18). He speaks of not rejecting the just cause of his male or female servants when they bring a complaint, and he makes it clear that his is a theological ethic: "How shall I act, since God will arise; since God calls one into account, how shall I answer Him?" (31:14). It is an ethic grounded in creation theology: "Surely in the belly the Creator of me created them [Job's servants], and He has formed us in the womb as one" (31:15). What this means, then, is that we must treat others justly out of respect for God's creation, since God is the Creator of all people, regardless of their class or stature. All are created in "the belly," which refers not just to the belly of a human being, but to the realm of God's cosmic rule (see Ps. 139:13, 15).

Job asserts that he has been just to the needy and the defenseless. His words in 31:16–17 are choked with emotion: "[I'll be damned] if I have turned away from the desires of the weak, extinguished the longings of the widow, eaten my morsels by myself, while the fatherless did not partake of it!" In the next verse he states, "For from my youth He has reared me like a father; so from the womb of my mother I will guide her [the widow]." In Job's appeal to creation a few verses earlier, he argues that he as a master treats his slaves respectfully because God is the Creator of them all "in the belly." Now Job moves from birth to parental nurture. He does not treat others unjustly, because God is the parent of all. Indeed, because God is father, Job has been father to the fatherless, and because God is mother, Job has been a mother, a guide to those who need guidance.

The book of Job recognizes as well that God is utterly transcendent and mysterious, and that the divine will may be unknowable. Yet, if that is the case, does human conduct, whether good or bad, matter at all? Does ethics matter if God is unknowable and God's will unknown? Job poses the question crudely, asking whether sinful conduct has negative consequences for God: "If I have sinned, what can I do to you, O guardian of humanity?" (7:20). Eliphaz later reframes the question to make an opposite point, asking how Job's good conduct might have a positive impact on God: "Is it a pleasure to Shaddai that you are righteous, or is it a benefit that your ways are blameless?" (22:3). Elihu deduces, however, as if responding to both formulations, that Job was wondering whether there is any use *for humans* to be in God's favor (34:9). These are questions of ethics when God is silent and hidden in the face of human suffering, and Elihu's own proffer is theologically profound and ethically principled:

> If you sin, how do you affect Him?
> If your transgressions are many, what do you
> do to Him?
> If you are righteous, what do you give Him?
> Or what does He receive from your hand?
> Your wickedness is for people like yourself,
> So your righteousness is for human beings. (35:6–8)

To Elihu, ethics has consequences not for oneself, but for others in the human race. Just as one's wickedness affects others, so too one's righteousness affects others. Thus, Elihu advocates an ethic that is not self-interested: righteous conduct is not for one's own benefit, nor is it even for God's sake. Rather, one acts ethically simply for the common good.

See also Creation Ethics; Justice, Retributive; Old Testament Ethics; Suffering; Theodicy

Choon-Leong Seow

Joel

The short but complex book associated with the prophet Joel has generated much scholarly discussion on a variety of issues, such as the date of the book, the nature of the locust invasion (real or symbolic), the unity of the book, and the relevance of its message. Particularly challenging is the prophet's insistence on judgment and punishment without ever specifying the transgression of the people. The placement of the book between Hosea and Amos may be due more to its thematic affinity than chronological proximity. In the absence of specific information, it is likely that the parameters for the date of the book lie somewhere between the sixth and fourth centuries BCE. The two-part division in the book (1:1–2:27; 2:28–3:21), each part with a contrasting message, tone, or mood, need not entail different authorship. The first part may be seen as relating to a crisis and resolution as experienced by the prophet's community, while the remainder of the book may be seen as presenting the prophet's broader vision for the future.

From an ethical perspective, three themes deserve mention. First, Joel sees a close connection between people's lives and the environment. When nature/land is affected, people's lives are affected, and the reverse would be true as well. The root cause for this is the lack of proper relationship to God. The assurance of new life in terms of economic renewal (2:18–27) is the result of Yahweh's response to the crisis. Second, in the passage on the outpouring of Spirit, Joel offers a vision that is barrier-breaking. The promise of the prophet is for the empowering of "all flesh" (2:28). By further specifying the recipients—sons and daughters, old and young, male and female servants—the prophet reinforces the idea that the outpouring of the Spirit knows no discrimination based on sex, age, or class. Third, Joel goes on to say that the Spirit is given for the purpose of prophesying and receiving dreams and visions. The recipients of the Spirit will be a nation of prophets. The use of the terms *dreams* and *visions* shifts the focus to something that is essential to prophecy. Prophecy often is understood merely as social critique or ethical urging. Joel goes one step beyond in calling for a broader vision. In its fundamental sense, prophecy is the ability to see the invisible—an alternative vision. The prophet Joel's vision is barrier-breaking as it seeks to redefine social perceptions, attitudes, and structures, thereby paving the way for a new ethic.

See also Ecological Ethics; Egalitarianism; Judgment; Justice, Retributive; Old Testament Ethics; Reward and Retribution

Bibliography

Barton, J. *Joel and Obadiah*. OTL. Westminster John Knox, 2001; Birch, B. *Hosea, Joel, and Amos*. WestBC. Westminster John Knox, 1997; Crenshaw, J. *Joel*. AB 24C. Doubleday, 1995; Mason, R. *Zephaniah, Habakkuk, Joel*. OTG. JSOT Press, 1994; Wolff, H. *Joel and Amos*. Trans. W. Janzen, S. McBride, and C. Muenchow. Hermeneia. Fortress, 1977.

D. N. Premnath

John

The identity of the author of the Fourth Gospel remains obscure. An author appears in the text as the "disciple" (21:24), but little can be verified about this witness. The dominant view among NT scholars is that John is the product of communal development of tradition, whoever its final redactor might have been.

Rather than seeing John's Gospel as a source for ethics, many have accused John of loving Christians and hating Jews. John is charged with characterizing Jews as children of the devil and as unbelievers (8:44–45). Granted, in the history of interpretation John has been shamefully used against Jewish people. But is such usage of John appropriate? Nowhere does John mention hating Jews. Hatred is expressed only the other way around: the world hates Jesus and his followers. Furthermore, when Jesus tells some Jews that they are from their father the devil, he does not characterize Judaism. Specific Jewish characters are not the Jewish people; rather, they are some Jews who are actually identified earlier as believers (8:31). This text is quite important for Johannine ethics because, for John, what one is and does derives from a relationship with a parent: either the devil or God. The text characterizes behavior, not Jews or "the Jewish people." Furthermore, against the notion that John is anti-Jewish, Jesus is called "king of the Jews" (19:19), and he dies for the nation in order to gather dispersed Israelites (11:51–52).

One approach to biblical ethics focuses on moral law. For John, law should not be broken (7:23). However, law alone is insufficient. It must be interpreted and practiced appropriately, and it is subject to misuse (19:7). Many interpreters take Jesus' reference to "your law" in 8:17; 10:34 as distancing Jesus from the Jewish law. More likely, just as Moses appeals to Israelites on the basis of the "Lord your God" (e.g., Deut. 4:10), Jesus appeals to his interlocutors on the basis of their fundamental obligation to their own law. But in such a case the law reveals deficiencies more than produces rectitude. Furthermore, grace and truth go beyond law (1:17). The fact that the story of the woman caught in adultery (7:51–8:11) does not appear in the earliest and best manuscripts has not kept it from being used as a basis for qualifying law with mercy (see 7:23).

For many interpreters, John is more attuned with grounding living in principles, particularly belief, truth, and love. In fact, love becomes a "new commandment" from Jesus (13:34). But in light of other metaphors (shepherd and sheep, vine and branches), belief, truth, and love hardly remain "principles"; rather, they point to believing, truth, and love as relationships.

Emulating characters is difficult in John in that the characters frequently are ambiguous (Nicodemus affirms Jesus' identity and signs but does not understand his teaching or receive his testimony [3:1–14]), faulty (a man whom Jesus heals gives him away [5:15]), unable to understand (Peter refuses to let Jesus wash his feet [13:8–10]), and disloyal (Peter denies Jesus [18:25–27]). According to many translations, however, in washing his disciples' feet Jesus gives an "example" (*hypodeigma* [13:15]) for how they should live. Although *hypodeigma* frequently means "example," here it evokes considerations surpassing an example to be imitated. The foot-washing is to be understood only in the future (Jesus' resurrection?). A lack of understanding is rarely problematic for imitation. Moreover, the anticipated outcome is mutuality, not one-way imitation. Against a Jewish background, *hypodeigma* may be rendered "revelatory pattern."

John provides bases for critiquing social norms. Jesus' interaction with a Samaritan woman contravenes norms of gender and ethnicity (John 4:1–42). Sabbath controversies likewise imply critiques of norms. Jesus rejects the marginalization of a man born blind as a social anomaly ("sin" [9:1–3]). John also undermines imperialism. At Jesus' trial Pilate asks a basic Johannine question: "Where are you from?" (19:9). Given the thematic development of Jesus' origin, his response subordinates imperial power to God.

John's portrayal of reality is heavily symbolic. Reality is viewed in terms of sharp oppositions: light/darkness, above/below, truth/falsehood, eternal life/death. On the negative side, visual, spatial, and temporal dimensions of reality imply complicity in evil: "And this is the judgment, that the light has come into the world, and people loved darkness rather than light because their deeds were evil" (3:19). Human behavior is influenced by relationships with such dimensions of reality.

The positive axis of these oppositions corresponds to a relationship with God in which God is the source, motivation, and empowerment for ethics: "But those who do what is true come to the light, so that it may be clearly seen that their deeds have been done in God" (3:21). When people ask, "What must we do to perform the works of God?" (6:28), Jesus presents himself as the middle term through which human beings live in a relationship with God.

One purpose of John is to engender an encounter with Jesus (20:31). Ethics as the fruit of a relationship with Jesus and with God is inseparable from this encounter. Repeatedly, this relationship is described as "following," but other metaphors reflect encounters with Jesus and living in a mutuality with him. The good shepherd knows his own, and his own know him (10:14). Jesus is the vine; his disciples are the branches (15:5). He abides in them and they in him, and this relationship bears fruit (15:4).

See also Anti-Semitism; Love, Love Command; New Testament Ethics

Bibliography

Carter, W. *John: Storyteller, Interpreter, Evangelist*. Hendrickson, 2006; Hays, R. *The Moral Vision of the New Testament: Community, Cross, and New Creation: A Contemporary Introduction to New Testament Ethics*. HarperSanFrancisco, 1996; Matera, F. *New Testament Ethics: The Legacies of Jesus and Paul*. Westminster John Knox, 1996; Rensberger, D. *Johannine Faith and Liberating Community*. Westminster, 1988; Schneiders, S. *Written That You May Believe: Encountering Jesus in the Fourth Gospel*. Crossroad, 2003; Thompson, M. *The God of the Gospel of John*. Eerdmans, 2001.

Robert L. Brawley

1–3 John

The Johannine Epistles proclaim the person and work of Jesus Christ and the relationship of the reader to him and to the Father. God is both light and love, and God's love is demonstrated through Jesus' sacrifice, which forgives sins (1 John 4:7–11). This sacrifice is the means by which believers live in love, truth, and purity with God and one another. God's love enables those who immerse their lives in God to resist sin and to be like God in character during this life (1 John 3:9). In addition, remaining within the sphere of God's love allows believers to live without fear of death and final judgment (1 John 4:17–18). All three of the epistles emphasize the importance of walking in the truth of one's relationship with Christ (1 John 3:18; 2 John 4; 3 John 4).

These epistles exhort readers to live ethically because of their relationship with God. The foremost aim of believers is to live a life that can be described as "walking with God." In 1 John, this life is made available through the atoning sacrifice of Jesus Christ (2:2), his advocacy for those who sin, including both believers and the whole world (2:2), and by the confession of sin (1:9). The same sacrificial blood that allows believers to walk with God also enables the believer to live in right relationship with others (1:7). It is the believers' relationship with Jesus and through Jesus with the Father that enables them to live in justice, love, truth, and purity (significant themes in the Johannine Epistles). Jesus becomes the source for loving God and loving fellow believers.

Those who want to know if they are living a life that is immersed in God should look to their own actions (1 John 3:14, 18). Love of God is evidenced through obedience rather than solely by verbal affirmation (1 John 2:3). Believers are to obey the "word of God," understood as the command to love God and other believers (1 John 4:21) as well as the instruction to follow the exemplary way of Jesus' sacrifice (1 John 2:6; 3:16). Believers demonstrate their love of God by obeying God's command to love their fellow believers. This is demonstrated in hospitality (2 John 10; 3 John 6) and by the sacrifice of one's life on behalf of others, if needed (1 John 3:16). Conversely, believers demonstrate their true allegiances, with all that is apart from God ("the world"), when they engage in hateful behavior toward others.

Speech is also a significant ethical topic of these epistles. In 1 John a contrast is established between those who make false claims about their relationship with God and the failure to live by the truth, and 2 John is concerned about those who deceive the church (v. 7). The truth of statements is determined by the lifestyle of the speaker (1 John 1:6) and by the assertions that the speaker makes about Jesus (1 John 2:22–23), particularly Jesus' incarnation and his relationship to the Father.

In 1 John there are abundant contrasts between love and hate, light and darkness, truth and lying. In a similar vein, 1 John indicates that those who confess their sins are forgiven and cleansed by God (1:8) and also claims that those who know God do not sin (2:1; 3:6, 9). This apparent contradiction has been the source for significant discussions about whether believers sin. Catholic tradition and many Protestant traditions assert that believers attain perfection either at death or upon entrance into heaven. This understanding attends well to the act of confession on the part of believers but does not easily explain the meaning of 1 John 3:6–9, with its emphasis on the sinless believer. The Wesleyan tradition claims that it is possible for believers to reach perfection in this life by being completely immersed in God's love and glory. This understanding attends well to 1 John 3:6–9 but has to assert that the confession referred to in 1 John 1:8 happens at conversion. The seeming contradiction contrasts the hope that believers will abide in God to such an extent in this life that they will not sin with the reminder that Jesus' sacrifice and advocacy are available for believers also if they have need.

The Johannine Epistles call believers to right relationship with God and others through the work of Jesus. This includes loving others, speaking truth and resisting deceit, imitating Jesus, practicing hospitality, and avoiding all that is counter to God. In the mingling of love, truth, and obedience comes the assurance of relationship with God as God's children.

See also Deception; Hospitality; Love, Love Command; New Testament Ethics; Perfection; Sanctification; Truthfulness, Truth-Telling; Wesleyan Ethics; World

Bibliography

Smalley, S. *1, 2, 3 John*. WBC 51. Word, 2007; Wesley, J. "The Great Privilege of Those That Are Born of God." Pages 431–43 in *The Works of John Wesley: Sermons*, ed. A. Outler. Abingdon, 1984.

Ruth Anne Reese

Jonah

Commanded by God to proclaim divine judgment to the Assyrian city Nineveh, Jonah refuses. He flees by ship, but he is jettisoned by its sailors when they learn that he is the cause of the storm that is threatening them. Rescued when swallowed by a large fish, Jonah prays for deliverance and is deposited on dry ground. God reissues the Nineveh assignment, and Jonah obeys. His words are few but effective. The city turns from its evil ways, and the destruction threatened does not happen. The book ends inconclusively with Jonah and God discussing the nature of mercy.

The most pressing ethical questions concern relations with opponents: God with sinners (here, Ninevites and Jonah); Jews (here, Jonah) with oppressors.

The book makes clear that God threatens the Ninevites due to their (unspecified) evil. Clearer still, God responds to Ninevite repentance and defers punishment. For the ancients, God serves as explanatory factor for events poorly understood. Here, punishment is threatened, mercy shown.

Commentators vary widely about Jonah's feelings toward those to whom he preaches. Granting that he declined his assignment at first, there is no suggestion that his eventual preaching was grudging or resentful. He preaches five Hebrew words: laconic but sufficient. We are not told Jonah's response when Nineveh responded to his preaching. Any certitude that Jonah wished ill to Israel's enemy is misplaced until chap. 4. With preaching and repentance accomplished, Jonah becomes displeased, though Hebrew syntax leaves the object of his anger ambiguous. He complains to God about divine graciousness, providing it as the reason for his initial flight. Jonah takes shelter outside Nineveh, in a hut, shaded by a vine. But when a worm eats the vine and the sun beats down on Jonah, he prays in anger again. God speaks with him, asking a question, offering an analogy. God probes by analogy the nature of divine mercy, asking rather than telling Jonah how mercy may be relevant. The story ends with God's question to Jonah, whose nonresponse prompts the reader to ponder why God might show concern. Scholars confirm that the story is about compassion without agreeing on the relevance of what God has said.

Many (more Christians than Jews) hold that the book's point is that Jews ought to be more open to gentiles. But others have recently argued that the book, written plausibly after the destruction of the city of Nineveh (612 BCE), might reflect worry by the citizens of postexilic Jerusalem, who knew that their own city, like Nineveh, had been both rebuked for its sins and reprieved by God. If Nineveh could collapse even after being spared, might the same fate be in store for Jerusalem? How could they avoid a fate that might be deserved but was dreaded? How can Jerusalem's citizens learn God's ways, even if all they have are clueless prophets?

Finally, with so many questions open in a book that seems at first glance simple, readers may recognize that their interpretive choices are ethically self-diagnostic. If Jonah emerges as a disobedient cynic, grudging mercy, sulking over God's goodness, that suggests what a reader wants to see. If the prophetic character is constructed more respectfully, as someone caught amid poor choices and hoping to make the best of what falls his way while remaining in prayerful dialogue with God, that is more promising.

See also Old Testament Ethics; Repentance

Bibliography

Green, B. *Jonah's Journeys*. Liturgical Press, 2005; Sasson, J. *Jonah*. AB 24B. Doubleday, 1990.

Barbara Green

Joshua

Few biblical books present readers with challenges as varied and vexing as does the book of Joshua. The overall structure seems simple enough: a theological prologue (1:1–18); an account of Israel's conquest of the land (2:1–12:24); an overview of the allotment, delineation, and occupation of tribal territories (13:1–21:45); and a closing collection of miscellaneous materials (22:1–24:33). The content of the book, however, raises multiple perspectives on what happened and how the events are to be understood. Chief among these is the clash between materials that present Israel's occupation as a conquest of the entire land through victories over helpless Canaanites (e.g., 10:28–12:24; 21:43–45), and others that describe vast tracts of land outside Israel's possession and a more robust resistance from the indigenous peoples (e.g., 13:2–6; 17:14–18; 19:47–48).

The book's disparate perspectives are the result of a long and complex process of composition that was not completed probably until Israel's return from exile in Babylon. Joshua, in short, bears the traces of Israel's theological reflection on its traditions of violent origins and of the nation's thinking through and recasting the traditions in light of its experience with God. Remarkably, conflicting perspectives and memories have not been harmonized but rather have been allowed to stand in tension with each other in the canonical text.

Theological and Moral Tensions

Joshua presents Israel's occupation of Canaan as a campaign of invasion, conquest, and extermination initiated by God and prosecuted in obedience to divine commandments. The Lord is prominent in the book as the divine warrior, one of the most ancient and ubiquitous images of God in the OT. In this role, the Lord confirms his faithfulness and demonstrates his power to fulfill his promises to Israel's ancestors. The Lord's victories over the opposing forces give him claim to the land by right of conquest. This claim in turn establishes the foundation for the affirmation that the Lord gives the land to Israel and determines what areas each of its tribes and clans will settle. For its part, Israel achieves success as it responds to God's initiative, acts in unity with God and within itself, and strictly observes the words of Moses. The conquest of the land, therefore, combines militant triumphalism with doxology, particularly in the Deuteronomistic speeches that open the book (1:1–18) and the accounts of victories over cities and kings (6:1–27; 8:1–29; 10:6–12:24).

Other texts, however, display uneasiness with the ostensive triumphalism of the conquest narrative and subtly undercut its claims. Three anecdotes precede each of the first three battle accounts at Jericho, Ai, and Gibeon (2:1–24; 7:1–26; 9:1–27). The three stories follow a parallel structure that centers thematically on exposing what is hidden. The first and third present encounters with indigenous peoples who praise Israel's God and display exemplary Israelite virtues (Rahab and the Gibeonite emissaries), while the second relates a sacrilege committed by a pedigreed Israelite (Achan). Read together, the three stories put a human face on both perpetrators and victims and challenge the ethnic separatism that demonizes Canaanites and sanctifies Israelites. The stories work together with summary comments that recast Israel's battles as defensive operations against increasingly aggressive kings (5:1; 9:1–2; 10:1–5; 11:1–5) and with a sophisticated reworking of the conquest narrative that gradually recasts the kings of Canaan, rather than its peoples, as the hostile force that Israel must overcome in the land.

At a fundamental level, Joshua is a narrative of origins that, on the one hand, lays claim to a homeland and a distinctive destiny and, on the other, constructs national identity over against the indigenous other (the peoples of the land). Joshua depicts Israel's encounter with difference and tests three primary identity markers: ethnicity, territory, and religious observance. In the course of the narrative each proves unable to provide a stable foundation on which to ground identity and action. Although ethnic exclusivity finds expression through Joshua's warnings that Israelites must keep their distance from Canaanites (23:1–16), the portrayals of Rahab and the Gibeonites oppose this notion of identity by presenting the reader with Canaanites who praise Israel's God and display exemplary Israelite virtues. These depictions, along with the reports of aliens within Israel (6:25; 8:30–35; 9:27), counter the sense that the nation is or should be ethnically homogenous. A similar dynamic holds true for territorial identity. Although boundaries define the extent of Israel's land and enclose tribal inheritances, few areas exhibit territorial integrity. Multiple references to unoccupied land and surviving peoples belie a simple correspondence between people and land. Finally, instances of Israelite disobedience and bickering over right religious practice counter depictions of meticulous obedience to divine commands, highlighting the difficulties involved in interpreting them correctly (e.g., 7:1–12; 22:10–34).

The difficulty of discerning divine priorities amid conflicting imperatives comes to a head when Joshua, twice, must decide whether to honor an oath to spare the lives of Canaanites (2:12–14; 6:22–25; 9:15–27). In both cases Joshua rules that Israel must keep the oath, even though doing so directly violates the commands of Moses that dictate how Israel must deal with the indigenous inhabitants (cf. Deut. 7:1–6; 20:16–18). In so doing, Joshua implicitly elevates mercy above the strict application of the law. As the narrative moves toward its conclusion, devotion to the one God emerges as the sole defining characteristic of the people of God. Joshua concludes with a climactic scene of covenant renewal (24:1–28), which portrays Israel as a people who choose the God who has chosen them.

Joshua as a Resource for Ethical Reflection

Joshua is a difficult and problematic book for Christians living in an age haunted by memories of genocidal conflicts and programs of colonization. It has, in many cases, directly or indirectly shaped the thinking and action of those who identify with biblical Israel. Given Christian complicity with such enterprises, grounded in declarations that "God is with us," would it not be safer to ignore this book's account of a warlike God who commands extermination and ethnic cleansing?

Modern theological reflection on Joshua generally has attempted to defuse its violent theology by placing the book within a historical and developmental framework. This allows one to read the book as a primitive expression of Israel's religious thought that has minimal relevance when set against other biblical texts that reflect a more mature ethical sensibility. It has also been argued that the prosecution of war in Joshua reflects a more thoughtful and humane prosecution of war when set against the brutal societies of the ancient Near East. Within a theology of progressive revelation, God's participation in the conquest has been viewed as a necessary divine accommodation that no longer applies in light of God's full revelation in Jesus Christ. These and other similar approaches effectively discredit strategies that use Joshua in support of violent or exclusionary agendas.

Recent study of Joshua has opened new trajectories by recognizing its narrativity and taking seriously its conflicting theological perspectives. Postcolonial readers of Joshua have seen in the book a biblical portrayal of the violence and dispossession that they have experienced at the hands of imperial powers. Other readers have noted the interplay of opposing perspectives within the book, one that advances claims to territory by right of conquest and another that undercuts these claims and exposes the rhetoric of militant nationalism. Read as narrative, Joshua does not so much constitute a template for the extraction of moral principles as it does a testimony of God's involvement in the life of a nation, one that draws readers into a long and contentious conversation about what it means to live as God's people in a violent world.

The patristic metaphor of Scripture as a mirror, which reflects our beauty and ugliness, offers a powerful point of reference for reading Joshua in the contemporary context. In this sense, Joshua reflects a nation that both constructs and critiques a narrative of origin configured by convictions of divine election and destiny. Joshua does not mute the militant triumphalism that infuses Israel's memories of violent origins, as the convictions it articulates had become fundamental components of Israel's national identity. It does, however, bring these sentiments under a subtle and powerful criticism that unmasks the perspectives, commitments, and rhetoric that emanate from them. Joshua therefore constitutes a vital theological resource for every nation that, like Israel, seeks to come to terms with the violence of its past and to rethink its own narratives of exclusion and imperialism.

See also Colonialism and Postcolonialism; Conquest; Deuteronomistic History; Holy War; Land; Old Testament Ethics

Bibliography

Creach, J. *Joshua*. IBC. John Knox, 2003; Goetz, R. "Joshua, Calvin and Genocide." *ThTo* 32 (1975): 263–74; Hawk, L. "Conquest Reconfigured: Recasting Warfare in the Redaction of Joshua." Pages 145–60 in *Writing and Reading War: Rhetoric, Gender, and Ethics in Biblical and Modern Contexts*, ed. B. Kelle and F. Ames. SBLSymS 42. Society of Biblical Literature, 2008; idem. *Joshua*. Berit

Olam. Liturgical Press, 2000; Nelson, R. *Joshua*. OTL. Westminster John Knox, 1997; Polzin, R. *Moses and the Deuteronomist: A Literary Study of the Deuteronomistic History*. Seabury, 1980; Prior, M. *The Bible and Colonialism: A Moral Critique*. BibSem 48. Sheffield Academic Press, 1997; Warrior, R. "A Native American Perspective: Canaanites, Cowboys, and Indians." Pages 135–43 in *Voices from the Margin: Interpreting the Bible in the Third World*, ed. R. Sugirtharajah. 3rd ed. Orbis, 2006.

L. Daniel Hawk

Jubilee

Jubilee was a yearlong sabbatical every half century in ancient Israel devoted to ecological, economic, and social rest, release, and redemption.

Biblical Jubilee

Leviticus and Deuteronomy. Deuteronomic law stipulates every seventh year as a period of debt remission (Heb. *šĕmittâ*; Gk. *aphesis* [Deut. 15:1–2]), including the emancipation of Israelite slaves, male or female (Deut. 15:12–18). The goal of this sabbatical legislation envisions liberal sharing in the land's bounty, graciously given by the redemptive "LORD your God," such that "there will be no one in need among you" (Deut. 15:4; cf. Acts 4:34).

In the regulations of Lev. 25, the septennial sabbatical primarily provides ecological rest for the land: complete suspension of fresh sowing in the fields, pruning of vineyards, and reaping of harvests (vv. 1–5). Intensifying the seventh-year respite, the regulations also call for a supersabbatical every fiftieth year, proclaiming "liberty [Heb. *dĕrôr*; Gk. *aphesis*] throughout the land to all its inhabitants" and heralding by sound of a trumpet (Heb. *šôpar*) a year of "jubilee" (Heb. *yôbēl*, lit., "ram's horn") (vv. 8–10). In addition to rest for the land (vv. 11–12), the Jubilee stipulates (1) return of property to its original owners and clans (vv. 13–17); (2) redemption of sold and foreclosed property (vv. 25–28); and (3) release of those forced into service because of extreme poverty (vv. 39–43). In the years preceding the Jubilee, debtors should not be charged interest (vv. 36–37), and land must be bought and sold justly and equitably (vv. 14–17 ["you shall not cheat one another"]).

On the calendar the Jubilee Year begins, significantly, on the Day of Atonement (Lev. 25:9), suggesting the "return to cosmic purity" (see Kawashima) or reestablishment of God's "very good" order for all creation (cf. Gen. 1:1–2:4). As with the Deuteronomic sabbatical, motivation for the Levitical Jubilee remains theologically rooted in God's exclusive proprietorship of the land ("the land is mine; with me you are but aliens and tenants" [Lev. 25:23]) and God's redeemed people ("my servants whom I brought out from the land of Egypt" [Lev. 25:55]).

Isaiah and Luke. In the context of exile, the latter chapters of Isaiah envision the people's restoration to their homeland as a new, climactic (eschatological) Jubilee. As the Lord's Spirit-anointed messenger, the prophet proclaims good news of "liberty [Heb. *dĕrôr*; Gk. *aphesis*] to the captives . . . release to the prisoners . . . the year of the LORD's favor" (Isa. 61:1–2)—that is, the Jubilee Year. Here God provides not so much the motives for the community's liberation/restoration of the land and one another as the means for realizing such liberation/restoration afresh: this is a new exodus (including God's "vengeance" against Israel's oppressive enemies [Isa. 61:2b]), inspiring the people's enactment of future Jubilees.

At the outset of his public ministry in Luke's Gospel, Jesus announces the immediate ("today") fulfillment of Isaiah's Jubilee vision, citing the text of Isa. 61:1–2a (minus the "vengeance" component in v. 2b) spliced with another liberation line from Isa. 58:6 (lit., "to send [out] the oppressed in liberty/freedom [Gk. *aphesis*]") (Luke 4:18–21). Jesus further glosses the Jubilee image with the restorative miracles of Elijah and Elisha on behalf of a poor Sidonian widow beset by famine and a powerful Syrian officer afflicted with leprosy (Luke 4:25–27). Jesus thus heralds a universal Jubilee across boundaries of territory, ethnicity, gender, and socioeconomic status as the programmatic goal of his mission. The balance of Luke's narrative abundantly illustrates Jesus' commitment to liberating the oppressed, including, in the manner of Elijah and Elisha, feedings, healings, and restoration of needy widows, lepers, and "foreign" officials (Luke 5:12–16; 7:1–17, 21–22; 9:10–17; 17:11–19). Moreover, the Levitical link between the Day of Atonement and the Jubilee Year crystallizes in Jesus' mediating the remission/forgiveness (*aphiēmi*, *aphesis*) of debts/sins against God and one another (Luke 5:17–26; 7:36–50; 11:4; 23:34; 24:47). Thus, as well as being universal, Jesus' Jubilee is as holistic, integrating spiritual, physical, psychological, social, economic, and ecological liberty.

Practical Jubilee

Although case law in Lev. 27:16–25 and Num. 36:1–4 suggests that the Jubilee was regarded as an actual duty and not merely a utopian ideal, we cannot be certain how often a full Jubilee Year was enacted in Israel's history. The Hebrew prophets' regular tirades against social oppression, exploitation, and unjust distribution of land and wealth intimate a frequent flouting of Jubilee principle and practice. For the Jubilee to work, landlords, slave owners, employers, financial brokers, and other controllers of means of production must buy into the communitarian vision and "release" their accumulative stranglehold on material and human resources. But both history and theology teach that the powers that be do not let go easily or naturally—every fiftieth year or any year. And even among the well intentioned, a host of practical, bureaucratic entanglements complicate a Jubilee agenda. The declaration of the Great Jubilee of the year 2000 by Pope John Paul II admirably called for a worldwide renewal of reconciliation, forgiveness, and charity. But, as with all Jubilees in the current era, it was up against the juggernaut of a staggeringly complex global economy driven by multinational and geopolitical corporate interests.

But however difficult the practical outworking of Jubilee might seem today, the theological foundations remain clear and firm in the creator and redeemer God. Since earth and all its "fullness" belong to God (Ps. 24:1) in perpetuity, all God's creatures, not least human beings, are tenants on God's property and directly responsible to God for just and equitable ecological management. Moreover, as redeemed servants of the forgiving God fiercely committed to liberty from all forms of oppressive enslavement, we must readily "forgive/release [*aphiēmi*] everyone indebted to us" (Luke 11:4) and resist tendencies to hoard God's bounty and dominate God's children.

See also Debt; Ecological Ethics; Economic Ethics; Koinonia; Land; Loans; Poverty and Poor; Property and Possessions; Sabbath; Wealth

Bibliography

Kawashima, R. "The Jubilee Year and the Return of Cosmic Purity." *CBQ* 65 (2003): 370–89; Kinsler, R., and G. Kinsler. *The Biblical Jubilee and the Struggle for Life: An Invitation to Personal, Ecclesial, and Social Transformation*. Orbis, 1999; Leiter, D. "The Year of Jubilee and the 21st Century." *Brethren Life and Thought* 47 (2002): 164–86; North, R. *The Biblical Jubilee . . . after Fifty Years*. AnBib 145. Editrice Pontificio Biblico, 2000; Ringe, S. *Jesus, Liberation, and the Biblical Jubilee: Images for Ethics and Christology*. Fortress, 1985; Sanders, J. "From Isaiah 61 to Luke 4." Pages 46–69 in *Luke and Scripture: The Function of Sacred Tradition in Luke-Acts*, ed. C. Evans and J. Sanders. Fortress, 1993; idem. "Sins, Debts, and Jubilee Release." Pages 84–92 in *Luke and Scripture: The Function of Sacred Tradition in Luke-Acts*, ed. C. Evans and J. Sanders. Fortress, 1993.

F. Scott Spencer

Jude

Jude is a small jewel of pastoral theology, giving guidance to a community in danger of falling out of step with the apostolic faith. This apostasy is described more as an ethical corruption than a doctrinal drift, but both are present. As elsewhere in the NT, "the faith once delivered" refers to more than a synopsis of apostolic teaching; it also incorporates a significant ethical component. Doctrinal corruption and ethical corruption are inseparable twins, always present together.

The source of the corruption is a new group of leaders in the church. These teachers have been accepted as members of the community (v. 12), but Jude is committed to exposing them as immoral corrupters of the community who teach unsound doctrine, plainly seen in the illicit lifestyle that they practice and promote (v. 4). To clarify the danger that these teachers pose to the community, Jude likens them to three reprehensible exemplars from the history of Israel: Cain, Balaam, and Korah (v. 11). In contemporary Jewish apocalyptic literature these three were depicted as deceivers who led Israel astray. Jude intimates that the fate of some in the community will mimic those in Israel who were party to the exodus but died in the desert for their unbelief (v. 5). The pastoral impulse behind this threat of judgment is to clarify the seriousness of the corruption in their midst and to facilitate a return to apostolic beliefs and praxis.

See also Eschatology and Ethics; Judgment; Moral Formation; New Testament Ethics; Sanctification; Vice; Virtue(s); Virtue Ethics

Bibliography

Bauckham, R. *Jude, 2 Peter*. WBC 50. Word, 1983; Green, G. *Jude and 2 Peter*. BECNT. Baker Academic, 2008; Reese, R. *2 Peter and Jude*. THNTC. Eerdmans, 2007.

J. de Waal Dryden

Judges

The book of Judges portrays the disintegration of a nation that has lost its center. In vivid contrast to the unified Israel that triumphs and occupies the land described in Joshua, Judges begins with a depiction of a nation fragmented into tribes, each preoccupied with its own territory (1:1–36). It then moves immediately to a divine rebuke for covenantal disobedience (2:1–5), the death of the leader who has unified the people (2:6–10), and a programmatic introduction that presents the era as a constant cycle of apostasy, chastisement, and deliverance (2:11–23).

The core of the book comprises accounts of the judges that God raised up to deliver Israel (3:1–16:31). The term *judge* does not here necessarily entail judicial authority but rather refers to the individual's mission to bring justice via deliverance to oppressed Israel. The first of these, Othniel, is rendered as the paradigmatic savior but without elaboration (3:7–11). Subsequent judges exhibit a quirk or flaw that, with each one, becomes increasingly grotesque and destructive. Ehud is left-handed (and thus, suggestively, sinister), which enables him to assassinate a Moabite tyrant behind closed doors (3:12–30). Deborah is a "mother in Israel" who gloats in bloodthirsty detail over the death of Sisera at the hands of Jael, a woman who sheltered the Canaanite commander, gave him milk, tucked him in, and then shattered his skull while he slept (4:1–5:31). Gideon arises from humble beginnings but barely averts intertribal conflict, constructs an ephod that leads Israel into idolatry, and sires a son, Abimelech (meaning "my father is king"), who attempts to make himself king (6:11–9:57). Jephthah, the son of a prostitute, sacrifices his daughter to fulfill a vow and participates in intertribal warfare (11:1–12:7). Samson is an impetuous loner, obsessed with danger and forbidden women, who rallies no one to the cause and enacts his deeds of deliverance out of a desire to get revenge on the Philistines (13:1–16:31).

The book ends with two narratives that depict the dissolution of the fundamental social bonds that configure tribal Israel. The first begins with Micah, a man who steals a huge sum of silver from his mother. The story then relates the dedication of silver to the Lord in the form of an idol and the installation of a family member as priest, and features a Levite who sells his services to the highest bidder and a dispossessed tribe (Dan) that wipes out a town outside its allotted territory (17:1–18:31). The second reports a mob attack on travelers, the gang rape of a young woman and her dismemberment by her Levite lover (he is hardly a lover [husband instead?], she is a secondary wife), the near annihilation of Benjamin by the other tribes, the destruction of an Israelite town for its nonparticipation in the conflict, and the kidnapping of women who are celebrating a religious festival (19:1–21:25).

Judges concludes with a comment that summarizes the spirit of the times: "In those days there was no king in Israel; all the people did what was right in their own eyes" (21:25 [cf. 17:6; 18:1; 19:1]). The statement is provocatively ambiguous. Does it imply that a tribal society was unworkable and thus infer that monarchy is a preferable social configuration? Or does it comment on the anarchy that ensued when Israel rejected the Lord as king (cf. 1 Sam. 8:7)? Viewed as social commentary, the statement illumines the contesting perspectives about Israel's polity (the kin-based society of tribal Israel and charismatic leadership versus the mediating institutions of dynastic monarchy) that constitute an important dynamic throughout the book. Viewed as theological commentary, it links Israel's persistent refusal to accord the Lord his rightful place at the center of communal life with the degeneration of Israelite leadership and society.

Faced with Israel's recalcitrance, the Lord repeatedly displays his supremacy by accomplishing his saving purposes in spite of the failings of his chosen deliverers. Difficult for many readers is the fact that imbuement of the Lord's spirit empowers judges to deliver Israel but does not result in the transformation of their moral or spiritual dispositions. Moreover, none of the judges succeed in restoring Israel to long-term devotion to God. Rather, the judges themselves are enmeshed in the nation's persistent attempts to chart its own destiny apart from the claims of the Lord. God is also drawn into the cycle through repeated attempts to restore Israel and, it seems, must even use surreptitious means to initiate deliverance through his chosen leaders (a case in point being the narrator's comment that Samson's infatuation with a Philistine woman "was from the Lord; for he was seeking a pretext to act against the Philistines" [14:4]).

The social consequences of "doing what is right in one's own eyes" (as opposed to the Lord's) are portrayed in stark and often symbolic terms. The perversion of fundamental values figures prominently in many accounts, with shocking effect. Deborah and Jael express their "motherly" attributes in bloodthirsty ways. Gideon the idol-destroyer becomes an idol-maker. Jephthah kills his own daughter. A Levite throws his concubine to a threatening mob after tenderly wooing her. (Women, it should be noted, bear the brunt of the violence that breaks out as the fabric of Israelite society unravels.) The symbolic threads converge in Samson, the personification of Israel, whose story is propelled by the interplay of forbidden sex, danger, and death.

As a whole, Judges draws an inseparable and reciprocal connection between devotion to God, strong central leadership, and national unity and well-being. It thus presents modern secular societies with a cautionary tale about the central importance of religious faith and the consequences that may ensue when faith in God is shunted to the periphery.

See also Narrative Ethics, Biblical; Old Testament Ethics

Bibliography

Bal, M. *Death and Dissymmetry: The Politics of Coherence in the Book of Judges*. CSHJ. University of Chicago,

1988; Block, D. *Judges*. NAC. Broadman & Holman, 2002; Brettler, M. "The Book of Judges: Literature as Politics." *JBL* 108 (1989): 395–418; Exum, J. "The Centre Cannot Hold: Thematic and Textual Instabilities in Judges." *CBQ* 52 (1990): 410–31; Schneider, T. *Judges*. Berit Olam. Liturgical Press, 2000.

L. Daniel Hawk

Judgment

Christian creeds profess a belief in Christ's return to judge the living and the dead. This foundational belief rests on the concept of judgment that emerged in the developing traditions of Israel and the early Christians. This survey will illustrate this developmental concept of judgment.

Judgment in the Old Testament

Judgment (Heb. *mišpāṭ*) is connected to the covenant between God and the people of Israel. In selecting Israel as the chosen people, God entered a covenant relationship with them as Lord and Judge. The various laws in the Torah expressed God's will for the way Israel was to remain true to this covenantal relationship. Consequently, God's judgment related to the way Israel remained faithful or unfaithful to this covenant relationship.

As Israel's partner in the covenant, God is first and foremost the defender of his people. When Israel appeals to God's judgment, it is more to his mercy and compassion (*ḥesed*) than to his role as judge. When David had the opportunity to harm Saul, David refused to do so, leaving judgment to God: "May the LORD judge between me and you! May the LORD avenge me on you; but my hand shall not be against you" (1 Sam. 24:12). God judged on behalf of David and delivered him from his enemies (2 Sam. 18:31). Throughout Israel's history, God's judgment gave priority to defending the poor and outcasts of the society. Since they had no one to defend them, God's judgment defended them: "For the LORD your God is God of gods and Lord of lords, the great God, mighty and awesome, who is not partial and takes no bribe, who executes justice for the orphan and the widow, and who loves the strangers, providing them food and clothing" (Deut. 10:17–18). Often the psalms call on the Lord to vindicate the petitioner: "Judge me, O LORD, according to my righteousness and according to the integrity that is in me" (Ps. 7:8).

God's judgment of Israel also involves punishment. The book of Ezekiel focuses exclusively on this aspect of God's judgment (Ezek. 5:7–12). The prophets often use the imagery of court proceedings to illustrate what has gone wrong in the covenant relationship. God appears not so much in the role of judge who metes out judgment, but as the one who accuses Israel for the ways the nation has turned from the covenant: "Hear, O heavens, and listen, O earth; for the LORD has spoken: I reared children and brought them up, but they have rebelled against me" (Isa. 1:2). The book of Job provides deeper insight into God's judgments. Convinced of his innocence, Job pleads with God to hear his case and explain his sufferings (Job 30:16–23). God responds by pointing to the mystery of his ways (Job 38:1–41:34), and Job discovers new insight into God's judgments. Since humans cannot fathom the depth of God's actions and decisions, Job submits to the mysterious nature of God's judgments: "Therefore I have uttered what I did not understand, things too wonderful for me, which I did not know" (Job 42:3).

God is also judge of the nations of earth: "But the LORD sits enthroned forever, he has established his throne for judgment. He judges the world with righteousness; he judges the peoples with equity" (Ps. 9:7–8). Some postexilic prophets prophesied a final judgment that would encompass the sinners of the entire world and those who caused suffering for God's people. The prophet Isaiah envisages God judging the world by fire (Isa. 66:16). In the apocalyptic literature between the two Testaments the concept of a judgment on all nations of the earth becomes prominent, and speculations develop regarding the nature of this judgment. As the earth is brought to a destructive end, God's Messiah, or "one like a Son of Man," arrives to pass judgment on those who have died and those who are alive (Dan. 7:13–14).

Judgment in the New Testament

The NT writings continue Israel's thought on God's judgment (Gk. *krinō* [verb], *krisis* [noun]). In Jesus' preaching in the Synoptic Gospels the concept of judgment appears more frequently in Matthew and Luke than in Mark. Judgment often takes on the meaning of condemnation, whereby Jesus' opponents, such as the Pharisees, are threatened with a judgment that embraces being condemned to hell: "You snakes, you brood of vipers! How can you escape being sentenced to hell [*apo tēs kriseōs tēs geennēs*]" (lit., "from the judgment of Gehenna" [Matt. 23:33]).

Jesus' preaching also announced a second coming of the Son of Man to bring about God's kingdom in its fullest state. As in Israel's apocalyptic texts, the future judgment is described in catastrophic terms of cosmic destruction that initiates the end and a judgment on the righteous and the wicked. Probably the most memorable of Jesus' parables embracing the end times is that of the parable of the judgment of the nations

(Matt. 25:31–46). Although the word *judgment* (*krisis*) does not occur in this parable, the imagery is clearly evident in the separation of those who have acted in the name of Jesus from those who have not. The basis for their separation rests not on the fulfillment of legal obligations, but rather on living out the law of love of neighbor in the manner of Jesus, who demonstrated love especially for the less fortunate of society.

In the Gospel of John, the focus is not on the future, but on present judgment. A certain paradox emerges regarding the judgment. On the one hand, God sent his Son not to judge the world, but to save it (John 3:17). Jesus himself reiterates the same thought: "I do not judge anyone who hears my words and does not keep them, for I came not to judge the world, but to save the world" (John 12:47). On the other hand, Jesus does say, "I came into this world for judgment" (John 9:39). This paradox finds its resolution in understanding that people, in the very act of rejecting faith in Jesus, pronounce judgment on themselves. The act of believing or not believing in Jesus is one of self-judgment.

Foundational to Paul's thinking is God's judgment arising from Adam and embracing the whole human race (Rom. 5:16). All who are in Christ Jesus escape this universal condemnation (Rom. 8:1) through the effects of Christ's death. The Spirit communicates these effects to the believer: "For those who live according to the flesh set their minds on the things of the flesh, but those who live according to the Spirit set their minds on the things of the Spirit" (Rom. 8:5). For Paul, a future judgment is also imminent. Paul calls this coming judgment "the day of the Lord" (2 Cor. 1:14; 1 Thess. 5:2). On that day believers in Christ Jesus will be saved, while those who follow wickedness will experience God's wrath (Rom. 2:7–8). Of special importance in examining Paul's understanding of God's judgment is his acknowledgment that it is beyond our understanding: "O the depth of the riches and wisdom and knowledge of God! How unsearchable are his judgments and how inscrutable his ways!" (Rom. 11:33).

For the book of Revelation, the concept of judgment lies in the trajectory of Israel's apocalyptic traditions and paints a frightening picture of God's judgment at the end of time. Central to God's final judgment of humanity is how they have led their lives (Rev. 20:12). Those who had remained true to the word of God cry out for God's judgment on those who persecuted them: "Sovereign Lord, holy and true, how long will it be before you judge and avenge our blood on the inhabitants of the earth?" (Rev. 6:10). The book of Revelation also acts as a reminder to believers to persevere in their commitment to Christ. The letters to the seven churches (Rev. 2:1–3:22) challenge them to remain ever faithful. To the church at Ephesus the Son of Man says, "Remember then from what you have fallen; repent, and do the works you did at first" (Rev. 2:5).

Summary

This survey of the concept of judgment in the biblical writings shows numerous aspects. A central focus does emerge, however, within the context of a covenantal relationship with the God of Israel and in the relationship of the believer to the person of Jesus Christ. Just as the writings of the people of Israel stress the need to remain faithful in their relationship with the God of the covenant, so the followers of Jesus are also called to fidelity in their relationship with him. This fidelity is illustrated through the imitation of Jesus' life (Matt. 25:31–46) and in belief in the person of Jesus (Gospel of John). The Scriptures stress this central vision, this way of life, which is led in relationship to God (the people of Israel) or to Christ (NT). One's actions bear witness to this relationship.

The biblical writers use graphic imagery in describing the last judgment. These images belong to the realm of the biblical world, but the eschatological vision remains central to the biblical belief: God's judgment lies outside history and brings history to an end. A final judgment remains essential to proclaim God's triumph over evil. If evil is not finally overcome, then evil is as eternal as God is. From the beginning of time, humans have rejected God and have been judged worthy of condemnation (Rom. 5:16–18). No one is able to restore this relationship with God. The Son of God came as a human being and through his death condemned sin and liberated humans from sin's effects (Rom. 8:3). For those who have become God's children (John 1:12), there is nothing to fear on the final day of judgment. As the Johannine writer eloquently says, "God is love, and those who abide in love abide in God, and God abides in them. Love has been perfected among us in this: that we may have boldness on the day of judgment, because as he is, so are we in this world" (1 John 4:16–17).

See also Covenant; Eschatology and Ethics; Fidelity; Justice, Restorative; Justice, Retributive

Bibliography

Hays, R. *The Moral Vision of the New Testament: Community, Cross, and New Creation; A Contemporary Introduction to New Testament Ethics.* Harper SanFrancisco, 1996; Travis, S. *The Limits of Divine*

Retribution in New Testament Thought. Hendrickson, 2009; von Balthasar, H. Urs. *The Last Act*. Vol. 5 of *Theo-Drama: Theological Dramatic Theory*. Trans. G. Harrison. Ignatius Press, 1998.

Patrick Hartin

Judith

The book of Judith presents many ethical problems. In saving her people from near certain destruction, the heroine (her name means "Jewish woman") flirts with and seduces the enemy commander, tells him lies and ironic half-truths, gets him drunk, chops off his head and has it put on public display, and sets off thirty days of plundering in the enemy's camp. The book appears to be a case of the end (Israel's salvation) justifying the means (Judith's deceit and violence).

The book is best interpreted as a historical fiction. There is no record of any city named Bethulia, or anything like the crisis described in the first half of the book, or a woman named Judith who saved her people in this dramatic way. The basic text is the Greek version found in the LXX, though the book may have been composed in Hebrew or Aramaic. Although not very accurate as history, the book is noteworthy for the literary skill with which the story is told—lively characters, complex plot, intricate structure, frequent shifting of scenes, skillful use of irony, and a final hymn.

Its most obvious biblical model is the story of Jael, the woman who in Judg. 4–5 saves ancient Israel by hammering a tent peg into the head of the enemy general Sisera. The irony is that the violence committed by Israel's enemies is overcome violently by a most unlikely instrument, the hand of a woman. Also central to the story is the biblical principle that Israel will prosper as long as it avoids sin but will be punished severely when it sins (see Deut. 30:15–20).

Judith does not appear until almost halfway through the book. The first seven chapters describe the crisis facing Israel: whether to remain faithful to the God of Israel or to worship the foreign king. As part of his program to exert sovereignty over many peoples and nations, Nebuchadnezzar (a Babylonian ruling over the Assyrians) commissions his general Holofernes (a Persian name) to bring Israel and its neighbors into line. The campaign is intended to show that Nebuchadnezzar alone is worthy of worship (3:8; 6:2) and so to test Israel's faith in its God. The people of Bethulia in the meantime are engulfed in fear. When Holofernes cuts off their water supply, the only strategy that their leader Uzziah can suggest is to wait five days for "the Lord our God" to act on their behalf (7:30).

God does act dramatically through the unlikely person of the rich and beautiful widow Judith. She criticizes the people of Bethulia for putting their God to the test and assures them that she is going to do "something that will go down through all generations of our descendants" (8:32). In prayer she asks God to make her "deceitful words" bring harm upon Israel's enemies (9:13). After beautifying herself, she lies her way into the enemy's camp and leads Holofernes on with ironic promises that he interprets positively but that she uses to disguise her real intentions.

The major theological theme of the book is captured in the phrase "the hand of a woman" (16:6). This is a reversal of expectations about the right of military conquerors to abuse women as part of the spoils of warfare. Judith shows that God can foil Israel's enemies and bring about good for his people by the most unlikely of instruments, the hand of a widow. The final hymn celebrates Judith's victory over Holofernes in a graphic way: "Her sandal ravished his eyes, her beauty captivated his mind, and the sword severed his neck" (16:9).

The inclusion of the book of Judith in the Catholic and Orthodox Christian canons of Scripture has led to its frequent use as a starting point for literary and artistic representations. There are many depictions of Judith in illustrated Christian Bible manuscripts, and she has been the subject of films, opera, and poems. Her slaying of Holofernes has attracted the attention of portrait artists for whom the combination of sex, violence, and religion has proved irresistible. In some circles Judith was viewed as a prefigurement of Mary the mother of Jesus. Medieval Jewish midrashim linked her story to Hanukkah, thus anticipating modern scholarly hypotheses about its origin in Maccabean times.

See also Deuterocanonical/Apocryphal Books; Feminist Ethics

Bibliography

Craven, T. *Artistry and Faith in the Book of Judith*. SBLDS 70. Scholars Press, 1983; Harrington, D. *Invitation to the Apocrypha*. Eerdmans, 1999, 27–43; Moore, C. *Judith*. AB 40. Doubleday, 1985; Stocker, M. *Judith, Sexual Warrior: Women and Power in Western Culture*. Yale University Press, 1998; VanderKam, J., ed. *"No One Spoke Ill of Her": Essays on Judith*. SBLEJL. Scholars Press, 1992.

Daniel J. Harrington

Justice

The Hebrew noun *mišpāṭ* often is translated as "justice" in the OT. Its semantic range, however, is quite broad. It may be translated as "judgment," "verdict," "law or statute," and in the plural it can refer to a code or body of law. Its translated nuance can be determined only in context. Somewhat oddly, there is no real equivalent to this Hebrew term in the Greek of the NT.

All Hebrew nouns are derived from verbal roots and find their semantic foundation there. The verbal root in question here is *špṭ*, which has as its basic meaning "to exercise powers of governance." In the OT it is most often rendered as "to judge," but its meaning is by no means limited to the judicial or juridical. It can apply to exercise of the processes of governance in civil or religious contexts, in judicial or executive capacity. It is, however, usually linked to offices of governing authority, and these vary in different OT periods. Thus, this verb could represent governing authority for a key figure such as Moses, or an office such as king or judge, or someone adjudicating disputes such as elders at the gate. In the book of Judges, the series of military leaders through the tribal period are said to "judge" Israel, but this is less a reference to judicial activity alone than to leadership in general. There is strong evidence that the verb refers to actions that help restore balance or wholeness (*shalom*) to community and, when exercised by God, reference a strong divine moral influence in the structure and governance of creation itself.

Major areas of semantic use for the verb *špṭ* include the following:

1. To exercise governing power—that is, to act as a ruler. This is, of course, seen of kings (1 Sam. 8:20). It may also be power wielded by the congregation of Israel or by designated individuals in roles of leadership as *šōpēṭ* (Deut. 1:16; Judg. 16:31; 1 Sam. 7:15–17).
2. To decide cases of controversy. This may be in civil, domestic, or religious arenas; it may be local, tribal, or national in context. Although bodies of law and statutes exist, these gain authority only as persons exercise authority to give judgment—that is, to exercise governing authority.
3. God, in covenant with Israel as a religious community, ultimately as judge, ruler, and governor of the entire world. Abraham appeals to this role in pleading for Sodom and Gomorrah (Gen. 18:25); God is distinguished from other gods by the ability to exercise authority justly (Ps. 82); even David appeals to God's role in finally vindicating him before Saul ("May the Lord therefore be judge, and give sentence [*špṭ*] between me and you. May he see to it and plead my cause, and vindicate [*špṭ*] me against you" [1 Sam. 24:15]).

Far more frequent in the OT is the use of the noun *mišpāṭ*, which is the foundation for understanding Hebrew concepts of authentic, faithful exercise of governing authority. It is found in contexts as varied as the family, judicial structures, the royal court, commerce, and religious offices and institutions. For Israel, all these arenas are governed by God's exercise of *mišpāṭ*, against which human efforts to embody this governing principle are measured. Thus, by measure against God's "justice" human exercise of "justice" can be judged faithful or unfaithful in a moral sense.

Many authorities cite more than a dozen distinct usages of *mišpāṭ*, and the English words used to translate it likewise have a wide range. But most suggest that if any one word can be used to represent the concept of *mišpāṭ* in its multiple contexts, it is the word *justice*. Instead of making a long list of nuanced meanings here, I will attempt a description of two major arenas within which "justice" appears in the OT and suggest meanings that it carries therein.

First, many uses of *mišpāṭ* reflect a judicial or legislative concept. Justice can be used for an ordinance, a statute, or a regulation giving clear guidance regarding social behavior on familial, cultic, economic, or social matters (Exod. 15:25; Lev. 5:10; Deut. 6:1). The plural form (*mišpāṭîm*) can indicate a code of laws or legislation recognized by the community (Deut. 5:1). Since many of these references are found in the legal texts of the Pentateuch, they function to make "justice" or "just ordinances" a concrete manifestation of the demands and obligations made by God's covenant with the people of God from Israel to the present.

It follows that the appeal is to "justice" when a case of dispute is brought before a magistrate (judge, elder, king, or even God) to render a "just" decision. BDB lists 204 instances of this usage. Solomon asks God to enable him to "hear justice" in a case brought before him (1 Kgs. 3:11). In every period of Israel's life there were structures for hearing disputes and rendering judgments, and justice is the concept that guards the integrity of such hearings at every level (Exod. 18; 1 Kgs. 10; 2 Chr. 19; Ps. 9; Hab. 1).

The term for "justice" sometimes seems to refer to matters of entitlement or rights in ancient Israel. For example, in Deut. 18:3–5 there is an enumeration of payments and food intended for the support of priests referred to as their *mišpāṭ*. Strangers and orphans, because of their vulnerability, are singled out for special instructions not to deprive them of "justice" (Deut. 24:17 [we will return to this matter with the prophets]). The right of a firstborn son to inherit is his *mišpāṭ* (Deut. 21:17), and Jeremiah exercised his right (*mišpāṭ*) to inherit land (Jer. 32:6–15).

Justice is the principle that guards the integrity of the judicial and administrative order of the land, whether applied to magistrates, leaders, or kings. Favoritism or bribes pervert justice (Deut. 16:18–20) and cannot be tolerated.

The recognition of justice as an expression of governing authority means that it does not always appear as a high moral claim. It may simply recognize who has the power to determine the exercise of authority. Thus, when Samuel, on the instruction of God, enumerates the oppressive practices of kings in 1 Sam. 8:11–18, it is called the "*mišpāṭ* of the king" (in v. 11 the NRSV blandly translates, "the ways of the king"). When David was serving the Philistines and left no one alive to tell the king of Gath that he was double-dealing, it is described as "his *mišpāṭ* all the time he lived in the country of the Philistines" (NRSV: "his practice").

Justice sometimes, in a legal context, refers to a penalty or a sentence rendered against violators of the just order (Prov. 21:15). Jeremiah 26:11, 16 refer to a "*mišpāṭ* of death," meaning a "sentence of death." By the same token, justice can represent the clearance or vindication of someone unjustly accused whose name is cleared, as Job is attempting to do: "I have set out my case [*mišpāṭ*]" (Job 13:18).

Second, justice appears more as a moral principle or ideal in the way it is used by the prophets and in the book of Psalms. Throughout the prophetic books and in the liturgical materials of the Psalter, the term *mišpāṭ* seems to function as a desired commitment to a moral principle that may find expression in relationship to leaders, offices, and institutions but is also generally applicable and directed to the social relationships of the community at every level. Justice functions as an ethical norm to measure and critique the interactions between individuals and social groupings in the Israelite community. Undoubtedly, there is a relationship to the use of justice to describe governance and legal concerns in the Pentateuch, but the understanding of justice has transcended the boundaries of what is required legally or magisterially by formal institutions and offices. Some representative texts are Pss. 9:7–12; 10:17–18; 82:3–4; 106:3; Isa. 1:11–17; 5:7; 10:2; Jer. 22:3, 15–16; Amos 5:7, 21–24; Mic. 6:6–8.

A measure of the broadened use of justice as a moral ideal is the frequency with which the term *mišpāṭ* is used in parallel with the term *ṣĕdāqâ* ("righteousness"): thirty-seven times, mostly in the psalms and the prophets. Righteousness relates to wholeness in relationships at every level of human community and is measured by the well-being of all parties rather than by adherence to formal rules, laws, or codes. "Happy are those who observe justice, who do righteousness at all times" (Ps. 106:3). "Let justice roll down like waters and righteousness like an ever-flowing stream" (Amos 5:24). Taken together, justice and righteousness represent the moral mandate laid on the community of God's people to incorporate these qualities into the character of the community so fundamentally that moral action is characterized by these same qualities. Justice and righteousness describe persons and behaviors that seek wholeness and well-being for all, that seek equity in all social interrelationships, and that do not seek advantage at the expense of another's disadvantage.

Especially in the psalms and prophets, but also true throughout the OT, it is clear that the foundation for any human exercise of justice is the understanding that the identity and the action of God are characterized by justice. One of the fundamental roles of God in Israelite understanding is that God is judge of all the earth. Abraham appeals directly to this role in his effort to plead mercy for Sodom and Gomorrah (Gen. 18:25). God is both the source and the champion of justice by virtue of creating the world and establishing justice as foundational to God's desire for all creation (Ps. 99:1–4). Justice is one of God's own attributes. "Righteousness and justice are the foundation of his throne" (Ps. 97:2). Since God is creator, ruler, and judge of all the earth, God's justice cannot be exercised in terms of narrow interests but rather is universal in its scope. This is part of what distinguishes Israel's God from the claims of other gods in surrounding cultures. Psalm 82 is remarkable, picturing a heavenly council of the gods in which Israel's God takes his stand and accuses the other gods of judging unjustly and showing "partiality to the wicked" (v. 2). Israel's God then proclaims justice as due to even the weakest and most vulnerable of the society (vv. 3–4) and claims that failing to meet the standard of justice means that the gods of other nations are not gods at all and are destined to die like mortals (vv. 6–7). The psalm ends by praising God as judge of all the earth (v. 8).

It therefore is God's justice that models the practice of justice in human community. Justice is a divine attribute alongside holiness, righteousness, steadfast love, and compassion. "The LORD of hosts is exalted by justice, and the Holy God shows himself holy by righteousness" (Isa. 5:16). "Let those who boast boast in this, that they understand and know me, that I am the LORD; I act with steadfast love, justice, and righteousness in the earth, for in these things I delight, says the LORD" (Jer. 9:24). Even God's exercise of the role as judge of all the earth characterizes divine judging not by sheer power and authority but by a concern for fairness and equity governed by other divine attributes. "He judges the world with righteousness; he judges the peoples with equity" (Ps. 9:8).

The framework for mediating justice as a divine quality and practice to the human exercise of justice is the establishment of covenant relationship between God and God's people. The Hebrew word for "covenant" (*bĕrît*) means "agreement" or "contract," but it takes on special meaning when applied to the agreement between God and Israel, and by extension between God and God's people in every age. God initiates the covenant relationship, but covenant implies mutual commitment. That commitment carries obligations, and in the biblical understanding of covenant God models the qualities of that commitment and its obligations. God shows justice, love, compassion, and righteousness to Israel and all creation, and covenant understandings expect God's people to reflect those same qualities in all their relationships. Law codes and formal obligations for leaders and members of the community may give concrete expression to those qualities, but it is the exercise of those qualities, not formal obligatory practice, that matters most to God. This finds constant expression in the prophets. God is not pleased by formal pious practices of worship and prayer if justice is not present and practiced. "I hate, I despise your festivals, and I take no delight in solemn assemblies. . . . But let justice roll down like waters, and righteousness like an ever-flowing stream" (Amos 5:21, 24). "Bringing offerings is futile; incense is an abomination to me. New moon and sabbath and calling of convocation—I cannot endure solemn assemblies with iniquity. . . . Cease to do evil, learn to do good; seek justice, rescue the oppressed, defend the orphan, plead for the widow" (Isa. 1:13, 16–17).

When God's justice (and other divine covenant qualities) is matched by Israel's justice (and other covenantally mandated qualities), the result is *šālôm*, "wholeness." Although never fully realized, *šālôm* is made visible to the degree that justice is done, righteousness shown, faithfulness demonstrated, and steadfast love returned in response to God.

As the passage from Isa. 1, noted above, shows, God is also portrayed, especially in the prophets and psalms, but also in the law codes, as having a special regard for and care of the poor, the dispossessed, the weak, and the vulnerable (see Ps. 10:17–18). Deuteronomy 15:7–11 builds this special regard for the poor and the needy into the divine mandate of covenant responsibility. In the prophets and the psalms, it is the requirement to do justice that serves as the guardian of this obligation.

Justice for the poor, the weak, and the vulnerable is not a moral demand to grant privilege. The prophets' call to do justice asks for fair practices, nonexploitation, and granting of full participation in the social order (Amos 2:6–7; 8:4–6). The poor have claims on full participation in the goodness of God's creation, and God desires that they be treated justly. In this sense, the call for justice for the poor comes close to recognizing the rights of the poor. God's people are thus critiqued: "They know no limits in deeds of wickedness; they do not judge with justice the cause of the orphan, to make it prosper, and they do not defend the rights of the needy" (Jer. 5:28).

Thus, when there are those who feel exploited by others or denied their just participation in the life of the community, they appeal to God as judge and defender of justice to vindicate them and ensure that justice is done. This is seen especially in psalms of lament where appeal is made to God in time of suffering at the hands of enemies who treat others unjustly. The petitioner often asks that the right to justice be restored (e.g., Ps. 146:7–9). When justice is denied, it is God who can restore it. "From the heavens you uttered judgment [*dîn*]; the earth feared and was still when God rose up to establish judgment [*mišpāṭ*], to save all the oppressed of the earth" (Ps. 76:8–9). God's justice aims to establish a social order in which inequities are replaced by equal regard and care for all. "He raises the poor from the dust, and lifts the needy from the ash heap, to make them sit with princes, with the princes of his people" (Ps. 113:7–8).

A text that captures much of the biblical spirit of justice as a central covenant obligation in partnership with God is Mic. 6:1–8. This passage is set up as a dramatic court scene. God has gone to court with Israel. The prophet recounts the scene as an intermediary in the legal proceeding to confront Israel with its breach of covenant obligation. Creation itself is summoned as judge and witnesses (vv. 1–2). God gives first testimony, claiming to have acted toward Israel with "saving acts" (vv. 3–5). Then Israel's voice gives cynical testimony, asking, "With what shall I come before the LORD?" and making exaggerated claims that not even "ten thousands of rivers of oil" or the offering of one's own "firstborn" would be enough (vv. 6–7). The prophet's answer and the verdict in the mock court case form a classic statement of the moral demand of covenant relationship with God, and a fitting witness to the central role of justice in the moral claims that covenant makes on God's people: "He has told you, O mortal, what is good; and what does the LORD require of you but to do justice, and to love kindness, and to walk humbly with your God?" (v. 8).

See also Justice, Distributive; Justice, Restorative; Justice, Retributive; Old Testament Ethics; Peace

Bibliography

Barton, J. *Ethics and the Old Testament*. Trinity Press International, 1998; Birch, B. *Let Justice Roll Down: The Old Testament, Ethics, and Christian Life*. Westminster John Knox, 1991; Boecker, H. *Law and the Administration of Justice in the Old Testament and in the Ancient Near East*. Augsburg, 1980; Epsztein, L. *Social Justice in the Ancient Near East and the People of the Bible*. Trans. J. Bowden. SCM, 1986; Gossai, H. *Justice, Righteousness, and the Social Critique of the Eighth-Century Prophets*. AUS 7/41. Peter Lang, 1993; Mott, S. *Biblical Ethics and Social Change*. Oxford University Press, 1982; Wright, C. *An Eye for an Eye: The Place of Old Testament Ethics Today*. InterVarsity, 1983.

Bruce C. Birch

Justice, Distributive

Justice provides the standard for right behavior in social relationships. "I will use justice as a plumbline and righteousness as a plummet" (Isa. 28:17 NEB). Distributive justice provides the standard for the distribution of the benefits of living in society. Retributive justice, in contrast, provides the standard for the assignment of penalties for violating the standards of the society.

Every society has a conception of justice, but the conception of justice varies between societies and between political ideologies of the same society. Accordingly, the biblical understanding of justice is crucial for those who look to it for moral guidance. The understanding of justice is consistent throughout the various literary genres of the Bible. The NT presupposes the OT view of justice; this is most directly seen in Jesus' statement that justice is one of the most important parts of the law (Matt. 23:23; cf. 2 Tim. 3:16).

The pervasiveness of justice in the Bible can be veiled by traditional terminology used for the key terms in English translations. The Hebrew *ṣĕdāqâ* and its corresponding Greek term, *dikaiosynē*, often are translated as "righteousness." Likewise, the Hebrew *mišpaṭ* and the Greek *krima* or *krisis* often are rendered as "judgment." A reliable rule of thumb is that when "righteousness" or "judgment" is found in the context of social distribution or social conflict, "justice" would be a better translation. Often these terms for justice are used in combination, as in Isa. 28:17. In that case, one of the terms can be rendered by something like "what is right."

Continuity with Love

Not all are agreed that justice is an extension of love. In a tradition in theology that may go back to Philo of Alexandria, justice and love are considered as separate poles. The result often is an interpretation of justice that is predominantly retributive, thus emphasizing justice as impartial; benefit rights are then denied as belonging to love, not justice.

Distributive justice, however, is closely related to loyal love (*ḥesed* [e.g., Hos. 10:12]) and love (*'ahăbâ* [e.g., Deut. 10:18]). This connection of loyal love to justice applies also to government (Ps. 89:14; Prov. 20:28; Isa. 16:5).

Distribution according to Needs

Theories of distributive justice differ in the standard for the assignment of benefits. They may be distributed according to worth, merit, ability, work, or the agreements that one has made. Biblical justice gives priority to distribution according to basic needs. Needs become rights, since they are to be met by the whole community. In Lev. 25:35 we read, "If members of your people become poor and their power wavers with you, you shall make them strong [*ḥāzaq*]" (in the Hiphil, causative conjugation). The basic needs to be met include not only matters indispensable for subsistence (such as food, clothing, and shelter [e.g., Deut. 10:18; Isa. 58:2, 7]) but also the possession and control of the resources that are preconditions for meeting those needs, such as land (as means of production [e.g., Isa. 65:21–22]), secondary means of production (Job 24:3), due process of law (Exod. 23:1–3, 6–8), and freedom from subjugation (Lev. 25:39–42; Deut. 23:15–16).

Justice is repeatedly associated with those from groups characterized by such needs: the poor, widow, orphan, resident alien, sick or differently abled, captive, slave, or wage worker. Their restoration is often to the disadvantage of the wealthy and powerful (e.g., Luke 1:51–53).

Restoration to Community

Distribution according to needs can also be described as a restoration to community, since the human being in Scripture is viewed as one who belongs in community (e.g., Ps. 107:36; Eccl. 4:9–12).

Being deprived of basic needs restricts a person's ability to participate in community; "their power wavers *with you*" (Lev. 25:35). The responsibility "to make them strong" again is so "that they may live beside you" (Lev. 25:36). Deprivation of rights can mean falling out of the economic or political community. There are other dimensions of community as well. When people are shunned because of some social characteristic, they are losing their place in the social community (e.g., Prov. 14:20).

Deliverance

Justice is repeatedly associated with the language of deliverance (e.g., Ps. 76:9). Justice describes the deliverance of people from political and economic oppressors (Judg. 5:11), slavery (1 Sam. 12:7), and captivity (Jer. 51:10). Justice is not mere alleviation; it sets people back on their feet, restores them to community, and ends oppression (Pss. 10:15–18; 68:5–10). Justice as deliverance from oppression is demanded of the government (Ps. 72:1, 4; Jer. 21:12; 22:2–3). Such justice is foundational to political rule (Prov. 29:14) and is universally required (Dan. 4:27). It is central to the work of the coming messianic king (e.g., Isa. 11:4–5; Ezek. 34:15–16, 23–24).

Justice as restoration to community and deliverance helps explain why justice language (*dikaiosynē*) is used for salvation through Christ as a person is restored to the divine community and delivered from sin and death (e.g., Rom. 3:22–26).

Taking Up the Cause of the Oppressed

Justice in Scripture is not described in abstract, ethical language. It comes as a command of God, for whom justice is a chief attribute (e.g., Pss. 99:4; 103:6; 146:5–9). The people of God are commanded to carry out justice because God does justice (Deut. 10:18–19; Jer. 22:15–16).

Justice is such a central duty of the children of God that God's provision of reconciliation to God will not be provided unless justice characterizes their actions (Isa. 1:11–20; Jer. 7:4–7; Amos 5:15, 21–24; Mic. 6:6–8; cf. Prov. 21:3; Matt. 5:23–24; Jas. 1:27).

See also Covenant; Covenantal Ethics; Justice, Restorative; Justice, Retributive

Bibliography

Birch, B. *Let Justice Roll Down: The Old Testament, Ethics, and the Christian Life*. Westminster John Knox, 1991; Lebacqz, K. *Justice in an Unjust World: Foundations for a Christian Approach to Justice*. Augsburg, 1987; Miranda, J. *Marx and the Bible: A Critique of the Philosophy of Oppression*. Orbis, 1974; Mott, S. "The Challenge of Biblical Justice." Pages 74–88 in *A Christian Perspective on Political Thought*. Oxford University Press, 1993; idem. "God's Justice and Ours." Pages 58–81 in *Biblical Ethics and Social Change*. Oxford University Press, 1982; Snaith, N. *The Distinctive Ideas of the Old Testament*. Westminster, 1946; Vawter, B. "A Tale of Two Cities: The Old Testament and the Issue of Personal Freedom." *JES* 15 (1978): 261–73; Weinfeld, M. *Social Justice in Ancient Israel and in the Ancient Near East*. Fortress, 1995.

Stephen Charles Mott

Justice, Restorative

The term *restorative justice* was coined in the 1970s to describe a way to respond to crime that focuses primarily on repairing the damage caused by the criminal act and restoring, insofar as possible, the dignity and well-being of all those involved. From modest Mennonite beginnings in Canada and the United States, restorative justice has grown into an international social movement for the promotion of collaborative and reparative approaches to dealing with offending and its consequences. It has had an impact on judicial thought and practice in many countries, perhaps most notably in New Zealand, where it forms the cornerstone of the entire juvenile justice system.

As it has developed and spread, restorative justice has also diversified. It now embraces a wide variety of programs and processes in the criminal justice domain, some of which have been adapted from reconciliation practices in indigenous societies. The principles of restorative justice have also been extended into other fields of conflict resolution, including school discipline, workplace disputes, neighborhood conflicts, and the resolution of historical injustices and human-rights abuses. The historic Truth and Reconciliation Commission in post-apartheid South Africa was expressly founded on a commitment to restorative justice.

Restorative justice may be distinguished from more conventional approaches to criminal justice in four main ways. First, restorative justice centers on a distinctive process whereby all those affected by an incident of wrongdoing (victims, offenders, and their families and supporters) come together, in a safe and controlled environment, usually with trained facilitators, to share their feelings and opinions truthfully and resolve together how best to deal with the aftermath. The process is dialogical and democratic and is concerned principally with clarifying the harm that has been suffered and determining how best it can be remedied.

Second, restorative justice prioritizes a distinctive set of values or moral principles in addressing the impact of offending. Of particular importance are the principles of accountability, respect, truth-telling, humility, collaboration, and mutual care. Restorative justice aims to hold offenders accountable, not simply to the law, but directly to those whom they have injured, and to underscore their obligation to put right the damages or losses that they have inflicted. When offenders truthfully confess their wrongdoing, when they listen respectfully to their victims as they recount their suffering, and when they honor their obligation to make restitution, significant steps are taken to restoring the dignity and well-being of the victims.

This leads to a third distinctive feature of restorative justice: it places a special emphasis on the rights and needs of victims. Historically, the Western criminal justice system has given scant attention to victims. The overwhelming emphasis has been on the punishment of offenders and the preservation of the state's interests. Victims are almost incidental to the judicial process since, technically speaking, the designated "victim" of the offense is the state, not the actual person injured. Restorative justice, by contrast, makes victims key players in the process. Time is allocated for them to speak in detail of their experience and to clarify what type of reparation or restitution will best help them to recover. Victimization, by its very nature, is an experience of disempowerment; restorative justice seeks to reempower victims by giving them a direct role in the disposition of their case.

Finally, restorative justice has a particular way of conceptualizing crime and justice. Crime is conceived not simply as the breaking of laws, but as the hurting of people and the damaging of relationships. Similarly, justice is understood not principally as the administration of punishment or the balancing of deed and desert, but as the restoring of relationships and the healing of hurts. There is still a valid place for punishment in the justice system, as a mechanism for clarifying society's moral boundaries, for protecting the vulnerable, and for eliciting repentance from offenders. However, from the perspective of restorative justice, it is not the pain of punishment that ultimately satisfies the demands of justice but rather the vindication of victims, the healing of hurts, and the mending of broken relationships.

There is a deep resonance between restorative justice theory and key emphases in biblical teaching on justice, crime, punishment, and reconciliation. At a macrolevel, the metanarrative of the Bible as a whole tells of God's restorative response to human sin and rebellion. God does not rest content with punishing sin, but works instead, through the election of Israel and supremely through the death and resurrection of Christ, to undo the damaging consequences of evil and to restore peace to the entire created order (Rom. 8:18–30; Rev. 21:1–5). God's commitment to restore humanity and the world in this way is, for the biblical writers, fundamentally a demonstration of God's justice or God's righteousness (the terms are virtually synonymous). Justice in the Bible is not an abstract norm; it is wholly to do with relationships and with restoring relationships when they are broken. God is shown to be just because God remains steadfastly loyal to his covenant people, despite their faithlessness (Rom. 3:1–9). God's people display justice or righteousness insofar as they remain loyal to God. This entails obeying God's law, including its multitudinous injunctions to practice justice and mercy in all their dealings with one another.

Within this overarching narrative, there are many individual stories of restoration as well as countless injunctions relating to repentance, confession, forgiveness, restitution, and reconciliation. There is a pronounced restorative dimension to OT criminal law. For many crimes, the typical penalty was restitution, together with varying levels of compensation depending on the seriousness of the injury and the intent of the offender (Exod. 22:1, 4, 7, 9; Lev. 6:1–7; Num. 5:5–8; Prov. 6:30–31; cf. Luke 19:8). In every case redress went to the victim, not to the state, and the overarching concern was the renewal of *shalom*, peace, in the community.

The NT teaching on justice has a strongly restorative character. The restoring impulse of divine justice is supremely shown in the life, death, and resurrection of Christ (Rom. 1:16–17; 3:21–31; 5:1), and the beneficiaries of such justice are expected to show a persistent dedication to justice and restoration when wrongdoing occurs in their midst (Matt. 5:21–26; 18:15–17; 1 Cor. 6:1–8; cf. 2 Cor. 2:5–11). "My friends, if anyone is detected in a transgression, you who have received the Spirit should restore such a one in a spirit of gentleness" (Gal. 6:1).

See also Crime and Criminal Justice; Justice, Retributive; Punishment; Reconciliation; Reparation; Restitution; Reward and Retribution

Bibliography

De Gruchy, J. *Reconciliation: Restoring Justice*. SCM, 2002; Johnstone, G., and D. Van Ness, eds. *Handbook of Restorative Justice*. Willan, 2007; Marshall, C. *Beyond Retribution: A New Testament Vision for Justice, Crime, and Punishment*. Eerdmans, 2001; idem. *The Little Book of Biblical Justice*. Good Books, 2005; Van Ness, D., and K. Strong. *Restoring Justice: An Introduction to Restorative Justice*. 3rd ed. LexisNexis, 2006; Zehr, H. *Changing Lenses: A New Focus for Crime and Justice*. 3rd ed. Herald Press, 2005; idem. *The Little Book of Restorative Justice*. Good Books, 2002; Zehr, H., and B. Toews, eds. *Critical Issues in Restorative Justice*. Willan, 2004.

Christopher Marshall

Justice, Retributive

Reference to retributive justice is commonplace in both popular and philosophical debates on crime and punishment. Yet the concept itself is dogged with ambiguity and imprecision; it has been described as one of the most misunderstood ideas in criminal jurisprudence. Such confusion is also reflected in discussions on the place of retributive justice in the Bible.

The word *retribution* (from Lat. *retribuere*) simply means "repayment"—the giving back to another what is deserved, whether in terms of reimbursement, reward, or reproof. Usually the term is used in the negative sense of punishment for wrongful deeds rather than in the positive sense of reward for good behavior. When the word is used in isolation, it tends to evoke the idea of vengeance or retaliation, and brutal retaliation at that. When it is paired with the word *justice*, however, it implies a more measured delivery of punishment as due recompense for wrongdoing. Nonetheless, the nuance of revenge is never far from view. Consequently, some ethicists speak of retributive justice with approval, others with disapproval. Those who disapprove of retributive justice regard it as virtually synonymous with vengeance and reject the whole notion as primitive and barbaric. Punishment, some insist, is defensible only on utilitarian grounds (i.e., if it produces better outcomes than does lack of punishment). Those who approve of retributive justice, however, sharply distinguish retribution from revenge and contend that retributive considerations alone are capable of justifying punishment in moral terms and of excluding the possibility of excessive or vicarious punishment.

There are several versions of retributivism as a penal philosophy, but they share at least four fundamental ideas. The first is the notion of "guilt." Individuals, as free moral agents, are responsible for their actions, and the choice that individuals make to do wrong creates objective moral and/or legal guilt. From this flows the concept of "desert." Punishment is justified only when it is personally deserved, and, when it is deserved, punishment is all but obligatory to meet the demands of justice. The third idea is "proportionality." In order to be just, the severity of the penalty must be commensurate with the seriousness of the crime. The fourth idea is "denunciation" or "censure." The purpose of punishment is not primarily to hurt or correct or deter the offender, but rather to bear witness to the constraints imposed by the moral and legal order and to rectify the moral imbalance created by the transgression.

The singular strengths of retributive justice as a theory of punishment are its capacity to restrict punishment to the guilty party alone and to prohibit disproportionate penalties from being employed (even though correlating punishments to crimes is far from an objective science). Retributivism rightly insists that moral blameworthiness is the sine qua non for the just imposition of punitive pain; there is never a justification for vicarious or collective or exemplary punishment. This point furnishes a significant obstacle to theories of atonement that depend on the notion of substitutionary punishment.

However, retributivist theory also has limitations. Moral guilt may be an essential prerequisite for justified punishment, but it is rarely a sufficient justification, since society deems it neither expedient nor morally imperative to punish every moral infraction. Only a limited (and culturally variable) number of transgressions are singled out for penal redress. This calls into question the retributivist principle that punishment is a requirement of justice if the moral balance is to be restored. Why should punishment be the only kind of repayment that satisfies the demands of justice? Confession, repentance, and restitution are equally capable of vindicating society's moral standards, and in everyday life these frequently suffice. The analogy of family life is instructive: only abusive parents feel compelled to punish every misdemeanor of their children; a truly just parent recognizes that in most cases a gentle rebuke or an apology or a change of conduct is all that is necessary to restore the right. At a theoretical level, then, retributive justice is better able to tell us when not to punish (i.e., when the party is innocent) than when or why we must punish. The latter cannot be determined solely on moral grounds, but only by taking into account circumstantial and utilitarian considerations as well.

There is a definite theme of retribution in biblical teaching on justice. At the most basic level, the Bible recognizes that human deeds carry inescapable consequences; there is an inbuilt law of recompense in the universe that "you reap whatever you sow" (Gal. 6:7 [cf. Ps. 7:15; Prov. 1:32; 26:27; Eccl. 10:8]). In addition, the four retributive concepts of guilt and atonement, desert, proportionality, and denunciation or censure are widely attested in the OT legal system and undergird moral and theological teaching in the NT as well (see Marshall 120–27). Similarly, since God is just, and God's judgments are never capricious, biblical accounts of divine judgment on sin, both within history and at the end of time, may also be regarded as demonstrations of retributive justice. The canonical record ends with an affirmation of the retributive principle of just deserts: "See, I am coming soon; my reward is with me, to repay according to everyone's work" (Rev. 22:12).

It would be false to conclude, however, that biblical teaching on justice is wholly controlled by the notion of impersonal retribution. Justice in the Bible is not an abstract metaphysical principle; it has an intrinsically relational character. It describes what is needed to create, sustain, and restore healthy relationships in the covenant community. Criminal offending is considered wrong because it breaches covenant commitments and because the wrongful deeds themselves unleash a disordering power in the community that could trigger a chain reaction of ruin and disaster unless it is arrested. One way of arresting this negative power, especially in situations of very grave interpersonal and religious offending, was by redirecting the destructive consequences of the deed back on to the perpetrator by way of judicial or divine punishment. The punishment served simultaneously to dramatize the catastrophic consequences of evil deeds and to "purge the evil from Israel" (Deut. 17:12). When this happened, justice was vindicated not by the act of punishment per se, but by the fact that the community had, by means of the punitive action, been delivered from evil and restored to wholeness.

Yet both biblical law and biblical narrative show that retributive punishment was not invariably required in order to secure or satisfy justice. Repentance, atonement, restitution, and forgiveness are constantly solicited and frequently celebrated in Scripture as alternatives to retribution (Exod. 34:6–7; Ps. 103:3, 10; Ezek. 33:11; Mic. 7:18). Christian believers in particular are expressly summoned to forgo retribution or retaliation in favor of forgiveness and reconciliation and to leave issues of ultimate justice to God (Matt. 5:38–48; Rom. 12:17–21; 1 Pet. 2:21–23). God's retributive wrath may sometimes be activated providentially through human agents and institutions (Rom. 13:4; 1 Pet. 2:14). But repeatedly in the biblical record, and supremely in the events of the Christian gospel, "mercy triumphs over judgment" (Jas. 2:13) as the means of vindicating justice by restoring right relationships. God's justice is retributive inasmuch as it is never prejudiced, arbitrary, or impulsive and is always morally attuned to human deeds and deserts (Rom. 2:1–16). But what ultimately "shows" or "proves" God's justice (Rom. 3:26) is not the ineluctable imposition of retribution on sinners, but rather the restoration of relationship made possible by "his grace as a gift through the redemption that is in Christ Jesus" (Rom. 3:24).

See also Crime and Criminal Justice; Justice; Justice, Restorative; Moral Agency; Punishment; Restitution; Revenge; Reward and Retribution

Bibliography

Burnside, J. "Retribution and Restoration in Biblical Texts." Pages 132–48 in *Handbook of Restorative Justice*, ed. G. Johnstone and D. Van Ness. Willan, 2007; Koch, K. "Is There a Doctrine of Retribution in the OT?" Pages 57–87 in *Theodicy on the Old Testament*, ed. J. Crenshaw. IRT 4. Fortress, 1983; Marshall, C. *Beyond Retribution: A New Testament Vision for Justice, Crime, and Punishment*. Eerdmans, 2001; Moule, C. F. D. "Punishment and Retribution: An Attempt to Delimit Their Scope in New Testament Thought." *Justice Reflections* 8, no. 60 (2005): 1–20; Peels, H. *The Vengeance of God: The Meaning of the Root NQM and the Function of NQM-Texts in the Context of Divine Revelation in the Old Testament*. OtSt 31. Brill, 1995; Talbot, T. "Punishment, Forgiveness, and Divine Justice." *RelS* 29 (1993): 151–68; Travis, S. *Christ and the Judgment of God: Divine Retribution in the New Testament*. Marshall & Pickering, 1986; Zehr, H. *The Little Book of Restorative Justice*. Good Books, 2002.

Christopher Marshall

Justification, Moral

Moral justification seeks to provide good reasons for moral acts or claims. The reasonableness of an act or claim may be shown by making an appeal to principles, rules, virtues, and/or goals, such that the reasons for doing a particular act outweigh the reasons against a particular act. Different people will emphasize to varying degrees and in different combinations these different considerations. Moral justification can also be grounded within a particular moral narrative. In this case, to act inconsistently with the constructed narrative is to act in a morally unjustifiable way. Further, moral justification has two general audiences: justification within a particular moral community and justification to those who stand outside the moral community. Broadly stated, moral justification raises the question of to whom and for what does a moral account need to be given within a particular context. Moral justification can be given and received by way of a combination of relationships including oneself, another person, a community, and God.

The Bible itself can be used as a source for moral justification in connection to these various relationships; however, the Bible holds various levels of authority among ethicists as a basis for moral justification and can be used as a guiding framework or can supply concrete moral solutions, depending on the particular Christian tradition and the specific moral issue. The Bible certainly plays a particularly critical role in moral justification for Protestant ethicists, has maintained an important place among Orthodox ethicists, and has increasingly been an important resource for Roman Catholic ethicists since Vatican II.

Two important aspects of moral justification in relationship to the Bible can be posed as questions. First, is the issue raised directly in the Bible? Second, how much does the historical context differ from the contemporary situation? For example, some moral issues, such as human cloning, are never specifically discussed in the Bible. Other issues, such as care for the poor, are clearly raised. In regard to historical context and contemporary situation, one highly debated question is the issue of homosexuality. Some ethicists argue that scriptural passages are quite clear about the immorality of homosexuality. Other ethicists argue that a more historically critical approach reveals a quite different understanding of sexuality from our own time, justifying homosexuality.

Finally, there is no general consensus on how the Bible relates to other sources of moral justification such as reason, human experience, and tradition. There is a strong integration of the Bible with tradition by Roman Catholic and Orthodox ethicists, and the experience of the marginalized in relationship to the Bible is important for liberationist ethicists. Rationality, while significant for ethicists, is increasingly challenged in its ability to justify universal moral claims due to a greater awareness of pluralism.

See also Narrative Ethics, Biblical; Narrative Ethics, Contemporary; Orthodox Ethics; Roman Catholic Moral Theology; Virtue Ethics

Bibliography

Birch, B., and L. Rasmussen. *Bible and Ethics in the Christian Life*. Rev. ed. Augsburg, 1989; Cosgrove, C. *Appealing to Scripture in Moral Debate: Five Hermeneutical Rules*. Eerdmans, 2002; Curran, C., and R. McCormick, eds. *The Use of Scripture in Moral Theology*. RMT 4. Paulist Press, 1984; McDonald, J. *Biblical Interpretation and Christian Ethics*. NSCE. Cambridge University Press, 1993.

Mark A. Tarpley

Just-Peacemaking Theory

Just peacemaking is the recently developed paradigm for the ethics of peace and war, alongside the historic paradigms of just war and pacifism. The older paradigms debate whether war is justifiable; just peacemaking focuses discussion on the proactive practices that prevent war and create peace.

Growing Awareness among Church Leaders

After the horrors of World War II many worked to develop practices to prevent a repeat of such devastation or worse, especially with nuclear weapons. Leaders in major church denominations in the United States saw that these practices of peacemaking were working to prevent wars and should be made widely known and supported. In the 1980s four book-length statements by major church denominations in the United States said that just war and pacifism do not provide adequate tools for guiding public debate about war and peace; we need a widely known new paradigm that enables Christians to resonate with one another in public discussion, thereby prodding governments to engage in practices that make for peace.

In *The Challenge of Peace*, the United States Conference of Catholic Bishops said,

> Recognition of the Church's responsibility to join with others in the work of peace is a major force behind the call today to develop a theology of peace. Much of the history of Catholic theology on war and peace has focused on limiting the resort to force in human affairs [just-war theory and pacifism]; this task is still necessary, . . . but it is not a sufficient response.
>
> A fresh reappraisal which includes a developed theology of peace will require contributions from several sectors of the Church's life: biblical studies, systematic and moral theology, ecclesiology, and the experience and insights of members of the church who have struggled in various ways to make and keep the peace in this often violent age. (§§23–24)

Methodists (*In Defense of Creation*), Presbyterians (*Peacemaking: The Believers' Calling*), and the United Church of Christ (*The Just Peace Church*) issued a similar call.

Accordingly, twenty-three interdisciplinary scholars from numerous denominations, Catholic and Protestant, joined together and worked successfully to develop an agreed new paradigm in 1998, and thirty scholars published the third edition in 2008 as *Just Peacemaking: The New Paradigm for the Ethics of Peace and War*. They include both just-war theorists and pacifists, who disagree on whether war is ever justified but agree that the ten practices of just peacemaking are effective in preventing many wars and are obligatory for people and governments to support. They agree it is time to do more than discuss whether we approve of a war; we need to gather public discussion around these practices that actually work to prevent war. Subsequently, the Evangelical Lutheran Church in America in *For Peace in God's World*, the Christian Reformed Church of North America in the adoption of its report "War and Peace," the Protestant Church of Germany in *Aus Gottes Frieden leben—für gerechten Frieden sorgen*, and the German Catholic Church in *Gerechter Friede* also shifted the emphasis from whether to justify war to advocacy of just peace and its practices. All are saying that, without a widely known paradigm with agreed practices that make peace and prevent war, public debate is vague and unclear about the effective alternatives to the drive to war.

The Ten Practices of Just Peacemaking

The ten practices in the just-peacemaking paradigm are grouped under themes of transforming initiatives, working for justice, and building community:

Peacemaking Initiatives

1. Support nonviolent direct action.
2. Take independent initiatives to reduce threat.
3. Use cooperative conflict resolution.
4. Acknowledge responsibility for conflict and injustice; seek repentance and forgiveness.

Justice

5. Advance democracy, human rights, and religious liberty.
6. Foster just and sustainable economic development.

Love and Community

7. Work with emerging cooperative forces in the international system.
8. Strengthen the United Nations and international efforts for cooperation and human rights.
9. Reduce offensive weapons and weapons trade.
10. Encourage grassroots peacemaking groups and voluntary associations.

The authors of *Just Peacemaking: The New Paradigm for the Ethics of Peace and War* urge that, in discussions of just-peacemaking theory, it is important to name practices specifically; otherwise, we fall back into the vagueness of being generally in favor of peace while failing to support the specific practices that make peace. They point out that the ten practices constitute a unified and agreed paradigm, not merely ten chapters by different authors. The ten practices are the result of five years of dialogical work, and the practices as well as the chapters defining them are the unanimous consensus of the diverse authors.

The authors explicitly state that they come to the ten practices of just peacemaking from deeply held faith commitments but also from empirical realism, as the ten practices are showing themselves to work empirically in decreasing wars, which is shown in the research of political scientists as well as the experience of recent history. They appeal to persons and groups of various faiths to join with them in supporting these specific, realistic, effective peacemaking practices. In 2008, thirty leading Muslim, Jewish, and Christian scholars, working with support from the United States Institute of Peace, agreed to this joint statement: "We all believe that Just Peacemaking is the best option to resolve human conflicts and actively work towards the elimination of the conditions that lead to violence. . . . We all agree to mine our own religious traditions to further develop the Just Peacemaking practices" (http://www.usip.org/files/resources/sr214.pdf).

Scriptural Reasoning with Analogical Contextualization

The first four peacemaking practices are initiatives based on a discipleship understanding of Christ's way as the authoritative model for ethical practice, with emphasis on his call to disciples to follow humbly his way of peacemaking. Paul's letters advocate initiatives for overcoming divisions within churches and divisions between Jews and gentiles. The Gospels see Jesus embodying God's love for all humankind, and the Sermon on the Mount portrays Jesus' way of confronting evil not by violence but through transforming initiatives (Stassen, ed., *Just Peacemaking*, 19–22).

This emphasis on peacemaking initiatives is based especially on the discovery that throughout the Sermon on the Mount the climax of each teaching is always a transforming initiative. Accordingly, a Christian ethic of peacemaking should include not only prohibitions but also transforming initiatives of deliverance from the destruction of war. Therefore, just peacemaking sees peace as something to be achieved not merely by refraining from war, but also by taking peacemaking initiatives. It is rooted in the heart of the biblical understanding of God's grace, which takes dramatic initiatives in coming to us, speaking in the burning bush (Exod. 3:1–4), pouring love into us in Jesus Christ while we were God's enemies (Rom. 5:1–21), and bringing God's delivering presence in Jesus.

In explaining the Sermon on the Mount as transforming initiatives, and referring to Glen Stassen's 1992 book *Just Peacemaking: Transforming Initiatives for Justice and Peace*, the authors of *Just Peacemaking: The New Paradigm for the Ethics of Peace and War* signal that the just-peacemaking ethic was actually first inspired by scriptural interpretation. Stassen's book grew out of the discovery that the structure and the theme of Jesus' Sermon on the Mount are not twofold "antitheses" but rather are threefold "transforming initiatives," and that this is echoed in Paul's Letter to the Romans. This discovery was first published in a series of articles in the 1980s, and then in the 1992 book on just peacemaking. So the scriptural discovery preceded and led to the ethic of just peacemaking.

For example, Matt. 5:21–26 commands someone involved in a relationship of anger or hostility to go to the adversary and make peace. There is no command not to be angry; the command is to go, talk, and make peace, which was crucial in Jesus' time of increasing conflict. What is the analogous practice in our context? Just peacemaking answers that the practice is conflict resolution with adversaries. And if Christ is Lord over all of life, this suggests practicing conflict resolution in marriages and families, in church relations, in work relationships, and in disagreements with nations such as the former Soviet Union, North Korea, and Iran. The historical context in 1980 and 1992, as just peacemaking was developing, required practicing conflict resolution in talks with the Soviet Union that helped end the Cold War and decrease the threat of nuclear destruction.

A second example is Matt. 5:33–42, where Jesus commands the transforming initiatives of turning the cheek of equal dignity, giving cloak as well as coat, going the second mile, and giving and lending to a beggar. These are nonviolent confrontations that seek a transformed, more peaceful relationship. What would be the analogous practice in our time? Just peacemaking answers that Mohandas Gandhi's and Abdul Gaffar Khan's practice of nonviolent direct action in India's struggle for independence, Martin Luther King Jr.'s similar practice in the civil rights struggle, and practices of nonviolent direct action spreading worldwide are clear analogies of Jesus' teaching for our historical context. But there is also the practice of independent initiatives, which worked to achieve a nuclear test ban in the Eisenhower and Kennedy administrations and since, and to reduce by one-half the number of nuclear weapons as the Cold War was ending. Scriptural interpretation, combined with the hermeneutical method of analogical contextualization, led to the development of the just-peacemaking paradigm.

Similarly, Jesus' and Paul's teaching against judging, but instead taking the logs out of our own eyes, connected directly with the practice of acknowledging our own responsibility for conflict and injustice and seeking repentance and forgiveness. Historically, governments had resisted apologizing for their errors, fearing that it indicated weakness. However, Dietrich Bonhoeffer, directly influenced by his own interpretation of the Sermon on the Mount in his book *Discipleship*, and then German churches initiated this practice after the Holocaust and World War II. Subsequently, the German government, followed by other governments, has begun apologizing, sometimes initiating reparations payments, as those made to Japanese Americans badly mistreated during World War II. In South Africa's Truth and Reconciliation Commission and in Rwanda this practice has greatly decreased the hostility that might have boiled over into new violence.

The next two just-peacemaking practices are practices of justice. The four basic words for *justice* in Hebrew and Greek are repeated 1,060 times in the Bible, more than almost any other term. The biblical prophets repeatedly insist that returning to God and practicing justice is the way to prevent the destruction of war. Jesus identifies with this prophetic message and calls those in authority and the wealthy to repent for neglecting justice, faithfulness, and mercy, and for covering their sins with temple sacrifices while neglecting the poor, the powerless, and widows and orphans (he cites Jer. 7:11 as he ejects the money traders from the temple). As Isaiah proclaimed justice based on God's compassion for those suffering injustice, so also did Jesus.

The final four practices are based on Jesus' teaching that all on whom God shines sun and drops rain, even one's enemies, are to be included in the community of neighbors and on his interaction with a Samaritan woman (John 4:5–30) and a Syrophoenician woman (Mark 7:24–30). Love must be understood realistically, not sentimentally, acting in concrete ways to create community interaction and covenant community. In the present context, this suggests participative and inclusive community development at local, ecclesial, and international levels.

See also Conflict; Deterrence, Nuclear; Forgiveness; Imitation of Jesus; Justice; Just-War Theory; Pacifism; Peace; Reparation; Restitution; Sermon on the Mount; Violence; War

Bibliography

Christiansen, D. "Catholic Peacemaking 1991–2005: The Legacy of Pope John Paul II." *RFIA* 4, no. 2 (2006): 21–28; Fuller Theological Seminary. "The Long Reach toward Just Peacemaking." *Theology News & Notes* (Spring 2009): http://documents.fuller.edu/news/pubs/tnn/2009_Spring/index.asp; Stassen, G. *Just Peacemaking: Transforming Initiatives for Justice and Peace*. Westminster John Knox, 1992; idem, ed. *Just Peacemaking: The New Paradigm for the Ethics of Peace and War*. 3rd ed. Pilgrim Press, 2008; idem et al. "Resource Section on Just Peacemaking Theory." *JSCE* 23, no. 1 (2003): 169–284; Thistlethwaite, S. "New Wars, Old Wineskins." Pages 264–79 in *Strike Terror No*

More: Theology, Ethics, and the New War, ed. J. Berquist. Chalice Press, 2002; Thompson, J. "Humanitarian Intervention, Just Peacemaking and the United Nations." Pages 83–93 in *The Return of the Just War*, ed. M. Aquino and D. Mieth. SCM, 2002; United States Conference of Catholic Bishops. *The Challenge of Peace: God's Promise and Our Response*. United States Catholic Conference, 1983; United States Institute of Peace, http://www.usip.org/files/resources/sr214.pdf.

Glen H. Stassen

Just Wage

"Wage" refers to the payment given or received for work performed. "Just wage" refers to payment given and received in a timely fashion that is proportionate to the work done. Both the OT and the NT include numerous texts that demand just wages for workers and condemn employers who fail to provide them. Although these texts cannot legitimately be used without qualification to support a specific economic system or civil law regarding wages in contemporary societies, they do provide Christians with an important biblical concern—the just treatment of workers—that can be used to evaluate economic systems and laws regarding wages.

Wage as Metaphor for Divine Action

Some biblical passages use the word *wage* metaphorically to describe God's response to the action of humans. Hence, Paul says that death constitutes the payment humanity receives for its sinfulness: "The wages of sin is death" (Rom. 6:23). The parable of the laborers in the field depicts God's unmerited grace by referring to wages that exceed expectations (Matt. 20:1–16). Elsewhere, Paul says that those who sow in the mission field "will receive wages according to the labor of each" (1 Cor. 3:8), clearly referring to divine reward rather than monetary earnings. Wage or recompense can also refer to something tangible given by God to those whose actions merit reward. For example, God gives the land of Egypt to Nebuchadnezzar as "the wages for his army" and "the payment for which he labored" (Ezek. 29:19–20).

Just Wage as Compensation for Labor

The Bible contains numerous passages regarding the giving of fair wages by employers to their workers. Mosaic law, for instance, includes the demand to pay wages at the end of each day to protect laborers, including immigrants, from abuse and to help them survive (Lev. 19:13; Deut. 24:14–15). There are also pronouncements of judgment in the OT against those who do not give fair wages (e.g., Jer. 22:13). In the NT, the writer of James says that the very wages that were unjustly withheld from workers cry out along with the harvesters who were cheated (Jas. 5:4). One text admonishes wage earners (specifically, soldiers) to be satisfied with their wages (Luke 3:14); however, since this admonition is set alongside concerns for treating people justly by sharing food and clothing, for not collecting more than the required taxes, and for not extorting money through false accusations, the admonition cannot be rightly understood as telling people to be satisfied with poor wages. The OT and the NT are consistently concerned with treating laborers fairly by paying a just wage. In fact, the familiar claim that "the labourer is worthy of his hire" (Luke 10:7 KJV) summarizes the message in both Testaments regarding fair wages: a worker should be given a fair wage in proportion to the work done.

Contemporary Debates regarding Just Wage

None of these passages from Scripture, taken individually or collectively, can lead Christians to say definitively that one economic system (e.g., socialism versus capitalism) or that a particular law (such as one that promotes the concept of a minimum wage) is supported by the Bible. Although the Bible speaks of God's concern for economic justice, it does not teach economics per se. Furthermore, the various economic systems familiar to ancient Israelites and to the early church were often vastly different from what we encounter in contemporary societies today. Nevertheless, Christians can be informed by the Bible when evaluating the effectiveness of a particular economic system or law. Christians may differ regarding which types of laws or economic systems best serve to provide a just wage to laborers. What is not debatable, however, is that the Bible exhorts Christians to care about laborers and that they receive a just wage. Indifference on this issue is clearly unbiblical.

See also Business Ethics; Capitalism; Economic Ethics; Exploitation; Justice; Work

Bibliography

Glickman, L. *A Living Wage: American Workers and the Making of Consumer Society*. Cornell University Press, 1997; John Paul II. *On Human Work*. United States Catholic Conference, 1981.

Nancy J. Duff

Just-War Theory

The expression "just war" refers to a two-thousand-year-old continuing tradition of Western moral reflection concerning war and peace. In the just-war tradition "war is always judged twice" (Walzer 21). First, there is judging the justifications for, or the justifiability of, going to war—whether waging war is the right thing to do. Second, there is judging the justifications for, or the justice of, the means for fighting in war—whether war is conducted rightly. The Latin phrases for these two judgments are *jus ad bellum* ("justice to war") and *jus in bello* ("justice in war"). Over the course of time, the just-war tradition has developed ethical criteria for making these moral judgments, which seek to constrain might according to standards of right.

Moral Criteria for Judging War

While there is no official, single index of moral criteria, ten commend themselves, and these are named in parentheses in the two lists below. The first eight judge *jus ad bellum*, and the last two judge *jus in bello*.

Waging war is justifiable:

1. when it is in response to the perpetration of a real injury (just cause);
2. when it is declared by legitimate public authority (legitimate authority);
3. when the legitimate authority prosecuting the war has righteous intentions (right intention);
4. when the goal of waging war is to restore a situation of peace with justice (goal of peace);
5. when war is undertaken only after exhausting other reasonable means of peaceful settlement (last resort);
6. when the overall damage caused by war will not exceed the original injury suffered (proportionality of ends);
7. when there is a reasonable hope that the purpose for going to war can be successfully accomplished (probability of success);
8. when there is a public declaration of the reasons for waging war (public declaration).

The conduct of war is justifiable:

1. when war does not target noncombatants (noncombatant discrimination);
2. when war uses only means proportional to the value of the target (proportionality of means).

The moral criteria for waging and conducting war, while varied, have a certain coherence about them. Still, important questions surface. How do the criteria conflict with one another in the real world? If so, what then? Do any criteria have priority over others? How completely must each or all of the criteria be met? What happens, for instance, with right intention when faced with mixed motives, which is surely an all-too-human occurrence? What happens when people do not have enough information to assess whether criteria have been met? What happens when those with knowledge about a situation lie, deceive, or are simply mistaken? Who holds whom accountable to the criteria? What happens when one party to a conflict does not follow just-war criteria? Since the just-war tradition has developed within Western civilization, what is its value and standing within other great global civilizations and within international law?

A Tradition of Judging War

The criteria for judging war are important, and yet the just-war tradition cannot be reduced to criteria alone. Traditions develop over long periods of time and are full-bodied, with characteristic ways of thinking, feeling, speaking, acting, and relating with peculiar attitudes, beliefs, loyalties, and habits of mind and heart. The just-war tradition is a prudential moral tradition requiring experience, wisdom, and practice to weigh matters of varying moral densities, and thus it steers a middle way between absolutism and relativism. Relations between peoples, nation-states, and social movements are messy, and complexities arise. It is tempting, but not wise, to expect more precision out of this prudential moral tradition than the complex matters at hand permit (Cook 32).

There are ambiguities associated with the just-war tradition due to the different contexts and time periods out of which it has developed and because different terminologies have been used. Most important, however, there are ambiguities "because of the expectations of many persons today regarding war, expectations that are transferred to the just war idea" (Johnson xxi). These transferred expectations have largely come from three other influential traditions dealing with questions of war and peace: war realism, holy war/crusade, and pacifism. The expectations that have been transferred from war realism and holy war/crusade have led to serious misunderstandings of the just-war tradition and how it judges war. The just-war tradition holds a strong presumption for peace. It seeks to restrain war, and it therefore holds certain things in common with the varieties of pacifism. It is important to consider how a unified theory and tradition of just peacemaking and just war might be forged (Simpson 33–36, 79–90).

Classical Footsteps of the Just-War Tradition

Marcus Tullius Cicero (106–43 BCE) left the first footprint of the just-war tradition. He made a brief case for just war in *On Duties* when he rebuked his own state, Rome, for too often waging war for the unjustifiable reasons of establishing supremacy and gaining glory. He placed war within the natural law of self-preservation in the face of another's violent aggression. The natural right to repel force with force in order to secure peace is "the only righteous grounds for going to war" (Simpson 40). He also criticized Rome for waging war without first exhausting discussion, thus inaugurating the criterion of "last resort." Finally, he cited many examples in which conducting war using proportional means contributed to an eventual sustainable peace.

Bishop Ambrose of Milan (339–97 CE) read Cicero extensively, considered him a righteous pagan, and passed on his key moral insights to Western Christianity. Ambrose stressed that defending the weak and the oppressed is a key aspect of justice in his famous maxim, "Whoever does not ward off a blow to a fellow man, when he can, is as much at fault as the striker" (Simpson 41). By emphasizing the failure to protect as the moral equivalent of war, he influentially extended the natural law principle, "Do no harm."

Bishop Augustine of Hippo (354–430 CE) is the most important figure in the historical development of the just-war tradition. He placed the first three moral criteria within the overall goal of establishing peace anchored in justice. He also stressed right intention by arguing that wars of desire are unjust, and only wars of necessity are justifiable. Even wars of necessity are limited in what they can be expected to accomplish, and they should not be waged in order to create the city of God here on earth. He was a prodigious interpreter of the Scriptures and carefully used common distinctions between self-defense as private citizens and public officials defending others to help Christians understand how followers of Jesus, who had told his disciples to turn the other cheek, may participate in a just war. Augustine rooted his moral reasoning in love and compared a just war with a father who in love disciplines a son who persists in wrong.

Augustine, however, also opened a crack in the conceptual door of the ethics of war and peace that centuries later would be pried open farther to argue for the Crusades. As bishop, he had to deal with numerous Christian heretics, including the Donatists, who at times violently persecuted other Christians. He advised the ruler Boniface that it was within his political office to wage war not only to secure the love and protection of neighbor commanded in the second table of the Decalogue but also to secure the love of God commanded in the first table and thus to defend right worship and doctrine.

Johannes Gratian (mid-twelfth century) gathered together thousands of authoritative theological, moral, legal, and civil statements that often seemed quite disconnected from one another at best and mutually contradictory at worst. He arranged them into a comprehensive, ordered whole, *The Concord of Discordant Canons*, or the *Decretum*. He produced the *Decretum* because a law is not really a law until it has been promulgated. He made Augustine's moral reasoning on war and peace the centerpiece of the just-war tradition. Gratian's collection of canon law (ecclesiastical law governing the Roman Catholic Church) was the standard text until the twentieth century and served both church and government during medieval times, when often they were seamlessly joined.

Thomas Aquinas (1225–74) was a university theologian who gave the tradition its scholarly status. In *Summa theologiae* he took Augustine's thinking, honed on the streets of a working bishop who offered practical moral counsel to political rulers, and worked it into a brief, ordered, and authoritative text for the university.

Thomas considered war under two topics: first under charity, whose principal action is to love, and second under religious orders. After defining charity, he dealt with the vices that oppose charity, including war. He begins his examination of war, as he begins every topic in the *Summa*, by posing a question: "Is it always sinful to wage war?" He thereby presumes war's sinfulness; any other judgment regarding war would have to meet rigorous criteria. He then enumerates legitimate authority, just cause, and right intention, with accompanying quotations from Augustine, as the three necessary moral criteria that establish the bar in order for a war to be considered just. Thomas's list set these three criteria in stone as the mainstay of the tradition from this time on.

By setting the topic of war also under religious orders, however, Thomas Aquinas legitimated the Crusades. First, he agreed with Augustine that temporal authority can be used to maintain right worship. Second, he argued that the church under the pope and bishops can bear the sword through the soldiering of religious orders, something that Augustine did not contemplate. Third, he took the book of 1 Maccabees to provide the biblical framework. Finally, he argued that military crusading can be a legitimate religious penance for wrongdoing.

Transforming Footsteps of the Just-War Tradition

Martin Luther (1483–1546) brought the just-war tradition into the thinking of the Protestant

Reformation by using Augustine's distinction between wars of desire and wars of necessity, and he advised that even just wars of necessity should be waged "with repentance." He used the distinction between law and gospel to argue against a reemerging pacifist interpretation of Scripture. Importantly, he also criticized Augustine's legacy of promoting the use of the sword by political authorities to restrain heresy, although in 1543 he himself would atrociously backslide when it came to the Jews in Germany, who rejected Jesus' divinity. He criticized any crusade against the Muslim Ottoman Empire as "idolatry and blasphemy" (Simpson 57). Finally, he supported what today is called "selective conscientious objection," whereby a soldier may refuse to serve in a particular war because it is manifestly unjust. In such cases, "We must obey God rather than any human authority" (Acts 5:29).

Francisco de Vitoria (1483–1546) was a Spanish Roman Catholic theologian who founded the School of Salamanca. Emperor Charles V sought Vitoria's advice regarding the "discovery" and military rule of the so-called New World. First, Vitoria viewed the native people as indeed being the owners of this "new" world, and therefore Spain had no property rights of discovery. Second, according to the criterion of just cause, he argued that Spanish imperial expansion violated just war. Third, he rejected holy war and the proposition that the pope has temporal authority to use the sword to convert the native people. "Difference of religion is not a cause of just war" (Simpson 60). Fourth, he introduced a new insight into the criterion of legitimate authority. While the legitimate sovereign has the right to declare a justifiable war, others also have a right to discern whether the sovereign ought to declare war, since notoriously sovereigns always think that they have a just cause. Finally, Vitoria gave considerable attention to the situation of noncombatants and to the treatment of prisoners of war and thus paved the way for the further development of *jus in bello* criteria, even though today people would not agree with him on each of his judgments on these matters.

Hugo Grotius (1583–1645) was a Dutch jurist who anticipated the coming era of international relations and is often called the "father of international law." He wrote *On the Law of War and Peace* during the Thirty Years' War (1618–48), paving the way for the Westphalian era. He placed just-war reasoning firmly on a natural-law basis while minimizing the reliance of the just-war tradition upon Scripture, Christian faith, and the church fathers. Famously, he sought an argument for just war "even if we should concede that which cannot be conceded without the utmost wickedness, that there is no God" (Simpson 63). Following Cicero, he made his appeal to natural law through the mediation of the law of nations—*jus gentium*—a common recognition among many or all nations of some fundamental moral insights. These commonly accepted moral insights signaled, but did not guarantee, that the insights disclosed natural law.

Grotius focused just cause on self-defense, although he included two other traditional just causes: the recovery of property or debt, and deterrent punishment for a committed offense. He located legitimate authority in the association of free persons who make up a state. This modern concept of sovereignty depends more on the quality of public procedures than on the personal moral character of the ruler under God's judgment. He redefined the purpose of the public declaration of war to be less about warning the enemy and more about placing a state's rationale for waging war up for public scrutiny and accountability by the community of nation-states. He sought to hold powerful nations more internationally accountable for meeting just-war criteria. Such public accountability places a very high bar on preemptive war, puts a check on so-called preventive wars whereby "the possibility of being attacked confers the right to attack [which] is abhorrent to every principle of equity" (Grotius, *On the Law of War and Peace* 2.1.17), and strengthens the obligation of selective conscientious objection. Finally, Grotius united in a single work the criteria of *jus ad bellum* and *jus in bello* with extensive analyses of proportionality of means and noncombatant immunity of civilians. He concluded his analysis of *jus in bello* with a treatment of the natural law of good faith even between enemies in order to bring about a lasting peace, and even when one party exercises bad faith.

The Just-War Tradition and International Humanitarian Law

The work of Grotius and his followers led to the development of the "international humanitarian law" of war and peace beginning in the mid-nineteenth century. The International Committee of the Red Cross (ICRC) highlighted the right of soldiers to medical attention and the right of medical and relief personnel to noncombatant immunity. In 1863 the United States created the Lieber Code, which first codified in law the *jus in bello* criteria even though it was only a US code. In 1864 Switzerland convened twelve states in Geneva (the United States chose not to participate) to adopt the first Geneva Convention regarding *jus in bello*. The Hague Conventions of 1899 and 1907 were convened to adopt *jus in bello* criteria and also ratified the Geneva Conventions.

In 1945 the United Nations Charter confirmed the Westphalian principle of sovereign, equal, and inviolable nation-states, included the just-war criterion of just cause restricted to defense alone, and declared the planning, preparing, initiating, or waging of war of aggression to be "crimes against peace." In 1949 the United Nations convened four Geneva Conventions and their three Additional Protocols. These form the core of international humanitarian law and *jus in bello*, establish the fiduciary and protective role of the ICRC, and set the international benchmarks for "war crimes" and "crimes against humanity." The question of humanitarian intervention has intensified since the 1990s, and the United Nations is developing the "Responsibility to Protect" protocol in order to respond collaboratively to conscience-shocking situations.

See also Deterrence, Nuclear; Force, Use of; Holy War; Just-Peacemaking Theory; Military Service; Pacifism; Peace; Violence; War

Bibliography

Cook, M. *The Moral Warrior: Ethics and Service in the U.S. Military*. State University of New York Press, 2004; Elshtain, J. *Women and War*. Basic Books, 1987; Johnson, J. *Just War Tradition and the Restraint of War: A Moral and Historical Inquiry*. Princeton University Press, 1981; Simpson, G. *War, Peace, and God: Rethinking the Just-War Tradition*. Augsburg Fortress, 2007; Walzer, M. *Just and Unjust Wars: A Moral Argument with Historical Illustrations*. 3rd ed. Basic Books, 2000.

Gary M. Simpson

K

Killing

Killing, or offending the life of another being, whether human or animal, is a surprisingly complex topic in Scripture considering the Decalogue's injunction against it. While the Hebrew verb *rāṣaḥ*, found in Exod. 20:13; Deut. 5:17 and translated as "kill" (KJV) and "murder" (NRSV), refers to the taking of a human life, the biblical witness in regard to all forms of killing reveals that the Bible presents varied accounts of killing, ranging from God's command to kill to God's suffering and overcoming state-sponsored killing in Jesus' resurrection. Throughout, God is presented as the only rightful taker of life.

Attending to Scripture

The Bible addresses killing in some form from cover to cover. Genesis 1:30 states that God gave all animals green plants for food, implying that they, including human beings, need not kill to eat. Israel's prophets echo this presentation of the goodness of creation in images of a peaceful kingdom where predator and prey will be at peace during the reign of the Messiah (Isa. 11:6–9; 65:25). Just as there was no killing in the beginning, the Bible suggests that there will be no killing at the end. Indeed, Paul in Rom. 8 writes that the whole of creation will benefit from Jesus' defeat of sin and death through his resurrection: "Creation itself will be set free from its bondage to decay and will obtain the freedom of the glory of the children of God" (Rom. 8:21). The book of Revelation ends with a vision of God dwelling with humankind in the new Jerusalem, where God "will wipe every tear from their eyes. Death will be no more; mourning and crying and pain will be no more" (Rev. 21:4). While the Bible is bookended by visions of cosmic peace where killing has no place, it remains to be seen how killing figures in the history of God's people.

The treatment of killing in the opening chapters of Genesis reveals the contours of killing's role throughout the OT. Immediately after Adam and Eve's expulsion from Eden, each of their two sons engages in a form of killing: Abel sacrifices a sheep, and Cain murders Abel. God approves of Abel's act and condemns Cain's, beginning a long history where killing is variously considered. The story of Noah in Gen. 6–9 continues to develop these themes. Because of the corruption and reign of violence on the earth "by all flesh" (Gen. 6:11–13), God decides to kill all creatures apart from the remnant saved on the ark. In this second creation story, God figures as both the giver and the taker of life, highlighting the priority of God over life. However, this narrative also emphasizes God's intentions for creation. God instructs Noah and his family to care for the animals in the ark by bringing all the necessary food with them (Gen. 6:21–22); the residents of the ark are not to eat one another. This example of human stewardship surprisingly concludes with Noah's sacrificial offerings of each of the clean animals (Gen. 8:20). This act of offering (and its necessary killing) pleases God, and God promises never again to destroy all creatures, despite the ongoing reality of human wickedness. With this new start, God allows humans to take animal life for food but forbids the eating of blood. Moreover, God prohibits human bloodshed and mandates that any creature, whether human or animal, who kills a human shall be put to death (Gen. 9:1–7).

With the conclusion of the Noah story, five ethical dimensions related to killing in the OT come into focus:

1. God sometimes kills humans and animals directly—for example, through the flood (Gen. 7:17–24), plagues (Exod. 7–12), and so forth.
2. God commands some human killing—for example, capital punishment for various infringements of the law (Exod. 21:12–17) and the ban in some acts of warfare (Deut. 20:10–18).
3. God allows for the killing of animals for food after the flood, but for Israel this killing is highly limited by dietary laws (Lev. 11).

4. God favorably accepts animal sacrifice as a form of worship and orders the liturgical and sacrificial life of Israel.
5. God forbids unauthorized killing, such as murder. The Hebrew word *rāṣaḥ*, found in the Decalogue's prohibition of murder, is also used to describe unintentional killing (Deut. 4:41–43; 19:1–13), thereby emphasizing the importance of preserving life.

Throughout the OT, killing is an act that is highly circumscribed. Although God authorizes and directs some killing, it is clear that the legitimacy of taking a life depends on God's prescription. For Israel, killing takes two primary forms: obedience to God's commands, and the sacrifice of animals in worship.

The NT witness radicalizes the trajectory found in the OT. In the Sermon on the Mount, Jesus teaches nonviolence and love for enemies (Matt. 5:38–48). He rejects bloodshed as a means to prevent his death, forgoing armed intervention (Matt. 26:51–53). Jesus allows himself to be wrongfully killed, thereby embodying the peaceful kingdom that he preaches throughout his life. In Jesus' death and resurrection, God inaugurates a new regime where God transforms killing and death. As a result of the age that has dawned with Christ, Paul echoes Jesus' call to love and care for enemies, rejecting vengeance and evil (Rom. 12:14–21). The letter to the Hebrews describes Jesus' death as a complete and perfect sacrifice, positing an end to the Jewish sacrificial system (Heb. 10:1–18). With Jesus fulfilling both Israel's law (Matt. 5:17–18) and worship, Jesus nullifies the main reasons for killing, according to the OT.

However, some NT passages also raise the question of licit killing. In Rom. 13 Paul famously defends the right of governing authorities to bear the sword. Acts 15 records the early church's decision to allow gentile converts to adhere to the more general rules about the eating of meat given to Noah in Gen. 9:1–7. Paul similarly affirms eating meat and allows for Christians to eat meat offered to idols provided this witness does not diminish others' faith (Rom. 14; 1 Cor. 8; 10:14–31).

Killing and the Christian Tradition

While the logic of Jesus' fulfillment presses in the direction of Christian nonviolence, Christians have arrived at varying conclusions about killing. The eating of meat persisted in the early church, though Christian practices of fasting and asceticism developed that involve either lifelong or periodic disciplines of abstinence from meat. Christians have also debated humankind's rightful relationship with animals, with many understanding God's accordance of human dominion in Gen. 1:26–28 to authorize the killing of animals for human benefit. Given modern treatment of animals in industrial agriculture and scientific research, many Christians are raising questions about just appropriation of animals and a reassessment of humanity's task of "dominion."

Debates about rightful killing of humans have played a more prominent role in the Christian tradition. During the period of the early church, Christian martyrs embraced death and life with Christ, allowing themselves to be persecuted and killed. Christian teaching until the fourth century promoted pacifism. Few Christians participated in the military prior to the year 170, and many of those who did serve after the late second century did so in a civic or administrative capacity. With the growing acceptance of Christianity by the Roman Empire, Christian teaching began to allow for participation in warfare and killing on behalf of the state in order to preserve justice and obtain peace. Augustine offered a full account of just-war reasoning in the fifth century, and this position has been the dominant one in the Christian tradition, though at various points in time some Christians have advocated for the legitimacy of holy war while others have urged a return to Christian pacifism. As Christians assumed responsibility for protecting the civic order, they also engaged in capital punishment. The assumption that Christians would exercise civic responsibilities continued with the Reformation, as Luther's treatise on secular authority makes clear. Christian pacifists have questioned Christians' engagement with the state and the legitimacy of killing for the sake of justice. Christians continue to forbid killing at the personal level, though debates about this prohibition have raged within bioethics.

See also Abortion; Animals; Ban, The; Bioethics; Capital Punishment; Death and Dying; Euthanasia; Force, Use of; Holy War; Infanticide; Justice, Retributive; Just-War Theory; Martyrdom; Military Service; Murder; Pacifism; Peace; Sanctity of Human Life; Suicide; Ten Commandments; Vegetarianism; Violence; War

Bibliography

Augustine. *City of God*. Trans. H. Bettenson. Penguin Books, 2003; Bainton, R. *Christian Attitudes toward War and Peace*. Abingdon, 1960; Hauerwas, S., and J. Berkman. "A Trinitarian Theology of the 'Chief End' of 'All Flesh.'" Pages 62–74 in *Good News for Animals? Christian Approaches to Animal Well-Being*, ed. C. Pinches and J. McDaniel. Orbis, 1993; Hays, R. *The Moral Vision of the New Testament: Community, Cross, and New Creation; A Contemporary Introduction to New Testament Ethics*. HarperSanFrancisco, 1996; Luther, M. "Secular Authority: To What Extent It Should Be Obeyed." Pages

363–402 in *Martin Luther: Selections from His Writings*, ed. J. Dillenberger. Doubleday, 1962; Verhey, A. *Remembering Jesus: Christian Community, Scripture, and the Moral Life*. Eerdmans, 2002. Webb, S. *Good Eating*. Brazos, 2001; Yoder, J. *The Politics of Jesus: Vicit Agnus Noster*. 2nd ed. Eerdmans, 1994.

Sarah Stokes Musser

Kingdom of God

In all of Jesus' teaching no idea is more important, more central, or more resonant than the kingdom of God. The kingdom of God is also a vital concept in the Scriptures of Israel (which Christians call the Old Testament). By referring to the kingdom, both Jesus and prophets before him focused on God as the king of the universe, the fundamental force behind all that is, and on God's role in shaping human experience. Jesus embraced this prophetic principle and gave it his own unique meaning.

The promise of the kingdom is that people will finally come to realize divine justice and peace in all that they do. People will put into action with one another the righteousness they see in God. So the kingdom is a matter of vision, of perceiving God at work both in the present and in the future, but it is also a matter of ethics. Jesus made the kingdom of God the center of his preaching as well as of his activity, and it remains the pivot of Christian theology.

Whether in present experience or in hope for the future, the kingdom of God was celebrated in ancient Israel in five ways, all closely related. The book of Psalms clearly reflects this celebration of the kingdom, and Jesus also taught that the kingdom could be known in these ways. Because the kingdom is a power within human beings, and not an entity alien to them, to understand it requires more than a simple definition. Instead, both the psalms and Jesus referred to the kingdom according to how its force could be perceived and how that force would shape all human life.

First, the kingdom of God is behind the whole of created life, the creativity that makes life possible, but at the same time it is beyond the immediate comprehension of any living thing. For that reason, the psalms portray the kingdom as so near as to seem present in time and tangible and yet ultimate and distant from the point of view of what its full disclosure will be like:

> Say among the nations, "The LORD is king!
> The world is firmly established;
> it shall never be moved.
> He will judge the peoples with equity." (Ps. 96:10)

All peoples are finally to know, when God judges, the truth that is even now celebrated and sung by some people. Those who sing, the group that joins in order to recite this psalm, recognize now, not just in the future, that "the world is firmly established; it shall never be moved." The wonderful order of the universe invites the psalmic community to rejoice in God's power in the present and to anticipate his full revelation in the future.

Second, just as the kingdom cannot be contained by time, it being a reality both in the present and the future, so also it is transcendent in space. The usual setting of Israel's praise is in the temple, where the psalms typically were sung, but every part of the creation will come to acknowledge what is known there:

> All your works shall give thanks to you, O LORD,
> and all your faithful shall bless you.
> They shall speak of the glory of your kingdom,
> and tell of your power,
> to make known to all people your mighty deeds,
> and the glorious splendor of your kingdom.
> Your kingdom is an everlasting kingdom,
> and your dominion endures throughout all
> generations. (Ps. 145:10, 13)

All creatures are to give thanks to the Lord, but it is his faithful in particular who are said to bless him. What is rehearsed in the temple, the "might of the awesome deeds" of God, is to be acknowledged by humanity as a whole (Ps. 145:6).

Third, the kingdom is an insistent force of justice that will ultimately prevail. The kingdom is ever righteous, but it attains to a consummation:

> Break the arm of the wicked and evildoers;
> seek out their wickedness until you find none.
> The LORD is king forever and ever;
> the nations shall perish from his land. (Ps.
> 10:15–16)

The punishment of the wicked is the dark side of the blessing of the poor; the vindication of the meek, the fatherless, and the oppressed (Ps. 10:17–18) requires a reversal in the fortunes of those who do evil in order to be realized.

Fourth, human entry into the kingdom depends on what people do. Psalm 24 poses and answers a question that is central to the religion of Israel as reflected in the biblical tradition:

> Who shall ascend the hill of the LORD?
> And who shall stand in his holy place?
> Those who have clean hands and pure hearts,
> who do not lift up their souls to what is false,
> and do not swear deceitfully. (vv. 3–4)

The point is that purity is effected by one's ethical behavior as well as by the practices of purification (such as bathing and abstention from sexual intercourse) that conventionally were requisites for ascending the mount of the temple.

Fifth, Ps. 47 evokes how the recognition of God is to radiate from Zion when it identifies "the people of the God of Abraham" as "the princes of the peoples":

> The princes of the peoples gather as the people of
> the God of Abraham.
> For the shields of the earth belong to God;
> he is highly exalted. (v. 9)

Israel is the nucleus of the larger group of those who recognize the God of Abraham. From its center, the power of the kingdom is to radiate outward to include within its recognition peoples beyond the usual range of Israel.

Jesus articulated all five of these ways of seeing God's kingdom because he understood that they conveyed the mystery of the kingdom. He taught his disciples to pray to God, "Your kingdom come" (Matt. 6:10; Luke 11:2), because he hoped for it to be fully present to all people. In Aramaic, he really said that the kingdom "will" come; he was not merely wishing for it to come. In the same way that God's presence can be sensed now, he taught, his followers should also welcome its coming in the future.

Jesus' belief that the kingdom is transcendent, capable of displacing other powers, comes through clearly in one of his most famous sayings: "If it is by the spirit of God that I cast out demons, then the kingdom of God has come to you" (Matt. 12:28; cf. Luke 11:20). For Jesus, exorcism was not an esoteric or magical practice but a matter of confronting evil with the power of divine justice. He typically called demons "unclean spirits." For Jesus, people taken on their own were as clean as God had made Adam and Eve. If a person became unclean or impure, it was not because of contact with exterior objects. Instead, impurity was a disturbance in one's own spirit, the "unclean spirit" that made a person want to be impure. To his mind, uncleanness arrived not from material contagion but rather from the disturbed desire that people conceive to pollute and do harm to themselves. Uncleanness had to be dealt with in the inward, spiritual personality of those afflicted. Jesus believed that God's Spirit was a far more vital force than the unclean spirits that disturbed humanity. Against demonic infection a greater, countercontagion could prevail, the positive energy of God's purity.

Entry into the kingdom is also the dominant image in Jesus' famous statement about wealth: "It is easier for a camel to go through the eye of a needle than for someone who is rich to enter the kingdom of God" (Mark 10:25; cf. Matt. 19:24; Luke 18:25). This dedication to justice, the third dimension of the kingdom, leads on naturally to the fourth: Jesus needed to cope with the issue of defilement as one member of Israel (with a certain set of practices) met with another member of Israel (with another set of practices). To deal with that question, a single aphorism of Jesus was precisely designed: "There is nothing outside a person that by going in can defile, but the things that come out are what defile" (Mark 7:15). Finally, in the course of Jesus' occupation of the temple, Mark has Jesus articulate the dimension of the kingdom's radiance: "Is it not written, 'My house shall be called a house of prayer for all the nations'? But you have made it a den of robbers" (Mark 11:17).

In Jesus' teaching, the five coordinates of the kingdom become the dynamics of the kingdom, the ways in which God is active with his people. Because God as kingdom is active, response to him is active, not only cognitive. The kingdom of God is a matter of performing the hopeful dynamics of God's revelation to his people. For that reason, Jesus' teaching was not merely a matter of making statements, however carefully crafted and remembered. He also engaged in characteristic activities, a conscious performance of the kingdom, which invited Israel to enter into the reality that he also portrayed in words. Once experience and activity are taken to be the terms of reference of the kingdom, what one does is also an instrument of its revelation, an aspect of its radiance. Jesus' awareness of that caused him to act as programmatically as he spoke, to make of his total activity a parable of the kingdom.

One of the most profound challenges of Jesus' teaching as a whole is that the kingdom of God is not merely for him to perform, but also for all who perceive it. Both the perception of the kingdom and the imperative to act on one's perception are developed by a type of speech well known within Judaism at the time of Jesus: the parable. The Hebrew term rendered by Greek *parabolē* and English "parable" is *māšāl*, which basically refers to a comparison. For that reason, the genre as a whole is an exploration of metaphorical possibilities, as is evidenced, for example, in the book of Proverbs (which in Hebrew is called *mišlê*, illustrating that the term *māšāl* has a wider sense than any single term in English conveys).

The book of Ezekiel represents the wide range of meaning involved. In the name of the Lord, the prophet says, "There is nothing for you in parabling [*mōšlîm*] this parable [*māšāl*]: 'The fathers ate sour grapes, and the children's teeth stand on edge'" (Ezek. 18:2 [translation mine]). Evidently, there is no requirement of a strong narrative element within the metaphorical image for the "parable" to stand as such. Its gist is transparent, and that is precisely what the prophet is objecting to and refuting. Yet within the same book a parable is developed in such an elaborate way that it may be styled an allegory (complete with explanation) in which the fate of Israel between Babylon and Egypt is addressed by comparison to two eagles and a sprig of cedar (Ezek. 17). It is fortunate the chapter includes interpretation because this particular parable (translated as "allegory" at 17:2 in the NRSV) is complicated, opaque, and unrealistic. Nathan's parable of the ewe lamb in 2 Sam. 12:1–15 is a more successful development of narrative allegory and interpretation, and it is not in the least surprising that David got the point of the parable, because a certain didacticism is evident here (as in the narrative parable in Ezek. 17).

Jesus was known as a master of the parable genre in its full extent, from simple adage to complicated, sometimes even surreal, narrative. For that reason, it is only to be expected that the parabolic tradition will have been the outcome of considerable embellishment during the course of transmission. The interest here is not in attribution but in the depth and range of the development of the genre.

Taxed with the charge that his exorcisms were performed by the power of Satan, Jesus replied with the observation that no kingdom or home divided against itself can stand (Matt. 12:24–25; Mark 3:22–25; Luke 11:15–17). That double maxim is devastating enough to have lived on within proverbial tradition of many languages (with a meaning usually unrelated to its original context), but the Gospels also add a parable with a narrative element: the comparison with attempting to rob a strong man's house (Matt. 12:29; Mark 3:27; developed more fully in Luke 11:21–22). Such examples instance not only the range of the genre but also the ease with which one sort of parable might be associated with another. (For that reason, unlike some recent treatments, no hard-and-fast distinction is suggested here between simple, embellished, and narrative parables; a single *māšāl* can easily participate in several features of the genre overall.) The narrative element that was perennially an option within the genre is exploited, complete with an interpretation of the allegory in the parable of the sower (Matt. 13:3–8, 18–23; Mark 4:3–8, 13–20; Luke 8:5–8, 11–15). Although no less didactic than the parable in Ezek. 17, here a certain vivid mastery is instanced.

Rabbinic parables offer analogies to those of Jesus. In a parable of Johanan ben Zakkai (*b. Šabb.* 153a), a king invited his servants to a feast without announcing the hour of the meal. Wise servants attired themselves properly and waited at the door of the king's palace. Foolish servants expected definite signs of the meal's preparation and went about their work until they should see them. When the king suddenly summoned the servants, the wise servants enjoyed a fine meal, while the foolish, work-soiled servants were made to stand and watch.

The motif of a festal banquet is central within Jesus' parables and sayings, and the Matthean parable of the wedding feast (Matt. 22:1–14; cf. Luke 14:16–24) especially invites comparison with that of ben Zakkai. Matthew's subplot concerning the appropriate wedding garment (22:11–13) provides another point of similarity. Still, the meanings generated by the two parables are distinctive. Where ben Zakkai speaks of servants who either are or are not prudent in their assessment of the king's capacity, Jesus speaks of guests invited to a feast who respond with extraordinarily bad and finally violent behavior that is answered in kind. Beneath that distinction, of course, there is a thematic similarity. The readiness to accept and act upon the invitation is called for, especially since the king is none other than God. But each parable urges a particular kind of response upon the hearer. Ben Zakkai's narrative involves dropping normal obligations to await God's promised banquet, while Jesus' parable of recalcitrant guests is more fraught in its warning against obstinacy.

Perhaps most important, comparison with rabbinic parables reveals what often has been overlooked: surrealism is possible within the genre, from Ezekiel through Jesus and on to ben Zakkai. Parables are not just lively stories taken from nature; the point often can turn on what is striking, peculiar, or unpredictable. Even in Jesus' parables of growth, elements of hyperbole are plain. In the narrative of the man, the seed, and the earth (Mark 4:26–29), action is abrupt and unmotivated. The man sleeps for no apparent reason, and he puts in his sickle "immediately"; the seed sprouts in no stated time, and the earth produces "as of itself." Similarly, mustard seed becomes a "tree" (Matt. 13:31–32; Luke 13:18–19) or makes "big branches" (Mark 4:30–32) without an interval of time being indicated. The point lies in the contrast between beginning and result, miraculous transformation rather than predictable process. The hyperbolic comparison of start and finish is evident also in the parable of the leaven (Matt. 13:33; Luke 13:20–21). The parables of the hidden treasure and of the pearl (Matt. 13:44–46) are surprising rather than hyperbolic when they concern the discovery of what is valuable, but the reaction of those who find them, in selling everything to acquire them, is exaggerated. In these cases, also, ethical themes are especially conveyed by the least realistic motifs.

Like the prophets, Jesus taught his hearers how to see as well as how to act on the basis of what they saw. Vision—the capacity to perceive God actively at work—is the prophetic foundation of calling people to work with God. In the Judaism of Jesus' time it was said that every Israelite, every day, took up "the yoke of the kingdom of heaven" (*m. Ber.* 2.2). The underlying image puts Israelites in the role of beasts of burden, yoked in harness in order to discharge the duties for which they were intended. Then, if they do in fact accept obedience, they prove themselves innocent of the accusation leveled at them by Isaiah: "The ox knows its owner, and the donkey its master's crib; but Israel does not know, my people do not understand" (Isa.1:3).

The moment of yoking oneself to God's kingdom was at the time of reciting one of the principal texts of Judaism, the Shema:

> Hear, O Israel: the LORD our God, the LORD alone. You shall love the LORD your God with all your heart, and with all your soul, and with all your might. Keep these words that I am commanding you today in your heart. Recite them to your children and talk about them when you are at home and when you are away, when you lie down and when you rise. (Deut. 6:4–7)

When asked about the "first commandment" in the Torah, of course, Jesus cited this one (Mark 12:29–30). In addition, in a famous saying he urged his followers to learn from him, "because my yoke is easy, and my burden is light" (Matt. 11:30). The motif of the "easy" (or "good" [Gk. *chrēstos*]) yoke is a shared metaphor that links Jesus with the rabbinic language that emerged in documents from the second century and later.

But in this case as in others, the sharing of language, when viewed contextually, reveals vital differences. The rabbinic "yoke" connects the Israelite to the Torah; Jesus' "yoke" links the disciple to God's kingdom. Profound lines of cleavage, and of controversy, emanate from that distinction. In Jesus' conception, this divine presence was the force behind the kingdom of God. As he said to Peter, James, and John just before his transfiguration, "There are some standing here who will not taste death until they see that the kingdom of God has come with power" (Mark 9:1 [cf. Matt. 16:28; Luke 9:27]). In the Jewish tradition of this time, both Moses and Elijah were thought to have been immortal; like Elijah taken up in God's chariot, Moses too was believed to have gone alive into heaven. This saying of Jesus about those who lived in God's presence, people such as Moses and Elijah (but also, in Jesus' view, Abraham, Isaac, and Jacob), showed the way for humanity as a whole. "The kingdom of God has come with power" expresses in a single phrase how Jesus anticipated that God would definitively transform the world as human beings can know the world.

Genuine transformation is a frightening prospect. It involves altering all the usual points of reference that people use to know who they are, where they are, and what they can do to improve their lives. "The kingdom of God has come with power" refers to a complete alteration of conventional reality. The phrase resonates with works that depict the apocalyptic dissolution of both social institutions and the tangible, physical world. The final chapter of the book of Zechariah, for example, predicted that Israel would envelop all the nations in an ultimate sacrifice on Mount Zion in the midst of warfare, destruction, earthquake, and plague. The Aramaic version of the book sets out that apocalypse in language like Jesus':

> *And the kingdom of the LORD shall be revealed* upon all *the inhabitants of* the earth; at that *time they shall serve before the LORD with one accord, for* his name *is established in the world; there is none apart from him.* (*Targum Zechariah* 14.9 [departures from the Hebrew text in italics])

To Jesus, this expectation was not merely a matter of symbolism or an expectation that could be passively awaited. Instead, he acted upon the apocalyptic scenario of transformation in order to actively join God in establishing his kingdom. His last public action—his intervention in the normal operation of the temple in Jerusalem—enacted the prophecy of Zechariah, particularly in its Aramaic version: "And there shall never again be a *trader* in the *sanctuary* of the Lord of hosts at that *time*" (*Targum Zechariah* 14.21b).

Putting those words into practice also put Jesus into direct opposition to Caiaphas, the high priest who had authorized the selling and buying inside the temple to which Jesus objected violently. He intervened with force and threw out both the vendors and their animals (Matt. 21:12–17; Mark 11:11–18; Luke 19:45–48; John 2:13–20).

This act is the key to why Jesus was crucified by the Romans, who had put their prestige behind the status quo in the temple. Although almost every claim ever asserted about Jesus has been subject to dispute, the fact of this forceful intervention is a matter of historical fact. More important than the details of Jesus' action for an understanding of the prophetic force he wished to unleash, however, is the total vision of which Zechariah's prophecy of the cleansing of the temple of commerce is a part. Jesus assimilated Zechariah's vision into his own and made it a programmatic part of his action.

Three key texts in Zechariah set out characteristic concerns of Jesus' message:

> Thus says the Lord of hosts: I will save my people from the east country and from the west country; and I will bring them to live in Jerusalem. They shall be my people and I will be their God, in faithfulness and in righteousness. (8:7–8)

> These are the things that you shall do: Speak the truth to one another, render in your gates judgments that are true and make for peace, do not devise evil in your hearts against one another, and love no false oath; for all these are things that I hate, says the Lord. (8:16–17)

> Thus says the Lord of hosts: The fast of the fourth month, and the fast of the fifth, and the fast of the seventh, and the fast of the tenth, shall be seasons of joy and gladness, and cheerful festivals for the house of Judah: therefore love truth and peace. (8:19)

Very often an ancient misunderstanding arises in the minds of modern readers of the Bible. A false contrast portrays "the God of the Old Testament" as violent and vengeful, while Jesus preached "the God of mercy." But Jesus also was willing to resort to violence, and these prophecies of Zechariah, themselves in line with other prophetic messages in the OT, show that Jesus was directly inspired by the prophets.

When Jesus said, "Many will come from east and west and will eat with Abraham and Isaac and Jacob in the kingdom of heaven" (Matt. 8:11 [cf. Luke 13:29]), he echoed Zechariah (8:7–8). When he spoke of love of God and love of neighbor as summing up the Torah (Matt. 22:34–40; Mark 12:28–34; Luke 10:25–28), he developed a principle that Zechariah had stated (8:16–17). When he offended many of his contemporaries in Judaism by insisting that feasting, not fasting, was to be the rule in the kingdom of God (Matt. 9:14–17; Mark 2:18–22; Luke 5:33–39), he was announcing the new prophetic era (Zech. 8:19) of rejoicing.

By better understanding where Jesus' teaching came from, how it derived from the prophetic tradition that fed his vision and encouraged his demand for justice and ethical action, we can also better see where it was intended to lead his followers. With the prophets before him, Jesus not only insisted on righteousness from individuals but also wanted communities to live by just judgment. Zechariah summarized centuries of the prophetic imperatives when he said, "Thus says the LORD of hosts: Render true judgments, show kindness and mercy to one another; do not oppress the widow, the orphan, the alien, or the poor; and do not devise evil in your hearts against one another" (7:9–10).

In Zechariah's prophecy, as in Jesus' Sermon on the Mount, there is no such thing as requirements for individuals that are separate from human behavior in community. How could there be, when love is at the foundation of the prophetic ethic? That is why, in Zechariah's imperative, God moves from what the community must do ("render true judgments") to what individual Israelites must accomplish ("show kindness and mercy to one another"). Both parts of this single imperative to righteousness appear in the plural: Zechariah, like Moses before him and Jesus after him, is addressing his message to people in their totality, living in community and also conscious of themselves as individuals.

See also New Testament Ethics; Parables, Use of in Ethics

Bibliography

Chilton, B. *Pure Kingdom: Jesus' Vision of God*. SHJ. Eerdmans, 1996; Grappe, C. *Le Royaume de Dieu: Avant, avec et après Jésus*. MdB 42. Labor et Fides, 2001; Jeremias, J. *Das Königtum Gottes in den Psalmen: Israels Begegnung mit dem kanaänaischen Mythos in den Jahwe-König-Psalmen*. FRLANT 141. Vandenhoeck & Ruprecht, 1987; idem. *The Parables of Jesus*. SCM, 1963; McKnight, S. *A New Vision for Israel: The Teachings of Jesus in National Context*. SHJ. Eerdmans, 1999; Weiss, J. *Jesus' Proclamation of the Kingdom of God*. Fortress, 1971.

Bruce Chilton

1–2 Kings

The books of 1–2 Kings recount the history of Israel and Judah from the end of David's kingship until the Babylonian exile in 587 BCE. After presenting an account of the accession and rule of Solomon and the subsequent division of the kingdoms, these books proceed to describe in varying degrees of detail the reigns of each of the Israelite and Judean monarchs, giving special attention to the kings' and people's religious practice and describing the fall of Israel to Assyria and Judah to Babylonia as the direct result of apostasy from exclusive worship of Yahweh. As part of the larger Deuteronomistic History, 1–2 Kings reflect the ethical and theological concerns of Deuteronomy.

Narrative criticism has shown significant potential in uncovering the ethical concerns and issues of narrative texts by focusing on the attitudes of the narrator or "implied author" toward characters and their actions (Wenham 5–15). This kind of analysis focuses our attention less on discussion of specific moral problems than on the characters' fundamental moral makeup and the process of their ethical formation, inviting readers to reflect on the complexity of the characters' moral lives and then on their own lives and ethical dispositions (Barton 71–74).

In 1–2 Kings the narrator gives more attention to Solomon than to any other individual, portraying him as a multifaceted character who appears to be the model of the ideal ruler yet who, in the end, is undone by his own excess. Early in the story, the new king seems almost too good to be true, not only replicating the obedience of his father, David (1 Kgs. 3:3), but also asking God for an "understanding mind" and the ability to "discern between good and evil" instead of wealth or long life (1 Kgs. 3:6–9). Thus, Solomon understands that ruling with equity, fairness, and discernment goes to the heart of what it means to be a wise leader. Undergirding these qualities is a sense of genuine humility and reliance on God, which Solomon further acknowledges in his prayer of dedication over the temple, where he asks that God forgive the people's sins when they pray in or toward the temple (1 Kgs. 8:33–34, 46–53). Finally, Solomon's wisdom leads, as promised by God (1 Kgs. 3:13), to the accumulation of great wealth, which attests to that wisdom and enables him to build a temple unparalleled for its opulence (1 Kgs. 5–6).

Ironically, though, this great wealth becomes a symbol of the excess that leads to Solomon's downfall. Right on the heels of the account of Solomon's wise judgment, the story raises a red flag with its mention of forced labor, as well as the subsequent description of the massive provisions that the royal administration must demand from its citizens (1 Kgs. 4:1–28). Because the construction of the temple requires the use of forced labor (1 Kgs. 5:13–18), Solomon's building of this magnificent house for God is accomplished only on the backs of his people. Moreover, Solomon's accumulation of horses (1 Kgs. 4:26; 10:26) points to overreliance on military might at the expense of trust in God, and his pursuit of national security through marriages to a thousand women and subsequent worship of their gods (1 Kgs. 11:1–8) leads to the Davidic-Solomonic line's loss of the whole nation except for the tribe of Judah. All this is exactly what Deuteronomy has already warned against in describing the king as a custodian of the law who is not to exalt himself above his people (Deut. 17:14–20). The story of Solomon, then, presents the reader with the opportunity to reflect on virtues in leadership such as wisdom, justice, discernment, humility, and reliance on God, especially in contrast to the dangers of excess, pride, and reliance on self.

The requirements of Deut. 17 that the king subject himself to the Torah and teach the people to do the same also lie behind the accounts of the other rulers in 1–2 Kings, even if those accounts are not as detailed as the Solomon story and generally describe the rulers as unambiguously good or bad rather than lingering over the complexities of their moral character. When Naboth refuses to sell to King Ahab the vineyard that is part of Naboth's ancestral inheritance, for instance, the king seems to accept, albeit reluctantly, that according to the law he has no recourse, but Jezebel, his wife, places herself and Ahab above the law by having Naboth falsely accused of a capital offense and put to death so that Ahab can then seize the property (1 Kgs. 21).

For the most part, though, the evaluations of Israel's and Judah's kings revolve around how well they conform to the requirements for religious practice set out in Deuteronomy, particularly the command to worship Yahweh only. Josiah, for instance, is the Deuteronomist's great hero for hearing the law and taking immediate steps to make sure that he and the people are following it, leading to his great religious reforms that centralized worship in Jerusalem and eradicated all hints of idolatry (2 Kgs. 22–23), while Manasseh reverses all of Hezekiah's reforms, leading to the downfall of the kingdom (2 Kgs. 21). More often the text includes little more than a brief formulaic evaluation of the ruler, indicating, for instance, whether he followed in the ways of David (1 Kgs. 14:8; 15:3, 11). Thus, the main concern is whether each king follows the divinely given Torah and teaches his subjects to do the same, and there is little gray area in the author's evaluations. While these accounts might seem best to support an ethic of divine command, one could perhaps also say that it is a matter of virtue and character for a ruler to subject himself to the law and thus put himself on a par with his subjects rather than simply consider himself as the giver of and authority over law.

The other important characters in 1–2 Kings are the prophets, who announce the consequences of disobedience to the Torah, speaking words of criticism to those who hold great power (e.g., Ahijah speaking to Solomon and Jeroboam [1 Kgs. 11:29–33; 14:7–14]; Elijah against the prophets of Baal [1 Kgs. 18]; Micaiah speaking to Ahab

[1 Kgs. 22]). At the same time, part of what makes these prophetic narratives difficult from the perspective of ethical consideration is that the text makes no explicit remarks about the morality of acts such as Elijah's slaughter of Baal's prophets, Micaiah's initial deception of the two kings, the violence resulting from Jehu's coup (which is criticized sharply in the next century by Hosea), and Elisha's cursing of some children who had taunted him so that a bear comes and mauls them (2 Kgs. 2:23–24).

Narrative analysis seems to bear fruit in the use of 1–2 Kings for moral reflection, as it helps to highlight virtues and character, especially in the rich and multidimensional portrayal of complex characters such as Solomon.

See also Deuteronomistic History; Deuteronomy; Narrative Ethics, Biblical; Old Testament Ethics

Bibliography

Barton, J. *Understanding Old Testament Ethics: Approaches and Explorations*. Westminster John Knox, 2003; Wenham, G. *Story as Torah: Reading the Old Testament Ethically*. OTS. T&T Clark, 2000.

Craig Vondergeest

Koinonia

Koinonia (Gk. *koinōnia*) refers to participation, fellowship, or community. In the NT it occurs frequently in regard to the mutuality of relationships shared among the followers of Christ.

The concept of koinonia is amply illustrated by Luke in the book of Acts, which notes what was typical of the church by observing that believers devoted themselves to "fellowship" (2:42); that is, "those who believed all joined in solidarity and held all things in common. They would sell their property and possessions and distribute them to everyone according to each person's need" (2:44–45 [translation mine]). This does not mean that fellowship is merely to be identified with economic sharing, but rather that economic sharing puts on display the unity of the believers. The picture that Luke allows is not one of a "common purse," however, nor of total renunciation as a prerequisite for discipleship. Selling what one has is customary within the community that Luke depicts, but such giving is voluntary, oriented toward addressing the plight of the needy.

This portrait is furthered in another summary statement in Acts in which Luke reflects on the early church's attitude and practices regarding possessions, observing that "there was not a needy person among them" (4:34). In Acts 2 "partnership" or "sharing" was the immediate consequence of belief and baptism. Here in Acts 4 proclamation of the resurrection is situated between dual references to economic koinonia (4:32–34a), interpreting the community of goods as a tangible expression and substantiation of the resurrection of Jesus from the dead. Borrowing from Deut. 15:4, Acts 4:34 pictures believers as God's people restored in new exodus. Moreover, it was proverbial that "friends hold all things in common" (e.g., Aristotle, *Eth. nic.* 9.8.2 §1168b); accordingly, Acts portrays discipleship as friendship with the needy.

On a grander scale, when the believers in Judea suffered because of famine, the disciples in Antioch provided economic support (Acts 11:27–30). Counterexamples drive home what is at stake here. When Ananias and Sapphira masquerade as persons committed to sharing all things, they fall under judgment (Acts 5:1–11). When, under the apostles' leadership, certain widows are ignored during the daily distribution of food, leadership of the mission church passes from them to others (Acts 6:1–7).

The language of koinonia is more pervasive in Paul's letters. The apostle refers to the believers' relationship with Christ and the Spirit as a "fellowship" (e.g., 2 Cor. 13:13; Phil. 3:10–14) and grounds his appeal for unity among believers in the reality of their koinonia with God (e.g., 1 Cor. 1:9–10). The Lord's Supper is both an expression of fellowship with Christ and a means by which participation in Christ is cultivated, as well as an expression and means of koinonia among those who share in the supper (1 Cor. 10:16–17). For this reason, the presence of (especially socioeconomic) divisions at the table is particularly heinous: such a supper does not honor the Lord (1 Cor. 11:17–22 [note the language of "have"/"have not" in v. 22]). Paul also uses the language of koinonia with reference to the collection for the saints in Jerusalem, drawing on the language of reciprocity: "For if the Gentiles have come to share in their spiritual blessings, they ought also to be of service to them in material things" (Rom. 15:27). Accordingly, the collection was the gospel in practice, a concrete manifestation of the partnership of the churches, Jew and gentile (2 Cor. 8–9).

Koinonia, then, is both gift and vocation—a manifestation of the gospel in the lives of believers and a call to embody the gospel in terms of the common life of the community of believers. As vocation, koinonia is less a list of things to do and more a disposition of openhandedness to the grace of God and to the needs of others. Accordingly, it has rightly served as the impetus for initiatives toward ecumenicity, for numerous local experiments with living (e.g., community-based farms, neighborhood development, shared households), and for various forms of economic relief (whether among friends, in interchurch relations, or across political boundaries). The basis and exemplar of koinonia is Jesus Christ—in his incarnation (e.g., 2 Cor. 8:9), in the nature of his self-giving on the cross (e.g., 1 Cor. 11:23–26), and in his resurrection (e.g., Acts 4:32–34).

See also Collection for the Saints; Poverty and Poor

Bibliography

Dupont, J. "Community of Goods in the Early Church." Pages 85–102 in *The Salvation of the Gentiles: Essays on the Acts of the Apostles*. Paulist Press, 1979; Fuchs, L. *Koinonia and the Quest for an Ecumenical Ecclesiology: From Foundations through Dialogue to Symbolic Competence for Communionality*. Eerdmans, 2008; González, J. *Faith and Wealth: A History of Early Christian Ideas on the Origin, Significance, and Use of Money*. Harper & Row, 1990; Panikulam, G. *Koinōnia in the New Testament: A Dynamic Expression of Christian Life*. AnBib 85. Biblical Institute Press, 1979.

Joel B. Green

L

Labor *See* Work

Lamentations

In the midst of Lam. 3 (vv. 25–39), where the poem's speaker ("the man" [Heb. *haggeber*] of v. 1) considers Judah's traditional teachings about how to cope with suffering (see Dobbs-Allsopp 119–22), comes the commendation "to give one's cheek to the smiter, and be filled with insults" (v. 30). Emmanuel Levinas, perhaps the twentieth century's foremost thinker of "the other," finds in this verse (Levinas, *Otherwise*, 111) insights that prove central to his account of subjectivity and the self, which, stated simply, is "suffering for the other" (Gibbs 56). Key among these insights is the idea of vulnerability, that "aptitude . . . for 'being beaten,' for 'getting slapped'" (Levinas, *Humanism*, 63), a susceptibility to trauma and persecution that makes possible the extraordinary human capacity "to pass from the outrage undergone to the responsibility for the persecutor . . . from suffering to expiation for the other" (Levinas, *Otherwise*, 111). To suffer in such a way, "by the other," is to take care of that other, to "bear him, be in his place, consume oneself by him. All love or hatred of one's fellow man as a thoughtful attitude supposes this prior vulnerability" (Levinas, *Humanism*, 64).

As ever, Levinas is a thinker of lived experience, and here one suspects that the insight reached bears the imprint of his own survival of the Shoah, that time in which even those most cherished of Enlightenment notions of self—as autonomous, free, rational—could not deflect the embodied vulnerability that ultimately subsists and envelops the self "from top to toe and to the very marrow" (Levinas, *Humanism*, 63). This analysis of persecution, intentionally extreme, still is intended to say something about the self's ordinary relations to the other; indeed, the entire middle section of Lam. 3 (vv. 25–39) is rendered in an expansive and inclusive voice such that the poem's audience may more readily assimilate the perspective(s) on suffering being scrutinized (see Dobbs-Allsopp 122). And yet the insight gained is one that the experience of persecution would surely teach, rendering brutally apparent the outer limits of a self's autonomy, freedom, and rationality. Nevertheless, in Levinas there is no glorification or "deliberate seeking of suffering or humiliation" (Levinas, *Humanism*, 63), no drawing "from suffering some kind of magical redemptive virtue" (*Otherwise*, 111); the alluding swerve away from the "turning of the *other* cheek" in the Gospels is patent (Matt. 5:39; Luke 6:29) (see Gibbs 56–57). For Levinas, suffering in itself is "precisely an evil" and "useless" and in the other "unforgivable to *me*" (Levinas, *Entre nous*, 92–94). Indeed, it is this perspective, as achieved (in this instance) through the experience of the Shoah, that leads Levinas to proclaim the end of theodicy: such suffering—"suffering for nothing"—"renders impossible and odious every proposal and every thought that would explain it by the sins of those who have suffered or are dead" (Levinas, *Entre nous*, 98).

Levinas's choice of texts by which to think these issues through is far from serendipitous. Lamentations is one of the Bible's more antitheodic works (Dobbs-Allsopp 27–33; see also Braiterman). In fact, one of the more poignant expressions of antitheodic sentiment in Lamentations comes in 3:42. Having contemplated several traditional poses toward suffering, including the "tending of the cheek" in v. 30, the speaker confronts Judah's God, "We have transgressed and rebelled, and you have not forgiven," thus refusing, rather acutely, any suggestion that the suffering experienced by "the man" of Lam. 3 (and the community whom he personifies and ventriloquizes) is finally containable by notions of sin, guilt, or theodicy. Renewed lamentation and complaint follow, counterpointing and countermanding wisdom's presumptuous grasp of human suffering (see Dobbs-Allsopp 122–28). Levinas is adamant that the only way that suffering's "congenital uselessness" can take on meaning is when it is "suffering *in me*, my own experience of suffering," "a suffering for the suffering . . . of someone else" (Levinas, *Entre nous*, 94).

This, for Levinas, is the very essence of human "subjectivity," a responsibility for the other in "the form of the total exposure to offense in the cheek offered to the smiter" (Levinas, *Otherwise*, 111).

The book of Lamentations, like so much biblical literature, does not present itself textually as a treatise on morality. And thus whatever ethical sensibilities are to be gleaned from it requires readerly interventions, acts of reading intent on engaging matters of ethical interest. Levinas's reading of (and with) Lam. 3:30 is one such act of ethically interested reading. It is a spectacular act of such a reading, in fact, as this one biblical verse lies at the "centerpiece" of Levinas's argument in *Otherwise than Being* (xlvii). But there are more verses in Lamentations—many more, in fact, and myriad contemporary moral concerns toward which to read them.

See also Exile; Old Testament Ethics; Poetic Discourse and Ethics; Suffering; Theodicy

Bibliography

Braiterman, Z. *(God) after Auschwitz: Tradition and Change in Post-Holocaust Jewish Thought*. Princeton University Press, 1998; Dobbs-Allsopp, F. W. *Lamentations*. IBC. John Knox, 2002; Gibbs, R. *Why Ethics? Signs of Responsibilities*. Princeton University Press, 2000; Levinas, E. *Entre nous: On Thinking-of-the-Other*. Trans. M. Smith and B. Harshav. Columbia University Press, 1998; idem. *Humanism of the Other*. Trans. N. Poller. University of Illinois Press, 2003; idem. *Otherwise than Being; or, Beyond Essence*. Trans. A. Lingis. M. Nijhoff, 1981.

Chip Dobbs-Allsopp

Land

Land was not property, at least not in the majority of the world's cultures, until recent times. Water (springs, streams, rivers, lakes, shores, bays, reefs) must be considered along with land and is also not just property. Land is much more than a commodity and often is understood in other than economic categories. Land is context, environment, symbol, identity, and habitat. Land is the repository of the ancestors, the reminder of narratives, the inheritance of the current generation, the promise of the future generation, and thus a site of social life. The relationship between land and ethics, then, is elementary: the ethics of land ownership and land use is foundational to human relations. Thus, the abuse of land rights reveals ethical breaches in human relations.

From the beginning, land has been symbol and part of the relationship between God and humans, and between humans and humans. The separation and drying of the land has been part of the process of linking God to humans in the salvation story (Gen. 1:9). The same process of separating waters and drying the land marked the exodus from the land of slavery (Exod. 14:21) as well as Israel's entrance into the promised land (Josh. 4:18, 22). The exiles were comforted with the promise that God would be with them when they walked through the waters (Isa. 43:2), and the remnant were reminded that God had brought them through the sea on dry land (Neh. 9:11). Being on the dry land is a symbol of being in a saving relationship with God (Lev. 25:23), while being down in the sea symbolizes a broken relationship with God (Jonah 1:13; 2:10).

The health of society is linked to the land in an ecosystem broader than modern scientists imagine. Much of the teaching of Leviticus and Deuteronomy takes the ethical stance that human behavior exists in a feedback relationship with the land. Thus, if the people remain faithful to Yahweh, "the land will yield its fruit" (Lev. 25:19; 26:4; cf. Deut. 11:17). But when people mistreat one another and stray from Yahweh, then the land is defiled or polluted (Lev. 18:25; 19:29; 25:33–34; Deut. 21:23). The land will fail to produce (Deut. 11:17), and finally the land will "vomit out her inhabitants" (Lev. 18:25). The land was a personal agent in the complex relationship between God and God's people, so much so that the people's sin and guilt became the land's sin (Deut. 24:4; Ezek. 14:13; Hos. 1:2). In fact, the land is able to rest (Judg. 3:11), to cry out (Job 31:38), and to mourn (Jer. 12:4; Hos. 4:3; Joel 1:10; Zech. 12:12). The land is a source of identity, and the loss of the land means the loss of identity (Ps. 137:4) (see Rynkiewich, "Strangers").

Walter Brueggemann argues that relationship to the land has always identified the people of Israel, who were homeless with only a promise, then landed with a blessing and a warning, and finally exiled with only the hope of return. Israel's relationship with the land forms a framework for ethics that affects how society treats the marginalized, women, others (boundary maintenance), the economy (particularly agricultural practices), and the environment.

Expanding on Brueggemann's insights, Norman Habel argues that in the OT there is not one ideology of land but a variety of ideologies. Most hierarchical are the theocratic ideology, in which God owns all the land and makes conditional grants to some, and the royal ideology, in which the king is God's representative with the right to appropriate the wealth of the land. More populist are the agrarian theology, in which God is the landowner and the people are tenants who must adhere to the contract to act with justice; and the ecological ideology, in which the land is God's heritage to be cared for just as God's people must be cared for. Most promising as a framework for ethics in our time is the immigrant ideology, in which the land is host and the people are guests. Habel takes the case of Abraham, who is to be a blessing, not a usurper, to the nations of the land (Habel 122). Appropriately, Abraham defends the nations in prayer and in battle, shares the resources without appropriating the land, discovers and encourages the fear of God among the Canaanites, and pays too much for the only field that he acquires. Abraham is a good guest.

Habel's analysis highlights the contrast between a biblical theology of land and the capitalist ideology of land that was shared by the state and the church during most of the colonial era (1500–1960). When Scripture was used at all, the part of the narrative most often deployed by the colonizers was the discovery ideology, in which the land was considered to have no occupants and thus be "waste and vacant," and the conquest ideology, in which the land was considered to be occupied by people who were similar to the Canaanites in the time of Joshua—that is, sinners whose time of destruction had come. In these ways, land was claimed for God and country. The church, inasmuch as it served as an arm of colonialism, also took land under these premises. Thus, in Latin America the church was among the largest of landowners in late colonial times. For example, a major part of the Mexican revolution involved divesting the church of the ownership of land. "The Lerdo Law, or Law of Disamortization of 25 January 1856, ordered church corporations to dispose of their real estate, to be sold to tenants or at public auction"; this led to civil war and the eventual loss of the wealth of the church estimated at "something between $100 million and $150 million" (Lynch 581).

The land ownership of the Catholic Church in Latin America is a well-known incident, but in fact many missions, Protestant and Catholic, have a dark history of land acquisition (see Rynkiewich, "Land Acquisition"). Although the early church seemed to own neither land nor building, the development of communities was accompanied by the development of canon law. By 341, the Council of Antioch ruled that a bishop should govern church property in order to dispense funds to those in need and to support the clergy and workers in the church (Roche 197). The current code of canon law says, "The following ends are especially proper to the Church: to order divine worship; to provide decent support for the clergy and other ministers; to perform the works of the sacred apostolate and of charity, especially towards the needy" (Roche 198). There was a conservative period, beginning in 1891 with Pope Leo XIII's *Rerum novarum*, in which charity for the poor could be provided out of what people had left over after they provided for themselves in the manner in which they had grown accustomed. This was reversed in Vatican II, and once again the church was obliged to help the poor from its property and not from its surplus (Roche 201–2).

The ideology of the churches in mission, until fairly recently, failed to consider that other local ideologies of land might exist. For many, land is incorporated into an ecological whole. Land, insofar as it might be considered separately, was the property of the ancestors, the living, and the yet to be born (Paroi). Land was the site of exchange with the spirit world, with neighbors and enemies, and with plants and animals. As such, land could not be bought and sold. Yet, prominent in the colonial production of new economies has been the commodification of land—that is, the process of assigning monetary value to land—thereby carving land out of the web of social and spiritual relations around it and casting land into the arena of market exchange. This perception of land has been resisted by indigenous people constructing local theologies of land—for example, Ilaitia Tuwere for Fiji.

During the colonial era, missionaries tended to follow colonial law, which privileged colonizers. Sometimes land was given to entice a mission to start a station in a particular location. More often, in exchange for a handful of trade goods, someone's signature could be obtained on a piece of paper, and that would suffice for colonial law courts (see Rynkiewich, "Land Acquisition"). This has raised a number of ethical issues as well as engendered many court cases.

The following generic case demonstrates some of the ethical problems in colonial and mission land acquisition and use. A church in the German colony of New Guinea acquired a piece of land in 1912 (under the German colonial administration), citing purposes of worship and ministry. As others settled near the church, a town grew up. When the Germans were repatriated after World War I, Australians from the same denomination took up the land and proved the deeds (written pieces of paper) in the Australian courts, which decided in a series of cases in the late 1920s and early 1930s that the acquisition process used by the Germans was valid and no further appeals would be heard. The town continued to grow. Although the town was taken by the Japanese during World War II, the Australians came back and established colonial law. At the time of independence for Papua New Guinea (1975), the actions of the Germans and the Australians were ratified regarding title to land. The local church now wants to sell the property and move to the outskirts of town, but the business wanting to purchase the land will pay a huge price because the land is now prime downtown real estate. The descendants of the original owners are complaining that the land was originally given to the church for the good of the people, not so the church could make money on it. Their argument is that if the church does not need the land, then the descendants want the land back.

There are multiple ethical issues here. How much land does a church need to operate? What kind of legal relationship with the owners of the land serves the church's purposes best? What claim do the descendants of the original owners have when the land appears to have been purchased? Is it permissible for the church to make a profit from selling land? Should unused land be given back, and how can land restitution occur?

In the West, related ethical issues continue to arise. What rights do individuals have in land, and what rights are reserved for various levels of society? What is the meaning of "public lands," and what kinds of land use are appropriate? What obligations do corporations have in cases of land use (mining, drilling, waste management), and what rights does the government retain? How does the government set priorities for land use? Recent incidents of dams breaking at mine waste sites and spilling pollutants into streams and rivers have raised the issue of the threat to watersheds, plant life, and wildlife posed by industrial activities.

The notion that even private ownership of land conferred ethical obligations can be traced to Aldo Leopold and the posthumous publication of his *Sand County Almanac* in 1949. Contemporary writers such as Wendell Berry continue to recover the understanding, common among indigenous peoples, that land is one agent in a complex ecosystem that reduces dichotomies such as physical/spiritual, individual/group, private/public, personal/corporate.

In this era of globalization more ethical issues about land and land use are raised. With oil reserves dwindling and politics threatening to restrict access, the United States has turned to biofuels as one alternative source of energy. That decision has initiated a debate about whether it is more ethical to use land for food production (directly as grain for human consumption, or indirectly as grain for consumption by animals, which then are for human consumption) or for biofuel production. Other emerging issues center on the loss of good farming land to urbanization and industrialization, and the looming conflict over water resources as we enter an era where there is no more prime cropland and the world population is at a point where we need all the fields and all the water that we have to grow food crops or herd livestock. In the coming era planning and zoning become more than local issues, though there are ethical issues at that level as well. The ethics of land use and its impact on public health and the public good is coming into sharper focus as we press the remaining land and water resources.

Finally, following the cycle of Israel's story, landlessness defines the economic and social condition of an increasing percentage of the world's population. Whereas traditional tenure guaranteed every member of land-owning social groups (lineages, clans, villages, etc.) access to land, colonial and neocolonial dispossession of local landowners (whether by force or by the commodification of land for the marketplace) threatens to make paupers of the last indigenous landowners on earth. Some economists, such as Hernando de Soto, argue that land rights should be privatized so that landowners will be able to capitalize their holdings by using them as collateral for bank loans. Theoretically, it might work, although there are many problems in determining ownership in a tenure that recognizes a variety of land rights, not all held by the same person. Beyond that, nearly every time this has been tried in the past it has led to the loss of land by private small holders who default on their bank loans and then lose their land to the bank. What looks on paper like economic development ends up in reality with an increase in landlessness.

See also Capitalism; Colonialism and Postcolonialism; Conquest; Creation Ethics; Ecological Ethics; Economic Development; Food; Globalization; Natural Rights; Population Policy and Control; Poverty and Poor; Property and Possessions; Resource Allocation; Urbanization; World Poverty, World Hunger

Bibliography

Berry, W. *Unsettling of America: Culture and Agriculture*. Sierra Club Books, 1977; Brueggemann, W. *The Land: Place as Gift, Promise, and Challenge in Biblical Faith*. 2nd ed. Fortress, 2002; de Soto, H. *The Other Path: The Invisible Revolution in the Third World*. Harper & Row, 1989; Habel, N. *The Land Is Mine! Six Biblical Land Ideologies*. Fortress, 1995; Leopold, R. *A Sand County Almanac*. Ballantine Books, 1986 [1949]; Lynch, J. "The Catholic Church in Latin America, 1830–1930." Pages 527–96 in *The Cambridge History of Latin America*, vol. 4, ed. L. Bethell. Cambridge University Press, 1986; Paroi, H. "Melanesian Spirituality of Land." Pages 168–93 in *Land and Churches in Melanesia: Issues and Contexts*, ed. M. Rynkiewich. Melanesian Institute, 2001; Roche, G. "Church Law and Policy on Land." Pages 194–209 in *Land and Churches in Melanesia: Issues and Contexts*, ed. M. Rynkiewich. Melanesian Institute, 2001; Rynkiewich, M. "Land Acquisition during the German Era." Pages 250–76 in *Land and Churches in Melanesia: Issues and Contexts*, ed. M. Rynkiewich. Melanesian Institute, 2001; idem. "Strangers in a Strange Land: Theologies of Land." Pages 210–32 in *Land and Churches in Melanesia: Issues and Contexts*, ed. M. Rynkiewich. Melanesian Institute, 2001; Tuwere, I. *Vanua: Towards a Fijian Theology of Place*. University of the South Pacific, Institute of Pacific Studies; College of St. John the Evangelist, 2002.

Michael A. Rynkiewich

Latino/Latina Ethics

The nomenclature and designation of Latino/Latina requires special attention not only as part of the definition process but also because it describes a particular group of people for whom their name is intrinsically connected to their self-identity and social location. The term *Latino/Latina* has been appropriated and embraced primarily by persons from Latin America living in the United States and, to a certain extent, as a reaction to the term *Hispanic*. For many, the term/label *Hispanic* is an imposition from the government and the dominant group in their attempt to group all persons who have a present or historical connection to the Spanish language and/or to Latin America. However, those to whom this label was assigned have reacted to it in a negative fashion: first, because it is an imposition, a name they did not choose; second, because, for some, the term seems to be semantically (and otherwise) associated with European colonizers. The root of the words *Hispanic* and *Spain* are related etymologically, emphasizing European dominance and culture while denying the important contributions of autochthonous groups present in Latin America before the arrival of Spaniards. Moreover, the term *Hispanic* seems to exclude immigrants from Brazil, since they do not speak Spanish yet are indeed from Latin America; the term *Latino/Latina* is mindful of their presence and includes them as part of the group.

At the same time, the term *Latino/Latina* has its own share of difficulties. First, the question of gender inclusiveness is raised because "Latino" is a masculine noun, and for this reason it is applicable only to men—hence, the necessity of also using "Latina" to include all persons, male and female. The second difficulty has to do with its origin and connection to Latin America, seemingly excluding persons from Spain and sometimes those who have been in the United States for more than one generation who do not think the term *Latino/Latina* represents them well. Finally, both terms tend to neglect the fact that persons in the United States of the first or second (or more) generations tend to identify with their particular country of origin; thus, the attempt to group them together oversimplifies the cultural differences of each group based on their country of origin/ancestry (see De La Torre and Aponte). Furthermore, other names and labels have their own idiosyncrasies—for example, *Chicano*, *Pocho*, *Californio*, *La Raza*—and important cultural distinctions between Central America, Mexico, and South America. For this article, the term *Latino/Latina* will be employed because it seems to encompass a wider audience and is relevant to academic and ecclesiological discussions.

Ethical and Social Diversity

The discussion of proper nomenclature shows the multiple facets and difficulties of trying to categorize several distinctive groups by one common name; it also shows the rich history and diversity of such groups. The task is even more complicated in trying to define and concretize the way Latinos/Latinas develop their moral reasoning and build ethical systems. For some, this very exercise goes against the "character" of Latinos/Latinas, since the methodological approach is an imposition and another form of colonizing persons from Latin America. Although this reactionary tendency is understandable and justifiable, the core of the argument serves as the foundation to elaborate Latino/Latina ethics. In other words, by reacting against the establishment, Latinos/Latinas build their own ethical method and explain their reality and construct their moral and social meaning.

Precisely because their ethical and moral reasoning is grounded in their present and past reality, no particular method and system will be able to offer a comprehensive and accurate description of each group under the Latino/Latina umbrella. Nevertheless, there are common themes and realities that serve as the framework of reference and ethical interpretation of the Latino/Latina community. These common elements will be analyzed here as a way to offer a representation of trends and systems of ethical inquiry, though never attempting to offer a "one-size-fits-all" ethical approach.

Common Themes

For the great majority of Latinos/Latinas, the migration experience is relevant and crucial. Departure from one's country of origin, for whatever reason, is a dramatic experience that creates major cultural and ethical tensions that result from the collision of at least two lifestyles, two worldviews. Suddenly, what was normal and appropriate may not be so in the "new" culture. Not only are practices and lifestyles at odds but also the whole person is classified as "alien"; documented or undocumented does not matter, since immigrants and their culture become aliens and "strangers in a foreign land." It is precisely this biblical motif that becomes and represents one of the common themes in Latino/Latina ethics. For second and subsequent generations of Latinos/Latinas who have not experienced this type of migration, cultural and emotional connections to the land of their ancestors remain an important factor in their self-identity.

For these reasons, Latinos/Latinas are faced with ethical and moral dilemmas almost daily: How do Latinos/Latinas determine what is good and right in the face of conflicting cultural claims and traditions? Do they give preference to moral values embraced by their ancestors? Should they embrace a "new" morality, which intuitively seems opposite to their initial reaction, for the sake of "fitting in" and social acceptance? In responding to these questions, Latinos/Latinas have a bicultural advantage (sometimes referred to in the literature as, e.g., "mestizaje," "sato," "hybridity"); they are self-critical of their own culture, and at the same time they critically analyze the dominant culture and its effects. The advantage consists in that members of the dominant culture often take for granted and embrace dominant values without questioning, simply because such values are assumed to be de facto moral absolutes, whereas Latinos/Latinas tend to examine the effectiveness of the "old" and "new" values in response to their reality as aliens and their basic needs.

The "bicultural advantage," however, is perceived by the dominant culture as a hindrance, as disloyalty, or as an unwillingness to contribute to the well-being of society. Christian Latino/Latina ethicists respond by appealing to the Scriptures and highlighting the importance of being "strangers in a strange land." Images of exile, dual citizenship, resident aliens, and welcoming strangers and foreigners offer a positive moral foundation and affirmation of the advantages of being bicultural. Working with these and other prominent themes, they suggest that the foundation of the Christian faith is precisely grounded in this premise: Christians are called to live as resident aliens (e.g., Lev. 19:34; Eph. 2:19; 1 Pet. 2:11). Since Christians are considered to be citizens of the kingdom of God, and since their loyalty is to God above all other kingdoms and social systems, they are called to examine and critically analyze these political organizations and their moral values in the light of the "foreign" experience and "alien" paradigm. It is here that the general call to Christians and the Latino/Latina experience find a common denominator that allows Latinos/Latinas to offer a perspective that is more than theoretical; it is a way of life, which in turn becomes the ethical/moral lens of their endeavors.

It is this moral lens that leads to and constitutes another important common theme in Latino/Latina ethics. This has to do with experiences in response to daily, real-life struggles, as opposed to theoretical and case studies. The practicality of the moral lens plays an important role for Latinos/Latinas because they are responding to ethical dilemmas that are not abstract or philosophical, but rather on many occasions involve life-or-death decisions that must be made. Although some consider this approach to be a form of utilitarian and pragmatic ethics, a closer look reveals that this is not the case. By responding to daily struggles, moral decisions made by Latinos/Latinas are not based on a cost-benefit analysis or on the simple empirical measure of the consequences of one's action. Rather, protection of life, family, and care are key aspects. Describing the Spanish term *lo cotidiano* as referring to the response of women to their daily struggles and their shared experiences, María Isasi-Díaz makes the following observation,

> In *mujerista* theology *lo cotidiano* has made it possible to appeal to the daily lived-experience of Hispanic women as an authentic source without ignoring social location. On the contrary, *lo cotidiano* makes social location explicit, for it is the context of the person in relation to the physical space, ethnic space, social space. Furthermore, *lo cotidiano* for Latinas points both to the struggle (*la lucha*) against the present social order and to the liberating alternative which constitutes the core of our historical project: community (*la comunidad*). This means that *lo cotidiano* constitutes the arena where Hispanic women are confronted by the groups of which they are members. This makes it possible for them to judge their own personal understandings, aspirations, ambitions, projects, and goals in their lives. So, *lo cotidiano* is where morality begins to play a role for Latinas. *Lo cotidiano* becomes the lived-text in which and through which Hispanic women understand and decide what is right and good, what is wrong and evil. (Isasi-Díaz 71)

Ismael García points out the importance of response to daily struggles but also responds to critics who insist on labeling this approach as utilitarian and pragmatic:

> The Hispanic focus on intimate relationships and our sensitivity to the needs of others cement our conviction that we have moral obligations beyond those defined in

> terms of rights and impartial universal laws. Within the family and the comunidad [community] it is not the language of beneficence and utility, nor the language of law, rights, and contracts between free agents that makes moral sense, but the language of commitment, mutual dependence, care, love, and compassion that communicates what is morally required. In these contexts obligation and responsibility take precedence over right. (García 44)

These two authors, as well as others, explain the importance of practical and moral responses to daily struggles, but they also highlight another common theme in Latino/Latina ethics by pointing out the hermeneutical and ethical importance of community. Latinos/Latinas offer a critique, as "strangers in a strange land," of the highly individualistic and privatized approaches to reading Scripture and pursuing goodness, particularly the way these have been rooted in the United States. For Latinos/Latinas, the task of moral discernment is not a private affair or an individual matter; for them, community plays an important role in the shaping of values—that is, in character formation. Extended family as well as traditions and religious practices embraced by communities at large not only constitute an important moral guide but also are significant in decision-making processes. The Latino/Latina moral agent is mindful not only of the personal and private implications of any given response to a moral dilemma but also of the connections and responsibilities to the agent's community.

In a similar fashion, while many in the United States regard biblical interpretation as a private exercise and regard individualistic hermeneutics as acceptable, Latinos/Latinas reject this notion and offer a communal, family-oriented reading of Scripture. For them, experiences of exile and migration have both private and corporate consequences. Based on their shared experiences, Latinos/Latinas cannot remain "neutral" in the face of suffering and discrimination. In facing acts of injustice, Latinos/Latinas, those who have personally experienced these situations and those who have not, are members of one family, and they respond to these acts as one community regardless of their private and personal connections. Furthermore, in reading Scripture, they point out that from the OT to the Gospels and the rest of the NT, God constitutes a community to reach out to other communities, not in an individual fashion but rather as corporate manifestation of God's work. It is in community that God's creative work is expressed, a community that is in harmony with the rest of creation. It is by constituting one community that God reaches all other communities/nations; in Christ, believers embrace a community of faith and are members of the family of God. These and other images are crucial in biblical interpretation for Latinos/Latinas as they strive to maintain the familial and communal aspects as relevant and essential in their attempt to replicate the values embraced by their original communities, which now in many cases are many miles away.

Key Figures

Without a doubt, the key figures and representatives of this ethical expression are the millions of persons who have embarked on the journey of migration to the United States. Latinos/Latinas who have arrived in this land—some before the arrival of the *Mayflower*, others as recently as the beginning of each new day—struggle to make sense of their new paradigm of living as "strangers in a strange land"; these are the main figures and representatives of this form of moral reasoning.

In exploring these stories and listening to their voices, some Latinos/Latinas have developed academic works in which they have been able to challenge common assumptions as well as create a hearing for the voices of the millions often ignored. These pioneers represent these voices, and they have opened a new path for new generations with their work and commitment to serve the Latino/Latina population. Among these pioneers are men and women, Protestant and Catholic, who have studied Christian ethics and have presented a new voice in their field. Among them are Ada María Isasi-Díaz, a Cuban American recently retired from Drew University, who dedicated the majority of her work to representing women's voices in dealing with daily struggles; Ismael García, a Puerto Rican who teaches at Austin Presbyterian Seminary and who used an important film, *My Family/Mi Familia*, to develop and explain a model for ethics from a Hispanic perspective; Eldin Villafañe, also from Puerto Rico, who teaches at Gordon-Conwell Theological Seminary and has concentrated his studies in developing a Pentecostal ethic; and, more recently, Miguel De La Torre, a Cuban American teaching at Iliff School of Theology, who has addressed a wide range of issues from immigration to human sexuality.

These authors represent broadly the ethical thinking, hermeneutical approaches, and character development of Latinos/Latinas as summarized and presented in this article.

See also Exile; Liberationist Ethics; Praxis

Bibliography

De La Torre, M. *Doing Christian Ethics from the Margins*. Orbis, 2004; De La Torre, M., and E. Aponte. *Introducing*

Latino/a Theologies. Orbis, 2001; Fernández, E. *La Cosecha: Harvesting Contemporary United States Hispanic Theology (1972–1998)*. Liturgical Press, 2000; García, I. *Dignidad: Ethics through Hispanic Eyes*. Abingdon, 1997; Isasi-Díaz, A. M. *En la Lucha—In the Struggle: A Hispanic Women's Liberation Theology*. Fortress, 1993; idem. *La Lucha Continues: Mujerista Theology*. Orbis, 2004; idem, *Mujerista Theology: A Theology for the Twenty-first Century*. Orbis, 1996; Villafañe, E. *The Liberating Spirit: Toward an Hispanic American Pentecostal Social Ethic*. University Press of America, 1992.

Hugo Magallanes

Law

The Bible often portrays God as issuing commands and laws, beginning already in the book of Genesis. God's first acts of creation involve commands to all creation, "Let there be light" (Gen. 1:3), and specifically to humans, "Be fruitful and multiply, . . . have dominion" (Gen. 1:28). The first divine command that humans disobey is the prohibition against eating the fruit of the tree of the knowledge of good and evil in the garden of Eden, leading to the expulsion of the humans from Eden (Gen. 2:17; 3:14–24). God's law and commands continue throughout the Bible, functioning both as a vehicle of divine blessing and as an instrument of divine judgment.

Law in the Pentateuch

The Bible's legal material is concentrated in the Pentateuch (Genesis through Deuteronomy), the first five books of the Bible. The terms used for laws include "statutes and ordinances" (Lev. 18:5), "commandments" (Exod. 20:6), "decrees" (Deut. 6:20), and "law," *tôrâ* (Deut. 4:44). The term *tôrâ* came to be an important and inclusive term within the biblical understanding of law. Deuteronomy used the term to designate the laws within its book (4:44) and then even more expansively to include the entire book and its wide variety of genres: narratives, speeches, curses, blessings, poems, and legal material ("the book of the law [*tôrâ*]" [31:26]). Jewish tradition eventually used the word *tôrâ* as a designation for the whole of Genesis through Deuteronomy (Neh. 8:1–2; Sirach, prologue; cf. Matt. 5:17).

The core meaning of *tôrâ* includes not only "law" but also "instruction" or "teaching." The teaching function of biblical law is illustrated by the frequent inclusion of motivational clauses along with the laws that seek to persuade and provide good reasons why the reader or hearer ought to obey the law in question (Exod. 20:8–11; 23:9; Lev. 19:2; Deut. 7:12–16).

The Bible locates the primary giving of God's law to Israel at Mount Sinai, the "mountain of God," in Exod. 20–Num. 10. At Mount Sinai, God established a covenant with the Israelites as God's chosen people, forming them into "a priestly kingdom and a holy nation" (Exod. 19:6) as they traveled from the slavery of Egypt to the freedom of Canaan. God's covenant obligations or laws functioned as expressions of gratitude to God for the good things that God had done for Israel. Thus, the narrative prologue to the Ten Commandments reminds Israel of what God had already achieved for Israel: "I am the LORD your God, who brought you out of the land of Egypt, out of the house of slavery" (Exod. 20:2). The ten commands that follow constitute the basic obligations of Israel, teaching Israel how to live into its already established identity as the freed people of God (Exod. 20:3–17).

A number of law codes follow the Ten Commandments within the Pentateuch:

1. the so-called Book of the Covenant or Covenant Code, which contains case law with significant parallels to other ancient Near Eastern law, especially the Code of Hammurabi, but also contains important adaptations that reflect ancient Israel's experience and theology (Exod. 20:22–23:19);
2. a set of cultic laws given by God after Israel's rebellious act of making a golden calf that mark a new covenant, rooted in the mercy and forgiveness of God (Exod. 34:6–7), and repeat certain laws from the Covenant Code focused on the proper worship of God and the avoidance of idolatry (Exod. 34:10–26);
3. the Priestly Code, which focuses on maintaining the holiness of the tabernacle or tent of God's presence in the midst of the Israelites as well as the holiness of the priests and the proper qualities and quantities of the sacrifices that they regularly offered to God (Lev. 1–16);
4. the Holiness Code, which expands the expectation of holiness beyond the Priestly Code to include the whole Israelite camp (not just the tabernacle), the whole land of Canaan when they live there, and the entire Israelite people (Lev. 19:1–2), both priests and laypersons (Lev. 17–26);
5. miscellaneous laws in Num. 1–10 (while still at Mount Sinai) and other laws in Numbers given by God as Israel left Sinai and continued its wilderness journey (Num. 15; 18; 19; 28–30; 35);
6. the Deuteronomic Code, which is presented as Moses' last words that he taught to a new generation of Israelites before his death and

includes new laws as well as reinterpretations of the several earlier laws from the Covenant Code in Exod. 20:22–23:19 (Deut. 6–26).

Although these varied collections of biblical laws contain numerous parallels to other law codes in the ancient Near East, they also reflect many unique features. They are unique in mixing together laws concerning everyday social, political, and economic life (Exod. 22:1–14) with laws concerning religious life and worship (Exod. 23:12–19). In the context of a largely polytheistic culture surrounding Israel, biblical laws are unique in their strong emphasis on the worship of Israel's one God alone and the prohibition of the worship of images or idols (Exod. 20:3–6; 22:20; 23:13). The biblical laws originate as words from God, whereas other ancient Near Eastern law codes typically originate not with the gods but rather with human kings.

In the conclusion of the book of Deuteronomy, Moses wrote down the "book of the law" and instructed the Levitical priests to read aloud the book of the law in the hearing of all Israel every seven years (Deut. 31:9–13). This ongoing life of the "book of the law" in Israel's history is suggested by the narrative of the finding of the "book of the law" during temple renovations in the reign of King Josiah, likely some version of the book of Deuteronomy (2 Kgs. 22) and Ezra's public reading of the "book of the law of Moses" after the exiles' return to Jerusalem (Ezra 8). The ongoing role of the law in Israel's family life is also suggested by the instruction to parents to recite and teach the laws of Deuteronomy to their children every day "when you lie down and when you rise" (Deut. 6:6–9). Daily meditation on God's law became a practice of religious devotion associated with joy, delight, freedom, mercy, and blessing (Pss. 1; 119).

Law in the Prophets

The OT prophets rarely cited specific laws in their announcements of the coming judgment of God upon Israel and its leaders. However, the prophets clearly based God's judgment on Israel's repeated disobedience of God's will as generally embodied in God's law, especially focused on the worship of false gods and on social injustice (Isa. 5; Jer. 7:8–11; 11:1–17; Hos. 4:1–3). The prophets criticized Israel's life of worship, sacrifice, and ritual when it was not combined with concern for God's justice for widows, orphans, and the poor (Isa. 1:10–17; 58:6–12; Amos 5:21–24; Mic. 6:6–8). As a result, the prophets blamed Judah's exile to Babylon and the destruction of Jerusalem and its temple on Israel's disobedience of God's law (Isa. 42:24–25).

Law in the New Testament

In the NT, "law" usually refers to the commandments and laws that were given to Moses at Mount Sinai, although at times it also refers to the Pentateuch as a whole ("the law and the prophets" [cf. Matt. 5:17; Luke 24:27]) or even to the whole of Jewish sacred Scripture (John 10:34; 12:34; 1 Cor. 14:21). The NT witness affirmed that the law and the prophets found their fulfillment in Christ (Matt. 5:17; Luke 24:44). Indeed, the law (the Pentateuch) itself testified to righteousness by faith "apart from law" (Rom. 3:21). In the NT, one focus of the call to obedience included the commandments of Moses (especially for the Gospel of Matthew), but more important, obedience involves "believing in" and "following" Jesus, who carried forward but also reinterpreted Mosaic law. An inner biblical dialectic exists between Jesus as fulfilling the law of Moses (Matt. 5:17–19) and Jesus as one who is sovereign over the law and able to reinterpret it (Matt. 5:21–48; Mark 2:23–28; Luke 6:1–11; John 7:22–24). For example, Jesus declared that what makes someone impure or unclean is not what goes into the person (a reference to the food laws in Lev. 11) but rather what comes out from the human heart in words and actions (Matt. 15:11, 17–20; Mark 7:19). Jesus challenged the Jewish scribes and their interpretation of the Sabbath law, declaring himself "lord of the sabbath" (Luke 6:1–11). Jesus reinterpreted a number of OT commandments in his Sermon on the Mount (Matt. 5:17–48).

According to Rom. 1:16, the core of the apostle Paul's mission was to proclaim to gentiles the gospel of "the power of God for salvation to everyone who has faith" in Christ alone apart from works of the law (i.e., apart from observing all the laws of Moses in the Pentateuch, including circumcision [cf. Rom. 3:21–26; see also Acts 15:1–35]). For Paul, God's law functioned to guard the welfare of human beings as a temporary custodian or "disciplinarian" until Christ came (Gal. 3:25). The law continues to serve as a mirror by which God convicts all humans, both Jews and gentiles, as sinners, since "all have sinned" against God's law (Rom. 3:23). Even gentiles had requirements of the law "written on their hearts," so that no one has an excuse (Rom. 2:15; cf. 1:20). The law reveals sin and drives the sinner to trust not in works of the law but instead in God's forgiveness and mercy through the death of Jesus, who "died for the ungodly" (Rom. 5:1–11).

Yet Paul could also speak positively about the continuing role of the law in terms of obeying "Christ's law" (1 Cor. 9:21), which was summarized by the command to "love your neighbor as yourself" (Rom. 13:8, 10; Gal. 5:14). Although those who follow Christ are in one sense free from living under the law, they are in another sense bound in obedience to Christ and the law of love. All things may be lawful, "but not all things are beneficial" (1 Cor. 6:12; see also Rom. 14:1–15:13).

Law and Ethics

The biblical traditions of laws, commandments, and instructions offer a complex and varied set of resources for reflecting on the relationship of law and ethics. A few observations may be made. The biblical witness affirms God as the source of biblical law. Yet the variety of law codes and their distinctive and sometimes conflicting content invite caution and careful interpretation, sensitivity to narrative context, and comparison with other biblical laws, narratives, wisdom material, prophetic oracles, and the combined witness of both Testaments before making definitive pronouncements about the clear will of God. The Bible itself also testifies to the need for ongoing interpretation of laws and customs in the face of new circumstances and contexts (Num. 27:1–11; Matt. 5).

Moreover, the laws and commandments of the OT often represent the minimum expectations of obedience to God and boundaries of behavior beyond which God's people should not go (the prohibitive commandments, such as "You shall have no other gods," "You shall not murder," and the like). But these minimum legal standards within the OT do not fully encompass the deeper and more positive ethical ideals that both OT and NT witnesses urged upon their communities of faith: to love God with passion and urgency in every aspect of one's life (Deut. 6:5–9; 10:12; Mark 12:30), to love one's neighbor as oneself (Lev. 19:18; Luke 10:25–37; Gal. 5:14), and "to do justice, and to love kindness, and to walk humbly with your God" (Mic. 6:8 [cf. Col. 3:12]). The OT and the NT also testify that whatever human love of God and neighbor humans can muster is itself a gift of God (Deut. 30:6), motivated by the prior and overflowing love, generosity, and mercy of God (Deut. 30:6; John 15:1–17). "We love because God first loved us" (1 John 4:19).

See also Antinomianism; Covenant; Divine Command Theories of Ethics; Good Works; Law, Uses of; Law and Gospel; Legalism; Love, Love Command; Moral Law; Priestly Literature; Sermon on the Mount; Ten Commandments; Torah

Bibliography

Dunn, J. D. G. *Jesus, Paul, and the Law: Studies in Mark and Galatians*. Westminster John Knox 1990; Levenson, B. *Deuteronomy and the Hermeneutics of Legal Innovation*. Oxford University Press, 2002; idem, *Legal Revision and Religious Renewal in Ancient Israel*. Cambridge University Press, 2010; Sanders, E. P. *Paul, the Law, and the Jewish People*. Fortress, 1983; Schreiner, T. *The Law and Its Fulfillment: A Pauline Theology of Law*. Baker, 1998; Thielman, F. *The Law and the New Testament: The Question of Continuity*. Crossroad, 1999; Wenham, G. "The Gap Between Law and Ethics in the Bible." *JJS* 48 (1997): 17–29. Wright, D. *Inventing God's Law: How the Covenant Code of the Bible Used and Revised the Laws of Hammurabi*. Oxford University Press, 2009.

Dennis T. Olson

Law, Civil and Criminal

Civil and criminal law and judicial processes for their enforcement are addressed most explicitly in the books of Exodus and Deuteronomy, with selected parallels in Leviticus. Exodus and Deuteronomy offer comprehensive visions of a cohesive society constituted by the covenant that God established with the people of Israel. The maintenance of civil order is essential to covenant faithfulness, and such order requires viable systems of civil and criminal law. These texts presume premodern social, economic, and political arrangements, and they authorize legal standards and punitive measures that are morally problematic for contemporary readers, such as qualified endorsements of slavery and impositions of the death penalty for sexual misconduct and idolatrous religious practices. Despite context-related limitations, these resources retain their pertinence for present-day social concerns because they challenge us to engage legal issues in a fashion that fosters social justice and advances a substantive vision of the common good.

The Biblical Context of Civil and Criminal Law

Accounts of civil and criminal law in Exodus and Deuteronomy are incorporated into extended lists of the statutes, laws, and ordinances that ordered the lives of the people of Israel, including shared ritual practices, dietary codes, and standards of purity (Exod. 20:22–23:19; Deut. 12–25). The normative foundation for these statutes is provided by the Ten Commandments or Ten Words (*dĕbārîm*) of the Lord (Exod. 20:1–17; Deut. 5:6–21), and they are reinforced by narratives of Israel's formation as a covenant people. Statutes in Exodus reflect an earlier source known as the Covenant Code (Exod. 20:22–23:19), which contains a substantial number of case laws that were widely operative within the larger Mesopotamian region.

(Hanson [53–56] sees the Covenant Code as an ancient source that contributed to the subsequent formulation of the Ten Commandments. Pleins [51–54], however, views the Ten Commandments as the most ancient source, with the Covenant Code functioning as an early commentary representing the values of peasant farmers over against the interests of monarchs and aristocratic classes.) These resources attest the openness of biblically grounded faith perspectives to common features of human experience (cf. Exod. 21:1–36; 22:1–17). At the same time, the Covenant Code begins and ends with "Yahwistic teachings"—that is, distinctive instructions that the Lord provided for the people of Israel. Opening verses reiterate condemnations of idolatry and graven images recorded in the Decalogue (Exod. 20:22–26) and elaborated in the so-called Ritual Decalogue (Exod. 34:12–26). Concluding Yahwistic teachings emphasize communal values with deep roots in Israel's covenant heritage (Exod. 22:18–31; 23:1–19), providing a moral framework for civil and criminal law.

Deuteronomy recasts the resources in Exodus with emphasis on covenant-making as a living, ongoing process (cf. Deut. 5:1–3), and it places special emphasis on God's steadfast love for his people despite their persistent disobedience. (Praise for God's steadfast love is a prominent theme in Psalms, especially Pss. 119; 136; see also Pss. 89; 106; 107; 118.) The people are summoned to love God in return with heart, soul, and strength, fully embracing the Lord's words in their own lives (Deut. 6:4–9). Legal codes are necessary for maintaining order among a stubborn and disobedient people, but covenant faithfulness extends well beyond the rigorous enforcement of civil law. This theme is reiterated throughout Deuteronomy (Deut. 10:12–13, 15–16; 11:13, 16, 18; 13:3; 26:16; 30:3, 10, 16). Similarly, the prophet Jeremiah announces the Lord's promise of a new covenant with Israel and Judah, a covenant in which the law of the Lord is placed within them and written on their hearts (Jer. 31:31–33); and the prophet Ezekiel declares the Lord's promise of new hearts of flesh to replace their stubborn hearts of stone (Ezek. 11:19–20).

Within the context of Jerusalem's postexilic reconstruction, Leviticus incorporates a significant number of the statutes contained in Exodus and Deuteronomy into what is known as the Holiness Code (Lev. 17–26). This code focuses on sacrificial rites, the consecration of priests, and standards of purity and holiness, yet it is also the original source of the commands to the people of Israel to love neighbors and strangers living among them as they love themselves (Lev. 19:17–18, 33–34; cf. Deut. 10:19).

Issues Addressed by Civil and Criminal Law

Treatments of civil and criminal law in Exodus, Deuteronomy, and Leviticus cover five types of issues:

1. class and property matters, including honest commercial transactions;
2. loans and debts;
3. physical assaults and interpersonal conflicts;
4. abominable sexual acts;
5. unacceptable religious practices.

The first set of issues is the most complex. Many items are addressed not by civil law but rather by moral imperatives: an insistence on just weights and measures (Deut. 25:13–16), repudiations of deceit and fraud (Deut. 25:13–16; cf. Lev. 6:2), mandates for the prompt payment of wages to workers (Deut. 24:14–15), and calls for Sabbath rest (Exod. 23:10). The needs of the poor receive special attention. Farmers must not harvest their crops to the borders, and they must leave gleanings in the field and fruit that falls to the ground so that the poor can acquire resources for their nutrition (Lev. 20:22). In the Sabbath year farmers must leave their fields fallow and allow the poor and wild animals to gather for themselves what grows naturally (Exod. 23:10–11; cf. Lev. 25:1–7). People with means are urged to be generous and openhanded to those in need (Deut. 15:4, 11). Following the harvest, they are to offer tithes to support priests and Levites and to provide for the needs of strangers, widows, and orphans (Exod. 23:19). They must in no case wrong or suppress strangers or abuse widows and orphans (Exod. 22:21–24 [the texts cited from Exodus stem from Yahwistic teachings in the Covenant Code]).

Criminal statutes related to class and property issues overlap with Mesopotamian case laws. Rather than elaborating detailed rules, they provide examples of cases that are equivalent to theft or to the abuse of a neighbor's lands and animal herds: stealing a neighbor's ox or sheep (Exod. 22:1); allowing animal herds to graze in a neighbor's field or causing a fire in that field (Exod. 22:5–6); placing one's goods, including animals, in the care of a neighbor and later discovering that those goods have been stolen (Exod. 22:7–8, 10). The last case required a judge's investigation of the neighbor's level of responsibility. Persons guilty of crimes related to property matters are punished with judicial orders of restitution—that is, payments to victims that compensate for their losses. Leviticus reports the case of a man who lied about having found a neighbor's lost property, keeping it for himself. The law required that he return the property with an additional payment equivalent to one-fifth of its value (Lev. 6:2–7). Exodus mentions a possible dispute over the ownership of a particular object—an animal, clothing, or some lost thing. Both parties are summoned to come before God, and the one whom God condemns must pay the neighbor double for the disputed property (Exod. 22:9). This verse reflects Mesopotamian case laws, so originally it could have referred to judicial actions informed by an oracle. A variant of this practice could have been incorporated into Israel's practices, given the prominence of Levites and priests in judicial processes (cf. Deut. 17:8–13). The general message is that people must honor property placed in the hands of others: returning an animal that has strayed (Exod. 23:4), leaving boundary markers in place for lands held by others (Deut. 19:14), setting burdened donkeys free, and caring for a neighbor's fallen donkey (Deut. 22:1–3).

Interest charges on loans are unequivocally condemned, a standard that can be confusing for contemporary readers because it contradicts taken-for-granted practices in market economies (Exod. 22:25–27; Lev. 25:35–38; Deut. 24:10–13). In ancient Israel there were no precedents for loans to facilitate business investments or to enable consumers to extend payments on costly yet enduring products, such as automobiles and houses. Loans were simply a means to enable desperately poor people to survive, at least for a time. Persons with means were urged to lend money to the poor, especially fellow community members in need, and to do so without charging interest, and they were obliged to remit all debts every seventh year (Deut. 15:12). They were also prohibited from demanding an object from a borrower as a "pledge" that the loan will be repaid, unless the object should be returned within a day (Exod. 22:27; Deut. 24:10–13). The example cited is a garment that the borrower needed for cover while sleeping. The presumption is that those who borrow money have no possessions that are not urgently needed in their daily lives.

The worst-case scenario for the poor was submission to an extended period of indentured servitude, a domestic version of slavery. Such servitude could be viewed as an ancient equivalent of contemporary declarations of bankruptcy, where people endure substantial losses under conditions that enable them to reconstruct their lives. Hebrew servants and their family members were to be provided with basic needs, and they were to be released at the beginning of the seventh year (Lev. 25:39–46; Deut. 15:12). Moreover, their master must not send them away empty-handed (Deut. 15:13–14). Leviticus stresses the Year of Jubilee, which occurs in fifty-year cycles (Lev. 25:8–12). In that year all debts are released, servitude ends, and people may return to lost lands. There are provisions that permit a servant and family to choose to remain in bondage for the remainder of their lives, for bondage to a just and caring master might give them security that they could not otherwise achieve (Exod. 21:2–6; Deut. 15:16–17). A father could also sell his own daughter as a slave, provided the master planned to take her as a wife (Exod. 21:7–11). There were important conditions: if the master is not pleased with the daughter, he must let her be redeemed; if he designates her for his son, he must treat her as a daughter; and if he takes another wife, he must not diminish her share of resources or deny her marital rights. If these conditions are not met, the daughter must be set free without any payment of money. Slavery had a different meaning for foreigners captured in war, for they and their heirs could be held as slaves throughout their lifetimes (Lev. 25:44–46; Deut. 20:10; 21:10–14). A similar policy was subsequently embraced in the United States when owners of landed estates purchased African slaves who had been forced into the slave trade following their defeat in tribal wars.

Statutes that address physical violence and sexual misconduct are more straightforward. These actions are explicitly treated as crimes, and the death penalty is imposed for intentional killing (Exod. 21:12–14; Lev. 24:17, 21); kidnapping (Exod. 21:16; Deut. 24:7); assaulting or cursing parents (Exod. 21:15–17); and abominable sexual practices, including adultery, incest, lying with an animal, and lying with a male as with a female (Exod. 22:19; Lev. 20:10–21; Deut. 22:13–21). There are no references to sexual acts between women, presumably because such acts were less public and because they entailed no waste of "seed" needed for procreation. Texts in Exodus, Leviticus, and Deuteronomy do not directly stress the urgency of endogamous marriage practices, though this theme was central to the postexilic reform agenda of Ezra and Nehemiah, who demanded that husbands dismiss their foreign wives and children borne by those wives (Ezra 9–10; Neh. 9:1–3; 13:23–30). The death penalty is also mandated for idolatry, sorcery, defamations of the Lord's name, and false prophecy (Exod. 22:18; Lev. 20:1–3, 27; 24:16; Deut. 12:13; 13:5, 12; 17:2–5). Why are all of these practices punished with the death penalty? The apparent reason is that they violated the covenant calling of the people of Israel: death and kidnapping deprived people of life and freedom; sexual misconduct threatened the patriarchal structure that preserved kinship bonds vital for their collective identity; and idolatry was a blatant betrayal of God, who had formed them as a covenant people.

Less serious forms of physical assault and sexual misconduct are addressed as well. Relevant texts in Exodus reflect Mesopotamian case laws. Those who unintentionally kill others can avoid death by fleeing to a specified refuge city, which provided an asylum where a fair judicial hearing could take place (Exod. 21:12–14; Deut. 4:41–43; 19:1–13; cf. Num. 35:9–12). When an individual strikes another in a quarrel, causing an injury from which recovery is possible, the assailant must reimburse the injured person for time lost during recovery (Exod. 21:18–19). Perpetrators of permanent injuries are subjected to comparable harm, "life for life, eye for eye, tooth for tooth, hand for hand, foot for foot, burn for burn, wound for wound, stripe for stripe" (Exod. 21:23–25). If a slave owner strikes a slave, and the slave dies immediately, the owner must be punished; but if the slave survives for a time, there is no punishment because the slave is the owner's property (Exod. 21:20–21). A slave who suffers a permanent injury—a lost eye or tooth—must be set free (Exod. 21:26–27). If individuals engaged in a fight accidentally injure a pregnant woman, causing a miscarriage, the person responsible for the injury must pay the woman's husband an amount determined by a judge (Exod. 21:22). A man who seduces a virgin must pay the father fifty shekels of silver and take her as his wife (Exod. 22:16; Deut. 22:28–29). If a man rapes a woman in town and she does not cry out for help, she is guilty of adultery and faces death along with the man; if the rape occurs in the countryside, only the man will be punished, since no one could hear the woman's cry for help (Deut. 22:23–27). These cases provide examples of conditions that might mitigate the seriousness of the crimes committed. There are no parallel examples for actions that violate the Lord's holiness.

Just Judicial Processes

Texts in Exodus and Deuteronomy provide standards for fair judicial processes. Local elders initially bore primary responsibility for dealing with criminal acts that merited the death penalty, such as murder, adultery, or incest. Local judges were subsequently appointed by the people to examine more complex cases, cases that required discriminating judgments of guilt and accountability with determinations of appropriate penalties (Deut. 16:18–20). Cases involving conflicts between family networks or tribes were referred to Levitical priests working with an assigned judge in the "place" (i.e., the Jerusalem temple), for cases of this kind normally could not be resolved at local levels (Deut. 17:6–7). (Wilson [42–45, 48–51] directs attention to two cases in the book of Judges that involved conflicts between tribes: the trial of Achan for stealing precious objects from Jericho [Judg. 7], and the trial of men from the tribe of Benjamin who raped and killed a Judahite woman from Bethlehem who was a Levite's concubine [Judg. 19–21].) Judges presided over trials, questioned witnesses, evaluated relevant information, and reached concluding judgments regarding levels of guilt or innocence. Where the death penalty was not required, they determined appropriate penalties. There were no provisions for juries, legal prosecutors, or defense attorneys. Affected persons or their family members had to take initiatives of their own to address wrongdoing. False and malicious witnesses and all forms of bribery were condemned (Exod. 23:1). At least two witnesses were required to substantiate a capital crime (Deut. 17:6–7; 19:15–16), and witnesses were cautioned against going along with a majority, because they were obliged to speak the truth (Exod. 23:6). Finally, justices were called to judge with justice, showing no partiality that disadvantaged the poor, or strangers, widows, and orphans (Exod. 23:2–6; Lev. 19:15; Deut. 10:19; 16:18–20; 17:8–13).

The central message is that civil and criminal laws derive their authority and their authenticity from fundamental covenant commitments: honoring God's glory; embracing God's steadfast love and loving God in return; maintaining stability and order; laboring for the material well-being and physical security of the people, including strangers living among them; offering special care for the vulnerable and protecting them from exploitation, especially the poor, widows, and orphans; and reinforcing marital bonds that undergirded the identity of the people.

Transformative New Testament Visions

The NT bears witness to founding events in the formation of a new people of God in Jesus Christ, generating ethnically diverse faith communities with only marginal social standing and virtually no direct access to centers of power and authority. There are no systematic assessments of civil and criminal law, though community members are instructed to honor governing authorities and to obey existing laws, provided those laws did not violate their basic faith commitments (Rom.

13:1–7; 1 Pet. 2:13–17). In subtle and indirect ways, however, NT texts provide a reminder that legal procedures are by no means the ideal system for maintaining social order. They are at best an unavoidable and imperfect backup system.

The cultivation of strong communal bonds among people with diverse ethnic and cultural roots and varied class and status positions in the larger society was an essential component of the emerging Christian mission. Yet this inclusive vision also generated serious divisions and conflicts, especially within family networks. Matthew and Luke report Jesus' acknowledgment that such divisions were directly linked to his mission (Matt. 10:34–39; Luke 12:51–53). Paul's gentile mission led to similar strains (1 Cor. 12–13). Members of emerging faith communities were urged to address their conflicts and difficulties not by resorting to legal procedures (Matt. 5:21–26; 1 Cor. 6:1–8), still less by retaliation (Matt. 5:38–42). Instead, they were to undertake personal initiatives to heal, renew, and strengthen their relationships with one another. Where they could not resolve their conflicts at an interpersonal level, they were to seek the help and guidance of the larger community (Matt. 18:15–20). Equally important, they were encouraged to extend their internal practices of conflict resolution into the wider social world, reaching out in love even to their enemies and persecutors (Matt. 5:43–44; Luke 6:27–28; Rom. 12:14–24). (For contemporary reflections on these themes, see Stassen; Cahill; Shriver.) These concerns underscore the necessity of a vibrant civil society for sustaining social order and for bestowing authority on civil and criminal law. The law cannot be maintained by force alone.

Also, while affirming the "enduring authority of the law and the prophets" in his Sermon on the Mount (Matt. 5–7), Jesus moved beyond strictly legal definitions of acceptable human behavior. He emphasized the vital role of feelings, passions, and desires in human interactions, with particular attention to the harm they can inflict on others: outbursts of anger, lustful gazes at a woman, obsessions with material well-being, intense desires to please people with status and power, and compulsive concerns for one's own righteousness and self-esteem. Passions such as these can lead to actual violations of the law. Anger can impel a violent assault. A lustful gaze can result in rape or some form of sexual abuse. Desires for earthly treasures can render us careless about property that belongs to others and totally unconcerned with the needs of poverty-stricken neighbors. Drives to please prominent people can dispose us to say what we think they want to hear instead of speaking the truth. Preoccupation with our own righteousness can generate hypocrisy and judgmental attitudes toward others. Passions such as these are contributing factors to forms of behavior that civil and criminal laws are designed to constrain: murder, rape, adultery, incest, theft, deceit, false testimony, and unjust judgment. We cannot constrain our passions simply by an act of the will, yet moral commitments to uphold the law do obligate us to take steps to address the impact that our feelings and desires have on our actual behavior. Jesus' counsel is practical. Reach out to a brother or sister in an effort to resolve the conflict that provoked anger. Put an end to inappropriate approaches to a woman. Simply speak the truth so that swearing becomes irrelevant, letting your yes be yes and your no be no. Set aside hypocritical judgments of others by removing the "log" from your own eye before attending to the "speck" in the eye of a neighbor. Acknowledge the transience and emptiness of "earthly treasures" and reorient your life to God's coming kingdom. In short, we honor the authority of the law and the prophets by fully embracing them in our hearts.

Jesus' final word is about compassion, mercy, and forgiveness. Although he sets extremely high expectations, he declares compassion and mercy as well. In the Lord's Prayer we are called to acknowledge our debts to others—that is, obligations that we have not fulfilled. We are also instructed to forgive those who are indebted to us (Matt. 6:9–13). Jesus' emphasis on mercy and forgiveness renders problematic forceful demands for the death penalty contained in the Pentateuch, especially for crimes other than homicide or murder. John 7:53–8:11 provides a striking example. The scribes and Pharisees brought to Jesus a woman who had committed adultery. They asked Jesus what should be done with her, given Moses' instructions that such a woman be stoned to death. Jesus said that the first stone must be cast by someone among them who is without sin. The scribes and Pharisees then left the scene, one by one. Jesus asked the woman, "Has no one condemned you?" She answered, "No one, sir." Jesus said, "Neither do I condemn you. Go your way, and from now on do not sin again."

The NT resources do not repudiate civil and criminal law, nor do they deny the need for such law. However, they call for ongoing human efforts to address divisions, conflicts, injuries, and wrongdoing without relying solely on judicial processes or penal codes, especially the death penalty. The Gospels, of course, portray Jesus' own crucifixion as based on spurious charges of blasphemy declared by temple priests with backing by false witnesses. Although Pilate was not convinced that Jesus had done anything wrong, he was pressured to carry out his crucifixion (Matt. 26:57–68; 27:11–26; Mark 14:53–65; 15:1–15; Luke 23:1–25). This event has at least fostered skepticism about the death penalty, except perhaps in cases where a convicted criminal has clearly been shown to be a serious threat to society.

See also Capital Punishment; Covenant; Crime and Criminal Justice; Economic Ethics; Law; Loans; New Testament Ethics; Old Testament Ethics; Sermon on the Mount; Ten Commandments

Bibliography

Cahill, L. *Love Your Enemies: Discipleship, Pacifism, and Just War Theory*. Fortress, 1994; Hanson, P. *The People Called: The Growth of Community in the Bible*. Westminster John Knox, 2001; Pleins, J. *The Social Vision of the Hebrew Bible: A Theological Introduction*. Westminster John Knox, 2001; Shriver, D., Jr., *An Ethic for Enemies: Forgiveness in Politics*. Oxford University Press, 1995; Stassen, G. *Just Peacemaking: Transforming Initiatives for Justice and Peace*. Westminster John Knox, 1992; Wilson, R. *Sociological Approaches to the Old Testament*. GBS. Fortress, 1984.

Thomas W. Ogletree

Law, Uses of

Law is a prominent religious and moral category in both Judaism and Christianity. In the OT, God's law embodies the covenantal relationship between God and God's people (Exod. 19:5–6; Deut. 10:12–15). It sets the people of God apart and provides guidance for their relationships with God and one another. The law, therefore, is a cherished gift that promotes flourishing (Ps. 19:7–11). The witness concerning the law in the OT is not singularly positive, however. Through the prophets, God enters suit against the people for blatantly ignoring or hypocritically misusing the law (Jer. 2:4–13; Isa. 1:2–20; Mic. 6:1–8). It is turned from a source of life and flourishing to condemnation and alienation.

The NT is also ambivalent about the law. Matthew reports that Jesus came "not to abolish but to fulfill" the law, calling his followers to a higher righteousness that "exceeds that of the scribes and Pharisees" (Matt. 5:17–20). In Mark, however, Jesus preaches freedom from scrupulous observance of legal regulations, associating it with the hypocrisy of the Scribes and Pharisees (Mark 7:1–13). For Paul, the law is good, but due to sin, it brings judgment and death rather than life and joy (Rom. 7:7–13; 2 Cor. 3:7–18). The authority of the law is superseded by Christ, who brings justification by faith, life in the Spirit, and adoption as children of God (Gal. 3:19–4:7).

A similar ambivalence can be seen in the heritage of Christian reflections on the uses of the law. For Thomas Aquinas, the natural law, available to all human beings through reason, is a necessary but insufficient guide for human existence. It provides trustworthy direction concerning their natural end as rational and social animals. The higher, supernatural end of human beings, however, is a gift of grace available only through Jesus Christ (*ST* I-II, qq. 90–95). Martin Luther, who emphasizes the depth of human sinfulness, understands the law negatively. First, it convicts people of their sinfulness before God (theological use); second, it restrains human licentiousness through the fear of punishment (civil use) (*Commentary on Galatians* 3:19; 4:3). Through grace, the true Christian is set free from the burden of the law to love God and neighbor. John Calvin's understanding of the law includes these negative uses but also a more positive, third use of the law, which he considers its principal and proper purpose: "to learn more thoroughly each day the nature of the Lord's will to which they aspire, and to confirm them in the understanding of it" (*Institutes* 2.7.12).

Throughout Scripture and the Christian heritage, God's law has been understood and used in a variety of ways that complement and conflict with one another: it is a guide for right relationship with God and one another, it condemns people for departing from God's will, it provides minimal but necessary measures to maintain order, and it is used by hypocrites and sinners as a tool of oppression and injustice.

See also Covenant; Judgment; Law; Legalism; Sin

Timothy A. Beach-Verhey

Law and Gospel

The biblical words *law* and *gospel* often appear in a tandem or dialectical relationship to each other. Paul in particular used these terms in his Letters to the Galatians and the Romans to summarize God's two ways of speaking with the world.

The concept of law focuses on God's gracious will that all creatures, especially humans, live gratefully in right relationship with God, with one another, and with the whole creation. God's word of law commands and structures right relationships, obligates obedience to God's law, and holds humans accountable to God's will. In Paul's view, God speaks law to all the peoples of the world through codes like the Ten Commandments and also to the particular ancient people of Israel through specific commands meant only for them in their time and place. The concept of gospel focuses on God's promise to everyone centered in Jesus Christ to liberate and redeem the world from sin, death, and the devil. As Jesus promises, "So if the Son makes you free, you will be free indeed" (John 8:36).

Key theologians have used these tandem terms to express the heart of Christian theology. Ambrose (339–97), bishop of Milan, picked up on the contrast between law and gospel. Augustine (354–430), bishop of Hippo, also drew on the distinction between law and gospel in light of Paul's contrast between "letter" and "spirit" when Augustine opposed the teaching of Pelagius that people could achieve righteousness by obeying God's commandments.

Martin Luther (1483–1546) and his confessional followers employed law and gospel in a comprehensive fashion to clarify the Reformation's confession of the chief teaching of the Christian faith, justification by faith alone. The ungodly are justified by their faith in the gospel of Jesus Christ and not by doing good works prescribed by the law.

Luther noted that God designed two uses for the law. First, God orders and preserves society by restraining sin and evil and by promoting the well-being of social and environmental life (the law's civil or political use [cf. Exod. 20:1–17]). Second, God accuses sinners of unrighteousness and shows them their need for a savior (the law's theological or spiritual use [cf. Rom. 3:20]). While Luther had much to say about the civil use of law and its implications for social ethics, he also considered the theological use to be God's chief purpose of the law because it prepares sinners for their savior. The law is, therefore, "dynamic" in that it powerfully affects human reality. Philip Melanchthon (1497–1560) and John Calvin (1509–64), two other key Reformation theologians, also emphasized law and gospel. In contrast to Luther, both acknowledged a third use of law that serves as the supreme guide for Christian living. The status of a third use of the law has remained a point of contention between those who follow Luther's thinking and those who follow that of Melanchthon and Calvin.

Luther emphasized the "dynamic" character of gospel as a living voice through the power of the Holy Spirit. The gospel thereby embodies both report and address characteristics. As report, the gospel always says something centrally about Jesus Christ—for instance, he was born of the Virgin Mary. As address, the gospel affects human reality by creating, forming, and sustaining the church as the body of Christ, God's new creation that lives already now in anticipation of the final coming of God to redeem all creation. As address, the gospel takes the form of the unconditional promise to justify the ungodly, to use Paul's language, and this promissory dynamic creates the living and active faith of the people of God on earth. This Jesus Christ is for you; he forgives your sins and you now belong to him.

The dynamic character of law and gospel leads to their "hermeneutic" quality; that is, law and gospel govern Christian speaking and living. Law and gospel are the background grammar, so to speak, so that Christians through words and deeds communicate Jesus in the world as God's ultimate good news. Communicating God's law generally follows an "if . . . then . . ." conditional grammar. For instance, if you kill your neighbor, then God considers you a murderer. Communicating gospel follows the "because . . . therefore . . ." grammar of an unconditional promise. For instance, because Jesus died for you, therefore you are a child of God. Or, because Jesus ends the law's accusation of your sin, you are free to live in the power of the Holy Spirit. Thus, Luther's hermeneutical warning: "See to it, therefore, that you do not make a Moses out of Christ" (Luther 360).

Bibliography

Althaus, P. *The Theology of Martin Luther*. Fortress, 1966; Ambrose, *On the Duties of the Clergy*. *NPNF*[2] 10. Eerdmans, 1966; Augustine. *On the Spirit and the Letter*. http://www.newadvent.org/fathers/1502.htm; Calvin, J. *Institutes of the Christian Religion*. Trans. F. Battles. Ed. J. McNeill. LCC 20, 21. Westminster, 1960; Gritsch, E., and R. Jenson. *Lutheranism: The Theological Movement and Its Confessional Writings*. Fortress, 1976; Kolb, R., and T. Wengert, eds. *The Book of Concord: The Confessions of the Evangelical Lutheran Church*. Fortress, 2000; Luther, M. *Luther's Works*. Vol. 35. Concordia, 1960.

Gary M. Simpson

Leadership, Leadership Ethics

Leadership plays a necessary and valuable role within organizations and society. It is a complex practice grounded in beliefs, values, and self-awareness, all of which affect how a leader leads. Increasingly, there is need for robust dialogue about good leadership because it is crucial to building healthy organizations and societies in which people can do good work and flourish. Scripture is a reference point for the leader in any context, but how to read biblical texts in a manner that leads to responsible, ethical leadership requires careful consideration.

Studies on leadership that include Scripture often focus on the individual rather than the organizational or cultural side of the role. Character studies featuring prominent biblical personalities, such as Jesus, Moses, David, and Paul, investigate their values and best practices. Another popular approach summons scriptural support for formulaic step-plans or how-to's for personal leadership development, organizational strategies, vision shaping, the use of power, and so on. Jesus was the CEO of his early movement, Nehemiah an entrepreneur, Moses an organizational leader, and David the exemplar of leadership character development. The fundamental flaw in all these studies is that their authors assume that the culture, societal norms and values, perceptions of reality and experience, organizational culture, and economic realities found in Scripture are essentially similar or identical to the worlds of contemporary readers. The Bible becomes a "handbook" for practices and ethical decision-making or a set of universal principles that provides rules for engagement. Although appealing in its simplicity and seeming respect of the authority of the text, this model fails because it is anachronistic and does not acknowledge the historical, cultural, and linguistic issues involved. A thoughtful approach to the moral life for leadership in this century must be based upon a different use of Scripture.

Need for a Model of Scriptural Interpretation

Scripture is socially located. Its meaning is tied to the context in which it was composed. The NT was written within the historical, social, and linguistic context of the eastern Mediterranean from roughly 45 CE to 100 CE. (The OT is, of course, much older.) The leadership issues that surfaced within this emergent religious movement were those of a loosely affiliated collection of small house churches, not unlike the guilds, associations, and Jewish synagogues of the ancient world. A large gulf stands between the leadership needs of these ancient communities and those of contemporary megachurches, publicly traded companies, or nonprofit organizations. The issues that arise in today's complex organizations and economy were not encountered in the ancient world and certainly not within the early Christian communities; thus, they were never addressed in Scripture.

Any discussion of leadership ethics with a view toward today's society must work from a more sophisticated model of interpretation. Three aspects of NT interpretation are important to follow: (1) engage in a historical-cultural exegesis of the text; (2) reflect on how this ancient text relates to our current situation; and (3) allow the interpretation of the text to shape our practices. Rather than reducing the text to a set of universal principles or rules, we are interested in the manner in which these early communities of faith, encoded in the scriptural documents, wrestled with ethical issues of their day. This then provides a model for us today. As many have argued, the process is similar to performing improvisational solos in jazz music. The musician improvises within the constraints of the specific song. In this case of reading Scripture with a view toward leadership, the constraints are the narrative theological worlds set by the text, which frame the complex issues that we confront as we seek to live out our lives in a manner faithful to the history of God's work in the world and within the kingdom of God.

Defining Reality

A key function of leadership is to define reality. Leadership that is explicitly Christian ought to base itself in a theological worldview and understanding of salvation history. This grand narrative profoundly shapes how a person leads, for within it are the beliefs and values that undergird good leadership, and it serves to frame ethical decisions and practices. And while we may not find "the five keys" to being an amazing CEO within the NT, the NT will shape the major theological concepts that ought to provide the structure for ethical discourse.

An example of the relationship of theology to practice occurs in Rom. 14:1–5. The issues that arose in these early Roman Christian communities were the result of the conflict between Jewish and gentile believers over how closely to adhere to OT law, dietary regulations, and so on. Paul's argument is rooted in his theology and understanding of God. Because there is one God, who is impartial, welcoming them all into one believing community (Rom. 3:27–31), they should all welcome one another. Paul's admonition flows from a vision of reality that has been informed by a theological vision, his understanding of God, and the grand narrative of God's work in the world in Christ. This affects his conception of diversity, their corporate identity, and the grounds for membership and acceptance. Paul's leadership is expressed by shaping these early communities with this vision and practice. Ethical decision-making is fundamentally rooted in good theology. Leadership, whether intentional or not, presents a view of reality to those within the organization that has a profound effect on moral life and practices.

What It Means to Be Human

Leadership occurs within the context of people and relationships; ultimately, we lead people. One may not speak of leadership apart from followership. A leader has the responsibility to create an organization or team that fulfills the mission of the organization with excellence and yet also is a place where people can flourish. To accomplish these aims, a thoughtful understanding of people (anthropology) is necessary.

The events and their consequences that occurred in the garden of Eden remain with us today. Scripture is honest about the capacity of humanity for good and evil, and in contrast to a modern understanding, we all share that capacity.

Leaders of all types of organizations are presented a challenge. How can they lead in such a way as to create space for the best of humanity to be realized while recognizing that both individuals and organizations have the capacity for the opposite? Whereas Scripture frames our understanding of the human condition, it is left to us to create structures and organizations that provide healthy boundaries that limit the impact of the fall, while at the same time enabling the beauty of humanity its fullest expression. Texts such as Gen. 1:26–28 (divine mandate and human dignity), 2 Cor. 5:16–21 (Paul's motif of new creation), and 1 Pet. 3:13–17 (seeking the public good) provide a way into a theological model that allows for such.

One of the most neglected aspects of leadership ethics is conversation about the responsibility of ensuring that organizational processes and values support the full functioning and development of people within it. Ethics too often has been associated solely with grievance processes or risk mitigation. In healthy organizations, transparency, honesty, authenticity, and integrity are the norm. Contractual arrangements are grounded in covenant, trust, grace, and love. Each of these aspects is present within a Christian theological world that is supported in Scripture but not explicit. Further, leadership plays a crucial role in shaping organizational values and culture, designing bounded systems, processes, workloads, buildings, workspaces, and other elements of organizational life that develop and utilize people. Leaders balance the efficiency and productivity necessary to remain sustainable.

Leadership ethics reflect and are grounded in the life and values of the community. For people of faith, this also means that Scripture plays an important role in shaping the ethical framework. The ethical discourse that surrounds leadership on this level is akin to improvisation rooted in Scripture. The turbulence and change that organizations of all kinds face today demand leaders for whom Scripture and theology are intimate friends.

See also Authority and Power; Ecclesiology and Ethics; Institution(s); Professional Ethics

Bibliography

Benedict XVI. *Encyclical Letter Caritas in Veritate of the Supreme Pontiff Benedict XVI to the Bishops, Priests and Deacons, Men and Women Religious, the Lay Faithful, and All People of Good Will on Integral Human Development in Charity and Truth*. Libreria Editrice Vaticana, 2009; Clarke, A. *Serve the Community of the Church: Christians as Leaders and Ministers*. Eerdmans, 2000; Gill, D. *It's about Excellence: Building Ethically Healthy Organizations*. Executive Excellence Publishing, 2008; Hays, R. *The Moral Vision of the New Testament: Community, Cross, and New Creation; A Contemporary Introduction to New Testament Ethics*. HarperSanFrancisco, 1996; Stassen, G. *Kingdom Ethics: Following Jesus in Contemporary Context*. InterVarsity, 2003; Williams, R. *Stewards, Prophets, Keepers of the Word: Leadership in the Early Church*. Hendrickson, 2006.

Richard Beaton

Legalism

In theological and ethical discourse, "legalism" is used negatively to describe rigorous checklist adherence to a standard or law. Frequently, legalism focuses on microethical issues, but it can also afflict those who are concerned with macroethics. A merit-based view of salvation is also termed legalism with a quid pro quo approach to obedience and blessing. Legalists can seem sanctimonious, calculating, inflexible, and even hypocritical to those who do not keep the same standards.

Obedience in Scripture is not synonymous with legalism. While the nature of God's covenant relationship with Israel sets out obligations for Israel to fulfill, Israel's call is wholly gracious. Torah makes obedience the appropriate response to God's election, but the temptation to turn obedience into a legalistic calculation in which the minimum standards are met is constant whenever observance of the law is paramount. Thus, the prophets accuse Israel of outward observance but missing the heart of God (e.g., Isa. 29:13). Torah observance reaches its zenith at the Qumran community, which considered itself to be the righteous remnant. Even here, however, outward obedience was to be matched by inward desire.

Both Jesus and the Pharisees were concerned with lives of holiness, but they take different views on boundary markers. For the Pharisees, holiness and purity require separation. Their halakah is viewed by Jesus as burdensome legalism (Matt. 11:28–30; 23:4). However, Jesus does not repudiate Torah; he demands a greater righteousness than that of the scribes and Pharisees (Matt. 5:20) and sums it up in the two Great Commandments (Matt. 22:36–40), neither of which can be reduced to a performance list. Jesus' halakah interprets Torah in a way that goes beyond the legalism of boundary maintenance.

Paul proclaims freedom from the abuse of the law conceived of as a barrier to God's gracious calling of the gentiles. He opposes those who would require the gentiles to undergo circumcision in order to become full-fledged members of God's covenant people (Gal. 5:1–12). However, a contrast drawn between law and gospel is untenable. Paul does not eliminate the law; he transposes it to another key: the law of Christ, the Spirit-enabled obedience of those in the new covenant relationship through Christ (2 Cor. 3:6).

The continuing call for the people of God to be holy leads to ethical reflection on how this call is expressed, but too often this has hardened into a narrow and unattractive legalism epitomized by a pernicious list of "dos and don'ts" by which the state of grace is measured. Boundary markers remain, but those that reflect contingent circumstances addressing microethical issues too easily become the traditions of the elders (see Mark 7:1–4). Legalism must be resisted as a distortion of the gospel, but at the same time the affirmation must be maintained that the call of God to be holy issues in transformed lives of grace-enabled faithful obedience in Christ from a heart filled by the love of God.

See also Antinomianism; Holiness; Torah

Bibliography

Barclay, J. *Obeying the Truth: A Study of Paul's Ethics in Galatians.* SNTW. T&T Clark, 1988; Barrett, C. K. *Freedom and Obligation: A Study of the Epistle to the Galatians.* SPCK, 1985; Dunn, J. D. G. *Christian Liberty: A New Testament Perspective.* Paternoster, 1993; Rosner, B., ed. *Understanding Paul's Ethics: Twentieth-Century Approaches.* Paternoster, 1995; Wenham, G. *Story as Torah: Reading the Old Testament Ethically.* T&T Clark, 2000.

Kent Brower

Lesbian Rights *See* Homosexuality

Letter of Jeremiah

The Letter of Jeremiah provides warnings about the folly of idolatry to Jews facing the prospect of exile to Babylon. The idea that Jeremiah wrote to the exiles is found in Jer. 29. The content echoes material in Jer. 10. Its polemic against idolatry has biblical roots in Deuteronomy, Deutero-Isaiah, and various psalms. In the Greek manuscript tradition it appears as a separate composition between Lamentations and Ezekiel, while in the Latin manuscript tradition it is chapter 6 in the book of Baruch. The primary text now is the Greek version, though it may have been composed in Hebrew. It may have originated at almost any time between the sixth and the first centuries BCE.

The text purports to be a copy of a letter that Jeremiah sent to Jews who were to be exiled to Babylon. The prophet warns that in Babylon they will be exposed to "gods made of silver and gold and wood" and exhorts them to remain faithful to worship of the God of Israel. The main point is captured by the advice, "But say in your heart, 'It is you, O Lord, whom we must worship' " (v. 6).

The body of the letter (more like a sermon) consists of ten warnings against idolatry, which here is defined as worshiping what are claimed to be images of gods. The thrust of the critique is that these images are helpless, useless, lifeless, and powerless. They cannot do what the real God does, so their devotees are misguided. Each unit ends with something like a refrain that affirms that these idols are not gods at all and therefore do not deserve "fear" of the Lord.

This letter-sermon clearly was intended to encourage Jews who found themselves in settings where they were exposed to cults other than their own Jewish form of worship. It insists that participation in such cults is foolish and useless and bears witness to strong Jewish convictions about monotheism in the Second Temple period. It was written from the viewpoint of a Jew whose own religion prohibited physical representations of God (see Exod. 20:4–5; Deut. 5:8–9). The author does not pretend to give an objective picture of the cults to which his fellow Jews might be exposed. At no point does he try to get into the heads and hearts of the devotees of those cults or to imagine that the various representations of the gods might be intended as visible symbols of the divine. For this reason, this text can present problems for Jews and Christians today attempting to engage in dialogue with other religions. Yet such attacks against the folly of idolatry are common in Second Temple Judaism (e.g., Bel; Wis. 13–15), rabbinic Judaism (the *'Abodah Zarah* tradition), and early Christianity (Rom. 1:18–32; 1 Cor. 8–10; Jas. 2:19; 1 John 5:21).

See also Deuterocanonical/Apocryphal Books; Exile; Idolatry; Jeremiah

Bibliography

Barton, S., ed. *Idolatry: False Worship in the Bible, Early Judaism and Christianity.* T&T Clark, 2007; Harrington, D. *Invitation to the Apocrypha.* Eerdmans, 1999, 103–8.

Daniel J. Harrington

Leviticus

The third book of the Pentateuch, Leviticus, is comprised of two major sections. The first section (chaps. 1–16) is largely concerned with ritual instructions and laws having to do with ancient Israel's cultic practices, and as such, it clearly reflects the influence of writers and redactors affiliated with the Priestly (P) tradition. The second section (chaps. 17–26) is concerned less with ritual than with moral and ethical behavior in the community of Israel. This block of texts is collectively known as the Holiness Code, and it seems to reflect a later Priestly perspective than that found in the first section of Leviticus. Because the Holiness Code's focus is explicitly on ethics in ancient Israel, it is treated in a separate entry in this dictionary. Leviticus 27 is included by many scholars as a part of the Holiness Code, whereas others see it as a separate, concluding chapter to the book.

The P material in Lev. 1–16 does not share the Holiness Code's concern that holiness be "democratized" to the whole community of Israel. Indeed, James Watts has recently suggested that Leviticus was preserved in Israel primarily as an apology for the hegemony of the Aaronide priesthood. In the P material, the maintenance of distinctions between holy and common, clean and unclean, as well as the teaching of Torah, are the purview of Israel's priests (Lev. 10:10–11). Ethics in the P material (and often in the Holiness Code) is not explicit, but rather implicit in the worldview of the Israelite cult.

Ritual Ethics

William Brown has suggested that in ancient Israel, morality and ethics were inseparable from cosmology. We can discern some key aspects of the priestly worldview inherent in Leviticus from other P texts in the Pentateuch. Genesis 1 makes it clear that the maintenance of proper boundaries within the created order is paramount for the priests: God creates, as it were, biospheres on days 1–3, and days 4–6 parallel them as the biospheres are filled with appropriate entities (the ruling lights, plants, animals, humans). Rhythmic cycles of times and seasons are established as integral to the proper functioning of the cosmos. Space too was sacred, as the detailed instructions for the building of the tabernacle (Exod. 25–27) illustrate. Breaches of the created order and its rhythms risk allowing the ingress of the "formless void" (*tōhû wābōhû* [Gen. 1:2]) of chaos that God bounded and organized at creation. Leviticus encodes this "ethos of the cosmos" in a kind of ritual ethics, wherein the regular practice of rituals allows the practitioner to literally embody the priestly worldview by understanding one's own body and life as a microcosm of the created order.

It was the job of the Israelite priesthood to recognize and maintain the proper boundaries of the created order so that Yahweh might continually reside in Israel's midst, enthroned within the holy of holies, the most sacred sector of the sanctuary (Lev. 16:2). The departure of Yahweh would mean the breakdown of the created order, so the maintenance of the sanctuary's holiness was of supreme importance. In the priestly worldview, people, places, things, and times could be either holy or common and either ritually clean or unclean, and these statuses were "contagious" to each other. That which was holy must be kept separate from that which was either common or ritually unclean, lest they pollute each other in catastrophic ways (see Lev. 10:1–2; Num. 16:35; 1 Chr. 13:9–10).

Yet the living of everyday life necessitates that people and things move back and forth between cleanness and uncleanness, holiness and commonness. Ordained priests (see Lev. 8–9) mediated between God and the people by employing rituals to facilitate the safe transition between the states of holy/common and clean/unclean. Jacob Milgrom has suggested that "life versus death" is the governing paradigm whereby the priests determined cleanness versus uncleanness. Thus, Leviticus attempts to delineate clearly when one is in danger of proximity to death, such as the loss of life force (e.g., menses [Lev. 12], semen [Lev. 15]), or contact with corruption (e.g., corpses [Lev. 22:4], leprosy [Lev. 13:1–46], or rot in fibers or walls [Lev. 13:47–59; 14:33–38]), and then to provide a ritual pathway back to the safety of life. The dietary laws in Lev. 11 are an effort to restrict humans' killing for food to a small selection of species and give the necessary death a ritualized context intended to show reverence for the animal's life—that is, its blood (Lev. 17:11, 14)—which belongs to God. Some rituals were designed to cleanse an impure person or thing (e.g., Lev. 4:1–5:13) or provide a means by which one could make reparation to God for sin (e.g., Lev. 5:14–6:7 [MT 5:14–26]). The ritual for Yom Kippur (Lev. 16) provides a means by which accreted sins within the community can be removed from the sanctuary, ensuring that it remains habitable for Yahweh. Still other rituals mark the recognition of sacred times and seasons (Lev. 23), and some seem intended solely for positive interaction between an individual and Yahweh (e.g., Lev. 3).

Leviticus in the Present Day

The ethical significance of Leviticus today necessitates an understanding of the book's motivations more than rote observation of its laws and rituals. In practical terms, it is impossible today to live by many of the laws and rituals found in Leviticus.

The sanctuary that Leviticus presupposes as God's earthly dwelling place is no longer extant. The blood sacrifice was done in the service of maintaining a harmonious world order, whereas to us, the two concepts stand in direct conflict. The Israelite priests' tasks of maintaining people and things within strict categories may lead to isolation or prejudice in today's world. Yet the often arcane laws and rituals of Leviticus were intended to provide guidelines for the care of the natural world, to strengthen interpersonal relationships within the Israelite community, and to allow for regular interaction with God. We humans need rituals to help us frame our lives in meaningful ways: bar/bat mitzvahs, baptisms, weddings, and funerals are our versions of Leviticus's rites of passage. There is much of value, even for those who do not follow a strict kosher diet, in the mindfulness of our fellow creatures' lives inherent in the laws of *kashrut*. The priests' goal of keeping the world as closely aligned as possible with God's "very good" creation (Gen. 1:31) is still a worthy one, especially in light of present-day concern for our beleaguered environment. A constant awareness of God's presence in Israel's midst is the ontological foundation of Leviticus's ritual and ethical views; people of faith today can share this foundation, even if our praxis is modified.

See also Atonement; Clean and Unclean; Creation Ethics; Food; Holiness; Holiness Code; Old Testament Ethics; Priestly Literature; Reparation; Sanctuary

Bibliography

Balentine, S. *Leviticus*. IBC. John Knox, 2002; Brown, W. *The Ethos of the Cosmos*. Eerdmans, 1999; Grabbe, L. *Leviticus*. OTG. Sheffield Academic Press, 1993; Milgrom, J. *Leviticus*. 3 vols. AB 3, 3A, 3B. Doubleday, 1991–2001; idem. *Leviticus: A Book of Ritual and Ethics*. CC. Fortress, 2004; Nelson, R. *Raising Up a Faithful Priest: Community and Priesthood in Biblical Theology*. Westminster John Knox, 1993; Watts, J. *Ritual and Rhetoric in Leviticus: From Sacrifice to Scripture*. Cambridge University Press, 2007.

Robin C. McCall

Libel

Libel usually refers to written falsehood that intends to mislead or damage another's reputation. It is not an expressly biblical concept, but in modern jurisprudence it is grouped with slander, its spoken equivalent. Biblically, both should be seen as species of false witness and are typically used when referring to people more so than to events. The Decalogue prohibition of false witness is specifically "against your neighbor" (Exod. 20:16; Deut. 5:20; cf. Prov. 24:28). Libel differs from false teaching or heresy, which sometimes is equated with blasphemy (as in 1 Tim. 1:20). Libel differs from slander not primarily in its being written as opposed to spoken, but in its being fixed, whether in print or in another medium. Its falsehood is therefore more likely to become a matter of the historical record than false speech, which is temporary, even though its effects may persist.

Nevertheless, traditionally, it is not necessary for a claim to be false in order to be considered libelous. True statements that custom and proper decorum would normally keep private may be considered slanderous or libelous upon their public airing. This idea that there is more to the ethics of speech than merely truth or falsehood points to the ways that speaking is governed by customs that elaborate the kinds of contexts in which some claims are permitted and others are not, regardless of their truth. Dietrich Bonhoeffer thus surmised that a statement is true not just as a matter of objective content, but through the conditions under which it is uttered (Bonhoeffer 358–67).

See also Slander; Speech Ethics; Ten Commandments; Truthfulness, Truth-Telling

Bibliography

Bonhoeffer, D. *Ethics*. Touchstone, 1995.

Craig Hovey

Liberation

The word *liberation* appears rarely in English Bibles (see Esth. 4:14 NET; Ezek. 46:16 MSG). However, the proclamation of liberty and release appears often, and the concept of liberation is deeply rooted in the Bible and is an essential component in ethical and theological discourses of the Christian message and life.

In the biblical narrative, God liberates people from social and political oppression, as well as from the bondage of sin, from temptations and attacks of the evil one, from dangerous places, and from death itself. God's "liberative" acts deliver those who are suffering and/or experiencing persecution. When humans are subjected to these conditions, God intervenes on their behalf to bring about wholeness, justice, equality, and full participation in the affairs of their respective communities; at the end, through these actions, God liberates those who were oppressed and/or in bondage. The basic premise of God's "liberative" acts is to protect human dignity, restore oppressed persons to full participation in the decision-making process in their communities, and bring all components of society into harmony.

God's liberation process is intrinsically connected to the creation narrative, in which "in the beginning" there is a sense of perfect harmony in all aspects and with all participants of the universe (Gen. 1). In this original organization of the universe and society in general, oppression does not exist. Furthermore, it is not just the absence of oppression that makes it perfect; it is also the way in which all components of creation—humans, animals, vegetation, and the universe in general—interact with one another in perfect harmony. Each component is dependent on the other in a system of equality and perfect social and environmental balance. It is this picture-perfect image that God's "liberative" acts are attempting to replicate now in a fallen world, in which humans use and abuse their freedom of will to disrupt this balance and to promote their self-centered agenda by subjecting others to suffering and persecution. In this fallen world, not only are humans the perpetrators but also the forces of evil and the evil one are at work, oppressing and persecuting persons to ultimately destroy them.

Under these circumstances, God's liberation for Christians is a call to restore the original harmony in all aspects of the universe and to restore the original order by renouncing evil, denouncing oppressive forces and structures, and confronting evil forces. God's liberation is a general call to all humanity and a particular appeal to Christians to change their ways and the oppressive structures that they have created, which produce destructive results. God's liberation is also an invitation to all humans to trust in Christ as the model and source for holistic (spiritual, physical, social, and personal) deliverance that leads to an abundant life.

The biblical narrative affirms that God desires liberation, and that liberation is an essential component of the biblical message in general and the Christian message in particular. The challenge posed by this understanding concerns the means of obtaining liberation. Some prefer to take a "spiritual" approach and simply make liberation equal to spiritual salvation, which is liberation from personal and private sins. In this way, liberation is a private practice commonly expressed through the sinner's prayers. At the other extreme, some see liberation as limited to political and social actions to promote equality and social justice. Hence, liberation is concerned with social change and transformation, its goal being to transform social structures and systems that create, maintain, and promote corporate practices that prevent some members of society from full participation in the decision-making processes in their respective communities. Both representations fall short of an accurate interpretation of God's liberation in the biblical narrative, simply because this dichotomy does not exist in the Scriptures. Although there are particular instances in which liberation seems to be centered on social transformation, such as the Jubilee Year, the exodus narrative, and prophetic discourses such as Rom. 8:20–22, there are other passages, such as Ps. 33; Rom. 8:1–2; 10:9–11, in which their common interpretation seems to affirm a spiritual liberation. Despite these polarized notions and interpretations, the biblical narrative as a whole begins and ends with a state of perfection, which sets the framework of reference for God's liberation. Thus, God's liberation is intrinsically connected to the creation narrative, in which all aspects of the human being and society are crafted in perfect harmony, and to the eschatological images of the book of Revelation, in which the promise of perfect harmony comes to fruition. Then, the "in-between" time is precisely God's call to liberate—that is, to resemble the perfect harmony described at the beginning and at the end of the biblical narrative. God's liberation, then, encompasses all aspects of the human being and all elements of the universe and society.

Finally, recent developments in ethical and biblical scholarship have highlighted another area in which liberation plays an important role by pointing out the need for liberation from ideological oppression. In this sense, an ethic of liberation questions those who are in control of interpretive processes and the dissemination of what is considered the dominant/predominant biblical interpretation. The assumption here is that those who are in power or belong to the dominant group, consciously or unconsciously, incorporate their self-centered agenda in their interpretations, which leads to the marginalization and oppression of groups and individuals whose interpretations are ignored and seen as erroneous simply because they are not part of the dominant norm. But even this case is included and addressed in God's liberation when it is grounded in the creation and apocalyptic narratives as described above, leading to, in this case, ideological harmony, tolerance, and mutual respect.

See also Emancipation; Freedom; Jubilee; Liberationist Ethics; Slavery

Bibliography

Gutiérrez, G. *Teología de la Liberación: Perspectivas*. CEP, 1971; Novak, M. *Will It Liberate? Questions about Liberation Theology*. Paulist Press, 1986; Segundo, J. *Liberación de la Teología*. Ediciones C. Lohlé, 1975; Sobrino, J. *Spirituality of Liberation: Toward Political Holiness*. Trans. R. Barr. Orbis, 1988.

Hugo Magallanes

Liberationist Ethics

Liberationist ethics, also known as liberative ethics, is a methodology of ethical analysis contextualized in the lived experiences of marginalized and disenfranchised communities attempting to employ liberative praxis over and against the normative Eurocentric tendency of philosophizing on and about ethical paradigms. Since the start of the twentieth century, Euroamerican ethicists distanced themselves from discussions concerning the implementation of praxis as a response to unjust social structures. They gradually moved toward discourses on the nature of ethics and the definition of virtues and the good. In effect, Eurocentric ethics became more a task of explaining what is ethical rather than which ethical praxis should be engaged.

By contrast, those engaged in liberative ethics attempt to reconcile academic and theological propositions through praxis as a manifestation of pastoral concerns. In short, it is an ethics of doing, of vigorous involvement in the daily life struggles and concerns of the disenfranchised.

For Christian communities, liberationist ethics is based on the message of Christ, which stresses liberation from all forms of human oppression, specifically social, economic, political, racial, sexual, environmental, and religious. In effect, Christian liberative ethics is not so much what is said in bearing witness to the good news of the resurrection but rather what is done to and with those still trapped by the social forces of death.

Liberationist ethicists, facing the inhumanity of marginalized communities, struggle not with God's existence but rather with God's character. Who is this God whom we claim to exist? God is understood as a God who (1) imparts life and opposes death; (2) acts in history; (3) sides with the oppressed, making a preferential option for them; (4) is deeply concerned with justice; and (5) knows, through Christ's crucifixion, what it means to experience unjust suffering at the hands of religious and state authorities. This understanding of God's character becomes the basis upon which liberative ethics is constructed.

While not dismissing the importance of the spiritual, liberative ethics employs whatever social-scientific tools are available that can help explain the reality of the oppressed. Without succumbing to rigid theories such as Marxism, postcolonialism, and postmodernism, liberationist ethicists are comfortable using such theories without embracing their worldviews if they provide insight into the causes of oppression and make suggestions concerning the implementation of praxis. Doing liberationist ethics becomes the process of marginalized communities integrating faith with the struggles and hardships of their daily sociopolitical life. Such a process does not produce faith; rather, it is a response to inhuman conditions. We call this response "liberative praxis," the doing of ethics.

Defining Liberation

Use of the word *liberation* connotes salvation, salvation from sins—not just the personal sins an individual might commit, but just as importantly, the social sins inflicted upon marginalized communities. Oppression and poverty are an expression of sin. There exists awareness that social structures are designed to exploit certain groups of people (usually along race, ethnic, and gender lines) so that a minority group can live a life of power and privilege. Known as "structural sins," these sociopolitical mechanisms are legitimized and normalized by the dominant culture. These oppressive structures are recognized as dispensing institutional violence toward the marginalized even though no immediate physical repressive acts take place. Nevertheless, the lack of physical restraints does not mean that economic violence ending in death is not occurring. Sin, committed by individuals or communities, breaks relationship with God. Liberation is not just for those oppressed; it is also for their oppressors, who are as much in need of salvation/liberation from structural sins as the oppressed.

The first praxis toward liberation involves the raising of consciousness—that is, to view and define reality not through the paradigms constructed and taught by the dominant culture but rather through those developed in the grass roots of marginalized communities. The goal is not to convince the "nonbeliever" to believe a certain set of doctrines to obtain salvation but rather to convince those who have been conditioned to see themselves as nonpersons that they have worth and dignity. Liberative ethics becomes the process of consciousness-raising and self-determination, which usually is prevented from occurring due to prevailing structures of oppression.

Goals of Liberative Ethics

The oppressed today are, like Jesus, being crucified so that the powerful can enjoy abundant life. They are indeed the crucified people. The ultimate goals of Christian liberative ethics become assisting these crucified people, as well as those who crucify them, to assume the task of becoming new creatures in Christ. To that end, liberative ethics seeks (1) liberation from all forms of exploitation,

(2) a more humane and dignified life for both oppressed and oppressors, (3) the abolition of all forms of injustices, and (4) a new society based on the biblical teachings of love and justice. In short, liberative ethics works toward establishing the principles of God's kingdom on earth—principles based on the biblical concepts of justice and love, which comprise the two major components of liberative ethics. To love the Lord your God and your neighbor like yourself is to do justice before God and foster justice with your neighbor. The doing of justice is a manifestation of love, so that liberative ethics becomes love in action.

Because Jesus is still among the people, the kingdom that he preaches is not some future event in the hereafter; it is in the here and now. Liberative ethics designed to bring about the kingdom, out of a sense for love and a commitment to justice, attempts to move beyond social reform. For many, the present social structures are rooted in such oppressive presuppositions that they simply cannot be reformed. They must be changed through an ethics that fosters social revolution that radically challenges and dismantles the prevailing political and economic structures.

Methodology of Liberative Ethics

The underlying problem with Eurocentric ethics is that moral reasoning is done from the realm of abstractions. Ethics has less to do with "what you do" than "how you think." The commitment is more to abstract thought than to praxis. When Eurocentric ethics engages in praxis, it is done deductively, starting first with some sort of theory or truth (based on the Bible, or church doctrine, or the writings of a formative ethicist), then moving toward an action taken as a second step. Thus, praxis is shaped by theory. But theories and truths are social constructs that can mask the power and privilege of the one doing the defining of reality. Liberative ethics reverses this methodology, so that theory is shaped by praxis. The doing of liberative ethics is the starting point, with theory or truth being formed by the faith community reflecting on the consequences of the committed praxis. This is understood through what has come to be known as the "hermeneutical circle." This hermeneutical circle is based on the circular paradigm of "seeing, judging, acting." The hermeneutical circle begins with the lived experiences endured within oppressive social structures, and then it proceeds by working out a theory and course of action geared to save (liberate) those negatively affected by the prevailing structures. This "acting" step in the liberative model is considered to be the "first act," upon which reflection and contemplation lead to what is called "theology." Hence, Christian theology becomes the "second act," a reflection on Christian ethics.

For Christians, liberative ethics is Christ-centered, where the character of God is best revealed in the personhood of Christ. This Christ is a liberator from all forms of oppression/sin. As such, Jesus can never belong to the oppressors. The advocates of militarism, capitalist triumphalism, and the present distribution of the global resources may claim a Christian faith, but their actions that cause death and oppression serve as proof of their denial of the Christian message of life and liberation. In short, Jesus Christ can never be part of, or belong to, the oppressors. Solidarity with the oppressed demonstrated in the participation of liberative ethics becomes the litmus test to one's fidelity to the mission of Christ. To fail to engage in liberative ethical praxis that brings about justice is to deny Christ and the kingdom that he advocates.

The Role of the Bible

Among most liberationist ethicists, the biblical text plays an authoritative role in the formation of moral agency. Rejecting both Eurocentric liberal and conservative methodologies of biblical interpretation, the liberationist reads the Scriptures with the goal of understanding the text from the perspective of marginalized communities. If the Bible is "the book of life," then what precepts are within its pages to assist the oppressed to live the abundant life promised by Christ (John 10:10)? Many of the tenets associated with liberationist thought are shaped by particular books, such as Exodus, where God enters history to liberate the slaves; by the Prophets, where God demands that justice flow for the disenfranchised; and by the Gospels, where Jesus, in the ultimate act of solidarity, takes his place among the crucified people of history.

Liberationists employ a hermeneutic of suspicion when reading the Bible. They are conscious of how biblical readings done from positions of power and privilege shape interpretations that justify lifestyles unresponsive to justice. Likewise, they are aware that their own interpretations are influenced by their social location. Nevertheless, a hermeneutical preferential option is claimed by the oppressed. Because they know what it means to survive in the dominant culture and are aware of what it means to live within marginalized communities, they have a greater grasp of reality than those who do not know what it means to live in marginality. Thus, the oppressed have a truer and more relevant interpretation of the biblical text.

Movements

Originally, liberationist religious thought was a Latin American Catholic response to the brutal right-wing dictatorships and military juntas of the region sponsored by the US government. For many of these early developers of liberationist thought, the poverty and oppression they were witnessing in their homeland was a by-product of US imperialism ushering in the global expansion of the economy and the multinational corporations benefiting from that expansion. A religious and ethical response to this structural sin is what came to be known as "liberation theology."

The theological and ethical paradigms developed were based on the initiative of implementing the conclusions of Vatican II (1962–65) and its documents (specifically *Gaudium et spes* [1965]) within a Latin American context. By 1968, a conference was held at Medellín, Colombia, to discuss the implementation of Vatican II within Latin America. Working within the church, many came to the realization that the official church was closely linked to the established political order—a relationship that needed to be broken if liberation was to flourish. The ethical praxis that arose as a response to oppressive structures caused by the collusion of state and church developed at the grass roots of the community seeking liberation.

Christian "base communities" became the grassroots, faith-based entities from which liberative ethical perspectives were developed and implemented. In these faith communities the dispossessed gathered to discover how their Christian faith could be lived out to create a more just society. Because the faith community can never be neutral in the presence of oppressive structures, it must be incarnated among the oppressed through the ethical act of choosing to live in solidarity with the oppressed. As the church evangelizes the oppressed, sharing the good news that God is a God of life and because of God's love they have worth and dignity, the church is in turn evangelized by the oppressed, who remind the church of its mission as the body of Christ. Thus, the church becomes both a sign and instrument of liberation. Choosing to participate in liberative ethics becomes a proactive option made for, with, and by the marginalized.

Ethics are never developed in a cultural vacuum. All ethics are a reflection of the social location and theological beliefs (or disbeliefs) of a given people. Liberationist ethics is no different. It is indigenous to specific communities, seriously considering the local cultural settings of the group desiring to implement a liberative ethical response to oppressive structures. As such, liberationist ethics cannot be exported from community to community as if it were a commodity. Soon, Protestants were developing their own version of liberative theological work. Besides crossing Christian denominational lines, liberative ethics were also being developed by other faith traditions as rooted in their own faith communities. Jews, Muslims, Hindus, Buddhists, humanists, and others were soon developing their own liberationist theology and ethics.

Types of Liberative Ethical Movements

Because liberative ethics is contextualized within specific communities, many types exist. Below are but a few examples, with a brief description of what makes them distinctive from other types of liberative ethics.

African: Unlike the liberative ethics in Latin America, which have focused on economic, social, and political oppression, Africans also stress racial oppression, specifically in South Africa, where the focus was on apartheid. Another salient characteristic is the African appreciation for indigenous religions. For some, liberation also includes liberation from nonindigenous religions such as Christianity and Islam.

African American: Liberative ethics takes the form of making the gospel relevant to the black community's daily struggle against white supremacy. It is rooted in a response against slavery, Jim Crow and Jane Crow, and the consequences felt today from these historical institutions. Black liberative theology and ethics are articulated especially in the teachings of Martin Luther King Jr. and Malcolm X, and are contemporaries to the Latin American project.

Native American: The exodus story, foundational in liberative thought, of a God who liberates slaves and brings them to the promised land is problematic to a people who, like the Canaanites, were invaded, subjected to genocide, and dispossessed of their land by those worshiping this same God. Here the focus is on how native peoples can recover an identity that was systematically decimated by an invading culture so that they can establish, as sovereign entities, liberation in the form of freedom to self-determination.

Asian: Christianity is a minority faith on the diverse religious continent of Asia, leading to a liberative ethics based on Buddhist, Hindu, Confucian, and Taoist principles. Asian liberative ethics encompasses all religions. Many Asians participating in liberative ethics also stress a liberation from a narrow Western view of history. In India, dalit theology has focused on dismantling the caste system, while in South Korea minjung becomes a struggle for human rights by basing theological and ethical constructs on those who have no rights, the downtrodden and oppressed.

Feminist: Not to be confused with feminism, which at times focuses more on gaining equal opportunities at the echelons of power, feminist liberative ethics challenges patriarchy with the aim of liberating not just women, but all oppressed groups. There is a refusal to simply surmount existing economic and political oppressive structures. With a focus on misogynistic structures, an attempt is made to create a just society for women and the rest of society by challenging the dominant structures in place.

Hispanic: Attention is given to the diversity of this ethnic group and its unique mixture (mestizaje) of races, cultures, languages, and religious beliefs. An emphasis is placed on cultural oppression that leads to ethnic discrimination as witnessed in immigration policies, language ordinances, or economic standing in society in the United States. Although seen as recent arrivals, many Latina/Latinos occupied the lands (for those with indigenous ancestors) prior to the existence of the United States. Others are victims of "manifest destiny," as their lands were taken (in the southwestern United States) or conquered for imperialist purposes (especially in the Caribbean and South America), and now they find themselves in the center of the empire.

Womanist: A profound realization exists that women of color must face the prevailing sexism of their community as well as the prevailing racism of white feminists. The liberative ethics that women of color develop attempts to deal with the oppression experienced by the two communities to which they belong.

See also African American Ethics; Class Conflict; Colonialism and Postcolonialism; Feminist Ethics; Imperialism; Justice; Kingdom of God; Latino/Latina Ethics; Liberation; Oppression; Praxis; Preferential Option for the Poor; Race; Racism; Solidarity; Women, Status of

Bibliography

Bonino, J. *Toward a Christian Political Ethics*. Fortress, 1983; De La Torre, M. *Doing Christian Ethics from the Margins*. Orbis, 2004; Krammer, C. *Ethics and Liberation: An Introduction*. Orbis, 1988; Schubeck, T. *Liberation Ethics: Sources, Models, and Norms*. Fortress, 1993; Townes, E. *Embracing the Spirit: Womanist Perspectives on Hope, Salvation, and Transformation*. Orbis, 1997.

Miguel A. De La Torre

Libertinism

In the context of early Christianity, *libertinism* is a term used by scholars to refer to a philosophy of freedom from moral constraints. According to some interpreters, a group of libertines based in the churches of Corinth practiced sexual license in the name of freedom from the Mosaic law and all other social conventions. This group has been described as gnostic, or incipiently so, on the assumption that gnostic rejection of the physical world as evil led gnostics to be libertine when it came to behaviors involving the body (notably sexual activity). However, close examination of what evidence we have about the gnostics (from the second century and later) supports the conclusion that they tended to be ascetics, not libertines. It is possible that some at Corinth, likely under the influence of Hellenistic dualism (which sharply distinguished the soul and the body, depreciating the latter), interpreted Paul's teaching about freedom from the Mosaic law to be absolute freedom (see 1 Cor. 6:12; 10:23). They sought to demonstrate their liberty by, for example, eating meat offered to idols and perhaps even practicing various kinds of sexual freedom. One widely held interpretation is that at least some believers at Corinth styled themselves "the spiritual ones" and devalued the body on the theory that their true selves were purely spirit. A consequence of this thinking was that they did not consider things done in the body to be important. From the standpoint of an ethics of the body, they appeared libertine.

The term *libertine* is also associated with *antinomian* ("against law," referring to a philosophy of living without any moral regulation). In Rom. 3:8 Paul suggests that some of his detractors accuse him of teaching a gospel that is antinomian or libertine. He denies it (see also Rom. 6:1–2). The basis of their charge is his gospel of justification apart from the law and probably also his preaching that God's grace abounds freely to those under sin's power. In Rom. 5:20 Paul writes of the situation of those under the law that "where sin increased, grace abounded all the more," and in Rom. 6:1 he asks a rhetorical question that likely reflects the charge of antinomianism: "What then are we to say? Should we continue in sin in order that grace might abound?" Paul's answer is that freedom from the law happens through dying with Christ in baptism, a union with Christ that entails a renewed moral life (Rom. 6:2–19).

See also Antinomianism; Body; 1 Corinthians; Dualism, Anthropological; Freedom; Romans; Sex and Sexuality

Bibliography

Thiselton, A. "Realized Eschatology at Corinth." *NTS* 24 (1978): 510–26.

Charles H. Cosgrove

Life, Sanctity of *See* Sanctity of Human Life

Life Support *See* Bioethics

Liturgy and Ethics

The academy has seen a renewed interest in the connections between liturgy/worship and ethics/Christian living since the mid-1970s. Yet this connection pervades the Christian Scriptures. In Scripture, action is rooted in identity: the guidelines for what one does follow from who one is or claims to be. And in Scripture, one's identity is determined primarily by who one worships, to which god one belongs. In other words, in Scripture, worship is the root of ethics and supplies the criteria of judgment necessary for discerning proper action and the shape of the life of individuals and communities.

Old Testament

Some explorations of Scripture and ethics search for discrete precepts or rules that can be distilled from canonical texts (e.g., the Ten Commandments, the Sermon on the Mount). Such an approach, however, is foreign to the way Scripture understands ethics (a category that is anachronistically applied to Scripture). Rather, ethics—better, what one is to do, how one is to live, how a community is to live together—is rooted in identity. For example, Jews welcomed strangers not primarily because it was a universally right thing do (in fact, it could be quite dangerous), but because they were Jews, they were God's people, who themselves "were once strangers in the land of Egypt" (Exod. 23:9; Lev. 19:34).

In Scripture, moreover, identity is rooted in worship: who one worships determines who (or whose) one is. Not only strangers but also slaves, the Israelites were liberated by God not simply to be free from the Egyptians; they were liberated to become God's people, to become the people who worship only Yahweh (e.g., Exod. 3:18; 7:16). This relationship between worship and identity is signaled in a number of ways. It was established liturgically, in the rite of the paschal lamb, whose blood marked the Israelites' identity as those to be "passed over" when the final plague visited Egypt. It was sustained liturgically in the annual celebration of the Passover and other holy days wherein the Israelites reaffirmed their identity, celebrated God's mighty deeds, repented of their sins, and restored right relationship with God and one another.

Further, it shapes the Mosaic covenant, where guidelines for worship and living are inseparably intertwined. The Decalogue (often misidentified as a code of ethics) is fundamentally liturgical, beginning as it does with injunctions regarding right worship: "I, the Lord, am your God, who brought you out of the land of Egypt, that place of slavery. You shall not have other gods besides me" (Exod. 20:2–3 NAB). The entire first table of the Decalogue focuses on worship—idols, God's name, the Sabbath. Worship, then, is the larger overarching and necessary context for understanding the remaining commandments in the Decalogue. Likewise, the 613 commandments in the Torah are a similarly integrated complex of injunctions about worship and life. Right relationship, right action, right form of communal life, the OT proclaims, can follow only from Israel's right relationship with God.

Finally, the purpose of this action and life is worship—to give glory to God. The commandments are for God's people. They distinguish Israel from the peoples among whom Israel finds itself. They trace what life looks like in a community that worships only God. How Israel lives bears witness to God's power, presence, and truth. And when done rightly, it gives glory to God.

Of course, the very first thing the Israelites do after receiving the covenant is commit idolatry (Exod. 32). This becomes the overarching theme of the OT: Israel's continued idolatry, the consequences, and God's continued call for Israel to return to right worship. Certainly, the Israelites, both individually and corporately, violate many if not all of the commandments of the Torah. They commit adultery, kill, exploit the poor, fail to care for widows and orphans, and more. But the authors of Scripture make clear that this failure to follow the commandments and live in right relationship with one another follows from their worship of their neighbors' false gods and their failure to properly worship Yahweh. The prophets never uncouple the connection between right worship and right living (e.g., Isa. 58:1–14; Hosea).

New Testament and the Early Church

The NT continues the story of Israel and shares the moral logic of the OT. Thus, worship and ethics are again inseparable. In Jesus' temptations in the desert, the fundamental question is one of idolatry, which he finally answers decisively with a version of the Shema, an OT liturgical practice that orients all life toward the worship of Yahweh (Matt. 4:10). When asked to identify the greatest commandment, Jesus again begins with the Shema: "You shall love the Lord your God . . ." (Matt. 22:37). In the Gospels, Israel once again finds itself oppressed with its religious and political leadership engaging in the externals of religious ritual but worshiping in fact at the altars of idols, particularly the power of the Roman Empire. Thus, the hearers of the prophetic proclamation are called to repent, to turn again to God, to live under God's kingship again, for as in Egypt, "the kingdom of God is at hand" (Mark 1:15).

To live as God's people—to worship, love, and trust God—leads to distinctive and countercultural economic, social, and political practices. Thus, God's people will care for those along the wayside (Luke 10:25–37), forgive (John 7:53–8:11), give away all their possessions (Matt. 19:16–24), love enemies (Matt. 5:44), make peace (Matt. 5:9), and more (see Matt. 5–7). Such is the distinctive witness of those who now follow Jesus (Matt. 16:24), God incarnate, as the Israelites followed Yahweh in the desert.

As in the OT, liturgical practice remains key for orienting all of life toward the worship of God. Echoing events of the exodus, the blood of Christ spilled in the passion on the Passover establishes the new covenant and demarcates God's people from those who worship other gods. Those baptized into his "name" (cf. the Decalogue) are grafted into God's people, the church, be they Jew or gentile. They are sustained in their identity as the body of Christ in the sharing of the Eucharist. This liturgical participation calls and shapes them to imitate individually and corporately God incarnate, the Christ, in whom they participate.

Yet as with the Israelites, the early church falls into idolatry and false worship. Destructive factionalism stems from idolatrous claims to "belong" to baptizers rather than to Christ (1 Cor. 1–4); it is the "double-minded" who wish to be friends with God and the world who meet the greatest censure (Jas. 1:8; 4:8); even the appearance of idolatry is cautioned against (Acts 15:29; 1 Cor. 8:4–13). And the cause for one of Paul's most extensive liturgical discussions is the scandalous continuation of economic divisions in the context of the Lord's Supper (1 Cor. 11:17–34). Constructively, liturgical language becomes the idiom for Christian living—Christians are called to become a "living sacrifice" (Rom. 12:1–2)—and the paschal referent of that sacrifice becomes the repeated warrant: for reconciliation (2 Cor. 5:17–20), caring for the poor (Gal. 2:10), loving one's enemies (Matt. 5:44), and more. In short, the shape of the life of the Christian community is to follow from its identity as Christ's body sustained through participation in a panoply of communal and liturgical practices (1 Cor. 11:1; Phil. 2:5–11) (see Yoder).

Contemporary Context

These connections between worship and the Christian life continue through most of Christian history. From the martyrs to the monastics and the saints, the Christian tradition is replete with those concerned not simply with doing good in the world, making right decisions, or even living upright, moral lives. Rather, the tradition is peopled with exemplars primarily concerned with being united with Christ via prayer and liturgy and thereby living in the form of Christ in the world.

With the advent of nominalism and voluntarism in the fourteenth century, Luther's notion of "the two kingdoms," and the Enlightenment, this connection was severed, and "morality" became a separate sphere of inquiry, a realm of individual decision-making for which "rational" (i.e., universal) justifications must now be discovered. Yet, a return to Scripture and tradition complicates this notion of morality as well as other conventional assumptions—for example, that a sustainable theological distinction can be made between issues in "social" ethics (e.g., poverty) as opposed to "personal" ethics (e.g., sexuality).

A Christian ethic that seeks to take Scripture and tradition seriously must grapple with the almost constant witness of Scripture and tradition that the norms for Christian living derive from one's identity as a member of God's people, of Christ's body, the church, and that the primary question for any ethic is this: who or what does one worship (Hauerwas and Wells)?

See also Ecclesiology and Ethics; Idolatry

Bibliography

Hauerwas, S., and S. Wells, eds. *The Blackwell Companion to Christian Ethics*. Blackwell, 2006; Saliers, D., E. Anderson, and B. Morrill. *Liturgy and the Moral Self: Humanity at Full Stretch*. Liturgical Press, 1998; Searle, M. "Liturgy and Social Ethics: An Annotated Bibliography." *SL* 21 (1991): 220–35; Spohn, B. *Go and Do Likewise: Jesus and Ethics*. Continuum, 2000; Yoder, J. *Body Politics: Five Practices of the Christian Community before the Watching World*. Herald Press, 2001.

M. Therese Lysaught

Living Will *See* Bioethics

Loans

In the contemporary world, "to lend" typically refers to the practice of granting someone the use of something with the expectation that it be returned, or of giving someone the use of money with the explicit agreement that it will be repaid with interest. Although the worlds of Israel and the early church knew such practices, lending in the Bible has a different emphasis. Here, lending typically takes the form of generosity to the needy, and in the NT in particular, economic relations, including lending, should avoid the demands of obligation and reciprocity.

Lending in the Old Testament

Three texts in the Pentateuch introduce key parameters for understanding lending in the OT. The first is Exod. 22:25: "If you lend money to my people, to the poor among you, you shall not deal with them as a creditor; you shall not exact interest from them." The mention of the poor indicates that the text does not refer to regular commercial loans, even though it speaks of money and not goods in kind. It is possible to imagine successful Israelite farmers borrowing to enlarge their herds, for example, but the OT does not refer to such loans. Rather, it presupposes a situation in which, for example, a farmer's harvest has failed and he needs to borrow to feed his family and/or buy seed for the next year.

The Hebrew term for "interest" is *nešek* (literally, "bite"). Other passages use the words *tarbît* and *marbît* (literally, "increase") with similar meaning. Older English translations (e.g., the KJV) understand the words to refer to "usury" (i.e., excessive interest, however that may be defined), but this is mistaken. The text forbids any lending to the poor at interest. Many English translations also introduce the idea of charging interest or the idea of usury into the use of the verbs *nāšā'/nāšâ* and related nouns, though in themselves these verbs simply refer to lending. But Exod. 22:25 does tell people not to behave like lenders (*nōšîm*) when they lend (*lāwâ*) money. It looks as if *lāwâ* refers to lending in general, in the way that an ordinary person might lend something to a friend, whereas *nāšā'/nāšâ* refers to something more formal or commercial, which by its nature would likely involve interest.

Nevertheless, it would be possible for creditors to keep the regulation concerning lending at interest yet still treat debtors oppressively. Lenders are not to take the necessities of life as pledges, such as an ox or ass, a garment, a millstone, or an infant (Deut. 24:6, 17; Job 22:6; 24:3, 9). One oppressive lender is the man who insists on taking away a widow's children (so that they can work for him) because of the family's debt (2 Kgs. 4:1). A story in Neh. 5 concerns oppressive lending; it may refer to charging interest or to other actions such as foreclosing on loans. It alludes to two reasons for debt: crop failure and imperial taxation. These two stories also make clear the results of default. One may forfeit fields, orchards, and houses, and/or one may end up in "slavery"—that is, temporary indentured labor (not chattel slavery).

A second key text, Lev. 25:35–37, expands on the point in Exod. 22:25, referring to the poor as "your kin" and referring to the need to "fear [better, 'revere'] your God." It also refers to lending food, which makes more explicit the kind of predicament, such as a poor harvest, that the texts are concerned to regulate. People who are doing well are expected to lend freely to the needy and to accept payment in the form of labor or the eventual repayment of the debt in money that the person had earned through labor. So debtors would seek to work their way back to solvency by committing themselves to indentured labor for a set period or to paid employment in relation to someone who did have land—the equivalent to getting a job rather than the norm of being self-employed.

A third text, Deut. 23:19–20, makes explicit that people must not impose interest on any form of loan, while also permitting Israelites to impose interest on loans to foreigners, as one does not have to remit a foreigner's debts in the Sabbath Year (Deut. 15:3). This is an example of a number of obligations that did not apply to foreigners. It did not imply that usury was acceptable in relation to foreigners; the OT says nothing about usury per se. It may presuppose that loans to foreigners were commercial loans; a foreigner who was in need would be covered by the provisions for the resident alien.

Beyond the Pentateuch, Prov. 28:8 promises that people who augment their wealth by lending at interest gather it "for people who are kind to the poor"; that is, they will not see the profit themselves. Psalm 15 asks who may sojourn in God's tent—that is, stay in God's presence. Its answer includes the general requirement of a life of integrity and truthfulness, and also some concrete expectations such as avoiding slander, keeping oaths, refusing bribes, and not lending money at interest. The prophet Ezekiel speaks in similar terms in listing obligations that people should fulfill if they wish God to treat them as righteous, such as not worshiping by means of images, defiling their neighbors' wives, robbing people, or lending at interest (Ezek. 18:8, 13, 17). Ezekiel implies that people were not fulfilling these obligations, and later he makes explicit that the well-to-do rulers in Jerusalem have committed many of the wrongs that he lists, including this one (Ezek. 22:12).

This draws our attention to the fact that we cannot draw inferences from the law of Moses regarding actual Israelite practice. The OT histories include no reference to Israel's ever having implemented the teaching about the Sabbath Year or the Jubilee Year, let alone lending without charging interest, and they include a number of criticisms of Israel regarding such matters. Yet we may mislead ourselves in expecting that Israelite practice would necessarily be expected to conform literally to Moses' teaching, as if it were some kind of law. Christians, at least, tend to understand Moses' teaching as "law," but the word *tôrâ* has broader meaning. Although it includes regulations that look designed for quasi-legal literal implementation, other material looks more like concrete embodiments of a style of life whose point we would miss if we took it legally; that is, we might fulfill the law's letter but not its inner demand. Thus, the ban on charging interest would indeed have been intended for literal implementation, but when we ask about its implications for us in a different social context, we must also look at it in the light of its stated rationale—for example, its concern for the poor. On the one hand, in more commercial contexts and in a competitive situation, people might charge interest on commercial loans without infringing the baseline concerns underlying this teaching. On the other hand, where lending to needy people or needy nations is a way of making money, this would seem in conflict with the principles of the Torah.

Exodus 22:25 begins, "If you lend . . . ," but it does presuppose that lending will occur. To refuse to lend would contravene other exhortations regarding concern for the needy. The point is explicit in Deut. 15, which urges people to lend generously. Righteous people do well in life and therefore are in a position to give and to lend and thus to be a blessing (Ps. 37:25–26). Things go well for the person who deals generously and lends (Ps. 112:5).

Lending in the New Testament

In the first-century Mediterranean world, the world of the NT, the government and landowners were sustained by a population, the overwhelming majority of whom drew their livelihood from agricultural activities. Much of this world, then, was analogous to the world of the OT in its traditional agrarian character. Surprisingly, even though debt was a prominent feature of the world of which the Gospels speak, the practice of lending is rarely mentioned. The onerous nature of overwhelming debt is portrayed in Matt. 18:23–35. The only reference to lending on interest is found in a parable that portrays a man distributing assets to his slaves and expecting that in his absence they will turn a profit (Matt. 25:14–30 // Luke 19:11–27). One slave, however, takes the money assigned to him out of circulation and is berated for not at least collecting interest (Matt. 25:27; Luke 19:23). If anything, this parable only adds to a generally negative portrait of lending with interest, since this advice comes from someone otherwise characterized as a fraud with exploitative business practices.

The Greek term for lending and borrowing, *daneizō* ("to lend" in the active voice, "to borrow" in the middle voice), appears in the NT only three times. Thus, Jesus urges his followers to lend to whoever asks for a loan (Matt. 5:42), extends this directive even to enemies, and instructs that those who lend should be "expecting nothing in return" (Luke 6:34–35). Here and elsewhere, Jesus underscores the importance of relationships not determined by strict reciprocity, even teaching his disciples to ask God to "forgive us our sins, for we ourselves forgive everyone indebted to us" (Luke 11:4). Similarly, Paul urges followers of Christ to avoid falling under the control of creditors or entangling themselves in relationships of obligation that would detract from their devotion to one another (Rom. 13:8).

Lending after the Bible

Through the first millennium, the church affirmed the OT notion that lending on interest was disapproved, on the continuing presupposition that lending was an aspect of care for the needy. In practice, lending on interest was tolerated as long as rates were not excessive, but in the impoverished conditions of fourth-century Cappadocia leading Christian voices spoke forcefully against lending and borrowing money. Even though lenders were known to exceed the upper limits set on interest rates (12 percent), interest charged was less lucrative than the lands and property gained when the poor defaulted on their loans. In his sermon "On Usury," Basil urges the poor not to borrow and rails against lenders who increased their opulence at the price of the suffering poor. Instead, lending ought to take the form of a gift to the poor, which would be seen as lending to God (see Prov. 19:17).

In the second millennium, commerce began to develop in new ways, and the practice of lending on interest became prevalent, initially despite the church's opposition. In due course, however, the church conformed itself to secular practices and provided a theological rationale for it. In fifteenth-century Italy, for example, public pawnshops developed with Franciscan support to offer loans to the poor more cheaply than those offered by regular moneylenders, charging a very low interest designed simply to cover expenses. In 1516 the Fifth Lateran Council approved these. As years went by, these pawnshops began also to lend for commercial purposes at higher rates.

Unbound by the course of discussion within the medieval church and perceiving that the OT was concerned with caring for the poor and not with commercial loans, John Calvin removed the ban on lending at interest, with safeguards that predictably were conveniently forgotten. In due course, the Roman Catholic Church also removed its ban on lending at interest. More seriously, as the capitalist world developed, the point that biblical perspectives on lending were tied to care of the needy was lost. In Victorian Britain the cooperative and building society movements attempted to recover it. In effect, the customers of the cooperative were the shareholders, while building societies worked by attracting safe investments from people who hoped eventually to buy a house and lending the money to people who were already in a position to do so.

Clearly, the focus of the scriptural material is on the predicament of needy people. Lending is a way to care for the needy, not a way to make money.

See also Almsgiving; Capitalism; Charity, Works of; Economic Ethics; Exploitation; Greed; Jubilee; Poverty and Poor; Profit; Resource Allocation; Wealth

Bibliography

Gnuse, R. *You Shall Not Steal: Community and Property in the Biblical Tradition*. Orbis, 1985; Goldingay, J. *Israel's Life*. Vol. 3 of *Old Testament Theology*. InterVarsity, 2009; González, J. *Faith and Wealth: A History of Early Christian Ideas on the Origin, Significance, and Use of Money*. Harper & Row, 1990.

John Goldingay and Joel B. Green

Lottery *See* Gambling

Love, Love Command

The Scriptures contain diverse yet mutually enriching perspectives on the love commands. These perspectives reflect a range of diverse social contexts, from Deuteronomy's comprehensive social construction of Israel's covenant legacy to Paul's counsel for marginal faith communities in an alien social environment.

Love Commands in the Old Testament

Deuteronomy displays the grounding of Israel's covenant calling in God's unrelenting love for his people and in his summons for them to love him in return (Deut. 4:35–39). A pivotal text is Deut. 6:4–5: "Hear, O Israel: The LORD is our God, the LORD alone. You shall love the LORD your God with all your heart, and with all your soul, and with all your might." The Hebrew word for "heart" has cognitive and volitional connotations, embracing "heart" and "mind"; "soul" suggests the depths of the self, and "might" expresses the full investment of our energies.

Building on the Ten Commandments, Deuteronomy provides an extensive list of statutes, laws, and ordinances that specify the requisites of social and political order, including a virtual constitution that establishes a division of powers between executive, legislative, and judicial processes designed to hold monarchs accountable to covenant standards (Deut. 17). Deuteronomy repeatedly stresses God's love for his people, including strangers living among them (Deut. 10:15, 18–19; 30:3), and it calls for heartfelt commitments by the people to uphold covenant faithfulness (Deut. 10:12–13, 16, 18–19; 11:13, 16, 18; 13:3; 26:16; 30:2, 10, 16). These themes reflect Jeremiah's vision of a new covenant that the Lord will engrave on the hearts of his people (Jer. 31:33–34) and Ezekiel's declaration that the Lord will give his people new hearts of flesh more responsive to his Spirit (Ezek. 36:26–27). Leviticus is the original source of the commands to love neighbors and resident aliens in the same way as one loves oneself (Lev. 19:18, 34). These commands are integrated with ritual observances and holiness codes designed to sustain the distinctive identity of the people of Israel. Neighbors are fellow members of the people of Israel, and aliens are to be welcomed as citizens, for the people of Israel survived as aliens in the land of Egypt.

Love Commands in the Synoptic Gospels

The Synoptic Gospels emphasize the unity of the commands to love both God and neighbor, though they represent these commands in distinctive ways. In Mark's narrative a scribe asks Jesus which commandment is first of all. Jesus responds by citing the command to love God with heart (*kardia*), soul (*psychē*), mind (*dianoia*), and strength (*ischys*), using four Greek terms in order to capture the richness of the Hebrew word for "heart" (Mark 12:30). Luke retains the same four terms, but Matthew omits the reference to "strength." Jesus then names a second command: love your neighbor as you love yourself. The scribe affirms Jesus' words, declaring that these commands are more important than burnt offerings and sacrifices (Mark 12:28–34). The scribe's observations are reinforced in Matthew's citation of Jesus' contention that ritual practices must not take precedence over "weightier matters of the law: justice and mercy and faith," words that capture the prophetic substance of Jesus' teachings (Matt. 23:23).

In Matthew's version of this exchange Jesus declares that all of the law and the prophets depend on the two Great Commandments (Matt. 22:34–40). This statement illumines his earlier claim that he had not come to abolish the law but rather to fulfill it, so that "not one letter, not one stroke of a letter, will pass from the law until all is accomplished" (Matt. 5:18). As the Sermon on the Mount makes clear, Jesus' reading of the law and the prophets is by no means focused on legalistic details, nor did he offer a comprehensive reading of the Ten Commandments. Instead, he provided a model for critical reflection on the moral substance of the law, one that emphasizes the importance of our feelings, needs, and desires and also our concrete interactions with our fellow human beings. Jesus suggests that explosive anger, harmful insults, lustful gazing, and deceitful oaths violate the underlying spirit of commands that prohibit murder, adultery, and a false witness against a neighbor. He urges his followers to take concrete steps to address these deeper problems, especially to seek ways of rebuilding broken relationships (Matt. 5:21–37) (see Stassen and Gushee 125–48).

Jesus also cites the Golden Rule: "In everything do to others as you would have them do to you," a rule that in Matthew he explicitly links to "the law and the prophets" (Matt. 7:12 [cf. Luke 8:31]). Jesus' teachings on the law are fully compatible with the spirit of Deuteronomy, which summons us to embrace God's commands in our hearts. In the Sermon on the Mount Jesus expands the reach of commands to love neighbors and strangers by urging us to love even our enemies and persecutors (Matt. 5:43–48; cf. Rom. 12:14–21). These words have inspired bold initiatives in peacemaking, conflict resolution, and restorative justice (see Cahill; Shriver; Stassen).

Jesus further challenges his followers to rise above the law of retribution, a law that mandates punishments for evildoers equivalent to the harm that they have caused. He directs special attention to the abusive practices of persons who wield power over others, and he calls for creative and potentially life-transforming moral responses to those practices: when someone strikes you on the right cheek, turn the other as well; when someone sues you for your coat, surrender your cloak as well; and if someone forces you to go one mile, go a second as well (Matt. 5:38–42). We are encouraged to accommodate such demands but to do so in ways that expose their lack of moral legitimacy (see Stassen and Gushee; Wink).

Luke places Jesus' discussion of the love commands in the context of his journey to Jerusalem, associating them with his broader Galilean mission (Luke 10:25–37). A lawyer stands up to test Jesus, asking what he must do to inherit eternal life. Jesus asks the lawyer how he read the law. The lawyer names the two Great Commandments, essentially describing them as one. Jesus assures the lawyer that by observing these commands he will live. The lawyer then asks, "Who is my neighbor?" Jesus responds by telling the parable of the good Samaritan. A priest and then a Levite walked past a man who had been seriously injured by thieves. A Samaritan showed him compassion, offering direct aid, taking him to an inn, and providing financial resources for his care. Jesus asks the lawyer which of the three men had been a neighbor to the victim, and the lawyer names the one who showed compassion. The parable does not explain who qualifies as a bona fide neighbor; instead, it discloses how good neighbors act. This parable has received special attention because it conveys an obligation to offer care as we are able for any and all of our fellow human beings, including strangers, enemies, and persecutors. Neighbor love becomes a universal principle that informs all aspects of our lives (see Nygren; Outka; Santurri and Werpehowski; Vacek).

Love Commands in the Gospel of John

The Gospel of John offers a christological transfiguration of the love commands. It begins with a declaration of God's love for the world, a love manifest in the gift of his only begotten Son (John 3:16). Jesus' own teachings on love are elaborated in his final conversations with his disciples as he prepares them to continue his mission. He begins by declaring his oneness with the heavenly Father. Those who believe in him believe in the Father, who sent him into the world (John 12:44); those who see him see the Father, who sent him as light into the world (John 12:46); those who hear him hear the words of the Father, who commands him to speak (John 12:49). He summarizes these claims by stating, "I am in the Father and the Father is in me" (John 14:10), a reality manifest in his good works.

Jesus then stresses his unity with his disciples, assuring them that he will not leave them desolate, even when the world no longer sees him. "You will see me," he promises them, and "because I live, you also will live" (John 14:19). "On that day you will know that I am in my Father, and you in me, and I in you" (John 14:20), for "the Father himself loves you, because you have loved me" (John 16:27). Jesus urges them to abide in him and in his love just as branches abide in a vine. They will then bear much fruit, and they will glorify the Father, though without him they can do nothing (John 15:1–11).

In the context of these conversations Jesus delivers a "new commandment": "Love one another just as I have loved you"; by practicing such love, they will be known as his disciples (John 13:34–35). Jesus' self-giving love now replaces traditional references to self-love as the standard for mutual love among his followers. Jesus observes that there is no greater love than a readiness to "lay down one's life for one's friends" (John 15:13). Jesus further states that he will no longer call his followers "servants" (*douloi*), for now they have become his friends (*philoi*) (John 15:15). The reference to friends explains why the Greek word for "love among friends," *philia*, sometimes appears in the Gospel of John alongside the more common NT term for "love," *agapē*. Jesus calls his followers "friends" because he has made known to them all that he has received from the Father (John 15:15). He promises that the Father will send them "another Advocate," the Holy Spirit, after he has departed from them (John 14:16). The Spirit will teach them all things, guide them into the truth, and refresh their memories about all that he has said to them (John 14:26). Empowered by the Spirit, they will do not only the works that he has done but also even greater works by continuing to abide in his love (John 14:12). They will keep his commandments, and the Father will love them (John 14:21). Jesus reminds his followers that the world will hate them just as it has hated him (John 15:18–25), for servants are not greater than their master. Even though the world's hatred has no legitimate cause, people who kill Jesus' followers may still believe that they are serving God (John 15:18–25; 16:2). These words prepared Jesus' followers for times of suffering and persecution.

Finally, in his private prayers Jesus states that he is praying not for the world but rather for those whom the Father has given him. They belong to the Father because they are the ones through whom he will be glorified (John 17:9–10). The Gospel of John characterizes Jesus' own crucifixion as his glorification (John 17:1–5). By enduring the world's hatred, Jesus' friends will be glorified as well—a message that parallels Jesus' words of blessing for the persecuted in his Sermon on the Mount (Matt. 5:11–12). Jesus also prays for those who will come to believe in him through the testimonies of his friends (John 17:20). Earlier he had spoken of "other sheep" not of his fold, sheep that he would gather into one flock with one shepherd—an apparent reference to gentile converts (John 10:16). Jesus prays that those who believe in him will become perfectly one, just as he and the Father are one (John 17:21–22), which underscores the urgency of communal solidarity for those who continue Jesus' mission. Their bonds will disclose to the world the truth that the Father sent them into the world, and that he loves the world just as he loves his only Son (John 17:23–26).

Epistles attributed to John reiterate many of these themes, stressing mutual love, caring responses to brothers and sisters in Christ who are in need, and a resolve to abide in the love of God (1 John 3:11–18, 23–24; 4:7–12, 16–21). Jesus' reference to the "new commandment" of mutual love (John 13:34) is qualified in 1 John, for this commandment has been disclosed from the beginning (1 John 2:7; cf. 2 John 4–6). The commandment is new in the sense that "the darkness is passing away and the true light is already shining" (1 John 2:8). The epistle adds, "Whoever loves a brother or sister lives in the light, and in such a person there is no cause for stumbling. But whoever hates another believer is in the darkness, walks in the darkness, and does not know the way to go, because the darkness has brought on blindness" (1 John 2:10–11).

Love Commands in the Letters of the New Testament

Paul's reading of the love commands is informed by his account of the Spirit of life in Jesus Christ. He makes no specific reference to the command to love God, giving central place to notions of faith, trust, and faithfulness. Even so, he does address his Corinthian readers as those who love God, citing multiple texts from Isaiah (1 Cor. 2:9; cf. Isa. 52:15; 64:4; 65:16). He also describes love for God as a sign that one is known by God (1 Cor. 8:3). Even the command to love neighbors is seldom mentioned, though Paul does state in his Letter to the Galatians, "The whole law is summed up in a single commandment, 'You shall love your neighbor as yourself'" (Gal. 5:14). He urges members of the Galatian community to become servants of one another lest they bite and devour one another (Gal. 5:15), and he calls for patience in addressing potentially divisive conflicts, for without such patience the church will not flourish.

Of central importance in Paul's letters are his persistent calls for mutual love within concrete faith communities, building upon the image of the church as the body of Christ. This message is introduced in 1 Cor. 12–13 and reiterated in Rom. 12. While different parts of the body have distinctive functions, Paul observes, they remain dependent upon one another as a condition of their effectiveness. In a similar manner, members of the body of Christ also have diverse gifts. There are apostles, prophets, teachers, healers, servants, leaders, and speakers in various tongues. All of these gifts can play roles in building up the body of Christ, but without love they become meaningless, even provoke divisions and conflicts within the body (1 Cor. 12:27–31; cf. Rom. 12:4–8). Paul especially emphasizes limitations in the gift of "speaking in tongues," for without an interpreter such speaking amounts to unintelligible noise (1 Cor. 14). Paul's central message is that members of the body must not compete with one another, still less foster conflicts that fragment the church. Instead, they must embrace one another in a love that is patient and kind, a love that "bears all things, believes all things, hopes all things, and endures all things" (1 Cor. 13:7). Faith, hope, and love are the enduring gifts of the Spirit, and love is the most important gift of all (1 Cor. 13:8–13). In his letter to the church in Rome Paul also calls for contributions to the "needs of the saints" and "hospitality to strangers" (Rom. 12:13).

Paul most clearly linked neighbor love to the fulfillment of the law in his Letter to the Romans. The text in Romans is distinctive in several ways. First, Paul's reference to the second love command follows his more general counsel regarding respect and honor for governing authorities (see Rom. 13:1–7). Second, he introduces his comments by emphasizing mutual love: "Owe no one anything, except to love one another" (Rom. 13:8). Third, he articulates the love command in two ways: initially as love for "another" (*ton heteron* [Rom. 13:8]) and subsequently as love for "the neighbor" (*ton plēsion* [Rom. 13:9]). Love for another conveys a love without limits, embracing all human beings, while love for neighbors directs attention to persons with whom we have ongoing relationships. Paul's language parallels the commands cited in Leviticus to love one's neighbors and to love resident aliens (Lev. 19:18, 34). Fourth, Paul states that by loving another we fulfill the law. He then lists selected mandates from the second table of the Ten Commandments: do not commit adultery, do not kill, do not steal, do not covet; he adds the phrase "and any other commandment," an apparent reference to commands similar in substance to those cited (Rom. 13:9–10). Read in context, Paul's words suggest parallels between the commands that he mentions and elements of Roman law, which he earlier identified as the law of the gentiles (Rom. 2:14–15). He does not refer to the first table of the Ten Commandments, for Rome could not be trusted to prevent idolatry, restrain vain religious expressions, or honor the Sabbath.

Given Paul's claims that Christ is the end of the law (Rom. 10:4), and that the law of the Spirit of life in Christ has replaced the old written code (Rom. 7:6), how could he also speak of mutual love, love for another, and neighbor love as fulfilling the law? Paul's purpose here is to assure his readers that the law did have continuing importance for sustaining social order, and that Roman authorities bore responsibility for enforcing the law. In so doing, they were not a terror to good conduct, but only to what is bad. Thus, Rom. 12–13 dramatizes fundamental differences between life within churches and respect for governing authorities. At the same time, Paul urges the faithful to extend the love that formed their life in Christ into the wider social world, offering blessings to those who persecuted them, refusing to repay anyone evil for evil, and renouncing vengeance—principles that echo Jesus' teachings in the Sermon on the Mount. He further calls them to provide food and drink for enemies who are hungry or thirsty. They must never be "overcome with evil," but rather they must "overcome evil with good" (Rom. 12:14–21).

Other epistles in the NT reinforce teachings on the love commands in the Synoptic Gospels and the Pauline Epistles. The Epistle of James displays connections between Matthew's treatment of the enduring authority of the law and Paul's references to freedom from the law in Christ Jesus. "Show me your faith apart from your works," James declares, "and I by my works will show you my faith" (Jas. 2:18). Faith without works, James insists, is "barren," even "dead" (Jas. 2:17, 20, 26). Citing Lev. 19:18, James further insists that by loving our neighbors we fulfill the law (Jas. 2:8). This epistle especially condemns acts of favoritism toward the wealthy and neglect for those in need (Jas. 2:1–7), and it stresses the urgency of addressing internal conflicts within faith communities (Jas. 4:1–3). It calls for "wisdom from above" that is "peaceable, gentle, willing to yield, full of mercy" (Jas. 3:13–17). First Peter reiterates Paul's emphasis on mutual love and the sharing of gifts within faith communities (1 Pet. 1:22–23; 4:7–11), and it combines calls for "unity of spirit" (1 Pet. 3:8) within the body of believers with appeals to show regard for governing authorities (1 Pet. 2:13–17). Second

Peter lists virtues that reflect Paul's account of the fruit of the Spirit (2 Pet. 1:5–7).

Conclusions

The love commands disclose the roots of substantive moral teachings in God's compassionate love. Human beings are summoned not simply to submit to God's dominion, but to love God passionately in return. Special attention is given to communal solidarity among people who have a distinctive calling within God's larger purposes, including the people of Israel and a new people of God taking form in Jesus Christ. Communal solidarity does not imply closed communities but rather underscores the social bonds essential for sustaining a wider mission. These communities also were expected to remain open to others, welcoming "strangers" and "aliens" into their common life. In Jesus' Sermon on the Mount and in Paul's letter to the Romans the faithful are further summoned to extend practices of mutual love into the wider social world, embracing even their enemies and persecutors. Thus, neighbor love entails commitments to peacemaking and conflict resolution, fostering more constructive relationships among people who have been formed by diverse social and cultural practices. Such initiatives exemplify the universal scope of the love commands.

See also Covenant; Enemy, Enemy Love; Fruit of the Spirit; Golden Rule; Grace; Imitation of Jesus; Mercy; Neighbor, Neighbor Love; Self-Love

Bibliography

Cahill, L. *Love Your Enemies: Discipleship, Pacifism, and Just War Theory*. Fortress, 1994; Furnish, V. *The Love Command in the New Testament*. Abingdon, 1972; Nygren, A. *Agape and Eros*. Trans. P. Watson. University of Chicago Press, 1982 [1953]; Outka, G. *Agape: An Ethical Analysis*. Yale University Press, 1972; Santurri, E., and W. Werpehowski, eds. *The Love Commandments: Essays in Christian and Moral Philosophy*. Georgetown University Press, 1992; Shriver, D., Jr. *An Ethic for Enemies: Forgiveness in Politics*. Oxford University Press, 1995; Stassen, G. *Just Peacemaking: Ten Practices for Abolishing War*. Pilgrim Press, 1998; idem, *Just Peacemaking: Transformative Initiatives for Justice and Peace*. Westminster John Knox, 1992; Stassen, G., and D. Gushee. *Kingdom Ethics: Following Jesus in Contemporary Contexts*. InterVarsity, 2003; Vacek, E. *Love Human and Divine: The Heart of Christian Ethics*. Georgetown University Press, 1994; Wink, W. *Violence and Nonviolence in South Africa: Jesus' Third Way*. New Society Publishers, 1987.

Thomas W. Ogletree

Loyalty

Loyalty is the virtue or practical disposition of being faithful to an intrinsically valued association or attachment. Typically, loyalty involves potential cost to the individual or group seeking the advancement or well-being of the object of loyalty. In contemporary theological writing, "fidelity" and "faithfulness" are often used interchangeably with "loyalty."

The object of loyalty is debated in the philosophical literature. For Josiah Royce, the proper object of loyalty is a cause that transcends the individual. Others contend that loyalty is a relational concept whose proper objects are particular persons, collectivities, organizations, and social groups. Still others contend that we can be loyal to virtually anything to which we can become attached or devoted.

Whether loyalty is a virtue is also debated. The difficulty here is twofold: first, one can be loyal to a bad or evil person or cause (e.g., Nazism); second, under some accounts of loyalty, judgment is suspended once one has become loyal to an object. It seems best to view loyalty as a virtue, however. Many commendable qualities of character, including conscientiousness, courage, and imagination, can be in the service of improper ends. Moreover, notions such as "loyal opposition" and "loyalty to the office" (but not to the tyrant filling the office) allow for loyalty that is tied to ongoing critical judgment. Like other virtues, loyalty also encompasses both feelings and practical dispositions to action. There is often a strong feeling of devotion associated with loyalty, but loyalty is demonstrated in action, particularly in sticking with the object of loyalty where there is risk or cost involved. Loyalty cannot stand alone as a guiding principle or determinative quality of character. For instance, lacking prudence or practical wisdom, loyalty is easily misplaced or misdirected.

Our experience is of many loyalties, not a single loyalty. For example, loyalty to a job or employer, which requires staying late at work, may conflict with loyalty to a child, which includes attending the school play. As this example suggests, multiple loyalties are part of our everyday experience, and resolution of conflicting loyalties is neither straightforwardly decided nor determined once and for all.

Perhaps the most discussed conflicting loyalties are between those directed to God and to the state. Loyalty to God should take priority over loyalty to the state, but in practice, the majority Christian position in the West, at least since Constantine, has assumed that loyalty to God nearly always means loyalty, and obedience, to the state (Rom. 13; 1 Pet. 2:13–17 have figured heavily here). Anabaptists, Quakers, the Confessing Church, and many liberation theologians would be among those questioning too easy an alignment of our loyalties to God and state. James Gilman suggests that swearing loyalty oaths to any auxiliary authority is a form of betrayal (cf. Matt. 5:33–37). He follows Victor Paul Furnish in distinguishing between being "subject" to authorities and "obeying" them. The Christian virtue of loyalty requires the former, not the latter.

In the medieval and early modern periods, loyalty was primarily associated with the oath or pledge of allegiance sworn by the subordinate in the hierarchical order. This usage helps to explain why Anabaptist and Quaker refusals to swear an oath met violent opposition. Their refusal was perceived in part as an act of disloyalty or treason. That medieval legacy may also help explain the dominant modern usage of loyalty in association with political parties and patriotism.

Regarding Scripture, Katharine Doob Sakenfeld argues that the Hebrew term *ḥesed* is often best captured by the English word *loyalty*. In the OT, loyalty emerges out of already existing relationships, assumes that the stronger owes an act of loyalty to the weaker or marginalized member of the relationship, and is fundamentally grounded in God's uncoerced faithfulness. David and Jonathan, and Ruth and Naomi are among the paradigmatic examples of human loyalty. Although *loyalty* is not a NT word, the phenomenon and notion is everywhere apparent, including in its breach. One thinks, for instance, of Christ's loyalty to God in the garden of Gethsemane, the women's loyalty to Christ at the cross and tomb, Peter's disloyal denial of Christ, and God's loyalty to Christ in the resurrection.

See also Authority and Power; Covenant; Fidelity; Government; Integrity

Bibliography

Gilman, J. *Fidelity of Heart: An Ethic of Christian Virtue*. Oxford University Press, 2001; Niebuhr, H. R. *Radical Monotheism and Western Culture: With Supplementary Essays*. Westminster John Knox, 1993; Ramsey, P. *The Patient as Person: Explorations in Medical Ethics*. 2nd ed. Yale University Press, 2002; Royce, J. *The Philosophy of Loyalty*. Macmillan, 1908; Sakenfeld, K. D. *Faithfulness in Action: Loyalty in Biblical Perspective*. Fortress, 1985.

Joseph J. Kotva Jr.

Luke

Luke's Gospel is anonymous, although the tradition has associated this writing with Luke, Paul's sometime companion (mentioned in, e.g., Phlm. 24). Assuming that Luke was the author of this Gospel and further that this Luke was in fact Paul's companion offers little to the interpreter. More productive is careful engagement with the text of Luke, together with comparison with Luke's sources (usually regarded as including Mark's Gospel and a sayings source known as Q) and Acts (Luke's second volume). For example, as a unit, Luke-Acts emphasizes the use of possessions as demonstrative of one's relationship with God.

Luke 4:18–19 maps Jesus' program in words borrowed from Isa. 58:6; 61:1–2: good news for the poor, release to captives, sight for the blind, freedom for the oppressed. Another programmatic Lukan text defines Jesus' ministry as the good news of God's kingdom (4:43). From the kingdom's centrality, it follows that "blessed are you poor" is thematic: "yours is the kingdom of God" (6:20). When God rules, the marginalized move from disdain in the social order to blessedness.

Often overlooked is that the Roman Empire as context permeates Luke. Luke 3:1–2 portrays the way the empire trickles down from the emperor through governors, client kings, and elite collaborators. Luke 22:25–26 explicitly presents God's kingdom as an alternative to the empire. Jesus says to his disciples, "The kings of the nations lord it over them; and those in authority over them are called benefactors. But not so with you." The woes to the rich, satisfied, and prominent (6:24–26) fit an imperial context where they correspond to elite collaborators. The first woe (6:24) is not a reversal but an astounding devaluation of status and possessions: "You have received your consolation." But does the God who inverts the woes of the poor and for whom nothing is impossible (1:37) invert the woes of the rich? God is kind to the ungrateful and the wicked (6:35)—the types to whom Jesus addresses the woes.

Division into winners and losers is a false dichotomy in Luke, as people under judgment have the possibility of entering God's kingdom. Does Jesus cultivate opponents like gardeners cultivate fig trees so that they might bear fruit (13:6–9)? In the parable of the prodigal son (15:11–32), the father with his older son is like a gardener cultivating a fig tree. Does the older son change and rejoice over the return of his disgraced brother? Is Jesus persuasive? At least some scribes agree with him in 20:39.

Some interpreters charge Luke with anti-Semitism. But early on, John the Baptist contrasts the offspring of vipers with true children of Abraham; furthermore, the God for whom nothing is impossible can make stones (even offspring of vipers) into Abraham's children (3:7–8). Repeatedly, controversy stories are open-ended and anticipate that opponents may become God's children. Moreover, marginalized people are continually reintegrated into Judean society.

One approach to Scripture and ethics identifies five ways biblical materials inform ethics: (1) moral law, (2) principles, (3) analogies to contemporary situations, (4) understanding of the world and human beings, and (5) understanding of God. But in Luke these all point more to the source, motivation, and empowerment for ethics than to explicit directives for praxis.

(1) Luke is weak in appeals to moral law for ethics. The law informs piety more than ethics (1:6; 2:22, 27).

(2) The lawyer in 10:25–37 epitomizes the law as love of God and neighbor embedded in each other. But his question "Who is my neighbor?" quibbles with definitions, anticipates no action, and shows that principles as such do not translate into ethics.

(3) Analogies with Jesus' followers enable readers to discover characters with whom they identify primarily in their deficiencies and in whom they can witness the realization of God's rule, but hardly people they should emulate. If one looks for characters to emulate, then Mary's positive response in her trouble, perplexity, and fear (1:29–30, 38) qualifies her as one of the best. But in the immediate story of Jesus' birth and also in the larger story of the restoration of God's people, the issue is how *God* is at work in human trouble, perplexity, and fear. When the disciples oppose bringing infants to Jesus, readers can hardly imitate them; nevertheless, they are part of a concrete demonstration of how God's rule is being realized (18:15–17).

(4) The understanding of the world and human beings and (5) the understanding of God invade each other. The narrator's perspective is that who humans are and what they do depend on who the God with whom they are in relationship is and what this God does. This emphasis anticipates ethics—not directives but a relationship with God as mediated through Luke that is the fountain for praxis. This is not to neglect action by hiding behind something that precedes ethics; rather, relationship with God bears fruit, often in ways that God's children cannot anticipate. In the parable of the so-called good Samaritan, love of God means love of neighbor (10:25–37). Loving God bears fruit in the Samaritan's actions that are dangerous (brigands are threatening) and that unexpectedly cross social, ethnic, and religious boundaries. Reality is transformed because the understanding of the world and a relationship with God invade each other. Not only does praxis determine relationships; relationships underlie praxis.

See also Acts; Kingdom of God; New Testament Ethics; Parables, Use of in Ethics

Bibliography

Burridge, R. *Imitating Jesus: An Inclusive Approach to New Testament Ethics*. Eerdmans, 2007; Carter, W. *The Roman Empire and the New Testament: An Essential Guide*. Abingdon, 2006; Fowl, S., and L. Jones. *Reading in Communion: Scripture and Ethics in Christian Life*. Eerdmans, 1991; Hays, R. *The Moral Vision of the New Testament: Community, Cross, and New Creation; A Contemporary Introduction to New Testament Ethics*. HarperSanFrancisco, 1996; Matera, F. *New Testament Ethics: The Legacies of Jesus and Paul*. Westminster John Knox, 1996.

Robert L. Brawley

Lust

As one of the seven deadly sins, lust is most often associated with inordinate or self-indulgent sexual cravings. However, lust can also be understood more broadly to describe any disproportionate or obsessive desire (e.g., lust for power) that prevents an individual from flourishing. Scripture addresses the risks of sexual lust for human fulfillment and relationships, and it also provides a foundation for considering the theological importance of this broader sort of lust, which theologians sometimes call "concupiscence." It is important to note that in both cases, the scriptural texts do not challenge all forms of desire, but specifically desires that are excessive and damaging to the soul.

Attending to Scripture

One of the best-known scriptural passages concerning lust comes from the Sermon on the Mount. Jesus tells his listeners, "You have heard that it was said, 'You shall not commit adultery.' But I say to you that everyone who looks at a woman with lust has already committed adultery with her in his heart" (Matt. 5:27–28). Jesus' condemnation of lust initially seems to be an intensification of the laws of the Torah, but many scholars suggest that Jesus is actually clarifying the laws' original intent. His references to "looking" on someone with lust and committing adultery in one's "heart" echo several OT texts that challenge the faithful to hold themselves accountable for their eyes and heart. Some of these texts do not relate explicitly to lust (see Num. 15:39; Prov. 21:4; Ezek. 6:9; 18:6; 20:7–8), but others more clearly remind us that we are accountable for our desires. Ecclesiastes 11:9, for example, encourages youth to pursue the desires of their hearts and eyes but cautions that God will judge their desires and actions. Job 31:9 similarly speaks of the heart's potential to be enticed by a woman.

Although these passages hold us accountable for our desires, they do not suggest that all forms of desire are bad. Instead, they challenge forms of desire that are damaging to our own ability to flourish and that impede the exercise of love for our neighbor. In Matt. 5:28 Jesus is explicating God's commandments concerning neighbor love, and it is in this context that he denigrates specific forms of sexual desire. John Paul II's *Love and Responsibility* (1981) distinguishes sinful lust from other forms of desire by explaining that lust treats another human as an object rather than a subject. Sexual desire within properly ordered relationships allows for mutuality between the persons in the relationship such that both are active subjects in sexual intercourse. Sexual lust that objectifies another person is problematic because it limits our ability to pursue a life consistent with God's intentions for us, a life in which we genuinely and authentically practice love toward others.

Scriptural passages witnessing to less explicitly sexual understandings of lust similarly emphasize the ways in which a disordered desire can be threatening to our relationship with God. Perhaps the most significant of these passages is Rom. 7 (particularly 7:5–6, 14–25), in which Paul describes his struggles against sin. This passage characterizes sin as a force that dwells within us and enslaves our wills, compelling us toward evil actions. Even after conversion, Paul suggests that there is a conflict between the life for God that the Spirit reveals to us and the "life of the flesh," a set of disordered compulsions against which we struggle. The life of the flesh that holds us "captive" leads us toward actions that run counter to God's service and limits our ability to do "what is right," even if we wish to do so. This notion of sin as a force that damages us by "bear[ing] fruit for death" gives rise to the idea, maintained by several historical thinkers, that the Christian life is partly characterized by a struggle against "concupiscence," which involves any sort of inordinate and damaging desire (sexual or nonsexual) that interferes with a moral agent's spiritual growth.

Christian Tradition

Augustine is known for speaking negatively about the pervasiveness of lust in human sexual experience. At many points in his writings he argues that the only real good that comes from sexual intercourse is the procreation of children; he even suggests that when humans have intercourse, they are taking part in the "evils" of lust for the sake of the "good" of children. But many scholars suggest that a closer look at Augustine's account of lust indicates not that he sees sexual activity as inherently negative, but rather that he is aware that in all human activity people will at times have to struggle against desires that have potential to harm themselves or that harm others. Augustine understands this harmful concupiscence as a sort of possessive "grasping" for other people or things. To free ourselves from this negative grasping, Augustine explains, we should transform our way of loving by "clinging" to Christ (Schlabach). Augustine believes that regenerate Christians will be subject to concupiscence, but that they should strive not to consent to its temptations (Augustine, *Grat.* 5; *Perf.* 44).

In contrast to Augustine, Thomas Aquinas affirms that some forms of concupiscence are "natural" and therefore morally legitimate (*ST* I-II, q. 30, a. 3). Some scholars therefore believe that Thomas allows for a more positive understanding of sexual pleasure than Augustine does. At the same time, Thomas echoes Augustine in recognizing that when concupiscence leads us to objectify someone else, it damages our relationships. In order to practice "true friendship," we must wish the good for another person for that person's own sake. Conversely, we practice concupiscent love, not genuine friendship, when we form and foster relationships for the primary reason of promoting our own happiness or pleasure (*ST* I-II, q. 26, a. 4).

Contemporary Application

In contemporary times, Christianity often is characterized as upholding a negative view of sexual desire or pleasure. However, this brief consideration of lust suggests not that Christian teachings reject all forms of sexual desire, but rather that they challenge obsessive forms of sexual and nonsexual desire that are destructive and that impede human relationships. Lust is one of the "deadly sins" precisely because it undermines our abilities to live in the manner for which God created us.

See also Adultery; Desire; Passions; Pornography; Sermon on the Mount; Seven Deadly Sins; Sexual Ethics

Bibliography

John Paul II. *Love and Responsibility*. Trans. H. Willetts. Farrar, Straus & Giroux, 1981; Schlabach, G. "'Love Is the Hand of the Soul': The Grammar of Continence in Augustine's Doctrine of Christian Love." *JECS* 6 (1998): 59–92.

Elizabeth Agnew Cochran

Lutheran Ethics

Martin Luther (1483–1546) and those Reformation confessors who followed his lead have given Lutheran ethics its basic shape and thrust (Kolb and Wengert). These original Lutherans confessed the Apostles' Creed, the Nicene Creed, and the

Athanasian Creed as catholic Christians who upheld the trinitarian faith. Traditions of Lutheran ethics exhibit a trinitarian dynamic and scope and regard Luther's originating theological and ethical reflections more as a prototype that can be critically explained and constructively extended within new historical realities than as an archetype that must be rigidly replicated. Luther himself took this prototypical approach to previous traditions of Christian moral reflection.

Justification and Love of Neighbor

All things Lutheran characteristically spring from the doctrine of justification by faith alone as the chief teaching of the Christian trinitarian faith. God through the power of the Holy Spirit justifies the ungodly only by their faith in Jesus Christ alone as their righteousness and not by any righteousness merited through doing good works prescribed by the law. Living morally, therefore, does not initiate, constitute, or contribute to one's basic righteousness in God's sight. Rather, ethical life is the fruit, consequence, and outgrowth of justifying faith in Christ. Luther was fond of quoting Jesus in the Sermon on the Mount, "A good tree produces good fruit" (Matt. 7:17), thereby steering a path between the ditches of legalism on one side and libertinism on the other. "Faith working through love" (Gal. 5:6) means that "faith alone" frees Christians for "love alone" for the neighbor (Luther, *Luther's Works*, 40:9). Because faith alone justifies, loving the neighbor does not become a stepping-stone to gain merit for oneself, and therefore the neighbor is not instrumentalized. This is the heart of Luther's critique of the instrumental love that he saw as rampant in medieval Christianity. Rather, Christians become "a Christ to my neighbor," for as Christ has "put on" our reality, so also we "put on" the neighbor's reality (Luther, *Luther's Works*, 31:367, 371). In this way, a neighbor-oriented moral imagination constitutes the blazing core of Lutheran ethical reflection.

Law and Gospel

The teaching of justification by faith alone comports with the distinction between law and gospel. Luther developed a kind of shorthand based on Paul's eschatological distinction between two ages in Adam and in Christ in Rom. 1–5. God's law tells us what we are to do and not to do, which is the law's first (civil or political) use, and also shows us our sin and our need for a savior, which is the law's second (theological or spiritual) use. In the gospel we are told what God in Christ through the power of the Holy Spirit has done, is doing, and will do for and with the world. The law governs through constituting social life, making demands, issuing commands, and enforcing them coercively through dissuading and rewarding consequences. The gospel governs through making promises that create, sustain, and consummate the communion of the church through the free gift of the Holy Spirit.

Two Kingdoms

That the law governs our temporal life and the gospel governs our spiritual life is often referred to as the teaching of the two kingdoms. Luther's teaching concerning the two was more dynamic than the static notion of "kingdom" may connote. A better formulation would be this: God's two ways of governing the one world. Especially when preaching, Luther used the metaphor of God's two hands. God's left-hand rule comes through law; God's right-hand rule comes through gospel (Luther, *Sermons*, 63). As Luther famously noted, "Both [governments] must be permitted to remain; the one to produce righteousness, the other to bring about external peace and prevent evil deeds. Neither one is sufficient in the world without the other" (*Luther's Works*, 45:92). This distinction and coordination guards against two menaces: ecclesial theocracy, which tries to "Christianize" earthly temporal rule, and autonomous secularism, which aspires to rule the world arbitrarily without any reference to God's will expressed through law and justice.

Creation and Law

By highlighting the distinction between God's left-hand and right-hand ruling, Lutheran ethics first upholds the gospel as God's free and unconditional promise of salvation, and second it safeguards God's law as the gift that restrains sin and evil and promotes social justice, earthly peace, and a flourishing creation even as the law also always shows sinners their need for repentance and for a savior. Lutheran ethics pays close attention, therefore, to creation and the first use of the law because this is the arena where our neighbors together with all creatures, indeed with the earth itself, live their daily lives. In this way, Lutheran ethics acknowledges that a deep sacredness endows the "secular world," and in this sacred secularity it is a proper concern for both Christians and the church to engage in civil righteousness with all people of good will for the sake of the common good.

Orders of Creation

Lutheran ethics takes notice of the comprehensive enduring (but not eternal) patterns or structures of human relationality, sometimes referred to as the orders of creation or orders of preservation or divine mandates. Luther used various terms: "orders," "ordinances," "institutions," or "estates." In his day there were three main enduring orders: church, government and civil affairs, and marriage and family (Luther, *Luther's Works*, 37:364–65). The commands of God's law are always situated within the broader context of these ordinances. While these estates are also always corrupted due to sin and evil, God uses them nevertheless as "masks of God" to carry out the divine work of preserving and promoting a flourishing, just, and peaceable social life (Luther, *Luther's Works*, 1:11–12; 13:197; 14:112–15; 26:94–96; 45:330–31). Earlier generations of Lutheran ethicists too often viewed the orders of creation as rigidly fixed and statically hierarchical, but Lutheran ethical reflection during the last century has attended more prudently to the historical nature of God's continuing creativity—*creatio continua*—and thereby has explored the dynamic character of these creational ordinances. In this way, Lutheran ethics promotes life together in Christ as critical participation with God in the social-cultural-natural world of the neighbor.

Because God continually creates earthly life, Lutheran ethicists since Luther's time have regularly identified work and the economy as a fourth great differentiated institution within creation. The widespread flourishing of global civil society in the late twentieth and early twenty-first centuries suggests itself as an emerging enduring order of God's creative activity, which awaits vigorous Lutheran ethical reflection. In the first half of the twentieth century the concept of the orders of creation was notoriously abused by some Lutherans under German Nazism, who used the concept to justify a totalitarian state immune from any prophetic critique by the church or any other entity. At other times some have misused the concept to justify the subordination of women to men, and of one race or culture to another leading to slavery and colonization. Most Lutheran ethicists today severely criticize these abuses by way of critical reflection on God's will for justice.

Natural Law, Reason, and Scriptures

Luther critically appropriated the Western Christian tradition of natural-law moral reasoning pioneered by Augustine and Aquinas. He routinely cited the apostle Paul's affirmation in Rom. 2:15 that the peoples of the world have God's law "written on their hearts" (Luther, *Luther's Works*, 35:161–74) and thereby have access to moral insight through their God-given reasoning capacities. Says Luther, "God is a gentle and wealthy Lord. . . . Thus he casts great intelligence, wisdom, languages, and oratorical ability among the godless, too, so that His dear Christians look like mere children, fools and beggars by comparison" (*Luther's Works*, 13:198). Luther and the Lutheran confessors thereby "praise natural law and natural reason as the source from which all written law has come and is issued" (Luther, *Luther's Works*, 13:160; see Kolb and Wengert 121–24). They also knew full well that human reason always also stands under the sign of sin, and that great wisdom, critical care, and community-wide moral conversation are needed in order to discern and establish right and just laws within nations based on natural law. They urged Christians to learn from the best of "worldly wisdom" from the likes of Demosthenes and Aristotle, Ulpian and Cicero (Luther, *Luther's Works*, 13:199). For this reason, Lutherans characteristically have had high regard for liberal arts, the humanities, and education in the sciences. In this vein, Lutheran ethics has critiqued modern forms of instrumental reason; developed critical, narrative, and communicative forms of rationality; and promoted the rise of expansive empathy.

Luther held that the sacred Scriptures themselves often reflect and record the natural law that God has woven into the fabric of creation. The Decalogue, the two Great Commandments, and the Golden Rule are especially poignant scriptural formulations of natural law. However, the Scriptures also contain countless moral laws that are simply instances of moral reasoning applied to the particular circumstances of ancient Israel and that do not bind people in quite different contexts. Luther noted that even the Decalogue itself contains such applied reasoning, especially in the Sabbath law, in the commandment regarding images, and in the inclusion of women under property. Luther therefore argued famously, "One must deal cleanly with the Scriptures. From the beginning the Word has come to us in various ways. It is not enough simply to look and see whether God has said it; rather we must look and see to whom it has been spoken, whether it fits us. That makes all the difference between night and day. . . . You must keep your eye on the Word that applies to you, that is spoken to you" (*Luther's Works*, 35:170). For this reason, Luther argued, people have an unequivocal obligation to follow scriptural law only when it "agrees with the natural law" (*Luther's Works*, 35:165, 168, 172–73). When Lutheran ethics takes its bearings from Luther and the Lutheran confessions, the threshold for indisputable moral obligation is natural law, not biblical law. This distinguishes Lutheran ethics from other prevalent Protestant ethical traditions that focus or fixate on biblical law, though some Lutherans have, in an uncharacteristically Lutheran manner, considered biblical moral law per se as unquestionably binding.

Vocation and Ordinary Life

Luther understood and urged Christian sanctification through his redefined concept of Christian vocation. In Western medieval Christianity the notion of vocation had primarily come to mean being called out of an ordinary life in the world into a "higher" religious order as a priest, monk, or nun whereby one could better attain Christian perfection. By contrast, Luther taught vocation as the call to serve one's neighbor through a wide range of everyday stations, offices, and places of responsibility, including one's positions in the family, like father or mother; in the workplace or on the farm, like employers and employees; in the city, like officers or citizens; or in the church, like pastors and laity. In these places of responsibility Christians are called to do good works that tangibly help real neighbors in their everyday lives. Luther often urged people, therefore, to stay in their ordinary places of responsibility rather than to enter monasteries or utopian communes. For Lutheran ethics, "service to God is indeed service to our neighbor" (Luther, *Luther's Works*, 43:129). Lutheran moral imagination radically revalues ordinary life with a liberated Christian laity.

Luther himself offered ethical reflections on various vocations, stations, and offices, often on the affairs of government and political life. When his own soon-to-be prince wondered whether a Christian could occupy that office, Luther argued that a Christian could answer a call to occupy public offices that included a legitimate use of force under the moral criteria of natural law with the purpose of protecting the most vulnerable among us and all of us in our vulnerabilities from harm, exploitation, and oppression (*Luther's Works*, 45:81–129). He regularly reminded rulers that administering law means going beyond its mere letter and using moral and political wisdom (Gk. *epieikeia*; Lat. *aequitas*) to judge according to the circumstances of a case (*Luther's Works*, 45:118–19; 46:102).

Lutheran ethicists have criticized Luther's own moral-political wisdom especially on two occasions. In the mid-1520s the peasants were suffering under various oppressive political policies. Luther initially took up their cause and presented their grievances to the princes. However, when the peasants turned to violence in the name of Christian freedom, he feared all-out social chaos and advised the princes to squash the revolt with overwhelming force (*Luther's Works*, 46:3–86). In the early 1540s, toward the end of his life, Luther advised the princes to use force to "rid" the Jews from Germany because they had violated the second commandment against blasphemy by publicly rejecting Jesus' divinity (*Luther's Works*, 47:121–306). Although earlier in his life he had rejected any legitimate use of force against blasphemy or false teaching, here he atrociously violated his own earlier and better ethical reflections.

Luther and Lutheran ethics generally have upheld the basic tenets of the just-war tradition because it conforms to the distinction between law and gospel (see Luther, *Luther's Works*, 46:87–137, 155–206). Further, Luther advanced just-war reasoning by vehemently criticizing holy war, or crusade, which had come to be seen as justifiable. On the basis of Acts 5:29 ("we must obey God rather than human authority"), he also supported selective conscientious objection to an unjust war (*Luther's Works*, 44:100). In the 1520s Luther had rejected any armed resistance against the emperor even if the emperor was systematically committing gross injustice (*Luther's Works*, 45:57–129). By the late 1530s he had changed his mind, and on the basis of natural-law reasoning and constitutional law he recognized a right of armed resistance against the emperor to be carried out by lesser magistrates. This set in motion Lutheran resistance theory, which Calvinist political theorists then developed further.

When poverty became rampant, Luther urged towns and villages to set up community chests to care for the poor (*Luther's Works*, 45:159–94). This advocacy for social welfare sprouted resilient roots within the Lutheran cultures of Scandinavia and Germany. When princes ruled arbitrarily in order to gain "honor, power, luxury, [and] selfish profit," Luther insisted that they "make and administer just laws so that the poor, the wretched, the widows, the orphans are not oppressed, but have their rights and can keep them." It was in this way that rulers become "partakers of divine majesty." He also admonished the bishops of the church not to "lie down and snore in their office," but rather to rebuke their unjust rulers "boldly and openly" (*Luther's Works*, 13:49–57). Famously, Luther recommended that princes should put a bread loaf rather than a lion on their coat of arms, thereby underscoring distributive justice (Kolb and Wengert 450).

When the medieval church promoted vows of celibacy as a higher form of Christian life, Luther espoused the moral beauty of married sexuality and urged priests, monks, and nuns to marry (*Luther's Works*, 44:243–400; 45:11–50). When, in the spirit of Augustine, Christians viewed earthly life as "the solace of our misery," Luther promoted not only the use but also the "enjoyment," of daily bread, music and other arts, and conviviality (Kolb and Wengert 449–52). When children became stuck in ignorance and drudgery, Luther encouraged towns to establish schools and persuaded parents to educate their children (*Luther's Works*, 46:207–58). When rich bigwigs monopolized the economy and fleeced the commoners, Luther condemned unjust wages and proposed government policy to counter exploitative business and banking practices (*Luther's Works*, 45:231–310).

Trinitarian Character

The trinitarian character of Lutheran ethics honors the Holy Spirit's creation of faith in Christ with the pulse of love seeking justice responsibly in the life of one's neighbor. It respects God's creation, dignifies ordinary daily life, critically values social institutions, and acknowledges the moral wisdom and empathetic reason that God provides for the protection of the most vulnerable and for the flourishing of all creation. During the last half century or more, contemporary Lutheran ethicists from within a host of global indigenous contexts have taken up this tradition of moral reflection and brought it critically and constructively to bear on myriad contemporary questions.

See also Anti-Semitism; Celibacy; Golden Rule; Government; Just-War Theory; Law, Uses of; Law and Gospel; Libertinism; Natural Law; Ten Commandments; Vocation

Bibliography

Althaus, P. *The Ethics of Martin Luther*. Trans. R. Schultz. Fortress, 1972; Bloomquist, K., and J. Stumme, eds. *The Promise of Lutheran Ethics*. Fortress, 1998; Bonhoeffer, D. *Ethics*. Fortress, 2005; Forell, G. *Faith Active in Love: An Investigation of Principles Underlying Luther's Social Ethics*. Augsburg, 1959; Kolb, R., and T. Wengert, eds. *The Book of Concord: The Confessions of the Evangelical Lutheran Church*. Fortress, 2000; Lazareth, W. *Christians in Society: Luther, the Bible, and Social Ethics*. Fortress, 2001; Lindberg, C. *Beyond Charity: Reformation Initiative for the Poor*. Fortress, 1993; Luther, M. *Luther's Works*. Vols. 1–30 edited by J. Pelikan, 31–54 by H. Lehman. 55 vols. Concordia/Fortress, 1955–86; idem. *Sermons of Martin Luther: The House Postils*. Ed. and trans. F. Klug. Vol. 1. Baker, 1996; Wingren, G. *Luther on Vocation*. Trans. C. Rasmussen. Muhlenberg Press, 1957.

Gary M. Simpson

Lying

See Truthfulness, Truth-Telling

M

1 Maccabees

Composed between the years 130 and 100 BCE, 1 Maccabees documents the Jewish struggle for independence from their Seleucid overlords following a brutal persecution by Antiochus IV Epiphanes. The book's drama revolves around the priestly family of Mattathias, known to history as the Maccabees or Hasmoneans. They liberate and purify the Jerusalem temple, free the occupied citadel, expand their nation's borders, and establish a new dynasty to rule over Judea. The book of 1 Maccabees aims to legitimate this dynasty's claim to the high priesthood and kingship and to unite its readers through common identity and values.

Among the moral sources of 1 Maccabees, "the law" holds a primary place. Scrolls of the law and obedience to it are proscribed during the persecution (1:56–57), but the resisters carry a Torah scroll with them, perhaps even searching in it for guidance as they prepare for battle (3:48–54). Judas musters troops "according to the law," following the prescriptions of Deut. 20:5–8 (3:56). The law contains not only statutes (2:21) but also moral exemplars. When the king's messenger commands Judeans to sacrifice on an alien altar, Mattathias kills messenger and sacrificer alike (2:24–25). The narrator reports, "Thus he burned with zeal for the law, just as Phinehas did against Zimri son of Salu" (2:26). In his last testament to his sons, Mattathias exhorts them to imitate not only Phinehas (2:54) but also Abraham (2:52 [cf. Gen. 15; 22]) and Joseph (2:53 [cf. Gen. 39:7–10; 41:38–45]).

Mattathias similarly urges his sons to imitate Joshua (2:55), Caleb (2:56 [cf. Num. 13:30]), David (2:57), and Elijah (2:58 [cf. 1 Kgs. 19:10, 14]). Each models piety as well as military leadership or militant zeal. Mattathias also invokes the examples of Hananiah, Azariah, Mishael (2:59 [cf. Dan. 3]), and Daniel (2:60 [cf. Dan. 6]). Elsewhere, "the holy books" provide encouragement (12:9).

Among specific practices targeted in the persecution, 1 Maccabees identifies sacrifice, Sabbath and feast days, circumcision, and purity laws (1:45–49, 60–63). Regarding idolatry, Mattathias counters the king's command with God's, declaring, "We will not obey the king's words by turning aside from our religion to the right hand or to the left" (2:22). The question of Sabbath observance is more complex. Early in the persecution a thousand women, children, and men flee to the desert (2:31, 38). Seleucid soldiers prepare to attack them on the Sabbath but first call them out, promising to spare them if they will obey the king's command (2:32–33). The Jews choose death rather than obey the king or violate the Sabbath (2:34–36). Learning of the massacre, Mattathias and his friends weigh Sabbath observance against the cost of human life, resolving to fight on the Sabbath to defend their lives and laws (2:39–41).

The book of 1 Maccabees contributes to moral discourses regarding just war (*jus ad bellum*), Sabbath observance, and conflict between divine commands and laws of the state.

Morally problematic features of the text also demand serious engagement. The call to arms in 1 Maccabees exceeds the charge to defend people and laws, aiming also at vengeance (2:67–68; 9:40–42; 13:6). Defense of the law extends to killing sinners (2:44; 9:73; 14:14). Mattathias and his comrades forcibly circumcise young boys (2:46). As their wars shift from defense to offense, his sons raze and plunder neighboring cities (5:51, 65–68; 10:84; 11:61; 12:31). Labeling certain inhabitants of Judea as "lawless" justifies their extermination (2:44; 3:5–6; 7:5; 9:23, 58, 69; 11:25; 14:14), while references to the hatred and aggression of "the nations" justify expansion (12:53; 13:6). The Judeans surrender their autonomy to this rhetoric of security through radical othering, shouting to Simon, "Fight our battles, and all that you say to us we will do" (13:9). Finally, as Jonathan and Simon broker alliances with Seleucids and Romans, they enter a world of political patronage fraught with deception and manipulation (12:43–48; 16:18–22). The favors that they exchange are costly: they kill one hundred thousand inhabitants of Antioch to aid a king who will betray them (11:41–53). They too trade moral autonomy for an illusion of power and self-determination. Readers do well to look at their own alliances and count the cost.

See also Deuterocanonical/Apocryphal Books; 2 Maccabees; Sabbath

Bibliography

Collins, J. *Daniel, First Maccabees, Second Maccabees.* OTM 15. Michael Glazier, 1981; idem. "The Zeal of Phinehas: The Bible and the Legitimation of Violence." *JBL* 122 (2003): 3–21; Hieke, T. "The Role of 'Scripture' in the Last Words of Mattathias (1 Macc 2:49–70)." Pages 61–74 in *The Books of the Maccabees: History, Theology, Ideology*, ed. G. Xeravits and J. Zsengellér. JSJSup 118. Brill, 2007; Schwartz, D. "The Other in 1 and 2 Maccabees." Pages 30–37 in *Tolerance and Intolerance in Early Judaism and Christianity*, ed. G. Stanton and G. Stroumsa. Cambridge University Press, 1998.

Anathea Portier-Young

2 Maccabees

The book of 2 Maccabees details events in Jerusalem between 175 and 160 BCE. Jerusalem's priests trade ancestral traditions for "Greek glories" (4:15). A tableau of horrors follows: slaughter, slavery, the temple profaned, Jewish faith outlawed (5:11–6:11). The stories of nine martyrs occupy the book's center (6:18–7:42). With God's help (8:23–24; 10:1), Judas Maccabeus and his brothers lead an army against the oppressors, liberate the city, purify the temple (10:1–5), and finally defeat the enemy general Nicanor (15:27–36).

In the moral economy of 2 Maccabees, God defended the temple and people of Jerusalem when they obeyed God's law (3:1; 8:36). When they abandoned it (4:16–17), God disciplined them (6:12–17; 7:32–33). The willing deaths of martyrs atoned for the people's sins, effecting a turning point for the nation (7:38; 8:3–5). Living and dead alike intercede with God through prayer (3:15–21; 7:37; 10:4; 12:42; 15:12–14). Sacrifice gains God's mercy for an enemy (3:32–33) and atones for the sins of the dead (12:40–46). God's justice works through human and supernatural agents (1:15–17; 3:24–34; 4:38) and through illness and calamity (9:5–11). Punishment frequently "fits" the crime (4:16, 26, 38; 8:25; 9:6, 10).

The law and ancestral traditions prescribe a way of life, including sacrificial worship, diet, Sabbath, and circumcision. For these and for "temple, city, country, and commonwealth," the book's heroes are willing to die (13:14). When the law appears secure, Judas makes peace terms with a view to what is *sympheron*, or advantageous (11:15; cf. 12:12; see also Aristotle, *Eth. nic.* 9.3 §1004b30–31). Here and elsewhere in the book (6:20, 27, 31; 7:12; 15:12) the narrator may show the influence of Greek moral philosophy.

The book of 2 Maccabees gives special attention to the moral reasoning of the martyrs. When Eleazar refuses to eat pork, he is encouraged to save his life by pretending. He refuses on the grounds that the young would mistake his action and be led astray by his example (6:24–25 [note later discourses on "scandal"—e.g., Thomas Aquinas, *ST* II-II, q. 43]). The seven brothers who give their bodies to death are emboldened by belief in resurrection, valuing eternal life over the present one (7:9, 11). Their mother encourages them with words from the Song of Moses, alluding to the belief that God will vindicate God's people "when their power is gone" (Deut. 32:36). She deduces God's power to restore life from her experience of the mystery of conception and gestation (7:22–23 [cf. Eccl. 11:5]). In a similar vein, she instructs her youngest son to observe heaven and earth and deduce from them God's life-giving power, so that he should not fear death (7:28–29). The stories of these martyrs have inspired many in multiple religious traditions and may be considered the book's most profound moral legacy.

The book also tells of Razis, a confessing Jew who took his own life when the enemy came to arrest him (14:37–46). The Donatist bishop Gaudentius cited Razis's example in support of his own plans for suicide. In a letter to Dulcitius (*Ep.* 204), Augustine countered that Razis's actions were "great" but not "good." In Augustine's view, the book offers Razis's example not for imitation but for judgment.

The book of 2 Maccabees asserts that God fought on the side of Judas and his army, in many cases claiming divine support for actions that violate modern understandings of just conduct in war (*jus in bello*). Judas sets fire to villages at night (8:6–7); burns alive an enemy who has taken refuge in a house (8:33; cf. 10:37); takes revenge by night on refugees (12:6); slaughters the people of Caspin, Carnaim (where women and children have been sent for refuge), and Ephron (12:16, 26–27); and mutilates the dead body of Nicanor to display his head, tongue, and arm as proof of God's help (15:30–35). Serious engagement with 2 Maccabees requires that we confront these and similar claims and actions not only in the text but also in the world we inhabit today.

See also Deuterocanonical/Apocryphal Books; 1 Maccabees; Martyrdom; War

Bibliography

Doran, R. *Temple Propaganda: The Purpose and Character of 2 Maccabees.* CBQMS 12. Catholic Biblical Association of America, 1981; Ego, B. "God's Justice: The 'Measure for Measure' Principle in 2 Maccabees." Pages 141–54 in *The Books of the Maccabees: History, Theology, Ideology*, ed. G. Xeravits and J. Zsengellér. JSJSup 118. Brill, 2007; Heard, W. "The Maccabean Martyrs' Contribution to Holy War." *EvQ* 58 (1986): 291–318; Schwartz, D. *2 Maccabees*. CEJL. De Gruyter, 2008; van Henten, J. *The Maccabean Martyrs as Saviours of the Jewish People: A Study of 2 and 4 Maccabees*. JSJSup 57. Brill, 1997.

Anathea Portier-Young

3 Maccabees *See* Orthodox Ethics

4 Maccabees *See* Orthodox Ethics

Magic *See* Divination and Magic

Malachi

The book of Malachi provides very little information about the prophet. Even the name *Malachi* has been the subject of debate as to whether it is a proper name or a prophetic title. Most scholars assign a date in the Persian period, sometime after the rebuilding of the temple in Jerusalem (515 BCE). From a literary perspective, two features stand out. First, the book is unique within the prophetic corpus in the way it deftly employs a series of imaginary discourses to communicate its message. In this regard, the intersection of the priestly and the prophetic in Malachi is noteworthy. The priestly aspect has to do with the main message: the concern for adherence to the Torah. The prophetic aspect has to do with the mode in which it is presented. The major portion of the book (1:6–3:24) is an excellent example of priestly instruction presented in the form of a prophetic disputation. Second, the literary parallels between the opening words of Malachi and Zech. 9:1; 12:1 have raised the issue of the book's status as an independent work. But the literary integrity, prophetic creativity, and theological sophistication displayed in the materials strengthen the case for an independent status.

The book opens on an affirmative note that God still loves Israel. For Malachi, God's love is the source of renewal and sustenance for the people. God's love is the basis of hope and the reason for the proper ethical response. In the rest of the book Malachi exposes the barriers to renewal. The longest section in Malachi (1:6–2:9) is a complex piece that reflects the rivalry between priestly groups. The prophet offers an indictment on the Aaronide priests for improper ritual practices and for usurping the role of the Levitical priests as providers of instruction and judgments. Malachi's own allegiances become clear in his explicit support of the role of the Levitical priests within the society. From an ethical perspective, the book's pointed exploration of the connection between worship and ethical/moral practices is of lasting value. Of primary importance to Malachi is the preservation of the covenant relationship between God and Israel, especially the obligation on the part of Israel to follow the stipulations, whether in regard to married family life (indictment against mixed marriages and divorces in 2:10–16) or support of cultic life (insistence on full payment of tithes in 3:6–12).

See also Covenant; Old Testament Ethics

Bibliography

Brown, W. *Obadiah through Malachi*. WestBC. Westminster John Knox, 1996; Floyd, M. *Minor Prophets, Part 2*. FOTL 22. Eerdmans, 2000; Nogalski, J., and M. Sweeney, eds. *Reading and Hearing the Book of the Twelve*. SBLSymS 15. Society of Biblical Literature, 2000; Petersen, D. *Zechariah 9–14 and Malachi*. OTL. Westminster John Knox, 1995.

D. N. Premnath

Malice

Malice is the desire or intent to inflict pain, injury, or distress on another person, particularly without legal or ethical justification or excuse. In English translations of the NT, the Greek word *kakia* often is translated as "malice," "wickedness," or "evil," and it regularly appears in Pauline lists of virtues and vices (Rom. 1:29; Eph. 4:31; Col. 3:8). Malice here serves as an all-inclusive vice, like anger, describing an attitude or inclination that can lead to further sinful thought and behavior. Within the NT, the presence of malice indicates a disordered relationship with God (Acts 8:22) and is placed in juxtaposition to the new life in Christ (Col. 3:8; Titus 3:3; 1 Pet. 2:1), which is marked by grace and goodwill. The worldly ubiquity of malice is acknowledged, but its insidiousness is presented as a particular danger to the relationships that are central to Christian community. It is a contaminating presence that cannot be ignored (1 Cor. 5:8). In the OT, malice or evil often is seen as resident in the human condition, a result of human free will (Gen. 6:5), and a constant presence among the community's oppressors (Ps. 73:8), which is redeemed within the community by the wisdom of God (Prov. 9:10).

Within the discipline of moral theology, considerations of malice attend to the place of intention in determining the relative morality in particular human action, as in debates concerning violence inherent in just-war theory and euthanasia.

Various moral theories allow the possibility that killing in wartime or killing to relieve mortal suffering does not necessarily require an act of malice. The classical foundation is provided by Augustine's political philosophy, which held that some types of violence, such as coercion by the state, are not malicious but are justifiable if they emanate from a rightly ordered will—that is, one ordered toward the will of God. Thomas Aquinas too regarded malice as a defect of the will that can move one to choose evil despite knowledge of the good. Malice renders control of the passions ineffective, yet the one who acts with malice retains culpability. Protestant thinkers likewise have focused on what Martin Luther called the "bondage of the will," which is transformed only by God's agape and faith in Christ. Contemporary virtue ethics, as compared to utilitarianism or deontological theories, continues to focus on the connection of virtue and vice with the will and moral agency, although not exclusively. Rather than locating the morality of a particular action through examination of obligation, duty, or consequence, it is determined by issues of character, such as maliciousness or benevolence.

See also Evil; Intention; Vice; Vices and Virtues, Lists of

Bibliography

Crisp, R., and M. Slote, eds. *Virtue Ethics*. Oxford University Press, 1997; Ogletree, T. "Agents and Moral Formation." Pages 36–44 in *The Blackwell Companion to Religious Ethics*. Blackwell, 2005; Stump, E., and N. Kretzmann, eds. *The Cambridge Companion to Augustine*. Cambridge University Press, 2001; Sweeney, E. "Vice and Sin (Ia IIae, qq. 71–89)." Pages 151–68 in *The Ethics of Aquinas*, ed. S. Pope. Georgetown University Press, 2002.

Gary B. MacDonald

Mammon *See* Wealth

Manipulation

The word *manipulation* signifies a means of control by which persons are intentionally influenced in secretive and often sinister ways to serve the purposes and advantages of others. As a form of power, manipulation aims to control and direct the actions and decisions of others who often are unaware of being manipulated. As a more subtle form of power, manipulation can be used by individuals who possess no identifiable legitimate power or control. For example, in asymmetrical relationships, such as between children and adults, and subordinates and superiors, manipulation can be a means to obtain desired results for those lacking more formal means of achieving their ends. In situations of oppression, manipulation may be one of the few means available to avert further harm and to simply survive. In general, however, manipulation is a morally dubious use of power because of its subtlety in concealing motives, its use of other persons as objects and means to other ends, and its proclivity to capitalize on the vulnerabilities of others.

Manipulation uses morally suspicious strategies to influence persons by concealing the motives and ends of the manipulator. The means of manipulation can be cognitive or emotional (Wartenberg 111), involving tactics such as omitting or skewing information, lying and deception, fomenting fear and hatred, and promising reward or threatening punishment. These tactics are designed to diminish the awareness and consciousness of those being manipulated. This also makes manipulation an ethical concern because people are viewed as objects and means to the ends of other persons and purposes. Manipulation violates basic principles such as respecting the dignity, freedom, and agency of others. In Kantian ethics, treating persons as means rather than ends themselves is a violation of human freedom and will, autonomy and rationality. While Christian ethicists may share these concerns, a moral evaluation of manipulation is also informed by virtues such as honesty, justice, fairness, truth-telling, communal obligations, and responsibility for others, especially for the "least of these," the powerless and the marginalized. Moral assessment is particularly called for in Christian ethics because manipulation often capitalizes on the vulnerabilities of others.

Manipulation can also be exercised through things such as education, advertising, political campaigning, fund-raising, and even religion, where the tactics may be the same, such as omitting and skewing information, lying and deception, and capitalizing on fears. Indoctrination may be a form of manipulation in education. Political advertising can manipulate the fears and sentiments of voters by distorting opponents' records and policies. Fund-raising can manipulate people into giving money for the hope of reward and promises of future gain. Religion can be a tool of manipulation to shape persons' perceptions of God and to direct their actions in particular directions.

Reflections on Scripture can help readers make moral assessments about manipulation, its exercise, purposes, and effects. One of the best known examples is David's manipulation of Uriah, recorded in 2 Sam. 11. David, after his brazen use of power to sexually exploit Bathsheba, now needs to manipulate Uriah in ways that will serve his purposes, because Bathsheba is pregnant with David's child. In his desire to convince Uriah that the child is his own, David begins to draw the unaware Uriah into his plan (11:6–8). David rewards Uriah by allowing him to return home, hoping that Uriah will then have reason to think that he is the father of the child Bathsheba is carrying. David also sends a gift to Uriah. The narrative provides a delightful irony and subversion to David's manipulative power. Although Uriah may appear to be vulnerable to manipulation, he does not go home but instead stays on duty with the ark and his fellow soldiers (11:9–11). Uriah does not do what David influenced him to do. David again attempts to manipulate Uriah to return to Bathsheba, but again Uriah does not return home (11:12–13). The narrative ends with the ramping up of power after manipulation's failure. Since manipulation failed to achieve David's desired end, he resorts to the overt and abusive use of his political power for his own gain (11:14–27).

See also Authority and Power; Deontological Theories of Ethics; Ends and Means; Honesty

Bibliography

Bowman, R. "The Complexity of Character and the Ethics of Complexity." Pages 73–97 in *Character and Scripture: Moral Formation, Community and Biblical Interpretation*, ed. W. Brown. Eerdmans, 2002; Cave, E. "What's Wrong with Motive Manipulation?" *ETMP* 10 (2007): 129–44; Häring, B. *Manipulation: Ethical Boundaries of Medical, Behavioral, and Genetic Manipulation*. St. Paul Publications, 1975; Wartenberg, T. *The Forms of Power: From Domination to Transformation*. Temple University Press, 1990, 110–12.

Wyndy Corbin Reuschling

Mark

The author of the Gospel of Mark is anonymous, although early tradition held that Mark wrote Peter's memoirs. The name *Mark* appears in a later title rather than the text. This is the earliest Gospel, and its sources are unknown. Interpreters have used methods such as the following for deriving ethics from Mark.

Extracting norms for judging people and events. In Sabbath controversies, human welfare takes precedence over Sabbath restrictions; stated positively, it is lawful to do good on the Sabbath (3:4). Sabbath legality no longer proscribes activity but prescribes redemptive activity. The commandment is still valid, but it alone is not decisive. Similarly, the rich man's use of possessions in 10:17–23 qualifies keeping commandments.

Determining bases for evaluating motivation, purposes, and objectives. As an act of faith, a bleeding woman violates social norms and touches Jesus to be made well (5:25–34). Out of compassion, Jesus feeds the hungry (6:34–44; 8:1–9). Jesus teaches forgiveness as a basis for relationships with others and with God (11:25).

Cultivating virtues. In the Aristotelian tradition, some interpreters look for virtues to practice to build character. Does perseverance in suffering strengthen faith and facilitate moral development (e.g., 4:19)? Is sacrifice to the point of death vicarious for others (8:34–35)?

Discovering Jesus' ethical teachings. After a discussion with some stereotyped Pharisees, Jesus teaches that a man who sends his wife away and marries another commits adultery (10:11). But more than teach about life, Jesus restores life (3:1–5). Further, rather than repeat Jesus' teachings, recipients and witnesses of Jesus' healings bear testimony to Jesus' activity as God's doing.

Finding critiques of people, systems, and structures that perpetuate injustice, and envisioning justice. Jesus' programmatic proclamation of the advent of God's kingdom (1:15) means, on the one hand, a critique of other kingdoms. On the other hand, if God rules, then ethical correlates are predicated of humans who live under God's rule. Restorations of the "unclean" to normal society (like the Gerasene demoniac [5:2–15]) implicitly critique social marginalization. Conversely, restorations of marginalized people to the social order dramatize God's rule. Mark evaluates negatively the execution of John the Baptist under Herod Antipas and Herodias, who are collaborators with the Roman Empire, and who see their elite status as exempting them from social propriety and as empowering them to execute John over a grudge (6:17–29). Following Jesus is an alternative to rulers of imperial systems (10:42–45). The high priestly party consists of ruling elites (who inevitably collaborate with the empire) against whom Jesus makes a claim on the temple (11:15–18; 12:1–12). Similarly, Jesus critiques scribal abuse of legal systems (12:38–40) and anticipates that following him will cause retribution from imperial collaborators—councils, synagogues, governors, and kings (13:9–20). This materializes immediately in his crucifixion implicating the governor, scribal systems, and the high priestly party (14:1–15:31).

Locating ethics in God's will for humanity and the world. The parable of the sower in 4:3–20 presents living under God's rule as analogous to seed in good earth that stands over against seed in unproductive soil—that is, over against evil. Similarly, living under God's rule is like the earth producing a harvest from growing seed (4:28–29).

Living in response to God. Mark points beyond its own story for living. First, Mark elicits a relationship with God that transcends its own narrative. When Jesus and a scribe agree that the greatest commandment is to love God and neighbor (12:28–34), Mark evokes a relationship with God that is inseparable from a relationship with other people. Mark also anticipates readers who will encounter God in reading the narrative. Living in response to God is not arbitrary, as it is subject to communal confirmation and has to do with the God characterized in Mark and the biblical tradition on which it draws. Because relationships with God are the source, motivation, and empowerment for praxis, ethics means giving up knowing in advance what one is to do. Praxis deriving from God also goes beyond Mark's story because it is impossible to know what love looks like until one confronts concrete situations. An instance is Jesus' "Abba" prayer that he may derive his behavior from the God to whom he is related as a son to a father (14:35–36). Some interpreters take this prayer as an example for imitation, but if so, it is noticeably ineffective for the disciples who fall asleep while Jesus is at prayer.

The Gospel of Mark points beyond itself because it anticipates following Jesus into the future beyond the end of the story. On the one hand, Mark is full of failure. The disciples regularly miss the mark; a widow casts all her livelihood into the temple treasury (12:41–44), but the very next verses inform readers about the temple's destruction (13:1–2); a woman anoints Jesus royally but for his burial (14:3–9); when Jesus is arrested, his gathering of followers disintegrates when they run away (14:27, 50). On the other hand, over against this failure and collapse, God remains Lord in a world that can turn into chaos. Further, Mark points to disciples following the risen Jesus beyond the end of the story (16:7).

Interpreters tend to characterize God by values. For instance, God is a God of justice. True enough, but the God of Mark's Gospel is primarily a God who acts and whose power gives life. This power of God at work beyond the end of Mark is the good earth out of which the seed bears fruit.

See also Imitation of Jesus; Kingdom of God; New Testament Ethics; Parables, Use of in Ethics

Bibliography

Burridge, R. *Imitating Jesus: An Inclusive Approach to New Testament Ethics*. Eerdmans, 2007; Fowl, S., and L. Jones. *Reading in Communion: Scripture and Ethics in Christian Life*. Eerdmans, 1991; Hays, R. *The Moral Vision of the New Testament: Community, Cross, and New Creation; A Contemporary Introduction to New Testament Ethics*. HarperSanFrancisco, 1996; Matera, F. *New Testament Ethics: The Legacies of Jesus and Paul*. Westminster John Knox, 1996; Via, D. *The Ethics of Mark's Gospel—in the Middle of Time*. Fortress, 1985.

Robert L. Brawley

Markets

Twentieth-century Christian ethics was preoccupied with the question of markets, especially the question of whether Christianity supports a socialist, capitalist, or mixed economy. Socialism assumed that markets should be planned and controlled, primarily by some state mechanism. Capitalism assumed that markets work best when freed from any interference—governmental, ecclesial, or moral. The "efficient markets theory" assumed that markets, if left to themselves, readjust to form the most efficient distribution of goods. Theologians debated whether they should throw themselves behind socialism, as many liberation theologians affirmed, or behind capitalism, as most neoliberal (or neoconservatives) affirmed. Many progressive liberals affirmed some kind of mixed economy such as "democratic capitalism" or "Keynesian" models of governmental influence. Once the Berlin Wall collapsed in 1989, the debate changed. Some suggested that we were now at the "end of history," and that, like it or not, everyone, even the pope, was now a capitalist. Both major political parties in the United States implemented strategies for the deregulation of the market based on the "efficient market thesis." This was a heady time of optimism, where some economists argued that, left to itself, the Dow Jones would rise to 30,000. Then came the recession of 2008, which shook the confidence of even the most ardent defender of the "efficient market" dogma.

Twenty-first-century theologians and economists seem less assured of any specific market proposal. Movements for neoconservatism or state-sponsored socialism are both in disarray. Progressive liberalism appears to be on the ascendancy, although no one knows the proper proportion of government interference and free-market exchange. We find ourselves in unstable times. It is not the first time this has happened, nor will it be the last.

The uncertainty of "markets" should not produce fear or undue anxiety among Christians. Although the negative consequences of such instability for the poor requires an attentiveness to their plight consistent with the traditional understanding that the patrimony of the church exists primarily for them, nonetheless the fact that markets cannot, and will never, provide security reminds us of what truly matters, which we see in the Gospel of Luke. It begins with Mary proclaiming that God has "filled the hungry with good things, and sent the rich away empty" (Luke 1:53). Those who trust in riches, who think that they secure life, are depicted as foolish. Jesus reaffirms this when he refuses to use his power to turn stones into bread, citing Moses' words, "One does not live by bread alone" (Luke 4:4). We then find three stories about the security of wealth. First is the rich ruler (Luke 18:18–25). He is saddened and cannot abide by Jesus' command to sell all that he has and give the proceeds to the poor. Jesus' denunciation of the rich causes anxiety even for his disciples. Who could obey this command? Jesus' response to the disciples gives hope: "There is no one who has left house or wife or brothers or parents or children, for the sake of the kingdom of God, who will not get back very much more in this age, and in the age to come eternal life" (Luke 18:29–30).

Does Jesus seek poverty? Does he say no to life? These passages in Luke gain intelligibility after the pentecostal miracle of Acts 2:43–47; 4:32–37. The true pentecostal miracle is a "common" life where teaching and possessions are held in common (*koinōnia*). Here we see the beginning of the fulfillment of Jesus' promise to the disciples in Luke 18:29–30. This is the "market" to which Christians are called.

What Christian advocates for socialism, capitalism, or mixed economies assume in common is that it is the vocation of Christians to determine which market should rule. It assumed "the Christian century," where the task of the church was to rule. In a post-Christian context that assumption, for better or worse, no longer works. Perhaps the Christian response to markets has less to do with which one they advocate for or against and more with how they make the church, and then by witness and analogy all of God's creation, embody the pentecostal miracle.

See also Capitalism; Ecclesiology and Ethics; Economic Ethics; Koinonia; Poverty and Poor; Wealth

D. Stephen Long

Marriage and Divorce

Marriage is the joining of two lives in a "one flesh" union to be characterized by fidelity. A "one flesh" union is both a mutual and exclusive sexual union and a sharing of the whole of life. Divorce is the sundering of that "one flesh" union.

Attending to Scripture

According to Mark, some Pharisees asked Jesus whether it is lawful for a man to divorce his wife (Mark 10:2). Moses, after all, had allowed it (Deut. 24:1–4), and every rabbi worth his salt had some interpretation of this law. But Jesus swept the law aside and reminded them of the story of creation. The law, he told them, was given "because of your hardness of heart" (Mark 10:5). The story, he said, is that "God made them male and female" (Mark 10:6 [cf. Gen. 1:27]), and "For this reason a man shall leave his father and mother and be joined to his wife, and the two shall become one flesh" (Mark 10:7–8 [cf. Gen. 2:24]).

Already at the beginning of the story there is marriage. God made of the one, two, so that the two might be one. "It is not good that the man should be alone" (Gen. 2:18). Marriage is a good gift of God. It is a story of an embodied relationship, a "one flesh" union of male and female, marked by mutuality, equality, and fidelity. It included from the beginning delight in the flesh, companionship, and the blessing of children. The two were at home in their flesh, "naked and . . . not ashamed" (Gen. 2:25); at home with each other, vulnerable and not anxious; and at home with God, the giver of life and love and joy. And from the beginning commitment was the way to love into the future, the way to give a future to their present love, binding not only Adam to Eve and Eve to Adam, but also binding present and future together. Their love would have a history. Their relationship would endure, either as fidelity or as betrayal. The story forms people to be ready to keep their promises, forms them to resist infidelity and divorce—so Jesus remembered the story, in any case.

Creation, however, is only the beginning of the story. Marriage continued, but it did so under the shadow of human sin and the curse that came in its wake. The vulnerability of nakedness, once an occasion for delight and mutuality, became an occasion for shame (Gen. 3:7). The equality and communion of marriage fell under the curse of patriarchy, and to the promise and blessing of children was joined the pain of the curse (Gen. 3:16).

Human sin might have smashed the cosmos back to chaos—and marriage along with it—but the grace of God would not let sin have the last word. Far as the curse is found, so far the grace of God would reach to restore and to bless, including marriage. The first sign of hope is this: "Now the man knew his wife Eve, and she conceived and bore Cain, saying, 'I have produced a man with the help of the LORD'" (Gen. 4:1). Later, the grace of God made its power felt in Sarah's "laughter" (her "Isaac" [see Gen. 17:19; 21:6]); in Joseph's fidelity against the temptations of Potiphar's wife; in the tender affection of Boaz and Ruth and in their fecundity; in the forgiveness and faithfulness of Hosea to Gomer; in the mutual passion of the two lovers in Song of Songs.

These signs of God's grace, however, came in the midst of a fallen world, a world of patriarchy and polygamy, pain and barrenness, infidelity and jealousy. Polygamy was practiced by some in ancient Israel, notably by the patriarchs and by the kings, but by how many is uncertain. Patriarchy deeply shaped practices of marriage, rendering women passive and reducing them to property. Men "married," but women were "given in marriage." The strict prohibition of adultery (Exod. 20:14), which is defined as a man having sexual intercourse with a married or engaged woman (Lev. 20:10), did not eliminate infidelity. In such a world Moses made a concession to divorce and to remarriage following divorce (Deut. 24:1–4). It too was an exclusively male prerogative.

Marriage (and divorce) came to be used as an analogy for the covenanted relationship of God and the people of God (e.g., Jer. 3:1–5; Ezek. 16; 23; Hos. 1–3; Mal. 2:13–16 [see Sampley]). These several texts suggest that the relationship of marriage was to be monogamous. Israel was to have no other gods, and God had chosen Israel as God's own. The relationship was to be marked by delight and desire, by mutual love (in Hos. 2:16 it is noteworthy that the wife calls her husband her "man," not her "master"). And it is to be marked by fidelity. Unfaithfulness was accepted as grounds for divorce, but "I hate divorce, says the LORD" (Mal. 2:16).

And so, evidently, did Jesus. That is where we began this account. When asked whether it is lawful for a man to divorce his wife, Jesus remembered the story of creation and drew this startling conclusion: "Therefore what God has joined together, let no one separate" (Mark 10:9). Divorce is not what God intended. It is a mark of our fallenness, an effect of the curse. When God's own sovereignty is at hand, when God's good future is making its power felt, the concession that Moses offered is no longer the finally decisive thing. Instead, "Whoever divorces his wife and marries another commits adultery against her; and if she divorces her husband and marries another, she commits adultery" (Mark 10:11). This remark is noteworthy for at least three reasons. First, women are regarded as agents in marriage and divorce no less than men. In the law and in patriarchy only men were regarded as agents, and in Deut. 24:1–4 only men could divorce their wives. This equal standing of men and women is a new thing, not found in the law, but found in the good future that Jesus announced and made present. Second, a man can commit adultery against his wife. In the law adultery was an offense against a man's property, a matter of taking another man's property. Technically, a man could not commit adultery against his wife but only against other men. But in Jesus' word a stunning new world of sex and marriage is created, a world where the wife is not simply property but rather is a partner, a partner who has the same rights over her husband that her husband has over her (cf. 1 Cor. 7:3–5). This too is a new thing. Third, of course, this remark calls those who would follow Jesus to renounce divorce. God's good future does not make its power felt in divorce.

The point of Jesus' word to the disciples was not to provide a new Torah, not to establish a new and extremely rigorous statute. The point was to announce the good future of God and the ways it already makes its power felt not only in singleness and celibacy but also in sexual relationships of equality and mutuality, where husband and wife are "one flesh," joined to each other in an embodied and enduring relationship. The power of God makes itself felt when husband and wife are "one flesh" and in their glad faithfulness when their marriage endures. The power of sin makes itself felt in divorce and in the patriarchal hegemony of husband over wife. God's purpose from the beginning is revisited and restored. Marriage is still the embodied love of a man and a woman that expresses and sustains both intimacy and continuity, that signals a covenant undertaken in vows and carried out in fidelity.

If those who would follow Jesus are to renounce divorce, then Christians may ask, and must ask, whether they may ever choose divorce. To begin to answer that question, we should note that we face the problem of diversity here. Matthew, Luke, and Paul handle the question of divorce somewhat differently.

Matthew, for example, tells the story that Mark told somewhat differently (Matt. 19:1–12). According to Matthew, the Pharisees ask whether it is lawful for a man to divorce his wife "for any cause" (Matt. 19:3); they ask, in effect, for Jesus to comment on the legal dispute about the interpretation of Deut. 24:1–3. Then Matthew artfully changes the order of Jesus' reply found in Mark. Jesus first takes up the Genesis texts and gives the Markan conclusion, "Therefore what God has joined together, let no one separate" (Matt. 19:6). Then the Pharisees cite Deut. 24:1, and Jesus responds, as in Mark, by saying that it is a concession to the hardness of their hearts, but he does not for that reason brush aside either the law or the necessity of interpretation. Instead, he interprets the law in the light of God's intentions. The law holds (see Matt. 5:17–20; 23:23), and Jesus is its best interpreter (see Matt. 9:9–13; 12:1–8). He gives a legal (halakic) interpretation for his community, an interpretation similar to the interpretation by Rabbi Shammai (*m. Giṭ* 10.10): "Whoever divorces his wife, except for unchastity, and marries another commits adultery" (Matt. 19:9 [cf. Matt. 5:32]). Because this is an interpretation of the Torah, it does not, as in Mark's version, make women agents in marriage and divorce, and it omits the stunning point that a man could commit adultery against his wife.

This passage is indeed a legal ruling. Should we, then, revise our renunciation of divorce in order to make allowance for men to divorce their wives "for unchastity" (for *porneia*, the precise meaning of which is disputed)? But what of Paul's words in 1 Cor. 7:10–16? Paul too cites the "command" of the Lord "that the wife should not separate from her husband . . . and that the husband should not divorce his wife" (1 Cor. 7:10–11), but he does not use that command as the basis for a legal ruling. Instead, faced with the concrete problem of whether marriage to an unbeliever can be dissolved, he exercises discernment. He offers the church his own advice ("I say—I and not the Lord" [1 Cor. 7:12]). On the basis of "one flesh" the couple is "holy" if one of the partners is (1 Cor. 7:14); therefore, the Christian wife or husband should not divorce an unbelieving spouse (1 Cor. 7:12–13). But if the unbelieving partner initiates divorce, then Paul's advice is to "let it be so," for "it is to peace that God has called you" (1 Cor. 7:15).

One other new thing may be traced to Jesus. In the good future of God, Jesus said, "they neither marry nor are given in marriage, but are like angels in heaven" (Mark 12:25 pars. [cf. Matt. 19:10–12]). That was something new, and suddenly singleness and celibacy were an option, an option signaled by Jesus' own singleness. Marriage was no longer a duty of Torah or a necessary condition for human fulfillment and divine approval.

So too Paul honored celibacy as a "gift" (*charisma*) of God (1 Cor. 7:7). It was not, however, as some Corinthian enthusiasts evidently understood it, a new requirement of truly Christian devotion. It was not a necessary condition for spiritual fulfillment and divine approval. Marriage was, in the light of God's good future, no longer a duty, but it remained a legitimate option on the way to that future. Although marriage may belong to the order of things that will pass out of existence (1 Cor. 7:31), in the present context of temptations to immorality, marriage may be the prudent option (1 Cor. 7:2). Moreover, Paul honored marriage too as a "gift" (1 Cor. 7:7) and as a place where the new order of things can make its power felt. The new identity and community owned in baptism prompted a retrieval of marital relationships of mutuality and equality, a renewal of creation. The full mutuality and equality of the marriage partnership in 1 Cor. 7, including the sexual aspects of that partnership (7:3–5), is stunning. It was hardly surprising, of course, that in the first century Paul should say, "The wife does not have authority over her own body, but the husband does" (1 Cor. 7:4). Patriarchies past and present have always welcomed and treasured that line. But that Paul should continue then in the first century to say, "Likewise the husband does not have authority over his own body, but the wife does" (1 Cor. 7:4), was stunning, and it shattered patriarchal traditions. The mutuality of authority, of ruling and submitting, within the partnership of marriage is itself a token of God's good future, a sign that the curse is being lifted, an indication of a future in which there is "no longer male and female."

Within marriage, moreover, sexual intercourse was not merely tolerated but rather was encouraged. Paul had accepted the Corinthian slogan, "It is well for a man not to touch a woman" (1 Cor. 7:1); celibacy is good. But marriage is also good, and within marriage "not to touch" your spouse is definitely not good. The sort of "spiritual marriage" that some Corinthians were attempting, and sometimes imposing on a partner, was not good. "Do not deprive one another," Paul says, "except perhaps by agreement for a set time, to devote yourselves to prayer" (1 Cor. 7:5). Sex is good, even in this chapter of Paul's letter where celibacy is called "better," and good sex gestures "one flesh," the unity and the mutuality and the equality of partners committed to each other and to God. Neither Christian identity nor Christian marriage requires asceticism.

Indeed, the Pastoral Epistles explicitly reject asceticism. Some of those whom the author opposed evidently had forbidden marriage (1 Tim. 4:3). These epistles condemn such teaching and the dualism behind it, for "everything created by God is good" (1 Tim. 4:4). In opposition to these heretics the author seems even to retreat from the Pauline recognition of celibacy as a gift and an option, for he evidently makes marriage a requirement for ecclesiastical office ("husband of one wife" [1 Tim. 3:2, 12; Titus 1:6 RSV]). It is possible, however, that "married only once" was directed not against the celibate but rather against those who engaged in the degenerate Hellenistic practice of successive brief marriages.

Ephesians retrieves the analogy of marriage and the covenanted relationship of God and God's people, rendering an analogy between marriage and the relationship of Christ and Christ's church (Eph. 5:25–33). This "one flesh" union is "a great mystery," and the author applies it to Christ and the church (Eph. 5:31–32).

The Tradition and Scripture

"Let marriage be held in honor by all" (Heb. 13:4). The early church always held marriage in honor. To be sure, there grew up in the early church a preference for celibacy, and marriage was regarded as being somewhat less holy in comparison to it. Certainly, the curse of patriarchy was not easily overcome. And some theologians, among them Augustine, were suspicious of delight in the sexual union of marriage, as though intercourse could be employed but not enjoyed. Nevertheless, the church honored marriage both in its theological reflection and practice, resisting various forms of dualism that would have insisted on celibacy.

Theological reflection on marriage ranges widely, from "sacrament" in the Catholic tradition to a "social estate" in Lutheran reflection, from a "covenant" binding spouses to each other and to God in the Calvinist tradition to "a little commonwealth" for the common good of the partners and the glory of God in some Anglican reflections. Accounts of marriage as a sacrament reach back to Ephesians and its identification of the "one flesh" union of marriage as "a great mystery" (*mysterion*), and yet further back to Hosea's use of marriage as a prophetic symbol of God's covenant with Israel. Others have been adamantly opposed to such an account of marriage as a sacrament. John Calvin, for example, called the transformation of marriage into a sacrament "a den of abominations" (*Institutes* 4.19.37). A good deal depends, of course, on how "sacrament" is defined. Some who use the language mean to insist only that Christian marriage is not to be reduced to something natural and secular but rather participates in the new order of God's new covenant. Calvin's polemic was aimed especially at what he regarded as the assertion of an excessive ecclesiastical jurisdiction over marriage. However, he hardly surrendered marriage to an arena of privacy inaccessible to the discipline of the Christian community.

The discipline of the church with respect to divorce has also ranged widely. The Orthodox Church typically has followed Basil's recommendation of "pastoral prudence" (*oikonomia*), permitting divorce in some circumstances. The same "pastoral prudence" is on display in the liturgy for remarriage after divorce in the Orthodox Church, which recognizes that such relationships are marked by our fallenness even while it blesses and consecrates the marriage. Protestants too typically have permitted divorce and remarriage, but on a spectrum that moves from a legalistic use of the concessions by Matthew and Paul to a surrender of discipline to the private decision of the parties. Roman Catholics have insisted on the indissolubility of Christian marriage but have allowed annulment of an unconsummated marriage, divorce of a recently baptized Christian from a nonbaptized spouse who is unwilling to continue the relationship with the Christian (the "Pauline privilege"), and other divorces as long as they are not of two Christians (the "Petrine privilege").

Contemporary Applications

Mark, Matthew, and Paul remembered Jesus' word about marriage and divorce, and each of them remembered it faithfully and creatively. They received and modified the tradition so that Jesus and his word could be remembered and performed in their own communities. None of them individually nor all of them combined into some elusive harmony should be read as a timeless code to settle directly and immediately contemporary questions about particular choices concerning marriage and divorce. But all of them are a part of the whole Scripture that the churches read and struggle to perform even as they face new challenges. Those challenges are many.

The "sexual revolution" now seems more commonplace than revolutionary, but still we struggle to find a way between promiscuous license and dour asceticism, between liberalism and legalism, a way to honor both sexuality and marriage with both sobriety and delight. Expectations of marriage as a gateway to human fulfillment may be extravagant and idolatrous, and when dashed, they may be one reason for the prevalence of divorce. Perhaps Protestants should retrieve an appreciation of the "gift" of celibacy. The phenomenon of "serial marriages" retrieves the degenerate Hellenistic practice of successive brief marriages and should be challenged by the discipline of the church. And, of course, there is the question of "gay marriage." Perhaps the Orthodox ritual for the remarriage of divorced persons can provide a model here as well as a reminder that even in a world of fallen sexuality, fidelity and mutuality can be a mark of God's good future. We need not regard divorce as good or homosexual acts as good in order to acknowledge fidelity and mutuality between divorced and homosexual persons as good. If we allow divorce in a world such as this for the sake of protecting marriage and marriage partners, and remarriage after divorce, then perhaps we should also consider blessing homosexual unions for the sake of nurturing fidelity and mutuality and protecting the homosexual partners.

The greatest challenge, however, may be to recover a practice of mutual admonition within the churches concerning marriage and divorce. Members of Christian churches too frequently regard these matters simply as private matters, as "no one else's business." Personal responsibility is not to be disowned, but it is to be exercised in Christian community, attentive to the voices of the community attentive to Scripture.

Scripture is not a timeless code for marriage and divorce, but in Christian community it is somehow the rule of our individual lives and of our common life. We set the stories of our lives, including the stories of our singleness and of our marriages, alongside the story of Scripture to be judged, challenged, formed, re-formed, and sanctified. Fidelity to this text and to its story does not require (or permit) us to read Mark (or any other particular text) like a timeless moral code. We do not live in Mark's community (or in Matthew's or Paul's), but we do live in memory of Jesus, and we test our lives and our readings for fidelity. Fidelity requires creativity. And creativity licenses the formation of rules and judgments concerning divorce that need not be identical to Matthew's concession or Paul's, but that respect both the vows of marriage and the partners of a marriage, safeguard both the delight and the vulnerability of sexuality, protect vulnerable partners, and honor God's creative and redemptive intentions.

So, for example, in a world such as this—still, sadly, not yet God's good future—although divorce is never to be celebrated as a good in itself or as a way God's good future makes its power felt, a Christian community may acknowledge that divorce sometimes may be necessary to protect either marriage itself or one of the marriage partners. For example, it might (and perhaps should, given God's promise to protect the weak and defend the humiliated) permit divorce in cases of abuse. Or, taking a cue from the just-war tradition, the Christian community might insist that divorce be "a last resort." Fidelity to Scripture and to its story surely does require a disposition not to divorce, even when the law (or a self-interested and patriarchal reading of the law) would permit it. It chastens any effort to read the text of Deuteronomy or the texts of Matthew and Paul as if they provide easily accessible justifications for divorce.

Divorce should not be the last word, not even of this article. Let the last word rather be a celebration of marriage as God's gift, a celebration of a covenant that is a fit analogy for God's faithful love, a celebration at a wedding at Cana of Galilee long ago (John 2:1–11). "Let marriage be held in honor by all" (Heb. 13:4).

See also Adultery; Asceticism; Celibacy; Homosexuality; Polygamy; Sex and Sexuality

Bibliography

Hays, R. *The Moral Vision of the New Testament: Community, Cross, New Creation; A Contemporary Introduction to New Testament Ethics*. HarperSanFrancisco, 1996, 347–78; Sampley, J. *And the Two Shall Become One Flesh: A Study of Traditions in Ephesians 5:21–33*. SNTSMS 16. Cambridge University Press, 1971. Verhey, A. *Remembering Jesus: Christian Community, Scripture, and the Moral Life*. Eerdmans, 2002, 212–42; Witte, J., Jr. *From Sacrament to Contract: Marriage, Religion, and Law in the Western Tradition*. Westminster John Knox, 1997.

Allen Verhey

Martyrdom

Martyrdom refers to being put to death for one's belief in God. The root word of *martyrdom*, Greek *martys*, originally meant "witness," in the sense of one who testifies before a court. *Martys* occurs throughout the NT, but only a handful of cases refer to a witness who dies (Acts 22:20; Rev. 1:5; 2:13; 3:14; 11:3; 17:6). The first Christian work that clearly uses "martyr" (and "martyrdom") to refer to someone who dies for the faith is *Martyrdom of Polycarp*, around 150 CE. Thus, the concept of dying for God or faith predates the development of the more specific terminology of martyrdom.

The biblical message about martyrdom is not univocal. Although the OT does not overtly encourage martyrdom, it presents those who die for their faithfulness, from Abel to Zechariah, in a sympathetic manner. The Second Temple texts 1–2 Maccabees recount the deaths of Jewish believers under Antiochus Epiphanes with a reverence that inspires imitation (see especially 2 Macc. 6–7). In the NT, martyrdom is presented in a variety of ways. First, Jesus' sacrificial death on the cross serves as the prototype and impetus for later suffering and death on account of one's faith. Jesus' teaching about martyrdom is more practical than theological; he foresees martyrdom as a probability for his closest disciples (Matt. 24:9–13; Mark 13:9–13; Luke 21:12–19) and a possibility for his other followers (Matt. 16:24–28; Mark 8:34–38).

Several NT writers depict martyrdom positively, exalting the deaths of faithful forerunners (including Jesus) to encourage perseverance under persecution (1 Thess. 2:14–16; cf. Heb. 11; Jas. 1:2–4; 1 Pet. 2:19–25; Rev. 1:5; 6:9–11; 11:1–13; 20:4). Paul also reflects a more cautious view of martyrdom in his Letter to the Philippians when he contemplates dying but decides that remaining alive would benefit them more greatly (Phil. 1:21–26).

Since the earliest years of the church, Christians under persecution have struggled with ethical questions such as these: Should a Christian seek martyrdom? Should martyrs receive special rewards for their sacrifices? Ignatius, a second-century bishop, believed so fervently that dying for God would help him "attain to God" that he pleaded for Roman believers not to impede his death so he might become a true disciple through martyrdom (Ign. *Rom.* 2). Although the Bible does not explicitly encourage the pursuit of martyrdom or promise greater rewards to those who die for their faith, the descriptions of martyrs as blessed (cf. Matt. 5:10–11) and reigning with Christ (Rev. 20:4) have fueled questionable ethical practices throughout church history, such as the cultic veneration of martyrs and the zealous pursuit of martyrdom. However, interpreting the biblical message about martyrdom as situational encouragement for believers under persecution rather than as universal example or promise of reward will allow the church to faithfully maneuver through the ethical dilemmas raised throughout the history of Christian martyrdom.

See also Ars Moriendi Tradition, Use of Scripture in; Cruciformity; Faith; Suffering

Bibliography

Castelli, E. *Martyrdom and Memory: Early Christian Culture Making*. Columbia University Press, 2004; Droge, A., and J. Tabor. *A Noble Death: Suicide and Martyrdom among Christians and Jews in Antiquity*. HarperSanFrancisco, 1992; Frend, W. H. C. *Martyrdom and Persecution in the Early Church: A Study of a Conflict from the Maccabees to Donatus*. Blackwell, 1965.

Jennifer Garcia Bashaw

Masturbation *See* Sexual Ethics

Materialism

The word *materialism* admits a variety of meanings. In philosophical terms, materialism can refer to the belief that matter is all that exists. In Marxist analyses of history the phrase "historical materialism" has a particular nuance, identifying the ultimate cause and driving force of human events to be economic in nature. In ethical discourse, however, materialism refers to the notion that the accumulation (and perhaps the display) of material resources is an ideal pursuit. To say that an individual or a culture is materialistic is to say that either is unduly consumed with the quest for material goods.

The Scriptural Witness

In general, the biblical tradition is thoroughly positive in its assessment of material existence, for the writers of Scripture frequently emphasize the goodness of the material world. In the creation narrative that opens the book of Genesis, for example, God's delight in the material world is accentuated by the oft-repeated phrase "it was good" (*kî-ṭôb*) as a summary for God's own reaction to the work of creation (Gen. 1:4, 10, 12, 18, 21, 25; cf. in Gen. 1:31 the emphatic *wĕhinnēh-ṭôb* ["it was very good"]). God's call of Abram in Gen. 12 includes an implied promise of land (Gen. 12:1–3), and the struggle to claim this blessing becomes a central motif in the unfolding story of Israel (cf. Gen. 17:1–8; 26:2–5; 35:9–12; Deut. 1:8; Josh. 23:1–16). The promised land is frequently identified as a "land flowing with milk and honey," a phrase that emphasizes the fruitful life that the people of God will enjoy through God's blessing (e.g., Exod. 3:8; Lev. 20:24; Num. 13:27; Deut. 6:3). Yet the affirmative perspective on material existence in the OT is by no means limited to the creation accounts and Israel's possession of land. With an emphasis on the cosmic dimensions of material existence, on the one hand, several psalms extol the handiwork of God in nature, reflecting an appreciation of the natural world and highlighting the extent to which the earth and all that is within it display the glory of God (e.g., Pss. 8:3–9; 19:1–6; 104). On the other hand, Song of Songs offers a narrower perspective on the joy of material existence through its reflection on the pleasure of physical love between a man and a woman.

This positive estimation of the material world continues in the NT. Jesus' proclamation and embodiment of the kingdom of God—seen in exorcisms, healings, and the supply of food for the hungry, among many miraculous demonstrations of divine power—includes both physical restoration and the provision of material resources (see Matt. 12:28 // Luke 11:20). Moreover, Jesus teaches his disciples to pray for daily bread (Matt. 6:11 // Luke 11:3), and his death is commemorated by his earliest followers through the celebration of a common meal (1 Cor. 11:17–34; cf. Mark 14:22–26 pars.). Indeed, from a theological perspective, the doctrine of the incarnation itself is a radical affirmation of material existence. The Christian claim that the advent of Jesus represents "the Word become flesh" (John 1:14) stands at odds with any docetic or gnostic rejection of the physical world as inherently tainted by sin. Not surprisingly, the biblical canon as a whole is punctuated with an eschatological vision of the new heaven and the new earth (Rev. 21–22), a picture of the beauty of material existence that stands in deep continuity with the OT stress on God as creator of the world.

Yet in spite of this characteristically affirmative outlook on the goodness of the material world, the Bible consistently maintains that it is the Creator, not the creation, that is worthy of human worship and allegiance. Since the accumulation of possessions offers the temptation to trust in one's own resources rather than in God, who is the source of all things, materialism in Scripture is often associated with idolatry. Moreover, since the biblical tradition strongly highlights the extent to which material resources are to be used to provide for the needs of others, materialism in Scripture is also frequently connected with economic injustice.

Materialism and idolatry. In both Testaments—to say nothing of noncanonical Jewish and Christian literature from the ancient world—there is often a close relationship between the accumulation of possessions and idolatry. At a basic level, both materialism and the worship of foreign gods involve focused attention on objects made of silver and gold, elements often associated with idol worship in the OT (Deut. 29:17; Pss. 115:4; 135:15; Isa. 2:7–8, 20; Jer. 10:1–5; Ezek. 7:19; Dan. 5:23; 11:8; Hos. 8:4; Philo, *Spec. Laws* 1.22–23). More substantively, materialism is associated with idolatry because the powerful and the wealthy are more prone to trust in themselves rather than God. Numerous biblical texts warn against the dangers of placing one's confidence in riches as opposed to the faithful Creator. With reference to the assessment of evildoers by the righteous, Ps. 52:7 makes the point explicitly, for the righteous will declare, "See the one who would not take refuge in God, but trusted in abundant riches, and sought refuge in wealth!" (cf. Ps. 49:6; Prov. 11:28). Similarly, Prov. 18:10–11 employs the metaphor of the name of the Lord as a strong tower that stands in contrast to "the wealth of the rich [which] is their strong city." Conversely, the poor have an advantage over the rich in that those of lesser means are more apt to trust in God (Pss. 9:18; 14:6; 22:26; 40:17; 68:10; Isa. 66:2).

This theme is continued in the NT. For example, in the parable of the rich fool, Jesus warns against the foolishness of material hoarding and the dangers of economic autonomy: the man's plans to "relax, eat, drink, and be merry" from his abundance are thwarted when his life is taken from him (Luke 12:16–21). Jesus himself exhibits a dependence on God that leads him to a kind of itinerant homelessness (Matt. 8:20 // Luke 9:58), and he charges his disciples to engage in missional activity with minimal resources (Mark 6:7–11 // Matt. 10:1–16 // Luke 9:1–5). Greed is labeled as idolatry in two NT vice lists (Eph. 5:3–5; Col. 3:5–9). The notion that possessions threaten trust in God is stated most directly in 1 Tim. 6:17–19, a passage that challenges the wealthy to depend on God instead of the uncertainty of material abundance: "As for those who in the present age are rich, command them not to be haughty, or to set their hopes on the uncertainty of riches, but rather on God who richly provides us with everything for our enjoyment. They are to do good, to be rich in good works, generous, and ready to share, thus storing up for themselves the treasure of a good foundation for the future, so that they may take hold of the life that really is life" (cf. Matt. 6:19–21 // Luke 12:33–34). Several verses earlier, in 1 Tim. 6:10, Paul reminds Timothy that materialism produces evil and is a danger for faith: "For the love of money [*philarguria*] is a root of all kinds of evil, and in their eagerness to be rich some have wandered away from the faith and pierced themselves with many pains" (cf. Heb. 13:5–6).

Materialism and injustice. The text of 1 Tim. 6:17–19 points toward another sense in which materialism is problematic from a biblical perspective: the desire for and the accumulation of possessions works against the ideals of communal sharing and social justice. The tenth commandment, for example, prohibits coveting as a violation against the covenant community (Exod. 20:17); this summary commandment proscribes an attitude that might lead to a breach of any or all of the other nine commandments. Material goods are not ends in themselves, but rather should be employed wisely and generously to provide assistance to the marginalized.

Many biblical writers link the pursuit of prosperity with oppression of the needy. Israel's prophets often assert that the wealth of the ruling elite has come at the expense of the poor (e.g., Isa. 3:14–17; 10:1–2; Jer. 2:34; Amos 2:6–8; 4:1; 8:4–6; Zech. 7:9–11). Also in the NT is the accumulation of possessions coupled with economic injustice. The book of James is perhaps most direct in this accusation: "Come now, you rich people, weep and wail for the miseries that are coming to you. Your riches have rotted, and your clothes are moth-eaten. . . . You have condemned and murdered the righteous one, who does not resist you" (Jas. 5:1–2, 6 [cf. Luke 6:24]). Similarly, Rev. 17–18, with its image of Rome as a whore, offers a profound critique of the exploitative character of the Roman imperial economy. Part of what makes Rome a harlot, the author suggests, is that she dresses luxuriously (cf. Rev. 17:4 with 18:16) by using others for her own economic benefit. In the list of imported luxuries in Rev. 18:11–13 is a depiction of Rome as the ultimate consumer city, the port of destination for these opulent goods traded by merchants. That the final item on the list of imported goods is tragically described as "human beings sold as slaves" (TNIV) is to be seen as a protest against the dehumanizing nature of the imperial consumption, and it is this economy that readers are warned to "come out of" earlier in the chapter (Rev. 18:4). Those who actively resist the temptations of this harlot may find themselves like the believers in Smyrna: materially poor yet spiritually rich (Rev. 2:8–11).

The opposite of materialism, of course, is to employ possessions that God has provided for the benefit of others. Scripture is consistent in its affirmation that those with material wealth have a responsibility to share their resources with those of lesser means (e.g., Lev. 25:8–55; Deut. 14:22–29; 15:1–11). Other legal traditions in the OT highlight God's special concern for the marginalized. The prohibition in Exod. 22:25 against lending at interest to the poor, for example, is designed to protect the interests of the vulnerable, not to maximize profit for the lender. In the NT, the members of the early church seem frequently to have pooled resources for the purpose of assisting those in need (Acts 2:44–45; 4:32–35; 6:1–7; Phil. 4:10–20; Rom. 12:6–8). Paul's efforts to organize a financial contribution for impoverished believers in Jerusalem among the largely gentile congregations of his mission stand as an exemplary episode of mutual assistance within the nascent Christian church (1 Cor. 16:1–4; 2 Cor. 8:1–9:15; Rom. 15:25–32).

Contemporary Reflection

Studies show that many American Christians are acutely concerned about materialism (Wuthnow; Smith, Emerson, and Snell). Yet most of those same believers are also participants in a consumerist economic system that stands in serious tension with the witness of Scripture. Studies of charitable practices and spending behaviors among American believers inspire little confidence that the church is winning the battle against materialism: on average, American Christians give somewhere around 3 percent or less of (pretax) income to religious and charitable causes. The power of advertising, the pressure to conform to consumptive spending practices, the temptation to find happiness and security in material possessions—all these offer significant challenges to those who want to affirm, with Scripture, the goodness of the material world and yet do not desire to bow down at the altar of mammon. With the rise of laissez-faire capitalism as the dominant global economic system, these challenges have perhaps become even more daunting.

The worldwide financial crisis of 2008 unfortunately illustrates the difficult nature of the problem. The international economic meltdown was caused by any number of factors: excessively negligent governmental regulation of financial markets; mass consumer greed; unscrupulous and predatory lending practices; overspending in both the private and public sectors. Yet at least in the United States recommendations to emerge from the recession were pinned, to a significant degree, on the return of consumer spending. This was hardly an environment conducive to the questioning, let alone the avoidance, of materialism.

The church is called to embody a faith that denies the world's claim that the accrual of material possessions is an ideal pursuit. Christian ethics must maintain a balance between an affirmation of the goodness of the material world and a willingness to critique the idolatrous and greedy accumulation of material goods.

See also Capitalism; Consumerism; Economic Ethics; Greed; Idolatry; Wealth

Bibliography

Hudnut-Beumler, J. *In Pursuit of the Almighty's Dollar: A History of Money and American Protestantism*. University of North Carolina Press, 2007; Murove, M. "Moving beyond Dehumanization and Greed in the Light of African Economic Ethics—A Statement." *R&T* 15 (2008): 74–96; Rosner, B. *Greed as Idolatry: The Origin and Meaning of a Pauline Metaphor*. Eerdmans, 2007; Sider, R. *Rich Christians in an Age of Hunger*. 5th ed. Thomas Nelson, 2005; Smith, C., M. Emerson, and P. Snell. *Passing the Plate: Why American Christians Don't Give Away More Money*. Oxford University Press, 2008; Wuthnow, R., ed. *Rethinking Materialism: Perspectives on the Spiritual Dimension of Economic Behavior*. Eerdmans, 1995.

David J. Downs

Matthew

The author of the Gospel of Matthew is anonymous. The author does not appear in the text but in a later title. Scholars generally consider this Gospel a third-generation witness to Jesus that includes among its sources the Gospel of Mark and a sayings source known as Q. This view has led some to attempt to isolate material from the historical Jesus or from developments between Jesus and Matthew as sources for ethics. For example, some have concluded that Jesus opposed divorce, but Matthew contains a development whereby divorce is forbidden "except for adultery." Recognizing the narrative nature of Matthew, however, other scholars have shifted their emphasis to the Gospel's final form as a source for ethics. Still there are multiple approaches to how Matthew serves the enterprise of ethics. This article deals particularly with extracting principles, imitating role models, the hermeneutics of suspicion, character formation, and deriving ethics from a relationship with God.

One approach is grounded in the commandments to love God and neighbor, because "on these two commandments hang all the law and the prophets" (22:40). As central as the two commandments are, they point to Scripture as a whole ("all the law and the prophets"). Thus, they are part of a grand plot reaching back to Abraham in which God makes promises, such as blessing all the people of the earth, and acts to keep these promises alive.

Conventionally, the double "love commandment" is supplemented with Jesus' teachings, especially the Sermon on the Mount, parables, and direct commands. A long tradition takes the Beatitudes (5:3–12) as exhortations, although no imperatives occur until 5:12: "Rejoice and be glad" (in the midst of opposition). The outcome is a love ethic, an intensification of the law (e.g., broadening the interpretation of murder), and specific instructions on things such as divorce, with the assumption that Jesus' sayings interpret God's unchanging will.

Another approach takes characters as role models. This is reflected in the popular platitude "What would Jesus do?" On the one hand, Jesus demonstrates living under God's rule. The same is true of other characters, such as the Canaanite woman (15:22–28). But ordinarily the characters are too flawed to be role models. After Peter confesses Jesus as the Messiah and Son of God, for example, he plays a satanic role (16:13–23). But this case also shows that the norms of the narrative enable readers to distinguish Peter's appropriate from his inappropriate praxis. On the other hand, to make Jesus a role model presents readers with unattainable challenges (teacher, healer, divine agent). Further, Matthew's Jesus repeatedly surprises. What would Jesus do? Matthew's readers should probably confess, "We cannot say, because he would surprise us."

A hermeneutics of suspicion asks if Matthew's rhetoric may be a part of sustaining injustices. Does Matthew give a derogatory portrayal of the Jews (e.g., 27:25)? Are women portrayed passively, and is their prominence among the followers of Jesus suppressed (e.g., 10:2–4)?

Such approaches tend to isolate commandments, God's will, role models, and suspicious perspectives from the framework of God's reign. Matthew establishes this framework early. It appears in the proclamation of John the Baptist (3:2). Then 4:17 is programmatic: "From that time Jesus began to proclaim, 'Repent, for the kingdom of heaven has come near.'" Henceforth, Jesus proclaims God's kingdom. When he begins the Sermon on the Mount nine verses later, he is interpreting God's kingdom. If the Beatitudes are taken as exhortations, they no longer reflect instances of God's rule, and rather than the outcome of God's rule, they become conditions for entering God's kingdom.

The communal nature of these relationships is an important part of several approaches to ethics in Matthew, including character ethics. Character ethics holds that the community's use of Scripture shapes the character of people who are nurtured in its life. Someone steeped in Matthew's story will likely have an orientation toward life quite distinct from the prevailing culture.

Another option is that Matthew mediates encounters with God out of which the community lives. For these relationships Matthew uses particularly kinship language: a "Father" in relationship with children who are brothers and sisters. Agricultural metaphors also reflect these relationships ("trees bearing fruit"). Beginning with these relationships means that ethics in Matthew is not merely determining appropriate praxis but is preeminently a matter of the source, motivation, and empowerment for living. When God is the source, motivation, and empowerment, living appropriately is the fruit of God's rule. For example, when God is parent, God's children love their enemies (5:45).

In several cases Matthew speaks of "righteousness" (*dikaiosynē*). On the one hand, this means a right relationship with God, and its other side is ethics. But English poses difficulties in representing *dikaiosynē*, because it also means "justice." So seeking *dikaiosynē* also means seeking justice. Additionally, seeking justice alone may be inadequate. Joseph, on the basis of justice (1:19), wishes to put Mary away quietly. His motivation is not deficient, but his understanding of God's purposes is, and so he intends to act at cross-purposes with God. Consequently, God informs Joseph what the divine purposes are. Thus, God's rule is not only the motivation or empowerment for praxis but also a source beyond what may be written. Because ethical praxis depends on God, ethics remains open to God's future.

Finally, justice has a particularly acute meaning in the context of the Roman Empire, which claimed to have established justice in the world. Imperial rule operated through collaboration of client kings and local elites, such as Herodian rulers and the Judean council. For Matthew, the rule of God is an alternative to this system that Rome called justice.

See also Anti-Semitism; Beatitudes; Imitation of Jesus; Kingdom of God; Love, Love Command; New Testament Ethics; Sermon on the Mount

Bibliography

Burridge, R. *Imitating Jesus: An Inclusive Approach to New Testament Ethics*. Eerdmans, 2007; Carter, W. *Matthew and the Margins: A Sociopolitical and Religious Reading*. Orbis, 2000; Fowl, S., and L. Jones. *Reading in Communion: Scripture and Ethics in Christian Life*. Eerdmans, 1991; Hays, R. *The Moral Vision of the New Testament: Community, Cross, and New Creation; A Contemporary Introduction to New Testament Ethics*. HarperSanFrancisco, 1996; Wink, W. *Engaging the Powers: Discernment and Resistance in a World of Domination*. Fortress, 1992.

Robert L. Brawley

Media, Ethical Issues of

The term *media* refers to a wide range of instruments used in mass communication, including newspapers, books, magazines, radio, television, cinema, audio recordings, video games, and the ever-expanding resources of the internet (e.g., the world wide web, email, and social networking sites). Collectively, these instruments use words and/or images to inform, educate, entertain, and shape individuals and groups, with each instrument capable of serving multiple and sometimes conflicting purposes. As instruments of mass communication, these resources are inherently connectional; they bring those responsible for their creation, production, distribution, regulation, and use into contact with one another, regularly placing them at cross-purposes with one another. And all this occurs within larger sociocultural and political-economic systems that both shape and are shaped by the media and its uses, making the instruments of media both highly visible cultural artifacts (and therefore open to cultural analysis, as per the work of the Frankfurt school or Marshall McLuhan, for instance) and significant shapers of culture (and therein useful as tools for cultural analysis). Given the ranges of instruments, purposes, persons, and contexts involved, the variety of ethical issues associated with the media is almost endless, and the responsibilities and values that pertain in one context may bear either no relation or sit in diametric opposition to the responsibilities and values that pertain in another. Complexity rules the day.

Given this complexity, it is remarkable how little explicit attention is given to the ethical issues that come up with regard to the media, especially within the context of religious ethics. This is due, in part, to the capacity of the various agents connected to the media to self-police and thereby to gain the credibility associated with self-regulating professions such as medicine or law. It is due, in part, to a complex set of laws and regulatory agencies that oversee the various instruments of mass communication. It is due, in part, to the difficulties of reflexivity—that is, of using media instruments to explore and describe the ethical issues associated with the media. And, probably most significantly, it is due to a diffused set of culturally shaped tacit understandings between the creators and users of media instruments about those instruments and their use. We expect, for instance, supermarket tabloids, leading newspapers, historical fiction novels, and television docudramas to maintain different relationships to (and even understandings of) truthfulness. Or we imagine that images of violence as portrayed by the evening news, the latest video game, and an action-adventure movie are likely to have different formative impacts on the minds of younger viewers. Indeed, many of the most visible debates about ethics in the media occur when one of these tacit understandings seems to have been violated. Whether these are also the most significant debates about ethics in the media is a different and much more complicated question.

In Western cultures, ethical issues in the media tend to congeal around several dominant debates. These include the following:

- *The right to privacy versus the right to know.* Manifestations of this debate include arguments about access to government and military documents or plans (some of which may contain sensitive, confidential, or classified information); access to the private lives of public persons (as when paparazzi attempt to get unguarded pictures of celebrities for publication); and the public broadcasting or representation of private and/or secret ceremonies, decontextualizing them and draining deeply significant symbols of their meaning.
- *Freedom of speech versus the effect of objectionable or manipulative materials on (often vulnerable) audiences.* Are there particular

types and degrees of censorship that are appropriate with regard to the distribution and display of materials that are pornographic, violent, or reinforcing of stereotypes? If so, how are these determined, and by whom? Should the creation or display of some materials (e.g., pornography involving minors) be prohibited regardless of who sees it? Should there be restrictions on whom advertisers attempt to reach or how they attempt to reach audiences (e.g., in the use of data mining by internet search engines)?

- *Journalistic rights versus journalistic responsibilities.* What rights do journalists have to keep their sources secret or to be protected when reporting from dangerous settings? Do they have corresponding responsibilities to share sources or information where lives or property may be at risk? Whose responsibility are journalists who either embed themselves with military groups or freelance in violent areas? How much deception is appropriate on the part of journalists in attempts to get a story? And does the advent of the 24/7 news cycle (the "CNN effect") inevitably blur the line between responsible reporting and sensationalism?
- *Objectivity versus bias.* Although audiences expect (and may even insist on) bias when some media sources explore controversial topics, they also expect objectivity in presenting multiple perspectives on those topics by other media sources. Questions arise, though, when those audiences' perspectives shape their various senses on what counts as "objective," when media sources choose to report only some pieces of agreed-upon data, or when media sources mix attempts to inform an audience with attempts to persuade that same audience. And what is the media's responsibility to name or convey all the perspectives on a given topic even if some of those perspectives are held by only a very few people on the basis of convictions that are not, themselves, objectively discernible?
- *Economic considerations versus social welfare.* It has become a truism that a free press (i.e., one that is not controlled by external state forces) is essential to create and maintain an informed public. Yet media organs are expensive to run and generally are for-profit enterprises; as such, they have the responsibility to shape their programming according to the good of their shareholders and the desires of the market. The tensions between economic and social considerations express themselves in the use of advertising that not only displays but also shapes markets; in media outlets buying stories or bribing sources to get stories; in the questioned right of the media, especially internet service providers, to restrict the information that their customers can access; in the power of media corporations to influence regulatory agencies or favor the perspectives of their stockholders; and in the social value of particular social groups, including religious groups, to develop and maintain separate media sources as alternatives to "mainstream media."

Each area of ethical concern, and indeed each topic within them, admits to different resources for exploration and resolution. These resources (e.g., obligations toward truth-telling, obedience to the civil law, concern for vulnerable populations) are as old as media itself and include significant religious and scriptural points of traction. Indeed, one growing set of methodological questions concerns the proper role(s) of religious voices speaking on cultural matters in pluralist societies, especially in light of how religion and religious voices often are the subjects of investigations by the media.

See also Accountability; Autonomy; Confidentiality; Deception; Globalization; Honesty; Information Technology; Libel; Manipulation; Privacy; Public Theology and Ethics; Slander; Social Contract; Truthfulness, Truth-Telling

Bibliography

Bittner, J. *Mass Communication*. 6th ed. Allyn & Bacon, 1996; Habermas, J. *The Theory of Communicative Action*. Trans. T. McCarthy. 2 vols. Beacon Press, 1985; Institute for Advanced Studies in Culture of the University of Virginia. "Politics and the Media." *The Hedgehog Review* 10, no. 2 (2008): 96–104; McLuhan, M. *Understanding Media: The Extensions of Man*. MIT Press, 1994; Postman, N. *Amusing Ourselves to Death: Public Discourse in the Age of Show Business*. Penguin Books, 1986; Silk, M. *Unsecular Media: Making News of Religion in America*. University of Illinois Press, 1998; Thayer, L. *Ethics, Morality, and the Media: Reflections on American Culture*. Hastings House, 1980.

Mark Douglas

Medical Ethics *See* Bioethics

Meekness

The biblical terms and concepts translated by the English word *meekness* can be summarized as submissive humility before a trustworthy, redeeming God, demonstrated through gentleness and kindness toward others. In contemporary usage, though, the word *meekness* has almost disappeared except as a pejorative describing those who are shy, fearful, or weak.

The word *meekness* translates the Greek *prautēs*, as in, for example, Jas. 1:21: "welcome with meekness [*prautēs*] the implanted word." The same concept is found in adjectival form in Matt. 21:5: "Look, your king is coming to you, humble [*praus*], and mounted on a donkey." The term is most famously used in the Beatitudes (Matt. 5:5) as a plural adjective describing those ready for the coming reign of God: "Blessed are the meek [*praeis*], for they will inherit the earth."

Matthew 5:5 is essentially a quotation from Ps. 37:11: "But the meek shall inherit the land" (cf. 37:29). These meek ones are contrasted sharply with the wicked, who prosper now but "will soon fade like the grass, and wither like the green herb" (37:2). This psalm is a response to the problem of evil, as seen from below—why the wicked prosper and the righteous have only "a little" (37:16). The psalmist's answer is that "soon" God will bring justice, and the meek will be vindicated.

The Hebrew root words that the LXX usually translates with "meek" and with "poor," "afflicted," and "humble" include *ʿānâ*, *ʿānî*, and *ʿānāw*. The term usually refers to the lowly, servants, social inferiors, the suffering, the poor, and the powerless. Psalm 37 makes the pivotal move of connecting material and social poverty with the posture of piety before God and linking (excessive?) prosperity with wickedness (cf. Matt. 5:3; Luke 6:20–26).

If the reference to meekness in the Beatitudes is an intentional echo of Ps. 37, Matt. 5:5 can be seen as an eschatological claim: the justice long promised to the righteous, trusting meek has now begun. That day in which God would vindicate the poor with justice is dawning through the work of Jesus.

It is interesting that God is never described as "meek" in the OT. However, Jesus describes himself as both "meek" (*praus*) and "humble in heart" in Matt. 11:29 (*praus* translated as "gentle" in the NRSV). This comforting word comes in the context of the invitation, "Come to me, all you that are weary and are carrying heavy burdens, and I will give you rest" (Matt. 11:28). Matthew quotes Zech. 9:9 to describe the nature of Jesus' kingly entry into Jerusalem (Matt. 21:5). Both the humility and afflictions suffered by Jesus culminate at the cross.

Jesus, the God-man, therefore redefines divinity by embracing meekness, embodies the eschatological promise in which justice comes to the pious meek, and calls forth a community characterized by meekness before God and gentle kindness toward neighbor (see Gal. 5:22–23; 6:1; Eph. 4:2; Col. 3:12; Jas. 1:21; 3:13, 17; 1 Pet. 3:15).

See also Beatitudes; Eschatology and Ethics; Humility; Sermon on the Mount

Bibliography

Good, D. *Jesus the Meek King*. Trinity Press International, 1999.

David P. Gushee

Mennonite Ethics *See* Anabaptist Ethics

Mental Health

The concept of mental health is complex and open to numerous interpretations even within the same society. At one level, mental health can be defined simply as the absence of mental illness. This way of looking at mental health sits well with highly medicalized cultures such as those in the West. Mental illness is perceived as an identifiable "blemished spot" within an individual. The task of psychiatry is to identify that spot (diagnosis) and to use its particular techniques and technologies to restore the person to mental health (treatment). Problems arise with this definition for people with enduring forms of mental illness. Here such a definition of mental health means that whole groups of individuals are always and will always be perceived as mentally unhealthy and thus defined primarily as objects of treatments aimed at controlling symptoms of illness rather than as persons who have positive potential to grow and develop even in the midst of their illness.

Health as an Ideal

An alternative approach is to see mental health as an ideal concept. A good example of this approach is found in the World Health Organization's definition of health: "A state of complete physical, mental, and social well-being and not merely the absence of disease and infirmity." According to this definition, mental health is a holistic concept that is deeply tied in with physical and social health. As such, it is an ideal concept that pertains to the perfect health of whole persons in the whole of their worlds. This definition seems to overcome the deficits in the medical model's approach by opening health in general and mental health in particular to a more person-centered perspective that locates whole persons within the fullness of their lives. However, there are dangers with such an ideal formulation of mental health. First, according to this definition everybody is and always will be unhealthy. If the medical approach tends to enforce a state of permanent ill health on people with long-term mental health problems, the ideal approach does the same thing, this time for all people. No one has complete health in the way the definition describes; health is always an ideal that one is striving toward but can never be achieved. This observation resonates deeply with inflated expectations of Western systems of care for mental health. Recent advancements in medical technology and pharmacology, and the ever-increasing interest in counseling and psychotherapy, have given the impression that absolute health in general and mental health in particular are not only an aspiration, but also technically possible. Because it is perceived as possible, perfect health is assumed to be the right of every person. However, the natural limitations of medicine and psychiatry mean that such ideals and aspirations remain unachievable.

Perhaps more important, where absolute health becomes an absolute value, there is a danger that health and a model of ideal humanity become inextricably intertwined and confused. If to be fully human becomes equated with being totally healthy, in this idealist sense, then any health deficit will be understood as a deficit of personhood. This becomes particularly dangerous in forms of mental illness that are highly stigmatized (schizophrenia or dementia) and within which questions around the nature of personhood become crucial.

The Recovery Movement

An important recent development within conversations about mental health comes from the Recovery Movement. This movement was initiated by people experiencing mental health problems who wanted to push against understandings of mental health that alienated and excluded people with enduring forms of mental illness. Within the recovery model of mental health, the focus is on the person in the context of the whole of one's life. Mental health is not measured by the presence or absence of mental illness; the criterion is not the absence of symptoms or the reduction of inpatient admissions. Rather, success is measured by how well a person is able to pursue the things that give purpose and meaning to life. It begins with the obvious but profound realization that people diagnosed with mental illness are first and foremost human beings. The task of the process of recovery and the movement toward mental health is to find ways to move toward living fully as a human being even in the midst of serious mental illness. This movement does not deny the pain and difficulty of mental illness. It simply states that it is possible to be healthy—that is, to pursue those goals that give meaning and purpose to life—even in the midst of mental illness.

Health as Shalom

How, then, might we understand mental health from the perspective of Christian theology? One way is by focusing on the biblical concept of *shalom*. *Shalom* is perhaps the closest match we have in Scripture to our contemporary word *health*. The Hebrew term *šālôm* occurs more than two hundred times in the OT. The basic meaning of this word is "peace." However, throughout the OT, *šālôm* covers well-being in the widest sense of the word, and as such it means considerably more than simply the absence of war, anxiety, or distress. This peace is defined not by an absence, but rather by a presence.

The root meaning of the word *šālôm* is "wholeness, completeness, well-being." To be in *šālôm*—to be healthy—is to be in right relationship with God (Ps. 72:7; Isa. 32:17). The presence of illness is not what makes a person healthy or unhealthy; it is the presence of God that brings health. It is Yahweh himself who is the source and giver of *šālôm*. Indeed, one of the covenant names that Gideon used when he built his altar at Ophrah is "Yahweh is *shalom*" (*yhwh šālôm* [Judg. 6:24]). True *shalom*, then, comes in and from God. It is a gift rather than an achievement. To flourish in all of one's relationships is to find *shalom*; this is health in its mental and physical dimensions. *Shalom* has several secondary meanings, encompassing health, security, friendship, justice, prosperity, righteousness, and salvation, all of which are necessary for wholeness and well-being.

In the NT, we find a similar dynamic with regard to Jesus. In the same way as in the OT "Yahweh is *shalom*," so also the apostle Paul informs his readers in Eph. 2:14 that Jesus is *shalom*. This assertion that *shalom* is a common purpose of the Trinity becomes even more clear in the light of Gal. 5:22, where Paul asserts that the Spirit also is the bearer and sharer of *shalom*. It is important to notice throughout that *shalom* is not a distant utopian ideal. *Shalom* is a person. *Shalom* is not a political ideal, a sociological movement, or a medical possibility. *Shalom* is a personal gift from a relational God to his fallen creation. The concept of *shalom* therefore is seen to be both a goal and a holistic process that is initiated and sustained by God as God seeks to deal with the relational alienation of creation.

Mental Health as Shalom

Focusing on the concept of *shalom* allows us to draw what is good from the medical, idealist, and recovery models but also goes some way toward overcoming their shortcomings. Mental health as *shalom* certainly includes the quest for alleviating symptoms and minimizing distress. As such, it includes the need for psychiatry, psychotherapy, and pharmacology. However, it places these disciplines under the service of God. In other words, the idea of mental health as *shalom* requires that those techniques and practices used by healthcare practitioners be sanctified and grafted into God's *shalom*. This puts contemporary practices of care for mental health in a different frame. For example, the primary goal of symptom control ceases to be viewed simply as a movement away from illness toward health; rather, in line with the goals of the Recovery Movement, it is now framed as a way of enabling people to flourish in their relationships with God, self, and others. Medication and therapy now have spiritual rather than simply therapeutic goals.

The recovery approach might be criticized for focusing on self-actualization and a search for meaning and purpose that is vague and open. If we shift into a theological frame, we are able to take the basic principles and align them within a context that focuses on God. Now mental health is determined by the presence or absence of relationships with God, self, and others. Recovery is now perceived as discovering who one is in God and in community even in the midst of long-term mental illness within which a person can learn to live well. The ideal becomes, to an extent, attainable now and in the future.

Understood from this theological perspective, mental health, at least for Christians, requires an interdisciplinary approach wherein all of the mental health professions can come together to enable a person to experience and to live in *shalom*. Mental health, then, is that process of learning to live well with God even in the midst of the most difficult of mental illness.

See also Health; Healthcare Ethics; Healthcare Systems in Scripture

Bibliography

Aggleton, P. *Health*. Routledge, 1990; Barth, K. *Church Dogmatics* Vol. III/4. Ed. G. Bromiley and T. Torrance. T&T Clark, 1961; Brueggemann, W. *Living toward a Vision: Biblical Reflections on Shalom*. United Church Press, 1976; Deegan, P. "Recovery: The Lived Experience of Rehabilitation." *Psychosocial Rehabilitation Journal* 11, no. 4 (1988): 11–19; Moltmann, J. *God in Creation: An Ecological Doctrine of Creation*. SCM, 1985, 271–75; Swinton, J. *From Bedlam to Shalom: Towards a Practical Theology of Human Nature, Interpersonal Relationships and Mental Health Care*. Peter Lang, 2000; Wilkinson, J. *Health and Healing: Studies in New Testament Principles and Practice*. Handsell Press, 1980; World Health Organization. "Constitution of the World Health Organization, Annex I." Pages 459–72 in *The First Ten Years of the World Health Organization*. World Health Organization, 1958.

John Swinton

Mental Illness *See* Mental Health

Mercy

Mercy is relenting pity demonstrated when one could harm or rightly punish another. Pardon, clemency, and other relief from cruelty or penalty often are identified as exercises of mercy.

Mercy in Scripture

The Hebrew words *raḥam* and *ḥûs* are most frequently translated as "mercy." In contrast to *ḥesed*, these terms connote a discrete surge of sympathy (Gen. 43:30; 1 Kgs. 3:26). The forcefulness and power asymmetry of *raḥam* are illustrated in Joseph's turbulent reaction to recognizing Benjamin (Gen. 43:30). The word *ḥûs* is also rendered as "pity" or "compassion" (Job 19:21).

Multiple OT sources announce the integration of mercy and wrath in God's justice (Exod. 34:6–7; cf. Num. 14:18; Neh. 9:17; Ps. 103:8; Jer. 32:18). On these accounts, mercy tracks God's assistance to trustworthy partners, openness to repentant offenders, and reluctance to utterly crush the human subjects of covenant justice. While anger calls attention to breaches of covenant, mercy performs mitigating and teleological functions in the administration of penalty.

Balancing mercy and punishment is a delicate act, however. Oriented toward the injured, mercy and judgment occupy complementary jurisdictions. Relief from cruelty entails active defeat of offending agents. In Mic. 6:8 human judges are expected to demonstrate impartial attention to the poor; mercy and justice are to be partners. Directed toward offenders, God's openness to repentance in the imposition of punishment seems to put mercy and judgment in conflict. Jonah's frustration with God's mercy to the repentant portrays mercy as a subtraction from desert (Jon. 4:2).

Similarly prizing integrative approaches, the NT writers follow the LXX in using the roughly synonymous terms *eleeō* and *oiktirmos* to translate both *raḥam* and *ḥesed*. *Splanchna* is also used, designating visceral emotional response.

Jesus shows mercy to those struck by illness, poverty, and demonic possession. The Synoptic writers self-consciously depict Jesus as fulfilling covenant promises, subsequently extending covenant boundaries beyond the Jewish people. Thus, when the diminished and possessed experience repair from

Jesus, it is counted as an eschatologically significant exercise of God's mercy (Matt. 10:41; Mark 5:19). The concomitant judgment against those who would prevent the afflicted from receiving God's mercy comports with the complementary scheme hinted at above. Reciprocity of mercy, under the threat of judgment, accordingly becomes a rule for community life (Matt. 6:14; Jas. 2:13).

Paul also uses covenantal imagery, especially in Romans, invoking God's free jurisdiction over his mercy to explain the Jewish rejection of Jesus (Exod. 33:19, quoted in Rom. 9:15). Emphasizing God's freedom highlights mercy's conflict with judgment and punishment. Arguing from God's redeeming work in Jesus, Paul charges the entire Christian community with the exercise of tender mercy (Phil. 2:1), while Jesus in Luke-Acts similarly extends the duty to act compassionately toward neighbors (Luke 10:37).

Mercy in Theology and Philosophy

Cultivation of mercy figures as a moral excellence across expressions of the Christian tradition. Latin Christianity favors a forensic model, emphasizing the victory of mercy over judgment. Eastern Orthodoxy focuses more on God's healing, interpreting mercy on integrative lines. Thomas Aquinas draws on an integrative model, resonating, some argue, in John Calvin. Martin Luther ties mercy with the churchly realm, assigning justice to the princely. Enlightenment moral sense theorists treat varieties of pity as morally crucial, while Immanuel Kant prioritizes desert, consigning mercy to the supererogatory.

In contemporary liberation theology, Jon Sobrino uses the parable of the good Samaritan to argue that a "principle of mercy" ought to ground Christian theology. In a complementary scheme for mercy and judgment, relief for the poor and judgment against their oppressors are primary for the church. Discussion of mercy has also been prominent in philosophy of punishment. Some argue that context sensitivity is reducible to robust justice; others resist equating justice with punishment. On a similar note, approaches using the concept of restorative justice recently have made progress in viability and sophistication. The relationship between mercy and justice remains a fecund site of investigation and argument, particularly in the relationship between religious traditions and legal theory.

See also Compassion; Empathy; Forgiveness; Grace; Law; Love, Love Command

Bibliography

Murphy, J. "Repentance, Punishment, and Mercy." Pages 143–70 in *Repentance: A Comparative Perspective*, ed. A. Etzioni and D. Carney. Rowman & Littlefield, 1997; Schweiker, W. "Criminal Justice and Responsible Mercy." Pages 181–205 in *Doing Justice to Mercy: Religion, Law, and Criminal Justice*, ed. J. Rothchild, M. Boulton, and K. Jung. University of Virginia Press, 2007; Sobrino, J. *The Principle of Mercy: Taking the Crucified People from the Cross*. Orbis, 1994; Stendahl, K. "Judgment and Mercy." Pages 147–54 in *The Context of Contemporary Theology: Essays in Honor of Paul Lehmann*, ed. A. McKelway and E. Willis. John Knox, 1974.

Christopher Dowdy

Micah

The book of Micah alludes to the specifics of societal oppression in singular ways, even as it expresses anger at such injustice in some of the most striking expressions of emotion in the prophetic literature. The heading (1:1) locates Micah in Judah in the eighth-century BCE during the time of Isaiah.

The exploitation of the vulnerable took the form of expropriating land (2:2, 8–9), deceit in the marketplace (6:10–12), and the perversion of justice by the powerful (3:9–10; 7:3). The prophet deplores the social violence (7:2), at one point likening the attitudes and actions of the leaders to stripping meat off the bone for soup (3:2–3). Leaders of all kinds, political and religious, were on the take (3:11). The prophets, who should have protested, preferred to give messages that their listeners craved (2:11; 3:5). The entire social and familial order had been contaminated (7:5–6).

As in other prophetic books, acceptable worship of God is inseparable from ethics. Idolatry was but one component of a misconstrued faith (1:5–7; 5:12–14). In a hypothetical exchange with the people, God exposes their obduracy. They believed that extravagant offerings could regain divine favor, but what the good God requires is this: "to do justice, and to love kindness, and to walk humbly with your God" (6:1–8).

The mention of the "good" in 6:8 points to the fact that God seeks a people of character who would manifest those ethical commitments toward others. Yet the leaders exhibit the very opposite of what God demanded. Therefore, in the broader national judgment that had been decreed, they are especially singled out for their personal transgressions and for leading the nation to ruin (2:3–5; 3:4, 12; 6:13–16; 7:4).

The book demonstrates that a passion for justice is accompanied by deep emotions. These emotions include righteous anger at injustice, expressed in powerful imagery (e.g., 3:2–3, 6–7), as well as profound pain at present suffering and at the horror that will be endured in the judgment. As he contemplated what was coming, Micah writhed in agony (1:8; 7:1) and hoped that the repentance of the people would be equally profound (1:10–16; 4:9–10). The assurance of his integrity and mission (3:8) was inseparable from a love for the nation, and this was grounded ultimately in God's compassion (7:18–20).

The recognition that this social world had earned divine condemnation is not the final prophetic word in Micah. It looks forward to national restoration (2:12–13; 4:6–8, 13; 5:3–9; 7:11–17) and offers a compelling pastoral image of peace (4:4–5).

See also Exploitation; Humility; Idolatry; Justice; Mercy; Old Testament Ethics

Bibliography

Brueggemann, W. *The Prophetic Imagination*. 2nd ed. Fortress, 2001; Carroll R., M. D. "A Passion for Justice and the Conflicted Self: Lessons from the Book of Micah." *JPsyC* 25, no. 2 (2006): 169–76; idem. "'He Has Told You What Is Good': Moral Formation in Micah." Pages 103–18 in *Character Ethics and the Old Testament: Scripture and Moral Life*, ed. M. D. Carroll R. and J. Lapsley. Westminster John Knox, 2007; Heschel, A. *The Prophets*. Harper & Row, 1962; Premnath, D. *Eighth Century Prophets: A Social Analysis*. Chalice, 2003.

M. Daniel Carroll R. (Rodas)

Military Service

Military service is one of the most divisive moral issues in Christianity. Throughout much of the OT, God is conceived as the leader of Israelite armed forces (Exod. 15:3). Soldiering is a religious task marked by ritual purity and lack of interest in the spoils of war. Soldiering is not, however, uncritically idealized in the OT. Even King David is, on one account, prevented from building the temple because of his participation in shedding blood in wars (1 Chr. 22:6–9).

The NT contains similar tensions. The Sermon on the Mount often is interpreted as pacifistic because of its emphasis on peacemaking and injunctions to turn the other cheek and to love one's enemy (Matt. 5:1–7:28). Jesus' renunciation of worldly rule, his acceptance of suffering in the crucifixion, and his rebuke of his disciples' use of the sword are also often cited as supporting a prohibition on Christian military service (Matt. 4:8–10; 16:21; 26:52–53). The NT does not, however, unambiguously condemn military service. Several NT texts present positive images of soldiers and omit any suggestion that converts are required to leave behind military vocations (Matt. 8:5–13; Mark 15:39; Luke 3:14; 7:1–10; Acts 10:1–18). Other texts, though not addressing Christian military service, suggest that earthly authorities should be respected as participating in God's providence (Rom. 13:1–7; 1 Pet. 2:13–17).

Early Christian positions on military service vary widely. Church fathers provide many reasons for opposing Christian military service: rejection of idolatrous military ceremonies, repugnance toward Rome, aversion to bloodshed, and adherence to the command of Christ. But some also found reasons to allow Christian support for the Roman military. Clement of Alexandria allowed military service at least for Christians at early stages in their spiritual development. Tertullian, though prohibiting direct military service for Christians, argued that Christians still were responsible Roman citizens because their prayers for "brave armies" and Roman stability advanced the interests of the empire (Holms 40).

As Christianity grew, Christians took on more responsibility for public order in the empire. From the mid-170s, evidence suggests that a significant number of Christians populated the Roman army. Eventually, a consensus developed around the acceptance of military service. Constantine's conversion often is seen as the watershed event in this development.

The primary challenge for those who defend Christian military service has been to articulate how the commands of the Sermon on the Mount fit within their positions. Some have argued that these commands, though valid in the eschaton, are not meant to be applied to contemporary history. Others have argued that these injunctions apply only to people acting as private citizens, that they hold only in cases of self-defense, or that these commands concern internal dispositions rather than outward action. Most Christian just-war thinkers have wished to maintain the command to love one's enemy and have argued that just-war obligations in some sense grow out of this requirement.

With notable exceptions during the Crusades, most who accept military service have also retained a prohibition on direct military service for Christian clergy. Reasons for this prohibition vary. Some claim that military service distracts from the "higher things" on which the clergy should be focused. Others have argued that participation in the spilling of blood detracts from the purity necessary to the delivery of the sacraments. In most cases, theologians have allowed indirect military service to clergy members, including service through prayer and participation in aiding wounded soldiers.

The Christian consensus on military service broke down with the rise of the Reformation.

Whereas Reformers such as Luther and Calvin continued the tradition of defending military service, Mennonites and Quakers came to reject Christian military participation. Given the endurance of this debate throughout the history of Christianity, Christians are likely to continue the argument into the foreseeable future.

See also Anabaptist Ethics; Just-Peacemaking Theory; Just-War Theory; Pacifism; Political Ethics; Sermon on the Mount; War

Bibliography

Biggar, N. "Specify and Distinguish! Interpreting the New Testament on 'Non-Violence.'" *SCE* 22 (2009): 185–98; Cahill, L. *Love Your Enemies: Discipleship, Pacifism and Just War Theory*. Fortress, 1994; Childress, J. "Moral Discourse about War in the Early Church." *JRE* 12 (1984): 2–18; Hays, R. *The Moral Vision of the New Testament: Community, Cross, and New Creation; A Contemporary Introduction to New Testament Ethics*. HarperSanFrancisco, 1996; Holms, A., ed. *War and Christian Ethics: Classic and Contemporary Readings on the Morality of War*. Baker Academic, 2005; Johnson, J. *The Quest for Peace: Three Moral Traditions in Western Cultural History*. Princeton University Press, 1987.

Kevin Carnahan

Moderation *See* Temperance

Money *See* Wealth

Monism, Anthropological

There are many kinds of monism. They are united by their attribution of oneness or singularity to some particular area of inquiry. For example, some philosophers have claimed that, despite appearances of plurality, there is really only one thing or substance—the universe or nature—manifesting itself in diverse ways. (Thus, in the seventeenth century, Benedict Spinoza defended a kind of monism in his *Ethics*, a work that today's readers would scarcely recognize as having anything to do with ethics as we know it.) In religion, monism is the view that there is but one God, despite the multiplicity of religions and despite that single Deity's manifold appearances across religions. With respect to anthropology, monism is the view that human beings are a unified, single entity—a view that amounts to a rejection of dualism, according to which human beings are joint entities consisting of body and soul (see, e.g., Corcoran; Murphy; van Inwagen).

Many erroneously identify monism (in all its permutations) with reductionism. Although there are many different kinds of reductionism (e.g., explanatory, theoretical, ontological, methodological), all are united in the claim that some higher-level entity or class of entities can be reduced to a more fundamental entity/entities or class of entities. For example, in the sciences some might claim that biology can be reduced to chemistry, and chemistry to physics. A kind of ontological reductionism might claim, for example, that consciousness and peculiarly mental phenomena can be reduced to and are nothing but neurophysiological phenomena.

With respect to anthropological monism, one might be a materialistic monist with respect to substance (i.e., human beings are one, wholly physical thing) but a nonreductionist with respect to consciousness and mental phenomena (i.e., consciousness, free will, and so on are irreducible to the neurophysiological phenomena from which they emerge) (see Murphy). Although it is conceivable and involves no logical inconsistency for one to be an immaterial monist (i.e., to claim that human beings are a single, immaterial soul that exemplifies physical properties), nearly all monists are in fact materialistic monists who assert that human beings are one, single, physical thing manifesting emergent mental properties.

The terms *holism* and *nonreductive physicalism* often are used to refer to the materialistic monism of the sort considered here. Central to nonreductive physicalism and holism is the notion of top-down causation. Put simply, top-down causation is the idea that higher-level properties or features of a system can causally affect lower-level features and components of that same system. In essence, this denies the claim that all a system's features and properties are determined by that system's most basic material constituents and thus amounts to a denial of reductionism. In anthropology, the idea has been employed to defend free will within the context of a materialistic monism, holism, or nonreductive physicalism. If you have ever considered whether it is the firing of neurons that made you perform some action or whether your decision to perform some action caused your neurons to fire in the first place, you have pondered the issue of top-down causation.

Free will and moral responsibility have been elements of Christian anthropology and ethics from its earliest days. To the extent that human moral responsibility requires free will (a claim that is contested by some [e.g., Pereboom]), reductionism must be denied. Therefore, to the extent that Christian philosophers and theologians want to defend materialistic anthropologies those anthropologies must be nonreductive in nature.

See also Body; Dualism, Anthropological; Humanity; Self

Bibliography

Corcoran, K. *Rethinking Human Nature: A Christian Materialist Alternative to the Soul.* Baker Academic, 2005; Murphy, N. *Bodies and Souls, or Spirited Bodies?* CIT. Cambridge University Press, 2006; Pereboom, D. *Living without Free Will.* CSP. Cambridge University Press, 2001; Spinoza, B. *Ethics.* Trans. W. White. Rev. A. Stirling. Wordsworth Editions, 2001; van Inwagen, P. *Material Beings.* Cornell University Press, 1995.

Kevin Corcoran

Monogamy *See* Marriage and Divorce

Moral Absolutes

An "absolute" ethical value carries the idea of something being good, or even obligatory, regardless of circumstances or anything that might be said against it. Thus, an absolute rule is one that we are obligated to follow, whatever the context or consequences. Many of the guidelines in Scripture are framed in absolutist terms—for example, the Ten Commandments. The Hebrews who first received the Mosaic law viewed it as a moral absolute, and deviation from these laws brought severe consequences for the offender (see Lev. 10:1–2; Deut. 4:1–14; 2 Sam. 6:6–7). At the same time, there are biblical instances of God blessing the efforts of people even when those efforts include otherwise forbidden actions such as lying—for example, the Hebrew midwives to the king of Egypt (Exod. 1:15–21) and Elisha to the Arameans (2 Kgs. 6:8–23).

Simple guidelines are useful for everyday living, and unqualified commands to perform (or refrain from performing) certain actions do serve this function. Still, Jesus emphasized that the moral worth of an action cannot be separated from the attitude that motivates the act. Note, for example, his reference to the Pharisees as "whitewashed tombs" (Matt. 23:26–28). Jesus' discussions of specific OT laws raise further questions about their status as moral absolutes. In commenting on the requirement to keep the Sabbath holy, he emphasized that its ultimate purpose was for human flourishing: "The sabbath was made for humankind, and not humankind for the sabbath" (Mark 2:27). Accordingly, the healing of a crippled woman, or even the well-being of an ox, takes precedence over the guideline to rest on the Sabbath (Luke 13:10–16).

Such contextualizing of biblical directives raises the question of which rules, if any, we should think of in absolute terms. We might identify very general guidelines that should govern our attitudes and actions without exception—for example, the commands to love God and neighbor (Mark 12:29–31). Also, prohibitions against certain, more specific actions—for example, rape, incest, torture of animals—seem absolute inasmuch as there are no imaginable contexts in which such actions might be linked to a greater good.

Other actions, such as killing, are less plausibly viewed as always wrong. For example, we would not ascribe moral blame to a pilot who ditches a plane in a rural farming community, thereby killing a number of residents, in order to avoid crashing into a more heavily populated city. In an attempt to account for this kind of action, while still maintaining a commitment to moral absolutes, one might return to very general principles (e.g., loving one's neighbor) and allow that the pilot rightly followed these general principles. Or, one might attempt to list all the specific criteria by which killing (which is sometimes permissible) is distinct from murder (which is never permissible). One then absolves the pilot of wrongdoing on the grounds that his or her actions did not meet the conditions for murder. However, in adopting this approach, which is common within debates on such issues as just war and euthanasia, the relevant question is not so much whether moral absolutes exist; rather, it is whether we can identify the relevant contextual considerations under which murder is to be distinguished from justifiable killing.

See also Deontological Theories of Ethics; Discernment, Moral; Intention; Moral Law; Norms; Right and Wrong

Bibliography

Geisler, N. *Christian Ethics: Options and Issues.* Baker, 1989; Ramsey, P. *Deeds and Rules in Christian Ethics.* Charles Scribner's Sons, 1967.

Kevin Kinghorn

Moral Agency

Moral agency is the ability to exercise responsibility in ethical decision-making—that is, to make decisions in the light of assumed or explicit ethical norms. According to much of Scripture, humans are moral agents because they are formed for relationship with God and with their neighbors.

In general, the broad outlines of two forms of moral agency can be discerned in the OT. In the first, persons are assumed to be capable of choosing the good and rejecting what is bad, whereas in the second, persons are depicted as incapable of choosing the good. Although both ways of thinking about moral agency are present in the OT, the first type is by far the more prevalent; in most texts people are assumed to be born with the capacity to choose the good. The second view, that people are born incapable of choosing the good, appears in a significant minority of texts. We will examine these two views in turn.

In the first type of moral agency, found in most of the extant traditions from ancient Israel (narrative, priestly, covenantal, prophetic, wisdom, etc.), not only are humans assumed to be capable of making reasoned choices and of being responsible for the choices they make but also they are relentlessly exhorted to act on that capacity by making choices that are morally responsible to God and to neighbor. This is transparent in the story of Gen. 2–3, which sets the canonically dominant pattern for moral agency. In part, the story expresses the writers' struggle to understand how humans developed into moral persons, how they came to inhabit the strange terrain of being both like other animals in their finitude and like God in their capacity for moral discernment. The story in the garden is concerned to show how humans came to possess their apparent freedom to make moral decisions—their moral agency—which in the writers' view is a characteristic peculiar to human beings, and also to show how fraught with consequences are human moral decisions.

The exact content of "good" and "bad" was left rather vague in Genesis. But once God has initiated the covenant with Israel at Sinai, ambiguity is, for the most part, swept away. Many traditions thus zealously urge that all choices be made in accordance with the revealed will of God (i.e., with Torah). Nowhere is this clearer than in the covenantal traditions of Deuteronomy and in prophetic calls to repentance, where the capacity to choose between obedience and disobedience is foregrounded. The basic picture of humans as capable of making, and indeed as being expected to make, moral decisions for the good and bearing responsibility for those decisions is thus pervasive in much of the OT. The emphasis on the human capacity to freely make choices that accord with the divine will, the urgency of the call to choose responsibly, and the gravity of the consequences of choosing rightly or wrongly—these characteristics pervade and are central to these Israelite traditions. In the normal course of reading, one is hardly aware of the anthropology that underlies these texts; the type of moral agency is so obvious and uncontested that most readers assume it.

Less prevalent but still present in the Bible are those materials that depict this version of moral agency as at least partially suppressed. In these texts, the idea that humans are inherently capable of discerning the good and choosing it comes under intense scrutiny, and sometimes it crumbles. The loss of human moral agency in these texts is often attended by a concomitant stress on God's initiative to effect human moral transformation (e.g., Jer. 31:31–34). This second, less common, type of moral agency is found in certain parts of the narrative traditions (Gen. 6:5), in traces of Deuteronomy (Deut. 30:6), a few penitential psalms (Pss. 51; 106), elements of the wisdom tradition (especially Proverbs), strands of Isaiah (especially Deutero-Isaiah), parts of Jeremiah (Jer. 13:23; 17:19), and especially parts of Ezekiel, in which the two types produce a considerable creative tension, mentioned below in a bit more detail.

On the one hand, human beings in the book of Ezekiel appear in a number of texts (chaps. 3; 14; 18; 33) as capable of orienting themselves to the good (Torah for Ezekiel); yet on the other hand, in some texts (e.g., chaps. 11; 16; 20; 23; 24:11–13) their capacity for moral agency is either implicitly or explicitly denied. Out of the conflict between these competing views Ezekiel fashions a third type of moral self that finds its origin in God (as opposed to humanity in the previously dominant articulation) and whose form is knowledge (as opposed to action in the previously dominant articulation). Thus, a shift is perceptible in Ezekiel, away from an anthropocentric and action-centered view of moral agency, and toward a view that is theocentric and knowledge-centered (glimpses of this type, which is still inchoate, are perceptible in, e.g., 36:26–36; 37:1–14).

The knowledge that takes on primary significance in this new form of moral agency is of two types: both knowledge of God and knowledge of self are necessary. The tension in Ezekiel's anthropology may be seen as a reflection of a profound crisis in Ezekiel's view of the moral self. Ultimately for him, the self is given its identity first, and the knowledge of that identity enables right action to follow. In other words, action discloses one's identity instead of determining that identity.

For the most part, Judaism between the fifth century BCE and the first century CE believed that, while humans were highly unlikely to choose the good, they were not, strictly speaking, incapable of doing so (with the notable exception of certain sectarian groups that stressed inherent moral incapacity). Like the OT, much of the NT assumes that people can choose the good (and so can choose to believe that Jesus is the Christ, or not), but Paul is a notable exception. J. Louis Martyn has argued persuasively that Paul, like Ezekiel, understands the moral agency of human beings to be inherently and irredeemably corrupted, such that only the power of God in Christ working in and through humans makes any choosing of the good possible. As in Ezekiel and the OT as a whole, a certain tension thus runs throughout the NT regarding the extent to which humans are capable of making moral decisions and the extent to which they rely on the agency of God to empower them.

See also Accountability; Free Will and Determinism; Moral Formation

Bibliography

Barclay, J., and S. Gathercole, eds. *Divine and Human Agency in Paul and His Cultural Environment.* LNTS 335. T&T Clark, 2008; Lapsley, J. *Can These Bones Live? The Problem of the Moral Self in the Book of Ezekiel.* BZAW 301. De Gruyter, 2000; Martyn, J. "Epilogue: An Essay in Pauline Meta-Ethics." Pages 173–83 in *Divine and Human Agency in Paul and His Cultural Environment*, ed. J. Barclay and S. Gathercole. LNTS 335. T&T Clark, 2008.

Jacqueline E. Lapsley

Moral Development

Western civilization has made numerous attempts to formulate theories of moral development, most of which derive from a particular view of the nature of persons (see Hoffman 124–34). One set of theories reflects the doctrine of original sin associated with early Christian theology, especially the writings of Augustine and reflected later in Puritanism. This perspective regards human nature as fundamentally depraved and posits that a sense of moral obligation is best acquired through restrictive socialization. This formulation is reflected in psychoanalytic thought that stresses prohibitions and punishment, repression of hostile and erotic impulses, and internalization of societal norms via parental correction. Strong identification with parents coupled with anxiety over losing acceptance or love fosters moral behavior. Religious proponents within this stream find biblical support in the assumed nature of authority exercised by God and subsequent derivative authority given to parents (Heb. 12:7–11) and to governing authorities (Rom. 13:1–7). Discipline may be justified on the basis that to spare the rod is to spoil the child (Prov. 13:24).

Similarly, theories of social learning posit that moral development occurs when a child witnesses a model, either punishment for misbehavior or reward for desired behavior, and then comes into alignment accordingly. Closely related are theories of attribution that move the locus of control within as the child attributes compliance to something that he or she has personally willed.

An opposite cluster of theories derives from the doctrine of innate purity usually credited to Jean-Jacques Rousseau (Lerner 13). Children are viewed as inherently good yet vulnerable to societal corruption. A rough parallel can be found in the thought of Jean Piaget. Though not assuming innate purity, Piaget regards a child's unilateral respect for adults as interfering with moral development. He advocates unsupervised peer interaction, mutual respect, perspective-taking, and trust in the naturally evolving cognitive capacities to create moral obligation. Given this social context, children between the ages of ten and twelve will progress from moral judgments based on material consequences to judgments based on intention. Scripturally, this view may be less tied to particular passages, associated with an anthropologically optimistic view, and focused on mutuality as a relational ideal.

An affiliate tradition emerged from Immanuel Kant that seeks to derive universal, impartially applied principles of justice (Hoffman 123). Kant inspired Lawrence Kohlberg (and Piaget before him) to postulate that a person acquires moral norms through a series of stages by actively constructing them. The catalyst is disequilibrium created by the inadequacy of one's current way of resolving a moral dilemma and exposure to more adequate reasoning. This stream includes information-processing views that offer a stage-like progression in a person's behavior control skills from external control by caregivers, to self-control and compliance in the caregivers' absence, culminating in self-directed moral behavior.

Kohlberg's original claim was that his stages represented qualitatively different patterns of thought, were universally applicable across cultures, and were invariantly sequenced. Adopting this framework for interpreting Scripture, one might suggest stage-like growth in the people of God. Mount Sinai, shrouded in smoke and thunder, hosts the giving of the Decalogue under threat of punishment (Kohlberg's first stage, punishment and obedience). Israel's later strict adherence to the law in remediation of exile reflects Kohlberg's fourth stage, law and maintenance. Finally, Jesus' principled reasoning in the Sermon on the Mount coupled with demonstration of communal life suggests higher, postconventional stages whereby existing moral codes and systems are questioned. Biblical scholars may also find resonance with Piaget's and Kohlberg's conceptualizations of justice and questions regarding how goods should be distributed, property owned, punishments allocated, and fair treatment adjudicated.

Successors to Kohlberg offer modifications to his original theory. Carol Gilligan writes that in authentic moral dilemmas (abortion) women show preference for an ethic of care as opposed to abstract and hypothetical justice-reasoning. This position suggests that moral development may proceed along more than one trajectory. Likewise, Vanessa Siddle Walker and John Snarey contend against Kohlberg's claim of universality, reasoning that race matters in the way people reason through moral dilemmas. Hoffman contends that cognitive principles are inadequate motivators and proposes empathy as necessary to compel and supplement principled, pro-social behavior.

Craig Dykstra offers an alternative to Kohlberg's juridical morality, contending that the unity of virtue called for in Christianity is broader than justice and assumes a covenantal relationship with God. Moral growth is not primarily determined by rational consensus or gained by perspective-taking in abstract social conflicts. Rather, the immediacy of how one acts depends on one's underlying moral vision of reality. Dykstra's visional ethics posits that transformation in how we see the world comes not by subjecting it to objective manipulation but by authentic encounter with the mystery of it. Repentance, prayer, and service enable a more accurate seeing of the world and our way of being in it.

A fourth view is utilitarianism, generally credited to David Hume and Adam Smith (Hoffman 222–23). Utilitarian theory holds that a moral act or decision maximizes happiness or well-being for all. As theories emerge from societal traditions, this position may presuppose communal interdependency and binding relational ties. Based in an ethic of high regard for the other rather than in personal development, utilitarianism may have some connection with "looking not to one's own interests but to the interests of others" (Phil. 2:4). However, utilitarianism seems out of step with Jesus' willingness to leave the ninety-nine for the sake of the one as well as other scriptural imperatives to sacrifice in order to redeem.

See also Children; Humanity; Individualism; Moral Formation; Utilitarianism

Bibliography

Dykstra, C. *Vision and Character: A Christian Educator's Alternative to Kohlberg*. Paulist Press, 1981; Gilligan, C. *In a Different Voice: Psychological Theory and Women's Development*. Harvard University Press, 1993; Hoffman, M. *Empathy and Moral Development: Implications for Caring and Justice*. Cambridge University Press, 2000, 128–34; Kohlberg, L. "Stages of Moral Development as a Basis for Moral Education." Pages 23–92 in *Moral Education: Interdisciplinary Approaches*, ed. C. Beck et al. University of Toronto Press, 1971; Lerner, R. *Concepts and Theories of Human Development*. McGraw-Hill, 1986, 11–32; Piaget, J. *The Moral Judgment of the Child*. Free Press, 1965; Siddle Walker, V., and J. Snarey. *Race-ing Moral Formation: African American Perspectives on Care and Justice*. Teachers College Press, 2004.

Chris A. Kiesling

Moral Formation

Moral formation is generally understood as the development of character to meet the tests and achieve the ends of the moral life. One biblical writing that is especially concerned with this subject is Proverbs. Proverbs 1 instructs the child ("my son") that his parent's teaching contains the foundational knowledge of wisdom (compare 1:1–4 with 1:8). The chapter goes on to offer a motivating reason for seeking wisdom, warning that the way of sinners leads to death (1:17–19), and it announces that wisdom comes by receiving instruction ("hearing") in an attitude of reverence toward God (1:5–7). The assumption that education is the primary means of moral formation was axiomatic throughout the ancient Near East. The words used in Proverbs to describe what one acquires through the forming process reflect this: "wisdom" (*ḥokmâ*), "instruction" (*mûsār*), "understanding" (*hābîn*), "insight" (*bînâ*), "knowledge" (*da'at*). Education in these things comes through listening to and observing parents and teachers, who, at their best, are examples to be emulated. Moreover, Proverbs appears to be structured in ways that suggest a process of formation: the opening chapters address the child under the tutelage of parents; the closing chapter addresses a responsible adult (a king) who has acquired wisdom from the sages but is not beyond constructive advice from his wise mother; the teaching in between perhaps also suggests pedagogical processes from beginning stages to later ones (so Brown).

Proverbs in most places assumes an air of confidence about the path from acquiring wisdom to doing righteousness and being rewarded with honor and success. Other wisdom books register doubt and concern. In Job, the experience of a divorce between righteousness and reward is explored as a problem of divine justice; in Ecclesiastes, the value of what one gains through wisdom is questioned. In these books, instruction takes a turn into the hard questions, uncertainties, and intellectual challenges of the moral life, without giving way to radical skepticism, cynicism, or nihilism. Ecclesiastes ultimately advises reverence for God and affirms the reliability of divine justice (Eccl. 12:13–14); Job's last speech concedes God's inscrutable superiority, and a final prose section (no doubt a later addition) vindicates Job as a righteous man whom God rewards in the end. This debate reflects a fundamental assumption found throughout the Bible: the promise of reward is a primary motivator to moral goodness, whether it is the inherent rewards of success and honor that are structured (by God) into the way the world works or future rewards bestowed by God after death.

According to the book of Deuteronomy, God's wisdom is given in the law (4:5–8). The words of the commandments are to be repeated by parents to children, talked about throughout the day, inscribed on foreheads (or headbands), hands, domestic doorposts, and the city gates (6:7–9). To choose the law (*tôrâ* is "instruction") is to choose life, as Deut. 30:15–20 puts it. Psalms 1 and 119 celebrate the success of those who choose life by making the law the focus of their lives.

The belief that moral formation depends on education in the law remained an enduring tenet of ancient Judaism throughout the Second Commonwealth period, and the moral influence of devotion to the law was understood in a variety of ways: making obedience second nature (Josephus, *Ag. Ap.* 2.178; Philo, *Embassy* 211), keeping the mind from idolatry (*L.A.B.* 22.4), training reason to regulate the passions (4 Maccabees; Philo), banishing evil spirits that might tempt one away from devotion to God (*T. Iss.* 7.7 in the light of 5.1; CD-A 16.4–5). But a pessimistic note is struck in *4 Ezra* regarding the power of the law to reform sinners (*4 Ezra* 3.20–22; cf. 9.31), and an emphatic rejection of the belief that the law plays a positive role in moral formation appears in Paul.

In Paul's view, the power of sin overwhelms any positive moral influence of the Mosaic law and even uses the law to incite wrongdoing (Rom. 7:7–24; 8:3–4; Gal. 3:21–22). Moral formation comes about not by devotion to the law but rather through a process of transformation carried out by the Spirit. Those who are "in the Spirit" are able "by the Spirit" to destroy wrongdoing in their lives ("put to death the deeds of the body" [Rom. 8:13]). They renew their minds (Rom. 12:2) by meditating not on the law but on "the things of the Spirit" (Rom. 8:5–6; cf. Phil. 4:8). By contrast, in the book of James the transformative word of God appears to be equated with (or at least closely associated with) the Mosaic law as a "perfect law of freedom" (1:18, 22–25). Those who look into this law as in a mirror and keep their gaze constant by joining hearing with doing are blessed.

Noticeably absent from the NT is the widespread Greek idea that ethics is a matter of pursuing "the good" through the cultivation of "virtues" that make the achievement of the good possible. Aristotle's "mean" (*mesotēs*) never appears; nor does a rationally determined "good" (*to agathon*); nor is "happiness" (*eudaimonia*) its goal. The purpose of the moral life is to obey God: to please God (1 Thess. 2:4), to be holy (1 Pet. 1:15), to keep God's commandments (Mark 12:28–34 pars.; John 13:34; 1 Cor. 7:19; Rom. 13:8), to keep the commandments of Jesus (Matt. 28:20; cf. 1 Cor. 9:21; Gal. 6:2), and so forth. The term *virtue* (*aretē*) appears occasionally as a human trait (Phil. 4:8; 2 Pet. 1:5) but does not seem to be a dominant concept. The Stoic idea that practice (*askēsis*) becomes habit (*ethos*) to form character (*ēthos*) is not found (or even hinted at) in the NT.

Here and there we find language suggesting that the moral life is a process of growth (e.g., Rom. 6:19; 1 Thess. 3:12–13; 4:9–10; 2 Thess. 1:3; 2 Pet. 1:8), and that it requires discipline (1 Cor. 9:24–27; 1 Pet. 1:13). It is assumed that the church has a role in the individual's growth through instruction, encouragement, and corrective discipline, which is evident from the fact that the NT letters include exhortation and also direct church leaders to exercise the role of moral and spiritual instruction (1 Thess. 5:11, 14; 1 Tim. 1:3–5; 4:13). In some circles the (Jewish) Scriptures are read aloud for "training in righteousness" so that believers may be "equipped for every good work" (2 Tim. 3:16–17). Moreover, moral teaching is not only by word but also by personal examples to be imitated (1 Cor. 11:1; Phil. 3:17; 4:9; 2 Thess. 3:7–9; 1 Tim. 4:12; 2 Tim. 3:10–11; Heb. 6:12; 13:7; 1 Pet. 5:3). Above all, Christ is to be imitated (1 Pet. 2:21). One purpose of the Gospels is to present Christ as the chief example of the life that God approves.

According to long-standing Jewish tradition, God disciplines the wayward by bringing suffering and misfortune on them (e.g., *Pss. Sol.* 3.4). This idea appears in the book of Hebrews (12:1–11), which teaches that even Jesus was morally perfected through suffering (5:7–10). Paul shares this idea (2 Cor. 12:7–10), but he also thinks that character is formed through undeserved suffering (Rom. 5:3–4), sharing Christ's sufferings and thus becoming conformed to the crucified Christ (Phil. 3:10). The idea of character formation through undeserved suffering (trials) is found also in Jas. 1:2–4; 1 Pet. 4:1–2.

Most important for NT writers is that God in Christ makes moral formation possible. Believers die to sin in baptism (Rom. 6:2); through the agency of the apostles, Christ is "formed" in them (Gal. 4:19); they are raised to "newness of life" (Rom. 6:4); "reborn" (1 Pet. 1:22–2:3; 1 John 4:7–12); they have the Spirit as a power of moral guidance (Rom. 8:1–11; 2 Cor. 3:18; Gal. 5:16–26); they are taught and directed by God in the ways of righteousness (1 Thess. 4:9; 2 Thess. 3:5). In short, God gives them everything they need for a new moral life (2 Pet. 1:3).

See also Character; Discipline; Habit; Moral Development; Moral Psychology; Sanctification; Suffering; Virtue Ethics

Bibliography

Barton, J. *Understanding Old Testament Ethics: Approaches and Explorations*. Westminster John Knox, 2003; Brawley, R., ed. *Character Ethics and the New Testament: Moral Dimensions of Scripture*. Westminster John Knox, 2007; Brown, W. "The Pedagogy of Proverbs 10:1–31:9." Pages 150–82 in *Character and Scripture: Moral Formation, Community, and Biblical Interpretation*, ed. W. Brown. Eerdmans, 2002; Carroll R., M. D., and J. Lapsley, eds. *Character Ethics and the Old Testament: Moral Dimensions of Scripture*. Westminster John Knox, 2007; Lee, M. *Moral Transformation in Greco-Roman Philosophy of Mind: Mapping the Moral Milieu of the Apostle Paul and His Diaspora Jewish Contemporaries*. Mohr Siebeck, 2011; Meeks, W. *The Moral World of the First Christians*. Westminster, 1986.

Charles H. Cosgrove

Moral Law

Philosophers often use the term *moral law* in a restricted sense as designating Immanuel Kant's categorical imperative, but for Christian ethicists, the term refers in a broad sense to divine directives for human action and disposition and for the institutions shaping those actions and dispositions. The moral law is articulated in the Ten Commandments and has as its twin foci "You shall love the LORD your God with all your heart, with all your soul, and with all your might" (Deut. 6:5) and "You shall love your neighbor as yourself" (Lev. 19:18; cf. Matt. 22:37–39). The purpose of the moral law is righteousness, the *shalom* in which people love, glorify, and delight in God, and where they flourish together as stewards of God's good creation. The moral law defines the fitting response of humans to God as creator, and of the people of God to God as redeemer and covenant keeper with Israel and the church.

In treating the unity of God's law in the Bible, it has been common to distinguish the moral law from ceremonial and judicial laws. Although the NT puts an end to OT ceremonial and judicial laws, it fulfills the moral law (Matt. 5:17) (see Thomas Aquinas, *ST* II-I, qq. 100–105; John Calvin, *Institutes* 2.7.16). Recent biblical scholarship questions clear divisions among these forms of law in the Bible while it acknowledges the distinction. Lutheran approaches to ethics often stress the differences between OT and NT law, so that the natural law and Ten Commandments (OT) direct life in the temporal kingdom according to norms (justice) different from those of the Sermon on the Mount (NT) governing life in the spiritual kingdom (mercy). Catholic and Calvinist ethics stress the unity of old and new law. John Calvin criticizes the saying that the perfection of the law of the gospel "far surpasses the old law" as in many ways "a most pernicious opinion" (*Institutes* 2.8.7). Christ gave no new law; he gave the best interpretation of the old law. So too Thomas Aquinas argues that the new law and the old law have the same end, subjection to God, and that the old law contains the new law within itself as a seed contains the plant it will become (*ST* II-I, q. 107, a. 1, 3).

The moral law has a complex relationship to gospel in Christian ethics. In his treatise "On the Freedom of the Christian," Martin Luther stresses the contrast between law and gospel, command and promise, works and faith. In its civic function, the moral law is the foundation for justice in the temporal kingdom. In its spiritual, and primary, function, the moral law evokes in us a deep sense of guilt and utter despair of ever being able to achieve God's righteousness. Since despair of works-righteousness is the necessary condition for true faith, the moral law prepares the way for faith's apprehension of the good news of the gospel of God's mercy and forgiveness.

Calvin also affirms a civil and spiritual use of God's law. But for Calvin, the "third and principal use" of God's law is as a guide and goad for "believers in whose hearts the Spirit of God already lives and reigns." Meditating on God's law rouses believers to obedience. The law is to the sinful flesh "like a whip to an idle and balky ass, to arouse it to work" (*Institutes* 2.7.12). Following Calvin's emphasis, the Heidelberg Catechism gives extensive treatment to the Ten Commandments in its third section, on gratitude, not in its first section, on sin.

As the law of God the Creator, the moral law is "natural" to human nature. As such, it overrides and stands in judgment on the positive laws of the state and is closely associated with natural law and human rights. The moral law as "natural law" is manifest both in scriptural revelation and in practical reason and human conscience. Paul says that what God's law requires of gentiles is "written on their hearts, to which their own conscience also bears witness" (Rom. 2:15). Thomas Aquinas defines natural law as rational participation in the eternal law whereby human beings apprehend the first principles of the moral life (seek good, avoid evil) and discern moral implications of rational patterns found in natural entities and processes

(*ST* II-I, q. 94). So too Calvin associates natural law with conscience, civil law, equity, and duties to society (*Institutes* 2.8.1).

Calvin affirms the traditional notion of the Ten Commandments as clarifying the natural law, but he severely restricts the salvific efficacy of reason, conscience, and natural law working apart from faith and biblical revelation. In sinful humans knowledge of natural law includes traces, or fleeting senses, of duty to God and neighbor. Fallen human beings neither clearly grasp nor properly heed this knowledge. God and their own consciences justly condemned them for failing to do what they know they should do. For Calvin, this inability is especially true of the first table of the law governing true worship. Humans have more understanding of the second table since they are more closely related to civil society. But here too vice and concupiscence often hold sway over observance of natural law.

The moral law as natural law provides a basis for cooperation of Christians with non-Christians in the major institutions of society. Marriage and family, business and commerce, culture and the arts, politics and international cooperation all have core purposes traceable to God as the Creator and discernible by human reason. Catholics view these in light of the doctrine of natural law, Lutherans see them as orders of creation, and Calvinists interpret them as spheres of social interaction. In the first half of the twentieth century, Dietrich Bonhoeffer, Karl Barth, and Helmut Thielicke rejected creation-oriented interpretations of the social order, grounding it instead in Christology. But in the latter half of that century to the present time there has been a resurgence of natural-law thinking in Catholic and Protestant circles (Porter; Finnis; VanDrunen; Stackhouse).

See also Law, Uses of; Law and Gospel; Love, Love Command; Lutheran Ethics; Natural Law; Reformed Ethics; Roman Catholic Moral Theology; Ten Commandments

Bibliography

Finnis, J. *Natural Law and Natural Rights*. Corrected ed. Clarendon, 1999; Porter, J. *Natural and Divine Law: Reclaiming the Tradition for Christian Ethics*. Eerdmans, 1999; Stackhouse, M. *God and Globalization*. Continuum, 2007; VanDrunen, D. *Natural Law and the Two Kingdoms: A Study in the Development of Reformed Social Thought*. Eerdmans, 2010.

Douglas J. Schuurman

Moral Psychology

The term *moral psychology* carries different connotations in different disciplines. Within modern psychology it refers generally to inquiry into moral development and moral decision-making. Within modern philosophy it often describes any conceptual inquiry concerned with the interface of human nature and the moral, therefore spanning contemporary disciplines such as philosophy of mind, ethics (particularly virtue ethics), and philosophical psychology. Historically, it has been used in reference to particular thinkers (one may read, for example, of the "moral psychology of Aristotle"), but any such taxonomy is retrospectively applied: the early church fathers knew nothing of modern disciplinary boundaries and freely wrote about what we would term "moral psychology" (e.g., Ambrose's *Jacob and the Happy Life*, Augustine's *Literal Commentary on Genesis*, and Gregory of Nyssa's *Life of Moses*) in their works of biblical exegesis.

None of the biblical texts, of course, speak of moral psychology per se, nor does Scripture give any empirical-scientific account of moral development in the way that Jean Piaget, Lawrence Kohlberg, and Carol Gilligan, for example, have attempted to do in our time. But as exemplified in the patristic tradition, Christian exegetes over time have consistently found the Bible to be a thoroughgoing witness to moral psychology, at least insofar as each of the biblical texts, in diverse ways, describes embodied moral agents in hopeful but imperfect relationship with God, who is the source and ground of morality and moral law. But in describing how the human moral agent is constituted, Christian exegetes have traditionally interpreted Scripture alongside the regnant contemporary psychologies. All of the aforementioned patristic treatises, for example, draw heavily on Stoic and neo-Platonic anthropology; Thomas Aquinas's *Summa theologiae* draws heavily on Aristotle; John Calvin's *Institutes* show the marked influence of Renaissance-era Platonism; even Karl Barth arguably drew on modern theories of self-in-relation in the psychological reflections in *Church Dogmatics* III/2. In our own time, conservative Protestant thinkers such as Jay Adams, invoking *sola scriptura*, have attempted to articulate psychologies that rely only on Scripture and not on modern psychological theory, but the possibility and the advisability of this have been questioned even by other evangelical scholars (e.g., Stanton Jones). Most contemporary Christian moral-psychological writers understand themselves to be bringing Scripture into conversation with the modern psychologies; in doing so, they participate in a very long-standing exegetical tradition.

However, Scripture can aid interpretation of the modern psychologies as well. In our own time, for example, biblically informed thinkers such as Don Browning, Paul Vitz, and Stanton Jones have argued that the modern psychotherapies and theories of moral development are never "value neutral" because they cannot avoid depicting, at least generally and implicitly, the shape of the morally excellent life. The light of theology, according to these thinkers, exposes as false the amoral pretensions of modern scientific psychology.

See also Character; Discernment, Moral; Moral Development; Moral Formation

Bibliography

Adams, J. *Competent to Counsel*. Baker, 1970; Browning, D. *Religious Thought and the Modern Psychologies*. 2nd ed. Fortress, 2004; Jones, S., and R. Butman. *Modern Psychotherapies: A Comprehensive Christian Appraisal*. InterVarsity, 1991; Vitz, P. *Psychology as Religion: The Cult of Self-Worship*. 2nd ed. Eerdmans, 1994.

Warren Kinghorn

Motive(s)

Motive is intention spurring a person to act in certain ways. It is the more or less rational connection of cause and effect in the minds of agents leading them to seek preferred outcomes and frequently is used in assigning praise or blame for initiating, not preventing, or omitting an action (both morally and legally). Most often, motive is understood as the expression of a reasoning process drawing on values, affections, passions, and/or tastes. Motive is best conceived not using a mere nominal categorization of good versus bad intention but rather as a matter of degrees within those two categories, especially since motives can be "mixed." For classical Christians, a wrong act without a wrong motive may or may not be defined as a sin, depending on the degree of culpability for knowledge of consequences, but an evil motive is always sinful even without the successful initiation of an act.

In the history of Christianity the most significant debates about motive have centered on whether the prior activity of God has so shaped the hearts and thereby the motives of individuals such that they are not genuinely free to act. If God is the first and final cause and all other causes spring directly and without modification from his prior action, then free self-determination of moral course seems absent. This leads to justice and soteriological questions about what is due each person. For many Christians, some degree of self-motivation seems to be necessary to generally hold a person morally responsible for his or her actions, and to specifically make damnation and salvation just. Responses to those concerns include the following: no one is due heaven; divine justice is defined by consistency with God's will, not by equitable treatment per se; and moral action can be free even if the motive is not entirely so. Regardless of the position taken on freedom of the will, classical Christianity includes the assumption that sin has tainted all motives to at least some degree, unless the Spirit graciously intervenes.

The author of the *Didache* asserted that passions can corrupt motivation and that such is un-Christlike double-mindedness. Most consideration of motive in the pre-Constantinian period concluded the same, with conversion sometimes understood as the gracious appropriation of the motive of incarnational servanthood, which in turn directs moral choices toward Christlike purity. For Augustine, the motive to act is determined by the affections, with the affections being ordered or prioritized loves. The responsibility for motivation, then, is pushed back to a prior consideration of the degree of human participation in the acceptance or rejection of God's gracious reordering of love (a matter on which Augustine seems to shift in his writings). Thomas Aquinas endorsed freedom of the will, allowing that the motives of an individual arise from the internal rational discourse of the mind as it seeks its own ultimate fulfillment, with the properly motivated Christian seeking his or her created end (*telos*) of glorifying God.

During the Reformation, Martin Luther spoke of the bondage of the human will, so that all natural motives rise out of spiritual confusion. John Calvin insisted that humans were predestined to serve God's ends, so that even if motivation might "freely" spring from the inclinations of the heart, those inclinations were so shaped by God that there was no freedom beyond acquiescing to the divine purpose. Anabaptists tended to emphasize the motivation generated by a vision of the kingdom to come that compelled the committed believer to choose the moral standard mirrored in the suffering of Christian martyrs.

Jonathan Edwards emphasized the affections as the source of moral inclinations, with the saved individual motivated by appreciation for divine benevolence and drawn toward God by his beauty, then "willing" in accordance with that attraction. Edwards engaged in the broader secular debates about will and motive as well as responded to the Arminians. Some of the principal secular figures were Spinoza, Hume, and Locke; many of the secularists favored determinism analogous to the machine or a complete epistemological uncertainty, with those holding either position denying a significant role for free motive. The Arminian revivalists, best represented by John Wesley, often argued that motivation arose from the reasonable processes of the mind engaging the will and the affections within the individual, thus a free choice, even while God graciously initiated the change that allowed motivation for the good.

A generation later, Charles Finney asserted that individuals could freely choose God, motivated by their own need for God, and subsequently could work toward living with pure motives in all actions (especially those having to do with justice). In reaction to the Second and Third Awakenings, various strong predestinarian groups developed, such as the Hard-Shell Baptists, that all but removed the concept of self-chosen motivation, even to the extent that some became antimissionary and antievangelistic. As the nineteenth century went on, in reaction to both stagnant traditionalism and to Enlightenment mechanistic philosophy, a position totally contrary to the predestinarian developed as Christian existentialism, with Søren Kierkegaard and Fyodor Dostoevsky the key figures. The desire to define oneself compels free, radically individualistic choice. Such is motivationally pure only if one "wills one thing"—that is, freely chooses what God chooses for the individual.

At the end of the nineteenth century and into the twentieth, the concept of motive was increasingly shaped by psychological theories; while some have been similar to existentialism, many are rooted in psychoanalysis, reductionist scientism, and behaviorism, all of which denied a significant role for self-controllable motivation and free will. Revivalist evangelicalism in the twentieth century generally has allowed that individual moral agents have free motives, although corruptingly tainted by sin before accepting Christ. Old-line Protestants, following a more existentialist line, generally have argued that the individuals should "be" themselves, motivated to act in accordance with the true self. Liberationist theologians, while not denying the morality of individual motivation, have emphasized the significance of the social location of the actor as a motivating factor in choice.

Disagreements about the nature of motive arise as texts such as Matt. 18:14; Luke 13:3–5; John 3:16; 2 Pet. 3:9 are juxtaposed with those seemingly indicating not only God's omniscience but also his implemented sovereignty, such as some of the passages about God hardening the heart, as with Pharaoh, and those in Romans. Jesus stated that actions come out of the heart, indicating the motivation from the inner self (Matt. 12:33–37; 15:10–20). The reference in Matt. 5:8 to "pure in heart" seems to be to pure motive.

See also Affections; Desire; Freedom; Free Will and Determinism; Intention; Moral Agency; Responsibility

James R. Thobaben

Murder

In the Bible, murder is the intentional killing of one human being by another outside the boundaries of legally prescribed or communally sanctioned execution or killing. Since humans bear the image of God, the severe guilt from a wrongful death adheres to an individual or community until it is removed through some means of legal or cultic resolution, usually execution of the murderer (Gen. 9:5–6; Num. 35:16–18; Deut. 19:5, 11; 1 Kgs. 2:32). In the case of an unsolved murder, a special ritual involving the community's elders and a heifer or cow was used to absolve the lingering blood guilt of the nearby community (Deut. 21:1–9).

The central legal prohibition of murder in the OT is contained in one of the Ten Commandments (Exod. 20:13; Deut. 5:17), translated sometimes more narrowly as "you shall not murder" (NRSV) or more broadly as "you shall not kill" (RSV). The Hebrew verb *rāṣaḥ* used in the commandment denotes any intentional or premeditated killing of another human that arises out of personal feelings of hatred or malice (Num. 35; Prov. 22:13; Isa. 1:21; Hos. 6:9). Someone who had accidentally killed another person could find sanctuary by living in one of six designated cities of refuge (Exod. 21:12–14; Num. 35:6–32; Deut. 12:1–14; 19:8–10; 1 Kgs. 1:50–53; 2:28–34).

A number of narratives illustrate various dimensions of the prohibition of wrongful killing. God mercifully suspended the death penalty in the Bible's first murder when Cain killed his brother, Abel (Gen. 4:1–16). The sons of Jacob deceitfully murdered all the Canaanite men of the city in revenge for Shechem's rape of their sister Dinah (Gen. 34). The young Moses killed an Egyptian foreman who was beating an Israelite slave (Exod. 2:11–15). A young Israelite priest, Phinehas, killed an Israelite man and Midianite woman with a spear in the context of Israelite apostasy with a foreign god (Num. 25:1–18). Taken together, the narratives raise the complex issues of capital punishment, the role of vengeance, violence in defense of the oppressed, and the use of violence in interreligious conflict.

The ways in which violence begets violence are illustrated in King David's insidious plot whereby he has one of his own soldiers, Uriah the Hittite, killed in battle in order to cover up his adulterous affair with Uriah's wife, Bathsheba (2 Sam. 11–12). The prophet Nathan announced that God's judgment on David's act of violence would be that "the sword will never depart from your house" (2 Sam. 12:10).

Jesus' Sermon on the Mount significantly expanded the commandment against murder to cover not only acts of physical violence but also expressions of anger or verbal insults directed against "a brother or sister" (Matt. 5:21–26). The human propensity toward anger, vengeance, and violence (Gen. 4:23–24) is overcome in the death of Jesus, who refused to inflict violence and vengeance on those who arrested and killed him (Matt. 5:38–42; 26:51–53; Rom. 12:17–21).

See also Capital Punishment; Killing; Revenge; Sanctity of Human Life; Ten Commandments; Violence

Bibliography

Barmash, P. *Homicide in the Biblical World*. Cambridge University Press, 2005; Miller, P. "Protecting Life." Pages 221–70 in *The Ten Commandments*. Westminster John Knox, 2009; Olson, D. "Violence for the Sake of Social Justice? Narrative, Ethics and Indeterminacy in Moses' Slaying of the Egyptian (Exod. 2.11–15)." Pages 138–48 in *The Meanings We Choose: Hermeneutical Ethics, Indeterminacy and the Conflict of Interpretations*, ed. C. Cosgrove. JSOTSup 411. T&T Clark, 2004.

Dennis T. Olson

Mutual Aid

Israel's practice of mutual aid was mandated systematically in God's commands to remit debts every seventh year and celebrate Jubilee every fiftieth year (see Deut. 15; Lev. 25) so that there "be no one in need among you" (Deut. 15:4). Forgiving debts marked community renewal in Israel's postexilic restoration (Neh. 5). This was Israel's systematic practice of justice that ensured the community's *shalom*.

The Lord's Prayer includes forgiveness of debts (Matt. 6:12). The early Christian church exemplifies two models of mutual aid. After Pentecost the believers had all things in common (Acts 2:42–45; 4:32–37). A second and more durable model of mutual aid consisted of collecting money from wealthier Jewish-gentile Christian churches throughout Asia Minor and Macedonia for the poorer Jewish Christians in Jerusalem. Paul speaks extensively of this relief gift (2 Cor. 8–9), grounding it in "the grace given me by God" (Rom. 15:15). Paul prays that this "offering of the Gentiles may be acceptable, sanctified by the Holy Spirit" (Rom. 15:16).

Both groups, the Jerusalem poor and the gentiles with material resources, give and receive (Rom. 15:25–27). Justin Meggitt says of this mutuality,

> Firstly, it was aimed at promoting *material well being*. It was initially undertaken to achieve a tangible end: *the relief of the economically poor in the Jerusalem church*. . . . Secondly, it was thoroughly *mutual* in its character. *It was in no sense an individual or unilateral undertaking for any of those involved*. Paul emphasises that *all* the members of the church were contributors as, indeed, were *all* the communities (we hear of no exceptions). It was not intended to be the work of a few wealthy members or congregations. And it was premised on the assumption of *mutual interdependence*. It was not a one-off act of charity. *The material assistance given was understood as something that would, in time, be returned, when the situation was reversed*. (Meggitt 159)

Paul died for this cause (Acts 21:7–14). His relief gift crowned his mission, exemplifying gentile and Jewish unity in Christ.

Mutual aid, with charity, continued in the early church through deacons (Acts 6:1–6). "In A.D. 251, the church in Rome had a massive program of care for the widows and the poor. The church . . . had 1,500 people on its roll for support. Bishop Cornelius was aided by six presbyters, seven deacons, seven more sub-deacons, and ninety-four people in minor roles" (Swartley 32). Church fathers speak of mutual aid and charity, grounded in creation, redemption, koinonia, and justice (see Swartley 29–34).

Mutual aid and charity continued in the church, with growing institutionalized forms. Sixteenth-century Anabaptists practiced mutual aid at the cost of life, especially for those "on the run" to escape persecution (see Jeni Hiett Umble, John D. Roth, and Mary S. Sprunger in Kraybill and Swartley 103–67). In the twentieth century, many Protestant denominations, including Mennonites and Brethren, combined mutual aid with insurance (property, auto, and health), which with high cost and exclusions compromised mutual aid, thus raising irresolvable ethical dilemmas.

See also Collection for the Saints; Debt; Generosity; Koinonia; Loans

Bibliography

Kraybill, D., and W. Swartley, eds. *Building Communities of Compassion: Mennonite Mutual Aid in Theory and Practice*. Herald Press, 1998; Meggitt, J. *Paul, Poverty and Survival*. SNTW. T&T Clark, 1998, 157–64; Swartley, W. "Mutual Aid Based in Jesus and Early Christianity." Pages 21–39 in *Building Communities of Compassion: Mennonite Mutual Aid in Theory and Practice*, ed. D. Kraybill and W. Swartley. Herald Press, 1998.

Willard M. Swartley

N

Nahum

Strong anti-Assyrian sentiment coupled with a nationalist fervor has been a source of discomfort and uneasiness among interpreters of this OT book. The book has one overriding concern. It prophesies and even takes delight in the impending fall of Nineveh. The deft use of diverse literary forms such as the partial acrostic poem (where each strophe begins with a letter of the alphabet) in 1:2–8, the "woe" oracle in 3:1–7, and the oracle of salvation in 3:14–20 creates a powerful impact. One is also struck by the prophet's ability to create sights and sounds through words and images (3:2).

No explicit information is provided on the date of the prophet's activity. Based on internal clues, one can assume a time frame somewhere between the fall of Thebes in 663 BCE (3:8) and the fall of Nineveh in 612 BCE, which the book predicts.

The book opens with a poem celebrating the coming of Yahweh, intended as an assurance to Judah (1:2–15). Yahweh's wrath and vengeance are directed against Nineveh. The assault on Nineveh is envisioned and rendered with graphic detail and force (2:1–13). Chapter 3 continues the indictment of Nineveh for its deceitful and wanton behavior.

From an ethical perspective, the uneasiness that many experience in reading the book and its message may stem from two things. First, God is portrayed as wrathful and avenging. Second, the divine wrath is directed against Assyria, a foreign nation. Both aspects bristle with theological and ethical questions. How does one reconcile the merciful versus vengeful depictions of God? How does one reconcile the anti-Assyrian stance and tirade expressed here with the more inclusive and merciful perspective in the book of Jonah (Jon. 4:2, 11)? These issues must be sorted out against the backdrop of Nahum's overall theological frame of reference. Nahum operates with an overarching sense of God's sovereignty over not just Judah but all nations. Anyone or anything contrary to the purposes of God will not go unchallenged. Forces that promote evil, tyranny, and violence will be brought under divine judgment. Assyria of antiquity was one such force known for its brutality and ruthlessness toward its enemies. Recognizing this helps to put into perspective Nahum's tirade. Part of the ethical challenge of the book concerns our responsibility and response to the persistence of evil, tyranny, violence, and injustice beyond our own borders. In our world of complex geopolitical realities and loyalties, a careful consideration and nuanced response may be necessary. The book of Jonah's emphasis on the merciful and redemptive purpose of God (Jon. 4:10–11) offers an alternative to divine justice and thus a different resolution to evil.

See also Anger; Jonah; Justice, Retributive; Old Testament Ethics; Punishment; Reward and Retribution

Bibliography

Brown, W. *Obadiah through Malachi*. WestBC. Westminster John Knox, 1996; Floyd, M. *Minor Prophets: Part 2*. FOTL 22. Eerdmans, 1999; Roberts, J. *Nahum, Habakkuk, and Zephaniah*. OTL. Westminster John Knox, 1991.

D. N. Premnath

Narrative Ethics, Biblical

Since Wayne Booth published *The Company We Keep: An Ethics of Fiction* (1988), the idea that ethics is central to our engagement with literature and, conversely, that literature is central to our engagement with ethics has enjoyed renewed life among a wide range of thinkers (to say nothing of the larger discussion of the importance of narrative in the moral life more generally [e.g., Alasdair MacIntyre]). Among them, Martha Nussbaum (*Love's Knowledge*; *Upheavals of Thought*) and Adam Zachary Newton (*Narrative Ethics*) have articulated quite different but generative ways of thinking about narrative ethics—that is, about the way in which literature, especially fiction, shapes our ethical reflection. Nussbaum, working in the Aristotelian tradition, shows some kinship to Booth but nonetheless makes the distinctive claim that every form of speaking, every style, expresses moral commitments, and readers need to attend to these as much as to moral content.

Newton, by contrast, works out of categories from Emmanuel Levinas (the "Saying" and the "Said") and is interested in performative ethics, in how the narrative implicates us in what we have heard.

In biblical studies a number of scholars have found Nussbaum's and Newton's work stimulating for engaging the Bible's narrative traditions ethically, among whom Carol Newsom especially stands out. How does the narrative genre of stories inform our ethical engagement with them? In her monograph *The Book of Job: A Contest of Moral Imaginations*, and as part of a much larger argument, Newsom first offers a Nussbaumian reading of Job 1–2: the moral imagination articulated in the prose tale is one of tremendous beauty and art that sublimely resolves contradictions between Job's grief and his continuing praise of God. Yet she then offers a Newtonian reading of the same narrative that places readers as ethically implicated observers of a scientific laboratory experiment, with Job as the unwilling object of deep physical and emotional pain for he knows not what purpose. The tension between these readings (in Levinasian language, a tension between the "Saying" and the "Said"), which cannot be resolved, is broken only by the interruption of the wisdom dialogue that erupts in Job 3.

See also Narrative Ethics, Contemporary

Bibliography

Newsom, C. *The Book of Job: A Contest of Moral Imaginations*. Oxford University Press, 1999; Newton, A. *Narrative Ethics*. Harvard University Press, 1995; Nussbaum, M. *Love's Knowledge: Essays on Philosophy and Literature*. Oxford University Press, 1990.

Jacqueline E. Lapsley

Narrative Ethics, Contemporary

This article narrates the concerns that produced a narrative turn in Christian ethics, delineates five enduring insights of narrative Christian ethics, and concludes with a sketch of prospects.

The significance of narrative in Christian ethics is complex and contested. For this reason, narrative ethics is neither a method nor a tradition. There is no consensus description of narrative ethics, notwithstanding James McClendon's confident claim that it is "the discovery, understanding, and creative transformation of a shared and lived story" whose focus is Jesus and his kingdom (McClendon 330). McClendon does represent a powerful trajectory among some Christian ethicists of recognizing that the gospel, the Scriptures, the church, and discipleship have essential narrative dimensions that are morally determinative for Christian life. Any ethic that consciously attends to the moral significance of those dimensions can be understood as narrative ethics.

Development

The most important impetus to rediscover the moral significance of narrative was Karl Barth. His rediscovery of "The Strange New World within the Bible" did not produce a self-consciously narrative method, but his *Church Dogmatics* was exhaustively engaged with theological redescription of the scriptural story seen through a christological lens. This had three significant effects in Barth that endure in narrative ethics. First, because Scripture's narrative world knows no disjunction between knowing God and the good, Barth refused to separate dogmatics from ethics. Likewise, narrative ethics is a form of theology. Second, Barth eschewed modernist justifications of theology in favor of dogmatic display of the God who speaks and acts in the biblical story. Likewise, proponents of narrative ethics attend to biblical and ecclesial narratives as a way to display Christian conviction rather than justify it (Hauerwas; McClendon). For them, this attends to truthfulness while avoiding foundationalism; for opponents of narrative ethics, this is the same fideism that they ascribe to Barth. Third, because Scripture narrates a story in which we find ourselves already participants, Barth's theologizing has the effect of telling us into the story. Likewise, narrative ethics has suggested that the biblical story truly renders the world (Frei), and that through conversion we find ourselves baptized into God's story (Loughlin). The enduring impact of these three features of Barth's theology on all subsequent development cannot be overestimated.

Another impetus for interest in narrative was H. Richard Niebuhr's discussion of "The Story of Our Life" in *The Meaning of Revelation*. There Niebuhr asserted that in order "to say truly what it stands for," the church is compelled to tell "the story of its life," a story that is "irreplaceable and untranslatable" (Hauerwas and Jones 23). Taken together, these claims suggest that Christian ethics is the delineation of how the story of Christ communicates, shapes, illuminates, and guides Christian community and living instead of the idealization of "Christ" into various social stances vis-à-vis "culture." The potential of Niebuhr's suggestion was largely untapped, however, as most of those who consciously extended his interest in story did so in the vein of a phenomenological analysis of the universality of narrative consciousness (e.g., Crites in Hauerwas and Jones) rather than of a thick description of the Christian story's catholic particularity.

Theology's narrative turn (c. 1970) inaugurated a lively and diverse conversation about the significance of story in Christian ethics. Narrative appeared to promise a way beyond the impasse of deontology's abstract universalism and utilitarianism's decontextualized decisionism. At its height (mid-1980s), there was a proliferation of publishing on narrative in relation to almost everything: revelation, character, identity, community, virtue, conviction, Christology, and hermeneutics. By the turn of the millennium, enthusiasm for narrative had faded in most quarters (including MacIntyre) but had matured among a particular constellation of ecclesial ethicists (e.g., Hauerwas; McClendon; Spohn; Wells) into five enduring contributions.

Key Achievements

Alasdair MacIntyre begins *After Virtue* with "a disquieting suggestion" that we have amnesia. This trope helps delineate the five key insights of narrative ethics. When the unfortunate amnesiac awakens at the beginning of the story, he wants to know: How did I get here? What's going on? Who am I? How should I think and feel about what's happening? What should I do now? Answering these crucial questions requires both telling stories and engaging narrative skills. The amnesiac can do neither and thus is left bereft and bewildered, unable to (1) historicize the present moment, (2) contextualize situation and decisions, (3) identify and characterize self and others, (4) perceive and feel the situation truly, and (5) enact a hopeful future. Let us consider each of these in turn.

The turn to narrative came in the context of dissatisfaction with Christian ethics enmeshed in quandaries and enamored with universality. A key strategy was to historicize the present moment by telling the story of how things came to such an impasse. In *After Virtue* and two sequels, MacIntyre narrates how we came to such dire moral straits. Likewise, John Milbank and Hans Frei offered magisterial eclipse narratives (for theology and hermeneutics, respectively). All these thinkers seek to illuminate the dead ends of modernity by narrating the mistakes that got us here.

Although these thinkers are strongly associated with the narrative turn, the viability of narrative ethics does not depend on the convincingness of their stories. Whether MacIntyre, Milbank, and Frei got their history right or not, it remains true that the Christian story situates ethical action, renders moral identity, forms character, and directs Christian life. What their work does demonstrate is the first enduring insight of narrative ethics: narrative is intrinsic to our rationality. It is more basic than either explanation or understanding (Milbank). We rightly have other modes of moral discourse, but none of them finally leaves narrative behind. Immanuel Kant's effort to throw off self-incurred tutelage for the heady freedom of enlightenment is, covertly, a story about jettisoning story.

A second enduring insight is that narrative has an essential role in human agency. An ethics focused solely on deciding and acting is incomplete or even false, precisely because it ignores the way we situate, orient, and explain our actions within stories that describe "what is going on." MacIntyre put it famously: "I can only answer the question 'What am I to do?' if I can answer the prior question 'Of what story or stories do I find myself a part?'" (MacIntyre 216). What makes a given action both intelligible and intentional is that it fits within a narrative account of the situation. Retrospectively, narratives make actions intelligible by fitting them within the interplay of other actions, intentions, and circumstances. Prospectively, narratives are how we imagine and enact intentions. Thus, we continuously read the lives of others, and read and author our own lives, by narrating what is going on; understanding and intending are both narrative skills.

Both claims inescapably raise questions of truth. Any action can be rendered intelligible by multiple stories, some of which are mutually exclusive (as phenomena such as lying and self-deception prove). So recognizing that choices sit within and are made intelligible by stories is insufficient. The goal of narrative ethics is not mere intelligibility, but truthfulness. The good life requires that we be claimed by and live within a truthful story. The criteria of truthfulness will be generated from within the story, not from a so-called objective point outside the gospel (Hauerwas and Jones 184–90). The core of a truthful story is that we are never more than coauthors of our own lives.

Third, narrative identifies and characterizes. Answering the question "Who?" typically begins with a name, but finally it requires a story. For example, Yahweh is the "God who brought you out of the land of Egypt." Stories thus differentiate one from another by narrating the unique circumstances and settings of who did what to whom. But more intrinsically, stories display how identity simultaneously changes and persists through time. It takes a story to display adequately the change in identity that conversion occasions, and it takes a story to display adequately the constancy of identity that fidelity and integrity entail. Narrative is the necessary display of both constancy and change in moral identity over time, such that continuity and transformation of identity are simultaneously possible. Narrative renders the changeable persistence of identity through time.

Narrative ethics focuses not on the generic power of story to render identity, however, but rather on the particular display of the identity of God, Israel, church, and the saints. Narrative ethics recognizes the primacy of God's story for rendering God's identity truthfully, and thereby for discovering the true or proper identity of disciples, church, and world. Each disciple's story nests within the church's story, which nests within Christ's story. Thus, God's identity already stipulates fitting goals, choices, actions, and dispositions for church and disciple so identified by, with, and in Christ.

Although God's full identity encompasses the entire scriptural story, there is a "master story" that is central: for Jews the exodus, and for Christians the paschal mystery—the life, death, and resurrection of Jesus (Goldberg). Narrative ethics works with a consciously christological hermeneutic of both Scripture and the moral life. The quintessential display of this is Yoder's *Politics of Jesus*, a book that irrevocably ties the story of Jesus' nonviolent fidelity to cruciform, ecclesial discipleship. Thus, the gospel not only identifies God but also thereby convokes and characterizes a peculiar people of God who live conformed to God's story. For both church and disciple, Christ is our life (Col. 3:4).

Much of narrative ethics attends to the way story displays character. Although character can indicate no more than a flat persona in a plot, it typically indicates that persona's unique congeries of qualities and traits as well. Character names those perduring yet changeable qualities of desiring, feeling, thinking, and acting that give our personhood enduring and recognizable shape. Thus, narrative ethics dovetails nicely with virtue ethics, since stories are finally necessary to display the full meaning of characteristics such as patience and hope and to show how such qualities take shape in particular lives. Although narrative ethics is not intrinsically wedded to virtue theory, many of its major proponents have favored both (Hauerwas; MacIntyre; McClendon; Spohn). In the end, narrating is more basic than describing or explaining character.

This leads to the fourth insight: narratives not only display our character but also shape it. Indeed, narratives shape moral seeing, feeling, imagining, and acting. This is not just the trite observation that we become who we are through what we do and what we suffer, the story of our life's actions and passions. It is the deeper insight that the stories we hear, learn, and live function as lenses through which we see God and self and world. Such stories specify appropriate (and forbidden) desires; they tutor our emotions and shape our affections; they carry, convey, and advocate particular goals and goods; they imagine our world and all its interrelations. And thus, they shape the agent who acts in encompassing ways.

Moral formation and imagination can be funded by everything from children's stories and parables (Spohn) to novels and biography. Although these various genres hold genuine potential for moral reflection, the core of a properly narrative Christian ethics must be the particular stories of the Christian faith rather than a literary type. Thus, narrative ethics' proper domain will be the Scriptures (Colwell), particularly the story of Jesus (Spohn; Hauerwas), along with narrative display of that story in the lives of the saints (Hauerwas, *With the Grain*).

The scriptural story, as it communicates patterns of God's way in, with, and for the world, forms dispositions and fosters imagination, thereby shaping and guiding our perceptions and passions. Stanley Hauerwas has emphasized the development of skills and habits in the church, by and through which we make the story of Jesus our own. William Spohn has emphasized the formation of moral imagination and perception through the interplay of stories of Jesus, virtue ethics, and practices of spirituality. John Colwell argues that what stories do in general—draw us into their world and reshape us—the biblical story does in particular through the promised action of the Holy Spirit.

The final enduring insight of narrative ethics is that it renders a coherent account of how we go on in hope, because it sets our finite stories within the encompassing gospel of divine justice and mercy. Readers follow a story by continually integrating what comes next with their emerging sense of the final ending and shape of the whole; the episodic dimension continually reinterprets and is interpreted by the configural (Ricoeur). As we read so we live, with and from this constant interplay of memory and hope. We perceive, imagine, decide, and act not in isolated moments, but rather with a constant sense of the ending toward which we go and thus of the overall shape of that story that we are becoming. If the story we follow is limited to ourselves or even to our communities, then we confront the twofold futility of a past and future bound in sin and fraught with tragedy. Only when our story is incorporated into Christ's story is our life redeemed by the comedy of resurrection, reconciliation, and rejoicing.

Samuel Wells has schematized the full story in which we live as a five-act play: creation, Israel, Christ, church, and consummation. This plotting of the story establishes the pure gratuity of the story's beginning, middle, and end and places both church and disciple in the finite freedom of covenant life. The church risks patient hope and courageous love because it believes that Christ's resurrection already determines the ending that has not yet fully come. Dwelling in the story of the ascended rule of the risen Servant delivers the church from taking responsibility for the story's end and binds the church to servant love of neighbor and enemy.

Prospects

Salient criticisms of narrative ethics point to perennial dangers as well as promising developments. One danger is to make story, or a theory about narrative theory, more basic than an encounter with Christ and enlivening by the Holy Spirit. Thus, at its worst, narrative ethics risks reducing God to mere story (Murphy). At its best, however, narrative ethics has discovered the power of worship to narrate a living encounter with the triune God. This liturgical deepening of narrative ethics holds much promise.

The other perennial danger is that attention to narrative may focus on personal understanding rather than ecclesial embodiment. Thus, at its worst, narrative ethics risks valorizing saving knowledge of God's story for individuals. At its best, however, narrative ethics is mitigating this threat by attention to analogies with performance (Hauerwas, *Performing the Faith*) and drama (Wells). This dramaturgical deepening of narrative ethics holds much promise as well.

See also Character; Ecclesiology and Ethics; Eschatology and Ethics; Liturgy and Ethics; Moral Formation; Narrative Ethics, Biblical; Teleological Theories of Ethics; Virtue(s); Virtue Ethics

Bibliography

Colwell, J. *Living the Christian Story: The Distinctiveness of Christian Ethics*. T&T Clark, 2001; Frei, H. *The Eclipse of Biblical Narrative: A Study in Eighteenth and Nineteenth Century Hermeneutics*. Yale University Press, 1974; Goldberg, M. *Jews and Christians, Getting Our Stories Straight: The Exodus and the Passion-Resurrection*. Trinity Press International, 1991; Hauerwas, S. *The Hauerwas Reader*. Ed. J. Berkman and M. Cartwright. Duke University Press, 2001, chaps. 5, 7–12, 15, 17; idem. *Performing the Faith: Bonhoeffer and the Practice of Nonviolence*. Brazos, 2004; idem. *With the Grain of the Universe: The Church's Witness and Natural Theology*. Brazos, 2001; Hauerwas, S., and L. Jones, eds. *Why Narrative? Readings in Narrative Theology*. Wipf & Stock, 1997; Loughlin, G. *Telling God's Story: Bible, Church and Narrative Theology*. Cambridge University Press, 1996; MacIntyre, A. *After Virtue: A Study in Moral Theory*. 3rd ed. University of Notre Dame Press, 2007; McClendon, J. *Ethics*. Vol. 1 of *Systematic Theology*. Rev. ed. Abingdon, 2002; Milbank, J. *Theology and Social Theory: Beyond Secular Reason*. 2nd ed. Wiley-Blackwell, 2006; Murphy, F. *God Is Not a Story: Realism Revisited*. Oxford University Press, 2007; Ricoeur, P. *Time and Narrative*. Trans. K. McLaughlin and D. Pellauer. Vol. 1. University of Chicago Press, 1984; Spohn, W. *Go and Do Likewise: Jesus and Ethics*. Continuum, 2003; Wells, S. *Improvisation: The Drama of Christian Ethics*. Brazos, 2004.

D. Brent Laytham

Nationalism

Christianity's relationship to nations and to nationalism is complex in part because the very notion of "nation" has changed over time. Christians have always had to negotiate their relationship to the ruling powers, of course, but the development of the modern nation-state in the seventeenth century introduced complex new questions concerning the relationship of the people of God to the nations. In recent years that relationship has been a contested question in Christian ethics and has been implicated in an assortment of other important issues, such as war, patriotism, justice, and the law.

Scripture itself portrays a shifting relationship that develops from the early Hebrews and the nations to the Jews in captivity to the early church under Roman rule. The victory of Constantine in the fourth century and subsequent political developments in Roman Christianity and Eastern Orthodoxy represented an important change from Christianity's previous relationship to Roman imperial power. In the Middle Ages the Holy Roman Empire was at once intimately tied to and frequently in tension with papal power. On the heels of the Reformation came the modern nation-state, which was regarded as the solution to the so-called wars of religion. The wars that followed the Reformation began as religious conflicts with political dimensions but became political conflicts with religious dimensions. Further changes in the relationship of Christianity to nations and to nationalism were wrought by the Enlightenment and its appeals to a secular rationality. And recently the rise of globalization has brought still other changes to this relationship. Within each period the "nation" and hence "nationalism" indicate different arrangements. The following material first surveys the scriptural and historical articulations of the nation and nationalism and then outlines the ethical issues that surround contemporary ethical reflection about nationalism.

Scripture

In the OT, Hebrew *ʿam* and *gôy* are the two most common expressions to denote "nation." Both *ʿam* and *gôy* are used to refer both to Israel and to foreign nations in contrast to Israel. The term *ʿam* is rendered "people" and "nation." It indicates personal relations and is used to refer to common ancestry and a nation belonging to a deity. The primary aspects of *gôy* seem to include common language, government, and territory. The OT, however, never precisely specifies requirements for Israel's or other nations' existence as a *gôy*. "Nation" here should not be confused with modern conceptions. Yahweh promises Abraham that his descendants will become a *gôy* and will be given a land of their own (Gen. 12:2; cf. 17:5; 18:18). Israel's deity-nation association was uniquely established and maintained independent of the people's presence in a particular land. Thus, even under Egyptian enslavement the Hebrews are Yahweh's people (Deut. 26:5), whom Yahweh eventually delivers from slavery (Deut. 4:34–38; cf. Exod. 15:21).

When the OT refers to the Hebrews among the nations, it generally refers to Yahweh's people as a nomadic people who wandered amid other peoples who worshiped other gods. Upon settlement in the promised land, the Hebrews instituted kingdoms under the rubric of Israel (1 Sam. 8:5, 19). Four successive empires captured Israel, and the Hebrews lived under political captivity (Lev. 26:38; Ps. 106:27; Ezek. 11:16). Strict prohibitions discouraged the nomadic Hebrews from intermingling with the other nations' allegiances to foreign gods. In the context of Israel and the institution of a theocratic kingship, faithfulness to God is largely expressed by faithfulness as a nation as embodied in the kings of Israel. In captivity the Hebrews oscillate between intermingled cultural life and struggling to remain distinct from their captors (Ezra 9:2). As these political circumstances regarding "the nations" change in the OT, the Hebrews, as Yahweh's people, also change, and the drama of the OT turns on the faithfulness of God's people in the midst of various arrangements of relating to political power.

The NT historically takes place within the context of the fourth captivity as Israel simultaneously languishes and thrives under Roman conquest. In the NT *ethnos* and *laos* can denote "nation." As with the comparable OT terms, these terms can have a general sense, referring to all nations including Israel, as well as a specific sense, referring to gentiles in distinction from Jews and/or Christians. *Laos* more frequently refers to Israel as well as the Christian church as God's people. When applied to the Christian church, *laos* takes on a new sense (Rom. 9; Titus 2:14; Rev. 18:4; 21:3). One's identification with God's people is redefined from common ancestry via natural birth/Torah observance to common ancestry via spiritual rebirth/baptism into Christ. Paul identifies those who are in Christ as the seed of Abraham, and he emphasizes the importance of the unity of the Christian church as one *laos* (Gal. 3:26–28; cf. 1 Cor 12:13; Col. 3:11). He critiques what we might call the "nationalism" of those Jewish Christians who refused table fellowship with gentile Christians on the basis of their different natural ancestries to the neglect of their common ancestry in Christ (Gal. 2:11–16).

Church History

In the early years of the Christian church, Christianity related to the Roman authorities as politically disconnected local house churches within a colossal military and political empire. As Christianity developed and grew in numbers and influence, this empire related to the church in varying degrees of persecution and accommodation. In the fourth and fifth centuries, the church and the political state became increasingly intermixed, and their respective boundaries began to blur within the developments of Eastern and Western Christian empires. Augustine's *City of God* is only one, though perhaps the most ambitious, of many treatises meant to address this relationship theologically. According to Augustine, the state seeks after goods commensurate to its order and hence can be related to the church around the question of earthly, or what he called "temporal," goods. However, the state could not procure lasting goods, even as Rome claimed the moniker of "the eternal city." In this way, Augustine aligned Christians with the state on the question of earthly goods but also postured Christians as pilgrims attached only temporarily to those goods and the state. It was specifically the Roman Empire's claim of ultimate, universal legitimacy that put it at odds with Christianity, making unconditional allegiance to the empire morally problematic. The fragile relationship between Christians' eternal home, as Augustine described it, and their temporary sojourn in the earthly city was maintained in many different expressions through the long decline of the Roman Empire and imperial Christendom.

The eclipse of Christian imperial life created room for new political realities as the empire's decline rapidly expedited new forms of political existence. Most notably, the development of secular space free of religious control answered a rallying cry after the so-called wars of religion. Whether the wars of religion produced or were produced by the emerging secular state is itself internal to the ethics of nationalism, for how one grants nationalism ethical value depends on how one answers that question. In the centuries that followed, the nation-state was born as an idea internal to the most creative of modern inventions. Enlightenment thinkers contrasted the nation-state with a mythical "state of nature" (a place forlorn of the state's political order) in order to portray the nation-state as not only beneficial but also necessary. Akin to the Roman Empire's claim of ultimate, universal legitimacy, the nation-state's self-avowed universality condones any action impelled by national interests as if the continual existence of the nation-state itself becomes a moral justification. It is in this context that the relationship between Christians, whose loyalty remains with God, and the nation-state, which demands loyalty as well, becomes difficult to negotiate. Rather than being situated as wandering Jews "among the nations," as captive Christians under the Romans, or as imperial Christendom, God's people today live as citizens of nations, hold "nationalities," and imagine the world, and their lives within it, as organized around the idea of the nation as a political, economic, and social reality. The advent of globalization, which is only now coming to the fore, names a state of affairs wherein these nations themselves have become organized by forces, such as market capitalism, themselves larger and more powerful than nations; globalization suggests that nations themselves may give way to new realities.

The Ethics of Christian Relationships to Nations

The issue of Christianity's relationship to the nation and to nations has become contested in contemporary Christian ethics largely due to this rather circuitous history wherein many different ways of relating to political powers ensue. Given this long and complex history, various models of this relationship have been formulated, often deemed "ethical" over against others. However, one would be hard-pressed in suggesting that Scripture and the traditions emanating from church history speak of one model. In this vein, paradigms regarding the ethics of nationalism within the modern nation-state vary to a great degree. Because Christian Scripture and tradition testify to so many different models of nations and relations to the nations, Christian faithfulness can be mapped onto many different approaches.

In recent years, debates have followed on Christian ethicist Stanley Hauerwas's rejection of a paradigm articulated by Reinhold Niebuhr, who believed that the contemporary church could appropriate Augustine's "two cities" politics in order to situate Christianity to the nation-state in the terms of tragedy. Niebuhr utilized Martin Luther in order to imagine nationalism in what he considered Augustinian terms. For Niebuhr, the church and nation could relate for mutual good, though not without a fair amount of ambivalence regarding those goods. For example, the church's conceptions of justice could humanize the nation and impel its actions for the sake of justice. However, this also meant that the church recognized the nation, and its tools of coercion, as necessary and "realistic" rather than as good: the nation can *do* good, if properly encouraged by Christianity, but this does not mean that it *is* good, since its goods are always, as Augustine said, directed only to the temporal order. In this vein, nationalism named positive favor toward the state but always within bounds; ultimate loyalty did not belong to the state. This clearly is not the blank-check patriotism that obeys the nation by way of a blind faith that unfolds in the most virulent modes of nationalism: imperialism, xenophobia, totalitarianism, and so on. If Niebuhr allowed nationalism, it was a careful nationalism that could never presume crusade-like status or undermine loyalty to God.

Hauerwas followed fellow ethicist John Howard Yoder in affixing Christian discipleship to the issue of pacifism and, through the ethics of war, came to articulate the most sustained critique of nationalism. For Hauerwas and Yoder, the Christian church is not opposed to the nation but is axiomatically contrasted to the world, whose violence indicates its disobedience. The church's relationship to the nation, then, follows the nation's ability or inability purposefully to obey God. In this line of thought, when the nation's rebellion against God expresses itself by way of its anxious violence, then nationalism as favor toward that rebellion names idolatry. Rather than a wholesale disavowal of nationalism, Yoder's ethics grant space for nationalism if nationalism can be understood as an encouragement of the nations toward greater obedience to God. In contrast, Hauerwas rejected Niebuhrian allowance for nationalism, disavowing the kinds of accommodation that he associated with Niebuhr's realism and even came to develop a broad critique of the secular theorists who conceptualized the nation-state in the first place. Instead, he named the church as a polis that required its own nationalism rivaling nationalism to the nation-state as a counterallegiance. Today, this argument continues, and Jeffrey Stout's recent work has attempted to reimagine the nation-state beyond the terms of ethicists such as Yoder or Hauerwas. Rather than positing nation and church as rivals, thinkers such as Stout have tried to imagine the kinds of mutuality, last suggested by Niebuhr, that grant allowance for the Christian church's positive relationship with and participation within liberal democracies.

See also Civil Disobedience; Colonialism and Postcolonialism; Government; Idolatry; Imperialism; Institution(s); Kingdom of God; Loyalty; Political Ethics

Bibliography

Arendt, H. *The Origins of Totalitarianism*. Harcourt Brace Jovanovich, 1973; Augustine. *The City of God against the Pagans*. Ed. R. Dyson. Cambridge University Press, 2002; Cavanaugh, W. *Theopolitical Imagination*. T&T Clark, 2003; Hauerwas, S., and R. Coles. *Christianity, Democracy, and the Radical Ordinary: Conversations between a Radical Democrat and a Christian*. Cascade Books, 2008; Niebuhr, R. *Love and Justice: Selections from the Shorter Writings of Reinhold Niebuhr*. Ed. D. Robertson. Westminster John Knox, 1992; Stout, J. *Democracy and Tradition*. Princeton University Press, 2004; Yoder, J. *The Politics of Jesus: Vicit Agnus Noster*. 2nd ed. Eerdmans, 1994.

Lindsay K. Cleveland and Jonathan Tran

Natural Law

The term *natural law* is widely misunderstood and therefore feared by those reluctant to consider it, as well as often misconstrued and misapplied by many supposed supporters of this ancient ethical tradition. The term *natural law* has often functioned as a shibboleth dividing Roman Catholic and Protestant ethical approaches to Christian moral living. Catholics, especially in their magisterium (the official Roman Catholic Church teaching authority of the pope and bishops), have grounded their approach to concrete moral issues using natural-law theory that one hopes would be both accessible and convincing not only to Christians but also to all men and women of goodwill. Contemporary human-rights discourse also shares a similar objective, even though its own methodologies may vary.

The classic Protestant hesitation with the natural law is that our human reason that we would use to reflect on and apply the natural law in our lives is clouded or corrupted by the fall of our first parents and therefore is a rather untrustworthy aid to ethical discernment. Thus, to rely on the natural law for Christian ethical analysis would be a bit like continuing to use a computer program that one knows has been infected by a virus: the program might still "work" to a degree, but one can never be sure of the results obtained or if other files might in turn be corrupted.

Protestant theologians often thought it sounder to go directly and principally to Scripture for moral guidance, and *sola scriptura* (Scripture alone) was advanced as the principal resource for moral reflection, especially as opposed to a secular natural-law theory and/or church "tradition" that was not somehow contained in the Bible. For their part, Catholics certainly recognized the deleterious effects of sin on humanity, but the traditional Catholic response was that although human reason certainly was affected by the fall, it was not totally destroyed and therefore could be used. Church tradition, especially as interpreted by the magisterium, would serve as a balance and quality control check for overly individualistic and erroneous interpretations of the natural law.

Thomas Aquinas (1225–74) spoke of the natural law as "law by analogy." Thus, while it has some of the same characteristics of law, it is not, strictly speaking, a law in the sense of a physical law of nature or a civil law enacted by a legislator. Thomas spoke of the natural law as the human participation in God's eternal law, and he saw it written directly by God onto our human hearts in our conscience (*lex indita non scripta*). The natural law is the means by which human beings live out authentically the particular nature that God has given them. Another way of saying much the same thing is to look on the natural law as one aspect of God's loving providential care of humans—a way to exercise our God-given free will for our own good. In this perspective, then, to follow in conscience the dictates of the natural law simply means trying to be faithful to the fullest expression of true humanity that has been shown us in Jesus Christ. This view echoes Irenaeus's famous dictum *Gloria Dei vivens homo* ("The glory of God is the human person fully alive" [*Haer.* 4.20.7]). Living according to the natural law corresponds to promotion of true human values that at the same time will give God glory and best express God's will for humankind.

Natura-law theory has two main premises, one ontological and one epistemological. The ontological premise is the assertion that in some real sense there is an objective moral order—a rightness and wrongness of moral actions that contribute to our goodness or wickedness. This moral order exists independently of our individual wishes or desires, and if we wish to be truly happy and flourish, then we must live according to our authentic human nature. In short, the natural law is nothing other than a reflection on this true human nature.

But how do we know precisely what this natural law requires? This involves the second premise of natural-law theory: the assertion that in some way (albeit partial and open to the possibility of error) we can discover this natural law and hold ourselves to it. This is the function of conscience, which is aided by *recta ratio* (right reason). Thomas Aquinas distinguishes between two types of *recta ratio*, which he calls "speculative reason" and "practical reason." Unfortunately, his use of this vocabulary is quite different from contemporary usage of these two words, and probably on this account there is some confusion and misunderstanding on some key points in his natural-law theory. For him, "speculative" does not mean "future conditional," and "practical" does not mean "utilitarian" or "pragmatic." Instead, in his view, "speculative reason" aims at the discovery of abstract truth and principles that will be universally valid, whereas "practical reason" works toward applying those principles in the best possible way to a concrete situation. Thomas's first universal principle of the natural law is *Bonum est faciendum et prosequendum et malum vitandum* (*ST* I-II, q. 94, a. 2), which should be translated not as the imperative "Do good and avoid evil," but rather as the indicative "The good is to be done and fostered and evil is to be avoided." The correct grammatical mood is crucial, since he sees the natural law as essentially a process of discovery and application in individual conscience through our God-given faculty of reason, not simply as a matter of blind obedience to arbitrary moral laws.

It is all well and good to say "Foster the good and avoid the evil," but what does that mean in concrete situations? Here Thomas suggests a twin speculative and practical reason-based discovery process of moving from general first-order "universal" principles of the natural law down to concrete applications of these principles. For example, the principle "Drive safely" is an abstraction that is universally binding. Even in fleeing from a catastrophe we would seek to drive as safely as possible, given the circumstances and relative risks. It is this judgment of how fast to drive that is the work of "practical reason." Other things being equal, we could say that we should follow the posted speed limit, but we recognize quite legitimate circumstances in which it is morally acceptable to exceed that posted limit (e.g., a medical emergency). Thus, the principle "Obey the speed limit" is one based in practical reason, and while it may be generally true, it is not universally valid. This kind of middle-level principle (or middle axiom), Thomas says, is a *lex valet ut in pluribus*, which means that it is a law (*lex*) that holds (*valet*) in most, but not all, cases (*ut in pluribus*). Yet this middle axiom is also fully part of the natural law.

The last level of moral principles in Thomas's view of the natural law is what he calls "concrete material norms," and these are the specific applications of practical reason to a particular situation. If "Drive safely" is a universal principle, and "Obey the speed limit" is a middle axiom, then the specific limit "30 mph" is an example of a concrete material norm. We recognize that "30 mph" is not a one-size-fits-all automotive ethical velocity dictate, and that, depending on time and other circumstances, going faster or slower would be the best moral application of the universal natural-law principle of "Drive safely," and along with the middle axiom "Obey the speed limit," even the occasional morally sanctioned violation of the concrete material norm "30 mph" is part of the natural law.

Thus, some aspects of the natural law can and do change according to circumstances, or what Thomas calls "contingency," and involve the use of the virtue of *epikeia*—that is, trying to find the most fitting ethical response to a given set of circumstances. Finding this fitting response should not be misunderstood as moral relativism or situation ethics; rather, it is a recognition that the objective nature of the moral order itself shows that the natural law is not an inflexible static law such as the laws of nature or mathematics and thus necessarily will demand different applications for differing circumstances. Most applications of the natural law come through individual conscience-based exercise of a combination of speculative and practical reason, which are expressed in what we call "prudential judgments." Thus, Thomas recognizes and accepts that different persons can come to different conclusions about what is the wisest and best choice to make in a particular circumstance. Moral decision-making is not like mathematical reasoning. This key point of the natural law is not well grasped by some opponents who do not want to use the natural law in their moral discernment because they misjudge the natural law to be something inflexible that would not take into account true human subjectivity.

But what about the classic objection to the natural law, namely, that our human reason often is weak and too susceptible to error and rationalization? Would it not be better to trust in a safer moral guide such as Scripture rather than to rely on unaided human reason? Thomas recognizes this problematic and clearly admits that while the more general principles of the natural law might be known and accepted by all people of good will, the more we descend to the level of concrete applications, the more our judgments made through practical reason will be affected not only by "contingency" (differing circumstances) but also by "fallibility"—that is, the very real human tendency for error and self-deception (*ST* I-II, q. 94, a. 4). There is no quick-and-easy fix to this very real problem, and this is where individual and collective efforts at forming and informing our consciences are crucial aspects of living out authentically our human moral lives. Scripture too is an indispensable aid to this process, but history has taught us that the same discernment processes, with the real possibilities of error and self-deception, exist likewise in trying to answer the moral questions of what we ought to do, whether formulated in the terms of a natural-law discourse or a scripturally based inquiry of what God would have us to do.

See also Conscience; Discernment, Moral; Moral Law; Right and Wrong; Roman Catholic Moral Theology; Sin; Teleological Theories of Ethics

Bibliography

Bretzke, J. *A Morally Complex World: Engaging Contemporary Moral Theology*. Liturgical Press, 2004; Cromartie, M., ed. *A Preserving Grace: Protestants, Catholics, and the Natural Law*. Eerdmans, 1996; Crowe, M. *The Changing Profile of Natural Law*. Martinus Nihoff, 1977; Curran, C., and R. McCormick, eds. *Natural Law and Theology*. RMT 7. Paulist Press, 1991; Fuchs, J. *Moral Demands and Personal Obligations*. Trans. B. McNeil. Georgetown University Press, 1993; Gustafson, J. *Protestant and Roman Catholic Ethics: Prospects for Rapprochement*. University of Chicago Press, 1978; Porter, J. *Natural and Divine Law: Reclaiming the Tradition for Christian Ethics*. Eerdmans, 1999; Traina, C. *Feminist Ethics and Natural Law: The End of the Anathemas*. Georgetown University Press, 1999.

James T. Bretzke, SJ

Natural Rights

The admonition to "do the right" is part and parcel of biblical ethics (Mic. 6:8). The notion of "natural rights," however, emerges only in late twelfth-century canonical jurisprudence. The progeny of natural law (see Rom. 1:19–21; 2:14–15), natural rights refer, inter alia, to a subject's essential powers, liberties, claims, or entitlements. In the complex genealogy of rights, the most influential interpretation, from which our modern human rights derive, views natural rights as subjective claims imposing correlative duties upon others to act or refrain from acting. Natural claim-rights (that is, natural rights that entail responsibilities on others regarding the one holding the right) tell us what is "naturally" right or lawful.

Under the influence of nominalism, modern liberal theories of rights are marked by rationalism, individualism, and voluntarism. In modern social-contract theories, the natural liberties of sovereign selves, rather than divine sanction, become the basis of political legitimacy. How, then, does the modern idiom of natural rights relate to biblical conceptions of divinely mandated justice (*mišpāṭ*) or covenant fidelity (*ṣĕdāqâ*)?

Christian and Jewish interpreters typically appeal to the doctrine of the *imago Dei* (Gen. 1:26–27). Created in the divine image, persons are irreducibly valuable prior to their particular social roles, legal status, ethnicity, race, or gender. Their divinely bestowed dignity is permanent, irreplaceable, and inalienable. Respecting persons equally as moral agents, in turn, enjoins respect for the basic conditions or capabilities of their exercising agency. These capabilities become the basis of natural or human rights, which as such enjoy presumptive priority over other moral and nonmoral claims.

Modern Roman Catholic social teaching, for instance, recognizes not only civil-political liberties or immunities from interference by others but also positive claim-rights to security and subsistence, including basic rights to nutrition, healthcare, shelter, education, and so forth. Guaranteeing such basic rights against standard threats, moreover, imposes duties not only of forbearance but also of structural protection and provision. Although differences persist regarding the "natural" grounding, extension, and implementation of rights' regimes, a consensus supports what the preamble of the Universal Declaration of Human Rights (1948) calls our common "faith in fundamental human rights." Indeed, in the wake of the Shoah, human rights have become a lingua franca, defining the moral and legal minima of justice for religiously pluralist polities like those of the West.

Such polities need not embrace the Bible in their public reasoning. Yet "faith in fundamental human rights" is not, for that reason, disenchanted. In this consensus, distinctive biblical doctrines of creation, covenant, redemption, and neighbor love (Lev. 19:18; Matt. 19:19; Luke 10:27) provide both ultimate justification for natural rights and rich interpretative resources (narratives, parables, tropes, etc.) in redeeming rights claims (e.g., Walter Harrelson's interpretation of the Decalogue). So too, prophetic biblical injunctions inspire persons such as Martin Luther King Jr. and communities to uphold the fundamental rights of the most vulnerable. Rights let us proclaim the "good news to the poor" today, in our hearing (Luke 4:21).

See also Civil Rights; Deontological Theories of Ethics; Human Rights; Image of God; Natural Law

Bibliography

Harrelson, W. *The Ten Commandments and Human Rights*. Fortress, 1980; Shue, H. *Basic Rights: Subsistence, Affluence, and U.S. Foreign Policy*. 2nd ed. Princeton University Press, 1996; Tierney, B. *The Idea of Natural Rights: Studies on Natural Rights, Natural Law, and Church Law, 1150–1625*. EUSLR 5. Scholars Press, 1997; Wolterstorff, N. *Justice: Rights and Wrongs*. Princeton University Press, 2008.

William O'Neil, SJ

Necromancy

Necromancy is the act of calling up ghosts of the dead either to appease a troublesome ghost or, more commonly in the OT, to consult a ghost for advice or information that the dead, or at least particular dead, were presumed to have. The practice was common throughout the entire ancient Near East and continued into the Hellenistic and Roman periods and beyond. The Deuteronomic and Priestly law codes strictly prohibited necromancy (Lev. 19:31; 20:6, 27; Deut. 18:10–11), as well as related mourning rites for the dead (Lev. 21:1–5; Deut. 14:1), but those prohibitions seemed to have had little effect on actual practice during most periods of Israelite history. Saul suppressed the practice, as did Josiah's reform (1 Sam. 28:3, 9; 2 Kgs. 23:24) and perhaps other reform movements, but the practice simply went underground until the political pressure abated. The practice was alive and well in Isaiah's time (Isa. 8:19), was supported by Manasseh (2 Kgs. 21:6), and reappeared even in the postexilic Judean community (Isa. 57:3–9).

The biblical vocabulary for necromancy suggests that normally it was carried out through the help of an expert medium who could be either male or female (Lev. 20:27). The term *ʾôb* may be related to Hittite *a-a-pi*, which designates the sacrificial pit used in the necromancy ritual, but in Hebrew the term appears to refer to a ghost who has taken up residence in the medium. Leviticus 20:27 speaks of a man or woman in whom there is an *ʾôb* or *yiddĕʿōnî*. The medium's control over the ghost is emphasized by the designation of the female medium as a *baʿălat-ʾôb*, "the possessor/mistress of a ghost" (1 Sam. 28:7).

The second term, *yiddĕʿōnî* (from the root *yādaʿ*, "to know"), characterizes the resident ghost or in other texts the medium who controls the ghost as a "knowing one." It is unclear why the ancients attributed special knowledge to the dead. If one were consulting the dead about conditions in the underworld, the attribution of such knowledge to the dead would be understandable, and if one were consulting a dead prophet such as Samuel, his ability to give a prophetic oracle as a ghost would simply be an extension of the knowledge that he possessed while living. It is likely, however, that the attribution of special knowledge to the dead was the result not of rational reflection but simply a first principle, only secondarily rationalized if at all. Other terms for the ghost are *ʾiṭṭîm* (Isa. 19:3 [a false plural loanword from Akk. *etimmu*, "ghost"]), *ʾĕlōhîm* (normally "god" but clearly "spirit" or "ghost" in 1 Sam. 28:13; Isa. 8:19), and *hammētîm*, "the dead" (Deut. 18:11; Isa. 8:19).

We know little about the actual process of necromancy in Israel. By analogy with more detailed descriptions of necromantic rituals in Greek and Hittite sources, we might assume that the Israelite mediums dug a small pit in the ground, set food offerings around or in it to lure the hungry ghosts, and recited incantations to summon up the desired ghost. The recitation of these incantations appears to have been done in a kind of chirping or muttering fashion similar to bird sounds, perhaps because the dead were thought to speak in that manner (Isa. 8:19; 29:4). What role the medium's resident ghost played in this process and how one isolated the particular ghost to which one wanted to speak from the host of ghosts that might come up for the food offerings is unclear. The most detailed account of necromancy in the Bible is Saul's summoning of the dead Samuel (1 Sam. 28), but this is a literary account intended to be humorous, and it is hard to know how closely it corresponded with actual practice. Did the paying client actually see and talk to the ghost, or was it only the medium who saw the ghost, described the ghost to the client, and then facilitated the communication between client and ghost? Or, as has been suggested with regard to Greek and Roman necromancy, did the medium simply prepare the site where the client then slept and received the message from the dead by dreams? Or were there, in fact, a range of practices? Without more evidence it is impossible to say.

Why Israel's religious authorities attempted to prohibit the practice is not as clearly articulated as one might wish, though it is clear that such arcane knowledge was seen as an attempt to bypass the prophetic word, which was the appropriate way to gain directions for life (Deut. 18:9–22). The dead as *ʾĕlōhîm* ("gods") may have also been seen as idolatrous rivals to Yahweh as sources for knowledge (Isa. 8:19–20). Isaiah casts the Egyptian consultation of their idols as parallel to their consulting the dead (Isa. 19:3). But, if we may judge from the surrounding cultures, such interaction with the dead was also dangerous, both for the participants in such rituals and even for innocent nonparticipants. The restless dead could disturb the living, in extreme cases even take possession of the living, and in the surrounding cultures there were rituals for putting these roaming dead to rest. One did not need anyone disturbing (cf. 1 Sam. 28:15) or stirring up the dead who were at rest. Moreover, the potential for using the dead in black magic against the living was a concern in the surrounding cultures, and it may have been a concern in Israel. An obscure passage in Ezekiel refers to women who use divination, wristbands, and veils to hunt down the lives of the innocent (Ezek. 13:17–23). Whether their practice had any connection to necromancy is unclear, but it cannot be entirely ruled out.

See also Divination and Magic

Bibliography

Lewis, T. *Cults of the Dead in Ancient Israel and Ugarit.* HSM 39. Scholars Press, 1989; Ogden, D. *Greek and Roman Necromancy.* Princeton University Press, 2001; Schmidt, B. *Israel's Beneficent Dead: Ancestor Cult and Necromancy in Ancient Israelite Religion and Tradition.* Eisenbrauns, 1995.

J. J. M. Roberts

Nehemiah

The book of Nehemiah continues the narrative about the reconstitution of Judah that begins in the book of Ezra. The stories of Ezra and Nehemiah compose a coherent narrative (Ezra 7–Neh. 13) that begins with the Persian king Artaxerxes commissioning Ezra to teach the Torah in Judah and continues with the same king appointing Nehemiah to two successive terms as governor of Judah (Ezra 7:25–26; Neh. 2:5–8; 5:14; 8:9; 13:6–7). The book of Nehemiah consists of four parts: (1) Nehemiah rebuilds Jerusalem and its walls while releasing Judahite debt slaves (1:1–7:72a), (2) Ezra and the Levites lead the people in a covenant renewal ceremony (7:72b–10:40), (3) Nehemiah oversees the repopulation of Jerusalem and the dedication of the city walls (11:1–12:43), (4) Nehemiah later enforces some of the covenant stipulations (12:44–13:31). The narrator interweaves the careers of the protagonists by noting Nehemiah's support for Ezra's Torah teaching, on the one hand, and Ezra's participation in Nehemiah's dedication of the city walls, on the other (8:9; 11:36).

The collaboration between Ezra (mission in 458 BCE) and Nehemiah (governor beginning in 445 BCE) is a literary construct; yet by making Ezra and Nehemiah contemporaries in Jerusalem, the narrator portrays them as partners who redefined the postexilic community of Judah by separating the authentic descendants of preexilic Israel from all outsiders. Each leader establishes the community boundaries by a distinctive activity: Ezra teaches the Torah, and Nehemiah constructs the city walls. The synergy of the two endeavors is apparent when the Judahites voice their commitment to disassociate from other peoples within the confines of the walls that they had reconstructed (Neh. 6:15; 9:2; 10:29; cf. 13:3). The identification of the authentic community as consisting of the families of Judah and Benjamin who returned from exile and severed all family ties from the people of the land carries forward a central thesis from the book of Ezra (Neh. 7:6–72a; cf. Ezra 1:5; 2:1–70; 4:1; 6:16, 21; 9:1; 10:9, 11).

A first-person report, the so-called Nehemiah Memoir, highlights the social reforms that Nehemiah initiated in each term: first, his cancellation of debts and release of Judahite slaves (5:1–13), and subsequently, his securing the tithes for the Levites, closing markets on the Sabbath, and protesting marriages to foreigners (13:4–31). The covenant renewal ceremony in Nehemiah constitutes the climax of the broader Ezra-Nehemiah narrative (7:72b–10:40). The postexilic community defines itself by Torah observance. The choreography of the covenant renewal suggests a movement toward greater egalitarianism within the community even as it becomes more exclusionary toward outsiders. The Torah passes in succession from Ezra to the heads of the ancestral clans and finally to the whole assembly (8:2–3, 13; 9:2–3). The assembly consists of women and children as well as men (8:3; 10:29–30).

The covenant commitments to fallowing the land every seventh year and canceling debts are matters of social justice (Neh. 10:31). The produce of the seventh year belongs to the poor (Exod. 23:10–11). The rule governing indemnity specifically demands the release of pledges that debtors had consigned to their creditors as security for loans (Deut. 24:10). Such pledges could range from a garment to a piece of real estate (Exod. 22:24–26; Neh. 5:3–4). However, the immediate context in Ezra-Nehemiah indicates that the pledge in question is a child who works as a debt slave for the creditor in order to repay a loan that his or her parents had transacted with a creditor (cf. 2 Kgs. 4:1; Isa. 50:1). Such arrangements had precipitated the social and financial crises that provoked Nehemiah to demand the release of Judahite slaves and the cancellation of debts (Neh. 5:1–13). The covenant renewal secured the possibility of indebted Judahite families to regain their social integrity as well as the possession of their ancestral properties. The participation of children in the covenant renewal suggests the priority of enfranchising the sons and daughters who had been debt slaves (Neh. 5:5; cf. 8:3; 10:29–30). In this way, the book of Nehemiah touches on the human rights of children.

See also Covenant; Exile; Ezra; Old Testament Ethics

Bibliography

Blenkinsopp, J. *Judaism, the First Phase: The Place of Ezra and Nehemiah in the Origins of Judaism*. Eerdmans, 2009; Duggan, M. *The Covenant Renewal in Ezra-Nehemiah (Neh. 7:72b–10:40): An Exegetical, Literary, and Theological Study*. SBLDS 164. Society of Biblical Literature, 2001; Grabbe, L. *Yehud: A History of the Persian Province of Judah*. Vol. 1 of *A History of the Jews and Judaism in the Second Temple Period*. T&T Clark, 2004.

Michael W. Duggan

Neighbor, Neighbor Love

Loving one's neighbor is central to Jewish and Christian ethics. The context within which this command comes is the Holiness Code of Leviticus: "You shall not take vengeance or bear a grudge against any of your people, but you shall love your neighbor as yourself: I am the Lord" (19:18). Although the importance that Christians place on this injunction is clear, the exact meaning of the text is less so. A proper theological and ethical interpretation of the command to love one's "neighbor" as oneself must deal with three questions: What does "neighbor" mean? What does it mean to "love" the neighbor? And what does it mean to love the neighbor "as yourself"?

Attending to Scripture and Early Jewish Conceptions

Neighbor. In the OT, the Hebrew word often translated as "neighbor" (*rēaʿ*) primarily involves some form of closeness, whether physical (Exod. 11:2; Judg. 6:29), social (Prov. 19:6), or ethnic (Exod. 2:13). There is good reason to understand *rēaʿ* in Lev. 19:18 as pertaining to the neighbor who is related by virtue of the covenant. Although this would naturally focus the view on loving (primarily) other Israelites, the discussion just prior to 19:18 involves more specifically care for the "poor and the alien" (19:10), as well as the deaf and the blind (19:14).

Even though Lev. 19:18 centers on loving within the community (and addressed outsiders only insofar as treatment of resident aliens was fair), the meaning of neighbor as kin (see "kin" in 19:17) was galvanized and treated by some as a command to avoid improper associations in early Judaism. Ben Sira observes that it is natural and proper to associate with one's own kind, to love your own "neighbor" (Sir. 13:15 [Gk. *plēsion*]). Allying with the wrong kinds of people is an abomination. Jesus criticizes the interpretation of Lev. 19:18 that exaggerates this bifurcation by seeing love of neighbor as promoting hatred toward enemies (Matt. 5:43). Enemies should be loved and treated as objects of prayer. Indeed, in Luke 10:25–37 Jesus turns a discussion about how to *identify* a neighbor into one about how to *be* a loving neighbor—that is, showing mercy and compassion to anyone in need, despite social and ethnic distance.

Love. In the Levitical context, loving is not simply an emotion; rather, it is characterized by doing the opposite of the preceding prohibitions in Lev. 19:10–17: looking after the needy, showing generosity toward laborers, having compassion for people with disabilities. The nature of these prohibitions reflects a working out of the Ten Commandments as a model for covenantal obedience with regard to the treatment of others. In the NT, Jesus commanded his disciples to love one another as he demonstrated love for them (John 15:12). The kind of love that Jesus gave is understood as a commitment to the other that may even lead to death (John 10:15; Eph. 5:2; 1 John 3:14).

Paul encouraged pleasing one's neighbors to strengthen them and to tolerate any inconveniences (Rom. 15:1–3). More radically, he described neighbor love as a disposition similar to being a slave to another person (Gal. 5:13–14). Similarly, James calls Lev. 19:18 the "royal law" that particularly discourages prejudice against the poor (Jas. 2:1–13).

As yourself. The part of Lev. 19:18 that adds "as yourself" to the idea of loving the neighbor is open to several interpretations, but the most likely one has two aspects. The first involves seeking the highest good for the other as one naturally pursues what is best for oneself. The second is that Israelites should treat (and love) one another in the same way that they expect to be treated as ones who were equally made in God's likeness and who were equally freed by God from Egypt (see *Sipre Qodashim* 4.12).

In the Synoptic Gospels, Jesus encourages self-denial as a prerequisite for obedience (Matt. 16:24; Mark 8:34; Luke 9:23). Jesus is not promoting self-neglect here, though, but rather prioritizing the needs of others at a great cost to self. This is similarly expressed by Paul when he discourages the Philippians from working for selfish gain or pride (Phil. 2:3–4).

Ethical Implications

Two elements of the foregoing discussion are especially relevant to modern ethical discussions, one individual and one political. As for the former, picking up again the discussion of the role of "self" in loving the neighbor, it is commonly debated what relationship "I" have to "you" or "them." Garth Hallett outlines and assesses six models of Christ's "neighbor-love": self-preference, parity (i.e., equal benefit), other-preference, self-subordination, self-forgetfulness, and self-denial. Of these, he reasons that the most faithful model to the Christian tradition is self-subordination, which does not take the route of the last two models, which refrain from seeking one's own benefit at all. Instead, self-subordination allows for the consideration of one's own benefit, but it must never be to the disadvantage of another. The personal good can be sought out if that benefit could not be passed on to another or if another would not be limited or adversely affected in any way because of it. If one is inclined to agree with Hallett, Lev. 19:18 resists the idea that one loves the other and cannot seek out a happy life for oneself. This is particularly relevant to those who promote an ethic in which personal mistreatment and abuse should not be opposed.

The political aspect of neighbor love involves the problem of violence and warfare. Although a number of scriptural texts and theological issues are often brought to bear on this subject, it at least involves the basic concerns of love for neighbor and love for enemies. Does love for enemies exclude the physical resistance of them for a just cause? Does love for neighbor as a scriptural ideal mark out the church as a peaceable community that imitates Christ's humility and his refusal to act according to the vengeful and retributive nature of the fallen world? Although the basic moral thrust of the biblical idea of neighbor love is perspicuous, its application on this issue is more opaque.

Conclusion

To borrow and rework a well-known metaphor, the command "Love thy neighbor" is like an ocean: shallow enough that almost anyone can grasp its basic meaning, yet deep enough that its moral implications and applications are nearly bottomless. It stands within the heritage of Christianity as not just one of the two great love commandments affirmed by Jesus, but the necessary complement to the ideal of loving God. However one interprets this command to love of neighbor ethically, the struggle undoubtedly is over the center of the moral vision of the Bible itself.

See also Covenantal Ethics; Cruciformity; Enemy, Enemy Love; Golden Rule; Love, Love Command; Self-Denial; Self-Love

Bibliography

Cahill, L. *Love Your Enemies: Discipleship, Pacifism, and Just War Theory*. Fortress, 1994. Furnish, V. *The Love Command in the New Testament*. Abingdon, 1972; Goldingay, J. *Israel's Life*. InterVarsity, 2009; Gorman, M. *Cruciformity: Paul's Narrative Spirituality of the Cross*. Eerdmans, 2001; Hallett, G. *Christian Neighbor-Love: An Assessment of Six Rival Versions*. Georgetown University Press, 1989; Hays, R. *The Moral Vision of the New Testament: Community, Cross, and New Creation; A Contemporary Introduction to New Testament Ethics*. HarperSanFrancisco, 1996; Milgrom, J. *Leviticus 17–22*. AB 3A. Doubleday, 2000; Perkins, P. *Love Commands in the New Testament*. Paulist Press, 1982; Swartley, W., ed. *The Love of Enemy and Nonretaliation in the New Testament*. Westminster John Knox, 1992.

Nijay K. Gupta

New Testament Ethics

New Testament Ethics as a Discipline

Since the formation of a Christian Bible in the third and fourth centuries, preachers and teachers of the church have appealed to the Bible's authority in moral instruction and as a basis for Christian ethics. Only in the past 150 years or so has "New Testament ethics" been a subject distinct from theology or separate from the task of giving practical instruction to the church. Prior to the nineteenth century, attention to biblical teaching on moral subjects was found in works of theology, in separate treatises on ethics, and in a wide variety of other churchly writings devoted to instructing the faithful, but separate works on the subject of NT ethics scarcely existed. Certainly this was the case if NT ethics denotes a historical treatment of earliest Christian morality in its original environment as reflected by the writings that came to make up the NT. In a book published in 1899 on NT ethics, Hermann Jacoby remarked that he knew of only one antecedent to his historical approach to the subject, Albrecht Thoma's *Geschichte der christlichen Sittenlehre in der Zeit des Neuen Testaments* (1879). Thoma himself was aware of no prior study of first-century Christian morality in which the author treated the subject using modern historical methods. Perhaps these authors were unaware of George Matheson's *Landmarks of New Testament Morality* (1888) and like works or did not regard them as sufficiently historical in the rigorous "scientific" sense.

Some who study NT ethics use the terms *ethics* and *morality* as rough equivalents; others distinguish the two by defining ethics as rational reflection on moral questions. Wayne Meeks finds it helpful to conceive "morality" as "a pervasive but, often, only partly conscious set of value-laden dispositions, inclinations, attitudes, and habits," and "ethics" as a "reflective, second-order activity, morality made conscious" (Meeks, *Origins*, 4). A number of scholars have stressed that the NT contains little that can be described as "ethics" in this more precise sense, although NT morality can be analyzed for its underlying logic. For example, by attending to the often unspoken or only briefly expressed rationales that inform moral exhortation in the NT, one can work out something of the implicit ethics of the NT.

Although the word *ethics* is a plural noun, it is often used as a singular concept. As a result, it is not immediately clear whether "New Testament ethics" is a plural or singular subject. Today, most scholars recognize that the NT does not express a single "ethic," and studies of NT ethics typically are careful to describe the diversity of moral teachings and assumptions in the NT writings. Some (but not all) studies also make it a point to synthesize this diversity into some sort of unity.

Interest in a synthesis almost invariably involves the assumption that the use of the NT for Christian ethics is compromised if its various writings present no more than a jumble of diverse and even contradictory views. It is generally agreed, however, that unity is not immediately evident and needs to be demonstrated (or even "constructed"), and that the NT cannot be treated as a "rule book" with immediate applicability to contemporary moral questions. Conscientious use of the NT requires due attention to the variety of views and perspectives in its writings and the historical and cultural distance between its times and later times. That distance calls for some sort of hermeneutical translation or mediation.

This way of conceiving NT ethics reflects the highly influential biblical theology program of Johann Philipp Gabler (1753–1826), which continues to shape the way Christian scholars think about their role as academics. Gabler's program consisted of three basic parts: (1) historically sensitive interpretation of the various books of the Bible, treating each in its own terms; (2) synthesis of the results of this historical descriptive work, with the aid of general concepts; and (3) theological construction for contemporary life, carried out primarily by theologians who make use of the syntheses provided them by biblical scholars. The staying power of Gabler's program is especially evident in Richard Hays's *Moral Vision of the New Testament*, in which he proposes and carries out four tasks: the descriptive, the synthetic, the hermeneutical, and the pragmatic. Hays assumes the normative concept of "New Testament," seeks to show that there is a unity (with diversity and variety) in the NT's "moral vision," and engages himself in the constructive task (hermeneutical and pragmatic) of developing normative proposals for the contemporary church.

Not all treatments of the subject attempt to synthesize the ethical views of the NT, much less to tackle the question of how to use the NT in contemporary moral debate. A common approach is to confine the task to describing the moral instruction and assumptions of individual writings or "authorships" (Mark, Luke-Acts, the Pauline corpus, the Johannine writings, etc.). This approach, exemplified by Frank Matera's *New Testament Ethics*, may be termed narrowly historical because it does not attend to questions inherent to the use of the "New Testament" as Scripture. This is not to say that those who take a more narrowly historical approach to NT ethics are uninterested in the practical use of the NT, much less that they do not regard these writings as Scripture. Nevertheless, the narrowly historical approach reflects a certain ambiguity about whether the subject of NT ethics is the NT writings interpreted on their own terms and in their original historical settings before there was a NT, or whether "New Testament ethics" is an inherently theological and confessional concept that cannot be treated without certain assumptions about the nature of Scripture. The observation of this ambiguity becomes important when we consider that the moral teachings of the NT writings are also studied historically by those interested in giving an account of early Christian morality in general. Wayne Meeks uses the NT writings in this way in *The Origins of Christian Morality* and *The Moral World of the First Christians*. If one were to abstract from these books only what Meeks says about the NT writings, would that abstraction amount to "New Testament ethics"? Or is "New Testament ethics" something different, a subcategory of a theological discipline, analogous to the way in which Gabler conceived biblical theology as a subcategory of a broader theological task?

Another ambiguity touching the concept of NT ethics is whether it properly includes the ethics of the historical Jesus as distinct from the ethics of Jesus in the Gospels. Modern critical study of the NT distinguishes the historical Jesus from later portraits of him. Should descriptions of NT ethics include reconstructions of the ethics of the historical Jesus? In fact, the ethics of Jesus is included as a separate subject in books on NT ethics by Allen Verhey, Wolfgang Schrage, Rudolf Schnackenburg, and Russell Pregeant. But others (e.g., Hays, Matera) restrict themselves to the NT writings without offering separate reconstructions of Jesus' ethics. Hays explains that his book is not about the historical development of early Christian ethics but rather concerns the question of how the NT witnesses should shape the life of the church (Hays 158–59).

Hays's position is not the only one available to those who approach NT ethics as a theological discipline in service of Christian ethics. One can make a theological case that the historical Jesus is the proper presupposition of NT ethics and hence that the study of NT ethics should begin with the historical Jesus. This way of putting the matter recalls a famous mid-twentieth-century debate between Rudolf Bultmann and his student Ernst Käsemann. Bultmann argued that the historical Jesus is the presupposition of NT theology but not himself (his activity and teachings as reconstructed by scholarship) part of that theology (or of Christian theology generally). Käsemann insisted that the church has a legitimate interest in discovering the historical relation between the Jesus of history and the Jesus of the NT (the "Jesus of faith"), even if it would be wrong to make a reconstructed historical Jesus not only primary but also superior in authority to the Jesus of the NT. Certainly, there is no contradiction in the idea that both Jesus himself and the writings of the NT are authoritative for the church and should be taken together as foundations for Christian ethics, however their relationship is conceived and however difficult it may be to reconstruct the historical Jesus.

Those who are explicit about their theological assumptions and commitments sometimes explain why they begin with Jesus (e.g., Verhey), but some books on NT ethics that make the historical Jesus their first topic proceed as if no explanation were needed. The reason, no doubt, is that the history of NT scholarship, with its momentous turn to rigorous historical methods in the nineteenth century, led to a conception of the field of NT study as including three subjects: the historical Jesus and his mission, the formation of the early church (including the oral tradition), and the NT writings. Hence, Rudolf Schnackenburg's *Moral Teaching of the New Testament* (1962) begins with Jesus, moves to the early church, and then examines the individual NT authors.

Method in New Testament Moral Reasoning

Orientation to example. In deliberative rhetoric, where the aim is to persuade the audience to adopt a certain course of action, proof from example (Gk. *paradeigma*, Lat. *exemplum*) is a typical form of argument. Paul's Letters often move into a deliberative mode; hence, it is not surprising that his exhortation sometimes includes examples and calls for "imitation" (*mimēsis*). Paul gives brief narrative summaries of Christ's exemplary action and presses believers to behave in similar ways (Rom. 15:3; 2 Cor. 8:9; Phil. 2:6–11). He also urges his churches to imitate him (1 Cor. 4:16–17; 10:31–11:1; Gal. 4:12; Phil. 3:17; 4:9; 1 Thess. 1:5–6) and regards others as worthy of imitation as well (2 Cor. 8:1–6; 1 Thess. 2:14; cf. 1 Tim. 4:12). The unity of word and example is evident in his admonition "Keep on doing the things that you have learned and received and heard and seen in me" (Phil. 4:9). Or as he puts it in 1 Cor. 4:17, Timothy will "remind you of my ways in Christ Jesus, as I teach them everywhere in every church." The Greek term for "ways" (*hodoi*) in this passage reflects the Hebrew sense of *halakah*, a word that means "walking" and was used to express teaching about right living. This idea is also found in 2 Pet. 2:21 ("way of righteousness"). In other places Paul uses a Greek word for "walking" (*peripateō*) to convey an ethical meaning: "walking in love" (Rom. 14:15); "walk in newness of life" (Rom. 6:4; see also Rom. 13:13; 2 Cor. 12:18; 1 Thess. 2:12). In the same vein, Acts refers to the gospel as "the Way," which shows how closely the message was associated with a way of living (Acts 9:2; 19:9, 23; 22:4; cf. Matt. 21:32; Mark 12:14). These terms for "walking" and "way" can be used of right ways of living and thinking (as in nearly all the preceding examples) or wrong ways (as in Acts 14:16; 1 Cor. 3:3; Phil. 3:18; Jas. 5:20).

Early Christians would have assumed that one purpose of the Gospels, as history or biography, was to display Jesus as a model to be imitated. This ancient way of understanding the Gospels is evident in Justin Martyr's description of early Christian worship. After lengthy reading of the "memoirs of the apostles" (Gospels) or the prophets, Justin says, the president of the church gets up and urges the people to imitate the good things that they have heard (*1 Apol.* 66.3–4). The unity of a teacher's word and example was axiomatic for ancient Mediterraneans (see, e.g., Quintilian, *Inst.* 2.2.8). Readers—hearers—of the Gospels would have taken for granted that Jesus teaches them through his word and his example. The unity of these two is especially evident in the Gospel of Matthew, where key terms help the reader see the correlations between Jesus' teachings and his actions (cf., e.g., 5:5 with 11:29; 5:7 with 9:27; 5:39 with 26:52). Regarded in this light, the closing command to make disciples of all peoples, "teaching them to obey everything that I have commanded you" (28:20), means to instruct others in Jesus' commandments as preserved in his teachings and exemplified in the stories about what he did and how he lived.

Orientation to the particular. In the Greco-Roman philosophical tradition, moral analysis focuses on the nature of things and particularly "the good" inherent to the nature of the human being. That "good" is rationally determined, with the help of experience and observation. The good in this general and abstract sense is not the focal point of moral understanding for the NT writers. In only one place is the question of "the good" posed in anything like a general way: in the Matthean version of the story of the rich young man, Jesus responds, "Why do you ask me about what is good?" Jesus goes on to give not an abstract definition of the good but rather an admonition that the man should keep the commandments, sell his possessions, and follow Jesus (Matt. 19:16–22). Is this admonition meant for everyone or only for this man or those like him? However we answer this question, it is evident that Jesus' response speaks in the concrete and particular.

It is the nature of the example to be concrete and particular, but often the example cannot be imitated unless one first grasps its principle(s). This suggests that the implicit principles of moral examples in the NT should be regarded as primary material for constructing NT ethics. We are encouraged in this direction by the fact that examples often are given to illustrate or explain concepts. The parable of the merciful Samaritan is offered to define the concept of "love" as an obligation to the "neighbor" (Luke 10:25–37). The "grace" (kindness, generosity) of "our Lord Jesus" is explained through a description of how he became "poor" in order to make others "rich" (2 Cor. 8:9). In Heb. 11, "faith" (as a moral-spiritual disposition) is defined with a series of examples from Scripture. In Phil. 2 Paul offers the example of Jesus to sum up a set of qualities that the Philippians are to embody with one another: love, humility, unity, other-centeredness. Modern scholars have characterized Jesus' exemplary behavior in the Gospels (notably in his miracle-working and table fellowship) as "boundary-crossing" and animated by a special concern for the "marginalized." These concepts represent modern conceptual distillations of what are seen as implicit principles governing Jesus' mission.

Modes of moral reasoning. The NT writings contain moral exhortation but rarely take up ethical issues in reflective ways or offer comments about method in moral reasoning. Stoic philosophers, for example, were interested in debating the precise role to be given to precepts in moral thinking and exhortation (see, e.g., Seneca, *Ep.* 94). Nothing like this is found in the NT. The most sustained moral instruction appears in the Sermon on the Mount, but without articulation of informing assumptions. Only in Paul do we meet moral arguments where rationales are given, in his treatment of various topics in 1 Corinthians and in his counsel in Rom. 14–15 about issues between the "weak" and the "strong."

Using modern categories, we can ask whether the reasoning in and behind the NT conceptions of moral decision-making is primarily consequentialist (judgments in concrete cases based on best outcomes as evaluated by normative principles), deontological (judgments governed by moral rules without regard for consequences), virtue-based (judgments governed by good character), or some combination of these. But we get an idea of the methods of NT writers only by observing what they do. One finds teaching that seems to reflect a consequentialist approach in 1 Cor. 7:1–16 (advice about whether to marry or separate based on outcomes) and instruction that appears to assume a deontological approach in Mark 10:2–9 (a rule about divorce). Exhortations to imitate exemplars arguably belong to a virtue-based approach, especially since the NT writers take for granted that exemplars are found not only in Scripture but also in life as formative influences in community. It probably is fair to say that all the NT writers took for granted that moral formation depends on imitating good examples in Scripture and in life. It is also clear that disagreements about proper behavior were debated with recourse to a variety of modes of argument: appeal to authority (personal authority, rules, the Mosaic law, common opinion), appeal to character, and appeal to principles (including consequences judged by principles).

The NT writers expected the near end of the world, and most if not all believed that the new age (new creation, kingdom of God) had already begun in provisional ways. Animated by this eschatological consciousness, some early church leaders sought to live out in the present the ideals that they ascribed to the dawning future age. Paul was one such leader, although he also sought to restrain the tendencies of those (such as certain members of the churches at Corinth) who wished to live as if the new creation had already fully arrived. His declaration that in Christ the distinctions between Jew and Greek, male and female, slave and free come to an end (Gal. 3:28) seems to have influenced his understanding of the social order that ought to prevail in the church, making him something of an egalitarian. But he was a consistent champion of full equality in the present when it came to only one of these social relations: the equality of gentile with Jew. Moreover, in the NT generally, eschatological references in moral exhortation are almost always threats of future punishment or promises of reward; only occasionally do they entail explicit appeals to new norms based on a vision of the future kingdom or new creation.

Integrated conceptions of the New Testament's moral vision. Modern interpreters interested in offering integrated descriptions of NT ethics have tended to focus on combining two main voices: Jesus and Paul. "Jesus" means the historical Jesus, the Jesus of the Synoptic Gospels, the Jesus of all four Gospels, or a portrait drawn on historical-Jesus research and the Gospels. "Paul" is usually restricted to the undisputed letters. Other parts of the NT are incorporated into the synthesis with various degrees of emphasis and attention to how well they fit into an ethical vision compounded of Jesus and Paul.

Integrating Jesus and Paul usually entails correlating Jesus' message of the kingdom ("reign") of God with Paul's understanding that a "new creation" has dawned in Christ. The Gospels frame Jesus' teaching by ordering it within the story of his journey to death and resurrection. Paul's Jesus, who willingly gave up his life out of obedience to God and merciful concern for others, seems to jibe with the other-centered Jesus of the Gospels, who embodies in action the values of the kingdom and who dies for what he said and how he lived. "Love" is the primary ethical principle for the Jesus of the Gospels and the Jesus of Paul, a love that Paul and the Gospels define as self-sacrificial and directed toward all human beings. Debate continues regarding the sense in which love is a primary moral norm in the NT and how far each writing or author is committed to an ethic based on love.

See also Consequentialism; Deontological Theories of Ethics; Imitation of Jesus; Kingdom of God; Moral Formation; Virtue Ethics

Bibliography

Burridge, R. *Imitating Jesus: An Inclusive Approach to New Testament Ethics*. Eerdmans, 2007; Hays, R. *The Moral Vision of the New Testament: Community, Cross, New Creation; A Contemporary Introduction to New Testament Ethics*. HarperSanFrancisco, 1996; Keck, L. "Rethinking 'New Testament Ethics.'" *JBL* 115 (1996): 3–16; Matera, F. *New Testament Ethics*. Westminster John Knox, 1996; Meeks, W. *The Moral World of the First Christians*. Westminster, 1986; idem. *The Origins of Christian Morality: The First Two Centuries*. Yale University Press, 1993; Pregeant, R. *Knowing Truth, Doing Good: Engaging New Testament Ethics*. Fortress, 2008; Schnackenburg, R. *The Moral Teaching of the New Testament*. Trans. J. Holland-Smith and W. O'Hara. Herder, 1965 [1962]; Schrage, W. *The Ethics of the New Testament*. Trans. D. Green. Fortress, 1988 [1982]; Verhey, A. *The Great Reversal: Ethics and the New Testament*. Eerdmans, 1984.

Charles H. Cosgrove

Nihilism

Nihilism is an epistemological assertion with ontological and ethical implications. Nothing of significance can be known. Existence has no discernible objective purpose or *telos* and, as differentiated from existentialism, can have no real subjective purpose either. Essentially, nihilism is intellectually generated anomie. To make any claim about what is right or wrong, good or bad, is utterly pointless.

Nihilist-like arguments have been made since antiquity (e.g., Gorgias, Pyrrho, arguably Nagarjuna), but it was not until after the Enlightenment that the position gained cultural prominence in the West, growing out of the epistemological skepticism of Hume and others and in reaction to romanticism, traditional Christianity, and the rise of the middle class. The term *nihilism* first came to prominence following its use by Ivan Turgenev in *Fathers and Sons* (1862). Nihilist concepts often have been presented at the boundary of philosophy and literature.

Søren Kierkegaard describes the aesthete as one who lives a shallow life, focusing on the trivial to numb the existential pain of meaninglessness and despair. Such a person is a practical nihilist. Eventually, an attempt to live the ethical life may follow, yet even that will end in failure, and then three options are presented: accept actual nihilism, kill oneself, or take the leap of faith.

In *Notes from Underground*, Fyodor Dostoevsky portrays a man who despises the inability of others to recognize that their lives are as pointless as his own, which ironically initially provides him some satisfaction. He obtains temporary pleasures in sensation, seeks prestige by not moving out of the way of others on a sidewalk, and attempts a humane relationship, finally concluding that neither a loving relationship nor dominating another can provide purpose or satisfaction. The story ends with the man observing himself, taking notes about his meaninglessness, as he spirals further down into nihilism, concluding that his observing, his note-taking, and his life are nothing.

Friedrich Nietzsche used a provocative metaphoric writing style and aggressive denunciation of opponents to establish a nihilist-like position, but as "life-affirming" for those willing to be defiant in the face of eternal meaninglessness. Tragic reality can be overcome through personal will to power by the *Übermensch*, rejection of slave status (especially as manifest in the slave religion of Christianity), and resigned recognition of the endless cycle of eternal return.

The character Kurtz in Joseph Conrad's *Heart of Darkness*, having sought satisfaction in the extreme violence of the ivory trade, finally becomes a charismatic megalomaniac attempting to rule by his own standards of morality—a mixture of Kierkegaard's ethical stage and Nietzsche's *Übermensch* or perhaps Dostoevsky's Underground Man but with power. Eventually, he concludes that even control of others is pointless, since superiority makes no sense if there is no way to determine the basis of desire, righteousness, or despicability. Choosing between ever-deepening melancholia and what is essentially an anomic suicide, the character's life ends. The juxtaposed figure in the story, Marlow, goes through a similar process, concluding finally to take a leap of faith, not toward the Christian God, but to what appears to be Westernized Buddhism.

As in the past, contemporary expressions of nihilism are more often found in the visual arts, music, and literature than in formal philosophy and, as in the past, often marked by a tone of mockery of those who do "believe" or cynicism about human relationships. In the visual arts, early twentieth-century Dada was self-described as "anti-art," and more recent efforts using mundane, vulgar, or surreal representations portray all images as misrepresentations and meaningless. The lyrical claims in some contemporary music and non sequitur dialogue in absurdist drama offer a deconstructionism that logically concludes in nihilism, in deconstruction deconstructed.

In ancient Israel, nihilist-like thought had no significant place, given the strong emphasis on an intervening and caring Deity. Ecclesiastes hints at some nihilistic concepts but concludes with resigned affirmation of God. Psalms 14 and 53 indicate that although some believe that "there is no God," they should be dismissed as "fools" who will finally find themselves filled with dread, or anomic despair.

James R. Thobaben

Nonviolence *See* Pacifism

Norms

Moral norms are standards by which we measure conduct. Modern moral theories have attempted to determine norms by the rational consistency of an action in itself (sometimes called "deontology") or by a calculation of the various consequences of an action (utilitarianism or consequentialism). Both sets of theories have set out to achieve a certainty of norms that is analogous to mathematics and the natural sciences. Ironically, the failure to meet these standards of disinterested objectivity has contributed to moral relativism, the view that all "norms" serve cultural, class, or individual interests. The biblical approach is quite different. In Scripture, the final measure and norm of human life is a personal and self-giving ("interested") God.

Human beings are made in the image of God (Gen. 1:27). With God as the measure of the image, the temptation of Eden carries a bit of irony: "When you eat of [the fruit of the tree] your eyes will be opened, and you will be like God, knowing good and evil" (Gen. 3:5). The sin of Adam and Eve can be seen as an attempt to be what they are created to be: "like God." But they are tempted to fulfill the image in the wrong way: by making and being the measure (self-making) rather than being the representative and image of God. At Sinai, God calls Israel to be a "kingdom of priests, a holy nation" (Exod. 19:6). The call is to be set apart by God and to live in a way that is faithful to God—that is, faithful to the divine measure, to be holy as God is holy (Lev. 11:44; 19:2; 20:7, 26). In the Gospel of Matthew, Jesus revitalizes this call to holiness (Matt. 5:48) to be the salt of the earth, the city on the hill, and a light for others (Matt. 5:13–16).

The desire to have a king in Israel, to be like the nations, is interpreted as a threat to the faith of the people in the kingship of God (1 Sam. 8:1–9). When Saul is anointed to be Israel's first king, the prophet Samuel warns the people that their destiny as a nation and the fate of their kings will hinge on their vocation as a people. The king and all of Israel are bound to the commands of God (1 Sam. 12:13–15). The prophetic witness in Israel is based on this covenant and calling. The imperative for Israel is to walk in God's ways and keep God's commands (1 Kgs. 2:4). David repents when Nathan pronounces judgment on his sins. His adultery (with Bathsheba) and murder (of Uriah) are likened to a rich man stealing from the poor. He has scorned the word of the Lord

(2 Sam. 12:9, 14). Here we find a web of prophetic denunciations: unfaithfulness to God—rejecting the commands, abusing the poor, and committing acts of false worship (Jer. 7:5–11; Amos 2:4–8; Mic. 6:3–8). Alternatively, the prophetic message of hope proclaims the faithfulness of Israel and the restoration of its vocation as a people: the lowly will be lifted up, the land will be free of oppression and injustice, the covenant with God will be renewed, the people will worship the Lord in truth, and foreigners will come to the Lord (Isa. 54–56). God will be proclaimed as king and, at last, the ruler of all life (Isa. 52:7).

In the NT, the prophetic promises and Israel's vocation are found in Jesus. Jesus is the righteousness of God and the faithfulness of Israel (Matt. 3:11–4:11). Paul proclaims that new life is offered through the dying and rising of Christ: "He died for all, so that those who live might live no longer for themselves, but for him who died and was raised for them. . . . So we are ambassadors for Christ, since God is making his appeal through us" (2 Cor. 5:15, 20). Jesus gathers and restores the people: in lifting up the lowly (Luke 4:16–21); in the calling and sending out of disciples (Mark 1:16–20; 6:7–13, 30–32); in eating with sinners and Pharisees (Luke 7:36–50); in healing and restoring the lost to common life (Matt. 8:1–4; Luke 19:1–10); in showing a new way of reconciliation and peace (Matt. 5–7); and, of course, in the cross and resurrection, which orders all things to God (Phil. 2:6–11). In short, Jesus is Lord. Therefore, he is worshiped and imitated. The norm of life is given in God incarnate, the divine and human person, who is God's righteousness and the fulfillment of our call to be holy as God is holy.

By understanding this biblical norm, the basic problems of "obligation" and "moral law," for modern moral theory, come into view. Moral norms become arbitrary and ultimately incoherent apart from a lawgiver who is also the fulfillment and purpose of human life. Apart from God as "measure" and "end" of human life, the moral rationality that holds together law, moral obligations, virtue, and human flourishing eventually disintegrates. This profound insight was made over a half century ago by Elizabeth Anscombe.

See also Consequentialism; Deontological Theories of Ethics; Imitation of Jesus; Incarnation; Justification, Moral

Bibliography

Anscombe, E. "Modern Moral Philosophy." *Philosophy* 33 (1958): 3–19.

David Matzko McCarthy

Numbers

The book of Numbers, the fourth book of the OT, derives its name from the two census lists that number the people in each of the twelve tribes of Israel during their wilderness journey to the promised land of Canaan (chaps. 1; 26). These two census lists mark two different generations of Israelites, one old and rebellious and the other new and hopeful. Numbers moves from Israel's obedient preparations for the march from Mount Sinai to Canaan (chaps. 1–10), to an abrupt series of increasingly serious rebellions against God and Moses by the old generation (chaps. 11–20), to glimpses of hope in the midst of the dying out of the old generation (chaps. 21–25), to the rise of a new generation standing with hope on the edge of the promised land (chaps. 26–36).

Israel's Second Great Sin: Refusing God's Gift of the Land

Israel's idolatrous worship of the golden calf in Exod. 32 was its first great sin in its wilderness journey from Egypt to Canaan. Israel's second great sin is presented in the spy story in Num. 13–14. The Israelites refuse to accept God's gift of the land of Canaan because they fear the power and size of the Canaanite enemy. God's reaction is initially a plan to destroy all the Israelites, but then God relents in response to Moses' intercession and appeal to God's merciful character (14:10–19).

However, severe consequences also result from Israel's lack of trust in God. God resolves that the old wilderness generation will have to wander in the wilderness for an additional thirty-eight years until they all die out in the wilderness. Only their children as a new generation of Israelites will be allowed to enter into the land of Canaan (14:20–35).

Challenging Ethical Issues in Numbers

The book of Numbers contains one of the most blatant examples of patriarchy and gender inequality in the Bible: the legal case of a wife suspected of adultery (5:11–31). The law allows a husband who suspects his wife of adultery to bring that charge against her even though he has no evidence. The wife is subjected to a humiliating public ritual involving a trial of ordeal. The wife, however, has no right to bring a similar charge against her husband.

Another ethically challenging text in Numbers is the story of the priest Phinehas, who kills a Midianite woman and Israelite man as punishment for Israel's entanglement with Midianite women and the worship of their foreign gods (25:1–18). Later in Numbers, God commands Israel to engage in a holy war against the Midianites because they tempted Israel away from the worship of Israel's God (31:1–54). These texts have been used in the history of biblical interpretation to legitimate the use of violence and holy war as a weapon of religious intolerance.

Positive Ethical Resources in Numbers

The book of Numbers also provides some positive ethical resources for the community of faith. God's ultimate will for his people is expressed by the benediction or blessing that God commands the priests to place upon the people of Israel (6:22–27).

The two narratives of chapter 11 and chapter 12 affirm the wisdom of the wide distribution of authority and leadership among many parts of the community (see 11:16–30) and, at the same time, the importance of maintaining Moses' authority as a central leader. The two stories together suggest the wisdom of a dialogical balance between distributed and centralized authority in the structure of community governance.

The story of the foreign prophet Balaam in chaps. 22–24 affirms God's ability to work through and accomplish his purposes through a foreign religious leader such as Balaam. God's sovereignty is clear as he unravels the plans of the Moabite king to curse Israel and instead ensures the blessing of Israel by the prophet Balaam.

The case of the five daughters of Zelophehad in chaps. 27 and 36 illustrates the need for ongoing reinterpretation of earlier laws and traditions in the face of new contexts and circumstances.

See also Adultery; Authority and Power; Blessing and Cursing; Feminist Ethics; Holy War; Old Testament Ethics; Violence

Bibliography

Bach, A. "Good to the Last Drop: Viewing the Sotah (Num. 5.11–31) as the Glass Half Empty and Wondering How to View It Half Full." Pages 26–54 in *The New Literary Criticism and the Hebrew Bible*, ed. J. Exum and D. Clines. JSOTSup 143. JSOT Press, 1993; Collins, J. "The Zeal of Phinehas: The Bible and the Legitimation of Violence." *JBL* 122 (2003): 3–21; Olson, D. *Numbers*. IBC. Westminster John Knox, 1996; Sakenfeld, K. "In the Wilderness, Awaiting the Promised Land: The Daughters of Zelophehad and Feminist Interpretation." *PSB* 9 (1988): 179–96.

Dennis T. Olson

Oaths

An oath is the strongest possible confirmation of the truthfulness of a statement about what has transpired ("assertive oaths") or a promise about one's future actions ("promissory oaths"). In Scripture, oaths nearly always invoke (at least implicitly) divine witness (Gen. 31:50; Jer. 42:5) to the veracity of a statement as well as divine retribution (1 Sam. 3:17; 14:44) should the statement prove false or the promise empty. Rabbinic literature and biblical scholars often distinguish between oaths and vows, but there is considerable overlap in practice. Both forms include promises about future actions, but oaths also include statements about present or past situations.

Oaths and vows are evident throughout the OT and play a variety of roles. Many OT figures swear oaths, including Abraham (Gen. 21:22–34), Jacob (Gen. 25:33; 28:20), Joseph (Gen. 50:5), Hannah (1 Sam. 1:11), David (1 Sam. 20:17), Ezra (Ezra 10:5), and Nehemiah (Neh. 13:25). Vows are found at times of distress (Gen. 28:20–22) and as expressions of thanksgiving (Ps. 116:16–18). Oath formulations include "As the Lord lives" (Ruth 3:13; 1 Sam. 19:6; 1 Kgs. 1:29; Jer. 4:2; Hos. 4:15) and "the Lord shall be between me and you" (1 Sam. 20:42). People swore by God's name (Neh. 13:25), by God's faithfulness (Isa. 65:16), and by the Lord (Gen. 24:23; 2 Sam. 19:7; 1 Kgs. 2:42). The practice of swearing by other gods came under attack by the prophets (Jer. 12:16; Amos 8:14; Zeph. 1:5).

It is difficult to overstate the importance of oaths in the OT. To swear by God's name can be a sign of faithful attachment to God (Deut. 6:13; 10:20; Isa. 48:1; Jer. 12:16). Swearing truthfully and faithfully is associated with God's blessing (Ps. 24:4; Isa. 65:16). Oaths were legally and morally binding, even if offered foolishly or rashly (Num. 30:2; Deut. 23:21–23; Eccl. 5:4–5; cf. Judg. 11:29–40). An oath by the accused could settle a dispute for which there were no witnesses (Exod. 22:11). By contrast, there is strong condemnation of false oaths offered in legal, business, and civil affairs (Lev. 6:3; 19:12; Jer. 5:2; 7:9; Mal. 3:5). In situations of crisis or mistrust, swearing indicated that the parties would honor their promises and refrain from harming each other (Josh. 2:12; Judg. 15:12; 1 Sam. 24:21).

Interestingly, God is depicted as swearing an oath to David (Pss. 89:3; 132:11). God swears by his eternal life (Deut. 32:40), holiness (Ps. 89:35; Amos 4:2), person (Isa. 45:23; Amos 6:8), and power (Isa. 62:8). In a cultural context where oaths play such a prominent role, God's swearing likely adds to the listener's confidence in God's intentions and promises, quite apart from the oaths adding to the truthfulness or reliability of God's words (cf. Heb. 6:13–18).

The difficulty for Christian ethics appears with Matt. 5:33–37, the fourth "antithesis" in the Sermon on the Mount. Robert Guelich contends that we see both "assertive" (v. 33a) and "promissory" (v. 33b) oaths in view when the text begins with the familiar OT concerns that "you shall not swear falsely" but rather "carry out the vows you have made to the Lord" (cf. Lev. 19:12; Num. 30:2; Deut. 23:21–23; Ps. 50:14). The difficulty is that rather than underline the importance of honoring oaths, Jesus prohibits any type of swearing (Matt. 5:34), specifically rejecting several types of oath formulas popular in that day—swearing by heaven, earth, Jerusalem, or one's head (vv. 34–36)—and demanding instead a straightforward yes or no (v. 37).

What are we to make of this passage? James 5:12 offers a similar "no oath" statement: "Above all, my beloved, do not swear, either by heaven or by earth or by any other oath, but let your 'Yes' be yes and your 'No' be no, so that you may not fall under condemnation." In the early church, Matt. 5:33–37 usually was interpreted as literally prohibiting all oaths, as seen in Justin, Irenaeus, Tertullian, Origen, Clement of Alexandria, and John Chrysostom. However, this position of "no oaths" became increasingly problematic as the church was accepted by and then directly connected with the state. Augustine developed a theological apology for oaths, noting that Paul gave thoughtful application of oaths, and that the oath was useful to both state and neighbor. This has remained the basic position of the Catholic Church. The Reformers and later Protestant Christianity typically have affirmed oath-taking, especially when ordered by the state, but also in situations where God's honor or neighbor well-being are at stake. Martin Luther rejected an individual's initiating an oath but taught that the state's command to swear must be obeyed. Arguments in favor of oath-taking, both Catholic and Protestant, are also often tied to the sinful nature of society and the unreliability of ordinary speech.

While most of the church accommodated oath-taking, an alternative position is seen in the rejection of swearing in the Middle Ages by the Cathari and Waldensians, later by the Hussites and Bohemian Brethren, and then especially by the Anabaptists. Most Anabaptist leaders and groups entirely rejected oath-taking. Article 7 of the Schleitheim Confession concerns Christ's abolishing all swearing for his followers. Because oath-taking often was seen as essential to the state's survival, the Anabaptist refusal to swear often met a harsh response from Catholic Church authorities, the Reformers, and state rulers alike. It is among the reasons that many early Anabaptists were imprisoned, tortured, and executed. Indeed, on the basis of their refusal to swear, Mennonites were denied civil and voting rights in some countries up until the first decades of the nineteenth century. Quakers too rejected the oath and often were imprisoned due to their refusal to swear loyalty oaths. Mennonites, Hutterites, Amish, and Quakers still abstain from the oath, instead offering a simple affirmation that they will tell the truth or do their duty.

The arguments by these groups against oath-taking are of several types. First, the refusal to take an oath often is seen as a matter of straightforward obedience to Christ's command. Second, oath-taking runs against true reverence for God: we should not endeavor to control or manipulate God into guaranteeing our speech. Third, since human beings are finite and sin-prone, it is presumptuous to assert such confidence in our ability to be truthful that we invoke God as witness and call upon God's judgment. The contingencies of human existence are such that we may not be able to carry out the content of an oath, no matter how well intended. Fourth, oath-taking undermines our confidence in everyday speech by teaching us that we are required to be truthful only in certain limited situations. Fifth, if we are honest in our daily dealings and speech, then the oath is unnecessary, but if we cannot be counted on to speak truthfully in such matters, then there is no reason to trust the veracity of the oath taker. Interestingly, secular humanists, atheists, and agnostics now add a different argument: they should not be required to invoke a divine witness whose existence they doubt or deny. Such swearing goes against their conscience and implicitly involves them in what they believe to be a lie.

Additional biblical interpretation sheds limited light here. Most commentators do not believe that Jesus abolished oath-taking. They point to Matt. 23:16–22, where Jesus does not explicitly reject oath-taking but instead attacks a corrupt oath-taking system in which swearing by symbols for God's name were claimed to be nonbinding. Commentators also point to Paul's taking of various oaths and vows (2 Cor. 1:23; Gal. 1:20; Phil. 1:8) and to Heb. 6:13–20, where the practice is cited without criticism. Other commentators argue that Matt. 5:34–36 shows that Jesus prohibited "promissory" oaths, not "assertive" oaths. However, some commentators, such as Ulrich Luz, contend that the history of interpretation of Matt. 5:33–37 is one of efforts to evade its demand, and that the "nonconformists," such as Anabaptists and Quakers, come closest to the text. Luz also contends that vv. 34–36 show that Jesus was particularly concerned with the sanctification of God's name; that is, both truth-telling and God's holiness are in view.

What most commentators agree on is that in requiring of us a simple yes or no, Jesus is calling us to straightforward and truthful speech at all times. Many commentators also agree that the broader setting of the Sermon on the Mount is more focused on what kind of people and practices are consistent with the inbreaking reign of God than with a new set of legal restrictions. Thus, Glen Stassen and David Gushee are at least partially correct when they contend that the central issue is less about whether we should swear oaths in court than how we become truthful people.

See also Promise and Promise-Keeping; Speech Ethics; Vows

Bibliography

Guelich, R. *The Sermon on the Mount: Foundation for Understanding*. Word, 1982; Luz, U. *Matthew 1–7: A Continental Commentary*. Trans. W. Linns. Fortress, 1992; Stassen, G., and D. Gushee. *Kingdom Ethics: Following Jesus in Contemporary Context*. InterVarsity, 2003.

Joseph J. Kotva Jr.

Obadiah

Two things about the book of Obadiah stand out. First, a book comprising only twenty-one verses has generated significant scholarly literature over the years. Second, part of the reason for the interest in the book, notwithstanding its anti-Edom polemic, may be the incorporation of some key prophetic themes within a span of twenty-one verses. The prophet touches on some familiar themes/motifs such as the day of Yahweh (v. 15), judgment against foreign nations (vv. 15–16), Zion theology (vv. 17, 21), retributive justice of God (v. 15), promise of repossessing the land (vv. 19–20), and the ultimate rule of Yahweh (v. 21). There are also echoes of prophecies from Joel (2:32) in verse 17 and Jeremiah (49:7–22) in verses 1–11. The imagery of the cup of wrath found in Jer. 49:12 also appears in verse 16. The relationship of Obadiah to other oracles against Edom found in Amos 1:11 and Jer. 49:7–22, among others, deserves closer scrutiny. Suggestions for the historical stimulus for the book have ranged from the preexilic conflict as reflected in 2 Kgs. 8:20–22 to a late postexilic context contemporaneous with Malachi or Joel. The most likely scenario seems to point in the direction of the catastrophe of 587 BCE.

Obadiah can be divided into two parts. Verses 1–15 describe judgment against Edom for its attitude and action toward Judah. Verses 16–21 take on a more general tone in that they are addressed to the "nations" about the impending judgment coupled with the promise of restoration for Judah. Three aspects of the Edomites' role draw the prophet's ire. First, although the Edomites did not initiate the action, they simply stood by and watched as the enemies carried out their assault against Judah (v. 11a). The ethical challenge of Obadiah here is this: we may not be guilty of inflicting oppression and violence, but have we chosen simply to watch as violence and oppression continue? Second, after being bystanders, the Edomites became participants in the act (vv. 11b, 13c, 14). Finally, to add insult to injury, they gloated over the misfortune of Judah (vv. 12a, 13b [cf. Ezek 35:10–15]).

From an ethical perspective, it is hard to condone or justify the xenophobic outlook presented in the book. But this must be put into perspective in light of Obadiah's emphasis on the sovereignty of God over not just Judah but over all nations. God's sovereignty manifests itself in the form of God's justice. God will not let evil go unpunished. As the focus shifts from Edom (v. 1) to the nations (v. 15), the message becomes broader to include all forces counter to God's purposes. Obadiah's word of hope to the victims is that in the end evil will be punished.

See also Judgment; Justice, Retributive; Old Testament Ethics

Bibliography

Barton, J. *Joel and Obadiah*. OTL. Westminster John Knox, 2001; Ben Zvi, E. *A Historical-Critical Study of the Book of Obadiah*. BZAW 242. De Gruyter, 1996; Mason, R. *Zephaniah, Habakkuk, Joel*. OTG. JSOT Press, 1994; Raabe, P. *Obadiah*. AB 24D. Doubleday, 1996.

D. N. Premnath

Obedience

See Divine Command Theories of Ethics

Obligation

In the field of ethics, the concept "obligation" is foundational. Since ethics is the art or science of investigating, enhancing, and furthering the most morally justifiable human behavior, the question "What is it that I or we ought to do?" is fundamental in ethics. The term *ought* is, in this respect, equivalent to *obligation*. If we are to act upon some sort of notion of rightness as to our actions or attempt to achieve some sort of goodness in our human acts and not to act simply upon instinct, then we are obliged to attempt to discern better human action(s) and subsequently to act upon those discoveries. Indeed, in terms of comparative ethics, few systems of morality adjudge human action as being merely the expression of human preferences generating no consequences whatsoever and avoiding all ties of responsibility.

Human biology, reproduction, and nurturance are themselves grounded in the notion of obligation. Female humans feed babies by means of their mammary glands. Some would say they ought to, or they are obliged to, by human anatomy. This is, of course, an instrumental understanding of the word *ought* rather than a moral one, but it is useful in illustrating that despite the cynicism of the modern world, our very createdness suggests some specific courses of human action.

Moving beyond this simple biological illustration, one that might even be accounted for as instinctive and therefore not even consensual, the world of obligation looms before us uncharted and limitless. Human interactions, both interactions among individuals and between individuals and social groups, suggest an endless stream of responses. Accordingly, it is difficult to determine precisely what it is that anyone is obliged to do, yet all groups have an understanding of obligation and engage in the reciprocities that it demands.

Here one may turn toward human capacities to ground moral claims. Jürgen Habermas has determined that humans are basically communicative creatures, and that language is structured to enable its speakers and users to understand each other and, more important, to understand themselves.

Indeed, Habermas maintains that human consciousness is tied to the use of language and to the process of understanding and being understood.

Thus, human existence is an experience of relationship and mutuality. Again, in a large world, the character, shape, and functioning of those relationships and mutuality take on endless forms. Nonetheless, this is perhaps a beginning point for understanding the term *obligation.*

If we are to be human, we are obliged both to understand ourselves and others and to have them understand us. Understanding is a process of discerning meaning, and meaning is again tied to the ongoing process of individual and corporate human behavior as acted out over time. We act and speak in order to express ourselves and to elicit preferable responses. We are born into an already created world, and all of our initial actions are responses to the prior actions of our nurturers and the world in which they and we live. All of our knowledge is, accordingly, socially given. In short, human action, whether intentional or nonintentional, is essentially responsive.

In regard to a theological understanding of obligation, H. Richard Niebuhr characterizes human action as response. For him, humanity is *Homo dialogicus* (Niebuhr 56). Human response is most important not between human individuals and groups, or between groups and other groups, but between humanity and God. Niebuhr sees that God is the divine initiator, the creator of all relationships with humanity. It is God who acts, directs, and gives meaning. We are to find our meaning in relationship with God.

The apostle Paul echoes this same sentiment in Rom. 14:7–9: "We do not live to ourselves, and we do not die to ourselves. If we live, we live to the Lord, and if we die, we die to the Lord; so then, whether we live or whether we die, we are the Lord's. For to this end Christ dies and lives again, so that he might be Lord of both the dead and the living." For the Christian, then, as previously mentioned, in a primitive survival sense, obligation comes, in part, out of our humanity, but even this obligation can be overridden by our obligations to God. Christ's action of dying for us, for our redemption, obligates us to Christ and to God and to the divine mission. It is here that we are obliged and find our deepest meaning in this world and the next.

Further, it is this divine obligation that challenges and qualifies all the other relationships, relationships to other people and to human institutions, principalities, and powers. Robert Jewett points out that in the writings of Paul the understanding of divine obligation superseded and undermined the Roman notions of obligation and law. It is this highest obligation to God that brings Christians, upon occasion, into conflict with all other obligating organizations. The Romans did, of course, learn to discern and to despise this notion of Christian obligation and promptly began to persecute and execute Christians. History demonstrates, however, that the Roman power and notion of obligation was, in time, subjugated to the Christian one by the blood of the martyrs and the conversion of the emperors.

Now, in a modern world, we stand in the shoes of our Christian ancestors. Numerous organizations and causes call to us to respond and sometimes claim that humans are obliged to act in a variety of ways. Frequently, we do so because we must. Even Jesus admonished us, "Give to the emperor the things that are the emperor's" (Mark 12:17). Yet all of these demands are relativized and modified by the prior and ultimate action and demands of God. Thus, for example, some pacifists withhold a portion of their taxes so as to fulfill a divine obligation to God to avoid furthering national wars.

Finally, then, one way of understanding ethics in general and Christian ethics in particular is to examine and analyze how we are to balance, constrain, and fulfill our obligations to others in ways that harmonize, recognize, and fulfill our prior, superior obligations to God. Since obligations change constantly, and we are never relieved of our obligations to God, Christian ethics is an ongoing, never-ending struggle as well as a way of life. We are obligated to engage in the process of discerning our ultimate obligations and then to fulfill these obligations.

See also Collective Responsibility; Deontological Theories of Ethics; Neighbor, Neighbor Love; Responsibility; Rights

Bibliography

Allen, J. *Love and Conflict: A Covenantal Model of Christian Ethics.* Abingdon, 1984; Dworkin, R. *Taking Rights Seriously.* Harvard University Press, 1978; Elazar, D. *Covenant and Polity in Biblical Israel: Biblical Foundations and Jewish Expressions.* Transaction Publishers, 1995; Glennon, F., G. Hauk, and D. Trimiew, eds. *Living Responsibly in Community: Essays in Honor of E. Clinton Gardner.* University Press of America, 1997; Habermas, J. *The Theory of Communicative Action.* Trans. T. McCarthy. Beacon Press, 1987; Jewett, R. "Response: Exegetical Support from Romans and Other Letters." Pages 58–71 in *Paul and Politics: Ekklesia, Israel, Imperium, Interpretation; Essays in Honor of Krister Stendahl*, ed. R. Horsley. Continuum, 2000; MacIntyre, A. *After Virtue: A Study in Moral Theory.* University of Notre Dame Press, 1981; Niebuhr, H. R. *The Responsible Self: An Essay in Christian Moral*

Philosophy. Harper & Row, 1963; Sandel, M. *Liberalism and the Limits of Justice*. 2nd ed. Cambridge University Press, 1998; Walzer, M. *Spheres of Justice: A Defense of Pluralism and Equality*. Basic Books, 1983.

Darryl Trimiew

Obscenity

The word *obscenity* refers to behaviors, images, or descriptions that offend accepted cultural norms. In the Western tradition of political liberalism and democracy, obscenity usually emerges as an issue of free speech. Since maximizing individual freedom is central in modern Western societies, access to pornography, images of graphic violence, and other questionable, provocative, or obscene behavior are often legally protected.

The Bible has a different ethical focus, which is faithfulness to God rather than maximizing individual freedom. In the NT, freedom in Christ means both liberation from oppression (cf. Luke 4:16–19; Isa. 61:1–2) and freedom from sinful desires and habits. This means that freedom is more than the exercise of individual choice or the unimpeded expression of desire. True freedom comes through conversion of desire away from sin toward obedience to God. Thus, the Bible prohibits certain desires and behaviors while encouraging others. For example, Eph. 5:3–4 says, "Fornication and impurity of any kind, or greed, must not even be mentioned among you. . . . Entirely out of place is obscene [*aischrotēs*], silly, and vulgar talk." Similarly, Colossians exhorts believers to "die" to unrighteous desires: "You have died and your life is hidden with Christ in God. . . . Consider the members of your earthly body as dead to immorality, impurity, passion, evil desire, and greed, which amounts to idolatry" (Col. 3:3, 5 NASB).

The association of immoral desires and practices with idolatry in Colossians is interesting when read against the backdrop of Exodus, where prohibitions regarding idolatry are part of God's emancipation of Israel from slavery in Egypt. In Exod. 20:2–3, God says to Israel, "I am the LORD your God, who brought you out of the land of Egypt, out of the house of slavery. You shall have no other gods before me." In a similar way, the "idolatry" of immoral pleasures is not fitting to God's people because they have been set free from sin. Paul's exhortation "to consider yourselves dead to sin" (Rom. 6:11; cf. Col. 3:3, 5) is part of a larger refrain about new life in Christ, which challenges Christians to move beyond mere religious rules to a genuine conversion of their desires. Thus, the author implores the readers, "Why do you submit to regulations, 'Do not handle, Do not taste, Do not touch'? All these regulations refer to things that perish with use; they are simply human commands and teachings. These have indeed an appearance of wisdom in promoting self-imposed piety, humility, and severe treatment of the body, but they are of no value in checking self-indulgence [*plēsmonēn tēs sarkos*]" (Col. 2:20–23).

Early Christians such as Justin Martyr argued for the superiority of Christianity over paganism by contrasting the righteousness and holiness of the Christian God with obscenities committed by pagan deities. Whereas pagan gods committed profane acts of lust and "in their loves with men did such things as it is shameful even to mention," Justin described the God of Christian worship as "impassible" and "never goaded by lust" (*1 Apol.* 25). Justin condemns raising children for prostitution, self-mutilation for the purposes of sodomy, and selling one's own child or wife as a sex slave, which he describes as part of pagan ritual (*1 Apol.* 27). He asks how pagan gods who exhibit the same destructive passions and obscene desires as wicked humans can be worthy of worship. Similarly, Augustine observes how pagan ritual coincided with violent gladiator fights and lurid theatrical shows that were celebrated in the name of one or more gods. He argues that although "the gods themselves sternly commanded, indeed almost extorted, the production of such shows," the Romans should never have "worshipped gods whom they thought of as wishing to have theatrical obscenities devoted to their honor" (*Civ.* 2.8, 13).

The charge of obscenity was a two-way street, however, and Christians had to defend and explain themselves. The Christian practice of worshiping a crucified criminal and ritually eating of his body and drinking of his blood was offensive to Romans. In Roman society, crucifixion was reserved for slaves and the most despised of the empire. Explaining Christian practices became the task of Christian apologists such as Tertullian, who defended the Eucharist by saying, "Our feast explains itself by its name. The Greeks call it *agapē*. . . . With the good things of the feast we benefit the needy. . . . It permits no vileness of immodesty. The participants, before reclining, taste first of prayer to God" (*Apol.* 39). For converts to Christianity, seeing the cross as the peaceful sign of God's reign required considerable faith. Becoming Christian meant rejecting certain cultural norms of Roman society while learning to see the previously "obscene" as the revelation of God.

See also Desire; Freedom; Sin

Chanon R. Ross

Old Testament Ethics

The Meaning of "Old Testament Ethics"

There are two fundamental ways to understand the phrase "Old Testament ethics." One is to focus on the descriptive task of identifying what might have been the moral beliefs and behavior of the people of God as a whole, or of various groups within Israel, at any one historical period or across OT times. From this perspective, the study of OT ethics consists of those efforts to reconstruct the ethics of ancient Israel by certain textual methods and through historical, sociological, anthropological, and comparative studies. The emphasis is on the multiplicity of ethical perspectives within the text and on the social settings, theological sources (such as covenant, the law, wisdom), and ideologies of those who may have produced this material. There is disagreement over whether a largely coherent ethical framework undergirds the OT's various appreciations of moral matters, and scholars have offered different hypotheses regarding the possible development of Israel's ethical views.

The second way to understand the phrase "Old Testament ethics" is to focus on the normative task of discerning what the OT can contribute to moral life today as part of Christian Scripture. The NT certainly invites such considerations (note, e.g., 1 Cor. 10:11; 2 Tim. 3:16–17; Heb. 11). The goal is to bring the OT to bear on the modern world. While the research interests of descriptive approaches may be utilized (if and how this is done will depend on the individual author), the purpose is to offer ways in which the text can demonstrate its contemporary relevance to believing communities and to the world. The OT is embraced in some measure as a trustworthy guide and a foundational authority for the practice of the Christian faith. The significance of its authority, however, is a topic of debate.

The Authority of the Old Testament

Historically, the authority of the OT was assumed by the Christian church. There were occasional exceptions to this consensus, the most famous being the stance of Marcion of Sinope (c. 85–160 CE), who rejected the entire OT and those sections of the NT that he thought reflected Jewish influence. In contrast, the generalized confidence in the OT's authority was grounded in the conviction that it was the word of God. In spite of theological disagreements about its teaching and how it should be interpreted, the consensus was that the OT was divine revelation and thus indispensable and supremely relevant to believers, the church, and the greater society. Those of more conservative persuasions continue to articulate the inspiration of the OT in similar ways.

Recently, some have reformulated the concept of the authority of the Bible (and of the OT). Instead of the traditional view of the OT's authority as being an ontological quality—that is, a property inherent in the text—biblical authority is explained as a functional reality. From this perspective, the Bible is taken as a unique collection of witnesses to the presence and work of God that the church authorizes as the primary resource for its moral life. Faith communities recognize its enduring value in shaping Christian character and conduct. An ontological stance may accept this view as complementary to its own, but many see it as an alternative to those classic conceptions. The concern is that this different focus on the concept of biblical authority can open the way for more significant input from sources other than the Bible, such as philosophy and the social sciences. It also allows for weighing what parts of the Bible may no longer manifest the redeeming designs of God and need not be accepted as binding.

There also are those who are strongly suspicious of the ethical authority of the OT. Its positions on ethical dilemmas are said to be dated and overly constrained by the worldview and mores of its cultural settings. This historical argument can be accompanied by a range of ideological critiques, which include disparaging the OT as politically nationalistic, hopelessly misogynistic, ethnically exclusive, problematic in its portrayal of the violence of its characters and of God, and insensitive to the plight of the disabled, animals, and the created order (Rodd; O'Brien). These perceptions reflect a hermeneutics of suspicion that often reads "against the grain" of textual meaning to question the unspoken agendas and embedded prejudices that lie hidden beneath the surface.

These kinds of doubts have generated several types of responses. One has been to revisit the OT and to begin to recover or rehabilitate pertinent ethical voices within the text that have been ignored (e.g., women's stories, the impulses toward peace). Another outcome has been to reinterpret texts that have been misunderstood and thus misused in ethical discourse to support harmful positions, whether consciously or not (e.g., gender issues, racial apartheid, the disregard of ecology). A third result has been to reassess problematic passages and concepts within the scope of the larger canon, where they can find development or complementary perspectives. We will return to this point below. All of these efforts ascribe authority to the OT and value its ethical lessons in whole or in part.

The most extreme option is to reject the OT's teachings and, in some cases, the God who is revealed therein. The goal of various scholars is to resist vigorously what it presents about life and the deity. Those who accept the OT as Scripture cannot endorse this overly critical judgment. This does not mean that none of the negative observations has any merit. A thoughtful position on the authority of the OT must be able to respond to legitimate concerns about its ethical content with the necessary complexity and erudition. These challenges have spurred reflection on the nature and role of language (especially of metaphor), the history of interpretive practices, and the complexity of the theological world of the OT—all of which have led to richer and more nuanced conceptions of its authority as Scripture.

Another key topic related to the authority of the OT is the characterization of its relationship to the NT within the Christian canon. This is fundamental to articulating how the OT can and should speak to the church as Scripture. These theological and hermeneutical issues have occupied theologians for two millennia. Some of the more important questions are these: What kind of continuity exists between the people of God of each Testament, and is it of such a degree that the OT moral demands have abiding value (the Israel-church question within Christian theological systems)? How is OT law to be understood as an ethical resource in light of the coming of Jesus, the implications of the cross for salvation and life, and the inauguration of the kingdom of God (the "third use of the law" debate and the law/gospel tension)? Can the OT be used as a discrete and separate ethical resource with direct application to contemporary moral discourse, or must its teaching and insights be run through a NT or Christian theological grid? Is there development of ethical perspectives as one moves from the OT into the NT? If so, does that mean that NT teaching qualifies, complements, and/or supersedes the OT perspective on a given subject? Does the NT itself offer any guidelines for the appropriation of the OT, and if so, should they have normative status? A full-orbed biblical ethics will incorporate decisions on these and other foundational matters into its methodological framework.

Approaches to Old Testament Ethics

If the OT is accepted as a suitable ethical resource, then it is incumbent to sort out the way(s) it is utilized for the moral life of faith communities today. Approaches to appropriating the text can be divided into three broad categories. These categories are not mutually exclusive classifications, and some approaches do not fit neatly into a single grouping, but this taxonomy can serve as a heuristic tool for sorting out the use of the OT for ethics. Because of the biblical focus of this volume, this survey emphasizes contemporary formulations by biblical scholars instead of those of theologians, both past and present, whose appropriation of the Bible for ethics has been quite sophisticated (e.g., Augustine, Luther, Barth, Bonhoeffer, O'Donovan).

Focusing on what is "behind the text." To say that certain approaches concentrate on what is "behind the text" means that they are less interested in what appears in the final, or canonical, form of the OT and more interested in uncovering background matters pertinent to the ethics of ancient Israel. These can be of two kinds, both of which essentially are efforts at reconstruction. Some investigate the historical and culture setting, others the hypothetical editorial history of the text.

Studies that locate the ethics of the OT within the moral world of its day compare its moral worldview and demands with those of surrounding cultures (Weinfeld). This has been done especially in regard to OT law, in particular legislation related to slavery, the poor, and issues concerning women (e.g., marriage, sexuality, and inheritance). Depending on the topic at hand, the OT is perceived as mirroring the limitations of its time or as humanizing the treatment of the vulnerable and eliminating the privileging of certain social hierarchies before the law. Positive assessments of the OT vis-à-vis the ancient Near East point to the enduring significance of the underlying principles of its ethics.

Another comparative approach, which moves beyond these synchronic juxtapositions and evaluations, suggests the possibility of an engagement with the "natural morality," or commonly accepted mores, of Israel's context (Rogerson). The ethical commitments of the people of God would have had points of both agreement and disagreement with these widely shared values. At the same time, Israel's ethics were grounded in its particular "imperatives of redemption"—that is, those demands based on God's unique gracious acts on their behalf, like the exodus (e.g., Exod. 22:21 [22:22 MT]; 23:9). These imperatives, in turn, found concrete expression in Israel's laws through "structures of grace," those social and economic measures intended to incarnate that redemption in their society; that is, there would have been overlap with surrounding cultures as well as distinctiveness in the ethical values and arrangements of Israel. For the church, the cross of Christ is the redemptive act that makes claims on how Christians are to act toward others and configure their lives. The concomitant structures of grace on behalf of the needy within faith communities obviously will look different in the twenty-first century than they did millennia ago in ancient Israel. The "natural morality" model can encourage Christians to work with those of other persuasions, who hold similar moral commitments, to seek to pass legislation and establish social structures and organizations in modern society that might approximate God's ideals. In other words, the OT law in many ways is largely context-specific; it is not to be imitated, although the processes of engagement with the broader context can be instructive. The peculiar ethics of the people of God in any time and place can connect at some level in constructive ways with the broader world, even as it follows its own narrative.

Other studies try to better comprehend the socioeconomic situation and dynamics of ancient Israel within which the ethics recorded in the OT functioned. The social sciences have been a primary tool to analyze the text and archaeological evidence and propose explanatory models. Several of the more prominent include the theories of rent capitalism and the tributary mode of production, both of which are based on the claim that the monarchy triggered the rise of latifundia (landed estates controlled by economic and political elites). A recent suggestion is that Israel essentially functioned as a peasant economy, even as its political structure changed. Society functioned according to kinship and patronage, with their culturally accepted mutual expectations and obligations between the various social strata. Even though that world of patronage is quite different from most contemporary societies, what is constant across the OT and what carries over the centuries is the divine demand for justice. This moral value will be worked out differently than it was in ancient times, but it remains the calling of the people of God (Houston).

A second kind of "behind the text" research concentrates on ascertaining the stages of the literary production of the OT. These critical textual efforts can be combined with sociological work on the plausible sociohistorical contexts of the authors and tradents of each step in that process. The OT, it is claimed, is an anthology of the ethical agendas of multiple social forces from different time periods as well as of competing points of view from the same settings. The implications that are drawn from these textual and historical reconstructions vary. Some believe that the original textual layers represent a higher ethical commitment to the vulnerable, which was neutralized to some degree by the later additions (Gottwald). Others find a different lesson in the incongruities and possible contradictions: awareness of this mixture of views makes it impossible to assign a consistent ethical point of view to the text. Its very complexity is a witness to the struggles of the moral discourse within Israel. The pluralism of the OT's ethics fits nicely with the ethos of postmodern culture (Pleins).

At least three comments are in order. First, these efforts at historical, social, and textual reconstruction can be of great value, but sometimes the intricacy of the argumentation and the level of scholarship required to comprehend the given model can make this work inaccessible to the broader Christian public. Their possible contribution to the ethical thinking of the church is diminished, if not negated. Second, the viability of these hypotheses is heavily dependent on the success of the particular reconstruction proposed, which is only as convincing as the quality of the data and their interpretation or the suitability of the applied social theory and the skill with which it is used. New developments and discoveries can impact what may have once been confident conclusions. Third, background studies need not serve the kinds of reconstruction programs cited here. Some provide information about sociocultural, economic, and political contexts to final form or canonical approaches, which use this material to provide a realistic historical backdrop to their work instead of a detailed critical reconstruction of the world of Israel or of the OT text.

Systems approaches. Several types of approaches fall under this rubric. One is to privilege a part of the OT. It is not uncommon to hear, for instance, of a "prophetic voice" in reference to a powerful reformer such as Martin Luther King Jr., or of a "prophetic church" or movement, also in connection with social issues. These people and organizations are identified with the posture of the prophetic literature, its denunciation of the oppression of the vulnerable, and the scathing critique of the powerful. Most often appeal is made to the eighth-century BCE prophets Isaiah, Micah, and Amos.

Historically, prominence has been given to the law (especially the Ten Commandments). This has been true especially in the Reformed tradition and is in part a legacy of John Calvin's Geneva and his *Institutes of the Christian Religion*. Emphasis on the law regularly is combined with the notion of the "cultural mandate," based on Gen. 1:26–28, that champions bringing all aspects of human life under the sovereign rule of God and his Christ. Examples that follow this trend include Oliver Cromwell's commonwealth in Britain and the Puritan experiment of the seventeenth century, and Abraham Kuyper's "sphere sovereignty" construct in the Netherlands in the late nineteenth and early twentieth centuries and his theological heirs who share a transformationalist view of Christian culture. A strain within Reformed circles that achieved some notoriety in the 1980s was a movement called "theonomy," which sought to apply OT law and its penalties to secular society (Bahnsen). This stress on the law as the substratum of OT ethical teaching also finds expression of a different sort in the work of Walter Kaiser. Grounded in exegesis of the Hebrew text and not in dogmatic theology, Kaiser believes that universal ethical principles can be extracted from individual laws through the "ladder of abstraction" and then applied today.

Christopher Wright also accentuates the law through a paradigm approach. A paradigm, on this view, is a transcendent set of beliefs and values that are the basis of a worldview and the organization of society. Wright postulates that there are three components of the OT's paradigm for ethics, and that these can be expressed in triangular fashion. The three angles are the theological (God), the social (Israel), and the economic (the land). This arrangement explains Israel's ethical lens for arranging and evaluating its socioeconomic life, but it can also be projected paradigmatically to encompass humanity and creation, typologically to NT parallels within the church, and eschatologically to the promise of a redeemed world at the end of time. The premier example of his method is the Jubilee (Lev. 25), which finds its echoes, respectively, in sinful humanity's life in rebellion against God in a fallen creation, in the generous sharing within the Christian community, and eventually in the restoration of all things in the new heavens and earth.

This approach makes several helpful contributions. First, Wright takes seriously the tangible realities dealt with by OT legislation, as well as the details of the laws themselves—their rationale and pragmatic impact. Those laws express God's lasting ethical demands in a way appropriate to that ancient society. Those demands necessarily would take a different shape in the legislation and socioeconomic structures suitable to other circumstances and eras. The law was a concrete paradigm that could not be duplicated, even as it was instructive to non-Israelite peoples (Deut. 4:5–8). Second, the paradigm concept and the interconnected triangles demonstrate a continuity of God's moral will across time. Third, Wright's proposal considers how the NT takes up and develops OT material. Thus, he is able to offer a comprehensive ethics that encompasses all of Scripture.

Literary and canonical approaches. These studies pay special attention to the final form, or canonical shape, of the OT. They often appeal to literary theory to probe the power of texts—that is, how texts impact the moral imagination of readers. Good literature, when engaged properly, can shape ethical views through plot, the depiction of scenes, the portrayal of characters, and by stirring emotions. Readers witness, and can vicariously enter into, the ethical decision-making taking place within a text and at some level participate in its motivations, struggles, and consequences. Literature also can attune readers to the darker side of reality within their own lives and societies, as well as present a world of possibilities for change. It can become a training ground, in other words, in ethical discernment and the nurturing of the virtues. Although these studies may employ research on backgrounds, the primary concern is the text itself.

The fact that the OT is both literature and Scripture adds immeasurable weight to this potentially powerful process of reading. Because it is literature with divine authority, reading of this text carries greater urgency. That Scripture is the text of a community adds further impetus to a virtue ethics orientation, because ideally the Christian church should provide the context for the requisite ethical growth and the presence of exemplars, who would echo and reinforce that reading. Literary approaches have been used with much profit in OT narratives (Perry) and the prophets (Brueggemann)—indeed, in the breadth of OT genres (Brown; Carroll R. and Lapsley).

Interest in the canon and its significance for theological interpretation and ethics has increased in the last few decades. The issues concerning the canon are many and diverse (Bartholomew et al.), but there are several ramifications for ethics that deserve mention. To begin with, the multiple ethical voices within the canon can be handled in several ways within moral discourse. Some trace trajectories in ethical views across the Scripture from the OT to the NT and see changes from restrictive formulations to more life-affirming possibilities.

This tack has been applied to various topics, such as the institution of slavery, the role of women, and war (Swartley). The breadth and diversity of the canon also provide a comprehensive appreciation of moral issues. For instance, there are several dimensions of the OT's awareness and treatment of the problems of poverty: the law demonstrates the need for legislation related to debt, the provision of food, and fairness in legal proceedings; narratives depict the painful plight of the needy; the wisdom literature points out that some of the poor have only themselves to blame, while at the same time declaring their worth before God and encouraging the wise person to be charitable; the prophets rail against systemic injustice that perpetuates poverty and proclaim the hope of a future of plenty when poverty will be no more. Each slice of the canon contributes to a fuller ethical perspective, which would be diminished by concentrating on only one or a few of the pieces.

Second, emphasis on the canon reconnects ethics with Christian communities. This is a pragmatic observation in that this is the only text that the vast majority of Christians will ever read or know for moral discourse. A canonical focus has ecclesiastical importance as well. It places ethics within the long history of interpretation of the Scripture for ethics, and that history becomes a resource of ethical reflection. It also allows for ethics to be linked, as it was very emphatically in the OT, with liturgy, because the centrality of moral thinking within the canon can be incorporated into the worship of the church. Finally, a canonical approach to ethics will benefit greatly from its relationship to the resurgence of theological interpretation of Scripture. These creative studies are recovering readings of Scripture that have much to teach the church, discovering new insights from which OT ethics has much to gain.

Conclusion

The field of OT ethics is as fascinating as it is complex. Debates concerning its moral authority and about how best to appropriate it for ethics will continue, even as they have for centuries. The fact that these discussions persist is proof of the OT's enduring value for ethics.

See also New Testament Ethics

Bibliography

Bahnsen, G. *Theonomy in Christian Ethics*. Rev. ed. P&R, 1984; Bartholomew, C., et al. *Canon and Biblical Interpretation*. SHS 7. Zondervan, 2006; Barton, J. *Understanding Old Testament Ethics*. Westminster John Knox, 2003; Birch, B. *Let Justice Roll Down: The Old Testament, Ethics, and Christian Life*. Westminster John Knox, 1991; Brown, W. *Character and Scripture: Moral Formation, Community, and Biblical Interpretation*. Eerdmans, 2002; Brueggemann, W. *The Prophetic Imagination*. 2nd ed. Fortress, 2001; Carroll R., M. D., and J. Lapsley, eds. *Character Ethics and the Old Testament: Moral Dimensions of Scripture*. Westminster John Knox, 2007; Gottwald, N. "Theological Education as a Theory-Praxis Loop: Situating the Book of Joshua in a Cultural, Social Ethical, and Theological Matrix." Pages 107–18 in *The Bible in Ethics: The Second Sheffield Colloquium*, ed. J. Rogerson, M. Davies, and M. D. Carroll R. JSOTSup 207. Sheffield Academic Press, 1995; Houston, W. *Contending for Justice: Ideologies and Theologies of Social Justice in the Old Testament*. LHBOTS 428. T&T Clark, 2006; Kaiser, W., Jr. *Toward Old Testament Ethics*. Zondervan, 1983; O'Brien, J. *Challenging Prophetic Metaphor: Theology and Ideology in the Prophets*. Westminster John Knox, 2008; Perry, R. *Old Testament Story and Christian Ethics: The Rape of Dinah as a Case Study*. PBM. Paternoster, 2004; Pleins, J. *The Social Visions of the Hebrew Bible: A Theological Introduction*. Westminster John Knox, 2001; Rodd, C. *Glimpses of a Strange Land: Studies in Old Testament Ethics*. OTS. T&T Clark, 2001; Rogerson, J. *Theory and Practice in Old Testament Ethics*. Ed. M. D. Carroll R. JSOTSup 405. T&T Clark, 2004; Swartley, W. *Slavery, Sabbath, War, and Women: Case Issues in Biblical Interpretation*. Herald Press, 1983; Weinfeld, M. *Social Justice in Ancient Israel and in the Ancient Near East*. Fortress, 1995; Wright, C. *Old Testament Ethics for the People of God*. InterVarsity, 2004.

M. Daniel Carroll R. (Rodas)

Omission, Sins of

A sin of omission is the failure to do what one has the obligation, opportunity, and ability to do on behalf of another. "Anyone, then, who knows the right thing to do and fails to do it, commits sin" (Jas. 4:17).

Biblical Considerations

Many biblical moral commands are framed negatively in terms of what one must not do—for example, murder, adultery, theft (Exod. 20:13–15). Sometimes morality is wrongly reduced to such "sins of commission."

However, within the Decalogue itself two commands are framed positively: "Remember the sabbath day, and keep it holy" (Exod. 20:8) and "Honor your father and mother" (Exod. 20:12). The behaviors required by such commands are not explicit; they have a certain open-ended quality to them.

Scripture certainly contains hundreds of negative commands specifying banned behavior. However, Scripture is most notable for its sweeping, positive injunctions, perhaps best summarized in the commands to love God and love neighbor (Deut. 6:5–8; Lev. 19:18; Matt. 22:34–40 pars.).

A moral vision built around positive, inexhaustible commands invariably creates space for the category of sins of omission, understood as the failure to live out the obligations of love of God and neighbor in various dimensions of life.

Sins of omission are suggested strongly in passages such as the parable of the good Samaritan (Luke 10:25–37), where the Samaritan's active service to the wounded stranger is contrasted sharply with the omissions of the priest and Levite. The judgment scene in Matt. 25:31–46, involving the sheep and the goats, rather terrifyingly conditions admission to the eternal kingdom on acts of service to "the least of these" and therefore to Jesus. Those on the wrong side of such judgments are condemned simply for their failures to act.

Jesus' woes to the scribes and Pharisees include condemnation for focusing on minutiae rather than "the weightier matters of the law: justice and mercy and faith" (Matt. 23:23). This serves as a reminder that ethics at its most profound involves weighing the relative significance of various paths of action in cases where no option is "wrong," but some are more significant than others.

Being faced with inexhaustible commands before which we fall short can create moral despair, but Scripture instead instructs believers toward humility, repentance, and recommitment (see Matt. 7:1–5). Continual challenges are created by practical questions related to how stringently such commands must be interpreted amid the realistic limits and countervailing obligations that we all face.

Contemporary Applications

Studies of Christian behavior toward Jews during the Holocaust raised the issue of sins of omission quite acutely. Millions of Jews went to their deaths in part because their Christian neighbors did nothing to help them. This is the problem of the "bystander."

The issue surfaces in contemporary bioethics around end-of-life care, with questions related to when it is appropriate not to intervene to save or lengthen a life, and whether there is a morally significant distinction between hastening death and letting death come.

See also Accountability; Love, Love Command; Sin

Bibliography

Barnett, V. *Bystanders: Conscience and Complicity during the Holocaust*. Praeger, 2000.

David P. Gushee

Oppression

In the biblical narrative, "oppression" carries a twofold meaning. First, it denotes a situation in which persons are subjected against their will to hardships placed on them by others and/or are made to live under deplorable conditions simply because they are considered inferior and/or marginal based on norms established by those in control of society. Second, spiritual oppression, though often ignored by Western thinkers, is also part of the biblical narrative. Spiritual oppression refers to "spiritual warfare" in which God and demonic forces battle for dominion and control of the human mind and body. When one is being attacked by the forces of "spiritual wickedness" (see 2 Cor. 10:3–5; Eph. 6:12), such state is described as spiritual oppression. God reacts to both situations of oppression in a similar fashion, taking a proactive approach promoting the necessary changes to overcome oppression.

When it comes to social and political oppression of groups or particular individuals, God intervenes by sending prophets and messengers to call leaders to correct their ways by protecting those of lowly and marginal status and by promoting social equality. Although the statements against oppression are clear, there is no consensus about how one overcomes oppression. Ethicists and Bible scholars alike have offered a wide range of interpretations, from passive forms of pacifism to full military intervention justified by just-war theory. The common denominator in these approaches is God's call for action to promote comprehensive reform, which includes the transformation of individual oppressors, the reorganization of social structures to protect the vulnerable, and the creation of a new system that strives to offer restoration to the oppressed and attempts to prevent situations of oppression in the future. Again, even when there is disagreement about how to bring oppression to an end, the biblical narrative indicates that oppression must be addressed at all levels of society. In our complex global society oppression is not a simple "rich versus poor" dynamic; rather, it is present in a global web of social, ethnic, and racial connections as well as political and financial interests that make the task of identifying the oppressor and oppressed quite difficult. Nevertheless, the divine mandate is clear and encompasses all aspects of society, which under our circumstances requires a constant and careful examination of all factors, social structures, and social institutions that keep some members of society from enjoying all the privileges and full participation in the decision-making process. And it is precisely these notions that constitute the norm in defining oppression; that is, any social structures, individuals, and/or institutions that prevent groups or individuals from fully participating in the life of society should be considered as oppressive, and something must be done in response to God's call to correct the situation.

As for spiritual oppression, a common response is to try to deal with these matters separately from the social and political aspects explained above; however, such a dichotomy does not seem to be supported by biblical references. In fact, the classic text commonly used to exemplify oppression is the narrative of Israel's exodus from Egypt, and to read this narrative only from a sociopolitical perspective would be a mistake, as much as it would be to read it as simply being about pure spiritual liberation. The reality of oppression encompasses the social and personal aspects of the person, the spiritual and corporate realities of societies and institutions. Furthermore, in looking at the life and ministry of Jesus, we see that the distinctions between the physical (personal/private) and the corporate (social/political) do not exist. In the Gospels, Jesus has the power to overcome physical oppression by healing and feeding individuals who are sick and hungry, while at the same time he challenges religious leaders to change their ways by being inclusive and extending God's grace to all and not just to some. The kingdom of God as proclaimed by Jesus is comprehensive, including individual, social, spiritual, and physical aspects (Luke 4:16–20), and offers liberation from all forms of oppression. For this reason, oppression must be addressed from a perspective that is both systemic and individual. Oppression finds its root cause in sinful human tendencies that often result in individual and corporate oppression, both of which God rejects, calling for comprehensive reformation of both the individual and society.

See also Institution(s); Liberation; Liberationist Ethics; Powers and Principalities

Bibliography

Gutiérrez, G. *Las Casas: In Search of the Poor of Jesus Christ*. Orbis, 1993; LeFevre, P., and W. Schroeder, eds. *Pastoral Care and Liberation Praxis: Studies in Personal and Social Transformation*. Exploration Press, 1986; Sobrino, J. *No Salvation Outside the Poor: Prophetic-Utopian Essays*. Orbis, 2008.

Hugo Magallanes

Organ Transplants *See* Bioethics

Original Sin *See* Sin

Orphans

A key theme in the biblical drama is God's passionate concern for those who are vulnerable to exploitation or neglect, and the many references to orphans highlight this attentiveness. Orphans' welfare therefore provides a centering concern for any ethics claiming to be biblical. Whether or how the welfare of orphans and similar groups informs discussions of ethics and policy provides an important measure of how Scripture-shaped our moral imaginations actually are. Rather than providing an ideological or political agenda, concern for the vulnerable centers our ethics and demands that we attend to their needs just as God, our Parent, attends to us all (Matt. 6:26–33).

Biblical Commands concerning Orphans

The OT contains numerous references to orphans and God's insistence that they be protected (Deut. 10:17–19; Exod. 22:22–24; Pss. 10:14, 18; 68:5; 146:9; Hos. 14:3; Zech. 7:10). Like the widows with whom they are often grouped, they lacked male advocates in a patriarchal society and thus were exposed to multiple levels of legal, emotional, economic, and social deprivation. The pattern here follows many others in Scripture: divine interest in this group's welfare means that those who follow Yahweh must enact that concern or else incur God's wrath (Exod. 22:22–24; Isa. 1:23–24). Genuine faith focuses on the powerless and tends them as their own. If a people wishes to please God and pursue his favor, they must embody this as expressed in the commands of Deut. 24:17–22.

Understood within the larger context, this text expresses a moral sentiment that links God, the vulnerable, and the larger community. These interconnections typify the seamlessness in Scripture between God's character and our ethics, God's command and our welfare. Discerning specific rules for behavior—"You shall not deprive a resident alien or an orphan of justice. . . . When you gather the grapes of your vineyard, do not glean what is left; it shall be for the alien, the orphan, and the widow" (Deut. 24:17, 21)—is often considered the central concern of ethics. Yet rather than merely floating abstractly as principles or guidelines for morality, scriptural commands find their sensibility within the larger story of salvation. Right telling of this narrative in word and in deed requires clear and accurate understanding of the actors, both God and humankind.

Yahweh acts consistently as compassionate redeemer, the deliverer and upholder of the forgotten (Deut. 24:18). As Yahweh acted to rescue Israel and redeem them, God's people respond in kind, imitative of divine character. It is not simply Yahweh's past actions but rather a constant covenantal relationship of dependence on this God who makes care for the powerless a win-win situation for everyone. Embodying Yahweh's deliverance and protection of the unsheltered, Israel glorifies God by revealing this goodness to others and trusting that such loving-kindness favors those who obey these commands. God sustains not only the obviously exposed such as the widow and orphan; in truth, all humankind rests on divine provision. In this way, care of the vulnerable provides opportunities not for philanthropy from on high, but rather for recollection of our humble status before Yahweh and for openness to further blessings and gifts (Deut. 14:29).

In the NT, there are few references to orphans. Instead, the language for enacting the care for the weak shifts to that of children as representative of the "least of these" (Mark 9:36; 10:13–15; Luke 9:48), as they often were invisible or exploited within the larger culture. The interconnectedness of God's blessings and embodied compassion remains consistent, for those who receive children are honored as those who unexpectedly welcome Christ himself (Mark 9:35–37). Indeed, the OT description of true faithfulness as imitative of God's character continues in the NT. As the Letter of James forcefully states, "Religion that is pure and undefiled before God, the Father, is this: to care for orphans and widows in their distress, and to keep oneself unstained by the world" (1:27).

Church Tradition

While concern about orphans could be understood as largely symbolic of God's interest in the marginalized, Christians have recognized this as a literal call to the parentless that has been exemplified in various ages, from care of children in Byzantium to the orphanages of George Müller in Victorian England. Current interest in foster care and adoption often includes "social orphans" who lack functional families and the security that these provide. The present global crises of millions of children due to neglect, warfare, disease (particularly the AIDS pandemic), food instability, and political and economic corruption remind us of the timelessness of ancient witnesses' warnings that these "least" still cry out to God and God's people for justice. Orphans also remain emblematic of those easily exploited as laborers in agriculture, domestic service, or the sex trade and others who are exposed to violence, abandonment, or various forms of mistreatment.

Welcoming Orphans as Gifts

Sometimes attention to orphans fosters an attitude of arrogance or pity. However, Scripture commands us to share with the orphan out of the gifts that come from God's hand; doing so tames fears that foster greed and self-indulgence. But such solidarity also recalls our mutual fragility as mere creatures who utterly depend on the graciousness of God. In this sense, doing justice for orphans never reinforces societal hierarchy or exclusive community, but rather disrupts them. As in ancient Israel, orphans offer an opportunity to remember and enact God's redemptive action by opening our table to name them as "family" and thus make them a focus of our ethical concern.

See also Aliens, Immigration, and Refugees; Children; Family; Foster Care; Justice; Reproductive Technologies; Widows

Bibliography

Brueggemann, W. "Vulnerable Children, Divine Passion, and Human Obligation." Pages 399–422 in *The Child in Christian Thought*, ed. M. Bunge. Eerdmans, 2001; Foster, G., C. Levine, and J. Williamson, eds. *A Generation at Risk: The Global Impact of HIV/AIDS on Orphans and Vulnerable Children*. Cambridge University Press, 2005; Gundry-Volf, J. "The Least and the Greatest: Children in the New Testament." Pages 29–60 in *The Child in the Bible*, ed. M. Bunge. Eerdmans, 2008; Herzog, K. *Children and Our Global Future: Theological and Social Challenges*. Pilgrim Press, 2005; Miller, T. *The Orphans of Byzantium: Child Welfare in the Christian Empire*. Catholic University Press, 2003; UNICEF. "The State of the World's Children 2006: Excluded and Invisible." http://www.unicef.org/sowc06/pdfs/sowc06%5Ffullreport.pdf; Vogt, P. "Social Justice and the Vision of Deuteronomy." *JETS* 51 (2008): 35–44.

Erin Dufault-Hunter

Orthodox Ethics

The Orthodox Church

The Orthodox Church is the second-largest Christian communion in the world today, comprising approximately 225 million to 300 million adherents to the faith. While Orthodox Christians can be found throughout the world, areas in which the Orthodox Church is the primary religious community are Belarus, Bulgaria, Cyprus, Georgia, Greece, Romania, Russia, Serbia, and Ukraine. The Orthodox Church is organized into a family of autocephalous (i.e., self-governing) ecclesial bodies, which include the churches of Constantinople (Istanbul), Alexandria, Antioch, Jerusalem, Russia, Serbia, Romania, Bulgaria, Georgia, Cyprus, Greece, Poland, the Czech lands and Slovakia, Albania, and America.

The Orthodox Church professes itself to be the one, holy, catholic, and apostolic church, locating its origins in the life and work of Jesus Christ and his apostles and continuing to the present day. For Orthodox Christians, the unity of the church is located not within an office or a sacred text but instead in a common faith that unites people of different languages, ethnicities, and generations. This common faith is believed to be the pure revelation of Jesus Christ, which is possessed by the church as a fruit of the Spirit of Truth. This deposit is given expression principally through sources such as the Holy Scripture, the first seven ecumenical councils, the canons of the church, the writings of the saints, the hymnology and prayers of the church, and the holy icons.

While the Orthodox Church and those who follow the Roman Catholic faith hold a common history of the first millennium, the division between the East and West was a gradual process that culminated in the year 1054 with what is commonly referred to as the Great Schism. Important historical markers in the life of the Orthodox Church since 1054 include the fall of the Byzantine Empire to the Muslim Ottoman Empire in 1453, Greek independence in 1821 from the Muslim Ottoman Empire, the rise of communism in Eastern Europe resulting in the martyrdom of millions of Orthodox Christians in the twentieth century, and the millennial anniversary of the conversion of the Slavs in 1988. Important figures in the history of the Orthodox Church include Gregory the Theologian, John Chrysostom, Maximus the Confessor, Symeon the New Theologian, Gregory Palamas, and Nikodemus of the Holy Mountain. More contemporary figures living in the twentieth century include Silouan the Athonite, Nikolai Velimirovich, and Justin Popovich.

One particularly important contemporary point with respect to the Orthodox Church is that Orthodox ethics, in general, stands relatively independent of the theological movements of the Western Christian tradition, including Scholasticism, the Protestant Reformation, and the Enlightenment. Consequently, the Orthodox Church represents to Western Christianity an alternative approach to understanding the relationship between Scripture and ethics.

Deification and Ethics

One of the most distinctive aspects of the Orthodox Church is its approach to ethics. Ethics is supported not by the strength of reason but through the pursuit of deification. Orthodox Christians understand deification as the soteriological process by which Christians undergo an ethical and anthropological transformation of the whole person, becoming all that God is by grace. As such, ethics is rooted in a personal God who is wholly transcendent and yet is disclosed to the human person through personal transformation within the liturgical and ascetical life of the church. Important here is that the liturgical and ascetical life of the church does not simply contribute to an understanding of ethics but rather forms the basis by which ethics is undertaken. Consequently, ethics is primarily the fruit of an unmediated experience of God in pursuit of deification.

Consequently, knowledge of God and knowledge of the ethical life are arrived at through a nondiscursive, noetic knowledge within the context of the transformation of the human person. For Orthodox Christianity, the *nous* is understood as the faculty of the soul that governs the person and mediates the person's relationship with God. The *nous* can also be described as the eye of the soul. Thus, an ethicist is one who through prayer, fasting, almsgiving, keeping vigil, prostrations, love of neighbor, and love of God undergoes purification and engages in a participatory knowledge of God through God's uncreated energies. It is through turning to God in repentance with an open heart that ethical knowledge is derived. At the same time, the importance of intellectual rigor is not to be denied in its ability to assist in the pursuit of deification or to provide clarity in ethical understanding. However, intellectual rigor can never form the foundation of arriving at ethical knowledge.

Orthodox Ethics

At the heart of ethical living is the pursuit of deification. The phrase "God became human so that humans may become gods [by grace]"—stated in various forms by important theologians including Irenaeus of Lyon, Athanasius the Great, Gregory the Theologian, Maximus the Confessor, and Gregory Palamas—provides the framework within the Orthodox tradition for understanding the ethical life. From the beginning of creation, a pilgrimage of growth and transformation for Adam and Eve was initiated within the divine economy. The first created humans were called to engage this process of growth and transformation in paradise in an ascent to God, yet they failed. Despite God's ongoing effort to call back creation, a stronger remedy was required, which was the Word of God taking on human nature, human experience, and, ultimately, human death and making them life-giving.

Through God's own assumption and deification of our human nature, human experience, and death in Christ, the principle upon which humanity returns to God is established. Further, this work of Christ as the new beginning and the second Adam, fulfilling the work of the first Adam, sets in place the basis by which Orthodox ethics is understood. Through the putting on of Christ in baptism, persons are integrated back into the path of deification offered through the life and work of Christ. The ethical life, then, is characterized by the cultivation of the grace given at baptism in pursuit of deification through the liturgical and ascetical life of the church. Stated differently, the ethical life is the personal appropriation of the work of Christ. The Orthodox ethical life, consequently, is aimed at holiness through right worship and right belief within the liturgical and ascetical life of the church.

Within this context, rules, goals, and virtues are reframed within the liturgical and ascetical life of the church. The ethical life is measured with respect to one's proximity to God. Virtues are understood as the uncreated energies of God in which the fruit is deification. The virtues are the result of a synergistic relationship between the human person and God and demonstrate the health of the soul. Vice, conversely, is sickness of the soul and reveals a person's spiritual distance from God. Rules, including the commandments and canons, are boundaries between life in the Spirit and spiritual death. The goal is always deification. The result is that the exemplars of Orthodox ethics are those who have made progress in the pursuit of deification through the liturgical and ascetical life of the church and that which is ethical leads to an encounter with the Truth, who is the triune God revealed in Jesus Christ.

Scripture and Tradition

This understanding of ethics relocates the Orthodox Church's understanding of Scripture within the soteriological framework of deification. Consequently, sacred tradition, here, is not restricted to the teachings and practices that are passed down over time in the life of the church. Sacred tradition, in the Orthodox understanding, is more fully and properly understood as the continued union and indwelling of the Holy Spirit in the church. Sacred tradition, then, at its core possesses the deifying life of Christ that gives birth to the revelatory and deifying experience of the saints. This experience of the saints, in turn, is given expression through Scripture, ecumenical councils, canons, writings of the saints, the hymnology and prayers of the church, and holy icons.

Scripture, then, possesses in it this revelatory and deifying experience of the saints from which it is borne out and points toward. For this reason, Orthodox Christians view Scripture as a whole, unified by the same life-giving Spirit with the highest ethic revealed in Jesus Christ. Further, Scripture is the product of a synergistic relationship between the working of the Holy Spirit and the author of the text in which the text maintains the personal character of the author in light of his experience of God and his historical circumstances. This understanding also points to the fact that the Scripture itself is not the revelatory and deifying experience; rather, it witnesses to the revelatory and deifying experience of the evangelists in which all Christians are called to participate. Thus, while the scriptural text witnesses to the divine truth, it also possesses the limitations of finite reality as part of the created world. Such an approach has several important implications.

First, Scripture is iconic in that it always points beyond itself to the divine Truth—the triune God revealed in Jesus Christ. Scripture, then, fundamentally exists within a soteriological context. In John 20:30–31 the evangelist writes, "Now Jesus did many other signs in the presence of his disciples, which are not written in this book. But these are written so that you may come to believe that Jesus is the Messiah, the Son of God, and that through believing you may have life in his name." Second, the Scripture arises out of the life of the church and stands in service of the church. To separate Scripture and the church would be a grave error. This point is particularly clear in the way in which the Orthodox Church has historically located its use of Scripture within the context of the liturgical worship of the church. As such, Scripture does not contain the whole of divine revelation, which can only be possessed by the church—that is, the body of Christ.

Consequently, third, it is only in the church through the living sacred tradition of the church that the Scripture can be properly understood. Because Scripture is born out of the deifying experience of the church, it is through the pursuit and acquisition of this same deifying experience that the mysteries of Scripture can be penetrated and understood. This truth is often referred to as acquiring the "mind of Christ" or the "mind of the Fathers" as a prerequisite for proper interpretation. On this point, Athanasius writes, "But for the searching and right understanding of the Scriptures there is need of a good life and a pure soul, and for Christian virtue to guide the mind to grasp, so far as human nature can, the truth concerning God the Word. One cannot possibly understand the teaching of the saints unless one has a pure mind and is trying to imitate their life" (*Inc.* 57).

Scripture in Ethics

Scripture and ethics have as their common basis, then, an experience of God in the pursuit of deification within the liturgical and ascetical life of the church. To remove Scripture or ethics from this soteriological framework would be to distort their foundations, their proper understanding, and their proper relationship to each other. Consequently, Orthodox ethics and Scripture are born out of a participatory knowledge of God and point Orthodox Christians toward this participatory knowledge of God in pursuit of deification.

Within this context, Orthodox ethicists view Holy Scripture as a primary resource within the sacred tradition of the church for understanding how one should pursue the ethical life in light of an Orthodox ethicist's own pursuit of deification. Here, the continuity of the life of the church is maintained in which that same Holy Spirit that guided the authors of Scripture is opening the heart of the Orthodox ethicist in turning to understand the Scripture and its ethical implications for Christian living.

At the same time, Orthodox ethicists do not use Scripture as an autonomous resource that is capable of standing outside of sacred tradition. Scripture is always interpreted within the context of the sacred tradition of the church. Consequently, in interpreting Scripture, the hermeneutical principle applied to Scripture is the living sacred tradition of the church. Scripture is read and understood within the pursuit of deification in one's own Christian life in adopting the "mind of Christ" guided by the writings, hymns, and liturgical prayers of those who have been recognized by the church as authoritative.

Such an approach, however, does not suggest that the proper way to deal with contemporary ethical problems is merely to read what a particular saint said in the fourth century about a particular biblical passage and that will resolve the ethical question in our own contemporary context. Rather, the aim in using Scripture is to enter into the same stream of sacred tradition that gave birth to these writings within their own historical context. Thus, the task is to discern what writings and interpretive methods are relevant in producing a creative and authentic response to our own historical situation within this same stream of sacred tradition. This approach also means that any ethical instruction today can never contradict the teaching of Scripture.

In light of the basic hermeneutical principle of sacred tradition, some general principles of exegetical method that are generally agreed upon by Orthodox ethicists include the following:

1. The life and work of Christ are the key that unlocks the meaning of all Scripture.
2. The pursuit of purity of heart through repentance and a turning to God in the life of the church is a critical precondition for an authentic interpretation of the text.
3. The aim and purpose of interpreting Scripture is always oriented toward the ethical life, which is the same as the pursuit of deification.
4. Only within the life of the church can Scripture be fully and properly interpreted, because it is within the church that a continuity of the working of the Holy Spirit can be found.
5. Methods of interpretation can vary as long as they authenticate the aim of the ethical life, which is the pursuit of deification.
6. Authority for proper interpretation ultimately rests within the apostolic tradition, which continues in the life of the church up to the present.

Given these general principles of interpretation, Orthodox ethicists make use of a wide range of biblical texts and methods. Such methods include typological, allegorical, and literal levels of interpretation that are witnessed to throughout the life of the church. Regarding the use of specific biblical critical methods such as philological criticism, literary criticism, and other forms of biblical criticism, generally speaking, Orthodox ethicists are open to using these methods, recognizing that these are simply tools for understanding the text that can be appropriated within an Orthodox framework.

Orthodox ethicists have much work to do today in responding to the many and diverse challenges presented in the world, ranging from new technologies to growing complex economic and ecological questions, to the ever-deepening discussions in the medical community. Scripture continues to play an important role in understanding how to respond to these contemporary challenges. The challenge for Orthodox ethicists is to properly discern within the living out of the liturgical and ascetical life of the church precisely how to manifest this same divine Spirit that has been manifested in every generation with the continued aim of the restoration and healing of the entire world.

Bibliography

Behr, J. "Scripture, the Gospel, and Orthodoxy." *SVTQ* 43, nos. 3–4 (1999): 223–48; Breck, J. *Scripture in Tradition: The Bible and Its Interpretation in the Orthodox Church*. St. Vladimir's Seminary Press, 2001; Engelhard, H., Jr. *The Foundations of Christian Bioethics*. Swets & Zeitlinger, 2000; Florovsky, G. *Bible, Church, Tradition: An Eastern Orthodox View*. Vol. 1 of *The Collected Works of Georges Florovsky*. Nordland, 1972; Ford, M. "Seeing, but Not Perceiving: Crisis and Context in Biblical Studies." *SVTQ*

35, nos. 2–3 (1991): 107–25; Keselopoulos, A. *Man and the Environment: A Study of St. Symeon the New Theologian*. Trans. E. Theokritoff. St. Vladimir's Seminary Press, 2001; idem. *Passion and Virtues according to St. Gregory Palamas*. St. Tikhon's Seminary Press, 2004; Mantzarides, G. *The Deification of Man*. Trans. L. Sherrard. St. Vladimir's Seminary Press, 1984; Nellas, P. *Deification in Christ: Orthodox Perspectives on the Nature of the Human Person*. Trans. N. Russell. St. Vladimir's Seminary Press, 1997; Stylianopoulos, T. *The New Testament: An Orthodox Perspective*. Vol. 1 of *Scripture, Tradition, and Hermeneutics*. Holy Cross Orthodox Press, 1997; idem, ed. *Sacred Text and Interpretation: Perspectives in Orthodox Biblical Studies*. Holy Cross Orthodox Press, 2006; Ware, T. *The Orthodox Church*. Penguin Books, 1993.

Mark A. Tarpley

P

Pacifism

What position should Christians hold with regard to the use of violence in conflict resolution? This question and one closely related to it—what should the Christian position be regarding participation in war?—have arisen consistently throughout the history of the Christian tradition. On the one hand, passages such as the Sermon on the Mount, with its injunctions not to resist an evil person and to "turn the other cheek" (Matt. 5:38–39), have been taken by many to mean that violence is not an acceptable tool for Christians to use or be involved with. On the other hand, there are many instances where the OT records God as commanding his people to engage in war against certain kinds of enemies (e.g., various cases in the book of Joshua). So what are Christians to do? Should they set aside the nonviolence of Jesus? Or is Jesus' own apparent commitment to nonviolence in the Gospels intended by God to be an example for engaging evil and violence?

Before taking up this question directly, it is important to clarify terms and to address a common confusion around the concept of pacifism. First, contrary to what many believe, the term *pacifism* does not name a single position but rather points to a constellation of positions that have to do with resisting the use of violence. Perhaps no one made this fact clearer than John Howard Yoder did in his book *Nevertheless: A Meditation on the Varieties and Shortcomings of Religious Pacifism*. Yoder explores in excess of twenty-five different ways in which different groups have understood what it means to be a pacifist. Yoder was a committed pacifist, but he held his position critically, and so he critically examined these different forms of pacifism.

Second, when one engages in popular debate on the topic, those who oppose the pacifist position erroneously conflate pacifism with passivism. Those who make this mistake often critique pacifism by implying that the pacifist argues that we should stand idly by while evil is being perpetrated in the world. If pacifists really were passivists, then this critique would be valid, but they are not. Yoder once commented that pacifists rule out only one option when it comes to considering the Christian response to evil, namely, the use of violence as a means of conflict resolution.

A third, but less common, mistake occurs when someone claims that the pacifist position stands at the opposite end of the spectrum from the just-war position. In reality, the pacifist and the just-war theorist agree that some limits must be put on the deployment of violence and war as tools for resolving conflict. The pacifist, of course, limits the use of violence much more strictly than does the just-war theorist. However, both the pacifist and the just-war theorist actually stand at the opposite end of the spectrum from the crusader, who tends to see little or no limits on the use of war to accomplish one's ends.

Historically speaking, the data confirm that the early church was predominantly pacifist. Prior to the year 200 CE, the Christian tradition was overwhelmingly pacifist, with several examples of individuals martyred for their unwillingness to take up arms. Although there was some slight movement away from this after 200 CE, the church remained predominantly pacifist until the time of Constantine. Once Christians gained an emperor sympathetic to their cause and willing to welcome them into the corridors of power, the access to imperial power changed the outlook on the acceptability of deploying violence in defense of the state. After Constantine, the church had a vested interest in the success of the state and thus came to view the use of power differently. The debate continues as to whether this change was a positive aspect of having access to power or was a basic betrayal of the call to embody Jesus' mandate to be peacemakers.

Biblically speaking, the early parts of the OT do not present a position that is embodied in the commitments of contemporary pacifists. Hence, one is faced immediately with the question of how to present a consistent biblical hermeneutic that allows one rightly to conclude that God calls us to lives of nonviolence. While one need not affirm

Vernard Eller's argument at every point, in *War and Peace: From Genesis to Revelation* he presents a strong case for understanding the unfolding of the biblical narrative in a way that explains why, by the time we get to Jesus, the expectation is that Christians will embrace the nonviolent example of the one whom they call the Prince of Peace. In summary form, Eller's thesis is that the biblical narrative tells the story of how God progressively weans his children away from the use of violence to the point that they can see in the model of Jesus one who shows what it means to overcome evil through suffering.

To explore Eller's argument, consider the extent to which early narratives in Genesis convey a picture of humanity that sees no problem with using violence. Even in some of these narratives, though, the readings that seem to affirm the use of violence are not without ambiguity. For example, in Gen. 10:9–10 we come across the character Nimrod. The common translation of the passage observes that Nimrod was a mighty warrior before the Lord, with the implication that God is either pleased with Nimrod the warrior or, minimally, is not particularly concerned by him. However, Eller is more inclined to the translation given by Jacques Ellul: "Nimrod was a violent man, upon whom God kept a close eye." The difference is immediately obvious in that the alternative translation problematizes the use of violence in ways the more popular translation obscures. Nimrod is not the mighty warrior upon whom God looks with favor; he is the one who easily appeals to violence, and so God must keep an extra close watch on him.

Another example of a text that can easily be misread is the injunction in Exod. 21:23–25 to repay "life for life, eye for eye, tooth for tooth, hand for hand, foot for foot, burn for burn, wound for wound, stripe for stripe." At first reading, this seems to warrant the use of violence to respond to violence. However, one has to take the time to situate this passage in its historical setting. It was not unusual for people to repay an evil by visiting a much greater evil on their enemies. If you kill a member of my clan, then I come after not only the killer but also all of your clan. This injunction to repay eye for eye, tooth for tooth, and so on actually moves away from unrestrained violence. God is limiting the response that one can make to injury brought about by another. No longer are people to exact unrestrained vengeance on an enemy; instead, God now expects that the repayment of evil for evil will be limited to an "in-kind" degree of evil. This is consistent with Eller's claim that God is moving his people, step by step, away from violence.

Throughout the first half of the OT Eller sees God conducting a series of movements away from the use of violence. The first can be seen in the example in the preceding paragraph. The next step is when God steps in and says, in effect, "You can go to war, but only when I say so." This next move is exemplified in the example of Gideon and his three hundred soldiers (Judg. 7). In essence, God is allowing war, but only on his terms and in a way that makes it clear that God is doing the fighting. We need not see this progression as linear, with no sliding back into the old patterns from time to time; rather, we should see it as a progression that moves, even if sometimes irregularly, through these steps with a major transition when we get to late Isaiah. For example, in Isa. 53 we have the image of the suffering servant, central for us in a number of ways. First, it is evident that the suffering servant is an important character who embodies God's way of interacting with the world. Second, the way of interacting with evil embodied is best characterized as overcoming evil through suffering, through allowing evil to spend itself against us and thus undermining it by neither resisting evil nor confronting it with "in-kind" responses.

It becomes particularly significant for followers of Jesus that of the different strands evident in the OT, the one that Jesus picks up and models is the way of the suffering servant, the one who overcomes evil by allowing it to do its worst to him. The cross, then, becomes the ultimate symbol of overcoming evil through suffering. If God had wanted to demonstrate that war was an acceptable tool for the accomplishment of his ends, the evil perpetrated against the children of Abraham by the Romans would have justified violent response. However, even in the midst of such violent abuse, Jesus models the way of peace and resists the call of the Zealots to take up arms and fight against the Romans. The arc described by Eller, then, is now complete. The suffering servant, who is at once Son of God and Son of Man, is now the one who has been weaned from the use of violence against others and instead shows what it means to resist the temptation to respond in violence even to the point of his own death.

Christian pacifists encourage us to look radically at what it means to conduct oneself in the world, and the implications for the field of ethics are enormous. If God calls us to lead lives embracing nonviolence, then Christians must more aggressively offer alternative means for engagement with evil. Without the church modeling an alternative, the temptation to deploy our weapons of violence against enemies will be too hard to resist. As Yoder insisted, if we were as committed to spending resources to identify nonviolent ways of overcoming evil as we seem to be in spending resources to use violence to overcome evil, many new and creative solutions and strategies would undoubtedly be identified.

The pressing question from an ethical standpoint is whether the pacifist position is the one that followers of Jesus should take as normative: must all Christians be pacifists in order to faithfully embody the faith? Minimally, it seems right to observe that the pacifist arguments and their appeal to Scripture must be taken seriously. Too much hinges on the conclusion that one draws at this point. If faithfully following Jesus requires pacifism, then we must rethink what Dwight Eisenhower called the "military-industrial complex." The amount of resources invested in militaries around the world, to a very real degree, limits the availability of resources available for other priorities, such as feeding the poor, providing healthcare for those who otherwise could not access it, providing basic infrastructure to support development, and so on. Additionally, if pacifism is to be seen as normative, then we must take nonviolent peacemaking strategies far more seriously than people, governments, and other institutions tend to do.

One of the ethical dilemmas that pacifists must face is how to deal with evil. Often pacifism is understood, and rightly so, as a position first and foremost about how one deals with international conflict. The pacifist simply is unwilling to so easily deploy military force. It is particularly troubling to the Christian pacifist that in the United States, for example, the demographic most willing to support war is the one that self-identifies as Christian. The nonpacifist may reasonably inquire of the pacifist what course of action should be taken if military engagement is wrong. It is at this point that the subtle nuances of the variety of pacifist positions are too easily overlooked. It is worth noting that the three most significant pacifist voices of the last century (Mohandas Gandhi, Martin Luther King Jr., and John Howard Yoder) believed that the deployment of a police force within society was an appropriate measure. They did not see this as inconsistent with their pacifist beliefs. In fact, near the end of his life, Yoder was considering what it would look like to have an international police force that could be deployed to deal with international conflict, observing the kinds of rules of engagement that police forces follow.

Stepping back from the level of international conflict, one might also consider the ethics implied for our day-to-day interactions if we take more seriously the pacifist call to nonviolence. How might we deal with social injustices, for example? Even a cursory study of the lives of King and Gandhi shows the extent to which the ethic of nonviolent resistance was built into all that they did. Both men found powerful symbolic ways to draw attention to the plight of oppressed people, but both consistently resisted the temptation to "repay evil for evil," even when they and their followers were being abused. Minimally, Christians need to ask themselves how the pacifist ethic ought to permeate their everyday lives so that the easy appeal to customary power paradigms is resisted in favor of more faithful imitation of the cross of Jesus—willing to suffer ourselves rather than to cause suffering to others.

See also Anabaptist Ethics; Force, Use of; Imitation of Jesus; Just-Peacemaking Theory; Just-War Theory; Peace; Security; Sermon on the Mount; Violence; War

Bibliography

Brown, D. *Biblical Pacifism*. Evangel Publishing House; Herald Press, 2003; Dombrowski, D. *Christian Pacifism*. Temple University Press, 1991; Eller, V. *War and Peace: From Genesis to Revelation*. Wipf & Stock, 2003; Hauerwas, S. The *Peaceable Kingdom: A Primer in Christian Ethics*. University of Notre Dame Press, 1991; Merton, T., ed. *Gandhi on Non-Violence: A Selection from the Writings of Mahatma Gandhi*. New Directions Publishing, 1965; Sider, R. *Non-Violence: The Invincible Weapon?* Word, 1989; Stassen, G. *Just Peacemaking: Transforming Initiatives for Justice and Peace*. Westminster John Knox, 1992; Trocmé, A. *Jesus and the Nonviolent Revolution*. Orbis, 2004; Wink, W. *Jesus and Nonviolence: A Third Way*, Fortress; Roundhouse, 2003; Yoder, J. *Nevertheless: A Meditation on the Varieties and Shortcomings of Religious Pacifism*. Herald Press, 1971; idem. *The Politics of Jesus: Vicit Agnus Noster*. 2nd ed. Eerdmans, 1994.

Charles E. Gutenson

Pain *See* Suffering

Parables, Use of in Ethics

Paul offers an epitome of Christian ethics: "Live your life in a manner worthy of the gospel of Christ" (Phil. 1:27) and "Let the same mind be in you that was in Christ Jesus" (Phil. 2:5). Characteristic of the Gospels is that Jesus "began to teach them many things in parables" (Mark 4:2), and the parables have been and remain a rich resource for discipleship and ethical reflection. The challenge is to describe how they so function in the Gospels and how they can be continually appropriated.

Speaking in Parables

"Parable," from the Greek *parabolē*, entails placing things side by side for the sake of comparison.

In the LXX, *parabolē* normally translates the Hebrew *māšāl*, which embraces various literary forms. Parables, then, would include proverbs (1 Sam. 10:12; Prov. 1:1, 6; 26:7–9), riddles (Judg. 14:10–18), taunt songs (Mic. 2:4; Hab. 2:6), oracles (Num. 23:7, 18), and metaphors and allegories (Isa. 5:1–7; Ezek. 17:2–24). In the Gospels, parabolic material includes proverbs (Luke 4:23), examples (Luke 12:16–21), similitudes (Luke 5:36–39), similes (Matt. 13:33), allegory (Matt. 25:1–13), as well as the more familiar narrative parables (Luke 10:25–37; 15:11–32).

The wide use of the term *parable* has spawned a major problem of interpretation of the nature and function of parables, with the distinction between parable and allegory occupying center stage. The word *allegory* (from Gk. *allēgoreō*, "to speak otherwise than one seems to speak") is defined as "description of a subject under the guise of some other subject of aptly suggestive resemblance" (*Oxford English Dictionary*). It has been applied to biblical passages such as Isa. 5:1–7, the infidelity of the people described as an unfruitful vineyard, or to a whole book, such as Song of Songs. In the NT itself, parables are interpreted as allegories (Matt. 13:36–43; Mark 4:13–20). Allegory quickly became a dominant characteristic of parable interpretation throughout church history. For example, in reflecting on the parable of the good Samaritan (Luke 10:29–37), Augustine identifies the man who went down from Jerusalem to Jericho as Adam; Jerusalem is the state of original happiness; Jericho represents human mortality; the Samaritan is Christ; the inn is the church; the innkeeper is Paul; and so on (Dodd 1–2). Allegory interprets details independent of their literary and historical context. It is also coded language for insiders that illustrates or supports the previously held beliefs of a definite group. Although the rejection of allegory became a keystone of parable interpretation, often there was a failure to distinguish between interpreting nonallegorical material in an allegorical manner and allegory as a vital literary genre. Fruitful interpretation can take place as well through an allegorical retelling of a parable that remains faithful to the originating meaning of the parable.

With the rise of historical criticism, allegorical interpretation fades, due especially to the influence of Adolf Jülicher, whose two-volume study marked a new era in parable research. From an understanding of *parabolē* as found in Greek rhetoric, Jülicher argued that parables were extended similes, whereas allegories were developed metaphors. In a simile, the point of comparison is clearly indicated by "like" or "as" (e.g., Luke 11:44), whereas metaphor is a compressed simile in which something is "transferred" or carried over (the literal meaning of *metapherō*) from one sphere to another, as in "The eye is the lamp of the body" (Matt. 6:22). Jülicher calls metaphor "inauthentic speech" that obscures rather than illustrates truth.

According to Jülicher, every parable is composed of an "image" (*Bild*) and the "reality part" (*Sache*), what the image points to. The focus of his position is that each parable has only one point of comparison. The individual details or characters in a parable have no meaning outside the parable (e.g., in Luke 15:11–32, the father does not stand for God, nor the elder brother for the Pharisees), and the point of comparison is one of the widest possible moral application.

Although subsequent scholarship rejected many of Jülicher's interpretations principally because of the rigidity of the single-point approach, the minimizing of OT background of Jesus' teaching, and the neglect of similarities between Jesus and early rabbinic teachers, Jülicher anticipated the major strains of parable research in the twentieth century: concern for parable as a literary form, parables as an entrée to kingdom proclamation, and, later, the self-understanding of Jesus, and the ethical relevance of parables.

The most influential interpreter of the parables in the twentieth century was Joachim Jeremias. With almost unparalleled knowledge of first-century Palestine, Jeremias sheds light on the details of daily life that provide the material for the parables. More significantly, he carefully analyzes the changes that the parables underwent as they moved from the setting in the life of Jesus through the missionary proclamation of the early church and to their final incorporation into the Gospels. For example, parables are allegorized (Matt. 13:36–43; Mark 4:14–20); parables addressed originally to opponents are directed to church leaders (Matt. 18:10–14; Luke 15:1–7); details are embellished, and OT allusions are added.

Jeremias's study of the parables, then, becomes a full-scale study of the message of Jesus. He rejected "realized eschatology," as advocated by C. H. Dodd, and proposed "inaugurating eschatology"—that is, in the process of realization. The definitive revelation of God's reign has begun in Jesus; its full effect lies in the future. Jeremias's view prevailed both as a faithful exegesis of Jesus' parables and of Christian eschatology in general.

Although Dodd did not stress the ethical implication of the parables beyond their urgent call to conversion, Jeremias sketched the major ethical demands of Jesus by grouping particular parables under headings such as "God's Mercy for Sinners," "It May Be Too Late," "The Challenge of the Hour," and "Realized Discipleship." Klyne Snodgrass adopts a similar approach in the most recent comprehensive study of the parables.

In the last third of the twentieth century, concern for the form and literary quality of the parables prevailed over their use to reconstruct the teaching of Jesus. Along with concern for the parables as the key to the teaching of Jesus, the other major focus of parable research has been concern for their literary nature. This owes much to Dodd's inductive description of parable "as a metaphor or simile drawn from nature or common life, arresting the hearer by its vividness or strangeness and leaving the mind in sufficient doubt about its precise application to tease it into active thought" (Dodd 5). These qualities of metaphoric language, realism, paradox, and open-ended summons to personal engagement became the focus for subsequent discussion.

Seminal works by Amos Wilder and Robert Funk viewed parables primarily as poetic rather than rhetorical forms where an appreciation of metaphor provided a key to a new vision of the parables. Metaphor, they noted, by the often surprising equation of dissimilar elements—for example, "You are the salt of the earth" (Matt. 5:13)—produces an impact on the imagination that cannot be conveyed by discursive speech. With Funk and Wilder, metaphor has moved from literary trope or figure to a theological and hermeneutical category; it is especially suited to express the two necessary qualities of all religious language, immediacy and transcendence. A religious experience, that sense of awe in the face of the holy or of being grasped by mystery, is immediate and personal and, in great religious literature, is expressed in concrete, physical imagery.

The parables of Jesus are more exactly "metaphoric" rather than metaphors, since metaphor involves the combination of two distinct images joined in a single sentence, whereas the Gospel parables generally are extended narratives. They combine narrative form and metaphoric process (Ricoeur). Focus quickly shifted to a "narrative" reading of parables. Again, Wilder was a leader. He argued that in telling about God's reign "in story," Jesus continued the narrative legacy of biblical revelation. In reading the stories of Jesus, a Christian realizes that life is "a race, a pilgrimage, in short, a story" (Wilder 65).

Ethics and the Parables

The formal characteristics of parables themselves have ethical implications. Jesus used realistic images from daily life that caught his hearers' attention by their vividness and narrative color. Yet his parables have a surprising twist; the realism is shattered, and the hearers knew that something more was at stake than a homey illustration to drive home a point. The parables raise questions, unsettle the complacent, and challenge the hearers to reflection and inquiry.

Illustrations from daily life. In the parables of Jesus the life of ordinary people from a distant time and culture comes alive in a way found rarely in ancient literature. Jesus was familiar with a rural Galilean milieu: outdoor scenes of farming and shepherding, and domestic scenes in a simple one-room house (Luke 11:5–8). Jesus sees life through the eyes of the *ʿănāwîm*, the poor and humble of the land. This creates an obstacle for the modern urban reader and poses challenges to historians and archaeologists to help us understand better the cultural context of the parables. The realism of the parables means also that Jesus places the point of contact between God and humans within the everyday world of human experience. Jesus does not proclaim the kingdom in "God language"; rather, he summons his hearers to realize that their destinies are at stake in their "ordinary, creaturely existence, domestic, economic, social" (Wilder 82).

Novelty and paradox. The realism of the parables is but one side of the coin. The novel twists in Jesus' stories make his hearers take notice. The harvest is not just bountiful, but extravagant (Mark 4:8); the mustard seed is the smallest of seeds, yet it becomes the "greatest of all shrubs" (Mark 4:31–32). The vineyard owner paying first those hired last (Matt. 20:8) makes the reader suspect that something strange is about to happen. A major key to the "meaning" of a given parable appears when the realism begins to break down.

Parables express a paradox, a seeming absurdity that conceals a deeper truth. Their fundamental message is that things are not as they seem; you must have your tidy image of reality shattered. The good Samaritan is not primarily an illustration of compassion and loving-kindness to the suffering, but rather a challenge to see as good those whom we would call enemy. The strange and paradoxical character of the parables is a counterpart to Jesus' association with, and offer of mercy and grace to, tax collectors and sinners, those thought to be beyond the pale of God's concern. Similarly, Paul Ricoeur notes that parables operate in a pattern of orientation, disorientation, and reorientation. Their hyperbolic and paradoxical language presents an extravagance that interrupts our normal way of viewing things and presents the extraordinary within the ordinary. The parables dislocate our project of trying to make a tight pattern of our lives, which Ricoeur feels is akin to the Pauline "boasting" or justification by works.

An open-ended challenge. In their transmission the parables received different applications and interpretations. Appended to the enigmatic parable of the unjust steward is a parade of interpretations, joined mainly by catchwords (Luke 16:8b–13). Other parables have appended sayings that are found in a number of different contexts (e.g., Matt. 25:13 = Mark 13:35; Matt. 25:29 = Mark 4:25; Matt. 13:12; Luke 8:18). The audience shifts; parables originally addressed to opponents are directed to the church (Matt. 18:1, 12–14; Luke 15:2–7). In their original form, the parables of Jesus may have ended at the narrative conclusion (e.g., Matt. 13:30; 18:34) or with a question or challenge (e.g., Matt. 20:15; 21:31; Mark 4:9). The meaning of a given parable often is elusive: is the point of the parable of the pearl (Matt. 13:45–46) the search, the joy of finding, or the willingness to risk all? Both in the early church and in subsequent history, the parables are "polyvalent." They demand and receive different interpretation from different audiences. Although exegesis may determine the parameters of misinterpretation of a given parable, it can scarcely exhaust the potentialities for fruitful interpretation and application.

Parables are open-ended; they are invitations waiting for a response. The parable does not really exist until it is freely appropriated. The response of the reader or hearer in a real sense creates the meaning of the parable. Parable is a form of religious discourse that appeals not only to the imagination or to the joyous perception of paradox or surprise but also to the most basic of human qualities, freedom. Jesus chose a form of discourse that put his life and message at the risk of free human response.

Appropriating the parables for Christian ethics is an aspect of the larger issue of the relation of Scripture and ethics. Fundamentally, the parables are an aspect of "remembering Jesus," and through preaching and study they form the conscience of Christian communities (Verhey 22–26; 286–87). The parables provide a storehouse of images that counter distorted images flooding our consciousness (Spohn 60–64). The poor, the disabled, and marginal are not to be hidden or neglected but are to be welcomed for dinner (Luke 14:16–24); women are not to be seen as powerless victims when a widow claims her rights before a corrupt judge (Luke 18:1–8); remembering Jesus is to follow the trajectory of the church through the ages as it retells and adapts the parables of Jesus.

Parables likewise contain clear exhortations to discipleship, warnings about failure, examples of virtues and vices; they nurture Christian attitudes and dispositions and enrich the imagination of believers. Although from a cultural milieu strange to most people today, they have a universal quality that, through reflective analogy, can shape the values of a Christian community. Experiencing and extending forgiveness "from one's heart" is a fundamental Christian challenge (Matt. 18:23–35), and the claims of justice should not limit generosity (Matt. 20:1–16). Christians still long for a God who reaches out in a surprising manner to the prodigal and the dutiful and risks the good of the majority to seek out the lost (Luke 15:1–32); blindness to the destitute at one's doorstep is a stain on Christian faith (Luke 16:19–31). The shock that the threatening outsider can actually be a "good Samaritan" who heals and gives life can overturn fixed prejudices and correct false values (Luke 10:25–37). The Gospels continue to teach many things in parables.

See also Eschatology and Ethics; Kingdom of God; New Testament Ethics

Bibliography

Blomberg, C. *Interpreting the Parables*. InterVarsity, 1992; Dodd, C. H. *The Parables of the Kingdom*. Charles Scribner's Sons, 1961; Donahue, J. *The Gospel in Parable: Metaphor, Narrative, and Theology in the Synoptic Gospels*. Fortress, 1988; Funk, R. *Language, Hermeneutic, and the Word of God: The Problem of Language in the New Testament and Contemporary Theology*. Harper & Row, 1966; Hultgren, A. *The Parables of Jesus: A Commentary*. Eerdmans, 2002; Jeremias, J. *The Parables of Jesus*. Trans. S. Hooke. Scribner, 1972; Jülicher, A. *Die Gleichnisreden Jesu*. 2 vols. Wissenschaftliche Buchgesellschaft, 1969 [1899]; Kissinger, W. *The Parables of Jesus: A History of Interpretation and Bibliography*. Scarecrow Press and American Library Association, 1979; Perrin, N. *Jesus and the Language of the Kingdom: Symbol and Metaphor in New Testament Interpretation*. Fortress, 1976; Ricoeur, P. "Biblical Hermeneutics." *Semeia* 4 (1975): 27–148; Scott, B. *Hear Then the Parable: A Commentary on the Parables of Jesus*. Fortress, 1989; Snodgrass, K. *Stories with Intent: A Comprehensive Guide to the Parables of Jesus*. Eerdmans, 2008; Spohn, W. *Go and Do Likewise: Jesus and Ethics*. Continuum, 1999; Verhey, A. *Remembering Jesus: Christian Community, Scripture, and the Moral Life*. Eerdmans, 2002; Wilder, A. *Early Christian Rhetoric: The Language of the Gospel*. Harvard University Press, 1972.

John R. Donahue

Pardon *See* Forgiveness

Parenthood, Parenting

The story of parenting in Scripture is appropriately confounding. The first instance of the Hebrew word most simply associated with "love" appears in what is arguably the most morally fraught passage in the Bible: a divine command for a parent to sacrifice his own child. The word that the NRSV translates as "love" in the command to Abraham is *āhab*: "Take your son, your only son Isaac, whom you love, and go to the land of Moriah, and offer him there as a burnt offering on one of the mountains that I shall show you" (Gen. 22:2). Centuries of interpreters (some of them parents, all of them once children) have struggled over the meaning. It has been little solace to most that God required only Abraham's obedience, not his obedience unto Isaac's death.

The Danish theologian Søren Kierkegaard donned a silent pseudonym (Johannes de Silentio) to speak of this story in *Fear and Trembling* (1843). Central to de Silentio's queries is the conflict in commands. Could sacrifice ever be consonant with parental love? If Abraham is, in a proleptic way, responsible to God's command to love one's neighbor (Lev. 19:18), even to love the alien in his midst (Lev. 19:34), would he not be responsible for loving his son Isaac? Here the wording of the command in Gen. 22 is crucial. Abraham is to take his "only" son, the son whom he did "love." As Kierkegaard mimes the unspeakable, Abraham was simultaneously to love his son and to draw the knife. If Abraham had not loved Isaac, and had been all too able to envision his own life without his child, the story might still be horrific, but sadly common.

Here is part of the trouble. Isaac is not Abraham's "only son." Isaac may be Abraham's only *beloved* son, but Isaac has an older brother, Ishmael. What to do with this twist in the story? Placed as it is in a series of stories, does the command now include a form of divine irony? The first direct scriptural reference to parental love is thus multiply fraught. The father of faith, apparently able to will the unspeakable, seems also to have willfully misplaced a child.

Hagar faced the terror of her son's exposure. Ishmael was not an orphan; he had a mother, who raged for his sake, even to God. In this, Hagar may be a role model for those who attend closely to scriptural stories of parents. Lament is an apt response to two stories on the way into the abyss that is Judges. Abraham escapes the torture of killing Isaac. Jephthah does not do so with his daughter (Judg. 11:29–40). "And Jephthah made a vow to the Lord, and said, 'If you will give the Ammonites into my hand, then whoever comes out of the doors of my house to meet me, when I return victorious from the Ammonites, shall be the Lord's, to be offered up by me as a burnt offering.'" Returning victorious, his daughter greets him "with timbrels and with dancing." Within two months, she suffers "according to the vow" that her father had made. The "whoever" required for victory turns out to be Jephthah's own daughter. We do not know whether her father actually loves her, only that she is a virgin. This story echoes as the master of the house in Judg. 19 offers his "virgin daughter" to assuage the "base fellows" at his door. In Judg. 11, the virgin daughter symbolically replaces Isaac as a sacrifice; here in Judg. 19, the virgin daughter is to replace an endangered guest in her father's house. The guest's concubine is sent out—a nonvirgin in exchange for a guest and a virgin. By the close of Judges, she has been ritually dismembered, and the young women of Shiloh have been taken as booty for the Benjaminites. Those who hear are to lament, as "in those days there was no king in Israel; all the people did what was right in their own eyes" (Judg. 21:25).

Could a king be the answer to the violent chaos against daughters, sons, virgins, and concubines? In the Septuagintal order of OT books, Ruth follows the ominous last line of Judges, quoted just above. The movement from chaos to kingship is interrupted by a childless woman who does what is right in God's eyes. During this menacing time "when the Judges ruled," there is also a famine, and a mother is left as a nonparent, with only two daughters-in-law (and foreign ones at that). Ruth resolves to bind herself to Naomi, willing to be aligned with a widow whose deity seems bleakly behind on keeping up with his own children. (The story has been a scriptural word [Ruth 1:16–17] for many twentieth-century weddings in the United States. The mix of marital promise, overpriced dresses, and carefully chosen invitation lists is not quite the right setting for the story, but perhaps it testifies nonetheless.) Ruth adopts a parent who is not her own kin, whose history is marked by tragic loss and whose future has no prospects. The great-grandmother of David adopts a deity whose children, in the canonical sweep of the story, are awash in bloody violence. In the small scope of Ruth's story, this same deity has failed to protect the man who was supposed to be the father of her children. Given all of this, those who hear the story might rightly hope that Naomi will give her daughter praise as they enter Bethlehem. Naomi gives her testimony, one that may resonate with children who care for bereft parents. With Ruth beside her, Naomi laments that she has returned home *empty* (Ruth 1:21). The scriptural word on parenting here involves death, tenacity, lament, bitterness, and, eventually, new life.

Readers of the NT are duly warned that Jesus' ministry may do more to break than to bind bonds of blood and marriage (see, e.g., Matt. 10:16–23, 34–39). Even so, key miracle stories included in the canonical Gospels involve the petitions of a parent on behalf of a cherished child. Apparently, belief in the resurrection did not preclude for early Christians a deep, embodied attachment to their earthly children in this life. Perhaps the women and men around Jesus recognized in him the strength of Elijah, who, after being saved by crows, saved the widow of Zarephath's son (1 Kgs. 17). Faith emboldened one mother to approach Jesus to heal her child (Matt. 15:22–28). She sacrifices what might be called her dignity and risks the scorn of Jesus' disciples. The Canaanite mother comes to Jesus, begging him to heal her daughter. The disciples urge Jesus to send her summarily away. Whose child is this parent? To whom does she belong? Jesus notes that she is not a sheep of Israel, and that she is not among the children to whom he was sent. She engages in brilliant rabbinic commentary: "Even family dogs are allowed to receive scraps from children's plates. Throw me and my daughter a scrap," she counters, and thus she opens the way for Jesus' ministry to dogged gentiles.

How is God parental? The story of the prodigal son (Luke 15:11–32) may be read helpfully alongside the story of Joseph, another beloved son of an extravagantly loving parent (Gen. 37–50). Joseph's brothers are so jealous of Jacob's love for Joseph that they sell Joseph into slavery. Through trickery, Joseph is able simultaneously to save, humble, and forgive his brothers. In what remains one of the most memorable lines in Scripture, Joseph unravels and reweaves a story of parental error and fraternal treachery: "Even though you intended to do harm to me, God intended it for good, in order to preserve a numerous people, as he is doing today" (Gen. 50:20).

God's intention of good for God's own "little ones" (see Gen. 50:21) is unwaveringly resilient, but such grace may also offend. Obedient sheep may resent the willful stupidity of a sibling who takes their protector off into the wilds. Jesus revisits the ramification of parental favor in the Lukan story. A father behaves with foolish extravagance, running joyfully, unceremoniously toward a son who smells of swine. The forgiving father does not permit the lost son even to complete his prepared apology. The father interrupts the son's attempt to humble himself, by calling those around him to prepare for a celebratory feast. One refuses. The older son names himself a "slave," situating himself in a position spared of the younger son by his father's sheer grace. The foolish son, who has "devoured" the family's goods, is given a fatted calf. But the one who has been "working like a slave" is not sent away hungry. The father tells the older son, "You are always with me, and all that is mine is yours." The newly found sheep are fed, the wayward "little ones" spared. But this changes nothing regarding the older, obedient children. They are, as ever, always with God, and all that is God's is theirs.

What of the prodigal daughter? The story that Jesus tells in Luke makes clear that sleeping with prostitutes is akin to sleeping with pigs. The association soils. This may take the reader back to questions raised earlier. Isaac is spared. A virgin daughter and a concubine are brutally sacrificed. Ishmael, although fiercely defended by his mother, is expelled and forgotten by his father. To consider parenting in Scripture is to come up against fraught danger and violent error. For many, it brings up a question that songwriter and biblical commentator Michelle Shocked asks in her song "Prodigal Daughter." What of the virgin, and what of the prostitute? What of the concubine and her child? The wayward son receives a party, but "when a girl goes home with the oats he's sown, it's draw your shades and your shutters. She's bringing such shame to the family name, the return of the prodigal daughter." In John 7:53–8:11, Jesus calls the religious leaders up short when they are determined to stone the adulterous daughter of Israel. Was that enough? Has it been enough to protect fallen daughters and ill-begotten sons? Shocked's song imagines that the prodigal son receives a "tall drink of water," while "there's none in the cup, cause he drank it all up, left for a prodigal daughter." Here, with the Canaanite woman, dogged believers are called to trust that the crumbs, the dregs, will be enough.

See also Child Abuse; Children; Family; Love, Love Command

Bibliography

Bunge, M., ed. *The Child in the Bible*. Eerdmans 2008; Trible, P. *Texts of Terror: Literary-Feminist Readings of Biblical Narratives*. OBT. Fortress, 1984; Weems, R. *Just a Sister Away: A Womanist Vision of Women's Relationships in the Bible*. LuraMedia, 1988; Wheeler, S. *What We Were Made For: Christian Reflections on Love*. Jossey-Bass, 2007.

Amy Laura Hall

Passions

The passions (Eng. *passion* is derived from Gk. *pathos*) were understood in classical thought as movements of the soul toward the sensuous good or away from sensuous evil. Although closely linked to the modern concept of emotion, the passions are correlative to particular ancient theories of human nature and must be understood in the context of these theories.

Plato (427–347 BCE), perhaps drawing on the earlier psychology of the Pythagoreans, posited a threefold division in the soul of the living person: the appetitive part, the seat of sensuous desire; the spirited part, the seat of courage; and the rational part, the seat of reason, which ruled the other two as a charioteer directing two horses (*Resp.* 4; *Phaedrus*). Plato's pupil Aristotle (384–322 BCE) proposed a modified view in which the soul was united to the body as its "form" or "actuality" (*entelecheia*) and was composed in humans of the vegetative soul, the seat of growth and reproduction shared with all forms of life; the sensitive soul, the seat of sensation, perception, and sensual desire, shared with the animals; and the rational soul, unique to humans and endowing humans with their capacity for reason (*De an.* 2–3). Aristotle held that habituation into the intellectual and moral virtues or excellences (*arētai*) is necessary for the attainment of a flourishing life in which reason rightly orders the desires, or passions, of the soul. Both the later works of Plato and Aristotle's philosophy held that the passions were a part of well-lived embodied human life; the goal was not to extirpate the animal passions but rather to moderate them under the control of reason.

The various Stoic writers generally both carried on and intensified the Platonic-Aristotelian teaching that the well-lived moral life is characterized by habits of excellence (or virtue) that demonstrate the mastery of reason over animal desire. For the Stoics, virtue became the supreme good, to be pursued for its own sake regardless of external circumstances. "Virtue," wrote Cicero (106–43 BCE), "is self-sufficient for a happy life" (*Tusc.* 5.1); because "troubled movements and agitations of the soul, roused and excited by ill-considered impulse, in scorn of all reason, leave no portion of happy life behind them" (*Tusc.* 5.6), the virtuous person, for the Stoics, is to strive for the ideal of *apatheia*, complete freedom from the controlling influence of the passions, or at least *eupatheiai*, passions that are rightly ordered by reason.

How did the NT writers incorporate and change the classical (and, in particular, the Stoic) account of the passions? First, they inherited in Israel's Scriptures a textual tradition that not only imparted "passion" language to God (e.g., Ps. 6:1) but also implicitly authorized expressions of fear, desperation, joy, and praise in liturgical contexts. The songbook of the Second Temple period, the book of Psalms, became the songbook of the early church, and the cries of Job and the prophets were understood as the church's cries. Unlike the Stoics, therefore, the early Christians understood themselves to be covenanted in Christ to a God who transcended (fallen) nature and to whom lament, and not just praise, could be offered.

Despite this, Greek philosophy became well established in some strands of Jewish life and literature in the centuries before Christ (e.g., Wisdom of Solomon), and the influence of pagan philosophy is evident particularly in the Pauline Epistles and the Pastoral Epistles. The term *epithymia*, used in pagan philosophy to connote carnal desire, is occasionally used in a morally neutral way (e.g., Luke 22:15; 1 Tim. 3:1 [verb *epithymeō*]), but overwhelmingly it is used to describe the desires of "the flesh" (Gal. 5:24; 1 Pet. 2:11), which entice the moral agent away from holiness. But the repeated scriptural condemnations of "the world" (e.g., 1 John 2:15–17) and "the gentiles" (e.g., 1 Thess. 4:5) should not obscure the fact that contemporary Stoic moralists too would have condemned most of the behaviors that appear in the various Pauline taxonomies of vice (e.g., Rom. 1:18–32; 1 Cor. 6:9–10; Gal. 5:19–21).

Despite this resonance with pagan virtue theory, however, the life, passion, death, and resurrection of Jesus Christ imparted to the NT writers an understanding of the virtuous life that would have been unthinkable to the writers of pagan antiquity. Christ, after all, suffered; the early Christians therefore could understand their own suffering as participation in the suffering of Christ and their own victory over sin as participation in Christ's resurrection. The pagan ideals of *apatheia* or abstract "virtue" could not be understood apart from participation in Christ; because of this, the moral injunctions of the NT become richly narrative. Whereas Cicero wrote in praise of virtue, Paul wrote in praise of "the surpassing value of knowing Christ Jesus my Lord," adding that "I want to know Christ and the power of his resurrection and the sharing of his sufferings by becoming like him in his death" (Phil. 3:8, 10). Participation in Christ becomes, for the early Christians, what virtue was to the Stoics: the way to freedom from ensnaring and enslaving bondage to that which is not true and good.

Understanding the life of Christ as the moral life of excellence, the early Christians were forced to retain a place for the passions in their moral psychology. Jesus wept, for example, and so impassioned expressions of grief, however different in practice from those of "others . . . who have no hope" (1 Thess. 4:13), could not be dismissed as intrinsically evil. Christ suffered for others, and so suffering for the sake of others became morally intelligible for Christians as well (Col. 1:24–29). But much more than the exemplar of the Christian moral life, Christ also became, in a deeply participatory way, its internal logic. Paul writes that the "flesh with its passions and desires [*epithymiai*]" has, in Christ, been crucified (Gal. 5:24), and in its place is life "by the Spirit," a life in which the passions are rightly ordered (Gal. 5:22–23). The Ephesians, likewise, having been "made alive together with Christ" (Eph. 2:5), are enjoined to "put away . . . your old self, corrupt and deluded by its lusts [*epithymiai*]" and "clothe yourselves with the new self, created according to the likeness of God in true righteousness and holiness" (Eph. 4:22–24). The author of 1 Peter similarly enjoins believers, as a result of Christ's passion, to "live for the rest of your earthly life no longer by human desires [*epithymiai*] but by the will of God" (1 Pet. 4:2).

In all of these NT texts it is clear that the passions are not to be abandoned, ignored, or suppressed but rather transformed by grace into Christ's passions, such that the Christian loves what Christ loves, hates what Christ hates, suffers when Christ suffers. The Christian life, that is, is to be characterized not by the absence of desire but rather by desire rightly directed. In Augustine's memorable words, "The citizens of the Holy City of God, as they live by God's standards in the pilgrimage of this present life, feel fear and desire, pain and gladness in conformity with the holy Scriptures and sound doctrine; and because their love is right, all these feelings are right in them" (*Civ.* 14.9).

See also Affections; Desire; Emotion; Lust; Suffering; Vices and Virtues, Lists of; Virtue Ethics

Bibliography

Brueggemann, W. *The Psalms and the Life of Faith*. Fortress, 1995; Nussbaum, M. *The Therapy of Desire: Theory and Practice in Hellenistic Ethics*. Princeton University Press, 1994.

Warren Kinghorn

Patience

In contemporary parlance, patience involves waiting calmly and hopefully. It implies endurance through time that is neither hurried nor anxious. The NT also links patience (usually expressed by the verb *makrothymeō* or the noun *makrothymia*) with calmly waiting for the appointed time. "Be patient, therefore, beloved, until the coming of the Lord. The farmer waits for the precious crop from the earth, being patient with it until it receives the early and the late rains. You too must be patient" (Jas. 5:7–8).

Perhaps because of its distance from earth's rhythms, contemporary Western culture hurries time, demanding quick results. So patience is increasingly difficult but increasingly necessary. Two strong theological pathways lie open for reclaiming patience. First, the Bible describes God as patient, which affects how we conceive it in ourselves. Second, the Christian virtue of patience has long been understood as protective; it keeps us from inordinate sorrow when we suffer evil.

Patience is attributed to Christ in 1 Tim. 1:16: "I received mercy so that in me, as the foremost [sinner], Jesus Christ might display the utmost patience, making me an example to those who would come to believe in him for eternal life." Christ does not press his justified case against Paul, the putative author of 1 Timothy; what is more, he extends time for Paul to respond to his grace. Christ's patience adds time to mercy, deepening it.

Paul writes similarly in Romans, "What if God . . . has endured with much patience the objects of his wrath that are made for destruction . . . in order to make known the riches of his glory?" (Rom. 9:22–23). God's patience here supports the complete biblical story; space is opened for it precisely as God is both merciful and patient. So Karl Barth ruminates, "The fact that He [God] has time for us is what characterises His whole activity towards us as an exercise in patience. Included in this exercise of patience is both God's mercy and punishment, God's salvation and destruction, God's healing and smiting. This all takes place in the course and service of the revelation of His Word. By it all Israel is instructed in the divine Word. . . . God always, and continually, has time for Israel" (Barth 417). For Barth, the very existence of the long biblical narrative is a decisive sign of God's patience. In that narrative God's word has gone out and will not return to him void. Meanwhile, he waits, enduring, as Cyprian notes, humanity's profanity and idolatry, hurled as insult.

Barth's broad reflections bundle related theological notions. He includes *anochē*, usually translated "forbearance" (Rom. 2:4), in his expansive treatment of divine patience. By contrast, Thomas Aquinas delimits patience narrowly as a human virtue. As one of the nine fruits of the Spirit (from Gal. 5:22–23), patience differs from another fruit: long-suffering. When troubled, the mind's good disposition is strengthened "first, by not being disturbed whenever evil threatens: which pertains to 'patience'; secondly, by not being disturbed, whenever good things are delayed; which belongs to 'long suffering'" (*ST* I-II, q. 70, a. 3). Thomas likewise distinguishes patience from perseverance, which is about "persisting long in something good until it is accomplished" (*ST* II-II, q. 137, a. 1).

If these distinctions appear overly fine, they function well when gathered into the cardinal virtue of fortitude (or courage), of which patience, perseverance, and long-suffering are parts. Conceived narrowly, fortitude strengthens us in the face of fear; more broadly, as a cardinal virtue, fortitude holds us fast as we struggle with difficult things. As a part of fortitude, patience specifically protects us from ill effects of the passion of sorrow.

Sorrow can paralyze. According to Thomas, it can deprive us of the power to learn, burden our souls, and weaken all our activities (*ST* I-II, q. 37). Inordinate sorrow collapses time into itself, such that progress on life's journey seems impossible. Sorrow can cause us to lose track of where we are going; patience preserves us on our way. "Patience . . . is that by which we tolerate evil things with an even mind, that we may not with a mind uneven desert good things, through which we may arrive at better" (Augustine, *Pat.* 2). Patience not only weathers the passage of time; it actually keeps time, which sorrow can obliterate.

In this way patience connects to the theological virtues of hope and love. Hope "places us in a narrative in which our suffering can be endured and accordingly made part of our life" (Hauerwas and Pinches 122). Time, the gift of a patient God, now can be lived "toward hope." Moreover, charity equips us to await the beloved's response, as God waits for us. It gives her time. "Love is patient" (1 Cor. 13:4).

The model of patience for Christians is always Jesus Christ, who endured for us the greatest sorrow. Yet James also recalls the patience of the prophets, who in the face of suffering spoke the truth (5:10). Job similarly models endurance (*hypomonē*) (5:11). This extended list suggests we learn patience best as we remember the saints who have gone before. Knowing sorrow, these ones nonetheless endured until the end: protected by patience, given in love, and steered by hope.

See also Courage; Fruit of the Spirit; Hope; Virtue(s); Virtue Ethics

Bibliography

Barth, K. *Church Dogmatics*. Vol. II/1. Trans. A. Mackay et al. T&T Clark, 1978; Hauerwas, S., and C. Pinches. *Christians among the Virtues: Theological Conversations with Ancient and Modern Ethics*. University of Notre Dame Press, 1997, 113–28, 166–78.

Charles R. Pinches

Patriotism *See* Nationalism

Peace

Peace (Heb. *šālôm*; Gk. *eirēnē*) is a dominant moral quality and goal in Scripture. Seeking peace by oppressing others (as the *pax Romana* did) is not what either OT *šālôm* or NT *eirēnē* represents.

Šālôm occurs about 250 times in the OT, and *eirēnē* about 100 times in the NT. *Šālôm*, iridescent in meaning, means "wholeness" or "well-being." *Šālôm* may denote (material) prosperity (Pss. 37:11; 72:1–7; 128:5–6; 147:14; Isa. 66:12; Zech. 8:12), ethical relationships (Zech. 8:19), or an eschatological vision of peace among nations, anticipating the "Prince of Peace" (Isa. 9:2–7; Zech. 9:9–11; cf. Isa. 2:2–4; Mic. 5:4–5). Old Testament scholars emphasize different, though complementary, meanings for *šālôm*: material, physical well-being within a social context of human relations (von Rad); relationship with God, inherent to salvation (Eisenbeis); one's state or condition in life (Westermann; Gerleman; Yoder 1–8).

Šālôm also denotes a correct order of life that reflects creation's purpose for human life (Schmid; Steck). God's divine judgment, even in war, intends to restore *šālôm*. Whatever blocks Yahweh's order for the world, materially or relationally, is the foe and antithesis of *šālôm*. Shalom cannot be understood apart from Yahweh-war, wars in which humans trust God for victory over enemies. God fights such wars to establish and maintain the creation order against chaos (Exod. 14:14; Pss. 29; 68; 89:7–18 [Ollenburger]) and to fulfill divine promises to Israel. The king was authorized to defend God's *šālôm* order against injustice and oppression.

Perry Yoder proposes a moral dimension in *šālôm*, standing against oppression, deceit, fraud, and injurious actions. *Šālôm* contrasts to deceit (Pss. 34:14; 37:37; Jer. 9:8), denotes innocence from moral wrongdoing (Gen. 44:17; 1 Kgs. 5:12), and is paired with justice (*mišpāṭ* [Isa. 59:8; Zech. 8:16–19]) and righteousness (*ṣĕdāqâ* [Ps. 72:7; Isa. 60:17]). *Šālôm* often is paired with healing (Isa. 53:5; 57:18; Jer. 8:15; 14:19; 33:6–9), and its cognate *šālēm* is best translated "health." Thus *šālôm* may describe health (Ps. 38:3 [MT 38:4]) or prosperity (37:11 NRSV) as well as tranquility or quietness of spirit (Ps. 119:165). Some form of "Peace [*šālôm*] be with you" is a common greeting

(Judg. 6:23; 19:20; 1 Sam. 25:6; Pss. 122:7–8; 125:5; 128:6). The treasured Aaronic benediction, "The LORD bless you and keep you," ends with "the LORD . . . give you peace [*šālôm*]" (Num. 6:24–26).

The Lord is *yhwh šālôm* (Judg. 6:24; cf. *yhwh rōp'ekā* ["Lord your healer"] in Exod. 15:26). God ultimately is the source of peace (1 Kgs. 2:33; Isa. 52:7; 60:17; 66:12) and promises a new "covenant of peace" (Isa. 54:10; Ezek. 34:25; 37:26; Mal. 2:5–6), in which "the effect of righteousness will be peace" (Isa. 32:17); "righteousness and peace will kiss each other" (Ps. 85:10) (see Wolterstorff). Peace is paired also with God's unfailing love and faithfulness (Ps. 85:7–13).

Although *war* is not an antonym of *šālôm*, the latter flourishes in times of peace, achieved often by negotiated treaties between nations (Deut. 20:10–12; Josh. 9:15; 10:1, 4; Judg. 4:17; 1 Sam. 7:14; 1 Kgs. 5:12). The wars of the kings, however, were waged mostly not "in the name of God's order of righteousness and peace but rather in the name of an imperialistic ideology" (Hanson 351). Israel's royal ideology collides with Isaiah's *šālôm*, for the nation's wars obstruct *šālôm*. Isaiah instead calls for quiet trust in God (Isa. 7:3–9; 8:6; 30:15). Deutero-Isaiah affirms new visions of *šālôm* (Isa. 52:7–10), including Israel's servant suffering (Isa. 53:5, where "whole" translates *šālôm*), God's sovereignty, and "a renewal of creation to its divinely intended wholeness" (Hanson 359). In postexilic Israel, however, internal community strife and excluding neighbors subvert this vision. "Beating swords into plowshares" (Isa. 2:4; Mic. 4:3) is eclipsed by an apocalyptic view that defers *šālôm* beyond history's horizon and "inflicts stinging defeat on outsiders even as it imbues the insiders with paradisiacal blessing" (Hanson 361).

Eirēnē in secular Greek sources is comparatively narrow in meaning. It contrasts to war, describing the tranquility and prosperity that follow victory in war. In classical Greek literature *eirēnē* may refer to a sociopolitical condition or to the Greek goddess Eirene. The historians Herodotus (*Hist.* 1.87) and Thucydides (*Pel. War* 2.61.1) speak of peace as a desirable sociopolitical condition, for humanitarian and political reasons. A statue of Eirene was erected on the Agora in Athens in 375 BCE, and thereafter the annual celebration of the peace treaty between Sparta and Athens in 375 BCE began with offerings to Eirene. But Eirene never emerged beyond the status of a minor goddess in Greco-Roman culture. Erich Dinkler cites Harald Fuchs: "Although she is peace, she is not the one that brings peace" (Dinkler 86).

Complementing Eirene as a significant minor deity in the Greek-speaking East, Augustus introduced into the Latin West the Pax cult in order to balance the older Roman Concordia cult. Concordia was directed to internal policy, Pax to imperial policy. Through this relationship, *eirēnē* in *pax Romana* sought pacification of foreign nations to enable concord and harmony at home. Erecting the Altar of Peace to Augustus on the Field of Mars in Rome in 9 BCE discloses the means of *pax Romana*: wars to subjugate the nations. Vespasian's Peace Temple, built in 75 CE, celebrates Rome's victory over the Jews, depicted on the famous Arch of Titus.

Pax Romana promised prosperity and order with one worldwide Greco-Roman language and culture. These features superficially accord with Hebrew *šālôm*. But the people subjugated under *pax Romana* suffered oppression in Rome's "golden age" of prosperity, thus mocking *šālôm* (Wengst 7–51).

The degree of influence that classical Greek *eirēnē* had on NT writers is unclear (Dinkler), for NT uses of *eirēnē* clearly extend OT *šālôm* (the LXX translates *šālôm* with *eirēnē*). The word *peace* occurs in every NT book except 1 John, with the majority of occurrences (sixty-five) in Paul and Luke-Acts. In the NT Epistles *eirēnē* joins "grace" (*charis*) as a recurring salutation. Theologically toned, the *eirēnē* greeting evokes gratitude for God's salvation and the faith community (Mauser 107–8). Studies of NT theology and ethics often miss or marginalize peace—a curious anomaly (Swartley, *Covenant of Peace*, 3–8, 431–70). While nonviolence, widely noted, seeks to correct injustice, peacemaking seeks positive initiatives to overcome evil with good.

Whereas worship of Eirene celebrated destruction of enemies, NT *eirēnē*, God's gift, reconciles former enemies through Christ, killing the enmity (Eph. 2:15–16). Like *šālôm* in the OT, *eirēnē* in the NT joins other important theological and ethical motifs (kingdom of God, salvation, Christology, ecclesiology, mission) and moral imperatives: love of enemy, nonretaliation, reconciliation.

Each Gospel has its distinctive peace/peacemaking emphasis. Jesus' pronouncement, "Blessed are the peacemakers [*eirēnopoioi*]" (Matt. 5:9) characterizes Jesus' proclamation of the kingdom (Matt. 4:17, 23), calling people to righteousness/justice (*dikaiosynē* in the Beatitudes [Matt. 5:6, 10]) and exhorting, "Love your enemies" (Matt. 5:44). Peacemaking and love of enemy mark identity as God's children. The Sermon on the Mount has fourteen triads, each one culminating in a positive initiative that breaks the cycle of human violence. Each seeks to transform the situation, person, and/or relationship. These transforming initiatives make peace, empowered by God's grace-based deliverance, echoing Isaiah (Stassen, "Fourteen Triads," 308; Stassen and Gushee 125–45).

Jesus calls his disciples to be at peace with one another (Mark 9:50), contrasting the kingdom ethic to the disciples' rivalry and aspirations to greatness (Mark 9:33–34; 10:35–37). Humble service contrasts to the gentile rulers' domination (Mark 10:41–45). Jesus' ministry encounters fierce opposition. Hence, "I have not come to bring peace, but a sword" (Matt. 10:34 [cf. "division" in Luke 12:51]) describes Jesus' battle against Satan; Jesus' kingdom collides with Satan's dominion (Mauser 44–45).

In Luke's Gospel *eirēnē* occurs fourteen times, mostly in content not in the other Gospels, and with structural significance. Three occur in the birth narratives: Zechariah concluding his prophecy with "to guide our feet into the way of peace" (1:79); angels proclaiming "peace on earth" at the birth announcement of the Savior-Messiah (2:14); Simeon blessing God for "dismissing your servant in peace" (2:29). Five occur at the beginning and ending of Luke's long travel narrative (three in 10:5–6; two in 19:38–42). The first three (in the mission of the seventy) announce the kingdom/gospel come near. For the ending inclusio, "peace in heaven" (19:38) is antiphonal to "peace on earth" (2:14), and it concludes with Jesus' judgment plea, "If you, even you, had only recognized on this day the things that make for peace!" (19:42). The risen Jesus greets his disciples, saying, "Peace be with you" (24:36).

Luke's *eirēnē* continues into Acts, occurring seven times: four uses pertain to ecclesial dimensions (7:26; 9:31; 10:36; 15:33), three to *pax Romana* contexts (12:20; 16:36; 24:2). Peter summarizes Jesus' ministry with "preaching (proclaiming) peace by Jesus Christ—he is Lord of all" (10:36 *evangelizomenos eirēnē*, quoting Isa. 52:7 LXX *evangelizomenou akoēn eirēnēs, hōs evangelizomenos agatha*, translating Heb. *mĕbaśśēr mašmîa šālôm*). Luke's *eirēnē* is not an apologetic for Rome's *pax Romana* of "peace and security" (see 1 Thess. 5:3). Neither courting nor condemning Rome, Luke's *eirēnē* establishes an alternative politics of peace and justice.

In John's Gospel, Jesus bestows *eirēnē* on his disciples as gift (14:27; 16:33) in the context of the world's hatred. As risen Lord he greets them three times, "Peace be with you," which frames his breathing of the Holy Spirit into them (20:19, 21, 26).

Of Paul's forty-four uses of *eirēnē*, ten occur in Romans and eight in Ephesians. Paul coins a virtually unique appellation, "God/Lord of peace" (Rom. 15:33; 16:20; 1 Cor. 14:33; 2 Cor. 13:11; 1 Thess. 5:23; 2 Thess. 3:16; Phil. 4:9 [cf. Heb. 13:20]). With the appellation of "warrior" (*ʾîš milḥāmâ*, "man of war") for God in the OT (Exod. 15:3) rendered "God crushes war" by the LXX, the trajectory culminates in Paul's striking "God of peace," consonant with the OT *šālôm* vision. This appellation links Paul's doctrinal emphases to peacemaking (Swartley, *Covenant of Peace*, 210).

God's peacemaking unites humans to God in justification and joins alienated parties into one new body through the cross (Rom. 5:1–10; Eph. 2:14–18; Col. 1:20). Reconciliation complements peacemaking (Rom 5:1–10; 2 Cor. 5:17–20). Jesus' followers are to live peaceably (Rom. 12:18; 14:19; Eph. 4:3; 2 Tim. 2:22). The "peace of God . . . will guard your hearts and your minds in Christ Jesus" (Phil. 4:7). Peace is a fruit of the Spirit (Gal. 5:22) manifesting God's reign (Rom. 14:17) and the new Spirit order of "life and peace" (Rom. 8:6). "The God of peace will shortly crush Satan under your feet" (Rom. 16:20) blends peace with battle (cf. Eph. 6:15, quoting Isa. 52:7).

Hebrews describes Jesus as king of peace, king of righteousness, after the order of Melchizedek (Heb. 7:1–3). In several places the NT Epistles call for believers to seek and pursue peace (Rom. 14:19; 2 Tim. 2:22; Heb. 12:14; 1 Pet. 3:11, quoting Ps. 34:14). According to James, righteousness/justice is the fruit harvest of sowing peace by using peacemaking means (Jas. 3:18).

Peace in the NT has divine-human, human-human, sociopolitical, cosmic, and inner personal dimensions (see Peter Stuhlmacher's "Twelve Theses on Peace in the New Testament" in Swartley, *Covenant of Peace*, 472–74). Peace is God's gift first and foremost, but it is also a task, seeking peace within Christ's body and witnessing to peace in the world (Mauser; Luz). Forgiveness leads to peacemaking, and reconciliation is its fruit.

Numerous peacemaking initiatives, strategies, and community models contribute to peace, such as Glen Stassen's ten peacemaking practices to abolish war and promote peace through justice, love, and community. These practices include nonviolent action and reducing threat, offensive weapons, and weapons trade. Other paths to peace include peacemaking education in schools, including conflict resolution and other peace-building activities; teaching peacemaking in churches; forming peace-living communities such as Reba

Place Fellowship (Evanston, IL), the Simple Life Community (Philadelphia), and the New Song Community Church (Sandtown, Baltimore); and national budgets funding peacemaking.

Seeking peace requires truth-telling; renouncing greed, oppression, and violence; sharing wealth; persevering in diplomacy in international relationships; and putting politics in service of human need. Outstanding contributors to peacemaking, in varied contexts, include Martin Luther King Jr., Oscar Romero, Thomas Merton, Desmond Tutu (who chaired the Truth and Reconciliation Commission in South Africa), Mother Teresa, and Jean Vanier. Numerous people and efforts have made significant contributions to peace praxis in peace-building and restorative justice (Sawatsky).

See also Beatitudes; Enemy, Enemy Love; Forgiveness; Fruit of the Spirit; Holy Spirit; Justice; Justice, Restorative; Just-Peacemaking Theory; Kingdom of God; Love, Love Command; Reconciliation; Righteousness; Sermon on the Mount

Bibliography

Brawley, R., ed. *Character Ethics and the New Testament: Moral Dimensions of Scripture.* Westminster John Knox, 2007; Dinkler, E. "*Eirene*—The Early Christian Concept of Peace." Pages 71–120 in *The Meaning of Peace: Biblical Studies*, ed. P. Yoder and W. Swartley, trans. W. Sawatsky. 2nd ed. SPS 2. Institute of Mennonite Studies, 2001; Eisenbeis, W. *Die Wurzel shalom im Alten Testament.* BZAW 133. De Gruyter, 1969; Gerleman, G. "*Die Wurzel šlm.*" ZAW 85 (1973): 1–14; Hanson, P. "War and Peace in Hebrew Scripture." *Int* 38 (1984): 363–83; Harris, D. *Shalom! The Biblical Concept of Peace.* Baker, 1970; Hauerwas, S. *The Peaceable Kingdom: A Primer in Christian Ethics.* University of Notre Dame Press, 1983; Hays, R. *The Moral Vision of the New Testament: Community, Cross, New Creation; A Contemporary Introduction to New Testament Ethics.* HarperSanFrancisco, 1996; Kremer, J. "Peace—God's Gift: Biblical-Theological Considerations." Pages 21–36 in *The Meaning of Peace: Biblical Studies*, ed. P. Yoder and W. Swartley, trans. W. Sawatsky. 2nd ed. SPS 2. Institute of Mennonite Studies, 2001; Luz, U. "The Significance of the Biblical Witnesses for Church Peace Action." Pages 237–55 in *The Meaning of Peace: Biblical Studies*, ed. P. Yoder and W. Swartley, trans. W. Sawatsky. 2nd ed. SPS 2. Institute of Mennonite Studies, 2001; Mauser, U. *The Gospel of Peace: A Scriptural Message for Today's World.* SPS 1. Westminster John Knox, 1992; Ollenburger, B. "Peace and God's Action against Chaos in the Old Testament." Pages 70–88 in *The Church's Peace Witness*, ed. M. Miller and B. Gingerich. Eerdmans, 1994; Sawatsky, J. *Justpeace Ethics: A Guide to Restorative Justice and Peacebuilding.* Cascade Books, 2008; Schmid, H. H. *Šalom: "Frieden" in Alten Orient und in Alten Testament.* SBS 51. Verlag Katholisches Bibelwerk, 1971; Stassen, G. "The Fourteen Triads of the Sermon on the Mount." *JBL* 122 (2003): 267–308; idem. ed. *Just Peacemaking: The New Paradigm for the Ethics of Peace and War.* 3rd ed. Pilgrim Press, 2008; Stassen, G., and D. Gushee. *Kingdom Ethics: Following Jesus in Contemporary Context.* InterVarsity, 2003; Steck, O. H. *Friedensvorstellungen im Alten Jerusalem: Psalmen, Jesaja, Deuterojesaja.* Theologischer Verlag, 1972; Swartley, W. *Covenant of Peace: The Missing Peace in New Testament Theology and Ethics.* SPS 9. Eerdmans, 2006; idem, ed. *The Love of Enemy and Nonretaliation in the New Testament.* SPS 3. Westminster John Knox, 1992; von Rad, G. "Shalom in the Old Testament." *TDNT* 2:402–6; Wengst, K. *Pax Romana and the Peace of Jesus Christ.* Trans. J. Bowden. Fortress, 1987; Westermann, C. "Peace (*Shalom*) in the Old Testament." Pages 37–70 in *The Meaning of Peace: Biblical Studies*, ed. P. Yoder and W. Swartley, trans. W. Sawatsky. 2nd ed. SPS 2. Institute of Mennonite Studies, 2001; Wolterstorff, N. *Until Justice and Peace Embrace: The Kuyper Lectures for 1981 Delivered at the Free University of Amsterdam.* Eerdmans, 1983; Yoder, P. "Introductory Essay to the Old Testament Chapters: *Shalom* Revisited." Pages 1–14 in *The Meaning of Peace: Biblical Studies*, ed. P. Yoder and W. Swartley, trans. W. Sawatsky. 2nd ed. SPS 2. Institute of Mennonite Studies, 2001.

Willard M. Swartley

Pedophilia

Pedophilia (or paedophilia) is sexual attraction to children (i.e., persons under the age of legal consent for sex). The term *pedophile* comes from the Greek words *pais* (genitive *paedos*) ("child") and *philia* ("love"). Pedophilia includes both the desire to act in a sexual manner toward children and the actual act of abusing children. Pedophilia is unquestionably harmful to children and leads to significant psychological distress and damage, such as chronic anxiety, lack of trust, poor self-esteem, sexual dysfunction, and problems with intimacy and emotional bonding.

Pedophiles are usually but not exclusively male and may or may not be attracted to both adults and children. While pedophilia may be monstrous in its acts and consequences, those who engage in such practices may appear quite normal. Pedophiles can be friends, family, strangers, workmates, and so forth. Although pedophiles often attempt to justify their actions by appeals to love and a desire for meaningful relationship, the power dynamics between adults and children make it impossible for a child to give informed consent. Pedophiles use various methods to groom and gain the trust of children and to make them more vulnerable to abuse (e.g., the incitement of guilt around sexual acts: "It is really your fault"). Because the power dynamic is so central to the practices of pedophilia, all acts of pedophilia are necessarily abusive. This is why societies consider pedophilia to be unacceptable legally, socially, and morally.

Pedophilia usually is very difficult to treat. At a medical level, the treatment options tend to be a combination of psychotherapeutic and/or pharmacological intervention. Both are helpful insofar as they can help to reduce both the urge and the compulsive thinking associated with pedophilia. However, pedophiles are notorious for not responding to treatment regimes. Thus, treatment is necessarily long-term and often is unsuccessful.

From the perspective of theology, ethics, and pastoral care, pedophilia raises important issues. What is a Christian response to pedophiles? Should Christians forgive them? Is it true that the grace and forgiveness of God are open to all people? Ultimately, whether or not a pedophile can find forgiveness and a right relationship with God is God's judgment alone. However, in the interim, forgiveness may not be possible for survivors of child sexual abuse. Great care is therefore necessary in interpreting Jesus' words on the necessity of practicing forgiveness (e.g., Matt. 18:21–35).

If Jesus' command is to love God, and then to love neighbor and oneself, then clearly, loving one's enemies (if that is even a possibility for survivors) does not mean putting oneself in danger. From the perspective of the church community, it also cannot mean pressuring people to engage in the practice of forgiveness if it damages their relationship with God and self.

Similarly, while the church as a community may have a call of compassion to both survivor and perpetrator, the readmission of the perpetrator to the community is a point of dispute. The key question is this: would allowing the perpetrator back into the community help or hinder the survivor in regard to loving God, neighbor, and self? If the answer is that it would hinder the survivor, then it is the responsibility of the church community to explore other ways of ministering to perpetrators that do not involve forced encounters with survivors and, equally important, do not put other children in the church community at risk. The pastoral and ethical challenge, then, is this: how can abusers be given the opportunity to find repentance and forgiveness without these very actions exacerbating the abuse that has already been perpetrated on survivors?

See also Abuse; Child Abuse; Children; Sexual Abuse; Sexual Ethics

Bibliography

Berlin, F. "Treatments to Change Sexual Orientation." *American Journal of Psychiatry* 157 (2000): 838–39; Dorr, D. "Sexual Abuse and Spiritual Abuse." *The Furrow* 51, no. 10 (2000): 523–31; Jenkins, P. *Pedophiles and Priests: Anatomy of a Contemporary Crisis*. Oxford University Press, 2001; Rigali, N. "Church Responses to Pedophilia." *TS* 55 (1994): 124–39; Rosemary, K. *After Disclosure: A Non Offending Parent Reflects on Child Sexual Abuse*. Westview Press, 2006; Swinton, J. "Battling Monsters and Resurrecting Persons: Practicing Forgiveness in the Face of Radical Evil." Pages 130–78 in *Raging with Compassion: Pastoral Responses to the Problem of Evil*. Eerdmans, 2007.

John Swinton

Penance

Penance names an act or practice that is an acknowledgment of one's sins and an attempt to make amends. Although no amount of penance can make amends for offenses against God, God nonetheless accepts the penitential efforts of human beings and in his grace and mercy offers them forgiveness. Penance is meant to be transformative for the sinner, as it is an opportunity to grow closer to God. Among Christians, penance has been regarded as part of the conversion to living a more Christoform life. Penance is a persistent theme throughout all of Scripture, and the penitential acts and practices in the Bible include, among other things, the rending of garments, the wearing of sackcloth and ashes, fasting, weeping, confessing sins, prayer, almsgiving, and bearing suffering well.

Old Testament

The OT contains many instances of penance, performed by individuals and by entire peoples. Penance is often indicated by the signs that were also associated with mourning; in particular, the wearing of sackcloth and ashes indicates sorrow for sin and for the temporal punishment of sin. These penitential acts demonstrated repentance from sin and sorrow for its consequences.

The OT Historical Books provide several examples of kings performing penitential acts, often on behalf of their people. King Ahab, when confronted by Elijah about his sins and impending punishment from God, rends his clothes, fasts, and dons sackcloth (1 Kgs. 21:27; see also 2 Kgs. 19:1). Following his adultery with Bathsheba and murder of her husband, Uriah, King David responds to Nathan's confrontation by confessing, "I have sinned against the Lord" (2 Sam. 12:13). David fasts, hoping to avert the punishment foretold by Nathan, and Ps. 51 exhibits David's repentance in poetic form as he prays for forgiveness from his sin. Likewise, when he sins by taking a census of the people Israel against the will of God, David confesses the sin and asks for God's mercy. He and the elders are described as clothed in sackcloth as they pray for the deliverance of Jerusalem (1 Chr. 21:16).

Penance by an entire people is beautifully described in the book of Jonah. When called to repentance, the Ninevites don sackcloth and ashes, proclaim a fast, and pray to God for his forgiveness (Jon. 3:5–8). As a group, they desire to make amends for their sins and together perform outward penitential acts as a testimony to this commitment. The people of Israel are also frequently depicted as participating in penitential acts. In Nehemiah, they are described as fasting and in sackcloth, with earth upon their heads, confessing their sins (Neh. 9:1–2; see also Esth. 4:1–3). Prophets such as Hosea, Jeremiah, and Ezekiel call for the repentance of the Hebrew people as a group (Jer. 26:3, 12; Ezek. 18:30; Hos. 14:1).

New Testament

Although the NT contains numerous references to acts of penance, the word *penance* itself does not occur. However, the Greek noun *metanoia* (verb, *metanoeō*), which indicates a turning away from something, is usually translated as "repent," as in both Jesus' and John the Baptist's calls for repentance (Matt. 3:2, 8; 4:17; Mark 1:15). *Metanoia* highlights the interior dimension of penitential acts. Penance is not meant to be merely exterior; in fact, this is criticized by Jesus (see Matt. 6:16; Luke 18:10–14; cf. Isa. 58:1–7; Joel 2:13). At the same time, however, external acts of penance continue into the NT. Jesus warns against doing penitential acts hypocritically (giving alms, praying, fasting), but he does not proscribe such acts (Matt. 6:2–18). When questioned about why his disciples do not fast, Jesus replies that they will fast when he is taken away from them (Mark 2:18–20 pars.). Indeed, the book of Acts contains several examples of fasting (Acts 9:9; 13:2; 14:23), as well as almsgiving (Acts 10:2–4, 31). Although such acts are not always penitential, there is often a connection, as indicated by *Did.* 15.5–7.

The penitential act of confessing sins again connects the interior and exterior, this time by external verbalization of one's internal identification of sin. Those baptized by John the Baptist are described as "confessing their sins" (Matt. 3:6; Mark 1:5). This is echoed in Acts, as new believers "confessed and disclosed their practices" (Acts 19:18). Hence, it is not merely that exterior acts of penance must be matched by a fitting interior disposition but also that interior *metanoia* must be matched by embodied acts of penance, such as verbalizing one's sins or any of the acts named above.

In Imitation of Christ

Acts of penance in the Christian tradition are to be done in imitation of Christ, in such a manner that unites sinners' penitential suffering with the passion of Christ. By undertaking penance, the sinner and the entire church seek to be converted to a more Christoform life. Sins ordinarily turn the sinner away from God, while acts of penance use sins as a way for the sinner to return to God and grow closer to God.

See also Confession; Penitence; Practices; Repentance

Bibliography

Anderson, G. "Redeem Your Sins by the Giving of Alms." *Letter and Spirit* 3 (2007): 39–69; Thomas Aquinas, *Summa theologiae* III, q. 85.

Maria C. Morrow

Penitence

The word *penitence* (from Lat. *paenitentia*, "regret") refers to remorse for wrongdoing or sin, and commitment to change one's actions or life, via objective, disciplinary practices.

Penitence is thickly intertwined with Christianity. The call to repentance is a major theme in the Christian Scriptures. Yet, the shape of penitence throughout most of Christian history differs significantly from the scriptural witness. To relate penitence and Christian ethics today requires looking anew at penitence in Scripture.

In Scripture

Two terms convey repentance in the OT: *nāḥam* and *šûb*. The word *nāḥam*, whose root means "to breathe strongly," translates as "pity, compassion, grief, regret, comfort"; *šûb* means "to turn, return, be restored." Thus, in the OT repentance refers to fully embodied, affective acts of the whole person, a sense captured in the penitential psalms (Pss. 6; 32; 38; 51; 102; 130; 143). Here, repentance is bodily, evoking illness and mourning. Beyond remorse, penitence connotes voluntary concrete actions that enact bodily punishment and publicly signal the authenticity of repentance. Both individuals and groups "proclaim a fast" (e.g., 2 Chr. 20:3) and "repent in sackcloth and ashes" (e.g., Job 42:6; Jon. 3:5). The endpoint is a return to the Lord (Deut. 30:2).

Although Genesis is rife with sin, conflict, and intrigue, actual remorse or penitence enters the story only with the Mosaic covenant and the complex practice of sin offering (Exod. 29:14–46; see also Leviticus; Deuteronomy). The first sin for which atonement must be made is Israel's sin against the Lord at the foot of Mount Sinai (Exod. 32). The nature of this first repented sin is key: idolatry. Personal, individual sin certainly is present in the OT, but most calls for repentance concern Israel's turning toward other gods. Most acts of penitence follow a call to the people of Israel to "re-turn," as a people, to(ward) God, and to turn toward a different way of life, living as members of the people of God (Lev. 5:5; 1 Kgs. 8:47–48; 2 Chr. 6:37–38; Ezek. 14:6; Jeremiah; Hosea).

Idolatry, although committed by individuals (e.g., Solomon in 1 Kgs. 11), is understood primarily as a sin of the people of Israel as a whole and penitence a corporate act (Ezek. 18:30). The sin offering in the Levitical code is largely a corporate penitential practice, conducted by the priest for individuals' sins but also for the general sinfulness of the priest and the people (the Ninevites extend penitence even to the animals [Jon. 3:8]).

The NT continues these themes, with some shifts. The Greek verb *metanoeō* derives from the roots *meta* ("with, after, behind") and *noeo* ("to perceive with the mind, understand") and suggests a sense of changing one's mind, captured in Paul's phrase about having "the mind of Christ" (1 Cor. 2:16). The Greek verb *epistrephō* connotes particularly a return to the worship of God or conversion. From the beginning of the Gospels, the hearers of the prophetic proclamation are urged, "Repent, for the kingdom of heaven has come near" (Matt. 3:2; 4:17; cf. Mark 1:15). The audience—the people of Israel—is called to return to God; later, the gentiles are called to become part of that people in the church. This call to repentance reverberates throughout the NT. Penitential acts, however, are scarce (except perhaps the woman who anoints Jesus with oil [Luke 7:36–50]), for the ultimate penitential act, the sin offering, has been made in Christ. The task of the Christian and the *ekklēsia* is less to engage in penitence than to live as (a member of) Christ's body. The Christian and the church are called to turn their minds—that is, their whole self, their life together—toward the one true God by living as God's people.

Tradition and History

Yet, turning one's whole mind, self, and life toward God proved as difficult for the early church, and throughout the rest of the Christian tradition, as it did for Israel. At particular issue was apostasy under persecution (a form of idolatry): can one who has publicly renounced faith in Christ return to God's people? Some said no (the Donatists), while others said only after rigorous penance (Augustine), and then only once (Tertullian). Thus, in the second century penitential practices emerged (also for murder and adultery) designed to test and reshape the sinner's allegiances; they were imposed by church authorities and could extend over a period of years. To sin was to worship falsely; penitence required public demonstration of repentance and willingness to live as a Christian in order to be admitted again to true worship—that is, participation in the sacrament of Communion.

With Constantine, the identity of the church as a distinct people of God becomes ambiguous and the function of penitential practices shifts. Christianity and penitence become almost coextensive. Penitence loses its corporate character and its link to idolatry, focusing on individual penitence for individual sins. First within monastic communities, then through the practice of auricular confession beginning in the fifth century, penitence becomes the primary mode of Christian practice for laity. Formative, punitive, and expiatory penitential practices remain extensive in rigor and time, resulting in infrequent reception of the Eucharist by the laity. The relationship between penitence and money contributes to the Reformation and Protestant rejection of penance as a sacrament (though certainly not a rejection of penitence itself). The Catholic Counter-Reformation reemphasizes the connection between penitence, the Eucharist, and the Christian moral life in creating the discipline of moral theology (Mahoney).

Penitence and Christian Ethics

Beyond Lenten observance, penitence today is largely suspect as repressive, body-denying, or an expression of works-righteousness. Yet Scripture's constant call to turn away from false gods remains relevant, and the tradition's connection between penitential practices and renewed living suggests that penitence is important for Christian ethics both intellectually and practically.

1. Primary questions of Christian ethics are these: Which artifacts of culture (democracy, money, medicine) have become false gods? Which specters (terrorism, death) are worshiped, even if that worship is manifested as fear?
2. Christian ethics becomes a form of grieving for the sin of idolatry and corollary sins (violence, injustice, etc.) committed in service of false gods. It names the sins, laments, and prophetically calls Christians and the church to repent.
3. Following Scripture, Christian ethics maintains that right worship is the point of the Christian life, and that right living, wisdom, and right discernment are of a piece with right worship with being a member of God's people.
4. Following the Christian tradition, Christian ethics highlights how centuries-old practices of penitence form critical skills: confession is training in truthfulness, naming false gods is training in seeing a situation in new ways, doing penance (e.g., fasting) trains bodies to detach from participation in practices that serve false gods that are clamoring for our attention.

See also Confession; Idolatry; Liturgy and Ethics; Penance; Practices; Repentance; Sin

Bibliography

Hauerwas, S., and S. Wells, eds. *The Blackwell Companion to Christian Ethics*. Blackwell, 2006, 1–50, 95–109; Mahoney, J. *The Making of Moral Theology: A Study of the Roman Catholic Tradition*. Oxford University Press, 1987.

M. Therese Lysaught

Perfection

Scripture presents tensions regarding notions of moral and religious perfection. On the one hand, many texts emphasize the inability of humans to live free from sin. For example, 1 Kgs. 8:46 states plainly, "There is no one who does not sin" (cf. Eccl. 7:20; Lam. 3:39). The NT picks up on this theme in Rom. 3:23 ("All have sinned and fall short of the glory of God") and 1 John 1:8 ("If we say that we have no sin, we deceive ourselves, and the truth is not in us"). Such verses suggest that sinless perfection may be impossible for humans.

On the other hand, several texts command the imitation of God, implying that humans should at least attempt some level of godlike perfection. In Lev. 19:2, God decrees, "You shall be holy, for I the LORD your God am holy." Likewise, in Matt. 5:48, Jesus tells the crowds, "Be perfect, therefore, as your heavenly Father is perfect." Throughout the ages, interpreters have wrestled with whether and how individuals might be able to obey such commandments in light of human sinfulness.

Many within the Reformed tradition maintain that, although one should strive toward sinless perfection, it is not possible in this life. Others, such as John Wesley, argue that a degree of perfection can be received as a gift of divine grace. Wesley agrees with Reformers that achieving absolute perfection is impossible on earth. Yet, he stresses that humans could be perfected in the sense that love reigns in their hearts and they avoid voluntary transgressions against known laws of God. The early church voiced arguments similar to both the Reformers (e.g., Augustine) and Wesley (e.g., Gregory of Nyssa).

Biblical notions of perfection differ in some respects from modern conceptions. Both the Hebrew words related to the root *tmm* and the Greek words related to *telos* have areas of semantic overlap with the English *perfection*, but their basic meaning is "completion." Thus, the OT uses words from *tmm* in reference to the completion of different types of actions (e.g., Josh. 3:17) and to the type of sacrifice that God expects—one "without defect" (e.g., Exod. 12:5). When the OT uses these words in reference to morality, it refrains from calling specific characters "complete" or "perfect," save a few notable exceptions (e.g., Noah, David, Job). Psalms and Proverbs speak on generic levels of those who are "complete," associating them with the "upright" (*yšr* [e.g., Ps. 37:37]) and the "righteous" (*ṣdq* [e.g., Prov. 20:7]), in contrast to those who are "crooked" (*ʿqš* [e.g., Prov. 28:18]). The OT suggests that "completeness of the heart" (*tm-lbb*) may not necessarily entail sinless perfection (Gen. 20:4–6; 1 Kgs. 9:4).

Greek words related to *telos* also have to do with "completion." Many texts using these words speak of the completion of either an activity (e.g., Luke 2:39) or a period of time (e.g., Matt. 24:6). When applied in the ethical sphere, these words can refer to the final goal, outcome, purpose, or result of one's actions. As Rom. 6:22 puts it, "But now that you have been freed from sin and enslaved to God, the advantage you get is sanctification. The end [*telos*] is eternal life." These words can also refer to moral maturity and completeness. Thus, in 1 Cor. 14:20, Paul admonishes his readers not to be "children" (*paidia*) in their thinking but rather to be "mature" (*teleioi*) (cf. Heb. 5:12–6:1).

Given the emphasis on human sinfulness in Scripture, the qualifications that Wesley and others have placed on the type of ethical perfection they envision, and the differences between biblical terms and modern conceptions of perfection, it may be useful to abandon the language of "perfection" while retaining the biblical concepts of *tmm* and *telos*, understood in the senses of "completeness," "maturity," and "integrity."

Indeed, in recent times many have been reluctant to embrace different types of perfection. Psychologically, the quest for perfection in oneself and others often is seen as problematic. In her study of the emotions, Martha Nussbaum denounces ideals of perfection both as unattainable and as failing to do justice to human contingency and frailty. Regarding medical genetics, Joel Shuman raises concerns about modernist notions of perfection that drive technological and scientific progress. Philosophically, Kenneth Burke characterizes humanity as "rotten with perfection," showing how individuals seek to perfect the negative (e.g., Hitler's characterization of Jews as the perfect enemy). Although many ethical systems retain a teleological focus, the quest for human perfection in this life frequently meets with skepticism.

See also Eschatology and Ethics; Holiness; Sanctification; Sin; Teleological Theories of Ethics; Wesleyan Ethics

Bibliography

Bounds, C. "The Doctrine of Christian Perfection in the Apostolic Fathers." *WesTJ* 42 (2007): 7–27; Burke, K. *Language as Symbolic Action: Essays on Life, Literature, and Method*. University of California Press, 1966; Gregory of Nyssa. "On Perfection." Pages 93–124 in *Saint Gregory of Nyssa: Ascetical Works*. FC 58. Catholic University of America Press, 1967; Nussbaum, M. *Upheavals of Thought: The Intelligence of Emotions*. Cambridge University Press, 2001; Schlimm, M. "The Puzzle of Perfection: Growth in John Wesley's Doctrine of Perfection." *WesTJ* 38 (2003): 124–42; Shuman, J. "Desperately Seeking Perfection: Christian Discipleship and Medical Genetics." *Christian Bioethics* 5 (1999): 139–53; Wesley, J. "Christian Perfection" [Sermon 40]. Pages 97–124 in *Sermons II: 34–70*, ed. A. Outler. Vol. 2 of *The Works of John Wesley*, ed. A. Outler et al. Bicentennial ed. Abingdon, 1985; idem. "Thoughts on Christian Perfection." Pages 283–97 in *John Wesley: A Representative Collection of His Writings*, ed. A. Outler. LPT. Oxford University Press, 1964.

Matthew R. Schlimm

Persecution

Persecution occurs when a group or individual inflicts physical, emotional, or social suffering on another individual or group because of who they are or what they believe. The biblical witness both describes the persecution of people(s) and prescribes warning and encouragement to its readers who are in the midst of persecution or may face it in the future. Most occurrences of persecution in the OT concern Israel and the persecution that they experienced as a nation or as faithful individuals at the hand of enemies. The OT writings present this persecution in two ways: as an impetus for God to show mercy (Judg. 2:18; 1 Sam. 9:16) and as a means for God to enact judgment (Neh. 9:27; Lam. 1:4–5). Persecution is also a common complaint of the prophets (Jer. 15:15) and psalmists (Pss. 10:2; 119:84–86, 150) who seek God's deliverance and comfort. The Second Temple texts 1–4 Maccabees recount the terrible persecution of the Jewish people under Antiochus Epiphanes (see especially 2 Macc. 6–7). The book of 4 Maccabees in particular defends the value of faithfulness in persecution, attributing virtue to those who suffer it willingly (5:22–23; 6:16–19; 10:10–11).

In the NT, persecution is presented in a variety of ways. The Gospels depict the persecution that Jesus would face, detailing it in Jesus' predictions of his death (Matt. 16:21; Mark 8:31; Luke 9:22; John 5:16) and in the passion accounts. The NT also records the persecution of the early church, at the hand of the preconversion Paul (Acts 9:1–2; 22:4–5; 1 Cor. 15:9) and other authorities (Acts 8:1; 11:9; 13:50; 20:22–23; 1 Thess. 1:6–7; 3:2–4, 7; 2 Tim. 3:10–12; Heb. 10:32–33; Rev. 1:9).

Jesus' teaching about persecution serves as a warning to his disciples, who would face trials because of their faith (Matt. 10:23; Luke 11:49–50; 21:12; John 15:18–21; 16:33), and as a comfort for those who would endure suffering for God (Matt. 5:10–12). Perhaps the most radical teaching that Jesus hands down concerning persecution is in Matt. 5:44: "But I say to you, Love your enemies and pray for those who persecute you." Paul, in his apostolic encouragement to the churches, wrote stirring accounts of his own persecution in order to inspire believers to stand strong and endure persecution and hardships (Rom. 5:3–5; 8:35; 2 Cor. 1:6; 12:9–10). The overall NT message about persecution focuses on exhorting believers to persevere under persecution and concentrate on the benefits of suffering for Christ (Acts 14:22; 2 Thess. 1:4; 2 Tim. 1:8; 2:3; 4:5; 1 Pet. 5:8–10).

Persecution has plagued the church since its inception. From the Jewish persecution of the earliest believers to the oppression of Christians under communist regimes, Christianity has always experienced suffering at the hands of persecuting authorities, largely because minority groups are easy to target. However, when Christianity has not been the minority, it often has turned from persecuted into persecutor, inflicting suffering on various religious groups, especially Jews, and even on its own members. This ethical injustice is not supported by the NT message about persecution, but may stem from the OT portrayal of God using persecution as a way to judge or discipline Israel. When Christians, whether corporately or individually, act as self-appointed judges of other religions or peoples and persecute on behalf of God, they corrupt the central message of the Bible and misrepresent the person of Jesus, who endured persecution and instructed his followers to persevere in righteous suffering, not prescribe or inflict it.

See also Cruciformity; Martyrdom; Suffering

Bibliography

Frend, W. H. C. *Martyrdom and Persecution in the Early Church*. Baker, 1981.

Jennifer Garcia Bashaw

Persistent Vegetative State *See* Bioethics

1 Peter

The Epistle of 1 Peter presents a banquet of ethical material, with numerous ethical admonitions and injunctions concerning issues such as household codes, Christian identity and lifestyle in a pagan society, and deference to the state. But it would be a mistake to see this epistle as simply an inchoate reservoir of ethical teachings. In fact, these ethical materials are signposts that lead to recognizing a coherent intentionality in the epistle. First Peter is an example of wisdom literature. It is written to shape the character of beleaguered Christian communities in northern Asia Minor, to encourage practical dependence on God, displaying his holy and gracious character through deepening expressions of love in the community and sustaining moral integrity toward those outside.

First Peter is an example of a paraenetic epistle, a prominent form of wisdom literature in the Greco-Roman philosophical schools. As an integrated piece of wisdom, it combines the ethical materials mentioned above with other themes that provide an intellectual context and affective motivations for considered moral action. For example, the typical wisdom theme of the "two ways" is prominent in 1 Peter, especially as related to the dichotomy of preconversion life (denigrated as "futile" in 1:18) and postconversion life (characterized by purity, love, obedience, and incorruptibility in 1:14–23). In addition, the Christology of the epistle is almost exclusively devoted to portraying Jesus as an exemplar of one who, out of reverent devotion to God, courageously maintained his moral integrity in the face of unjust suffering (2:21–25). This shaping of Christology to contextualize and motivate moral action is typical of the theology of the epistle as a whole, which is organized according to pragmatic more than systematic concerns. Theology serves the purpose of wisdom—to orient communal life toward a world where a righteous "way of life" (*anastrophē*) is comprehensible, laudable, and desirable. Whether in Christology, eschatology (1:13), or the new birth (1:3), doctrinal teaching moves immediately to practical implication and serves the paraenetic wisdom agenda of shaping communal life in its concreteness.

First Peter is addressed to Christian churches under threat, ostracized for their distinct beliefs and lifestyle and for their lack of conformity to normative social practices. Experiencing the pain of social rejection and alienation, they are simultaneously tempted toward conformity, isolation, and retaliation. It is in this context that the author encourages these churches to retain their Christian identity and to continue to "do good." To many this call to do good has seemed a strange response to persecution, but for our author, the greatest challenge of suffering is not despondency but vice. The moral challenges of suffering, the corruption of character and corporate life, the temptations to vengeance, isolation, and selfishness are the main targets that the author has in view in writing to these careworn Anatolian churches. So it is not surprising that from the start (1:6) the author interprets their persecutions through the image of a refining fire (another archetypal wisdom theme). In this way, sufferings have the potential of becoming a means of salvation (1:9), producing a strengthened faith that is worth more than gold (1:7). This process, however, is not automatic. Suffering has the power to refine character only when it is met with actions that reflect both the holiness and hospitality of God.

Social persecution is a dangerous challenge to the corporate identity and distinctive lifestyle of these Christian communities. The defining and retention of corporate identity is thus a key component in the author's agenda. Incorporating images from the OT, the author defines corporate identity in terms of the electing love of God. They are a people chosen by God, a people defined by the fact that they have been shown mercy (2:9–10). Their identity arises not from themselves or from the surrounding culture but from the free love of God. Their lives, corporate and individual, are defined by this reality. The consequence of this is that they are social aliens and exiles (2:11)—a distinct society but not separate unto itself, a community that is recognizably different but not hostile, possessing what has been called "soft difference" (Volf). It is out of this unique identity, as a community called by God, that their new life of righteousness that reflects the character of God receives its form and impetus.

See also Eschatology and Ethics; Government; Household Codes; New Testament Ethics; Persecution; Suffering; Vice; Vices and Virtues, Lists of; Virtue(s)

Bibliography

Achtemeier, P. J. *1 Peter*. Hermeneia. Fortress, 1996; Dryden, J. *Theology and Ethics in 1 Peter: Paraenetic Strategies for Christian Character Formation*. WUNT 2/209. Mohr Siebeck, 2007; Green, J. B. *1 Peter*. THNTC. Eerdmans, 2007; Volf, M. "Soft Difference: Theological Reflections on the Relation between Church and Culture in 1 Peter." *Ex auditu* 10 (1994): 15–30.

J. de Waal Dryden

2 Peter

Like 1 Peter, this epistle adopts the modes of ancient paraenetic epistles and offers wisdom to a Christian community at a perilous crossroads. The nascent danger is false teachers leading the community away from the apostolic faith. But, perhaps surprisingly, this danger is defined in almost exclusively moral terms. The false teachers are "creatures of instinct" (2:12), who "have eyes full of adultery" and "hearts trained in greed" (2:14). Here, as elsewhere in the NT, heterodoxy and heteropraxis are two sides of the same coin, distinguishable but inseparable. Where one is present, the other is assumed. So while these false teachers are denounced as "ignorant blasphemers" (2:12), the emphasis of the epistle is on the moral threat that they pose, having the ability to "entice unsteady souls" (2:14).

The author's main agenda is not merely to protect the church from false teachers but to lead them in a path of flourishing, where their faith produces recognizable fruits of righteousness and love. This is why the body of the letter begins with its stair-stepping catalog of virtues in 1:5–7: faith, goodness, knowledge, self-control, endurance, godliness, mutual affection, and love. The chief aim of the epistle is the inculcation of these (and other) Christian virtues as a means of and a sign of growth and maturity in Christian character (Charles). The false teachers are an obstacle to this process of sanctification and are denounced as such.

Typical of ancient paraenetic literature, the concern in 2 Peter is with the process of maturation (what the Stoics called *prokopē*), the author using rhetorical techniques that foster the adoption of virtues and the repudiation of vices—for example, the rhetorical strategy of the "two ways," a staple in ancient wisdom literature. In this epistle we have a host of such contrasts. The false teachers, who deceive and corrupt, are contrasted with the apostles, who have given a true witness of Christ that leads to righteousness and glory. The false teachers are associated with archetypal evil characters from the OT, like Balaam, while those who remain faithful to Christ are identified with archetypal characters of faith, like Noah, "a herald of righteousness" (2:5). The false teachers are "waterless springs" (2:17) that lead to destruction, whereas faithfulness to the apostolic witness leads to the "new heaven and the new earth in which righteousness is at home" (3:13). The point of these contrasts is to clarify choices. The author exposes the magnitude of the disparity between them and the apostolic faith in order to force a choice between the two; it is no longer possible to befriend both. In this way, the author safeguards this community from a lethal danger to its progress in the faith.

See also Eschatology and Ethics; New Testament Ethics; Vice; Vices and Virtues, Lists of; Virtue(s)

Bibliography

Bauckham, R. *Jude, 2 Peter*. WBC 50. Word, 1983; Charles, J. *Virtue amidst Vice: The Catalog of Virtues in 2 Peter 1*. JSNTSup 150. Sheffield Academic Press, 1997; Green, G. *Jude and 2 Peter*. BECNT. Baker Academic, 2008.

J. de Waal Dryden

Philemon

Philemon is both the shortest of Paul's letters and the only one in which, primarily, just one person is addressed. Philemon was the patron of a house church (probably in Colossae), a man well known by Paul, and perhaps one of the apostle's own converts (v. 19). The letter, written from prison in an unnamed location, is an appeal on behalf of Philemon's slave Onesimus, who has wronged his master in some unspecified way. There is no evidence to support the traditional view that he was a fugitive from Philemon's household who subsequently was confined in the same prison from which Paul was writing. Yet somehow the two were in touch during the apostle's imprisonment, and he converted Onesimus to the gospel (v. 10).

There is no deliberate theological exposition or argumentation in this letter, and the theological grounding of the appeal to Philemon must be largely inferred. The inferences, however, are not difficult to draw. Paul addresses Philemon, first of all, not as the master of Onesimus but as his (the apostle's) friend and co-worker (v. 1), the patron of a house church (v. 2), and a person who has shown "love for all the saints" and "faith toward the Lord Jesus" (v. 5; cf. v. 7). When, therefore, Paul goes on to say that his appeal to Philemon is made "on the basis of love" (v. 9), presumably he is thinking both of God's love that elicits faith and the love through which that faith is actualized in the lives of believers (see Gal. 5:6 NRSV mg.), like Philemon himself.

It is specifically the circulation of love within the believing community (the *koinōnia* of faith [v. 6]) that is on view here. Throughout, Paul uses kinship terms to describe the relationships that bind the members of this community together: Paul's conversion of Onesimus makes the apostle his "father" and the convert a "son" (v. 10); Timothy is "the brother" (v. 1) and Apphia is "the sister" (v. 2); Philemon is not only Paul's "beloved friend," "co-worker," and "partner [*koinōnos*]" (vv. 1, 17) but also his "brother" (vv. 7, 20); and Paul hopes that Philemon will regard Onesimus as a "beloved brother," even as he himself does (v. 16). At several important points in the letter the phrases "in Christ" (vv. 8, 20), "in the Lord" (vv. 16, 20), and "in Christ Jesus" (v. 23) identify the sphere within which this whole network of relationships exists and is sustained.

The content of Paul's appeal for Onesimus (vv. 9–10) is not provided in the form of a directive until v. 17: "So if you [Philemon] consider me your partner, welcome him as you would welcome me." The convert, Onesimus, is to be accepted as a partner in the faith, "no longer as a slave" but as a "beloved brother," both in the workaday world and in the community of faith ("both in the flesh and in the Lord") (v. 16). Above all, the apostle wants to bring about reconciliation between these men, and he well understands that this will require a complete transformation of their relationship, even if their legal relationship as slave and master remains unchanged. But also, Paul strongly hints that when Philemon has accepted Onesimus as a Christian brother, he should allow him to resume his ministry, now on Philemon's behalf, with the imprisoned apostle (v. 13).

Paul writes with the authority of an apostle; he is "bold enough in Christ to command" (v. 8), and he expects Philemon's "obedience" (v. 21). Yet, his appeal is not based on this authority. He neither confronts Philemon with apostolic demands nor invokes the teaching of Jesus or the words of Scripture about mercy and compassion. He bases his appeal, rather, on the love that is constitutive of Christian community, through which its members are partners "in Christ" and brothers and sisters in the family of faith. Because reconciliation cannot be coerced, Paul leaves it to Philemon himself to determine what "good" he is called to do "for Christ" in the case of Onesimus.

In this letter one sees the apostle engaged in a "ministry of reconciliation" (see 2 Cor. 5:18). Although the parties most directly involved are a master and his slave, slavery itself is not Paul's subject. It is doubtful whether he or any other first-century Christian could have envisioned a political order without the institution of slavery, for it was one of the foundations of the social and economic stability of the Roman Empire (hence the instructions to masters and slaves in Eph. 6:5–9; Col. 3:22–4:1; cf. 1 Pet. 2:18–25). Moreover, even if Christians could have envisioned the abolition of slavery, they would have been powerless to bring it about. Thus, although the apostle may be hinting that Onesimus deserves manumission ("knowing that you will do even more than I say" [v. 21]), he remains silent on the injustice of slavery as an institution. This is also true when, elsewhere, he counsels slaves to gain their freedom if they have the opportunity (see 1 Cor. 7:21 NRSV mg.).

Nonetheless, for Paul, the institution of slavery belongs to the old age that is "passing away" (1 Cor. 7:31), for in God's "new creation," already inaugurated in Christ (2 Cor. 5:17), "there is no longer slave or free" because all are one in Christ (Gal. 3:27–28; cf. 1 Cor. 12:13; Col. 3:11). Paul's appeal to Philemon is, in effect, a summons to allow this new reality to work its transforming power in his relationship with Onesimus.

See also New Testament Ethics; Reconciliation; Slavery

Bibliography

de Vos, C. "Once a Slave, Always a Slave? Slavery, Manumission and Relational Patterns in Paul's Letter to Philemon." *JSNT* 82 (2001): 89–105; du Plessis, I. "How Christians Can Survive in a Hostile Social-economic Environment: Paul's Mind Concerning Difficult Social Conditions in the Letter to Philemon." Pages 387–413 in *Identity, Ethics, and Ethos in the New Testament*, ed. J. van der Watt. BZNW 141. De Gruyter, 2006; Osiek, C. *Philippians, Philemon*. ANTC. Abingdon, 2000, 133–46.

Victor Paul Furnish

Philippians

Writing from prison, Paul informs the Philippian Christians of his present circumstances and expectations, challenges them to be united and steadfast in their faith in the face of opposition from outsiders and dissension within their own community, and expresses appreciation for the financial assistance they had sent to him by way of Epaphroditus.

Standing at the theological and rhetorical center of Philippians is the "Christ hymn" (2:6–11), which tells the cosmic story of Christ's taking the form of a "slave" who is "obedient to the point of death" (2:6–8) and of God's subsequent exaltation of him to be the "Lord" of all creation (2:9–11). When Paul calls on his church to be of the "same mind" as Christ (2:5), he does not mean that it should take the earthly Jesus as its moral "role model." He is urging that its moral reasoning be informed and guided by the outlook that led Christ to "humble" himself and become "obedient" to God's will (2:6–8). The Christ-mindedness that Paul calls for as he introduces the hymn (2:5) is summed up in the immediately preceding appeal: "Let each of you look not to your own interests, but to the interests of others" (2:4 [cf. Rom. 15:2–3]). This is a call for selfless, serving love (2:2 [cf. 1 Cor. 13:5]), which Paul had earlier named along with "knowledge and full insight" as critical for discerning "what is best" (1:9–10).

In addition to the definitive instance of Christ's self-giving, the letter offers several lesser examples of what it means to "look . . . to the interests of others": Timothy, "genuinely concerned for your welfare" (2:20–22); Epaphroditus, "your . . . minister to my need" (2:25, 29–30); and Paul himself, "Whatever gains I had, these I have come to regard as loss because of Christ" (3:4–11). The charge to "imitate" Paul and those who live according to his "example" (3:17) is, therefore, but another way of summoning the church to be of the "same mind" as Christ (so also 4:1, "stand firm in the Lord"). It is a summons to "know Christ and the power of his resurrection" as Paul knows these, by "sharing . . . his sufferings" and "becoming like him in his death" (3:10).

The general appeals for unity, selflessness, and steadfastness likely were prompted by several particular concerns that Paul had about the Philippians. One was the opposition that these believers were continuing to face from outsiders. The apostle declares that even though they are already citizens of heaven, where Christ reigns as Lord (3:20), for the time being they are also citizens of this world, with continuing responsibilities for its welfare. Despite the risks, it is not apart from society but within it that they are both called and empowered to live in a manner "worthy of the gospel" (1:27–2:18). Moreover, Paul does not hesitate to commend, where he can, moral qualities and actions that were widely affirmed in the Greco-Roman world (4:8; cf. 4:5a, where "everyone" includes nonbelievers).

Paul is concerned, further, about a dispute between two leading members of the congregation, Euodia and Syntyche (4:2–3). Their conflict must have been consequential, or Paul would not have singled it out for attention. With an implicit appeal to the selflessness of Christ (2:6–11), he urges these women to "be of the same mind in the Lord" (4:2) and then requests a respected third party to help effect their reconciliation (4:3).

This moral outlook is evident also in the way Paul expresses gratitude for the congregation's financial support (4:10–20). Departing from the usual practice, he does not accept their help as a gift that needs to be reciprocated. He describes it, rather, as "a fragrant offering, a sacrifice acceptable and pleasing to God" (4:18). The ancient social conventions of giving and receiving served to protect the interests of each party to the relationship. Paul, however, views the Philippians' gift differently: acting with the mind of Christ, they had looked not to their "own interests" but to the "interests of others" (cf. 2 Cor. 8–9).

See also Cruciformity; New Testament Ethics

Bibliography

Fee, G. *Paul's Letter to the Philippians*. NICNT. Eerdmans, 1995; Fowl, S. *Philippians*. THNTC. Eerdmans, 2005; Hooker, M. "Philippians." Pages 467–549 in *The New Interpreter's Bible*, vol. 11, ed. L. Keck. Abingdon, 2000; Meeks, W. "The Man from Heaven in Paul's Letter to the Philippians." Pages 329–36 in *The Future of Early Christianity: Essays in Honor of Helmut Koester*, ed. B. Pearson et al. Fortress, 1991.

Victor Paul Furnish

Plagiarism

See Information Technology

Play

Play is a God-given human activity that, along with worship, work, feasting, and other activities, is both a present participation in the goodness of creation and an anticipation of the playful life of the future kingdom of God.

Because play is not "serious," its theological and ethical significance often is undervalued, especially when a "work ethic" (with its conviction that productivity, hard work, and deferred pleasure are signs of high morality) has been a cornerstone of Western society for more than 250 years. This work ethic has supported the Newtonian/Cartesian idea of the world as a "machine," thus supporting industrial and technological development in a capitalist context. This, ironically, then created a consumerist society that questions the presuppositions of the ethic that brought it about. If work is the spirit of capitalism, then play is the spirit of consumerism.

In reality, work and play are complementary, and each has its social role. The opposite of play is not work but depression. A culture that defines people solely according to work will be productive, ordered, and rational but potentially lacking in imagination, creativity, free relationships, joy, and pleasure.

A play ethic thus relates to both the conduct of specific activities and those attitudes that influence other dimensions of life, including work, worship, community, and the purpose of life. An ethic of play may, for example, be associated with worship not only through specifically playful activities (such as music and dance [Exod. 15:20]) but also as an attitude toward worship standing in contrast to a "work ethic" (with liturgy as "the work of the people of God" and an emphasis on duty and responsibility rather than grace and gratitude). Different styles of worship can be interpreted in terms of different forms of play (reflecting variously a preference for wordplay, experiential games, mystery, acting, or musical play).

Play has intrinsic qualities that enhance human experience. Although play does not produce "things," it does generate pleasure, joy, and laughter and is a reminder that life is not justified by works but is a gracious gift. The six days of work at creation are followed by the most holy day of nonwork—that is, a time of appreciation and enjoyment of the created order (as wisdom personified delighted in playing in the created world [Prov. 8:30–31]). Play creates friendship and community and enables people to be happier. Play stresses freedom and spontaneity (even when there is extensive preparation) and far from being a distraction from education is fundamental to it. Playing allows for testing, exploring, and learning in a safe environment. It develops the creativity and imagination essential to art, music, problem-solving, and forming scientific hypotheses. Play is essential to ongoing human re-creation and a healthy life.

Play can be distorted and sinful when it involves greed, violence, unhealthy competitiveness, selfishness, sexual immorality, the denigration of others, or the destruction of the environment, or when it is excessively costly, wasteful of time, or obsessive. The difficulties involved in determining what is appropriate should encourage teaching about the necessity of a biblical ethic of play. Such an ethic exists as a part of the created order and is enhanced by an understanding of the eschatological new creation pictured in terms of song (Rev. 14:2–3), dance (Jer. 31:4), feasting (Rev. 19:9), and play (Zech. 8:5).

See also Capitalism; Consumerism; Creation Ethics; Humanity; Sabbath; Work

Bibliography

Johnston, R. *The Christian at Play.* Eerdmans, 1983; Kane, P. *The Play Ethic: A Manifesto for a Different Way of Living.* Macmillan, 2004; Moltmann, J. *Theology of Play.* Harper & Row, 1972.

Brian G. Edgar

Pluralism

The "fact of pluralism" is that liberal societies are composed of peoples with divergent moralities, religions, worldviews, and so forth. To some, this fact poses the "problem of pluralism"; the problem is that they think pluralistic societies lack adequate cultural stability or moral reserves. Others, however, believe that there is no problem; the "fact of pluralism" is to be celebrated, for it serves certain goods and does not require a unifying ideological grounding.

There have been various responses to the "problem of pluralism." Some, such as social theorists John Rawls and Robert Bellah, have attempted to draw unifying foundations for pluralism from pluralistic culture itself. For Rawls, the upshot is the ethic of "political liberalism." Political liberalism entails a substantive theory of justice. It also requires that, when arguing about constitutional issues or coercive law, participants in liberal societies speak in terms that are equally accessible to all citizens. Thus, religious arguments are ruled out. While some Christians find Rawls's theory useful, some critique him for privatizing religion and for presupposing that people can and should alienate themselves from the particularities of their own lives and traditions. Some cite passages such as Matt. 5:13–14 and Luke 13:21 to show that any acceptable political theory must allow Christians to participate in society *as Christians* to serve as salt, light, or yeast for the world.

Robert Bellah's project is more robust than that of Rawls in that Bellah finds within American society a civil religion, not just a common political ethic. According to Bellah, civil religion includes patriotic rituals, saints, holidays, and scriptures. America's civil religion borrows from Christian and classical Greco-Roman cultures, but is sufficiently independent to ground a limited pluralism within American society. Bellah's position overlaps with some Christian communitarian tendencies, but it has been criticized for restraining prophetic critique of culture and ultimately of running into the problem of cultural idolatry.

Some Christians share Rawls's and Bellah's concerns about pluralistic society but are less optimistic about saving pluralistic society through its own resources. One theological response has been to advocate distancing the church from liberal pluralism (the world) and emphasizing instead the unified body of Christian believers (the church). This has been a tendency among Anabaptists, early fundamentalists, and premillenial dispensationalists. Following this tendency does not necessitate complete social withdrawal. The Christian community can continue to interact as a "witness" to the world. Still, some Christians question whether such positions advocate sufficiently for justice in broader human society, and they challenge the implied social dualism of such positions, which may deny the sovereignty of God over sacred and secular modes of life (see Rom. 13; 1 Pet. 2:13–14).

A different theological response has been to emphasize the sovereignty of God over all of life. Accordingly, these Christians have sought to reform pluralistic society by (re)claiming Christian cultural hegemony over society. This has been attempted in various ways, of course. Some, such as the English Christendom Group and many members of the Religious Right, have advocated for limited social pluralism within the context of an officially Christian culture. Pre–Vatican II Catholicism and Protestant reconstruction and dominion theologies represent more totalizing approaches, seeking to enforce upon Western society determinate forms of natural or OT law. Some Christians have accused theologians who hold these positions of Constantinianism—that is, the corruption of Christianity that occurs when the religion is directly linked with coercive ideology or power. In pushing for a Christianization of society, these theologians fail, some claim, to recognize that Christ's kingdom is "not of this world" (John 18:36).

In contrast to those who attempt in one way or another to solve the "problem of pluralism" are those who deny that pluralism needs any unifying ideological grounding. Among these are some epistemic pluralists. Epistemic pluralists assert that multiple apparently contradictory claims can be simultaneously true. Such a position is represented in the theology of religions by John Hick's "religious pluralism." According to Hick, all major religious traditions are equally valid approaches to "the Real"—a tradition-transcendent term for ultimate reality. Social pluralism is not a problem for the religious pluralist since all disagreements (at least all religious disagreements) are only apparent. More traditional Christian theologians of religion, often citing texts such as John 14:6, have challenged Hick. They begin with the presupposition that Christianity has the uniquely true framework for describing God and the world.

One need not embrace epistemic pluralism in order to find that there is hope for social pluralism without unifying ideological foundations. Some Christians have defended social pluralism on what they take to be uniquely true Christian grounds while denying that pluralistic society needs to accept these grounds in order to have stability. On this account, each particular group must, if it is to accept pluralism, articulate its own reasons for accepting pluralistic society. These Christians may (or may not) offer Christian reasons within public debate, but they do not presuppose that society at large will accept Christian arguments. In such a pluralistic society, arguing effectively in the public sphere may require translating Christian ideas or arguing on non-Christian grounds. These groups face criticisms from those who hold that they are compromising Christian faith by potentially abandoning Christian language in public debate or, in some instances, by acquiescing to non-Christian cultural norms.

It should also be noted that, although many locate the problem of pluralism in terms of how "the Christian" should relate to "pluralistic society," Christianity itself is marked by significant levels of social pluralism. This pluralism is reflected in denominationalism and embodied in the Bible itself, with its four Gospels and multiple apparently contradictory commands on subjects such as divorce (Matt. 5:31–32; 19:9; Mark 10:11–12; Luke 16:18; 1 Cor 7:10–11). As an ecumenical problem, Christians have responded to intra-Christian pluralism in many of the same ways that Christians and others have dealt with wider social pluralism. Models from intra-Christian debate have at times influenced approaches to broader social pluralism. The future may see further exchanges of strategies as Christians and others navigate an increasingly pluralistic world.

See also Democracy; Ecumenism; Political Ethics; Public Theology and Ethics; Religious Toleration; Tolerance

Bibliography

Markham, I. *Plurality and Christian Ethics*. NSCE 4. Cambridge University Press, 1994; Stout, J. *Democracy and Tradition*. Princeton University Press, 2004; Wolterstorff, N., and R. Audi. *Religion in the Public Square: The Place of Religious Convictions in Political Debate*. Rowman & Littlefield, 1997.

Kevin Carnahan

Poetic Discourse and Ethics

W. H. Auden once remarked that of the two questions that interested him most when reading a poem, one was "broadly speaking, moral" (51): What kind of person inhabits the poem? What notion of the good life is on display? Yet, in the fifty-plus years since Auden's statement very little attention has been given to the general topic of poetry and ethics, and even less to the subject with respect to biblical verse more specifically. What follows, then, is by necessity a precursory statement on the topic, distinctly probative. And, in fact, the focus here is considerably narrower still. Ethical thinking over the years has preferred the expanded space afforded by narrative, philosophical discourse, and the like, and poetry has been commonly thought of as an irrational genre; yet there can be no doubt that poems often have proved an especially effective medium for asserting knowledge, for thinking (Vendler 1–9; von Hallberg 105–42). The nexus of poetry and wisdom is quite old, as the most cursory of encounters with the biblical book of Proverbs will attest. But such assertions of truth or knowledge or wisdom are not the primary interest here. While biblical poetry, like all language arts, cannot do without semantics, without propositional content, it is the potential differences of poetry's *way(s)* of saying, especially in its lyric mode (see Dobbs-Allsopp), and how these can affect ethical thinking that hold most of the attention in this article. My claim, echoing Robert von Hallberg (107), is that the (lyric) poetry of the Bible has at its "ready disposal" resources (figures, dialogue, line play, rhythm) that are conventionally less accessible to other genres and thus provide biblical poems with the capacity to open on to and stage ethical thought differently. Several examples may be offered by way of illustration.

We begin by focusing the potential gains to be had from nonlinear, nonepistemic thinking. In counterdistinction to a process of thinking in which a chain of ideas is marshaled into a "single steady trend moving toward a unified conclusion" (von Hallberg 110), lyric poems in the Bible (as elsewhere) often proceed by fits and starts, intuitive surmise, leaping over gaps, moving via juxtaposition and paradox, and generally following prosodic structures of one kind or another. And as a consequence, happily, thinking is as often as not led in directions that otherwise might not be explored, and auditors are provided with warrants for valuing certain dispositions other than by a chain of argument (see Altieri 267; von Hallberg 120).

The poetry of Lamentations is strongly paratactic in nature, which the poet exploits to good effect in shaping a response to the radical suffering caused by the 586 BCE destruction of Jerusalem. Ideas and images are routinely juxtaposed to each other without being logically linked or scripted. This forces readers to consider each idea on its own and then in relation with those most contiguous to it. Individual claims are allowed to surface and be experienced on their own, but they are also ultimately required to be considered as a part of a larger whole, which acts as a strong deterrent to the domination of any single perspective. In Lam. 1:5 we read, "Yahweh has made her [Jerusalem] suffer." The line break after "suffer" ensures that the reader contemplates this startling statement. Yahweh did not "punish" or otherwise "reprimand" personified Jerusalem, but rather intentionally caused her pain. The second line of the couplet then shifts the perspective slightly: "for the multitude of her transgressions." In other words, Jerusalem's "transgressions" precipitated Yahweh's actions, and thus our original aversion to Yahweh's behavior is mollified somewhat, but only somewhat, as we are still haunted by Yahweh's suffering-causing activity. The last couplet exploits this slippage one final time: "her children have gone away, captives before the foe." Yahweh's infliction of suffering on Jerusalem ultimately results—though the link is only implicit in the concatenation of lines—in the exile of the city's children. The image of children (however figurative) being forcefully taken into captivity evokes feelings of empathy and compassion and, ultimately, anger. Whatever guilt there is on Jerusalem's part cannot, ever, rationalize the suffering of innocent children (figures matter ethically too).

Here, then, is a wonderful example of how the poet's paratactic style shapes the ethical outlook sponsored. The attribution of sin and the reality of suffering both have their own claims to make, but neither can ultimately be considered in isolation from the other. Human responsibility must ultimately be owned and the consequences of past actions assumed, but sin, no matter how severe, can never justify human suffering. Beyond the unique perspective on the question of suffering and sin achieved through this manner of putting things (it is neither wholly Deuteronomistic nor prophetic in ideology), such a paratactic style, especially when employed regularly as throughout Lamentations, has the potential to habituate in readers a process of reflection and thinking that demands constant attention to, and interpretation and reinterpretation of, individual details, words, images, propositions; it stresses responsiveness and attention to complexity and discourages the search for single and all-encompassing answers. The time and circumstances of the poet of Lamentations likely did not permit the formulation of simple and singular solutions, and the poet's paratactic habit of thought is generally reflective of and isomorphic to this. But such a style and the view of life and learning that it sponsors may hold attraction even for those of us who read these poems belatedly. At the very least, it exemplifies a productive way for thinking (even ethically) other than through logic and abstraction.

In the short but rich Ps. 133 there is, on a certain reading (Dobbs-Allsopp), a strong valorization of family—kindred dwelling together (v. 1). But this is never argued for logically. Instead, it is simply declaimed. The only warrants provided are aesthetic, what is "good" and "beautiful" about family is likened to "precious oil" (v. 2) and the most bountiful dewfall (v. 3); and theological, the poem's one bit of significant sound play (*gam*, *šām*, *hāʿôlām*; *nāʿîm*, *ʾaḥîm*, *ḥayyîm*; *mah-*, *mah-*, *habbĕrākâ*) linking the opening couplet (v. 1) and closing triplet (v. 3b) and in the process identifying family as the premier site (the literal "there" [*šām*] of v. 3) of Yahweh's blessing. Here, then, we have a good example of how a poem's prosodic structures can give way to ethical insight just as productively and effectively as logic or narrative. Of course, much also depends on our readerly decision to ask ethical questions of this psalm, to embed it, for example, in a larger discussion about what constitutes a good life. There is no such thing as a given or neutral ethical point of view. All ethics, in the end, are cultural constructs. And while the positive ethical evaluation often conveyed by *ṭôb* ("good" [e.g., Gen. 2:17; 3:5, 22; 1 Kgs. 8:36; Isa. 7:15]) might be taken to invite a certain ethical curiosity about this psalm, there is otherwise nothing explicitly moral about it.

And this is true too of most poems in the Bible. In these cases, whatever ethical sensibilities are to be derived from their reading(s) is the responsibility of the reader, the decision to think the psalm (in this instance) through with ethical matters chiefly in mind. And even in those places where it seems that biblical poems may be advocating specific ethical positions—as, for example, in the valorization of family life—such approbations are themselves culturally and historically motivated, and taking them up into other cultural contexts requires, at the very least, negotiating the differences that always accompany historical existence, differences, say, between what constituted a typical family household in Iron Age Israel (Meyers) and what constitutes the same today in North America—the two are by no means identical. So even when contemporary readers are won over to a perspective advocated in an ancient biblical poem, as well we might be in the case of Ps. 133, there will always be more ethical work to do should we also then want to bring that perspective (e.g., a valuing of family) to bear on our own lives. If ethics is always a constructive endeavor, it is also never-ending.

A final example to consider is the general topic of the emotions. That emotion and passion—whether in the agonizing (and angry) cry of radical suffering (Ps. 22:2), or the expressed ecstasy of sublime devotion (Ps. 9:3), or the irresistible desire of one newly in love (Song 4:6)—figure prominently and frequently in biblical poems is readily apparent (see Ryken 123–24). I would add only that this being so is entirely consistent with the strong propensity of lyric poems the world over and throughout the ages to traffic in the emotions. The ethical implications of such lyric prizing of emotion are not insignificant. Two stand out. First, there is a tacit validation of the emotional, the affirmation that the passions are part and parcel of our makeup as human beings. Indeed, we as readers are forced to engage this poetry at an emotional level, and so emotions are made visible as topics for critical discourse and thinking. Second, one of the truths toward which emotionally charged and evocative verse spurs us is the recognition of how impoverished would be our thinking and reasoning were it unaccompanied by feeling and emotion. Emotions "embody some of our most deeply rooted views about what has importance" (Nussbaum, *Fragility of Goodness*, 69–70), views that could be easily lost if we fail to attend routinely and intentionally to the emotional. Philosophers and scientists alike are now beginning to (re)appreciate how crucial the emotions are for the health and well-being of the human creature (Damasio; Nussbaum, *Upheavals of Thought*). To have a discourse, therefore, so routinely charged with emotion, where engagement with the passions is easy and comfortable (however unessential), as with so many moments in Psalms or Lamentations or the Song of Songs, is also a very good thing, something to cherish and nourish. Cold, hard logic is no guarantee of right thinking, ethical or otherwise.

If there has been little attention recently given to the general topic of biblical poetry and ethics, it is not for the lack of substantive material with which to work. Even this necessarily abbreviated consideration of a small handful of examples is sufficient to make clear the wealth of still mostly untapped potential that awaits any ethical line of inquiry into this poetic corpus. In the "how" of a biblical poem's saying there are resources for ethical thinking not so readily available to other genres or modes of discourse. Formal and stylistic choices are matters, as Alan Shapiro observes, "fraught with extraliterary judgments, biases, commitments that have moral as well as aesthetic implications" (1). In fact, to ignore "the sound and evocative power of words . . . and other rhythmic devices, associated images, repetitions, archaisms and grammatical twists" (Langer 259) in biblical poems is to miss much of how this predominantly nonnarrative kind of poetry (see Alter 27) means and to settle, ultimately, for a much impoverished moral worldview.

See also Lamentations; Old Testament Ethics; Psalms; Song of Songs

Bibliography

Alter, R. *The Art of Biblical Poetry*. Basic Books, 1985; Altieri, C. "Taking Lyrics Literally: Teaching Poetry in a Prose Culture." *New Literary History* 32 (2001): 259–81; Auden, W. H. *The Dyer's Hand, and Other Essays*. Vintage Books, 1989; Damasio, A. *Descartes' Error: Emotion, Reason, and the Human Brain*. G. P. Putnam, 1994;

Dobbs-Allsopp, F. W. "Psalm 133: A (Close) Reading." *JHS* 8 (2008). http://www.arts.ualberta.ca/JHS/Articles/article_97.pdf; idem. "The Psalms and Lyric Verse." Pages 346–79 in *The Evolution of Rationality: Interdisciplinary Essays in Honor of J. Wentzel van Huyssteen*, ed. F. Shultz. Eerdmans, 2006; Langer, S. *Feeling and Form: A Theory of Art Developed from Philosophy in a New Key*. Routledge & Kegan Paul, 1953; Meyers, C. "The Family in Early Israel." Pages 1–47 in *Families in Ancient Israel*, by L. Perdue et al. Westminster John Knox, 1997; Nussbaum, M. *The Fragility of Goodness: Luck and Ethics in Greek Tragedy and Philosophy*. Cambridge University Press, 1986; idem. *Upheavals of Thought: The Intelligence of Emotions*. Cambridge University Press, 2001; Ryken, L. *The Literature of the Bible*. Zondervan, 1974; Shapiro, A. *In Praise of the Impure: Poetry and the Ethical Imagination; Essays, 1980–1991*. Northwestern University Press, 1993; Vendler, H. *Poets Thinking: Pope, Dickinson, Whitman, Yeats*. Harvard University Press, 2004; von Hallberg, R. *Lyric Powers*. University of Chicago Press, 2008.

Chip Dobbs-Allsopp

Political Ethics

The biblical writings themselves are shaped by and at times explicitly critique particular political contexts. Thus, the figure of Moses is represented as a functionary of God, bringing national liberation to the people of Israel. The development of monarchy in Israel is both lauded and critiqued (Judg. 21:25; 1 Sam. 7). Prophetic and priestly strains fought over whether the values of society should be defined primarily by temple worship (associated with the monarchy in Jerusalem) or by concerns about social justice.

In later years, as Assyria and Babylon came to dominate the region, Israel's monarchy came under increasing pressure. Jeremiah, following the prophetic strain, set the stage for the continuation of Judaism in exile by emphasizing obedience to covenantal commands over temple worship. The priestly emphasis would return again after the Babylonian exile, adapted to the political limitations of a vassal state, in the books of Ezra and Nehemiah. This emphasis, however, was destined to wane with the last destruction of the temple in 70 CE.

The exilic and postexilic periods also witnessed the development of political and eschatological messianism. Many in Israel looked forward to the emergence of a new king (messiah, "anointed one") who would lead Israel to national independence. Others believed that the injustices of history had become so dire that God would end present history and bring a new creation marked by covenantal justice. Cyrus, the Persian ruler who ended the exile, became the only foreign ruler to be given the title of messiah (Isa. 45:1). Later oppressive occupation by Hellenistic and Roman political powers, however, led to new yearnings for an indigenous messianic figure. These messianic hopes fueled many Jewish revolutionary movements, which ended in the destruction of Jerusalem.

Jesus was born into a period marked by Jewish political diversity. Pharisees, Sadducees, revolutionaries, and other Jewish reform movements took different approaches to Roman authority, temple worship, Hebrew law, and Hellenistic culture. As the leader of a reform movement who was received as a messianic figure, Jesus' actions and teachings no doubt had political implications. Although there is little agreement across Christian history on the content of Jesus' politics, efforts to recover the politics of Jesus have been at times a significant impetus for various Christian political movements.

The followers of Jesus took up messianic language but modified the meaning significantly to fit the activities of Jesus, who was neither conquering king nor a mediator of the immediate end of unjust history. Early evangelists such as Paul tended to lower the ritual requirements of Hebrew law, opening the way for a Christian community that incorporated significant segments of Greco-Roman society.

Early Christian community was shaped by the need to locate itself in relation to imperial Rome. Several factors pushed Christians to distance themselves from the empire. Apocalyptic literature, especially Revelation and Daniel, portrayed empires as demonic. Jesus himself had clashed with Pilate and was crucified on a Roman cross. Christians were also subject to varying levels of persecution from the Roman Empire. Still, several other factors led Christians to emphasize the continuity between their community and imperial power. From the OT came images of Moses as lawgiver and David as ideal king. Texts such as Rom. 13 and 1 Pet. 2:13–17 drew on the Hebrew wisdom tradition, suggesting that worldly rulers participated in God's sovereignty over the world (e.g., Prov. 8:15; 21:1; 24:21). Christ's teachings on taxation also appeared to carve out a legitimate place for imperial power (Matt. 17:24–27; Mark 12:13–17 pars.).

Patristic Developments

The reflections of early church fathers reveal diverse approaches to these tensions. Irenaeus saw the Roman Empire as the means of God's judgment against evil, but he believed that in the end times it would come under judgment itself as a tool of the antichrist. For Tertullian, Christians were distinguished from other citizens by their rejections of idolatry and military service, but their prayers for the stability and success of Rome's armies and governors made them ideal citizens. Origen imagined a progressive conversion in which the peace of God would sweep over the world through the empire.

Constantine's conversion to Christianity set the stage for new possibilities. Seeing Constantine's arrival as God's means of converting the empire, Eusebius cast Constantine as the new Moses and the ideal Platonic philosopher-king. The violence necessary under his rule was simply a means to spread the peace of God.

Not all Christians agreed. After Rome was sacked in 410, Augustine came to a more dour view of imperial Christianity. In *The City of God*, Augustine explored the nature of the *saeculum*, the period between the first and second advents of Christ. In this period, Augustine found, there could be no truly peaceful or just society. Such society could come only when all ordered themselves toward the true God. In the *saeculum*, society is an irreducible mixture of Christians (citizens of the city of God), ordered by love of God, and non-Christians (citizens of the earthly city), ordered by love of self. The two cities have opposed ultimate ends, but they overlap in the use of a set of common worldly goods. As such, the Christian partakes in (and can forcibly defend) the relative "peace of Babylon" that exists in the *saeculum* and may encourage the increase of relative justice in society (see Jer. 29:7). Ultimately, however, the maintenance of order in the *saeculum* via worldly government and the coming of perfect order in the kingdom of God are matters of God's inscrutable action.

After the collapse of Rome, eastern and western branches of empire and church gradually drifted apart. Eastern Christianity tended to conceive of church and empire as facets of a single community. In the West, church and worldly society tended to be seen as separable but related political communities. In the next centuries, the principal struggles for power arose between the leaders of these communities: popes and kings.

Medieval Developments

Shortly after the fall of Rome, Pope Gelasius I articulated an influential doctrine of ecclesiastical and political authority. Christ, Gelasius wrote, was both king and priest. For the rest of history, humans are humbly confined to one or the other role. Though advised by the pope, the king's judgment was sovereign in matters of state. As the "vicar of Christ" in the line of Peter, the pope ruled in matters of religion, for only the priest could "bind and loose" the sins of humanity (see Matt. 16:18–19; cf. John 20:22–23; 21:16–17).

Throughout the medieval period, Gelasius's model would be almost universally acknowledged in the West, but it was rarely practiced. Kings assumed powers to call church councils, tax clergy, and appoint bishops. King Charlemagne was even called the "new Constantine" and was said to rule "in the place of God." Popes also grew in power. Pope Gregory VII claimed sovereignty over all of Christendom. As Bernard of Clairvaux had written, the two swords (see Luke 22:38, 49–51; John 18:10–11), one of spiritual judgment and one of temporal judgment, both belong to the pope, who wields the spiritual sword directly and the temporal sword via the pope's command to temporal authorities. The church expanded its wealth during this period, locating itself as the apostolic guarantor of the purse of Christ (see John 12:6; Acts 2:44–45). Popes also came to grant indulgences for worldly political activities, such as the Crusades.

The late medieval period witnessed the rise of the Scholastic, Franciscan, and Conciliar movements. Scholasticism grew out of the Western rediscovery of Aristotle, which led to a new injection of classical Greek thought in Christian theology. Thomas Aquinas, the paradigmatic Scholastic, emphasized the continuity between pre- and postlapsarian existence. Especially important was Thomas's stress on the goodness of the natural law (see Rom. 2:14), which is theoretically accessible to all people. Whereas Christianity prior to Thomas tended to see hierarchical government as a consequence of sin, Thomas saw humans as naturally political animals marked by natural inequalities. Politics was a good and natural part of life. The secular ruler was, on Thomas's account, not only to punish evil but also to order the society toward the procurement of virtue and the realization of social justice and the common good.

The Franciscan movement was arrayed against the growing worldly wealth and militarism of the church (and occasionally against Aristotelian naturalism). Drawing on the commands given to the apostles in Matt. 10:5–10, Franciscans challenged the church to embrace missional poverty, pacifism, and service. This protest would have echoes throughout the rest of Christian history.

In 1303, the excommunicated King Philip IV captured and humiliated Pope Boniface VIII, proving that papal power was not sufficient to restrain the armies of France. This set the stage for the growth of the idea that the jurisdiction of the church was strictly nontemporal. Philip's appeal to church councils to justify his position against the pope foreshadowed a slow process of democratization that would work its way through both worldly and ecclesiastical societies. Drawing upon Roman republicanism and Aristotelian natural law, theologians came to locate worldly political community as the ground of worldly sovereignty. Similar ideas came to be applied to the Christian church in the Conciliar movement. The Christian community was the ground for the priestly sovereignty of the pope. For support, Conciliarists drew upon the biblical image of the Christian community as a diversified body and upon the idea that the Holy Spirit is active within the community of Christianity (see Acts 20:21; 1 Cor. 1:2; 12:12–27).

Renaissance, Reformation, and Modernity

By the time of the Renaissance, European Christianity was quite diverse. A revival of Thomism led scholars to explicitly expand "natural rights" to non-Christian persons (e.g., Native Americans encountered by Spanish conquistadores), develop the framework of international law, expand the role of worldly political society in grounding state sovereignty, and systematize just-war thought. At the same time, Christian humanists drew upon their Franciscan roots to ridicule the naturalism of the Thomists and the failures of society in realizing the gospel ideals of pacifistic self-sacrificial service.

In the Reformation, Martin Luther parted from the humanists by deploying his Augustinian-inspired "two kingdoms" theology. Luther's love-infused "kingdom of God" was paralleled by an equally robust, violence-driven "kingdom of the world." These two kingdoms had clearly separate jurisdictions. Within the kingdom of God, the word of God taught the true faith and imputed righteousness to sinners. In the kingdom of the world, the temporal ruler was authorized to restrain evil (see Rom. 13:1–7) by enforcing the laws of nature (paralleling the moral precepts of the Ten Commandments) but had no ecclesial role. The Christian was first a member of the kingdom of God but ought to participate in the authorized use of force to restrain evil.

Menno Simons's Anabaptist movement followed Luther's ethic for the kingdom of God but rejected the obligation to participate in the restraint of evil. Reclaiming an imminent eschatology, Mennonites relied on the ban (communal shunning) to maintain the order of the church and upon God's action to order and end the worldly reign of evil.

John Calvin also took and modified Luther's scheme. The law, Calvin concluded, not only convicted people of sin and restrained the wicked (two functions that Luther admitted) but also educated the elect. This was one of several ways in which Calvin stressed the complementary character of the two kingdoms in ways that Luther did not. Calvin favored a civil administration that enforced certain levels of (Calvinist) orthodoxy on the populace.

Neither Luther nor Calvin was a democrat. Still, many ideas from the Lutheran and Calvinist traditions contributed to the rise of democracy. Luther's attacks on papal authority easily transferred to attacks on temporal monarchy. Calvin endorsed the role of "lesser magistrates" to counter the power of tyrants. Calvinist Huguenots would develop this idea and link it to the idea that worldly sovereignty was granted via a "covenant" with political society.

After the Reformation, religious wars broke out across Europe. A series of treaties periodically ending these wars established a system of sovereign states. At the same time, Enlightenment thinkers set out to justify political authority without problematic appeals to denominational authorities. John Locke famously argued that sovereignty was granted on the basis of a social contract. Human beings, Locke posited, are originally free and equal in relation to one another inasmuch as all of them exist as the creations and property of God. As such, humans have natural rights (which can be known independent of revelation), and worldly government is formed by individuals who establish a social contract for the purpose of protecting these natural rights. As long as one's neighbors are trustworthy, upstanding participants in society, the ideal Christian disposition toward those of other religious affiliation is properly one of toleration.

Beyond Modernity

For the most part, modernity witnessed a decline of violent conflicts over Christian doctrine. The Roman Catholic Church maintained its opposition to democratization and religious freedom until the middle of the nineteenth century. But this trend was reversed at Vatican II. This council stands in the middle of a renaissance of Catholic political theology, embodied in the social encyclicals from *Rerum novarum* (1891) to the present. Within this tradition, the Roman Catholic Church has defended workers' rights against laissez-faire capitalism and has defended rights to private property against communist theory. It has also articulated the doctrine of subsidiarity, according to which, larger institutions (such as governments) should intercede only in issues where individuals and smaller institutions cannot realize the common good under their own power. An extension of this position has been used to argue for a stronger form of international government.

Among Protestants, social activism on issues of slavery, feminism, and alcoholism was notable throughout the late eighteenth and nineteenth centuries. The late nineteenth century witnessed the beginnings of the split between fundamentalism and liberalism in Protestant American Christianity. Within fundamentalism, theologians tended to claim that the Bible consisted in a set of original principles from which all moral/political truths ought to be deduced. With dwindling support from mainline denominations, the rise of premillenial dispensationalism, and the embarrassment of the Scopes trial, many fundamentalists withdrew from political activity. Fundamentalism has continued, however, to spin off politically significant movements. In the latter half of the twentieth century the neofundamentalist Religious Right emerged in the culture wars in American politics. This movement has tended toward a Calvinist model of society, has wielded significant political power, and has come under criticism for its association with the Republican Party.

On the other side of the divide, liberal Protestantism tended to combine confidence in providential progress with a high appraisal of the prospects of scientific advancement, especially in social theory. In the United States, this gave rise to the social gospel movement. This movement rejected post-Reformation individualism and sought to recover an appreciation for the OT prophets who proclaimed God's judgment on social structures. The central idea in moral theology, their leaders claimed, was the idea of the kingdom of God. It was the obligation of Christians to participate in the progressive realization of this kingdom of ultimate justice and equality through a peaceful restructuring of political and economic society.

In the early part of the twentieth century, liberal Protestantism came under attack. In Germany, Karl Barth drew upon the apostle Paul to challenge liberal Protestantism's confidence in social development. For Barth, faith in the progress of society appeared to be a faith in something other than God's unique act in Christ. By World War II, Barth's anti–natural law, "neoorthodox" theology allowed the German Confessing Church to resist the cultural pressure of Nazism.

In America, Reinhold Niebuhr took up the neoorthodox critique of liberal Protestantism and pointed it squarely at the social gospel movement. Unlike Barth, however, Niebuhr (like Emil Brunner and Dietrich Bonhoeffer) found ways to maintain qualified respect for a natural law mediated through the social order within history. Other post-Barthian traditions such as postliberalism and radical orthodoxy have wedded Barth's antinaturalism (in the form of robust claims for the uniqueness of the Christian language) with high ecclesiology. This has resulted in calls within these traditions for either neo-Mennonite tensions with the world or a return to Christendom.

The twentieth century also saw the rise of a variety of liberation theologies. Drawing from the biblical emphasis on poverty and contemporary Marxism, early liberation theologians emphasized God's "preferential option for the poor" (see Matt. 5:3; Luke 6:20; 2 Cor. 8:9), which they interpreted as a call to solidarity with impoverished peoples. Liberation theology soon diversified as it was taken up by black, feminist, womanist, and mujerista theologians. In general, however, these theologies have maintained emphasis on the themes of liberation (see Exodus; Gal. 5:1) and the realization of kingdom justice and equality for oppressed groups (see Gal. 3:28).

See also Anabaptist Ethics; Authority and Power; Common Good; Democracy; Economic Ethics; Government; Lutheran Ethics; Nationalism; Natural Rights; Public Theology and Ethics; Social Contract; Subsidiarity, Principle of; Theocracy

Bibliography

Gutiérrez, G. *A Theology of Liberation: History, Politics, and Salvation*. Trans. and ed. C. Inda and J. Eagleson. Orbis, 1973; Hatch, N. *The Democratization of American Christianity*. Yale University Press, 1989; Locke, J. *Two Treatises of Government*. Cambridge University Press, 1988; Murray, J. *We Hold These Truths: Catholic Reflections on the American Proposition*. Sheed & Ward, 1960; Niebuhr, R. *The Nature and Destiny of Man: A Christian Interpretation*. 2 vols. LTE. Westminster John Knox, 1996; O'Donovan, O. *The Desire of the Nations: Rediscovering the Roots of Political Theology*. Cambridge University Press, 1996; O'Donovan, O., and J. Lockwood. *From Irenaeus to Grotius: A Sourcebook in Christian Political Thought*. Eerdmans, 1999; Rauschenbusch, W. *A Theology for the Social Gospel*. Westminster John Knox, 1997; Yoder, J. *The Politics of Jesus: Vicit Agnus Noster*. 2nd ed. Eerdmans, 1994.

Kevin Carnahan

Polygamy

The term *polygamy* denotes a person having more than one spouse at one time. The term *polyandry* denotes a woman having more than one husband, *polygyny* a man having more than one wife, and *communal marriage* multiple husbands being in relationship with multiple wives.

Western cultures, under the influence of the NT and centuries of Christian and European tradition, have rejected polygamy theologically, morally, and legally. And yet it exists in many parts of the world, creating challenges when Western missionaries encounter polygamous cultures. Meanwhile, the weakening of Christian cultural hegemony in the West has begun to create the conditions for a questioning of any inherited norm in relation to marriage.

Biblical Considerations

Christian ethics has taught that monogamy reflects God's design for marriage. The argument is that monogamy was established by God in creation (Gen. 2:18–25), reaffirmed by Christ in his teachings about marriage (Matt. 19:3–12 // Mark 10:2–12), and echoed in the later NT when it touches on marriage (1 Cor. 6:16; 7:1–2; Eph. 5:22–33; 1 Tim. 3:2). The turn early in the church's history toward a sometimes pessimistic and ascetic approach to sexuality, in which celibacy competed with monogamous marriage as the highest expression of Christian discipleship, moved the church even farther away from any acceptance of polygamy.

Certainly the tradition has recognized that polygamy (technically, polygyny) is recorded in numerous stories of the OT, such as the ancestor narratives of Gen. 12–36, in the stories of Lamech (Gen. 4:19), Gideon (Judg. 8:30), Elkanah (1 Sam. 1:1–2), and Joash (2 Chr. 24:1–3), and in the sad, lengthy tales of David and Solomon. Yet Christian leaders have been quick to note that polygamy is not explicitly endorsed, only described, and that its effects quite often were problematic if not disastrous. Polygamy seems to have been the preserve of exceptionally powerful and wealthy men whose sprawling households of wives and half-related children often were filled with favored and disfavored wives and children and vexed by the inevitable intrigues, jealousies, and hard feelings (the problem was sufficient to prompt legislation regulating how disfavored wives and children were to be treated [Deut. 21:15–17]). Solomon's polygamy comes in for special opprobrium as the avenue through which idolatry infected Israel at the height of its power. Maintenance of such a massive household also contributed to Solomon's exploitative use of power and violation of Israel's older, more egalitarian traditions (see 1 Kgs. 11).

The practice of concubinage, also recorded frequently in the OT (Gen. 16:3; 30:3; Judg. 19:1), in which the man enjoyed sexual access to a woman who did not have the status of "wife" to him, leaving him free to bed other women, has been even more objectionable in Christian thought.

The setting aside of divine permission or concession for polygamy and concubinage, if such had ever really been permitted, has been taken by most Western Christians as clear from the prior and subsequent biblical evidence. Rejection of this interpretation of Scripture historically has been confined to heterodox groups such as the Mormons.

As Christian thinking about marriage turned in more modern times in more personal, relational, and companionate directions, polygamy became even more unthinkable. The interpersonal intimacy sought in marriage seems entirely incompatible with the maintenance of multiple simultaneous marriages. And it did not take a well-developed form of feminism for modern Christians to oppose polygamy as oppressive to women and as a venue for male sexual license—organized adultery.

Contemporary Challenges

Christians in nations still practicing polygamy have struggled with the issue of whether monogamy should be treated as a nonnegotiable element of Christian morality. For the church to bring people to Christian faith and then demand that they shatter the polygamous relationships to which they were committed strikes many as a damaging practice that does more harm than good—especially, for example, to women and children who are abandoned by new Christian converts. One solution, offered by John Pobee for the African setting, suggests that in such situations those new Christians who are already polygamists should be permitted to continue existing relationships as long as they care for the wives and children that they have and create no new marriages. The unmarried and those with one wife must not enter into polygamous unions. This approach gradually eases polygamy out of the church, if not the culture.

The Western setting is, if anything, even more interesting. Marriage, understood as a sexually exclusive lifetime covenant between one adult man and one adult woman, the God-given locus for adult male/female companionship, sexual expression, procreation, and childrearing, is a legacy of Christian civilization. For centuries it was both taught by the churches and enforced by the state. Even when states disestablished Christianity, as in the United States, a deep cultural establishment continued that worked its way into both law and culture.

Late-twentieth-century developments in Western cultures have shattered the cultural hegemony of Christianity and therefore of the Christian understanding of marriage. Marriage is no longer the privileged locus for sexual expression; procreation and childrearing happen routinely outside of marriage; many adults live together without benefit of marriage; some press for sex between adults and children; many marriages are not sexually exclusive; at least 40 percent of all marriages end in divorce; many people marry two, three, or more times; and gays, lesbians, and bisexuals enter into marriage or marriage-like relationships. Western law continues to evolve to make room for greater and greater personal freedom to enter into whatever adult sexual and romantic partnerships might be desired. Eventually, the state may abandon any regulatory efforts in this arena, although there are strong social reasons to continue to regulate marriage.

In this context, the centuries-long cultural and legal rejection of polygamy undoubtedly will be challenged. It might be said that Western cultures are already in one sense "polygamous," since most adults do have multiple partners or spouses over the course of a lifetime. Christian marriage, as classically understood, may soon exist only within the countercultural reality of the local church.

See also Adultery; Family; Marriage and Divorce; Sexual Ethics; Women, Status of

Bibliography

Pobee, J. *Toward an African Theology*. Abingdon, 1979.

David P. Gushee

Poor *See* Poverty and Poor

Population Policy and Control

Since ancient times, human cultures have regulated population numbers by way of societal norms for marriage, child rearing, and inheritance. Today, population growth is a global issue as human numbers exceed seven billion. Developing nations, on average, have higher population growth rates and thereby very youthful demographics, which can strain resource availability, including schools, jobs, and medical services. Poor nutrition and excess child mortality often accompany rapid population increase. A few developed countries, primarily in Europe, have average family sizes smaller than necessary to replace their current populations. Low rates of growth also have economic impacts, such as reducing the available labor pool and raising the proportion of elderly citizens. Environmentalists and economists have argued over the ultimate carrying capacity of the planet, and whether human technology can compensate for greater stresses on the world's water, agricultural, and energy resources.

Although to some the Bible may appear to offer unified instruction concerning human population growth, texts applicable to the topic are historically varied and complex. The oldest biblical books describe a herding culture, centered on family camps. The influence of urbanization on biblical narratives increases through time, as does the impact of empire building. In the ancient world, norms and practices encouraging large families and population growth included the following: marrying at a young age, taking multiple wives and concubines, avoiding sexual intercourse during menstruation, valuing children as agricultural labor, and offering children in marriage to build economic or military relationships with other clans. Among the historic practices limiting family size and population growth are the following: marrying at an older age, sexual abstinence outside marriage, monogamy, breastfeeding infants for more than a year, and formal schooling for children. The latter strategies often improve survivorship of individual children. Extended breastfeeding delays ovulation, for example, and prevents an additional child from being conceived while the mother is already stressed with a new baby.

The Creation

In Gen. 1:22 God, having created the sea creatures and the birds, "blessed them, saying, 'Be fruitful and multiply, and fill the waters in the seas.'" God affirms the animals' compliant response and says that it is "good," implying that reproduction is intended to be a blessing. In Gen. 1:28 God extends the blessing to Adam and Eve, saying to them, "Be fruitful and multiply, and fill the earth and subdue it." Some interpreters treat this passage as a command, effective in perpetuity, to produce large families. The gift of reproduction, however, is shared among the animals and humankind and is not an instruction to overwhelm or displace other creatures. Texts such as Ps. 104 invoke God's care for the earth's biota and their offspring as evidence for the continuing providential activity of God.

Hebrew Family Structure

Genesis 13:8–13 recognizes the importance of carrying capacity, such as avoiding overgrazing and of sharing land, when Lot moves his flocks to the Jordan Valley and Abram takes his to Canaan. In the third millennium BCE, having a son was important to continuing the family name and to providing care for aging parents. When Sarai was barren, Abram had sexual intercourse with her maidservant Hagar in order to begin a family. Hagar bore Ishmael, and after three men, identified as angels, visit their camp, Sarah (renamed) gives birth to Isaac (Gen. 16–21). God affirmed, "Abraham shall become a great and mighty nation, and all the nations of the earth shall be blessed in him" (Gen. 18:18). The Bible reports that polygamy led to jealousy and internal disagreements within families, such as the strained relationships between Rachel and Leah (Gen. 29–30) or among David's wives and concubines and their offspring (2 Sam. 13). Solomon's many marriages with foreign women are portrayed as luring him to make offerings to their false gods (1 Kgs. 11).

Despite the value awarded to children, OT texts model loving treatment for the childless and discourage selling one's own children into slavery. Elkanah gave his wife, Hannah, who was barren, a double portion of meat when he sacrificed "because he loved her" (1 Sam. 1:5). She ultimately becomes the mother of the prophet Samuel. Deuteronomy 24:19–22 requires resource sharing with widows and orphans, who are allowed to glean the fields of those more fortunate. Care for the aged is encouraged by Exod. 20:12, which instructs, "Honor thy father and mother." Isaiah 56:4–5 promises eunuchs who keep the covenant "a monument and a name better than sons and daughters."

War, Invasion, and Deportation

The OT responds to population crises, such as famine, war, and deportation. Joseph's eleven brothers, with the survival of their families at stake, were forced to travel to Egypt in search of food during famine (Gen. 40–47). The invasions of the Assyrians and the Babylonians resulted in the deportation and dispersal of ten of the tribes of Israel. Jeremiah describes the return of a "remnant" of the nation to their homeland. The general perspective in the face of these continuing forced population depletions is pronatalist. Biblical norms encourage mercy to outsiders and sojourners, while not depleting the population-supporting agricultural resources of the countryside during war.

The New Testament

The Gospels, in contrast to the family narratives of Genesis, place little emphasis on childbearing, while frequently addressing the worth of children and care for the ill or widowed. In the Roman realms of the first century CE, fathers exposed unwanted female or disabled children and sold children into slavery to settle debts. Caesar Augustus, worried about staffing Rome's armies, however, established pronatalist policies, encouraging larger family sizes, while discouraging abortion and abandonment of healthy infants. Jesus, in opposition to Roman norms, treated children as valued souls and not merely as economic commodities or future soldiers. Jesus says, "Let the little children come to me" (Luke 18:16), implying all are welcome in his kingdom.

The Gospels provide no information about the children of Christ's disciples and imply that the early church did not have hereditary leadership. The NT encourages recruitment of new Christians via evangelization from all ethnicities and from those with and without families. One of the first non-Palestinian converts was the Ethiopian eunuch, a Jewish proselyte baptized by Philip on the desert road (Acts 8:26–40). He returned to Africa to found the Ethiopian church. Some potential Christians, including many soldiers and slaves, had predetermined life paths without families. Still controversial apocalyptic texts suggest the first Christians believed that the numbers of those entering the kingdom were already determined (Rev. 14). Rodney Stark has argued that Christianity spread rapidly both because it addressed the social issues of the empire and bridged class boundaries, and because Christians had high fertility rates. While committed to caring for their own children, the first Christians adopted orphans, saved infants from exposure, and helped to feed the poor.

Interpretation

Today, those denominations and sects that are predominantly rural, partially isolated from the greater culture, or living in communities composed of their coreligionists, such as Hasidic Jews and the Amish, are more likely to take a pronatalist position, affirming high birth rates and family size. Those denominations or sects that are liberal or highly integrated with other religious groups are more likely to be nonnatalist, believing that each family should make its own decision about childbearing. Historically, some Christian sects have been strongly antinatalist, practicing complete celibacy. The Shakers, or United Society of Believers in Christ's Second Appearing, lived on communal farms, did not marry, and replenished their numbers by adopting orphans. Today's Christians and Jews largely continue to agree that care for children, respect for the elderly, just sharing of the earth's resources, and concern for the poor are key themes of biblical ethics.

See also Bioethics; Birth Control; Childlessness; Children; Family; Procreation

Bibliography

Bouma-Prediger, S. *For the Beauty of the Earth: A Christian Vision for Creation Care*. Baker Academic, 2001; Bratton, S. *Six Billion and More: Human Population Regulation and Christian Ethics*. Westminster John Knox, 1992; Stark, R. *The Rise of Christianity: How the Obscure, Marginal Jesus Movement Became the Dominant Religious Force in the Western World in a Few Centuries*. HarperSanFrancisco, 1997.

Susan Power Bratton

Pornography

For Christians in a technological and media-saturated age, pornography presents one of the most common moral struggles as well as one of the most shameful and thus least discussed. Although the numbers are difficult to track, approximately forty million people in the United States view pornography every year; the global pornography industry generates approximately $100 billion per year, producing $13 billion in US revenue. Pornography comprises roughly 25 percent of all internet search-engine requests. As with any ethical issue, Christians seek guidance from many sources, particularly Scripture. Despite availability of sexually explicit art in cultures in which they were written, the Scriptures remain relatively silent on this topic, at least in the forms in which we encounter it today. However, Scripture does provide guidance for understanding and addressing this issue, especially as it shapes our moral imaginations and expectations of the goods at which sex and sexuality aim.

The "Sin" of Pornography

The root of the first part of the word *pornography* is the Greek *pornē*, "female slave or prostitute." The related verb *porneuō* occurs in many texts in the NT and is translated variously as "immorality," "fornication," or "lust" (e.g., 1 Cor. 5:1; Gal. 5:19–21; Col. 3:5–6). Given the understanding of sin as a distortion of God's good intention, pornography must be contrasted against the background of sexuality as described in Gen. 2:18–25. Sexuality there involves a celebration of sameness and difference, with a creative power that binds people together as inspirited bodies. The destructive nature of pornography is, then, understood as a twisting of God's good gift into a means of violating, dominating, or controlling others, or of users themselves becoming enslaved, warped, or driven by pornography.

A major reason why pornography is such an important ethical issue today is the internet. Therapist and researcher Al Cooper describes a "triple-A engine" that has produced an explosion of explicit material in the "pornosphere": accessibility, affordability, and anonymity. Addiction, a related and important aspect of such proliferation, can be defined in different ways, but it includes many hours of viewing (e.g., more than ten hours per week); increased appetite, desire, or tolerance; compulsivity; or harm to self or others, including marital difficulties. Some psychologists suggest that the combination of fantasy and isolation contribute to such addictive behavior; this is not surprising, given a traditional Christian perspective of sexuality as aiming at human bonding and friendship. Despite the shame, this addiction should be treated like any other addiction, with professional help and support in a caring community. However, most research indicates that a relatively small percentage of viewers (2–8 percent) are addicted to pornography.

Pornography needs to be distinguished from erotica, which is acceptable to many Christians. Some Christians define the difference between the two as the muddy but real line between material that expresses committed and affectionate sex (erotica) and that which portrays degrading, violent, or dehumanizing sexual acts (pornography). How such material shapes the viewer depends not only on its objective content but also on the character of the participant(s). From this perspective, the biblical book Song of Songs qualifies as erotic but not pornographic. Although sexually explicit, films may highlight the vacuous or destructive nature of uncommitted sex. Whether individuals find such material inappropriate or sexually stimulating depends on their maturity as well as their worldview. For Christians, then, determining if something qualifies as pornographic requires an honest analysis of the material's effect on those involved, including those who produce it. Given these parameters, some Christians might support the use of erotica for masturbation while prohibiting pornography for such use.

Gender and Pornography

Although the use of pornography is most often assumed to be a problem for men, the "triple-A engine" has made sexually explicit material more accessible to women; studies indicate that 30 to 60 percent of women view or download pornography. Some feminists have argued stridently against the harmful effects of pornography, but others have argued for equal use. It appears, however, that women and men interpret and respond to such material differently. For example, some studies indicated that women bring what they are seeing and doing online into their sexual relationships, while men are more apt to utilize such material in isolation. In contrast to the experience of most men, pornography sometimes negatively affects women's body image, with an increasing number pursuing physical augmentation (Albright 185).

For many women, sexual fantasy takes a form other than use of material strictly understood as pornography, such as romance novels or sexual banter. Although more socially acceptable, this relational or emotional stimulation parallels men's arousal by physically beautiful, pleasing, or malleable women. Pornography in this broader sense draws people away from the actual relationships and into an unreal world devoid of the demands and rewards of committed sexual affection.

Like prostitutes purchased for pleasure, divorced from the complexities and fruitfulness of committed sexual relationships, pornography demands nothing from us but our own preferences; we re-create the other as a mirror image of our own desires apart from their uniqueness. Its allure lies in the control of persons and situations in a manner that denies the other's dignity, needs, or desires. This dominating stance makes impossible a Christian sexuality that trains us to offer ourselves to one another in life-giving, life-sustaining ways. At its worst, pornography—especially that involving children, rape, or other violence—scars and deforms our individual and social moral imaginations. Pornography illustrates the antithesis of Gen. 2:23–25, where sexuality is celebrated as mutual vulnerability by which the other makes claims on us yet also frees us to be more fully and joyfully human.

See also Exploitation; Prostitution; Sex and Sexuality; Sexual Ethics

Bibliography

Albright, J. "Sex in America Online: An Exploration of Sex, Marital Status, and Sexual Identity in Internet Sex Seeking and Its Impacts." *JSexR* 45 (2008): 175–86; Balswick, J. K., and J. O. Balswick. "Pornography and Erotica." Pages 275–93 in *Authentic Human Sexuality: An Integrated Christian Approach*. IVP Academic, 2008; Paul, P. *Pornified: How Pornography Is Damaging Our Lives, Our Relationships, and Our Families*. Holt, 2006; Sheldrake, P. "Desire and Sexuality." Pages 77–100 in *Befriending Our Desires*. Darton, Longman & Todd, 2001.

Erin Dufault-Hunter

Possessions *See* Property and Possessions

Poverty and Poor

Concern for the poor is present throughout the biblical tradition. Although the OT sometimes uses "the poor" as a pious metaphor for those who must depend on God (see Pss. 40:17; 86:1), most often the term refers to those who find themselves on the margins of society because of their economic situation, which leaves them open to exploitation (e.g., Pss. 10:2; 72:12; 109:31). The prophetic tradition usually portrays poverty as the result of actions taken by people of means to deprive the vulnerable of their share of the bounty that God gave to Israel. The prophets condemned the economic exploitation made possible by the corruption of the ancient Israelite legal system. They announced divine judgment on the social, economic, and political system that, they insisted, created poverty (e.g., Isa. 1:21–26; Amos 4:1–4). Deuteronomy maintains that there would be no poor in Israelite society if the people observed the norms of traditional Israelite morality (Deut. 15:4–5). Still, Deuteronomy recognizes that poverty does exist in Israel (15:11), so it calls for Israelites to be generous to the poor (15:7) and suggests strategies to ensure that poverty would never become a permanent feature of Israelite society (15:12–14). Those who wish to follow Jesus are to sell their goods and give the proceeds to the poor (Matt. 19:21). Paul urged generosity toward the poor of Jerusalem (1 Cor. 16:1–3; cf. Rom. 15:26).

At first glance, the needs of poor people and the injustice they experience do not appear to be a central concern of the Torah. Various Hebrew words that are rendered in English as "poor" or "needy" occur fewer than twenty times in the first five books of the Bible. Yet this statistic does not tell the whole story. The narratives of the Torah include stories of how wealthy people can use their economic power as an advantage in their dealings with those whose social standing is marginal because of their poverty. The stories about Hagar illustrate the vulnerability of the poor (Gen. 16; 21:1–21). Sarah and Abraham used their servant Hagar to meet their needs. She provided Abraham with an heir whom Sarah claimed as her child according to the customs of the day. But when Hagar's presence and service were no longer necessary and when she and her child were deemed troubling following the birth of Isaac, Abraham simply sent them away at Sarah's insistence. But God saved Hagar and her son Ishmael from certain death and promised to make of him "a great nation" (Gen. 21:18).

The story of Pharaoh's enslavement of Jacob's descendants living in Egypt is another case in point. This Egyptian king, who "did not know Joseph" (Exod. 1:8), exemplifies those who use their power to oppress people and thereby "make" poverty. God, of course, took the side of the poor Hebrew slaves against their Egyptian masters. Through Moses, God freed the slaves and brought them to a land where they enjoyed freedom and prosperity (Deut. 8:7–10).

The laws of the Torah serve not only to specify the rights of poor people but also to regulate how more successful Israelites are to deal with those on the margins of the ancient Israelite economy. For example, people who have completed service as bond slaves in repayment of a debt are not simply to be left to their own devices after regaining their freedom. The former slaves are to be given "gifts" that will enable them to make a fresh start (Deut. 15:13–14). Without such help, former slaves would eventually find that their newly reacquired freedom brought them to the same kind of destitution that led them into bond slavery in the first place. The Deuteronomic law, then, sought to break the cycle of poverty that kept the poor in economic dependency.

The call for justice on behalf of poor people and the announcement of judgment on their oppressors are central concerns of prophetic preaching. Ancient Israel's prophets were not economic theorists or social critics, but still they were convinced that the traditional moral values of ancient Israel were being violated by people of means for their own enrichment. The prophets sought to make Israel appreciate the consequences of the injustice that infested the ancient Israelite social and economic system. The poor were created by the rich who, in their greed, disregarded the norms of traditional Israelite morality (Jer. 5:27; Ezek. 45:9; Amos 3:9; Hab. 2:9; Mal. 3:5). The prophets believed that the actions of those who oppressed people with no economic power and social standing would bring divine judgment on Israel. The prophets were certain that God called them to announce the inevitability of that judgment.

The preaching of the prophets often included intense criticism of the monarchy and associated institutions, especially the judicial system that facilitated the oppression of the poor (Isa. 5:23; Jer. 22:13–17; Amos 5:7; Mic. 3:9–11). Prophetic criticism was directed also at wealthy landowners. Ancient Israel witnessed the gradual concentration of land in the hands of a few and the creation of a great number of landless farmers who were reduced to hiring themselves out as agricultural workers to survive (Isa. 5:8; Ezek. 22:29; Mic. 2:1–3; Hab. 2:5–6). Also, the crops grown on the land taken from the poor were olives and grapes, since oil and wine made from these crops were valuable commodities. Less land was devoted to the cultivation of grains, which were the staples of the ancient Israelite diet. The result was that the price of grain rose, thus creating a cycle of poverty. The landless poor could not afford to buy grain, and so they became more indebted to the wealthy landowners. Merchants who defrauded their customers and thereby made life more difficult for the poor also heard their practices condemned by the prophets (Isa. 3:14; Jer. 5:27; Hos. 12:7–8; Amos 8:5; Mic. 6:10–11). The economic system during the monarchic period guaranteed the continuation of poverty in Israel and so was the object of prophetic invectives.

The wisdom literature (e.g., Job, Proverbs, Ecclesiastes) deals with the theme of the poor, but its way of approaching this motif differs markedly from that of the Torah and the prophets. The origins of the wisdom tradition lie in the upper classes of ancient Israelite society. It is not surprising that one does not find the moral outrage at the oppression of the poor in the wisdom literature that one finds in prophetic literature, though the sages did regard the existence of poverty as an affront to God (Prov. 14:31). Ancient Israel's sages address the sons of society's upper class and warn them against laziness and inattention that will inevitably lead to poverty (Prov. 10:4). According to the sages, success demands a disciplined life. The book of Proverbs makes no connection between the problems faced by the poor and the actions of the wealthy, because it looks at the question of poverty not as a social or moral problem in Israelite society but as a potential threat to the well-being of Judah's elite. The sages assume that people "choose" poverty by failing to follow the advice of the elders and teachers to live a disciplined life. A fundamental assumption of the wisdom tradition is that actions have consequences and that these consequences are quite predictable. If experience has taught people anything, it is that poverty comes to those who are lazy and unproductive (Prov. 13:18; 20:13; 23:21; 28:19). Still, like the Torah and the prophets, the wisdom tradition also calls its readers to be generous toward the poor (Prov. 19:17; 22:9).

The book of Psalms is replete with references to the "poor and needy." It is sometimes difficult to determine if the poor of the psalms are the economically poor or if the poor have become a metaphor pointing to the pious in ancient Israelite society. It appears that at times the language of social and economic stratification and conflict become simply a convention in some psalms to speak about the community of Israel as a whole or about a group of the pious within the community. The psalms consistently portray God as the protector and deliverer of the poor (e.g., 9:12, 18; 10:14; 35:1; 68:10; 69:33; 107:41; 109:31; 113:7; 140:12; 147:6; 149:4). Those who experience exploitation ask for God's protection and strength in their conflict with the rich (12:1; 69:33) because the poor are those who depend on God (10; 25; 34; 37; 82). The poor turn to prayer in the midst of their oppression because they believe in God's love and fidelity (69:13–15; 86:5, 15). They pray that God will vindicate them, establishing justice according to God's righteousness (35:23–24; 140:12). Because the biblical tradition regards material poverty as an evil, the book of Psalms is able to appropriate and reinterpret the vocabulary of poverty to speak about the life situations faced by the pious, whether they are poor or not.

When the NT speaks of "the poor," however, it speaks both of the "working poor" and the genuinely destitute. Members of both groups had little social status and no political power in the first-century Roman world. They existed on the margins of society and were vulnerable to exploitation at the hands of the wealthy. The apocalyptic perspective that helped shape the preaching of Jesus effects a noticeable shift in the assessment of poverty. Indeed, the poor are the fortunate ones given the reversal of fortunes that will happen when the reign of God begins (Matt. 5:3; Luke 6:20). Nevertheless, the Gospels do not idealize poverty, nor do they suggest that the poor have special access to God. But having no significant possessions, being without political power, and having no social standing eliminate one type of temptation to dismiss Jesus' call to repentance: the temptation that comes with the self-sufficiency brought by wealth (Matt. 19:24; Luke 12:16–21). While the Gospels recognize the injustice that gives rise to poverty, they hold that this injustice will be redressed in the world to come rather than in this world. Still, the Gospels do not imply that poverty can be ignored or that its existence must be fatalistically accepted.

Responding to Jesus' calls to repentance enables the disciples to hear the call for justice that comes from ancient Israel's prophetic tradition. It impels the disciples to sell what they have in order to give to the poor (Matt. 19:21). Indeed, one way for the wealthy to give a tangible sign of their repentance is for them to distribute their goods to people in need. An essential component of a proper response to Jesus' preaching is action that will benefit the poor (Luke 19:8). Generosity toward the poor, then, is a mark of an authentic disciple. The Gospels present the life and teaching of one who was able to live without the security that comes with political power, social status, or material possessions. They challenge his followers to do the same—to be content living on the margins—because the poor are blessed: the kingdom of God belongs to them (Matt. 5:3; Luke 6:20).

Paul gives no evidence of any spiritualization of poverty. For the apostle, the poor are simply those in need. He showed particular concern for the church of Jerusalem because so many of the faithful were in need there (Rom. 15:26; 1 Cor. 16:3). He also advised people to follow his example by supporting themselves from their work (1 Cor. 4:12; 1 Thess. 4:11) and by being happy with a less than comfortable existence.

The Epistle of James provides the single example of a NT author displaying the passion of the Hebrew prophets (5:1–6). James decried the economic stratification and marginalization of the poor that were evident in some Christian communities (2:2–6). James assumed that the Christian life ought to be characterized by a type of solidarity that should make social injustice and the marginalization of the poor unthinkable.

The biblical tradition is unanimous in asserting that material economic poverty should not exist. Poverty is clearly not in accord with the divine will, since God has provided all that is necessary for people to live a good life. Although the tradition is not unanimous in its explanations for the origin of poverty, it does suggest that poverty results from human decision-making. Poverty is not an inevitable feature of human existence. Poverty exists because people allow it to exist. Although sometimes these decisions can be laid at the feet of the poor themselves (e.g., Prov. 10:4), the predominant assertion made by the tradition is that the avarice and greed of the wealthy lead them to unjustly deprive some people of their essential needs (Isa. 10:2). There is no question that the Scriptures recognize the evil of economic oppression. In the face of this oppression, the tradition affirms that God is the protector of those who are unjustly deprived of their access to the bounty of the earth and the fruits of their labor (Jer. 20:13).

Both the OT and the NT pay attention to the people who are unable to control their own destiny because of their lack of economic independence. Without the power that wealth gives, poor people are especially vulnerable to exploitation and oppression. The biblical tradition also finds the experience of the poor people to be an apt metaphor for the universal need for salvation. Poor people have no other choice but to depend on God. Nevertheless, while the Bible uses poverty as a metaphor to speak about the status of all human beings before God, it never overlooks the injustice that creates the poor. At the same time, the biblical tradition does not idealize the poor as having some sort of special access to God (see Jer. 5:4). Although the Bible uses the cries of the poor to speak about the universal human need for God, it does not confer an aura of holiness around the poor, nor does it understate the need to overcome the forces that create and sustain injustice and oppression.

Indeed, the Bible recognizes the evil of economic oppression and asserts that God hears the cry of the poor. The challenge that the biblical tradition offers believers is to imitate the character of God and stand with the poor in their struggle to overcome the oppression that they experience in their lives. Believers cannot acquiesce in the degradation and exploitation of the poor and oppressed. They will endeavor to end the marginalization and alienation of the poor. Today, standing with the poor is most often a political act, though there is room for expressing solidarity with the poor by individual acts of benevolence such as almsgiving. Still, those who stand with the poor today are resisting the structures of society that institutionalize poverty. This resistance takes different forms: public advocacy, lobbying, protesting, and other forms of political action. The biblical tradition pushes believers beyond simple benevolence toward poor people and beyond radical pronouncements and scathing criticism of unjust economic systems. Of course, the gospel calls believers to conversion, not revolution. It takes genuine conversion before one can really stand with the poor, before one can become an authentic instrument of justice, liberation, and reconciliation.

Finally, the biblical tradition does not allow believers to leave social justice to secular political structures. The community of faith should model a type of society founded on solidarity rather than on competition between social and economic classes. The church must take action on behalf of the poor. Without such actions, the community of faith loses its reason for existence, as the people of ancient Israel and Judah discovered. The very existence of poverty is evidence that the church has not been living up to its responsibilities for "there shall be no poor among you" (Deut. 15:4).

Too often, texts such as Deut. 15:11, "there will always be poor people in the land" (NIV [cf. Matt. 26:11; Mark 14:7; John 12:8]), have been read as evidence that poverty is part of the natural order of things. But when these texts are read against the wider backdrop of the entire biblical tradition, it becomes clear that not poverty but mutual concern and support are to be the normal pattern of the community's life. The Bible does not demand that believers adopt any particular economic system. The biblical tradition serves to animate believers to respond to poverty with imagination, creativity, and generosity. Believers recognize that poverty is the creation of those who do not live according to the ideals of the Torah and the gospel, and they are confident that with God's help they can overcome the selfishness and sin that are the obstacles preventing people from standing with the poor so that the biblical ideal can become a reality: "there should be no poor among you" (Deut. 15:4 NIV).

See also Almsgiving; Collection for the Saints; Economic Ethics; Exploitation; Generosity; Greed; Justice; Koinonia; Property and Possessions; Sloth; Solidarity; World Poverty, World Hunger

Bibliography

Hoppe, L. *There Shall Be No Poor among You: Poverty in the Bible.* Abingdon, 2004; Lohfink, N. *Option for the Poor: The Basic Principle of Liberation Theology in Light of the Bible.* BIBAL, 1987; Pixley, J., and C. Boff. *The Bible, the Church and the Poor.* Orbis, 1989; Vaage, L., ed. *Subversive Scriptures: Revolutionary Christian Readings of the Bible in Latin America.* Trinity Press International, 1997; West, G. *The Academy of the Poor: Towards a Dialogical Reading of the Bible.* Sheffield Academic Press, 1999.

Leslie J. Hoppe, OFM

Power *See* Authority and Power

Powers and Principalities

In Paul's Letters and elsewhere in the NT we find references to "principalities," "powers," "authorities," "rulers," "thrones," "dominions," and "elemental spirits of the universe" (see, e.g., Rom. 8:38; 1 Cor. 2:6, 8; 15:24; Gal. 4:3, 8–9; Eph. 1:21; 3:10; 6:12; Col. 1:16; 2:8, 10, 15; 1 Pet. 3:22). Although there is ongoing debate about the precise meaning of these titles, comparisons with contemporary apocalyptic literature (e.g., *1–2 Enoch*, *Jubilees*, *Testament of Levi*, *Testament of Solomon*) and other sources (e.g., Greek magical papyri) suggest that they refer to distinct classes of supernatural agents who exercise a domain of authority over structural aspects of society and creation. Given that the NT provides no information regarding the specifics of these classifications, it has become common for contemporary theologians to refer to the whole realm simply as "the principalities and powers" or, even more simply, as "the powers."

Background

A number of historical factors contributed to the development of the conception of the powers in Paul's thought and in that of the apocalyptic writers of his day, but scholars generally agree that its origins can be traced back to the OT. In keeping with other ancient Near Eastern cultures, ancient Hebraic authors believed that the earth was surrounded and perpetually threatened by forces of chaos, usually depicted as personified waters (Job 38:6–11; Ps. 104:7–8; Prov. 8:27–29) or cosmic monsters (Job 9:13; 26:12–13; 40–41; Pss. 74:10–14; 87:4; Isa. 51:9–10). Moreover, despite their creational monotheism, OT authors generally assumed that a multitude of lesser gods exist alongside Yahweh. Some of these are aligned with God and form his divine council and heavenly army, but others work at cross-purposes with Yahweh and must be fought against. Indeed, as with their Near Eastern neighbors, ancient Jews believed that these gods were involved in their earthly battles (Judg. 11:21–24; 2 Sam. 5:23–24; cf. 2 Kgs. 6:15–18) (Boyd, *God at War*, 73–142). Biblical authors are uniformly confident that Yahweh is ultimately sovereign over the forces of chaos and rebellious gods that oppose him. However, his victory is celebrated as something praiseworthy precisely because these foes are so formidable (König 46).

Owing to a number of historical factors, the OT's view that Yahweh does battle against cosmic forces of evil and rebel gods began to play an increasingly central role in the theology of many Jews in the two centuries leading up to Christ. Undoubtedly, several centuries of living under an often-oppressive pagan regime contributed to an intensified sense of cosmic evil among many Jews (Russell 237–38). In addition to this, some scholars argue that this development was partly influenced by Zoroastrianism and possibly other pagan influences (e.g., astrology, magic), though theories of pagan influence such as these have come under strong criticism and now enjoy less academic favor than they once did. Whatever the causes, in the two centuries leading up to the time of Christ we find many Jews depicting the world as engulfed in spiritual warfare as well as an explosion of speculations about the numbers, names, domains of authority, histories, and particular battles of angels and other cosmic agents.

Something of this intensification and increased specification of the powers against which Yahweh fights is reflected in the book of Daniel. At one point, we read that God dispatched a heavenly messenger in response to Daniel's prayer. However, the angel was detained for twenty-one days by "the prince of the kingdom of Persia," which most scholars conclude was a divine power that had jurisdiction over this particular nation but was working at cross-purposes with God. In response, "Michael, one of the chief princes," came to resist the prince of Persia and free the messenger (Dan. 10:13). After the angel successfully delivered his message, he told Daniel that he must "turn to fight against the prince of Persia," after which "the prince of Greece will come," referring to a different power with a different jurisdiction (Dan. 10:20). This intensified and detailed awareness of the spiritual realm is a characteristic of apocalyptic literature and forms the primary background of Paul's understanding of the powers.

The Powers in Paul's Theology

In keeping with the creational monotheism that runs throughout the biblical literature, Paul sees the powers as originally belonging to God's good created order (Col. 1:15–17). Yet, as in the apocalyptic literature of the time, Paul for the most part depicts the powers in negative terms. Indeed, to the extent that they work against God's purposes in the world, Paul and other NT authors view them as belonging to Satan's rebel kingdom. Going beyond anything found in noncanonical apocalyptic literature, the NT depicts Satan as the head of a vast army of rebel agents, including the powers, fallen angels, and demons (Ling 12–22; Yates 99). Satan is thus spoken of as "the ruler [*archōn*] of the power [*dynamis*] of the air" (Eph. 2:2), "the ruler [*archōn*] of this world" (John 12:31; 14:30; 16:11), and "the god of this age" (2 Cor. 4:4), who controls the entire world (1 John 5:19), owns and dispenses all the authority of the world's governments (Luke 4:5–7; cf. Rev. 13), and deceives the nations (Rev. 14:8; 18:3; 20:3, 8) (Boyd, *God at War*, 180–84).

Jesus came to defeat Satan and the powers and deliver humans and all creation from their oppressive reign (Heb. 2:14; 1 John 3:8; cf. Gal. 4:3–9). Failing to understand the "secret wisdom of God," the powers helped bring about Christ's crucifixion only to discover that this very act brought about their own demise (1 Cor. 2:6–8; cf. John 13:27; Col. 2:15) (Boyd, "Christus Victor View," 36–38). Because Christ's death and resurrection in principle defeated the powers and enthroned Christ "far above" them (Eph. 1:19–21), all who are "in Christ" are empowered to live free from their oppression (Col. 2:20) and make known "the wisdom of God . . . to the rulers and authorities in the heavenly places" (Eph. 3:10).

At the same time, reflecting the "already but not yet" tension of the NT's eschatology, Paul and other authors are aware that Christ's victory over the powers will be fully manifested only when Christ returns and God's reign is fully established (e.g., 1 Cor. 15:24; Eph. 1:10). Until this time, the powers remain active, and believers must continually struggle against them (Eph. 6:12; cf. Gal. 4:9) while having the assurance that whatever else the powers are capable of doing, they cannot separate believers from the love of Christ (Rom. 8:38–39).

Contemporary Theology and the Powers

Throughout much of its history, the church has made little of the powers as a distinct category of supernatural agents. This changed rather dramatically in the twentieth century as theologians wrestled with the horror of two world wars and with national, systemic, and institutional evil on an unprecedented scale. Theologians such as Heinrich Schlier, Hendrik Berkhof, G. B. Caird, and, more recently, Walter Wink have employed the language of the powers to articulate the manner in which nations, governments, social movements, corporations, and other institutions (e.g., "the military industrial complex") often take on a demonic life of their own and wreak a destructive influence that goes far beyond what any individual caught up into these social structures would want or be capable of. Many contemporary theologians interpret the apocalyptic depiction of the powers as supernatural agents to be a quasi-mythological way of expressing the "inner essence" and quasi-autonomous reality of corporate wholes (e.g., Wink, *Naming the Powers*, 104–5). Others, however, argue for the importance of retaining the view of the powers as transcendent agents without denying their close identifications with structural aspects of society and creation (e.g., Boyd, *God at War*, 272–76; Arnold 169–82).

This renewed appreciation for the centrality of the NT's concept of the principalities and powers has led some to construe Jesus' life, ministry, death, and resurrection as a sustained nonviolent revolt against the powers and as the model that the body of Christ is to emulate as we struggle "not against enemies of blood and flesh, but against the rulers, against the authorities, against the cosmic powers of this present darkness, against the spiritual forces of evil in the heavenly places" (Eph. 6:12) (Weaver; Yoder; Wink, *The Powers That Be*, 63–111; Boyd, "Kingdom"). Among other things, the contemporary reinvigoration of the NT's concept of the powers is helping Christians today wake up to and resist the demonic pull of structural evils such as nationalism, militarism, racism, classism, consumerism, and individualism.

See also Eschatology and Ethics

Bibliography

Arnold, C. E. *Powers of Darkness: Principalities and Powers in Paul's Letters*. InterVarsity, 1992; Boyd, G. "Christus Victor View." Pages 23–66 in *The Nature of the Atonement: Four Views*, ed. J. Beilby and P. Eddy. InterVarsity, 2006; idem. *God at War: The Bible and Spiritual Conflict*. InterVarsity, 1997; idem. "The Kingdom as a Political-Spiritual Revolution." *CTR* 6, no. 2 (2008): 23–41; Caird, G. B. *Principalities and Powers: A Study in Pauline Theology*. Clarendon, 1956; König, A. *New and Greater Things: Reevaluating the Biblical Message on Creation*. University of South Africa, 1988; Ling, T. *The Significance of Satan*. SPCK, 1961; Russell, D. *The Method and Message of Jewish Apocalyptic*. Westminster, 1964; Weaver, J. *The Nonviolent Atonement*. Eerdmans, 2001; Wink, W. *Naming the Powers: The Language of Power in the New Testament*. Fortress, 1984; idem. *The Powers That Be: Theology for a New Millennium*. Doubleday, 1998; Yates, R. "The Powers of Evil in the New Testament." *EvQ* 52 (1980): 97–111; Yoder, J. *The Politics of Jesus: Vicit Agnus Noster*. 2nd ed. Eerdmans, 1994.

Greg Boyd

Practices

In his study of the history of the idea of "theory and practice," Nicholas Lobkowicz distinguished between the lived realities of theory and practice and various theories about theory and practice (xii–xiii). Thinking about practices, religious or otherwise, has the same kind of complexity associated with it. Practices themselves are observable phenomena of particular kinds of teleological human action in specific historical and communal contexts. Theories about practices aim to provide interpretive and normative frameworks for understanding or criticizing these forms of human activity. Yet such a distinction may be too neat and tidy in that it overlooks the perplexing fact that practices and theoretical perspectives used to guide or to observe them are always deeply intertwined. Merely attempting to define what counts as a practice for purposes of observation (i.e., its boundaries, substantial elements, and function or purpose) always arises from a perspective imbued with normative theory about what constitutes the nature of a practice or practices by some observer (Dewey 491–92). Similarly, whatever perspective informs the observer's notion of practice inevitably arises out of experience with a distinct constellation of practices.

In recent decades many Christian scholars and ecclesial leaders have developed a strong interest in religious practices as a generative source for various creative intellectual and practical initiatives. This emphasis on religious practices draws from wider discussions about practice in the fields of philosophy, ethics, theology, cultural anthropology, and sociology. Much of the contemporary discussion about religious practices emphasizes the importance of fostering the development of high-commitment Christian "contrast communities" that offer a clear witness to Jesus Christ and the core values of the Christian life over and against the prevailing corrupt, secular, or anti-Christian values and practices of the larger society.

Definitions

Contemporary Christian scholars and ecclesial leaders use the term *practice* in a variety of ways. In one common usage, it refers to an entire pattern of behaviors and interactions to describe the entirety of the Christian life, akin to the practice of medicine or law. In this usage, the sum total of skills, theories, histories, cases, and judgments constitutes the practice of Christian discipleship. Often, this usage implies a bias toward concrete, communal action over and against merely abstract theological reflection that is disconnected from the life of the church or individual Christian actions in a particular social and cultural context.

A second usage of the term *practice* by Christian scholars and ecclesial leaders is not so much an entire way of religious or professional life as a coordinating center for a constellation of interrelated constituent religious activities. Recent work by Craig Dykstra, Dorothy Bass, and several of their colleagues uses the term in this way. As an example, the practice of testimony might include the activities of preaching, teaching, and various kinds of faith-oriented conversation without being reducible to any one of these discrete activities (see Long). In this way of handling the idea of practice, the Christian life of individuals and communities is made up of many overlapping and interlocking teleological behaviors sustained over time, each of which coordinates several discrete and related actions.

The various discussions of religious practices related to the second usage of the term *practice* tend to be influenced by the neo-Aristotelian virtue ethics of Alasdair MacIntyre, who defined a practice as "any coherent and complex form of socially established cooperative human activity through which goods internal to that form of activity are realised in the course of trying to achieve those standards of excellence which are appropriate to, and partially definitive of, that form of activity, with the result that human powers to achieve excellence, and human conceptions of the end and goods involved, are systematically extended" (175).

MacIntyre's notion of practice emphasizes that practices are communal, progressive, and teleological. Many Roman Catholics and Protestants have found MacIntyre's approach compatible with traditional theological understandings of the nature, character, and purpose of the Christian life (Bass 30 n. 11). Some religious appropriations of MacIntyre's definition of practices tend to deemphasize both the role of abstract or dogmatic theology and the centrality of the priest or minister; in contrast, the focused religious formation of the community as a whole as it engages in certain prescribed practices takes center stage. Dogmatic theology and the clergy both continue to play meaningful roles, but only insofar as they support the formational and witnessing dimensions of the religious practices of the Christian community.

Christian scholars and ecclesial leaders who use the term *practice* in this second orientation guard against latent or overt anti-intellectualism, which can arise from the foregrounding of practice and action, by highlighting the ways in which practices contain, convey, and cultivate theory. The theological reflection promulgated in a religious-practices approach often is held up as superior to other forms of theological theory because it is grounded in, disciplined by, and tethered to the actual life of the Christian community. Further, it is asserted that theological theory arising out of religious practices recovers an older, traditional conception of theology that is inherently and pervasively practical in character (see Charry; Farley 85–102).

A third usage of the term *practice* among Christian scholars and ecclesial leaders refers to a narrowly defined or focused form of activity. In this usage, religious practices have to do with active engagement in a certain discrete pattern of action. For example, one might engage in specific focused actions extended over periods of varying lengths of time, such as reading the Bible, praying, fasting, or offering acts of compassion. The emphasis in this way of using the term lies in the concretion of action. Practice and concrete action in this usage are so closely related as to be virtually identical.

A fourth usage of the term *practice* by Christian scholars and ecclesial leaders arises out of Marxian and Marxist notions of praxis (Marx 154–65). This term usually signifies something of the complex, reciprocal interplay between theory and practice, particularly with respect to the effects of social class, race, gender, or sexual identity on human flourishing. Those who draw on critical social theory criticize the MacIntyre-inspired approach to religious practices for focusing too much on the Christian community itself and not attending sufficiently to wider issues of justice and compassion in relation to society at large. The lack of a significant place for critical social theory has raised concern that a religious-practices approach bears an inherently conservative agenda that, in the end, merely supports the social, political, and economic status quo. Instead of a Neo-Aristotelian approach to religious practices, some Christian scholars and ecclesial leaders express a strong preference for the Marxist-inspired notion of "praxis" that intends to contribute to the fundamental reorganization of societal structures in the direction of justice, equality, and compassion.

Engaging discussions about religious practices in an effective and constructive manner requires a certain degree of clarity about the ways in which terms such as *practice* and *religious practices* are used. Clarity about the language employed in discussions of practice is essential, but it is not sufficient for robust analysis or for constructive proposals. Additionally, some attention must be given to a range of tensions associated with religious practices.

Tensions Related to Religious Practices

The Christian scholar or the ecclesial leader who wishes to embrace or analyze a religious-practices approach to lived realities of Christian communities in relation to their internal and external relations must negotiate a series of tensions connected with religious practices, including the relationship of theory and practice, the interplay of uniformity and diversity, and the connection between communal and individual engagement. First, one must address the tension between theory and practice. Borrowing from Immanuel Kant's famous dictum about the necessary interplay of percepts and concepts in the production of thought, we can say that theories without practices are empty, and practices without theories are blind (Kant 193). In the end, theory and practice must and always do go together. Specifying the exact nature of their interplay provides the central challenge for negotiating this tension.

Traditional Protestant emphases on the primacy of divine revelation, the centrality of Scripture, and the initiative of God often have combined to yield an "applied theory" approach to religious practices. In this view, the truth of the divinely inspired and biblically attested gospel message shapes Christian practice. The arrow of influence moves unidirectionally from theory to practice. In this very traditional and often conservative orientation little attention is given to the complexities of context, whether of the biblical text, the theological vision, or the "target" of contemporary ecclesial or society action; the contours of divine revelation provide the determining factor in this orientation to theory and practice.

Another approach to the relationship between theory and practice envisions a multivalent and multilayered reciprocal interplay between them. Often drawing from notions of praxis derived from critical social theory, this approach espouses a bidirectional influence between theory and practice: practices shape theories just as much as theories shape practices. This approach emphasizes the dynamic interrelationship of theory and practice. In this view, often found in liberal Protestantism, the vicissitudes of context and the challenges of hermeneutics tend toward both a mitigation of substantive and metaphysically normative claims and a decided preference for contemporary experience as the determinative norm.

An additional way to approach the tensive relationship between theory and practice gives primacy to practice, maintaining that practice gives rise to theory or that practice is in some significant way "theory laden" (Browning 6). Prosper of Aquitaine provided one of the earliest articulations of this approach when, in arguing for the primacy of prayer and worship in the development of doctrine, he contended that the pattern of prayer (*lex orandi*) gives rise to the pattern of belief (*lex credendi*) (Kavanagh xii; see also Schmemann). This way of negotiating the tension holds that all doctrine—at least that which pertains to the life and flourishing of the church—arises from, can be resolved back into, and ultimately serves religious practices.

Second, any engagement with religious practices must attend to and negotiate tensions between uniformity and diversity. Religious practices derive their normative character from Scripture and various ecclesial traditions. The authoritative teachings and narratives of Scripture determine both the range of possible religious practices that are consonant with the core vision and ethical norms of the Jewish and Christian traditions and their normative shape. Similarly, but in a usually subordinate manner, particular religious traditions also contribute to the shaping of normative character of religious practices. The boundaries of orthopraxis arising from biblical interpretation and from awareness of accumulated tradition provide the terms within which communities of faith should engage in particular religious practices, largely without regard to contexts or circumstances. Much of the formal and informal teaching that takes place within religious communities focuses on inducting the faithful and their children into normatively prescribed patterns of engagement with religious practices.

Religious practices as engaged by actual communities and individuals do not take place in abstraction from historical, social, cultural, political, geographical, and economic realities. The actual instantiation of religious practices by communities and individuals always varies to some degree from the prescribed norms of Scripture and tradition. Context and the idiosyncrasies of practitioners always determine the ways in which actual people appropriate and engage in religious practices (see de Certeau). Michel de Certeau, in *The Practice of Everyday Life*, provided a helpful distinction between "strategies" and "tactics." For de Certeau, strategies are the imposed norms of the powerful and the established on the weak or the subjected; tactics, by contrast, are the improvised, ad hoc, and often artful appropriations of imposed strategies by the weak and objectified. In relation to religious practices, de Certeau's distinction illuminates how actual religious practitioners appropriate the norms imposed by Scripture and tradition in ways that often are unique, messy, and ad hoc. Theologian Kathryn Tanner similarly observes about practices that they are "quite open-ended, in the sense of being rather undefined in their exact ideational dimensions and in the sense of being always in the process of re-formation in response to new circumstances" (229–30). The implications of this distinction make clear that religious practices can never be fully understood solely in relation to their normative aspect as derived from Scripture and tradition; religious practices are always a pastiche of the uniformly normative and the contextually diverse. Any treatment of religious practices that attends to only one aspect of this tension will distort their genuine complexity and richness.

Third, any analytical or constructive focus on religious practices must attend to the connection between communal and individual engagement. Communities of faith serve as both seedbeds and stewards of religious practices across centuries and even millennia. Religious practices belong primarily to communities. Most religious practices grow out of and support the ongoing vitality of religious communities. Prior to appropriation by individuals, religious practices find expression in communal contexts, usually in corporate worship or liturgy.

At the same time, communities are made up of individual adherents and their networks of kinship and friendship. While religious communities are always more than the sum total of their individual members, they are never less than the aggregation of those unique persons. Each adherent of a religious community participates in a religious practice in a way that makes sense to him or her, given the specifics of life narrative, personality, gender, likes and dislikes, racial and ethnic identity, economic circumstances, and cultural affinities. No one person engages in a practice in exactly the same way as another person, even if the outwardly observable behavior may appear identical. The meaning made and the particular instantiation of any given religious practice varies from person to person within a religious community.

It should be noted that not every person who engages in one or more religious practices identifies with a particular religious community. Through the widespread availability of information via print, visual, and digital media, not to mention word of mouth and informal observation, many people who lack affiliation with a particular religious community engage in religious practices of various kinds. For example, many people pray and read Scripture who have no membership in any religious community. The recent phenomena of globalization, the digital revolution, and the marbling of cultures have produced significant numbers of people who claim to be "spiritual without being religious" (Eck 4–5). Decoded, this phrase often means that religiously unaffiliated people engage in one or several religious practices in order to find self-fulfillment, meaning, or transcendent experience apart from particular religious communities.

A closely related phenomenon has come into increasing prominence in the contemporary situation: people who appropriate and engage in religious practices from multiple religious traditions. With the greater awareness, access, and curiosity that comes with globalization, ease of migration, multireligious families, and the digital revolution, many individuals who continue to claim primary affiliation with one particular religious community experiment with engagement in selected particular religious practices of other communities within one's own religion or of religions other than one's own. Hybridity and creative juxtaposition of religious practices from a dazzling array of religious sources have emerged as significant themes in the contemporary situation. Such a changed and rapidly changing situation presents new challenges for traditionally bounded religious communities, particularly in relation to the issue of uniformity and normativity in relation to religious practices.

Religious Practices in Relation to Scripture and Ethics

Religious practices play a key role in both Scripture and ethics. Normative practices central to both the Jewish and the Christian traditions derive primarily from Scripture. Narratives, paraenetic material, and wisdom literature provide the norms and range of acceptable variations for religious practices of these religious communities.

Similarly, religious practices play a key role in Christian ethics. Ethical visions and norms exert shaping influence on the range and norms of practices pertinent to Christian communities and individuals in particular times and places. While religious practices play some role in every approach to Christian ethics, the Aristotelian-inspired "virtue ethics" orientation to Christian ethics makes religious practices central to the enterprise (see Hauerwas).

Religious practices have to do with more than simply the contents or subject matter of Scripture and ethics. The enterprise of reading and interpreting Scripture through the ages has given rise to a significant set of religious practices. Particular religious practices for reading Scripture devotionally, liturgically, homiletically, scholarly, ethically, and politically have emerged over time. As with Scripture, participation in the discipline of Christian ethics has given rise to distinctive practices and attendant norms for interpreting and responding to moral problems or situations.

Scripture and ethics considered conjointly in their interplay in relation to religious practices have a complex history. For example, scriptural teachings and norms have given rise to many of the practices associated with Christian ethics. Further, for Christian ethics, Scripture provides the primary aims, norms, and guidelines for analysis, evaluation, and construction of ethical visions or programs. Conversely, reflection in the area of Christian ethics has shed considerable light on the meaning of Scripture. A practices perspective frequently has opened up new levels of insight into key or difficult passages of Scripture. Sometimes, as in the cases of the issues of slavery and of the roles of women in church and society, ethical reflection has challenged traditional interpretations of texts and brought to light deeper readings of texts.

Strengths and Weaknesses of a Practices Approach

A religious-practices emphasis in relation to Christian life and belief affords a range of benefits for both academy and religious communities. Primarily, this approach makes central lived realities of Christian community and individual discipleship. It underscores the importance of action, commitment, and embodiment in Christian belief and life. Further, it provides something of a check on tendencies toward abstraction and decontextualization associated with certain idealist forms of theological reflection. It also tends to emphasize the central role of the entirety of the Christian community, not just members of the clergy or Christian academics.

At the same time, a religious-practices approach to Christian life and belief has some significant weaknesses. By putting so much emphasis on the action of communities and individuals, it perpetually runs the risk both of slipping into a "works righteousness" orientation to Christian faith and of deemphasizing the central importance of divine action in human life. A further risk associated with a religious-practices approach involves the devaluation of contemplation, beauty, and serendipitous dimensions of Christian belief and life.

Conclusion

The religious-practices approach to Christian belief and life that has emerged in recent decades has fostered much richness in various branches of theological study, not the least in the fields of Bible and ethics, and in the life of local churches. It has inspired deeper insight into Scripture and has opened up renewed appreciation for the contours of Christian faith as expressed in the patterns of life in Christian communities. Despite some limitations and dangers, the recent emphasis on religious practices promises to function as a fecund source of creativity in biblical studies and Christian ethics for the foreseeable future.

See also Character; Ecclesiology and Ethics; Habit; Hospitality; Liturgy and Ethics; Praxis; Teleological Theories of Ethics; Virtue(s); Virtue Ethics

Bibliography

Bass, D., ed. *Practicing Our Faith: A Way of Life for a Searching People*. Jossey-Bass, 1997; idem. *Receiving the Day: Christian Practices for Opening the Gift of Time*. Jossey-Bass, 2000; idem. "Ways of Life Abundant." Pages 21–40 in *For Life Abundant: Practical Theology, Theological Education, and Christian Ministry*, ed. D. Bass and C. Dykstra. Eerdmans, 2008; Browning, D. *A Fundamental Practical Theology: Descriptive and Strategic Proposals*. Fortress, 1991; Charry, E. *By the Renewing of Your Minds: The Pastoral Function of Doctrine*. Oxford University Press, 1997; de Certeau, M. *The Practice of Everyday Life*. Trans. S. Rendall. University of California Press, 1984; Dewey, J. *Logic: The Theory of Inquiry*. Holt, 1938; Dykstra, C. *Growing in the Life of Faith: Education and Christian Practices*. Geneva Press, 1999; Eck, D. *A New Religious America: How a "Christian Country" Has Become the World's Most Religiously Diverse Nation*. HarperSanFrancisco, 2001; Farley, E. *The Fragility of Knowledge: Theological Education in the Church and the University*. Fortress, 1988; Hauerwas, S. *The Hauerwas Reader*. Ed. J. Berkman and M. Cartwright. Duke University Press, 2001; Kant, I. *Critique of Pure Reason*. Trans. P. Guyer and A. Wood. Cambridge University Press, 1998 [1787]; Kavanagh, A. *The Shape of Baptism: The Rite of Christian Initiation*. SRRCC 1. Pueblo, 1978; Lobkowicz, N. *Theory and Practice: History of a Concept from Aristotle to Marx*. University of Notre Dame Press, 1967; Long, T. *Testimony: Talking Ourselves into Being Christian*. Jossey-Bass, 2004; MacIntyre, A. *After Virtue: A Study in Moral Theory*. 3rd ed. University of Notre Dame Press, 2007; Marx, K. "The German Ideology: Part I." Pages 146–200 in *The Marx-Engels Reader*, ed. R. Tucker. 2nd ed. Norton, 1978; Schmemann, A. *Introduction to Liturgical Theology*. Trans. A. Moorhouse. 3rd ed. St. Vladimir's Seminary Press, 1986; Tanner, K. "Theological Reflection and Christian Practices." Pages 228–42 in *Practicing Theology: Beliefs and Practices in Christian Life*, ed. M. Volf and D. Bass. Eerdmans, 2002.

Gordon Mikoski

Praxis

The term *praxis* signifies a complexity and multiplicity of meanings. Its most traditional definition has been "practice" or "action." Aristotle is believed to have been the first to use *praxis* as a philosophical term. For him, *praxis* referred to the public activity in which free men (not women or children) engaged within the political realm. Convinced that pure reason was insufficient in achieving knowledge, Aristotle saw praxis combining rational reflection with activity within the polis. In effect, praxis was the ideal mean between practical reason and virtuous action. Praxis was further nuanced by Augustine, who attempted to balance praxis (a life of practicing Christian deeds) with contemplating the afterlife. As medieval times began, *praxis* ceased to mean "how we ought to live" and instead referred to how we must live in our present temporary sojourn through this earth as we prepare for the eschatological hope. With the rediscovering of Aristotle in the twelfth century, Thomas Aquinas attempted to reconcile Aristotelian thought with Christianity by making practical truth an extension of theoretical truth. As such, praxis became the application of theory. By the nineteenth century, thinkers such as Karl Marx further developed the concept of praxis as a practical response to the economic consequences of industrialization. Praxis was a way of knowing and a way of affecting reality. Through praxis, the proletariat could claim their role as "historic subjects."

Today, the term *praxis* usually is connected with theologies of liberation, theologies that seriously considered Marx's challenge for a "philosophy of praxis." Praxis attempts to move beyond practice or action toward a lifestyle that demonstrates how the gospel of Christ is to be lived. Christianity becomes what we do, more so than what we believe. In the doing of justice, theology is developed as a reflection of the doing. Rather than having action flow from theological thought (the deductive norm common within most Eurocentric theological traditions), praxis occurs when theological reflection is brought to bear on the liberating actions committed. And while the ultimate hope may be a messianic perfect justice, for now, such justice serves as a touchstone for Christian praxis in the quest for God's will.

For those engaged in praxis-based theologies, knowing what is "truth" remains insufficient for the Christian life. The dichotomy between theology and practice is collapsed as the understanding of theology moves beyond faith formulas or dogmas. The purpose of theology is praxis, the doing of theology, known as "orthopraxis" (correct action). Thus, there exists a greater emphasis on orthopraxis than on "orthodoxy" (correct doctrine). More important than developing philosophical abstract concepts about the things of divinity, those engaged in praxis-based theologies strive to ascertain the meaning of human existence by being faithful to God's calling in God's overall objective of redeeming creation from the power of sin, with sin being understood as private and corporate oppressive acts that cause alienation from God and community. The starting point for orthopraxis is found within the space and experience of disenfranchised people. The purpose of doing theology, or orthopraxis, is not to grasp mystery but rather to change the structures causing oppression for the hope and sake of possibly liberating those who live under the yoke of injustices.

For liberationists, to be a Christian is to do justice-based praxis via a three-stage process involving a seeing-judging-acting methodology. Praxis marks the start of theological reflection for the purpose of achieving emancipatory transformation of oppressive social structures and situations. Because praxis is political, it seeks liberation from sin, specifically the corporate sins responsible for oppressive structures. This liberative praxis, as synthesis of the dialectical relationship between theory and practice, is conducted by and for the oppressed participating freely within the polis. To walk with and be committed to the oppressed is to discover Christ, who is present among them. Praxis, according to Gustavo Gutiérrez, can be understood as (1) "socio-political-economic," an expression of the oppressed breaking away from the subjugation caused by these structures; (2) "historical-utopian," an intention of the oppressed to determine their own destiny; and (3) "Christian," an interpretation of liberation as freedom from sin (personal and communal) and as communion, based on love, with God and neighbor.

Theologies arising in the United States that seek liberation from oppressive structures that emerge from Asian American, black, feminist, Latino/Latina, and Native American communities usually are praxis-based. These theological expressions become the reflection of the praxis in which the faith community engages, a praxis in which the goal is to bring about liberation from both corporate and individual sins. For these communities, to do theology is to participate in the actions of God, actions motivated by God's love and best illustrated in the figure of Jesus the Christ. Such praxes are both prophetic (engaging the oppressive structures of the dominant culture) and pastoral (consciousness-raising among the disenfranchised as a form of empowerment).

See also Liberationist Ethics; Practice

Miguel A. De La Torre

Prayer of Manasseh *See* Orthodox Ethics

Preferential Option for the Poor

The phrase "preferential option for the poor" became popular at the Second General Conference of Latin American Bishops in Puebla, Mexico, in 1979; however, some historians and theologians find its origin at the previous Episcopal Conference in Medellín, Colombia, in 1968, where Gustavo Gutiérrez, one of the advisers to the Medellín meeting, gave a presentation delineating the foundations for his theology, which was labeled as "theology of liberation." A few years later, his presentation became a book published in English in 1973 under the title *A Theology of Liberation: History, Politics, and Salvation*, in which he explains this phrase. Regardless of its historic origin, Gutiérrez was clear about its theological origins; for him, the phrase is grounded in pastoral care—that is, pastoral care and concern for those who are poor. For this reason, the phrase "preferential option for the poor" has always been grounded in pastoral theology, which seeks practical ecclesiological and pastoral ways to respond to poverty-stricken parishioners in the context of Latin America. Thus, the preferential option for the poor is much more than an abstract theological concept; it is a call to action and a challenge to the church and society to respond to the cry of the needy by changing the circumstances and structures that keep the poor in deplorable conditions, unable to satisfy their most basic needs.

Although the phrase is practical in nature and requires action, it is also grounded in significant biblical and theological reflection. The basic premise and foundation of the phrase are rooted in God's character and God's protection of "the least." For those who embrace the preferential option for the poor, God is always on the side of the poor—the least, the marginal, and the powerless. For them, there is clear evidence that God favors the poor by offering special attention, care, and protection to them. But it is this very point that leads many to criticize this theological approach as unfair because of its favoritism of the poor, which the word *preferential* seems to imply. The notion that God favors the poor raises concerns for some who affirm that God has no favorites (Rom. 2:11). Furthermore, others think that portraying God's character as opting for the poor denies the universality and inclusiveness of God's divine love and grace. If God demonstrates special care and affection for the least, one is led to think that God cares more for the poor than other groups. These two points of view are crucial in denying the moral significance and claims of the preferential option for the poor.

In responding to this type of criticism, Gutiérrez and other liberation theologians highlight the importance of the practical aspects of the words *preference* and *option* in the controversial phrase and in their theology. Also, they point out the importance of their social context as the starting point. It is clear that their initial arguments are centered in responding theologically and pastorally to the needs of the poor in Latin America; however, they do not separate their context from the core and centrality of their moral claims. For Gutiérrez and other theologians, when God favors the poor, it does not mean that God overlooks the rich and powerful, nor does it mean that God's love for wealthy and powerful persons is placed at a lower level than God's love for the poor. For them, the explanation is simple and is centered on distributive justice based on need. They argue that God favors, protects, and opts for the poor because they have greater needs, both immediate and long-range. By contrast, the argument that God should care for each person equally regardless of economic and social condition would affirm and portray God as one who overlooks those who are dying (because their basic needs are not met) for the sake of treating everyone equally. For Gutiérrez and other theologians, such a view is inconsistent with God's character as depicted in the Scriptures, since divine justice is a response to human need. In their interpretation, God's character is such that God cannot (and will not) remain neutral or inactive in the face of negligence and destitution; God works proactively and cares and protects the poor because they are in need and nobody is caring for them.

God's action is twofold: it provides immediate relief to the poor and it denounces the oppression that is at work in society, social structures, and local churches in the form of failure to care for the poor. In this interpretation, God's action does not mean that God opts for and/or favors the poor by excluding the rich and powerful; the opposite is true. By reaching out to the least, God is being "all inclusive," which is demonstrated in this very action. In other words, if God is able to love the least, those at the very bottom of society, then by doing so God is proving the universality of divine grace and love extended to all; that is, by reaching the bottom, God has reached everyone from the top down. Furthermore, God's action and call include both the poor and the rich; for the poor, God takes action to fulfill their needs, while God calls the rich to share their wealth with those in need.

Thus, the preferential option for the poor is the result of conscientious study of the Scriptures in the face of poverty in Latin America. However, many in other contexts who have followed this approach have identified the powerless in their societies and have provided practical responses by challenging social structures and by promoting a needs-based justice.

See also Liberation; Liberationist Ethics; Oppression; Poverty and Poor

Bibliography

Gutiérrez, G. *Evangelización y Opción por los Pobres*. Ediciones Paulinas, 1987; idem. *A Theology of Liberation: History, Politics, and Salvation*. Trans. and ed. C. Inda and J. Eagleson. Orbis, 1973; Segundo, J. *Liberation of Theology*. Trans. J. Drury. Orbis, 1976.

Hugo Magallanes

Prejudice

Prejudice is an attitude, judgment, or feeling about a person, either positive or negative, that emerges from stereotypic beliefs held about the group to which the person belongs. Stereotypes drive prejudice because they involve generalizations that are factually incorrect in that people from out-groups do not uniformly possess the same characteristics. Discrimination, the behavioral manifestation of prejudice, involves responding to a person on the basis of the person's group membership, not the individual facts about the person. Thus, stereotypes lead to the discriminatory behavior that manifests prejudice (Jones).

Negative Prejudice in the Bible

Some of the discussion about prejudice and biblical ethics concerns the degree to which biblical teachings contain or endorse prejudicial attitudes about various groups in society. For example, the so-called curse of Ham in Gen. 9:20–27 was used as a justification for antiblack sentiment and slavery for generations. In this text, Ham fails to cover his father Noah's exposed, drunken body, and in response Noah curses Ham's son Canaan to slavery. Racist interpretations of the story extended this curse to all of the black peoples listed in the adjacent Table of Nations in Gen. 10, though that account concerns the relationships among the peoples in the ancient Near East and especially the relationship of Israelites to Canaanites, and never makes an association between skin color and slavery. Although Canaanites stand in opposition to Israelites, one scholar notes that other voices in the tradition undermine this view, pointing out that the characterization of named Canaanites in the conquest narrative is strikingly positive (Davis). In the NT, Jesus' caustic and stereotypic attitude toward the Canaanite woman in Matt. 15:22–29 // Mark 7:25–29 generates no little interpretive uneasiness, though the episode may represent a critical moment in which Jesus learns about the broader scope of his mission from "the least of these" (cf. Matt. 7:5) (Scott). Titus 1:12–13 describes a stereotypic generalization about Cretans, and 1 Tim. 2:12–14, which makes a similar sweeping statement about the gullibility of women, is the subject of endless debate in some circles.

Scriptural Teaching against Negative Prejudice

Many see teaching about the poor and other marginalized segments of Israelite society as analogous to and representative of biblical attitudes against prejudice. In this vein, the OT concern with attitudes toward aliens or foreigners in ancient Israel is especially important. The consensus in nineteenth- and twentieth-century scholarship is that the *gēr* ("alien"; LXX: *prosēlytos*) is a non-Israelite living within Israelite territory, though more recent scholarship disputes the exact identity of *gērîm* (Bultmann; Ramírez Kidd). The *gēr* often appears in the triad "*gēr*, widow, orphan," where it is associated with a concern for social justice relative to the most helpless members of society (Deut. 10:17–19; 14:29; 24:17–21; 27:19; cf. Exod. 12:48; 22:21; 23:9; Lev. 19:10, 34; Ezek. 47:22–23; Isa. 14:1). In the NT, Jesus models concern for the poor and marginalized throughout the Gospel narratives (Matt. 5:3 // Luke 6:20; Matt. 19:16–22 // Mark 10:17–22 // Luke 18:18–23; Mark 12:41–44 // Luke 21:1–4), and Luke's emphasis on the poor is prominent throughout (e.g., Luke 4:16–19; 14:12–14, 21; 19:1–10). His treatment of Samaritans in six episodes is especially pertinent to the subject of prejudice, given traditional hostility between Israelites and Samaritans (Luke 9:51–56; 10:25–37; 17:11–19; Acts 1:8; 8:4–25; 15:3), and the ethnicity of the exemplar of the good neighbor in the parable of the good Samaritan would have been particularly shocking in this regard. Paul is also sensitive to the power dynamics that accompany manifestations of negative prejudice. His mediation of disputes in the community between the strong and the weak, and the haves and the have-nots, is invariably addressed to the powerful (Rom. 14:14–23; 1 Cor. 8:9–12; 10:28; 11:18–22). According to Paul, attitudes of superiority and inferiority threaten the functioning of the church as the body of Christ (1 Cor. 12:21–26), and his description of the unity of a multicultural people in Christ figures prominently in contemporary reflection on racial and ethnic prejudice in modern society and in the church (Gal. 3:28; cf. Eph. 2:11–22). Finally, in the General Epistles, Jas. 2:1–13 has one of the most explicit injunctions against prejudice or partiality in the NT, describing it as a violation of the "royal law" that has eschatological consequences (Felder).

See also Discrimination; Racism

Bibliography

Bultmann, C. *Der Fremde im antiken Juda: Eine Untersuchung zum sozialen Typenbegriff "ger" und seinem Bedeutungswandel in der alttestamentlichen Gesetzgebung.* FRLANT 153. Vandenhoeck & Ruprecht, 1992; Davis, E. "Critical Traditioning: Seeking an Inner Biblical Hermeneutic." *AThR* 82 (2000): 733–51; Felder, C. "Partiality and God's Law: An Exegesis of James 2:1–13." *JRT* 39 (1982–83): 51–69; Hays, J. *From Every People and Nation: A Biblical Theology of Race.* InterVarsity, 2003; Jones, J. *Prejudice and Racism.* 2nd ed. McGraw-Hill, 1997; Ramírez Kidd, J. *Alterity and Identity in Israel: The "ger" in the Old Testament.* BZAW 283. De Gruyter, 1999; Scott, J. "Matthew 15.21–28: A Test-Case for Jesus' Manners." *JSNT 63* (1996): 21–44.

Love L. Sechrest

Pride

Pride is a central concept in Christianity. It is one of the seven deadly sins, often regarded as the most basic description of sin and as the fount of all other sins. It represents powerfully the nature of our condition before God and reminds us of how our sin is acted out in our relationship to God, to one another, to creation, and to ourselves. Pride has been variously defined as inordinate self-esteem, boasting, rebellion, and more, but if we allow ourselves to be instructed by Scripture, we will hold any definition loosely so that the narrative guides our discernment of pride.

Pride may be observed in the attitudes and behavior of humankind. Reinhold Niebuhr pursues this course with power and insight. He examines manifestations of pride following a traditional catalog of pride of power, knowledge, and virtue, deriving from the last an additional manifestation of spiritual pride. Niebuhr's exposition and analysis expose the phenomena of pride in persons and society. But beyond claiming biblical warrant for pride being the basic sin, Niebuhr rarely draws from Scripture. Niebuhr's account is a powerful phenomenological account of sin as pride, but for all its insight, it does not give us a full scriptural account.

If we are to think biblically about pride, we may be guided by two approaches. One approach submits to the passages where pride is explicitly named and described, usually with an accompanying declaration of God's judgment. We may call this the exegetical-theological approach. Another approach submits our inquiry to stories of pride in persons and societies that also describe God's judgment. We may call this the narratological approach.

In the exegetical-theological approach, we have a number of passages to turn to, especially in the OT. There the most instructive verses are found in Proverbs (8:13; 11:2; 13:10; 14:3; 16:18; 29:23). In these passages pride is tied to folly, teaching us that the proud make a basic error in their judgment of reality and in measuring one's place within the world that God has created. As a result of this error in judgment and perception, the proud contribute to disorder, breeding contention and furthering the development of evil ways in creation. In Proverbs we learn also that pride manifests itself bodily, in haughty eyes and lips. These descriptions may be extended as figures of speech, but we must not lose the physical reference. Pride shows itself outwardly in the appearance of proud lips as well as the speech that comes from those lips, in the cast of proud eyes as well as the way that the world is viewed through those eyes. Finally, in Proverbs we learn also that Yahweh's order in creation, wisdom itself, works against the proud and brings them to destruction. This declaration occurs in the midst of recognizing the apparent prosperity and success of the proud. (See also Ps. 73. Proverbs and this psalm teach us the limitations of a phenomenological account of pride.) But those instructed in wisdom know that the divine order bestows blessing and life on those who fear Yahweh and submit themselves to wisdom. The proud do not fear Yahweh and do not submit themselves to wisdom. They are already in Sheol.

In the narratological approach, we have many stories in the OT. Although the word *pride* does not occur in the passage, Gen. 3 provides a piercing account. There, our first parents exalt themselves and by their actions declare themselves to be creators, not creatures ("you will be like God" [Gen. 3:5]). This prideful act disorders God's creation. It breaks the proper relationship between the Creator and the creature, thus bringing death to humans. It breaks our proper relationship to one another, thus introducing conflict and mistrust. Pride also disorders our relationship to the rest of creation, as God describes both the increase in birth pains as we seek to fulfill the mandate to fill the earth and the toil that will be required for us to rule over the rest of creation. Finally, pride disorders each person's relationship to self, dividing each individual so that each is ashamed. This narrative reveals to us the fundamental brokenness of the sin of pride and indicates the devastating trajectory that self-exaltation works out in the history of creation.

To this narratological approach Karl Barth adds a significant development: an extended narratological-christological practice of interpretation. In following this practice, Barth demonstrates its power to witness to God's work in our world. Here the emphasis is not on the human predicament but rather on God's gracious revelation of our predicament and his redemptive work in Christ. After submitting ourselves to this story, we can turn to our lives in the world and see the work of pride with greater clarity, depth, and breadth in the context of God's work in Christ.

For Barth's narratological-christological practice of interpretation, the sin of pride is best exposed by the coming of Jesus Christ. In this act, God the Son humbles himself to become human. In contrast to human self-exaltation that is the entrance of sin, God's self-humbling brings reconciliation. What could be more revelatory of human pride than this act of God? And what could be more prideful—and sinful—than unbelief in this act of God? In the light cast by this coming of the Son we see most fully the pride of human beings: not in pride that rejects God's order in turning to folly rather than wisdom, or in our self-exaltation as creators rather than creatures, but in our unbelief in the salvation accomplished for us and revealed to us in the self-humiliation of God in Christ. Here is the pride of humankind fully exposed to the judgment of God's grace.

One more aspect of Barth's exposition must be noted for us to understand more fully the sin of pride in the church's tradition. As a complement to the sin of pride, Barth exposits the sin of sloth as the mirror image of pride. Whereas pride is the self-exaltation of the human being, sloth is the self-abasement of the human being. Both are sins that misconstrue the relationship between God and humanity and thus between humanity and all else. Valerie Saiving persuasively argues that we must not concentrate so completely on pride as sin that we miss its mirror image, sloth.

At this point, we may be able to understand why Christianity regards pride as sinful and humility as righteous, in contrast to Aristotle, Nietzsche, and others who regard pride as a virtue and humility as a vice. For Christians, the exaltation of the human is accomplished by God in Christ. We may, then, boast in Christ, as Paul does, but we do so with a humility that is not feigned but arises from faith in Christ that properly orients our lives to God and redeems us from self-exaltation and self-abasement.

See also Cruciformity; Humility; Meekness; Self; Seven Deadly Sins; Sin; Sloth

Bibliography

Augustine. *Concerning the City of God against the Pagans*. Trans. H. Bettenson. Penguin Books, 1972; Barth, K. *Church Dogmatics*. Vol. IV/1, §60.2. T&T Clark, 1956; Bonhoeffer, D. *Creation and Fall: A Theological Exposition of Genesis 1–3*. Ed. J. de Gruchy. Trans. D. Bax. Fortress, 1997; Cassian, John. *The Conferences*. ACW 57. Paulist Press, 1997; Lewis, C. S. "The Great Sin." Pages 121–28 in *Mere Christianity*. HarperCollins, 2001; Niebuhr, R. *Human Nature*. Vol. 1 of *The Nature and Destiny of Man: A Christian Interpretation*. LTE. Westminster John Knox, 1996; Saiving, V. "The Human Situation: A Feminine View." Pages 25–42 in *Womanspirit Rising: A Feminist Reader in Religion*, ed. C. Christ and J. Plaskow. Harper & Row, 1979; Thomas Aquinas. *Summa theologiae* II-I, q. 84; Waltke, B. *Proverbs*. 2 vols. NICOT. Eerdmans, 2004–5.

Jonathan R. Wilson

Priestly Literature

The Priestly material in the OT principally comprises the book of Leviticus, broadly understood (the "Priestly" and "Holiness" material); the framework of the rest of the Pentateuch (e.g., parts of Genesis, parts of Exodus and Numbers); as well as the book of Ezekiel, again broadly understood, since it shows considerable Priestly influence, among other texts. The Priestly material is routinely considered of little ethical import by modern readers due to its interest in the arcane details of Israelite worship of Yahweh, Israel's God, and due to its intense focus on the arrangement of time and space that supports appropriate worship. Despite these apparent handicaps, the Priestly material is of considerable interest for ethics. The Priestly writers understood a unitary cosmos in which human actions have cosmic import, and thus questions of ethics are always at least implicitly present and of vital importance.

The Priestly worldview is shaped by a particular concern for the sanctity of time and space (e.g., the emphasis on divisions of time and space in Gen. 1, a Priestly text). In the Pentateuch time is divided into three distinct periods, each of which is marked by an everlasting covenant. The primeval period is marked by the covenant with Noah in Gen. 9, the ancestral period is marked by the covenant with Abraham in Gen. 17, and the Mosaic period is marked by the Sinai covenant (see Exod. 31:12–17 for Sinai as a perpetual covenant). For the Priestly writers, worship is the central experience, and within that framework the presence of God within the sanctuary is of utmost importance. The sanctuary is a microcosm of the cosmos, which is why the details concerning the building of the tabernacle at the end of Exodus are so important (Exod. 35–40). God is present with the people by tabernacling with them—that is, being present along the journey with them in a kind of movable tent. The people are identified as a worshiping community; that is the core of their identity. They are called the *ʿēdâ*, the congregation that worships Yahweh.

The Priestly writers ground worship in the structures of creation as a whole; thus, each of the many details of the tabernacle is sacred and is an outward and visible sign of the invisible presence of God. It is a sacramental vision of worship that may appear to be in some tension with idolatry but is always carefully nonrepresentational. The sacred details of the tabernacle mediate the presence of God and make it possible for God to be present with the people in a way that maintains the necessary boundaries between the holy, the common, and the unholy. When the boundaries between these categories are inappropriately transgressed, God's continued presence with the community is jeopardized, and with it the welfare of the community is endangered.

In the Priestly worldview, a distinct order reigns, and when certain things (e.g., food, bodily fluids) cross boundaries without due ritual, the order of the world itself is disturbed. This attention to order helps to explain the regulations pertaining to food, sex, menstrual blood, and so forth. In Gen. 1, for example, the text records that God made the sky and things that fly in the sky, the sea and things that swim in the sea, and the land and things that crawl on the land. These things are separated from one another in the order of creation itself, and so, in the Priestly view, they should remain separate. But many things found in creation pose challenges to the Priestly worldview. Consider a lobster: it lives in the sea, but it does not look like a fish; it does not have fins and scales (indeed it looks more like a giant bug that should live on the land) (see Lev. 11:9–12). In the Priestly worldview, lobster and other shellfish break the boundaries of the "natural" order and therefore are defiling to eat. Likewise, wearing garments made of two different fabrics breaks boundaries and invites chaos (Lev. 19:19). So also with human sexuality: in the Priestly worldview, there are men and women, and all are assumed to be heterosexual (the priests did not imagine anyone being created "homosexual"), and so all sexual activity should be heterosexual; to do otherwise crosses boundaries and invites chaos (Lev. 18:22) (though the priests only address male-to-male homosexual acts; lesbian activity does not seem to be in view, though women having sex with animals is a concern [Lev. 18:23]). In working with the Priestly material ethically, it is important not to extract a topic (e.g., food, sex, clothing) from its Priestly context in order to establish an ethical norm for our own time. Rather, it is worth considering how to engage the Priestly writers in a way that respects the distance between this ancient worldview and the present but still seeks points of connection with integrity.

The world envisioned in Leviticus is an orderly world, created and shaped by God's purposes; a ritual world, in which creation itself is established, sustained, and restored through liturgies of worship (i.e., worship in the sanctuary keeps chaos at bay); a relational world, wherein God invites humanity to share in responsibility for sustaining and restoring the divine purposes for the world. A crucial question for ethics is this: how are human beings invited to participate in God's purposes for the world? As shown by Jacob Milgrom, a scholar of the Priestly material who has drawn attention to its rich potential as a resource for ethical reflection, the people's continuing participation in the sanctuary's cultic worship plays a vital role in keeping the forces of chaos at bay. Cultic ritual keeps the sanctuary clean, and the whole people are part of this effort. The specific role of the priests is to organize and officiate in worship, and also to teach the Torah to the people so they will know how to avoid sin, but it is the people who recognize when they have sinned and who bring their offerings to the sanctuary on the proper occasion.

The assumption is that God's world is subject to sin and disorder. Yet when human beings commit certain kinds of sins, it is not the sinner who becomes unclean, but rather the sanctuary itself is defiled: pollution, like an invisible, airborne miasma, adheres to the edifice. Milgrom likens this process to Oscar Wilde's story *The Picture of Dorian Gray*, in which the main character's sins adhere not to the man himself but instead to his hidden portrait. So the Israelite sanctuary is akin to the painting in the attic that is deteriorating hideously on account of the sins of the man below, who bears no outward sign of sin. The entire sanctuary, of course, is holy, but it is also increasingly holy as one approaches the most holy place, the inner sanctum where God is understood to be most present ("the holy of holies"). If what is holy is defiled by impurity, and if that builds up long enough, God will abandon the sanctuary, and so the people, and so the whole world. And if God abandons the sanctuary, the people, and the world, chaos will break in and overwhelm the whole world. Thus, maintaining category distinctions is crucial to maintaining order, keeping chaos at bay, and so keeping God with the people. If the sanctuary becomes too polluted with this miasma produced by sin, God will abandon it, with the resulting breach in the community's life with God.

The consequences of such a failure, the failure to keep the sanctuary relatively free of pollution, are catastrophic for the world. So the Priestly worldview believes that Israel is performing a service on behalf of the world (here one might recall the promise to Abraham in Gen. 12 that through his descendants all the families of the earth would be blessed). The entire community, not just the priests, must participate in keeping the sanctuary as pollution-free as possible; the life of the community depends on the extent to which this responsibility is shared. When they sin, the people must bring their gifts to the priest at the sanctuary, and through their sacrifice the sanctuary can be adequately cleansed of the miasma, and the community will thrive.

In order to see what Priestly ethics might look like with a specific text, consider the case of Lev. 4 and the problem of unintentional sins. Leviticus 4, like most of the book, is taken up with the problem of sin and its effects. Leviticus 1–3 deals with voluntary gifts brought to the sanctuary, whereas Lev. 4–5 prescribes mandatory gifts for the expiation of sin. These chapters are addressed to the entire people, not simply to the priests. In Lev. 4 the issue is unintentional sins, unwittingly committed. What can be done about them? The chapter moves through these on a case-by-case basis: when a priest unknowingly sins (4:3–12), a certain sacrifice is prescribed (bull); when the whole congregation unknowingly sins (4:13–21), there is another sacrifice (bull, but with elders involved); and so on, until, at the end of the list, bringing up the rear, is the ordinary person who sins unknowingly (4:27–31). This case, the ordinary person who sins unknowingly, is of particular interest for ethics.

As noted above, sin is not about what it does to the individual; it is the sanctuary that requires attention. The blood of the sacrifice is the ritual detergent, cleansing the altar. Forgiveness is a byproduct of the sinner's effort to address sin, but the sinner's forgiveness is not of primary importance. The sinner brings a gift to the priest in order to repair the relationship with God and to help the community to prosper. So in Leviticus, sin is not individual in the first instance; it is about the health of the life of the community, about whether the community as a whole will thrive. The sinner is forgiven for the sin, but the need for forgiveness arises from the effect of the sin on the sanctuary, not from impurity of the self. This focus on the welfare of the community and the ethical import of unintentional sins led Milgrom to this comment about the purification offering of Lev. 4: "If only this ritual were fully understood and implemented, it could transform the world" (*Leviticus: A Book of Ritual and Ethics*, 33).

See also Clean and Unclean; Ezekiel; Holiness Code; Leviticus; Old Testament Ethics

Bibliography

Balentine, S. *The Torah's Vision of Worship*. OBT. Fortress, 1999; Milgrom, J. *Leviticus 1–16*. AB 3. Doubleday, 1991, 253–63; idem. *Leviticus: A Book of Ritual and Ethics*. CC. Fortress, 2004, 8–16, 30–33.

Jacqueline E. Lapsley

Prison and Prison Reform

Prisons (also called penitentiaries, penal institutions, and adult correctional facilities) are state or federal facilities of confinement for convicted criminals, especially felons. In contrast to prisons, jails (also called jailhouses and lockups) are places where individuals awaiting trial, or going through the process of trial, or convicted of misdemeanor offenses are confined. Jails sometimes serve as places of provisional imprisonment post trial.

Prisons and Christian Social Ethics

Today more than 2.3 million persons occupy US prisons and jails, which are supervised by a variety of federal, state, and local jurisdictions. This number represents the highest per capita incarceration rate in the country's history. Writing for the National Criminal Justice Commission, Steven Donziger reported, "Since 1980, the United States has engaged in the largest and most frenetic correctional buildup of any country in the history of the world" (Donziger 31). Indeed, with just 6 percent of the world's population, the United States now holds 25 percent of its prisoners at a cost of about $60 billion per year.

The basic reasons for the increase in the number of US residents being imprisoned appear to be (at least) five: (1) the development of legislation (since the 1970s) requiring mandatory minimum sentencing as a cornerstone of corrections public policy; (2) the nationwide declaration of a "war on crime," specifically the "war on drugs," since the 1980s; (3) the economic profit generated by increased imprisonment; (4) an ever-increasing social policy commitment to incarceration as a tool of social maintenance and control; and (5) new immigration policies since the mid-1990s that target specific nationalities (e.g., Arabs, Haitians, Jamaicans, Cubans, and Mexicans) while emphasizing enforcement and detention over individualized justice, personal transformation, and social services (Miller). Taken as a whole, these developments represent interrelated dimensions of a "prison industrial complex"—that is, a set of bureaucratic, economic, political, and media-driven interests that encourage increased spending on incarceration.

For over three decades now a social policy that some describe as "mass imprisonment," which issues in a variety of "collateral" and/or "invisible" consequences, has significantly transformed the nation's family and community dynamics (Mauer and Chesney-Lind 1–2). The increased scale of incarceration has an impact that extends far beyond individual prisoners and their families, including the exacerbation of racial divisions, and economic and social risk for the most vulnerable of the nation's residents (children, the poor, the mentally ill, the drug addicted). Incarceration on such a large scale also poses fundamental questions of justice/fairness and citizenship in a democratic society.

Before and since the tragic events of 9/11, the United States has been commonly and widely cited by various international human rights organizations for the torturing and other inhumane treatment of prisoners. Amnesty International has reported that the United States is one of just four nations performing 97 percent of the world's state-sponsored executions, the other three nations being China, Iran, and Vietnam.

Attending to Scripture and Theological Ethics

Critical sources for much Christian contemplation and practice around prisons and prison reform lie in Scripture and theological ethics. These sources guide Christian discernment concerning the ultimate restorative and transformative relationships toward which the Christian narrative aims.

Stanley Hauerwas has rightly suggested that "ontological intimacy" refers to the Christian understanding that literally nothing exists outside God, since God makes the entirety of the finite realm *ex nihilo*, through an act of purest and gentlest generosity. Therefore, all of creation should be understood as participating in the power of God's being. This means that all that is related through bonds of ontological intimacy should aim to exist in communion because all that is rooted in a more primordial communion with God as modeled in history by God self-revealed in Jesus Christ (Hauerwas 111–12). Paul Tillich might have expressed the theological drive of ontological intimacy as an "ontology of love," which essentially drives humanity toward "the reunion of the separated" (Tillich 57). Such an intimacy speaks of humanity's primordial interconnectedness.

Clues about what such an intimacy entails for Christian praxis in the context of prisons and prison reform can be discerned in God's self-unveiling as the lowly born, tortured, spat upon, beaten, and crucified Jesus Christ of Nazareth. These sufferings were not ends in themselves; they were misery-filled consequences of Jesus' living toward the restorative/transformative end of ontological intimacy. The way of this humiliated Jesus has been demonstrated for us in a gospel tradition that aims at the restoration of love in human relationships, as expressed in notions of grace-soaked penance, forgiveness, and reconciliation. The grace modeled for Christians in the Jesus tradition is a profound love and concern for others that speaks of our primal interrelatedness, our radical mutuality for the cause of liberation from the wages of what many Christians know as "sin."

The birth, life, death, and resurrection of Jesus challenge Christians to consider the implications of ontological intimacy in the formation of Christian community in relation to those whom societal authorities condemn as criminals. As Christians contemplate their individual and collective relationships with society's prisons and prison reform, they ought not neglect noting the companionship of Jesus in close proximity to the condemned, as well as the important companionship and comfort offered to the human Jesus as he suffered the same abuse, the same pain, and the same death throes as the criminals who hung from crosses with him (Barth 78): "They crucified Jesus there with the criminals, one on his right and one on his left" (Luke 23:33). On a cross, and today in Holy Communion, God upsets the logic and power of violent retribution by forgiving humanity for its sin, including humanity's own grand execution of God's Son, Jesus Christ. Christians must contemplate the implications of such a narrative for Christian thinking about prisons and prison reform.

Prison Reform

Central to Christian theological perspectives on prison reform is the requirement of discerning the difference that Jesus makes for Christian participation in society's understanding and meting out of punishment. Christians must continually struggle with how best to embrace the praxis of criminal justice as an expression of a politics of better hope for society. This better hope should connect the Christian worship of God to a radically reconfigured reality of social justice ushered into human history by God's self-unveiled love in the person of Jesus Christ. Hauerwas has rightly suggested that although society does not share the Christian faith and therefore cannot be expected to live as Christians ought to live, this in no way means that a sectarian demarcation should be established indicating what Christians cannot ask of the societies in which they reside. Christians should actively model the countercultural politics of Jesus as a contribution to the societies in which they live. This means that Christians contemplating prisons and prison reform must continuously affirm the radical nature of Christian penance, forgiveness, and reconciliation in the service of humanity's primordial communion of interrelatedness with God and with one another, including those "others" viewed as the criminals among us. Christian forgiveness and reconciliation must be viewed as more primary than punishment.

Christian efforts toward prison reform must consider scriptural, theological, and moral foundations grounded in penance, forgiveness, and reconciliation. These foundations are displayed in distinctive, virtue-inspired principles and practices (e.g., faith, hope, love, patience, courage) that restore and transform society for the better. Broadly conceived, virtue-inspired principles and practices that restore and transform may include restorative justice efforts as well as various (preventative) systemic alternatives to large-scale imprisonment and harsher punishments.

"Restorative justice" is a phrase that encompasses a variety of programs and practices based on an "alternative framework for thinking about wrongdoing" (Zehr 5). Restorative justice is community-based and deals with offenders through a victim-oriented process of restoration (see, e.g., Zehr 24). Restorative approaches to criminal justice, in opposition to retributive frameworks, reject the idea that the infliction of pain will vindicate wrongdoing. While it is not unusual for victims (or their surrogates) and offenders to meet at some point during a process of restorative justice, forgiveness and reconciliation are not primary goals. Nonetheless, the context does provide a setting where some degree of either or both might occur. It should be noted that its practitioners do not necessarily view restorative justice as an alternative to the state's normal criminal justice process. In some felony cases (e.g., rape, murder, domestic violence) the framework may prove less useful or desirable, although sometimes the usefulness of restorative justice has been apparent in such cases. At base, restorative justice as an alternative lens through which Christians might engage prison reform expresses values that comport to a better Christian vision for society. Such values include a respect for all persons, enemies included. It is an approach to justice that acknowledges both the individuality and radical interconnectedness of all persons, for better or for worse.

Today activists such as Christian Parenti, Angela Y. Davis, and Christian ethicist T. Richard Snyder (alongside scores of other US residents, Christian and non-Christian alike) offer possible ways forward in providing concrete alternatives to current criminal justice practices in the United States. Parenti recommends, in regard to criminal justice, "less." Specifically, he recommends "less policing, less incarceration, shorter sentences, less surveillance, fewer laws governing individual behaviors, and less obsessive discussion of every lurid crime, less prohibition, and less puritanical concern with 'freaks' and 'deviants'" (Parenti 242). Davis argues for "abolitionist alternatives" to prisons. Abolitionist alternatives to prisons constitute a foreshadowing of the better society that people of goodwill hope to build. Davis contends that hope for the future of justice-making requires an abolitionist approach that would eventually "remove the prison from the social and ideological landscape of our society." Davis's abolitionist perspective insists that society not search for prisonlike substitutes for the prison, "such as house arrest safeguarded by electronic surveillance bracelets." Rather, she invites society to imagine a constellational continuum of alternatives to imprisonment—for example, the "demilitarization of education at all levels, a health system that provides free physical and mental care to all, and a justice system based on reparation and reconciliation rather than retribution and vengeance" (Davis 107). Finally, Snyder's contribution to prison reform is his suggestion that some focus be placed on the proposition that society itself is a significant cause of crime through its creation and advocacy of the very conditions that make crime possible. Snyder asserts, "Certainly the one who has committed a criminal act is in need of forgiveness from the victim and the larger society that has been harmed. But so too is the society in need of forgiveness for having created and permitted crime-generative communities to exist" (Snyder 110–11). If Snyder is correct, Christians must pay attention to the distinction between the habilitation of prisoners and the rehabilitation of offenders: "If the lack of habilitation is a reality, then those responsible for this condition are as much in need of forgiveness as is the perpetrator of any specific crime" (Snyder 111).

As Christians continue to reflect upon where they stand on deeply difficult and complex issues surrounding criminal justice, the challenge is this: whatever the reform-minded efforts may have brought to the issue of prison and prison reform, it is scripturally, theologically, and morally imperative that Christians exemplify their witness by remembering themselves to be a living testimony to the difference that Jesus' birth, life, death, and resurrection make in the society and world.

See also Capital Punishment; Crime and Criminal Justice; Forgiveness; Justice, Restorative; Law, Civil and Criminal; Reconciliation; Reparation; Restitution

Bibliography

Barth, K. "The Criminals with Him." Pages 75–84 in *Deliverance to the Captives: Sermons and Prayers by Karl Barth*. Harper, 1961; Davis, A. *Are Prisons Obsolete?* Seven Stories Press, 2003; Donziger, S., ed. *The Real War on Crime: The Report of the National Criminal Justice Commission*. HarperPerennial, 1996; Hauerwas, S. *A Better Hope: Resources for a Church Confronting Capitalism, Democracy, and Postmodernity*. Brazos, 2000; Logan, J. *Good Punishment? Christian Moral Practice and U.S. Imprisonment*. Eerdmans, 2008; Mauer, M., and M. Chesney-Lind, eds. *Invisible Punishment: The Collateral Consequences of Mass Imprisonment*. New Press, 2002; Miller, T. "The Impact of Mass Incarceration on Immigration Policy." Pages 217–18 in *Invisible Punishment: The Collateral Consequences of Mass Imprisonment*, ed. M. Mauer and M. Chesney-Lind. New Press, 2002; Parenti, C. *Lockdown America: Police and Prisons in the Age of Crisis*. Verso, 1999; Snyder, T. *The Protestant Ethic and the Spirit of Punishment*. Eerdmans, 2001; Tillich, P. *Love, Power, and Justice: Ontological Analyses and Ethical Applications*. Oxford University Press, 1954; Zehr, H. *The Little Book of Restorative Justice*. Good Books, 2002.

James Samuel Logan

Prisoners of War

Many ancient Near Eastern wars involved the capture of prisoners, and the OT refers to this practice on many occasions, especially in conjunction with the Babylonian exile (frequently using cognates of the root *šbh*, "take captive"). There are significant variations on what captives suffered. On some occasions, prisoners of war were killed (2 Chr. 25:12; cf. Amos 9:4) or faced life-threatening conditions (Neh. 1:2–3). Texts such as 2 Chr. 28:15 suggest that prisoners of war were deprived of food, clothing, and drink (cf. Isa. 20:4). Frequently, they were forced into labor (e.g., Judg. 16:21). To prevent escape, captors blinded, imprisoned, enchained, and fettered prisoners (e.g., Isa. 52:2; Jer. 52:11; Nah. 3:10). Forced migrations were also considered a form of imprisonment (e.g., Isa. 42:22; 61:1). Becoming a prisoner of war frequently entailed profound emotional trauma (Ps. 137:1–3; Isa. 20:4; Jer. 13:17; 22:22; 30:10; Ezek. 16:52–53) and placement among the lowest social strata (cf. Exod. 12:29). Yet, some prisoners of war were shown compassion by their captors (1 Kgs. 8:46–50; 2 Chr. 30:9; Ps. 106:46). A number were even allowed a degree of self-autonomy (cf. Jer. 29:4–7). In some cases, prisoners were freed or permitted to return home at a later time, particularly when battles had ended (2 Kgs. 25:27–29; Ezra 3:8; 8:35; Neh. 8:17; cf. Isa. 49:25; Jer. 29:14; 41:14; 46:27; 52:31–33).

The NT contains few references to those taken captive in war. Luke 21:24 and Rev. 13:10 mention captives alongside those killed by the sword, much like a variety of passages in the OT (e.g., Ezra 9:7; Jer. 15:2; 43:11; Ezek. 30:17; Dan. 11:33; Amos 4:10).

Ethically, several texts are of key importance. In line with Deuteronomistic theology, many passages describe war and captivity as the result of sinfulness (e.g., Deut. 28:41; 2 Chr. 6:36; Ezra 9:7; Jer. 20:6; Lam. 1:5, 18). Numerous texts also describe God as ultimately responsible for freeing individuals from captivity (e.g., Jer. 29:14).

Other texts condemn making individuals into prisoners of war (e.g., 2 Chr. 28:8–15; Jer. 30:16), anticipating divine judgment for those who do so. Meanwhile, Deut. 21:10–14 permits the capture of female prisoners of war, but it appears to deter their mistreatment.

Finally, although the *ḥerem* texts are ethically problematic (i.e., advocating the annihilation of all the inhabitants of an opposing city or tribe [e.g., Deut. 20:17]), these texts can be interpreted as a way to counteract those who would go to war simply for personal gain, such as the acquisition of forced labor provided by prisoners of war.

One of the most significant texts for ethics today is the oracles of Amos against the nations (1:3–2:3), which have resonances with the Geneva Conventions, condemning a variety of inhumane actions that are, at least by modern standards, war crimes. Among the crimes Amos denounces is the capture and enslavement of others through war (1:6–7). Although the Bible is hardly monolithic, it contains voices that condemn crimes against humanity, including the mistreatment and imprisonment of individuals in times of war.

See also Ban, The; Conquest; Deuteronomistic History; Exile; Slavery; War

Bibliography

Barton, J. "Amos's Oracles against the Nations: A Study of Amos 1:3–2:5." Pages 77–129 in *Understanding Old Testament Ethics: Approaches and Explorations*. Westminster John Knox, 2003; Elman, P. "Deuteronomy 21:10–14: The Beautiful Captive Woman." *Women in Judaism* 1, no. 1 (1997): http://wjudaism.library.utoronto.ca/index.php/wjudaism/article/viewArticle/166; Gelb, I. "Prisoners of War in Early Mesopotamia." *JNES* 32 (1973): 70–98; Goodnick, B. "She Shall Mourn." *JBQ* 32 (2004): 198–201; Schlimm, M. "Teaching the Hebrew Bible amid the Current Human Rights Crisis: The Pedagogical Opportunities Presented by

Amos 1:3–2:3." *SBL Forum* 4, no. 1 (2006): http://www.sbl-site.org/publications/article.aspx?articleId=478; Van der Toorn, K. "Judges XVI 21 in the Light of the Akkadian Sources." *VT* 26 (1986): 248–53.

Matthew R. Schlimm

Privacy

Privacy involves the state of being alone, free from the purview or intrusion of others. Respect for privacy is a fairly recent topic in philosophical discourse. Only after the rise of industrialism and the expansion of technology in the late nineteenth century did American jurists Thomas Cooley and Louis Brandeis famously argue for legal recognition of a right to privacy, which they defined as the "right to be let alone."

Recent technologies and policies have raised privacy concerns: "full body scan" airport security devices; electronic surveillance of telephone, internet, and other communications to fight terrorism; wiretaps and infrared, X-ray, and video security cameras to fight crime; and medical, academic, and financial record-keeping and tracking in vast bureaucratic systems. The US political controversies over the legality of contraception, abortion, sodomy, and gay marriage followed in the wake of the Supreme Court's 1965 determination that a "right to privacy" exists within the Constitution. Justice William Douglas's landmark majority opinion in *Griswold v. Connecticut* located this right in "penumbras" emanating from specific guarantees of the Bill of Rights that "give them life and substance."

The Bible is a poor resource for the modern concept of privacy. Scripture emphasizes that various interactions were held "in private" or "privately." These include Joseph weeping upon meeting his brother Benjamin in a private room (Gen. 43:30), Saul's command that his servants communicate to David in private (1 Sam. 18:22), multiple private discussions between Jesus and his followers (Matt. 17:19; 24:3; Mark 4:34; 7:33; 9:28; 13:3; Luke 9:10; 10:23; John 11:28), and Paul's meeting with the Jerusalem church leaders (Gal. 2:2). These passages reflect a respect for human dignity in which the parties communicate freely in mutual trust.

Jesus also encouraged his followers to both pray and do good deeds in private (Matt. 6:3–6). An implication of his commands is that relative to an omniscient God, nothing is private. Any attempt, however, to construct a theory of privacy based on these and other biblical texts would be forced.

Advances in those technologies that expand the possibilities of mass surveillance can present challenges to the right to privacy. The ancient distinction between the public sphere and the private household chronicled by Hannah Arendt is at some risk of disappearing.

James Rule observes that the central ethical issue in the extension of surveillance is "the tension between the essentially utilitarian logic of *efficiency* with the Kantian logic of *rights*" (27). He posits that "the only limits to endless erosion of privacy are those created by human intervention—that is, by laws and policies that 'just say no' to endless extension of institutional surveillance" (xv). The challenge for biblical ethicists is to formulate arguments to counter the constant pressures to encroach on privacy.

See also Confidentiality; Individualism; Information Technology; Rights

Bibliography

Arendt, H. *The Human Condition*. University of Chicago Press, 1958; Nissenbaum, H. *Privacy in Context: Technology, Policy, and the Integrity of Social Life*. Stanford Law Books, 2010; Rössler, B., ed. *Privacies: Philosophical Evaluations*. Stanford University Press, 2004; Rule, J. *Privacy in Peril: How We Are Sacrificing a Fundamental Right in Exchange for Security and Convenience*. Oxford University Press, 2007; Warren, S., and L. Brandeis. "The Right to Privacy." *Harvard Law Review* 4 (1890): 194–200; Westin, A. *Privacy and Freedom*. Atheneum, 1967.

Lawrence M. Stratton

Procreation

According to the first creation story in Genesis, God created humankind in his image, "male and female he created them" (Gen. 1:27), linking human sexual differentiation to our reflection of God. Because the sexual union of man and woman can generate new life, procreation partakes in God's creative profligacy. Moreover, biological offspring literally instantiate the Christian conception of marriage as a union in which man and woman are made one flesh (Gen. 2:24; Matt. 19:5–6). God told the first humans, "Be fruitful and multiply, and fill the earth and subdue it" (Gen. 1:28). Accordingly, procreation is a form of faithful service to God.

However, not all Christians are called to procreate; there are "eunuchs for the sake of the kingdom" (Matt. 19:12). While Scripture generally regards fertility as a blessing and involuntary childlessness as a curse (see Ryan), Eugene Rogers argues that childless Christian couples can witness to the fact that resurrection, not procreation, ensures the survival of the human species.

Scripture includes stories of procreation under uncommon or socially undesirable circumstances.

Sarah, for example, conceived in her old age (Gen. 17:15–21; 18:1–15; 21:1–7), and Mary became pregnant while betrothed to a man who was not the biological father of her child (Matt. 1:18–25; Luke 1:26–38). Key scriptural stories of procreation reveal God's providential governance of history. The genealogies of Jesus in Matthew (1:1–17) and Luke (3:23–28) illustrate as much. Matthew's genealogy notably includes women with complex social or moral status who nevertheless help to prepare the way for the Lord. They point to the power of grace to make all things work for our good.

A number of moral questions surround procreation. What circumstances make morally ideal conditions for procreation? Under what conditions is it morally acceptable, even advisable, to limit or otherwise regulate births or to promote conception through medical and technological interventions? Related ethical issues include the utilization of medical resources for assisted reproduction and to care for significantly premature infants, the donation or sale of gametes and gestational labor, as well as genetic diagnosis of and experimentation on embryos and fetuses.

The Scriptures assume and generally endorse a procreative context of heterosexual marital coitus. Christian ethicists disagree regarding the moral character of reproductive ventures that depart from this context. Historically, Christian tradition viewed the procreative potential of human sexuality as a given feature of God's creative order that morally constrains our freedom regarding procreation. Some early Christian thinkers claimed that procreation provides moral justification for intercourse. Augustine believed that original sin was transmitted through the concupiscence that inevitably accompanied intercourse. Today the conviction "in sin my mother conceived me" (Ps. 51:5 NASB) is more likely rendered in terms of the social reproduction of selfhood.

Christian thinkers accorded increasing importance to the unitive value of sexual relations. Some ethicists argue the "procreationism" of traditional Christian sexual ethics devalues the unitive dimension of sex and casts nonprocreative (infertile, same-sex, postmenopausal) sexual relations as inferior. Christine Gudorf contends that procreationism encourages us to think of penile-vaginal penetration as the only "real" sex act and all other forms of sexual activity as foreplay or perversion. Official Catholic moral teaching holds that every genital sexual act must refrain from deliberately separating the procreative potential and unitive expression of sex. Ethicists such as Margaret Farley and James Nelson argue that sexual relations ought generally to be fruitful, but not every genital sexual encounter needs to be open to the possibility of generating new life; moreover, sexual relations that are nonprocreative can be fruitful in other ways. They and others find theological, ethical support for nontraditional forms of procreation and family formation in salvation history, particularly God's hospitality to Israel, Jesus' inauguration of a new order that transvalues human kinship, and Christian liberty under this new order. Those who affirm such values but worry about tendencies to regard procreation and sexual relations as contingently related through human preferences rather than linked in a divinely created order emphasize the moral weight of human embodiment.

See also Birth Control; Childlessness; Children; Conception; Family; Reproductive Technologies

Bibliography

Congregation for the Doctrine of the Faith. *Donum Vitae: Instruction on Respect for Human Life in Its Origin and on the Dignity of Procreation.* Catholic Truth Society, 1987; Farley, M. *Just Love: A Framework for Christian Sexual Ethics.* Continuum, 2006. Gudorf, C. *Body, Sex, and Pleasure: Reconstructing Christian Sexual Ethics.* Pilgrim Press, 1995. Nelson, J. *Embodiment: An Approach to Christian Sexuality and Christian Theology.* Augsburg, 1978; Rogers, E., Jr. *Sexuality and the Christian Body: Their Way into the Triune God.* Blackwell, 1999; Ryan, M. *Ethics and Economics of Assisted Reproduction: The Cost of Longing.* Georgetown University Press, 2003.

Darlene Fozard Weaver

Profanity *See* Speech Ethics

Professional Ethics

Professional ethics involves moral reflection on the activities of professions, including the principles, codes of ethics, and other guidelines by which professional guilds guide their members. These codes and principles can be used to prepare and evaluate those wishing to enter the profession, to monitor those already within it, and, in cases of violations of the principles or codes, to discipline offenders or even remove them from the profession.

Historically, the professions were limited to attorneys, physicians, and clergy. Over time, other occupations (e.g., engineering, nursing, counseling) took on both the label "profession" and a predictable array of characteristics often shared in common by professional occupations, including concerns about ethics.

Professionals have specialized knowledge and skills particular to the activities of the profession. Physicians, for example, have specialized medical knowledge and skills necessary to care for patients. Professionals normally engage in activities for the common good. Professions are characterized, in part, by their moral complexity; the particular activities of the professional bring with them particular moral questions that call for moral deliberation and discernment.

Professionals are often described as bearing great responsibility, in part because of the serious and even dangerous consequences if they fail to carry out their professional activities properly (e.g., physicians bear responsibility for people's health, and attorneys for their legal rights). In part because of the gravity of these responsibilities, professionals normally undergo a long period of training (including formal education and often residency programs or internships) as well as a formal examination or evaluation. At the completion of this period of training and examination professionals often are formally approved or licensed by the professional guild. In some disciplines (e.g., law, medicine, ministry), new professionals take an oath or formally enter into a covenant. For example, attorneys are sworn in by a judge; pastors are ordained; many physicians and nurses take an oath.

The professional guild sets standards not only to train those wishing to enter the profession but also to monitor, guide, and hold accountable those already in the profession. To this end, professional organizations often develop guidelines and codes of ethics and professional conduct that are directed at the activities of the profession and that delineate formal processes for disciplining those who fail to meet the standards.

Throughout this process as members are trained, monitored, and disciplined by their guilds, ethics is central. Many professions now require ethics courses and examinations as a part of their training period as well as continuing education in ethics. For example, most law schools now require courses in professional responsibility and ethics. Almost all states require aspiring attorneys to pass an examination on professional responsibility and ethics either as a part of the bar exam or in a separate national exam based on the American Bar Association's codes concerning professional and judicial conduct. The oath required of attorneys includes promises with ethical import. Moreover, attorneys in most states are required to take regular continuing education courses in the field of ethics throughout their careers.

There is often a link between a profession and the state. For example, US physicians must be licensed by their states after completing certain educational requirements and passing a licensing exam. Many other healthcare workers, including mental health professionals, must be licensed by the state before they are allowed to practice. The role of the state in the guilds is not without controversy. For example, what is the proper role for public officials, who ordinarily have no medical training, in policing medical guilds whose members have highly specialized training? For this reason, state licensing normally follows certification by a professional association.

Ethical issues are often at the center of the formal guidelines and codes of many professions. For example, physicians, attorneys, and counselors are enjoined to honor confidentiality. Attorneys must be zealous advocates for their clients (within the limits of the law), even when they have moral qualms about their clients' activities. Journalists are directed to protect the names of confidential sources. Physicians must respect the autonomy of their patients. In many professions, practitioners are enjoined to keep strict professional boundaries and refrain from sexual activity with clients.

The ethical rules and principles of professional codes are ordinarily related to the particular activities of that profession. If a given principle is not followed, then the activities of the profession are in some way hindered. For example, professional guilds often insist that their members maintain confidentiality not simply because it is wrong to break someone's trust but also because confidentiality is necessary for the proper functioning of their particular profession. For example, if clients think that their attorneys might disregard confidentiality, they could be discouraged from giving their attorneys all the information necessary to defend them. The guild, the interests of its clients, and even the entire judicial system could suffer.

In another example, journalists do not ordinarily reveal the names of anonymous sources because it undermines the field of journalism; if sources did not believe that agreements of anonymity would be honored, they would be less likely to reveal information. This principle stands at the heart of journalism. Even when ordered by courts to reveal the names of sources, many journalists refuse because of the professional standards of their fields, standards that are included in the codes of ethics of organizations such as the United States Society of Professional Journalists.

These rules sometimes admit exceptions and limits. For example, many states and some professional organizations require certain professionals to break confidentiality in cases of suspected child abuse and neglect. Moreover, although attorneys are to be zealous advocates for their clients, they are held to the limits of the law and certain standards of the court. In these cases both the rules and their exceptions are driven by ethical concerns.

Many of these examples deal with the relationships between professionals and their clients. Professional ethics codes and guidelines also address the relationships between professionals and colleagues. For example, many clergy codes of ethics recommend or even require that pastors not return to their previous churches to offer pastoral services such as weddings and funerals unless invited by the current pastor. If new pastors do not have the opportunity to marry and bury the people in their congregations, their work as pastors will be diminished and churches and their members will suffer. Professional ethics can also be addressed to the responsibilities that professionals have to their guilds, to the particular institutions in which they work, to particular areas of public life (e.g., attorneys to the judicial system and doctors to healthcare), and to the larger public good.

Professional guilds and professional ethics have been the subject of much criticism (Campbell; Kultgen; Reeck). Critics have charged, for example, that guilds give so much weight to the relationships between professionals and their clients, their colleagues, and the institutions paying their salaries that they neglect to address sufficiently their responsibilities to the larger society and the public good. Critics have called for greater realism about professional guilds, asking whether they function as institutions for the public good or, primarily, for the good of a self-interested elite. By extension, are professional ethics, including the ethical codes and guidelines of various professional organizations, directed more toward fostering moral activity for the common good or protecting the guild?

Professional guilds and their codes have also been criticized for being conservative by nature. As professional guilds have exercised control over who can become members and can practice the profession, have they at times been guilty of racism, sexism, and classism? For example, as the medical profession began requiring formal training for physicians, many women were no longer able to practice. Moreover, the American Medical Association originally prohibited women from membership.

Similarly, it could be argued that professional guilds are elitist, setting up two tiers of occupations: professional and nonprofessional. This could be a particularly troubling concern for Christian professionals, particularly but not exclusively Protestants. If a Christian group has historically rejected a two-tiered model with those professing religious vocations somehow standing above those in other occupations, then it is awkward to turn around and affirm another two-tiered system where professionals somehow stand above nonprofessionals.

Critics have also argued that professional guilds tend to be reactive. Many professional codes have been written or revised in the wake of scandals and lawsuits. It is common for professional associations to include attorneys in the writing and revising of codes and policies so that the guild and its officers can limit their legal liability. If an organization tends to shape itself and its policies in response to scandals and legal concerns, how are its mission and self-identity changed?

Further, guilds and their professional guidelines have tended to focus heavily on ethical rules and principles while neglecting other aspects of moral reflection. For example, professional ethics tends to give little attention to the moral virtues needed for particular professions and how those virtues are to be formed. Professional guilds often neglect teleological questions in ethics. What is the larger goal toward which the profession and its members are working? How do the activities promote that good? How might the guild form aspiring and established professionals toward the pursuit of that good?

These various concerns may be rooted in a final criticism of professional guilds and their moral discourse. The concept of the profession as well as many of the classic professions themselves emerged from the Christian church. As James Wind put it, "It may not be too much to say that for much of the history of the west, the church was the mother of the professions" (Wind 171). The word *profession* itself comes from the Latin *profiteri*, meaning "to confess," and was associated with the profession or pledge that Christians took on entering a religious order. Many guilds previously drew on the language and worldview of Scripture and Christian theology. Over time, most professional guilds, with the exception of clergy, distanced themselves from the language, worldview, and cultural history from which the professions emerged, rendering them increasingly secularized.

This distancing or separation of professional guilds from religious language is understandable, given the tremendous religious and cultural diversity within the professions. At the same time, this move leaves the professional guilds with an oddly shallow moral discourse. Dennis Campbell has argued that the moral discourse of the professions is weakened without substantive theological underpinnings, and that Christian professionals should consider their religious traditions as sources for moral reflection on their professional lives. One could add that all professionals, not just Christian professionals, might benefit in their professional reflection from the wisdom of various religious traditions and frameworks, not just Christian ones.

Professionals who seek Jewish and Christian language to support their moral reflection as professionals could turn to many different biblical ideas. The language of covenant has often been used to reflect on professional ethics (Campbell; Reeck; Mount; May). The covenants throughout Scripture, particularly in Genesis and Exodus, form a resource for professionals. The mandate to seek justice and care for the poor, found throughout both the OT and the NT and in many other sacred texts, could provide an antidote to any tendency within the professions to become overly focused on the more narrow interests of the guild and its members. Moreover, biblical mandates to work on behalf of the poor might challenge professionals to reconsider their own goals and those of their professions. Others have turned to the concept of vocation or calling as a resource for professional ethics (Mount; Reeck). Christian and Jewish reflections on work would also be relevant to professional ethics. For example, the papal encyclical *Laborem exercens* (*On Human Work*) draws on the first chapters of Genesis to ground its claim that work is a central part of human life, and that as humans work they participate in God's creative work in the world. Although *Laborem exercens* focuses not on the professions specifically but rather on work generally, these reflections on human nature and human participation in God's work in the world could help provide grounding for moral reflection on the professions.

Of course, all of these biblical ideas—covenant, vocation, justice, and human work as participation in God's work—are not limited to the professions. These concepts are just as fitting for a bricklayer as an engineer, for a homemaker as an attorney. All of these activities can be a participation in God's work, all have value, all are important for the common good, all bear moral import, all can be a means to glorify God. When the professions are considered in light of a larger discussion of a Christian or Jewish theology of work, clear distinctions between the various professions and between professional and nonprofessional occupations fall away. As Christian and Jewish professionals turn to their own religious traditions as resources, they may find that their identity as professionals is overshadowed by their larger vocation as faithful people who seek to do God's will in all parts of their lives, including their employment.

See also Business Ethics; Confidentiality; Covenant; Healthcare Ethics; Justice; Vocation; Work

Bibliography

Campbell, D. *Doctors, Lawyers, Ministers: Christian Ethics in Professional Practice*. Abingdon, 1982; John Paul II. *On Human Work*. United States Catholic Conference, 1981; Kultgen, J. *Ethics and Professionalism*. University of Pennsylvania Press, 1988; Lebacqz, K. *Professional Ethics: Power and Paradox*. Abingdon, 1985; May, W. *The Physician's Covenant: Images of the Healer in Medical Ethics*. Westminster John Knox, 2000; Mount, E., Jr. *Professional Ethics in Context: Institutions, Images, and Empathy*. Westminster John Knox, 1990; Reeck, D. *Ethics for the Professions: A Christian Perspective*. Augsburg, 1982; Wind, J. "Ministry and Profession: The Paradoxical Relationship." *CurTM* 11, no. 3 (1984): 168–75.

Rebekah Miles

Profit

Profit is an advantage generated beyond the effort required to achieve the related goal. While profit can be understood as any such excess gain, the term is typically used in business to denote the net financial return after all relevant expenses have been taken into account. Ethical questions associated with such return should be informed by Scripture's emphases on economic stewardship, proper human motivation, economic responsibility, and appropriate policies for the generation of profit.

Genesis 1:28; 2:15 indicate that humans share in God's rule, with the expectation that the whole of creation will flourish as humans work with and care for its resources. Within this divine delegation of economic responsibilities, profit may serve as one measure of responsible trusteeship for God's resources. The industrious woman of Prov. 31 is praised as an example of wise entrepreneurial choices that illustrate such good stewardship. Still, the NT has multiple warnings about human motivations related to financial return. Jesus observes, "You cannot serve God and wealth" (Matt. 6:24), and "It is easier for a camel to go through the eye of a needle than for someone who is rich to enter the kingdom of God" (Mark 10:25). Paul writes, "The love of money is a root of all kinds of evil" (1 Tim. 6:10). These passages indicate that commitment to God and love for God's kingdom should provide the primary framework within which financial rewards should be sought. Profit-making can be appropriate if kingdom goals are cultivated and if biblical values are honored in the processes by which profit is achieved.

The Bible also describes how those with financial gain have direct responsibilities for other people's needs. In Lev. 19:9–10, when land and crops were principal forms of wealth, God commands productive Israelites to leave the crop's remainder for the poor. Similarly, Paul encourages generosity by the well-supplied Corinthians, so that "the one who had much did not have too much, and the one who had little did not have too little" (2 Cor. 8:15). Scripture teaches that economic profits should spread beyond those who directly generate them so that an entire community can flourish because of a fair balance between abundance and need. Finally, God retains the right, through his human agents, to alter economic structures within which profit is generated. The Jubilee Year, as recorded in Lev. 25:23–28, required that, without cost, land revert to its original owner after fifty years. While profits could be sought, the policies under which profits were generated could also be altered periodically to mirror God's concerns for equitable access to the resources of production.

The market economy of the twenty-first century differs substantially from that of the biblical era. Several millennia of economic experience and change have now created a global network for economic transactions. Amid perennial moral questions about the human motivation for seeking profits, the scope of every person's economic stewardship has become worldwide. In such an economy profits are needed for business survival, growth, and other healthy economic outcomes. Profits are now generated by multiple economic strategies, through individuals, small partnerships, multilateral contracts, or large corporate entities, and related stewardship for them must be considered from multiple vantage points. But each entity generating profits should distribute fair gains to the various constituencies that participated in the generation of profits. Balancing their proportionate claims with Christian justice, prudence, and wisdom is a significant challenge.

See also Almsgiving; Benevolence; Business Ethics; Capitalism; Cost-Benefit Analysis; Debt; Economic Development; Economic Ethics; Greed; Justice, Distributive; Markets; Tithe, Tithing; Trade

Bibliography

Bakke, D. *Joy at Work: A Revolutionary Approach to Fun on the Job*. PVG, 2005; De Pree, M. *Leadership Is an Art*. Doubleday, 1989; Miller, D. *God at Work: The History and Promise of the Faith at Work Movement*. Oxford University Press, 2007; Pollard, C. *Serving Two Masters? Reflections on God and Profit*. HarperCollins, 2006; Stackhouse, M., D. McCann, and S. Roels. *On Moral Business: Classical and Contemporary Resources for Ethics in Economic Life*. Eerdmans, 1995.

Shirley J. Roels

Promiscuity *See* Sexual Ethics

Promise and Promise-Keeping

To make a promise is to intend or will in the present a particular future. In keeping a promise, persons allow the intended future to affect choices or decisions in the present. Promise-making and promise-keeping are important to human identity because they are closely connected to personal integrity and interpersonal trust. Promising is also crucial to community life and shared undertakings. Nevertheless, the practice is difficult because of the unpredictability of the future, human fickleness, and a variety of intervening circumstances.

Because of the importance of promises to social life and because of the mysterious ways that promising connects the present and the future, philosophers over the centuries have given the topic significant attention. It is an important aspect of discussions of duty, contract, and morality in general. In the Scriptures, promises are associated with covenants, vows, oaths, and fidelity. The God of the Bible makes and keeps promises and expects followers to do the same. In the Christian theological tradition there is some attention to promising, but much more emphasis is given to fidelity, faithfulness, and covenant, and rarely do contemporary philosophical and theological literatures intersect on these themes.

The Features, Forms, and Challenges of Promising

While philosophers have disagreed over whether the obligation to keep promises is conventional or natural, promising is generally understood to create a moral obligation. As John Searle has written, "To recognize something as a promise is to grant that, other things being equal, it ought to be kept" (51). The Kantian tradition has viewed promise-keeping as a duty of perfect obligation, allowing no exceptions. In contrast, a utilitarian emphasis on producing the most good can undermine the practice because persons are expected to continually evaluate whether, by breaking a promise, they might accomplish more good than by keeping it.

Although a commitment to keeping promises helps to foster interpersonal trust, predictability in human relationships, and the possibility of cooperative efforts, most philosophical discussions have also explored excusing conditions or circumstances under which a person is released from a promise. These include situations when it is impossible to sustain or fulfill the promise, when a promise "no longer fulfills the purposes of the larger commitment it was meant to serve," and when "another obligation comes into conflict with, and supersedes, the commitment-obligation in question" (Farley 84). In other circumstances, promises are conditional or limited and therefore anticipate the possibility of release. Because of the nature of promising, most moral traditions reject "inconvenience" as an excusing condition, even for minor promises.

Inability to fulfill a promise does not necessarily eliminate responsibility or obligation, and persons often are expected to find alternative ways to keep or redeem the promise. A commitment to fulfilling a promise, however, does not change an otherwise evil or morally reprehensible action into a good or right one.

The practice of promising is always located in a larger context of commitments and responsibilities, and the unfinished nature of many of our stories makes promising both necessary and complicated. Particular promises are never made in a vacuum, and in attempting to keep them, humans sometimes struggle with conflicting commitments, frailty, and finitude.

Promises take different forms; some are formal and are articulated as vows, covenants, or contracts. Promises are generally bilateral or multilateral and involve reciprocal relationships and mutuality. Vows can be unilateral, and they do not necessarily require explicit commitments from another party. Vows taken in marriage, baptism, ordination, and citizenship often are accompanied by ceremonies, witnesses, and historic traditions.

Other promises are informal but basic to everyday interactions and relations: "I'll be home at four to take care of the children." Some promises are explicitly spelled out, while others are implicit, setting up expectations that are not fully articulated but form the fabric of everyday fidelity.

Especially during times of transition or significant uncertainty about the future, promises can be conditional, taking the form of "if . . . then . . ." While more limited, such promises are also generally less stable. Contemporary understandings of promises often are both conditional and limited; they are more contractual than covenantal. Covenantal commitments anticipate mutual fidelity and enduring responsibility. Contracts build into the promise the possibility of its breach and the subsequent consequences, tied to whether there is satisfaction for one or both parties. Contractual arrangements for business transactions and relations are important, but contracts are not a fully adequate framework for understanding the most important promises in our lives.

Contemporary culture places a high value on an individual's freedom and capacity to make choices. In this environment, making promises is difficult because keeping options open is seen as an important dimension of freedom. Promises and commitments necessarily foreclose some good opportunities while they open up other ones.

Although institutions often are criticized for their inflexibility, they also can be appreciated as expressions of fidelity over time, embodying promises and providing a framework for consistency to help persons persevere even when perseverance is inconvenient or unsatisfying. Promises constrain behavior, but they also act as anchors so that humans are able to pursue what is most desired or valued.

Promising is an important dimension of personal and interpersonal integrity. Human beings rely on and make subsequent decisions in light of the promises made to them. A person who regularly breaks promises or lightly dismisses them is viewed as unreliable and increasingly untrustworthy. In some situations, broken promises are experienced as deep betrayals.

Promise-Making and Promise-Keeping in the Bible

The God of Scripture has made promises to followers and lives in covenantal relationship with them (e.g., Deut. 7:8–11). God's covenants or promises are central to the history and theology of the Bible, and God's character is deeply connected to steadfast love and fidelity (e.g., Exod. 34:6; Pss. 36; 136; Jer. 9:24). The people of God are formed by a promise-keeping God into a community of promise (e.g., Ps. 105:42–45). In Genesis, promises and covenants frame God's early dealings with humans; much later, Jesus is presented as the fulfillment of God's promises. Paul says that in Christ, "every one of God's promises is a 'Yes'" (2 Cor. 1:20).

In commissioning his disciples, Jesus assures them that he will be with them always, "to the end of the age" (Matt. 28:20). Jesus' promise never to leave or forsake his followers is invoked to strengthen their fidelity, holiness, and freedom from fear (Heb. 13:5–6). Peter assures believers that the gift and challenge of the "precious and very great promises" of God will allow them to become "participants of the divine nature," and that they can trust the promise of his coming. Jesus is not slow, but rather patient, in fulfilling his promise (2 Pet. 1:4; 3:1–13).

The Scriptures and Christian tradition affirm the importance of keeping promises and vows.

Those who walk blamelessly and do right "stand by their oath even to their hurt" (Ps. 15:4). Thomas Aquinas advises, "For one to be accounted faithful one must keep one's promises" (*ST* II-II, q. 88, a. 3). Those who have freely made vows to God should perform them. Deuteronomy 23:21–23 warns that "whatever your lips utter you must diligently perform," while also allowing that individuals might rightly refrain from vowing in the first place.

Within the Scriptures, this affirmation of promising and promises is richly nuanced. Fidelity to God relativizes other fidelities and shapes the promises that ought to be made and kept. In Matt. 5:33–37 Jesus commends a lifestyle rooted in both truthfulness and fidelity when he warns followers not to make oaths or to swear by heaven or earth. A person's veracity and faithfulness should not need to be shored up by taking an oath.

A certain humility and trust before God are appropriate, given the ambiguity of making plans and promises when the future is both uncertain and unknowable. James 4:13–17 acknowledges that humans neither know nor control the future and cannot do so even by the plans or promises that they make. While it is possible to reduce the future's uncertainty by making and keeping commitments, we cannot eliminate it entirely.

Several biblical stories illustrate the danger of making or keeping rash promises. Jephthah makes a vow to God that is foolish, and his keeping of it has devastating consequences (Judg. 11:29–40). The story of Herod and John the Baptist is a shocking example of a promise that should neither have been made nor kept. Herod, in response to her "pleasing" dance, promises his wife's daughter anything she might ask for. When she asks for the head of John, on a platter, Herod complies with the morally outrageous request "out of regard for his oaths and for the guests" (Matt. 14:1–12; Mark 6:21–29). To count a rash promise more important than the life of "a good and holy man" reinforces the picture of Herod as weak and evil.

Making and keeping promises is profoundly important, but the content of those promises is significant as well. The practice is deformed when persons are faithful to the wrong things. For example, loyalties to close-knit groups such as gangs can include strong structures of promising, but the object of fidelity is misplaced. Augustine's insight into rightly ordered love, that persons should love God first and all else in relation to that love, helps to order our lesser fidelities.

A wariness of the allure and danger of certain promises is built into baptismal formulations that ask candidates, "Do you renounce the devil and all his empty promises?" Though necessarily accompanied by practices of humility, truthfulness, and forgiveness, promising is crucial to the Christian life and to understanding the deepest and most costly expressions of fidelity in marriage, family, vocation, and martyrdom.

See also Covenant; Duty; Fidelity; Forgiveness; Integrity; Marriage and Divorce; Oaths; Obligation; Truthfulness, Truth-Telling; Utilitarianism; Vows

Bibliography

Arendt, H. *The Human Condition*. University of Chicago Press, 1958, chaps. 33–34; Atiyah, P. *Promises, Morals, and Law*. Oxford University Press, 1981; Farley, M. *Personal Commitments: Beginning, Keeping, Changing*. Harper & Row, 1986; Rawls, J. *A Theory of Justice*. Belknap Press, 1971, 344–50; Robins, M. *Promising, Intending, and Moral Autonomy*. CSP. Cambridge University Press, 1984; Ross, W. *Foundations of Ethics*. Clarendon, 1939, 87–113; idem. *The Right and the Good*. Clarendon, 1930, 16–47; Searle, J. "How to Derive 'Ought' from 'Is.'" *PR* 73 (1964): 43–58; Smedes, L. "The Power of Promising." *Christianity Today* (Jan. 21, 1983): 16–19; Vitek, W. *Promising*. Temple University Press, 1993.

Christine D. Pohl

Propaganda

The term *propaganda* came into use when in 1622 Pope Gregory XV established the Sacra Congregatio de Propaganda Fide (Sacred Congregation for the Propagation of the Faith). The modern connotation of propaganda as a deliberate attempt to coerce and manipulate perception became prevalent during World War I, when governments employed various forms of media to promote domestic war efforts while demonizing enemies.

The Roman Empire used architecture, public ceremonies, religious events, public inscriptions, sculptures, and other propaganda to build up the image of the empire and its emperor. The Romans, through their propaganda, were able "to exploit a political and spiritual vacuum that made their imperial subjects much more susceptible to the sophisticated offerings of their conquerors. . . . It provided a moral philosophy and a cultural aesthetic that was adopted by the local peoples" (Jowett and O'Donnell 54). In the ancient world coins were an especially important instrument of propaganda because they indicated economic power and authority and reached a wider audience than any other medium.

The Herodians and Pharisees attempted to trap Jesus with a question about paying taxes to Caesar (Mark 12:13–17 pars.). On the one hand, had Jesus openly opposed taxation, that would have marked him as an enemy of the state and allowed for his arrest. On the other hand, had he endorsed taxation, that would have evoked condemnation from the Jewish populace. They regarded taxation as acceptance of Roman rule and as idolatry because Roman coins featured images of the emperor. In response to their question, Jesus asks for a denarius, which featured the image of Caesar and the inscription "Tiberius Caesar Augustus, Son of the Divine Augustus." When the Pharisees and Herodians acknowledge the image and inscription on the denarius as belonging to Caesar, Jesus responds, "Give to Caesar the things that are Caesar's, and to God the things that are God's" (Mark 12:17 NET). Jesus effectively avoids their trap by distinguishing between Caesar, whose divine status is merely inscribed on coins, and the true God of the Jews, who has no need for such propaganda.

Rome's spectacle entertainments were another important use of propaganda. Roman politicians and dignitaries sponsored gladiator fights, exotic animal hunts, public executions, and other "attractions" to display the military might of Rome to tens of thousands in the Colosseum and in similar venues. Early Christians objected to both the violence of the spectacles and the way they cultivated desires in the spectators. Augustine described the effects of this propaganda on spectators: "As soon as he saw the blood, he at once drank in savagery and did not turn away. His eyes were riveted. He imbibed madness . . . he found delight in the murderous contest and was inebriated by bloodthirsty pleasure. He was not the person who had come in, but just one of the crowd" (*Conf.* 6.7.13). In his catechetical lectures Quodvultdeus warned catechumens, "The very one who is delighted by such a spectacle has lost his empty soul" (*First Homily on the Creeds* 2.1–4). Similarly, Tertullian (*The Shows*), Cyprian (*On the Public Shows*), and Irenaeus counseled their congregations against participation in this powerful form of propaganda.

See also Deception; Government; Manipulation; Media, Ethical Issues of

Bibliography

Jowett, G., and V. O'Donnell. *Propaganda and Persuasion*. 4th ed. Sage, 2006; Lasswell, H., D. Lerner, and H. Speier, eds. *The Symbolic Instrument in Early Times*. Vol. 1 of *Propaganda and Communication in World History*. University Press of Hawaii, 1979.

Chanon R. Ross

Property and Possessions

From the beginning, the Bible devotes significant attention to possessions. The narratives of the patriarchs keep account of the flocks and herds that accompany the wanderings of Abraham and his descendants, and these are repeatedly referred to as evidence of divine blessing. Later, when agriculture replaces nomadic herding as a way of life, property comes to include land as well as livestock, and houses and fields are added to the inventory. Certainly this positive depiction of prosperity rules out certain attitudes toward property. There can be neither gnostic rejection of matter as tainted nor any pure asceticism that flatly equates material comfort with spiritual corruption. These and related motifs in Scripture, coupled with the values and inclinations of our own society, have given rise to a contemporary school of thought that understands wealth as an essential sign of God's favor. Some claim it as a central aspect of the welfare that God desires for the faithful, to be actively pursued as such. But the biblical witness is much more various than this suggests and much more ambivalent in its attitude toward possessions. We will return to this question after a summary review of canonical sources.

Paralleling the patriarchal stories of expanding household wealth are the covenant law and prophetic materials that associate well-being, including abundance and material security, with righteousness and fidelity (e.g., Deut. 11:13–15). (They correspondingly threaten disaster, poverty, and suffering as the consequence of faithlessness to God.) Framed in the legal and prophetic texts in terms of the covenant fidelity and well-being of Israel as a whole (e.g., Lev. 26:3–5), in the later wisdom tradition they become promises of abundance addressed to individuals based on their personal righteousness and favor with God. This strand can be represented by a couple of examples: "The blessing of the Lord makes rich" (Prov. 10:22); "Prosperity rewards the righteous" (Prov. 13:21). Because of the close links between piety, moral rectitude, and practical prudence in this material, one finds in Proverbs a related strand of material that treats wealth and abundance as the natural reward of diligence and sound judgment—for example, "A slack hand causes poverty, but the hand of the diligent makes rich" (Prov. 10:4). Taken alone, these elements of the tradition seem consistent with the views of the popular "prosperity gospel."

But these are not the only biblical perspectives on wealth, even within the books cited above. Alongside Deuteronomy's promises of abundance and Isaiah's visions of grain and oil and tribute flowing into Jerusalem stand dire warnings. They caution against the temptation to trust in abundance and forget the God who provides it (Deut.

32:10–18), and they offer vigorous denunciations of those whose wealth turns them to idolatry (Isa. 2:7–8). Even the wisdom tradition is far from univocal. Proverbs can speak of ill-gotten riches (Prov. 10:2) and of the "deceptive wages" of the wicked (Prov. 11:18 NIV). The psalms that promise that those who fear the Lord "will abide in prosperity" (Ps. 25:13) are matched by those that lament the success of the ruthless and powerful and the impoverishment of the righteous (Ps. 10:1–6). If wealth and prosperity can be viewed as divine blessings on the righteous and as the natural result of hard work and sagacity, they can also be viewed as constant temptations to idolatry and as the tools and frequently the fruit of injustice and oppression. The prophets denounce the avid pursuit of wealth. Jeremiah declares, "Everyone is greedy for unjust gain" (Jer. 6:13), and "Their houses are full of treachery; therefore they have become great and rich" (Jer. 5:27). Zechariah pronounces judgment on those who accumulate wealth while ignoring the poor: "Just as, when I called, they would not hear, so, when they called, I would not hear, says the Lord of hosts, and I scattered them with a whirlwind among all the nations that they had not known. Thus the land they left was desolate" (Zech. 7:13–14).

The NT displays the same diversity and complexity of views about possessions, with both substantial overlap and significant departures from the OT. The theme of wealth as an occasion of idolatry, something that tempts its possessors to trust in economic security rather than in God, remains prominent. Along with explicit instruction equating covetousness with idolatry (Col. 3:5), multiple passages in the Pastoral Epistles warn against the love of money. In 1 Timothy the author goes so far as to call such love "a root of all kinds of evil" (1 Tim. 6:10). There are also multiple sayings of Jesus that address the problem of devotion to riches, including the blunt pronouncement "You cannot serve God and wealth" (Matt. 6:24; Luke 16:13).

Also brought forward from the OT is the suspicion of wealth as frequently being the result of injustice and the means of corruption. Luke repeatedly announces the coming reign of God in terms of the vindication of the poor over against the rich (e.g., Luke 1:53; 4:18), and the book of Revelation similarly identifies the saints as victims of economic oppression, whereas the whore of Babylon and her allies are wealthy and overindulged (e.g., Rev. 2:9; 17:3–4; 18:3, 23–24). Perhaps most vivid of all is the Letter of James, which contains a withering attack on the wealthy who hoard money while others are in want and use their economic power to exploit and cheat the poor, compromising the systems of justice (Jas. 5:1–6).

Particular to the NT is the concern with property and possessions as barriers to following Christ. The story of a particular well-off individual called to follow Jesus and refusing to do so appears with variations in all three Synoptic Gospels (Matt. 19:16–22; Mark 10:17–22; Luke 18:18–23). In all three versions it is the fact of his many possessions that keeps him from heeding the call, and he departs grieving for the life he cannot embrace. The parable of the sower, likewise in all three Synoptic Gospels, makes a similar point: the "riches and pleasures of life" (Luke 8:14) choke off the seed of the gospel and prevent its coming to fruition.

Finally, ownership of property in the NT is regarded as a call to responsibility for the well-being of the whole community, ultimately extending even to enemies. Believers are to share the means of bodily support with those in need and thus show their love to be more than words on the tongue (1 John 3:16–18). The early community in Acts offers an example of property held in common and distributed according to need (Acts 4:32–37). Elsewhere, the practical aim of sharing within the church is said to be "balance" or "equity" between those who have abundance and those who are in want (2 Cor. 8:13), but its touchstone is the overflowing generosity of Christ, who "for your sakes became . . . poor, so that by his poverty you might become rich" (2 Cor. 8:9). We are to do good to all as it lies in our power and explicitly to provide for the needs of our enemies, giving them food and drink as need requires (Rom. 12:20). The weight and the seriousness of these obligations are indicated in Matt. 25:31–46, where material care for the needy serves as the test of discipleship and the gate of heaven.

It is worth noting what does not come forward into the NT, which is much of the wisdom literature's confidence that faithfulness will bring prosperity. It remains that those who trust in God are promised the things they need to sustain their faithful service, but the emphasis is on necessities, not wealth. And numerous countertexts (e.g., Heb. 11:32–40), not to mention the Passion Narrative itself, make it difficult to maintain that fidelity will consistently find a material reward, or that material prosperity is an essential part of what God wants for faithful people. Similarly, the strand of wisdom literature that counts prosperity the reliable result of diligence and so to be taken as a mark of good character finds little validation in the NT. Traces of it remain in the insistence that those who expect to eat must continue to work and contribute to the community, and in the admonition that the former thieves take up work so that they may contribute to the poor.

The Bible gives us rich and theologically profound themes to guide our thinking regarding the accumulation, use, and distribution of property and possessions. The nuance, variety, and depth of its witness resist codification into simple rules about what one might earn, or own, or keep. At the same time, it provides powerful barriers against wholesale accommodation to consumer culture and its ethos of endless accumulation. Any version of the gospel that equates the fullness that God promises and desires for all with a celebration of personal wealth in the face of the dire poverty of millions of the world's inhabitants cannot stand as a credible response to the whole witness of Scripture.

See also Capitalism; Collection for the Saints; Consumerism; Economic Ethics; Greed; Idolatry; Koinonia; Land; Materialism; Poverty and Poor; Resource Allocation; Stewardship; Tithe, Tithing; Wealth

Bibliography

Cavanaugh, W. *Being Consumed: Economics and Christian Desire*. Eerdmans, 2008; Johnson, L. *Sharing Possessions: Mandate and Symbol of Faith*. Fortress, 1981; Wheeler, S. *Wealth as Peril and Obligation: The New Testament on Possessions*. Eerdmans, 1995.

Sondra E. Wheeler

Proselytism

Proselytism is the practice of gaining converts to a religious sect. Proselytizers promote a change in Christian denominations as well as interreligious conversion. In most cases, the term *proselytism* has a negative connotation, implying coercive methods or impure motives. Most Christians today who actively engage in sharing the message of the gospel prefer to speak of their work as evangelism, witness, or mission. These categories are considered more holistic or legitimate than proselytism. However, some theologians and legal experts argue that the distinction between proselytism and "authentic evangelism" is somewhat arbitrary and ought to be replaced with a conversation about proper versus improper proselytism.

Scriptural Origins

The term *proselytism* is derived from the Greek *prosēlytos* ("proselyte"). In the LXX, *prosēlytos* is used to translate the Hebrew for a "stranger" who chose to live among the people of Israel and to embrace the requirements of the law. The Jews did not actively engage in proselytism until after the Babylonian exile, but generally they welcomed proselytes and treated them with respect. The NT contains only four references to proselytes (Matt. 23:15; Acts 2:11; 6:5; 13:43), always reflecting Jewish and not Christian proselytizing efforts. Matthew 23 depicts Jesus condemning scribes and Pharisees who lead proselytes astray through an erroneous interpretation of Jewish law. This lone negative reference is not a denunciation of proselytism as such but rather of the practice when accompanied by false teaching. The three passages in Acts indicate that Jewish proselytes were among the most receptive to early Christianity.

In the Great Commission (Matt. 28:19) Jesus urges his followers to "make disciples of all nations." New Testament scholars who take this command seriously affirm that Jesus was issuing a call to evangelize and not proselytize. They also observe that neither Paul nor the other apostles spoke of their work as proselytism. Yet those who draw a sharp line between evangelism and proselytism may be ignoring the complex nature of the issue today, particularly with regard to intra-Christian proselytism. It is difficult to draw clear parallels with Scripture on this issue because early Christian conversion did not involve the vast range of denominational choices we face today.

Tension between Proselytism and Ecumenism

Contrasting proselytism with evangelism has been the focus of ecumenical efforts to achieve some consensus on the problematic features of proselytism. In 1995, a joint working group between the Roman Catholic Church and the World Council of Churches (WCC) published *The Challenge of Proselytism and the Calling to Common Witness*. This document urges evangelizing Christians to avoid using coercive or manipulative marketing techniques such as unfairly representing other Christian communities and providing material benefits in an attempt to convert a vulnerable portion of the population. A more recent WCC statement on proselytism, published in 1997, urges Christian churches to "renounce proselytism as a denial of authentic witness and an obstruction to the unity of the church." These statements highlight the ongoing tension between proselytism and ecumenism.

Because of the human desire for power and influence, proselytism can indeed be corrupted by colonialist ambitions and "the tendency toward empire-building" (Bosch 415). The numerical growth of one's denomination is a powerful motive for seeking converts. In the process, the reality of divine grace is de-emphasized and denominational membership is affirmed as essential to salvation. However, from the perspective of the zealous proselytizer, an ecumenical impulse toward unobjectionable evangelism overlooks the importance of building Christian faith communities and focuses too much on individual conversion. These proselytizers promote a rigorous and even competitive intrareligious dialogue. They suggest that the leaders of more established churches resist proselytism based on a fear of competition and a desire to retain ecclesiastical influence rather than on an uncorrupted desire for Christian unity.

Legal and Political Issues

Religious institutions with deep historical roots in a country often claim the legal right to retain or maintain their religion (Kerr 12). This is true especially for Muslims and Orthodox Christians. Orthodox views are influenced by a lingering resentment over the history of Catholic and Protestant proselytizing efforts. Some laws that restrict proselytism have a legitimate purpose in protecting citizens from fraud and extortion, such as when radical religious groups promise susceptible individuals eternal life in exchange for their life savings. Yet more often than not, laws that restrict proselytizing and other activities of younger churches amount to little more than the establishment of a preferred state religion.

International norms for religious freedom clash with Muslim teachings as well as with the efforts of established Christian churches to control proselytism through legal or political means. The Universal Declaration of Human Rights, adopted in 1948 by the United Nations, affirms religious freedom as a universal human right. From this perspective, the United Nations seeks to protect the rights of minorities, celebrate religious pluralism, discourage the abuse of political power, and support the separation of church and state.

Conclusion

Disagreement over the ethical nature of proselytism will continue as long as religious groups embrace missionary work as a God-given mandate. However, we can hope for some consensus regarding what falls into the category of "improper proselytism." We can agree that proselytism should never be subsidized by tax dollars. Other inappropriate motives and methods can also be collectively denounced, such as insensitivity to the beliefs and practices of an indigenous culture, uncharitable representations of other religious groups, and coercive practices that mock genuinely ecumenical efforts. Whether classified as proselytism or evangelism, the good news must always be shared "with gentleness and reverence" (1 Pet. 3:16).

See also Conversion; Ecumenism; Evangelism; Manipulation

Bibliography

Bosch, D. *Transforming Mission: Paradigm Shifts in Theology of Mission.* Orbis, 1991; Joint Working Group between the Roman Catholic Church and the World Council of Churches. *Seventh Report.* WCC Publications, 1998; Kerr, D. "Christian Understandings of Proselytism." *IBMR* 23 (1999): 8–12, 14; World Council of Churches. *"You Are the Light of the World": Statements on Mission by the World Council of Churches, 1980–2005.* WCC Publications, 2005.

Paul D. Miller

Prostitution

Prostitution is the provision of sexual services in exchange for some form of payment. In the ancient world, as today, it was a tolerated but socially dishonorable occupation. The prostitute is an ambiguous figure, simultaneously desired and despised.

Any attempt to offer an ethical assessment of prostitution must consider not only the activity of prostitutes but also that of their clients and of the people who act as third parties providing prostitutes (pimps, brothel owners, and those involved with sex trafficking). It must also consider the economic and social dynamics that enable the business of prostitution to function in the way that it does (and these will not be identical everywhere).

There are numerous contingent ethical issues raised by the sex trade that go beyond questions of sexual ethics. Various studies from different countries have shown that prostitutes are often threatened, violently assaulted, raped, and even murdered. The danger of disease is also ever present. In addition, a host of issues surround the way in which states deal with prostitutes via legislation, the police, and the courts. Ethical issues also surround the routes into prostitution; people become prostitutes for many different reasons, but common ones include poverty, homelessness, the need to feed a drug addiction, and coercion by criminal gangs (with a growing number of children forced into prostitution). Prostitutes are, in varying degrees and in different ways, both victims (albeit not always innocent victims) and moral agents.

Although some people, especially at the upper end of the market, choose prostitution because it is what they want to do and their experience of it does not involve violence and coercion, various studies show that the majority of prostitutes in both the developed and developing world do not wish to bc prostitutes.

A biblical-ethical assessment will need to consider biblical texts beyond those directly dealing with prostitutes and to ponder biblical themes such as the *imago Dei*, sin (structural and individual), a general sexual ethic, the importance of the body, freedom and slavery, social justice, God's solidarity with the broken, and redemptive love. This short article is restricted to biblical texts directly relating to prostitution and therefore falls short of this fuller discussion.

It has been common in scholarship to see two kinds of prostitute in biblical times: sacred (*qĕdēšâ*) and secular (*zônâ*). The cultic prostitute was thought to perform sex acts as part of the ritual in a fertility cult. A growing number of biblical scholars now argue that the *qĕdēšâ*, though a pagan cultic functionary, was not a "cult prostitute" (Bird). Thus the present discussion will ignore the probably mythical cult prostitute.

Although prostitution was socially disapproved of in Israel, biblical laws did not forbid it. This gap between ethical ideal and legislation is worth reflecting on. What the laws forbade was fathers selling their daughters into prostitution, presumably to pay off debts (Lev. 19:29). This has implications for the contemporary sex trade. The law also forbade priests from marrying prostitutes, but this seems to be because they were not virgins (and possibly the paternity of priestly descendants was the critical issue) (Lev. 21:7, 13–14). This standard was not applied to nonpriests. The daughter of a priest was forbidden to become a prostitute lest she defile both herself and her father (Lev. 21:9). Finally, the Deuteronomic law forbade the use of money earned from prostitution for the payment of a religious vow (Deut. 23:18). The honoring of vows was taken very seriously, and it is possible that some women resorted to prostitution to pay them. All the aforementioned laws presuppose that a woman who prostitutes herself, even if unwillingly (Lev. 19:29), ritually "defiles" herself, and this implies that the activity is antithetical to ritual holiness.

The place of prostitutes in OT narrative traditions is interesting. Tamar, Judah's daughter-in-law, was not a prostitute, but she pretended to be one in order to lure Judah to impregnate her on behalf of her dead husband (Gen. 38). The story reveals Judah's double standard and ultimately vindicates Tamar.

Rahab is presented in a very positive light (Josh. 2:1–14). She is a female Canaanite prostitute, but she trusts in Israel's God and shows *ḥesed*, covenant love, by assisting the people of Israel in their attack on Jericho. For this loyalty she was spared and her descendants lived in Israel (Josh. 6:17–25). In the NT, Rahab is honored as one of the ancestors of David and of Jesus (Matt. 1:5). She is upheld as a model of faith (Heb. 11:31) and as one who was justified by her works of faith (Jas. 2:25–26).

In 1 Kgs. 3:16–28 we read of two prostitutes who came to Solomon in a dispute over whose child was dead and whose still living. The story is told to show Solomon's wisdom in settling an argument in which the only evidence is the word of one prostitute against another. It is interesting that prostitutes had access to the king to settle a dispute, and that Solomon's strategy is predicated on the assumption that the real mother of the living baby will be a good mother, willing to give up her child rather than see it killed by being divided in half.

What is intriguing about these stories is that, while they are parasitic upon a stereotype of prostitutes as corrupt and untrustworthy people, they go some way toward undermining such stereotypes. The stories challenge us to see prostitutes as real people—daughters, mothers, sisters. Also interesting is that men such as Judah (Gen. 38) and Samson (Judg. 16:1), who used prostitutes, though implicitly disapproved of, were not thereby written off.

The wisdom literature sought to persuade its (male) audience not to use prostitutes. The reasoning is quite pragmatic: an addiction to prostitution is very expensive, and a man will lose his economic resources that way (Prov. 29:3; Sir. 9:6; 19:2). That said, the price of no-strings sex with a prostitute is cheap compared to the price of sex with a married woman (Prov. 2:16–19; 5:1–20; 6:25–26).

Wisdom literature aims to help men to be aware of, and to resist, the seductive words used by prostitutes and adulteresses (Prov. 7:1–27). As such, it trades off stereotypes, being disinterested in looking behind those words to the reasons why women might be resorting to them. The strategy has its place in persuading men not to use prostitutes, but it also has its obvious limitations.

The biblical prophets' references to prostitution are almost entirely metaphorical. Prostitution became the major sexual metaphor used to signify Israel's infidelity to Yahweh (Jer. 2:19–21; 3:1–3; 13:27; Ezek. 16; 23; 43:9; Hos. 4:6–19; 5:1–4; 6:6–11; 9:1–3). The metaphor is also picked up in various narratives, laws, and psalms (e.g., Exod. 34:15–16; Num. 15:37–41; Deut. 31:16–71; Judg. 2:17). However, the image is not simply Israel as a whore but rather Israel as a wife who acts as a whore. The use of prostitution rather than straightforward adultery as the key metaphor for apostasy probably was intended to (1) accentuate the number of her "sexual partners" (idols); (2) highlight that the infidelity was motivated by the expected "fee" (material blessings); and (3) suggest her shameless attitude toward her shameful behavior (Jer. 2:23). The metaphor trades off negative attitudes toward prostitution combined with the horror at inexplicable infidelity toward a good and faithful husband.

In the NT, Jesus says that the prostitutes and tax collectors who repented at John the Baptist's teaching are akin to a son who said that he would not do his father's will but then did it (Matt. 21:28–32). He told the Jewish leadership, "The tax collectors and the prostitutes are going into the kingdom of God ahead of you" (Matt. 21:31). Here, Jesus was not endorsing the validity of prostitution; indeed, the power of the saying depends on its undesirability (even prostitutes are ahead of priests and Pharisees!). However, he was implicitly rejecting the idea that prostitutes were inherently lewd and was welcoming repentant prostitutes into God's kingdom. This open approach is reinforced by the story of Jesus' attitude toward the woman (quite possibly a prostitute) who cleaned his feet with her tears in Simon the Pharisee's house (Luke 7:36–50). His forgiving attitude toward those who had used prostitutes in the past might be inferred from the parable of the prodigal son (Luke 15:13, 30).

The most theological argument in Scripture against the use of prostitutes is found in 1 Cor. 6:9–20. Paul is opposing those who think that all that matters is the spirit, and that what one does with one's body is ethically irrelevant. Paul's view of the body is grounded in a Jewish understanding of the goodness of material creation and of its ultimate resurrection. Consequently, the body is integral to our identity and holiness. To have sex with a prostitute is to sin:

1. *against Christ*. To sleep with a prostitute (who represents the alienated cosmos) is to join Christ with that prostitute, thereby blurring fundamental identity boundaries, and to deny Christ's ownership of our bodies (vv. 13–15).
2. *against oneself*. Paul sees the sexual act as one that involved the whole person, not simply body parts (vv. 16–18).
3. *against the Holy Spirit*. The body is a temple of God's Spirit, and to use it for sexual immorality is to "pollute" that temple (v. 19).

Clearly, all the biblical texts, both OT and NT, view prostitution as an ethically problematic activity. At the sexual level, this is grounded in the view that sexual activity should be restricted to marriage. The Bible has a consistently negative view of the practice of prostitution, though without allowing negative stereotypes of prostitutes to remain unchallenged and while granting prostitutes certain rights and welcoming prostitutes who wish to follow Yahweh. The Bible also consistently opposes the use of prostitutes but does not write off those who have used prostitutes.

The biblical writers say little about the ethical issues surrounding the routes into prostitution, the treatment of prostitutes by the state, and violence against prostitutes. However, the wider biblical materials do provide rich resources for Christians today who are alert to such issues. A contemporary biblical-ethical analysis of prostitution must engage in such broader reflections and position itself "against prostitution but for prostitutes."

See also Adultery; Body; Image of God; Sex and Sexuality; Sexual Ethics; Sin; Slavery

Bibliography

Bird, P. "The Harlot as Heroine: Narrative Art and Social Presupposition in Three Old Testament Texts." Pages 197–218 in *Missing Persons and Mistaken Identities: Women and Gender in Ancient Israel*. Fortress, 1997; idem. "'To Play the Harlot': An Inquiry into an Old Testament Metaphor." Pages 219–36 in *Missing Persons and Mistaken Identities: Women and Gender in Ancient Israel*. Fortress, 1997.

Robin Parry

Proverbs

The book of Proverbs directly addresses questions concerning ethics and the moral life. It is an anthology of "wisdom" material that includes long instructional poems (chaps. 1–9); collections of short, pithy sayings commonly thought of as "proverbs" intermingled with direct admonitions (chaps. 10–29); and other instructional material, including an acrostic poem (chaps. 30–31).

The poems in Prov. 1–9 deploy the metaphor of the "two ways" to speak of the possibilities of moral life: the way of wisdom and righteousness leads to life; the way of folly and wickedness leads to death. These poems exhort the reader to forsake the way of folly and follow the way of wisdom. Wisdom's value, or desirability, in the poems is persistently and metaphorically highlighted in terms of material riches (e.g., 2:4; 3:14–16; 8:10–11) and erotic attraction (e.g., 4:6, 8–9; 7:4). Wisdom is more valuable than wealth and offers not merely literal, material riches, but the "enduring wealth" of virtue (8:18) and is personified for the book's presumed original young, male audience as a desirable and marriageable woman (Yoder).

Yet, Proverbs recognizes that life's two divergent paths may not always appear so different from each other; it speaks of the enduring value of wisdom's way, but also of the powerful (if superficial) attraction of the way of folly and wickedness. The "sinners" who follow this way, for example, also hold out a promise of (ill-gotten) "precious wealth" to the one who would join them (1:10–19). Likewise, Prov. 1–9 not only personifies wisdom as a virtuous and desirable woman; these chapters also speak of another desirable woman: the strange or foreign woman, who, on a literal reading of the text, is best understood as an adulteress, potentially able to seduce the addressee (e.g., 2:16–19; 5:3–23). The adulteress, however, is symbolically linked with folly, which is later also personified as a woman (9:13–18). Together, the strange woman and Woman Folly constitute the mirror image of Woman Wisdom (9:1–6; cf. 1:20–21; 7:10–12). They represent all that belongs to the dangerous, wrong way.

By deploying images of desirable women and valuable material wealth in relation to the ways of wisdom and folly, Prov. 1–9 undertakes the moral task of training the desires of its addressee along the better of the two paths. Although wealth and erotic fulfillment are pleasing and can afford temporary advantage, neither, according to the sages of Proverbs, is ultimately as desirable as wisdom. The pursuit of these and other lesser goods, the text suggests, ought to be subordinated to the pursuit of wisdom and appropriately ordered by wisdom's virtues.

The precise content of the virtues that constitute wisdom's way, however, is only minimally sketched in Prov. 1–9. The short sayings, or "proverbs," and admonitions of Prov. 10–29, by contrast, address a spectrum of topics relevant to daily life that together comprised the themes of moral discourse in ancient Israelite wisdom traditions: right and wrong speech, diligence and slothfulness, wealth and poverty, the rich and the poor, and so forth.

Folklorists who have studied the proverbs of a range of cultures have demonstrated that the oral "performance" (or use) of such sayings in everyday settings regularly serves important moral purposes—in ethical instruction, decision-making, legal reasoning, and promoting the prized values and virtues of the culture in which they are current. However, the precise meaning, and hence moral import, of any proverbial saying is dependent on the concrete context in which it is uttered. When it is divorced from its oral context, a proverb becomes rootless and loses its full connotation. Wolfang Mieder has gone so far as to claim that "a proverb in a collection is dead" (Mieder 892) because, by definition, a proverb that is written in a book is devoid of its oral context.

If Mieder is correct that a proverb in a collection is dead, certain problems for understanding the book of Proverbs arise, since this text in large part consists precisely of proverbs in collections. Some commentators advocate "recontextualizing" the sayings of Proverbs for today's world (Bergant) and suggest that readers of the book today consider their own lives and apply any biblical proverbs that might prove to illumine those contexts.

Recontextualizing biblical proverbs is one way in which the contemporary ethical import of aspects of the book of Proverbs might be recognized and made accessible. Yet, scholars have long debated whether the sayings of Proverbs are the kind of oral, folk proverbs with which Mieder and other folklorists are concerned, or whether they represent the literary production of learned sages. If the sayings of Proverbs are not the kind of proverbs normally deployed in oral contexts, any recontexualizing can appear artificial and awkward.

In fact, it is likely that the sayings of Proverbs are not mere transcriptions of the oral, proverbial wisdom of the folk of ancient Israel and Judah, but rather are tropes that have been consciously shaped by the literary hand of professional scribes. Hence, they reflect and promote the virtues and moral perspectives of an intellectual elite, though not necessarily an economic or political elite.

Thus, in order to understand the moral landscape of Proverbs, it is most productive to consider the book's literary character. In this regard, the prologue in Proverbs (1:2–6) provides a hermeneutical cue for understanding both the book's moral purpose and how the text's literary features relate to the book's instruction. These verses indicate that Proverbs is concerned with instilling in its addressee intellectual virtues that it calls "wisdom," "instruction," and "insight" (v. 2); the social virtues of "righteousness, justice, and equity" (v. 3); and practical virtues such as "shrewdness" (v. 4). A close examination of 1:2–4 (see Sandoval) also indicates that v. 3 stands at the pinnacle of the passage's poetic structure, suggesting that the sages who constructed Proverbs particularly prized social virtue.

If vv. 2–4 of the prologue outline the content of Proverbs' teaching, vv. 5–6 signal how Proverbs' instruction will be presented by means of tropes (NRSV: "proverbs"), figures, and riddles. The book's moral discourse therefore is not a discourse that can be comprehended in merely literal terms; it requires readers who will thoughtfully examine its figurative dimensions.

Considering Proverbs' teaching within the literary horizon sketched by the prologue is important because the book sometimes is characterized as a simple guide to success. This understanding is largely due to an overly literal reading of the book's retributive rhetoric, which appears simplistically to promise good things to those who pursue wisdom's way and bad things to those who stray onto folly's path. The book's association of wealth with wisdom, for instance, often is thought to suggest that the one who finds wisdom should inevitably be rewarded with literal, material riches. Similarly, because the text also relates specific virtues (e.g., diligence) with images of material wealth, and certain vices (e.g., sloth) with images of material lack, sayings such as "A slack hand causes poverty, but the hand of the diligent makes rich" (10:4) sometimes are thought to "blame the poor" for their poverty and to congratulate the wealthy for their virtue. Since Proverbs also recognizes the real social advantage that wealth often provides the rich (10:15; 18:23; 22:7), many likewise believe that the book's moral bias is in favor of the economic elite. Yet, because the text also insists that poor be treated with kindness and justice, some have characterized much of the book's moral discourse as ambiguous.

However, by recalling that Proverbs is likely the product of a scribal (intellectual) elite, and that the prologue communicates the sages' preference for social virtue or justice (1:3) via figurative language, modern readers can approach the text in a meaningful manner while avoiding the extremes of literalism or acquiescence to the book's apparent moral ambiguity.

Readers can achieve this by, on the one hand, recognizing that Proverbs' retributive rhetoric, even if it ought not to be understood in a simple, literal manner, does suggest a correlation between the attainment of wisdom and good things, or a "good life," and by, on the other hand, identifying another important moral-theological claim made in the book: wisdom's close relationship to creation. According to Prov. 8:22–31, wisdom is intimately related to Yahweh's act of creation and might be said to infuse creation itself. Hence, those who attain wisdom's virtues and thus align themselves with the genuine nature of the wisdom-infused cosmos ought not be surprised if they reap real-life well-being.

Proverbs 8:22–31 is furthermore significant because here wisdom is personified as a woman and is arguably presented as a divine being whom Yahweh "acquired" (NRSV: "created"), perhaps as a consort, at "the beginning of his work" (v. 22). She both preexists creation (8:23–26) and is present at the moment of creation (8:27–29), if not actively creating with Yahweh as a "master worker" (8:30). As an independent and creative being beside the male Yahweh, Woman Wisdom has proved a remarkably generative image for much feminist ethical and theological work.

See also Old Testament Ethics; Wisdom Literature

Bibliography

Bergant, D. *Israel's Wisdom Literature: A Liberation-Critical Reading*. Fortress, 1997, 78–107; Mieder, W. "The Essence of Literary Proverb Studies." *Proverbium* 23 (1974): 888–94; Sandoval, T. *The Discourse of Wealth and Poverty in the Book of Proverbs*. BIS 77. Brill, 2006; Yoder, C. *Wisdom as a Woman of Substance: A Socioeconomic Reading of Proverbs 1–9 and 31:10–31*. BZAW 304. De Gruyter, 2001.

Timothy J. Sandoval

Prudence

In the OT, especially its sapiential literature, prudence is depicted as the practical wisdom possessed by the person who is able to apply knowledge to everyday life. Prudence is a particularly important theme in the book of Proverbs, the announced purpose of which is to provide instruction leading to wise and disciplined conduct, "doing what is right and just and fair" (Prov. 1:3 NIV). Since wisdom "dwells together" with prudence (Prov. 8:12), the latter is virtually synonymous with the learned patterns of "knowledge and discretion" that ultimately stem from the proper fear of the Lord (Prov. 1:7). The prudent person "acts out of knowledge" (Prov. 13:16 NIV), gives thought to ways and steps taken (Prov. 14:8, 15), shows an ability to foresee evil and avoid it (Prov. 22:13), chooses words carefully (Prov. 12:23), and overlooks insults (Prov. 12:16). The prudent person is often contrasted starkly with the fool. Prudence is presented as a matter of the heart that transforms moral character: "The heart of the discerning acquires knowledge; the ears of the wise seek it out" (Prov. 18:15 NIV). The prudent person displays a fundamental coherence and consistency of words, emotions, desires, and actions. This sort of integration of personal character is consistent with other biblical accounts of godliness or upright character (e.g., the Shema in Deut. 6:5). According to Proverbs, practical wisdom is gained gradually in the context of instruction and correction from parents and wise elders in the community and shows itself in openness to correction (Prov. 15:5; 16:21).

The Bible sometimes uses prudence in a different and basically negative sense to refer to shrewdness or craftiness in managing one's worldly affairs. For example, the serpent in the garden of Eden is "more crafty" or "cunning" than any other animal (Gen. 3:1; cf. 1 Sam. 23:22; Ps. 83:3). Guile and duplicity are routinely condemned as aberrant forms of "worldly prudence" that contradict righteous living.

In the NT, the typical Greek term for prudence (*phronēsis*) appears rarely (Luke 1:17; Eph. 1:8). Yet there are occasional echoes of the OT's endorsement of the prudent person. In various places the NT affirms the value of shrewd practical judgments in everyday life and praises those who make well-calculated decisions in mundane and practical matters. A clear example is when Jesus concludes his teaching in the Sermon on the Mount by extolling the "wise" (Gk. *phronimos*, "prudent") person who built a house on rock (Matt. 7:24). Just as a practically sensible person sees the folly of building on sand, so the spiritually sensible person will build an understanding of life on the words of Jesus. Similarly, Jesus says that he is sending his disciples out as sheep among wolves, therefore they should be "prudent" as serpents and harmless as doves (Matt. 10:16). The "prudent" virgins know how to manage daily affairs more effectively than the foolish virgins (Matt. 25:1–13). Another parable commends the prudent or "sensible" stewards (Luke 12:42; 16:8) for acting shrewdly in managing resources.

In classical antiquity, the crucial distinction is between *sophia* as theoretical wisdom having to do with the mind and knowledge, and *phronēsis* as practical wisdom dealing with life and conduct. Prudence is classified as one of the cardinal virtues. Stoic thinkers such as Cicero and Seneca identified goodness with wisdom. For Aristotle, prudence is truth "concerned with action in relation to the things that are good for human beings" (*Eth. nic.* 1140b20). It is the virtue required for all the other virtues. In the Christian tradition, the church fathers gave prudence relatively little treatment. Augustine recast the cardinal virtues as forms of Christian love, according to which "prudence is love discerning well between what helps it toward God and what hinders it" (*Mor. eccl.* 15.25). Drawing heavily on Aristotle, the moral theology of Thomas Aquinas gives prominence to prudence as "right practical reason," which is "a virtue or developed ability which enables an agent to make and carry out good decisions" (Westberg 3). Reflecting the Thomistic tradition, the Catechism of the Catholic Church (par. 1835) holds that prudence "disposes the practical reason to discern, in every circumstance, our true good and to choose the right means for achieving it."

See also Cardinal Virtues; Character; Proverbs; Virtue(s); Wisdom Literature

Bibliography

Augustine. *The Morals of the Catholic Church*. Kessinger, 2005; *Catechism of the Catholic Church*. Rev. ed. Burns & Oates, 1994, paragraphs 1806, 1835; Thomas Aquinas. *ST* II-II, qq. 47–56; Westberg, D. *Right Practical Reason: Aristotle, Action and Prudence in Aquinas*. Clarendon, 1994.

Jeffrey P. Greenman

Psalm 151 *See* Orthodox Ethics

Psalms

The Psalter manifests the implicit connection between ethics and prayer through its explicit focus on the Torah, the law. Indeed, the very structure of the Psalter reveals a concern for the law, for the five books of the Psalter (Pss. 1–41; 42–72; 73–89; 90–106; 107–150) reflect the fivefold division of the Torah (Genesis, Exodus, Leviticus, Numbers, Deuteronomy). Thus, in its final form, one could understand the Psalter as the law of God in song. Within this framework, numerous individual psalms describe the benefits of living according to the law and the overall necessity of righteous (i.e., orderly) living. Psalm 19, for example, exhorts the faithful to act in ways that preserve the order God has established at creation (vv. 1–6). Just as God has created the world by bringing order to chaos, God created the faithful community by ordering it through the law (vv. 7–14). Individuals and communities can participate in God's creative and ordering work; by living in accordance with the law, the faithful help preserve and sustain the order that God has imposed upon the world.

Many psalms focus on the theme of living righteously—that is, keeping the law (e.g., Pss. 15; 24; 37; 73). Among them, Ps. 1 has pride of place. As the introduction to the Psalter, it sets the agenda for all that follows. The first verses of this psalm reveal that a clear choice faces all individuals regarding how they will live in relationship to God and the world. One option is to live with and like the wicked (1:1), yet such a life leads inexorably to destruction (1:4–5, 6b). The other option is to live righteously and enjoy the rich blessings of God as a result (1:2–3, 6a). Given the extreme consequences of these options, it may seem surprising that the psalm names only one specific activity that characterizes the righteous life: meditating on the law (v. 2).

Modern readers often understand meditation as the process of entering into a state of silence, tranquility, solitude—even transcendence. However, the Hebrew verb *hāgâ* (translated "meditate" in the NRSV) actually suggests none of these connotations. Rather, *hāgâ* has a broad semantic range that includes numerous modes of speaking: uttering, reciting, growling, murmuring, and even singing (LeFebvre). To meditate on the law (Ps. 1:2) is to use a variety of forms of speech to talk to God and about God's justice. That is to say, the essence of meditation on the law is prayer; and framed this way, the entire Psalter becomes an extended meditation on the law. In light of Ps. 1, one discerns that the Psalter presents an ethic of prayer. Prayer is the sole foundation of righteous behavior, informing and shaping every action in the lives of the faithful. Right actions rely on constant dialogue with God.

In the Psalter, this dialogue appears in beautiful and arresting poetry, set in a variety of genres (individual and communal laments, hymns, songs of thanksgiving, etc.). Taken together, these prayers give expression to the profound joys and deep sorrows that accompany a life lived honestly in relationship with God. Yet there remains a significant challenge for those who seek to live out the ethic of prayer that the psalms embody. Many psalms reflect a fear of the violence of the wicked enemies and contain prayers for Yahweh to provide both salvation from and retribution against the enemies. The violent pleas of the psalmist—for example, that God slay the wicked (Ps. 139:19) or shatter the heads of the enemies (Ps. 68:21)—create unease among many modern readers, for these passages seem to blur the line between salvation from enemies and retribution against enemies. One wonders if it is right for the psalmist to pray this way.

There have been many suggestions for how Christians should understand the psalms that curse the enemies and invoke God's violent actions against them—the so-called imprecatory psalms. Erich Zenger has helpfully outlined a number of the proposals (13–22). Some interpreters have considered these psalms to reflect a pre-Christian or anti-Christian Judaism that is utterly contrary to Jesus' teaching of love for one's enemies (Matt. 5:4; Luke 6:27, 35). This supersessionist viewpoint has led to the dismissal of certain psalms altogether or at least to the practice of reading only selected verses of problematic psalms so as not to acknowledge the psalmists' desire for God to act violently against the enemies. The sad irony is that such supersessionism has actually motivated and ostensibly justified brutal acts of violence by Christians against Jews.

In response to this, an increasingly common trend is to find ways to reclaim the psalms of imprecation as appropriate and even vital elements of Christian piety. According to one line of thinking, violent thoughts that go unacknowledged can degrade and pollute the relationship between God and the faithful. Praying honestly requires voicing these feelings, so these psalms function as a form of theological catharsis for those who suffer greatly (McCann 115). Such catharsis is a necessary step in healing. Similarly, Patrick Miller has suggested that psalms of imprecation are valuable for Christian faith and practice in that they represent a simultaneous "letting go" and "holding back." The prayers validate the experience of suffering and acknowledge the need for retribution, even as the psalmists restrain their emotions by praying the violence rather than executing violence themselves (Miller 200). Thus, these psalms in fact present a radical ethic of nonviolence. By placing violence in the context of prayer, the psalmists reject the right of human retribution and trust in God alone to bring about justice (Firth 141).

These responses to the problem of violence in the psalms have merit, but questions remain. It is difficult to maintain that the psalms categorically reject any act of retribution by humans against humans. While the Psalter commonly pictures Yahweh as the one who would execute violence on the enemies, in several cases humans are the ones meting out violence (e.g., Pss. 18; 149). Whether one understands this violence as execution of divine justice or vengeance, these psalms suggest that such human violence somehow serves the will of a righteous, judging God.

A community's patterns of prayer reflect and inform its behavior. Thus, someone who prays for blessings of widows, orphans, and the downtrodden (Ps. 146:8–9) also will be inclined to minister to the needs of these people just as God does. Likewise, it is reasonable to assume that someone who prays for God to execute violence on evil oppressors may be motivated to act as God's agent and inflict violence if and when that is possible. Violent prayers may ultimately have a deleterious effect on the community if they lead to the assumption that one can act as God's agent and mete out divine retribution.

At this point, the antiphonal nature of the psalms becomes critical to understanding their ethic of prayer. In ancient Israel, as today, prayers uttered within a community prompt the community's "Amen!" (e.g., Deut. 27:19–26; 1 Chr. 16:36;

Pss. 41:13; 72:19; 89:52; 106:48; Jer. 28:6); that is, the community can serve as a moderator of the prayers, confirming some prayers with its amen and withholding its amen from other prayers, when, for example, the violence of the prayer does not suit the actual situation of the supplicant. A faithful and sensitive community affirms that it is better to pray that God would act violently against the enemies than it is for supplicants to do violence and take matters into their own hands. Yet the community is also aware that prayers shape behavior. And violent prayers can be as dangerous as they are healing. Thus, for every prayer in the psalms, particularly for violent ones, a community serves a critical role, regulating and affirming the prayers with its amens.

See also Old Testament Ethics; Poetic Discourse and Ethics

Bibliography

Firth, D. *Surrendering Retribution in the Psalms: Responses to Violence in the Individual Complaints*. PBM. Paternoster, 2005; LeFebvre, M. "Torah Meditation and the Psalms: The Invitation of Psalm 1." Pages 213–25 in *Interpreting the Psalms: Issues and Approaches*, ed. D. Firth and P. Johnston. InterVarsity, 2005; McCann, J. *Theological Introduction to the Book of Psalms: The Psalms as Torah*. Abingdon, 1993; Miller, P. "The Hermeneutics of Imprecation." Pages 193–202 in *The Way of the Lord: Essays in Old Testament Theology*. Eerdmans, 2007; Wenham, G. "The Ethics of the Psalms." Pages 175–94 in *Interpreting the Psalms: Issues and Approaches*, ed. D. Firth and P. Johnston. InterVarsity, 2005; Zenger, E. *A God of Vengeance: Understanding the Psalms of Divine Wrath*. Westminster John Knox, 1994.

Joel M. LeMon

Public Theology and Ethics

The term *public theology*, understood as the basis of social ethics, is quite new. However, the traditional claim that key dimensions of theology can and should be accepted publically as the best grounding for such an ethic is very old. It is rooted in the biblical doctrines of creation, sin, covenantal law, providence, prophetic witness, salvation in Christ, and an eschatology that entails the realization of the kingdom of God. The essential reason that these doctrines should be accepted is simply that these key themes and claims of theology are true, and not only true for believers. Martin Marty, the noted church historian, first used the new term in relation to the work of the leading Christian ethicist of the twentieth century, Reinhold Niebuhr. It was later adopted and expanded by theologian David Tracy, who drew also on the earlier work of Protestant sociologist Ernst Troeltsch, and Catholic moral philosopher John Courtney Murray. They had documented the ways in which such doctrinal teachings influenced social, political, economic, familial, and professional ethics that were woven into the fabric of cultural life and accepted by believers and nonbelievers alike as enabling human flourishing. The idea was adopted also by European scholars such as Jürgen Moltmann and Wolfhart Pannenberg and spread over the years so that in 2007 the Global Network for Public Theology was formed, and the *International Journal for Public Theology* was established.

Today the term *public theology* applies to those aspects of theology that are both informed by the interaction of biblical insights with philosophy, the sciences, and the world religions, and intended to shape the ethics that guide the common life. Historic leaders of Christian thought who have addressed social questions are taken as models of public theology, and their texts can be identified as the "classics" of this tradition—for example, Augustine's *City of God*, Thomas Aquinas's *Summa theologiae* (part II-II), Martin Luther's writings on Christianity and society, John Calvin's *Institutes*, Abraham Kuyper's *Lectures on Calvinism*, Emil Brunner's *Christianity and Civilization*, as well as the many texts produced by missionary, Puritan, social gospel, social encyclical, civil rights, and liberation movements.

In these writings and movements, theological matters are addressed both to the churches and to all those who are instrumental in forming and/or reforming the hearts and souls of persons and the shape of ecclesiastical organizations and civil society. And the warrants, explicit or implicit, for doing so are taken from what has become known as the "quadrilateral." That is, they appeal to Scripture, tradition, reason, and experience, especially where they overlap, mutually support or correct possible misuses of one or another, and foster compelling arguments as to what we ought to believe about why things are as they are and about how we ought to live.

It is perhaps not surprising that such a term would appear in the twentieth century, for it was a time when new technologies, secular philosophies, and nationalist-driven expansion culminated in colonialism (prompting intense decolonialization movements), two world wars, and the threat of a cold war with nuclear weaponry hovering over regional conflicts. These threatened much of public life as it had been conventionally understood in particular contexts, following the principles of national sovereignty. These also reflected a newly vigorous internationalization of political, cultural, and economic institutions (now called "globalization") in which a new public was created, wider than most people previously imagined (and against which many reacted). Thus, the attempt to find more universal, genuinely ecumenical and catholic, yet orthodox, evangelical, and just ways of speaking theologically and ethically to guide the increasingly common life was urgent. On the one hand, the new awareness of pluralism led to neosectarian reactions against the modern world and to the recognition that the age of politically established national creeds, especially in Christian Europe, is over—although the residues of similar structures remain in some contexts and have analogies in societies shaped by the traditions of other world religions. On the other hand, in Christian cultures both sectarian particularity and politically enforced confessions make theology a private matter of this or that community, which Christian public theology has always aspired to surpass from very early in its history (see the "great commission" of Matt. 28:18–20).

In this regard, it may be useful to contrast public theology with the several concepts with which it is sometimes confused. Sociologist Will Herberg used the term *civic religion* to describe what Protestantism, Judaism, and Catholicism in the United States shared as the religious aspects of "Americanism," although he was also clear that each "root" of this shared canopy of conviction retained its own distinctive faith and practice. Later, sociologist Robert Bellah published one of his famous essays on "civil religion," which had similar overtones. Such views can help us to describe the operating value system in a particular culture, and any theology or ethic seeking to address social or cultural issues should be clear about this matter. But these views of the ethos often are used to celebrate these values because they are "ours," to solidify the collective consciousness of the nation. Thus, critics have wondered whether civic religion and civil religion are forms of chauvinism, merely a worshiping of Western culture.

In contrast to these common-denominator features within a particular society and the tendency to project that culture into the heavens, public theology intends to identify universally valid dimensions of biblical and doctrinal sources, of the world's philosophical wisdom, and of general ethical principles to evaluate the validity of these operating values, and to call for the reform, revision, or refinement of them and of the convictions on which they rest as necessary. Of course, to do so convincingly it must also make a plausible case in public discourse that it can identify what is universally valid in biblical and extrabiblical sources and be willing to be corrected if or when it is shown that its claims are not and cannot be universally valid.

Yet, public theology as it was developed over the centuries has taken quite seriously the ways in which religion in general and specific doctrines operate in a culture, in contrast to some dogmatic traditions that focus more exclusively on the particularities of the faith and treat all religion(s) as idolatrous social or cultural inventions no matter what the consequences of such dogmas render. From the standpoint of at least some forms of public theology, religion as it is believed and practiced in a cultural ethos may well contain the relative incarnation of revelatory insights, authentic faith, and valid ethical elements that need defending or refining, not rejection. It takes the comparative and critical assessment of these factors and of their consequences very seriously and holds that it demands nuanced quadrilateral analysis, using all the theological and ethical methods to confirm or challenge their authenticity.

The idea of public theology is also challenged by those who argue that philosophy is a more universal human mode of public discourse, and that theology is always dependent on a particular religion that is closed to outsiders. But advocates of public theology argue that some particulars in fact bear and reveal the universal more adequately than others. Further, this kind of theology at its best includes the concerns of philosophy, but it understands them within a larger framework that involves attention to claims about the self-disclosure of the love and justice of *theos*—the basis that is held to be deeper and broader than any humanist love of wisdom by itself can discover. Theology always, sometimes unwittingly, selectively uses philosophy as its servant and considers the philosophy of religion a close cousin; however, philosophy does not always include consideration of God and sometimes excludes it as a problem, if not nonsense.

Another contrast with public theology is "political theology," in some senses a sister discipline. This contrast is based in the conviction that although a political order is necessary in every social order, the public is prior to the republic. The fabric of civil society, of which religious faith and organization ordinarily form the core, is more determinative of and normatively more important for politics than politics is for society, religion, and morality. Public theology and ethics, as widely seen, differ from political theology and ethics precisely in this: public theology tends to adopt a social theory of politics, whereas political theology inclines to a political view of society. The latter view is most common in imperial, authoritarian, and totalitarian contexts and tends to see political activity or government as the comprehending institution of society. Politics, in this view, is dedicated to the accumulation, organization, and exercise of coercive power for the sake of the enforcement of the edicts of a ruling party. It may do so in a benevolent way, but it is ever concerned with gaining a monopoly of power to guide, limit, or command every subject or citizen and every other institution in a geographical territory, with the threat of the use of force standing behind its actions. Yet, since no regime can long rule by naked force alone, it seeks legitimacy. That is, it seeks a recognition that its possession and use of its power are spiritually and morally, or at least legally, authorized by the religious ideology that it seeks to establish.

However, a social theory of politics sees political parties, governmental polities, and official policies as profoundly shaped by the more primary powers in society—those spheres of life that exist morally, spiritually, and socially prior to the formation of political orders. In this view, political orders, regimes, and dynasties come and go; they are always necessary, but they are also artifacts of those cultural, intellectual, social, technological, and economic spheres of life built on values and interests that are prior to government, and to which every government is, sooner or later, accountable. If a government unduly attempts to control these spheres of social life, they will foment resistance, revolution, and attempts to transform the ruling parties or the form of government altogether. Further, a public theology is predisposed to embrace those social theories that recognize how much these spheres of the common life are shaped by religion and constitute the true public, which government exists to protect, aid, and allow to flourish. It is on this basis that we can say that the purpose of government is "public service," where the public supplies the source of the legitimacy that any regime needs to survive. The shorthand slogan of this view is this: "Piety predetermines polity, and polity predetermines policy."

The idea is that faith should not only address believers gathered under the steeple in regard to their private beliefs and behaviors as children of God and in regard to their life together as members of a community of believers; it should also address their lives and actions as participants in families, schools, communities, corporations, cultural organizations, and service and advocacy groups in the so-called secular institutions of civil society. These often are treated by Catholic doctrines of a God-given "natural law" and by the Reformed traditions of "common grace" or "general revelation." Both imply a public theology. The biblical sources to which both public theologies turn are many, each laden with elements of a universal ethic.

The stories at the beginning of the Bible are intended to establish that life is a gift of God, that humans are made in the image of God, that all persons have a dignity and capabilities that ought not to be wantonly violated, that humanity has a cultural mandate to care for the earth and form civilization responsibly, and that all must acknowledge that we are not always faithful in how we treat these gifts of grace. The grand story of the exodus is a paradigmatic statement against sinfulness, oppression, and exploitation, and of how God commissions all who gain enough liberation from these betrayals of grace to participate in the ordering of life in societies around universal first principles of right and wrong and ultimate purposes of the common good. The narratives of leadership by priests and kings and the oracles of the prophets repeatedly warn humanity of the consequences of infidelity and injustice, and the wisdom literature shows that valid insight can come from sources outside our primary religious and cultural traditions. And from this historical experience comes the expectation and promise of redemption by a messiah.

And in the NT, it is not only Jesus and the disciples who bear the good news of the gospel that the Messiah has come; repeatedly, the crowds are witnesses, even though some turn away and some turn against that message. Even more, the parables used to convey the theological and ethical message about a historical transformation of the common life were drawn from areas of public life—weddings, working, trading, fishing, healing, trials, teaching, preaching, sharing, feasting, debating—that Jesus presumes can be publically understood. And both Paul and Peter anticipate missionaries and preachers of all generations who go to the peoples of the world everywhere with both the insights of the faith and the drive to help people, which generate missions of education, medicine, just legal systems, and technological and economic development, even if they also carry with them the perils of imperialism, which can be overcome only by a better global public theology than some have had.

See also Common Good; Natural Law; Pluralism; Political Ethics

Bibliography

Atherton, J. *Public Theology for Changing Times*. SPCK, 2000; Bellah, R. "Civil Religion in America." *Dædalus* 96, no. 1 (1967): 1–21; Bolt, J. *A Free Church, A Holy Nation: Abraham Kuyper's American Public Theology*. Eerdmans, 2001; Breitenberg, E., Jr. "To Tell the Truth: Will the Real Public Theology Please Stand Up?" *JSCE* 23, no. 2 (2003): 55–96; Browning, D., and F. Schüssler Fiorenza, eds. *Habermas, Modernity, and Public Theology*. Crossroad, 1992; Cady, L. *Religion, Theology, and American Public Life*. State University of New York Press, 1993; Casanova, J. *Public Religions in the Modern World*. University of Chicago Press, 1994; Fergusson, D. *Community, Liberalism, and Christian Ethics*. NSCE. Cambridge University Press, 1998; Herberg, W. *Protestant, Catholic, Jew: An Essay in American Religious Sociology*. Rev. ed. Anchor Books, 1960; Himes, M., and K. Himes. *Fullness of Faith: The Public Significance of Theology*. Paulist Press, 1993; Lovin, R. *Christian Faith and Public Choices: The Social Ethics of Barth, Brunner, and Bonhoeffer*. Fortress, 1984; Moltmann, J. *God for a Secular Society: The Public Relevance of Theology*. Fortress, 1999; Niebuhr, R. *The Nature and Destiny of Man: A Christian Interpretation*. 2 vols. Charles Scribner's Sons, 1949–51; Schindler, J. *Christianity and Civil Society: Catholic and Neo-Calvinist Perspectives*. Lexington Books, 2008; Simons, R. *Competing Gospels: Public Theology and Economic Theory*. E. J. Dwyer, 1995; Stackhouse, M. *Public Theology and Political Economy*. Eerdmans, 1984; Tracy, D. *Blessed Rage for Order: The New Pluralism in Theology*. Crossroad, 1991; Wijaya, Y. *Business, Family, and Religion: Public Theology in the Context of the Chinese-Indonesian Business Community*. Peter Lang, 2002; Wuthnow, R. *Christianity and Civil Society: The Contemporary Debate*. Trinity Press International, 1996.

Max L. Stackhouse

Punishment

Punishment may be defined as the deliberate infliction, by a recognized authority, of an unpleasant or painful experience on a person, such as the deprivation of something greatly valued, like freedom or money or even life itself, as the sequel to a perceived offense and corresponding in some way to the action that evoked it. The need to punish wrongdoing often seems self-evident, but because the calculated imposition of suffering on another human being is typically an evil, punishment stands in need of moral justification. What entitles us to add the pain of punishment to the pain already caused by the offense? This question is particularly challenging for Christian ethics because the NT expressly calls on believers not to repay evil with evil but rather to overcome evil with good (Matt. 5:38–48; Rom. 12:14–21).

Two main sets of approaches have been taken to justify the legitimacy of punishment as a social institution: retributivist and utilitarian. The former appeals to moral considerations, in particular the concept of just deserts. Where an offense has been committed, the offender intrinsically deserves to be punished; no further grounds are needed to justify punishment. The latter approach appeals to efficacy considerations. Punishing wrongdoers is justifiable only where it yields better results than not punishing them. Some utilitarian theories stress the role of punishment in reforming offenders; others give primacy to deterrence; still others emphasize its value in incapacitating criminals and protecting the innocent. Each account has strengths and weaknesses, and each can claim some biblical warrant, which is not surprising given the diversity of biblical teaching on the topic.

The validation of punishment as a means of rehabilitation first emerged in the late eighteenth century and became increasingly popular during the nineteenth and twentieth centuries. As it took hold, it contributed significantly to mitigating the severity of criminal law. Brutal physical punishments, such as torture, mutilation, transportation, and execution, were progressively supplanted by prolonged periods of incarceration as a more humane and effective way of dealing with criminals. The modern penitentiary, as the name suggests, was devised with the goal of encouraging penance in inmates by a combination of hard work, strict discipline, and solitary reflection.

The concern for rehabilitating wrongdoers resonates deeply with biblical teaching on repentance and renewal. God's punishments of Israel frequently are said to be given in order to encourage repentance (Lev. 26:14–33; Deut. 4:24–31; 1 Kgs. 8:33–34; Ps. 78:34; Jer. 31:18), though, perhaps tellingly, the strategy does not always work in practice (Isa. 9:13; 42:25; Jer. 2:30; 5:3; Dan. 9:13; Amos 4:6–11; Zech. 1:1–6). The reformative intent of punishment is also evident in the NT (1 Cor. 5:5; 2 Cor. 2:6–8; 1 Tim. 1:19–20; Heb. 12:7–11). It is important to realize, however, that punishment can only ever serve as an invitation to change. Inflicting pain on a person does not, of itself, amend character, and it seriously risks doing the opposite. One reason why rehabilitationism has fallen out of favor in recent penal thought is that it has signally failed to reduce recidivism. For this reason, and for other ethical considerations, punishment is better understood as a potential occasion for rehabilitation rather than its essential rationale.

Another utilitarian way of justifying punishment is by appealing to its effect in deterring further offending, whether by the individual concerned ("specific deterrence") or by others in the community ("general deterrence"). Here punishment is more about dissuading offending rather than reforming offenders. Such dissuasion helps to protect the innocent, which sometimes is cited as a separate justification for punishment. A frequent defense of imprisonment is that it incapacitates predatory individuals, thus preventing additional victimization.

Scripture is filled with admonitions for the protection of the innocent, and the Bible seems to recognize a deterrent dimension to punishment. The outcome of the death penalty for rebellion in ancient Israel was that "all the people will hear and be afraid, and will not act presumptuously again" (Deut. 17:13 [cf. Deut. 13:11; 21:21; Rom. 13:3–5]). A similar concern underlies instructions relating to church discipline in 1 Timothy: "As for those who persist in sin, rebuke them in the presence of all, so that the rest also may stand in fear" (1 Tim. 5:20 [cf. Acts 5:11]).

The deterrent effect of punishment, however, is susceptible to a number of constraints. Deterrence works best with certain kinds of crime (those involving rational premeditation and promising material gain) and with certain sections of the population (those normally inclined to be law-abiding citizens); it has not been shown to work for crimes of passion or with people predisposed to offending by debilitating personal or social circumstances over which they feel they have little control.

All such utilitarian justifications for punishment are rejected by the retributivist approach, which appeals solely to its character as deserved recompense. On this view, wrongdoing creates a moral or social imbalance that can be rectified only by reciprocating with punishment.

There is undoubtedly a retributive dimension to biblical teaching on punishment. This is especially apparent in the restriction of punishment to the guilty party alone (Deut. 24:16; 2 Kgs. 14:6; Ezek. 18:4) and in the requirement that the penalty be proportionate to the crime (Exod. 21:23–24; Lev. 24:19–22; Deut. 19:21; 25:3). At the same time, there is a uniquely religious or ritual dimension to OT jurisprudence that transcends retributive calculations. This feature needs to be factored in when assessing the relevance of biblical texts to contemporary social ethics. Also to be factored in is the rhetorical or pedagogical intent of biblical laws that seem to prescribe excessively harsh punishments for certain behaviors.

New Testament texts on punishment fall into two main categories: those that refer to punitive practices in wider Roman and Jewish society (e.g., Mark 13:9; John 16:2; Acts 4:3; 12:2–3; Rom. 13:2–4; 1 Pet. 2:14) and those that describe disciplinary actions within the community of faith (e.g., Matt. 18:15–20; 1 Cor. 5:1–8, 11, 13; 6:1–11; 2 Cor. 2:5–11; 7:5–13; 10:6; Gal. 6:1; 2 Thess. 3:14–15; 1 Tim. 1:19–20; 2 Tim. 3:1–5). In the latter case, physical or financial punishments are never imposed as a means of church discipline; penalties range from private admonition, to public rebuke, to expulsion from the community. In every case, it can be shown that the goal of such punishment was to clarify the moral demands of discipleship and to summon repentance from offenders and their reintegration into the community.

See also Capital Punishment; Crime and Criminal Justice; Excommunication; Justice, Restorative; Justice, Retributive; Penance; Prison and Prison Reform; Restitution; Reward and Retribution

Bibliography

Golash, D. *The Case against Punishment: Retribution, Crime Prevention, and the Law*. New York University Press, 2005; Gorringe, T. *God's Just Vengeance: Crime, Violence and the Rhetoric of Salvation*. CSIR 9. Cambridge University Press, 1996; Hoyles, J. *Punishment in the Bible*. Epworth, 1986; Logan, J. *Good Punishment? Christian Moral Practice and U.S. Imprisonment*. Eerdmans, 2008; Marshall, C. *Beyond Retribution: A New Testament Vision for Justice, Crime, and Punishment*. Eerdmans, 2001; Moberly, J. *The Ethics of Punishment*. Faber & Faber, 1968; Redekop, P. *Changing Paradigms: Punishment and Restorative Discipline*. Herald Press, 2007; Wood, C. *The End of Punishment: Christian Perspectives on the Crisis in Criminal Justice*. St. Andrews Press, 1991.

Christopher Marshall

Q

Quality of Life

"Quality of life" is a phrase used to designate the broadest measures of well-being of an individual or community. It may be used, for example, in the consideration of the impact that graffiti or a park or street lighting may have on neighborhood crime rates. Nevertheless, quality-of-life considerations are most often raised in the context of medical care (especially end-of-life care decisions), and that is the usage considered here.

Contemporary Situation

Quality-of-life considerations frequently are involved with decisions to forgo medical treatments that may prolong one's life but risk rendering its quality unacceptable and with decisions to undergo medical treatments to enhance the quality of one's life but risk either significantly diminishing the quality of life or shortening life itself. Medicine's abilities to cure disease and to preserve life often are attended by risks, great or small, of some harm, great or small, that diminishes a person's potential for full flourishing. Decisions about treatment have always posed such problems—even the ancients risked blindness to have their cataracts removed. Recent medical technologies, however, have pressed this question as sharply as possible: do efforts to prolong life sometimes force us into living a life of untenable suffering?

Recognizing that illness and health always involve a patient who is part of a complex web of social commitments, personal aspirations, and religious convictions, medical professionals have begun to include considerations of a patient's social, psychological, financial, and spiritual well-being in their treatment decisions and care plans. Yet the growing inclusion of quality-of-life considerations in medical care decisions prompts both relief and concern. Where they are perceived as a change from a problematic tendency—medical professionals focusing on pathologies rather than patients, on strictly medical attributes of health absent psychological, social, and spiritual ones—quality-of-life considerations are welcomed as enhancing patient care, particularly when those considerations are congruent with respect for the autonomy of patients and with palliative care (so Beauchamp and Childress; Shuman). Medicine is oriented toward the health of the patient, and the richest possible understanding of health (including so-called quality-of-life measures) is to be welcomed as enhancing the practice of medicine.

Where such considerations intersect with life-or-death decisions, however, they seem to some to destabilize basic political and medical commitments to the innate value of life. The more negative the assessment of an individual's quality of life, the less that life will appear to be worth preserving; thus, some worry that quality-of-life assessments are wrongly used to justify the selective nontreatment (or passive euthanasia) of disabled individuals and the abortion of "defective" fetuses. While there is anecdotal and sociological evidence for such practices (see Rapp; Verhey), a more serious concern is the absence in Western political theory of any robust commitment to the moral standing of the individual or to the protection of the vulnerable that might put a check on the tendency to devalue disabled life (so Reinders). A decision not to treat may be perfectly congruent with a vigorous respect for life, especially when it is the proposed treatment, rather than the continuation of life, that is judged onerous; nonetheless, the concern that certain deaths will become too readily accepted seems apt.

Scripture and Tradition

Scripture does not, of course, address the minutiae of medical care decisions with any specificity. But even the broader question of how to account for nonmedical factors when making medical care decisions has no obvious analogue in Scripture.

The Scriptures do evidence a profound concern for all aspects of human flourishing. Torah instructs the Israelites to care for their neighbors, particularly the vulnerable members of society, in every possible way: through basic economic justice (Exod. 23:9; Lev. 19:13, 35–36; Deut. 25:15), through care for neighbors' property in their stead (Exod. 22:5; 23:4–5), through restitution for negligence or wrongdoing (Exod. 22:1–14; Lev. 6:1–7; Num. 5:5–8), through addressing systemic poverty (Lev. 25), and through generous and effective aid to the needy (Exod. 25:25–27; Lev. 19:9–10). The prophetic tradition continues these concerns, setting Israel's and Judah's political misfortunes in the context of their practices of social injustice (see, e.g., Isa. 58; Amos 5:10–15; Mic. 2–3; 6–7).

Similarly, the healing ministries of Jesus and the early church testify to a holistic understanding of human health and well-being. The evangelists highlight the importance of the relief of human suffering—economic (Mark 10:21 pars.; Luke 16:19–31; Acts 2:44–45), social (Mark 2:15–17 pars.; Luke 15:11–32; 19:1–10), physical (Matt. 4:23; 9:22; 10:1; 15:32)—in the ministry of Jesus and the early church and are notably attentive to the relationship between these modes of suffering (cf. Mark 5:25–26 // Luke 8:43; Luke 13:16; 17:11–19; John 9). The impulse throughout the Christian tradition to improve the quality of human life through personal and institutional means (almsgiving, friendship, forgiveness and reconciliation, hospitals, schools, the rule of law) evidences an understanding of these Scriptures as exemplary and authoritative.

In Scripture, life and its flourishing are good gifts of God the creator and redeemer. Yet Scripture does not present life as an absolute good or a life utterly free from suffering as a worthy (much less possible) goal. While human life, in all its fullness, is to be protected and enjoyed, many things are to be preferred to a life free from suffering, and some are to be preferred to life itself. The crucial tension is between eternal life and earthly life (Mark 8:35–36 pars.), and the follower of Christ is instructed to forsake all manner of temporal well-being, including life itself, for the sake of eternal life (see, e.g., Matt. 10:28, 39; and the hyperbolic 5:29–30; 18:8–9; Luke 9:23; John 15:19–20; Acts 4:34–35; 5:41; 1 Cor. 5:1–5; Heb. 10:34; cf. Matthew's emphasis on heavenly reward in 5:12; 6:1–6, 16–18; 10:41–42).

Yet to take these Scripture passages, or Paul's effusive desire simply to "be with Christ" (Phil. 1:20–22), as warrant to hasten death, either one's own or another's, in the face of a reduced quality of life is to misunderstand them. Death is yet an evil; it is a conquered enemy, and it is to be preferred to apostasy or unrighteousness, but it has not become, as Francis of Assisi sees it, a "sister," nor is it anywhere in Scripture to be preferred to a suffering life.

See also Abortion; Ars Moriendi Tradition, Use of Scripture in; Bioethics; Death and Dying; Euthanasia; Happiness; Sanctity of Human Life

Bibliography

Beauchamp, T., and J. Childress. *Principles of Biomedical Ethics*. 6th ed. Oxford University Press, 2009; Rapp, R. *Testing Women, Testing the Fetus: The Social Impact of Amniocentesis in America*. Routledge, 1999; Reinders, H. *The Future of the Disabled in Liberal Society: An Ethical Analysis*. Notre Dame University Press, 2000; Shuman, J. *The Body of Compassion: Ethics, Medicine, and the Church*. Westview Press, 1999; Verhey, A. "Jesus and the Neonates: The Death of Infant Doe." Pages 345–58 in *Reading the Bible in the Strange World of Medicine*. Eerdmans, 2003.

Sarah Conrad Sours

R

Race

Race is an arbitrary categorization that frequently classifies humans into groups according to genetic heritage. However, given that many scholars consider the idea of race as a biological reality to be unwarranted, race is now theorized as an anthropological construct. Certainly, racial delineations vary from culture to culture, and it is clear that definitions of race depend on social, cultural, geopolitical, and ideological criteria. Therefore, discussing race is difficult because of its multiple meanings, as well as the continued factor of racial prejudice and the extreme practices that result from it. Broadly, racial identification resides in visible characteristics such as skin pigmentation, facial features, and/or hair texture. However, race theory of this nature first took root only as recently as the conquest of the New World. When the English colonists first landed in North America, rather than describe the vastly differing indigenous populations that they encountered as different peoples, cultures, or tribes, they began to make categorizations according to skin color. While physical differences among people had been previously rarely referred to as a matter of great importance, now race emerged on a black/white scale.

The sociopolitical construction of the idea of race served as a precursor to an economic policy. Europeans were not always the world's dominant power, and many Europeans were enslaved. In fact, white slavery facilitated the dualistic defining of race. Enslaved women from Eastern Europe became symbols of beauty, giving rise to the first claims of the supremacy of whiteness. As early as the late fifteenth century, the colonial conquests advanced the idea of white dominance, conflating "white" skin pigmentation with the presumed superiority of white political and economic power for arranging reality. With this thinking, the "enlightened" peoples of Europe colonized the "primitive" peoples of Africa, Asia, Australia, and the Americas, conveniently facilitating the removal of land from some and the forced displacement from land of others. Celebrating the Anglo-Saxons as embodying manliness, beauty, liberty, and individualism, English settlers slowly defined blacks as slaves and whites as free, establishing arbitrary legal and judicial definitions of race. The white race was linked to freedom, whereas blackness was tied to enslavement.

Additionally, the moral views and practices of the dominant group became the standard applied to all, and those who appeared not to share the standard were deemed lesser beings who could be subjected to bondage. Prejudice against slaves became racial prejudice against nonwhites, most intensely against blacks. Throughout the nineteenth and early twentieth centuries, whiteness expanded as immigrants and their children actively attempted to situate themselves within the new nation as "true" Americans. Noteworthy is the emblematic identification of the Irish. First considered nonwhite, they eventually joined Jewish, Italian, Russian, and Polish immigrants to be categorized as fully white, a status unattainable for African Americans.

Although race is a social construction and difficult to define, people do in fact find it useful and use the idea of race both unconsciously and intentionally. Often race has been used interchangeably with ethnicity to describe identity. Racial and ethnic identities are essential aspects of individual and communal identity. Behavior and ideological attitudes that form cultural traditions become available to persons through religious, familial, neighborhood, and education communities. These shared practices sustain racial identification. An individual acknowledges his or her identity as a racialized person through deliberate concurrence with particular concepts, attitudes, and behaviors. However, these better represent ethnic practices. Neither African Americans nor European Americans are a race in the anthropological sense. Each is a population group, highly mixed in racial stock and ancestry. Ethnic consciousness increasingly replaced notions of white racial difference as new biological sciences demonstrated the genetic similarities of all humans. Eliminating the biological distinctions reveals controlling social, economic, and political conditions that disproportionately privilege some and disadvantage others.

The concepts of race and ethnicity remain important means for critically understanding the breakdown in society resulting from assumptions that certain practices of goodness, wisdom, or integrity have become identified as the prerogative of one ethnic or racial group. The practices of those privileged as representative of what is deemed normative cultural or ethnic identity often have appeared invisible, and white males of European descent were taken as the de facto template for defining humanity. Flaws rooted in historical inequities and long-standing cultural stereotypes imply only certain human opinions, goals, or behaviors appropriately define humanity. Socially constructed standards, however, rendered any deviance as ontologically determined rather than chosen against valid, though alternative, priorities or assumptions. The assumption that racial identity establishes behavior ignores environmental, social, and cultural factors and holds that observable physical categorization provides a biological delineation of predetermined social and moral behavior traits. Consequently, racial labels function erroneously in society as predictors of ethical behavior and intellectual capacity.

In recent years, race theorists have focused on whiteness as a category of constructed identity, giving attention to the idea of a racialized identification for those of white ethnicity. This is an important development because it helps us understand in a far more comprehensive way racialized identification as more than ethnic identity. A survey of intellectual, cultural, social, and legal history explains notions of difference among people groups from ancient empires to the present. Ancient societies did not divide people according to physical features, relying instead on religion, status, class, and language. These societies enslaved others as a result of war or debt.

Only recently has a theological account of race entered the collective consideration. One aspect of the genesis of the modern problem of whiteness resides in the theopolitical wrestling of the Western world with the so-called Jewish question. In order to understand the modern problem of race, this position seeks a full account of modernity's struggle to alienate itself from Jewish history, thereby integrating race, religion, and the discourse about the modern state. In this approach, theology is acknowledged as a contributor to the process by which humans came to be viewed as racial beings.

Rather than begin with the European encounter with Native Americans and Africans, new arguments contend that modernity's racial imagination originated in the process by which Christianity was severed from its Jewish roots. Viewing Jews as an alien, inferior race, this reasoning likewise implied the natural supremacy of white European peoples and the corresponding superiority of Christianity over Judaism. A connection with Christianity was born of the success of the European conquests that generated an assumption that God ordained white domination. The association of whiteness and good continues to hold significant influence in contemporary imagination. A scriptural imagination prompts reconsideration of these "superstitions" of whiteness/blackness.

Arguments for a binary racial construction of reality have been attributed to biblical accounts such as the mark of Cain, the curse of Ham/Canaan, and the table of nations (Gen. 4:1–16; 9:20–27; 10). In none do we explicitly find either a dehumanization of the other or the signification of physical difference as identification of position. Paradoxically, the mark of Cain is neither promised to his descendants nor an indicator of his oppression; it was a sign of his divinely protected status. In a scriptural epistemology, the ideological systems of knowledge constructed on race emerge as a result of a distortion of God's intended design. From this vantage point, racial identification is an errant exhibition of sin defined as anthropocentric concentration; it is a divisive human creation that distorts God's design of humanity created in the divine image. The suggestion of the biblical witness gives rise to the notion of one race of humanity. Since classifications of persons by color (categories of race) do not exist in the witness of the biblical narrative, it holds that they will not exist in the new creation. Too often, Christian identity is qualified by a racial or ethnic identifier, ignoring the claim that Christ's death has restored the nature of all humankind to its identity as a facsimile of the Creator. This redemption provides the ability to move beyond the racial framework with a Christian theology of Israel grounded in the nonracial flesh of Jesus. Transcending the binary categories of blackness and whiteness, a scriptural imagination restores God's covenantal relationship with the Jews as the anti-gnostic and nonracist canopy under which all true Christians should live. Race is fundamentally a theological issue, and eradication is a sign of God's reconciling work in Christ.

See also Anti-Semitism; Apartheid; Civil Rights; Culture; Ethnic Identity, Ethnicity; Freedom; Humanity; Human Rights; Prejudice; Racism; Rights

Bibliography

Bantum, B. *Redeeming Mulatto: A Theology of Race and Christian Hybridity*. Baylor University Press, 2010; Carter, J. *Race: A Theological Account*. Oxford University Press, 2008; Gossett, T. *Race: The History of an Idea in America*. Schocken, 1965; Jacobson, M. *Whiteness of a Different Color: European Immigrants and the Alchemy of Race*. Harvard University Press, 1998; Painter, N. *The History of White People*. W. W. Norton, 2010; Snowden, F., Jr. *Before Color Prejudice: The Ancient View of Blacks*. Harvard University Press, 1983.

Joy Jittaun Moore

Racism

Racism, the most destructive form of prejudice, dehumanizes those who are different. Some of the most violent expressions of racist violence have been perpetrated against blacks in South Africa and in the United States and elsewhere in the African diaspora, and against Jews in Nazi Germany. Racism is based on a biological notion of race, wherein there is an assumption that real or imagined physical, mental, and moral characteristics are transmitted genetically and are therefore permanent. Racism assumes the hierarchical ordering and rejection of other races and the ideas, customs, and practices associated with them. Studies in the United States show that racial attitudes toward blacks are more negative than attitudes toward Hispanics, Asians, legal and undocumented immigrants, and whites. They also reveal that minorities sometimes internalize the same biases as majority groups, thus having prowhite or antiminority bias even with respect to their own group (a phenomenon called "internalized racism").

"Institutional racism" restricts the choices, rights, mobility, and access of other racial groups to needed social and material resources. Systemic racism considers the way that material, attitudes, emotions, habits, and practices are embedded in social institutions, including power imbalances, the accumulation of intergenerational wealth, and the long-term maintenance of major socioeconomic deficits for other races. Given the decline of explicitly demeaning language and symbols, "aversive racism" occurs when a subject feels or expresses discomfort, uneasiness, disgust, or fear in the presence of blacks or other racialized minorities or in discussing race issues. "Symbolic racism" blends antiblack feeling and traditional American moral values in a way that results in support for the racial status quo. Symbolic racism assumes that blacks and others violate the values of self-reliance, work ethic, obedience, and discipline and expresses resentment for "special favors" (e.g., affirmative action) and rejection of the idea that there is continuing discrimination in society. Proponents of this view maintain that by operating out of symbolic racism, privileged people are able to maintain prejudicial stereotypes that normalize their own cultural values and oppose social policies aimed at improving the status of underprivileged groups without having to feel as if they are racists. Opponents insist that this concept is unfair, that such traditional values constitute empirical goods that are inherently beneficial for society.

The Bible does have examples of nationalism and ethnocentrism that may be equivalent to racism, but there are other theological currents that forcefully counter it. The second creation account in Gen. 2:4–24 emphasizes the equality of all people, and Gen. 1:27 denies racial superiority, since all are created in God's image, a conclusion that flies in the face of racial separation and homogeneous congregations. Although neither story specifically mentions race, some deduce a Middle Eastern ethnicity for the first humans from the setting in Mesopotamia, though modern genetics places the first humans in sub-Saharan Africa. The so-called curse of Ham (Gen. 9:18–27) is an example of a text that has been interpreted through a racist lens, used often in antebellum defenses of slavery and white supremacy. In the story, Ham, Noah's son, sees his father's genitals as Noah lies in a drunken stupor. When he wakes, Noah does not curse Ham, but curses Canaan, Ham's son, to slavery. Racist interpretations extended this curse to all of the black peoples listed in the adjacent Table of Nations in Gen. 10, despite the lack of connections between these peoples and the Canaanites. The text is actually a curse against Canaanites as Israel's perennial enemies, and while it may be true that the curse on Canaan is racist and legitimizes slavery of Canaanites, it is also true that there has never been a full-scale enslavement of Canaanites. Indeed, many hold that historically Israel emerged as a nation from within Canaan.

The historical writings in the OT have tendencies toward both the exclusion and inclusion of outsiders in Israel. Some maintain that the Deuteronomistic History espouses a concern for religious purity from a relatively late date in Israel's history, but other traditions counter the anti-Canaanite theme, as does a consideration of the ethnic formation and composition of Israel. To begin with, there is no more exclusivistic practice than the *ḥerem*, the complete ethnic cleansing and annihilation commanded in Deut. 7:2. Although we cannot excuse or justify a practice that is so offensive to modern sensibilities, it is still important to note that the *ḥerem* was not unique to Israel in the ancient Near East. In Scripture, the *ḥerem* has a theological basis: destruction was not mandated for all enemies, only those who would lead the Israelites to worship of other gods (Deut. 20:10–18). Indeed, Scripture also sanctions death for Israelite cities that abandon God (Deut. 13:12–18). Many think that by the time the Deuteronomistic History was written, the different Canaanite peoples mentioned in the history had long since disappeared. Indeed, independent of controversies about dating these historical texts, even the "conquest" narrative in Joshua reflects the presence of numerous Canaanites still living in the land: Gibeonites (chaps. 9–10), Geshurites and Maacathites (13:13), Anakim (14:12), Jebusites (15:63), and Canaanites (16:10; 17:12; cf. Judg. 1).

Against this exclusivist tendency, we can note that Deuteronomy makes special provisions for "resident aliens" along with widows and orphans in a concern for social justice (Deut. 24:17–22; 14:28–29). Resident aliens (*gārîm*) have the same rights as citizens (16:9–12; 24:14–15) and may participate in the Passover when circumcised (Exod. 12:48), though foreigners who have not assimilated religiously (*nokrîm*) are excluded. The blended Israel that celebrates Passover perhaps represents a partial fulfillment of the promise to Abraham (Gen. 12:3). Old Testament narratives about the formation and composition of Israel also counter the exclusivist tendency. The "mixed crowd" of Israelites that emerged from Egypt included Egyptians and other ethnic peoples (Exod. 12:38). Moreover, it is difficult to differentiate Israelites from Canaanites, especially considering the instances of foreigners who become joined to Israel in the narratives, such as Rahab (Josh. 2:10–14) and the Gibeonites (Josh. 9:3–27). Also, many individuals in David's kingdom were non-Israelites, such as Uriah the Hittite (2 Sam. 23:29); David's bodyguards, the Cherethites and Phelethites (2 Sam. 15:13–18); the Cushite messenger in 2 Sam. 18:19–33; and Orna, a Jebusite from whom David purchased the land for the temple (2 Sam. 24; 1 Chr. 21).

Biblical passages about marriage in the OT also reflect both inclusive and exclusive tendencies. On the one hand, among the patriarchs, Judah and Simeon marry Canaanites, while Joseph marries an Egyptian. Numbers 12 provides an implicit sanction of intermarriage when it condemns Miriam and Aaron in their opposition to Moses' marriage to a Cushite (i.e., Ethiopian). Some surmise that the opposition was principally in reaction to the wife's skin color, since Miriam is afflicted with leprosy, a whitening skin disease, as a punishment (Num. 12:10–16), though others speculate that a power struggle was at issue. On the other hand, in order to prevent idolatry, Israel was forbidden from marrying Canaanites (Exod. 34:15–16; Deut. 7:1–4; Josh. 23:12; cf. Deut. 21:10–14). In addition, Ezra-Nehemiah expands the prohibition in Deut. 7 against marrying Canaanites by prohibiting marriage to any non-Israelites (Ezra 9–10; Neh. 13:25; cf. Mal. 2:10–16).

Many have taken note of the universalism in Isa. 2:2–4 (cf. Pss. 67; 86:9–10; 117:1–2; Isa. 19:19–25; 45:14; 49:6; 66:18–24; Mic. 4:1–3). Even more compelling, however, is the idealized image of *shalom* in Isa. 11:1–9, where creatures who are naturally predator and prey live in peace, an image that showcases the horizontal dimension of *shalom* as opposed to an almost exclusive focus on the vertical. Interpretations of references to Cushites in the prophetic literature have sometimes reflected racial bias. Earlier interpreters of Amos 9:7 see an unfavorable comparison between Israel and Cush; now interpreters see Cush as an example of a powerful nation that will ultimately belong to God. Jeremiah 13:23 does not reflect negatively on the skin color of Cushites, but rather only maintains that Israel's sin has become an unchangeable part of its nature.

In the Gospels and Acts, most attention is focused on Luke-Acts, with its six Samaritan episodes (Luke 9:51–56; 10:25–37; 17:11–19; Acts 1:8; 8:4–25; 15:3), a concentration that is significant, given the traditional animosity between Israelites and Samaritans. Luke's focus on Jesus' ministry to outsiders and the mission to gentiles in Acts begins in Luke 2:31–32, where Simeon alludes to the universalism in Isa. 49, continues in Luke 3:23–4:30, wherein the genealogy emphasizes Jesus as a representative of all humanity, and is boldly proclaimed in Luke 4:18–19 with a quotation of Isa. 61. The parable of the good Samaritan (Luke 10:25–37) explicitly counters racism and ethnic prejudice, since the hero is a Samaritan who helps an injured man in contrast with the religious leaders who bypass him. Jesus shows that loving one's neighbor transcends racial and cultural boundaries, and the episode challenges hatred and stereotypes of the "other," illustrating that faithfulness to Jesus means taking action. Many interpret Pentecost in Acts 2 as a reversal of the Tower of Babel episode in Gen. 11:1–9, which explains the origins of languages and cultures as a consequence of sin, though others caution against this. The ambiguity may be seen in the fact that Peter's appeal to Joel 2:31 ("Everyone who calls on the name of the Lord shall be saved") occurs in a speech addressed to "men of Judea and all who live in Jerusalem." Other episodes in Acts point to the diversity of the early church: the apostles resolve the conflict over the feeding of the Hellenistic Jewish widows by adding Hellenistic leaders to oversee the activity (Acts 6:1–6); the Ethiopian eunuch is regarded as the first gentile convert among a people who live at the farthest reaches of the known world (Acts 8:26–39); through the conversion of Cornelius, a Roman centurion, Peter learns that God shows no partiality (Acts 10:34–35); and the presence of Simeon called Niger (Acts 13:1) suggests that the church at Antioch had multicultural members and leadership from the beginning (cf. Acts 11:19–20). In the Fourth Gospel, Jesus ignores gender, ethnic, and social boundaries in his encounter with a female Samaritan sinner (John 4:1–42). More strikingly, John 10:16 places great weight on the importance of the formation of a unified community that includes "other sheep that do not belong to this fold" in the context of the discourse on the good shepherd. Indeed, John 17:20–23 discusses the goal of Jesus' mission as unity between God, Jesus, and his followers.

In the Pauline Epistles, Gal. 3:28 is the centerpiece of reflection on racism in the biblical materials (cf. Col. 3:1–11), which teaches that access to God is no longer through ethnic identity or adherence to law. The verse stresses unity in Christ beyond racial, gender, and socioeconomic stratification, not the obliteration of differences. Paul addresses the issue of diversity within unity in 1 Cor. 12:12–30, where the "body of Christ" metaphor illustrates the interdependence among the individual members of the body, a dynamic that may be applied to modern racial relations as well. Ephesians 2:11–22, possibly even more commonly cited than Gal. 3:28, develops Paul's theology of race relations in Christ, attaching enormous significance to human fellowship in the work of Christ. While Eph. 2:11–12 is written from a Jewish perspective of "superiority over gentiles," Eph. 2:14–15 depicts Jesus as the peacemaker who ends hostility and brings *shalom* in the new humanity. Here we see human relationships as the purpose of Christ's incarnation and death; Jews and Greeks are united in order that the new humanity may then be presented to God for reconciliation.

See also Anti-Semitism; Apartheid; Discrimination; Ethnic Identity, Ethnicity; Humanity; Image of God; Prejudice; Race; Slavery

Bibliography

Bonilla-Silva, E. *White Supremacy and Racism in the Post-Civil Rights Era*. Lynn Rienner, 2001; Byron, G. *Symbolic Blackness and Ethnic Difference in Early Christian Literature*. Routledge, 2002; DeYoung, C., et al., eds. *United by Faith: The Multiracial Congregation as an Answer to the Problem of Race*. Oxford University Press, 2003; Feagin, J. *Systemic Racism: A Theory of Oppression*. Routledge, 2006; Hays, J. *From Every People and Nation: A Biblical Theology of Race*. InterVarsity, 2003; Hodge, C. *If Sons, Then Heirs: A Study of Kinship and Ethnicity in the Letters of Paul*. Oxford University Press, 2007; Isaac, B. *The Invention of Racism in Classical Antiquity*. Princeton University Press, 2004; Jones, J. *Prejudice and Racism*. 2nd ed. McGraw-Hill, 1997; McKenzie, S. *All God's Children: A Biblical Critique of Racism*. Westminster John Knox, 1997; Rodríguez, R. *Racism and God-Talk: A Latino/a Perspective*. New York University Press, 2008; Sadler, R. *Can a Cushite Change His Skin? An Examination of Race, Ethnicity, and Othering in the Hebrew Bible*. T&T Clark, 2005; Sechrest, L. *A Former Jew: Paul and the Dialectics of Race*. T&T Clark, 2009; Sharp, D. *No Partiality: The Idolatry of Race and the New Humanity*. InterVarsity, 2002; Snowden, F. *Before Color Prejudice: The Ancient View of Blacks*. Harvard University Press, 1983.

Love L. Sechrest

Rape

Rape is commonly understood as an act of sexual violence in which one person forces another to have sexual intercourse. Modern definitions of rape emphasize the female victim's lack of consent. By contrast, rape in the biblical world and the ancient Near East assumes an androcentric and group-oriented perspective. It is understood primarily as a crime against another male or group of males related to the victim. The woman's consent does play a critical role, however, in determining the extent of the offense and the subsequent punishment of the perpetrator.

The primary sources for understanding rape in the biblical world come from legal and narrative materials in the OT. Scholars identify Deut. 22:25–27, 28–29 as rape laws. There are also three biblical narratives that depict rape: Gen. 34; Judg. 19; 2 Sam. 13. Scholars sometimes have included other texts such as 2 Sam. 11:2–5 (David and Bathsheba) or prophetic texts such as Hos. 2:2–3 within their discussion of rape in the Bible. However, the Deuteronomic laws and three biblical rape narratives use vocabulary and describe dynamics that unambiguously identify these passages as rape texts.

In Hebrew, the verb for rape is *ʿinnâ*, which has the broader meaning of "oppress" or "commit violence against." In the context of sexual relations, the word is used in combination with other verbs of force to describe the act of rape. Within the three narrative texts, the narrator and characters use the word *nĕbālâ*, meaning "disgraceful thing," to make judgments on the perpetrator and the rape itself. This term connotes a serious breach of social mores and boundaries and occurs primarily within the idiom "to do a disgraceful thing in Israel" (Gen. 34:7; Judg. 20:6; 2 Sam. 13:12).

Deuteronomy 22 contains legislation that deals with various forms of sexual contact, including adultery and rape. Within these laws, a woman's marital status—married, engaged, or not engaged—is a determining factor in understanding the nature of the crime and the extent of the punishment. If a man has sexual relations with a woman who is married or engaged, the offense is handled as adultery, regardless of whether the man raped the woman. The punishment for the offending male is death. The woman is also put to death if she consented to the sexual encounter in question. In the case of rape, the woman is not punished (v. 26). Similar to other laws in the ancient Near East, a woman's consent is tied to whether she cries out for help. The context of the sexual encounter also determines female consent. If the act occurs in a town and the woman does not cry out, the offense is considered to be consensual, presumably because someone would have heard a woman's cries if she had resisted (v. 23). If, however, the crime occurs in the open country, the woman is innocent, since she might have cried out with no one to hear her (v. 27). In a case where a man rapes an unbetrothed woman, he is required to pay the bride price to the woman's father because the offense is considered to be a financial loss for the father. The perpetrator is required to marry the woman without the possibility of divorce (v. 29). Though by modern standards this penalty is problematic for the woman, the law seeks to protect the female victim's financial future.

There are three rape narratives in the OT: Shechem's rape of Dinah, daughter of Jacob (Gen. 34), a violent mob's gang rape of an unnamed concubine in Gibeah (Judg. 19), and the rape of Tamar, daughter of David, by her half-brother, Amnon (2 Sam. 13). In each of these stories the progression of events moves from the initial rape of the woman to escalating violence among men to some form of social fragmentation. The shared progression points to cultural configurations of rape within honor/shame societies. The use of the term *nĕbālâ* ("disgraceful act") in all three rape narratives points to the shame-inducing character of the offense in biblical culture. The offended males and their larger social groups respond to the act of rape as a challenge to their honor. Thus, the initial offense of rape escalates into retributive cycles of violence among men. The resulting social fragmentation subtly leads the reader of these narratives to pass negative judgment on the subsequent male responses to rape.

See also Abortion; Abuse; Feminist Ethics; Sexual Abuse; Violence

Bibliography

Pressler, C. *The View of Women Found in the Deuteronomic Family Laws*. BZAW 216. De Gruyter, 1993; Yamada, F. *Configurations of Rape in the Hebrew Bible: A Literary Analysis of Three Rape Narratives*. SBL 109. Peter Lang, 2008.

Frank Yamada

Reconciliation

Reconciliation is in the apostle Paul's proclamation at the very heart of the Christian gospel, rooted as it is in (1) God's love and purpose, (2) Christ's ministry and death, and (3) what appear to be the earliest Christian confessions.

The Language of Reconciliation

The Greek verbs *katallassō* and *diallassō* ("to reconcile") and the Greek noun *katallagē* ("reconciliation") are compound forms built on the verb *allassō* ("to alter, change") and the noun *allos* ("other"), and so they basically mean "to make otherwise" and connote "a change of relationship or situation." They appear frequently in Greek writings to signify a change of circumstances or relationships in the political, social, familial, and/or moral spheres of life. However, they played no part in the cultic expiatory rites of the Greco-Roman world and are almost entirely absent in Greek religious writings, for pagan religions did not think of relations between divinity and humanity in terms of personal nearness. Only Sophocles, who was one of the three great tragic poets of the fifth century BCE, in depicting the humiliation and suicide of the warrior Ajax, speaks about a person reconciling himself to the gods (*Aj.* 744), but he says nothing about how such reconciliation was accomplished.

There are no equivalents to the language of reconciliation in Hebrew or Aramaic. The closest terms in the OT as well as in the later rabbinic codifications (the Jewish Talmud and its associated tractates) are the verbs *kapher* and *raṣer*, which mean "to please, appease, satisfy, placate." When used in the context of a wrongdoer placating by some act of restitution a person who had been wronged, these verbs may be seen as connoting certain features that correspond, at least to some degree, to the idea of "reconciliation," though without any change of personal relationships or of emotional feelings necessarily being involved.

The somewhat parallel Greek verb *epistrephō* ("to turn, turn around, turn back, return") is used in a purely secular fashion in Judg. 19:3 LXX with reference to a Levite "returning his concubine to himself." The noun *diallagē* ("reconciliation") appears in Sir. 22:22; 27:21 with respect to friends being reconciled (cf. the use of the verb *diallassō* in Matt. 5:24 with respect to a person being reconciled to a brother or a sister). In *m. Yoma* 8.9 it is said, "For transgressions that are between man and God, the Day of Atonement effects atonement; but for wrongs that are between a man and his fellow, the Day of Atonement effects atonement only if he [the wrongdoer] has appeased his fellow" (i.e., only if a form of reconciliation has taken place between the two parties, as instigated by the wrongdoer).

Reconciliation as a Religious Term among Jews

A religious use of the term *reconciliation* appears first among Jews in 2 Maccabees, where the writer prays, "May [God] hear your prayers and be reconciled [*katallassō*] to you [the Jewish addressees], and may he not forsake you in the time of evil" (2 Macc. 1:5). Later in that same writing the writer expresses the common Jewish belief that after God has chastened his people because of their sins—and so when he becomes, in effect, reconciled to his people—the Jerusalem temple will be restored to its former glory (2 Macc. 5:20; 7:33). Further, after the early successes of Judas Maccabeus against the Seleucids, the author of 2 Maccabees tells his readers that the Israelite warriors "made common supplication and implored the merciful Lord to be wholly reconciled [*katallassō*] with his servants" (2 Macc. 8:29). Josephus also twice uses the terminology of reconciliation (both as a noun and as a verb) in a religious manner: first, in telling his Roman readers that he had declared at the close of his address to the Jewish insurgents of his day, "The Deity is reconciled [*eudiallaktos*] to those who confess and repent" (*J.W.* 5.415); second, in reporting that Samuel, at a time of King Saul's "contempt and disobedience," pleaded with God "to be reconciled [*katallassō*] to Saul and not angry with him" (*Ant.* 6.143).

Paul's Use of the Concept and Language of Reconciliation

It was Paul, however, who focused on the concept of reconciliation in his Christian theology and made the language of reconciliation central in his preaching to gentiles in the Greco-Roman world. The term appears in very significant portions of his letters and is used by him almost entirely in a theological sense. The noun *katallagē* appears four times (Rom. 5:11; 11:15; 2 Cor. 5:18, 19); the verb *katallassō* five times (Rom. 5:10 [2x]; 2 Cor. 5:18, 19, 20); the verb *apokatallassō* (an emphatic form with a prepositional prefix) three times (Eph. 2:16; Col. 1:20, 22). Only one secular use occurs in Paul's Letters, when he exhorts a wife who may have thoughts about separating from her husband: "If she does separate, let her remain unmarried or else be reconciled [*katallassō*] to her husband" (1 Cor. 7:11).

Somewhat surprisingly, language about reconciliation does not appear in any of the other writings of the NT, and is rare in the extant Christian writings of the second century. Among the earliest extant Christian writers, it therefore may be considered especially Pauline. Yet by the form, content, and context in which this reconciliation terminology is used in 2 Cor. 5:19 ("In Christ God was reconciling the world to himself, not counting their trespasses against them, and entrusting the message of reconciliation to us"), it may be postulated that Paul was actually quoting a portion of early Christian confessional material here in this verse, for the statement of 2 Cor. 5:19 evidences a certain balance of structure; is introduced by the particle *hoti* (a so-called *hoti recitativum*), which Paul and other NT writers often used to introduce a quotation from some traditional material; incorporates in a formal manner the essence of Christian proclamation; and serves as the linchpin or central feature of what else is said by way of exposition in 2 Cor. 5:18, 20.

It probably is best, therefore, to surmise that Paul came to know this language of reconciliation in a vital manner because of its inclusion in some early Christian confessional material, and that he appreciated it as being most expressive of what he had personally experienced in his relationship with God through the work of Christ and the ministry of God's Spirit. Further, it may be postulated that he made this relational and personal soteriological language central in his preaching to gentiles in the Greco-Roman world simply because he believed it to be more theologically significant, more culturally meaningful, and more ethically compelling than many of the forensic soteriological expressions of traditional vintage that were used among both Jews and Jewish Christians.

Paul always makes two important theological points when he speaks of reconciliation. First, contrary to a Jewish understanding of reconciliation, where God is spoken of as being reconciled to his people or situations (as in the references from the LXX, Josephus, and the rabbinic writings cited above), Paul always speaks of God as the subject of the verb *katallassō* and never its object. That is, in Paul's proclamation it is always God who reconciles "people" and "the world," and never the reverse (Rom. 5:10: "we were reconciled to God"; Rom. 5:11: "our Lord Jesus Christ, through whom we have now received reconciliation"; Rom. 11:15: "the reconciliation of the world"; 2 Cor. 5:18: "God, who reconciled us to himself"; 2 Cor. 5:19: "in Christ God was reconciling the world to himself"). Second, God's reconciliation of people and the world is based on the work and faithfulness of Jesus Christ and never on what people might do in their attempts to please God or by their own faithfulness (note, in the context of Paul's discussions of reconciliation, texts such as Rom. 5:10: "We were reconciled to God through the death of his Son"; 2 Cor. 5:15: "[Christ] died for all, so that those who live might live no longer for themselves, but for him who died and was raised for them"; 2 Cor. 5:21: "[God] made [Christ] to be sin who knew no sin, so that in him we might become the righteousness of God").

Paul's language of reconciliation is inclusive in its applications, since it refers not only to the reconciliation of "people" (Rom. 5:10–11; 2 Cor. 5:18) but also to the reconciliation of "the world" (Rom. 11:15; 2 Cor. 5:19). Further, his teaching with respect to reconciliation has reference not only to what God has already accomplished (Rom. 5:10; 2 Cor. 5:19) but also to what he presently is accomplishing in the believer's life (2 Cor. 5:17) as well as to what he will yet bring about both for those who have responded positively to him and for his entire creation (Rom. 5:10–11; 8:19–25). Yet inherent in Paul's proclamation of reconciliation—reconciliation has been provided by God, is a present reality for those who turn to him in faith, and will be fully brought about for all his people and all his creation—is what may be called "the twofold absurdity" of the Christian gospel: (1) reconciliation with God comes about by means of death (i.e., objectively, the physical death of Jesus of Nazareth, God's Messiah, but also subjectively, the "death" of a person's self-reliance before God, and so a turning to God in complete trust in him alone); and (2) "the ministry of reconciliation," both in its proclamation and its exemplary practice, has been delegated by God to finite humans, who themselves have been reconciled to God (2 Cor. 5:18b, 19b).

The Ministry Component and Ethical Compulsion of Reconciliation

Paul's teaching regarding reconciliation includes a ministry component, for not only has God reconciled people to himself but also he has "entrusted the message of reconciliation to us" (2 Cor. 5:18). So we who have been reconciled to God and are experiencing in an initial measure that reconciliation are commissioned as "ambassadors for Christ" and therefore are called by God to "entreat" all people "on behalf of Christ" to be "reconciled to God" (2 Cor. 5:20).

Likewise, there is a vitally important ethical compulsion in Paul's teaching about reconciliation. For just as being loved by God we are motivated to love, and just as being forgiven by God we are motivated to forgive, so being reconciled by God to himself we are motivated "on behalf of Christ" to be agents of reconciliation to people individually and to the world inclusively. God's love for us is expressed in our love for others; God's forgiveness of us takes bodily form in our forgiveness of others. So also God's reconciliation of us to himself and to others compels our involvement in working for the reconciliation of others, whatever their needs and as God directs us, whether that involvement manifests itself almost unconsciously or quite deliberately. To divorce in practice an ethic of reconciliation from the doctrine of reconciliation is, sadly, to deny them both.

A Brief Summation in Light of Some Current Discussion

The traditional forensic soteriological terms *justification*, *expiation*, and *redemption* were quite well known to both Jews and Jewish Christians (so, quite rightly, the emphases of Ed Sanders, James Dunn, and others and the so-called New Perspective on Paul). However, the relational, participationist, personal soteriological expressions "reconciliation," "peace with God," "in Christ," "in the Spirit," and "Christ by his Spirit in us," which Paul highlights in Rom. 5–8, are realities known only through divine encounter and personal acquaintance (so the emphases of Ralph Martin and Seyoon Kim). Both the forensic set of terms and the relational, participationist, personal set of expressions are important for a fuller understanding of the "good news" of the Christian gospel. Yet at the heart of the Christian message—at least as proclaimed by Paul in his gentile mission, and so by extension to most people today—is the relational, participationist, and personal proclamation of God's reconciliation to himself of sinful and rebellious people through the work of Christ and the ministry of the Holy Spirit.

See also Atonement; Forgiveness; Salvation

Bibliography

Breytenbach, C. *Versöhnung: Eine Studie zur paulinischen Soteriologie*. WMANT 60. Neukirchener Verlag, 1989; Denney, J. *The Christian Doctrine of Reconciliation*. Hodder & Stoughton, 1917; Fitzmyer, J. "Reconciliation in Pauline Theology." Pages 155–77 in *No Famine in the Land: Studies in Honor of John L. MacKenzie*, ed. J. Flanagan and A. Robinson. Scholars Press, 1975; Goppelt, L. "Versöhnung durch Christus." Pages 147–64 in *Christologie und Ethik: Aufsätze zum Neuen Testament*. Vandenhoeck & Ruprecht, 1968; Käsemann, E. "Some Thoughts on the Theme 'The Doctrine of Reconciliation in the New Testament.'" Pages 49–64 in *The Future of Our Religious Past: Essays in Honor of Rudolf Bultmann*, ed. J. Robinson, trans. C. Carlston and R. Scharlemann. SCM, 1971; Kim, S. *The Origin of Paul's Gospel*. Eerdmans, 1982, 19–20, 311–15; Marshall, I. H. "The Meaning of 'Reconciliation.'" Pages 117–32 in *Unity and Diversity in New Testament Theology: Essays in Honor of G. E. Ladd*, ed. R. Guelich. Eerdmans, 1978; Martin, R. *Reconciliation: A Study of Paul's Theology*. Rev. ed. Academie Books, 1989; Taylor, V. *Forgiveness and Reconciliation: A Study in New Testament Theology*. Macmillan, 1941.

Richard N. Longenecker

Redemption *See* Atonement

Reformed Ethics

From the beginning, the Reformed tradition was a diverse, even ambiguous movement, developing in different communities around several influential leaders, including John Calvin (1509–64), but also other formative figures, finding support in many countries and taking on a variety of local forms. It was a confessional tradition, without any central structures of authority to determine uniformity in faith, polity, and life. Even the confessions and their corresponding church orders were diverse and local.

The story of Reformed ethics is therefore complex. It became the story of ethical developments in many countries and continents: for example, Switzerland, France, and Germany; but also the Netherlands and Belgium and many churches worldwide affected by their church life and theology; Britain, especially Scotland, and again many churches under their influence; churches in eastern Europe, including Hungary, and others; the United States and Canada, and their pervasive presence in the world; many churches in Africa, including western, central, and southern Africa; churches in many societies in Asia, such as Indonesia and South Korea, in addition to many others; and regions in Latin America.

It is impossible to do justice to this richness. Many of these churches are members of the World Alliance of Reformed Churches (WARC, after 2010 the World Communion of Reformed Churches), including churches mostly from Calvinist, Presbyterian, and Congregationalist origins, but also others with diverse historical backgrounds. These churches do not share any common confessional tradition or any structure of authority that could guarantee identity and uniformity. During the 1920s, the world body considered the possibility and necessity of one common Reformed confession and asked Karl Barth for advice. He strongly rejected the idea as against the nature of being Reformed, and he specifically referred to ethical challenges of the time, to which they would not have a common response.

The term *Reformed* refers to a further complicating characteristic, namely, its changing historical nature, summarized in the slogan "A Reformed church is continuously being reformed according to God's Word." Even within the particular churches, major shifts can be observed regarding morality. The tradition is very sensitive to context, culture, and history. The Reformed faith has often been held responsible, whether with praise or blame, for contributing to major historical changes—for example, the birth of modernity, democratic culture, notions of human dignity, and the free-market economy. At the same time, however, it has been deeply transformed by these developments. The story of Reformed ethics in any specific society today is therefore not only one of diversity but also one of change. Accounts of Reformed ethics in the Netherlands during the twentieth century, for example, describe how an influential, even dominant, Reformed subculture and way of life disappeared completely.

Calvin's Ethics

The importance of Calvin's own views for the tradition should not be overestimated. Still, his work illustrates several typical later trajectories. Different ethical voices would appeal to different ethical approaches already present here. Debates about Reformed ethics often take the form of appeals to Calvin against Calvin, or Calvin against (some form of) Calvinism.

Calvin was deeply concerned with the implications of faith for life, as his major work, called an instruction in the Christian religion or piety, demonstrates. His concern was that the gospel should be purely proclaimed but "also heard." Calvin was primarily a pastor, and through his activities and writings—sermons, commentaries, lectures, Bible studies, letters, treatises, but also his involvement in public life, local and international politics, social services, poverty relief, education, and legal affairs—he sought to assist the faithful in what he saw as the Christian life.

His key conviction was that we do not belong to ourselves (1 Cor. 6:19–20). This knowledge brings both comfort and claim. In the tradition this conviction remained central, almost as summary of Reformed ethics. It is the theme of the Heidelberg Catechism (1563), an influential and formative (spiritual, doctrinal, and ethical) confessional document; it was key in the convictions behind the Theological Declaration of Barmen (1934), the founding document of the Confessing Church in Nazi Germany; it is the opening motif in the Brief Statement of Faith (1993) of the Presbyterian Church (USA); it is the recurring refrain of the Debrecen litany (1997), drafted by the WARC to challenge economic injustice and ecological destruction.

Still, both the conviction itself and the integral relationship between comfort and claim became controversial. Questions regarding self-love, self-denial, and self-sacrifice, whether personal or communal (nation, country), led to intense debate. Conflicts regarding gospel and law, the third use of the law, justification and sanctification, grace and gratitude, freedom and responsibility, became commonplace.

Calvin developed this conviction in a trinitarian way, leading to a complex description of the Christian life—before the face of the gracious Father; in growing unity with Jesus Christ; through the active work of the Holy Spirit. For him, all these were important. Ethical themes therefore appear in several theological contexts in his work. Accordingly, his followers often emphasized different trajectories. Three such theological contexts in Calvin had major histories of reception.

First, at the heart of his discussion of our knowledge of God as gracious Father, he deals with God's moral law and argues that it is summarized in the Decalogue (*Institutes* 2.8). He searches for positive intent behind each commandment, applying them to ethical issues of his day. In Reformed history this approach became common, raising controversies regarding natural-law approaches to ethics and the need for Scripture in discerning the divine moral law. Of special importance is his claim that believers should respect the dignity of others, irrespective of who they are and what they do, since we should recognize in them both the image of God and our own flesh.

Second, he describes the Christian life when discussing our knowledge of God in Jesus Christ and the nature of justification and sanctification (*Institutes* 3.6–10). Already during his own day, this section was published separately. It became an important resource for Reformed ethics. Belonging to God, we are called to lives of self-denial, searching for righteousness in relation to others and piety in relation to God; to take up our cross as followers of Jesus, accepting our sufferings and trusting in God's power, learning patience and experiencing God's consolation; to meditate on the future life, not in order to escape the present but rather to come to proper estimation of life, receiving perspective and priorities; to enjoy and appreciate God's wonderful gifts to delight and sustain, support and empower us for our daily lives of service and love (Leith).

Third, he gives an influential depiction of "Christian freedom" (*Institutes* 3.19), originally introducing his discussions of church polity as well as civil government. His views of the visible church and of public life rest on his understanding of freedom—again a formative tradition in Reformed ethics. Following Luther's treatise on Christian freedom as well as Galatians, he adds a far-reaching argument concerning the *adiaphora*, defending the freedom to be indifferent toward the indifferent (Douglass). This critical potential often would liberate Reformed believers from established practices and institutional forms regarded by others as divinely ordained and unchangeable. Barth would describe evangelical ethics as an ethics of freedom.

Since Calvin, any of these three approaches could be emphasized at the cost of the others, contributing to the ambiguous history of reception. Some construct ethics primarily on the basis of the moral law, using notions such as natural law, general revelation, and common grace; some concentrate on personal ethics, emphasizing discipleship and meditation; others argue for social ethics and public responsibility.

Reformed Ethics in History

Even a brief historical overview of Reformed ethics is impossible. Hopefully, a few representative illustrations can highlight some typical features.

Since the earliest days, instruction played a formative role in Reformed piety, whether through catechisms, sermons, or writings. The teaching, study, and instruction of Scripture became central. Confessions such as the Heidelberg Catechism deeply influenced Reformed life (Verhey). Application of the Decalogue as moral law became widespread. Preaching probably was the most important discipline and practice in Reformed ethics. Biéler famously studied Calvin's social and economic thought by analyzing his sermons.

The first Calvinist ethics came from a jurist, Lambertus Danaeus (1577), providing an instructive illustration of what would often happen. The humanist background, already present in Calvin, is developed further, together with philosophical influences, from both Aristotle and Stoicism—characteristic of humanist and philosophical influences later. The changing mentality of the times—a strong sense of social crisis and an awareness of the falling apart of the social order, and therefore the urgent need for social reconstruction—motivates Danaeus's work, as will often become the case again when social crises lead to ethical revisioning. In the work itself, his legal training and interests combine with fundamental theological convictions—again typical of later developments in which legal thought and theological conviction regularly combine (Strohm, *Ethik*).

Reformed thought contributed greatly toward the separation between church and state and the development of legal systems based on human dignity and rights (Witte) and independent from the influence of institutional church and religion (Strohm, *Calvinismus*).

At the dawn of the modern period, Friedrich Schleiermacher's philosophical ethics provides a helpful distinction among three approaches, focusing, respectively, on goods (values, visions), virtues (character, moral agency), and duties (norms, rules, principles, decisions). In terms of this distinction, different Reformed ethical traditions show different preferences, with important implications for the role of Scripture in their respective approaches. Some concentrate on broader visions and worldviews and use Scripture accordingly, in so-called social, political, or public theology and ethics. Some concentrate on the personal life of believers as moral agents and emphasize virtues and character, again reading Scripture accordingly, in so-called individual ethics. Some concentrate on moral decisions and the role of norms and rules and mine Scripture for that purpose, often leading to so-called scriptural principles, to the direct application of texts to moral dilemmas, even to so-called moralism and legalism. Depending on their experience, people may identify Reformed ethics with any one of these approaches and its respective role for Scripture, but all three have been dominant in Reformed history, exemplified by different communities.

Some illustrations may suffice. In the Netherlands, Abraham Kuyper created a comprehensive worldview (called "neo-Calvinism") with a lasting impact on culture and specific subcultures in many places in the world (Heslam). In South Africa, for example, this legacy was important both in the justification of the apartheid worldview and in the struggle against this ideology (Boesak; de Gruchy).

Influential public theologians and ethicists in North America, such as Reinhold Niebuhr, H. Richard Niebuhr, Paul Lehmann, and James Gustafson, made their contributions standing within the tradition of Reformed ethics. Gustafson, for example, takes three theological tenets from this tradition: the sense of a powerful Other (in Calvinist terms, God's sovereignty), the centrality of piety or religious affections for morality (for him, the Calvinist affections of dependence, gratitude, obligation, remorse, possibility, and direction), and the recognition that all human activity should be related to what we can discern about God's purposes (which is why his ethics is "theocentric," based on "theology as a way of construing the world").

From Europe, Karl Barth had a large influence. Based on his earlier work, some regard his ethics as a form of arbitrary decision-making, but it is more adequately understood as a comprehensive attempt to live within "the moral ontology" or "world" of Scripture (Webster), which even includes attention to personal ethics of virtues and character (Mangina).

A century ago, Ernst Troeltsch made an influential argument for the significance of Reformed Protestantism for modernity. Following Max Weber's thesis about the foundational role of Calvinist ethics for the free-market economy (and Georg Jellinek's even earlier thesis about the Calvinist origins of modern notions of religious freedom), he extended that to other spheres of public life, including individualism and democratic culture. Such theses remain contested. As genealogical claims ("Calvinism caused . . .") they are difficult to maintain, but as indications of deep affinities they remain instructive.

Characteristics of Reformed Ethics

Although difficult and controversial, some characteristics of Reformed ethics can be discerned. It is, first, already typical that ethics is so central. Interest in the Christian life—in discipleship, sanctification, the third use of the law, respect for human dignity, calling, covenant, social life, public responsibility, political participation, issues of freedom and justice, democracy and social well-being, culture, scholarship, education—belongs integrally to the Reformed vision. Some close link between Scripture and ethics is taken for granted. Scripture is confessed and read as normative (sometimes even as trustworthy, sufficient, and clear), not only for matters of faith but also of life.

It is, second, characteristic that this passion for ethics flows from theological and confessional convictions. There are noteworthy exceptions (arguing that ethics should be general, philosophical, and natural, not based on or expressed in the language of faith), but the overall picture is rather that doctrine and faith are integrally related. This often implies that theology in a narrow sense (a particular view of God) plays a decisive role in the particular view of ethics. Barth and Gustafson offer an illustration. Agreeing on the crucial importance of the doctrine of God for ethics, Gustafson radically differs from Barth's particular view of God (namely, revealed in Christ and therefore trinitarian and salvific). The spectrum of theological possibilities is obviously rich and complex and therefore also the use of Scripture, supporting pictures of God and providing ethical orientation.

Third, the term *Reformed* points to the self-critical willingness to be examined anew and, if needed, transformed in the light of Scripture. This self-understanding often made Reformed ethics deeply historical and contextual. It implies that ethical convictions and practices are seen as temporary, for now and for the time being, never final, but based on present insight. This makes notions such as realism (Reinhold Niebuhr), responsibility (H. Richard Niebuhr), vocation ("here and now"), discerning God's will (the early Barth), and reading and responding to the context (Lehmann) popular in Reformed ethics—all underlining the historical responsibility to discern and respond—rather than notions of obedience or loyalty to authority. For the way Scripture is read and heard, this has major implications, with the emphasis on hearing and responding to the "living Word," often in a communal way. The congregation, believers together, those studying and reading Scriptures in communion, are seen as the locus of interpretation.

Fourth, it is characteristic that such continuous renewal according to Scripture can refer either to believers, to the church, or to society. Drawing practical implications for all three—for personal life, for the visible church, and for political and public spheres—has always been integral to Reformed ethics. Accordingly, the message of Scripture can be construed differently in order to provide orientation for such embodiment; popular Reformed motives are, for example, gratitude, discipleship, being raised to new life and dying of the old self, the kingdom of God, the lordship of Jesus Christ, and the prophetic role of the church. Such a prophetic attitude often means commitment to social justice, typical of WARC since its inception, until its Accra Declaration (2004) regarding economic injustice and ecological destruction.

Finally, Reformed people are described as "people of the Book," underlining Scripture's importance. The two elementary spiritual practices in the tradition have been worship, where Scripture, through exposition and teaching, is central, and the meditative reading and study of Scripture, whether privately, in households, or in groups. Scripture, including the OT, is regarded as authoritative and often described as the Word of God. In confessing Scripture's authority for faith and life, the Reformed tradition shows several distinctive emphases, including an affirmation of the need for interpretation; a stress on scholarly exegesis; attention to Scripture as a whole, stressing both diversity and unity; acknowledging some scopus, thrust, or message; respecting the role of tradition; taking the fellowship of believers seriously; regarding preaching, teaching, and study as central for edification; and emphasizing the guidance of the Spirit.

Bibliography

Biéler, A. *Calvin's Economic and Social Thought.* Ed. E. Dommen. Trans. J. Greig. World Alliance of Reformed Churches, World Council of Churches, 2006; Boesak, A. *The Tenderness of Conscience: African Renaissance and the Spirituality of Politics.* Sun Press, 2005; de Gruchy, J. *Liberating Reformed Theology: A South African Contribution to an Ecumenical Debate.* Eerdmans, 1991; Douglass, E. *Women, Freedom, and Calvin.* Westminster, 1985; Gustafson, J. *Ethics from a Theocentric Perspective.* 2 vols. University of Chicago Press, 1981–84; Heslam, P. *Creating a Christian Worldview: Abraham Kuyper's Lectures on Calvinism.* Eerdmans, 1998; Leith, J. *John Calvin's Doctrine of the Christian Life.* Westminster John Knox, 1989; Mangina, J. *Karl Barth on the Christian Life: The Practical Knowledge of God.* Peter Lang, 2001; Strohm, C. *Calvinismus und Recht: Weltanschaulich-konfessionelle Aspekte im Werk reformierter Juristen in der frühen Neuzeit.* SLMAHR 42. Mohr Siebeck, 2008; idem. *Ethik im frühen Calvinismus: Humanistische Einflüsse, philosophische, juristische und theologische Argumentationen sowie mentalitätsgeschichtliche Aspekte am Beispiel des Calvin-Schülers Lambertus Danaeus.* AK 65. De Gruyter, 1996; Verhey, A. *Living the Heidelberg: The Heidelberg Catechism and the Moral Life.* CRC Publications, 1986; Webster, J. *Barth's Moral Theology: Human Action in Barth's Thought.* Eerdmans, 1998; Witte, J. *The Reformation of Rights: Law, Religion and Human Rights in Early Modern Calvinism.* Cambridge University Press, 2007.

Dirkie Smit

Refugees *See* Aliens, Immigration, and Refugees

Rehabilitation of Offenders *See* Prison and Prison Reform

Religious Toleration

Religious toleration is respect, freedom, and nondiscrimination of a person or idea with regard to religion. In most modern cultures tolerant respect for a person's religion or religious ideas implies disagreement with that religion; tolerant freedom and nondiscrimination imply freedom and nondiscrimination under a system of laws, formal or informal, legal or moral.

Today, religious toleration can create acute problems. Complex cultures that implicitly endorse one religion but give legal freedoms to many create difficulties for indigenes to fully commit to one religion as a matter of faith but tolerate others as a matter of principle.

Scripture and Religious Toleration

In the world of Scripture, religious toleration was an issue of a different sort for two reasons. First, the traditional societies of Scripture tended toward more religious homogeneity. With respect to religion, the OT people of God made decisions that reflected communality rather than individuality. Religion was synonymous with tribe. Second, their basic stance toward other tribes' gods was henotheistic. The reality and, sometimes, even the beneficence of other tribes' gods were not in question; the real issue was the relative power of other gods vis-à-vis Yahweh. In the confrontation with Baal, Elijah's belief was that Yahweh was stronger than Baal, not that Yahweh was real and Baal was not. The issue was not toleration of mistaken belief but rather confrontation with the powers.

This is not to say that the idea of toleration is absent in the OT. But when the idea was introduced, it tended to be transcendent, a divine prerogative or a kingly right. Toleration (the word and its derivatives appear rarely in English translations) had the feeling of patient endurance on the part of one more powerful and perhaps more mature than regular individuals. In Psalms, for example, the phrase "His mercy endures forever," which appears more than forty times, has a sense of God's toleration for human foibles—his forgiveness will always be available.

In the NT we sense a move toward the modern idea of toleration. It is accompanied by a social shift toward empire, and within empire, nationhood. Within Roman political boundaries and the scope of Greek philosophical influence many religions existed. Romans managed religious differences; Greeks debated them. In Jesus' teaching an ethic emerged that emphasized patience and endurance and love on the part of individuals with one's neighbors (and even enemies).

The church fathers played to both the Roman political mentality and the Greek philosophical one. Justin Martyr attempted to place Christian teachings within the Greek debate over *logos*, while other fathers, such as Clement and Tertullian, saw the other religions as the wayward creations of God's former viceroys (McDermott). As God's underlings, these "angels" got some things right and some things wrong. In both cases, the other religions were to be tolerated as either slightly mistaken or insufficiently religious creations of lesser beings.

Toleration in the Christian Tradition

One does not have to page through very much of church history to see that religious toleration has not always, or even often, been seen as a virtue. Augustine, Thomas Aquinas, and John Calvin are only the most well-known of Christian leaders who come out in favor of persecution rather than toleration of religious difference. The reasons for such persecution vary, ranging from attempts to punish heretics, to dominate marginal populations, to protect the purity of the faithful. Although most of these church teachers definitely run against the ideal of modern advocacy for religious toleration, an enduring lesson emerges: religious toleration is never absolute. It is probably safe to say that all Christian communities have taken Jesus' teachings of loving one's neighbor as a call for some level of religious toleration, but no Christian communities have taken toleration to include all religious deviancy. Mistaken belief sometimes can be tolerated, evil cannot.

Religious toleration is a historical product of the Enlightenment, with its emphasis on the value and worth of human rationality and agency. The modern understanding of religious toleration is an intellectual product of John Locke, who wrote *A Letter Concerning Toleration*. Locke wrote within the context of the emerging European nation-state and the accompanying phenomenon of established Christian churches. Early modernity found itself free of the hegemony of the Holy Roman Empire, but not totally free of alliances between church and state. Countries with established churches, paid for and supported by governments, raised inevitable issues of freedom of religion for free churches and minority faiths.

Continental philosophy's creation of the idea of the autonomous self did much to shift the locus of discussions of religious tolerance from the arena of tribe/empire/state responsibility to individual human rights, where it is mostly discussed today. The idea of religion being a freely chosen option by individuals with identity and agency has been much of the reason why the issue of religious toleration is such an important one.

Contemporary Applications

In assessing where we are as a Christian community today in grappling with this issue, we find it not at all difficult to return to the biblical text for resources to inform our discussions. Jesus' ethical teachings particularly lend themselves to be used as rationales and supports for dealing with religious toleration issues. His teachings anticipate the Enlightenment and Lockean emphasis on individual human religious rights without abandoning the importance of grappling with political religious responsibilities.

The growing prevalence of democratic pluralisms as political forms of choice means that religious toleration on both the political level and the individual level will continue to be important. We live in an age when the separation of church and state has become almost complete, and in such a social scenario the rights and privileges of individuals to practice their religion will raise the issue of how those rights relate to the sometimes competing rights of others. In such a setting it is probably helpful to see the spectrum of possible positions on the issue of religious toleration to include four settings:

acceptance tolerance intolerance persecution

Although it might be tempting to consider religious tolerance as a private and/or communal attitude toward those of other religions, the reality is that religious tolerance usually moves us toward actions of acceptance, and that religious intolerance usually moves us toward acts of persecution.

See also Enemy, Enemy Love; Freedom; Human Rights; Persecution; Tolerance

Bibliography

Locke, J. *The Second Treatise of Government; and, A Letter Concerning Toleration*. Dover Publications, 2002; McDermott, G. *God's Rivals: Why Has God Allowed Different Religions?* IVP Academic, 2007; Zagorin, P. *How the Idea of Religious Toleration Came to the West*. Princeton University Press, 2003.

Terry C. Muck

Remarriage *See* Marriage and Divorce

Reparation

Reparation is usually the act of a culpable party providing compensation for wrongs done to an offended party. The Bible speaks to the issue of reparation, specifically and in general terms, in numerous accounts. For example, Exod. 22 deals specifically with reparation for theft, damage to crops, false judgments, sexual irresponsibility, and the lending of money. According to Hebrew law at that time, not only were perpetrators required to pay back what was stolen (or the equivalent of what was stolen) but also they sometimes were required to go beyond the original value and double or even quadruple the value of what was stolen. By extracting ethical guidelines from the Exodus passage, we can reason that when injustices occur that can be handled through reparation, acts of reparation should be taken very seriously.

The reparation principle continues into the NT period as affirmed by Jesus. In Jesus' interaction with Zacchaeus, the tree-climbing tax collector, the latter admits to his extortion. He then offers to give half of his possessions to the poor and specifically to pay back four times the amount to those whom he had cheated. Zacchaeus's actions, which were within the parameters of the requirements in Exod. 22, appear to have pleased Jesus immensely. Jesus' response was to tell Zacchaeus that he had found salvation that day (Luke 19:8–9), no doubt invoking the promise of Isa. 58:6–8 to those who free the oppressed, feed the hungry, help the homeless, and cover the naked. As that prophetic OT passage reports, the promise of a salvific experience awaits such people who make these reparations: "Then your light shall break forth like the dawn, and your healing shall spring up quickly; your vindicator shall go before you, the glory of the LORD shall be your rear guard."

Reparation fits broadly in Scripture under the universal principle of Jubilee and its accompanying theological construct *shalom*. The Hebrew noun *šālôm* ("well-being, wholeness, perfection of God's creation, prosperity, peace") is used 225 times in the OT. The functional Greek equivalent in the NT, *eirēnē* ("restoration of relationship, wholeness, healing, peace"), is used 94 times. The Hebrew verb *šālam* ("to repay in full, make obligatory restitution, repay for loss, restore, be at peace, make peace, fulfill a vow, bring to completion, accomplish the goal") is used 117 times in the OT. The concept of *shalom* encompasses a whole range of descriptors, but certainly reparation is included in order to make things right in God's *shalom* purview.

Jesus' proclamation of Jubilee was an affirmation of the ethical principle of reparation. When Jesus announced to the synagogue at Nazareth that Jubilee was now a reality (Luke 4:18–21), at the least it meant that those who were oppressed and treated unjustly would in some way be compensated. The Jubilee was seen as the fulfillment and realization of God's intended *shalom* kingdom. Jesus' words reflected the fulfillment of those principles, specifically those mentioned in Isa. 61:1–2. One can argue, at least in general terms, that Jesus' mother understood something about justice and reparation within its Jubilee context. The onset of Jubilee fulfillment is the occasion about which Mary sang in Luke 1:51–53: "He has shown strength with his arm; he has scattered the proud in the thoughts of their hearts. He has brought down the powerful from their thrones, and lifted up the lowly; he has filled the hungry with good things, and sent the rich away empty."

How do we distinguish reparation from the broader theme of justice and *shalom*? Reparation becomes the specific actions taken to ensure that God's intended *shalom* kingdom is continued. It is the enduring effort to make compensation for what has been taken. Acts of reparation are unambiguous and should have a direct relationship to the offense. For example, if land has been stolen, then land plus other compensation should be given to the offended party in order to compensate for the loss of capital in the land.

On a national level, the ethical practice of reparation has not often been utilized. Since numerous nations now exist on lands that many argue have been wrongly taken from and rightfully belong to indigenous peoples, it would be an awkward situation for the colonizer to make reparation to the colonized. Still, arguably, the responsibility exists for those who claim to live according to principles founded on Scripture.

The world has observed prominent instances of attempted reparation in the past century. Germany made monetary reparation to the Allied nations after World War I and to Israel for claims regarding the Jewish Holocaust. More recently, the United States made monetary reparation to survivors of the Japanese internment camps that occurred during World War II.

In recent history, reparation has been a hotly contested topic in America. Among African Americans, the case of reparations has been introduced to assist descendants of slavery. Others argue that social programs that favor African Americans, such as minority hiring preferences, constitute reparation. Native Americans, who, arguably, have lost more than anyone, have not received reparations for the loss of the American continents. The same is true for the Aboriginal people of Australia, the Maori people of New Zealand, and many other indigenous groups who have been colonized.

See also Colonialism and Postcolonialism; Jubilee; Justice; Justice, Restorative; Reconciliation

Bibliography

Brown, W. *The Ethos of the Cosmos: The Genesis of Moral Imagination in the Bible*. Eerdmans, 1999; Brueggemann, W. *The Land: Place as Gift, Promise, and Challenge in Biblical Faith*. Fortress, 1977; idem. *Peace*. Chalice Press, 2001; Habel, N. *The Land Is Mine: Six Biblical Land Ideologies*. Fortress, 1995; Memmi, A. *Colonization and the Colonized*. Beacon Press, 1991; Powers, E. *Signs of Shalom*. United Church Press, 1973; Swartley, W. *Covenant of Peace: The Missing Peace in New Testament Theology and Ethics*. Eerdmans, 2006; Wright, R. *Stolen Continents: Five Hundred Years of Conquest and Resistance in the Americas*. Houghton Mifflin, 1992; Zehr, H. *The Little Book of Restorative Justice*. Good Books, 2002; Zinn, H. *A People's History of the United States: 1492–Present*. Harper Collins, 2003.

Randy S. Woodley

Repentance

The notion of repentance is closely related to the concept of "conversion," and signifies in the OT and the NT a turning from whatever hinders one's radical orientation to God, together with a turning to God in wholehearted devotion and faithfulness.

The concepts of "repentance" and "conversion" have become associated especially with the Christian faith, but these are not particularly NT terms, nor in the ancient world are these concepts peculiar to early Christian proclamation and literature. In the OT, "to turn" (*šûb*) is used especially with reference to Israel, and thus the demand for repentance emerges from its covenantal basis in God's initiative and call. Accordingly, the term is often translated "to return." Form-critical work has demonstrated a basic pattern for the prophetic call to repentance (see Steck): (1) rehearsal of Israel's unfaithfulness; (2) a reference to divine patience; (3) at times, a reference to Israel's rejection of God's messengers, the prophets; (4) the call to repentance; and (5) at times, warnings or promises tied to the people's response to the message of repentance (e.g., Jer. 7; Zech. 1:3–6; Mal. 3). This pattern evidences a central motif found elsewhere in the OT—namely, that God's people may serve as agents for the conversion of others, but they themselves have a continuous need for conversion. Repentance centers especially on turning away from idolatry and might explicitly include remorse and confession of sin, as well as turning to God in love and obedience and, thus, restoration of covenantal relations.

As in Greek literature more widely, so in the NT, the concept often is signaled by the terms *metanoia* ("change of mind") and its verbal form, *metanoeō* ("to change one's course"), or *epistrophē* ("turning [toward]") and its verbal form, *epistrephō* ("to turn around"). Practically from the coining of terms connoting "repentance," their primary sense has centered on a "change in thinking." However, this sense expands to "a change of mind, heart, view, opinion, or purpose," often in tandem with feelings of remorse due to the perception of having acted or thought wrongly, inappropriately, or disadvantageously. This is a reminder that, in antiquity, "knowing" and "thinking" were typically collocated with a person's dispositions, one's habits of thinking, feeling, believing, and behaving. Moreover, repentance, if it were genuine, would be accompanied by a will to make right the wrong committed or to change the situation that eventuated in the wrongdoing, and a concomitant alteration of future behavior. In the wider literature of antiquity, repentance was sometimes the result of divine and/or human chiding. Ultimately, repentance would lead to forgiveness and reconciliation.

Repentance is prominent in the Synoptic Gospels and Acts, much less so in the NT Epistles. In the Gospels of Matthew, Mark, and Luke, repentance is central to the message of Jesus' precursor, John, to the mission of Jesus himself, and to the proclamation of Jesus' followers when they are sent out, two by two. John's message of repentance receives its urgency on account of his expectation of the immediate arrival of the Messiah, whose advent would mark eschatological judgment. Reliance on Jewish ancestry was out of the question, replaced in John's preaching by an emphasis on an authentic, thoroughgoing reorientation of life around God's purpose (Matt. 3:1–12; Mark 1:1–8; Luke 3:1–20). For Matthew and Mark, Jesus' opening words tie the inbreaking, imperial rule of God to the necessity of repentance and faith (Matt. 3:17; Mark 1:15). Luke too portrays Jesus' mission as one of calling sinners to repentance (Luke 5:27–32). The disciples, sent by Jesus to extend his missionary activity, "went out and proclaimed that all should repent" (Mark 6:12). The vocabulary of repentance is also prominent in the book of Revelation (2:5, 16, 21–22; 3:3, 19; 9:20–21; 16:9, 11) where, as often in the Synoptic Gospels, it is associated above all with judgment. Repentance in the NT is also associated with heavenly rejoicing (Luke 15:7, 10) and with divine patience and graciousness (e.g., 2 Tim. 2:25; 2 Pet. 3:9).

Although some have attempted to draw a distinction in early Christian proclamation between repentance and conversion—with "repentance" expected of the Jewish people, "conversion" of gentiles—such a distinction cannot be maintained. In part, this is because this terminology is associated in antiquity with both the crossing of religious boundaries (as would be the case with gentiles) and with going deeper into one's own religion (as would be the case with Jews who followed Jesus as Messiah, for whom "conversion" would have required embracing a christocentric interpretation of their religion). Moreover, the call to leave idolatry addressed to gentiles (e.g., Acts 17:22–31; 1 Thess. 1:9–10) has its ready parallels in Israel's own history, in prophetic calls to turn from idolatry (e.g., Hosea).

As a response to the Christian message, repentance is developed most fully in the Acts of the Apostles and then in the first volume of Luke's two-part work, the Gospel of Luke. In this respect, Peter's call for response to the Christian message in the context of the Pentecost address (Acts 2:14–41) is programmatic: "Repent, and be baptized every one of you in the name of Jesus Christ so that your sins may be forgiven; and you will receive the gift of the Holy Spirit" (2:38). Indeed, repentance is often mentioned explicitly as an appropriate response to God's salvific work (cf. Acts 3:19; 5:31; 11:18; 17:30; 20:21), and Paul can summarize the content of his message as calling on both Jews and gentiles that they "should repent and turn to God and do deeds consistent with repentance" (Acts 26:20).

At the close of Peter's sermon in Acts 2, baptism is the medium by which repentance comes to expression as well as the sign that forgiveness has been granted. This collocation of repentance and baptism is not at all surprising, given the identification of baptism in the ministry of John the Baptizer as "a baptism of repentance" (Luke 3:4; Acts 13:24; 19:4; cf. Mark 1:4; Matt. 3:11). For John, repentance is marked by behavior that grows out of and demonstrates that one has indeed committed oneself to service in God's purpose (cf. Luke 3:1–20; Acts 26:20; Matt. 3:8). The examples Luke provides in his portrait of John urge the down-to-earth, relational, and socioeconomic contours of "fruits worthy of repentance": sharing with those who lack clothing and food, honesty in financial transactions (Luke 3:7–14; these behaviors are displayed by Zacchaeus in Luke 19:10). Not surprisingly, baptism in Acts has as its consequence, among other things, economic sharing (e.g., 2:41–47) and the extension of hospitality (e.g., Acts 10:47–48; 16:14–15, 28–34)—practices, then, that help to fill out the meaning of "fruits worthy of repentance."

If repentance is something people are called "to do," however, this is only because of the prior work of God. Thus, for Luke, repentance itself is the gracious gift of God—as Peter announces in Jerusalem, "When God raised up his servant, he sent him first to you, to bless you by turning each of you from your wicked ways" (Acts 3:26). Repentance is thus both active and passive—both divine gift (passive) and call (active) (e.g., Luke 5:31–32; Acts 5:31; 11:18).

See also Conversion

Bibliography

Goodman, M. *Mission and Conversion: Proselytizing in the Religious History of the Roman Empire*. Clarendon, 1994; Nave, G., Jr. *The Role and Function of Repentance in Luke-Acts*. SBLAB 4. Society of Biblical Literature, 2002; Steck, O. *Israel und das gewaltsame Geschick der Propheten: Untersuchungen zur Uberlieferung des deuteronomistischen Geschichtsbildes im Alten Testament, Spätjudentum und Urchristentum*. WMANT 23. Neukirchener Verlag, 1967; Wright, C. "Implications of Conversion in the Old Testament and the New." *IBMR* 28 (2004): 14–19.

Joel B. Green

Reproductive Technologies

Infertility is a human problem. Sarai (Sarah), Rachel, Hannah, and Elizabeth suffered from infertility (Gen. 11:30; 18:11; 29:31; 30:1; 1 Sam. 1:1, 5–6; Luke 1:7). Reproductive technologies have been developed to respond to the problems of infertility. One-third of the cases are male-related, one-third female-related, and the other cases have no specific medical issue. The problem for men and women is either with the delivery system or the quality of sperm, eggs, or womb, or with the act of sexual intercourse.

Biological Issues in Reproductive Technologies

Male reproductive technologies relate to problems of penetration, ejaculation, low sperm count, and poor sperm mobility or quality. Surgery or drugs may help. Specific reproductive technologies for men use artificial insemination by the husband (AIH), which requires masturbation. The sperm is washed, selected, and implanted using intracytoplasmic sperm injection (ICSI). Many Christians, especially Roman Catholics, regard masturbation as a selfish, self-centered, pleasure-giving, incomplete activity specifically condemned in the sin of Onan (Gen. 38:9). Yet some Catholic theologians argue that this particular act of masturbation, having the purpose of bringing about a pregnancy, is justifiable. Many Protestants have no problem with masturbation and understand the sin of Onan to be his failure to obey the levirate law rather than simply "spilling the seed." The sperm is delivered artificially, and that may be condemned as "unnatural" because it separates the procreative and unitive aspects of sexual intercourse.

If the quality of the sperm is poor, a donor may be used. Artificial insemination by donor (AID) involves a third party. Some regard this as adultery. Although an act of sexual intercourse is not needed for this process, there is a life-creating intrusion by an external, third party. This raises questions about who is the father, and the United Kingdom has made a legal ruling that the father is the genetic rather than the social father. This may have a deep psychological impact on the husband and his relationships with his wife and any resultant children. The donor usually is paid for his services or simply donates altruistically. Ethical questions include how donors should be selected, whether parents should have any role in that selection, and whether donors should be anonymous or have any responsibility for their progeny. Do children have the right to know the identity of their biological parents? It may be medically crucial to know one's genetic inheritance. Most clinics and countries keep careful records to enable genetic but not personal tracing.

Female reproductive technologies are responses to problems with conceiving or carrying a child. Surgery may relieve problems (e.g., blocked fallopian tubes). Gamete intrafallopian transfer (GIFT) and zygote intrafallopian transfer (ZIFT) allow transfer of eggs or even fertilized eggs directly into the fallopian tubes. These technologies relate to in-vitro fertilization (IVF), which fertilizes eggs outside the womb in a petri dish, versus in-vivo fertilization, which happens in the human body.

Eggs may be harvested from the woman seeking fertility treatment often using "superovulation," producing many more than one egg as in the normal monthly cycle. Egg donors may be family or friends donating altruistically, or women receiving fertility treatment for donation or for payment. Moral and legal issues include payment, the impact of the health and well-being of the donor, the relationship and responsibilities between a third party and the infertile couple, the selection of the donor and of the egg or embryo, the understanding of parenthood, and the regulatory role of government or professional organizations.

Superovulation produces more embryos than are needed. Selection, whether of sex or genetic characteristics, is normal. The number and quality of embryos replaced can lead to situations like that of Nadya Suleman (the so-called Octomom), who gave birth to octuplets in 2009. Selective reduction is sometimes used to reduce the number of embryos in the womb even if it involves killing some. Spare embryos may be donated or frozen for future use. Freezing creates new dilemmas. Years after the death of her husband, Diane Blood gave birth to two children by using sperm collected from him while he was in a coma. Freezing and defrosting may have long-term negative effects on resultant children. Many claim that experimentation on embryonic genetic material may solve fertility and genetic problems and produce cures for everything from cancer to Alzheimer's disease using embryonic stem cells. Governments debate what kind of legislation and regulation should oversee experimentation on human material. In the United States, financial support for research has been a key regulative tool. In the United Kingdom and Australia, governments created regulative bodies to supervise legislation protecting human material in experimentation. This includes control of transspecies experimentation. The creation of hybrids, part human and part animal, may offer an alternative source of organs and material for transplantation ranging from pancreatic islets to kidneys and hearts.

New technologies enable the extraction of follicles that will become eggs from aborted female embryos. Public reaction has been negative, expressing the "yuck" factor of the parent of a child being an aborted fetus. Egg donors may be carefully selected for the likely genetic characteristics. This creates a market for eggs from women considered to be intellectually, artistically, or athletically gifted or physically beautiful, paralleled by the selection of similarly qualified males as sperm donors. Women may be paid up to thirty thousand dollars for their eggs, but there is deep unease that babies, eggs, sperm, and women's bodies are commodities for sale. Some clinics offer treatment to women who are unable to pay in return for their eggs to be used for others. Coercion of women who are vulnerable, in financial need, or desperate for children seems inevitable.

In-vitro fertilization makes it possible to select which embryos may be placed. In countries such as India and China, where male offspring are generally preferred, gender selection is used. In the United Kingdom and the United States it often is possible to select gender in cases involving gender-related diseases or predispositions to diseases. How far should we go to select embryos when trying to produce desirable traits or rule out genetic disabilities?

For women unable to carry a pregnancy to term, reproductive technologies have made it possible to insert embryos into surrogate mothers. Women who "rent" or "sell" their wombs receive expenses or payment. The "Baby M" case, in which the surrogate mother refused to release the baby into the custody of the sperm-donor father and his wife, demonstrated the problems between natural and social parents even when legal contracts are involved. Feminists are uneasy about the potential pressures on women, though some argue that female autonomy and freedom of choice are fundamental.

Fertility technologies can be used not only for infertile married couples but also for single women and gay and lesbian couples wanting to have children. Clinics make judgments regarding who is eligible for infertility treatment and decide the moral bases of such judgments.

Ethical Issues in Reproductive Technologies

New reproductive technologies have created new moral questions. What is a parent? Traditional understandings of family, inheritance, and genetics have been replaced by social parental roles. Adoption has been the model for reproductive technology, but it seeks to put right what has gone wrong. In infertility technology, we are not simply putting right but rather are creating entirely new situations. For many, natural law and what is natural exclude the artificial intrusion into the personal and marital arenas. As we use certain medical procedures, our experience of what we consider normal and natural constantly changes.

Christians are divided over reproductive technologies, some seeing them as challenges to human dignity, human relationships, and God-given natural limits, others seeing them as God-given knowledge and expertise for overcoming disease and restoring human fertility to God's initial purpose. As God blessed many infertile women, modern reproductive technologies fulfill his divine intention for marriage (Gen. 1:28).

Practically reproductive technologies cost anywhere from five hundred to thirty thousand dollars. The success level ranges widely, depending on selectivity. Producing a baby is more difficult than creating a pregnancy. In general, the rate of success is about 25 percent. Given overpopulation and widespread hunger, should we spend so much on techniques with such low success rates?

These practical moral questions raise key issues of justice. Who pays for such treatment? Is it fair that only the wealthy have access to such technologies?

The Scriptures emphasize the value, worth, and dignity of human life from the earliest stage, but they were written long before modern biological understanding and reproductive technologies. The psalmist, Isaiah, Jeremiah, and the Gospel writers assume that God is involved in human origins from the very start, and the whole Bible stresses the sanctity of human life (Ps. 139:13–16; Isa. 49:1, 5; Jer. 1:5; Luke 1:31). Accordingly, embryos must be protected. This will set limits to how reproductive technology works and what are the consequences.

Modern surgical and genetic developments enable us to put right what has gone wrong. In a fallen world, infertility is not unusual but is growing. We can help married couples fulfill God's purpose of being fruitful and multiplying (Gen. 1:28), but we must consider the financial, social, and moral cost of such technologies.

Marriage and sexual expression are fundamental to human well-being. Reproductive technologies can threaten the human bonds between husband and wife by the intrusion of a third party and by the artificial separation of procreation from sexual expressions of love.

Parenthood, family, and familial relationships are under pressure from reproductive technologies. Secrecy and anonymity of donors are unwise both from medical and genetic points of view, as well as impacting the health of any children so conceived as they mature and want to know their biological parent.

Christians do not believe that there is a right to have a child, certainly not by any and all means. Rather, there is a freedom to have children, and reproductive technology can help fulfill that freedom. Society must set limits to the availability of reproductive technologies. Medical associations stress that for the healthy development of children there should be both a father and mother, raising questions about the artificial creation of single, gay, and lesbian parents. There is a key difference between situations that just happen and deliberately creating less-than-ideal situations.

Scripture stresses responsibility to God and to one another as human beings (Rom. 14:12; Gal. 6:2). Any use of reproductive technologies that undermines the responsibility of individuals and couples must be rejected. There is no technological imperative: availability does not require usage.

Ethical reflection on reproductive technology must evaluate motivation for its use. Wanting to help a married couple have a child of their own is different from helping a single woman have the experience of becoming a mother by artificial insemination. The means that we use have moral implications. Many Christians would regard masturbation as a legitimate means in helping a couple conceive when the husband is unable to inseminate his wife naturally, but it is another matter when we produce far more eggs than are used, destroy eggs or embryos regarded as "flawed," or experiment on human embryos thinking that the end or possibility of producing a medical advance justifies the means of abusing human being and human beings. Secular society argues that the embryo is at best a potential human being rather than a human being with potential. Trying to produce medical cures for those suffering from crippling diseases justifies all kinds of offshoots from reproductive technologies, ranging from embryonic stem-cell and genetic manipulation to cloning and hybrid creation. Each means must be assessed, as must the principles on which we act. Christians believe that humans are made in the image of God and have a fundamental value, worth, and dignity that must be preserved (Gen. 1:26–27; 9:6). Therefore, we cannot act in ways that undermine and degrade human beings and use them as commodities, means for our own ends, or as sacrifices for others. When a child is unable to give consent for medical treatment, the parents and professionals act in the best interests of the child. We must do the same in reproductive technologies. The principle of other love drives many in medicine, but that love must be aware of the consequences.

The short- and long-term consequences of reproductive technologies compel us to be extremely careful about what we do, how we do it, and what might happen if we fail to regulate and control our practices. Part of being human and living in a fallen world is that we must learn to live with limits.

See also Adoption; Bioethics; Childlessness; Family Planning; Infertility; Resource Allocation; Sanctity of Human Life

Bibliography

Jones, D. *Brave New People: Ethical Issues at the Commencement of Life*. InterVarsity, 1984; idem. *Manufacturing Humans: The Challenge of the New Reproductive Technologies*. InterVarsity, 1987; Lammers, S., and A. Verhey, eds. *On Moral Medicine: Theological Perspectives in Medical Ethics*. 2nd ed. Eerdmans, 1998; Rae, S. *Brave New Families: Biblical Ethics and Reproductive Technologies*. Baker, 1996.

E. David Cook

Resistance Movements

One potentially fruitful way to read the Bible is as a dramatic series of faith-based resistance movements commissioned by God to counter the rise of idolatrous conquest states, from the first city-states arising in Mesopotamia (the "tower of Babel" civilization that Abraham left behind in Genesis) to the Mediterranean empire of Rome (the "beast" denounced by John in Revelation). The entire history of the people of Israel was lived out at the (often violent) crossroads of the perennial empires of the ancient Near East (Egypt, Assyria, Babylon), while the birth of Jesus coincided with the appearance of the greatest emperor to yet bestride the globe: Caesar Augustus. The Bible's most formative social movement—the Hebrew prophetic tradition begun in Elijah and Elisha and culminating for Christians in the ministries of John the Baptist and Jesus of Nazareth—could similarly be interpreted as a domestic resistance movement arising to counter Israel's own attempts to become a superpower: the Davidic monarchy that reached its sudden apogee in Solomon's Jerusalem temple-state before rapidly fragmenting into short-lived northern and southern kingdoms. The contrasting strategies of resistance to the second-century BCE Greek overlord Antiochus Epiphanies IV mapped out by the books of Daniel and Maccabees subsequently staked out the parameters of a postexilic anti-imperial politics of Jewish apocalypse.

Exodus and exile, the two crucibles that bookend the faith story of Israel, were struggles either to be liberated from an enslaving empire (Egypt) or to live counterculturally within one (Babylon). The Moses-led campaign of the ten plagues, culminating in the battle of the Red Sea (Exod. 1–15), crystallized an anti-imperial "Yahweh war" tradition among the Hebrews that featured reliance on divine nature miracle, and even "girl power," rather than kings, generals, chariots, and conventional armies (examples of biblical "girl power" include the prophetic songsters Miriam, Hannah, Elizabeth, and Mary; the battle-tested judge Deborah; the secret agent Rahab; the opportunistic assassin Jael; the savior queen Esther; the foreign great-grandmother of the great king, Ruth; the patriarch-confronting Tamar; and the peace negotiator Abigail). Its mantra was "Not by might, not by strength, but by my Spirit says the LORD" (Zech. 4:6). This unprecedented way of fighting was carried forward by Joshua in the Jubilary (i.e., 7 x 7) "protest march/jam session" that brought the Canaanite fortress of Jericho tumbling down and was continued by the charismatic guerrilla commanders Deborah, Gideon, and Samson. Strong echoes of this populist impulse continued even in the transition to an Israelite monarchy, via the dire warnings of the last judge, Samuel, about the reenslavement that having a "king like the other nations" would bring (1 Sam. 8) and the "upside-down kingdom" victory of the youngest son, slingshot-toting shepherd boy David over Goliath, the greatest Canaanite commando of all.

Jeremiah's letter to the exiles (Jer. 29) quintessentially outlined the tactics for the Jews' exilic struggle of subversive, countercultural, synagogue-shaped, and *shalom*-seeking polity without a king. The contemporaneous exemplars of the "servants" and "tremblers" of Yahweh (Isa. 55–65) and the "wise ones" of Daniel became paradigmatic for Jews living under imperial occupation of one kind or another ever since, including the first-century CE Galilean Jews who came to understand Jesus of Nazareth as Israel's Messiah. In contrast, the zealously violent approach to resistance mastered for a time by the Maccabees did not "make the cut" of the Hebrew canon, a hermeneutical decision confirmed by the ultimate political failure of their many imitators (armed Jewish rebellions immediately prior to and following the reign of Herod the Great; the Sicarii; the disastrous Jewish revolts against Rome of 66–73 and 132–135 CE).

Following the lead of John Howard Yoder, whose trailblazing book *The Politics of Jesus* could have just as easily been titled *The Politics of Paul* because half of the book references Pauline Letters, scholars such as Jacob Taubes, Daniel Boyarin, James Dunn, and N. T. Wright have increasingly come to see the itinerant church-planting ministry of Paul (and other NT apostles) as representing a kind of counterimperial "politics" as well. Here the subversive *shalom*-seeking of Jeremian exiles was extended to include reconciliation with gentile enemies, even a Roman centurion such as Cornelius (Acts 10). It would seem more than a coincidence that John the Baptist, Jesus, Stephen, Peter, Paul, James, and other leading lights of the NT were all executed as subversives under the rule of Rome and its client kings. The book of Revelation (whose author, John, apparently was exiled by Rome to the island of Patmos [1:9]) is the most explicit among NT writings in its call to conquer the "beast" of a violently exploitative and emperor-worshiping Roman Empire by fighting a (willing-to-die-but-not-to-kill) resistance "war of the Lamb." It could be said that the underground (and periodically persecuted) church of the first three centuries CE did indeed conquer the Roman Empire, nonviolently and from within, using just such an approach (if then paradoxically capitulating to a "Christianized" empire cult of its own).

Following the rise of an imperial Christendom in the fourth century CE, marginal sects arising from within Christianity itself, often branded as heretics, could be seen as resisters to this new state-church synthesis, from Donatists, the desert fathers and mothers, Benedictines, and Celtic Christians in the early medieval period, to later medieval renewal movements such as the Waldensians, Cathars, Franciscans, Lollards, Hussites, Czech Brethren, Beguines, Brethren of the Common Life, and, finally, the Radical Reformation Anabaptists (and their Free Church descendants and cousins: Mennonites, Amish, Hutterites, Brethren, Baptists, Quakers, Moravians, Disciples of Christ, Adventists, Pentecostals). Continuing this venerable tradition of dissident discipleship, Christian groups have also been prominent in a wide variety of liberation struggles in the modern period—for example, the Anglo-American abolitionist and women's suffrage movements, the African American civil rights campaign, the South African antiapartheid movement, Catholic base communities in Latin America, "people power" in the Philippines, and anticommunist struggles across Eastern Europe.

See also Civil Disobedience; Colonialism and Postcolonialism; Dissent; Freedom; Imperialism; Liberationist Ethics; War

Bibliography

Borg, M. *Conflict, Holiness, and Politics in the Teachings of Jesus.* Trinity Press International, 1984; Brueggemann, W. *The Prophetic Imagination.* 2nd ed. Fortress Press, 2001; Crossan, J. *The Historical Jesus: The Life of a Mediterranean Jewish Peasant.* HarperSanFrancisco, 1991; Driver, J. *Radical Faith: An Alternative History of the Church.* Pandora Press, 1999; Ellul, J. *The Meaning of the City.* Trans. D. Pardee. Eerdmans, 1970; Freyne, S. *Jesus, a Jewish Galilean: A New Reading of the Jesus-Story.* T&T Clark, 2004; Gottwald, N. *The Tribes of Yahweh: A Sociology of the Religion of Liberated Israel, 1250–1050 B.C.E.* Orbis, 1979; Herzog, W. *Parables as Subversive Speech: Jesus as Pedagogue of the Oppressed.* Westminster John Knox, 1994; Horsley, R. *In the Shadow of Empire: Reclaiming the Bible as a History of Faithful Resistance.* Westminster John Knox, 2008, idem, ed. *Jesus and the Spiral of Violence: Popular Jewish Resistance in Roman Palestine.* Harper & Row, 1987; idem, ed. Lind, M. *Yahweh Is a Warrior: The Theology of Warfare in Ancient Israel.* Herald Press, 1980; Mendenhall, G. *The Tenth Generation: The Origins of the Biblical Tradition.* Johns Hopkins University Press, 1973; Myers, C. *Binding the Strong Man: A Political Reading of Mark's Story of Jesus.* Orbis, 1988; Sharp, G. *The Politics of Nonviolent Action.* Porter Sargent, 1973; Stringfellow, W. *An Ethic for Christians and Other Aliens in a Strange Land.* Word, 1973; Wink, W. *Engaging the Powers: Discernment and Resistance in a World of Domination.* Fortress, 1992; Wright, N. T. *Jesus and the Victory of God.* Fortress, 1996; Yoder, J. *For the Nations: Essays Public and Evangelical.* Eerdmans, 1997; idem. *The Politics of Jesus: Vicit Agnus Noster.* 2nd ed. Eerdmans, 1994.

Kent Davis Sensenig

Resource Allocation

In a world of too many people and not enough food or other natural resources, humans need to allocate limited resources carefully. Ecologists and economists have suggested various schemes based on some form of justice and fairness. These schemes respond to human needs and outline the responsibilities of societies and individuals to provide for themselves and each other. The problem of resource allocation is magnified in natural disaster, famine, and war, where triage is often used to decide which people should be fed, treated, and cared for and in what order. When the *Titanic* was sinking and lifeboats were in short supply, "women and children first" was a basic form of resource allocation. Today, resource allocation is especially important in the area of healthcare provision, determining how to allocate limited healthcare resources in a world of overpopulation and increasing life expectancy.

Healthcare systems are under pressure because of our ability to keep alive people who in previous generations would have died, to extend the life of those near death, and to treat illnesses that previously were untreatable. The pressure continues to increase because of the rising cost of medical technologies and medicines as well as the development of new treatments and the rising number of people without medical insurance in the United States.

Resource allocation relies on the diverse strategies of delay, dilution, diversion, and the discouraging or denying of treatment. Healthcare economists have introduced the concept of the "quality-adjusted life year" (QALY) to present a more objective, scientific basis for healthcare decisions. This calculation compares different treatments and individuals, predicting how long persons might live and the quality of their lives should they be treated. These calculations generally favor the young and healthy over the elderly and the sick, who, consequently, are less likely to receive treatment.

Currently, governments, insurance companies, doctors, and patients have some say in resource allocation by the decisions they make and the practices they follow. The kinds of criteria used in medical moral decision-making range from personal preference on grounds of age, sex, or relationship; merit (giving people what we think they deserve in terms of social worth and past, present, or future contribution to society); or a host of other considerations—for example, the patient's ability to pay, the likely success of treatment in terms of increased life expectancy or quality of life, equality (everyone receives the same treatment or same sum of money for healthcare), or the need or urgency of the situation (where life-threatening, emergency care will trump nonurgent, elective procedures).

The dangers in many systems of resource allocation are those of reductionism (reducing the person to a unit or to his or her disease), materialism (considering only the physical body), determinism (treating people as machines), and depersonalization and dehumanization (ignoring the whole person in the entirety of his or her context, physical, psychological, social, and spiritual).

Specifically Christian approaches to resource allocation are holistic and begin with God, whose image the human family bears and to whom humans are ultimately responsible (e.g., Gen. 1:27–28). The consistent witness of Scripture is that God's aim for humanity is *shalom*—health, well-being, and peace—and that this is achieved only in the context of dispositions and practices of justice and mercy (e.g., Mic. 6:8). This has immediate influence on criteria in resource allocation. Additionally, Scripture emphasizes the dignity and worth of individual persons and the responsibility of all to protect the weak and vulnerable. In biblical visions of the new heaven and earth, all are restored to perfect humanity and harmony (e.g., Isa. 35; Rev. 21–22). In their contributions to the difficult challenges involved in allocation of limited resources, Christians will reflect on the importance of the human body in the incarnation and resurrection of Christ and the renewed, transformed bodies of humanity in God's ultimate reign in eternity.

See also Healthcare Ethics; Human Rights; Image of God

Bibliography

Kilner, J. *Who Lives? Who Dies? Ethical Criteria in Patient Selection*. Yale University Press, 1990; Lammers, S., and A. Verhey, eds. *On Moral Medicine: Theological Perspective in Medical Ethics*. Eerdmans, 1998.

E. David Cook

Responsibility

In contemporary parlance, "responsibility" is most often used as a synonym for "accountability." Retrospectively, it is used to allocate blame or praise, as well as punishment or reward, for a specific action or outcome. Prospectively, it is used to assign certain roles, activities, or outcomes to particular persons or groups of persons. In both legal and philosophical circles, therefore, it gives rise to fundamental questions about requirements for accountability. In philosophical circles the concept of responsibility often provokes discussions of the minimal requirements for moral agency, including the nature and possibility of free will. In legal debates it leads to related questions about mitigating conditions that limit accountability, such as immaturity or mental incapacity.

Even though the term *responsibility* did not come into use until the late eighteenth century, it is generally understood as a fundamental facet of human morality. Although the term does not appear anywhere in Scripture, scholarly examinations have focused their exploration of responsibility on biblical notions of accountability. Because modern society has an individualistic orientation, special attention has been paid to concepts of collective responsibility in Scripture. In the ancient Near East, accountability was a social rather than a personal phenomenon. Commendation and blame, rewards and punishments, devolved to entire social groups, including future generations. So children inherited the rewards and punishment of their parents, and entire groups were held accountable for the actions of their members (Exod. 20:5–6; 34:7; Deut. 5:9–10; Josh. 7:1–26). That such a notion of collective responsibility was still current in Jesus' time is evident in the narrative about the man born blind (John 9:2). It also had significance for Paul's understanding of both sin and salvation: "Therefore just as one man's trespass led to condemnation for all, so one man's act of righteousness leads to justification and life for all" (Rom. 5:18). Notions of individual responsibility are also present in Scripture (Deut. 24:16; Prov. 24:12; Ezra 14:20; Jer. 31:30). Because the notion of collective responsibility flies in the face of modern assumptions about moral agency and autonomy, it has been the focus of attention.

Amid the struggle against National Socialism in Germany, Dietrich Bonhoeffer, a Lutheran theologian and ethicist, developed a christocentric model of responsibility to loosen the rigid moral requirement to obey the designated authorities without jettisoning a sense of moral obligation. He argued that a responsible human agent is characterized by both freedom and relationship. Humans are bound to one another and to God; therefore, moral responsibility is always a matter of deputyship, acting for the sake and on behalf of another. Jesus Christ is the perfect model of human responsibility: complete surrender of oneself for the sake of the other. Responsible persons do not impose a foreign ideal or law upon recalcitrant reality, but rather conform themselves to reality as it is realized in Jesus Christ, who has taken all of reality unto himself.

Criticizing the legalism of the modern Roman Catholic Church (particularly the role of the manuals in ecclesiastical life), Bernard Häring, a German Catholic theologian, used the language of responsibility to emphasize the fundamentally relational character of religion and ethics. Religion entails a "response" to the presence and power of God. It is a dialogue between the person and God that establishes a personal relationship. Salvation, in this sense, is communion with the living God. Like religion, morality is primarily relational. It entails relationships of mutual responsibility in the light of a fundamental response to God. Salvation is a social reality, which includes personal relationships of responsibility with God and all God's creation. Häring does not reject the place of law and command in the religious or moral life; rather, he renews their significance and depth by embedding them in the existential, relational context of personal response to God and neighbor.

H. Richard Niebuhr, a Reformed theologian and ethicist, provided the most sustained and systematic development of the language of responsibility in mid-twentieth-century theology and ethics. Without dismissing the significance of deontological and teleological approaches to ethics, he found them wanting. Neither the pursuit of ends nor obedience to law properly captures the social and reflexive nature of human moral existence. Humans are not autonomous agents, but rather are relational beings, more acted upon than acting. The metaphor of responsibility captures the social and contextual nature of human activity. From this perspective, human moral activity is more a matter of doing the fitting or appropriate thing in the given context than obeying a timeless law or pursuing an ultimate goal. Discerning the "fitting" thing requires an interpretation of what is going on and how to respond properly. It also assumes accountability in a continuing relationship of responsibility with the realities with which the agent contends. Human morality is, therefore, not judgment about discrete, atomic acts or decisions, but rather a dialogic process of revising, reorienting, and reacting within the context of a continuing relationship with the realities that one encounters.

Without losing contact with the commonsense meaning of responsibility, these three twentieth-century theologians developed and enriched its significance in ways that are consistent with modern realities but also alleviate some of modernity's weaknesses. In response to excessive formalism and idealism in moral and religious theory, the idea of responsibility provides a way to reconcile fact and value, the real and ideal, the spiritual and the material. In response to the association of the modern ideals of freedom and equality with individualism and autonomy, the language of responsibility provides a means to recover the social nature of human existence and a concern for the common good apart from premodern models of hierarchy. More recent explorations of the idea of moral responsibility in theology and ethics have placed it in conversation with related, but distinct, concepts of moral realism. What they share is the idea that human moral activity takes place in the context of realities that limit and shape human moral possibilities. Where they differ is in how those realities should be understood and interpreted: are they the negative forces that resist and limit moral and religious possibilities, or are they the positive realities that press humanity toward more responsible moral and religious existence. The former camp, the moral realists, seems more indebted to Max Weber and his use of the term *responsible* (as well as Reinhold Niebuhr), while the latter camp, moral responsiblists, follows more closely in the tradition of Bonhoeffer, Häring, and H. Richard Niebuhr.

While biblical scholars, attentive to the common usage of the term *responsibility*, have identified and explored cognate terms in the biblical literature, the rich possibilities for dialogue between biblical studies and theological ethics in this arena have not been realized. Mutual instruction between theological ethics and biblical studies concerning the concept of responsibility will take place not at the level of common terminology, but rather through an exploration of fundamental questions of human relationship to God, one another, and all reality—the sort of approach associated with the broad sweep of biblical theology.

See also Accountability; Collective Responsibility; Equality; Freedom; Individualism; Moral Agency; Reward and Retribution

Bibliography

Bonhoeffer, D. "History and the Good." Pages 224–62 in *Ethics*, ed. E. Bethge, trans. N. Smith. Macmillan, 1965; Buckers, H. "Kollektiv- und Individualvergeltung im Alten Testament." *TGl* 25 (1933): 273–86; Gamwell, F., and W. Schweiker. "Realism and Responsibility in Contemporary Ethics: Introduction." *JR* 73 (1993): 473–637; Gustafson, J. "The Place of Scripture in Christian Ethics: A Methodological Study." Pages 121–45 in *Theology and Christian Ethics*. United Church Press, 1974; Gustafson, J., and J. Laney, eds. *On Being Responsible: Issues in Personal Ethics*. Harper & Row, 1968; Häring, B. *General Moral Theology*. Vol. 1 of *The Law of Christ: Moral Theology for Priests and Laity*. Trans. E. Kaiser. Newman Press, 1963; Niebuhr, H. *The Responsible Self: An Essay in Christian Moral Philosophy*. Harper & Row, 1963; Robinson, H. "The Hebrew Conception of Corporate Personality." Pages 49–62 in *Werden und Wesen des Alten Testaments: Vorträge gehalten auf der internationalen Tagung alttestamentlicher Forscher zu Göttingen vom 4.–10. September 1935*, ed. P. Volz, F. Stummer, and J. Hempel. BZAW 66. Töpelmann, 1936; Weber, M. "Politics as a Vocation." Pages 115–28 in *Max Weber: Essays in Sociology*, ed. and trans. H. Gerth and C. Mills. Oxford University Press, 1958; Zank, M. "'Where Art Thou?' Biblical Perspectives on Responsibility." Pages 63–76 in *Responsibility*, ed. B. Darling-Smith. Lexington Books, 2007.

Timothy A. Beach-Verhey

Rest *See* Sabbath

Restitution

In its simplest definition, *restitution* means paying back for any loss, damage, or injury. Justice is satisfied when the offender repays the loss caused by the offense. Restitution is a commutative concept, or one that involves exchange, that focuses in contemporary usage more on the restoration of the offended party than on punishing the offender, although elements of both persist.

Within the Jewish and Christian traditions, restitution takes its basic cues from the Decalogue commandment "You shall not steal." Inherent in this command is a respect for both persons and property and the recognition that this respect is both spiritually and politically effective. Numerous legal codes and examples of restitution-based justice follow this command. Exodus 22, for example, demands restitution payments for a host of offenses ranging from thievery to allowing one's livestock to graze in a neighboring field. This passage deals primarily with property rights, which in Exodus includes both slaves and women. It is not an exhaustive account of restitution; instead, it represents properties that most directly affect the agrarian ways of life.

While the passage in Exodus applies most specifically to property owners, Lev. 25 extends restitution to the poor and to those who have been victimized by economic hardships. In this passage, the kinsman redeemer and the Jubilee Year are instituted to reorient the economic balance of the Hebrew people, a balance that orients much of the Hebraic and Jewish law traditions. The book of Ruth provides one of the clearest narratological examples of the kinsman-redeemer clause, where the unlikely Boaz assumes the role and redeems Naomi's family line. The resultant marriage of Naomi's daughter-in-law Ruth to Boaz results in the birth of Obed, the grandfather of David (Ruth 4:21). The Jubilee Year also relates to restitution and its ability to balance society because special provisions were to be made to forgive debts and return lands to families that had lost them. Although we have no historical evidence that Israel ever enacted any such Jubilee Year, the idealistic concept still permeates Judaic self-perceptions. For the Israelites, the Jubilee served as a reminder that Yahweh was the rightful owner of the land (Lev. 25:23).

The NT also provides examples of restitution. So, for example, when Paul writes to Philemon, he promises to repay all of Onesimus's debts (Phlm. 18). And Jesus' parable of the servant whose debts were forgiven by the king but who failed to forgive his own debtor recalls the Jubilee imagery (Matt. 18:23–35). Perhaps the clearest example is in Luke 19:1–10, which describes the Jewish tax collector Zacchaeus, who, upon his encounter with Jesus, vows to repay fourfold anyone he has wronged. Both the Mosaic laws and these NT passages deal with the returning of things to their intended order and serve as Christian justifications for restitution theology, wherein restitution plays a crucial role in the doctrines of atonement and creation. Further continuity exists between the passages in Exodus and Luke on the issue of overcompensation by the guilty party. Just as Zacchaeus pledged to pay back fourfold, the Exodus passage demands a minimum of double the value of stolen property and a maximum of the thief's life.

This precedence for overcompensation raises an interesting question for contemporary moral conceptions of restitution. Since excess repayment is required to satisfy justice, restitution is supplementary in character (Santi 89). Excess compensation, then, serves a function beyond the mere restoration of original damages; it emphasizes the guilt associated with the infraction and exacts a punishment to make amends for the guilt of the crime (Santi 90). Restitution in this sense encroaches on retributive or punitive forms of justice. Opponents of this view focus instead on the ideal of "pure restitution." This ideal focuses on the offended party and the desire for compensation rather than on any desire to see the offender suffer punishment (Kaufmann 55; Barnett 289). The victim remains the focal point of pure restitution as the paid damages by the offender are extracted in accord with "common sense" (Barnett 287–88).

While biblical precedent for restitution focuses primarily on individuals and families, the principles of restitution within ethical discourse apply to larger entities as well. With land restitution, for example, corporations and governments justify and maintain their rights to occupy the lands that they inhabit. The apartheid government in South Africa upheld laws, including issues of restitution, that overwhelmingly privileged white inhabitants. Many of these laws were justified by the white Voortrekkers' literal application of Exodus and by the presumptuous notion that South Africa was their "promised land." Such literal interpretations of the OT proved insufficient for answering post-apartheid questions about the nature of private ownership, how historic imbalances should be rectified, and the feasibility of land redistribution (Vorster 686). Since Israelite land ownership had numerous manifestations in Israelite history, Scripture is useful for current ethical analysis if we can discern its underlying principles (Vorster 689).

The most powerful nations today exist as a direct result of their colonial exploits, which forcibly removed, subjugated, or killed indigenous inhabitants. This realization has raised complex ethical questions among postcolonial scholars. What would restitution look like if colonial nations followed the principles of restoring lands to their original inhabitants? How might nations approach restitution when repayment for damages would bankrupt nations? If the lands were returned, what further restitutions would have to be made for the damages caused by the desolation of indigenous families and by the desolation of the land itself as a result of industrialization? Finally, if political and economic realities make the overcompensation of indigenous peoples unfeasible, theological ethicists must determine what form of restitution is feasible in light of its scriptural mandates.

See also Apartheid; Colonialism and Postcolonialism; Jubilee; Justice, Restorative; Justice, Retributive; Reparation; Ten Commandments; Theft

Bibliography

Barnett, R. "A New Paradigm of Criminal Justice." *Ethics* 87, no. 4 (1977): 279–301; Kaufmann, W. *Without Guilt and Justice: From Decidophobia to Autonomy*. P. H. Wyden, 1973; Santi, E. "Latinamericanism and Restitution." *Latin American Literary Review* 20, no. 40 (1992): 88–96; Vorster, J. "The Ethics of Land Restitution." *JRE* 34 (2006): 685–707.

Aaron Conley

Resurrection

The Greco-Roman world accepted the "immortality of the soul" and the "transmigration of souls" but never the "resurrection of the dead." In the religion of Israel (as presented in the OT) there arose a set of convictions that focused on the eternal nature of God's covenant with his people and the attendant expectation that God somehow would sustain relations with his people even after their deaths. During the period of Second Temple Judaism (c. 200 BCE–120 CE) there came to expression a number of various understandings of what "resurrection of the dead" meant. It was, however, God's resurrection of Jesus that both established and clarified for Christians their belief in the resurrection of the dead, with the result that the recently past bodily resurrection of Jesus, together with the present spiritual resurrection of believers in Jesus and the future physical resurrection of Christ's own at his parousia (return, second coming), became the cornerstone of Christian hope in the writings of the NT and the central proclamation of the Christian church.

The English word *resurrection* translates the Greek noun *anastasis*. In its basic sense, resurrection denotes restoration to existence or life after a period of decline, oppression, or obscurity (as with the nation or a group of people) or after an interval in the realm of the dead (as with a person or people). The English expression *raise up* translates the Hebrew verb *qûm* and the Greek verbs *anistēmi* and *egeirō*. The noun *anastasis* (or *exanastasis*) and the verbs *anistēmi* and *egeirō* appear throughout the NT for both the historical resurrection of Jesus and the resurrection of people in the eschatological future.

Convictions about the Continuance of God's Covenantal Relations with His People Even after Their Deaths

There are stories in the OT of people being brought back to life after their deaths (1 Kgs. 17:17–24; 2 Kgs. 4:18–37; 13:20–21). However, these are not, strictly speaking, resurrection accounts; they are miracle stories about resuscitation, revivification, or reanimation. The people in these stories were restored to their former lives, not to a new life or to the life of the new eschatological order, and so (evidently) they had to die again. There are also stories of certain righteous individuals who were taken up by God into heaven without dying (Gen. 5:22–24; 2 Kgs. 2:1–12). But again, these are not resurrection accounts; they are stories of translation into God's presence without the experience of death.

The imagery of being raised up by God is used primarily in the OT for the restoration of the nation Israel in the eschatological future—that is, of God's people with whom he had established his covenant. In Isa. 44:21–26, for example, God is portrayed as declaring that he has not forgotten the nation Israel and, in particular, as saying of Jerusalem, "It shall be inhabited," and of the cities of Judah, "They shall be rebuilt, and I will raise up their ruins." In Isa. 49:6 the eschatological servant's mission will include the task "to raise up the tribes of Jacob and to restore the survivors of Israel." In Hos. 6:2 the prophet assures his people, "After two days he will revive us; on the third day he will raise us up, that we may live before him." In Amos 9:11 there are included within God's promises regarding the nation's eschatological future these words: "On that day I will raise up the booth of David that is fallen, and repair its breaches, and raise up its ruins, and rebuild it as in the days of old." And throughout the prophecy of Ezekiel such a raising up of the nation is graphically portrayed by various dramatic actions and symbolic figures, particularly by the vision of the valley of dry bones in Ezek. 37 and the attendant visions of restoration in Ezek. 40–48.

Among righteous Israelites, however, there was also the hope that God somehow would continue relations with his people individually even after their deaths. It was a hope based on their convictions about divine justice and the fulfillment of God's covenant. Thus Job could declare, "I know that my Redeemer lives, and that at the last he will stand upon the earth; and after my skin has been thus destroyed, then in my flesh I shall see God" (Job 19:25–26). And David could exclaim, "My heart is glad, and my soul rejoices; my body also rests secure. For you do not give me up to Sheol, or let your faithful one see the Pit" (Ps. 16:9–10). Likewise, the Korahites are credited with proclaiming, "God will ransom my soul from the power of Sheol, for he will receive me" (Ps. 49:15).

Among the latter prophets, such individualist convictions about God's justice and the eternality of his covenant were developed to apply to the life of the nation, as in these words of Isaiah: "Your dead shall live, their corpses shall rise. O dwellers in the dust, awake and sing for joy! For your dew is a radiant dew, and the earth will give birth to those long dead" (Isa. 26:19 [cf. Ezek. 37:1–14; Hos. 6:1–2]). Further, these basic convictions began to be developed in ways that had not only national but also universal significance, as in this prophecy of Daniel: "At that time Michael, the great prince, the protector of your people shall arise. There shall be a time of anguish, such as had never occurred since nations first came into existence. But at that time your people shall be delivered, everyone who is found written in the book. Many of those who sleep in the dust of the earth shall awake, some to everlasting life, and some to shame and everlasting contempt" (Dan. 12:1–2).

Developments during the Period of Second Temple Judaism

Expectations regarding the future state of the dead were in flux during the period of Second Temple Judaism. Immortality doctrines were rampant. Some of these immortality teachings were clothed in resurrection language, others in astral imagery, others in terminology that paralleled expressions used in speaking about reincarnation and the transmigration of souls, and still others in distinctly Grecian anthropological terms. Hopes for some type of resurrection of the dead also became increasingly prominent during this time.

What can be said about these developments and particularly about the relationship of resurrection and ethics? (1) Passages such as *1 En.* 22.1–14; 25.4–22; 90.28–42 suggest a resurrection and gathering of righteous Jews into an earthly messianic kingdom, with some type of transformation of the righteous taking place. (2) Second Maccabees 7:1–41; 14:37–46 and *1 En.* 51.1–5; 61.5; 62.14–16 present fairly explicit statements regarding the expectation of a future physical resurrection of the dead. (3) *Fourth Ezra* 7.32–38; 14.35 and *2 Bar.* 49.1–3; 50.1–51.16 spell out in quite explicit detail Jewish hopes with regard to the nature of a future resurrection body. (4) *Sibylline Oracles* 4.175–191 presupposes a similar doctrine of the resurrection of the dead as found in *4 Ezra* 7.32–38 and *2 Bar.* 50.1–51.16.

God's Resurrection of Jesus as the Basis for the Christian Belief in the Resurrection of the Dead

Although Jews understood that the nation corporately and righteous people individually would suffer, with hope that both the nation and the dead would somehow be raised up or resurrected in the eschatological future, there was little if any expectation that the Messiah would suffer death or need to be resurrected from the dead. Only in *4 Ezra* 7.28–31, written sometime about 100 CE, is there any reference in the writings of Second Temple Judaism to the death and subsequent resurrection of the expected Jewish Messiah. Jewish hopes for the future were expressed, at least in the great majority of cases, without any thought of either the Messiah's death or the Messiah's resurrection.

Jesus, however, is portrayed in all four canonical Gospels as speaking repeatedly about his approaching death at Jerusalem and his resurrection three days afterward (Mark 8:31–32 pars.; 9:31–32 pars.; 10:33–34 pars.; see also Mark 9:9 pars.; 14:58 pars.; 15:29 pars.; Matt. 12:40; 17:9; 26:61; John 2:19–22). And all four evangelists focus on Jesus' death and resurrection as being the most crucial and significant features of his ministry, not only in the concluding chapters of their respective Gospels but also by way of anticipation in all that they set out earlier. The resurrection of Jesus is, in fact, the high point of the four NT Gospels. For God's resurrection of Jesus from the dead vindicates all that Jesus believed, said, and did, and so it is the definitive answer to the cross.

The resurrection of Jesus, itself an intrinsically eschatological event, was the impetus for the christological thinking of the early church and the content of most of its preaching. Further, it is the proper beginning for all distinctly Christian teaching about the ethical lives of those who commit themselves to Christ and for all distinctly Christian teaching about what they may legitimately expect regarding the future. For it is the message about Christ's resurrection that informs his followers as to what kind of resurrection lives they are to live presently as his people and assures them that they will share in Christ's resurrection and glory in the future.

The Message of the Resurrection in the New Testament

As in the OT, there are stories in the NT of people being brought back to life after death (Mark 5:35–43; John 11:30–44; Acts 9:36–42; as well as the amazing report in Matt. 27:52–53). But as with the similar OT instances, these are not, strictly speaking, resurrection accounts; they are miracle stories about the resuscitation, revivification, or reanimation of people who were restored to their former lives and (evidently) had to die again. The proclamation of Jesus' resurrection, however, has to do with the defeat of death and the inauguration of the messianic age, while the promise of a future general resurrection has to do with the completion of the salvation that God effected through the saving work of Jesus.

God's resurrection of Jesus, together with the implications of this momentous event for the eschatological resurrection of the dead, is the central affirmation of the Christian message as given throughout the book of Acts. The mandate given by Jesus to his followers was to be "my witnesses" (Acts 1:8), and that mandate is further explicated as being "witness to his resurrection" (Acts 1:22). The preaching of Peter focuses on God having raised Jesus from the dead, to which events the apostles were commissioned to be the accredited "witnesses" (Acts 2:32; 3:15). The accounts of the trials of Peter and John before the Jerusalem authorities begin with the council's accusation that the apostles were "proclaiming that in Jesus there is the resurrection of the dead" (Acts 4:2) and end with the apostolic statement "The God of our ancestors raised up Jesus, whom you had killed by hanging him on a tree. . . . And we are witnesses to these things" (Acts 5:30–32). Paul's own conversion resulted from being confronted by the resurrected, ascended, and heavenly Jesus (Acts 9:3–5). Peter's preaching to the Roman centurion Cornelius had as its high point the proclamation that "God raised [Jesus] on the third day and allowed him to appear, not to all the people but to us who were chosen by God as witnesses" (Acts 10:40–41). Paul's preaching in the synagogue at Antioch of Pisidia had as its major content the resurrection of Jesus from the dead (Acts 13:32–37), and his message to the Athenians is epitomized as being "the good news about Jesus and the resurrection" (Acts 17:18). Further, in his defenses before Jewish and Roman courts Paul is portrayed as declaring that the central issue for which he was being tried was "the hope of the resurrection of the dead" (Acts 23:6).

The importance of the resurrection in Acts is rivaled only by the significance of the death of the Messiah within the divine purpose, alongside which it often appears. Luke, the author of Acts, wanted readers always to keep in view the nexus between Jesus' death and Jesus' resurrection. But while always emphasizing the importance of the death of Christ in the divine program of redemption, Luke must also be seen to have been particularly concerned to present the apostolic response to Jesus' resurrection and its redemptive implications—a concern that appears not just in his giving a narrative about the apostles' witness to Jesus as having been resurrected by God from the dead but also in presenting that narrative itself as a witness to Jesus' resurrection and an explication of its significance for the realization of God's redemptive purposes.

Implications, Future and Present, for the Lives of Christians

Three types of resurrection statements appear in the NT. First, there are statements regarding the bodily resurrection of Jesus Christ from the grave to immortality, as in "We know that Christ, being raised from the dead, will never die again; death no longer has dominion over him" (Rom. 6:9). Second, there are statements having to do with the present spiritual resurrection of believers in Christ, which is from slavery to sin to newness of life, as in "We have been buried with him by baptism into death, so that, just as Christ was raised from the dead by the glory of the Father, so we too might walk in newness of life" (Rom. 6:4 [see also Rom. 6:6, 13, 17; Col. 2:12). Third, there are statements declaring a future physical resurrection of believers from death to immortality, as in "The dead will be raised imperishable, and we will be changed" (1 Cor. 15:52). In all three of these types of statements the resurrection of the dead has to do with the raising of a person from the dead to a new and permanent life in the presence of God. Such a definition applies first of all to the resurrection of Jesus Christ himself, but it also applies to the present ethical lives of believers in Christ Jesus and to their future experiences of death, resurrection, transformation, and exaltation at the time of Christ's eschatological parousia, his eagerly awaited second coming or presence.

Paul includes in 1 Cor. 16:22 what appears to have been a cry that arose within the worship of the early Jewish Christian church: "Our Lord, come!" (Aramaic: *marana tha*). And John closes his apocalypse in Rev. 22:20 with the words of "the one who testifies to these things," Jesus Christ: "Surely I am coming soon" (*Nai, erchomai tachy*);

and then he immediately expresses the church's response: "Amen. Come, Lord Jesus!" (*Amēn, erchou kyrie Iēsou*). It is this parousia of Christ that Christians look forward to with expectation, for included among the events of his second coming will be their own resurrection, with its resultant transformation into an immortal life and its exaltation into the very presence of Jesus Christ the Son and God the Father. Of all of that, however, there is nothing that can be done by Christians, for that time is known only to God and will be worked out only by God. All that followers of Jesus can do with respect to his parousia and their own physical resurrection is await that time with eagerness and prepare for it with earnestness.

With respect, however, to the new spiritual resurrection that believers in Jesus Christ have received by faith, there is much that they can do by way of coming to appreciate more and more their new resurrection life, being constantly open to the needs and situations of others, and seeking the direction of God's Spirit as to how they can effectively express that new resurrection life today. For as the apostle Paul has written, Christians need always to recognize that "just as Christ was raised from the dead by the glory of the Father," so they are called to "walk in newness of life" (Rom. 6:4).

Christian ethical living springs from the new resurrection life given by a loving God, on the basis of the life, death, and resurrection of Jesus Christ and through the ministry of God's Holy Spirit. So the Christian life, while awaiting a future resurrection, must always be understood as the present experience of a new type of spiritual resurrection life—a life given by God through the work of Christ and the ministry of God's Spirit, and a life to be lived out in ways that glorify God, respond to the work of Christ, follow the guidance of the Holy Spirit, and serve others in representing the resurrected Christ.

See also Eschatology and Ethics; Hope

Bibliography

Harris, M. *From Grave to Glory: Resurrection in the New Testament*. Zondervan, 1990; idem. *Raised Immortal: Resurrection and Immortality in the New Testament*. Eerdmans, 1985; Longenecker, R., ed. *Life in the Face of Death: The Resurrection Message of the New Testament*. MNTS 3. Eerdmans, 1998; Marshall, I. H. "The Resurrection in the Acts of the Apostles." Pages 92–107 in *Apostolic History and the Gospel: Biblical and Historical Essays Presented to F. F. Bruce on His 60th Birthday*, ed. W. Gasque and R. Martin. Eerdmans, 1970; idem. "The Resurrection of Jesus in Luke." *TynBul* 24 (1973): 55–98; Martin-Achard, R. *From Death to Life: A Study of the Development of the Doctrine of the Resurrection in the Old Testament*. Oliver & Boyd, 1960; Nickelsburg, G., Jr. *Resurrection, Immortality, and Eternal Life in Intertestamental Judaism*. HTS 26. Harvard University Press, 1972; O'Donovan, O. *Resurrection and Moral Order: An Outline for Evangelical Ethics*. Eerdmans, 1986; Perkins, P. *Resurrection: New Testament Witness and Contemporary Reflection*. Doubleday, 1984; Stuhlmacher, P. "The Resurrection of Jesus and the Resurrection of the Dead." *ExAud* 9 (1993): 19–30; Wenham, D. "The Resurrection Narratives in Matthew's Gospel." *TynBul* 24 (1973): 21–34.

Richard N. Longenecker

Retribution *See* Reward and Retribution

Revelation, Book of

According to D. H. Lawrence, "The Apocalypse of John is, as it stands, the work of a second-rate mind. It appeals intensely to second-rate minds in every country and every century" (12). Apparently, many Christians agree. Finding the book strange and disturbing, most Christian communities rarely read the final book of the Christian canon. Christians who are serious about changing this world find escapist interpretations of Revelation irrelevant. The book is left to fanatics waiting for the world to erupt, while real Christians go about the ministry of Jesus.

Yet, according to the first words of Revelation, Jesus is both the subject and the mediator of the book: "[The] Revelation of Jesus Christ" (1:1). During the mid-1980s Allan Boesak, a Christian preacher and critic of South Africa's apartheid, was allowed one book, the Bible, during months of solitary confinement. Boesak later wrote, "Somehow, I don't know why, I turned to the words of John of Patmos, and for the first time I began to understand. The power of his testimony forever changed my life" (13). For him, the book is precisely for Christians who are serious about the ministry of Jesus to change this world. But how are we to read this work? The present article discusses the book's genre, the book's social setting, and the use of the book in ethics.

A Liturgical Apocalypse: Revelation's Unique Genre

Although the book of Revelation starts with the Greek word *apokalypsis* ("apocalypse"), its genre is not easy to distinguish. The work refers to itself as a "prophecy" (1:3; 22:7, 10, 18, 19). Yet seven letters are tucked into the first part, and it begins and ends like a first-century epistle (1:4–7; 22:21). Between chapters 4 and 19, sixteen hymns burst through the narrative (Aune 314–17; Harris 4–16). Consequently, most scholars see the book as a hybrid of some sort. For Elisabeth Schüssler Fiorenza, the apocalyptic and liturgical elements serve the book's prophetic goals (164–70). Other scholars emphasize the overarching epistolary format or the characteristics that it shares with other apocalypses.

This generic complexity provides an important key to the interpretation of the book and its ethical implications. If a genre is not merely a mold into which content is poured but rather is inseparable from meaning, then these forms carry various theological perspectives and show the complex nature of the book (Bakhtin; Morson and Emerson 271–305). For example, apocalyptic literature emphasizes a view of God far removed from human experience and in control of the entire cosmos. Typically, the apocalyptic seer must stand far off and watch the mighty actions of God taking place throughout the universe and into the future. In contrast, Christian liturgy embraces a God-with-us who is present in earthly worship experiences. John shows these views of God as they continually collide and collaborate. Using the book to shut down such a "surplus" of theological meaning is fundamentally opposed to the book's very nature (Haloviak 21–108).

Revelation's Social Setting: Ordinary People Resisting Rome

Studies in the book of Revelation still wrestle with many disputed issues, including date of authorship, the author's identity, the work's intended audience(s), and the overall social situations of people living in the province of Asia during the first century CE of the Roman Empire.

Recent studies on provincial imperial cults and life in the major cities of the province of Asia provide a helpful corrective to the assumption, no longer held by most scholars, that Christians underwent harsh persecution during the reign of Domitian (81–96 CE). However, the provincial imperial cult did permeate every aspect of life in the major cities of the Roman provinces (Friesen 23–131). Purchasing food in the marketplace, eating meals in a trade guild banquet, and participating in the regular festivals, games, and intercity competitions all held major implications for one's social status. Although it might be rare for a Christian to be dragged before a Roman provincial leader for refusing to worship at a local shrine, the degree to which a follower of Jesus could participate in city life required daily decisions (Thompson 37). The author of Revelation takes a firm stand against assimilating into Roman culture.

The reality of the provincial imperial cult, along with internal controversies (2:6, 14, 15, 20) and tensions with the local Jewish communities in the cities (2:9; 3:9), posed difficult choices for the first recipients of John's Apocalypse. The book is a call to resist Rome (the "beast" [13:1–18]; the "harlot" [17:1–18]) and all who blur the lines between Rome and the Lamb (like "Jezebel" [2:18–29]). Members of local congregations who chose to join in the songs of Revelation became witnesses who were willing to lay down their lives rather than compromise with the culture in which they found themselves (11:4–13).

Apocalypse Now and Then: The Book of Revelation's Moral Vision

The Apocalypse, this work of generic (theological) complexity that was originally situated in liturgical experiences calling worshipers to resist the dominant culture, invites readers today to consider its resources for the moral life. The book weaves together worship and ethics. The liturgical moments surround the unfolding drama. After Christians worship, additional action is required: contemporary beasts must be confronted (13:1–18), the collaboration of church and state must be denounced (13:11–17), and the seduction of wealth must be resisted (17:1–18:18). Human lives may not be labeled a commodity to be traded (18:11–13), but rather must be deeply valued in the worshiping community's ongoing commitment to the "healing of the nations" (22:2).

Typically, ethicists considering the use of Scripture in the moral enterprise focus on moral obligations, societal values, or personal virtues. However, the category of moral vision must also be considered. Although last in the NT canon, the book of Revelation should be first in terms of ethical discourse. "Before the message there must be the vision, before the sermon the hymn, before the prose the poem" (Wilder 1). The book of Revelation provides a moral vision that "is a revolution in the imagination. It entails a challenge to view the world in a way that is radically different from the common perception" (Collins 283). The book's future vision—an earth made new (21:1–5)—shapes moral vision, compelling its readers to transform the world.

See also Eschatology and Ethics; Liturgy and Ethics; New Testament Ethics

Bibliography

Aune, D. *Revelation 1–5*. WBC 52A. Word, 1997; Bakhtin, M. "The Problem of Speech Genres." Pages 60–102 in *Speech Genres and Other Late Essays*, ed. C. Emerson and M. Holquist. University of Texas Press, 1986; Bauckham, R. *The Theology of the Book of Revelation*. NTT. Cambridge University Press, 1993; Boesak, A. *Comfort and Protest: The Apocalypse from a South African Perspective*. Westminster, 1987; Collins, J. *The Apocalyptic Imagination: An Introduction to Jewish Apocalyptic Literature*. 2nd ed. Eerdmans, 1998; Friesen, S. *Imperial*

Cults and the Apocalypse of John: Reading Revelation in the Ruins. Oxford University Press, 2001; Haloviak, K. "Worlds at War, Nations in Song: Dialogic and Moral Vision in the Hymns of the Book of Revelation." PhD diss., Graduate Theological Union, 2002; Harris, M. "The Literary Function of Hymns in the Apocalypse of John." PhD diss., Southern Baptist Theological Seminary, 1989; Lawrence, D. H. *Apocalypse*. Heinemann, 1931; Morson, G., and C. Emerson. *Mikhail Bakhtin: Creation of a Prosaics*. Stanford University Press, 1990; Schüssler Fiorenza, E. *The Book of Revelation: Justice and Judgment*. 2nd ed. Fortress, 1998; Thompson, L. "Ordinary Lives: John and His First Readers." Pages 25–47 in *Reading the Book of Revelation: A Resource for Students*, ed. D. Barr. RBS 44. Society of Biblical Literature, 2003; Wilder, A. *Theopoetic: Theology and the Religious Imagination*. Fortress, 1976.

Kendra Jo Haloviak

Revenge

The Bible treats revenge as both an appropriate desire and a threat to communal stability. In the ancient world, revenge was motivated primarily by family honor. Thus, Jacob's sons slaughter the men of a neighboring city in retaliation for the rape of Dinah, appealing to their family's honor (Gen. 34:25–27). At the same time, biblical narratives realistically show how acts of revenge initiate cycles of increasing violence. After God decrees sevenfold vengeance against anyone who kills Cain—ironically, to prevent someone from taking revenge for Abel—Cain's descendant Lamech threatens seventy-sevenfold vengeance for wrongs done to him (Gen. 4:23–24). Absalom's murder of Amnon, in retaliation for the rape of his sister Tamar, begins a series of events that nearly destroys the house of David (2 Sam. 13–20). By contrast, the refusal to seek revenge is portrayed as exemplary in the cases of Joseph and his brothers (Gen. 50:15–21) and David and Saul (1 Sam. 24; 26).

Vengeance is identified as a divine attribute in the OT (Ps. 94:1; Nah. 1:2). God takes revenge against Israel's enemies, who are also God's enemies (Deut. 32:35–36; Ps. 8:3; Isa. 47:3; Jer. 51:36). God also seeks revenge against his own people for covenant violations that offend divine honor (Lev. 26:25; Ps. 99:8; Jer. 5:9, 29; Ezek. 24:8). The NT likewise portrays God as taking vengeance on those who reject Christ (2 Thess. 1:8; Heb. 10:30). In some texts, God authorizes humans to act as agents of divine vengeance, often through military action (Num. 31:2; Josh. 10:13; 2 Kgs. 9:7), and Exod. 21:20 describes the legal penalty for murdering a slave as a divinely sanctioned act of vengeance (Heb. *nāqam*, "avenged"; NRSV: "punished").

The tendency in biblical texts, however, is to curtail and discourage revenge. The *lex talionis* in Exod. 21:22–27 limits actions of revenge by a standard of proportionality (cf. Jer. 50:15). Numbers 35:16–28 commands the establishment of cities of refuge, where persons who have unintentionally killed someone may escape "the avenger [*gō'ēl*, redeemer] of blood," who is otherwise authorized to execute murderers. Renunciation of revenge against other Israelites is joined with love of neighbor in Lev. 19:18, which Jesus quotes in the Synoptic Gospels as the second greatest commandment (Matt. 22:39; Mark 12:31; cf. Luke 10:27). Jesus also expands the *lex talionis* in the Sermon on the Mount to dismiss revenge as inappropriate for his followers (Matt. 5:38–39). Appealing to Deut. 32:35, Paul suggests that human acts of revenge encroach on the divine prerogative for vengeance (Rom. 12:19).

This last verse helpfully bridges some competing claims without completely resolving their complexity. It honors the desire for revenge, which at best results from a longing for justice, but also recognizes that human actions are necessarily inadequate and often have unintended outcomes; consequently, the resolution of wrongs is deferred to God, upon whom all hopes for justice ultimately rest. Appropriate models for this attitude are individuals in the OT who pray for God to exercise vengeance for them (Ps. 79:10; Jer. 11:20) and criticize God for failing to do so (Ps. 44:13–16).

See also Violence

J. Blake Couey

Reward and Retribution

Biblical teaching on reward and retribution is grounded in the basic conviction that human deeds carry inescapable moral consequences. Sometimes these consequences are experienced as the automatic outcome of the deeds themselves: "Can fire be carried in the bosom without burning one's clothes? Or can one walk on hot coals without scorching the feet?" (Prov. 6:27–28). At other times the consequences are imposed from outside as secondary rewards or punishments, whether directly by God (e.g., Isa. 40:10; 59:12–19; 62:11; Rom. 12:19) or by human agents (e.g., Rom. 13:3–4). Both cases attest to the existence of an underlying law of recompense in the universe according to which good deeds deserve and bring reward, and evil deeds deserve and bring retribution. "Misfortune pursues sinners, but prosperity rewards the righteous" (Prov. 13:21).

It is on the basis of this retributive principle that Paul, in Rom. 1:18–32, is able to diagnose the moral, social, and physical evils that afflict the human condition as an outworking of divine wrath on human sin and rebellion. In rejecting dependence on God and surrendering to the lie of idolatry, humankind has fallen victim to degenerative processes that, in reality, are visible expressions of God's "handing over" of people (1:24, 26, 28) to "receive back in their own persons" (1:27) the consequences of their actions. The thought here is not so much one of God meting out personally tailored punishments in payment for every individual transgression but rather of God withdrawing his protective hand so that humanity reaps the deleterious consequences of its chosen way of life (cf. Rom. 5:12–21).

Of course, as the biblical writers often recognize, the operation of this law of just recompense is not always evident in human experience. "Why do the wicked live on, reach old age, and grow mighty in power?" Job protests (Job 21:7). "How often is the lamp of the wicked put out? How often does calamity come upon them? How often does God distribute pains in his anger?" and "Who repays them for what they have done?" (Job 21:17, 31 [cf. Jer. 12:1–2]). The problem of theodicy—the justification of God's goodness, faithfulness, and power in the face of evil—arises precisely from the fact that the law of recompense does not always work out in practice. The wicked prosper and the righteous suffer, and neither can be simplistically construed as their just deserts (cf. Luke 13:1–5; John 9:2–3).

Sometimes the biblical authors anticipate an imminent historical reversal to rectify the problem of such injustice. But Israel's own experience of defeat, exile, and continuing subjection to foreign powers stubbornly defied this hope, and so attention increasingly shifted to a final, definitive revelation of divine justice at the end of the age where God would visit retribution on evildoers and confer rewards on the righteous. This expectation permeates NT literature from start to finish. The final day of reckoning will be "the time for judging the dead, for rewarding your servants . . . and for destroying those who destroy the earth" (Rev. 11:18). On that day "there will be anguish and distress for everyone who does evil . . . but glory and honor and peace for everyone who does good" (Rom. 2:9–10).

There is no uniform conception of final judgment and its consequences in the NT, but a common scenario emerges. At the end of the age all people, both "the righteous and the unrighteous" (Acts 24:15; John 5:28–29), will appear before the judgment seat of God or Christ, where each will receive a verdict "according to what has been done in the body, whether good or evil" (2 Cor. 5:10; cf. Matt. 25:31–46; Rom. 2:6–11; 14:10; Rev. 20:11–15; 21:5–8). A separation will occur. The righteous will depart into eternal life. For them there will be "rewards" or "prizes" or "treasure in heaven" (Matt. 5:12, 46; 6:1–6, 16–21; 10:41; 19:28–29; 20:1–16; 24:46–47; 25:21, 23; Mark 9:41; 10:21, 28–30; Luke 6:23, 38; 12:33–34; 14:12, 14–15; 18:28–30; cf. 1 Cor. 3:5–15; 4:4–5; 2 Cor. 5:10; Phil. 3:12–16; Eph. 6:8–9; Col. 3:24–25; Heb. 10:35; 2 John 8). The wicked, however, "will go away into eternal punishment" (Matt. 25:46; cf. 10:28; 13:30; Mark 12:9; Luke 13:9, 22–30; John 3:36; 5:28–29). In the Gospels Jesus speaks frequently of Gehenna or a place of outer darkness and unquenchable fire where there will be "weeping" and "gnashing of teeth" among those excluded from salvation (Matt. 5:22, 29–30; 8:11–12; 10:28; 13:41–42, 50; 18:8–9; 22:13; 23:15, 33; 24:51; 25:30; Mark 9:42–48; Luke 12:4–5; 13:28–29). He also indicates that judgment will fall not just on individuals but on cities and nations as well (Matt. 10:15; 11:21–24; 21:43–44; 23:35–38). Many other NT texts speak of the terrible loss that the wicked will face, described variously as an experience of "wrath," "vengeance," "repayment," "tribulation and distress," "fire," and, most often, of "destruction," "death," or "disintegration." Final judgment, then, is depicted as a matter of God assessing and recompensing human works, sometimes with the hint of varying degrees of reward (Mark 10:29–30; 1 Cor. 3:10–15; Eph. 6:8; cf. Luke 12:47–48).

It is important, of course, to recognize the figurative and connotative nature of such language. The basic thought is that earthly actions have transcendent significance and will receive appropriate recognition from God. But a wide range of images and metaphors from the world of human relations is used to express the process of assessment and its outcome. God has a treasury, keeps books, hires and fires, pays wages, harvests crops, herds animals, hands down sentences, scourges slaves, gives rewards, refines metal, confers prizes in athletic contests, holds feasts, bestows inheritances, and so on. Notions of reward or repayment are commercial metaphors for the intensification of relationship with God granted to the redeemed. (What greater reward could there be?) To envisage some kind of quantifiable material benefits is to imply that something can be added to the bliss of knowing God. Conversely, the metaphors of judicially imposed punishments and torments for the condemned are metaphors intended to capture the horror involved in being excluded from relationship with God. (What greater punishment could there be?) To imagine some corner of the cosmos where the lost suffer endless or prolonged retribution is to miss the figurative nature of these utterances as well as to create profound theological and moral problems.

Theologically, the imagery of God evaluating human deeds and dispensing appropriate rewards and punishments underscores the reality and importance of human freedom and moral responsibility. The battle between good and evil is deadly serious, and to casually or deliberately dally with evil in this life is fraught with eschatological danger. The imagery also safeguards God's personal involvement in dealing with evil and the inherent justness and integrity of his judgment, "for God shows no partiality" (Rom. 2:11). At the same time, it must be remembered that the revelation of God's saving righteousness in Christ shows that God is not somehow controlled by the impersonal norm of strict retributive justice. On the one hand, salvation comes by "grace as a gift" (Rom. 3:23–24; Eph. 2:8–10); it is never merited or deserved as a reward for good behavior. It is wholly gratuitous, an act of restorative rather than retributive justice. On the other hand, the lost typically are treated as a single category who suffer the same fate. There is little hint of varying severities of punishment according to individual merit. This perhaps suggests that final judgment should be understood not as God suspending his mercy to give sinners what they finally deserve but rather as respecting the choices they have made to forgo participation in the kingdom of God. The loss they experience is self-inflicted, not retributively imposed.

See also Crime and Criminal Justice; Eschatology and Ethics; Free Will and Determinism; Judgment; Justice, Restorative; Justice, Retributive; Punishment; Theodicy

Bibliography

Blomberg, C. "Degrees of Reward in the Kingdom of Heaven?" *JETS* 35 (1992): 159–72; Charette, B. *The Theme of Recompense in Matthew's Gospel.* JSNTSup 79. JSOT Press, 1992; Marshall, C. *Beyond Retribution: A New Testament Vision for Justice, Crime and Punishment.* Eerdmans, 2001; Reiser, M. *Jesus and Judgment: The Eschatological Proclamation in Its Jewish Context.* Fortress, 1997; Snodgrass, K. "Justification by Grace—to the Doers: An Analysis of the Place of Romans 2 in the Theology of Paul." *NTS* 32 (1986): 72–93; Travis, S. *Christ and the Judgment of God: Divine Retribution in the New Testament.* Marshall & Pickering, 1986; Van Landingham, C. *Judgment and Justification in Early Judaism and the Apostle Paul.* Hendrickson, 2006.

Christopher Marshall

Right and Wrong

The first moral statement made in the Bible is the voice of God declaring his creation "good." The culmination of creation is the forming of Adam (and Eve), crafted in God's image, capable of reflecting his goodness, prohibited from and yet free to taste fruit from the tree of the knowledge of good and evil. The categories of good and evil, with their accompanying terms *righteousness* and *wickedness*, become the preferred and most frequently used ethical categories of the biblical writers after humanity exercises its freedom in rebellion. Right and wrong are introduced presupposing a moral universe, constituted and upheld by a God whose essential nature is both just and good. For an individual, ruler, or nation to align with God's righteousness, heed his commands, and walk in his ways is to do right. To ignore his way and succumb to the deceptions of the evil one, to self-betrayals, or to harming others is to do wrong. Because God is free from moral evil (see Oden), and because evil is a distortion of good and not a dual force in the universe, God alone serves as judge in the affairs of humanity, vindicating the innocent and serving justice on the abuser.

An early illustration of this moral ordering for fallen humanity is found in the story of Adam and Eve's offspring. The Lord has regard for Abel's offering but not for Cain's. Seeing the angry and downcast face of Cain, the Lord extends, "If you do what is right, will you not be accepted? But if you do not do what is right, sin is crouching at your door; it desires to have you, but you must master it" (Gen. 4:7 NIV). Cain will not fare well at this task and, symptomatic of the rest of fallen humanity, consequentially will live in fearful wandering outside of Eden, with the only hope for continued life resting in that which God provides.

The summons to do right is given legislative expression in the OT moral code. Following the decisive triumph over Pharaoh's army at the Red Sea, and after providing sustenance for their wilderness journey, God promises Israel exemption from the plagues Egypt suffered if they will heed his commands and "do what is right in his sight" (Exod. 15:26). This warning and promise, embedded in the events of exodus and deliverance, serves as prologue to the Ten Commandments—commandments that structure relational life for the emerging nation. Right and wrong, emanating from the essence of God's character and manifested in his laws, further ground the teachings of wisdom literature (e.g., to heed wisdom is to be led in the pathway of right [Prov. 4:11]) and originate the declarations of the prophets (e.g., the Lord "declares what is right" [Isa. 45:19]).

Readers of the OT will note the recurrence of the phrase "do what is right in the sight of the

Lord." God's sight is equivalent to his being—both expressions of the immanence of God (Tozer 59). The converse of doing right in the eyes of the Lord is not simply doing wrong, but doing what is right in one's own eyes. The summative statement of the book of Judges, "all the people did what was right in their own eyes" (21:25), is coupled with the reality that there was no king in Israel, the presumption being that when God as the source of moral authority is removed, a nation decays into self-referential indulgence. Hence, biblical theologians may find suspect contemporary theories of right and wrong that attribute morality solely to parental socialization, peer interaction, legal instruction, empathic concern, or evolutionary biology and/or those derived from philosophical proposition or rationalistic principle. These may enhance and inform the moral image in whose likeness humans are created, but all of them are limited in themselves and are likely to err detached from transcendent moorings.

Yahweh, the all-seeing, omniscient God of moral rectitude is thus often summoned when one is accusing or being accused; "May the Lord judge between us" is invoked to ensure vindication. Such is the case when Sarah contends with Abram over the contempt she senses from the impregnated concubine Hagar (Gen. 16:5). In like manner, Jepthah pleads his case against an Ammonite king (Judg. 11:27), as does David when he is uncertain about the loyalty of the Benjamites and Judahites (1 Chr. 12:16–17). The plea for God to witness a wrong suffered and to uphold a right cause is echoed in Jeremiah's lament (Lam. 3:59) and in the cry of the psalmist before his enemies (Ps. 9:4). In the NT, Paul encourages slaves, confident that their masters will receive just recompense (Col. 3:25).

During the era in which Israel establishes a monarchy, the biblical writers evaluate every king historically on the criterion of whether they did evil in the sight of the Lord or walked in his ways. These judgments anticipate that when the true king comes, not only will he do right in God's sight and fulfill God's word but also he will in fact *be* the very word of God made flesh.

Although the NT writers seldom make use of the terms *right* and *wrong*, the revelation, teachings, passion, and resurrection of Jesus establish NT ethics. Two passages are illustrative. First, Peter and John are arrested for proclaiming Jesus' resurrection and salvation and are ordered to stop. Their defense, "Whether it is right in God's sight to listen to you rather than to God, you must judge" (Acts 4:19), suggests that right action under God's reign may be distinct from conventional legality. Second, as recipients of the exemplary suffering of Christ, followers are called on to suffer wrong, endure hardship, do right, and trust God for the final vindication of all justice (1 Pet. 4:12–19).

See also Conscience; Good, The; Moral Development; Moral Formation

Bibliography

Oden, T. *Life in the Spirit*. Vol. 3 of *Systematic Theology*. HarperSanFrancisco, 1994; Tozer, A. W. *The Pursuit of God*. WingSpread, 1993.

Chris A. Kiesling

Righteousness

The basic biblical meaning of the term *righteousness* (Heb. *ṣdq*; Gk. *dik-)* is multivalent, describing appropriate actions and attitude in the context of relationships. Difficulty arises, however, when the term is translated into English by two words, *justice* and *righteousness*, which connote fairness and retribution, on the one hand, and virtuous living, on the other. The word *justice* has a legal ring to it, suggesting the pursuit of rights and equity before the law rather than the concept of restorative justice, which is an apt summation of the goal of OT justice (Heb. *mišpāṭ*). Discussion is further complicated by extensive scholarly debate over the meaning of the "righteousness of God." While the biblical perspective is that all human righteousness ultimately stems from God, righteousness as a foundation for ethics has to do with how humans live in relationship, whether it is with God or the created order.

In the OT "righteousness" is also paralleled with "blameless" (Heb. *tāmîm*; Gk. *teleios* [see Gen. 6:9; Ps. 7:9]). Blameless living is living according to the purpose of the Creator, in harmony with fellow creatures and with integrity, openness, and obedience toward God. The concept of *tāmîm*/*teleios* connotes blamelessness, not flawlessness, so that human righteousness is not to be understood as a performance target. For instance, "Noah was a righteous man, blameless in his generation; Noah walked with God" (Gen. 6:9). Thus, the defining characteristic of the righteous in the OT is their relationship to God and obedience to his commands, making righteousness essentially a relational concept that issues in behavior according to the standards of God. Conversely, disobedience breaches relationship beyond human repair.

Justice (*mišpāṭ*) and righteousness (*ṣĕdāqâ*) often are paired in the prophets' stinging critique of Israel's unfaithfulness. Isaiah laments that the city "that was full of justice, righteousness lodged in her" is full of murderers (Isa. 1:21);

God "expected justice, but saw bloodshed; righteousness, but heard a cry!" (Isa. 5:7). When judgment is executed, God "will make justice the line, and righteousness the plummet" (Isa. 28:17). But Israel is to be just and holy because God is "exalted by justice, and the Holy God shows himself holy by righteousness" (Isa. 5:16). The call for Israel to amend its ways is similarly described: "Let justice roll down like waters, and righteousness like an ever-flowing stream" (Amos 5:24). This brings peace (*shalom*), the direction of God's good purposes for his entire created order.

Degrees of righteousness may also be noted. Jacob acknowledges that Tamar has acted more righteously than he (Gen. 38:26). Wickedness, its opposite, is variously called "sin" (Heb. *ḥaṭṭāʾt*; Gk. *hamartia*) or "unrighteousness" (Gk. *adikia*, *asebeia* [in the LXX *adikia* also translates Heb. *ḥāmās*, "violence"]). All of this supports the view that righteousness with respect to humans describes appropriate behavior and attitude toward others. Essentially, righteous acts build covenant community, and unrighteous actions destroy it.

The holy people of God usually are designated as "the righteous" in the wisdom tradition and frequently as a synonym for Israel as God's chosen people. The contrast between the righteous and the wicked is pronounced; Psalms and Proverbs particularly juxtapose the two ways of wickedness and righteousness (see especially Prov. 10). Wickedness often is associated with the oppression of God's people.

The NT also frequently speaks of righteous people. The birth narratives in both Matthew and Luke demonstrate late Second Temple piety at its best. Joseph is "a righteous man" (Matt. 1:19); Zechariah and Elizabeth are "righteous before God, living blamelessly" (Luke 1:6); the ministry of their son John was to turn the people "to the wisdom of the righteous, to make ready a people prepared for the Lord" (Luke 1:17), and he will be described later as "a righteous and holy man" (Mark 6:20). Zechariah prophesies that the coming of Jesus would enable God's people to "serve him without fear, in holiness and righteousness" (Luke 1:74–75); Simeon is a "righteous and devout" worshiper of God (Luke 2:25).

In Matthew's Gospel Jesus is baptized by John in order to "fulfill all righteousness" (Matt. 3:15), signifying Jesus' full identification with his people in their need. He blesses those who "hunger and thirst after righteousness" because they will be filled (Matt. 5:6). The disciples' righteousness must exceed that of the Pharisees (Matt. 5:20). On the surface, this demand seems performance-driven, but its context shows that the greater righteousness is that which emulates God: "Be perfect, therefore, as your heavenly Father is perfect" (Matt. 5:48). It penetrates beneath rules and commands, getting to the heart of Christian ethics, which is single-minded devotion to God and undifferentiated love of neighbor (Matt. 5:45–47). Those who seek first the kingdom of God and God's righteousness (Matt. 6:33; cf. Rom. 14:17) have their priorities correct.

Even with these statements, however, there is no sense of righteousness being attained independently of a right relationship with God. The whole basis of these demands is the renewal of the covenant relationship in which the law is written on the heart. That is why Jesus explicitly indicates that he has come to call not the righteous but rather sinners (Mark 2:17). Although irony may play a part in this statement, the implication is that there are righteous people before God; the purposes of God in Christ are to bring back those who have strayed from the path of righteousness, the sinners.

One of Paul's major concerns is to explain how the righteousness of God displayed in his covenant faithfulness first to Israel and then to the entire created order is being worked out in the life, death, resurrection, and ascension of Christ. Paul also shows how the dire condition of humanity, alienated from God and helpless to rescue itself, is remedied only through the righteousness of God personified in the faithful obedience of Jesus. In that sense, God's righteousness is more than covenant faithfulness. In fact, "the righteousness of God, God's saving activity, is none other than Christ himself" (Southall 205), as Paul himself explicitly states in 1 Cor. 1:30. Only through participating in Christ's righteous obedience and through his atoning death are people brought into the sphere of God's righteousness, in contrast to the enslavement to sin and unrighteousness that is their current condition (Rom. 6:13–19). Human performance cannot restore this marred relationship with God; rather, the initiative and the action are God's, and the restoration is received as a free gift (Rom. 3:24). The unrighteous are brought into this new relationship through faith in the faithfulness of Christ and his atoning sacrifice. Human boasting therefore is excluded (Rom. 3:27; cf. Phil. 3:9): "For by grace you have been saved through faith, and this is not your own doing; it is the gift of God" (Eph. 2:8).

Paul is equally adamant that righteous living is essential to the holy people of God. Paul sees his apostolic purpose as engendering "the obedience of faith among all the Gentiles for the sake of his name" (Rom. 1:5), and he offers thanks for what "Christ has accomplished through me to win obedience from the Gentiles, by word and deed" (Rom. 15:18). Believers are chosen in Christ "before the foundation of the world to be holy and blameless before him in love" (Eph. 1:4) and are "created in Christ Jesus for good works, which God prepared beforehand to be [their] way of life" (Eph. 2:10).

This theme runs through the remaining NT Letters as well. In 1 John readers get a particularly pointed reminder that the test of identity is observable righteousness: "If you know that [Christ] is righteous, you may be sure that everyone who does right has been born of him" (1 John 2:29 [cf. 1 John 3:10]). James links good works inextricably with faith. Some see a tension here between Paul and James, but the "faith versus works" debate is based on a false dichotomy. God justifies the ungodly—that is, puts them into a right relationship with himself (Rom. 3:21–26)—but the consequence of this is that believers are "to present [themselves] to God as those who have been brought from death to life, and present [their] members to God as instruments of righteousness" (Rom. 6:13).

See also Covenant; Holiness; Justice, Restorative; Legalism

Bibliography

Campbell, D. *The Quest for Paul's Gospel: A Suggested Strategy*. JSNTSup 274. T&T Clark, 2005; idem. *The Rhetoric of Righteousness in Romans 3.21–26*. JSNTSup 65. JSOT Press, 1992; Carson, D., P. O'Brien, and M. Seifrid, eds. *The Paradoxes of Paul*. Vol. 2 of *Justification and Variegated Nomism*. WUNT 2/181. Mohr Siebeck, 2004; Hill, D. *Greek Words and Hebrew Meanings: Studies in the Semantics of Soteriological Terms*. SNTSMS 5. Cambridge University Press, 1967; Przybylski, B. *Righteousness in Matthew and His World of Thought*. SNTSMS 41. Cambridge University Press, 1980; Seifrid, M. *Christ, Our Righteousness: Paul's Theology of Justification*. NSBT 9. Apollos, 2000; Southall, D. *Rediscovering Righteousness in Romans: Personified dikaiosynē within Metaphoric and Narratorial Settings*. WUNT 2/240. Mohr Siebeck, 2008; Wright, N. T. *Justification: God's Plan and Paul's Vision*. SPCK, 2009; Ziesler, J. *The Meaning of Righteousness in Paul: A Linguistic and Theological Enquiry*. SNTSMS 20. Cambridge University Press, 1972.

Kent Brower

Rights

In contemporary international life the idea of rights has become a dominant way of speaking of justice. This is so in spite of ambiguities in the history of the idea and the variety of its definitions, warrants, and applications. The most significant reason for the impact of this idea is that in 1948 the newly formed United Nations issued the Universal Declaration of Human Rights. It was written in reaction to the dehumanizing policies of the Nazi and fascist governments during World War II. This declaration begins its preamble by stating that the "recognition of the inherent dignity and of the equal and inalienable rights of all members of the human family is the foundation of freedom, justice, and peace in the world." It goes on to list the major rights that each person has in principle, such as the right to life, liberty, and security; to freedom from slavery, cruel punishment, and arbitrary arrest; to freedom of religion, thought, and association; and to marry, work, and have access to education.

This declaration was followed by two international "covenants" and several "conventions," and many of the principles were written into the constitutions of the many states emerging from colonial rule. The covenants were on civil and political rights and on social and economic rights. The former, advocated especially by the democratic West, had to do with the liberties that should be guaranteed to each citizen. The latter, advocated especially by the socialist East, had to do with guarantees that the state should provide for all citizens. After long and disputatious negotiations, both were finally approved in 1966 and were followed by various conventions, such as those against torture and genocide. In addition, postcolonial countries included versions of these rights in their new constitutions. Although these civil rights are unevenly enforced, they serve as standards that hover over the actual legal codes, governmental policies, and judicial practices around the world.

Simply recalling these events of the last century invites us to inquire into the roots of the idea of rights and their social implications. The claim that every person is endowed with an "inherent dignity" has not been obvious to all. Clearly, it is a normative claim about what ought to be. People ought to be treated with dignity, even if an equal and inalienable dignity is not based on empirical evidence. After all, people are not equal in stature, maturity, strength, ability, looks, intelligence, character, health, emotional stability, social contribution, and so on. Some have argued that the idea of rights can be rooted in basic concepts of natural law, and for many centuries the idea of nature was connected with a sense of a perceivable right order and normative purpose known by unaided reason. However, the modern Darwinian view of natural law does not attest to some inherent dignity in humans any more than the bloody record of exploitation and conflict in every culture reveals a natural moral logic of history. Thus, post-Darwinians argue that the idea of rights points to higher moral principles rooted in a worldview that includes transempirical, usually theistically given, norms of justice.

No known culture, to be sure, is without some definition of "rights"; those of the head of the family, of the firstborn son, of the slave owner, of the king, or of members of a tribe or caste have been variously honored in many societies since time immemorial, and these have been seen as "natural." Such "rights" have to do with the privileges of "status" in a particular culture. Further, in those societies where social differentiation is advanced, certain rights are office-related: police have the right to arrest perpetrators of crime, judges have the right to consign convicted criminals to imprisonment, doctors can be granted the right to perform surgery on patients, political authorities can be given the right to tax the public, and certain stakeholders have a right to make claims on a corporation. Beyond these rights of status or function, only some cultures and societies are guided by worldviews that affirm principles of justice and demand recognition of universal, equal, and inalienable rights that regulate, restrict, or guide rights of status or office.

Categories of rights can be further refined. Already mentioned are "civil" rights, which are those rights found in a system of traditional practices or established in codes of a particular civil order, and "human" rights, which are those ethical principles of justice understood to stand over every cultural, social, or governmental institution. In both civil and human rights, some are entitlements; they indicate the propriety of a claim to a privilege, good, or service that someone must deliver, such as a right to a fair wage. Some are freedoms; they indicate a liberty that cannot be forbidden or compelled by others, such as a right to convert to another religion. Still others are pleas for the recognition and rectification of discriminations against a distinct group, such as the rights of women, ethnic minorities, and homosexuals. There are also rights that can be withheld under certain conditions in contrast to those that are inalienable, such as the right of a nonregistered citizen to vote in contrast to the right of free speech. Another use of the term *rights* requires that we distinguish between those things that are never justifiably right to do, such as genocide, and those things that generally are wrong but arguably right to do in certain circumstances, such as tyrannicide. We must also note debates about whether rights can be assigned to nonpersons, such as animals or the environment generally.

How did such clusters of rights develop, what are their roots, and what are their warrants? We must address these questions in view of the fact that some (MacIntyre; Strauss) argue that the idea of rights is false in the first place. Some see the origin of rights in the Enlightenment's attempt to develop a cosmopolitan ethic on the basis of a humanist ideal of reason (Henkin; Rawls). However, the historical evidence is quite clear, if not universally acknowledged, that the modern ideas of rights evolved in those cultures most deeply rooted in the biblical traditions, even if parts of these traditions have also at times ignored or violated human and civil rights. It is also quite clear that the influence of the biblical tradition is indirect; that is, theologians and jurists selectively drew from classical philosophical and jurisprudential concepts of rights and adopted, adapted, modulated, and reinforced some of their insights on the basis of themes drawn from scriptural sources (Jellinek; Wolterstorff). Many who hold this view also recognize that the principles of human rights based in these fused foundations have been widely adopted by people from other traditions once the principles were discovered and articulated.

New studies have shown the influence of the French Catholic moral philosopher Jacques Maritain and the Lebanese Protestant political leader Charles Malik on the drafting of the United Nations Universal Declaration of Human Rights (Glendon), and others have documented the influence of Protestant and Orthodox leadership working with Jewish rabbis and Catholic bishops both in forging the declaration and in mobilizing religious communities in support of it (Nurser). Further, comparative studies reveal that the social and legal infrastructure for the support of human and civil rights is strongest in those countries where reform-oriented Judaism, Catholicism, and Protestantism have had the greatest social impact (Stackhouse; Witte). And recently, intellectual historians have documented the long and deep Christian traditions that generated the idea of human rights (Tierney; Hass), while older social historians have stressed the political and legal impact of minority, sectarian, independent, and free church groups in advocating them (Troeltsch; Woodhouse).

Although some Christian thinkers question the embrace of human rights, since such an expression does not appear in the Bible, most see motifs in the biblical texts that support the affirmation of human rights and the inclusion of civil rights in all legal codes (Harrelson; Smylie). The references are many, but the most important themes can be briefly summarized. Humanity (males and females of all races equally) is created in the image and likeness of God. Thus, each person has a bestowed dignity and, with it, a mandate and right to participate in the creation of culture and society. This requires for most a capacity for reason, will, and affection. These are not always rightly used, and their misuse inexorably leads to violence, disaster, and slavery. Yet, covenantal promises of providential care and salvation are given by God along with universally valid moral laws governing personal and social behavior. Further, covenanted communities of faith and specific people—prophets, priests, political leaders—are called to instruct the soul and ethically guide the common life. Moreover, Christians believe that in Jesus the covenantal promises are fulfilled, and that true prophecy, faithful ministry, and the Prince of Peace, who regulates all enduring political possibilities, invite all who seek the relative justice attainable in history to embrace and actualize human rights in every sphere of life.

See also Civil Rights; Comparative Religious Ethics; Government; Humanity; Human Rights; Image of God; Natural Law; Natural Rights

Bibliography

Bucar, E., and B. Barnett, eds. *Does Human Rights Need God?* Eerdmans, 2005; Glendon, M. *The World Made New: Eleanor Roosevelt and the Universal Declaration of Human Rights*. Random House, 2001; Gustafson, C., and P. Juviler, eds. *Religion and Human Rights: Competing Claims?* M. E. Sharp, 1999; Harrelson, W. *The Ten Commandments and Human Rights*. Rev. ed. Mercer University Press, 1997; Hass, G. *The Concept of Equity in Calvin's Ethic*. Wilfred Laurier University Press, 1997; Henkin, L. *The Age of Rights*. Columbia University Press, 1990; Jellinek, G. *Die Erklärung der Menschen- und Bürgerrechte: Ein Beitrag zur modernen Verfassungsgeschichte*. Duncker & Humblot, 1895; Nurser, J. *For All Peoples and All Nations: The Ecumenical Church and Human Rights*. Georgetown University Press, 2005; Smylie, R. *Life in All Its Fullness: The Word of God and Human Rights*. American Bible Society, 1992; Stackhouse, M. *Creeds, Society, and Human Rights: A Study in Three Cultures*. Eerdmans, 1984; Strauss, L. *Natural Right and History*. University of Chicago Press, 1950; Tierney, B. *The Idea of Natural Rights: Studies on Natural Rights, Natural Law, and Church Law, 1150–1625*. EUSLR 5. Scholars Press, 1997; Troeltsch, E. *The Social Teaching of the Christian Churches*. Trans. O. Wyon. Harper & Row, 1932; Witte, J., Jr., and J. van der Vyver, eds. *Religious Human Rights in Global Perspective*. 2 vols. Martinus Nijhoff, 1996; Wolterstorff, N. *Justice: Rights and Wrongs*. Princeton University Press, 2007; Woodhouse, A., ed. *Puritanism and Liberty*. University of Chicago Press, 1932.

Max L. Stackhouse

Rights, Animal *See* Animals

Rights, Human *See* Human Rights

Roman Catholic Moral Theology

Although many different definitions have been given over time, Roman Catholic moral theology corresponds to "Christian ethics" in the Protestant tradition and essentially is the sustained reflection in conscience on the part of both the individual and the Christian community on how best to understand and live out their new identity in light of God's definitive revelation of God's own self and the true nature of humanity that is found in Jesus Christ. In short, moral theology should be nothing more, nor less, than the individual's and the community's best efforts to understand and live out Paul's articulation of the gospel message in 2 Cor. 5:16–21:

> From now on, therefore, we regard no one from a human point of view; even though we once knew Christ from a human point of view, we know him no longer in that way. So if anyone is in Christ, there is a new creation: everything old has passed away; see, everything has become new! All this is from God, who reconciled us to himself through Christ, and has given us the ministry of reconciliation; that is, in Christ God was reconciling the world to himself, not counting their trespasses against them, and entrusting the message of reconciliation to us. So we are ambassadors for Christ, since God is making his appeal through us; we entreat you on behalf of Christ, be reconciled to God. For our sake he made him to be sin who knew no sin, so that in him we might become the righteousness of God.

Theological anthropology is the first task of moral theology. In other words, how do we answer the question, who am I, and what sort of person should I strive to become in the light of who we consider God to be? Building on these foundational reflections, moral theology is the discipline that further aids the individual and the community in discerning the most appropriate virtues and actions that will best live out Christian identity.

In early church history there was a very close connection between the disciplines of moral theology and Christian spirituality, but unfortunately for both a split eventually occurred, and spirituality tended to move more in the direction of asceticism and withdrawal from the secular world, while moral theology became increasingly preoccupied with sin, especially as seen in terms of individual actions. During the early Middle Ages, academic moral theology increasingly focused on helping priests counsel penitents in the sacrament of penance. A case-method approach was widely adopted that developed into the practice of casuistry that would list typical scenarios of a particular "sin," then list the relevant moral principles involved and the relative culpability of the penitent, and finally propose an adequate penance to be given. Regrettably, several related stresses came to dominate both the discipline of moral theology and its practice.

The first of these was conceiving of morality as somehow separable from the character of the moral agent. This led in turn to delineation of the so-called *fontes moralitatis* (fonts of morality), which were the action in itself, the intention of the agent in performing the action, and the circumstances in which the act was performed. Since the last two elements (intention and circumstances) were both highly unique and subjective, in effect the focus of moral analysis devolved to an excessive degree onto the *finis operis* (end of the action) of the so-called objective nature of the act. Certain types of these acts were then further described as being an *intrinsece malum in se* (intrinsically evil) and thus always wrong, regardless of intention and/or circumstances. Other actions were considered always to have "grave matter" and therefore potentially resulting in mortal sin if committed with sufficient awareness and freedom by the individual. Many of these actions were connected with sex, and the corresponding moral principle was that there was never *parvitas materiae in Sexto* (no "light" matter in the sixth commandment of the Decalogue [the seventh in Orthodox and Protestant Christian traditions]), and so each and every action involving sexuality, from heavy kissing to full intercourse, ran the serious risk of being classified a mortal sin—that is, the definitive breaking of the relationship with God, which would send the individual to hell unless he or she were reconciled and forgiven in the sacrament of penance. Moral theology for several centuries then became largely caught up with sin and less and less with the positive thrust of living out the gospel message.

Connected with this preoccupation with sin and moral acts in the sixth commandment was a theology of marriage that looked rather askance at sexuality and its expression between a husband and wife. Dating back to Augustine, there was a definite uneasiness about sexual pleasure unless it could be "justified" by the good of conception of offspring (*bonum prolis*) (see *Coniug. adult.* 2.12 [Gen. 38:8–10]). Augustine and many of his successors thought that sexual intercourse between husband and wife done without directly willing to have a child conceived of the specific sexual encounter was at least venially sinful, though he did allow that one of the ends of marriage was a *remedium concupiscientiae* (remedy for sexual desire).

The growth of the discipline of canon law in the Middle Ages became so linked to moral theology, especially in the administration of the sacraments of penance and marriage, that often the two disciplines were treated as if they were indistinct, and an ethos of legalism increasingly infused the teaching of moral theology in the seminaries. The classic textbook model of this era, which persisted almost up to the Second Vatican Council (1962–65), was the so-called moral manual, usually written in Latin and used in most seminaries around the world. A theological method grounded primarily in Neo-Thomism, coupled with the moral reasoning of simple probabilism (a weighing of a spectrum of likely or "probable" opinions about the morality of an act), characterized most of these manuals. Although the list of authors is long, the actual differences were slight among the works of some better-known manuals of Fathers Scavini, Gury, Ballerini-Palmieri, Genicot, Lehmkuhl, Noldin, Tanquerey, Goepfert, Jone, Vermeersch, Arregui, Healy, and Zalba. Arregui's well-known moral compendium serves as a good example of the popularity of this sort of moral manual: it went through fourteen editions by the time of his death in 1942, and a further ten posthumously (revised by Zalba). Although the manuals listed Scripture, along with tradition and the magisterium (official teaching of the pope and bishops), as one of the primary sources for moral theology, the Bible was used sparingly and largely in a proof-texting mode to buttress arguments drawn from a Neo-Thomistic natural-law analysis. The usual manualist approach was intentionally regressive in that it started with the current teaching of the magisterium at that particular time on a given issue and then worked back to Scripture and the tradition to demonstrate how this teaching was harmonious and constant through the ages.

In the 1930s, 1940s, and 1950s, moral theology, though still dominated by the manualist tradition, began to face some of the modern problems posed by the rise of totalitarianism, two world wars, rapid growth in technology, and dramatic advances in medicine. The magisterium, especially in the numerous writings and discourses of Pius XI (1922–39) and Pius XII (1939–58), addressed many of these issues, and several Roman-based moralists, such as Francis Hürth at the Pontifical Gregorian University, were called on to aid the pope in the drafting of these writings, while elsewhere other moral theologians, such as John Ford and Gerald Kelly in the United States and Marcelino Zalba in Europe, sought to integrate this new magisterium in their treatment of contemporary moral theology.

Genuine adaptation and innovation marked much of the work in social ethics, and for over a century now, papal encyclicals have often been seen to be more in the vanguard for social theory grappling with the most troubling and contentious economic and political issues of the day, ranging from the publication of Leo XIII's landmark 1891 encyclical on labor, *Rerum novarum*, followed in turn by Pius XI's 1931 social encyclical, *Quadragesimo anno*, and his attack on Nazism in 1937 (*Mit brennender sorge*); John XXIII's *Mater et magistra* (1961) and *Pacem in terris* (1963); Paul VI's *Populorum progressio* (1967); and John Paul II's *Laborem exercens* (1981), *Sollicitudo rei socialis* (1987), and *Centesimus annus* (1991). The latter two in particular sought to raise concerns about free-market capitalism following the decline and fall of the communist bloc.

In the area of sexual ethics, though, the tack often taken was viewed as a retrenchment and has occasioned perhaps the most acrimonious debates among moral theologians. *Casti connubii*, Pius XI's 1930 encyclical on Christian marriage, severely condemned as "shameful and intrinsically vicious" (§54) any use of artificial contraception by married couples. This encyclical was partially a response to the more benign toleration of artificial contraception given by Anglicans in their Lambeth Conference earlier that same year. The next pope, Pius XII, in his famous "Address to Midwives on the Nature of Their Profession" (1951), recognized as morally licit the practice of periodic continence by married couples, the so-called rhythm method, in order to avoid conception. His successor, John XXIII (1958–63), created a special pontifical commission to study the issue of regulation of births in light of changes in world population and the invention of nonbarrier methods of contraception that seemed less morally problematic than the traditional condom or diaphragm. The special pontifical commission, using the moral principle of totality, overwhelmingly voted in 1965 to recommend a change in the official teaching. However, when Paul VI finally published his encyclical *Humanae vitae* (1968), he reiterated the traditional rejection of contraception, stating that each and every marital act must be open to the possibility of procreation (§14).

In other areas, the period marked by the Second Vatican Council was a major watershed in nearly every area of the church's life and theology, and the impact on moral theology was considerable. The traditional moral manual largely disappeared, and the texts that replaced these tried more earnestly to respect the council's mandate that Scripture truly become the "soul of theology," and that the discipline of moral theology, "nourished more on the teaching of the Bible, should shed light on the loftiness of the calling of the faithful in Christ and the obligation that is theirs of bearing fruit in charity for the life of the world" (*Optatam totius* §16). The theology of Karl Rahner had a tremendous bearing not only on the council but also in virtually every theological field. Rahner's theological anthropology highlighted the distinctively "personal" characteristics of human nature of each individual. Within each person, Rahner argued, are two distinct levels of freedom operative: a core, or "transcendental," freedom in which each person expresses his or her fundamental orientation toward or away from God, and another level, which he termed the "categorical," related to those existential acts and choices that constitute the bulk of human daily moral life. The ramifications of this notion of the human person and different levels of freedom helped redefine an understanding of "mortal sin" in terms of a "fundamental option" toward God that would change less often or easily as had once been thought. Although misunderstood and criticized by some, the fundamental option theory actually tried to take more seriously the reality of personal sin and its effect on a person's life.

Another important development in post–Vatican II moral theology concerns the "knowability" of universal moral norms and their application in concrete situations. A related concept, still debated, concerns the precise nature of "intrinsically evil acts"—that is, human actions that are in each and every instance always objectively sinful and therefore may never be countenanced regardless of any extenuating circumstances. Richard McCormick proposed using the concept of a "virtually exceptionless norm" to replace the notion of intrinsic evil, since it would be largely impossible to foresee for all time and situations whether a particular action (e.g., "abortion" or removal of an ectopic fetus) would always have the exact same moral meaning.

These twin issues of moral norms and intrinsically evil acts came to the fore principally in the fields of sexual and biomedical ethics, with such thorny problems of the moral liceity of artificial contraception, artificial insemination, and in-vitro fertilization. Relative to this ongoing debate on the precise nature of concrete fundamental moral norms and intrinsically evil acts in value-conflict situations is the development of a moral theory usually called "proportionalism," which argued that especially in double-effect actions in which there are both good and bad consequences, the moral rightness or wrongness of causing or permitting of evils depends on the presence or absence of "proportionate" reason. If such proportionate reason is present in the act, then the human intention bears on it, not on the evil caused. The theory of proportionalism is still a matter of much lively debate, with a large number of theologians taking positions pro or con.

Another change in post–Vatican II moral theology involves the shift from a "classical" worldview to a more nuanced historical consciousness. A classicist view of nature is largely deductive and stresses the eternal, the universal, the immutable aspects of human nature and natural moral law. In contrast to this classicist paradigm, a worldview that is more conscious of the historical and cultural aspects of human nature is more inductive and therefore accents more the concrete and particular, the individual and personal, cultural and historically conditioned elements that may change and that may not be as universalizable. This attention to the "how" and "where" of moral theology necessarily involves greater attention to inculturation and contextualization, ecumenical ethics, and cross-cultural ethics in a global arena. No doubt the discipline of moral theology will continue to develop in meeting these challenges.

Bibliography

Bretzke, J. *A Morally Complex World: Engaging Contemporary Moral Theology*. Liturgical Press, 2004; Curran, C., et al., eds. *Readings in Moral Theology*. 15 vols. Paulist Press, 1979–2009; Davis, H. *Moral and Pastoral Theology*. 8th ed. 4 vols. Sheed & Ward, 1959; Fuchs, J. *Christian Morality: The Word Became Flesh*. Georgetown University Press, 1987; Gallagher, J. *Time Past, Time Future: An Historical Study of Catholic Moral Theology*. Paulist Press, 1990; Gula, R. *Reason Informed by Faith: Foundations of Catholic Morality*. Paulist Press, 1989; Häring, B. *Free and Faithful in Christ: Moral Theology for Priests and Laity*. 3 vols. St. Paul Publications, 1978; Hogan, L. *Confronting the Truth: Conscience in the Catholic Tradition*. Paulist Press, 2001; Mahoney, J. *The Making of Moral Theology: A Study of the Roman Catholic Tradition*. Clarendon, 1987; McCormick, R., and P. Ramsey, eds. *Doing Evil to Achieve Good: Moral Choice in Conflict Situations*. Loyola University Press, 1978; Noonan, J., Jr. *A Church That Can and Cannot Change: The Development of Catholic Moral Teaching*. University of Notre Dame Press, 2005.

James T. Bretzke, SJ

Romans

This letter, addressed to a church that Paul had not founded, was dispatched from Corinth shortly before the apostle headed east with an offering from his gentile congregations for the Jewish Christians of Jerusalem (15:25–27, 30–31). His aims were to gain support for a projected mission to Spain (1:8–15; 15:23–24, 28–29, 32) and to address the problem of reported tensions between Jewish and gentile Christians in the imperial capital (14:1–15:6). These objectives account for Romans being the most deliberately and comprehensively theological of Paul's Letters. The apostle has laid out with special care the principal affirmations of his preaching and emphasized that the gospel is good news for gentiles as well as for Jews. As a result, the letter's argument also anticipated his impending trip to Jerusalem, where his gentile mission was being seriously questioned.

In the body of Romans Paul deals, in turn, with humanity's plight (1:18–3:20), contending that "all have sinned and fall short of the glory of God" (3:23), God's saving grace (3:21–8:39), God's faithfulness (chaps. 9–11), and God's claim (12:1–15:6). His premise, stated in 1:16–17, is that the gospel (God's power for salvation) reveals God's justice ("righteousness") "through faith for faith," not only to Jews but also to gentiles. Concluding (15:7–13), he reiterates this universal scope of God's saving power, identifying Christ as "a servant of the circumcised on behalf of the truth of God in order that he might confirm the promises given to the patriarchs, and in order that the Gentiles might glorify God for his mercy" (15:8–9).

In accord with his belief in the universality of both humanity's sin and God's mercy, Paul identifies Christ's death for the "ungodly" and "sinners" as proof of God's unconditional love, an eschatological event of saving power (5:1–11). Baptism into Christ's death marks the crucifixion of one's "old self," deliverance from sin, and a transformed life under the dominion of grace (6:1–14). The first and most fundamental imperatives of the letter appear in this context, joined with a reference to the believers' new, eschatological existence: "No longer present your members to sin as instruments of wickedness, but present yourselves to God as those who have been brought from death to life, and present your members to God as instruments of righteousness" (6:13). Subsequently, Paul describes this new life as indwelt and guided by the Spirit (8:1–27).

The summons for believers to present themselves to God is reiterated in 12:1–2, where Paul introduces the ethical appeals that follow as grounded in the gospel that he has been expounding. Those who have been brought "from death to life" and granted a renewed mind are called to "discern" (*dokimazō*) what God regards as "good and acceptable and perfect." Paul's verb points to a process of inquiry, critical reflection, analysis, and testing that seeks to determine what God's will requires. It is clear from both the general appeals in chaps. 12–13 and the specific counsels in 14:1–15:6 that he regards the "norming norm" of moral discernment to be not God's law as conveyed in the Torah but rather God's love revealed in Christ (12:9–10; 14:15). Viewed through the lens of faith, all of the commandments of the law are perceived as summed up in the single commandment to love one's neighbor as oneself (13:8–10; cf. Gal. 5:13–14).

The appeals in 12:3–13, focused on conduct within the believing community, echo the apostle's comments in 1 Cor. 12–14 about membership in the body of Christ and its upbuilding in love. Most, if not all, of the counsels in 12:14–21 deal with the conduct of believers in relation to nonbelievers, including the church's opponents. Here again, love appears as the "norming norm": "Do not be overcome by evil, but overcome evil with good" (12:21).

One of the most difficult and debated passages in Romans is 13:1–7, which concerns the responsibility of Christians toward the governing authorities. Although some interpreters argue that Paul urges complete and unquestioning obedience to the state, there is better evidence for the view that he calls for compliance with its laws only in some limited sense. This passage may be seen as extending his appeal to live peaceably with all people (12:18); now he includes the governing authorities. He urges respect for these officials and the laws that they administer because he believes that God has authorized them for the specific purpose of rewarding those who do good and punishing those who do evil. He does not consider how believers should respond if the authorities prove unfaithful, unwise, or unjust in fulfilling this task. It is especially important that, like all of the counsels in these chapters, his call to good citizenship is fundamentally qualified by the introductory appeals: believers are to present their transformed lives unconditionally to God and not be conformed to this present age.

Only in 14:1–15:6 does Paul address an issue specific to the Roman church. The ("strong") gentile Christian majority despised the ("weak") Jewish Christian minority for abstaining from meat and observing special holy days, while the latter passed judgment on the former because they did not do so (cf. 1 Cor. 8:1–11:1). The apostle charges each group to "welcome" the other because both have been welcomed by God, and God alone will be their judge (14:2–4, 10–13). He believes, nonetheless, that the "strong" bear a special responsibility for the "weak": "If your brother or sister is being injured by what you eat, you are no longer walking in love. Do not let what you eat cause the ruin of one for whom Christ died" (14:15 [cf. 15:1–4]).

See also Government; New Testament Ethics; Righteousness

Bibliography

Betz, H. "The Foundations of Christian Ethics according to Romans 12:1–2." Pages 55–72 in *Witness and Existence: Essays in Honor of Schubert M. Ogden*, ed. P. Devenish and G. Goodwin. University of Chicago Press, 1989; du Toit, A. "Shaping a Christian Lifestyle in the Roman Capital." Pages 167–97 in *Identity, Ethics, and Ethos in the New Testament*, ed. J. van der Watt. De Gruyter, 2006; Keck, L. *Romans*. ANTC. Abingdon, 2005.

Victor Paul Furnish

Ruth

The book of Ruth tells the story of Naomi, an Israelite woman living in Moab whose husband and two sons have died, and of her faithful daughter-in-law Ruth, who forsakes her Moabite homeland and religious traditions for the uncertainties of life in Judah. Through a series of events, both fortuitous and orchestrated, Ruth ends up marrying Naomi's kinsman Boaz and bearing a son. At the end of the story both Naomi and Ruth are restored to the fullness of family and community life, with Naomi cradling the child considered her grandson.

Like most stories, the book of Ruth does not engage ethics explicitly; rather, the ethics espoused and affirmed must be discerned within the narrative itself. Engaging the book of Ruth by means of narrative ethics allows one to perceive that this short story is surprisingly rich in its ethical vision.

Unlike much of the rest of the Bible, God's role in the story is muted—only Ruth's conception of a son at the end is directly attributed to God's action (4:13); the story focuses instead on the actions of human beings. Nonetheless, the characters consistently invoke God's blessing on others in prayer, and these prayers are crucial for understanding the connection between life with God and life lived in community. Most of the characters lead God-centered lives, and the richness of that fundamental relationship empowers them to enact blessings for others through their own works of loving-kindness. The health of the community depends quite directly on the health of the people's relationship with God.

The story begins with famine and death and ends in the bounty of the harvest and the birth of a child who represents the hope of the future. Boaz and Ruth's acts of loving-kindness redeem Naomi; taking initiative to enact God's blessings, they weave her back into a full life, surrounded by a community marked by care and joy for all generations.

The story connects intertextually with OT legal material. Boaz keeps the laws that allow the poor to glean after the harvesters (Lev. 19:9–10; 23:22; Deut. 24:19–22) and keeps the spirit of the laws of levirate marriage and land redemption (see Sakenfeld 57–61). Many commentators posit a postexilic date for the book and have observed that the inclusion of a Moabite woman in the ancestral line of David flies in the face of postexilic laws against intermarriage (Ezra 10; Neh. 13), thus creating an intertextual conversation about the role of foreign women in Israel.

In the OT, the book immediately follows Judges, and the contrast in ethos is startling. Whereas Judges ends with a vision of the devastation effected when the community of faith is disconnected from God, Ruth offers a vision of the redemption possible when the community centers its prayers on God and its acts of loving faithfulness on those in need of restoration.

Bibliography

Lapsley, J. *Whispering the Word: Hearing Women's Stories in the Old Testament*. Westminster, 2005, 89–108; Sakenfeld, K. D. *Ruth*. Interpretation. Westminster, 1999.

Jacqueline E. Lapsley

S

Sabbath

The Sabbath was instituted shortly after Israel gained freedom from Egyptian slavery (Exod. 16:23–30). In Gen. 2:2–3, however, God already established the Sabbath on the seventh day of creation. Commands to observe the Sabbath appeal to God's hallowing that day at creation, Israel's deliverance from bondage, and freedom for all, including slaves and animals, to rest from labor and celebrate joyfully (Exod. 20:8–12; Deut. 5:12–15). The seventh-year sabbatical and the fiftieth-year Jubilee express God's Sabbath grace (Lev. 25; Deut. 15).

Jesus and his disciples observed the Sabbath (Mark 1:21; Luke 4:16; 23:56b), although Jesus tangled with the Pharisees over Sabbath laws. Willy Rordorf holds that Jesus attacked the Sabbath itself, not just the Pharisaic laws "fencing" the Sabbath (Rordorf 15). Jesus healed on the Sabbath, allowing physical exertion on that day: taking up one's mat and walking (John 5:2–12), plucking grain (Mark 2:23–28), and washing in a pool (John 9:1–12). Jesus' Sabbath actions spiraled into mortal conflict with the religious leaders.

Jesus explains his Sabbath practices as life-affirming: "The sabbath was made for humankind; and not humankind for the sabbath," and therefore "the Son of Man is lord even of the sabbath" (Mark 2:27–28). In speech and action Jesus fulfills the Sabbath, bringing rest to the weary (Matt. 11:28–29) with human liberation.

Sabbath practices among early Christians differed. Paul counsels that no one should judge another over observance of Jewish festivals and Sabbaths, for these "are only a shadow of what is to come, but the substance belongs to Christ" (Col. 2:16–17). Luke highlights Jesus fulfilling what the Sabbath signifies (quoting Isa. 58:6; 61:1–4 in Luke 4:18–19). In the book of Acts, however, Paul's custom is Sabbath observance (Acts 17:2); he regularly goes to the synagogue (Acts 13:14, 44; 16:13; 18:4). The believers' custom of gathering on the first day, the "Lord's Day," is attested in Rev. 1:10 (see also *Did.* 14.1), and began early (Acts 20:7; 1 Cor. 16:2), likely pre-Pauline (Rordorf 218).

Differences in Sabbath observance among Christians continued. Some sources relegate Sabbath observance to Judaism and urge celebration of the Lord's Day only, the spiritual fulfillment of Sabbath (Ign. *Magn.* 9.1–3; Clement of Alexandria; Origen; Justin; Irenaeus); other sources urge both Sabbath observance and Sunday Lord's Day gatherings (Ebionite and Nazorean Christians; Syriac sources) (Ekenberg 651–53).

The Sabbath is God's temple in time (see Heschel 79–83). Seventh-day Adventists and several Christian minorities continue Sabbath observance, worshiping on the seventh day, Saturday. They appeal to second-century apostate influences causing the switch to Sunday: anti-Judaism, the influence of sun cults in pagan Roman religion, and growing authority in the church of Rome to change the day (Bacchiocchi). Constantine legalized Sunday rest (March 3, 321 CE). The case for three different positions on observance has been argued by various writers: Sabbath/Seventh Day observance; Sunday Lord's Day worship; and All-Days-Holy (Swartley 65–95).

Increasing numbers of Christians recognize the importance of keeping the Sabbath in today's pressured societies. Marva Dawn identifies four dimensions of Sabbath-keeping crucial to faithful Christian living, each with ethical import: "ceasing," to deepen our repentance from self-planning our future; "resting," to strengthen faith, breathing God's grace; "embracing," to apply faith practically to our values and friendships; and "feasting," to celebrate the joy of God's love and the Sabbath's foretaste of the age to come (Dawn 203). Similarly, the Sabbath enables us to discover "the rhythms of rest and delight" (Wirzba). In Sunday worship we participate in God's re-creation, marked by joy, peace, hospitality, and love, renewing allegiance to Christ (Wirzba 48–49). Sabbath renews work, home, economics, education, environment, and worship (Wirzba 91–165). Sabbath-keeping is essential for *shalom* wholeness.

The Sabbath and the Lord's Day point us toward God's "eighth day" of eternal bliss.

See also Creation, Biblical Accounts of; Jubilee; Play; Time, Use of; Work

Bibliography

Bacchiocchi, S. *From Sabbath to Sunday: A Historical Investigation*. Pontifical Gregorian University Press, 1977; Carson, D., ed. *From Sabbath to Lord's Day: A Biblical, Historical, and Theological Investigation*. Zondervan, 1982; Dawn, M. *Keeping the Sabbath Wholly: Ceasing, Resting, Embracing, Feasting*. Eerdmans, 1991; Ekenberg, A. "Evidence for Jewish Believers in 'Church Orders' and Liturgical Texts." Pages 640–58 in *Jewish Believers in Jesus: The Early Centuries*, ed. O. Skarsaune and R. Hvalvik. Hendrickson, 2007 [contains other pertinent articles]; Heschel, A. *The Sabbath: Its Meaning for Modern Man*. Farrar, Straus & Giroux, 1951; Rordorf, W. *Sunday: The History of the Day of Rest and Worship in the Earliest Centuries of the Christian Church*. Trans. A. Graham. Westminster, 1968; Swartley, W. *Slavery, Sabbath, War, and Women: Case Issues in Biblical Interpretation*. Herald Press, 1983; Wirzba, N. *Living the Sabbath: Discovering the Rhythms of Rest and Delight*. Brazos, 2006.

Willard M. Swartley

Sadomasochism *See* Sexual Ethics

Salvation

The word *salvation* appears relatively rarely in the Christian Scriptures. The term, however, unites other concepts into an ultimate eudaemonism: a concern for eternal human flourishing that has its roots in present deliverance from sin, violence, and evil.

Given the numerical symbolism of the book of Revelation, it should not surprise us that "salvation" (*soterion*) occurs three times there (Rev. 7:10; 12:10; 19:1). Each use shares a common setting—a great sound in the heaven proclaims "salvation" in praise of God. Those robed in white "from every nation, from all tribes and peoples and languages" (Rev. 7:9) are no longer in "the great ordeal" (v. 14a). "Salvation" involves movement—the One on the Throne moves those dressed in white from suffering to human flourishing through the "blood of the Lamb" (v. 14b). They now worship the One on the Throne and the Lamb who "will guide them to springs of the water of life" (v. 17b). The time of this movement is ambiguous. The translation of "have come out" of the NRSV (v. 14) masks the present participle—"These are the ones who are coming out of the great ordeal."

The second use occurs after Satan and his minions are thrown from heaven to the earth. A great heavenly voice declares: "Now have come the salvation and the power and the kingdom of our God and the authority of his Messiah" (Rev. 12:10). "Salvation" quells the war in heaven (Rev. 12:7) "by the blood of the Lamb and by the work of their testimony, for they [the saints] did not cling to life even in the face of death" (v. 11). The third occurrence follows the downfall of Babylon (Rev. 18:1–24). The judgment of the "whore" on earth (Rev. 19:2) gives a reason for the heavenly multitude to ascribe "salvation and glory and power to our God" (Rev. 19:1), a salvation celebrated in the "marriage supper of the Lamb" (19:7). Salvation entails a movement from violent conflict to peace and flourishing. In salvation God moves the faithful from the violence of this world to find their end in God eternally through Christ's nonviolent overcoming of the evil of this age.

The Pauline use of "salvation" possesses a similar underlying structure. "Salvation" is a present, continuous reality. The verb "to save" occurs twice in the present passive participial form to indicate "those who are being saved" (1 Cor. 1:18; 15:2). This "salvation" arises from participation in the gospel (1 Cor. 15:1–2a); its end lies still ahead of the believer when "the last enemy to be destroyed is death" (1 Cor. 15:26) so that "God may be all in all" (1 Cor. 15:28). "Salvation" has a sense of deliverance, whether release from present-day affliction (Phil. 1:19; 2 Cor. 1:6) or future judgment (Phil. 1:28). It calls for believers to "work out your own salvation" in the tension between one's present "salvation" and the future deliverance at the culmination of all things (Phil. 2:12; see also 1 Thess. 5:8–9; 2 Cor. 7:10). As James Dunn writes, "Paul's understanding of salvation as a process has frequently been summed up as a tension between the 'already' and the 'not yet.' The process character is clear from the consistent way he speaks of salvation itself as *a goal still to be attained*, the final good" (Rom. 5:9–11) (Dunn 93).

The eudaemonistic tension is creative, not vicious, because "salvation" has already fully occurred in the gospel—the life, death, and resurrection of Jesus Christ (1 Cor. 15:1–2; see also Eph. 1:13). The centrality of "salvation" for Paul appears in the "thesis statement" of the Epistle to the Romans: "I am not ashamed of the gospel; it is the power of God for salvation to everyone who has faith, to the Jew first and also to the Gentile" (Rom. 1:16–17). Because "salvation"—the human flourishing that arises out of deliverance from sin, death, and Satan—has already happened, it is continuously happening in the believer through participation in the life, death, and resurrection of Jesus by faith in baptism (see Rom. 6:1–11; Gal. 2:19–20; 3:26–4:7).

Because the gospel happened "in accordance with the scriptures," Paul reached into the ancestral Jewish writings to articulate his understanding of "salvation." Paul describes God's salvation in Christ through his use of Isa. 49:8 (2 Cor. 6:2), Isa. 28:16 (Rom. 10:10–11), and Joel 2:32 (Rom. 10:12–13). First Peter shares this background presupposition—"Concerning this salvation, the prophets who prophesied of the grace . . . when it testified in advance to the sufferings destined for Christ and the subsequent glory" (1 Pet. 1:10–11). "Salvation" in Christ found its intelligibility through the Prophets. These writings "are able to instruct you for salvation through faith in Jesus Christ" (2 Tim. 3:15).

The Gospel of John, then, should not surprise us when we read that "salvation is from the Jews" (John 4:22). The Gospel of Luke develops this Jewish context for the use of "salvation" in the Jewish psalms spoken by Mary (Luke 1:47) and Zechariah (Luke 1:69, 77) and in quotations from Isaiah (Luke 2:30; 3:6). These provide the matrix for the introduction of Jesus as "Savior" by the angels at his birth. Jesus himself represents and enacts salvation (see Luke 19:9–10).

In Luke "salvation" is moving through the "narrow door" (Luke 13:23) where the one who loses one's life will save it (Luke 9:24; 17:33). Jesus himself embodies this saying on the cross, ironically recognized by the mockers who deride him (Luke 23:35, 37, 39). "Salvation" becomes fully visible in the resurrection of Jesus (see Acts 4:10–12; 13:26–41), Jesus' bodily flourishing that exceeds his crucifixion. For Luke "salvation" marks God's rescue of humans within and beyond the present suffering of this age through the suffering and resurrection of Jesus, all interpreted through the words of the Jewish prophets.

It is helpful to turn to the OT to grasp how the NT uses the term *salvation*. Early Christians did not read the Hebrew text but the Old Greek translations. Translators used the Greek *soterion* to translate two Hebrew roots and related terms: *ysh'*, deliverance, and *shlm*, peace/flourishing. The Old Greek version had already brought together the two concepts of deliverance and flourishing into the one Greek term, *soterion*. We find the use of *soterion* and related terms particularly concentrated in three loci: within the book of Isaiah, the sacrificial sections of the Torah, and the book of Psalms.

Prophetic "salvation oracles" arose within Judah following the destruction of Jerusalem by the Babylonians, oracles incorporated into the book of Isaiah following earlier oracles of judgment. As Claus Westermann stated, "The prophecies of salvation constitute a bridge to the life of a 'remnant' in the land of their ancestors after return from exile" (269). The history of the formation of the book of Isaiah, therefore, placed an interpretive context for reading the text. As a complete scroll, the book provides a narrative world in which the prophetic sayings have been given a new interpretation by shifting the literary context of the original oracles (see Childs). Salvation entails a movement from sin and judgment to a restoration for the fullness of life.

"Salvation" in Isaiah looks to the future even in the first half of the book (Isa. 12:2–3; 25:9, 26:1; 33:2, 6). The middle of the book declares the nearness of God's salvation, as God declares Zion's time of judgment past (Isa. 40:5 Old Greek; 45:17; 46:13). The speech shifts to first person (49–53). God announces that God will spread "salvation" to the nations through a first-person speaker (Isa. 49:6–8; 51:6–8; 52:7–10). The next concentration of the term comes in Isa. 60–62 (60:6, 16, 18; 61:10; 62:1). "Salvation" looks to a future renewed Zion as the center of the nations. The "salvation" from exile has occurred; "salvation" as the flourishing of "Zion" still stands in the future.

A new third-person voice connects these two notions of salvation. Isaiah 53:12 speaks of the suffering and execution of the first-person voice of Isa. 49–52. The narrator nonetheless looks for a future in which "I [the Lord] will allot him [the servant] a portion with the great and he shall divide the spoil with the strong; because he [the servant] poured out himself to death, and was numbered with the transgressors" (Isa. 53:12). The "servant of the Lord" accomplished salvation as deliverance; his death and future open into the future flourishing of Jerusalem (Isa. 60–62). The Isaiah Scroll looks to salvation, a present deliverance from past judgment for God's "servants" through a suffering "servant" that leads into a future flourishing Zion that includes gentiles.

The Torah moves from deliverance to flourishing in its use of *soterion*. Within narrative sections, salvation as "deliverance" predominates. Moses assures Israel that the Lord will deliver/save Israel from the pursuing Egyptian army (Exod. 14:13); the song following the demise of the Egyptian army states that the Lord "has become my salvation" (Exod. 15:2). "Salvation" in the Torah therefore also describes positively a particular type of sacrifice: the "salvation offering"—or as the NRSV translates the phrase, "the sacrifice of well-being" (see, for instance, Lev. 3).

It is a celebratory sacrifice, barbequed lamb with pan bread to be consumed in thanksgiving (Lev. 7:11–18), personally brought before the Tent of Meeting and shared with the officiating priest (Lev. 7:28–36). One participates in eating the body and bread of the "sacrifice of salvation" in thanksgiving. Salvation as deliverance brings Israel into the salvation-sacrifice of flourishing.

Soterion finally appears regularly within the Greek book of Psalms. The NRSV commonly translates the term as *deliverance* or *safety*—a present rescue from danger *and* the subsequent flourishing. God's "salvation" reaches into the lives of individuals (Ps. 69:29) and Israel (Ps. 85:1–4). "Salvation" can take on an undetermined future sense in some psalms (see, e.g., Pss. 12:5; 14:7; 37:39; 40:10; 85:4, 9; 119:41, 81, 123, 153, 174). In one case "salvation" even takes the individual beyond death (Ps. 69:19–20). As Schaper writes, Ps. 69 (MT) "was reinterpreted according to contemporary Jewish rules of textual hermeneutics, and its message now became that of an exodus even from within the boundaries of death" (90). "Salvation" in the Greek Psalter can involve God rescuing an individual and Israel now, in the future, and beyond death.

Salvation entails both a negative aspect (salvation from) and a positive aspect (salvation for). Positively and negatively, the word overcomes artificial dichotomies that have entered Christian ethical discourse from the early modern period on. Negatively, God saves from evil, personal *and* social; from suffering, individual *and* political; from death—even in its midst. Positively, salvation is both present *and* eternal; both within suffering *and* ultimately the cessation of suffering; both personal *and* communal; both deliverance and forgiveness from the past *and* healing and purity in the present and future. The negative and the positive characteristics of "salvation" set those "saved" apart from the perpetuators of sin, violence, death, and oppression within creation and in eternity. The concept thus is closely related to "sanctification" and "holiness" in the Christian Scriptures.

Salvation in the Christian Scriptures requires a eudaemonistic ethic—a concern for human deliverance leads to subsequent flourishing. Humans may flourish in the present, even amid suffering, but always look to an eschatological end that exceeds the suffering of "this age." The hinge for this flourishing, present and future, is Jesus Christ, who himself is God's salvation. Jesus defines the nature of the flourishing of human life on the other side of deliverance in his resurrection.

See also Eschatology and Ethics; Happiness; Liberation; Sanctification

Bibliography

Childs, B. "The Canonical Shape of the Prophetic Literature." *Int* 32 (1978): 46–55; Dunn, J. D. G. *New Testament Theology: An Introduction*. Abingdon, 2009; Schaper, J. *Eschatology in the Greek Psalter*. WUNT 2/76. Mohr Siebeck, 1995; van der Watt, J., ed. *Salvation in the New Testament: Perspectives on Soteriology*. NovTSup 121. Brill, 2005; Westermann, C. *Prophetic Oracles of Salvation in the Old Testament*. Trans. K. Crim. Westminster John Knox, 1987.

John W. Wright

1–2 Samuel

The books of Samuel were one book in the ancient Hebrew manuscripts, and they narrate the stories that move Israel from a loose tribal association to a small monarchy in the eleventh century BCE. Modern scholars understand these books as part of a larger edited narrative that tells Israel's story from entry into the land of Canaan to the destruction of Jerusalem and the start of the Babylonian exile in 587 BCE—that is, the books of Joshua through 2 Kings (excluding Ruth, which was placed after Judges in later Bibles). This narrative is edited together from multiple sources to form a continuous narrative. The process for this was complex and its description disputed, but almost all agree that some materials date close to the events of the period described, and that the process of editing and collecting was completed by editorial comments and shaping from a Deuteronomistic editor responsible for the final collection from Joshua to 2 Kings seeking to explain and interpret the end of Israel's history in exile.

The books of Samuel open in a time of internal and external crisis in Israel. The closing stories and final verse of the book of Judges suggest a situation of moral anarchy, as "there was no king in Israel" (Judg. 21:25). This is compounded by a story at the beginning of 1 Samuel that tells of corruption in the house of Eli, who with his impious sons served as priests for the sanctuary of the ark of the covenant in Shiloh (1 Sam. 2:11–17). The internal moral crisis is related to a crisis of leadership, and the birth of the prophet Samuel and the song of his mother, Hannah (1 Sam. 1:1–2:10), suggest that God is at work to answer the central question of the books of Samuel: "Who will lead Israel?"

The internal crisis is matched by an external threat in the form of the Philistines, Israel's aggressive and militaristic neighbors on their southern coast. This becomes a crisis threatening Israel's extinction when the Philistines invade Israelite territory, capture the ark, and occupy all of Israel's territory west of the Jordan River (1 Sam. 4–6). Such a threat is a factor behind the elders' demand for Samuel to "appoint for us . . . a king to govern us, like other nations" (1 Sam. 8:5) and the call and anointing of Saul to lead Israel against the Philistines (1 Sam. 9–10).

The remainder of 1–2 Samuel is dominated by three major figures whose stories are intertwined and overlapping: Samuel, the prophet who anointed the first two kings of Israel; Saul, Israel's first king, whose story ends in a tragic suicide; and David, Israel's second king, described as the "man after God's own heart" (1 Sam. 13:14) who later betrays his own promise by committing adultery and murder to satisfy his own desire (2 Sam. 11). Especially in 1 Samuel some stories seem to reflect a negative attitude toward kingship as a sinful rejection of God's rule, while other stories see kingship as the gift of God, probably reflecting the existence of a similar tension when kingship began for Israel.

The books of Samuel, like other narrative traditions in the OT, have not often been treated as material with significant theological or ethical importance. More attention has been paid to material with overt moral content, particularly if it addresses the norms of moral conduct. The books of Samuel usually are treated simply as historical narration of an important period of events establishing kingship in ancient Israel, and discussion often focuses on the reliability of its testimony.

The stories of 1–2 Samuel are actually better treated as historically realistic narrative with an intense theological testimony to God's providence as the true source of power in a transformative period of Israel's life. These narratives are not dispassionate history writing, but neither are they the saga-like narratives of the Pentateuch, where God is likely to appear and act as an overt character in the story. In the books of Samuel divine providence operates through human events and personalities, but the narration makes it quite clear that God is at work in and through the characters and events of the stories (see, e.g., 2 Sam. 5:10; 11:27b).

Several themes with theological and ethical significance can be identified in the books of Samuel:

1. In the course of transformative events in ancient Israel, God is at work subverting the usual arrangements of human power. Hannah's song at the beginning of the narrative (1 Sam. 2:1–10) and David's song at the end (2 Sam. 22:2–51) witness to God as one who overturns the world's customary power arrangements. God can allow the ark of the covenant to be captured by the Philistines and yet bring them low through the "hand of the Lord" without any human agency (1 Sam. 4–6). God can look on the heart and choose an eighth son, just a boy (1 Sam. 16:1–13), to become Israel's greatest king and the "man after God's own heart" (1 Sam. 13:14), yet who later will be confronted and judged by God's prophet (2 Sam. 12:1–15).
2. The nature of leadership of God's people requires more than personal charisma and human skill. Both Saul and David are legitimized not through their own power and authority or by the recognition of their abilities by the people. They are anointed by God's prophet and receive the indwelling of God's spirit as a result (1 Sam. 10:1–8; 16:13), so that even their achievements are understood in the narrative as manifestations of the power of God's spirit. That recognition of God's providential working through events is more crucial than human skill or power is clear in David's own statement during his retreat from Jerusalem during Absalom's rebellion: "If I find favor in the eyes of the Lord, he will bring me back" (2 Sam. 15:25).
3. There is a moral valuation attached to the contrast in the stories of the books of Samuel between the ability to receive power as God's gift and the exercise of power as a matter of grasping for oneself. David's early story shows a man of prayer constantly grateful for the providential gifts of God (1 Sam. 16–2 Sam. 10), but tragic consequences result from his use of power to grasp the objects of his own desire by taking Bathsheba and murdering her husband, Uriah (2 Sam. 11–18). Saul comes to his tragic end largely because he, constantly pursuing his own desire to control events, falls victim to his inability to trust what God is doing. His own anger, envy, and violence are his undoing (see 1 Sam. 18).

The books of Samuel are not occupied with the ethics of conduct made explicit through commandment, law, or admonition. The expression of divine will is not overt and direct. The narratives of Samuel are reflective of an ethics of character, which focuses on the working of divine providence in partnership with the workings of personality and power. We experience the successes and failures of moral character in these appealing and all-too-human characters and come away wiser in our efforts to perceive the workings of God's providence in our own lives.

See also Deuteronomistic History; Old Testament Ethics

Bibliography

Birch, B. "The First and Second Books of Samuel." Pages 947–1383 in vol. 2 of *The New Interpreter's Bible*, ed. L. Keck. Abingdon, 1998; idem. *Let Justice Roll Down: The Old Testament, Ethics, and Christian Life*. Westminster John Knox, 1991, pp. 198–239; Brueggemann, W. *David's Truth in Israel's Imagination and Memory*. Fortress, 1985; idem. *Power, Providence, and Personality: Biblical Insight into Life and Ministry*. Westminster John Knox, 1990.

Bruce C. Birch

Sanctification

The concept of sanctification brings together a constellation of terms in the Bible originating in the Hebrew root *qdš* and the Greek word *hagios*. English versions translate these terms with words having Latin (*sanct-*) or Germanic (*holi-*) roots. The basic meaning is "to set apart." The NT presupposes the use of "holiness" or "sanctification" in the OT. As Hannah Harrington observes, "Christianity owes to its Jewish parent its strong emphasis on ethical goodness as a component of holiness, its imitation of the divine model for the acquisition of holiness, and its dependence on the divine word as a guide for becoming holy" (205–6).

The first instance of *qodeš/hagios* in the Bible appears in the book of Exodus. The "holy ground" from which God summons Moses (3:5) becomes the site of God's call to deliver Israel (3:7–10). Before the Passover, God tells Moses to convoke a "holy" (NRSV: "solemn") assembly (12:16) as a "day of remembrance" (12:14). Likewise, Israel must "sanctify" (NRSV: "consecrate") their firstborn to God (13:2, 12) as a visible remembrance of God's deliverance. Sabbath, the seventh day, is "sanctified" in the wilderness (16:23) to remember the original order of God's good creation (see also 20:8). Sanctification becomes a means of remembrance.

The center of the sanctification of Israel comes in the covenant and the law (Exod. 19:1–24:18). God says, "If you obey my voice and keep my covenant, you shall be my treasured possession out of all the peoples. Indeed, the whole earth is mine, but you shall be for me a priestly kingdom and a holy nation" (19:5–6). The law is to set Israel apart from the nations as a witness to the God of Israel. Israel's sanctification becomes the goal of the law as the law becomes the means to exhibit Israel's God to the world.

Israel's sanctification requires a sanctified space, the tabernacle (Exod. 25–31; 35–39). The tabernacle itself has gradations of holiness, sanctified spaces within the sanctified space (26:33). At the very center is "the mercy seat on the ark of the covenant" (26:34). Physical barriers set the tabernacle apart. To enter it, one must wear holy clothing, and those who can wear such clothing are priests (28:3–4, 36, 40–43). The altar itself, upon which the priests cook the sacrificial meat, becomes set apart (29:37). God takes what humans set apart in obedience to the divine command and completes its sanctification with his own glory so that "they shall know that I am the LORD their God, who brought them out of the land of Egypt that I might dwell among them; I am the LORD their God" (29:44–46; cf. 40:34–38).

The book of Leviticus describes the goods that pass into and through the tabernacle. Only parts of sacrifices reserved for compensation for the priests (see 2:2–3, 10; 6:14–18; 7:1–6) and special donations (22:2–4, 6–7, 9–10, 12, 14, 15–16, 32) are "holy." The priests are commanded to "distinguish between the holy and the common, and between the unclean and the clean" (10:10); they must remain visibly set apart (see 21:6, 7, 8, 12, 15, 22, 23). Unclean and clean fall within a system of ensuring that the space remains functional as "set apart."

Leviticus further shows how Israel is also set apart for God through observing commandments involving diet, Sabbath observance, eating sacrifices as prescribed, caring for the poor, and sexual practices (see chaps. 11; 19–20, especially 11:44–45; 19:2, 8, 24, 30; 20:7–8). Participation in particular festivals and economics sanctifies Israel as well (see 23:2–4, 7–8, 20–21, 24, 27, 35–37; 25:5, 10, 12). The people of Israel must consecrate themselves to their God. As they do, God sanctifies them in their difference from the world to show his glory: "You shall be holy to me; for I the LORD am holy, and I have separated you from the other peoples to be mine" (20:26).

God prohibits Moses and Aaron from entering the promised land because of their refusal to sustain God's holiness in the wilderness (see Num. 20:12; 27:14). Deuteronomy 14:2 makes explicit what has been implicit previously in the Torah, that God's election of Israel is their sanctification: "You are a people holy to the LORD your God; it is you the LORD has chosen out of all the peoples on earth to be his people, his treasured possession" (see also 7:6; 26:19). The struggle of Israel to be holy as their God is holy (see Josh. 24:19) dominates the narrative that follows until Judah loses their land (see 2 Kgs. 25). Israel's sanctification remains commanded but unfulfilled.

The OT prophetic books, particularly Isaiah and Ezekiel, thicken the moral content and hope for the future sanctification of Israel. In the book of Isaiah, the God of Israel, the Holy One, "shows himself holy by righteousness" (5:16). Following God's judgment on Judah, the book speaks of a "Holy Way" "for God's people" to "come to Zion with singing" (Isa. 35:8, 10). Within the narrative structure of the book, God opens this Holy Way to a promised future Zion (chaps. 60–62). In this new Jerusalem Israel will be called "The Holy People, The Redeemed of the LORD" (62:12). After judgment, the Holy One of Israel leads the elect from exile through a Holy Way to an eschatological end in which they finally are made a "Holy People" (cf. Exod. 19:6).

The book of Ezekiel has a similar underlying narrative. Following exile from the land, Ezekiel looks to the future for Israel's sanctification. God declares that he has been the sanctified space, "a sanctuary to them for a little while in the countries where they have gone" from which God will regather them (11:16–17). God will gather them on his "holy mountain," promising, "I will manifest my holiness among you in the sight of the nations" (20:40–41; see also 28:25). God tells Israel that he will display his holiness through sprinkling "clean water upon you, and you shall be clean. . . . A new heart I will give you, and a new spirit I will put within you. . . . I will put my spirit within you, and make you follow my statutes and be careful to observe my ordinances" (36:23–27). This future is imaged through a future temple (chaps. 40–48) where Israel may participate in the sacrifices "and so communicate holiness to the people" (46:20). God will manifest his holiness through restoring the elect within a new temple.

The OT presents the sanctification of Israel as an unfinished but future task. The prophets look to a future in which Israel might be holy as their God is holy. This underlying narrative sets the stage for the use of sanctification in the NT.

In the Gospels Jesus is identified as "the Holy One of God" (Mark 1:24; Luke 4:34; John 6:69), and he teaches his disciples to pray to God, "Hallowed be your name" (Matt. 6:9; Luke 11:2). In John 17 Jesus prays that the Father will sanctify Jesus' followers "in truth; your word is truth" (v. 17). The sanctification of the believers depends upon Jesus sanctifying himself (v. 19), a reference to Jesus' voluntary death. Sanctification sets the disciples apart from the world to sustain their witness in unity as they are sent into the world (v. 18). Their sanctification arises from their participation in the love shared between the Father and the Son that sets the believers apart from the world for the sake of the world (vv. 21, 23).

The Pauline epistles, Hebrews, and 1 Peter provide the center of the NT's teaching on sanctification. Frank Matera observes, "The Pauline tradition portrays the church as a sanctified community, the body of Christ, the temple of God because it begins with Christ's redemptive death and resurrection. . . . For those who have been redeemed live in a sanctified community as they wait for the coming of their Lord" (448). All believers are in one sense already "sanctified" as they are baptized "into Christ Jesus" (see Rom. 6:3), so Paul addresses his letters to the "the saints." Yet, believers are to become what they have already been made through their own consecration: "Present your members as slaves of righteousness for sanctification" (Rom. 6:19; see also 6:22). Paul exhorts believers to an ethical distinctiveness as "set apart," much as the tabernacle was kept set apart as "pure": "Let us cleanse ourselves from every defilement of body and of spirit, making holiness perfect in the fear of God" (2 Cor. 7:1; see also 1 Cor. 3:17). Just as the tabernacle possessed degrees of holiness, so does the life of believers, who participate in God's holiness in Jesus Christ, "who became for us wisdom from God, and righteousness and sanctification and redemption" (1 Cor. 1:30). The sanctified life has a final end: "May [the Lord] so strengthen your hearts in holiness that you may be blameless before our God and Father at the coming of our Lord Jesus with all his saints" (1 Thess. 3:13). "Entire sanctification" prepares the believer to be kept "sound and blameless at the coming of our Lord Jesus Christ" (1 Thess. 5:23). As with the tabernacle, sanctification is completed by God, who takes the human consecration and fulfills it: "The one who calls you is faithful, and he will do this" (1 Thess. 5:24).

Later Pauline Epistles develop Paul's thought. Ephesians extends the call to holiness into the very eternal plan of God for human beings: "The God and Father of our Lord Jesus Christ . . . chose us in Christ before the foundation of the world to be holy and blameless before him in love" (1:3–4). Christ becomes the temple: "In him the whole structure is joined together and grows into a holy temple in the Lord; in whom you are also built together spiritually into a dwelling place for God" (2:21–22).

Hebrews likewise describes sanctification in OT imagery. Jesus becomes the high priest who sanctifies others (see 9:1–23): "The one who sanctifies and those who are sanctified all have one Father" (2:11). As the sacrifice himself, Jesus sanctifies those who participate in him: "For by a single offering he has perfected for all time those who are sanctified" (10:14; see also 13:12). Nonetheless, the sanctification of believers is not necessarily complete. Discipline comes so that "we may share his holiness" (12:10). The "apartness" that arises from participation in Christ again has an eschatological end: "Pursue peace with everyone, and the holiness without which no one will see the Lord" (12:14).

The Letter of 1 Peter interprets the beginning of the Sinai narrative, at Exod. 19:5–6, to develop its concept of sanctification. Sanctification comes in fulfillment of God's purpose in the giving of Torah through Christ: "You are a chosen race, a royal priesthood, a holy nation, God's own people, in order that you may proclaim the mighty acts of him who called you out of darkness into his marvelous light" (2:9). The Christian life forms desires profoundly different from the society around them: "Do not be conformed to the desires that you formerly had in ignorance. Instead, as he who called you is holy, be holy yourselves in all your conduct; for it is written, 'You shall be holy, for I am holy' " (1:14–16). To accomplish this end, the letter exhorts believers, "In your hearts sanctify Christ as Lord" (3:15).

Sanctification requires a "set apartness" from the "the nations" or "the world." Sanctification names the fulfillment of the divine law in the formation of the church and its particular members—those who live the fullness of God's deliverance from the evil and sinfulness of the world in preparation for participation in the eschatological end of all things in God. Ultimately centered in Jesus Christ by the Holy Spirit, sanctification names the process and the result of how the triune God moves the saints to their eschatological end; it characterizes the subsequent visible witness of the body of Christ in its moral and political difference from the nations, for the sake of the nations. Participation in the love that names the eternal unity between the Father and the Son, sanctification names the work of the Holy Spirit that cleanses the human life from sin and refills it with this love. Ethically, sanctification speaks of the reforming of the church's and the believer's desires from that given by the sinfulness of the world to that which God intended for human beings in their creation. The "sanctified difference" that results from this process ultimately takes on a Christoform shape in the believer, the true end of human life, but lives that look very different from the virtues, character, and practices of "the world."

See also Holiness; Salvation

Bibliography

Harrington, H. *Holiness: Rabbinic Judaism and the Graeco-Roman World*. RFCC. Routledge, 2001; Matera, F. *New Testament Theology: Exploring Diversity and Unity*. Westminster John Knox, 2007.

John W. Wright

Sanctity of Human Life

To speak of the sanctity of human life is to assert that all human lives are equally precious to God and are to be respected as such. As the French Catholic philosopher Jacques Maritain often pointed out, the sanctity and rights of human life ultimately rest in the fact that Christ became incarnate as a human creature, not as some other sort of creature. The doctrine of the incarnation involves God taking on human flesh in the person of Christ. Karl Barth wrote, "The respect of life which becomes a command in the recognition of the union of God with humanity in Jesus Christ has an incomparable power and width" (Barth 339). God became human and, in doing so, affirmed human life as unconditionally special and worthy of the gift of eternal life.

In addition to the incarnation, the sanctity of life has roots in Gen. 1:26–27, where human beings are described as created in the image of God to take caring dominion over other species. Being in the divine image, human life is to be especially protected (Gen. 9:6), and justice for the poor is required. Human beings are to be respected simply by virtue of being members of the human species and enjoying the special blessing of God.

The doctrine of the sanctity of life is grounded also in the idea of a human "soul" or "point of contact" between the human and God such that a unique relational reality exists that other species do not have. To our knowledge, nonhuman species do not pray.

Finally, the Christian tradition understands "pro-creation" as a participation in divine creation, whereby as humans we are involved in the creative action of God. "Pro-creation" is a very different concept than "re-production," for the former implies higher theological purpose in life's biological creation, whereas the latter is entirely secular and devoid of higher meaning. From the very beginning, a human life is deemed a part of divine creative action and, as such, is loved by God.

Human dignity is based in the prior assertion of the sanctity of life, and from this flow the ideals of rights and justice that define Western civilization. There is a dignity, significance, and sacredness that sets human life apart from other biological life and that warrants its special protection regardless of circumstance or condition. The Christian tradition has built its robust practice of civilization and moral decency on this lofty view of human worth;

as this view has deteriorated, the destruction of human life has become trivialized. In response, Christian thinkers have exhorted a "consistent ethics of life" that precludes abortion, infanticide, mercy killing, suicide, capital punishment, and the destruction of human lives generally, with the exception of carefully justified war.

Protestant ethicist Paul Ramsey extrapolated from the idea of the sanctity of life his classic arguments against the neglect of imperiled infants born with cognitive disabilities. Famously, Helen Prejean has extended the sanctity of life to arguments against execution; Jean Vanier has distinguished himself in the founding of L'Arche, a faith-based international program for the care of persons with developmental cognitive deficits. Quaker concerns with the fate of the mentally ill undergirded the emergence of compassionate and "moral treatment" in the 1820s (Tomes). Christian interest in persons with dementia has resulted in assisted-living reforms to humanize and dignify the lives of the deeply forgetful (Post). Concerns with economic justice, global poverty, AIDS prevention and treatment, access to healthcare, and adoption as an alternative to abortion are extrapolations from the bedrock principle that every human life has a special significance against the background of divine love, creation, and incarnation.

The Enlightenment philosopher Immanuel Kant attempted to base human dignity on rational autonomy, but this foundation fails to protect those in whom rationality has faded or developed only in small part. The idea of the sanctity of life has been challenged by philosopher Peter Singer, who denounces it as a form of "speciesism." As a result, Singer sanctions abortion, mercy killing, killing of the elderly, and infanticide, as long as these practices are carried out without causing pain. In the final analysis, his failure to appreciate the depth of the idea of the sanctity of life rests on metaphysical assumptions.

Some critics have attacked the idea of the sanctity of life on the grounds that proponents espouse a medical vitalism in which every possible means must be used to extend the lives of the terminally ill. In general, however, the ethic of the sanctity of life has included profound appreciation for hospice and options for palliative care as well as for distinctions between ordinary and extraordinary care. As Barth asserted, the sanctity of life does not make life "a second God."

In the absence of a robust sense of the sanctity of life, civilization cannot thrive. The secular alternatives neither adequately protect life nor commit us to its flourishing. Increasingly, the perennial idea of the sanctity of life, which has given to the world much of its moral progress, becomes more plausible as wanton violence has become routine and casual.

See also Abortion; Capital Punishment; Dementia; Disability and Handicap; Euthanasia; Healthcare Ethics; Humanity; Human Rights; Image of God; Incarnation; Killing; Suicide; War

Bibliography

Barth, K. *Church Dogmatics*. Vol. III/4. T&T Clark, 1961; Post, S. *The Moral Challenge of Alzheimer Disease: Ethical Issues from Diagnosis to Dying*. 2nd ed. Johns Hopkins University Press, 2000; Ramsey, P. *Ethics at the Edges of Life: Medical and Legal Intersections*. Yale University Press, 1978; Singer, P. *Writings on an Ethical Life*. Ecco Press, 2000; Tomes, N. *The Art of Asylum-Keeping: Thomas Kirkbride and the Origins of American Psychiatry*. University of Pennsylvania Press, 1994; Vanier, J. *Becoming Human*. Paulist Press, 1998.

Stephen Post

Sanctuary

Attending to the Scriptures

While the English word *sanctuary* can refer either to a sacred space or to a place of refuge, the Hebrew terms (*qōdeš, miqdāš*) designated the temple, where some aspect of God "dwells" among the Israelites. Because of God's presence, human action in the temple was regulated according to purity stipulations.

Temple architecture demarcated spheres of holiness. In the holy of holies and the courtyard that immediately surrounded it only the best materials could be used, and only certain priests could officiate. Nonpriests used outer courtyards, where the materials could be less "pure." All human participants in ritual had to be purified as well. One thing that contaminated a person was contact with a corpse (Num. 19:11–22). Because of this, slaying a person within a temple precinct was forbidden.

Priests maintained the purity of a sacred precinct by serving as judges of purity cases. Deuteronomy 17 assigns judicial duties to Levites, and Exod. 28 describes the use of the ephod in judicial decisions. Priests had the authority to kill anyone who attempted desecration of the sanctuary and to conduct trials decided by ordeal. They were also authorized to protect innocent people by providing them sanctuary or safety. In that way, the sacred space became also a place of refuge. In 1 Kgs. 1:50–53 we read of Adonijah's attempt to find safety within a sacred area until he has been rightfully judged (see also 1 Kgs. 2:28–34).

Biblical law, moreover, required the creation of cities run by Levitical priests that served as sites of refuge (see Exod. 21:13; Num. 35:9–15; Deut. 4:41–43; 19:1–13). There were six of these "cities of refuge," three on each side of the Jordan River. If the elders decided that the accused was innocent or that a death was accidental, the priests would protect the accused until the death of the high priest. This refuge was available not only for Israelites but also for resident aliens.

Although there is no mention of sanctuary as refuge in the NT, it was practiced in both ancient Greece and Rome. Within the postbiblical period, evidence of sanctuary first appears in the Edict of Toleration (313 CE), which identified certain churches as exercising legitimate sanctuary. These churches followed biblical principles: sanctuary lasted until due process could be carried out. The Justinian version of sanctuary (535 CE) notes that its purpose was to protect the security of the victims of injustice, and it often was used to protect people in the lower classes. It was applicable only for certain crimes, although in England in the early Middle Ages churches did have the right to grant mercy from execution to the guilty through restitution and penance. As time progressed, however, the right of sanctuary became increasingly limited until it was abolished by James I in 1625.

The Sanctuary Movement

The call for sanctuary was renewed by churches in the 1980s with the birth of the Sanctuary Movement. This movement combines the concept of sanctuary with the biblical teachings on the treatment of resident aliens and strangers. The OT offered significant legal protection for resident aliens. Although this practice of protection is found in other ancient Near Eastern law codes, the laws in the Pentateuch suggest that ancient Israel was more benevolent toward this social group. One of the clearest and most comprehensive statements protecting resident aliens is Lev. 19:33–34.

Although the NT does not mention sanctuary, some texts do focus on the treatment of "strangers." In Matt. 25:34–46 final judgment is based in part on how one has treated the stranger. Here the stranger, who needs shelter and safety, is associated with the hungry and thirsty—that is, those lacking basic human necessities. This stranger is someone with no local social ties and therefore particularly vulnerable to victimization. The parable of the good Samaritan features someone helping one such stranger (Luke 10:30–37).

Members of the Sanctuary Movement used these biblical texts in defense of their illegal offer of shelter to refugees from El Salvador and Guatemala. The Sanctuary Movement began formally in 1982 when several churches formed an underground railroad for these refugees. Under President Ronald Reagan, the United States, which provided military support to the ruling party in El Salvador, did not recognize these people as political refugees. Churches that opposed this policy offered asylum until such time as due process could be restored in their homelands. They argued that God's law, the command to offer sanctuary to the innocent and provide shelter to vulnerable strangers, outweighed civil law.

In the United States a number of people assisting in these efforts were arrested and convicted. In Latin America Christians acting on behalf of political prisoners were killed. Eventually these regimes fell, and the Sanctuary Movement receded into the background.

Churches have remained involved in immigration issues in this country. The New Sanctuary Movement asserts that the global economy renders countries such as the United States responsible for the economic injustice that compels many people to flee their homelands. Groups working in the New Sanctuary Movement aid illegal immigrants by leaving food and water in the deserts through which many enter the United States. They do so as a way to fulfill the biblical proscription to feed the hungry, provide water for the thirsty, and shelter the stranger.

See also Aliens, Immigration, and Refugees; Hospitality

Bibliography

Coutin, S. *The Culture of Protest: Religious Activism and the U.S. Sanctuary Movement*. Westview, 1993; Crittenden, A. *Sanctuary: A Story of American Conscience and the Law in Collision*. Weidenfeld & Nicolson, 1988; Cunningham, H. *God and Caesar at the Rio Grande: Sanctuary and the Politics of Religion*. University of Minnesota Press, 1995; Golden, R., and M. McConnell. *Sanctuary: The New Underground Railroad*. Orbis, 1986; MacEoin, G., ed. *Sanctuary: A Resource Guide for Understanding and Participating in the Central American Refugees' Struggle*. Harper & Row, 1985.

Corrine Carvalho

Science and Ethics

The Relations between Science and Ethics

The word *science* is understood in various ways. Science is broadly defined as a systematic body of knowledge. In that spirit, during medieval times theology was called the "queen of the sciences" because major thinkers, especially Thomas Aquinas, integrated revelation and natural reason to provide comprehensive accounts of the nature and being of God, relations between God and his creatures (including angels, humans, and animals), and between God and the world at large. Since the time of the scientific revolution of the seventeenth century, science is now understood in a more specific and more limited fashion. It refers to the systematic study of natural phenomena via rational empirical methods. More pointedly, it also refers to particular branches of such specialized knowledge, wherein the exploration of empirical phenomena leads to replicable and predictive generalizations according to basic principles and covering laws. In many fields of science, such principles and laws are rigorously formulated in mathematical terms. Thus, physics and chemistry are often viewed as "hard" sciences, while other fields, especially some social sciences, may be viewed as "softer" to the degree that they resist mathematical exposition. Moreover, in contrast to classical and medieval conceptions of science, modern science is characterized by a methodological reductionism: more complex natural phenomena are most appropriately explained in terms of underlying more basic components, processes, or mechanisms. The movement from a classical, primarily Aristotelian science to the modern scientific perspective, therefore, reflects a fundamental shift from a broadly teleological approach that focuses on an appeal to the final ends or purposes of entities to a perspective that views the world largely in mechanistic terms (Dijksterhuis). And although much recent discussion in the life sciences and in ecology eschews efforts to reduce biology, without remainder, to the laws of physics and chemistry that underlie the emergence of life, earlier metaphysical notions of teleology have not been reintroduced.

Ethics is defined as a systematic reflection on morality. Although the terms *morality* and *ethics* are often used synonymously, the latter is a more restrictive term: morality designates first-order experiences of moral choice and action, while ethics is a second-order reflection on the moral reasoning that informs and justifies such choices and behaviors. There are several types of ethics. Metaethics analyzes the status of moral terms—for example, the meanings of right and wrong, good and bad, virtue and obligation. Descriptive ethics, often done by anthropologists and ethnographers, provides accounts of the moralities of different communities and cultures in order to identify moral diversity or commonality, often depending on the predilections of the observer. Normative ethics focuses on the moral norms that should guide our moral choices and actions. In contrast to descriptive ethics, normative ethics is prescriptive in its intent; it seeks to justify particular moral choices and actions, often in situations of ambiguity or conflict. The issues raised by considerations of science and ethics generally fall within the domain of normative ethics.

The relations between science and ethics are best assessed by considering the epistemic warrants for scientific activity, as well as possible constraints on it. During much of the twentieth century, claims were made that science, as a rational activity that seeks to discover and systematize facts about natural phenomena, is entirely (or nearly) "value free," and that normative issues arise not with science itself but only with the technological applications of scientific knowledge. That stance held sway for several decades among scientists themselves, among philosophers known as positivists, and to significant extent among the public at large. Nonetheless, the insufficiencies of positivism have become clear over time. As its central tenet, positivism limited valid knowledge to the findings of logic and to claims that could in principle be scientifically verified. But it became evident, especially with the influence of the later Wittgenstein (see his *Philosophical Investigations*), that there are existential forms of justified belief (i.e., knowledge) that are warranted on extrascientific grounds, and that scientific knowledge is only one avenue for experiencing the world. For example, there are forms of experience and humanistic reflection upon them that, while unscientific, are nonetheless meaningful and appropriate objects of knowledge. Moreover, science itself cannot claim to be value-neutral. Philosopher of science Thomas Kuhn, in his seminal work *The Structure of Scientific Revolutions*, pointed out the inevitable contextuality of scientific paradigms and the importance of social and psychological factors in the acceptance of new theories. Others have noted that the scientific method necessarily presupposes certain epistemic norms about the forms and sources of knowledge to which it accords legitimacy (e.g., Rollin). Moreover, the technological applications of scientific research are inherently ethical. Given their size and scale, many modern technologies are necessarily the objects of societal deliberation and collective funding, and virtually all such technologies (e.g., nuclear energy, genetic engineering, nanotechnology) offer both benefits and risks that require careful ethical assessment.

Science and Ethics in a Theological Context

In the Christian tradition, the fundamental theological warrants for science as an appropriate activity are twofold: God is the creator of the world and humankind, and we are made in God's image and likeness. The meanings associated with humans as imagers of God in the Christian tradition include capacities that in some respects mirror the attributes ascribed to God and at the same time reflect our distinct status in the created order. Central to these interpretations are two dominant strands: our rationality as self-conscious and free creatures, and our dominion over creation. Both emphases provide the warrant for science as an activity to explore the created world, as well as to derive appropriate benefits from dominion over the world and its resources. But both emphases are also problematic. Rationality is not, in the first instance, the mere capacity to reason about means to any and all ends. Theologically, judgments about appropriate means require a prior acceptance of, and reasoning about, God's creative and sustaining purposes, which provide the general framework for particular moral judgments, including judgments about science and technology. And the concept of dominion is often misconstrued as the exercise of mastery or control, whereby nature is reduced to the merely manipulable object of human desire. As recent discussions in ecotheology remind us, the value of nature, though not independent of human agency and judgment, is not thereby reducible to its instrumental use by humans. Instead, a rational sense of dominion will include an appreciation and affirmation of the integrity of all creation, which maintains its own "goodness" as an aspect of God's creating and sustaining will.

Within an expressly theological context, science emerges as our rational inquiry into the patterns of God's order, as well as our partnership with God as stewards and cultivators of the natural world. One finds, classically in Augustine and Thomas Aquinas, and notably in the writings of believing scientists since the time of the seventeenth century, a strong affirmation of what has come to be called the "Two Books" tradition about the sources of our knowledge of God (Barbour). In Scripture, the first book, God provides, through the history of Israel and the coming of Christ, God's self-revelation as Father, Son, and Spirit. Nature, the second book, also provides its own witness to the patterns of God's creative, ordering, and sustaining will as revealed in nature and its regularities. This natural knowledge of God, available to all persons of goodwill, is a central theme of Jewish wisdom literature and is also fundamental to Paul's judgment about the universal moral accountability of all humans (see Rom. 1). Preeminently in the Scholastic tradition, Thomas Aquinas spoke of certain naturally available facts about the world that bespeak God as creator and orderer as "preambles" to faith, accessible to all persons by the light of natural reason (*ST* I, q. 2, a. 2).

Theologically construed, the relations between science and ethics pose several concerns. First, the warrants for science as a rational inquiry into nature, including human nature, necessarily raise prior questions about "created nature" itself. What is the status of nature as the handiwork of God? What are the connections between nature as currently "given" and God's original purposes in creation? What have been the effects of sin on the natural order and, perhaps more crucially, on the efficacy and appropriateness of human rationality in exploring that order? Second, what are the scriptural warrants for, and limits on, human responsibility in exploring and controlling created nature when analyzed according to the broad norms of conservation, stewardship, and created cocreation? Third, of what relevance are various metaphors, especially that of "playing God," to debates about human interventions into and alterations of the created order? Finally, what areas of current and prospective scientific and technological exploration raise specific ethical concerns within a theological framework of interpretation and assessment?

The Status of Created Nature

It is inaccurate to speak of a univocal Christian perspective on the warrants for, and limits on, the scientific study of nature and the appropriate applications of technology, since a range of perspectives and assessments can be identified both within and across various traditions. At the same time, several shared Christian emphases serve to distinguish these perspectives, writ large, from secular approaches. That general distinctiveness is hardly surprising; one would expect that the idea of *created* nature, interpreted in light of God's purposes, would transform nonreligious accounts of nature as an independent domain, with possible implications for judgments about the appropriateness of particular scientific and technological pursuits.

Consider the range of Christian perspectives on created nature, with implications for the legitimacy of particular scientific and technological pursuits. Nature may be viewed as intrinsically valuable ("God saw everything that he had made, and indeed, it was very good" [Gen. 1:31]). This perspective situates humans as stewards of creation, according to God's initial purposes. At the same time, nature may also be seen as fundamentally disordered as the result of sin. In light of the deleterious effects of the fall on both external nature and human reason, this emphasis may reinforce the importance of humility and caution in dealing with nature.

Alternatively, accounts that view nature as a relatively trustworthy source of insight may emphasize the appropriateness of human beings responsibly working as partners with God's good purposes. For example, in traditional Roman Catholic moral theology, reasoning about the appropriate pursuit of human goods establishes a set of natural law–based duties. Catholic perspectives are often judged to be conservative because natural tendencies and forms of human flourishing have traditionally been interpreted in relatively static fashion. However, a number of recent Catholic discussions have proceeded in more historicist terms, with an emphasis on the dynamics of human responsibility in an evolutionary universe (e.g., Fitzgerald).

In historical contrast to the traditionally positive appraisal of nature in the Roman Catholic tradition, classical Protestant thought has been less prone to appeal to nature as a source of moral insight because of its disordered character as the result of sin and because of the moral ambiguities that attend human efforts to alter or reconstruct natural givens. This more literally conservative vision emphasizes the need to be responsible stewards of the orders of creation, as well as the likelihood of human hubris in the desire to deny our finitude (e.g., Hanson; Niebuhr). Here, the metaphor of "playing God" is invoked in largely negative fashion as the illegitimate effort of humans to usurp God's prerogatives by confusing remediable suffering with the conditions of our creaturehood. Such traditional cautions, however, are countered in recent Protestant discussions by an emphasis on a more positive and capacious role for humans in repairing, restoring, and even improving created nature. Some perspectives (Hefner; Peters) emphasize the duties incumbent on human beings as "created cocreators" of the human future with God. From this vantage point, the dialectic between the fall and creation is interpreted in far more optimistic terms, with the emphasis on the goodness of a continuously evolving creation rather than the depravity of the human condition. Here, the metaphor of "playing God" is invoked quite positively as an appropriate celebration of human creativity, which is seen as the primary attribute of humans as imagers of God.

The Art of Technology Assessment

There are three broad levels of inquiry at which the effects of technology can be analyzed (McKenny). At a first level, discussion focuses, either currently or prospectively, on particular devices and techniques. A second level of discourse considers the range of social practices that are altered by the introduction of new technologies. At this level, we are assessing not simply a particular invention or technique, but the ways that its introduction reframes our cultural understandings. At a third level are broad discussions of technology as an entire way of relating to the world. At this level, one finds analyses and, quite often, critiques of technology for its characteristic willingness to reduce the natural world to the malleable object of human mastery. All three levels are of interest to both secular and theological ethical analysis, but the second level is perhaps the most fruitful way to focus the distinctive concerns posed to, and the distinctive contributions offered by, theological perspectives on science, technology, and ethics. At this level, the central normative issues that arise are not simply whether it is appropriate to alter nature or to what extent, but more complex questions about how nature is being altered and toward what end. Thus, ethical judgments about which technologies should be pursued or forgone will invariably be linked to other broad understandings, including perspectives on God's creative and sustaining purposes, the appropriate relations to be maintained between nonhuman and human nature, the scope of justified human responsibility, and basic issues of justice in the distribution of likely benefits and burdens of new technologies.

Four broad areas of technology have been the subjects of significant recent theological discussion and debate: reproductive technology, somatic-cell nuclear transfer (cloning), developments in genetic therapy and enhancement, and human-machine incorporation technologies (Lustig, Brody, and McKenny). The particulars of these debates are beyond the scope of this article, but a number of theological ethical concerns emerge as common themes in the various discussions. First, the ways that nature is perceived will influence judgments pro or con. Is nature, as a given, linked closely to God's creative and ordering will, with the subsequent emphasis primarily on conservation or restoration as our duties of stewardship? Alternatively, is nature viewed in more dynamic and open-ended fashion, with a subsequent emphasis on remaking the world as the appropriate expression of human partnership as created cocreators? Second, and obviously linked to the first question, what central themes in Christian anthropology do we bring to bear on our reflections about particular technologies? To what extent has sin affected the natural order, including our own natural capacities to identify and accomplish the good? In light of such judgments, what implications follow concerning our interventions into, and alterations of, the natural world, including the physical basis of our own humanity? Where does the burden of proof lie in decisions about whether to encourage, regulate, or ban certain types of research activity? Finally, as a matter of theological method, how does the Christian tradition best honor the integrity of its own deepest convictions when assessing issues in science and technology? Given its understandings of God's purposes and of human nature, in a particular case, which of several strategies—prophetic resistance, thoughtful accommodation, or creative reinterpretation—emerges as the most appropriate expression of traditional Christian commitments?

See also Artificial Intelligence; Bioethics; Creation Ethics; Ecological Ethics; Humanity; Image of God

Bibliography

Barbour, I. *Religion and Science: Historical and Contemporary Issues*. Rev. ed. HarperOne, 1997; Cahill, L., ed. *Genetics, Theology, and Ethics: An Interdisciplinary Conversation*. Crossroad, 2005; Dijksterhuis, E. J. *The Mechanization of the World Picture: Pythagoras to Newton*. Trans. C. Dikshoorn. Princeton University Press, 1986; Fitzgerald, K. "The Need for a Dynamic and Integrative Vision of the Human for the Ethics of Genetics." Pages 79–96 in *Genetics, Theology, and Ethics: An Interdisciplinary Conversation*, ed. L. Cahill. Crossroad, 2005; Hanson, M. "Indulging Anxiety: Human Enhancement from a Protestant Perspective." *ChrBio* 5 (1999): 121–38; Hefner, P. *The Human Factor: Evolution, Culture, and Religion*. Fortress, 1993; Kuhn, T. *The Structure of Scientific Revolutions*. 3rd ed. University of Chicago Press, 1996; Lustig, A. "Are Enhancement Technologies 'Unnatural'? Musings on Recent Christian Conversations." *AJMG* 151C (2009): 81–88; Lustig, A., B. Brody, and G. McKenny, eds. *Religion, Biotechnology, and Public Policy*. Vol. 2 of *Altering Nature*. PM 98. Springer, 2008; McKenny, G. "Technologies of Desire: Theology, Ethics, and the Enhancement of Human Traits." *ThTo* 59 (2002): 90–103; Niebuhr, R. *The Nature and Destiny of Man*. 2 vols. Prentice-Hall, 1964; Peters, T. *Playing God? Genetic Determinism and Human Freedom*. 2nd ed. Routledge, 2003; Rollin, B. *Science and Ethics*. Cambridge University Press, 2006; Wittgenstein, L. *Philosophical Investigations*. Prentice-Hall, 1973.

B. Andrew Lustig

Security

The complex of definitions surrounding the term *security* reveals its usefulness, diverse applications, and slipperiness as a term. One can speak of physical security (e.g., freedom from the threat of harm), metaphysical security (comfort in one's relationship with God), psychological security (self-confidence), political security (the ability of a state to protect its citizens), economic security (freedom from concerns about changes in the market, a deposit that one gives as collateral toward the fulfillment of a pledge), and so on. One can locate security concerns at individual, family, community, nation, state, international, and global levels and apply it to contexts as diverse as military strength, adequate food supplies, the tenure system in higher education, the protection of personal information shared via the internet, systems of economic security for retirees, and the use of home alarm systems to protect property and people. Across all these definitions, levels, and contexts, however, are shared basic connotations about a sense of freedom to pursue one's purposes and protection from the vicissitudes of life.

Although most of these meanings and contexts are addressed both in Scripture and by Christian ethicists, the primary foci of attention have been national and personal security, in part due to their emphases in the OT and NT, respectively.

National security concerns the ability of a nation to protect itself from both external and internal threats. Those threats can take many forms—for example, famine, disease, political instability, invasion—but nations have tended to focus security concerns on their ability to maintain sovereignty. Painting in the broadest of strokes, we might order the history of national sovereignty as a long age of sequential empires followed by an era of unstable equilibrium in which many states attempted to coexist through balance of power arrangements, which itself has been replaced by projects of collective security in which states band together to ward off the threats of either opposing collectives (as in the Cold War) or nonstate actors. It is a question of current investigation as to whether we are entering yet another era. Spanning a longer period of time and giving special attention to the relation between God and Israel, the OT repeatedly connects national security to national fidelity: when Israel is faithful to its God, it exists as a state; when it pursues its own plans for power and security, it falls. The prototypical example here comes in Proto-Isaiah, in which Israel seeks to maintain its own security by making alliances with surrounding nations against the growing threat of the Assyrian Empire. God sides against Israel for its failure to trust in divine protection, and the result is exile.

Coming together during a time of Roman occupation, the NT radically deemphasizes the importance of national security, building instead a vision of security that can be found only by participation in the kingdom of God. Neither force of arms nor economic power can ensure safety, and in most NT examples such an approach to security is treated not only as a refusal to trust God but also as a failure to understand the transience of this life and the dangers of those who would destroy body and soul. Thus, Matt. 10:28 warns, "Do not fear those who kill the body but cannot kill the soul; rather fear him who can destroy both soul and body in hell," and Luke 12:16–21 treats the rich man who builds bigger barns as a fool for not being aware of his own impending death.

As the church came into closer contact with sources of political power, eventually becoming a political power itself with responsibilities for those within and around it, it found itself in the awkward position of attempting to reformulate its thoughts on security in such a way as to maintain consistency with its early teachings while supporting those institutions that promoted security. Never reaching consensus on either the value or the direction of such reformulations, Christians nevertheless have developed a wide-ranging literature that analyzes the importance and limitations of pursuing security, whether of persons or communities, bodies or souls.

Several tensions recur throughout these analyses of security. Are we more secure when we are independent or when we are interdependent? Must we make trade-offs between structures that promote freedom and those that ensure security, and if so, how thoroughgoing must those trade-offs be and what justifies them? Do political manifestations of religion make states less secure, or, given the apparent permanence of religious inclinations in people, does the squelching of such political manifestations have the effect of promoting instability? Given both the inevitability of death and the responsibilities of faithful stewardship, how important ought security be to any of us in the first place?

See also Economic Ethics; Freedom; Government; Property and Possessions

Mark Douglas

Self

At its most basic level, the self is the subject or referent of the English word *I*, when that word figures in such thoughts as these: "I am not feeling well today" or "I hope we get some rain today." The human self is, in the first instance, that which is not feeling well and, in the second instance, that which hopes for rain. What is the nature of the self? Is the human self a material being, an immaterial being, or a compound of both? Is the human self the sort of thing that endures or persists through time and change, or is what we think and call the same human self actually a concatenation of many selves bound together by overlapping psychology or consciousness? In the Christian tradition, questions about the nature of the human self include questions not only about its metaphysical nature, whether it is material or immaterial, but also about its origins, purpose, and end, whether the self can survive death, as well as questions about how the human self is related to God and to the rest of nature, and its moral obligations both to other human selves and the natural world more broadly.

The relation of soul and body became a subject of intense theological speculation from the earliest days of the church, and such speculation continues to this day. Marcion of Pontus (c. 84–160), an early thinker who eventually was excommunicated from the church for his views of Scripture and his denial of the incarnation of Christ, posited a stark dualism of soul and body. Marcion's rejection of the incarnation stemmed largely from his outright contempt for the material world.

Manichaeus of Manes (c. 216–76) described the cosmos as being embroiled in a battle of good and evil, where the good is spiritual and the evil is material. With respect to the human self, Manichaeus viewed the good spiritual soul as being trapped in the evil material body.

Augustine of Hippo (354–430), who went to great lengths to reject the moral dualism of Manichaeus (spiritual/immaterial good versus material evil), nevertheless retained a metaphysical dualism of soul and body, as did Thomas Aquinas (1225–74), John Calvin (1509–64), and even, it has been argued, Karl Barth (1886–1965). Although each retained a dualist view of the human self, their "holistic dualism" of "embodied souls or ensouled bodies" differed in important respects from the straightforward dualism of thinkers such as Plato and René Descartes, both of whom seem to have identified the human self with an immaterial soul housed in a material body.

Although the majority of Christians and Christian thinkers continues to embrace some form of dualism (for recent book-length defenses of dualism, see Taliaferro; Hasker; Moreland and Rae; Cooper), some are embracing various forms of anthropological physicalism. Among Christian philosophers, Peter van Inwagen, Trenton Merricks, Lynne Baker, and Kevin Corcoran defend views of the human self as a wholly physical object with no nonphysical parts such as an immaterial soul. According to van Inwagen and Merricks, human selves are human animals or physical organisms. What most would identify as the biological body of a human person or self, van Inwagen and Merricks identify as the self itself. Both, however, believe in the Christian doctrine of resurrection of the body, and neither denies that God and the angels are immaterial or nonphysical selves. Lynne Baker and Kevin Corcoran, however, defend a "constitution view" of the human self, according to which the human person or self is a wholly physical object but not the object that is one's body or organism. According to Baker and Corcoran, the human self is constituted by one's organism without being identical with that organism.

Among contemporary theologians who defend versions of a "nonreductive physicalism" are Nancey Murphy and Joel Green. Nonreductive physicalists deny the existence of immaterial souls (hence the "physicalism" part in nonreductive physicalism), and the "nonreductive" part refers to a denial that our mental lives can be reduced to, or are wholly and exhaustively, the outworkings of neurochemical discharges inside our heads.

It has been argued that views of the human self that emphasize the centrality of embodiment, whether holistic dualism or nonreductive physicalism, make more sense of the Christian doctrines of creation, incarnation, and resurrection of the body than do their dualist counterparts, and they can also help to ground Christian moral obligations to steward the earth and its nonhuman inhabitants, to feed the hungry, clothe the naked, and so on.

Although the metaphysical nature of the human self in Christian theology and philosophical theology has received no small amount of attention, it is the identity, flourishing, and destiny of the human self that receives the most attention and concern in the Scriptures (e.g., Gen. 1–2), as well as in Christian theology itself. In this regard, God is understood as triune, three persons or selves—Father, Son, and Holy Spirit—in intimate, trinitarian relations. And the scriptural portrait of authentic human selfhood is likewise relational insofar as it consists in a fully embodied life rightly—that is, ethically lived in relation to God, neighbor, and the rest of the terrestrial world. The identity of the human self, therefore, is to be found in relation to God and others, and it is in the context of these embodied relations that humans flourish, both now and forever.

See also Body; Dualism, Anthropological; Humanity; Image of God; Monism, Anthropological

Bibliography

Baker, L. *Persons and Bodies: A Constitution View*. CSP. Cambridge University Press, 2000; Cooper, J. *Body, Soul, and Life Everlasting: Biblical Anthropology and the Monism-Dualism Debate*. Eerdmans, 2000; Corcoran, K. *Rethinking Human Nature: A Christian Materialist Alternative to the Soul*. Baker Academic, 2006; Green, J. *Body, Soul, and Human Life: The Nature of Humanity in the Bible*. Baker Academic, 2008; Hasker, W. *The Emergent Self*. Cornell University Press, 2001; Merricks, T. *Objects and Persons*. Oxford University Press, 2003; Moreland, J., and S. Rae. *Body and Soul: Human Nature and the Crisis in Ethics*. InterVarsity, 2000; Murphy, N. *Bodies and Souls, or Spirited Bodies?* CIT. Cambridge University Press, 2006; Taliaferro, C. *Consciousness and the Mind of God*. Cambridge University Press, 2005; van Inwagen, P. *Material Beings*. Cornell University Press, 1995.

Kevin Corcoran

Self-Denial

The term *self-denial* rarely appears in Scripture, but Jesus attests to its significance as a Christian virtue: "If any want to become my followers, let them deny themselves and take up their cross and follow me" (Mark 8:34 pars.). Such close proximity to the cross places self-denial at the heart of the Christian moral imagination. Pauline theology elaborates this cruciform theme when noting that "all of us who have been baptized into Christ Jesus were baptized into his death" (Rom. 6:3). Baptism marks the person as dying and rising with Christ so that it is "no longer I who live, but it is Christ who lives in me" (Gal. 2:20).

In the early church, taking up one's cross meant martyrdom. Later, ascetics took up the cause of self-denial by fleeing civilization and its comforts for the desert, where they committed themselves completely to God. During the Middle Ages, monasticism maintained the ideal of self-denial for the sake of Christ through vows of poverty, chastity, and obedience. In the Reformation era, self-denial emerged from the monastery, becoming the religious responsibility of all Christians rather than the supererogatory practice of the spiritual elite. For John Calvin, the sum of the Christian life was denial of self (*Institutes* 3.7.1–10). For Martin Luther, God's grace through Jesus Christ liberated Christians from self-concern, allowing them to serve God and neighbor wholeheartedly. Within Protestantism, self-denial was no longer reserved for those who fled civilization and its rewards; it became a general norm for all Christians amid their various roles and responsibilities.

Throughout the ages, many have cautioned against confusing the virtue of Christlike self-denial with the vices of self-hatred and world-rejection. In the modern era, however, the virtue of self-denial itself came under scrutiny from both inside and outside the Christian fold. In the nineteenth century, Friedrich Nietzsche condemned Christianity as a slave morality, born of resentment, which delegitimized the heroic, assertive morality of the natural aristocracy in favor of the servile passivity of the masses. In the twentieth century, many feminist and liberation theologians have argued that, although the virtue of self-denial may critique the sinful pride of the powerful, it also reinforces structures of inequality by encouraging oppressed groups to embrace self-abnegation. They have disparaged self-denial as a Christian virtue, favoring mutuality as a more profound and appropriate Christian ideal.

In an age characterized by a culture of self-interested individualism as well as structures of social and economic inequality, self-denial is both an important part of the Christian witness and a concept open to potential misuse and abuse. A proper understanding of this Christian virtue requires renewed attention to the cross as a model for the Christian life. After all, Jesus neither preached nor practiced asceticism and self-abnegation (cf. Luke 5:33–35). Rather, he proclaimed, in word and deed, self-denial for the sake of a higher cause, "the year of the Lord's favor" (Luke 4:14–21).

See also Asceticism; Cruciformity; Martyrdom; Self-Love

Bibliography

Daly, L., ed. *Feminist Theological Ethics: A Reader*. Westminster John Knox, 1994; Luther, M. *The Freedom of the Christian*. Fortress, 2008; Nietzsche, F. *Thus Spoke Zarathustra: A Book for All and None*. Cambridge University Press, 2006; *The Rule of St. Benedict in English*. Ed. T. Fry. Vintage Books, 1998.

Timothy A. Beach-Verhey

Self-Esteem

William James described self-esteem as "the ratio of our actualities to our supposed potentialities." By this he meant that we gain our global sense of self-esteem through our ability to positively evaluate successes within aspects of our lives that have personal significance, and to live comfortably with those aspects of our lives within which we have less success but which have less personal significance. In this understanding, self-esteem is assumed to be a global concept—that is, a concept that impacts a person across the board in all areas of life. However, it is possible to have good self-esteem in one area of one's life and to have less in another. So, for example, I may gain much self-esteem from being a good father but have less self-esteem when it comes to being faithful in my prayer life or in my spiritual devotions. Self-esteem is thus seen to have both global and particular aspects to it. George Mead developed an idea originally put forward by Charles Cooley: the self as a "looking-glass self." By this he means that it is the ways in which individuals appraise significant others that enable them to gain or lose self-esteem. In this understanding, the attitudes and values of significant others are internalized and used to construct one's sense of self and self-esteem. Self-esteem is thus perceived to be a matter of perception: it is how you perceive yourself in the "looking glass" of significant others (and society) that adds or takes away from your self-esteem.

Theologically, self-esteem is a complicated idea that sits in the tension between self-praise and humility. Theologians such as Reinhold Niebuhr have associated self-esteem with self-love, pride, and original sin. However, to attribute esteem to the self is not necessarily an act of sin or pride. Jesus commands self-love, aligning it as a vital dimension of loving God and neighbor (Luke 10:27). To love one's self is to recognize one's status as made in the image of God. While humility remains a primary mark of discipleship (Phil. 2:3), self-love is clearly an important aspect of living life in all of its fullness (John 10:10). However, the love of self is not a personal achievement. It is not self-actualization or the bringing to fruition of our hidden potential. Self-esteem relates to the internalization and recognition of God as the primary "significant other," the acknowledgment of God's love and grace for all people (John 3:16) and the embodiment of that love in the lives of the Christian community. It is God's love and grace that provide the global basis for self-esteem, and faithful Christian friendship that provides a conduit for discovering a positive image of the self (John 15:15).

Self-esteem is thus seen to be both gift and action: a recognition of the value that one has in the eyes of God and the ongoing action of allowing that knowledge to form us in ways that protect us from assessments of ourselves that are overly negative. Such an understanding allows us to encounter disappointment in ourselves (negative self-esteem in aspects of our lives) but always to recognize such disappointment in the sure and certain knowledge that, at the global level, God's love remains a primary and continuing source of self-esteem. Maintaining self-esteem at the global and particular levels and dealing with the inevitable fluctuations in both is thus seen to be an integral aspect of healthy spiritual development.

See also Humility; Love, Love Command; Meekness; Pride; Self-Love

Bibliography

Cooley, C. *Human Nature and the Social Order*. Scribner's, 1902; James, W. *The Principles of Psychology*. 2 vols. Dover, 1950 [1890]; McGrath, J., and A. McGrath. *Self-Esteem: The Cross and Christian Confidence*. Crossway, 2002;

Mead, G. *Mind, Self, and Society: From the Standpoint of a Social Behaviorist.* University of Chicago Press, 1934; Niebuhr, Reinhold. *The Nature and Destiny of Man: A Christian Interpretation.* Scribner's, 1941.

John Swinton

Self-Harm

Self-harm is the act of deliberately inflicting some form of physical injury to oneself. It is also sometimes called "self-injury," "self-mutilation," or (less often and causing far more stigma) "parasuicide." Self-harm can be done by actions directly injuring one's body, by putting oneself in dangerous situations, or by neglecting aspects of one's life and person. Examples of self-harm include cutting, burning, picking, scratching, biting, hitting, banging the head, and pulling hair. Self-harm also includes things such as deliberately putting oneself at risk, self-neglect, substance abuse, overdosing, self-poisoning, and disordered eating (behaviors related to anorexia and bulimia but not diagnosable as an eating disorder).

It is not possible to make blanket statements about the reasons for engaging in self-harm. The reasons are as diverse as the people engaging in it. Moreover, the same person may engage in self-harm for different reasons at different times. Nevertheless, there are rationales for self-harm commonly cited by those who do so. Self-harm can provide escape or distraction from feelings of emotional pain or from the physical manifestation of those feelings. Again it may be that the act of self-harming, rather than being an escape from such feelings, actually provides a physical manifestation of feelings. Self-harming also provides escape from feelings of emptiness or unreality. It is an effort to overcome feelings of numbness; self-harm enables people at least to feel *something*—anything. It seeks relief from overwhelming anger or/and emotional or physical tension. It provides physical expression of inexpressible emotional or physical tension. It satisfies the feeling that one deserves to be punished. It is an effort to eliminate bad memories; seeing blood flow or feeling flesh burn may be like watching bad things being flushed away, particularly in relation to abuse. It provides a means by which one feels to be in control; often, the choice of how and when to inflict self-harm is the only thing that such persons feel they have any control over in their lives.

From the perspective of those engaging in self-harming behaviors, it may be easier to state what self-harm is not. It is not an attempt to get attention. Most people who self-harm actually try to hide their injuries. Self-harm is also not "just" a failed suicide attempt. Many people who harm themselves see it as a way of actually staying alive, using it as a means to stave off suicidal feelings and thoughts or to prove to themselves that they are actually still alive (this is linked to the feelings of numbness).

Reflecting theologically on the experience of self-harm requires care and sensitivity. For example, the Gerasene demoniac in Mark 5:1–20 certainly seems to offer an example of self-harming. He appears to be in a good deal of emotional pain that manifests itself in loud expressions of deep sorrow, feelings of alienation, confusion over identity, and a desire to self-harm. However, while there are similarities, it would be an error to associate self-harm with demonic possession. At heart, self-harm is best understood as a form of communication within situations in which a person feels deep hurt and/or confusion, anger, sadness, and isolation but discovers that none of it can be spoken; it is too much for language to articulate. This, combined with feelings that no one can or will hear their words, leads sufferers to a different form of language. The behavior, as noted, should not be seen as an effort to get attention. Rather, it can be more helpful to think of it as a *need* for attention, as a desperate attempt to communicate deep emotional wants and needs that people do not know how to begin to communicate in words. Pastorally, the task is to learn to listen to the language of self-harm. Jesus took time to learn the name of the Gerasene demoniac. He recognized his need and heard him in all of his fullness. Pastorally, like the apostles struggling to understand the meaning of Jesus' scars (Luke 24:36–42), the task is to learn the meaning of wounds, actions, silence, and scars so that genuine healing becomes a possibility and hope becomes a reality.

See also Abuse; Body; Harm; Mental Health

Bibliography

Alderman, T. *The Scarred Soul: Understanding and Ending Self-Inflicted Violence.* New Harbinger Publications, 1997; Johnstone, L. "Self-Injury and the Psychiatric Response." *Feminism & Psychology* 7 (1997): 421–26; McLane, J. "The Voice on the Skin: Self-Mutilation and Merleau-Ponty's Theory of Language." *Hypatia* 11, no. 4 (1996): 107–18; Miller, D. *Women Who Hurt Themselves: A Book of Hope and Understanding.* Basic Books, 2005; Pattison, E., and J. Kahan. "The Deliberate Self-Harm Syndrome." *American Journal of Psychiatry* 140 (1983): 867–72; Rieth, S. "Scriptural Reflections on Deafness and Muteness as Embodied in the Healing Journeys of Adult Survivors of Sexual Abuse." *JPastT* 3 (1993): 39–52; Strong, M. *A Bright Red Scream: Self-Mutilation and the Language of Pain.* Viking, 1998.

John Swinton, Jay Brownlee, and Elizabeth Lynch

Selfishness

In modern discourse, the opposition of selfishness to altruism is sometimes taken to be the first problem to be faced in ethical reflection: before I can begin to consider what moral obligations I might have to others, I must give an account of why I should recognize any obligation to anyone other than myself (Woolcock).

In recent decades this problem has been given a new twist by evolutionary biologists theorizing the origins of human and animal behavior in neo-Darwinian terms. Their point of departure is some theoretical work famously popularized by Richard Dawkins in *The Selfish Gene*. This offers evolutionary explanations of altruism, defined by biologists as behavior by one individual that enhances others' chances of survival and reproduction at the expense of the individual's own. As theorists from Darwin on have recognized, altruistic behavior is an evolutionary puzzle: an inherited predisposition to "lay down one's life for one's friends" (John 15:13) would seem, by definition, less likely to be passed on to future generations than a predisposition to selfish behavior, yet altruistic behavior is observed in many species of animal, including some insects. The theory of "kin selection" states that if the beneficiaries of the altruistic behavior are close kin, they are likely to share many of the same inherited characteristics, so if their survival and reproductive chances are sufficiently enhanced by the behavior, a "gene for" altruism could survive and spread in the population. The concept of "reciprocal altruism" extends the discussion beyond kin, essentially offering a sophisticated theoretical argument that a strategy of "You scratch my back and I'll scratch yours" can enhance the survival and reproductive chances of both parties.

In the literature on evolution and ethics, distinctions are not always clearly observed between (1) explaining the phenomena of moral behavior, (2) investigating whether and to what extent evolution has given humans either a natural understanding of moral norms or a natural capacity for moral behavior, and (3) inferring moral norms from supposed facts about human evolution. This literature has also been criticized for, among other things, a simplistic and overly determinist view of the link between genes and behavior, speculative theorizing supported by relatively little hard evidence, and a proneness to ideological bias (e.g., Rose and Rose). With these caveats, how might a biblically rooted theological ethic respond to evolutionary accounts of selfishness and altruism?

In terms of explanation, kin selection and reciprocal altruism end almost exactly where a Christian understanding of neighbor love begins: "If you love those who love you, what credit is that to you? For even sinners love those who love them. . . . But love your enemies, do good, and lend, expecting nothing in return" (Luke 6:32–35). Christians are not, of course, the only ones who have noticed this, and various evolutionary explanations of "genuine" (i.e., nonreciprocal, nonkin) altruism have been proposed. None, however, commands a general consensus, and more generally, opinion is divided on whether, and to what extent, either our moral understanding or our moral behavior has evolutionary roots.

The literature on evolution and ethics is also divided on the extent to which human evolution has given us either a natural capacity for altruism or a natural understanding of right and wrong, and on whether moral norms concerning altruistic behavior can be inferred from an understanding of its evolution origins. Christian responses vary as well. Some authors, particularly those taking some form of natural-law approach, hold that evolution has given us a natural "moral sense" (Arnhart), or that an evolutionary account of human nature "makes a modest but real contribution" to our understanding of the content of moral obligations such as neighbor love (Pope 249). Few of these authors, though, would suggest that evolutionary insights can be incorporated uncritically into a Christian ethic. Others are more suspicious of any claim that either a natural moral understanding or a natural capacity for moral behavior results from human evolution. Those influenced by Karl Barth, for example, might suspect that reliance on natural moral understanding or goodness will turn out to be a form of pride, which will simply alienate us from the God on whom we must rely for the true knowledge and strength that we need (Messer, chaps. 4–5).

In a Christian ethic, the problem of selfishness and altruism must in any case be reframed. The concept of altruism is a secularized and arguably distorted version of what the Christian tradition understands by the love of neighbor. As Alasdair MacIntyre (228–29) has argued, the opposition of selfishness to altruism presupposes a peculiarly modern view of ourselves as individuals whose interests are always potentially in competition with those of others. In a Christian perspective, which connects our love for our neighbor with our love for God (Mark 12:28–34 pars.) and presents both as responses to, and reflections of, God's love for us, the shortcomings of the concept of altruism become clear. To use "altruism" as a category with which to describe either God's love for us or ours for God seems to imply that God has interests that are potentially in conflict with those of his human creatures—a very odd way, to say the least, to speak of the God whom Christians worship.

If this is correct, then the command "You shall love your neighbor as yourself" (Lev. 19:18; Mark 12:31) should not be read through the lens of selfishness and altruism. Certainly, the love that is commanded is self-giving and potentially costly; that is clear, if we are called to reflect a divine love made visible in Jesus Christ, who laid down his life for his friends (cf. John 15:13). But it is not best understood in terms of a competition in which either my interests trump my neighbor's (selfishness) or vice versa (altruism). Nor is the kind of self-love condemned in texts such as 2 Tim. 3:2 adequately characterized as selfishness in this distinctively modern sense. It is better understood as an aspect of idolatry, in which the love and devotion that properly belong to God are misdirected to that which is not God, with destructive results. Appreciating this might also help us to understand those voices in the Christian tradition that have held that there can be a rightly ordered love of self (e.g., Thomas Aquinas).

See also Agape; Altruism; Golden Rule; Individualism; Justification, Moral; Love, Love Command; Neighbor, Neighbor Love; Self-Love

Bibliography

Arnhart, L. "The Darwinian Moral Sense and Biblical Religion." Pages 204–20 in *Evolution and Ethics: Human Morality in Biological and Religious Perspective*, ed. P. Clayton and J. Schloss. Eerdmans, 2004; Dawkins, R. *The Selfish Gene*. Oxford University Press, 1976; MacIntyre, A. *After Virtue: A Study in Moral Theory*. 2nd ed. Duckworth, 1985; Messer, N. *Selfish Genes and Christian Ethics: Theological and Ethical Reflections on Evolutionary Biology*. SCM, 2007; Pope, S. *Human Evolution and Christian Ethics*. NSCE 28. Cambridge University Press, 2007; Rose, H., and S. Rose, eds. *Alas, Poor Darwin: Arguments against Evolutionary Psychology*. Jonathan Cape, 2000; Thomas Aquinas. *ST* II-II, q. 25, a. 4; Woolcock, P. "The Case against Evolutionary Ethics Today." Pages 276–306 in *Biology and the Foundation of Ethics*, ed. J. Maienschein and M. Ruse. CSPB. Cambridge University Press, 1999.

Neil Messer

Self-Love

Self-love has maintained an ambiguous yet key presence in Christian ethical discourse from early church leaders through contemporary ethicists and theologians. Most classical Christian theologians, including Augustine and Thomas Aquinas, locate the flourishing of self, the fulfillment of a natural self-love, in direct relationship with love for God. They posit that a proper love for self as God's creation would lead to the glorification of and right relation with God. These theologians stress Jesus' summary of the laws of Israel with his commandment to love God and neighbor as self (Matt. 22:37–40; Mark 12:29–31; Luke 10:27). They also highlight mutual relations within the Trinity as a model for reciprocal relations between self, God, and neighbor. Catholic traditions have maintained this thread despite the minority who practice asceticism, or self-denial, to achieve spiritual perfection.

The Protestant Reformation brought new emphasis on God's sovereignty, extravagant grace, and human depravity, dissolving the direct link between love of God and self-love. Further, the salvific role of faith separated the moral life from one's status before God, with ultimate import placed on Christ's self-sacrificial love. Thus, self-love came to be held in suspicion and associated with negative characteristics such as selfishness, egocentrism, narcissism, pride, and vanity. Anders Nygren not only regarded self-love as entirely pernicious but he also viewed it as the basic human moral problem. Reinhold Niebuhr also equated self-love with pride and original sin. Some Protestant thinkers emphasize biblical accounts of excessive, negative self-love, such as Sarah's expulsion of Hagar (Gen. 21), Jacob's theft of Esau's birthright (Gen. 25), and David's murder of Uriah (2 Sam. 11), as well as general exhortations against self-seeking (Ps. 119:36; 1 John 2:12). They note, moreover, that the Pauline Letters particularly privilege models of humility and self-denial (1 Cor. 13:5; Phil. 2:3).

While many modern and contemporary theologians and ethicists have cast self-love in a more neutral light, seeking balance among love of self, God, and neighbor, they often functionally elevate God and neighbor, with self-love assuming the lowest priority and self-sacrificial love for God and neighbor idealized. Feminist theologians, such as Judith Plaskow, Beverly Harrison, and Darlene Fozard Weaver, have argued that constant self-abnegation violates women by reinforcing their second-class status; indeed, they regard self-denial as often women's sin. Christian feminists suggest a retrieval and update of classical Catholic teachings by rejecting any oppositional or separate relations between love of self, God, and neighbor.

Self-love as conceived in this way assumes a prominent role in certain ethical frameworks. Virtue, narrative, liberation, and feminist ethics concern themselves with self-flourishing within communal contexts. These models do not set autonomy or self-sufficiency as ideals but do seek to wed self-flourishing and communion to the common good within a theological framework, rendering self-love and morality inextricably intertwined.

See also Happiness; Love, Love Command; Neighbor, Neighbor Love; Pride; Self-Denial; Selfishness

Bibliography

Augustine. *Confessions.* Trans. H. Chadwick. Oxford University Press, 1991; Niebuhr, R. *The Nature and Destiny of Man: A Christian Interpretation.* Scribner's, 1941; Nygren, A. *Agape and Eros.* Trans. P. Watson. SPCK, 1953; Plaskow, J. *Sex, Sin, and Grace: Women's Experience and the Theologies of Reinhold Niebuhr and Paul Tillich.* University Press of America, 1980; Weaver, D. *Self Love and Christian Ethics.* NSCE 23. Cambridge University Press, 2005.

Julie Mavity Maddalena

Sermon on the Mount

The Sermon on the Mount (Matt. 5:1–7:12) is the largest block of Jesus' teaching in the NT and the most frequently referred to teaching in the church's early centuries (Kissinger 6). Surely, Jesus' Great Commission (Matt. 28:19–20), calling us to make disciples and teach them "to obey everything that I have commanded you," especially includes these teachings.

Ways of Interpreting that Lead to Evasion

Yet something is wrong. Harvey McArthur shows an enormous amount of rationalizing, evading, and accommodating in the usual ways of interpreting the Sermon on the Mount:

1. *Literal interpretation applied universally and absolutely.* Love is nonviolent, sacrificial, self-emptying, dying to self and rising to walk in newness of life, practicing servanthood in community. But many interpret the sermon idealistically: never be angry, never resist evil, merely allow whatever injustice is done to us. This strikes people as impossible in real life, so they call it "hard teachings" and devise ways to evade Jesus' teachings.
2. *Hyperbole.* Clearly Jesus uses hyperbole in Matt. 5:29: "If your right eye causes you to sin, tear it out and throw it away." But this applies only to the passages that are hyperboles. It is no excuse for watering down and rationalizing away the sermon, which is intended quite directly and seriously.
3. *General principles.* Surely, "Go also the second mile" applies to our context even if no Roman soldier requires us to carry his pack one mile. Therefore, many derive principles from what Jesus teaches concretely and apply them to today's context. But human nature often dilutes Jesus' command into a vague principle that loses its concrete meaning. A historically concrete hermeneutic will see Jesus' teachings in their full historical concreteness, anti-Roman hostility and all, without reducing them to a thin principle, and will carry the full concrete story over to our present situation, letting it take concrete shape in our historical context, with our own particular hostilities.
4. *Double standard.* As Constantinian Christianity compromised with the world, the notion developed that many of Jesus' teachings were only for monks who were seeking perfection, not for laypeople. Luther criticized the medieval double-standard ethic severely but did not see how he could advocate not resisting evil. So he split public and secular life from inner and private life and said that in public life, "You do not have to ask Christ about your duty. Ask the imperial or the territorial law." Others have similarly split actions from attitudes and said that the sermon applies to attitudes but not to actions.

   The result of these false splits was to block Jesus' teachings from real application and to render the gospel impotent in dealing with pogroms against Jews, the Holocaust, slavery, segregation, world hunger, economic injustice, and nuclear idolatry. It renders the public realm secularized, opens the door to rationalizing, and violates Jesus' first basic principle, which is that we are to serve God wholeheartedly and not money or other gods.

   By contrast, the Sermon on the Mount splits those who actually do Jesus' commands and have their house built on the rock from those who do not do them and are headed to destruction. There is no third category for those who have good attitudes but do not do the teachings.
5. *Repentance.* This view considers the Sermon on the Mount, the Ten Commandments, and the ethical teachings of the Bible as law and opposes this to gospel. The Sermon on the Mount brings us to repentance because we cannot live up to it, but once we repent and accept forgiveness, we are free without the law, without actually doing what the sermon says.

   This opens the door to a wide field of rationalizing and blocks the sermon from actually guiding our lives. Surely, the sermon does bring us to repentance when it is taken seriously, and the more we live by forgiveness, the more we can take the sermon seriously without flinching, even though we fail at times. Those who actually do these teachings have their house built on the rock (Matt. 7:16, 21, 24).

Peter Stuhlmacher points out that the NT throughout assumes the incumbency and practicality of the commands of Jesus; they are to be obeyed by Christians. Paul himself says that keeping the commands of God and obeying the law of Christ are essential for Christians (Rom. 8:3–8; 1 Cor. 7:19; 9:21; Gal. 6:2).

6. *Interim ethic* (Albert Schweitzer) and *dispensationalism* (J. N. Darby). Jesus expected the end of history to come very quickly and so intended his absolute love ethic only for the short interim before the end of history. We know, however, that history did not end that way, and so we have to fashion an ethic with more realism in it.

   Or, we know that Jesus' ethic was intended for a future dispensation, an ideal world without sin, where there is peace, not for us in our time. For now, we need an ethic not based on Jesus' teaching that only those who do the will of God as Jesus teaches it enter the kingdom of heaven. Strangely, this agrees with the liberal Schweitzer that God's kingdom is not already at hand, already happening, but is totally future, and so we need to live by another ethic than that of Jesus.

   But in fact the Sermon on the Mount is based on a realistic view of the world, where we know poverty, anger, murder, lust, idolatry, deceit, hate, hypocrisy, beams in our eyes, people taking each other to court and to severe punishment, judgment and self-righteousness, captivity to mammon (money), people not following the narrow path and going to their destruction. Where did anyone get the idea that Jesus was teaching only for an ideal world with no sin in it? He was teaching for a world that needs God's deliverance. God is already forgiving, already being merciful, already feeding the hungry, already speaking through Jesus, already shining his sun and sending his rain on the just and the unjust. Jesus nowhere said that his ethic was valid only if God would end the world soon. His ethic was based on God's nature, presence, and righteousness—a present reality.

The Sermon on the Mount as Transforming Initiatives of Deliverance

Until recently, the Sermon on the Mount usually was interpreted idealistically as antitheses, as if it prohibited being angry, lustful, and so on. Then it was seen as high ideals or hard teachings. So it was evaded, as noted above, or simply not preached or taught.

In fact, the structure of the Sermon on the Mount in Matt. 5:21–7:12 is not dyadic antitheses; rather, it is triadic transforming initiatives of proactive deliverance: not "hard teachings," but the way of deliverance. The consistent pattern is this: first, traditional righteousness; second, diagnosis of a vicious cycle; third, transforming initiatives that perform like mustard seeds of the reign of God breaking in.

Matthew 5:21–26 begins by citing the traditional righteousness, "You shall not murder." Second, Jesus diagnoses the vicious cycles of being angry and calling someone a fool. These are expressed in Greek participles diagnosing an ongoing practice. The NT gives no command against being angry; Jesus became angry at times (Matt. 21:12–13; 23; Mark 3:5). Third, Jesus commands us that when there is anger, we should go to our adversary and make peace. This is not a high-ideal prohibition but rather the realistic way of deliverance.

Matthew 5:27–30 begins with "You shall not commit adultery." The vicious cycle consists of looking at a woman with lust (expressed with a participle in the Greek text). Then comes the transforming initiative: "If your right eye causes you to sin, tear it out and throw it away." This is a dramatic exaggeration for impact, a hyperbole. I suggest that it means "Cut out the practice that is leading you to be looking with lust," such as meeting this woman secretly or looking at pornography.

Matthew 5:38–42 begins with the traditional teaching about retaliating with an eye for an eye. Then comes the diagnosis and proscription of the vicious cycle, which should be understood as "not to be retaliating revengefully by evil means." The apostle Paul also gives the teaching that way in Rom. 12:17–21. Translating Jesus' words in Matt. 5:39 as "Do not resist an evildoer" does not fit the Greek; does not fit Jesus' practice of resisting Pharisees, money changers, and Peter (Matt. 16:23); and misinterprets Jesus as teaching impossible ideals.

Then comes the climax, the four transforming initiatives. (1) Turning the other cheek is not merely complying with injustice. In Jewish culture, where there was no soap, it was forbidden to touch someone with your left hand, which was used for personal hygiene. So a right-handed slap on the right cheek was a backhanded insult, saying, "You dog! You nothing!" Turning the left cheek was turning the cheek of equal dignity. It was a nonviolent initiative confronting the injustice. (2) In biblical teaching, if you took someone's coat as collateral for a loan, you had to return it every night so that the owner had something warm to sleep in when it got cold. If a greedy person unjustly sues for the coat, and you give your cloak as well, you stand there naked, confronting the greed nonviolently, hoping that the embarrassment leads to repentance. (3) When the Roman soldier forces you to carry his pack one mile—a symbol of unjust foreign occupation—you go a second mile, probably conversing on the way as Matt. 5:21–26 suggests, nonviolently confronting the injustice. (4) When a beggar begs for money, thereby confronting you with your greed, give, but also lend. Jesus never teaches mere compliance with something that you are forced to do; he always teaches a nonviolent transforming initiative aimed at a relationship of justice and peacemaking.

Matthew 5:43–48 begins by relating a traditional teaching from the Dead Sea Scrolls: "You shall love your neighbor and hate your enemy." This vicious cycle fails to exceed the righteousness of the tax collectors and gentiles. The transforming initiative is to love your enemies and pray for your persecutors "so that you may be children of your heavenly Father," who includes the just and the unjust in his gift of sunshine and rain.

The sentence that climaxes the first six transforming initiatives in English translations is "Be perfect, therefore, as your heavenly Father is perfect" (Matt. 5:48). Idealism interprets this as a mandate to live up to high ideals. However, it makes no sense biblically to say "as your heavenly Father lives up to high ideals"; there is no ideal above God for God to live up to. Jesus is saying that God is complete or inclusive in love, giving sun and rain to the unjust as well as the just. What Jesus means is this: "Be complete (in your love), as your heavenly Father is complete in loving enemies." Luke 6:36 agrees: "Be merciful, just as your Father is merciful."

Matthew 5:21–7:12 follows this threefold pattern consistently for fourteen teachings, with one exception. (Note that Jesus' genealogy in Matt. 1:2–17 is three times fourteen generations, with one exception.) In all fourteen teachings the main verb in the first part is consistently a future or a subjunctive; the vicious cycle is always expressed with a continuous-action verb (participle, infinitive, or indicative); the transforming initiative is always expressed as an imperative, always an initiative of deliverance, never an idealistic prohibition. This much consistency surely is intentional: Jesus' teachings are grace-based transforming initiatives of deliverance, not idealistic antitheses.

The NRSV mistranslates Matt. 7:13–14 idealistically, as if Jesus teaches that the road is "easy" that leads to destruction, and the road is "hard" that leads to life. The Greek text, however, contrasts a wide road with a narrow road. Jesus says, "My yoke is easy, and my burden is light" (Matt. 11:30). A life of truthfulness, love, peace, and sobriety is actually an easier life than one of deceit, hate, violence, and drunkenness.

See also Beatitudes; Kingdom of God; Matthew

Bibliography

Allison D. C., Jr. *Studies in Matthew: Interpretation Past and Present*. Baker Academic, 2005; Carter, W. *What Are They Saying about Matthew's Sermon on the Mount?* Paulist Press, 1994; Guelich, R. *The Sermon on the Mount: A Foundation for Understanding*. Word, 1982; Hendrickx, H. *The Sermon on the Mount*. Rev. ed. Geoffrey Chapman, 1984; Kissinger, W. *The Sermon on the Mount: A History of Interpretation and Bibliography*. Scarecrow Press, 1975; Lapide, P. *The Sermon on the Mount: Utopia or Program for Action?* Trans. A. Swidler. Orbis, 1986. McArthur, H. *Understanding the Sermon on the Mount*. Harper, 1960; Stassen, G. "The Fourteen Triads of the Sermon on the Mount: Matthew 5:21–7:12." *JBL* 122 (2003): 267–308; idem. *Living the Sermon on the Mount: Practical Hope for Grace and Deliverance*. Jossey-Bass, 2006.

Glen H. Stassen

Seven Deadly Sins

The seven deadly sins traditionally are listed as pride, envy, wrath, avarice, sloth, gluttony, and lust. This precise group of sins does not appear in the Bible. There are few points of commonality between the seven deadly sins and key passages that delineate the varieties of sin (e.g., Prov. 6:6–19; Matt. 15:19–20; Rom. 1:28–32; Gal. 5:19–21; Col. 3:5–8; 2 Tim. 3:2–4; 1 Pet. 4:2–5; 2 Pet. 2:12–22). The seven sins often are understood as the negative implications of the command to love one's neighbor as oneself.

The categories came to prominence in the monastic context as part of the struggle against disruptive passions and the cultivation of virtue. This tradition may stem from the monks' early reflection on Luke 11:24–26, in which an exorcised evil spirit joins up with "seven other spirits more evil than itself" before possessing another person. Evagrius of Pontus's ascetical writings expound the spiritual dynamics of "eight kinds of evil thoughts" (gluttony, impurity, avarice, sadness, anger, acedia or sloth, vainglory, and pride) and recommend mental, spiritual, and physical disciplines to combat them. John Cassian's instruction manual for monks provides extensive exposition of the same eight in order to explain "the roots and natures of sins" to help those seeking purity of heart. Explicit battle against these seven enemies (sometimes allegorically linked with driving out the seven powerful nations listed in Deut. 7:1) was essential to spiritual progress. Gregory the Great reduced the number from eight to the traditional seven, reorganized the sequence, added envy to the list, and elevated pride to the principal vice as the "queen of sins" and "root of all evil." He also suggested a close psychological progression between the vices. The other deadly sins spring from the "poisonous root" of pride, which begets envy, which generates anger, which deteriorates into melancholy, which turns into avarice, which produces gluttony, which in turn fosters lust. In this way, the seven underlying dispositions are shown to be the "capital" sins, since they stand at the head of other sins that proceed from them.

In medieval theology, explaining the rationale for the traditional scheme (why there were seven, why these particular vices, why a certain order within the sequence) became a standard topic. For example, Thomas Aquinas argues that pride, gluttony, lust, and avarice express disordered human inclinations toward specific created goods, while sloth, envy, and anger represent the substitution of true goods for false ones (*ST* I-II, q. 84).

The seven deadly sins played a central part in penitential and catechetical literature throughout the medieval period, but their importance diminished dramatically for Protestants after the Reformation, partly owing to their lack of biblical foundation. The seven deadly sins have held a firm place in the imagination of Western culture, providing a shared moral vocabulary for evil, ranging from Dante's *Divine Comedy* (c. 1300), Chaucer's "Parson's Tale" (c. 1390 [unversified epilogue to *The Canterbury Tales*]), and Hieronymus Bosch's painting *The Seven Deadly Sins and Four Last Things* (1485), to Kurt Weill and Bertolt Brecht's satirical ballet *Seven Deadly Sins* (1933), C. S. Lewis's poem "Deadly Sins" (1964), and films such as *Se7en* (1995).

See also Anger; Gluttony; Greed; Jealousy and Envy; Lust; Passions; Pride; Sin; Sloth; Vice; Vices and Virtues, Lists of

Bibliography

Bloomfield, M. *The Seven Deadly Sins: An Introduction to the History of a Religious Concept, with Special Reference to Medieval English Literature*. Michigan State College Press, 1952; Bossy, J. "Moral Arithmetic: Seven Sins into Ten Commandments." Pages 214–34 in *Conscience and Casuistry in Early Modern Europe*, ed. E. Leites. Cambridge University Press, 1988; Cassian, J. *Monastic Institutes*. Saint Austin Press, 1999; Evagrius of Pontus. *The Monk: A Treatise on the Practical Life* [*Praktikos*]. Pages 91–114 in *Evagrius of Pontus: The Greek Ascetic Corpus*, trans. and ed. R. Sinkewicz. OECS. Oxford University Press, 2006; Fairlie, H. *The Seven Deadly Sins Today*. University of Notre Dame Press, 1979; Gregory the Great. *Morals on the Book of Job*. Vol. 3, part 2, book 31. J. H. Parker, 1850; Wenzel, S. "The Seven Deadly Sins: Some Problems of Research." *Speculum* 43 (1968): 1–22.

Jeffrey P. Greenman

Sex and Sexuality

The terms *sex* and *sexuality* can be confusing, especially as used in the twenty-first century. Most people now concede that sex as gender—that is, as what constitutes masculinity or femininity—is strongly influenced by cultural and historical context and thus is socially constructed. Although related concepts of sex as maleness and femaleness are rooted in biological difference and therefore are less fluid, among contemporary theologians the ethical significance of our dimorphism remains under discussion, particularly with regard to issues such as homosexuality and women's roles in church and society. The term *sex* also signifies intercourse or other physically intimate interactions.

Most broadly, sexuality connotes the fact that our humanity entails embodiment; we are created with a profound desire to be physically, socially, psychologically, and emotionally intimate with one another. However, in modernity sexuality attained heightened importance. For example, despite continued controversies over Sigmund Freud's work, his focus on sexual drive unalterably shaped assumptions and discussions about the centrality of sex in our relationships; now many assume that sexuality (including but not limited to sexual preference and orientation) is key to our personal identity and thus to our fulfillment as humans. Neither gender nor personal sexual identity as we now understand them is a major concern of the biblical world, and thus we cannot demand Scripture to address such issues directly. Nonetheless, Scripture offers both guidance and caution as we approach sex and sexuality from our own sociohistorical context.

The Church's Teaching on Sex and Sexuality

Many assume that the Christian tradition has a negative, prudish, and unenlightened view of sex. In fact, the inheritance in the Western church is quite mixed; even Augustine, who often is blamed for this trend, is not consistent in his views. Although there is no shortage of offensive statements about women specifically and human sexuality generally, over the millennia theologians have consistently affirmed at least two aspects of God's created order related to this topic/issue.

First, men and women together image God in their difference and sameness. In this sense, Christianity acknowledges what current discussions of gender often note: our sex remains important even though also fluid and perhaps mysterious. Second, this unity of persons most commonly involves physical expression that flourishes in a faithful and fruitful marriage. These convictions spring from the creation narrative in Gen. 1:26–31, which is clear that God created women and men together in his image and likeness. Despite difficulties of interpretation and application of Scripture in our own era, these basic insights provide contours for discussing sex and Christian ethics.

Scriptural Resources for Sex and Sexuality

Although the first creation narrative in Genesis and a few other OT texts, such as Song of Songs, provide a positive account of sex and sexuality, Scripture speaks surprisingly little about these topics. In contrast to the focus on sexual sin in some Christian circles, or on sexual satisfaction in others, the Bible remains relatively uninterested in the morality of sex per se (as opposed, e.g., to consistent and ample calls for justice for the poor across both Testaments). This in itself should temper our postmodern tendency to grant too much to sexual expression, either as dangerous to true spirituality or as crucial for human fulfillment.

The NT writers, despite a socioreligious inheritance that emphasized marriage, family, and limited roles of women in faith communities, offer new proposals for understanding sex and sexuality, such as a concern for women's welfare in divorce (Mark 10:2–5) and the affirmation of their role in the early church (e.g., Acts 16:14–15; Rom. 16:3, 7). Paul's reiteration of the baptismal formula in Gal. 3:28, "There is no longer . . . male and female; for all of you are one in Christ Jesus," beckons us to live now as "new creation" established by the risen Christ (2 Cor. 5:17–18). Although gender difference clearly remains, it no longer sustains enmity or supports hierarchy.

Rather, the members of this richly diverse community care for one another, and thus the community witnesses to the transforming power of God (1 Cor. 12:12–27). Marriage provides a commonly chosen context in which believers practice such love, as it habituates us to fidelity, patience, and cooperation. Sexual intercourse ritualizes and enhances this partnership of unity in difference and, if it is to be fulfilling, requires seeking not only one's own pleasure but also that of the other. Although church tradition consistently affirms that sexual intercourse is limited to marriage for unitive and procreative purposes, the NT rarely mentions the importance of childbearing in marriage (see 1 Tim. 2:15; 5:14); welcoming children is but one way that marriages enact the Christian community's commitment to hospitality and openness to the stranger.

However, unlike the OT, which presents sexual difference as being primarily for sexual expression in intercourse, the views expressed in the NT, particularly those of Jesus and Paul, take a different approach (Matt. 19:11–12; 1 Cor. 7:8, 32–33). In this alternative community women and men partner for the sake of the kingdom. "Healthy" sexuality does not necessitate being "sexually active"; celibacy becomes an expression of fidelity to God's good work in the world, not a denial of God's gift or intention for creation.

Conclusion

The Genesis story contains seeds of the good news of Christ's salvation of men and women together in the new creation, but the fall and its aftermath remind us of the force of sexuality and thus its potential before Christ's return to be used as a weapon rather than as a means of intimate affection or faithful love. Rather than mutually tending God's creation, the intimacy of man and woman fractures amid shame (Gen. 3:7) and blame (Gen. 3:12–13); mutuality gives way to hierarchy (Gen. 3:16). More than encouraging stories of partnership, Scripture contains disturbing stories of how sex easily becomes a weapon or opportunity for greedy self-indulgence (Judg. 16:18–19; 19:22–20:7; 2 Sam. 11; Mark 6:17–28).

Scripture's witness regarding sex and sexuality is more complex than delineating roles for men and women or rules for sexual behavior. Instead, Scripture recognizes that our physicality—our gendered nature as well as our biological, social, psychological need to be intimate with others—is given in the creation itself. As such, our sex and sexuality provide occasions for faithfulness in our relationship to God and neighbor. In doing so, Scripture still speaks prophetically to our culture and reminds us that God intends our sexuality as a resource for the community as well as a source of personal joy. Yet it realistically cautions us that our own or others' sin often warps our sexuality. Like food and taste, sex and sexuality are not simplistically good or bad. Rather, for sex to nourish and sustain our relationships, we must control our desires and temper our drives. If we do so, we can savor and delight in our sexuality, giving thanks to the God who offers such rich gifts.

See also Body; Celibacy; Gender; Homosexuality; Image of God; Sexual Ethics; Women, Status of

Bibliography

Balswick, J. K., and J. O. Balswick. *Authentic Sexuality: An Integrated Christian Approach*. IVP Academic, 2008; Grenz, S. "Theological Foundations for Male-Female Relationships." *JETS* 41 (1998): 615–30; Hollinger, D. *The Meaning of Sex: Christian Ethics and the Moral Life*. Baker Academic, 2009; May, W. "Four Mischievous Theories of Sex: Demonic, Divine, Casual, and Nuisance." Pages 186–95 in *Perspectives on Marriage: A Reader*, ed. K. Scott and M. Warren. 3rd ed. Oxford University Press, 2006; Roberts, C. *Creation and Covenant: The Significance of Sexual Difference in the Moral Theology of Marriage*. T&T Clark, 2007; Trible, P. *God and the Rhetoric of Sexuality*. Fortress, 1978; Volf, M. "Gender Identity." Pages 167–90 in *Exclusion and Embrace: A Theological Exploration of Identity, Otherness, and Reconciliation*. Abingdon, 1996.

Erin Dufault-Hunter

Sex Discrimination

Sex discrimination refers to prejudice or favoritism that prevents some people from gaining employment or access to resources or excludes them unfairly because of gender.

Male domination of women contradicts God's original intention for humankind as described in the creation narratives of Genesis. In Gen. 1:27–31 God creates both men and women in the image of God and commands them to "be fruitful and multiply" and to cooperatively share dominion over all creation, which God has given to them. Genesis 2 describes how humankind is incomplete without both sexes. God shapes Eve from Adam so that he might have "bone of my bones and flesh of my flesh" (v. 23); their relationship is intimate, and in their nakedness they "were not ashamed" (vv. 21–25). However, these blessings are lost with the onset of sin. Rather than subdue the earth and enjoy its fruit, Adam suffers painful toil because the earth will produce "thorns and thistles" for him (Gen. 3:18). Rather than fruitfully multiplying throughout the earth, childbirth becomes ridden with pain and difficulty. Adam and Eve no longer share the same intimacy, but now hide their shame with clothing (Gen. 3:7). She is no longer his helpmate, and they no longer share in the task of dominion as equals because she has become the object of his rule (Gen. 3:16). Ultimately, their original glory as the image of God is tarnished by their rebellious desire to become "like God" (Gen. 3:5, 22).

In the rest of the OT, men generally occupy positions of authority and power over women, with some exceptions (Judg. 4–5; 1 Kgs. 19:1–2). However, the OT is full of stories of women resisting male domination and exerting power in other ways. In the NT, equality becomes an important theme. Christ teaches his disciples not to "lord it" over one another (Luke 22:25–26) but rather to be the servant of all. Equality is part of the "new creation" begun in Christ, who restores humankind to the image of God. For example, Col. 3:10–11 describes the work of Christ as renewing in humankind "the image of its creator" so that "there is no longer Greek and Jew, circumcised and uncircumcised, barbarian, Scythian, slave and free; but Christ is all and in all!" Similarly, Gal. 3:28 reads, "There is no longer Jew or Greek, there is no longer slave or free, there is no longer male and female; for you are all one in Christ Jesus." Categories previously used to subject, discriminate, and unjustly favor some people are brought into the unifying work of Christ.

However, these passages of Scripture stand in tension with others such as 1 Tim. 2:11–15, which subordinates women to men because "Adam was formed first, then Eve; and Adam was not deceived, but the woman was deceived and became a transgressor." Other passages, such as 1 Cor. 11:2–16; Eph. 5:21–33; 1 Pet. 3:1–7, exhibit similar tensions.

Tensions also appear in the tradition. Thomas Aquinas says that it is "not right for woman to be subject to man's contempt as his slave" (*ST* I, q. 92, a. 3), but he also says that "economic or civil subjection whereby the superior makes use of his subjects for their own benefit and good" preceded the fall and constituted God's original intention for men and women (*ST* I, q. 92, a. 1). Thomas also differentiates men from women in saying that the image of God resides in woman insofar as she is a human being, but in her individual nature she is "defective and misbegotten" and therefore "naturally subject to man" because in man "the discernment of reason predominates." However, he acknowledges that this perspective is in tension with Gregory of Nyssa, who argued that God's original intention was equality between men and women (*ST* I, q. 92, a. 1). Gregory argued that the "power" of the image of God extends to both men and women, and that "they equally bear in themselves the divine image" (*Op. hom.* 16.17). Similarly, Augustine said that woman was "not defective but natural," and that men and women are equally in need of redemption (*Civ.* 22.17).

Recent theology has emphasized the equality of men and women as equal bearers of the image of God, and feminist theology has assessed how social structures discriminate against women and perpetuate patriarchy. These contemporary insights have led to critical reflection on the ways Christian Scripture and tradition have been shaped by dominant patriarchal cultures. However, contemporary theology has recovered important elements of resistance to patriarchy in Scripture and tradition (like those mentioned here) that should continue to inform the church's struggle against sex discrimination.

See also Discrimination; Equality; Gender; Image of God; Sexual Harassment; Women, Status of

Bibliography

Tucker, W. "Women in the Old Testament: Issues of Authority, Power, and Justice." *ExpTim* 119 (2008): 481–86.

Chanon R. Ross

Sexism *See* Sex Discrimination

Sexual Abuse

Sexual abuse is the uninvited, nonconsensual touching, penetration, or violent assault or threat of assault of the buttocks, anus, breasts, vagina, or penis. It is a general category encompassing rape (marital, stranger, acquaintance, date, gang), domestic or intimate partner violence, spousal abuse, child sexual abuse, incest, sexual harassment, and sexual/ized violence. It is an act of violence, hatred, and aggression in which a person becomes the victim of another person's violent sexualized behavior. Injuries involve psychological, spiritual, and physical trauma. Regarded as an "unmentionable sin," sexual abuse violates the bodily integrity of another and thereby denies a person's choice to determine one's own boundaries and activities (Fortune). Sexual abuse denies the principle of consent, in which a person is fully informed about his or her options, has the right to say no and to have that choice respected, and has the power and agency to determine how to participate. Women and children are the primary targets of sexual abuse by men, although men are also victims, women are assailants, and sexualized violence happens in same-sex relationships.

Sexual abuse involving single victims most often occurs by someone known and assumed to be trustworthy, such as a friend, family member, spouse, or acquaintance. Most media stories of sexual abuse cover assaults by unknown men, giving the impression that sexual abuse most often occurs in relationships not assumed to be safe. On a mass scale, rape has long been a tool of war (Barstow).

Scripture

There are no direct scriptural admonitions against sexually abusing adults or children. The OT includes several stories of explicit sexual abuse, but there are no such references in the NT.

Old Testament scholar Phyllis Trible recognized that like art, the Bible reflects both the holiness and horrors of life. The OT contains several "texts of terror" in which sexual abuse is prominent. In Gen. 19:1–11, Lot refuses to turn out his two male guests/angels so that the men of Sodom could "know them" and offers his daughters in their place. Similarly, in Judg. 19:22–30, a Levite man offers his virgin daughter and concubine to be raped, protecting the sojourning man. The men of the city gang rape the concubine, leaving her for dead. In both narratives, many commentators recognize breaking the code of hospitality as the central violation. In Gen. 34 Dinah is raped and abducted by Shechem, and in 2 Sam. 13:1–22 Tamar is raped by her half-brother Amnon. In these stories, Tamar is the only victim who vocalizes her personal protest and shame. Additional texts of terror include Hagar's forced intercourse with Abraham (Gen. 16:1–6), Abraham's (Gen. 20) and Isaac's (Gen. 26:6–11) offerings of their wives for nonconsensual sex, Queen Vashti's refusal to consent to King Ahasuerus's orders (Esth. 1:10–22), and Potiphar's wife's threat of a false rape charge against the nonconsenting Joseph (Gen. 39:6b–23). In three texts—Jer. 20:7; Lam. 5:11; Zech. 14:2—rape serves as a metaphorical device to warn the Israelites concerning impending or past devastation. The Deuteronomistic laws concerning sexual relations include descriptions of nonconsensual sexual encounters (Deut. 22:23–28) and the punishments that ensue.

Scriptural Interpretation and Cultural Beliefs

Where the Bible records acts of coercive sexualized behavior, many commentators maintain that the prohibitions and negative outcomes lie not in the nonconsensual acts themselves or in the harm done to the women, but in crossing relational and class codes, endangering the community, and violating the codes of hospitality. Feminist and womanist scholars argue that biblical interpretations, reflecting patriarchal and racial standards of the day, ignore sexual abuse as a significant interpretive lens for these narratives. Susanne Scholz contends that interpretations of the rape of Dinah include views of rape as punishment for the woman's behavior or as sign of immature love. In some cases, the admonitions about sexual abuse are determined by the prohibition in Lev. 18:6–18 of sexual contact between persons related by blood, as in Amnon's rape of Tamar. Some have taken the narratives of violence and approached them as erroneously redacted love stories. In her book *The Red Tent*, Anita Diamant presents a midrash of Gen. 34 as a story of forbidden love between Dinah and Shechem.

Sexual Abuse and Christian Tradition

Early Christian theologians provided only a few overt references to sexual abuse. In *The City of God*, Augustine asserted, contrary to notions held by church leaders such as Jerome, that consecrated virgins raped by the invaders who sacked Rome should not commit suicide (Pellauer). This countered the Roman practice of suicide in the face of dishonor. Augustine's task was a complex one, for he believed that, while the consecrated virgin rape victims deserved to live, he also held that if victims experienced "lust or pleasure" in the act of the assault, it was not rape. This form of blaming the victim found its basis in the virgin martyr tradition, where it was understood that women could be miraculously rescued from sexual assault if they were steadfast in their prayers (Schroeder). In 1902, twelve-year-old Maria Goretti "successfully" fought off a rapist before she was stabbed to death. As she died, she forgave her murderer. Protecting her virginity, even to her death, led to her canonization as a martyred Christian woman of virtue. This confusion of sexual abuse and sexual activity became the standard for the virtuous Christian woman.

This concept of female virtue had a dangerous side. From the mid-sixteenth to the mid-seventeenth centuries, the *Malleus Maleficarum* (*The Hammer of Witches*) became a basic text for the Inquisition and the guide for uncovering witches and witchcraft. Women who were suspected of demon possession underwent violations of their bodies as church officials attempted to purge them of the devil.

Contemporary Issues

In the 1960s and 1970s, women's consciousness-raising groups and women's crisis services were among the few groups talking about sexual abuse. In the twenty-first century, practitioners, scholars, and faith communities have the opportunity to work collaboratively on these complex issues. Reports and charges of clergy sexual abuse have forced the church to take responsibility for its own complicity in this "unmentionable sin." Stories of child sexual abuse lift up questions about parental versus states' rights. Lesbian/gay/bisexual/transgendered communities work with law enforcement agencies and medical services to raise awareness of intimate partner violence and the assaults by members of their communities. Those who work on reproductive rights have collaborated with antiviolence services for women as they seek to make interventions possible after rape. Those concentrating on intimate partner violence and acquaintance rape know that date-rape drugs make it even harder for survivors to identify and prosecute perpetrators. The high rate of sexual assaults in men's prisons forces us to recognize that sexual abuse is not just a woman's issue. Technology that brings us closer together also makes predatory behavior more problematic. This is especially true with children and youth. We teach them about "stranger danger" in social networks (e.g., Facebook and MySpace), where identities are easily hidden and parental monitoring is harder. The ubiquitous presence of cell phones makes stalking behavior more common as youth and adults can keep track of someone's every move. The rise of "sexting" (sexually explicit text messaging) among youth and young adults adds a level of complexity to the understanding of relational consent. As we turn our eyes to the wider world, we learn about additional forms of sexual abuse. Female genital mutilation is an ongoing practice in many countries, and the trafficking of young girls and women as sex slaves has become an issue for domestic violence shelters in the United States. The systematic sexual abuse of Korean "comfort women" by the Japanese during World War II and the existence of rape camps in Bosnia and Herzegovina during the 1990s Balkan wars are painful examples of rape as a tool of war.

Sexual abuse is an act of aggression and violence that devastates individuals, families, communities, and nations. Attending to the suffering victims/survivors and eliminating sexual abuse means moving our approach from a "tactful mention of an awkward subject" to a justice issue of biblical proportions.

See also Child Abuse; Incest; Pedophilia; Pornography; Prostitution; Rape; Sexual Ethics; Sexual Harassment; Spousal Abuse; Violence; Virginity

Bibliography

Barstow, A., ed. *War's Dirty Secret: Rape, Prostitution, and Other Crimes against Women*. Pilgrim Press, 2000; Diamant, A. *The Red Tent*. Picador, 1997; Fortune, M. *Sexual Violence: The Unmentionable Sin*. Continuum, 1983; Pellauer, M. "Augustine on Rape." Pages 207–41 in *Violence against Women and Children: A Christian Theological Sourcebook*, ed. C. Adams and M. Fortune. Continuum, 1995; Scholz, S. *Rape Plots: A Feminist Cultural Study of Genesis 34*. Peter Lang, 2000; Schroeder, J. *Dinah's Lament: The Biblical Legacy of Sexual Violence in Christian Interpretation*. Fortress, 2007; Trible, P. *Texts of Terror: Literary-Feminist Readings of Biblical Narratives*. Fortress, 1984; West, T. *Wounds of the Spirit: Black Women, Violence and Resistance Ethics*. New York University Press, 1999.

Kristen J. Leslie

Sexual Ethics

Within both churches and larger society sexual ethics has become a vigorously contested area of morality. Steeped in a highly sexualized society that promotes "responsible" sexual activity as healthy, many Christians seem unconvinced that intercourse or other genital contact should be reserved for marriage or even limited to committed relationships. They debate whether Scripture can offer guidance for contemporary sexual practice, given its seeming affirmation of patriarchy and lack of awareness of alternative orientations such as homosexuality and bisexuality. Many question Christianity's credibility when speaking about sexual morality, since historically it has exhibited patriarchal attitudes, renounced desire, and focused on negative prohibitions. Simultaneously, there is widespread concern in both secular and religious circles about the consequences of shifts in sexual behavior, such as high rates of abortion, divorce, teenage pregnancy, and sexually transmitted diseases. Technology presents previously inconceivable challenges to sexual ethics, such as internet pornography and reproductive medicine.

The demoralization of sex within this chaotic context highlights an inherent difficulty in a Christian ethic that seeks to be biblical, attentive to church tradition, socially relevant, and prophetic. Can we separate timeless truth in Scripture from what is culture-specific? If not, how can we proceed with any sense that we are being faithful to God in our own era? Sexual ethics provides a case study for how to embody Christian morality. Despite some obvious difficulties of utilizing Scripture for sexual ethics, we must interpret our sacred texts and then enact them within radically different sociohistorical circumstances. This requires making judgments about what central texts or stories should fashion sexual ethics as distinctively Christian and then how these Scriptures provide the contours for a discussion of what sex is "for" from within the tradition. Application of such teaching takes place within a society impacted by sociohistorical shifts that provided fertile soil for renegotiations of sexual morality. Despite the difficulty of doing so, we must articulate an overarching theological understanding of sexual ethics for our time that affirms concrete practices and encourages faithfulness to the gospel.

Christianity's Mixed Sexual Legacy

Augustine profoundly influenced moral theology for future generations in the Western church (the medieval Catholic church and all the churches that stemmed from it). Although sometimes caricatured as entirely negative about sexuality, his writings are somewhat inconsistent, as they are dependent on his audience and purpose, and his views develop over time. A lasting legacy was Augustine's assertion that original sin passes on through intercourse. However much he insisted on the good of rightly ordered loves, whether in marriage or in celibacy, such a link tainted future views of sexuality and erotic desire. Protestant theologians such as Martin Luther and John Calvin affirmed desire within marriage, with Luther the most effusive, as when he states that men and women were created to "come together with pleasure [*Lust*] and love [*Liebe*], willingly and gladly with all their hearts" (Luther 304). Many modern theologians, from Karl Barth to Pope John Paul II, emphasize our embodiment and sexuality as a part of the good of creation.

Despite attempts to correct this tainted view of sexuality, much of Christian history only begrudgingly affirms sex within marriage as a means of channeling lust. Although important exceptions and correctives can be gleaned from this tradition, moral theology is too easily read as renouncing sexuality rather than redeeming it. Christians therefore must learn from contemporary insights regarding sexuality while insisting that theological and biblical resources inform and critique them.

Challenges for Using Scripture for Sexual Ethics

Although it would be reassuring to claim that it is univocal about sexual ethics, the Bible at first glance appears alternatively cavalier about the topic and violently reactionary. If we look to Scripture primarily for rules or specific texts to govern sexual behavior, Deut. 22 provides a vivid example of how problematic this can be. The chapter contains sexist and lenient penalties regarding payment of the father when a virgin is raped or violated (vv. 28–29), mandates public proof of a young girl's virginity if accused by her husband and her death by stoning if she fails the test (vv. 13–21), and lists laws prohibiting only male adulterous behavior (v. 22). Given Scripture's historical and cultural context, it is not self-evident how certain stories or behaviors in the OT, such as Tamar's seduction of her father-in-law in Gen. 38:1–30 or the polygamy of the patriarchs, should guide our moral theology.

The NT also proves challenging as a source of all-encompassing laws for sexual behavior because much of what is acceptable or forbidden is assumed by general prohibitions, such as the one against *porneia* ("sexual immorality, lust, fornication"). At particular points we have examples of *porneia*: a man taking his father's wife (1 Cor. 5:1), visiting prostitutes (1 Cor. 6:13), or committing adultery (1 Thess. 4:3–4). These do not exhaust its meaning, as the term appears in lists along with greed or uncleanness (e.g., Gal. 5:19–21; Eph. 5:3–5; Col. 3:5–6) without elaboration and appears to be shorthand for sexually immoral behavior, often related to the sin of idolatry.

Jesus' command that a man is not to look lustfully at a woman (Matt. 5:28) uses a different word, *epithymeō*. Aware that women often were viewed as possessions and were vulnerable to abuse through male rights of divorce, he forbids the greedy, objectifying stares that signal the beginning of such sinful cycles (Matt. 5:31–33). Divorce generally is forbidden in the NT (Luke 16:18), but various exceptions can be made (Matt. 5:32). Concerning homosexual behavior, interpretations and implications of Rom. 1, especially verses 22–27, vary considerably. On the one hand, some argue that this passage's appeal to nature does not apply to homosexuals, who are naturally oriented to persons of the same gender; others insist that this text reveals cultural biases similar to Deuteronomy above. On the other hand, some argue that Paul's theological argument here clearly indicates that only male-with-female sexuality lies within God's intention. Nonetheless, most scholars agree that this text's central interest is not sexuality per se but rather idolatry and the consequences of exchanging our worship of God for something or someone else. Though applicable to sexual ethics, Paul's warning against idolatry pertains to all areas of morality.

Rather than begin by seeking rules for constraints of behavior, Christians should consider overarching concerns of the OT and the NT regarding sexuality and its expression in order to determine core theological concerns regarding God's created purposes. Rules, guidelines, and principles then become means of accepting God's salvation through the disciplining and shaping of our desires rather than through merely negative prohibitions disconnected from the story of creation and redemption. Though influenced by historical factors, contemporary forms of life and specific sexual practices must seek to habituate ordinary people into the holiness that has always been humankind's truest end. Such holiness also fosters a humility befitting our limited understanding and continued reliance on the Spirit for moral wisdom.

Scriptural Resources for Sexual Ethics

Creation stories center our ethics, imparting insights regarding God's character and human nature; they also identify the problem—what went awry—and how to address this new reality. In addition to Gen. 1–3, a brief consideration of Song of Songs provides a vivid vision of sexual love and corrects the stream of theology that overemphasizes the dangers of concupiscence. Such a celebration of sexuality would not be Christian unless juxtaposed against a NT text that models how God's work in Christ recasts and relativizes all relationships, including sexual ones.

Genesis 1–3. The first creation account emphatically affirms the goodness of creation, including humans as gendered, embodied creatures (Gen. 1:27, 31). The second account describes how God, from the mud, sculpted Adam, who becomes a living being by the gift of God's spirit, blown into his nostrils (Gen. 2:7). Made from the dust of the earth, humans image God as physical, material creatures (Gen. 1:27); our physical life cannot be divorced from our spiritual life. We read these stories poorly if we overly spiritualize our sensuality or embrace desire apart from the constraints of our Creator.

Importantly, Jesus (e.g., Matt. 19:5) and Paul (1 Cor. 6:16; Eph. 5:31) return to the second creation story when discussing marriage as covenant, particularly Gen. 2:24: "Therefore a man leaves his father and his mother and clings to his wife, and they become one flesh." They considered the unitive purpose of sexuality to remain unaltered by circumstances or culture; God's intention persists despite the propensity for human sinfulness to become embedded in patriarchal social arrangements or in dominating, abusive intimate spaces. Jesus' and Paul's quoting of this passage also appears to be a reference to the larger context of this creation story, as the phrase "for this reason" refers to the humorous yet evidently sexually charged discovery of the woman as like yet unlike man in Gen. 2:23. Recent discussions of this passage ask whether it renders homosexual practices unnatural and therefore outside the goodness of the created order. This is a serious hermeneutical issue, and thoughtful Christians must wrestle with the text's application to this issue with care.

However, taken from within its Israelite sociocultural context (in which homosexuality would have been unacceptable and gender distinctiveness a given), Gen. 2:23 celebrates the nature of sexual differences between man and woman. Remarkable given the patriarchal culture in which the story was told and preserved, the text asserts that such differences can press us toward relational communion and mutual enjoyment rather than the hierarchy and cycles of enmity recounted in the following chapters of Genesis. When placed within the larger salvation story, the text underscores that in God's design, humans must join together despite (or because of?) potentially divisive differences such as gender in order to be God's image on the earth.

This intention for communion is also stated directly in Gen. 2:25, in which man and woman were "naked, and were not ashamed." Together, these conceptions of community and vulnerability provide a crisp encapsulation of sexual differentiation and expression at its best. Such differences aim at a mutual embrace of someone different from ourselves, a hospitality that reflects God's broader intention for humanity to relate to one another and God's self without restraint or fear; we long to be seen for who we are ("naked") yet remain unembarrassed by this revealing, even admiring, gaze of another. This pithy description of Edenic unity also reminds us why sexual morality is inherently contentious and emotionally evocative. We can indeed experience this acceptance and care of another distinctively (though not solely) in sexual expression, and this is at the heart of human sexuality generally. We are created for an intimacy in which another rejoices in our uniqueness. We are "known," as the biblical euphemism revealingly describes sexual intercourse, rather than rejected, shamed, dominated, or abused.

Song of Songs. This sometimes playful, sometimes serious poem unabashedly rejoices in the erotic love of a woman and her lover. It mentions God in only one verse (Song 8:6). As sacred text, it was often considered merely an extended analogy of how much God loves us "like" a man and woman love each other. However, it stretches credibility to ignore the evident erotic content of Song of Songs as merely symbolic. Particularly because certain strains of the tradition remain reticent to embrace sensuality, this sacred text provides a corrective. Indeed, its ability to inform our relationship with the divine requires that we honestly assess the text on the level of human-human love before asking what it might mean for divine-human love.

While this is a complex and rich poem that deserves careful study, certain features remain clear. First, sensuality and appreciation of another's beauty (male and female) become a source of deep satisfaction, a cause of celebration among lovers. The poem's expressions of fulfillment, the pleasure and pain of teased desire, and the aching longing for physical touch reinforce the joyful power of requited love. Even in a bent world, lovers can cross the divide of differences and experience the God-given goodness of sexual pleasure. Yet the poem also alludes to difficulties for lovers, from overcoming annoyances (e.g., Song 5:2–3) to the realization that devotion to another can be dangerous, particularly for women (e.g., Song 5:5–7). Overall, the poem affirms the intentions of our Creator for sexuality to blossom amid mutual affection; within such a relationship, passion empowers us to embrace another despite our vulnerability and relish the grace of self-discovery found in such sacred spaces.

***1 Corinthians* 7.** In 1 Corinthians Paul wrestles with the practical difficulties of responding to the all-encompassing claim of Christ within the messiness of life lived with others. Although Western Christians might feel more at home in Song of Song's celebration of *eros*, sections of this letter by Paul offend our cultural sensibilities or cause us to wonder if his own sexual or marital experiences were negative (see, e.g., 1 Cor. 7:1, 7). Like most of Paul's writings regarding relationships between women and men, interpretation of 1 Cor. 7 remains contested. But Paul also surprises us. Writing from a Jewish tradition in which a woman became the possession of her husband in marriage, he equally commands men and women to offer themselves sexually to each other (1 Cor. 7:4–5) and thus to model the self-offering love of Christ. He proposes limits on sexual expression but also recognizes its place within certain boundaries as a way of keeping ourselves centered on God. Paul rejects a vision of sexuality that separates it entirely from the physical, including his earlier contention that intercourse with a prostitute makes one flesh of two (1 Cor. 6:16); what we do with our bodies matters for our spiritual lives. Our bodily desires therefore are not self-interpreting or ends in themselves; they must be harnessed so that they honor God's intention for us in our divine and human relationships. Paul wisely notes that denial of sexuality can be just as distracting from our devotion to God as overindulgence (1 Cor. 7:5).

Paul's ethics reflect his context, especially his sense that "the appointed time has grown short" (1 Cor. 7:29), but are remarkable, as in his unwillingness to quote inflexible rules regarding marriage, continence, and divorce. Instead, his central interests are pastoral, as in his balancing of concern for the salvation of unbelievers (1 Cor. 7:14) and for believers' freedom from marital anxiety or stress (1 Cor. 7:32–35). He responds creatively, seeking to attend to human needs as well as divine interests (e.g., 1 Cor. 7:5, 8). Specific concerns arise as the "present form of this world is passing away" (1 Cor. 7:31), and Paul invites us to live now aware that we are destined for a place in which we remain gendered and embodied creatures and yet do not marry (cf. Mark 12:25). Marital arrangements and sexual intimacy remain relative goods (1 Cor. 7:29–31) because it is only in giving ourselves wholly to God that we, like the lovers in Song of Songs, find our true end.

Sociohistorical Shifts

Reasons for contentiousness over sexual morality in the West are complex, but certainly they correlate to significant sociohistorical shifts that make heterosexual marriage and the procreation of children less central to societal survival. That is, before the industrial era, the family was the center of production. The survival of individuals and communities required that most people marry and produce children, and social forces and mores reinforced fidelity to a partner and to one's extended kinship group. Marriage was not only a religious issue but also a pragmatic one. Arranged not for reasons of romantic interest, marriages were negotiated by families for partnership, economic sustainability, kinship survival, and political or social power. Women were valued as bearers of children, and men as laborers. Romantic love might develop within such arrangements, but it did not serve as the basis for them. Families often took into account concerns about companionability and character when they linked their families and thus their welfare through marriage. In non-Western societies in which marriages still are arranged or in which families have a strong say regarding mates, these dynamics remain important.

A tectonic shift occurred in the West in the postindustrial era as families shifted from centers of production to centers of consumption, and the so-called traditional nuclear family became the norm rather than extended families that depended on one another for economic support and survival. In addition, recent advances in nutrition and medicine mean that we are living longer, demanding more of lifelong fidelity or providing reasons for delaying marriage. Lower infant mortality rates decrease the necessity of bearing multiple children, who are also no longer crucial to economic and social stability as a source of cheap labor and social security. In many industrialized capitalist societies it is now possible to economically survive and thrive as a single, unattached individual.

Many have noted that reproductive choice, widespread divorce, feminism, freedom to date, multiple sexual experiences, and the like become possible only if supported by these dramatic cultural movements. Overall, these changes cumulatively shifted emotional and friendship ties from a larger network within a community to the privatized space of a home, with accompanying demands on intimate relationships and heightened expectations of sexual fulfillment within them. Paralleling these developments, sexuality in modernity became an aspect of personal identity in ways previously unimaginable. It is not surprising that the definition of homosexuality as an orientation rather than as a set of behaviors does not occur until the late 1800s.

Many Christian ethicists want to rescue sexuality from what they feel is an overly negative view of sex and physical intimacy in the tradition, often blaming (perhaps unfairly) the influence of Augustinian anti-concupiscence as a major cause. Yet most recognize that for all its faults, the tradition has linked healthy sexual morality to social and familial goods, particularly the raising of children, as an aspect of the fruitfulness at which human intimacy aims. Sexuality has largely become unmoored from these larger concerns and narrowed into a matter of individual interests and self-expression; this worries the spectrum of Christian ethicists from liberal to conservative. Many want to recapture the public or social purpose of marriage and seek public support for its stability and longevity, whether legalizing (or denying) same-gender unions or passing laws that require premarital counseling and render divorces more difficult to obtain. There is also considerable concern and debate about how to articulate limitations for adolescents, with some promoting purity movements while others speak about responsibility and justice. In all of this, Christian ethicists struggle to affirm certain cultural shifts (such as sexuality as gift, women's rights, or marriage as mutual friendship) while reasserting in some form the traditional conviction that long-term, committed, monogamous relationships provide the best soil for healthy and fertile sexuality.

Conclusion: Holy Sexuality That Is Wholly Sexual

Across both Testaments, sexuality—what we do with our bodies, especially as we relate to others—is one of the many ways in which we practice fidelity to God. Although we will disagree about what specific practices should or should not be affirmed, we can agree that our sexuality falls within the purview of God's concern. Bucking trends that consider this a private matter or separate from obedience or spirituality, Christians must insist that faithful sexuality is both personally chosen and communally supported. For example, if Christians are commonly engaging in sexual intercourse apart from committed relationships or marriage, this reveals our failure to provide coherent and compelling reasons for restraint. Loyalty to spouses is also an expression of our loyalty to God, so that marital infidelity is never merely a deeply painful betrayal of one other person. Such disloyalty often shatters a community and places children at risk. The failure of marriages and the ripple effect that this causes also expose demanding and chaotic social pressures on marriage as well as the failure of churches to support long-term covenants and provide help amid conflict.

Responding to our context, we can learn from teachings of the past, even as we seek to correct some of them from our historical perspective. Despite gender biases and other prejudices, our tradition speaks prophetically into our culture, as in its consistent affirmation of celibacy. Whether for a season or for a lifetime, celibacy reflects not a rejection of sexuality per se but rather the possibility that devotion to God can produce joy even though, as with all love, it also entails hardship. Christian ethics always demands self-control and training of our desires, including but not exclusively our sexual ones, so that our character conforms to that of Christ, and we are thus better able to love God and neighbor.

Embracing our sexuality, in whatever form this takes as single or married, physically intimate with another or not, recognizes that God created us for relationship. Our spirituality cannot be divorced from our physical life with others. Scripture reminds us that sex is powerful in life-giving and life-denying ways. Despite current rhetoric, sex can never be "safe," because by its very nature it exposes us, opens us to shame or intimacy, fruitful partnership or fearful domination. Our embodiedness requires us to take seriously the need for guidelines that acknowledge that what we do with our bodies matters deeply for our formation as people, for good or for ill. Sex and sexuality are indeed gifts, but they are much more than this. Even pagans did not simply celebrate sexuality; they also recognized its explosive power (consider the stories of the Greek gods or Homer's poetry). As those claiming to be shaped by the scriptural narrative, Christians should acknowledge that sexuality is never merely natural but rather must be ordered from within the Christian narrative so that we can be made whole by God's grace.

Scripture reminds us that sexuality is at its worst when merely utilitarian—solely for our own pleasure, for the conception of heirs, for dominating others. Sexual passion is at its best when it is harnessed so that we are freed to love others faithfully and pursue other important goods. Erotic passion burns without consuming us within intimate commitments marked by the deep satisfaction of mutually self-forgetting, self-offering love. Expressed or restrained, disciplined Christian sexuality sustains and nourishes us for the work of faith, hope, and love.

Arguments to ignore limitations once broadly accepted in the Christian tradition (such as moves to view sexual intercourse as a private matter between mature, consenting adults; to accept homosexual unions; to understand marriage as primarily an avenue for emotional, sexual, or psychological fulfillment) must make theologically coherent and biblically informed arguments. Those arguing against these trends must do likewise. All sides must take seriously calls in the NT for Christlike humility and graciousness toward those with whom we deeply disagree. To fail to do so is to reject the task of moral discernment as a mandate for the church in every age. Most important, facile or blustering arguments cannot support the weight of a sexual ethic that is holy, that witnesses in faithful living that we are most truly free to flourish in obedience to Christ, or of a sexual ethic that is wholly integrated, that understands our sexuality as a crucial aspect of our humanity embraced and redeemed in Christ.

See also Adultery; Celibacy; Divorce; Feminist Ethics; Gender; Homosexuality; Idolatry; Marriage and Divorce; Pornography; Prostitution; Sex and Sexuality

Bibliography

Clark, E., ed. *St. Augustine on Marriage and Sexuality*. Catholic University of America Press, 1996; Coontz, S. *Marriage, a History: How Love Conquered Marriage*. Penguin, 2006; Dawn, M. *Sexual Character: Beyond Technique to Intimacy*. Eerdmans, 1993; Grenz, S. *Sexual Ethics: An Evangelical Perspective*. Westminster John Knox, 1990; Hauerwas, S. *The Stanley Hauerwas Reader*. Ed. J. Berkman and M. Cartwright. Duke University Press, 2001, 481–504, 603–22; Hays, R. *The Moral Vision of the New Testament: Community, Cross, New Creation; A Contemporary Introduction to New Testament Ethics*. HarperSanFrancisco, 1996, 46–59, 347–406; Hefling, C., ed. *Our Selves, Our Souls, and Bodies: Sexuality and the Household of God*. Cowley Publications, 1996; Luther, M. "On Marriage Matters." Pages 259–320 in *The Christian in Society III*. Vol. 46 of *Luther's Works*, ed. R. Schultz. Fortress, 1967; Miles, C. *The Redemption of Love: Rescuing Marriage and Sexuality from the Economics of a Fallen World*. Brazos, 2006; Sheldrake, P. *Befriending Our Desires*. Ave Maria Press, 1994; Tipton, S., and J. Witte Jr., eds. *Family Transformed: Religion,*

Values, and Society in American Life. Georgetown University Press, 2005.

Erin Dufault-Hunter

Sexual Harassment

Sexual harassment is the use of one's authority or power, either explicitly or implicitly, to coerce another into unwelcome sexual relations, to punish another for her or his refusal, or to create a hostile, intimidating, or offensive work environment through verbal or physical conduct of a sexual nature. Women continue to be the most common targets of male harassment. Examples of sexual harassment include pornography posted in the workplace or sent through email, sexually explicit comments meant to degrade, jokes based on sexual stereotypes, and requests by professors for sex in exchange for grades. The "cultural custom" quality of sexual harassment means that the primary hurdle to eliminating it remains proving that it is in fact a problem. The widespread trivializing of sexual harassment fuels those who would engage in it and ensures that this degrading treatment can continue.

Sexual harassment takes many forms: intentional individual harassment, pseudoromantic individual harassment of a selected person, intentional group harassment (wolfpack mentality), unintentional or unenlightened harassment, harassment threatening economic or educational conditions, paraphilic harassment (e.g., voyeurism or exhibitionism), and harassment as a prelude to a more serious act (Cooper-White).

Sexual harassment can be humiliating, leaving a woman with a heightened sense of wariness and a lack of trust in this and similar relationships. Victims of even mild forms of sexual harassment may question their safety, worrying about whether a harasser's conduct is merely a prelude to violent sexual assault (*Ellison*). Relying on sexual stereotypes, harassers play by the rules of the "shame game," in which they tacitly expect victims and bystanders to collude with the degrading behavior by "playing along," submitting, or remaining quiet (MacKinnon). Because consensual sexual interactions are generally relegated to the private sphere, confronting (nonconsensual) harassment challenges the presumed rules of engagement by forcing private or unnamed male privilege into the public for scrutiny. A victim who challenges these rules is accused of failing to recognize the harassing behavior as humorous, as unintentional, or as something to which she consented.

Scripture

There are no direct biblical edicts pertaining to sexual harassment, and yet the Bible presents several examples of people using coercive power to gain access to sexual relations or to create a hostile environment based on sex. In 2 Sam. 11–12 David abuses his power by sending Bathsheba's husband, Uriah, to the front lines of battle to be killed so that David can have Bathsheba for himself. Nathan, citing the story of a rich man robbing a poor man of a lamb, accuses David of abusing his power and compromising his moral authority. In Gen. 39:6a–23 Potiphar's wife threatens a false charge of attempted rape against Joseph unless he agrees to have intercourse with her. In the apocryphal book of Susanna, Susanna is sentenced to death by two men who, in an attempt to coerce her into having sex with them, falsely charge her with infidelity. While not all directly related to unwanted sexual advances, there are many biblical stories in which an authority figure misuses his power, harms someone of lesser power, and creates a hostile working environment, such as in Ezek. 34, where shepherds are accused of stealing from the flock they are charged to protect, using the gains to meet their own needs.

The Just Community

Sexual harassment in the workplace, school, church, and the public taints the important work in these spaces. It violates one's sense of safety and compromises one's relational world. Sexual harassment works against the goals of a just community. The ubiquitous nature of sexual harassment makes it difficult to eradicate. The greatest legal progress in addressing inappropriate sexualized behavior in the workplace has occurred because these "mundane" private interactions are understood to be public violations with economic consequences.

Today, legal and ethical debates on sexual harassment include questions about what constitutes sexual harassment, growing rates of sexual harassment despite laws prohibiting it, failures in law enforcement, the connection between racism and sexual harassment, and questions of free speech.

See also Authority and Power; Professional Ethics; Sex Discrimination

Bibliography

Cooper-White, P. *The Cry of Tamar: Violence against Women and the Church's Response*. Fortress, 1995; *Ellison v. Brady*. 924 F.2d 872. United States Court of Appeals, Ninth Circuit, 1991; MacKinnon, C. *Sexual Harassment of Working Women: A Case of Sex Discrimination*. Yale University Press, 1979; "Prohibited Employment Policies/

Practices." U.S. Federal Equal Employment Opportunity Commission (http//www.eeoc.gov/laws/practices/index.cfm); West, T. "The Harms of Sexual Harassment." *ASCE* 19 (1999): 377–82.

Kristen J. Leslie

Sexuality *See* Sex and Sexuality

Shalom *See* Peace

Shame

Shame is a feeling or perception that one experiences after breaking a cultural norm or transgressing social boundaries. Shame and its counterpart, honor, are key social values that undergird the thinking of ancient Mediterranean peoples, including the authors of the biblical texts. Within these cultures, shame has both positive and negative aspects. In a positive sense, shame is related to a person's proper awareness of social norms and standards. Such a person possesses shame. The modern expression "Have you no shame?" captures the idea that a person might lack this capacity. Shame also has a negative component. When a person or a group does something socially inappropriate, or when someone is challenged by another and is unable to rise to that challenge, the resulting status for that person or group is shame. For example, when someone fails to act in accordance with accepted boundaries of public engagement—for example, speaking to one's elders disrespectfully, challenging a social superior, using inappropriate speech—the resulting status for that person is shame. Similarly, if one tribe of peoples taunts another group or that other group's gods, and the mocked group fails to respond, the second group has been humiliated and experiences shame. In both cases, the court of approval for these examples is the larger social order. Shame is not synonymous with modern understandings of guilt, which emphasize an individual person's feelings of unworthiness after doing something wrong. Ancient societies were group-oriented or dyadic, and thus the individual's identity was rooted in a person's reputation in relationship to others. Shame emphasizes this more social component.

The vocabulary for shame in both the OT and the NT assumes this broader context of honor/shame culture in the ancient Mediterranean world. In the OT, the Hebrew roots *bwš* and *klm* and their corresponding verbs and nouns connote humiliation, embarrassment, and a loss of face in the larger social sphere. The concept of shame and shaming are important interpretive keys for understanding much of the prophetic literature and the psalms, where this vocabulary is used often. Thus, when the psalmist cries out in lament to God in the face of persecution, it is not simply for relief; rather, the appeal is for God to minimize shame and preserve the petitioner's honor: "O my God, in you I trust; do not let me be put to shame; do not let my enemies exult over me" (Ps. 25:2). In a similar way, when the prophets proclaim divine judgment on a nation, the end result is humiliation and dishonor: "So shall the king of Assyria lead away the Egyptians as captives and the Ethiopians as exiles, both the young and the old, naked and barefoot, with buttocks uncovered, to the shame of Egypt" (Isa. 20:4). Moreover, it is God's honor that is at stake when Israel or Judah acts disobediently or is unfaithful to the terms of the covenant. In this way, divine judgment is the deity's way of preserving honor or saving face among the nations and their gods.

In the NT, the Greek verb *aischynō* ("to be ashamed, disgraced") and the noun *aischynē* ("shame, disgrace"), along with other words from the root *aisch-* (e.g., *kataischynō* and *epaischynomai*, both meaning "to be ashamed"), also presuppose this larger sociocultural understanding of shame. Paul, for example, appeals to those in early Christian communities to hold fast to their faith in the face of social rejection. Therefore, he boldly proclaims, "I am not ashamed [*epaischynomai*] of the gospel; it is the power of God for salvation to everyone who has faith" (Rom. 1:16); and he encourages followers to persevere, since the Scriptures proclaim, "No one who believes in him will be put to shame" (Rom. 10:11). In this way, NT writers adopt earlier biblical themes of divine judgment, framing God's execution of justice for the faithful in terms of the preservation of divine reputation, including the establishing of God's eschatological reign over the earth—a final and complete vindication of God's honor.

It is important that theologians and interpreters of the Bible recognize how biblical authors understood shame. Ideas such as honor and shame remind the contemporary interpreter that the Bible is working from a worldview that is different from a modern contemporary context. In the cultures of the ancient Near East and the Greco-Roman world, virtues and morality are not only related to the composition of a person's nature; they are connected to the reputation of others. How one acts reflects positively or negatively upon the character of one's God and the community to which one belongs. Thus, prophetic words of judgment in the OT are not simply political or theological statements about how humans have strayed into error. They are culturally specific descriptions of the shameful incongruity that results from the moral failures of a social order or the humiliation that accompanies a nation's devastating destruction at the hands of a conquering enemy. Similarly, oracles of salvation are not simply statements about a person's ontological redemption. They are witnesses to the preservation of God's honor and glory in the earth through this person's or nation's circumstances. Moreover, early Jewish and Christian eschatological hope is tied directly to the cultural values of honor and shame, because within these traditions the destiny of humanity is inextricably tied to God's final vindication, when "every knee shall bow, every tongue shall swear" to the goodness and justice of God's reign in the earth (Isa. 45:23; cf. Rom. 14:11; Phil. 2:10–11).

See also Guilt

Bibliography

Bechtel, L. "Shame as a Sanction of Social Control in Biblical Israel: Judicial, Political, and Social Shaming." *JSOT* 49 (1991): 47–76; deSilva, D. *Honor, Patronage, Kinship and Purity: Unlocking New Testament Culture*. InterVarsity, 2000; Malina, B. *The New Testament World: Insights from Cultural Anthropology*. 3rd ed. Westminster John Knox, 2001.

Frank Yamada

Sick, Care of the *See* Care, Caring

Sin

Colloquially, the omnibus term *sin* denotes any violation of some moral standard. This moralistic usage has significant roots in a theological tradition long dominant in the West (Augustine, Martin Luther, Reinhold Niebuhr) that relies on a legal/juridical metaphor. Since Abelard, a distinction with regard to intention has also been a factor, so that a given act may be deemed wrong or harmful without rising to the level of sin because the agent lacked the requisite intent. Sin, in this view, is violation of the law of God.

Not surprisingly, the biblical view involves a much more sophisticated and nuanced understanding of human behavior. The task of outlining the biblical concept of sin immediately confronts the problem of language and culture, a problem complicated by the fact that the Bible communicates in two unrelated languages and reflects cultural settings that stand in a complicated relationship to one another. The description of the biblical notion of sin must account for the semantics of the Hebrew concept, on the one hand, and Koine Greek, on the other. Careful attention must be given to subtlety and substance.

Remembering that usage carries greater weight than etymology, the point of departure is a survey of biblical terminology. Biblical Hebrew and Greek exhibit vocabulary for human wrongdoing too extensive for detailed discussion here. Nonetheless, a few terms appear in frequencies and contexts that suggest their centrality. The most common terms in both the OT and the NT derive from the realm of archery and connote the image of "missing the mark" (Heb. *ḥṭ'*, verb and related noun more than 580 times; Gk. *hamart-*, about 270 times [see, e.g., Judg. 20:16; 1 Pet. 2:20]). Especially in the wisdom literature, the term can refer to "bumblers, losers" (see Eccl. 9:18). The NT equivalent renders the full range of Hebrew "sin" vocabulary, suggesting that in Koine Greek the term lost contact with its origins to a degree, although significantly, Paul uses *hamartanō* once to parallel "falling short (of an objective)" (*hystereō* [Rom. 3:23]). Notably, one does not usually "miss the mark" intentionally but rather as the result of incapacity or error. Both the OT and the NT employ other terms denoting willful transgression. The image underlying the Hebrew term *pš'* (verb and related nouns more than 130 times), which appears in contexts involving property crimes (e.g., Gen. 31:36; Exod. 22:8) or political rebellion (e.g., 1 Kgs. 12:19; 2 Kgs. 1:1; 3:5, 7; 8:20), seems to be the breach of relationship. It appears in concentrations in the Deuteronomistic History and the prophetic literature emphasizing Israel's persistent rebelliousness and apostasy. New Testament equivalents (e.g., *parabainō, hyperbainō*) refer to similar acts of rebellion. A final key term in the OT underscores the inadequacy of the crime-and-punishment model in accounting for the holistic relationship between agent, act, and aftereffect. From a root that means "to bend, twist, contort" (e.g., Isa. 24:1; Lam. 3:9), the noun *'āwôn* occurs in three overlapping usages describing (1) the wrongful act as "perversion" (in this sense, usually translated "iniquity" in English), (2) the twisted condition of the agent created by the act ("guilt"), and (3) the perversion of the agent's environment produced by the iniquitous act (also usually translated "guilt"). Although the NT does not reserve a term for this aspect of sin, the Hebrew notion echoes in passages such as Paul's discussion of God "handing" humanity "over" to its sin (Rom. 1–2) and Jesus' discussion of the maturation of sin into consequences (Matt. 23:36; Luke 11:51).

This survey of biblical vocabulary for sin points to the Bible's comprehensive understanding. First, the crime-and-punishment model, though insufficient alone, corresponds roughly to one aspect of the biblical idea. The prophets and the Deuteronomistic History view Israel's long history of sin as violation of its covenant with Yahweh—a covenant with established, clear standards. Indeed, for the Deuteronomistic History, Israel's fundamental covenant violation was the breach of relationship inherent in transgressions against the supreme commandment of fidelity to Yahweh. Similarly, texts in 1 John (2:22–23; 4:2–3; 5:10) and in Hebrews (6:4–6; 10:26–27) deal with the renunciation of relationship with God through Jesus Christ. The failure to recognize Jesus or, having recognized him, to willfully deny him is sin.

What, however, does this model have to say about people who do not stand in Israel's covenant relationship or who have not been introduced to Jesus? Can infants and young children be charged with willfully violating the covenant or with rejecting relationship with God through Jesus Christ? The portrayal of early humankind in Genesis offers key insights. Traditional Western readings emphasize the first pair's rebellion against the divine command. A closer examination reveals a much more complex and subtle situation. The Bible explicitly points to the moral naïveté of the first pair: they did not yet know good and evil. Like infants and small children, they did not yet possess the capacity for moral judgment necessary for "willful rebellion." The text details Eve's thought process: the fruit was beautiful and apparently edible and had the capacity to bestow Godlikeness—the very faculty of moral judgment necessary as a prerequisite in a juridical model. Subsequent texts in the primal history confirm that this desire to transcend humanity's proper boundaries is fundamental to the human predicament: Cain stubbornly substitutes his own criterion for God's; at Babel, humanity seeks to "make a name" by literally climbing to heaven. In a midrash-like meditation on Gen. 3 (Eccl. 3:11–22), the preacher offers a somewhat forlorn commentary. Human beings, made in the image of God, are able to emulate divinity ("eternity in the hearts of men" [3:11 NIV]) but are unable by God's design, nonetheless, to transcend the limits of creatureliness. In the NT, Paul echoes this line of thought in Rom. 1. Combining the prophetic/Deuteronomistic and creation/wisdom traditions, he portrays the human condition as the refusal to worship the true God revealed throughout nature in favor of elevating the creature to divine status—a violation of the created order. In sum, a basic component of human sin is dissatisfaction with the limits of creatureliness, a desire to be more than human, a concupiscent hunger for autonomy.

As feminist theologians have pointed out, however, the model of sin as prideful egocentrism fails both to account for the full range of human behavior and experience and to reflect the comprehensive biblical witness. The biblical vocabulary for "sin" already implies that sin can also involve the opposite of overreaching, namely, underachieving—"sloth," to use the language of medieval theology, or "loss of self," as feminists and others sometimes put it. The Bible attests to the human tendency to shrink back from the attainment of proper goals (see, e.g., Num. 11:4–6; 14:2–4). On some occasions, Jesus, aware that human beings can prefer disability over the challenges and responsibilities that come with wholeness, pointedly asks infirm persons whether they wish to be healed (Mark 10:51; John 5:6). Expectedly, the notion of sin as a failure to mature dominates the wisdom literature. This tradition views wisdom, the order in God's creation (Prov. 8:22–31), as God's gift readily available to any who seek it (Prov. 2:1–6). The objective of authentic humanity is harmony with this wisdom. Therefore, failure to seek it and live in accordance with it, the failure to mature, constitutes sin. Proverbs 8:36 states pointedly that "those who miss [*ḥṭ'*] me [i.e., 'wisdom'] injure themselves" (cf. Prov. 1:24–25, 29–33). The NT Letters of 2 Peter (2:4–22) and Jude (vv. 5–18) inveigh against a group of "false teachers" (early libertine/antinomian gnostics?) who encourage subhuman or animalistic behavior (2 Pet. 2:12; cf. Jude 10). Both letters cite episodes in the primal history involving the intermarriage of angels and human women (Gen. 6:1–4) and the atrocious intentions of the men in Sodom and Gomorrah (Gen. 19) as examples of the kind of boundary-crossing (human/divine) that violates the proper order. The inference defines the behavior and attitudes advocated by the false teachers as a transgression of the boundary between human and animal, an abandonment of the nobility of humanity's status as beings created in God's image.

Paul's view of the human condition hinges on the contention that the proper objective of human life is full humanity as modeled and made possible in Jesus Christ—a view consistent with John's understanding of the incarnation. Indeed, Paul describes salvation as transformation into the image of God in Christ (Rom. 8:29; 1 Cor. 15:49; 2 Cor. 4:4–6; Col. 1:15–20; 3:10). Consequently, Paul's understanding of sin involves the assertion, explicit in Rom. 3:23, that human beings universally "miss the mark" (*hamart-*) by "falling short" (*hyster-*) of the "glory of God" (a near synonym in Paul for "image of God" [see 1 Cor. 11:7; cf. 2 Cor. 3:18; 4:4, 6]). Sin, then, can be manifest either in overreaching or in falling short of proper humanity.

Motivating the human propensity to overreach or underachieve is a basic mistrust of God and God's order of creation. In Eden, the serpent insinuates that God has withheld something good from humankind. With half-truths sowing seeds of doubt and mistrust, the serpent seduces the first pair to undervalue their humanity. Indeed, the Bible consistently defines the antidote to sin as believing/trusting in God, implying that the problem is mistrust, seen in events such as the Israelites "murmuring" (e.g., Exod. 15:24) and "rebelling" (e.g., Deut. 1:26, 43; Ps. 78:17) against God for bringing them into the wilderness to die and the prophetic accusations against Israel for trusting falsely in untrustworthy idols (Isa. 40:18–20; Jer. 2:11–13; Hos. 2:5, 8), political alliances (Isa. 7:4; Jer. 2:36b–37; Ezek. 29:16), and military might (Isa. 31:1; Jer. 5:17; Hos. 10:13). Similarly, wisdom literature warns against trust in untrustworthy sources such as wealth (e.g., Ps. 49:6; cf. Job 31:24), military strength (Ps. 44:6), princes (Ps. 146:3), and oneself (Prov. 3:5). Conversely, it encourages trust in God as solely reliable (e.g., Ps. 4:5; Prov. 3:5).

Although Jesus had little to say about sin in terms of a systematic definition, his message compares repentance of sin to trust in the good news (Mark 1:15). He offers a child's trust in his or her father as a model for the trust in God that is key for entry into the kingdom of God (Mark 10:14 pars.) and defines anxiety as a lack of trust in God's determination to provide (Matt. 6:25–34; Luke 12:22–30 [cf. the mistrust of Adam and Eve]). Indeed, Jesus identifies the only sin beyond forgiveness as mistrust of God's presence (Mark 3:28–30 pars.). John and Paul reduce the issue to its essence. In John, Jesus asserts boldly, "For you will die in your sin unless you believe that I am he" (John 8:24). Paul's entire argument in Romans revolves around the proclamation of God's absolute reliability (e.g., Rom. 3:21–22), the essence and foundation of the gospel. Mistrust is sin.

Perhaps the chief shortcoming of the crime-and-punishment model involves its view of sin as an act discrete from its real-world effects. For this model, the issue involves whether an intentional violation of the law has been committed. The remedy involves the willingness of the divine judge to pardon. Meanwhile, however, the real damage done to the sinner and the sinner's environment survives. Much that is clearly wrong lies outside the purview of redemption.

In contrast, both the Bible and common experience demonstrate that sin has a quasi-objective character. It creates its own reality in the world, a reality that cannot be remedied by a mere pardon. The Deuteronomic case of a corpse discovered in the open countryside (Deut. 21:1–9) attests to ancient Israel's concern that wrong be addressed even when the wrongdoer cannot be identified. Similarly, the Priestly manual specifically discusses the need to address "unintentional sin" (Lev. 4:1–6:7), wrong committed "accidentally" and "unknowingly." After having become aware of the wrong, the perpetrator must effect restoration and restitution. The priority for the ancient Israelite priest was not pardon for the wrongdoer but healing of the injury inflicted, the restoration, as far as possible, of wholeness and balance. Although Jesus' teaching, especially in the Sermon on the Mount, insists on the unity of intention and action, it should not be taken as a reversal of the Priestly determination to deal with the quasi-objective nature of sin. Indeed, Jesus expresses not the reverse, but the converse view, that even apparently "good" deeds such as prayer and almsgiving can be tainted by improper motivations. The case of the man blind from birth recounted in John 9 offers significant insights into Jesus' attitude toward the real-world quality of sin. Resisting the disciples' desire to assign guilt, Jesus moved directly to rectify the harm. In defiance of common sense, the Western church has for far too long ignored the everyday, real-world manifestation of sin. From an ethical standpoint, the church's inconsistent view of sin as largely a question of intention has left it poorly equipped to deal with real pain that may result from error, inattention, or recklessness. A Priestly approach to sin focuses on damage and restoration; notably, for Jesus, throughout his ministry, forgiving sin and healing physical conditions were but aspects of a holistic redemption.

The biblical concept also incorporates the sphere around the individual sinner. It insists on the organic relationship between deed and consequence. The Hebrew term *ʿwn*, which can denote the act, the condition of the sinner produced by the act, or the effects of the act in the broader world, points to this continuum of sin. This holistic view is perhaps best expressed in the Bible's language for punishment and forgiveness. Since sin perverts reality (Isa. 59) such that the aftermath lingers far beyond the originating moment (Hos. 13:12), it "twists" conditions in which others must live (cf. Josh. 22:17, 20).

Indeed, the maturation of sin in its consequences constitutes the central principle of the moral order that God incorporated into creation (Gen. 15:16; Ezra 9:6–7; Ps. 38:4; Matt. 23:29–36; Luke 11:47–51; Gal. 6:7). Thus, the Bible contradicts the crime-and-punishment model regarding the notion that God "punishes" sinners. Instead, the Hebrew expression regularly translated "God punished" relies on the organic principle for its force. God "visits guilt/consequences on [the orginator]" (*pqd ʿāwôn ʿal* [e.g., Exod. 20:5; Lev. 18:25; Num. 14:18; Deut. 5:9; 2 Sam. 3:8; Ps. 89:32; Isa. 13:11; Jer. 25:12; Lam. 4:22; Amos 3:2]). In other words, God's role in "punishment" is either to actively enforce the moral order (e.g., Lam. 1:2–14, especially v. 14; Hos. 8:13) or simply to allow events to take their natural course (e.g., Amos 1:3, 6, 9, where Amos announces God's intention not to "turn it back"—that is, not to reverse the natural course of events). In the NT, Paul also describes the human condition as the result of how God has "given [human beings] up" or "handed [them] over" (*paradidōmi*) to the consequences that they have chosen (Rom. 1:24, 26, 28) and offers the proverbial statement of the principle (Gal. 6:7; cf. Jesus' statement in Matt. 26:52).

If the penalty for sin consists in its organic maturation, forgiveness must also address sin's aftereffects loosed in the world. In fact, the most common terminology in the OT refers to "bearing (away)," "covering," "removing," or "washing away, cleansing from" sin. Of these, the image of "bearing" sin predominates. The language conveys the image of reality twisted such that simply to pardon its perpetrator would have no effect on the continued virulence of the contagion. The NT also prefers verbs that connote "removal" (the verb *aphiēmi* forty-four times, the noun *aphesis* fifteen times), "covering" (a range of terms [e.g., Rom. 4:7; Jas. 5:20; 1 Pet. 4:8]), "redeeming" (e.g., Titus 2:14), and "washing/cleansing" (again, a range of terms [e.g., Acts 15:9; 22:16; 1 Cor. 5:7; 6:11; Eph. 5:26; Titus 3:5; Heb. 1:3; 9:14, 22, 23; 1 John 1:7, 9; 2 Pet. 1:9]).

The Bible's account of the series of family crises with national import that followed David's adulterous and murderous affair with Bathsheba exemplifies the poisonous nature of sin (2 Sam. 12–19; 1 Kgs. 1–2). Although Nathan assures a repentant David of God's pardon, David's subsequent indulgence and passivity encourage three of his sons in succession to replicate behaviors modeled by their father. David's sin came to fruition not as a God-imposed penalty but as the organic result of sin left to flourish.

In sum, the Bible sees sin as fundamental mistrust of God's constant benevolence, a mistrust manifest in the effort to exceed human limitations or to shirk the wonder of being fully human. These behaviors do real harm to the agent and to the world, perverting it such that, in a practical form of original sin, it contorts circumstances in which others must subsequently act. An approach to ethics informed by this comprehensive understanding of sin will be alert to failures to recognize human limitations as evident in unbridled scientific and technological development (e.g., thalidomide, reproductive technologies). It will take into account the implications of the failure to exercise full humanity involved in addictions and educational choices or to encourage full humanity involved in decisions on public policy. Given affinities with the insights of developmental psychology, it will take seriously the welfare of infants and young children as essential for the development of the basic trust necessary for mature ethical behavior. Finally, it will address the systemic nature of sin, recognizing the manner in which structures embody and perpetuate harm and wrong.

See also Forgiveness; Intention; Pride; Seven Deadly Sins

Bibliography

Biddle, M. *Missing the Mark: Sin and Its Consequences in Biblical Theology*. Abingdon, 2005; Dunfee, S. "The Sin of Hiding: A Feminist Critique of Reinhold Niehbuhr's Account of the Sin of Pride." *Soundings* 65 (1982): 316–27; McFayden, A. *Bound to Sin: Abuse, Holocaust and the Christian Doctrine of Sin*. CSCD 6. Cambridge University Press, 2000; Mercadante, L. *Victims and Sinners: Spiritual Roots of Addiction and Recovery*. Westminster John Knox, 1996; Murphy-O'Connor, J. *Becoming Human Together: The Pastoral Anthropology of St. Paul*. Liturgical Press, 1982; Park, A. *The Wounded Heart of God: The Asian Concept of Han and the Christian Doctrine of Sin*. Abingdon, 1993.

Mark E. Biddle

Singleness

The OT gives a more positive assessment of married life than it gives to singleness, while the NT considers marriage the norm but evaluates singleness as having equal worth. It is important to remember that in both Testaments, salvation comes from God without regard to one's marital status.

Old Testament

When considering the OT views on singleness and marriage, we must remember that ancient Israel was a kinship-based society with no concept of the nuclear family or of the social construct of singleness that we have today. Unmarried individuals, for instance, did not establish independent households and live alone. In Hebrew culture, men and women were expected to marry, primarily to ensure the family line by bearing children, and remaining childless was considered a disgrace (Gen. 16:4; 1 Sam. 1:5–6; Ps. 127:3–5). Marriage and sexuality within marriage were celebrated (Eccl. 9:9), and remaining unmarried well into adulthood is rarely mentioned. Women are portrayed as especially vulnerable if they did not marry. A father could sell his daughter as a concubine (Exod. 21:7–11), and if a single woman was the victim of rape, she could find herself married to her attacker (Exod. 22:16–17; Deut. 22:28–29). Divorced or widowed women needed to find a father, brother, or new husband to protect them (Deut. 24:1–4). The OT, however, includes some positive references to single women and men. Promises are made to single women and eunuchs (Isa. 54:1; 56:5), prophets often admonish the people for not taking care of widows (Isa. 1:23; Ezek. 22:7; Mal. 3:5), and God even called Jeremiah not to marry, albeit as a sign of imminent punishment for Israel (Jer. 16:1–4).

New Testament

In the NT, marriage is represented as the norm, but singleness is portrayed as equally valued in the church. Jesus was single, counseled celibacy for some (Matt. 19:10–12), and shifted emphasis from the family to the community of faith (Matt. 12:50; Luke 18:29–30). Paul states a personal preference for the state of singleness (1 Cor. 7:28, 36, 39–40). Philip's four unmarried daughters are described as actively involved in prophecy with no negative connotations for being single women (Acts 21:9).

The Church

The church has historically tended to elevate either the state of marriage or the state of singleness as superior. The early church fathers, for instance, considered singleness and celibacy to be morally superior, whereas today being married and having children is the expected norm for Christian men and women in the church. If, however, what is promised in heaven signifies what we value today, the contemporary church should consider the claim in the NT that there is no marriage in the age to come (Matt. 22:30). More important, however, the contemporary church should remember that the Bible consistently affirms, in both Testaments, that salvation comes from God alone, independent of one's marital status.

See also Celibacy; Family; Widows

Nancy J. Duff

Sirach

Sirach (or Ecclesiasticus) is a wisdom book written by the Jewish sage Jesus Ben Sira in the late third or early second century BCE. The book did not make it into the Jewish and Protestant canons, but it is part of the Roman Catholic OT. In these reflections, Ben Sira presents pithy sayings and longer theological discourses as he addresses a group of pupils negotiating the complex circumstances of the Hellenistic age. This colorful advice constitutes the longest postexilic sapiential work.

In terms of ethics, Sirach encourages upright behavior in the tradition of the book of Proverbs, but with a major innovation: the author explicitly links wisdom and Torah. Earlier sages in ancient Israel had discussed Wisdom and the virtuous life without mentioning the Mosaic covenant, but Ben Sira brings these together. For example, "If you desire wisdom, keep the commandments, and the Lord will lavish her upon you" (1:26).

The sage includes a great deal of discussion on financial matters, offering advice on how to handle money and remain faithful to God. Favorite topics include the intricacies of the marketplace, borrowing and lending, relations between rich and poor, and the practice of almsgiving. Of particular interest is Ben Sira's belief that "riches are good if they are free from sin" (13:24). The sage is dubious of this possibility, since he also states, "A merchant can hardly keep from wrongdoing, nor is a tradesman innocent of sin" (26:29). Yet it is noteworthy that Ben Sira does not categorize material assets as inherently evil. His ambivalence about money appears to stem, at least in part, from the fact that he educated young scribes who were destined to serve the elite classes.

Family relations also receive attention in this instruction. Ben Sira affirms the Decalogue by highlighting the need to honor one's parents (3:1–16). He also has an extended discourse on the good wife and the bad wife (25:13–26:27) and emphasizes the anxiety that daughters may bring (42:11). His discussion includes harsh language that goes beyond the patriarchal ethos of Israel's wisdom tradition. For example, "Any iniquity is small compared to a woman's iniquity" (25:19). In his instruction on such matters, Ben Sira focuses on the shame that ensues from disreputable behavior, and it is likely that he was influenced by Greek ideas of honor and shame.

On the issue of moral agency, Ben Sira urges his listeners to take responsibility for their actions: "Do not say 'It was the Lord's doing that I fell away'; for he does not do what he hates" (15:11). According to certain maxims in this book, God places human beings in the power of their "inclination" (15:14), and it is up to each person to practice "fear of the Lord" by leading a righteous existence and making the correct decisions. Elsewhere, he appears to contradict this logic by claiming that wisdom is created "with the faithful in the womb" (1:14). There is an unresolved tension between free will and determinism in Sirach.

Ben Sira's ethics are also famous for his interpretation of the creation story in Gen. 2–3. When alluding to this narrative and explaining God's creative acts, the sage declares, "He filled them with knowledge and understanding, and showed them good and evil" (17:7). According to the sage's interpretation, moral discernment was not a forbidden fruit, but an essential gift imparted to the first humans. In addition, Ben Sira appears to understand human sin and death in the context of the Adam and Eve story: "From a woman sin had its beginning, and because of her we all die" (25:24). Yet he is inconsistent on this point, since he argues elsewhere that death is a "decree" from God (41:3–4) rather than a punishment for Eve's transgression.

Finally, this instruction deals extensively with death and cultivating a good name. Like the author of Ecclesiastes, Ben Sira endorses a *carpe diem* mentality (e.g., 14:16), since he does not believe in the immortality of the individual soul. At the same time, he exhorts his pupils to cultivate a positive reputation among their contemporaries. Many sayings represent the core belief that the best way to achieve happiness and to secure a lasting future for one's offspring is through a good name. Such a goal can be met by upright, pious behavior (i.e., "fear of the Lord").

See also Deuterocanonical/Apocryphal Books; Wisdom Literature

Bibliography

Collins, J. *Jewish Wisdom in the Hellenistic Age*. Westminster John Knox, 1997, 23–111; Skehan, P., and A. Di Lella. *The Wisdom of Ben Sira*. AB 39. Doubleday, 1987.

Samuel L. Adams

Slander

Slander is a sin of speech that involves reporting information about someone else in order to discredit that person. The information usually is false or distorted, or it could possibly have a shade of truth. Motivated by jealousy, quest for power, money, job advancement, or personal dislike, the slanderer desires to sway public opinion against a rival. As Ezek. 22:9 describes them, slanderers "shed blood," and Jas. 4:2 likens slander to "murder." Slander is lying with sinister intention.

By its inclusion as the ninth of the Ten Commandments, slander is immortalized as one of humanity's worst sins not just against others, but against God as well (Exod. 20:16). The ultimate slander occurs in the formality of public court, where the slanderer offers an untrue report under oath. Jewish thinkers describe slander as "more vicious than transgressions which are called 'great'" (*Midrash Psalms* 12.2), and as the Greek orator Isocrates explains, "It causes liars to be looked on with respect, innocent men to be regarded as criminals, and judges to violate their oaths" (*Antidosis* 18–19).

Jeremiah and Ezekiel list slander as one of the prevalent activities in Israel for which God will bring destruction and exile (Jer. 6:28; 9:4). Psalm 101:5 and Prov. 21:28 forecast the condemnation of slanderers.

Slander is the most commonly named speech sin in the NT, occurring at least eighteen times, appearing on most of the sin lists. In Rom. 1:30, Paul points at slander as a sin of people who do not recognize God. In Col. 3:8, slander is one of the old ways of life that believers are to leave behind. In 2 Tim. 3:3, slander epitomizes the evil of people in the last days, and in 1 Pet. 2:1 slander is one of the childish behaviors that serious believers are implored to grow out of into mature living. "Slanderer" is one of the names for Satan in the Bible (Job 1:6–11; Rev. 12:10).

James 4:11–12 indicates that slanderers elevate themselves into a position that only God can occupy, since they choose to act as if the clear teaching against slander in God's law does not apply to them. More is at stake than ignoring OT law, because the passage implies that slanderers are violating Jesus' teaching to love their neighbors (note "neighbor" in 4:12; cf. Luke 10:27).

Augustine observes that any speech intended to deceive misappropriates the gift of speech that God has given people for good. Despite the speaker's perception of having good intentions—even slanderers might consider their actions as covertly bringing about a greater good certainly for themselves but maybe also for the good of society—no good can come of slanderous speech (Griffiths 89–93).

Certainly believers, then, are not to slander. However, they can also be proactive against slander by standing up for the integrity of people who are being slandered and also by exposing and confronting the slanderer.

See also Libel; Speech Ethics; Ten Commandments; Truthfulness, Truth-Telling; Vices and Virtues, Lists of

Bibliography

Baker, W. *Personal Speech-Ethics in the Epistle of James*. WUNT 2/68. Mohr Siebeck, 1995; idem. *Sticks and Stones:*

The Discipleship of Our Speech. InterVarsity, 1996; Griffiths, P. *Lying: An Augustinian Theology of Duplicity*. Brazos, 2004.

William R. Baker

Slavery

Slavery as a socioeconomic institution permeated the ancient Near East and the Roman Empire. In Israel and early Christianity distinctive Judeo-Christian humanitarian ethics regulated slavery practices.

Three types of slavery existed in Israel: by birth or purchase Hebrews served fellow Hebrews as security against poverty, Hebrews took non-Hebrews as slaves through purchase or capture in war, and Hebrews sold themselves to non-Hebrews as security against debt. In the first type slaves were eligible for sabbatical and Jubilee benefits (Exod. 21:2–6; Lev. 25:10, 38–41). In the second type slaves were circumcised and sworn into covenant membership (Gen. 17:9–14, 23; Deut. 29:10–15) but were not eligible for sabbatical and Jubilee benefits (Lev. 25:44–46). In the third type slaves could be redeemed; freedom was mandatory in a Jubilee year (Lev. 25:47–55). Participation in Sabbath rest and religious festivals was normative for all slaves.

The humanitarian impulse regulating slavery among the Hebrews, compared to practices of contemporary nations, was grounded in God's deliverance of Israel from slavery in Egypt (Deut. 15:15; cf. Lev. 25:42–43). Prophetic ethics criticized slavery practices, forbidding King Ahaz to enslave Judean captives (2 Chr. 28:8–15), calling Israelites to "break every yoke" and "let the oppressed go free" (Isa. 58:6), and declaring Israel's exile to be God's punishment for not granting slaves sabbatical release (Jer. 34:8–20). Eschatological hope foresaw God's Spirit poured out on both male and female slaves (Joel 2:29; cf. Acts 2:18).

Although slavery practice prevailed in first-century culture, Roman and Jewish (Matt. 24:45–51; 25:14–30; 26:51; Luke 7:1–10; 12:37–46), Jesus proclaimed release for the oppressed (Luke 4:18–19) and turned conventional culture on its head, measuring greatness by the humble service of others. Jesus identified his mission as serving (Mark 10:42–45), giving himself for the life of the world (John 6:51). He emptied himself of his divine prerogative and took upon himself the form of a slave (Phil. 2:7).

Slavery functions as a metaphor of the Christian life. Due to multivalent meanings of slavery in the Roman world (where a slave's rise to power surfaced in Greco-Roman novels and history—e.g., King Cyrus of Persia), Paul uses "slave of Christ" (Rom. 1:1; Gal. 1:10; Phil. 1:1) to enhance his status and authority or "slave of all" (1 Cor. 9:19) to lower himself to identify with slaves (Martin). Murray Harris, however, contends that the metaphor "slave(s) of Christ/God," in more than forty uses, designates divine ownership and devotion to Christ or God as Lord. The NT Epistles regulate the conduct of slaves and masters, with slaves usually addressed first, showing their significant standing in the Christian community (Eph. 6:5–9; Col. 3:22–4:1; 1 Tim. 6:1–2; Titus 2:9–10; 1 Pet. 2:18–19). Jesus Christ's liberating gospel abolishes status distinctions between slave and free in the Christian community (1 Cor. 12:13; Gal. 3:28; Col. 3:11). Slaves and masters alike are accountable to the Lord Jesus, thus jettisoning temporal slavery by the reality of new creation, in which all believers are slaves of Christ. Paul's Letter to Philemon transforms slavery. Paul instructs Philemon to receive his runaway slave Onesimus back as a brother "both in the flesh and in the Lord" in the same way he would receive Paul himself (Phlm. 16–17). Affirming the equality of slave and free, the Christian gospel subverts the social institution. Moral philosopher Epictetus, among other writers, expressed similar thought: no essential difference exists among humans, whatever their social status (Glancy 30–31).

Western imperialism developed a flourishing slave trade in the seventeenth and eighteenth centuries. Slavery was abolished in the nineteenth century, first in Britain and then in the United States, which had been key beneficiaries of the slave trade's economic prosperity, purchasing West Africans for slaves as chattel. In hot debates over scriptural sanction and economic necessity, both in England and the United States, abolitionists appealed to broad moral scriptural principles while slavery proponents legitimated slavery practice by citing scriptural texts that condoned slavery (Swartley 31–64; Wayland and Fuller). Richard Fuller's voice represented pro-slavery views, contending that Scripture does not condemn slavery but only abuses of slavery. Francis Wayland, a gracious and patient correspondent, argued that we must recognize Scripture's gradual revelation, and if "slavery is inconsistent with the principles of the Gospel, it is wrong" (Wayland and Fuller 78). Indeed, slavery contradicts the principles of the gospel. Some abolitionists, but not Wayland, unpersuasively distinguish between the humane nature of OT servitude and the insufferable slavery conditions in the United States (Barnes, in Swartley 40–41).

David Torbett's analysis of Horace Bushnell and Charles Hodge is fascinating. Bushnell opposed slavery but maintained Anglo-Saxon superiority; Hodge regarded slavery as scriptural but decried the conditions in Southern slavery. The debate had no resolution (Swartley 58–64). Evangelicals zealously voiced both sides (Torbett 25–31; Weld, in Swartley 38, 39, 41–42). Moses Stuart's interpretation, Quaker and Mennonite witness (Swartley 53–56), and slaves' use of Scripture (Swartley 56–58) offered alternatives.

English Quaker Josiah Wedgewood's plea, echoed later by ex-slave William Wells Brown, "Am I not a man and brother? Ought I not then to be free?" led to a situation in which "slaves were reframed, re-described and re-presented as 'brothers' and 'men,' so they could be found in the love-commandment, the parable of the Good Samaritan, the parable of the sheep and the goats, and elsewhere, whatever might be said in texts more explicitly concerned with slaves and slavery" (Barclay 14). This reframing of the slave as a person in God's image spurred the abolition of slave trade in the British Parliament in 1807, though owning slaves continued until 1833. William Wilberforce's courageous leadership, together with William Pitt and earlier prophetic voices (Clarkson, Sharp, Ramsey) and the writings of ex-slaves Olaudah Equiano and Quobna Ottobah Cugoano, ended this hellish treatment of "Negroes" (Hochschild 30–40, 135–36). It took a tragic civil war in the United States to bring about President Lincoln's Emancipation Proclamation in 1863. Slavery put biblical interpretation and moral sensibility through the fiery furnace.

Great Britain's bicentennial of the abolition of the transatlantic slave trade took place in 2007, and around this time Wilberforce's fight against slavery was popularized in film and biography, especially utilizing the theme of "Amazing Grace," the hymn authored by former slave trader John Newton after his conversion. On July 29, 2008, the US House of Representatives made a first formal apology to African Americans for slavery and its subsequent racist social consequences. Sojourner Truth's lifework shines (Stetson).

Slavery continues today, with twenty-eight million people worldwide trapped in slave bondage, from sex trafficking to forced labor (prompting a 2008 global church conference). Poverty victims are most vulnerable. Slavery, in whatever time and place it occurs, violates Christ's gospel and human dignity.

See also African American Ethics; Civil Rights; Emancipation; Equality; Freedom; Human Rights; Image of God; Jubilee; Liberation; Natural Rights; Philemon

Bibliography

Barclay, J. " 'Am I Not a Man and a Brother?' The Bible and the British Anti-Slavery Campaign." *ExpTim* 119 (2007): 3–14; Glancy, J. *Slavery in Early Christianity*. Oxford University Press, 2002; Harris, M. *Slave of Christ: A New Testament Metaphor for Total Devotion to Christ*. InterVarsity, 1999; Hochschild, A. *Bury the Chains: Prophets and Rebels in the Fight to Free an Empire's Slaves*. Houghton Mifflin, 2005; Martin, D. *Slavery as Salvation: The Metaphor of Slavery in Pauline Christianity*. Yale University Press, 1990; Stetson, E. *Glorying in Tribulation: The Lifework of Sojourner Truth*. Michigan State University Press, 1994; Swartley, W. *Slavery, Sabbath, War, and Women: Case Issues in Biblical Interpretation*. Herald Press, 1983; Torbett, D. *Theology and Slavery: Charles Hodge and Horace Bushnell*. Mercer University Press, 2006; Wayland, F., and R. Fuller. *Domestic Slavery Considered as a Scriptural Institution*. Ed. N. Finn and K. Harper. Mercer University Press, 2008 [1847].

Willard M. Swartley

Sloth

One of the seven deadly sins, "sloth" (Gk. *akēdia*) generally is understood to mean "apathy" or "laziness." Some passages in Scripture, especially in the book of Proverbs, emphasize the problems brought about by physical idleness or laziness (Prov. 12:24–27; 15:19; 18:9; 19:15, 24; 21:25; 22:13; 24:30; 26:13–16; Eccl. 10:18). It is more frequently the case, however, that discussions of sloth emphasize the dangers of spiritual weariness. As the idea of sloth developed within the Christian tradition, theologians increasingly came to highlight the challenges that sloth poses to spiritual development. Sloth is considered to be sinful because, in its most severe form, it represents a refusal to embrace the joy that comes from God and a resistance to celebrating and returning God's love.

Sloth in the Scriptures

The Scriptures generally associate *akēdia* with a lack of watchfulness or attentiveness to the possible activity of God in one's life. In the Septuagint the word *akēdia* appears in Ps. 119:28 (118:28 LXX) in connection to the soul's weariness or torpor: "My soul is weary with *akēdia*" (TNIV). Although the word does not appear in the NT, theologians perceive several Gospel stories to caution against the vice. When Christ leaves the disciples in Gethsemane to pray, their falling asleep might be thought to represent sloth (Matt. 26:40–45). Several of Christ's parables and teachings can be read as exhortations against sloth as well: the fig tree will be cut down unless it bears fruit (Luke 13:6–9), the servant who buries his talent is chastised (Matt. 25:24–30), the man who does not wear the proper garment to a wedding is expelled from the event (Matt. 22:11–14), the people whose hearts have grown "dull" and who have "shut their eyes" are unable to understand Christ's teachings (Matt. 13:13–17). Christ calls his followers to exercise vigilance in a manner that will allow them to be open to God's activity in their lives.

Sloth in the Christian Tradition

Akēdia appears in many early writings of the Christian tradition as a physical weariness that interferes with a monk's spiritual growth. During the medieval period, Christian authors came to emphasize the risks that *akēdia* poses to each Christian's spiritual development and to describe *akēdia* increasingly in spiritual terms. In some early lists of the "deadly sins" *akēdia* was treated as a different sin from *tristitia* ("sorrow"). But medieval theologians such as Thomas Aquinas defined *akēdia* as a particular kind of *tristitia*. This sorrow is sinful for two reasons. First, *akēdia* is a feeling of sadness about God's goodness, and Thomas explains that it is sinful to be sorrowful about such a great spiritual good. Second, *akēdia* is sinful because it causes us to be lazy. According to Thomas, *akēdia* is a sorrow that "so weighs upon man's mind, that he wants to do nothing" (*ST* II-II, q. 35, a. 1).

This connection of sloth to sorrow might raise questions about whether Christian theology condemns all feelings of depression or discouragement. Thomas's response to this issue is reassuring: it is possible for Christians to feel themselves to be struggling against sloth without actually succumbing to its temptations. He also reminds his readers that there are times in Scripture when Christ feels great sorrow. Not all sorrow is slothful or sinful.

See also Seven Deadly Sins; Sin

Bibliography

North, J. "*Akedia* and *Akedian* in the Greek and Latin Biblical Tradition." Pages 387–92 in *Studia Evangelica*, vol. 6, ed. E. Livingstone. Akademie Verlag, 1973; Wenzel, S. *The Sin of Sloth: Acedia in Medieval Thought and Literature*. University of North Carolina Press, 1960.

Elizabeth Agnew Cochran

Social Contract

The term *social contract* refers to a political claim about the state that arose out of the mixture of rising capitalism, Enlightenment understandings of the natural order and human nature, and fear of the unfettered passions that led to war after war in seventeenth- and eighteenth-century Europe. The social contract is a deontological assertion about social relations. Because everyone has "interests" in personal well-being, individuals can band together for common ends. Although the terms are sometimes used synonymously, social contracts differ from community-creating covenants in emphases, with contracts relying more on legality (and using deontological reasoning), and covenants relying more on the character of the covenantal partners (virtue teleological reasoning). Social contracts generally are assumed to be generated in a natural state of potential conflict or extreme uncertainty among strangers. John Rawls and Robert Nozick are two major contemporary theorists of social contract. The three foundational theorists of social contract are Thomas Hobbes, John Locke, and Jean-Jacques Rousseau.

Hobbes found that life without appropriate governance is "solitary, poor, nasty, brutish and short." Indeed, this state of nature is a war of all against all. The only logical solutions are continuing escalation in arms, which is finally against one's own interests, or formation of a social contract and ceding of self-sovereignty. The new ruler is Leviathan, who takes the combined sovereignty of the contract makers and uses force to protect the individuals from the most dreaded of aversions, a violent death.

Locke, however, did not favor a contract that protected only life at the cost of losing freedom. His proposed social contract is one in which sovereignty remains with the individual, bound to other individuals for protection of life, liberty, and property. Locke's social contract assumes prior existing natural rights—a concept derived from natural-law theory but without the assumption of a shared telos; instead, each individual sets a personal telos limited by the contract and others' rights. Property is necessary for seeking that individual telos (or what Thomas Jefferson later calls "the pursuit of happiness").

Rousseau thought that the natural state was original innocence, but that individuals were corrupted by society. While one might seek to return to a state of nature, it is so improbable as to be considered generally impossible. As an alternative, a social contract can be formed that will allow the fulfillment of one's purpose (understood as appropriate self-love) while restraining selfish self-love for one's own sake and the sake of others. Individual sovereignty is ceded to the general will, which, as opposed to Locke, is not the cumulative total of all the contract makers' sovereignty but is actually a whole that is more than the sum of the parts. The danger of such understandings is that those who do not agree with what is deemed the general will are considered either ill or subversive.

Social contract, in this specific sense, does not exist in Scripture. Rather, most social agreements in the OT are based on tribal affiliation, including relations of suzerainty and rules of hospitality. Something approaching a social contract, though without assumptions of individual autonomy or liberty, can be found in the Deuteronomic "original agreement" between God and his people. In particular, sections describing the role of political and legal authorities that require fairness by judges, limitation on the authority of the king, and protection of sojourners indicate some civil significance for all humans expressed in a legal agreement among the people and with God (Deut. 16:18–20; 17:14–20; 24:17–18). This interpretation, centuries later, played a role in Enlightenment theories of social contract when Puritan Samuel Rutherford, in *Lex, Rex* (1644), claimed that a constitutional monarchy, a contract between citizens and the government expressed in the regent, was both divinely intended and divinely limited, as evidenced by God's restraint on royal prerogative when the people asked for a king like other nations had, but Yahweh gave them one constrained by divine law (1 Sam. 8). This argument was later used and expanded by Locke.

In the NT, the political language of lordship is that of shared sovereignty or contract agreement. Further, the dominant image of the gathered Christian community is familial and covenantal, not contractual. Still, one basis of social contract can be found in the NT assertion of universal human worth to God. The notion of human rights exists in a nascent form, and Paul's plea on the basis of his Roman citizenship indicates how rights might be used under a social-contract arrangement. Still, modern political structures are not described in the text of the NT, nor is there any specific enumeration of negative rights or entitlement claims (positive rights) protected by social contract.

See also Covenant; Deontological Theories of Ethics; Government; Natural Law

James R. Thobaben

Social Service, Social Ministry

Social ministry is ministry to and with persons and communities that addresses their societal context, the needs of the whole person, and personal and social reform and renewal.

The biblical warrants for social ministry include the many injunctions to care for the poor and hungry, widows and orphans, as well as the broader mandate to combine justice and mercy. The parable of the good Samaritan (Luke 10:29–37) stands out, including its prophetic social critique. In addition, Jesus' own calling "to serve rather than be served" (see Mark 10:45) and his uniting the good news of God's reign with healing and social reintegration also provide guidance. In the OT, prophets speak to the responsibilities of those in power and of the whole people of God, putting political and economic matters under God's sovereignty. Both Testaments present the values and virtues of individuals and communities, seen in times of disaster and cooperative action. The NT provides four basic dimensions of ministry: *kergyma* (proclamation), *leitourgia* (worship), *koinōnia* (community), and *diakonia* (caring for physical needs), which is most linked to social ministry.

In earlier times, corporal works of mercy would address physical circumstances caused by social as well as natural factors (e.g., wars and war-related famines, enslavement, deportation). Diaconal service would still include agents of a faith community providing healthcare and institutions such as hospitals. Social services today link persons to a range of institutions that meet a variety of individual, familial, and communal needs; the dimension of ministry lies in the intent to serve the whole person in community and in so doing to reflect the imperatives of love and justice. Government "ministries" provide much of the social services in most developed countries.

Broadly speaking, social service ministries or social ministries help those who are disabled or disadvantaged. Both Testaments judge individuals and communities by their care for the "widows and orphans" and the "halt and the lame." Prophets and saints criticized the "faithful" for neglecting the disadvantaged. Sometimes these prophets went on to organize groups dedicated to specific forms of social ministry. At times, these groups have become institutions, some of which later were secularized.

In 1955, when the churches of the United States were entering into a time of postwar prosperity, the National Council of the Churches of Christ produced a comprehensive three-volume study, *Churches and Social Welfare*. Social welfare work was seen to include social service, social education and action, and social research. Reports from fourteen denominations summarized work in these areas, often drawing on traditions of immigrant mutual aid, circumstances of political and economic strength, particular theological inspiration (often by "social gospel" leaders; the 1908 Social Creed is specifically mentioned three times), and historic commitment (such as the Quakers' involvement in prison ministry and penal reform). Chapters in these volumes reflect strategically on the various levels of explicitly Christian influence that may accompany the provision of specific services, the need to protect human dignity without resorting to paternalism, the mixture of preventive and remedial concern, and the degree to which the church's role as social conscience may make it a critic of government and private institutions. Administration and funding challenges are also considered: "The basic objective must be continued development of strong, well equipped, well supported institutions under the influence of the Protestant churches" (Bachmann, Cayton, and Nishi 3:79).

The earlier ideas of the social gospel about social ministry brought social-science values and professionalism to a wide range of social work and ministry: settlement houses, YMCAs and YWCAs, specialized orphanages and therapeutic schools, homes for older persons, provision of counseling and training on family life and childrearing, help for immigrants, the training of volunteers to do direct service, and the training of ministers and priests to understand the need for social welfare and social workers. Temperance, antigambling, and public health/nutrition initiatives were meant to prevent tragedy, degradation, and family breakup; the transformation of rescue missions into rehabilitation centers, the rise of church-based counseling centers with clinical pastoral training of various forms—all spoke to a holistic understanding of salvation and health. The relatively recent development of "parish nurse" programs speaks to a bridging role for the church between its members and complex medical institutions and to the continuum between salvation and health in the community of the congregation.

In the 1960s, concern for racial justice led to the question of whether direct action, including demonstrations and protests, could be a form of social ministry. Between four hundred and five hundred Protestant ministers went to Hattiesburg and several other Mississippi towns in 1964 and volunteered their help with voter registration and various kinds of teaching. Although these efforts aroused tensions and exposed local residents to physical risks from some parts of the community, they persisted in a sometimes symbolic witness for justice and solidarity, crossing not only racial but also class lines. Participants themselves were profoundly changed as they sought to change the social climate and horizon for African Americans. A study by Nile Harper of what some called "servant ministry" or a "ministry of presence," based on seventy-four in-depth survey responses by Presbyterian ministers, showed that few lost their pulpits, and most were family men with an average of three young children. Harper more recently charted the work of "religious collaborative working for social transformation" involving ranges of stakeholders and community-building strategies.

In the more recent period in the United States, some services and institutions directed to serve particular racial-ethnic populations have changed focus, seeking to meet new demographic or educational needs. The "deinstitutionalization" of the mentally ill, facilitated by new medications, led to more homeless persons beginning in the 1970s. Very basic services, such as food banks and clothing distribution, have been needed to face the rise of homelessness of more than one million citizens starting in the 1980s. Prison ministry has also been increasingly needed to meet the vast numbers of persons convicted of drug-related offenses, sometimes connected to addiction and mental illness.

The role of welfare itself became widely debated; critics of dependency alleged that government support weakened families and benefited social service providers. Critics also pointed to the stagnation of real wages, deindustrialization, and persistent levels of unemployment, particularly in inner cities. Critics such as John McKnight, though supportive of government social welfare provision, pointed to the lack of actual care in the treatment of caseloads of clients and to the development of disempowered "client neighborhoods." Scholarly debate has identified sophisticated forms of "blame the victim" and "unintended consequences" in dealing with an "underclass" dimension of persistent poverty in areas abandoned by all but mandated service providers and struggling public schools. The "feminization of poverty" has also been noted in the growth of households headed by mothers; the absent fathers are often poor as well, but the focus is more on the high proportion of impoverished children.

Since the 1990s, some churches have adapted the broad language of "public ministry" rather than "urban" or "rural" ministry to address the combination of service and advocacy for services and social change needed. Communitarian ethics seeking the common or public good is invoked, capacity-building is a goal, and cultural creativity is encouraged. Although more US citizens will have medical insurance after the healthcare legislation enacted in 2010, advocacy is still needed in many areas of social service for availability, adequacy, accessibility, affordability, and accountability (Miller and Burggrabe).

Dieter Hessel's *Social Ministry* offers a comprehensive vision of social ministry as a liberating dimension of ministry learned from struggles for social change from the 1960s. This approach lifts up the benefits of social involvement for churches that are sometimes fearful of being "political." He argues for coalitional and organizing strategies that link particular caring action with larger social analysis, including reflection on the church's own situation as a community and an institution. The range of experts is also expanded to include not only the established and credentialed but also the affected and change agents, including independent prophets. Rather than be trapped in the private sphere in its own "downward mobility," the church and its members are given confidence to address the public order and its dysfunctions and to sustain these efforts without "burnout" or isolation. He contrasts a constructive opposition to all forms of abandonment and scapegoating with a crusading style that can confuse public piety with social righteousness. This vision of social ministry, then, combines the pastoral and the prophetic, seeks to build congregational sustainability, addresses lifestyle change for ecojustice and wider sustainability, and appeals to real interests and personal needs while at the same time putting them in a shared context. Social ministry provides a dimension of corporate responsibility to enhance the vocation of every Christian concerned to be part of the "salt and light" described in Matt. 5:13–16.

See also Charity, Works of; Common Good; Justice; Neighbor, Neighbor Love; Poverty and Poor; Welfare State

Bibliography

Bachmann, T., H. Cayton, and S. Nishi, eds. *Churches and Social Welfare*. 3 vols. National Council of the Churches of Christ in the U.S.A., 1955; Findlay, J., Jr. *Church People in the Struggle: The National Council of Churches and the Black Freedom Movement, 1950–1970*. Oxford University Press, 1993; Harper, N., *Journeys into Justice: Religious Collaboratives Working for Social Transformation*. Bascom Hill, 2009; idem. *Social Conflict and Adult Christian Education*. General Division of Parish Education, Board of Christian Education, United Presbyterian Church U.S.A., n.d.; Hessel, D. *Social Ministry*. Rev. ed. Westminster John Knox, 1992; Miller, K., and J. Burggrabe. "A Health Crisis and a Healing Ministry." Pages 205–20 in *Envisioning the New City: A Reader on Urban Ministry*, ed. E. Meyers. Westminster John Knox, 1992.

Christian Iosso

Sociobiology *See* Science and Ethics

Sociology of Religion

Sociology is a social science that uses quantitative (e.g., surveys) and qualitative (e.g., personal interviews) tools to study how human beings relate to one another within a society or subculture. The discipline assumes that people both shape and are shaped by their environment. Sociology of religion is a branch of this larger discipline that studies how people put their beliefs about the sacred into practice as they interact with others, particularly through institutions and systems (political, economic, family, church, etc.). In this sense, the sociology of religion affects theology and ethics, as it concerns itself with the behavior of individuals and groups and the beliefs that inform those actions. Because the discipline focuses on the practical impact of religion, it presses beyond discussions of beliefs as mere abstractions and instead steers us to faith's moral and pragmatic importance.

The founders of sociology devoted much effort to the study of religion because of its unquestioned significance for providing meaning. However, many sociologists believed Max Weber's prediction of religion's demise, claiming that it would fade in a "disenchanted world" in which science, technology, bureaucracy, and other aspects of modernization reigned. This secularization theory continues to provide useful insights but is now tempered by religion's vitality in much of the world, including the Global South and industrialized nations such as the United States.

One of the major concerns of sociologists of religion has been the definition of religion itself. There are two major schools of thought, each associated with pioneers in sociology. Influenced by Émile Durkheim, some emphasize the function of religion within a culture or group, usually with an eye to how faith supports a particular moral outlook or helps control behavior. Durkheim and many after him viewed religion as inherently conservative of the status quo. Others, taking their cue from Max Weber, stress the substance or content of a faith tradition and the ways that beliefs influence patterns of relationships and forge ethical frameworks. For theological ethics, understanding how beliefs function in society as well as their substance is crucial.

In Rom. 12:1–2 Paul warns of subtle encroachments of society upon Christian beliefs; he commands a renewal of mind that bears fruit in moral transformation. Sociologists provide "sensitizing concepts" or theories regarding various aspects of culture that influence us, such as race, ritual, gender, identity, power, individualism, community, and class. Revealing how faith commitments intersect experience, sociology provides tools for understanding our cultural milieu and its influence on us, as well as for measuring faith's impact on our world.

Bibliography

Bellah, R., et al. *Habits of the Heart: Individualism and Commitment in American Life*. 3rd ed. University of California Press, 2007; Dillon, M., ed. *Handbook of the Sociology of Religion*. Cambridge University Press, 2003; Emerson, M., and C. Smith. *Divided by Faith: Evangelical Religion and the Problem of Race in America*. Oxford University Press, 2001; Wuthnow, R. *Acts of Compassion: Caring for Others and Helping Ourselves*. Princeton University Press, 1993.

Erin Dufault-Hunter

Sodomy

The term derives from *Sodom* (Heb. *sĕdōm*; Gk. *Sodoma*), the name of an ancient biblical city located in the southern portion of the Dead Sea corridor, which, according to Gen. 19:24–28, was destroyed along with the neighboring city of Gomorrah by Yahweh.

Although the exact nature of Sodom's sin(s) is never made clear in the Genesis account, most interpreters have linked it to the licentious behavior that its men display toward Lot's guests. In Gen. 19:4–9, the men of Sodom demand that Lot turn over his male guests so that they "may know them." Since the Hebrew word for "know" (*yāda'*) has sexual connotations (e.g., Gen. 4:1; 1 Sam. 1:19), the men appear to be demanding sexual intercourse with Lot's guests, an act expressly forbidden in Lev. 18:22; 20:13.

The notion that Sodom was destroyed because of its sexual perversion is made more explicit in 2 Pet. 2:6–10 and Jude 1:7, although the precise meanings of *aselgeia* ("licentiousness" [2 Pet. 2:7]), *epithymia miasmou* ("depraved lust" [2 Pet. 2:10]), and *sarx hetera* ("unnatural lust" [Jude 1:7]) do not necessarily refer to homosexual intercourse. In light of Gen. 18:1–8; 19:1–4, 8, it is a violation of the rule of hospitality and protection to traveling strangers, which was a crucial ethical mandate in that time. Josephus (*Ant.* 1.11.1), Ezek. 16:49–50, and Wis. 19:13–17 speak of Sodom's callous disregard of the poor and the stranger as being the primary cause of its destruction.

See also Homosexuality; Hospitality; Rape; Sexual Ethics

Bibliography

Gagnon, R. *The Bible and Homosexual Practice: Texts and Hermeneutics*. Abingdon, 2002; Helminiak, D. *What the Bible Really Says about Homosexuality*. Alamo Square Press, 2000.

Nicholas Read Brown

Solidarity

When the term *solidarity* is employed, many different ideas and practices come to mind, most frequently the independent trade union founded in 1980 by Lech Wałesa in Poland during the communist regime or the more recent *Marcha en Solidaridad con los Inmigrantes* (Immigrant Solidarity March) in 2008. These two historical events reflect a desire to represent the cause of a group or groups that are under distress or find themselves at risk in a marginalized situation. In this sense, solidarity promotes active, public participation to bring attention and change in favor of the group at risk. From this point of view, the moral responsibility of those who enter into solidarity with the group at risk is to identify actively with them and raise awareness of their current conditions, to pressure governmental authorities to intervene on behalf of those who are facing calamities and injustices, and to teach society as a whole about the plight of those at risk.

From a Christian perspective, solidarity goes beyond active participation and raising awareness; solidarity is grounded in the practice and principle of loving our neighbor, which in the biblical narrative is extended to our enemies (Matt. 5:44; Rom. 12:14). Entering into solidarity with the vulnerable and with those who have been wronged does not deny the importance of loving the enemy. Rather, solidarity is an empathic movement toward the protection of the least—the vulnerable and those who have been wronged. Loving the enemy, as a product of solidarity, is a call for transformation; loving the enemy is a call to self-identification with the least, just as committed persons work on behalf of the least and as silent bystanders are moved to action by practices of solidarity. Solidarity implies a self-transformative process in which everyone involved, oppressed and oppressors alike, place themselves in the condition and situation of "the other" out of love and respect. Solidarity represents a practice of sacrificial love and self-denial by everyone involved.

First, this practice of solidarity will lead those who are perceived as enemies to learn and see firsthand the consequences of their actions and the implications for the victims. Second, this practice will move silent bystanders by presenting them with a direct glimpse of suffering and distress, and also by confronting them with the comforts of their own and of the perpetrators' privileged positions. And finally, solidarity for those in vulnerable positions will lead to transformation in terms of equality, respect, and full participation in the decision-making process, which in turn will bring about social change. In terms of moral responsibility, the first two groups are responsible to make the initial move toward solidarity; that is, they, moved by the principle and practice of love for the neighbor, are responsible to self-identify with the vulnerable. Reality from a privileged position does not reflect life for everyone; the reality of the vulnerable is an integral part of everyone's life, and it becomes a daily call to solidarity.

The biblical narrative provides examples of this expression of solidarity, but one in particular addresses the three groups described above. Acts 2:42–47 is a community where solidarity is well represented. In this community there were some members in privileged positions—those who had possessions—and they were moved to sell their property and "break bread together" with everyone, but particularly taking care of the basic needs of those who did not have these means. At the same time, these practices serve as a testimony to "silent bystanders" who are perplexed by the actions of solidarity and are led to join this group. And of course the vulnerable, whose basic needs had not been met, now receive, each according to need.

See also Koinonia; Neighbor, Neighbor Love; Praxis

Bibliography

Bilgrien, M. *Solidarity: A Principle, an Attitude, a Duty? Or the Virtue for an Interdependent World?* AUS 7/204. Peter Lang, 1999; Horrell, D. *Solidarity and Difference: A Contemporary Reading of Paul's Ethics*. T&T Clark, 2005; Isasi-Díaz, A. "Solidarity: Love of Neighbor in the 1980s." Pages 31–40 in *Lift Every Voice: Constructing Christian Theologies from the Underside*, ed. S. Thistlewaite and M. Engel. Harper & Row, 1990.

Hugo Magallanes

Song of Songs

Of all biblical literature, Song of Songs may well be the least obvious site for an ethically oriented kind of criticism. Indeed, these poems' exquisite reveling in the erotic escapades of two young lovers outside the bounds of marriage, if anything, is likely to put Song of Songs beyond the ethical pale for many with traditionally oriented pieties. Yet, let us consider 4:1–7. In its essence this section offers a poetic rendition of a boy gazing at a girl. In the conceit of the so-called *wasf* (in Arabic literature, a genre in which an extended description of a person or other object is elaborated), the poem follows the boy's line of vision, as it were, as he admires one part of his beloved's body after another, moving from her head, topped with long, flowing dark hair, down to her gazelle-like breasts. At the very least, the poem provides a wonderful literary site from which to enter the discussion initiated by Laura Mulvey in 1975 about the "male gaze." But there is more here. This poem's staging of the "male gaze" has something positive of its own to contribute to the conversation. Gazing is never neutral, and far too frequently males looking at females even in the Bible results in violence perpetrated against the woman (e.g., Dinah in Gen. 34), though female gazing is not necessarily innocent either, as evidenced by the Shulammite's own stares in Song of Songs, which occasionally overwhelm her beloved (4:9; 6:5).

Still, not all gazing is of a kind; not all gazing, even by men, is destructive. These poems are a case in point. Here tone, however intangible and nebulous a quality, forever resisting precise specification, is absolutely critical. There is little doubt as to the loving nature of this boy's gaze. He is, after all, the one whom the girl's "soul loves" (3:1–4) and in whose eyes she finds "well-being" (*šālôm* [8:10])—a gazing, in other words, that is not only not malignant but also is judged by this girl to be life-enhancing. Here, then, in 4:1–7 we have the kind of "male gaze" that a woman can honor and enjoy, "one where the desire to discover her beauty is linked to a desire to discover her otherness, both sexually and personally" (Lambert, cited in Steiner 219). Worries over the hurt and violation that can result from the "male gaze" are real, well documented, and not to be lightly dismissed. But males are also capable of gazing lovingly, or so these poems would provoke us to believe—a not insignificant moral insight.

Song of Songs does not wear its ethics on its sleeves. After all, it is a sequence of love poems and not a treatise on the moral life. In this, it is very much like most of the Bible, in fact, where moral concerns are mostly not presented explicitly as points of textual interest. Therefore, whatever ethical sensibilities are to be gleaned from these poems require acts of reading, as in the much (too) abbreviated reading of 4:1–7 here, intent on engaging matters of ethical interest.

Not all is fair game, of course. Song of Songs, by dint of its subject matter—love—will open on to some moral issues more seamlessly, more readily, than others, and the book's own cultural particularity will itself always demand ethical negotiation. Moreover, readers will want to remain ever attuned to the lyricism of this poetry's underlying medium of discourse (see Dobbs-Allsopp), as not all that is of moral relevance is given propositionally in such poems (e.g., tone can have an ethical uptake). But in the end, the project of reading Song of Songs toward specifically ethical ends is a wonderfully open project that awaits only the decision to put these age-old love poems into conversation with the moral issues of the day. The possibility of a loving male gaze as provoked in the foregoing reading of 4:1–7 is offered as but one example of what may be achieved through such an ethically interested kind of criticism. There are many more poems in Song of Songs to read, and myriad moral concerns toward which to read them.

See also Old Testament Ethics; Poetic Discourse and Ethics

Bibliography

Dobbs-Allsopp, F. W. "Psalms and Lyric Verse." Pages 346–79 in *The Evolution of Rationality: Interdisciplinary Essays in Honor of J. Wentzel van Huyssteen*, ed. F. Shults. Eerdmans, 2006; Mulvey, L. "Visual Pleasure and Narrative Cinema." *Screen* 16, no. 3 (1975): 6–18; Steiner, W. *Venus in Exile: The Rejection of Beauty in Twentieth-Century Art*. Free Press, 2001.

Chip Dobbs-Allsopp

Sorcery *See* Divination and Magic

Speech Ethics

The ethics of human speech is concerned with the many ways words are used, their effects, and the intentions that lie behind them. But it is not sufficient simply to begin with the phenomenon of human speech, since Christian thought generally has located our speaking as an antiphonal response to God's, in creation and supremely in Jesus Christ. It is therefore necessary to specify what human speech is *for* before being able to name its corruptions. Broadly, two chief purposes for speech are worship and instruction.

In worship, the psalms orient human words to God's ways by locating our praise, despair, adoration, longing, entreaty, and lament within Israel's liturgy and hymnody. In singing the psalms, gentile Christians were joined to Israel's life by learning the appropriate ways to address God even while all Christians (Jewish and gentile) needed to reckon with God's new speech in and as Christ. It is not surprising, then, that the principal corruptions of speaking lie in false worship (heterodoxy) and the denial of God. According to Jas. 3:2, one who is able to avoid offense in speaking is a perfect person, but because "all of us make many mistakes," those whose speaking arguably has the greatest impact and is presumed closest to intending truth—teachers—are subject to severe judgment.

Both purposes highlight how the Bible seems to side with critics of modernity's notorious yearning after detachment when it touches on the theme of speech ethics, for the modern ideal champions distance from objects of worship and objects of instruction alike. Speech's corruptions may be viewed as various kinds of separations.

Falsification and Silence

The most obvious separation is between speaking and doing—hypocrisy, of which Jesus repeatedly accuses the scribes and Pharisees (e.g., Matt. 6:5; 22:18; 23:13; Mark 7:6). When speech is false, it betrays an unwillingness either to face or to trust the truth that, for Christian thought, is often synonymous with a distorted approach to confession. The Bible forbids lying, understood as both a strictly legal act (Exod. 20:16; Deut. 19:18) and an indication of a wicked heart (Ps. 15:2) subject to God's judgment (Ps. 5:6). The first contradicts the legal obligation to tell the truth, and the second contradicts the restless heart's true end.

In its effects, a lie offends against the way things are, which usually involves those who are wrongly included in the lie. This other is paradigmatically one's neighbor, although this becomes reconfigured in the NT because of the work of Christ, wherein the justification for not wronging the neighbor owes to the fact that one's self and one's neighbor are now members of each other (Eph. 4:25).

Consider the story of Rahab. Rahab is commended for her aid of Israel's spies not because she lied to protect them, but because she showed them welcome and mercy (Josh. 2; 6:17; Heb. 11:31). Quite apart from Rahab's hiding of the spies, however, what about the act of spying? For Thomas Aquinas, the act of "laying ambushes" seems to intend to deceive even though it is unproblematic for God to command Joshua to do it (Josh. 8:2) because it is a concealment carried out not by speech or by breaking a promise (see below) but through silence and thus is not, properly speaking, deception, particularly if it serves the ends of justice as in a just war (*ST* II-II, q. 40, a. 3). When challenged about whether one may lie to a murderer, Immanuel Kant agreed that although it is impermissible to lie, silence might be the response most faithful to truthfulness.

Verity and Its Guarantees

Where the Bible addresses the issue of truth-telling, it sometimes seems inconsistent on swearing oaths. Oaths are sometimes positively enjoined (Deut. 6:13) or simply presupposed as an important element of human speech (Heb. 6:16). God swears an oath to uphold his promise to Abraham (Gen. 22:16; Heb. 6:17). But Jas. 5:12 emphatically prohibits swearing and mandates "let your 'Yes' be yes and your 'No' be no," agreeing with Jesus' teaching that sets in opposition truthful speech and the speaking of oaths (Matt. 5:34, 37). Such prohibitions are not even primarily concerned with the speaking of false oaths. This is because even an oath that is honored betrays a separation in transferring moral obligation away from the more fundamental need always to speak truthfully (as when not under oath) and places it on the oath's promise. Keeping the oath then risks becoming more important than telling the truth except insofar as the former fulfills the latter.

In contemporary reflection, actions that are accomplished by speaking (such as promising) are often understood according to J. L. Austin's nomenclature as "performative." Promising and oath-taking perform the actions they speak. "I promise to" does not refer to something that I do; it is something I do when I speak it. Such performances, however, may still go wrong when there is a contradiction between what one is doing by speaking (promising) and what one is doing by means of speaking (covering one's tracks, for instance, or reassuring the other party that one can be trusted). An oath that is employed "without necessity and due caution" (Thomas Aquinas, *ST* II-II, q. 89, a. 2) trades in this kind of contradiction. An oath that invokes God as a witness (as "so help me God"), but either intends merely to placate the listener or else is spoken concerning frivolous matters, still performs the promise to speak truthfully in its meaning even while contradicting itself by the manner in which it is enacted.

Even though perjury seeks to hold together forces of separation (telling the truth and the promise to do so), its method accomplishes this by joining two other forces that ought to be kept separate. Perjury is possible only in the presence of an oath, without which deceptive speech simply constitutes lying. In practice, Christians who have refused to take oaths out of fidelity to certain biblical injunctions not to do so have often discovered a link between sovereign-judicial power and the requirement for oath-taking that supersedes the requirement to speak truthfully. This is because perjury can justify official punishments only after speech is brought within the regulatory schema of sovereignty. Jesus' teaching against oath-taking, then, may be seen as a way of freeing speech from the official demands of those who hold power, thus also disconnecting truth from power itself.

God's Name in Vain

Returning to the purposes of human speech, we note that if truth is disconnected from human sovereign power in the biblical warnings against oath-taking, it is for the purpose of reestablishing an appropriate concern that human speech be used properly of God. In his sermons on the psalms, Augustine understood adoration to be the paradigm of truthful speech, returning the gift of speech to its giver; adoration is the proper use of God's name (*Enarrat. Ps.* 98.9).

Speaking God's name in vain (Exod. 20:7; Deut. 5:11), therefore, is not identical with speaking words that fail to accomplish something. Indeed, it belongs to adoration not to be concerned at all with accomplishments precisely through its giving words back. Rather, using God's name in vain robs God's name of its power. It attempts to do with words alone what can come only from God. Adoration is speech marked foremost by its prodigality and so by its trust that God can link speech with effects. God can swear by God's own name (Heb. 6:13) because his power to keep promises is identical with his power to make them. Humans, on the other hand, are limited with making promises that depend on the continuing presence of God's name to their promises in order for them to be true.

Connected to God's power, human speech will forgo many of the connections with speech's effects, such as preeminently in the example of Jesus, who entrusted the outcome of his suffering to God rather than return abuse with abuse (1 Pet. 2:22–23). Commenting on John 8:44, Augustine refers to "the father of lies" as one who chose to "live according to his own self," eminently not returning words to God as speech (*Civ.* 14.3). Self-worship and autonomy are therefore nearly synonymous with lying, keeping one's words for oneself. Consequently, God's name is used improperly when it becomes merely another name for the self; it is the speech of idolatry.

By contrast, instruction must continually submit itself to correction in its attempt to be true. The NT and early Christian association of proper authority (the church rather than the self) with avoiding heresy underscore that right teaching about God involves more than getting the facts right. It involves the persistent openness to challenge because, as Augustine understood, teaching is also confession in both senses, and, as James said, "all of us make many mistakes."

God's Speech

It is perhaps less immediately clear how affirmation of Jesus Christ as the word of God yields an ethic for human speech. If adoration of God is the paradigm for human speech, then when people speak to one another about God's acts, they adore God through proclaiming the gospel. In this way, the proclamation of the gospel is itself also a form of the word of God. But it is truly proclamation only when human words yield to God's own speaking in human speech, where "God Himself gives Himself to it as its theme" (Barth 95). As a teacher of God's kingdom, Jesus proclaimed the word of God (e.g.,

Luke 5:1), even though Christianity was not content with a Jesus who simply brings God's communication to the world or symbolizes an antecedent message. Rather more fundamentally, from its earliest theology (e.g., John 1), the church asserted that Jesus *is* the communication of the Father to us.

The fact that the Word became flesh (John 1:14), that God has materially become a word-presence in the world, enables the preaching of the gospel to be the gospel just as speech about Jesus must in some way be said to deliver Jesus himself (see Acts 17:3; contrast with 1 John 1:5). Moreover, because the church (as at Pentecost with tongues of fire [Acts 2]) is a speaking agent of Jesus-talk and is likewise the body of Christ that speaks of him, Jesus witnesses to his own status as God's good news—there is no other possible conclusion—sacramentally both from within the church and as the church. The Holy Spirit (as Spirit of the risen Christ) is precisely a witness to Christ in Christian testimony about him in this sense.

This Christology entails a speech ethic for the church. Its speaking of God is always disciplined by a provisionality appropriate to the freedom of its subject and the nature of its words as living, and so simultaneously both given to and wrested from human control. For this reason, Augustine understood the confession of sin to be the paramount human posture of speech for those who endeavor to "do the truth" (John 3:21). This speaking accuses one's own evil works and does not work to achieve self-forgiveness, but instead seeks God's forgiveness (*Tract. ev. Jo.* 12, on John 3:6–21). Such self-criticism arises not out of lack of faith in God or even of words, but rather out of faith that human words will be most truthful when the ultimacy of their meanings and intentions is given back to God to be the word of God, since Jesus Christ himself, as the Word, will always be the one capable of speaking about God most truthfully.

See also Blasphemy; Blessing and Cursing; Confession; Dishonesty; Honesty; Hypocrisy; Libel; Oaths; Promise and Promise-Keeping; Slander; Truthfulness, Truth-Telling; Vows

Bibliography

Austin, J. L. *How to Do Things with Words*. Clarendon, 1962; Barth, K. *Church Dogmatics*. Vol. I/1. T&T Clark, 1936; Griffiths, P. *Lying: An Augustinian Theology of Duplicity*. Brazos, 2004; Hovey, C. *Speak Thus: Christian Language in Church and World*. Cascade, 2008.

Craig Hovey

Spousal Abuse

On the face of it, abuse of any sort is, by definition, unethical, let alone unchristian. Yet one of the difficulties faced by Christian women and some men is that they are indeed victims of brutality in their most intimate relationships, and that too often the church in its understanding of its tradition and texts has been complicit to terror, injury, and cycles of aggression. Spousal abuse can be physical (e.g., strangling, beating, kicking, shoving, throwing objects, slapping, rape, or murder) or emotional and psychological (e.g., ridiculing, demeaning, shaming, withholding affection, blaming, or threatening). In order to combat injustice and misuse of Scripture, central concerns of the gospel, such as renouncing violence while pressing for reconciliation and transformation, must be applied to Christian marriage.

History and the (Mis)use of Texts

Two recurring scriptural topics (as well as the interpretation and application of them) must be considered: violence against women and commands for wives to submit to husbands. For many feminists and others, such texts indicate that the Bible at worst supports violence against women, especially wives, or at least justifies some forms of abuse and nonintervention by the church.

Several stories of brutality toward women occur in the OT (e.g., Judg. 11:30–39; 19:22–30; 2 Sam. 13; Ezek. 16:35–43; 23:25–35). On closer examination, interpretation of these "texts of terror," as well as the history of their interpretation, proves far from self-evidently misogynistic. Despite their disturbing content, from within the larger context of Scripture and many precritical interpreters, these stories do not support spousal abuse or cruelty toward women (Trible xiii–8; Thompson 222–53). However, awareness of ways women have been abused must inform how such texts are read, preached, and applied.

Careful consideration of texts calling for the submission of women (Eph. 5:22; Col. 3:18; 1 Pet. 3:1, 6) must be taken up elsewhere. However, even interpreters who read such verses as affirming males as the sole leaders in families and the church note that the NT clearly prohibits misuse of such authority. Instead, true authority finds its model in the servanthood and self-giving love of Christ (e.g., Mark 10:41–45; Eph. 5:25). In addition, only the most questionable interpretation and application of Scripture would twist commands for willing submission into justifications for violence or cruelty. The NT seems quite aware of the propensity for just such misapplications, and most texts that affirm authority also contain explicit corrections to misuse (Col. 3:19; 1 Pet. 3:7), while others strongly forbid harmful speech (Jas. 3:6, 9–10).

If the prohibition of divorce has often kept spouses in abusive situations without recourse, Christians must be mindful that the oft-quoted words of God in Mal. 2:16, "For I hate divorce," cannot be separated from what immediately follows: God also hates "covering one's garment with violence." That some continue to distort Scripture in order to justify spousal abuse attests to the insidious nature of violence and the need for consistent repentance, renewal of our marriage vows, and communal commitment to their fulfillment.

Response of the Church Today: Keeping Vows

Spousal abuse not only violates an individual victim but also ravages the covenant of marriage itself, affecting families, society, and the community charged with sustaining promises of faithful love. In most forms of Christian marriage, the vows contain something similar to those found in the *Book of Common Prayer* (1979): "I take you to be my wife/husband, to have and to hold . . . for better or worse . . . until we are parted by death."

These simple vows remind us not just of the seriousness of our promise to remain with one person and to refrain from sexual infidelity. The vows themselves—"to have and to hold"—are dense and rich concepts that not only indicate unity (1 Cor. 7:4) but also charge us to engage in a lasting embrace that protects, provides, and cares for the other. These promises forbid manipulation or force against another who has now become one with us through this sacramental act (Gen. 2:24; Eph. 5:31). In addition, the church and witnesses to the ceremony promise to do their best to sustain the couple, to aid them in their fidelity to these vows. This includes actively promoting healing from wrongs done to each other, from minor ways we fail to cherish each other to infidelities of all kinds, including abuse. One irony of our sin is that love and hate remain closely linked, and we too often injure (or are injured by) those with whom we are most intimate, thus creating a deep wound and shattering the bonds of trust. Churches and friends must continue to speak truthfully about spousal abuse, calling for repentance and reconciliation.

In an age in which egalitarian and companionate marriages have become a widely accepted goal, Christian marriage continues to serve as a kiln that fires individuals into a community marked by the loving-kindness of the God who unites them (John 13:34–35; Eph. 5:21). Spousal abuse by a man or woman twists a sacrament meant to sustain us in mutual affection and the love of God and neighbor into an evil that reveals humankind's propensity to choose violence over humility and fury over forgiveness, even with those whom we have promised to guard and nurture. In the face of the sin of spousal abuse, Christians call one another back to the intentions of marriage and the vows made to one another, refusing to allow either victims or perpetrators to languish alone or covenants to disintegrate into testimonies of infidelity and fear.

See also Covenant; Feminist Ethics; Headship; Household Codes; Marriage and Divorce; Sexual Abuse; Violence; Women, Status of

Bibliography

Adams, C., and M. Fortune, eds. *Violence against Women and Children: A Christian Theological Sourcebook*. Continuum, 1995; Green, J. *1 Peter*. THNTC. Eerdmans, 2007; Kroeger, C., and N. Nason-Clark. *No Place for Abuse: Biblical and Practical Resources to Counteract Domestic Violence*. InterVarsity, 2001; McClure, J., and N. Ramsay. *Telling the Truth: Preaching about Sexual and Domestic Violence*. United Church Press, 1998; Thompson, J. *Writing the Wrongs: Women of the Old Testament among Biblical Commentators from Philo through the Reformation*. Oxford University Press, 2001; Trible, P. *Texts of Terror: Literary-Feminist Readings of Biblical Narratives*. Fortress, 1984.

Erin Dufault-Hunter

State, The *See* Government

Stealing *See* Theft

Stewardship

In the Christian faith, the word *stewardship* usually refers to the management of one's life, possessions, and resources in a manner that reflects the conviction that these are trusts from God. The concept is broad and, at its widest, becomes virtually synonymous with discipleship, encompassing all aspects of Christian living. The emphatic notion of stewardship, however, lies in the claim that all things belong to God.

The term *stewardship* is loosely derived from biblical narratives featuring persons who are described as "stewards"; typically, these are people who live in a place that they do not own, making full use of (but also taking care of) things that do not belong to them. Abraham had a steward, a servant "who had charge of all that he had" (Gen. 24:2). Joseph was a steward of Potiphar in Egypt (Gen. 39:1–6) and then later had a steward of his own (Gen. 44:1–5). In the NT, stewards (sometimes called "managers") are mentioned in Matt. 20:8; Luke 8:3; John 2:8.

Most important, Jesus tells stewardship parables about travelers who go on journeys and leave others in charge of their possessions (Matt. 21:33–43; 24:45–51; 25:14–30; cf. Luke 16:1–10). Typically, these parables provide examples of "good stewards" and "bad stewards." Thus, a simple ethical paradigm emerges: people live in the world as stewards of God, entrusted with caring for all that God so generously allows them to use, and they are accountable to God for whether they prove to be good stewards or bad ones.

Beyond this obvious point, however, a deeper level of understanding is often obtained. What theologians derive from Jesus' parables (and other biblical literature) is that bad stewardship is not just a matter of negligence or carelessness. The root cause of bad stewardship is a fundamental misunderstanding or false claim regarding ownership. Thus, in one of Jesus' stories, wicked tenants (stewards) try to retain control of a vineyard that they apparently have decided belongs to them (Matt. 21:33–41). So, Christian ethicists often maintain that a fundamental problem with humans is that they fail to realize that God is only allowing them to use what still belongs to God.

The biblical teaching of stewardship challenges human presumption while simultaneously allowing that human beings are uniquely entrusted with caring for everything God has made (Gen. 1:28; Ps. 8:6). They are granted dominion (Gen. 1:26), but apart from God they are only dust (Gen. 3:19); they bring nothing into this world and take nothing out of it (Job 1:21), they possess nothing that is not a gift (1 Cor. 4:7), and they must be called again and again to remember this (Deut. 8:12–18).

Theological Basis

The theological basis for stewardship derives first and foremost from a doctrine of creation. The psalmists and other biblical writers make explicit that recognizing God as creator involves an affirmation that all things belong to God: "The earth is the LORD's and all that is in it, the world, and those who live in it" (Ps. 24:1 [cf. Neh. 9:6])."Know that the LORD is God. It is he that made us, and we are his" (Ps. 100:3). In the NT, Jesus Christ is connected with this work of creation (John 1:2–3), and a similar conclusion is reached: "All things have been created through him and for him" (Col. 1:16).

A further basis for the theological and ethical notion of stewardship lies in the biblical doctrine of redemption. Paul puts it this way: "You are not your own, for you were bought with a price" (1 Cor. 6:19–20). The "price" to which Paul refers is the blood of Jesus Christ. Jesus gave his life as a "ransom for many" (Mark 10:45), and those who have been saved from death and hell are now to live for Christ, who died for them (2 Cor. 5:15). This construal is essentially a development of covenant theology that, in the OT, grounded what we would now call "stewardship doctrine" in redemption as well as in creation. In both Testaments, the significant point is that belonging to God (or to Christ) is viewed not as a response to redemption (something we owe God for redeeming us) but rather as the essential content of redemption (belonging to God = what it means to be redeemed). It is not payback for salvation; it *is* salvation. God's declaration to Israel, "I will be your God, and you shall be my people" (Lev. 26:12 [cf. Jer. 11:4; 30:22]), is but one expression of ownership as redemption. The essential point of this affirmation was not that people were obligated to God for freeing them from bondage (although that also would be true) but that the God who had freed them from bondage was willing to take ownership of them, and that through belonging to this God the people would experience redemption in an ongoing and permanent sense.

A similar perspective is articulated in a third theological basis for stewardship: the doctrine of the reign (or kingdom) of God. Jesus spoke often of God's kingdom as something that was near (Mark 1:15), something that people could seek (Matt. 6:33), something that they could enter (John 3:5), something that was among them (Luke 17:21). By speaking of God's kingdom in such terms, Jesus meant to emphasize that people do not have to die and go to heaven in order to live in a realm of power ruled by God. Already, in this life, God is ready and willing to rule human lives. Jesus called this message "the gospel," and he expected it to change people's lives, to make a difference in how they thought and behaved (Mark 1:15; see also Isa. 52:7).

Finally, stewardship is also grounded in the biblical doctrine of the sovereignty of God and, in the NT, in the related concept of the lordship of Christ. Jesus is to be acclaimed as Lord from birth (Luke 2:11) to parousia (Phil. 2:11), which means (at least) that to be a Christian is to be a person who names Jesus Christ as being in charge of one's life. Such servitude, furthermore, is presented not as oppressive, but as an experience of "rest" (Matt. 11:28–30).

From the above, two overall conclusions should be obvious. First, stewardship in the Bible is always 100 percent. While the notion of the "tithe" and other forms of "percentage giving" become relevant with regard to discussions about how specific assets are to be allocated for God, the transcendent concern is that people belong to God in totality, and that they are to regard all that they have as gifts from God to be used in accord with God's will.

Second, stewardship is presented throughout the Bible as both obligation and privilege, with emphasis on the latter. God has appointed the followers of Jesus to be the "light of the world" and the "salt of the earth," the people whose good works will inspire others to glorify the Father in heaven (Matt. 5:13–16).

Expressions of Stewardship

Stewardship takes a variety of forms in the contemporary church, applicable to various aspects of life under God. The following are representative.

Stewardship of physical bodies emphasizes care for one's physical self. A favored biblical basis is found in Paul's teaching that human bodies are temples of the Holy Spirit (1 Cor. 6:19–20) that may be offered to God as living sacrifices (Rom. 12:1). Such teaching opposes gnostic tendencies to evaluate what is fleshly or bodily in a negative way; it also places concern for matters such as nutrition, exercise, dental care, stress management, and substance abuse within the sphere of religious ethics.

Stewardship of time deals with time management in a manner analogous to concerns involving money taken up under the rubric of financial stewardship (see below). The concern in Christian ethics is not only with whether one's time is being used productively but also with whether it is being spent in ways that accord with the divine will.

Stewardship of families views issues connected with marriage, parenting, and other aspects of family life from a perspective that understands one's family to be a gift and trust from God. The difficult sayings of Jesus claiming that love for him must take priority over love for one's family members (Matt. 10:37; Luke 14:26; cf. Mark 10:29 pars.) are key in these discussions: one does not belong to one's parents or spouse or children; one belongs only to God. Healthy family relationships arise within contexts in which the basic identity and security of all persons are established via their preeminent relationship with Christ. Additional texts relevant to these concerns include the Ten Commandments (Exod. 20:1–17), various teachings of Jesus (Mark 7:9–13; 10:2–12), and the household codes found in certain NT letters (Eph. 5:21–6:9; Col. 3:18–4:1; 1 Tim. 2:8–15; 5:1–2; 6:1–2; Titus 2:1–10; 1 Pet. 2:13–3:7).

Stewardship of the gospel derives from the notion that God has entrusted Christians with the gift of a message of salvation and charged them with the task of spreading that word to all (1 Cor. 4:1; 1 Pet. 4:10; cf. Matt. 28:18–20). It is through human beings that God continues to reconcile the world through Christ (2 Cor. 5:18–20).

Stewardship of the earth involves a host of issues connected with caring for the planet or physical environment that God has created (Gen. 1:26; Ps. 8:6): conserving water and soil; recycling paper, aluminum, and other products; preserving wetlands and rain forests; preventing pollution, adverse erosion, radical climate change, or the unnecessary extinction of species; and much more. In a basic sense, environmental stewardship understands dominion (Gen. 1:26–28) to imply responsibility as well as privilege and thus a commitment to preserve the integrity of God's world for future generations. Beyond this basic call for conservation, however, many ethicists append concern for equity (fair distribution of resources) and efficiency (avoidance of waste or exploitation, regardless of whether adverse effects are discernible). The science of ecology, furthermore, has impacted environmental ethics dramatically in recent years, such that many ethicists now maintain that previous concerns for conservation were inevitably anthropocentric, viewing humans as the only aspect of creation to possess intrinsic value and viewing nature as possessing only instrumental value. The trend in modern environmental ethics is toward viewing all aspects of creation (plants, animals, humans, soil, water, air, etc.) as tightly integrated into a biotic community that, as a whole, is viewed as inherently good (Gen. 1:31) and, as a whole, has been reconciled to God through Christ (Col. 1:20).

Stewardship of finances receives by far the most attention in religious communities. At least five areas of concern are worth noting:

1. *Acquisition of money.* Negatively, people are to avoid earning money in dishonest ways (Lev. 19:35–36; Deut. 25:13–16; Prov. 10:2; Jer. 17:11; Amos 8:5–6; Luke 3:13–14); in ways that inflict hardship on others, especially the poor (Exod. 22:25–27; Lev. 25:35–37; Amos 2:6–7; 5:11; Luke 20:47; Jas. 5:1–6); or in ways that allow the acquisition of material things to become an end in itself (Isa. 5:8; Luke 12:15–21). Positively, work is to be encouraged (2 Thess. 3:10–12) and, indeed, viewed as a vocation from God.
2. *Regard for money.* The Bible has much to say about attitudes toward money. Wealth may be considered a gift from God (Deut. 8:12–14, 17–18), but money should not become a prime source for joy and meaning in life (1 Tim. 6:10), nor should it exercise a controlling influence (Matt. 6:24). Beyond this, the Bible counsels against greed (Matt. 6:19;

Luke 12:15), covetousness (Exod. 20:17), envy (Matt. 20:1–15), and anxiety over material concerns (Matt. 6:25–33), encouraging instead a sense of trust and gratitude (Phil. 4:6). The biblical ideal is contentment: satisfaction with what one has, whether much or little (Phil. 4:11–12).

3. *Management of money*. This is not a prominent concern in the Bible, but there is general counsel against both hoarding money (Luke 12:16–21) and squandering it (Luke 15:11–16); doing nothing at all with money is also condemned (Matt. 25:14–30). Modern ethicists discern a number of issues for believers who want to manage their money in ways pleasing to God: avoiding unnecessary debt is a key factor; asking questions concerning the ethical criteria for including a company in one's investment portfolio also come into play.
4. *Use of money*. Christian ethics teaches that all money is to be used in ways that accord with God's will. A distinction is sometimes made between necessities and luxuries; the latter are not to be avoided altogether, but frugal limitation is encouraged. This notion derives from the somewhat paradoxical teaching of Scripture that does not typically discount the enjoyment of affluence per se but does encourage frugality, sharing (Luke 3:11; Acts 4:32–37), and even divestment (Mark 10:17–22).
5. *Giving*. Christian stewardship teaches that believers are not only to use all of their money in ways pleasing to God; they are also to give away a generous portion of that money. The OT refers often to tithing (an offering of 10 percent), but the manner in which tithes were determined and allocated seems to have varied over time (Lev. 27:30–33; Num. 18:20–32; Deut. 14:22–29; Neh. 10:32–39; Mal. 3:8–10). Most modern ethicists do not regard the tithe as binding on Christians (Gal. 3:23–26), though they may still commend it as a traditional benchmark. More often, two types of Christian giving are identified as normative for all believers. First, Christians are to support their religious communities with gifts proportionate to their assets and circumstances (2 Cor. 8:3, 12–13; 9:7). The presentation of such offerings as an act of worship expresses the church's theology (derived in part from 1 Chr. 29:14) that believers are not simply helping the institution to pay its bills but are returning to God a symbolic portion of what in fact belongs to God. Second, believers are expected to offer generous and sacrificial gifts that go well beyond mere support for their local congregation. Such gifts correspond loosely to the giving of alms in the Bible, and they might be made to individuals or institutions or to any number of charitable causes (Matt. 5:42; 6:2–4; Acts 20:35).

See also Almsgiving; Body; Creation Ethics; Ecological Ethics; Economic Ethics; Generosity; Greed; Loans; Property and Possessions; Time, Use of; Tithe, Tithing; Wealth

Bibliography

Blomberg, C. *Neither Poverty nor Riches: A Biblical Theology of Material Possessions*. Eerdmans, 1999; Brattgård, H. *God's Stewards: Theological Study of the Principles and Practices of Stewardship*. Augsburg, 1963; Clinard, T. *Responding to God: The Life of Stewardship*. Westminster, 1980; Hall, D. *The Steward: A Biblical Symbol Come of Age*. Rev. ed. Eerdmans, 1990; Hoge, D., et al. *Money Matters: Personal Giving in American Churches*. Westminster John Knox, 1996; Kantonen, T. *A Theology of Christian Stewardship*. Muhlenberg, 1956; Kauffman, M. *Stewards of God*. Herald Press, 1975; Powell, M. *Giving to God: The Bible's Good News about Living a Generous Life*. Eerdmans, 2006; Reumann, J. *Stewardship and the Economy of God*. Eerdmans, 1991; Vallet, R. *The Steward Living in Covenant: A New Perspective on Old Testament Stories*. Eerdmans, 2001.

Mark Allan Powell

Submission and Subordination

As a topic within biblical ethical discourse, the English words *submission* and *subordination*, and their related verbal forms, translate the Greek term *hypotassō*, which defined and regulated the behaviors and attitudes appropriate to a system of social, political, and cosmic relationships in ancient Greco-Roman culture and to some degree in the social world of Hebrew culture. This regulatory language conforms to the top-down, vertical orientation of relationships of power, prestige, responsibility, and obligation in antiquity. Moreover, in the cultural contexts that shaped worldviews and social behavior of the communities and individuals responsible for the biblical writings, power and authority typically ran along patriarchal lines.

In recent decades, as themes of the American culture wars have been embraced and engaged by advocates of a variety of discourses (liberation, feminist, postcolonial, gender/queer), as well as, at a more popular level, by certain church leaders, the language of subordination and submission has been assessed for both historical and contemporary relevance. It remains central within the lexicon of reactionary traditionalists in conservative evangelical churches in discussions about family and the role of women in ministry, where it is often insisted that biblical social configurations (in marriage, family, and church leadership) are valid for all time.

Against the background of these trends, there are two immediate issues to address. The first is exegetical: the range of meanings that *hypotassō* might express in biblical use and the influence of any broader theological impulses that would guide an understanding. The second is hermeneutical and relates to the adoption of biblical-ethical patterns to modern situations: what is the bearing of this relation-shaping language embedded in an ancient culture on similar relationships in another culture?

Biblical Usage: The Range of Relationships; Diversity of Meaning

The lexicons offer as the basic definition of *hypotassō*, our key Greek word, "to order under." This is the sum total of the root, *tassō* ("I order or arrange"), plus the preposition *hypo* ("under"). The assumptions and architecture of Greco-Roman culture fostered and reinforced the sense of a top-down, vertical organization of power and prestige structures.

The OT usage of the concept (with the key Greek term in the LXX) is not widespread. A scattering of LXX texts commends submission to God as the human obligation (Pss. 36:7 [37:7 ET]; 61:2 [62:1 ET]; 2 Macc. 9:12). Submission to the messianic reign is endorsed in Ps. 8:7 (8:6 ET); Dan. 7:27. Elsewhere the tradition endorses submission to kings and rulers (3 Macc. 1:7). But within the biblical tradition, reflection on the appropriate postures and roles within social relationships is largely a NT phenomenon for which the theme in Greco-Roman ethical thought, "concerning the household," supplied the language of submission and subordination.

As the NT takes up the concept, it repeats and enlarges certain OT themes. But early Christian writers were engaged to some degree in the discourse of Hellenized Roman culture that had assimilated Greek categories. In this context, the hierarchically shaped "ordering under" becomes the frame for thinking about much of the cosmic and social organization that defined society and the church.

In the cosmic and eschatological scope, God has (or will) put all things, including angels, under subjection to Christ (1 Cor. 15:27; Eph. 1:22; Phil. 3:21; Heb. 2:5). The human response entails submission to God (Jas. 4:7) and the acknowledgment that the churches are in subjection to Christ (Eph. 5:24). In the cosmic-eschatological scheme of things, Christ also will be subjected to God (1 Cor. 15:28). Though stated only once, the advice of Eph. 5:21, "Be subject to one another out of reverence for Christ," has that flavor of eschatological promise.

But eschatology and the limits of historical reality create an ambiguous tension in the succeeding instruction to wives to be in subjection to their husbands (Eph. 5:21–22; so also Col. 3:18; Titus 2:5; 1 Pet. 3:1). A similar dissonance with eschatological aims occurs in the subordinating of women/wives to men in the worship setting (1 Cor. 14:34; 1 Tim. 2:11). In the case of slaves being subordinate to masters (Titus 2:9; 1 Pet. 2:18; otherwise the regulatory term is *obey*: Eph. 6:5; Col. 3:22) or children to parents (Luke 2:51, of Jesus; "obey" is preferred: Eph. 6:1; Col. 3:20), hierarchy may seem more a matter of common sense. Yet in general, this system of hierarchical arrangements of authority and power—the human as subject to the ruling authorities (Rom. 13:1; Titus 3:1; 1 Pet. 2:13), male householders in dominance over wives and slaves—though explored uniquely within a growing Christian theology or ideology, reflects preconceptions about cosmology and the subdivine place of human beings in the ethical and religious thought of the Greco-Roman milieu (e.g., Epictetus, *Diatr.* 3.24.65). Language and concept were a part of the larger worldview, and the confrontation of emerging Christian theology and values with the prevailing worldview often promised more than was immediately delivered.

Narrowing the Focus: Social Relationships in a Hierarchical World

Within the empire of the first century CE, the household (*oikos*) continued to be held up as the fundamental unit of the social structure. This paradigm reached back to Greek reflection on the nature of human society that took shape in the dominant theme, discussed by Aristotle and others, "on the household" (*peri oikonomias*). Aristotle (*Pol.* 1253B.1–3) begins his discussion of the city from the starting point of household management: "For every city is composed of households"; for this reason, innovations, disturbances, evidence of poor management, and so on attracted the attention of conservative-minded observers. By Roman times, the emperor was conceived of as the father of a great household (the entire empire), and many functions and positions in relation to the state were described with terms that took their root from *oikos* (*metoikoi*/*paroikoi*, "resident aliens"; *katoikoi*, "military colonists"; *oikonomos*, "administrator"). The household, from macro- and microperspectives, exerted a shaping influence on order and organization.

In the world in which the NT Letters were written, both the social structure and the physical structures of the ancient household reflected the hierarchical system. Relationships were clearly defined. The father/*kyrios* ("master") was the head of the household. The conception of the household according to clearly defined reciprocal (but not equal) pairs is traditional from before Aristotle, who expressed the system clearly: "master and slave, husband and wife, father and children" (Aristotle, *Pol.* 1.1253b 6–7). One related to one's counterpart either with authority or in subjection. The houses of the era were built in ways that expressed the system, so that, for example, the locations of the slaves generally were kept separate from those of the masters. Protocol for household activities also signified status: in the symposia held by householders, slaves might serve the guests, and women might attend the meals but would sit upright, not recline like the men, and they would depart before discussions began.

All of this is to say that the rather rigid way of defining the core relationships in society in top-down terms—subordination and submission—was reinforced and protected, and deviations were regarded as a threat to the respectability and the good order of the empire itself. Although the system of relationships within which human beings carried on life (cosmic, political, social, familial) was regarded in a holistic sense, it was mainly at the level of the basic human relationships, traditionally ordered along vertical lines of authority and status, where the impact of the Christian gospel reveals, at some points anyway, a cautious reconfiguration. In this household frame, at macro- and microlevels, the language of submission served as a compass. It was especially at the microlevel of Christian households where the penetration of the Christian gospel, with its emphasis on freedom and equality, began to test the long-accepted assumptions about authority and roles appropriate to the relational divisions.

New Testament Household Codes and the Language of Submission and Subordination

The ethical interest in the household in Greek and Roman society eventually gave rise to the operational language (submission, subordination, obedience) and various didactic delivery systems through which the values could be transmitted (e.g., Aristotle's relational pairings).

One of these didactic mechanisms, which appears several times in the NT, has come to be called "household code." These codes resemble forms occurring in the secular discussions (especially Colossians and Ephesians resembling Aristotle), but no exact literary source, as such, has been found for the NT household codes (Col. 3:18–4:1; Eph. 5:22–33; 1 Pet. 2:13–3:7; see also Rom. 13:1–7; 1 Cor. 14:33–34; 1 Tim. 2:8–15; 5:1–2; 6:1–2; Titus 2:1–3:8). With some variation from code to code, we find the pairings of husband/wife, parents/children, householder/slave under consideration and the directional verb "to be subject/subordinate to" is in play (with a preference for "obey" [*hypakouō*] in some cases [Eph. 6:1, 5; Col. 3:20, 22]). Observance of the state is equally in view in Rom. 13; 1 Pet. 2; Titus 3.

Although some earlier scholars viewed this adaptation of secular forms as evidence of the secularization of Christian ethics, there is a noticeable "Christianizing" reformulation of the teaching on social relationships. With some variation (as implementation and experimentation of gospel freedom experiences an accordion-like fluctuation from one setting to the next), NT application of the tradition of the household code reflects a degree of fairness and justice absent from Greco-Roman reflection, and all relationships, attitudes, and status/authority within them are mitigated by the presence of "the Lord" (e.g., Eph. 5:21–22, 26; 6:1, 4; Col. 3:18, 20, 22).

Grasping the meaning of the submission/subordination thrust in NT household (and civic) ethics requires some reflection on the didactic function of the household style of teaching, as well as the meaning of submission/subordination within it. By taking up the form, Christian writers effectively entered the broader social conversation "concerning the household," at whatever stage that discourse had reached by this time. The question is this: why was the early church compelled to engage in this discourse about the household?

We note first the variety. Use of the household code in a variety of letters and situations suggests that the search for a single specific function is futile. Ranging from their appearance in Colossians and Ephesians, to 1 Peter, to the later Pauline or post-Pauline writings, the most that can be discerned is an overarching concern for basic household and social structures that perhaps were under stress. But no single sort of stress seems evident. The codes probably were applied for a range of reasons, and those suggested by scholars (for mission, to quiet unrest or enthusiasm, as a defense apologetic) undoubtedly will apply, in varying combinations, in most instances. But generally, the conservative and respectable ethics that the code tended to endorse (relationships configured in vertical terms, even if moderated by Christian values) reflects in all settings an awareness of the expectations of society and the desire to order Christian life according to accepted standards. Public respectability is therefore one of the goals of this teaching. And both the ethical lexicon employed (*hypotassō* and "obedience") and the form of the teaching seek to maintain a dialogue with and engagement in the wider society.

All well and good, but did embracing the accepted ethical language and echoing widely accepted values entail a surrender (patriarchalist or otherwise) of an original equality impulse inspired by the gospel (Gal. 3:28)? After all, the "Christian" moderation of the household ethics noted above might seem nothing more than the deceptive measures taken by conservatives bent on baptizing a status quo that privileged the powerful in the church. Many have staged this argument with force. And it should not be too quickly dismissed.

But the ambiguity or openness of the language itself has sometimes been passed over too quickly. On the one hand, a range of usage is apparent in the NT, and in cases where human relationships are in view, any sense of rigid hierarchy is moderated somewhat by the note of willingness (expressed in the middle voice) in the act of submitting (cf. the range of meanings for *hypotassō* in Rom. 8:20; 13:1; 1 Cor. 15:27–28; Eph. 5:21–22; Col. 3:18). On the other hand, the term *hypotassō* itself contains creative instability or polyvalence. Goppelt (*Variety and Unity*) argues that the basic sense of the word group was derived from its root (*taxis*, "order"; or *tassomai*, "to order oneself") and less so from the prefix (*hypo*, "under"), and that contextual considerations would decide the specifics of the organizational structure (expectations and freedoms) in view. This opens up hermeneutical possibilities that Goppelt finds underlying NT household code employment. The writers urged, by means of the traditional form and language, Christian engagement in all walks of life "according to society's rules for playing the game." For Goppelt, what was at stake was ensuring a missional Christian presence in society and allaying any impulse to flee from what might have been perceived as a hostile environment.

Whether this is an overly optimistic evaluation of the subordination ethic in the NT, Goppelt's observations, along with the theological mitigation of social verticality supplied by softer language, middle voice, and dominical oversight, recommend a hermeneutical strategy. A Christian ethics concerned with the church's presence in the world could plot a trajectory through time and cultures that fosters a robust and ongoing conversation about issues such as relational subordination. The conversation would necessarily include several voices: the early gospel ideal of equality (emerging in the equality tradition of Rom. 10:12; Gal. 3:28; 1 Cor. 12:13; Col. 3:11), the eschatological reality of a preliminary experience of salvation, and the embedded, situated, and therefore limited locations of the church(es) in any and all historical and cultural contexts.

This conversation can at least be imagined in the first churches. Most agree that Paul has social change in mind by shaping a theology of gospel impact around the tradition that he cites in Gal. 3:28 (Rom. 10:12; 1 Cor. 12:13; Col. 3:11). But apparently Paul did not appropriate the equality tradition under any illusion that its radical pronouncements could be instantaneously implemented. His own reluctance to dismantle the existing social framework (see, e.g., 1 Cor. 14; Philemon) argues instead that we take seriously two convergent realities for Paul: his own cultural embeddedness and the inconsistencies, vis-à-vis the gospel, that might result from this, and, more positively, a subtler sense of missiological motivation. On the one hand, the equality tradition announces the initiation of the liberating and equalizing intentions of the gospel, and a trajectory is detectable. This must be the implication of the tradition's citation in Galatians, where he establishes the theological case for actual and historical equality of Jew and gentile. On the other hand, the view that this text is a straightforward declaration calling for the immediate eradication of all social distinctions is too simple. The diversity of approaches to women and slaves in the Pauline tradition (1 Cor. 11:3–16; 14:33–35; see also 1 Cor. 7:21; 1 Tim. 2:11–15; 6:1–2; Philemon) suggests that a number of factors would come into play to determine the timing and degree of the equality change that could be implemented in any given context.

This might suggest a fairly carefully conceived missiological hermeneutic. But probably it is more accurate to say that although such a hermeneutic may emerge from time to time as Paul or other NT writers address the social relationships, in fact their social embeddedness presents them with conservative defaults (patriarchal and actually inimical to equality) that they sometimes fall back on in times of community crisis or uncertainty.

Cultural forces and assumptions are ever-present factors in the formulation of ethics from Scripture, and a process of negotiation is evident in mechanisms such as the household codes. New

Testament writers seem to have viewed their world and its structures as a part of God's design. They could encourage the church to "submit to" the institutions of the world (Rom. 13:1; 1 Pet. 2:13) and through generally accepted conduct to bear witness within it (1 Thess. 4:11–12; 1 Tim. 3:7; 6:1). But in tension with this view was the conviction (though perhaps primitive) that the world is an evil force opposed to God. The church was to resist its influence and policies (Rom. 12:2; 1 John 2:11–17); yet, it was also to inhabit the social space and be a redemptive presence. The NT household codes reflect social and cultural awareness and could have been deployed to activate and justify the conservative defaults, but they stop short of advocating conformity as an end in itself. We can imagine that Paul or some other NT figure would have equivocated in redressing the inequalities of slavery out of concern that the culture would regard such activism as a threat. In other cases, community dysfunction may have been corrected by return to or reinforcement of default settings, slowing movement toward equality. Both ways of negotiating with culture may seek peaceful coexistence, even if only one of the ways is progressive.

Theological forces were also at work shaping NT perceptions of the social world. How did NT conception(s) of salvation affect movement toward gospel equality? Feminists in the tradition of Elisabeth Schüssler Fiorenza interpret salvation as liberation in history. The church's remit is to actualize it now. But there is another picture of salvation, often characterized with the phrase "already and not yet," that is a combination of aspects of salvation to be realized progressively in this life and aspects to be fulfilled only with the full arrival of the eschaton (resurrection, the final victory over sin). From this latter progressive perspective, the achievement of equality for women or freedom of slaves may be realized in history at different paces in different situations. The factors determining the balance between speed of realization and caution in experimentation could well include the degree of social readiness to absorb innovative shock. Experimentation with equality might need to move in concert with cultural trends. And what is possible in this respect in one culture (e.g., Western) may not be immediately possible in another (e.g., Muslim).

It may be argued that submission or subordination is the appropriate human response or posture within certain authority contexts or relationships. Few would dispute this in the case of the human relationship with God, church leadership, legitimate political leaders, or in the case of children to parents. In such cases, the ordering of the relationship can be understood, in the present imperfect age, in terms of the responsibility of the "higher" to protect, lead, govern, and so forth, and the dependence of "the lower" on "the higher" for these things. But even in such cases, the exercise of leadership after the model of Jesus Christ—sacrificial, empowering, nurturing, other-centered—would utterly transform the meaning of subordination or submission. In other cases, where status and honor were assigned arbitrarily to one member of the traditional pairs on the basis of race, dominant gender, or the power that came from relative wealth, citizenship, or conquest, gospel freedom seeks a level playing field, and subordination or submission becomes the responsibility of each member of the relationship now pledged by faith to serve the other.

Engagement with the NT writings finds space for submission and subordination to achieve each of these ethical outcomes. The biblical writings reveal only the beginnings of experimentation with gospel freedom. Gentile elevation within the messianic community, at least in the Pauline arena, was a nonnegotiable, seismic development in this direction. But any program of equality that would level relationships determined culturally by submission/subordination (slaves, women/wives) was either barely under way, resisted or halted by cultural conservatives, or being implemented with extreme caution. Where responsiveness to legitimate leadership and structure can be defined (cautiously) by submission and subordination, the godly exercise of leadership mitigates any sense of loss (prestige, status) by the way it honors and elevates those under leadership's influence. What remains and applies to all believers is mutual and consensual subordination and submission as the posturing of individuals who respect one another and seek one another's best.

See also Authority and Power; Egalitarianism; Equality; Family; Feminist Ethics; Headship; Household Codes; Leadership, Leadership Ethics; Slavery; Women, Status of

Bibliography

Balch, D. *Let Wives Be Submissive: The Domestic Code in 1 Peter*. SBLMS 26. Scholars Press, 1981; Goppelt, L. *A Commentary on 1 Peter*. Ed. F. Hahn. Trans. J. Alsup. Eerdmans, 1993, 162–82; idem. *The Variety and Unity of the Apostolic Witness to Christ*. Vol. 2 of *Theology of the New Testament*. Ed. J. Roloff. Eerdmans, 1982, 161–74; Hartman, L. "Some Unorthodox Thoughts on the 'Household Code' Form." Pages 219–32 in *The Social World of Formative Christianity and Judaism: Essays in Tribute to Howard Clark Kee*, ed. J. Neusner et al. Fortress, 1988; Pilch, J., and B. Malina, eds. *Biblical Social Values and Their Meaning: A Handbook*. Hendrickson, 1993, 125–26;

Schüssler Fiorenza, E. *In Memory of Her: A Feminist Theological Reconstruction of Christian Origins*. Crossroad, 1983; Webb, W. *Slaves, Women and Homosexuals: Exploring the Hermeneutics of Cultural Analysis*. InterVarsity, 2001; Wells, S. *Improvisation: The Drama of Christian Ethics*. Brazos, 2004.

Philip H. Towner

Subsidiarity, Principle of

The principle of subsidiarity insists on two points: first, in a well-ordered social body the different parts of that body, whether individuals or groups or institutions, help one another; second, the larger and higher parts ought not assume or replace the authority and responsibilities of the lesser parts but rather should provide help (*subsidium*) to them. This principle has played a significant role in Roman Catholic political thought for more than a century.

Emmanuel von Kettler (1811–77), the influential bishop of Mainz, seems to have been the first to name this principle and to articulate it. Pope Leo XIII used it (without naming it) in *Rerum novarum* (1891). Out of pastoral concern for "the condition of labor" he opposed both laissez-faire capitalism, with its excessive and atomistic individualism, and the socialist vision of equality among citizens engineered by an all-powerful state. Against them both he offered the vision of the social body as an organism with its many different parts helping to achieve the common good. That social body would be ordered hierarchically, but it would observe the aforementioned two points in the principle of subsidiarity. When Pope Pius XI issued *Quadragesimo anno* (1931) to celebrate the earlier encyclical's fortieth anniversary, the principle appeared explicitly.

The principle itself, then, is more than a century old, but it may be regarded as an evolution of the political thought of Thomas Aquinas. Thomas had received the political thought of Augustine, which had emphasized the state as a postfall institution authorized by God to remedy injustice and to remove dangers to the community. Romans 13:1–7 had held a central place in that tradition. But Thomas also received the Aristotelian vision of a well-ordered state as capable to define and to realize the common good, a good that included harmoniously the smaller communities and individuals with their particular goods. Aristotle's vision required a larger and more positive role for the state. Thomas followed Aristotle on that point, while preserving the Augustinian insistence that the state is authorized and answerable to God, answerable now not simply for restraining evil but for achieving the common good.

The principle would continue to evolve in the political thought of Catholics such as Jacques Maritain. It would influence, and be influenced by, liberal-democratic political thought. Today, for example, the principle can be found in the Maastricht Treaty of the European Union (1991), article 3b: "In areas that do not fall within its exclusive competence, the Community shall take action in accordance with the subsidiarity principle."

See also Authority and Power; Common Good; Government; Institution(s); Political Ethics; Roman Catholic Moral Theology

Bibliography

Hinze, C. "Commentary of Quadragesimo anno (After Forty Years)." Pages 151–74 in *Modern Catholic Social Teaching: Commentaries and Interpretations*, ed. K. Himes. Georgetown University Press, 2004; Maritain, J. *Man and the State*. University of Chicago Press, 1951; O'Donovan, O., and J. Lockwood O'Donovan. *Bonds of Imperfection: Christian Politics, Past and Present*. Eerdmans, 2004, 225–45; Schuck, M. "Early Modern Roman Catholic Social Thought." Pages 99–125 in *Modern Catholic Social Teaching: Commentaries and Interpretations*, ed. K. Himes. Georgetown University Press, 2004.

James Keenan, SJ

Suffering

The Latin roots of the word *suffering* imply being weighed down. In what follows, "suffering" refers to something physical, mental, emotional, or spiritual that a person must bear or endure. Suffering includes pain, death, punishment, hardship, disaster, grief, sorrow, care, loneliness, injury, loss, shame, disgrace, bodily injury or discomfort, and disease. In the Bible, the ultimate suffering is death (e.g., Deut. 30:15–19; Rom. 5:12; 1 Cor. 15:21–26). Although there is biblical reflection on the suffering of creation (e.g., Rom. 8:19–23), creation's suffering being interpreted as caused by human sin (Gen. 3:17–18), and reflection on divine suffering (Hosea, Jeremiah, the NT), the focus in the following discussion is on the primary concern of the biblical witness: human suffering. Moreover, although both the OT and the NT require the faithful to care for the suffering of others, the center of attention in what follows here concerns biblical references to sufferers themselves.

Typically, theological discussions of suffering occur in the context of considerations of theodicy: how to put together the experience of suffering with a conviction that God exists and is good, omnipotent, and omniscient. These discussions include the assumption that suffering is undeserved. Among the myriad biblical references to suffering are those concerned with innocent suffering, and some of these references do draw attention to the issue of theodicy. Others, as we will see, do not.

One significant distinction between the NT and the OT involves perspectives on innocent suffering. Undergirding the entire NT is the conviction that Christ's innocent suffering has transformative power. Consequently, whereas the OT struggles with theodicy, the NT by and large accepts, even claims, the paradox of the justice of God and innocent suffering. (Acceptance of this paradox is, of course, foreshadowed in portions of the OT.) That theodicy is not a NT focus is indicated by Paul's claim that his gospel, while proclaiming the risen Christ, is at the same time "the word of the cross" (1 Cor. 1:17–18); the four Gospels' emphasis on Christ's suffering and death; and the consistent focus in almost all of the NT writings (James is an exception) on Christ's suffering and death as key to the revelation of God's justice. Rather, the NT ponders various ways in which believers may benefit from and partake in Christ's innocent suffering for the sake of their own and the world's salvation.

Throughout both Testaments there are also, of course, references to suffering that is deserved, in which case the matter of the justice of God is not at issue. Instead, these passages understand God's righteousness to be revealed precisely in God's initiating or allowing suffering as a consequence of human guilt.

Old Testament

Innocent suffering. *Innocent suffering challenges faith in the justice of God.* Certain portions of the OT ponder the matter of innocent suffering in the context of theodicy. The book of Job, for instance, raises the problem of innocent suffering. Job is portrayed as a man who fears God and avoids evil (1:1), a man who has fulfilled both the spirit and the letter of the law (1:3–5). Nevertheless, Job suffers intensely. The book offers no purpose or reason for innocent suffering; instead, it gives one of the most graphic and timeless presentations of it and thus serves to pose vividly the matter of theodicy. Like Job, Ecclesiastes raises the problem of innocent suffering. In Ecclesiastes' case, the riddle is presented in this way: if God is responsible for all things under the sun, then God must also be responsible for suffering and death (Eccl. 3:1–10). Ecclesiastes asks why the righteous suffer while the wicked prosper (see also 3:16; 4:1–3; 9:11–12). Ecclesiastes finds, as does Job, that the problem cannot be solved and concludes that if there is wisdom to be had on this most profound of human problems, it is not wisdom to which humans have access (1:16–18). The best that humans can do is to fear God (Eccl. 12:13–14). Some of the psalms also ask the same question (e.g., Ps. 88:13–18).

Innocent suffering does not challenge God's justice. Interestingly, certain references to innocent suffering do not serve to challenge God's justice. For instance, to our minds it may appear unjust that the whole nation of Israel experienced a three-year famine, although it was only the nation's representative, "Saul and his blood-stained house" (2 Sam. 21:1 TNIV), who are said to be at fault. This instance of the suffering of the nation is recounted without comment on the matter of theodicy.

Various other OT passages appear undisturbed about the paradox of innocent suffering and God's righteousness. For instance, the endurance of suffering may be understood to bear witness to God's righteousness (Ps. 22; Isa. 50:4–10) or bring one closer to God (Pss. 16; 17; Jer. 15:15–21).

Likewise, substitutionary innocent suffering (Isa. 52:13–53:12; see also Exod. 32:32; Zech. 11:4–17) is not understood to challenge God's goodness or justice but rather is regarded as used by God for the sake of others.

When evil is identified as the cause of suffering, there is a corresponding certainty that God will vindicate it (Ps. 94:1–3; Isa. 57:1–13; Hab. 3:16–19). At times, the very intensity of suffering is regarded as evidence that God's vindication (the eschaton) is at hand (Isa. 24:17–23; 26:1–21; Dan. 12:2), when evil will finally be vanquished.

In these passages innocent suffering does not challenge faith in God's justice; rather, it seems to intensify trust in God's power and righteousness.

Deserved suffering. While in portions of the OT evil is understood as the cause of suffering, in other portions God is regarded as the source of suffering. The justice of God is not at issue in such references, since divinely inflicted suffering is seen as the appropriate consequence for disobedience.

The Bible presents certain instances of human beings inflicting suffering on one another as occurring under God's direction (e.g., Lev. 26:27–33). Likewise, God may be understood as the source of sickness (Ps. 38:1–8). God's justice is not called into question when suffering is regarded as the consequence of wickedness (Pss. 9:16; 39:11). Whereas knowledge and wisdom, love, life and prosperity are the rewards of lives filled with love for God (Deut. 30:8–10; Prov. 22:4), the opposite results accrue when God is disobeyed. It is essential to give loyalty only to God and God's law (Deut. 8:11–20) and to care for the poor and needy (Ps.

9:18). When these commands are disobeyed, suffering is the consequence.

Divinely inflicted suffering is understood as being justified on the basis that God's righteousness demands retribution for disobedience. For example, the Israelites will be punished when they give their allegiance to other gods (Deut. 18:13–22; Jer. 4:4; Lam. 1:18–2:22; Hos. 8:11–13; 9:3–6; 12:11–12; Amos 8:1–12).

Closely related to this is the idea that God legitimately uses afflictions to discipline (Job 5:17; Ps. 94:12; Prov. 3:11; Isa. 26:16; Jer. 2:30; 30:14; 31:18; Hos. 5:1–2; 7:12; 10:10; Zeph. 3:7), and that God rightly uses suffering to refine or test (Job 23:10; Ps. 66:10; Isa. 48:10; Zech. 13:9). Some of the psalms evidence an acceptance that God afflicts in order to renew faithfulness in either an individual (Pss. 6:1–4; 38:1–4) or the nation (Ps. 118:18). We see something similar in Proverbs (15:10).

New Testament

The NT's primary focus is on the meaning of believing in an innocent and crucified Messiah. In part because the texts of the NT are written on the basis of faith in the transformative power of Christ's innocent suffering, which suffering is understood to reveal God's righteousness, compared to the OT there is little focus on theodicy. In fact, several NT passages present an apology for the fittingness of believers' suffering (e.g., 1 Cor. 4:8–13; 2 Cor. 11:21–33), without at the same time regarding that suffering as either divine retribution or discipline (although there are also a few references to deserved suffering in this vein). The NT is concerned less with theodicy than with a theology of suffering.

In addition to confidence in the revelation of the justice of God precisely in Christ's innocent suffering, the lack of attention to theodicy may also be attributed to the NT's basic conviction that "all are under the power of sin" (Rom. 3:9); that is, no one is innocent. Even though believers in Christ are released from sin's power and so from condemnation (Rom. 8:1), justified by God's grace as a gift through the redemption that is in Christ Jesus (Rom. 3:24), the NT is clear that believers are still affected by sin. Belief in Christ liberates from sin's mastery, but it does not kill sin itself. The influence (although not the mastery) of sin or the devil (1 Pet. 5:8–9) remains until Christ's return. This understanding also contributes to the NT's acceptance of present suffering.

Given the NT's convictions that Christ's innocent suffering reveals God's faithfulness, that even those "in Christ" are not innocent but are still in battle with sin, and that the death and resurrection of Christ inaugurate but do not fully institute the time when evil is vanquished, the NT accepts the fact that for various reasons believers suffer.

The suffering of believers is understood in several ways: as a means of strengthening faith, as a sharing in the human condition in this time of waiting for God to complete the healing of creation, and as a necessary sharing in the suffering of Christ.

Deserved suffering. References to deserved suffering can be divided into two categories: suffering that disciplines the faithful, and suffering that punishes the disobedient.

Deserved suffering of the faithful. There are a few references to suffering as disciplining, testing, and refining Christians (Jas. 5:13–20; 1 Pet. 4:12). God may use trials to help purify (1 Pet. 1:7) and strengthen in hope (Rom. 5:3–5) the believer.

Deserved suffering of the unfaithful. God's wrath visits suffering on the disobedient. God's wrath exhibits itself either as God now giving up those who do not acknowledge the destructive behaviors that they desire (Rom. 1:18–31) or as a present threat of future judgment (Mark 13:3–27; 1 Thess. 1:10; Rev. 6:9–11). Even believers are warned of future suffering if they do not abide in Christ (John 15:6) and remain faithful (Heb. 6:4–8).

Suffering due to the time of waiting for Christ's return. Since creation is still in a state of groaning for liberation (Rom. 8:18–23), suffering continues, even for those "in Christ." Paul, for instance, recounts without apology his experience of a physical affliction (Gal. 4:13). Suffering will continue until Christ's return, when the ultimate suffering, death, will finally be defeated (1 Cor. 15:26).

Suffering in conformity with Christ. Followers of Christ are enjoined to share in (Rom. 8:17; Phil. 3:8–10; Rev. 1:9) or emulate Christ's manner of suffering (1 Pet. 4:1–2, 13; Rev. 7:14). Jesus tells his disciples that just as it is required that he suffer and die (Mark 8:31), so his disciples must deny themselves, take up their cross, and lose their lives for his sake (Mark 8:34–38). Christ's suffering was at the hands of sinners (Heb. 12:3); consequently, followers of Jesus can expect unjust treatment (Mark 13:9), at times understood as occasioned by the devil (Rev. 2:9–10). Luke-Acts presents Jesus' suffering and death as the model for his followers (see the similarities between Jesus' death in Luke and that of Stephen in Acts 6–7). Hebrews 12:1–13 is best understood as encouraging endurance in suffering, with Jesus as the paradigm of obedience in the midst of extreme suffering.

Paul provides the earliest firsthand reflection on sharing in Christ's sufferings, which sufferings he understood as being for the sake of others (2 Cor. 1:5–6). Paul considered it essential for believers in Christ to share in Christ's suffering and be conformed to Christ's death (Phil. 3:10). According to Paul, the resurrection of believers depends on their suffering in conformity with Christ (Rom. 8:17; Phil. 3:10–11). Such suffering, since it is done "in Christ" and in conformity with Christ's death, is neither self-inflicted nor morbid. It is, instead, unbidden and part of the package of being "in Christ"; it leads to life and liberation both for self and others, just as did Christ's suffering and death. Believers' suffering in conformity with Christ is understood by Paul and other NT writers as redemptive, both for themselves (Rom. 8:17; Phil. 3:10–11; Jas. 1:2–18) and for creation (Rom. 8:18–23; Rev. 12:11–12).

Here we see the joining of reflection on the suffering self and care for the suffering of others. The conviction of the NT writers that the redemption of the world's suffering is achieved by Christ's suffering leads to the conviction that the suffering of others, and even of creation, will be relieved as believers in Christ suffer in conformity with Christ.

See also Cruciformity; Death and Dying; Discipline; Evil; Job; Judgment; Justice, Retributive; Martyrdom; Persecution; Punishment; Sin; Theodicy

Bibliography

Crenshaw, J., ed. *Theodicy in the Old Testament*. Fortress, 1983; Croy, N. *Endurance in Suffering: Hebrews 12:1–13 in Its Rhetorical, Religious, and Philosophical Context*. SNTSMS 98. Cambridge University Press, 1998; Fretheim, T. *The Suffering of God: An Old Testament Perspective*. Fortress, 1984; Jervis, L. *At the Heart of the Gospel: Suffering in the Earliest Christian Message*. Eerdmans, 2007; Lindström, F. *Suffering and Sin: Interpretations of Illness in the Individual Complaint Psalms*. ConBOT 37. Almquist & Wiksell International, 1994; Milazzo, G. *The Protest and the Silence: Suffering, Death, and Biblical Theology*. Fortress, 1992; Robinson, H. *Suffering, Human and Divine*. Macmillan, 1939; Sanders, J. *Suffering as Divine Discipline in the Old Testament and Post-Biblical Judaism*. Colgate Rochester Divinity School, 1955; Talbert, C. *Learning through Suffering: The Educational Value of Suffering in the New Testament and Its Milieu*. Liturgical Press, 1991.

L. Ann Jervis

Suicide

Suicide is the voluntary and intentional killing of oneself. Given the negative valuation of suicide in much of the Christian tradition, many will be surprised that Scripture contains no explicit condemnation of suicide. Nevertheless, Scripture formed community and character in ways that required the rejection of suicide as a viable option.

Attending to Scripture

The Bible contains the stories of five or six suicides: of Abimelech in Judg. 9:50–56; of Saul in 1 Sam. 35:1–5 and 2 Sam. 1:5–16; of Ahithophel in 2 Sam. 17:23; of Zimri in 1 Kgs. 16:18–19; of Samson in Judg 16:23–31 (although commentators differ about whether to regard Samson's action as suicide); and, most famously, of Judas in Matt. 27:3–10. There is in addition one story of a suicide prevented (the jailer at Philippi in Acts 16:25–29). In none of these do we find an explicit condemnation or prohibition of suicide, nor do we find in Scripture a moral rule that articulates and substantiates the conviction that suicide is prohibited. To be sure, there is the commandment "thou shalt not kill" (Exod. 20:13 KJV; also Deut. 5:17), but the word for "kill" is best understood as "wrongful killing" or "murder" (so the NRSV), and the question remains whether suicide should be considered "wrongful killing." Other passages have sometimes been cited against suicide, for example, Gen. 9:5–6 (especially important to talmudic discussions of suicide) with its prohibition against "shedding the blood" of one made in God's image; Deut. 30:19, with its instruction to "choose life"; the "patience" of Job, who endured great suffering; the prevention of the suicide of the Philippian jailer; and 1 Cor. 6:19 with its reminders that our bodies are temples of the Spirit and that we are not our own. Those who have challenged the Christian tradition's prohibition of suicide have sometimes appealed to John 15:13 and 1 John 3:16, which invoke the example of Christ as one who "lays down his life" (notably John Donne), and to 2 Cor. 5:1–8 and Phil. 1:21–23, understood as stating a preference for death as a means to attain the fullness of salvation.

The Tradition and Scripture

Some have taken the lack of an explicit condemnation of suicide either to whisper an implicit approval or to shout a divine indifference to suicide (Williams, Battin). Such arguments from silence frequently regard tradition's condemnation of suicide as the innovation of Augustine. Darrel Amundsen has shown, however, that Augustine, although the first Christian theologian to discuss suicide thoroughly (most famously in *The City of God* 1.17–27), was hardly an innovator. His condemnation of suicide stood in the tradition of Justin Martyr, Clement of Alexandria, Tertullian, Lactantius, Ambrose, and others. To be sure, while Ambrose and others permitted suicide to women who had no other way to preserve their chastity, Augustine, although prepared to excuse such women, did not justify even such suicides. But there was a consensus that suicide was forbidden. Indeed Ambrose, Augustine's mentor, states the common assumption that "holy Scripture forbids a Christian to lay hands on himself" (*Concerning Virgins* 3.7.32).

What allowed—or required—that assumption? Augustine can cite the suicide of Judas (1.17), the commandment against killing (1.20, calling attention to the fact that it does not add "your neighbor"), and the "patience" of Job (1.24), but behind both such citations and the assumption itself was a biblical account of life and death. The story of Scripture, stories of creation and fall and redemption, stories of a cross and of an empty tomb, determined the significance of life and death for Christians. It required—and requires—a dialectic in the dispositions toward life and death.

On the one hand, life belongs to the creative and redemptive cause of God. The signs of it are God's own breath at the beginning, a rainbow and God's sanction against the "shedding of blood" after the flood, a commandment at Sinai, and finally the resurrection. Therefore, life was recognized and celebrated as a good against which one may not turn without turning against the cause of God. Acts that aim at death do not fit the story; they do not cohere with devotion to the cause of God or with gratitude for the gifts of God. To intend one's own death is forbidden by the story.

On the other hand, life is not the ultimate good. It is not to be regarded as a "second god" (Barth 392). Jesus walked a path steadily and courageously that led to his death; therefore, Christians may not live as though survival were the law of their being. Sometimes life must be risked, let go, given up. The refusal to risk death for the sake of the faith is not a sign of faithfulness but of idolatry. And if life is not the ultimate good, neither is death the ultimate evil. It need not be feared finally, for death is not as strong as the promise of God. This dialectic is captured in the distinction between suicide and martyrdom and in the juxtaposition of the refusal to kill oneself and the willingness to die for the faith.

The traditional condemnation of suicide intensified in the Middle Ages, and the sanctions against it grew more severe. Indeed, there can be little doubt that the tradition has been guilty of excess, as presumptuous about God's judgment and as despairing of God's mercy as Judas had been. In part because of such excesses the tradition has been challenged both from within the Christian community and from others outside of it. John Donne's work *Biathanatos* (1608, published posthumously in 1647) was among the first and most famous of these challenges. Donne examined Scripture and found there "no abomination of self-homicide" (2.5.1). He argued that suicide could be done to the glory of God, that Christ's "laying down his life" was a form of suicide, and that God could command suicide in the prompting of one's conscience. In the early twentieth century suicide came to be regarded less as an individual choice and more as a function of social organization (Émile Durkheim) or of mental illness (Sigmund Freud). These "scientific" views interpreted suicide as the outcome of conditions for which the person had no moral responsibility. Later in the century suicide would come to be regarded as a "cry for help," a manipulative but sometimes effective act to communicate to another the need to change the circumstances of the one attempting suicide.

Contemporary Application

In the late twentieth century the moral issue surfaced again in the bioethical controversies concerning suicide and assisted suicide (see Verhey). The distinctions between killing and allowing to die and between suicide and accepting death have been challenged. Utilitarianism, for example, which looks at consequences rather than at intentions, has questioned the distinction since either way the consequence is the same: someone is dead. The distinction, however, still fits the story of Scripture. As the martyrs "bore witness" to the story not by choosing death but by being ready to endure death for the sake of God's cause in the world, today in more mundane and commonplace ways some terminally ill Christians still bear witness to the story by their readiness to die but not to kill. They may refuse both the offer of assisted suicide and the offer of treatment that may prolong their days but only by rendering those days (or months or years) less apt for their tasks of reconciliation with enemies or fellowship with friends or simply fun with their families. Their comfort is still that they are not their own but belong to God, the giver of life, from whom not even death can separate them. And their comfort is still their courage.

It will not be sufficient to shout a prohibition against suicide or assisted suicide, even one formed out of Scripture's story. What is required is not law but a powerful and creative word of grace, some little signal that one is permitted to live, not obligated to live, even while it gives no permission to kill, some token that one is also permitted to die, not obligated to die, even while it gives no permission to live on at all costs.

See also Bioethics; Death and Dying; Martyrdom

Bibliography

Amundsen, D. W. "Suicide and Early Christian Values." Pages 70–126 in *Medicine, Society, and Faith in the Ancient and Medieval Worlds*. Johns Hopkins University Press, 1996; Barth, K. *Church Dogmatics* III/4. T&T Clark, 1961; Battin, M. P. *Ethical Issues in Suicide*. Prentice Hall, 1982; *John Donne's Biathanatos: A Modern Spelling Edition*, ed. M. Rudick and M. P. Battin. Garland, 1981; Verhey, A. "Judas, Jesus, and Physician Assisted Suicide." Pages 304–44 in *Reading the Bible in the Strange World of Medicine*. Eerdmans, 2003; Williams, G. *The Sanctity of Life and the Criminal Law*. Alfred A. Knopf, 1957.

Allen Verhey

Sunday *See* Sabbath

Supersessionism

Supersessionism is a contested term, often confused with the separation of Christianity from Judaism or conflated with Christian anti-Judaism or anti-Semitism. Here, we follow a narrow definition that represents the dominant postbiblical Christian view that the church has superseded the synagogue or the Jewish people as the people of God. Supersessionism is the outcome of the ecclesiological struggle between the synagogue and the church, for each defines itself as the singular people of God. As Christianity formed within Judaism, it slowly became clear that the synagogue and the church had mutually exclusive ecclesiologies. The synagogue claimed the inheritance of the sacrificial cult, and the church claimed the inheritance of both the synagogue and the cult. The Christians claimed that the church, not the synagogue, now constitutes the people of God.

The church's claim is supersessionist if the Jewish people truly were the people of God until Jesus, but are no longer. The word *supersessionism* is anachronistic when applied to the NT, however, because the communities had not yet separated. The linguistic awkwardness, however, does not obscure the fact that that claim is taking shape in the texts that became Christian Scripture.

Jews based their claim to election on Scripture. Those who would become Christians also considered themselves the people of God. We have here mutually exclusive ecclesiologies. Redefining the people of God began long before the communities separated and Christianity gained political power.

New Testament

The seeds of supersessionism are visible early on. Ephesians 2:15–16 is sure: "[God] has abolished the law with its commandments and ordinances, that he might create in himself one new humanity in place of the two, thus making peace, and might reconcile both groups to God in one body through the cross, thus putting to death the hostility through it." Ephesians 2:19 refers to the church as the "household of God," implying that the Jewish people are not.

Paul

Paul is ambivalent about the theological status of non-Christian Jews. He invents the great reversal of Jews and gentiles in what would later be called the "economy of salvation." Two texts, Rom. 9:6–8 and Gal. 4:22–31, establish the new ecclesiology, and Rom. 9–11 is the locus classicus of Paul's Israelology. Not all will agree with the following reading, but it has been highly influential. Non-Christian Jews, Paul argues, are descended from Esau, not Jacob. "For not all Israelites truly belong to Israel, and not all of Abraham's children are his true descendants; but 'It is through Isaac that descendants shall be named for you [gentiles]' " (Rom. 9:6–7). The children of the promise of Gen. 12:3b are not, or at least now are not, the Jewish people, but those who follow Jesus are.

In Rom. 11:1, 29 Paul denies that God has rejected his people, but in Rom. 11:15 he speaks of their rejection. A key to understanding the seeming contradiction is in Rom. 11:25–26: "I want you to understand this mystery: a hardening has come upon part of Israel, until the full number of the Gentiles has come in. And so all Israel will be saved." The hardening and punishment of being cut off are only temporary. Paul expected Jews to enter the church eventually because, as he says at Gal. 6:16, the church is now the Israel of God. Those who cling to the law are now rejected but will be restored when they enter the church, the Israel of God.

Paul enacts the great reversal of gentiles and Jews as the people of God again in Galatians, where he reinterprets the women characters of Gen. 16. Just as Jacob is not the father of Jewish Israel, so Sarah is not the mother of Jewish Israel through Isaac and Jacob, but "Hagar . . . corresponds to the present Jerusalem, for she is in slavery with her children. But the other woman corresponds to the Jerusalem above; she is free, and she is our mother" (Gal. 4:25–26). Jewish Israel is the enslaved children of Hagar, and the gentiles are the free children of Sarah, the children promised to Abraham.

The Gospels

In the Gospels, Judaism and Christianity have not yet separated, but the basis for separation and the seeds of ecclesiological supersession have sprouted. The Beatitudes, for example, and the great banquet in Matt. 25 propose the new ecclesiology. The people of God are the humble and meek who seek peace and righteousness and are persecuted because they confess Jesus. When the nations are gathered and the sheep separated from the goats, the judgment is a moral accounting. Those who have visited prisoners, clothed the naked, and fed the hungry experience eternal life, while those who did not "go away into eternal punishment" (Matt. 25:46). At both its beginning and end, Matthew's Gospel defines a new people of God ethically. Election is no longer of a people, but rather is of those who follow Jesus. They have displaced Jews who cling to the traditions of the rabbis. Ethical conduct determines one's eternal fate.

John's Gospel displays the fight to redefine Israel at its most bitter moment. Dualist light/darkness imagery enacts the struggle between Jews who accept Jesus and those who do not. Tension runs so high that Jesus claims that Jews who are not persuaded by his claim that God sent him are not the descendants of Abraham (John 8:31–59). This intensifies Paul's reversal of Jews and gentiles as descendants of Esau, Jacob, Hagar, and Sarah, respectively, and reports it as live interchange. The one sent by God opposes those who claim to be the children of Abraham by birth but who now are the children of the devil (John 8:44) because they do not accept Jesus.

Hebrews

In the book of Hebrews, Jesus is not simply a revivification of the prophets (1:1–3), the angels (1:5–2:18), Moses (3:1–6), and the priesthood (4:14–7:28); he is superior to all of them and eclipses the lot. His sacrificial death replaces the sacrificial system. He is both the single priest and the single victim forever. This also is a step toward supersessionism. Both communities agree that the sacrificial system has been replaced, but the church claims that it, not the synagogue, is the proper place to worship God. The church is an upstart.

Summation

The texts noted here are moving toward ecclesiological supersessionism by reinterpreting Scripture, redefining the sacrifices as Christ, and redefining Israel's holy days and festivals, long before the two communities separated. There is not, however, a simple replacement; rather, it is sublation. The original is preserved, even as it is transformed, lifted up, and fulfilled in the new. Preserving Israel as the church grounds later claims that the church is the new or true Israel.

Consequences

Judaism never accepted its ecclesiological disenfranchisement. The theological argument turned violent as early as the stoning of Stephen, but, of course, Christians later gained the upper hand. The supersessionist implications of the new ecclesiology play out in subsequent centuries. Whether *supersessionism* is the best word to capture the ecclesiology may be argued, but its consequences were serious.

The supersessionist seeds blossomed into a vibrant body of *adversus Judaeos* literature. Jewish claims to election were refuted repeatedly, initially to establish and then to maintain Christian supremacy. Christianity's negative Israelology was unchallenged until after World War II.

Cracks in the Christian Israelology began to appear as early as Augustine, however. Romans 11:28–29 enabled him to recognize an enduring albeit limited place for the Jews in salvation history (Fredricksen 119). Thomas Aquinas is cautious, but, like Augustine, he says that Jews should not be killed for their refusal of Christ (Hood). Karl Barth found an enduring role for the Jews as those elected to rejection for the sake of the church, following Rom. 11:28 (Sonderegger). These somewhat more positive Israelologies remain within classic Cyprianic ecclesiology of *extra ecclesiam nulla salus* (no salvation outside the church), however. Paul van Buren, disagreeing with his teacher Karl Barth on this matter, stepped out of supersessionist ecclesiology to write the first completely positive Christian Israelology. It fully embraces the Jewish "no" to Jesus, arguing that God has not rejected the Jews, even temporarily, as Paul seems to suggest, or partially, as suggested by Augustine and those following him. R. Kendall Soulen followed van Buren's lead.

Ethical Reflection

The ecclesiological disagreement endures. Jews polemicized against Christian claims (Lasker), but often they paid the price for resisting Jesus. The sad consequence of exclusivist ecclesiology harnessed to political and legal power raises ethical questions. One is whether Christians are morally responsible for their treatment of Jews. Beneath that, a theological question arises. Are Christian theology and Scripture implicated in that history? If so, is Christian treatment of Jews and Judaism simply a regrettable bit of Christian history that was overcome by the modern notion of religious toleration in the West and the demise of Christendom? Alternatively, can the problem be remediated by arguing that the church misunderstood Paul and so the problem is sociological? Further, is there a theological problem here that theology should address regardless of the political remediation of the consequences of exclusivist ecclesiologies?

Ecclesiological exclusiveness is currently out of favor in some Jewish and Christian quarters because it disrespects self-definition. Again, classic Jewish ecclesiology is also exclusive, but Jews never had the political opportunity to act on it, and its "low" soteriology did not make converting Christians a pressing matter. Ecclesiological exclusiveness is not limited to Judaism and Christianity, however. The question raised is whether unseemly historical consequences of theological doctrine constitute an adequate warrant for theological reconstruction.

See also Anti-Semitism; Ecclesiology and Ethics

Bibliography

Fredriksen, P. "Augustine and Israel: *Interpretatio ad litteram*, Jews, and Judaism in Augustine's Theology of History." Pages 91–110 in *Engaging Augustine on Romans: Self, Context, and Theology in Interpretation*, ed. D. Patte and E. TeSelle. Trinity Press International, 2002; Hood, J. *Aquinas and the Jews*. University of Pennsylvania Press, 1995; Lasker, D. *Jewish Philosophical Polemics against Christianity in the Middle Ages*. Littman Library of Jewish Civilization, 2007; Lasker, D., S. Stroumsa, and J. Niehoff-Panagiotidis. *The Polemic of Nestor the Priest: Qiṣṣat mujādalat al-usquf and Sefer Nestor ha-Komer*. 2 vols. Ben-Zvi Institute for the Study of Jewish Communities in the East, 1996; Lloyd, K. *Polemic in the Book of Hebrews: Anti-Semitism, Anti-Judaism, Supersessionism?* Pickwick, 2006; Longenecker, B. "On Israel's God and God's Israel: Assessing Supersessionism in Paul." *JTS* 58 (2007): 26–44; Sonderegger, K. *That Jesus Christ Was Born a Jew: Karl Barth's "Doctrine of Israel."* Pennsylvania State University Press, 1992; Soulen, R. *The God of Israel and Christian Theology*. Fortress, 1996; van Buren, P. *A Theology of the Jewish-Christian Reality*. 3 vols. University Press of America, 1995.

Ellen T. Charry

Swearing *See* Speech Ethics

T

Taxation

Primal communities often had specified labor or products that each person was to contribute to the well-being of the community. More complex societies (ancient empires, modern states) have designated agents (publicans, tax collectors) to exact a portion of produce (grain, wine, salt, etc.), to organize conscripted labor (corvée, military draft), or to demand monetary payments for governmental services.

No society can survive without a political order and civil bodies such as families, businesses, and guilds to provide the services and constructions that allow civilization to flourish. To be sure, warlords have established regimes on the basis of booty taken in battle. However, regimes built on the loot of perpetual war are unstable, although they can, for a time, use their might to aggrandize their dynasty, tribe, class, or religion. Eventually, however, taxes are required, as governments ordinarily are not wealth-producing units per se; rather, they get their stable resources from fees, tolls, duties, tributes, or "donations" from families or profitable institutions—that is, taxation.

The OT record tells us that after the exodus and conquest, when Israel began to develop a stable society, the people demanded a centralized government. Samuel is called upon to anoint a king, but he warns against the price in taxes and forced labor that would likely have to be paid (1 Sam. 8). Still, God commands Samuel to do so. Thus, Saul and then David are anointed kings and develop their rule on the basis of booty (see 2 Sam. 8). Later, Solomon predictably introduces taxes, forced labor, and various duties (1 Kgs. 5:13–18; 10:14–19).

The NT record reflects that taxes were levied by imperial Rome, which ordered a census so that it could know whom and how much to tax (Luke 2:1–3) through tax collectors; by the appointed ethnarch (Luke 2:2), who collected the tribute; and by the priests who collected a temple tax (Matt. 17:24–27). Resentment of taxes and tax collectors was deep in NT times and cultures, as it is everywhere.

A key incident that has been debated for two millennia is the response of Jesus to those who were seeking to trap him into saying that the gospel he advocated entailed disloyalty to political authority (Matt. 22:15–22 pars.). Some Pharisees and Herodians ask Jesus about paying taxes to Rome, and he replies, "Give back to Caesar what is Caesar's, and to God what is God's" (Matt. 22:21 TNIV). This response affirms a positive duty to "worldly," even pagan, governments, while putting this duty in a context that makes government subject to a higher authority. The regimes of the earth are not intrinsically sacred, for they are subordinate to God whether they know it or not. They have a claim on our resources because they are commissioned by God to constrain evil and serve the common good, but they are limited by God's justice and the duty to be merciful and uncorrupted—points reinforced by Paul (Rom. 13:1–6) and Peter (1 Pet. 2:13–17), among others.

See also Economic Ethics; Government; Political Ethics

Bibliography

González, J. *Faith and Wealth: A History of Early Christian Ideas on the Origin, Significance, and Use of Money*. Harper & Row, 1990; Verhey, A. *Remembering Jesus: Christian Community, Scripture, and the Moral Life*. Eerdmans, 2002; Webber, C., and A. Wildavsky. *A History of Taxation and Expenditures in the Western World*. Simon & Schuster, 1986.

Max L. Stackhouse

Tax Evasion *See* Taxation

Technology

Technology takes many shapes. Things such as water heaters, cell phones, intercontinental ballistic missiles, high-definition television, and hybrid cars belong to the large family called "technological artifacts." In addition to artifacts, technology includes infrastructure (e.g., roadways, water and sewage lines, fiber-optic phone lines, Wi-Fi transponders)—systems of technologies that enable the artifacts to function while the system itself remains, for the most part, out of sight and under the moral radar. Further, technology connotes a certain form of life, one not simply auxiliary to the existing social structure but also contributing to its very form (hence, the phrase "technological age"). Finally, technology also includes a particular mode of productive reasoning that vies for cultural dominance over both practical and theoretical reasoning.

The moral challenges surrounding technology are exacerbated by the fact that new technologies are appearing at an exponential rate, threatening to outstrip the pace at which Christians can evaluate them. Further, Christians find little explicit treatment of technology in the Bible. Consequently, Christian moral reflection on technology requires examining the moral qualities of particular technologies in detail, describing the most germane biblical resources, and learning to distinguish Christian moral reasoning itself from the kind of reasoning that technocentrism engenders.

Evaluating Technology's Moral Qualities

Many technological achievements, such as CAT scans and air conditioning, are good things, while some of their by-products, such as toxic waste and global warming, are not. Very frequently, a given technology turns out to be a mixed bag. Innovations in communication (e.g., telephone, internet) that enable frequent and instantaneous contact with a broad range of people may also have adverse effects. This same technology may increase the physical distance that people maintain from one another, which in turn may weaken the bonds of family and friendship. Further, technology often opens up new possibilities for daily life while rendering opaque other, equally legitimate behaviors. For example, in 2007 there were more televisions per home in the United States than there were people. The ubiquity of television tends to preempt leisure reading. Finally, one must consider how technology shapes what people come to expect as culturally "normal." Not only are we coming to expect fast internet connection as a basic human right but also we increasingly champion the subtler technological values of rapid innovation, standardization, and quantification, as well as taking efficiency as the superior metric and novelty as the only recognizable form that progress takes. In light of the ambiguity of these so-called values, it is difficult, if not impossible, to say whether technology is uniformly positive or negative. It is clear, however, that technology is not inherently neutral; it plays a determinate role in shaping the lives of producers, users, and losers (e.g., those who do not own cars but still breathe the smog [see Staudenmaier]).

Technology and Scripture

The biblical canon was closed well before the first major technological revolution in the West (c. twelfth–thirteenth centuries). Despite the obvious presence in the Bible of useful artifacts such as axes and chariots, there is little evidence that technology shaped biblical culture on the same scale that it shapes culture today. So, it is unsurprising that the Bible does not directly discuss technology. Nevertheless, there are three distinct senses in which technology can be "good" or "bad" in light of Scripture.

First, some technological artifacts are tools that aid human flourishing. A hammer, for example, can extend human power to build without necessarily undermining human community (murder by a hammer blow notwithstanding). Similarly, the apostle Paul's missionary journeys were facilitated by a simple yet pervasive form of technology: roads built by the Romans. Tools such as hammers and infrastructures such as roadways are genuinely good insofar as they facilitate human community. Some technologies are also good because they resonate with Christian evangelism and discipleship. And some technologies are good for both reasons. For example, novel methods of water extraction embody Christ's mercy toward people in drought-stricken areas and prosper their communities.

Second, "technological" denotes a centuries-long revolution resulting in an entirely new form of life. Consider the mechanical clock (thirteenth century), which found its first home among Benedictine monks who sought greater precision in devotional life. By the fourteenth century, the mechanical clock had transformed Western life, opening up new possibilities for regularizing labor relations and standardizing production outside the monastery, thereby setting the stage for the rise of market economies. In this way, a technological artifact that was intended to function solely as a tool precipitated changes on such a vast scale that the entirety of Western culture is no longer a "tool" culture but a "technological" one.

Finally, technology can be evaluated in terms of what Scripture calls "powers and principalities" (e.g., Rom. 8:38; Eph. 3:10; 6:12; Col. 1:16; 2:15). Providing order to the chaos of fallen creation and structuring our shared postlapsarian human life, the powers play an important role in the story of salvation history. Indeed, they play a part in the story of God's redemption of humanity and, in that way, are in service to God. At the same time, these powers are also part of fallen creation and thereby had to be conquered by Christ's life, death, and resurrection, thereby relativizing their importance to God's reign (Col. 2:15). The powers serve a limited purpose and thus are "good" to the extent that they are properly ordered toward God's kingdom. But when they become an end in themselves, the powers engender disorder and constitute a dangerous idolatry. The powers seem to be limitless in number: "They include all institutions, all ideologies, all images, all movements, all causes, all corporations, all bureaucracies, all traditions, all methods and routines, all conglomerates, all races, all nations, all idols" (Stringfellow 205).

Despite their variety, the powers share similar features: they are able both to enslave human beings (typically by distortion and manipulation of language) and to take on a life of their own. However, not all powers are alike. Some powers are "unredeemed," while others are "in the process of being redeemed." Consequently, Christians are admonished to communally discern the workings of the powers, cooperating where these support the reign of Christ and resisting when they overstep their bounds (1 Cor. 12:8–10; Col. 1:15–17) (Wink).

As a power, technology is seen to be a life-shaping set of forces within the contemporary world. For example, the telephone and its global infrastructure did not simply appear overnight as an answer to a specific human need. Despite advantages that are now visible from hindsight, potential users at that time had to be convinced of its utility and, consequently, to accept (however unconsciously) the remolding of their lives that use of the telephone would precipitate. On the one hand, the telephone promotes the idea that communication is mere information transfer, since it disables face-to-face conversation, whether the interlocutor is across the country or across the hall. Consequently, the nuances provided by nonverbal communication are lost, and miscommunication frequently results (an effect that surely is intensified by email). On the other hand, we enjoy rapid access to emergency services and can transact important business instantly over enormous distances. Once again, it is a mixed bag (Schultze). However, viewing technology as a power readies Christians to see it in relation to the preeminence of Christ's kingdom, judging its potential benefits in light of Christian discipleship and its drawbacks in terms of its demands for idolatrous allegiance.

Technology and Modes of Reasoning: Technē and Phronēsis

Closely linked with technology as a community-shaping power is the widespread acceptance of a technological mode of thinking. Technological advances have affected the ways people understand cause and effect within the world. When cause and effect are as immediately and directly related as the push of a button or the flip of a switch, we are easily bewitched by the idea that the same pattern of easy cause and instant effect holds for social and spiritual worlds. We crave techniques for "managing" (i.e., manipulating) others. The search for techniques is a mark of "productive reasoning." By nailing together pieces of wood, the builder produces a picket fence. Cause and effect are immediately related. The builder hits the nail, the nail pierces and conjoins the wood, and, picket by picket, a fence is produced. The carpenter's pattern of reasoning, called *technē* by the Greeks, from which we get the word *technology*, emphasizes production and is suited for things that are externally (or mechanically) related to their causes. Productive reasoning (*technē*) approaches the world in terms of efficiency, mechanical causation, one-size-fits-all, speed, and numerical measurability. That is, certain actions are pursued as "good" precisely because they improve efficiency and increase output.

Most of human life, especially the moral or communal sphere, cannot be "nailed" together. We cannot fix a family the way we repair the fence, because the "pieces" of a family are not mechanically related. Rather, they are related contextually and reciprocally. In other words, the character of each family member (as for every human being) varies slightly with surroundings. Over time, small changes in character that arise in response to context and the actions of others begin to accumulate in the form of habits that become more and more permanent. In the case of the fence, a picket is and always will be just a picket. Although productive reasoning works for mechanical systems, it is not suited for dynamic systems such as the social world. An entirely different mode of reasoning, one marked by practical wisdom (*phronēsis*), is needed for knowing how to respond wisely and appropriately to human surroundings. In contrast to productive reasoning's quest for technique, practical reasoning takes deliberation over uncertainties and genuine contingencies as the primary way human beings navigate life together.

The church needs believers who are skilled in practical reasoning. The NT uses *phronēsis* and its cognates forty-eight times (thirty-four times in Pauline corpus [e.g., Rom. 8:5; 1 Cor. 13:11; 2 Cor. 13:11; Gal. 5:10; Phil. 1:7]). Practical reasoning involves making judgments about technology not on the basis of its productive value but in light of the purpose, or telos, of human existence as revealed by the gospel. This goal guides human life by asking, what sort of people should we be? Certain technologies may be found to be beneficial at certain times and places (e.g., computers that aid in Bible translation), while at other times they might engender a corrupting influence (e.g., violent video games to attract adolescents to a youth group). Even the use of technology within Christian worship requires us to ask, what sort of people are we becoming by using this technology? Churches everywhere are employing a plethora of technologies in their sanctuaries, from computerized slideshows on large projection screens to the complete control over sound, light, and temperature. These innovations allow more people to see and hear, but some have asked whether these technologies also change the character of worship.

The question, what sort of people are we becoming? must be considered by the church because technology, from nanobots to wind turbines, structures community life. Christian moral discernment about technology depends on conversation across the church (and across the ages), a communal conversation in which participants "have the same mind [*phroneō*] . . . that was in Christ Jesus" (Phil. 2:5), thereby eclipsing mere *technē*.

See also Information Technology; Powers and Principalities; Prudence

Bibliography

Borgmann, A. *Power Failure: Christianity in the Culture of Technology*. Brazos, 2003; Conway, R. *Choice at the Heart of Technology: A Christian Perspective*. Trinity Press International, 1999; Jardine, M. *The Making and Unmaking of Technological Society: How Christianity Can Save Modernity from Itself.* Brazos, 2004; Schultze, Q. *Habits of the High-Tech Heart: Living Virtuously in the Information Age*. Baker Academic, 2002; Staudenmaier, J. "The Politics of Successful Technologies." Pages 150–71 in *In Context: History and the History of Technology; Essays in Honor of Melvin Kranzberg*, ed. S. Sutcliffe and R. Post. Leigh University Press, 1989; Stringfellow, W. *A Keeper of the Word: Selected Writings of William Stringfellow*. Ed. B. Kellerman. Eerdmans, 1994; White, S. *Christian Worship and Technological Change*. Abingdon, 1994; Wink, W. *Naming the Powers: The Language of Power in the New Testament*. Fortress, 1984.

Derek C. Hatch and Brad J. Kallenberg

Teleological Theories of Ethics

Teleological ethical theories deal with questions of the proper end or goal of human moral action. The English word *teleology* is rooted in the Greek word *telos*, meaning "goal" or "end." There are a variety of teleological theories of ethics, though they break down broadly along two lines: those concerned with the proper understanding of the purpose of human life and the attainment of that purpose, and those concerned with the consequences of human action, which seek to bring about morally good consequences.

Teleological Moral Theories

Teleological ethics is usually distinguished in moral theory from deontological ethics, which understands morality as arising from concepts of duty or obligation, and from virtue ethics, which conceives of morality primarily as a matter of character and habituation. However, teleological theories encompass a broad spectrum of goal-oriented ethical thought, in some cases coupled with deontological concepts, and in some cases making use of aspects of virtue theory. Thus a hard-and-fast distinction between teleological theories and these others cannot be maintained.

Teleological ethical theories can be subdivided into two broad types: consequentialist and natural-law theories. Consequentialist theories understand the telos of moral action to be concerned primarily with the outcomes of actions—in particular, whether moral actions result in some kind of good effect. Natural-law approaches to teleology, though, are not specifically concerned with outcomes, but rather with whether moral actions conform to the natural end for which human beings are created. Natural-law ethics therefore are primarily concerned with elaborating what kinds of behaviors most fully allow humans to achieve their natural inner potential to become who they are meant to be.

Consequentialist Moral Theories

Consequentialist moral theories are concerned with the outcome or result of moral actions. The morality of an action is evaluated, in other words, based on its consequences. Actions that produce putatively good consequences are deemed to be morally good actions. Consequences, in turn, are considered to be good to the degree that they result in the increase of overall happiness for those affected by the action.

Happiness is defined in a variety of ways, though the mainstream of consequentialist ethics usually has defined happiness in terms of pleasure. Such theories are thus understood to be hedonic, rooted in pleasure. However, another common definition of happiness conceives of it as being rooted not in pleasure per se but rather in the achievement of preferences. In other words, we are happy or not to the degree that we do or do not achieve our desired plans or goals.

The most prominent consequentialist moral theory is utilitarianism. Founded by British philosopher Jeremy Bentham (1748–1832), utilitarianism is based on seeking to achieve the greatest good for the greatest number of people, what Bentham terms the "principle of utility" or the "greatest-happiness principle."

Bentham's theory assumes that it is possibile to calculate the morality of actions based on precise measurements of the total pleasure or pain that they would cause. Such calculations are based on what would be good in the aggregate for all of those affected by an action, and thus the act that produces the most happiness over unhappiness is morally preferable, even if some of those affected are actually made unhappy by the act. The question, for Bentham, is not whether any particular individuals are made happy, but whether a greater number are made happy than are made unhappy.

Bentham applied his moral theory across a broad range of topics, from economics to law and politics to prison reform. Though influential, his work also is controversial, suggesting that it is possible to determine moral action precisely by the calculation of pleasure and pain. Subsequent utilitiarians refined and modified his proposal in an attempt to account for these controversies. His most influential successor is John Stuart Mill (1806–73).

Mill's utilitarianism built upon the foundation laid by Bentham but is qualified in several ways. First, he distinguishes, as Bentham did not, between qualitatively different kinds of pleasures, arguing that the pursuit of some pleasures is more morally worthwhile than the pursuit of others. Second, Mill emphasizes the role of personal liberty in morality, arguing that the greatest-happiness principle should not undermine individual choice and self-determination.

In *Utilitarianism* Mill argues that not all pleasures should be evaluated equally, nor are all people equally competent to evaluate which pleasures are preferable to others. Rather, intellectual pleasures are to be preferred to more mundane pleasures. Only those who have experienced both are in a position to make such an evaluation. Mill writes, "It is better to be a human being dissatisfied than a pig satisfied; better to be Socrates dissatisfied than a fool satisfied" (Mill 164). The greatest good for the greatest number, therefore, entails the pursuit of higher versus lower pleasures and also the creation of circumstances that would enable people to do so.

In *On Liberty* Mill makes a further refinement to the utilitarian argument, saying that individual liberties, insofar as they do not directly affect others, should not be curtailed or limited, even if the exercise of those liberties might harm those who exercise them. This puts a strong limitation on the application of utilitarian principles to the degree that the greatest good for the greatest number might require interference with individual liberty. However, Mill still argues that moral action is oriented toward achieving the greatest good for the greatest number.

This points to an important distinction between act and rule versions of consequentialism. Act consequentialism evaluates the morality of particular actions on the basis of whether their results are likely to produce happiness, whereas rule consquentialism evaluates moral actions on the basis of whether they conform to a general rule that, if followed, would tend to produce greater happiness. Bentham's brand of utilitarianism is often understood to be a form of act consequentialism, while Mill's is generally understood to be a form of rule consequentialism.

The key element of utilitarianism that distinquishes it from other brands of consequentialism is its emphasis on *aggregate* happiness; that is, its concern is with the overall happiness within society as a consequence of moral actions and policies. Egoistic consequentialism, by contrast, is concerned with whether the consequences of an action tend to increase the happiness of the individual performing the act, irrespective of what effect it may have on others.

Natural-Law Theory

Natural-law theory is concerned with the natural goal or end of human action rather than with particular consequences. Whereas utilitarianism is by and large hedonic, natural-law theory is eudaemonistic, concerning itself with human flourishing that results from a life lived in correspondence with its created end.

The tradition of natural law extends back to the Stoics, whose view of natural law bore much in common with more deontological conceptions of morality. Thomas Aquinas, combining the Stoic understanding of natural law with an Aristotelian conception of the nature of the good and a Christian theological framework, created a theory of natural law that was fundamentally teleological in its orientation, emphasizing the natural ends for which human beings were created and the overarching goals of human flourishing and the vision of divine perfection. Thomas's conceptualization of the natural law stands at the foundation of Catholic moral theology.

Thomas's argument in the *Summa theologiae* echoes Aristotle's argument at the beginning of *Nicomachean Ethics*, that all action is oriented toward an end, which is valued either for its own sake or for the sake of something else. Those things that are valued for their own sake are intrinsically good. Aristotle argued that the highest human good was happiness, which in *Politics* is conceived of as being constituted by life in a good society. However, in *Nicomachean Ethics* Aristotle argues that true happiness is finally found in contemplation.

In *Summa contra Gentiles* Thomas argues that all moral agents strive toward achieving their goals or ends, which they understand to be goods. But the final end or good toward which all things strive is the knowledge of God.

Teleological Moral Theory and Other Ethical Theories

Moral theories, both practically and in conceptual terms, cannot be neatly separated from one another. The actual process of moral discernment often combines elements of a variety of moral theories in arriving at a conclusion as to which course of action most fully conforms to the requirements of morality. Beyond this, however, it is not always possible to easily separate moral theories from one another. While a few may represent a more or less "pure" form of the theory, in most cases both the history of their development and their actual theoretical underpinnings reveal elements of other theories.

This can be seen in both the consequentialist and natural-law approaches to teleological ethics. Both approaches incorporate elements of Aristotelian ethics. In the case of consequentialist ethics, the emphasis on happiness as the goal of human action can be seen as grounded in Aristotle's arguments in the first section of *Nicomachean Ethics*, although the early utilitarian conception of happiness as reducible to pleasure is a departure from the Aristotelian framework. Similarly, natural-law theories, particularly insofar as they are grounded in the work of Thomas Aquinas, also take much from Aristotle, in particular his understanding of the nature of virtue.

Natural-law theory also has a strongly deontological dimension, which can be traced back to the Stoic ethical tradition of natural law. This deontological dimension of natural-law ethics can be seen in Kant's approach to ethics, as well as the understanding of natural rights that grounds much of liberal political theory, particularly that of Locke and Montesquieu. In the same vein, some interpretations of virtue theory interpret it not in terms of natural ends that can be said to be human in a universal sense, but rather belonging to particular classes, communities, or contexts.

A strictly deontological moral theory, such as Kant's, claims to understand moral action as wholly independent of its aims or consequences, asserting that pure principle ought to govern moral action, regardless of its outcomes. However, Kant's understanding of deontological ethics is itself rooted in a transcendental consequentialism, in which it is the consequences of the hypothetical universalization of a course of action that render it moral or immoral. In *Critique of Judgment* Kant develops his own account of teleology, in which the human capacity for morality renders humanity as the ultimate end of the natural world.

Teleological Ethics in Biblical Context

In the biblical setting, morality is rooted in the sovereign will of God; God's will often is expressed in that context as having as its objective the well-being of creation in general, and human beings in particular. This theme appears as early as the creation narratives in Genesis, where the natural world is seen as an expression of God's creative power, and where human beings are created for the end of caring for and enhancing God's creation. Human beings are also created for one another in a teleological sense: the man and the woman are each other's "end," companions created by God for the sake of each other's well-being.

In Gen. 2 God commands Adam and Eve not to eat from the tree of the knowledge of good and evil, which can be interpreted as an expression of God's teleological will for humanity: our natural end is to be free from such knowledge. By the same token, God's command is given a consequentialist edge, as God instructs them, "For in the day that you eat of it you shall die" (Gen. 2:17).

Throughout the OT, the commands of God are frequently understood in a teleological manner. In a positive sense, this is understood in terms of the covenant relationship between God and Israel, whereby God promises to shower blessings on Israel in return for their faithfulness. For example, God commands the Israelites, "Choose life so that you and your descendants may live, loving the Lord your God, obeying him, and holding fast to him; for that means life to you and length of days, so that you may live in the land that the Lord swore to give to your ancestors, to Abraham, to Isaac, and to Jacob" (Deut. 30:19–20). In a negative sense, however, the prophets often concern themselves with the evil consequences of unjust and idolatrous practices on the part of the Israelites, particularly with regard to the impoverishment and exploitation of the weak and vulnerable, but also with regard to the possibility that the abandonment of faithfulness to God will lead God to forsake Israel.

New Testament ethics, insofar as it is rooted in the Jewish moral teaching from which it emerged, is also teleological in its emphasis on obedience to the law of God for the sake of human well-being and the maintenance of community. However, the apocalyptic strain in Jesus' teaching radicalizes both the telos toward which moral action is oriented and the kind of behavior appropriate to it. Thus, Jesus commands his disciples to concern themselves with the kingdom of God rather than worldly things, as that is the imminent end to which their behavior should be directed. Concerns such as wealth, status, and kinship obligations are relativized to the coming of God's imminent reign. Thus, human well-being is understood in the teaching of Jesus to be both continuous with what was taught in the OT but also recontextualized in light of the oncoming eschaton.

A similar emphasis appears in Paul's teaching. However, Paul was concerned with the maintenance of the community of Christ's followers during the time of the parousia, and thus from a practical standpoint he had to make moral determinations for the purposes of preserving and expanding the integrity of the church. Thus, in his letters he frequently admonishes the community to do that which serves the goal of strengthening, rather than weakening, the bonds of the ecclesial community.

Finally, there is a consequentialist dimension to NT ethics as well, insofar as Jesus' teaching is encapsulated in the dictum "In everything do to others as you would have them do to you" (Matt. 7:12). This moral formulation has implications in terms of both the consequences of one's actions and the nature of reciprocity. The consequences of the actions that we cause to befall on others should be those that we would wish to befall on us as well. This presents a moral test to be considered when contemplating our actions: to what degree would I want the consequences of this action to fall on me alone? As a guide to moral action, it requires that we take account of the consequences of our actions for others and for ourselves.

See also Consequentialism; Deontological Theories of Ethics; Golden Rule; Good, The; Happiness; Natural Law; Utilitarianism; Virtue Ethics

Bibliography

Aristotle. *Nicomachean Ethics*. Trans. T. Irwin. 2nd ed. Hackett, 1999; idem. *Politics*. Trans. E. Baker. Oxford University Press, 2009; Bentham, J. "From *An Introduction to the Principles of Morals and Legislation*." Pages 65–112 in *Utilitarianism and Other Essays*, by J. S. Mill and J. Bentham. Ed. A. Ryan. Penguin Books, 1987; Cicero. *On Duties*. Trans. M. Griffin. Cambridge University Press, 1991; Kant, I. *The Critique of Judgement*. Trans. J. Meredith. Oxford University Press, 1978; Mill, J. S. *On Liberty and Utilitarianism*. Bantam Classics, 1993; Thomas Aquinas. *Nature and Grace: Selections from the Summa theologica of Thomas Aquinas*. Trans. and ed. A. Fairweather. LCC. Westminster, 1954; idem. *St. Thomas Aquinas on Politics and Ethics: A New Translation, Backgrounds, Interpretations*. Trans. and ed. P. Sigmund. Norton, 1987.

Scott Paeth

Temperance

Temperance is the harmonious self-regulation of appetites and desires, principally the physical appetites for food, drink, and sex. Commonly referred to as "moderation" or "self-control," temperance has long been considered one of four cardinal virtues, along with justice, courage, and wisdom. Yet of the four, it is the least known, and often it is associated with the temperance movements of the nineteenth century that discouraged the use of alcoholic beverages.

Classical Origins

Temperance originated in the Greek *sōphrosynē*, a term whose richness outstrips any single English definition. A particularly Greek virtue, temperance, in Plato's conception, included self-knowledge, self-restraint, self-government, harmony, and internal order. In his *Republic*, Plato saw temperance as the virtue of the masses, who voluntarily accept the rule of the wise; this is a social analogy for the rule of reason over the bodily appetites. Temperance is often depicted as a charioteer controlling the horse that pulls his chariot.

In his quest to more explicitly demarcate the fields and limits of each virtue, Aristotle narrowed the sphere of temperance to the bodily appetites of food, drink, and sex. However, a form of temperance runs throughout Aristotle's ethical thought, as his definition of virtue as a mean between two extremes. Aristotle is also the first to distinguish between temperance and continence (*enkrateia*), which is the determined self-control of one's appetites. This lesser virtue lacks the harmonious agreement of the appetites that characterizes temperance.

Scriptural Transitions

Scriptural temperance is something of a chimera. *Sōphrosynē* in the NT Epistles is most readily expressed by mental clarity and sobriety (derived directly from its roots, "sound mind"). The Gerasene demoniac is restored to his right mind (Mark 5:15), and Paul commends being in one's right mind to strengthen the brethren (2 Cor. 5:13). Believers should be serious and self-disciplined (1 Pet. 4:7), as well as teachable (Titus 2:4). Temperance is a requirement for bishops (1 Tim. 3:2; Titus 1:8) and is linked with knowledge, endurance, and godliness (2 Pet. 1:6). And Paul's counsel of sober self-assessment as a path to unity within the fellowship (Rom. 12:3) echoes the sociopolitical role of temperance in Plato's *Republic*.

However, it is as self-control that temperance emerges most prominently in Scripture and in ongoing Christian thought. Translations of *sōphrosynē* as "self-control" (Titus 2:2, 5) and "self-discipline" (2 Tim. 1:7) notwithstanding, this development hinges largely upon the association of temperance with *enkrateia*, a term with deep connections to willpower and restraint. As a gift of the Spirit, temperance is manifested when one has "crucified the flesh with its passions and desires" (Gal. 5:23–24). This is a departure from the classical position, in which virtue was the cause, not the result, of ethical purity.

Development in the Christian Tradition

The temperance inherited by the church fathers was not the vibrant virtue of Greece. Harmony and balance were gradually supplanted by an increased emphasis on its ascetical components. In their hands, temperance became virtually synonymous with sexual conduct, purity, and especially virginity—an important distinction of Christians living in a pagan world. Augustine retained this notion of temperance while also recalling its status as a cardinal virtue.

It is not until Thomas Aquinas that temperance appears in anything resembling its classical form. Locating the Aristotelian virtues in the love of (and for) God, temperance now creates a fitting proportion within the appetites and a wholesome delight in objects of pleasure, which results in a beautiful tranquillity of the soul.

Wesleyan temperance retains these positive aspects, but with a renewed emphasis on asceticism. John Wesley spoke of temperance as "using rather than abusing the world," the voluntary abstention from all things that do not lead to God. For Wesley, temperance was associated with meekness, patience, gentleness, and long-suffering; it was also coupled with fasting, mortification, and self-denial. As the asceticism of the church shifted its attention from sexuality to alcohol, the formation of the temperance movements of the nineteenth century gave temperance its most recent association, one that dominates our perception of the virtue to this day.

Contemporary Applications

The current understanding of and appreciation for temperance is a faint shadow of its rich history; it is the sole cardinal virtue to be essentially lost from the modern moral lexicon. It may be asked whether salvaging temperance for today's world is profitable, or advisable, or even possible. Certainly, its reclamation would take substantial effort. Yet doing so might provide a fresh conversation partner for contemporary moral discussions. Scholars are increasingly willing to expand the scope of the virtue beyond the triad of food, drink, and sex, applying it to discussions of, for example, resource consumption and the environment.

Consumption is naturally connected to temperance. Humans are by definition consumers in that we must consume to live; yet we have now become a people who live to consume. Modern appetite has come untethered from its basis in actual need and now drifts upon the tides of media-generated excess. Needs and wants are increasingly difficult to distinguish, and advertisers encourage us to conflate the two categories at will. With its dual emphasis on self-knowledge and self-control, temperance moves us beyond the extremes of strict asceticism and heedless gluttony and into a thoughtful assessment of actual needs. Similarly, our relationship to the created world is one of necessity; we must draw from it in order to live. Yet our connection to nature grows increasingly frail as we separate ourselves from the sources of the goods that we consume. Temperance eases our impact on the planet by lessening our drain on the world's resources.

In a world thrown out of balance and overrun by excess, it does little good to offer imbalanced alternatives. What are needed, rather, are responses that flow from a centered posture of harmony and order. Temperance is a very promising possibility.

See also Asceticism; Cardinal Virtues; Continence; Fruit of the Spirit; Virtue(s)

Bibliography

Aristotle. *The Nicomachean Ethics*, book 3; Curzer, H. "Aristotle's Account of the Virtue of Temperance in Nicomachean Ethics III.10–12." *JHP* 35 (1997): 5–25; North, H. *Sophrosyne: Self-Knowledge and Self-Restraint in Greek Literature*. Cornell University Press, 1966; Pieper, J. *The Four Cardinal Virtues: Prudence, Justice, Fortitude, Temperance*. Trans. R. Winston et al. University of Notre Dame Press, 1966; Plato. "Charmides." Pages 639–63 in *The Complete Works of Plato*, ed. J. Cooper. Hackett, 1997; Thomas Aquinas. *Summa theologiae* II-II, qq. 141–56.

Maria Kenney

Temptation

The word *temptation* usually carries a negative sense as enticement to sin. It is, however, not the same as sin. The word *testing* is used as a neutral term denoting practically anything that demands a religious or moral choice. The very existence of temptation implies that to choose good or evil matters. It also concretizes the reality of the struggle between good and evil.

Temptation in the Old Testament

In the Genesis account of the temptation and fall of Adam and Eve, the serpent is presented as the tempter who is "more crafty than any other wild animal that the LORD God had made" (Gen. 3:1). Adam and Eve were persuaded by the serpent to doubt the word of God, and they succumbed to sin by disobeying God's command not to eat the fruit of the tree of knowledge of good and evil (Gen. 3:1–8). This primordial story of the first human sin shows that temptation to sin arises both from within (the fruit was good for food, a delight to the eyes, and made one wise) and from without (the tree itself, and the serpent that aimed to mislead them).

Cain, instead of keeping his envy and rage at bay, was taken over by his own murderous desire into violence against his brother, Abel (Gen. 4:1–8). The sons of God saw that the daughters of human beings were good (Gen. 6:2). This description is reminiscent of that of Eve in the garden. God saw that the inclination of the human heart was only evil continually (Gen. 6:5).

Israel is called to respond in fidelity to the initiation of the covenant God. The wilderness generation was tempted to sin in putting God to the test by questioning his sovereignty and fidelity (e.g., Num. 14:22–23; Ps. 95:9). The same situation was repeated when Israel in the promised land worshiped other gods and ignored God's commands (Deut. 6:10–25). The tenth commandment accentuates one's inner disposition of covetousness that can lead to the violation of others seen in the previous commandments. Moses thus exhorted the Israelites to circumcise the foreskin of their heart (Deut. 10:16), a theme picked up by Jeremiah (Jer. 4:4). This foreshadows God's promise to put his law within his people and write it on their hearts (Jer. 31:33; cf. Ezek. 36:26). How one is being tempted to sin is brought up most vividly in Proverbs, where Woman Folly is portrayed as a harlot enticing men to sin (Prov. 9:13–18). The harlot promises to fulfill their desires, but the destiny of those being led astray is nothing but death.

Temptation in the New Testament

Jesus gains victory over temptation and Satan by appealing to the word of God (Matt. 4:1–11 // Luke 4:1–13). He resisted the temptation to satisfy his own desire, to perform a miraculous act, to assert his authority that would guarantee accomplishment of his mission. Jesus triumphed over the devil by rejecting all his suggestions, demonstrating his fidelity and submission to God. He was tested in every respect, but he did not sin (Heb. 4:15). This qualifies him as the merciful and faithful high priest, bringing all believers to the throne of grace to receive mercy and grace (Heb. 4:16). His submission to the will of the Father through trials to the point of crucifixion proves that he is perfect, securing eternal salvation for all who obey him (Heb. 5:9; cf. 12:2). Those who endure trials to the end will be saved (Matt. 24:13).

When Peter tried to dissuade Jesus from the path to the crucifixion, Jesus said to him, "Get behind me, Satan! You are a stumbling block to me; for you are setting your mind not on divine things but on human things" (Matt. 16:23). Peter, like anyone else, can ally himself with Satan at any particular moment if he refuses to see things from the perspective of God (cf. 2 Cor. 11:14–15). Both Luke and John see the betrayal of Jesus by Judas Iscariot as the working of the devil in him (Luke 22:3; John 13:2). Believers are to be wary of the wiles of the devil (Eph. 4:27; 6:11).

The structures of human existence can ally themselves with the principalities and powers to hold people hostage, luring them to come under their power in opposition to the authority of God (2 Cor. 4:4; Gal. 4:3; Col. 2:8, 20). The whole world is seen as ruled by the devil (1 John 5:19). In James, the world represents everything aligned against God (4:4). Those allying themselves with the devil are "united in yielding their power and authority to the beast" (Rev. 17:13). The primeval and supernatural source of all opposition to God will eventually be thrown into the lake of fire (Rev. 20:10).

Human desires are not intrinsically evil, for they too are created by God. Human beings, however, are responsible for controlling them. James insists that God never tempts people to do evil, as that is contradictory to God's own nature (Jas. 1:13). The voluntary nature of the desire is underlined when James says that the desire is "one's own" (Jas. 1:14). The evil desire is personified as one who lures and entices people into sin when they yield to inner temptation in the testing situation. James vividly portrays the process using the imagery of procreation: desire conceives and gives birth to sin, which, when fully grown, gives birth to death (Jas. 1:15). It is out of one's own inner cravings that envy and selfish ambition come (Jas. 3:15–16; 4:1). The lure of temptation often achieves its aim via deception, deluding one's conscience, distracting one's commitments, eventually resulting in surrender to the slavery of one's own passion (2 Pet. 2:19).

Jesus teaches that out of the human heart come evil intentions that issue in such things as fornication, theft, murder, adultery, avarice, wickedness, deceit, licentiousness, envy, slander, pride, and folly (Mark 7:21–23). This corresponds to Paul's idea of "the mind that is set on the flesh," which is "hostile to God" (Rom. 8:7). Out of the desire of the flesh come the works of the flesh: fornication, impurity, licentiousness, idolatry, sorcery, enmities, strife, jealousy, anger, quarrels, dissensions, factions, envy, drunkenness, carousing, and other such things (Gal. 5:19–21). Greed stands out as the root of all kinds of evil (1 Tim. 6:9–10); it is idolatry (Eph. 5:5; Col. 3:5). All human beings are under the slavery of sin. This is evident in the fact that people often cannot resist the temptation to do what they know is morally wrong, succumbing to the working of their evil desires (Rom. 7:14–20).

Desire can and must be managed, but it is never obliterated. Peter warns believers that "the desires of the flesh" wage war against their lives (1 Pet. 2:11). John exhorts believers not to love the world and all that is in the world—the desire of the flesh, the desire of the eyes, the pride in riches (1 John 2:15–17). Human desire can lead people astray (2 Pet. 2:3, 10, 18; 3:3). For Paul, it is through the power of the risen Christ in the working of the Spirit of life that the power of sin is broken (Rom. 8:1). Life in obedience to the law can be achieved by means of the Spirit, the divine agent of good. Only for those led and guided by the Spirit can the law of Christ be fulfilled in the Christian community (Gal. 5:13–15, 22–24). For their part, humans must keep alert and exercise self-control, for Satan can use all sorts of things to lead people into temptation (1 Cor. 7:5; 1 Pet. 5:8). God, who is always faithful, will provide the way out for his people so that they may endure every trial and triumph over temptation (1 Cor. 10:13).

For James, the only way to counteract the influence of the evil inclination that entices one to sin is by the gracious gift of the word of truth from God, through which a renewed people of God comes into existence (Jas. 1:18). Conversion does not completely eradicate the evil inclination, but with the implanted word and the wisdom from above, the renewed people of God can be freed from the power of the evil inclination so that they can love God wholeheartedly (Jas. 1:5, 21, 25). They must submit themselves to God and resist the devil, and the devil will flee from them (Jas. 4:7). Eventually, it is by God's grace that people can overcome temptations: "he gives all the more grace" (Jas. 4:6).

See also Desire; Fidelity; Moral Formation; Vices and Virtues, Lists of

Bibliography

Cheung, L. *The Genre, Composition and Hermeneutics of the Epistle of James*. PBTM. Paternoster, 2003; Gerhardsson, B. *The Testing of God's Son (Matt. 4:1–11 & par.): An Analysis of an Early Christian Midrash*. ConBNT 2. Gleerup, 1966; Wa Gatumu, K. *The Pauline Concept of Supernatural Powers: A Reading from the African Worldview*. PBM. Paternoster, 2008.

Luke Leuk Cheung

Ten Commandments

Although brief, the Ten Commandments (sometimes called the "Ten Words," from the Greek *deka logoi* [Exod. 34:28; Deut. 10:4 LXX], hence also the "Decalogue") have been crucially important in the history of ethical reflection in the Jewish and Christian traditions, and they continue to have significant normative power in most Jewish and Christian communities today. They occur twice in the first five books of the Bible, in both cases as a series of commands said to be authored directly by God (Exod. 31:18; Deut. 4:13). They are the first and only commandments that the whole people of Israel hear directly from God, as opposed to the rest of the Sinai legislation, which is mediated by Moses (Deut. 5:4, 22). The commandments are numbered slightly differently in various traditions. For example, Jewish traditions include as the first commandment (or word) what in Christian traditions is identified as the prologue ("I am the LORD your God, who brought you out of the land of Egypt, out of the house of slavery"), and the Jewish, Lutheran, and Catholic traditions combine into the first commandment (no other gods) what the Reformed tradition has taken to be two separate commands (no other gods, and no images).

In the first appearance of the Decalogue (Exod. 20:1–17), Israel is being formed as a people at Sinai, whereas later Moses is recalling that formative moment for the people just before they enter the land of Canaan (Deut. 5:6–21). The text makes no claim that the Ten Commandments constitute the complete will of God, but their placement within the narrative suggests that they possess an ethical priority. In both contexts the Decalogue is set apart from the rest of the legislation that follows it. Furthermore, many readers have long understood the Book of the Covenant in Exod. 20–23 and the legislation in Deut. 12–26 as a kind of explication and unfolding of the Ten Commandments, which precede them. These larger bodies of legal material show how the commandments actually function in the life of the community—that is, how they work in real-life situations that the community encounters.

Within the history of interpretation of the Ten Commandments, many scholars and interpreters have understood them as a summary of the moral law. As early as the first century CE, Philo of Alexandria, for example, understood the Torah (i.e., all the laws) to be an elaboration of the Ten Commandments. The Reformers in the sixteenth century paid special attention to the Decalogue as a source for ethical reflection. Martin Luther organized his commentary on Deuteronomy around the Ten Commandments because he understood that book to be an elaboration of them, and John Calvin understood each commandment broadly, interpreting each of the so-called negative commandments positively. The commandment against killing, for example, is appropriately understood as a command to promote the neighbor's well-being. In this way, the Ten Commandments come to exert their moral force on nearly every aspect of life. In a similar way recently, Patrick Miller proposes that a moral "trajectory" emerges from each commandment, thus indicating the broad swath of the moral life that the Decalogue encompasses.

The so-called prologue (the first "word" in the Jewish tradition) is crucial to understanding the Ten Commandments, even though typically it is not considered part of the Decalogue by most Christians: "I am the Lord your God, who brought you out of the land of Egypt, out of the house of slavery" (Exod. 20:2; Deut. 5:6). This divine self-presentation reveals the character of God as one who saves, who is gracious. Its position at the head of the commandments is vital to understanding them as coming not from an abstract deity, but rather from Yahweh, with whom Israel is already in relationship and whose character has already been revealed as one who acts for his people. The prologue is, then, intimately connected to the first commandment ("You shall have no other gods before me"). Based on the truth of the prologue, of who this God is, the people are not to have any other gods. And the first commandment, together with the prologue, serves as the foundation upon which all the others stand. They affirm unequivocally that the vertical, divine-human relationship is prior to, and sustaining of, all horizontal relationships among human beings. Given the importance of the prologue to a correct understanding of the rest of the commandments, excising it (for purposes of posting in public places, for example) violates the intent of the commandments. And it is in light of God's gracious action to save that human moral action to fulfill the commandments becomes intelligible. The twentieth-century theologian and ethicist H. Richard Niebuhr, for example, outlined an understanding of human moral action as the "response to God's redeeming action." People are set free from past bondage, and this is how they respond to that new freedom. So the commandments describe how a free people respond to freedom in that new identity.

The people are to obey the Ten Commandments not simply because God commands them to do so, but rather because obeying them is beneficial; that is, adherence to them makes it possible for the community to flourish. The commandments are meant to be not a burden, but a gift. The mere presence of the motivation clauses (e.g., persons are to honor their parents "so that your days may be long in the land that the Lord your God is giving you" [Exod. 20:12]) suggests that the commandments are neither arbitrary nor designed for the sake of having people obey. The motivation clauses suggest, rather, that from God's point of view, the commandments are not self-evident. God seeks to persuade the people that this way of life is attractive. Some tension thus exists between the deontological approach to ethics, with its emphasis on duty, and the motivational clauses in the commandments. It is good and valuable to obey these commandments, not simply a duty to do so. The commandments are also rational and sensible in and of themselves; that is, they are good for human life. In short, by giving these laws, God seeks to persuade the people that this way of life is a good one; obedience to the commandments is not only a recognition of the claim laid upon the people and an appropriate response to the gracious activity of the one who commands but also is inherently life-giving (they are "for our lasting good" [Deut. 6:24]).

The first commandment, "You shall have no other gods before me," is the foundation upon which all the other commandments rest, and also is the one that is automatically violated when any of the others is violated. The first commandment requires total and undivided trust and commitment to Yahweh, Israel's deity. Other potential claimants for meaning, value, and devotion are numerous ("other gods") and seductive, but they must be resisted. Patrick Miller spells out some of the implications of the first commandment: "The oneness of the reality that grounds existence, God, is what keeps life from being chaotic and divided beyond the limits of human management. In the face of the multiple pulls and dimensions of human life and experience, human existence is held together and in order by that one and absolute object of our allegiance and loyalty" (Miller 23). The commandment is intelligible only in light of the prologue; that is, it is only after God has acted graciously on Israel's behalf that God makes this claim of obedience. Grace precedes the law. But the first commandment is also closely connected to the prohibition on images that follows in the second commandment (in Reformed numbering) insofar as it has the double meaning of prohibiting the fashioning of images of Yahweh and also of other gods. The latter is subsumed under the first commandment; the former, however, is likely where the emphasis lies: human-made images of the divine being are excluded forever. God alone chooses the mode of divine revelation.

This article has insufficient space to deal with each commandment in turn, but here a few observations about the sixth commandment are offered because it has proved especially fascinating yet nettlesome to interpreters, with important implications for ethics. The commandment is variously translated somewhat narrowly as "You shall not murder" (e.g., NRSV) or more broadly as "You shall not kill" (e.g., RSV). Yet neither of these is entirely appropriate to the Hebrew text; indeed, there is no way to satisfactorily translate the Hebrew verb *raṣaḥ* into English, as it came to mean different things in different contexts over the course of time in ancient Israel (see, e.g., Num. 35:6–34; Deut. 19:3–13; Josh. 20:3–9; and related narratives, especially 1 Kgs. 21). Lengthy analysis of these and many other related texts reveals that the commandment against killing prohibits not just these acts of violence but also the prior emotions and attitudes that feed them. So while Jesus explicitly interiorizes the commandment in the Sermon on the Mount (Matt. 5:21–26), control of one's passions in service to the preservation of life was already in view in the original context(s) of the sixth commandment. "You shall not hate in your heart anyone of your kin" (Lev. 19:17).

In giving Israel the commandments at Sinai (and they are a gift), God seeks to form a community that will thrive in its relationship with God and with one another. But to achieve this end, the commandments cannot simply be promulgated; they must be taught and interpreted for each new generation. When the young are taught the commandments, they are first reminded of the gracious character and identity of the God who commands, and then they are instructed in the commandments themselves (Deut. 6:20–25). The centrality of the commandments for the life and faith of the community is indicated by the way in which Scripture equates the covenant itself with the commandments (Deut. 4:13; 9:11). Many interpreters understand them to function in a way akin to the US Constitution, as a founding document that must be reinterpreted by and for each new generation. In the NT, Jesus offers an authoritative interpretation of the Ten Commandments so that their radical intention, with their true force and compass, is made clear for all to see.

See also Covenant; Law; Old Testament Ethics

Bibliography

Braaten, C., and C. Seitz, eds. *I Am the Lord Your God: Christian Reflections on the Ten Commandments*. Eerdmans, 2005; Brown, W., ed. *The Ten Commandments: The Reciprocity of Faithfulness*. LTE. Westminster John Knox, 2004; Miller, P. *The Ten Commandments*. IRSC. Westminster John Knox, 2009.

Jacqueline E. Lapsley

Terrorism

Although there is no internationally agreed upon definition of *terrorism*, the term generally refers to attempts to manipulate or control a noncombatant population through violence or the threat of violence or other means of causing great fear. Scholars of modern terrorism often describe the Jewish Sicarii of the first century as early terrorists. The Sicarii used assassination, kidnapping, property destruction, and other forms of violence against the Herodians, Sadducees, and Jewish aristocracy who collaborated with Rome (Josephus, *Ant*. 20.172, 187–188; *J.W.* 2.264–265). The Sicarii played an important role in the Jewish revolt of 66 CE. The relationship of the Sicarii to the Zealots is not entirely clear, but they were similar if not identical movements against Roman occupation (see Horsley).

The terrorism of the Sicarii was a response to the terror that Rome visited on the Jewish people. The Jewish people lived under threat of Roman persecution, and all resisters to Roman rule were publicly executed. The Jews were caught between the terror of Rome and the terrorism of the Sicarii. Like the Sicarii, Jesus proclaimed the imminence of the kingdom of God (Mark 1:15), but he rejected violent resistance to Rome. Ultimately, his confrontation with Rome transformed the cross, the symbol of Rome's reign of terror, into the symbol of God's reign of peace.

Early Christian martyrs such as Ignatius of Antioch and Polycarp embodied the teachings and example of Christ. Because they refused to worship Caesar, they, and many other early Christians, were victims of state terrorism and torture. Like Christ, they were mocked and killed as part of public exhibitions designed to display Rome's power over its enemies. However, Christian martyrs saw the public setting of Roman gladiator shows and other spectacle entertainments as an opportunity to testify about Christ's reign of peace and hope. As Robin Darling Young observes, "Christian communities invaded those spectacles [entertainments] and turned them to their own purposes, as athletes in games they did not invent and as officiants in sacrifices they set up against the sacrificial civic religion of the Romans" (Young 12–13). They did not passively accept Rome's terror but rather engaged it with creative and courageous witness. Tertullian, who converted to Christianity because of the martyrs' witness, wrote to Scapula, proconsul of Carthage, "In the time of [Christianity's] seeming overthrow, it is built into a greater power. For all who witness the noble patience of its martyrs . . . are inflamed with desire to examine the matter in question; and as soon as they come to know the truth, they straightaway enroll themselves its disciples" (*Scap.* 5).

Ultimately, Christianity outlasted the terror of Rome's persecutions. Today, the challenge is not responding to terrorism with violence, which merely perpetuates and imitates its fear; rather, the task is to creatively and courageously engage it with the gospel of peace. As Augustine observes, the key lesson of the martyrs' witness is that "righteousness puts all things, evil as well as good, to good employment" (*Civ.* 8.4).

Bibliography

Horsley, R. "The Sicarii: Ancient Jewish Terrorists." *JR* 59 (1979): 435–58; Young, R. *In Procession before the World: Martyrdom as Public Liturgy in Early Christianity*. Marquette University Press, 2001.

Chanon R. Ross

Test-Tube Babies *See* Reproductive Technologies

Theft

Theft is the wrongful appropriation of what belongs to another.

Attending to Scripture

Scripture consistently condemns theft. It is prohibited, of course, in the Decalogue: "You shall not steal" (Exod. 20:15; Deut. 5:19). It is prohibited also in the Holiness Code (Lev. 19:11, 13). It appears in the prophetic catalog of Israel's sins in Hos. 4:2 and in the list of Judah's sins in Jer. 7:9. The NT echoes that condemnation in citations of the Decalogue (Mark 10:19 pars.; Rom. 13:9) and in catalogs of wrongs (1 Cor. 6:10; 1 Pet. 4:15).

Stealing is a crime, and as a crime it warrants punishment. The legal tradition of the OT stipulates certain penalties. The punishment for stealing (or "kidnapping") a person is death (Exod. 21:16; Deut. 24:7). The punishment for stealing animals is that "the thief shall make restitution" (Exod. 22:1), fourfold for a slaughtered sheep, twofold for an animal found alive (Exod. 22:1, 4). A thief who is unable to make restitution "shall be sold for the theft" (Exod. 22:1). The punishment for stealing money or goods is twofold restitution (Exod. 22:7). These punishments are relatively mild compared to those in the Code of Hammurabi, which stipulated the death penalty for various thefts and for thieves unable to make restitution, and which stipulated tenfold restitution as the norm. Even so, the OT condemnation of theft is clear and consistent.

The commandment "You shall not steal" is a perennial favorite of the propertied class. The rich cherish both the authorization that it seems to afford to their possessions and the protection that it evidently provides against any who would take them away, including (and especially) the poor. The economically powerful frequently have read the commandment in self-serving ways, defending their tight-fisted grip on their own prosperity and security as a faithful performance of the law of God. The biblical account of theft, however, provides an alternative reading; it does not simply pronounce God's benediction on those who would use the prohibition of theft to protect their possessions and to keep them from the poor.

There are many different kinds of theft, as Scripture makes clear. It is not just that various objects (people, animals, goods) can be stolen, but also that there are various means of wrongfully appropriating what belongs to another. To be sure, there is the sort of theft to which the poor and powerless are tempted, the use of violence or stealth to take what one needs. The Bible never condones such theft, but it does understand it: "Thieves are not despised who steal only to satisfy their appetite when they are hungry" (Prov. 6:30; the next verse makes it clear, however, that such a thief is still to be punished). But there are also the subtler forms of stealing that Scripture discerns among the rich and powerful. It is a kind of theft when merchants "deal falsely" (Lev. 19:11 [hard on the heels of the commandment against theft], 35–36; Deut. 25:13–16), when they "make the ephah small and the shekel great" (Amos 8:5). It is a kind of theft when the rich withhold the wages of the poor (Lev. 19:13 [again, hard on the heels of the commandment against theft]; Deut. 24:14–15), when the rich get richer at the expense of a decent wage for laborers or by taking advantage of slaves. It is a kind of theft when judges take bribes (1 Sam. 8:3; Amos 5:12), subverting justice for the poor. In Samuel's farewell address he insists that he is not guilty of a whole catalog of kinds of theft. "Whose ox have I taken? Or whose donkey have I taken? Or whom have I defrauded? Whom have I oppressed? Or from whose hand have I taken a bribe to blind my eyes with it?" (1 Sam. 12:3).

What makes all such theft wrongful in Scripture? Theft is, of course, conventionally regarded as a violation of property rights. And, of course, if there were no property rights, there could be no theft. Indeed, the very presence of the command against stealing in Scripture allows the inference that Scripture accepts property rights. Scripture, however, sets property rights in the context of God's more fundamental claims as the creator and redeemer of all things. "The earth is the LORD's and all that is in it" (Ps. 24:1). The land is God's (Lev. 25:23, which authorized the Jubilee regulations concerning the redistribution of the land every fifty years). Its produce is God's (recognized in the Feast of Firstfruits), and "the cattle on a thousand hills" are God's (Ps. 50:10). Property is recognized and protected, but all property is finally regarded as a gift of God, a loan over which we have only the rights of stewardship. That stewardship demands not only gratitude to God but also loyalty to the cause of God. And the cause of God includes provision for the poor and powerless. Thus, it is a kind of theft when the wealthy do not recognize that what they call "their own" is really God's and a call to justice and generosity. It is a kind of theft when the rich ignore and dismiss the legitimate claims of the poor upon them, when they do not share with the needy what is due them by God's justice.

Theft is wrongful also because it violates the trust between human beings. By its violence or its secrecy, by its dishonesty or by its "fine print," theft breaks faith with other human beings in order to enrich oneself. It can prompt suspicion and anxiety, resentment and the desire for revenge. Also, this commandment is "summed up in this word, 'Love your neighbor as yourself' " (Rom. 13:9).

Finally, theft is wrongful as an expression of the malformation of the self, as an expression of the heart's distorted desires. So we read in Mark 7:21, for example, "For it is from within, from the human heart, that evil intentions come: fornication, theft, murder" (cf. Matt. 15:19). It is an expression of the greed that is idolatry (Eph. 5:5; Col. 3:5), the idolatry that looks to mammon instead of God for one's hope and security. Little wonder, then, that in describing the contrast of the "old self" and the "new self," Ephesians gives this example: "Thieves must give up stealing; rather let them labor and work honestly with their own hands, so as to have something to share with the needy" (Eph. 4:28).

The Tradition and Scripture

The Christian church has a rich tradition concerning the prohibition of theft. That tradition too, for all of its great variety, consistently condemns theft. Some (e.g., Thomas Aquinas) did argue that in extreme circumstances of urgent need one could justifiably appropriate what belonged to another. But such arguments were carefully hedged and usually acknowledged that theft per se is a wrongful activity. On the one hand, such arguments gave no license to the idea that the possessions of someone whose needs have been met may be happily and justifiably appropriated by another. On the other hand, the tradition gave no license to the piling up of wealth while others were in need.

Attention to the social significance of wealth and property, to the duties of love and covenant in communities where there was need, and to the temptations of greed and idolatry characterized the tradition from the beginning. Theft was never a matter of merely legal entitlement. Property rights were never absolute. The prohibition of theft was seldom simply put in the service of those relatively well-off members of the community who wanted to protect themselves from the poor; rather, it was regularly put in the service of the call to provide for the needy. Ambrose, for example, in a short work titled *Naboth*, reflected on the story of Ahab's greedy theft of Naboth's small plot of land (1 Kgs. 21) and sadly complained that the story has "perennial application." The avaricious rich find ways, clever or vicious, to seize the goods of the poor. Ambrose concluded that the rich should give alms as a form of restitution to the poor, as simply "handing over to him what is his." Basil had argued that if those who have the means to help the needy fail to do so, they should be regarded as "thieves" (*Homily on Luke* 12.18). Thomas Aquinas said the same (*ST* II-II, q. 66).

There are numerous such examples in the tradition, but it may be useful to consider one other example, John Calvin, who, because of Max Weber, often has been associated with "the spirit of capitalism" (see Weber's *The Protestant Ethic and the Spirit of Capitalism*). The commandment prohibits theft, to be sure, but Calvin, in *Commentaries on the Four Last Books of Moses* and in *Institutes of the Christian Religion*, warns against the moral minimalism that would prohibit theft by violence while it calls "prudent" the one "who takes in the simple, and insidiously oppresses the poor" (Calvin 111). Such moral minimalism serves self-righteousness, but God "pronounces all unjust means of gain to be so many thefts" (Calvin 111). "There are many kinds of theft," he says (*Institutes* 2.8.45), and he begins to list them—theft by violence, by fraud, through craftiness, through flatteries—but he stops his list-making to generalize. The commandment prohibits "all those arts" whereby we take what belongs to our neighbor. And "all those arts" include legal means, court action of one sort or another. What is due another is not simply a matter of legal entitlement, and there can be legal theft. God "sees the intricate deceptions with which a crafty man sets out to snare one of simpler mind. . . . He sees the hard and inhuman laws with which the more powerful oppresses and crushes the weaker person" (*Institutes* 2.8.45).

According to Calvin, "We will duly obey this commandment, then, if content with our lot, we are zealous to make only honest and lawful gain; if we do not seek to become wealthy through injustice, nor attempt to deprive our neighbor of his goods to increase our own; if we do not strive to heap up riches cruelly wrung from the blood of others; if we do not madly scrape together from everywhere, by fair means or foul, whatever will feed our avarice or satisfy our prodigality" (*Institutes* 2.8.46).

The commandment against theft finally invites us to "do justice." "Since injustice is an abomination to God, we should render to each man what belongs to him" (*Institutes* 2.8.45). The commandment itself, of course, or for that matter the Decalogue, does not mention justice. But Calvin confidently reports that the purpose of the command is nothing other than justice, and that any injustice is a form of theft. And this is justice: "Let us share the necessity of those whom we see pressed by the difficulty of affairs, assisting them in their need with our abundance" (*Institutes* 2.8.46). That principle of justice is familiar enough as Paul's principle in 2 Cor. 8:14, and it is at work in Calvin's treatment of theft.

> Since all men are born for the sake of each other, human society is not properly maintained, except by an interchange of good offices. Wherefore, that we may not defraud our neighbours, and so be accounted thieves in God's sight, let us learn . . . to be kind to those who need our help, for liberality is a part of righteousness. . . . Those who have abundance do not enjoy their possessions as they ought, unless they communicate them to the poor for the relief of their poverty. (Calvin 126)

Contemporary Applications

Arthur Hugh Clough, in his poem "The Latest Decalogue," satirized contemporary applications of the commandment against theft: "Thou shalt not steal; an empty feat / when 'tis so lucrative to cheat." Contemporary applications would do better to use the prohibition of theft not as a way to secure either the possessions or an easy conscience for the rich but rather as an invitation to an economic justice that serves both God and the poor.

See also Greed; Jubilee; Justice; Just Wage; Loans; Property and Possessions; Stewardship; Ten Commandments

Bibliography

Calvin, J. *Commentaries on the Four Last Books of Moses: Arranged in the Form of a Harmony*. Vol. 3. Eerdmans, 1950; Shewring, W. *Rich and Poor in Christian Tradition: Writings of Many Centuries Chosen, Translated and Introduced*. Burns, Oates & Washbourne, 1948; Verhey, A. "Calvin and the 'Stewardship of Love.'" Pages 157–74 in *The Ten Commandments for Jews, Christians, and Others*, ed. R. Van Harn. Eerdmans, 2007.

Allen Verhey

Theocracy

The term *theocracy* derives from the Greek word *theokratia*, meaning "reign of God." The Jewish historian Josephus first used it to distinguish the government of ancient Israel from the monarchies, oligarchies, and republics of other peoples (*Ag. Ap.* 2.165). But Josephus's usage is imprecise, for he fails to distinguish whether it refers to the actual rule of God, any polity intended to mediate a god's rule, or a particular form of Israel's polity. Similar imprecision plagues contemporary usage.

Scripture

The Bible is thoroughly theocratic in that it witnesses to God's sovereignty over all creation and all nations and longs for that reign to be fully realized on earth, beginning with the people of God. In the sense that the word *theocracy* refers to the actual rule of God, all societies are part of a theocracy; the question is whether "the nations conspire" (Ps. 2:1) against God's rule or willingly confess that "Jesus Christ is Lord" (Phil. 2:11).

In the OT Yahweh is affirmed as sovereign, not only as ruler of Israel (Ps. 72) but also as ultimate ruler of all nations (1 Sam. 5:3–4; Ps. 82) and the entire creation (Job 38–39).

God's rule over Israel is recognized from its political birth, when God rescues Israel from Egyptian captivity (Exod. 15:18). God's rule is mediated through a variety of polities, first through the prophetic and priestly leadership of Moses and Aaron, who deliver God's law to the people (Exod. 20:1–20) and inquire of the Lord for particular guidance (Exod. 18:15–16; 28:30). Although the form of mediation changes during the periods of Joshua and Eleazer (Num. 27:18–21), the judges (Judg. 2:6–16), the monarchy of Israel (2 Sam. 7), and later periods of exile and restoration (Ezra 7:25–28), the law and the offices of prophet, priest, and king are of continuing importance.

A mark of Israelite theocracy is that human rule, authority, and will are carefully distinguished from those of God. Fittingly, Israel's exemplary leaders are noted for their humility (Num. 12:3) and repentance (2 Sam. 12:13; Isa. 6:5).

Although the goals of God's rule in Israel (Exod. 19:6; Isa. 2:2–4) are not fully realized, hopes for this realization, often bound up with expectations of a Davidic messiah, fill the visions of the prophets (Isa. 11:1–10; Zech. 14:16).

Central to the theocratic vision of the NT is the phrase at the center of Jesus' preaching, "the kingdom of God," which, he announces, is breaking into the life of Israel (Mark 1:15). By taking upon himself the mantles of prophet, priest, and king of Israel (Mark 14:65, 58, 62) as well as the authority of the Torah (Matt. 5:17), and by symbolically gathering the twelve disciples around himself, Jesus claims that God's promised reign is being mediated through and realized in himself. But given the surprising signs of this inbreaking kingdom (Luke 7:18–23), his qualification "My kingdom is not from this world" (John 18:36), and his crucifixion and resurrection, it is clear that Jesus' theocratic rule is not a simple replacement of Caesar (Matt. 22:15–22; 26:52–54). The NT writers understand that eventually all will bow before Christ (Phil. 2:9–11; Rev. 7:9–10), but until that time the reign of God in and through Christ and the Spirit is evidenced in part through the qualities and practices of the church (Acts 4:23–35). Christians are the body of Christ with Christ as its head (1 Cor. 12:27; Col. 1:18), ruled not by coercive power (Matt. 20:25–27) but rather through the authority of the Spirit (Gal. 5:16) and through the discipline of the community (2 Thess. 3:14–15; Heb. 13:17).

The Christian Tradition and the Modern West

Given the nature of Christ's reign, it is not surprising that Christians disagree about whether coercive political power might be wielded by Christians, and how Christians might best rule those in and out of the church. Such questions became especially pressing when Christianity became a state-sponsored religion during the reign of Theodosius I (379–95). As Christian political thought such as that found in Augustine's *City of God* developed, it contributed to a diversity of theocratic Christian societies, ranging from the Carolingian empire to Calvin's Geneva to pacifist Anabaptist communities.

As religious and political leadership was distinguished in the West, especially in the wake of modern political theorists such as John Locke and Thomas Hobbes, the term *theocracy* often was defined in light of an assumed separation between religion and the state and then used to point to societies, such as European monarchies or Puritan New England, without a strict separation. In contemporary parlance, *theocracy* often is a pejorative term, conjuring images of tyrannical rule by leaders claiming God's authority or according to doctrinaire interpretations of sacred texts. But some contemporary Christian scholars call for a reconsideration of what God's sovereignty means for political thought and the relationship of the church to the state, sometimes using the term *theocracy* favorably.

See also Government; Kingdom of God; Old Testament Ethics; Political Ethics

Bibliography

Augustine. *Concerning the City of God against the Pagans*. Trans. H. Bettenson. Penguin Books, 1972; Calvin, J. *Institutes of the Christian Religion*, book 4, chapter 20; Harvey, B. "Insanity, Theocracy, and the Public Realm: Public Theology, the Church, and the Politics of Liberal Democracy." *ModTh* 10 (1994): 27–57; Mettinger, T. *In Search of God: The Meaning and Message of the Everlasting Names*. Fortress, 1988; Milbank, J. *Theology and Social Theory: Beyond Secular Reason*. Blackwell, 1990; O'Donovan, O. *The Desire of the Nations: Rediscovering the Roots of Political Theology*. Cambridge University Press, 1999; O'Donovan, O., and J. Lockwood O'Donovan, eds. *From Irenaeus to Grotius: A Sourcebook in Christian Political Thought*. Eerdmans, 1999; Verhey, A. *Remembering Jesus: Christian Community, Scripture, and the Moral Life*. Eerdmans, 2002; Yoder, J. *The Royal Priesthood: Essays Ecclesiological and Ecumenical*. Eerdmans, 1994.

David L. Stubbs

Theodicy

The English word *theodicy* is derived from the Greek words for "God" and "justice." Theistic thinkers use this term as an attempt to explain why God, as defined by traditional Christian theism, permits the occurrence of evil—a term also used synonymously with pain and suffering. Many nontheists generally feel that the existence of evil is, at the very least, incompatible with the existence of God. Others have argued that the probability of God's existence is very low given the reality of evil. Hence, evil is seen as evidence against God's existence.

Responses to these charges are sometimes regarded as theodicies. For example, Alvin Plantinga's "free will defense" tries to show that there is no logical inconsistency between the existence of God and the existence of evil. He notes that if indeed God exists and has created significantly free creatures, then their freedom necessarily implies that they are capable of moral good as well as moral evil. Unfortunately, such creatures choose moral evil in the exercise of their freedom. Hence, it is not logically impossible for evil to exist in a world created by God.

Other major theodicies also postulated include Augustinian theodicy, soul-making theodicy, and process theodicy. Augustine of Hippo began by contending that evil is not a thing; it is the absence of something: the good. God created everything originally good, including human will. However, humans became corrupt when they misused their free will by disobeying God's commandments. Augustine does not adequately explain how something originally good eventually became corrupt. For him, it is simply a mystery.

The soul-making theodicy originally was stated by the bishop Irenaeus in the second century; in modern times, it was reformulated by the philosopher-theologian John Hick. Both Irenaeus and Hick contend that evil exists for the purpose of enabling God's free-willed creatures to become increasingly mature in character. However, Hick takes this view further, contending that the ultimate goal of evil is to perfect every human being, thereby entailing the salvation of all people. This form of religious pluralism has been criticized by some thinkers who wonder whether the salvation of all humans will also include those unrepentantly dedicated to evil.

Process theodicy was articulated by Alfred North Whitehead. Despite contending that God is very powerful, Whitehead argued that God does not have all the power. For example, God cannot guarantee his own welfare, for he meets real resistance from his own creatures. Moreover, God would not use coercive power to manipulate creatures with free will. He would be preempting their freedom if he did so. Rather, God uses persuasive power. Whitehead's view of God has been criticized because it diminishes the hope that God will someday defeat evil. His view offers little or no assurance that such a victory is forthcoming.

Several passages of Scripture (e.g., lament psalms) are concerned with suffering and evil, but it is the book of Job that places the question of the goodness of God and the suffering of the righteous squarely in the center. As Marilyn McCord Adams has pointed out, the manner in which God answers Job suggests that divine reasons for Job's suffering are beyond his cognitive grasp. After Job's lengthy and searing requests to know the meaning of his suffering, God tells Job, in the speech from the whirlwind (Job 38–41), how little he understands. God is not simply the God of order, but also of chaos, and God is the God of all that lies outside Job's imagined world, as well as what lies within. Rather than explain why Job was suffering, God instructs him on the extent of divine omnipotence and then eases his pain, thereby allowing him to experience divine goodness.

See also Cruciformity; Evil; Job; Suffering

Bibliography

Adams, M. "Horrendous Evils and the Goodness of God." Pages 365–81 in *Philosophy of Religion: Selected Readings*, ed. D. Basinger et al. 3rd ed. Oxford University Press, 2007; Newsom, C. *The Book of Job: A Contest of Moral Imaginations*. Oxford University Press, 2003; Peterson, M., ed. *The Problem of Evil: Selected Readings*. University of Notre Dame Press, 1992; Plantinga, A. *God, Freedom, and Evil*. Eerdmans, 1977.

Joseph B. Onyango Okello

1–2 Thessalonians

The letters of 1–2 Thessalonians address rather different circumstances and take rather different approaches to ethics. The primary occasion of 1 Thessalonians is Timothy's report to Paul that the churches in that city are remaining faithful despite persecutions and some confusion about what happens to believers who die before the second coming of Christ. Paul responds by interpreting their persecution as a sign of their faithfulness and by assuring them that the dead will participate fully in the resurrection. In 2 Thessalonians Paul seeks to combat an overrealized eschatology that claims that some Christians have already experienced a second coming that gives the participants spiritual superiority. This has led some who make this claim to quit their jobs and demand pay from the congregation for their work within the church. This letter argues that the second coming remains a future event, and that Christians must live their lives in the light of its judgment.

1 Thessalonians

Paul's answer to the Thessalonians' questions about persecution initiates his discussion of ethics in this letter. He asserts that God's people historically have experienced persecution, and that his readers have adopted a faithful manner of life in imitation of those earlier people of God. Paul explicates the proper manner of life more by way of examples than specific instruction. He says that they have become imitators of him, Christ, earlier believers, and perhaps the prophets, and he exhorts them to follow such examples. Then he notes that they have become examples to others. Imitation is a significant element of the way ethics is taught and encouraged in 1 Thessalonians.

Paul defines God's will for believers as sanctification, being made holy (4:3, 7). One motivation he identifies for living a holy life is that the believer might be found guiltless at judgment. Indeed, the letter's most concentrated section on ethics leads into Paul's discussion of eschatology. He says that it is necessary for believers to live in a way that pleases God, and that such behavior distinguishes them from unbelievers.

However, this ethic does not remove believers from the world. Instead, they are to be concerned about how unbelievers perceive them (4:11–12; 5:15). They should exemplify the virtues of self-sufficiency and peacefulness. In this way, living properly pleases God and ameliorates, perhaps even invites in, their neighbors.

More often, though, 1 Thessalonians emphasizes innerchurch relations. Paul's ministry provides an example for the Thessalonians because his life among them was not only honest but also gentle and self-giving (2:1–12). The concluding exhortations also focus on relations among church members, how they are to treat leaders, the disorderly, and the weak. Thus, the ethic of this letter is strongly inner-directed.

Although 1 Thessalonians is focused on two problems that are not directly ethical, ethics plays a large role in the letter. How one lives is a central element in its teaching about persecution and eschatology. There is little explicit instruction about particular behaviors, but proper living is seen as a central part of what it means to be a believer. Not only will behavior be important at judgment but also it is a part of God's will for them. Since proper living includes both innerchurch relations and relations with outsiders, the whole of the believer's life is to be formed by imitation of Christ.

2 Thessalonians

Perhaps it is the continuing disadvantage or persecution experienced by the Thessalonians that leads 2 Thessalonians to emphasize the judgment and punishment coming on unbelievers. Retribution for those troubling the church is a central theme of the thanksgiving and other parts of this letter. It asserts that judgment against such people has already begun because they are the people who will believe the false wonders that Satan empowers (2:8–12).

Conversely, 2 Thessalonians gives being found not guilty at judgment a central place in motivating its readers to live ethically. Still, God's call and love empower believers to live for God. Indeed, God's call includes the expectation that the believer will live a sanctified/holy life (2:13–14). The lives of Paul and other faithful leaders exemplify the holy living believers are to imitate (3:6–7), but prior apostolic instruction is the basis for determining what constitutes ethical living. Christians who fail to live by the expected standards, however, are not relegated to the ranks of the unbelievers destined for destruction. Such errant believers remain part of the family of believers, and they must be set apart from the community but not treated as enemies. Rather, the church is to nurture their return to full fellowship (3:14–15). Like other Pauline Letters, 2 Thessalonians links ethical living and doing good works with correct teaching; only those who believe the right doctrine will be able to live ethically (2:15–17).

The conduct of the "disorderly" (the "idle" of 3:6–15) flows from their overrealized eschatology. Asserting that their experience of a spiritual coming of Christ gives them superior spiritual blessings and abilities, they quit their jobs, impose themselves as ministers on this church, and demand salaries. This letter rejects their eschatology and understanding of spirituality by telling the church not to support them. Proper conduct for ministers follows the apostolic example of giving of oneself for the good of the church, and it does not include demanding deference and pay.

The letter of 2 Thessalonians contains few instructions about what constitutes proper living, expecting its readers to know what behavior the apostolic tradition requires. It focuses more on assessment at judgment than on motivations based on believers' new identity as God's children or one's place in Christ. The latter kinds of motivations are not absent from 2 Thessalonians, but they do play a much smaller role than in other Pauline Letters.

See also Eschatology and Ethics; Good Works; Holiness; Judgment; New Testament Ethics; Sanctification; Work

Bibliography

Donfried, K. *Paul, Thessalonica, and Early Christianity*. Eerdmans, 2002; Furnish, V. *1 Thessalonians, 2 Thessalonians*. ANTC. Abingdon, 2007; Getty, M. "The Imitation of Paul in the Letters to the Thessalonians." Pages 277–83 in *The Thessalonian Correspondence*, ed. R. Collins. BETL 87. Leuven University Press, 1990; Malherbe, A. *Paul and the Thessalonians: The Philosophic Tradition of Pastoral Care*. Fortress, 1987; Still, T. *Conflict at Thessalonica: A Pauline Church and Its Neighbours*. JSNTSup 183. Sheffield Academic Press, 1999.

Jerry L. Sumney

Time, Use of

In Western societies people increasingly complain about the busyness of life and the pace of change. Leisure time is being steadily eroded, and even children are feeling under duress. Ways of measuring time have also become more exact and numerous.

Except on occasions such as sowing and harvesting, fleeing or fighting enemies, the Bible does not reflect the same sense of pressure or haste, but it does recognize the brevity and transience of life. Although the Bible does not contain our precise measurements of time, it speaks in terms of "a short time," "immediately," "a while," and "after some time." And although it does not have names for weekdays, it distinguishes days numerically and refers to "the next day," "a few days," and "the seventh day." Like us, it demarcates dawn, morning, midday, dark, and evening, as well as watches during the night. It also refers to days, weeks, months, seasons, and years.

General Perspective on Time

First, time is a divine gift. Too often today we take time for granted, as a human resource or as simply another commodity to be consumed. In the Bible, however, time is viewed as a gift from the Creator. God is the author of time, including its ongoing and dependable daily rhythms (Gen. 1:3–2:3; 8:22; Zech. 14:7). God also imprints a weekly pattern on time by sanctifying the seventh day (Gen. 2:2). Periodic events throughout the year also spring from the divine provision of natural cycles or historical interventions (Lev. 23:4–44). Yet God also reckons time by means of the inner connection between events that fulfill his purposes. Consequently, for God a thousand years can seem like one day (Ps. 90:4; 2 Pet. 3:8).

Second, time is under God's control. Today we also too often consider time to be at our disposal, to be organized and scheduled, measured and distributed, invested and spent, as we choose. According to the Bible, however, God is the one who controls time throughout our lives. Both the beginning and the end of life are in God's hands (Job 1:21), as is the entire destiny of both individuals and peoples (Ps. 139:16; see also Job 7:6; Ps. 31:15). We must not forget this and assume that we have control over what happens (Jas. 4:13–16). Instead, we should remain constantly aware that everything depends on God's will (1 Cor. 16:7).

Responsible Use of Time

We must discern how to use time responsibly because (1) it is limited and structured in character, (2) we are faced with a range of responsibilities and possibilities, and (3) sin is able to affect our choices. The following four biblical guidelines can help us make wise decisions about its use.

First, there is an appropriate point and length for every significant aspect of our lives—for example, its main stages, significant experiences, basic responsibilities, and primary relationships. So Eccl. 3:1–8 identifies birth and death, starting and ending projects, beginning and completing a search, collecting and discarding possessions, crying and laughing, speaking and keeping quiet, embracing and holding at a distance, mourning and dancing, approaching and withdrawing, waging war and making peace.

Other texts indicate that there is a proper season for household (Gen. 29:7) and work (Isa. 28:24–25) activities, residing and traveling (Deut. 2:14), feasting and going hungry (Judg. 14:12; Ps. 37:19), menstruation (Lev. 15:25) and marriage (1 Sam. 18:19), youth (Ezek. 16:22) and old age (Job 5:26). There are also times of temptation (Luke 8:13) and refreshment (Acts 3:20), distress (Nah. 1:7) and healing (Jer. 8:15), joy and adversity (Eccl. 7:14), affliction (Lam. 1:17) and salvation (Isa. 49:8). Although we may not always know the outcome of marking these times and may often find life burdensome and enigmatic (Eccl. 3:9–11), we remain responsible for apportioning our time wisely.

Second, there is a rhythm to our use of time that we must respect and honor. Because God has given us the daily rhythm of wakefulness and sleep, we should draw boundaries around how much we work. To do otherwise suggests that God has not given us the time we need to accomplish his purposes, that we fail to trust that he works for us even while we sleep, and that we are ungrateful for the daily present of rest that he gives us (Ps. 127:1–2).

Although since the coming of Christ we no longer have to observe Sabbath obligations, we should follow the example of Jesus in alternating periods of activity and rest (Mark 6:31), and of the early Christians in gathering with fellow believers on "the first day of the week" (Acts 20:7), though we cannot be fully certain if this happened every Sunday or just on appointed Sundays. Whatever the case, it is important not to neglect meeting to exhort and admonish one another regularly (Heb. 10:25).

Third, there is a need to avoid ways of using time that divert us from our main priorities. We should identify when and where evil is active, how it seeks to tempt us, and what we can do to defend ourselves. This entails "redeeming" time that would otherwise be spent unfruitfully (Eph. 5:15–17). This is a call not to busyness, as some modern translations suggest (e.g., "making the most of the opportunity"), but to a judicious use of time, one that "seeks first the kingdom of God" rather than an anxious quest for material security (Matt. 6:33).

Given the fact that our life on earth is limited, we should also "number" our days (Ps. 90:12). Those who try to extract more and more out of time to further their business or financial interests "do not even know what tomorrow will bring" (Jas. 4:14). Similarly, those who seek to ensure themselves against whatever the future may bring forget that how long they live is entirely in God's hands (Luke 12:16–20). Instead, we should acknowledge that all our projections of the future are subject to accordance with God's will (1 Cor. 16:7), for although our plans are many, it is only "the purpose of the LORD that will be established" (Prov. 19:21).

Fourth, there are certain moments of time that contain an immediate opportunity or challenge. This is what is meant by the importance of recognizing the meaning of "today" (Ps. 95:7–11). Sometimes even religious leaders failed to recognize the significance of events taking place around them, as when Jesus was teaching (Luke 12:56) and crucified (1 Cor. 2:7–8) in their midst. We should therefore be aware of what "hour" it is and that our full salvation is drawing nearer (Rom. 13:11–12), even if we do not know exactly when Jesus will return (Acts 1:6–7).

Practical Guidelines about Time

The Bible provides five further insights into helping us to discern the appropriate use of time.

First, we ought undertake our work diligently (Eccl. 9:10), but we should do so from a position of basic restfulness in Christ concerning our worth and identity rather than restlessly seeking to achieve or gain recognition through what we do (Matt. 11:28–30; Heb. 4:1–3a, 10–11). All too easily we can seek to justify ourselves to ourselves, others, or God through our work.

Second, we must always be ready to meet an unexpected call for help (Luke 10:25–37), but the mere existence of a need or an opportunity does not necessarily mean that we have a responsibility to meet it. Much depends on what we are capable of at the time (Mark 1:35–39; 2 Cor. 2:12–13). Since we cannot attend to everything, we require a clear sense of what falls inside or outside the boundaries of our God-given vocation (Rom. 15:20).

Third, we should avoid idleness (2 Thess. 3:11–13), but we should not fall into the opposite error of too much busywork. It is not the number of things we accomplish but rather their quality, according to the measure of Christ, that ultimately will last (1 Cor. 3:11–15). This is all too easily forgotten in an age that tends to value quantity instead.

Fourth, to some extent it is responsible to organize our time so that we can fulfill our responsibilities to God and others, but the more we are engaged in future planning, the more flexible we must be (1 Cor. 16:5–9). The reason for this is that we do not always know in advance what further variables or circumstances may arise.

Fifth, all of us have a role to play in fulfilling our divinely given calling, but we should remember that none of us is indispensable (1 Kgs. 19:15, 18). The danger here is the temptation to develop a "messianic complex" about our role in God's purposes.

See also Sabbath; Work

Bibliography

Banks, R. *The Tyranny of Time: When 24 Hours Is Not Enough*. Wipf & Stock, 1997; Barr, J. *Biblical Words for Time*. SBT 33. SCM, 1962; Burns, L. *Busy Bodies: Why Our Time-obsessed Society Keeps Us Running in Place*. Norton, 1993; Cullmann, O. *Christ and Time: The Primitive Christian Conception of Time and History*. Rev. ed. Westminster, 1964; De Vries, S. *Yesterday, Today, and Tomorrow: Time and History in the Old Testament*. Eerdmans, 1975; Hochschild, A. *The Time Bind: When Work Becomes Home and Home Becomes Work*. Metropolitan Books, 1997; Marsh, J. *The Fulness of Time*. Nisbet, 1952; McCullough, E., and R. Calder, eds. *Time as a Human Resource*. University of Calgary Press, 1991; Rifkin, J. *Time Wars: The Primary Conflict in Human History*. Simon & Schuster, 1987; Wolff, H. "The Old Testament Concept of Time." Pages 83–92 in *Anthropology of the Old Testament*. SCM, 1974.

Robert Banks

1–2 Timothy

Although 1 Timothy and 2 Timothy typically are grouped, along with Titus, as part of a single corpus known as the Pastoral Epistles, each document addresses a particular situation. Therefore, the moral issues dealt with and the potential contribution of each letter to contemporary ethical reflection differs due to the diverse rhetorical aims of each composition. Here, the two letters to Timothy will be treated separately. Although both letters often are considered by most scholars to be pseudonymous writings, the implied author of the texts is Paul, whether or not he is the real author.

1 Timothy

The first letter of Paul to Timothy is predominantly concerned with the threat of opponents who are advocating "different doctrine" (1:3). These false teachers, two of whom are identified by name in 1:20, are accused of devoting themselves to "myths and endless genealogies" (1:4), of forbidding marriage and demanding abstinence from certain foods (4:3), and of triggering controversy within the congregation that leads to envy, dissension, slander, suspicion, and division (6:3–5).

In light of this challenge, Paul offers his "loyal child in the faith" (1:2) instruction regarding church life (2:1–3:16; 5:1–6:2) and teaching on Timothy's own duties as a believer and leader (4:1–16; 6:3–21). Some of the ecclesiological directives in 1 Timothy draw on conventional Hellenistic ethical discourse (cf. the qualities for church leadership in 3:1–12 with Onasander, *Strat.* 1). Yet often Paul's ethical instructions are given explicit theological grounding. For example, the critique of those who imagine that "there is great gain in godliness" is rooted in the understanding that those who brought nothing into the world will take nothing out of it (6:6–7). Therefore, the rich in the present age should share generously with others (6:17–19). Similarly, the rejection of the ascetic practices of the opponents is warranted by a theology of the goodness of creation (4:4). Whereas the opponents insist on an ethical asceticism that takes believers away from the world, Paul calls Timothy, and by extension all believers, to a deep engagement with the world.

This coherence between the church and the world in 1 Timothy is highlighted by the metaphor of the *ekklēsia* as the "household of God" (3:15). The structures of the household become the structures of the church (5:1–6:2). On the one hand, this metaphor runs the risk of encouraging the church simply to accept or endorse the patriarchal values of the Greco-Roman household. This seems to be the case regarding the instructions given to men and women in the context of prayer and worship in 2:8–15, a text in which the restrictions on the role of women in worship stand in some tension with the other Pauline Letters (e.g., Rom. 16:7; 1 Cor. 11:2–16; Gal. 3:28; but cf. 1 Cor. 14:33–36). On the other hand, 1 Timothy consistently reflects a desire to protect and maximize the effectiveness of the church's witness in the world (e.g., 2:1–7). For those tempted to become frustrated with the somewhat conservative social ethic represented in 1 Timothy, perhaps recognition that this ethic is rooted in a missional concern to guard the church's public witness to the gospel will temper discontent with the perspective articulated in the letter.

2 Timothy

The letter of 2 Timothy is a testamentary epistle from the apostle Paul to his "beloved child" Timothy (1:2). Paul is in prison at the time of the letter's composition (1:8, 15–18), quite likely facing the prospect of his death (4:6–8). An important theme in 2 Timothy is that of Paul's exhortation to his younger associate to remain faithful to the testimony about the Lord at a time when Timothy seems tempted to be shamed by the gospel. Timothy's wavering commitment seems to be due, at least in part, to perceptions about Paul's own weakness as a prisoner of Christ (1:6–2:7) and to the threat of conflict from within the church (1:15–16; 2:14–26; 3:1–9, 13; 4:3–5). Thus, Paul's testament aims at encouraging and challenging Timothy in the face of the younger man's shame and in response to the danger of false teaching.

One way that Paul accomplishes his goal is by highlighting examples of faithful witness. These examples include the sincere faith of Timothy's grandmother and mother (1:3–5; 3:14); the model of Paul's own suffering as a prisoner for the Lord (1:8–14; 2:9; 3:10–12; 4:6–8); the willing service of Onesiphorus, who was not ashamed of Paul's chains (1:15–18); the images of the solider, athlete, and farmer that demonstrate persistent commitment in the pursuit of a specific goal (2:3–6); and the paradigm of Christ's own vicarious suffering (2:11). Negatively, Hymenaeus and Philetus are singled out as those who have "swerved from the truth by claiming that the resurrection has already taken place" (2:18; cf. 3:8). Thus, Paul's call for Timothy to remain steadfast in his commitment to the gospel is warranted by a series of models of faithful commitment. Perhaps the most important example is found in Christ's own faithfulness on behalf of those who have died and will live with him (2:8–13). If the moral requirements in 1 Timothy reflect a context of (relatively) positive relations between church and world, 2 Timothy speaks more directly to believers facing marginalization and hostility because of their adherence to the gospel. In 2 Timothy, as in other texts in the NT, cruciform ethics are shaped by the experience of suffering.

See also Cruciformity; Household Codes; New Testament Ethics; Titus

Bibliography

Aageson, J. *Paul, the Pastoral Epistles, and the Early Church*. Hendrickson, 2008; De Villiers, P. "Heroes at Home: Identity, Ethos, and Ethics in 1 Timothy within the Context of the Pastoral Epistles." Pages 357–86 in *Identity, Ethics, and Ethos in the New Testament*, ed. J. van der Watt and F. Malan. BZNW 141. De Gruyter, 2006; Scholer, D. "1 Timothy 2.9–15 and the Place of Women in the Church's Ministry." Pages 98–121 in *A Feminist Companion to the Deutero-Pauline Epistles*, ed. A.-J. Levine and M. Blickenstaff. FCNTECW 7. T&T Clark, 2003; Young, F. *The Theology of the Pastoral Letters*. NTT. Cambridge University Press, 1994, 24–46.

David J. Downs

Tithe, Tithing

The giving of a tenth of property or produce was a widespread practice in ancient cultures. The few references to tithing in the OT and the NT reflect varying practices during different historical periods. The focus here is not on the history of tithing, but rather on the diverse purposes prescribed in the texts (Tate 154–56).

Tithing before Moses. Only two instances of "tithing" are found in the patriarchal narratives: Abram (Gen. 14:18–24) and, conditionally, Jacob (Gen. 28:10–22).

Tithing in the Mosaic law. Three major purposes were to be served by tithing as prescribed in the law: (1) the tithes that went for the upkeep of the Levites, who themselves tithed to support the priests (Lev. 27:30–33; Num. 18:21–29); (2) a (second?) festival tithe (Deut. 14:22–27); and (3) a triennial welfare tithe for the Levites, foreigners, orphans, and widows (Deut. 14:28–29). In fact, the community's covenant obedience was to be demonstrated by their care for the poor (Deut. 26:12–15). If these various tithes are taken as being cumulative (a matter of scholarly debate, even though Judaism appears to have assumed it to be so), then the annual "tithes" for the Israelites could have amounted to more than 20 percent of their annual income (Köstenberger and Croteau 63–64).

Tithing after Moses. One of the consequences of political and/or religious renewal (as under Hezekiah and Nehemiah) was a restored emphasis on giving, which included the tithe (2 Chr. 31:5–12; Neh. 10:34–39; 13:4–13; though see the critique in Amos 4:1–5 and the situation in Mal. 3:6–12).

Tithing in the NT. While tithing was widely practiced in Judaism, one may be surprised to discover the meager attention given to it in the NT (e.g., Heb. 7:1–10). The most significant passages present Jesus as neither commanding nor prohibiting tithing but rather, resonating with Amos, condemning the Pharisees and scribes who were scrupulous in tithing but negligent in upholding more important matters of the law (Matt. 23:23 // Luke 11:42; cf. Luke 18:9–14).

The ethics of tithing today. The varied patterns of tithing in the OT point to a broad-based socioeconomic ethic expected of Israel in support of the temple, the priesthood, and the impoverished. Today, a case could be made for tithing to serve as a helpful benchmark for Christians, as long as one heeds the caution that legalistic tithing can hardly express the radical demands of stewardship placed on disciples by Jesus' revolutionary teachings about sharing possessions and the generosity manifested by and expected of early Christians (Acts 2:45; 4:32, 36–37). A reasonable extrapolation is to build an ethical paradigm taking tithing into consideration along with other socioeconomic prescriptions, such as for the Sabbath Year (Deut. 15:1–11), the Jubilee (Lev. 25), and Paul's collection for the poor in Jerusalem (1 Cor. 16:2; 2 Cor. 8–9).

See also Almsgiving; Collection for the Saints; Economic Ethics; Koinonia; Stewardship; Wealth

Bibliography

Davis, G. "Are Christians Supposed to Tithe?" *CTR* 2 (1987): 85–97; Goldingay, J. "Jubilee Tithe." *Transformation* 19 (2002): 198–205; Köstenberger, A., and D. Croteau. " 'Will a Man Rob God?' (Malachi 3:8): A Study of Tithing in the Old and New Testaments." *BBR* 16 (2006): 53–77; Tate, M. "Tithing: Legalism or Benchmark?" *RevExp* 70 (1973): 153–61.

Jacob Cherian

Titus

The Letter to Titus, ostensibly written by the apostle Paul to a younger ministry associate in Crete, focuses on the necessity of sound teaching and virtuous living in light of the threat of false instruction within the Christian community. The author is alarmed about "rebellious people, idle talkers and deceivers," particularly those of a group that he labels "the circumcision" (1:10). It is likely that the opponents of the author, like those addressed in Galatians, were encouraging gentile believers to abide by the Torah (1:13–15; 3:9).

Unlike Paul in Galatians, however, the author of Titus does not engage in a sustained theological and hermeneutical debate with the views of his opponents. Instead, the false teachers are condemned (1:15–16; 3:9), and Titus is encouraged to teach "sound doctrine" (2:1) and to exhort various groups within the churches to live respectable lives. Qualifications for elders (1:6) and overseers (1:7–9) are articulated in terms that emphasize a leader's honorable character in domestic, interpersonal, and ecclesiastical settings. Similarly, the author adapts the literary form of "household code" in order to urge older men (2:2), older women (2:3–5), younger men (2:6–8), and slaves (2:9–10) to virtuous living that will not compromise Christian witness in the world. Moreover, the entire Christian community is exhorted "to be subject to rulers and authorities, to be obedient, to be ready for every good work, to speak evil of no one, to avoid quarrelling, to be gentle, and to show every courtesy to everyone" (3:1–2). This appeal for obedience to secular authorities corresponds to other NT texts that counsel subordination to political rulers as an aspect of Christian mission (cf. Rom.

13:1–7; 1 Pet. 2:12–17). Yet while these instructions in Titus are framed in terms that largely correspond to contemporary Greco-Roman virtues, the paraenesis is also rooted in the author's insistence that the grace of God and eschatological expectation of the future appearance of Jesus lead believers to "good deeds" (2:11–14; 3:3–8).

That Titus is viewed by a majority of NT scholars as a pseudonymous composition, written in Paul's name after the apostle's death, raises moral questions related to its interpretation for some. If the document perpetuates a deception (although a case can be made that Titus is not pseudonymous), does this literary fiction violate the claims of truth and trustworthiness made within the text itself (1:1, 12–13; 3:8)? The answer to this question rests in part on whether the practice of pseudonymity in antiquity was an accepted literary device. Some who concede the pseudonymous nature of Titus locate the practice not in deception but rather in the actualization of an earlier authoritative tradition in a new setting, with similar examples occurring in Jewish apocalyptic, prophetic, and wisdom traditions (e.g., Deutero-Isaiah, *Psalms of Solomon*).

See also Household Codes; New Testament Ethics; 1–2 Timothy; Vices and Virtues, Lists of

Bibliography

Donelson, L. *Pseudepigraphy and Ethical Argument in the Pastoral Epistles*. HUT 22. Mohr Siebeck, 1986; Meade, D. *Pseudonymity and Canon: An Investigation into the Relationship of Authorship and Authority in Jewish and Earliest Christian Tradition*. WUNT 39. Mohr Siebeck, 1986; Young, F. *The Theology of the Pastoral Letters*. NTT. Cambridge University Press, 1994, 24–46.

David J. Downs

Tobit

The book of Tobit tells the story of a Jewish family living during the Assyrian deportation. Tobit, the title character, is an upright man. Early in the story, Tobit gives proper burial to one of his people who has been murdered. Afterward, he must sleep outside, where bird droppings fall in his eyes, causing him to go blind. Tobias, Tobit's son, leaves to retrieve money deposited in a far-off city, accompanied by the angel Raphael, disguised as a human. Tobias, with Raphael's instructions, survives a threatening large fish, thwarts a demon, marries, and returns home with great wealth. Tobias also, using a reserved part of the fish, cures Tobit's blindness. At the end, Raphael reveals his true angelic identity, and Tobit sings a hymn about the future of Jerusalem. After Tobit dies, Tobias witnesses the destruction of Assyria at the hand of Media.

The book of Tobit contains many ethical exhortations, but at a deeper level it struggles with how God treats those who do or do not act with righteousness.

Tobit the character is an exemplar of ethical practice. Introduced as a righteous one who did many acts of charity, Tobit tithed appropriately and alone among the exiles traveled to Jerusalem for festivals. Tobit's actions, such as feeding the hungry and clothing the naked, are for those of his tribe. Tobit provides proper burial for one of his kin, a righteous act that ironically results in his blindness. The book's most pressing issue arises in the fact that Tobit suffers because of his righteousness.

The book of Tobit has two major sections of ethical instruction (chaps. 4; 14). Although the beginning of the book mentions the law of Moses (1:8), the "commandments" (4:19) in Tobit show little interest in specific laws but instead advocate boilerplate sapiential instruction such as the importance of almsgiving (4:5–11), sexual purity (4:12–13), and fair treatment of workers (4:14–19). Such admonitions recall many parts of Proverbs or Sirach and also emulate the wisdom of Ahikar, a well-known sage in the Assyrian court whom Tobit names as a relative (1:21–22; 14:10). More important than the specifics of Tobit's ethical instructions is their conceptual underpinning that God will repay a righteous life with blessing: "Do not turn your face away from anyone who is poor, and the face of God will not be turned away from you" (4:7). Such a close connection between act and consequence leads most scholars to call the book "Deuteronomic," meaning that it draws on a well-established theological formulation that finds its source in Deuteronomy.

Despite Tobit's assertions that God repays people according to their actions, the arc of Tobit's character questions such a conclusion. The trajectory of the narrative has its own rhetorical force, one that undermines confidence in such a close connection between act and consequence. At the beginning, Tobit has no recourse in explaining his predicament other than that he (or his ancestors) has sinned (3:1–6). At the end of the book, Raphael reveals his angelic identity and the "whole truth" (12:11) about Tobit's predicament: God's role in the story was different from that which Tobit had assumed. This revelation impinges directly on the purported connection between act and consequence. It may be tempting to posit that deeds, whether just or unjust, breed commensurate repayment, but reality is much more complex. Tobit's sight returns at the end, but the original problem for Tobit's family is that they live under foreign rule and are subject to the whims of gentile kings. This situation is not resolved at the end of the book. Some scholars suggest that the healing of Tobit's blindness anticipates the future restoration that is to come to the Jewish people as a whole. Such a reading is possible but not necessary. One can also suggest that the inconclusive ending intends to question the efficacy of Tobit's ethical program. In such a scenario, the book of Tobit asks a question: is righteousness really a guarantor of God's blessing? Earlier in the story, Tobit was profoundly sure that God repays people according to their actions, but at the end, after Raphael's revelation, he is less so: "Turn back, you sinners, and do what is right before him; perhaps he may look with favor upon you" (13:6). What the NRSV translates as "perhaps" might better be rendered as "who knows?" Thus, at the end, Tobit's disposition is marked by epistemological humility. The ethical norms do not wane; they are constantly upheld. They may not, however, be used to leverage God toward blessing.

See also Deuterocanonical/Apocryphal Books; Deuteronomistic History; Theodicy

Micah D. Kiel

Tolerance

Tolerance is a patient or respectful attitude toward persons of differing religion, culture, or status, or toward their beliefs or actions. Etymologically, the word *tolerance* suggests a kind of endurance or forbearance; thus, it implies restraint in the face of a morally, politically, or religiously significant difference that might otherwise prompt opposition or interference. Tolerance is advocated or legislated particularly where it is historically lacking or as a preventive measure in the face of religious or cultural pluralism.

Contemporary Uses

Christian history and tradition often are used as the foil against which the virtues of tolerance are to be made clear. Eusebius's demonizing of Constantine's political enemies, Justinian's discrimination against pagans and heretics, the atrocities of the Crusades and the Inquisition, and the so-called Wars of Religion in Europe are adduced as proof that intolerance (especially religious intolerance) promotes coercion and violence. (For a more nuanced reading of the political theology of the ancient, medieval, and Reformation churches, see O'Donovan and O'Donovan.)

Broadly, tolerance purports to recognize political, social, moral, or religious difference without punishing it (one does not need to "tolerate" those with whom there is assumed general agreement). The management of religious difference in pluralistic societies is of particular concern: though the actual policies may differ by country, policies of religious toleration are enjoined as a means of avoiding or lessening violence or conflict. Tolerance may be offered as an alternative both to whatever is deemed intolerant (coercion, persecution, repression) and to participation or cooperation. If one cannot persuade (i.e., secure the free consent of) one's political or religious opponent, one tolerates the differences from which the conflict arose without necessarily supporting or advancing them.

Yet tolerance is advocated (or criticized) with such variety and imprecision that it is difficult to specify what is being described. To identify concrete practices of toleration is even more difficult. The same word may refer to the proscription of sectarian identity markers and arguments from public life or, quite the opposite, to the protection of the right to publicly forward such arguments or display such identity markers. Thus, for example, in France or Turkey the hijab is banned as, itself, a marker of religious intolerance, while in the United States the right to wear the hijab is protected in the name of religious tolerance. The creation of an allegedly tolerant space might be said to depend on the celebration of differences that are in danger of causing conflict, or on the exclusion of anything that highlights such differences. Thus, a school might mark all its students' religious holidays in the name of tolerance, or it may ban any such celebration for the same reason. It may be considered intolerant to interfere with unwelcome behavior or speech or, to the contrary, to fail to interfere when such behavior or speech seems itself to promote intolerance. Thus, does one promote tolerance by associating with one's bigoted nephew, or instead by disowning him in order not to endorse his intolerance? Does one tolerate a sister-in-law's beliefs by letting her handle her business affairs in peace, or rather does one counsel her on nondiscriminatory hiring?

Neither is tolerance universally recognized as a virtue. Some suspect that tolerance perpetuates the sorts of power inequities that it purports to mitigate (so Jakobsen and Pellegrini). Others object that tolerance seems to preclude any substantive agreement on the sorts of goods on which true community depends. So, a gathering of people who merely tolerate one another may be pacific but may yet lack the kind of community that makes for a truly just society.

Scripture

One struggles to find a useful entry point into Scripture on this matter. In Scripture, religious pluralism is not a good, nor its maintenance a virtue. Indeed, OT proscriptions of idolatry on pain of capital punishment (e.g., Exod. 22:18, 20; Deut. 13) and the commands to exterminate the Canaanites (Deut. 7:1–6; Josh. 6:17; 8:1–2) provided rich sources for self-justification among persecution-minded religious and political reformers. While peacekeeping and graciousness among factions are vital practices within the NT church (e.g., Rom. 14–15; 1 Cor. 1:10–17; Gal. 5:16–26; 1 John 4:7–21) and for the sake of witness (e.g., John 13:34–35; 1 Cor. 10:31–33), the NT writers evidence little concern for the protection of alternative religious practice or belief. Attitudes toward non-Christian Jews (e.g., Matt. 21:33–44; 23; Luke 20:9–19; John 9) are especially troubling (and have been used as warrant for disturbing attitudes and policies throughout Christendom).

Even within the church, tolerance is only sometimes considered a virtue. Paul exhorts the Romans and the Corinthians to bear controversy with peace and mutual love (Rom. 14–15; 1 Cor. 8–10), and his instructions to the Galatian churches are at least as attentive to their unity as their orthodoxy (Gal. 5). The topics that he addresses (food laws, Sabbath observance, circumcision) were not insignificant within the fledgling church, and his counsel to prefer unity to doctrinal and ethical correctness requires practices of patience and forbearance in the midst of serious conflict. Yet he castigates those who tolerate flagrant immorality within the church (1 Cor. 5), and he presents the remedy, excommunication, in the starkest possible terms: it is a handing over to Satan (1 Cor. 5:5). How one distinguishes between situations that call for tolerance and those that call for renunciation is not entirely clear.

If tolerance as such has an ambiguous value within the biblical text, other biblical concepts are clearer, as well as more clearly relevant to political stability or peacemaking among individuals. Humility, for example, is an important biblical theme, both in contexts that suggest personal virtue (Pss. 18:27; 37:11; Prov. 22:4; Isa. 66:2; Luke 17:7–10; 1 Pet. 5:5–6) and in those that deal with conflict (1 Cor. 1–3; Phil. 2:1–13; Jas. 4:1–12). Founded both on concern for the other and awareness of one's status before and relative to God, biblical humility addresses many of the same issues and situations that proponents of tolerance seek to address.

Likewise, the NT rejection of violence, even in the face of evil or persecution, is explicit and absolute (e.g., Matt. 5:38–42; Rom. 12:17–21) (see Hays 329–36). Even where it cannot be agreed that a particular behavior, belief, policy, or person should be "tolerated," the NT witness argues persuasively that the situation ought to be approached without recourse to violence.

Peacemaking itself is good in NT texts, and those with whom there might be conflict can only benefit when Christians take seriously Paul's counsel: "If it is possible, so far as it depends on you, live peaceably with all" (Rom. 12:18). Although such general prescriptions for peacemaking (Rom. 12:17–21; Titus 3:1–2; Heb. 12:14) offer little guidance in particularities, their universal scope offers, at the very least, a presumption in favor of peacemaking wherever potential conflict arises. The peaceableness that is learned and practiced within the church might also be practiced among those with whom one does not necessarily share faith in Christ, and the richness of the biblical concept of peace (*shalom*) has many advantages over such pallid substitutes as tolerance.

See also Anti-Semitism; Just-Peacemaking Theory; Peace; Pluralism; Racism; Religious Toleration

Bibliography

Hays, R. *The Moral Vision of the New Testament: Community, Cross, and New Creation; A Contemporary Introduction to New Testament Ethics.* HarperSanFrancisco, 1996; Jakobsen, J., and A. Pellegrini. *Love the Sin: Sexual Regulation and the Limits of Religious Tolerance.* New York University Press, 2003; O'Donovan, O., and J. O'Donovan, eds. *From Irenaeus to Grotius: A Sourcebook in Christian Political Thought, 100–1625.* Eerdmans, 1999.

Sarah Conrad Sours

Tongue *See* Speech Ethics

Torah

The ethics of Torah is a predominantly Jewish ethical perspective shaped by obedience to biblical laws and commandments as an expression of Israel's covenant relationship with God. Torah ethics encompasses not only the biblical commandments but also the subsequent interpretations and clarifications of the biblical commandments and teachings in the writings of ancient and medieval rabbinic Judaism.

The Meaning of Torah

Understanding the ethics of Torah begins with a survey of the varied meanings of the Hebrew term *tôrâ* in the Bible and subsequent Jewish and Christian traditions. The term *tôrâ* often is translated as "law," but it may better be understood more broadly as "teaching" or "instruction."

The word is used in the Bible and subsequent religious traditions to mean a variety of things. It can refer to specific priestly instructions concerning rituals ("This is the *tôrâ* [NRSV: "ritual"] of the burnt offering [Lev. 6:9]; "This is the *tôrâ* [NRSV: "law"] in cases of jealousy" [Num. 5:29–30]). More generally, *tôrâ* can refer to the whole body of instruction taught by priests (Ezek. 22:26; Mal. 2:6–9). Leviticus 10:11 uses the Hebrew verb *yārâ* ("teach"), which lies at the root of the noun *tôrâ*, to describe the teaching function of priests (see also Jer. 18:18; Ezek. 7:26). Also, *tôrâ* can designate the story or "teaching of the Lord" concerning God's deliverance of Israel from Egypt that is to be remembered in every generation in association with the Festival of Unleavened Bread and Passover (Exod. 13:9).

Torah is used most frequently in the Bible alongside other terms that signify the commandments and laws that Israel is to obey as an expression of its covenant relationship and obligations before God (Exod. 24:12; Lev. 26:46; Neh. 9:13–14; Ps. 78:10; Jer. 44:10). Priests are not the only teachers of *tôrâ*. The prophet Isaiah associates *tôrâ* with the words of the prophets and the servant of God (Isa. 8:16, 20; 42:4, 21; 51:4). The wisdom and instructions of the sages in biblical books such as Proverbs and Ecclesiastes that were derived as much from human observation and experience as divine revelation can also be called *tôrâ* (Prov. 1:8; 3:1; 4:2; 6:20, 23; 28:9; 31:26). This facilitated the blending of biblical laws and commandments with wisdom sayings and proverbs into a broad category of *tôrâ* as inclusive of the divine will and all normative traditions that ancient Israelites were called to follow or obey (Pss. 1:2; 19:7–10; 119:1).

Torah, Deuteronomy, and the Pentateuch

Another variation in the meaning of *tôrâ* arose with its use in the book of Deuteronomy, which is the only book of the Bible that refers to itself as *tôrâ* (1:5; 4:8, 44; 17:18–19; 27:3, 8, 26; 28:58, 61; 29:28; 31:9, 11, 12, 24; 32:46) and as "this book of the *tôrâ*" (29:20; 30:10; 31:26). Some have associated the meaning of *tôrâ* in this context with a law code in connection with the book's common name, "Deuteronomy." The name "Deuteronomy" comes from the Greek (Septuagint) translation of the Hebrew phrase in Deut. 17:18 that commands every king of Israel to study "a copy of this *tôrâ*." The Greek translates this phrase as *deuteronomion touto*, "this second [or 'repeated'] law," with the Hebrew *tôrâ* translated by the Greek word *nomos*, meaning "law." This Greek rendering of *tôrâ* as *nomos* and the subsequent Latin translation *lex* ("law") led to Christian misunderstandings that the Torah meant legalism.

Although *tôrâ* likely referred at some earlier stage in the composition of the book of Deuteronomy primarily to its central law code of Deut. 12–26, the term *tôrâ* came to be applied to the many different sections and genres included in the whole book of Deuteronomy (law codes, narratives, exhortations, poetry, blessings). The term *tôrâ* thus encompassed the whole set of diverse catechetical or formational literature within Deuteronomy that Moses is portrayed as writing down in "the book of the *tôrâ*" of Moses. This "book of the *tôrâ*" was to be regularly read out loud to the people, studied, and obeyed (Deut. 17:18; 31:9–13, 24–29). As the book of Deuteronomy was joined with the books of Genesis through Numbers, the term *tôrâ* was extended to include all five books of Genesis through Deuteronomy (the Pentateuch) as the central revelation of God to God's people Israel (Ezra 3:2; 7:6; Neh. 8:1–18; Mal. 4:22; Sirach, prologue; Matt. 5:17; Luke 24:44; Rom. 3:21).

Oral and Written Torah

The written Torah is portrayed in Scripture as mediated from God to Moses on Mount Sinai (Exod. 20:18–21; Deut. 5:22–33) and written down in the "book of the *tôrâ*" (Exod. 24:4; Deut. 31:9, 24–26). Rabbinic Judaism claimed that a second, orally transmitted Torah was given by God to Moses, which was transmitted orally from generation to generation alongside the written Torah. This oral Torah comprised an authoritative collection of rabbinic interpretations (legal halakah and midrashic haggadah) on biblical laws and texts that was not written down until after the destruction of the second temple, beginning with the Mishnah in the second century CE. Additional rabbinic commentaries known as the Gemara elaborated on the Mishnah and eventually were gathered together with the Mishnah into the Talmud by the sixth century CE. The Talmud itself exists in two versions: the Jerusalem Talmud and the more comprehensive Babylonian Talmud. The oral Torah involves a massive legal and ethical commentary tradition that is approximately fifty times larger than the biblical Torah of the Pentateuch.

The oral Torah fulfilled two functions. First, it addressed what seemed to be contradictory elements in the several diverse law codes and narratives of the Bible and sought to harmonize them. Second, the oral Torah filled in perceived gaps left by sometimes sparse biblical laws in order to facilitate the practical implementation of biblical commandments in everyday life and ritual practice. The need for ongoing interpretation of biblical law is suggested internally within the OT itself in the story of the daughters of Zelophehad when, far from Sinai, Moses consults with God about a legal quandary involving daughters inheriting their father's land (Num. 27:1–11). Law always required ongoing interpretation. Thus, "Torah" came to be used in various ways to designate the Pentateuch, the whole OT or Tanakh, the Bible and the Talmud together, and, most broadly, the entire body of authoritative Jewish traditions and interpretations taken as a whole.

The written and oral Torah are the source for what Jewish tradition (most notably, the medieval Jewish interpreter Rambam) had specified as a definitive list of 613 commandments (*mitzvot*) that are rooted in Scripture and that form the primary obligations for people of Jewish faith. These commandments touch upon all facets of a person's life, including religious obligations, relationships with others, Sabbath observance, Jewish festivals, marriage and sexuality, judicial and financial matters, practices of ritual purity, and the like. Obedience to these many commandments, however, is animated overall by the spirit of the central Jewish confession of the Shema, which commands the people of God to "love the LORD your God with all your heart, and with all your soul, and with all your might" (Deut. 6:4–6). One of the most important obligations of Torah ethics and one of the most important expressions of the love of God is the recitation, study, and ongoing interpretation of the Torah itself as commanded in Deut. 6:6–9.

Before Creation: The Preexistent Torah and Israel's Holiness

Some Second Temple Jewish traditions (Sir. 24:23; Bar. 3:9–4:4) merged the concept of Torah with the image of personified "Woman Wisdom," which was the first of God's created works (Prov. 8:22–23, 29–31). In their view, the Torah was the architectural blueprint from which God constructed the world (*Gen. Rab.* 1:1). The wisdom of Torah was woven into the fabric of all creation with all of its blessings available to those who studied, discerned, and obeyed the teachings of Torah. Theoretically, Torah was available for all to obey. But practically, it was only with God's giving of the Torah to Moses and the chosen people at Mount Sinai that the Torah was revealed in all its fullness. Israel thereby took on the responsibility as God's chosen people to actualize the blessings of Torah through intentional obedience to God's precepts and teaching revealed at Mount Sinai. Israel was God's "priestly kingdom and holy nation" whose obedience to Torah mediated the blessings of God to the whole of God's world (Exod. 19:5–6).

The Sabbath

This view of the Torah as an embedded potentiality in creation that only became fully actualized through Israel's obedience of God's revealed Torah at Sinai was well illustrated in the rabbinic tradition with the Sabbath commandment. God rested on the seventh day of creation (Gen. 2:2–3) and thereby made the Sabbath holy long before the commandment to obey the Sabbath is given at Sinai (Exod. 20:8–11). No human observed the Sabbath rest until God gave the command to Israel in the manna story in Exod. 16 and in the Ten Commandments in Exod. 20:8–11. Only then did the Torah's law to observe Sabbath rest become actualized into the world of human activity and obedience.

Observance of the Sabbath became an especially important element of Jewish identity during and after the Babylonian exile with the destruction of the Jerusalem temple. Thus, the Priestly creation story in Gen. 1, often dated to the exilic or postexilic period in Israel's history (post–587 BCE), placed the Sabbath as the high point of its creation story on the last or seventh day of creation. Other ancient Near Eastern creation stories often concluded their accounts with the climactic building of a palace for the appointed king of the nation. In Gen. 1, the Sabbath becomes "a palace in time" that in some way replaced the physical temple and palace that had existed in space within the walls of Jerusalem (Heschel).

Along with the commanded observance of a Sabbath day of rest, the Torah contains a large number of commands to observe and celebrate numerous festivals throughout the year that commemorate events and stories essential to Jewish identity and remembrance. For example, detailed instructions for how each generation is to observe the Passover meal every year are woven into the narrative account of the rescue of the Israelite slaves from their bondage in Egypt (Exod. 12–13). All Israelites were also to attend three pilgrimage festivals in Jerusalem every year, according to Deut. 16:16 (the Festival of Unleavened Bread, the Festival of Weeks, the Festival of Booths). These festivals had roots in the agricultural calendar of harvest. The alignment of one's life and use of time with God's prescribed calendar is a means to become attuned to the sacred rhythms built into God's creational order (Fishbane).

Holiness and Purity, Justice and Righteousness

The theme of the holiness of Israel as specially set apart from the other nations was grounded in the holiness of Israel's God (Lev. 19:2). Israel's law was also unique and set apart, unique in its justice and wisdom in comparison to all the other laws of other nations (Deut. 4:5–8). The Priestly tradition in the Torah, especially the book of Leviticus, prescribes an extensive symbolic system of boundaries within creation intended to separate one kind from another. Whenever such boundaries were crossed, ritual impurity resulted. God and anything associated with God were holy and had to be kept away from the profane. For humans, a serious contamination arose when the boundary between death and life was crossed or blurred: a living person who touched a corpse became unclean (Lev. 22:4; Num. 5:2). Many other conditions involving food or bodily secretions or other improper mixtures could render a person impure. Uncleanness was a condition that every person encountered at numerous times in life, sometimes unavoidably so. For example, attending a parent's funeral is an obligation, and yet doing so made the mourner ritually impure by virtue of being in the same room as a corpse. Certain prescribed rituals could restore an impure person to a ritually pure state over time.

Intermingled among the laws of purity and impurity in the Torah are laws involving a whole range of human activities, realms, and endeavors, from business and commerce to marriage and sexuality, to care of the land, to kindness to one's neighbor, to punishment of sinners. Particularly in the Holiness Code of Lev. 19–26, the concern for holiness extends not just to priests but to all God's people and to the land of Israel as well. The Torah or Pentateuch of Genesis through Deuteronomy is a complex anthology of diverse narratives, multiple law codes, and other diverse traditions, all of which are understood in an ethics of Torah as resources for teaching and guiding the reader in the wide range of relationships, both human and divine.

Promise and Obedience

Christians have sometimes mistakenly characterized Jewish law or Torah observance as legalism. However, strong voices within the OT portray the obedience of the Torah as a joyful gift that offers freedom, delight, mercy, joy, and blessing to those who follow the ways of Torah (Ps. 119). At the definitive event of the giving of the Torah at Mount Sinai, the Ten Commandments make clear that Israel is already God's chosen and rescued people simply because God graciously loved Israel and selected Israel as God's "firstborn son" before the law was ever given (Exod. 4:22–23). God rescued Israel from Egyptian slavery before the first of the Ten Commandments was revealed (Exod. 20:2). Reaching back to Abraham and Sarah, God had promised to make of them a great nation, and God was committed to that covenantal promise (Gen. 12:1–3; 15:1–21; Exod. 3:7–10). The commandments of Sinai thus express the rules of the household of God to which Israel already belongs by the mercy and love of God, who chose Israel as a heritage (Deut. 32:8–9) from among all the other nations (Deut. 9:4–7). For the OT and Jewish Torah ethics, the promises of God and obedience to Torah exist in a synergistic bond of mutuality: "Promise leads to obedience, but obedience renews the promise" (Levenson 152).

Another dialectic emerges in the affirmation of the ability of God's people to obey the commandments of the Torah, on one hand, and the seeming inability of God's people to obey God's law, on the other. Thus, the commandments are "not too hard for you," and "the word is very near to you" (Deut. 30:11–14). At the same time, Moses says to Israel, "For I know well how rebellious and stubborn you are" (Deut. 31:26–29 [cf. Deut. 9:6–9; Josh. 24:19–22]). Israel is able to obey the law, and yet Israel often seems unable to be obedient. Therein lies one of the mysterious complexities of the divine-human relationship.

See also Deuteronomy; Exodus; Genesis; Holiness; Holiness Code; Law; Leviticus; Numbers; Old Testament Ethics; Sabbath; Ten Commandments

Bibliography

Fishbane, M. *Sacred Attunement: A Jewish Theology*. University of Chicago Press, 2008; Harvey, W. "Torah." Pages 160–72 in *The Blackwell Reader in Judaism*, ed. J. Neusner and A. Avery-Peck. Blackwell, 2001; Heschel, A. *The Sabbath: Its Meaning for Modern Man*. Farrar, Straus & Giroux, 1979; Levenson, J. *Creation and the Persistence of Evil: The Jewish Drama of Divine Omnipotence*. Princeton University Press, 1994; Neusner, J. *The Theology of the Oral Torah: Revealing the Justice of God*. McGill-Queen's University Press, 1999; Ratheiser, G. *Mitzvoth Ethics and the Jewish Bible: The End of Old Testament Theology*. T&T Clark, 2007; Silver, D. *Judaism and Ethics*. Ktav, 1970; Sweeney, M. *Reading the Hebrew Bible after the Shoah: Engaging Holocaust Theology*. Fortress, 2008.

Dennis T. Olson

Torture

The United Nations Convention against Torture (1985) defines its subject as "any act by which severe pain or suffering, whether physical or mental, is intentionally inflicted upon a person" by or at the instigation of a public official for purposes such as interrogation or intimidation.

This convention, as well as earlier international agreements, requires that "no one may be subjected to torture or to cruel, inhuman, or degrading treatment." No exceptions are recognized. The United States is a signatory to this convention, and torture is banned by US criminal law as well.

The American Debate

Torture suddenly surfaced as a moral issue in the United States during the presidency of George W. Bush (2001–9). Apparently unrelated incidents of prisoner abuse in various theaters of the "war on terror" turned out to have been linked to one another by secret administration policy decisions and legal judgments that permitted increasingly harsh treatment of prisoners, ostensibly for interrogation.

While the Bush administration denied that it was authorizing torture, a public debate broke out over the question of whether torture per se could be morally justified. Majorities in public opinion polls said that torture was permissible at least on rare occasions. This disturbing debate crept into the Christian community. Opponents of any torture for national security found themselves locked in bitter debates with those who either denied that the United States was torturing or that it would be wrong for the nation to torture.

Biblical Considerations

Since there is no explicit ban on torture in Scripture, Christian opponents of torture ground their arguments in human dignity, human rights, and the sanctity of life. Some also argue on national character and national security grounds. For example, torture damages the soul of the torturer and the nation that tortures, and in the end it weakens rather than enhances national security.

Christian proponents of at least "aggressive" or "enhanced" interrogation techniques generally argue from just-war theory's acceptance of calibrated uses of coercion and force to protect the innocent from harm. Many cite Rom. 13:1–7 as authorization of the "sword" of government violence to deter and punish evil and protect the community.

It has become clear to antitorture advocates that a more deeply christological grounding for their position is needed. Closer study of the passion narratives in the Gospels reminds observers that Jesus himself was tortured by the state for national security reasons. Jesus took on human flesh and suffered cruel mistreatment in his own body; in a sense, whatever is done to a human body is done to the body of Jesus. He taught that what we do to the least of these, or fail to do on their behalf, we do to him (Matt. 25:31–46). And he contrasted the good Samaritan, who rescued his beaten and bleeding neighbor, with the religious leaders who passed by on the other side of the road (Luke 10:25–37).

See also Abuse; Authority and Power; Cruelty; Enemy, Enemy Love; Force, Use of; Human Rights; Just-War Theory; Sanctity of Human Life

Bibliography

Gushee, D., J. H. Zimmer, and J. D. Zimmer, eds. *Religious Faith, Torture, and Our National Soul*. Mercer University Press, 2010.

David P. Gushee

Trade

Trade is the exchange of goods and services, generally through some form of market mechanism, such as a monetary or barter system. Trade represents the basic means by which capitalist economic systems function. In the biblical context, *trade* is an expansive term covering a variety of occupations and groups of occupations, as well as the general practice of commercial exchange.

In the OT, trade takes place in the context of Israel's relationships with its neighbors and allies. A number of major land trading routes went through Palestine, which was also home to several important seaports.

In the NT era, trade relationships were to a large degree normalized within the Roman Empire by an improvement in the systems of roads, the standardization of currency, and the emergence of Greek as a standard trading language throughout much of the empire. The imperial system ameliorated problems such as piracy and banditry to some degree but at the same time levied high taxes, the collection of which often was poorly regulated, making trade more difficult.

Several ethical issues arise from the discussion of trade in the biblical context. The most common was the problem of exploitation and injustice. The prophets frequently railed against the economic exploitation of widows, orphans, and the poor as the result of injustice on the part of the wealthy and powerful. The crimes of which Israel was accused often were explicitly economic, involving the expropriation of land, the victimization of debtors, and the exploitation of the vulnerable.

This theme continues into the NT. Economic exploitation is a strong subtext of Jesus' preaching, reflecting as it does the mistreatment of the poor and colonized by the economically powerful. Thus, for example, the admonition in Matt. 5:40, "If anyone wants to sue you and take your coat, give your cloak as well," is rooted in the economic hardships faced by debtors from whom creditors could demand even the clothes on their backs.

At the same time, trade also was held up as a virtue in many biblical texts, and shrewd traders were subjects of Jesus' parables. For example, Matt. 25:14–30, the parable of the talents, uses trade and investment as a metaphor for spreading the gospel. Similarly, Matt. 13:44–46 offers two short parables using the world of trade metaphorically to describe the gospel, each involving the selling of assets for the sake of buying something of far greater value. Both Jesus' followers and many who listened to his preaching were drawn from the ranks of merchants, traders, and businesspeople, for whom such parables carried a great deal of significance.

At the same time, however, Jesus condemns the trade within the temple walls, implying that it is an act of blasphemy that diminishes what should be a holy place. However, it is clear even in this context that the target is not trade in general, but only trade that is an affront to the worship of God.

See also Capitalism; Economic Development; Economic Ethics; Markets

Bibliography

Wink, W. *Engaging the Powers: Discernment and Resistance in a World of Domination.* Fortress, 1992.

Scott Paeth

Trinity

Although Scripture does not explicitly state trinitarian doctrine, the majority of the Christian theological tradition has consistently held that a faithful reading of Scripture affirms that God is triune. In Scripture there are places where all three trinitarian members are mentioned (e.g., Matt. 28:19; Luke 10:21; Gal. 4:6). Many others name at least two members (e.g., Matt. 11:27; Mark 8:38; Luke 3:22; John 1:18; 2 Pet. 1:17). In each case, the language clearly intends to portray the trinitarian members as distinct persons. Although trinitarian doctrine is only nascent in Scripture, there is substantial scriptural warrant to see it as a faithful expression of what is implicitly conveyed.

Many consider ambiguous the precise meaning of many of the claims that Jesus made regarding his relationship to God, and the church from the earliest period found itself struggling to articulate that relationship. Was this Jesus a messianic claimant, albeit a very impressive one? Or was he more than that, somehow the incarnation of the God of Abraham, Isaac, and Jacob? For his early followers, this was no mere abstract question. Rather, concrete liturgical realities drove the church to address it: the early Christians found themselves drawn to pray to and in the name of Jesus, an expression of piety normally reserved for God alone. Within the NT itself one finds the triple invocation that Jesus instructs his followers to use in baptism. They were to baptize "in the name of the Father, and of the Son, and of the Holy Spirit" (Matt. 28:19). Such matters drove the church to undertake theologizing that, by the end of the fourth century, had resulted in the doctrine of the Trinity.

It is worth noting that there were other theoretical options open for articulating an understanding of Jesus and his relationship to God. The canonized position affirmed one person in two natures (one divine, one human) without affirming a third type of being who was neither truly and fully God nor truly and fully human. Although the doctrine of two natures was not finalized until later, it was evident in the creedal affirmation from the Council of Constantinople (381): "We believe in one Lord, Jesus Christ, the only Son of God, eternally begotten of the Father, God from God, Light from Light, true God from true God, begotten, not made, of one Being with the Father." The early church unambiguously affirmed the deity of Jesus, the Son.

With recognition of duality in God, passages such as those noted above raised similar questions about the Holy Spirit. On this, the creed states, "We believe in the Holy Spirit, the Lord, the giver of life, who proceeds from the Father [and the Son]. With the Father and the Son he is worshiped and glorified. He has spoken through the Prophets." With this creed, then, the church canonized a central part of its doctrine of God. It had now determined how to understand the biblical references to Father, Son, and Holy Spirit. These three persons are one God.

Historically speaking, the difficulty that this opened was how to be faithful to the biblical witness of three distinct entities while at the same time being faithful to the strong monotheism of the antecedent Hebrew faith. For example, the Shema states, "Hear, O Israel: The Lord our God, the Lord is one" (Deut. 6:4 TNIV). Compared to the polytheism of many ancient Near Eastern religions, the Israelitic faith was consistently and explicitly monotheistic. The doctrine of God defended by the early Christians certainly sounded to some as a slip back into polytheism.

Perhaps the most common challenge to the trinitarian doctrine is that it is incoherent. How can God be "one" of something and "three" of something at the same time? However, this question is rooted in a fundamental misunderstanding of what the doctrine actually claims. The precise meaning of the terms *person* and *substance* evolved during the period between the Council of Nicea (325) and the Council of Constantinople (381). By the time of the latter, it is clear that the terms are being used to describe different things. The term *person* came to be identified with the three members of the Trinity: Father, Son, and Spirit are persons. The term *substance* came to mean the underlying "stuff" that constitutes the three persons. The claim was not, then, that there are both one God and three Gods to be worshiped (thus, rejecting polytheism), nor are there both one person and three persons. The claim was that there is, in the one God, one of one thing (substance) and three of another thing (persons).

In *On Not Three Gods*, Gregory of Nyssa (c. 335–94) responds to the question why speaking of three persons does not affirm three Gods. He uses two different analogies to answer the question. The first is the analogy of human persons to divine persons. The second involves comparing gold coins to the one material, gold, that makes up the coins.

Consider Peter, James, and John. It is customary for us to speak of these three, who share a common human nature, as being three humans. If it is acceptable to speak of those who share a common human nature as being three humans, why should we not speak of Father, Son, and Spirit, who share a common divine nature, as being three Gods? Gregory argues that we engage in a common abuse of language: saying that there are many humans is a customary abuse of language, and that it would be much the same thing as saying that there are many human natures. Thus, there are many who have shared in the nature—many disciples, say, or apostles, or martyrs—but the human in them all is one because the term *human* belongs not to the nature of the individual as such but rather to that which is common.

The term *human* refers not to individual persons but rather to the common nature that they share, Gregory argues. So, it actually is a mistake to speak of multiple humans. Gregory develops the argument by observing that this customary abuse of language might be excused on the basis that humans, though sharing a common nature, still undertake the actions that they engage individually. So, for example, where there are multiple lawyers practicing, each one engages in his or her own cases with individual goals and objectives. Thus, while humans share a common nature, they engage independently in their activities. This is where the application of language that we use with regard to humans breaks down when applied to God. The members of the Trinity always are completely engaged in the works that they undertake. As Gregory says in *On Not Three Gods*,

> But in the case of the divine nature we do not similarly learn that the Father does anything by Himself in which the Son does not work conjointly, or again that the Son has any special operation apart from the Holy Spirit; but every operation which extends from God to the Creation, and is named according to our variable conceptions of it, has its origin from the Father, and proceeds through the Son, and is perfected in the Holy Spirit.

This customary abuse of language, when it occurs with regard to speaking about human persons, does not create a great deal of confusion. However, with regard to the divine nature, this error can falsely create the image of a multiplicity of Gods.

In the second analogy Gregory discusses the difference between gold coins and the gold from which the coins are made. Take three gold coins. We can handle each of them separately, and thus we can rightly speak of three different coins. However, the gold that makes up each one of the three coins is the same. So, one must rightly speak of the individual coins; however, at the same time, one must also recognize that in each case there is only one subtance, gold. Similarly, in the doctrine of the Trinity, there are three individual persons who share a common underlying substance. The one God of the Christian faith is concretely realized in three identifiable persons who share a common divine nature. Thus, on the one hand, the church explicitly denied the existence of three distinct Gods, and on the other hand, it denied the existence of one divine person who merely was manifest in different forms.

Systematic theologian Wolfhart Pannenberg notes that when the doctrine of the Trinity wanders far from the center of the Christian understanding of God, the implications of trinitarian theology quickly are lost, and the doctrine, while piously affirmed, easily becomes viewed as something optional or, worse, as an outright hindrance and stumbling block to Christian faith. Why does the doctrine really matter? What, then, are the implications of the trinitarian doctrine?

First, the doctrine of the Trinity provides instructive content to the claim in the creation account that human persons are created in the image of God. The doctrine of the Trinity helps us to see that first and foremost human persons have been created for relationship, and not just any kind of relationship, but deeply intimate relationships characterized by self-giving love. The image of God that we bear, then, is not first an expression of the divine rationality but rather is first an expression of the divine relationality.

Second, Richard of St. Victor held that the doctrine of the Trinity helps us to see that, at the very core of what is real, there exist persons united forever in relationships of perfectly self-giving love. There are no realities in this universe more basic than this. Richard went so far as to observe that the trinitarian doctrine was essential to understanding what it means to love unselfishly, since, he argued, on the one hand, where there are only two persons, love may be self-centered as one or the other of the lovers may hold too tightly to the other in a selfish way. On the other hand, he claimed, when three persons are in relationships of perfect love, self-centeredness is overcome because each lover must love both the others and desire them to love each other. The Christian doctrine of God, with its trinitarian structure, Richard argued, is central to properly understand the divine love that we are to imitate.

Third, the Christian tradition has held that in Jesus the second person of the Trinity unites with human nature to bring about one person who is both fully human and fully divine. If there were not some differentiated unity within the divine life, it would radically undermine the claim that God himself appears in human history in human form.

Finally, the doctrine of the Trinity reminds us that the inner life of God serves as a model for how human societies are to be. Their relationality is to be rooted in the sort of unselfish love modeled by the trinitarian persons—a love that the early church captured by saying that each person of the Trinity gave himself without reservation to the other two. The biblical injunctions to love our neighbor as ourself, to place the interests of others above our own, and to open ourselves to welcome the stranger are concrete expressions of what it means to imitate the inner life of God.

To expand on the implications of the doctrine of the Trinity for ethics, consider that Scripture consistently drives us to think more highly of others than ourselves (see, e.g., Phil. 2:1–12). The command to interact with our neighbors in ways that elevate their interests over our own is not some abstract command that God gives; it is an extension of having been created in the image of the triune God. We are to embody the sorts of relationships in our interactions with others that are modeled for us in the inner life of God. Given God's particular care for those on the margins and otherwise at risk in our societies, it is not surprising that this care for others is often expressed in the form of care for "the least of these." The trinitarian doctrine, then, provides a theological backstop for the biblical injunctions to express special care for "the least of these."

One interesting expression of what can be called a "for the other" ethic is found in Lev. 19. Contained in this short passage are many of the most fundamental ethical injunctions of Scripture, including those expressed in the Ten Commandments—both those focused on our obligations to God and those focused on our ethical obligations to one another. The gleaning laws are included here as well as others that would fall well within the realm of what we might today call "social justice." What is interesting about this particular passage is the extent to which these commands are directly connected back to God and his holiness. In various places throughout this chapter the writer has God saying things such as "For I am the Lord your God" and "For I the Lord your God am holy." To get the proper nuance of the use of the term *holy* in many places in Scripture, one has to realize the extent to which it is a relational term. And, as we have just seen, when God's relationality is discussed, it is only properly understood when connected with the trinitarian doctrine.

Finally, the Son is sent into the world to free us from sin, and the Holy Spirit is sent to indwell and to empower Christians to live as God expects. So, the trinitarian doctrine provides a basis for understanding the relational nature of God and its implications for us and for understanding that the divine persons, though united in their actions, have different foci for their work. The Son frees us from the guilt and horror of our sins, while the Spirit living within us provides empowerment both to hear God's commands and to live them out faithfully. In sum, the doctrine of the Trinity is ripe with implications for our moral lives, and we rightly ground our ethical discussions there.

See also Holy Spirit; Image of God; Incarnation

Bibliography

Augustine. *The Trinity*. Trans. E. Hill. Ed. J. Rotelle. New City Press, 1991; Basil the Great. *On the Holy Spirit*. Trans. D. Anderson. St. Vladimir's Seminary Press, 1980; Hanson, R. *The Search for the Christian Doctrine of God: The Arian Controversy, 318–381*. Baker Academic, 2005; LaCugna, C. *God for Us: The Trinity and Christian Life*. HarperSanFrancisco, 1993; Moltmann, J. *The Trinity and the Kingdom: The Doctrine of God*. Trans. M. Kohl. Fortress, 1993; Olson, R., and C. Hall. *The Trinity*. GT. Eerdmans, 2002; Pannenberg, W. *Systematic Theology*. Vol. 1. Eerdmans, 1991; Peters, T. *God as Trinity: Relationality and Temporality in Divine Life*. Westminister John Knox, 1993; Rahner, K. *The Trinity*. Trans. J. Donceel. Herder & Herder, 1970; Turcescu, L. "The Lesser Trinitarian Treatises II." Pages

61–78 in *Gregory of Nyssa and the Concept of Divine Persons*. Oxford University Press, 2005.

Charles E. Gutenson

Truthfulness, Truth-Telling

Truthfulness is a matter of being straight with our words. Truth-telling has the character of witness. It can be risky. It unmasks falsehoods (sometimes dominant and compelling points of view) while giving testimony to the truth. James, in his epistle, exhorts teachers to be true in their words, but the wisdom applies to the power of the word for all of us. Truthfulness in our words and truth-telling as witness to God's word are essential to living out faithfulness to God.

> For all of us make many mistakes. Anyone who makes no mistakes in speaking is perfect, able to keep the whole body in check with a bridle. If we put bits into the mouths of horses to make them obey us, we guide their whole bodies. Or look at ships: though they are so large that it takes strong winds to drive them, yet they are guided by a very small rudder wherever the will of the pilot directs. So also the tongue is a small member, yet it boasts of great exploits. How great a forest is set ablaze by a small fire! (Jas. 3:2–5)

The exhortation on the use of words in Jas. 3:1–12 flows smoothly from the preceding discussion in Jas. 2:14–26 of faith and works. The point of Jas. 2:14–26 is that faith is active and brought to completion through works (2:22). But the examples of faithful works, Abraham (2:21–23) and Rahab (2:25), seem to be inopportune. In these traditional tropes, the "works" of Abraham (the binding of Isaac) and Rahab (concealing Joshua's spies) include equivocation on the one hand, and deception on the other. When on the way to the place where Isaac will be bound for sacrifice, Isaac asks his father about the sheep to be offered. With well-crafted ambiguity, Abraham withholds an important bit of information from him. "God himself will provide the lamb for a burnt offering" (Gen. 22:8). The drama of their journey and Abraham's exemplary faith hinges on Abraham's belief that Isaac is the promised son, whom God provides, and now the offering to be given back to God. In Josh. 2:1–24, Rahab harbors and aids the escape of Israelite scouts in Jericho. She disobeys her own king and lies outright to those who pursue the Israelite spies (Josh. 2:5). Are these the faithful deeds to which James refers?

In order to attend to the complications of truth-telling in the Bible, we should expand the basic point of Jas. 3, that truthfulness is the rudder of faithfulness. Developing the Pauline theme of new life in Christ (2 Cor. 5:17), the letters to the Colossians and the Ephesians ask us to put lying and falsehood behind us: "Do not lie to one another, seeing that you have stripped off the old self with its practices and have clothed yourselves with the new self, which is being renewed in knowledge according to the image of its creator" (Col. 3:9–10). Ephesians 4 draws, as well, on the Pauline themes of the unity of the body and the diversity of gifts. Living as the body of Christ, the community can be free from the winds of "deceitful scheming" (Eph. 4:14). "But speaking the truth in love, we must grow up in every way into him who is the head, into Christ, from whom the whole body, joined and knitted together by every ligament with which it is equipped, as each part is working properly, promotes the body's growth in building itself up in love" (Eph. 4:15–16).

In 1 Cor. 8, Paul takes up this relationship between truthfulness and love when dealing with the problem of eating meat sacrificed to idols. The truth is that idols represent nothing real: "We know that 'no idol in the world really exists,' and that 'there is no God but one'" (8:4). With this knowledge comes the freedom to eat meat that has been sacrificed to so-called idols. However, knowledge of the truth ought not lead to pride. "We are no worse off if we do not eat, and no better off if we do" (8:8). Paul argues that the Christian community, especially the "strong," when choosing their behaviors, must take into account the inferior knowledge of the "weak." Some are not free from a false belief about idols, and eating meat used in pagan ceremonies would, for them, be an act of defilement, a wound to their faith. By eating meat offered to idols, those with knowledge of the truth would be using their knowledge to destroy the faith of brothers and sisters for whom Christ has died (8:11). "What is at stake is the salvation of a member of the Christian family. A sibling must not be lost" (Collins 324). Salvation in Christ is the central truth that guides the use of our knowledge in word and deed.

Truthfulness in our words, we might say, is necessary but not self-sufficient if we are to witness to the truth. We need faith in God's way. In Matt. 5–7, the Sermon on the Mount, Jesus teaches about the fulfillment of the law and the righteousness of the kingdom (5:17–20). He requires radical dependence on God and trust in the way of the kingdom—the way of justice, peace, and reconciliation. Jesus includes instruction on the truthfulness of our words (5:33–37). The people of God's reign need no props and oaths to guarantee their truthfulness. There are no particular occasions when they ought to call on God as their witness.

Their words ought to be true on every occasion. There are no times when they need to hedge with circumlocutions. They ought to witness to God in all their words. "Let your word be 'Yes, Yes' or 'No, No'; anything more than this comes from the evil one" (5:37). The double "yes" and double "no" have been interpreted by some, ironically, to mean that Jesus provides an acceptable oath (saying "yes, yes") in his rejection of traditional oaths (Luz 317). The context (the higher righteousness) and the concluding line (about the evil one) make this interpretation unlikely. "Duplication of the word as a rule provides intensification in Greek as well as in Semitic languages. 'Yes, yes' means nothing but a true yes, a yes which is valid and has solidity" (Luz 318). Within the context of Matt. 5–7, being bound by one's words is understood to be an act of dependence on God (cf. Matt. 5:3–12). It is confidence in Jesus' proclamation of the kingdom.

Dependence on and confidence in God are found in the parable of the dishonest steward in Luke 16:1–13. On the surface, the parable appears to recommend self-serving dishonesty. The complicated commentary on the parable in vv. 8b–9, 10–12, 13 indicates that even "Luke and the pre-Lukan tradition experienced as much difficulty understanding the parable as did succeeding generations" (Donahue 163). The parable begins as the manager is summoned to his wealthy master and released from service for squandering the rich man's property. Before the termination takes effect, the manager quickly decides on a course of action so that "people may welcome me into their homes" (16:4). "So, summoning his master's debtors one by one, he asked the first, 'How much do you owe my master?' He answered, 'A hundred jugs of olive oil.' He said to him, 'Take your bill, sit down quickly, and make it fifty'" (16:5–6). After the manager reduced the amount due on other accounts, "his master commended the dishonest manager because he had acted shrewdly" (16:8a). Why would the master commend the manager for cheating him further? Even though the debtors benefit from his actions, why would they welcome the scoundrel into their homes? How is it that the commentary on the parable concludes with "You cannot serve God and wealth" (16:13)? Does not the manager successfully serve wealth?

Recent biblical research presents a case that the dishonest manager is deceitful in squandering his master's property but law-abiding when he acts shrewdly (sensibly and prudently) in rewriting the debtors' promissory notes. As in the case of Zacchaeus (Luke 19:1–10), it is the just and faithful use of wealth that accords with God's hospitality and salvation. The logic of the parable—the conversion of the dishonest steward—makes sense in the context of rules that develop from Jewish legal prohibitions against charging interest on a loan (Exod. 22:25; Lev. 25; Deut. 23:19–20). A tradition had developed in Judaism that allowed the charging of interest by another name. "If, for example, the contract stated that $100 was to be lent at 6 percent interest, the contract was usurious. If, however, the projected rate of interest was written into the original loan, then there was no usury in the technical sense" (Donahue 165). Thus, if a contract stated a loan in the amount of $106 but the borrower received only $100, it would appear to be lawful. Here we have the source of the manager's dishonesty: "People of respect and authority would avoid tainting their hands by direct dealing. The finances and skirting of the law were managed by their stewards, who could be called 'stewards of injustice'" (Donahue 165).

In the Lukan parable, there is a debt of one hundred jugs of oil, which is reduced to fifty, and we can imagine the manager bringing a good profit to his master and lining his own pockets as well. The manager's shrewd and praiseworthy action is this: by rewriting the promissory notes, he denies himself an acceptable loophole and the income that goes with it. He sets the books right. He takes decisive action "to sacrifice his own gain" and to depend instead on upright and honest dealings (Donahue 165). He makes, perhaps, an honest man of his master as well. For these reasons, he will be praised by his master (16:8) and welcomed into the homes of the debtors (16:4). He will be making friends through his dishonest wealth (16:9) not by additional dishonesty or by the favors that money can buy, but rather by his faithfulness to God's law. By his faithfulness, he will be welcomed "into the eternal homes" (16:9).

The deep connection between truth and faith is basic to the gospel. The themes of light and darkness, for example, are woven through the Gospel of John. Jesus is the light (1:9; 9:5), disciples are called to walk in the light (8:12; 12:35), and those whose deeds are evil "[love] darkness rather than light" (3:19). "But those who do what is true come to the light, so that it may be clearly seen that their deeds have been done in God" (3:21). In the Synoptic Gospels, faith and dependence on God provide an orientation that opens us to the truth about Jesus as the Christ. Parables are comparisons that illuminate the truth of the kingdom, but when they fall on unbelieving ears, their teachings become obscure (Matt. 13:10–15; Mark 4:11–12). In

Mark's Gospel, blindness is a motif woven through Jesus' three passion predictions. Knowing the truth requires trust, not only in Jesus but also in the way of the cross. Within the framework of healing the blind (8:22–26; 10:46–52), the disciples fail to understand the implications of Peter's declaration that Jesus is the Messiah (8:27–33). Jesus must suffer and die (8:31), and discipleship means denying oneself and taking up the cross (8:34). "Whoever wishes to become great among you must be your servant, and whoever wishes to be first among you must be slave of all. For the Son of Man came not to be served but to serve, and to give his life a ransom for many" (10:43–45).

Such truthfulness requires conversion and faith. This is the call of the Hebrew prophets as well as the Gospels; when bound by our lies, we do not know God (Jer. 9:1–5). The call to truthfulness is a call to repentance and faith in God, to "prepare the way of the LORD" (Isa. 40:3). This biblical understanding of truthfulness and the suffering that comes with truth-telling are different from typically modern frameworks. It certainly is not utilitarian; that is, the so-called good of lying is not determined by favorable results of falsehoods. Biblical truth-telling is not deontological; that is, truthfulness is not judged as an abstract norm apart from context. Rather, truthfulness and truth-telling are the ways of faithfulness to God. God's word is true, and we are called to be faithful in our lives and in our words.

A good example of this approach is found in the life of André Trocmé, who, with the people of Le Chambon, hid and rescued Jews in Nazi-occupied France. Trocmé was deeply concerned with truth-telling, of witnessing to the truth by resisting the falsehoods of the Nazis. On one occasion, he accepted imprisonment rather than sign an oath of allegiance to the Vichy government. Another time, he risked arrest when he decided not to use the false identification papers at his disposal. In order to avoid falsehood in harboring Jews, he and the people of his village organized their activities in such a way that they would not have to lie. When asked if Jews were in the village, Trocmé said, "Yes." When asked their names and whereabouts, he honestly said (the equivalent of), "No" or "You are welcome to look" (Hallie). The people of Le Chambon also performed symbolic acts of truth-telling that pointed to Nazi falsehoods, such as publically refusing to honor the Vichy flag. They risked their lives for the truth.

Extreme situations are full of ambiguities, and the risks of truth-telling ought not to be used to justify lying. It has been a habit in modern ethics to take extreme situations as the norm for the ordinary ("Would you lie if there was a gun at your child's head?"). In contrast, the biblical norm is God's faithful word. Trocmé and the people of Le Chambon did practice deception, specifically in forging identification cards and the like. But the falsehoods weighed heavily on their consciences. They would agree with Augustine, the most rigorous of the church fathers on truthfulness and lying. When commenting on the deceptions of Rahab, Augustine notes that her hospitality is exemplary, not her deceit; lies are not to be imitated. Likewise with Abraham (Gen. 12:13; 20:2; 22:8), as well as Isaac (26:7) and Jacob (Gen. 27), his equivocation is part of the frailty of the human drama of faithfulness. Our character flaws are overcome by God's promises, so that Abraham's hedge to Isaac ironically (and despite himself) points to the truth. Jacob uses deception to attain the birthright, but amid his clever dealings and desire for the father's blessing there is human foolishness (Bandstra 111–20). We see what Jacob, who is in the middle of things, does not; we know that God will provide. Jacob is our representative in this regard. When we are tempted to commit acts of deception that are senseless and unnecessary, we need to stop to remember and to have faith that God's promises are true.

See also Dishonesty; Honesty; Hypocrisy; Oaths; Parables, Use of in Ethics; Speech Ethics; Vows

Bibliography

Augustine. "Against Lying." Pages 481–500 in vol. 3 of *Nicene and Post-Nicene Fathers*, ed. P. Schaff. Eerdmans, 1956; Bandstra, B. *Reading the Old Testament*. 2nd ed. Wadsworth, 1999; Collins, R. *First Corinthians*. SP 7. Liturgical Press, 1999; Donahue, J. *The Gospel in Parable: Metaphor, Narrative, and Theology in the Synoptic Gospels*. Fortress, 1988; Hallie, P. *Lest Innocent Blood Be Shed: The Story of the Village of Le Chambon and How Goodness Happened There*. HarperPerennial, 1994; Luz, U. *Matthew 1–7*. Trans. W. Linss. CC. Fortress, 1989.

David Matzko McCarthy

Two Kingdoms *See* Lutheran Ethics

Tyranny

In modern usage, the word *tyranny* refers to the arbitrary and (broadly) absolute rule of a single person or small group of people over others. During antiquity, the term held fewer negative connotations (the word *tyrant*, e.g., was used as a synonym for *king* among ancient Greeks), largely due to the preponderance of rulers who came into power either by seizing it or inheriting it from someone who had seized it—the very conditions likely to produce tyrants. Nonetheless, both Plato and Aristotle thought of it as the worst form of government, but principally because it was the negative expression of the best form of government, namely, benevolent kingship. According to Aristotle, kings worked for the interests of their state and its people, whereas tyrants pursued their own interests.

There are few uses of the terms *tyrant* or *tyranny* in English translations of Scripture. The NRSV of the Protestant canon, for instance, uses the word *tyrant* only five times (Isa. 13:11; 29:5, 20; 49:24, 25) and never uses the word *tyranny*, although both terms appear repeatedly in the various books of Maccabees. This is due partly to the predominance of kingdoms and empires among the forms of government during its writing, and partly to the relative absence of discussions of statecraft in Scripture. Scripture does, however, portray tyrannous actors throughout, including many among the various kings of Israel and Judah.

Among the more complex ethical questions related to tyranny is whether anyone has a right (or even a duty) to commit tyrannicide, the assassination of a tyrant. The OT includes at least two examples of tyrannicide: Ehud taking the life of King Eglon of Moab (Judg. 3:15–25), and Jehu taking the life of Joram (2 Kgs. 9:14–26). The NT injunction in Rom. 13:1–7 to be subject to governing authorities makes tyrannicide difficult to justify. However, Thomas Aquinas allowed it by claiming that it could not be seditious, since the tyrant himself was guilty of sedition. Likewise, Martin Luther and John Calvin allowed for it during those instances in which a tyrant prevented the practices of "true religion." The most famous recent case of a Christian involved in tyrannicide was Dietrich Bonhoeffer's participation in the plot to kill Adolf Hitler. In all cases, however, the risks of tyrannicide are that the assassin acts in opposition to God's governing will and that the current tyranny is replaced by something even worse (e.g., another tyranny or anarchy).

One of the claimed advantages of democracies over other forms of government is that they make tyranny less likely because the people are involved in the project of governance. This advantage is multiplied in constitutional democracies by adherence to the rule of law rather than the arbitrary will of a few or even the majority of the people. Thus, Christian ethicists since at least the Enlightenment have been interested in promoting such democracies and in determining if and when tyrannicide is justified.

See also Authority and Power; Democracy; Government; Political Ethics

Mark Douglas

U

Unemployment *See* Work

Urbanization

Biblical history begins in a garden but ends with a garden in the center of a cubic city. The city of God in the book of Revelation is a communal human reflection of the communicating, productive nature of the Godhead, expressed first in the village, then the town, then the city. These progressions of migration and city building we call "urbanization."

Twentieth-Century Urban Explosion

An explosion of megacities in the last century has led to the urban millennium. In the year 2000 there were 433 new megacities with a population over 4 million and 6,600 cities over 100,000. This is largely the result of technological advances in the sanitary and health fields, enabling people to live longer, and of advances in productivity, enabling people to live better.

Pushed from rural land by overpopulation, warfare, deforestation, appropriation of lands, and pulled toward cities by the good life seen on television, education, access to medical care, and the possibility of jobs, more than one billion people have migrated in the last decade. The majority migrate from cohesive tribal or peasant communities via dispossession and poverty into the disorganization of slums and *favelas*, without rights to land and legal status. They are employed in the "informal sector" with poorly paid part-time jobs. Industrial growth ranges from 1 to 4 percent, whereas population growth ranges from 6 to 12 percent. In the last generation the children of the slums have increasingly become children of the streets, and drug addiction has escalated so that many slums are now controlled by drug gangs. But a global middle class of one billion (out of the three billion people found in cities) has also emerged with their distinctive consumer goods—their jeans, their cars, their iPods.

Urban Theological Approaches

Urban background to the early church. The context of the early church was largely urban. Richard Batey describes Sepphoris, a Roman city only four miles from Nazareth, suggesting the potential impact of Greek and Roman urban culture on the earliest Jesus movement. Focusing on the Pauline mission and churches, Wayne Meeks describes first-century urban churches across the empire.

Comprehensive urban theologies. Jacques Ellul's *The Meaning of the City* is the most comprehensive urban theology of the last century. Harvie Conn explored historical responses by the church to the city, as it interacted with the cosmopolis of the Roman Empire, the theopolis of Christendom, the megalopolis, and now the global city. His integrated work with Manuel Ortiz includes exegesis of many biblical books in their relationship to the city.

Urban conversational theologies. Most urban practitioners deal with theologies of context, focusing on particular issues rather than urbanization as a whole. Urban theologies tend to be eclectic, crossing theological divides, incarnational in style, based on story (Grigg, "Transformational Conversations"), engaged with oppression that causes poverty, and integrating justice and proclamation.

Urban mission studies and postmodern cities. Church planters on the frontlines of non-Christian religions have developed a stream of responses to urbanization, emphasizing the incarnational and evangelistic formation of holistic churches as a primary goal. Since these responses deal with poverty as a primary context, they draw on urban economic theories (de Soto), focus on the holistic church among the poor (Grigg, *Companion to the Poor*), and relate urban anthropological studies to church growth (Hiebert and Meneses).

A second stream is essentially British and American, where the institutional church already exists as a significant player in a highly government-funded context of meeting social needs within cities (Bakke).

These perspectives draw on urban studies derived from the comprehensive sociology of Max

Weber in *The City* (1958) and further developed by the "Chicago School." They emphasize urbanism as a way of life, migration, family and kinship, class, ethnicity, and urban places and spaces. Urban planners and geographers highlight other issues of infrastructure, transportation, or public services. Newer works related to the emergence of postmodern cities are being produced (Dear).

Some theologians (Linthicum; Tonna) explore these structural issues, but as scores of new cities spring up in the desert sands of the East and a thousand new cities are planned for China, there is little theological engagement with the underlying ethics of urban growth and design represented in urban planning and thinking.

The Nature of God Predicts the Nature of Urbanization

What is the nature of godly urbanization? From the first chapters of Genesis, we can predict the nature of today's cities. This is because cities grow out of the collective nature of humankind, which itself reflects the very nature of God, as God is described in Gen. 1.

Cities also grow toward the nature of God's city, as expressed in the apocalyptic visions of the city of God in Revelation. Beginning with Augustine's *City of God*, this theme has always been one of defining Christian utopias, of envisioning the "good" city.

The narratives in Gen. 4 and Gen. 11 complement these optimistic themes, with a more somber perspective on the city of collective fallen humanity, for these first cities are built in rebellion against God. Cain, cursed by God to be a wanderer, builds a city in defiance. His heirs later build Babel, a city where humans determine to reach God by their own patterns, a city that God steps in to destroy.

Redemption history has been described as the history of struggle between these two cities, the city of God and the city of humanity. The two cities are symbolized in Revelation by Jerusalem, the city of *shalom*, where God has set his presence, and by Babylon, the city of opulent oppression, the city against God. The outcome of the ongoing spiritual warfare is the triumph of the city of God with the violent overthrow of Babylon by God himself (Rev. 18). Then the bride of Christ, which is the city of God, is fully revealed in all its glory (Rev. 21).

God of creation: Cities of creativity. The Spirit's presence before creation lends credence to the importance of prayer and the work of Spirit-filled believers in creation of cities. Humankind also reflects God's capacity to create something out of nothing. Cities that can innovatively copy and improve on items they import, then reexport them, are cities that grow economically.

God the communicator: Cities as centers of media and academe. In the silence of Gen. 1, we hear a recurrent voice (vv. 3, 6, 9, 14, 20, 24, 26), an ongoing creative process. Here is the basis of a present focus on the incarnate word in the urban church and the preached word of God as source of the creation of the city. Humans seek to communicate, so cities become the center of television, internet, and radio.

God of the aesthetic: City as environment. The city is also to be aesthetically pleasing, just as the garden was good. It is to be ecologically integrated, and humanity is to manage it. Geographers and mathematicians currently utilizing fractal analysis in urban studies perceive a hand outside of humankind generating patterns into which urban growth falls. The end of urban demography is predicted when the Scriptures speak of a cubic city, one thousand stadia high, long, and wide.

God also holds the people of this city accountable for their spatial relationships. A theology of urban planning flows from God's care and provision, and God's delegation of managerial responsibility.

The creation of Adam from dust requires our humanness to remain connected to the environment. The disconnection of tribal people from their land, of migrants from basic necessities of life, and of youth from their fathers—these realities help to create the dissonances leading to youth gangs, a neurotic society, and teen suicide. Restoring healthy environments is an essential activity of the Godhead and of followers of Christ.

God as community: City as managed community. The city is also relational. God says, "Let *us* make." As in the Godhead, there is the companionship that works itself out in many areas: entertainment, sports, media, family life, and recreational activities.

God structures: City as productive structure. In the first three days recorded in Genesis, God creates form out of formlessness, then fills the form with life. City planning and city management should be a reflection of that godly activity, for cities are centers of structures. For example, the agricultural system is based in rural cities; banking structures built off the production of the land are also based in cities. The mandate given to manage resources leads to issues of efficiency and productivity, patterns of decision-making, and the spatial form and function of the city. God creates things to be fruitful, and from this comes wealth. The city is a center of productive economic growth.

Secularization and urbanization. The godly city in the book of Revelation centers on the King of kings and his light-giving, and it is watered by the river, symbolic of the life-giving Holy Spirit. Thus, one aim of developing a city in which the church is growing (as with its other healthy systems) is that its worshiping nature become centrally illuminating and life-giving to city systems.

There has been significant sociological literature on the increase in secularization during urbanization. It became the basis of Harvey Cox's urban theology in *The Secular City*. The expansion of urban fundamentalist and experiential religions is increasingly evident.

Oppression and justice. The prophets speak of justice in the city. Where is there a city that is incrementally just over time and space, where there is a sense of fairness in the distribution of resources?

In highly oppressive cities, where poverty results from exploitation, Christians become active in defending the poor, in seeking justice, and in creating systems of justice. This work in most contexts is incremental and localized as the church expands rapidly among the poor of the slums, and as the rich and middle class seek to transfer wealth to the needy. Christian theologies and practices of community organization result in political processes reaching toward transformation of power relationships (Linthicum).

See also Creation Ethics; Economic Development; Globalization; Humanity; Poverty and Poor; Property and Possessions

Bibliography

Bakke, R. *A Theology as Big as the City*. InterVarsity, 1997; Batey, R. *Jesus and the Forgotten City: New Light on Sepphoris and the Urban World of Jesus*. Baker, 1991; Conn, H., and M. Ortiz. *Urban Ministry: The Kingdom, the City, and the People of God*. InterVarsity, 2001; Cox, H. *The Secular City: Secularization and Urbanization in Theological Perspective*. Macmillan, 1965; Dear, M. *The Postmodern Urban Condition*. Blackwell, 2000; de Soto, H. *The Other Path: The Economic Answer to Terrorism*. Trans. J. Abbott. Harper & Row, 1989; Ellul, J. *The Meaning of the City*. Trans. D. Pardee. Attic Press, 1997; Greenway, R., and T. Monsma. *Cities: Missions' New Frontier*. Baker, 1989; Grigg, V. *Companion to the Poor*. Authentic Media, 2004; idem. "Transformational Conversations." Pages 20–32 in *The Holy Spirit and the Postmodern City: Transformative Revival among Auckland's Evangelicals and Pentecostals*. Urban Leadership Foundation, 2009; Hiebert, P., and E. Meneses. *Incarnational Ministry: Planting Churches in Band, Tribal, Peasant and Urban Societies*. Baker, 1995; Linthicum, R. *City of God, City of Satan: A Biblical Theology of the Urban Church*. Zondervan, 1991; Meeks, W. *The First Urban Christians: The Social World of the Apostle Paul*. Yale University Press, 1983; Soja, E. *Postmodern Geographies: The Reassertion of Space in Critical Social Theory*. Verso, 1989; Tonna, B. *Gospel for the Cities: A Socio-Theology of Urban Ministry*. Trans. W. Jerman. Wipf & Stock, 2004; Weber, M. *The City*. Trans. and ed. D. Martindale and G. Neuwirth. Free Press, 1958.

Viv Grigg

Usury *See* Loans

Utilitarianism

In moral decision-making there are at least two broad approaches: deontology and consequentialism. Deontologists judge actions according to their conformity with a particular law or rule. Consequentialists judge actions primarily by the consequences that the act produces or the goals toward which it tends. A consequentialist sometimes is willing to advocate breaking a law for the sake of achieving a greater good.

Utilitarianism is a special kind of consequentialism associated with Jeremy Bentham and John Stuart Mill. Contemporary scholars tend to summarize the main principles of utilitarianism in one of two related ways. First, utilitarianism sometimes is associated with seeking the "greatest good for the greatest number," so that an action is understood to be moral if it benefits more people than it harms. Second, classic utilitarianism sometimes is described in terms of the maximization of happiness (or pleasure): an act is moral when it leads to the most possible happiness for an individual or community. Both of these definitions presume that the goodness of an act is understood in terms of its "utility," its tendency to produce good outcomes.

Utilitarian Reasoning in Scripture

Many scriptural texts run counter to utilitarian reasoning. The dominant witness of the NT is that all humans are equal and all life is worth preserving. Galatians 3:28 affirms the equality of all persons in Christ, and throughout the Gospels Jesus speaks of God's care for each individual person. The story of the sheep and goats speaks to God's concern for and identification with those humans who are part of the "least" significant spheres of society (Matt. 25:31–46). Jesus interacts with social outcasts (Matt. 9:10–13; Mark 2:13–17; Luke 5:27–32; 19:1–10; John 4:7–39), treats children with special care (Matt. 19:13–15; Mark 10:13–16; Luke 18:15–17), and praises the actions of a shepherd who leaves ninety-nine sheep in order to find the one that is lost (Matt. 18:10–14; Luke 15:3–7). The idea that the good of some persons can be sacrificed for the sake of a greater number of people is at odds with these texts' emphasis upon care for all persons. The only exception is in the case of sacrificing one's own good for others. Jesus commends the self-sacrifice of one's life for the sake of friends as the greatest love (John 15:13), and such love is exemplified in Christ's own actions, the actions of a shepherd who lays down his life for his sheep (John 10:14–18).

The witness of Scripture is more complicated, however, when one thinks of utilitarianism in terms of happiness. Certainly, in the Christian understanding, the moral life does not necessarily lead to short-term pleasure or happiness, and it may in fact lead to martyrdom. But Scripture and the tradition simultaneously affirm that a moral life should produce its own kind of fulfillment and happiness consistent with the ends for which God created us; it is expected that Christians will ultimately find joy and contentment in a relationship with God. The Puritan pastor Jonathan Edwards preached his first sermon, "Christian Happiness," arguing that God loves us so much that God created moral laws to coincide with the things that ultimately will make humans joyful. For this reason, Edwards believed, it is appropriate to speak of Christian morality as leading to happiness. The quality of this happiness, however, is different from the happiness upheld by some forms of utilitarianism. It is perhaps more appropriate to speak of Christian happiness in terms of joy than in terms of pleasure, for pleasure is a quality that may be fleeting or temporary.

Contemporary Application

Several arguments in twentieth-century Christian ethics rely upon a type of consequentialist reasoning. In the 1970s, Roman Catholic theologian Richard McCormick and Protestant theologian Paul Ramsey collaborated on an edited volume called *Doing Evil to Achieve Good*. This book signified a consensus among many American ethicists that it is impossible to avoid doing evil, on some level, when addressing certain moral dilemmas that arise in healthcare ethics and in the ethics of war and peace. Both Ramsey and McCormick advocated a method for addressing these dilemmas that many scholars call "proportionalism." This method allows for the moral permissibility of actions that produce evils in certain circumstances when the evils are outweighed by compelling goods. Many contemporary ethicists continue to advocate proportionalist reasoning, contending that it is the only authentic way to address certain situations in which evil outcomes are unavoidable. However, proportionalism has come under significant critique from other scholars who insist that certain moral norms should never be compromised.

See also Consequentialism; Deontological Theories of Ethics; Double Effect, Principle of; Happiness; Teleological Theories of Ethics

Bibliography

Edwards, J. "Christian Happiness." Pages 294–307 in *Sermons and Discourses 1720–1723*, vol. 10 of *The Works of Jonathan Edwards*, ed. W. Kimmach. Yale University Press, 1992; McCormick, R., and P. Ramsey. *Doing Evil to Achieve Good: Moral Choice in Conflict Situations*. Loyola University Press, 1978.

Elizabeth Agnew Cochran

V

Values, Value Judgments

Values are guiding principles and enduring beliefs within a community about that which is good and desirable and that which is not. Values are ascriptions of worth that emerge from personal, institutional, cultural, and religious norms. As such, values assign worth to an object, a state of being, an action, humans, and so forth. Values include an ethical evaluation pertaining to specific social issues or social conditions. Value judgments are the application of values to pursue identified ends and goals. Value judgments depend on implicit understandings of value theory, a clarification of what possesses worth or value. Thus, values, value judgments, and value theory are interwoven.

Christian Accounts of Values and Value Judgments

Christianity traditionally holds central the values of unconditional love, hope, righteousness, forgiveness, truth, compassion, justice, honoring God, the renunciation of violence, and the rejection of excessive materialism (e.g., Matt. 5:43–45; 22:36–40; Mark 10:21; 12:32–34; Luke 6:26–28). These Christian values correspond to believers' attempts to follow Jesus' life and work. Such values, though, also have a context within Christian Scriptures that must be carefully examined. Significant interpretive questions emerge here regarding the religious, historical, and socioeconomic context of the earliest churches in formulating such value judgments and what weight these value judgments should carry for Christians today.

Indeed, the role of the Christian Scriptures in the formation of values is complex. Some scholars see the Scriptures as a source of divine command whereby accounts of what humans should value are clear and distinct (Mouw 32). For other scholars, the Scriptures provide a singular value trajectory—for example, "love"—toward which humans must aim (Fletcher 57). Another argument here is that the Scriptures provide pluralistic accounts of values and as such must be described, contextualized, interpreted, and applied (Hays 4–7). Finally, some scholars contend that the Scriptures as interpreted and practiced by Christian communities themselves become central in the formation of specific values, such as the practice of nonviolence in the earliest church, and how such values might be properly embodied by Christians today (Yoder 1–7).

Several matrices have emerged within the Christian tradition to adjudicate issues of values and value judgments. Protestant evangelicals widely embrace both the unity and normativity of the Scriptures in articulating values and value judgments. Such accounts emphasize the pervasive impact of sin on human judgment, reason, and cognition and thus the need for divine revelation to make known the values that humans should embrace (Mouw 32). Many Roman Catholic approaches focus on natural-law traditions. Catholic natural-law traditions argue that all rational persons can, with the aid of God, both know and act on universally held values. Other Catholic accounts fuse the natural-law tradition, direct engagement with the Christian Scriptures, and phenomenological insights regarding the human person in order to clarify values and value judgments (John Paul II 3–11).

Narrative theologians argue against both evangelical and natural-law approaches and contend that values are rooted in the Christian narrative and its communal interpretation of Christian Scriptures and practices (Hauerwas 17–28). Postmodernist theologians reject arguments that values can be known through universal reason available to all humans; instead, postmodernist theologians contend that humans know and act on values through linguistically and socially constructed realities (Vanhoozer 166–67). Process theologians have stressed the creativity of both God and humans in constructing emerging accounts of value as a response to the evolutionary and relational nature of the cosmos. Thus, values are by the nature of the cosmos dynamic and subject to change (Suchocki 155). Feminist theologians emphasize the patriarchal construction of values both in the Christian Scriptures and in present societies. As such, both ancient and contemporary values that dehumanize and enslave women and men require critique, reassessment, and enlightened engagement (Ruether 213). Liberationist theologians have stressed accounts of values that utilize empirical data to assess unjust social and class formations in contemporary society. Liberationist theologians see values as rooted in the trajectories of Christian Scriptures that point toward God's hope for the liberation of humans from oppression. As such, personal freedom, community, and solidarity with the outcast of society emerge as central values for liberationist theologians (Gutiérrez 193–94). Still other theologians construe values as expressing the relationship of being to being. Here, "value exists in the reciprocal relations which beings realizing potentiality have to other beings. In this situation every good is an end and every good a means" (Niebuhr 105).

Some recent Christian movements have defined "family values" as the promotion and upholding of the nuclear family, sexual abstinence outside of marriage, the rejection of same-sex behavior, prayer in public schools, the rejection of all forms of abortion, the rejection of stem-cell research, and more generally as the conflict between Christian and non-Christian value judgments. Several scholars have challenged such interpretations of values: "Today's phrase *family values* connotes a solidarity in family identity that the first Christians found highly suspect, if not condemnable" (Cahill 18).

Other Christian accounts of values and value judgments in the twentieth century have been supplemented, enriched, and challenged by ecumenical engagement with other living religious traditions. Mainline expressions of the Abrahamic religions of Judaism and Islam focus on the values of loving-kindness, learning and wisdom, honoring God, remembrance, repentance and forgiveness, justice, purity, and righteousness. Buddhism generates values based on the Four Noble Truths and the Eightfold Path. As such, one's views, intentions, speech, action, livelihood, efforts, mindfulness, and concentration are focused on the true nature of reality, and as such are dedicated to the eradication of hatred, greed, and falsehood (Dalai Lama 31).

All of these religious approaches to values and value judgments emerged in the twentieth century alongside both the tremendous hopes for the advancement of society (through science, education, human rights, etc.) and the fears associated with the vast destruction of society (through war, genocide, human-rights violations, famine, population explosions, and environmental degradation).

Economic, Sociological, and Other Accounts of Values

Christian notions of values and value judgments interact with and are shaped deeply by nonreligious accounts (and vice versa). Christian theologians were deeply shaped by Stoic, Platonic, and Aristotelian intellectual traditions that played important roles in determining values. Modern secular accounts of values have profoundly shaped these conversations, including the capitalism of Adam Smith, the democratic ideals of Thomas Jefferson, the utilitarianism of Jeremy Bentham and John Stuart Mill, the socialism of Karl Marx, the skepticism of Friedrich Nietzsche, the social Darwinism of Herbert Spencer, and the pragmatism of John Dewey. Moreover, more recent notions of economic value in the twentieth century have challenged traditional Christian understandings of value judgments. The economist Gary Becker has argued that values are fully explained by utilizing the economic notions of market equilibrium, stable preferences, and the maximization of behavior (Becker 1–14). Such economic accounts of values and value judgments have shaped modern society pervasively and profoundly.

Sociological interpretations of economic well-being (including technological change, improving health and life expectancy, rising incomes, rising educational levels, etc.) also have illuminated significantly both values formation and value judgments. Indeed, improvements in socioeconomic conditions have been linked to a shift from premodern traditional values to the values of industrialized societies that emphasize personal choice, freedom of personal expression, and the democratization of society. Longitudinal data presented in the World Values Survey sheds significant light on contemporary understandings of values and value judgments in light of religious affiliation, economic and social development (or underdevelopment), gender, country of origin, race, and so on (Inglehart and Welzel 135–48).

Finally, evolutionary and naturalistic accounts of value judgments enlighten both the universal nature of certain values (e.g., disgust for "foul" or "foreign" objects) and the progression of certain values (e.g., attitudes toward slavery [Hauser 406, 421]). Likewise, quantitative approaches to value judgments have proved remarkably important in understanding how humans process and form values. Quantitative testing can illuminate the highly subjective nature of value judgments, the cognitive biases that plague the formation and articulation of values, and the universal value codes seemingly present in all human societies (Kahneman and Tversky; Hauser 2–15).

Philosophical Distinctions in Values and Value Judgments

Philosophical qualifications of values and value judgments are important here. Philosophical monism argues that only one supreme value exists. This might refer to a singular ethical or religious approach supplying value or to one supreme value within a system of ethics. Philosophical pluralism, in contrast, argues that multiple values exist. A pluralistic approach might contend that many value systems exist, or that multiple values emerge within a particular ethical system.

Values can also be described as universal (applicable and discernible everywhere) or relative (dependent on cultural or historical realities). Important arguments here on the relativity of values have framed many seminal philosophical exchanges. Other important distinctions in value theory include notions of intrinsic value (things or persons having value "in themselves") and extrinsic value (value as derivative from something else). Moreover, when two values cannot be compared using a common framework, they are described as incommensurable. For example, the values of fidelity and equality might be incommensurable if no common standard exists for measuring these (Rolston 98–102, 111–15, 151, 186–89).

Value judgments, then, include the act of putting values to work. Value judgments can be epistemic, aesthetic, prudential, moral/ethical, religious, and so forth. A value judgment is a determination of worth and can be clarified by a rigorous examination of the hierarchy of values that emerges as humans affix importance to objects, states of being, humans, and so on. Value judgments may conflict. Thus, a mechanism for sorting and assigning a hierarchy of values is helpful to provide coherence (Rolston 186–87).

See also Comparative Religious Ethics; Cross-Cultural Ethics; Deontological Theories of Ethics; Natural Law

Bibliography

Becker, G. *The Economic Approach to Human Behavior*. University of Chicago Press, 1976; Cahill, L. *Family: A Christian Social Perspective*. Fortress, 2000; Dalai Lama. *The Essential Dalai Lama: His Important Teachings*. Ed. R. Mehrotra. Penguin Books, 2006; Fletcher, J. *Situation Ethics: The New Morality*. Westminster, 1966; Gutiérrez, G. *The Power of the Poor in History*. SCM, 1979; Hauerwas, S. *The Peaceable Kingdom: A Primer in Christian Ethics*. University of Notre Dame Press, 1983; Hauser, M. *Moral Minds: How Nature Designed Our Universal Sense of Right and Wrong*. Ecco, 2006; Hays, R. *The Moral Vision of the New Testament: Community, Cross, and New Creation; A Contemporary Introduction to New Testament Ethics*. HarperSanFrancisco, 1996; Inglehart, R., and C. Welzel. *Modernization, Cultural Change, and Democracy: The Human Development Sequence*. Cambridge University Press, 2005; John Paul II. *The Splendor of Truth: Veritatis Splendor, Encyclical Letter*. United States Conference of Catholic Bishops, 1993; Kahneman, D., and A. Tversky. "Choices, Values, and Frames." Pages 1–16 in *Choices, Values, and Frames*, ed. D. Kahneman and A. Tversky. Cambridge University Press, 2000; Moore, G. *Principia Ethica*. Ed. T. Baldwin. Rev. ed. Cambridge University Press, 1993; Mouw, R. "Biblical Imperatives." Pages 31–33 in *From Christ to the World: Introductory Readings in Christian Ethics*, ed. W. Bolton, T. Kennedy, and A. Verhey. Eerdmans, 1994; Niebuhr, H. "The Center of Value." Pages 100–113 in *Radical Monotheism and Western Culture: With Supplementary Essays*, ed. J. Gustafson. Westminster John Knox, 1970; Rolston, H. *Environmental Ethics: Duties to and Values in the Natural World*. Temple University Press, 1988; Ruether, R. *Sexism and God-Talk: Toward a Feminist Theology*. Beacon Press, 1983; Suchocki, M. *The End of Evil: Process Eschatology in Historical Context*. State University of New York Press, 1988; Vanhoozer, K. *Is There a Meaning in This Text? The Bible, the Reader, and the Morality of Literary Knowledge*. Zondervan, 1998; Yoder, J. *When War Is Unjust: Being Honest in Just-War Thinking*. Augsburg, 1984.

Daniel E. McFee

Vegetarianism

The term *vegetarianism* was not coined until the nineteenth century, but as a practice, vegetarianism was widespread in the ancient world. The Greek philosopher Pythagoras, who lived in the sixth century BCE, is thought to have been the first Western vegetarian, and esoteric groups associated with his name carried on this dietary practice well into the first several centuries of the Christian era. Several church fathers, including Tertullian and Clement of Alexandria, not only referred to the Pythagorean diet but also developed a Christian version of vegetarianism as an alternative to it.

Church fathers who defended a plant-based diet did so on several grounds. First, they were indebted to Greek medical philosophy that attributed sexual and physical aggression to the consumption of meat, especially the blood in meat. Second, they argued that Adam and Eve were vegetarians in the garden of Eden, since the animals were tame and there was no violence in paradise (Gen. 1:30). Third, they argued that God granted permission for humans to eat meat only after the flood, when Noah and his descendants had to eat animals out of necessity (Gen. 9:1–4). Moreover, this permission was an accommodation to the fallen state of humankind. Fourth, they argued that the Jewish dietary law was evidence of a compromise between the peaceful diet of the garden of Eden and the gluttonous and cruel diet of the fall. Fifth, they argued that the council at Jerusalem, at which Paul and Peter divided their missionary responsibilities, kept in place the ban on consuming blood that was central to the Jewish diet (Acts 15:19–21). Sixth, and finally, they argued that the kingdom that God promised for the end times would include harmonious relations between people and animals, thus implying that vegetarianism was an appropriate way to anticipate the eschaton (Isa. 11:6–9).

Remarkably, all of these arguments were submerged in church history only to reappear in the nineteenth century, when many Christian groups rediscovered vegetarianism and began promoting it for both theological and medical reasons. The modern case for vegetarianism is, thus, rooted in the earliest Christian theologians.

Vegetarianism was never required as the daily diet for believers in the early church for a variety of reasons. First, it was associated with dualistic heretical groups such as gnostics and the Manichaeans. These groups identified the eating of meat with the consumption of fallen spirits embedded in animals, and they treated a plant-based diet as a work of merit necessary for the cleansing of the soul. They also were influenced by Eastern versions of reincarnation, which might have been one of the rationales behind Pythagoras's version of vegetarianism. Second, the early church was trying to distance itself from the more legalistic aspects of the Jewish tradition and, as a missionary movement, was not interested in erecting new barriers to fellowship. Third, many theologians argued that Jesus intended to free his followers from the more cumbersome aspects of Jewish legislation.

Nevertheless, vegetarianism remained as a sign of holiness, as demonstrated by two features of early Christianity. First, the church expected believers to fast on Fridays, a practice that slowly permitted the consumption of fish but no other animal flesh. The church also required a meatless diet for the period of Lent. Second, vegetarianism became the common diet of monasticism, with Benedict requiring it for monks in his rule, with the exception of the elderly and the ill.

See also Asceticism

Bibliography

Hobgood-Oster, L. *Holy Dogs and Asses: Animals in the Christian Tradition*. University of Illinois Press, 2008; Linzey, A. *Animal Theology*. University of Illinois Press, 1995; Webb, S. *Good Eating*. Brazos, 2001; Young, R. *Is God a Vegetarian? Christianity, Vegetarianism, and Animal Rights*. Open Court, 1999.

Stephen H. Webb

Vice

The concept of vice is best elucidated with reference to the concepts of virtue and sin. The most prominent accounts of virtue in the history of Christian ethics have roots in Platonic, Aristotelian, and Stoic thought. According to these schools, a virtue (Gk. *aretē*; Lat. *virtus*) is a good habit of the soul that is acquired over time as one seeks to respond well to the circumstances of life. It is an interior state that disposes one to think, feel, and act in ways that exhibit good human functioning. Ancient philosophers analyze vice in less detail than they do virtue. Vice (Gk. *mochthēria* or *kakia*; Lat. *vitium*) is generally conceived as virtue's contrary, as a bad habit of the soul. It is a habit that disposes one to think, feel, and act in disordered and dysfunctional ways. Whereas virtue is caused directly by choosing to respond to situations in ways that one judges to be fine, vice is usually caused less directly by consenting to weaknesses and failures within the self. A vice is typically caused by repeatedly avoiding moral knowledge, failing to recollect and apply the knowledge one has, or applying it in a self-deceived and self-serving manner because one is motivated by appetites or emotions that are not governed by reason.

Ancient philosophers reveal that vice is self-defeating. When one is in the grip of a vice, one behaves in ways that are contrary to the laws of nature, most notably the laws of human nature, which determine what is and is not possible for humans and what is necessary for human flourishing. One fails to serve as one's own master, and one becomes, instead, a slave to objects outside oneself and to the desires and pleasures that these objects evoke. Medical metaphors are prevalent in this ethical literature. Under the influence of a vice, one's soul becomes sick. The moral philosopher is imaged as a physician whose role is to heal the sick soul, or to help the soul heal itself, through the application of prescribed rational therapies, including critical reflection on what is most important in life.

In Christian ethics, as in Greco-Roman philosophical ethics, vice is conceived relative to virtue. It is conceived also relative to sin. A sin is an act that violates the law of reason, the law of God, or both. The repetition of a sinful act leads predictably to a vice, but a vice is more than a disposition to act badly; it is an interior state that can involve the corruption of every aspect of one's moral agency. Augustine and Thomas Aquinas have contributed much to Christian thinking about virtue and vice. For Augustine, a virtue is a form of well-ordered love. It is a tendency, made possible by the indwelling of the Holy Spirit, to adhere to God as one's highest good. It is a tendency also to interact with finite goods only as required to help oneself and others to love God. A vice, by contrast, is a form of disordered love. It is a tendency to occupy oneself with attractions of the temporal order and thereby to become conformed to this world. It is a tendency to be subject to things that one ought, through the power of reason and the grace of God, to make subject to oneself (see Augustine, chaps. 11–15).

For Thomas Aquinas, a virtue is a habit of excellent human operation. Some virtues, acquired through the exercise of natural human powers, orient one to function in ways that contribute to natural happiness or flourishing. Other virtues, infused or inspired by God, orient one toward a higher, supernatural happiness or flourishing; they extend the powers of one's moral agency in ways that allow one to participate more fully in the life of God. Acquired and infused virtues both orient one to think, feel, and act in accordance with the law of reason, which reflects the eternal law, the governing principle of the universe. Infused virtues also dispose one to operate in accordance with laws revealed in Scripture, most notably the law of love. Vices, however, are acquired habits that dispose one to function poorly, in ways that are contrary to one's true nature, contrary to right reason, contrary to the revealed laws of God, and thus contrary to the well-being of oneself and others, in this life and in the life to come. Following Pope Gregory I, Thomas identifies seven principal vices: pride, envy, anger, sloth, greed, gluttony, and lust (*ST* II-I, q. 55; qq. 62–63; q. 71; q. 84, a. 4).

Augustine, Thomas Aquinas, and other thinkers of the Christian tradition are informed not only by philosophy but also by the Bible. Biblical images or metaphors highlight the personal and social degradation associated with vice. One image involves a tree and its fruit, which calls to mind the story in which Adam and Eve eat of the forbidden fruit in the garden of Eden (Gen. 3). This choice of the first humans leads not only to their expulsion from paradise but also to the degeneration of the human race. In the prophetic literature, the image of the tree and its fruit functions in a different, but related, way. Hosea, for example, says that Israel was intended to become a grapevine or a fig tree that bore good and bountiful fruit, but it became instead a barren vine with dried-up roots (Hos. 9:10–17). The people of God had loved what was lifeless, and they had become what they loved. Similarly, Jeremiah says that God planted Israel as a choice vine, but the people had turned their backs on God. In pursuing what was worthless, their lives had become worthless (Jer. 2:5, 20–23). Unless they turned their faces toward God, they would be incapable of life-affirming attitudes and actions.

Agricultural imagery appears in the NT as well. Even before Jesus begins his ministry proper, John the Baptist warns the crowds that an ax stands ready to cut down trees that do not bear fruit (Matt. 3:10; Luke 3:9), a position echoed later by Jesus (Luke 13:5–9). In the Gospel of John, Jesus claims that he is the true vine, and only branches that grow from him will be well cultivated and productive of good fruit (John 15:1–8). In Matthew and Luke, Jesus warns that bad trees can be expected to bear bad fruit (Matt. 7:15–20; 12:33; Luke 6:43–45). In much the same way, bad hearts—those with misplaced attachments or allegiances (Matt. 6:19–20; Luke 12:33–34)—can be expected to yield bad behavior.

Another biblical metaphor for vice concerns servitude or slavery. New Testament literature identifies the problem of spiritual slavery and proclaims Jesus' role as lord and liberator. The image of Jesus as liberator is particularly important for Matthew, who draws subtle parallels to the Torah to help his audience understand Jesus as a new Moses who has come to set them free from their slavery to sin (Matt. 5–7). New Testament writings explain that one can be a slave either to God or to things of this world, but not to both (Matt. 6:24; Luke 16:13; Rom. 6:16–22). Anyone who submits to the power of money or sensory pleasure rather than to the power of God becomes trapped by that choice. One's desires and pleasures become disordered; they distort perceptions, condition reasoning, and lead to the commission of the same error again and again. Paul explains to the gentiles in Rome that they, like others, have had access to the truth of life from the beginning, but they have disregarded it (Rom. 1:18–32). They have turned away from God and toward idols, and God has let them suffer the natural consequence of their choice, which is to become enslaved to their passions.

Paul distinguishes between slavery to Christ and slavery to the elemental powers of the universe (Gal. 4:1–7). Whereas slaves to Christ live according to the Spirit and produce life-giving fruits (Gal. 5:22–24), slaves to the other powers live according to the flesh and produce death-bearing works (Gal. 5:19–21). Probing the moral psychology of vice, Paul suggests that vice is the product of interior conflict and weakness of will: "I can will what is right," he says, "but I cannot do it. For I do not do the good I want, but the evil I do not want is what I do. Now if I do what I do not want, it is no longer I that do it, but sin that dwells within me" (Rom. 7:18–20). As one becomes more accustomed to vice, one cares less about doing what is right; one simply surrenders to one's strongest impulses.

Finally, the Gospels depict Jesus not only as a lord whom the people are to serve and a savior who sets them free but also as a healer. Jesus heals diseases and disabilities of all kinds (Matt. 15:30–31). He casts out evil spirits (Matt. 8:28–34; Mark 5:1–20; Luke 8:26–39). He brings the dead back to life (John 11:1–44). He depicts tax collectors and other sinners as sick people, and himself as their physician (Matt. 9:10–12; Mark 2:15–17; Luke 5:29–31). With such passages in mind, we could describe a vice as a habit that weakens certain powers of the soul, causing a loss of moral function. It could be described as a spirit-possession in which destructive appetites take over the self and undermine one's ability to pursue and enjoy what is good. It could be characterized as a state of spiritual deadening or darkness, for anyone who becomes attached to objects that turn out to be harmful, yet feels powerless to overcome these attachments, can fall into despair. Christian ethics can appeal to stories of miraculous healing to dramatize not only the debilitation of vice but also the idea that persons who succumb to vice must rely on a power greater than themselves to return them to a state of well-being.

See also Character; Evil; Habit; Idolatry; Moral Psychology; Seven Deadly Sins; Sin; Vices and Virtues, Lists of; Virtue(s)

Bibliography

Augustine. *The Catholic and Manicheaean Ways of Life*. Trans. D. Gallagher and I. Gallagher. Catholic University of America Press, 1966; Cicero. *Tusculan Disputations*. Trans. J. E. King. Rev. ed. LCL. Harvard University Press, 1945; Nussbaum, M. *The Therapy of Desire: Theory and Practice in Hellenistic Ethics*. Princeton University Press, 1994; Seneca. *Moral Essays*. Vols. 1–2. Trans. J. Basore. Harvard University Press, 1985–90.

Diana Fritz Cates and Jordan Smith

Vices and Virtues, Lists of

Vice and virtue lists refer to the ancient literary form, adapted by biblical writers, in which authors group together dispositions and/or actions to be avoided or embraced. Thus, when the apostle Paul describes the "fruit of the Spirit" as "love, joy, peace, patience, kindness, generosity, faithfulness, gentleness, and self-control" (Gal. 5:22–23), this catalog of virtues fits broadly within an established literary form in the Greco-Roman world.

Context

To the extent that any religion or philosophical system focuses on the cultivation of praiseworthy deeds and the avoidance of immoral actions, inventories of acceptable and unacceptable behavior are customary. Antecedents for and parallels to the biblical vice and virtue lists are found in numerous ancient sources. In the Greco-Roman world in particular, a rich tradition of philosophical reflection on the nature and demonstration of virtue (*aretē*) is the context for the development of the distinct literary form of the virtue and/or vice list. Plato's famous classification of the four cardinal virtues (*aretai*) as wisdom (*phronēsis*), temperance (*sōphrosynē*), justice (*dikaiosynē*), and courage (*andreia*) set the stage for a converse listing of four vices in Hellenistic philosophical writings, particularly in the Stoic tradition (e.g., Plato, *Resp.* 4.427–445). These cardinal vices are typically identified as folly (*aphrosynē*), licentiousness (*akolasia*), injustice (*adikia*), and cowardice (*deilia*), although the fourfold scheme of virtues and vices frequently is divided and expanded. Lists of virtues and vices can run into the dozens and even hundreds (see Aristotle, *Virtues and Vices*; Cicero, *Tusc.* 4.11–38; Diogenes Laertius, *Lives* 7.54). In the Hellenistic world, therefore, virtue and vice catalogs emerged as a literary form that played an important role in moral exhortation and instruction.

Numerous writings from ancient Israel emphasize sin and obedience, yet no precise examples of the fixed literary form of Hellenistic virtue and vice lists are found in the OT. Prophetic denunciations of Judah and Israel's disobedience in Jer. 7:9 and Hos. 4:1–2 do itemize transgressions against the Decalogue (cf. Prov. 6:16–19; 8:13), but these are catalogs of sinful behavior against the Decalogue and not reflections on virtue and vice as character traits. In Jewish literature of the Second Temple period, however, catalogs of virtue and vice become increasingly common, reflecting the influence of Hellenistic thought and literary patterns on Jewish authors (see, e.g., Wis. 8:7; 14:22–27; 4 Macc. 1:2–4; 5:23–24; *T. Reu.* 3.3–8; *T. Levi.* 17.11; Philo, *Sacrifices* 20–33; *Alleg. Interp.* 1.86–87). Related to the virtue and vice lists, though not identical to the literary form, is the "two ways" motif that emphasized the sharp division between the way of life and the way of death (see Deut. 30:19; Prov. 2:12–15; Jer. 21:8; Sir. 21:10; 1QS 3.13–4.26; *Did.* 1–6; *Barn.* 18–21).

Biblical Vice and Virtue Lists

Formal vice and virtue lists are found throughout the NT, sometimes in polysyndetic form (i.e., repetition of a conjunction [1 Cor. 6:9–10]) and sometimes in asyndetic form (i.e., no conjunction [Gal. 5:22–23]). Although some would include more and some fewer passages, the following texts generally are seen as representatives of this literary form in the NT:

Virtue Lists: 2 Cor. 6:6–7a; Gal. 5:22–23; Eph. 4:2–3, 31–5:2, 9; Phil. 4:8; Col. 3:12; 1 Tim. 3:2–4, 8–10, 11–12; 4:12; 6:11, 18; 2 Tim. 2:22–25; 3:10; Titus 1:8; 2:2–10; Heb. 7:26; 1 Pet. 3:8; 2 Pet. 1:5–7 (cf. Matt. 5:3–11; 1 Cor. 13:4–7; Jas. 3:17)

Vice Lists: Matt. 15:19; Mark 7:21–22; Luke 18:11; Rom. 1:29–31; 13:13; 1 Cor. 5:10–11; 6:9–10; 2 Cor. 12:20–21; Gal. 5:19–21; Eph. 4:31; 5:3–5; Col. 3:5–9; 1 Tim. 1:9–10; 6:4–5; 2 Tim. 3:2–4; Titus 1:7; 3:3; 1 Pet. 2:1; 4:3, 15; Rev. 9:21; 21:8; 22:15 (cf. Luke 18:11)

These ethical catalogs perform a variety of rhetorical functions in the NT writings. Some vice lists highlight the depravity of humanity in general (Matt. 15:19; Mark 7:21–22; Rom. 1:29–31; 1 Tim. 1:9–10), while others emphasize or establish ethical boundaries between inheritors of the kingdom of God and "the immoral of this world," as Paul puts it in 1 Cor 5:10–11 (cf. Rom. 13:13; 1 Cor. 6:9–10; Eph. 5:3–5; Col. 3:5–9; 1 Pet. 4:3, 15). Several ethical lists serve to encourage virtuous behavior by exhorting readers to exhibit certain general qualities (Phil. 4:8; 1 Pet. 2:1; 3:8) or by reminding believers of the characteristics of their old lives in contrast to the new existence that they have in Christ (2 Cor. 12:20–21; Gal. 5:19–23; Eph. 4:31; Col. 3:12; Titus 3:3; 2 Pet. 1:5–7). Thus, the call to "clothe yourselves with compassion, kindness, humility, meekness, and patience" (Col. 3:12b) is immediately preceded by a reminder of the new identity that God's chosen saints have received in Christ (Col. 3:11–12a). Particularly in the Pastoral Epistles, which contain the highest concentration of ethical lists in the NT, the focus of virtue and vice catalogs is on identifying qualities appropriate for ecclesiastical leaders (1 Tim. 3:1–12; 4:12; 6:11, 18–19; 2 Tim. 2:22–25; 3:10; Titus 1:7; 2:2–10 [cf. 2 Cor. 6:6–7a]) while at the same time denouncing as immoral the false teachers who are opposed in the letters (1 Tim. 6:3–5; 2 Tim. 3:2–4 [cf. Rev. 9:21; 21:8; 22:15]). The virtue list in Heb. 7:26 ("For it was fitting that we should have such a high priest, holy, blameless, undefiled, separated from sinners, and exalted above the heavens") is distinctive in that it is primarily christological in nature.

The biblical vice lists, combined with the continuing influence of Platonic and Aristotelian philosophical reflection on the nature of virtue and vice, led to fertile contemplation of virtue and vice among Christian writers of the patristic and medieval periods. Augustine (354–430), for example, emulated his teacher Ambrose (339–97) in adding to the four cardinal virtues in pagan thought (wisdom, temperance, justice, courage) three distinctively theological virtues taken from 1 Cor. 13:13: faith, hope, and love (see *Mor. eccl.* 15.25; cf. 1 Thess. 1:3; 5:8). For Augustine, the four classical virtues of Greek philosophy are simply expressions of the highest Christian virtue, namely, love. The Christian tradition of the "seven deadly sins," well represented in Chaucer's *Parson's Tale*, has its origins in pastoral considerations of vice offered by writers such as John Cassian (ca. 360–435) and Pope Gregory the Great (ca. 540–604). In the modern period, an emphasis on natural law within Catholic theology and the rejection of the stress on virtue among nineteenth-century liberal Protestantism by Karl Barth and other neoorthodox theologians led to a turn away from virtue as a key theme of Christian ethics. Yet, with a renewed awareness of virtue ethics among Protestant theologians after Alasdair MacIntyre's groundbreaking work and in response to Stanley Hauerwas's ethical proposals, and with an increased interest in integrating Scripture more deeply into the rich tradition of moral theology among Catholics (especially after Vatican II's *Optatam totius* 16), the virtue and vice lists in the NT, along with the philosophical strands on which they draw, should once again spark reflection on the importance of character in the formation of Christian communities.

See also Cardinal Virtues; Faith; Fruit of the Spirit; Seven Deadly Sins; Sin; Vice; Virtue Ethics; Virtue(s)

Bibliography

Aune, D. *The New Testament in Its Literary Environment*. Westminster, 1987; Charles, J. *Virtue amidst Vice: The Catalog of Virtues in 2 Peter 1*. JSNTSup 150. Sheffield Academic Press, 1997; Colish, M. *The Stoic Tradition from Antiquity to the Early Middle Ages*. 2 vols. SHCT 34–35. Brill, 1990; Harrington, D., and J. Keenan. *Jesus and Virtue Ethics: Building Bridges between New Testament Studies and Moral Theology*. Sheed & Ward, 2002; MacIntyre, A. *After Virtue: A Study in Moral Theory*. 3rd ed. University of Notre Dame Press, 2007; McEleney, N. "The Vice Lists of the Pastoral Epistles." *CBQ* 36 (1974): 203–19.

David J. Downs

Violence

Although definitions of violence are controversial, a provisional definition is "a forceful action that intends to cause unwanted injury to another." This definition is tight enough to exclude some events (a fierce storm, a forceful collision in a football game) while including others (both physical and psychological actions that injure others, violence against nonhumans) and remaining silent on still others (a failed assassination attempt—must an act be successful to be violent?).

Scripture describes a wide range of violent actions beginning with Cain killing Abel (Gen. 4) and ending with the judgment of the dead (Rev. 20). These actions are bookended by visions of a peaceable kingdom: the garden of Eden before sin and the new Jerusalem after the final judgment. Between beginning and ending, violence is sometimes commanded, sometimes permitted, sometimes discouraged, sometimes prohibited, and sometimes absorbed. In general, violence is far less accepted in the NT than in the OT, but as with all generalizations, this one does not hold in all instances. For example, in the NT soldiers are commended, Jesus expels vendors from the temple, Ananias and Sapphira die as a result of their attempt to deceive Peter, and violent judgment is repeatedly threatened.

Given the OT's long history and range of characters and events, it is no surprise that it speaks with many voices about violence. God acts violently and calls Israel to do so as well, but God also calls for restraint. David is a man of God and a soldier, but because of the blood on David's hands, God refuses to allow him to build the temple. Jeremiah prophesies violence, and Isaiah prophesies the peaceable kingdom. Building a consistent ethic about violence or nonviolence from OT texts would involve an unsupportable degree of selectivity.

Whether one can build a compelling argument that the NT ethic forbids violence is still a point of debate within Christian ethics. At the very least, there is a strong presumption against violence that not only grows out of Jesus' and Paul's teachings (e.g., Matt. 5; Rom. 12–13) but also is evinced by Jesus' actions, especially leading up to and including his crucifixion, and by the actions of members of the early church, such as Stephen, who endured martyrdom.

As the church became more established, especially after Christianity became a legal religion in the Roman Empire, its theological interpretations of violence and nonviolence grew in complexity. Would not the same arguments about love of neighbor that led Christians to help others lead them to get involved if those others were being attacked? Would not the commandment in Rom. 13:1 that Christians be subject to governing authorities lead them to serve those authorities if necessary, including as members of the military? The church developed increasingly intricate arguments about when violence was justified and when it was not: it is justified in defense of another but not in self-defense; justified if motivated by love but not if motivated by anger or bloodlust; justified if decreed by a ruler but not if pursued for personal reasons; justified for soldiers but not for priests. As these justifications developed, the arguments for and against such justifications developed as well. Fourth-century monastics, medieval Franciscans, participants in the radical Reformation, and present-day peace churches have all developed theological arguments against the use of violence.

In the face of nuclear weapons, terrorism, and genocide, among other horrors, there has been a renewed interest in questions about whether and when violence can be justified. Moreover, the past several decades have seen a growing interest in the relation between religion and violence. Some (e.g., Regina Schwartz) have theorized a tendency toward violence among monotheistic religions; others (e.g., Sudhir Kakar) argue that religions promote in-group identities that make violence toward outsiders more likely. Some (e.g., Bruce Lincoln, Mark Juergensmeyer) argue that religious reasoning used to defend otherwise immoral actions has a "force multiplier" effect: religious violence is more acceptable and its magnitude is greater; still others (e.g., Rene Girard) have argued that religion, or rather a particular understanding of Christianity, reveals and thereby counteracts universal and subconscious tendencies for violence.

See also Abuse; Anabaptist Ethics; Capital Punishment; Cruelty; Enemy, Enemy Love; Force, Use of; Genocide; Government; Holy War; Just-Peacemaking Theory; Just-War Theory; Killing; Military Service; Murder; Pacifism; Rape; Sin; Terrorism; Torture; War

Bibliography

Arendt, H. *On Violence*. Harcourt, Brace & World, 1970; Ellul, J. *Violence: Reflections from a Christian Perspective*. Seabury, 1969; Hauerwas, S. *The Peaceable Kingdom: A Primer in Christian Ethics*. University of Notre Dame Press, 1983; Holmes, R. *On War and Morality*. Princeton University Press, 1989; King, M. L., Jr. *A Testament of Hope: The Essential Writings and Speeches of Martin Luther King, Jr.* Ed. J. Washington. Harper & Row, 1986; Niebuhr, R. *Love and Justice: Selections from the Shorter Writings of Reinhold Niebuhr*. Ed. D. Robertson. Westminster John Knox, 1992; Ramsey, P. *The Just War: Force and Political Responsibility*. Littlefield, Adams, 1983; Yoder, J. *The Politics of Jesus: Vicit Agnus Noster*. 2nd ed. Eerdmans, 1994.

Mark Douglas

Virginity

The OT contains no explicit discussions of virginity. Whether specific Hebrew terms denote "virgin" or "virginity" is debated. Gordon Wenham's argument that the Hebrew term *bĕtûlâ*, traditionally translated as "virgin," means "girl of marriageable age" is increasingly accepted. Old Testament views of virginity must be inferred from its narratives, poetry, and laws.

The OT depicts human sexuality as integral to God's good creation, divinely given that humankind might be "fruitful and multiply" (Gen. 1:28), and that persons need not "be alone" (Gen. 2:18). Asceticism, particularly lifelong virginity, is foreign to the OT. The ancient texts do recognize that sexual desire is a powerful force, with the potential to fracture familial, social, national, and even cosmic bonds; numerous biblical laws seek to channel sexuality within the family (Frymer-Kensky, "Virginity"). Given the patriarchal structure of ancient Israel, sexual restraint takes the form of male control of female sexuality.

Virginity was both expected and valued in girls prior to marriage (e.g., Gen. 24:16). Deuteronomy 22:20–21 mandates death for a bride whose family fraudulently claimed that she was a virgin. The amount of a bride-price that a groom paid to a girl's family apparently depended on her virginity (Exod. 22:17). Male control of women's sexuality was a matter of honor as well as economics (e.g., Gen. 34:31). Priestly legislation reflects yet another set of concerns; laws regulating whom priests and high priests may marry (Lev. 21:7, 13–14) treat virginity as a matter of purity and pollution.

The NT contains few references to virginity. The Greek term *parthenos*, like the Hebrew *bĕtûlâ*, is ambiguous, referring to a girl's age more than stressing her lack of sexual experience. Presumably, the NT authors assume that young women should remain virgins until they marry. The writers do not extol virginity as a lifelong state. Portrayals of Mary's virginity at the time of Jesus' birth have to do with the miraculous nature of his conception and his divine nature rather than with Mary's purity (Matt. 1:18–25; Luke 1:26–35). Paul's recommendation to remain unmarried (1 Cor. 7:36–38) relates to his conviction that Jesus' return is imminent.

Reflection on the contemporary ethical significance of the relatively scarce biblical references to virginity belongs within the broader discussion of sexual ethics and will vary, depending on one's views of the Bible, of biblical authority, and of how Scripture relates to other sources. However, such reflection should take account of the wide gap between modern and biblical cultures, including the patriarchal nature of Israelite and early Christian families, the youth of Israelite and early Christian girls at the time of their first marriages, and, in the case of the NT, the expectation of Jesus' imminent return. At the same time, ethical reflection will benefit from biblical insights that sexuality is God's good gift, and that faithfulness has to do with all spheres of life, including sex.

See also Celibacy; Sex and Sexuality; Sexual Ethics

Bibliography

Frymer-Kensky, T. "Law and Philosophy: The Case of Sex in the Bible." Pages 3–16 in *Jewish Explorations of Sexuality*, ed. J. Magonet. Berghahn Books, 1995; idem. "Virginity in the Bible." Pages 79–96 in *Gender and Law in the Hebrew Bible and the Ancient Near East*, by V. Matthews, B. Levinson, and T. Frymer-Kensky. JSOTSup 262. Sheffield Academic Press, 1998; Nelson, J., and S. Longfellow. *Sexuality and the Sacred: Sources for Theological Reflection*. Westminster John Knox, 1994; Wenham, G. "Betûlah, 'A Girl of Marriageable Age.'" *VT* 22 (1972): 326–48.

Carolyn Pressler

Virtue(s)

In recent decades, Christian ethicists have retrieved the tradition of virtue and the virtues that were somewhat present in the early church, central in the medieval church, and somewhat neglected during the time of the Protestant Reformation and modernity. Within biblical studies, this retrieval is beginning to have some impact but is still in its early stage. Some of the Christian ethicists leading the recovery of the virtue tradition are reading Scripture more attentively, and this promises further cross-fertilization between Christian ethics and biblical studies.

The recovery of the virtue tradition may sometimes be framed as the development of "virtue ethics," but great care must be taken with this language, because the virtue tradition does not merely add something called "virtue" to the work of Christian ethics. Rather, the virtue tradition reconceives "Christian ethics" to be concerned with our whole way of life as participation in and witness to the gospel.

The virtue tradition comes to us as a contested tradition with many disputes that may illuminate the work of Christian ethics even though they are unresolved. For example, what counts as a virtue? What is the relationship between virtue and the virtues? Can one be truly virtuous without having all the virtues? What is the purpose or telos of a human being that determines what counts as virtue? Which community defines purpose and virtue? What must a community be and how must it live in order to embody its conviction about the human telos and to form people who are virtuous?

Are the virtues unified? Is it always possible for people to act virtuously? If we fail to act virtuously, is it due to weakness on our part? Is it due to a failure of vision, an inability to see what we are to do? Or are there some (tragic) circumstances in which it is simply not possible to act virtuously, to do the good? Should Christians understand the virtues to be produced by an infusion of grace that transforms something already present within us or an impartation to us of something from the outside?

The word *virtue* translates the Greek *aretē*, which generally denotes excellence that comes from a thing fulfilling its purpose. Thus, a carpenter's hammer has *aretē*—excellence or "virtue"—when it fulfills its purpose in driving or pulling nails. In regard to humans, to have virtue is to live well as a human being. Virtue, in Christian understanding, is coming to the full maturity for which God made us and redeemed us in Christ.

The recovery of the virtue tradition has been driven in philosophy largely by the work of Alasdair MacIntyre. The seminal text is his *After Virtue*, which works within an Aristotelian virtue tradition. In his later book *Whose Justice? Which Rationality?* MacIntyre returns to Christian faith and locates virtue in the Thomist tradition. In theology, Stanley Hauerwas (Methodist) has been a driving force in the recovery of the virtue tradition, beginning with *Character and the Christian Life* and developed in numerous essays and collections. He is joined in this work by theological ethicists such as Gilbert Meilaender (Lutheran) and Jean Porter (Roman Catholic).

In the virtue tradition, the virtues describe a perduring way of life that characterizes our actions and our disposition. For example, persons marked by the virtue of truthfulness not only tell the truth but they are also disposed toward the truth, coming even to cherish the truth and truthfulness. They are truthful not out of duty, obedience to a rule, or conformity to social norms; they are truthful because through habituation they have become truthful people or, to put it biblically, because through conformity to Christ they have come to be in the truth and thus they know, love, and act truthfully.

Recent theological development of the virtue tradition draws a number of insights from MacIntyre that illuminate the work of theological ethics and the teaching of Scripture. If we understand the insights of the virtue tradition, then we will know that we are doomed to misunderstanding if we attempt an account of virtue and the virtues apart from all the elements of the tradition. More egregiously, we are doomed to moral frustration and failure if we seek to become virtuous apart from these other realities.

Perhaps the central insight in the virtue tradition is its teleological character. Teleology may be used in a number of ways in ethics. In the virtue tradition, telos identifies the purpose or end for which we are made. This telos may be conceived in different ways. Plato, Aristotle, Augustine, and Thomas Aquinas all give different accounts, but in the midst of these different accounts they all have the same understanding of the shape of living. They agree that whatever our telos is, it is given to us and in turn gives shape and meaning to our lives. Our telos is not something that we choose or create; rather, it is given to us, it is our destiny. Either we submit to our destiny and become fully human, or we rebel against our destiny, our telos, and become something other than fully human.

In the virtue tradition, a telos gives us a vision of who we are meant to be. Our way of life, our morality, carries us to where we are meant to be from where we presently are. For Christians, our telos may be identified as "the vision of God" by some theologians and as "conformity to Christ" by others. These and other Christian descriptions of our telos do not necessarily conflict with one another. What they give us, even in their diversity, is a vision of who we are created to be. Knowing ourselves as people saved by grace, we identify the life of discipleship as the way by which we participate now in our telos, which will be fulfilled through Christ's return, when "we will be like him, for we will see him as he is" (1 John 3:2); when we will know fully, even as we are known fully (1 Cor. 13:12); when we will see God face-to-face and be made fully human. For Christians, this teleological structure is eschatological. That is, our telos is always dependent on God and our relationship to God; our telos is never something that we possess or that is "natural" to us independent of our creaturely dependence on God.

When teleological thinking becomes eschatological, then the questions are not merely who are we now, who are we meant to be, and how do we get from where we are to where we are meant to be. When we recast the questions in eschatological terms, we ask what God is doing and how we are to participate in what God is doing so that by grace we become what we are created to be.

When we think eschatologically while we read Scripture, we find ourselves in the middle of a narrative about this very journey. For the virtue tradition, the narrative is essential for two reasons. First, narrative is essential to the intelligibility of our actions. That is, our lives make sense as they are claimed by God's work of redemption. This story is not just the narrative of an individual life, but of life within the story of God's people and all creation. This does not mean that all Scripture can be reduced to narrative. There are, obviously, other genres in Scripture—law, prophecy, poetry, and so forth. As a whole, however, Scripture narrates the work of redemption, within which our lives are meaningful and which gives rise to the virtues that mark people on that journey.

For Christians, the agent of this narrative is God. We become agents when we are caught up in this story through the Holy Spirit. In theological ethics there is considerable controversy over the relationship between human agency and divine agency. Some theologians accuse others of too great an emphasis on human agency. This may easily occur if we place too great an emphasis on the development of moral agency and character that can make us independent of God's continuing grace in our lives. Others are concerned that we have not rightly elucidated the sanctifying work of the Spirit that conforms us to Christ and makes us moral agents of the gospel.

This narrative of redemption is embodied in a living tradition, which MacIntyre describes as "an historically extended, socially embodied argument" (MacIntyre, *After Virtue*, 222). For Christians, this living tradition is not only the church but more so the continuing work of redemption through Christ, in which the church is caught up and to which it bears witness. It is this continuing reality that gives meaning to virtue and to the particular virtues that constitute Christian life.

With this recognition of the living tradition, we can then identify the church as the institution or community that is called to participate in the telos of all creation. Thus, the church is an institution called into being and sustained by the agency of God for the purpose of participating in the work of redemption and being a people to glorify God and bear witness to God's redemptive work.

The church fulfills its calling as an institution when it engages in practices that both participate in this telos and form people whose virtue is conformity to Christ by the work of the Spirit. In the virtue tradition, practices are shaped by an intentionality that draws its motivation and aims from the telos of the gospel. These practices also require and strengthen the social relationships that characterize a teleological community. Finally, these practices begin with a conception of the telos and the narrative of the gospel, but as the community engages in these practices, there is a deepening of the community's understanding of the telos and the narrative in which it participates.

The theological virtues are faith, hope, and love. They are theological because they are formed in us by the grace of God. The cardinal virtues are courage, temperance, justice, and fortitude. In the theological tradition, the cardinal virtues are transformed by the theological virtues so that they enable us to participate in God's redemptive work by the power of the Holy Spirit. As the Spirit incorporates us in Christ, other virtues appropriate to this work of redemption—such as meekness, mercy, and forgiveness—are formed in us.

In Scripture, there are very few passages where "virtue" is an appropriate translation of the Hebrew or Greek, but there are many biblical passages calling us to the formation of perduring character traits through practices (or habits) directed toward a telos that participates in God's redemptive work identified by the narrative of the gospel that forms a people.

In the OT, there is no Hebrew word directly equivalent to the Greek *aretē*, and even in the Greek translation of the OT (the LXX), the word *aretē* is used only in reference to the excellence of God. Nevertheless, we may find places in the OT where the virtue tradition illuminates the teaching of the texts. Moreover, we may also find in the OT some correctives to the virtue tradition.

Many narratives in the OT provide examples of the importance of virtues for living as God calls us to live. For example, we may observe that David sinned with Bathsheba and against Uriah not because he was ignorant of adultery and murder as contrary to life, but because he lacked the character, the virtues, that would keep him faithful to what he knew. This failure contrasts sharply with his steadfast faithfulness to God in the time between his anointing as king and his ascendancy to the throne on the occasions that he had opportunity to kill Saul and did not do so.

In the psalms, we have examples of virtue in the psalmist and among God's people. The practices of praise and lament before God incorporate the psalmist and the people into the work of redemption, form their character for faithful witness, and lead them more deeply into understanding and participating in their telos.

The closest that we come to the virtue tradition in the OT is the wisdom literature, especially Proverbs. In passages such as Prov. 2:1–11, we can see the telos, practices, community, and narrative of God's redemptive work. The acquisition of wisdom, which marks one's entire character (Prov. 1:2–6), begins and ends with "the fear of the

Lord" (Prov. 1:7) and sets the virtue of prudence firmly within the life of God's people and God's redemptive work.

In the prophets, the practice of covenant-keeping is participation in God's redemptive work that forms a people who are capable of remaining steadfast because of their vision of the telos for which we have been made. The call of Mic. 6:8 to "do justice, and to love kindness, and to walk humbly with your God" powerfully encapsulates this teaching.

In the NT Gospels, the Beatitudes (Matt. 5:3–12; Luke 6:20–23) may be read as descriptions of the character traits of those who are participating in the redemptive work of Christ. So, for example, we are blessed in our spiritual poverty because it is rooted in our knowledge that our only hope of salvation is Christ, not ourselves.

In the letters of the NT we find several lists that characterize the lives of Christians. Four of these lists single out the theological virtues of faith, hope, and love (1 Cor. 13:13; Col. 1:4–5; 1 Thess. 1:3; 5:8). The other lists cover a wide range of virtues (2 Cor. 6:6; Gal. 5:22–23; Eph. 4:23, 32; 5:9; Phil. 4:8; Col. 3:12; 1 Tim. 4:12; 6:11; 2 Tim. 2:22; 3:10; Jas. 3:17; 1 Pet. 3:8; 2 Pet. 1:5–7). There is no suggestion in these passages that there is a comprehensive list that would characterize the whole of Christian living. These "virtue lists" typically are accompanied by "vice lists."

Together, these lists affirm our growing in goodness not as a path to becoming virtuous in ourselves and independent of God, but as a path to becoming more fully reconciled and more faithful in our witness to God's redemptive work that enables us to participate now in our telos and be God's people. The whole of Scripture, illuminated by insights of the virtue tradition, teaches us the necessity of eschatological vision (telos) for our formation in faithfulness and, in doing so, calls us to virtues such as patience in awaiting full redemption and humility in knowing that it is only by God's grace that we are redeemed and made fully human by conformity to Christ through the power of the Holy Spirit.

See also Character; Habit; Moral Formation; Narrative Ethics, Biblical; Narrative Ethics, Contemporary; Practices; Teleological Theories of Ethics; Vices and Virtues, Lists of; Virtue Ethics

Bibliography

Aristotle. *Nicomachean Ethics*. Trans. C. Rowe. Oxford University Press, 2002; Burridge, R. *Imitating Jesus: An Inclusive Approach to New Testament Ethics*. Eerdmans, 2007; Charles, J. *Virtue amidst Vice: The Catalog of Virtues in 2 Peter 1*. JSNTSup 150. Sheffield Academic Press, 1997; Hauerwas, S. *Character and the Christian Life: A Study in Theological Ethics*. TUMSR 3. Trinity University Press, 1975; Hauerwas, S., and C. Pinches. *Christians among the Virtues: Theological Conversations with Ancient and Modern Ethics*. University of Notre Dame Press, 1997; Kenneson, P. *Life on the Vine: Cultivating the Fruit of the Spirit in Christian Community*. InterVarsity, 1999; MacIntyre, A. *After Virtue: A Study in Moral Theory*. 2nd ed. University of Notre Dame Press, 1984; idem. *Whose Justice? Which Rationality?* University of Notre Dame Press, 1988; Meilaender, G. *The Theory and Practice of Virtue*. University of Notre Dame Press, 1984; Porter, J. *The Recovery of Virtue: The Relevance of Aquinas for Christian Ethics*. Westminster John Knox, 1990; Thomas Aquinas. *Treatise on Happiness*. Trans. J. Oesterle. University of Notre Dame Press, 1983; idem. *Treatise on the Virtues*. Trans. J. Oesterle. University of Notre Dame Press, 1984.

Jonathan R. Wilson

Virtue Ethics

Virtue ethics emphasizes the development of moral excellence in terms of character qualities called virtues. Virtues are (1) habituated dispositions involving both an affective desire for the good and the skill to both discern and act accordingly; (2) learned through practice within a tradition (i.e., a historical community with a rich account of the "good"); and (3) directed toward this tradition's particular conception of the good (making virtues "teleological"). From a Christian perspective, virtue ethics is an ethics of discipleship, which emphasizes the development of the habits, practices, and wisdom necessary to pursue the "good" exemplified by Christ. Reading Scripture is such a practice: disciples are formed by reading with more mature members of the church and thus gradually develop virtues and skilled judgment necessary to faithful interpretation.

In contrast, much contemporary ethical discourse focuses on decisions in hard cases or moral quandaries. Such ethics of decision stress defending a difficult choice by appealing to universal principles of obligation (deontological ethics) or to calculations of utility (consequentialism). In virtue ethics, the question, what kind of people ought we to be? takes priority over the question, what are we to do? Virtue ethics is more concerned with truthful description of the moral life than with the theoretical construction of a normative system. A virtues approach does not reject law or rules but suggests that the application of moral rules requires the prior cultivation of good habits and skilled reflexes (namely, virtues). Correlatively, morality is the development of character through an entire life, not simply the ability to rationally discern the right course of action on a particular occasion.

Classical Virtue

Many, if not all, premodern societies in the West assumed an ethics of virtue. The moral life was conceived in terms of the development of the attributes necessary for pursuit of the "good," the telos or purpose of life as understood within the tradition. The character of the person was expected to be shaped by and oriented toward the good of the whole. In ancient Israel, the people were called to righteousness in a joint covenant with God. But the golden age of Athens (fourth century BCE) provided the most thorough explication of "virtue."

Aristotle's *Nicomachean Ethics* defined virtues as habitual dispositions that incline the human person to act in accordance with the good. Such dispositions are acquired through the practice of acting well under the tutelage of mentors and involve a sincere desire for the good, not merely acting rightly despite contrary desires. Virtues are of two distinct types: the intellectual habits of skillful thinking (in solving problems, in responding to other people, in making things) and character habits that incline one not only to do the right thing but also to behave in the right manner. Phronesis, the intellectual virtue that perfects the practical reasoning toward the good, is absolutely central to this account (Gk. *phronēsis*; Lat. *prudentia*). Through the right exercise of practical reason and aided by the other virtues, the prudent person is able to recognize what goods are worth pursuing as well as what it might mean to act with excellent character in a particular situation. Phronesis can be distinguished from mere cleverness because the clever may figure out the means to an end but fail to know which ends are worthwhile. Phronesis, like all the virtues, is ordered toward the "good" and requires cultivation.

Aristotle calls the ultimate telos, or end, to which all the virtues are oriented *eudaimonia*, usually translated as "human flourishing" or "happiness." In theological terms, it is closest to "blessed," which in the OT means "able to walk well" (cf. use of the Heb. *ʾšr* in Mal. 3:12, where the Piel verb means "to bless," while in Prov. 9:6 the Qal form of *ʾšr* means "to walk straight"; this double entendre is present in the fifty-two occurrences of "blessed" in the book of Psalms and is repeated by Jesus some forty-six times). Human living aims at this ultimate good in the sense that this good is identical to what human life is for. However, virtue acquisition may be foiled: individuals often are confused about their true end and may be habituated into vices rather than virtues.

Virtue lists vary from society to society because the concept is tied to what a given community holds to be the chief good for human beings. For example, ancient Greeks understood the telos of the virtues to be the perfection of citizens for their particular function in the society through obedience to one's teachers and the fostering of friendship. Aristotle, and Plato before him, advocated those particular virtues necessary to life in the Greek city-state, the polis, at a time when the older heroic list of virtues appeared to be breaking down with the disappearance of clan life. Aristotle's teacher Plato identified four linchpin or cardinal virtues: courage, temperance, justice, and prudence. Both men were resisting what they saw as increasing pluralism and moral decline in Greek culture. Yet both were rightly accused of elitism. In particular, Aristotle's account condoned the social hierarchy of his culture. Slaves and artisans kept their place, and few had the leisure for the sort of philosophical contemplation that was presumed to be the noblest human endeavor. As we will see, Christians borrowed the language of virtue but substituted a radical vision of the good society (Luke 4:18–19).

Early Christian Virtue

Although the Greek term *aretē* ("excellence, virtue") is rare in NT usage (Phil. 4:8; 1 Pet. 2:9; 2 Pet. 1:3, 5), biblical authors presumed that the moral life is a matter of development and growth. The biblical authors assumed that a person of good character is more apt to have a right reading of Scripture and must be formed within the body of Christ to desire and rightly perceive what is true and good. God, and thus love and desire for God, is central to Christian accounts of virtue. Early Christians overturned Hellenistic assumptions about the telos of human life, insisting that human purpose and ultimate good is found in Christ. As the phrase "in Christ" is closely related to "the body of Christ" (Eph. 4:12), the human good was said to be found *in ecclesiam*, in the congregation of believers that is Christ's body, for that is where Christ sent his Spirit. The early church also stressed different virtues than did its classical forebears: patience, humility, obedience, and, especially, Christlike love. The martyr, rather than the heroic warrior, was the model of courage. And care for the marginalized rather than preserving class distinction was the model of justice. These virtues were understood to be the by-product of both grace and the practice of discipleship.

Like Aristotle, early Christians understood virtues to be habitual dispositions involving the perception of and desire for human "good," which for

Christians is ultimately found in God. Discipleship in the NT requires a love of the good that goes beyond an ethic of obligation or mere obedience (e.g., Sermon on the Mount) and results in seeing a "whole new world" (*kainē ktisis* [2 Cor. 5:17]). John speaks of "abiding" with Christ as necessary to perceive the glory of Christ and the nearness of the kingdom of God. This abiding bears "fruit," namely, the life of discipleship shaped by love after the pattern of Christ (John 15:7–17).

There are several lists of character traits or virtues in the NT letters (e.g., 2 Cor. 6:3–10), including Paul's triad of faith, hope, and love (1 Cor. 13:13), which came to be called the "theological virtues" by later Christians. Yet, for early Christians, mature discipleship in the "Way" of Christ (Acts 9:2; 19:9) was not simply the human acquisition of godly habits but rather a gift of God's grace that must be cultivated through worship and the other social practices of the church. As a free gift of God, these practices comprise the Way and constitute (in part) the free gift of salvation. Conversion, particularly in the Pauline writings, may initially appear sudden but thereafter requires the ongoing growth of sanctification. Paul argues that sanctification is both a result of God's grace and requires cultivation of gifts of the Spirit (Gal. 5:16–24; Eph. 4:1–5:2; see also 2 Pet. 1:3–8). These are gifts in that they come from God, but they function as virtues and can develop over time. Sanctification involves not only a habitual disposition toward acting well but also the ability to discern the good. The author of Hebrews distinguishes between new converts and mature Christians. Only the latter are ready for solid food because they have been "trained by practice to distinguish good from evil" (Heb. 5:14; cf. 1 Cor. 2:14–3:1). To borrow Aristotle's terminology, such persons are skilled in the exercise of practical reason.

Paul himself explicitly uses cognates for "practical wisdom" (*phron-*) thirty-four times, ten times in Philippians alone. (Interestingly, the usage in Philippians is aimed at corporate achievement, whereby the church as a unit is to display the same skillful practical wisdom as Christ himself [Phil. 2:2, 5].) In addition, Paul employs the other Greek term for wisdom, *sophia*, which he lists as one of the gifts of the Spirit (1 Cor. 2:13; 12:8). This may have been a bit confusing for some first-century readers. For Greek-speakers since Plato, *sophia* connoted the skill of theoretical reasoning (math, logic, etc.), but *phronēsis* ("intelligence") was the term used for practical wisdom. But somewhere along the way, usage was reversed; "wisdom" came to indicate one who lives well, while "intelligence" referred to someone who was merely smart. An important contributor to this change is the fact that the Pauline corpus never refers to theoretical reasoning but only to practical reasoning (i.e., deliberation about how, when, and in what manner to act) and its correlative skill, *phronēsis*. Indeed, the mystery is solved simply by noting that Paul is employing not the classical Greek notion of *sophia* but that of the Greek translation of the OT (the LXX). Paul's use of *sophia*, like its Hebrew counterpart *ḥokmâ*, is something that is both a gift of God (Job 38:36) and something for human beings to seek and progressively acquire (Prov. 4:5, 7). Thus, in the NT, wisdom is a gift that goes beyond natural reason, and it is also the fruit of a life of faith and prayer oriented to God and must be embodied as the imitation of Christ (1 Pet. 2:21). Of course, the gifts are fully realized only eschatologically. Nevertheless, in the meantime their cultivation within the gathered body of Christ is real, albeit incomplete (1 Cor. 1–2; Eph. 1:7–9; Col. 1:9–14; 3:14–16).

The early church drew heavily on the concept of Christianity as a "way," distinct from other forms of social life because of its orientation to the kingdom of God as the true telos of human life. New Christians were expected to spend an entire year (and in some cases as many as three years) preparing for baptism. They learned the tenets of the faith but also were expected to begin developing in the likeness of Christ; sin committed after baptism was understood to be particularly grievous. The retraining of desires and cultivation of virtue were essential. To this end, the practices of the church, particularly worship, formed the Christian in love of God and the habits of faithful discipleship. By the fourth century, Augustine argued explicitly that the love of God was the true telos of human life—all our actions are directed toward this end—but that we err because our desires have been disordered such that we settle for lesser goods. For Augustine, virtue is conformance of our desires to love of God, and love is the form of all of the virtues, including the cardinal virtues identified by Plato.

Virtue in Medieval Christianity

Medieval moral theology also stressed the cultivation of virtue within a life of discipleship. Although Thomas Aquinas (d. 1174) is sometimes misunderstood as a natural philosopher, his moral theology is a reworking of Aristotle in light of Scripture and early Christian discipleship. In the medieval university, philosophy and the other disciplines were assumed to be at the service of theology and knowledge of God. Thomas was first of all a monk and a member of the Dominican Order of Preachers. His *Summa theologiae* is the most important systematic account of Christian virtue ethics. Drawing on Paul, Thomas identified wisdom and the theological virtues (i.e., faith, hope, and love or "charity") as gifts of grace and argued that charity (*caritas*, love) is the "form" that shapes and directs the other virtues toward union with God as our true end.

For Thomas, like centuries of Christians before him, the virtues are habituated dispositions involving a desire for the good. Yet he distinguishes between infused and acquired virtues. Acquired virtues are oriented toward natural ends and habituated through acting in accordance with the good, while infused virtues are oriented toward our supernatural end, eternal union with God. Although the infused virtues, which genuinely inhere in the person, require cultivation through prayer and worship, they receive their beginning as a directly imparted divine gift. Thomas argues that the theological virtues of faith, hope, and love are infused, but *prudentia* (practical wisdom) and the other virtues may be acquired through practice, through divine gift, or some combination of the two.

Thomas held that moral virtue requires an intellectual grasp of the good and a capacity to apply practical reason in concrete situations. Every human action is, in this sense, a moral act. Some may be trivial, while others are monumental. But insofar as an act is deliberate (as opposed to being absentminded, such as scratching one's chin), it is moral because it aims at some perceived good. Problems arise when we are mistaken about what is good and what is not. Such a mistake amounts to a failure in practical reasoning. Thomas attributes this clouding of judgment to sin, the propensity toward selfishness, self-deception, and independence from God. *Prudentia* (what Paul, writing in Greek, called *phronēsis*), as a gift from God, is an antidote (in part) for the effects of sin. As a natural intellectual virtue, *prudentia* requires practice, memory, and teachability as well as seasoned judgment. For Thomas, *prudentia* is best cultivated within a community. Alongside a naturally developed trait, the infused gift of *prudentia* also aids in practical reasoning. Infused wisdom via the indwelling Spirit is manifest as an affinity for the good. In sum, wisdom as a natural virtue can judge rightly in ordinary practices, such as in medicine or architecture, but wisdom as a gift of the Spirit is additionally necessary to judge according to God as the highest cause and end. Thus might one opt for death by martyrdom over bodily health and still be choosing wisely.

Thomas structures his discussion in the *Summa theologiae* around the classical cardinal virtues of courage, temperance, justice, and prudence, but he adds to these the theological virtues of faith, hope, and love (Gk. *agapē*; Lat. *caritas*). For Thomas, following Augustine, *caritas* is the form of both intellectual and character virtues, including *prudentia*, because love is necessary for knowing what human life is for: eternal union with God. In his commentary on Paul's prayer that love might abound in the church with "knowledge and all discernment" in Phil. 1:9, Thomas writes,

> Does knowledge arise from charity [*caritas*]? . . . Charity is the Spirit, of whom it is said in John (16:13): "When the Spirit of truth comes, he will guide you into all the truth." The reason for this is that when a person has a habit, if that habit is right, then right judgment of things pertaining to that habit follows from it; but if it is corrupted, then false judgment follows. . . . Now all things that are done by us must be informed with charity. Therefore, a person with charity has a correct judgment both in regard to things knowable; hence [Paul] says, "with knowledge," by which one recognizes the truth and adheres to the truths of faith . . . and in regard to things to be done; hence [Paul] says, "and all discernment." (*Comm. Phil.* 1.2)

Thus, receptivity to grace through the practices of prayer and worship is crucial to medieval moral theology. In addition to the cultivation of virtues as acquired habits, the moral life requires an infusion of grace that directs the other virtues by imparting a love of God, which is the *telos* of the other virtues.

Modern Eclipse and Recovery of Virtue Ethics

Eighteenth-century Enlightenment philosophers sought a certain foundation for knowledge in objective "truths" accessible to the autonomous individual and apart from traditional teaching and communal practices. In this environment, virtue ethics was replaced by various systems of theoretical reasoning that claimed an objective, universal foundation for morality but in fact more often led to competing and irreconcilable positions. In a seminal 1958 essay, G. Elizabeth Anscombe highlighted the unexpected breakdown of modern theoretical attempts to describe moral obligation. She suggested that once the sense of moral authority of God was lost in philosophy or was excluded from argument, theorists found it impossible to move from the "is" of brute facts to the "ought" of moral obligation. Subsequently, contemporary Westerners tended to see morality as a matter of subjective choice among a range of possible values and beliefs despite philosophers' (Locke, Kant,

Mill, Rawls, etc.) perennial attempts to author a universally compelling account of ethics.

Alasdair MacIntyre, in *After Virtue*, argues that this state of affairs precludes any rational resolution of moral disputes; discussions of moral obligation reduce to attempts at persuasion. As an example, MacIntyre describes the lack of consensus on the meaning of "justice" in Western culture. Does justice consist in equality ensured by the redistribution of goods and opportunity or in the protection of private property and ownership earned by hard work? These rival ways of conceiving justice result in competing claims about morality of taxation, which cannot be easily resolved by an obviously circular appeal to "justice." MacIntyre argues that contemporary thought is missing any shared agreement on the purpose, or *telos*, of human life, which in turn would provide a shared meaning to terms such as *justice*, *obligation*, and the *good*. He calls for a return to an ethics of virtue as a way forward in recovery of these concepts.

Implicit communal agreement concerning what the good is and which habits are virtuous derives from at least three kinds of sources. First, there are narratives both factual (e.g., history) and figural (e.g., the parable of the good Samaritan) that exemplify what human life is for. Second, there are social practices (for Christians, the list includes evangelism, prayer, worship, caring for the needy, etc.) that embody what human life is for. Third, there are explicit statements taken by a tradition to be definitive of their identity (e.g., creeds, confessions). Thus, virtues are those skillful habits that enable one to live in ways that "fit" the authoritative stories, that faithfully extend the constitutive practices and emblematize the traditional identity. Of course, each individual is on a journey to learn well these three identity markers. Along the way, individuals may become confused about what human life is for (e.g., accumulating wealth) and thus unwittingly be habituated into vices (e.g., miserliness) rather than virtues.

Discipleship as Moral Formation through Practices

MacIntyre's work reflects a broader interest in recovering virtue as an approach to both philosophical ethics and moral theology in the late twentieth century. A more theologically specific version of MacIntyre's vision has been voiced by Stanley Hauerwas, who advocates an ethics of discipleship rather than an ethics of decision. Like MacIntyre, Hauerwas stresses the importance of tradition and practices of particular communities in formation of the virtues. Some contemporary Christian virtue ethicists utilize a virtue approach with less emphasis on Christian particularity. Jean Porter, for instance, uses the Thomistic account of practical reason in an attempt to bring together ethics of virtue with deontological ethics. Others appeal to virtue as a complement to utilitarian or deontological decisionist ethics, arguing, for instance, that virtue is necessary to be a competent judge in these theories or emphasizing particular virtues, such as "care for others," that seem to be undervalued by other approaches. In contrast to these attempts to reconcile virtue with philosophical theories, Hauerwas stresses the importance of embodied traditions for the development of virtue. He argues that Christians develop virtuous dispositions through communal practices and stories. Reading Scripture is such a communal practice, learned within the church, not simply private devotion. It requires virtue but also contributes to the cultivation of virtue and moral vision.

Hauerwas describes practices as communal ways of life developed over time and extended from one generation to the next. There is no virtue "in general," but only specific virtues within particular traditions with specific accounts of the human *telos*. Like his theological forebears, Hauerwas uses "virtue" to denote publicly visible relational habits rather than a hidden psychological state. Virtue is acquired through ongoing imitation of those who have mastered the virtue-cultivating practice. In an ethics of Christian discipleship, the master is Christ, yet secondarily, disciples also learn to recognize excellence of practice by observing and imitating those who are more mature in the faith (1 Cor. 4:16; 11:1; Phil. 3:17; 1 Thess. 1:6; 2:14; 2 Thess. 3:7, 9; Heb. 6:12; 13:7). To follow Christ is not simply to imitate specific acts but also to aspire to an entire life of wisdom and moral virtue. Worship, reading Scripture, prayer, feeding the hungry, and the like are specific practices that are central to the broad task of community formation or disciple-making. Through these practices, faithful disciples become habituated in the virtues, learn to desire what is good, and thus make wise, prudent judgments about moral action. Especially through the practice of communal worship (i.e., abiding with Christ) followers of Christ become open to the grace of the infused virtues and spiritual gifts.

All practices have goods that are best known by those who practice well. For instance, Jesus condemns those who pray in order to gain the respect of others (Matt. 6:5), an external good, rather than communion with God, a good that is knowable only to those who pray well (making communion with God a good internal to the practice of prayer).

Ultimately, Christian practices are oriented to God as our true end. Christian narratives, both biblical and historical, provide a context that makes sense of our practices and exemplifies the *telos* of human life as understood within the Christian tradition. To return to an earlier example, the Christian practice of reading Scripture as a communal story trains disciples to understand their Christian identity in the context of the scriptural witness and subsequent story of the church. Scripture is paradigmatic for the ethics of discipleship, but reading well requires wisdom. And wisdom is not a habit that Christians are prone to develop in isolation. Rather, only by learning to read Scripture together, especially in the context of worship, can Christians become more skilled at hearing and living the gospel as their story.

See also Cardinal Virtues; Character; Conversion; Habit; Moral Formation; Narrative Ethics, Biblical; Narrative Ethics, Contemporary; Practices; Prudence; Sanctification; Teleological Theories of Ethics; Vice; Vices and Virtues, Lists of; Virtue(s)

Bibliography

Anscombe, G. "Modern Moral Philosophy." *Philosophy* 33 (1958): 1–19; Crisp, R., and M. Slote, eds. *Virtue Ethics.* Oxford University Press, 1997; Fowl, S., and G. Jones. *Reading in Communion: Scripture and Ethics in Christian Life.* Wipf & Stock, 1998; Hauerwas, S., and C. Pinches. *Christians among the Virtues: Theological Conversations with Ancient and Modern Ethics.* University of Notre Dame Press, 1997; Hays, R. *The Moral Vision of the New Testament: Community, Cross, and New Creation; A Contemporary Introduction to New Testament Ethics.* HarperSanFrancisco, 1996; MacIntyre, A. *After Virtue: A Study in Moral Theology.* University of Notre Dame Press, 1984; Mattison, W., III. *Introducing Moral Theology: True Happiness and the Virtues.* Brazos, 2008; McClendon, J., Jr. *Ethics.* Vol. 1 of *Systematic Theology.* Abingdon, 1986; McInerny, R. *Ethica Thomistica: The Moral Philosophy of Thomas Aquinas.* Catholic University of America Press, 1997; Murphy, N., et al., eds. *Virtues and Practices in the Christian Tradition: Christian Ethics after MacIntyre.* Trinity Press International, 1997; Porter, J. *Moral Action and Christian Ethics.* NSCE 5. Cambridge University Press, 1995; Thomas Aquinas, *Commentary on Saint Paul's First Letter to the Thessalonians and the Letter to the Philippians.* Magi Books, 1969; Verhey, A. *Remembering Jesus: Christian Community, Scripture, and the Moral Life.* Eerdmans, 2004.

Nikki Coffey Tousley and Brad J. Kallenberg

Virtues and Vices, Lists of

See Vices and Virtues, Lists of

Vocation

In contemporary usage the term *vocation* (or *calling*) has a range of meanings. Most generally and simply, it is a synonym for occupation or job. In high school, students are introduced to the term as a way of distinguishing students on a college preparatory track from those taking vocational classes, which prepare them to enter the workplace immediately following graduation. For young people with more education and therefore more occupational options, the term *vocation* sometimes is associated with choosing a career that suits their abilities, inclination, and training. In this case, it is used as an exhortation to select an occupation that they will find intrinsically satisfying and valuable rather than extrinsically rewarding in terms of social status or financial compensation. In religious contexts, this basic range of meanings is sanctified by a sense that God has a particular occupation in mind for each person. The added religious dimension does not alter the understanding of vocation in any significant way because most Christians assume that God intends them to do work for which they are well suited and that they will find satisfying.

The contemporary use of the term *vocation* bears only a tangential resemblance to its biblical meaning. In Scripture, vocation or calling is associated more closely with election than with occupation. In the OT, God calls (*qārāʾ*) those whom God chooses or elects (*bāḥar*). For example, "But you, Israel, my servant, Jacob, whom I have chosen [*bāḥar*], the offspring of Abraham, my friend; you whom I took from the ends of the earth, and called [*qārāʾ*] from its furthest corners, saying to you, 'You are my servants, I have chosen [*bāḥar*] you and not cast you off' " (Isa. 41:8–9). As this passage makes clear, biblical notions of election and calling have less to do with receiving a divine reward than a divine commission to participate in God's purpose in the world. In addition to calling the whole people of Israel, God calls individuals—for example, Moses (Exod. 3:1–12), Abraham (Gen. 12:1–4), Samuel (1 Sam. 3:1–14), and prophets (Isa. 6:1–13; Jer. 1:2–10). Those who are called are summoned to become servants of God in the world. So, for example, God calls the people of Israel to be a "priestly kingdom and a holy nation" (Exod. 19:6), and God blesses Abraham so that "through him all the nations of the world might be blessed" (Gen. 12:4). In each case, the call is to serve God and God's purposes in the world. Like the contemporary understanding of vocation, the biblical idea of calling includes certain roles or responsibilities. Far from corresponding with a particular secular occupation or job, however, the biblical concept draws people toward participation in God's cosmic reign.

The NT builds upon this fundamental understanding of vocation. Jesus "calls" (*kaleō*) disciples to leave their occupations and social roles behind in order to follow him (Mark 1:19–20). Those who are not ready and willing to leave everything immediately are considered unworthy of discipleship (Matt. 22:1–7; Luke 9:59–62). God's call demands a joyful and immediate commitment of one's whole life in service to God and God's purposes. Paul uses the language of calling to designate salvation and the mode of life that grows out of it. He exhorts the Thessalonians to "lead a life worthy of God, who calls [*kaleō*] you into his own kingdom and glory" (1 Thess. 2:12), and he begs the Ephesians to "lead a life worthy of the calling [*klēsis*] to which you have been called [*kaleō*]" (Eph. 4:1). In other words, Christians are called to live in a manner consistent with the reconciliation embodied in and brought about through the life, death, and resurrection of Jesus Christ. Again, there is a corporate as well as an individual dimension to calling. Those who follow Christ are the *ekklēsia*, "those called out."

Persons' occupations have little bearing on their Christian calling. In fact, when Paul does relate worldly occupations and the Christian calling, it is simply to encourage Christians to remain in and be content with the status that they had when they were called to Christ. "Let each of you lead the life that the Lord has assigned, to which God has called you" (1 Cor. 7:17). Here Paul seems to use the term *call* in relation to a person's occupation or worldly standing, whether the person is married or single, Jew or gentile, slave or free. What he intends to communicate, however, is not the significance of worldly occupations and status but rather their insignificance. "Circumcision is nothing and uncircumcision is nothing; but obeying the commandments of God is everything" (1 Cor. 7:19). In Scripture, whether OT or NT, "calling" is always God's gracious call to become God's own, to be those called out (*ekklēsia*), in order to bear witness to and serve God's creative and redemptive purposes in the world.

The early church maintained this sensibility, by necessity as much as design. In the Roman Empire, becoming a Christian required subordinating one's worldly standing to a divine calling. Christians were considered a threat to the social order because of their refusal to participate in the pagan practices insinuated in every aspect of social, economic, political, and family life. Following Christ guaranteed not only occasional and intermittent persecution but also relentless and persistent constriction of one's social and economic opportunities. When Christianity became legal in the empire, and eventually its official religion, some Christians rejected the comforts of legitimacy, retreating to the desert in order to maintain an absolute and unwavering commitment to God alone. These early ascetics continued to conceive of God's calling as requiring a rejection of the world and all its mundane temptations. Just as the martyrs provided a model of Christian vocation in the face of Roman persecution and exclusion, so the desert fathers, such as Antony, were admired for their singular commitment to God in Christ. The medieval church maintained this pattern as well, associating calling or vocation with the "religious" life of priests, monks, and nuns. Again, vocation was seen as the complete commitment of one's whole self to God and God's purposes in the world. The vows of poverty, chastity, and obedience liberated the "religious" from worldly goods, allowing them to respond to God's call wholeheartedly. Like the martyrs and the desert fathers before them, they provided a model of the Christian life to which all ought to aspire, but that only a few could claim: wholehearted commitment to God and God's purposes in the world.

The Protestant Reformation in the fifteenth and sixteenth centuries revolutionized the language of vocation and calling. Martin Luther did not reject the sense that calling required a complete commitment to God and God's purposes, but he saw these purposes as consistent with rather than in conflict with worldly goods. Rather than rejecting the obligations and blessings of family and society for the sake of God's call, Luther assumed that God's call was realized within the context of these other roles, responsibilities, and goods. Furthermore, he assumed that God's calling was for everyone, not just a select few. The distinction that the church had made between the "spiritual estate" and the "temporal estate" was illegitimate. All Christians were equally called, and every aspect of life was an appropriate context for serving God and neighbor. Rather than closing the monasteries, therefore, it might be better to say that Luther's intention was to turn the whole world into a monastery. All people in all walks of life were called to participate wholeheartedly in God's purposes amid their worldly commitments. In whatever "stand" or station, a Christian should endeavor to "give myself as a Christ to my neighbor, just as Christ offered himself to me; I will do nothing in this life except what I see is necessary, profitable, and salutary to my neighbor, since through faith I have an abundance of all good things in Christ" (Luther).

The Calvinist wing of the Protestant Reformation further accentuated the egalitarian and inner-worldly impulses with which Luther imbued the notion of Christian vocation. However, the Reformers were not satisfied simply to sanctify the mundane; they wanted to transform it. Puritans such as William Perkins identified two aspects of vocation: the general and the particular. The former is the common calling to the Christian faith and life, while the latter is the particular context within which it takes place. According to Perkins, these two aspects cannot be separated; the general calling to love God and neighbor can be realized only in the context of the particular Christian's life, relationships, and responsibilities. Moreover, "That we may the better joyne both our callings together, wee must consider the maine end of our lives, and that is, to serve God in the serving of men in the works of our callings. . . . [God's] pleasure is that men should be his instruments, for the good of one another" (Perkins). Max Weber, Ernst Troeltsch, and other prominent sociologists properly identify the Protestant notion of vocation as an important factor in the modern transformation of the political, economic, social, and familial spheres. However, their emphasis on the influence of its egalitarian and inner-worldly aspects often ignores the centrality of service to God and neighbor in the Protestant vision of vocation.

Modern individualism and materialism in contemporary economic, political, and social spheres are not the unambiguous realization of Protestant vocation but rather are its distortion and corruption. Contemporary uses of the term *vocation*, whether emphasizing occupation generally or fulfilling work more specifically, depart from its more robust and radical meaning. A culture of self-interested individualism has subverted the true meaning of vocation, absorbing it into a preoccupation with self-reliance and personal satisfaction. Contemporary use of the terminology would do well to recall these words of William Perkins: "He abuseth his calling, whosoever he be that against the end thereof, imployes it for himself, seeking wholly his own, and not the common good. And that common saying, 'Every man for himselfe, and God for us all,' is wicked, and directly against the end of every calling or honest kind of life" (Perkins).

Recovering the biblical and theological heritage of the term *vocation* may rejuvenate its radical and transformative implications. At the heart of Christian calling is Christ's gracious and demanding invitation to follow him. The only appropriate response is to commit oneself wholeheartedly to God and God's purposes in the world. All things—occupation, family, social standing, personal satisfaction—must be subordinated to this absolute and ultimate responsibility. In a society characterized by personal and social fragmentation, such a calling comes not only as a daunting command but also as a joyful opportunity. It offers a vision of the integrity of life that reveals the interdependence and unity of all creation within the providence of God's gracious sovereignty, which the current culture of individualism masks and distorts as profoundly as Roman imperialism did in the first century.

See also Covenant

Bibliography

Babcock, G. *The Way of Life: A Theology of Christian Vocation*. Eerdmans, 1998; Luther, M. "The Freedom of the Christian." Pages 261–316 in *Three Treatises*. Rev. ed. Fortress, 1970; Meilaender, G., ed. *Working: Its Meaning and Limits*. University of Notre Dame Press, 2000; Perkins, W. "A Treatise of the Vocations or Callings of Men, with Sorts and Kinds of Them, and the Right Use Thereof." Pages 35–57 in *Puritan Political Ideas, 1558–1794*, ed. E. Morgan. Bobbs-Merrill, 1965; Placher, W., ed. *Callings: Twenty Centuries of Christian Wisdom on Vocation*. Eerdmans, 2005; Schuurman, D. *Vocation: Discerning Our Callings in Life*. Eerdmans, 2004; Troeltsch, E. *The Social Teaching of the Christian Churches*. Trans. O. Wyon. 2 vols. Westminster John Knox, 1992; Weber, M. *The Protestant Ethic and the Spirit of Capitalism*. Trans. T. Parsons. Routledge, 1992.

Timothy A. Beach-Verhey

Vows

In the Bible, a vow is a promise spoken directly to God by a petitioner who offers to dedicate property, self, or other persons to God on the condition that God fulfill the request made by the individual. Vows were made by individuals, typically were spoken in private prayer to God, did not require mediation by religious officials, and usually involved situations of great distress. Thus, the making of vows operated largely within the arena of popular religious devotion apart from official or formal worship. However, payments of vows often were done in the context of communal worship and praise in thanksgiving for God's fulfillment of the vow's request (Pss. 22:25; 50:14; 116:12–19). Priests also played a role in certifying that sacrificial animals offered as payment for vows were without blemish (Lev. 22:18, 21; Mal. 1:14). When a vow involved the promise to dedicate a person to serve God (as in 1 Sam. 1:22), the one who made the vow had the option to redeem the person by paying a fee to the priests. The amount of the fee was adjusted according to the age and gender of the individual being redeemed and the economic capability of the one paying the fee (Lev. 27:1–8).

In general, making a vow to God was considered a solemn commitment that should not be broken (Num. 30:2; Deut. 23:21–23; Eccl. 5:4–5). However, there were exceptions. Most women in biblical times were seen as being under the guardianship of a male, typically father or husband. Thus, if a woman made a vow to God and her husband or father disapproved, he had a right to nullify the vow if he acted promptly to do so. Otherwise, the woman's vow would stand (Num. 30:1–16). This provision reflects the imbalance of power and rights between men and women in ancient Israel.

People called "Nazirites" formed a special category of individuals whose lives were devoted in service to God by a vow made by oneself or by someone else (often a parent). Certain vows of abstinence were associated with Nazirites during their time of service: they would not drink wine or eat grapes, cut their hair, or touch a corpse (Num. 6:3–6). If a Nazirite inadvertently violated one of these vows, certain ritual actions and sacrifices could restore the status of the Nazirite. Other rituals also marked the end of the Nazirite's term of service if the vow was for a temporary period (Num. 6:9–21). Other Nazirites retained their status throughout their lifetimes, from birth until death (Judg. 13:5; 1 Sam. 1:11).

Examples of Nazirites include the prophet Samuel, son of Hannah (1 Sam. 1:11; 3:19–21), and the warrior-judge Samson (Judg. 13:5). Interestingly, Samson's mother assumed some of the Nazirite vows of abstention (wine, strong drink, unclean food), while Samson only had to keep his hair uncut (Judg. 13:4–5). Samson's revelation of this one secret of his extraordinary strength to Delilah led to his downfall (Judg. 16:16–21).

Some scholars argue that the Nazirite vow may have played a role in the understanding of Jesus and his ministry. Jesus is called a "Nazorean" in Matt. 2:23, perhaps a double-voiced allusion to his hometown of Nazareth and his dedication to God as a Nazirite. The apostle Paul is portrayed as ending the term of his own "vow" by allowing his hair to be cut (Acts 18:18). Paul also paid the redemption fee for four other individuals who ended their Nazirite vows by having their heads shaved (Acts 21:15–27). Thus, the practice of making vows seems to have been known in early Christian communities, and it has continued as a practice of religious devotion throughout the church's history.

Two other OT figures make noteworthy vows to God. Jacob made a vow after seeing a nighttime vision of angels ascending and descending from the heavens at Bethel and hearing God's promise to bless him. In grateful response, Jacob vowed to give God a tenth of his possessions and to worship God if God continued to protect him (Gen. 28:10–22). In a more negative portrayal, the judge Jephthah recklessly vowed to offer as a burnt offering to God "whatever" came out of the door of his house when he returned from battle if God granted him victory against the Ammonites (Judg. 11:29–40). Presumably, Jephthah had expected an animal to emerge from the house, but instead his own daughter came out on his return. Jephthah viewed his vow as irrevocable and thus felt that he had no choice but to offer his only child as a burnt sacrifice, even though biblical law allowed paying a fee in order to redeem a child from a vow (Lev. 27:1–8). Other biblical laws also associated the practice of child sacrifice with the worship of other gods (Lev. 18:21; 20:2–5; Ezek. 20:31).

The biblical treatment of vows to God raises a number of ethical issues. The use of vows appears to put God under obligation and may appear to function as a crass bribe to move God to some desired action. "If God will do *x*, then I will offer God *y*." This would seem to contradict the claim that God "takes no bribe" (Deut. 10:17). But biblical vows offer not so much a payment or a bribe as a token of desperate need by someone in distress and as a sign of anticipatory thanksgiving if and when God fulfills the request. The biblical witness also balances the seriousness of any commitments or vows that a person makes to God with some degree of reasonable flexibility in how the vow is fulfilled in light of the desperate circumstances in which vows often are made. The biblical vows do suggest God's willingness to take into consideration the prayers and pleas of his people in distress and at times to be moved by them in response.

One of the most troubling vows in the Bible is associated with the holy war laws, in which God commands the Israelites to "annihilate" the Canaanites and their towns as they approach the promised land (Deut. 20:16–18). In Num. 21:2 the Israelites make a vow to God. If God grants them a military victory against the Canaanite king of Arad and his troops, then the Israelites pledge to "utterly destroy" the Canaanites' towns and dedicate everything in them to God. The text reports that God "listened to" the Israelites' vow and then gave them the victory. This use of the vow is entangled with the ethical perplexities associated with the broader theme of holy war in the Bible, especially in the book of Joshua.

See also Holy War; Oaths; Promise and Promise-Keeping

Bibliography

Berlinerblau, J. *The Vow and the "Popular Religious Groups" of Ancient Israel: A Philological and Sociological Inquiry*. JSOTSup 210. Sheffield Academic Press, 1996; Cartledge, T. *Vows in the Hebrew Bible and the Ancient Near East*. JSOTSup 147. JSOT Press, 1992; Olson, D. "Dialogues of Life and Monologues of Death: Jephthah and Jephthah's Daughter in Judges 10:6–12:7." Pages 43–54 in *Postmodern Interpretations of the Bible: A Reader*, ed. A. K. M. Adam. Chalice Press, 2001.

Dennis T. Olson

War

The term *war* as used in Scripture generally refers to armed conflict between contending nations, though it can also function metaphorically to convey a deep conflict within a person (e.g., Paul says, "I see in my members another law at war with the law of my mind" [Rom. 7:23]). In both Testaments it may either refer to or imply a cosmic conflict between God and the forces that oppose God. Given not only its longer historic narrative and greater length but also its continued focus on the nation of Israel, it is unsurprising that the vast majority of references to war as armed conflict occur in the OT. Also unsurprising is the attention that Christians give to NT texts in developing their theological understandings of war and peace. Given not only scriptural multivocality but also the degree to which judgments about war are always densely related to the cultures in which they arise, the development of multiple theological traditions within Christianity is unsurprising as well.

War in the Old Testament

War and the threat of war are constant features of the OT; so too, however, is the search for peace. Genesis 14 describes the first instances of war named in the Bible. Various kings from the area's city-states have waged war against one another and, in the process, the victorious kings have taken Lot hostage. Abram pursues them with 318 "trained men" and routs them in the night. Abram's victory leads the priest-king Melchizedek to bless him and to suggest that Abram keep the spoils but give him the persons whom Abram has brought back. Abram refuses, claiming that he must rely on the generosity of God rather than kings. The chapter encapsulates many of the themes surrounding war through the rest of the OT: the politics of disputed land and contested crowns, the impact of being chosen by God and its concomitant implications for fidelity and purity (a purity that extends to the slaughter of enemies), the removal and recovery of a people from the land and the question of who fights for whom in those processes.

Three central types of war are described in the OT: wars of conquest, civil wars, and defensive wars. Within each type there are varied images of war and peace. During the wars of conquest, for instance, God restricts who fights, when to fight, and how to fight in some places (Deut. 20) while casting aside all restrictions in others (Deut. 7; 1 Sam. 15:3). Both images, however, assume that Israel can fight and will win because God fights with them.

Living between conquest and exile, David personifies the tensions between commands to fight and visions of peace: revered as warrior-king and favored by God in battle but, in 1 Chr. 22:8, not allowed to build the temple because of the blood on his hands. Isaiah calls for Israel neither to fight nor to make alliances with neighboring countries but rather to allow God to protect them; some of the most profoundly peaceful and moving images, notably that of the peaceable kingdom in Isa. 11:1–9, occur here. Yet even a clear vision of peace like that in Isa. 2:1–4, with its famous promise that the nations "shall beat their swords into plowshares, and their spears into pruning hooks," is matched by the call in Joel 3:10, in different historical circumstances, to "beat your plowshares into swords, and your pruning hooks into spears." The range of perspectives on war and peace in the OT reinforces the importance of exegetical work that is sensitive to both historical contexts and political-theological assumptions.

During the intertestamental period, the variety of images and perspectives on war and peace continued to expand, sometimes opposing earlier images and sometimes extending them. The LXX, for instance, repeatedly replaces the description of God as a warrior with that of God as the one who destroys war (cf. the LXX of Exod. 15:3; Isa. 42:13 with the MT). The Qumran scrolls not only include martial images but also expand warfare to a cosmic level, focusing on the battle between light and darkness. And the Maccabean revolt led some

Jews to refine their vision of war (paradoxically, partially Hellenizing it) in light of their struggles against the Seleucid Empire. All these images and perspectives were alive and active during the centuries immediately surrounding the formation of the NT and played various roles in shaping it.

War in the New Testament

New Testament references to war, especially calls to war, are considerably more rare than in the OT. This is partly for pragmatic and historical reasons: in spite of the desires of Zealots who hoped that Jesus was a military leader, war against Rome by first-century Jews was not a viable option. During the period of Jesus' ministry an uneasy peace existed among Zealots, isolationists such as the Essenes, Jewish accommodationists to Roman authority, and Rome. Since the NT writers and their comunities lacked either a state to defend or the power to defend it, the far more tangential role of war in NT visions of political engagement is unsurprising.

However, the relative paucity of attention to or encouragement toward war in the NT is not simply a result of historical context. It is also a product of Jesus' emphasis on peace in his teachings as developed by NT writers. Most notably in Matthew, Jesus repeatedly preaches nonviolence and nonresistance: be peacemakers, turn the other cheek, love your enemies, and do not resist evil. Obviously, such injunctions are hard to square with acts of war. Equally so are his actions as interpreted by the early church. Not only his repeated acts of comfort and healing, including healing those outside of the covenant community, but also his willingness to die on the cross rather than call on legions of angels to defend himself (Matt. 26:53) reinforce his emphasis on peace and his claim in John 18:36 that his kingdom is not of this world. Paul reiterates Jesus' call not to resist evil and argues for the priority of love (Rom. 12:9–21). Other NT Letters are replete with the call for Christians to pursue peace and rely on the grace of the "God of peace" that was made manifest in Jesus, whose work, as described by Col. 1:20, is to make peace through the reconciliation of all things to God via his death on the cross.

Yet, although the NT leans heavily toward a pacifist position, it is not entirely univocal on the matter. Jesus tells Peter that those who take up the sword will die by the sword (Matt. 26:52) but also tells the disciples that those who lack swords should sell their cloaks to buy them (Luke 26:36). He tells them that wars and rumors of wars are "but the beginning of the birth pangs" (Matt. 24:8). Paul writes that the governing authorities have been instituted by God and serve God through their use of the sword against evildoers (Rom. 13:1–4). A number of military men (the centurion in Luke 7:1–10, Cornelius in Acts 10) are treated favorably in the NT, and Heb. 11 includes the great warriors of Israel among the cloud of witnesses to the faith. Martial metaphors are scattered throughout the NT, including those concerning the armor of God (Eph. 6:14–17; 1 Thess. 5:8). Moreover, some NT scholars (Otto Betz, Ragnar Leivestad) have emphasized Jesus' adoption and use of the warrior God vision of the OT for his own use, claiming to be a messianic warrior in battle against the forces of evil.

The book of Revelation, in which fifteen of the twenty-five NT uses of the noun *polemos* ("war") and verb *polemeō* ("to wage war") occur, adds further complexity to the matter. The book's apocalyptic imagery promotes a vision of cosmic conflict in which the forces of evil make war against the Lamb of God, whose weapon is the word/sword. Notable in its absence, however, is any actual battle between the King of kings and the armies of darkness arrayed against him: they gather for battle but are summarily vanquished (Rev. 19:19–21). The book's metaphorical character has allowed Christians to use it both in support of martial violence and against all acts of violence, including war.

Interpreting the OT through the lens of Jesus' teachings and actions, the early church probably was exclusively pacifist. As of the second century, soldiers were refused baptism, though whether this was because of their connection to violence or to the cult of the emperor is not entirely clear. Nor is it clear whether the early church's pacifism was due more to its tenuous place in the Roman Empire or to its theological convictions. The evidence of martyrs willing to die, though not to kill, for the faith does not settle the case, and scholarly arguments on such matters are ongoing. We know that by the third century, soldiers were being baptized, if only because we have the writings of early church fathers, such as Tertullian, who were vehemently opposed to their baptisms.

Traditions of Theological Reflection on War and Peace

Constantine's victory at the Battle of Milvian Bridge in 312 CE signaled a watershed moment for the church and its understandings of war and peace. Not only did it lead to the Edict of Milan in 313 CE, which made Christianity a legal religion (rendering moot pragmatic concerns about the church making itself a target for persecution), but also Constantine connected his military victory to the Christian faith. Within seventy-five years, Christianity would become the official religion of the empire, making the questions of what to do with soldiers in the church and church participation in war even more pressing.

Five approaches to the questions were variously pursued, each by way of emphasizing a distinction between acceptable and unacceptable behavior: (1) one could fight in battle if motivated by love and a desire for justice but not if driven by hate or love of violence; (2) one could fight on behalf of others but not on one's own behalf; (3) one could fight in battles called for by the rulers of the state but not in private skirmishes; (4) one could fight if one's station in life did not require living according to a higher moral standard (i.e., soldiers could fight, priests could not); (5) one could fight if one was not a part of the church but not once one had joined the church. These distinctions would continue to play themselves out in the development of the three dominant traditions of theological reflection on war and peace.

Pacifism. Pacifism was the ethic closest to that of Jesus as he is described in the Gospels; it is also probably the closest to that of the early church. Like all traditions, it is not a single approach, however. John Howard Yoder names more than twenty varieties of pacifism. For the sake of convenience, these might be reduced to three broad categories. The first, emphasizing nonresistance and practiced by the historic peace churches (e.g., Mennonites, Amish), begins in the conviction that obedience to Jesus' commandment to love our enemies trumps all other considerations in moral reasoning about war and peace, including any consequentialist calculations about making things come out right. God in Christ has already done everything necessary to ensure that things come out right; such calculations, therefore, signal a lack of faith in God's work and a refusal to live into Christian eschatological hope as well as a failure to love others properly. The second, best seen in the nonviolent resistance projects of the civil rights movement as shaped by Martin Luther King Jr. (relying on Gandhi's idea of *satyagraha*), argues not only that pacifism is faithful to Jesus' vision of the kingdom of God but also that nonviolent resistance has the effect of changing the hearts of those who see it practiced and, therein, the political, social, and military structures that support war. It sees pacifism not only as faithful but also as effective. The third, sometimes called "technological pacifism," argues that modern weapons of war cannot be used in just ways, and therefore we must be pacifists. This latter form is not so much a principled pacifism as a conclusion that follows from a particular approach to just-war arguments. These three categories attend closely to the moral persuasiveness of NT writings, but they are criticized for failing to adequately account for human behavior between Jesus' resurrection and his return and for allowing some coercive practices (including the use of force by, e.g., the police) while refusing to create space for the violence of war.

Holy war. Born of the conviction that God fights for the good and against evil and calls Christians to do the same, the tradition of holy war relies on its dualistic vision of the world (good/evil; us/them; victory/defeat) to drive a vision of war without limits. Restraints on conduct are ignored, and the only rule in a crusade is to win by utterly defeating the enemy. Interestingly, then, it shares with pacifism the conviction that war is hell. Although certainly (and regrettably) there have been historical manifestations of this approach to war within Christianity (including, most obviously, the Crusades of the Late Middle Ages), and although some contemporary fundamentalisms, especially of the premillenial dispensationalist variety, support it, holy war cannot be theologically justified. Its dualisms deny basic Christian claims about the fundamental goodness of creation (which remains even after the fall), the intrinsic value of all human life, and the continued and free work of God to order, sustain, and transform the world.

Just war. Although precursors to the just-war tradition appear in the OT and Roman law, it enters Christianity most apparently after Constantine, especially in the work of Ambrose and Augustine. It assumes that violence in war must be justified but also can be justified as human beings attempt to make sense of how to live between Jesus' resurrection and his return. Such justification emphasizes human responsibility for doing justice and assumes that Christians have some political power. Possible justifications have included national self-defense, the support of an aggrieved nation, and the punishment of wrongdoing. Like all traditions, it changes over time; after the sixteenth century, it finds its legal center in the development of international law and its theological/moral center in the just-war criteria. *Jus ad bellum* criteria pertain to justifications for going into war and generally include demands for legitimate authority, just cause, right intention (and announcement of that intention), last resort, reasonable hope of success, and proportionality. *Jus in bello* criteria pertain to fighting justly and generally include right intention, proportionality, and discrimination. Recent work has included questions about *jus post bellum* criteria. Seeing even war as a rule-governed activity that can lead to social stability, the just-war tradition recognizes both human failings and human possibilities this side of eternity and seeks to limit warfare while claiming that some goods do accrue through warfare. Significantly harder to justify on NT grounds, and given the presumption against taking human life, critics point to the way just-war theory can be used to rationalize rather than justify war, question the way the criteria are applied, and highlight its limitations in the face of modern weaponry and the way it can be co-opted by realist/Clausewitzian arguments.

James Childress has argued that rather than thinking of the pacifist and just-war traditions as opposed to each other, we ought to recognize that they need each other. Presupposing the common starting points that human life is valuable and war is bad, just warriors need pacifists to remind them of that starting point and keep them honest, while pacifists need just warriors to supply them with the criteria by which to rule out particular wars (and, perhaps, to keep them safe). This argument, though, has faced criticisms from both perspectives.

Contemporary Problems and Projects

Faced with changes in political and economic systems, technology, and war itself (see, e.g., John Mueller's argument that the age of conventional war has come to an end and is being replaced by criminal activity), and frustrated by the limitations of the traditions to adequately address those changes, a number of ethicists have developed new projects in thinking about war and peace from a Christian perspective. Perhaps the best known of these is the "just-peacemaking" project, developed by Glen Stassen and others, which seeks to develop international practices that would make war unnecessary. Given the advent and distribution of modern weapons of mass destruction, the changing face of geopolitics and its attendant global economic disparities, the proliferation and power of nonstate players and terrorism, the return to public consciousness of religio-ethnic violence, and increasingly critical concerns about the environment, all these traditions and projects face important and difficult tests of fidelity and viability today and into the foreseeable future.

See also Conflict; Conquest; Conscientious Objection; Conscription; Deterrence, Nuclear; Dirty Hands; Enemy, Enemy Love; Force, Use of; Genocide; Government; Holy War; Just-Peacemaking Theory; Just-War Theory; Military Service; Pacifism; Peace; Prisoners of War; Terrorism

Bibliography

Elshtain, J. *Women and War*. University of Chicago Press, 1995; Gat, A. *War in Human Civilization*. Oxford University Press, 2006; Hauerwas, S. *Performing the Faith: Bonhoeffer and the Practice of Nonviolence*. Brazos, 2004; Holmes, A. *War and Christian Ethics: Classic and Contemporary Readings on the Morality of War*. Baker Academic, 2005; Joas, H. *War and Modernity*. Trans. R. Livingstone. Blackwell, 2003; Johnson, J. *Can Modern War Be Just?* Yale University Press, 1984; Miller, R. *War in the Twentieth Century: Sources in Theological Ethics*. Westminster John Knox, 1992; Mueller, J. *The Remnants of War*. Cornell University Press, 2004; O'Donovan, O. *The Just War Revisited*. CIT 2. Cambridge University Press, 2003; Ramsey, P. *The Just War: Force and Political Responsibility*. Rowman & Littlefield, 1968; von Clausewitz, C. *On War*. Ed. and trans. M. Howard and P. Paret. Princeton University Press, 1976; Walzer, M. *Just and Unjust Wars: A Moral Argument with Historical Illustrations*. Basic Books, 1992; Yoder, J. *When War Is Unjust: Being Honest in Just-War Thinking*. Orbis, 1996.

Mark Douglas

Wealth

The Witness of Scripture

Scripture contains an abundance of material devoted to the topic of wealth. Yet, although the biblical writers speak consistently about wealth, they do not speak about wealth consistently. The variety of voices and perspectives within the canon means that the Bible's treatments of wealth and possessions cannot easily be synthesized. Here the data will be summarized in six categories, with the recognition that these representative divisions are illustrative and not exhaustive (see Wheeler 107–34).

Wealth as the result of God's blessing. With the biblical acknowledgment that God's creation of the material world is good comes the recognition that material possessions are gifts from God intended for use and enjoyment. In the Pentateuch, for example, God's promise of deliverance from Egypt is repeatedly framed with reference to the people's relocation to a fruitful "land flowing with milk and honey," a pledge of communal success in an agrarian context (e.g., Exod. 3:8; Lev. 20:24; Num. 13:27; Deut. 6:3). The blessing of land, however, is associated with the confession that all the earth ultimately belongs to Yahweh (Lev. 25:23; cf. Ps. 24:1: "The earth is the LORD's and all that is in it"). The theological conviction that Israel's land and possessions are held in trust on behalf of God places certain responsibilities on those who steward these material goods in the present. Custody of the land is a gift from God, given to the people at the time of their exodus from Egypt. Therefore, this divine blessing entails the duty of caring for the marginalized: "You shall not wrong or oppress a resident alien, for you were aliens in the land of Egypt" (Exod. 22:21; cf. 22:22–27; 23:9; for a similar expression of the idea that national prosperity should be followed by generosity to the less fortunate, see Deut. 15:1–8).

The prophets also frequently articulate visions of future redemption in terms of abundance and agricultural prosperity (e.g., Isa. 60:6–18; Jer. 33:1–9). Even the book of Revelation, which contains one of the most stinging indictments of luxurious excess in the entire canon (17:1–18:24), is punctuated with an eschatological picture of material blessing for the people of God in the new heaven and new earth (21:1–22:22). Thus, the biblical tradition emphasizes the inherent goodness of both the created order and the enjoyment of material blessings as an aspect of God's creation.

If most of the texts in this category stress the collective dimensions of God's blessing, there is also a strand of the OT that tends to individualize these promises, so that personal prosperity becomes a sign of divine favor: "Who, then, are those who fear the LORD? He will instruct them in the ways they should choose. They will spend their days in prosperity, and their descendants will inherit the land" (Ps. 25:12–13 TNIV; cf. Prov. 10:22; 13:21, 25). That this notion of righteousness bringing riches is muted, if not altogether absent, in the NT witness is an important factor in the attempt to develop a biblical perspective on wealth and possessions.

Wealth as a resource for meeting human needs. Related to the affirmation of the inherent goodness of material possessions is the concept that those with wealth have a responsibility to share their resources with those in need. The legal traditions in the OT, for example, contain numerous provisions such as the poor tithe, the sabbatical year, and the Jubilee—all designed to provide assistance for the disadvantaged (e.g., Deut. 14:22–29; 15:1–11; Lev. 25:8–55; cf. Sir. 4:1–10). Indeed, a frequent refrain in the Deuteronomic legislation centers on the responsibility of the community to care for the marginalized, particularly resident aliens, orphans, and widows (Deut. 14:29; 16:11, 14; 26:12–13; cf. Job 22:9; Ps. 68:5; Isa. 10:1–3). Adherence to the commandments is said in Deut. 15:4 to lead to an absence of the needy among the people of God.

In the NT, the book of Acts contains several examples of resource sharing within the early church. Picking up on the refrain of Deut. 15:4, the author of Acts notes that the result of the refusal of members of the messianic community in Jerusalem to claim private ownership of possessions, holding instead all things in common, was that "there was not a needy person among them" (4:32–35; cf. 2:44–45; 6:1–7). The NT Epistles provide numerous instances of, or calls for, the provision of material relief for those in need within the community of faith (e.g., Rom. 12:6–8; Phil. 4:10–20; Jas. 2:15–16). Paul's efforts to organize a financial contribution for impoverished believers in Jerusalem among the largely gentile congregations of his mission stands as an exemplary episode of mutual assistance within the nascent church (Rom. 15:25–32; 1 Cor. 16:1–4; 2 Cor. 8:1–9:15). The author of 1 John aptly summarizes the christological foundation for this kind of beneficence: "We know love by this, that he laid down his life for us—and we ought to lay down our lives for one another. How does God's love abide in anyone who has the world's goods and sees a brother or sister in need and yet refuses help?" (1 John 3:16–17). Thus, an important strand in the biblical tradition is the notion that those who receive the blessing of material abundance have an obligation to share with those of lesser means.

Wealth as a reward for labor. A third thread, found particularly in the wisdom literature in the OT and the Apocrypha, emphasizes wealth as the outcome of diligent or prudent work. Conversely, a lack of resources is occasionally seen as the result of idleness: "The lazy do not roast their game, but the diligent obtain precious wealth" (Prov. 12:27; cf. 8:18, 21; 10:4; 12:11, 24; 13:4; Sir. 2:12). This notion is at least partially reflected in 2 Thess. 3:6–13, a passage that encourages work and warns against idleness for members of the Christian community.

Wealth as a temptation to idolatry. Whereas the three previous categories tend to view wealth in relatively positive light, the next three emphasize the perils of riches. Numerous texts in Scripture underscore, for example, the close relationship between wealth and idolatry. Here the danger of wealth is found particularly in (1) the ability of affluence to foster self-reliance rather than trust in God; and (2) the close connection between prosperity and the worship of pagan gods (Deut. 32:10–18; Isa. 2:5–18; Jer. 5:7–8; Ezek. 7:19–24; Hos. 2:5–9). Indeed, greed, idolatry, and sexual immorality form a kind of unholy triumvirate in Jewish assessment of pagan vice. Wealth is transitory and will mean nothing on the day of judgment (Ps. 49:10–20; Prov. 11:4, 28; 23:1–5; Eccl. 5:10–12; 5:1–6; Matt. 6:19–21; 1 Tim. 6:6–7; Jas. 1:9–11). Jesus' declaration that one "cannot serve God and wealth" emphasizes the enslaving, idolatrous power of wealth (Matt. 6:24 // Luke 16:13). Similarly, the parable of the rich fool in

Luke 12:16–21 identifies the imprudence of an economic autonomy that ignores God. In both Colossians and Ephesians, the connection between greed and idolatry is explicit: greed *is* idolatry (Eph. 5:5; Col. 3:5; cf. 1 Tim. 6:17–19).

This connection between wealth and idolatry relates to an important aspect of the Bible's language about wealth and its converse, poverty: in the ancient world wealth and poverty were not merely economic categories. Since economic activities in antiquity were deeply embedded in social relationships, to be wealthy was as much to enjoy cultural privilege, social power, and elite status as it was to possess money. Conversely, to be poor was to be marginalized, shamed, and excluded, quite often because of a lack of financial resources, but not exclusively so. This is perhaps best illustrated in the Gospel of Luke, where the rich (*plousios*, *plouteō*) often are identified as those with power and honor (1:53–54; 6:24–26; 14:12; 16:19–31; 21:1), while the poor (*ptōchos*) often are the socially excluded and dispossessed (4:18; 6:20; 7:22; 14:13, 21; 16:20, 22; 21:3; but cf. 18:22; 19:8, where the poor are recipients of alms) (see Green). To the extent that the wealthy possess power and prestige, they are perhaps particularly prone to the temptation of trusting in the idol of their own resources.

Wealth as the product of injustice. If the previous tradition stresses the spiritual threat of wealth, the next accentuates the extent to which wealth can stem from and perpetuate social injustice. Particularly in the prophetic tradition, wealth is frequently associated with dishonest gain (Mic. 6:10–14) or oppression of the poor (Eccl. 5:8; Isa. 10:1–4; Amos 2:6–8; 4:1; cf. Exod. 23:6). Zechariah 7:9–10 stands as an apt summary of much of the prophetic witness: "Thus says the LORD of hosts: Render true judgments, show kindness and mercy to one another; do not oppress the widow, the orphan, the alien, or the poor; and do not devise evil in your hearts against one another." Instead of unjust treatment of the poor, the people of God are consistently called to defend the cause of the needy. Psalm 72 is a royal psalm that voices the hope that the king will reflect God's justice on the earth: "Give the king your justice, O God, and your righteousness to a king's son. May he judge your people with righteousness, and your poor with justice. May the mountains yield prosperity for the people, and the hills, in righteousness. May he defend the cause of the poor of the people, give deliverance to the needy, and crush the oppressor" (Ps. 72:1–4).

In the NT too the accumulation of wealth often is associated with economic injustice. The parable of the rich man and Lazarus offers an evocative commentary on the dangers faced by the wealthy if they neglect the responsibility to demonstrate justice for the poor (Luke 16:19–31). Perhaps more than any other NT book, James accuses the rich of economic oppression (5:1–6), and it defines "pure and undefiled religion" as "to care for orphans and widows in their distress, and to keep oneself unstained by the world" (1:27). James's passionate denunciation of the rich is matched by the critique of the exploitative and dehumanizing nature of Roman imperial commerce found in Rev. 18:1–24. These texts that speak against the unjust pursuit and accumulation of wealth are, of course, protests against contingent abuses. Yet this biblical tradition ought to cause all those who possess (relative) wealth to think about the ways in which material prosperity and social power might result from and maintain unjust economic structures.

Wealth as an obstacle to discipleship. Related to the previous motif, a notable theme in the NT is that attachment to wealth can serve as a stumbling block to following Jesus. This notion is exemplified in Jesus' encounter with a rich man in Mark 10:17–31 (cf. Matt. 19:16–22; Luke 18:18–23). The man is saddened when Jesus instructs, "Sell what you own, and give the money to the poor, and you will have treasure in heaven; then come, follow me" (10:21). Jesus' response to the man's grief and departure acknowledges the difficulty of discipleship for the wealthy: "How hard it will be for those who have wealth to enter the kingdom of God!" (10:23). Similarly, in the parable of the sower, "the lure of wealth" is one of the thorns that choke the seed and prevent its growth (Mark 4:1–19, especially vv. 18–19; cf. 1 John 2:15–17; Rev. 3:14–22). Conversely, dispossession of goods sometimes signals faithful discipleship (Mark 10:28–31; cf. Mark 1:16–20; Matt. 9:9; 13:44–46; Luke 19:1–10).

The Tradition and Scripture

There is an equally great diversity represented among the early Christian authors of the second century and beyond who grappled with Scripture's witness as it bears on pecuniary matters. One point of unanimity among all church fathers, however, is the common assumption that faith and finance are intimately intertwined. This perspective, of course, is one that the patristic writers inherited from biblical tradition. Although today one sometimes observes—at least in practice, if not in pronouncement—a sharp division between theology and economics, no single important Christian author of the first several centuries of the Common Era advocates such a separation. Those who desire that their beliefs and practices be shaped by the teachings of Scripture, and those who wish to live under the moral authority of the OT and the NT, will necessarily have to wrestle with economic questions, for the questions are raised first and constantly within the Bible itself. Any individual, church, or tradition that fails consistently to identify economic issues as central to the understanding and embodiment of the Christian faith is simply unfaithful to the testimony of Scripture.

Given the number of harsh pronouncements against wealth found in Scripture, it is not surprising that as the church gradually rose in social prominence and collected a greater number of prosperous believers in the second and third centuries, thoughtful Christians began to wrestle with the implications of the Bible's teachings on wealth. Clement of Alexandra (c. 150–211/216), for instance, penned what is probably the first extended reflection on the problem of wealth for believers. His treatise *Quis dives salvetur* ("Who Is the Rich Man Being Saved?") is an extended homily on Mark 10:17–31 aimed at demonstrating to rich Christians in Alexandria that salvation is possible for the wealthy. Clement interprets Jesus' command to dispossess goods allegorically, so that what one must abandon is not money but rather the desire for, and excessive attachment to, material goods. Such an understanding of this difficult text has been quite popular in Christian history. Clement does, however, advocate both unostentatious living for the wealthy as the outer form of interior detachment (see *Paed.* 3.10–11) and giving alms to the poor (*Quis. div.* 32). In his discussion of almsgiving, Clement suggests that it is possible for the rich to purchase eternal reward through the giving of money to the destitute in the present life. Clement's is an important early voice in the development of the doctrine known as "redemptive almsgiving," the notion that providing material assistance to the poor redeems (or cancels or cleanses) sin. Aside from Clement, advocates of redemptive almsgiving include such documents and church fathers as *2 Clement* (16.1–4), *Didache* (4.5–8), *Epistle of Barnabas* (19.9–11), *Shepherd of Hermas* (51.5–9), Cyprian (*Works and Almsgiving*), Ambrose (*Hel.* 20; 76), and Augustine (*Enchir.* 67; 69; 70). This solution conveniently allowed the rich to maintain the bulk of their wealth while also providing tangible financial assistance to the poor.

Voices more radical than Clement's can be found. The preaching of John Chrysostom, for example, is at times quite sharp in its assessment of the dangers of wealth and abuses perpetuated by the wealthy. Even more extreme is the development of the monastic tradition, with its emphasis on voluntary poverty and asceticism. The success of the monastic movement probably played a part in discouraging the church from serious reflection on the spiritual and ethical issues associated with wealth, for monastics could aspire to practices of limited and shared possessions, while the majority of believers were free to accumulate wealth of their own, sharing some of it with the religious and some of it with the involuntary poor.

In the twentieth century, advocates of the social gospel and liberation theology, along with certain strands of Catholic social teaching and evangelicals who emphasize biblical traditions of justice, have drawn upon the Bible to offer significant challenges to the self-interested accumulation of wealth that forms the basis of the modern capitalist system. However, proponents of the so-called prosperity gospel, both in the United States and increasingly in the developing world, have focused on one relatively minor strand in the scriptural witness to claim that material prosperity, including financial success, will accompany the faithful.

Any attempt to come to terms with Scripture's teaching on wealth and possessions must take into account the diversity of the canonical witness. There is no easy way to synthesize the various traditions. One approach would insist that economic ethics, or moral decisions about things such as wealth, must be rooted in the larger story of God's creativity and salvific action narrated in the witness of Scripture.

Yet, this canonical diversity can be seen as a good thing. The diversity of Scripture can be used to help articulate different messages to different audiences in different contexts. There are times when the harsh prophetic denunciations issued by Isaiah and James will need to serve as a grave warning to rich Christians whose careless and selfish pursuit of wealth is defrauding and perhaps even murdering the poor. There are times when believers will need to be reminded that wealth can lead to idolatry, that wealth is portrayed in Scripture as an anti-God power that threatens to enslave the people of God (e.g., Luke 16:13). And there are times when followers of Jesus will need to be reminded of the powerful way in which wealth can be used to meet the material needs of others, when those with an abundance of possessions will be invited to participate in a sharing of goods aimed at providing financial relief for the poor—an endeavor itself modeled after the self-giving love of Jesus Christ (2 Cor. 8:9).

See also Almsgiving; Economic Ethics; Generosity; Idolatry; Jubilee; Justice, Distributive; Koinonia;

Liberationist Ethics; Loans; Poverty and Poor; Property and Possessions; Stewardship; Tithe, Tithing

Bibliography

Blomberg, C. *Neither Poverty nor Riches: A Biblical Theology of Possessions*. InterVarsity, 1999; Coleman, S. *The Globalisation of Charismatic Christianity: Spreading the Gospel of Prosperity*. Cambridge University Press, 2000; González, J. *Faith and Wealth: A History of Early Christian Ideas on the Origin, Significance, and Use of Money*. Wipf & Stock, 1990; Green, J. "Good News to Whom? Jesus and the 'Poor' in the Gospel of Luke." Pages 59–74 in *Jesus of Nazareth: Lord and Christ*, ed. J. Green and M. Turner. Eerdmans, 1994; Holman, S. *God Knows There's Need: Christian Responses to Poverty*. Oxford University Press, 2009; idem, ed. *Wealth and Poverty in Early Church and Society*. Baker Academic, 2008; Lindberg, C. *Beyond Charity: Reformation Initiatives for the Poor*. Fortress, 1993; Rosner, B. *Greed as Idolatry: The Origin and Meaning of a Pauline Metaphor*. Eerdmans, 2007; Wheeler, S. *Wealth as Peril and Obligation: The New Testament on Possessions*. Eerdmans, 1995.

David J. Downs

Welfare State

The welfare state is a nineteenth- and twentieth-century model for social, political, and economic organization in which a government takes actions to foster the well-being of its citizens. Services might include education, healthcare, retirement pensions, libraries, poverty relief, and other "safety nets" to ensure basic quality of life. Usually found in highly developed democratic economies, the welfare state represents a theoretical middle way between Marxism and laissez-faire capitalism, arising in response to the historical shortcomings of both. It seeks to foster social unity while not unduly hindering economic growth. It has been most fully embraced in continental Western Europe, but also to lesser degrees in the United Kingdom, Australia, Canada, the United States, and Japan.

Attending to Scripture

One looks in vain for direct references to the welfare state in the Bible. Although a nonnegotiable command to love one's neighbor in response to God's love is present in both the OT and the NT, neither one gives directions on exactly how to implement this love. The main argument among Christians with regard to the welfare state model involves the question of where God places the responsibility to care for the poor and otherwise needy: is it upon individuals or upon governmental institutions?

The Torah's audience is the nation of Israel. God directs them not to be "tight-fisted" toward the needy but rather to "give liberally and be ungrudging" about it (Deut. 15:7, 10). God commands them to leave some food in their vineyards and fields for the alien, widow, and orphan to take (Deut. 24:19–22). They are commanded to treat resident aliens kindly (Lev. 19:34) and to support relatives when they fall on hard times (Lev. 25:35–37). They are not to exploit the poor by lending money to them at interest. Obedience to these commands ensures the well-being not only of the vulnerable but also of Israel as a nation (Lev. 26:3–13). Such teachings rest on a concept of *ṣĕdāqâ* as an act of justice, righteousness, and duty to God rather than simple "charity" (as usually translated).

The NT demonstrates a continuing interest in the Jewish concern for the poor and vulnerable. In the Gospels, Mary sings that God "has filled the hungry with good things, and sent the rich away empty" (Luke 1:53). Jesus introduces himself as one who "brings good news to the poor" (Luke 4:18), and he urges a rich man to give all his money to the poor (Mark 10:21). He says that only those who feed the hungry, give drink to the thirsty, welcome the stranger, clothe the naked, and visit the sick and imprisoned will inherit the kingdom of God; those who do not will suffer eternal punishment (Matt. 25:31–46). Three times Jesus tells Peter to feed and care for his flock (John 21:15–17). Jesus discouraged greed and hoarding, encouraged generous giving, and even took the paying of taxes in stride (Matt. 22:21), and the early churches appear to have followed this example. The writer of Acts claims that there was no private ownership in the earliest church, and God punished those who refused to share (Acts 2:42–47; 4:32–5:11). Similarly, Paul urges wealthy Christians to follow Jesus' lead by becoming poor and sending their money to poorer Christians (2 Cor. 8:1–15). This does not mean that the early apostles looked kindly upon idleness or freeloading: "Anyone unwilling to work should not eat" (2 Thess. 3:10). One NT writer wished that "the church not be burdened" with widows who are young or who have family members to care for them, "so that it can assist those who are real widows" (1 Tim. 5:16).

Jesus' parable of the good Samaritan (Luke 10:25–37) provides an example of the inherent difficulties in applying the Bible to social life. According to one interpretation, the moral of the parable is that God's people should alleviate suffering, even for complete strangers. If relieving suffering is the thrust of the parable, this task might rightly be taken up by state policymakers in response to a community's mandate. Another reading, however, sees this parable as a directive for individuals to love their neighbors. If individual love is the main point, then it would be a mistake for a government to take charge of caring for the poor, thereby hindering individuals from performing acts of charity. Jesus said, "You always have the poor with you" (Matt. 26:11; John 12:8), so the eradication of poverty-related suffering may not be of utmost importance for Christians on a large scale. In short, the Scriptures are clear that love of neighbor is among God's top priorities for humankind, but they offer no explicit policy prescriptions for modern nation-states.

The Tradition and Scripture

In the fifth century, Augustine made a distinction between the city of God, in which love of God is the law, and the city of humans, in which self-love and natural law are the rule. One might then argue that government should focus on public matters, while the church takes care of the poor. A simple distinction between church and state does not work here, however, since Augustine saw self-love and love of God coexisting in both the church and the earthly city. In the sixteenth century, John Calvin followed Augustine's lead in distinguishing church and government, but he too saw them working together harmoniously with several overlapping goals rather than one overpowering the other. The church in Calvin's Geneva boldly intervened in the economic lives of its citizens: lending at exorbitant interest rates was forbidden, work was divided evenly among local businesses, and offenders against economic justice could be called before the consistory and excommunicated (Valeri). Thus, Christians have a long tradition of partnerships between government and church; the "separation of church and state" is an idea born in the modern period.

The Christian socialist and social gospel movements of the late 1800s and early 1900s did much to offer Christian justification for welfare models. Proponents turned their gaze from saving souls to what they saw as a more important plan: saving society as a whole. An editorial in a 1912 issue of *The Biblical World* states, "The world will never be saved by the salvation of individuals, simply because the greatest of its sins are not individual sins at all. As individuals we are kind and just, as a society we are heartless and tyrannical." In the twentieth century, liberation theologians called upon Christians to put practices of social justice at the center of their theology. In 1986 the National Conference of Catholic Bishops in the United States reminded their audience that "the justice of a society is tested by the treatment of the poor."

In the twenty-first century, the "welfare state" is often invoked as a negative, attacked by Christians who believe "that God ordained government to protect a nation through strong defense and to enforce fundamental laws" but not to "regulate the economy, intervene in the parental responsibility for educating children, or help people who can help themselves" (Zweir and Smith 938). Implicit are two important beliefs: first, markets work perfectly (or nearly so) to ensure that each person gets his or her due; second, individuals, families, and churches can help needy people more effectively and efficiently than governments can (Murray). Opponents of government safety nets generally cite reasons of paternalism and infringements on individual freedoms (i.e., government-mandated charity). Some even characterize safety nets as theft, in that the state unjustly steals from the wealthy through taxation while rewarding the undeserving with handouts (Williams).

Contemporary Application

Conventional wisdom holds that conservative Christian theologies are linked to conservative economic opinions, and liberal theologies are related to liberal economic opinions. Sociologists have found, however, that support for social spending correlates more closely to race, class, and political affiliation than to theology or biblical interpretation (Pyle). The Bible provides mixed messages; Israel saw itself as a sovereign nation, whereas early Christianity was forged in a context in which the "kingdom of God" apparently had little to do with earthly power. One may argue that biblical instructions on the redistribution of wealth were directed to individuals or faith communities rather than governments. Christians might agree that God creates scarcity as "the occasion for God to provide for us through each other" (Barrera xv) but still disagree over the best means of instituting those provisions.

Two and a half centuries of capitalism reveal that it is highly effective at fostering the growth of wealth. However, this growth tends to accumulate exponentially in the pockets of the few while disproportionately afflicting society's weakest members with its unintended consequences. A government depends on the work of all its citizens and therefore has a responsibility to all of its citizens. Human beings "are uneven beneficiaries of . . . grace," and individual humans' capacities usually are not earned but rather are a matter of "enabling forces beyond [their] control" (Beckley 17), namely, good birth. More often than not, wealthy people are those who were born into wealth and/or born into families that enabled them to build the social capital needed to succeed in their economic context. If wealth is a gift from God, enabled by stable government, then it should be shared. When private sharing lags, taxation and redistribution can constitute an effective backup plan for ensuring the basic needs of vulnerable individuals and the overall health of society.

See also Capitalism; Charity, Works of; Common Good; Democracy; Economic Ethics; Government; Loans; Political Ethics; Poverty and Power; Taxation; Wealth

Bibliography

Barrera, A. *God and the Evil of Scarcity: Moral Foundations of Economic Agency*. University of Notre Dame Press, 2005; Beckley, H. "Moral Justifications for the Welfare State." *ASCE* 21 (2001): 3–22; Berman, S. *The Primacy of Politics: Social Democracy and the Making of Europe's Twentieth Century*. Cambridge University Press, 2006; Galbraith, J. K. *The Affluent Society*. Houghton Mifflin, 1958; Murray, C. "A Plan to Replace the Welfare State." *Wall Street Journal*, March 26, 2006, A16; National Conference of Catholic Bishops. *Economic Justice for All: Pastoral Letter on Catholic Social Teaching and the U.S. Economy*. United States Catholic Conference, 1986; Pyle, R. "Faith and Commitment to the Poor: Theological Orientation and Support for Government Assistance Measures." *SocRel* 54 (1993): 385–401. "The Social Gospel." Editorial in *BibW* 40 (1912): 147–51; Valeri, M. "Religion, Discipline, and the Economy in Calvin's Geneva." *SCJ* 28 (1997): 123–42; Williams, W. "Bogus Rights." *The Washington Times*, Feb. 14, 2006; Zweir, R., and R. Smith. "Christian Politics and the New Right." *ChrCent* 97, no. 32 (Oct. 8, 1980): 937–41.

Kathryn D. Blanchard

Wesleyan Ethics

Relevance and Background Information

John Wesley was an important figure in eighteenth-century England, and in many ways his work and ministry remain influential in the twenty-first century as well. Many denominations consider him instrumental and foundational to the point that his methodological approach and theology have become the center for their organization and rules of faith. Furthermore, one of the fastest-growing Christian expressions, Pentecostalism, is closely associated with the Wesleyan movement. For these reasons, there is no doubt that John Wesley's contributions to the church have been significant, and his influence still relevant today. And perhaps what is even more significant is the way in which Wesley made an impression in his world and ours. In a traditional way, theologians promote their ideas by organizing them into categories, writing about them, and then publishing them; although we know that Wesley was a highly organized and methodical person, and even though he wrote extensively, he did not organize his ideas in a systematic fashion as did some of his predecessors such as John Calvin and Martin Luther.

It is precisely this nontraditional approach that is fascinating and raises the question of how a theologian who never wrote systematic theology became so influential in defining core theological concepts. The same can be said when it comes to the field of ethics: what do we mean by "Wesleyan ethics" in light of the fact that John Wesley never wrote or published an ethical treatise per se? It is precisely in attempting to answer such questions that one begins to realize the importance of the method itself as opposed to the "systematic" results. In fact, in exploring ethical theories, one could characterize Wesley's method and approach as character ethics and/or virtue ethics because his focus is on the tangible actions and their moral value as well as the character traits in life and ministry that resemble those of Christ. It is evident that Wesley developed an ethical system that was quite different from the logical organization of abstract moral ideals and philosophical notions typically embraced by traditional academic sources and often removed from their pastoral applicability. Although it is likely that Wesley was aware of these philosophical categories, it is of significant importance to know that he placed particular emphasis on the pastoral and ecclesiological practices as the ethical standard. For these reasons, it is important to explore Wesley's method because it seems that the method itself becomes the focal point of Wesley's ethics, and by exploring it one will become acquainted with Wesley's conclusions, ministerial practices, and moral admonitions to his followers and nonfollowers alike. Furthermore, a careful analysis of Wesley's methodological approach will offer insights into his hermeneutical practices and his moral views with regard to humankind and its goodness and wickedness.

Wesley's Methodology: An Obedient Response or Moved by a Higher Call?

In attempting to answer this question, one is required to explore Wesley's life, ministerial work, and writings to determine the reasons and principles underlying his methodological approach and the consistency of it. Beginning with his life, and based on his own recollection and interpretation, the first notable aspect is his life-changing experience at Aldersgate, which he described thus:

> I felt my heart strangely warmed. I felt I did trust in Christ, Christ alone for salvation: And an assurance was given me, that he had taken away my sins, even mine, and saved me from the law of sin and death. I began to pray with all my might for those who had in a more especial manner despitefully used me and persecuted me. I then testified openly to all there, what I now first felt in my heart. (Wesley 1:103)

Wesley's popular account of his experience at Aldersgate shows that there was a paradigm shift in his belief system, whereby at the personal level he placed his trust in Christ alone and became certain of Christ's work in his life in terms of deliverance from the law of sin and death. The language of deliverance and its connection to the legal motif are an important aspect in exploring Wesley's ethical approach. By his own account, Wesley seems to indicate that before the Aldersgate moment he was following a legal approach to the Christian life; in a way, he felt obligated to fulfill his Christian duty, and thus his ethical reasoning can be labeled as deontological. If this is true, Wesley's primary reasons for his actions and even his missionary work were grounded in a sense of duty and obligation. But after Aldersgate, Wesley seems to be moved by a higher impulse, and the first indication of this shift is his first action. He prayed for those who "used" him and "persecuted" him, which raises questions. Did he not pray for them before this occasion? If he did, what was he asking God to do with them? Perhaps in his strict legalistic sense and following his duty, Wesley did not feel compelled to pray for his enemies; but after his personal transformation, Wesley seems to have developed a sense of moral responsibility for his enemies, not out of a deontological imposition, but rather in response to God's work in his life. God accepted him, welcomed him, and gave him peace in his heart, while he considered himself an enemy of God! Now, as a response to God's radical love and embrace, Wesley wants to do the same for all people, including praying for his enemies and publicly testifying to these actions—not a private practice, but rather a private and public expression of God's love in his life.

Wesley's Aldersgate experience is indicative of a theological and ethical paradigm shift in which Wesley was moved by God's love to love others in an attempt to replicate God's character and acceptance demonstrated to him. And for this reason, his ethical reasoning may be described in Christian ethics as character or virtue ethics. Furthermore, his ministerial work and his writings seem to corroborate this fundamental shift in his methodological approach. For example, before Aldersgate, Wesley practiced personal spiritual disciplines and became quite active in social work, but reflecting on these years at Oxford as a member of the Holy Club, Wesley wrote,

> More especially, we call upon those who for many years saw our manner of life at Oxford. These well know that "after the straitest sect of our religion we lived [like] Pharisees"; and that the grand objection to us for all those years was, the being righteous overmuch; the reading, fasting, praying, denying ourselves,—the going to church, and to the Lord's table,—the relieving the poor, visiting those that were sick and in prison, instructing the ignorant, and labouring to reclaim the wicked,—more than was necessary for salvation. These were our open, flagrant crimes, from the year 1729 to the year 1737. (8:29)

Therefore, and by his own admission, his work during the Oxford years reflected a legalistic (Pharisaic) and deontological tendency as his ethical and moral impulse, which reiterates the methodological shift and the striking contrast in his life and ministry. Wesley's emphasis on integrating personal experience and convictions with public and social manifestations of them is not just the basis for his personal morality and ethical paradigm; Wesley also takes this approach to critique the philosophers of his time, as stated in one of his sermons:

> But how great is the number of those who, allowing religion to consist of two branches,—our duty to God, and our duty to our neighbour,—entirely forget the first part, and put the second part for the whole,—for the entire duty of man! Thus almost all men of letters, both in England, France, Germany, yea, and all the civilized countries of Europe, extol humanity to the skies, as the very essence of religion. To this the great triumvirate, Rousseau, Voltaire, and David Hume, have contributed all their labours, sparing no pains to establish a religion which should stand on its own foundation, independent on any revelation whatever; yea, not supposing even the being of a God. So leaving Him, if he has any being, to himself, they have found out both a religion and a happiness which have no relation at all to God, nor any dependence upon him. It is no wonder that this religion should grow fashionable, and spread far and wide in the world. But call it humanity, virtue, morality, or what you please, it is neither better nor worse than Atheism. Men hereby wilfully and designedly put asunder what God has joined,—the duties of the first and the second table. It is separating the love of our neighbour from the love of God. (7:270–71)

In this paragraph, although Wesley uses deontological language, he offers a critique of the humanistic ethical and philosophical methods that promote an anthropocentric view of life and place value in being "good" to others for their sake. For Wesley, this approach is flawed because it ignores God as the main source of love and goodness, and God's nature and character, which are centered in the importance of relationships—with God and with one another. Wesley's emphasis on relationships and God as the ultimate source of love provides the core of his ethical system.

Wesleyan Ethics: Key Elements

Although love of God and love of neighbor are general themes in John Wesley's sermons and journal entries, in a detailed look at these general themes one can easily identify unique elements and contributions that in turn provide the foundation for his view of theology and ethical systems. Such elements are the image of God in humans, universal grace and salvation, personal and social holiness, and the importance of free human will.

The image of God, according to Wesley, is the central point of understanding salvation and the human condition after the fall of humankind. Wesley uses the image of God to highlight the state of perfection and the harmony present between the Creator and all created beings, of which humans are an important part. The image of God provides the moral framework of reference to evaluate our existence. Evidence of this is found in Wesley's sermon "The New Birth," in which he says,

> Why must we be born again? What is the foundation of this doctrine? The foundation of it lies near as deep as the creation of the world; in the scriptural account whereof we read, "And God," the three-one God, "said, Let us make man in our image, after our likeness. So God created man in his own image, in the image of God created he him. Not barely in his natural image, a picture of his own immortality; a spiritual being, endued with understanding, freedom of will, and various affections; nor merely in his political image, the governor of this lower world, having "dominion over the fishes of the sea, and over all the earth"; but chiefly in his moral image; which, according to the Apostle, is "righteousness and true holiness." In this image of God was man made. "God is love": Accordingly, man at his creation was full of love; which was the sole principle of all his tempers, thoughts, words, and actions. God is full of justice, mercy, and truth; so was man as he came from the hands of his Creator. God is spotless purity; and so man was in the beginning pure from every sinful blot. (6:66)

For Wesley, the original state of creation depicts God's character in relationship to the universe and particularly to humans, and it is this depiction that provides the point of departure and arrival—departure in the sense in which it provides the initial setting of the narrative, a state of perfect harmony later marred by the fall of humanity, and arrival in providing the target and ultimate goal for the Christian community as part of the redemption and restoration of the current (and temporal) social order and personal condition. In this way, Wesley argues that the goal of salvation (and holiness) is precisely the restoration of the perfect and harmonious state, the point of arrival and departure; thus, our responsibility is to reflect, to the best of our ability and relying in God's grace, this general state of moral perfection, but particularly "the moral image of God," which is, according to Wesley, fulfilled in loving God and neighbor. However, this fulfillment requires human action, intentionality, and willingness to do so; it is something that occurs not by divine imposition, but rather implies the use of human free will in using it in accordance with God's will and character.

For Wesley, humans are morally accountable for their actions because they have a choice between accepting God's invitation and following their fallen desires. Again, the image of God through prevenient grace makes this possible, when God provides grace (prevenient and irresistible) to all humans; they acquire moral attributes and the capacity to discern between the choices above. Wesley affirms that God is the author of this work, but he also affirms that it requires human participation in the form of a moral choice. At the same time that Wesley's concept of prevenient grace makes humans morally responsible for their choices, it also makes them valuable and worthy of dignity and respect. If all humans have a glimpse of the moral image of God, and if all humans have received God's grace, then there is something intrinsically good in them. And finally, if God sees value in each of them, then in our deliberations and actions we should express the same kind of appreciation, respect, and protection for the dignity of all humans because of their God-given condition.

Following his methodological approach, Wesley affirms that all humans have the potential to be saved, and those who already are saved have an additional moral responsibility: to strive and move toward Christian perfection. The word *perfection* in moral theory is a difficult and controversial one that leads to wide-ranging views; however, for Wesley the term is grounded in love and in relationships—in the practical aspects, not so much in the theoretical ones. Wesley places a second stop in the journey toward the point of arrival, which he indentifies as Christian perfection, entire sanctification, or holiness (he uses other terms, but these more frequently). In this second stop, the Christian is moved by God's grace to follow and reflect God's character in demonstrating divine love, not only accepting God's love in a personal way but also applying the same redemptive love toward others and, in doing so, looking for ways to alleviate the social conditions of those in need. Again, this aspect is personal, but also it is social; it requires the support of the Christian community, and it implies actions that move Christians to enter relationships with all other creatures, as was reflected in the original state. Thus, Wesleyan ethics is not simply another theory about moral choices; rather, it is a bold challenge to live a life that reflects God's character in community for the well-being of the community at large, always striving and moving toward the point of arrival and departure as the moral framework of reference.

See also Holiness; Love, Love Command; Neighbor, Neighbor Love; Perfection; Salvation; Sanctification; Virtue Ethics

Bibliography

Dunning, H. *Christian Ethics in Wesleyan Perspective: Reflecting the Divine Image*. InterVarsity, 1998; Long, D. S. *John Wesley's Moral Theology: The Quest for God and Goodness*. Kingswood, 2005; Marquardt, M. *John Wesley's Social Ethics: Praxis and Principles*. Abingdon, 1992; Weber, T. *Politics in the Order of Salvation: New Directions in Wesleyan Political Ethics*. Kingswood, 2001; Wesley, J. *The Works of John Wesley*. 3rd ed. 14 vols in 7. Baker, 1998.

Hugo Magallanes

White Privilege *See* Racism

Widows

A widow is a woman who has outlived her husband and not remarried.

Widows in Scripture

Although the word *widow* and its cognates appear in the Bible 115 times (NRSV), widows have been understudied among biblical scholars. No overall picture of the widow in her ancient Hebrew or Greco-Roman contexts exists. Interestingly, the NRSV has no references to "widower." In a patriarchal society, where the father was head of the household and women were in some sense the property of the husband, a man did not suffer "widowerhood." Either he had more than one wife or he soon found another. A husband's loss of his spouse did not have for him the economic effect that it had on widowed women.

In ancient patriarchal kin-group societies, the two expected roles for females were as a virgin in her father's house and later as a wife married into the household of her husband and father-in-law. In each case, she had a male or males to provide for her economically and a social system in which to belong. A woman was not always considered a widow unless both husband and father-in-law were deceased (Hiebert 128).

In the OT a woman with no male protector lost not only her financial security but also her social connections. In a culture organized by family systems she was truly marginalized. At least sixteen of the OT references to widows link them with orphans and resident aliens, the latter also lacking a local kin group for socioeconomic support. Yahweh becomes their male advocate, calling on the larger Hebrew community to look after them (see Exod. 22:22; Deut. 10:18; 14:29; 16:11, 14; 24:17, 19–21; 25:7; 26:12–13).

The prophets reinforce these laws. A godly Israelite will care for widows and orphans (Isa. 1:17, 23; 10:2; Jer. 7:6; 22:3; 49:11; Ezek. 22:7; Zech. 7:10; Mal. 3:5). Laments from Psalms, Job, and Lamentations back this up (Job 24:21; 31:16, 18; Pss. 68:5; 94:6; 146:9; Lam. 5:3).

For a young woman widowed without children, levirate marriage as described in Deut. 25:5–10 provided a communal, patrilineal solution (see Gen. 38; Ruth 4). The woman will remain in the family (Deut. 25:5). Her husband's brother will marry her, and her first son will be considered the son of the deceased man.

Since the OT understanding of widowhood implies a woman bereft of her socioeconomic kin group, the term *widow* could apply to any female in similar circumstances, such as divorced women. Since the OT is silent on the effects of divorce upon women, perhaps they are already considered to be widows. Divorce (see Deut. 24:1–4) may have been prevalent because purity laws and honor/shame values held women responsible for nearly any sexual behavior outside of marriage.

However, descriptive texts about widows present them as the opposite of helpless victims. Tamar (Gen. 38), Naomi and Ruth (Ruth), and Abigail (1 Sam. 25) come across as intelligent, resourceful women who go after what they want and achieve it. Boldest of all is the heroine Judith, a widow who saved her people by seducing and then beheading Holofernes, their Assyrian oppressor (Jdt. 8–16).

The importance of belonging to a kinship group, however patriarchally structured, for economic support continues in the NT. The plight of any unattached woman—widowed, divorced, or forced into prostitution—was potentially desperate. According to Jesus, scribes were "devouring widows' houses" (Mark 12:40; Luke 20:47).

Of the Gospels, however, only Luke discusses widows with the same concern shown in the OT. With his interests in both women and economics, Luke depicts widows as the exemplary poor, depending on God alone for help (i.e., 2:37; 4:25–26; 7:12; 21:2–3) and being resourceful in getting their needs met (18:1–6). Luke introduces other women, some "sinners" and others, who appear as independent women in their own right (e.g., 7:36–8:3).

Such inclusiveness carries into Luke's second volume, where the believing community now shares possessions so that "there was not a needy person among them" (Acts 4:34). As in the community begun by Jesus, widows, the divorced, former prostitutes, and other unattached women are no longer poor and marginalized but rather are full members in the fictive kinship group. The work of widows is highlighted in, for example, the raising of Tabitha (Acts 9:36–41). A community of production as well as consumption is in view, where the disciple Tabitha appears to employ a group of widows in her tailor shop. Rather than receiving handouts, they are contributing members of the believing community, not dependent on a male head of household.

That not all single women were poor and helpless is also attested in 1 Cor. 7, where Paul counters cultural traditions by preferring that the unmarried and widows remain single as he is (1 Cor. 7:8) so that they can focus more on "the affairs of the Lord" (1 Cor. 7:32). Paul's circle of friends and co-workers includes a number of women named without reference to a male (e.g., Rom. 16:1, 6, 12, 15; 1 Cor. 1:11; Phil. 4:2).

Widows surface in 1 Timothy, a manual of church discipline structured as a letter from Paul, though it appears to be set in Ephesus at a later time than Paul. Here, prescriptions restricting women may attest to their rising leadership in that church. The writer forbids women to teach (1 Tim. 2:12) and severely limits the definition (and therefore support) of "widows" (1 Tim. 5:3–16).

Accordingly, the term *widow* in the Bible has different connotations, depending on literary and cultural contexts. One of the one hand, in a patriarchal, patrilineal, clan-based society, women without male relatives to support them usually are poor and socially marginalized. The larger community is expected to care for them. On the other hand, for women with sufficient means, widowhood could encourage resourcefulness and bring new freedom and independence. According to Acts, in a Jesus community where goods were shared, none were in need. Thus, widows (all unattached women) were no longer objects of charity or pressured to marry for economic support and thus were able to assume honorable roles of service and leadership.

Widows in Contemporary Culture

In contrast to ancient societies, modern women in the West benefit from the democratic concept of "all people created equal," which derives at some level from Gen. 1 and the inclusiveness of Jesus' gospel. In a democracy, however imperfect, women have more choices and a wider range of roles. Thus it is not possible to make a one-to-one application of either prescriptive or descriptive texts about widows in today's world.

However, many nations of the world today are not democracies. As a gender, the majority of women are disadvantaged in authoritarian, patriarchal cultures. The global people of God are called to care for "widows, orphans, and resident aliens," which today translates into women and dependent children without male support, and also refugees, the majority of whom are women and children. Christians should support both religious and secular organizations working to relieve the plight of these three groups of needy people. For example, it is now recognized that the well-being of a society advances most quickly when its girls are educated, and microfinancing has been far more successful among women than men because women spend their profits on their children's welfare.

Democracies are far from perfect as well. Economically, women's earning power and wealth lag behind those of men. When a divorce occurs, the man's income usually rises, but the woman's usually falls.

What of widows in the United States? When a husband dies, the American widow's disposable income decreases by 30 percent. The rate of poverty (calculated as 50 percent of median income) among those aged sixty-five and older increases among racial minorities, the more advanced in age, and those living alone. More women in all these categories are poor—African American women at three times the rate of white women, the poorest being Hispanic women living alone. Moreover, poverty among the elderly in the United States is higher than in other industrialized countries, again with the poverty rate more advanced in the case of elderly women (Matcha 226).

Reasons for the feminization of poverty still reflect a male-dominated society. They include (1) economic dependence of women on men, (2) family and work history prior to retirement, (3) division of labor where women take time off for children and elder care, (4) discrimination in the workforce, and (5) costs of caring for an ill spouse.

Although a liberal democracy offers more choices and opportunities for single women, our social structures still privilege males and feminize poverty. Women living alone (or with dependent children) would be helped by belonging to a caring community, preferably not as objects of charity but rather in a reciprocal relationship of social and economic sharing.

The law and the prophets still cry out to warn the people of God that their righteousness depends on their concern and care for "the least of these"—widows, orphans, refugees. In each changing cultural context our task is to discern who they are and how best to care for them.

See also Charity, Works of; Marriage and Divorce; Poverty and Poor; Singleness; Women, Status of

Bibliography

Finger, R. *Of Widows and Meals: Communal Meals in the Book of Acts*. Eerdmans 2007; Frick, F. "Widows." Pages 197–99 in *Women in Scripture: A Dictionary of Named and Unnamed Women in the Hebrew Bible, the Apocryphal/Deuterocanonical Books, and the New Testament*, ed. C. Meyers. Eerdmans 2001; idem. "Widows in the Hebrew Bible: A Transactional Approach." Pages 139–51 in *A Feminist Companion to Exodus and Deuteronomy*, ed. A. Brenner. FCB 6. Sheffield Academic Press, 1994; Hiebert, P. " 'When Shall Help Come to Me?' The Biblical Widow." Pages 125–41 in *Gender and Difference in Ancient Israel*, ed. P. Day. Fortress, 1989; Hillier, S., and B. Barrow. *Aging: The Individual and Society*. Wadsworth, 2007; Matcha, D. *The Sociology of Aging: An International Perspective*. Sloan Publishing, 2007; Thurston, B. *The Widows: A Women's Ministry in the Early Church*. Fortress, 1989.

Reta Halteman Finger

Will, Free *See* Free Will and Determinism

Wisdom Literature

The ethics of wisdom literature in the OT moves in a linear direction from the traditional scribal wisdom of Proverbs, to the critical wisdom texts of Job and Ecclesiastes, to the transformation into apocalyptic and rabbinic teachings. Thus, there were transmutations in the understanding of morality among the ancient sages and scribes of Israel due to historical and social changes from the eighth century BCE to the third century CE.

The Ethics of Traditional Sages and Scribes

Although family and tribe have been viewed by some as the earliest social setting of traditional wisdom, a more likely view is that the canonical and other sacred texts originated in the royal court during the period of the first temple and continued an association with the ruling classes, kings, and, later, Zadokite priests and governors even into the rule of imperial Rome in the early centuries CE. The sages and scribes presented discourse and insights of sapiential ideology that included their views of God, the cosmos, and human nature, behavior, and society. This ideology was transmitted through the generations of wisdom schools at court, then the temple, and finally the *beit midrash* (i.e., "house of interpretation") associated with the synagogue. Sapiential instruction was largely for the education of children of both the aristocracy and the bureaucrats, although by the third century BCE a more democratized wisdom emerged. While it is not true of the later texts of Sirach and Wisdom of Solomon, a more democratized wisdom characterizes the rabbinic literature that included the Mishnah, Tosefta, midrashim, and the Palestinian and Babylonian Talmuds. The social ideology that included moral teachings was routinized textually and was passed down through the generations that experienced an everchanging culture. Any possible egalitarian features of premonarchic Israel were eliminated in favor of the establishment of classes based on hierarchy and power until the last two centuries BCE.

Proverbs. Traditional sages and scribes compiled the seven collections of the book of Proverbs from the eighth to the third centuries BCE and concluded with an introductory instruction (1:2–7) and a final poem (31:10–31). They engaged in their search for knowledge in the world by beginning with the affirmation of "the fear of God." "The fear of God" represented the foundational belief that God was the Creator who established a divine cosmic and social order, brought life into existence, and oversaw and maintained this order through the principle of retribution. This did not operate automatically, but rather was orchestrated by God. All life was good—that is, was filled with blessings and joy—except for that of the wicked and the fool, who experienced punishment and at times even destruction.

The wise of Israel sought out patterns of unchanging phenomena, categories of physical, anthropological, biological, and zoological classifications in the world, and political, social, and economic systems of human construction established by divine creation and guidance. This order (*ṣĕdāqâ*), considered to be part of the cosmic structure established by the Creator to orchestrate and govern the world, became the basis for human institutions and actions. Israelite society, with political and economic control in the hands of the rulers, was understood as grounded in this divine order of the cosmos. Any disturbance of the social order by foolish or criminal behavior was condemned as threatening to disrupt the world and thus was an abomination against God and disobedience to divinely selected leaders. Wealth, especially as gained through the accumulation of property, was viewed as one of the rewards of the righteous and wise, since their actions were in harmony with the cosmic order. By contrast, poverty was generally considered to be the consequence of foolish and/or wicked behavior. This ideology of the traditional sages was understood to be self-evident and was read into their perception of God, the cosmos, and humankind. Through their writings in the various sapiential forms, the sages clearly supported the social worlds in the periods of the first and second temples.

An important metaphor is Woman Wisdom in Proverbs 1; 8–9. She is an itinerant teacher who offers life to her followers, a queen of heaven who chooses and directs kings, and the firstborn of God who was present, perhaps active, at creation. She becomes the image of divine transcendence and immanence in a world where God is increasingly remote.

Ben Sira. Ben Sira (c. 200 BCE) was a scribal interpreter of Scripture who taught in an academy (perhaps a Torah school of the temple in Jerusalem or a synagogue school), a scholar of Scripture, and a sage who compiled a list of his teachings, poems, and hymns into a book that underwent later redaction, the book of Sirach. He operated a wisdom school for the children of the wealthy, scribes, political bureaucrats, and aspiring teachers and taught many of the same ethical instructions found in Proverbs' traditional wisdom, except that now he fashioned wisdom, the Torah, and salvation history into a new theological synthesis.

Ben Sira equates wisdom with the Torah and even considers himself an inspired prophet. The equating of wisdom and Torah and the sage as the teacher and interpreter of the law are strong indications that the sages are professionals under the oversight of the temple priests. Thus, he emphasizes the importance of the support of the priests and especially the high priest (notably Simon II), as well as the observance and performing of the rituals of the temple cultus.

Ben Sira likely attended and later taught in a Jewish school in Jerusalem connected to the temple or a synagogue. The synagogue became a place of assembly for the local community, a house of worship, and often, if a *beit midrash* was attached, a location for study, including a formal school. He was an interpreter of earlier texts that became Scripture and was familiar with Greek philosophy, in particular Stoicism. Ben Sira's virtuous sage is described within an aretology in Sir. 38–39 as a loyal servant to God and an ambassador to foreign lands who has cultivated speech and possesses wisdom. Further, the primary virtue is the "fear of Yahweh," expressed in piety, faith in the creator and sustainer of the cosmos, trust in the providential guide of human history, and obedience to the revealed commandments. As the divine potter who creates humanity from the earth, God fashions both the nature and destiny of humans. Making use of Gen. 1:26–28, Ben Sira tells of humans as created in the divine image who rule over the other creatures that fear them. Rulers receive from God the gift of wisdom in order to rule justly. Created to possess freedom of will, humans acquire their knowledge of the Creator through the "fear of God," which they receive in the womb and is equated with reflection on and living according to the commandments.

Personified wisdom is a dominant theme for Ben Sira. Wisdom is the first of God's acts of creation and permeates cosmic and social reality. Wisdom also is given to the sages in order to understand both God and the world. With this knowledge, the sage is able to interpret correctly the Torah and thus to live a moral life. This cosmic wisdom also becomes the divine inspiration that fills the heart of the sage and teaches youth how to behave in order to experience well-being. As the means of divine immanence, Woman Wisdom is the agent of God in revitalizing creation, while just and wise acts of humans strengthen this cosmic order.

In his encomium known as the Praise of the Pious (Sir. 46–50), Ben Sira focuses on noble heroes whose qualities enhanced their character, deeds, and prestige and thus are to be remembered. It is because of their deeds and virtues that their descendants will continue for all times.

Qumran and the moral life. The texts from the Judean Desert indicate that wisdom literature was copied, newly written, and transmitted to the members of a community whose founders, including the enigmatic Teacher of Righteousness, were opponents of the Zadokite priesthood. The Qumran community looked forward to their installation as the legitimate priests, led by a priestly messiah who would control the temple, and also to the return of a royal descendant of David who would rule as the surrogate of God from Jerusalem over the "heavens and earth."

Many of the wisdom texts found in Qumran not only teach the proper course of the moral life but also project a theological worldview from an apocalyptic perspective. Their ethos for this approaching time was shaped by study of the ancestors, the composition of commentaries on prophets, the engagement in piety and ritual cleansing designed to prepare them for worship and the final days and the restoration of the purified cosmos and temple, the knowledge of sacred things, and a prescribed moral behavior of avoiding sins of laziness, greed, impatience, and sexual promiscuity.

Their ethical emphasis was placed on the gift of divine wisdom, which enabled them to know the proper behavior that prepared them for the final conflict between the "Children of Light" and the "Children of Darkness." This wisdom could be known through study and reflection on sacred texts. The order of the cosmos is revealed to and known by only the elect, including the recipients of the instruction who are to reflect on and learn from divine revelation. These apocalyptic sages appropriate the ethical dualism of Proverbs to divide humans into two groups of good/righteous and evil/sinful. This dualism is also projected to a cosmic level. The wisdom of the sectarians is also pedagogical, for its purpose is to teach people the commandments and virtues of piety, study, meditation, sexual purity, hospitality and sharing with the poor, and control of the passions. Once actualized in speech and behavior, these virtues lead to well-being and the future exaltation of the righteous.

Wisdom of Solomon. The final sapiential, canonical/deuterocanonical wisdom book, Wisdom of Solomon, was likely written by a sage or rhetor to a Jewish audience in Alexandria at the time of Rome's control of Palestine and Egypt (30 BCE and following). The book appears to reflect a period of persecution when Egyptian Jews were experiencing a pogrom conducted by Hellenists (Greeks, Egyptians, and possibly some apostate Jews), probably in about 38 BCE.

Traditional wisdom is given new shape in the form of a paraenetic address by linking Jewish wisdom, apocalyptic, the exodus from Egypt, and Greek popular philosophy. This exhortatory speech encourages faithful Jews to maintain their loyalty to their ancestral traditions in the face of persecution, to persuade apostate Jews to return to their religion, and to convince Hellenes of the superiority of Jewish religion and the moral life. The rhetor used both Greek rhetorical and literary features and popular philosophical ideas from a variety of sources. These included the Stoic understanding of the Logos and the four cardinal virtues, the Platonic teaching of the immortality of the soul and the corruptibility of the flesh that hindered the moral life, and Wisdom's guidance of the heroic leadership of unnamed ancestors whose deeds and virtues led to salvation.

This teacher combines creation and redemption into a new theological synthesis. Central to redemption are the elements of justice and wisdom. The divine spirit (Sophia) that permeates creation and dwells within the souls of the righteous and pure (Wis. 7:27) is the architect of all things and guides and delivers the righteous throughout history (Wis. 10:1–11:1). The "good" is understood as virtue and is to be actualized in human behavior. The cardinal virtues are self-control, prudence, justice, and courage, found also in Stoicism. Reason, not the passions, is the highest aspect of human nature for both Stoics and the rhetor, and moral human beings should realize it to control the passions and to follow consistently the ordered world. The life of virtue is to conform to the natural order, which permeates the cosmos and is present in human nature.

The Ethics of the Critical Sages and Scribes

The collapse of traditional wisdom occurred due to the transformation of the sociopolitical order initiated first by the Babylonians (587–539 BCE) and then by the Ptolemies (200–31 BCE). These conquests and oppressive rules brought traditional teaching into disrepute. With the fall of the monarchy, some of the sages continued in the role of counselors, but now they advised the governors appointed by the foreign kings or the temple priests. Others provided instruction in wisdom schools, likely attached either to the temple or to local political institutions. The poetic book of Job likely was composed in the context of a wisdom school, especially since the dialogues make use of the disputation, a sapiential form in which sages debate the authenticity of a teaching. In this case, the principle of retribution grounded in the justice of God is the object of contention. Qohelеth, who was a teacher of the "people" (Eccl. 12:9–14), also likely taught in a wisdom school. This text may have been written as late as the beginning of the third century BCE for a school of scribes by a famous but unidentified sage. This teacher takes on the fictional role of being the "son of David," likely Solomon, who, like Egyptian pharaohs of the Middle Kingdom addressing their successors from the dead, instructs his students in critical wisdom.

Job. The earlier of two canonical texts representing critical wisdom is Job (sixth century BCE). The ideology of the previously uncontested values and affirmations in traditional wisdom is represented by the "friends of Job," who argue that God is a just deity, sure to reward the righteous and punish the wicked. They are inflexible dogmatists. Job, represented as a man of great wealth and status who lost everything, contends that God is a destructive tyrant who seeks capriciously to destroy both creation and the wise and righteous. The justice of God and retribution are assailed. In the concluding theophany, Yahweh first attempts to intimidate Job with power and knowledge but, failing that, admits that he struggles with chaos (Behemoth and Leviathan) for rule over the earth. This strengthening of the power of chaos into a contestant for kingship over the cosmos is a step toward the development of a satanic power.

The prose narrative is an early example story of traditional wisdom prior to the Babylonian captivity (Job 1–2; 42:7–17). This tale is taken by the exilic poet of Job and appended to the poetic dialogue as a prologue and epilogue in which the traditional Job is pious and just and maintains his faith in spite of extreme suffering. Once the poetry and prose are connected, the epilogue concludes, incidentally, that Yahweh is angry with Eliphaz and his two friends for not having spoken "correctly" about him. This rereading of the older, traditional tale of Job suggests that the poet has affirmed the authenticity of Job's repudiation of retribution and the unchallenged justice of divine rule in his speeches with his friends and in his direct challenge of Yahweh. It is unlikely that Job repents. Rather, Job continues to adhere to his condemnation of an unrighteous Yahweh and feels sorry for humankind, who must suffer under the divine yoke. It is in the epilogue that Yahweh is the one who repents, or changes his behavior, when he condemns his three supporters and honors Job with his restoration.

Qoheleth. Several centuries later, in the book of Ecclesiastes, a sage who came to be known only by his office, "Qoheleth" ("one who assembles"), argues against any assertion that the political and social order are ruled over by righteous rulers, and that cosmic rule is presided over by a just deity. His opponents probably were temple scribes and apocalyptic sages, the former of which looked to the past and the Jerusalem cultus as the guarantee of divine favor, while the latter looked to the future as a time of a "new heaven and new earth" when divine salvation and the exaltation of Israel and the righteous would occur. For Qoheleth, any hope in a just social and political order in the present world is repudiated by his own experience. This sage teaches that the behavior of the unknown God is unpredictable, even capricious, although he remains a power to be feared (Eccl. 5:7). The one teaching that Qoheleth offers about God is that one should "fear him." Yet this is actual terror, not faith in a just God of creation. For Qoheleth, it is better to go to the temple to listen than it is to offer the sacrifices of fools and to make unwise vows. Qoheleth does not totally negate the validity of temple worship, but he does stress the fear and trembling that should accompany any who engage in its activities.

Qoheleth argues not only against the justice of God, the principle of retribution, and cosmic and social embodiments of order, but also against a final judgment in which the righteous will be vindicated and the wicked punished. He also denies the teaching that wisdom will enable one to know when and how to act successfully. For him, both the righteous and the wicked, along with the wise and the foolish, face the same fate: death. From death there is no escape, and the tomb is humanity's eternal home. The one boon of human existence, provided by God to anesthetize the pain of suffering and despair, is the joy that one may experience. Joy becomes the basis of Qoheleth's moral system, occurring seven times in the literary structure: joy in one's activities and labor, eating and drinking (a symposium?), and one's spouse. But joy and life are quickly fleeting. Qoheleth does not articulate a program of social justice, but rather is resigned to passive acceptance.

Conclusion

As wisdom transitioned to apocalyptic, the direction of history finally became the end of the present order and the beginning of a "new heaven and new earth." As wisdom's teachings were incorporated into rabbinic texts, they supplemented ethical instruction. Wisdom's social location moved from the court, to the temple, to the synagogue, to the apocalyptic community. The tradition developed from an elitist one for behavior in the court and service to the monarch to a more democratized setting in which the marginalized, such as the Essenes of Qumran, became the elect of God.

See also Dead Sea Scrolls; Deuterocanonical/Apocryphal Books; Ecclesiastes; Job; Old Testament Ethics; Proverbs; Sirach; Wisdom of Solomon

Leo G. Perdue

Wisdom of Solomon

Wisdom of Solomon is a sapiential text composed in Greek and written in Alexandria, Egypt, perhaps in the early first century CE. The author does not identify himself, but clearly he is an educated Jew who is familiar with Greek philosophy. The book combines hortatory language in the spirit of earlier instructions with certain philosophical ideas. It also reflects the fractured relations during this period between the large Jewish community in Alexandria and the Greeks and native Egyptians. Wisdom of Solomon can be divided into three distinct sections: the "book of eschatology" (1:1–6:21), the "book of wisdom" (6:22–10:21), and the "book of history" (11:1–19:22).

The ethics of Wisdom of Solomon focuses on the promise of eternal life for the righteous and the failure of the wicked to recognize the possibility of such reward. According to the author, the wicked believe that life is fleeting, and therefore they say to themselves, "Let us take our fill of costly wine and perfumes" (2:7). The callous behavior of these sinners also involves oppressing the righteous, since the righteous ones are so overtly pious and accuse the wicked of disobeying the law (2:12–13). Yet such wicked persons have been "blinded" by foolishness and have not "discerned the prize for blameless souls" (2:21–22), which is eternal life.

The righteous ones, however, will be vindicated. Their souls are in "the hand of God" (3:1), and although they will appear deceased to the wicked category, God has "tested" them and deemed them worthy of immortality (3:1–7). The ethical dualism of Wisdom of Solomon is therefore predicated on postmortem reward for the righteous, and this is a major innovation for a Jewish instruction. Earlier works such as Ecclesiastes and Sirach had dismissed the possibility of individual immortality as fanciful (the promise of eternal life is extended in Daniel and sections of *1 Enoch*).

It should be noted that the afterlife in Wisdom of Solomon does not involve resurrection, but rather the survival of the righteous "soul" after death. The concept of the undying soul is influenced by the author's understanding of Platonic philosophy.

In the second section of the book the author praises Wisdom as a spirit "who passes into holy souls and makes them friends of God, and prophets" (7:27). Within this framework, which is indebted to Middle Platonism, the figure of Wisdom is an entity representing God on earth, "a spotless mirror of the working of God" (7:26). Only through this intervening force can humans be set on the proper path (9:13–18). This middle section culminates in a description of how Wisdom has worked through Israel's forebears. From Adam to Noah to Abraham, the author maintains, it is Wisdom who rescues the righteous on behalf of God (10:1–21). This retrospective has a didactic function: these familiar stories serve as a model that righteous believers will be saved from precarious circumstances by the gracious intervention of God.

In the concluding "book of history," the author speaks directly to God, and the central topic is idolatry. The author excoriates the ancient Canaanites and Egyptians by recounting the exodus narrative, and this is undoubtedly a polemic against the non-Jews (both Greeks and Egyptians) living in Alexandria. The polemic serves a function within the author's ethical framework, since he encourages fellow Jews to be steadfast in their convictions and religious practices, even in the face of difficult opposition. In the midst of this polemic against idolatry and infanticide, it is noteworthy that the author of Wisdom of Solomon affirms the fairness of God: "For you love all things that exist, and detest none of the things that you have made, for you would not have made anything if you had hated it" (11:24). Despite the author's palpable concern for the situation of Jews in Alexandria, he cites the philanthropic nature of God (using the Greek word *philanthrōpia*) toward all humanity.

Wisdom of Solomon is an important book for ethics because it appeals vividly to eschatological deliverance as a means of instilling righteous behavior on earth. Subsequent Jewish and early Christian texts would follow suit. This text is also a pivotal example of how Torah piety could be merged with the insights of Hellenistic philosophy. A more elaborate example of this is found in the writings of Philo, another Alexandrian Jew from the same general period.

See also Deuterocanonical/Apocryphal Books; Eschatology and Ethics; Wisdom Literature

Bibliography

Collins, J. *Jewish Wisdom in the Hellenistic Age*. OTL. Westminster John Knox, 1997, 178–221; Winston, D. *The Wisdom of Solomon*. AB 43. Doubleday, 1979.

Samuel L. Adams

Witchcraft *See* Divination and Magic

Women, Status of

Women have had lower social status than men in almost all documented cultures, or a woman's status has been linked to that of her husband or father, with church and Scriptures more often than not reflecting their associated cultures. Behind this there is undoubtedly a mass of reasons, from the biological to the religious. Much attention has been paid to the social constructions of reality associated with gender in all countries and ages. Nevertheless, there is also a strong biological component to this lower status. Our closest cousins, the chimpanzees, are patriarchal. All primates share a highly stratified social organization. Thus, the importance of status and of gender inequity in human society has deep evolutionary roots.

Humans, however, have never been creatures of instinct alone. They have unique capacities to change and to control biological impulses. Indeed, Christians have always claimed, in different ways, that some of our deepest desires and inclinations are far from ideal; they are fallen. What is the case by nature need not necessarily be a guide to what should be the case. Nevertheless, the lower status of women has become encoded in social mores and religious worldviews. Thus, although humans have the capacity to challenge deeply embedded tendencies, they have done so widely only in recent centuries, perhaps because the burdens of bearing and rearing children have been too overwhelming until the advent of the age when the use of effective means of contraception became widespread.

In Greek culture, for instance, although some Greek women achieved unusual success, the accepted hierarchy was this: free men, women, and then slaves of both sexes. Plato's utopian world, described in *The Republic*, elevated women to a nearly equal status with men, although Aristotle sees women as having a subordinate deliberative faculty and slaves as having none. Aristotle's basic premises have had deep resonances in Christian theology and church life. Thomas Aquinas, for instance, quotes Aristotle's term for women, "the misbegotten male," but defends God's creation of women and argues for a modified form of complementary equality between the sexes.

Hebrew women also had a status linked to that of their husband or clan. Thus Sarah, Rebecca, and Rachel are named and are of importance because of their links to the patriarchs. In general, however, the status of women in Israel was mixed. Genesis 1:26–27 could be interpreted as giving women status equal to that of men, both being image bearers of God. In practice, however, and often in law, men controlled a wife or daughter (the word for *husband* was *baal* or "lord"), and women's status was significantly formed by the patterns of polygamous marriage, where the changing favor of the husband shaped everyday life and expectations. In Exod. 21:7; 22:16–17; Lev. 27:6 we have examples of laws that assume that women, especially daughters, are under the control of men, and that girls are of lesser value than boys.

In Christian theology, the primary legitimating story of this lesser role for women has been the Genesis account of Adam and Eve, and especially the "fall" story in Gen. 3. From Tertullian to Augustine to Luther, Eve was blamed for the fall, and this, together with Gen. 3:16, has been used to construct a picture of women as easily deceived and needing both to make amends for this original sin and to be overseen by men lest they lead others astray. Tertullian called every woman an Eve, and he accused women collectively of seducing Adam, whom even the devil could not seduce. The linking of women to evil reached new heights in the witch trials and executions of medieval and early modern Europe and the Americas.

There are, however, other possible readings of Gen. 3. This chapter can be read as a remarkably wise account of origins in which blame is equally accorded to woman, man, and serpent. Genesis 3:17–19 is never read as prescriptive. For centuries, men and women have labored to overcome the difficulties of bringing life and nourishment from the soil. Genesis 3:16, however, is sometimes read prescriptively as giving the justification for a husband's, and sometimes all men's, dominance of a woman. Feminism, then, can be seen as a parallel of farming, working to counteract the natural fallen tendencies of the human and created order.

Moreover, women have not been absent from history. There have always been exceptional women. In the Scriptures we see this in the stories of Deborah, Ruth, Esther, and Mary, among others. Important also are the marginal women who turn up in the genealogy of Christ, hinting that the deeper message of Scripture is against the grain of the surface interpretation.

Change has come slowly in human societies and in the church. Ironically, marked changes came with the deconstruction of powerful religious legitimating stories in the Enlightenment and following. Thus, human rights came to prominence in the eighteenth and nineteenth centuries, even if the counterauthoritarian roots lie in the Reformation. Throughout the nineteenth century, women in First World countries campaigned for suffrage, encouraged in the end by the success of the struggle against slavery. Nevertheless, the move to a more scientific and rational society did not always lead to a higher status for women. In general, men became the guardians of the new scientific and technological order. Again and again the rules for intellectual prowess and moral development were controlled and defined by men. More mystical and sometimes more intuitive ways of knowing were displaced by the heavy emphasis on evidence and rational thought alone. Women's work often moved from the home to the alienating environment of the factory, or women became isolated in the home as guardians of the domestic moral order.

Religion, though, was not always problematic. The Bible often was a book of liberation, and faith has provided a motivation to keep up the struggle. Much of the use of the Bible that had proved effective in the abolitionist movements was applicable also to women. The overall message of Scripture is one of liberation. Within the church, this struggle was focused first on the right to preach and to ordination and was bolstered by a reading of Scripture through the lenses of Gen. 1:26–27 and Gal. 3:28, texts that speak of radical equality before God in spite of the tradition. Although women preached and have spoken out in times of revival, there was no concerted women's leadership until the nineteenth century. In the United States, Oberlin College in Ohio, whose second president was Charles Grandison Finney, admitted women and blacks to its programs in 1834 and 1833, respectively. The first woman to be ordained in a mainline denomination, Antoinette Brown (ordained 1853), was a graduate of Oberlin.

Margaret Bendroth has documented the trends and backlashes that have accompanied the struggle of women to have an equal place in the church. By the end of the nineteenth century, women were gaining ground and were being accepted into positions of authority and teaching in many of the more populist denominations. The twentieth century saw a backlash against women in positions of authority, a phenomenon that was to recur whenever the church was in danger of being "feminized." In 1996 the Roman Catholic Church closed down all conversation on the issue of women's ordination. The author of this edict was Cardinal Joseph Ratzinger, now Pope Benedict XVI. There was also an extraordinary turnaround among Southern Baptists in the American South. Fundamentalists took over this huge denomination in the 1980s, and women's rights to ordination and the pulpit were systematically overturned. In mainline churches, on the whole, women have won the right to be ordained, although this was won for women in the Church of England only in 1993.

Throughout church history the Holy Spirit has shown that the gifts of the Spirit are never related to gender. At times of revival women have led and contributed, most equally with men, speaking, prophesying, and healing in the more informal context that revival brings. This was particularly evident in John Wesley's Britain, where women's manifest gifts, including those of his mother, convinced him that women should be allowed to lead. And it was in rising tides of revival in more sectarian churches that women thrived in nineteenth-century America.

Progress, however, is not linear. In the late twentieth century, evangelical and fundamentalist churches have seen a resurgence of the notion of headship in family and church (taking literally 1 Cor. 11:3–16); men must have the ultimate authority in these areas. By some estimates, 90 percent of evangelical families ascribe either literally or symbolically to headship ideals. Paradoxically, others have pointed to the deeply subversive nature of some otherwise conservative women's groups such as *Women Aglow*. These women depend on the Spirit for guidance and for mutual support and solidarity that is similar in many ways to feminist groups.

In society as a whole, women in First World countries have made significant progress toward equal pay and opportunity, yet inequities persist in spite of greater success in formal education by women. In all societies, however, deeper evidence of unequal status for women persists; women are more likely to be poor, to be the victims of violence, to be raped, and to be marginalized. In many countries these differences are acute. Wartime or recession has quickly brought about a decline in women's status and security.

Feminist theology has continued through the twentieth century and beyond to advocate a radical equality in status. Feminism has pointed to the uplifting of marginal women in the salvation narrative. Christ reversed and so resisted traditional gender mores. A woman affirmed his mission with gifts of oil and love where others were uncomprehending. Feminist theology has named the silences, imagined where women must have been, and discovered texts and interpretations hitherto ignored.

The depth of patriarchy in human society, and extending even beyond humans to the animal world, gives cause for thought. For some, this is God's order and should not be broken, and the ills of society may be placed at the door of feminism. For others, the persistence of patriarchy and the associated lower status of women are linked to the problem of evil. Indeed, Gen. 3:16 suggests that imbalance between the sexes has the same kind of ongoing and persistent negative effect as human alienation from nature. If this is the case, then the status of women will continue to be a matter of concern in church and in society.

See also Creation Ethics; Egalitarianism; Equality; Feminist Ethics; Gender; Headship; Image of God;

Sex Discrimination; Sexual Harassment; Submission and Subordination

Bibliography

Bendroth, M. *Fundamentalism and Gender: 1875 to the Present.* Yale University Press, 1993; Brasher, B. *Godly Women: Fundamentalism and Female Power.* Rutgers University Press, 1998; Gallagher, S. *Evangelical Identity and Gendered Family Life.* Rutgers University Press, 2003; Griffith, H. *God's Daughters: Evangelical Women and the Power of Submission.* University of California Press, 1997; Hardesty, N. *Women Called to Witness: Evangelical Feminism in the Nineteenth Century.* Abingdon, 1984; Neft, N. *Where Women Stand: An International Report on the Status of Women in 140 Countries, 1997–1998.* Random House, 1997; Schüssler Fiorenza, E. *In Memory of Her: A Feminist Theological Reconstruction of Christian Origins.* Crossroad, 1983; Torjesen, K. *When Women Were Priests: Women's Leadership in the Early Church and the Scandal of Their Subordination in the Rise of Christianity.* HarperSanFrancisco, 1993; Trible, P. *Texts of Terror: Literary-Feminist Readings of Biblical Narratives.* Fortress, 1984.

Nicola Hoggard Creegan

Work

Scripture provides no full-blown theological ethic of work, but it does offer consistent themes from which an ethic of work can be (and have been) formed. These themes include the following:

1. Work is good. God works and created humans to work.
2. Work is toil and pain, and its produce is fleeting.
3. People are enjoined to work. Refusal to work is a vice; hard work is a virtue.
4. People are commanded to stop work—their own work and that of others in their household—on the Sabbath.
5. Through their work, humans are able to feed themselves, their families, and others who cannot support themselves by their own work (e.g., orphans and elderly), to give alms, and to make offerings.
6. Those who mistreat workers or fail to pay fair wages to them are under judgment.

From the earliest chapters of Genesis, one can see the central place of work in the created order. In creating the world, God is engaged in work, speaking into being the stars and the moon, the earth and its creatures, fashioning the first human from the dust of the ground. The psalmist describes the heavens using the language of artistry; the heavens are "the work of [God's] fingers" (Ps. 8:3). God's continuing providential care for creation has the character of work. When God finds Adam and Eve hiding in the garden, the first thing God does after talking with them is make garments from animal skins and clothe them (Gen. 3:21).

Throughout both Testaments, God is described using words drawn from ordinary human occupations—from the lowliest and most menial to the highest and most exalted. God is a shepherd caring for his sheep, protecting them from wolves, seeking the lost, and binding the wounds of the injured (Ezek. 34:12–31; John 10:11–18). God is a housekeeper sweeping her home in search of the lost coin (Luke 15:8), and a vinedresser tending and pruning the vine (John 15:1–2). God is a potter shaping his people (Isa. 64:8), a builder, and a watchman (Ps. 127:1). God is both the mother panting in labor (Isa. 42:14) and the midwife who takes the child from its mother's womb (Ps. 22:9). God is a judge (Gen. 18:25; Ps. 94:2; Isa. 33:22; Jas. 4:12), a king enthroned (Pss. 5:2; 29:10; Isa. 43:15), and a warrior who is mighty in battle (Exod. 15:3; Ps. 24:8).

In Gen. 2, this God who works creates humans for work. God, observing creation, sees that there is no one "to till the ground." God places the first human in the garden for a specified purpose: "to till it and keep it." In the Gen. 1 account of human creation, God gives humans the mandate to subdue the earth and have dominion over it. These texts have been used repeatedly in Christian reflections on work. St. Simeon the New Theologian, for example, wrote, "In the beginning man was created with a nature inclined to work, for in paradise Adam was enjoined to till the ground and care for it, and there is in us a natural bent for work, the movement toward the good" (Louth and Conti 61).

Christian ambivalence about work is also rooted in these first chapters of Genesis. Adam, created for work in the first two chapters, is placed in a new relationship to work in the third chapter. After Adam eats of the fruit of the forbidden "tree of the knowledge of good and evil," God speaks: "Cursed is the ground because of you; in toil you shall eat of it all the days of your life; thorns and thistles it shall bring forth for you; and you shall eat the plants of the field. By the sweat of your face you shall eat bread until you return to the ground" (Gen. 3:17–19). John Chrysostom wrote that, when God turned Adam's work to toil, God was, in effect, saying, "I will ensure you pass the whole time with pain so that this experience may prove a brake on your getting ideas above your station, and . . . that everything you do is achieved only by sweat so that under pressure from these you may have continual guidance in keeping to limits and recognizing your own makeup" (Louth and Conti 95).

The ambivalence about work does not stop with the expulsion from the garden at the end of Gen. 3. In the opening verses of Gen. 4, Adam and Eve's elder son, Cain, "a tiller of the ground," is angry with his younger brother, Abel, "a keeper of sheep," because God "had regard" for the offering from Abel's labor but not from Cain's (Gen. 4:2–5). A few verses later, when a jealous Cain takes Abel into his fields and slays him, God, in language reminiscent of, though even stronger than, Gen. 3:17–19, tells Cain that he is cursed from the very ground, "which has opened its mouth to receive" Abel's blood. "When you till the ground, it will no longer yield to you its strength" (Gen. 4:10–12).

The idea of work as toil and pain is found elsewhere in Scripture and in church history. The book of Ecclesiastes is a classic case in point. Human toil is a prime example of the vanity of human life. The author of Ecclesiastes reflects on the work of his life: "Then I considered all that my hands had done and the toil I had spent in doing it, and again, all was vanity and a chasing after wind, and there was nothing to be gained under the sun" (Eccl. 2:11). Both human work and the gain of that work are ultimately fleeting. But Ecclesiastes is not totally negative about work. Toil, along with eating and drinking, are gifts of God: "This is what I have seen to be good: it is fitting to eat and drink and find enjoyment in all the toil with which one toils under the sun" (Eccl. 5:18).

Work, however fleeting, is praised in Ecclesiastes and elsewhere in Scripture, especially Proverbs. When Prov. 31 extols the "capable wife" who surpasses all other women, most of the verses are given over to her work; she buys fields, makes clothing, sells merchandise, and "works with willing hands" (Prov. 31:10–31). Proverbs admonishes the "lazybones" to follow the example of the hard-working ant, or else "poverty will come upon you like a robber" (Prov. 6:8–11). Here and elsewhere in Scripture reluctance to work is linked with its consequence, poverty (Prov. 28:19). It is put even more bluntly in 2 Thessalonians: "Anyone unwilling to work should not eat" (2 Thess. 3:10). The faithful are exhorted instead to "earn their own living" (2 Thess. 3:12).

In Scripture, injunctions to work stand alongside injunctions to stop work on the Sabbath. God, who had worked for six days creating the world, stopped work on the seventh day and blessed and "hallowed it" (Gen. 2:1–3). God insists that God's people honor the Sabbath by stopping work, both their own and that of others in their household, including servants and slaves (Exod. 16:23–30; 20:8–11; Deut. 5:12–15). Even when Jesus breaks the Sabbath, he does not deny the command but rather points to the law to show that exceptions may be made (Mark 3:1–6; John 7:23).

Humans work for practical ends. Working is linked in Scripture with gaining food to eat (Gen. 3:17–19; Ps. 128:2; 2 Thess. 3:10). Through their work, people are able to feed not only themselves and their households but also those unable to support themselves by their labor. The injunction to care for the needy who are unable to provide for themselves runs throughout Scripture. Farmers are not to harvest the edges of their fields or "gather the gleanings" or "strip [their] vineyard bare," so that the poor can gather the remainder (Lev. 19:9–10; 23:22; cf. Deut. 24:19). And in Eph. 4:28, work is recommended so that workers may "have something to share with the needy." Jesus uses the story of the rich fool (Luke 12:16–21) as a warning for those who focus on gaining and storing excess riches for their use alone.

Thomas Aquinas picks up on these two purposes of work—to eat and to give to the needy—and adds two additional purposes: "the removal of idleness" and the "curbing of concupiscence" (*ST* II-II, q. 187, a. 3). Work also allowed people to bring to the temple as an offering the "first fruits" of their harvest (Exod. 23:19; 34:26; Deut. 26:1–11).

Many texts in Scripture call for fair treatment of workers, especially in their wages (Deut. 24:14–15; Jer. 22:13; Lev. 19:13). Those who mistreat workers or fail to pay fair wages are under judgment. Through the prophet Malachi, God says, "Then I will draw near to you for judgment; I will be swift to bear witness against . . . those who oppress the hired workers in their wages, the widow and the orphan" (Mal. 3:5). According to James, the rich who hoard their wealth and fail to pay wages to their workers are under judgment. "Come now, you rich people, weep and wail for the miseries that are coming to you" (Jas. 5:1). The cries of the unpaid harvesters and of the unpaid wages themselves have "reached the ears of the Lord of hosts" (Jas. 5:4). Jesus tells a story of a just and generous landowner who not only pays his workers the wages due them, but even pays a full day's wage to those who worked only its last portion (Matt. 20:1–15).

Most Christian treatments of work—from Thomas Aquinas to Martin Luther to John Calvin to John Paul II—share in common some basic claims about work rooted in the Scriptures reviewed here: work is a good gift of God; humans serve God and others through their labor; faithfulness to God is the primary task for Christian life, outweighing any particular occupation; humans are to be just and fair in their work; the faithful have responsibilities to the poor that can be fulfilled in many ways, including through human work and through the sharing of the produce of that work; and householders have a particular obligation to provide the basic necessities for themselves and their households.

The Christian tradition has also contained disagreements about work, the most famous perhaps being the relative value of the work of those taking religious vows (priests, monks, and nuns) and those engaged in "secular" occupations. This argument, often addressed in Protestant treatments of work, has been framed as a clash between Roman Catholics and Protestants. Certainly, when Martin Luther rejected the idea that the work of those taking religious vows was somehow higher than ordinary work such as farming, soldiering, and parenting, he was responding to a claim common in the medieval church. Even on this once-disputed point, however, there is now much common ground. Many recent Roman Catholic statements are glowing in their appraisals of ordinary labor and insist that through work humans participate in God's creative work in the world.

Despite all these agreements, there have been and still are many points of disagreement. Christians may agree that work is good and still disagree about whether certain forms of employment—for example, the military or the weapons industry—are acceptable. Christians may agree that work is an important part of human life and disagree about whether people have a "right to work" or who is responsible for providing employment. Christians may value the labor of caring for children and homes alongside other kinds of labor outside the home and disagree strongly about the relative roles and responsibilities of mothers and fathers in fulfilling these tasks. Christians may generally agree that employers should be just and fair to their employees but disagree about the particulars—for example, what a fair wage is, or what just working conditions are, or whether it is just for a small group to own and control the means of production.

John Paul II's 1981 papal encyclical, *On Human Work*, is a classic example of this move from broader, shared claims about work found in Scripture to more specific and contested claims. Although the document draws on many of the biblical texts reviewed here, the key texts are the first chapters of Genesis, especially 1:26–28, where humans are created in God's image and instructed to "fill the earth and subdue it" (John Paul II 9–22). This text is the grounding for John Paul II's claim that "work is a fundamental dimension of human existence on earth" (John Paul II 9). As humans work, they fulfill the command of God to subdue and have dominion, and they reflect "the very action of the creator of the universe." Reflections on human work and policies concerning work should focus primarily on the subject of work, which is the person who is working, and only secondarily on the object of aspects of work, which is the means of production, technology, the product or its economic value. To give greater value to the objective aspects is a "reversal of the order laid down" in Genesis. Humans are not "instruments of production," but rather the "subject of work and its true maker and creator" (John Paul II 16).

Drawing from these Genesis texts and many others, John Paul II insists on the dignity of the worker and the centrality of work in human life and then moves from these broad claims to insist on particular rights, including the right to employment, to working conditions beneficial for the workers' health and "moral integrity," and to a fair "family wage"—that is, a wage by which a worker can support a family (John Paul II 37–52). The recommendation of a family wage, as well as "grants to mothers," would allow mothers to focus their attention on home and family—a responsibility uniquely theirs, according to John Paul II.

On Human Work also calls for other workers' rights: healthcare benefits, medical care in case of accidents on the job, the right to form unions and strike, regular days off and vacation time, unemployment benefits, pensions for the elderly, and insurance in the event of disability. Moreover, people who are disabled have the right to employment fitting to their capabilities. People should also have the right to seek work in other countries, and immigrants should be given the same employment protections and rights as citizens.

Nations bear responsibility not only to secure these rights for workers in their own countries but also to enact policies fair for workers in other countries. Wealthier states, for example, sometimes fix tariffs disadvantageous to, and even exploitative of, workers in poorer countries. Officials, both national and international, are responsible for acting "against unemployment" by strategic planning and collaboration, so that people around the world who are able to work can find employment.

The most radical claim of *On Human Work* is perhaps not its policy proposals, but rather its theological claim that, through their work, humans join in the redemptive work of Christ. "By enduring the toil of work in union with Christ crucified for us, man in a way collaborates with the Son of God for the redemption of humanity" (John Paul II 59). In recent treatments of work, many Protestants still argue against the old two-tiered vision of religious and secular work found in the medieval church. It is ironic, then, that work is described in more glowing terms in this papal encyclical than in many recent treatments by Protestants, many of whom would hesitate to describe human labor as a means of participating with Christ in redemption. Perhaps the greater temptation today is not a two-tiered model overvaluing religious occupations at the expense of secular ones; the greater temptation, for Roman Catholics and Protestants alike, may be to substitute for the old two-tiered system a new one that, in effect if not by intention, gives greater value to work that garners more money and prestige. This substitution is not only out of keeping with most Christian and Jewish appraisals of work; it is their antithesis.

See also Just Wage; Professional Ethics; Sabbath; Vocation

Bibliography

Arendt, H. *The Human Condition*. University of Chicago Press, 1958; Heschel, A. *The Sabbath*. Farrar, Straus & Giroux, 1951; Jensen, D. *Responsive Labor: A Theology of Work*. Westminster John Knox, 2006; John Paul II. *On Human Work*. United States Catholic Conference, 1981; Louth, A., and M. Conti, eds. *Genesis 1–11*. ACCS 1. Routledge, 2001; Volf, M. *Work in the Spirit: Toward a Theology of Work*. Oxford University Press, 1991.

Rebekah Miles

World

Although the term *world* can be broadly conceived, it tends to have three connotations in Scripture: the world as all of creation, the human inhabitants of the earth, and (specifically in the NT) the current eschatological phase of the world.

Scriptural Portraits of the World

In the OT, the emphasis is repeatedly made that the Lord, the God of Israel, is the sole creator and owns everything in the world (Ps. 24:1). Although he made the world and its inhabitants and deemed them "very good" (Gen. 1:31), the cancerous effects of sin frustrated this divine orderliness and brought enmity and chaos to nature and humanity (Gen. 4–11).

Israel was called by God to be a priestly kingdom (Exod. 19:5–6) to fulfill God's promise to bless all the families of the earth through Abraham's descendants (Gen. 12:3). Thus, on the one hand, Israel had a responsibility to stand near outsiders and call forth for all people (and even nonhuman elements of creation) to recognize and praise the Lord (e.g., Pss. 33:8; 49:1; 96:11; Isa. 43:9). On the other hand, the response and temptations of the world often were deleterious as Israel witnessed the wickedness of the nations, fell prey to their enticements of idolatry and immorality, endured their mistreatment, and prophesied their demise (e.g., Isa. 13:11; Jer. 25:1–15; Nah. 1:1–11).

In the NT, the same tension exists where the inhabitants of the world are characterized as evil and vapid, enticing and polluting the people of God (Matt. 13:22; Luke 12:30; 1 John 2:15–18). Indeed, James defines pure and undefiled religion in terms of caring for the needy and keeping oneself "unstained by the world" (Jas. 1:27). In the Pauline corpus there is a strong eschatological edge to this tension, where the present evil age of the world and the new age ushered in by the Christ event presently overlap, and one must vigilantly resist the conforming pressures of the former (Rom. 12:2; cf. 1 Cor. 7:31; 2 Cor. 4:4). According to the Pastoral Epistles, Paul sent for Timothy to come soon because his former companion, Demas, abandoned him on account of his "love with this present world [age]" (2 Tim. 4:10).

Paul advocated a distinct moral disassociation from outsiders, but he did not encourage a physical separation (1 Cor. 5:9–10). Like other NT authors, and ostensibly in line with Jesus' own teaching, Paul encouraged a benevolent attitude toward unbelievers and praised the success of the gospel in reaching far-flung regions of the world (Rom. 1:8; Phil. 2:15; cf. Matt. 5:14; John 1:29; 3:16–17; Acts 22:15).

The letter of 1 Peter offers perhaps a prime example of the challenge that early Christians encountered vis-à-vis society at large. It is apparent that the letter's recipients were experiencing some kind of persecution (1:6–7). In the face of the options of accommodation (1:14; 2:1, 11) or resistance (3:9, 13–17; 4:15), a different path was drawn out by the author, who, again, depicted the people of God as holy priests (2:5, 9) who have a separate and special identity in God but also bear the responsibility of serving and caring for the world (2:9b; cf. 2:12).

Creation itself plays an important role throughout Scripture as one groaning in bondage (Rom. 8:21). Yet it hopes for renewal and prosperity through God's hands in anticipation of the revealing of the children of God (Rom. 8:19), whose care for creation in the present is a foretaste of God's promise of full restoration. Although Scripture does refer to the formation of a new heaven and new earth (Isa. 65:17–22; 2 Pet. 3:13; Rev. 21:1), this does not necessarily involve the complete destruction of creation. Rather, many scholars have understood such language as analogous to that of the resurrected human body, where the newness does not cancel out a continuity of identity and even substance (John 20:27).

The Ethics of Engaging the World

The scriptural depiction of the relationship between the people of God and the world at large is complex. Various Christian communities, therefore, have conceived of the appropriate stance toward society differently. From a sociological perspective, Bryan Wilson's taxonomy of sectarian responses to the world is helpful: conversionists trust that God will change the world through personal transformation; revolutionists imagine an overturning of societal structures; introversionists isolate their community from outsiders, abandoning the world as hopelessly corrupt; reformists seek to affect the world socially and politically with God's aid; utopianists try to restructure the world; thaumaturgists look for God's supernatural actions to save the world; manipulationists tend to see divine power as an instrument for worldly blessing and benefit; a final response would simply be acceptance of the world as it is (i.e., complete accommodation).

Christian groups, in various locales and periods of history, could be categorized according to virtually all these types—for example, evangelical Christians often fit the conversionist model, faith-healing groups are thaumaturgical, and introversionists could be exemplified in radical monastic communities.

Although one might focus on the psychological dimensions of these lifestyle choices and the crafting of personal and group identity, it is particularly appropriate for us to consider the moral implications of these models with respect to the world. On the extreme of introversion, the group has become insular and has left the world to its own vices. The sect takes no interest in serving outsiders. On the other end of the spectrum is the acceptance and acquiescent position that is fully immersed in the world and does not resist its norms and moral ills. Most Christian churches and communities tend to stand somewhere between these poles, and the tension lies precisely in how to construct a distinctly Christ-centered identity within society while avoiding the temptation to obsequiously accommodate. The answer, again, seems to lie in the scriptural image of the royal priesthood whereby the church finds its identity within the kingdom and kingship of Jesus Christ while serving as priests, bringing God to the world and the world to God (see Gupta).

The Ethics of Creation Care

Ecological concerns are ubiquitous today in a way unimaginable in generations past for many reasons, not the least of which is the depletion of natural resources. There is a common belief among some Christians (and also represented more widely particularly in American society) that God will destroy the earth, and thus its growing barrenness is a sign of the imminent apocalypse. Therefore, giving regard to the earth and sustaining it with a view toward long-term productivity and fertility, for some such thinkers, is vain and perhaps merely a secular agenda.

However, in recent decades dissenting voices have arisen among Christian scholars. Terence Fretheim, through a close reading of Gen. 1–2, argues that, while humanity does appear to be prominent in these narratives, God chooses to create through the participation of various created elements rather than working alone. Fretheim refers to this as a relational model, where there is an intentional and chosen interdependence. He also reasons that it is a mistake to use the verb "subdue" (Gen. 1:28) as the biblical viewpoint of human interaction with creation, since the Hebrew word *wĕkibšuhâ* in that verse is more properly understood to mean "and bring order out of continuing disorder" (Fretheim 52–53). Finally, in relation to the world and God's act of creation, Fretheim opposes the assumption that the earth is for humans and at their disposal. The natural world and its elements are "creatures" in the same way humans are "creatures"—God created them for his own purposes and pleasure. Therefore, instead of referring to human stewardship of the earth, Fretheim prefers the notion of human partnership or servanthood.

Newer ecological readings of other biblical texts are being pursued as well. For example, Barbara Rossing proposes that the crisis of creation in Revelation is not the need to purge an evil natural world, but rather is the desire to see an end to the exploitation of the earth and its inhabitants. Thus, judgment is pronounced on those who are destroying the earth (Rev. 11:18).

Beyond the academy, there are many signs that Christians worldwide are taking an interest in ecological concerns. The publishing of *The Green Bible* by HarperOne in 2008 signals an interest in such a version of Scripture, which is made of recycled paper and presents in green lettering verses and passages that relate to God's care for creation.

A number of Christian environmentalist groups have emerged in recent years, such as the Evangelical Environmental Network, A Rocha, and the Au Sable Institute of Environmental Studies.

Conclusion

The world is in the center of the view of the God of Scripture, who made his creation good. Although his world had become corrupted by human sin, God desired, through Christ, to use his own creatures to work toward its redemption (2 Cor. 5:19). Thus, Christians are called by Scripture to serve this world of human and nonhuman constituents as priests, servants who carry out the divine will and act as mediators between the one God and his creation.

See also Creation Ethics; Ecological Ethics; Salvation; Worldliness

Bibliography

Adams, E. *Constructing the World: A Study in Paul's Cosmological Language*. SNTW. T&T Clark, 2000; Bartholomew, C., et al., eds. *A Royal Priesthood? The Use of the Bible Ethically and Politically*. Zondervan, 2002; Fretheim, T. *God and World in the Old Testament: A Relational Theology of Creation*. Abingdon, 2005; Gupta, N. "A Spiritual House of Royal Priests, Chosen and Honored: The Presence and Function of Cultic Imagery in 1 Peter." *PRS* 36 (2009): 61–76; Horrell, D. "Ecological Criticism." Pages 192–98 in *Searching for Meaning: An Introduction to Interpreting the New Testament*, ed. P. Gooder. Westminster John Knox, 2008; Moltmann, J. *God in Creation: A New Theology of Creation and the Spirit of God*. Harper & Row, 1985; Rossing, B. "For the Healing of the World: Reading Revelation Ecologically." Pages 165–82 in *From Every People and Nation: The Book of Revelation in Intercultural Perspective*, ed. D. Rhoads. Fortress, 2005; Tonstad, S. "Creation Groaning in Labor Pains." Pages 141–49 in *Exploring Ecological Hermeneutics*, ed. N. Habel and P. Trudinger. SBLSymS 46. Society of Bibical Literature, 2008; Volf, M. *Exclusion and Embrace: A Theological Exploration of Identity, Otherness, and Reconciliation*. Abingdon, 1996; Wilson, B. *Magic and the Millennium: A Sociological Study of Religious Movements of Protest among Tribal and Third-World Peoples*. Heinemann, 1973.

Nijay K. Gupta

Worldliness

The term *worldliness* refers to an undue preoccupation with the physical and temporal things of this world, such as wealth, pleasure, and success, to the detriment of one's spiritual life. A worldly attitude is spiritually damaging not because the world is intrinsically evil—it is, after all, created, loved, inhabited, and ultimately redeemed by God (John 1:10; 3:16)—but rather because it focuses on the physical without reference to the spiritual (1 Cor. 10:31), on the present without thought of God's purposes for the future (2 Pet. 1:4), and on the self without consideration of others or God (Luke 9:23).

The idea of a worldly approach to life derives from the "world" (*kosmos*) being understood as the sum total of physical things (Acts 17:24), then, by extension, as the arena of human life and activity (Matt. 4:8), and finally, as a fallen and sinful world alienated from God and under the power of the ruler of this world (John 14:30). This world does not know God (John 1:10); it is a realm of unbelief, and at the heart of it is the world's rejection of Christ (1 Cor. 2:8).

Some attitudes and activities, such as murder, theft, and lying, are sinful by definition, but worldliness involves activities and relationships that are not intrinsically wrong but can become the means by which a person is seduced away from a spiritual life. Although it can be a distortion of any good, worldliness most often involves a preoccupation with wealth and what it can buy in this world, or an inappropriate desire for success or status, or the distortion of relationships in order to gain power or sexual gratification at the expense of others. A more spiritually fulfilling approach stores up "treasures in heaven" (Matt. 6:19–20), finds "success" in union with God (John 15:5), and develops right relationships with God and neighbor (Rom. 13:9).

Worldliness is more spiritually dangerous than many other, more overt sins, because it involves an interior attitude and an external behavior concerning activities that are potentially good. This means that it can be justified to others or rationalized to oneself. The worldly person is not so obviously depraved or wicked as much as self-absorbed, probably complacent and comfortable, and lacking a passion for the spiritual life.

Overcoming worldliness means rejecting or overcoming the evil world (Rom. 12:2; Titus 2:12; Jas. 4:4), but it also means developing a true worldliness that is a result of being sent into the world by Christ (John 17:18). The world is the place where the gospel bears fruit (Col. 1:6). Overcoming worldliness means deepening one's relationship with God and living by the Spirit (Rom. 8:5). This involves developing essential disciplines (whether the traditional disciplines of poverty, chastity, and obedience or others such as simplicity, fidelity, and service), enhancing personal virtues (such as those listed in Gal. 5:22–23), and engaging in spiritual practices (including prayer, contemplation, worship, and community life).

See also Desire; Materialism; Vice; Wealth; World

Bibliography

Bonhoeffer, D. *The Cost of Discipleship*. Trans. R. Fuller. Rev. ed. Macmillan, 1959; Foster, R. *Money, Sex and Power: The Challenge of the Disciplined Life*. Harper & Row, 1985; Mouw, R. *Called to Holy Worldliness*. Fortress, 1980;

Outler, A., and R. Heitzenrater, eds. *John Wesley's Sermons: An Anthology*. Abingdon, 1991; Packer, J. *A Quest for Godliness: The Puritan Vision of the Christian Life*. Crossway Books, 1990; Ramsey, M. *Sacred and Secular: A Study in the Otherworldly and This-Worldly Aspects of Christianity*. Harper & Row, 1965; Wimbush, V. *Paul, the Worldly Ascetic: Response to the World and Self-Understanding according to 1 Corinthians 7*. Mercer University Press, 1987.

Brian G. Edgar

World Poverty, World Hunger

The United Nations Development Programme (UNDP) *Human Development Report 2005* states, "One in five people in the world—more than 1 billion people—still survive on less than $1 a day, a level of poverty so abject that it threatens survival" (UNDP 24). Former Brazilian president Luiz Inácio da Silva (elected in 2002 and again in 2006) compares hunger to a weapon of mass destruction. "Hunger is actually the worst of all weapons of mass destruction, claiming millions of victims every year. Fighting hunger and poverty and promoting development are the truly sustainable ways to achieve world peace. . . . There will be no peace without development, and there will be neither peace nor development without social justice" (UNDP 74). Clearly, world poverty and hunger are moral issues that face both those who suffer from it and those who have the capacity to respond to it.

Today, per capita income is the standard economic indicator of wealth and poverty. To calculate this figure, we divide the annual gross domestic product (GDP) by national population (GDP is the total of government expenditures, business investment, consumption, and net exports). For example, Canada has a per capita income of $30,677, whereas Honduran per capita income is $2,665 (UNDP 340). Per capita income, however, is a crude measure that does not account for vast inequities in education, health, infant mortality, ecological degradation, and so forth. To account for these additional variables, the UN measures human well-being with sharper tools, such as human development indicators (HDI). Human development indicators measure the length and health of one's life, one's knowledge, and standard of living (UNDP technical note 1, 340). At present, Norway has the highest rank on the HDI scale, and Niger the lowest (UNDP 340). The index of sustainable economic welfare is also used to show how economic development impacts the environment.

Although contemporary measures of poverty vary, a starting point is the lack of material goods. The particular goods may vary from culture to culture, but their absence inevitably creates hunger and other types of deprivation. This definition of the poor as lacking basic goods is seen in biblical literature via the Hebrew term *ʿănāwîm*. Other Hebrew terms broaden this meaning: *dal* ("cut off from property"), *miskēn* ("contemptible"), *rāš* ("having lost all"), *ʾebyôn* ("yearning"), *dak* ("depressed"), and *mak* ("downtrodden") (*Leviticus Rabbah* 34.6). In the NT, the Greek term *ptōchoi* gathers up these meanings. In addition, *ptōchoi* sometimes is grouped with other conditions that alienate a person from community, such as lameness, sickness, blindness, and hunger (Green). There are approximately one hundred references to "the poor" and "poverty" in the Bible. Related terms such as *wealth* and *possessions* make the issue of poverty a prominent theme in Scripture.

Although the Bible does not directly establish policies for modern nations or individuals regarding poverty, it does provide standards, examples, virtues, and goals regarding the poor and the hungry. God cares for his creation, especially his human children. God's desire is that they love him and their neighbor and care for creation. To thrive as God's image-bearer in the world requires a minimal standard of sustenance. Creation does produce sufficient goods for the basic needs of all; none need go hungry. Creation does not, however, produce sufficient goods to satisfy the desires of all. Thus, scarcity results not from the inadequacy of creation or from God's neglect but rather from the way goods are distributed. How goods ought to be allocated is a question of distributive justice. Various criteria for just distribution are proposed: equality, need, proportionality, ability to pay, contribution to output, and so on. That is, a person might lay claim to goods because he or she is equally human, or has great need, or contributed to the production of goods. The Bible does not specify a theory of distributive justice. In many cases in Scripture, however, it is clear that God hears the cries of the poor and the hungry as just claims to scarce goods. Although it is theoretically possible that God might have designed a world without scarcity, he did not; instead, God entrusted humans with the task of caring for their fellows. By alleviating the hunger and poverty of others, Christians exhibit the virtues and justice of God. Viewed this way, poverty is not merely the problem of an individual who has too few resources; rather, it is a societal and moral issue indicating that relationships with God, humans, or nature have become broken or perverse. In short, poverty and hunger are results of individual and corporate sin, not the inadequacy of creation or the malevolence of God.

The essential mark of social justice in ancient Israel was its treatment of the poor. The king had final authority in this matter and was instructed to stand up for the poor (Ps. 72; Prov. 29:14). It was not only obedience to law that God desired, but an attitude of care as well. "If there is among you anyone in need . . . do not be hard-hearted or tight-fisted toward your needy neighbor. You should rather open your hand, willingly lending enough to meet the need, whatever it may be" (Deut. 15:7–8). Yet the Bible also recognizes that poverty can be the result of foolishness or laziness (Prov. 6:10; 13:4; 20:4).

Jesus' ministry stressed the importance of restoration for the poor. His inaugural sermon in the Nazareth synagogue uses portions of Isaiah and proclaims, "The Spirit of the Lord is upon me, because he has anointed me to bring good news to the poor. He has sent me to proclaim release to the captives and recovery of sight to the blind, to let the oppressed go free, to proclaim the year of the Lord's favor" (Luke 4:18–19). Jesus' concern for the poor was evidenced in word and deed. His miracles provided food for the hungry, restored sight to the blind, and brought health to the sick. His teachings showed the folly of hoarding goods or putting trust in wealth. The fact that the kingdom of God was "at hand" in his very person relativized the importance and value of all the world's goods.

Jesus' teachings were delivered in an agricultural society in which a few members had great wealth and most lived in relative poverty. Clearly, his words did not directly address modern, worldwide poverty. Rather, he sought to instruct his listeners about their responsibility toward their own poor neighbors. But when asked, "Who is my neighbor?" Jesus responded with the parable of the good Samaritan, showing that a neighbor is one who can and does serve the needy. And when questioned about judgment day, Jesus said, "Then the king will say to those at his right hand, 'Come, you that are blessed by my Father, inherit the kingdom prepared for you from the foundation of the world; for I was hungry and you gave me food, I was thirsty and you gave me something to drink, I was a stranger and you welcomed me, I was naked and you gave me clothing, I was sick and you took care of me, I was in prison and you visited me'" (Matt. 25:34–36). Explaining how this could be, the king adds, "Truly I tell you, just as you did it to one of the least of these who are members of my family, you did it to me" (Matt. 25:40). Jesus himself was among the poor of his society, and serving the poor serves him.

As the church developed, care for its poor was a major concern. As Paul spread the gospel throughout Aegean cities, he collected offerings for the poor in the Jerusalem church. The early church was a tiny minority within the Roman Empire and lacked resources to combat poverty and hunger outside its own doors. But by the mid-fourth century CE, when the church became dominant in the empire, it was renowned for its beneficence. Even the pagan Roman emperor Julian wrote, "The impious Galileans [Christians] support not only their own poor but ours as well" (quoted in Pohl 44).

Liberation theologians refer to God's concern for the poor as "the preferential option for the poor." Gustavo Gutiérrez writes, "The question of poverty is a question of the very meaning of life and the collective course of humanity. Poverty is the result of a system which institutionalizes privileges for some and poverty, humiliation, and death for others" (Gutiérrez, "Violence of a System," 93). In Scripture, the poor often were the oppressed, and their poverty was a direct result of injustice. Widows, orphans, and foreigners were particularly vulnerable because only adult male citizens had legal standing in ancient Near Eastern societies.

As there were many causes for poverty and hunger in the ancient Near East, so were there many solutions. Within Scripture are prescriptions for direct aid for the hungry, offerings, laws enacted to protect the poor from harm, restoration of property, freedom from debt and slavery, and proper attitudes. Today, direct relief, attitudinal shifts, glad giving, distributional justice, political advocacy, development and relief projects, and business entrepreneurship that creates jobs may be appropriate responses to poverty and hunger.

Globalization enables us to be the neighbor of many, be they the poor in India, sub-Saharan Africa, or elsewhere. The poor do have responsibility for their own actions, but all Christians and all churches are challenged by Scripture to distribute their own goods in keeping with God's demands for justice and mercy. As seen in Matt. 25, one's actions toward the poor and the hungry entail ultimate consequences.

See also Economic Development; Economic Ethics; Globalization; Jubilee; Justice, Distributive; Liberationist Ethics; Peace; Poverty and Poor; Preferential Option for the Poor

Bibliography

Barrera, A. *God and the Evil of Scarcity: Moral Foundations of Economic Agency*. University of Notre Dame Press, 2005; Green, J. "Good News to Whom? Jesus and the 'Poor.'" Pages 59–74 in *Jesus of Nazareth, Lord and Christ: Essays on the*

Historical Jesus and New Testament Christology, ed. J. Green and M. Turner. Eerdmans, 1994; Groody, D., ed. *The Option for the Poor in Christian Theology*. University of Notre Dame Press, 2007; Gutiérrez, G. *A Theology of Liberation: History, Politics, and Salvation*. Orbis, 1973; idem. "The Violence of a System." *Concilium* 10, no. 140 (1980): 93–100; Pohl, C. *Making Room: Recovering Hospitality as a Christian Tradition*. Eerdmans, 1999; United Nations Development Programme (UNDP). *Human Development Report 2005*. New York, 2005; Van Til, K. *Less than $2.00 a Day: A Christian View of World Poverty and the Free Market*. Eerdmans, 2007.

Kent A. Van Til

Z

Zechariah

The book of Zechariah presents the words of a prophet and the response of the Jewish community living in the early phase of the restoration of Judah after the devastating Babylonian exile (late sixth–early fifth century BCE).

The book draws heavily on earlier OT ethical traditions. It is dominated by intertextual links to earlier prophets (see 1:4–6; 7:7, 12), especially Isaiah, Jeremiah, and Ezekiel, while also drawing from key Deuteronomic and Priestly traditions.

The Deuteronomic vision of repentance found in Jeremiah dominates the prose sermon material in Zech. 1:1–6; 7:1–8:23. The initial call in 1:3 ("return to me") emphasizes that repentance is fundamentally a renewal of relationship between Yahweh and people, with the following citation of the earlier prophets in 1:4 ("return from your evil ways") reminding the reader that such covenantal renewal has ethical implications. The character of the misdeeds is identified in 7:9–10; 8:16–17 as social injustice through manipulation of the courts. The Deuteronomic vision of covenantal blessing/curse underlies the ardent call of both Zechariah and his predecessors, reminding the people that disobedience incites the disciplinary curse of Yahweh, while obedience results in God's blessed reward. Ethical transformation is encouraged through the threat of discipline (7:11–14; 8:14) and the promise of blessing (8:1–13, 15, 19–23) delivered through the prophetic voice (1:4–6; 7:12b–13).

The night visions in 1:7–6:15 represent the predominantly positive divine response to the people's initial repentance in 1:6b. Yahweh promises to return, rebuild the city, restore its prosperity, and renew its social structures. The cry of the angel in the first night vision expresses the Jewish community's moral outrage over the enduring destruction and seeming lack of punishment of their exilic abusers (Babylon). God's promise is to punish those nations (1:14–15; cf. 1:18–21; 2:6–13; 6:1–8). Yahweh's declaration of the election of Jerusalem and Joshua and provision of clean priestly clothing signal a new start for both community and priestly leadership. Nevertheless, there are enduring ethical concerns within the community: in particular, social injustice through manipulation of the courts (5:1–4) and idolatry introduced from Babylon (5:5–11). The flying scroll in 5:1–4 suggests a role for the written Torah in ethical transformation. Unethical behavior will be treated severely by Yahweh, as his legal curse destroys the lives of offenders (5:4) and heavenly messengers remove idolatrous objects from the land (5:9–11).

Interspersed among the main oracles in Zech. 9–14 are a series of short pericopes focusing on ethical crises within Judah, especially related to its leaders, who are accused of divining through idols (10:1–3), abusing the vulnerable (11:4–16), and deserting their leadership post (11:17). These crises reach a climax in the purging of 13:7–9, which finally produces a remnant able to embrace Yahweh in covenantal relationship. The eschatological vision of the oracles in Zech. 12–14 looks to Yahweh's punishment of the nations and their submission to his rule from Jerusalem through pilgrimage to the Feast of Tabernacles. In addition, these oracles envision the purification of Judah and Jerusalem, with the community grieving over their offenses against Yahweh (12:10–14) and eradicating false prophecy (13:3–6). This response is made possible by Yahweh's provision of a spirit of grace and supplication (12:10). Yahweh will also intervene directly, providing a fountain able to cleanse from sin and impurity and removing both idols and false prophets from the land (13:1–2). The book concludes with a vision of the ceremonial holiness usually associated with the temple, its personnel and utensils, now characterizing all of Jerusalem and Judah (14:20–21).

Zechariah expands the ethical vision beyond Haggai's limited vision of temple reconstruction to include issues related to injustice, idolatry, and imperial compromise. Its introduction is an important reminder that ethical response must be founded on covenant relationship.

See also Old Testament Ethics

Bibliography

Boda, M. *Haggai, Zechariah*. NIVAC. Zondervan, 2004; idem. "Zechariah: Master Mason or Penitential Prophet?" Pages 49–69 in *Yahwism after the Exile: Perspectives on Israelite Religion in the Persian Era*, ed. B. Becking and R. Albertz. STR 5. Van Gorcum, 2003; Boda, M., and M. Floyd, eds. *Bringing Out the Treasure: Inner Biblical Allusion in Zechariah 9–14*. JSOTSup 370. Sheffield Academic Press, 2003; idem, eds. *Tradition in Transition: Haggai and Zechariah 1–8 in the Trajectory of Hebrew Theology*. Continuum, 2009; Cook, S. *Prophecy and Apocalypticism: The Postexilic Social Setting*. Fortress, 1995; Larkin, K. *The Eschatology of Second Zechariah: A Study of the Formation of a Mantological Wisdom Anthology*. CBET 6. Kok Pharos, 1994; Petersen, D. "Zechariah's Visions." *VT* 34 (1984): 195–206; Tollington, J. *Tradition and Innovation in Haggai and Zechariah 1–8*. JSOTSup 150. JSOT Press, 1993.

Mark J. Boda

Zephaniah

The genealogical introduction to this book, unusually long for a prophetic book, places the prophetic activity of Zephaniah in the reign of King Josiah of Judah (640–609 BCE). The connection to "Cushi" in the genealogy raises the intriguing possibility of an African ancestry for the prophet, which in turn may explain the longer introduction for the purpose of stressing legitimacy. For a relatively short composition, the book manages to pack a range of themes that echo the messages of some earlier prophetic figures. Readers may recognize familiar themes such as indictment against wayward religious behavior (1:4–6; 2:10–11), invectives against incompetent and venal leadership (1:8–9; 3:3–4), indignation against social injustices (1:10–13), call for repentance (2:1–3), the idea of the remnant (2:7, 9b; 3:8–13), the day of Yahweh (1:14–16), God's sovereignty over the nations (2:4–9a), and a picture of future salvation (3:14–20). Aside from these familiar themes, in arranging the materials, Zephaniah also incorporates the familiar threefold pattern of judgment against Judah (1:2–18; 3:1–8), judgment against the nations (2:4–15), and salvation for Judah (3:9–13). Like Amos and Joel, the prophet explicitly develops the concept of the day of Yahweh to frame his prophecies. But Zephaniah never loses sight of the specific reasons for God's judgment such as social injustices. Here one recognizes the prophet's affinity with the eighth-century BCE prophetic voices.

From an ethical perspective, some key emphases are worthy of note. The image in the opening lines of the book sets a powerful tone. God's wrath will sweep away the creation in its entirety. The all-inclusive nature of the destruction is indicated by references to creatures that populate the heavens, the earth, and the sea. But the ones responsible for the calamity are the humans. From an ecological perspective, the point that can be extrapolated is that the sinful and destructive behavior of humans drags down the rest of the creation.

Scholars have long recognized the paraenetic character of Zephaniah. The exhortation to embrace life-saving faith and conduct, and the admonition to abandon destructive beliefs and action, form the core of the book's emphasis. Although the prophet talks about life-saving and life-negating conducts, the primary emphasis is on turning to God. The prophet goes to the root of the issue. True devotion to God will result in proper ethical behavior. Obedience to the law may fulfill the letter of the covenant relationship, but the vitality of the relationship derives from a vibrant and genuine attunement to God. Zephaniah recognizes the deeper theological basis of the prophetic ethical urging.

See also Old Testament Ethics

Bibliography

Berlin, A. *Zephaniah*. AB 25A. Doubleday, 1994; Mason, R. *Zephaniah, Habakkuk, Joel*. OTG. JSOT Press, 1994; Roberts, J. *Nahum, Habakkuk, and Zephaniah*. OTL. Westminster John Knox, 1991; Sweeney, M. *Zephaniah*. Hermeneia. Fortress, 2003.

D. N. Premnath

LIST OF ENTRIES

SCRIPTURE INDEX

Old Testament

Exodus

Leviticus

Numbers

Deuteronomy

Proverbs

Jeremiah

Lamentations

Ezekiel

Daniel

Hosea

Joel

Amos

Obadiah

Jonah

Micah

Nahum

Habakkuk

Old Testament Apocrypha

New Testament

Mark

John

1 Corinthians

Ephesians

Philippians

Colossians